Contents

Front section 1–24

Introduction 6
Where to go 8
When to go 10
Things not to miss 13

Basics 25–96

Getting there 27
Visas and red tape 35
Information, websites and maps 37
Insurance 38
Health 40
Costs, money and banks 44
Getting around 47
Accommodation 57
Eating and drinking 61
Communications 67
The media 69
Opening hours, holidays and festivals 70
Sports and outdoor pursuits 73
Crime, police and personal safety 80
Work 82
Travellers with disabilities 86
Travelling with children 89
Gay and lesbian Australia 91
Women and sexual harassment 93
Directory 95

Guide 97–1172

1. Sydney and around 99
2. Coastal New South Wales and ACT 263
3. Inland New South Wales ... 353
4. Southeast Queensland 411
5. Tropical Queensland and the Reef 481
6. Outback Queensland 577
7. Northern Territory 629
8. Western Australia 709
9. South Australia 801
10. Melbourne and around 899
11. Victoria 971
12. Tasmania 1063

Contexts 1173–1229

History 1175
Australia's indigenous peoples 1188
Wildlife 1193
Australian film 1198
Australian music 1207
Books 1215
Australian English 1227

Advertisers 1231-1236

Small print & Index 1237-1256

◀◀ Children holding Australian flag, Western Australia, ◀ Dirt road, Northern Territory

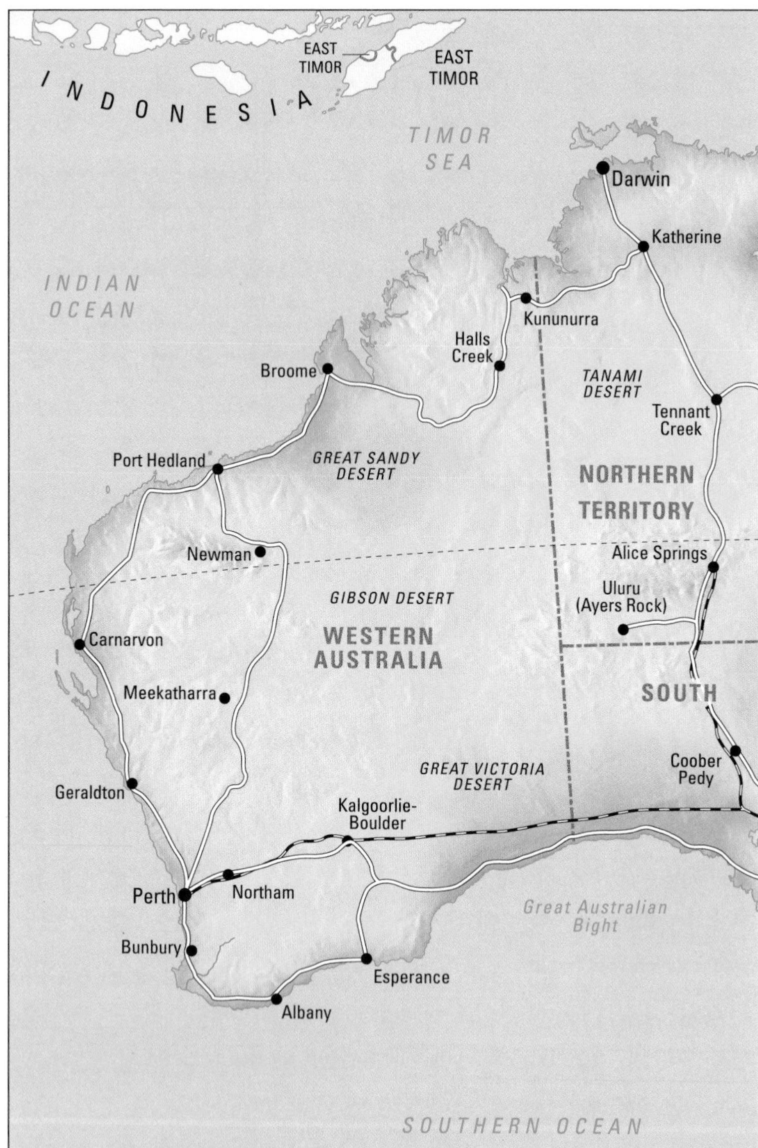
INDONESIA
EAST TIMOR
EAST TIMOR
TIMOR SEA
Darwin
Katherine
INDIAN OCEAN
Kununurra
Halls Creek
Broome
TANAMI DESERT
Tennant Creek
Port Hedland
GREAT SANDY DESERT
NORTHERN TERRITORY
Newman
Alice Springs
Uluru (Ayers Rock)
GIBSON DESERT
WESTERN AUSTRALIA
Carnarvon
Meekatharra
SOUTH
Coober Pedy
GREAT VICTORIA DESERT
Geraldton
Kalgoorlie-Boulder
Perth
Northam
Great Australian Bight
Bunbury
Esperance
Albany
SOUTHERN OCEAN
0
800km

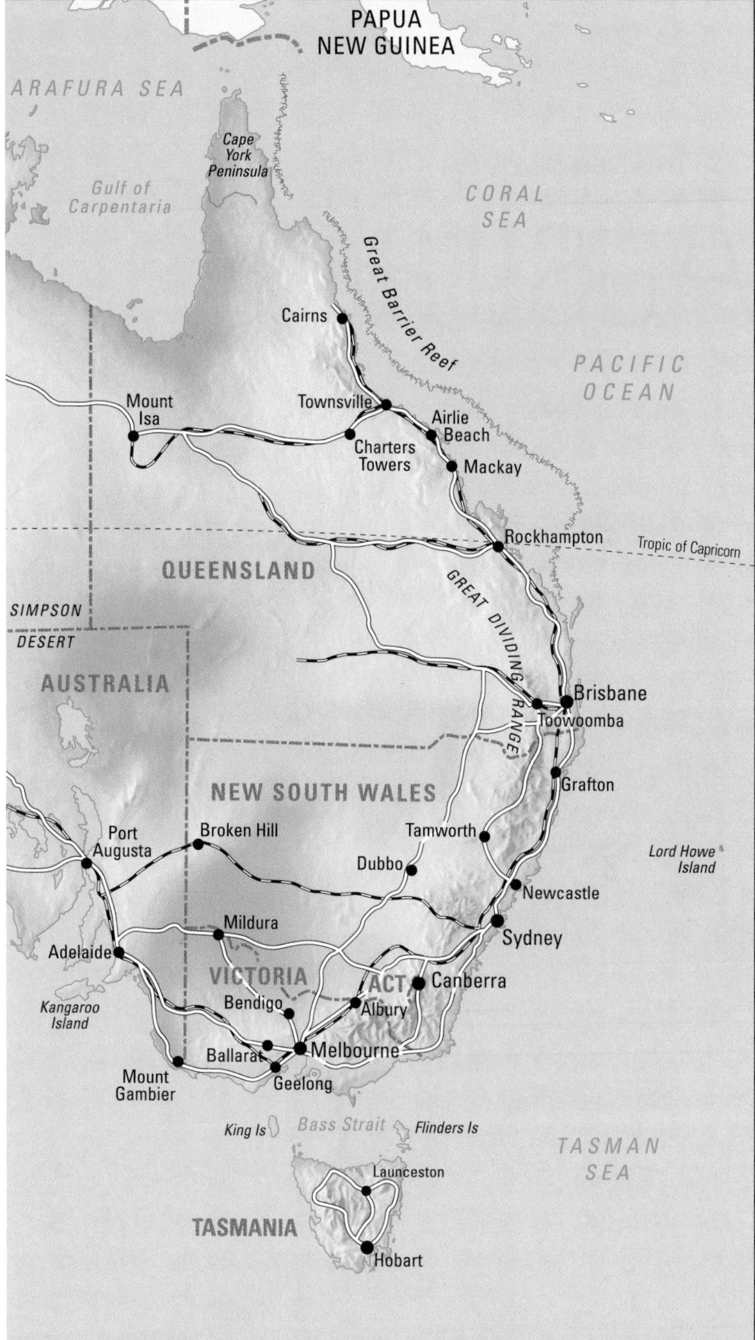
PAPUA
NEW GUINEA
ARAFURA SEA
Cape
York
Peninsula
Gulf of
Carpentaria
CORAL
SEA
Great Barrier Reef
Cairns
PACIFIC
OCEAN
Mount
Isa
Townsville
Airlie
Beach
Charters
Towers
Mackay
Rockhampton
Tropic of Capricorn
QUEENSLAND
GREAT DIVIDING RANGE
SIMPSON
DESERT
AUSTRALIA
Brisbane
Toowoomba
Grafton
NEW SOUTH WALES
Port
Augusta
Broken Hill
Tamworth
Lord Howe
Island
Dubbo
Newcastle
Mildura
Sydney
Adelaide
VICTORIA
ACT
Canberra
Kangaroo
Island
Bendigo
Albury
Ballarat
Melbourne
Mount
Gambier
Geelong
King Is
Bass Strait
Flinders Is
TASMAN
SEA
Launceston
TASMANIA
Hobart

Introduction to Australia

Australia is massive, and sparsely peopled: in size it rivals the USA, yet its population is just twenty million. It is an ancient land, and often looks it: in places, it's the most eroded, denuded and driest of continents, with much of central and western Australia – the bulk of the country – overwhelmingly arid and flat. In contrast, its cities – most of which were founded as recently as the mid-nineteenth century – express a youthful energy.

The most memorable scenery is in the Outback, the vast desert in the interior of the country west of the Great Dividing Range. Here, vivid blue skies, cinnamon-red earth, deserted gorges and other striking geological features as well as bizarre wildlife comprise a unique ecology – one that has played host to the oldest surviving human culture for up to seventy thousand years (just ten thousand years after *Homo sapiens* is thought to have emerged from Africa).

This harsh interior has forced modern Australia to become a **coastal country**. Most of the population lives within 20km of the ocean, occupying a suburban, southeastern arc extending from southern Queensland to Adelaide. These urban Australians celebrate the typical New World values of material self-improvement through hard work and hard play, with an easy-going vitality that visitors, especially Europeans, often find refreshingly hedonistic. A sunny climate also contributes to this exuberance, with an outdoor life in which a thriving beach culture and the congenial backyard "barbie" are central.

▲ Baby smoking ceremony, Kimberley

While visitors might eventually find this *Home and Away* lifestyle rather prosaic, there are opportunities – particularly in the Northern Territory – to gain some experience of **Australia's indigenous peoples** and their culture, through visiting ancient art sites, taking tours and, less easily, making personal contact. Many Aboriginal people – especially in central Australia – have managed to maintain a traditional lifestyle (albeit with modern accoutrements), speaking their own languages and living according to their law. Conversely, most Aboriginal people you'll come across in country towns and cities are victims of what is scathingly referred to as "welfare colonialism" – a disempowering consequence of dole cheques and other subsidies combined with little chance of meaningful employment, often resulting in a destructive cycle of poverty, ill health and substance abuse. There's still a long way to go before black and white people in Australia can exist on genuinely equal terms.

Fact file

- With an area of eight million square kilometres, Australia is the **sixth largest country** in the world.
- The **population** stands at just twenty million, of whom some 85% live in urban areas, mainly along the coast. About 92% of the population are of European origin, 2% Aboriginal and about 6% Asian and Middle Eastern.
- Much of Australia is arid and flat. One-third of the country is **desert** and another third is steppe or semi-desert. Only six percent of the country rises above 600m in elevation, and its **tallest peak**, Mount Kosciuszko, is just 2228m high.
- Australia's main **exports** are fossil fuels, minerals, metals, cotton, wool, wine and beef, and its most important **trading partners** are Japan, China and the US.
- Australia is a **federal parliamentary** state (formally a constitutional monarchy) with two legislative houses, the Senate and the House of Representatives. The chief of state is the British Monarch, represented by the Governor-General, while the head of government is the Prime Minister.

Where to go

For visitors, deciding where to go can mean juggling with distance, money and time. You could spend months driving around the Outback, exploring the national parks, or hanging out at beaches; or you could take an all-in two-week "Reef, Rock and Harbour" package, encompassing Australia's outstanding trinity of "must sees".

Both options provide thoroughly Australian experiences, but neither will leave you with a feeling of having more than scraped the surface of this vast country. The two big natural attractions are the two-thousand-kilometre-long **Great Barrier Reef** off the Queensland coast, with its complex of islands and underwater splendour, and the brooding monolith of **Uluru** (Ayers Rock), in the Northern Territory's Red Centre. You should certainly try to see them, although exploration of other parts of the country will bring you into contact with more subtle but equally rewarding sights and opportunities.

The **cities** are surprisingly cosmopolitan: waves of postwar immigrants from southern Europe and, more recently, Southeast Asia have done much to erode Australia's Anglocentrism. Each Australian state has a capital stamped with its own personality, and nowhere is this more apparent than in New South Wales where glamorous Sydney has the iconic landmarks of the Opera House and Harbour Bridge. Elsewhere, the sophisticated café society of Melbourne (Victoria) contrasts with the vitality of Brisbane (Queensland). Adelaide, in South Australia, has a human-scale and old-

▲ bills, Darlinghurst, Sydney

▲ Yarra Ranges, Victoria

fashioned charm, while Perth, in Western Australia, camouflages its isolation with a leisure-oriented urbanity. In Hobart, capital of Tasmania, you'll encounter fine heritage streetscapes and get a distinct maritime feel. The purpose-built administrative centre of Canberra, in the Australian Capital Territory, often fails to grip visitors, but Darwin's continuing revival enlivens an exploration of the distinctive "Territory".

Away from the suburbs, with their vast shopping malls and quarter-acre residential blocks, is the transitional "bush", and beyond that the wilderness of the **Outback** – the quintessential Australian environment. Protected from the arid interior, the **east coast** has the pick of the country's greenery and scenery, from the north's tropical rainforests and the Great Barrier Reef to the surf-lined beaches further south. The east coast is backed by the Great Dividing Range, which steadily decreases

Outdoor activities

Though there's fun to be had in the cities, it's really the great outdoors that makes Australia such a special place. Its multitude of national parks – around a thousand in total – embrace everything from isolated beaches and tropical rainforest to the vast wildernesses of the bush and the Outback. Visitors are spoilt for choice when it comes to getting out and about, with a huge range of outdoor pursuits on offer – everything from diving off the Great Barrier Reef or white-water rafting Tasmania's Franklin River to hot-air ballooning over Alice or even skiing in the Australian Alps. Perhaps the best way to see something of the great outdoors, and certainly the cheapest and the most popular, is bushwalking. You'll find trails marked in every national park. For more see p.76.

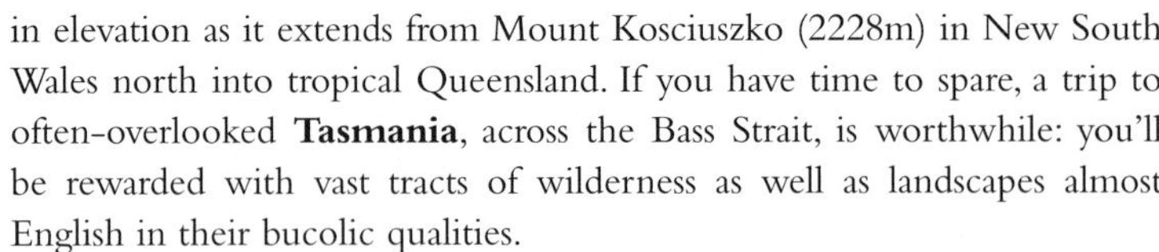

in elevation as it extends from Mount Kosciuszko (2228m) in New South Wales north into tropical Queensland. If you have time to spare, a trip to often-overlooked **Tasmania**, across the Bass Strait, is worthwhile: you'll be rewarded with vast tracts of wilderness as well as landscapes almost English in their bucolic qualities.

When to go

Australia's **climate** has become less predictable in recent times, although like the rest of the planet the country has rarely had stable weather patterns over the last few thousand years. Recently observed phenomena, such as an extended drought in the eastern Outback, the cyclic El Niño effect, and even the hole in the ozone layer – which is disturbingly close to the country – are probably part of a long-term pattern.

Visitors from the northern hemisphere should remember that, as early colonials observed, in Australia "nature is horribly reversed": when it's winter or summer in the northern hemisphere, the opposite season prevails Down Under. Although this is easy to remember, the principle becomes harder to apply to the transitional seasons of spring and autumn. To confuse things further, the four seasons only really exist in the **southern half of the country** outside of the tropics. Here, you'll find reliably warm summers at the coast with regular, but thankfully brief, heatwaves in excess of 40°C. Head inland, and the temperatures rise further. Winters, on the other hand, can be miserable, particularly in Victoria, where the short days add to the gloom. Tasmania's highlands make for unpredictable weather all year round, although summer is the best time to explore the island's outdoor attractions.

In the **coastal tropics**, weather basically falls into two seasons. The best time to visit is during the hot and cloudless Dry (from April to November), with moderate coastal humidity maintaining a pleasant temperature day and night and cooler nights inland. In contrast, the Wet – particularly the "Build Up" in November or December before the rains commence – can be very uncomfortable,

▲ Bondi Beach

with stifling, near-total humidity. As storm clouds gather, rising temperatures, humidity and tension can provoke irrational behaviour in the psychologically unacclimatized – something known as "going troppo". Nevertheless, the mid-Wet's daily downpours and enervating mugginess can be quite intoxicating, compelling a hyper-relaxed inactivity for which these regions are known; furthermore the countryside – if you can reach it – looks its best at this time.

▲ Road train

Australia's **interior** is an arid semi-desert with very little rain, high summer temperatures and occasionally freezing winter nights. Unless you're properly equipped to cope with these extremes, you'd be better off coming here during the transitional seasons between April and June, or October and November.

Aboriginal art

Aboriginal art has grown into a million-dollar industry since the first canvas dot paintings of the central deserts emerged in the 1970s. Though seemingly abstract, early canvases are said to replicate ceremonial sand paintings – temporary "maps" fleetingly revealed to depict sacred knowledge. In the tropics, figurative bark and cave paintings are less enigmatic but much older, though until recently they were ceremonially repainted. The unusual x-ray style found in the Top End details the internal structure of animals. The Northern Territory – and Alice Springs in particular – are the best places to look; for tips on buying Aboriginal art as well as didgeridoos, see pp.684–686.

In general, the **best time to visit** the south is during the Australian summer, from December to March, though long summer holidays from Christmas through January mean that prices are higher and beaches more crowded at this time. In the tropical north the best months are from May to October, while in the Centre they are from October to November and from March to May. If you want to tour extensively, keep to the southern coasts in summer and head north for the winter.

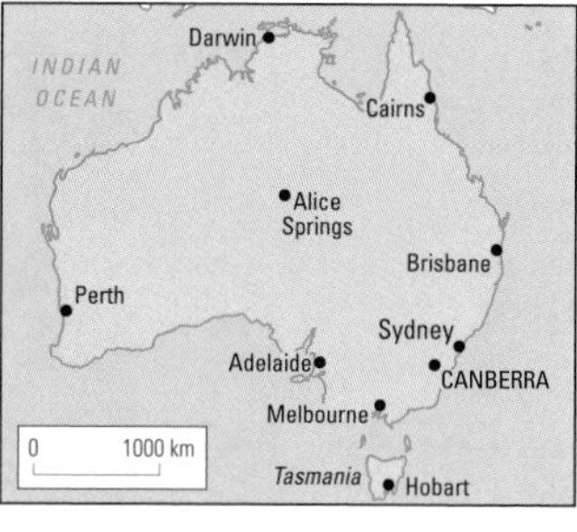

Average temperatures (°C) and rainfall (mm)

		Jan/Feb		Mar/Apr		May/Jun		July/Aug		Sept/Oct		Nov/Dec	
Adelaide	°C	28	27	25	22	18	16	14	15	17	21	22	25
	mm	20	20	25	45	65	70	65	60	55	40	25	20
Alice Springs	°C	36	35	32	27	22	21	19	21	25	30	32	35
	mm	35	40	25	20	25	25	20	20	10	25	30	35
Brisbane	°C	27	27	26	25	23	21	23	22	24	25	26	27
	mm	160	160	150	80	70	60	55	50	50	75	100	140
Cairns	°C	31	31	30	29	28	25	25	27	27	28	30	31
	mm	400	440	450	180	100	50	30	25	35	35	90	160
Canberra	°C	27	25	23	20	15	13	12	13	15	18	22	25
	mm	55	50	50	45	50	30	30	50	50	70	65	65
Darwin	°C	31	30	31	32	31	30	30	31	32	32	33	32
	mm	400	430	435	75	50	10	5	10	15	70	110	310
Hobart	°C	21	21	20	17	14	12	11	12	15	18	19	20
	mm	50	45	50	55	50	45	50	50	55	55	50	50
Melbourne	°C	26	26	24	21	16	15	14	15	17	19	21	20
	mm	45	50	55	60	55	50	50	50	55	65	55	55
Perth	°C	30	30	28	25	22	20	19	19	20	22	25	28
	mm	10	15	25	50	125	185	175	145	80	75	25	20
Sydney	°C	25	25	24	23	20	17	16	17	19	22	23	24
	mm	100	105	125	130	125	130	110	75	60	75	70	75

things not to miss

It's not possible to see everything that Australia has to offer in one trip – and we don't suggest you try. What follows is a selective taste of the country's highlights: great places to visit, outstanding national parks, spectacular wildlife and lively festivals. They're arranged in five colour-coded categories, which you can browse through to find the very best things to see, do and experience. All entries have a page reference to take you straight into the guide, where you can find out more.

01 Uluru (NT) Page **703** • Uluru, otherwise known as Ayers Rock, is a sacred site for Aboriginal people, and a magnet for tourists the world over.

02 Humpback whales (Qld) Page **471** • Saved from extinction by a ban on whaling, humpback whales migrate up the Queensland coast each June–October to calve around the Whitsundays' warm tropical waters.

03 Sailing in the Whitsundays (Qld) Page **512** • There's fantastic sailing and diving – and whale-watching in season – in the idyllic white-sand Whitsunday Islands.

04 Skiing in the Snowy Mountains (NSW) Page **299** • The Snowy Mountains have the best skiing in Australia.

05 Bushtucker Page **62** • Witchetty grubs and wattle seeds, possum-tail soup and rooburgers – a few restaurants around the country are now experimenting with bushtucker.

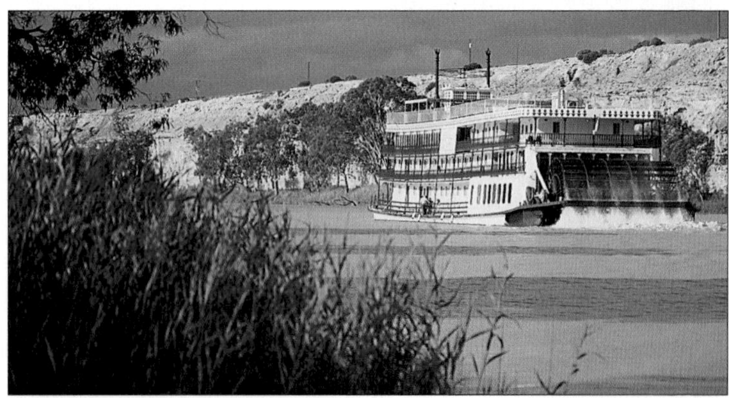

06 Boating on the Murray River (SA) Page **866** • By far the best way to see the great brown Murray River is to get out on the water – hop on a paddle-steamer, splash about in a canoe or rent a houseboat.

07 Coober Pedy (SA) Page **883** • The underground homes, shops and churches of Coober Pedy – where temperatures soar to over 50°C in summer – are the most enduring symbol of the harshness of Australia's Outback.

08 The Sanctuary at Mission Beach (Qld) Page **532** • Rainforest retreat par excellence, with stilt cabins at tree level surrounded by fifty acres of steamy coastal jungle.

09 The Franklin River (Tas) Page **1166** • White-water rafting is the only way to explore the wild Franklin River, one of the great rivers of Australia.

10 Fraser Island (Qld) Page **474** • The giant dunes, freshwater lakes and sculpted coloured sands of the world's largest sand island form the backdrop to exciting 4WD safaris.

11 Aussie Rules football at the MCG (Vic) Page **921** • Taking in a game at the venerable Melbourne Cricket Ground (MCG) is a must for sports fans.

12 Lake Eyre (SA) Page **893** • This massive saline lake, topped by a glaring salt crust and walled by red dunes, creates a harsh, unforgettable landscape.

13 Tree kangaroos (Qld) Page **556** • North Queensland's tropical rainforest is home to two species of tree kangaroo, which forage at night on the forest floor but spend the days crashed out in the canopy. Spot them at Yungaburra in the Atherton Tablelands.

14 Renting a campervan Page **51** • Invest in a good map and experience the freedom of the road, stunning national parks and the seclusion of Australia's Outback equipped with all your creature comforts.

15 Beer Can Regatta, Darwin (NT) Page **646** • Wacky boat races in sea craft made entirely from beer cans, held in early August.

16 Diving at the Great Barrier Reef (Qld) Page **486** • Come face-to-face with stunning coral and shoals of curious fish.

17 Kangaroo Island (SA) Page **849** • Unspoilt Kangaroo Island boasts fantastic coastal scenery and excellent wildlife-spotting opportunities.

18 Kakadu National Park (NT) Page **648** • Australia's largest national park is a vast World Heritage-listed wilderness with an amazing diversity of wildlife.

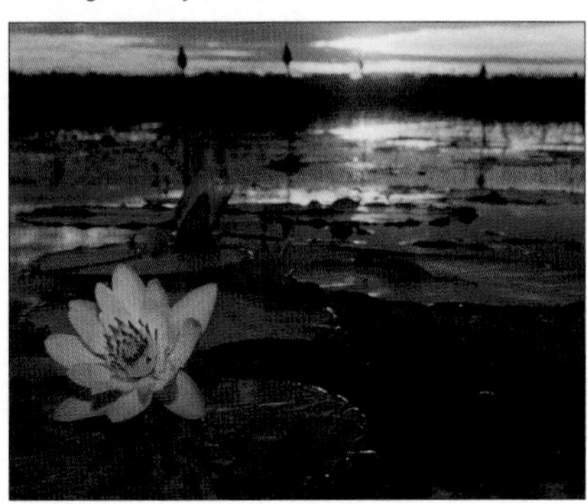

19 Sydney Opera House performance (NSW) Page **130** • Take in a performance at one of the world's busiest performing arts centres – interval drinks certainly don't have such spectacular harbour views anywhere else in the world.

20 Kings Canyon in Watarrka National Park (NT) Page **698** • The hike around the canyon's rim takes you past exposed lookouts, domed outcrops and a secluded waterhole that's great for a dip on a hot day.

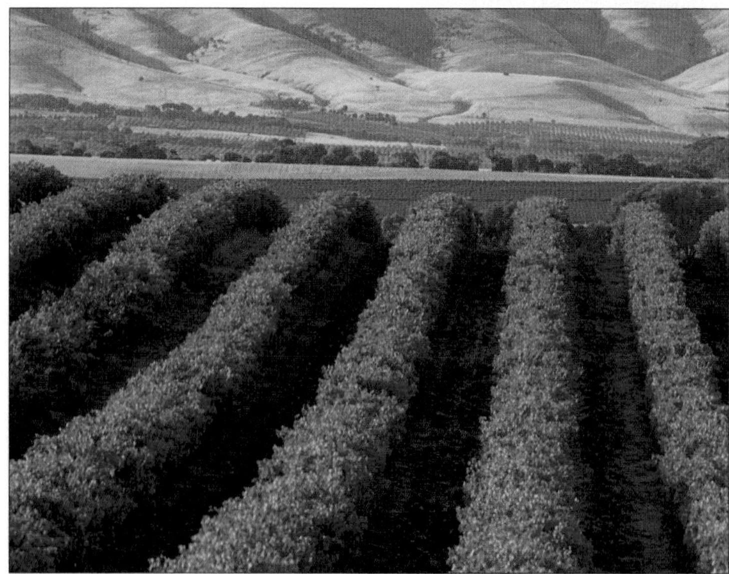

21 Barossa Valley wineries (SA) Page **834** • Australia's premier wine-producing region, just 50km from Adelaide, is a great place to stop over and unwind.

22 Crocodiles (NT) Page **650** • Head up north to see the Territory's growing population of fearsome crocs.

23 Melbourne Cup (Vic) Page **73** • Melbourne's 144-year-old horse race brings the entire country to a standstill around the radio or TV.

24 Wilpena Pound (SA) Page **889** • Fantastic hikes amid spectacular scenery at the famous elevated basin of Wilpena Pound in the Flinders Ranges National Park.

25 The Great Ocean Road (Vic) Page **977** • On two wheels or four, the 280-kilometre ride along the rugged, surf-battered cliffs bordering the Great Ocean Road comes straight out of a road movie.

26 Climbing Sydney Harbour Bridge (NSW) Page **131** • Scale the bridge for adrenaline thrills and great vistas – or walk or cycle across it for free.

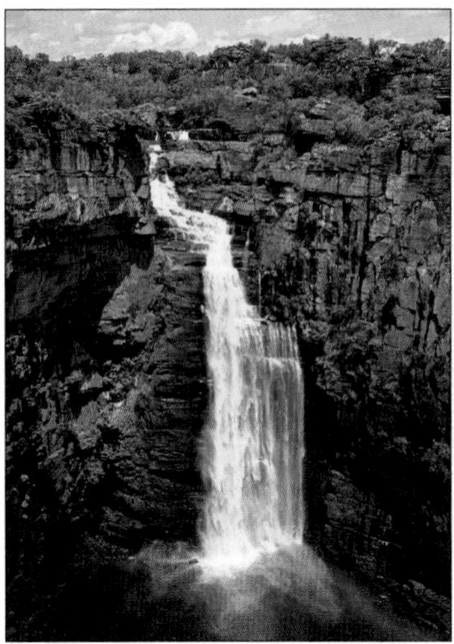

27 The Kimberley (WA) Page **789** • Regarded as Australia's last frontier, the Kimberley is a sparsely populated, untamed wilderness that contains some stunning landscapes.

28 Giant termite mounds (NT) Page **660** • These impressively huge towers – up to four metres tall – are a regular feature of the Top End.

29 Karijini National Park (WA) Page **776** • The water-carved gorges of the Karijini National Park make a dramatic backdrop for challenging canyoneering adventures.

30 Manly Ferry (NSW) Page **108** • The short ferry trip from Circular Quay to the surfing mecca of Manly takes in picture-postcard views of Sydney Harbour.

31 Tall Timber Country (WA) Page **741** • The primeval karri forests of the so-called Tall Timber Country are one of WA's greatest natural sights. Get a bird's eye view from the Tree Top Walk.

32 The Strzelecki, Birdsville and Oodnadatta tracks (SA) Pages **892** & **894** • Making the most of the journey is what counts – the fabled Outback routes to Oodnadatta, Birdsville and Innamincka are still real adventures.

33 Aboriginal Dance Festival at Laura (Qld) Page **568** • Electrifying celebration of Aboriginal culture, held in June in odd-numbered years.

34 Atherton Tablelands (Qld) Page **551** • With its majestic rainforest, crater lakes and abundant wildlife, you could spend days exploring the Atherton Tablelands.

35 Broken Hill (NSW) Page **397** • Pay a visit to the Royal Flying Doctor Service and the School of the Air headquarters at NSW's historic outback mining town and thriving arts centre.

36 Birdsville Races (Qld) Page **594** • Birdsville Hotel is the focus for the annual Birdsville Races, when five thousand people descend on the tiny desert township in Queensland's Outback for a weekend of drinking, horse racing and mayhem.

37 Mutawintji National Park (NSW) Page **409** • Red, barren earth laced with ancient galleries of Aboriginal rock art, secluded gorges and quiet waterholes.

38 Wilsons Promontory National Park (Vic) Page **1038** • Victoria's most popular national park, "The Prom" boasts some superb coastal scenery and bushwalks.

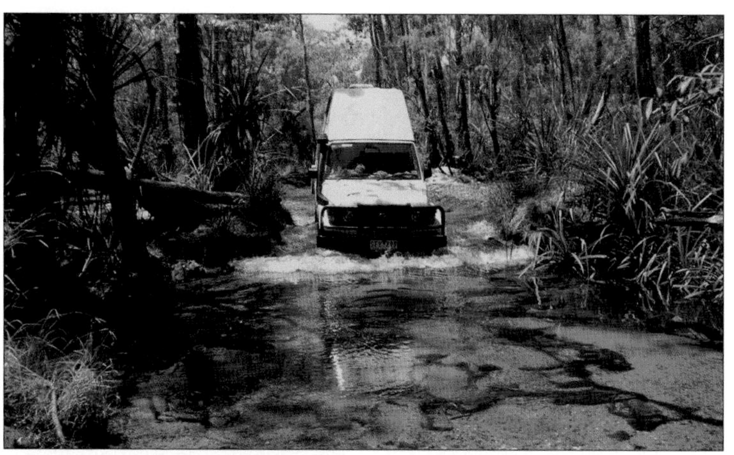

39 Rent a four-wheel-drive Page **51** • Adventure off-road from Queensland's Cape York (p.563) to the Territory's Central Deserts (p.694) or WA's Kimberley (p.798).

40 Hiking through Carnarvon Gorge (Qld) Page **589** • With its Aboriginal art sites and magical scenery, a day-hike into the Carnarvon Gorge takes some beating.

41 Blue Mountains (NSW) Page **236** • World Heritage listed, the Blue Mountains, just west of Sydney, get their name from the blue mist of fragrant eucalyptus oil hanging in the air all year round.

42 Bondi Beach (NSW) Page **167** • Beach, surf and café culture; Sydney's famous beach has something for everyone.

43 Mardi Gras (NSW) Page **196** • The irreverent Oxford Street parade, from dykes on bikes to the Melbourne marching boys, ends the summer season.

44 Canoeing up the Katherine Gorge (NT)

Page **666** • Hop on a cruise or paddle a canoe through the dramatic orange cliffs of the Katherine Gorge – you won't have it to yourself, but it's still hugely enjoyable.

45 Overland Track in Cradle Mountain-Lake St Clair National Park (Tas) Page **1162** • The 80-kilometre Overland Track is Australia's greatest extended bushwalk, spread over five or more mud- and leech-filled days of physical, exhilarating exhaustion.

Basics

Basics

Getting there 27

Visas and red tape 35

Information, websites and maps 37

Insurance 38

Health 40

Costs, money and banks 44

Getting around 47

Accommodation 57

Eating and drinking 61

Communications 67

The media 69

Opening hours, holidays and festivals 70

Sports and outdoor pursuits 73

Crime, police and personal safety 80

Work 82

Travellers with disabilities 86

Travelling with children 89

Gay and lesbian Australia 91

Women and sexual harassment 93

Directory 95

Getting there

Few will be surprised to learn that flying is the main way of getting to Australia. You can fly pretty much every day to the main east coast cities from Europe, North America and Southeast Asia. Airfares always depend on the season, with the highest fares being the two weeks either side of Christmas, when the weather is best in the main population centres (note, however, that you can get a good bargain if you fly on Christmas Day itself). Fares drop during the "shoulder" seasons – mid-January to March and mid-August to November – and you'll get the best prices during the low season, April to June. Because of the distance from most popular departure points, flying on weekends does not alter the price.

To cut costs, use a **specialist flight agent** or a **discount agent,** who may also offer special student and youth fares as well as travel insurance, rail passes, car rental, tours and the like. Some agents specialize in **charter flights**, which may be cheaper than anything available on a scheduled flight, but again departure dates are fixed and withdrawal penalties are high. If Australia is only one stop on a longer journey, you might want to consider buying a **Round-the-World** (RTW) ticket. Some travel agents sell prepackaged RTW tickets that will have you touching down in about half a dozen cities and Australia is frequently part of the regular eastbound RTW loop from Europe. See "Fares" for more details on RTW tickets.

Booking flights online

Many airlines and discount travel websites offer you the opportunity to book your tickets online, cutting out the costs of agents and middlemen. Good deals can often be found through discount or auction sites, as well as through the airlines' own websites.

Online booking agents and general travel sites

ⓦ**travel.yahoo.com** Incorporates a lot of Rough Guide material in its coverage of destination countries and cities across the world, with information about places to eat, sleep etc.
ⓦ**www.cheapflights.com** Flight deals, travel agents, plus links to other travel sites.
ⓦ**www.cheaptickets.com** Discount flight specialists.
ⓦ**www.dialaflight.co.uk** Website useful for tracking down bargains, plus telephone sales for scheduled flights.
ⓦ**www.etn.nl/discount.htm** A hub of consolidator and discount agent Web links, maintained by the non-profit European Travel Network.
ⓦ**www.expedia.com** Discount airfares, all–airline search engine and daily deals.
ⓦ**www.flyaow.com** Online air travel info and reservations site.
ⓦ**www.hotwire.com** Bookings from the US only. Last-minute savings of up to forty percent on regular published fares. Travellers must be at least 18 and there are no refunds, transfers or changes allowed. Log-in required.
ⓦ**www.lastminute.com** Offers good last-minute holiday package and flight-only deals.
ⓦ**www.priceline.com** Name-your-own-price website that has deals at around forty percent off standard fares. You cannot specify flight times (although you do specify dates) and the tickets are non-refundable, non-transferable and non-changeable.
ⓦ**www.skyauction.com** Bookings from the US only. Auctions tickets and travel packages using a "second bid" scheme. The best strategy is to bid the maximum you're willing to pay, since if you win you'll pay just enough to beat the runner-up regardless of your maximum bid.
ⓦ**www.travelocity.com** Destination guides, best deals for car rental, accommodation and lodging as well as fares. Provides access to the travel agent system SABRE, the most comprehensive central reservations system in the US.
ⓦ**www.travelshop.com.au** Australian website offering discounted flights, packages and insurance for Australia and your onward journey.

Getting there from Britain and Ireland

The market for **flights** between Britain and Australia is one of the most competitive in the world, and in real terms prices are still as low as ever.

Modern aircraft can now reach the north Australian coast from London in just fifteen hours' flying time, though in practice the journey to Sydney or the other eastern cities takes a minimum of 21 hours including stopovers. If you break the journey in Southeast Asia or North America, getting to Australia need not be the tedious, seat-bound slog you may have imagined. There are no direct flights from Ireland.

A word of warning: don't actually buy your ticket until you're sure that you've been granted a **visa** (see "Visas and red tape" for more details). Visa in hand, you'll next need to decide where you want to fly to in Australia, where you would like to stop en route (or on the way back) and whether you want to use flights to get around once you're there. Sydney and Melbourne are served by the greatest number of airlines, and carriers such as Qantas offer the same price to fly to any east-coast city between Cairns and Adelaide; flights to Darwin and Perth are around £100 cheaper, but you'll spend at least that much on the overland journey to the east coast. An **open-jaw ticket** (flying into one city and out from another) usually costs no more than an ordinary return.

Direct scheduled flights depart from London's two main airports, Gatwick and Heathrow, although Singapore Airlines has daily flights from Manchester to Singapore which connect with onward flights to Sydney.

Tourists and those on one-year working visas are generally required by Australian immigration to arrive with a ticket out of the country, so **one-way tickets** are really only viable for Australian and New Zealand residents. If you've purchased a return ticket and find you want to stay longer or head off on a totally different route, it's sometimes possible to cash in the return half of your ticket (though you'll make a loss on the deal) at the travel agent where you bought it: either post it back to them or arrange for someone in the UK to do it on your behalf.

Fares

The cheapest fare you're likely to find is around £550 return, available during the **low-season** months of April to June, though special offers can go as low as £450; if you insist on flying with Qantas, BA or Singapore Airlines, expect to pay from around £800 for a flight in this off-peak period with special offers sometimes taking prices down to £600. The **most expensive time to fly** is in the two weeks before Christmas, when you'd be lucky to find anything for less than £1000 return: to stand a chance of getting one of the cheaper tickets, aim to book at least six months in advance. Prices also go up from mid-June or the beginning of July to the middle of August coinciding with the peak European holiday times. In between times (the **shoulder seasons** of mid-Aug to Nov and mid-Jan to March) you should expect to pay around £700 (or up to £950 with one of the prestige airlines).

With Qantas you can fly from **regional airports** at Aberdeen, Belfast, Edinburgh, Glasgow, Manchester or Newcastle to connect with your international flight at Heathrow. There is no extra charge from Manchester, but you'll pay a **supplement** from the others.

An excellent alternative to a long direct flight is a **multi-stopover ticket**, which can cost the same or just a little more than the price of an ordinary return; check airlines for routings. Unusual routes are inevitably more expensive, but it's possible to fly **via South America** with Aerolineas Argentinas, which offers stops in Buenos Aires and Auckland – at least £925 return – or **via Africa** with South African Airways, which offers return fares via Johannesburg to Perth and Sydney from around £1000, with the added bonus of discounted internal flights to many other African destinations. You can also often get good deals **via Japan** on All Nippon Airways and Japan Airlines.

More expensive, but even better value, **Round-the-World (RTW) tickets** incorporating Australia provide a chance to see the world on your way to and from down under. RTW flights come prepackaged in a tantalizing variety of permutations, with stopovers chiefly in Asia, the Pacific and North America, but you can pretty much devise your fantasy itinerary and get it priced. A good agent should be able to piece together sector fares from various airlines: providing you keep your itinerary down to three continents prices range from around £850 for a simple London–Bangkok–Sydney–LA–London deal to well over £1000 for more complicated routings. It's also possible to incorporate substantial overland segments for variety. A sample itinerary London–Nairobi–overland to Johannesburg–Perth overland to Broome–Alice Springs overland to Melbourne–Bali–Hong Kong–Bangkok–London costs from around £860.

Most of the routings **from Ireland** involve a stopover in London and transfer to one of the airlines listed below. Fares in low-season are usually around the €890 mark, and €1160 in high season. There are often good deals on Olympic Airways from Dublin via Greece. Singapore Airlines has flights ticketed through from Dublin, Shannon or Cork via London to Singapore and Sydney, while Malaysian Airlines also goes from all three Irish airports via Kuala Lumpur. The three airports are also served by the affiliated British Airways and Qantas: all their flights to Australia have a Dublin–London add-on included in the price. For youth and student discount fares, the best first stop is Usit (see below).

With an international ticket from any participating airline (certainly Qantas and British Airways), you may be tempted to buy a **Qantas Boomerang Pass**. But before you do, read about internal flights in "getting around"; you may find the Pass not such a good deal.

Airlines

Aerolíneas Argentinas Ⓣ020/7290 7887, Ⓦwww.aerolineas.com.ar/uk.
Air New Zealand Ⓣ0800/028 4149, Ⓦwww.airnz.co.uk.
All Nippon Airways (ANA) Ⓣ0870/ 837 8866, Ⓦwww.ana.co.jp.
British Airways Ⓣ0870/850 9850, Eire Ⓣ1890/626 747. Ⓦwww.britishairways.com.
Emirates Ⓣ0870/243 2222,Ⓦwww.emirates.com.
Garuda Indonesia Ⓣ020/7467 8600, Ⓦwww.garuda-indonesia.co.uk.
Japan Airlines Ⓣ0845/774 7700, Ⓦwww.jal.co.jp/en.
KLM Royal Dutch Airlines Ⓣ0870/243 0541, Ⓦwww.klm.com.
Korean Air Ⓣ0800/0656 2001, Eire Ⓣ01/799 7990, Ⓦwww.koreanair.uk.com.
Malaysia Airlines Ⓣ0870/607 9090. Eire Ⓣ 01/676 1561. Ⓦwww.malaysia-airlines.com.
Olympic Airlines Ⓣ0870/606 0460, Eire Ⓣ01/608 0090, Ⓦwww.olympicairlines.com.
Qantas Airways Ⓣ0845/774 7767, Ⓦwww.qantas.com.au.
Royal Brunei Airlines Ⓣ020/7584 6660. Ⓦwww.bruneiair.com
Singapore Airlines Ⓣ0870/608 8886, Eire Ⓣ 01/671 0722, Ⓦwww.singaporeair.com.
South African Airways Ⓣ020/7312 5000, Ⓦwww.flysaa.com.
Thai Airways Ⓣ0870/606 0911, Ⓦwww.thaiairways.com.
United Airlines Ⓣ0845/8444 777, Ⓦwww.ual.com.

Discount travel agents

Austravel Ⓣ0870/166 2020,Ⓦwww.austravel.net. Specialists for flights and tours to Australia with nine shops in the UK. Issues ETAs and traditional visas for an administration fee of £17.
Bridge the World Ⓣ0870/814 4400,Ⓦwww.bridgetheworld.com. Specialists in RTW tickets, many with Australian components, with good deals aimed at the backpacker market.
Flightbookers Ⓣ0800/082 3000, Ⓦwww.ebookers.com. Low fares on an extensive range of scheduled flights and other travel services.
Flynow.com Ⓣ0800/066 0003, Ⓦwww.flynow.com. Large range of discounted tickets.
Oz Flights Ⓣ0870/747 11 747, Ⓦwww.ozflights.co.uk. Good deals on southeast Asian airlines.
North South Travel Ⓣ01245/608 291, Ⓦwww.northsouthtravel.co.uk. Competitive travel agency, offering discounted fares worldwide – profits are used to support projects in the developing world, especially the promotion of sustainable tourism.
Quest Worldwide Ⓣ0870/442 3542, Ⓦwww.questtravel.com. Specialists in RTW and Australian discount fares.
STA Travel Ⓣ0870/1600 599, Ⓦwww.statravel.co.uk. Specialists in low-cost flights and tours for students and under-26s, though other customers welcome. Over sixty branches around the UK and over 450 worldwide.
Trailfinders Ⓣ0845/058 5858, Ⓦwww.trailfinders.com. Excellent for multistop and RTW tickets, including some unusual routings via South Africa, the Pacific and the US. Well-informed and

efficient – visa service available at the Kensington High St branch. Also has branches in Brisbane, Cairns, Melbourne, Perth and Sydney.
Travelbag ⓣ0800/082 5000, ⓦwww.travelbag.co.uk. Well-established long-haul travel agent (now part of ebookers) with a good reputation for Australian coverage.

Irish agents

Australia Travel Centre ⓣ01/804 7188, ⓦwww.australia.ie. Specialists in long-haul flights.
Trailfinders Dublin ⓣ01/677 7888, ⓦwww.trailfinders.ie. One of the best-informed and most efficient agents for independent travellers; produces a very useful quarterly magazine worth scrutinizing for RTW routes.
Usit Dublin ⓣ01/602 1904, ⓦwww.usit.ie. Student and youth specialists for flights, accommodation and transport.

Packages and organized tours

There are relatively few traditional **package holidays** available – nobody's going to fly all the way to Australia just to spend a couple of weeks in a hotel by a beach – but if your time is short and you're reasonably sure of what you want to do, it may not be a bad idea to prebook some of your accommodation, tours and vehicle rental. Many companies offer minimal packages, consisting of a flight with some accommodation and a couple of tours. Full "see-it-all" packages can work out quite expensive and the pace can be rather exhausting, but they aren't bad value, considering what you'd spend anyway.

Many of the Australian specialists also offer such things as bus and train passes (see "Getting around"), discounted hotel vouchers and the like – all of which are worth considering. Some discount flight agents also arrange tours and accommodation – check out Austravel and Trailfinders, among others.

Package tours and specialist operators

Australian Pacific Touring ⓣ020/8879 7444, ⓦwww.aptours.co.uk. Comprehensive range of Australia-wide tours including a 28-day "Rock, Kakadu, Reef" coach tour from £4205 per person twin share. Accommodation and meals and international flights included.
Contiki ⓣ020/8290 6422, ⓦwww.contiki.com. Big-group, countrywide bus and four-wheel-drive tours for fun-loving 18- to 35-year-olds. All transport (excluding flights to Australia) and most meals covered; plenty of additional excursions (climbing, diving, etc) at extra cost. From £109 for a 4-day Sydney and around, to a 25-day Sydney to Darwin via the east coast from £1259.
Explore Worldwide UK In UK; ⓣ01252/760 000, in Dublin; ⓣ01/677 9479, ⓦwww.explore.co.uk. Bus and 4WD tours ranging from an 18-day East Coast Adventure (£1745), to a 31-day 'Australia Explorer' for around £2245 and all with flights from UK.
P&O ⓣ0845/355 5333, ⓦwww.pocruises.com. Once-yearly 100-day cruises to Australia via Suez and back via Cape Town from £8733 or a RTW cruise through the Panama and Suez canals for £7534 for 80 days.
Qantas Holidays ⓣ0990/673464, ⓦwww.qantas.com.au/qantasholidays. Quality packages from undoubted Australian experts. Car and campervan rental, accommodation and sightseeing passes, rail holidays, cruises, coach transport, city packages and tours can all be priced in.
Travelbag ⓣ0800/082 5000, ⓦwww.travelbag.co.uk. Everything from flights to car and campervan rental, farmstays and coach and 4WD tours all over the country. Flights extra.
Travelmood ⓣ0800/066 0004, ⓦwww.travelmood.com. Part of flynow.com. Flights, quality accommodation, car and campervan rental as well as tailor-made itineraries, bus passes, tickets and package tours.
World Expeditions ⓣ0800/074 4135, ⓦwww.worldexpeditions.co.uk. Australian-owned adventure company; small-group active wilderness holidays; cycling, canoeing, rafting, 4WD excursions, walking and camping. All expeditions are graded according to difficulty.

Getting there from the US and Canada

From Los Angeles it's possible to fly non-stop to Sydney in fourteen and a half hours. Qantas, United, Air Canada and Air New Zealand all operate direct to the east coast of Australia. Flying on a national Asian airline will most likely involve a stop in their capital city (Singapore, Tokyo, Hong Kong, etc) and if you're travelling from the west coast of North America to the east coast of Australia you'll probably find their fares on the Pacific route somewhat higher than their American and Australian competitors. However, if you're travelling from the east coast of North America with Perth, say, as your destination, a carrier such as Singapore Airlines or Malaysia Airlines with a transatlantic routing may offer the best value, especially as new low-cost Asian airlines have forced prices down. Flights leave the west coast of the US in the evening, and there are good connections from most North American cities.

Many of the major airlines offer deals whereby you can make **stopovers** either at Pacific Rim destinations such as Tokyo, Honolulu or Kuala Lumpur or at a number of exotic South Pacific locations. Either there will be a flat surcharge on your ticket or they may offer you a higher-priced ticket allowing you to make as many stops as you like, within certain parameters, over a fixed period of time.

But the best deal, if you don't mind planning your itinerary in advance, will most likely be a **Circle Pacific** or a **Round-the-World** (RTW) ticket from a discount outfit.

Fares

Sample lowest standard **scheduled fares** for low/high seasons are approximately as follows: **to Sydney or Melbourne** from Chicago or New York (US$1250/1780); Los Angeles or San Francisco (US$1050/1650); Montréal or Toronto (CDN$1500/2500); Vancouver (CDN$1300/2450); **to Perth** from New York, Los Angeles or San Francisco (US$1850/2450); Vancouver, Toronto or Montréal (CDN$2050/3100). The price of an **open-jaw ticket** (flying into one city and returning from another) should be approximately the average of the return fares to the two cities. If your destination is on the west coast you might also want to check out the Qantas Boomerang Pass which offers coast-to-coast return flights in Australia starting at around US$208 (US$104 one-way); see "Getting Around", for more on this.

Round-the-World (RTW) and **Circle Pacific** tickets can be very good value. A sample RTW **itinerary** would be: Los Angeles–Sydney–Singapore-Bangkok–Delhi–Mumbai (Bombay)–Paris–London–Los Angeles (US$2530); or New York–Tokyo–Hong Kong–Bangkok–Singapore–Jakarta–Yogyakarta–Denpasar (Bali)–Darwin, overland through Australia, Sydney–Kuala Lumpur–London–Amsterdam–New York (US$3250). Sample **Circle Pacific** routes are: Los Angeles–Tokyo–Kuala Lumpur–Singapore–Perth–Sydney–Los Angeles (US$2800); and New York–Hong Kong–Bangkok–Bandar Seri Begawan (Brunei)–Perth, overland through Australia, Sydney–Kuala Lumpur–Tokyo–Los Angeles/ New York (US$3360).

Charter flights to Australia are offered by companies such as Jetset (who will only take bookings through a travel agent). Fares may slightly undercut those on scheduled flights, but this is offset by more restrictions to contend with, so check conditions carefully.

Airlines

Air Canada ⓣ1-888/247-2262, ⓦwww.aircanada.ca.

Air New Zealand US ⓣ1-800/262-1234, Canada ⓣ1-800/663-5494, ⓦwww.airnz.co.nz, ⓦwww.airnewzealand.com, ⓦwww.ca.airnewzealand.com.

Cathay Pacific ⓣ1-800/233-2742, ⓦwww.cathay-usa.com.

Malaysia Airlines ⓣ1-800/552-9264, ⓦwww.malaysiaairlines.com.

Qantas Airways ⓣ1-800/227-4500, ⓦwww.qantas.com.

Singapore Airlines ⓣ1-800/742-3333, Eastern Canada ⓣ1-800/387-0038, Western Canada ⓣ1-800/663-3046, ⓦwww.singaporeair.com.

United Airlines international ⓣ1-800/538-2929, ⓦwww.united.com.

Discount flight agents, travel clubs and consolidators

Air Brokers International ⓣ1-800/883-3273, ⓦwww.airbrokers.com. Consolidator and specialist in Round-the-World and Circle Pacific tickets.

Airtech ⓣ212/219-7000, ⓦwww.airtech.com. Standby seat broker; also deals in consolidator fares.

Airtreks.com ⓣ1-877-AIRTREKS or 415/977-7100, ⓦwww.airtreks.com. Round-the-World and Circle Pacific tickets. The website features an interactive database that lets you build and price your own round-the-world itinerary.

Educational Travel Center ⓣ1-800/747-5551 or 608/256-5551, ⓦwww.edtrav.com. Student/youth discount agent.

STA Travel ⓣ1-800/781-4040, ⓦwww.sta-travel.com. Worldwide specialists in independent travel; also student IDs, travel insurance, car rental, rail passes, etc.

Student Universe ⓣ1-800/272-9676 or ⓣ1-617/321-3100, ⓦ**www.studentuniverse.com.** Competitive student travel specialists, no card or membership required.
TFI Tours ⓣ1-800/745-8000 or 212/736-1140, ⓦ**www.tfitours.com.** Consolidator with consistently good deals on flights and accommodation.
Travel Cuts Canada ⓣ1-800/667-2887, US ⓣ1-866/246-9762, ⓦ**www.travelcuts.com.** Canadian student-travel organization with offices in many North American cities.
Travelers Advantage ⓣ1-877/259-2691, ⓦ**www.travelersadvantage.com.** Discount travel club; annual membership fee required (currently $1 for two months' trial).
Worldtek Travel ⓣ1-800/243-1723, ⓦ**www.worldtek.com.** Discount travel agency with offices in several Eastern and Midwestern states.

Package tours

Organized tours of Australia are usually tailored for those short on time and long on funds; that said, even independent travellers may want to build their stay around one or two planned activities arranged through a tour company. Several of the operators listed offer so-called city **stopovers/city modules**, providing, for instance, two nights' accommodation, and perhaps a day-tour, costing from US$185 to US$450 depending on the location and time of year. Though **fly-drive deals** don't always make sense in sprawling Australia, they're worth considering if you plan to explore just one part of the country closely. Typical prices for the smallest class of car work out at around A$45–75 per day. And even if a package tour is the furthest thing from your mind, before you leave home you may want to check out tour or specialist operators for rail or bus passes (see "Getting around" for some of the options).

Tour operators

AAT King's ⓣ1-800/353-4525, ⓦ**www.aatkings.com.** Offers a wide selection of escorted and independent tours, the best of which are 4WD Wilderness Safari tours and camping adventures.
Abercrombie and Kent ⓣ1-800/554-7016, ⓦ**www.abercrombiekent.com.** Offers 8- to 21-day high-end tours, ranging from basic tours (including Sydney, Melbourne and the Great Barrier Reef) to more extensive ones (including Tasmania and the Outback). Also specializes in family tours and customized itineraries. Extensions available to Papua New Guinea, New Zealand and Fiji.
Adventure Center ⓣ1-800/228-8747 or 510/654-1879, ⓦ**www.adventurecenter.com.** Customized tour service, offering Australian excursions lasting 3 to 28 days. Tours include 4WD safaris, nature and wildlife tours, Aboriginal culture tours, 18-to-35 group tours, car rentals, camel safaris and rainforest lodges.
Adventures Abroad ⓣ1-800/665-3998 or 604/303-1099, ⓦ**www.adventures-abroad.com.** Small-group cultural/historical/nature interest tours. A choice of multi-country South Pacific and Australia specific tours. Two weeks in Australia from US$3460 (land only).
Asia Transpacific Journeys ⓣ1-800/642-2742, ⓦ**www.asiatranspacific.com.** Long-established outfit with a wide range of customized itineraries and group tours including nature, adventure and Aboriginal rock art.
ATS Tours ⓣ1-800/423-2880, ⓦ**www.atstours.com.** Huge Australian and New Zealand specialist; dive deals, fly-drives, city stopovers, rail/bus passes, motel vouchers and other add-ons.
Australian Pacific Tours ⓣ1-800/290-8687 or 416/234-9676, ⓦ**www.aptours.com.** General interest escorted tours along with cruising and safari packages; specializes in coach tours (US$1500–7100 land only) and fully independent travel.
Contiki Tours ⓣ1-866/CONTIKI, ⓦ**www.contiki.com.** 18- to 35-year-olds-only tour operator. Their 14-day beaches and reefs tour starts at $1070 (land only).
Cross-Culture ⓣ1-800/491-1148 or 413/256-6303, ⓦ**www.crosscultureinc.com.** Well-balanced all-inclusive group tours; a 15-day tour, including flights from Los Angeles, starts at $6200.
Destination World ⓣ1-888/345-4669, ⓦ**www.destinationworld.com.** Offers a wide variety of tours, from budget to expensive. Off-the-beaten-track tours include a pub-crawl on horseback and motorcycle tours. Also offers a wheelchair-accessible bus for disabled groups and motorhome rentals.
Goway Travel ⓣ1-800/387-8850, ⓦ**www.goway.com.** Specialists in travel down under, with airfare deals, independent land bookings, fully escorted tours, over-50s vacations, bus tours, hostel passes, camping safaris, cruises, rail, fly-drives and group arrangements.
Maupintour ⓣ1-800/255-4266, ⓦ**www.maupintour.com.** Variety of South Pacific tours, including 15 days in Australia, or 24 days in Australia, New Zealand and Tasmania (US$2730–6430 land only).
Nature Expeditions International ⓣ1-800/869-0639, ⓦ**www.naturexp.com.** Fifteen-day educational/nature-focused tour

including Sydney, Uluru, Great Ocean Road, Blue Mountains National Park, Alice Springs and the Great Barrier Reef, led by professional guides (US$5040 land only).

Qantas Vacations US ⓣ1-800/348-8145, ⓦwww.qantasvacations.com. Offers a variety of special travel deals to cities (Sydney/Melbourne), the Great Barrier Reef and the Outback, plus Fiji or New Zealand extensions.

REI Adventures ⓣ1-800/622-2236, ⓦwww.rei.com/travel. Adventure tour operator. Their 15-day reef and rainforest trip includes diving, white-water rafting, hiking and mountain biking starting at $2800 (land only).

Swain Australia Tours ⓣ1-800/227-9246 or 610/896-9595, ⓦwww.swainaustralia.com. Customized tours to meet individual travel needs and budgets, from $1400, including tours specifically designed for families.

Tauck World Discovery ⓣ1-800/788-7885, ⓦwww.tauck.com. Upmarket guided group tours of two to three weeks, with optional extensions to Fiji.

United Vacations ⓣ1-888/854-3899, ⓦwww.unitedvacations.com. Varied assortment of individual tours, city-break packages, and multi-city excursions.

Wilderness Travel ⓣ1-800/368-2794 or 510/558-2488, ⓦwww.wildernesstravel.com. High-end specialists in hiking and wildlife adventures; a ten-day tour of Tasmania, including a yacht cruise and luxury inns, starts at $3700 (land only).

Getting there from New Zealand

New Zealand–Australia routes are busy and competition is fierce, resulting in an ever-changing range of deals and special offers; your best bet is to check the latest with a specialist travel agent (see below) or the relevant airlines' websites. The recent influx of low-cost, no-frills airlines has meant a further price drop, with the likes of Christchurch-based Pacific Blue offering special "Happy Hour" fares daily, from one dollar plus tax. It's a relatively short hop across the Tasman Sea: flying time from Auckland to Sydney is around three and a half hours.

All the **fares** quoted below include tax and are for travel during low or shoulder seasons; flying at peak times (primarily Dec to mid-Jan) can add substantially to these prices. Ultimately, the price you pay for your flight will depend on how much flexibility you want; many of the cheapest deals are hedged with restrictions – typically a maximum stay of thirty days and a fourteen-day advance-purchase requirement. The New Zealand, web-based Freedom Air specializes in no-frills, low-cost trans-Tasman air travel, with flights from Auckland, Christchurch, Dunedin, Palmerston North and Wellington to Brisbane plus Melbourne, Sydney or Gold Coast flights from some destinations; there are few restrictions in how long tickets stay open and advance purchase has little effect on ticket prices, which are around $NZ480 return. Pacific Blue flies from Christchurch to Brisbane, Melbourne, Sydney and the Gold Coast, and from Wellington to Sydney and Brisbane for around NZ$500 return. Only Qantas, Air New Zealand, Freedom Air and Aerolineas Argentinas offer tickets that stay open for one year, while Polynesian and Malaysia Airlines offer tickets open for up to six months; there are also ninety-day tickets that fall between the two extremes in price. The cheapest regular thirty-day return fare from Auckland to Sydney is usually with Aerolineas Argentinas (also to Melbourne) for around NZ$350–$500 but flights tend to be heavily booked. Six-month return fares from Qantas, United, Emirates or Air New Zealand to Brisbane, Melbourne and Sydney are around $850–1000, Cairns $1000, Perth $1300 and Brisbane $830. Whether you fly from Wellington or Christchurch generally makes no difference to the fare. Outside peak season, when the airlines often have surplus capacity, they may offer promotional fares, which can bring prices down to as low as $550 for a thirty-day return from Auckland to Brisbane.

Open-jaw tickets – which let you fly into one city and out of another, making your own way between – can save a lot of back-tracking and don't add hugely to the total fare. For example, flying into Cairns and out of Sydney, or vice versa, with Qantas or Air New Zealand, costs from $900. You may also find additional internal flight deals when buying your main ticket.

If you're taking in Australia at the beginning (or end) of your grand tour, you can usually add one or two Australian stops at negligible extra cost, since many airlines go via Australian gateway airports anyway.

Airlines

Aerolineas Argentinas ⓣ09/379 3675, ⓦwww.aerolineas.com.au
Air New Zealand ⓣ0800/737 000, ⓦwww.airnewzealand.co.nz
Freedom Air ⓣ0800 600 500, ⓦwww.freedom.co.nz
Malaysia Airlines ⓣ09/373 2741, ⓦwww.malaysiaairlines.com
Qantas ⓣ09/661 901, ⓦwww.qantas.com.au
Pacific Blue ⓣ0800 670 000, ⓦwww.flypacificblue.com
Polynesian Airlines ⓣ09/309 5396, ⓦwww.polynesianairlines.com
Thai Airways ⓣ09/377 3886, ⓦwww.thaiair.com

Specialist travel agents

Flight Centre 350 Queen St, Auckland ⓣ09/358 4310 or ⓣ0800/243544, ⓦwww.flightcentre.co.nz. Competitive discounts on airfares and a wide range of package holidays and adventure tours. Also has branches nationwide.
Holiday Shoppe 27–35 Victoria St West, Auckland, plus 79 other branches around the country ⓣ09/379 2099 or ⓣ0800/808480, ⓦwww.holidayshoppe.co.nz. One of New Zealand's largest travel agencies brought about by a merger between the former Budget Travel and the Holiday Shoppe. Good for budget airfares and accommodation packages.
STA Travel 187 and 267 Queen St, Auckland ⓣ09/366 6673 or ⓣ0508/782 872, ⓦwww.statravel.co.nz. Fare discounts for students and those under 26, as well as visas, student cards and travel insurance. Also branches nationwide.

Packages and tours

There's a huge variety of holidays and tours to Australia available in New Zealand; call any of the travel agents listed above. The holiday subsidiaries of airlines such as Air New Zealand and Qantas package short **city-breaks** (flight and accommodation) and **fly-drive deals** for little more than the cost of the regular airfare. On the other hand, if romping around the Outback is a high priority, check out any available **adventure tours** as they can be a good way of covering a lot of ground in a short time and getting you to remote places that would otherwise be inaccessible without your own transport. Itineraries range from 14 to 39 days and concentrate on exploring remoter regions, as well as classic rainforest-and-reef trips; prices (not including airfare from New Zealand) start at $1750 and go up to $5000 for extended journeys.

Getting there from Southeast Asia

A satisfying way of reaching Australia and really getting some impression of the distance you've come is to travel **overland through Southeast Asia**, or at least have a stopover en route. This is a very popular route for travellers en route to Australia from Europe, or vice versa, especially Australian backpackers heading in the other direction at the start of their trip. Southeast Asia isn't as straightforward or relaxing as Australia (and you'll need to take appropriate health precautions), but it's a fascinating region and is unlikely to make a big dent in your budget. It also shouldn't make too much of a difference to the price of your plane ticket, since many Asian airlines stop in Bangkok, Singapore, Jakarta, Denpasar or Kuala Lumpur on the way to Australia, and breaking your journey is either free or possible for a small extra charge. If you want to go overland on the route detailed below between Bangkok and Bali, rather than just stop over, you could buy a Round-the-World ticket with an overland component. If you do buy a one-way ticket from Bali, you will still need to be in possession of a return ticket out of Australia to get through immigration, probably best routed via Bangkok.

Bangkok is a popular starting point for an overland route, with return flights available from around £350–400 in the UK and US$750 in the US. From Bangkok an inexpensive bus service leaves twice daily for the 2000-kilometre ride to **Singapore**, though it's a gruelling 48-hour trip unless you make a stop or two along the way; a more comfortable option is the International Express train from Bangkok to Padang Besar on the Thai–Malaysia border (1 daily; 23hr) and then the KMBT train from Butterworth (3hr south) to Singapore via Kuala Lumpur (4 daily; 6hr); you will usually need to stay overnight in Butterworth or Penang to connect with the KMBT train but at least a few days is recommended. Book both journeys a day or two in advance to be sure of a seat; the combined price for first class is UK£27/US$50, but considerably cheaper second- and third-class fares are available. Of course, you could instead go in luxury on the Eastern and Oriental Express, modelled on the original Orient Express; the 41-hour journey via Kuala Lumpur costs from UK£960/US$1730 per person.

From Singapore, you can cross to the **Indonesian islands** of Sumatra or Kalimantan (Indonesian Borneo) and from there island-hop via local buses and ferries southeast through to Java and Bali, from where you can take a short flight to Darwin in Australia's Northern Territory. From Denpasar (Bali), Qantas flies to Darwin twice weekly and daily to Sydney and Brisbane from Denpasar and Jakarta, while Malaysia Airlines flies direct from Bali to Darwin. Qantas subsidiary, Australian Airlines flies three times a week from Denpasar to Sydney, twice a week to Melbourne and once to Perth. Garuda has twice-weekly flights to Darwin, and flies from Denpasar several times a week to Adelaide, Brisbane and Sydney and daily to Melbourne and Perth.

Allow at least a month travelling overland from Bangkok to Bali, but be aware that there is still political and social unrest right through Indonesia, including Bali, and travel through some of these regions may not be wise or even possible. Check the websites below for the latest information.

Ⓦ **www.dfat.gov.au** Australian Department of Foreign Affairs.

Ⓦ **www.fco.gov.uk** British Foreign and Commonwealth Office.

Ⓦ **www.fac-aec.gc.ca/menu-en.asp** Canadian Foreign Affairs Department.

Ⓦ **http://travel.state.gov/travel/warnings.html** US State Department Travel Advisories.

Visas and red tape

All visitors to Australia, except New Zealanders, require a visa or Electronic Travel Authority (ETA) to enter the country; if you're heading overland, you'll obviously need also to check visa requirements for the countries en route. You can get visa application forms from the Australian high commissions, embassies or consulates listed below. Citizens of the US can get visa application forms from the Washington, Los Angeles and Ottawa offices and from the embassy Internet sites.

Far simpler for nationals of the UK, Ireland, the US, Canada, Malaysia, Singapore, Japan and most European countries who intend to stay for **less than three months**, is to get an **ETA** (Electronic Travel Authority), valid for multiple entry over one year. Applied for online, it replaces the visa stamp in your passport (ETAs are computerized) and saves the hassle of queuing or sending off your passport. ETAs can be applied for on the Web with a credit card for A$20 (see the Australian government websites below or go directly to Ⓦwww.eta.immi.gov.au) or are available from travel agents and airlines at the same time as you book your flight. In this case an additional fee may be levied on top of the cost of your ETA – in the UK around £17.

Citizens of other countries and visitors who intend to stay for longer than three months should apply for a **visitor visa**, valid for **three to six months**. You'll need to complete an application form and lodge it either in person or by post to the embassy or consulate. It costs A$65 (or the equivalent in your country) and takes up to three weeks to process. If you think you might stay more than three months, it's best to get the longer visa before departure, because once you get to Australia extensions cost A$160. Once issued, a visa usually allows multiple entries, so long as your passport is valid.

An important condition for all holiday visa applications is that you have **adequate funds** both to support yourself during your stay – at least A$1000 a month – and eventually to get yourself home again. If you're visiting immediate family who live in Australia – parent, spouse, child, brother or sister – you can apply for a **Sponsored Family Visitor Visa (A$65)**, which has fewer restrictions.

Twelve-month **working holiday visas** are easily available to British, Irish, Canadian, Dutch, German, Japanese and Korean single people aged 18–30, though exceptions are made for young married couples without children. Unless you see your future in planting sugar cane, it is not a chance to further your career, since the stress is on casual employment: you are meant to work for no more than three months at any one job. You must arrange the visa before you arrive in Australia, and several months in advance. Working visas cost A$170; some travel agents such as Trailfinders in the UK (see p.29) can arrange them for you.

Young **American citizens** wishing to work in Australia might consider the **Special Youth Program**, designed to allow young people (aged 18–30) to holiday while working in short-term employment over a four-month period. Membership of the scheme costs US$550, and applications can be made through BUNAC (Ⓣ203/264-0901, Ⓦwww.bunac.com), Camp Counselors (Ⓦwww.ccusa.com) or Council/CIEE (Ⓦwww.ciee.org).

Note that having a visa is not an absolute guarantee that you'll be allowed into Australia – immigration officials may well check again that you have enough money to cover you during your stay, and that you have a return or onward ticket. In extreme cases they may refuse entry, or more likely restrict your visit to a shorter period.

Australia has strict **quarantine** laws that apply to fruit, vegetables, fresh and packaged food, seed and some animal products, among other things; there are also strict laws prohibiting drugs, steroids, firearms, protected wildlife and associated products. Those over 18 can take advantage of a **duty-free allowance** on entry of 1 litre of alcohol and 250 cigarettes or 250g of tobacco.

Australian embassies and consulates abroad

For the full list visit Ⓦwww.dfat.gov.au/missions/index.html

UK

London Australian High Commission, Australia House, Strand, London WC2B 4LA Ⓣ020/7379 4334, Ⓦwww.australia.org.uk.

Ireland

Dublin Australian Embassy, Fitzwilton House, Wilton Terrace, Dublin 2 Ⓣ01/ 664 5300, Ⓦwww.australianembassy.ie.

USA

Washington Australian Embassy, 1601 Massachusetts Ave NW, Washington, DC 20036 2273 Ⓣ202/797-3000, Ⓦwww.austemb.org. With consulates (no visa enquiries) in Atlanta, Chicago, Denver, Detroit, Honolulu, Houston, Los Angeles, Miami, New York and San Francisco.

Canada

Ottawa Australian High Commission, Suite 710, 50 O'Connor St, Ottawa, ON K1P 6L2 Ⓣ613/236-0841,Ⓦwww.ahc-ottawa.org. Consulates also in Toronto and Vancouver (no visa enquiries).

Netherlands

The Hague Australian Embassy. Carnegielaan 4, The Hague 2517 KH Ⓣ 070 310 8200, Ⓦwww.australian-embassy.nl

New Zealand

Auckland Australian Consulate-General, Level 7, PriceWaterHouseCoopers Tower 186–194 Quay Street, Auckland Ⓣ09/921 8800, Ⓦwww.australia.org.nz. Also 72-76 Hobson St, Thorndon, Wellington Ⓣ04/473 6411.

Indonesia

Bali Australian Consulate, Australian Consulate-General, Jalan Hayam Wuruk No 88B, Tanjung Bungkak, Denpasar, Bali 80234 Ⓣ0361/241 118, Ⓦwww.dfat.gov.au/bali

Jakarta Australian Embassy, Jalan HR Rasuna Said Kav C15–16, Jakarta Selatan 12940 Ⓣ021/2550 5555 , Ⓦwww.austembjak.or.id

Malaysia

Kuala Lumpur Australian High Commission, 6 Jalan Yap Kwan Seng, Kuala Lumpur 50450 Ⓣ2146 5555, Ⓦwww.australia.org.my. Also consulates (no visa enquiries) in Penang, Sabah and Sarawak.

Singapore

Singapore Australian High Commission, 25 Napier

Rd, Singapore 258507 ⓣ065/6836 4100, ⓦwww.singapore.embassy.gov.au

South Africa

Pretoria Australian High Commission, 292 Orient Street, Arcadia, Pretoria 0083 ⓣ12/342 3781, ⓦwww.australia.co.za. Also consulates – but no visa service – in Johannesburg and Durban.

Thailand

Bangkok Australian Embassy, 37 South Sathorn Rd, Bangkok 10120 ⓣ02/287 2680; ⓦwww.austembassy.or.th.

Information, websites and maps

Australian tourism abroad is represented by the Australian Tourist Commission, who produce the annual, glossy *Australia, A Traveller's Guide*, which gives an excellent introduction. It details the country region by region, offers travel tips and ways of getting around and has a useful directory of addresses. You can also get information on the Internet at the Tourist Commission's website ⓦwww.australia.com.

More detailed information is available by the sackful once you're in the country. Each state or territory has its own **tourist authority**, which operates information offices throughout its own area and in major cities in other parts of Australia – some are even represented abroad (those with London offices are detailed below). A level below this are a host of regional and community-run **visitors centres** and **information kiosks**. Even the smallest Outback town seems to have one – or at the very least a pamphlet rack at the local service station – while larger places will often have two or more rival offices. Remember though, most of these associations only promote subscribing or advertising members – the information they supply is not comprehensive or impartial, as anyone in the tourist business is likely to be involved with a tourism association.

It's also worthwhile asking **fellow travellers** about places they've been to. **Hostels** tend to act as information points, with **notice boards** where you'll find local bus schedules, offers of cheap excursions or ride shares, and comments and advice from people who've already passed this way.

Finally, most tourist hotspots will have a **travellers centre**. The most widespread of these organizations are Backpackers World Travel ⓦwww.backpackers-world.com.au; World Wide Workers ⓦwww.worldwideworkers.com; and Travellers Contact Point ⓦwww.travellers.com.au; all have branches in New South Wales, Victoria and Queensland. Once you've signed up with them, they can help you find work and prebook travel and accommodation as you move around; you also get discounted phone and Internet rates, cheap drinks at selected pubs, use of notice boards and help with work.

State government and tourist website

For a list of state tourist and government websites check out ⓦwww.australia.org.uk/qna/html/state%20offices.htm

Australia online

General

ⓦwww.ozemail.com.au/atie/index.html
The Australian Travel Information Exchange gives an easy-to-read overview of key destinations, resorts, tour operators and transport services.

ⓦwww.australianexplorer.com
Comprehensive travel information website.

ⓦ**www.oztravel.com.au**
Online database of hotels, tours, car rental and other travel services.
ⓦ**www.walkabout.fairfax.com.au/**
Better than average directory including travellers' tales, links and not too much commerce.

Newspapers

ⓦ**www.theage.com.au** – The Age
ⓦ**www.smh.com.au** – Sydney Morning Herald
ⓦ**www.theaustralian.news.com.au** – The Australian

Weather

ⓦ**www.abc.net.au/news/australia/weather**
ⓦ**www.bom.gov.au/weather**

Maps

If you want to obtain maps before you go, the Rough Guide **map of Australia** (1:4,500,000) is handily printed on rip- and waterproof paper. Also finely produced are GeoCenter (including NZ) and Nelles, both 1:4,000,000, with good topographical detail: the Nelles (printed in northern and southern halves on both sides of the sheet) includes additional detail of major city environs. The Bartholomew and the new Globetrotter (both 1:5,000,000) are the best of the rest.

In Australia UBD (ⓦwww.ubd.com.au), Gregory's, (ⓦwww.gregorys-online.com), HEMA (ⓦwww.hemamaps.com.au), Westprint (ⓦwww.westprint.com.au) and the state-produced AusMap publish national, regional and city maps of varying sizes and quality. HEMA produces scores of regional and themed maps and atlases covering the entire country many times over. Cities, states, national parks, fishing, hiking, 4WD and wine are some of the many themes covered. BP and the state motoring organizations have regularly updated **touring guides** to Australia, with regional maps, listings and details of things to see and do – something for the back shelf of the car rather than a backpack.

If you're a member of a **motoring organization** or automobile association, there's a chance you'll have reciprocal rights with the Australian equivalent and be entitled to **free maps** and other discounted services. Each state has its own organization (they're listed in the Australian Tourist Commission's guide) and most are excellent – you'll need to bring proof of membership along to take advantage.

Insurance

If you're entitled to free emergency healthcare from Medicare (see "Health" for details of reciprocal arrangements), you may feel that the need for the health element of travel insurance is reduced, but check carefully what is included (ambulance trips, among other things, will not be reimbursed). In any case, some form of travel insurance can help plug the gaps and will cover you in the event of losing your baggage, missing a plane and the like.

A typical travel insurance policy usually provides cover for the loss of baggage, tickets and – up to a certain limit – cash and cheques, as well as cancellation or curtailment of your journey. Most of them exclude **"high-risk" activities** unless an extra premium is paid: depending on the insurer, these can include water sports (especially diving), skiing or even just hiking; check carefully that any policy you are considering will cover you in case of an accident. Many policies can be chopped and changed to exclude coverage you don't need – for example, sickness and accident benefits can often be excluded or included at will. If you do take medical coverage, ascertain whether

Rough Guides travel insurance

Rough Guides has teamed up with Columbus Direct to offer you travel insurance that can be tailored to suit your needs.

Readers can choose from many different travel insurance products, including a low-cost backpacker option for long stays; a short break option for city getaways; a typical holiday package option; and many others. There are also annual multi-trip policies for those who travel regularly, with variable levels of cover available. Different sports and activities (trekking, skiing, etc) can be covered if required on most policies.

Rough Guides travel insurance is available to the residents of 36 different countries, with different language options to choose from via our website – Ⓦwww.roughguidesinsurance.com – where you can also purchase the insurance.

Alternatively, UK residents should call Ⓣ0800 083 9507; US citizens Ⓣ1-800 749-4922; and Australians Ⓣ1 300 669 999. All other nationalities should call Ⓣ+44 870 890 2843.

benefits will be paid as treatment proceeds or only after return home, and whether there is a 24-hour medical emergency number. When securing baggage cover, make sure that the per-article limit – typically under £500 – will cover your most valuable possession. If you need to **make a claim**, you should keep receipts for medicines and medical treatment, and in the event you have anything stolen, you must obtain an official written statement from the police.

Before spending out on a new policy it's worth checking whether you are already covered: some all-risks home insurance policies, for example, may cover your possessions against loss or theft when overseas, and many private medical schemes such as BUPA or PPP include cover when abroad, including baggage loss, cancellation or curtailment and cash replacement as well as sickness or accident. Bank and credit cards often have certain levels of medical or other insurance included and you may automatically get travel insurance if you use a major credit card to pay for your trip (check the small print on this, though, as it may not be of much use).

In Canada, provincial health plans usually provide partial cover for medical mishaps overseas, while holders of official student/teacher/youth cards in Canada and the US are entitled to meagre accident coverage and hospital inpatient benefits. Students will often find that their student health coverage extends during the vacations and for one term beyond the date of last enrolment.

Health

Australia has high standards of hygiene, and there are few exceptional health hazards – at least in terms of disease. No vaccination certificates are required unless you've come from a yellow-fever zone within the past week. Standards in Australia's hospitals are also very high, and medical costs are reasonable by world standards. For general health information while in Australia, check out ®www.travmed.com.au.

The national healthcare scheme, **Medicare**, offers a reciprocal arrangement – free essential healthcare – for citizens of the UK, Ireland, New Zealand, Italy, Malta, Finland, the Netherlands and Sweden. This free treatment is limited to public hospitals and casualty departments (though the **ambulance** ride to get you there isn't covered); at GPs you pay up front (about $40 minimum) with two-thirds of your fee reimbursed by Medicare (does not apply to citizens of New Zealand and Ireland).

Collect the reimbursement from a Medicare Centre (many branches) by presenting your doctor's bill together with a **Medicare Card.** This card is available from any Medicare Centre. Anyone eligible who's staying in Australia for a while – particularly those on extended working holidays – is advised to obtain one. Applicants need to bring their passport and the National Health documents of their country. Dental treatment is not included: if you find yourself in need of dental treatment in one of the larger cities, try the dental hospital, where dental students may treat you cheaply or for free.

The sun

Australia's biggest health problem for fair-skinned visitors is also one of its chief attractions: **sunshine**. A sunny day in London, Toronto, or even Miami, is not the same as a cloudless day in Cairns, and the intensity of the Australian sun's damaging ultraviolet rays is far greater. Whether this is because of Australia's proximity to the **ozone hole** is a matter of debate, but there's absolutely no doubt that the southern sun burns more fiercely than anything in the northern hemisphere, and you need to take extra care.

Australians of European origin, especially those of Anglo-Saxon or Celtic descent, could not be less suited to Australia's outdoor lifestyle, which is why two out of three Australians are statistically likely to develop **skin cancer** in their lifetime, the world's worst record. About five percent of these will develop potentially fatal **melanomas**, and about a thousand die each year. Looking at the ravaged complexions of some older Australians (who had prolonged exposure to the sun in the days before there was an awareness of the great dangers of skin cancer) should be enough to make you want to cover yourself with lashings of the highest factor sun block (SPF 35+), widely used and sold just about everywhere. Sunscreen should not be used on babies less than six months old: instead, keep them out of direct sunlight. What looks like war paint on the noses of surfers and small children is actually **zinc cream**; the thick, sticky waterproof cream, which comes in fun colours, provides a total blockout and is particularly useful when applied to protruding parts of the body, such as noses and shoulders.

These days, Australians are fully aware of the sun's dangers, and you're constantly reminded to "**Slip, Slop, Slap**", the government-approved catch-phrase reminding you to slip on a T-shirt, slop on some sun block and slap on a hat – sound advice. Pay attention to any moles on your body: if you notice any changes, either during or after your trip, see a doctor; cancerous melanomas are generally easily removed if caught early. To prevent headaches and – in the long term – cataracts, it's a good idea to wear **sunglasses**; look for "UV block" ratings when you buy a pair.

The sun can also cause **heat exhaustion** and **sunstroke**, so as well as keeping well covered up, stay in the shade if you can. Drink plenty of liquids: on hot days when walking, experts advise drinking a litre of water an hour – which is a lot to carry. Alcohol and sun don't mix well; when you're feeling particularly hot and thirsty, remember that a cold beer will actually dehydrate you.

Wildlife dangers

Although **mosquitoes** are found across the whole of the country, malaria is not endemic; however, in the tropical north there are regular outbreaks of similarly transmitted Ross River Fever and Dengue Fever, chronically debilitating viruses which are potentially fatal to children and the elderly. Outbreaks of Ross River Fever are now occurring as far south as Tasmania, which is reason enough not to be too blasé about mozzie bites. Aeroguard and Rid are the popular brands of insect repellent.

The danger from other **wildlife** is much overrated: snake and spider bites are an essential part of the perilous Outback myth, and crocodile and shark attacks are widely publicized – nonetheless, all are extremely rare. There are always scares, though dangers present in other countries are mercifully absent in Australia: rabies is relatively unknown here. However, it's best to err on the side of caution and, for instance, never handle bats, should you have the opportunity.

The way to minimize danger from **saltwater crocodiles** (which actually range far inland; see p.650) is to keep your distance. If you're camping in the bush within 100km of the northern coast between Broome (WA) and Rockhampton (QLD), make sure your tent is at least 50m from waterholes or creeks, don't collect water at the same spot every day or leave any rubbish around, and always seek local advice before pitching up camp. Four-wheel drivers should take extra care when walking creeks prior to driving across.

Snakes almost always do their best to avoid people and you'll probably never see one. They're more likely to be active in hot weather, when you should be more careful. Treat them with respect, and it's unlikely you'll be bitten: most bites occur when people try to catch or kill snakes. Wear boots and long trousers when hiking through undergrowth, collect firewood carefully, and, in the event of a confrontation, back off. **Sea snakes** sometimes find divers intriguing, wrapping themselves around limbs or staring into masks, but they're seldom aggressive. If **bitten** by a snake, use a crepe bandage to bind the entire limb firmly and splint it, as if for a sprain; this slows the distribution of venom into the lymphatic system. Don't clean the bite area (venom around the bite can identify the species, making treatment easier), and don't slash the bite or apply a tourniquet. Treat all bites as if they were serious and always seek immediate medical attention, but remember: not all snakes are poisonous, not all poisonous snakes inject a lethal dose of venom every time they bite, and death from snakebite is rare.

Two **spiders** whose bites can be fatal are the **Sydney funnel-web**, a black, stocky creature found in the Sydney area, and the small **redback**, a relative of the notorious black widow of the Americas, usually found in dark, dry locations all over Australia (i.e outdoor toilets, among shrubs, under rocks and timber logs), although they are less common in colder regions like Tasmania. Both are prolific in January and February when there is the greatest danger of bites. Treat funnel-web bites as for snakebites, and apply ice to redback wounds to relieve pain; if bitten by either, get to a hospital – antivenins are available. **Other spiders, centipedes** and **scorpions** can deliver painful wounds but generally only cause serious problems if you have allergies.

Ticks, mites and **leeches** are the bane of bushwalkers, though spraying **repellent** over shoes and leggings will help keep these pests away in the first instance.

Ticks are poisonous – spring is the time when they produce the most toxins during feeding – and attach themselves to long grass and bushes, often latching on to passing animals that brush against them.

Ticks can cause paralysis and death in people but the most common complaint to humans is local discomfort and allergic reactions. However, the Paralysis Tick, a native of Australia, is found from Cairns to Lakes

Entrance and is a life-threatening parasite of both man and animals. This tick is very common and regularly causes paralysis in dogs and cats.

Check yourself over after a hike: look for local stinging and swelling (usually just inside hairlines) and you'll find either a tiny black dot, or a pea-sized animal attached, depending on which species has bitten you. Use fine-pointed tweezers and grasp it as close to the skin as possible, and gently pull the tick out, trying to avoid squeezing the animal's body which will inject more venom. Seek medical attention if you are not successful. A lot of bushwalkers advocate dabbing kerosene, alcohol or insect repellent on the ticks before pulling them out but the official medical advice is don't – it will cause the ticks to inject more toxins into the host's body. Mites cause an infuriating rash known as "scrub itch", which characteristically appears wherever your clothes are tightest, such as around the hips and ankles. Unfortunately, there's not much you can do except take antihistamines and wait a day or two for the itching to stop. Leeches are gruesome but harmless: insect repellent, fire or salt gets them off the skin, though bites will bleed heavily for some time.

More serious is the threat from various types of **jellyfish** (also known as stingers or sea wasps), which occur in coastal tropical waters through the summer months. Two to watch out for are the tiny irukandji and the saucer-sized box jellyfish, though both are virtually invisible in water. Irukandji have initially painless stings, but their venom causes "irukandji syndrome" which can be fatal. Its symptoms are somewhat similar to those of decompression illness: elevated heart rate and increased blood pressure; in addition to that, excruciating pain, anxiety and an overwhelming sense of doom and dread. Box jellyfish stings leave permanent red weals, and the venom can cause rapid unconsciousness and even kill, by paralyzing the heart muscles, if the weals cover more than half a limb. Treat stinger victims by dousing the sting area (front and back) with liberal amounts of **vinegar** – which you may find in small stands on affected beaches, such as North Queensland. Never rub with sand or towels, or attempt to remove tentacles from the skin – both could trigger the release of more venom; apply mouth-to-mouth resuscitation if needed, and get the victim to hospital for treatment. Whatever the locals are doing, **don't** risk swimming anywhere on tropical beaches during the **stinger season** (roughly Oct to May) – stinger nets don't offer any protection against the tiny irukandji which pass through the mesh designed to stop the box jellyfish. Specific reef hazards are covered at the start of the chapter on Queensland's tropical coast.

For more background on Australian fauna, see "Wildlife".

Other health hazards

Australia has one of the lowest rates of **AIDS** infection in the world, largely because the population caught on very early to the need for safe sex, which has been promoted heavily. Infected needles are a danger, not only among intravenous drug users but also from ear-piercing and tattooing. You'll find AIDS helplines listed in the major cities in this guide.

Other health hazards are far less pressing. **Tap water** is safe to drink everywhere. It doesn't always taste good, but bottled water is commonly available. One thing to watch out for in the hot and humid north is **tropical ear**, a very painful fungal infection of the ear canal. Treatment is with ear drops and if you think you might be susceptible, use them anyway after getting wet.

Although you're unlikely to find yourself in the path of a raging **bushfire**, it helps to know how to survive one. If you're in a car, don't attempt to drive through smoke but park at the side of the road in the clearest spot, put on your headlights, wind up the windows and close the air vents. Although it seems to go against common sense – and your natural instincts – it's safer to **stay inside the car**. Lie on the floor and cover all exposed skin with a blanket or any covering at hand. The car won't explode or catch on fire, and a fast-moving wildfire will pass quickly overhead. If you smell or see smoke and fire while **walking**, find a cleared rocky outcrop or an open space: if the terrain and time permits, dig a shallow trench – but in any event, lie face down and cover all exposed skin.

Websites

Ⓦ **http://health.yahoo.com** Information on specific diseases and conditions, drugs and herbal remedies, as well as advice from health experts.
Ⓦ **www.tmvc.com.au** Contains a list of all Travellers' Medical and Vaccination Centres throughout Australia, New Zealand, Singapore and South Africa, plus general information on travel health.
Ⓦ **www.istm.org** The website of the International Society for Travel Medicine, with a full list of clinics specializing in international travel health.
Ⓦ **www.tripprep.com** Travel Health Online provides an online-only comprehensive database of necessary vaccinations for most countries, as well as destination and medical service provider information.
Ⓦ **www.fitfortravel.scot.nhs.uk** Scottish NHS website carrying information about travel-related diseases and how to avoid them.

Travel clinics in the UK and Ireland

British Airways Travel Clinics 213 Piccadilly, London W1 (Mon–Fri 9.30am–5.30pm, Sat 10am–4pm, no appointment necessary); 101 Cheapside, London EC2 (hours as above Mon–Fri only, appointment required) Ⓣ0845/600 2236, Ⓦwww.britishairways.com/travel/healthclinintro). Vaccinations, tailored advice from an online database and a complete range of travel healthcare products.
Communicable Diseases Unit Gartnaval General Hospital, The Brownlee Centre, Glasgow G12 0YN. Outpatients Ⓣ0141/211 1074. Travel vaccinations including yellow fever.
Dun Laoghaire Medical Centre 5 Northumberland Ave, Dun Laoghaire, Co Dublin Ⓣ01/280 4996, Ⓕ280 5603. Advice on medical matters abroad.
Hospital for Tropical Diseases Travel Clinic 2nd Floor, Mortimer Market Centre, off Capper St, London WC1E 6AU (Mon–Fri 9am–4.30pm by appointment only; Ⓣ020/7388 9600; a consultation costs £15 (which is waived if you have your injections here). A recorded Health Line (Ⓣ09061/337 733; 50p per min) gives hints on hygiene and illness prevention as well as listing appropriate immunizations.
Liverpool School of Tropical Medicine Pembroke Place, Liverpool L3 5QA Ⓣ0151/708 9393, Ⓦwww.liv.ac.uk/lstm. Walk-in clinic Mon–Fri 9am–noon; appointment required (MonThurs) for yellow fever jab.
Malaria Helpline 24-hour recorded message providing general information and prevention tips. Ⓣ0891/600 350; 60p per minute.
Nomad Pharmacy surgeries 40 Bernard St, London WC1N; and 3–4 Wellington Terrace, Turnpike Lane, London N8 0PX (Mon–Fri 9.30am–6pm Ⓣ020/7833 4114 to book vaccination appointment). Advice is free if you go in person, or their telephone helpline is Ⓣ09068/633 414 (60p per minute). They can also give information tailored to your travel needs.
Trailfinders Immunization clinics (no appointments necessary) at 194 Kensington High St, London W8 7RG (Mon–Fri 9am–7pm, Sat-Sun 10am–6pm) Ⓣ020/7938 3939, Ⓦwww.trailfinders.com/london.htm.
Travel Health Centre Department of International Health and Tropical Medicine, Royal College of Surgeons in Ireland, Mercers Medical Centre, Stephen's St Lower, Dublin Ⓣ01/402 2337. Expert pre-trip advice and inoculations.
Travel Medicine Services PO Box 254, 16 College St, Belfast 1 Ⓣ028/9031 5220. Offers medical advice before a trip and help afterwards in the event of a tropical disease.
Tropical Medical Bureau Grafton Buildings, 34 Grafton St, Dublin 2 Ⓣ01/671 9200, Ⓦhttp://tmb.exodus.ie. Provides online travel health advice and booking for their vaccination clinics located throughout Ireland.

In the US and Canada

Canadian Society for International Health 1 Nicholas St, Suite 1105, Ottawa, ON K1N 7B7 Ⓣ613/241-5785, Ⓦwww.csih.org. Distributes a free pamphlet, "Health Information for Canadian Travellers", containing an extensive list of travel health centres in Canada.
Centers for Disease Control 1600 Clifton Rd NE, Atlanta, GA 30333 Ⓣ1-800/311-3435 ; Ⓦwww.cdc.gov. Publishes outbreak warnings, suggested inoculations, precautions and other background information for travellers. Useful website plus International Travelers Hotline on Ⓣ1-877/FYI-TRIP.
International Association for Medical Assistance to Travellers (IAMAT) 417 Center St, Lewiston, NY 14092 Ⓣ716/754-4883, Ⓦwww.lamat.org and 40 Regal Rd, Guelph, ON N1K 1B5 Ⓣ519/836-0102. A non-profit organization supported by donations, it can provide climate charts and leaflets on various diseases and inoculations.

AIDS organizations

AFAO (Australian Federation of AIDS Organisations), PO Box 51, Newtown, NSW 2042 Ⓣ02/9557 9399, Ⓦwww.afao.org.au; AIDS Trust of Australia, PO Box 1030, Darlinghurst, NSW 2010 Ⓣ02/9310 0610.

International SOS Assistance 3600 Horizon Boulevard, Suite 300, Trevose, PA 19053, ⓣ1-800/523-8930, Alarm Center 1-215-942 8226, ⓦwww.internationalsos.com. Members receive pre-trip medical referral info, as well as overseas emergency services designed to complement travel insurance coverage.
MEDJET Assistance ⓣ1-800/963-3538, ⓦwww.medjetassistance.com. Annual membership program for travellers ($175 for individuals, $275 for families) that, in the event of illness or injury, will fly members home or to the hospital of their choice in a medically equipped and staffed jet.
Travel Medicine ⓣ1-800/872-8633, ⓦwww.travmed.com. Sells first-aid kits, mosquito netting, water filters, reference books and other health-related travel products.
Travelers Medical Center 31 Washington Square West, New York, NY 10011 ⓣ212/982-1600. Consultation service on immunizations and treatment of diseases for people travelling to developing countries.

In Australia and New Zealand

Travellers' Medical and Vaccination Centres 27–29 Gilbert Place, Adelaide, SA 5000 ⓣ08/8212 7522; 1/170 Queen St, Auckland ⓣ09/373 3531; 5/247 Adelaide St, Brisbane, Qld 4000 ⓣ07/3221 9066; 5/8–10 Hobart Place, Canberra, ACT 2600 ⓣ02/6257 7156; 2/95 Nerang St, Southport (Gold Coast), Qld 4215, ⓣ07/5526 4444; Sandy Bay Rd, Sandy Bay, Hobart, Tas 7005 ⓣ03/6223 7577; 2/393 Little Bourke St, Melbourne, Vic 3000 ⓣ03/9602 5788; 45 Stirling Hwy, Nedlands, WA 6009 ⓣ08/9386 4511; Level 7, Dymocks Bldg, 428 George St, Sydney, NSW 2000 ⓣ02/9221 7133; Shop 15, Grand Arcade, 14–16 Willis St, Wellington ⓣ04/473 0991.

Costs, money and banks

If you've travelled down from Southeast Asia you'll find Australia expensive on a day-to-day basis, but fresh from Europe or the US you'll find prices comparable or cheaper, especially with (often) advantageous exchange rates. Australia is well set up for independent travellers, and with a student, YHA or a backpackers' card (see "Accommodation") you can get discounts on a wide range of transport and entertainment.

Australia's currency is the Australian dollar, or "buck", divided into 100 cents. The colourful plastic notes with forgery-proof clear windows come in $100, $50, $20, $10 and $5 denominations, along with $2, $1, 50¢, 20¢, 10¢ and 5¢ coins. There are no longer 1¢ or 2¢ coins, but prices are regularly advertised at $1.99 etc and an irregular bill will be rounded up or down to the closest denomination, which can be confusing at first.

At the time of writing, the Australian dollar is very strong with over-the-counter exchange rates of A$2.46 for £1; A$1.32 for US$1; A$1.07 for CDN$1; and A$0.92 for NZ$1. To give an example of how the dollar fluctuates, in 2003 the rates were around A$2.90 for £1; A$1.75 for US$1; A$1.15 for CDN$1; and A$0.95 for NZ$1. To check the latest exchange rate, log onto ⓦwww.oanda.com.

Some basic costs

If you're prepared to camp you might get by on as little as $50 a day, but you should count on around $70 a day for food, board and transport if you stay in hostels, travel on buses and eat and drink fairly frugally. Stay in motels and B&Bs (assuming you're sharing costs), and eat out regularly, and you'll need to budget $110 or more: extras such as scuba-diving courses, clubbing, car rental, petrol and tours will all add to your costs.

Hostel **accommodation** will set you back $18–25 a person for a dorm room (and sometimes more for the classier joints), while a double room in a motel costs $50–110, bearing in mind that quality varies and less touristy places or highway motels can be much cheaper. Finally, a moderate hotel costs $75–120. **Food**, on the whole, is good value: counter meals in pubs and café mains often start from $12; restaurant mains cost between $15 and $30 depending on the standard, and many let you BYO (Bring Your Own) wine or beer. Buying your own ingredients is not always the cheapest way to eat in the bigger cities, where there's sure to be a range of budget diners and Asian food halls (with a bowl of noodles for around $8), but overall you'll save; meat and fresh seasonal produce are generally inexpensive. **Drinking** out will set you back around $3 for a small glass of draught beer, $4–6 for a bottled brew, and local wine by the glass starts at $4 for an ordinary drop but expect to pay at least $7 for something choicer. Beer is good value bought in bulk from a "bottle shop" – a "slab" of beer (24 cans) costs around $30; a decent bottle of wine will set you back from $14, with vin ordinaire from as little as $8.

Given the size of the country, **transport** can make a major dent in your budget and is perhaps the area in which you're most likely to overspend. **Pre-planning** helps – an open-jaw plane ticket, for example, saves you having to get back to where you started, or pay a little extra for an international flight that gives you some discounted internal fares. There is also a huge variety of **bus and train passes** available overseas (see "Getting Around" for more on the options available). **Driving** yourself may not always save money but it does give you a great deal more flexibility. Finding passengers willing to share costs is one way to minimize expenses and is usually not too difficult – try the notice boards at hostels and other meeting places. Buying a used car will, realistically, set you back $4000 or more for a mechanically sound vehicle with a reasonable resale value (see p.53 for more advice), but even $2000 might buy something that will get you around – if not in the greatest of style. Renting a car costs $40–70 a day; the longer you rent for, the cheaper the price. Fuel, with substantial local variations, averages 90¢–$1.10 a litre; cheaper than in the UK, dearer than the US, but vast distances see it used up fast.

Youth and student discounts

Once obtained, various official and quasi-official **youth/student ID cards** soon pay for themselves in savings. Full-time students are eligible for the International Student ID Card (ISIC, ⓦwww.isiccard.com), which entitles the bearer to special air, rail and bus fares and discounts at museums, theatres and other attractions. For Americans there's also a health benefit, providing up to $5000 in emergency medical coverage and $100 a day for 60 days in hospital, plus a 24-hour hotline to call in the event of a medical, legal or financial emergency. The card costs $22 for Americans; CDN$16 for Canadians; NZ$20 for New Zealanders (AU$18 in Australia itself); and £7 in the UK. If you're no longer a student, but are 26 or younger, you still qualify for the International Youth Travel Card, which costs the same price and carries the same benefits, while teachers qualify for the International Teacher Card (same price and some of the benefits). All these cards are available in the US from STA, Travel CUTS or Travel Abroad offices and, in Canada, from Hostelling International (see "Getting there" & "Accommodation" for addresses) and Travel CUTS; in Australia and New Zealand from STA; and in the UK from STA and other student travel outlets. Once you are in Australia, purchasing either an **International YHA Card** or **VIP Backpacker Card** will give you discounts on not just the relevant hostel accommodation, but a host of transport, tours, services, entry fees and even meals; they're worth getting even if you're not planning to stay in hostels. See "Accommodation" for prices and details.

Travellers' cheques

Travellers' cheques, such as those sold by American Express and Travelex, can still be a good way to bring your funds into Australia, as they can be replaced if lost or stolen (remember to keep a list of the serial numbers separate from the cheques). Australian dollar travellers' cheques are ideal as theoretically they're valid as cash and so shouldn't attract exchange fees, though smaller businesses may be unwilling to take them, but you can always change them for free at the local offices. Travellers' cheques in US dollars and pounds sterling are also widely accepted, and banks should be able to handle all major currencies. It's worth checking both the rate and the commission when you change your cheques (as well as when you buy them), as these can vary quite widely – many places charge a set amount for every cheque, in which case you're better off changing relatively large denominations. You'll need your passport with you to cash travellers' cheques.

The usual fee **to buy travellers' cheques** is one or two percent, though this fee may be waived if you buy the cheques through a bank where you have an account. Make sure to keep the purchase agreement and a record of cheque serial numbers safe and separate from the cheques themselves. In the event that cheques are lost or stolen, the issuing company will expect you to report the loss forthwith to their head office in Australia; most companies claim to replace lost or stolen cheques within 24 hours.

Credit and debit cards

Credit cards are a very handy back-up source of funds, and can be used either in ATMs or over the counter. MasterCard and Visa are the most widely recognized; you can also use American Express, Bankcard and Diners Club. Remember that all cash advances are treated as loans, with interest accruing daily from the date of withdrawal; there may be a transaction fee on top of this. However, you may be able to make withdrawals from ATMs in Australia displaying the Cirrus-Maestro symbol and be able to pay for goods via EFTPOS (see below), using your debit card, which is not liable to interest payments, and the flat transaction fee is usually quite small – your bank will be able to advise on this. Make sure you have a personal identification number (PIN) that's designed to work overseas.

Visa TravelMoney

A compromise between travellers' cheques and plastic is **Visa TravelMoney**, a disposable pre-paid debit card with a PIN which works in all ATMs that take Visa cards. You load up your account with funds before leaving home, and when they run out, you simply throw the card away. You can buy up to nine cards to access the same funds – useful for couples and families travelling together – and it's a good idea to buy at least one extra as a back-up in case of loss or theft. There is also a 24-hour Australia-wide toll-free customer assistance number (Ⓣ1800 125 161). The card is available in most countries from branches of Travelex. For more information, check the Visa TravelMoney website at http://international.visa.com/ps/products/vtravelmoney.

Banks and exchange

The unfortunate closure of local banks throughout much of Australia means you will no longer necessarily find a branch of one of the main **banks** in every town, though there will be a local agency which handles bank business – usually based at the general store, post office or roadhouse – though not necessarily a 24-hour ATM machine. The best policy is always make sure you have some cash on you before leaving the bigger towns, especially at weekends. The major banks, with branches countrywide, are Westpac (Ⓦwww.westpac.com.au), ANZ (Ⓦwww.anz.com.au), the Commonwealth (Ⓦwww.commbank.com.au) and the National Australia Bank (Ⓦwww.national.com.au); you can search their websites for branch locations. For banking hours, see "Opening hours, holidays and festivals".

Bureaux de change are only found in major tourist centres and airports; they are often open daily with more extended hours than banks, but due to their scarcity and the fact that ones outside of the airports are often closed on Sundays, you should try to change money during banking hours. All **post offices** act as Commonwealth or National Australia Bank agents which means there's a fair chance of changing money even in the smallest Outback settlements – withdrawals at these places are often limited by a lack of ready cash, however, though less remote post offices may have EFTPOS facilities (see below).

If you're spending some time in Australia, and plan to work or move around, it makes life a great deal easier if you **open a bank account**. To do this you'll need to take along every piece of ID documentation you own – a passport may not be enough, though a letter from your bank manager at home may help – but it's otherwise a fairly straightforward process. The Commonwealth Bank and Westpac are the most widespread options, and their **keycards** give you access not only to ATM machines but also anywhere that offers **EFTPOS** facilities (Electronic Funds Transfer at Point of Sale). This includes many Outback service stations and supermarkets, where you can use your card to pay directly for goods; some of them will also give you cash (ask for "cash back"). Note, all Australia Post outlets offer Commonwealth banking services. Bear in mind that **bank fees and charges** are exorbitant in Australia; most banks allow only a few free withdrawal transactions per month (depending on who you bank with – it's well worth shopping around before you open an account), and there are even bigger charges for using a competitor's ATM machine, as well as monthly fees.

Wiring money

Having **money wired** from home is never convenient or cheap, and should be considered a last resort.

You can make arrangements with either MoneyGram International (ⓦwww.moneygram.com) through Travelex offices or Western Union (ⓦwww.westernunion.com) through American Express offices.

It's also possible to have money wired directly from a bank in your home country to a bank in Australia, although this is somewhat less reliable because it involves two separate institutions. If you go down this route, your home bank will need the address of the branch bank where you want to pick up the money and the address and fax number of the head office, which will act as the clearing house; money wired this way normally takes two working days to arrive, and costs around £25/US$40 per transaction.

Getting around

Australia's huge scale makes the distances, and how you cover them, a major feature of any stay in the country. In general, public transport will take you only along the major highways to capital cities, the bigger towns between them, and popular tourist destinations; to get off the beaten track you'll have to consider driving, either by buying or renting your own vehicle. Regular long-distance bus, train and plane services can be found under "Travel details" at the end of each chapter, with local buses and trains covered in the main text.

However you decide to travel, check out the route on a map first, as it's very easy to underestimate **distances and conditions** – you may well be letting yourself in for a three-day bus or train journey, or planning to drive 500km on bad roads. Bear in mind what the **weather** will be doing too; you don't necessarily want to head into central Australia in a battered old car during the summer, or into the northern tropics in the wet season.

Planes

Flying between major destinations, you've a choice between Qantas, Jetstar and Virgin Blue.Elsewhere, **regional routes** are served by smaller airlines such as Kendell, who cover New South Wales, Victoria, South Australia and Queensland; and state-based companies such as Airlines of South Australia, Hazelton in NSW, Sunstate in Queensland and Skywest in WA. While these smaller airlines' fares appear costly, consider the time and money you'll spend on a long bus or train journey.

If you expect to be flying a fair amount, you can save costs **before you leave** home as some airfares to Australia allow you to buy a set number of internal flights at a substantial discount if booked with your international ticket. Qantas' **Boomerang Pass**, which must be purchased before arrival, divides the country into three zones and requires you to book at least two flights (and a maximum of ten) from £100/US$155 for single-zone fares, and £125/US$195 for multiple-zone flights across Australia. Two further zones include New Zealand and the South Pacific. You pay according to how many zones your flight crosses. As long as you have purchased the minimum number of flights before arriving in Australia, you can purchase additional flights at the same rates, up to the maximum ten allowed. Note though that the Boomerang Pass is not always as good value as it sounds: check Qantas Internet rates first. At the time of writing Virgin Blue do not offer air passes but there are always very good last-minute and other special deals on their website.

You may also be able to get further **student and pensioner reductions**: Qantas **backpacker fares** are available to anyone with a YHA or VIP card (see "Accommodation"); you buy a minimum of three flights and get a substantial discount – a useful adjunct to an open-jaw ticket.

Another type of flight offered all over Australia is brief **sightseeing** or joyrides. Everything is covered, from biplane spins above cities to excursions to the Great Barrier Reef and flights over well-known landscapes. A good example is a flight from Alice Springs to Ayers Rock in a small plane which enables you to visit the Rock in a day, but also observe the impressive central Australian landforms from the air. Bill Peach Journeys (ⓣ02/9693 2233, ⓦwww.aircruising.com.au) offers a twelve-day tour by air which takes in the main sights from A$12,000 and includes absolutely everything.

Major domestic airlines

Jetstar ⓣ13 15 38, ⓦwww.jetstar.com.au
Qantas ⓣ13 1313, ⓦwww.qantas.com.au
Virgin Blue ⓣ13 6789, ⓦwww.virginblue.com.au

Trains

The populous southeast has a reasonably comprehensive service: interstate railways link the entire east coast from Cairns to Sydney, and on to Melbourne and Adelaide. The two great (or perhaps just long) journeys, include the twice weekly **Indian–Pacific** (Perth–Sydney; 66hr; one-way, seat only A$252, A$513/conc; sleeper A$805, A$1250/conc; luxury sleeper with meals A$1178, A$1640/conc), and the seasonally twice weekly **Ghan** (Adelaide–Darwin; 47hr; one-way, seat only A$440, A$220/conc; sleeper A$1390, A$834/conc; luxury sleeper with meals A$1830, A$1244/conc). The rail service, Trainways (ⓣ13 21 47, ⓦwww.trainways.com.au) has concessionary fares, which work out only around fifteen percent more than a bus. To get the student/backpacker concessionary fares all you need is an easily obtained YHA or VIP card (you need never set foot in a hostel) or an ISIC student card. Remember though, this is not a European-style high-speed network; journey times are similar to those of buses.

On the overnight Ghan and Indian–Pacific a twin-share "Red Kangaroo" sleeper service provides washing facilities and converts from a day lounge into a sleeper, while "Gold Kangaroo" lays on an en-suite cabin and all meals for the full "Orient Express" treatment. Either of these options is well worth considering for the full two-and-a-half day trawl from Sydney to Perth if you have something against flying. The seat-only option is a reclining chair with generous legroom and a reading light, with access to a lounge and buffet, videos and showers. With a pair of Gold Kangaroo tickets between capitals and/or Alice, you get the offer of **motorail** car transportation for just A$99 – something that's really caught on with southerners wanting to tour the Centre or Top End with their own vehicles, but enjoy the train ride there.

Other than these, there are a couple of inland tracks in Queensland – to Mount Isa,

Longreach and Charleville, plus the rustic Cairns–Forsayth run and isolated Croydon–Normanton stretch – and suburban networks around some of the major cities. Only around Sydney does this amount to much, with decent services to much of New South Wales. There are no passenger trains in Tasmania.

The advantages of travelling by train rather than bus are comfort and (usually) a bar; disadvantages are the slower pace, higher price and potential booking problems – Queensland trains, for instance, travel at about 60kph and require a month's advance booking during the holiday season. The famous long-distance journeys can also be booked solid, so you'd be wise to reserve a place before you leave home if this is a major part of your plans (Rail Australia agents are listed on p.50).

Rail passes include Rail Australia's (Ⓦwww.railaustralia.com.au) **Great Southern Rail Pass** ($590/$450 conc), which must be bought before you arrive in Australia and lets you loose without limit on their routes described above for a six-month period. To be sure that you can make full use of your pass, it's advisable to book your route when you buy it. Other passes are also available from Rail Australia, while Western Australia, Victoria, New South Wales and Queensland also have their own passes available through main stations, but check any travel restrictions before buying – interstate routes do not overlap as far as passes are concerned.

Buses

With the good deals on the train fares outlined above, as well as online flights and popularity in campervan rental, **bus travel** is in decline amongst overseas travellers in Australia. It's almost certainly the cheapest way to get around but there's a lot to be said against spending your trip squirming through the night in a cramped seat while a grumpy driver glares at you for daring to use the toilet. Even though the **bus network** reaches much further than the train network, routes follow the main highways between cities, and may mean arriving or departing at smaller places in the middle of the night. And services are not daily as you might think, especially in Western Australia with only one bus a week to Adelaide. The buses are about as comfortable as they can be, with reclining seats, air-conditioning, toilets and videos: the real problem is having all these things work for the entire duration of your trip. If possible, try and plan for a stopover after every twenty hours – if you try stoically to sit out a sixty-hour marathon trip, you'll need a day or more to get over it and the roadhouse food you'll have survived on. **Discounts** (ten percent, or fifteen percent if you buy your ticket before entering Australia) are available on many fares if you have a YHA, ISIC or recognized backpacker card such as VIP (see p.59), or if you are a pensioner.

The major **interstate bus company** on the mainland is **Greyhound/McCafferty's** (Ⓣ13 14 99, Ⓦwww.greyhound.com.au) which covers the entire country. Along the east coast, there's also **Premier Motor Service** (Ⓣ13 34 10; Ⓦwww.premierms.com.au), which calls in everywhere along the highway between Melbourne and Cairns, plus Countrylink (Ⓣ13 22 32; Ⓦwww.countrylink.nsw.gov.au), while in WA Integrity Coach lines (Ⓦwww.integritycoachlines.com.au) runs from Perth as far as Port Hedland. **Tasmania** is thoroughly covered by Tasmanian Redline Coaches and Tassie Link.

Fares vary according to the popularity of the route and quality and speed of the road, and, though competing companies offer similar rates, special offers can slash prices – it's always worth shopping around. Sample direct one-way fares from Sydney are: Adelaide $141 (24hr), Alice Springs $353 (49hr), Brisbane $100 (16hr), Cairns $317 (2 days), Darwin $590 (3 days 3hr), Melbourne $64 (12hr) and Perth $405 (3 days 12 hrs). Return fares are, at best, only marginally cheaper than two singles, while fares for slower indirect routes (mainly between Sydney and Adelaide and onward, via Melbourne) may be cheaper.

A good value option for bus travellers is to buy a **pass**, though bear in mind that you won't save money over shorter routes and that passes are **nonrefundable** – tie yourself into a specific schedule and you'll be unable to change your plans. Greyhound offers a range of over twenty passes lasting between one and twelve months covering **preset routes**, on which you can break your journey as often as you like and travel in any direction, but are not allowed to backtrack. Sample fares include the six month Melbourne–Cairns "Sunseeker" pass for $481, $433/conc; a one year "Best of the East" which circuits via everywhere between Adelaide, Uluru, Alice Springs, Mount Isa, Cairns, Sydney and Melbourne for $1200, $1080/conc; and the "All Australian" pass for $2458, $2212/conc. Year-long **kilometre passes** are more flexible, giving you unlimited travel up to 20,000 kilometres in any direction until you have used up the distance paid for – these work out upwards of just over 10¢ per kilometre. Tasmania has its own passes offered by Tassie Link (Ⓦwww.tigerline.com.au). Their coverage is not comprehensive, but the passes do also give a third off Tasmanian Redline Coaches' services; passes cost from $172 for seven days' travel within a ten-day period, to $280 for 21 days' in a thirty-day period.

Driving

Having **your own vehicle** really allows you to explore Australia, filling the public transport void away from the cities and allowing you to get to the national parks, the isolated beaches and the ghost towns that make the country such a special place. If your trip is a long one – three months or more – then **buying a vehicle** may well be the cheapest way of seeing Australia. On shorter trips you should consider **renting** – if not for the whole time, then at least for short periods between bus rides, thereby allowing you to explore an area in depth.

Most foreign **licences** are valid for a year in Australia. An International Driving Permit (available from national motoring organizations) may be useful if you come from a non-English-speaking country. **Fuel prices** start at around $1 per litre for unleaded, with diesel about 5 percent more: prices increase by ten to fifteen percent along the Outback highways and can double at remote communities or on stations. The **rules of the road** are similar to those in the US and UK. Most importantly, **drive on the left** (as in Britain), remember that seatbelts are compulsory for all, and that the **speed limit** in all built-up areas is 50kph or less. Outside built-up areas, maximums are around 110kph on long, isolated stretches – except in the Northern Territory, where common sense is your only limit between towns. Whatever else you do in a vehicle, avoid **driving when you are tired** – get out of the car every two hours and **don't drink alcohol**; random breath tests are common even in rural areas, especially during the Christmas season and on Friday and Saturday nights. One rule that might catch you out in town is that **roadside parking** must be in the same direction as the traffic, in other words don't cross oncoming traffic to park on the right; it helps keep the streets tidy.

Main **hazards** are boredom and fatigue, losing control on dirt roads, and animal collisions – a serious problem everywhere (not just in the Outback) at dawn, dusk and night-time. Driving in the Outback is by far the most dangerous tourist pursuit in Australia and every year several people get

Train and bus representatives abroad

Trainways

UK International Rail Ⓣ0870 751 5000 Ⓦwww.international-rail.com.

US ATS Tours Ⓣ1-888/751-5170 Ⓦwww.atstours.com.

Canada Goway Travel, Toronto Ⓣ800-387-8850, Ⓦwww.goway.com, also in Vancouver Ⓣ800-387-8850.

South Africa Holiday Tours Ⓣ21 683 2221, Ⓦwww.holidayholdings.co.za.

Greyhound/McCafferty's

UK and Ireland Contact one of the travel agents listed in "Getting there", such as STA Travel, Usit or Trailfinders.

US Swain Australia Tours Ⓣ1-800/227-9246,Ⓦwww.swainaustralia.com.

Canada Goway Travel (see above).

killed in single-vehicle rollovers or head-on collisions, particularly Europeans on short see-it-all holidays in cumbersome 4WDs or motorhomes. Beware of fifty-metre-long **road trains**: these colossal trucks can't stop quickly or pull off the road safely, so if there's the slightest doubt, get out of *their* way; only overtake a road train if you can see well ahead and are certain that your vehicle can manage it. On dirt roads be doubly cautious, or just pull over for a rest and let the road train get ahead.

Roads, Outback driving and breakdowns

Around the cities the only problem you'll face is inept signposting, but the quality of interstate main roads – even Highway 1, which circles the country – isn't always great, and some of the minor routes are awful. **Conditions**, especially on unsealed roads, are unpredictable and some roads will be impassable after a storm, so always seek reliable advice (from the local police or a roadhouse) before starting out. Make it clear what sort of vehicle you're driving and remember that their idea of a "good" or "bad" road may be radically different from yours. Some so-called "4WD only" tracks are easily navigable in ordinary cars as long as you take it easy – high ground clearance, rather than four driven wheels, is often the crucial factor.

Rain and flooding – particularly in the tropics and central Australia – can close roads to all vehicles within minutes, so driving through remote regions or even along the coastal highway in the wet season can be prone to delays. The stretches of highway between Broome and Kununurra and Cairns to Townsville are notorious for being cut by floods during the summer cyclone season. Several remote and unsealed roads through central Australia (the Sandover and Plenty highways, the Oodnadatta, Birdsville and Tanami tracks, and others) are theoretically open to all vehicles in dry winter weather, but unless you're well equipped with a tough car, don't attempt a crossing during the summer, when extreme temperatures place extra strain on both driver and vehicle.

On **poor roads and dirt tracks**, the guidelines are to keep your speed down to 80kph, stick to the best section and never assume that the road is free from potholes, eroded cattle grids, sand, rocks or oncoming traffic. Long corrugated stretches can literally shake the vehicle apart – check radiators, fuel tanks and battery connections after rough stretches; reducing tyre pressures slightly softens the ride but can cause the tyres to overheat making them more prone to punctures. Windscreens are often shattered by flying stones from passing traffic, so slow down and pull over to the left. Fine "bulldust" obscures potholes and other hazards and invades the car.

At all times carry plenty of **drinking water** and **fuel**, and if you're heading Outback tell someone reliable your timetable, route and destination so that a rescue can be organized if you don't report in. Carry a detailed **map** and don't count on finding regular signposts. In the event of a **breakdown** in the Outback, always **stay with your vehicle**: it's more visible to potential rescuers and you can use it for shade; in any case, you risk finding it stripped when you return with a tow truck if you're stranded on an isolated road. If you are off a main track, as a last resort, burn a tyre or anything plastic – the black smoke will be distinctive from the average bushfire.

Car, 4WD and campervan rental

To **rent** a car you need a full, clean driver's licence; usually, a minimum age of 21 is stipulated by the major car-rental companies, rising to 25 for 4WDs and motorcycles (see below). Check on any mileage limits or other restrictions, extras, and what you're covered for in an accident, before signing. The multinational operators Hertz, Budget, Avis and Thrifty have offices in the major cities, but outside the big cities lack of competition makes their **standard rates** expensive at $70–90 a day for a sedan; long-term rental, specials and even plain bargaining can bring this down to a more affordable level. National has offices in Melbourne, Brisbane, Cairns, the Gold Coast and Surfers Paradise, and Holiday has several branches throughout the country. **Local firms** – of which there are many in the cities – are almost always better value, and the bottom-line "rent-a-bomb" agencies go as low as $30 a day; however, these places often have restrictions on how far away from base you're allowed to go. A city-based non-multinational rental agency will supply new cars for around **$45 a day** with unlimited kilometres.

One-way rental might appear handy, but is usually very expensive: at least $200 extra for the drop-off fee. If you're simply trying to get from one place to another, you could try offering to relocate any vehicles they may have from other cities (ie returning someone else's one-way rental). As a rule, cars are needed in the southern cities as the Wet hits the tropics towards the end of the year. To reserve a rental car from the UK, USA or Canada, contact the companies listed below.

Four-wheel drives are best used for specific areas rather than long term, as rental and fuel costs are steep, starting at around $120 a day. Some 4WD agents actually don't allow their vehicles to be driven off sealed roads, so check the fine print first. **Campervans** and **motor homes** are more popular than ever as the idea of a road trip across Australia becomes possible with rates over 28 days or more from $50 a day for a two-berth campervan in low season (up to $175 high season) with unlimited kilometres – amazing value when you consider the independence, comfort and the saving on accommodation costs. And one-way rental is not necessarily penalised with campervan agencies. Like cars, campervans can be limited to sealed roads but they give you the chance to create your own tour of a lifetime across Australia. Vehicles are cleverly designed and converted – sometimes too cleverly; you can get pretty cranky spending all day *and* all night in the same compact vehicle. High-roof or pop-top models are more tolerable but don't expect to be happy to spend weeks on end in a campervan. Remember, too, that the sleeping capacity stated in the adverts is an absolute maximum, which you wouldn't want to endure for too long. Furthermore in the tropics the interior will never really cool enough overnight unless you leave the doors open – which brings the bugs in. Consider sleeping outside under a mozzie dome or inner tent.

For **4WD campervans**, the high-roofed Toyota Troop Carriers used by Britz, Apollo and Kea, to name a few, are a tough all-terrain vehicle fitted with 180-litre fuel tanks that will only be stopped off-road by your experience or the height of the roof. With these models it's important to understand the operation of the free-wheeling hubs on the front axle to engage 4WD – many a Britz camper and the like has become bogged by tourists who didn't engage 4WD correctly. The only drawback with this popular model is the high fuel consumption of around 7kpl. Lighter 4WD utes fitted with a cabin and a pop-up roof or roof rents can't really take the same hammering but will be more economical, while the large Isuzu-based six-berthers look chunky but would really be a handful off-road and use even more fuel. With all these 4WD campers it's vital to appreciate the altered driving dynamics of an already high vehicle fitted with a heavy body. In the hands of overseas renters they regularly topple when an inexperienced driver drifts off the road, overcompensates and rolls over.

Prices for 4WD campers start around A$140 a day in the low season up to $250 in the high season for a long trip, mid-January to June, in the low season. In addition to the big companies listed below, several smaller or local outfits buy in high-mileage, ex-rental vehicles to rent on at low prices. Branches of the big rental chains and local firms for all types of vehicles are detailed in "Listings" sections throughout the Guide.

Car reservations

Autos Abroad Ⓦwww.autosabroad.co.uk – in the UK Ⓣ0870 066 7788.
Avis Ⓦwww.avis.com – in the UK Ⓣ0870/0100 287; in Eire Ⓣ021/428 1111; in the US Ⓣ1-800/230-4898; in Canada Ⓣ1-800/272-5871; in New Zealand Ⓣ0800/655 111.
Budget Ⓦwww.budget.com – in the UK Ⓣ0800/153 9170; in Eire Ⓣ90/662 7711; in the US Ⓣ1-800/527-0700; in Canada Ⓣ800/268 8900; in New Zealand Ⓣ0800/283 438.
Hertz, Ⓦww.hertz.com – in the UK Ⓣ0870/844 8844; in Eire Ⓣ01/676 7476; in the US Ⓣ1-800/654-3131; in Canada Ⓣ1-800/263-0600.
Holiday Autos – in the UK Ⓣ0870/400 0011; Ⓦwww.holidayautos.co.uk; in Eire Ⓣ01/872 9366, Ⓦhttp://ireland.holidayautos.com
Kemwel Holiday Autos Ⓦwww.kemwel.com – in the US Ⓣ1-877/820-0668.
National Ⓦwww.nationalcar.com – in the US Ⓣ1-800/CAR-RENT.

Campervan and motor home reservations

Apollo Motorhome Holidays ⓣ1800 777 779, ⓦwww.apollocamper.com.au. A full range of campervans and motorhomes, from 2-6 berth and 4WD bushcampers.
Britz Campervan Rentals ⓣ1800 331 454, ⓦwww.britz.com. Long-established company whose high-roofed Bushcampers are a common sight all around the country. These 4WD models are built and equipped to a high standard with long-range fuel tanks and even a kitchen sink and outdoor shower. Britz also offer half-day 4WD training courses for around $200 that first-time off-roaders should consider good insurance. Maui (ⓦwww.maui-rentals.com, part of the Britz group), specialise in campervans and motor homes holding from two to six people.
Campervans.com ⓣ0800/917 4347, ⓦwww.campervans.com. UK-based agent for many of the campervan rentals listed here.
Kea Campers ⓣ1800/252 555, ⓦwww.keacampers.com. Sydney-based outfit with a similar range of campers and motorhomes.
NQ Rentals ⓦwww.nqrentals.com.au, ⓣ1800/079 529 – in the UK ⓣ0800/899 558; in the US ⓣ1-800/308 2075; in Canada ⓣ1-800/378 7019. Cairns-based campervan company with a comprehensive range of vehicles to suit your needs and agents in all major mainland cities and abroad.

Buying a car

Buying a used vehicle needn't be an expensive business and a well-kept car should resell at about two-thirds of the purchase price at the end of your trip. If you're lucky, or a skilful negotiator, you might even make a profit. A good place to evaluate vehicle prices and availability on the Web is at ⓦwww.autotrader.com.au.

If you don't know your axle from your elbow but are not too gullible, **car yards** can provide some advice: in Sydney, they're the most common place to buy a used vehicle, and some even cater specifically to travellers (see p.207) – but don't forget you're dealing with used-car salesmen whose worldwide reputation precedes them; a **buy-back guarantee** offered by some car yards and dealers is usually a guarantee to pay you a fraction of the car's potential value. Assuming you have a little time and some mechanical knowledge, you'll save money by buying **privately**. **Backpackers' notice boards** in

Best secondhand buys

Big-engined, mid-1980s Holden Kingswood or Ford Falcon station wagons are popular travellers' cars: cheap, roomy, reliable, mechanically simple and durable, with spares available in just about any city supermarket, roadhouse or wrecker's yard. At the bottom end, $2000 plus some luck should find you some kind of old car that runs reliably. Chances are, if a vehicle has survived this long, there's nothing seriously wrong with it and you should be able to nurse it through a bit further. Real bargains can also be secured from travellers desperate to get rid of their vehicle before flying out. Ideally, though, you should plan to pay at least **$4000** in total for a sound, and well-equipped vehicle. Manual transmission models are more economical than old automatics, with the four-speed versions superior to the awkward, three-speed, steering-column-mounted models. Smaller and less robust, but much more economical to run, are old Japanese station wagons or vans like Mazda L300s (also in 4WD version), suitable for one or two people. Any city backpackers' notice board will be covered in adverts of vehicles for sale.

Four-wheel drives are expensive and, with poor fuel economy and higher running costs, worth it only if you have some actual off-highway driving planned; to do that you can't buy an old wreck. Toyota FJ or HJ Land Cruisers are Outback legends, especially the long-wheelbase (LWB) models: tough, reliable and with plenty of new and used spares all over the country. If nothing goes wrong, a diesel (HJ) is preferable to a petrol (FJ) engine, being sturdier and more economical – although all Toyota engines, particularly the six-cylinder FJs, seem to keep on running, even if totally clapped out. The trouble with diesels is that problems, when they occur, tend to be serious and repairs expensive. Generally, you're looking at $8000 for a twenty-year-old model.

main exit points from Australia are the best places to look. One of the great advantages of buying from a **fellow traveller** is that you may get all sorts of stuff thrown in – jerry-cans, camping gear and many of the spares listed below. The disadvantage is that the car may have been maintained on a backpacker's budget.

A **thorough inspection** is essential. **Rust** is one thing to watch for, especially in the tropics where humidity and salt air will turn scratches to holes within weeks – look out for poorly patched bodywork. Take cars for a spin and check the engine, gearbox, clutch and brakes for operation, unusual noises, vibration and leaks; repairs on some of these parts can be costly. Don't expect perfection, though: worn brake pads and tyres, grating wheel bearings and defective batteries can be fixed inexpensively, and if repairs are needed, it gives you a good excuse to haggle over the price. All tyres should be the same type and size. If you lack faith in your own abilities, the various state automobile associations offer rigorous **pre-purchase inspections** for about $100, which isn't much to pay if it saves you from buying a wreck – and plenty of people do.

If you're buying privately (or from an unscrupulous dealer) you should also check the requirements of the state transport department: in most states you'll need a **roadworthiness certificate** to have the vehicle transferred from its previous owner's name to yours. This means having a garage check it over; legally, the previous owner should do this, and theoretically it guarantees that the car is mechanically sound – but don't rely on it. You then proceed to the local Department of Transport with the certificate, a receipt, your driver's licence and passport; they charge a percentage of the price as stated on the receipt to register the vehicle in your name. WA-registered cars are a special case because a new roadworthy certificate is not necessary when the car is sold, as is sensibly but expensively the case in other states. This means that cars with WA plates are much easier to sell on wherever you are (as long as you keep the WA registration). You get some really clapped-out bangers still on the road in WA until the police slap an "unroadworthy" ticket on them.

If the annual **vehicle registration** is due, or you bought an interstate or deregistered vehicle ("as is", without number plates), you'll have to pay extra for registration, which is dependent on the engine size and runs into hundreds of dollars. Note that cars with interstate registration can be difficult to sell: if possible, go for a car with the registration of the state where you anticipate selling. Registration includes the legal minimum third-party personal **insurance**, but you might want to increase this cover to protect you against theft of the vehicle (for around $120), or if you've bought something more flash go the whole way with comprehensive motor insurance. Joining one of the **automobile clubs** for another $70 or so is well worth considering, as you'll get free roadside assistance (within certain limits), and discounts on road maps and other products. Each state has their own, but membership is reciprocal with overseas equivalents.

Equipping your car

Even if you expect to stick mostly to the main highways, you'll need to carry a fair number of **spares**: there are plenty of very isolated spots, even between Sydney and Melbourne. For ordinary cars, the cheapest place to **buy spares** is at a supermarket – head for the racks of any branch of K-Mart or Coles. A **tow rope** is a good start; passing motorists are far cheaper than tow trucks. In addition – and especially if your vehicle is past its prime – you should have a set of spark plugs, points, fuses, fuel filters (for diesels), fan belt and radiator hoses – you need to check and maybe replace all these anyway. A selection of hose clamps, **radiator sealant**, water-dispersing spray, **jump leads**, tyre pump/compressor and a board to support the jack on soft ground will also come in handy. Again, if the car is old, establish its engine oil consumption early on; a car can carry on for thousands of kilometres guzzling oil at an alarming rate, but if the level drops too much the engine will cook itself. If you're confident, get a *Gregory's* workshop manual for your vehicle; even if you're not, carry a copy and the above spares anyway – someone might help who knows how to use them. A ten-litre or bigger fuel container is also useful in case you run out.

Four-wheel driving: some hints

The Outback is not the place to learn how to handle a 4WD and yet this is exactly where many tourists attracted by driving a tough off-road vehicle, do so. In late 2002 a solo German tourist was rescued by chance after waiting a week on the 1900-km-long Canning Stock Route in WA, almost out of water and fuel. A novice four-wheel driver, he assumed his bushcamper was an unstoppable, all-terrain machine until he got bogged in a saltpan through lack of experience. Take all the spares listed on p.54, plus a shovel, hi-lift jack and gloves. In addition to the many "how to" manuals easily found in bookshops, if you're planning a long off-road tour, *Explore Australia by Four-Wheel Drive* (Viking) will suit recreational drivers. The following basic hints should help; see also the advice on creek crossings on p.571.

- Be aware of your limitations, and those of your vehicle.
- Know how to operate everything – including free-wheeling hubs (where present) and how to change a wheel – before you need it.
- Always cross deep water and very muddy sections on foot first.
- Don't persevere if you're stuck – avoid wheel spin (which will only dig you further in) and reverse out. Momentum is key on slippery surfaces such as mud, sand and snow – as long as you're moving forward, however slowly, resist the temptation to change gear, and so lose traction.
- Reducing tyre pressures down to 1 bar (15 lb psi) dramatically increases traction in mud and sand, but causes tyre over-heating so keep speeds down. Carry a compressor or reinflate as soon as possible.
- If stuck, clear all the wheels with your hands or a shovel, create a shallow ramp (again, for all wheels), engage four-wheel-drive, lower pressures if necessary, and drive or reverse out in low-range second.
- Keep to tracks – avoid unnecessary damage to the environment.
- Driving on beaches can be great fun, but is treacherous – observe other vehicles' tracks and be aware of tidal patterns.
- Consider a rented satellite phone for remote travel (see "Communications").

Before you set off, check battery terminals for corrosion, and the battery for charge – buy a new one if necessary and don't risk money on a secondhand item. Carry **two** spare tyres. In fact, one of the best things you can do is start a long road trip with six new tyres, oil, filters, and radiator coolant, as well as points (if present) and plugs on a petrol engine. **Off-road drivers** in remote regions should add to the list a puncture repair kit, bead breaker and tubes – and know how to use them. Keeping tyres at the correct pressure and having a wheel balance/alignment will reduce wear.

Motorcycling

Motorcycles, especially large-capacity trail bikes, are ideal for the Australian climate, although long distances place a premium on their comfort and fuel range. Japanese trail bikes, like Yamaha's XT600, sell for around $4000 and allow 100kph on-road cruising, are manageable on dirt roads and have readily available spares. A bike like the **Honda** XL650V Transalp is heavier but has a much smoother engine and fairing which add up to better long-range comfort and reasonable gravel manners.

If it's likely that you'll return to your starting point, look out for dealers offering **buy-back** options which guarantee a resale at the end of your trip; bikes can be more difficult to sell privately than cars. Whether you're planning to ride off or on the bitumen, **plenty of water**-carrying capacity is essential in the outback. **Outback night-riding** carries risks from collisions with wildlife from which a rider always comes off badly; all you can do is make sure your lights and brakes are up to it and keep your speed down to under 100kph.

Motorcycle **rental** has become widely available from the main southern cities. All types of models are available but for extended touring you can't beat something like a BMW GS1150: comfortable, economical and a pleasure to ride loaded, two-up, day in, day out (although tyre choice will be critical for unsealed roads and it weighs a ton). Among other outlets, 1150s are available from Ⓦwww.carconnection.com.au from around AU$120 a day, or at a flat rate of AU$5500 for three months (plus various deposits and bonds). The *Adventure Motorcycling Handbook* (Trailblazer) is a definitive manual for preparation and riding off the beaten track and includes a regional rundown of Australia's Outback tracks.

Hitching

The gruesome 1992 "backpacker murders" changed Australian attitudes to hitching forever. What proved most shocking was the seemingly indiscriminate choice of victims: men and couples seemed as likely a target as lone women, allaying several hitchhiking myths. The official advice is **don't**: with so many affordable forms of transport available, there's no real need to take the risk.

If you must do it, **never hitch alone**, and always avoid being dropped in the middle of nowhere between settlements. In rural areas people seem more willing to stop, but long, isolated stretches of road don't make this the safest country to hitch in; as usual, **women** are at greatest risk. Remember that you don't have to get into a vehicle just because it stops: choose who to get in with and don't be afraid to ask questions before you do get in, making the arrangement clear from the start. Ask the driver where he or she is going rather than saying where you want to go. Try to keep your pack with you; having it locked in the boot makes a quick escape more difficult.

A much better method is lining up lifts through **backpackers notice boards** (though this means sharing fuel costs). This option gives you the chance to meet the driver in advance, and – as a fellow traveller – they will most likely be stopping to see many of the same sights along the way. In out-of-the-way locations, roadhouses are a good place to head, as the owners often know of people who'll be heading your way.

The best way to ensure your **safety**, apart from exercising your judgement and common sense, is to make concrete arrangements before your departure and stick to them. Hostel managers are well aware of the possible danger to young women departing across the Outback with new acquaintances or undertaking work on remote stations, and will gladly receive – or better still – make calls to ensure your safe arrival.

Accommodation

Finding somewhere to bed down is rarely a problem, even in the smallest of places. However, on the east coast it's a good idea to book ahead for Christmas, January and for the Easter holidays, as well as for long weekends, especially when big sporting events are held (see "Opening hours, holidays and festivals"). In some places (the Gold Coast, for instance) there can be price rises and room shortages even at ordinary weekends.

Watch out for the term "**hotel**", which in Australia generally means a pub or bar. Although they were once legally required to provide somewhere for customers to sleep off a skinful – and many still do provide accommodation – the facilities are not necessarily luxurious. Those highlighted in this Guide do offer decent rooms, though the majority of them are still primarily places to drink, can be loud and drunken, and are not usually enticing places to stay.

The other side of this coin is that many places that would call themselves hotels anywhere else prefer to use another name – hence the reason for so many motels and resorts, and in the cities "private hotels" or (especially in Sydney and Melbourne) "boutique hotels" that tend to be smaller and more characterful places to stay, run along guesthouse lines. There are also a growing number of bed and breakfast places (B&Bs) and farmstays where you can join in with farm life.

Other categories of accommodation worth looking into are the huge array of excellent hostels and "backpackers", caravan parks that offer accommodation in the form of permanent on-site vans and cabins or chalets as well as campervan facilities and tent spaces, and self-catering apartments or, in country areas, cabins and cottages.

Hotels and motels

Cheaper Australian **hotels** tend to be basic – no TV, and shared bathrooms and plain furnishings – and aren't always the best choice for peace and quiet. In country areas hotels are often the social centre of town,

Accommodation price codes

All the accommodation listed in this book has been categorized into one of eight **price codes**, as set out below. These represent the cost of the **cheapest** available **double** or twin room **in high season**; single rooms are generally about two-thirds the price of doubles. Hostels and backpackers' accommodation mainly have beds in dormitories. Where this is the case the price stated is in dollars per dorm bed per night in high season. However, in addition, they quite often provide inexpensive single and double rooms for which we have provided the price code. For units, cabins and vans the code covers the cost of the entire unit, which may sleep as many as six people.

In the lower categories, most rooms will be without private bath, though there's usually a washbasin in the room. From code ❹ upwards you'll most likely have private facilities. Remember that many of the cheaper places may also have more expensive rooms with en-suite facilities.

❶ Under $35
❷ $35–55
❸ $55–80
❹ $80–110
❺ $110–150
❻ $150–200
❼ $200–250
❽ $250 and upwards

especially on Friday and Saturday nights. But with double rooms at around $50–70 and singles from $40 (often with breakfast included), they can be better value – and more private – than hostel accommodation.

Motels are typically a comfortable, bland choice, often found en masse at the edge of town to catch weary drivers, and priced on average upwards of $70 for a double room with TV and bath, not including breakfast. They rarely have single rooms, but they may have larger units for families, often with basic cooking facilities.

In cities, you're far more likely to come across a hotel in the conventional sense. The cheaper of these may well describe themselves as "**private hotels**" to distinguish themselves from pubs, the decisive factor being the absence of a public bar. Some of these, especially in inner cities, can be rather sleazy, but others are very pleasant family-run guesthouses. Double rooms might cost anything from $60 and up, and there are often singles available at about two-thirds of the price. More expensive hotels are much as you'd expect: in the cities most of them are standard places with all the usual facilities, aimed at the business community; in resorts and tourist areas they're more like upmarket motels. Prices might be anything from $150 to $300 or more in five-star establishments: a typical city three-star will probably cost you above $120. Similar places in a resort or country area charge $100 or more.

There are numerous nationwide hotel and motel chains that give certain guarantees of standards, among them familiar names such as Best Western and Travelodge, as well as Australian ones such as Budget, Golden Chain and Flag. All have directories of their members, which you can use to plan ahead. While you might find it rather restrictive to use them for your whole stay, they offer dependable facilities and can be used to ensure that you have a reservation on arrival, or at anywhere else you know you'll be spending some time.

Resorts and self-catering apartments

You'll find establishments calling themselves **resorts** all over Australia, but the term is not a very clearly defined one. At the bottom end, price, appearance and facilities may be little different to those of a motel, while top-flight places can be exclusive hideaways costing hundreds of dollars a night. Originally the name implied that the price was all-inclusive of accommodation, drinks, meals, sports and anything else on offer, but this isn't always the case. These places tend to be set in picturesque locations – the Barrier Reef islands swarm with them – and are often brilliant value if you can wangle a stand-by or off-season price.

Self-catering or self-contained units, apartments or country cabins can be a very good deal for families and larger groups. The places themselves range from larger units at a motel to purpose-built apartment hotels, but are usually excellent value. Cooking facilities are variable, but there'll always be a TV and fridge; linen (generally not included) can sometimes be rented for a small extra charge.

Farmstays and B&Bs

Another option in rural areas are **farmstays** on working farms and **B&Bs** or **guesthouses**, the last two predominantly in the south and east. Both offer a more homely atmosphere, though B&Bs especially can be anything from someone's large home to your own colonial cottage – ask what the "breakfast" actually includes. Farmstays are even more variable, with some offering very upmarket comforts while at others you make do with the basic facilities in vacant shearers' quarters; their attraction is that they are always in out-of-the-way locations, and you'll often get a chance to participate in the working of the farm, or take advantage of guided tours around the property on horseback or by 4WD.

Hostels

There's a huge amount of **budget accommodation** in Australia, and though the more shambolic operations don't survive for long, standards are variable. Official **YHA youth hostels** are pretty dependable – if often relatively expensive – and in most places their regimented rules and regulations have been dropped in the face of competition, especially from the firmly established **VIP Backpacker Card** network, whose membership card is as useful and widely known as the YHA. Another established network of backpacker hostels is **Nomads** which also issues a membership card entitling holders to plenty of discounts.

At their best, hostels and backpackers' accommodation – both names are widely used, and don't necessarily imply membership of an organization – are excellent value and are good places to meet other travellers and get on the grapevine. There's often a choice of dormitories, double or family rooms, plus bike rental, kitchen, games room, TV, Internet access, a pool and help with finding work or organizing trips. Many have useful notice boards, organized activities and tours. At their worst, their double rooms are poorer value than local hotel accommodation, and some are simply grubby, rapid-turnover dives – affiliation to an organization does not ensure quality. Hostels charge $16–30 or more for a dormitory bed, with doubles – if available – from around $45.

Most establishments, being either hygienically minded or forced by local council regulations, prohibit the use of personal sleeping bags and instead provide all bedding needs, but it might be a good idea to carry at least a sheet sleeping bag for the few hostels which still don't provide linen.

Youth hostel associations

In England and Wales

Youth Hostel Association (YHA) Trevelyan House, Dimple Rd, Matlock, Derbyshire DE4 3YH ⓣ01629/592 600, ⓦwww.yha.org.uk. Annual membership £14; under-18s £7; family £27 (one-parent family £14); group £14; lifetime £200 (or five annual payments of £41).

In Scotland

Scottish Youth Hostel Association 7 Glebe Crescent, Stirling FK8 2JA ⓣ0870/155 3255, ⓦwww.syha.org.uk. Annual membership £6, under-18s £2.50.

In Ireland

An Óige 61 Mountjoy St, Dublin 7 ⓣ01/830 4555, ⓦwww.irelandyha.org.
Annual membership €20; under-18s €10; family €40; lifetime €100.

Hostel passes

If you're travelling on a budget, it's well worth laying your hands on at least one of the following **hostel passes**, which give you cheaper rates – around ten percent off – on accommodation at member hostels, and also entitle you to a wide range of other discounts on everything from bus tickets and tours to phone calls, museum entry fees and meals.

Probably of most use in Australia is a **VIP Backpacker Card**, which doubles as a rechargeable eKit phone card with a few dollars' worth of phone calls factored into the price of the card ($32 for one year, $44 for two years). Anyone can obtain it from member hostels in Australia or over the Net at ⓦwww.backpackers.com.au (add $6 for postage and handling). At present there are around 140 member hostels around the country, and your card will also be valid at a score more in New Zealand and Fiji.

Another organization that works along similar lines is **Nomads**; their card, which also doubles as a rechargeable phone card, costs $29, and can be bought at their hostels in Australia or on the Web at ⓦwww.nomadsworld.com. Their network comprises about 70 hostels in Australia, many of them in old pubs, a few of them "working hostels" in country areas specializing in harvest work, and there are also affiliated hostels in New Zealand, Fiji, and a few other countries.

Yet another option is an **International YHA card**, available through your national youth hostel association before you leave home, or you can purchase a one-year Hostelling International card in Australia for $35. Australian residents can, of course, also join in Australia but must pay $52. YHA Membership and Travel Centres can be found in Sydney, Darwin, Brisbane, Cairns, Adelaide, Hobart, Melbourne and Perth, at many YHA hostels, and on their website ⓦyha.com.au. Australian YHA hostels number about 140, with thousands more worldwide.

Hostelling International Northern Ireland 22–32 Donegall Rd, Belfast BT12 5JN ⓣ028/9032 4733, ⓦwww.hini.org.uk. Adult membership £13; under-18s £6; family £25; lifetime £75.

In the US

Hostelling International-American Youth Hostels (HI-AYH) 8401 Colesville Rd, Suite 600, Silver Spring, MD 20910 ⓣ301/495-1240, ⓦwww.hiayh.org. Annual membership for adults (18–54) is $28, for seniors (55 or over) is $18, and for under-18s and groups of ten or more, is free. Lifetime memberships are $250.

In Canada

Hostelling International/Canadian Hostelling Association 75 Nicholas St, Ottawa, ON K2P 1C3 ⓣ613/569-1400, ⓦwww.hostellingintl.ca. Individual Adult membership costs $35, membership is free for under-18s and you can become a lifetime member for $175.

In Australia

Australia Youth Hostels Association 422 Kent St, Sydney ⓣ02/9261 1111, ⓦwww.yha.com.au. Adult membership rate $52 (under-18s, $19) for the first twelve months and then $37 each year after.

In New Zealand

New Zealand Youth Hostels Association Level 1, Moorhouse City, 166 Moorhouse St, Christchurch ⓣ03/379 9970 or 0800/278 299; ⓦwww.yha.co.nz. Adult membership $40 for one year, $60 for two and $80 for three; under-18s free; lifetime $300.

Camping, caravan parks and roadhouses

Perhaps because Australian hostels are so widespread and inexpensive, simple tent **camping** is an option little used by foreign travellers. **National parks** and nature reserves have a host of camping grounds. Depending on the location, they'll have an amenities block with flushing toilets, hot and cold showers plus a barbecue and picnic tables, or nothing at all. Australia has some remarkably hard ground, as well as lots of sand, so vital **equipment** includes ground mats and a range of pegs – some wide for sand, others narrow for soil. A hatchet for splitting firewood is light to carry and doubles as a hammer. Fuel stoves are recommended, but if you do build a fire, make sure it doesn't get out of control – and always observe any fire bans. In national parks, **bushcamping** is often the only option for staying overnight: some park sites have hot showers, drinking water, a barbeque and toilets; others provide absolutely nothing. Prices depend on state policy and site facilities, and you'll usually need a permit from the local NPWS (National Parks and Wildlife Service) office, details of which are given throughout the Guide. Payment will be either by **self-registration** (fill in a form, put it into an envelope together with the required money, and drop it off in a box on the camp ground), or a park ranger will do the rounds and collect the money.

Camping rough by the road is not a good idea, even if you take the usual precautions of setting up away from the roadside and avoiding dry riverbeds. If you have to do it, try and ensure you're not too visible: having a group of drunks pitch into your camp at midnight is not an enjoyable experience. Animals are unlikely to pose a threat, except to your food – keep it in your tent or a secure container, or be prepared to be woken by their nocturnal shenanigans.

All over Australia, **caravan parks** (sometimes called holiday parks) are usually extraordinarily well-equipped: in addition to an amenities block and a coin-operated laundry, very often you'll get an ironing board, a camp kitchen, a coin-operated gas barbecue, a kiosk and a swimming pool, maybe even a children's playground, tennis court and a boat-launching ramp. If you are travelling without a tent, renting an on-site van (with cooking facilities but shared facilities) is a cheap, if somewhat basic, accommodation option, whereas cabins usually come with cooking facilities and an en-suite bathroom. In some upmarket caravan parks, cabins can even be slightly more expensive than a motel room, but as they are larger and better equipped, they are a good choice for families or groups travelling together.

Expect to pay $10–18 per tent for an unpowered site, or $36–90 for a van or cabin, depending on its location, age, size and equipment. Highway **roadhouses** are similar, combining a range of accommodation with fuel and restaurants for long-distance travellers.

Eating and drinking

Australia is almost two separate nations when it comes to food. In the cities of the southeast – especially Melbourne – there's a range of cosmopolitan and inexpensive restaurants and cafés featuring almost every imaginable cuisine. Here there's an exceptionally high ratio of eating places to people, and they survive because people eat out so much – three times a week is not unusual. Remote country areas are the complete antithesis of this, where the only thing better than meat pies and microwaveable fast food are the plain, straightforward counter meals served at the local hotel, or a slightly more upmarket bistro or basic Chinese restaurant.

Traditionally, Australian food found its roots in the English overcooked-meat-and-three-veg "common-sense cookery" mould. Two things have rescued the country from its culinary destitution: **immigration** and an extraordinary range of superb, locally produced fresh **ingredients** that not even the most ham-fisted chef could ruin. Various ethnic cuisines are briefly discussed below, but in addition to introducing their own cuisine, immigrants have had at least as profound an effect on mainstream Australian food. "Contemporary Australian" cuisine is an exciting blend of tastes and influences from around the world – particularly Asia and the Mediterranean – and many not specifically "ethnic" restaurants will have a menu that includes properly prepared curry, dolmades and fettuccine alongside steak and prawns. This healthy, eclectic – and above all, fresh – modern Australian cuisine has a lot in common with California cooking styles, and both go under the banner of "East meets West" or "Fusion" cuisine.

Australian food

Meat is plentiful, cheap and excellent: steak forms the mainstay of the pub counter meal and of the ubiquitous **barbie**, or barbecue – as Australian an institution as you could hope to find. Even if no one invites you along to one, you can still enjoy a barbie: free or coin-operated electric barbecues can be found in car parks, campsites and beauty spots all over the country. As well as beef and lamb, you may also find **exotic meats**, especially in the more upmarket restaurants. Emu, buffalo, camel and witchetty grubs may be served, but the two most common are kangaroo, a rich, tender and virtually fat-free meat, and crocodile, which tastes like a mix of chicken and pork and is at its best when simply grilled. At the coast, and elsewhere in specialist restaurants, there's tremendous **seafood**: prawns and oysters, mud crabs, Moreton Bay bugs (small crustaceans) and yabbies (sea- and freshwater crayfish), lobsters, and a wide variety of fresh- and seawater fish – barramundi has a reputation as one of the finest, but is easily beaten by sweetlips or coral trout.

Fruit is good, too, from Tasmanian apples and pears to tropical bananas, pawpaw (papaya), mangoes, avocados, citrus fruits, custard apples, lychees, pineapples, passion fruit, star fruit and coconuts – few of them native, but delicious nonetheless. **Vegetables** are also fresh, cheap and good, and include everything from European cauliflowers and potatoes to Chinese bok choy and Indian bitter gourds. Note that aubergine is known as eggplant, courgettes as zucchini and red or green peppers as capsicums.

Vegetarians might assume that they'll face a narrow choice of food in "meatocentric" Australia, and in the country areas that's probably true. But elsewhere most restaurants will have one vegetarian option at least, and in the cities veggie cafés have cultivated a wholesome, trendy image that suits Australians' active, health-conscious nature.

Finally, a word on **eskies** – insulated food containers varying from handy "six-pack" sizes to cavernous sixty-litre trunks capable of refrigerating a weekend's worth of food or beer. No barbie or camping trip is complete

Bushtucker

The first European colonists decided that the country was not "owned" by the **Aborigines** because they didn't systematically farm the land. As many frustrated pastoralists later came to realize, this was a direct response to Australia's erratic seasons, which don't lend themselves to European farming methods with any degree of long-term security. Instead, Aborigines followed a **nomadic lifestyle** within extensive tribal boundaries, following seasonal game and plants and promoting both by annually burning off grassland.

Along the coast people speared turtles and dugong from outrigger canoes, caught **fish** in stone traps, piled emptied oyster shells into giant middens, and even co-operated with dolphins to herd fish into shallows. Other animals caught all over the country were possums, snakes (highly prized), goannas, emus and kangaroos. These **animals** were thrown straight onto a fire and cooked in their own juices, and their skins, bones and fat were sometimes used as clothing, tools and ointment respectively. More meagre pickings were provided by honey and green ants, water-holding frogs, moths and various grubs – the witchetty (or *witjuti*) being the best known. Foot-long ooli worms were drawn out of rotten mangrove trunks and tiny native bees were tagged with strands of spider web and then followed to their hives for honey; another sweet treat was mulga resin, picked off the tree trunk.

Plants, usually gathered by women, were used extensively and formed the bulk of the diet. The cabbage palm, sea almond, mangrove seeds, pandanus and dozens of fruits, including tropical coconuts, plums and figs, all grew along the coast. Inland were samphire bush, wild tomatoes and "citrus", grasstree hearts, cycad nuts (very toxic until washed, but high in starch), native millet, wattle seeds, waterlily tubers, nardoo seeds (a water fern), fungi, macadamia nuts, quandongs, and bunya pine nuts – the last had great social importance in southern Queensland, where they were eaten at huge feasts. In Queensland's far north you'll find one of the few surviving traditional styles of cooking, the Torres Strait Islander *kup maori* – meat and vegetables wrapped in banana leaves and roasted in an underground oven.

It's tempting to taste some bushfoods, and a good few city **restaurants** are now experimenting with them as ingredients; otherwise you'll need expert guidance, as many plants are poisonous. A few **tours** and safaris (particularly in the Northern Territory) give an introduction to living off the land; for further reading, try *Bush Tucker: Australia's Wild Food Harvest* by Tim Low.

without a couple of eskies. The brand name "Esky" has been adopted to describe all similar products.

Ethnic food

Since World War II wave after wave of immigrants have brought a huge variety of ethnic cuisines to Australia: first North European, then Mediterranean and most recently Asian.

Chinese

Chinese restaurants were on the scene early in Australia – a result of post-goldrush Chinese enterprise – and Sydney, Melbourne and Darwin have Chinese connections dating back to the 1850s. The Chinese restaurants you'll find in most of the country tend to be rather old-fashioned and heavily reliant on MSG, but they're often the only alternative to Australian food. In contrast, the Chinatown area of big cities will provide a chance to sample some regional Chinese dishes as well as the usual Cantonese fare.

Two specialities served in Chinese restaurants are *yum cha* (or dim sum), lots of little titbits such as steamed buns and dumplings served from trolleys; and steamboat, an Asian version of fondue. Both are tasty and extremely good value for money – especially for a group.

Other Asian cuisines

Since the 1970s a new wave of immigrants from Southeast Asia has further energized

Australian cuisine. **Vietnamese** restaurants not only offer some of the cheapest meals anywhere, they also come with the freshest of ingredients: accompanying most meals is a plate of red chillies, lemon wedges and crunchy beansprouts.

There are numerous **Malaysian** and **Indonesian** restaurants and market stalls, where hearty noodle soups and satays with hot peanut sauce are served up. Hawker-style stalls in city food courts often serve *laksa*, a huge bowl of hot and spicy coconut-milk-based soup full of noodles, tofu and chicken or prawns.

The biggest success of them all, however, are the **Thai** restaurants, and it's hard to believe that they've been around for less than twenty years. Dishes can be fiery, yet subtly flavoured, with ingredients such as basil, lemongrass, garlic, chilli and coriander.

Because so much fresh seafood is available in Australia, **Japanese** food is more accessible – and less expensive – that it is in many other countries. There may not be a large Japanese population, but there are a huge number of Japanese visitors, and plenty of places catering for them (you'll find lots on the Gold Coast and in Cairns, for example).

Mongolian barbecues sound like a short-lived novelty but in fact are quite good: an unusual, fast and inexpensive complement to the already diverse Asian food culture. Thinly sliced meat or seafood is added to a selection of sliced vegetables and stir-fried in a soy-type sauce before your eyes on a giant wok – a Mongol warrior's shield is said to have been the original cooking utensil.

Italian – and coffee

The **Italian** influence on Australian cooking has been enormous. Second in number only to the English as an ethnic group, the Italians brought with them their love of food, which was a perfect complement to the Australian climate and way of life, and from the 1950s pizzerias, espresso and *gelati* bars, and the then-exotic taste of garlic, were conquering palates countrywide. One particularly Australian metamorphosis is **focaccia**, now a staple of every city café and even beginning to make an appearance in country towns.

Infamous Australian foods

Chicko Roll Imagine a wrapper of stodgy dough covered in breadcrumbs, filled with a neutered mess of chicken, cabbage, thickeners and flavourings, and then deep fried. You could only get away with it in Australia.

Damper Sounding positively wholesome in this company, "damper" is the swagman's staple – soda bread baked in a pot buried in the ashes of a fire. It's not hard to make after a few attempts – the secret is in the heat of the coals and a splash of beer.

Lamington A chocolate-coated sponge cube rolled in shredded coconut.

Pavlova (pav) A dessert concoction of meringue with layers of cream and fruit; named after the eminent Russian ballerina. Made properly with fresh fruit and minimum quantities of cream and sugar, it's not bad at all.

Pie floater The apotheosis of the meat pie; a "pie floater" is an inverted meat pie swamped in mashed green peas and tomato sauce; found especially in South Australia. Floaters can be surprisingly good, or horrible enough to put you off both pies and peas for life.

Vegemite Regarded by the English as an inferior form of Marmite and by almost every other nationality with total disgust, Vegemite is an Australian institution – a strong, dark, yeast spread for bread and toast.

Witchetty grubs (*witjuti*) About the size of your little finger, witchetty grubs are dug from the roots of mulga trees and are a well-known Australian bush delicacy. Eating the plump, fawn-coloured caterpillars live (as is traditional) takes some nerve, so try giving them a brief roasting in embers. They're very tasty either way – reminiscent of peanut butter.

Australia can also thank the Italians for elevating **coffee** to a pastime rather than just a hot drink. Nowadays every suburban café has an espresso machine, and it's not just used to make cappuccino. Other styles of coffee have adopted uniquely Australian names: a "flat white" is a plain white coffee, a "cafe latte" is a milkier version usually served in a glass (like cappuccino without the froth), a "long black" is a regular cup of black coffee, and a "short black" is an espresso – transformed by a splash of milk into a macchiato. ("Espresso" is also a brand of instant coffee, so ask for a short black if you're after the genuine article.) A cappuccino costs around $3.

Other European and Middle Eastern

Melbourne is Australia's food capital, with its legendary **Greek** population among the many European influences in the city. As well as taverna-style Greek restaurants, souvlaki bars, with spiced lamb rotating on a spit, abound. **Turkish** and **Lebanese** takeaways use a similar ingredient for their spicy filled rolls, while some Turkish places also offer *börek*, small, simple but spicy variants on a pizza. Lebanese restaurants are especially good for vegetarians, with falafel rolls (pitta bread stuffed with chickpea patties, hummus and tabbouleh) making an inexpensive, filling meal.

Central European influences are most obvious in baking, particularly in Melbourne, where there is a large **Jewish** community made up of immigrants from prewar Poland, and there are also a few **Polish** restaurants serving solid, peasant-style dishes. **German** influences are most prominent around Adelaide – as well as at deli counters throughout the country, where you'll find an abundance of Australian-made small goods and sausages.

Places to eat

Restaurants are astonishingly good value compared with Britain and North America, particularly as many restaurants are **BYO** (bring your own): you buy your own wine or beer and bring it with you – you're rarely far from a **bottle shop** (the Australian term for an off-licence or liquor store). The restaurant will charge a corkage fee, usually small – around $1–2, which works out cheaper than paying the restaurant wine prices. Some licensed restaurants also allow BYO wine, but if you add their steep corkage fee to the price of your bottle, you might as well stick to their wine list. You should have no problem finding an excellent two-course meal in a BYO restaurant for $25 or less, though a main course at a moderate restaurant is around $16–21. There are also lots of excellent **cafés and coffee shops** – Italian ones, continental patisseries/ bakeries, and places that serve English-style Devonshire (cream) teas and cakes. In the cities and resorts, cafés will be open from early in the morning until late at night, serving food all day; in the country, they may stick more or less to shop hours.

The **hotel** counter meal is another mainstay, and at times may be all that's available: if it is, make sure you get there in time – meals in pubs are generally served only from noon to 2pm and again from 6 to 8pm, and rarely at all on Sunday evening. The food – served at the bar – will be simple but substantial and inexpensive (usually around $14 or less): steak, salad and chips, and variations on this theme. Slightly more upmarket is the hotel **bistro** or restaurant in a motel, where you sit down to be served much the same food; these places often have a help-yourself salad bar, too, which is always a good alternative for vegetarians. Usually the most expensive thing on the menu is a huge steak for $15–20.

Fast food is widely available, with all the usual burger, pizza and chicken places offering a quick bite for as little as $6. Fish (usually shark or snapper) and chips can be excellent in coastal regions. In cities and bigger resorts you'll find fantastic fast food in **food courts**, often in the basements of office buildings or in shopping malls, where dozens of small stalls compete to offer Thai, Chinese, Japanese or Italian food as well as burgers, steaks and sandwiches. On the road, you may be reduced to what's available at the roadhouse, usually the lowest common denominator of reheated meat pies and microwaved ready meals.

Drinking

Australians have a reputation for enjoying a drink, and **hotels** (also sometimes called taverns, inns, pubs and bars) are where it mostly takes place. Traditionally, public bars are male enclaves, the place where mates meet after work on their way home, with the emphasis more on the beer and banter than the surroundings (see also "Women travellers"). While changing attitudes have converted many city hotels into comfortable, relaxed bars, many Outback pubs are still pretty spartan and daunting for strangers of either sex, but you'll find barriers will come down if you're prepared to join in the conversation.

Friday and Saturday are the serious party nights, when there's likely to be a band and – in the case of some Outback establishments – literally everybody for a hundred kilometres around jammed into the building. **Opening hours** vary from state to state; they're usually 11am to 11pm, but are often much later, with early closing on Sunday. Some places are also "early openers", with hours ranging from 6am to 6pm.

For **take-out** sales (known in Australia as take-away), liquor stores or off-licences are known as bottle shops. These are usually in a separate section attached to a pub or supermarket – in some states, you can't buy alcohol from supermarkets or grocery stores. There are also **drive-in** bottle shops attached to pubs where locals can load bulk purchases directly into the boot of their car; these solve the question of parking, though aren't totally the lazy option as you normally have to get out of the car to make your selection. If you plan to visit Aboriginal communities in the Outback, bear in mind that some of them are 'dry'. Respect their regulations and don't take any alcohol with you, even if members of the communities ask you for 'grog'.

Beer

As anyone you ask will tell you, the proper way to drink **beer** in a hot country such as Australia is ice cold (the English can expect to be constantly berated for their warm beer preferences) and fast, from a small container so it doesn't heat up before you can down the contents. Tubular foam or polystyrene **coolers** are often supplied for **tinnies** (cans) or **stubbies** (short-necked bottles) to make sure they stay icy. Glasses are always on the small side, and are given confusingly different names state by state. The standard ten-ounce (half-pint) serving is known as a **pot** in Victoria and Queensland, and a **middie** in New South Wales and Western Australia, where the situation is further complicated by the presence of fifteen-ounce **schooners**. A **carton** or **slab** is a box of 24–30 tinnies or stubbies, bought in bulk from a bottle shop and always cheaper when not chilled (a "Darwin stubby", with typically Territorian eccentricity, is two litres of beer in an oversized bottle).

Australian beers are lager- or pilsner-style, and even the big mass-produced ones are pretty good – at least once you've worked up a thirst. They're considerably stronger than their US equivalents, and marginally stronger than the average British lager at just under five percent alcohol. Each state has its own **label** and there are fierce local loyalties, even though most are sold nationwide: Fourex (XXXX; see p.426) and Powers in Queensland; Swan in Western Australia; Coopers in South Australia; VB in Victoria; Tooheys in New South Wales; and Boags in Tasmania. Almost all of these companies produce more than one beer – usually a light low-alcohol version and a premium "gold" or bitter brew. There are also a number of smaller "boutique" breweries and specialist beermakers: Tasmania's Cascade, WA's Redback or Matilda Bay, Cairns' Draught and Eumundi from Queensland are more distinctive but harder to find. Fosters is treated as a joke in Australia, something that's fit only for export. Larger bottle shops might have imported beers, but outside cities (where Irish pubs serve surprisingly authentic-tasting Guinness) it's rare that you'll find anything foreign on tap.

Wines and spirits

Australian **wines** have long been appreciated at home, and it's not hard to see why; even an inexpensive bottle (around $12) will be better than just drinkable, while pricier varieties compare favourably with fine French wines – though some critics complain that Australian reds have become a bit too "woody" in recent years. If you're new to Australian wines, you'll always find Yalumba, Lindemans, Hardy's and Wolf

Aussie wine on the Net

Boutique Wines ⓦ www.boutiquewines.com.au.
Links to all those vineyards you've probably never heard of.
Hardy's ⓦ www.hardys.com.au.
Lindemans ⓦ www.lindemans.com.au.
Penfolds ⓦ www.penfolds.com.au.
Wines of Distinction ⓦ www.australianwines.com.au.
Maps and a description of the most important Australian wine regions, lots of links to other websites and FAQs about how to best serve and drink wine.
Yalumba ⓦ www.yalumba.com.

Blass will give satisfaction, but the secret is to be adventurous: you're extremely unlikely to be disappointed. Even the "chateau cardboard" four-litre bladders or wine casks that prevail at parties and barbecues are perfectly palatable. Whatever the colour, a mid-range bottle of wine will set you back about $16.

The biggest wine-producing **regions** are the Hunter Valley in New South Wales and the Barossa Valley in South Australia, but you'll find smaller commercial vineyards as far north as Kingaroy in Queensland and in southwest Western Australia; all are detailed in the text of the Guide. If you buy at these places you'll be able to sample in advance, though there's occasionally a charge for tasting to discourage overly enthusiastic visitors from just trying everything and then moving on elsewhere (see the box on "Wine tasting tips" on p.836). Most bottle shops will, in any case, have a good range of very reasonably priced options.

The Australian wine industry also makes port and brandy as a sideline, though these are not up to international standards. Two excellent dark **rums** from Queensland's sugar belt are well worth tasting, however: the sweet, deliciously smoky Bundaberg (see p.488) and the more conventionally flavoured Beenleigh. They're of average strength, normally 33 percent alcohol, but beware of "overproof" variations, which will have you flat on your back if you try to drink them like ordinary spirits.

Soft drinks

Various colas, Sprite, 7-Up, Fanta and a couple of home-produced brands – Bundaberg ginger beer and Cascade's Tasmanian apple juice – are the **soft** alternatives to alcohol. Bottled **fruit juices** come in every style, and in recent years, **juice bars** have sprung up, like the proverbial mushroom, in all the major cities and larger country towns, serving freshly squeezed juices made from all kinds of familiar and not-so-familiar fruits. There's also a range of **spring waters** from several sources along the Great Dividing Range – a relief at times from the heavily chlorinated tap water. Sickly **flavoured milk** is another national institution: every store's fridge will be packed with different-flavoured cartons.

Communications

Australia may be far away to some, but efficient international communication has enabled the visitor from abroad to be in contact wherever they are. To ensure you're not waking somebody up when phoning, see "Directory" for the relevant time zone.

Mail

Every town of any size will have a **post office**, and where there isn't one there'll be an **Australia Post agency**, usually at the general store. Post offices and agencies are officially open Monday to Friday 9am to 5pm. Agencies might have an hour off during the day for lunch or close early, and big city GPOs sometimes open late or on Saturday morning. Out in the country it's rare to see postboxes, so you'll usually have to take your mail to the nearest post office or agency.

Domestically, the mail service has a poor reputation, at least for long distances: it will take a week for a letter to get from Wittenoom (WA) to Wagga Wagga (NSW), though major cities have a guaranteed express delivery service to other major cities – worth the expense for important packages. On the other hand **International mail** is extremely efficient, taking four to five working days to the UK, four to six to the US and five to seven to Canada. Stamps are sold at post offices and agencies; most newsagencies sell them for standard local letters only. A standard letter or postcard within Australia costs 50¢; printed aerogrammes for international letters anywhere in the world cost 95¢; postcards cost $1.10 and regular letters start at $1.80 to the US, Canada, or Europe. If you're sending anything bigger in or outside Australia, there are many different services: get some advice from the post office. Large **parcels** are reasonably cheap to send home by surface mail, but it will take up to three months for them to get there. Economy Air is a good compromise for packages that you want to see again soon (up to 20kg) – expect a fortnight to Europe. To get more information on letter and parcel postage rates, and expected delivery waits, go to ⓦwww.austpost.com.au and click on "postage calculator".

Although the Internet has made this service rather redundant, you can receive mail at any post office or agency: address the letter to **Poste Restante** (add "GPO" or "Central Post Office" for cities, unless you have the address of a particular branch), followed by the town, state and post code. You need a passport or other ID to collect mail, which is kept for a month and then returned; it's possible to get mail redirected if you change your plans – ask for a form at any post office. Some smaller post offices will allow you to phone and check if you have any mail waiting.

Most **hostels** and **hotels** will also hold mail for you if it's clearly marked, preferably with a date of arrival, or holders of Amex cards or travellers' cheques can have it sent to American Express offices.

Phones

The two major phone operators in Australia are Telstra and Optus, though all public phones are Telstra-operated and their coverage is wider. However, their rates, on a day-to-day basis, are pretty similar. Post offices (but not agencies) always have a bank of **telephones** outside; otherwise head for the nearest bar or service station – you'll even find solar-powered, satellite-connected booths in the Outback. Public telephones take coins or **Telstra phonecards**, which are sold through newsagents and other stores. Many bars, shops and restaurants have **orange** or **blue payphones**; watch out for these as they cost more than a regular call box. Whatever their type, payphones do not accept incoming calls.

Creditphones accept most major credit cards such as Amex, Visa and Diners International, and can be found at international and domestic airports, central locations in major cities, and many hotels. You can make free **reverse charge** calls using the 1800-REVERSE.

Rates for calls within Australia from a public phone are cheapest daily from 7pm to 7am, and from a private phone Monday to Friday and Sunday from 7pm to midnight, and Saturday from 4pm to midnight. **Local calls** are untimed, allowing you to talk for as long as you like; this costs around 17¢ on a domestic phone, though public phones may charge 50¢. Many businesses and services operate **free call numbers**, prefixed ⓣ1800, while others have six-digit numbers beginning ⓣ13 that are charged at the local-call rate. Numbers starting ⓣ1900 (and occasionally ⓣ0055, though these have mostly been phased out) are private information services (often recorded), costing between 38¢ and $5.50 a minute; a message introduction will be charged at 16.5¢ (40¢ from public phones) when you'll be alerted to the exorbitant charge before being given the choice to proceed.

International calls are charged at a flat per minute rate depending on the country called, whatever the hour or day of the week that the call is made. All incur a connection fee of 22¢, then it costs 37.4¢ per minute to the UK; 31¢ to the US; 44¢ for Canada; and 31¢ for New Zealand. If you plan to speak for a while, you can save money by buying half-hour blocks to all the above countries for $6.60 by dialling ⓣ0018 (instead of the standard ⓣ0011), then the country code and number. Hang up within the first minute and you only pay a $2 connection fee, otherwise you'll be charged for the full half hour: speak for over thirty minutes and you'll pay double. **Phonecards** can be a far cheaper way to call cross-country or abroad. Various brands are available such as *Say G'day* or Go Talk, but all require a minimum of 40¢ to call the local centre, after which you key in your scratch number and telephone number. Rates are incredible, as little as 5¢ a minute with Go Talk, if you call from one of the urban centres listed on the card.

It's also possible to pop into Woolworths and buy a **pre-paid mobile phone** for as little as $99 including a pay-as-you-go SIM card with $25 credit that lasts three months. Or you can just buy the pre-paid SIM cards alone in various denominations for your own handset – UK-sourced units work fine. Telstra is the

Operators and international codes

Operator services

Local Directory Assistance ⓣ1223
National Directory Assistance ⓣ12 455
International Directory Assistance ⓣ12 455
Operator ⓣ1234
International Operator ⓣ1234

International calls

To call Australia from overseas dial the international access code (ⓣ00 from the UK or New Zealand, ⓣ011 from the US and Canada), followed by ⓣ61, then the area code minus its initial zero, and finally the number. To dial out of Australia it's ⓣ0011, followed by the country code, then the area code (without the zero, if there is one), followed by the number:

Ireland ⓣ0011 353
UK ⓣ0011 44
New Zealand ⓣ0011 64
US and Canada ⓣ0011 1

Country direct

Ireland
Telecom free call ⓣ1800 881 353

Canada
Teleglobe free call ⓣ1800 881 490

New Zealand
Clearfree call ⓣ1800 124 333
Telecom free call ⓣ1800 881 640

UK
BT operator free call ⓣ1800 881 440
BT automatic free call ⓣ1800 881 441
Mercury free call ⓣ1800 881 417

US
AT&Tfree call ⓣ1800 881 011
LDDS Worldcomfree call ⓣ1800 881 212
MCI free call ⓣ1800 881 100
Sprint free call ⓣ1800 881 877

main provider and with the widest coverage, but does not include unpopulated areas in the north and west of the country. Vodafone is a long way behind on cross coverage but may work out cheaper solely for urban use.

As anywhere in the world, mobile phone reception will drop off in remote areas. A solution offering guaranteed reception (but at call rates several times higher) is a **satellite phone**. Little bigger than a conventional GSM, they can be rented from Ⓦwww.rentasatphone.com.au in Perth (among other places) from around $20/day and can run both GSM as well as the special satellite SIM cards.

The Internet

Public Internet access is widespread across Australia. Wherever you travel in the country, keeping in touch via the Web is easy and cheap. In the cities **Internet cafés** are everywhere, typically charging $3–6 an hour with concessions as well as happy hours early in the morning. Many places to stay – especially **hostels** – also provide terminals for their guests at similar rates (hotels will charge more) although some places – notably Ayers Rock Resort – still opt for the user-reviled coin-op booths, while at some YHAs you buy a card that works like a phone card. Otherwise, try **local libraries**, who almost always provide free access, though time is generally limited to one hour and you'll have to sign up in advance on a waiting list.

Out in the country, if not at a shop or roadhouse, then even the smallest one-horse town will have a **Telecentre** – a council or privately-run outlet, although opening times can be pretty provincial too. Throughout the Guide, you'll find Internet locations have been identified, where available.

The media

The Murdoch-owned *Australian* is Australia's only national daily (that is, Monday to Saturday) newspaper; aimed mainly at the business community, it has good overseas coverage but local news is often built around statistics. The *Australian Financial Review* is the in-depth business and finance paper to buy. Each state (or more properly, each state capital) has its own daily paper, the best of which are two Fairfax-owned papers, the *Sydney Morning Herald* and Melbourne's venerable *The Age* – both available across the southeast (the two papers share similar content in their weekend-edition magazines). For the websites of these three papers, see "Information, websites and maps". There are also more leisurely populist Sunday-only papers in most capital cities, such as Sydney's *Sun-Herald*.

Local papers are always a good source of listings, if not news. You should be able to track down some **international papers**, or their overseas editions – British, American, Asian and European – in the state capitals. The weekly *Time Australia* and *The Bulletin* are the current-affairs **magazines**. If you're interested in wildlife, pick up a copy of the quarterly *Australian Geographic* (related only in name to the US magazine) for some excellent photography and in-depth coverage of Australia's remoter corners, or the quarterly *Australian Wildlife* magazine published by the Wildlife Preservation Society. There are some excellent glossy Australian-focused adventure travel magazines, too, like the quarterly *Wild*, while the beautifully produced and written quarterly *40° South* concentrates on all things Tasmanian (it's hard to track down; see Ⓦwww.fortysouth.com.au for details). You'll find Australian versions of all the fashion mags, from *Vogue* to *Marie Claire*, plus enduring publications like the *Australian Women's Weekly* (now monthly), which is well-known for its excellent recipes. The excellent *Australian Gourmet Traveller* celebrates both fine food and travel, while *Donna Hay Magazine* and the new *ABC Delicious* concentrate on the gastronomic side of things. Gossipy magazines like *Who Weekly* feature the lowdown on the antics of international and Australian celebs. On a different note, the Australian version of *The Big Issue*, produced out of Melbourne, is called *The Big Issue Australia* and has been operating since 1996. Vendors are homeless, ex-homeless or long-term unemployed and make half of the cover price.

Australia's first **television** station opened in 1956 and the country didn't get colour television until 1974 – both much later than other Westernized countries. Australian television isn't particularly exciting unless you're into sport, of which there's plenty, and commercial stations put on frequent commercial breaks – with often annoyingly unsophisticated advertisements – throughout films. There are Australian content rulings, which mean that there are a good amount of Australian dramas, series and soap operas, many of which go on to make it big overseas, from *Neighbours* and *Home and Away* to *The Secret Life of Us*. However, there's a predominance of American programmes and lots of repeats. Australian TV is also fairly permissive in terms of sexual content compared to the programming of Britain or North America. There are three predictable commercial stations: Channel Seven; Channel Nine, which aims for an older market with more conservative programming; and Channel Ten, which tries to grab the younger market with some good comedy programmes including *Good News Week* and the irreverent talk show *The Panel*. In addition, there is also the more serious ABC – a national, advertisement-free station still with a British bias, showing all the best British sitcoms and mini-series – and the livelier SBS, a government-sponsored, multicultural station, which has the best coverage of world news, as well as interesting current-affairs programmes and plenty of foreign-language films. In more remote areas you won't be able to access all five channels and often only ABC and one commercial offering are receivable. There are now 38 pay TV stations, though the **pay-TV** culture is not firmly established yet as in other countries, and even expensive hotels often still only have terrestrial TV.

The best **radio** is on the various ABC stations, both local and national. ABC Radio National – broadcast all over Australia – offers a popular mix of arty intellectual topics, and another ABC station, 2JJJ ("Triple J"), a former Sydney-based alternative rock station, is aimed at the nation's youth and is available across the country in watered-down form.

Opening hours, holidays and festivals

Shops and services are generally open Monday to Friday 9am to 5pm and until lunchtime on Saturday. In cities and larger towns, many shops stay open late on Thursday or Friday evening – usually until 9pm – and all day on Saturday, and shopping malls, department stores and larger stores are now often open all day Sunday as well.

In remote country areas, **roadhouses** provide all the essential services for the traveller and, on the major highways, are generally open 24 hours a day. **Tourist offices** – even ones well off the beaten track – are often open every day or at least through the week plus weekend mornings; urban information centres are more likely to conform to normal shopping hours.

Tourist attractions such as museums, galleries and attended historic monuments are often open daily, though those in rural communities may have erratic opening hours. Practically without exception all are closed on Good Friday and Christmas Day. Specific opening hours are given throughout the Guide.

Banking hours are Monday to Thursday 9.30am to 4pm, Friday 9.30am to 5pm. A recent change in the law has made Saturday bank opening legal, though it's not yet fully in practice. In country areas some banks may have more limited hours, such as lunchtime closures, or some agencies may be open later, and some big-city branches might also have extended hours. ATMs are generally open 24 hours.

Holidays

Contrary to popular opinion and Australia's commendably relaxed interpretation of the work ethic, there are surprisingly few nationwide **public holidays** – and even when you add in the state ones (two or three per state), Australia lags behind most European countries in having official days off. State holidays are listed in the capital city accounts of each state or territory. National holidays are New Year's Day, Australia Day (26 Jan), Good Friday, Easter Monday, Anzac Day (25 April; see Canberra), Queen's Birthday (10 June, except WA), Christmas Day and Boxing Day (26 Dec, except SA). Perhaps to compensate for this dearth, when a public holiday falls on a weekend, Australians tend to take the following Monday off.

Watch out for **school holidays**, when seaside resorts can be transformed into bucket-and-spade war zones, national park campsites are full to overflowing, and the roads are jammed with station wagons full of holidaying families. Dates vary from year to year and state to state but all schools (except Tasmania) have four terms. Generally people are on the move for six weeks from a week before Christmas to the end of January or beginning of February (January is worst, as many people stay home until after Christmas), two weeks around Easter, another couple of weeks in late June to early July and another two weeks in late September to early October. The minor exceptions to this general pattern are Queensland and the Northern Territory, which both begin summer holidays a week earlier in mid-December, and far west New South Wales, where students return a week later than the rest of the state, in early February. The state with the greatest variation to this general pattern is Tasmania, which has an eight-week summer break, going back to school in mid-February. There are only three terms, with a short Easter break and two other fortnight-long holidays in early June and early September. January and Easter are the busiest periods when you are likely to find accommodation booked out.

Festivals

The nationwide selection of festivals listed below all include, necessitate and are in some cases the imaginative product of, prolonged beer-swilling. Why else would you drive to the edge of the Simpson Desert to watch a horse race? More seriously, each mainland capital tries to elevate its sophistication quotient with a regular celebration and showcase of art and culture, of which the biennial Adelaide Arts Festival is the best known.

Besides the major events listed below, there's a host of smaller, local events many of which are detailed throughout the Guide. Also, all cities and towns have their own agricultural "shows" which are high points of the local calendar. The Christmas and Easter holiday periods, especially, are marked by celebrations at every turn, all over the country.

January

Sydney Festival NSW. Three weeks of festivities take place all over the city – in parks, theatres and cinemas – with something for absolutely everyone, from new film and outdoor jazz to contemporary art and current events lectures. Ⓦ www.sydneyfestival.com.au.

Telstra Tamworth Country Music Festival NSW. Last week. Seven days of Slim Dusty and his ilk, culminating in the Australian Country Music Awards. Ⓦ www.telstra.com/countrywide/countrymusic.

February

Sydney Gay and Lesbian Mardi Gras NSW. Sydney's proud gay community's festival begins at the end of February and lasts three weeks, ending with an extravagant parade and an all-night dance party. Ⓦ www.mardigras.org.au.

UWA Perth International Arts Festival WA. Early February–early March. Australia's oldest and largest arts festival, attracting renowned international artists, performers and attendees to indoor and outdoor events all over the city. Ⓦ www.perthfestival.com.au.

March

Adelaide Arts Festival SA. Starts first week. The country's best-known and most innovative arts festival (biennial, in even years), including one of the largest literary festivals in the world; not to be missed. Ⓦ www.adelaidefestival.org.au.

Australian Grand Prix Melbourne, VIC. First or second weekend. Formula One street racing which follows a week of partying; formerly held in Adelaide, now relocated to Albert Park in Melbourne. Ⓦ www.grandprix.com.au.

Womadelaide SA. First weekend. Part of the Womad festival circuit, featuring world music, folk, blues and jazz. Ⓦ www.womadelaide.com.au.

Moomba Waterfest VIC. Mid–March. A long weekend of partying in Melbourne, beginning and ending with fireworks, with lots of water-based fun on the Yarra River in between.

April

Barossa Valley Vintage Festival SA. Begins Easter Monday. Biennial (odd years) Germanic week-long festival set in the country's viticultural heart. Ⓦ www.Barossa-region.org/vintagefestival.

Melbourne International Comedy Festival VIC. Opening on April Fools' Day, comics from around the world gather at bars, halls and theatres around the city for three weeks. Ⓦ www.comedyfestival.com.au.

May

Bangtail Muster Alice Springs, NT. First Monday of the month. Wacky parades and Outback silliness, with all proceeds going to the Alice Springs Youth Centre.

June

Sydney International Film Festival NSW. Mid-June. Also an important film festival, running for over two weeks and based at the glorious State Theatre. Ⓦ www.sydneyfilmfestival.org.

Barunga Cultural and Sports Festival Beswick Aboriginal Land, NT. Mid–June. This three-day festival offers a rare and enjoyable opportunity to encounter Aboriginal culture in the NT. No alcohol.

Laura Dance and Cultural Festival, Cape York, QLD. Third weekend. Three-day, alcohol-free celebration of authentic Aboriginal culture. Biennial in odd-numbered years.

July

Voyages Camel Cup Alice Springs, NT. Second Saturday. Camel-racing down the dry Todd River. Ⓦ www.camelcup.com.au.

Darwin Beer Can Regatta NT. Third Sunday. Mindil Beach is the venue for the recycling of copious empties into a variety of "canstructed" seacraft. Also a thong-throwing contest; Territorian eccentricity personified.

Melbourne International Film Festival VIC. Mid–July to early August. The country's largest and most prestigious film festival, lasting two weeks. Ⓦ www.melbournefilmfestival.com.au.

August

Mount Isa Rodeo Mount Isa, QLD. Second or third weekend. Australia's largest rodeo – a gritty, down-to-earth encounter with bulls, horses and their riders. Ⓦ www.isarodeo.com.au.

September

AFL Grand Final Melbourne, VIC. Third Saturday. Huge, testosterone-charged sporting event. The Australian Football League final is held at Melbourne's MCG and is accompanied by lots of beer drinking and celebrating, depending on which team wins. Ⓦ www.afl.com.au.

Bathurst 1000 Road Races Bathurst, NSW. Second weekend. Australia's premier weekend of car and bike street racing. Ⓦ www.bathurst1000.com.au.

Birdsville Races QLD. First weekend. Once a year the remote Outback town of Birdsville (population 120) comes alive for a weekend (Fri and Sat) of drinking and horse-racing – a well-known and definitive Australian oddity. Ⓦ www.birdsvilleraces.com.

Energex Brisbane Festival Brisbane, QLD. Huge, biennial (even years) month-long festival featuring performing arts, food and drink, music, writing and children's events topped off with fireworks. Ⓦ www.brisbanefestival.com.au.

Shinju Matsuri Festival Broome, WA. Ten days in September. Probably the most remote big festival, but this doesn't stop the town being packed for WA's annual Oriental-themed pearl festival. Ⓦ www.shinjumatsuri.com.

October

Artrage Perth, WA. Contemporary and cutting-edge performance arts festival taking place in Perth, Fremantle and Midland the whole month long.

Entry into all events is A$60. Ⓦ www.artrage.com.au.

Henley-on-Todd Regatta Alice Springs, NT. Third Saturday. Wacky races in bottomless boats running down the dry Todd riverbed; the event is heavily insured against the river actually flowing. Ⓦ www.henleyontodd.com.au.

Manly Jazz Festival Sydney, NSW. First weekend. Mainly free three-day community jazz festival featuring artists from all over the world.

Melbourne International Arts Festival VIC. Mid–Oct. Two-week celebration of visual, performing and written arts in venues all over the city; lots of international and Australian "big names". Ⓦ www.melbournefestival.com.au.

November

Melbourne Cup Flemington Racecourse, VIC. First Tuesday. Australia's Ascot, a 130-year-old horse race which brings the entire country to a standstill around the radio or TV. Ⓦ www.melbournecup.com.

December

Christmas Day Sydney, NSW. For travellers from the northern hemisphere, turkey on the beach is an awesome concept – on Sydney's Bondi Beach, it's coupled with a lot of alcohol, making this public holiday a raucous riot. Sadly, though, the days of free partying are long gone and the organized festivities are a ticket affair only.

New Year's Eve The fireworks display from Sydney Harbour Bridge is a grand show, and a fine example to the rest of the world of how to welcome the New Year. To get the best views along the water's edge you'll need to get there when it's still light.

Rolex Sydney–Hobart Yacht Race Sydney, NSW. Crowds flock to the harbour to witness the start of this classic regatta which departs Sydney on Boxing Day and arrives in Hobart three days later. Ⓦ www.rolexsydneyhobart.com.

Sports and outdoor pursuits

Australians are sports mad, especially for the ostensibly passive spectator sports of cricket, Aussie Rules football, rugby (league or union), tennis or any type of racing, from cockroach to camel. No matter what it is, it'll draw a crowd – with thousands more watching on TV – and a crowd means a party. Even unpromising-sounding activities such as surf lifesaving and yacht racing (the start of the Sydney to Hobart race just after Christmas is a massive social event) are tremendously popular.

It's hard to escape sport in Australia: people talk about it all the time; sporting news fills up the newspapers; events and commentary are constantly broadcast on TV and radio; and it's a huge source of national pride. The wintertime **football** (footy) season in Australia lasts from March to September; in summer **cricket** is played from October to March.

Footy comes in several varieties. Before World War II, **soccer** was played by British immigrants but with postwar immigration it was branded as "ethnic", as new clubs became based on the country of origin of the players: Australian Rules (see below) was considered the game "real Australians" played. Before the National Soccer League's (NSL) competition was disbanded in 2004, more than fifty percent of the NSL's former twelve clubs had evolved from communities of postwar immigrants – mainly Italians, Greeks and Yugoslavs. The former chairman of Soccer Australia (now rebranded Football Federation Australia), David Hill, believed that their fervent nationalism marginalized the game; his mid-1990s ban on clubs that included national flags in their logos won support as well as accusations of the pursuance of a policy of "ethnic cleansing". The new A-League competition, set to begin in August 2005, with eight teams from Australia and New Zealand, is the latest attempt to promote national rather than localised, politicised interest in the sport. The best players invariably head off to play overseas but can usually be seen in Australia's national team, the Socceroos. **Rugby union** is also very much a minority interest domestically. However, the introduction of a Super 12 competition, involving teams from Australia, New Zealand and South Africa, has generated a much greater interest in what was formerly an elitist sport, and the national team, the Wallabies, are hugely popular.

Australian Rules ("Aussie Rules") football dominates Victoria, Tasmania, South Australia and Western Australia. It's an extraordinary, anarchic, no-holds-barred, eighteen-a-side brawl, most closely related to Gaelic football and known dismissively north of the Victorian border as "aerial ping pong". The ball can be propelled by any means necessary, and the fact that players aren't sent off for misconduct ensures a lively, skilful and, above all, gladiatorial confrontation. Aussie Rules stars have delightful sobriquets such as "Tugger" and "Crackers", and their macho garb consists of tiny butt-hugging shorts and bicep-revealing tank tops. The game is mostly played on cricket grounds, with a ball similar to that used in rugby or American football. The aim is to get the ball through the central uprights for a goal (six points). There are four 25-minute quarters, plus lots of time added on for injury. Despite the violence on the pitch (or perhaps because of it), Aussie Rules fans tend to be loyal and well behaved. Victoria has traditionally been the home of the game, and Victorian sides are expected to win the AFL Flag, decided at the Grand Final in September, as a matter of course.

In New South Wales and Queensland **Rugby League** attracts the fanatics, especially for the hard-fought **State of Origin** matches. The thirteen-a-side game is one at which the Australians seem permanent world champions, despite having a relatively small professional league. Formerly run by the Australian Rugby League (ARL), the game was split down the middle in 1996, when Rupert Murdoch launched Super League in an attempt to gain ratings for his Foxtel TV station. It quickly became obvious that the game could not support two separate competitions, and in 1997 they united to form the National Rugby League (NRL). Rugby League is *the* football code in Sydney, and the majority of the fifteen NRL teams are based there. One of the sadder consequences of this media-inspired revolution has been the loss of some of the traditional inner-city clubs through mergers. Many people also resent the way in which this one-time bastion of working-class culture has been co-opted by pay TV.

Summertime **cricket** is a great spectator sport – for the crowd, the sunshine and the beer as much as the play. Every state is involved, and the three- or four-day Sheffield Shield matches of the interstate series are interspersed with one-day games and internationals, as well as full five-day international test matches.

The international competition that still arouses greatest interest is that between Australia and England – **The Ashes**. Having been around for over 120 years, this is perhaps the oldest rivalry between nations in international sport. The "**trophy**" competed for has an interesting provenance: in 1882 an Australian touring side defeated England at the Oval in South London by seven runs, and the *Sporting Times* was moved to report, in a mock obituary, that English cricket had "died at the Oval... deeply lamented by a large circle of sorrowing friends". The funeral ceremony involved the cremation of a set of bails, which were then preserved in a funerary urn. Each time the two countries compete, this is the trophy that is up for grabs (though the urn itself never actually leaves Lord's cricket ground in London) and a new crystal trophy actually goes to the winners.

Minor sports are followed with no less avid attention, and there are plenty of them, including horse racing and trotting, motor racing, swimming, athletics, tennis – you name it. One peculiarly Australian institution is the **surf carnival**, when teams of volunteer lifesavers demonstrate their skills – this makes for a great day out on the beach. **Surfing** itself can also be a competitive sport, with the Eastertime World Championships held at Bell's Beach, southwest of Melbourne, and November's Margaret River Classic, south of Perth, both good opportunities to catch some wave-riding action. Inland, many rural towns have a **speedway track** occupying a tract of waste-land, where at weekends motor-headed hoons demonstrate their dirt-tracking skills in souped-up utes or motorbikes; a dusty, noisy and merry focus for the entire community and passers-by.

Outdoor pursuits

Though the cities are fun, what really makes Australia special is the great outdoors: the vast and remote wilderness of the bush,

Melbourne 2006 XVIII Commonwealth Games

15–26 March

In 1956, the Victoria capital Melbourne hosted the Olympic Games. Then rival city Sydney stole Melbourne's Olympic-city claim to fame in 2000. Now Melbourne is fighting back in the sport-hosting supremacy stakes with the 2006 XVIII Commonwealth Games. Comparisons will be made to Manchester, England, hosts of the 2002 games, and expectations are sure to be set for the 2010 games in Delhi, India. Melbourne already has excellent sporting facilities and most of the Games' venues already exist – though some will be upgraded and redeveloped. The **Melbourne Cricket Ground (MCG)** will witness the opening and closing ceremonies and the marathon's start and finish.

Originally known as the British Empire Games, the Commonwealth Games were first held in 1930 in Hamilton, Ontario, Canada. They've been held every four years since, except during WWII and its aftermath (1942 and 1946). Eleven countries and 400 athletes competed in 1930; in 2006, 71 countries and 4,500 athletes will compete. Sports represented are aquatics (diving, swimming, synchronised swimming), athletics (marathon, track and field, walking), badminton, basketball, boxing, cycling (track, road, mountain biking), gymnastics (artistic, rhythmic), hockey, lawn bowls, netball, rugby 7s, shooting (clay target, full bore, pistol, small bore), squash, table tennis, triathlon and weightlifting. Elite Athletes with a Disability (EAD) events are integrated into the schedule. The Commonwealth Games Federation website Ⓦwww.thecgf.com has more background information, while for the latest details check out the Melbourne 2006 website Ⓦwww.melbourne2006.com.au.

Head offices/Ticketing contacts

Tickets, at various price levels, start from around $A20 and rise to $A280. For Australian residents, the ticket ballot for purchase of tickets closed in late-April 2005, but tickets for leftover seats are usually sold at the time of the Games. Residents of other competing Commonwealth nations should approach their local Commonwealth Games Association for ticketing information. There are links for these, and other Commonwealth country ticket contacts, on the official website Ⓦwww.melbourne2006.com.au. Non-Commonwealth residents, such as US residents, need to register on the Melbourne 2006 website to receive information about ticketing.

Canada Executive Worldwide Travel Ⓣ613/236 5555.

England Commonwealth Games Council for England Ⓣ020/8676 3543, Ⓦwww.cgce.co.uk

New Zealand Premier Events Groups Ⓣ09/307 0770, Ⓦwww.premiereventsgroup.com

Northern Ireland Commonwealth Games Council for Northern Ireland Ⓣ028/9071 6558.

Scotland Commonwealth Games Council for Scotland Ⓣ01786/466 480, Ⓦwww.cgcs.org.uk

South Africa Seekers Sports Travel Ⓣ011/790 0454, Ⓦwww.travel.co.za

Wales Commonwealth Games Council for Wales Ⓣ01269/850 390.

the legendary Outback, and the thousands of kilometres of unspoilt coastline. There's tremendous potential here to indulge in a huge range of outdoor pursuits – hiking, fishing, surfing, diving, even skiing – especially in the multitude of national parks that cover the country. Further information on all of these is available from local tourist offices, which publicize what's available in their area; from Parks Australia, which has detailed maps of parks with walking trails, climbs, swimming holes and other activities; to specialist books. In addition, virtually any activity can be done as part of an organized excursion, often with all the gear supplied. If you want to go it alone you'll find plenty of places ready to rent or sell you the necessary equipment. Before indulging in adventure activities, check your insurance cover (see "Insurance").

As with any wilderness area, the Australian interior does not suffer fools, and the coast conceals **dangers** too: sunstroke and dehydration are risks everywhere, with riptides, currents and unexpectedly large waves to be wary of on exposed coasts. In the more remote regions isolation and lack of surface water compromise energetic outdoor activities such as bushwalking or mountain biking, which are probably better practised in the cooler climes and more populated locations of the south.

Bushwalking

Bushwalking in Australia doesn't mean just a stroll in the bush, but refers to self-sufficient hikes, from a day to a week or longer. It's an increasingly popular activity nationwide, and you'll find trails marked in almost every national park, as well as local bushwalking **clubs** whose trips you may be able to join.

It's essential to be **properly equipped** for the conditions you'll encounter – and to know what those conditions are likely to be. Carry a **map** (often on hand at the ranger station in popular national parks), know how the trail is marked, and stay on the route. If your trip is a long one, let someone know where you're going, and confirm to them that you've arrived back safely – park rangers are useful contacts for this, and some will insist on it for overnight walks which may require registration. One point worth noting is that in national park areas the estimated duration of a given walk is often exaggerated – certainly in the Territory and WA: you can comfortably divide the indicated time by half or more. On formed tracks a walking speed of 3–4kph is average. The essentials, even for a short walk, are adequate clothing including a wide-brimmed hat, enough food and, above all, **water**. Other useful items include a torch, matches or lighter, penknife, sun block, insect repellent, toilet paper, first-aid kit, and a whistle or mirror to attract attention if you get lost. A lot of this gear can be rented, or bought cheaply at disposal stores, which can often also put you in touch with local clubs or specialists.

Long-distance tracks exist mostly in the south of the country, with Tasmania's wilderness areas being perhaps the most rewarding bushwalking location; the eighty-kilometre **Overland Track** from Cradle Mountain to Lake St Clair is one of the country's best-known trails. On the mainland, the **Blue Mountains**, a two-hour train ride from Sydney, the **Snowy Mountains** further south, and Victoria's spectacular **Grampians** are all popular regions for longer, marked walks.

South Australia's **Flinders Ranges**, 300km north of Adelaide, are accessible along the **Heysen Trail** from the Fleurieu Peninsula, the walk into the thousand-metre-high natural basin of Wilpena Pound being the highlight. In temperate southwestern WA, the 960-kilometre **Bibbulmun Track**, an old Aboriginal trail passing through the region's giant eucalypt forests, was completed in 2002 from Albany to Kalamunda near Perth. In the same year the 220-kilometre **Larapinta Trail**, along the McDonnell Ranges west of Alice Springs was also completed; an initially strenuous hike out of Alice Springs that should only be attempted in winter. Queensland's rainforested coastal strip offers plenty more opportunities for walks, including the **Lamington** area in the south, and around northern **Atherton Tablelands** and **Hinchinbrook Island**.

Throughout the text of the guide, we mention specialist bushwalking guides and maps which are relevant. Two of Australia's best-regarded bushwalkers are John Chapman and Tyrone T. Thomas, and both publish

Bush essentials

Four things above all:

Fire The driest continent on earth is covered by vegetation which has evolved with regular conflagrations, and is always at risk from bushfires. Three times in the last ten years Sydney was ringed with burning bushland, and during the terrible bushfire season of 2002/2003 a large part of the Alpine region in Australia's southeast was ablaze for almost two months, wreaking havoc on bush and forests, animals and people. Only a few human lives were lost, however, mainly owing to the skills, resilience and determination of the fire fighters and local residents. Even in wet years, there's a constant red alert during summer months. Always use an established fireplace where available, or dig a shallow pit and ring it with stones. Keep fires small and make absolutely sure embers are smothered before going to sleep or moving on. **Never discard burning cigarette butts** from cars. Periodic total fire bans – announced in the local media when in effect – prohibit any fire in the open, including wood, gas or electric barbecues, with heavy fines for offenders. Check on the local fire danger before you go bushwalking – some walking trails are closed in the riskiest periods (summer – Dec, Jan & Feb – in the south; the end of the dry season – Sept/Oct – in the north). If driving, carry blankets and a filled water container, listen to your car radio and watch out for roadside fire danger indicators. If the worst happens, there are practical ways of surviving a bushfire. See "Health", for potential bushwalking hazards and advice on how to deal with them – including ways to survive if caught in a bushfire.

Water Carry plenty with you and do not contaminate local water resources. In particular, soaps and detergents can render water undrinkable and kill livestock and wild animals. Avoid washing in standing water, especially tanks and small lakes or reservoirs.

Waste Take only photographs, leave only footprints. That means carrying all your rubbish out with you – never burn or bury it – and making sure you urinate (and bury your excrement) at least 50m from a campsite or water source.

Hypothermia In Tasmania, where the weather is notoriously changeable, even in summer, prepare as you would for a walk in Scotland.

a range of **walking guides**. Try to get hold of the latest edition of Chapman's rigorously updated *Bushwalking in Australia*, which details 25 of the country's best bushwalks.

Water sports

The oceans and seas around Australia are a national playground and are not just for lying by or playing volleyball on the beach. Always take local advice on the waves, which must be treated with respect. If possible, **swim** from a patrolled beach, between the flags: raise one hand if you get into difficulty, and clear the water if a siren sounds – it could signal dangerous waves, a shark sighting or a swarm of bluebottles (stinging jellyfish).

Enjoying the water doesn't necessarily involve any special effort or equipment, but if you want it, there are plenty of activities on offer. Probably the easiest to get into is **surfing**, starting with body-surfing and progressing to boogie-boards (small boards that you lie on) and then on to full-scale surfboards. Surfing is popular everywhere, but don't expect the local surfie community to be too friendly at first – they're often very cliquey. Seaside hostels often have boards which they loan out free. **Windsurfing** and **sailing** are also extremely popular, and you'll be able to rent equipment and get instruction in almost any resort, though some of the best sailing in the country can be found around Queensland's Whitsunday Islands or off WA's West Coast. Other water sports include **white-water rafting**, **sea-kayaking** and **canoeing**.

The Great Barrier Reef is one of the world's great **scuba-diving** meccas, with some other lesser-known but excellent sites

Australia's top dive sites

Bougainville Reef Coral Sea, Great Barrier Reef, QLD. Exceptional in every way: kilometre-deep coral walls, clear water, and both reef and pelagic life in abundance. Live-aboard trips from Cairns and Port Douglas.

Cod Hole Great Barrier Reef, QLD. Where the giant potato cod and divers meet. Live-aboard trips from Cairns.

Geographe Bay WA. The *HMS Swan* was sunk to make a recreational diving wreck just off Cape Naturaliste, a couple of hours south of Perth.

Lord Howe Island NSW. The world's southernmost reef surrounds one of the world's most beautiful islands. Flights from Brisbane and Sydney.

Ningaloo Reef WA. Whale sharks come through from April to June, but there's great diving all year, in places right off the beach. Tours from Exmouth or Coral Bay.

Port Lincoln SA. South Australian waters are one of the last bastions for the poorly understood Great White shark. Trips out from Port Lincoln use shark cages.

Seal Rocks NSW. Hosts a great grey nurse convergence every so often, a chance to be surrounded by these fierce-looking but largely harmless sharks. Trips from Foster or Tuncurry.

Yongala Shipwreck QLD. Huge fish and the remains of a 100-metre-long passenger liner which went down in an early-twentieth-century cyclone. Trips from Townsville and Cairns.

around the country – such as West Australia's Ningaloo Reef – beginning to attract attention. Dive facilities in Australia are of a high standard, and scuba courses are not that expensive, though if you simply want to try it once there are plenty of people offering closely supervised "resort dives". Good **rental gear** is widely available, but if you're bringing your own, check for compatibility problems; yokes are the Australian norm, so if your first-stage fitting is DIN (likely in Europe and the UK), you'll need an adaptor. **Snorkelling** is the low-tech alternative, and still allows you to get dramatically close to the aquatic life around a reef.

Fishing is an Australian obsession, conducted on rivers and lakes, off piers or small boats ("tinnies"), or out at sea where – if your bank balance is up to the challenge – marlin and other game fish are caught. Again, all the equipment – even boats – can be rented in most good fishing areas. Barramundi, renowned for its fighting qualities, is the thing to go for up north. Bear in mind that recreational **fishing licenses** may be required depending on the state or territory; check the government website of the relevant state in "Information, websites and maps" for further details.

Other pursuits

Alice Springs' wide-open spaces make it the country's **hot-air-ballooning** capital and also the main base for **camel treks** into the surrounding desert.

More regular riding, on **horseback**, is offered all over the country – anything from a gentle hour at walking pace to a serious cattle roundup. **Cycling** and **mountain biking** are tremendously popular too, as well as being a good way of getting around resorts; just about all hostels rent out bikes, and we've listed other outlets throughout the Guide.

Australia's wilderness is an ideal venue for extended **off-road driving** and **motorbiking**, although permission may be needed to cross station- and Aboriginal-owned lands, and the fragile desert ecology should be respected at all times. Northern Queensland's Cape York and WA's Kimberley are the most adventurous destinations, 4WD-accessible in the dry season only. The great **Outback tracks** pushed out by explorers or drovers, such as the Warburton Road and Sandover Highway and the Tanami, Birdsville and Oodnadatta tracks, are actually two-wheel driveable in dry conditions, but can be hard on poorly

National parks

The Australian Government federal **Department of the Environment and Heritage (DEH)** is tasked with protecting and conserving the nation's natural environment (and aspects of its cultural heritage). Its mandate includes dealing with international problems such as whaling, and making decisions about the Australian Antarctic Division. Under the DEH, Parks Australia (itself under the Director of National Parks) manages Commonwealth reserves including six **Commonwealth national parks**, three of which are jointly managed by traditional Aboriginal owners – Booderee in Jervis Bay Territory, and in the Northern Territory, Uluru-Kata Tjuta and Kakadu – while the remaining three protect unique island eco-systems, including Norfolk Island National Park. The DEH also manages the Australian National Botanic Garden in Canberra and botanic gardens at Booderee and Norfolk Island, as well as a number of marine protected areas.

Each state and territory has their own protected area management authority; departmental names vary from state to state, but Australians tend to generically dub them as the **National Parks and Wildlife Service** (NPWS) which is how we refer to them in the Guide.

The thousand-odd **national parks** range from suburban commons to the Great Barrier Reef, and from popular hiking areas within striking distance of the big cities to wilderness regions which require days in a 4WD simply to reach. They protect everything within their boundaries: flora, fauna and landforms as well as Aboriginal art and sacred sites, although not always to the exclusion of mineral exploitation, as in Karijini in WA or Kakadu in the Territory.

Entry and camping **fees** are variable. Some parks or states have no fees at all, some charge entry fees but often don't police the system, some charge for use of camping facilities, while others require permits bought in advance; each state or territory usually offers a pass which makes it cheaper if you want to visit many national parks and for longer periods, but unfortunately no national pass is available. If you're camping you can usually pay on site, but booking ahead might be a good idea during the Christmas, Easter and school holidays. Some parks have cabin accommodation, either self-catering or bunk-style with a camp kitchen, but nearby resorts or alternative accommodation are always independently run. For details on the names and vagaries of each state or territory's system, consult the websites listed below.

Commonwealth: Department of the Environment and Heritage (DEH) Ⓦ www.deh.gov.au

Australian Capital Territory Environment ACT Ⓦ www.environment.act.gov.au

New South Wales NSW National Parks and Wildlife Service (NPWS) Ⓦ www.nationalparks.nsw.gov.au

Northern Territory Parks and Wildlife Commission of the Northern Territory Ⓦ www.nt.gov.au/ipe/pwcnt

Queensland Environmental Protection Agency (EPA)/Queensland Parks and Wildlife Service Ⓦ www.epa.qld.gov.au

Victoria Parks Victoria Ⓦ www.parkweb.vic.gov.au

South Australia National Parks and Wildlife SA Ⓦ www.environment.sa.gov.au/parks

Tasmania Tasmania Parks and Wildlife Service Ⓦ www.parks.tas.gov.au

Western Australia Department of Conservation and Land Management (CALM) Ⓦ www.calm.wa.gov.au/national_parks

prepared vehicles. Getting right to the tip of Queensland's eight-hundred-kilometre-long Cape York Peninsula will definitely require a 4WD or trail bike; while the Kimberley's notoriously corrugated Gibb River Road in WA is also popular in the Dry.

Finally, you may not associate Australia with **skiing**, but there's plenty of it in the 1500-metre-high Australian Alps on the border of Victoria and New South Wales, based around the winter resorts of Thredbo, Perisher, Falls Creek and Mount Hotham. Europeans tend to be sniffy about Australian skiing, and certainly it's limited, with a season that lasts barely two to three months – from the end of June until end of September, if you're lucky – and very few challenging runs. The one area where it does match up to Europe is in the prices. On the other hand it's fun if you're here, and the relatively gentle slopes of the mountains are ideal for **cross-country skiing**, which is increasingly being developed alongside downhill.

Crime, police and personal safety

Australia was once populated with criminals condemned to "Transportation across the seas." However, the rehabilitation programme seems to have worked — Australia today can pride itself on being a relatively safe country, although increasingly it is following the American trend in gun-related incidents.

This is not to say there's no petty crime, or that you can leave normal caution behind, but there is less violent crime and theft in Australia, even in the big cities, than in most of Europe or North America, and even "heavy" downtown areas can appear pretty tame. One place where **violence** is commonplace is at the ritual pub "blue" (fight), usually among known protagonists on a Friday or Saturday night in smaller, untouristed towns. Strangers are seldom involved without at least some provocation.

You're more likely to fall victim to a fellow traveller or an opportunist: **theft** is not unusual in hostels and many therefore provide lockable boxes. But if you leave valuables lying around, or on view in cars, you can expect them to be stolen. Exercise caution, don't forget common-sense, street-wise precautions, and you should be fine; in cities at night stay in areas that are well lit and full of people, look like you know where you are going and don't carry excess cash or anything else you can't afford to lose.

Police and the law

Australia's **police** – all armed – have a poor public image and perhaps as a result tend to keep a low profile; you should have no trouble in your dealings with them. Indeed you'll hardly see them, unless you're out on a Friday or Saturday night when they cruise in search of drink-related brawls.

Things to watch out for, most of all, are **drugs**. A lot of marijuana is grown and its use is widespread, but you'd be foolish to carry it when you travel, and crazy to carry any other illicit narcotic. Each state has its own penalties, and though a small amount of grass may mean no more than confiscation or an on-the-spot fine, they're generally pretty tough – especially in Queensland. When you **cross state borders** you may find that your vehicle will be **searched** – not just for "firearms, pornography or drugs" but also for fruit and fresh produce, which often cannot be carried from one state to the next, to minimize the spread of plant pests and viruses. You'll see huge bins at the side of the road as you approach a state border line: dump any perishables here before crossing over. Driving in general makes you more likely to have a confrontation of some kind, if only for a minor traffic infringement: **drunk driving** is taken extremely seriously, so don't risk it – random breath tests are common around all cities and larger towns.

Lesser potential problems are **alcohol** – there are all sorts of controls on where and when you can drink, and taking alcohol onto Aboriginal lands can be a serious offence; smoking, which is increasingly being banned in public places; and nude or **topless** sunbathing, which is quite acceptable in many places, but absolutely not in others – follow the locals' lead.

If for any reason you are **arrested** or need help (and you can be arrested merely on suspicion of committing an offence), you are entitled to contact a friend or lawyer before answering any questions. You could call your consulate, but don't expect much sympathy. If necessary, the police will provide a lawyer, and you can usually get legal aid to settle the bill.

Australia is becoming increasingly tough on immigrants, and recent reports include a heightened level of police raids on businesses for people working either on tourist visas or on expired working visas. If you're caught working illegally, you will have any visa cancelled and will be asked to leave the country immediately; you may be taken into detention if immediate arrangements cannot be made. Furthermore, you will be forbidden to re-apply for a working visa for three years, but even after this time period it is extremely unlikely that you would be granted another visa under normal circumstances. Employers can be fined up to A$10,000 for employing illegal workers, and soon will also be liable for prosecution.

Prejudice and the traveller

Given Australia's record on its treatment of the Aboriginal population, the history of the White Australia policy, and the passing popularity of the One Nation party founded by Pauline Hanson on a partly racist agenda, it comes as little surprise to find that this is a nation where **racial prejudice** is ingrained. As a **black traveller** you're likely to attract attention when you don't particularly want it, and be unable to get it when you do – even to the extent of being refused service in an Outback bar or being unable to flag down a cab in a city. Certainly in remote areas, where Aboriginal people are still treated as second-class citizens at best, black travellers may have an uncomfortable time.

Asians are generally more accepted (in Australia, "Asian" usually means Southeast Asian – the Indian and Pakistani populations are negligible) than most other non-white foreigners in Australia, although they have often been a target of envy, due to high numbers of skilled and qualified Asian workers taking Australian jobs. Recently, a strong undercurrent of anti-Asian feeling – never too far below the surface in Australia's European history – has reared its ugly head.

Nevertheless, Australia does have powerful anti-discrimination laws. Any racial discrimination can be reported to the **Human Rights and Equal Opportunities Commission**, which has offices in each state capital (listed in the "Government" section at the front of the *White Pages* phone book). Although you might not have time (or the desire) to go through the lengthy complaints process, the threat is a useful one, as their powers are considerable. Just don't expect a country policeman to help you – many are part of the problem rather than the solution.

Emergencies

Ⓣ000 is the free **emergency telephone number** to summon the police, ambulance or fire service.

Work

Most visitors' visas clearly state that no employment of any kind is to be undertaken during a visit to Australia. However, if you've succeeded in getting a Working Holiday Visa (see "Visas and red tape") and are prepared to try anything – officially for no more than three months at a time – there are plenty of possibilities for finding work. Work Oz (@www.workoz.com) can help with paperwork and contacts. There are also organized work programmes – both paid and voluntary (see p.85)

In practice this means that the only jobs officially open to you are unskilled, temporary ones. The **National Harvest Labour Hotline** (Mon–Fri 9am–5pm; ⓣ1800 062 332 ⓦ www.jobsearch.gov.au/harvesttrail) has information about harvesting or farm-labouring jobs and will put you in touch with potential employers. There is no centralized agency for casual work, such as bar or restaurant, construction and factory work. A good place to start searching, however, is **Travellers' Contact Point** (ⓣ1800 647 640; ⓦwww.travellers.com.au), which has a branch in Sydney and Cairns. Services include a job notice board, skills testing, CV updating and help with the required paperwork. You can view the jobs posted online by their recruitment agency, travellers @work at ⓦwww.taw.com.au. The travel centre **Backpackers World** also runs an employment agency (ⓣ1800 676 763; ⓦwww.backpackersworld.com.au), with branches all over Australia except South Australia and Tasmania. Quite a few hostels run their own employment agency or have a permanently staffed **employment desk**. Some charge a membership fee – about $40 a year. All of these places will help with all aspects of working, from organizing tax file numbers to actually getting you jobs. In addition, more specialized employment **agencies** are worth a try in the cities if you have a marketable skill (computer training, accountancy, nursing, cooking and the like). They might have better, higher-paid jobs on their books, though they may be looking for full-time or at least longer-term commitment. Newspaper job ads are also worth checking out, especially in smaller local papers. And finally, fellow travellers, hostel staff in smaller hostels, and notice boards may be the best source of all, especially in remote areas. This is where you'll find out about local opportunities. The hostels themselves may occasionally offer free nights in lieu of cleaning work – or even pay you for jobs that involve a bit more skill. Some of the hostels in the big cities or in country towns where there is a lot of harvesting work also arrange employment.

Significant long-term unemployment is prevalent in Australia, and the days of legendary wages for relentless hard work in mines, on the roads or on prawn trawlers are long gone. Some people still manage to work illegally, but **visa checks** at small businesses and in the major harvest areas (they really do happen) as well as tax reforms have made this much harder than it used to be. See "Police and personal safety".

Seasonal picking and harvesting work

Listed below are the major **harvest seasons** around the country. Once you're into the harvest season it's possible to move with it around the country, from one product to another, as many people do. There may be lesser harvests and other work in all of these places at any time. Just remember that crop picking is hard work for low wages (which usually are paid on a commission basis) – if you're bad at it and don't pick much, you'll put in a lot of effort for virtually nothing. It's also worth noting that harvest work often is on farms or plantations that are quite some distance away from a town. In some cases, employers or a workers' hostel in a near-by town or settlement will provide transport to and from work – sometimes, but not always, free of charge. In other cases you will be given some basic accommodation on the farm; sometimes you may even be required to pitch your own tent

New South Wales

Summer November–April, peaking in February, in the central eastern district around Bathurst, Dubbo and Orange; orchard and other fruits, cotton, onions and asparagus.
Year-round The north coast around Coffs Harbour; bananas.

Queensland

Summer December–March, around Warwick, inland on the NSW border; stone and orchard fruits, grapes.
May–December The central coast around Bowen; fruit and vegetables, especially mangoes at the end of the year.
May–November The northern coast around Ayr, Tully and Innisfail; sugar cane, bananas and tobacco.
Year-round The southern central coast around Bundaberg and Childers; all kinds of fruit and vegetables.

Western Australia

October–June The southwest; grapes and orchard fruits (February–April), plus tractor-driven grain harvesting.
March–November The west coast from Fremantle to Carnarvon; crayfish, prawn and scallop fishing and processing.
May–October The northeast around Kununurra; fruit and vegetable picking and packing.

South Australia

February–April The Barossa Valley; grapes.
Year-round The Riverland; picking, pruning and packaging citrus and soft fruits.

Victoria

Summer November–April, peaking in February, in central northern areas around Shepparton, and also along the Murray River (Mildura, Swan Hill and, to a lesser extent, Echuca); orchard fruits, tomatoes, tobacco, grapes and soft fruits.

Tasmania

Summer December–March; orchard and soft fruits, grapes.

Organized work programmes

To streamline the process of procuring a working visa, getting to Australia and orienting yourself on arrival, there are several packages aimed at working travellers. BUNAC organizes a **Work Australia** programme that can be combined with their North American programmes, with departures from London between August and December and from Los Angeles in September and October. Work Oz assists with the paperwork and arranges accommodation packages. See pp.84–85 for contact details of these and other organizations.

Teaching English

There are two options: find or prepare for finding work **before you go**, or just wing it and see what you come up with while you're out there, particularly if you already have a degree and/or teaching experience. Teaching English – often abbreviated as **ELT** (English Language Teaching) or **TEFL** (Teaching English as a Foreign Language) – is the way many people finance their way around the greater part of the world; you can get a CELTA (Certificate in English Language Teaching to Adults) qualification before you leave home. Certified by the RSA, the course is very demanding and costs about £1,000 to £1,100 for the month's full-time tuition; you'll be thrown in at the deep end and expected to teach right away. The British Council's website, Ⓦwww.britishcouncil.org has a list of English-teaching vacancies.

Useful publications and websites

Another pre-planning strategy for working abroad, whether teaching English or otherwise, is to get hold of Overseas Jobs Express (Premier House, Shoreham Airport, West Sussex BN43 5FF; Ⓣ01273/699 611, Ⓦwww.overseasjobs.com), a fortnightly publication with a range of job vacancies, available by subscription only. Vacation Work also publishes books on summer jobs abroad and how to work your way around the world; call Ⓣ01865/241 978 or visit Ⓦwww.vacationwork.co.uk for their catalogue. Travel magazines like the reliable *Wanderlust* (ⓦwww.wanderlust.co.uk. Every two months) have a Job Shop section which often advertises job opportunities with tour companies, while ⓦwww.studyabroad.com is a useful website with listings and links to study and work programmes worldwide.

Study and work programmes

From the UK and Ireland

BTCV 36 St Mary's St, Wallingford, Oxfordshire OX10 0EU ⓣ01491/839 766, ⓦwww.btcv.org. One of the largest environmental charities in Britain, with branches across the country, also has a programme of national and international working holidays (as a paying volunteer), ranging from dry-stone walling in Japan to turtle monitoring in Turkey; comprehensive brochure available.

BUNAC (British Universities' North America Club) 16 Bowling Green Lane, London EC1R 0QH ⓣ020/7251 3472, ⓦwww.bunac.org. Organizes working holidays in Australia and New Zealand, among other countries, for students, typically training placements with companies.

Earthwatch Institute 57 Woodstock Rd, Oxford OX2 6HJ ⓣ01865/311 600, ⓦwww.earthwatch.org. Long-established non-profit international charity with offices in Oxford, USA (Boston), Melbourne and Tokyo. Its 50,000 members and supporters are spread across the US, Europe, Africa, Asia and Australia and volunteer their time and skills to work on environmental and archeological research projects worldwide (140 projects in around 48 countries). Participation is mainly as a paying volunteer (pricey) but fellowships for teachers and students are available.

Field Studies Council Overseas (FSCO) Montford Bridge, Shrewsbury SY4 1HW ⓣ01743/852 150, ⓦwww.fscoverseas.org.uk. Respected educational charity with over 25 years' experience of organizing specialized holidays with study tours visits worldwide. Studies have included ecology in the Canadian Rockies, flora of New Zealand, and plants and birds of Andalucia. Group size is generally limited to 8–15 people. Overseas Experiences brochure available.

International House 106 Piccadilly, London W1V 9NL ⓣ020/7518 6999, ⓦwww.ihlondon.com. Head office for reputable English-teaching organization which offers TEFL training leading to the award of a Certificate in English Language Teaching to Adults (CELTA), and recruits for teaching positions in Britain and abroad.

From the US

American Institute for Foreign Study River Plaza, 9 West Broad St, Stamford, CT 06902-3788 ⓣ1-800/727-2437, ⓦwww.aifs.com. Language study and cultural immersion for the summer or school year, as well as au pair and Camp America programs.

Association for International Practical Training 10400 Little Patuxent Pkwy, Suite 250, Columbia, MD 21044 ⓣ410/997-2200, ⓦwww.aipt.org. Summer internships for students who have completed at least two years of college in science, agriculture, engineering or architecture.

Bernan Associates 4611-F Assembly Dr, Lanham, MD 20706 ⓣ1-800/274-4888, ⓦwww.bernan.com. Distributes UNESCO's encyclopedic *Study Abroad*.

BUNAC USA PO Box 430, Southbury CT 06488 ⓣ1-800/GO-BUNAC, ⓦwww.bunac.org. Offers young US and Canadian students the chance to work in Australia, New Zealand or Britain. Visa support, flights, job information, help with setting up a bank account, and accommodation on arrival is provided.

Council on International Educational Exchange (CIEE) 205 E 42nd St, New York, NY 10017 ⓣ1-800/2COUNCIL, ⓦwww.ciee.org/study. The non-profit parent organization of Council Travel, CIEE runs summer, semester and academic-year programs in Australia and New Zealand (among many other countries) and can also arrange six-month work permits for currently enrolled or recently graduated students in Australia. They provide leads, but it's up to you to find the work. CIEE also runs volunteer projects in 30 countries in Africa, Europe, Latin America, Asia and North America.

Earthwatch Institute 3 Clock Tower Place, Suite 100, Box 75, Maynard, MA 01754 ⓣ1-800/776-0188 or 978/461-0081, ⓦwww.earthwatch.org. See left.

Elderhostel 75 Federal St, Boston, MA 02110 ⓣ1/877-426-8056, ⓦwww.elderhostel.org. An extensive worldwide network of educational and activity programs, cruises and homestays for people over 60 (companions may be younger). Programs generally last a week or more and costs are in line with those of commercial tours.

Experiment in International Living ⓣ1-800/345-2929, ⓦwww.usexperiment.org. Summer program for high-school students. Same organisation as World Learning, see below.

HarperCollins Perseus Division ⓣ1-800/242-7737. Publishes *International Jobs: Where They Are, How to Get Them.*

Peace Corps 1111 20th St NW, Washington, DC 20526 ⓣ1-800/424-8580, ⓦwww.peacecorps.gov. Places people with specialist qualifications

Tax

In recent years employers have been threatened with huge fines for offering cash-in-hand labour and, as a result, it's difficult to avoid paying **income tax**, which is levied at 29 percent for earnings under about $26,000 per annum and deducted at source. To become part of the system you'll need a **tax file number** (form available at post offices or taxation offices), which is pretty easy to obtain on presentation of a passport with relevant visa. Your employer will give you a couple of weeks' grace, but not much more – if you don't have a number, after that you'll be taxed at 49 percent. Nowadays it's hard to claim a tax **rebate**, no matter how little you earn; however, it's worth a try, and possibly a visit to a tax adviser.

or skills in two-year postings in many developing countries. Special Youth Program covers one four-month period in Australia, with an age restriction of 18–30 and a cost of US$365, through Work Experience Down Under, including two nights' accommodation in Sydney and work support. You have to pay the fee even if you have a job already lined up, and you have to fly on their specially arranged (and priced) twice-monthly flights from Los Angeles. The Australian embassy also insists that you have US$500 a month available to you and proof of funds before departure.

Volunteers for Peace 1034 Tiffany Rd, Belmont, VT 05730 ⓣ802/259-2759, ⓦwww.vfp.org. Non-profit organization with links to a huge international network of "workcamps", two- to four-week programs that bring volunteers together from many countries to carry out needed community projects. Most workcamps are in summer, with registration in April–May. Annual membership including directory costs $20. Programs worldwide.

World Learning Kipling Road, PO Box 676, Brattleboro, VT 05302 ⓣ802/257-7751, ⓦwww.worldlearning.org. Its School for International Training (ⓣ1-800/336-1616, ⓦwww.sit.edu) runs accredited college semesters abroad, comprising language and cultural studies, homestay and other academic work. Programs in 40 countries.

In Australia

ATCV (Australian Trust for Conservation Volunteers) 18/142 Addison St, Marrickville, NSW 2204. ⓣ02/9564 1244 or 1800 032 501. There are 24 offices in Australia; ⓦwww.atcv.com.au. Volunteer work (unpaid) on conservation projects across Australia; about $20 a day charged for food and accommodation. The projects are usually four to six weeks long.

Visitoz Springbrook Farm, MS 188 via Goomeri, 4601, Queensland ⓣ07/4168 6106, ⓦwww.visitoz.org. Provides work on farms and stations and rural hospitality for all those who would like to work in the bush and have the experience of a lifetime. Previous experience is not required. There are more than 980 employers who provide work all over Australia throughout the year. Those coming in direct from overseas are met at the airport, get assistance with obtaining a tax file number and other paperwork sorted out. Participants must attend a four-day preparation and orientation course and during this period a job is chosen from a few suitable ones offered. Work is guaranteed and driving licences are necessary for 95 percent of the jobs. Offices in the UK, Sweden, Germany, Holland, the USA and Canada.

Work Oz Kings House, 14 Orchard St, Bristol BS1 5EH ⓦwww.work.oz.com. An organization owned and run in Australia and Britain by ex-Australian high commission staff, designed to assist 18–30 year old British, Irish, Canadian, Dutch, German, Japanese, Maltese and US citizens who want to work in Australia with a working holiday visa. They assist with visa application, employment in Australia, pre-book hostel accommodation prior to arrival, arrange pick-ups from the airport and arrange travel insurance.

WWOOF (Willing Workers on Organic Farms) 2166 Gelantipy Rd, W Tree, Buchan, VIC 3885 ⓣ03/5155 0218, ⓕ03/5155 0342, ⓦwww.wwoof.com.au. Wwoofing is a great way to experience a side of Australia that you'd never see if you just worked in an office and then beachbummed your way up the east coast. As you are not paid cash, a work visa is not required: you put in about half a day's work at your host's place in exchange for full board and lodging, and the rest of the time is yours to go exploring. You are expected to stay at least two nights; everything else is negotiable. The *Australian WWOOF Book* lists about 1200 organic farms and 100 non-farm hosts (such as organic nurseries and greengrocers, alternative schools). By ordering the book you become a member; the membership includes a basic work insurance for one year ($50 single, $60 for any two people travelling together). The book is available over the Internet (add $5 for postage and handling) as well as from some backpacker hostels and travel shops such as Backpackers World and branches of Student Uni Travel. WWOOF also publishes another book for people who would like to visit such places and stay there for a while without working: *WWOOF Australia's Communities, Retreats and Bed and Breakfast Book* ($15) which can also be ordered online.

Travellers with disabilities

The vast distances between Australia's cities and popular tourist resorts present visitors with mobility difficulties with a unique challenge but, overall, travel in Australia for people with disabilities is rather easier than it would be in the UK and Europe.

The federal government provides information and various nationwide services through the **National Information Communication Awareness Network** (NICAN) and the **Australian Council for the Rehabilitation of the Disabled** (ACROD) – see p.87 for contact details. The **Australian Tourist Commission** offices provide a helpline service and publish a factsheet, *Travelling in Australia for People with Disabilities*, available from its offices worldwide (see "Information, websites and map").

Disability needn't interfere with your sightseeing: the attitude of the management at Australia's major tourist attractions is excellent, and they will provide assistance where they can. For example, you'll find you can view rock art at Kakadu National Park, do a tour around the base of Uluru (Ayers Rock), snorkel unhindered on the Great Barrier Reef, go on a cruise around Sydney Harbour, and see the penguins at Phillip Island.

Planning a holiday

There are **organized tours and holidays** specifically for people with disabilities (including mobility, hearing, vision and intellectual restrictions). Some arrange travel only, some organize travel and accommodation, and others provide a complete package – travel, accommodation, meals and carer support. This last type, as well as catering fully for special needs, provides company for the trip. The contacts below will be able to put you in touch with any specialists for trips to Australia; several are listed in the Australian Tourist Commission factsheet. If you want to be more independent, it's important to become an authority on where you must be self-reliant and where you may expect help, especially regarding transport and accommodation. It is also vital to be honest – with travel agencies, insurance companies and travel companions. Know your limitations and make sure others know them. If you do not use a wheelchair all the time but your walking capabilities are limited, remember that you are likely to need to cover greater distances while travelling (often over rougher terrain and in hotter temperatures) than you are used to. If you use a wheelchair, have it serviced before you go and carry a repair kit.

Read your **travel insurance** small print carefully to make sure that people with a pre-existing medical condition are not excluded. And use your travel agent to make your journey simpler: airline and bus companies can cope better if they are expecting you, with a wheelchair provided at airports and staff primed to help. A **medical certificate** of your fitness to travel (provided by your doctor) is also extremely useful; some airlines and insurance companies may insist on it. Make sure that you have extra supplies of medication – carried with you if you fly – and a prescription including the generic name in case of emergency.

Several **books** give a good overview of accessible travel in Australia, and include: *Smooth Ride Guides: Australia and New Zealand*, *Freewheeling Made Easy* (FT Publishing), which lists support organizations, airports and transport, specialist tour operators and places to visit and stay; *Easy Access Australia* (Easy Access Australia Publishing), which has information on all the states, with maps, and a separate section with floor plans of hotel rooms; and *A Wheelie's Handbook of Australia* ($19.95 plus $5 postage and handling; available from Colin James, PO Box 89, Coleraine, Victoria 3315).

Useful contacts

Ⓦ www.wheelabout.com and Ⓦ www.accessibility.com.au both have lists of accommodation and transport in Australia for people with disabilities as well as Access Maps of major Australian cities.

In the UK and Ireland

All Go Here Ⓦ www.everybody.co.uk. Provides information on accommodation suitable for disabled travellers throughout the UK, including Northern Ireland.

Holiday Care 5th Floor, Surrey House, 4 Bedford Park, Croydon, Surrey CRO 2AP, Ⓣ 0845/124 9971, Minicom Ⓣ 0845/124 9976, Ⓦ www.holidaycare.org.uk. Provides free lists of accessible accommodation abroad – European, American and long-haul destinations – plus a list of accessible attractions in the UK. Information on financial help for holidays available.

Irish Wheelchair Association Blackheath Drive, Clontarf, Dublin 3 Ⓣ 01/833 8241, Ⓕ 833 3873, Ⓔ iwa@iol.ie. Useful information provided about travelling abroad with a wheelchair.

RADAR (Royal Association for Disability and Rehabilitation) 12 City Forum, 250 City Rd, London EC1V 8AF Ⓣ 020/7250 3222, Minicom Ⓣ 020/7250 4119, Ⓦ www.radar.org.uk.

Tripscope The vassal centre,Gill Avenue, Bristol BS 16 2QQ, Ⓣ 0845/7585 641, Ⓦ www.tripscope.org.uk. This registered charity provides a national telephone information service offering free advice on UK and international transport for those with a mobility problem.

In the US and Canada

Access-Able Ⓦ www.access-able.com. Online resource for travellers with disabilities.

Mobility International USA 451 Broadway, Eugene, OR 97401, voice and TDD Ⓣ 541/343-1284, Ⓦ www.miusa.org. Information and referral services, access guides, tours and exchange programmes. Annual membership $35 (includes quarterly newsletter).

Society for Accessible Travel & Hospitality (SATH) 347 5th Ave, New York, NY 10016 Ⓣ 212/447-7284, Ⓦ www.sath.org. Non-profit educational organization that has actively represented travellers with disabilities since 1976.

Travel Information Service Ⓣ 215/456-9600. Telephone-only information and referral service.

Twin Peaks Press Box 129, Vancouver, WA 98661 Ⓣ 360/694-2462 or 1-800/637-2256, Ⓔ twinpeak@pacifier.com. Publisher of the *Directory of Travel Agencies for the Disabled* ($19.95), listing more than 370 agencies worldwide; *Travel for the Disabled* ($19.95); the *Directory of Accessible Van Rentals* ($12.95); and *Wheelchair Vagabond* ($19.95), loaded with personal tips.

Wheels Up! Ⓣ 1-888/389-4335, Ⓦ www.wheelsup.com. Provides discounted airfare, tour and cruise prices for disabled travellers, also publishes a free monthly newsletter and has a comprehensive website.

Australia

ACROD (Australian Council for Rehabilitation of the Disabled) PO Box 60, Curtin ACT 2605 Ⓣ 02/6282 4333; Suite 103, 1st Floor, 1–5 Commercial Rd, Kingsgrove 2208 Ⓣ 02/9554 3666, and offices in other states. Ⓦ www.acrod.org.au. Regional offices provide lists of state-based help organizations, accommodation, travel agencies and tour operators.

DIRC (Disability Information Resource Centre) 195 Gilles St, Adelaide, SA 5000 Ⓣ 08/8236 0555.

Disability Advocacy Service Shop 1A, 63 Railway Terrace, Alice Springs, NT 0871 Ⓣ 08/8953 1422.

Disability Information Victoria PO Box 295, Malvern, Victoria Ⓣ 1300/650 865.

NICAN (National Information Communication Awareness Network) PO Box 407, Curtin, ACT 2605 Ⓣ 02/6285 3713 or 1800 806 769, Ⓦ www.nican.com.au. A national, non-profit, free information service on recreation, sport, tourism, the arts, and much more, for people with disabilities. Has a database of 4500 organizations – such as wheelchair-accessible tourist accommodation venues, sports and recreation organizations, and rental companies who have accessible buses and vans.

Paraplegic and Quadriplegic Association 208 Wellington Rd, Collingwood, Victoria Ⓣ 03/9415 1200, Ⓦ www.paraquad.asn.au. Serves the interests of the spinally injured; offices in each state capital.

Travellers Aid Support Centre 2nd Floor, 169 Swanston St, Melbourne, VIC 3000 ⓣ 03/9654 7690.

Accommodation

Much of Australia's tourist accommodation is well set up for people with disabilities, because buildings tend to be built outwards rather than upwards. New buildings in Australia must comply with a legal minimum **accessibility standard**, requiring that bathrooms contain toilets at the appropriate height, proper circulation and transfer space, wheel-in showers (sometimes with fold-down seat, but if this is lacking, proprietors will provide a plastic chair), grab rails, adequate doorways, and space next to toilets and beds for transfer. There are, of course, many older hotels which may have no wheelchair access at all or perhaps just one or two rooms with full wheelchair access. Most hotels also have refrigerators for medication which needs to be kept cool.

The best place to start looking for accommodation is the *A–Z Australian Accommodation Guide* published by the Australian Automobile Association (AAA) – the umbrella organization for state- and territory-based motoring associations that rate accommodation. They also offer some specialized services, a centralized **booking service** and a repair service for motorized wheelchairs, with reciprocal rights if you are a member of an affiliated overseas motoring organization. The guide is available from any of the state organizations; NICAN also has access to their database via computer, so you can choose your accommodation over the phone. Many travel shops and bookshops have accommodation guides which detail places that have wheelchair access.

The greatest range of accessible accommodation is found in the more densely populated areas of Australia – especially the east coast. In the **cities**, the big chain hotels have rooms with wheelchair access. Some of the smaller hotels do provide accessible accommodation, and a large proportion of suburban motels will have one or two suitable rooms. In the **country** there are fewer specially equipped hotels, but many motels have accessible units; this is particularly true of those that belong to a chain such as Choice Hotels – consult their directories or website ⓦ www.choicehotels.com.au for locations. The newest YHA **hostels** are all accessible, and there has been an effort to improve facilities throughout; accessible hostels are detailed in the YHA *Handbook*, or contact them direct (see "Accommodation"). **Caravan parks** are also worth considering, since some have accessible cabins. Others may have accessible toilets and washing facilities. Many **resorts** are also fully designed and equipped for wheelchair travellers, though in all cases, it's best to check in advance what facilities are available.

Transport

Interstate **buses** are generally not an option, though interstate **trains** can accommodate wheelchairs and give assistance for other disabilities; for enquiries about services in Queensland, New South Wales and Victoria call ⓣ 13 2232, for elsewhere phone ⓣ 1800 888 480. However, the most convenient ways of getting around are by plane and car. The two domestic airlines Qantas and Virgin Blue (see "Getting around") have services to help people with disabilities; Qantas staff undergo special disability-awareness training and on international flights their aircraft carry the sky chair and are equipped with a larger toilet cubicle.

Of the major car-rental agencies, Hertz and Avis offer **vehicles with hand controls** at no extra cost, but advance notice is required. Reserved **parking** is available for vehicles displaying the wheelchair symbol (available from local council offices) in all major centres. There is no formal acceptance of overseas parking permits, but states will generally accept most home-country permits as sufficient evidence to obtain a temporary countrywide permit in Australia. Parking charges and designated spaces differ from state to state (call NICAN for further information). A specially adapted **taxi service** operates from all the major national airports, booked in advance on freecall ⓣ 1800 043 187; in addition every capital city has wheelchair-accessible taxis. Some suburban rail services can be used with a wheelchair: Melbourne's Metlink leads the way – call (ⓣ 1800 800 120). Minibuses in some cities have either a hoist or a ramp for rental (call NICAN for further information – see p.87).

All capital cities and most regional centres produce **mobility maps** showing accessible paths, car parking, toilets and so on, which can be obtained from local councils. Other cities have gone further and their tourist authorities produce comprehensive books such as *Access Brisbane* and *Darwin City without Steps*, while ACROD in New South Wales publishes *Accessing Sydney* (available from them at Suite 103, 1st floor, 1–5 Commercial Rd, Kingsgrove NSW 2208). *Easy Access Australia – A Travel Guide to Australia* ($27.45) is a comprehensive guide written by the wheelchair-user Bruce Cameron for anyone with a mobility difficulty. It is available from all good bookstores ISBN 0-9577510-1-X) or from the author: PO Box 218, Kew, Vic 3101, Ⓣ0407/317 397, Ⓕ03/9853 900; Ⓔbruceeaa@vicnet.net.au Ⓦwww.easyaccessaustralia.com.au.

Travelling with children

Australians have an easy-going attitude to children and in most places they are made welcome. With plenty of beautiful beaches, parks and playgrounds, travelling with children in Australia can be great fun.

Getting around

Most forms of **transport** within Australia offer child concessions. Throughout the country, **metropolitan buses** and **trains** give discounts of around fifty percent for children and many allow children under 4 or 5 to travel free. Most **interstate buses** offer around twenty percent off for children under the age of 14.

Long-distance train travel is limited in Australia. It's also a slower and more expensive option, but if you're travelling with small children, it does have the advantage of sleepers and a bit more freedom of movement. **Domestic airlines** offer discounts of around fifty percent of the full adult fare, for children between 2 and 11 years. However, it's worth checking for adult discount deals which are likely to be even cheaper. Infants usually travel free of charge.

Otherwise, there's always the option of **self-drive**. Car rental is reasonably priced, and motorhomes and campervans are also available for rental. They're an excellent way of seeing Australia and make it possible to camp rough in some spectacular national parks, as well as the many caravan parks, which offer power, amenities and often a pool and activities room. In most cases babies and very young children can camp for free. It's important to remember (especially when travelling with children) that Australia is a huge place and that driving outside of the major cities almost always involves long distances. Take plenty of activities for the car – music, books, magnetic games, cards and, if you don't like your children's taste in music, let them bring their own headsets. Stop regularly for breaks: most towns in Australia have public playgrounds which are a great way for young kids to let off steam.

Accommodation

Many **motels** give discounts for children and some offer a baby-sitting service – it's worth checking when you book. The Novotel chain allows two children up to the age of 16 to stay for free (Ⓦwww.accorhotels.com.au/novotel). If you like the idea of a quiet whinge-free bushwalk or cocktails by the pool, most **resorts** have kids' clubs, organized children's activities and baby-sitting services.

Although initially more expensive, **self-contained accommodation** can prove cheaper in the long run as it's possible to cook your own meals. With young children this is often the best way to relax, without worrying about tired, grumpy behaviour in restaurants. Unless your children are older and very well-behaved, avoid **B&Bs** wherever possible. They're inevitably dotted with breakables and usually call for quiet and restraint that isn't possible with young children.

These days **youth hostels** are not exclusively for young backpackers and most provide affordable family rooms – some en-suite. A few of the more modern hostels are positively luxurious, most are in fabulous locations, and in cities they're usually conveniently close to the city centre. They all have communal kitchens, lounge areas and television and there's usually plenty of books and games.

Aside from camping, the most economical way to see Australia is to stay in some of the thousands of **caravan parks** in Australia. Most have on-site vans or self-contained cabins at very reasonable rates for families. Check with information centres for caravan park listings.

Eating out

Things have moved on in Australia and, in the cities especially, many of the more atmospheric upmarket **restaurants** are welcoming to children, often providing high-chairs, toys, blackboards, drawing materials and a reasonable children's menu. Otherwise, there are still plenty of the standard fast-food outlets, which often have enclosed play areas, and children are allowed in the dining section of pubs for counter meals. Most country towns in Australia have pubs and some have RSL clubs (Returned Servicemen's League), which are a good cheap way to feed the family on basic pub food and make a welcome change from the greasy hamburgers, chips, meat pies and steak sandwiches sold practically everywhere.

Kids' gear

Car and van rental companies provide **child safety seats**. Taxis will also provide child seats if you request them when making a booking, although there may be a longer wait. Airlines will allow you to carry a pram or travel cot for free, and it's possible to rent baby equipment from some shops – check the local *Yellow Pages* for listings. When planning a sightseeing day that involves a lot of walking, check with the tourist attraction to see if they rent out pushchairs, as this can make the difference between a pleasant and an awful day out.

Activities

Most tours and entry fees for tourist destinations offer **concession rates** for children and many also offer family tickets. If you have two or more children these will usually work out substantially cheaper. Museums often have special children's areas and during school holidays many run **supervised activities**, along with programmes that include storytelling and performances (check "Opening Hours, holidays and festivals" for school holiday dates). In most states the National Parks and Wildlife Service runs entertaining and educational ranger-led walks and activities during the school holidays. The walks are free, but there's usually a park entrance fee. Check at information centres or with NPWS in each state for timetables and fees.

Sun care

The Australian **sun** is ferocious, making it essential to combine outdoor activities with sensible skin care. A broad-spectrum, water-resistant sunscreen (minimum SPF of 30) is essential; see "Health" for more on sunscreens. There's a "no hat, no play" policy in school playgrounds and most kids wear legionnaire-style caps, or broad-brimmed sun hats, which are cheap and easy to find in surf shops and department stores. All sunglasses in Australia are UV-rated and most kids also wear UV-resistant lycra swim tops or wetsuit-style all-in-ones to the beach. The Cancer Council Australia has shops in most Australian cities selling a high-quality and colourful range of all these items; for locations consult Ⓦwww.cancer.org.au.

Helpful publications

For general tips and anecdotes pick up the latest copy of Lonely Planet's *Travel With Children*, by Cathy Lanigan and Maureen Wheeler. More specifically there are excellent guidebooks to what to do with kids in Sydney (*Sydney For Under Fives* by Seana Smith),

Melbourne (*Melbourne For Kids* by Deb Morris and Jean Nankin) and Tasmania (*It's a Kids' Life* by Wendy Nielson and Avril Priem), which are eagerly snapped up by local parents. In Sydney look for *Sydney's Child* (Ⓦwww.sydneyschild.com.au), a free monthly magazine listing kids' activities in and around the city and advertising a range of services including babysitting. Spin-offs *Canberra's Child* (Ⓦwww.canberraschild.com.au), *Melbourne's Child* (Ⓦwww.melbourneschild.com.au), *Brisbane's Child* (Ⓦwww.brisbaneschild.com.au) and *Adelaide's Child* (Ⓦwww.adelaideschild.com.au) have the same format and the websites include some of the content. All can be picked up at libraries and major museums. In other states, most tourist information centres will be able to help with suggestions for planning a child-friendly itinerary.

Gay and lesbian Australia

Year by year Australia grows in popularity as a Queer destination. Even as far back as 1832 a Select Committee of the British Parliament noted the popularity of "alternative lifestyles" among the colonists. Today, the beautiful people flock down under, lured by the conducive climate and laid-back lifestyle and eager to hang out with the homeboys on balmy beaches and sun-kissed city streets.

Despite its reputation as a macho culture, Australia revels in a large and active **scene**: you'll find an air of confidence and a sense of community that is often missing in other countries – and, what's more, it's friendly and accessible.

The colonists transported English **law** to Australia, but in 1972 South Australia was the first state to enact **decriminalization**, followed the next year by the ACT and Northern Territory. Surprisingly, Victoria and New South Wales (generally thought of as liberal states) delayed similar legislation until the 1980s. Less surprisingly, Queensland took the plunge only in 1991, while it took a decade of constant petitioning from the Tasmanian Gay and Lesbian Rights Group, and pressure from the Federal Government and the UN Human Rights Committee for the law to change in Tasmania in 1997. In Western Australia there's still an **age of consent** of 21, whereas the ages of consent in ACT and Victoria (both 16), SA and Tasmania (both 17), are the same as the heterosexual age. In the Northern Territory and NSW, the homosexual age of consent is 18. In Queensland, the age of consent for homosexuals depends on the sexual act practised, with anal sex outlawed until 18 but otherwise 16. Sex between women is either not mentioned in state laws or is covered by the heterosexual age. The foreign partner in a **de facto** gay relationship can apply to immigrate to or permanently reside in Australia, a much better situation than in many countries, but the current battle the gay and lesbian lobby groups are waging is to make same-sex relationships as completely equal in the eyes of the law as heterosexual ones, in terms of marriage, parenting, next of kin rights, superannuation and age of consent.

Today, Australia is testimony to the power of the **pink dollar**, and there's an abundance of gay venues, services, businesses, travel clubs, country retreats and the like. Given the climate, the scene obviously makes use of sun and sport, and while it's far from limited to the tan and toned muscle crowd, if you want to make the most of a thriving community, it's a good idea to pack your swimming, snorkelling and clubbing gear.

Australian dykes are refreshingly open and self-possessed – a relief after the more closed and cliquey scene in Europe. The flip side of their fearlessness is the predominance of S&M on the scene. Maybe the climate has something to do with it, but you'll see a good deal of tattoos and pierced flesh around. Dyke and gay scenes are nothing if not mercurial, and Australia is no exception. We've done our best to list bars, clubs and meeting places, but be warned that venues open, change their names, change hands, shut for refurbishment, get relaunched at a new address and finally go out of business with frightening rapidity.

Where and how to go

Sydney is the jewel in Australia's luscious navel. Firmly established as one of the world's great gay cities – only San Francisco can really rival it – it attracts lesbian and gay visitors from around the world. And if this can be overwhelming at times (the gossip alone has been known to drive people to the other side of the continent), Australia has plenty more to offer. Melbourne closely follows the scene in Sydney, but for a change of pace, take a trip to Brisbane and the Gold Coast. Perth, Adelaide and Darwin all have smaller, quieter scenes.

Away from the cities, things get more discreet, but a lot of **country areas** do have very friendly local scenes – impossible to pinpoint, but easy to stumble across. Australians on the city scene are a friendly bunch, but in a small country town they get really friendly, so if there's anything going on you'll probably get invited along.

The **Outback** covers the vast majority of the Australian continent and is, in European terms, sparsely populated. Mining and cattle ranching are the primary employers and they help to create a culture not famed for its tolerance of homosexuality. Tread carefully: bear in mind that Ayers Rock may be 2000km from Sydney as the crow flies, but in many ways it's a million miles away in terms of attitudes.

Each chapter of this Guide has specific gay and lesbian listings, with a wealth of information – see in particular the box on pp.196–197, which has all you need to know to join in Sydney's Mardi Gras celebrations.

Gay and lesbian contacts

Personal contacts

Guys 4 Men Ⓦwww.australia.guys4men.com. A personals service providing exactly what its name suggests.

Pinkboard Ⓦwww.pinkboard.com.au. Popular long-running Australian website featuring personal ads and classifieds sections with everything from houseshares, party tickets for sale, employment and a help and advice section. It's free to run your own personal or classified.

Press and multimedia

Each major capital has excellent free gay newspapers, like the *Sydney Star Observer* (Ⓦwww.ssonet.com.au) and the *Melbourne Community Voice* (Ⓦwww.mcv.net.au) that give the local lowdown. Otherwise, check out:

ALSO Foundation Ⓦwww.also.org.au. Based in Victoria, they have a good website with an excellent nationwide business and community directory.

DNA Ⓦwww.dnamagazine.com.au. National glossy – an upmarket lifestyle magazine for gay men.

Gay Australia Guide Ⓦwww.gayaustraliaguide.bigstep.com. Handy general guide. Information on where to stay, what to do, nightlife and community groups – covers Sydney and the state capitals.

LOTL (Lesbians on the Loose) Ⓦwww.lotl.com. A monthly publication available at lesbian and gay venues.

Pink + Blue Ⓦwww.pinkandblue.com.au. A useful online gay and lesbian lifestyle magazine.

The Pink Directory Ⓦwww.thepinkdirectory.com.au or contact Pink Publishing Australia, PO Box 1005, Potts Point NSW 1335 Ⓣ02/8356 9733, Ⓕ9225 9763. Launched in 2001, this is an online and print directory of gay and lesbian business and community information.

Tourist services

International Gay and Lesbian Travel Association Ⓣ1-800/448-8550 or Ⓣ1-954/776-2626, Ⓦwww.iglta.org. Trade group with lists of gay-owned or gay-friendly travel agents, accommodation and other travel businesses.

GALTA (Gay and Lesbian Tourism Australia) Ⓦwww.galta.com.au. An online resource and non-profit organization set up to promote the gay and lesbian tourism industry. Website has links to accommodation, travel agents and tour operators, and gay and lesbian printed and online guides.

Q Beds Ⓦwww.qbeds.com. An online accommodation directory and booking service for gay- and lesbian-owned, -operated or -friendly businesses.

Travel agents

Gay Travel ⓦ www.gaytravel.com. Online travel agent, concentrating mostly on accommodation.

Harvey World Travel, 70 Glen Osmond Rd, Parkside, Adelaide, SA 5063 ⓣ 08/8274 1222, ⓔ parkside@harveyworld.com.au

Tearaway Travel 1st Floor, 155 Commercial Road, South Yarra, Melbourne, VIC 3141 ⓣ 03/9827 4232, ⓦ www.tearaway.com

Women and sexual harassment

The stereotyped image of the Aussie male is of a boozy bloke interested in sport, his car and his mates, with his wife or girlfriend a poor fourth. The Australian ethos of "mateship" traditionally excluded women – the hard, tough life of the early days of white settlement, when women were scarce, fostered a male culture that's to some extent still current. Another legacy of pioneering times is the reputation of Australian women for being robust and practical.

In the main **cities**, attitudes are generally enlightened and "new men" are gaining ground, but in the more remote **country and Outback** areas, the older attitudes are more tenacious and sexual harassment can be commonplace – if rarely threatening. Men driving by in cars, in particular, are notorious for shouting out crude comments and sexual remarks as a woman walks by, and catcalling from groups of men in the street can be intimidating.

Sexual equality and attitudes

In public life, Australia has one of the best records for **sexual equality** in the world. It was the second country to give women the vote (after New Zealand in 1893), and the fact that this happened a year after federation in 1901 shows that the intention was for women to take a full role in the new nation. In the 1970s and 1980s Australia kept pace with the worldwide **feminist movement** (indeed, with Germaine Greer, it helped lead it): the first big milestone – equal pay for equal work – was finally achieved in 1974. Equal opportunities legislation and affirmative action schemes for employment have been widely adopted: today, non-sexist language is the norm for newspapers and officialdom.

However, corresponding changes in attitudes have not always kept pace with all of this. At about the same time that women achieved equal pay, the **public bars** of hotels, which had traditionally refused to serve women, were being stormed by women's groups. Today, a woman can be served a drink anywhere in the country, but the way that Australian pubs are set up – with two separate bars – continues to reflect the old bias; you'll still see signs saying "Ladies' Lounge", and if you want to go to the women's toilets you'll have to walk a long way from the public bar. **Outback and country** pubs are still very much male bastions, and any woman travelling on her own would do well to avoid them, thus escaping the full blast of misogyny.

Travelling solo

Avoiding pubs is all very well, but **hotels** are often the cheapest and sometimes the only places to stay in **small towns**. The major drawback is that pub accommodation is often full of single male workers from other towns, or old men who are permanent boarders, so roaming corridors late at night in search of the toilet can be an unpleasant experience. That said, the management is usually friendly, and most country pubs are family-run. **Bed and breakfast** establishments and **guesthouses** provide a more homelike, friendly environment, unlike the inevitably impersonal **motels** where a stay can be a potentially lonely experience. **Caravan parks** and **campsites** tend to be safe, family-dominated environments and are a good bet if you have your own transport – and sleeping bag. In larger towns and cities, **hostels** are where you're most likely to meet like-minded women travelling alone. Easy-going Australian attitudes mean that dorms in backpackers' hostels (never YHA hostels) are often mixed-sex. There's usually at least one female-only dorm and if this is really important to you, you should ask about it in advance or when you check in.

Best of all for making contact with locals and generally getting involved are **farmstays** (which needn't be expensive if you stay in shearers' quarters and the like) or the experience of being a WWOOF (Willing Workers on Organic Farms; see "Work"). Before going to work or to stay on remote **Outback stations**, try to find out as much about the set-up as possible – you could end up being the only woman among a group of men.

Rape and serious trouble

If the worst happens, it's best to contact a **Rape Crisis Line** before going straight to the police; all major cities have them and there's always a free-call line if you're in the country. Women police officers form a large part of the force, and in general the police deal sensitively with sexual assault cases.

To **avoid** physical attack, don't get too relaxed about Australia's friendly, easy-going attitude. The usual defensive tactics apply. In the cities at night, buses and trams are generally safer than trains – on the train, always sit next to the guard in the carriage. Pick somewhere to stay that's close to public transport so you don't have to walk far at night – an area with busy nightlife may well be safer than a dead suburban backstreet. If you're going to have to walk for long stretches at night, take a cab unless the streets are busy with traffic, restaurants and people.

The 1992 "backpacker murders" of hitching travellers just outside Sydney prove that it's not only in remote areas or when travelling alone that **hitchhiking** is dangerous – and that even male company is no safeguard. Hitching is doubly inadvisable for women and, with the wide variety of inexpensive transport options available, is hard to justify. If you must do it, never do it alone – and heed the general advice and warnings given in "Getting around".

Women's contacts

All the major cities have good **women's contacts**, from resource centres and information lines to health centres where you can often get free pregnancy testing and other help. There's also a lively culture of women's galleries and bookshops; as well as stocking the works of the hundreds of great Australian women writers (see "Books"), they'll have copies of feminist journals and good notice boards which often have information about **women-only accommodation**. Lesbian magazines also carry ads for women's bed and breakfasts and the like – you don't have to be gay to stay. In March, **International Women's Day** provides an excuse for a month-long series of women's events in the cities, culminating in enthusiastically attended street marches.

Specific women's contacts are listed in the city accounts of this Guide. For more, check out the White Pages under "Women"; alternatively, the Citizen's Advice Bureau in each city should be able to refer you to relevant organizations.

Directory

Electricity Australia's electrical current is 240/250v, 50Hz AC. British appliances will work with an adaptor for the Australian three-pin plug. American and Canadian 110v appliances will also need a transformer.

Emergencies Dial ⓣ000.

Gambling Australians are obsessive about gambling, though legalities vary from state to state. Even small towns have their own race-tracks and there are government TAB betting agencies everywhere; you can often bet in pubs too. Many states have huge casinos and clubs, open to anyone, with wall-to-wall one-armed bandits (poker machines or "pokies"); there are also big state lotteries.

Laundries Known as laundromats, these are rare outside urban centres. Hostels always have a laundry with at least one coin-operated washing machine and a dryer, as do most caravan parks, holiday units and a lot of motels. Five-star hotels, of course, will do it for you.

Public toilets In civic-minded Australia, public facilities can be found in all towns and cities; they are usually amazingly clean and well supplied with toilet paper and even soap. In country areas, they are located in parks and/or at council and tourist offices, and in the cities you'll find them in shopping arcades, train stations and department stores. Most roadhouses offer showers as well as toilets, usually for a small payment.

Seasons Don't forget that in the southern hemisphere the seasons are reversed. Summer lasts from November to February, winter from June to September. But of course it's not that simple: in the tropical north the important seasonal distinction is between the Wet (effectively summer) and the Dry (winter) – for more on their significance to travellers see p.637.

Student cards As an overseas student traveller, you need an International Student Identity Card (ISIC card) – well worth having (if you're eligible) for discounts on travel, tours, museum entry, etc. If you apply for one before you leave you can also get a discount on your return flight. Otherwise in Australia they cost $18 from any branch of STA Travel. Equally useful is a YHA or VIP membership card (see p.59) which can be obtained by backpackers of any age or status, and are available online or from travellers' centres throughout Australia.

Tax A Goods and Services Tax (GST) of ten percent was introduced in 2000, and caused a general across-the-board price hike. Visitors can claim GST refunds for goods purchased in Australia as they clear customs, providing individual receipts exceed $300 and the claim is made within thirty days of purchase.

Time zones Australia has three time zones: Eastern Standard Time (TAS, VIC, NSW, QLD), Central Standard Time (SA, NT) and Western Standard Time (WA). Eastern Standard Time is ten hours ahead of GMT (Greenwich Mean Time) and fifteen hours ahead of US Eastern Time. (When it's 10pm in Sydney, it's noon in London, 7am in New York and 4am in Los Angeles – but don't forget daylight saving, which can affect this by one hour either way.) Central Standard Time is thirty minutes behind Eastern Standard, and Western Standard two hours behind Eastern. Daylight saving (Oct–March) is adopted everywhere except QLD, NT and WA; clocks are put forward one hour.

Tips Tipping is not customary in Australia, and cab drivers and bar staff don't generally expect anything. In fact, cab drivers often round the fare down rather than bother with change. In cafés and restaurants you might leave the change – only very fancy establishments expect ten percent.

Weights and measures Australia has been fully metric since the early 1970s and is thoroughly adapted to kilometres, kilograms, litres and degrees Celsius. Shoe sizes are unique to Australia, while dress sizes are the same as in the UK (US 8 is equivalent to Australian 10).

Guide

Guide

1. Sydney and around 99–262
2. Coastal New South Wales and the ACT 263–352
3. Inland New South Wales 353–410
4. Southeast Queensland 411–480
5. Tropical Queensland and the Reef 481–576
6. Outback Queensland 577–628
7. Northern Territory 629–708
8. Western Australia 709–800
9. South Australia 801–898
10. Melbourne and around 899–970
11. Victoria 971–1062
12. Tasmania 1063–1172

Sydney and around

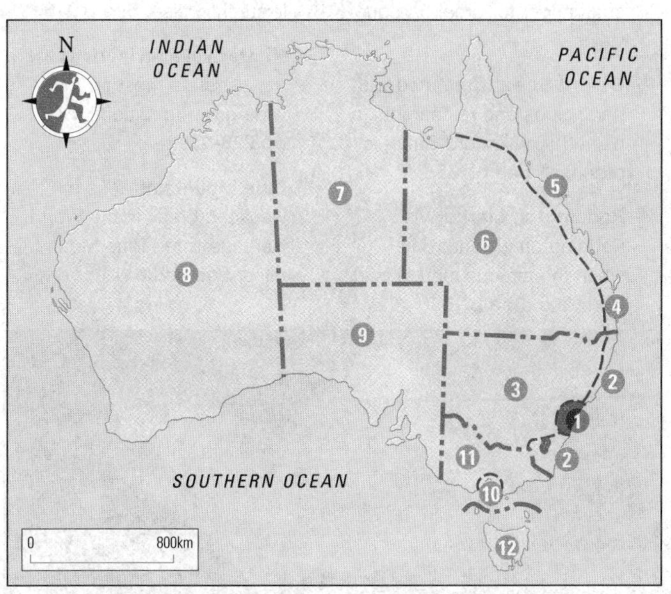

CHAPTER 1

Highlights

* **Opera House performance** Admire the stunning exterior of this Australian icon, or better still, take in a performance. See p.127
* **Manly Ferry** The ferry trip out to Manly, with its un-beatable views of the harbour, is a must. See p.128
* **Climbing Sydney Harbour Bridge** Climb the famous coathanger for great harbour views. See p.131
* **Oxford Street** Crammed with bars, clubs and restaurants, a night out on Oxford Street is essential. See p.155
* **Paddington Market** Visit Paddington on Saturday, when the famous market is in full swing. See p.155
* **Bondi Beach** Bold, brash Bondi is synonymous with Australian beach culture. See p.166
* **Mardi Gras** The biggest celebration of gay and lesbian culture in the world. See pp.196–197
* **Cruising on the Hawkesbury River** Explore the pretty Hawkesbury River on a leisurely cruise. See p.216
* **Hunter Valley wineries** One of Australia's most famous wine-growing regions. See pp.228–229
* **Blue Mountains** Take a weekend break in the World Heritage-listed Blue Mountains. See p.236

△ Sydney Opera House

Sydney and around

Flying into **Sydney** provides the first snapshot of Australia for most overseas visitors: toy-sized images of the Harbour Bridge and the Opera House, tilting in a glittering expanse of blue water. The Aussie city par excellence, Sydney stands head and shoulders above any other in Australia. Taken together with its surrounds, it's in many ways a microcosm of Australia as a whole – if only in its ability to defy your expectations and prejudices as often as it confirms them. A thrusting, high-rise business centre, a high-profile gay community and inner-city deprivation of unexpected harshness are as much part of the scene as the beaches, the bodies and the sparkling harbour. The sophistication, cosmopolitan population and exuberant nightlife of Sydney are a long way from the Outback, and yet Sydney has the highest Aboriginal population of any Australian city, and bushfires are a constant threat.

The area around – everything in this chapter is within day-trip distance – offers a taste of virtually everything you'll find in the rest of the country, with the exception of desert. There are magnificent **national parks** – Ku-Ring-Gai Chase and Royal being the best known – and native wildlife, each a mere hour's drive from the centre of town. While further north stretch endless ocean **beaches**, great for surfers, and more enclosed waters for safer swimming and sailing. Inland, the **Blue Mountains**, with three more national parks, offer isolated bushwalking and scenic viewpoints. On the way are historic colonial towns that were among the earliest foundations in the country – Sydney itself, of course, was the very first. The commercial and industrial heart of the state of New South Wales, especially the central coastal region, is bordered by **Wollongong** in the south and **Newcastle** in the north. Both were synonymous with coal and steel, but the smokestack industries that supported them for decades are now in severe decline. This is far from an industrial wasteland, though: the heart of the coal-mining country is the **Hunter Valley**, northwest of Newcastle, but to visit it you'd never guess, because this is also Australia's oldest, and arguably its best-known, wine-growing region.

Sydney

The 2000 Olympics were a coming-of-age ceremony for **SYDNEY**. The impact on the city was all-embracing, with fifty years' worth of development

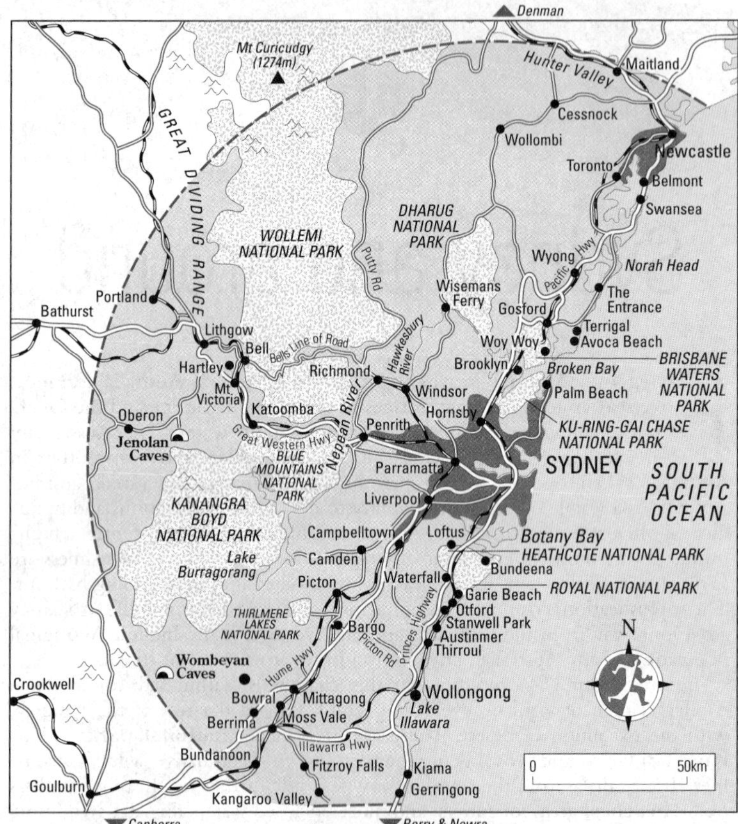

compressed into four years under the pressure of intense international scrutiny. Transport infrastructure was greatly improved and a rash of luxury hotels and waterside apartments added themselves to the skyline. The City of Sydney Council spent $200 million to improve and beautify the city streets, public squares and parks, and licensing laws changed too, creating a European-style bar culture. Sydney now has all the vigour of a world-class city, with the reputation of its restaurants in particular turning the lingering cultural sneers to swoons. It seems to have the best of both worlds – twenty minutes from Circular Quay by bus, the high-rise office buildings and skyscrapers give way to colourful inner-city suburbs where you can get an eyeful of sky and watch the lemons ripening above the sidewalk, while to the centre's north and south are corridors of largely intact bushland where many have built their dream homes. During every heatwave, however, bushfires threaten the city, and sophisticated Sydney becomes closer to its roots than it sometimes feels. In the summer, the city's hot offices are abandoned for the remarkably unspoilt beaches strung around the eastern and northern suburbs.

It's also as beautiful a city as any in the world, with a **setting** that perhaps only Rio de Janeiro can rival: the water is what makes it so special, and no introduction to Sydney would be complete without paying tribute to one of the world's great **harbours**. Port Jackson is a sunken valley which twists inland to meet the fresh water of the Parramatta River; in the process it washes into a hundred coves and bays, winds around rocky points, flows past the small harbour islands, slips under bridges and laps at the foot of the Opera House. If Sydney is seen at its gleaming best from the deck of a harbour ferry, especially at weekends when the harbour's jagged jaws fill with a flotilla of small vessels, racing yachts and cabin cruisers, it's seen at its most varied in its lively neighbourhoods. Getting away from the city centre and exploring them is an essential part of Sydney's pleasures.

It might seem surprising that Sydney is not Australia's capital: the creation of Canberra in 1927 – intended to stem the intense rivalry between Sydney and Melbourne – has not affected the view of many Sydneysiders that their city remains the true capital of Australia, and certainly in many ways it feels like it. The city has a tangible sense of history: the old stone walls and well-worn steps in the backstreets around The Rocks are an evocative reminder that Sydney has more than two hundred years of white history behind it.

Some history

The early history of Sydney is very much the history of white Australia, right from its founding as a penal colony, amid brutality, deprivation and despair. In January 1788 the **First Fleet**, carrying over a thousand people, 736 of them convicts, arrived at **Botany Bay** expecting the "fine meadows" that Captain James Cook had described eight years earlier. In fact what greeted them was mostly swamp, scrub and sand dunes: a desolate sight even for sea-weary eyes. An unsuccessful scouting expedition prompted Commander Arthur Phillip to move the fleet a few kilometres north, to the well-wooded Port Jackson, where a stream of fresh water was found. Based around the less than satisfactory Tank Stream, the settlement was named **Sydney Cove** after Viscount Sydney, then Secretary of State in Great Britain. In the first three years of settlement, the new colony nearly starved to death several times; the land around Sydney Cove proved to be barren. When supply ships did arrive, they inevitably came with hundreds more convicts to further burden the colony. It was not until 1790, when land was successfully farmed further west at **Parramatta**, that the hunger began to abate. Measure this suffering with that of the original occupants, the **Eora Aborigines**: their land had been invaded, their people virtually wiped out by smallpox, and now they were stricken by hunger as the settlers shot at their game – and even, as they moved further inland, at the Eora themselves.

By the early 1800s Sydney had become a stable colony and busy trading post. Army officers in charge of the colony, exploiting their access to free land and cheap labour, became rich farm-owners and virtually established a currency based on rum. The **military**, known as the New South Wales Corps (or more familiarly as "the rum corps"), became the supreme political force in the colony in 1809, even overthrowing the governor (mutiny-plagued Captain Bligh himself). This was the last straw for the government back home, and the rebellious officers were finally brought to heel when the reformist Governor **Lachlan Macquarie** arrived from England with forces of his own. He liberalized conditions, supported the prisoners' right to become citizens after they had served their time, and appointed several to public offices.

By the 1840s the transportation of convicts to New South Wales had ended, the explorers Lawson and Blaxland had found a way through the Blue Mountains to the Western Plains and **gold** had been struck in Bathurst. The population soared as free settlers arrived in ever-increasing numbers. In the Victorian era, Sydney's population became even more starkly divided into the **haves** and the **have-nots**: while the poor lived in slums where disease, crime, prostitution and alcoholism were rife, the genteel classes – self-consciously replicating life in the mother country – took tea on their verandahs and erected grandiloquent monuments such as the Town Hall, the Strand Arcade and the Queen Victoria Building in homage to English architecture of the time. An outbreak of the plague in The Rocks at the beginning of the twentieth century made wholesale slum clearances inevitable, and with the demolitions came a change in attitudes. Strict new vice laws meant the end of the bad old days of backstreet knifings, drunken taverns and makeshift brothels.

Over the next few decades, Sydney settled into comfortable **suburban living**. The metropolis sprawled westwards, creating a flat, unremarkable city with no real centre, an appropriate symbol for the era of shorts and knee socks and the stereotypical, barbecue-loving Bruce and Sheila – an international image which still plagues Australians. Sydney has come a long way since the parochialism of the 1950s, however: skyscrapers at the city's centre have rocketed heavenward and constructions such as the **Opera House** began to reflect the city's dynamism. The cultural clichés of cold tinnies of beer and meat pies with sauce have long been tossed out, giving way to a city confident in itself and its culinary attractions too. Today, Sydney's citizens don't look inwards – and they certainly don't look towards England. Thousands of immigrants from around the globe have given Sydney a truly cosmopolitan air and it's a city as thrilling and alive as any.

Arrival

The dream way to **arrive** in Sydney is, of course, by ship, cruising in below the great coathanger of the Harbour Bridge to tie up at the Overseas Passenger Terminal alongside Circular Quay. The reality of the functional airport, bus and train stations is a good deal less romantic.

By air

Sydney's **Kingsford Smith Airport**, referred to as "Mascot" after the suburb where it's located, near Botany Bay, is 8km south of the city (international flight times ⓣ13 12 23, ⓦwww.sydneyairport.com.au). Domestic and international terminals are linked by a free shuttle bus if you're travelling with Qantas (every 30min), or you can take the KST Sydney Airporter bus for $4; see box opposite for **buses** into the city. The **Airport Link** underground railway connects the airport to the City Circle train line in around fifteen minutes (Mon–Fri every 10min, Sat & Sun every 15min; one-way $11; to compete with taxis, there's a group fare for four people of $18 to Central Station, $24 to City Circle line stations; ⓦwww.airportlink.com.au). A return Airport Link transfer is part of the SydneyPass tourist transport package (see p.112); you can purchase one at the Sydney Visitor Centre (below). A **taxi** will cost $32 to $36 from the airport to the city centre or Kings Cross.

Bureau de change offices at both terminals are open daily from 5am until last arrival with rates comparable to major banks. On the ground floor (arrivals) of the international terminal, the **Sydney Visitor Centre** (daily 5am until last arrival; ⓣ02/9667 6050) can arrange car rental and onward travel – it's licensed to sell train and bus tickets – and **book hotels** anywhere in Sydney and New South Wales free of charge and at stand-by rates. Most hostels advertise on an adjacent notice board; there's a freephone line for reservations, and many of them will refund your bus fare; a few also do free airport pick-ups.

By train and bus

All local and interstate **trains** arrive at **Central Station** on Eddy Avenue, just south of the city centre. There are lockers and left luggage at the "country trains" section of the station, and showers at the volunteer-run **Travellers' Aid** on Platform 1 (Mon–Fri 8am–2.30pm; shower $3, with towel $5, bed $2 per hour). From outside Central Station, and neighbouring **Railway Square** you can hop onto nearly every major bus route, and from within Central station you can take a CityRail train to any city or suburban station (see "City transport" on p.106).

All **buses** to Sydney arrive and depart from Eddy Avenue and Pitt Street, bordering Central station. The area is well set up with decent cafés, a 24-hour police station and a huge YHA hostel as well as the **Sydney Coach Terminal** (daily 6am–10pm), which also has luggage lockers ($7–12 per 24hr, depending on size). The **Traveller's Information Service** (Ⓣ02/9281 9366) in the coach terminal can make hotel **accommodation bookings** and there are free phones for hostel reservations; pick-up is usually free (from Bay 14). You can purchase coach tickets and passes from the Information Service as well as Sydney Passes (see box, p.112), and arrange harbour cruises and other tours. Greyhound Australia also has separate ticket offices/departure lounges on Eddy Avenue.

Airport buses

State Transi

State Transit no longer offers dedicated airport buses but there is a daily commuter route heading east and west: the Metroline #400 goes frequently to Bondi Junction via Maroubra and Randwick in one direction, and to Burwood in the other (tickets cost a maximum of $4.80).

Shuttle services - Sydney area

KST Sydney Transporter Ⓣ02/9666 9988, Ⓦwww.kst.com.au. Private bus service dropping off at hotels or hostels in the area bounded by Kings Cross and Darling Harbour. Service leaves when the bus is full ($9 one-way, $14 return). Bookings three hours in advance for an accommodation pick-up to the airport.

Super Shuttles Ⓣ02/9311 3789, Ⓦwww.supershuttle.com.au. Minibus service (quick call-out service) to and from the city and eastern beaches - Bondi, Coogee, Randwick, Clovelly and Bronte - and dropping off at all hostels, motels and hotels ($12 one-way). Book an accommodation pick-up 24 hours in advance to return to airport.

Surface To Air Ⓣ02/9913 9912, Ⓦwww.surfacetoair.com.au. Minibus service to the city and the northern beaches - including Manly, Whale Beach and Palm Beach - dropping off at accommodation. Book in advance by phone or email giving the day, time and flight and they will designate a waiting point. Manly $28, Palm Beach $55 (cheaper rates for couples and groups).

Coach and shuttle services - central coast and south coast

Aussie Shuttles Ⓣ1300 130 557, Ⓦwww.ben-air.com.au. Pre-booked door-to-door service to accommodation anywhere on the central coast ($55–$65, cheaper rates for couples and groups), and to Newcastle ($95).

Premier Motor Service Ⓣ13 34 10, for bookings outside Australia Ⓣ02/4423 5244, Ⓦwww.premierms.com.au. Departs daily at 9.45am and 3.30pm, plus Monday to Friday at 7.45am from the domestic terminal, fifteen minutes later from the international terminal, to south coast towns as far as Bega ($53), the 9.45am and 3.30pm services continuing on to Eden ($60). Bookings necessary.

Information

There are three **Sydney Visitor Centres** offering comprehensive information, free accommodation and tour booking facilities, and selling tourist transport tickets and sightseeing passes. The Sydney Visitor Centre at the international airport terminal is detailed on p.104. The other two are centrally located at 106 George St, The Rocks, just behind the Museum of Contemporary Art; and at Darling Harbour, beside the IMAX cinema (both daily 9.30am–5.30pm; ⓣ02/9240 8788 or 1800 067 676; ⓦwww.sydneyvisitorcentre.com). Free **maps** and brochures can be picked up at all three, including the very useful *Sydney: The Official Guide*. Tourism New South Wales (Tourist Information Line ⓣ13 20 77, ⓦwww.visitnsw.com.au) runs the **City Host information kiosks** (daily 9am–5pm) at Circular Quay (on the corner of Pitt and Alfred streets), Martin Place and Town Hall providing brochures, maps and face-to-face information. There's also a tourist office at Manly.

Several free monthly **listings magazines** are worth picking up at tourist offices: the weekly *Where Magazine* is best for general information; the quarterly *This Week in Sydney* is also useful; and *TNT Magazine* is the best of an array of publications aimed at **backpackers**, giving the lowdown on Sydney on the cheap.

City transport

Sydney's **public transport network** is reasonably good, though the system relies heavily on buses, and traffic jams can be a problem. There are **State Transit Authority (STA)** buses, trains and ferries, and a privately run light rail and monorail system to choose from, plus plenty of licensed taxis. Trains stop running around midnight, as do most regular buses, though several services towards the eastern and northern beaches, such as the #380 to Bondi Beach, the #372 and #373 to Coogee and the #151 to Manly, run through the night. Otherwise a pretty good network of **Nightride buses** follows the train routes to the suburbs, departing from Town Hall station (outside the Energy Australia Building on George St) and stopping at train stations (where taxis wait at designated ranks); return train tickets, Railpasses and Travelpasses can be used, or buy a ticket from the driver. For stays of more than a few days, a weekly STA **Travelpass** is a worthwhile investment (see box on p.112). For public transport information, routes and timetables call ⓣ13 15 00 (daily 6am–10pm; ⓦwww.131500.com.au).

Smartvisit Card

All three Sydney Visitor Centres sell the **See Sydney & Beyond Smartvisit Card** (ⓣ1300 661 711, ⓦwww.seesydneycard.com) which comes in one-, two-, three- and seven-day versions (to be used over consecutive days) with or without a transport option (one-day $65/$80, two-day $109/$145, three-day $139/$195, seven-day $199/$265; cheaper children's passes are available) and includes admission to forty well-known attractions in Sydney and the Blue Mountains as well as a range of discounts. If an action-packed, fast-paced itinerary is your thing the card can be good value and it's certainly a convenient way to by-pass the queues. To work out whether it's worth buying one decide what you want to see, check the entry prices in our Guide and compare the total amount to the price of a card, and work out a realistic schedule.

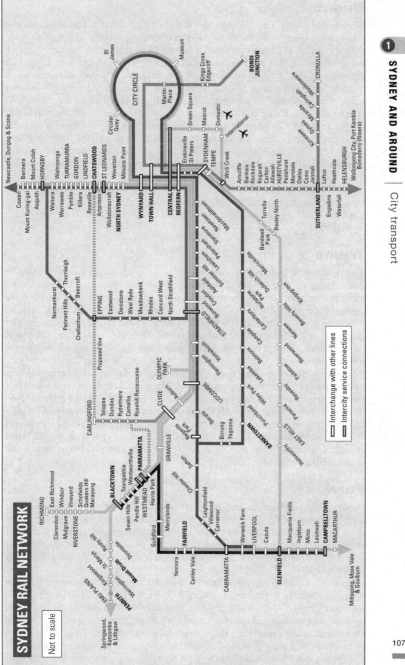

SYDNEY RAIL NETWORK

Not to scale

Newcastle, Dungog & Scone
Cowan
Berowra
Mount Kuring-gai
Mount Colah
Asquith
HORNSBY
Waitara
Wahroonga
Warrawee
TURRAMURRA
Pymble
GORDON
Killara
LINDFIELD
Roseville
CHATSWOOD
Artarmon
ST LEONARDS
Wollstonecraft
Waverton
NORTH SYDNEY
Milsons Point
WYNYARD
TOWN HALL
CENTRAL
REDFERN

Circular Quay
St James
CITY CIRCLE
Museum
Martin Place
Kings Cross
Edgecliff
BONDI JUNCTION

Normanhurst
Thornleigh
Pennant Hills
Beecroft
Cheltenham
EPPING
Eastwood
Denistone
West Ryde
Meadowbank
Rhodes
Concord West
North Strathfield

CARLINGFORD
Proposed line
Telopea
Dundas
Rydalmere
Camellia
Rosehill Racecourse

RICHMOND
East Richmond
Clarendon
Windsor
Mulgrave
Vineyard
RIVERSTONE
Schofields
Quakers Hill
Marayong

Springwood, Katoomba & Lithgow
EMU PLAINS
PENRITH
Kingswood
Werrington
St Marys
Mount Druitt
Rooty Hill
Doonside
BLACKTOWN
Seven Hills
Toongabbie
Pendle Hill
Wentworthville
WESTMEAD
PARRAMATTA
Harris Park
GRANVILLE
CLYDE
Auburn
OLYMPIC PARK
LIDCOMBE
Berala
Regents Park
Flemington
Homebush
STRATHFIELD
Burwood
Croydon
Ashfield
Summer Hill
Lewisham
Petersham
Stanmore
Newtown
Macdonaldtown

Guildford
Merrylands
Yennora
FAIRFIELD
Canley Vale
Chester Hill
Sefton
Leightonfield
Villawood
Carramar
CABRAMATTA
Warwick Farm
LIVERPOOL
Casula
GLENFIELD
Macquarie Fields
Ingleburn
Minto
Leumeah
CAMPBELLTOWN
MACARTHUR
Mittagong, Moss Vale & Goulburn

Birrong
Yagoona
BANKSTOWN
Punchbowl
Wiley Park
Lakemba
Belmore
Campsie
Canterbury
Hurlstone Park
Dulwich Hill
Marrickville

Holsworthy
EAST HILLS
Panania
Revesby
Padstow
Riverwood
Narwee
Beverly Hills
Kingsgrove
Bexley North
Bardwell Park
Turrella

Erskineville
St Peters
SYDENHAM
TEMPE
Green Square
Mascot
Domestic
International
Wolli Creek
Arncliffe
Banksia
Rockdale
Kogarah
Carlton
Allawah
HURSTVILLE
Penshurst
Mortdale
Oatley
Como
Jannali
SUTHERLAND
Kirrawee
Gymea
Miranda
Caringbah
Woolooware
CRONULLA
Loftus
Engadine
Heathcote
Waterfall
HELENSBURGH
Wollongong City, Port Kembla
Bomaderry (Nowra)

Interchange with other lines
Intercity service connections

Buses

Within the central area, **buses**, hailed from yellow-signed bus stops, are the most convenient, widespread mode of transport, and cover more of the city than the trains. With few exceptions buses radiate from the centre with major interchanges at Railway Square near Central station (especially southwest routes), at Circular Quay (range of routes), from York and Carrington streets outside Wynyard station (North Shore), and Bondi Junction station (eastern suburbs and beaches). **Tickets** can be bought on board from the driver and cost from $1.60 for up to two distance-measured sections, with the maximum fare at $5.20; $2.70 (up to five sections) is the most typical fare. Substantial discounts are available with TravelTen tickets and other travel passes (see box on pp.112–113); these must be validated in the ticket reader by the front door. Bus **information**, including route maps, **timetables** and **passes** is available from handy booths at Carrington Street, Wynyard; at Circular Quay on the corner of Loftus and Alfred streets; at the Queen Victoria Building on York Street; at Bondi Junction bus interchange; and at Manly Wharf. For detailed timetables and route maps see Sydney Buses' website Ⓦwww.sydneybuses .nsw.gov.au.

Trains

Trains, operated by **CityRail** (see Sydney Rail map), will get you where you're going faster than buses, especially at rush hour and when heading out to the suburbs, but you need to transfer to a bus or ferry to get to most harbourside or beach destinations. There are six train lines, mostly overground, each of which stops at Central and Town Hall stations. Trains run from around 5am to midnight, with **tickets** starting at around $2.20 single on the City Loop and for short hops; buying off-peak returns (after 9am and all weekend) means you can save up to forty percent.

Automatic ticket vending machines (which give change) and barriers (insert magnetic tickets, otherwise show ticket at the gate) have been introduced just about everywhere. On-the-spot fines for fare evasion start from $200 and transit officers patrol frequently. All platforms are painted with designated "nightsafe" waiting areas and all but two or three train carriages are closed after about 8pm, enforcing a cattle-like safety in numbers. Security guards also patrol trains at night. At other times, if the train is deserted, sit in the carriage nearest the guard, marked by a blue light.

Ferries

Sydney's distinctive green-and-yellow **ferries** are the fastest means of transport from Circular Quay to the North Shore, and indeed to most places around the harbour. Even if you don't want to go anywhere, a ferry ride is a must, a chance to get out on the water and see the city from the harbour. There's also a speedy **hydrofoil**, the JetCat, which reaches Manly in half the time, but with less charm.

There are ferries going off in various directions from the wharves at Circular Quay (see Sydney Ferries map); cruises depart from Jetty 6. The last ferry service from Circular Quay to Manly is at 7pm after which time the faster JetCats operate until midnight, 11pm on Saturdays. Other ferry routes, such as those to Parramatta and Pyrmont Bay, also operate only until early evening, while ferries to locations including Neutral Bay and Balmain continue to around 11.30pm. Except for the Manly Ferry, services on Sunday are greatly reduced and often

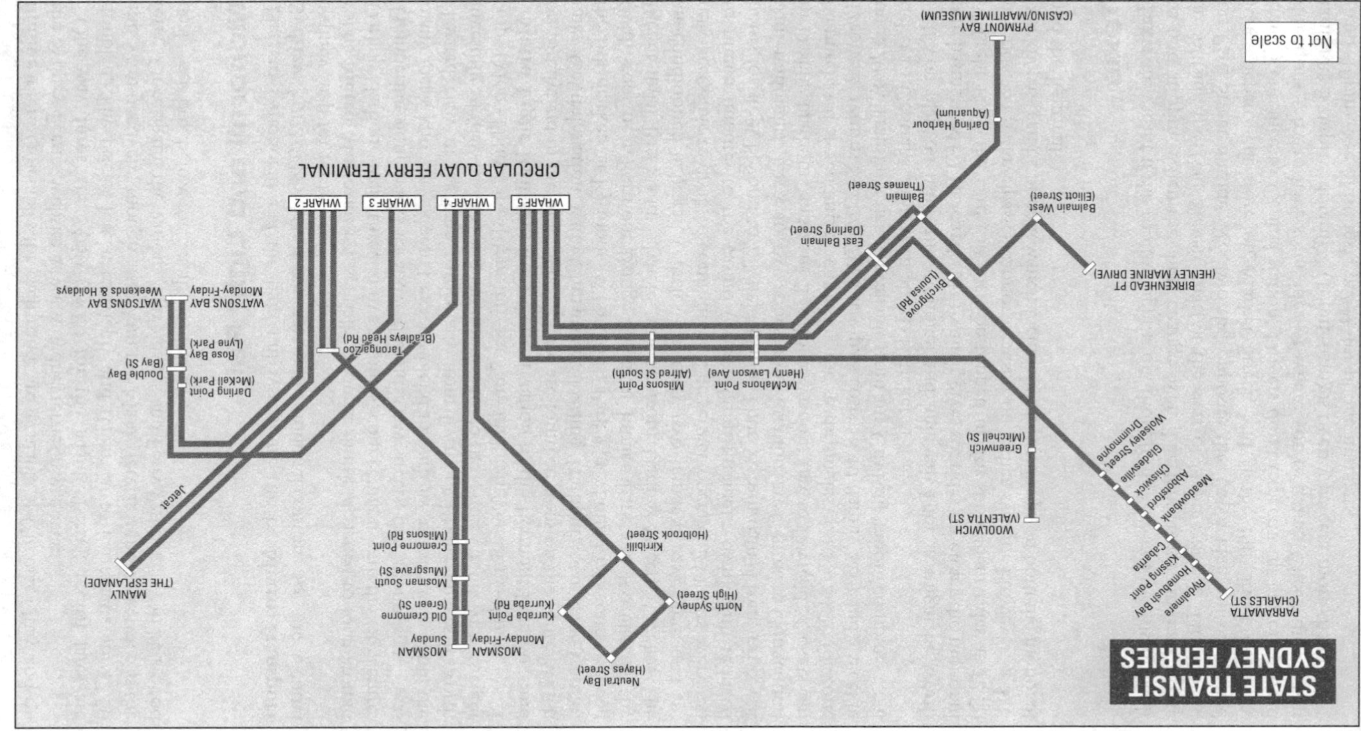
STATE TRANSIT
SYDNEY FERRIES
Not to scale
PARRAMATTA (CHARLES ST)
Rydalmere
Homebush Bay
Kissing Point
Cabarita
Meadowbank
Abbotsford
Chiswick
Gladesville
Wolseley Street, Drummoyne
WOOLWICH (VALENTIA ST)
Greenwich (Mitchell St)
BIRKENHEAD PT (HENLEY MARINE DRIVE)
Balmain West (Elliott Street)
Birchgrove (Louisa Rd)
Balmain (Thames Street)
East Balmain (Darling Street)
Darling Harbour (Aquarium)
PYRMONT BAY (CASINO/MARITIME MUSEUM)
McMahons Point (Henry Lawson Ave)
Milsons Point (Alfred St South)
North Sydney (High Street)
Kirribilli (Holbrook Street)
Neutral Bay (Hayes Street)
Kurraba Point (Kurraba Rd)
MOSMAN Monday-Friday
MOSMAN Sunday
Old Cremorne (Green St)
Mosman South (Musgrave St)
Cremorne Point (Milsons Rd)
Taronga Zoo (Bradleys Head Rd)
WHARF 5
WHARF 4
WHARF 3
WHARF 2
CIRCULAR QUAY FERRY TERMINAL
Darling Point (McKell Park)
Double Bay (Bay St)
Rose Bay (Lyne Park)
WATSONS BAY Monday-Friday
WATSONS BAY Weekends & Holidays
MANLY (THE ESPLANADE)
Jetcat

finish earlier. Timetables for each route are available at Circular Quay and on the Sydney Ferries website Ⓦwww.sydneyferries.nsw.gov.au.

One-way **fares** are $4.50 ($5.80 for the Manly Ferry); return fares are doubled. The pricier JetCat to Manly and RiverCat to Parramatta are $7.50 and $7 respectively, though after 7pm the Manly JetCat is the same price as the ferry. Once again, the various Travelpasses and FerryTen tickets can be a good deal – see box below for details.

Monorail and Light Rail

The city's monorail and the light rail system are run by **Metro Transport Sydney** (Ⓣ02/9285 5600, Ⓦwww.metromonorail.com.au; see the Central Sydney map for more details on routes).

The **Metro Monorail** is essentially a tourist shuttle designed to loop around Darling Harbour every three to five minutes, connecting it with the city centre. Thundering along tracks set above the older city streets, the "monster rail" – as many locals know it – doesn't exactly blend in with its surroundings. Still, the elevated view of the city, particularly from Pyrmont Bridge, makes it worth investing $4 (day-pass $8) and ten minutes to do the whole circuit with its eight stops (Mon–Thurs 7am–10pm, Fri–Sat 7am–midnight, Sun 8am–10pm).

Metro Light Rail runs from Central station to the Pyrmont Peninsula and on to Lilyfield in the inner west. There are fourteen stops on the route, which links Central station with Chinatown, Darling Harbour, Star City Casino, the fish markets at Pyrmont, Wentworth Park's greyhound racecourse, Glebe (with stops near Pyrmont Bridge Road, at Jubilee Park and Rozelle Bay by Bicentennial Park) and Lilyfield, not far from Darling Street, Rozelle. The air-conditioned light rail vehicles can carry two hundred passengers, and are fully accessible to disabled commuters. The service operates 24 hours every ten to fifteen minutes to the casino (every 30min midnight–6am) with reduced hours for stops beyond to Lilyfield (Mon–Thurs & Sun 6am–11pm, Fri & Sat 6am–midnight). There are two zones: zone 1 stations are Central to Convention in Darling Harbour, and zone 2 is from Pyrmont Bay to Lilyfield. Tickets can be purchased at vending machines by the stops; singles cost $3/$4.20 for zone 1/zone 2, returns $4.60/5.70, a day-pass costs $8.40 (family $20) and a weekly one $20. A TramLink ticket, available from any CityRail station, combines a rail ticket to Central station with an MLR ticket.

If you plan on using the monorail and light rail a lot, it might be worth purchasing a **METROcard** ($18) which gives six rides on either the monorail or Light Rail; the card can then be topped up for subsequent rides at $2.50 per ride. STA travelpasses cannot be used on either system. However, a $28 weekly pass can be bought which includes unlimited trips on both the monorail and the light rail.

Taxis

Taxis are vacant if the rooftop light is on, though they are notoriously difficult to find at 3pm, when the shifts change over. The four major city **cab ranks** are outside the *Four Seasons Hotel* at the start of George Street, The Rocks; on Park Street outside Woolworths, opposite the Town Hall; outside David Jones department store on Market Street; and at the Pitt Street ('country trains') entrance to Central station. Drivers don't expect a tip but often need directions – try to have some idea of where you're going. Check the correct tariff rate is displayed: tariff 2 (10pm–6am) is twenty percent more than tariff 1 (6am–10pm). See "Listings", p.209, for phone numbers.

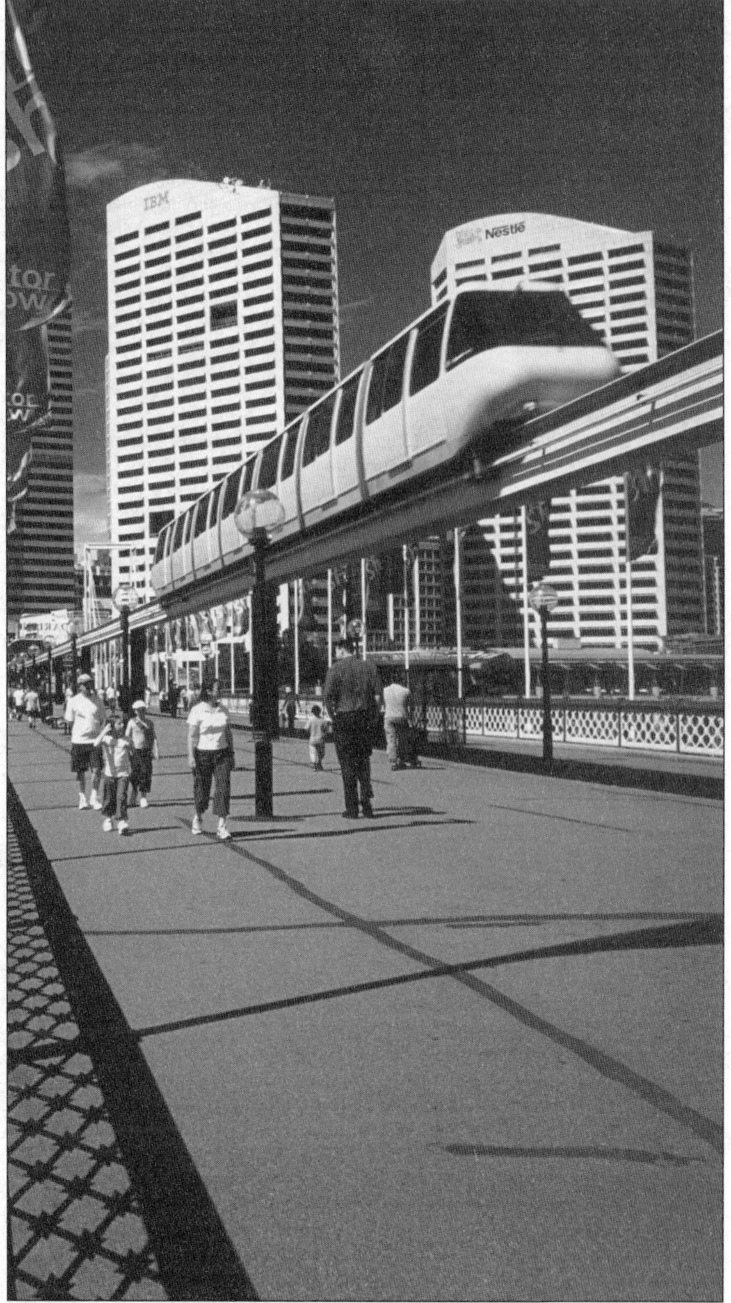

△ Monorail, Pyrmont Bridge

Travel passes

In addition to single-journey tickets, there's a vast array of **travel passes** available. The most useful for visitors are outlined below; for more **information** on the full range of tickets and timetables, phone the Transport Infoline or check out their website (daily 6am–10pm; ⓣ13 15 00, ⓦwww.131500.com.au).

Passes are sold at most **newsagents** and at **train stations**; the more tourist-oriented Sydney Passes and Sydney Explorer Passes can be bought at the airport (from the Sydney Visitor Centre and the STA booth in the international terminal and from State Transit ground staff in the domestic), at State Transit Info booths, from the Sydney Visitor Centre in The Rocks and Darling Harbour, and at some Countrylink offices as well as at train stations.

No travel pass includes the Airport Line stations (Green Square, Mascot, Domestic Airport and International Airport). An extra Gate Pass (COST) must be purchased to exit from these two stations; however, you can purchase a Gate Pass on arrival without being fined.

Tourist passes

Sydney Explorer Pass (one-day $36) comes with a map and description of the sights, and includes free travel on any State Transit bus within the same zones as the Explorer routes. The red **Sydney Explorer** (from Circular Quay daily 8.40am–5.22pm; every 18min) takes in all the important sights in the city and inner suburbs, via 26 hop-on-hop-off stops. The blue **Bondi Explorer** (daily from Circular Quay 9.15am–4.15pm; every 30min) covers the waterside eastern suburbs (19 stops include Kings Cross, Paddington, Double Bay, Vaucluse, Bondi, Bronte, Clovelly and Coogee). A **two-day ticket** ($62) allows use of both bus services over two days in a seven-day period.

Sydney Pass (three-, five- or seven-day passes within an eight-day period; $100/$130/$150) is valid for all buses and ferries including the above Explorer services, the ferry and JetCat to Manly, the RiverCat to Parramatta, a return trip to the airport valid for two months with the Airport Link train (buy the pass at the airport on arrival). It also includes three narrated harbour cruises, one of them in the evening, travel on trains within the central area, and discounts at many attractions.

Bus, train and ferry passes

Travelpasses allow unlimited use of buses, trains and ferries and can begin on any

Accommodation

There are a tremendous number of places to stay in Sydney, and fierce competition helps keep prices down. Finding somewhere to stay is usually only a problem just before Christmas and throughout January, in late February/early March during the Gay Mardi Gras, and at Easter: at these times **book ahead**. All types of accommodation offer a (sometimes substantial) discount for **weekly bookings**, and may also cut prices considerably during the **low season** (from autumn to spring, school holidays excepted).

The larger **international hotels** in The Rocks and the Central Business District (CBD) charge $200 and upwards for a double room. The least expensive hotels in the city centre, often above **pubs** and sharing bathrooms, start from $100. Rates in Kings Cross are much cheaper, with rooms in **private hotels** available for $60 (sharing a bathroom) and around $85 en suite and in three- or four-star hotels at around $110–160. **Motels**, such as ones we've listed in Glebe and Surry Hills, charge around $100. An increasing number of day of the week. Most useful are the **Red Travelpass** ($32 a week), valid for the city and inner suburbs, and inner harbour ferries (not the Manly Ferry or the RiverCat beyond Meadowbank); and the **Green Travelpass** ($40), which allows use of all ferries – except JetCats before 7pm. Passes covering a wider area cost between $44 and $54 a week, and monthly passes are also available.

DayTripper tickets ($15) are also available for unlimited travel on all services offered by CityRail, Sydney Buses and Sydney Ferries and they can even be purchased on board buses and ferries.

Bus and ferry passes

The **Blue Travelpass** ($29 a week) gives unlimited travel on buses in the inner-city area and on inner-harbour ferries but cannot be used for Manly or beyond Meadowbank; the **Orange Travelpass** ($36 a week) gets you further on the buses and is valid on all ferries; and the **Pittwater Travelpass** ($49 a week) gives unlimited travel on all buses and ferries. These Travelpasses start with first use rather than on the day of purchase.

Bus

TravelTen tickets represent a 30 percent saving over single fares by buying ten trips at once; they can be used over a space of time and for more than one person. The tickets are colour-coded according to how many sections they cover: the Brown TravelTen ($21.30), for example, is the choice for trips from Leichhardt to the city, while the the Red TravelTen ($27.90) is the one to buy if you're staying at Bondi. In addition, there's a two-zone bus-only travel pass for $29.

Ferry

FerryTen tickets, valid for ten single trips, start at $28.50 for Inner Harbour Services, go up to $42.90 for the Manly Ferry, and peak at $62.50 for the JetCat services.

Train

Seven Day RailPass tickets allow unlimited travel between any two nominated stations and those in between, with savings of about twenty percent on the price of five return trips. For example, a pass between Bondi Junction and Town Hall would cost $22.

mid-range "boutique" hotels and **guesthouses** are smaller, more characterful places to stay, charging upwards of $150. **Serviced holiday apartments** can be very good value for a group, but are heavily booked.

Despite the number of **hostels** all over Sydney and the rivalry between them, standards are variable and, in Kings Cross especially, can be very low. As the scene changes rapidly, it's worth getting the latest news from other travellers. Rates (which should include bedding) can range from $20 to $30 depending on the number of dorm beds, the hostel standard and location. Rates rise in summer and fall in winter. Doubles average around $65, and $85 for an en suite; weekly rates usually save the cost of a night's stay. All hostels have a laundry, kitchen and common room with TV unless stated otherwise. Office hours are restricted, so it's best to arrange an arrival time.

For longer stays a **flat-share** can be an alternative to hotels or hostels. Saturday's real-estate section of the *Sydney Morning Herald* is the first place to look, or try café notice boards, especially in King Street in Newtown, Glebe Point Road in Glebe or Hall Street, Bondi Beach (the window of the health food store at 29 Hall St is crammed with house-share notices aimed at travellers). The average shared-house room price is around $150 a week (usually two weeks in advance, plus a bond (deposit) of four weeks' rent; you'll usually need to get hold of at least your own bedroom furniture and linen). Sleeping With The Enemy, 373 Bulwara Rd, Ultimo (ⓣ02/9211 8878, ⓦwww.sleepingwiththeenemy.com) organizes travellers' (aimed at under-28s) house-shares in fully equipped inner-city terraces but sharing a room with up to five others (from $120 per week for a one-month stay).

The nearest **campsites** to the centre are in the suburbs of Rockdale, 13km south of the city, and North Ryde, 14km northwest (see box below).

Where to stay

The listings below are arranged by area. For short visits, you'll want to stay in the **city centre** or the immediate vicinity: The Rocks, the CBD and Darling Harbour have the greatest concentration of expensive hotels and now also several backpackers' hostels, while the area around Central station and Chinatown, known as Haymarket, has some cheaper, more downmarket places and an ever greater concentration of hostels led by the huge YHA. **Kings Cross** is still hanging on as a travellers' centre, with more backpackers' accommodation and cheaper hotels (some with a few dorm beds) than elsewhere; there are also some upmarket choices too. The area is falling out of favour as travellers head for the newer hostels in town to avoid the sleaze and the all-night partying, concentrated on Darlinghurst Road, the hardcore red-light strip. Despite this, Kings Cross remains a lively and convenient base; it's only a ten-minute walk from the city and has its own train station, and the leafy Victoria Street and the backstreets have a contrastingly pleasant atmosphere and seem almost a world away. The adjacent suburbs of **Woolloomooloo**, **Potts Point** and **Elizabeth Bay** move gradually upmarket, a little less accessible, but quieter. To the west, leafy and peaceful **Glebe** is another slice of prime travellers' territory, featuring several backpackers' and a number of small guesthouses.

Campsites around Sydney

The three caravan parks listed below are the closest sites to the centre. Camping rates rise in the peak season and cost from $25–30 for two people in an unpowered site to $30–36 for a powered site; expect to pay $5 less at less popular times.

Lakeside Caravan Park Lake Park Rd, Narrabeen, 26km north of the city ⓣ02/9913 7845, ⓦwww.sydneylakeside.com.au. Great spot by Narrabeen Lakes on Sydney's northern beaches. Free gas BBQs, camp kitchen and a nearby shop. Minimum two-night stay in a range of cabins and modern two-bedroom villas; all are en suite and linen is included. Bus #190 or #L90 from Wynyard station and then a ten-minute walk. Cabins ❺, villas ❻–❼.

Lane Cove River Tourist Park Plassey Rd, North Ryde, 14km northwest of the city ⓣ02/9888 9133, ⓦwww.lanecoverivertouristpark.com.au. Wonderful bush location beside Lane Cove National Park, right on the river, in Sydney's northern suburbs. Great facilities include a bush kitchen (with fridge), TV room and swimming pool. Train to Chatswood then bus #550 or #551. Sites are at the top end of the price range. En-suite cabins ❹.

Sheralee Tourist Caravan Park 88 Bryant St, Rockdale, 13km south of the city ⓣ02/9567 7161. The cheapest and closest option to the centre. Small park with camp kitchen. Train to Rockdale station and then a ten-minute walk.

For longer stays, consider somewhere further out, on the **North Shore**, where you'll get more for your money and more of a feel for Sydney as a city. **Kirribilli**, **Neutral Bay** or **Cremorne Point**, only a short ferry ride from Circular Quay, offer some serenity and affordable water views as well. Large old private hotels out this way are increasingly being converted into hostels, particularly on Carabella Street in Kirribilli. **Manly**, tucked away in the northeast corner of the harbour, is a seaside suburb with ocean and harbour beaches, just thirty minutes from Circular Quay by ferry. It has a concentration of hostels and also more upmarket accommodation; the beachside **eastern suburbs** of **Bondi** and **Coogee** offer similar places to stay and are closer to the city.

The Central Business District (CBD)

Hotels & B&Bs

Central Park 185 Castlereagh St, City ⓣ02/9283 5000, ⓦwww.centralpark.com.au. Small chic hotel in a great position in the midst of city bustle right near Town Hall and Hyde Park. Studios have king-size beds and smart and spacious bathrooms with bathtub. Smaller standard rooms are still a good size although minus the tub; all come with sofa, desk, air-con and well-equipped kitchenette. Tiny daytime lobby café. 24hr reception. Light breakfast. Rooms ❺, studios ❻

Corus 7–9 York St, City ⓣ02/9274 1222. Central position for both the CBD and The Rocks. This 22-storey four-star hotel has the usual motel-style rooms but excels with its spacious studios, which come with kitchen area, CD player, voicemail and safe. Small gym; 24hr room service; pleasant café-brasserie. Rooms ❻, studios ❼

Grand Hotel 30 Hunter St, City ⓣ02/9232 3755, ⓦwww.grandhotel.citysearch.com.au. Close to Wynyard station, with several floors of accommodation above one of Sydney's oldest (but not necessarily nicest) pubs, which opens until 3am Thurs–Sat. Rooms, sharing bathrooms, are fine – all brightly painted, with colourful bed covers, lamps, fridge, kettle, TV, fan, heating and ceiling fans. ❹

Intercontinental 117 Macquarie St, City ⓣ02/9230 0200, ⓦwww.intercontinental.com. The old sandstone Treasury building forms the lower floors of this 31-storey, five-star property, with stunning views of the Botanic Gardens, Opera House and harbour. The café-bar is the perfect place for everything from champagne to afternoon tea, and there are three other eateries, a cigar divan, and a pool and gym on the top floor. All this comes at a price, of course: $290 city view and $400 harbour view. ❽

Hostels

base Backpackers 477 Kent St, City ⓣ02/9267 7718, ⓦwww.basebackpackers.com. This huge 360-bed hostel in a great location near Town Hall station has recently undergone a name change and complete refurbishment. Single girl travellers can enjoy the *base* "Sanctuary" concept; a women-only section featuring all the home comforts from hairdryers in the bathrooms to free Aveda hair care products and feather pillows. Well-furnished rooms and dorms (four-, six-, eight- and ten-bed) with shared bathrooms all have air-con. It's well set up with the usual facilities plus Internet access and a solarium for that all-year tan. Dorms $26–34, rooms ❹

Sydney Backpackers Victoria House, 7 Wilmot St, City ⓣ02/9267 7772 or 1800 88 77 66, ⓦwww.sydneybackpackers.com. Very central choice off the George Street cinema strip. Clean and spacious, although lacking a little in atmosphere; staff encourage sociability and there's a comfortable, colourful common room with cable TV, books and Internet access. Small but clean kitchen. Four-, eight-, ten- and twelve-bed dorms – one en-suite dorm on every floor – and spacious doubles and twins; all have air-con, cable TV, fridges and lockers. Dorms $27–34, rooms ❹

The Rocks

Hotels & B&Bs

Lord Nelson Brewery Hotel Cnr Argyle and Kent streets, The Rocks ⓣ02/9251 4044, ⓦwww.lordnelson.com.au. B&B in a historic pub dating from 1841. The smart colonial-style rooms are mostly en suite and come with all mod-cons. Price varies according to size and position: best is the corner room with views of Argyle St. Serves beer brewed on the premises, plus bar food daily and upmarket meals from its first-floor brasserie (lunch

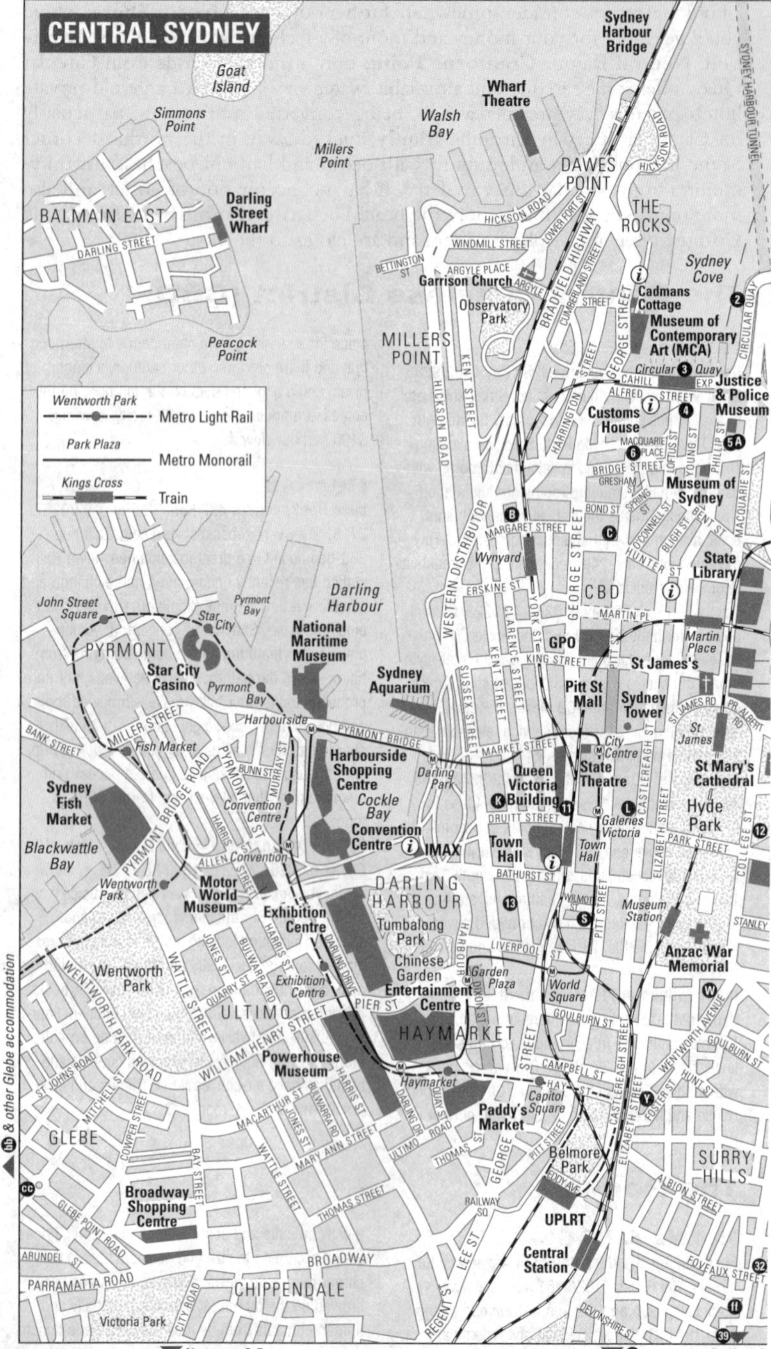
CENTRAL SYDNEY
Goat Island
Simmons Point
Millers Point
Walsh Bay
Wharf Theatre
Sydney Harbour Bridge
SYDNEY HARBOUR TUNNEL
HICKSON ROAD
DAWES POINT
THE ROCKS
BALMAIN EAST
Darling Street Wharf
DARLING STREET
WINDMILL STREET
LOWER FORT ST
BETTINGTON ST
ARGYLE PLACE
Garrison Church
ARGYLE
BRADFIELD HIGHWAY
CUMBERLAND STREET
Sydney Cove
Cadmans Cottage
Observatory Park
MILLERS POINT
Museum of Contemporary Art (MCA)
CIRCULAR QUAY
Peacock Point
KENT STREET
HARRINGTON STREET
GEORGE STREET
Circular Quay
CAHILL EXP
Justice & Police Museum
Wentworth Park
Metro Light Rail
Park Plaza
Metro Monorail
Kings Cross
Train
ALFRED STREET
Customs House
MACQUARIE PLACE
LOFTUS ST
YOUNG ST
PHILLIP ST
BRIDGE STREET
GRESHAM ST
SPRING ST
Museum of Sydney
MACQUARIE ST
BOND ST
MARGARET STREET
O'CONNELL ST
BLIGH ST
BENT ST
WESTERN DISTRIBUTOR
Wynyard
HUNTER ST
State Library
Darling Harbour
ERSKINE ST
CBD
MARTIN PL
John Street Square
Pyrmont Bay
Star City
PYRMONT
Star City Casino
National Maritime Museum
Sydney Aquarium
YORK ST
CLARENCE STREET
KENT STREET
SUSSEX STREET
GPO
KING STREET
Martin Place
St James's
Pitt St Mall
Sydney Tower
PITT ST
ST JAMES RD
PR. ALBERT RD
St James
Harbourside
PYRMONT BRIDGE
BANK STREET
MILLER STREET
Fish Market
PYRMONT STREET
MURRAY ST
BUNN ST
MARKET STREET
City Centre
Harbourside Shopping Centre
Darling Park
Queen Victoria Building
State Theatre
St Mary's Cathedral
Sydney Fish Market
PYRMONT BRIDGE ROAD
Convention Centre
Cockle Bay
CASTLEREAGH STREET
Hyde Park
DRUITT STREET
Galeries Victoria
ELIZABETH STREET
COLLEGE ST
Blackwattle Bay
HARRIS ST
ALLEN ST
Convention
Convention Centre
IMAX
Town Hall
Town Hall
PARK STREET
Wentworth Park
Motor World Museum
DARLING HARBOUR
BATHURST ST
Exhibition Centre
WILMOT ST
PITT STREET
Museum Station
STANLEY
Tumbalong Park
LIVERPOOL ST
Anzac War Memorial
Wentworth Park
WATTLE STREET
JONES ST
BULWARRA RD
DARLING DRIVE
Chinese Garden
HARBOUR ST
Garden Plaza
World Square
QUARRY ST
Exhibition Centre
Entertainment Centre
DIXON ST
WENTWORTH PARK ROAD
ULTIMO
PIER ST
GOULBURN ST
WENTWORTH AVENUE
HAYMARKET
WILLIAM HENRY STREET
CASTLEREAGH STREET
GOULBURN ST
Powerhouse Museum
CAMPBELL ST
ST JOHNS ROAD
MITCHELL ST
Haymarket
HAY ST
HUNT ST
COWPER STREET
MACARTHUR ST
QUAY ST
Capitol Square
FOSTER ST
Paddy's Market
DARLING DR
ULTIMO ROAD
GLEBE
MARY ANN STREET
THOMAS ST
PITT STREET
Belmore Park
SURRY HILLS
Glebe accommodation
BAY STREET
WATTLE STREET
GEORGE STREET
EDDY AVE
ALBION STREET
Broadway Shopping Centre
THOMAS STREET
RAILWAY SQ
UPLRT
GLEBE POINT ROAD
LEE ST
Central Station
ARUNDEL ST
BROADWAY
FOVEAUX STREET
PARRAMATTA ROAD
CHIPPENDALE
CITY ROAD
Victoria Park
REGENT ST
DEVONSHIRE ST
Newtown & Enmore
Redfern &

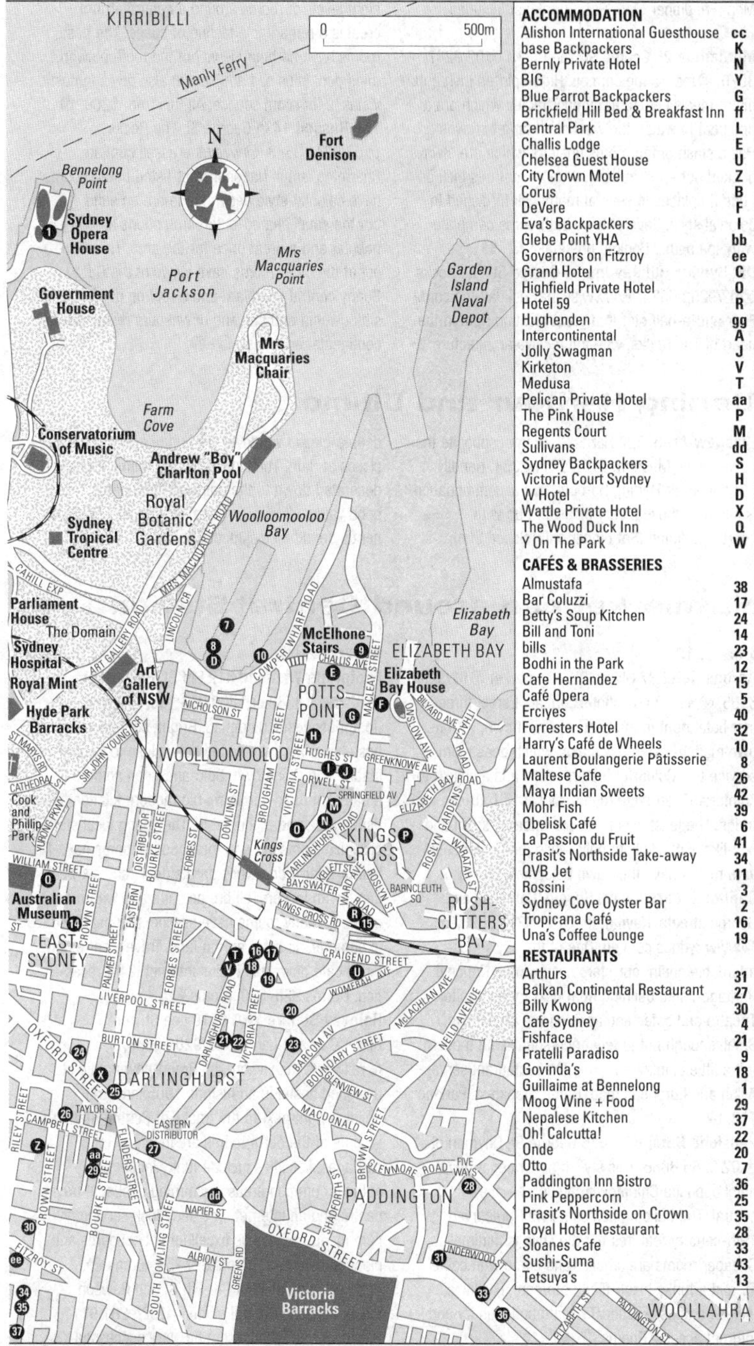
ACCOMMODATION
Alishon International Guesthouse cc
base Backpackers K
Bernly Private Hotel N
BIG Y
Blue Parrot Backpackers G
Brickfield Hill Bed & Breakfast Inn ff
Central Park L
Challis Lodge E
Chelsea Guest House U
City Crown Motel Z
Corus B
DeVere F
Eva's Backpackers I
Glebe Point YHA bb
Governors on Fitzroy ee
Grand Hotel C
Highfield Private Hotel O
Hotel 59 R
Hughenden gg
Intercontinental A
Jolly Swagman J
Kirketon V
Medusa T
Pelican Private Hotel aa
The Pink House P
Regents Court M
Sullivans dd
Sydney Backpackers S
Victoria Court Sydney H
W Hotel D
Wattle Private Hotel X
The Wood Duck Inn Q
Y On The Park W
CAFÉS & BRASSERIES
Almustafa 38
Bar Coluzzi 17
Betty's Soup Kitchen 24
Bill and Toni 14
bills 23
Bodhi in the Park 12
Cafe Hernandez 15
Café Opera 5
Erciyes 40
Forresters Hotel 32
Harry's Café de Wheels 10
Laurent Boulangerie Pâtisserie 8
Maltese Cafe 26
Maya Indian Sweets 42
Mohr Fish 39
Obelisk Café 6
La Passion du Fruit 41
Prasit's Northside Take-away 34
QVB Jet 11
Rossini 3
Sydney Cove Oyster Bar 2
Tropicana Café 16
Una's Coffee Lounge 19
RESTAURANTS
Arthurs 31
Balkan Continental Restaurant 27
Billy Kwong 30
Cafe Sydney 4
Fishface 21
Fratelli Paradiso 9
Govinda's 18
Guillaime at Bennelong 1
Moog Wine + Food 29
Nepalese Kitchen 37
Oh! Calcutta! 22
Onde 20
Otto 7
Paddington Inn Bistro 36
Pink Peppercorn 25
Prasit's Northside on Crown 35
Royal Hotel Restaurant 28
Sloanes Cafe 33
Sushi-Suma 43
Tetsuya's 13
KIRRIBILLI
0 500m
Manly Ferry
N
Fort Denison
Bennelong Point
Sydney Opera House
Mrs Macquaries Point
Port Jackson
Garden Island Naval Depot
Government House
Mrs Macquaries Chair
Farm Cove
Conservatorium of Music
Andrew "Boy" Charlton Pool
Royal Botanic Gardens
Woolloomooloo Bay
Sydney Tropical Centre
CAHILL EXP
MRS MACQUARIES ROAD
Parliament House
The Domain
Sydney Hospital
Royal Mint
ART GALLERY ROAD
LINCOLN CR
COWPER WHARF ROAD
McElhone Stairs
CHALLIS AVE
ELIZABETH BAY
Elizabeth Bay
Elizabeth Bay House
Art Gallery of NSW
Hyde Park Barracks
NICHOLSON ST
POTTS POINT
MACLEAY STREET
BILYARD AVE
ITHACA ROAD
ONSLOW AVE
ST MARYS RD
SIR JOHN YOUNG CR
WOOLLOOMOOLOO
HUGHES ST
GREENKNOWE AVE
CATHEDRAL ST
ORWELL ST
ELIZABETH BAY ROAD
SPRINGFIELD AV
Cook and Phillip Park
YURONG PKWY
BROUGHAM
VICTORIA STREET
DOWLING ST
DISTRIBUTOR
BOURKE STREET
FORBES ST
DARLINGHURST ROAD
KINGS CROSS
Kings Cross
ELIZABETH GARDENS
ROSLYN GDNS
WARATAH ST
WILLIAM STREET
Australian Museum
CROWN STREET
EASTERN
BAYSWATER
KELLETT ST
WARD AVE
ROSLYN ST
BARNCLEUTH SQ
KINGS CROSS RD
RUSH-CUTTERS BAY
EAST SYDNEY
PALMER STREET
FORBES STREET
CRAIGEND STREET
WOMERAH AVE
McLACHLAN AVE
NEILD AVENUE
LIVERPOOL STREET
OXFORD STREET
BURTON STREET
DARLINGHURST ROAD
VICTORIA STREET
BARCOM AV
BOUNDARY STREET
GLENVIEW ST
DARLINGHURST
MACDONALD
TAYLOR SQ
CAMPBELL STREET
EASTERN DISTRIBUTOR
RILEY STREET
CROWN STREET
BOURKE STREET
FLINDERS STREET
BROWN STREET
SHADFORTH ST
GLENMORE ROAD
FIVE WAYS
PADDINGTON
NAPIER ST
DOWLING STREET
FITZROY ST
ALBION ST
GREENS RD
SOUTH DOWLING STREET
UNDERWOOD
Victoria Barracks
WOOLLAHRA
ELIZABETH ST
PADDINGTON ST
40
SCG, 41, 42 & 43
Bondi, Paddington Market & Centennial Parklands
gg

Mon–Fri, dinner Mon–Sat). Breakfast included. ⑤–⑥

Mercantile 25 George St, The Rocks ⓣ02/9247 3570, ⓔmerc@tpg.com.au. High-spirited Irish pub; bistro meals served at outdoor tables which are a fine spot to watch the weekend market crowds. Has a stash of fab rooms upstairs which are always booked out – get in early. Original features include huge fireplaces in several rooms, all furnished in colonial style. Several have bathrooms complete with spa baths. Cooked breakfast. ④–⑤

Old Sydney Holiday Inn 55 George St, The Rocks ⓣ02/9252 0524, ⓦwww.sydney.holiday-inn.com. Four-and-a-half star in a great location right in the heart of The Rocks, with impressive architecture: eight levels of rooms around a central atrium creates a remarkable feeling of space. The best rooms have harbour views but the rooftop swimming pool (plus spa and sauna) also gives fantastic vistas. 24hr room service. All this from $260. ⑧

The Russell 143A George St, The Rocks ⓣ02/9241 3543, ⓦwww.therussell.com.au. Charming, small National Trust-listed hotel. Rooms have colonial-style decor; some are en suite but the small shared-bathroom options are very popular and a great price for the area. The priciest of the other rooms have views of the Quay. Sunny central courtyard and a rooftop garden, sitting-room and bar, and downstairs restaurant for continental breakfast. ⑤–⑦

Darling Harbour and Ultimo

Glasgow Arms 527 Harris St, Ultimo, opposite the Powerhouse Museum ⓣ02/9211 2354. Handily positioned for Darling Harbour, this accommodation is situated above a very pleasant pub with courtyard dining (Sat dinner only, closed Sun); double-glazed windows are handy now the bar closes at 3am. The high-ceilinged rooms – nicely decorated down to the polished floorboards – are good value, all with en-suite, air-con and TV. Continental breakfast included. ⑤

Haymarket and around Central Station

Hotels

Aarons Hotel 37 Ultimo Rd, Haymarket ⓣ02/9281 5555, ⓦwww.aaronshotel.com.au. Large, three-star hotel right in the heart of Chinatown, with its own modern café downstairs; which does room service too. Colourful feature-walls add a splash to comfortable en-suite rooms, all with TV, air-con and fridge. The least expensive are internal, small and box-like, with skylight only, while the pricier courtyard rooms have their own balconies. ⑤

Capitol Square Capitol Square, Campbell and George streets, Haymarket ⓣ02/9211 8633, ⓦwww.rydges.com.au. One of the city's most affordable chain four-stars occupying a National Heritage-listed building right next to the Capitol Theatre and cafes and across from Chinatown. Small enough not to feel impersonal, with modern – if a little chintzy – rooms. The restaurant serves Asian and European food. Buffet breakfast. Parking $18. ⑥

Pensione Hotel 631–635 George St, Haymarket ⓣ02/9265 8888. This stylish new budget private hotel opposite Chinatown couldn't be more central. The building has some well-preserved 19th-century features but the style is minimalist. Cheaper rooms are smaller and come with cable TV and a funky black-tiled bathroom. Facilities include a guest kitchen/TV room and laundry and Internet access. Rooms ④–⑤

Hostels

Footprints Westend 412 Pitt St, Haymarket ⓣ02/9211 4588 or 1800 013 186, ⓦwww.footprintswestend.com.au. Bright, contemporary hostel in a large renovated hotel close to Central station and Chinatown. Spic-and-span common areas with funky furniture, big modern kitchen and dining area and a pool table. The young local staff organize nights out and tours. Some rooms have TV and/or mini-fridge while dorms (four- and six-bed) come with lockers; all are en suite and with nice bedding. Many rooms have air-con: request these in summer, as there are no fans. Travel centre and small café downstairs, plus Internet. 24hr reception. Dorms $28–$30, rooms ③

Railway Square YHA 8–10 Lee St, cnr Upper Carriage Lane ⓣ02/9281 9666, ⓔrailway@yhansw.org.au. Brand-new architect-designed hostel in an historic 1905 industrial building right next to the tracks of Central Station – some of the dorm rooms are in actual train carriages. Facilities include funky indoor and outdoor common areas, swimming pool/spa, travel centre and an Internet café and kiosk serving light meals, as well as excellent noticeboards and planned activities. Dorms $27–33, rooms ④.

Sydney Central YHA Cnr Pitt St and Rawson Place, opposite Central station ⓣ02/9281 9111, ⓔsydcentral@yhansw.org.au. Very successful YHA in a centrally located listed building transformed into a huge and snazzy hostel with over 550 beds – which are almost always full so you'll need to book well in advance. Hotel-like facilities but still very sociable. Spacious four- and six-bed dorms and twins sharing bathrooms or en-suite twins and doubles. Wide range of amenities, including employment desk, travel agency, rooftop pool, sauna, and BBQ area. 24hr reception. Licensed bistro plus a cute, very popular basement bar, *Scubar*. Some parking available. Maximum stay fourteen days. For longer stays, the YHA also has a "working holidaymaker hostel" at Dulwich Hill (ⓣ02/9550 0054). Dorms $28–$33, rooms ❸–❹

wake up! 509 Pitt St, opposite Railway Square and Central station ⓣ02/9264 4121, ⓦwww.wakeup.com.au. Trendy mega-backpackers' complex (over 500 beds) with a vibrant interior inside an early-twentieth-century corner building. Very styled, right down to the black-clad staff in the huge intimidating foyer with its banks of Internet terminals. Rooms, some en suite, are light-filled, well furnished and above all serviceable. Dorms – four-, six-, eight- and ten-bed – have lockers. Facilities include a huge modern kitchen with gigantic windows overlooking busy Railway Square, a streetside café and an underground late-opening bar and eatery. Dorms $24–$33, rooms ❸–❹

Kings Cross and around

Hotels

Bernly Private Hotel 15 Springfield Ave, Kings Cross ⓣ02/9358 3122, ⓦwww.bernlyprivatehotel.com.au. This clean budget hotel, which also has a few dorms, is one street back from the seedy heart of the Cross but has good security, 24hr reception, and courteous staff. Private rooms have air-con, TV, sink and fridge and are either en suite or share bathrooms. Tidy kitchen, TV lounge and big sunroof with deck chairs and fantastic views across the harbour to the Bridge and Opera House. Good single rates. Dorms $22–$25, rooms ❸

Challis Lodge 21–23 Challis Ave, Potts Point ⓣ02/9358 5422, ⓦwww.budgethotelssydney.com. Budget accommodation in a wonderful old mansion with polished timber floors throughout. In a great location on a quiet, tree-filled street a short walk from Woolloomooloo and Kings Cross, and a step away from some of the area's trendiest cafés and restaurants. All rooms have TV, fridge and sink; guest laundry. Rooms ❷, en suite ❸, with balcony ❹

DeVere 44–46 Macleay St, Potts Point ⓣ02/9358 1211, ⓦwww.devere.com.au. Comfortable three-star hotel in a great position close to cafés, restaurants and transport. Third- and fourth-floor rooms have stunning views of Elizabeth Bay; studios with kitchenette available. Some rooms have balconies and spas; all are air-con. There's also a breakfast room (buffet-style), guest laundry and 24hr reception. Rooms ❺, studios ❻

Highfield Private Hotel 166 Victoria St, Kings Cross ⓣ02/9326 9539, ⓦwww.highfieldhotel.com. Swedish-run, clean, modern and secure budget hotel. Rooms are well equipped with fans, heating and sinks but a little dark. Also three-bed dorms. Tiny kitchen/common room with TV, microwave, kettle and toaster; no laundry but a laundrette just a few doors up. Dorms $23, rooms ❸

Hotel 59 59 Bayswater Rd, Kings Cross ⓣ02/9360 5900, ⓦwww.hotel59.com.au. Small hotel (just eight rooms) reminiscent of a pleasant European guesthouse; benefits include a friendly owner, small but tastefully decorated air-con rooms, a quiet leafy location that's just out of the bustle, and a downstairs café where delicious full cooked breakfasts are served. Very popular, so book in advance. One family room (sleeps four) with small kitchenette. Outdoor courtyard. B&B. Rooms ❹, studio ❺

Regents Court 18 Springfield Ave, Potts Point ⓣ02/9358 1533, ⓦwww.regentscourt.com.au. Small hotel, raved about by international style mags for its fab fit-out, this place is a little piece of glam without an outrageous price tag. Classic designer furniture, and each apartment-style room has a sleek kitchen area, air-con and TV/video. Instead of a bar, there's a well-chosen wine list downstairs (at bottle-shop prices), and help-yourself coffee and *biscotti*. Small but elegant rooftop kitchen and BBQ area, amongst potted citrus trees. ❼

Victoria Court Sydney 122 Victoria St, Kings Cross ⓣ02/9357 3200, ⓦwww.victoriacourt.com.au. Boutique hotel in two interlinked Victorian terraced houses; very tasteful and quiet though decor is overly floral. En-suite rooms with all mod cons, some with balconies; buffet breakfast included and served in the conservatory. Secure parking a bonus. ❺

W Hotel The Wharf, 6 Cowper Wharf Rd, Woolloomooloo ⓣ02/9331 9000, ⓦwww.whotels.com. Luxury hotel with bags of smooth contemporary style and fantastic service and facilities, right on the water in a redeveloped wharf alongside a ritzy apartment complex and a marina. The lobby is spacious and striking in design; the lush *Water Bar* is one of Sydney's trendiest watering holes, and the rest of the wharf is lined with some of Sydney's best restaurants and cafés. 24hr room service; day spa, indoor heated pool and gym. ❽

Hostels

Blue Parrot Backpackers 87 Macleay St, Potts Point ⓣ02/9356 4888, ⓦwww.blueparrot.com.au. In a great position in the trendy (and quieter) part of Potts Point and with helpful staff, this converted mansion is sunny, airy, brightly painted and tastefully furnished. The huge courtyard garden out back has wooden furniture and big shady trees. Mostly six- and eight-bed dorms; one four-bed dorm but no doubles or twins. Common room with cable TV and free Internet. Dorms from $25.

Eva's Backpackers 6–8 Orwell St, Potts Point ⓣ02/9358 2185, ⓦwww.evasbackpackers.com.au. Recommended family-run hostel away from Darlinghurst Road's clamour; feels safe and friendly. Colourful and clean rooms and common areas, well set up with fans, mirrors and lamps. Four-, six-, eight- and ten-bed dorms; four-beds are en suite. Peaceful rooftop garden with table umbrellas, greenery, BBQ area and fantastic views over The Domain. The guest kitchen/dining room, positioned at street level, feels like a café and is conducive to socializing, though this isn't a "party" hostel. Dorms $25, rooms ❸

Jolly Swagman 27 Orwell St, Kings Cross ⓣ02/9358 6400, ⓦwww.jollyswagman.com.au. Vibrant, long-established hostel geared towards the louder, livelier backpacker. Organised social events range from sports teams to pub crawls; in-house travel centre, good noticeboards and work connections. Along with the usual communal facilities, every room has its own fridge and lockers; four- to six-bed dorms. Cheap licensed café with Internet access out front. 24hr reception. Dorms $24, rooms ❸

The Pink House 6–8 Barncleuth Square, Kings Cross ⓣ02/9358 1689 or 1800 806 385, ⓦwww.pinkhouse.com.au. Attractive Art Deco mansion with big dorms – up to eight-bed – and a few doubles, some with sink and shower but none with toilet. All the expected amenities plus cable TV in the common room and garden courtyards with BBQ. Friendly and very peaceful but also close to the action. Dorms $24, rooms ❷

The Wood Duck Inn 49 William St, East Sydney ⓣ02/9358 5856 or 1800 110 025, ⓦwww.woodduckinn.com.au. Hostel run by two switched-on brothers in a great spot right by Hyde Park at the quieter end of William Street. Don't be put off by the dingy, endless flights of concrete steps: they emerge into the nerve centre, a sunny rooftop with fantastic park and city views, all-day reception-cum-bar, outdoor tables and BBQ, a small but functional kitchen, laundry and a TV-cum-dining room with quirky surfboard tabletops. The dorm-only accommodation below has polished floors, citrus-coloured walls, high ceilings and fresh flowers in the hall. Spacious dorms come with fans, good beds and cage lockers. Lots of activities, including free lifts to the beach. Good security. Dorms $20–22.

Surry Hills, Darlinghurst, Paddington and Woollahra

BIG 212 Elizabeth St, Surry Hills ⓣ02/9281 6030, ⓦwww.bigonelizabeth.com. Stylish 140-bed part-boutique hotel, part-hostel in a lousy location opposite the railway line but a five- to ten-minute walk to Central station, Chinatown and Oxford Street. Sunny rooms have extra-thick glass, good curtains and contemporary decor in natural colours; all are air-con with TV and video. The lobby, with designer lounges and Internet terminals, doubles as the common area with a high-tech guest kitchen to the side. An organic café serves breakfast through dinner (plus $5 specials). Four-, six- and eight-bed dorms; rates include linen, towels and breakfast (pancakes, fresh scones, juice). Roof-terrace BBQ area. Guest laundry. Dorms $24.50, rooms ❺

City Crown Motel 289 Crown St, cnr of Reservoir St, Surry Hills ⓣ02/9331 2433, ⓦwww.citycrownmotel.com.au. A fairly typical motel but in a great location. The en-suite units are air-con with free in-house movies. One self-catering apartment, sleeping six, is available. Some parking space ($15 extra): enter on Reservoir St. Rooms ❹, apartment ❼

Hughenden 14 Queen St, Woollahra ⓣ02/9363 4863, ⓦwww.hughendenhotel.com.au. Old-fashioned Victorian-era guesthouse, built in 1876 and decorated to retain the old-world charm, including features such as servants' bells and black marble fireplaces. Situated opposite Centennial Park and close to Paddington's shops and the sports stadiums. Expensive en-suite singles and doubles, prices depend on size of room. Hot breakfast included. ❺–❼

Gay and lesbian accommodation

You shouldn't encounter any problems booking into a regular hotel, but here are several places that cater to a gay clientele or are gay-friendly. Other particularly welcoming places in our general listings include *BIG* (p.120), *DeVere* (below), *Kirketon* (below), *Medusa* (below), *Sullivans* (below) and *Victoria Court* (p.119).

Brickfield Hill Bed & Breakfast Inn 403 Riley St, Surry Hills ⓣ02/9211 4886, ⓦwww.brickfieldhill.com.au. In a terrace house, five minutes' walk from Oxford Street, this gay-owned and -operated ornate four-storey terrace recalls a bygone Victorian era, with antique-style furnished rooms, window drapes, chandelier lights and four-poster beds. Mixed. Cheaper rooms share bathrooms. Breakfast optional $10 extra. Rooms ❹, en suite ❺.

Chelsea Guest House 49 Womerah Ave, Darlinghurst ⓣ02/9380 5994, ⓦwww.chelsea.citysearch.com.au. Tastefully decorated terrace house in the quieter leafy backstreets of Darlinghurst. Standard en-suite doubles, plus deluxe rooms with king-sized beds including a couple of suites ($185–195); singles ($94) share bathrooms but have sinks. Light breakfast served in the courtyard. B&B from ❺.

Governors on Fitzroy 64 Fitzroy St, Surry Hills ⓣ02/9331 4652, ⓦwww.governors.com.au. Long-established gay B&B in a restored Victorian terrace just a few blocks from Oxford Street. The six guest rooms – big and well-appointed – share bathrooms but have their own basin. A full cooked breakfast is served in the dining room or the garden courtyard. Guests – mostly men – can also meet and mingle in the spa. B&B ❺.

Pelican Private Hotel 411 Bourke St, Darlinghurst ⓣ02/9331 5344, ⓦwww.pelicanprivatehotel.iwarp.com. Comfortable budget accommodation in one of Sydney's oldest gay guesthouses, a short walk from Oxford Street. The mid-nineteenth-century sandstone building's tree-filled garden is an inner-city oasis and the communal kitchen (with help-yourself breakfast) here make it even more sociable. Appealing, good-sized, well-furnished rooms have fans, TV and fridge, but share bathroom facilities. Extra $5 for a cooked breakfast in the hotel's street-front café. ❸

Wattle Private Hotel 108 Oxford St, cnr Palmer St, Darlinghurst ⓣ02/9332 4118, ⓦwww.sydneywattle.com. You can't get any closer to the action at this long-established gay-friendly hotel. The decor in the spacious well-appointed air-con, en-suite rooms has recently been contemporarised; in-room facilities include VCR/DVD (extensive library to choose from). The best room is on the roof, opening out to the rooftop garden with city and harbour views. Deluxe spa rooms available, including a pricey King Spa Suite ($389). Rooms from ❹

Kirketon 229–231 Darlinghurst Rd, Darlinghurst ⓣ02/9332 2011, ⓦwww.kirketon.com.au. A lively location and top in the fashion stakes, thanks to the big name Australian designers who created the swish and very understated interiors. Stylish bars including *Fix*, and a top contemporary restaurant, *Salt*, beckon on the ground level, while the rooms (costing from $169) come with toiletries by Aveda. Beautiful staff, slick service. Room service and free parking. ❻

Medusa 267 Darlinghurst Rd, Darlinghurst ⓣ02 9331 1000, ⓦwww.medusa.com.au. This boutique hotel is a modernist's dream, set in a grand heritage mansion and decorated with a mix of cutting edge and dramatic furniture and fittings. The seventeen rooms all have a balcony, CD player and microwave, with chaise lounges and access to the stunning interior courtyard for the deluxe rooms. Glamorous and attentive staff. Specials available. ❼

Sullivans 21 Oxford St, Paddington ⓣ02/9361 0211, ⓦwww.sullivans.com.au. Medium-sized contemporary-style private hotel in a trendy location, run by staff tuned into the local scene (free guided walking tour of Paddington included). Comfortable, modern en-suite rooms with TV and telephones. Free (but limited) parking, garden courtyard and swimming pool, in-house movies, free Internet access, free guest bicycles, fitness centre, laundry, 24hr reception, tour-booking service, and a café open for a huge and delicious breakfast. ⑤

Y On The Park 5–11 Wentworth Ave, Darlinghurst ⓣ02/9264 2451, ⓦwww.ywca-sydney.com.au. Great location just off Oxford St near Hyde Park for this YWCA (both sexes welcome); recently renovated, the hostel is surprisingly stylish and caters to every level of traveller. Rooms have all you'd expect in a good hotel. En-suite, shared-bathroom or self-catering studios, and deluxe rooms even come with a pamper pack and plunger coffee. Good value singles and four-bed dorms (made-up beds with towel, no bunks). No common kitchen, but facilities include a café (7am–8pm), and a laundry. Light breakfast. Dorms $33, rooms ④

Inner west: Glebe and Newtown

Alishan International Guesthouse 100 Glebe Point Rd, Glebe ⓣ02/9566 4048, ⓦwww.alishan.com.au. Restored Victorian mansion in a handy spot at the bottom of Glebe Point Road. Rather bland but very clean en-suite, motel-style rooms plus one furnished in Japanese fashion (minus an actual futon), and some four- and six-bed dorms. Facilities include a kitchen, spa, an airy common room, garden patio and BBQ area. Internet access available. A spacious family room sleeps six. Despite having dorms, this is a peaceful, not party, option. Dorms $25–$33, rooms ④

Australian Sunrise Lodge 485 King St, Newtown ⓣ02/9550 4999, ⓦwww.australiansunriselodge.com. Inexpensive and well-managed small private hotel well positioned for King Street action but with good security. Single and double rooms, some en suite, come with TV, fridge and toaster. Ground floor rooms are darker, smaller and cheaper – better option are the sunny rooms on the top two floors, all with cute balconies. En-suite family rooms also available. Guest kitchen. ③

Billabong Gardens 5–22 Egan St, off King St, Newtown ⓣ02/9550 3236, ⓦwww.billabonggardens.com.au. In a quiet street but close to the action, this long-running purpose-built hostel is arranged around a peaceful inner courtyard with swimming pool, and has excellent communal facilities. Clean dorms (four- to six-bed; some en suite), single ($49), twin and double rooms and motel-style en suites. Daily $5 charge for the popular undercover car park. Dorms $23–$25, rooms ③

Check Inn 146 Glebe Point Rd, Glebe ⓣ02/9660 7711, ⓔcheckinglebe@pubboy.com.au. Reasonably priced motel right in the heart of Glebe. On three floors (no lift), with a rooftop courtyard with city views, BBQ and a pool. Very light, spacious and clean air-con rooms with plain, recently updated decor. 24hr reception. Parking included. ④

Glebe Point YHA 262 Glebe Point Rd, Glebe ⓣ02/9692 8418, ⓔglebe@yhansw.org.au. Reliable YHA standard with helpful staff who organize lots of activities. The hostel sleeps just over 150 in a mix of private rooms – no en suites – as well as four- and five-bed dorms. Facilities include the usual plus a pool table, luggage storage and roof terrace with city views. Dorms $24–$28, rooms ③

Glebe Village Backpackers 256 Glebe Point Rd, Glebe ⓣ02/9660 8133 or 1800 801 983, ⓦwww.glebevillage.com. Three large old houses with a mellow, sociable atmosphere – the generally laid-back guests socialize in the leafy streetside fairy-lit garden. Staffed by young locals who know what's going on around town. Doubles and twins plus four, six-, ten- or twelve-bed dorms. Dorms $26–$30, rooms ③

Tricketts Bed and Breakfast 270 Glebe Point Rd, Glebe ⓣ02/9552 1141, ⓦwww.tricketts.com.au. Luxury B&B in an 1880s mansion. Rooms – en suite – are furnished with antiques and Persian rugs, and the lounge, complete with a billiard table and leather armchairs, was originally a small ballroom. Also a self-contained one-bedroom garden apartment with its own verandah. Delicious, generous and sociable breakfast. ⑥

Wattle House Hostel 44 Hereford St, Glebe ⓣ02/9552 4997, ⓦwww.wattlehouse.com.au. Top-class small, cosy and clean hostel in a restored terrace house on a quiet street. Four-bed dorms and well-furnished doubles. Pretty gardens and an outdoor eating area make staying here extra pleasant, and there's even a library room. Rates include linen and towels. Very popular, so book in advance. Dorms $27, rooms ④

Bondi Beach

Bondi Beachhouse YHA 63 Fletcher St, cnr Dellview St, Bondi ⓣ02/9365 2088, ⓔbondi@intercoast.com.au. Actually closer to Tamarama Beach than Bondi, in a former student boarding house – international students still stay, hence the buffet-style breakfasts and

Holiday apartments

The following places rent out apartments, generally for a minimum of a week. All are completely furnished and equipped – though occasionally you're expected to provide linen and towels: check first. Many hotels (some called apartment hotels) and all hostels also have self-catering facilities – see main listings for details.

Enoch's Holiday Flats ⓣ02/9388 1477, ⓕ9371 0439. One-, two- or three-bedroom apartments, all close to Bondi Beach, sleeping four to six people. $500–2000 weekly, depending on the size and season.

Manly National 22 Central Ave, Manly ⓣ02/9977 6469, ⓕ9977 3760. One- and two-bedroom apartments for up to four people; swimming pool; linen not supplied. One-bedroom $580–700 weekly, two-bedroom $980.

Medina Executive Apartments Head office, Level 1, 355 Crown St, Surry Hills ⓣ02/9360 1699 or 1300 300 232, ⓦwww.medinaapartments.com.au. Upmarket studio or one-, two- and three-bedroom serviced apartments with resident managers and reception in salubrious locales. City locations – Lee St near Central station, Kent St and Martin Place in the CBD, King St Wharf at Darling Harbour; inner-city and eastern suburbs – Chippendale, Surry Hills, Paddington, Double Bay and Coogee; and lower North Shore – Crows Nest and North Ryde. All include undercover parking. From $750 weekly upwards.

The Park Agency 190 Arden St, Coogee ⓣ02/9315 7777, ⓦwww.parkagency.com.au. Spacious, well-set-up studio and one-, two- and three-bedroom apartments near the beach from $800 per week for the smaller units, and $800–1200 per week for the larger properties. Cheaper quarterly leases available. All fully furnished including washing machine and linen.

Raine and Horne 255 Miller St, North Sydney ⓣ02/9959 5906, ⓦwww.accommodationinsydney.com. Modern executive fully furnished apartments fitted out by interior designers, on the leafy North Shore: North Sydney, Kirribilli, Milsons Point and McMahons Point. Studios from $550, one-bed from $675, two-bed from $800, three-bed from $1500 per week. All have TV, video, CD player, telephone; several have spas, pools or gyms. Cheaper rates for one month or more. The one-off cleaning fee is pricey: $120 for studios and one-bedders, $220–$320 for larger apartments.

Sydney City Centre Serviced Apartments 7 Elizabeth St, Martin Place ⓣ02/9233 6677, ⓦwww.accommodationsydneycity.com.au. Fully equipped, open-plan studio apartments sleeping up to three; kitchenette, laundry, TV, video, fans; basic, but in an excellent location. A good choice for long-stayers, as they rent out for a minimum of thirteen weeks. $250–$350 weekly.

dinners at cut-rate prices. Painted vibrant citrusy colours and with a sunny internal courtyard with BBQ, and a rooftop deck with fabulous ocean views. The Art Deco building has spacious high-ceilinged dorms (four-, six- and eight-bed, with lockers) and rooms – some en suite, with fridges and kettles – all have ceiling fans. Bag one of the beach-view rooms which go for the same price. Lots of local info; free surf talks. Dorms $27, rooms ❸, en suite ❹

Bondi Sands 252 Campbell Parade, Bondi Beach ⓣ02/9365 3703, ⓦwww.bondisands.com. Budget hotel across from the northern end of the beach. Fantastic views from its oceanfront rooms and the rooftop common area – with tables and chairs, a BBQ, and a handy kitchen and laundry. All rooms share bathrooms but have sinks; pricier oceanfronts are well furnished and with queen-size beds. Also four-bed dorms. Very popular, so book in advance. Dorms from $24, rooms ❸

Bondi Serviced Apartments 212 Bondi Rd, Bondi ⓣ02/8837 8000 or 1300 364 200, ⓦwww.bondi-serviced-apartments.com.au. Good-value serviced motel studio apartments halfway between Bondi Junction and Bondi Beach. Air-con units, recently decorated, with clean modern furniture, TV, telephone, kitchen and a balcony with sea view. Cheaper older-style apartments without views. Rooftop pool. Cheaper weekly or monthly rates. Parking included. ❹–❺

Noah's Backpackers 2 Campbell Parade, Bondi Beach ⓣ02/9365 7100 or 1800 226 662, ⓦwww.noahsbondibeach.com. Huge hostel opposite the beach has marvellous ocean views from the rooftop deck with a BBQ area and convenient kitchen. Beach-view rooms with sink, TV, fridge, fan and lockable cupboard plus four-, six- and eight-bed dorms. Clean, well-run but with cramped bathrooms. Bar, TV room (wide-screen TV) and pool table; greasy-spoon food available. Excellent security. Dorms $24, rooms ❸

Ravesi's 118 Campbell Parade, cnr of Hall St, Bondi Beach ⓣ02/9365 4422, ⓦwww.ravesis.com.au. Most rooms at this small hotel have glorious ocean views. The facade is pure 1914, but rooms have minimalist Asian-style decor. Most second-floor rooms have French windows onto small balconies; split-level and penthouse suites have spacious balconies. No views from smaller standard rooms, but great value at $125. All rooms have ceiling fans plus air-con. Large, popular bar at ground level and first-floor restaurant. ❺–❼

Coogee

Coogee Bay Boutique Hotel 9 Vicar St, Coogee ⓣ02/9665 0000, ⓦwww.coogeebayhotel.com.au. Newer hotel attached to the rear of a pub, the older, sprawling *Coogee Bay Hotel*. Rooms – all with balconies, half with ocean views – look like something from *Vogue Interior*, luxurious touches include marble floors in the bathrooms. Cheaper rooms in the old hotel heritage wing are noisy at weekends but are just as stylish; several offer splendid water views. Parking included. 24hr reception. The pub, one of the busiest in Australia, has an excellent brasserie, several bars and a nightclub. ❺–❼

Dive Hotel 234 Arden St, Coogee Beach ⓣ02/9665 5538, ⓦwww.divehotel.com.au. A wonderful small hotel in a renovated former boardinghouse opposite the beach; features include Art Deco tiling and high, decorative-plaster ceilings. A pleasant, bamboo-fringed courtyard (with BBQ and discreet guest laundry) opens out from the spacious breakfast room for buffet-style breakfasts. Larger two rooms at the front have splendid ocean views; one at the back has its own balcony. All have funky little bathrooms, CD players, cable TV, queen-size beds and a handy kitchenette with microwave and crockery. Free Internet access. ❻

Surfside Backpackers Coogee 186 Arden St, Coogee ⓣ02/9315 7888, ⓦwww.surfsidebackpackers.com.au. On Coogee's main drag, above *McDonald's* and opposite the beach, Coogee's largest hostel tends to attract a drinking, party crowd – try elsewhere for quiet. Modern facilities and great views from its high balconies, but a bit of a concrete tower-block feel, and not as clean as it should be. Mostly eight-, ten- or twelve-bed dorms, though some four-beds available. Doubles outside the peak periods only. Dorms $22–28, rooms ❸

Wizard of Oz Backpackers 172 Coogee Bay Rd, Coogee ⓣ02/9315 7876, ⓦwww.wizardofoz.com.au.Top-class hostel run by a friendly local couple in a big and beautiful Californian-style house with a huge verandah and polished wooden floors. Spacious, vibrantly painted dorms with ceiling fans, and some well-set-up doubles. TV/video room, dining area, modern kitchen, good showers and big pleasant backyard with BBQ. Same couple run the *Coogee Beachside Budget Accommodation* at 178 Coogee Bay Rd which has one-bedroom apartments sleeping up to four with linen supplied. Dorms $22–28, rooms ❸ apartments ❹–❻

North Shore

Cremorne Point Manor 6 Cremorne Rd, Cremorne Point ⓣ02/9953 7899, ⓦwww.cremornepointmanor.com.au. Huge restored federation-style villa. Nearly all rooms are en suite, except for a few good-value singles (from $52) which have own toilet and sink, and all have TV, fridge, kettle and a fan; some pricier rooms have harbour views. One family room has its own kitchen. Guest balcony also has great views. Communal kitchen and laundry. Light breakfast. Reception sells bus and ferry passes and books tours. ❺–❻

Elite Private Hotel 133 Carabella St, Kirribilli ⓣ02/9929 6365, ⓦwww.elitehotel.com.au. Bright place surrounded by plants offering good rooms with sink, TV, fridge and kettle; some dearer ones have a harbour view and most share bathrooms. Small communal cooking facility but no laundry; garden courtyard. Only minutes by ferry from the city (to Kirribilli Wharf) and near Milsons Point train station. Cheaper weekly rates. ❸–❹

Glenferrie Lodge 12A Carabella St, Kirribilli ⓣ02/9955 1685, ⓦwww.glenferrielodge.com. Another made-over Kirribilli mansion: clean, light and secure with 24hr reception. Three-share dorms and single, double or family rooms (all shared bathroom). Some pricier rooms have their own balcony and harbour glimpses but guests can also hang out in the garden and on the guest verandahs. Facilities include a TV lounge, laundry and dining room; buffet-style $7 dinner. Light breakfast. Ferry to Kirribilli Wharf or train to Milsons Point. Dorms $35, rooms ❹–❺

North Shore Hotel 310 Miller St, North Sydney ⓣ02/9955 1012, ⓦwww.smallanduniquehotels.com. Two-storey mansion with balconies in a quiet location opposite a park; within walking distance (10–15min) of the cafés and restaurants of North Sydney and Crows Nest. En-suite rooms or family studios sleeping four, all with air-con, TV, fridge and tea and coffee making facilities. Shared kitchen and laundry facilities; breakfast available. ❹–❺

Manly and the northern beaches

Avalon Beach Hostel 59 Avalon Parade, Avalon ⓣ02/9918 9709, ⓔgunilla@avalonbeach.com.au. At one of Sydney's best – and most beautiful – surf beaches, this hostel has seen better days, but its location and atmosphere still make it worth considering. Built mainly of timber, it has an airy beach-house feel with breezy balconies and plenty of greenery and rainbow lorikeets to gaze at. Warming fireplaces make it conducive to winter relaxation as well. The hostel could be cleaner, however, and bathroom facilities are stretched at peak times. Dorms (four- and six-bed) and rooms have storage area and fans. Boat trips on Pittwater can be organized; surfboard rental available. Excellent local work contacts. Dorms $20–22, rooms ❷

Manly Backpackers Beachside 28 Raglan St, Manly ⓣ02/9977 3411, ⓦwww.manlybackpackers.com.au. A modern and purpose-built two-storey "hostel with lifestyle" one block from the surf. One of the few hostels in Manly that manages to be both clean and fun, this place has free Internet access, a spacious well-equipped kitchen and outside terrace with BBQ and is good at organising group activities. Attracts long-stayers. Twin and double rooms – some en suite – plus small three-bed dorms (six-bed is largest). Best dorm at the front with a balcony. Dorms $22, rooms ❷

Manly Pacific Sydney 55 North Steyne, Manly ⓣ02/9977 7666, ⓦwww.accorhotels.com. Beach-front, multi-storey, four-star hotel with 24hr reception, room service, spa, sauna, gym and heated rooftop pool. You pay well for it all, and more for an ocean view, which is spectacular. Rooms ❼

Palm Beach Bed and Breakfast 122 Pacific Rd, Palm Beach ⓣ02/9974 1608. ⓔbandb@palmbeachsydney.net. Incredibly friendly and slightly quirky B&B (antique cars are scattered about the front lawn). All rooms have balconies and water views of either Pittwater or the Pacific and the emphasis is on relaxing and unwinding in this leafy setting. Four rooms with French themes have either en suite or shared bathroom. ❼

Periwinkle Guesthouse 18–19 East Esplanade, cnr Ashburner St, Manly ⓣ02/9977 4668, ⓦwww.periwinklemanlycove.com.au. Pleasant B&B in a charming, restored 1895 villa on Manly Cove. Close to the ferry, shops and the harbour and perfect for swimming, sailing or just listening to the lorikeets chatter. Rooms have fridge and fans; several en suites and larger family rooms available. Communal kitchen, laundry, courtyard with BBQ, and car park. Light breakfast. ❺–❻

Sydney Beachouse YHA 4 Collaroy St, Collaroy Beach ⓣ02/9981 1177, ⓦwww.sydneybeachouse.com.au. Purpose-built beachside hostel with a casual, relaxed attitude. Heated outdoor swimming pool, sundeck, BBQs, open fireplaces, video lounge and games and pool rooms. Four- to six-bed dorms plus several doubles (some en suite) and family rooms. Too far out for your entire Sydney stay (45min bus ride from the city), it's a good base for exploring the northern beaches – bikes are free for guests. Free use of boogie- and surfboards with surfing lessons for weekly guests. Other activities include didgeridoo lessons, kayaking and sailing. Free parking. Dorms $20–$26, rooms ❸

Cronulla Beach

Cronulla Beach YHA 40 Kingsway, Cronulla ⓣ02/9527 7772, ⓦwww.cronullabeachyha.com. No fuss hostel in this unpretentious, surf-oriented suburb, two minutes from the sand and even less to the shops and restaurants in Cronulla Mall. Also well situated for day-trips to the Royal National Park; the friendly live-in manager offers surf trips to Garie and drop-offs to Wattamolla. Surfboards, kayaks and bicycles for rent and free use of boogie boards. En suite rooms plus four- and six-bed dorms, all with fans and lockers. Facilities include Internet, pool table and a TV/video room. Friendly and small – but as it's so popular, plans for a big expansion are underway. Dorms $21–26, rooms ❸

The City

Port Jackson carves Sydney in two halves, linked by the Harbour Bridge and Harbour Tunnel. The **South Shore** is the hub of activity, and it's here that you'll find the **city centre** and most of the things to see and do. Many of the classic images of Sydney are within sight of **Circular Quay**, making this busy waterfront area on Sydney Cove a logical – and pleasurable – point to start discovering the city, with the **Sydney Opera House** and the expanse of the Royal Botanic Gardens to the east of Sydney Cove and the historic area of **The Rocks** to the west. By contrast, gleaming, slightly tawdry **Darling Harbour**, at the centre's western edge, is a shiny redeveloped tourist and entertainment area.

Circular Quay

At the southern end of Sydney Cove, **Circular Quay** is the launching pad for harbour and river ferries and sightseeing boats, the terminal for buses from the eastern and southern suburbs, and a major suburban train station to boot (some of the most fantastic views of the harbour can be seen from the above-ground station platforms). Circular Quay itself is always bustling with commuters during the week, and with people simply out to enjoy themselves at the weekend. Restaurants, cafés and fast-food outlets line the Quay, buskers entertain the crowds, and vendors of newspapers and trinkets add to the general hubbub. The sun reflecting on the water and its heave and splash as the ferries come and go make for a dreamy setting – best appreciated over an expensive beer at a waterfront bar. The inscribed bronze pavement plaques of **Writers' Walk** beneath your feet as you stroll around the Circular Quay waterfront provide an introduction to the Australian literary canon. There are short biographies of writers ranging from Miles Franklin, author of *My Brilliant Career*, through Booker Prize winner Peter Carey and Nobel Prize awardee Patrick White, to the feminist Germaine Greer, and quotable quotes on what it means to be Australian. Notable literati who've visited Australia – including Joseph Conrad, Charles Darwin and Mark Twain – also feature.

Having dallied, read, and taken in the view and the crush of people, you could then take to the water and either embark on a sightseeing **cruise** or enjoy a ferry ride on the harbour (see box p.128). Staying on dry land, you're only a short walk from most of the city-centre sights, along part of a continuous foreshore walkway beginning under the Harbour Bridge and passing through the historic area of Sydney's first settlement The Rocks, and extending beyond the Opera House to the Royal Botanic Gardens.

Besides ferries, Circular Quay still acts as a passenger terminal for ocean liners; head north past the Museum of Contemporary Art to Circular Quay West. It's a long time since the crowds waved their hankies regularly from the **Overseas Passenger Terminal**, looking for all the world like the deck of a ship itself, but you may still see an ocean liner docked here; even if there's no ship, take the escalator and the flight of stairs up for excellent views of the harbour. The rest of the terminal is given over to swanky restaurants and bars with fabulous views – *Aria*, *Wildfire* and *Cruise Bar* among them.

Leading up to the Opera House is the once-controversial **Opera Quays** development which runs the length of **East Circular Quay**. Since its opening locals and tourists alike have flocked to promenade along the pleasant colonnaded lower level with its outdoor cafés, bars and bistros, upmarket shops and Dendy Cinema, all looking out to sublime harbour views. The ugly apartment building above, dubbed "The Toaster" by locals and described by Robert Hughes, the famous expat Australian art critic and historian, as "that dull brash, intrusive apartment block which now obscures the Opera House from three directions", caused massive protests, but went up anyway, opening in 1999.

Customs House and the Justice & Police Museum

The railway and the ugly Cahill Expressway block views to the city from Circular Quay, cutting it off from Alfred Street immediately opposite, with its architectural gem, the sandstone and granite **Customs House**, which at the time of writing was undergoing its second multi-million dollar refurbishment in a decade, due for completion in mid-2005. First constructed in 1845, it was redesigned in 1885 by the colonial architect James Barnet to give it its current Classical Revival-style facade. On the ground floor a **City Exhibition Space** keeps pace with the development of Sydney with an up-to-the-minute detailed 500:1 scale model of the city set into the floor under glass and accompanied by a multimedia presentation. At the front of the building is a newly designed forecourt with *Young Alfred's* café offering alfresco seating, while the first three floors of the building house the City of Sydney's premier **public library** (Mon–Fri 8am–7pm, Sat 10am–4pm, Sun noon–4pm, closed public holidays). On the top floor is the only reminder of the building's previous incarnation, a pricey contemporary brasserie, *Cafe Sydney* (see p.179), which comes with wonderful Harbour Bridge views.

A block east of Customs House, on the corner of Phillip Street, the **Justice & Police Museum** is housed in the former Water Police station (Jan daily except Fri 10am–5pm; Feb–Dec Sat & Sun only 10am–5pm; $7; Ⓦwww.hht.net.au), an 1856 sandstone building with a particularly fine ironwork verandah. This social history museum focuses on law, policing and crime in New South Wales with several temporary themed exhibitions throughout the year. The permanent crime displays, including some truly macabre death masks and gruesome confiscated weapons, some of them murder implements, are shown within the context of a late-nineteenth-century police station and courtroom. There's also an interesting display on bushrangers.

Museum of Contemporary Art (MCA)

The **Museum of Contemporary Art** (daily 10am–5pm; free; free tours Mon–Fri 11am & 2pm, Sat & Sun noon & 1.30pm; Ⓣ02/9252 4033 for details of special exhibitions and events; Ⓦwww.mca.com.au), on the western side of Circular Quay with another entrance on George Street (no. 140), was developed out of a bequest by the art collector John Power in the 1940s to Sydney University to purchase international contemporary art. The growing collection finally found a permanent home in 1991 in the former Maritime Services Building, provided for peppercorn rent by the State Government. The striking Deco-style 1950s building is now dedicated to international twentieth-century art, with an eclectic approach encompassing lithographs, sculpture, film, video, drawings, paintings and Aboriginal art, shown in themed temporary exhibitions. The museum's superbly sited, if expensive, café has outdoor tables overlooking the waterfront.

The Sydney Opera House

The **Sydney Opera House**, such an icon of Australiana that it almost seems kitsch, is just a short stroll from Circular Quay, by the water's edge on **Bennelong Point**. It's best seen in profile, when its high white roofs, at the

Harbour cruises

There's a wide choice of **harbour cruises**, almost all of them leaving from Jetty 6, Circular Quay and the rest from Darling Harbour. Apart from the running commentary (which can be rather annoying), most offer nothing that you won't get on a regular harbour **ferry** for a lot less. The best of the ordinary trips is the thirty-minute ride to **Manly**, but there's a ferry going somewhere at almost any time throughout the day. If you want to splash out, take a **water-taxi** ride – Circular Quay to Watsons Bay, for example, costs $54 for the first passenger and then an additional $9 for each extra person. Pick-ups are available from any wharf if booked in advance (try Water Taxis Combined on ⓣ02/9555 8888, ⓦwww.watertaxis.com.au). One water taxi company, **Watertours**, located on Cockle Bay Wharf in Darling Harbour (ⓣ02/9211 7730, ⓦwww.watertours.com.au), even offer tours on their bright yellow taxis, from $12.50 for a speedy ten-minute, one-way spin under the Harbour Bridge to the Opera House (every 15min).

The **Australian Travel Specialists (ATS)** at Jetty 6, Circular Quay and the Harbourside Shopping Centre at Darling Harbour (ⓣ02/9211 3192, ⓦwww.atstravel.com.au) books all cruises. Those offered by State Transit – **Harboursights Cruises** (ⓣ13 15 00; ⓦwww.sydneyferries.nsw.gov.au) – offer the best value: choose between the Morning Harbour Cruise (daily 10.30am; 1hr; $18), the recommended Afternoon Harbour Cruise to Middle Harbour and back (Mon–Fri 1pm, Sat & Sun 12.30pm; 2hr 30min; $24), or the Evening Harbour Cruise (Mon–Sat 8pm; 1hr 30min; $22). Buy tickets at the Sydney Ferry ticket offices at Circular Quay. State Transit Authority (STA) cruises are also included in a Sydney Pass – see p.112.

Captain Cook Cruises at Jetty 6, Circular Quay (ⓣ02/9206 1122, ⓦwww.captaincook.com.au), the big commercial operator, offers a vast range of cruises on their very large boats including morning and afternoon "Coffee" Cruises into Middle Harbour (daily 10am & 2.15pm; 2hr 20min; $39), a lunch cruise (daily 12.30pm; 1hr 30min; buffet $57, one- or two-course $59–$69), a range of dinner cruises including the two-course Sunset Dinner (includes a drink; daily 5pm; 1hr 35min; $69) and Opera Afloat with opera singers accompanying a four-course dinner (daily 7pm; 2hr 30min; $99), and a Harbour Highlights Cruise (daily 9.30am, 11am, 12.45pm, 2.30pm, 4pm, 5.45pm; 1hr 15min; $20). Their hop-on-hop-off five-stop Sydney Harbour Explorer from Circular Quay (daily 9.30am–3.30pm; every 2hr; $25) circuits via the Opera House, Watsons Bay, Taronga Zoo and Darling Harbour.

same time evocative of full sails and white shells, give the building an almost ethereal quality. Some say the inspiration for the distinctive design came from the simple peeling of an orange into segments, though perhaps Danish architect **Jørn Utzon**'s childhood as the son of a yacht designer had something to do with their sail-like shape – he certainly envisaged a building which would appear to "float" on water. Despite its familiarity, or perhaps precisely because you already feel you know it so well, it's quite breathtaking at first sight. Close up, you can see that the shimmering effect is created by thousands of white tiles.

The feat of structural engineering required to bring to life Utzon's "sculpture", which he compared to a Gothic church and a Mayan temple, made the final price tag A$102 million, ten times original estimates. Now almost universally loved and admired, it's hard to believe quite how controversial a project this was during its long haul from plan, as a result of an international competition in the late 1950s, to completion in 1973. For sixteen years construction was plagued by quarrels and scandal, so much so that Utzon, who won the competition in 1957, was forced to resign in 1966. Some put it less kindly and say

Matilda Cruises, based in Darling Harbour (Aquarium Wharf, Pier 26; ⓣ02/9264 7377, ⓦwww.matilda.com.au), offers various smaller-scale cruises on sailing catamarans (engines mostly used), with big foredecks providing great views. Departures are from Darling Harbour (either at the Aquarium or King Street wharves) with pick-ups from Circular Quay twenty minutes later. Morning and afternoon cruises include tea, coffee and biscuits (10am & 3.05pm; 1–2 hrs; $27); there's a buffet on the Lunch Cruise (12.10pm; 2hr; $59), while the pricey Dinner Cruise allows you to dine on the foredeck (7.30pm; 2hr 30min; $99). Their hop-on-hop-off **Rocket Harbour Express Cruise** is a one-hour circuit stopping at Darling Harbour, the Opera House, Circular Quay West, Taronga Zoo and Watsons Bay (daily 9.30am–4.30pm; every hour; $22 includes refreshment; all-day ticket but one complete circuit only), while their ordinary ferry services include the Rocket Express, shuttling between Darling Harbour, the casino and Circular Quay every half-hour ($5.70 one-way, $10 return).

There are also a number of more romantic sailing options. **Svanen Charters**' (ⓣ02/9698 4456, ⓦwww.svanen.com.au) sailing ship, built in 1922, is moored at Campbells Cove, and offers harbour day-sails for $110, including morning tea and lunch, or longer overnight sails to Broken Bay, Port Hacking, Jervis Bay or Port Stephens (two nights $297, three nights $396). Sydney's oldest sailing ship, the **James Craig**, an 1874 three-masted iron barque, is part of the Sydney Heritage Fleet based at Wharf 7, Pirrama Rd, Pyrmont, near Star City Casino, and does six-hour cruises on Saturdays (10.30am–5pm; $193; over-12s only; morning and afternoon tea and lunch provided). **Sydney by Sail** (ⓣ02/9280 1110, ⓦwww.sydneybysail.com) offers the popular small-group, three-hour Port Jackson Explorer cruise (daily 1–4pm; $130) on board a luxury Beneteau yacht, departing from the National Maritime Museum, Darling Harbour (free entry to the museum included).

There are several options for more thrills (but noise pollution for the locals). **Ocean Extreme** (ⓣ0414 800 046, ⓦwww.oceanextreme.com.au) offers a hair-raising, forty-minute, small-group (maximum ten) "Adrenaline Tour" (daily 11am & 1pm; $90) on *Extreme 1*, an RIB (Rigid Inflatable Boat). At speeds of more than 100kph, the harbour scenery is mostly a blur. **Harbour Jet** (ⓣ1300 887 373, ⓦwww.harbourjet.com) offers the 35-minute "Jet Blast" (daily except Tues noon, 2 & 4pm from Convention Jetty, Darling Harbour; $60), on a boat which goes at speeds of 75kph, accompanied by blasting music.

he was hounded out of the country by politicians – the newly elected Askin government disagreeing over his plans for the completion of the interior – and xenophobic local architects. Seven years and three Australian architects later the interior, which at completion never matched Utzon's vision, was finished: the focal Concert Hall, for instance, was designed by **Peter Hall** and his team. However, Utzon now has a chance to have final say: in 1999 he was appointed as a design consultant to prepare a Statement of Design Principles for the building, which will become the permanent reference for its conservation and development. At the time of writing Utzon was continuing his consultancy with the Opera House and the first stage of the new masterplan, the **Reception Hall** opened to much acclaim in mid-2004. It represents the only space in the building ever built using the design of the original architect and is occasionally open to the public.

"Opera House" is actually a misnomer: it's really a performing arts centre, one of the busiest in the world, with five performance venues inside its shells, plus restaurants, cafés and bars, an Aboriginal artists' gallery, and a stash of upmarket souvenir shops on the lower concourse. The building's initial impetus, in fact, was as a home for the Sydney Symphony Orchestra, and it was designed with the huge **Concert Hall**, seating 2690, as the focal point; the smaller **Opera Theatre** (1547 seats), is used as the Sydney performance base for Opera Australia (seasons June–Nov & Feb–March), the Australian Ballet (mid-March to May & Nov–Dec) and the Sydney Dance Company. There are three theatrical venues: the **Drama Theatre** and **The Playhouse**, both used primarily by the Sydney Theatre Company, and the more intimate **The Studio**. There's plenty of action outside the Opera House too, with the use of the Mayan temple-inspired **Forecourt** and Monumental Steps as an amphitheatre for free and ticketed concerts – rock, jazz and classical, with a capacity for around 5000 people. Sunday is also a lively day on the forecourt, when the **Tarpeian Markets** (10am–4pm), with an emphasis on Australian crafts, are held.

If you're not content with gazing at the outside, **guided tours** are available: the Front-of-House tour gives an overview of the site, looking at the public areas and discussing the unique architecture (daily 9am–5pm; every 30min; 1hr; $23). Early morning backstage tours include access to the scenery docks, rehearsal rooms, technical areas and breakfast in the Greenroom (daily 7am; 2hr; $140; bookings on ⓣ02/9250 7250). These tours also visit the foyer of The Playhouse where two original Utzon models of the Opera House are displayed, alongside a series of small oil paintings depicting the life of **Bennelong**, the Iora tribesman who was initially kidnapped as little more than an Aboriginal "specimen" but later became a much-loved addition to Governor Arthur Phillip's household; Phillip later built a hut for him on what is now the site of the Opera House.

The best way to appreciate the Opera House, of course, is to attend an evening **performance**: the building is particularly stunning when floodlit and, once you're inside, the huge windows come into their own as the dark harbour waters reflect a shimmering night-time city – interval drinks certainly aren't like this anywhere else in the world. You could choose to **eat** at what is considered to be one of Sydney's best restaurants, *Guillame at Bennelong* (see p.179) overlooking the city skyline or take a **drink** at the *Opera Bar* on the lower concourse with outside tables and an affordable all-day menu (see p.189), plus there's a sidewalk café, a bistro and several theatre bars. Good-value **packages** which include tours, meals, drinks and performances can be purchased over the Internet or on site (ⓣ02/9250 7250, ⓦwww.sydneyoperahouse.com).

The Harbour Bridge

The charismatic **Harbour Bridge**, northeast of Circular Quay, has straddled the channel dividing North and South Sydney since 1932; today it makes the view from Circular Quay complete. The largest arch bridge in the world when it was built, its construction costs weren't paid off until 1988. There's still a toll ($3) to drive across, payable only when heading south; you can walk or cycle it for free. Pedestrians should head up the steps to the bridge from Cumberland Street, reached from The Rocks via the Argyle Steps off Argyle Street, and walk on the eastern side (cyclists keep to the western side). The ever-increasing volume of traffic in recent years proved too much for the bridge to bear, and a harbour **tunnel** (also $3 heading south) also crosses the river, starting south of the Opera House.

The bridge demands full-time maintenance, protected from rust by continuous painting in trademark steel-grey. Comedian Paul Hogan, of *Crocodile*

Dundee fame, worked as a rigger on "the coathanger" before being rescued by a New Faces talent quest in the 1970s. To check out Hoge's vista, you can follow a rigger's route and climb the bridge with **Bridge Climb**, who take specially equipped groups (maximum 12) to the top of the bridge from sunrise until after dark (minimum age 12; twilight climbs $225, Mon–Thurs day or night climbs $160, Fri–Sun day or night climbs $185; booking advised, particularly for weekends, on ⓣ02/8274 7777 or ⓦwww.bridgeclimb.com). Though the experience takes three and a half hours, only two hours is spent on the bridge, gradually ascending and pausing while the guide points out landmarks and offers interesting background snippets. The hour spent checking in and getting kitted up at the "Base" at 5 Cumberland St, The Rocks, and the grey Star Trek-style suits designed to blend in with the bridge, make you feel as if you're preparing to go into outer space. It's really not as scary as it looks – harnessed into a cable system, there's no way you can fall off. So that nothing can be dropped onto cars or people below, cameras cannot be taken on the walk (only your glasses are allowed, attached by special cords), limiting scope for one of the world's greatest **photo opportunities**. Though one group photo on top of the bridge is included in the climb price, the jolly strangers, arms akimbo, crowd out the background. To get a good shot showing yourself with the splendours of the harbour behind, taken by the guide, you'll need to fork out at least $16.

If you can't stomach (or afford) the climb, there's a **lookout point** (daily 10am–5pm; $8.50; ⓦwww.pylonlookout.com.au; 5min walk from Cumberland St then 200 steps) actually inside the bridge's southeastern pylon where, as well as gazing out across the harbour, you can study a photo exhibition on the bridge's history.

The Rocks

The Rocks, immediately beneath the bridge, is the heart of historic Sydney. On this rocky outcrop between Sydney Cove and Walsh Bay, Captain Arthur Phillip proclaimed the establishment of Sydney Town in 1788, the first permanent European settlement in Australia. Within decades, the area had become little more than a slum of dingy dwellings, narrow alleys and dubious taverns and brothels. In the 1830s and 1840s, merchants began building fine stone warehouses here, but as the focus for Sydney's shipping industry moved from Circular Quay, the area fell into decline. By the 1870s and 1880s, the notorious Rocks "pushes", gangs of "larrikins" (louts), mugged passers-by and brawled with each other: the narrow street named **Suez Canal** was a favourite place to hide in wait. Some say the name is a shortening of Sewers' Canal, and indeed the area was so filthy that whole streetfronts had to be torn down in 1900 to contain an outbreak of the bubonic plague. It remained a run-down, depressed and depressing quarter until the 1970s, when there were plans to raze the historic cottages, terraces and warehouses to make way for office towers. However, due to the foresight of a radical building workers' union which opposed the demolition, the restored and renovated **historic quarter** is now one of Sydney's major tourist attractions and, despite a passing resemblance to a historic theme park, it's worth exploring. It's also the best place, apart from the airport, to do tax-free shopping.

There are times, though, when the old atmosphere still seems to prevail: Friday and Saturday nights in The Rocks can be thoroughly drunken. New Year's Eve is also riotously celebrated here, to the backdrop of fireworks over the harbour. The best time to come for a drink is Sunday afternoon when many of the pubs here offer live jazz or folk music.

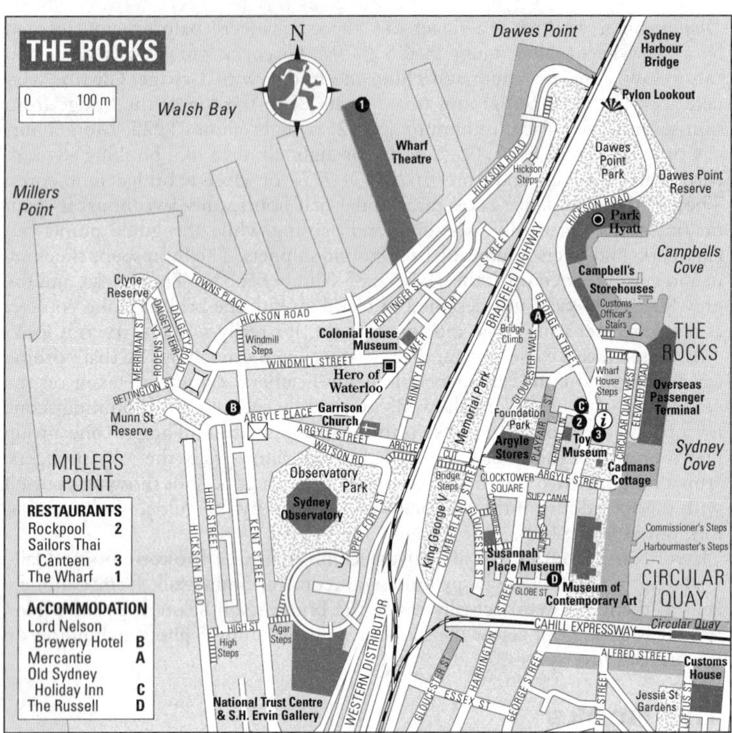

Information, tours and transport

The best place to start your tour of The Rocks is the **Sailors' Home**, at 106 George St, built in 1864 to provide decent lodgings for visiting sailors as an alternative to the brothels and inns in the area. The building housed sailors until the early 1980s but now contains the **Sydney Visitor Centre** (daily 9.30am–5.30pm, ⓣ02/9240 8788, ⓦwww.sydneyvisitorcentre.com), which at street level supplies tourist information (including a guided tour leaflet for $2.20). On the two galleried levels, information is provided about the history and sights of The Rocks along with a recreation of the original sailors' sleeping quarters. A great introduction to the area is the long-running **The Rocks Walking Tours**, starting from 23 Playfair St, Rocks Square (Mon–Fri 10.30am, 12.30pm & 2.30pm, Jan 10.30am & 2.30pm only, Sat & Sun 11.30am & 2pm; 1hr 30min; $19; ⓣ02/9247 6678, ⓦwww.rockswalkingtours.com.au).

The small sandstone house next to the information centre, at 110 George St, is **Cadmans Cottage**, the oldest private house still standing in Sydney, built in 1816 for John Cadman, ex-convict and Government coxswain. It's now the **National Parks and Wildlife Service** bookshop and information centre (Mon–Fri 9.30am–4.30pm, Sat & Sun 10am–4.30pm; ⓣ02/9247 5033, ⓦwww.nationalparks.nsw.gov.au), providing information about the Sydney Harbour National Park and taking bookings for trips to Fort Denison and other harbour islands that are part of the park.

The corner of Argyle and Kent streets, Millers Point, is a terminus for several useful **bus routes**; aim to head to here through The Rocks and then catch a bus back: routes #431–434 go along George Street to Railway Square and from there to varying locations including Glebe and Balmain, while #339 goes to the eastern beaches suburb of Clovelly via George Street in the city and Surry Hills.

Exploring The Rocks: from Campbells Cove to the Argyle Cut

Just exploring the narrow alleys and streets hewn out of the original rocky spur is the chief delight of The Rocks, a voyage of discovery that involves climbing and descending several stairs and cuts to different levels. A set of steps alongside the Sydney Visitor Centre leads down to the waterfront and the Overseas Passenger Terminal. Head north from here along the waterfront walkway to **Campbells Cove**, where the beautifully restored 1830s **Campbell's Storehouses**, once part of the private wharf of the merchant Robert Campbell, now house a shopping and eating complex. A replica of Captain Bligh's ship, the *Bounty*, is moored here between cruises, while a luxury hotel, the *Park Hyatt*, overlooks the whole area. Climb the **Customs Officer's Stairs** from Campbells Cove to Hickson Road, from where it's a short walk to Dawes Point beneath the Harbour Bridge, or browse in the road's **Metcalfe Stores**, another storehouses-turned-shopping complex, this time dating from around 1912. Exit onto George Street, where at weekends **The Rocks Market** (Sat & Sun 10am–5pm) takes over the entire Harbour Bridge end of the street with more than a hundred stalls selling bric-à-brac and arts and crafts mostly with an Australiana/souvenir slant.

There's more shopping at the **Argyle Stores**, on the corner of Argyle and Playfair streets, a complex of decidedly more tasteful and upmarket boutiques in a beautifully restored set of former bond stores arranged around an inner courtyard. The Argyle Stores is just near the impressive **Argyle Cut**, which slices through solid stone to The Rocks' other half, Millers Point. The cut took sixteen years to complete, carved first with chisel and hammer by convict chain gangs who began the work in 1843; when transportation ended ten years later the tunnel was still unfinished, and it took hired hands to complete it in 1859. Walk up the **Argyle Steps** and along the narrow, brick pedestrian walkway of peaceful **Gloucester Walk** – this was the very rocky spur the area was named after – to peep through greenery to gardens below. Remains of cottage foundations were discovered here and have been used as the basis for installations of sculptures of Victorian furniture in the tiny, delightful **Foundation Park**. En route back to the northern end of George Street the *Mercantile* is one of Sydney's best-known Irish pubs. Gloucester Walk also leads to the pedestrian entrance of the Harbour Bridge on **Cumberland Street**, the location of a couple of fine old boozers, the *Glenmore* and the *Australian*. From the latter, head down **Gloucester Street**; at nos. 58–64 is the **Susannah Place Museum** (Jan daily 10am–5pm; Feb–Dec Sat & Sun 10am–5pm; $7; Ⓦwww.hht.net.au), a row of four brick terraces built in 1844 and occupied by householders until 1990. It's now a "house museum" (including a recreated 1915 corner store), which conserves the domestic history of Sydney's working class.

The old wharves and Fort Denison

At the end of George Street, under the Harbour Bridge, **Dawes Point** separates Sydney Cove, on the Circular Quay side, from **Walsh Bay** and the old

Just for kids

There are two great **free attractions** in The Rocks aimed at children: **The Rocks Toy Museum**, just off Argyle Street on Kendall Lane (daily 10am–5.30pm; free), has two floors of collectable toys from the nineteenth through to the twentieth century, housed in a sandstone 1850s coachhouse; while next door, **The Puppet Cottage** puts on free weekend and school holiday puppet shows (11am, 12.30pm & 2pm; more information ⓣ02/9247 9137).

piers; the park here is a favourite spot for photographers. Looking out past the Opera House, you can see **Fort Denison** on a small island in the harbour: "Pinchgut", as the island is still known, was originally used as a special prison for the tough nuts the penal colony couldn't crack. During the Crimean Wars in the mid-nineteenth century, however, old fears of a Russian invasion were rekindled and the fort was built as part of a defence ring around the harbour. **Tours** from Circular Quay are booked through and leave from Cadmans Cottage (ⓣ02/9247 5033; daily 11.30am & 2.30pm, 3hr 30min, $22; brunch tours with a cooked meal in the fort's café included, Sat–Sun 9am, 3hr, $47).

Head a bit further along Hickson Road to the **Wharf Theatre** (Pier 4/5), home to the Sydney Theatre Company and the Sydney Dance Company. From the restaurant and its bar (see p.179) you can revel in the sublime view across Walsh Bay to Balmain, Goat Island and the North Shore. Guided tours, including the costume department and a peek at set construction, run on the first and third Thursday of the month (10.30am; 1hr; $8; bookings essential; ⓣ02/9250 1777, ⓦwww.sydneytheatre.com.au).

Millers Point and Observatory Park

Beyond the wharves, looking west towards Darling Harbour, **Millers Point** is a reminder of how The Rocks used to be – with a surprisingly real community feel so close to the tourist hype of The Rocks, as much of the housing is government- or housing association-owned. The area has its upmarket pockets, but for the moment, the traditional street-corner pubs and shabby terraced houses on the hill are reminiscent of the raffish atmosphere once typical of the whole area, and the mostly peaceful residential streets are a delight to wander through.

Reach the area through the Argyle Cut or from the end of George Street, heading onto **Lower Fort Street**. The **Colonial House Museum**, 53 Lower Fort St (daily 10am–5pm by arrangement only on ⓣ02/9247 6008; $1), takes up the bottom two floors of a residential terrace house (1883) where Shirley Ball has lived for over fifty years; her labour-of-love collection, crammed into six rooms, includes period furnishings, hundreds of photographs of the area, etchings, artefacts and models. Continue to wander up Lower Fort Street and stop for a drink at the **Hero of Waterloo** at no. 81, built from sandstone excavated from the Argyle Cut in 1844, then peek in at the **Garrison Church** (daily 9am–5pm) on the corner of Argyle Street, the place of worship for the military stationed at Dawes Point fort (the fort was demolished in the 1920s to make way for the Harbour Bridge) from the 1840s. Next to the church, the volunteer-run **Garrison Gallery Museum** (Tues, Wed, Fri & Sat 11am–3pm, Sun noon–4pm; free) is housed in what was once the parish schoolhouse and has a fascinating collection of historical photographs of The Rocks. Beside the church, **Argyle Place** has some of the area's prettiest old terrace houses.

From here, walk up the steps on Argyle Street opposite the church to **Observatory Park** with its shady Moreton Bay figs, park benches and lawns, for a marvellous hilltop view over the whole harbour in all its different aspects – glitzy Darling Harbour, and the newer Anzac Bridge in one direction and the older Harbour Bridge, with gritty container terminals, and ferries gliding by, in the other – and on a rainy day enjoy it from the bandstand which dominates the park. It's also easy to reach the park from the **Bridge Stairs** off Cumberland Street by the Argyle Cut.

The Italianate-style **Sydney Observatory** from which the park takes its name marked the beginning of an accurate time standard for the city when it opened in 1858, calculating the correct time from the stars and signalling it to ships in the harbour and Martin Place's GPO by the dropping of a time ball in its tower at 1pm every day – a custom which still continues. Set amongst some very pretty gardens, the Observatory is now a **museum of astronomy** (daily 10am–5pm; free; Ⓦwww.sydneyobservatory.com.au). A large section is devoted to the Transit of Venus, a rare astronomical event occurring about twice every century; it was the observation of this which prompted Captain Cook's 1769 voyage. The extensive exhibition of astronomical equipment, both obsolete and high-tech, includes the (still-working) telescope installed under the copper dome to observe the 1874 Transit of Venus. Another highlight, in the "Stars of the Southern Sky" section, are three animated videos of Aboriginal creation stories, retellings of how the stars came to be, from the Milky Way to Orion. Every evening you can view the southern sky through telescopes and learn about the Southern Cross and other southern constellations (times vary with season; 2hr tours include a lecture, film, exhibition, guided view of the telescopes and a look at the sky, weather permitting; $15; booking essential on Ⓣ02/9217 0485, usually up to a week in advance); the small planetarium is only used during night visits when the sky is not clear enough for observation.

Also in the park is the **National Trust Centre**, located in the former military hospital (1815) south of the Observatory, with a National Trust bookshop and café (both closed Mon). The rear of the building, purpose-built as a school in 1850 in neo-Regency style, houses the **S. H. Ervin Gallery** (Tues–Fri 11am–5pm, Sat & Sun noon–5pm; free; entry to special exhibitions $6; Ⓦwww.nsw.nationaltrust.org.au), the result of a million-dollar bequest by wool broker and art collector Ervin in 1978; around eight thematic exhibitions of Australian art each year focus on subjects such as Aboriginal or women artists.

City Centre

From Circular Quay south as far as King Street is Sydney's **Central Business District**, often referred to as the **CBD**, with **Martin Place** as its commercial nerve centre. A pedestrian mall stretching from George Street to Macquarie Street, lined with imposing banks and investment companies, Martin Place has its less serious moments at summer lunchtimes, when street performances are held at the little amphitheatre, and all-year-round stalls of flower- and fruit-sellers add some colour. The vast **General Post Office** (GPO), built between 1865 and 1887 with its landmark clock tower added in 1900, broods over the George Street end of the place in all its Victorian-era pomp. The upper floors have been incorporated into part of a five-star luxury hotel, the *Westin Sydney*; the rest of the hotel resides in the 31-storey tower behind. The old building and the new tower meet in the grand Atrium Courtyard, on the lower ground floor, with its restaurants, bars, classy designer stores, and the **GPO Store**, a gastronome's delight featuring a butcher, fish shop, deli, cheese room, wine merchant and greengrocer. The other end of Martin Place emerges opposite the old civic buildings on lower Macquarie Street. The cramped streets of the CBD itself, overshadowed by office buildings, have little to offer as you stroll through, though a crowd often gathers outside the **Australian Stock Exchange** opposite Australia Square at 20 Bond St to gaze at the computerized display of stocks and shares through the glass of the ground floor.

Museum of Sydney

North of Martin Place, on the corner of Bridge and Phillip streets, stands the **Museum of Sydney** (daily 9.30am–5pm; $7; ⓣ02/9251 5988 for exhibition details, ⓦwww.hht.net.au). The site itself is the reason for the museum's existence, for here from 1983 a ten-year archeological dig unearthed the foundations of the first Government House built by Governor Phillip in 1788 which was home to eight subsequent governors of New South Wales before it was demolished in 1846. The museum is totally original in its approach, presenting history in an interactive manner, through exhibitions, film, photography and multimedia, though you may come away feeling less well informed than you expected. A key feature of the museum are the special exhibitions – about four each year – so it's worth finding out what's on before you go.

First Government Place, a public square in front of the museum, preserves the site of the original Government House: its foundations are marked out in different coloured sandstone on the pavement. The museum itself is built of honey-coloured sandstone blocks, using the different types of tooling available from the earliest days of the colony right up to modern times: you can trace this development from the bottom to the top of the facade. Near the entrance, **Edge of the Trees**, an emotive sculptural installation, which was a collaboration between a European and an Aboriginal artist, attempts to convey the complexity of a shared history that began in 1788. Inside, on level 1, a video screen shows images of the bush, sea and sandstone Sydney as it was before the arrival of Europeans. Level 2, inside the **auditorium**, shows a fifteen-minute video explaining the background and aims of the museum; there are also recordings of Aboriginal people combined with video images to help the viewer reflect on contemporary experience. At the dark and creepy **Bond Store** on level 3, holographic "ghosts" relate tales of old Sydney as an ocean port. On the same level, a whole area is devoted to some rather wonderful **panoramas** of Sydney Harbour with views of the harbour itself from the windows.

There's also an excellent **gift shop** with a wide range of photos, artworks and books on Sydney and the expensive, licensed *MOS* **café** on First Government Place.

Sydney Sculpture Walk

The specially commissioned artworks of the **Sydney Sculpture Walk** – a City of Sydney Council initiative for the 2000 Olympics and the 2001 Centenary of Federation – form a circuit from the Royal Botanic Gardens, through The Domain, Cook and Phillip Park, the streets of the CBD, Hyde Park and East Circular Quay. One of the most striking of the ten site-specific pieces is Anne Graham's *Passage*, at the eastern end of Martin Place. At timed intervals, a fine mist emerges from grilles marking the outlines of an early colonial home which once stood here, creating a ghostly house on still days. A map showing the sculpture sites is available from Sydney Town Hall (p.138) or the City Exhibition Space (p.127) or there are details at ⓦwww.cityofsydney.nsw.gov.au.

Sydney Architecture Walks offers various **walking tours**, led by young architects, leaving from here every Wednesday and Saturday at 10.30am (2hr; $20; bookings ⓣ02/8239 2211, ⓦwww.sydneyarchitecture.org).

King Street to Liverpool Street

Further south from Martin Place, the streets get a little more interesting. The rectangle between Elizabeth, King, George and Park streets is Sydney's prime shopping area, with a number of beautifully restored **Victorian arcades** (the Imperial Arcade, Strand Arcade and Queen Victoria Building are all worth a look) and Sydney's two **department stores**, the very upmarket David Jones on the corner of Market and Elizabeth streets, established over 160 years ago, and Myers on Pitt Street Mall.

The landmark **Sydney Tower** (daily 9am–10.30pm, Sat until 11.30pm; viewing gallery and Skytour; $22; ⓦwww.sydneyskytour.com.au), or "Centrepoint" as it is still known to the locals, on the corner of Market and Pitt streets, a giant golden gearstick thrusting up 305m, is the tallest poppy in the Sydney skyline. The 360-degree view from the observation level is especially fine at sunset, and on clear days you can even see the Blue Mountains, 100km away. The observation deck is packaged with the **Skytour** on entry-lift level, a tacky forty-minute "virtual ride" introduction to a clichéd Australia. Unfortunately, the addition of Skytour has doubled the entry price to Sydney Tower and no single ticket is available; the best advice is to go straight to the top. You can see the same view, without the crowds and the entry ticket, at the **revolving restaurants** at the top of the tower; the tower revolution takes about seventy minutes and nearly all the tables are by the windows (bookings ⓣ02/8223 3800; $75 level 1 restaurant three-course dinner, Tues–Sat from 5.30pm; level 2 restaurant buffet, Mon–Sat lunch $42.50, Sun lunch $49.50, Mon–Sun dinner $52.50).

Nearby, several fine old buildings – the State Theatre, the Queen Victoria Building and the Town Hall – provide a pointed contrast. If heaven has a hallway, it surely must resemble that of the restored **State Theatre**, just across from the Pitt Street Mall at 49 Market St. Step inside and take a look at the ornate and glorious interior of this picture palace opened in 1929 – a lavishly painted, gilded and sculpted corridor leads to the lush, red and wood-panelled foyer. To see more of the interior, you'll need to attend the Sydney Film Festival (see p.200) or other events held here, such as concerts and drama, or you can take a guided tour (monthly 10.30am; 1hr 30 min; $15). Otherwise, pop into the beautiful little *Retro Cafe*, adjacent, for a coffee.

The stately **Queen Victoria Building** (abbreviated by locals to the QVB), taking up the block bounded by Market, Druitt, George and York streets, is another of Sydney's finest. Stern and matronly, a huge statue of Queen Victoria herself sits outside the magnificent building. Built as a market hall in 1898, two years before her death, the long-neglected building was beautifully restored and reborn in 1986 as an upmarket shopping mall with the focus on fashion: from the basement up, the four levels become progressively upmarket (shopping hours Mon–Sat 9am–6pm, Thurs until 9pm, Sun 11am–5pm; building open 24hr). The interior is magnificent, with its beautiful woodwork, gallery levels and antique lifts; Charles I is beheaded on the hour, every hour, by figurines on the ground-floor mechanical clock. From Town Hall station you can walk right through the basement level (mainly bustling food stalls) and continue via the Sydney Central Plaza to Myers Department Store, emerging on Pitt Street without having to go outside.

In the realm of architectural excess, however, the **Town Hall** is king – you'll find it across from the QVB on the corner of George and Druitt streets. It was built during the boom years of the 1870s and 1880s as a homage to Victorian England, the huge organ inside its Centennial Hall gives it the air of a secular cathedral. Throughout the interior different styles of ornamentation compete in a riot of colour and detail; the splendidly dignified toilets are a must-see. Concerts and theatre performances (see p.195) set off the splendiferous interior perfectly.

Down to Chinatown

Between Town Hall and Central station, **George Street** becomes increasingly downmarket, with sex shops side by side with discount stores. Along the way you'll pass Chinatown, in the area known as **Haymarket**, and a little further west is Darling Harbour. The short stretch between the Town Hall and Liverpool Street is for the most part teenage territory, a frenetic zone of **multiscreen cinemas**, pinball halls and fast-food joints, though the **Metro Theatre** is one of Sydney's best live-music venues (see p.192) and Planet Hollywood also attracts a keen stream of youngsters and tourists alike. The stretch is trouble-prone on Friday and Saturday nights when there are pleasanter places to catch a film (see cinema listings, p.199). Things change pace at Liverpool Street, where Sydney's **Spanish corner** consists of a clutch of Spanish restaurants and the Spanish Club.

Sydney's **Chinatown** is a more full-blooded affair than Spanish corner and probably the most active of the ethnic enclaves in Sydney. Through the ornate Chinese gates, **Dixon Street Mall** is the main drag, buzzing day and night as people crowd into numerous restaurants, pubs, cafés, cinemas, food stalls and Asian grocery stores. Towards the end of January or in the first weeks of February, Chinese New Year is celebrated here with gusto: traditional dragon and lion dances, food festivals and musical entertainment compete with the noise and smoke from strings of Chinese crackers. Friday nights are also a good time to visit, when a **night market** takes over Dixon and Little Hay streets (6pm–11pm). For a calmer retreat, on the edge of Chinatown at the southern fringes of Darling Harbour, is the serene **Chinese Garden** (see p.146).

The area immediately south of Chinatown is enlivened by Sydney's oldest market, bustling **Paddy's Market** (Thurs–Sun 9am–4.30pm), in its undercover home in between Thomas and Quay streets, next door to the Entertainment Centre. It's a good place to buy cheap vegetables, seafood, clothes, cheap souvenirs and bric-à-brac. Above Paddy's, the multilevel **Market City Shopping Centre** has a very modern Asian feel as well as some excellent outlet stores for discounted fashion. There's also a first-rate Asian food court, on the top floor next to the Reading multiscreen cinema.

The historic precinct: Hyde Park, College Street and Macquarie Street

Lachlan Macquarie, reformist governor of New South Wales between 1809 and 1821, gave the early settlement its first imposing public buildings, clustered on the southern half of his namesake Macquarie Street. He had a vision of an elegant, prosperous city – although the Imperial Office in London didn't share his enthusiasm for expensive civic projects. Refused both money and expertise, Macquarie was forced to be resourceful: many of the city's finest buildings were designed by the ex-convict architect Francis Greenway and paid for with rum money, the proceeds of a monopoly on liquor sales. Hyde Park was fenced off

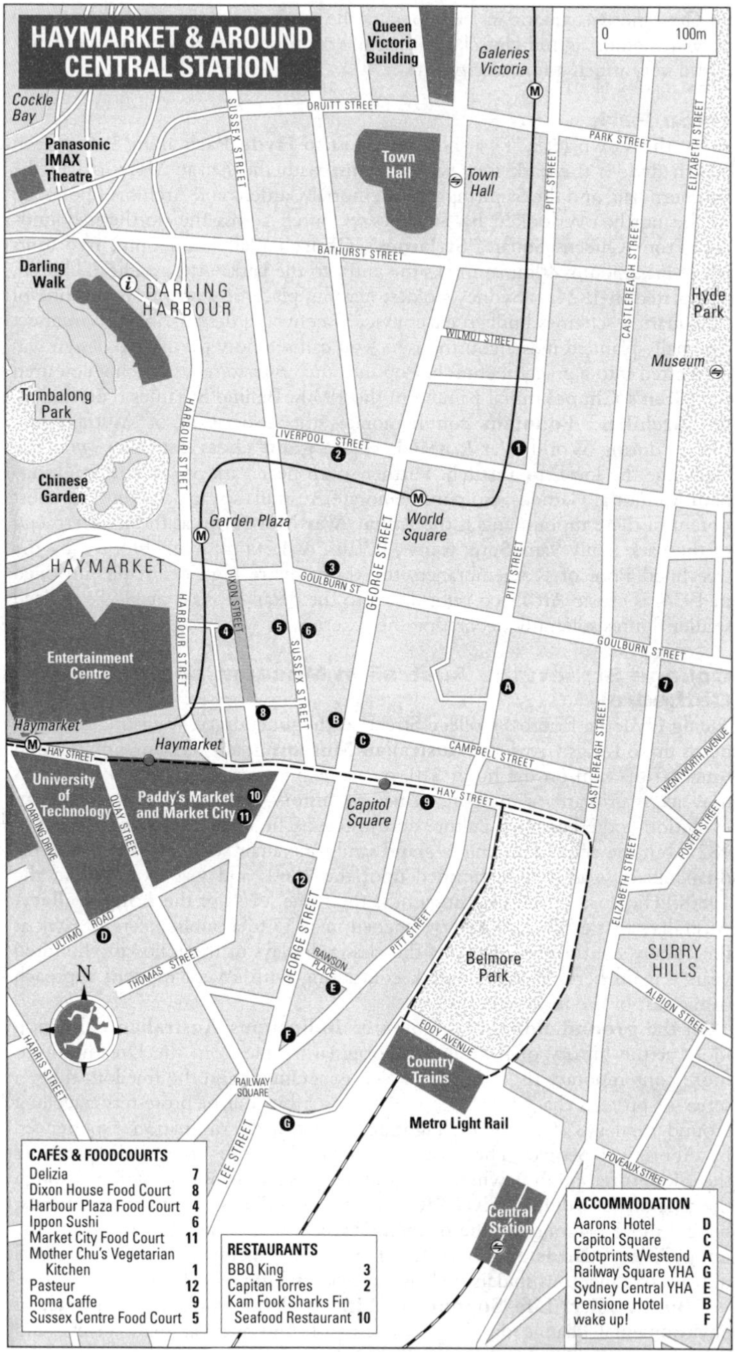

HAYMARKET & AROUND CENTRAL STATION
0 100m
Queen Victoria Building
Galeries Victoria
Cockle Bay
Panasonic IMAX Theatre
DRUITT STREET
SUSSEX STREET
PARK STREET
Town Hall
Town Hall
PITT STREET
ELIZABETH STREET
BATHURST STREET
CASTLEREAGH STREET
Darling Walk
DARLING HARBOUR
Hyde Park
WILMOT STREET
Museum
Tumbalong Park
HARBOUR STREET
LIVERPOOL STREET
Chinese Garden
Garden Plaza
World Square
GEORGE STREET
HAYMARKET
DIXON STREET
GOULBURN ST
GOULBURN STREET
Entertainment Centre
Haymarket
Haymarket
HAY STREET
CAMPBELL STREET
WENTWORTH AVENUE
University of Technology
Paddy's Market and Market City
Capitol Square
HAY STREET
DARLING DRIVE
QUAY STREET
FOSTER STREET
ULTIMO ROAD
THOMAS STREET
RAWSON PLACE
PITT STREET
Belmore Park
SURRY HILLS
ALBION STREET
N
HARRIS STREET
EDDY AVENUE
Country Trains
RAILWAY SQUARE
Metro Light Rail
LEE STREET
FOVEAUX STREET
Central Station
CAFÉS & FOODCOURTS
Delizia 7
Dixon House Food Court 8
Harbour Plaza Food Court 4
Ippon Sushi 6
Market City Food Court 11
Mother Chu's Vegetarian Kitchen 1
Pasteur 12
Roma Caffe 9
Sussex Centre Food Court 5
RESTAURANTS
BBQ King 3
Capitan Torres 2
Kam Fook Sharks Fin Seafood Restaurant 10
ACCOMMODATION
Aarons Hotel D
Capitol Square C
Footprints Westend A
Railway Square YHA G
Sydney Central YHA E
Pensione Hotel B
wake up! F

by Governor Macquarie in 1810 to mark the outskirts of his township, and with its war memorials and church, and peripheral museum and Catholic cathedral, is still very much a formal city park.

Hyde Park

From the Town Hall, it's a short walk east to **Hyde Park** along Park Street, which divides the park into two sections, with the Anzac Memorial in the southern half, and the Sandringham Memorial Gardens and Archibald Fountain in the north, overlooked by St James's Church across the northern boundary. From Queens Square, **St James's Church** (daily 9am–5pm; free tours Mon–Fri 2.30pm; 40mins) marks the entry to the park – the Anglican church, completed in 1824, is Sydney's oldest existing place of worship. It was one of Macquarie's schemes built to ex-convict Greenway's design, and the architect originally planned it as a courthouse – you can see how the simple design was converted into a graceful church. Pop into the crypt to see the richly coloured **Children's Chapel** mural painted in the 1930s. Behind St James train station, the **Archibald Fountain** commemorates the association of Australia and France during World War I; near here is a **giant chess set** where you can challenge the locals to a match. Further south near Park Street, the Sandringham Memorial Gardens also commemorate Australia's war dead, but the most potent of these monuments is the **Anzac War Memorial** at the southern end of the park (daily 9am–5pm; tours 11.30am & 1.30pm; free). Fronted by the tree-lined Pool of Remembrance, the thirty-metre-high cenotaph, unveiled in 1934, is classic Art Deco right down to the detail of Raynor Hoff's stylized soldier figures solemnly decorating the exterior.

College Street: the Australian Museum and St Mary's Cathedral

Facing Hyde Park across College Street, at the junction of William Street as it heads up to Kings Cross, the **Australian Museum** (daily 9.30am–5pm; 30min tours 10am–3pm on the hour; $10, special exhibitions extra; Ⓦwww.austmus.gov.au) is primarily a museum of natural history, with an interest in human evolution and Aboriginal culture and history. The collection was founded in 1827, but the actual building, a grand sandstone affair with a facade of Corinthian pillars, wasn't fully finished until the 1860s and was extended in the 1980s. The core of the old museum is the three levels of the **Long Gallery**, Australia's first exhibition gallery, opened in 1855 to a public keen to gawk at the colony's curiosities. Many of the classic displays of the following hundred years remain here, Heritage-listed, contrasting with a very modern approach in the rest of the museum.

On the **ground floor**, the impressive **Indigenous Australian** exhibition looks at the history of Australia's Aboriginal people from the Dreamtime to more contemporary issues of the "stolen generation" and the freedom rides, a series of protests that took place in 1965 by a bus full of protesters travelling around rural NSW towns highlighting the racial discrimination experienced by Aboriginal people. The ground-floor level of the Long Gallery houses the **Skeletons** exhibit, where you can see a skeletal human going through the motions of riding a bicycle, for example. Level 1 is devoted to **minerals**, but far more exciting are the disparate collections on level 2 – especially the Long Gallery's **Birds and Insects** exhibit, which includes chilling contextual displays of dangerous spiders such as redbacks and funnelwebs. Past this section the **Biodiversity: Life Supporting Life** exhibition looks at the impact of environmental change on the ecosystems of Australian animals, plants, and micro-organisms, around eighty percent of which do not naturally occur elsewhere, giving the country one of the highest levels of biodiversity. In the newer section, **Search and Discover** is aimed at both adults and children, a flora and fauna identification centre with Internet access and books to consult, while the **Human Evolution** gallery traces the development of fossil evidence worldwide and ends with an exploration of archeological evidence of Aboriginal occupation of Australia. A separate section, **More Than Dinosaurs**, deals with fossil skeletons of dinosaurs and giant marsupials: best of all is the model of the largest of Australia's megafauna, the wombat-like Diprotodon, who may have roamed the mainland as recently as ten thousand years ago.

Stanley Street, off College Street just south of the museum, has a cluster of cheap Italian cafés and restaurants, while nearby Crown Street features Sydney's version of the Hard Rock Cafe. North up College Street is Catholic **St Mary's Cathedral** (Mon–Fri & Sun 6.30am–6.30pm, Sat 8am–6.30pm; free tours Sun noon; 1hr), overlooking the northeast corner of Hyde Park. The huge Gothic-style church opened in 1882, though the foundation stone was laid in 1821. In 1999 the cathedral at last gained the twin stone spires originally planned for the two southern towers by architect William Wardell in 1865. The cathedral also gained an impressive new forecourt – a pedestrianized terrace with fountains and pools – with the consolidation of two traffic-isolated parks into the large **Cook and Phillip Park**. Its **recreation centre** (Mon–Fri 6am–10pm, Sat & Sun 7am–8pm; swim $5.50) has a fifty-metre swimming pool, gym and an excellent vegetarian restaurant. The remodelling also created a green link to The Domain.

Macquarie Street

Macquarie Street neatly divides business from pleasure, separating the office towers and cramped streets of the CBD from the open spaces of The Domain and the Royal Botanic Gardens. The southern end of Governor Macquarie's namesake street is lined with the grand edifices that were the result of his dreams for a stately city: Hyde Park Barracks, Parliament House, the State Library and the hospital he and his wife designed. The new Sydney – wealthy and international – shows itself on the corner of Bent and Macquarie streets in the curved glass sails of the 41-floor Aurora Place tower, designed by Italian architect **Renzo Piano**, co-creator of the extraordinary Georges Pompidou Centre in Paris.

Sandstone **Sydney Hospital**, the so-called "Rum Hospital", funded by liquor-trade profits, was Macquarie's first enterprise, commissioned in 1814 and therefore one of the oldest buildings in Australia. From here it is a short walk through the grounds to The Domain and across to the Art Gallery of New South Wales. One of the original wings of the hospital is now **NSW Parliament House** (Mon–Fri 9am–5pm; free half-hour guided tours: non-sitting days Mon–Fri 9.30am, 11am, 12.30pm, 2pm, 3pm & 4pm, sitting days Tues 1.30pm; ⓣ02/9230 2111 or ⓦwww.parliament.nsw.gov.au to check for parliamentary recesses), where as early as 1829 local councils called by the governor started to meet, making it by some way the oldest parliament building in Australia. Changing exhibitions in the foyer represent community or public sector interests and range from painting, craft and sculpture to excellent photographic displays. You can listen in on question time (Tues–Fri 2.15pm) when the parliament is sitting; book tickets in advance by telephone. The other wing was converted into a branch of the **Royal Mint** in response to the first Australian goldrush, and for some time served as a museum of gold mining; most of the building has now been taken over by NSW Historic Trust offices, but a café (Mon–Fri 8am–4pm; licensed) extends onto the balcony looking over Macquarie Street, and some interpretive boards detail the Mint's history.

Next door, the **Hyde Park Barracks** (daily 9.30am–5pm; $7), designed as convict lodgings by ex-convict Francis Greenway, was built in 1816, again without permission from London, to house six hundred male convicts. Now a museum of the social and architectural history of Sydney, it's a great place to visit for a taste of convict life during the early years of the colony: start at the top floor, where you can swing in recreations of the prisoners' rough hammocks. Computer terminals allow you to search for information on a selection of convicts' history and background – several of those logged were American sailors nabbed for misdeeds while in Dublin or English ports (look up poor William Pink). After the Barracks closed in 1848, the building was used to house single immigrant women, many of them Irish, escaping the potato famine; an exhibition looks at their lives, and there's a moving monument in the grounds erected by the local Irish community. Look out too for the excellent temporary historical exhibitions (Ⓣ02/9223 8922 for details).

The **State Library of New South Wales** (Mon–Fri 9am–9pm, Sat & Sun 11am–5pm, Mitchell Library closed Sun; free guided tours Tues 11am & Thurs 2pm) completes the row of public buildings on the eastern side of Macquarie Street. This complex of old and new buildings includes the 1906 sandstone **Mitchell Library**, with an imposing Neoclassical facade gazing across to the verdant Botanic Gardens. Its archive of old maps, illustrations and records relating to the early days of white settlement and exploration in Australia includes the original **Tasman Map**, drawn by the Dutch explorer Abel Tasman in the 1640s. The floor-mosaic in the foyer replicates his curious map of the continent, still without an east coast, and its northern extremity joined to Papua New Guinea. A glass walkway links the library with the modern building housing the General Reference Library. Free exhibitions relating to Australian history, art, photography and literature are a regular feature of its vestibules, while lectures, films and video shows take place regularly in the **Metcalfe Auditorium**, which holds free and ticketed events (Ⓣ02/9273 1770 or Ⓦwww.sl.nsw.gov.au for details and bookings). The glass-roofed **café** on level 7 (Mon–Fri 10am–4.30pm, Sat & Sun 11am–3.30pm) is airy with masses of plants; it's a relaxing, inexpensive spot for lunch or just coffee and cake. It's also worth browsing in the library's **bookshop** on the ground floor, for an impressive collection of Australia-related books.

The Domain and the Royal Botanic Gardens

The Cook and Phillip Park fills in the green gap between Hyde Park and **The Domain**, a much larger, plainer open space that stretches from behind the historic precinct on Macquarie Street to the waterfront, divided from the Botanic Gardens by the ugly Cahill Expressway and Mrs Macquarie's Road. In the early days of the settlement, The Domain was the governor's private park; now it's a popular place for a stroll or a picnic, with the Art Gallery of New South Wales, an outdoor swimming pool and Mrs Macquarie's Chair to provide distraction. On Sundays, assorted cranks and revolutionaries assemble here for **Speakers' Corner**, and every January thousands of people gather on the lawns to enjoy the free open-air concerts of the Sydney Festival (see p.202).

Art Gallery of New South Wales

Beyond St Mary's Cathedral, Art Gallery Road runs through The Domain to the **Art Gallery of New South Wales** (daily 10am–5pm, Wed till 9pm; free except for special exhibitions; free general tours Mon & Sat 1 & 2pm, Tues–Fri hourly 11am–2pm, Sun 11am, 1 & 2pm, ⓣ02/9225 1744, ⓦwww.artgallery.nsw.gov.au), whose collection was established in 1874. The original part of the building (1897) is an imposing Neoclassical structure with a facade inscribed with the names of important Renaissance artists, and principally contains the large collection of European art dating from the eleventh century to the twentieth; extensions were added in 1988, doubling the gallery space and providing a home for mainly Australian art. On level 1 is the **Yiribana Gallery**, devoted to the art and cultural artefacts of Aboriginal and Torres Strait Islanders; one of the most striking exhibits is the **Pukumani Grave Posts**, carved by the Tiwi people of Melville Island. A highly recommended half-hour performance here of dance and didgeridoo by an indigenous Australian (Tues–Sat noon) is well combined with the free one-hour tour of the indigenous collection (Tues–Sun 11am). Other highlights include some classic **Australian paintings** on level 4: Tom Roberts' romanticized shearing-shed scene *The Golden Fleece* (1894) and an altogether less idyllic look at rural Australia in Russell Drysdale's *Sofala* (1947), a depressing vision of a drought-stricken town. On level 5, the **photographic collection** includes Max Dupain's iconic *Sunbaker* (1939), an early study of Australian hedonism.

In addition to the galleries, there's an auditorium used for art lectures, an excellent bookshop, a coffee shop on level 2, and a restaurant on level 5 that attracts Sydneysiders for its food and atmosphere.

Mrs Macquarie's Chair and "the Boy"

Beyond the Art Gallery is the beginning of one of Sydney's most scenic routes – Mrs Macquarie's Road, built in 1816 at the urging of the governor's wife, Elizabeth. The road curves down from Art Gallery Road to Mrs Macquarie's Point, which separates idyllic Farm Cove from the grittier Woolloomooloo Bay. At the end is the celebrated lookout point known as **Mrs Macquarie's Chair**, a seat fashioned out of the rock. From here Elizabeth could admire her favourite view of the harbour on her daily walk in what was then the governor's private park. On the route down to the point, the **Andrew "Boy" Charlton Pool** is an open-air, saltwater swimming pool safely isolated from the harbour waters (daily Oct–April 6am–8pm; $5) on the Woolloomooloo side of the promontory, with views across to the engrossingly functional Garden Island Naval Depot. The "Boy", as the locals fondly call it, was named after the gold-medal-winning Manly swimmer, who turned 17 during the 1924 Paris Olympics. It's a popular hangout for trendy Darlinghurst types and sun-worshipping gays, even more so since its 2002 revamp. The much-glamorized pool now has its own café-restaurant, yoga, Pilates and kickboxing classes and a regular Thursday night **biathlon** (running and swimming) open to all competitors (6.30pm; ⓣ02/9358 6686 for more details).

The Royal Botanic Gardens

The **Royal Botanic Gardens** (daily 7am–sunset; free; ⓦwww.rbgsyd.gov.au), established in 1816, occupy the area between this strip of The Domain and the Sydney Opera House, around the headland on Farm Cove where the first white settlers struggled to grow vegetables for the hungry colony. While duck-ponds, a romantic rose garden and fragrant herb garden strike a very English air, look out for native birds and, at dusk, the fruit bats flying overhead (hundreds of the giant bats hang by day in the Palm Grove area near the restaurant) as the nocturnal possums begin to stir. There are examples of trees and plants from all over the world, although it's the huge, gnarled native Moreton Bay figs that stand out. The gardens provide some of the most stunning **views** of Sydney Harbour and are always crowded with workers at lunchtime, picnickers on fine weekends, and lovers entwined beneath the trees.

Many **paths** run through the gardens. A popular and speedy route (roughly 15min) is to start at the northern gates near the Opera House and stroll along the waterfront path to the gates separating it from The Domain, through here and up the **Fleet Steps** to Mrs Macquarie's Chair (see above). Within the northern boundaries of the park, the sandstone mansion glimpsed through a garden and enclosure is the Gothic Revival **Government House** (built 1837–45), seat of the governor of New South Wales, and still used for official engagements by the governor, who now lives in a private residence. The stately interior has limited opening hours (free guided tour every half-hour Fri–Sun 10am–3pm; 45min; ⓣ02/9931 5222 or ⓦwww.hht.net.au for more details) but you are free to roam the grounds (daily 10am–4pm). Further south, just inside the gardens at the end of Bridge Street, the **Conservatorium of Music** is housed in what was intended to be the servants' quarters and stables of Government House. Public opinion in 1821, however, deemed the imposing castellated building far too grand for such a purpose and a complete conversion, including the addition of a concert hall, gave it a loftier aim of training the colony's future musicians. Conservatorium students traditionally give free lunchtime recitals during term time in Recital Hall West (Wed 1.10pm).

Below the Conservatorium, the remaining southern area of the gardens has a herb garden, a cooling palm grove, a popular café by the duckponds, and the **Sydney Tropical Centre** (daily 10am–4pm; $2.20), where a striking glass pyramid and adjacent glass arc respectively house native tropical plants and exotics. At an entrance to the park in the southeast corner is the **visitors centre** (daily 9.30am–5pm), where free **guided tours** of the gardens commence (Dec–Feb daily 10.30am; 1hr 30min; March–Nov Mon–Fri 1pm; 40mins). If you're short of time, the **Trackless Train** runs through the gardens every twenty minutes (Mon–Fri 9.30am–5pm, Sat & Sun 9.30am–6pm; all-day hop-on-hop-off service $10) between the visitors centre and the entrance near the Opera House.

Darling Harbour and around

Darling Harbour, once a grimy industrial docks area, lay moribund until the 1980s, when the State Government chose to pump millions of dollars into the regeneration of this prime city real estate as part of the Bicentenary Project. The huge redevelopment scheme around Cockle Bay, which opened in 1988, included the building of the above-ground monorail – one of only a few in the world – as well as a massive new shopping and entertainment precinct. In many ways it's a thoroughly stylish redevelopment of the old wharves, and Darling Harbour and the surrounding areas of **Ultimo** and **Pyrmont** have plenty of attractions on offer: museums, an aquarium, entertainment areas, a shopping mall, an IMAX cinema, a children's playground, gardens, a casino, and a convention and exhibition centre. However, it's only recently that Sydneysiders themselves have embraced it. Sneered at for years by locals as tacky and touristy, it took the Cockle Bay Wharf development – an upmarket café, bar and restaurant precinct on the eastern side of the waterfront – and the most recent King Street

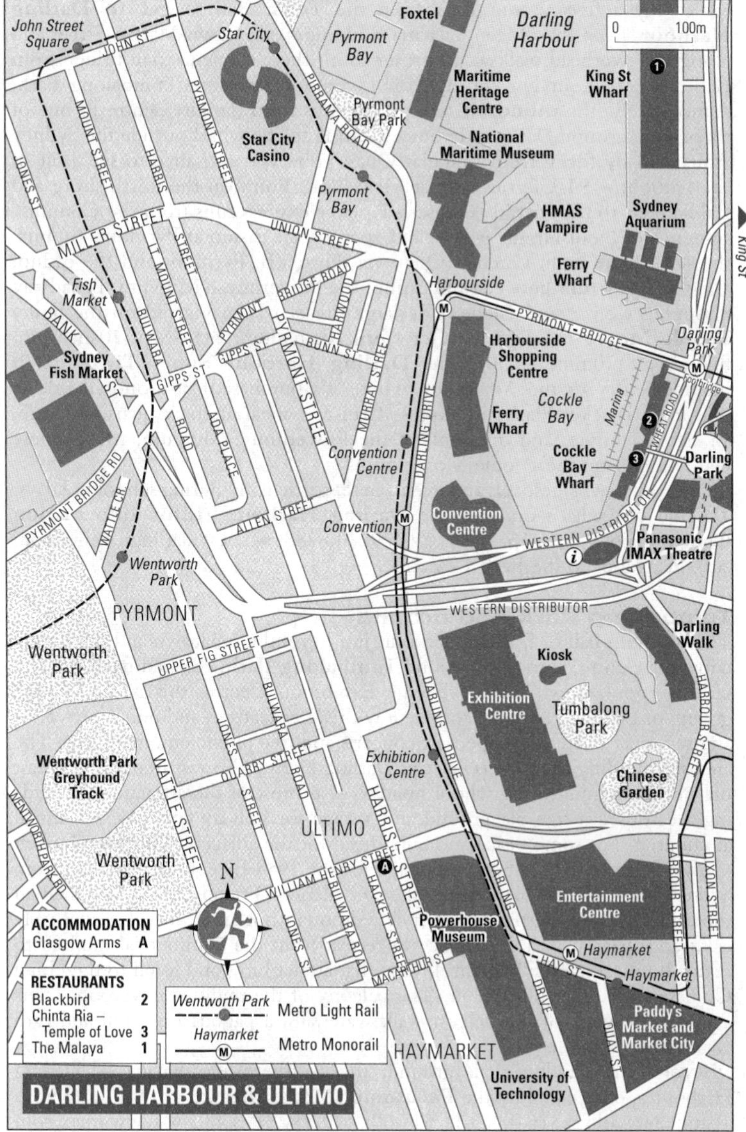

Wharf development to the north of the Aquarium – to finally lure locals in to the much-maligned area.

Behind the development, and accessible from it, is **Darling Park**, with paths laid out in the shape of a waratah flower. The western side of Darling Harbour is dominated by rather ugly modern chain hotels, ironically providing some of the view for the stylish Cockle Bay wharf diners.

It's only a five-minute walk from the Town Hall to **get to Darling Harbour**; from the Queen Victoria Building, walk down Market Street and along the overhead walkway. Further south there's a pedestrian bridge from Bathurst Street, or cut through on Liverpool Street to Tumbalong Park. Alternatively, the **monorail** (see p.110) runs from the city centre to one of three stops around Darling Harbour. Getting to the wharf outside the Sydney Aquarium by **ferry** from Circular Quay gives you a chance to see a bit of the harbour – STA ferries stop at McMahons Point on the north shore and Balmain en route. Matilda Cruises's Rocket Express runs from the Commissioners Steps, outside the MCA, and goes via the casino at Pyrmont. By **bus**, the #443 goes from Circular Quay via the QVB, Pyrmont and the casino, and the #449 runs between the casino, the Powerhouse Museum, Broadway Shopping Centre and Glebe. The large site can be navigated on the dinky **People Mover train** (daily: Oct–April 10am–6pm; May–Sept 10am–5pm; full circuit 20min; $3.50). The **Darling Harbour Super Ticket** ($62) includes entry to the Aquarium (where it's purchased), a monorail ride, a one-hour Rocket Harbour Express Cruise, a meal at the Aquarium's café, an IMAX movie, and discounts at the Powerhouse Museum, the Chinese Gardens and on the People Mover train.

There are always festivals and events here, particularly during school holidays. To find out what's on, visit the **Darling Harbour Visitor Information Centre** (daily 9.30am–5.30pm; Ⓣ02/9240 8788, Ⓦwww.darlingharbour.com.au), next door to the IMAX cinema.

Tumbalong Park and around

The southern half of Darling Harbour, just beyond Chinatown and the Entertainment Centre, is focused around **Tumbalong Park**, reached from the city via Liverpool Street. Backed by the Exhibition Centre, this is the "village green" of Darling Harbour, complete with water features and public artworks, and serves as a venue for open-air concerts and free public entertainment. The area surrounding the park is perhaps Darling Harbour's most frenetic – at least on weekends and during school holidays – as most of the attractions, including a carousel, a free playground and a stage for holiday concerts, are aimed at children. For some peace and quiet head for the adjacent **Chinese Garden** (daily 9.30am–5pm; $4.50), completed for the 1988 Bicentenary as a gift from Sydney's sister city Guangdong; the "Garden of Friendship" is designed in the traditional southern Chinese style. Although not large, it feels remarkably calm and spacious – a great place to retreat from the commercial hubbub to read a book, smell the fragrant flowers that attract birds and listen to the lilting Chinese music that fills the air. The balcony of the traditional tearoom offers a bird's-eye view of the dragon wall, waterfalls, a pagoda on a hill and carp swimming in winding lakes.

Beyond the children's playground, the Southern Promenade of Darling Harbour is dominated by the **Panasonic IMAX Theatre** (films hourly from 10am; 2-D films $16.00, 3-D $17.00; Ⓣ02/9281 3300, Ⓦwww.imax.com.au). Its giant eight-storey-high cinema screen shows a constantly changing programme from their 100-film library, with an emphasis on scenic wonders, the animal kingdom and adventure sports.

Sydney Aquarium

At the bottom of Market Street is **Pyrmont Bridge,** a pedestrian walkway across Cockle Bay, linking the two sides of the harbour. On the eastern side is the impressive **Sydney Aquarium** (daily 9am–9pm; $25, Aquarium Pass including STA ferry from Circular Quay $29.10; Ⓦwww.sydneyaquarium.com.au). If you're not going to get the chance to explore the Barrier Reef, the aquarium makes a surprisingly passable substitute. The entry level exhibits freshwater fish from the Murray Darling basin, Australia's biggest river system, but speed past these to get to the two underwater walkways, where you can wander in among sharks and watch gigantic stingrays gliding overhead. Another area features exotic species from the Great Barrier Reef, including a mass of glowing undulating Moon Jellyfish. Educational displays highlight the threats to the reef and its conservation. The Great Barrier Reef Oceanarium finishes with a huge floor-to-ceiling tank where you can sit and be mesmerized by the movement and colour of the underwater world while classical music plays. Alongside all the fish, there are also platypus, crocodiles, seals and Little Penguins on display. Removed here after becoming lost or injured, the seals at least seem to be enjoying themselves in their glass-walled outdoor pool, but the sad-looking penguins seem a little lost.

The National Maritime Museum and around

On the western side of Pyrmont Bridge the **National Maritime Museum** (daily 9.30am–5pm, Jan until 6pm; free entry to the museum, but you must purchase a $20 Big Ticket for guided tours of HMAS *Vampire*, the *James Craig* and HMAS *Onslow*; Ⓦwww.anmm.gov.au), with its distinctive modern architecture topped by a wave-shaped roof, highlights the history of Australia as a seafaring nation, but goes beyond maritime interests to look at how the sea has shaped Australian life, covering everything from immigration to beach culture and Aboriginal fishing methods in seven core-themed exhibitions. Highlights include the "Merana Eora Nora – First People" exhibition, delving into indigenous culture, and "Navigators – Defining Australia" which focuses on the seventeenth-century Dutch explorers. Outside several vessels are moored: the navy destroyer *Vampire*, and a submarine, HMAS *Onslow*, plus the beautifully restored 1874 square-rigger, the *James Craig* are permanently on display, while a collection of historic vessels, including a 1970s Vietnamese refugee boat, are rotated. The pleasant alfresco café here, which you don't have to enter the museum to use, has views of the boats. The bronze **Welcome Wall** outside the museum pays honour to Australia's six million immigrants.

Included in the museum entry is a behind-the-scenes tour of the **Maritime Heritage Centre** at Wharf 7, just beyond the museum off Pirrama Road and beside Pyrmont Bay Park, where conservation and model-making work takes place and some of the collection is stored. Also at the wharf, the Sydney Heritage Fleet's collection of restored boats and ships is moored, the oldest of which was built in 1888. Just nearby, the two-level **Harbourside Shopping Centre** provides opportunities for souvenir shopping: don't miss the first-floor **Gavala: Aboriginal Art & Cultural Education Centre** (daily 10am–9pm), the only fully Aboriginal-owned and -run store in Sydney (all profits go back to the artists), selling Aboriginal art, clothing, accessories and music.

Ultimo: the Powerhouse Museum and around

From Tumbalong Park, a signposted walkway leads to **Ultimo** and the **Powerhouse Museum** on Harris Street (daily 9am–5pm; $10, extra for special exhibitions, free 45min tour daily 11.30am & 1.30pm; Ⓦwww.phm.gov.au; monorail to Haymarket). Located, as the name suggests, in a former power station, this is arguably the best museum in Sydney, an exciting place with fresh ideas, combining arts and sciences, design, sociology and technology under the same roof – and even fashion, with the much-anticipated "Fashion of the

Year" display every November. There are several big temporary exhibitions on each year, with past popular themes as varied as "The Lord of the Rings" and "Audrey Hepburn, Woman of Style." The permanent displays are varied, presented with an interactive approach that means you'll need hours to investigate the five-level museum properly. The entrance level is dominated by the huge **Boulton and Watt Steam Engine**, first put to use in 1875 in a British brewery; still operational, the engine is often loudly demonstrated. The **Kings Cinema** on level 3, with its original Art Deco fittings, suitably shows the sorts of newsreels and films a Sydneysider would have watched in the 1930s. Judging by the tears at closing time, the **special children's areas** have proved a great success. On level 5, there's a licensed restaurant, with a more inexpensive courtyard cafeteria downstairs. The souvenir shop is also worth a browse for some unusual gifts.

Pyrmont: Star City Casino and the Sydney Fish Market

Frantic redevelopment is taking place at **Pyrmont**, which juts out into the water between Darling Harbour and Blackwattle Bay. The once dilapidated suburb was Sydney's answer to Ellis Island in the 1950s when thousands of immigrants disembarked at the city's main overseas passenger terminal, Pier 13. Today the former industrial suburb, which had a population of only nine hundred in 1988, is being transformed into a residential suburb of twenty thousand, housed in modern units and groovy renovated warehouses, paid for with A$2 billion worth of investment. With the New South Wales government selling A$97 million worth of property, this has been one of the biggest concentrated sell-offs of land in Australia. The area has certainly become glitzier, with Sydney's casino, Star City, and two TV companies – Channel Ten and Foxtel – based here. Harris Street has filled up with new shops and cafés, and the area's old pubs have been given a new lease of life, attracting the young and mobile. The approach to the spectacularly cabled **Anzac Bridge** (complete with statue of an Australian and New Zealand Army Corps soldier) – Sydney's newest – cuts through Pyrmont and saves between fifteen and twenty minutes' travelling time to Sydney's inner west.

Beyond the Maritime Museum, on Pyrmont Bay, palm-fronted **Star City** is the spectacularly tasteless 24-hour Sydney casino. As well as the casino, the building houses two theatres, fourteen restaurants, cafés and theme bars, souvenir shops, a convenience store and a nightclub. The casino interior itself is a riot of giant palm sculptures, prize cars spinning on rotating bases, Aboriginal painting motifs on the ceiling, Australian critters scurrying across a red desert-coloured carpet and an endless array of flashing poker machines. Dress code is smart casual. You can just wander in and have a look around or a drink, without betting. Nearby **Pyrmont Bay Park** is a shady spot to rest, and on the first Saturday of the month it hosts an early morning **Growers Market** (7–11am). To **get to the casino** bus #449 runs in a loop to and from Broadway in the city via the QVB to the casino and the Exhibition Centre in Darling Harbour, and the #443 runs from Circular Quay via Phillip and Market streets and the QVB. The Light Rail (see p.110) pulls in right underneath the casino.

The best reason to visit this area, though, is the **Sydney Fish Market**, on the corner of Pyrmont Bridge Road and Bank Street (daily 7am–4pm; Ⓦwww.sydneyfishmarket.com.au), only a ten-minute walk via Pyrmont Bridge Road from Darling Harbour. The market is the second-largest seafood market in the world for variety of fish, after the massive Tsukiji market in Tokyo. You need to visit early to see the **auctions** (Mon–Fri only, with the biggest auction floor on Friday; buyers begin viewing the fish at 4.30am, auctions begin 5.30am, public viewing platform opens 7am); buyers log into computer terminals to register their bids.

You can take away oysters, prawns and cooked seafood and eat picnic-style on waterfront tables watching the boats come in. Everything is set up for throwing together an impromptu meal – there's a bakery, the *Blackwattle Deli* with an extensive (and tempting) cheese selection, a bottle shop and a grocer. Alternatively, you can eat in at *Doyles*, the casual and slightly more affordable version of the famous *Doyles* fish restaurant at Watsons Bay; at the excellent sushi bar; or have dirt-cheap fish and chips or a crack-of-dawn espresso at the *Fish Market Cafe* (Mon–Fri 4am–4pm, Sat & Sun 5am–5pm). Retail shops open at 7am. The increasingly popular **Sydney Seafood School** (ⓣ02/9004 1111) offers seafood cookery lessons, from Thai-style to French provincial, plus a two-hour, early-morning tour of the selling floor (first Thurs of month; $20 includes a coffee).

To **get to** the fish market, take the Light Rail from Central to Fish Market station on Miller Street, or take bus #443 from Circular Quay or the QVB, and it's a five-minute walk from the corner of Harris Street and Pyrmont Bridge Road.

The inner west

West of the centre, immediately beyond Darling Harbour, the inner-city areas of **Glebe** and **Newtown** surround Sydney University, their vibrant cultural mix enlivened by large student populations. On a peninsula north of Glebe and west of The Rocks, **Balmain** is a gentrified former working-class dock area popular for its village atmosphere, while en route **Leichhardt** is a focus for Sydney's Italian community.

Glebe

Right by Australia's oldest university, **Glebe** has gradually been evolving from a café-oriented student quarter to more upmarket thirty-something territory with a New Age slant. Indeed, it's very much the centre of alternative culture in Sydney, with its yoga schools, healing centres and organic food shops. **Glebe Point Road** is filled with a mix of cafés with trademark leafy courtyards, restaurants, bookshops and secondhand shops as it runs uphill from **Broadway**, becoming quietly residential as it slopes down towards the water of Rozelle Bay. The side streets are fringed with renovated two-storey terraced houses with white-iron lacework verandahs. Not surprisingly, Glebe is popular with backpackers and offers several hostels (see "Accommodation", p.122). The **Broadway Shopping Centre** on nearby Broadway, but linked to Glebe by an overhead walkway from Glebe Point Road opposite one of the street's favourite cafés, *Badde Manors*, is handy if you're staying in the area, with its supermarkets, speciality food shops, huge food court, record, book and clothes shops and twelve-screen cinema.

Just before the beginning of Glebe Point Road, on Broadway, **Victoria Park** has a pleasant, heated outdoor swimming pool (Mon–Fri 6am–7.15pm, Sat & Sun 7am–5.45pm; $3.00) with attached gym and a sophisticated café. From the park, a path and steps lead up into **Sydney University**, inaugurated in 1850; your gaze is led from the walkway up to the Main Quadrangle and its very Oxford-reminiscent clock tower and Great Hall. You're welcome to wander round the university grounds, and there are several free museums and galleries to visit. Glebe itself is at its best on Saturday, when **Glebe Market** (10am–4pm),

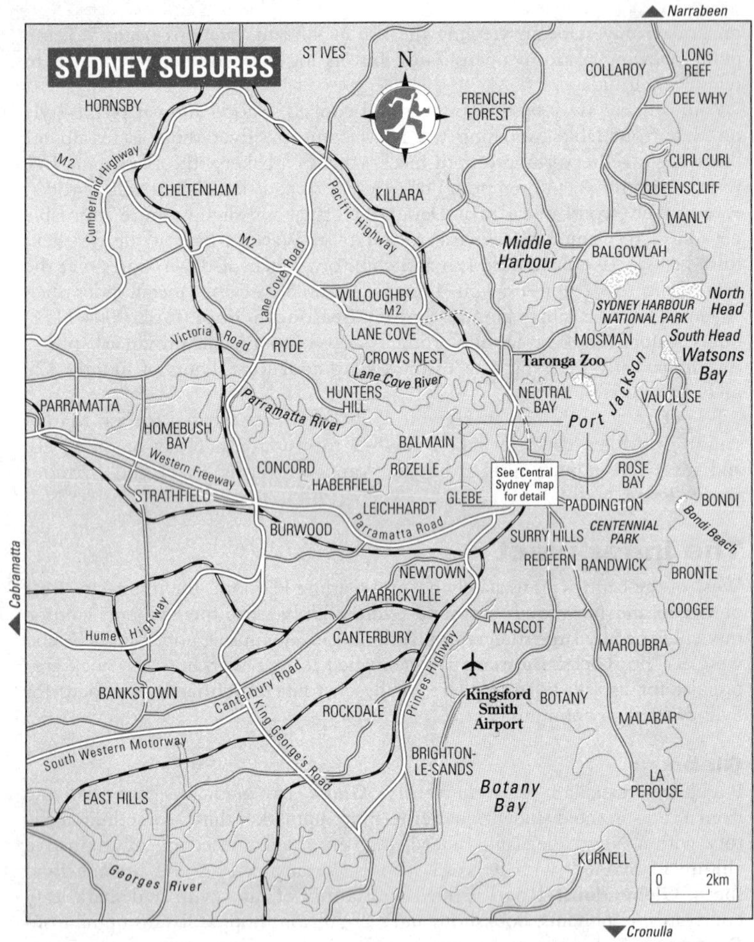

which takes place on the shady primary school playground on Glebe Point Road (opposite the *GNC Live Well* healthfood supermarket), is in full swing. On sale are mainly secondhand clothes and accessories, CDs, the inevitable crystals and a bit of bric-à-brac. At 49 Glebe Point Rd, you'll find the excellent **Gleebooks** – one of Sydney's best-loved bookshops. The original, now selling secondhand and children's books, is worth the trek further up to 191 Glebe Point Rd, past St Johns Road and Glebe's pretty park. Across the street and a couple of blocks further on is one of Sydney's best independent cinemas, the Valhalla, established in 1976. A few blocks on from here, the action stops and Glebe Point Road trails off into a more residential area, petering out at **Jubilee Park** with views across the water and Rozelle Bay's dilapidated (and soon to be replaced) container terminal. The pleasantly landscaped waterfront park, complete with huge, shady Moreton Bay fig trees and a children's playground, offers an unusual view of far-off Sydney Harbour Bridge framed within the cabled Anzac Bridge.

Buses #431, #433 and #434 run to Glebe from Millers Point, George Street and Central station; #431 and #434 run right down the length of Glebe Point Road to Jubilee Park, with the #434 continuing on to Balmain, while the #433 runs half-way turning at Wigram Road and heads on to Balmain. From Coogee beach, the #370 runs to Glebe via the University of NSW and Newtown. The Metro Monorail runs between Central station and Rozelle stopping at the "Glebe" stop, just off Pyrmont Bridge Road, and the "Jubilee" stop at Jubilee Park. Otherwise it's a fifteen-minute **walk** from Central Station up Broadway to the beginning of Glebe Point Road.

Newtown and around

Newtown, separated from Glebe by Sydney University and easily reached by train (to Newtown station), is another up-and-coming, inner-city neighbourhood. What was once a working-class district – a hotchpotch of derelict factories, junkyards and cheap accommodation – has transformed into a trendy, offbeat area where body piercing, shaved heads and weird fashions rule. Newtown is characterized by a large gay and lesbian population, and a rich cultural mix and a healthy dose of students and lecturers from the nearby university. It also has an enviable number of great cafés and diverse restaurants, especially Thai. The Dendy Cinema complex is a central focus, more like a cultural centre than just a film theatre, with its attached bookshop, excellent record store, and streetfront café, all open daily and into the night.

The main drag, gritty, traffic-fumed and invariably pedestrian-laden **King Street**, is filled with unusual secondhand, funky fashion and speciality and homeware shops and a slew of bookshops, old and new. For two weeks in June, various shop windows are taken over by young, irreverent and in-your-face art in the Walking the Street exhibition. The highlight of the year, however, is in November (second Sun) when the huge **Newtown Festival** takes over nearby Camperdown Memorial Park, with over 200 stalls and live music on three stages.

King Street becomes less crowded south of Newtown train station as it heads for a kilometre towards **St Peters** train station, but it's well worth strolling down to look at the more unusual speciality shops (buttons, ribbons, vintage records, Chinese medicine), as well as some small art galleries and yet more retro and funky new clothes shops. It's also stacked with culturally diverse restaurants including Singaporean, Japanese, Turkish and African, and closer to St Peters station are several colourful businesses aimed at the local Indian community. A couple of theatres and a High School for the Performing Arts give extra energy to this end of King Street.

Enmore Road stretching west from King Street, opposite Newtown station, is a similar mix of speciality shops and evidence of a migrant population – such as the African International Market at no. 2 and Amera's Palace Bellydancing Boutique at no. 83, and a range of restaurants from Swedish to Thai. It's generally much quieter than King Street, except when a big-name band or comedian is playing at the Art Deco **Enmore Theatre**, at no. 130. At the end of Enmore Road, Enmore Park hides the **Annette Kellerman Aquatic Centre** and its tiny heated 33-metre pool (Mon–Sat 5.30am–8.30pm, Sun 8am–6pm; $3.80). Beyond here, the very multicultural, lively but down-at-heel **Marrickville** stretches out, known for its Vietnamese and Greek restaurants.

Erskineville Road, stretching from the eastern side of King Street, marks the beginning of the adjoining suburb of **Erskineville**, a favourite gay address; the *Imperial Hotel* at 35 Erskineville Rd (see p.194), has long hosted popular drag shows, and is famous as the starting point of the gang in the 1994 hit film *The Adventures of Priscilla, Queen of the Desert.*

Buses #422, #423, #426 and #428 run to Newtown from Circular Quay via Castlereagh Street, Railway Square and City Road. They go down King Street as far as Newtown station, where the #422 continues to St Peters and the others turn off to Enmore and Marrickville. From Coogee beach, take the #370 bus to Glebe, which goes via Newtown. Alternatively, catch a **train** to Newtown, St Peters or Erskineville stations.

Leichhardt and Haberfield

It's almost an hour from The Rocks to Balmain by the #440 bus, via **Leichhardt**, Sydney's "Little Italy", where the famous **Norton Street** strip of cafés and restaurants runs off unattractive, traffic-jammed **Parramatta Road** (buses #436, #437 and #438 from George Street in the city will also take you here). Leichhardt is very much up and coming – shiny, trendy, Italian cafés keep popping up all along the strip, though its focus is the upmarket cinema complex, The Palace (which hosts a two-week Italian film festival in late October), with its attached record store, bookshop and Internet café and nearby shopping mall. Opposite, two-storey Beurkelow's bookstore sells both old and new books and has a café. Closer to Parramatta Road is the **Italian Forum**, an upmarket shopping and dining centre and showcase for all things Italian. However, the lively, much-loved and enduring *Bar Italia*, a fifteen-minute walk further down Norton at the extent of the tempting array of eateries, is still the best Italian café in Leichhardt (see p.182 for more details on cafés and restaurants in this area). The real heart of Italian Sydney, however, is a little further west on Ramsay St in **Haberfield**; one of Sydney's best pizzerias, *La Disfida*, is here at no.109, and the surrounding streets are full of decorative **Federation Style houses**, a classic Australian confection which spread around the country in 1901. To get to Haberfield, catch bus #436 from Leichhardt.

Rozelle to Balmain and Birchgrove

From Leichhardt, the #440 bus continues to **Darling Street**, which runs from **Rozelle** right down to Balmain's waterfront. Rozelle, once very much the down-at-heel, poorer sister to Balmain has emerged as a fully-fledged trendy area, with the Sydney College of the Arts and the Sydney Writers' Centre now based here in the grounds of the 61-hectare waterfront **Callan Park** on Balmain Road. Darling Street has a string of cafés, bookshops, speciality shops, gourmet grocers, restaurants, made-over pubs, and designer home-goods stores, and is at its liveliest on the weekend, when a huge **flea market** (Sat & Sun 9am–4pm) takes over the grounds of Rozelle Primary School, near the Victoria Road end. A leaflet, *Rozelle Walks* ($4.40) is available from Bray's Books in Balmain (see below).

To **get to Rozelle**, take bus #440 from George Street in the city or from Leichhardt. The Metro Light Rail from Central, Pyrmont or Glebe has a "Lilyfield" stop, about 500m from Balmain Road: follow Catherine Street and Grove Street to emerge opposite the Sydney College of the Arts campus.

Balmain, directly north of Glebe, is less than 2km from the Opera House, by ferry from Circular Quay to Darling Street Wharf. But, stuck out on a spur in the harbour and kept apart from the centre by Darling Harbour and Johnston's Bay, it has a degree of separation that has helped it retain its village-like atmosphere and made it the favoured abode of many writers and filmmakers. Like better-known Paddington, Balmain was once a working-class quarter of terraced houses that has gradually been gentrified. And though the docks at

White Bay no longer operate, the pubs that used to fuel the dockworkers still abound, and **Darling Street** and the surrounding backstreets are blessed with enough watering holes to warrant a pub crawl – two classics are the *London Hotel* on Darling Street and the *Exchange Hotel* on Beattie Street. Darling Street also rewards a leisurely stroll, with a bit of browsing in its speciality shops (focused on clothes and gifts), and grazing in its restaurants and cafés. The best time to come is on Saturday, when the lively **Balmain Market** occupies the shady grounds of St Andrews Church (7.30am–4pm), on the corner opposite the *London Hotel*. An assortment of books, handmade jewellery, clothing and ceramics, antiques, home-made chocolates, cakes and gourmet foods and organic produce are sold. The highlight is an eclectic array of food stalls in the church hall where you can snack your way from the Himalayas to Southern India.

On the Parramatta River side of Balmain, looking across to Cockatoo Island, Elkington Park is where you'll find the quaint **Dawn Fraser Swimming Pool** (March, April, Oct & Nov daily 7.15am–6.30pm, Dec–Feb 6.45am–7pm; $3.30), an old-fashioned harbour pool named after the famous Australian Olympic swimmer, a Balmain local. For long, stunning sunsets and wow-worthy real estate, meander from here down the backstreets towards water-surrounded **Birchgrove** on its finger of land, where Louisa Road leads to Birchgrove wharf; from here you can catch a ferry back to Circular Quay, or stay and relax in the small park on Yurulbin Point.

For a **self-guided tour** of Balmain and Birchgrove, buy a *Balmain Walks* leaflet ($2.20) from Balmain Library, 370 Darling St, or the well-stocked Bray's Bookshop, at no. 268. The most pleasurable way to **get to Balmain** is to catch a ferry from Circular Quay to Darling Street Wharf in Balmain East, where the #442 bus waits to take you up Darling Street to Balmain proper (or it's about a ten-minute walk). Buses #433 and #434 run out to Balmain via George Street, Railway Square and Glebe Point Road and down Darling Street; faster is the #442 from the QVB, which crosses Anzac Bridge and heads to Balmain Wharf. Birchgrove can be reached via ferry from Circular Quay or on the #441 from the QVB.

Goat Island

Just across the water from Balmain East, **Goat Island** is the site of a well-preserved gunpowder magazine complex. The sandstone buildings, including a barracks, were built by two hundred convicts between 1833 and 1839. Treatment of the convicts was harsh: 18-year-old Charles Anderson, a mentally impaired convict with a wild, seemingly untameable temper who made several escape attempts, received over twelve hundred lashes in 1835 and was sentenced to be chained to a rock for two years, a cruel punishment even by the standards of the day. Tethered to the rock, which you can still see, his unhealed back crawling with maggots, he slept in a cavity hewn into the sandstone "couch". Eventually Anderson ended up on Norfolk Island (see p.347), where under the humane prisoner reform experiments of Alexander Maconochie, the feral 24-year-old made a startling transformation. Today Goat Island is a part of Sydney Harbour National Park and accessible only by NPWS tour. **Heritage tours** (Wed & Sat 12.30pm; 2hr 30min; $19.80, child $15.40, family $61.60) and **Picnic tours** (Sun 11.30am; 3hr; $22, child $18, family $72) run to the island during the day. Not for the faint-hearted, the **Gruesome Tales tour** is run by torchlight and includes a light supper to settle frazzled nerves (Sat 6.45pm Nov–March, 5.45pm April–Oct; 3hr; $24.20; over 12s only). All tours depart from Cadmans Cottage in The Rocks and include the return ferry trip; bookings are essential (ⓣ02/9247 5033, ⓦwww.nationalparks.nsw.gov.au).

The inner east

To the **east**, **Surry Hills**, **Darlinghurst** and **Paddington**, once rather scruffy working-class suburbs, have long been taken over and revamped by the young, arty and upwardly mobile. **Kings Cross**, or "the Cross", is home to Sydney's red-light district as well as many of its tourists, while in adjacent **Woolloomooloo** container ships tie up at the docks in view of the newly renovated wharf. Further east, the Cross fades into the more elegant but tightly packed suburbs of **Potts Point** and **Elizabeth Bay**, which trade on their harbour views and proximity to the trendy restaurant province.

Surry Hills

Surry Hills, directly east of Central station from Elizabeth Street, was traditionally the centre of the rag trade, which still finds its focus on Devonshire Street. Rows of tiny terraces once housed its original poor, working-class population, many of them of Irish origin. Considered a slum by the rest of Sydney, the dire and overcrowded conditions were given fictional life in Ruth Park's *The Harp in the South* trilogy (see Contexts "Books"), set in the Surry Hills of the 1940s. The area became something of a cultural melting pot with European postwar immigration, and doubled as a grungy, studenty, muso heartland in the 1980s, fuelled by cheap bars and cheaper rent. By the mid-1990s, however, the slickly fashionable scene of neighbouring Darlinghurst and Paddington had finally taken over Surry Hills' twin focal points of parallel **Crown Street**, filled with cafés, swanky restaurants, funky clothes shops and designer galleries, and leafy **Bourke Street**, where a couple of Sydney's best cafés lurk among the trees. As rents have gone up, only **Cleveland Street**, running west to Redfern and east towards Moore Park and the Sydney Cricket Ground (see p.156), traffic-snarled and lined with cheap Lebanese, Turkish and Indian restaurants, retains its ethnically varied population.

Surry Hills is a short **walk** up a steep hill from Central (Devonshire St or Elizabeth St exit); take Fouveaux or Devonshire Street and you'll soon hit Crown, or it's an even quicker stroll from Oxford Street, Darlinghurst, heading south along Crown or Bourke streets.

A good time to visit Surry Hills is the first Saturday of the month when a lively **flea market**, complete with tempting food stalls, takes over the small Shannon Reserve, on the corner of Crown and Fouveaux streets, overlooked by the **Clock Hotel**. The hotel, which has expanded out of all recognition from its 1840s roots, is emblematic of the new Surry Hills, with its swish restaurant and bar. The artistic side of Surry Hills can be experienced nearby at the **Brett Whiteley Studio** at 2 Raper St (Sat & Sun 10am–4pm; by appointment Thurs & Fri ⓣ02/9225 1881; $7); walk about three blocks further south down Crown Street, and it's off Davies Street. Whitely was one of Australia's

Redfern

Just beyond Surry Hills, and only 2km from the glitter and sparkle of Darling Harbour, **Redfern** is Sydney's underbelly. Around the **Eveleigh Street** area, Australia's biggest urban Aboriginal community lives in "**the Block**", a squalid streetscape of derelict terrace houses and rubbish-strewn streets not far from Redfern train station – the closest Sydney has to a no-go zone. The Aboriginal Housing Company, set up as a co-operative in 1973, has had problems paying for repairs and renovation work. Recently the company began knocking down derelict houses and relocating people, which has upset many residents who want to keep the community together.

best-known contemporary painters with an international reputation by the time he died in 1992 of a heroin overdose at the age of 53; wild self-portraits and expressive female nudes were some of his subjects, but it is his sensual paintings of Sydney Harbour for which he is best known, painted from his home in Lavender Bay. In 1986 Whitely converted this one-time factory into a studio and living space, and since his death it has become a museum and gallery showing his paintings and memorabilia.

Darlinghurst, Paddington and Woollahra

Oxford Street, from Hyde Park to Paddington and beyond, is a major amusement strip. Waiting to be discovered, here and in the side streets, is an array of nightclubs, restaurants, cafés, pubs, cinemas and late-night bookshops. The Oxford Street shopping strip – many would argue Sydney's best for labels and funky style – starts at the corner of Victoria Rd in Darlinghurst and doesn't stop until the corner of Jersey Rd in Woollahra. Around **Darlinghurst**, Oxford Street is the focus of Sydney's very active gay and lesbian movement. Hip and bohemian, Darlinghurst mingles seediness with a certain hedonistic style. There's another concentration of cafés, restaurants and fashion on Liverpool Street, while Victoria Street is a classic pose strip with the legendary, street-smart *Bar Coluzzi* (see p.184)

At 148 Darlinghurst Rd, the impressive **Sydney Jewish Museum** (Mon–Thurs & Sun 10am–4pm, Fri 10am–2pm; $10; ⓣ02/9360 7999, ⓦwww.sydneyjewishmuseum.com.au) is housed in the old Maccabean Hall, a Jewish meeting point for over seventy years. Sixteen Jews were among the convicts who arrived with the First Fleet, and the high-tech, interactive museum explores over two hundred years of Australian Jewish experience. An introductory fifteen-minute film discusses anti-Semitism through the ages, and the Holocaust is covered in harrowing detail with Australian survivors' videotaped testimony. You can pick up the pamphlet *Guide to Jewish Sydney* from the museum.

Paddington, a slum at the start of the twentieth century, became a popular hangout for hipsters during the late 1960s and 1970s. Since then, the young professionals have taken over and turned Paddington into the smart and fashionable suburb it is today: the Victorian-era terrace houses, with their iron-lace verandahs reminiscent of New Orleans, have been beautifully restored. Many of the terraces were originally built in the 1840s to house the artisans who worked on the graceful, sandstone **Victoria Barracks** on the southern side of Oxford Street, its walls stretching seven blocks, from Greens Road to just before the Paddington Town Hall on Oatley Road. **Shadforth Street**, opposite the entrance gates, has many examples of the original artisans' homes. Though the barracks are still used by the army, there are free guided tours (Thurs 10am).

Crossing to the north side of Oxford Street the small, winding, tree-lined streets running off it are a pleasant place for a stroll, and offer a chance to wander into the many small art galleries or to take some liquid refreshment. Head via Underwood and Heeley streets to "**Five Ways**", where you'll find cafés, speciality shops and a typically gracious old boozer, the *Royal Hotel* (see p.186). Continuing east there are more shops along Elizabeth Street, while back on Oxford Street the main Paddington action of stylish boutiques and arty homeware stores attracts the "see and be seen" crowd. Always bustling, the area really comes alive on Saturdays, when everyone descends on **Paddington Market** (9am–4pm) in the church grounds at no. 395, opposite Elizabeth Street. The ever-expanding market sells everything from funky handmade jewellery to local artwork, as well as cheap fresh flowers and vintage clothes; you can even get a massage or a tarot reading between a cup of coffee and an organic sandwich.

Woollahra, along Oxford Street from Paddington, is even more moneyed but contrastingly staid, with expensive **antique shops** and **art galleries** along **Queen Street** replacing the fashion and trendy lifestyle focus of Paddington's shops. Leafy Moncur Street hides *jones the grocer* (at no. 68), where Woollahra locals gather for coffee at the long central table; it also sells stylishly packaged, outlandishly priced and utterly delicious groceries and gourmet treats.

Transport heading in this direction includes **buses** #380, #381 and #382 from Circular Quay which both run up Elizabeth Street in the city and along Oxford Street to Bondi Junction. The #378, from Central station, also heads along Oxford Street. Bus #389 from Circular Quay runs via Elizabeth and William streets in the city and along Glenmore Road and Hargrave Street, Paddington, to emerge on Oxford Street.

Centennial Parklands

South of Paddington and Woollahra lies the great green expanse of **Centennial Parklands** (daily sunrise to sunset; Ⓦwww.cp.nsw.gov.au), opened to the citizens of Sydney at the Centennial Festival in 1888. With its vast lawns, rose gardens and extensive network of ponds complete with ducks it resembles an English country park, but is reclaimed at dawn and dusk by distinctly antipodean residents, including possums and flying foxes. The park is crisscrossed by walking paths and tracks for cycling, rollerblading, jogging and horse riding: you can rent a bike or rollerblades nearby (see p.208) or hire a horse from the adjacent equestrian centre and then recover from your exertions in the café with its popular outside tables or, in the finer months, stay on until dark and catch an outdoor film with the Moonlight Cinema (see "Cinemas"). Adjoining **Moore Park** is incorporated under the banner of Centennial Parklands and has facilities for tennis, golf, grass-skiing, bowling, cricket and hockey; it's also home to the Sydney Cricket Ground and Fox Studios (see below). Pick up a free map of the Centennial Parklands from the Park Office (Mon–Fri 8.30am–5.30pm; Ⓣ02/9339 6699) near the café and easily reached from the Paddington gates off Oxford Street (opposite Queen Street). To get to the park you can take a **bus** from Central station (#372, #393 or 395) or from Elizabeth Street in the city, before Museum station (#L90, #391, #394 or #396; #394 and #396 extend to and from Circular Quay). Alternatively you could take a bus to Oxford Street, Paddington and then walk in via the Paddington gates or further along at the Woollahra gates (opposite Ocean Street).

The Sydney Cricket Ground (SCG)

The venerated institution of the **Sydney Cricket Ground (SCG)** earned its place in cricketing history for Don Bradman's score of 452 not out in 1929, and for the controversy over England's bodyline bowling techniques in 1932. Ideally, proceedings are observed from the lovely 1886 Members Stand, while sipping an icy gin and tonic – but unless you're invited by a member, you'll end up elsewhere, probably drinking beer from a plastic cup. Cricket spectators aren't a sedate lot in Sydney, and the noisiest barrackers will probably come from "the Hill" – or the Doug Walters Stand, as it's officially known. The Bill O'Reilly Stand gives comfortable viewing until the afternoon, when you'll be blinded by the sun, whereas the Brewongle Stand provides consistently good viewing. Best of all is the Bradman Stand, with a view directly behind the bowler's arm, and adjacent to the exclusive stand occupied by

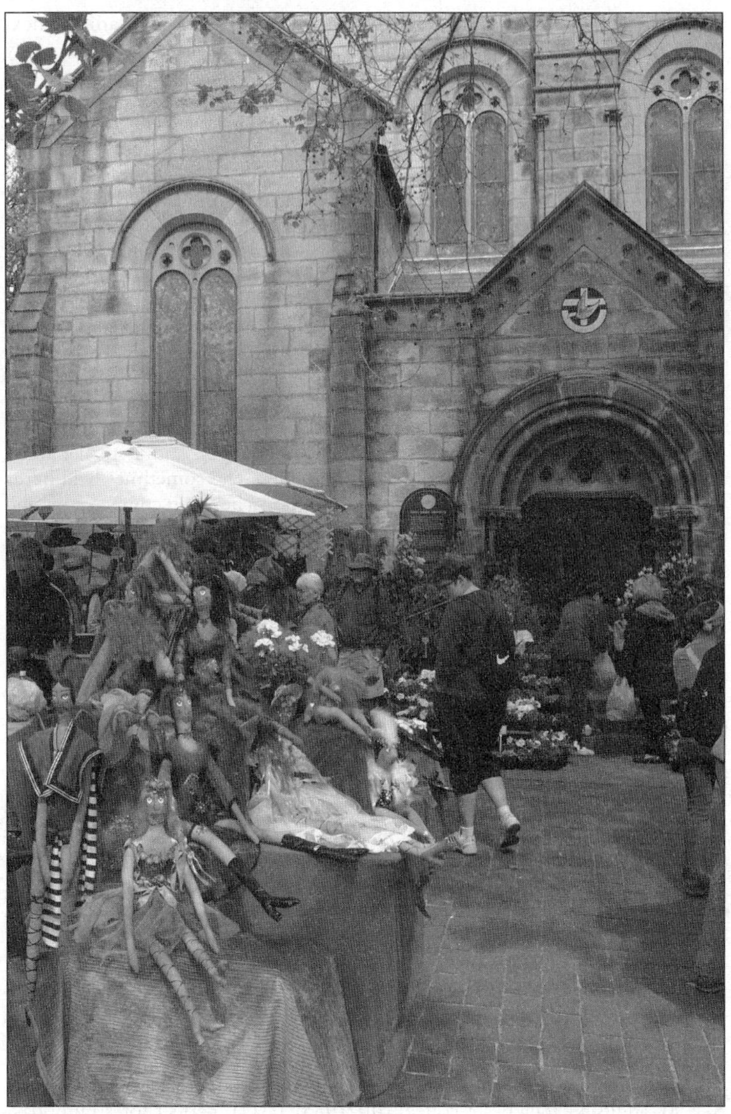

△ Paddington Bazaar, Paddington

members, commentators and ex-players. The Test to see here is, of course, **The Ashes**; the Sydney leg of the five tests, each for five days, begins on New Year's Day. For information, scores, prices and times, call ⓣ02/9360 6601. You can buy tickets for all matches at the gates on the day subject to availability, or purchase them in advance from Ticketek (ⓣ02/9266 4800, ⓦwww.ticketek.com.au). Die-hard cricket fans can go on a **tour** of the SCG on non-match days (Mon–Fri 10am & 1pm; 1hr 30min; $23.50; ⓣ1300 724

737, ⓦwww.scgt.nsw.gov.au), which also covers the **Aussie Stadium** next door, where the focus is on international and national rugby league and rugby union, and Aussie Rules football matches, when Sydneysiders come out to support their local team The Swans.

Fox Studios

Also within Moore Park, immediately southeast of the SCG, are the Murdoch-owned **Fox Studios** (ⓦwww.foxstudios.com.au), constructed at a cost of A$300 million within the old Showgrounds site, where the Royal Agricultural Society held its annual Royal Agricultural Show from 1882 until 1997, now held at Sydney Olympic Park (see p.234). The **Professional Studio**, opened in May 1998, takes up over half the site and has facilities for both film and television production, with six high-tech stages and industry tenants on site providing everything from casting services to stunt professionals. Films made here include *The Matrix* trilogy, *Mission Impossible II*, Baz Luhrmann's *Moulin Rouge*, and Episode I and II of the *Star Wars* saga. The **public areas** of the site are focused around a state-of-the-art, twelve-screen **cinema complex**, complete with digital surround-sound and VIP lounges, and a smaller four-screen arthouse cinema; international film premieres are sometimes held here.

The old **Show Ring**, once the preserve of wood-chopping competitions and rodeo events, is now used for everything from open-air cinema and circuses to the weekend craft market (Sat & Sun 10am–6pm), as well as the International Food Market (Fri from 6pm) and the fresh produce Farmers Market (Wed, Sat & Sun from 10am). The **Bungy Trampoline** (Wed–Sun 10am–6pm; $10) here is designed to give you the thrill of a bungy jump without the danger, and in winter there's an ice rink.

The Show Ring is adjacent to the gleaming shops, cafés, restaurants and bars of pedestrianized **Bent Street**. The twenty or so upmarket **shops**, including book and record shops, a young designers' clothes store and a bush outfitters, stay open daily until 10pm. The *Fox and Lion* has a traditional pub atmosphere and a beer garden looking onto the big outdoor screen showing music-video **Channel [V]**. The screen is outside the channel's live studio; free-to-attend shows are often being taped both inside and out (check ⓦwww.channelv.com.au for show times). There's a stand-up comedy venue, the *Comedy Store* (see p.199) and two music venues, *City Live* and the *Hordern Pavilion* (see p.192). Including the bars, there are fifteen **places to eat**: an eat-in gourmet deli, wood-fired pizza, Chinese seafood, noodles and classy contemporary Australian are among the choices.

The theme park area of Fox Studios, the Backlot, was a commercial failure, closing in 2001. However, there's still a lot to attract families including the mini-golf course by the old Backlot entrance (the film-themed murals are still there) and the indoor **Lollipops Playground** (Mon–Thurs 9.30am–7pm, Fri 9.30am–8pm, Sat 9am–8pm, Sun 9am–7pm; under-2s $8.90, 2–9 years $12.90, adults $4 includes a coffee; ⓣ02/9331 0811), perfect for a rainy day. Just outside are two free playgrounds and a carousel ($2.50).

To **get to Fox Studios** catch buses #339, #392, #394 or #396 from Central, Wynyard, or Town Hall.

Kings Cross and Potts Point

The preserve of Sydney's bohemians in the 1950s, **Kings Cross** became an R&R spot for American soldiers during the Vietnam war. Now Sydney's red-light district, it is still frequented by sailors from the ships docked in Woolloomooloo, and its streets are prowled by prostitutes, drug abusers, drunks, and homeless teenagers. Despite this, it is also a bustling centre for backpackers and other travellers, especially around leafy and quieter Victoria Street. The two sides of "the Cross" (as locals call it) coexist with little trouble, though some of the tourists seem a little surprised at where they've ended up, and it can be rather intimidating for lone women. However, the constant flow of people (and police officers) makes it relatively safe, and it's always lively, with bars and eating establishments open all hours.

Heading up **William Street** from Hyde Park and past Cook and Phillip Park and the Australian Museum, **Kings Cross** beckons with its giant neon Coca-Cola sign. By day, William Street looks quite grotty with its streams of fast and fumey traffic heading to the eastern and western distributors and its car rental firms; at night, hardcore transvestite streetwalkers and kerb-crawling patrons go about their business. However, with the new Cross City Tunnel easing traffic along here, there are long-term plans for William Street to become a European-style boulevard, tree-lined, traffic-calmed, and with wide pavements for café tables and strolling pedestrians. At the top of the hill, **Darlinghurst Road** is Kings Cross's "action zone". At weekends, an endless stream of suburban voyeurs emerge from the Kings Cross station, near the beginning of the Darlinghurst Road "sin" strip, and trawl along the streets as touts try their best to haul them into tacky strip-joints and sleazy nightclubs. The strippers and sleaze extend to the end of Darlinghurst Road at the El Alamein fountain in the paved Fitzroy Gardens, which though pleasant-looking, is the usual hangout of some fairly abusive drunks. It's much changed on Sundays when it's taken over by a small arts and crafts market. Generally, Kings Cross is much more subdued during the day, with a slightly hungover feel to it: local residents emerge and it's a good time to hang out in the cafés.

From Fitzroy Gardens, **Macleay Street** runs through quieter, upmarket **Potts Point** with its tree-lined streets, apartment blocks, classy boutique hotels, stylish restaurants, buzzy cafés and occasional harbour glimpses over wealthier Elizabeth Bay, just to the east; this is as close to European living as Sydney gets. The area was Sydney's first suburb, developed land granted to John Wylde in 1822 and Alexander Macleay in 1826. The grand villas of colonial bureaucrats gave way in the 1920s and 1930s to **Art Deco** residential apartments and in the 1950s big splendid hotels were added to the scene. The area is set to go more upmarket and more residential with the conversion of all the large hotels into luxury apartments.

You can get to Kings Cross by **train** or **bus** (#311, #324 or #325 from Circular Quay; #327 from Gresham St in the city), or it's not too far to walk; for a quieter route than William Street, you could head up from The Domain via Cowper Wharf Road in Woolloomooloo, and then up the McElhone Stairs to Victoria Street.

Woolloomooloo

North of William Street just below Kings Cross, **Woolloomooloo** occupies the old harbourside quarter between The Domain and the grey-painted fleet of the **Garden Island Naval Depot**. Once a narrow-streeted slum, Woolloomooloo is quickly being transformed, though its upmarket apartment developments sit uneasily side by side with problematic community housing, and you should still be careful at night in the backstreets. There are some lively pubs and some more old-fashioned quiet drinking holes, as well as the legendary **Harry's Café de Wheels** on Cowper Wharf Road, a 24-hour pie-cart operating since 1945 and popular nowadays with Sydney cabbies and hungry clubbers.

Next door, the once picturesquely dilapidated **Woolloomooloo Finger Wharf**, dating from 1917, is now a posh complex comprising a marina, luxury residential apartments, the cool *W Hotel* and its funky *Water Bar*, and some slick restaurants with alfresco dining. The general public are free to wander along the wharf and even go inside: there's a free exhibition space with a changing theme in the centre.

Woolloomooloo is best reached by foot from Kings Cross by taking the **McElhone Stairs** or the **Butlers Stairs** from Victoria Street; or from the Botanical Gardens by walking south around the foreshore from Mrs Macquarie's Chair; alternatively take bus #311 from Kings Cross, Circular Quay or Central station.

The Harbour

Loftily flanking the mouth of Sydney Harbour are the rugged sandstone cliffs of North Head and South Head, providing spectacular viewing points across the calm water to the city 11km away, where the Harbour Bridge spans the sunken valley at its deepest point. The many coves, bays, points and headlands of Sydney Harbour, and their parks, bushland and swimmable beaches are rewarding to explore. However, harbour beaches are not as clean as ocean ones, and after storms are often closed to swimmers (see p.166). Finding your way by ferry is the most pleasurable method: services run to much of the **North Shore** and to harbourfront areas of the **eastern suburbs**. The eastern shores are characterized by a certain glitziness and are the haunt of the nouveaux riches, while the leafy North Shore is very much old money. Both sides of the harbour have pockets of bushland which have been incorporated into **Sydney Harbour National Park**, along with five islands, two of which – Goat Island and Fort Denison – can be visited on tours (see p.153 and p.134); the other three – Shark Island, Clark Island and Rodd Island – are bookable for picnics but you must provide your own transport. The NPWS publishes an excellent free map detailing the areas of the national park and its many walking tracks available from Cadmans Cottage in The Rocks.

Elizabeth Bay to South Head

The suburbs on the hilly southeast shores of the harbour are rich and exclusive. The area around **Darling Point**, the enviable postcode 2027, is the wealthiest in Australia, supporting the lifestyle of waterfront mansions and yacht-club memberships enjoyed by some-time residents Nicole Kidman and Lachlan Murdoch. A couple of early nineteenth-century mansions, Elizabeth Bay House and Vaucluse House, are open to visitors, giving an insight into the life of the pioneering upper crust, while the ferry to **Rose Bay** gives a good view of the pricey contemporary real estate; the bay is close to beautiful **Nielson Park** and the surrounding chunk of Sydney Harbour National Park. At South Head, **Watsons Bay** was once a fishing village, and there are spectacular views from **The Gap** in another section of the national park. Woollahra Council (Ⓣ02/9391 7000, Ⓦwww.woollahra.nsw.gov.au) has brochures detailing three **waterside walks**: the 5.5-kilometre (3hr) **Rushcutters Bay** to Rose Bay harbour walk, which can then be continued with the eight-kilometre (4.5hr) walk to Watsons Bay, and the fascinating five-kilometre cliffside walk from Christison Park in **Vaucluse** (off Old South Head Road) to Watsons Bay and **South Head**, with shipwreck sites, old lighthouses and military fortifications along the way.

Buses #324 and #325 from Circular Quay via Pitt Street, Kings Cross and Edgecliff cover the places listed below, heading to Watsons Bay via New South Head Road; #325 detours at Vaucluse for Nielson Park. Bus #327 runs between Martin Place and Bondi Junction stations via Edgecliff station and Darling Point.

Elizabeth Bay and Rushcutters Bay

Barely five minutes' walk northeast of Kings Cross, **Elizabeth Bay** is a well-heeled residential area, centred on **Elizabeth Bay House**, at 7 Onslow Ave (Tues–Sun 10am–4.30pm; $7; bus #311 from either Railway Square or Circular Quay, or walk from Kings Cross station), a grand Regency residence with fine harbour views, built in 1835. Heading southeast, you're only a few minutes' walk from **Rushcutters Bay Park**, wonderfully set against a backdrop of the yacht- and cruiser-packed marina in the bay; the marina was revamped for the 2000 Olympics sailing competition. You can take it all in from the tables outside the very popular *Rushcutters Bay Kiosk*. The **tennis courts** at Rushcutters Bay Tennis Centre (daily 8am–11pm; courts $20 per hour, $24 after 4pm and on Sat & Sun; racket rental $3; bookings ⓣ02/9357 1675) are popular, and if you don't have anyone to play, the managers will try to provide a partner for you.

Double Bay and Rose Bay

Continuing northeast to **Darling Point**, McKell Park provides a wonderful view across to **Clarke Island** and **Bradleys Head**, both part of Sydney Harbour National Park; follow Darling Point Road (bus #327 from Edgecliff station). Next port of call is **Double Bay**, dubbed "Double Pay" for obvious reasons. The noise and traffic of New South Head Road are redeemed by several excellent antiquarian and secondhand bookshops, while in the quieter "village", some of the most exclusive shops in Sydney are full of imported designer labels and expensive jewellery. Eastern suburbs' socialites meet on Cross Street, where the swanky pavement cafés are filled with well-groomed women in Armani outfits. Double Bay's hidden gem is **Redleaf Pool** (daily Sept–May dawn–dusk; free), a peaceful, shady harbour beach enclosed by a wooden pier you can dive off or just laze on and there's an excellent café here. A ferry stops at both Darling Point and Double Bay; otherwise catch buses #324, #325 or #327.

A ferry to **Rose Bay** from Circular Quay gives you a chance to check out the waterfront mansions of **Point Piper** as you skim past. Rose Bay itself is a haven of exclusivity, with the verdant expanse of the members-only Royal Sydney Golf Course. Directly across New South Head Road from the course, waterfront **Lyne Park**'s **seaplane** service has been based here since the 1930s (see Sydney "Listings"). Rose Bay is also a popular **windsurfing** spot; you can rent equipment from Rose Bay Aquatic Hire (see Sydney "Listings").

Nielson Park and Vaucluse

Sydney Harbour National Park emerges onto the waterfront at Bay View Hill, where the 1.5-kilometre **Hermitage walking track** to Nielson Park begins; the starting point, Bay View Hill Road, is off South Head Road between the Kambala School and Rose Bay Convent (bus #324 or #325). The walk takes about an hour, with great views of the Opera House and Harbour Bridge, some lovely little coves to swim in and a picnic ground and sandy beach at yacht-filled **Hermit Point**. Extensive, tree-filled **Nielson Park**, on Shark Bay, is one of Sydney's delights, a great place for a swim, a picnic, or refreshment at the popular café. The decorative Victorian-era mansion, **Greycliffe House**, built for William Wentworth's daughter in 1852 (see below), is now the headquarters of Sydney Harbour National Park; if it's open (no regular hours) pop in for information on other waterfront walks. With views across the harbour to the city skyline, the park is a prime spot to watch both the New Year's Eve fireworks and the Sydney to Hobart yachts racing out through the heads on Boxing Day.

Beyond Shark Bay, Vaucluse Bay shelters the magnificent Gothic-style 1803 **Vaucluse House** and its large estate on Wentworth Road (Tues–Sun & public holiday Mondays 10am–4.30pm, grounds open daily 10am–5pm; $7), with tearooms in the grounds for refreshment. The house's original owner, explorer and reformer William Wentworth, was a member of the first party to cross the Blue Mountains. In 1831 he invited four thousand guests to Vaucluse House to celebrate the departure of the hated Governor Darling – the climax of the evening was a fireworks display which burned "Down with the Tyrant" into the night sky. To get here, walk from Nielson Park along Coolong Road (or take bus #325). Beyond Vaucluse Bay, narrow **Parsley Bay**'s shady finger of a park is a popular picnic and swimming spot, crossed by a picturesque pedestrian suspension bridge.

Watsons Bay and South Head

On the finger of land culminating in South Head, with an expansive sheltered harbour bay on its west side, and the treacherous cliffs of The Gap on its ocean side, **Watsons Bay** was one of the earliest settlements outside of Sydney Cove. In 1790 Robert Watson was one of the first signalmen to man the clifftop flagstaffs nearby and by 1792 the bay was the focus of a successful fishing village; the quaint old wooden fishermen's cottages are still found on the tight streets around Camp Cove. It's an appropriate location for one of Sydney's longest-running fish restaurants, *Doyles*, by the old Fishermans Wharf, now the ferry terminal (accessible by ferry from Circular Quay, or Rocket Harbour Express Cruise from Darling Harbour – see box on pp.128–129). In fact *Doyles* has taken over the waterfront here, with two restaurants, a takeaway, and a seafood bistro in the bayfront beer garden of *Doyles Palace Hotel*.

Spectacular ocean views are just a two-minute walk away through grassy Robertson Park, across Gap Road to **The Gap** (buses terminate just opposite – the #324, #325, and faster #L24 from Circular Quay, and the #L82 from Circular Quay via Bondi Beach), whose high cliffs are notorious as a place to commit suicide. You can follow a walking **track** north from here to South Head through another chunk of **Sydney Harbour National Park**, past the HMAS Watson Military Reserve. The track heads back to the bay side, and onto Cliff Street which leads to **Camp Cove**, a tiny palm-fronted harbour beach popular with families; a small kiosk provides refreshments.

Alternatively, reach Camp Cove by walking along the Watsons Bay beach and then along Pacific Street and through Green Point Reserve. From the northern end of Camp Cove, steps lead up to a boardwalk which will take you to **South Head** (470m circuit), the lower jaw of the harbour mouth affording fantastic views of Port Jackson and the city, via Sydney's best-known **nudist beach**, Lady Jane (officially "Lady Bay"), a favourite gay haunt. It's not very private, however: a lookout point on the track provides full views and ogling tour boats cruise past all weekend. From Lady Bay, it's a further fifteen minutes' walk along a boardwalked path to South Head itself, past nineteenth-century fortifications, lighthouse cottages, and the picturesquely red-and-white-striped Hornby Lighthouse.

The North Shore

The **North Shore** is generally more affluent than the South. **Mosman** and **Neutral Bay** in particular have some stunning waterfront real estate, priced to match. It's surprising just how much harbourside bushland remains intact here – "leafy" just doesn't do it justice – and superbly sited amongst it all is **Taronga Zoo**. A ride on any ferry lets you gaze at beaches, bush, yachts and swish harbourfront houses and is one of the chief joys of this area.

North Sydney and around

North Sydney has been associated with "pure fun" since the 1930s – beside the Harbour Bridge on Lavender Bay at **Milsons Point**, you can't miss the huge laughing clown's face that belongs to **Luna Park**. Generations of Sydneysiders have walked through the grinning mouth, and the park's old rides and conserved 1930s fun hall, complete with period wall murals, slot machines, silly mirrors and giant slippery dips, have great nostalgia value for locals. Luna Park was closed down for several years from the late 1980s until a grand reopening in January 1995 with a new clown's face. Unfortunately, the amusement park noise upset nearby residents, and the park spent the next few years opening and closing until in early 2004, rising like the proverbial phoenix from the ashes, the park reopened in its present form (Sun–Thurs 11am–6pm, Fri 11am–10pm, Sat 10am–11pm, longer hours during school holidays; individual ride tickets $3–5, unlimited-ride day pass $39). The ferry to Milsons Point Wharf from Circular Quay or Darling Harbour pulls up right outside (or train to Milsons Point station). Beyond the park a boardwalk goes right around Lavender Bay.

Right next door to Luna Park is Sydney's most picturesquely sited public swimming pool, with terrific views of the Harbour Bridge – the heated **North Sydney Olympic Pool**, Alfred South Street (Mon–Fri 5.30am–9pm, Sat & Sun 7am–7pm; $4.70). There's a indoor 25-metre pool as well as a 50-metre outdoor pool, a gym, sauna, spa, café, and an expensive restaurant, *Aqua*, overlooking the pool.

Beyond Luna Park and the pool, amongst North Sydney's impersonal corporate zone, is the Catholic Church-run **Mary MacKillop Place Museum**, 7 Mount St (daily 10am–4pm; $8.25; ⓦwww.marymackillopplace.org.au). Housed in a former convent, it provides a surprisingly broadminded look at the life and times of Australia's first saint-in-waiting (MacKillop was beatified in 1995 and is entombed here) and sainthood itself. For the full story, see the account in Coonawarra (on p.861), where the nun's charitable educational work began. Take the train to North Sydney station and head north along Miller Street for about five minutes.

Just east of the Harbour Bridge and immediately opposite the Opera House, **Kirribilli** and adjacent Neutral Bay are mainly residential areas, although Kirribilli hosts a great general **market** on the fourth Saturday of the month in Bradfield Park (7am–3pm), the best and biggest of several rotating markets on the North Shore (see "Markets"). On Kirribilli Point, the long-standing prime minister, native Sydneysider John Howard, lives in an official residence, **Kirribilli House**, snubbing Canberra, the usual PM's residence. Next door, Admiralty House is the Sydney home of the Governor General and where the British royal family stay when they're in town.

Following the harbour round you'll come to upmarket **Neutral Bay**. A five-minute walk from Neutral Bay ferry wharf via Hayes Street and Lower Wycombe Road is **Nutcote**, at 5 Wallaringa Ave (Wed–Sun 11am–3pm; $7), the former home for 45 years of May Gibbs, the author and illustrator of the famous Australian children's book, *Snugglepot and Cuddlepie*, about two little gumnuts who come to life; published in 1918, it's an enduring classic. Bush-covered **Cremorne Point**, which juts into the harbour here, is also worth a jaunt. Catch the ferry from Circular Quay and you'll find a quaint open-access sea pool to swim in by the wharf; from here, you can walk right around the point to Mosman Bay (just under 2km), or in the other direction, past the pool, there's a very pretty walk along **Shell Cove** (1km).

Mosman Bay: Taronga Zoo

Mosman Bay's seclusion was first recognized as a virtue during its early days as a whaling station, since it kept the stench of rotting whale flesh from the Sydney Cove settlement. Now the seclusion is a corollary of wealth. The ferry ride into the narrow, yacht-filled bay is a choice one – get off at Mosman Wharf – and fittingly finished off with a beer at the unpretentious *Mosman Rowers' Club* (visitors welcome).

What Mosman is most famous for, though, is **Taronga Zoo** on Bradleys Head Road, with its superb hilltop position overlooking the city (daily: Jan 9am–9pm; Feb–Dec 9am–5pm; $27, Zoo Pass including return ferry and entry $33.50; Ⓦwww.zoo.nsw.gov.au). The wonderful views and the natural bush surrounds are as much an attraction as the chance to get up close to the animals. The zoo houses bounding Australian marsupials, native birds (including kookaburras, galahs and cockatoos), reptiles, and sea lions and seals from the sub-Antarctic region. You'll also find exotic beasts from around the world, including giraffes. Established in 1916, the zoo's cages have new been replaced with more natural habitats. Taronga Zoo is currently part-way through a decade-long, major redevelopment programme and at the time of writing large areas of the zoo grounds were closed off. However, most of the zoo's creatures are still on show, although some of them are in temporary displays. The spectacular new **Asian Rainforest** exhibit is due to open in mid-2005 and includes a long-awaited new home for Taronga's elephants.

You can get close to kangaroos and wallabies in the **Australian Walkabout** area, and the **koala house** gives you eye-level views; to get closer, arrange to have your photo taken patting a koala. For a guaranteed **hands-on experience**, a VIP Aussie Gold Tour (daily 9.15am & 1.15pm; 1hr 30min–2hr; $57 includes zoo entry; book 24hr in advance on Ⓣ02/9969 2777) will give you and a small group a session with a zookeeper, guiding you through the Australian animals. Keeper talks and feeding sessions – including a free-flight bird show and a seal show – run through the day; details are on the map handed out on arrival.

The zoo is best reached by **ferry** from Circular Quay to Taronga Zoo Wharf (every half-hour). Although there's a lower entrance near the wharf on Athol Road, it's best to start your visit from the upper entrance and spend several leisurely hours winding downhill to exit for the ferry. State Transit buses still meet the ferries for the trip uphill, but a better option is to take the **Sky Safari** cable car included in the entry price. **Bus** #247 from Wynyard or the QVB also goes to the zoo.

Bradleys Head

Beyond the zoo, at the termination of Bradleys Head Road, **Bradleys Head** is marked by an enormous mast that once belonged to HMS *Sydney*, a victorious World War II Royal Australian Navy battleship lost (with all 645 hands) in 1941 off Australia's west coast after sinking a German raider. The rocky point is a peaceful spot with a dinky lighthouse and, of course, a fabulous view back over the south shore. A colony of ringtailed possums nests here, and boisterous flocks of rainbow lorikeets visit. The headland comprises another large chunk of **Sydney Harbour National Park**: you can walk to Bradleys Head via the six-kilometre Ashton Park **walking track** which starts near Taronga Zoo Wharf, and continues beyond the headland to Taylors Bay and Chowder Head, finishing at **Clifton Gardens**, where there's a jetty and sea baths on **Chowder Bay**. The now defunct military reserve which separates Chowder Bay from another chunk of Sydney Harbour National Park on Middle Head is now open to the public (see below), reached by a boardwalk from the northern end of Clifton Gardens. NPWS offers a monthly two-hour **bush food tour** of Bradleys Head (1st Sun of month 1.30pm; $13.20; bookings ⓣ02/9247 5033).

Middle Harbour

Middle Harbour is the largest inlet of Port Jackson, its two sides joined across the narrowest point at **The Spit**. The Spit Bridge opens regularly to let tall-masted yachts through – much the best way to explore its pretty, quiet coves and bays (see box pp.128–129). Crossing the Spit Bridge, you can walk all the way to Manly Beach along the ten-kilometre Manly Scenic Walkway (see p.173). The area also hides some architectural gems: the mock-Gothic 1889 bridge leading to **Northbridge**, and the idyllic enclave of **Castlecrag**, which was designed in 1924 by **Walter Burley Griffin**, fresh from planning Canberra and intent on building an environmentally friendly suburb – free of the fences and the red-tiled roofs he hated – that would be "for ever part of the bush". Bus #144 runs to Spit Road from Manly Wharf, taking in a scenic route uphill overlooking the Spit marina. To get to Castlecrag, take bus #207 from Wynyard.

Between Clifton Gardens and Balmoral Beach, a military reserve and naval depot at **Chowder Bay** blocked coastal access to both **Georges Head** and the more spectacular **Middle Head** by foot for over a century. Since the military's 1997 withdrawal from the site, walkers can now trek all the way between Bradleys Head and Middle Head. The 1890s military settlement is open to visitors as a reserve, and NPWS offers tours exploring its underground fortifications (2nd & 4th Sun of month 10.30am; 2hr; $13.20). You can reach the military reserve entrance from the northern end of Clifton Gardens (see below) or walk from Balmoral Beach.

The bush of Middle Head provides a gorgeous backdrop to **Balmoral Beach** on Hunters Bay. The shady tree-lined harbour beach is very popular with families. Fronting the beach, there's something very Edwardian and genteel about palm-filled, grassy Hunters Park and its bandstand, which is still used for Sunday jazz concerts or Shakespeare recitals in summer. The antiquated air is added to by the pretty white-painted **Bathers Pavilion** at the northern end, now converted into a restaurant and café (see "Eating and Drinking"). There are two sections of beach at Balmoral, separated by **Rocky Point**, a noted picnicking spot. South of Rocky Point, the "baths" – actually a netted bit of beach with a boardwalk and lanes for swimming laps – have been here in one form or another since 1899; you can rent sailboards, catamarans, kayaks, canoes and take lessons from Balmoral Sailing Club at the southern end of the beach (see p.209).

On the Hunters Bay side of Middle Head, tiny **Cobblers Beach** is officially **nudist**, and is a much more peaceful, secluded option than the more famous Lady Jane at South Head. The hillside houses overlooking Balmoral have some of the highest price tags in Sydney: for a stroll through some prime real estate, head for **Chinamans Beach**, via Hopetoun Avenue and Rosherville Road. To get to Balmoral, catch a ferry to Taronga Zoo Wharf then bus #238 via Bradleys Head Road, or after 7pm Mon–Sat the ferry to South Mosman (Musgrave Street) Wharf, then bus #233, or #257 via Military Road (#257 originates at Chatswood Station).

Ocean beaches

Sydney's **beaches** are among its great natural joys. The water and sand seem remarkably clean – people actually fish in the harbour – and at Long Reef, just north of Manly, you can find rock pools teeming with starfish, anemones, sea-snails and crabs, and even a few shy moray eels. In recent years, whale populations have recovered to such an extent that humpback and southern right whales have been regularly sighted from the Sydney headlands in June and July on their migratory path from the Antarctic to the tropical waters of Queensland, and southern right whales even occasionally make an unusual appearance in Sydney Harbour itself – the three southern right whales frolicking under the Harbour Bridge in July 2002 caused a sensation. Don't be lulled into a false sense of security, however: the beaches do have **perils** as well as pleasures. Some beaches are protected by special shark nets, but they don't keep out stingers such as bluebottles, which can suddenly swamp an entire beach; listen for loudspeaker announcements that will summon you from the water in the event of shark sightings or other dangers. Pacific **currents** can be very strong indeed – inexperienced swimmers and those with small children would do better sticking to the sheltered **harbour beaches** or **sea pools** at the ocean beaches. Ocean beaches are generally patrolled by **surf lifesavers** during the day between October and April (all year at Bondi): red and yellow flags (generally up from 6am until 6 or 7pm) indicate the safe areas to swim, avoiding dangerous rips and undertows. It's hard not to be impressed as **surfers** paddle out on a seething ocean, but don't follow them unless you're confident you know what you're doing. Surf schools can teach the basic skills, surfing etiquette and lingo: see "Surfing" in the listing sections. You can check daily **surf reports** on Ⓦwww.realsurf.com.

The final hazard, despite the apparent cleanliness, is **pollution**. Monitoring shows that it is nearly always safe to swim at all of Sydney's beaches – except after storms, when storm water, currents and onshore breezes wash up sewage and other rubbish onto harbour beaches making them (as signs will indicate) unsuitable for swimming and surfing. To check pollution levels, consult the Beachwatch Bulletin (Ⓣ1800 036 677, Ⓦwww.epa.nsw.gov.au).

Topless bathing for women, while legal, is accepted on many beaches but frowned on at others, so if in doubt, do as the locals do. There are two official nudist beaches around the harbour (see p.162 and p.165).

Bondi and the eastern beaches

Sydney's eastern beaches stretch from Bondi down to Maroubra. Heading south from Bondi, you can walk right along the coast to its smaller, less brazen but very lively cousin **Coogee**, passing through gay favourite **Tamarama**, family-focused, café-cultured **Bronte**, narrow **Clovelly** and **Gordons Bay**, the latter with an underwater nature trail. Randwick Council has designed the Eastern Beaches Coast Walk from Clovelly to Coogee and beyond to more downmarket

Maroubra, with stretches of boardwalk and interpretive boards detailing environmental features. Pick up a free guide-map detailing the walk from the council's Customer Service Office, 30 Francis St, Randwick (ⓣ02/9344 7006, ⓦwww.randwickcitytourism.com.au), or from the beachfront *Coogee Bay Kiosk*, Goldstein Reserve, Arden Street opposite McDonald's. It's also possible to walk north all the way from Bondi to South Head along the cliffs now that missing links in the pathway have been connected with bridges and boardwalk.

Bondi Beach

Bondi Beach is synonymous with Australian beach culture, and indeed the mile-long curve of golden sand must be one of the best-known beaches in the world. It's the closest ocean beach to the city centre; you can take a train to Bondi Junction and then a ten-minute bus ride, or drive there in twenty minutes. Big, brash and action-packed, it's probably not the best place for a quiet sunbathe and swim, but the sprawling sandy crescent really is spectacular.

Red-tiled houses and apartment buildings crowd in to catch the view, many of them erected in the 1920s when Bondi was a working-class suburb. Although still residential, it's long since become a popular gathering place for backpackers from around the world (see box below).

The beachfront **Campbell Parade** is both cosmopolitan and highly commercialized, lined with cafés and shops. For a gentler experience, explore some of the side streets, such as **Hall Street**, where an assortment of kosher bakeries and delis serve the area's Jewish community, and some of Bondi's best cafés are hidden. On Sunday the **Bondi Beach markets** (10am–5pm), in the grounds of the primary school on the corner of Campbell Parade and Warners Avenue facing the northern end of the beach, place great emphasis on groovy fashion and jewellery. Between Campbell Parade and the beach, **Bondi Park** slopes down to the promenade, and is always full of sprawling bodies. Along the promenade a **skate** and **BMX** park is popular with locals. The focus of the promenade is the arcaded, Spanish-style **Bondi Pavilion**, built in 1928 as a deluxe changing-room complex and converted into a community centre hosting an array of workshops, classes and events, from drama and comedy in the theatre and the Seagull Room (the former ballroom) to daytime dance parties and outdoor film festivals in the courtyard (programme details on ⓣ02/8362 3400, ⓦwww.waverley.nsw.gov.au). Downstairs in the foyer, photos of

Christmas Day on Bondi

For years backpackers and Bondi Beach on **Christmas Day** were synonymous. The beach was transformed into a drunken party scene, as those from colder climates lived out their fantasy of spending Christmas on the beach under a scorching sun. The behaviour and litter began getting out of control, and after riots in 1995, and a rubbish-strewn beach, the local council began strictly controlling the whole performance, with the idea of trying to keep a spirit of goodwill towards the travellers while also tempting local families back to the beach on what is regarded as a family day. Nowadays alcohol is banned from the beach on Christmas Day, and police enforce the rule with on-the-spot confiscations. However, a **party** is organized in the Pavilion and outdoors in its grounds, with a bar, DJs, food and entertainment running from 11am to 8pm. Around 3000 revellers cram into the Pavilion, while thousands of others – including a greater proportion of the desired family groups – enjoy the alcohol-free beach outside. In 2004, tickets for **Sunbeats** were $55 in advance from record stores or from Ticketek (ⓣ02/9266 4800, ⓦwww.ticketek.com.au).

Bondi's surf lifesavers

Surf lifesavers are what made Bondi famous; there's a bronze sculpture of one outside the Bondi Pavilion. The surf lifesaving movement began in 1906 with the founding of the Bondi Surf Life Bathers' Lifesaving Club in response to the drownings that accompanied the increasing popularity of swimming. From the beginning of the colony, swimming was harshly discouraged as an unsuitable bare-fleshed activity. However, by the 1890s swimming in the ocean had become the latest fad, and a Pacific Islander introduced the concept of catching waves or **bodysurfing** that was to become an enduring national craze. Although "wowsers" (teetotal puritanical types) attempted to put a stop to it, by 1903 all-day swimming was every Sydney-sider's right.

The bronzed and muscled surf lifesavers in their distinctive red and yellow caps are a highly photographed, world-famous Australian image. Surf lifesavers (members of what are now called Surf Life Saving Clubs, abbreviated to SLSC) are volunteers working the beach at weekends, so come then to watch their exploits – or look out for a surf carnival; lifeguards, on the other hand, are employed by the council and work all week during swimming season (year-round at Bondi).

Bondi's past are worth checking out, and there's an excellent **souvenir shop** (daily 9.30am–5.30am) which utilizes lots of old-fashioned Bondi imagery. A community-access **art gallery** (daily 10am–5pm) features changing exhibitions by local artists. In September, the day-long Festival of the Winds, Australia's largest **kite festival**, takes over the beach.

Surfing is part of the Bondi legend, the big waves ensuring that there's always a pack of damp young things hanging around, bristling with surfboards. However, the beach is carefully delineated, with surfers using the southern end of the beach. There are two sets of flags for swimmers and boogie-boarders, with families congregating at the northern end near the sheltered saltwater pool (free), and everybody else using the middle flags. The beach is netted and there hasn't been a shark attack for over forty years. If the sea is too rough, or if you want to swim laps, there's a seawater swimming pool (plus gym, sauna, massage service and poolside café) at the southern end of the beach under the **Bondi Icebergs Club** on Notts Avenue (Mon–Wed & Fri 6am–8pm, Sat & Sun 6.30am–6.30pm; $3.80). Part of the Bondi legend since 1929, members must swim throughout the winter, and media coverage of their plunge, made truly wintry with the addition of huge chunks of ice, heralds the first day of winter. The recently rebuilt clubhouse is a great place for a drink (see p.192). Below, Surf Lifesaving Australia offices have a small collection of memorabilia (Mon–Fri 10am–3pm; free).

Topless bathing is condoned at Bondi – a long way from conditions right up to the late 1960s when stern beach inspectors were on the lookout for indecent exposure. If you want to join in the sun and splash but don't have the gear, Beached at Bondi, below the lifeguard lookout tower, rents out everything from umbrellas, wetsuits, cozzies and towels to surfboards and boogie-boards and has lockers for valuables.

Reach Bondi Beach on **bus** #380, #L82 or #389 from Circular Quay via Oxford Street and Bondi Junction, or take the train to Bondi Junction station, then transfer to these buses or to the #361, #381 and #382.

Tamarama to Gordons Bay

Many people find the smaller, quieter beaches to the south of Bondi more enticing, and the oceanfront and clifftop **walking track** to Clovelly (about

2hr) is popular – the track also includes a fitness circuit, so you'll see plenty of joggers en route. Walk past the Bondi Icebergs Club on Notts Avenue (see above), round Mackenzies Point and through Marks Park to the modest and secluded **Mackenzies Bay**. Next is **Tamarama Bay**, a deep, narrow beach favoured by the smart set and a hedonistic gay crowd ("Glamarama" to the locals), as well as surfers; there's a popular café here. Tamarama is a fifteen-minute walk from Bondi or a 300-metre walk from the #380 bus stop on Fletcher Street, or take bus #360 or 361 from Bondi Junction.

Walk through Tamarama's small park and follow the oceanfront road for five minutes to the next beach along, **Bronte Beach** on Nelson Bay. More of a family affair with a large green park, a popular café strip and sea baths, it's easily reached on bus #378 from Central station via Oxford Street and Bondi Junction where you can also catch #361. The **northern end** has inviting flat-rock platforms, popular as fishing and relaxation spots, and the beach here is cliff-backed, providing some shade. The **park** beyond is extensive with Norfolk Island Pines for shade, electric barbeques, a **mini-train ride** ($3), here since 1947, and an imaginative children's playground. The secluded and peaceful Bronte Gully lies to the rear where kookaburras are a common sight and brightly coloured lorikeets are often seen bathing in the waterfall. At the **southern end** of the beach, a natural rock enclosure, the "Bogey Hole", makes a calm area for kids to swim in, and there are rock ledges to lie on around the enclosed sea swimming pool known as **Bronte Baths** (open access; free). Nearby, palm trees give a suitably holiday feel as you relax at one of the outside tables of Bronte Road's wonderful café strip (eight to choose from, plus a fish and chip shop).

From Bronte, it's a pleasant five-minute walk past the baths to **Waverly Cemetery**, a fantastic spot to spend eternity. Established in 1877, it contains the graves of many famous Australians, with the bush poet contingent well represented. **Henry Lawson**, described on his headstone as poet, journalist and patriot, languishes in section 3G 516, while **Dorothea Mackeller**, who penned the famous poem "I love a sunburnt country", is in section 6 832–833. Beyond here – another five-minute walk – on the other side of Shark Point, is the channel-like **Clovelly Bay**, with concrete platforms on either side and several sets of steps leading into the very deep water. Rocks at the far end keep out the waves and the sheltered bay is popular with lap-swimmers and snorkellers; you're almost certain to see one of the bay's famous blue gropers. You can rent snorkels up the road at Clovelly. There's also a free swimming pool. A grassy park with several terraces extends back from the beach and is a great place for a picnic. The divinely sited café is packed at weekends, and on Sunday afternoons and evenings the nearby *Clovelly Hotel* is a popular hangout, with free live music and a great bistro, or get rock-bottom-priced drinks and fab views at the Clovelly Bowling Club. To get to Clovelly, take **bus** #339 from Millers Point via Central station and Albion Street, Surry Hills; #360 from Bondi Junction; or the weekday peak-hour X39 from Wynyard.

From Clovelly it's best to stick to the road route along Cliffbrook Parade rather than rockhop around to equally narrow **Gordons Bay**. Unsupervised, undeveloped Gordons Bay itself is not a pretty beach, but another world exists beneath the sheltered water: the protected **underwater nature trail**, marked out for divers, is home to a range of sea creatures; diving and snorkelling gear can be rented at Clovelly. From here, a walkway leads around the waterfront to Major Street and then onto **Dunningham Reserve** overlooking the northern end of Coogee Beach; the walk to Coogee proper takes about fifteen minutes in all.

Coogee

While Coogee has a lively bar, café, restaurant and backpacker scene, and some big hotels, there's just something more laid-back, community-oriented and friendly about it compared to Bondi – and it's not totally teeming with trendies. With its hilly streets of Californian-style apartment blocks looking onto a compact, pretty beach enclosed by two cliffy, green-covered headlands, Coogee has a snugness that Bondi just can't match. Everything is close to hand: beachfront Arden Street has a down-to-earth strip of cafés that compete with each other to sell the cheapest cooked breakfast, while the main shopping street, Coogee Bay Road, running uphill from the beach, has a choice selection of coffee spots and eateries, plus a big supermarket.

The ugly high-rise *Holiday Inn* has spoilt the southern end of the beach, though its bar does have fabulous views over the water. Other 1990s developments were more aesthetically successful: the imaginatively modernized promenade is a great place to stroll and hang out. Between it and the medium-sized beach is a grassy park with free electric barbecues, picnic tables and shelters. The beach is popular with families (there's an excellent children's playground at the southern end) and travellers, as there's a stack of backpackers' hostels. However, one of Coogee's chief pleasures is its baths, beyond the southern end of the beach. The first, the secluded McIvers Baths, traditionally remains for women and children only and is known by locals as **Coogee Women's Pool** (volunteer-run; noon–5pm; entry by donation). Just south of the women's pool, the unisex **Wylies Baths**, a saltwater pool on the edge of the sea, is at the end of Neptune Street (Oct–April 7am–7pm; May–Sept 7am–5pm; $3.00) with big decks to lie on, and solar heated showers; it's a fine spot for the excellent coffee made at its kiosk.

Reach Coogee on **bus** #373 or #374 from Circular Quay via Randwick, or #372 from Central station; journey time from Central is about 25 minutes. There are also buses from Bondi Junction via Randwick: #313 and #314, and the #370 runs from Leichhardt via Glebe and Newtown.

Immediately south of Wylies, **Trenerry Reserve** is a huge green park jutting out into the ocean; its spread of big, flat rocks offers tremendous views and makes a great place to chill out. Probably the most impressive section of Randwick Council's **Eastern Beaches Coast Walk** commences here. The walk, sometimes on boards, is accompanied by interpretive panels detailing the surrounding plant- and bird-life. Steps lead down to a rock platform full of teeming rock pools, and you can swim in a large tear-shaped pool. It's quite thrilling with the waves crashing over – but be careful of both the waves and the dangerous blue-ringed octopus which are found here. At low tide you can continue walking along the rocks around Lurline Bay – otherwise you must follow the streets inland, rejoining the waterfront from Mermaid Avenue. Jack Vanny Memorial Park is fronted by the cliff-like rocks of Mistral Point, a great spot to sit and look at the water, and down by the water the **Mahon Pool**, a small, pleasant open-access sea pool, with waves crashing at the edge and surrounded by great boulders, has an unspoilt secluded feel. The isolated *Pool Caffe* across the road on Marine Parade makes a wonderful lunch or coffee spot.

Manly and the northern beaches

Manly, just above North Head at the northern mouth of the harbour, is doubly blessed with both ocean and harbour beaches. When Captain Arthur Phillip, the commander of the First Fleet, was exploring Sydney Harbour in 1788, he saw a group of well-built Aboriginal men onshore, proclaimed them

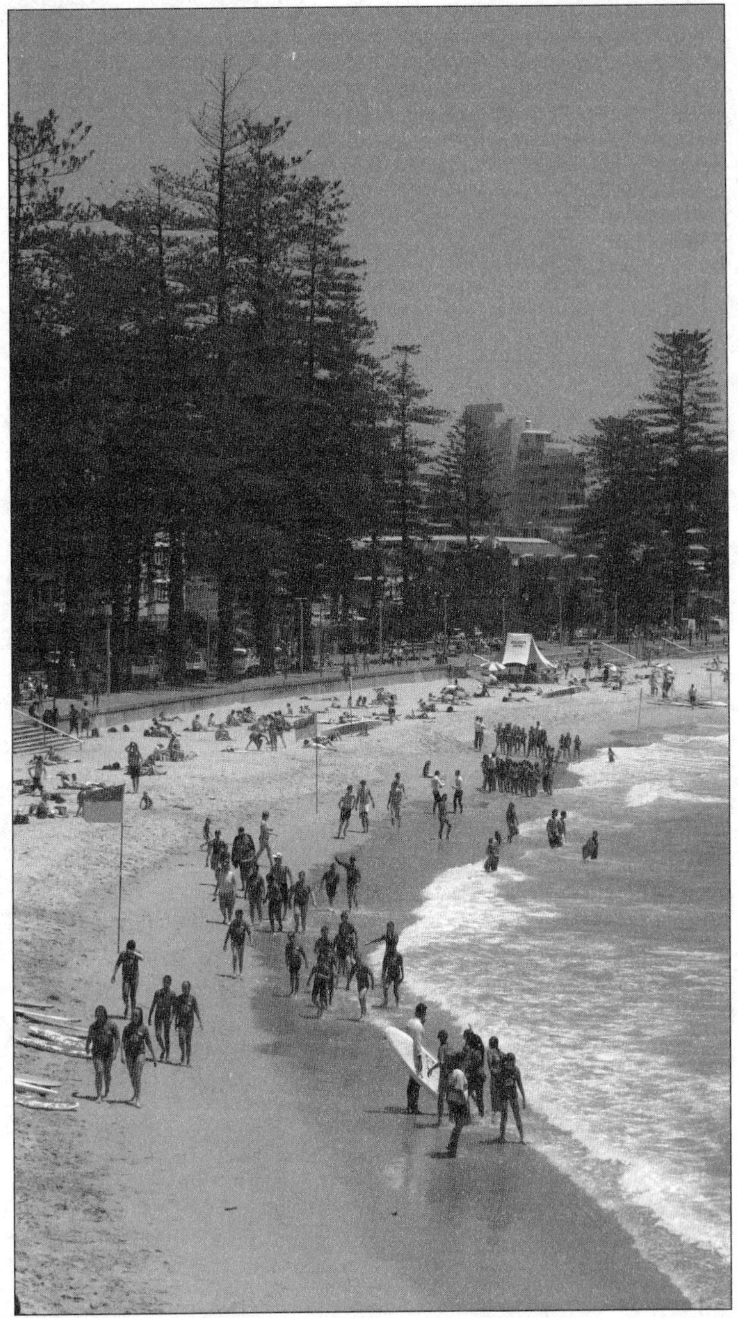

△ Manly beach

to be "manly" and named the cove in the process. During the Edwardian era it became fashionable as a recreational retreat from the city, with the promotional slogan of the time "Manly – seven miles from Sydney, but a thousand miles from care". An excellent time to visit is over the Labour Day long weekend in early October, for the **Jazz Festival** with free outdoor concerts featuring musicians from around the world. Beyond Manly, the **northern beaches** continue for 30km up to Barrenjoey Heads and **Palm Beach**. Pick up the excellent and free *Sydney's Northern Beaches Map* from the Manly Visitor Centre (see below). The northern beaches can be reached by regular **bus** from various city bus terminals or from Manly ferry wharf; routes are detailed throughout the text below.

Manly

A day-trip to Manly, rounded off with a dinner of fish and chips, offers a classic taste of Sydney life. The ferry trip out here has always been half the fun: the legendary Manly Ferry service commenced in 1854, and the huge old boats come complete with snack bars selling the ubiquitous meat pie. Ferries terminate at Manly Wharf in Manly Cove, near a small section of calm harbour beach with a netted-off swimming area popular with families. Like a typical English seaside resort, **Manly Wharf** had always housed a tacky funfair until a few years ago; now the wharf is all grown up with a slew of cafés and brand shops, including multicultural food stalls and a very swish pub, the *Manly Wharf Hotel*. You'll also find the **Manly Visitor Information Centre** (Mon–Fri 9am–5pm, Sat & Sun 10am–4pm, summer 10am–5pm; ⓣ02/9977 1088, ⓦwww.manlytourism.com.au; lockers $2) out the front. The wharf is now a hub for adventure activity: three watersports companies based here offer parasailing, kayaking and rigid inflatable boat tours through crashing surf to North Head; ask at the tourist office for details.

From the wharf, walk along West Esplanade to **Oceanworld** (daily 10am–5.30pm; $18.50; ⓣ02/8251 7877, ⓦwww.oceanworld.com.au), where clear acrylic walls hold back the water so you can saunter along the harbour floor, gazing at huge sharks and stingrays. Divers hand-feed sharks three times weekly (11am Mon, Wed & Fri) and there's always a range of shows and guided tours, including the Dangerous Australians show with local (and deadly) snakes and spiders. You can also dive amongst the **grey nurse sharks** _– which can grow up to 160kg – with Shark Dive Extreme (30min; qualified diver $175, unqualified diver $235; bookings ⓣ02/8251 7878). Opposite, the screams come from the three giant waterslides of **Manly Waterworks** (Oct to Easter Sat, Sun, school & public holidays 10am–5pm; 1hr $14.50, all day $19.50; height restriction 120cm or more). Between the slides and Oceanworld, the **Manly Art Gallery and Museum** (Tues–Sun 10am–5pm; $3.60), has a collection started in the 1920s of Australian paintings, drawings, prints and etchings, and a stash of beach memorabilia including huge old wooden surfboards and old-fashioned swimming costumes.

Many visitors mistake Manly Cove for the ocean beach, which in fact lies on the other side of the isthmus, 500m down **The Corso**, Manly's busy pedestrianized main drag filled with surf shops, cafés, restaurants and pubs. The ocean beach, **South Steyne**, is characterized by the stands of Norfolk pine which line the shore. Every summer, a beach-hire concession rents out just about anything to make the beach more fun, from surfboards to snorkel sets, and they also have a bag-minding service. A six-kilometre-long shared pedestrian and **cycle path** begins at South Steyne and runs north to Seaforth, past North Steyne Beach and Queenscliff. You can rent mountain bikes from Manly Cycles, a block

The Manly Scenic Walkway

The **Manly Scenic Walkway** follows the harbour shore inland from Manly Cove all the way back to Spit Bridge on Middle Harbour, where you can catch bus #180 back to Wynyard station in the city centre (20min). The wonderful eight-kilometre walk takes you through some of the area's more expensive neighbourhoods before heading into a section of **Sydney Harbour National Park**, past a number of small beaches and coves (perfect for stopping off for a dip), Aboriginal middens and some subtropical rainforest. The entire walk takes three to four hours but is broken up into six sections with obvious exit/entry points; pick up a map from the Manly Visitor Information Centre or NPWS offices (see p.209).

back from the Beach at 36 Pittwater Rd (☎02/9977 1189; 1hr $12, all day $25). For a more idyllic beach, follow the footpath from the southern end of South Steyne around the headland to Cabbage Tree Bay, with two very pretty, protected green-backed beaches at either end – **Fairy Bower** to the west and **Shelley Beach** to the east.

Belgrave Street, running north from Manly Wharf, is Manly's alternative strip, with good cafés, interesting shops, yoga schools and the Manly Environment Centre at no. 41, whose aim is to educate the community about the local biodiversity and the issues affecting it.

Ferries leave Circular Quay for Manly twice an hour, between about 6.30am and midnight (30min; $4.50; to 11pm Sun). Faster JetCat catamarans ($7.50) operate in the morning and evening on weekdays (Mon–Fri 6–9.25am & 4.20–8.30pm) and between 7.10am and 3.35pm on Sundays (from 6.10am Sat). After midnight, night buses #E71 and #E69 run from Wynyard station.

North Head

You can take in more of the Sydney Harbour National Park at **North Head**, the harbour mouth's upper jaw, where you can follow the short circuitous Fairfax Walking Track to three lookout points, including the **Fairfax Lookout**, for splendid views. A regular #135 **bus** leaves from Manly Wharf for North Head or if you have your own car you can drop in to the NPWS office (daily 9am–4.30pm), a kilometre or so before the lookouts, to pick up free information leaflets. Right in the middle of this national park is a military reserve with its own **National Artillery Museum** (Wed, Sat, Sun & public holidays 11am–4pm; $8) sited in the historic **North Fort**, a curious system of tunnels built into the headland – it takes up to two hours to wander through them with a requisite guided tour.

There's more history at the old **Quarantine Station**, on the harbour side of North Head, used from 1832 until 1984: arriving passengers or crew who had a contagious disease were set down at Spring Cove to serve a spell of isolation at the station, all at the shipping companies' expense. Sydney residents, too, were forced here, most memorably during the plague which broke out in The Rocks in 1900, when 1828 people were quarantined (104 plague victims are buried in the grounds). The site, its buildings still intact, is now looked after by the NPWS, which offers **guided history tours** (Tues, Thur, Sat, Sun 1.15pm; 1hr 30min–2hr; $11; booking essential on ☎02/9247 5033), giving an insight not only into Sydney's immigration history but the evolution of medical science in the last 170 years, often in gory detail. The tours, which co-ordinate with the #135 bus from Manly Wharf (bus fare extra), provide the only opportunity to get out to this beautiful isolated harbour spot with its views across to

Balmoral Beach. The very spooky night-time **ghost tours** (Wed & Fri–Sun 7.15pm; 3hr 15min; Wed $22, Fri–Sun $27.50; light supper included) are very popular; children under 12 have a less hair-raising, once-weekly Kids Ghost Tour (Fri 5.45pm; 2hr 15min; $13.20 child or adult; no supper). No public transport is available for the night-time visits.

Freshwater to Mona Vale

Freshwater, just beyond Manly, sits snugly between two rocky headlands on Queenscliff Bay, and is one of the most picturesque of the northern beaches. There's plenty of surf culture around the headland at Curl Curl, and a walking track at its northern end, commencing from Huston Parade, will take you above the rocky coastline to the curve of **Dee Why Beach** (bus #136, #146, #152, #158 or #169 from Manly Wharf; bus #178 from outside the QVB in the city). Dee Why provides consistently good surf, while its sheltered lagoon makes it popular with families. Beyond the lagoon, windsurfers gather around **Long Reef**, where the point is surrounded by a wide rock shelf creviced with rock pools and protected as an aquatic reserve – well worth a wander to peek at the creatures within. The long, beautiful sweep of **Collaroy Beach**, with a popular YHA (see p.125), shades into **Narrabeen Beach**, an idyllic spot backed by the extensive, swimmable and fishable **Narrabeen Lakes**, popular with anglers, kayakers and families; there's also a good campsite (see box on p.114). Both Collaroy and Narrabeen can be reached by bus #183 from Wynyard station and Manly Wharf and bus #190 from Central and Wynyard stations. Several other buses also go to Collaroy: the #151 from the QVB and Manly Wharf, the #187 from Millers Point in The Rocks, and the #156 and #159 from ManlyWharf.

Beyond Narrabeen, **Mona Vale** is a long, straight stretch of beach with a large park behind and a sea pool dividing it from sheltered **Bongin Bongin Bay**, whose headland reserve, and rocks to clamber on, make it ideal for children. A short drive inland from Mona Vale at Ingleside, in the middle of the Ku-Ring-Gai Chase National Park, the domed **Baha'i Temple** in extensive gardens at 175 Mona Vale Road (daily 9am–5pm, till 7pm in summer; Ⓦwww.bahai.org) is one of only seven in the world; the Baha'i faith teaches the unity of religion, and Sunday services (11am) read from texts of the world's main religions. To get to the temple, catch bus #159 from Manly Wharf or the #190 from Central or Wynyard stations to Palm Beach.

The Barrenjoey Peninsula: Newport to Palm Beach

After Bongin Bongin Bay the Barrenjoey Peninsula begins, with calm Pittwater on its western side and ocean beaches running up its eastern side until it spears into Broken Bay. **Newport** boasts a fine stretch of beach between two rocky headlands on its ocean side and the popular drinking spot the *Newport Arms* (see box on p.189), overlooking Heron Cove on its Pittwater side. Next door to Newport and nestled at the base of a steep cliff, unassuming **Bilgola Beach**, with its distinctive orange sand, is one of the prettiest of the northern beaches. From Bilgola Beach, a trio of Sydney's best beaches, for both surf and scenery, run up the eastern fringe of the mushroom-shaped peninsula: Avalon and Whale beaches are popular surfie territory, while the more fashionable Palm Beach caters to visiting celebs and Sydney identities getting away from the city.

Backed by bush-covered hills (where koalas can still be found), and reached by three kilometres of winding road, smallish **Avalon Beach** has a suitably secluded feel and is indeed a slice of paradise on a summer's day. A pleasing set of shops and eateries run at right angles from the beach on Avalon Parade; *Avalon Beach Cafe* at no. 23 is a good, moderately priced licensed café with a very contemporary feel, popular with the travellers who stay nearby at the hostel. The people of Avalon memorably rejected the proposed filming of a series of *Baywatch* in early 1999, though the beach did feature in a tacky *Baywatch* special.

Whale Beach, 8km further north via Barrenjoey Road and Whale Beach Road, is much less of a settlement, with the beach fronted by the inevitable Surf Life Saving Club and the classy *Whale Beach Restaurant* (ⓣ02/9974 4009; closed Mon & Tues), which also has a cheaper, very pleasant garden café. Continue following Whale Beach Road north to reach **Palm Beach** which, living up to its name, is a hangout for the rich and famous. To blend right in, you too can arrive Hollywood-style on a seaplane from Rose Bay (see p.161). Palm Beach residents aren't as concerned about the film cameras as their Avalon neighbours: the ocean beach, on the western side of the peninsula, leads a double life as "Summer Bay" in the famous, long-running Aussie soap *Home and Away*, with the picturesque **Barrenjoey Lighthouse** and bushcovered headland – part of **Ku-Ring-Gai Chase National Park** – regularly in shot. A steep walking path to the summit of **Barrenjoey Headland** from the car-park at the base takes twenty to forty minutes, rewarded by a stunning panorama of Palm Beach, Pittwater and the Hawkesbury River. The NPWS offers weekend tours of the sandstone lighthouse, which dates from 1881 (Sun every 30min 11am–3pm; 30min; gold coin donation).

The bulk of Ku-Ring-Gai Chase National Park (see p.125) is across Pittwater, and can be visited courtesy of Palm Beach and Hawkesbury River Cruises (ⓣ02/9997 4815). The **ferries** leave from the Wharf on the eastern, Pittwater side of the peninsula (11am–3.30pm, with a one-hour lunch break at Bobbin Head or Cottage Point; $32); they also offer general transport to Patonga (see p.219). Alternatively, the Palm Beach Ferry Service (ⓣ02/9918 2747) runs from Palm Beach Wharf via The Basin to Mackerel Beach reaching picnicking and camping spots on Pittwater (departing hourly Mon–Fri 9am–5pm, also Fri 8pm, Sat & Sun 9am–6pm; $10 return).

Beside the wharf, calm Snapperman Beach is fronted by yachts and a shady park. Across the road you can **eat** at *Barrenjoey House*, an upmarket guesthouse and restaurant. You can also dine well at popular *Ancora*, but for less cash, get fish and chips from the excellent milk bar and throw down a rug on the grass.

Bus #190 and #L90 run up the peninsula from Central via Wynyard to Avalon, continuing to Palm Beach via the Pittwater side; change at Avalon for bus #193 to Whale Beach. Bus #188 and #L88 go from Central and Wynyard to Avalon, and the #187 and #L87 run from The Rocks to Newport.

Botany Bay

The southern suburbs of Sydney, arranged around huge **Botany Bay**, are seen as the heartland of red-tiled-roof suburbia, a terracotta sea spied from above as the planes land at **Mascot**. Clive James, the area's most famous son, hails from Kogarah – described as a 1950s suburban wasteland in his tongue-in-cheek *Unreliable Memoirs*. The popular perception of Botany Bay is coloured by its proximity to an airport, a high-security prison (Long Bay), an oil refinery, a container terminal and a sewerage outlet. Yet the surprisingly clean-looking water is fringed by quiet, sandy beaches and the marshlands shelter a profusion of birdlife. Whole areas of the waterfront, at **La Perouse**, with its associations with eighteenth-century French exploration, and on the **Kurnell Peninsula** where Captain Cook first put anchor, are designated as part of **Botany Bay National Park**, and large stretches on either side of the Georges River form a State Recreation Area. **Brighton Le Sands**, the busy suburban strip on the west of the bay, is a hive of bars and restaurants and is something of a focus for Sydney's Greek community. Its long beach is also a popular spot for windsurfers and kiteboarders.

La Perouse

At least, is there any news of Monsieur de Laperouse?

Louis XVI, about to be guillotined, 1793

La Perouse, tucked into the northern shore of Botany Bay where it meets the Pacific Ocean, contains Sydney's oldest Aboriginal settlement, the legacy of a mission. The suburb took its name from the eighteenth-century French explorer, **Laperouse**, who set up camp here for six weeks, briefly and cordially meeting Captain Arthur Phillip, who was making his historic decision to forgo swampy Botany Bay and move on to Port Jackson. After leaving Botany Bay, the Laperouse expedition was never seen again.

A monument erected in 1825 and the excellent NPWS-run **La Perouse Museum** (Wed–Sun 10am–4pm; $5.50), which sits on a grassy headland between the pretty beaches of Congwong Bay and Frenchmans Bay, tell the whole fascinating story. Tracing Laperouse's voyage in great detail, the museum displays are enlivened by relics from the wrecks, exhibits of antique French maps and copies of etchings by the naturalists on board. The voyage was commissioned by the French king Louis XVI in 1785 as a purely scientific exploration of the Pacific to rival Cook's voyages, and strict instructions were given for Laperouse to "act with great gentleness and humanity towards the different people whom he will visit". After an astonishing three-and-a-half-year journey round South America, the Easter Islands, Hawaii, the northwest coast of America, and past China and Japan to Russia, the *Astrolabe* and the *Boussole* struck disaster – first encountering hostility in the Solomon Islands and then in their doomed departure of Botany Bay, on March 10, 1788. Their disappearance remained a mystery until 1828, when relics were discovered on Vanikoro in the Solomon Islands; the wrecks themselves were found only in 1958 and 1964. There is also an exhibition which looks at the Aboriginal history and culture of the area.

The surrounding headlands and foreshore have been incorporated into the northern half of **Botany Bay National Park** (no entry fee; the other half is across Botany Bay on the Kurnell Peninsula, see below). A **NPWS visitor centre** (ⓣ02/9311 3379) in the museum building provides details of walks including a fine one past **Congwong Bay Beach** to Henry Head and its lighthouse (5km round trip); ask about the "whale" Aboriginal rock carving. The idyllic verandah of the *Boatshed Cafe*, on the small headland between Congwong and Frenchmans bays, sits right over the water with pelicans floating about below. La Perouse is at its most lively on **Sunday** (and public holidays) when, following a tradition established at the start of the twentieth century, Aboriginal people come down to sell boomerangs and other crafts, and demonstrate snake-handling skills (from 1.30pm) and boomerang throwing. There are also tours of the nineteenth-century fortifications on **Bare Island** (Sat, Sun & public holidays 12.30pm, 1.30pm, 2.30pm & 3.30pm; $5.00; no booking required, wait at the gate to the island), joined to La Perouse by a thin walkway; the island was originally built amid fears of a Russian invasion and featured in *Mission Impossible II*. Across from the **Frenchmans Bay** beach and park there are a few places to eat on Endeavour Avenue, including the popular, casual and affordable *Paris Seafood Cafe* at no. 51, where you can also get take-away fish and chips.

To **get to** La Perouse, catch bus #394 or #399 from Circular Quay via Darlinghurst and Moore Park, or #393 from Railway Square via Surry Hills and Moore Park, or the #L94 express from Circular Quay.

The Kurnell Peninsula and Cronulla

From La Perouse, you can see across Botany Bay to Kurnell and the red buoy marking the spot where Captain James Cook and the crew of the Endeavour anchored on April 29, 1770 for an eight-day exploration. Back in England, many refused to believe that the uniquely Australian plants and animals they had recorded actually existed – the kangaroo and platypus in particular were thought to be a hoax. **Captain Cook's Landing Place** is now the south head of **Botany Bay National Park**, where the informative **Education Centre** (Mon–Fri 10am–4pm, Sat & Sun 9.30am–4.30pm; car fee $7.50; ⓣ02/9668 8431) looks at the wetlands ecology of the park and tells the story of Cook's visit and its implications for Aboriginal people. Indeed the political sensitivity of the spot which effectively marks the beginning of the decline of an ancient culture has led to the planned renaming of the park to Kamay-Botany Bay National Park, "Kamay" being the original Dharawal people's name for the bay. Set aside as a public recreation area in 1899, the heath and woodland is unspoilt and there are some secluded beaches for swimming; you may even spot parrots and honeyeaters. To get here, take the train to Cronulla and then Kurnell Bus Services route #987 (ⓣ02/9524 8977).

On the ocean side of the **Kurnell Peninsula** sits Sydney's most southern beach suburb and its longest stretch of beach – just under five-kilometres; the sandy stretch of Bate Bay begins at **Cronulla** and continues as deserted, dune-backed **Wanda Beach**. This is prime **surfing** territory – and the only Sydney beach accessible by train (40min from Central Station on the Sutherland line; surfboards carried free). Steeped in surf culture, everything about Cronulla centres on water sports and a laid-back beach lifestyle, from the multitude of surf shops on Cronulla Street (which becomes a pedestrianized **mall** between Kingsway and Purley Place), to the outdoor cafés on the beachfront and the surfrider clubs and boating facilities on the bay. Situated on a finger of land jutting into **Port Hacking**, Cronulla is blessed with both sheltered bay beaches and ocean frontage. Its rundown red-brick beach houses are fast becoming prime waterfront residential and commercial developments, giving it the feel of a Gold Coast resort, but at heart it's still just a down-to-earth outer suburb.

Sheltered **South Cronulla Beach** is just 300m from the train station: across Cronulla Street a small alleyway leads to shady Cronulla Park, which slopes down to the water. Protected from the wind and most tidal rips, South Cronulla is a favourite spot for families and can get very crowded. The waterfront *Cronulla Kiosk* is a magic spot for breakfast or lunch here while the unpretentious *Cronulla RSL* has ocean views from its wall-to-ceiling windows, which can be enjoyed with a cheap drink or meal. Head down Kingsway or follow the concreted walkway, The Esplanade, north along the rock platform and past a couple of delightful sea pools to reach the main beach, **North Cronulla**, where serious surfing is done; further north are **Elouera** and **Wanda** beaches. All four beaches have their own surf clubs with facilities and canteens.

The well-trodden footpath of **The Esplanade** follows the coastline around to **Bass and Flinders Point** (just under 3km) and beyond to Salmon Haul Bay and Hungry Point. At low tide the path can be followed right around the headland to Gunnamatta Park – a popular and sheltered barbeque spot with a sizeable amphitheatre, which in summer hosts performances. Its calmer inlet, **Gunnamatta Bay**, is filled with yachts and dinghies and is a good place to paddle a kayak or swim in the shark-netted ocean pool. You can also catch a ferry here from Tonkin Street Wharf to **Bundeena** (see p.253) – Tonkin Street is just behind the train station, if you want to get to it quickly.

Eating and drinking

If the way its chefs are regularly stolen to work overseas is any indication, Sydney has blossomed into one of the great restaurant capitals of the world, offering a fantastic range of cosmopolitan eateries, covering every imaginable cuisine. Quality is uniformly high, with the freshest produce, meat and seafood always on hand, and a culinary culture of discerning, well-informed diners. The restaurant scene is highly fashionable and businesses rise in favour, fall in popularity and close down or change names and style at an astonishing rate. For a comprehensive guide, consider investing in the latest edition of *Cheap Eats in Sydney* or the *Sydney Morning Herald Good Food Guide*. All New South Wales' restaurants are **non-smoking**, except for reception areas and outside tables.

Sydney's fully fledged **café culture** can be found most notably in Potts Point, Darlinghurst, Surry Hills, Glebe, Newtown, Leichhardt and the eastern beaches of Bondi, Bronte and Coogee.

There are many fascinating **ethnic** enclaves, representing Sydney's diverse communities, where you can eat authentic cuisines including: Jewish on Hall Street, Bondi Beach; Chinese – in Haymarket; Turkish and Indian on Cleveland Street, Surry Hills; Italian in East Sydney, Leichhardt and Haberfield; Portuguese on New Canterbury Road, Petersham; Greek in Marrickville and Brighton Le Sands; Indonesian on Anzac Parade, in Kingsford and Kensington. Much further out, reached by train, Cabramatta is very much a little Vietnam.

All restaurants in the following listings are **open** daily for lunch and dinner, unless otherwise stated, and the more specific café times are given (many are open early for breakfast, one of Sydney's most popular meals).

The City Centre and Circular Quay

The cafés and food stalls in the business and shopping districts of the city centre cater mainly for lunch-time crowds, and there are lots of **food courts** serving fast food and snacks. Check out the selection in the basements of the **Queen Victoria Building**, **Myers** department store on Pitt Street Mall, and the **MLC Centre** near Martin Place, and on the first floor of the **Hunter Connection** shopping arcade, 310 George St, opposite Wynyard station. The classiest is the foodie's paradise in the basement of the **David Jones** department store on Market Street. There are lots of great Italian espresso bars for quick coffee hits throughout the CBD. Many museums and tourist attractions also have surprisingly good **cafés** – notably the Museum of Contemporary Art, the Australian Museum, Hyde Park Barracks and the Art Gallery of New South Wales.

Cafés and brasseries

Café Opera *Hotel Inter-continental*, 117 Macquarie St, City ⓣ02/9240 1260. The buffet offered by the five-star *Inter-continental*'s *Café Opera*, groaning under the display of seafood, is legendary. Stuff yourself silly for $42 at lunchtime ($59 Sun, with live jazz), $48 at dinner ($54 Fri & Sat, $52 Sun) or $28.50 at supper (10pm Fri & Sat).

Obelisk Café Shop 1, 7 Macquarie Place, City. Fabulous spot for an outdoor café on a historic square with big shady trees, close to Circular Quay. Attracts a working crowd who plunge in for great coffee, *pizzetta*, sandwiches and salads. Mon–Fri 6am–5pm, Sat & Sun 9am–1pm.

QVB Jet Cnr York and Druitt streets, City. Very lively Italian café-bar, on the corner of the QVB building looking across to the Town Hall, with big, glass windows and outdoor seating providing people-watching opportunities. Coffee is predictably excellent, and the menu is big on breakfast. The rest of the day choose from pasta, risotto and soups, salads and sandwiches. Licensed. Mon–Fri 8am–10pm, Sat 9am–10pm.

Rossini Wharf 5, Circular Quay. Quality Italian fast food alfresco while you're waiting for a ferry or just watching the quay. *Panzerotto* – big, cinnamon-flavoured and ricotta-filled doughnuts – are a speciality. Pricey but excellent coffee. Licensed. Daily 7am–11pm.

Sydney Cove Oyster Bar Circular Quay East. En route to the Opera House, the quaint little building housing the bar and kitchen was once a public toilet, but don't let that put you off. The outdoor tables right on the water's edge provide a magical location to sample Sydney Rock Pacific oysters (around $17.50 for half a dozen), or just come for coffee, cake and the view. Licensed. Daily 11am–11pm.

Restaurants

Cafe Sydney Level 5, Customs House, 31 Alfred St, Circular Quay ⓣ02/9251 8683. Though the wide-ranging food here – from a Tandoori oven to French- and Italian-inspired dishes – has never been that highly rated, the views of the Harbour Bridge and Opera House from the balcony are jaw-dropping, plus service is great and the atmosphere is fun (the Fri night jazz is popular). Very much on the tourist agenda. Mains start from $24. Licensed. Closed Sun dinner.

Guillaume at Bennelong Sydney Opera House, Bennelong Point ⓣ02/9241 1999. French chef Guillaume Brahimi has fused his name with the Opera House's top-notch restaurant, housed in one of the iconic building's smaller shells; the huge windows provide stunning harbour views. For one splash-out, romantic meal in Sydney, come here. With mains at around $35 (elegant modern French fare), it's not *the* most expensive place in town and if you can't afford it you can opt for a drink at the bar. Lunch Thurs–Fri, dinner Mon–Sat.

Tetsuya's 529 Kent St, City ⓣ02/9267 2900, ⓕ02/9799 7099. Stylish premises – all Japanese timber interior, and a beautiful Japanese garden outside – of the internationally renowned chef Tetsuya Wakuda, who creates exquisite Japanese/French-style fare. The waiting list is a month ahead – worth it to sample his twelve-course *dégustation* menu ($175), described by local Sydneysiders as the "meal of a lifetime"; wine teamed with each course starts from $60; book by phone or fax. Licensed and BYO. Lunch Sat only, dinner Tues–Sat.

The Rocks

There are several good **pubs** in The Rocks (see pp.189–190), many of which serve some kind of food, but for the most part the area around the harbour has a choice of expensive restaurants, popular for business lunches, or trading on fantastic views.

Restaurants

Rockpool 107 George St, The Rocks ⓣ02/9252 1888. Owned by top chef Neil Perry, the raved-about seafood – blue swimmer crab omelette, mud crab ravioli – and other contemporary creations here make sure this place is still rated as one of Sydney's best dining spots. With mains mostly $54, definitely splurge material. Licensed. Closed Sat lunch, Sun & Mon.

Sailors Thai Canteen 106 George St, The Rocks. Cheaper version of the much-praised, pricey downstairs restaurant (bookings ⓣ02/9251 2466), housed in the restored Sailors' Home (see p.132). The ground-level canteen with a long stainless-steel communal table looks onto an open kitchen, where the chefs chop away to produce simple one-bowl meals. Licensed. Closed Sunday.

The Wharf Pier 4, Hickson Rd, The Rocks, next to

the Wharf Theatre ⓣ02/9250 1761. Enterprising modern food (lots of seafood), served up in an old dock building with heaps of raw charm and a harbour vista; bag the outside tables for the best views. Cocktail bar open from noon until end of evening performance. Expensive. Closed Sun.

Darling Harbour

The Cockle Bay Wharf restaurant precinct harbours some excellent quality food. Beyond Darling Harbour, you can eat fantastically well at the Sydney Fish Market (see p.148).

Restaurants

Blackbird Cockle Bay Wharf, Darling Harbour ⓣ02/9283 7835. Bar-restaurant with the feel of a funky American diner; sit on stools at the bar or couches out the back, or enjoy the water views from the terrace. Generous, good-value meals to suit all cravings – from dhal to spaghetti, noodles, salads, pizzas from a hot-stone oven, and breakfast until 4pm. Daily 7am–1am. Licensed. Inexpensive.

Chinta Ria – Temple of Love Roof Terrace, 201 Sussex St, Cockle Bay Wharf, Darling Harbour ⓣ02/9264 3211. People still queue to get in here (bookings lunch only) years after opening, as much for the fun atmosphere – a blues and jazz soundtrack, and decor which mixes a giant Buddha, a lotus pond and 50s-style furniture – as for the yummy Malaysian food. Licensed and BYO. Moderate. Open daily lunch and dinner.

The Malaya 39 Lime St, King Street Wharf, Darling Harbour ⓣ02/9279 1170. Popular, veteran Chinese-Malaysian place in swish water surrounds, serving some of the best, and spiciest laksa in town. Mains $18 to $25; licensed, no BYO.

Haymarket, Chinatown and around Central Station

The southern end of George Street and its back streets have plenty of cheap restaurants, of variable quality. Chinatown around the corner is a better bet: many places here specialize in *yum cha* (or dim sum as it's also known), and there are several late-night eating options. Inexpensive licensed Asian **food courts**, serving everything from Japanese to Vietnamese, and of course Chinese food, can be found in the Sussex Centre (1st floor, 401 Sussex St; daily 10am–9pm); Dixon House (basement level, corner Little Hay and Dixon streets; daily 10.30am–8.30pm); the Harbour Plaza (basement level, corner Factory and Dixon streets; daily 10am–10pm); but the best is on the top floor of the Market City Shopping Centre, above Paddy's Market at the corner of Ultimo Road and Thomas Street (daily 8am–10pm). A few blocks from Chinatown back toward the city centre, there's a good array of Spanish eateries on Liverpool Street, almost all of them boisterous and lively.

Cafés and foodcourts

Delizia 148 Elizabeth St, City. High-ceilinged Italian deli-café bustling with black-clad staff behind gleaming glass counters full of pasta and delicious salads; looks pricey, but nothing's over $10. A delightful secondhand literary bookshop is a haven out back, with café tables and sofas among the bookshelves. Popular for weekend breakfasts when most city cafés are closed. Mon–Fri 7am–6pm, Sat & Sun 8am–4pm.

Ippon Sushi 404 Sussex St, Haymarket. Fun, inexpensive Japanese sushi train downstairs, with a revolving choice of delectable dishes from $2 to $5.50 (depending on plate colour), and a proper restaurant menu upstairs. Inexpensive Licensed and BYO. Daily 11am–11pm.

Mother Chu's Vegetarian Kitchen 367 Pitt St, City. Taiwanese Buddhist cuisine in suitably plain surrounds, and true to its name, is family-run. Though onion and garlic aren't used, the eats here aren't bland. Inexpensive. Don't try to BYO – there's a no-alcohol policy. Closed Sat lunch & Sun.

Pasteur 709 George St, Haymarket. Popular Vietnamese cheap eat specialising in *pho*, rice noodle soup, served with fresh herbs, lemon and bean sprouts. Most noodles (mainly pork, chicken and beef) are $9, and there's nothing over $12. Refreshing pot of jasmine tea included. BYO. Daily 10am–9pm.

Roma Caffe 191 Hay St, Haymarket. The veteran *Roma* offers fabulous coffee, great breakfasts and a huge gleaming display of wicked Italian desserts, plus delicious focaccia, with every imaginable topping, and fresh pasta – try the home-made pumpkin tortellini. Inexpensive. Mon–Sat 8am–6pm.

Restaurants

BBQ King 18 Goulburn St, Haymarket ⓣ02/9267 2433. Late-night hangout of chefs, rock stars and students alike, this unprepossessing but always packed Chinese restaurant does a mean meat dish, as suggested by its name and the duck roasting in the window, but there's a big vegetarian menu too. Communal tables. Licensed. Inexpensive to moderate. Daily 11.30am–2am (last orders 1.30am).

Capitan Torres 73 Liverpool St, Haymarket ⓣ02/9264 5574. Atmospheric and enduring Spanish place specializing in seafood. Freshly displayed catch of the day and an authentic tapas menu, plus great paella. Sit downstairs at the bar or upstairs in the restaurant. Licensed. Inexpensive to moderate.

Kam Fook Sharks Fin Seafood Restaurant Level 3, Market City complex, Hay Street, Haymarket ⓣ02/9211 8988. The long name matches the size of this 800-seater Cantonese establishment, officially Australia's largest restaurant. You can eat some of the best *yum cha* in Sydney here, and you'll still have to queue for it on the weekend if you haven't booked, despite the restaurant's size. Moderate to expensive. Licensed. Mon–Fri 10am–5.30pm, Sat & Sun 9am–5.30pm.

Glebe

In Glebe you'll find both cheap and upmarket restaurants, ethnic takeaways, delis and a string of good cafés. **Glebe Point Road** is dominated by cafés – with a cluster of particularly good places at the Broadway end. Also check pub listings (p.190) for cheap Italian food at the characterful *Friend in Hand Hotel.*

Badde Manors 37 Glebe Point Rd, Glebe. Veteran vegetarian corner café with a wonderful light-and-airy ambience, eclectic decor and laid-back staff; still one of Glebe's best cafés and always packed, especially for weekend brunch. Yummy cakes and ice cream, and inexpensive and generous servings – nothing over $12.50. Mon–Fri 8am–midnight, Sat 8am–1am, Sun 9am–midnight.

The Boathouse on Blackwattle Bay End of Ferry Rd, Glebe ⓣ02/9518 9011. Atmospheric restaurant located in a former boatshed, with fantastic views across the bay to Anzac Bridge and the fishmarkets, opposite. Fittingly, seafood is the thing here (and this is one of the best places to sample some), from the six different kinds of oysters to the raved-about snapper pie. Very expensive (around $40 a main) but worth it. Licensed. Closed Mon.

Darbar 134 Glebe Point Rd, Glebe ⓣ02/9660 5666. An old sandstone building with a leafy courtyard provides a gorgeous setting for a surprisingly inexpensive – and delicious – Indian meal. Mains average $14–$16. Licensed & BYO. Closed Mon lunch.

Iku 25 Glebe Point Rd (also at 612 Darling St, Rozelle; 168 Military Rd, Neutral Bay; 279 Bronte Rd, Waverly; and 62 Oxford St, Darlinghurst). The original *Iku* at Glebe proved so popular it keeps branching out. Healthy – but delicious – macrobiotic meals and snacks, all vegetarian or vegan. Organic, pesticide-free coffee too. Meditative interior and outdoor dining area. Mon–Fri 11am–9pm, Sat 11am–7pm, Sun noon–7.30pm.

Toxteth Hotel 345 Glebe Point Rd, Glebe ⓣ02/9660 2370. Refurbished pub with a wonderful courtyard dining area complete with murals and mosaics, plus braziers to keep you warm in winter. The Italian- and French-run bistro has a small, simple menu of pub food – steaks ($19–$21), salads (niçoise to calamari salad, around $14), and burgers – as well as classier European dishes, from marinated sardines to duck à l' orange.

Vegetarian eating

Vegetarians are well catered for on just about every café menu, and most contemporary restaurant menus too. The following are specifically vegetarian: *Badde Manors* (see above), *Bodhi in the Park* (see p.184), *Green Gourmet* (see p.182), *Harvest* (see p.182), *Iku* (see above), Mother Chu's Vegetarian (see p.180) and *Maya Indian Sweets* (see p.183).

Newtown

On the other side of Sydney University from Glebe, **King Street** in **Newtown** is lined with cafés, takeaways and restaurants of every ethnic persuasion, particularly Thai. For gorgeous courtyard Thai dining check out also *Sumalee* at the *Bank Hotel* (see p.190).

Citrus 227 King St, Newtown. A Newtown café favourite: vibrant walls, friendly service, huge servings of delicious food – the Mediterranean-inspired chicken-breast burger and the steak sandwich are stand-outs – with nothing much over $12. Big fold-back windows bring in light and views of Newtown's unconventional inner-city dwellers, while retaining a bit of a distance from the fumes and throng. BYO. Mon–Thurs & Sun 8am–10pm, Fri & Sat 8am–midnight.

Green Gourmet 115 King St, Newtown. Loud and busy Chinese vegan eatery, which always has plenty of Asian customers, including the odd Buddhist monk. The devoted Buddhist owner's creativity is reflected in the divine tofu variations on offer. Order off the menu (mains around $14) or to get a taste of everything, there's a nightly buffet or *yum cha* at weekend lunch. The same owners run the excellent *Vegan's Choice Grocery* next door. Daily lunch and dinner.

Kilimanjaro 280 King St, Newtown. Long-running Senegalese-owned place serving authentic and simple dishes that span Africa – from West African marinated chicken to North African couscous. Casual and friendly atmosphere, with African art and craft adorning the walls. Inexpensive. BYO.

The Old Fish Cafe 239 King St, Newtown. This little corner place, decorated with strands of dried garlic and chilli, is pure Newtown: lots of shaven heads, body piercings, tattoos and bizarre fashions. Food is simple – mainly focaccia and mini pizzas – and the excellent raisin loaf goes well with a coffee. Daily 6am–7pm, later in summer.

Steki Taverna 2 O'Connell St, off King St, Newtown ⓣ02/9516 2191. Atmospheric and inexpensive Greek taverna, with live music and dancing at weekends – when you'll need to book. Pleasant courtyard. Licensed & BYO. Dinner Wed–Sun.

Thai Pothong 294 King St, Newtown ⓣ02/9550 6277. King Street's best Thai; excellent service and moderate prices (mains around $17). Essential to book on the weekend. Closed Mon lunch.

Thanh Binh 111 King St, Newtown ⓣ02/9557 1175. With a celebrated original in Cabramatta, the Vietnamese food at this Newtown offspring is just as fresh, delicious and inexpensive. Licensed and BYO. Closed lunch Mon–Wed.

Balmain, Rozelle and Leichhardt

Further west is **Leichhardt**, Sydney's "Little Italy", which has a concentration of cafés and restaurants on **Norton Street**, while the **Darling Street** strip of restaurants runs from **Rozelle** to upmarket **Balmain**.

Bar Italia 169 Norton St, Leichhardt. Like a community centre with the day-long comings and goings of Leichhardt locals, positively packed at night. The focaccia, served during the day, comes big and tasty, and coffee is spot-on. Some of the best *gelato* in Sydney; pasta from $9.50, and the extra night-time menu includes more substantial meat dishes. Shady courtyard out the back. BYO. Sun & Mon 10am–midnight, Tues–Thurs 9am–midnight, Fri 9am–1am, Sat 10am–1am.

Canteen 332 Darling St, Balmain. Airy, high-ceilinged café with whitewashed walls inside the old Working Men's Institute. Simple fare: generous baguettes, burgers and salads, and big cooked breakfasts particularly popular on weekends when customers spill onto the sunny outside tables. Mon–Fri & Sun 7am–5pm, Sat 6am–5pm.

Grappa 267 Norton St, Leichhardt ⓣ02/9560 6090. One of the liveliest restaurants in Little Italy, with an open kitchen, a huge dining area and gregarious staff. The wood-fired oven turns out tasty Italian sausage, pizza and pasta, plus there are more sophisticated mains ($20–35), including the signature slow-roasted duck. An extensive wine list – Italian and local – includes a section devoted to the namesake digestive liqueur. Licensed and BYO. Closed Sat lunch and all Sun.

Harvest 71 Evans St, Rozelle ⓣ02/9818 4201. Established in the 1970s, this vegan and vegetarian restaurant has kept up with the times, dipping into Vietnamese, Japanese, Italian and a whole range of cuisines. Delicious, moderately priced food (mains around $19), decadent desserts and great coffee. BYO. Dinner Tues–Sat.

Surry Hills and Redfern

Just east of Central station, **Cleveland Street** in Surry Hills, running down to Redfern, is lined with cheap Turkish, Lebanese and Indian restaurants, which are among the cheapest and most atmospheric in Sydney. **Crown Street** in Surry Hills is home to several funky cafés and some upmarket restaurants.

Cafés and pubs

Almustafa 276 Cleveland St, Surry Hills. Very homey Lebanese place and one of the stalwarts of the area, with low couches and cushions for relaxing in the traditional manner. Tasty home-style food – sample a wide range with a shareable meze platter. Belly dancing on weekends. BYO. Inexpensive. Closed lunch Mon–Wed; open until 12.30am Fri & Sat.

Erciyes 409 Cleveland St, Redfern ⓣ02/9319 1309. Among the offerings of this busy family-run Turkish restaurant is delicious *pide* – a bit like pizza – available with 22 different types of toppings, many vegetarian; take-out section too. Belly dancing Fri & Sat nights when bookings are essential. BYO. Inexpensive. Daily 10am–midnight.

Forresters Hotel 336 Riley St, Surry Hills. The *Forresters'* Sun–Wed tasty steak and chicken specials (and until 6pm Sat) have become a legend: a 300g scotch fillet or T-bone steak or a chargrilled chicken breast with mash and Asian greens (and a different sauce each day) for $5 all day. There's not much of a catch – you must buy a drink (wine by the glass and cocktails $5 Thurs–Sun). Other menu options include mussels and squid. The three-levelled pub itself is very pleasant with an unpretentious crowd. Inexpensive.

La Passion du Fruit 633 Bourke St, cnr Devonshire St, Surry Hills. Bright and friendly café with lively staff serving up some of the best brunches in town. Also salads, sandwiches and light meals. Inexpensive. Mon–Sat 8am–5pm.

Maltese Cafe 310 Crown St, Surry Hills. Established in the early 1940s, this café is known for its delicious (and ridiculously cheap at 80¢) Maltese *pastizzi* – flaky pastry pockets of ricotta cheese, plain or with meat, spinach or peas – to eat in or take away. Inexpensive. Mon 10am–8pm, Tues, Wed & Sun 8am–8pm, Thurs–Sat 8am–10pm.

Maya Indian Sweets 470 Cleveland St, Surry Hills. Cheap, authentic South Indian cafeteria-style restaurant serving exquisite vegetarian food: *dosas*, *chaat* salads, *paneer kulcha*, thalis and the like. Very popular with local Indian families, especially on weekends. A vast display of very sickly Indian sweets too. BYO. Daily 10am–10.30pm. The more upmarket version, *Maya da Dhaba* (ⓣ02/8399 3785; closed lunch Mon–Thurs) opposite at no. 431, also serves meat dishes.

Mohr Fish 202 Devonshire St, Surry Hills. Tiny but stylish fish-and-chip bar, with stools and tiled walls, packs in the customers. BYO. Moderate. Daily 10am–10pm.

Restaurants

Billy Kwong 355 Crown St, Surry Hills. Traditional Chinese cooking gets a stylish new slant at this restaurant owned by celebrity chef Kylie Kwong. The space itself – all dark polished wood and Chinese antiques but brightly lit and with contemporary fittings – complements the often adventurous combination of dishes and flavours. Mains start from $22. Licensed & BYO. Moderate to expensive. Dinner daily. No bookings so you'll have to queue.

Moog Wine + Food 413 Bourke St, Surry Hills ⓣ02/8353 8201. Tough choices abound at this stylish new restaurant with its red walls, funky seats and cool music selection, including which wine to chose from a list of 200 (30 of them by the glass), and what to eat from the spectacular modern Australian menu, with dishes such as rabbit confit or slow-cooked lamb wrapped in vine leaves. Moderate–expensive. Bookings essential. Dinner nightly.

Nepalese Kitchen 481 Crown St, Surry Hills ⓣ02/9319 4264. Peaceful establishment with cosy wooden furniture, religious wall hangings and traditional music. The speciality here is goat curry, served with freshly cooked relishes which traditionally accompany the mild Nepalese dishes, and simple but delicious *momos* (stuffed handmade dumplings). Vegetarian options, too. Lovely courtyard for warmer nights. Inexpensive. BYO. Dinner nightly.

Prasit's Northside on Crown 415 Crown St, Surry Hills ⓣ02/9319 0748. Be prepared for some great spicy Thai taste sensations amongst the bold purple colour scheme. Takeaway branch (395 Crown St) can squeeze diners out front on stools, with a few more places upstairs, though it's often a fairly rushed affair. Both BYO and inexpensive. Takeaway closed Mon; restaurant open lunch and dinner Tues–Sun.

Sushi-Suma 421 Cleveland St, Surry Hills ⓣ02/9698 8873. That this small, noisy Japanese restaurant is extremely popular with Japanese locals and visitors says it all, where you can watch the chef prepare your dish from fresh. Book a table to avoid disappointment. BYO. Inexpensive to Moderate. Lunch Tues–Fri, dinner Tues–Sun.

Darlinghurst and East Sydney

Oxford Street is lined with restaurants and cafés from one end to the other. **Taylor Square** and its surroundings is a particularly busy area, with lots of ethnic restaurants and several pubs. **Victoria Street** in Darlinghurst has a thriving café scene. East Sydney, where Crown Street heads downhill from Oxford Street towards William Street, has some excellent Italian restaurants and coffee bars – particularly on **Stanley Street**.

Cafés and pubs

Bar Coluzzi 322 Victoria St, Darlinghurst. Veteran Italian café that's almost a Sydney legend: tiny and always packed with a diverse crew of regulars spilling out onto wooden stools on the pavement and partaking in the standard menu of focaccias, muffins, bagels and of course coffee. Daily 5am–6pm.

Betty's Soup Kitchen 84 Oxford St, Darlinghurst. Soup is obviously the speciality here, with continually changing specials that makes for a cheap but filling meal, served with damper, but there's also all the simple things your ideal granny might serve: stews, sausages or fish fingers with mash, pasta, salads and desserts too. Delicious home-made ginger beer and lemonade. Nothing over $15. BYO. Daily noon–10.30pm, Fri & Sat to 11.30pm.

Bill and Toni 74 Stanley St, East Sydney. Cheap atmospheric Italian, where it's worth the queue up the stairs for the huge servings of simple homemade pasta and sauces. The café downstairs serves tasty Italian sandwiches (daily 7am–midnight). BYO. Inexpensive. Breakfast, lunch and dinner daily.

bills 433 Liverpool St, Darlinghurst. This sunny corner café-restaurant in the quieter, terrace house-filled backstreets of Darlinghurst, owned by celebrity chef Bill Granger, is one of Sydney's favourite breakfast spots: the ricotta hotcakes, huge muffins and deliciously creamy scrambled eggs top the morning list. Breakfast isn't cheap ($15 hotcakes), but is definitely worth it. The modern Australian lunches start at about $15. Mon–Sat 7.30am–3pm, Sun 8.30am–3pm. BYO. The moderately priced bistro-style *bills 2*, 359 Crown St, Surry Hills, is just as trendy and fun and also does dinner. Licensed.

Bodhi in the Park Cook and Phillip Park, College St, East Sydney ☎02/9281 6162; another branch at Capitol Square, 730–742 George St, Haymarket. Interesting Chinese vegetarian and vegan food, with the focus on delicious *yum cha*, which is served daily until 5pm. Well situated for the local galleries and museums or if you've been for a swim in the park's pool. Organic and biodynamic produce is used. Licensed. Inexpensive. Daily 11am–11pm.

Tropicana Café 227B Victoria St, Darlinghurst. The birthplace of the Tropfest film festival (see box on p.200), and still a hugely popular place to hang out and pose, on the weekend especially. The huge but cheap Trop salad could fuel you all day. Licensed. Daily 5am–11pm, Fri & Sat until midnight.

Una's Coffee Lounge 340 Victoria St, Darlinghurst. Cosy café that's been here for years dishing up schnitzel, dumplings, sauerkraut and other almost authentic German dishes that are cheap, plentiful and tasty. The big breakfasts are very popular and served till 2.30pm. BYO. Mon–Sat 6.30am–11pm, Sun 8am–11pm.

Restaurants

Balkan Continental Restaurant 209 Oxford St, Darlinghurst ☎02/9360 4970. For almost 40 years this bustling Croatian place has been chargrilling inside the front window and luring in Sydneysiders with traditional favourites like schnitzels and mixed grills, plus an extensive range of excellent fish and seafood. Balkan specialities such as *cevapci* (spicy skinless sausages) are worth a try but save room for dessert. Moderate. Lunch and dinner Wed–Mon. Licensed and BYO. There's another *Balkan Seafood* at Bent St, Fox Studios, Moore Park ☎02/9360 0097.

Fishface 132 Darlinghurst Rd, Darlinghurst ☎02/9332 4803. This is one place where size doesn't matter – it's tiny – and the excellent range of seafood and sushi speak for themselves. Everything is fresh: the fish and chips served in a paper cone, the pea soup with yabby tails or the sushi prepared before your eyes. Licensed & BYO. Moderate–expensive. Dinner Mon–Sat.

Govinda's 112 Darlinghurst Rd, Darlinghurst. Legendary among locals, this Hari-Krishna run restaurant-cum-cinema offers excellent, cheap Indian all-you-can-eat food for a bargain $15.90. Soup, lentils, curry and for an extra $4 a new release or classic movie on huge comfy couches thrown in at the attached cinema. Inexpensive. Dinner nightly from 6pm and two screenings at 7.30 and 9.30pm.

Oh! Calcutta! 252 Victoria St, Darlinghurst ☎02/9360 3650. Certainly not your grungy neighbourhood Indian: the interior was fitted out by a star interior decorator. *Oh! Calcutta!* keeps getting suitably exclamatory reviews for its authentic – and occasionally inventive – food. Dishes like quail and goat regularly appear beside more mainstream dishes. Try for a balcony table upstairs. Moderate. Licensed and BYO wine only. Lunch Fri only, dinner Mon–Sat.

Onde 346 Liverpool St, Darlinghurst. People keep returning to this French-owned restaurant, situated in a Darlinghurst side street, which serves outstanding and very authentic bistro-style food: soups and patés to start, mains such as steak and *frites* or *confit* of duck, plus a fish dish. Portions are generous, service excellent and desserts decadent. Licensed, and all wine is available by the glass. Moderate. Dinner nightly.

Pink Peppercorn 122 Oxford St, Darlinghurst ⓣ02/9360 9922. A place that keeps springing up on critics' favourites lists, lured by the unusual Laotian-inspired cooking – including the signature dish stir-fried king prawns and pink peppercorns. Licensed and BYO. Moderate. Dinner daily.

Kings Cross, Potts Point and Woolloomooloo

Many of the coffee shops and eateries in the Cross cater for the tastes (and wallets) of the area's backpackers, though there are also several stylish restaurants particularly in Potts Point. Many are also open late.

Cafes and pubs

Cafe Hernandez 60 Kings Cross Rd, Potts Point. Veteran Argentinian-run 24hr coffee shop. Relaxed and friendly with an old-time feel, you can dawdle here for ages and no one will make you feel unwelcome. Popular with taxi drivers and a mixed clientele of locals. Spanish food is served –*churros*, tortilla, *empanadas* and good pastries – but the coffee is the focus. Open daily.

Harry's Café de Wheels cnr Cowper Wharf Rd and Brougham St, Woolloomooloo. Sometimes there's nothing like a good old-fashioned pie and this little cart (open 24 hours) has been serving them up for over 60 years. Some gourmet and vegetarian options have made it onto the menu but the standard meat pie with mashed peas and gravy is still the favourite.

Laurent Boulangerie Pâtisserie The Wharf, 6 Cowper Wharf Rd, Woolloomooloo. Paris meets Sydney at this bakery-café: the gleaming glass counters hold a tempting array of pastries, filled baguettes and *croque-monsieurs*, while the woven outdoor seats could have been stolen from the nearest *boulevard*. Daily 7.30am–8pm.

Restaurants

Fratelli Paradiso 12–16 Challis Ave, Potts Point ⓣ02/9357 1744. This place has everything, from gorgeous wallpaper and a dark furniture fit-out to flirty wait staff and a diverse wine list. There's even an adjoining bakery which runs out of stock before lunchtime most days. And the food's amazing too – calamari, veal, pizzas and pastries – with a blackboard menu that changes daily. Licensed. Moderate. Breakfast and lunch daily, dinner Mon–Fri.

Otto The Wharf, 6 Cowper Wharf Rd, Woolloomooloo ⓣ02/9368 7488. *Otto* is the sort of restaurant where agents take actors and models out to lunch, or a well-known politician could be dining at the next table. Trendy and glamorous, with a location not just by the water but on the water. The exquisite Italian cuisine – very fresh seafood – coupled with friendly service and a lively atmosphere, is what keeps them coming back. Lunch summer daily, winter Tues–Sun. Licensed. Expensive. Dinner daily (Sun 6–8.30pm).

Paddington

As **Oxford Street** continues through Paddington, it becomes gradually more upmarket; the majority of restaurants here are attached to gracious old pubs and most have had a complete culinary overhaul and now offer far more than the steak and three veg option of times past.

Arthurs 260 Oxford St, Paddington. Paddington pizza institution recognised by its upside down sign out front – queueing to get in is mandatory (no bookings). Thin-crust pizzas, with a huge range of toppings (from around $14 for a small); fresh pasta dishes available too. Inexpensive to moderate. BYO. Mon–Fri 5pm–midnight, Sat & Sun noon–midnight.

Paddington Inn Bistro 338 Oxford St, Paddington. Busy upmarket pub-bistro with tasty tapas menu as well as more substantial meals, from risotto to imaginative salads, amongst a decor of textured glass, cushioned booths, polished concrete floors and fabric-lined walls. Packed on Saturdays, as it's opposite the market; popular pool tables upstairs. Licensed. Moderate.

Royal Hotel Restaurant *Royal Hotel*, 237 Glenmore Rd, off Five Ways, Paddington. Grand old triple-storey pub-restaurant serving some of the most mouth-watering steaks in Sydney, nonstop from noon to 11pm (9pm Sun). Eating on the verandah is a real treat, with views over the art gallery and Five Ways action below. Tables fill fast – no bookings. There's the *Elephant Bar* upstairs (see p.191). Moderate.

Sloanes Cafe 312 Oxford St, Paddington. The emphasis in this veteran café is on good, unusual vegetarian food, moderately priced, but some meatier dishes have slipped onto the menu, including a BLT with guacamole to die for; the fresh juice bar has always been phenomenal. The stone-floored dining room opens onto the street to check out all the Saturday market action, or for more peace eat out back under vines in the delightful courtyard. Breakfast and lunch served all day. Mon–Wed 7am–5pm, Thur–Sat 7am–10pm, Sun 7am–5pm. BYO.

Bondi and Watsons Bay

Bondi is a cosmopolitan centre with the many Eastern European and Jewish people giving its cafés a continental flair; there are also some fantastic kosher restaurants, delis and cake shops. The Bondi Beach area is full of cheap takeaways, fish-and-chip shops and beer gardens, as well as some seriously trendy cafés and restaurants. To the north, **Watsons Bay** is known for its famous seafood restaurant, *Doyles*.

Bondi Social 1st Floor, 38 Campbell Parade, Bondi Beach ⓣ02/9365 1788. You could easily miss the sandwich-board sign pointing you to this hidden gem, but once found a million-dollar balcony view of the beach awaits those wanting to escape the mêlée of the Campbell Parade pavement. The wood interior is rich and dim-lit at night; the mood promises romance and an interesting dining experience with a worldwide influence. Dinner mains $21–26. Licensed. Mon–Fri 5.30pm–11pm, Sat & Sun 9am–3.30pm (for brunch) and 5.30pm–11pm.

Bondi Tratt 34B Campbell Parade, Bondi Beach ⓣ02/9365 4303. Considering the setting, with outdoor seating overlooking the beach, not at all expensive. Come here to take in the view and the invariably buzzing atmosphere over breakfast, lunch and dinner, or just a coffee. Serves contemporary Australian and Italian food. Licensed and BYO. Cheap pasta deals from 5–7pm. Daily from 7am–10.30pm.

Brown Sugar 100 Brighton Boulevard, North Bondi. Groovy, relaxed little café tucked in a quiet residential street around the corner from the North Bondi set of shops. Music is funky, the staff suitably sweet. Locals straggle in for the very good breakfast menu: an interesting way with eggs, from green eggs (with pesto) to dill salmon eggs and the pancakes come with a week's supply of fruit. Lunch on toasted Turkish sandwiches, salad or pasta – the most expensive item is $14. Great coffee. Daily 7.30am–4.30pm.

Doyles on the Beach 11 Marine Parade, Watsons Bay ⓣ02/9337 1350; also *Doyles Wharf Restaurant* ⓣ02/9337 1572. The former is the original of the long-running Sydney fish-restaurant institution, but both serve great if overpriced seafood (but without the flair and inspiration of newer places) and have views of the city across the water. The adjacent pub serves pub-versions in its beer garden. A water taxi can transport you from Circular Quay to Watsons Bay. Expensive. Daily lunch and dinner.

Gertrude & Alice Cafe Bookstore 40 Hall St, cnr Consett Ave, Bondi Beach. Open daily from 8.30am until late into the night, it's hard to decide if *Gertrude and Alice*'s is more of a café or a second-hand literary bookshop. With small tables crammed into every available space, a big communal table and a comfy couch to lounge in, it can be hard for browsers to get to the books at busy café times. A homely hangout with generous, affordable serves of Greek and Mediterranean food, great cakes, great coffee and lots of conversation.

Hugo's 70 Campbell Parade, Bondi Beach ⓣ02/9300 0900. Smack amongst the parade of posers, surfers and travellers, this is contemporary Bondi – part café, part bar, part fine dining – with a casual, young and friendly flair. At weekends there's all-day brunch (9am–4pm; no bookings); while from 6pm every night white tablecloths and softly glowing lamps appear and everyone seems to be having noisy fun. Service is wonderful and honed for your comfort, including blankets for those chilly sea breezes if you sit outside. Portions are generous modern Asian and Mediterranean-slanted creations. Expensive (mains $30–39). Licensed.

Bronte, Clovelly and Coogee

South of Bondi, **Bronte**'s beachfront café strip is wonderfully laid-back, and **Coogee** has a thriving café scene.

Barzura 62 Carr St, Coogee ☎02/9665 5546. Fantastic spot providing up-close ocean views. Both a café and a fully fledged restaurant, with wholesome breakfast until 1pm, snacks until 7pm, and restaurant meals – like seafood spaghetti or grilled kangaroo rump – served at lunch and dinner. Unpretentious though stylish service encourages a large local crowd. Moderate; mains $13–26, pasta deals 5–7pm; licensed and BYO. Daily 7am–10pm.

The Beach Pit 211 Coogee Bay Rd, Coogee ☎02/9665 0068. Really enjoyable café-restaurant with Coogee's trademark informality and friendliness. Small but succulent menu has European and Asian influences and plenty of fish and seafood on offer; dishes are generous, well priced and presented, mains $13–21. You can breakfast here at the weekend too. Closed Tues & Wed.

Jack & Jill's Fish Café 98 Beach Street, Coogee ☎02/9665 8429. This down-to-earth fish restaurant is a local legend. Come here to enjoy delightfully cooked fish, from the basic battered variety to tasty tandoori perch. Prices $13–20 for mains. Tues–Sat from 5pm, Sun from noon.

Seasalt 1 Donnellan Circuit, Clovelly ☎02/9664 5344. Open-fronted café-restaurant, with fabulous views over the beach to cliffs, greenery and houses. *Seasalt* looks really smart, but it's the sort of casual beach place where you can come in sand-covered and have just a coffee, as well as the place to head for a full meal with wine. Cuisine is fresh and modern with a seafood basis; lunch mains range from $16 to $27, and dinner (fully clothed and groomed) from $19–27. Sophisticated, extensive breakfast packs them in at weekends. Takeaways from the small kiosk. Licensed. Mon–Fri 9am–3.30pm, Sat & Sun 8.30pm–4pm. Dinner Tues–Sat 6–10pm summer, Fri & Sat 6–10pm winter.

Sejuiced 487 Bronte Rd, Bronte. Delicious fresh juices, smoothies and frappés, combined with ocean and palm-tree views, make this tiny place a beauty to kick-start a summer's day. The "Morning Energiser" (beetroot, apple, ginger and carrot juice) ought to get you going, or there's all manner of other breakfast foods. Salads, soups and pasta are terrific too. Daily 6.30am–6pm.

Swell Restaurant 465 Bronte Road, Bronte ☎02/9386 5001. One of three Bronte café/restaurants to open in the evening down at the beach these days. Sit inside for the latest in sharp interiors, or out on the pavement for the million-dollar Bronte Beach view. There's plenty of competition alongside so prices are very reasonable for what you're getting. Dinner mains all $28. Daily 7am –10pm.

North Shore and Manly

Military Road, running from Neutral Bay to Mosman, rivals and perhaps outdoes all the gourmet streets south of the harbour. The string of excellent restaurants tends to be expensive, but there are a number of tempting pastry shops and well-stocked delis. **Miller Street**, which runs from North Sydney, has a great range of eateries around **Cammeray**. **Manly** offers something for every taste and budget; there's an upmarket food hall and food stalls on Manly Wharf, and loads of good cafés and restaurants on **Belgrave Street**, **Darley Street** and along **South Steyne**.

Café Steyne cnr South Steyne and Victoria Parade, Manly. The laid-back staff and customers epitomise the Manly vibe, and it's easy to spend time over the giant breakfast plates or tucking into the gourmet burgers. BYO. Mon–Fri 8am–9.30pm, Sat–Sun 7.30am–11pm.

The Bathers Pavilion 4 The Esplanade, Balmoral Beach ☎02/9969 5050. Indulgent beach-house-style dining in the former (1930s) changing rooms on Balmoral Beach. The very pricey restaurant and café double-act is presided over by one of Sydney's top chefs, Serge Dansereau. Fixed-price dinner menu in the restaurant starts from $90 for two courses (from $60 lunchtime). Weekend breakfast in the café is a North Shore ritual – expect to queue to get in (the restaurant has Sunday breakfast only, for which you can book) – while the wood-fired pizzas are popular later in the day. Licensed. Café daily 7am–midnight, restaurant lunch and dinner daily.

Maisys Cafe 164 Military Rd, Neutral Bay. Cool hangout on a hot day or night (open 24hr), with funky interior and music. Good for breakfast – from croissants to bacon and eggs – or delicious Maltese *pastizzi* plus soups, burgers, pasta and cakes. Not cheap, but servings are generous. BYO.

Out of Africa 43–45 East Esplanade, opposite Manly Wharf ⓣ02/9977 0055. The zebra skin seat covers and tribal spears, masks and colourful photos on the walls put you right in the mood for the "Couscous Royale", and other African speciality dishes, prepared traditionally. Live acoustic jazz funk and world music from 7.30pm Thurs. BYO. Moderate. Lunch Mon–Thurs, dinner daily.

Pacific Thai Cuisine 2nd floor, 48 Victoria Parade, cnr South Steyne, Manly ⓣ02/9977 7220. With crisp decor and fantastic views of the beach from its upstairs location, this inexpensive Thai restaurant offers a variety of fresh favourites as well as chef's specials such as Chu Chi Curry (red curry with kaffir lime leaves). Vegetarian options too. Licensed & BYO. Inexpensive to moderate.

Roger Fish Café Grill Shop 6, 2A Waters Rd, Neutral Bay ⓣ02/9953 6242. An interactive, fresh seafood experience: choose not only your preferred catch (from a changing menu of up to 26 choices), the cooking style, flavouring and even the thickness of the fillet. Personalised, yet still moderately priced, fish & chips. Licensed & BYO. Lunch and dinner daily.

Watermark 2A The Esplanade, Balmoral Beach ⓣ02/9968 3433. For a memorable Sydney meal, both for location and food, you can't go wrong here. Chef Kenneth Leung is well known for his fusion of Eastern and Western cooking styles and local ingredients, plus there are views right across the water, a terrace to dine on under the sun or stars (or sit by the fireplace in winter), a stylish interior and fabulous service. Very expensive; licensed. Breakfast, lunch and dinner daily.

Entertainment, nightlife and culture

To find out exactly **what's on** in Sydney, Friday's *Sydney Morning Herald* offers "Metro", a weekly entertainment lift-out, and the *Daily Telegraph* has the "Seven Days" pull-out every Thursday. In addition to these and the rather bland monthly programmes distributed by various tourist organizations (see p.106), there is a plethora of **free listings magazines** for more alternative goings-on – clubbing, bands, fashion, music and the like – which can be found lying around in the cafés, record shops and boutiques of Paddington, Darlinghurst, Glebe and Kings Cross: these include *Revolver* and *Drum Media* with their weekly band listings and reviews, and *3D World* and *Beat* covering the club scene. *City Hub*, a politically aware, free, weekly newspaper, also has an excellent events listing section and *TNT Magazine* has a "What's On In Sydney" section. The Sydney Citysearch **website** (ⓦwww.sydney.citysearch.com.au) has listings of film, theatre and music events.

The two main **booking agencies** are Ticketek (bookings ⓣ02/9266 4800, ⓦwww.ticketek.com.au) and Ticketmaster7 (bookings ⓣ13 61 00, ⓦwww.ticketmaster7.com). Ticketek outlets are at 195 Elizabeth St (cnr Park St), the State Theatre and the Theatre Royal. Ticketmaster7 outlets include the Capitol Theatre and the Entertainment Centre.

Pubs and bars

The differences between a restaurant, bar, pub and nightclub are often blurred in Sydney, and one establishment may be a combination of all these under one roof, with a place to suit any mood and taste. Sydney's bland pub wilderness has all but disappeared and you'll find a fashionable bar on almost every corner, offering everything from poetry readings and art classes to groovy Sunday afternoon jazz or DJ sessions. Not to be outdone, the traditional hotels are getting in renowned chefs and putting on food far beyond the old pub grub fare. Sydney has many Art Deco pubs, a classic 1930s style notably seen in the tilework; we've mentioned some of the best below.

The Rocks and CBD

Arthouse Hotel 275 Pitt St, City. A grand nineteenth-century School of Arts building converted inot a pub. The main bar, the *Verge*, is a converted chapel that makes for a dramatic drinks setting: high ceilings, polished wood floorboards, beautiful Victorian-era design, burning cauldrons and flowing material hanging from the ceiling. New and sometimes famous artworks are exhibited here and in the first-floor Dome Restaurant (mains $20–$36). *Arthouse* lives up to its name with free life-drawing classes in the library, art exhibitions, short-film screenings and guest DJs. Good-value lunchtime bar food in the *Verge*. Specials are moderately priced and taste great.

Australian Hotel 100 Cumberland St, The Rocks. Convivial corner hotel seemingly always full of Brits, the crowded outside tables face towards a sports centre under the Harbour Bridge, but it's the verandah upstairs that gives sweeping vistas of Circular Quay and the Opera House. Inside, original fittings give a lovely old-pub feel. Known and loved for its Bavarian-style draught beer brewed in Picton, plus delicious gourmet pizzas with toppings which extend to native animals – emu, kangaroo and crocodile.

Establishment 252 George St. Deluxe bar. The huge main room boasts an extraordinarily long marble bar, white pillars, high decorative ceilings, and an atrium and fountain at the back. Despite the size, it gets jam-packed, particularly on Thursday nights (when it's free champagne for ladies before 7.00) and Fridays, when the door policy is very strict. On-site ballroom, restaurants (the world-class *est*, with top chef Peter Doyle) and *Tank* nightclub (p.194), and thirty-odd luxurious hotel rooms. Level 4 is *Hemmesphere*, a sophisticated Moroccan-themed bar room with cushions and lavish couches, and a drinks list to match.

Harbour View Hotel 18 Lower Fort St, The Rocks. Sibling to the stately *Exchange Hotel* in Balmain, this three-storey renovated gem puts you right under the bridge – and close enough from the top balcony cocktail bar to raise a glass to the grey overall-clad Bridgeclimbers making their way back from the summit. The crowd is mixed, and better for it. Pricey but exceptional upstairs restaurant.

Hero of Waterloo 81 Lower Fort St, Millers Point, The Rocks. One of Sydney's oldest pubs, built in 1843 from sandstone dug out from the Argyle Cut (see p.134), this place has plenty of atmosphere and oozes history. Open fireplaces make it a good choice for a winter drink, and it serves simple meals.

Horizons Bar 36th Floor, *Shangri La Hotel*, 176 Cumberland St, The Rocks. Top-floor bar of the five-star *Shangri-La Hotel* has a stunning 270-degree view – the Opera House, Darling Harbour, Middle Harbour and Homebush Bay to the Blue Mountains. Mega-expensive lounge is worth it for the view – dress smart to get in. Daily noon–1am (Sun until midnight).

Opera Bar Lower Concourse Level, Sydney Opera House, Sydney. In summer you can't move for the

Legendary beer gardens

Many Sydney pubs have an outdoor drinking area, perfect for enjoying the sunny weather – the four listed below, however, are outright legends.

The Coogee Bay Hotel, Arden Street, Coogee. Loud, rowdy and packed with backpackers, this enormous beer garden across from the beach is legendary in the eastern suburbs. The hotel has six bars in all, including a big-screen sports bar for all international sporting events. Revellers can buy jugs of beer and cook their own meat from 9.30am till late.

Doyles Palace Hotel 10 Marine Parade, Watsons Bay. Still known to locals as the Watson's Bay Hotel, the beer garden here gives uninterrupted views across the harbour which you can enjoy with fresh fish and chips from the renowned *Doyles* kitchen or a steak from the outdoor BBQ.

Newport Arms Hotel 2 Kalinya St, Newport. Famous beer-garden pub established in 1880 with a huge deck looking out over Heron Cove at Pittwater. Good for families, with a children's play area. The bistro's Asian-influenced salads and big seafood servings complement a large wine list.

The Oaks Hotel 118 Military Rd, Neutral Bay. The North Shore's most popular pub takes its name from the huge oak tree which shades the entire beer garden. Cook your own (expensive) steak, or order a gourmet pizza from the restaurant inside.

people – a mix of concertgoers, tourists and office workers – but that's half the fun of this stunningly located bar with outside tables. Watch the ferries come in and have a drink next to one of the world's greatest buildings. Jazz on Sunday afternoons and a bar snack menu.

Darling Harbour, Haymarket and around

Cargo Bar 52–60 The Promenade, King Street Wharf, Darling Harbour. Multi-level bar with plenty of outdoor seating downstairs and sofas and stools upstairs. Views of Darling Harbour are quite dazzling at night when the lights of the hotels and casino glitter off the water. Drinks are not cheap, but yummy pizzas are satisfying.
Civic Hotel 388 Pitt St, cnr Goulburn St, Haymarket ⓣ02/8267 3186. Beautiful 1940s Deco-style pub, its original features in great condition. Upstairs, there's a glamorous dining room and cocktail bar with performance spaces offered to young artistic talent. Handy meeting point for Chinatown and George Steet cinema forays.
Pontoon Cockle Bay Wharf, Darling Harbour. Open-fronted bar with outside tables feels like one big lively beer garden, right on the water opposite the marina. Big umbrellas shade you from the sun for a daytime drink; pool tables inside. Attracts a young casual crowd, despite the upmarket restaurants surrounding it.
Scruffy Murphy's 43 Goulburn St. Rowdy, late-opening Irish pub with Guinness on tap, of course; phenomenally popular, particularly with travellers and ex-pats, who come for some hearty home-cooking too. Just around the corner from Central station. Closes around 3.30 or 4.30am most nights.
Slip Inn 111 Sussex St. Now famous as the place where Mary Donaldson met her Prince Frederick of Denmark, this huge three-level place has several bars, a bistro and a nightclub, *The Chinese Laundry*, overlooking Darling Harbour. Front bars have a pool room, while downstairs a boisterous beer garden fills up on sultry nights, with the quieter, more sophisticated *Sand Bar* beside it. Excellent wine list, with lots available by the glass; bar food includes Thai and pizzas.

Inner west: Glebe, Newtown, Balmain and Leichhardt

Bank Hotel 324 King St, next to Newtown station. Smart-looking pub open late and always packed with local arty residents and visiting musos. Pool table out front, cocktail bar out back and a great Thai restaurant, *Sumalee*, in the leafy beer garden.
Exchange Hotel cnr Beattie & Mullens St, Balmain. Classic Balmain backstreet corner pub, built in 1885, with a vast iron are lace balcony. There are four lively bars, including the themed *Safari Bar*, which always has something happening (trivia, live music, comedy and theatre) and the Bloody Mary Breakfast Club on Saturday and Sunday mornings (10am–3pm).
Friend in Hand 58 Cowper St, cnr Queen Street, Glebe ⓣ02/9660 2326. Character-filled pub in the leafy backstreets of Glebe, with all manner of curious objects dangling from the walls and ceilings of the public bar; a popular haunt for backpackers. Diverse entertainment in the upstairs bar (where you can also play pool) includes script-reading, poetry nights, backgammon championships and quizzes – call to check what's on when. On Saturday nights there's a piano player in the public bar. An Italian restaurant, *Cesare's No Names* (closed Sun lunch), with pasta from $10, is in the gazebo and beer garden.
Nag's Head Cnr Lodge St and St Johns Rd, off Glebe Point Rd, Glebe. Calling itself a "posh pub", this is a good place for a quiet drink – definitely no pokies. Decor and atmosphere is very much that of a British boozer: several imported beers on tap – Guinness, Boddingtons, Stella and Becks – and pints and half-pints available. Its bistro dishes up excellent steaks and other grills, and there's an extensive bar menu. Pool tables in the loft area upstairs.

Darlinghurst, Kings Cross and Woolloomooloo

The Bourbon 24 Darlinghurst Rd, Kings Cross. Established in 1968 when it was frequented by US soldiers on R&R, this infamous 24-hour Kings Cross restaurant and drinking hole has been given a swish new upgrade, which hasn't done much to deter some of its more colourful regulars. New terrace upstairs, a lounge bar out the back and the front opens up onto the street, (bistro daily noon to 10pm). Bands on every night (usually covers) and DJs playing retro 80s disco four nights a week. There may be a cover charge at weekends depending on the night.
Burdekin 2 Oxford St, Darlinghurst. Well-preserved Art Deco pub with several trendy bars on four

levels. The dimly-lit basement *Dug Out Bar* (from 5pm) is tiny and beautifully tiled, and has table service and generous cocktails, while the spacious, ground-level *Main Bar* sports dramatic columns and a huge round bar.

Darlo Bar *Royal Sovereign Hotel*, cnr Darlinghurst Rd and Liverpool St, Darlinghurst. Popular Darlinghurst meeting place, with a lounge-room atmosphere. Comfy colourful chairs and sofas have a 1950s feel, the crowd is mixed and unaffected, the drinks well-priced, and there's a popular pool table. At night you can order from menus of local eateries, and they'll fetch the food for you.

Green Park Hotel 360 Victoria St, Darlinghurst. A Darlinghurst stalwart, partly because of the stash of pool tables in the back room, but mainly because of the unpretentious vibe. The bar couldn't be more unassuming; there's nothing decorating the walls and humble bar tables with stools and a few lounges out the back accommodate the regular arty crowd.

Judgement Bar *Courthouse Hotel*, 189 Oxford St, Darlinghurst. Overlooking Taylor Square, the upstairs bar of this pub is often open 24hr. Totally undiscriminating – you may find yourself here in the wee hours among an assortment of young clubbers and old drunks – and drinks aren't pricey. Wakes up around 1am.

Kingsleys Alehouse Level 1, *Woolloomooloo Bay Hotel*, cnr Bourke St and Cowper Wharf Rd, Woolloomooloo ⓣ02/8353 1333. Commandeering the upstairs and verandah of the *Wolloomooloo Bay Hotel* and the gorgeous marina and harbour views that go with it, this sister to *Kingsleys Steak and Crabhouse* (ⓣ02/9331 7788) across the road prides itself on its impressive local and international beer selection. Set up inside like a beerhall, with long communal tables and dark floorboards, and the menu of hearty steaks, schnitzels and mussels fits right in. There's also great seafood platters ($40) in the bistro downstairs.

Soho Bar & Lounge *Piccadilly Hotel*, 171 Victoria St, Kings Cross. Trendy Art Deco pub on leafy Victoria Street. Ground-floor *Gold Room* bar is the most Deco, but locals head for the upstairs *Leopard Lounge* bar (Tues–Sun nights) to hang out on the back balcony, play pool and sample the seasonally updated cocktail menu. The attached nightclub, *Yu*, runs on Fri and Sat nights from 10pm to sunrise.

Surry Hills, Paddington and Woollahra

The Clock Hotel 470 Crown St, Surry Hills. This huge hotel has expanded out of touch with its 1840s roots (the landmark clocktower was only added in the 1960s). Upstairs, a swish restaurant and bar runs off the huge balcony; downstairs the booths and tables fill up quickly for after-work drinks and the four pool tables are ever popular.

Cricketers Arms 106 Fitzroy St, Surry Hills. Just down the road from the live music scene at the *Hopetoun* (see p.192), the *Cricketers* has an equally dedicated clientele. A young, offbeat crowd – plenty of piercings and shaved heads – cram in and fall about the bar, pool room, and tiny beer garden, and yell at each other over a funky soundtrack. Hearty bar snacks and a bistro (Tues–Sun 3–10pm).

Elephant Bar *Royal Hotel*, 237 Glenmore Rd, Paddington. The top-floor bar of this beautifully renovated, Victorian-era hotel has knockout views of the city, best appreciated at sunset (happy hour 6–7pm). The small interior is great too, with its fireplaces, paintings and elephant prints. As it gets crowded later on, people cram onto the stairwell and it feels like a party.

Lord Dudley 236 Jersey Rd, Woollahra. Sydney's most British pub, complete with fireplaces, fox-hunting pictures, dark wood furniture – and a dart-board. Thirty-six beers on tap including Newcastle Brown Ale. The bistro serves up hearty British fare and on winter afternoons you can while away the hours playing scrabble or backgammon in the comfy overstuffed chairs.

Bondi and Coogee

Beach Palace Hotel 169 Dolphin St, Coogee. Home to a young and drunken crowd, made up of locals, beach babes and backpackers. Features seven bars, two restaurants and a great view of the beach from the balcony under the distinctive dome.

Beach Road Hotel 71 Beach Rd, Bondi Beach. Huge, stylishly decorated pub with a bewildering range of bars on two levels and a beer garden. Popular with both travellers and locals for its good vibe. Entertainment, mostly free, comes from rock bands, DJs and a jazz supper club. Cheap Italian bistro, *No Names*, takes over the beergarden and has a set menu for $9; upmarket contemporary Australian restaurant upstairs.

Bondi Hotel 178 Campbell Parade, Bondi Beach. Huge pub dating from the 1920s, with many of its original features intact, seating outside and an open bar area where locals hang out with sand still on their feet. Sedate during the day but at night an over-the-top, late-night backpackers' hangout. Mon–Sat until 4am.

Bondi Icebergs Dining Room and Bar, 1 Notts Ave, Bondi Beach. Famous for its winter swimming club (see p.168), *Icebergs* is a fantastic place to soak up the views and atmosphere of Bondi Beach. The clubhouse was recently rebuilt at a cost of $10 million, and has fast become the place to be seen, Sunday afternoons being an especially big time to dress up and mingle with the beautiful, bronzed people sampling the 37 types of champagne on the terrace. The *Sundeck Café* within the club offers Mediterranean-style light meals all day, but the seafood-inspired menu here is divine, though expensive.

Live music: jazz, blues and rock

The live music scene in Sydney has passed its boom time, and pub venues keep closing down to make way for the dreaded poker machines. However, there are still enough venues to just barely nourish a steady stream of local, interstate and overseas acts passing through every month, peaking in summer with a well-established open-air festival circuit. Pub bands and clubs are often free, especially if you arrive early; door charge is usually from $5, with $25 the uppermost price for smaller international acts or the latest interstate sensation. Sunday afternoon and early evening is a mellow time to catch some music, particularly jazz, around town.

The **venues for major events**, with bookings direct or through Ticketek or Ticketmaster (see p.188), are the Entertainment Centre at Haymarket near Darling Harbour (enquiries and credit-card sales ⓣ02/9266 4800); The Hordern Pavilion at Driver Ave, Fox Studios (ⓣ02/9383 4063); the Capitol Theatre, 13 Campbell St, Haymarket (ⓣ02/9266 4800); the Enmore Theatre, 130 Enmore Rd, just up from Newtown (ⓣ02/9550 3666); the centrally located Metro Theatre, 624 George St (ⓣ02/9264 2666) and City Live (ⓣ02/9358 8000) at Fox Studios.

There are now several big outdoor rock concerts throughout spring and summer but Homebake and the Big Day Out are still the best. **Homebake** (around $80; ⓦwww.homebake.com.au) is a huge annual open-air festival in The Domain in early December with food and market stalls, rides and a line-up of over fifty famous and underground Australian bands from Spiderbait to Jet. The **Big Day Out**, on the Australia Day weekend (around $100; ⓦwww.bigdayout.com), at the showground at Homebush Bay, features big international names like Metallica, the Chemical Brothers, the Foo Fighters as well as big local talent like Powderfinger and Silverchair. Also see Festivals, pp.202–203, for the Manly Jazz Festival.

Annandale Hotel Cnr Nelson St and Parramatta Rd, Annandale, just before Leichhardt ⓣ02/9550 1078. A showcase for indie bands, from up-and-comers to headline international acts, through rock, funk, metal and groove, with a capacity of 450. Music Tues–Sat nights (door $5–12).

The Basement 29 Reiby Place, Circular Quay ⓣ02/9251 2797. This dark and moody venue is an institution that attracts the great and rising names in jazz, acoustic and world music as well as a roster of the world's most renowned blues performers. To take in a show, book a table and dine in front of the low stage, otherwise you'll have to stand all night at the bar at the back. Recorded broadcasts on the Internet on ⓦwww.thebasement.com.au.

Bridge Hotel 135 Victoria Rd, Rozelle ⓣ02/9810 1260. Legendary inner-west venue specializing in blues and pub rock, with some international but mostly local acts. Also good pub theatre and comedy nights.

Excelsior Hotel 64 Foveaux St, Surry Hills ⓣ02/9211 4945. Something of a muso's pub; jazz four nights a week, with residencies covering every style, from swing to avant garde (Mon–Wed 8pm; $5). Sunday evening from 6pm is usually a jamming session. Adjacent bistro. Bar until 3am Fri and Sat.

Hopetoun Hotel 416 Bourke St, cnr of Fitzroy St, Surry Hills ⓣ02/9361 5257. One of Sydney's best venues for the indie band scene, "The Hoey" focuses on new young bands: local, interstate and international acts all play in the small and inevitably packed front bar (Mon–Sat from 7.30pm; cover charge depends on the act, though sometimes free) and on Sunday there are DJs (5–10pm; $5). Popular pool room, drinking pit in the basement, and inexpensive little restaurant upstairs (meals from $5–$10). Closes midnight.

Rose of Australia Hotel 1 Swanson St, Erskineville ⓣ02/9565 1441. Trendy inner-city types mix with Goths, locals and gays to sample some favourites of the pub circuit. Line-up changes regularly, and bands play Fridays and Sundays on a rotational basis, so you can catch anything from an original rock act through to a country and western cover band. Music starts from 8.30pm (from 6.30pm Sundays) and is always free. The bistro is cheap (from $7) and the Rose Burgers are legendary.

Sandringham Hotel 387 King St, Newtown ⓣ02/9557 1254. "The Sando" features local and interstate indie bands, who play on the stage upstairs (Thurs–Sat 8.30pm–midnight, Sun 7pm–10pm; usually $5–$8, more well-known bands $12–$15).

Side On Cafe 83 Parramatta Rd, Annandale ⓣ02/9519 0055. Sydney's most interesting venue calls itself a "multi-arts complex" with a nightly programme running Thurs–Sun in an intimate café atmosphere. There's jazz (Fri & Sat) from popular trios to the latest experimental fusions; world music/latin (Thurs) and cabaret (Sun). Also an art gallery and sometimes film screenings and script readings. Book if you want to dine (ⓣ02/9516 3077); mains such as steak with roasted vegetables cost around $20. Door charge $10–15.

Soup Plus 1 Margaret St, cnr Clarence St, City ⓣ02/9299 7728. After more than 30 years at its old basement location, *Soup Plus* has upgraded and turned into a much larger music and dining venue. Still serving up live jazz with its bowls of $5 soup, the menu and the acts have expanded accordingly. Music Mon–Sat 7pm–11.30pm (Mon–Thur $8–$10, Fri & Sat nights $35 includes a two-course meal). Open for lunch too. Closed Sun.

Clubs

Many of Sydney's best clubs are at **gay** or **lesbian** venues, and although we've listed these separately on pp.194–195, the divisions are not always clear – many places have specific gay, lesbian and straight nights scheduled each week. A long strip of thriving clubs stretches from Kings Cross to Oxford Street and down towards Hyde Park. The scene can be pretty snobby, with door gorillas frequently vetting your style. Admission ranges from $5 to $30; many clubs stay open until 5am or 6am on Saturday and Sunday mornings. The year's big dance party is **Vibes on a Summers Day** in the Bondi Pavilion at the end of January (around $90; ⓦwww.vibes.net.au). There are also good clubs attached to several of the drinking spots listed on pp.188–192. Below are the bigger venues or places with something unusual to offer.

Club 77 77 William St, Kings Cross. The big nights are Thursday to Saturday at this intimate and relaxed club. Drinks are cheap and there's a swag of regulars who come here for the progressive and rare funk and house music. It also recently hosted the *Hellfire Club* during renovations, attracting a new crowd of fetishists and the curious. $5–$10.

Gas 467 Pitt St, Haymarket. One huge cutting-edge room downstairs where international DJs appear about once a month with a mezzanine level which acts as a viewing area over the dance floor, and chill-out lounges attached to get away from the hard house and trance which pervades most nights. Three bar areas. Thurs–Sun 10pm–6am. $15 Thurs, $20 Fri & Sat.

Globe Disco Lounge and Cocktail Bar 60 Park St, City. *Globe*'s cocktail-bar lounge is open 24 hours, and Thursday to Saturday from 10pm it's linked to a downstairs club section – you'll have to dress very cool to get past the door staff. Great place for soul, energetic house and hip-hop sounds Wed–Sat. $10–$15.

Home Cockle Bay Wharf, Darling Harbour. The first *really* big club venture in Sydney. The lavish *Home* can cram 2000 punters into its cool, cavernous interior. Also a mezzanine, a chill-out room, and outdoor balconies. Decks are often manned by big-name DJs, drinks are expensive, and staff beautiful. Packed with a younger crowd on Fridays for its flagship night Sublime, with four musical styles across four levels. On Saturdays, Together at Home plays progressive and funky house. Fri & Sat from 11pm til late. $25.

Le Panic 20 Bayswater Rd, Kings Cross. The old site of nightclub grandmother *Sugareef*, the extreme makeover shows *Le Panic* aims to be a one-stop-shop for late-night partying, with the sizeable dancefloor now surrounded by a swarthy bar and comfy booths. A private and exclusive lounge off to the side acts as a chill-out room.

Tank 3 Bridge Lane, off George St, City. This is for the glamorous industry crowd – fashion, music and film aficionados. If you don't belong, the style police will spot you a mile away. All very "funky" – from the house music played by regular or guest DJs to the mirrors and wash basins in the toilets. Three amazing bars and a VIP section. Attire is smart casual to funky street wear, but attitude and good looks override the dress code. Fri & Sat 10pm–6am. $15–$20.

Tantra 169 Oxford St, Darlinghurst. Alternating resident DJs and live musicians/percussionists ensure that there's always something new happening. The younger crowd comes on Fridays for the high-octane beats, while Saturdays are predominantly 25- to 30-year-olds. Fri & Sat 10pm–6am. $10–$30.

The World 24 Bayswater Rd, Kings Cross. With cheap drinks on Friday and Saturday nights and a relatively relaxed door policy, *The World* is popular with a fun, party-loving crowd of travellers, who jive to a pleasing mix of funk and house grooves in a pleasant Victorian-era building with a big front balcony. The atmosphere throughout is lively, if a little beery in the front bar. Fri & Sat noon–6am, Sun–Thurs noon–4am. Free.

Gay and lesbian bars and clubs

The last few years have seen a quiet diminishing of specifically gay and lesbian bars and due to Sydney's highly restrictive liquor licensing laws, the smaller venues vanish and the large ones just get bigger. One of the best things about Sydney's gay and lesbian scene is that it's concentrated in two areas so it's easy to bar hop: in the inner east around Oxford Street, Darlinghurst, including Surry Hills and Kings Cross, and in the inner west in adjoining Newtown and Erskineville. Those wanting a comfortable place to drink with a mixed clientele should also check out pubs already listed such as the *Green Park Hotel* (p.191), the *Darlo Bar* (p.190) and the *Burdekin* (p.190). Entry is free unless otherwise indicated.

Arq 16 Flinders St, cnr Taylor Square, Darlinghurst. Huge nine-hundred-person capacity, state-of-the-art club with everything from DJs and drag shows to pool competitions. Two levels, each with a very different scene: the *Arena*, on the top floor, is mostly gay, while the ground-floor *Vortex* is a quieter, less crowded mix of gay and straights, with pool tables. Chill-out booths, laser lighting, viewing decks and fishtanks add to the fun, friendly atmosphere. Sunday is the big night. Thurs–Sun from 9pm. Fri $10, Sat $20, Sun $5. Check website for specific events Ⓦwww.arqsydney.com.au.

Bank Hotel 324 King St, next to Newtown station. This stylish bar is a dyke favourite on Wednesday nights when the long-running women's pool competition (8pm) draws large crowds to socialize and maybe even compete. The back bar offers a stylish space to chill out and enjoy a cocktail while downstairs is one of Newtown's favourite Thai restaurants, *Sumalee*.

The Columbian Hotel 117 Oxford St, cnr Crown St, Darlinghurst. The latest and most popular addition to Oxford St, this mixed clientele bar is where people come to get revved-up in the evenings and renew their energy the day after. The downstairs bar offers an airy, comfortable space to drink, bop and chat with open windows onto the street. Upstairs (6pm–late) gets very crowded Thurs–Sun nights, attracting a hip and chilled crowd. The music is Hi-NRG upstairs, progressive house downstairs. Downstairs Mon–Sun 10am till late.

Exchange Hotel 34 Oxford St, Darlinghurst. In the downstairs *Phoenix* bar, Saturday night's *Crash* underground "alternative" dance club is mostly gay men dancing en-masse and shirtless, but on Sunday nights there's a happy mix of gays and dykes. After midnight it's at its peak and a more raunchy, bacchanalian crowd you won't find anywhere else on the strip (Sat & Sun from 10pm; $10 Sat, $5 Sun).

Flinders Bar 63–65 Flinders St, Darlinghurst. Recently reopened, revamped and welcoming a mixed crowd, this hotel offers a funky, sleek modern environment to drink or dance with friends. Once very popular with younger gays and their admirers, this bar is now much more an after-work drinks place and late-night groove lounge. It also boasts a Thai restaurant upstairs that serves meals from $7. Open Tues–Sun 3pm until late.

Imperial Hotel 35 Erskineville Rd, Erskineville Ⓣ02/9519 9899. Late-night gay and lesbian venue, with four bars including a popular, hot and sweaty dance floor in the basement (Fri & Sat progressive, commercial, Hi-NRG 11pm–6am for $5), and a riotous drag show line-up in the Cabaret Room

(Thurs–Sat; free; call for show times). Bingay (gay and lesbian bingo) is held Tuesday 8.30pm. The film *The Adventures of Priscilla, Queen of the Desert* both started and ended here; it was the *Imperial*'s finest hour, and the memories are kept alive in the photo-lined cocktail bar, the *Priscilla Lounge* (cabaret Fri & Sat 10.30pm; free). The drag shows are hilarious, inventive and constantly changing: expect anything from the gay-version of *Survivor* to the *Rocky Horror Drag Show*. Pool tables (free all day Mon & Sun) and music videos in the public bar. Mon–Thurs 3pm–2/3am, Fri & Sat 1pm–7am, Sun 1pm–midnight.

Manacle cnr Bourke & Flinders Streets, Surry Hills (enter from Patterson Lane, behind the *Taylor Square Hotel*). Currently gay Sydney's only regular hardcore, day recovery spot, this underground club full of chains and leather caters for all those who refuse to go home at 7am. Good mix of seasoned partygoers of every persuasion including drag queens. At night the bar serves as a popular leather and Levis bar and is the last remaining men-only bar in the neighbourhood offering pool tables and dim lighting. The night bar opens 7pm–3am Thurs–Sun. $5.

Midnight Shift 85 Oxford St, Darlinghurst. "The Shift", running for over twenty years, is a veteran of the Oxford Street scene. The *Shift Video Bar* is a large drinking and cruising space to a music-video backdrop; pool tables out back. Upstairs the revamped weekend-only club is a massive space with everything from a waterfall to a cutting-edge laser light show. It hosts drag shows (usually Fri nights), DJs and events; cover charge upwards of $10. Mainly men. Downstairs bar daily noon–6am, club Fri & Sat 11pm–7am; free.

Newtown Hotel 174 King St, corner Watkin Street, Newtown. A stalwart of the Sydney scene. Laid-back mix of Newtown lesbians and gays. Drag shows (Tues–Sat 10pm & 11pm, Sun 8.30pm & 9.15pm), and pool tables (free on Mon nights). A tiny dance floor – nightly DJs means it's always in action. The well-regarded *Linda's Backstage Restaurant* (Mon–Sat from 6pm) serves up delicious, very reasonably priced modern Australian fare. Upstairs, *Bar 2* is a quiet intimate space. Mon–Sat 11am–midnight, Sun 11am–10pm; *Bar 2* Wed–Sun 6pm–midnight.

Oxford Hotel 134 Oxford St, Darlinghurst. The ground-floor 24hr bar, once the macho pillar of the gay community, has now expanded offering a mixed open-to-the-street bar and café, with a pool table, hard music (and handbag) and a regular clientele – busier on Friday and Saturday nights. On the first floor, *Gilligans* is a very different scene, a popular cocktail bar which attracts a mixed crowd of gay boys, lesbians and the straight party set; happy hour 5–7pm; daily 5pm–3am. On the second floor, *Gingers* is a quieter, more elegant bar – decor is plush, and several small cosy rooms provide intimacy; open Thurs–Sat from 6pm.

Stonewall Hotel 175 Oxford St, Darlinghurst. With three action-packed levels, this pub is a big hit with young gays and lesbians and their straight friends. Theme nights like karaoke, celebrity drag, or dating games and DJs in the various different bars Wednesday to Saturday. Downstairs bar plays commercial dance music, the cocktail bar above accelerates with uplifting house, while the top-floor, weekend-only VIP Bar gets off on campy, "handbag" sounds (Fri & Sat 11pm–6am; free). Natural light and outside tables at ground level, where you can order a meal.

Taxi Club 40 Flinders St, Darlinghurst. It's a Sydney legend and famous (or notorious) for being the only place you can buy a drink after 10pm on Good Friday or Christmas Day, but don't bother before 2 or 3am, and you'll need to be suitably intoxicated to appreciate it fully. There's a strange blend of drag queens, taxi drivers, lesbians and boys (straight and gay) to observe, and the cheapest drinks in gay Sydney. An upstairs dance club (free) operates Friday and Saturday from 1am. Supposedly a members club but bring ID to show you're from out of town. 24hr except for a clean from 6am–9am.

Classical music, theatre and dance

Sydney's **arts scene** is vibrant and extensive. The Sydney Symphony Orchestra plays at the Town Hall, St James's Church or the Concert Hall at the Opera House while the Australian Ballet performs at the Opera House and the Capitol Theatre. The free outdoor performances in The Domain, under the auspices of the Sydney Festival, are a highlight of the year, with crowds gathering to enjoy the music with a picnic.

Concert halls

City Recital Hall Angel Place, between George and Pitt streets, City ⓣ02/8256 2222. Opened in 1999, this classical music venue right next to Martin Place was specifically designed for chamber music. Seats over 1200, but on three levels giving it an intimate atmosphere.

Gay and lesbian Sydney

Sydney is indisputably one of the world's great gay cities – indeed, many people think it capable of snatching San Francisco's crown as the Queen of them all. There's something for everyone – whether you want to lie on a beach during the warmer months (Oct–April) or party hard all year round. Gays and lesbians are pretty much accepted – particularly in the inner-city and eastern areas. They have to be – there's too many of them for anyone to argue. A big drawcard is the **Sydney Gay & Lesbian Mardi Gras**; the festival lasts for four weeks, starting the first week of **February**, kicking off with a launch in Hyde Park, followed two weeks later by a Fair Day in Victoria Park and culminating in the parade and party on the last weekend of February or the first weekend of March. The first parade was held in 1978 as a gay-rights protest and today, it's the biggest celebration of gay and lesbian culture in the world. In 1992, an unprecedented crowd of four hundred thousand, including a broad-spectrum of straight society, turned up to watch the parade and two years later it began to be broadcast nationally on television. Mardi Gras turned 27 in 2005 but for a while it looked like it wouldn't make it. By 1999, the combined festival, parade and party was making the local economy $100 million dollars richer and the increasing commercialization of Mardi Gras was drawing criticism from the gay and lesbian community. Its bubble burst in 2002, after financial mismanagement saw the Mardi Gras organization in the red to the tune of $500,000. Instead of throwing in the towel, the fundraising organization was rebuilt as the "New Mardi Gras"; although less cash-rich, New Mardi Gras is drawing on the resources and creativity of its talented community along with the desire to keep the festival going in order to revive the old Mardi Gras spirit.

But don't despair if you can't be here for Mardi Gras or the Sleaze Ball (the annual Mardi Gras fundraiser in late September/early October). The city has much more to offer. **Oxford Street** is Sydney's official "pink strip" of gay restaurants, coffee shops, bookshops and bars, and here you'll find countless pairs of tight-T-shirted guys strolling hand-in-hand, or checking out the passing talent from hip, streetside cafés. However, the gay-straight divide in Sydney has less relevance for a new generation, perhaps ironically a result of Mardi Gras' mainstream success. Several of the long-running gay venues on and around Oxford Street have closed down and many remaining attract older customers, as younger gays and lesbians embrace inclusiveness and party with their straight friends and peers or choose to meet new friends on the Internet instead of in bars. **King Street**, Newtown, and nearby **Erskineville** are centres of gay culture, while lesbian communities have carved out territory of their own in **Leichhardt** (known affectionately as "Dykehart") and **Marrackville**. The bar and club listings have not been split into separate gay and lesbian listings, as the scene thankfully doesn't divide so neatly into "them and us" but weekly event listings are included in the free magazines (see below).

If you've come for the sun, popular **gay beaches** are Tamarama (see p.169), Bondi (see p.167), and "clothing optional" Lady Jane, while pools of choice are Red Leaf harbour pool at Double Bay (see p.161) and the appropriately named Andrew "Boy" Charlton pool in The Domain (see p.143). The Coogee Women's Baths, at the southern end of Coogee Beach (see p.170) is popular with lesbians.

Mardi Gras, Sleaze and PRIDE

From a Queer perspective the best time of year to visit Sydney is still February, when the **Sydney Gay & Lesbian Mardi Gras** takes over the city. Four weeks of exhibitions, performances and other events – including the ten-day **Mardi Gras Film Festival** in mid-February showcasing the latest in Queer cinema – represent the largest lesbian and gay arts festival in the world, paving the way for the main event, an exuberant night-time **parade** down Oxford Street, when up to a half-a-million gays and straights jostle for the best viewing positions, before the Dykes on Bikes, traditional leaders of the parade since 1988, roar into view. Participants devote months to the preparation of outlandish floats and outrageous costumes at Mardi Gras workshops, and even more time is devoted to the preparation of beautiful bodies in Sydney's packed gyms. The parade begins at 7.30pm (finishing around 10.30pm), but people line the barricades along Oxford Street from mid-morning (brandishing stolen milk crates to stand on for a better view). If you can't get to Oxford Street until late afternoon, your best chance of finding a spot is along Flinders Street near Moore Park Road, where the parade ends. Otherwise, AIDS charity The Bobby Goldsmith Foundation (Ⓣ02/9283 8666, Ⓦwww.bgf.org.au) has around 7000 grandstand seats on Flinders St, at $65 each.

The all-night **dance party** which follows the parade attracts up to 25,000 people and is held in several differently themed dance spaces at Fox Studios in Moore Park (including a women's space, *G-Spot*). You may have to plan ahead if you want to get a **ticket**: party tickets ($125 in advance, or $140 at the gates) sometimes sell out by the end of January. The purchase of tickets used to be restricted to "Mardi Gras members" to keep the event Queer, with special provisions for visitors from interstate and overseas, but as the New Mardi Gras is rebuilding the old memberships and procedures no longer exist, tickets can be bought from Ticketek (Ⓣ02/9266 4800, Ⓦwww.ticketek.com.au) or for general enquiries contact the **New Mardi Gras office** (Ⓣ02/9568 8600, Ⓦwww.mardigras.org.au). Your local gay-friendly travel agent can also organize tickets. The **Sydney Gay & Lesbian Mardi Gras Guide**, available from mid-December, can be picked up from bookshops, cafés and restaurants around Oxford Street or viewed on line from their website.

Sydney just can't wait all year for Mardi Gras, so the **Sleaze Ball** is a very welcome stopgap in early October and acts as a fundraiser for the Mardi Gras organizers. Similar to the Mardi Gras party, it's held at the Fox Studios, and goes on through the night. Tickets, which cost around $110, are organized by New Mardi Gras and sold through Ticketek. The community centre **PRIDE** (Ⓣ02/9331 1333; Ⓦwww.pridecentre.com.au) have been organizing a similarly priced and over-the-top **New Year's Eve party** for the past decade, usually also at Fox Studios.

For those who miss the parties themselves, the **recovery parties** the next day are nearly as good; virtually all the bars and clubs host all-day sessions after the parties especially the lanes behind the *Flinders Bar*, which are packed with exhausted but deliriously happy party people.

Groups and information

Information The Bookshop, 207 Oxford St, Darlinghurst (Ⓣ02/9331 1103), is a good starting point for getting to know gay Sydney, with a complete stock of gay- and lesbian-related books, cards and magazines. The staff are friendly and ready to help in any way they can. You can pick up the free gay and lesbian weeklies *Sydney Star Observer* (Ⓦwww.ssonet.com.au) and *SX* (Ⓦwww.sxnews.com.au) and the monthly lesbian-specific *LOTL* (*Lesbians on the Loose*; Ⓦwww.lotl.com) from here and other venues and gay-friendly businesses in the eastern suburbs and inner west. These magazines will tell you where and when the weekly dance parties are being held, and where you can buy tickets.

Support networks Gay & Lesbian Counselling Service (daily 4pm–midnight; Ⓣ02/ 8594 9596). AIDS Council of NSW (ACON), 9 Commonwealth St, Surry Hills Ⓣ02/9206 2000. Albion Street Centre, 150–154 Albion St, Surry Hills Ⓣ02/9332 1090; counselling, testing clinic, information and library. Anti-Discrimination Board Ⓣ02/9268 5544.

Gay and lesbian Sydney (Contd.)

Travel agents

Specifically gay and lesbian travel agents seem to be almost a thing of the past in Sydney but most of the regular agencies in Oxford St will be able to help you with any travel promotions that are tailor-made to suit the gay or lesbian traveller.

Mardi Gras Travel level 10, 130 Elizabeth St ⓣ02/9268 2188, ⓦwww.redoyster.com. Offers tailor-made packages and trips for gay and lesbian groups or individuals.

See also p.121 for gay- and lesbian-friendly **places to stay**, and pp.194–195 for a lowdown on the **club scene** and listings of specifically gay and lesbian venues.

Conservatorium of Music Royal Botanic Gardens, off Macquarie St, City ⓣ02/9351 1263. Students of the "Con" give free lunchtime recitals every Wednesday at 1.10pm during term time in Recital Hall West. Other concerts, both free and ticketed (anywhere from $10 up to around $35) are given by students and staff here and at venues around town; a programme is available from the concert department. See p.144 for more details.

Eugene Goossens Hall ABC Centre, Harris St, Ultimo ⓣ02/9333 1500. Auditorium (320-seater) with state-of-the-art acoustics within the radio headquarters of the ABC, used for reasonably priced ABC Classic FM Recital Series and occasional free lunchtime concerts.

St James' Church King St, beside Hyde Park, City ⓣ02/9232 3022. St James' highly acclaimed chamber choir, whose repertoire extends from Gregorian chants to more contemporary pieces, can be heard on Sundays at 11am (plus 4pm last Sun of the month). St James' music programme also includes a series of free lunchtime concerts (Wed 1.15pm; 30min).

Sydney Opera House Bennelong Point ⓣ02/9250 7777. The Opera House is, of course, *the* place for the most prestigious performances in Sydney, hosting not just opera and classical music but also theatre and ballet in its many auditoriums. Forget quibbles about ticket prices (classical concerts from $50, ballet from $65, opera from $95) – it's worth going just to say you've been. See pp.122–130 for more details.

Town Hall Cnr Druitt and George streets, City ⓣ02/9265 9189. Centrally located concert hall (seats 2000) with a splendid high-Victorian interior – hosts everything from chamber orchestras to bush dances and public lectures.

Theatre and dance

Bangarra Dance Theatre Pier 4, Hickson Rd, Millers Point, The Rocks ⓣ02/9251 5333. Formed in 1989, Bangarra's innovative style fuses contemporary movement with the traditional dances and culture of the Yirrkala Community in Arnhem Land. Based at the same pier as the Wharf Theatre but performing at other venues in Sydney and touring nationally and internationally – call for the latest details.

Belvoir St Theatre 25 Belvoir St, Surry Hills ⓣ02/9699 3444. Highly regarded two-stage venue for a wide range of contemporary Australian and international theatre.

Capitol Theatre 13 Campbell St, Haymarket ⓣ02/9320 5000. Built as a deluxe picture theatre in the 1920s, the building was saved from demolition and beautifully restored in the mid-1990s. The 2000-seater now hosts big-budget musicals and ballet, watched from beneath its best feature, the deep-blue ceiling spangled with the stars of the southern skies.

Ensemble Theatre 78 McDougall St, Milsons Point ⓣ02/9929 0644. Hosts Australian contemporary and classic plays.

The Footbridge Theatre Parramatta Rd, University of Sydney, Glebe ⓣ02/9692 9955. Rich and varied repertoire, from *Cabaret* to Shakespeare.

Lyric Theatre Star City Casino, Pirrama Rd, Pyrmont ⓣ02/9657 9657. The place to see those big musical extravaganzas imported from the West End and Broadway. The casino's smaller theatre, the Star City Showroom, puts on more off-beat musicals – such as the *Rocky Horror Picture Show* – and comedy.

NAISDA Dance College 3 Cumberland St, The Rocks ⓣ02/9252 0199. Established in 1976, this famous training company for young Aboriginal and Islander dancers, based in The Rocks, puts on mid-year and end-of-year performances at the NAISDA Studios at the college; call for times.

The Playhouse, Drama Theatre and The Studio Sydney Opera House, Bennelong Point ⓣ02/9250 7777. The three theatrical venues at the Opera House, The Playhouse and Drama Theatre show modern and traditional Australian and international plays mostly put on by the Sydney Theatre Company, while the Studio, the Opera House's smallest venue (with the most affordable ticket prices), is flexible in design with a theatre-in-the-round format, and offers an innovative and wide-ranging programme of contemporary performance: theatre, cabaret, dance, comedy, and hybrid works.

Theatre Royal MLC Centre, King St, City (bookings through Ticketek ⓣ02/9266 4800). Imported musicals and blockbuster plays.

Wharf Theatre Pier 4/5, Hickson Rd, Millers Point, The Rocks ⓣ02/9250 1777. Home to the Sydney Dance Company and the highly regarded Sydney Theatre Company, producing Shakespeare and modern pieces. Atmospheric waterfront location, two performance spaces, and a good restaurant (see p.179), bar and café.

Fringe theatre, comedy and cabaret

As well as the venues listed below, also see the *Bridge Hotel* (p.192) which has Monday comedy nights and Tuesday improv and cabaret runs, and *The Imperial* (p.194) for its brilliant free drag shows.

New Theatre 542 King St, Newtown ⓣ02/9519 8958. Professional and amateur actors (all unpaid) perform contemporary dramas with socially relevant themes. Tickets $25.

NIDA 215 Anzac Parade, Kensington ⓣ02/9697 7613. Australia's premier dramatic training ground – the National Institute of Dramatic Art – where the likes of Mel Gibson and Judy Davis and Colin Friels started out, also offers student productions for talent-spotting. Tickets $25.

The Performance Space 199 Cleveland St, Redfern, opposite Prince Alfred Park ⓣ02/9698 7235. Experimental performances.

Stables Theatre 10 Nimrod St, Darlinghurst ⓣ02/9361 3817. Home theatre for the Griffin Theatre Company whose mission is to develop and foster new Australian playwrights.

Sydney Comedy Store Fox Studios, Driver Ave, Moore Park ⓣ02/9357 1419. International (often American) and Australian stand-up comics Thurs to Saturday; open mic nights Tues and new comics Wed. Bar open from 7pm, show 8.30pm. Meals aren't available inside, but the lively *Dog Gone Bar* offers meal discounts for *Comedy Store* ticket holders. Bookings recommended. Entry Tues & Wed $15, Thurs $20, Fri & Sat $27.50.

Cinemas

The commercial movie centre of Sydney is two blocks south of the Town Hall at 505–525 George Street where you'll find the two big chains – Hoyts (ⓣ02/9273 7431) and Greater Union (ⓣ02/9267 8666) under one roof. This is mainstream, fast-food, teenager territory and there are much nicer places to watch a film, especially at the locals in the list below. Other more pleasantly located Hoyts can be found at the Broadway Shopping Centre, on Broadway near Glebe (ⓣ02/9211 1911); and at the 12-screen Hoyts at Fox Studios (ⓣ02/9332 1300), where five of the screens have an upmarket La Premiere section aimed at couples with double seats (bookings ⓣ02/9332 1300 ext 5; $25–$30 includes soft drinks and popcorn). Hoyts arthouse option, the four-screen Cinema Paris ((ⓣ02/9332 1633), is also at Fox Studios. Another mainstream multiplex is bang in Chinatown, Reading Cinemas, at Level 3, Market City Shopping Centre, Haymarket (ⓣ02/9280 1202). Standard tickets cost around $15, but Tuesdays are reduced-price (around $10.50) at all of these cinemas and their suburban outlets, and Monday or Tuesday at most of the arthouse and local cinemas listed below.

In the summer, two open-air cinemas open up: from November to the end of March the **Moonlight Cinema**, in the Centennial Park Amphitheatre (Oxford Street, Woollahra entrance; Tues–Sun, films start 8.45pm, tickets from 7pm or bookings on ⓣ1300 551 908; $14.50), shows classic, arthouse and cult films; and throughout January and February, the **Open Air Cinema** (tickets from 6.30pm or bookings on ⓣ13 61 00; $19) is put up at Mrs Macquarie's Point in the Royal Botanic Gardens for a very picturesque film screening

Film festivals

The **Sydney Film Festival**, held annually for two weeks in **early June**, is an exciting programme of features, shorts, documentaries and retrospective screenings from Australia and around the world. Founded in 1954 by a group of film enthusiasts at Sydney University, the festival struggled with prudish censors and parochial attitudes until freedom from censorship for festival films was introduced in 1971. From the early, relaxed atmosphere of picnics on the lawns between screenings and hardy film-lovers crouching under blankets in freezing prefabricated sheds, it has gradually moved off-campus, to find a home from 1974 in the magnificent State Theatre (see p.137). Films are also shown at the wonderfully sited three-screen Dendy Quays in Circular Quay. The festival was once mainly sold on a subscription basis, but subscriptions now only apply to screenings at the State Theatre; the more provocative line-up of films at the Dendy Quays aims to attract a new, younger audience on a single or packaged ticket basis. Single **tickets** cost around $15, selected film packages of five to ten $12.50 each, eleven or more $11 each or if you can't decide, there are 10- or 20-film Flexi Passes for $120/$200; **subscriptions** for the State Theatre programme start from $170 for one week daytime only unreserved stalls seating, and go up to $290 for two weeks reserved dress circle night-time screenings. For more information, call or drop into the festival office at Level 5, 414–418 Elizabeth St, Surry Hills (Mon–Fri 9am–5pm; ⓣ02/9280 0511; bookings ⓣ02/9280 0611 or via ⓦwww.sydneyfilmfestival.org).

There are also two short film festivals in the summer with the sort of irreverent approach which once fuelled the Sydney Film Festival. Stars above and the sound of waves accompany the week-long **Flickerfest International Short Film Festival** (single ticket $14, season pass $120; ⓣ02/9365 6888, ⓦwww.flickerfest.com.au), held in the amphitheatre of the Bondi Pavilion in early January, and showcasing foreign and Australian productions, including documentaries. The **Tropfest** (ⓣ02/9368 0434, ⓦwww.tropfest.com) is a competition festival for short films held annually around the end of February; its name comes from the *Tropicana Cafe* (see p.184) on Victoria Street, Darlinghurst, where the festival began almost by chance in 1993 when a young actor, John Polsen, forced his local coffee spot to show the short film he had made. He pushed other filmmakers to follow suit, and the following year a huge crowd of punters packed themselves into the café to watch around twenty films. These days the entire street is closed to traffic to enable an outdoor screening, while cafés along the strip also screen the films inside. The festival has grown enormously over the years, and the focus of the event in Sydney has moved to The Domain, with huge crowds turning up to picnic and watch the free 8pm screening (plus live entertainment from 3pm), while outdoor screenings are held simultaneously in capital cities Australia-wide. The judges are often famous international actors and Polsen himself, still the festival's director, has made it as a Hollywood director with his 2002 film *Swimfan* and 2005 film *Hide and Seek*. Each state capital also screens the event simultaneously in venues ranging from cafés to parks. Films must be specifically produced for the festival and be up-to-the-minute – an item is announced a few months in advance of the entry date which must feature in the shorts. In 2005 it was "umbrella" – however you wanted to interpret it.

Other film festivals include the **World of Women (WOW) Film Festival** held over three days in late October at the Chauvel Cinema, Paddington (ⓦwww.FutureTrain.com.au/wift/wow); and a **gay and lesbian film festival** in late February as part of the Gay and Lesbian Mardi Gras.

– mainly mainstream recent releases and some classics. See box opposite for details of Sydney's annual film festivals.

Chauvel Twin Cinema Paddington Town Hall, cnr Oatley Rd and Oxford St, Paddington ⓣ02/9361 5398. Varied programme of Australian and foreign films plus classics at this cinephile's cinema. The $45 four-film pass or $100 ten-film pass can also be used at the Valhalla (see below). Discount on Mon and Tues.

Cremorne Orpheum 380 Military Rd, Cremorne ⓣ02/9908 4344. Charming heritage-listed, six-screen cinema built in 1935 with a splendid Art Deco interior and old-fashioned friendly service. The main cinema has never dispensed with its Wurlitzer organ recitals preceding Saturday night and Sunday afternoon films. Mainstream, and foreign new releases. Discount on Tues.

Dendy 261 King St, Newtown ⓣ02/9550 5699. Trendy four-screen cinema complex with attached café, bar and bookshop, shows prestige new-release films. The newer, three-screen Dendy Opera Quays, 2 East Circular Quay (ⓣ02/9247 3800) is superbly sited. Discount on Mon.

Govinda's Movie Room 112 Darlinghurst Rd, Darlinghurst ⓣ02/9380 5155. Run by the Hare Krishnas (but definitely no indoctrination), *Govinda's* shows two films every night from a range of classics and recent releases in a pleasantly unorthodox cushion-room atmosphere. The movie and dinner deal (all-you-can-eat vegetarian buffet) is popular – $15.90 for the meal with an extra $4 to see a movie. Buy your film ticket after you've ordered your meal, or you may miss out on busy nights. Film only is $10.90 but diners are given preference.

IMAX Theatre Southern Promenade, Darling Harbour ⓣ02/9281 3300. State-of-the-art giant cinema screen showing a choice of four films designed to thrill your senses; $16 for 2-D version, $17–$20 for 3-D. Screenings on the hour, 10am–10pm.

Palace Cinemas Chain of inner-city cinemas showing foreign-language, arthouse and new releases: Academy, 3A Oxford St, cnr South Dowling St, Paddington (ⓣ02/9361 4453); Verona, 17 Oxford St, cnr Verona St, Paddington (ⓣ02/9360 6099), with a bar; Norton, 99 Norton St, Leichhardt (ⓣ02/9550 0122), the newest with a bookshop and cybercafé. Discount Mon.

Valhalla 166 Glebe Point Rd, Glebe ⓣ02/9660 8050. The beloved Valhalla, Sydney's first alternative cinema (established in 1976), shows documentaries, foreign films, new-release independents and Australian films on two screens. Specialist evenings – including short film nights – draw in local filmmakers for screenings and discussions. No discount day, but $45 four-film or $100 ten-film passes can also be used at the Chauvel (above).

Art galleries and exhibitions

The Citysearch Sydney website (ⓦwww.sydney.citysearch.com.au) has comprehensive listings of art galleries and current exhibitions, while Friday's "Metro" section of the *Sydney Morning Herald* offers reviews of recently opened shows, or check out the useful *Artfind Guide* online (ⓦwww.artfind.com.au). Galleries tend to be concentrated in Paddington and Surry Hills, with a few smaller ones on King Street, Newtown.

Artspace The Gunnery Arts Centre, 43–51 Cowper Wharf Rd, Woolloomooloo ⓣ02/9368 1899. In a wonderful location, showing provocative young artists with a focus on installations and new media. Tues–Sat 11am–5pm.

Australian Centre for Photography 257 Oxford St, Paddington ⓣ02/9332 1455. Exhibitions of photo-based art from established and new international and Australian artists in two galleries. Emerging photographers are showcased on the Project Wall. There's a specialist bookshop, photography courses and a dark room for hire, plus the very good French-style *Bistro Lulu*. Tues–Sat 11am–6pm.

Australian Galleries: Painting & Sculpture 15 Roylston St, Paddington ⓣ02/9360 5177. Serene gallery exhibiting and selling contemporary Australian art, including works by Gary Shead, Jeffrey Smart and John Coburn. Mon–Sat 10am–6pm.

Australian Galleries: Works on Paper 24 Glenmore Rd, Paddington ⓣ02/9380 8744. Works for sale here include drawings by William Robinson, Brett Whiteley and Arthur Boyd, as well as prints and sketches by young Australian artists. Tues–Sat 10am–6pm, Sun noon–5pm.

Hogarth Galleries Aboriginal Art Centre 7 Walker Lane, Paddington ⓣ02/9360 6839. Extensive collection of work by contemporary Aboriginal artists, both tribal and urban, and special exhibitions. Tues–Sat 10am–5pm.

Ivan Dougherty Gallery Cnr Albion Ave and Selwyn St, Paddington ⓣ02/9385 0726. This is the exhibition space for the College of Fine Arts (COFA), University of NSW. The ten shows per year focus on international contemporary art with accompanying forums, lectures and performances. Mon–Sat 10am–5pm.

Josef Lebovic Gallery 34 Paddington St, Paddington ⓣ02/9332 1840. Renowned print and graphic gallery specializing in Australian and international prints from the nineteenth, twentieth and twenty-first centuries, as well as vintage photography. Wed–Fri 1–6pm, Sat 11am–5pm.

The Performance Space 199 Cleveland St, Redfern, opposite Prince Alfred Park ⓣ02/9698 7235. Experimental multimedia and plastic arts: installations, sculpture, photography and painting. Wed–Fri noon–6pm.

Ray Hughes Gallery 270 Devonshire St, Surry Hills ⓣ02/9698 3200. Influential dealer with a stable of high-profile contemporary Australian and New Zealand artists. Openings monthly, with two artists per show. Tues–Sat 10am–6pm.

Roslyn Oxley9 Gallery 8 Soudan Lane, off Hampden St, Paddington ⓣ02/9331 1919. Avant-garde videos and installations among the Australian and international offerings. Tues–Fri 10am–6pm, Sat 11am–6pm.

Festivals and events

The Sydney year is interspersed with festivals and events of various sorts that reach their peak in the summer. Check City of Sydney Council's online "What's On" section (ⓦwww.cityofsydney.nsw.gov.au) for details of events year-round, or its free weekly listings *City Life* comes out Wednesday and is available at the Town Hall and tourist offices.

The **New Year** begins with a spectacular **fireworks** display from the Harbour Bridge and Darling Harbour. There's a brief hiatus of a week or so until the annual **Sydney Festival** (ⓣ02/8248 6500, ⓦwww.sydneyfestival.org.au), an exhaustive and exhausting arts event that lasts for most of **January** and ranges from concerts, plays and outdoor art installations to circus performances. About fifty percent of the events are free and are based around urban public spaces, focusing on Circular Quay, The Domain, Darling Harbour, and Sydney Olympic Park; the remainder – mostly international performances – can cost a packet. The general programme is usually printed in the *Sydney Morning Herald* in October while a full eighty-plus-page programme is available nearer the time. From Boxing Day to the end of January, **Darling Harbour** hosts its own festival (see ⓦwww.darlingharbour.com.au), linked with the Festival of Sydney. Most of the attractions are aimed at children, but the very lively **Bacardi Latino Festival** is perfect for a balmy evening.

Australia Day on January 26 is a huge celebration in Sydney, with activities focused on the water (see Australia Day Council of NSW; ⓦwww.australiaday.com.au). Sydney's passenger ferries race from Fort Denison to the Harbour Bridge, there's the Tall Ships Race from Bradleys Head to the Harbour Bridge, a 21-gun salute fired from the Man O'War steps at the Opera House, and an aerial display of military planes. The **Australia Day Regatta** takes place in the afternoon, with hundreds of yachts racing all over the water, from Botany Bay to the Parramatta River. There are also free events at The Rocks, Hyde Park, and at Darling Harbour, where the day culminates at around 9pm with a fireworks display. In addition, many museums let visitors in for free. Besides all this, there are at least two outdoor rock concerts to choose from: **Yabun** (formerly 'Survival'), which celebrates Aboriginal culture and acts as an antidote to the mainstream white Australia Day festivities, is held at Redfern Oval (free; no alcohol allowed; contact Koori Radio on ⓣ02/9564 5904 or check ⓦwww.gadigal.org.au); while the **Big Day Out** (see p.192) is usually held that day at the Showground at Homebush Bay, featuring around sixty local and international bands and DJs.

Horse racing in Sydney

There are horse-racing meetings on Wednesday, Saturday and most public holidays throughout the year, but the best times to hit the track are during the **Spring and Autumn Carnivals** (Aug–Sept and March–April), when prize money rockets, and the quality of racing rivals the best in the world. The venues are well maintained, peopled with colourful racing characters, and often massive crowds. Principal **racecourses** are: Royal Randwick (Alison Rd, Randwick), which featured in *Mission Impossible 2*; Rosehill Gardens (James Ruse Drive, Rosehill); and Canterbury Park (King St, Canterbury), which has midweek racing, plus floodlit Thursday-night racing from September to March. Entry is around $10, or $15–20 on carnival days. Contact the Australian Jockey Club (Ⓣ02/9663 8400) for details of many other picturesque country venues to choose from. Every Friday the *Sydney Morning Herald* publishes its racing guide, "The Form". Bets are placed at TAB shops; these are scattered throughout the city, and most pubs also have TAB access.

An entirely different side of Sydney life is on view at the impressive summer **surf carnivals**, staged regularly by local surf lifesaving clubs; contact Surf Life Saving NSW (Ⓣ02/9984 7188, Ⓦwww.surflifesaving.com.au) for details.

At the end of **February** the city is engulfed by the **Sydney Gay & Lesbian Mardi Gras**. Another big event is the **Sydney Royal Easter Show** (Ⓦwww.eastershow.com.au), an agricultural and garden show in late **March/early April**, based at the Sydney Showground at Homebush Bay. For twelve consecutive days (with the second weekend always the Easter weekend) the country comes to the city for a frantic array of amusement-park rides, fireworks, parades of prize animals, a rodeo, and wood-chopping displays. In **May**, the week-long **Sydney Writers Festival** (mostly free; Ⓦwww.swf.org.au) takes place in the very scenically located Wharf Theatre complex.

The **Sydney International Film Festival** takes over many of the city's screens in **June** (see box on p.200). Every even-numbered year, the **Biennale of Sydney** takes place over six weeks from early June until mid-August, with provocative contemporary art exhibitions at various venues and public spaces around town and the **City to Surf Race**, a 14-km fun run from the city to Bondi, happens every **August**. Labour Day weekend in early **October** is marked by the **Manly International Jazz Festival**, with several free outdoor, waterfront events and a few indoor concerts charging entry. This is followed by the very Italian **Blessing of the Fleet** at Darling Harbour. In **November**, the coast between Bondi and Tamarama is transformed for two weeks by the magical **Sculpture By The Sea** exhibition (Ⓦwww.sculpturebythesea.com.au). The year is brought to a close by the **Sydney to Hobart Yacht Race**, when it seems that half of Sydney turns up at or on the harbour on December 26 to cheer the start of this classic regatta and watch the colourful spectacle of two hundred or so yachts setting sail for a 630-nautical-mile slog.

Shopping

Sydney's main shopping focus is the city centre, in the stretch between Martin Place and the Queen Victoria Building. Apart from its charming old nineteenth-century arcades and two **department stores**, David Jones and Myers, the city centre also has several modern multilevel **shopping complexes** where you can hunt down clothes and accessories without raising a sweat, among them Skygarden (between Pitt and Castlereagh streets) and Centrepoint on Pitt Street Mall, on the corner of Market Street. Much of the area from the QVB to the mall is linked by underground arcades which will also keep you cool.

Most stores are **open** Monday to Saturday 8.30am to 5.30pm, with Thursday late-night shopping until 9pm. Many of the larger shops and department stores in the city are also open on Sunday 10am to 5pm, as are shopping centres in tourist areas such as Darling Harbour. If you've run out of time to buy presents and souvenirs, don't worry: the revamped **Sydney Airport** is attached to one of the biggest shopping malls in Sydney, with outlets for everything from surfwear to R.M. Williams bush outfitters, at the same prices as the downtown stores. The Rocks is the best place for souvenir and duty- and GST-free shopping.

Fashion

Oxford Street in Paddington is the place to go for interesting fashion, with outlets of most Australian designers along the strip. You'll find more expensive designer gear in the city, at the Strand Arcade, 412 George St, and David Jones Department Store (see p.137). For striking street fashion check out Crown Street in Surry Hills, with places such as Wheels & Doll Baby at no. 259 and Dangerfield at no. 330, and King Street in Newtown running up to St Peters, where you'll also find cheaper styles, retro clothes and other interesting junk. To go with the outfits, funky Australian **jewellery** can be found in the Strand Arcade at Dinosaur Designs (also at 339 Oxford St, Paddington), and at Love and Hatred, both on Level 1.

For Australian **workwear** head for Gowings, a delightfully old-fashioned **menswear** department store on the corner of Market and George streets. This beloved Sydney institution, in business for over 135 years, has everything a bloke (and often a sheila) could want, from Bonds T-shirts to Speedo swimwear, Blundestone boots and a range of felt hats at the best prices in town. Two other branches are at 319 George St, near Wynyard station and 82 Oxford St, Darlinghurst. The quality **bush outfitters** R. M. Williams, with branches at no. 71 and no. 389 George Street, is great for moleskin trousers, Drizabone coats and superb leather riding boots. For the widest range of Akubra **hats**, check out Strand Hatters on the ground floor of the Strand Arcade. If it's interesting **surfwear** you're after, head for Mambo at Market City, Hay St, Haymarket (also at 17 Oxford St, Paddington; 80 The Corso, Manly; and 80 Campbell Parade, Bondi Beach) and an array of surf shops at Manly and Bondi Beach.

Arts and crafts

The Rocks is heaving with **Australiana** and **arts and crafts** souvenirs, from opals to sheepskin. Tourists flock to Ken Done's emporium here at 123 George St and 1–5 Hickson Rd (in the restored Australian Steam and Navigation Building) to buy his colourful designs, which feature Sydney's harbour, boats and flowers; there's a Done Art & Design store at the airport, too, and another at Market City.

The Rocks is also a focus for **Aboriginal art** (see also "Art Galleries and exhibitions", p.201): the Aboriginal and Tribal Art Centre, 1st floor, 117 George St, has a huge collection of traditional Aboriginal art from around Australia. However, the best place to buy Aboriginal art and crafts is the Aboriginal-owned and -run Gavala, in the Harbourside shopping centre in Darling Harbour. A great place to buy **boomerangs** is The Boomerang School, at 224a William St, Kings Cross, which has been run for over 40 years by Duncan MacLennon. The boomerangs sold here are mostly authentic, made by Aboriginal artisans from around Australia. Though insurance now precludes Duncan from his free boomerang-throwing lessons in a nearby park, he still promises to provide in-store tips.

Music and books

For a take-home sample of the **Australian music** scene in all its variety, from Aboriginal through to indie and jazz, head for the Australian Music Centre shop, Level 4, The Arts Exchange, 18 Hickson Rd, The Rocks, with very knowledgeable staff and a relaxed listen-before-you-buy policy.

One of the biggest **bookshops** in the city is the long-running, Australian-owned Dymocks, 428 George St, open daily, on several floors with an impressive Australian selection and a café. Book superstores include Kinokuniya in Galleries Victoria, on the corner of George and Park streets; Borders, 77 Castlereagh St, between King and Market streets; and Collins Superstore, Level 2, Broadway Shopping Centre near Glebe. Nearby, Gleebooks, 49 Glebe Point Rd, Glebe, is one of Australia's best bookshops, specializing in academic and alternative books, contemporary Australian and international literature, and is open daily until 9pm; book launches and other literary events are regularly held. Ariel has two large, lively and hip branches, one at 103 George St, The Rocks and the other at 42 Oxford St, Paddington; both branches open daily until midnight. Macleay Bookshop, 103 Macleay St, Potts Point (daily until 9pm), is a tiny and peaceful choice. **The Travel Bookshop** at 175 Liverpool St (closed Sun) is the place to head for maps, guides and travel journals, plus a good selection of Australiana. **Secondhand books** can be found at Glebe and Paddington markets, at Gleebooks Second Hand Books, 191 Glebe Point Rd (daily until 9pm); upstairs at Lesley McKays Bookshop, 346 New South Head Rd, Double Bay (the ground level, for new books, is open until midnight); and in the secondhand bookshops on King Street, Newtown – in particular check out the amazingly chaotic piles of books at Gould's Book Arcade, nos. 32–38 (daily 7am–midnight).

Food and drink

There are several handy **supermarkets** in the city centre with extended opening hours: one is in the basement of Woolworths on the corner of Park and George streets, above Town Hall station (Mon–Fri 6.30am–midnight, Sat & Sun 8am–midnight); and there are three small Coles supermarkets in the city; Wynyard station; 388 George St; and 580 George St in the Pavilion Central Shopping Centre (daily 6am–midnight), while the larger Coles in Kings Cross, at 88 Darlinghurst Rd, and on Broadway near Glebe are both also handy for travellers (all daily 6am–midnight). In the suburbs, large supermarkets such as Coles stay open daily until about 10pm or midnight, and there are plenty of (albeit overpriced) 24-hour convenience stores in the inner city and suburbs, often attached to petrol stations. For **delicatessen** items, look no further than the splendid food hall at David Jones (see p.178). The **Australian Wine Centre**, cnr George and Alfred streets, Circular Quay (Mon–Sat 9.30am–6.30pm, Sun 11am–5pm), sells more than a thousand **wines** from around Australia and even has an in-house wine bar.

Markets

The two best **markets** are the Paddington Market (9am–4pm) and Balmain Market (7.30am–4pm), both on Saturday, while the relaxed Glebe Market (10am–4pm), also on a Saturday, and flea market at Rozelle (Sat & Sun

9am–4pm) are also worth a look. The Rocks Market on George Street (Sat & Sun 10am–5pm), is more touristy but worth a browse, while Paddy's Market (Thurs–Sun 9am–5pm) in Haymarket near the Entertainment Centre and Chinatown, is Sydney's oldest, selling fruit and veg, deli products, meat and fish, plus large quantities of bargain-basement clothes and toys. There's also a series of alternating Saturday markets on the North Shore; the scenically sited Kirribilli Market (fourth Sat of month) is the best-known. Foodies should check out the series of **produce markets**: at Pyrmont Bay Park in front of the Star City Casino (first Sat of month 7–11am); at the Showring at Fox Studios (Wed & Sat 10am–4pm); and at Northside Produce Market at the Civic Centre, Miller St, North Sydney, between Ridge and McClaren streets (third Sat of month 8am–noon).

Listings

Airlines (domestic) Aeropelican (☎13 13 00) to Belmont or Williamtown, both nr Newcastle; Qantas, see address below (☎13 13 13), Australia-wide including Albury, Armidale, Ballina, Coffs Harbour, Dubbo, Lord Howe Island, Moree, Narrabri, Newcastle, Norfolk Island, Port Macquarie, Tamworth and Wagga Wagga; Regional Express (REX; ☎13 17 13) to Albury, Armidale, Ballina, Bathurst, Broken Hill, Dubbo, Griffith, Lismore, Merimbula, Mildura, Moruya, Narrandera, Orange, Parkes and Wagga Wagga; Big Sky Express (☎1800 008 759) to Inverell, Gunnedah, Taree, Grafton and Coonabarabran, plus Cooma during ski season; Air Link (☎02/6884 2435), to Dubbo, Mudgee, Lightning Ridge, Bourke, Cobar, Coonamble and Walgett; Jetstar (☎13 15 38) to Cairns, Gold Coast, Hamilton Island, Hobart, Launceston, Mackay, Rockhampton, Sunshine Coast and Whitsunday Coast; Virgin Blue (☎13 67 89) Australia-wide to all state capitals as well as much of coastal Queensland, and Coffs Harbour.

Airlines (international) Aeroflot, Level 24, 44 Market St ☎02/9262 2233; Aerolineas Argentinas, Level 3, 64 Clarence St ☎1300 131 744; Air Canada, Level 18, Australia Square, 264 George St ☎1300 655 767; Air New Zealand, Level 4, 10 Barrack St ☎13 24 76; Alitalia, 64 York St ☎02/9244 2400; British Airways, Level 19, AAP Centre, 259 George St ☎1300 767 177; Cathay Pacific ☎13 17 47; Continental, 64 York St ☎02/9244 2242; Delta, Level 9, 189 Kent St ☎02/9251 3211; Finnair, 64 York St ☎02/9244 2299; Garuda, 55 Hunter St ☎1300 365 330; Gulf Air, 12/403 George St ☎02/9244 2149; Japan Airlines, Level 14, 201 Sussex St ☎02/9272 1111; KLM, 13th floor, 115 Pitt St ☎1300 303 747; Korean Air, level 4, 333 George St ☎02/9262 6000; Lauda Air, Level 2, 1 York St ☎02/9251 6155; Malaysia Airlines, 16 Spring St ☎13 26 27; Olympic, 3rd Floor, 37–49 Pitt St ☎02/9251 1047; Qantas, 70 Hunter St, cnr Phillip St ☎13 13 13; Scandinavian Airlines, Level 15, 31 Market St ☎1300 727 707; Singapore Airlines, 17–19 Bridge St ☎13 10 11; Swiss International, Level 3, 117 York St ☎1300 724 666; Thai Airways, 75 Pitt St ☎1300 651 960; United, Level 6, 10 Barrack St ☎13 17 77.

Banks and foreign exchange Head offices of banks are mostly in the CBD, around Martin Place; hours are Mon–Thurs 9.30am–4pm, Fri 9.30am–5pm, with some suburban branches open later and on Saturday. American Express outlets include 105 Pitt St (Mon–Fri 9am–5pm; ☎1300 139 060); 296 George St (daily 8.30am–5.30pm); Quay Grand Hotel, Circular Quay East (Mon–Fri 9am–5pm, Sat & Sun 11am–4pm); lost or stolen traveller's cheques ☎1800 251 902. Money can also be exchanged at Travelex bureaux de change at the airport and several city locations including the Queen Victoria Building at Shop 64, Lower Ground Floor (Mon–Fri 9am–5.45pm, Sat 10am–3pm) and 37–49 Pitt St, near Central station (Mon–Fri 9am–5.15pm, Sat 10am–2.45pm; ☎02/9241 5722). UAE Money Exchange, Shop 175 Harbourside shopping centre, Darling Harbour (Mon–Fri 9.30am–9pm, Sat & Sun 10am–9pm; ☎02/9212 7124).

Camping equipment and rental Kent Street in the city behind the Town Hall (and near YHA headquarters) is nicknamed "adventure alley" for its preponderance of outdoor equipment stores; the best known is the high-quality Paddy Pallin at no. 507. Cheaper options include army surplus stores at the downtown ends of George and Pitt streets near Central station, and suburban K-Mart stores (closest stores to the city are at Spring St, Bondi

Cars: buying and selling

Sydney is the most popular place to buy a car or campervan in which to travel around Australia; the information below is specific to buying a car in NSW – for general background on buying and selling a car, see pp.53–55.

Before you start looking, it's a good idea to join the NRMA motoring association, 74 King St, City (Ⓣ13 21 32, Ⓦwww.mynrma.com.au; $49.50 joining fee plus $69.50 annual charge; overseas motoring association members have reciprocal membership); membership entitles you to roadside assistance and a reduced rate for a vehicle inspection of a potential purchase ($199; bookings Ⓣ13 11 22). The NRMA's website has an excellent "Motoring" section where you can find out market prices and cars for sale. The Office of Fair Trading's useful *The Car Buyers Handbook: Buying and maintaining a car in NSW* can be viewed online (Ⓣ13 32 20, Ⓦwww.fairtrading.nsw.gov.au), while the Roads and Traffic Authority (RTA; Ⓣ13 22 13, Ⓦwww.rta.nsw.gov.au) prints *The Guide to Purchasing a Secondhand Vehicle*. Thursday's *Weekly Trading Post* (or check Ⓦwww.tradingpost.com.au) has a big secondhand car section. The *Sydney Morning Herald*'s Friday "Drive" supplement has ads for secondhand dealers (most on Parramatta Rd from Annandale onwards) and private used cars for sale at the pricier end of the market. Demand to see a "pink slip" (certificate of roadworthiness) that is less than 28 days old. If you're serious about buying, contact REVS (Ⓣ02/9633 6333, Ⓦwww.revs.nsw.gov.au) to check if there are any payments owing or unpaid parking fines and call the RTA (above) to check registration is still current.

Sydney is well equipped with dealerships who will arrange to **buy back** the vehicle they've sold you at the end of your trip – expect to get thirty to fifty percent back. The two longest running are **Auto Becker**, 752 Parramatta Rd, Lewisham (Ⓣ02/9568 4455), who also offer a twelve-month warranty on most cars, and **Travellers Auto Barn**, 177 William St, Kings Cross (Ⓣ02/9360 1500, Ⓦwww.travellers-autobarn.com.au), with offices in Melbourne, Brisbane, Cairns, Perth and Darwin.

The **Kings Cross Car Market**, Kings Cross Car Park, Level 2, Ward Ave (daily 9am–6pm; Ⓣ02/9358 5000 or 1800 808 188, Ⓦwww.carmarket.com.au), is specifically aimed at travellers with help with paperwork and contract exchange provided. It's also one of the few places where you will be able to sell a car registered in another state. Dealers are barred, and fees for sellers are $60–$85 per week. Many of the vehicles come equipped with camping gear and other extras. Third-party property **insurance** ($260 for 3 months, $425 for 12 months) can be arranged – the NRMA often refuses to cover overseas travellers. It's worth checking the Car Market's website, where sellers can advertise for $20. **Paddy's Motor Market**, held on Sunday at Flemington Market opposite Flemington station, Austen Avenue entrance (8am–4pm; Ⓣ1300 361 589, Ⓦwww.paddysmotormarket.com.au; selling fees $55 for two Sundays), is better for buying than selling: if you're trying to sell a vehicle that's travelled around Australia, particularly if the clock is past 200,000km, local buyers won't be interested.

Junction and at the Broadway Shopping Centre, Bay St) or hostel notice boards. Only a few places rent gear, mostly based in the suburbs: try Alpsport, 1045 Victoria Rd, West Ryde (Ⓣ02/9858 5844) with weekend rental of a backpack for around $32, sleeping bag from $27, and tent from $30.

Consulates Embassies are all in Canberra (see p.282), and it's usually easier to call them when in difficulty than to go to the consulates in Sydney: Canadian, Level 5, 111 Harrington St Ⓣ02/9364 3000; New Zealand, Level 10, 55 Hunter St Ⓣ02/8256 2000; UK, Level 16, Gateway Building, 1 Macquarie Place Ⓣ02/9247 7521; US, Level 59, MLC Centre, 19–29 Martin Place Ⓣ02/9373 9200. For visas for onward travel, consult "Consulates and Legations" in the *Yellow Pages*.

Cycling Bicycles are carried free on trains outside of peak hours (Mon–Fri 6–9am & 3.30–7.30pm) and on ferries at all times. The Roads and Traffic Authority (RTA; Ⓣ1800 060 607) produces a handy fold-out map, *Sydney Cycleways*, showing both off-road paths and suggested bicycle routes, which they will post out. The best source of information, however, is the organization Bicycle NSW, based at Level 5, 822 George St (Mon–Fri 9am–5.30pm; ⓣ02/9281 4099). Two useful publications are *Bike It Sydney* ($13), which has backstreet inner-city bike routes, and *Cycling Around Sydney* ($25) which details 25 of the best rides; they also have free council and RTA bike route maps. Popular cycling spots are Centennial Park and the bike path which runs from Manly (see p.172). The international cycling activist group Critical Mass has a Sydney movement; on the last Friday of the month meet at the Archibald Fountain in Hyde Park for an hour-long mass ride through the city at 6pm. Recommended central bicycle shops include Clarence Street Cyclery, 104 Clarence St (ⓣ02/9299 4962); Woolys Wheels, 82 Oxford St, Paddington (ⓣ02/9331 2671); and Inner City Cycles, 151 Glebe Point Rd, Glebe (ⓣ02/9660 6605). The cheapest bike rental is at Cheeky Monkey Cycle Co, 456 Pitt St, near Central station (closed Sun; mountain bikes $25 day, $100 week; ⓣ02/9212 4460), and they also sell bikes and rent and sell cycle-touring equipment. Clarence Street Cyclery also rents mountain bikes ($65 per day, $100 per weekend), as does Inner City Cycles (open daily; $33 per 24hr, $55 per weekend). For a leisurely ride in the park, Centennial Park Cycles, 50 Clovelly Rd, Randwick (open daily; ⓣ02/9398 5027) rents bikes at hourly rates (mountain bikes $12 per hour, $32 per day; bikes for kids $10 per hour, $27 per day; tandems $18 hour, $50 day), as well as rollerblades ($15 per hour) and pedal cars ($25–$35 hour).

Disabled travellers See also "Travellers with Disabilities", p.86. Disability Australia, 52 Pitt St, Redfern, NSW 2016 ⓣ02/9319 6622. Spinal Cord Injuries Australia, PO Box 397, Matraville NSW 2036 (ⓣ02/9661 8855, ⓦwww.spinalcordinjuries.com.au) publishes the very useful *Access Sydney* ($10 plus postage). Most national parks have wheelchair-accessible walks, check ⓦwww.npws.nsw.gov.au. Post-Olympic improvements include many wheelchair-accessible train stations, check ⓦwww.cityrail.nsw.gov.au. All taxi companies take bookings on behalf of Wheelchair Accessible Taxis; for numbers, see "Taxis" below.

Diving One of the best places to dive is at Gordon Bay in Clovelly, and off North and South heads. Nearby Pro Dive Coogee, 27 Alfreda St, Coogee (ⓣ02/9665 6333), offers boat and shore dives anywhere between Camp Cove (Watsons Bay) and La Perouse (4hr double boat dive from $125–$169; double shore dive $105), plus dives all over Sydney. Aquatic Explorers, 40 Kingsway, under *Cronulla Beach YHA*, Cronulla (ⓣ02/9523 1518), does local weekend co-ordinated shore dives (free but gear rental costs $50–$75 per day) and also organizes boat dives, night dives and weekends away up and down the New South Wales coast. Dive Centre Manly, 10 Belgrave St, Manly (ⓣ02/9977 4355), offers shore dives to Shelley Beach, Fairlight, and Little Manly plus Harbord if conditions are good, and boat dives off North and South Head and Long Reef (boat dives 4 daily Fri–Sun; single boat dive $90, double $145; shore dives twice daily; single shore dive $75, double $90; rates include equipment). They also have a Bondi branch at 192 Bondi Rd (ⓣ02/9369 3855) offering shore dives at Camp Cove and North Bondi (double dive $95) and boat dives to South Head and Maroubra where there's a chance to see sharks. All of the above also offer dive courses.

Hospitals (with emergency departments) St Vincents Hospital, cnr Victoria and Burton streets, Darlinghurst ⓣ02/8382 1111; Royal Prince Alfred, Missenden Rd, Camperdown ⓣ02/9515 6111; Prince of Wales, Barker St, Randwick ⓣ02/9382 2222.

Immigration Department of Immigration, 26 Lee St, near Central station, City ⓣ13 18 81.

Internet access You can surf the Net for free at the State Library, Macquarie St, for up to an hour a day, but can't send emails. Global Gossip ($4 for 30min–1hr) has several offices including 790 George St, nr Central Station; 415 Pitt St, nr Chinatown (both daily 9am–11pm); 14 Wentworth Ave, next to Hyde Park (Mon–Fri 9am–6pm); 111 Darlinghurst Rd, Kings Cross (daily 8am–1am); 37 Hall St, Bondi (Mon–Thurs 9am–midnight, Fri–Sun 9am–11pm), they also offer cut-rate international calls and parcel post. *Phone Net Cafe*, 73–75 Hall St, Bondi (Mon–Fri 8am–10pm, to 9pm Sat & Sun; from $3.30 for 1hr) is a lively café haunt in its own right.

Left luggage There are serve-yourself lockers at Central station inside the country trains terminal; make sure you have $1 and $2 coins (daily 6.30am–9.30pm; $8/$6/$4 per 24hr depending on size). Also lockers at the airport and the Sydney Coach Terminal ($7– $12 per 24hr).

Libraries See the State Library, p.142 and City of Sydney Library, p.127.

Maps Map World, 280 Pitt St (ⓣ02/9261 3601, ⓦwww.mapworld.net.au) has Sydney's biggest selection of maps and travel guides; see also "Parks and wildlife", below.

Medical centres Broadway Medical Centre, 185–211 Broadway near Glebe (ⓣ02/9281 5085), general practitioners open Mon–Fri 9am–7pm, Sat & Sun 11am–5pm, no appointment necessary; Skin Cancer Centre, 403 George St (ⓣ02/9262 4877);

Sydney Sexual Health Centre, Sydney Hospital, Macquarie St (☎02/9382 7440 or 1800 451 624); The Travel Doctor, 7th Floor, 428 George St (☎02/9221 7133, Ⓦwww.traveldoctor.com.au).

Parks and wildlife information The NPWS, Cadmans Cottage, 110 George St, The Rocks (☎02/9247 5033, Ⓦwww.nationalparks.nsw.gov.au) is the information centre for Sydney Harbour National Park and books tours to its islands; they do not arrange camping permits. For these and information on other national parks around Sydney, go to The National Parks Centre, 102 George St, The Rocks (☎02/9253 4600). The Sydney Map Shop, part of the Surveyor-General's Department, 22 Bridge St (☎02/9228 6111) sells detailed National Park, State Forest and bushwalking maps of New South Wales.

Pharmacy (late-night) Crest Hotel Pharmacy, 60A Darlinghurst Rd, Kings Cross (daily 8.30am–midnight; ☎02/9358 1822).

Police Headquarters at 14 College St (☎02/9339 0277); emergency ☎000.

Post office The General Post Office (GPO) is in Martin Place (Mon–Fri 8.15am–5.30pm, Sat 10am–2pm). Poste restante is located at the post office in the Hunter Connection shopping mall at 310 George St (Mon–Fri 8.15am–5.30pm), opposite Wynyard station. Log your name in the computer to see if you have any post before queueing. Poste Restante, Sydney GPO, Sydney, NSW 2000.

Public holidays In addition to the Australia-wide public holidays (see Basics, p.71), the following are celebrated only in New South Wales: Bank Holiday – first Monday in August; Labour Day – first Monday in October; Queen's Birthday – first Monday in June.

Scenic flights Sydney Harbour Seaplanes, Rose Bay (☎02/9388 1978) can take you on a 15min scenic flight over Sydney Harbour and Bondi Beach ($125 per person, min 2, max 8), or the harbour and the Northern beaches ($195), or drop you off for lunch at Palm Beach or one of the Hawkesbury River restaurants ($395 including lunch).

Surfing The two best surf schools in Sydney, offering both individual and group lessons' are Lets Go Surfing (☎02/9365 1800) which also has its own surf store renting and selling boards at 128 Ramsgate Ave, North Bondi; and Manly Surf School (☎02/9977 6977) which covers the northern beaches.

Swimming pools Most pools are outdoors and unheated, and open from the long weekend in October until Easter. Those detailed in the text, with times and prices given, are: Cook and Phillip Park Aquatic and Leisure Centre, near Hyde Park (p.141); Andrew "Boy" Charlton in The Domain (see p.143); North Sydney Olympic Pool, North Sydney (p.163); Victoria Park, City Rd, next to Sydney University (p.149); the Annette Kellerman Aquatic Centre in Enmore (p.151); and the pool of champions, the Sydney International Aquatic Centre at Homebush Bay (p.234).

Taxis ABC ☎13 25 22; Legion ☎13 14 51; Premier ☎13 10 17; RSL ☎13 15 81; St George ☎13 21 66; Taxis Combined ☎02/8332 8888. For harbour water taxis call Taxis Afloat ☎02/9955 3222.

Telephones The unattended Telstra Pay Phone Centre, 231 Elizabeth St, City (Mon–Fri 7am–11pm, Sat & Sun 7am–5pm) has private booths; BYO change or phonecard. Global Gossip (see "Internet access" above) offers discount-rate international calls and Backpackers Travel Centre (see below) sells their own rechargeable discount phonecard.

Travel agents Backpackers World Travel, 234 Sussex St (☎02/8268 6001; Ⓦwww.backpackerstravel.net.au), does everything from international flights to bus passes; offices also at 91 York St (☎02/8268 5000), at 488 Pitt St near Central station (☎02/9282 9711), 212 Victoria St, Kings Cross (☎02/9380 2700), and 2b Grosvenor St, Bondi Junction (☎02/9369 2011). Flight Centre, 52 Martin Place (☎02/9235 0166), also at several other locations, offers cheap domestic and international air tickets. STA Travel has many branches, including Town Hall Square, 464 Kent St (☎02/9262 9763), or try Student Flights (☎1800 069 063), with several offices including 140 King St, Newtown, 50 Spring St, Bondi Junction and 185 Broadway near Glebe. Trailfinders is at 8 Spring St (☎02/9247 7666). YHA Travel, 422 Kent St (☎02/9261 1111) is a full travel agent and also has a branch at *Sydney Central YHA*, 11 Rawson Place off Eddy Ave (☎02/9281 9444), and offers an excellent range of Sydney tours.

Water sports Rose Bay Aquatic Hire, just near the waterfront at 1 Vickery Ave, Rose Bay (☎02/9371 7036), rents out catamarans ($40 first hour, $30 thereafter), kayaks ($20 per hour single kayak, $30 double) and motorboats ($60 for the first two hours, $15 for each subsequent hour). Balmoral Windsurfing, Sailing and Kayaking School, open Oct–April at the Balmoral Sailing Club, southern end of the Esplanade (☎02/9960 5344), rents out sailboards (from $40 per hour), offers sailboarding and Hobiecat dinghy sailing courses (both 4hr over 2 days; $245), as well as 5-day holiday courses for kids ($348). Northside Sailing School, Spit Bridge, Mosman (☎02/9969 3972) specializes in weekend dinghy sailing courses on Middle Harbour during the sailing season (Sept–April); tuition is one-on-one

($130 per 3hr lesson). Sydney by Sail, based at Darling Harbour (ⓣ02/9280 1110), has Learn To Sail programmes for yacht sailing throughout the year, from a Level 1 Introductory Course (12-hour 2-day course; $425) to a Level 4 Inshore Skipper Course (3-day, 2-night live-aboard; $695). Experienced sailors can charter the yachts from $400 per half-day. For other sailing courses and yacht rental contact the NSW Yachting Association (ⓣ02/9660 1266, ⓦwww.nsw.yachting.org.au). Natural Wanders Sea Kayak Adventures (ⓣ02/9899 1001) arrange sea-kayaking in the harbour: their most popular trip is the Bridge Paddle ($90; 4hr; suitable for beginners), from Lavender Bay near Luna Park, under the Harbour Bridge and exploring the North Shore; picnic brunch included.

Women Contact the Women's Information and Referral Service (Mon–Fri 9am–5pm; ⓣ1800 817 227) for information on International Women's Day events in March. For this and other women's organizations, services and referrals, also try The Women's Library, 8–10 Brown St, Newtown (Tues, Wed & Fri 11am–5pm, Thurs 11am–8pm, Sat & Sun noon–4pm), which lends feminist and lesbian literature. Jesse Street National Women's Library, housed in the Town Hall, 456 Kent St (Mon–Fri 10am–2pm), is an archive collecting literature detailing Australian women's history and writing. The Feminist Bookshop is in Orange Grove Plaza on Balmain Rd, Lilyfield (ⓣ02/9810 2666).

Work If you have a working holiday visa, you shouldn't have too much trouble finding some sort of work, particularly in hospitality or retail. Offices of the government-run Centrelink (ⓣ13 28 50) have a database of jobs. Centrelink also refers jobseekers to several private "Job Network" agencies, including Employment National (ⓣ13 34 44). The private agency Troys (Level 11, 89 York St; ⓣ02/9290 2955) specializes in the hospitality industry. If you have some office or professional skills, there are plenty of temp agencies that are more than keen to take on travellers: flick through "Employment Services" in the *Yellow Pages*. For a whole range of work, from unskilled to professional, the multinational Manpower is a good bet (ⓣ13 25 02). Otherwise scour hostel notice boards and the *Sydney Morning Herald*'s employment pages – Saturday's bumper edition is best.

Around Sydney

If life in the fast lane is taking its toll, Sydney's residents can easily get away from it all. Right on their doorstep, golden beaches and magnificent national parks beckon, interwoven with intricate waterways. Everything in this part of the chapter can be done as a day-trip from the city, although some require an overnight stay to explore more fully. See the box on p.212 for some of the huge variety of tours on offer.

North of Sydney the Hawkesbury River flows into the jagged jaws of the aptly named **Broken Bay**. The entire area is surrounded by bush, with the huge spaces of the **Ku-Ring-Gai Chase National Park** in the south and the **Brisbane Waters National Park** in the north. Beyond Broken Bay, the **Central Coast** between Gosford and Newcastle is an ideal spot for a bit of fishing, sailing and lazing around. **Newcastle** is escaping its industrial city tag and the attractive beach metropolis is coming up in the world, with a surfing, student, café and music culture all part of the mix. Immediately beyond are the wineries of the **Hunter Valley**.

Moving on from Sydney

Most **bus** services from Sydney depart from **Eddy Ave**, alongside Central train station, and tickets can be bought from the Sydney Coach Terminal, cnr Eddy Ave and Pitt St (daily 6am–10pm; ⓣ02/9281 9366) or direct from bus companies. There are four **interstate services**: Greyhound Australia has Australia-wide services (ⓣ13 14 99, ⓦwww.greyhound.com.au); Firefly Express (ⓣ1300

730 740, Ⓦwww.fireflyexpress.com.au), daily to Melbourne and connecting to Adelaide; Murray's (Ⓣ13 22 51, Ⓦwww.murrays.com.au; also from Strathfield station), to Canberra daily; while Pioneer Motor Service departs just around the corner at 490 Pitt St (Ⓣ13 34 10, Ⓦwww.premierms.com.au), heading to Cairns via the north coast, and to Melbourne via the south coast. Most bus services to **destinations within NSW** also depart from Eddy Ave: Keans (Ⓣ02/6543 1322), daily to the Lower and Upper Hunter Valley; Port Stephens Coaches (Ⓣ02/4982 2940 or 1800 045 949, Ⓦhttp://pscoaches.com.au), daily to Port Stephens via Newcastle outskirts; Selwoods (Ⓣ02/6362 7963, Ⓦwww.selwoods.com.au), daily to Orange via the Blue Mountains, Lithgow and Bathurst; Premier Motor Service (Ⓣ13 34 10, Ⓦwww.premierms.com.au; also available from the airport), daily to Bega via the south coast, with one service daily continuing on to Eden; Rover Coaches (Ⓣ02/4990 1699 or 1800 801 012, Ⓦwww.rovercoaches.com.au; also from Circular Quay and the airport), daily to Cessnock and Hunter Valley resorts. Prior's Scenic Express departs from Parramatta, Liverpool and Campbelltown train stations (Ⓣ02/4472 4040 or 1800 816 234), daily except Sat to the Southern Highlands and Kangaroo Valley, thence to Moruya or Narooma via the south coast including Batemans Bay and Ulladulla.

All out-of-town trains depart from the **country trains terminal** of Central station (information and booking 6.30am–10pm; Ⓣ13 22 32). There are Countrylink Travel Centres at these train stations: Central station on Eddy Ave (Ⓣ02/9379 4076; Ⓦwww.countrylink.nsw.gov.au); in the Queen Victoria Building Arcade at Town Hall station (Ⓣ02/9379 3600); Wynyard (Ⓣ02/9224 4744); Circular Quay (Ⓣ02/9224 3400) and Bondi Junction (Ⓣ02/9379 3777). The Indian Pacific, the Ghan and the Overland are now managed by Great Southern Railway (bookings Ⓣ13 21 47, Ⓦwww.gsr.com.au) but you can also book through Country Link offices. Interstate trains should be booked as early as possible, especially the Indian Pacific and Brisbane–Cairns trains.

The *Spirit of Tasmania* ferry from Sydney to Devonport in Tasmania leaves from Darling Harbour; see p.1069 for details.

The big four **car-rental companies**, with expensive new model cars, charge from $50 per day for a small manual, with much cheaper rates for five- to seven-day and longer rentals: Avis, airport (Ⓣ02/8374 2847) and 220 William St, Kings Cross (Ⓣ02/9357 2000); Budget, airport (Ⓣ13 27 27), and 93 William St, Kings Cross (Ⓣ02/8255 9600); Hertz (Ⓣ13 30 39), airport and elsewhere including cnr William and Riley streets, Kings Cross; Thrifty, airport (Ⓣ1300 367 227) and 75 William St, Kings Cross. There are cheaper deals with the popular Bayswater, 180 William St, Kings Cross (Ⓣ02/9360 3622), which has low rates but limited kilometres; Kings Cross Rent-a-Car, 169 William St, Kings Cross (Ⓣ02/9361 0637), which is open daily and has low rates; Daytona Rentals, 164 Parramatta Rd, Ashfield (Ⓣ02/9716 8777), which has slightly older cars at very good rates for weekly rentals all inclusive of insurance; and Rent-a-Ruffy, 29 Pittwater Rd, Manly (Ⓣ02/9977 5777), which has cheap, older-model cars but offering limited kilometres. Travellers Auto Barn, 177 William St, Kings Cross (Ⓣ02/9360 1500 or 1800 674 374), does cheap one-way rentals to Melbourne, Brisbane or Cairns but with a minimum ten-day hire.

There are many places renting **campervans** and **4WD**s. All Seasons Campervans, 77 Planthurst Rd, South Hurstville (Ⓣ02/9547 0100), offers a wide range of campervans, motorhomes, four-door sedans plus camping equipment, including free delivery to CBD accommodation, linen and sleeping bags. Britz Campervan Rentals, 653 Gardeners Rd, Mascot (Ⓣ02/9667 0402 or 1800 331

Tours from Sydney

Day-tours from Sydney range from a sedentary trip on a bus to a wildlife park to a day of canyoning in the Blue Mountains, and there are many overnight trips too. Listed below are a couple of regular bus-tour operators, but you'll almost certainly have a better time with one of the outfits who specialize in small-group tours, quite often with an emphasis on physical activities such as bushwalking, horse riding, white-water rafting or abseiling. **One-way tours** can be the next best thing to going by car: small groups in minibuses travel from Sydney to Melbourne (for example), taking detours to attractions along the way that you'd never be able to reach on public transport.

As well as booking direct on the numbers given, most of the tours listed below can be booked through YHA Travel (ⓣ02/9261 1111, ⓦwww.yha.com.au).

Day- and overnight trips around Sydney

AAT Kings ⓣ02/9518 6095, ⓦwww.aatkings.com. One of the largest operators, its big-group, sedentary bus tours cover city sights, wildlife parks, the Blue Mountains, Jenolan Caves, the Hawkesbury River and the Hunter Valley. Admissions and hotel pick-ups and drop-offs included in the price.

Oz Experience ⓣ02/9213 1766 or 1300 300 028, ⓦwww.ozexperience.com. Their active one-day tour to the Blue Mountains ($85) includes a three-hour mountain bike adventure along a bush track, a day and an evening bush walk, and a ride on the scenic railway. An overnight stay at *Katoomba YHA* is an optional extra or you can return the same evening.

Oz Trek ⓣ02/9666 4662 or 1300 661 234, ⓦwww.oztrek.com.au. Recommended active full-day tours to the Blue Mountains ($54), with a choice of three bushwalks (30min–1hr 30min). Small groups (max 21). The trip can be extended to overnight packages with either horse riding ($209), abseiling ($209), or a Jenolan Caves visit ($179–199). City, Glebe, Kings Cross, Coogee and Bondi pick-ups.

Waves Surf School ⓣ02/9369 3010 or 1800 851 101, ⓦwww.wavessurfschool.com.au. One- or two-day "Learn To Surf" trips in the Royal National Park, learning surfing technique and etiquette and beach safety, and with a chance to spot wildlife (one day with lunch $69; two days with meals, bushwalking and camping or sleep-on-board bus $189). Bondi, Coogee, Kings Cross and city pick-ups.

Wildframe Ecotours ⓣ02/9440 9915, ⓦwww.wildframe.com. Two full-day tours to the Blue Mountains (both $82). The Grand Canyon Eco-tour is for fit walkers as it includes a small-group bushwalk (max 16) through the Grand Canyon (5km; 3hr); BYO lunch in Katoomba. The Blue Mountains Bush Tour is more relaxed with several short bushwalks and BYO lunch in Blackheath. Kangaroo spotting promised on both trips. Kings Cross and city pick-ups.

454), has campervans, 4WD campers and camping gear, available one-way to Adelaide, Alice Springs, Brisbane, Cairns, Darwin, Melbourne and Perth. Travel Car Centre, 26 Orchard Rd, Brookvale (ⓣ02/9938 1129 or 1800 440 300), has been established for nearly twenty years and has hatchbacks, stationwagons, campervans and 4WDs available for long- or short-term rental. Travellers Auto Barn (ⓣ02/9360 1500; see above) offers budget campervan and 4WD bush-camper rentals. Also Australian Outback 4 Wheel Drive Hire Co, 184 Elizabeth St, City (ⓣ02/9281 9676) and Hertz Campervans, 1084–1088 Botany Rd, Botany (ⓣ02/9316 4188).

For secondhand **motorbikes** and rental, there's Bikescape, Unit 17, 566 Gardeners Rd, Alexandria (ⓣ1300 736 869, ⓦwww.bikescape.com.au), with

Wildspirit Adventure Company ⓣ02/9371 5859, ⓦwww.wildspirit.com.au. Exploring the Blue Mountains' deep canyons requires a thrilling mixture of abseiling down waterfalls, swimming through cave slots, bushwalking and rock-climbing. Wet canyoning is offered Oct–April, dry canyoning is available all year. Depending on the area and the number of abseils, trips range from $160 to $210. The most popular wet-canyoning trip is to Fortress Creek (grade 2; $160), near Leura, picking up Sydney 7am and returning 7pm.

Extended and one-way tours

Ando's Outback Tours ⓣ02/6842 8286 or 1800 228 828, ⓦwww.outbacktours.com.au. Popular five-day tour from Sydney to Byron Bay but getting well off the beaten track inland via the Blue Mountains, the Warrumbungles, Coonabarabran and Lightning Ridge ($435 all-inclusive; departs Sydney every Sun); includes a stay on the rural property of the true blue family who run the tours. Sydney return for $35. Finding farm work is a common bonus.

Autopia Tours ⓣ03/9419 8878 or 1800 000 507, ⓦwww.autopiatours.com.au. This excellent, long-established Melbourne-based tour company has a three-and-a-half-day Sydney to Melbourne tour via the Blue Mountains, Jenolan Caves, Canberra, the Snowy Mountains and Victoria's Alpine Way ($195; meals, accommodation and entry fees extra). Small-seater buses with the driver acting as guide.

Oz Experience See above. A cross between transport and tours that go a little off the beaten track, with a hop-on, hop-off component lasting six months; accommodation and meals not included. Scheduled routes include Sydney to Cairns in nine days ($420); Sydney to Brisbane via the Warrumbungles and Byron Bay in four days ($250); and Sydney to Melbourne in three days via the south coast, Canberra, the Snowy Mountains and Phillip Island ($225). There are also several Sydney to Byron Bay options encompassing beach, bush and rural experiences.

Pioneering Spirit ⓣ02/6685 7721 or 1800 672 422, ⓦwww.pioneeringspirit.com.au. Another tour (max 21 passengers) that heads to beach-heaven Byron Bay. This three-day excursion goes inland via the Hunter Valley for wine-tasting, back on the coast to Hat Head National Park, inland again to the Dorrigo World Heritage Area, returning to the coast at Coffs Harbour ($300 including breakfast, dinner, accommodation and entry fees; extra $35 for a Sydney return, usually Mon). Tours depart Tues; Central station, Kings Cross and Bondi pick-ups.

Waves Surf School See above. Four-day ($399; departs Tues) or five-day four-night ($479; departs Mon) surfing trips from Sydney to Byron Bay. Price includes gear, lessons, meals, and a mixture of beachside cabin accommodation and camping. Trips run Oct to mid-May. The five-day tour can be done in reverse (Byron to Sydney, departs Sat).

scooters from $75 per day and motorbikes from $115 (cheaper weekend and longer term rates available).

To the **west**, you escape suburbia to emerge at the foot of the beautiful World Heritage-listed **Blue Mountains**, while the scenic Hawkesbury–Nepean river valley is home to historic rural towns such as **Windsor**.

Heading **south**, the **Royal National Park** is an hour's drive away, while on the coast beyond are a string of small, laid-back towns – Waterfall, Stanwell Park, Wombarra – with beautiful, unspoilt **beaches**. The industrial city of **Wollongong** and neighbouring Port Kembla are impressively located between the Illawarra Escarpment and the sea, but of paltry interest to visitors, although more interesting spots cluster around. Inland, the **Southern Highlands** are covered with yet more national parks, punctuated by pleasing little towns such as **Bundanoon** and **Berrima**.

North

The **Hawkesbury River** widens and slows as it approaches the South Pacific, joining Berowra Creek, Cowan Creek, Pittwater and Brisbane Water in the system of flooded valleys that form **Broken Bay**. The bay and its surrounding inlets are a haven for anglers, sailors and windsurfers, while the surrounding bushland is virtually untouched. Three major **national parks** surround the Hawkesbury River: **Ku-Ring-Gai Chase** in the south, **Brisbane Waters** facing it across the bay, and **Dharug**, inland to the west.

The **Pacific Highway** up here, partly supplanted by the **Sydney–Newcastle Freeway**, is fast and efficient, though not particularly attractive until you're approaching Ku-Ring-Gai Chase; if you want to detour into the national parks or towards Brooklyn, don't take the freeway. The **rail** lines follow the road almost as far as Broken Bay, before they take a scenic diversion through the **Central Coast** passing Brooklyn, Brisbane Waters, Woy Woy and **Gosford** en route to **Newcastle**.

Ku-Ring-Gai Chase National Park

Ku-Ring-Gai Chase is much the best known of New South Wales' national parks and, with the Pacific Highway running all the way up one side, is also the easiest to get to. The bushland scenery is crisscrossed by walking tracks, which you can explore to seek out Aboriginal rock carvings, or just to get away from it all and see the forest and its wildlife. Only 24km from the centre of Sydney, the huge park's unspoilt beauty is enhanced by the presence of water on three sides: the Hawkesbury, its inlet Cowan Creek, and the expanse of Pittwater, an inlet of Broken Bay. From Palm Beach you can take a boat cruise (see p.175) through all these waters to the park's most popular picnic spot at **Bobbin Head**, with a colourful marina. At the **Kalkari Visitor Centre** (daily 9am–5pm), on the Ku-Ring-Gai Chase Road, you can pick up information about walks in the park or take a guided walk. The Birrawanna Walking Track leads from here for 1.5km to the park headquarters, which can also be approached by car further along Ku-Ring-Gai Chase Road. The NPWS **Bobbin Head Information Centre** (daily 10am–4pm; ⓣ02/9472 8949) is located inside the Art Deco *Bobbin Inn* which also has a very pleasant restaurant, popular for weekend breakfasts and Sunday afternoon jazz. There are four road entrances to the park and an $11 entrance fee for cars. Without your own transport, take a ferry to the Pittwater side from Palm Beach, or a train to Turramurra station and then Hornsby Bus #577 (ⓣ02/9457 8888 for times) to the Bobbin Head Road entrance; some buses continue down to Bobbin Head itself.

At the northeastern corner of Ku-Ring-Gai Chase National Park, West Head juts into the eastern shore of **Pittwater** – a deep, 10km-long sheltered waterway which enters Broken Bay from the south. From the West Head lookout, reached via West Head Road, there are superb views across to Barrenjoey Head and Barrenjoey Lighthouse at Palm Beach on the western shore of Pittwater. From West Head, the **Garigal Aboriginal Heritage Walk** (3.5km circuit) heads to the Aboriginal rock engravings and hand art, the most accessible Aboriginal art site in the park.

Koala patting and other wildlife

It is no longer legal to physically pick up and hold a koala in New South Wales' wildlife parks, but photo-opportunity "patting" sessions are still on offer. Below are several hands-on wildlife experiences around Sydney.

The **Koala Park Sanctuary** (daily 9am–5pm; $18; Ⓦwww.koalaparksanctuary.com.au) was established as a safe haven for koalas in 1935 and has since opened its gates to wombats, possums, kangaroos and native birds of all kinds. Koala-feeding sessions (daily 10.20am, 11.45am, 2pm & 3pm) are the patting and photo-opportunity times. Around 25km north of Sydney, not far from the Pacific Highway on Castle Hill Road, West Pennant Hills; train to Pennant Hills then bus #651 or #655 towards Glenorie (Mon–Sat).

One of Sydney's oldest wildlife reserves, **Waratah Park Earth Sanctuary** (Ⓣ02/9986 1788, Ⓦwww.waratahpark.com.au), sits in stunning bush scenery on the edge of Ku-Ring-Gai Chase National Park at the end of Namba Road in Duffys Forest. Waratah is most famous as the home of Skippy the bush kangaroo, television's marsupial star, and you can still see free-ranging Skippy look-alikes and visit the Ranger Station where most of the filming was done. The rest of the sanctuary can only be seen on a 90-minute guided bushwalk (advance bookings essential; 1.30pm, 3.30pm & 5.30pm, plus night-time walk, departing after sunset; $16.50). Around 36km north of Sydney, reached via Mona Vale Rd – it's signposted from Terrey Hills; train to Chatswood then bus #284 from stand "S" (Ⓣ02/9450 1236 for times).

At **Featherdale Wildlife Park** (daily 9am–5pm; $17.50; Ⓦwww.featherdale.com.au), patting koalas is the special all-day attraction. Located at 217 Kildare Rd, Doonside, 30km west of Sydney off the M4 motorway between Parramatta and Penrith; train to Blacktown station then bus #725.

The **Australian Reptile Park** (daily 9am–5pm; $20; Ⓦwww.reptilepark.com.au), 65km north of Sydney, just off the Pacific Highway before the Gosford turn-off, offers photographic opportunities with koalas, and has kangaroos roaming the park that you can tickle and hand-feed, though its real stars are the reptiles, with native Australian species well represented and visible all year round thanks to heat lamps in the enclosures. The highlights are Eric, New South Wales' largest saltwater crocodile, and the sizeable Perentie lizard of central Australia. Reptile shows twice a day. You can also watch snakes and funnel web spiders being milked for their venom for the Commonwealth Serum Laboratories. There's no public transport: tour available with AAT Kings (see p.212).

The only place to **camp** is The Basin (Ⓣ02/9974 1011 for bookings) on Pittwater, reached via the Palm Beach Ferry Service. Facilities at the site are minimal so bring everything with you. If you want to stay in the park in rather more comfort, there's a very popular **YHA hostel** (Ⓣ02/9999 5748, Ⓔpittwater@yhansw.org.au; dorms $23, rooms ❸; bookings essential and well in advance for weekends) at **Halls Wharf**. It's one of New South Wales' most scenically sited – a rambling old house surrounded by bush and with a verandah where you can look down onto the water; sailing lessons can also be arranged. Bring supplies with you – the last food (and bottle) shop is at Church Point where the **ferry** departs to Halls Wharf (last departure Mon–Fri 7pm, Sat & Sun 6.30pm; Ⓣ02/9999 3492 for times; $7.50 return).

Two direct buses run to Church Point: #E86 from Central station or #156 from Manly Wharf; it's then a ten-minute uphill walk. Alternatively the 24-hour Pink Water Taxi operates from Newport (Ⓣ02/96344791); bus #190 from Wynyard runs up the coast to Newport.

The Hawkesbury River

One of New South Wales' prettiest rivers, lined with sandstone cliffs and bush-covered banks for much of its course and with some interesting old settlements alongside, the **Hawkesbury River** has its source in the Great Dividing Range and flows out to sea at Broken Bay. For information about the many national parks along the river, contact the NPWS in Sydney (Ⓣ02/9247 5033) or at 370 Windsor Rd in Richmond (Ⓣ02/4588 5247). Short of chartering your own boat, the best way to explore the river system is to take a cruise (see box below); the River Boat Mail Run is the most interesting.

Upstream: Wisemans Ferry

The first ferry across the Hawkesbury River was opened by ex-convict Solomon Wiseman ten years after he was granted two hundred acres of river frontage in 1817, at the spot now known as **WISEMANS FERRY**. The crossing forged an inland connection between Sydney and the Hunter Valley via the convict-built Great North Road. Unfortunately, travellers on this

Exploring the Hawkesbury River system

Brooklyn, just above the western mass of Ku-Ring-Gai Chase National Park, and easily reached by train to Brooklyn station from Central station in Sydney and from Gosford, is the base for Hawkesbury River Ferries (Ⓣ02/9985 7566), whose River Boat Mail Run still takes letters, as well as tourists, up and down the river. Departures are from Brooklyn Wharf on Dangar Road (Mon–Fri 9.30am excluding public holidays; 4hr; $35 including morning tea; booking essential). Also on offer are two-hour coffee cruises towards the mouth of the river (Mon–Fri 1.30pm; $15, Sat & Sun 11am & 1.30pm; $20), which can be used as transport to Patonga (see p.219; $10 one-way).

Gosford's Public Wharf is the starting point for the MV *Lady Kendall* (Ⓣ02/4323 1655, Ⓦwww.starshipcruises.com.au), which cruises both Brisbane Water and Broken Bay (Mon–Wed, Sat & Sun, daily during school & public holidays, 10.15am & 1pm; 2hr 30min; $22; bookings essential).

Windsor is the base for the Hawkesbury Paddlewheeler (Ⓣ02/4575 1171, Ⓦwww.paddlewheeler.com.au) which has a good-value Sunday afternoon Jazz Cruise: live jazz and a BBQ lunch for $28 (12.30pm–3pm; advance bookings essential).

Woy Woy is also a port of call for the MV *Lady Kendall* (see above) at 10.40am and 12.10pm.

Boat and houseboat rentals and fishing charter

Barrenjoey Boating Services at Governor Phillip Park, Palm Beach (Ⓣ02/9974 4229) hires out **boats,** which seat up to six people (2hrs $40, 4hrs $55, 8hrs $90) and are perfect for fishing expeditions around the mouth of the Hawkesbury. The centre has a fishing shop and sells bait supplies and rods (no hire). Otherwise, if you're keen to **fish** and can get four people together, you can charter a boat, including all the gear and bait, plus a skipper who knows exactly where to go, with Fishabout Tours (Ⓣ02/9451 5420, Ⓦwww.fishnet.com.au/fishabout; $150 per person; 7hr) who have a great reputation on the Hawkesbury. **Houseboats** can be good value if you can get a group together, with prices starting from $530 a weekend and $960 a week for four people. The Sydney Visitor Centre in Sydney (Ⓣ02/9667 6050) has details of operators, or try Able Hawkesbury River Houseboats, on River Road in Wisemans Ferry (Ⓣ1800 024 979, Ⓦwww.hawkesburyhouseboats.com.au), or Ripples Houseboats, 87 Brooklyn Rd, Brooklyn (Ⓣ02/9985 5534, Ⓦwww.ripples.com.au).

isolated route were easy prey for marauding bushrangers and it was largely abandoned for the longer but safer coastal route. Today it's a popular recreational spot for day-trippers – just a little over an hour from Sydney by car, and with access to the **Dharug National Park** over the river by a free 24-hour car ferry. Dharug's rugged sandstone cliffs and gullies shelter Aboriginal rock engravings which can be visited only on ranger-led trips during school holidays; there's a camping area at Mill Creek (Gosford NPWS ⓣ02/4320 4203 for details of walks and camping; bookings for both essential at weekends and holiday periods). Open to walkers, cyclists and horse riders but not vehicles, the **Old Great North Road** was literally carved out of the rock by hundreds of convicts from 1829; you can camp en route at the Ten Mile Hollow camping area.

The settlement of Wisemans Ferry was based around Wiseman's home, Cobham Hall, built in 1826. Much of the original building still exists in the blue-painted *Wisemans Ferry Inn* on the Old Great North Road (ⓣ02/4566 4301; motel ❸, pub ❸–❹), with character **rooms** upstairs sharing bathrooms, and en-suite, motel-style rooms outside at the back. Bistro meals are served daily and there's entertainment on Sunday afternoons. Other accommodation in the surrounding area includes *Del Rio Riverside Resort* (ⓣ02/4566 4330, ⓦwww.delrioresort.com.au; en-suite cabins ❹), a campsite in Webbs Creek reached via the Webbs Creek car ferry, 3km south of Wisemans Ferry; facilities include a Chinese restaurant, swimming pool, tennis court and golf course. *Rosevale Farm Resort*, 3km along Wisemans Ferry Road en route to Gosford (ⓣ02/4566 4207; vans ❷, motel ❸), has less expensive camping and motel units – cheaper weekdays – in extensive bushland close to Dharug National Park.

Taking the ferry across the river from Wisemans Ferry, it's then a scenic nineteen-kilometre river drive north along Settlers Road, another convict-built route, to **St Albans**, where you can partake of a cooling brew (or stay a while) at a pub built in 1836, the hewn sandstone *Settlers Arms Inn* (ⓣ02/4568 2111; en-suite rooms ❺). The pub is set on two and a half acres and much of the vegetables and herbs for the delicious home-cooked food are organically grown on site (lunch daily, dinner Fri–Sun).

The Upper Hawkesbury: Windsor

About 50km inland from Sydney and reached easily by train from Central station via Blacktown, **Windsor** is probably the best preserved of all the historic Hawkesbury towns, with a lively centre of narrow streets, spacious old pubs and numerous historic colonial buildings. It's terrifically popular on Sundays, when a **market** takes over the shady, tree-lined mall end of the main drag, George Street, and the *Macquarie Arms Hotel* on Thompson Square, the grassy village green opposite, which claims to be the oldest pub in Australia, puts on live rock 'n' roll. Next door to the pub, the **Hawkesbury River Museum and Tourist Information Centre** (daily 10am–4pm; museum $2.50; ⓣ02/4577 2310, ⓦwww.hawkesburyweb.com) doles out local information. A Sunday cruise leaves from the jetty across the road from the tourist office (see box opposite). From Windsor, Putty Road (Route 69) heads north through beautiful forest country, along the eastern edge of the Wollemi National Park, to Singleton in the Hunter Valley.

From Richmond, just 7km northwest of Windsor, the **Bells Line of Road** (Route 40) goes to Lithgow via Kurrajong and is a great scenic drive; all along the way are fruit stalls stacked with produce from the valley. There's a wonderful view of the Upper Hawkesbury Valley from the lookout point at

Kurrajong Heights, on the edge of the Blue Mountains. Another scenic drive from Richmond to the Blue Mountains, emerging near Springwood (see p.237), is south along the Hawkesbury Road, with the **Hawkesbury Heights Lookout** halfway along providing panoramic views. Not far from the lookout, the modern solar-powered *Hawkesbury Heights YHA* (Ⓣ02/4754 5621; dorms $20), has six twin rooms with beds at dorm rates and more views from its secluded bush setting.

The Central Coast

The shoreline between Broken Bay and Newcastle, known as the **Central Coast**, is characterized by large **coastal lakes** – saltwater lagoons almost entirely enclosed, but connected to the ocean by small waterways. The northernmost, **Lake Macquarie**, is the biggest saltwater lake in New South Wales. People in a hurry can bypass the Central Coast altogether on the Sydney–Newcastle Freeway which runs some way inland, but to see a bit more of the coastal scenery and the lakes, stay on the older Pacific Highway which heads to Newcastle via Gosford and Wyong. A further detour would take you from Gosford to **Terrigal** and then right along the narrow coastal strip via **The Entrance** and **Budgewoi** to rejoin the Pacific Highway after Lake Munmorah. The fit and intrepid can get here by bike: from Manly, head up the northern beaches, hop on a ferry service from Palm Beach to **Ettalong** (ex-Palm Beach: 8 Mon–Fri 6.30am–5pm, 7 Sat, Sun from 7.30am; ex-Ettalong: 8 Mon–Fri 6am–5.40pm, Sat from 8am, Sun from 9.40am; $8 one-way; Ⓣ02/9918 2747, Ⓦwww.palmbeachferry.com.au), then continue up through Woy Woy and Gosford to the coast. You can also reach **Patonga** by ferry with Palm Beach and Hawkesbury River Ferries (Ⓣ02/9997 4815, Ⓦwww.sydneysceniccruises.com), departing Palm Beach daily at 11am (also 9am & 3.45pm holidays & weekends; $6.50 one-way) and returning from Patonga at 4.15pm (also 9.30am & 3pm holidays & weekends) and from Brooklyn with Hawkesbury River Ferries (see box on p.216). Otherwise, you can take a very scenic **train** route to Gosford or Woy Woy from Central station in Sydney, or come direct from Sydney airport with Aussie Shuttles (see "Airport buses" box on p.105).

Central Coast Tourism (Ⓣ1800 806 258, Ⓦwww.cctourism.com.au) offers **tourist information** on the whole region and accommodation bookings. Within the Central Coast area there's a well-developed **bus service** run by the private Busways (Ⓣ02/4392 6666) and The Entrance Red Bus Services (Ⓣ02/4332 8655). For **taxis**, call Central Coast Taxis (Ⓣ13 10 08).

Gosford and around

To get anywhere on the Central Coast, you need to go through **GOSFORD**, perched on the north shore of Brisbane Water and just about within commuting distance of Sydney. Its proximity to the city has resulted in uncontrolled residential sprawl along much of the Central Coast, which has put a great strain on the once-unspoilt lakes. Although there's plenty of accommodation in and around Gosford – details from **Central Coast Tourism**, near the train station at 200 Mann St (Mon–Fri 10am–4pm, Sat 10am–12.30pm; Ⓣ02/4385 4074, Ⓦwww.cctourism.com.au) – there's not much incentive to stay. See the box on p.215 for details of the **Australian Reptile Park**, just 10km southwest.

Brisbane Waters National Park ($7 cars), immediately south of Gosford, is the site of the **Bulgandry Aboriginal engravings**, which are of a style unique to the Sydney region, with figurative outlines scratched boldly into sandstone. The site, no longer frequented by the Guringgai people – whose territory ranged south as far as Sydney Harbour and north to Lake Macquarie – is 7km southwest of Gosford off the Woy Woy road. Tiny **Bouddi National Park** ($7 cars) is 20km southeast along the coast, at the northern mouth of Broken Bay, and is a great spot for bushwalking, with camping facilities at Putty Beach, Little Beach and Tallow Beach: book through the NPWS office at 207 Albury St, Gosford (ⓣ02/4320 4203), which also has information on both parks.

Surrounded by Brisbane Waters National Park, friendly, undeveloped **PEARL BEACH**, just over a 25-kilometre drive from Gosford via Woy Woy and Umina, is a small community which expands on weekends. There are holiday houses to rent, but no other accommodation. Besides the popular *Sit 'n' Chats Beach Cafe* (live jazz Sun noon–4pm) and a restaurant, *Pearls on the Beach* (licensed and BYO; bookings ⓣ02/4342 4400; closed Mon–Wed, no dinner Sun), there's a general store (daily 8am–6pm) also selling petrol, a real estate agent who can arrange holiday lets (ⓣ02/4341 7555, ⓦwww.pearlbeachrealestate.com.au; from $700 per week in peak season), and some tennis courts. The very pretty, sheltered beach, popular with families, has a relaxing open-access saltwater pool at one end. You can walk from the end of Crystal Avenue to the neighbouring beach settlement of **PATONGA** visiting the Mount Ettalong lookout for excellent views and the **Crommelin Native Arboretum** en route. The 45-minute walk is best undertaken on the last Sunday of the month when the **Patonga Beach market** is held (8am–4pm); by road from Pearl Beach, it's 2km southwest. Ocean Planet, 25 Broken Bay Rd, Ettalong Beach (ⓣ02/4342 2222, ⓦwww.oceanplanet.com.au; kayak rental from $30 half-day), does **kayaking trips** on Patonga Creek (10km; 7hr; $92.50) with pick-ups from Woy Woy station.

To get to Pearl Beach or Patonga, take the Busways bus #50–53 (ⓣ02/4392 6666) from Woy Woy station or the **ferry** to Patonga from Palm Beach or Brooklyn (see opposite).

Terrigal

Twelve kilometres southeast of Gosford, beautiful upmarket **TERRIGAL**, backed by bush-covered hills, is one of the liveliest spots on the Central Coast, a thriving beach resort with a strong café culture. The big curve of beach has a picturesque sandstone headland, and the sheltered eastern end, The Haven, where the boats moor, is popular with families. Much of the social life revolves around the five-star *Crowne Plaza Hotel*, with its grand marble lobby and pricey boutiques, which dominates one end of **The Esplanade**.

Terrigal is a popular spot for **water-based activities** and operators include Erina Sail 'n' Ski (ⓣ02/4365 2355; sailboarding lessons and rental); Sea Surf School (ⓣ02/4325 1870; private lesson $44 per hr); Central Coast Charters (ⓣ0427 665 544; ocean and river cruises, deep-sea and game fishing); Kincumber Water-ski School (ⓣ0414 685 005; first-timer $50 sessions); and Terrigal Dive School (ⓣ02/4384 1219; five-day diving courses $385, shore or boat dives $45 with your own gear, $85 everything provided).

Central Coast Tourism at Rotary Park, Terrigal Drive (daily 9am–5pm, May–Sept closed Sun; ⓣ02/4385 4430, ⓦwww.cctourism.com.au), is a good source of information on the whole region, and can make free **accommodation** bookings. If you're after a holiday unit (from around $400 weekly) contact Hunters Real Estate, 104 Terrigal Esplanade (ⓣ02/4384 1444, ⓔhuntrs@ozemail.com.au). *Crowne Plaza Hotel*, on the corner of Pine Tree Lane (ⓣ02/4384 9111, ⓦwww.crowneplaza.com; ⑦), has three restaurants, two bars, a nightclub, a pool, gym and tennis courts; all this costs from $285 per night, including buffet breakfast and champagne. The pleasant YHA-affiliated *Terrigal Beach Backpackers Lodge*, 12 Campbell Crescent (ⓣ02/4385 3330, ⓔjrpproperties@hotmail.com; dorms $25, rooms ❸), is only one minute's walk from the beach; boogie-boards are provided free. Upmarket motel accommodation is available at *Tiarri* (all rooms with own courtyard ⓣ02/4385 9564; ❹–❺), who also rent apartments ($350 to $895).

Terrigal has plenty of **cafés**: *Louvres*, 60 The Esplanade (daily 8am–9pm), is beachy but sophisticated with a lovely plant-filled courtyard; *Aromas on Sea* has the best position (and great coffee, or drinks from the hotel bar with your food), on the breezy terrace of the *Crowne Plaza* looking right over the beach (daily 8am–5pm) while the local favourite is the tiny *Patcinos*, a block back from the beach at 17 Church St, near the hostel. The best fish and chips are from *Fish Bonez*, 90 The Esplanade (take away or eat in), while *The Break*, on Pine Tree Lane behind the *Crowne Plaza*, specializes in gourmet pizzas; its fun, intimate bar is a good alternative to the *Crowne's* packed beer garden – the *Florida Beach Bar* – or its posh *Lord Ashley Lounge* upstairs. The **restaurant** scene is dominated by Thai eateries: two of the best are the stylish *Al-Oi Thai*, near the *Crowne Plaza* at 3 Kurrawyba Ave (ⓣ02/4385 6611) and the cheap and cheerful *N Thai Sing*, 84 The Esplanade (ⓣ02/4385 9700). *Letterbox* at 4 Ash Street, on the site of the original post office, has a modern Australian menu and a number of awards for its food.

To get to Terrigal, take Busways #67, #68 or #69 from Gosford station.

Avoca Beach and The Entrance

Six kilometres to the south of Terrigal, and altogether quieter, **AVOCA BEACH** is especially popular with surfers. A large, crescent-shaped and sandy beach between two headlands, it has its own surf lifesaving club and a safe children's rock pool. West of the beach are the still waters of **Avoca Lake**. Avoca's pleasant small-town atmosphere is enhanced by the Avoca Beach Theatre near the beach on Avoca Drive (ⓣ02/4382 2156), a little-changed, early-1950s cinema. You can **learn to surf** here with Central Coast Surf School (ⓣ02/4382 1020; 1hr lesson $25) and Aquamuse (ⓣ02/4368 4172), by the bridge in Heazlett Park, rents out pedal boats, bikes, kayaks and surf-skis to use on the lake. Limited overnight **accommodation** in Avoca includes self-contained cabins and villas in an upmarket, garden-set holiday resort, *The Palms*, Carolina Park, off The Round Drive (ⓣ02/4382 1227, ⓦwww.palmsavoca.com.au; ❹), which has swimming pools, spa, and games room. Otherwise, the best bet is to rent a holiday unit (from $450 per week) – call George Brand Real Estate (ⓣ02/4382 1311) for listings. For **eating**, grab fish and chips, gourmet and veggie burgers and Turkish bread sandwiches from the groovy, colourful *Burger Girls*, at the end of the main set of shops at 168 Avoca Drive (8.30am–9.30pm, closed Tues & Wed, daily school holidays), or there's fine dining at the expensive French-run *Feast* at Shop 3, 85 Avoca Drive (ⓣ02/4381 0707), at the end of the beach near the SLSC, with an open deck right over the beach. **To get here**, take Busways #65, #66 or #67 from Gosford station; #69 also links Terrigal and Avoca Beach.

Further north, Tuggerah and Munmorah lakes meet the sea at **THE ENTRANCE**, a beautiful spot with water extending as far as the eye can see. It's a favourite fishing spot with anglers – and with swarms of **pelicans**, which turn up for the afternoon fish-feeds daily at 3.30pm (free) at Memorial Park, near the visitor centre (see below). The beaches and lakes along the coast from here to Newcastle are crowded with caravan parks, motels and outfits offering the opportunity to fish, windsurf, sail or water-ski: although less attractive than places further north, they make a great day-trip or weekend escape from Sydney. Pro Dive Central Coast, 96 The Entrance Rd (Ⓣ02/4334 1559), arranges **scuba-diving** lessons, daily boat dives and rents out snorkelling and dive gear. The **Entrance Visitors Centre**, Marine Parade (daily 9am–5pm; Ⓣ02/4385 4430 or 1800 806 258, Ⓦwww.cctourism.com.au), has a free **accommodation** booking service. To get here by **bus**, take The Entrance Red Bus Services #21–23 from Gosford station or #24–26 from Tuggerah or Wyong stations.

Newcastle

NEWCASTLE was founded in 1804 for convicts too hard even for Sydney to cope with, but the river is the real reason for the city's existence: coal was and still is carried on it from the fields of the Hunter Valley, to be exported around the country and the world. The proximity of the mines encouraged the establishment of other **heavy industries,** though the production of steel here ceased in late 2000 and most of the slag heaps have been worked over, but the docks are still functional, particularly with the through traffic of coal from the Hunter Valley. Today Newcastle remains the world's largest coal-exporting port, and there may be a dozen or so bulk carriers queued off the beaches at one time; the city also has a reputation as being one of the most environmentally progressive places on earth.

New South Wales' second city, with a population of around a quarter of a million, Newcastle has long-suffered from comparison with nearby Sydney. However, for a former major industrial city, it's surprisingly attractive, a fact now being more widely recognized. The city is experiencing a **real estate boom**: hundreds of apartments and hotels have gone up, and old icons are being redeveloped, such as the once grand *Great Northern Hotel* on Scott Street, first built in 1938 and undergoing a $3 million facelift. Years of accumulated soot has been scraped off the city's stately buildings, riverside gardens have been created in front of the city centre, and a former goods yard has been converted into a waterside entertainment venue. The once blue-collar town is taking to tourism in a big way, trading particularly on its **waterside location** – the surf beaches are wonderful, and there are some more sheltered sandy beaches around the rocky promontory at the mouth of the Hunter River; the extraordinary dunes of Stockton Beach are just a ferry ride away. An alternative feel is provided by a big dose of **surf culture** – many surfwear- and surfboard-makers operate here, several champion surfers hail from the city, and the big contest is Surfest in March – and the large and lively student community. You might not choose to spend your entire holiday here, but it can be a good base for excursions, particularly for the wineries of the nearby Hunter Valley.

Arrival, public transport and information

If you're not driving, you'll arrive by train at Newcastle **train station**, right in the heart of the city on Scott Street, or by **bus** at nearby Watt Street.

Heading west from Newcastle train station, Scott Street eventually becomes Hunter Street, the city's main thoroughfare. Newcastle's hub is the pedestrianized, tree-lined Hunter Street Mall, with its department store, shops, fruit stalls and buskers, linked by a footbridge across to the harbour foreshore. From the mall, continuing west along Hunter Street, Civic train station marks the city's cultural and administrative district focused around City Hall and Civic Park. A short

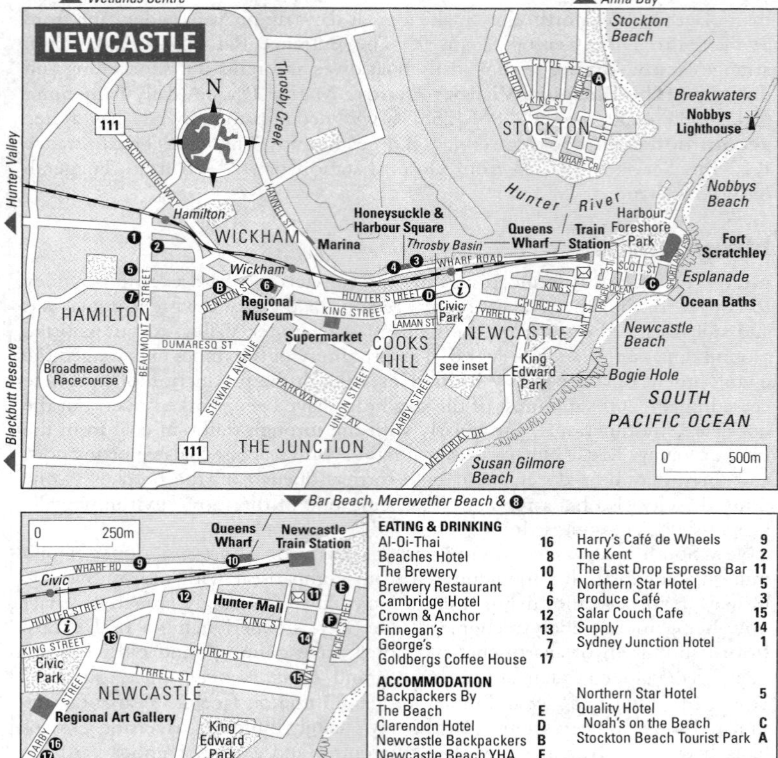

walk south of here, Cooks Hill is focused on café- and restaurant-lined Darby Street. It's easy to get around using Newcastle's **public transport** system, Newcastle Bus and Ferry Services (Ⓣ13 15 00 or Ⓦwww.newcastlebuses for information). Bus fares are time-based, allowing transfers (1hr $2.60; 4hr $5.10; all-day bus and ferry $7.80); all tickets can be bought on board. The one ferry operating goes to Stockton, departing from Queens Wharf (Mon–Sat 5.15am–midnight, Sun 8.30am–10pm; $1.90 one-way). Two passenger train lines have several suburban stops, the most useful heading towards Sydney, with handy stops at Civic for Darby Street and Hamilton for Beaumont Street (fares from $2.20 single). Weekly train-bus-ferry passes, available from selected newsagencies, start from $36.

You can familiarize yourself with the city sights on **Newcastle's Famous Tram** (Mon–Fri hourly 10am–1pm & 1.45pm, Sat & Sun hourly 10am–2pm; 45min; $12; Ⓣ02/4963 7954), the usual twee coach-done-out-as-a-tram deal, departing from Newcastle station; or get shown around Newcastle Harbour with **Moonshadow Cruises** (Nov to April Sat 2.30pm; 1hr 30min; $19; dinner cruises Wed, Fri & Sat 7pm; 3hr; from $59.50; licensed kiosk; Ⓣ02/4984 9388, Ⓦwww.moonshadow.com.au), based at the new Newcastle Cruising Yacht Club Marina, Hannel Street, Wickham, next to the Fisherman's Co-op; train to Wickham station, then a short walk.

The very helpful **Newcastle Visitors Information** (Mon–Fri 9am–5pm, Sat & Sun 9.30am–4.30pm; ⓣ02/4974 2999 or 1800 654 558, ⓦwww.visitnewcastle.com.au) at 361 Hunter St, opposite Civic station, can provide other local information and maps.

Accommodation

Backpackers By The Beach 34 Hunter St, cnr of Pacific St ⓣ02/4926 3472, ⓦwww.backpackersbythebeach.com.au. A fun and sociable hostel, with a street-level kitchen-cum-common room with big windows and outdoor tables set on an already lively, café-filled corner. Reached by utilitarian metal steps, there are three floors of dorms (four- and eight-bed, some en suite) and rooms. The rooms are clean, though perhaps due for renovation, and all have fans and colourful curtains. Free boards and bikes; loads of computers for Internet access. Dorms $24, rooms ❷

Clarendon Hotel 347 Hunter St ⓣ02/4927 0966, ⓦwww.clarendonhotel.com.au. This central 1930s Art Deco pub has been beautifully renovated and shows its original features in the bar downstairs. The stylish, vibrantly coloured rooms are totally contemporary and offer great value. Suites have kitchenettes. A bright café-bistro with a huge courtyard does good-value meals from breakfast on. Free parking. ❺

Newcastle Backpackers 42 & 44 Denison St, Hamilton ⓣ02/4969 3436 or 1800 333 436, ⓦwww.newcastlebackpackers.com. An outstanding home-style hostel in two houses; the more upmarket house has doubles, while the other has four- , six- and twelve-bed dorms – run by a friendly family, and with its own heated pool. Located 3km from the city centre and beach but only a few minutes' walk from lively Beaumont Street; bus #260 from the city, or call for a free pick-up. The owner runs people down to the beach most days and offers free surfing lessons (boogie-boards free, surfboards $15 per day). Dorms $21, rooms ❷

Newcastle Beach YHA 30 Pacific St, cnr King St ⓣ02/4925 3544, ⓔmail@newcastleyha.com.au. Fantastic hostel in an impressively restored, spacious old building complete with ballroom, huge staircases and a lounge with a fireplace and leather armchairs, a pool table and courtyard with BBQ, plus the usual facilities. Four-bed dorms, doubles, twins and family rooms. Just 50m from the surf and right in the centre of town; free surfboards and boogie-boards. Dorms $24–25, rooms ❸

Northern Star Hotel 112 Beaumont St, Hamilton ⓣ02/4961 1087. Pub accommodation in a great location on this restaurant- and café-lined street – though with bands downstairs nightly, this is not the place for light sleepers. All double rooms are en suite, spacious, clean and have fridges, TV, tea and coffee facilities and ceiling fans; cheaper shared-bath singles available for $55. ❹

Quality Hotel Noah's on the Beach Cnr Shortland Esplanade and Zaara St ⓣ02/4929 5181, ⓦwww.noahsonthebeach.com.au. Upmarket, modern multi-storey motel right opposite Newcastle Beach. Most rooms have ocean views. Room service. ❺

Stockton Beach Tourist Park Pitt St, Stockton Beach ⓣ02/4928 1393. Picturesquely sited campground right on the extensive beach; two camp kitchens. Two-minute ferry ride from the city. Cabins ❸, en-suite cabins ❹

The City

Newcastle has whole streetscapes of beautiful **Victorian terraces** that would put Sydney's to shame – pick up a free *Newcastle City of Heritage and Enterprise* map from the tourist office, or the *Newcastle Town Walk*, to guide you around some of the old buildings. A couple of buildings in **Newcastle Harbour Foreshore Park** show the trend for the city's wealth of disused public architecture: on one corner of the park stands the beautiful Italianate brick **Customs House**, now a popular pub. Nearby is the wooden two-storey **Paymasters House**, where you can sit with a coffee in its fine verandah café and contemplate the water. The restored **Queens Wharf**, a landmark with its distinctive observation tower, is located on the south bank of the Hunter River. It's linked to the city centre by an elevated walkway from Hunter Street Mall and boasts *The Brewery*, a popular and stylish waterfront drinking spot (see p.225). Further along the foreshore is the new **Honeysuckle** development, an assortment of renovated rail sheds, wharves, pristine walkways and smart new apartments centring on Harbour Square. You'll find a string of stylish café and restaurants here, and on Sunday there's a produce and craft market boasting some interesting food alternatives such as gourmet *pizzettas*.

Besides Newcastle's waterside attractions, a few other places might be of interest. The **Newcastle Regional Museum**, 787 Hunter St (Tues–Sun 10am–5pm, daily during school holidays; free), housed in what began as a brewery in the 1870s, focuses on the history of the mining and steel industries of the area; attached is the Supernova hands-on science centre, much the best thing about the museum (along with the **free Internet access** in the café on weekdays). If you're at a loose end, the **Newcastle Regional Art Gallery**, on Laman Street near Civic Park (Tues–Sun 10am–5pm; free), usually has an interesting temporary exhibition in addition to its permanent display. Alternatively, **Watt Space** on the corner of King and Auckland Streets in the city centre exhibits work by Newcastle University art students and is well worth a visit (Wed–Sun noon–6pm; free).

Beaches and wildlife reserves

The city centre, positioned on a narrow length of land between the Hunter River to the west and the Pacific Ocean to the east, has several popular and pleasantly low-key beaches close by. **Newcastle Beach**, only a few hundred metres from the city on Shortland Esplanade, has patrolled swimming between flags, a sandy saltwater pool perfect for children, shaded picnic tables and good surfing at its southern end. At the northern end, the beautifully painted Art Deco-style free **Ocean Baths** houses the changing pavilions for the huge saltwater pool, which has its own diving board.

Overlooking the water north of Newcastle Beach, **Fort Scratchley**, built in the 1880s, houses a maritime and military museum (generally Sat & Sun and public holidays noon–4pm but check on ⓣ02/4929 3066 as it's volunteer-run; free). Beyond the fort is the long, uncrowded stretch of **Nobbys Beach**, with a lovely old beach pavilion. A walkway leads to Nobbys Head and its nineteenth-century lighthouse.

If you follow Shortland Esplanade south from Newcastle Beach, you'll come to the huge expanse of King Edward Park, with good walking paths and cliff views over this rocky stretch of waterfront. One section of the rock ledge holds Australia's first man-made ocean pool, the **Bogie Hole** chiselled out of the rock by convicts in the early nineteenth century for the Military Commandant's personal bathing pleasure. The cliffs are momentarily intercepted by **Susan Gilmore Beach** – secluded enough to indulge in some nude bathing – then further around the rocks is **Bar Beach**, a popular surfing spot that's floodlit at night. The longer **Merewether Beach** next door has a fabulous ocean baths at its southern end and a separate children's pool; overlooking the beach is the *Merewether Beach Hotel*, a fine place for a drink.

Just two minutes by ferry from Queens Wharf across the Hunter River, the beachside suburb of **Stockton** is the starting point for the extensive, extraordinary **Stockton Beach**, which extends 32km north to **Anna Bay**. Two kilometres wide at some points and covered in moving sand dunes, some of which are up to 30m high, Stockton Bight, it's officially known, looks strikingly like a mini-desert and has been the location for a Bollywood film. It's become something of an adventure playground in recent years, with thrilling quad-bike tours offered by Sand Safaris (2hr; $129, pick-ups from Stockton ferry; ⓣ02/4965 0215, ⓦwww.sandsafaris.com.au) which also take in the 1974 shipwreck, the *Sygna Bergen*. You can sandboard down the dunes on the

4WD beach tours offered by Dawsons Scenic Tours (Ⓣ02/4982 0602; Ⓦwww.portstephensadventure.com.au; from $20; 1hr 30min tour; pick-ups from Anna Bay) or explore them on horseback with Horse Paradise Tours, based at Williamtown (Ⓣ02/4965 1877, Ⓦwww.users.bigpond.com/horseparadise; from 1hr beginner, $40).

Inland, **Blackbutt Reserve** is a large slab of bushland in the middle of Newcastle suburbia in New Lambton Heights about 10km southwest of the city (daily 9am–5pm; free; koala talks Sat & Sun 2.30pm, koala feeding daily 2–3pm); consisting of four valleys, it includes a remnant of rainforest, creeks, lakes and ponds and 20km of walking tracks to explore them. En route you'll see kangaroos, koalas, wombats, emus and other native animals in the reserve's wildlife enclosures. To get here from the city, take bus #222 or #224 to the Carnley Avenue entrance; for the entrances on Lookout Road you can take bus #363; the tourist office produces a helpful free map. Northwest of the city, the **Wetlands Centre**, Sandgate Road, Shortland (Mon–Fri 9am–3pm, Sat & Sun 9am–5pm; $5; Ⓣ02/4951 6466, Ⓦwww.wetlands.org.au), is situated on the wetlands of Hexham Swamp by Ironbark Creek and is home to a mass of birdlife. There are walking and cycling trails here, and you can rent canoes from tourist information. Reach the Wetlands Centre by train from Newcastle to Sandgate, from where it's a ten-minute walk.

Eating

The two streets to head for are **Darby Street**, close to the city centre, which has a multicultural mix of restaurants and some very hip cafés, as well as some secondhand bookshops and retro clothes stores to browse in between coffees; and **Beaumont Street** in Hamilton, 3km northeast of the city centre (train to Hamilton station or bus #260), with a concentration of Italian places, as well as Turkish, Lebanese, Japanese and Indian; it's jam-packed Friday and Saturday nights. Another good spot in the city centre is *Market Square Foodcourt*, upstairs in the Hunter Street Mall, with a range of food bars. Newcastle has the only franchise of the Sydney legend, *Harry's Cafe de Wheels*, an all-day, **late-night** pie-cart (Mon, Tues & Sun to 11pm, Wed & Thurs to 1am, Sat & Sun to 4am) stationed on Wharf Road near *The Brewery* (see below).

Al-Oi-Thai 133 Darby St Ⓣ02/4929 3610. Delicious traditional Thai food served in stylish surrounds. Justifiably popular. Lunch Wed–Sat, dinner Tues–Sun; BYO. Another branch at 50 Beaumont St, Hamilton (Ⓣ02/4969 1434).

Brewery Restaurant "The Boardwalk", 1 Honeysuckle Drive Ⓣ02/4929 5792. Not to be confused with *The Brewery* at Queens Wharf. The best regarded of the contemporary restaurants at the new Honeysuckle development concentrates on fresh seafood and modern bistro-style dishes. Closed Sun dinner.

George's 79 Beaumont St, Hamilton. The popular *George's* has a spacious (and very trendy) interior and also outside tables to check out the busy street action, but it still gets packed: the portions of great contemporary Australian food are huge, coffee is good and you can just come here for a drink. Licensed (and BYO). Daily 8am–10pm.

Goldbergs Coffee House 137 Darby St. This perennially popular Darby Street institution is big, buzzy and airy with modish green walls and polished wooden floors. The emphasis is on the excellent coffee, plus very reasonably priced eclectically modern meals. Also outside courtyard. Daily 7am–midnight. Licensed.

The Last Drop Espresso Bar 37 Hunter St. Great little café near the *YHA* which serves excellent coffee, fresh juices, frappés and smoothies and tasty gourmet sandwiches. Mon–Fri 7am–4pm, plus Nov–Feb Sat & Sun 7am–3pm.

Produce Café Honeysuckle Railway Buildings, Merewether Ⓣ02/4927 5366. Champion of the area's produce, this café uses local ducks, sourdough bread, organic milk and vegetables to rustle up gourmet breakfasts, sandwiches and delicious meals. Daily 7am–3pm.

Salar Couch Cafe 54 Watt St. Quirky, comfortable and relaxed café on the bottom floor of a terrace house: long communal tables, lounging couches and cushions, a fireplace, cool music (good live performances Sun from 3pm and every second Thurs night; ⓣ02/4927 5329 for details), free Internet access, books and games. Delicious food – nothing over $15 – from a spicy international menu. Tues & Wed 11am–5pm, Thurs 11am–10pm, Fri 11am to late, Sat 10am to late, Sun 10am–10pm.

Supply Cnr King & Watt St, around the corner from the *YHA*. With a light, modern and airy interior and groovy music playing, this is a good place to clear a hangover. Breakfasts, pastas, salads and dinner served at very reasonable prices. Daily 8am–10pm.

Entertainment and nightlife

The area known as "the cultural precinct", near Civic Park on King, Hunter and Auckland streets, is the location for three refurbished Art Deco venues; pick up a monthly calendar from the tourist office for details of what's on. The **Civic Theatre**, 375 Hunter St (ⓣ02/4929 1977) hosts mainly big-budget musicals and theatre productions. At the **University Conservatorium of Music** on Auckland Street (ⓣ02/4921 8900), there are often free lunchtime concerts as well as evening performances, while the grand **City Hall**, 290 King St (ⓣ02/4974 2948) has occasional classical music events such as the Australian Chamber Orchestra. Mainstream **cinema** is on offer at the three-screen Greater Union nearby at 183 King St (discount Tues $9; ⓣ02/4926 2233). Both arthouse and mainstream releases are shown around the corner at the three-screen Showcase City Cinemas, 31–33 Wolfe St, off Hunter Street Mall ($12.50; ⓣ02/4929 5019).

For **nightlife listings**, check out the listing supplement "TE" in Wednesday's *Post* or the fortnightly free music mag, *U Turn*. During term time, the students of Newcastle University add a lot of life to the city but there is always a thriving **live music** scene. One of the best venues in town for live bands is the uni's **Bar on the Hill** at Callaghan, 12km west of the city (ⓣ02/4921 5000; bus #260 or train to Warabrook Station) and the **Cambridge Hotel** at 789 Hunter St, West Newcastle (ⓣ02/4962 2459) is also a big venue for touring interstate and international bands. On Friday and Saturday nights the city pubs on Hunter Street and parallel King Street are lively and there are a few **nightclubs** – *Surf City* on adjacent Watt Street has a young crowd and is very popular, while near the harbour, *Fanny's*, 311 Wharf Rd, has a wild reputation.

Pubs and bars

Beaches Hotel Opposite Merewether Beach ⓣ02/4963 1574. With a huge beachfront beer garden this is popular all weekend and is *the* place to go on Sun nights when there are live bands (free).

The Brewery Queens Wharf, 150 Wharf Rd. Popular waterfront drinking hole with three bars – grab tables right on the wharf or on the upstairs balcony. Food from the busy bistro can be eaten outside (weekend breakfasts too). Live music or DJs Wed–Sun. Free.

Crown & Anchor 189 Hunter St. Well-known city boozer, with tables outside alongside the classic, beautifully tiled exterior. Popular balcony upstairs, overlooking the street. The nightclub, *Frost Bites* (Wed–Sun; free), specializes in lethal sno-cone alcoholic drinks.

Finnegan's Cnr Darby and King streets. Newcastle's obligatory Irish theme pub. Inevitably lively and popular, especially with travellers as they often put on free food nights to pack them in.

The Kent 59 Beaumont St, cnr Cleary St, Hamilton ⓣ02/4961 3303. Beautifully renovated old pub and music venue, which is busy most nights – pool comps, quizzes, karaoke, a rock duo Friday to Sunday nights, and Sunday afternoon jazz (4.30–8.30pm) – but with several refuges, including a plant-filled beer garden and a great bistro. No cover charge.

Northern Star Hotel 112 Beaumont St, Hamilton ⓣ02/4961 1087. Music in the back bar nightly from folk to jazz, blues and rock but Friday and Saturday are the big nights for up-and-coming Australian bands (10.30pm–1am; $6–10); other nights mostly free.

Sydney Junction Hotel 8 Beaumont St, Hamilton ⓣ02/4961 2537. "SJs", as the locals call it, is a young and lively pub in an equally animated strip – open to 1am most nights and until 4am Friday and Saturday. Bands – local and touring – and CD launches Thurs–Sat nights. Usually free but entry up to $15 for major gigs.

Listings

Banks and exchange American Express, 49 Hunter St ⓣ1300 139 060. Commonwealth Bank, 136 Hunter Street Mall (ⓣ02/4927 2777), has foreign exchange.

Car rental A.R.A ⓣ02/4962 2488; Thrifty ⓣ02/4942 2266.

Internet access *Internet Cafe*, 58 Lindsay St, off Beaumont St, Hamilton; daily 10am–10pm; $6.60 per hour); *Salar Couch Cafe* (see p.225); Newcastle Regional Museum (see p.224).

Left luggage At the train station (daily 8am–5pm; $1.50 per article).

Post office Newcastle GPO, 96 Hunter St, NSW 2300 (Mon–Fri 8am–5pm).

Supermarket Bi-Lo, cnr King and National Park streets; open 24hr.

Taxi Taxi Services Co-Op ⓣ02/4979 3000.

Travel agent Newcastle Travel, 68 Hunter St ⓣ02/4926 1855.

The Hunter Valley

New South Wales' best-known wine region is the **Hunter Valley,** an area long synonymous with fine **wine** – in particular its golden, citrusy **semillon** and soft and earthy **shiraz**. The first vines were planted in 1828, and some still-existing wine-maker families, such as the Draytons, date back to the 1850s. In what seems a bizarre juxtaposition, this is also a very important **coal-mining region**: in the **Upper Hunter Valley** especially.

By far the best-known wine area, though, is the **Lower Hunter Valley**, nestled under the picturesque **Brokenback Range** around the main town of **CESSNOCK** – even the town's jail and high school have their own vineyards. The town itself is uninteresting, and surprisingly unsophisticated given the wine culture surrounding it, though the main drag, Vincent Street, has been landscaped in an attempt to improve things, and it features some big old country pubs which you can stay at or eat in for a taste of Australian rural life. The wine-tasting area of **Pokolbin** is twelve to fifteen kilometres northwest, and has some very salubrious accommodation and a fine-dining scene, including the **Hunter Valley Gardens Village** (see p.232), whose gardens alone cost millions and include picnic grounds with BBQs.

The Pokolbin area can seem like an exhausting winery-theme park, with its hot-air ballooning, horse-and-carriage rides, wall-to-wall B&Bs, resorts and shops, and wineries offering tours, tastings and wine courses, all screaming out their attractions. To experience the real appeal of the Hunter Valley wine country with its charming bush and farming feel and its vast vineyards seemingly lost among forested ridges, red-soiled dirt tracks, and paddocks with grazing cattle, take the Lovedale/Wilderness Road area north of Cessnock, or visit towns such as Wollombi, 28km southwest; Broke, 35km northwest; Branxton, 22km north; and the still unspoilt Upper Hunter, west of Muswellbrook, with its marvellous ridges and rocky outcrops.

Pick up the excellent free *Hunter Valley Wine Country* guide with a handy pull-out map from the **Hunter Valley Wine Country Visitor Information Centre** (Mon–Thurs 9am–5.30pm, Fri & Sat Sun 9am–6pm, Sun 9am–4pm; ⓣ02/4990 4477, ⓦwww.winecountry.com.au), Main Road, Pokolbin, scenically sited amongst vineyards and with the pleasant, affordable *Wine Country Café*. If it's closed you can still pick up the free guides from a rack outside. Try to tour the wineries during the week; at weekends both the number of visitors and accommodation prices go up, and it can get booked out completely when there's a concert on in the valley. In late October Wyndham Estate (see p.229) hosts the night-time **Opera in the Vineyards** (bookings via Ticketek ⓣ02/9266 4800; tickets $72–$112; ⓦwww.wyndhamestate.com) on the banks of the Hunter River, followed a week later by a day of fine food, wine and

Hunter Valley wineries

Nearly 150 wineries cluster around the Lower Hunter Valley and there are less than twenty in the Upper Hunter; almost all offer **free wine tastings**. Virtually all wineries are open daily at least between 10am and 4pm, and many offer **guided tours**. These include: McWilliams Mt Pleasant Estate, Marrowbone Rd, Pokolbin (daily 11am; 45min $2.20); Hunter Resort, Hermitage Rd, Pokolbin (daily 11am & 2pm; 45min; $5, refunded on wine purchase; bookings ⓣ02/4998 7777); and at Drayton's, Tyrrell's, Wandin Valley, and Wyndham Estate, all detailed below.

The Hunter Resort also runs an excellent **wine course** (daily 9am–11am; $25; bookings essential) including a tour followed by a tasting-instruction tutorial; and Ivanhoe, Marrowbone Rd, Pokolbin, conducts free wine appreciation classes (daily 10.30am & 1pm; 45min) with hillside vineyard views from the balcony. There are **museums** at the famous Lindeman's, McDonalds Rd, Pokolbin (daily 10am–5pm), where Dr Lindeman first planted his vines in 1842; the swish Tulloch's (Debeyers Rd, Pokolbin), whose display includes early-twentieth-century photos by Australian photographer and family friend, Max Dupain; Reg Drayton Wines (cnr McDonalds and Pokolbin Mountains roads, Pokolbin); and a nineteenth-century "shop" museum at Oakvale (Broke Rd, Pokolbin), whose tasting area also sells **wine-related books**. Some impressive new **state-of-the art wineries** are worth checking out, too, including the space-station-like Hungerford Hill (Broke Rd, Pokolbin ⓣ02/4990 0711 with its fine-dining restaurant *Terroir* (mains $15–$32) and smart café. Enjoy fine panoramic **views** at Audrey Wilkinson (Debeyers Rd, Pokolbin) and Tinklers Vineyard (see p.233), from where you can continue to the Pokolbin Mountains Lookout. The award-winning Pepper Tree Wines, Halls Rd, Pokolbin, with its French-rustic feel, has beautiful **gardens**. Below are a few more of our favourites, but by meandering you'll discover your own gems.

Allandale Lovedale Rd, Pokolbin ⓣ02/4990 4526. Picturesque, medium-sized winery established in 1978. Set on a hill, with great views overlooking the vineyard and the Brokenback Range. All their wines are highly recommended but make sure you try their prize-winning Chardonnay. Mon–Sat 9am–5pm, Sun 10am–5pm.

Cruikshank Callatoota Estate Wybong Rd, Wybong, Upper Hunter Valley, 18km north of Denman ⓣ02/6547 8149. Owner John Cruikshank, a real character, has been making red wine here since 1974. All grapes are estate-grown and everything is done in-house including the bottling. The slow pace – only the well-regarded rosé is rushed off the shelves – and unpretentious cellar door suits the remote feel of the place whose vineyards nestle below bush-covered ridges. BBQ and picnic facilities, or light lunch available. Daily 9am–5pm.

Constable & Hershon. Gillards Rd, Pokolbin ⓣ02/4998 7887. Established in 1981 by two best friends, this small establishment feels like a personal dream come true (wine is made by contract winemaker Neil McGuigan; the owners visit on annual holiday from England). The 12-hectare vineyard under the Brokenback Ranges has five formal gardens – Sculpture, Camellia, Rose, Herb and Secret – and you're encouraged to wander around with a glass of semillon. Otherwise, weekdays at 10.30am the gardener leads a tour. After a stroll, there's an unhurried sit-down tasting. Daily 10am–5pm.

Drayton's Family Wines Oakey Creek Rd, Pokolbin ⓣ02/4998 7513. Friendly, down-to-earth winery, established in 1853. Everything from vine to bottling is still done here and the excellent tours (Mon–Fri 11am; 40min; free) show the whole process. A pretty picnic area with

music at **Jazz in the Vines** (ⓣ02/4933 2439, ⓦwww.jazzinthevines.com.au; tickets $35–$70) based at Tyrrell's vineyard (see p.229). In late November (and wood-fired BBQ overlooks a small dam and vineyards. Mon–Fri 8am–5pm, Sat & Sun 10am–5pm.

Peterson Champagne House Cnr Broke and Branxton roads, Pokolbin ☎02/4998 7881. The only Hunter Valley winery to specialise in sparkling wines, they also use their *méthode champenoise* expertise to produce for other wineries. The pretty duck-pond set stone building makes a pleasant tasting – and eating – spot: the *Magnum Café*'s fantastic, well-priced cooked breakfast (daily 9am–11am) can be teamed with some champers. For more indulgence, the Hunter Valley Chocolate Factory is right next door. Daily 9am–5pm.

Rosemount Estate Rosemount Rd, 8km west of Denman, Upper Hunter ☎02/6549 6400. Producer of some of Australia's best-known, award-winning wines. Its excellent brasserie at pub-food prices (lunch Wed–Sun, dinner Thurs–Sat) is a relaxing spot, with marvellous vineyard views. Also picnic tables and BBQs. Daily 10am–4pm.

Scarborough Gillards Rd, Pokolbin ☎02/4998 7563. Small, friendly winery has a reputation for outstanding wines' specializing in Chardonnay and Pinot Noir. Pleasantly relaxed sit-down tastings are held in a small cottage on Hungerford Hill with wonderful valley views. Daily 9am–5pm.

Tamburlaine McDonalds Rd, Pokolbin ☎02/4998 7570. The jasmine-scented garden outside provides a hint of the flowery, elegant wines within. Tastings are well orchestrated and delivered with a heap of experience. Daily 9.30am–5pm.

Tempus Two Broke Rd, Pokolbin. This huge, spectacular winery – all steel, glass and stone – looks worth every cent of its $7-million cost. A high-tech urban chic exterior – terrace, fountains and amphitheatre – meets a rural landscape of vineyards and dam, its contemporary designed interior continuing down even to the sinuous bottles with their distinctive pewter labels. Owned by Lisa McGuigan, of the well-known winemaking family, whose unique-tasting wines are the result of using lesser-known varieties such as Pinot Gris, Viognier and Marsanne. The attached Japanese-Thai *Oishi* (☎02/4993 3999) has surprisingly moderate prices (noodle soups $8, mains $16.50), and there's a lounge area where you can relax over an espresso. Daily 9am–5pm.

Tyrrell's Broke Rd, Pokolbin ☎02/4998 7509. The oldest independent family vineyards, producing consistently fine wines. The tiny ironbark slab hut, where Edward Tyrrell lived when he began the winery in 1858, is still in the grounds, and the old winery with its cool earth floor is much as it was. Beautiful setting against the Brokenback Range. One of the best. Mon–Sat 8am–5pm, with free tour 1.30pm.

Wandin Valley Estate Cnr Wilderness and Lovedale roads ☎02/4930 7317. Picturesquely sited on a hundred acres of vineyards with magnificent views across the Wategos and the Brokenback Ranges, especially from the balcony of the European-style *Bel Posto Café/Restaurant*; mains $17–$20; cellar-door priced wine. Free tours Sat & Sun 11am. Daily 10am–5pm.

Wyndham Estate, Dalwood Rd, Dalwood. A scenic drive through the Dalwood Hills leads to the Lower Hunter's northern extent, where Englishman George Wyndham first planted Shiraz in 1828. Now owned by multinational Pernod Ricard, there's an excellent guided tour (daily 11am; free) which covers the vines and winemaking techniques and equipment, including the original basket press. The idyllic riverside setting – grassy lawns, free BBQs – makes a great spot for picnics and the annual opera concert. Restaurant (☎02/4938 3444) and outdoor café. Daily 10am–4.30pm.

in early March), Bimbadgen Estate (see p.233), hosts **A Day on the Green**, a sunset concert in their amphitheatre, featuring the likes of Elvis Costello and

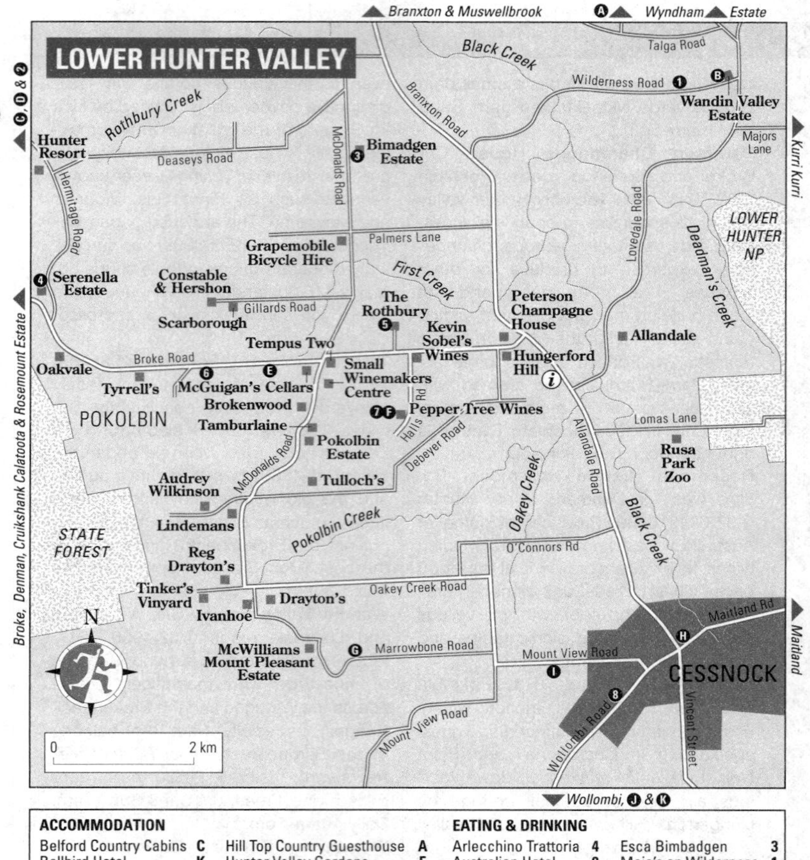

ACCOMMODATION				EATING & DRINKING			
Belford Country Cabins	C	Hill Top Country Guesthouse	A	Arlecchino Trattoria	4	Esca Bimbadgen	3
Bellbird Hotel	K	Hunter Valley Gardens	E	Australian Hotel	8	Mojo's on Wilderness	1
Cedar Creek Vineyard Cottages	J	Peppers Convent	F	Café Belltree	2	Robert's at Peppertree	7
Cessnock Hotel	H	Splinters Guest House	D	Café Enzo	6	Toby's Coffee House	5
Elfin Hill Motel	G	Valley Vineyards Tourist Park	I				
		Wandin Valley Estate	B				

Bryan Adams (tickets through Ticketek; $75–$100; Ⓦwww.adayonthegreen.com.au).

Other Hunter Valley activities include **hot air ballooning** – Balloon Aloft Australia offers sunrise champagne flights ($280, standbys $220; Ⓣ02/4938 1955 or 1800 028 568, Ⓦwww.balloonaloft.com). *Hill Top Country Guesthouse* (see p.232) offers cross-country **horse riding** on their 300-acre property ($45; 1hr 30min) and a 4WD wildlife-spotting tour ($30; 1hr), which leaves at dusk, when you're likely to see kangaroos, wallabies and wombats.

Getting there and around

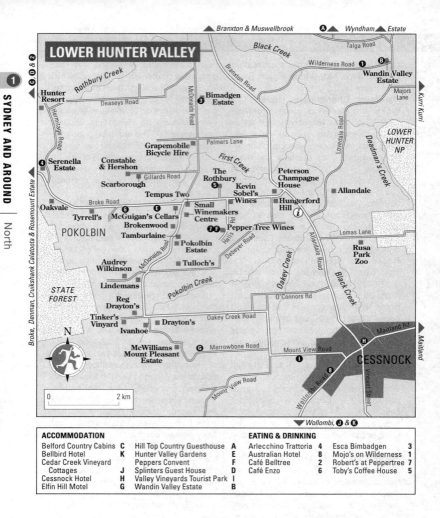

By car, the Lower Hunter Valley is two hours north of Sydney along the National Highway 1 (the F3), or for a more scenic route turn off the F3 towards Peats Ridge and drive via the **Wollombi Valley**. A meandering route from the Blue Mountains via **Putty Road** is popular with motorcyclists. Rover Coaches (ⓣ02/4990 1699, ⓦwww.rovercoaches.com.au) leaves daily from Sydney Airport, Central station and Circular Quay via Newcastle and Maitland to Cessnock and on to Pokolbin resorts. Keans (ⓣ02/6543 1322) goes from Central station to Scone via the Hunter Valley (once daily except Sat); stops include Kurri Kurri, Neath, Cessnock, Pokolbin and Muswellbrook. For the Upper Hunter, take a train to Newcastle where Sid Fogg's Coachlines (ⓣ02/4928 1088) heads daily to Maitland, Branxton, Singleton, Muswellbrook and Denman.

Before you think about driving and wine-tasting, consider the perils of drink-driving. Rover Coaches (above) offers a daily **hop-on-hop-off** Wine Rover service; stops include the tourist office, around eighteen wineries plus eating places (Mon–Fri; $35, Sat & Sun; $40). **Vineyard tours** are also an option, with a big range on offer. Many are exhausting return trips from Sydney (see box on pp.212–213), but several local operators offer day-trips from within the valley. The excellent, long-established Hunter Valley Day Tours (ⓣ02/4938 5031, ⓦwww.huntertourism.com/daytours) offers a wine-and-cheese tasting tour ($80 for Cessnock, Pokolbin and Maitland pick-ups; $95 from Newcastle; restaurant lunch included), with very informative commentary. The long-established, family-run, Hunter Vineyard Tours (ⓣ02/4991 1659, ⓦwww.huntervineyardtours.com.au) visits five wineries (Cessnock pick-up $50, Newcastle or Maitland $55; restaurant lunch $25 extra). Also recommended are Trek About 4WD Tours (ⓣ02/4990 8277, ⓦwww.hunterweb.com.au/trekabout; $44) and Aussie Wine Tours (ⓣ02/4991 1074, ⓦwww.aussiewinetours.com.au; $45 weekend, $40 mid-week), both supportive of small local wineries and flexible. Otherwise, you can **rent bikes** from Grapemobile, on the corner of McDonalds Road and Palmers Lane, Pokolbin (ⓣ0500 804 039, ⓦwww.grapemobile.com.au; $22 per day), or hire a **taxi** (Cessnock RadioCabs ⓣ02/4990 1111).

Hunter Valley accommodation

Since the Hunter Valley is a popular weekend trip for Sydneysiders, accommodation **prices** rise on Friday and Saturday nights and most places only offer two-night deals; the price-ranges below indicate the substantial mid-week to weekend variable. Advance **booking** is essential for weekends, or during the October–November string of events.

Belford Country Cabins 659 Hermitage Rd, Pokolbin ⓣ02/6574 7100, ⓦwww.belfordcabins.com.au. Family-run, fully equipped self-catering two- and four-bedroom wooden bungalows set in bushland. Comfy, spacious and clean cabins – renovated ones are quite stylish – each with its own barbecue. Games room with pool table, table tennis and TV; outdoor pool and playground. ❹–❺

Bellbird Hotel 388 Wollombi Rd, Bellbird, 5km southwest of Cessnock ⓣ02/4990 1094. Classic country pub, circa 1908, with wide iron-lace verandah and a bar full of rustic charm. Eat inexpensive no-frills bistro food in the pleasant beer garden; adjacent playground. All rooms share bathrooms. Mid-week light breakfast included (❸) or weekend cooked breakfast (❹).

Cedar Creek Vineyard Cottages Wollombi Rd, Cedar Creek, 10km northwest of Wollombi ⓣ02/4998 1576, ⓦwww.cedarcreekcottages.com.au. An idyllic choice away from the busy Pokolbin area on a 550-acre deer- and cattle-stocked farm. Run by Stonehurst Wines, whose tiny chapel-like tasting room, constructed from recycled materials, and wine from insecticide-free, handpicked, estate-grown grapes, illustrate the owners' philosophy. The self-catering cottages are made from recycled timber. Expect queen-sized beds, wood combustion stoves, ceiling fans, flowers on the table, TV, CD-player, comfy lounges, stylish decor, and a BBQ outside. Breakfast hamper, port and chocolate included; civilised noon check-out. ❺–❻

Cessnock Hotel 234 Wollombi Rd, Cessnock ⓣ02/4990 1002, ⓦwww.cessnockhotel.com.au. Renovated pub with a great bistro-cum-bar, the *Kurrajong Café*. Rooms all share bathrooms but they're huge with high ceilings, fans and really comfy beds. Big verandah to hang out on; cooked breakfast served in the café. ❸–❹

Elfin Hill Motel Marrowbone Rd, Pokolbin ⓣ02/4998 7543, ⓔelfinhill@hunterlink.com.au. Friendly, family-run hilltop motel with extensive views is particularly good value mid-week. Comfortable, modest timber-cabin-style air-con units; saltwater pool and tranquil BBQ area. Light breakfast included. Plans for a common room and guest kitchen. ❹–❻

Hill Top Country Guesthouse 288 Talga Rd, Rothbury ⓣ02/4930 7111, ⓦwww.hilltopguesthouse.com.au. Rural retreat on 300 acres of the Molly Morgan range, with fantastic views. Explore the property by foot, horse (see p.230), two-seater bush buggy ($60 per hour), mountain bike ($16.50 half-day), 4WD tour, or take a canoe on the dam ($35 per hour). The modern brick building has the feel of an old-fashioned guesthouse, with a piano, billiard table and wood fire in the communal rooms. Mock-antique-style bedrooms have TV; cheaper ones share bathroom. Also a large unit with a spa (❻–❼). Light breakfast included (lunch and dinner available). Rooms ❹–❺; en-suite ❺–❼

Hunter Valley Gardens Broke Rd, Pokolbin ⓣ02/4998 7854, ⓦwww.hvg.com.au. Resort set in extensive lakeside gardens, complete with a shopping mall and cafés and restaurants. The modern motel–hotel complex overlooks the vineyards, and has a popular Irish pub and bistro, *Harrigan's*, an Italian restaurant, a heated pool, spa, sauna, tennis courts and three accommodation standards: four-and-a-half-star *Tallawanta Lodge* with 72 rooms from $300; smart four-star motel-style *Harrigan's* (❼); and good-value self-contained one- and two-bedroom cabins at *Grapeview Villas* ❸–❺

Peppers Convent Halls Rd, Pokolbin ⓣ02/4998 7764, ⓦwww.peppers.com.au. The swankiest place to stay in the Hunter Valley, with a price to match (from $360 per night). The guesthouse, converted from an old convent, has heaps of cosy cachet, fireplaces and low beams. Part of the Pepper Tree winery (see box p.228), with wine tasting there and fine-dining at *Robert's Restaurant* (see p.233), just a stroll away. ❽

Splinters Guest House 617 Hermitage Rd, Pokolbin 02/6574 7118, ⓦwww.splinters.com.au. Built and run by an affable former woodwork teacher, the mezzanine-bedroomed cottages on this 25-acre property feature heaps of timber, slate floors, lead-light windows and New Guinea artefacts. And come with wood-combustion stove, leather armchairs and kitchen with espresso coffee machine (cook-your-own breakfast supplied). Also en-suite rooms ❺–❻ with a mini espresso-machine and an egg cooker (light breakfast included); everyone gets port and chocolate in their room. There's a covered BBQ area with fountain, a telescope, guest-lounge massage chairs, a practice golf green, gazebo, walking tracks, dogs and horses. Wineries and restaurant within wandering distance. Best value around, especially mid-week. Cottages ❺–❼

Valley Vineyards Tourist Park 137 Mount View Rd, 2km northwest of Cessnock ⓣ02/4990 2573, ⓦwww.valleyvineyard.com.au. High-standard campsite with kitchen, BBQ area, pool and on-site Thai restaurant. Cabins (BYO linen) have external en suites, cottages (linen included) internal. Cabins ❸–❹; cottages ❹–❺

Wandin Valley Estate Wilderness Rd, Lovedale ⓣ02/4930 7317, ⓦwww.wandinvalley.com.au. Two- to four-bedroom Tuscan-style villas on two levels situated on wonderful winery estate (see p.229), and owned by a former *A Country Practice* TV producer (set in fictional Wandin Valley). You can wonder from your villa through vineyards, where grazing kangaroos are a common sight at dusk. The huge cathedral-ceilinged villas are comfortable and stylish (though some bathrooms are disappointing), with everything from woodfires to wine books to read. Expect two bottles of wine and generous cook-your-own breakfast provisions. Portable BBQ, swimming pool and tennis court. ❼–❽

Eating and drinking

Many of the Hunter's excellent (and pricey) restaurants are attached to wineries or are among vineyards rather than in the towns (see box on pp.228–229), while the Hunter's large old pubs dish out less fancy but more affordable grub; see the "Accommodation" section above for bistro options. Every year over a mid-May weekend around eight wineries along and around the scenic Lovedale and Wilderness roads team up with local restaurants to host the **Lovedale Long Lunch** (ⓣ02/4930 7611, ⓦwww.lovedalelonglunch.com.au). The Hunter olive-growing industry has also taken off: check out the Hunter Olive Centre (Pokolbin Estate Vineyard, McDonalds Rd, Pokolbin; ⓣ02/4998 7524), where you can enquire about the weekend-long **The Feast of the Olive Festival** in late September. Other places where you can taste the local wares include The Hunter Valley Cheese Company at the McGuigan Cellars, Broke Road; the newer Binnorie Dairy, just across the road from the Hunter Resort (below), which specializes in soft fresh cheeses; and fresh farm produce at Tinkler's Vineyard, Pokolbin Mountains Rd; you can drink local-brewed beer at the Blue Tongue Brewery at the Hunter Resort (daily 7.30am–midnight). Just about every winery and accommodation place in the valley has a BBQ, so for picnic or self-catering supplies there's the large Coles **supermarket** in Cessnock, at 1 North Ave (Mon–Sat 6am–midnight, Sun 8am–8pm), or the small supermarket in the Hunter Valley Gardens Village. You can also get deli supplies from the Australian Regional Food Store at the Small Winemakers Centre on McDonalds Rd.

Arlecchino Trattoria Serenella Estate, Hermitage Rd, Pokolbin ☎02/4998 7120. Stylish interpretation of a trattoria, attached to the Cecchini-family-established winery. The wood-fired pizza ($10.50–$18) is worth the drive out here; a small but delicious menu includes pasta and risotto ($17), a few meaty mains ($24) and gelato. The dining room, with cool stone floors and crisp white tablecloths, overlooks a dam and vineyards from windows on three sides. Lunch Wed–Sun, dinner Wed–Sat.

Australian Hotel 136 Wollombi Rd, Cessnock. The excellent bistro at *The Australian* is popular with the locals, and the pub showcases the Hunter's coal-mining roots with mining paraphernalia and related art. Though some steaks hit the $25 mark, mains average between $15–$19, and the menu encompasses stir-fries, gourmet salads and vegetarian dishes.

Café Belltree Margan Family Winegrowers, 266 Hermitage Rd, Pokolbin ☎02/6574 7216. After twenty Tyrrell's vintages and six in France, winemaker Andrew Margan turns out some tasty wines, and the attached Mediterranean-influenced eatery is pretty good too. Dishes use seasonal, local produce, and a changing blackboard menu of share plates (around $20; wines served with a $5 corkage) adds to the convivial atmosphere. Most lunchtimes it's crowded and lively, and you'll need to book, despite the café appellation. The deck is a great spot to hang out and soak up the isolated bush feel with a cake teamed with a Toby's Estate Coffee in the quieter morning or afternoon. Daily 10am–5pm.

Café Enzo Peppers Creek Antiques, Broke Rd, Pokolbin. Relaxing courtyard café which feels like it's been lifted from the south of France; light Mediterranean menu ($14–$25) and excellent Italian-style coffee, or start the day here with a cooked breakfast. Though it's pricey, the spot is worth it. Mon & Tues 10am–4pm, Wed–Sun 9am–5pm.

Esca Bimbadgen Lot 21, McDonalds Rd, Pokolbin ☎02/4998 4666. With a squint this winery, complete with fountain and bell tower, could be in Europe. Its modern restaurant, however, is all timber and glass, reached via the working winery (make sure you taste the wines before dining), and with wonderful vineyard and mountain views from the balcony. Food, with mains around the $32 mark, is contemporary European, with veal, spatchcock and roast duck all on the menu. Lunch daily, dinner Wed–Sat.

Mojo's on Wilderness Wilderness Rd, Lovedale ☎02/4930 7244. A British Michelin-rated chef and his Australian chef-wife create the divine modern British/Australian food at this bush-set restaurant. Warm, local-art decorated interior, flowery courtyard with hillside views, cheerful staff and a laid-back vibe. Set dinner menu (2-course $48, 3-course $60) has suggested wines for each course, many from the Lovedale–Wilderness Road area and all available by the glass (lunch mains $17–$27). Popular all-day Sunday brunch (10am–3pm) with outstanding Eggs Benedict. Lunch & dinner Thurs–Mon.

Robert's at Peppertree Peppertree Winery, Halls Rd, Pokolbin ☎02/4998 7330. *Robert's* is a long-established Hunter Valley fine-dining institution, as much for the setting in a charming 1876 wooden farmhouse filled with flowers and antiques, and shaded by a huge peppertree, as for the French rustic-style food which is cooked in a wood-fired oven. Mains average $38.

Toby's Coffee House The Rothbury Estate, Broke Rd, Pokolbin. Upstairs, above the Rothbury Estate cellar door, this contemporary-style café's huge windows provide views over vineyards and bush to far-off hills. Focus is on the smooth, rich Toby's Estate Coffee to enjoy with a selection of great cakes and cookies. A simple all-day menu – shareable cheese plates from Binnorie Dairy ($20), antipasto plates ($17) or mugs of soup with a baguette ($6.50) – can be enjoyed with a glass of Rothbury Estate wine ($5.50). Daily 10.30am–3.30pm.

West

For over sixty years, Sydney has slid ever westwards in a monotonous sprawl of shopping centres, brick-veneer homes and fast-food chains, along the way swallowing up towns and villages, some dating back to colonial times. The first settlers to explore inland found well-watered, fertile river flats, and quickly established agricultural outposts to support the fledgling colony. **Parramatta**, **Liverpool**, **Penrith** and **Campbelltown**, once separate communities, are now satellite towns inside Sydney's commuter belt. Yet, despite Sydney's advance, bushwalkers will find there's still plenty of wild west to explore in the beauty of the **Blue Mountains**. Heading west, however, now starts for many travellers with a visit to the Olympic site at **Homebush Bay**.

Parramatta and Penrith

Situated on the Parramatta River, a little over 20km upstream from the harbour mouth, **PARRAMATTA** was the first of Sydney's rural satellites – the first farm settlement in Australia, in fact. The fertile soil of "Rosehill", as it was originally called, saved the fledgling colony from starvation with its first wheat crop of 1789. It's hard to believe today, but dotted here and there among the malls and busy roads are a few remnants from that time – eighteenth-century public

Sydney Olympic Park at Homebush Bay

The main focus of the 2000 Olympic events was **Sydney Olympic Park** at **Homebush Bay**. Virtually the geographical heart of the westward-sprawling city, Homebush Bay already had some heavy-duty sporting facilities – the State Sports Centre and the Aquatic Centre – in place. The **Sydney Olympic Park Authority (SOPA)** is turning Sydney Olympic Park into an entertainment and sporting complex with family-oriented recreation in mind, with events such as free outdoor movies, multicultural festivals and children's holiday activities. For details check Ⓦwww.sydneyolympicpark.nsw.gov.au.

The A$470-million Olympic site was centred around the 110,000-seat **Telstra Stadium**, the venue for the opening and closing ceremonies, track and field events, and marathon and soccer finals. And despite a A$68-million overhaul to reduce the number of seats to 83,500, it's still Sydney's largest stadium, though with a more realistic number for its use as an Australian Rules football, cricket, rugby league, rugby union, soccer and concert venue. Tours of the Stadium, with commentary, are available daily (hourly 10.30am–3.30pm; 30min tour $15, 1hr tour $26; turn up at Gate C but check it's a non-event day first by contacting Ⓣ02/8765 2360 or Ⓦwww.telstrastadium.com.au).

Just south of the stadium is the **State Sports Centre** (daily 9am–5pm; Ⓣ02/9763 0111, Ⓦwww.sscbay.nsw.gov.au), where you can visit the **NSW Hall of Champions**, devoted to the state's sporting heroes (same hours as centre; free; the Hall is closed when events are on at the State Sports Centre, so call before setting out); and the **Sydney International Aquatic Centre** (Nov–March Mon–Fri 5am–8.45pm, Sat & Sun 6am–7.45pm; April–Oct Mon–Fri 5am–8.45pm, Sat & Sun 6am–6.45pm; swim & spa $6).

On the south side of the site, you can watch tennis tournaments (the big one is the Medibank International, second week of January) or rent a court at the **Sydney International Tennis Centre** (Ⓣ02/8746 0777, Ⓦwww.sydneytennis.com.au), while on the north side, the 21,000-seat **Sydney Superdome** (Ⓣ02/8765 4321, Ⓦwww.superdome.com.au), which hosted the basketball, rhythmic gymnastics and paralympic basketball, is Sydney's basketball stadium and is also used as a concert buildings and original settlers' dwellings that warrant a visit if you're interested in Australian history. Today Parramatta is the headquarters of many government agencies and law firms.

It's a thirty-minute suburban train ride from Central station to Parramatta, but the most enjoyable way to get here is on the sleek RiverCat ferry from Circular Quay up the Parramatta River (1hr; $7 one-way). The wharf is on Phillip Street, a couple of blocks away from the helpful visitor centre within the **Parramatta Heritage Centre**, corner of Church and Market streets (daily 9am–5pm; ⓣ02/8839 3300, ⓦwww.visitsydney.org/parramatta), by the convict-built Lennox Bridge. The centre hands out free walking route maps detailing its historical attractions. From the ferry wharf, you can walk here in around ten minutes along the colourful paved Riverside Walk, decorated with Aboriginal motifs and interpretative plaques telling the story of the Burramatagal people. One block south of the visitor centre, the area around the corner of Church and Phillip streets has become an **"eat street"** with around twenty cafés and restaurants, including Filipino, Chinese, Malaysian and Japanese, reflecting Parramatta's multicultural mix. Parramatta's most important historic feature is the National Trust-owned **Old Government House** (Mon–Fri 10am–4pm, Sat & Sun 10.30am–4pm; $7) in **Parramatta Park** by the river. Entered through the 1885 gatehouse on O'Connell Street, the park – filled with native trees – rises up to the gracious old Georgian-style building,

venue. The Royal Agricultural Society Showground, taking up an extensive area at the very north of the site, hosts the annual Royal Easter Show (see p.203).

Opposite the Olympic site is the huge **Bicentennial Park**, opened in 1988; more than half is conservation wetlands – a boardwalk explores the mangroves and you can observe the profusion of native birds from a bird hide. There are around 8km of cycling and walking tracks and the Parklands Express Train Shuttle tours the wetlands on Sundays (12.30pm, 1.15pm, 2.15pm, 3pm & 3.45pm; 45min; $4.40), with four hop-on-hop-off stops. Further north, the green-friendly Athletes' Village is now a solar-powered suburb, **Newington**.

To get an overview of the site, there's an **observation centre** on the 17th floor of the *Novotel Hotel* (daily 10am–4pm; $4; ⓦwww.sydneyolympicparkhotels.com.au), on Olympic Boulevard between the Telstra Stadium and the Aquatic Centre. The *Novotel* is Olympic Park's social focus, with several places to eat and drink including the popular *Homebush Bay Brewery*.

Visiting the venues

The best way to get out to Olympic Park is to take a ferry up the Parramatta River: the **RiverCat** from Circular Quay ($6 one-way to Homebush Bay) stops off frequently en route to Parramatta. Otherwise, a direct **train** from Central to Olympic Park station runs four times daily weekdays (otherwise and at weekends change at Lidcombe station from where trains depart every 10min). You can get to some venues directly by **bus** from Strathfield train station: #401–404 run regularly to the Homebush Bay Olympic Centre, the State Sports Centre and the Athletic Centre via the Olympic Park ferry wharf. To get around the extensive site you can **hire bikes**, though on the weekend only ($12 hour, $22 half-day) from the **Sydney Olympic Park Visitor Gateway**, right next to Olympic Park station on the corner of Showground Road and Murray Rose Avenue (daily 9am–5pm; ⓣ02/9714 7888). The **Games Trail Tour**, a walking tour exploring the Olympic sites and stories leaves from outside the information centre (daily noon, 1.30pm & 3pm; no bookings necessary; $20; 1hr).

the oldest remaining public edifice in Australia. It was built between 1799 and 1816 and used as the Viceregal residence until 1855; one wing has been converted into a pleasant teahouse. One-and-a-half kilometres west to the end of Macquarie Street, then 300m south down Harris Street, the aptly named **Experiment Farm Cottage**, 9 Ruse St (Tues–Fri 10.30am–3.30pm, Sat & Sun 11am–3.30pm; $5.50), another National Trust property, was built on the site of the first land grant, given in 1790 to reformed convict James Ruse. On parallel Alice Street, at no. 70, **Elizabeth Farm** (daily 10am–5pm; $7) dates from 1793 and claims to be the oldest surviving home in the country. The farm was built and run by the Macarthurs, who bred the first of the merino sheep that made Australian wealth "ride on a sheep's back"; a small café here serves refreshments. Nearby **Hambledon Cottage**, 63 Hassall St (Wed, Thurs, Sat & Sun 11am–4pm; $4), built in 1824, was part of the Macarthur estate.

Continuing west, the Western Highway and the rail lines head on to **PENRITH**, the most westerly of Sydney's satellite towns, in a curve of the Nepean River at the foot of the Blue Mountains (on the way out here you pass **Featherdale Wildlife Park**; see box on p.215). Penrith has an old-fashioned Aussie feel about it – a tight community that is immensely proud of the Panthers, its boisterous rugby league team. The area is also the home of the extensive International Regatta Centre on Penrith Lakes, spreading between Castlereagh and Cranebrook roads north of the town centre, and used in the Olympics; at **Penrith Whitewater Stadium** you can go on a thrilling 90-minute **white-water rafting** session ($66; bookings ⓣ02/4730 4333, ⓦwww.penrithwhitewater.com.au). You can take in the splendour of the spectacular **Nepean Gorge** from the decks of the paddle-steamer *Nepean Belle* (range of cruises from $15 for 1hr 30min; ⓣ02/4733 1274, ⓦwww.nepeanbelle.com.au), or head 24km south to the **Warragamba Dam**, Sydney's water supply. The dam has created the huge reservoir of **Lake Burragorang**, a popular picnic spot with barbecues and a kiosk, and some easy walking trails through the bush.

The Blue Mountains region

The section of the Great Dividing Range nearest Sydney gets its name from the blue mist that rises from millions of eucalyptus trees and hangs in the mountain air, tinting the sky and the range alike. In the colony's early days, the **Blue Mountains** were believed to be an insurmountable barrier to the west. The first expeditions followed the streams in the valleys until they were defeated by cliff faces rising vertically above them. Only in 1813, when the explorers Wentworth, Blaxland and Lawson followed the ridges instead of the valleys, were the "mountains" (actually a series of canyons) finally conquered, allowing the western plains to be opened up for settlement. The range is surmounted by a plateau at an altitude of more than 1000m where, over millions of years, rivers have carved deep valleys into the sandstone, and winds and driving rain have helped to deepen the ravines, creating a spectacular scenery of sheer precipices and walled canyons. Before white settlement, the Daruk Aborigines lived here, dressed in animal-skin cloaks to ward off the cold. An early coal-mining industry, based in Katoomba, was followed by tourism which snowballed after the arrival of the railway in 1868; by 1900 the first three mountain stations of Wentworth Falls, Katoomba and Mount Victoria had been established as fashionable resorts, extolling the health-giving benefits of eucalyptus-tinged mountain air. In 2000 the Blue Mountains became a **UNESCO World Heritage Site**, joining the Great Barrier Reef;

the listing came after abseiling was finally banned on the mountains' most famous scenic wonder, the **Three Sisters**, after forty years of clambering had caused significant erosion. The Blue Mountains stand out from other Australian forests, in particular for the **Wollemi Pine**, discovered in 1994 (see p.242), a "living fossil" which dates back to the dinosaur era.

All the villages and towns of the romantically dubbed "**City of the Blue Mountains**" – principally Glenbrook, Springwood, Wentworth Falls, Leura, Katoomba and Blackheath – lie on a ridge, connected by the Great Western Highway. Around them is the **Blue Mountains National Park**, the state's fourth-largest national park and to many minds the best. The region makes a great weekend break from the city, with stunning views and clean air complemented by a wide range of accommodation, cafés and restaurants. But be warned: at weekends, and during the summer holidays, Katoomba is thronged with escapees from the city, and prices escalate accordingly. Even at their most crowded, though, the Blue Mountains always offer somewhere where you can find peace and quiet, and even solitude – the deep gorges and high rocks make much of the terrain inaccessible except to bushwalkers and mountaineers. Climbing schools offer courses in rock-climbing, abseiling and canyoning for both beginners and experienced climbers, while Glenbrook is a popular mountain-biking spot.

Transport, tours and information

Public transport to the mountains is quite good but your own vehicle will give you much greater flexibility, allowing you to take detours to old mansions, cottage gardens and the lookout points scattered along the ridge. **Trains** leave from Central station for Mount Victoria and/or Lithgow and follow the highway, stopping at all the major towns en route (frequent departures until about midnight; 2hr; $11.40 one-way to Katoomba, $14 off-peak day return). If you're dependent on public transport, Katoomba makes the best base: facilities and services are concentrated here, and there are **local buses** to attractions in the vicinity and to other centres. Blue Mountains Bus Co (Ⓣ02/4751 1077) has several commuter routes from Katoomba: to Blackheath; Mount Victoria (no service weekends); Echo Point and the Scenic World complex; Leura and Gordon Falls; Leura and Wentworth Falls; North Katoomba; and to Katoomba Aquatic Centre and Narrow Neck Rd. Buses run daily between about 7am and 6pm, roughly half-hourly; it costs $2.60, for example to get to Echo Point. Buses leave from Katoomba Street outside the *Carrington Hotel*, and opposite the *Savoy*.

The two Katoomba-based, hop-on, hop-off tour buses have offices by the train station exit on Main St; passes include discounts to some of the attractions en route. **Trolley Tours** (Ⓣ02/4782 7999 or Ⓣ1800 801 577, Ⓦwww.trolleytours.com.au), run by Blue Mountains Bus Co, is a minibus decked out like a tram, which does a scenic circuit with commentary from Katoomba to Leura around Cliff Drive to the Three Sisters and back, taking in attractions along the way (8 daily hourly approx 9.30am–5pm; $12 all-day pass is also valid on all ordinary bus routes, above). The **Blue Mountains Explorer Bus**, run by Fantastic Aussie Tours (Ⓣ02/4782 1866 or 1300 300 915, Ⓦwww.fantastic-aussie-tours.com.au), links Katoomba and Leura taking in all attractions (over thirty stops) in a red double-decker bus (departs Katoomba hourly 9.30am–4.30pm, last return 5.15pm; $25 all-day pass). There's no commentary with the Explorer Bus, but you get a 29-page guide with maps detailing bushwalk and sightseeing options.

The **Blue Mountains Information Centre** (Mon–Fri 9am–5pm, Sat & Sun 8.30am–4.30pm; Ⓣ1300 653 408, Ⓦwww.bluemts.com.au) is on the Great

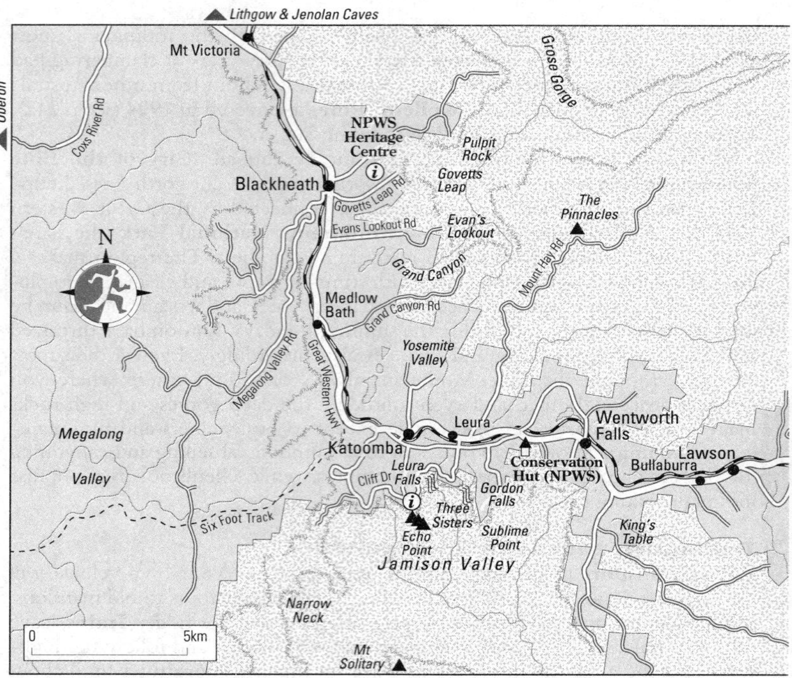

Western Highway at Glenbrook (see below), the gateway to the Blue Mountains. The centre has a huge amount of information on the area, including two free publications: the *Blue Mountains Wonderland Visitors Guide* (Ⓦwww.bluemountains wonderland.com), which has several detailed colour maps and bushwalking notes, and an events guide, *Imag Monthly*. The other official tourist information centre is at **Echo Point**, near Katoomba (see p.242); both offices offer a **free accommodation booking** service.

The **Blue Mountains National Park** has its main ranger station at Blackheath (p.244), where you can get comprehensive walking and camping information – there are car-accessible NPWS camping and picnic sites near Glenbrook, Woodford, Wentworth Falls, Blackheath and Oberon and bush camping is allowed in most areas. The only point where you must pay vehicle entry into the park is at Glenbrook ($7).

Glenbrook to Wentworth Falls

Off the busy highway and further on from the information centre (see opposite), **GLENBROOK** is a pleasant village arranged around the train station, with an adventure shop and a strip of cafés on Ross Street. The section of the **Blue Mountains National Park** here is popular for **mountain-biking** along the **Oaks Fire Trail** (it's best to start the thirty-kilometre trail higher up the mountain in **WOODFORD** and head downhill ending up in Glenbrook; bike rental is available at Katoomba, see p.249). The park entrance (cars $7) is just over a kilometre from the train station following Burfitt Parade then Bruce Road alongside the railway line as it heads back towards Sydney; about 200m

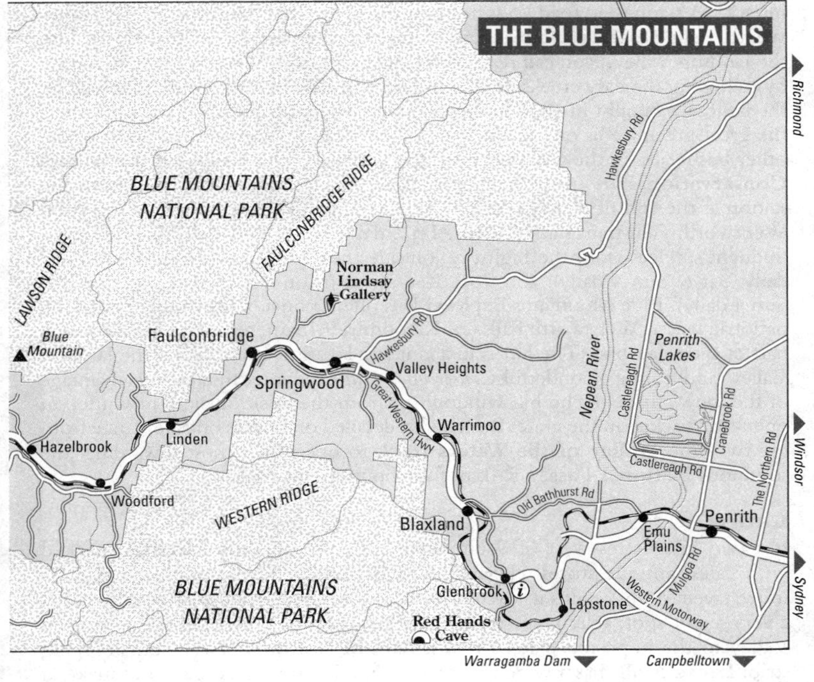

before the entrance you'll cross a railway bridge. Several bushwalks commence from the part-time NPWS office at the end of Bruce Rd (Sat & Sun, public and school holidays 8.30am–4.30pm, ⓣ02/4739 2950). In summer, head for the swimmable **Blue Pool** and **Jellybean Pool** (2km return; easy). One of the best walks from here is to see the Aboriginal hand stencils on the walls of **Red Hands Cave** (6km; 3hr return; medium difficulty). With a car or bike you can get there via road and continue to the grassy creekside Eoroka picnic ground (also camping) where there are lots of eastern grey kangaroos.

Eleven kilometres northwest of Glenbrook, **SPRINGWOOD**, the Blue Mountains' second largest town, with express train links to Sydney, has the feel of a commuter suburb but with several cafés, including the excellent *Bakehouse on Wentworth* (see p.247), and bushwalks in **Sassafras Gully** (8km circuit; easy). Three kilometres further west is **FAULCONBRIDGE**, where many artists and writers were first drawn to the mountains in the footsteps of Norman Lindsay, the controversial artist and poet (1879–1969), whose nude studies scandalized Australia in the 1930s and whose story was told in the 1994 film *Sirens*. From 1912, Lindsay spent a great part of his life at his 42-acre bush property, now owned by the National Trust as the **Norman Lindsay Gallery**. Set amongst extensive gardens at 14 Norman Lindsay Crescent (daily 10am–4pm; $9) it's well worth a visit, with the exhibition of paintings and drawings including some from his famous, enduring and very funny children's tale, *The Magic Pudding* (itself made into a film in 2001).

The small town of **WENTWORTH FALLS**, 23km further west, was named after William Wentworth, one of the famous trio who conquered the mountains in 1813. A signposted road leads from the Great Western Highway to the **Wentworth Falls Reserve**, with superb views of the waterfall tumbling down into the Jamison Valley. You can reach this picnic area from Wentworth train station by following the easy creekside 2.5km **Darwin's Walk** – the route followed by the famous naturalist in 1836 to the cliff edge where he described the view from the great precipice as one of the most stupendous he'd ever seen. Most of the other bushwalks in the area start from the national park's **Valley of the Waters Conservation Hut** (daily 9am–5pm; ⓣ02/4757 3827), about 3km from the station at the end of Fletcher Street. Blue Mountains Bus Co services run from Wentworth Falls train station (Mon–Fri 2 daily, Sat & Sun 4 daily), with more frequent services from the highway, outside the *Grand View Hotel* (Mon–Fri 7 daily, Sat & Sun 4 daily), and from Katoomba (Mon–Fri 10 daily, Sat 8 daily, Sun 4 daily). Blue Mountains Explorer Bus offers a once-daily shuttle bus to the national park at Wentworth Falls (ex-Katoomba 9.15am, returning at 5.25pm) as part of their day-pass. The hut is in a fantastic location overlooking the Jamison Valley, and from its wonderful *Conservation Hut Cafe* you can take full advantage of the views through the big windows or from the deck outside; in winter an open fire crackles in the grate. Bushwalks, detailed on boards outside, range from the two-hour **Valley of the Waters track** to one of the most rewarding, the strenuous **National Pass**, a 5.4km, four-hour circuit walk.

Leura

Just two kilometres west of Wentworth Falls, the wealthy **LEURA**, packed with cafés, antique stores, elegant boutiques and a hugely popular old-fashioned sweet shop, retains its own distinct identity and a village atmosphere. It's a very scenic spot: arriving by train, there are stunning views across the Jamison Valley to the imposing plateau that is **Mount Solitary**. The main shopping strip, **Leura Mall**, has a wide nature strip lined with cherry trees and makes a popular picnicking spot. In fact, Leura is renowned for its beautiful **gardens**, and nine are open to the public during the **Leura Gardens Festival** (early to mid-Oct; $16 all gardens, or $5 per garden; ⓦwww.leuragardensfestival.com.au). Open all year round, though, is the beautiful National Trust-listed **Everglades Gardens** (daily 9am–sunset; $6) at 37 Everglades Ave, 2km southeast of the Mall. There are wonderful Jamison Valley views from its formal terraces, a colourful display of azaleas and rhododendrons, an aboretum, and a simple tearoom. Just over a kilometre south of the Mall, the privately run **NSW Toy and Railway Museum** (daily 10am–5pm; $10, $6 garden only), 36 Olympian Parade, is within the Art Deco mansion Leuralla, set in twelve acres of gardens. Opposite, there's a separate entry fee to get into Olympian Park ($2) where a natural amphitheatre gives stunning Jamison Valley views. From the nearby **Gordon Falls** picnic area on Lone Pine Ave, Leura's mansions and gardens give way to the bush of the **Blue Mountains National Park**; it's an easy ten-minute return walk to the lookout over the falls or there's a canyon walk (two-hour circuit; medium difficulty) via Lyre Bird Dell and the Pool of Siloam which takes in some of the Blue Mountains' distinctive hanging swamps, an Aboriginal rock shelter and cooling rainforest. From Gordon Falls, a 45-minute bushwalk part-way along the Prince Henry Cliff Walk (see p.243) heads to **Leura Cascades** picnic area off **Cliff Drive** (the scenic route around the cliffs which extends from Leura to beyond Katoomba) where several bushwalks include a two- to three-hour circuit walk to the base of the much-photographed **Bridal Veil Falls**. To the east of Gordon Falls, Sublime Point Road leads to the aptly named **Sublime Point** lookout, with panoramic views of the Jamison Valley.

Katoomba and around

KATOOMBA, 103km west of Sydney, is the biggest town in the Blue Mountains and the area's commercial heart; it's also the best located for the major sights of Echo Point and the Three Sisters. There's a lively café culture on **Katoomba Street**, which runs downhill from the train station; the street is also full of vintage and retro clothes shops, secondhand bookstores, antique dealers and giftshops. When the town was first discovered by fashionable city dwellers in the late nineteenth century, the grandiose **Carrington Hotel**, prominently located at the top of Katoomba Street, was the height of elegance (an historian gives 1hr–1hr 30min tours of the hotel; $8; bookings ⓣ02/4754 5726). It's recently been returned to its former glory, with elegant sloping lawns running down to the street, half of which has been taken over by a new **town square**. Katoomba also boomed during the era of **Art Deco** and many cafés and restaurants feature the style, notably the famous **Paragon Cafe** at 65 Katoomba St (closed Mon), also known for its handmade chocolates and sweets.

Across the railway line (use the foot-tunnel under the station and follow the signs), a stunning introduction to the ecology of the Blue Mountains can be

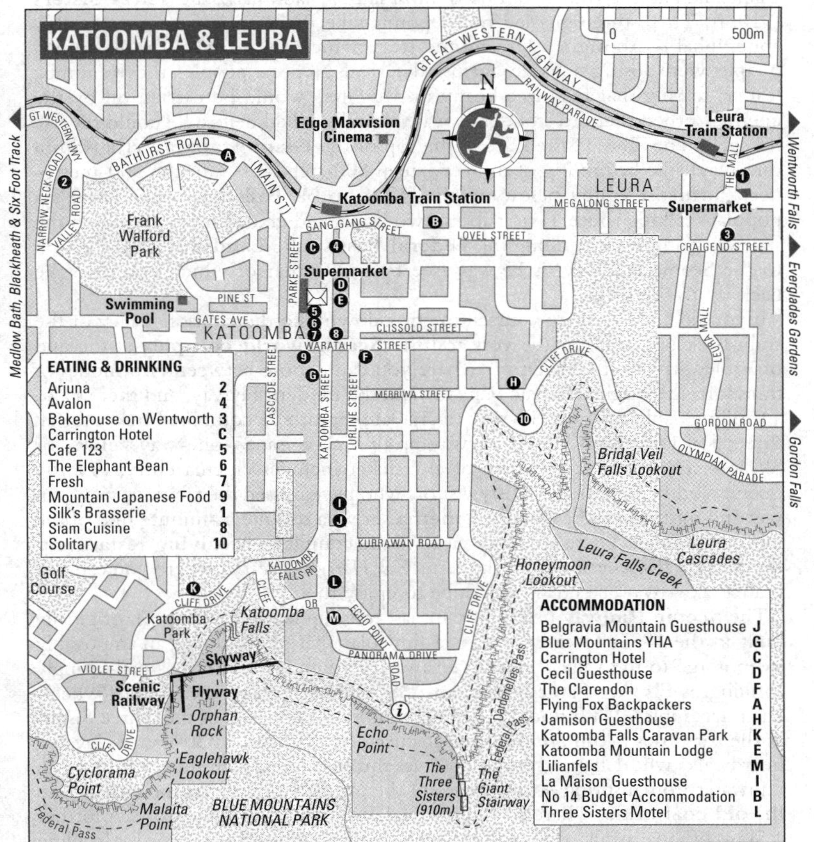

had at the **Edge Maxvision Cinema**, at 225–237 Great Western Highway (Ⓣ02/4782 8928, Ⓦwww.edgecinema.com.au), a huge six-storey cinema screen created as a venue to show *The Edge – The Movie* (daily 10.20am, 11.05am, 12.10pm, 1.30pm, 2.15pm & 5.30pm; $14.50). The highlight of the forty-minute film is the segment about the "dinosaur trees", a stand of thirty-metre-high **Wollemi Pine**, previously known only from fossil material over sixty million years old. The trees – miraculously still existing – survive deep within a sheltered rainforest gully in the **Wollemi National Park**, north of Katoomba, and they made headlines when they were first discovered in 1994 by a group of canyoners. Since the discovery, the first cultivated Wollemi Pine was planted in 1998 at Sydney's Royal Botanical Gardens.

A 25-minute walk south from the train station down Katoomba Street and along Lurline Street and Echo Point Road (or by tour or regular bus from outside the Savoy Theatre; see p.232) will bring you to **Echo Point**. From the projecting lookout platform between the **information centre** (daily 9am–5pm; Ⓣ1300 653 408, Ⓦwww.bluemts.com.au) and souvenir shops and eateries at the Three Sisters Heritage Plaza, breathtaking vistas take in the Kedumba and Jamison valleys, Mount Solitary, the Ruined Castle, Kings Tableland and the Blue Mountains' most famous landmark, the **Three Sisters** (910m). These three gnarled rocky points take their name from a – possibly apocryphal – Aboriginal Dreamtime story which relates how the Kedumba people were losing a battle against the rival Nepean people: the Kedumba leader, fearing that his three beautiful daughters would be carried off by the enemy, turned them to stone, but was tragically killed before he could reverse his spell. The Three Sisters are at the top of the **Giant Stairway** (1hr 45min one-way), the beginning of the very steep 800-step stairs into the 300-metre-deep **Jamison Valley** below, passing **Katoomba Falls** en route. There's a popular walking route, taking about two hours and graded medium, down the stairway and part way along the **Federal Pass** to the **Landslide**, and then on to the Scenic Railway or Flyway (see below), either of which you can take back up to the ridge.

If you do want to spare yourself the trek down into the Jamison Valley or the walk back up, head for the very touristy **Scenic World complex** at the end of Violet Street off Cliff Drive, where you can choose between two modes of transport, the original Scenic Railway and the modern Flyway, and there's also a thrilling cable car ride, Skyway (daily 9am–5pm; $25 combined ticket for all three; $14 for railway down, Flyway up or vice versa; $7 one-way railway or Skyway; Flyway $14; purchase of any ticket includes cinema entry; Ⓦwww.scenicworld.com.au). To satisfy visitors who have missed the fabulous views on wet and misty days, the **Scenic Cinema** shows a seventeen-minute film of the mountain sights. There are more views at the complex's **revolving restaurant**, the *Skyway Brasserie* and from the terrace at *Harry's Cafe-Bar* where you can just grab a take-away ice cream or coffee to enjoy them.

The **Scenic Railway** (every 10min; last train up leaves at 4.50pm), originally built in the 1880s to carry coal, is a funicular that glides down an impossibly steep gorge to the valley floor. Even more vertiginous, but not as nail-bitingly thrilling, is **Flyway** (same hours), an A$8 million, high-tech cable car (wheelchair accessible). With floor-to-ceiling windows, the views of the Three Sisters as the car drops 545m are really spectacular. At the base, a 330-metre elevated boardwalk (wheelchair accessible) weaves through forest – en route, drink clean rainwater from a spring – to the base of the Scenic Railway via the entrance to the **old coal mine**, where an audio-visual display tells the mine story. A further 1.5km of boardwalk on various levels, with interpretative boards detailing

△ Katoomba Flyway

natural features, are worth exploring, and there's access to longer bushwalks in the national park, including a 12km return walk (medium difficulty) to the **Ruined Castle**. Back up on the ridge, you can get your legs trembling again with the new **Skyway**, the state-of-the-art replacement for the rickety-looking cable-car contraption that had been plying its way 350m across to the other side of the gorge and straight back again since 1958. As if the bird's-eye view of Orphan Rock, the Three Sisters and Katoomba Falls weren't exhilarating enough, the new gondola has a glass floor which starts out opaque then becomes crystal clear, revealing the 270-metre drop to the ravines and waterfalls below. Though the price for a few anxious minutes is high, the thrill is worth it. A short walk from the Scenic World complex along Cliff Drive is the **Katoomba Falls picnic area** where there's a kiosk and several bushwalking options. The **Prince Henry Cliff Walk** (9km one way; 1hr 30min; easy) is a long, pleasant stroll along the plateau clifftop via Echo Point all the way to **Gordon Falls** (see p.240) with glorious lookouts along the way. A scenic drive following Cliff Drive southwest of Katoomba Falls leads to several other spectacular lookouts: Eaglehawk, the Landslide, and Narrow Neck – a great sunset spot, with views into both the Jamison and Megalong Valleys. The Blue Mountains Explorer Bus's **Cliff Tops and Valleys Tour** in an open-topped bus takes in these lookouts (included in the day-pass; 1hr; departs Scenic World hourly 11.45am–2.45pm). To get to Narrow Neck peninsula itself, a popular mountain-biking spot, take the unsealed, winding Glen Raphael Road. From here, the top of the **Golden Stairs** provides access down to a difficult 14km-return, eight- to ten-hour walking route to **Mount Solitary**, where you can bushcamp overnight (but take NPWS advice first). The track to Mount Solitary goes past the turn-off to the **Ruined Castle**, a six-hour medium to hard return walk from the Golden Stairs (or it can be reached via the base of Scenic World).

The Six Foot Track

The Six Foot Track Along the Great Western Highway, about 2.5km west of Katoomba train station, is the **Explorers Tree**, initialised by Blaxland, Lawson and Wentworth during their famous 1813 expedition. From Nellies Glen Road here is the start of the 42km **Six Foot Track** to the Jenolan Caves – two to three days, and you're advised to carry plenty of water – and shorter walks to Pulpit Rock and Bonnie Doon Falls. There are four basic **campsites** along the way, plus well-equipped cabins at Binda Flats (see p.251). Blackheath NPWS can provide more bushwalking and camping information. Blue Mountains Guides (ⓣ02/4782 6109, ⓦwww.bluemountainsguides.com.au) offers a **guided walk** along the track (3-day $550; tent camping). Otherwise, Fantastic Aussie Tours (ⓣ02/4782 1866 or 1300 300 915, ⓦwww.fantastic-aussie-tours.com.au) provides a daily transfer service for bushwalkers from Katoomba to the start of the track and a return service a few days later from Jenolan Caves (2hr; $50); you can leave cars in their depot. Tread Lightly Eco Tours (ⓣ02/4788 1229; see p.249) popular morning Wilderness Walk ($25) takes in some of the track. A more unusual way to do the track is to enter Australia's largest annual off-road marathon, the **Six Foot Track Marathon** held in March (more details at ⓦwww.coolrunning.com.au).

Medlow Bath and Blackheath

One train stop beyond Katoomba, and 6km further northwest along the Great Western Highway, the quiet village of **MEDLOW BATH** is based around the distinctively domed **Hydro Majestic Hotel**, built as an exclusive health resort in 1904 on an escarpment overlooking the **Megalong Valley**. The hotel had a meticulous make-over by the Mercure chain in 2000, and it's worth a stop-off to gaze at the interiors and the stunning bush views from the balcony beer garden – walk through the Megalong Room to get outside; you can take a drink out there anytime. The Megalong Room has the same view from its windows, but the buffet-style café is overpriced.

Five kilometres north of Medlow Bath along the Great Western Highway, there are more lookout points at **BLACKHEATH** – just as impressive as Echo Point and much less busy. One of the best is **Govetts Leap**, at the end of Govetts Leap Road (just over 2km east of the highway through the village centre), near the **Blue Mountains National Park** headquarters, the **Blackheath Heritage Centre** (daily 9am–4.30pm; ⓣ02/4787 8877). The two-kilometre **Fairfax Heritage Track** from the NPWS Centre is wheelchair- and pram-accessible and takes in the Govetts Leap Lookout with its marvellous panorama of the **Grose Valley** and Bridal Veil Falls. Many walks start from the centre, but one of the most popular, **The Grand Canyon** (5km; 3hr 30min; medium difficulty), begins from **Evans Lookout Road** at the south end of town, west of the Great Western Highway.

Govetts Leap Road and its shady cross-street, Wentworth Street, have lots of antique and craft shops, an antiquarian bookshop, and great cafés and restaurants. Ten kilometres southwest of Blackheath, across the railway line, the beautiful unspoilt **Megalong Valley** is reached via winding Megalong Road; it's popular for **horse riding** (see "Listings" p.249) and there are creeks with swimmable waterholes.

Mount Victoria and around

At the top of the Blue Mountains, secluded and leafy **MOUNT VICTORIA**, 6km northwest of Blackheath along the Great Western Highway and the last mountain settlement proper, is the only one with an authentic village feel. The great old pub, the *Imperial* (see below), is good for a drink or meal, and there's old-fashioned scones at the *Bay Tree Tea Shop* opposite. Mount Victoria is also fondly regarded for its tiny cinema, Mount Vic Flicks, in the public hall (see "Listings" p.249). Worth a browse are several antique and secondhand bookshops. Some short **walks** start from the Fairy Bower Picnic area, a ten-minute walk from the Great Western Highway via Mount Piddington Road.

Beyond Mount Victoria, drivers can circle back towards Sydney via the scenic **Bells Line of Road**, which heads east through the fruit- and vegetable-growing areas of Bilpin and Kurrajong to Richmond, with growers selling their produce at roadside stalls. On the way **Mount Tomah Botanic Garden** (daily: Oct–March 10am–5pm; April–Sept 10am–4pm; $4.40; Ⓦwww.rbgsyd.gov.au; no public transport) has been the cool climate outpost of Sydney's Royal Botanic Gardens since 1987. The popular Garden Restaurant (lunch daily; licensed; Ⓣ02/4567 2060; mains $30) with a pricey contemporary Australian menu has fantastic north-facing views over the gardens, Wollemi National Park and Bilbin orchards. Cheaper light lunches are also available and there's a kiosk, plus free electric barbecues and picnic tables. By car, you can continue west along the Bells Line of Road to the Zig Zag Railway at Clarence, just over 35km away (see p.250).

Accommodation

Accommodation rates rise on Friday and Saturday nights – aim to visit on weekdays when it's quieter and cheaper. The tourist offices at Glenbrook and Echo Point can book accommodation. **Katoomba** is the obvious choice if arriving by train, particularly for those on a budget since it has several **hostels** to choose from, but if you have your own transport you can indulge in some of the more unusual and characterful guesthouses in **Blackheath** and **Mount Victoria**. Several real estate agents rent out quite charming **holiday homes**: weekend rates average $300, but the weekly rate is often only $75 to $100 more (linen extra), so consider staying longer: contact Soper Bros, 173 The Mall, Leura (Ⓣ02/4784 1633, Ⓦwww.soperbros.com.au) or Raine & Horne, 66 Katoomba St, Katoomba (Ⓣ02/4782 2822, Ⓦwww.bluemts.com.au/raineandhorne/holiday.asp). There are two council-run **caravan parks**: *Katoomba Falls*, at Katoomba Falls Rd (Ⓣ02/4782 1835; en-suite cabins ❸) and *Blackheath*, at Prince Edward St (Ⓣ02/4787 8101; cabins ❷, en-suite ❸), you can **camp** at both of these, as well as in the grounds of *Flying Fox Backpackers* (see below), and in the bush at several NPWS sites (see p.238).

Hotels, motels and guesthouses

Carrington Hotel 15–47 Katoomba St, Katoomba Ⓣ02/4782 1111, Ⓦwww.thecarrington.com.au. When it opened in 1882, the *Carrington* was the region's finest. Now fully restored, original features include stained-glass windows, open fireplaces, a splendid dining room and ballroom, cocktail bar, snooker and games room, library and guest lounges. The spacious, well-aired rooms are beautifully decorated in rich heritage colours. Good-value budget rooms (❺) share bathrooms – there are masses of very private ones, with baths. Buffet breakfast. En-suite ❻–❽

Cecil Guesthouse 108 Katoomba St, Katoomba Ⓣ02/4782 1411, Ⓦwww.ourguest.com.au. Very central choice, set back from the main street. There are great views over the town and Jamison Valley from the common areas and some bedrooms (these ones go first). Very shabby but charming – an old-fashioned 1940s atmosphere with log fires, games room and tennis courts, plus modern touches such as the spa. Most rooms share bathrooms. Good single rates ($45–$55). Cooked breakfast included; dinner served if booked in advance. ❸–❹, en suite ❹

The Clarendon Cnr Lurline and Waratah streets, Katoomba Ⓣ02/4782 1322, Ⓦwww.clarendonguesthouse.com.au. Classic 1920s guesthouse on three levels, with its own cocktail bar and restaurant, and a music and cabaret programme (see p.247). Also heated pool, sauna, gym, open fires, games room and garden. Guesthouse rooms aren't flash but atmospheric in an old-fashioned way. Mostly en-suite, but budget rooms (with TV) without bathroom are available and exude a more faded charm. Also modern motel rooms along the front. ❹–❺

Glenella 56 Govett's Leap Rd, Blackheath ⓣ02/4787 8352. Guesthouse in a charming 1905 homestead with its own licensed restaurant (dinner Fri & Sat). Antique-furnished rooms, most en suite, but there are a few cheaper share-bathroom options ❺, en suite ❻

Imperial 1 Station St, Mount Victoria ⓣ02/4787 1233, ⓦwww.bluemts.com.au/hotelimperial. Nicely restored huge country pub with beautiful lead-lighting. Good-value, filling and tasty bistro meals. There are en suite rooms and spacious, pleasantly decorated guesthouse-style share-bathroom options, or more basic no-frills 'pub' style rooms. Breakfast included. Basic ❸–❹, en suite ❺

Jamison Guesthouse 48 Merriwa St, cnr Cliff Drive, Katoomba ⓣ02/4782 1206, ⓦwww.jamisonhouse.com. Built as a guesthouse in 1903, this seriously charming place has amazing, unimpeded views across the Jamison Valley. The feel is of a small European hotel, added to by the French restaurant downstairs, *The Rooster*, in a gorgeous dining room full of original fixtures (dinner daily, lunch Sat & Sun; set price menus: two-course $56, three-course $68) and with big picture windows. Upstairs, a breakfast room gives splendid views – provisions (and an egg cooker) come with the room – and there's a sitting room with a fireplace. All rooms en suite. ❺

Lilianfels Lilianfels Ave, Katoomba ⓣ02/4780 1200, ⓦwww.lilianfels.com.au. Spectacularly sited on the edge of the cliffs near Echo Point with stunning Jamison Valley views, the luxurious *Lilianfels* consists of the original 1889 mansion and a 1992 country house – with two restaurants and bars – set on two acres of landscaped gardens. Rooms are romantic but with contemporary style. There's a guest lounge with open fires, a reading room, billiards room, indoor and outdoor pools, a gym, spa treatments, tennis court and mountain bikes. ❽

La Maison Guesthouse 175–177 Lurline St, Katoomba ⓣ02/4782 4996, ⓦwww.lamaison.com.au. This modern place with its big foyer and large Asian-feel conservatory-style dining room (where the included buffet breakfast is served) feels more small hotel than guesthouse. With a four-star level of comfort in the spacious, conservatively decorated, well-furnished rooms (some with bathtubs in the en suites), and very obliging management, it's one of the best-value places in Katoomba, and in a good spot between the town centre and Echo Point. Also a garden and deck, guest spa and sauna. The same management run the cheaper *Belgravia Mountain Guesthouse* next door at no. 179 (ⓣ02/4782 2998), in a homely bungalow (light breakfast included). *La Maison* ❺, *Belgravia* ❹

Jemby-Rinjah Lodge 336 Evans Lookout Rd, 4km from Blackheath ⓣ02/4787 7622, ⓦwww.jembyrinjahlodge.com.au. Accommodation in distinctive one- and two-bedroom timber cabins (with own wood fires) in bushland near the Grose Valley. There's also a licensed common area whose focal point is the huge circular "fire pit"; a restaurant operates in here most Friday and Saturday nights (Fri Italian buffet $29, Sat two-course meal $35, three-course $45). Bushwalks organized for guests. Cabins sleep two to six people. ❻

Three Sisters Motel 348 Katoomba St, Katoomba ⓣ02/4782 2911. This unprepossessing-looking motel, with its small, old-style, red-brick motel units, has always been clean, well-equipped and well-run but rather basic. However, an interior upgrade means it's now three-and-a-half stars and extras include air-con and Foxtel. Excellent location near Echo Point. ❹

Victoria and Albert Guesthouse 19 Station St, Mount Victoria ⓣ02/4787 1241, ⓦwww.ourguest.com.au/victoria.albert.html. Built in 1914, this traditional guesthouse has lovely original fixtures. Rooms are large though a little run-down. Cheaper rooms share bathroom. Cooked breakfast. The dining area overlooks the garden with pool, spa and sauna. Bar and restaurant (dinner only; bookings essential). ❹, en suite ❺

Hostels

Blue Mountains YHA 207 Katoomba St, Katoomba ⓣ02/4782 1416, ⓔbluemountains@yhansw.org.au. Huge 200-bed YHA hostel right in the town centre. The former 1930s guesthouse has been modernized but retains its charming lead-lighted windows, Art Deco decor, huge ballroom and an old-fashioned mountain retreat ambience, with an open fire in the reading room, separate games room (with pool table), Internet access and a pleasant courtyard. Most rooms and some of the four-bed dorms are en suite (also 8-bed dorms). Mountain-bike rental for guests; tours can be booked. A dedicated information room has topographic maps; friendly reception staff are very helpful. Dorms $22–28, rooms ❸

The Flying Fox Backpackers 190 Bathurst Rd, Katoomba ⓣ02/4782 4226 or 1800 624 226, ⓦwww.theflyingfox.com.au. Colourfully painted, homely and comfortable bungalow near the station, with spacious dorms (6- to 10-bed; linen $1 extra) and lovely laidback doubles decked out with cushions and lamps (no en suites). Separate TV/video room, board games, Internet access, a small kitchen with free tea and coffee. Outside, there's a courtyard and a popular "chillout" hut with a fire, and a bush-outlook camping site ($12 per person). Camping gear is rented out at reasonable rates and the knowledgeable managers offer info on bushwalks and camping, and free transport to walks. Dorms $21, rooms ❸

Katoomba Mountain Lodge 31 Lurline St, Katoomba ⓣ02/4782 3933, ⓦwww.bluemts.com.au/kmtlodge. Friendly, family-run, central budget accommodation on three floors with great views from its verandah, TV room (with fireplace) and some bedrooms. Dorms (4- to 6-bed), and cute faded-kitsch doubles with window seats (one en-suite; most have TV); all heated with electric blankets. Small kitchen, large dining room, free tea and coffee, pleasant sundeck and BBQ area. Free broadband Internet access. Cheap breakfast and dinner available. Dorms $16–20, rooms ❸

No 14 Budget Accommodation 14 Lovel St, Katoomba ⓣ02/4782 7104, ⓦwww.bluemts.com.au/No14. This relaxed hostel in a charming restored former guesthouse – polished floors, cosy fire, and original features – is like a home away from home, run by an informative, friendly young couple who put in a lot of effort. Mostly twin and double rooms, some en suite, plus four-share dorms with comfy beds instead of bunks; all centrally heated. Peaceful verandah surrounded by pretty plants and valley views. Dorms $22, rooms ❸

Eating, drinking and nightlife

Cuisine in the Blue Mountains has gone way beyond the ubiquitous "Devonshire teas", with many well-regarded restaurants, and a real **café culture** in Katoomba and Leura. There are some great bakeries, too: top of the list is *Hominy*, 185 Katoomba St (daily 6am–5.30pm), with no eating area of its own, but the street's public picnic tables just outside. Also see p.240 for the *Conservation Hut Cafe* and accommodation listings for other eating options.

There are several **nightlife** options in Katoomba. The salubrious cocktail bar and cabaret room at *The Clarendon* (see p.245) hosts eclectic folk, blues, jazz, and world music (Thurs–Sat, sometimes Sun; $10–$45; dinner plus show extra $20–$25; bar 6pm, dinner 7pm, show 8.30pm). *Tris Elies Nightclub* beside the train station at 287 Bathurst Rd (ⓣ02/4782 4026; Wed 9pm–midnight, Thurs–Sat 9pm–3am) puts on Karaoke (Wed), jamming sessions (Thurs; $5), world, blues, rock music (Fri; $10), and eclectic club nights (Sat; $10–15), plus grill-style meals. On the other side of the tracks, opposite the station, the huge and now rather hip *Gearin Hotel* (ⓣ02/4782 4395) is a hive of activity, with several bars where you can play pool, see touring bands (Fri and Sat nights) or boogie at the club nights ($10). There's more mainstream action at *The Carrington*, below.

Arjuna 16 Valley Rd, just off the Great Western Highway, Katoomba ⓣ02/4782 4662. Excellent, authentic Indian restaurant. A bit out of the way but positioned for spectacular sunset views, so get there early. Good veggie choices too. BYO. Evenings from 6pm; closed Tues & Wed.

Avalon 18 Katoomba St ⓣ02/4782 5532. Stylish place with the ambience of a quirky café, in the dress circle of the old Savoy Theatre, with many Art Deco features intact. Beautiful views down the valley too – turn up for lunch or early dinner to see them. Moderately expensive menu, but generous servings and to-die-for desserts. BYO & Licensed. You can come here just for a drink. Lunch & dinner Wed–Sun.

Bakehouse on Wentworth 105 Wentworth St, Blackheath; The Mall, Leura; and Station St, Springwood. The original Blackheath outlet is a cottage-like bakery selling European-style and organic bread and yummy pies and pastries plus excellent coffee, with seating in the shady front courtyard. Phenomenally popular with locals, the *Bakehouse* has recently expanded to Leura (by the fire station) and Springwood (opposite the train station) with indoor seating and a relaxed café-culture feel at both new spots.

Carrington Hotel See above. The *Carrington* has a host of bars in and around the grand old building. *Champagne Charlies Cocktail Bar* has a decorative glass ceiling dome and chandeliers. You can order an understandably pricey drink and take it into one of the classic Kentia-palm-filled lounges or out onto the wonderful front verandah overlooking the lawns. Its really splendid *Grand Dining Room* has columns and decorative inlaid ceilings; the high tea buffet here on Sun is a treat (3–5pm; $16.50), or for dinner, mains are around $33 (also Fri night seafood and carvery buffet; $55). Cheaper drinks and a more lively atmosphere are found in the modern annexe next door, the *Carrington Bar* (live music Wed–Fri includes a piano player on Thurs night; bistro above), and the down-to-earth public bar, with a separate entrance on Main Street opposite the train station; there's a nightclub above, *The Attic* (Fri & Sat 10.30am–3am; $5).

Cafe 123 123 Katoomba St. White, bright modern place with a couple of outside tables and a counter with stools indoors does simple, inexpensive food that's as fresh and healthy as the decor: excellent juices, organic wheat-grass shots, sushi, sandwiches, focaccia and muffins. Coffee is freshly roasted. Daily 8.30pm–6pm.

The Elephant Bean 159 Katoomba St, Katoomba Small, squeezy cafe that serves the best coffee in Katoomba – choose from lots of coffee styles – and great all-day breakfasts with eggs everyway (or there's even a big vegan breakfast for $10.95). Other choices include the popular burgers for veggies or carnivores and gourmet sandwiches (all $10.95) and salads ($8.95). Not the place for cakes though, with only a couple of choices.

Fresh 181 Katoomba St, Katoomba. Spacious goldfish-bowl at the flat base of the main street, by the busy lane heading to the health food co-op, post office and supermarket, is the most popular café with locals, from cops to arty types. With an open kitchen, wooden interior, good music, sunny tables outside, and a big magazine stash. Superb gourmet pies, from Thai Vegetable to Rogon Josh ($4.50 take-away), big fruit muffins, and nearly the best coffee in town. Also Turkish bread sandwiches from $7 and blackboard lunch (around $12).

Mountain Japanese Food Shop 1, 43 Waratah St, Katoomba, behind the petrol station. This new Japanese joint is hugely popular, so much so that you have to get there early to snap up the sushi. Also noodle soups and dumplings. Mainly take-away, with few tables inside and out.

Il Postino 13 Station St, opposite the train station, Wentworth Falls. Great relaxed café in the original old post office – the cracked walls have become part of an artfully distressed, light and airy interior; outside tables on a street-facing courtyard. Menu is Mediterranean- and Thai-slanted, with plenty for vegetarians (nothing over $14). Excellent all-day breakfast featuring many pancake variations. BYO. Daily 8.30am–6pm.

Patisserie Schwartz 30 Station St, opposite the station, Wentworth Falls. Divine German-style pastries to eat in or take away – the perfect reward after a long bushwalk.

Silk's Brasserie 128 The Mall, Leura ⓣ02/4784 2534. Lunching at this smart high-ceilinged restaurant with its white tablecloths, Parisian-style bar and excellent service is actually better value than at some of the overpriced cafés on this strip. For little more than the price of a sandwich elsewhere, you could lunch here on veal and mushroom saffron ravioli with putanesca sauce for $17, and lunch mains peak at $22. At dinner the sophisticated European-style dishes, from confit of duck to Tasmanian salmon, range from $26–$33 (salad or vegetables extra $6). Divine desserts (around $18). Licensed, with many wines available by the glass.

Siam Cuisine 172 Katoomba St, Katoomba ⓣ02/4782 5671. One of three much-of-a-muchness Thai restaurants interspersed along Katoomba Street. This one is popular, inexpensive and offers cheap lunchtime specials. BYO. Closed Mon.

Solitary 90 Cliff Drive, Leura Falls ⓣ02/4782 1164. Perched on a hairpin bend on the mountains' scenic cliff-hugging road, the views of the Jamison Valley and Mount Solitary from this former kiosk, now modern Australian restaurant, are sublime. Expect beautifully laid tables, eager service, a well-chosen and reasonably priced wine list, jazz on the soundtrack, and fine food. There's a fireplace in the back room, and picnic tables outside which are popular for the weekend breakfast. Moderate to expensive. Lunch Sat & Sun, dinner Tues–Sat. Licensed.

Victory Cafe 17 Govetts Leap Rd, Blackheath ⓣ02/4787 6777. A very pleasant space in the front of an old Art Deco theatre now converted into an antiques centre; the café also houses a book stall. Gourmet sandwiches ($8.60) and café favourites (from $7 to $15) with an interesting spin; special mains such as Greek-style fish, and all-day breakfast, with also plenty for vegetarians. The Malaysian and Thai curry nights (Fri & Sat from 6pm; bookings essential) are very popular. BYO. Daily 8.30am–5pm, plus dinner Fri & Sat.

Vulcan's 33 Govetts Leap Rd, Blackheath ⓣ02/4787 6899. Raved-about restaurant housed in an early-twentieth-century bakery, where the wood-fired oven is put to use to produce sensational, seasonal food. Fantastic desserts, too, such as the trademark chequerboard liquorice and pineapple ice cream. Expensive, with mains around the $30 mark, though it's BYO, which makes it more affordable. Lunch & dinner Fri–Sun.

Listings

Adventure activities Australian School of Mountaineering, at Paddy Pallin, 166 Katoomba St (ⓣ02/4782 2014, ⓦwww.asmguides.com). Katoomba's original abseiling outfit offers daily day-long courses ($125), plus canyoning to Grand, Empress or Fortress canyons (9am daily Oct–May;

$135; also less frequent trips to other canyons), rock-climbing and bush-survival courses. Another long-established operator, High 'n' Wild Mountain Adventures, 3–5 Katoomba St (Ⓣ02/4782 6224, Ⓦwww.high-n-wild.com.au), has a good reputation for its beginners' courses in abseiling (full-day $135, half-day $85), canyoning (from $145), rock-climbing (full-day $159, half-day $109) and mountain biking (full-day $149, half-day $109), plus guided bushwalking and bushcraft courses. Both include lunch in full-day courses.
Bike rental The friendly Vélo Nova, 182 Katoomba St, Katoomba (Ⓣ02/4782 2800), has mountain bikes from $28 half-day, $50 full-day; ask in-store about the free guided bike rides which happen once a week. There's cheaper bike hire for guests at the *YHA*.
Bookshops There are several interesting second-hand bookshops on Katoomba St, Katoomba, and in Blackheath and Mount Victoria. The best place for new books is the very literary Megalong Books, 183 The Mall, Leura.
Bus services See p.237.
Camping equipment Paddy Pallin, 166 Katoomba St (Ⓣ02/4782 4466), sells camping gear and a good range of topographic maps and bushwalking guides and supplies, as does nearby Mountain Designs, 190 Katoomba St (Ⓣ02/4782 5999), or for cheap gear go to K-Mart (next door to Coles supermarket, Katoomba St). *Flying Fox Backpackers* (p.246) rents gear to guests.
Car rental Redicar, 80 Megalong St, Leura Ⓣ02/4784 3443, Ⓦwww.redicar.com.au.
Cinemas The Edge Maxvision Cinema, 225–237 Great Western Highway, Katoomba (Ⓣ02/4782 8928), shows new-release feature films on a giant screen ($12.50; cheap tickets $8.50 all day Tues), as well as *The Edge – The Movie*. Mount Vic Flicks, Harley Ave, off Station St, Mount Victoria (Ⓣ02/4787 1577), is a quaint local cinema in an old hall showing a fine programme of prestige new releases and independent films (Thurs–Sun, daily during school holidays; good-value $9 tickets, even cheaper $6 tickets Thurs morning).
Festivals Blue Mountains Music Festival Ⓦwww.bmff.org.au. Three-day mid-March festival of folk, roots and blues features Australian and international musicians on several indoor and outdoor stages ($135 whole weekend, $90 full-day ticket, $70 night ticket).
Horse riding Blue Mountains Horse Riding Adventures (Ⓣ02/4787 8688, Ⓦwww.megalong.cc; pick-ups from Blackheath), escorted trail rides in the Megalong Valley and along the Coxs River; beginners' one-hour Wilderness Ride ($40), experienced riders' all-day adventure along the river ($135). Werriberri Trail Rides offer horse riding for all abilities in the Megalong Valley (Ⓣ02/4787 9171; 2hr ride, including Katoomba pick-up, $70; pony rides from $5.50 for 5min).
Hospital Blue Mountains District Anzac Memorial, Katoomba Ⓣ02/4782 2111.
Internet access Katoomba Book Exchange, 34 Katoomba St, Katoomba ($2.60 15min, $8 1hr; Mon & Tues 10.30am–5pm; Wed–Sun 10am–6pm).
Laundry The Washing Well, K-Mart car park, Katoomba. Daily 7am–7pm.
Pharmacies Blooms Springwood Pharmacy, 161 Macquarie Rd, Springwood (Mon–Fri 8.30am–9pm, Sat 8.30am–7pm, Sun 9am–7pm; Ⓣ02/4751 2963); Greenwell & Thomas, 145 Katoomba St, Katoomba (Mon–Fri 8.30am–7pm, Sat & Sun 8.30am–6pm; Ⓣ02/4782 1066).
Post office Katoomba Post Office, Pioneer Place opposite Coles supermarket, off Katoomba St, Katoomba, NSW 2780.
Supermarket Coles, Pioneer Place off Katoomba St, Katoomba (daily 6am–midnight).
Swimming pool Katoomba Aquatic Centre, Gates Ave, Katoomba (Mon–Fri 6am–8pm, Sat & Sun 8am–8pm, winter weekends closes 6.30pm; Ⓣ02/4782 1748; swim $4.20), has outdoor, heated Olympic-sized and children's pools, plus an indoor attached complex which is open all year with heated 25m pool, toddlers pool, sauna, spa and gym.
Taxis Taxis wait outside the main Blue Mountains train stations to meet arrivals; otherwise for the upper mountains call Katoomba Radio Cabs (Ⓣ02/4782 1311) or for the lower mountains call Blue Mountains Taxi Cab (Ⓣ02/4759 3000).
Tours Most tours of the Blue Mountains start from Sydney; see box on pp.212–213. For the two hop-on-hop-off tour services from Katoomba see p.237. Fantastic Aussie Tours (see p.237) also does large-group coach tours to the Jenolan Caves: a day-tour (daily; $85–$92 with one cave entry), and a combined bushwalk and cave visit ($105), or adventure caving ($150); and a half-day 4WD tour taking in the Blue Mountains National Park ($92). The excellent Blue Mountains Walkabout (Ⓣ0408 443 822, Ⓦwww.bluemountainswalkabout.com) is an all-day (8-hour), off-the-beaten track bush roam (around 10km) between Faulconbridge and Springwood led by an Aboriginal guide; expect to look at Aboriginal rock carvings, taste bushtucker and swim in waterholes in summer ($95, BYO lunch; own train journey to Faulconbridge and ex-Springwood). Tread Lightly Eco Tours (Ⓣ02/4788 1229; Ⓦwww.treadlightly.com.au) offers recommended small-group, expert-guided half-day and full-day bushwalk and 4WD tours from Katoomba.

Trains Katoomba station general enquiries ☎02/4782 1902.
Travel agent Backpackers Travel Centre, 283 Main St, Katoomba ☎02/4782 5342, ⓦwww.backpackerstravel.net.au. Bookings for domestic buses, trains, flights and tours.

Lithgow and the Zig Zag Railway

En route to Bathurst and the Central West on the Great Western Highway, **Lithgow**, 21km northwest of Mount Victoria, is a coal-mining town nestled under bush-clad hills, with wide leafy streets, quaint mining cottages and some imposing old buildings. About 13km east of the town on the Bells Line of Road, by the small settlement of **Clarence**, is the **Zig Zag Railway**. In the 1860s engineers were faced with the problem of how to get the main western railway line from the top of the Blue Mountains down the steep drop to the Lithgow Valley, so they came up with a series of zigzag ramps. These fell into disuse in the early twentieth century, but tracks were relaid by rail enthusiasts in the 1970s. Served by old steam trains, the picturesque line passes through two tunnels and over three viaducts. You can stop at points along the way and rejoin a later train. The Zig Zag Railway can be reached by ordinary State Rail train on the regular service between Sydney and Lithgow, by requesting the guard in advance to stop at the Zig Zag platform; you then walk across the line to Bottom Point platform at the base of the Lithgow Valley. To catch the Zig Zag Railway from Clarence, at the top of the valley, you'll need to have your own transport. Zig Zag trains depart from Clarence daily (11am, 1pm & 3pm; from the Zig Zag platform add 40min to these times; $20; no bookings required; ☎02/6353 1795, ⓦwww.zigzagrailway.com.au). There are plenty of **motels** in and around Lithgow, especially on the Great Western Highway – and the **Lithgow Visitor Information Centre**, 1 Cooerwull Rd (daily 9am–5pm; ☎02/6353 1859; ⓦwww.tourism.lithgow.com), can advise on accommodation.

Kanangra Boyd National Park and the Jenolan Caves

Kanangra Boyd National Park shares a boundary with the Blue Mountains National Park. Further south than the latter, much of it is inaccessible but you can explore the rugged beauty of **Kanangra Walls**, where the Boyd Plateau falls away to reveal a wilderness area of creeks, deep gorges and rivers below. Reached via Jenolan Caves, three **walks** leave from the car park at Kanangra Walls: a short lookout walk, a waterfall stroll and a longer plateau walk – contact the NPWS in Oberon for details (38 Ross St; ☎02/6336 1972; $7 car entry). Boyd River and Dingo Dell camping grounds, both off Kanangra Walls Road, have **free bush camping** (pit toilets; no drinking water at Dingo Dell). You can get to **Oberon**, a timber-milling town and the closest settlement to Kanangra, by Countrylink bus from Mount Victoria (3 weekly).

The **Jenolan Caves** lie 30km southwest across the mountains from Katoomba on the far edge of the Kanangra Boyd National Park – over 80km by road – and contain New South Wales' most spectacular limestone formations. There are nine "show" caves with prices for a guided tour of each cave ranging from a pricey $15 to $27.50 depending on the cave (guided tours various times daily 10am–5pm; 1hr 30min–2hr). If you're coming for just a day, plan to see one or two caves: the best general cave is the Lucas Cave ($15; 1hr 30min), and a more spectacular one is the Temple of Baal ($22; 1hr 30min) while the extensive River Cave, with its tranquil Pool of Reflection, is the longest and priciest ($27.50; 2hr). Buying a ticket for two caves works out to be a better deal: for example, the Lucas combined with the Temple of Baal is $29.50. The system of caves is surrounded by the **Jenolan Karst Conservation Reserve**, a fauna and flora sanctuary with picnic facilities and walking trails to small waterfalls and lookout points. It and the caves are looked after by The Jenolan Caves Trust (ⓣ02/6359 3311, ⓦwww.jenolancaves.org.au), which also offers **adventure caving** in various other caves (2hr Plughole tour $55, 7hr Central River Adventure Cave tour $187.50).

There's **transport** to Jenolan Caves with Fantastic Aussie Tours (see p.237; 2hr; $50; departs Katoomba 10.30am; departs Jenolan Caves 3.45pm), designed as an overnight rather than a day-return service; otherwise the same company offers day-tours from Katoomba, as do several other operators (see "Listings" p.249), or there are many tours from Sydney (see box pp.212–213). You can actually **walk** from Katoomba to the Jenolan Caves along the 42-kilometre-long **Six Foot Track** (see box p.244).

The focus of the area, apart from the caves themselves, is the rather romantic *Jenolan Caves House*, a charming old hotel which found fame as a honeymoon destination in the 1920s and is now part of the *Jenolan Caves Resort* (ⓣ02/6359 3322, ⓦwww.jenolancaves.com). In the old hotel section, there's a good restaurant in the grand dining room (3-course dinner $45), a bar and a more casual bistro, plus recently refurbished en-suite rooms (❻, Sat night ❼), and cheaper share-bathroom versions (❺, Sat night ❼). The newer *Mountain Lodge* annexe has motel-style rooms and two- to three-bedroom units without the character (❺, Sat night ❼); family rooms sleep four to six in the *Gatehouse* (❸, Sat ❹; BYO linen), which has shared communal areas, including a kitchen. The Jenolan Karst Conservation Park has well-equipped cabins at Binda Flats, *Jenolan Caves Cottages*, reached by car from Jenolan Caves Road (sleep 6–8; ❹–❺; BYO linen), and there's a spacious simple campsite (no powered sites), in a rural and secluded spot 1.6km from the caves along the Jenolan River from where you can walk back to the caves; book both cabins and camping through Jenolan Caves Trust (see above). Other **places to stay** in the area include *Jenolan Cabins*, 42 Edith Rd, 4km west on Porcupine Hill (ⓣ02/6335 6239, ⓦwww.jenolancabins.com.au; ❹), whose reasonably priced, well-equipped two-bedroom timber cabins with wood fires accommodate six (BYO linen) – all with magnificent views over the Blue Mountains and Kanangra Boyd national parks and the Jenolan Caves Reserve; 4WD tours of the area are also offered (from $80 half-day including lunch).

South

Once you escape Sydney's uninspiring outer suburbs, the journey south is very enjoyable. Beyond Botany Bay and Port Hacking, the Princes Highway and the Illawarra railway hug the edge of the **Royal National Park** for more than 20km. South of the park, the railway and the scenic Lawrence Hargrave Drive (Route 68) follow the coast to **Wollongong**. Between here and Nowra, the ocean beaches of the Leisure Coast are popular with local holidaymakers, while fishermen, windsurfers and yachtsmen gather at **Lake Illawarra**, a huge coastal lake near Port Kembla. A few kilometres further down the coast is the famous, and often lethal, blowhole at **Kiama**.

Inland, west of Wollongong, Sydney's drinking water is stored in the Cataract and Cordeaux **reservoirs**, surrounded by picnic and leisure areas. Further southwest, past **Kangaroo Valley**, the softly rolling hills of the **Southern Highlands** are dotted with old country towns such as **Berrima** and **Bundanoon**, the latter overlooking the wild and windswept crags of **Morton National Park**.

Transport down south is good, with a frequent train service operating between Sydney and Nowra, stopping at most of the coastal locations detailed below. The main bus service is Premier Motor Service, which stops at Wollongong and Kiama en route to Bega and Eden (Ⓣ13 34 10, Ⓦwww.premierms.com.au). Greyhound Australia (Ⓣ13 20 30) has a daily Sydney–Melbourne coastal route which also stops at Wollongong and Kiama. There are also several local bus companies in the region detailed in the accounts below.

The Royal and Heathcote national parks

The **Royal National Park** is a huge nature reserve right on Sydney's doorstep, only 36km south of the city. Established in 1879, it was the second national park in the world (after Yellowstone in the USA). The railway between Sydney and Wollongong marks its western border, and from the train the scenery is fantastic – streams, waterfalls, rock formations and rainforest flora fly past the window. If you want to explore more closely, get off at one of the stations along the way – Loftus, Engadine, Heathcote, Waterfall or Otford – all starting points for walking trails into the park. On the eastern side, from Jibbon Head to Garie Beach, the park falls away abruptly to the ocean, creating a spectacular coastline of steep cliffs broken here and there by creeks cascading into the sea and little coves with fine sandy beaches; the remains of **Aboriginal rock carvings** are the only traces of the original Dharawal people. The ultimate trek is the spectacular 26-kilometre **Coastal Walk**, taking in the entire coastal length of the park. Give yourself two days to complete it, beginning at either Otford or Bundeena, camping overnight at the officially designated bushcamp at North Era (several other campsites were closed at the time of writing; check availability with the NPWS). The walk is gruelling as you mostly have to carry your own water; water is available at Wattamolla and Garie but it must be purified. Undertaking part of the route is also satisfying, such as the popular trail from **Otford** (which you can reach by train from Sydney) down to beachfront **Burning Palms** (2hr one-way; no camping). A good book to buy is the *Royal National Park on Foot* by Alan Fairley, and try to get a copy of the *Royal National Park* map; both are available at the NPWS Visitor Centre (see below). Escape Sydney Ecotours (Ⓣ02/9664 3047, Ⓦwww.escapecotours.com.au) operates unhurried small-group **tours** of the area: a one-day tour ($85) explores the diverse track to Burning Palms, while a two-day trek (Fri & Sat; $240; food, cabin accommodation and pick-ups included) will take you further afield; also half-day **whale-watching** trips in season (May–Aug: $40).

You can also drive in at various points ($11 car entry; gates open 24hr except at Garie Beach where gates close at 8.30pm). Coming in at the northern end, turning off the Princes Highway south of Loftus, you can visit the **NPWS Visitor Centre** (daily 8.30am–4.30pm; Ⓣ02/9542 0648, Ⓦwww.npws.nsw.gov.au), 2km from Loftus train station. The easy one-kilometre track from here to the Bungoona Lookout boasts panoramic views and is wheelchair-accessible. Cars are allowed right through the park, exiting at **Waterfall** on the Princes Highway or **Stanwell Park** on Lawrence Hargrave Drive. Not far south of the NPWS centre, **Audley** is a picturesque picnic ground on the Hacking River, where you can rent a boat or canoe for a leisurely paddle and where you'll find another **NPWS Visitor Centre**. Deeper into the park, on the ocean shore,

Wattamolla and **Garie beaches** have good surfing waves; the two beaches are connected by a walking track. There are **kiosks** at Audley, Wattamolla and Garie Beach.

There's a small, very basic but secluded YHA **youth hostel** inside the park 1km from Garie Beach (bookings essential; ⓣ02/9261 1111, ⓔbookings@yhansw.org.au; key must be collected in advance; dorms $13, rooms ❶), with no electricity or showers. The **bushcamp** at North Era requires a permit from the visitor centre; often full weeks in advance on weekends, you'll need to book and the permit can be posted out to you (which can take up to five days), or you can purchase it before leaving Sydney at the NPWS centre at 102 George St, Sydney (see p.209).

An interesting way to get here is by **ferry** to Bundeena from Cronulla (see p.177) at the Tonkin Street Wharf just below the train station: Cronulla and National Park Ferries (Mon–Fri hourly 5.30am–6.30pm, except 12.30pm but continuous during school holidays; Sat & Sun: Nov–March 8.30am–6.30pm, April–Oct to 5.30pm; returns from Bundeena hourly: Mon–Fri 6am–7pm, except 1pm; Sat & Sun: Sept–March 9am–7pm; April–Oct to 6pm; $4.50; narrated cruises 10.30am: Sept–May daily; June–Aug Mon, Wed, Fri & Sun; 3hr; $17.50; cruise bookings ⓣ02/9523 2990, ⓦwww.cronullaandnationalparkferrycruises.com) take 25 minutes to cross Port Hacking to the small town of **BUNDEENA** at the park's northeast tip. To begin the Coastal Walk from Bundeena, follow The Avenue and Lambeth Walk 1km to the national park gate. A shorter option is the pleasant half-day walk to pretty sheltered **Little Marley Beach** for a swim and a picnic (2hr one-way) – or head down a pathway to **Jibbons Beach**, a thirty-minute stroll which will take you past some Dharawal rock engravings, where faint outlines of a kangaroo, stingrays, whales and a six-fingered man can be seen (pick up the *Jibbon Aboriginal Rock Engravings Walk* map and leaflet from the café near the wharf). Just west of the town on the shores of the Hacking River is a NPWS **campsite**, the *Bonnie Vale Camping Ground* (no powered sites). There's a great café, a fish and chip shop and a sheltered little beach next to the ferry wharf.

Heathcote National Park, across the Princes Highway from the Royal National Park, is much smaller and quieter. This is a serious bushwalkers' park with no roads and a ban on trail bikes. The best **train** station for the park is Waterfall, from where you can follow a twelve-kilometre trail through the park (pick up a map from the Royal National Park visitor centre), before catching a train back from Heathcote. On the way you pass through quite a variety of vegetation and alongside several swimmable pools, the carved sandstone of the **Kingfisher Pool** making it the most picturesque, and there is a small, six-site, very basic camping ground beside it (no drinking water), and another one at Mirang Pool. **Camping** permits are available from the Royal National Park NPWS Visitor Centre (see p.252) or at The Rocks NPWS office (see p.209). By **car**, you can reach the picnic area at Woronora Dam on the western edge of the park: turn east off the Princes Highway onto Woronora Road (free entry).

South down the coast

For a **scenic drive from Sydney** – bush, coast and cliff views and beautiful beaches – follow the Princes Highway south, exiting into the Royal National Park after Loftus onto Farnell Drive; the entry fee at the gate is waived if you are just driving through without stopping. The national park route emerges above the cliffs at **Otford** beyond which the **Lawrence Hargrave Drive** (Route 68) continues to Thirroul.

At the time of writing, due to some dangerous rockfalls, the section between Coalcliff, south of Stanwell Park, and Clifton is closed for upgrading until early 2006. To access the picturesque coast and small towns beyond it's necessary to drive northwest to Helensburgh from Stanwell Park, take the F6 freeway south to precipitous Bulli Pass (see below), descend towards Thirroul and come back up the coast. The diversion is worth the effort.

A few kilometres from Otford is the impressive clifftop lookout on Bald Hill above **Stanwell Park**, where you're likely to see the breathtaking sight of **hang-gliders** taking off. The Sydney Hang Gliding Centre (Ⓣ02/4294 4294, Ⓦwww.hanggliding.com.au) offers tandem flights with an instructor for around $180 during the week, $195 weekends; the centre also runs courses (from $195 per day). At **Clifton** the *Imperial Hotel* is a must for an en-route drink, as it sits right on the cliff's edge. By the time you get to **AUSTINMER** you're at a break in the stunning cliffs and into some heavy surf territory. The down-to-earth town has a popular, very clean, patrolled surf beach that gets packed out on summer weekends. Across the road from the beach, there's delicious fish and chips at *Anne's Take Away and Coffee Shop* (but expect long weekend waits), or seek out the locals' secret, the *Fireworks Gallery Café* at 40 Moore Street, just back from the beach, for an impressive slice of home-cooked sticky date pudding in artistic surrounds.

There's impressive cliff scenery again as you pass through **Scarborough** (best seen from the historic *Scarborough Hotel*), **Wombarra** and **THIRROUL**. Thirroul is the spot where the English novelist D.H. Lawrence wrote *Kangaroo* during his short Australian interlude; the town and the surrounding area are a substantial part of the novel, though he renamed the then-sleepy village Mullumbimby. Thirroul is now gradually being swallowed up in the suburban sprawl of Wollongong; it's busy, with plenty of shops and cafés, including the excellent and appropriately literary *Oskar's Wild Bookstore & Coffee Bar* at 289 Lawrence Hargrave Drive. At the southern end of the beach, **Sandford Point**, as it's known (it's actually Bulli Point on maps) is a famous surfing break. A 60km cycle track runs from Thirroul south along the coast through Wollongong to Lake Illawarra. *The Beaches Hotel*, 272 Lawrence Hargrave Drive (Ⓣ02/4267 2288, rooms ❸, apartment ❺), is a modern, stylish pub complex that has one good-value spacious, colourful two-bedroom apartment, plus cheaper share-bathroom **rooms**; you can barbecue your own steaks in the popular beer garden or eat in the bistro; weekend bands (when accommodation can be noisy) and pool tables provide entertainment.

After Thirroul, Lawrence Hargrave Drive joins up with the Princes Highway going south into Wollongong (Route 60) or heading northwest, uphill to a section of the forested **Illawarra Escarpment** and the **Bulli Pass**. There are fantastic views from the Bulli Lookout, which has its own café, and further towards Sydney at the appropriately named **Sublime Point Lookout**. You can explore the escarpment using the **walking tracks** which start from the lookouts, and another extensive part of the **Illawarra Escarpment State Recreation Area**, about 10km west of Wollongong's city centre on Mount Kembla and Mount Keira.

Wollongong

Although it's New South Wales' third-largest city, **WOLLONGONG** has more of a country-town feel; the students of Wollongong University give it extra life in term time and it has a big dose of surf culture as the city centre is set right on the ocean. Eighty kilometres south of Sydney, it's essentially a working class industrial centre – Australia's largest steelworks at nearby Port Kembla looms unattractively over Wollongong City Beach but the **Illawarra Escarpment** (see above) rises dramatically beyond the city and provides a lush backdrop.

There's not really much to see in the **city centre** itself (concentrated between Wollongong train station and the beach), which has been swallowed up by a giant shopping mall on **Crown Street** but the regional art centre, the **Wollongong City Gallery**, on the corner of Kembla and Burelli streets (Tues–Fri 10am–5pm, Sat & Sun noon–4pm; free), shows changing exhibitions and has a permanent collection with an emphasis on contemporary Aboriginal and colonial Illawarra artists. If you continue east down Crown Street and cross Marine Drive, you'll hit **Wollongong City Beach**, a surf beach which stretches over 2km. Most locals choose the more salubrious **North Wollongong Beach** (bus #20 from the Crown Gateway bus interchange near City Mall). But in between the two beaches, sheltering beside Flagstaff Point, is the city's highlight, **Wollongong Harbour**, with its fishing fleet in Belmore Basin, a fish market, a few seafood restaurants, and a picturesque nineteenth-century lighthouse on the breakwater; there's also gentle swimming from its beach. At the end of October the **Viva la Gong festival** spices up the city with a sculpture exhibition along the seafront and events every night including circus, dance, music and the like.

Away from the centre, science and religion provide the most interest. North of the city centre, near the University of Wollongong at the southern end of **Fairy Meadow Beach** and next to Brandon Park, is the $6 million **Science Centre** on Squires Way (daily 10am–4pm; $10; Ⓦwww.uow.edu.au/science_centre; train to Fairy Meadow station, then a 10–15min walk), attractions include the state's best **planetarium** (daily shows noon & 3pm; 30min; laser concert Sat, Sun & school holidays 1pm; $2 extra per show; planetarium-only $6) and over a hundred themed kid-friendly hands-on exhibits. South of the centre the vast **Nan Tien Buddhist Temple**, the largest in Australia, is on Berkeley Road, Berkeley, reached from Sydney by train to Unanderra station and a twenty-minute walk, or by bus from Wollongong train station with John J. Hill Bus Co (Ⓣ02/4229 4911) or Rutty's bus #34 or #43 from Crown Gateway. The Fo Guang Shan Buddhists welcome visitors to the temple (Mon & Tues–Sun 9am–5pm) and offer a good-value $7 vegetarian lunch, weekend meditation and Buddhist activity retreats in peaceful and surprisingly upmarket guesthouse accommodation (Ⓣ02/4272 0500, Ⓦwww.nantien.org.au; ❹).

Practicalities

The best and cheapest way to get to Wollongong from Sydney by public transport is the frequent **train** from Central station which hugs the coast and stops at most of the small towns en route; Wollongong station is right in the centre just off Crown Street. Pioneer Motor Service has three to four **bus** services on weekdays and two a day at weekends (reservations Ⓣ13 34 10). **Wollongong Tourist Information Centre**, near the mall at 93 Crown St (Mon–Fri 9am–5pm, Sat 9am–4pm, Sun 10am–4pm; Ⓣ02/4227 5545, Ⓦwww.tourismwollongong.com), provides information and can advise on **accommodation**. The central *Boat Harbour Motel*, on the corner of Campbell and Wilson streets (Ⓣ02/4228 9166, Ⓦwww.boatharbour-motel.com.au; ❺), has comfortable and spacious rooms with balconies, some with sea views; more upmarket, and also with water views, is Wollongong's four-and-a-half-star *Novotel Northbeach*, 2–14 Cliff Rd, North Wollongong (Ⓣ02/4226 3555, Ⓦwww.novotelnorthbeach.com; ❼). The really friendly, colourful and home-like *Keiraleagh House*, 60 Kembla St (Ⓣ02/4228 6765, Ⓔkeiraleagh@backpack.net.au; dorms $18, rooms ❷), in an old converted mansion a few blocks back from the beach, has dorms (up to six-bed) as well as singles, and doubles (some en suite); rooms are comfy and clean with desks and an armchair. A garden with a barbecue area makes for happy mingling between the students, surfers and travellers who all stay here; free surfboards. The new **YHA hostel** at 75–79 Keira Street, near the intersection with Smith Street (Ⓣ 02/4229 1132; dorms $24, rooms ❸), is modern and lively with a central alfresco courtyard. Most rooms have en suite facilities and shared balconies. There's nowhere central to **camp**, but the two caravan parks to the north are right on the beach: *Corrimal Beach Tourist Park* is on Lake Parade in Corrimal, 6km north at the mouth of Towradgi Lagoon (Ⓣ02/4285 5688; en-suite cabins ❸); while *Bulli Beach Tourist Park* is 11km north of town on Farrell Road, Bulli (Ⓣ02/4285 5677; bungalows ❷, en-suite cabins ❸–❹).

Wollongong isn't really renowned for its **food**, which can be a bit hit or miss. There's a concentration of cafés on Crown Street near the tourist office (*Flame Tree Music Café*, at no. 89 and *Santana Books & Coffee*, at no. 53 are both worth checking out, as is *Elementary Organics*, at no. 47, with live music) and Corrimal and Keira streets, both intersecting Crown. *Namik's*, on the corner of Crown and Corrimal streets, is one of the best. Around the corner, *Litani's*, at 120 Corrimal St, is a relaxed BYO restaurant and coffee shop serving Lebanese and other Mediterranean dishes; its street-side courtyard is very popular. On Keira Street, well-regarded *Lorenzo's Diner* at no. 119 (Ⓣ02/4229 5633; lunch Fri, dinner Tues–Sat; licensed & BYO) serves top-notch contemporary Italian food, at surprisingly moderate prices, in a bold and stylish interior. *Caveau* at no. 122 (Ⓣ02/4226 4855; dinner Tues–Sat) has an excellent, very reasonably priced French-influenced menu, while *Monsoon* at no. 193 (Ⓣ02/4229 4588; lunch & dinner Tues–Sat) is a hip Vietnamese restaurant with an Australian slant. The front of the beachside Entertainment Centre is the setting for the *Five Islands Brewing Company*, where you can try at least ten delicious and varied ales with an imaginative bar menu. At North Beach you can enjoy juices and burgers at the recently restored art deco kiosk, or sit down in the funky interiors of *Diggies* right at the water's edge.

Kiama and around

Of the coastal resorts south of Sydney, **KIAMA** is probably the most attractive – though if you want more than a day- or overnight trip to the beach, you'd be better off continuing down to Nowra and beyond (see p.288). A large resort and fishing town, Kiama is famous for its star attraction, the **Blowhole**, a five-minute walk from the **railway station** on Blowhole Point. Stemming from a natural fault in the cliffs, the blowhole explodes into a waterspout when a wave hits with sufficient force. It's impressive, but also potentially dangerous: freak waves can be thrown over 60m into the air and have swept several over-curious bystanders into the raging sea – so stand well back. The **Kiama Visitor Information Centre**, nearby on Blowhole Point Road (daily 9am–5pm; Ⓣ02/4232 3322 or 1300 652 262, Ⓦwww.kiama.com.au), supplies details of other local attractions such as **Cathedral Rocks**, a few kilometres to the north, whose rocky outcrops drop abruptly to the ocean. About 15km south of Kiama is **Seven Mile Beach**, a stunning sweep of sandy beach with its own small oceanfront **national park**.

West of Kiama, a steep road leads to **Mount Saddleback Lookout**, from where on a clear day you can get an incredible view of the entire coast – from the Royal National Park in the north to Jervis Bay in the south. Beyond the lookout you can head north to join the Illawarra Highway, and follow that inland to **Macquarie Pass**, the gateway to the Southern Highlands. The **Macquarie Pass National Park** is one of the southernmost stands of Australia's subtropical rainforest; there's a car park on the road from where the Cascades Walk takes you on a two-kilometre loop through the forest to Cascades Waterfall. Alternatively, Jamberoo Mountain Pass Road heads to Robertson on the Illawarra Highway via the **Budderoo National Park** where the **Minnamurra Rainforest Centre** (park daily 9am–5pm, centre and *Lyrebird Cafe* 9am–4pm; boardwalk closes 4pm, track closes 3pm; ⓣ02/4236 0469; car entry $10 at Minnamurra only), has a wheelchair-accessible elevated loop boardwalk from the centre (1.6km return; 30min–1hr) through subtropical and temperate rainforest – you'll see cabbage tree palms, staghorn ferns and impressive Illawarra fig trees – and a viewing platform to **Minnamurra Falls**. You can continue halfway on a paved walk with some steep sections leading to the upper falls (2.6km return; 1.5–2hr). The impressive **Carrington Falls**, also within the park, are 8km east of Robertson by road, and are worth a detour: a turn-off from the Jamberoo Mountain Pass Road leads to lookout points over the waterfalls. Free **bushcamping** is possible in both Macquarie Pass and Budderoo national parks.

Otherwise if you want to **stay** in this area you'll find plenty of the usual motels strung out along the highway. There's an abundance of B&Bs and self-catering holiday units too; the tourist office (see above) has a comprehensive list and can book accommodation for free. Budget alternatives in Kiama include *Kiama Backpackers*, 31 Bong Bong St, very close to the train station and right near the beach (ⓣ02/4233 1881; dorms $22, rooms ❷), though it sometimes closes down in winter; and the *Grand Hotel*, on the corner of Manning and Bong Bong streets (ⓣ02/4232 1037; ❸), which has budget-priced, old-fashioned share-bathroom pub accommodation – the pub restaurant serves decent filling meals for lunch and dinner daily. The closest campsite to the centre is at *Blowhole Point Holiday Park* right near the blowhole (ⓣ02/4232 2707 or 1800 823 824; ⓦwww.kiama.net/holiday/blowhole; en-suite vans ❸), while *Easts Beach Caravan Park*, a couple of kilometres south of Kiama (ⓣ02/4232 2124 or 1800 674 444, ⓦwww.kiama.com.au/eastpark; en-suite cabins ❹), is on the beach with safe, sheltered swimming; the grassy park has a camp kitchen, playground and tennis courts. There are plenty of **places to eat** – Thai, Chinese, Italian and lots of cafés – with a concentration on Manning and Terralong streets. For a great coffee, the smart *esse*, 55 Collins Street (dinner bookings ⓣ02/4232 2811; from 10am, closed Tues, dinner Thurs–Sat; licensed & BYO) is a café by day and modern Australian restaurant by night. Sunday lunch is hugely popular at the relaxed *Zumo Restaurant*, 127 Terralong St (ⓣ02/4232 2222; lunch Sun only, dinner Wed–Sun; licensed & BYO), housed in an old building with lots of greenery and outdoor seating; food is adventurous and eclectic.

Gerringong, 10km south of Kiama, is wonderfully scenic, set against green hills with glorious sweeping beach views. Budget accommodation includes a **YHA hostel**, *Nestor House*, on Fern Street, just 250m from Werri Beach (ⓣ02/4234 1249; dorms $20, rooms ❸), or there's the *Werri Beach Holiday Park* (ⓣ02/4234 1285 or 1800 655 819; vans and en-suite cabins ❹), which benefits from a great location at the northern end of Seven Mile Beach, between Crooked River and the sand. The best café in town is *Gerringong Gourmet Deli*, 133 Fern St, which does divine fish and chips and gourmet burgers. Great views can be had at the *Sea Vista Café*, while non-meat eaters should head for the *Perfect Break Vegetarian Cafe*, further along at no. 115.

Inland: the road to Canberra

If you want to take your time getting to Canberra, there are a number of worthwhile diversions off the speedy South Western Motorway (M5), the main road inland which eventually joins up with the Hume Highway (Route 31). Camden Valley Way heads west from the motorway to **CAMDEN** on the Nepean River, where John Macarthur pioneered the breeding of merino sheep in 1805. The town still has a rural feel and several well-preserved nineteenth-century buildings, the oldest of which dates from 1816. En route, you'll pass **Mount Annan Botanical Garden** (daily: April–Sept 10am–4pm; Oct–March 10am–6pm; $4.40; ⓦwww.rbgsyd.gov.au). Actually the native-plant section of the Royal Botanic Gardens in Sydney, this outstanding collection of flora is the largest of its kind in Australia. Within the grounds, you can eat well at the idyllically sited *Gardens Restaurant* at outside tables surrounded by trees. A major attraction, it makes sense to book if you intend to dine (ⓣ02/4647 1363); there's also a kiosk in the park. The garden is 57km southwest of Sydney and can be reached from the M5 (Camden exit, then follow Tourist Drive 18 and look for signs) or by a combination of CityRail train to Campbelltown, and then Busways (ⓣ02/4655 7501).

From Camden, Remembrance Drive leads to **PICTON**, a small farming town cradled by hills; you can get here by train from Sydney or with Picton Coaches (ⓣ02/4677 1564) who run five coaches per day from Campbelltown or Narellen, via Bargo, Tahmoor and Thirlmere. Picton is a good spot for a drink in the shady beer garden of the 1839 sandstone *George IV Inn*, which brews its own beer by a traditional German method (and also serves up legendary seafood platters). Eleven kilometres south of Picton, the five connected freshwater lakes that make up **Thirlmere Lakes National Park** are named in the language of the Gandangarra Aborigines. Lake Couridjah is best for swimming, surrounded by unspoilt bushland and plenty of birdlife. Continuing along Remembrance Drive, it's 8km to the **Wirrimbirra Sanctuary** at **Bargo** (daily 8am–5pm; free; ⓣ02/4684 1112, ⓦwww.wirrimbirrasanctuary.com), a peaceful bushland spot run by the National Trust, with a field studies centre, a native-plant nursery, a visitor information centre and café (daily 7am–5pm), bushwalking trails, and pools to swim in, where you can engage in a bit of platypus-spotting at dawn or dusk if you stay over in the bunk-style cabins ($15 per person) or camp. You might also see wallabies, kangaroos, wombats, brush-tailed possums and goannas, along with 150 different species of birds. Without your own **transport**, you can get here by train from Sydney to Bargo and then walk a couple of kilometres.

The Southern Highlands

From Bargo, you can detour onto the Old Hume Highway, through the picturesque **Southern Highlands**, a favourite weekend retreat for Sydneysiders since the 1920s; the pretty Highlands towns are full of cafés, restaurants, antique shops and secondhand bookstores and there's an emerging wine industry. Visiting the wineries is a great way to enjoy the beautiful countryside of the area. The information centre at Mittagong can provide a map of all the local cellar doors. The cooler-climate wines produced here are building a good reputation, and a tour of the area is an excellent alternative to the better known Hunter Valley. The Southern Highlands is well served by **transport**, with a frequent train service between Sydney and Canberra stopping at Picton, Mittagong, Bowral, Moss Vale, Bundanoon and Goulburn. Priors Scenic Express (ⓣ02/4472 4040 or 1800 816 234) from Campbelltown train station on Sydney's western fringes (3.30pm daily except Sat) also goes to Mittagong and Bowral terminating in Nowra, while Berrima Coaches provides a local bus service (ⓣ02/4871 3211).

Marking the beginning of the Highlands is **MITTAGONG**, a small agricultural and tourist town 110km south of Sydney, mostly visited on the way to the limestone **Wombeyan Caves** (daily 8.30am–5pm; guided tours: one cave $15; two caves $21; all caves $26; 1hr 30min for each cave) in the nearby hills. The route to the five caves begins 4km south of the town off the highway and winds upwards for 65km on a partly unsealed road. The associated **campsite** near the caves (ⓣ02/4843 5976, ⓦwww.jenolancaves.org.au; cabins ❸, cottages ❹) is well run. For more on accommodation in the area – and a free booking service – contact **Tourism Southern Highlands** (daily 8am–5.30pm; ⓣ02/4871 2888, accommodation bookings on ⓣ1300 657 559, ⓦwww.highlandsnsw.com.au) in Winifred West Park on the Hume Highway; room rates in the area rise considerably on Friday and Saturday nights. Tourism Southern Highlands also has masses of information on bushwalks of varying lengths. Neighbouring **BOWRAL**, 6km southwest, is a busy, well-to-do town; its main strip, Bong Bong Street, is full of upmarket clothes and homeware shops and it has a good bookstore and a cinema. It was also the birthplace of cricket legend Don Bradman and cricket fans should check out the **Bradman Museum** (daily 10am–5pm; $8.50), on Jude Street, in an idyllic spot between a leafy park and the well-used cricket oval and club. It has a pleasant café with a garden terrace. Other good **places to eat** include *That Noodle Place*, 279 Bong Bong St (ⓣ02/4861 6930; lunch Fri–Sun, dinner Tues–Sun), a colourful and funky retro-styled place that serves really yummy Vietnamese, Thai and Chinese food (including *yum cha*); and further down the same street, on a lane beside the Empire Cinema complex, you can have the best coffee in town and excellent food at slick, city-style *Coffee Culture*.

The picturesque village of **BERRIMA** is 7km on from Bowral. The *Surveyor General Inn*, one of an excellent complement of well-preserved and restored old buildings, has been serving beer here since 1835. Inside the 1838 sandstone **courthouse**, on the corner of Argyle and Wiltshire streets (daily 10am–4pm; $6), is the **Berrima Visitor Centre** (same hours; ⓣ02/4877 1505), while across the road the still-operational **Berrima Gaol** once held the infamous bushranger Thunderbolt – and also has the dubious distinction of being the first place in Australia where a woman was executed. Continue up Wiltshire Street from the courthouse to get to the **River Walk**, the end of which is marked by a fine reserve with picnic tables – and camping too. Other **accommodation** includes a clutch of B&Bs in pretty, old stone cottages such as *Berrima Glen* (ⓣ02/4877 1164; ❺), and the *White Horse Inn* in the Market Place (ⓣ02/4877 1204, ⓦwww.highlandsnsw.com.au/whitehorseinn; ❹), a large, old 1832 sandstone hotel with accommodation in modern motel units in the garden. There are plenty of places to eat here – try *Café Fraiche* at 9 Old Hume Highway for coffee or cheap hearty meals, or *Elingrange* in the centre of town, an offshoot of the winner of Best Winery Restaurant 2004 at Eling Forest Winery, serving Italian-style fare and gelato. Three kilometres north of Berrima on the Old Hume Highway in the direction of Mittagong and worth a look is *Berkelouw's Book Barn & Cafe*, for secondhand and rare books and good **food** and coffee in a vast converted barn set amongst fields.

Five kilometres from **Moss Vale** on the Old Hume Highway is the turn-off south to **BUNDANOON**, famous for its annual April celebration of its Scottish heritage. Exploiting the autumnal atmosphere of mist and turning leaves, Bundanoon becomes Brigadoon for a day, overtaken by Highland Games – Aussie-style. But a nearby commmunity of Thai Buddhist monks at the **Sunnataram Forest Monastery** (visitors welcome; ⓣ02/4384 4262 or ⓦwww.sunnataram.org for details and directions) are providing a different cultural input by offering retreats and teaching programmes. Bundanoon is in an attractive spot set in hilly countryside scarred by deep gullies and with splendid views over the gorges and mountains of the huge **Morton National Park** (car fee $7) which extends east from Bundanoon to near Kangaroo Valley (see below). The park, and Bundanoon, have traditionally been a **cycling** mecca, with the long-established Ye Olde Bicycle Shop renting out bikes at very reasonable rates (Mon–Fri 9am–4.30pm, Sat & Sun 9am–5pm; $12.50 per hour, $18.50 half-day, $30 full-day; ⓣ02/4883 6043). A recommended evening activity – set off at sunset, armed with a torch – is a visit to **Glow Worm Glen**; after dark the small sandstone grotto is transformed by the naturally flickering lights of these tiny creatures. It's a 25-minute walk from town via the end of William Street, or an easy forty-minute signposted trek from Riverview Road in the park.

At the northeast edge of Morton National Park, 17km from Kangaroo Valley, **Fitzroy Falls** is a must-see. A short boardwalk from the car park takes you to the waterfall plunging 80m into the valley below, with glorious views of the Yarrunga Valley beyond. The **NPWS Visitor Centre** (daily 9am–5.30pm; entry fee $3 site visit, $6 all-day visit) has a buffet-style café with a very pleasant outside deck. Detailed information about walking tracks and scenic drives in the surrounding area is available and the office issues **camping** permits for the nearby bushcamp at Yarrunga Creek and the Gambells Rest camping ground (bookings essential ⓣ02/4887 7270) near Bundanoon, which has flush toilets and hot showers but no drinking water.

The Bundanoon **YHA hostel**, on Railway Avenue (ⓣ02/4883 6010; dorms $22, rooms ❷), is a spacious Edwardian-era guesthouse complete with open fireplaces and an outdoor spa (extra charge), and set on extensive grounds where you can also camp. A good-value **motel** with great facilities is the central *Bundanoon Country Inn* on Anzac Parade (ⓣ02/4883 6068; ❹). For more style, the elegant, antique-furnished *Tree Tops Country Guesthouse*, 101 Railway Ave (ⓣ02/4883 6372, ⓦwww.treetopsguesthouse.com.au; ❺), dates from 1910. Recommended **places to eat** are the *Old Post Office Cafe*, on Railway Parade, which doubles as a modern Australian restaurant on Saturday nights (dinner bookings ⓣ02/4883 6354; otherwise Wed–Sun 9am–5pm). The best coffee in town is served at the cute *Cafe de Railleur* attached to Ye Olde Bicycle Shop (see above). The *Bundanoon Hotel*, on Erith Street, opposite the station – on the other side of the railway tracks – is a very cosy British-style pub which serves up plain, affordable food in its tiny *Thistle* bistro (book Fri–Sun on ⓣ02/4883 6005; no food Mon & Tues).

Kangaroo Valley

Between Moss Vale and Nowra on the coast, **Kangaroo Valley** is a popular spot for weekenders from Sydney – a lovely, hidden valley situated between the lush dairy country of Nowra and the Southern Highlands. Continuing along the highway, a kilometre before entering the village, the picturesque old sandstone Hampden Suspension Bridge crosses the Kangaroo River; beside it is the large *Source Café* where you can sit beneath a vine-covered verandah, and the **Pioneer Settlement Museum Park** (daily 10am–4.30pm; $4) with an attached bushwalk and a **market** held in the grounds on the last Sunday of the month. Kangaroo Valley Safaris are based here for canoe hire and operate self-guided overnight canoe safaris along the Kangaroo River and Shoalhaven Gorge with a pickup service at the end of your journey (ⓣ02/4465 1502; ⓦwww.kangaroovalleycanoes.com.au). A service station here sells groceries. The very pleasant *Kangaroo Valley Escapes* just beside the bridge (ⓣ1300 559 977, ⓦwww.kangaroovalleyescapes.com.au; cabins ❹), is a great place to camp, complete with camp kitchen, or the en-suite timber cabins have everything from video to air-con; mountain bikes, canoes and kayaks for rent. In **KANGAROO**

VALLEY village itself, Moss Vale Road has several craft, antique and gift shops and a bookstore, plus lots of cafés – two of the best are *Cafe Bella*, at no. 151 and *Bounce* at no. 165 – but is dominated by the characterful old pub, the *Friendly Inn Hotel* at no. 159, which is overflowing on weekends. The area is prime **B&B** territory and *Tall Trees Bed and Breakfast*, 8 Nugents Creek Rd, 1km east from the Kangaroo Valley village (Ⓣ02/4465 1208, Ⓦwww.talltreesbandb.com.au; ❹–❺), has log fires and great views across the valley from its patio; the self-contained studio has a spa, wood fire and kitchen. Leaving the village the narrow and winding road climbs 700m up Cambewarra mountain and then descends to the coast with superb panoramas all the way.

You can get to Kangaroo Valley from Campbelltown train station on the outskirts of Sydney on Priors Scenic Express (Ⓣ02/4472 4040 or 1800 816 234); a half-hour stop is scheduled at Fitzroy Falls (see opposite).

Travel details

Sydney is very much the centre of the Australian transport network, and you can get to virtually anywhere in the country from here on a variety of competing services. The following list represents a minimum; as well as the dedicated services listed below, many places will also be served by long-distance services stopping en route.

Trains

Sydney to: Adelaide (Indian Pacific 2 weekly, Mon & Thurs 2.40pm; 27hr 30min); Brisbane (2 daily; 14hr 10min); Broken Hill (2 daily; 13hr); Canberra (2 daily; 4hr 10min); Dubbo (5 daily; 6hr 30min); Goulburn (8–10 daily; 3hr); Katoomba (22–30 daily; 2hr); Maitland (1 daily; 2hr 30min); Melbourne (2 daily; 11hr; plus daily bus/train Speedlink via Albury; 12–13hr); Murwillumbah (1 daily; 13hr 45min); Newcastle (20–25 daily; 2hr 30min); Perth (2 weekly, Mon & Thurs 2.40pm; 60hr); Richmond (18–25 daily; 1hr 15min); Windsor (18–25 daily; 1hr 15min); Wollongong (15–25 daily; 1hr 40min).

Buses

Sydney to: Adelaide (2–3 daily; 20hr); Albury (2 daily; 8hr 30min); Armidale (2 daily; 8hr 30min); Batemans Bay (3 daily; 5hr 20min); Bathurst (2–3 daily; 4hr); Bega (2–3 daily; 8hr); Bowral (5 weekly; 2hr 35min); Brisbane (8–12 daily; 15–17hr, with connections to Cairns and Darwin); Broken Hill (1 daily; 15hr 40min); Byron Bay (4–6 daily; 13hr 15min); Canberra (3 daily; 4hr); Cessnock (1 daily; 2hr 20min); Coffs Harbour (8 daily; 8hr 30min); Eden (4 daily; 8hr 30min–9hr 30min); Forster (1 daily; 5hr 30min); Glen Innes (2 daily; 10hr); Grafton (2 daily; 10hr); Melbourne (5 daily; 12–18hr); Mildura (2–3 daily; 16hr); Mittagong (5 weekly; 2hr 30min); Moss Vale (5 weekly; 2hr 45min); Muswellbrook (1 daily; 3hr 30min); Narooma (4 weekly; 8hr); Newcastle (8 daily; 3hr); Nowra (3 daily; 3hr–4hr 20min); Orange (1 daily; 4hr 15min); Perth (2–3 daily; 52–56hr); Port Macquarie (8 daily; 7hr); Port Stephens (1 daily; 4hr); Scone (1 daily; 3hr 50min); Tamworth (2 daily; 7hr); Taree (5 daily; 6hr); Tenterfield (2 daily; 11hr 30min).

Flights

Sydney to: Adelaide (20 daily; 2hr 30min); Albury (4–6 daily; 1hr 20min); Alice Springs (4 daily; 2hr 40min); Armidale (3–8 daily; 1hr 15min); Ballina (2–7 daily; 1hr 50min); Bathurst (3 daily Mon–Fri; 45min); Bourke (1 daily except Sat; 3hr 10min); Brisbane (20 daily; 1hr 15min); Broken Hill (1 daily except Sun; 2hr 30min); Cairns (15 daily; 2hr 40min); Canberra (20–25 daily; 35min); Cobar (2 daily Mon–Fri, 1 daily Sun; 2hr 25min); Coffs Harbour (6 daily; 1hr 15min); Cooma (1–2 daily; 1hr); Coonabarabran (1–2 daily; 2hr); Coonamble (1 daily except Sat; 2hr); Darwin (3 daily; 4hr); Dubbo (3–4 daily Mon–Fri, 1 daily Sun; 1hr); Glen Innes (1–3 daily; 1hr 25min); Grafton (1– 2 daily; 2hr); Griffith (2–3 daily except Sun; 1hr 25min); Gunnedah (1–2 daily; 1hr 10min); Hobart (20 daily; 1hr 30min); Inverell (1–2 daily; 1hr 55min); Lightning Ridge (1 daily except Sat; 3hr); Lismore (3–4 daily except Sun; 1hr 35min); Lord Howe Island (1 daily; 2hr); Melbourne (20 daily; 1hr 10min);

Merimbula (1–3 daily except Sun; 1hr 35min); Mildura (1 daily Mon–Fri; 2hr 40min); Moruya (2 daily Mon–Fri; 50 min); Mudgee (2 daily Mon–Fri, 1 daily Sat; 1hr); Narrandera (1 daily except Sun; 2hr); Newcastle (Mon–Fri 4 daily; 40min); Norfolk Island (4 weekly; 2hr 30min); Orange (2 daily except Sun; 45min); Parkes (Mon–Fri 3 daily; 1hr); Perth (20 daily; 4hr); Port Macquarie (6 daily; 1hr); Port Stephens (Mon–Fri 1 daily; 1hr); Tamworth (4–6 daily; 1hr); Taree (1–2 daily; 1hr); Uluru (2 daily; 3hr); Wagga Wagga (2–8 daily; 1hr 5min); Walgett (1 daily except Sat; 2hr 35min).

2

Coastal New South Wales and the ACT

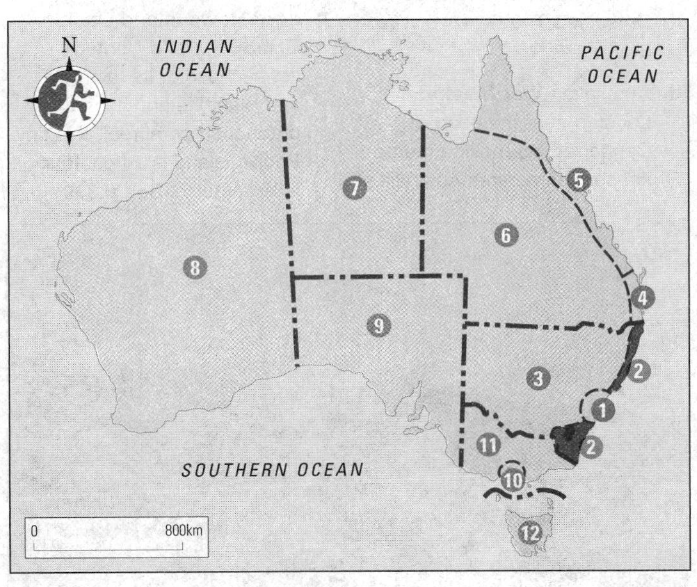

CHAPTER 2 Highlights

* **New Parliament House, Canberra** The stunning angular design of the New Parliament House is matched by its interior, which shows contemporary Australian design at its best. **See p.273**

* **The National Gallery, Canberra** Home to an extensive collection of Aboriginal art, plus iconic paintings such as the Ned Kelly series by Sidney Nolan and Russell Drysdale's *The Drover's Wife*. **See p.273**

* **Australian War Memorial** Located near the heart of Canberra, this moving memorial commemorates Australia's war dead from Gallipoli to Vietnam. **See p.276**

* **Snowy Mountains** Fine bushwalking in summer, and the best skiing in Australia in winter. **See p.298**

* **Byron Bay** New Age and alternative mecca with 30km of sandy beaches and fantastic diving – an essential stop on the backpacker circuit. **See p.325**

* **Lord Howe Island** On the UNESCO World Heritage list because of its rare bird and plant life and its virtually untouched coral reef, this tiny Pacific island is an ecotourist's paradise. **See p.339**

△ Byron Bay

2

Coastal New South Wales and the ACT

New South Wales is Australia's premier state in more ways than one. The oldest of the five states, and also the most densely populated, its six and a quarter million residents make up a third of the country's population. The vast majority occupy the urban and suburban sprawl which straggles along the state's thousand-plus kilometres of **Pacific coastline**, and the consistently mild climate and many beaches also draw a fairly constant stream of visitors, especially during the summer holiday season, when thousands of Australians descend on the coast to enjoy the extensive surf beaches and other oceanside attractions.

South of Sydney there's a string of low-key family resorts and fishing ports, great for water sports and fishing. To the **north** the climate gradually becomes warmer, and the coastline more popular – the series of big resorts up here includes **Port Macquarie** and **Coffs Harbour**, but there are also less-developed places where you can escape it all. One of the most enjoyable beach resorts in Australia is **Byron Bay**, which is just about managing to retain its slightly offbeat, alternative appeal, radiating from the still-thriving hippie communes of the lush, hilly **North Coast Hinterland**.

Just over 280km southwest of Sydney is the **Australian Capital Territory** (ACT), which was carved out of New South Wales at the beginning of the twentieth century as an independent base for the new national capital, **Canberra**, a city struggling to shed its dull image. Canberra is also the gateway to the **Snowy Mountains**, where the Great Dividing Range builds to a crescendo at **Mount Kosciuszko** (Australia's highest at 2228m), marking the peak of the Australian Alps, which offer skiing in winter and glorious hiking in summer.

Also included in this chapter are the Pacific islands far off the north coast of New South Wales: subtropical **Lord Howe Island**, 700km northeast of Sydney, and **Norfolk Island**, 900km further northeast and actually closer to New Zealand, inhabited by the descendants of the mutineers on the *Bounty*.

For details of the **rail network** in NSW – which runs from Sydney to Canberra; along the south coast from Sydney as far as Bomaderry; from Canberra to Eden; and from Sydney to Brisbane via the north coast – in Chapter 4.

QUEENSLAND
Coolangatta
Tweed Heads
Murwillumbah
Woodenbong
Nimbin
Byron Bay
Kyogle
Goondiwindi
Dumaresq
Bald Rock
Lismore
Lennox Head
Casino
Ballina
Mungindi
Tenterfield
Evans Head
Pacific Hwy
Clarence
Moree
Yamba
Gwydir Hwy
Warialda
Emmaville
Gwydir Hwy
Grafton
Newell Hwy
Inverell
Glen Innes
Bingara
Tingha Ben Lomond
Walgett
Wee Waa
NEW ENGLAND PLATEAU
New England Hwy
Guyra
NEW ENGLAND N.P.
Woolgoolga
Dorrigo
Coffs Harbour
Narrabri
Namoi
Bellingen
Mylestom
Uralla
Armidale
Bowraville
Nambucca Heads
Manilla
NEW ENGLAND
Walcha
Maclean
WARRUMBUNGLES
Oxley Hwy
Gunnedah
Tamworth
Oxley Hwy
Kempsey
Crescent Head
Coonabarabran
Nundle
Hwy
Port Macquarie
Quirindi
New England Hwy
Wauchope
Crowdy Head
Pacific
BARRINGTON TOPS N.P.
Gilgandra
Coolah
Murrurundi
Wingham
Taree
Gloucester
Scone
Merriwa
Forster-Tuncurry
Muswellbrook
Wallis Lake
Dubbo
Gulgong
Bulahdelah
Seal Rocks
Hunter
Myall Lake
Mudgee
Singleton
Port Stephens
Maitland
Cessnock
Nelson Bay
Newcastle
Parkes
Orange
Bathurst
Forbes
Lithgow
Katoomba
Cowra
SYDNEY
Camden
Picton
Young
Bargo
Crookwell
Wollongong
Bowral
Boorowa
Moss Vale
Robertson
Bundanoon
Cootamundra
Kiama
Hume Hwy
Olympic Way
Murrumbidgee
Goulburn
Berry
Yass
Nowra-Bomaderry
MORTON N.P.
Barton Hwy
Jervis Bay
Gundagai
BOODEREE N.P.
SOUTH PACIFIC OCEAN
Queanbeyan
Tumut
CANBERRA
Snowy Mts Hwy
Ulladulla
Braidwood
Tharwa
Princes Hwy
ACT
NAMADGI N.P.
Batemans Bay
Tumbarumba
DEUA N.P.
KOSCIUSZKO N.P.
Narooma
Murray
Cooma
WADBILLIGA N.P.
Tilba Tilba
Thredbo
Bermagui
Jindabyne
Monaro Hwy
Mt Kosciuszko (2228m)
Bega
Tathra
Candelo
Merimbula
Bombala
Eden
Snowy
BEN BOYD N.P.
VICTORIA
N
0
100 km

National parks in New South Wales

The **National Parks and Wildlife Service** (NPWS) has **entrance fees** to many of its parks – usually $6–15 per car and $4 for motorcycles (often on an honour system). If you intend to "go bush" a lot in New South Wales you can buy an **annual pass** for $60 ($30 for motorbikes), which includes all parks except Kosciuszko. Because of its popularity as a skiing destination, entrance to Kosciuszko is a steep $15 per car per day, perversely levied in summer too – so if you plan on spending any length of time here, or are going to visit other parks as well, consider the $80 annual pass which covers entry to all parks, including Kosciuszko. Passes can be bought at NPWS offices and some park entry stations, over the phone using a credit card (Ⓣ02/9253 4600 or 1300 361 967) or online (Ⓦwww.npws.nsw.gov.au); you can also download an order form from the website and send it (include your vehicle type and its registration number) by fax (Ⓕ02/9251 9192) or by mail to the National Parks Centre, PO Box N429, Grosvenor Place, NSW 1220.

You can **camp** in most national parks. Bushcamping is generally free, but where there is a ranger station and a designated campsite with facilities, fees are charged, usually around $6 per site. If the amenities are of a high standard, including hot showers and the like, or if the spot is just plain popular, fees can be as high as $18 per tent. Open fires are banned in most parks and forbidden everywhere on days when there is high danger of fire, and while there are often electric or gas barbecues in picnic areas, you'll need a fuel stove for bush camping.

Australian Capital Territory

The first European squatters settled in the valleys and plains north of the Snowy Mountains in the 1820s, though until 1900 this remained a remote rural area. When the Australian colonies united in the **Commonwealth of Australia** in 1901, a capital city had to be chosen, with Melbourne and Sydney the two obvious and eager rivals. After much wrangling, and partly in order to avoid having to decide on one of the two, it was agreed to establish a brand-new capital instead. In 1909, Limestone Plains, a plain south of Yass surrounded by mountain ranges, was chosen out of several possible sites as the future seat of the Australian government. An area of 2368 square kilometres was excised from the state of New South Wales and named the **Australian Capital Territory**, or **ACT**. The ACT officially included an adjunct at Jervis Bay (see p.289), on the coast south of Nowra, to give Australia's capital its own access to the sea and a naval base. The name for the future capital was supposedly taken from the language of local Aborigines: **Canberra** – the meeting place.

Canberra is situated on a high plain (600m above sea level). In summer, the average temperatures are 27°C maximum during the day and 12°C minimum at night; in winter they drop from an average of 12°C maximum during the day to freezing point (and below) at night. Spring and autumn can be really delightful, though. The mountain ranges to the west and south of the city rise to 1900m and are snow-covered in winter.

Canberra

In 1912 **Walter Burley Griffin**, an American landscape architect from Chicago, won the international competition for the design of the future Australian capital, **CANBERRA**. His plan envisaged a garden city for about 25,000 people based in five main centres, each with separate city functions, located on three axes: land, water and municipal. Roads were to be in concentric circles, with arcs linking the radiating design. Construction started in 1913, but political squabbling and the effects of World War I, the Depression and World War II prevented any real progress being made until 1958, when growth began in earnest. In 1963 the Molonglo River was dammed to form the eleven-kilometre-wide artificial **Lake Burley Griffin** that is the centrepiece of modern Canberra. Slowly, the **Civic Centre** began to live up to its name. The **population** grew rapidly, from fifteen thousand in 1947 to over one hundred thousand in 1967; today, it is more than three hundred thousand. accommodated in satellite towns – a sprawl that fostered Canberra's image as "a cluster of suburbs in search of a centre".

Inevitably, modern Canberra is mainly a place of civil servants and administrators, and the city is trying very hard to shake off its reputation as the domain of dull bureaucrats. It hasn't succeeded yet, however, and most Australians still regard Canberra as "pollie city" – a boring place where politicians and public servants live it up at the expense of the hard-done-by Australian taxpayer. They also complain about the city's contrived, neat-as-a-pin nature, and its baffling concentric streets, which can make driving here seem like a Kafka-esque nightmare.

The main reason to come to Canberra is for the national museums and institutions, top of the list being the **National Gallery**, the **War Museum** and the stunning **New Parliament House**. The city also has plenty of wide open spaces and many **parks** and gardens, with the impressive national institutions set in astonishingly well-groomed surroundings. And right on Canberra's doorstep are forests and **bushland**, with unspoilt wilderness just a bit further afield in the Brindabella Ranges and the Namadgi National Park. Sadly, in late 2002, this natural bush setting, combined with extreme drought conditions, precipitated Canberra's worst **bushfires** for fifty years. The area to the west of the city was hardest hit. Mount Stromlo Observatory was completely gutted and over five hundred homes were destroyed and four residents killed – the effects of the fires can still be seen today.

Canberra's **nightlife** - in term time at least – is alive and kicking. The two universities here (and the Duntroon Military Academy for officer material) mean there's a large and lively **student population** (good news for those who have student cards, as most attractions offer hefty discounts), and the city is also said to have more **restaurants** per capita than any other in Australia – which is saying something. Canberra also holds the dubious title of Australia's **porn capital**, due to its liberal licensing laws, which legalize and regulate the sex industry.

Arrival and information

Canberra's **airport**, about 7km east of the city, handles domestic flights only. Bus #80 ($5) runs on weekdays between the airport and the city centre; otherwise expect to pay around $20 for a taxi. The main **train station** is located southeast of the centre, on Wentworth Avenue in Kingston; from here, taxis are again the easiest way to get where you're going; trains also stop at the suburb of Queanbeyan, in New South Wales, where there's some cheap accommodation. Most interstate **buses** drop and pick up at the handy

Jolimont Centre, downtown at 65–67 Northbourne Ave; the modern centre has showers, lockers ($2), a TV room, snack bar, post office, Internet kiosk and a travel bookshop, which also offers everything from Australia-wide tours to Canberra city bus tickets, as well as some tourist information and maps. Additionally, the centre has ticket offices for the train, airline and bus companies. There is a free direct telephone line to the tourist office (see below), to taxi companies and to accommodation.

The **Canberra Visitor Information Centre**, the main tourist office, is inconveniently located about 2km north of the centre, at 330 Northbourne Avenue in Dickson (Mon–Fri 9am–5.30pm, Sat & Sun 9am–4pm; ⓣ02/6205 0044 or 1800 026 166, ⓦwww.canberratourism.com.au), reachable by bus #380; it books tours, transport and accommodation. More central is the **tourist information booth** on the ground floor of the Canberra Centre, a shopping mall on Bunda Street (Mon–Thurs & Sat 9am–5.30pm, Fri 9am–7.30pm, Sun 10am–4pm); it provides maps and information, but doesn't make bookings.

City transport

To appreciate the city, you ideally need a vehicle of some kind – things are very spread out, and at the weekend especially public transport is extremely limited. You'll find that the dispersed nature of Canberra means that you can easily **park** your car, often for free, at the main sights. Renting a **bike** to take advantage of the excellent network of bike paths is strongly recommended (see "Listings" on p.281). The handy hop-on-hop-off **double-decker bus**, (ⓣ0418 455099, ⓦwww.canberradaytours.com.au) circuits the major sights and routes; buses depart from 9.30am until 3.30pm (every 90min) from the Melbourne Building on Northbourne Avenue. Tickets ($20) are valid all day, and include obligatory running commentary from the driver. Note, however, that unless you're planning a relentless sightseeing spree, bus #34 covers many of the major tourist haunts for a fraction of the cost.

Municipal buses are run by Action. The **Off-Peak Daily** ($3.50; valid Mon–Fri 9am–4.30pm and after 6pm; Sat & Sun all day), purchased from the driver, is excellent value and can be used for as many journeys as you like. There's also a $6 pass which is valid all day. Other buses cover all of Canberra, including the satellite towns: for details, contact Action **timetable information** (ⓣ13 17 10, ⓦwww.action.act.gov.au).

Most Action buses start at the City Bus Interchange, at East Row just across Northbourne Avenue from the Jolimont Centre; you can buy tickets at the Newslink shop behind stand 9, or at most other newsagents. For ticketing purposes, the city is divided into three zones: North, South and Central – most sights are situated within the central zone. Besides the day-trip ticket (valid for all zones), you can pay a single zone, flat-rate fare ($2.40) or a single, all-zone fare ($5.40), both of which can also be bought on board; a ten-journey Faresaver ticket costs $21 for one zone (or $40 for all zones); a weekly ticket costs $23.50.

For a bit of kitsch fun, check out the very popular **Love Bus tours** of the adult entertainment industry, which include the National Museum of Erotica (information and bookings on ⓣ02/6262 9266, ⓦwww.lovebus.com.au).

Accommodation

One of the best accommodation locations is **Kingston**, a salubrious, café-filled suburb close to the train station, and within walking distance of the Parliamentary Triangle attractions. Canberra has a couple of excellent **hostels**, and out-of-term inexpensive B&B is available in several student halls of residence.

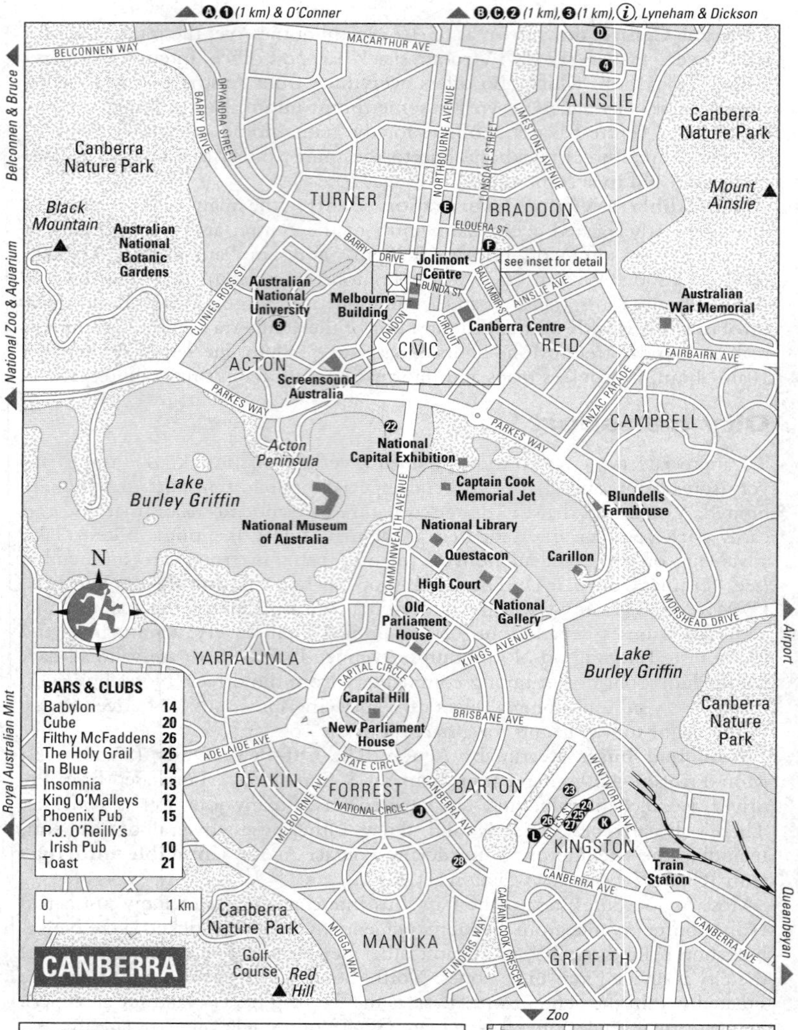

A, 1 (1 km) & O'Conner
B, C, 2 (1 km), 3 (1 km), i, Lyneham & Dickson
Belconnen & Bruce
National Zoo & Aquarium
Royal Australian Mint
Airport
Queanbeyan
Zoo

BELCONNEN WAY
MACARTHUR AVE
BARRY DRIVE
DRYANDRA STREET
NORTHBOURNE AVENUE
LONSDALE STREET
LIMESTONE AVENUE
AINSLIE
Canberra Nature Park
Canberra Nature Park
Mount Ainslie
Black Mountain
Australian National Botanic Gardens
TURNER
BRADDON
ELOUERA ST
BARRY DRIVE
Jolimont Centre
see inset for detail
BUNDA ST
BALLUMBIR ST
AINSLIE AVE
CLUNIES ROSS ST
Australian National University
Melbourne Building
Canberra Centre
Australian War Memorial
LONDON CIRCUIT
CIVIC
REID
FAIRBAIRN AVE
ACTON
Screensound Australia
PARKES WAY
ANZAC PARADE
CAMPBELL
PARKES WAY
Acton Peninsula
National Capital Exhibition
Lake Burley Griffin
Captain Cook Memorial Jet
Blundells Farmhouse
COMMONWEALTH AVENUE
National Museum of Australia
National Library
Questacon
Carillon
High Court
National Gallery
Old Parliament House
MORSHEAD DRIVE
N
YARRALUMLA
KINGS AVENUE
Lake Burley Griffin
CAPITAL CIRCLE
Capital Hill
New Parliament House
BRISBANE AVE
Canberra Nature Park
ADELAIDE AVE
STATE CIRCLE
DEAKIN
FORREST
BARTON
WENTWORTH AVE
MELBOURNE AVE
NATIONAL CIRCLE
CANBERRA AVE
GILES ST
KINGSTON
Train Station
CANBERRA AVE
0 1 km
Canberra Nature Park
MUGGA WAY
MANUKA
FLINDERS WAY
CAPTAIN COOK CRESCENT
GRIFFITH
CANBERRA AVE
Golf Course
Red Hill

CANBERRA

BARS & CLUBS

Babylon	14
Cube	20
Filthy McFaddens	26
The Holy Grail	26
In Blue	14
Insomnia	13
King O'Malleys	12
Phoenix Pub	15
P.J. O'Reilly's Irish Pub	10
Toast	21

ACCOMMODATION

Blue & White Lodge	B
Canberra City Accomodation	I
Canberra YHA Hostel	A
Chifley	E
City Walk Hotel	G
Civic Pub Backpackers	F
Crowne Plaza Canberra	H
Forrest Inn and Apartments	J
Medina Classic	L
Parkview Lodge	C
Tall Trees Motel	D
Victor Lodge	K

RESTAURANTS & CAFÉS

Ali Baba	9
ANU Union	5
Artespresso	23
Barocca Café	6
Bernadette's	4
The Blue Olive	7
The Café	22
Café Essen	9
Caffe della Piazza	9
Chairman and Yip	8
Delicateating	1
Fringe Benefits Brasserie	6
Gus Café	18
Iridium	17
Kingsland Vegetarian Restaurant	3
Lemon Grass Thai Restaurant	16
Little Saigon	11
Madame Woo	24
Montezuma's	I
Portia's Place	25
Silo	27
Tilley's Devine Café Gallery	2
Tosolini's	28
Zydeco	19

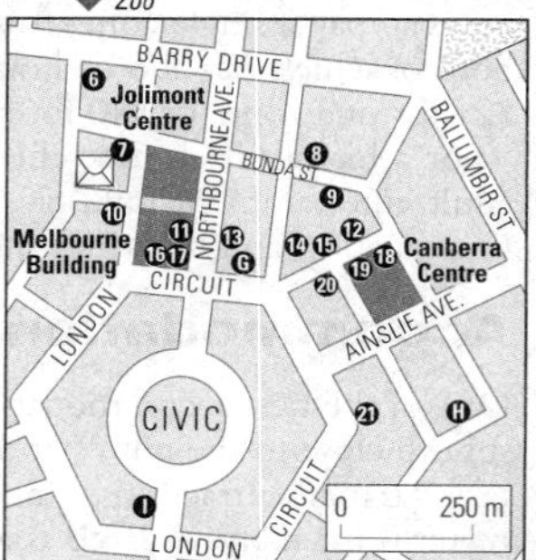

Hotels, motels and guesthouses

Blue & White Lodge 524 Northbourne Ave, Downer, 5km north of the city ⓣ02/6248 0498, ⓔblueandwhitelodge@bigpond.com. Recently refurbished B&B with well-equipped, en-suite rooms – TV, fridge, heating, air-con and tea-making facilities. Cooked breakfast included. Bus #39 or #50. ❹

Chifley 102 Northbourne Ave (ⓣ02/6249 6878, ⓦwww.chifleyhotels.com). Luxurious, professional and very easy to find, this chain clone has all you could wish for including gym, pool, restaurants and office.

Crowne Plaza Canberra 1 Binara St, Civic ⓣ02/6247 8999, ⓦwww.crowneplaza.com. Central, four-star hotel with all the conveniences you'd expect, including room service, swimming pool, sauna and gym. ❼

Forrest Inn and Apartments 30 National Circuit, Forrest ⓣ02/6295 3433, ⓦwww.forrestinn.com.au. Next to the pretty Serbian church, this modern, clean and clinical motel is lacking in atmosphere, but professionally run. Bus #35 or #36. ❹–❺

Medina Classic 11 Giles St, Kingston ⓣ02/6239 8100, ⓦwww.medinaapartments.com.au. Tasteful, upmarket one-, two- and three-bedroom, self-catering serviced apartments with fully equipped kitchens (except for a couple of smaller apartments). Facilities include laundry, swimming pool, spa, gym and undercover parking; bike rental available. Popular with families, and staff are friendly. Bus #39 or #84. ❻

Parkview Lodge 526 Northbourne Ave, Downer, 4km north ⓣ02/6249 8038, ⓦwww.mirandalodge.com.au. Good non-smoking B&B with off-street parking and en-suite rooms with TV and fridge (some also have spas). Bus #39 or #50. ❸

Tall Trees Motel 21 Stephen St, Ainslie (look for the "Best Western" sign) ⓣ02/6247 9200, ⓦwww.talltreesmotel.com. Pleasant, upmarket motel set in quiet shady grounds and offering various standards of en-suite room. Bus #38. ❸–❹

Hostels and college accommodation

ANU student accommodation ⓦwww.anu.edu.au. Bruce Hall ⓣ02/6267 4123, ⓔenquiries.bruce@anu.edu.au; Fenner Hall ⓣ02/6125 9000, ⓦwww.fenner.anu.edu.au; Ursula College ⓣ02/6279 4300, ⓦwww.anu.edu.au/res/Ursula/index.shtml; Burgmann College ⓣ02/6125 6087. Student accommodation located around the Australian National University campus in Acton, just west of the city centre. Most rooms are singles, but there are also a few twins. Dorms $35, rooms ❷

Canberra City Accommodation 7 Akuna St, Civic ⓣ02/6257 3999 or 1800 300 488, ⓦwww.canberracityaccommodation.com.au This cavernous, centrally located hostel heralds a new backpacking dawn (and a parking nightmare). Facilities include gym, bar, rooftop BBQ garden, laundry, Internet café, sauna, bike rental, cable TV, lockers in every room and 24hr check-in. Dorms $25, rooms ❸

Canberra YHA Hostel 191 Dryandra St, O'Connor ⓣ02/6248 9155, ⓔcanberra@yhansw.org.au. Friendly modern hostel with excellent facilities and a quiet air, situated about 4km out of town with lots of parking in a quiet bush setting. There's a small shop, Internet access and super-cheap bike rental; rates include linen. The congenial staff at reception (7am–10pm) run regular minibus pick-ups from town (call beforehand); otherwise it's a ten-minute trip on bus #35. Dorms $25, rooms ❷

City Walk Hotel 2 Mort St, City ⓣ02/6257 0124, ⓦwww.citywalkhotel.citysearch.com.au. Just across the road from the bus station (but don't even think about parking here), this spic-and-span place has a very central location and an excellent Irish bar downstairs (guests often get discounted beer). Facilities include a kitchen, Internet access and a common room with TV. Dorms $22, rooms ❸

Civic Pub Backpackers 8 Lonsdale St, Braddon ⓣ02/6248 6488. Canberra accommodation (dorms only) doesn't come any cheaper than this place. It's clean enough, though there are no kitchen or laundry facilities. Dorms $20.

Victor Lodge 29 Dawes St, Kingston, 4km southwest ⓣ02/6295 7777, ⓦwww.victorlodge.com.au. Small, friendly and very popular family-run hostel-cum-guesthouse, situated close to lots of good restaurants. The dorms are clean and bright, but the rooms are overpriced. Facilities include a well-equipped kitchen and BBQ area, laundry, TV room, Internet access and very reasonable bike rental, plus free city pick-ups and drop-offs. Bus #39, #80 or #84. Dorms $25, rooms ❹

Camping and caravan parks

Canberra Carotel Motel and Caravan Park Federal Highway, Watson, 7km north ⓣ02/6241 1377, ⓔinfo@carotel.com.au. Caravan park with a swimming pool and café, plus camping space. Bus #36. On-site vans ❷, cabins ❸

Canberra South Motor Park, Canberra Ave, Symonstone, 4km southeast ⓣ02/6280 6176, ⓦwww.csmp.net.au. Well equipped park on a little creek with air-con options and en-suite cabins. ❷

Crestview Tourist Park 81 Donald Rd, Queanbeyan, 17km east ⓣ02/6297 2443, ⓦwww.crestview.contact.com.au. Facilities here include camping space and cabins, plus a swimming pool and shop. ❷

White Ibis Tourist Village and Caravan Park 47 Bidges Rd, off the Federal Highway, Sutton, 14km north ⓣ02/6230 3433, ⓦwww.sydneycaravanparks.com.au. Good site with pool, cricket pitch, volleyball, basketball and tennis courts, plus a kiosk selling the essentials. Cabins ❹

The City

Canberra is a straightforward place to find your way around – though distances are such that only in the very centre will you want to do much walking, and even there it can be something of a test of fitness. The eleven-kilometre-wide **Lake Burley Griffin** pretty much marks the heart of the city, with several lakeside places of interest both north and south, including the **National Museum of Australia** right on the lake on the Acton peninsula. North of the lake is the city centre proper, the **Civic Centre**, or "Civic" for short, which houses shops, restaurants, cafés, pubs, cinemas and theatres, as well as the GPO. The campus of the **Australian National University** (ANU) is just to the west of the centre in the suburb of Acton, as is **Screensound Australia**, the old National Film and Sound Archive. Beyond Acton, the **National Botanic Gardens** sit at the flanks of the 806-metre **Black Mountain**, topped by the distinctive Telstra Tower and just one of many scattered sections of the **Canberra Nature Park**.

East of the centre is the **Australian War Memorial**, solemnly gazing back along monument-lined **Anzac Parade** to the **Parliamentary Triangle**, south of the lake, with the old Parliament House overlooked by the New Parliament House on Capital Hill. This political quarter, linked to the city centre by the **Commonwealth Avenue Bridge**, is where you'll find the government offices and national cultural institutions, and is the part of Canberra that is of most architectural interest. Fronting the lake, strung along King Edward Terrace, are four impressive modern public buildings: the **National Library**, **Questacon** (the National Science and Technology Centre), the **National Gallery** and the **High Court**. Most of the city's foreign embassies – intended to resemble the vernacular architecture of their home countries – cluster around **Yarralumla** and **Forrest**.

Questacon and the National Library

Crossing the Commonwealth Avenue Bridge from the city centre, you turn left onto King Edward Terrace. Immediately before you is **Questacon** – the National Science and Technology Centre (daily 9am–5pm; $14; ⓦwww.questacon.edu.au), a hands-on science museum which offers activities such as getting shaken by a simulated earthquake. There are some free interactive exhibits in the foyer if you just want a taste. A **three-in-one ticket** ($37), available at the visitors centre, will get you into Cockington Green (see p.285), the Australian Institute of Sport (see p.278) and Questacon.

Looming behind Questacon is the **National Library** (Mon–Thurs 9am–9pm, Fri & Sat 9am–5pm, Sun 1.30–5pm; ⓦwww.nla.gov.au; free), whose reading room has a comprehensive selection of overseas newspapers and magazines. There are also exhibitions of rare books in the foyer, like Captain Cook's journal from the *Endeavour*, as well as temporary exhibitions.

The High Court of Australia

From the library, it's a pleasant walk about 500m east along lakefront Parkes Place to the **High Court of Australia** (daily 9.45am–4.30pm; free), set in an appropriately grandiose, glass-fronted edifice with a stylized waterfall running alongside the walkway up to the entrance. Visitors can watch a short video which explains the court's function and examines two of its landmark cases: the 1983 ruling that saved Tasmania's wild Franklin River from damming; and its finding on the 1992 land rights case of Mabo versus Queensland – a momentous decision that overturned the British legal concept of *terra nullius* whereby Australia was considered uninhabited prior to white settlement in 1788. You can watch judgments while the court is in session.

The National Gallery

One of Canberra's major attractions is the **National Gallery** (daily 10am–5pm, tours at 11am & 2pm; free; Ⓦwww.nga.gov.au), immediately east of the High Court, to which it is linked by a footbridge. The collection includes art from every continent and includes work by Monet, Cézanne, Magritte and Tanguy, but the core of the collection is Australian.

The **Art of Aboriginal Australia and Torres Strait Islands** gallery is on the entrance level; the collection is extensive, ranging from traditional bark paintings from the Northern Territory to politically aware contemporary work in different media. The **Aboriginal Memorial 1988** pays homage to the Aboriginal people who since 1788 have lost their life, land and culture. The memorial, which looks at first glance like a forest of huge didgeridoos, comprises two hundred termite-hollowed logs representative of the culture's log coffins, painted with totemic designs by over forty artists from around Ramingining in Central Arnhem Land.

On the upper level is the excellent **Australian Art** gallery. Most striking are the 25 bushranger paintings in Sidney Nolan's celebrated *Ned Kelly* series, while there are also some Bret Whitleys, some samples of the nightmarish work of Albert Tucker and fine pieces by Arthur Boyde and the Aboriginal-influenced John Olson. Other works on permanent display include Russell Drysdale's *The Drover's Wife* (1945), probably his best-known painting, and American artist Jackson Pollock's *Blue Poles* (1950).

Outside is a living fern-tree sculpture by Australian artist Fiona Hall, and a mostly abstract **Sculpture Garden** overlooking Lake Burley Griffin. Also visible and audible across the water from here is the **Carillon** stranded on Aspen Island, whose three elegant bell towers and 53 bronze bells – ranging from tiny to huge – were a gift from the British government to mark Canberra's fiftieth birthday. It's pleasant to sit on the lawns under a shady tree by the lake and listen to the Carillon recitals (June–Aug Sun & Wed 12.30pm-1.20pm; Sept–May Mon, Wed, Fri & Sun 12.30pm–1.20pm). There are tours of the Carillon ($8) at 11.30am in winter and 12.30pm in summer. On summer evenings, concerts and other events, such as open-air film screenings, are sometimes held here to coincide with special exhibitions (ask at the tourist office for details).

The Old and New Parliament houses

Away from the lake, on King George Terrace at the foot of Capital Hill, is the **Old Parliament House** (daily 9am–5pm; $2; Ⓦwww.oph.gov.au), whose grounds became the site of a live-in Aboriginal protest for land rights – dubbed the **Tent Embassy** – for over six months in 1972. Twenty years later a second tent embassy was erected, and it remains here still, flying the Aboriginal flag. You'll be welcomed for a cup of tea and a (political) chat.

The simple white Neoclassical building of the Old Parliament House itself was the seat of government from 1927 until 1988; a **tour** of the "wedding cake" shows just how crowded and inconvenient the building actually was. You can walk into the old senate or house of representatives, take a leather seat and listen to one of the guides. The **National Portrait Gallery** (Ⓦwww.portrait.gov.au)

uses the building for exhibitions, and large portraits of many prime ministers hang on the walls. Outside, you can wander in the **Senate Rose Garden** or visit the **National Archives of Australia** on Queen Victoria Terrace, which has socio-historical exhibitions (daily 9am–5pm; free; Ⓦwww.naa.gov.au).

Built into the side of Capital Hill is the **New Parliament House** (daily 9am–5pm; free; Ⓦwww.aph.gov.au). The excellent guided **tours** are recommended, while the first-floor theatre screens hourly films about the construction of the building. The building (opened in May 1988) was the startling design of American-based architect Romaldo Giurgola, an Italian. Visitors and locals are generally impressed, but the unnecessarily large edifice still causes many an Aussie cheek to burn, not least that of former president Malcolm Fraser, who in 1997 described the building as "an unmitigated disaster" and "my one very serious political mistake". Whatever your views on the architecture and scope of the thing, you're free to walk over, loll on, and even roll down the grassy ramps covering the building.

Outside the ground-floor entrance level is a **mosaic** by the Aboriginal artist Michael Tjakamarra Nelson – a piece that conveys the idea of a sacred meeting place. Inside, the impressive **foyer** is dominated by grand marble staircases and over forty columns clad in grey-green and rose-pink marble, representing a eucalypt forest. The floors are made of native woods, and the walls feature marquetry panels detailing native plants.

Beyond the foyer, the **Great Hall** is dominated by a twenty-metre-high tapestry based on a painting by Arthur Boyd showing the opposing forces of life and death meeting in blackened trees set against a powerful sky. Other chambers are adorned with paintings by artists such as Albert Tucker, Sidney Nolan and Ian Fairweather, as well as portraits of political figures, photographs and ceramics. Important documents in the country's political history are also displayed.

When Parliament is in session – usually from seventy to eighty days a year – you can sit in the public gallery and watch the proceedings in the House of Representatives (the lower chamber of Parliament) or the Senate (the upper chamber of the legislature); **Question Time** in both chambers starts at 2pm, with the House of Representatives making for better viewing; to guarantee a seat at busy times (like budget day), book in advance on Ⓣ02/6277 4889.

The diplomatic quarters and the mint

A trip among the upmarket suburban homes in Canberra's diplomatic quarters – **Yarralumla** and **Forrest** – completes the political sightseeing tour. The consuls and high commissions were asked to construct buildings that exemplified the typical architecture of the countries they represent – look out for the eye-catching embassies of Thailand, Indonesia (with a small cultural centre), China and Papua New Guinea.

At the **Royal Australian Mint** (Mon–Fri 9am–4pm, Sat & Sun 10am–4pm; free; Ⓦwww.ramint.gov.au), a few kilometres to the southwest on Denison Street, Deakin, you can actually make your own money for twice the face value. It's fun, especially for kids.

Lake Burley Griffin

Back across Commonwealth Avenue Bridge, at the far western end of Lake Burley Griffin on Lady Denman Drive, is the **National Zoo and Aquarium** (daily 9am–5pm; $18.50; Ⓦwww.zooquarium.com.au). Visitors walk through tunnels of acrylic glass while sharks, stingrays and other creatures glide past, only an arm's-length away; outside there's a bear park, a monkey island, and kangaroos, lions, tigers (which you can feed), giraffes, emus and dingoes.

△ Lake Burley Griffin, Canberra

On the Acton Peninsula, the prime lakefront site of the old Royal Canberra Hospital is now home to the **National Museum of Australia** (daily 9am–5pm; free; Ⓦwww.nma.gov.au), housed in a controversial $100 million "anti-monumental" building – a postmodern riot, considered vibrant and playful by some, and simply crass by others. The exhibitions offer an interesting look at what it means to be Australian, warts and all; some claim that the museum trivializes white Australia and celebrates kitsch. The **Nation: Symbols of Australia gallery** features Victa lawnmowers and Hills Hoists (revolving clothes lines), while the bleak symbolism of an arid, treeless country is presented in the concrete **Garden of Australian Dreams**. There has been discomfort, too, at the **First Australians gallery**, which goes beyond boomerangs and canoes to tell the story of the "massacre" of Aboriginal people, the reserve system, black deaths in custody, and the "stolen generations". The **Tangled Destinies gallery** explores the relationship between land and people in Australia, while the **Horizons gallery**, subtitled "The Peopling of Australia since 1788", looks at the nation's migrant history. There are also quality temporary exhibitions (entrance fee payable) and **film screenings** in the evenings.

Just east of the Commonwealth Avenue Bridge, you'll pass the **National Capital Exhibition** at Regatta Point (daily 9am–5pm; Ⓦwww.nationalcapital.gov.au; free), comprising a small theatre plus displays and models depicting Canberra's development. Guided tours are available, though on windy days you have to beware of the spray from the **Captain Cook Memorial Jet** (10am–noon & 2–4pm, also 7–9pm during daylight saving), built in 1970 to mark the bicentenary of Captain Cook's "discovery" of Australia, which spurts a column of water 140m into the air.

Further east is one of the few historic buildings in the city: **Blundells Cottage** (daily 10am–4pm; $4; Ⓣ02/6257 1068, Ⓦwww.nationalcapital.gov.au), on Wendouree Drive in Kings Park, a little stone cottage, built in 1860, which was once part of a local farm.

The Australian War Memorial

To the east of the city, **Anzac Parade** is lined with individual memorials to every war Australia has been involved in, leading up to the **Australian War Memorial** (daily 10am–5pm; free; Ⓦwww.awm.gov.au). The grounds around the memorial are filled with top-class sculpture, while the interior has paintings by Arthur Streeton, among others, along with very realistic battle dioramas and military relics including huge naval guns and giant bombers, as well as countless films, sound and light shows, regular free tours and loads of information, artefacts, posters and photographs. The **Hall of Memory**, at the innermost part of the War Memorial, is beautifully built atop a hill in a Byzantine style intended to evoke the memory of Gallipoli. Look up at the ceiling to see one of the world's largest mosaics, depicting veterans of World War II, while the lovely blue stained-glass windows commemorate those who fought in World War I. In the centre is the tomb of the Unknown Australian Soldier, while over 100,000 names of the fallen are etched onto the walls outside, with poppies planted in the cracks.

ANU and Screensound Australia

The green and spacious **Australian National University** (ANU) campus is just west of the city centre in Acton. The two small **anthropological museums** at the Hope Building on Ellery Crescent are open to the public (Mon–Fri 9am–4pm; free), and there are also concerts and plays: for information call Ⓣ02/6125 5736 or see Ⓦwww.anu.edu.au.

The Anzacs

Travelling around Australia you'll notice that almost every town, large or small, has a war memorial dedicated to the memory of the Anzacs, the **Australia and New Zealand Army Corps**. When war erupted in Europe in 1914, Australia was overwhelmed by a wave of pro-British sentiment. On August 5, 1914, one day after Great Britain had declared war against the German empire, the Australian prime minister summed up the feelings of his compatriots: "When the Empire is at war so Australia is at war." On November 1, 1914, a contingent of twenty thousand enthusiastic volunteers – the **Anzacs** – left from the port of Albany in Western Australia to assist the mother country in her struggle.

In Europe, Turkey had entered the war on the German side in October 1914. At the beginning of 1915, military planners in London (Winston Churchill prominent among them) came up with a plan to capture the strategically important Turkish peninsula of the Dardanelles with a surprise attack near **Gallipoli**, thus opening the way to the Black Sea. On April 25, 1915, sixteen thousand Australian soldiers landed at dawn in a small bay flanked by steep cliffs: by nightfall, two thousand men had died in a hail of Turkish bullets from above. The plan, whose one chance of success was surprise, had been signalled by troop and ship movements long in advance; by the time it was carried out, it was already doomed to failure. Nonetheless, Allied soldiers continued to lose their lives for another eight months without ever gaining more than a foothold.

In December, London finally issued the order to withdraw. Eleven thousand Australians and New Zealanders had been killed, along with as many French and three times as many British troops. The Turks lost 86,000 men.

Official Australian historiography continues to mythologize the battle for Gallipoli, elevating it to the level of a national legend on which Australian identity is founded. From this point of view, in the war's baptism of fire, the Anzac soldiers proved themselves heroes who did the new nation proud, their loyalty and bravery evidence of how far Australia had developed. It was "the birth of a nation", and at the same time a loss of innocence, a national rite of passage – never again would Australians so unquestioningly involve themselves in foreign ventures. Today the legend is as fiercely defended as ever, the focal point of Australian national pride, commemorated each year on April 25, **Anzac Day**.

Within the grounds of the ANU campus, on McCoy Circuit, **Screensound Australia**, the old National Film and Sound Archive, houses the most comprehensive collection of Australian sound and screen recordings in existence, dating back to the 1890s. One of the highlights of a visit here is an interactive exhibition (Mon–Fri 9am–5pm, Sat & Sun 10am–5pm; free; Ⓦ www.screensound.gov.au) where special headphones tune in to the frequency of each display as you pass. A wild-card display of Australian TV ads features some real humdingers from the 1970s, and you can watch fascinating snippets from old newsreels in a small projection room.

Black Mountain and around

The **Australian National Botanic Gardens** (daily 9am–5pm; free; free guided tours daily at 11am & 2pm; Ⓦ www.anbg.gov.au/anbg), on the flanks of Black Mountain, have been planted with around six thousand species of native plants. The main entrance is on Clunies Ross Street, beyond the university area, and there's a **visitor information centre** (daily 9.30am–4.30pm) with leaflets for self-guided tours, displays and videos. While you're here, you should take the opportunity to drive or walk up to Black Mountain, which rises about 200m above Canberra and offers magnificent panoramic views of Canberra from the 66-metre-high viewing platform at the **Black Mountain Telstra Tower** (daily 9am–10pm; $3.30). The tower also has a revolving restaurant (Ⓣ1800 806 718) serving smorgasbord and modern Australian cuisine.

A couple of kilometres north of Black Mountain is the ultramodern, multi-million-dollar **Australian Institute of Sport** (AIS), on Leverrier Crescent in Bruce (daily 9am–5pm; tours 10am, 11.30am, 1pm & 2.30pm; $10.80; Ⓦwww.aisport.com.au; bus #431), a complex designed to churn out world-class athletes – which they do. You can see some in training (catch the gymnasts if you can), while the Sportex interactive sports exhibition gives you the chance to test your prowess at various sports. For an extra charge you can use the heated pool, spa, sauna, and tennis courts. A **three-in-one ticket** ($37), available at the visitors centre (see p.269), will get you into the Australian Institute of Sport, Cockington Green and Questacon.

Canberra Nature Park

The bush hills and ridges that intersperse Canberra's suburbs make up the **Canberra Nature Park**, which has many walking tracks to explore. You can pick up free maps from the visitors centre, or call the park headquarters for more information on Ⓣ02/6207 2113 (north) or Ⓣ6207 2087 (south); alternatively, visit Ⓦwww.environment.act.gov.au/general. From the Bruce/O'Connor Ridge section, across Belconnen Way from the Black Mountain area of the park, several walking tracks head through bushland, including one that runs right behind the youth hostel. Jerrabomberra wetlands offer another pleasant escape from the heat and are home to many waterbirds which you can watch from hides.

Eating

The pedestrian mall in **Civic** is well served with places to eat, while the areas of **Manuka** and **Kingston**, near New Parliament House, have gourmet café-delis and fine restaurants, particularly on Giles Street, which is a good spot for pizza or Chinese. Woolley Street in **Dickson** is the best suburban street to head for, crammed as it is with a variety of Asian restaurants, while Dickson Street Shopping Centre has a great selection of inexpensive multi-cultural eateries. **Cafés** are plentiful around the centre, with a particular concentration on Bunda Street. There's an excellent **food court**, serving a wide variety of cuisines, as well as a large **supermarket** on the ground level of the City Market shopping mall on the corner of Bunda Street and Ainslie Avenue. Canberra's many **clubs** (see p.281) also serve inexpensive meals in a typical Aussie atmosphere. Healthy **vegetarian** ingredients can be bought from Mount Creek Wholefoods, 14 Barker Street, Griffith. Most local buses go from the City Bus Interchange to the suburbs listed below (see "City transport", p.269).

Cafés

Ali Baba Cnr Garema Place and Bunda St. Simple Lebanese takeaway with outside tables. Daily to 10pm, very late Fri & Sat.

ANU Union Union Crescent, Acton. The students' union here has a restaurant, a café and a super-cheap bistro specializing in Asian food. BYO. Mon–Fri lunch and dinner.

The Blue Olive 56 Alinga St, Civic. Home-baked speciality breads and cakes, toasted Turkish sandwiches and ice-cold beer from the in-house bottle shop. Mon–Sat 7am–late.

The Café Barrine Drive, west of the Commonwealth Ave Bridge, next to Mr Spokes Bike Hire. In a lovely spot by the lake. Daily from 9am.

Café Essen Garema Arcade, Civic. Long-standing and much-loved gourmet coffee house with enormous, cheap and unusual brunches, all-day breakfasts and live music at the weekend. Daily from 7.30am.

Caffe della Piazza 19 Garema Place. This lively place has award-winning Italian coffee, focaccia, pizza and pasta and is a good place to people-watch, spilling out onto the square with tables set out on the pavement. Licensed. Daily from 8am.

Gus Café Bunda St, next to Center Cinema. Canberra's best café, this place serves inexpensive light meals, good pasta and fresh soups, with lots of choice for vegetarians. It's popular with students and an arty crowd, and there are magazines and newspapers to read, and outside tables under vines and a huge tree. Daily 7.30am–10.30pm, later at the weekend.

Iridium Cnr Northbourne Ave and London Circuit. This beautifully designed place offers interesting breakfast and dinner choices, and an all-day menu featuring the scrumptious artistry of its very own pastry chef. Perfect for post-club munchies. Mon–Thurs 7am–midnight, Fri–Sun 24hr.

Zydeco 173 City Walk. This airy café-restaurant offers a comprehensive breakfast menu, great coffee, and an Australian twist to the omnipresent focaccia. Tables outside. Mon–Sat 10am–late, Sun noon–6pm.

Restaurants

Artespresso 31 Giles St, Kingston ☎02/6295 8055. Executives plot global domination over barramundi and duck in this swanky bar-restaurant, which also has fine artworks on periodic display. Tues–Sat 12 till late.

Barocca Café Shop 6, 60 Marcus Clarke St ☎02/6248 0253. Modern Australian cuisine is the order of the day at this award-winning but reasonably priced restaurant. Bookings advised for evenings. Mon–Fri lunch and dinner.

Bernadette's Ainslie Shops, Wakefield Gardens, Ainslie ☎02/6248 5018. A friendly, sunny BYO vegetarian café with a pleasant terrace, in an unassuming suburb about ten minutes' walk from the main tourist office. The menu features huge focaccia sandwiches, pizzas (with vegan alternatives) and salads, as well as home baking to die for. Booking advised at night. Tues–Fri 11am–10pm, Sat & Sun 9am–10pm.

Chairman and Yip 108 Bunda St ☎02/6248 7109. This stylish and friendly Chinese restaurant is much more congenial than most of its Civic neighbours. The walls are adorned with Mao paraphernalia and a "workers lunch" costs $12.50. Lunch Mon–Fri, dinner daily.

Delicateating O'Connor Shopping Centre, Macpherson St. Trendy, delicatessen-style place leaning towards Italian cuisine, and conveniently located near the Canberra YHA hostel. Mellow-yellow walls and tables outside. BYO. Mon–Fri 10am–10pm, Sat & Sun 9am–10pm.

Fringe Benefits Brasserie 54 Marcus Clarke St ☎02/6247 4042. Stylish but pricey French restaurant with an extensive wine cellar. Closed Sun.

Kingsland Vegetarian Restaurant Shop 5, Dickson Plaza, 28 Challis St, Dickson (near the visitor information centre) ☎02/6262 9350. Earthy, reasonably priced veggie cuisine. Mon–Fri & Sun 11am–2.30pm & 5–10pm, Sat 5–10pm.

Lemon Grass Thai Restaurant 65 London Circuit ☎02/6247 2779. Award-winning but inexpensive Thai restaurant with an imaginative menu which is strong on fish and vegetarian dishes.

Little Saigon Cnr Alinga St and Northbourne Ave ☎02/6230 5003. Large, busy, cheap and tasty Vietnamese restaurant, with $7 lunchtime specials (which can be taken out). Best to book at weekends. Daily 9am–3pm & 5–10.30pm.

Madame Woo 38 Giles St, Kingston ☎02/6232 6932. This acclaimed pan-Asian restaurant takes in Japanese, Thai, Chinese and others – nibble *gyoza* dumplings before tucking into satay or red curry. Tues–Fri: lunch from noon, dinner from 5pm.

Montezuma's 197 London Circuit, next to *Canberra City Backpackers*. Loud, accommodating and popular Mexican, with live entertainment from Friday to Sunday. Licensed. Mon–Sat 5pm–late, also open for lunch Wed–Fri.

Portia's Place Shop 5, 11 Kennedy St ☎02/6239 7970. Authentic and inexpensive Chinese restaurant with good vegetarian options. Daily noon–2.30pm & 5pm–10.30pm.

Silo 36 Giles St, Kingston ☎02/6260 6060. A great, no-fuss and popular Italian place with pizzas and pasta, as well as meaty mains and cakes.

Tilley's Devine Café Gallery Cnr Brigalow and Wattle streets, Lyneham. Named after Tilley Devine, the Melbourne gangster's moll, this is no place to be on a diet. The cheesy melts, large portions and elegant surrounds make you want to sit back and loosen a few buttons.

Tosolini's Cnr Franklin and Furneaux streets, Manuka ☎02/6232 6600. Very popular, award-winning modern Australian–Italian eaterie in the city's most glitzy neighbourhood. Sunday brunch on the terrace is a must, as are the pastries. Tues–Sun noon–3pm & 6–10.30pm, plus weekend breakfast 8.30–11.30am.

Drinking, nightlife and entertainment

For information about upcoming events, the daily *Canberra Times* is your best bet; the most extensive **listings** are published every Thursday in the *Good Times* supplement. For details of bands and clubs, pick up a copy of the free monthly music magazines *BMA* or *3D World*, available from record shops, hostels and bars. The visitor information centre and most hotels also distribute the quarterly booklet *Canberra What's On*, which lists major cultural events. Up-to-date information can be found by calling the "Today and Tonight" events hotline on ⓣ02/6257 4347. The visitors centre (and web site, ⓦwww.canberratourism.com.au) also has extensive listings of venues.

Drinking and nightlife

The best **pub** is the tiny *Phoenix Pub*, 23 East Row, which attracts a grungey crowd and has feral live bands. *P.J. O'Reilly's Irish Pub*, at the corner of West Row and Alinga Street, has music nights. Similarly popular, and rather less forced, are *King O'Malleys*, at 131 City Walk, with outside tables, nightly live music (see ⓦwww.kingomalleys.com.au) and a hearty bill of fare; and *Filthy McFaddens* on Green Square in Kingston. Another good Kingston pub is *The Holy Grail*, also on Green Square; catering for a slightly older crowd, it hosts live music (Wed–Fri) and has a nightclub.

There are several **nightclubs** in Canberra, including *Babylon*, on the corner of Alinga Street and East Row, with two floors of dance music, disco and easy rock; and *Insomnia*, above *ICBM*, 50 Northbourne Avenue, where the city's public servants let their hair down. Of several **bars** and **dance venues**, *In Blue*, at the corner of Mort and Alinga streets, is worth a visit – downstairs is a vodka and cocktail bar (which also serves dinner from $7.50), upstairs a small dance floor which favours hip-hop and classic pop. *Cube*, 33 Petrie Plaza, is the city's main gay and lesbian club, playing techno and house as well as featuring drag shows. *Toast*, in the Boulevard Building on Akuna Street, is a studenty place with DJs and live acts.

Live music

The *ANU Union Bar* on Childers Street at the ANU campus in Acton is invariably the best place for **rock bands** of all sorts, with live Indie gigs, touring big-name bands and all-night raves at least a couple of times a week during term time (call ⓣ02/6249 2446 or visit ⓦwww.anuunion.com.au for details). The *Canberra Workers Club* in Civic (ⓣ02/6248 0399) hosts big touring bands, with cheap drinks until midnight.

The music you're most likely to hear in Canberra, however, is **jazz**. *Déjà Vu*, the upstairs bar at the *Casino Canberra*, 21 Binara Street, Civic (ⓣ02/6257 7074), regularly hosts big-name jazz bands, while there are more intimate performances on Sunday night from 7pm at the gay-friendly *Tilley's*, an ambient café-bar-gallery in Lyneham on the corner of Brigalow and Wattle streets (ⓣ02/6247 7753); more mainstream jazz is played on Thursdays and Sundays at *All Bar Nun*, near the YHA in O'Connor, and at the *Wig & Pen* on Alinga Street on Saturday nights.

Weekends see **folk and blues** at the *Pot Belly Bar*, Weedon Close, Belconnen; there's nightly **hardcore rock** and ear-splitting **metal** at *Rock Ape* in the Northside Fitness Centre, 20 Dickson Place, Dickson (ⓣ02/6257 8195), and anything from **world music** to **jungle** at the self-consciously cool *Mombasa*, 128 Bunda Street, Civic (ⓦwww.clubmombasa.com.au). The *Canberra Yacht Club*, Coronation Drive, Yarralumla, has more middle-of-the-road lounge-style entertainment on Friday night, featuring a singer and guitarist. **Classical music** performances are staged sporadically at the Canberra Theatre Centre, London Circuit (Ⓣ02/6257 2700, Ⓦwww.canberratheatre.org.au), and regularly at the Canberra School of Music, Llewellyn Hall, Childers Street, Acton (Ⓣ02/6249 5700, Ⓦwww.anu.edu.au).

Theatre and cinema

The main **drama** venue in the capital is the impressive Canberra Theatre Centre on London Circuit (see above). In addition to a broad range of plays, its several theatres also host concerts, dance performances and readings. Other, less mainstream, options include The Street Theatre (Ⓣ02/6247 1519, Ⓦwww.thestreet.org.au), on the corner of Childers Street and University Avenue, and a number of active independent theatre groups based at the Gorman House Arts Centre on Ainslie Avenue, Braddon (Ⓣ02/6249 7377, Ⓦwww.gormanhouse.com.au). *Tilley's* in Lyneham (see p.279 and p.280) also hosts cabaret programmes, as does the *School of the Arts Café*, 108 Monaro St, Queanbeyan (Ⓣ02/6297 6857), worth checking out for its new plays by fringe theatre groups, as well as its live music, bush poetry and comedy acts – all from Thursday to Saturday. There's inexpensive student theatre at the ANU Arts Centre, Union Court, ANU (Ⓣ02/6215 2419).

As for **cinemas**, the Center Cinema on Bunda Street (Ⓣ02/6249 7979, Ⓦwww.ronincinemas.com.au) is probably the best of the regular commercial choices, with an interesting programme and Saturday late shows at 11pm, while the Electric Shadows Cinema, Akuna Street (Ⓣ02/6247 5060, Ⓦwww.electricshadows.com.au), shows the best in world cinema, and has a bookshop and café-bar.

Clubs

Numerous **clubs**, most of which admit visitors, are one of the features of Canberra life. They often serve inexpensive meals, and may also organize live music, film evenings, parties or comedy shows – all in the hope of luring visitors to gamble their money away on the one-armed bandits. One of the biggest is the *Canberra Workers Club* on Childers Street (Ⓣ02/6248 0399): it boasts a bistro serving meals every day, regular discos, and darts and pool as well as pokies. The *Canberra Tradesmen's Union Club*, 2 Badham Street, Dickson (Ⓣ02/6248 0999, Ⓦwww.ctuc.asn.au/dickson.htm), has a sauna, gym and squash courts, an observatory with an astronomical officer on duty (dusk until about 12.30am), and a free Bicycle Museum (daily 9am–midnight); you can even dine in a restored tram, or have your hair cut in a 1920s-style barber shop. The attractions are all free, but children have to leave by 8pm, when the sinful poker machines rev up. The *Canberra Labor Club*, Chandler Street, Belconnen (Ⓣ02/6251 5522), serves meals daily and offers bingo as well as occasional disco or rock nights.

Listings

Airlines Qantas Ⓣ13 13 13; Regional Express Ⓣ13 17 13; Virgin Blue Ⓣ13 67 89.
American Express Centerpoint Arcade, cnr City Walk and Petrie Plaza Ⓣ02/6247 2333.
Banks The city branches of the bigger banks are open Mon–Thurs 9.30am–4pm, Fri until 5pm: ANZ, 25 Petrie Plaza; Commonwealth Bank, cnr London Circuit and Northbourne Ave; National Australia Bank, cnr London Circuit and Hobart Place; Westpac, 53 Alinga St.
Bike rental A pleasurable bicycle path goes all the way around Lake Burley Griffin. To rent a bike the most convenient place to head for is Mr Spokes Bike Hire (Ⓣ02/6257 1188; $10 per hour, summer only), right on the water at Barrine Drive, Acton. You can also check out Row 'n' Ride mountainbike tours, c/o Canberra South Motor Park, Canberra Ave Ⓣ02/6228 1264; $35 per half-day, $45 per day.
Books Smiths Alternative Bookshop is the antithesis of all things Canberrian, stocking interesting

fiction and cultural theory, as well as radical and left-leaning publications.

Buses For local bus information phone Action timetable information (ⓣ13 17 10), check out their website (ⓦwww.action.act.gov.au) or call at the kiosk at the City Bus Interchange, 11 East Row. Long-distance services, including state-owned Countrylink, use the Jolimont Centre, 65–67 Northbourne Ave, as their terminal. You can buy tickets here from the Jolimont Centre for direct services with Countrylink to Cooma, Eden and Cootamundra (ⓣ13 22 32); Greyhound Australia to Sydney, Brisbane, Melbourne and Adelaide (ⓣ02/6249 6006); and Murrays Coaches to Wollongong and south coast (ⓣ13 22 51).

Car rental Inexpensive deals are available from Network Car & Truck Rentals, 117 Redfern St, Macquarie (ⓣ02/6251 6626) and Rumbles Rent-a-Car, 11 Paragon Mall, Gladstone St, Fyshwick (ⓣ02/6280 7444). Others, mostly clustered on Lonsdale St in Braddon, with additional locations at the airport, are: Avis ⓣ02/6249 6088, airport ⓣ02/6249 1601; Budget ⓣ13 27 27; Hertz ⓣ02/6257 4877, airport ⓣ02/6249 6211 or 13 30 39; and Thrifty ⓣ02/6247 7422, airport ⓣ1300 367 227.

Embassies and high commissions There are over seventy in Canberra (all the following are in Yarralumla, unless otherwise stated): Britain, Commonwealth Ave ⓣ02/6270 6666; Canada, Commonwealth Ave ⓣ02/6270 4000; Germany, 119 Empire Court ⓣ02/6270 1911; Indonesia, 8 Darwin Ave ⓣ02/6250 8600; Ireland, 20 Arkana St ⓣ02/6273 3022; Malaysia, 7 Perth Ave ⓣ02/6273 1543; Netherlands, 120 Empire Circuit ⓣ02/6273 3111; New Zealand, Commonwealth Ave ⓣ02/6270 4211; Norway, 17 Hunter St ⓣ02/6273 3444; Papua New Guinea, 39–41 Forster Crescent ⓣ02/6273 3322; Singapore, 17 Forster Crescent ⓣ02/6273 3944; Sweden, 5 Turrana St ⓣ02/6270 2700; Switzerland, 7 Melbourne Ave, Forrest ⓣ02/6273 3977; Thailand, 111 Empire Circuit ⓣ02/6273 1149; USA, 21 Moonah Place ⓣ02/6214 5600.

Environmental contacts The Environment Centre, Kingsley St, Acton (ⓣ02/6247 3064, ⓦwww.ecoaction.net.au), is a library and archive on environmental topics as well as a book and gift shop (Mon–Fri 9am–5pm). The Wilderness Society Shop, 16 Garema Place (ⓣ02/6249 8011), is a book and gift shop with information about the local environment.

Festivals The big event of the year is the Canberra Festival – the anniversary of the city's foundation – celebrated with concerts, theatre, exhibitions, street parades and fireworks for ten days from the beginning of March. The Royal Canberra Show is an agricultural fair lasting three days over the last weekend in February, while the Floriade is a spring festival marked by floral displays, theatre and music, from mid-September to mid-October. Even more popular, though less feted by the tourist board, is the annual Summernats Car Festival in January (details on ⓣ02/6241 8111 or at ⓦwww.summernats.com.au), when revheads convene in Exhibition Park to compare modified street machines and compete at the world's only purpose-built burnout facility.

Galleries Good private galleries include the Chapman Gallery, 31 Captain Cook Crescent, Griffith (Wed–Sun 11am–6pm; ⓣ02/6295 2550), specializing in Aboriginal art; and the Beaver Galleries, 81 Denison St, Deakin (daily 10am–5pm; ⓣ02/6281 1315), for paintings, sculpture, jewellery and furniture.

Gay and lesbian Canberra Gayline ⓣ02/6247 2726 (nightly 6–10pm); Gay Contact ⓣ02/6257 2855 (same hours); Gaywaves Radio Mondays 92.9 FM.

Golf Royal Canberra Golf Club, Westbourne Woods, Yarralumla ⓣ02/6282 7000.

Horse riding Brindabella Valley Trails, 19 Sabine Close, Garran (ⓣ02/6281 6682), offers riding in the Brindabella Ranges close to Kosciuszko National Park.

Hospitals John James Memorial Hospital, Strickland Crescent, Deakin ⓣ02/6281 8100 (private); The Canberra Hospital, Yama Drive, Garran ⓣ02/6244 2222.

Internet access *On Line Café Canberra*, cnr London Circuit and Akuna St ⓣ02/6262 7427.

Markets Gorman House Markets, Gorman House Arts Centre, Ainslie Ave, Braddon (Sat 10am–4pm; bus #302, #303 or #385), is a community market where items such as pottery, hand-painted T-shirts, bric-à-brac and secondhand clothes are sold; Belconnen Markets, Lathlain St (Wed–Sun 8am–6pm), is a large fresh-food market featuring an organic grocery, seafood and poultry outlets, organic veggies, home-made jams, health foods, a naturopath and several cafés. Old Bus Depot Markets, Wentworth Ave, Kingston Foreshore (Sun 10am–4pm), is the big market in town and the only one indoors – high-quality handicrafts, great food, musicians and other entertainment make this a must if you're here on a Sunday.

Nature reserves Information on ACT parks and reserves from Canberra Nature Park (north ⓣ02/6207 2113, or south ⓣ02/6207 2087) and Environment ACT (ⓣ02/6207 9777, ⓦwww.environment.act.gov.au/general).

NRMA (National Roads and Motorists Association), 92 Northbourne Ave, Braddon, or Belconnen Mall, Belconnen ⓣ13 11 1. Publishes a very useful map of Canberra and the ACT, free to members.
Police ⓣ02/6256 7777.
Post office Alinga St, Canberra, ACT 2600 (Mon–Fri 9am–5pm; ⓣ02/6209 1680).
Scenic flights Canberra Flight Centre (ⓣ02/6257 6331) charges from about $60 per person for 30min–1hr.
Shopping Shopping hours are Mon–Thurs 9am–5.30pm, Fri 9am–9pm, Sat 9am–4pm, Sun 10am–4pm. In the city centre the shopping focus is on Bunda St and surrounding area, with department stores such as David Jones and Grace Bros, and the Canberra Centre shopping mall. There are late-opening supermarkets in the shopping centres of the satellite towns.
Taxis Canberra Cabs (ⓣ13 22 27) has wheelchair-accessible cabs; Queanbeyan Taxi Co-operative (ⓣ02/6297 3000). There is a taxi rank on Bunda St outside the Center Cinema.
Tours and cruises Murrays, the Jolimont Centre, 65–67 Northbourne Ave (ⓣ13 22 51), has half- and full-day bus tours around Canberra ($35); Canberra & Snowy Mountains Day Tours (ⓣ02/6249 6006) are similar, but also take in the Snowy Mountains ($75); Weird Canberra Ghost and History Tours (ⓣ02/9943 0167, ⓦwww.destinytours.com.au) take you on an eerie trip through Canberra's tunnels, haunted sites and scenes of murder ($49); Adventures on Rail (ⓣ/02 6284 2790, ⓦwww.arhsact.org.au) offer steam-train rides on the first Sunday of the month, Go Bush Tours (ⓣ02/6231 3023, ⓦwww.gobushtours.com.au) offer tours for small groups around the city, to the Snowy Mountains and to Namadgi National Park; Harley Rides 'r' Us (ⓣ02/6231 7231 or 1800 242 753) offers sightseeing trips in and around Canberra from the back of a Harley-Davidson from $66; Wild Things Tours (ⓣ02/6254 6303) runs six-hour tours into Namadgi National Park for guaranteed eastern grey kangaroo spotting and to see indigenous rock art ($85, including light lunch, park entrance, pick-ups and drop-offs); Southern Cross Cruises (ⓣ02/6273 1784, ⓦwww.cscc.com.au) offers one-hour scenic cruises, plus lunch and dinner cruises on Lake Burley Griffin; and Dawn Drifters (ⓣ02/6285 4450, ⓦwww.dawndrifters.com.au) will fly you over the city in a balloon (Mon–Fri $195 per person, weekends & holidays $230 per person), and then feed you breakfast when safely aground.
Trains The Xplorer train links Canberra and Sydney (3 daily; 4hr) via Queanbeyan, Bungendore, Goulburn, Bundanoon, Moss Vale, Bowral and Mittagong. Ticket sales and information at the Countrylink Travel Centre, Jolimont Centre, 65–67 Northbourne Ave, and at the train station in Kingston (all enquiries ⓣ13 22 32).
Travel agents Flight Centre, Lower Ground Floor, Canberra Centre (Mon–Thurs 9am–5.30pm, Fri 9am–8pm, Sat 10am–3pm; ⓣ13 16 00); STA Travel, Shop B6, Canberra Centre, Civic (Mon–Thurs 9am–5pm, Fri till 7pm, Sat 10am–2pm; ⓣ02/6257 7122).
Women Women's Information and Referral Centre, 6th Floor, FAI Insurance Building, 197 London Circuit (Mon–Fri 9am–5pm; ⓣ02/6205 1075, ⓦwww.act.gov.au/womensinfo).

Around Canberra

The residents of Canberra live with nature right on their doorstep, the numerous **picnic grounds** and **bushwalking trails** in the state reserves and national parks being only about half an hour's drive from the city centre. Be warned, though, that at the height of summer, when there is a high risk of **bushfires**, a total fire ban is declared and all the nature reserves and national parks are closed (call ⓣ02/6207 8600 to check). Bushland aside, the environs of the capital can also lay claim to historic **homesteads and villages**, private zoos, a former gold-mining town and a few **wineries**, some of them across the border in New South Wales.

South

Leaving the city behind, the Tharwa Road follows the course of the **Murrumbidgee River** as it approaches Tharwa. Thirty-two kilometres from Canberra, at the southern end of the Tuggeranong Valley, the convict-built **Lanyon Homestead** (Tues–Sun 10am–4pm; $7, admission to grounds free) dates back to the earliest European settlement of the region. Thoroughly refurbished by the National Trust, it now houses a small display outlining the history of the area before Canberra existed, but the real reasons to come are the house itself and the **Sidney Nolan Gallery** (Tues–Fri 10am–4pm, Sat & Sun 10am–5pm; $3) next door, where you'll find works by the famous Australian painter, including some of his *Kelly* and *Burke and Wills* series, alongside changing exhibitions of contemporary Australian art. There's no public transport out here.

Beyond the Lanyon Homestead and Tharwa, old cottages on the Naas Road, overlooking the river, house the galleries and antique shops of the **Cuppacumbalong Craft Centre** (Wed–Sun 11am–5pm). Nearby, a small, licensed café serves hearty meals and local cider, and there's also a spot where you can swim in the river.

Namadgi National Park

Namadgi National Park occupies almost half of the ACT, largely made up of wilderness areas in the west and southwest. Its mountain ranges and high plains, rising to 1900m, have a far more severe climate than low-lying Canberra and give rise to the Cotter River and many smaller streams. In the northwest, the Corin Road leads to Corin Dam, while in the south the partly surfaced Bobyan Road cuts right through the national park, emerging beneath the Snowy Mountains in the south. There are picnic grounds and bush campsites by the Orroral River and near Mount Clear in the south.

The **Namadgi Visitors Information Centre**, 3km south of Tharwa on the Naas Road (Mon–Fri 9am–4pm, Sat, Sun & public holidays 9am–4.30pm; Ⓣ02/6207 2900, Ⓦwww.environment.act.gov.au/general), has displays and videos about the park, and also provides guided tours on request, as well as detailed information on bushwalking tracks and emergency shelters in the remote areas.

West: Tidbinbilla Nature Reserve and Cotter Reserve

The small **Tidbinbilla Nature Reserve**, to the southwest of the city (daily 9am–6pm, till 8pm during daylight saving; $3; Ⓦwww.environment.act.gov.au/bushparksandreserves/tidbinbilla.html), is an enjoyable place with relatively easy walks and some wheelchair-accessible paths. The area around the park entrance and **information centre** (Mon–Fri 9am–4.30pm, Sat & Sun 9am–5.30pm; Ⓣ02/6205 1233) is home to kangaroos and wallabies in spacious bush enclosures, and you can also see koalas, lots of birds and corroboree frogs. Picnic grounds are dotted all along the sealed road leading through the reserve, and on long weekends and during the school holidays it's a busy place, especially popular with families.

The **Canberra Space Centre** on Discovery Drive in Tidbinbilla (visitors centre open daily 9am–5pm, till 8pm in summer; free; Ⓦwww.cdscc.nasa.gov) sounds like every child's dream, though in fact the displays of spacecraft and highly sensitive communications equipment are not as exciting as you might have hoped. Operated in conjunction with NASA, the purpose of the station is to pick up even the most obscure signals from outer space; there are only two others in the world with the same range as Tidbinbilla – one near Madrid, the other in Goldstone, California.

Southwest of here, Corin Road turns off the Tidbinbilla Road towards the **Corin Forest** (Sat & Sun 10am–5pm, also weekdays during school holidays

10am–4pm; Ⓦwww.corin.com.au) and reservoir, a popular recreation spot in the hills, with many walking trails, year-round bobsledding, picnic grounds and barbecue facilities. In winter you can ski on artificial snow and during school holidays special activities are organized for children.

Cotter Reserve

The **Cotter Reserve**, near the Cotter Dam, 22km west of the city, was badly hit by the 2002 bushfires. This had traditionally been a popular spot for short weekend outings, though the devastation that the fires wreaked meant that the reserve remained out of bounds at the time of writing; for latest details, contact the tourist office. On the way to the Cotter Reserve you pass the remains of the **Mount Stromlo Observatory** (Ⓦwww.mso.anu.edu.au/msovc), about 16km from Canberra, whose main dome housed the ANU's Department of Astronomy until it was gutted in the bushfires. The complex is currently being rebuilt.

North

Leaving Canberra by the Barton Highway to the north, the first place of interest is **GINNINDERA**, approximately 9km out, a rather consciously touristy village with a few arts and crafts shops and *The Green Herring* restaurant in a log hut. Just before Ginnindera, on Gold Creek Road, the **National Dinosaur Museum** (daily 10am–5pm; $8.50; Ⓦwww.nationaldinosaurmuseum.com.au) is not a big, government-run museum as the name might suggest, but a private collection of replica skeletons and some bones and fossils. Other local tourist attractions include **Cockington Green** (daily 9.30am–4.15pm; $13.50, children $7; Ⓦwww.cockington-green.com.au), a miniature model English village with a mini-train for kids to ride on; and the **Artgems Gallery** (daily 10am–5pm; free) in the village, with exhibits of paintings, gems (especially opals and crystals), and local arts and crafts. **HALL**, 3km north of Ginnindera, is a similar village with a few shops and a restaurant, and another Artgems Gallery.

More or less opposite the turn-off for Hall, the Wallaroo Road heads west towards the New South Wales border. Not far down the road, at Woodgrove Close, is Brindabella Hill Wines (Ⓣ02/6230 2583), where you can sample some of the local "cool climate" vintages. There are more **wineries** around **MURRUMBATEMAN**, north along the Barton Highway into New South Wales between Canberra and the large country town of Yass; full lists are available from the tourist office.

The Federal Highway

Northeast of Canberra, the Federal Highway crosses into New South Wales shortly after leaving the city. The first of the sights along this way is the **Bywong Gold Mining Town** (daily 9.30am–4.30pm; $8; Ⓦwww.bywonggold.citysearch.com.au), where a brief goldrush at the end of the nineteenth century has left shafts and some old mine workings. The gold-diggers' camp has been reconstructed with serious attention to historic detail, and it's well worth stopping in if you're passing by; you can also try your hand at panning, and there are picnic and barbecue areas.

The mining village is on Bungendore Road, further down which lies the attractive village of **BUNGENDORE**, with a pottery, woodturner, café and shops arranged around the village green. Heading on, you can circle back round to Canberra via Queanbeyan, or strike east, a scenic drive that takes you through **BRAIDWOOD** – which has more antiques and crafts shops, and a fine old hotel – towards the coast at Batemans Bay.

The south coast and Snowy Mountains

The **south coast**, with its green dairylands, is delightful in a quiet sort of way – an area for fishing, surfing or relaxing on the beaches, with no huge resorts or commercial developments. Inland are the **Snowy Mountains**, the Dividing Range's highest peaks, which have Australia's best skiing and, in summer, some fine bushwalking.

The direct route from Sydney to Melbourne via the inland **Hume Highway** (covered in chapter 3) passes close to Canberra and the Snowy Mountains. The coastal route, the **Princes Highway**, is slightly longer but much more attractive in terms of scenery. Give yourself two or more days if you want to appreciate the surf, the sandy beaches, and the mountains, valleys and forests that back this beautiful stretch of the coast. Most **buses** run via the Hume Highway, usually with a detour to Canberra; the **train** follows largely the same route.

The south coast

The **south coast** of New South Wales is relatively quiet and relaxed, its numerous bays, coastal lakes and inlets interspersed with unspoiled, sandy beaches, small fishing villages and seaside resorts. During the summer months, especially from Christmas to the end of January, the towns can get busy, especially the **Shoalhaven area** around **Nowra**, **Batemans Bay**, and **Merimbula**. But don't expect resort hotels and entertainment Queensland-style – it's all rather low-key and family-oriented, with a few wildlife and amusement parks to keep the children happy, and plenty of opportunities for traditional outdoor pursuits. Exposed parts on this stretch of the coast are battered by powerful waves that are perfect for **surfing**, while the calmer waters of the numerous coastal lakes, bays and inlets are suited for **swimming**, windsurfing, sailing or canoeing. There's great **fishing** too, in the rivers and lakes, as well as the inevitable deep-sea season, when game-fishers set out to tussle with marlin. Away from the ocean there's some superb, rugged scenery, great bushwalking and horse riding in the forest-clad, mountainous hinterland.

Most of the way down the coast from Sydney, the **Princes Highway** runs a few kilometres inland. Away from the towns, apparently obscure turn-offs from the highway often lead to beautiful and secluded beaches – it's worth taking some time to make your own discoveries. From **Canberra** there are three main routes to the coast: through Kangaroo Valley (see p.260), via Goulburn and Moss Vale (or Bundanoon); the Capital Highway to Batemans Bay; and the Snowy Mountains Highway to Bega via Cooma.

Transport links from Sydney, Canberra and Melbourne to the south coast include **trains** from Sydney as far as Bomaderry on the South Coast rail line and from Canberra to Eden with Countrylink (Ⓣ13 22 32); and **buses** along the Princes Highway from Sydney with Premier Motor Services (Ⓣ13 34 10, Ⓦwww.premierms.com.au) and Murray's (Ⓣ13 22 51, Ⓦwww.murrays.com.au).

Berry

Sixteen kilometres north of Nowra along the Princes Highway, and easily reached by train on the Sydney–Nowra route, **BERRY** is a historic small town with many listed buildings, surrounded by dairy country and green hills. The main drag, **Queen Street**, is packed with antique craft shops, cafés, restaurants and two very characterful country pubs. The town's popularity, enhanced by the wineries in the surrounding countryside and the beach just 6km away at **Gerringong** (see p.257), means that Berry get almost unbearably crowded on fine weekends, especially when the monthly market (first Sun of month) is on. The town's two **pubs** are attractions in themselves, at opposite ends of Queen Street. The boisterous *Great Southern Hotel* at no. 95 is a huge, spreading Outback-style bungalow pub with two lifesavers' boats on its tin roof. The wrap-around verandah, hung with pretty flowerbaskets, is a great place to relax and the beer garden has a fantastic enclosed playground. Inside, the pub is rammed with steer's horns, a coin-op emu and other Aussie bric à brac. The pleasantly sedate *Berry Hotel*, at no. 120, is an old coach-house and looks the part.

Practicalities

You can **stay** at both pubs in Berry. The motel units at the *Great Southern Hotel* (Ⓣ02/4464 1009, Ⓕ4464 1118; ❷) are as wackily decorated as the pub itself. The accommodation at the *Berry Hotel* (Ⓣ02/4464 1011, Ⓦwww.berryhotel.com.au ❸) gets booked out on Saturday nights, even the huge four-bedroom flat upstairs and the two-bedroom house (with kitchen) out the back. Other rooms, which are well furnished, share bathrooms. A more upmarket option is *The Bunyip Inn*, next door at 122 Queen Street (Ⓣ02/4464 2064, Ⓕ4464 2324; B&B ❺), set in an imposing National Trust-classified former bank with a lovely garden and swimming pool. The decor is elegant olde-worlde and every room is different (nearly all are en-suite); there's a picture of a Bunyip on the sign if you're wondering what they look like. Right opposite on the corner of Prince Alfred Street, the little *Postman's Ghost* (Ⓣ02/4464 3379, Ⓦwww.postmansghost.com.au, ❻–❼) is housed – guessably – in the old post office. The hefty four-poster beds sit solidly in rooms with every comfort, and breakfast is included.

There are lots of popular **gay and lesbian** weekend retreats in the surrounding area including *Spotted Gums Cottage* (Ⓣ02/4464 1779, Ⓔspotgum@shoalhaven.net.au; ❺), a one-bedroom self-contained cottage 3km out of town set on five acres of native gardens (with a barbecue), which has its own spa; expect champagne when you arrive and a breakfast basket for the morning.

There's a big choice of **places to eat** in Berry. The inexpensive bistro at the *Great Southern Hotel* serves nachos, fish and burgers, while there are affordable gourmet meals, from chargrilled steaks to pumpkin and sage torte in the pleasant covered courtyard at the *Berry Hotel*, plus a tapas bar out front. Sunday night roast is only $10. The moderately priced *Postman's Ghost* serves gourmet burgers and Thai salad for lunch and a famous fish pie for dinner. Opposite the *Berry Hotel*, *The Emporium Food Co* at 127 Queen Street serves affordable gourmet sandwiches, savoury pies and pastries and excellent coffee. A few doors down is the busy *Gourmet on Broughton Café* (daily 8am–3.30pm), good for ice creams and sandwiches. The *Delicious Food By Lisa* delicatessen also has an excellent reputation; it's on the corner of Alexander and Albert streets behind the main street. Also on Alexander Street, on the corner with Queen Street, vegetarians could head to the *Thai Berry* (noon–8pm, Fri & Sat till 9pm, closed Tues), where there are several non-meat choices on the spicy menu. Nearby on Queen Street is the friendly *HedgeHog Café*, which rustles up cooked breakfasts, croissants and the like.

There are many wineries **around Berry**, some with attached restaurants. The *Berry Hotel* can arrange tours ($15) to all of them. Coolangatta is one such, just 5km out of Berry, but the most highly regarded fine-dining is at the **Silos Winery** on the Princes Highway at Jaspers Bush (wine-tasting daily 10am–5pm; restaurant bookings Ⓣ02/4448 6082; lunch & dinner Wed–Sat, lunch Sun). The menu is European, with all mains under $30. There are luxury cottages here too (❻) with nice views of the vineyard.

Nowra-Bomaderry

Straddling the wide Shoalhaven River, some 20km south of Berry, the twin town of **NOWRA–BOMADERRY** is the local administrative centre. It's popular with rockclimbers, but the town itself has that "a highway runs through it" feeling and isn't the best place to stay. Bomaderry is situated north of the river, Nowra to the south. The Shoalhaven here is great for sailing, windsurfing and boating in general, while the coast, 13km away, is dotted with popular holiday settlements and numerous beaches. **Shoalhaven Heads** north of the river mouth, **Greenwell Point** in the south, **Huskisson** at Jervis Bay (see p.289) and **Bendalong** are all easily accessible on good roads, although public transport doesn't run out this way. Bounty Bus Tours (Ⓣ02/4421 2233, Ⓔbookings@bountymotorinn.com.au) will take you round the local wineries for about $20 each.

Practicalities

For further information on the beaches and local accommodation including winery-stays and country B&Bs, stop at the **Shoalhaven Visitor Centre**, at the corner of the Princes Highway and Pleasant Way, just after the road bridge between the two towns (daily 9am–4.30pm; Ⓣ02/4421 0778 or 1800 024 261, Ⓦwww.shoalhaven.nsw.gov.au).

Accommodation in Nowra includes an abundance of motels, and an ever-increasing choice of guesthouses, hostels and boutique B&Bs. One of the better motels is the *Riverhaven Motel* at 1A Scenic Drive (Ⓣ02/4421 2044, Ⓕ4421 2121; ❷); facilities include a kitchen and swimming pool, and rooms are en-suite and have microwaves. You can camp at the central, riverside *Shoalhaven Caravan Village*, Terrara Road, Nowra (Ⓣ02/4423 0770, Ⓔshoal_haven@optusnet.com.au; cabins ❷), with its own pool, tennis courts and bikes for rent. It's near the river but away from the highway – an Aussie classic with old Holdens on bricks, boats, flags and a good vibe.

There's not much by way of **restaurants** or **nightlife** in Nowra, but it does have one alternative hangout, the *Tea Club*, 46 Berry Street (Ⓣ02/4422 0900, Ⓔinfo@teaclub.com.au; closed Sun & Mon), a veggie café which caters for every leftish arty yearning: live bands, film screenings, artworks for sale, drumming workshops (Thurs) and alternative show nights (Sat). They also run monthly poetry and philosophy evenings (call for details). The *Riverhaven Motel* has a good café (Mon, Tues & Sun 8am–3.30pm) with decent food (mains for $12). If you need a seafood fix without the showtime thrills, the Co-op next to Shoalhaven River Bridge sells oysters caught by Jimmy Wildes, the reigning world oyster-opening champion. *Urban Eyes* (sushi) and *River Delhi* (sandwiches) by the bus terminal on Kingsbourne Street are popular lunch spots.

Jervis Bay

Just southeast of Nowra, the sheltered waters of **Jervis Bay**, by a political quirk, are technically part of the ACT, in order to provide Canberra with access to the sea. The area gets very busy on long weekends and holidays as it's easily driveable from Sydney, a fact reflected in local accommodation prices.

The focus of the town itself is the beachfront *Huskisson Hotel*, which has a good bistro and plenty of pool tables. **Sealife-watching tours** are available all year, and there's an eighty percent success rate of seeing whales and other marine life with Dolphin Watch Cruises, 50 Owen Street (Ⓣ02/4441 6311 or 1800 246 010, Ⓦwww.dolphinwatch.com.au), and Dolphin Explorer Cruises at number 62 (Ⓣ02/4441 5455 or 1800 444 330, Ⓦwww.dolphincruises.com.au). Dolphin tours leave at 11am and 1pm. June to November is the best time for whales. On the western shores of Jervis Bay, the very popular spot of **HUSKISSON** is a good base for **diving** into the pristine waters of the bay (it's actually the second most popular dive spot in Australia after the Great Barrier Reef). For details of one-off dives and packages, contact ProDive at 64 Owen Street (Ⓣ02/4441 5255, Ⓦwww.prodivejervisbay.com.au) or Seasports, 47 Owen Street (Ⓣ02/4441 5012, Ⓦwww.jbseasports.com.au).

The beautiful coast of **Booderee National Park**, at the southeast arm of the bay, is very popular, with its rugged cliffs facing the pounding ocean and tranquil beaches of dazzling white sand and clear water within the confines of the bay, while inland heaths, wetlands and forests offer strolls and bushwalks; details are available from the **visitor centre** (Ⓣ02/4443 0977) as you enter the park ($10). There's also great snorkelling from the park, with a chance of spotting a range of marine life including dolphins and sting rays, and around the nearby Bowen Island – a penguin colony. Note that the park is privately run by Wreck Bay Aboriginal Community and Environment Australia, and NPWS passes are not valid. The **Wreck Bay Aboriginal Community** organizes a summer cultural interpretation programme, Wreck Bay Walkabouts (bookings and information through the visitor centre), which covers diet and medicines, archeology and wildlife; alternatively, try the recommended Barry's Bushtucker Tours (Ⓣ02/4442 1168).

Jervis Bay Botanic Gardens (Mon–Fri 8am–4pm, Sun 10am–5pm, closed Sat; free), on Cave Beach Road, hosts specimens of plants from around Australia, including a pleasantly cool rainforest gully, and has a number of signed walks with interpretative boards (30–90min). Ten kilometres south of Nowra, down the turn-off for Huskisson, is the "emusing" **Marayong Park Emu Farm**, at 132 Jervis Bay Road (Wed–Sun 10am–4pm; Ⓦwww.emushop.com). Chicks hatch from August to December.

Practicalities

There are a couple of **campsites** at the Booderee National Park (bookings – essential in summer – through the visitor centre): the more secluded and small *Cave Beach* on Wreck Bay is the most sought-after site, despite its cold showers; the larger, more expensive *Greenpatch*, on a creek by Jervis Bay, has hot showers, and cars can be parked at each tent site. *Murray's Beach* is a one-kilometre walk further on, and thus quieter. There are two beachside campsites at Huskisson, including the council-run *Huskisson Beach Tourist Resort,* Beach Street (Ⓣ02/4441 5142 or 1300 733 027; cabins ❹–❺), which has a playground and tennis courts, and *Huskisson White Sands Tourist Park*, on the corner of Nowra and Beach streets (Ⓣ & Ⓕ02/4441 6025; cabins ❺).

Bushy Tail Caravan Park 29 Deakin St, Erowal Bay ⓣ02/4443 0468. The area's best caravan park, a short drive southwest in Erowal Bay, this large and easy-going place has good facilities and is literally hopping with 'roos – especially fun for kids. Cabins ❷
Huskisson B&B 12 Tomerong St, Huskisson ⓣ02/4441 7551, ⓦwww.huskissonb&b.com.au. Another friendly option in Huskisson, light and airy, and with a famously comfy bed in its one and only room. ❻
Jervis Bay Backpackers/Beach'n'Bush 16 Elizabeth Drive, Vincentia ⓣ02/4441 6880, ⓦwww.beachnbush.com.au. Set slightly outside town, this very homely and welcoming place has just four precious bunks, plus inexpensive rooms. Dorms $25, doubles ❶
Jervis Bay Guesthouse On the corner opposite Nowra and Beach Sts, Huskisson ⓣ02/4441 7658, ⓔinfo@jervisbayguesthouse.com.au. Overlooking the beach in Huskisson, this elegant and tastefully decorated beach house-style place has just four en-suite rooms, all with verandahs; two rooms have beach views and one has its own spa bath. ❻
The Paper Bark Camp Eco Resort 605 Woollamia Rd ⓣ02/4441 6066 or ⓣ4441 7299, ⓦwww.paperbarkcamp.com.au. Unusual luxury resort set in the middle of the bush, with accommodation in en-suite safari tents on stilts, huge beds, private verandahs, solar-powered lighting and a superb restaurant which is very inexpensive for what you get. It's better in summer than winter. Midweek and low-season deals are often available Full-board in tents ❽.
Woollamia Village Retreat 21 Pritchard Ave ⓣ02/4441 6108. The weirdest local accommodation option, set in a replica "old" village constructed out of various genuine bits of old timber and signs. All rooms have spas, and you can stay in the church, the post office or the general store. ❺

Ulladulla

In the 1930s many Italian fishermen settled in the small fishing village of **ULLADULLA**, and they're still a strong influence on this tranquil outpost – the traditional Blessing of the Fleet continues to be celebrated every Easter at the harbour breakwater. It's a beautiful area, dominated by the sandstone plateau of the **Morton National Park** to the west, one of the biggest and wildest national parks in NSW. The park presents a mostly inaccessible barrier, and although you can drive across it on horrifically corrugated dirt roads, it's strictly 4WD only in the wet. There's a good bushwalk to the top of the 719-metre-high **Pigeon House Mountain** in the Budawang Range in the park, where there are also aboriginal cave sites. The marked trail takes about four hours return and is accessed from the Princes Highway, via a turn-off (Coobyar Road) 8km south of Ulladulla.

There are attractive river mouths, beaches and lakes along the coast in both directions. Pretty **Lake Conjola** (10km to the north), **Lake Burrill** (5km to the south), and **Lake Tabourie** (13km to the south) are all popular with fishermen, canoeists and campers. **Mollymook**, 3km north of Ulladulla, has some sensational surfing sites and hiking trails. A few kilometres further on, the village of **Milton** is home to numerous antique shops, craft shops and cafés.

Practicalities

Tourist information is available from the Civic Centre on the highway (daily 9am–5pm; ⓣ02/4455 1269, ⓦwww.shoalhaven.nsw.gov.au). In terms of **activities**, there's swimming at the free seawater pool by the wharf, and open-water scuba courses run by Ulladulla Dive & Adventure, 211 Princes Highway (ⓣ02/4455 3029, ⓦwww.ulladulladive.com.au). Two boat dives plus gear costs $105. The local Budamurra Aboriginal community (ⓣ02/4455 5883, ⓦwww.budamurra.asn.au) has also constructed an interesting cultural trail, "One track for all", on Ulladula headland. Turn off the highway at North Street and keep going. Guided tours ($10) are offered by the Budamurra people, and include tips on boomerang throwing, didgeridoo playing and fire making, as well as some bush tucker.

Accommodation

Bannister's Point Lodge 191 Mitchell Parade ⓣ02/4455 3044, ⓦwww.bannisterspointlodge.com.au. Smart, modern B&B with a spa and licensed restaurant. It's a few suburbs north in Mollymook, right on the cliff edge. ❼

Beach Haven Holiday Resort Princes Highway, Ulladulla South ⓣ02/4455 2110. Boasts a beach-front location plus swimming pools, spa and tennis courts. On-site vans ❷, holiday apartments and cabins ❸

South Coast Backpackers, 63 Princes Highway ⓣ02/4454 0500, ⓦwww.southcoastbackpackers.com.au. Small backpackers with a lovely garden with hammocks for lazing. Staff provide lifts to Pigeon House Mountain, Jervis Bay and Murramarang National Park, and also have bikes and canoes for rent. Dorms $20, rooms ❷

Ulladulla Guesthouse Near the harbour at the corner of Burrill and South Sts ⓣ02/4455 1796, ⓦwww.guesthouse.com.au. Very smart guest-house complete with spa, sauna, a beautiful palm-fringed and heated saltwater swimming pool, art gallery and a restaurant serving top-notch French cuisine. No children. ❻–❼

Ulladulla Headland Tourist Park South St ⓣ02/4455 2457. More central and with smarter cabins than the *Beach Haven Holiday Resort*, though it's situated on the harbour rather than the beach. Camping spaces available, plus cabins. ❷

Eating

Bannister's Point Lodge 191 Mitchell Parade ⓣ02/4455 3044 The restaurant at *Bannister's Point Lodge* (see left) is one of the best in town, with award-winning food and a particularly good wine cellar.

Café Alfresco 10 Watson St. Great home-made soups, interesting salads and sandwiches. Open daily.

Elizans *Ulladulla Guesthouse*, near the harbour at the corner of Burrill and South Sts ⓣ02/4455 1796. This wonderful restaurant at the *Ulladulla Guesthouse* is open to non-residents and serves breakfasts and superb three-course evening meals accompanied by a carefully chosen wine list featuring local wines. Bookings essential.

The Fish Shop Six kilometres south of town, just before the bridge at Burrill Lake. The takeaways here are as fresh as you can get, and you can look around the Hot Glass Gallery next door while you wait for your order.

Harbourside Restaurant 84 Princes Highway ⓣ02/4455 3377. Specializes in modern Australian cuisine and fresh seafood. Open daily; licensed and BYO.

Supreeya's Corner of Deering and St Vincent Sts ⓣ02/4455 4579. If you fancy Thai food, this is the place to come. Also does takeaways and has a good selection of vegetarian options.

Tory's Seafood 30 Watson St ⓣ02/4454 0888. By the wharf, this excellent place has some of the best Italian food in town. Open daily for dinner plus Sun lunch.

Batemans Bay and around

BATEMANS BAY, at the mouth of the Clyde River and the end of the highway from Canberra, is a favourite escape for the landlocked residents of the capital, just 152km away. It's not the most exciting place on the coast, but since it's a fair-sized resort, there's plenty to do. Around Batemans Bay itself you can take a **cruise** on the Clyde River with one of several companies, including Merinda Cruises (ⓣ02/4472 4052); tours depart daily from the wharf and prices start at around $25 for a three-hour tour, including a lunch stopover upriver in the historic township of **Nelligen** with arts-and-crafts shops and a nice café. Alternatively, you can cuddle a wombat at the **Birdland Animal Park**, 55 Beach Road (daily 9.30am–4pm; $14).

From **MOGO**, 10km to the south, you can visit the open-air **Old Mogo Town Goldrush Theme Park** (daily 10am–4pm; $14; ⓦwww.oldmogotown.com.au), a reconstruction of a mid-nineteenth-century goldrush town near an old gold mine. **Mogo Zoo** (daily 9am–5pm; keeper talks and feeding twice daily at 10.30am & 1.30pm; $16.50, under-15s $9; ⓦwww.mogozoo.com.au) is much better than you might expect, and is open at night for a look at the big cats' nocturnal habits. Twenty-five kilometres south of Batemans Bay, just before **MORUYA**, a small, unsealed road turns off the highway to the west, heading through a pretty valley and then up over hills at the edge of the remote **Deua**

National Park to the former goldrush town of **Araluen** where, between 1868 and 1872, about fifteen thousand prospectors congregated in the hope of striking it lucky. Moruya itself has a pleasant **market** on Saturdays.

Practicalities

Batemans Bay Tourist Information is on Princes Highway, at the corner of Beach Road (daily 9am–5pm; ⓣ02/4472 6900 or 1800 802 528, ⓦwww.naturecoast-tourism.com.au).

There's a range of **restaurants** in Batemans Bay, mainly with fish- and seafood-based menus. Cheap and healthy luncheon fare – mugs of coffee and home-made savouries and cake – can be found at the *Good Food Café* on 45 Orient Street. On the Esplanade, *Seagulls* serves seafood and steaks and has sweeping waterfront views (ⓣ02/4472 0253; closed Tues), while the trendy and popular *Starfish Deli* also has a marine panorama and a modern menu, including a variety of wood-fired pizzas and lots of veggie dishes. *On the Pier*, on the opposite side of the bay by the bridge on Old Punt Road (ⓣ02/4472 6405), offers fine dining with fresh fish and is set on its own jetty. Also popular, and good for lunch, is *Monet's Cafe* on Orient Street near the post office. Best of all, however, is *Global Office* (ⓣ02/4472 5600) at the bowling club, 3 Vesper Street, which has top-notch food at a good price – so don't be put off by the name or the location.

Accommodation

As you'd expect of a resort, **accommodation** consists mainly of motels and a wide range of holiday units; most of the latter require a minimum week's booking during peak summer times. There are **campsites** just north of town at Pretty Beach, Pebbly Beach and Durras Beach, all in the Murramarang National Park, a small coastal strip popular not only with campers but also with kangaroos, which come here at dawn and dusk to frolic on the beach.

Shady Willows Holiday Park ⓣ02/4472 4972, ⓦwww.shadywillows.com.au. Close to town (though not to the beach), with cabins set amongst large gum trees – they're cosy, if a little too close to one another. There's also a clean and functional YHA hostel section. Dorms $22, cabins ❷–❸

Beechwood Court Bed & Breakfast 12 Beechwood Court ⓣ02/4472 9127). Modern, oceanfront place in quiet cul-de-sac. ❹

Clyde View B&B Nelligen, 15km north of Batemans Bay ⓣ02/4478 1019, ⓦwww.clydeviewbb-nelligen.com. Plush B&B which strikes just the right balance between bright modern decor and traditional-style fixtures. ❹

The Coachhouse Marina Resort Beach Rd 1km south of town ⓣ02/4472 4392 or 1800 670 715, ⓦwww.coachhouse.com.au. By the beach, with spacious self-contained bungalows with up to ten beds, plus a pool and tennis court – great for families, though lacking in atmosphere. ❹–❽

Mogendoura Farm ⓣ02/4474 2057, ⓦwww.southcoast.com.au/mogendoura. This working horse and cattle property on Hawdons Rd, 8km west of Moruya on the Moruya River, offers week-long cottage farmstays with horse riding, canoeing and bushwalking. Overnight stays are also occasionally possible. ❸

Murramarang Resort Murramarang National Park ⓣ02/4478 6355, ⓦwww.murramarangresort.com. In the national park just north of town. Bike and canoe rental is available, plus organized geology walks, lake rides and fishing cruises. Cabins and on-site vans. ❸

River Breeze Caravan Park Moruya ⓣ02/4474 2370, ⓦwww.riverbreeze.com.au. Excellent caravan park a five-minute walk from the coach stop on the Princes Highway in Moruya. Dorms $24, cabins (sleeping up to 4) ❸

Narooma and around

A small but expanding fishing village surrounded by beautiful beaches, bays and coastal lakes, **NAROOMA** lies at the heart of an area famous for its succulent

mud oysters. Southern right and humpback whales migrate past the bay between September and November, you can book **whale-watching** trips at the **Narooma Visitors Centre** on the highway (daily 9am–5pm; ⓣ02/4476 2881, ⓦwww.naturecoast-tourism.com.au). You've also got a decent chance of seeing whales and seals from the lookout at the end of Bar Rocks Road.

You can canoe on the **Wagonga Inlet** or sail to **Montague Island** – an offshore sanctuary for sea birds, seals and penguins. If you actually want to disembark at the island, you'll have to join a tour organized by the NPWS in Narooma (3hr; $70; ⓣ02/4476 2888, ⓕ4476 2757), since it's a protected wildlife reserve. Non-landing **cruises** cost from around $55 for a two-hour trip, plus $44 for a visit to Montague Island to see the seal colonies. The visitors centre also books scenic inlet cruises through the mangroves aboard the *Wagonga Princess*, a century-old pine ferry which winds its way in and out of secluded bays on the river, stopping off for a guided rainforest walk and oyster-tasting session (Wed, Fri & Sun at 1pm; $25 for a 3hr tour). **Diving** off Montague Island is organized year-round by Ocean Hut, 123 Princes Highway (ⓣ02/4476 2278; $60 for one dive, $75 for two plus $50 for gear hire); from January to April you might see grey nurse sharks and tropical fish, while from August to December there are seals.

In the first few days of October, don't miss the **Blues and Rockabilly Festival** (ⓦwww.bluesfestival.tv; $45–80 a day).

Practicalities

Good **motels** and resorts include the excellent *Forsters Bay Lodge*, 55 Forsters Bay Road (ⓣ02/4476 2319; ⓔforstba@acr.net.au; ❸) with great harbour views; and *Narooma Golfers Lodge*, 8 Bluewater Drive (ⓣ02/4476 2428; ❸), with great beach views. The budget option is *Ecotel* at 44 Princes Highway (ⓣ02/4476 2217, ⓦwww.ecotel.com.au; ❷). The village-sized, beachside *Island View Beach Resort*, on the highway 3km south of town (ⓣ02/4476 2600 or 1800 465 432, ⓦwww.islandview.com.au; campsites ❶, cabins ❸–❻) has luxury cabins (with Jacuzzis) as well as more basic accommodation, a heated pool, tennis courts and a barbecue area. There are also a couple of further-flung options (get directions from the visitor centre). *Pub Hill Farm*, Scenic Drive 4, 8km west of Narooma (ⓣ & ⓕ02/4476 3177, ⓦwww.pubhillfarm.com; ❹–❺), is a farm-style B&B with four large en-suite rooms (including one private garden room with log fire), and offers a baby-sitting service. The beautifully located *Clark Bay Farm* (ⓣ02/4476 1640, ⓦwww.clarkbay.com.au; ❹) offers disabled-access accommodation sleeping up to six. There's a nice pool too.

Local favourites for **dining** include *Lynch's Restaurant* on the Princes Highway (ⓣ02/4476 3002), serving excellent contemporary Australian cuisine and local oysters. There are several **bistros** at the marina on Riverside Drive at Forsters Bay, including the *Quarterdeck Marina* (ⓣ02/4476 2723) which has a Cajun flavour and is a popular music venue. *Rockwall Restaurant*, 107 Campbell Street, has well-priced à la carte seafood specials (ⓣ02/4476 2040; closed Sun & Mon), while *Casey's Café* at the top of the town's hill, on the corner of Canty and Wagonga streets (ⓣ02/4476 1241), is a bright, cheery establishment, serving healthy, hearty food with many veggie options and the best coffee in town. For something more special, you could try the oyster bar overlooking Forsters Bay in the Narooma Oyster Supplies shop on Riverside Drive (ⓣ02/4476 1256).

Narooma's **nightlife** doesn't extend much beyond the vast *Golf Club* on Ballingalla Street (daily 10am–10pm), with pool tables and poker machines. If you're in need of a film fix, visit the delightfully preserved Kinema picture theatre: an original 1920s **cinema** screening modern movies on Friday and

Saturday evenings and Sunday matinees (shows run daily except Mon during school holidays and the Dec/Jan holiday season,).

Central Tilba and Tilba Tilba

On your way south you'll pass through the picturesque mountain villages of **CENTRAL TILBA** and **TILBA TILBA**, just off the highway 10km south of Narooma. Central Tilba might just be the prettiest village in the south, set beautifully against the granite and wooded slopes of Mt Dromedary, and with shops selling crafts, jams, pickles and fudge everywhere. The area is also famous for its cheeses, and Central Tilba's hundred-year-old **ABC Cheese Factory** is open for visits and free tastings (Christmas to end Jan 9am-5pm, Feb to Christmas 10am–4.30pm). You could follow this up with some wine-tasting at **Tilba Valley Winery** (Mon–Sat 10am–5pm, Sun 11am–5pm), signposted off the Princes Highway 5km north of town. Situated on Corunna Lake, the working family vineyard and winery is an idyllic spot for a ploughman's lunch on the terrace or a picnic in the grounds overlooking a lake. Try the unusual local mead made at the winery before you leave. If you're feeling energetic, follow the walking trail which starts from Pam's Store in Tilba Tilba and leads through a forest to the summit of **Mount Dromedary**, almost 800m high. The hike there and back is about 11km (allow 5–6hr).

The *Dromedary* Hotel, on Bates Street in Central Tilba (Ⓣ02/4473 7223, Ⓕ4473 7229; ❸), is a historic pub with open fires; counter **meals** are served and **B&B** accommodation in simple rooms is available. *Two Story Bed and Breakfast* (Ⓣ02/4473 7290; ❹) is cosier, with many a frilly pillow, while a kilometre or so beyond town is *The Bryn* (Ⓣ02/4473 7385, Ⓦwww.thebrynattilba.com.au; ❺), a lovely spacious and scenic B&B in the hills. Back in town, the *Rose & Sparrow Café* and *Tilba Teapot* are the most atmospheric of several places offering cream teas and light **meals**.

Bermagui

Continuing south for a few kilometres along the main Princes Highway brings you to the turn-off to one of the best scenic detours along the coast, heading from Wallaga Lake to Tathra via **BERMAGUI**, 8km southeast from the highway, on both the Bermagui River and sheltered Horseshoe Bay. En route you'll pass **Jingarra Trail Rides** (Ⓣ02/4473 7529, Ⓦwww.jingarratrailrides.com), at the turn-off from the Princes Highway to Bermagui, where you can climb into the saddle for some horse riding ($30 for 1hr; $95 for 5hr plus lunch). Bermagui attracts **game-fishing** fanatics thanks to its associations with Zane Grey, the American writer of Westerns and a legendary marlin fisherman. There are several big-game fishing tournaments annually, and charter boats offer trips to catch black marlin, yellow-fin tuna and other big fish.

If you don't believe the tall stories, just take a look at the photos in the *Bermagui Hotel* on Lamont Street (Ⓣ02/6493 4206, Ⓔbermipub@bigfoot.com.au; dorms $25, doubles ❹, spa-doubles ❺), which has comfortable **rooms** and also serves good meals. *Flats Elite*, 84 Murrah Street (Ⓣ02/6493 4274, Ⓔflatselite@acr.com.au; ❸), is good value and backs onto the beautiful south lagoon wetlands, with pink galas perched about the place. The *Zane Grey Caravan Park* on Lamont Street (Ⓣ02/6493 4382; cabins ❹) is central, quiet and functional.

Eating choices include *Thai Kim* on Lamont Street (Mon–Fri 6pm until late; Ⓣ02/6493 4022) and the good *That Italian Mob* (Mon–Fri lunchtime, plus Wed–Sun 5.30pm till late; Ⓣ02/6493 3165). The *Saltwater Seafood Restaurant*

(Ⓣ02/6493 4328) is the best place to try Bermagui's legendary fish catches. Bermagui has its own tiny **Information Centre** by the *Bermagui Hotel* (daily 10am–4pm; Ⓣ02/6493 3054 or 1800 645 808).

Wallaga Lake and around

Some 5km north of Bermagui and 25km south of Narooma lies **Wallaga Lake**, one of the largest saltwater lakes on the Australian coast. The area around the lake is home to a thriving local **Koorie** community, who run their own Umbarra Aboriginal Cultural Centre (Mon–Fri 9am–5pm, Sat & Sun 9am–4pm; free; Ⓣ02/4473 7232, Ⓦwww.umbarra.com.au). The centre operates daily **tours** ($10–50) to local sacred sites, including Gulaga (Mount Dromedary), with hands-on activities such as face-painting with ochres, building bark huts and sampling bush tucker and traditional medicine. They also run cruises on Wallaga Lake, a wild and lovely place where flocks of black swans and pelicans perch on the sandbars as the tide washes in and out. On the road to Bermagui, in a terrific location backing onto the lake and a short bushwalk from the beach is *Wallaga Lake Park* (Ⓣ02/6493 4655, Ⓔwlp@acr.net.au; sites ❶, cabins ❸, flats sleeping six ❹). Unfortunately, prices triple at weekends.

For a quieter alternative to the highway, you can continue south along the coast road to Merimbula via Tathra. It's as pleasant a drive as you'll find in this area, crossing wooden bridges over pristine lagoons, traversing bush and beach. Not far out of Bermagui, unsealed tracks branch off the coast road to **Mimosa Rocks National Park**, where there are opportunities for bushwalking and swimming. There are NPWS **campsites** at Middle Beach, Picnic Point and Argannu Beach (details and bookings on Ⓣ02/4476 2888).

Bega and around

The area around **BEGA** is prime dairy country, with munching cows, lush green meadows and wide valleys. At the **Bega Cheese Heritage Centre**, Lagoon Street, North Bega (daily 9am–5pm; Ⓦwww.begacheese.com.au), you can try a few samples of the famous local cheese. Cheese apart, there's no great reason to come here. In town, the **Bega Family Museum** (Mon–Fri 10am–4pm), on the corner of Bega and Auckland streets, has regional memorabilia and photos. For more on local attractions, including the Grevillea Winery,

Burnum Burnum: Aboriginal activist

Wallaga Lake is the birthplace of one of Australia's most important Aboriginal figureheads, the elder named **Burnum Burnum**, an ancestral name meaning great warrior. He is best known for his flamboyant political stunts, which included planting the Aboriginal flag at Dover to claim England as Aboriginal territory in Australia's bicentennial year, 1988, in order to highlight the dispossession of his native country. He was born under a sacred tree by Wallaga Lake in January 1936. His mother died soon afterwards and he was taken by the Aborigines Protection Board and placed in a mission at Bomaderry, constituting one of the "stolen generation" of indigenous children removed from their families in this period. After graduating in law and playing professional rugby union for New South Wales, he became a prominent political activist in the 1970s. He was involved in various environmental and indigenous protests, including erecting the "tent embassy" outside the Federal Parliament in Canberra (see p.273), and standing twice, unsuccessfully, for the senate. Burnum Burnum died in August 1997 and his ashes were scattered near the tree where he was born.

check out the **Tourist Information Centre**, 91 Gipps Street (Mon–Fri 9am–4pm; ⓣ02/6492 2045, ⓔbegatic@acr.net.au).

There's **accommodation** at the *Grand Hotel*, 236 Carp Street (ⓣ02/6492 1122; ❷), which has motel-style rooms, as well as counter **meals** during the week; at the *Pickled Pear*, a beautifully restored three-room 1870s guesthouse at 62 Carp Street (ⓣ02/6492 1393, ⓦwww.ausac.com/ppear; ❹); and at *Bega Caravan Park* on the Princes Highway (ⓣ02/6492 2303; cabins and units ❸, on-site vans ❷).

Tathra

From Bega, you can peel off the Princes Highway to pick up the coast road at the small holiday and fishing village of **TATHRA**. **Accommodation** in Tathra ranges from the motel-style units at the *Tathra Hotel Motel* on Bega Street (ⓣ02/6494 1101; ❸) to the fantastic *Tanja Rural Retreat* on Barrabooka Road (ⓣ02/6494 0220, ⓦwww.tanjaruralretreat.com.au; ❻), an artist-owned B&B with gallery, three private cottages set in the bush and very good food. Alternatively, try the timber cottages at *Kianinny Cabins Resort* on Tathra Road, Tathra Beach (ⓣ02/6494 1990 or 1800 064 225, ⓦwww.kianinny.com.au; ❹), a family-oriented place with a saltwater pool (note that only weekly bookings are accepted at peak times). Finally, there's the *Tathra Beach Tourist Park* (ⓣ02/6494 1302, ⓦwww.tathrabeachtouristpark.com.au; on-site vans ❷, cabins ❸) on the beach towards Bermagui. The **tourist information centre** at Tathra Wharf (daily 9am–5pm; ⓣ02/6494 4062) also rents out fishing, diving and surfing gear, and has a decent café. There's a **maritime museum** upstairs (daily 8am–5pm; $2) which blurs the distinction between "attic" and "museum".

Just south of Tathra, the coastal **Bournda National Park** features stunning beaches, brackish lagoons and freshwater lakes: there are NPWS **campsites** at Hobart Beach on the southern end of Wallagoot Lake (book well ahead from Dec to Easter; ⓣ02/6495 5000).

Merimbula

The pretty township of **MERIMBULA** attracts a lot of holiday-makers from Victoria because of its accessibility, year-round temperate climate and good beaches. You can cruise Merimbula Lake (actually the wide mouth of the Merimbula River) and Pambula Lake with several different companies for around $20 for two hours: Sinbad Cruises (ⓣ02/6495 1686, or book at the tourist centre) is recommended for their interesting commentary on Aboriginal history and oyster cultivation, and they also do dinner cruises ($50). Merimbula Marina (ⓣ02/6495 1686, ⓦwww.merimbulamarina.com) offers dolphin-watching, jet-boating and, from September to early December, whale-watching tours. Cruises and boat rental can both be arranged at the **Tourist Information Centre** on Beach Street (daily 9am–5pm; ⓣ02/6497 4900, ⓦwww.sapphirecoast.com.au), where you can also ask about local **dive** operators (about $88 for two dives, plus $50 equipment hire). You've a chance in a million of seeing a whale under water, but it has happened.

Practicalities

There are several places to **eat** out, including the renowned *Waterfront Café*, on the promenade by the tourist office, which has a seafood and snack menu (ⓣ02/6495 2211). Also on the promenade, *The Peppered Pelican* serves steaks and scallops (but no pelican). *Wheelers* (ⓣ02/6495 6330), across the road from the golf club on the south side of town, serves excellent local oysters and there are several good Asian restaurants, including *Bahn Thai* at 17 Merimbula Drive

(☎02/6495 4555). *Costa's* (☎02/6495 4073) on Market Street has a $10 Italian lunch deal, but even better is the *Bowling Club* (☎02/6495 1306), which has generous $6.90 lunch deals with a choice of three excellent mains; they also serve a good feed for dinner too. Poshest is the *Wharf Restaurant* (☎02/6495 4446), right on the point at Fishing Wharf, with terrific seafood and views.

Though there are dozens of **motels** (❸) and **holiday apartments** in Merimbula, all of which tend to get heavily booked up during the summer holidays, when many places hike their rates considerably and holiday apartments accept only weekly bookings. The places listed below may have space at short notice. If you're stuck, try the free **phone booking service** run by the local Chamber of Commerce (☎1800 150 457), which covers all grades of accommodation.

Mandeni Resort Sapphire Coast Drive, 7km north ☎02/6495 9644 or 1800 358 354, Ⓦwww.mandeni.com.au. Fully equipped timber cottages in a bushland setting, sleeping up to six. Facilities include tennis courts, two swimming pools, a golf course and many walking trails. Two-night minimum stay. ❺

HC Resort Motor Inn 95 Merimbula Drive ☎02/6495 1587. The cheapest doubles in town, of a decent standard and with panoramic views. There are plenty of other reasonable and only slightly more expensive motels on this strip too if this place is full.

Holiday Hub Beach Resort Pambula Beach Rd ☎02/6495 6363, Ⓦwww.holidayhub.com.au. A serial award-winner, this is one of the best and most popular parks in Australia with superb and never-ending facilities and activities in the only real beachfront site in the area – excellent for kids. You can turn up for a site (❷) if you bring your own caravan, but you'll need to book months in advance (try 12) for a cabin (❹).

Merimbula Beach Cabins Short Point, Merimbula ☎02/6495 1216 or 1800 825 555, Ⓦwww.beachcabins.com.au. Bushland cabins by the beach with inspiring ocean views, half-court tennis, laundry and BBQ. ❸

Wandarrah Lodge YHA 8 Marine Parade ☎02/6495 3503, Ⓕ6495 3163. Modern, purpose-built youth hostel close to both the beach and lake. Facilities include two lounges, Internet access and a BBQ area. There's a generous free breakfast, lots of organized activities and outings (including free canoe rental), friendly, knowledgeable staff and a free pick-up service. $2 discount per night for three nights' stay or more. Dorms $22, rooms ❷

Eden and heading inland

EDEN, on Twofold Bay, is pretty much the last seaside stop before the Princes Highway heads south towards Victoria. In 1818 the first whaling station on the Australian mainland was established here, and **whaling** remained a major industry until the 1920s. For information on the local area, call in at the **Tourist Information Centre** on the highway (daily 9am–5pm; ☎ & Ⓕ02/6496 1953, Ⓦwww.sapphirecoast.com.au). You can also book **cruises** here on Twofold Bay and further out to sea – with luck you might see penguins, dolphins and, in winter, even whales. Cat Balou Cruises (☎02/6496 2027) offer excellent year-round dolphin-spotting cruises ($28 for 2hr), and seasonal whale-watching trips ($60 for 4hr).

Today Eden is touristy in a quiet sort of way, with good fishing, and there are plenty of reminders of the old days, the best of which is the **Killer Whale Museum** on Imlay Street (daily 9.15am–3.45pm; $6; Ⓦwww.killerwhalemuseum.com.au), which has an excellent display of giant whale bones, harpoons and boats, along with incredible but authenticated accounts of a man being swallowed by a whale and coming out alive fifteen hours later after an 800m deep dive. Yet stranger is the tale of "old Tom" – a killer whale, whose skeleton is on display – who used to lead whaling boats towards whale pods and help round them up.

Heading south from Eden, you become increasingly surrounded by the vast temperate rainforests that characterize southeastern Australia. Roads lead off the highway in both directions into the magnificent **Ben Boyd National Park**

(☎02/6495 5000), which hugs the coast to the north and south of Eden, offering good camping, walking and beaches. Inland, the summit of **Mount Imlay** can be reached via a three-kilometre walking track that starts at the picnic grounds at Burrawang Forest Road, 14km south of Eden. The steep, strenuous ascent is rewarded by a panoramic view over the coast and across the dense forests of the hinterland onto the Monaro plain. Camping and park passes can be obtained from the visitors centre in Eden.

Practicalities

There's a disproportionate number of good places **to eat** in Eden. *The Wheelhouse* (☎02/6496 3392), right on the wharf, keeps winning awards for its seafood (mains about $20), while *Bianca's* at the *Australasia Hotel* serves renowned modern Australian food. The *Café Lamplighter* at the *Coachman's Rest Motel* also has a very good reputation.

Accommodation

Australasia Hotel 160 Imlay St, Eden ☎02/6496 1600, Ⓦwww.g'daypubs.com/hotelaustralasia. Basic budget accommodation in an old pub. Dorms $25, rooms without en suite ❷, with en suite ❸

Bayview Motor Inn Princes Highway, Eden ☎02/6496 1242, Ⓔazalea@asitis.net.au. Simple, inexpensive motel with swimming pool and spa. ❸

Coachman's Rest Motel 81 Princes Highway (look for the "Best Western" sign) ☎02/6496 1900, Ⓦwww.bestwestern.com.au/coachmaneden. Professionally run place – clean and efficient and with good facilities, albeit rather characterless. ❹

Crown & Anchor Inn 239 Imlay St, Eden ☎02/6496 1017, Ⓦwww.crownandanchor.com.au. The best B&B on the south coast, set in a beautiful building full of tasteful artwork. All rooms are en suite and have expansive water views, while breakfast is served on the verandah or back deck looking out over the ocean. ❺–❻

Seahorse Inn just off the Princes Highway in Boydtown ☎02/6496 1361. A grand mock-Tudor-cum-Georgian inn offering B&B, with a tennis court, tearooms and restaurant. ❹

Twofold Beach Resort 7km south of Eden ☎02/6496 1572, Ⓔ2fold@austernet.com.au. This impressive-looking neo-Gothic hulk on a palm-fringed beach was being renovated at the time of research. Cabins and on-site vans ❸

Wonboyn Lake Resort 40km south of Eden ☎02/6496 9162, Ⓦwww.wonboynlakeresort.com.au. In a scenic location off the beaten track at Lake Wonboyn with swimming pool, spa, shop, boat-ramp, canoe and boat rental. There's also a beach nearby. ❹

The Snowy Mountains

The **Snowy Mountains** are just one section of the alpine highlands that spread across the southeast corner of the Australian continent, once gigantic volcanic peaks which have been eroded over millions of years to form the rounded, granite-strewn mountains of today. The Australian Alps sprawl from Mount Buller, Mount Bogong and Mount Beauty in northeast Victoria via the Crackenback Range in New South Wales to the township of Cooma; though it's a continuous massif, only the New South Wales section is strictly known as the Snowy Mountains. **Mount Kosciuszko**, at 2228m the highest mountain in Australia, is located close to the Victorian border in the far southeast. It was named in 1840 by the Polish-born explorer Paul Strzelecki after the Polish freedom fighter General Tadeusz Kosciuszko, and, although Strzelecki stressed he was "in a foreign country and on a foreign ground", he couldn't resist giving it its name "amongst a free people who appreciate freedom". The **Kosciuszko National Park**, which surrounds the peak, includes most of the Snowy Mountains region and almost everything of interest. To the north and east of **Cooma**

– the main approach to the range – the treeless, brownish-yellow **Monaro High Plain** is sheep country famous for the quality of its merino wool.

Compared to the high mountain ranges of other continents, the "roof of Australia" is relatively low and, despite the name, the flattened mountaintops lie below the line of permanent snow. After heavy snowfalls in winter, however (roughly from the end of June to the beginning of Oct), winter-sports fans from all over southeast Australia congregate at the **ski resorts** in the Mount Kosciuszko area – Perisher Blue Resort, Thredbo, Mount Selwyn and Charlotte Pass. The downhilling isn't world-class and the snow is rarely dry, but it's better than you might think, and if you're into back-country skiing, the Snowy Mountains offer a paradise of huge, empty valleys, snowgum forests and wildlife. **Accommodation prices** double in winter; in summer the towns and resorts are less crowded and there are fabulous walks through mountain scenery to be enjoyed. The accommodation prices given below are for the winter skiing season. Perisher and Selwyn almost completely close down in summer, but Thredbo operates ski-lifts throughout the year up to the mountaintops, from where you can bushwalk across the wildflower-covered high country. Other activities include mountain biking, horse trekking, fishing and white-water rafting in the crystal-clear mountain rivers.

The system of roads that made possible the existence of the townships and ski resorts was established by the **Snowy Mountains Hydroelectric Scheme**, which was begun in the 1950s. Many postwar immigrants from middle and southern Europe found their first jobs on the "Snowy"; some also lost their lives here. Twenty-five years and about $800 million later, in 1974 the project was completed: seven power stations now utilize the waters of the Upper Murrumbidgee, Tumut and Snowy rivers to generate electricity and provide New South Wales, the ACT and Victoria with power. The scheme's generating capacity is about eighteen percent of the total for southeast Australia, while the water of the redirected rivers is used for irrigation right across New South Wales, Victoria and South Australia.

Skiing and snowboarding in the Snowy Mountains

The easiest option for **skiing in the Snowy Mountains** is to arrange a **ski package** departing from Sydney – always check exactly what's included in the price. Be aware that snow conditions can let you down and that the resorts' interpretation of "good" conditions may not match yours, so check an independent source like the excellent Ⓦwww.ski.com.au (which also has links for accommodation) before you go.

Recommended operators include the Kosciuszko Accommodation Centre (Ⓣ02/6456 2022 or 1800 026 385), who can put together a basic low-season weekend package, including transport by bus, national park entry, ski rental, lift and lessons, and two nights' accommodation, dinner and breakfast for around $350; and Ski Kaos (Ⓣ02/9976 5555, Ⓦwww.skikaos.com.au) who offer similar deals minus food for $204.

The longest downhill runs are at Thredbo, while the Perisher/Blue Cow/Smiggins/Guthega complex (all one liftpass) is the largest and most varied. A one-day **ski-lift pass** starts from about $63 at Selwyn, $85 at Charlotte Pass and $83 at Thredbo and Perisher Blue; beginners' one-day group lessons cost $83. Resorts are generally child-friendly, particularly at Charlotte Pass where the homely and old-fashioned *Kosciuszko Chalet* (Ⓣ1800 026 369) offers free childcare throughout the ski season; Paddy Pallin at Jindabyne (Ⓣ02/6456 2922 or 1800 623 459, Ⓦwww.adventurepro.com.au/paljin) has several cross-country skiing sessions, including an easy three-hour introduction aimed at family groups.

Getting there and around

The **Snowy Mountains Highway** leads straight across the mountain ranges and through the national park from Cooma to Tumut and Gundagai. If you want to see more of the alpine scenery, head along the spectacular **Alpine Way**, turning off the highway at Kiandra in the heart of the park and heading via Khancoban and Geehi to Thredbo. In winter, check road conditions before driving anywhere; **snow chains** (you can hire them one-way) must be carried by two-wheel drives between June and October, and the roads might be closed altogether.

Bus services are far more frequent in winter than in summer – a **rental car** is strongly recommended for summer sojourns. Greyhound Australia (ⓣ13 14 99, ⓦwww.greyhound.com.au) has summer services four times weekly from Canberra to Cooma, Jindabyne, and Thredbo. Autopia Tours operates a year-round Melbourne–Sydney, three-day tour (ⓣ03/9419 8878 or 1800 000 507, ⓦwww.autopiatours.com.au; $195) via the Alpine Way, picking up and dropping off in Jindabyne. Additional winter-only bus services include Adaminaby Bus Service (ⓣ02/6454 2318) between Cooma, Adaminaby and Mount Selwyn ski resort. In winter, the cheapest option is to take the Snowliner Schoolbus ($13) from Cooma to Jindabyne. Perisher Blue Skitube (ⓣ02/6456 2010, ⓦwww.perisherblue.com.au/winter/skitube; see p.302 for more details) is a **railway** under the mountains, linking the ski areas of Bullocks Flat, Perisher Valley and Mount Blue Cow (though note that there is talk of suspending the service between October and June). Countrylink (ⓣ13 22 32) has a daily train from Sydney, with a coach connection on to Cooma ($70).

Cooma

Although **COOMA** functions mainly as a service centre for skiers, it's also an attractive place in its own right, with a number of fine old buildings, notably on Lambie and Vale streets, as well as the Geebung Polo Club, the inspiration for Banjo Patterson's famous poem of the same name. The visitors centre (see below) has a brochure detailing buildings of interest.

Many of the migrants who worked on the Snowy hydroelectric scheme in the 1950s – particularly those who arrived from central Europe – ended up settling here, making it a fairly cosmopolitan town. If you're interested in the history of the project and the technical details, check out the **Snowy Mountains Hydro Information Centre**, on the Monaro Highway in North Cooma (Mon–Fri 8.30am–5pm, Sat & Sun during school holidays 8.30am–2pm; ⓦwww.snowyhydro.com.au). The Snowy Mountains are traditionally regarded as prime **horse riding** country. The long-established Yarramba Trail Riding at Berridale, 34km southwest of Cooma (ⓣ02/6453 7204), offers escorted rides at $30 per hour or full-day picnic rides ($80), as well as extended camping safaris ($190 for two days).

Practicalities

The staff at **Cooma Visitors Centre**, Centennial Park (daily: June–Oct 7am–6pm; Nov–May 9am–5pm; ⓣ02/6450 1742 or 1800 636 525, ⓦwww.visitcooma.com.au) will just about vault over the counter in their eagerness to help you with information on Kosciuszko National Park, farmstays, horse riding and fishing safaris; they also offer a free accommodation-booking service and copies of the free monthly *Snowy Times*, which has detailed resort information and maps, plus listings of skiing prices and packages. The helpful Harvey World Travel **travel agency**, at 96 Sharp Street (Ⓣ02/6452 4677), can book flights out, provide details of bus services and arrange local tours. **Car rental** is available from Thrifty, 60 Sharp Street (Ⓣ02/6452 5300), and more cheaply from the Caltex service station at 223 Sharp Street (Ⓣ02/6452 1283).

Accommodation

Note that **accommodation** can be hard to come by during the ski season.

Bunkhouse Motel 28–30 Soho St Ⓣ02/6452 2983, Ⓦwww.bunkhousemotel.com.au. Basic but functional family-run backpackers with en-suite doubles. Dorms $25, rooms ❷

Royal Hotel Corner of Lambie and Sharp Sts Ⓣ02/6552 2132. Central hotel, built in 1858. Many of the rooms (shared bathrooms only) have French windows opening onto the huge wrought-iron balcony. ❷

Sovereign Inn 35 Sharp St Ⓣ02/6452 1366, Ⓦwww.sovereigninns.com.au. More luxurious than most places in Cooma, with a hotel-feel and large, tastefully furnished rooms. ❹–❺

Snowtels Caravan Park 286 Sharp St Ⓣ02/6452 1828, Ⓦwww.snowtels.com.au. This probably the best of the town's campsites, and also has on-site vans (❷), cabins (❸) and apartments (❹), plus a tennis court and communal kitchen.

White Manor Motel 252 Sharp St Ⓣ02/6452 1152, Ⓦwww.whitemanor.com. The town's best motel: smart and inexpensive. ❸–❹

Eating

Cooma is a good place to **eat**. The licensed *Sharp Food*, 122 Sharp Street, is a cosy place serving delicious soups and sandwiches, with outdoor dining in a pleasant courtyard at the back. *Grand Court Chinese Restaurant*, Snowstop village, Sharp Street (Ⓣ02/6452 4525), is also excellent, *The Lott Food Store* (Ⓣ02/6452 1414), 100m northwest of the visitors centre on Sharp Street, is a great café with sandwiches, coffee and cakes, as is the Lebanese *Rosie's Restaurant*, also on Sharp Street (Ⓣ02/6452 1366).

Kosciuszko National Park and around

The largest national park in New South Wales, **Kosciuszko National Park** extends 200km north to south, encompassing an area of some 6500 square kilometres. The scenery includes ten peaks above 2100m, forested valleys and a beautiful plateau with glacial lakes, as well as the headwaters of Australia's biggest river system, the Murray–Murrumbidgee. The main centres are the lakeside resort of **Jindabyne**, just outside the eastern boundary of the park, and the ski resort of **Thredbo**, 30km further west along the scenic Alpine Way, actually in the national park. Perisher and Mount Blue Cow can be reached via the Skitube from Bullocks Flat, roughly midway between Jindabyne and Thredbo, or you can drive round from Jindabyne.

If you're driving to Thredbo or Perisher, note that there's a **fee** of $16 per car per 24hr – so if you plan to stay a few days, the annual national park pass ($85; see p.267 for details) may be a good investment. Arriving by bus, you'll still have to fork out a one-off payment of $6.60. The **Snowy Region Visitor Centre** is within the **NPWS headquarters** in Jindabyne (daily: Dec–Feb 8.30am–5pm; Ⓣ02/6450 5600). This complex features red-gum interiors, a cinema, café, bus station and tourist information office with leaflets about walking trails in the national park, activities such as ranger-guided tours, details of campsites, as well as maps for sale and a display on the natural features of the park. There are also NPWS **ranger stations** at Perisher Valley (June–Aug only; Ⓣ02/6457 5214), Khancoban (Ⓣ02/6076 9373), Yarrangobilly (Ⓣ02/6454 9597) and Tumut (Ⓣ02/6947 7023).

Bushwalking in the park

Some of the country's most interesting and beautiful **bushwalking tracks** pass through the area. You might see echidnas, wombats or even a heavyweight 'roo crashing through the powder, while the snowgums themselves are beautiful, with multi-coloured bark in greens and yellows. One of the most accessible of these is the walking trail around **Mount Kosciuszko**. The **chair-lift** from Thredbo (see below) will take you up to Crackenback station on the edge of the plateau; the actual summit is 6.5km from here, though it seems barely higher than the surrounding country; alternatively you can walk 2km to **Mount Kosciuszko Lookout** for panoramic views. Perhaps the best walk, however, is the main range walk from Charlotte Pass to the lovely Blue Lake, and then up Kosciuszko via more glacial lakes. Alternatively, take the **Skitube** from Bullocks Flat on the Alpine Way to Perisher Valley and Mount Blue Cow (which has a bistro and art gallery), where more fine trails await. The weather up here is very fickle so pack a sweater and raincoat.

Jindabyne and Thredbo

A resort town at the man-made lake of the same name, **JINDABYNE**, 63km west of Cooma, is the jumping-off point for the ski resorts of Thredbo, a further 30km west, and Guthega, or up the Kosciuszko road to Smiggin Holes and Perisher Valley (these two are also accessible by the Skitube – Ⓣ02/6456 2010, Ⓦwww.perisherblue.com.au; $32 return). Jindabyne itself is entirely new, having been relocated when the Snowy Mountains Scheme dammed the Snowy River and drowned the first settlement. There's good fishing on the lake, and in summer you can also swim and sail – equipment is available to rent in the town.

From Jindabyne, the Alpine Way continues into the national park and up to **THREDBO**, a compact and attractive village, squeezed into a narrow valley beside the road and the Crackenback River, with alpine-style houses huddled against the mountainside. Unlike the other resorts, it's also reasonably lively in summer and – with its Crackenback **chair-lift** (daily 8.30am–4pm; $23 return) giving easy access to the high country – makes a good base for bushwalking and mountain biking which can be hired locally. The **Thredbo Resort Centre**, Friday Drive (Ⓣ1800 020 589, Ⓦwww.thredbo.com.au), can advise on chair-lift timetables and provide other tourist information. There are several annual events in the Thredbo calendar. Musical highlights include the three-day Thredbo **Blues Festival** in mid-January, the three-day **Global Music Festival** in March and the four-day **Jazz Festival** in early May.

Yarrangobilly Caves and Kiandra

The **Yarrangobilly Caves**, a system of about sixty limestone caves at the edge of a rocky plateau surrounded by unspoiled bushland, are one of the few specific sights in the park; they're 6.5km off the Snowy Mountains Highway near Kiandra, 113km northwest of Cooma and 70km south of Tumut. There are several guided tours daily to the **North Glory**, **Jersey** and **Jillabenan Caves** (all $13; Ⓣ02/6454 9597 for tour times). A fourth cave, the **South Glory Hole Cave** (daily 10am–4pm; $3), can be explored on a self-guided tour. From walking trails along the edge of the rock plateau there are panoramic views of the Yarrangobilly Gorge, and a steep trail leads from the Glory Hole car park to a thermal pool at the bottom of the gorge near the Yarrangobilly River. The spring-fed pool, which you can swim in (for free), has a constant year-round temperature of 27°C.

KIANDRA itself is a ghost town, but the Heritage Trail's detailed interpretive boards will help you find your way through the remaining ruins on this desolate, windswept spot – the extensive plains in the northern part of the park are too cold for any trees to survive. It's hard to believe that fifteen thousand prospectors camped here during the goldrush of 1860; the short-term rush left behind a town of about three hundred people who eked out a living mining and grazing.

Accommodation

In winter, **rooms** are at a premium – despite the plethora of holiday apartments and motels, accommodation is almost impossible to come by without a reservation. In summer, the situation is less dire, and you should have little difficulty finding somewhere in one of the resorts, or at motels on the fringes of the park, such as at Tumut in the north or even back in Cooma. Most accommodation in Thredbo can be **booked** through the Thredbo Resort Centre (see above) or Thredbo Accommodation Services (ⓣ1800 801 982, ⓦwww.thredboproperties.com.au); the Snowy River Information Centre in Jindabyne (ⓣ02/6456 2444) also handles accommodation bookings, and there is extensive information and a booking service online at ⓦwww.thredbo.com.au. Note that prices given below are for high season (winter), and that prices can drop dramatically in summer.

Budget

Alpine Inn Alpine Way, Khancoban ⓣ02/6076 9471. Motel-style accommodation (with parking) attached to a great pub and restaurant. ❸

Fishermen's Lodge Alpine Way, Khancoban ⓣ02/6076 9471. Under the same management as the *Alpine Inn*, this lodge caters to backpackers with inexpensive single rooms, plus activities such as horse riding and white-water rafting; they also rent out fishing gear, boats and canoes. ❶

Jindy Inn 18 Clyde St, Jindabyne ⓣ02/6456 1957, ⓦwww.jindyinn.com. Guesthouse-style place with large rooms and views of the lake from the verandah, plus a communal kitchen. ❸

Khancoban Lakeside Caravan Resort Alpine-Way, Khancoban ⓣ02/6076 9488, ⓦwww.uppermurray.com. Riverside location with great facilities including canoe hire. Good for kids. ❶–❺

Snowline Caravan Park Junction of Alpine Way and Kosciuszko Rd, Jindabyne ⓣ02/6456 2099, ⓦwww.snowline.com.au. The cheapest dorms in town, plus camping and cabins with good facilities, including spa, sauna, café-restaurant, tennis courts and boat rental. You can camp right on the lakeshore. Dorms $20, cabins ❸

Snowy Mountain Backpackers 7 Gippsland St, Jindabyne ⓣ02/6456 1500 or 1800 333 468, ⓦwww.snowybackpackers.com.au. Facilities include an Internet lounge, a good café with tasty food, massage, laundry, bikes for hire, a tour-booking desk and fantastic kitchens and common areas with comfy sofas. Full disabled access. Dorms $35, rooms ❹

Thredbo YHA Lodge 8 Jack Adams Pass, Thredbo ⓣ02/6457 6376, ⓦwww.yha.com.au. Central and purpose-built hostel with open fires and great views across the mountains. Dorms $23, rooms ❷

Moderate and expensive

Banjo Patterson Inn 1 Kosciuszko Rd, Jindabyne ⓣ02/6456 2372, ⓔbanjopatterson@ski.com.au. Tastefully decorated en-suite rooms with disabled access, balconies, cable TV and fridges. The inn itself has open fires, a laundry, bistro, nightclub, beer garden and communal cooking facilities. ❺

Bimble Gumbie Next door to *Crackenback Farm* ⓣ02/6456 2185, ⓦwww.bimblegumbie.com.au. This is the most characterful place in the mountains by a very long way, set in a tranquil cluster of lovely farmhouses backing onto the bush overflowing with art from every continent and century, The shelves are full of books, and you can bring your dog to the property. Excellent value, and not to be missed. ❸–❻

Crackenback Farm Halfway between Jindabyne and Thredbo on the Alpine Way ⓣ02/6456 2198, ⓦwww.crackenback.com.au. Plush, tasteful rooms in a very cosy replica farmhouse with pool, sauna, massage parlour and all the trimmings. The restaurant here (modern Australian) is one of the best in the region, and the bar boasts Australia's largest collection of schnapps. ❺

Kasees Lodge Banjo Drive, Thredbo ⓣ02/6457 6370, ⓦwww.kasees.com.au. An excellent motel with a pool, sauna (Finnish, if you appreciate the difference) and log fires. ❹

Kosciuszko Mountain Retreat Sawpit Creek, near the park headquarters ⓣ02/6456 2224, ⓦwww.kositreat.com.au. Tent sites, cabins and chalets sleeping six, set among a forest of snow gums with possums and 'roos padding about the clearings. Two-night minimum stay in high season. Chalets for two: high season ❽, low season ❹

Quality Resort Kosciuszko Rd, just out of town towards Thredbo ⓣ02/6456 2562, ⓔreservations @horisonsresort.com.au. This is the top spot in town, with self-contained apartments and all the facilities of a top hotel: gym, pool, beautician and a good, Chinese-influenced restaurant. ❻–❽

The Swagman's Rest 16km east of Jindabyne towards Berridale in the Alpine Way (turn off at the Equestrian Centre and fork right) ⓣ02/6456 7332, ⓦwww.swagmansrest.com.au. Luxurious, rustic farm chalets named after Banjo Patterson's famous poem of the same name. ❻

Thredbo Alpine Hotel Friday Drive, Thredbo ⓣ02/6459 4200, ⓦwww.thredbo.com.au. Large, luxury hotel complex in the centre of the village, close to the chairlift, home to wine bars and the resort's only nightclub. ❺

The north coast

The coast from Sydney **north to Queensland** is more densely populated and much more touristy than the southern coast, with popular holiday destinations strung along the coast north of Newcastle. **Port Stephens**, **Port Macquarie**, **Coffs Harbour** and the twin city of **Tweed Heads–Coolangatta**, straddling the state line, attract local tourists as well as overseas visitors. The subtropical part of the coast, from Coffs Harbour north, is more attractive: since the 1970s the area around **Lismore**, **Byron Bay** and **Murwillumbah** has been a favoured destination for people from the southern cities seeking an alternative lifestyle. This movement has left in its wake not only disillusioned hippie farmers (as well as a few who've survived with their illusions intact), but also a firmly established artistic and alternative scene.

As in the south, the **coastline** consists of myriad inlets, bays and coastal lakes, interspersed by white, sandy beaches and rocky promontories. Parallel to the coast, the rocky plateaus of the **Great Dividing Range** rise up from the plain; so steep is the eastern edge of this range that it defied even the efforts of the early foresters, so that to this day the hills remain densely wooded. A handful of townships still depend on the timber industry, but most forest areas are now protected as national parks or state forests. From the highlands, numerous streams tumble down from the escarpment in mighty waterfalls, and once on the coastal plain they flow together to form short, wide and fast-flowing rivers. In the fertile river valleys the predominant agricultural activity is cattle breeding, while in the north subtropical and tropical agriculture takes over, especially the cultivation of bananas.

In essence, the further you go, the better this coast gets – the northeast corner is one of the most scenic areas in the state and its remote country roads are well worth exploring. If the bigger coastal resorts are too touristy for your liking, there's no shortage of quiet, even lonely, beaches as you head further up, along with small fishing villages and virtually undiscovered sleepy hamlets inland. For bushwalkers there are vast areas of remote, rugged and wild terrain to explore in the national parks of the Great Dividing Range.

Getting up the north coast is easy, with frequent **train** and **bus** services between Sydney and Brisbane. There are also some excellent one-way tours from Sydney to Byron Bay (see box on p.213). In addition, Kirklands (ⓣ02/6622 1499) runs between Brisbane and Lismore via Surfers Paradise (see p.445), Tweed Heeds, Murwillumbah, Brunswick Heads, Byron Bay, Lennox Head and Ballina. The busy **Pacific Highway** which runs along the coast leaves something to be desired. Though it's gradually being upgraded and widened, with the addition of much-needed overtaking lanes, sections of this winding coastal road are still alarmingly narrow considering the weight of traffic and the big trucks that use it; bus services on the highway almost invariably run late. The inland route on the New England Highway (covered in chapter 3) is a faster alternative if you're heading straight for Brisbane from Sydney – many buses go this way too.

Port Stephens and the lakes

Just north of Newcastle, the wide bay of **Port Stephens**, which extends inland for some 25km, offers calm waters and numerous coves ideal for swimming, water sports and fishing, while the ocean side has good surf and wide, sandy beaches – **Stockton beach** actually has the largest sand dunes in the eastern Australian mainland. In January, thousands of families arrive to take their annual holiday in the "Blue Water Paradise", as the area has been dubbed. The main township of **NELSON BAY** is perched at the tip of the southern arm of the bay, together with the quieter settlements of **Shoal Bay**, **Soldiers Point**, **Fingal Bay**, **Boat Harbour** and **Anna Bay**. **Dolphin-watching** cruises are popular here, and you might also see whales as they migrate north from May to July. Most dolphin cruises leave from **Tea Gardens** on the northern arm of the bay (see p.306 for details of operators). There are also opportunities to go on bushwalks to spot **koalas** in the wild at **Tilligery Habitat**, 14 Tilligery Plaza, Tanilba Bay, on the Tilligery Peninsula (Mon–Sat 9.30am–4pm, Sun 10am–2pm; daily guided tours at 10.30am and 2pm; $15). The smaller beaches around the bay offer various other activities, including sea-kayaking, sand safaris and horse trekking.

Myall Lakes National Park and around

From Port Stephens the Pacific Highway continues north for about 40km to **BULAHDELAH**, a small town surrounded by bush-covered hills and rocky outcrops. About 20km before Bulahdelah, turn right onto Tea Gardens Rd for a heavenly drive along the Myall lakeshores. At **Mungo Brush**, an easy walking track (30min return) heads through the littoral rainforest – a variant adapted to salty and harsh seafront conditions, with a low canopy. A more challenging 21-kilometre walking track leads from here to **Hawks Nest**, on Port Stephens Bay and the Myall River, linked by a bridge across the river to Tea Gardens. The road eventually heads north via a toll ferry (daily 8am–6pm; $3) back to the highway via Bombah Point Rd.

Heading north towards the twin holiday towns of Forster–Tuncurry, you can turn east just after Bulahdelah onto the **Lakes Way** (tourist drive 6). This goes past Myall Lake and then Wallis Lake. Lakes Way is one of the better scenic routes; the road winds along gum trees, lake shores and reeds. Along here, at Bungwahl, a turn-off leads down mostly unsealed roads to **SEAL ROCKS**, a remote fishing village and the only settlement in the **Myall Lakes National Park**. Its national park status means it's unspoilt, and the small beach is truly beautiful, with crystal-clear waters marooned between two headlands. Seal Rocks' seasonal agglomerations of nurse sharks also make it one of the best dive sites in New South Wales; contact Forster Dive Centre (see p.306) to arrange a trip. There are also great waves here for surfing. **Sugar Loaf Point Lighthouse** (1875) is a ten-minute stroll away; the grounds (Tues & Thurs 10am–noon & 1–3pm) offer a fantastic view along the coast, and the lookout below leads down to a deserted, rocky beach.

North of Seal Rocks, the tiny **Booti Booti National Park** is located between Cape Hawke and Charlotte Head. The park encompasses many beaches, oceanside forests and – on the western boundary – Wallis Lake, an excellent boating and fishing spot. There's also a secluded camping site on the coastline near Seal Rocks. Ten kilometres further north, a bridge connects the twin towns of **FORSTER–TUNCURRY**, set on the spit of land that separates **Wallis Lake** from the ocean. The lake is very pretty, surrounded by trees and with bush-covered **Corrie Island** at its centre. Forster is famous for its **oysters**, and for its playful resident **dolphins**. The lake itself is superb for fishing and swimming, and you can rent dinghies, canoes and windsurfers. The local Aboriginal people, the Wallamba, take visitors on a tour of significant sites, while Tobwabba Gallery (Mon–Fri 9am–5pm in theory, if not always in practice; free) has some great traditional art.

Practicalities

Some Sydney–Brisbane **buses**, such as Busways (ⓣ02/4983 1560 or 1800 043 262), stop daily at Newcastle, Bulahdelah, Tea Gardens, Hawkes Nest and Forster. Greyhound Australia (ⓣ013 20 30) serves Newcastle, Bulahdelah and Forster. Between Newcastle and Sydney, Port Stephens Buses (ⓣ02/4982 2940, ⓦwww.psbuses.nelsonbay.com) stop daily at Nelson Bay, Shoal Bay and Fingal Bay, from where local buses run to Boat Harbour, Anna Bay and Soldiers Point.

Both the **Port Stephens Visitors Centre**, at Victoria Parade in Nelson Bay (daily 9am–5pm; ⓣ02/4980 6900 or 1800 808 900, ⓦwww.portstephens.org.au), and the well-organized **Great Lakes Visitors Centre** at Little Street in Forster (daily 9am–5pm; ⓣ02/6554 8799 or 1800 802 692, ⓦwww.greatlakes.org.au), can provide you with stacks of information and book accommodation and tours (including those run by local Aborigines). The Port Stephens Office handles everything south of Tea Gardens. The **NPWS** office is on Teramby Road in Nelson Bay (ⓣ02/4984 8200). **Dolphin/whale watching** jaunts are organized by several operators: Moonshadow Cruises (ⓣ02/4984 9388, ⓦwww.moonshadow.com.au; 3hr; $19) in Nelson Bay (they also run twilight dinner cruises); Amaroo Dolphin Watch (ⓣ0419 333 445; 2hr; $35) at Forster; and Simba II Cruises (ⓣ02/4997 1084, ⓔsimba@myallcoast.net.au; daily at 10am; 3hr; $18) at Tea Gardens. Much more satisfying than a motor cruise, however, are the environmentally-aware dolphin- and whale-watching trips ($20/$49 respectively) aboard *Imagine*, a fifteen-metre catamaran moored at Nelson Bay (ⓣ02/4984 9000, ⓦwww.portstephens.org.au/imagine). There are also sea-kayaking tours and trips to snorkel with dolphins (all bookable at the tourist office).

Forster Dive Centre, at 15 Little Street in Forster (ⓣ02/6555 4477), arranges **diving trips** at Seal Rocks. In Nelson Bay, try Pro Dive (ⓣ02/4981 4331, ⓔprodive@hunterlink.net.au) at D'albora Marinas, Teramby Road. Port Stephens 4WD tours, (ⓣ02/4984 4760, ⓔps4wd@hunterlink.net.au), 35 Stockton Street, Nelson Bay, run trips to Stockton beach's giant **sand dunes** – try sandboarding down sixty-degree slopes or sliding down a 30m high dune in the truck. Weirdest of all, you'll think you're on a sci-fi film-set when you see a row of black, metallic pyramids rising out of the sand – World War II anti-tank defences.

A good place to **eat** in Forster–Tuncurry is *The Oyster Rack* on Wharf Road, which serves great seafood (bookings advised ⓣ02/6557 5577). *Poet's Corner*, on Memorial Drive (ⓣ02/6557 5577; closed Tues), serves gourmet seafood on the wharf from 6.30pm, while *Merret's Restaurant* (ⓣ02/4984 2555), in Peppers Anchorage, just outside Kallaroo, is well worth the detour for its award-winning modern cuisine. There's fine dining and yacht-watching at *Sinclair's* (ⓣ02/4984 4444) on the marina in Nelson Bay.

Accommodation

There are scores of motels (❸) and even more holiday apartments to choose from in the area, though many insist on weekly bookings during the holiday season. If you want to stay in the national park itself, **camping** is the way to go. **Houseboats** are also an option at **Bulladellah** (weekend rates $390–1160; weekly rates $550–2000).

Dolphin Lodge YHA 43 Head St, Forster ⓣ & ⓕ02/6555 8155, ⓔdolphin_lodge@hotmail.com. Just three minutes from the beach, with en-suite doubles, dorms, a BBQ area, pool room, laundry and free use of bikes, fishing gear and surf- and boogie-boards. Dorms $23, rooms ❸

Halifax Holiday Park Beach Rd, Little Beach, 2km east of central Nelson Bay ⓣ02/4981 1522 or 1800 600 201, ⓔhalifax@beachsideholidays.com.au. A well-equipped beachside campsite with kitchen, BBQs and kiosk. Cabins ❷

Melaleuca Surfside Backpackers 33 Eucalyptus Drive, One Mile Beach ⓣ02/4982 1248, ⓦwww.baysholidaypark.com. Timber bungalows and tent sites with all amenities set in bushland on a surf-beach. Dorms $25, doubles ❸.

Mitchells Waterfront B&B 6 Mitchell St, Soldiers Point ⓣ02/4982 0402. Luxury en-suite rooms on the beach with verandahs overlooking the water and Yacaaba headlands. ❺

Myall Shores Ecotourism Resort Bombah Point, 16km east of Bulahdelah in the Myall Lakes National Park ⓣ02/4997 4495, ⓦwww.murramarangresort.com. Beautifully located four-star waterfront villas with campsite, restaurant and boat ramp. Bushwalks, canoes, 4WD tours and cruises are offered. Cabins ❹

Samurai Beach Bungalows YHA Frost Rd, cnr Robert Connell Close, Anna Bay ⓣ02/4982 1921, ⓦwww.yha.com.au. One of the best budget options in the Myall Lakes area, with four bungalows – and resident possum – set in rainforest and cabins arranged around an undercover "bush" kitchen. There are free boards and bikes, and surfing excursions to nearby beaches and other social activities are also offered. Port Stephens Buses from Sydney or Newcastle stop outside. Dorms $23, rooms ❸

Seal Rocks Camping Reserve Seal Rocks ⓣ02/4997 6164 or 1800 112 234. Small site just across from a great surf beach; all sites unpowered. Bookings essential during school holidays. Sites ❶

Shoal Bay Backpackers/Shoal Bay Motel 59–61 Shoal Bay Beachfront Rd, Shoal Bay ⓣ02/4981 0982, ⓔshoalbaymotel@bigpond.com. Beachfront motel with sauna and spa. Advance booking recommended. Dorms $23, rooms ❸

Smuggler's Cove Holiday Village 45 The Lakes Way, 2km south of Forster ⓣ02/6554 6666, ⓦwww.smugglerscove.com.au. This pirate-themed park has crazy golf, a pirate ship, pool, entertainment shows and games as well as smart, well-equipped cabins. Heaven for kids, and a spotless, efficent place for adults. ❸

A detour inland: Barrington Tops

Heading from Forster via Nabiac, Krambach and Gloucester takes you through the World Heritage-listed **Barrington Tops National Park** ⓦwww.barringtons.com.au). It's gentle hilly farming country up to the country town of **Gloucester**; about 40km beyond here, unsealed roads lead through the park – the Barrington Tops Forest Road towards Scone (see p.379), or the Gloucester Tops road to the park's southwestern section. You can also approach via the Hunter Valley from Maitland via Dungog. The closest you'll get to the park with public transport is on the train from Sydney or Newcastle to Dungog or Gloucester; *The Barringtons Country Retreat* (see p.308) offers free pick-ups from Dungog.

The Barrington Tops themselves are two high, cliff-ringed plateaus, **Barrington** and **Gloucester**, which rise steeply from the surrounding valleys. The changes in altitude within the park are so great – the highest points are Mount Barrington (1555m) and Polblue Mountain (1577m) – that within a few minutes you can pass from areas of subtropical rainforest to warm and cool temperate rainforest, and then to high, windswept plateaus covered with snow gums, meadows and subalpine bog. Up on the plateau, snow is common from the end of April to early October.

The **Great Lakes Visitors Centre** in Forster (see p.306) can help with specific routes or organized 4WD tours into the national park. There are plenty of picnic grounds and scenic **lookouts** in the park, plus several **campsites**, some of which are accessible only by 4WD. The main camping area, reached by car, is in the Gloucester River area, with barbecues, toilet (but no shower) and water ($7 per person). The easiest walks are in the south of the park. You don't need to book, but for more information contact the NPWS at 59 Church St, Gloucester (ⓣ02/6538 5300, ⓔgloucester@npws.nsw.gov.au). All other **accommodation** in the area is relatively plush and pricey. One of the closest places to the park itself is *Salisbury Lodges* (ⓣ02/4995 3285, ⓦwww.salisburylodges.com.au; ❻), at 2930 Salisbury Rd in Salisbury, 40km north of Dungog. This wilderness retreat has self-contained lodges with spa, fire, cooking/dining area and private balcony, as well as more basic chalets, also with self-catering facilities (though there's also a very good restaurant), in a gorgeous rainforest setting. A slightly cheaper alternative is *The Barringtons Country Retreat* on Chichester Dam Road, 23km north of Dungog (ⓣ02/4995 9269, ⓦwww.thebarringtons.com.au; ❺), which has a pool, spa and horse riding on offer (meals and self-catering deals are also available).

The Manning Valley: Taree and around

TAREE, on the Pacific Highway north of Forster–Tuncurry, is a quiet riverside town and the main centre of the fertile, scenic Manning Valley, especially good as a base for some gentle exploration of the hills, forests and beaches. The very helpful **Manning Valley Visitor Information Centre**, on the old Pacific Highway in Taree North (daily 9am–5pm; ⓣ02/6592 5444 or 1800 182 733, ⓦwww.manningvalley.info), has detailed leaflets describing forest drives, most of which lead up to the high plateau where waterfalls abound. Taree's main attraction, **river cruises**, are organized by Manning Valley River Cruises (ⓣ02/6553 2683, ⓦwww.manningrivercruises.com.au; 3–4hr; $30–40). There's the usual abundance of **motels** along the highway, including the wheelchair-friendly *Pacific Motel*, 500m north of town (ⓣ02/6552 1977; ❸), which has air-conditioned rooms and a swimming pool, and *Rainbow Gardens Motel*, 28 Crescent Ave (ⓣ/02 6551 7311; ❸), a friendly place with big complimentary breakfasts. The budget spots are *Fotheringham's Hotel* at 236 Victoria Street (ⓣ02/6552 1153; ❷), a pleasant old pub and restaurant; and *Twilight Caravan Park*, Pacific Highway, 3km north of town (ⓣ02/6552 2857, ⓔtwilight@tsn.cc; on-site vans ❶, cabins ❷).

There are a number of worthwhile detours along the route from Taree to Port Macquarie. One of the most impressive waterfalls on the whole coast is the 160-metre-high **Ellenborough Falls**, about an hour's drive northwest of Taree beyond Wingham on the Bulga Forest Drive – unsealed for much of the way. From the main Pacific Highway at Moorland, a road turns off to the small **Crowdy Bay National Park**, situated between Crowdy Head and the lofty Diamond Head, whose landscape includes heathlands, swamp, lagoons, woodlands, forests and sand dunes, all with prolific birdlife. Back on the Pacific Highway, there's a convenient tourist office fuelling drivers with free tea and coffee at **Kew**, between Taree and Port Macquarie; turn right at the *Kew Hotel* for the more interesting route that hugs the coast.

Port Macquarie

PORT MACQUARIE, a tangle of creeks, sandbars and ocean at the mouth of the Hastings River, was established in 1821 as a place of secondary punishment for convicts who had committed offences after arrival in New South Wales, as well as for hardened criminals from Britain. By the late 1820s, however, the spread of population meant that this was no longer an isolated outpost, so the penal settlement was closed and the area opened up to free settlers. As with many other northern coastal ports, however, the **harbour** was unreliable and its approaches difficult, so for more than a century the town failed to live up to its early commercial promise.

Prosperity finally came only with the tourism boom, which began in the early 1970s and shows no signs of abating; Port Macquarie is now one of the fastest-growing towns on the north coast of New South Wales, particularly popular with older people from the southern cities keen to spend their retirement years in a sunny place with what meteorologists have declared "Australia's best year-round climate". Long, sandy beaches start right in town and extend far along the coast, while the hinterland is dotted with forests and mountains. The town itself offers amusement parks, mini-zoos, nature parks, cruises on the Hastings River and connecting waterways, horse riding and, above all, water sports and fishing.

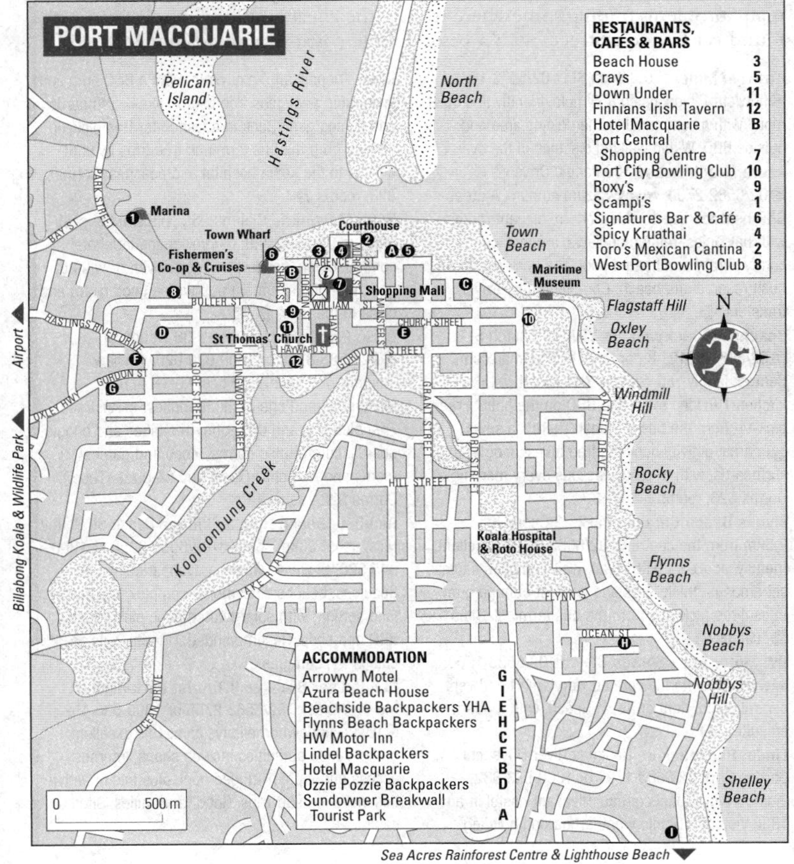

Arrival and information

Port Macquarie is well served by transport from Sydney, Tamworth (see p.380) and Brisbane, although not all **buses** make the detour from the Pacific Highway, so check carefully. Buses drop you off outside the tourist information office. Countrylink **trains** stop in Wauchope, 22km west, from where there's a connecting bus service (3 daily; ⓣ13 22 32). You can also **fly** to Port Macquarie from Sydney with Qantas (ⓣ13 13 13); the airport is about 6km west of town.

Horton Street is the main downtown street, running north to the Hastings River. The helpful **tourist information office** (Mon–Fri 8.30am–5pm, Sat & Sun 9am–4pm; ⓣ02/6681 8000 or 1300 303 155, ⓦwww.portmacquarieinfo.com.au), on the corner of Hay and Clarence streets, can book rooms and activities. The town's attractions and beaches are far flung, and transport isn't the best. You can **get around** town on Busways (ⓣ02/6583 2499, ⓦwww.busways.com.au), which also serves the Camden Haven area (#334), Bonny Hills, Lauriton and Wauchope (#335), Kempsey (#340). Otherwise, the best option is **cycling** (see p.312).

Accommodation

With sixty motels and holiday apartments in town, you're not going to have many problems finding somewhere to stay; the cheaper, older motels are mostly found on Gordon Street, with a basic double costing from around $60.

Arrowyn Motel 170 Gordon St ⓣ02/6583 1633, ⓔhowlettc@bigpond.com. Simple, friendly and quiet motel with a communal kitchen/dining area and outside BBQ. Within walking distance of the river. ❹

Azura Beach House 109 Pacific Drive ⓣ & ⓕ02/6582 2700, ⓦwww.azura.com.au. A great B&B near the beach with modern, elegant rooms with balconies, rainforest views, a guest lounge, comfy library and heated pool. The deck overlooks bush reserve and beach. Complimentary travel transfers. ❹

Beachside Backpackers YHA 40 Church St ⓣ02/6583 5512, ⓔportmaqyha@hotmail.com. Central, family-run, friendly YHA hostel, with kitchen/TV/video room and BBQ on the patio. Free pick-up from the bus terminal. There's a small gym area, activity booking, free bikes, boogie- and surfboards, with free surf lessons every morning. Dorms $23, rooms ❸

Flynns Beach Caravan Park 22 Ocean St, 2.5km from the centre ⓣ02/6583 5754. Excellent, friendly, eco-park with clean, well-equipped cabins set amongst thick ferns and a forest of huge gum trees. Free pick-ups from the bus terminal. Sites ❶, cabins ❸

HW Motor Inn 1 Stewart Steet ⓣ02/6583 1200, ⓦwww.hwmotorinn.com.au. Very smart and very central place, right on Town Beach, with modern en suites. ❺

Lindel Backpackers Hastings River Drive, cnr Gordon St ⓣ02/6583 1791 or 1800 688 882, ⓔlindel@midcoast.com.au. Pleasant hostel in an 1888 Victorian Gothic weatherboarded building. Clean, friendly and family-run, with a BBQ area and swimming pool, plus free use of bikes, surfboards and fishing gear. Book in advance for free pick-up service from the bus terminal; free trips by shuttle-bus to the koala hospital and beaches. Dorms $23, rooms ❷

Hotel Macquarie Clarence St, opposite the post office ⓣ02/6580 788, ⓔinfo@macquariehotel.com.au. Clean, good-value rooms with or without bath, in a huge, modern pub with a good bistro and close to the river. ❷–❸

Ozzie Pozzie Backpackers 36 Waugh St ⓣ02/6583 8133 or 1800 620 020, ⓦwww.nomadsworld.com. The best hostel in Port Macquarie, and one of the friendliest in Australia. Free pick-ups and drop-offs, free bikes and boogie-boards, comfortable dorms, video and games rooms and free chilli (Tues) and $6 pizza (Thurs). Dorms $22, rooms ❷

Rainbow Beach Holiday Village Beach St, Bonny Hills, about 23km south ⓣ02/6585 5655 or 1800 045 520, ⓦwww.sydneycaravanparks.com.au. Spacious, beachside camping complex in a bush-land setting, with solar-heated pool, playground, BBQ and shop. Recommended. On-site vans ❷, cabins ❸, cottages ❹

Sundowner Breakwall Tourist Park Right on the riverfront ⓣ02/6583 2755 or 1800 636 452, ⓦwww.sundownerholidays.com. This excellent park's varied amenities include shops, Internet access and a palm-fringed pool, plus lots of activities including surf trips. Good for families. Sites ❶, cabins ❷

The Town and around

Port Macquarie has a history of destroying reminders of its past, though a few buildings survive (you can get a historic walk leaflet at the visitor centre). The few surviving remnants include **St Thomas' Church** (1824–28; tours Mon–Fri 9.30am to noon, $1) on Hay Street and the **courthouse** on Clarence Street (Mon–Fri 10am–3.30pm; $2), built in 1869. The **Historical Museum**, opposite the courthouse (Mon–Sat 9.30am–4.30pm; $5), has an extensive and well-presented collection of documents and memorabilia dealing with the history of the Hastings River area; while the **Maritime Museum**, 6 William Street (daily 10am–4pm; $4), offers a history of the early navigators through artefacts, nautical paintings and model ships. The 1890s **Pilots Boatshed Museum** (Mon–Sat 10am–4pm; $1) at Town Wharf also has a small collection covering the history of maritime and river wrecks.

Several **river cruises** leave from the **Fishermen's Co-op** at the beach end of Clarence Street (see "Listings", p.312). The river foreshore provides a pleasant place for a peaceful sunset stroll and you can watch the pelican colony begging for tiddlers from the local anglers. Also in a maritime vein, you can step aboard the **Alma Doepel** (daily 10am–4pm; $3), a wonderfully restored timber sailing ship docked at Town Wharf. Perhaps the best of the local attractions, however, is the **Kooloonbung Creek Nature Reserve**, a large bushland reserve remarkably close to the town centre. From the entrance at the corner of Horton and Gordon streets, you step onto trails among casuarinas, mangroves and eucalypts, or sweat through a small patch of rainforest – it's amazingly easy to believe that you're lost in the wilderness of the bush, rather than minutes from the main road.

On the ocean-facing side of town are Port Macquarie's three flagged and patrolled **beaches**: Town Beach, Flynns and Lighthouse. The **Sea Acres Rainforest Centre** (daily 9am–4.30pm, free guided walks at regular intervals; $6), south of the town on Pacific Drive, is impressive, conveying an urgent environmental message about the fast-disappearing coastal rainforest of New South Wales. The centre comprises three different types of rainforest, which can be inspected at close quarters from a boardwalk. Take one of the fascinating and guided tours, unless you *really* know your monocotyledons from your dicotyledons.

Back towards the town centre, on Lord Street, **Roto House** is a fine nineteenth-century homestead, with Australia's oldest **koala hospital** in its grounds (both open Mon–Sat 9am–4pm, Sun 9am–1pm; $1; check feeding times on ⓣ02/6584 2180). Run and financed by volunteers, the hospital takes in sick koalas, as well as the inevitable road casualties. For yet more cuddly animals, the **Billabong Koala & Wildlife Park**, 61 Billabong Drive (daily 9am–5pm; $9.50), has emu chicks, cute kangaroos that can be hand-fed and koalas that can be patted and hugged.

There are also a few **wineries** in the area: Cassegrain Winery, on the Hastings River on Fernbank Creek Road off the Pacific Highway south of town (daily 9am–5pm; ⓣ02/6583 7777), has a particularly pleasant restaurant on a verandah overlooking the vineyards.

Eating, drinking and nightlife

There are plenty of places to **eat** in town; not surprisingly, seafood and fish predominate and the local oysters really must be tried. *Macquarie Seafoods*, centrally located on the corner of Clarence and Short streets, is the best place for takeaway fish and chips. You can also buy fresh fish and seafood from the **Fishermen's Co-op** at the end of Clarence Street in the Town Wharf area and cook it yourself.

Opposite the tourist information office, the streets leading down to the river offer several good **drinking** spots, notably the *Beach House*, right on the riverfront (which also has good and affordable seafood and pizzas). Of the town's **nightclubs**, *Down Under*, on Short Street next to Coles supermarket, is a perennial favourite – a tiny underground place for the over-30s. Alternatively, try the similar but tackier *Roxy's* in the Galleria Building on Williams Street.

Crays 74 Clarence St. Pricey waterfront restaurant offering fine local catch and shell fish; decent lunchtime deals.
Finnians Irish Tavern 97 Gordon St. Decent pub grub including things like nachos and steaks ($7–10), plus live music at weekends.
Macquarie Hotel Clarence St, opposite the post office. Large and inexpensive bistro meals, including fish and the ever-present pub steak.
Port Central Shopping Centre Clarence St, behind the tourist information office. The good-value food court on the second floor of this shopping centre has various choices including fresh, healthy fare from the *Pure and Natural Food Co.* and excellent coffee and cakes at *The Coffee Club* – both open daily.
Port City Bowling Club Corner of Owen and Church Sts ⓣ02/6583 1133. The giant daily lunchtime and evening buffet ($14–20) here is one of the best budget feeds in town.
Scampi's At the marina on Park St, just west of the town centre ⓣ02/6583 7200. One of the most enjoyable of the town's seafood restaurants. BYO. Dinner nightly, plus lunch in summer.
Signatures Bar & Café Bottom of Clarence St, close to Town Wharf. Good-value seafood platters, plus steaks and pizzas.
Spicy Kruathai Corner of Clarence and Hay Sts ⓣ02/6583 9043. Reasonably priced Thai seafood and stir-fries.
Toro's Mexican Cantina 22 Murray St. Tasty build-your-own burritos and tacos. Open evenings only.
West Port Bowling Club Buller St ⓣ02/6583 1499. Good two-course meals ($11) for those with large appetites and small wallets. Daily noon–8pm.

Listings

Bike rental Cycle De Sport ⓣ02/6584 4177, 2 Murray St, rents out bikes ($10 for 1hr, $15 for 2hr, $20 for 3hr or $30 per day).
Boat rental Settlement Point Boatshed ⓣ02/6563 6300, next to the Settlement Point Ferry, 2km north of the CBD on the Hastings River, rents out canoes ($6 per hr) and boats ($20 for 2hr or $60 per day).
Camel safaris Port Macquarie Camel Safaris ⓣ02/6583 7650, ⓔpmqcamels@telstra.easymail.com. Offers rides of up to an hour from Lighthouse Beach (daily except Mon & Thurs).
Car rental Hertz, Gordon St ⓣ02/6583 6599; Thrifty, corner of Horton and Hayward Sts ⓣ02/6584 2122.
Cruises *Port Venture* cruises up the Hastings River ($25–35; ⓣ02/6583 3058) and the Waterbus Everglade Tours ($25–59; ⓣ02/6583 8483, ⓦwww.cruiseadventures.com.au) offer trips through the everglades and a dolphin-spotting cruise in their glass-sided boats.
Hospital Port Macquarie Hospital, Wright's Rd ⓣ02/6581 2000.
Internet access Free at the library on Gordon St.
Police ⓣ02/6583 0199.
Post office At the Palm Court shopping centre, corner of William and Short Sts.
Surfing The Paradise Surf Centre at 228 Horton St ⓣ02/6583 6062 sells surfboards and gear. You can learn to surf with the Port Macquarie Surf School ⓣ02/6585 5453, ⓦwww.portmacquariesurfschool.com.au.
Taxis There's a taxi rank on Horton St. Alternatively call Port Macquarie Taxicabs ⓣ02/6581 0081; Wauchope Radio Taxicabs ⓣ02/6585 2100.
Water sports Several companies operate parasailing, fishing charters and jet-ski tours on the river and ocean, including Port Water Sports (ⓣ0412 234 509) and Sea Quest (ⓣ02/6583 3463).

Heading inland: Wauchope

Surrounded by forest 22km west of Port Macquarie lies the pretty little village of **WAUCHOPE** (pronounced "war-hope"), whose wide and sedate high street retains a classic pioneer's feel, with old painted signs and large stately buildings. Through working exhibits, the open-air museum of **Timbertown**,

3km from the village on the Oxley Highway (daily 9.30am–3.30pm; donation), depicts life as it must have been in the isolated timber settlements 150 years ago. Timber logs are pulled over muddy roads to saw-pits, where they are cut and shaped; the bakery bakes and sells bread fresh from the oven; and many other aspects of Victorian life are recreated. There's also a steamtrain ($7), paddleboat ($6) and horse-drawn carriage ($4). North of Wauchope, the **Wilson River Rainforest Reserve**'s picnic grounds are a popular destination for day-trippers from Port Macquarie. Another feature of Wauchope is the large separatist lesbian community that lives in the vicinity – something strangely absent from the tourist literature.

Basic pub **accommodation** and counter meals can be had at the *Hastings Hotel*, on the corner of High and Cameron streets (Ⓣ02/6585 2003; ❶), and there are slightly fancier rooms at the *Wauchope Motel*, 84 High Street (Ⓣ02/6585 1933, Ⓕ6586 1366; ❸). You can get to Wauchope daily with Busways (Ⓣ02/6583 2499).

The coast north to Nambucca Heads

The coastline between Port Macquarie and Nambucca Heads, 115km north, has some magical spots. **KEMPSEY**, though not one of them, is an important service town on the Macleay River, 49km from Port Macquarie. It is home to a prominent Aboriginal population, the **Dunghutti** people. Explorer John Oxley entered the Macleay River area in 1818, and the first white settlers moved in five years later, leading to prolonged conflicts with the Dunghutti until the 1860s, when Aboriginal reserves were established. The Dunghutti's ability to demonstrate continuous links with their land led in 1996 to a successful claim for native title for a portion of land at **CRESCENT HEAD**, 21km southeast from Kempsey along a good sealed road, although they held title only temporarily and have since received compensation for losing their native title rights to property developers in the area. The agreement was the first recognition of native title by an Australian government on the mainland and the first time that an Australian government negotiated an agreement with indigenous people to acquire their land.

There are a couple of wonderful waterfront **campsites** here: *Beachside Crescent Head Holiday Park* (Ⓣ02/6566 0261), which also has some very pleasant verandah-fronted wooden chalets (❸); and *Delicate Nobby Camping Ground* on point Plomer Rd (Ⓣ02/6566 0144, sites ❶, cabins ❸), set in extensive and secluded bushland, ten minutes' drive from the township.

Meandering back and then away from the Pacific Highway, you come to the coastal **Hat Head National Park** and the small town of **SOUTH WEST ROCKS**, perched on a picturesque headland. There's a plush timber luxury bungalow here, *Grass Trees Escape* (Ⓣ/02 9907 1440, Ⓦwww.grasstreesescape.com; ❺), and a good caravan park, the *Hat Head Holiday Park* (Ⓣ02/6567 7555; sites ❶, cabins ❸).

Three kilometres east on **Trial Bay**, the **Arakoon State Recreation Area** has as its centrepiece **Trial Bay Gaol** (daily 9am–4.15pm; $4). Classified as a public works prison in which prisoners could learn a trade, the gaol was considered progressive when it was established in 1886. Built from local granite, it's an impressive construction – the massive outer walls surround an extensive complex of buildings and are supported by high buttresses with four watchtowers. The prison was closed in 1903, but reopened during World War I when it was used as an internment camp for over five hundred prisoners of war, including Buddhist monks from Ceylon.

Further north, back on the Princes Highway and just before you reach the turn-off for Nambucca Heads, you'll pick up signs for **TAYLORS ARM**, famous for its pub, *The Pub with no Beer* (Ⓣ02/6564 2100, Ⓦwww.pubwithnobeer.com.au), of the popular Australian folk song. The pub still looks as it did when Slim Dusty and Gordon Parsons penned the song, though it now promises always to have the coldest and freshest beers on tap. It also serves up very good lunches and dinners at weekends and has rooms available (❹). Nearby is the wonderful *Bakers Creek Station* (Ⓣ02/6564 2165, Ⓦwww.bcstation.com.au; bunkhouses ❶, cabin tents ❷, cabins ❻), which has luxury cabins, bunkhouses and camping in its massive grounds. As well as accommodation, the station offers horse riding, canoeing and fishing as well as tennis and bushwalking; it also has its own restaurant, the *Billabong*, overlooking a sizeable lake.

Nambucca Heads and around

About 100km north of Wauchope on the Pacific Highway is the laid-back holiday town of **NAMBUCCA HEADS**. From the headlands near the town centre there are fantastic views of the mouth of Nambucca River, and of the seemingly endless sweep of sandy beaches that stretch both north and south from here. There's fishing, windsurfing and canoeing available amidst the gentler waters at the river mouth, and some excellent surf on the ocean beaches. Whales can be sighted from Scotts Head, a popular surfing spot, during their southern migration (July–Oct).

Nambucca Heads is on the main Sydney–Brisbane bus and train routes. Busways (Ⓣ02/6583 2499) runs between here and Macksville, Coffs Harbour and Bellingen daily. All Countrylink services along the north coast call at Nambucca Heads. Arriving **by train** you'll alight on Railway Road, about 3km north of the centre. The **visitor information centre** and **bus stop** is just off the Pacific Highway on Riverside Drive, at the southern entrance to town (daily 9am–5pm; Ⓣ02/6568 6954, Ⓦwww.nambuccatourism.com). You can book **accommodation** here; motels and apartments are generally better value here than in Port Macquarie and Coffs Harbour. The best place to stay is *Beilby's Beach House* at 1 Ocean Street (Ⓣ02/6568 6466, Ⓦwww.beilbys.com.au; ❸), a modern but homely B&B with a pool, good-value rooms and a great location overlooking the dramatic coastline, just a ten-minute walk from the shops. Alternatively, try the exceptionally well-located *White Albatross Holiday Resort* (Ⓣ02/6568 6468, Ⓦwww.whitealbatross.com.au; ❺); it's right on the lagoon and by the ocean beach, and also has a tennis court, café and children's playground. Next door, *The V-Wall Tavern* (Ⓣ02/6568 6394) serves beer, lunch and dinner overlooking the rivermouth and beach. *Byll's Café* (weekdays till 5pm, Sat till late; BYO) at the top of Wellington Drive serves breakfast, afternoon tea, baguettes, burgers and salads as well as more substantial meals. *Nirvana Sawadee* (Ⓣ02/6568 9622), opposite the tourist office, offers traditional Thai food making good use of fresh local seafood. Ten kilometres south of town in Macksville is the very popular *Bridge Café* – a 1950s-style milk bar offering burgers, sandwiches and home-made chocolates.

Heading inland from Nambucca, it's about half an hour's drive to the picturesque former timber town of **BOWRAVILLE**, where you can rest up in the old pub, now renovated to its former glory, and browse in a few arts-and-crafts shops and the jumble of Gleeson's Second Hand Store. *The Phoenix Gallery & Tea Rooms* is a pleasant refreshment stop. From here, you can travel on unsealed forest roads to the small, alternative town of **Bellingen** (see p.315), although it's more easily reached on the sealed road that turns off the Pacific Highway after Urunga.

The Bellinger River and around

URUNGA, 20km north from Nambucca Heads, is a pleasant beachside spot where the Bellinger and Kalang rivers meet the sea. From here you can walk right along the beach to nearby **MYLESTOM** (the turn-off is 7km further down the highway), an undeveloped backwater which occupies a stunningly beautiful spot on the wide Bellinger River. You can take advantage of its riverside setting at the **Alma Doepel Reserve**'s sheltered, sandy river beach, which has changing rooms and showers. Two minutes' walk to the east is a gorgeous sweep of surf beach – often gloriously deserted. You can walk along the beach to **Bundagen**, an alternative, environmentally friendly community that welcomes visitors and hosts frequent music and spoken-word evenings.

A great **place to stay** in Mylestom is the *North Beach Caravan Park* on Beach Parade (Ⓣ02/6655 4250; sites ❶, cabins ❷). Other **facilities** in Mylestom are limited: a post office with pies, supplies and EFTPOS, and two good, inexpensive restaurants, Chinese and Italian, at the North Beach Bowling Club (Ⓣ02/6655 4293).

Bellingen

Just after Urunga, the turn-off west heads through the verdant Bellinger River valley for 12km to **BELLINGEN** (Ⓦwww.bellingen.com), one of the prettiest and most characterful towns in New South Wales, with a strong alternative bent. It's full of arts-and-crafts, cafés and thriving small businesses. Just before town, the **Old Butter Factory**, a renovated dairy, holds a complex of several craft shops where you can check out the work of local artisans – the opal-jewellers are a fine sight. You can get a massage and float-tank session (Ⓣ0413 104 800; $65 for a 2hr combo pamper) if you call ahead. Bellingen also has an interesting monthly **market** (third Saturday of the month 7am–2pm) in Bellingen Park, with buskers, crafts and organic food stalls. There's more shopping at the **Hammond and Wheatley Emporium** on Hyde Street, a glorious old restored department store with an Aladdin's cave of locally produced jewellery, artefacts and artworks. Each year Bellingen hosts a lively **jazz festival** (Ⓣ02/6655 9345, Ⓦwww.midcoast.com.au/~belljazz) over the third weekend in August, followed by the three-day Global Festival of world music over the October long weekend. For a cooling break from crafts and culture, you can swim in the waterholes of the Bellinger and Never Never rivers.

Practicalities

The **Visitor Information Centre** (daily 9am–4pm, Sept–Feb until 5pm; Ⓣ02/6655 1522) is at the Old Butter Factory; otherwise, Traveland on Hyde Street (Ⓣ02/6655 2055) has details of rafting, bushwalking and other tours, and acts as an agent for Countrylink. Busways (Ⓣ02/6583 2499) operates a **bus** service to Coffs Harbour at 7.50am, 9.50am and 3pm.

The creekfront *Bellingen YHA Backpackers*, 2 Short Street (Ⓣ02/6655 1116, Ⓦwww.yha.com.au; dorms $26, rooms ❸), is perhaps the most pleasant YHA in Australia – a beautiful two-storey timber house with a huge balcony facing a rainforest island full of jacaranda trees that come alive at dusk with fruit bats; you can even sleep outdoors under a gazebo or lounge in the treehouse. Free pick-ups from Urunga train/bus station are available and they also have bikes for rent ($5 daily), tubing ($10), day/night canoe trips ($35), Internet access, trips to the Dorrigo rainforest ($25) and the alternative, mostly nudist, community on Bundagen Beach. Otherwise, there's the gay-friendly *Rivendell Bed and Breakfast*, centrally located at 12 Hyde Street (Ⓣ & Ⓕ02/6655 0060,

Ⓦwww.midcoast.com.au/~rivendell; ❹), where there's a pool. The *Koompartoo Retreat* (Ⓣ & Ⓕ02/6655 2326; ❺), at the corner of Rawson and Dudley streets at the southern edge of town, is a quieter option, with superb hardwood chalets, each with its own balcony, tucked away amongst five acres of rainforest rich in birdlife.

The town is full of great **cafés**. *Lodge 241*, an art gallery-cum-café on Short Street serves good coffee and delicious, wholesome lunches. The light and airy *Carriageway Café*, 75 Hyde Street (Mon 10am–4pm, Wed–Sun 10am–9pm, closed Tues), serves affordable mains and gourmet sandwiches; there's an art gallery upstairs. The spacious *Cool Creek Café* (open Mon & Thurs–Sun for dinner, plus Sat lunch) at 5 Church Street has a folky ambience and some veggie mains, as well as live music and poetry readings. *The Good Food Shop* next door has local wines, while next door to that is the early-opening *Swiss Patisserie & Bakery*. Two doors down, the *Boiling Billy* serves the best coffee in town. Finally, there's *McNally House* on Hyde Street (Ⓣ02/6655 0344; Tues–Sat dinner only), a BYO restaurant in a cute cottage, with a distinctly European menu.

The town has only one **pub**: the animated, heritage-listed *Federal Hotel* on Hyde Street, with live music (usually free) on Fridays and the third Saturday of each month. If you're very lucky, you might catch a rare piano performance by David Helfgott (whose life was dramatised in the 1996 film, *Shine*) somewhere in town.

Inland to Dorrigo

The Dorrigo road from Bellingen passes through farmland before winding steeply through the **Dorrigo National Park**, a startlingly beautiful rainforest remnant of an area that was once similarly heavily forested; the lure of the valuable Australian cedar – "red gold" – left most of the plateau cleared by the 1920s. One kilometre east of Dorrigo town, the **Dorrigo Rainforest Centre** (daily 9am–4.30pm) has a detailed interpretive display on rainforest plants and animals. The *Canopy Café* here has wonderful views and serves light lunches until 2.30pm and afternoon teas until 4pm. Starting at the visitor centre, the **Skywalk** is easily the most spectacular of the walks through the park and also the least strenuous; a wooden walkway extends high over the rainforest canopy, enabling you to look down on the forest and out over the surrounding landscape and distant hills. The walkway is open until 10pm so visitors can observe the forest's nocturnal creatures. Other trails lead to some of the park's best features, including a number of beautiful waterfalls; try the Wonga Walk (6.6km) through the rainforest past two waterfalls, or the Rosewood creek track (5.5km).

DORRIGO itself is a small country town with artistic leanings and an old-fashioned air typified by the kitsch 1950s Formica fittings of *Plateau Café* on Hickory Street, which serves scones and pots of tea. The *RSL* (Ⓣ02/6657 2924) just up the road is a good spot for lunch. There's plenty of **accommodation** here: the wide-verandahed *Hotel Dorrigo* (Ⓣ02/6657 2016; ❷) has basic hotel and fancier motel-style rooms (❸), some of them en-suite. For budget accommodation head to the homely, friendly *Dorrigo Backpackers*, 14 Bielsdown Street (Ⓣ02/6657 2431; dorms $23, doubles ❷); *Dangar Falls Lodge* near the magnificent Dangar waterfall at 175 Coramba Road (Ⓣ02/6657 1131) is a good **camping** option, and also has some double rooms (❸). There are also plenty of **farmstays** in the area; full details are available from the **tourist information service** at 36 Hickory Street (daily 10am–4pm; Ⓣ02/6657 2486).

The only way to get to Dorrigo on **public transport** is with Keans Bus Service (Ⓣ02/6543 1322), which runs via Bellingen. The bus follows the road west from Dorrigo cutting cross-country, past several more national parks, towards Armidale (see p.383).

Coffs Harbour and around

Back on the main coastal highway, **COFFS HARBOUR** – or "Coffs" – is set at a point where the mountains of the Great Dividing Range fall almost directly into the South Pacific Ocean, and also boasts glorious expanses of white-sand **beach** which stretch north from the town centre. The **Solitary Islands** offshore are good for diving, with fringing coral reefs and a plethora of fish. From June to November, you can also see migrating whales.

Arrival and information

All long-distance buses stop at the **bus station** on the corner of Maclean Street and the Pacific Highway; the **train** station (☎13 22 32) is by the harbour. You can fly to Coffs with Qantas (☎13 13 13); the **airport** is about

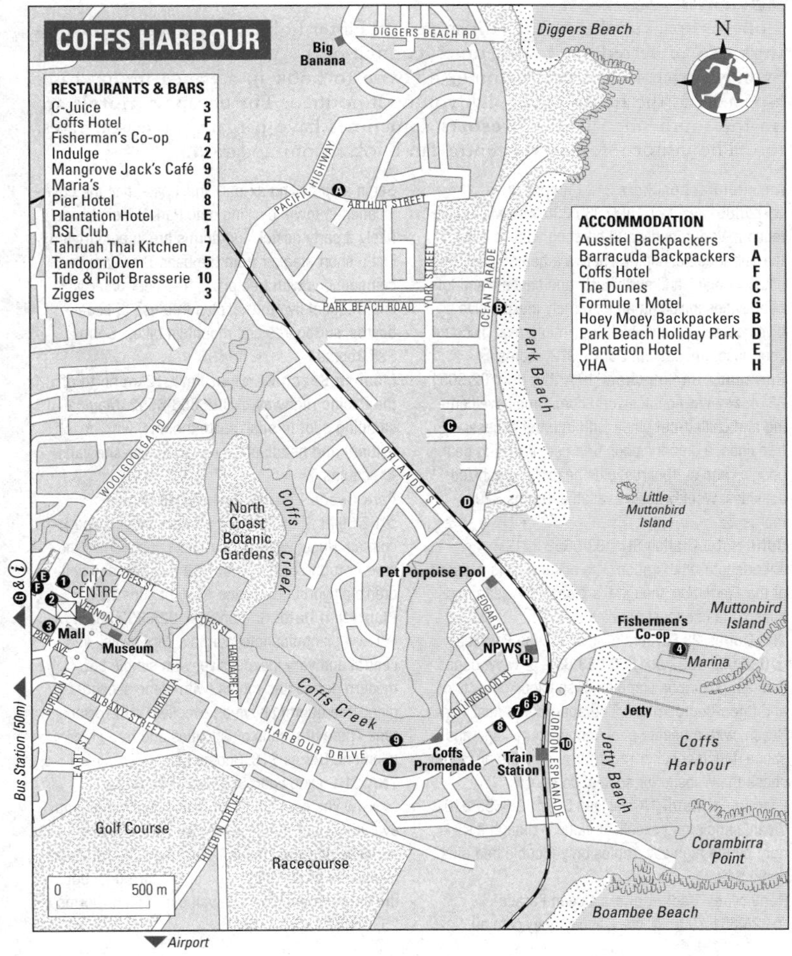

5km south of town; you can rent a car at one of the airport desks, take a taxi into town (about $10) or, if you've booked accommodation, arrange to be picked up. Coffs is rather spread out, and the half-hourly **bus** (run by Busways ⓣ02/6583 2499; timetables from the visitor information centre) which runs between the town centre, Coffs Jetty and Park Beach is barely adequate, so you may find yourself having to take taxis. Alternatively, you could rent a bike or car – see p.320.

The City Centre Mall, right in the centre off Grafton Street (as the Pacific Highway is called in town), is very much the heart of Coffs and most facilities and much of the accommodation are nearby. The **visitor information centre** (daily 9am–5pm; ⓣ02/6652 1522 or 1300 369 070, ⓦwww.coffscoast.com.au) is a few minutes' walk south of here. The NPWS has an office down at the marina (ⓣ02/6651 0900), providing information on the marine reserve and ranger tours of Muttonbird Island.

Accommodation

Coffs gets packed during the Christmas and Easter holidays, and weekly **bookings** are preferred (and sometimes compulsory). As trains and buses from Sydney arrive in the late evening, it's wise to book in advance in any case, especially as the **hostels** will pick you up if notified. The cheapest **motels** are on the south side of town; **resorts** sometimes have bargain off-season rates, too. The visitor information centre can book accommodation.

Aussitel Backpackers 312 Harbour Drive ⓣ02/6651 1871 or 1800 330 335, ⓦwww.aussietel.com. Very friendly and bursting with "all down the pub together" spirit. There's a heated pool, free bikes, boogie- and surfboards and canoes, and lots of activities including an extremely inexpensive dive course (during which they might also discount your accommodation). Dorms $22, rooms ❷

Barracuda Backpackers 19 Arthur St ⓣ02/6651 3514, ⓦwww.nomadsworld.com. Small, welcoming and chilled-out place with Internet access, free linen, a laundry, pool, free use of fishing gear, boogie- and surfboards, plus heaps of organized activities. Weekly deals available. Dorms $20, rooms ❷

Coffs Hotel Grafton St ⓣ02/6652 3817, ⓔcoffshotel@hot.net.au. The ocker Aussie cousin of the *Plantation*, though it's pleasantly clean and boasts the cheapest doubles in town.

The Dunes 28 Fitzgerald St, off Ocean Parade ⓣ02/6652 4522 or 1800 023 851, ⓦwww.dunes.com.au. Luxurious complex of spacious one-, two- and three-bedroom serviced apartments near Park Beach, with a heated pool, tennis courts, spa and sauna. Much cheaper rates for two nights or more; check the Website for special deals. ❹

Formule 1 Motel 1A Maclean St ⓣ02/6650 9101. Clean, simple and excellent value – though it's right by the highway. Triples only (double bed plus bunk) $49.

Hoey Moey Backpackers Ocean Parade ⓣ02/6651 7966, ⓔhoey@hoeymoey.com.au. Set in a sprawling ex-pub, this hostel has the best location in town, backing onto Park Beach. It's definitely a party hostel, and dorms are in a courtyard just a short stagger from the beer. There are pool competitions with free pizza, free beer on arrival and frequent live music, plus free use of boogie-boards, surfboards and mountain bikes. Dorms $25, rooms ❷

Moonee Beach Caravan Park 12km north off the Pacific Highway ⓣ02/6653 6552. Magical camping spot in bush surroundings, with beach, estuary and headlands to explore. On-site vans ❷, cabins ❸

Park Beach Holiday Park Ocean Parade ⓣ02/6648 4888, ⓦwww.parkbeachholidaypark.com.au. Huge, well-run campsite, just across the road from the beach, with BBQ facilities and children's playground. Cabins ❸, tent sites ❶

Plantation Hotel Grafton St ⓣ02/6652 3855, ⓦwww.plantationhotel.com.au. Very swish, very central and very inexpensive, with simple but modern dorms and rooms (with some second-night-free offers) above an excellent pub-restaurant. There are loads of activities and free entertainment. Dorms $18, Rooms ❷

YHA 51 Collingwood St ⓣ02/6652 6462, ⓦwww.yha.com.au. Giant space-age hostel with everything but atmosphere. The facilities are faultless and the staff will help sign you up for an avalanche of activities. The dorms are fine, but the en-suite doubles are well overpriced. Dorms 25, Doubles ❸

The Town

The small **Museum**, at 191A Harbour Drive (Mon–Fri & Sun 10am–4pm; $3), has a collection of relics and tools owned by early pioneers and cedar-cutters, as well as local Aboriginal artefacts of the **Gumbaingirr** people, whose territories extended from the Nambucca River north to the Clarence River, and inland to the foothills of the Great Dividing Range. From the museum, it's only a short distance to the magnificent **North Coast Botanic Gardens** (daily 9am–5pm), entered from Hardacre Street. These delightfully tranquil subtropical gardens are located on a triangle of land surrounded on two sides by **Coffs Creek** and feature a mangrove boardwalk and a slice of rainforest; guided walks are available. A charming **creek walk** and **cycle trail** begin just off Coffs Street in the town centre and head 5.4km to Muttonbird Island; the final thirty minutes are along the northern breakwater – detailed maps are available from the visitor information centre. **Coffs Promenade**, along the creek walk, off the High Street at the Coffs Jetty end, hosts crafts and speciality shops as well as an ice-cream parlour, a café and restaurant, the last two with outdoor tables overlooking the tranquil, tree-lined creek. You can rent bikes here (see p.320), as well as canoes ($15 per hr, $30 per half-day).

The **Fishermen's Co-op**, on the northern breakwater of the harbour, sells fresh fish; the wharf here is also the departure point for most cruises from Coffs (see p.320). Beyond the boat-filled marina is **Muttonbird Island Nature Reserve**, high enough to offer fantastic views of Coffs Harbour and the southern and northern beaches. There's plenty of birdlife too, with an interpretive walk describing the lifestyle of the migratory birds that come here to nest in summer. The best time to come is at sunset, when you can watch the muttonbirds return to their nests. You can sometimes see dolphins frolicking close to the island, but if you want to see domesticated dolphins and seals being put through their paces, visit the misleadingly named **Pet Porpoise Pool**, between Coffs Jetty and Park Beach (performances at 10.30am & 2.15pm; 1hr 30min; $22), where you can kiss a seal or feed a penguin. There's also a small aquarium with sharks.

Local banana plantations are evidence of Coffs subtropical climate, and the cultural influence of nearby Queensland becomes apparent, too, in tourist attractions such as the **Big Banana** (daily 9am–5pm; Ⓦwww.bigbanana.com), a huge, bright-yellow concrete banana, 3km north of Coffs on the Pacific Highway, advertising a "horticultural theme park". It's free to walk through the banana and look at displays dealing with early pioneer life in the district and Coffs Harbour's $70-million-a-year banana industry. There are monorail tours of the plantation (1hr 30min; $14), which show you packing sheds and hydroponics glasshouses, as well as a space station and an Aboriginal Dreamtime Cave. A newer attraction is a toboggan ride ($8), which whizzes 720m down through the steep hillside plantations. For the complete bananathon, stop in at the milk bar, which serves bananas in every conceivable way.

Eating, drinking and nightlife

C-Juice Near *Zigges*, The Mall. Good juices, smoothies, wraps and tofu.

Coffs Hotel Grafton St. The Thai–Aussie restaurant here offers pretty good fare at decent prices.

Fisherman's Co-op The Marina. Fish and chips to die for for just $8. Closes at 5.30pm.

Golden Crown 374 High St ⓣ02/6651 6787. Chinese food, with the emphasis on fish, to eat in or take away. Tues–Sat dinner only.

Mangrove Jack's Café 321 Harbour Drive (just off the road through a few shops) ⓣ02/6652 5517. Very pleasant spot with modern Australian cuisine, ice creams and a deck overlooking the river. Tues–Sat 7.30am–9.30pm, Sun & Mon 7.30am–5.30pm.

Maria's 368 High St (ⓣ02/6651 3000). Italian BYO with pasta, pizza and seafood chowders.

Pier Hotel At the ocean end of Harbour Drive, on the corner of Camperdown St. The bistro here has

good, inexpensive counter meals. Daily 7–9am, noon–2pm & 6–9pm,
Plantation Hotel Grafton St. The best-value food in town, with good meals (steak, pasta and so on) for just $6, as well as many other good choices, including Malaysian food.
Tahruah Thai Kitchen 366 High St ⓣ02/6651 5992. Tasty, mildly spicy stir-fries and coconut-flavoured dishes in a traditional family-run place.
Tandoori Oven 384 High St ⓣ02/6652 2279. Tasteful, marine-inspired decor and a menu to match, along with good-value vegetarian thalis.
Tide & Pilot Brasserie ⓣ02/6651 6888. Down at the marina, this place has some of the town's finest seafood and views.
Zigges On an arcade just off Harbour Drive, near the junction with Grafton St. Good city fodder – focaccia, large breakfasts, ice creams and decent cups of coffee.

Nightlife

Nightlife in Coffs is lively in summer, but very mainstream. There are generally **live bands** playing cover versions at some venue around town from Wednesday to Sunday, usually with free entry. The *Coffs* and *Plantation* hotels have DJs and bands several nights a week. *Indulge* (Fri & Sat) nightclub, on the corner of Grafton Street and Harbour Drive, charges about $10–15 (or free to guests at the *Plantation Hotel*). On Friday and Saturday nights the *RSL Club*, on the corner of Vernon and Grafton streets, has two live bands, free entry and very cheap drinks until 2am. The *Plantation Hotel* also puts on live music at weekends. For a contemplative drink overlooking the ocean, the verandah at the yacht club bar in the marina is hard to beat, and they've got a good stock of local wines.

Listings

Art Gallery City Gallery, on the corner of Coff and Duke Sts (ⓣ02/6648 4861; daily 10am–4pm; free) has some great photography on display.
Banks Commonwealth, 92 City Centre Mall; National, 42 City Centre Mall; Westpac, 137 Harbour Drive.
Bike rental Coffs Bike Hire, corner of Orlando and Collingwood Sts (ⓣ02/6652 5102), charges $25 a day; $40 for two days.
Buses Besides the interstate services, there's Ryan's Buses (ⓣ02/6652 3201), with services to Woolgoolga and Grafton; and Busways (ⓣ02/6583 2499), with services to Urunga, Bellingen and further afield.
Canoeing Bellingen Canoe Adventures (ⓣ02/6655 9955) organizes half- and full-day canoeing trips on the Bellinger River ($44/$88), including lunch; they also rent out canoes to those who would sooner go it alone (from $11 per hr).
Car rental Delta Europcar ⓣ02/6651 8558; Coffs Harbour Rent-a-Car ⓣ02/6652 5022; Hertz ⓣ02/6651 1899; Thrifty ⓣ02/6652 8622.
Cinema Coffs Cinema, Bray St ⓣ02/6651 6444.
Cruises Pacific Explorer ⓣ02/6652 7225, ⓦwww.pacificexplorer.com.au and Spirit of Coffs Harbour Cruises (ⓣ02/6650 0155) run whale-watching cruises from June to November, and regular cruises from December to May ($40).
Diving The Solitary Islands Marine Reserve, five islands and several islets north of Coffs, is the largest marine reserve in New South Wales; the mingling of tropical and temperate waters means that there's a huge variety of sealife (grey nurse sharks are a common sight), described in a range of excellent leaflets available from the visitor information centre or the Fisheries office at the marina. Jetty Dive Centre, 398 Harbour Drive, at the harbour (ⓣ02/6651 1611, ⓦwww.jettydive.com.au), offers dives for beginners and experienced divers costing from $115 for two dives for PADI qualified divers and from $195 for four-day PADI courses for the unqualified. All hostels arrange inexpensive snorkelling expeditions and scuba courses.
Horse riding Valery Trails, 20km southwest of Coffs, off the Pacific Highway at Bonville (ⓣ02/6653 4301, ⓔqwirk@mpx.com.au); rates include pick-up and return to Coffs. Closer to Coffs, Bushland Trails (ⓣ02/6649 4491) offers horse rides and overnight treks. Booking essential.
Hospital 345 Pacific Highway, opposite the junction with Isles Drive ⓣ02/6656 7000.
Internet access Half-hour slots are free at the library if you pre-book on ⓣ02/6648 4900.
Laundry Marina Laundrette (daily 8am–8pm) at the jetty has the best views whilst you wait for your whites.
Markets Sunday-morning markets are held at the Jetty Village Shopping Centre, at the jetty (8am–2pm), and in the Big W car park, cnr Castle and Vernon Sts (same hours).

Police 22 Moonee St ⓣ02/6652 0299.
Post office In the Palms Centre, off Harbour Drive, NSW 2450.
Sky diving Coffs City Skydivers (ⓣ02/6651 1167, ⓦwww.coffsskydivers.com.au) offers tandem dives from 10,000ft for $255 or a course (two jumps) for $630.
Surfing East Coast Surf School, based at Diggers Beach (ⓣ02/6651 5515, ⓦwww.eastcoastsurf school.com.au), is an excellent place to learn to surf in small groups. An introductory two-hour lesson costs $50 and five classes cost $180; includes surfboard and wetsuit. They also do excellent-value weekend (two-night) courses.
Taxi ⓣ13 10 08.
Tours Mountain Trails 4WD Tours (ⓣ02/6658 3333) is the main operator in town and runs half- and full-day 4WD adventures along remote tracks to banana plantations, waterfalls and the rain-forest, weekend trips to Dorrigo and mountain country, and wildlife tours at night; also has "bush tucker and Dreamtime" tours hosted by Mark Flanders, a local Aboriginal tour guide.
Travel agent Kelly Travel, cnr High and Moonee Sts (ⓣ02/6651 2747, ⓦwww.kellytravel.com.au), is a discount flight agent for Qantas and STA Travel.
White-water rafting There's rafting inland on the rainforested Nymboida river, though after a dry winter the rivers can be low. The best outfit is WOW, based a few kilometres inland at 1448 Coramba Rd, Coramba (ⓣ02/6654 4066), with trips at around $153 per day.
Wineries There are many wineries in the area – one pleasant place is Raleigh Winery, 36 Queen St, Raleigh (ⓣ02/6655 4388, ⓦwww.ralaighwines .com), half an hour's drive south of town.

Around Coffs Harbour

An hour's drive inland from Coffs, on Bushmans Range Road at Lowanna, 42km northwest, is **George's Gold Mine** (Wed–Sun 10am–3.30pm, daily during school holidays; $10), where you can take a tour of a gold mine and look at the old stamper battery that crushes the ore. There are also picnic grounds, barbecues and walking trails through the rainforest.

North of Coffs lie a string of fantastic sandy beaches. **Sapphire Beach**, 9km north, has an **environment centre** (daily 10am–5pm) with a relaxing café. **Moonee Beach Reserve**, 3km further, occupies beautiful bush surroundings with a winding creek that has safe swimming – but beware of strong currents at its mouth. The reserve has plenty of shade, picnic tables and barbecues, and there's also a caravan park here (see p.318), plus a small shop selling basic supplies, good fish and chips and hamburgers. About 8km further on, the relatively unspoilt **Emerald Beach** is popular with surfers; it's very picturesque, with a small island offshore.

At **WOOLGOOLGA**, another 10km or so north on the Pacific Highway, a gleaming white **temple** is evidence of the large Sikh population that settled here in the early 1970s. Woolgoolga is also a popular seaside holiday resort, with excellent surfing on the ocean beach, while the calmer waters of **Woolgoolga Lake** to the north offer swimming and boating opportunities. Eight kilometres north of Woolgoolga, **Corindi Beach** is the site of the **Yarrawarra Aboriginal Cultural Centre** (phone for opening hours and to book guided walks on ⓣ02/6649 2669), which provides a focus and employment for the **Gumbaingirr** people in the area. There's an arts-and-crafts shop, bush-tucker café, and a native bush-tucker medicine nursery with plants for sale. After Corindi Beach, the road turns inland towards Grafton; for more beaches, take the first turn off the Pacific Highway and follow a short road northeast for 6km to reach the coast again at **Red Rock** and the beginning of the **Yuraygir National Park** (see p.323).

Grafton and around

Between Woolgoolga and Ballina the Pacific Highway runs inland, and the unspoilt coast between the two towns consists of a series of national parks accessible by intermittent side roads. **GRAFTON**, an 83-kilometre drive along the Pacific Highway from Coffs Harbour, is a pleasant, leafy district capital on a bend of the wide **Clarence River**, which almost encircles the city and occasionally floods it. The "Big River" is the largest river system on the north coast. Northeast of Grafton, the river widens as it approaches the ocean and branches out into a network of waterways and channels. There are more than a hundred river islands, on many of which sugar cane is grown.

Grafton is a genteel, old-fashioned town with wide, tree-lined streets. The **Jacaranda Festival** (last week of Oct and first week of Nov) celebrates the town's jacaranda and flame trees, which come ablaze with purple, mauve and red blossoms in the spring, and there are many arts and sports festivals throughout the year. Out of festival time this is a quiet place, where the main attraction is cruising on the river or visiting some of the historic buildings preserved by the National Trust. **Schaeffer House**, 192 Fitzroy Street (Tues–Thurs & Sun 1–4pm; donation), has a collection of beautiful china, glassware and period furniture donated to the Trust over the years; on the same street at no. 158 is the **Grafton Regional Gallery** (Tues–Sun 10am–4pm; donation), which has some fine woodcarvings and local arts.

Practicalities

The very knowledgable staff at the **Clarence River Visitor Information Centre**, on the Pacific Highway at the corner of Spring Street, South Grafton (daily 9am–5pm; ⓣ02/6642 4677, ⓦwww.clarencetourism.com), can give you information on scenic drives, river cruises and the national parks that surround Grafton. Countrylink **train** services along the north coast stop at Grafton station, close to the river crossing in South Grafton, while **long-distance buses** stop nearby, close to the visitor information centre. The Countrylink office at the train station can provide timetables and make reservations. Busways (ⓣ02/6642 2954) runs regular hourly local buses as well as a Yamba and Iluka service. Ryans's Bus Service (ⓣ02/6654 1063) runs to Coffs Harbour.

There's some very inviting **accommodation** in Grafton, notably the *Roches Family Hotel*, 85 Victoria Street (ⓣ02/6642 2866; ❷), a very friendly 100-year-old pub offering the cheapest accommodation and the best food in town. The *Crown Hotel-Motel*, 1 Prince Street (ⓣ02/6642 4000, ⓦwww.crownhotelmotel.com; ❷), is just as old and friendly, though not quite as cheap, but with a beautiful riverfront location and nicer rooms. If you want a swimming pool, spa and all the mod-cons, check out the very welcoming and quiet *Country Comfort Fitzroy*, 27 Fitzroy Street (ⓣ02/6642 4477, ⓕ6643 1828; ❹). Quieter still is the homely *Rosary B&B*, 41 Bacon Street (ⓣ02/6642 2292, 0418 299 690; ❹), another beautiful, antique, federation house. For **camping**, head to the well-equipped *Gateway Village Holiday Park*, just north of Grafton at 598 Summerland Way (ⓣ02/6642 4225, ⓔgateway@hotkey.net.au; cabins ❹).

A good place to **eat** is *Georgie's Café* (closed Sun & Mon), at the Regional Art Gallery, but the best fare is at *Roaches Family Hotel*. Alternatively you can while away a very pleasant afternoon sitting on the balcony of the *Crown Hotel*, sampling the tasty bistro and watching the river roll by.

Around Grafton

From Grafton it's 47km northeast on the Pacific Highway, paralleling the Clarence River, to **MACLEAN**, a small delta town which proclaims its Scottish heritage with street signs in Gaelic. From the Maclean lookout on Wharf Street, 2km from the centre, there are panoramic views of the coast, bushland and river islands. While you're here, sample some of the much-feted local prawns from the Co-op. A few kilometres further north, you can turn east off the highway in the direction of the twin settlements of **YAMBA** and **ILUKA** – two very pretty holiday villages facing each other across the mouth of the river. Clarence River Ferries shuttle between the two communities (4 daily; $5; ⓣ02/6646 6423) and also cruise along the river.

In Yamba, far nicer than the many motels (❸) is the idyllic *Calypso Holiday Park*, right on the water in Harbour Street (ⓣ02/6646 8846; ❸), where there's a range of cabins and sites. *Yamba Pacific Hotel*, 1 Pilot Street (ⓣ02/6646 2466, ⓦwww.pacifichotelyamba.com.au; dorms $25, rooms ❷), right on the beach, is a pub with OK rooms and great live music (Thurs–Sun nights), as well as an excellent, inexpensive seafood restaurant overlooking the ocean. You can get to Yamba on several daily services with Busways (ⓣ02/6642 2954). This is also an outstanding place to **eat**.

A few kilometres south of Yamba is **Yuraygir National Park**, with several basic but attractive NPWS campsites (details from Grafton Visitor Information Centre) surrounded by isolated beaches and placid lakes. North of Iluka, between the town and Bundjalung National Park, the **Iluka Nature Reserve** contains a World Heritage-listed rainforest remnant, one of sixteen such areas in northern New South Wales. **Bundjalung National Park** itself has a long coastline on the Coral Sea, as well as the sheltered inland waterways of the Esk River; you can **camp** at Woody Head, (ⓣ02/6646 6134, bookings advised). Just north of Bundjalung, the town of **EVANS HEAD** has a range of accommodation and shops, plus boat rental outlets. The increasingly tropical climate begins to make its presence felt here, with sugar cane growing by the roadside.

West from Grafton, the **Gwydir Highway** takes you to Glen Innes, 160km away on the New England Plateau. En route it passes the rugged and densely forested adjoining **national parks** of Gibraltar Range and Walshpool. **Gibraltar Range** is an elevated plateau 1200m above sea level, scattered with huge granite outcrops and intersected by deep gorges, and is famous for its wildflower displays of Christmas bells and waratahs in late summer. There's a **visitors centre** on the highway at Dandahra Picnic Area and a gravel road leads from here into the park, where you'll find walking tracks, lookout points and waterfalls. **Walshpool National Park** is very remote, a wilderness park on the eastern escarpment of the New England Tableland. Its **rainforest** is worth visiting, and there are picnic facilities, walks and camping at Coombadjha Creek – reached via the Coombadjha Road off the Gwydir Highway, 88km from Grafton.

Ballina

The old port of **BALLINA**, at the mouth of the Richmond River, experienced a short-lived goldrush in the 1880s, but has few reminders of this era and is now mostly a holiday town, with some pleasant beaches and the opportunity to take river trips to Lismore (see p.334) and other destinations. Neither has it escaped the clutches of the "big things", with the **Big Prawn** marking the entrance to town on the highway from Grafton. Four kilometres north on Gallans Road, east of the Pacific Highway, the tea trees of the **Thursday Plantation** (daily 9am–5pm; free; ⓦwww.tphealth.com) produce the all-healing oil; the plantation – with a sculpture park in the grounds – makes for an interesting visit. One of the highlights of the town is the lively **market** (third Sunday of the month).

There's a cycling and walking track from the centre of town along the sea wall to the beach, a twenty-minute walk. In Las Balsas Plaza, on River Street, is the **maritime museum** (daily 9am–4pm; $1), which houses the *Atzlan*, a balsa raft which was sailed across the Pacific from Ecuador in 1973 as part of the Thor Heyerdahl-inspired Las Balsas expedition – the huge and striking raft is modelled on millennia-old technology and has a sail which some say was painted by Salvador Dali. The **tourist information centre** (Mon–Fri 9am–5pm; ⓣ02/6686 3484, ⓦwww.discoverballina.com) is in the same plaza, and can book accommodation, river cruises and other tours. **Accommodation** includes the historic *Ballina Manor*, a luxurious B&B at 25 Norton Street (ⓣ02/6681 5888, ⓦwww.ballinamanor.com.au; ❻), and the *Ballina Travellers Lodge Motel*, 36 Tamar Street (ⓣ02/6686 6737; dorms $25, rooms ❸), with a YHA hostel section; it's modern and family-run, with a swimming pool and free use of bicycles, fishing rods, boogie- and surfboards. *Shaws Bay Caravan Park*, 1 Brighton Street (ⓣ02/6686 2326; cabins ❸) backs onto the water, but if you have a car, the prime spot to pitch a tent is at *Flat Rock Tent Park* (ⓣ02/6686 4848), on the coast road 5km east of Ballina; right on the beach, this unspoilt site is for tents only and there's no electricity, so it's very peaceful – solar-heated hot showers supply a touch of comfort.

For tasty alfresco **food**, *Shellys on the Beach* at Shellys Beach has great ocean views and healthy, creative cooking; follow the bridge and sea wall 2km north of town. *Shaws Bay Hotel* has good cheap pub grub on the river, but the best feed is at *Spinnakers* in the RSL, 240 River Street, also right on the riverbank. Poshest of all is the *Ballina Manor Restaurant*. Ballina has quite a lively summer **nightlife**: the *Australian Hotel*, on the corner of Cherry and River streets, has jazz, piano music and a Saturday night disco, though backpacker types tend to gravitate towards the nightly craic at *Paddy McGintys* on River Street.

You can fly to Ballina from Sydney. By land, the town is connected by the long-distance Kirklands (ⓣ02/6622 1499) and Greyhound Australia (ⓣ13 14 99) **buses** to Brisbane via Lismore, Lennox Head and Evans Head. **Local services** include Blanch's (ⓣ02/6686 2144), to and from the airport, and to Lennox Head, Byron Bay and Mullumbimby. You can rent **bikes** from Jack Ransom Cycles, 16 Cherry Street (ⓣ & ⓕ02/6685 3485), and **cars** from Budget (ⓣ13 27 27) and Avis (ⓣ02/6681 4036); both have offices on Southern Cross Drive and at the airport.

Lennox Head

The best of the **surf beaches** are those around the small town of **LENNOX HEAD**, 11km north of Ballina, a relaxed resort with a small shopping centre, some good cafés and restaurants and a lively pub. Lennox rates among the best **surfing** spots in the world, and professionals congregate here for the big waves in May, June and July. Adding to Lennox Head's appeal is the calm, fresh water of **Lake Ainsworth** close to the beach; stained dark by the tea trees around its banks, it's a popular swimming spot for families seeking refuge from the crashing surf in the soft, practically medicinal water (it's effectively diluted tea tree oil).

There are a couple of inexpensive places **to stay** in town. *Lennox Head Beach House YHA*, 3 Ross Street (ⓣ02/6687 7636, ⓦwww.yha.com.au; dorms $24, rooms ❸), is ideally situated between the lake and the beach; massage (free short sessions on Thurs), reflexology and Bowen therapy are available in-house, and there are boards, fishing gear, bikes, windsurfers and paddle-skis for $5. Also in a prime position is the *Lake Ainsworth Caravan Park* on Pacific Parade (ⓣ02/6687 7249, ⓦwww.tropicalnsw.com.au/ballinavanparks; cabins ❸). *All Bad Backpackers*, on the corner of Rutherford and Ballina Streets (ⓣ02/6687 6600, dorms $20), feels more like a commune than a hostel – meals are communal and lager-louts are not welcome. If you hate the Byron party-vibe, you'll love it here – and vice versa. Most guests stay for months.

As for **food**, there's cheap but excellent pizza, pasta and salad at *Lennox Head Pizza* on Ballina Street (Ⓣ02/6687 7080), and delicious grub at *Mi Thai* a few shops further down. 7 *Mile Café* on Pacific Parade has popular Mediterranean food and a prime waterfront location. The *Lennox Point Hotel* serves excellent modern Australian food in a convivial atmosphere with water views; it also hosts bands on Thursday, Friday and Saturday nights.

Since Lennox Head is off the Pacific Highway, few long-distance **bus** services call here; the closest drop-off with Greyhound Australia is at nearby Ballina, from where the YHA will pick up guests free of charge. Premier, which runs services right along the east coast, stops in Ballina three times daily, from where there are local services to and from Byron Bay.

Byron Bay and around

Situated at the end of a long sweeping bay, the township of **BYRON BAY** boasts 30km of almost unbroken sandy beaches. Byron was first discovered by the surfies, then the hippies and more recently by better-heeled travellers – these days the town is a "must do" on the backpacker circuit. What once made the place special – the small-community feel, the free-for-all atmosphere, the barefoot hippies and the herbalists – is fast disappearing. Byron these days is still beautiful and undeniably good fun, but the ever-encroaching chain stores and the profusion of competing tie-dye therapies combine to make it, in summertime at least, about as alternative as MTV.

Arrival and information

If you come by **train** you'll arrive right in the heart of town on **Jonson Street**, the main thoroughfare. Not all north-coast **buses** stop at Byron Bay; those that

△ Byron Bay

Tours from Byron Bay

There are plenty of **tours** available to the rainforest, waterfalls and national parks in the hinterland around Byron Bay. All tours and activities can be booked at the Byron Bus & Backpacker Centre (see below). The following are some of the more specialist and unusual tour operators.

Byron Bay Eco Tours ⓣ02/6685 4030, ⓦwww.byronbayecotours.com. Informative rainforest tours ($85) by 4WD and on foot through the World Heritage-listed rainforest. Lunch included.

Byron Bay Sea Kayaks ⓣ02/6685 5830, ⓦwww.byronbayadventureco.com. Dolphin-watching from sea level in two-person boats; tours leave at 8.30am & 1.30pm (3.5hr; $60 including breakfast or afternoon tea).

Happy Coach ⓣ02/6685 3996. One of many Nimbin day tours ($25), taking in Minyon Falls and the rainforest and providing lots of local info.

Jim's Alternative Tours ⓣ02/6685 7720. Tours aimed at presenting a positive, accurate portrayal of the hinterland "back to the land" movement, with its communes devoted to organic agriculture and the simple life. The tours ($25) visit Nimbin and Minyon Falls, with opportunities for swimming. They can also take you to the Sunday markets at The Channon ($10) and Bangalow ($5), with more flexible times than other operators.

Mountain Bike Tours ⓣ1800 122 504, ⓦwww.mountainbiketours.com.au. Tours along a range of single-track trails through the rainforest which will satisfy both the casual cyclist and the rabid downhiller. A great way to see the bush. $88 for a full-day trip including lunch.

Surfari ⓣ1800 634 951, ⓦwww.surfaris.com. If you really want to learn to surf, this is a great way of doing it. For $499 you'll spend five days living with a crew of gnarly wave riders who will chuck you in the water every day until you get it.

do will also drop you here, or else a little way north near the junction of Jonson and Lawson streets (see p.331 for details of bus companies and booking agents). The closest **airports** are at Ballina, 39km south, or Coolangatta, 109km north in Queensland; Express Bus (ⓣ1800 626 222) serves Brisbane airport daily ($36), while Airport Transfers go to Coolangatta airport (ⓣ02/6685 7447; $36).

The helpful **Byron Bay Tourist Information Centre**, at 80 Jonson Street next to the train station (daily 9am–5pm; ⓣ02/6680 9271, ⓦwww.visitbyronbay.com), has an excellent range of printed information and a free booking service. A *Disabled Access Guide* is available from the Community Centre opposite. The **Byron Bus & Backpacker Centre**, next to the information centre (daily 7am–7pm; ⓣ02/6685 5517, ⓔbustop@lismore.com.au), books tours, activities, accommodation, bus tickets and does cheap car rental. There are other "information centres" along the street, but they're really geared up for selling adventure activities and tours.

Accommodation

During December and January especially, demand for accommodation in all categories far exceeds supply, and it's essential to book well in advance. There's a dedicated **accommodation** desk in the tourist information centre (daily 9.30am–5pm; ⓣ02/6680 8666, ⓦwww.byronbayaccom.net). The **hostels** in Byron Bay are among the liveliest in Australia, but prices and stress levels rise dramatically in summer due to overcrowding. Note that all the hostels reviewed below only have rooms with shared bathrooms. If you're part of a group, **holiday apartments** (booked through the accommodation desk at the

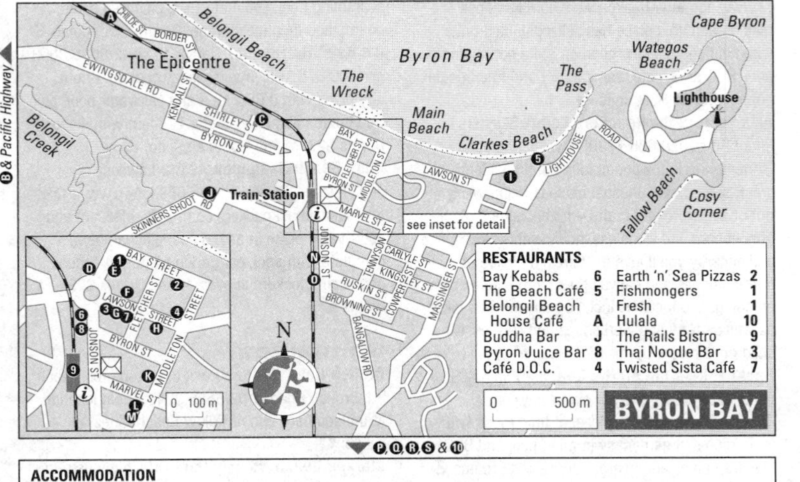

ACCOMMODATION

Aquarius Backpackers Motel	H	Byron Bay Bunkhouse	M	Great Northern Hotel	G
Arts Factory Backpackers Lodge	J	Byron Bay Rainforest Resort	P	Holiday Village Backpackers	N
Backpackers Inn on the Beach	C	Cape Byron Lodge	R	J's Bay YHA Hostel	L
Beach Hotel	E	Cape Byron YHA Hostel	K	Lord Byron Resort Motel	O
Belongil Beach House	A	Clarkes Beach Holiday Park	I	Main Beach Backpackers	F
Broken Head Holiday Park	Q	Dolphins Motor Inn	S		
Byron Bay Beach Resort	B	First Sun Holiday Park	D		

tourist office and real estate agents in town) might be a more practical option. If all places in town are full, try **Brunswick Heads**, about 18km further up the coast (see p.330), Lennox Head, about 12km south (see p.324), or the quiet town of **Mullumbimby** – known for its very potent marijuana – just inland.

Motels, hotels, guest-houses and apartments

Arcadia B&B 48 Cowper St ⓣ02/6680 8699. Just a few leafy streets up from the centre, this smart old B&B makes a homely, comfortable alternative to the town's hotels. ❺

Beach Hotel Cnr Jonson and Bay Sts ⓣ02/6685 6402, ⓦwww.beachhotel.com.au. This luxury waterfront hotel is a favourite amongst visiting Aussie celebs and has spacious, tasteful units with balconies and a heated pool and spa. ❽

Byron Bay Beach Resort Bayshore Drive, 3km north on the road to the Pacific Highway (turn off at the Byron Bay Industrial Estate) ⓣ02/6685 8000, ⓦwww.byronbaybeachresort.com.au. Lovely complex of serviced wooden chalets with kitchens, a pool, bar, restaurant, tennis courts and golf course. ❼

Byron Bay Rainforest Resort Broken Head Rd, Suffolk Park, 3.5km south, opposite the golf course ⓣ02/6685 6139, ⓔholiday@rainforestresort.com.au. Prize-winning resort designed to be completely accessible to people with disabilities. There are private one- or two-room cabins, fully equipped, with verandah and TV, as well as dorms ($22) set in rainforest close the beach and a swimming pool. Weekly rates available. Cabins ❼

Dolphins Motor Inn 32 Bangalow Rd, 1 km south ⓣ02/6680 9511, ⓦwww.byronbay.com/dolphins. Spacious motel units with verandah; most have kitchenettes, and there's also a pool. ❹

Great Northern Hotel Cnr Jonson and Byron Sts ⓣ02/6685 6454. Clean, no-frills pub rooms right above the main St and amongst the cheapest in town, though the noise from bands playing below makes it a place for confirmed night owls only. ❷

Lord Byron Resort Motel 120 Jonson St ⓣ02/6685 7444, ⓔlbyron@nor.com. Very smart place with air-con units plus swimming pool, spa, gym and tennis court. Some serviced apartments also available (with fans only). ❻

Hostels

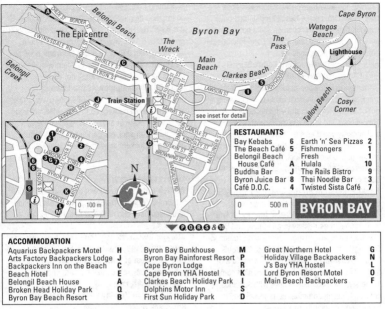

Aquarius Backpackers Motel 16 Lawson St ⓣ02/6685 7663 or 1800 028 909,

Ⓦ www.aquarius-backpackers.com.au. Close to Main Beach, this place has self-contained units with kitchenettes plus good en-suite dorms and a pool, BBQ area, café, bar, Internet and free boogie-boards. Dorms $26, units ❸
Arts Factory Backpackers Lodge Skinners Shoot Rd Ⓣ 02/6685 7709, Ⓦ www.artsfactory.com.au. Set in a wooden lodge in a bushland creek setting, this unusual place is a sprawling riot of sculpture and crafts – if you value a hippie atmosphere and sleepless, noisy nights over space and security you'll love it. There's a choice of dorms, tepees and canvas huts by the creek, plus camping, and facilities include pool and free bikes, as well as New Age workshops and classes. No children allowed. Dorms $28, huts ❸
Backpackers Inn on the Beach 29 Shirley St Ⓣ 02/6685 8231, Ⓦ www.byron-bay.com/backpackersinn. More pleasant than most, with large rooms, a garden, swimming pool and BBQ, plus free bikes and boards. Dorms $26, rooms ❸
Belongil Beach House Childe St Ⓣ 02/6685 7868, Ⓦ www.belongilbeachhouse.com. One of the best places in town, set in a beautiful complex in the style of a Balinese resort, with spacious, cool, high-ceilinged timber cottages around a landscaped garden. Dorms are en suite, and there are free bikes and boards, plus an excellent café. Dorms $25, rooms ❸, apartments ❹
Byron Bay Bunkhouse 1 Carlyle St Ⓣ 02/6685 8311 or 1800 241 600, Ⓔ byronbay@org.com.au. Large, rowdy hostel (dorms only). There's free breakfast and a nice deck, but the place isn't for the faint hearted. Dorms $23.
Cape Byron Lodge 78 Bangalow Rd Ⓣ 02/6685 6445, Ⓦ www.capebyronlodge.com. Simple, friendly place with the cheapest dorms in Byron, plus the usual bikes, boards and activities, though it's a bit out of town. Dorms $20, rooms ❸
Cape Byron YHA Hostel Cnr Middleton and Byron Sts Ⓣ 02/6685 8788, Ⓔ byronyha@nrg.com.au. Large, central hostel with extensive facilities, including a pool, free bikes, boogie-boards and pancakes, and two BBQ nights a week. The dorms are OK, but the bare doubles are overpriced. Dorms $25, rooms ❸
Holiday Village Backpackers 116 Jonson St Ⓣ 02/6685 8888 or 1800 350 388 (reservations only), Ⓕ 6685 8777. Clean, friendly and well-equipped backpackers, with a solar-heated swimming pool, spa and BBQs, plus free bikes, boards and luggage storage. Dorms $25, rooms ❸
J's Bay YHA Hostel 7 Carlyle St Ⓣ 02/6685 8853 or 1800 678 195, Ⓦ www.jsbay.com.au. Bright, airy place with a BBQ area and saltwater pool, plus free boards and bikes and a TV room with videos. Dorms $23, rooms (some en suite) ❸
Main Beach Backpackers Cnr Lawson and Fletcher Sts Ⓣ 02/6685 8695, Ⓦ www.mainbeachbackpackers.com. Safe, pleasant and good-value place in an old council chambers, complete with pool, car parking, Internet access and secure lockers in every room. Dorms $23, rooms ❸

Campsites

Broken Head Holiday Park 6km south on Beach Rd, Broken Head Ⓣ 02/6685 3245. Great location at the southern end of Tallow Beach. Sites ❶, cabins ❹
Clarkes Beach Holiday Park Off Lighthouse Rd Ⓣ 02/6685 6496, Ⓦ www.bshp.com.au/clarkes. Only 1km west of town, and right on the beach. All cabins are fully self-contained, with showers and toilets. Sites ❶, cabins ❺
Ferry Reserve Holiday Park Pacific Highway, Brunswick Heads, 35km from Byron Bay Ⓣ 02/6685 1872, Ⓦ www.bshp.com.au/ferry. Very pleasant campsite near the river, with a kiosk, BBQ, and self-contained and basic cabins as well as campsites. Sites ❶, cabins ❸
First Sun Holiday Park Lawson St Ⓣ 02/6685 6544, Ⓦ www.bshp.com.au/first. Excellent central location on Main Beach. Cabins range from basic to fully self-contained. Sites ❶, cabins ❸
Maca's Camping Ground Main Arm Rd, near Mullumbimby, 35km from Byron Bay Ⓣ 02/6684 5211. Bush campsite with communal kitchen and dining room, plus laundry. Tents for rent. Vans ❷, sites ❶
Suffolk Park Holiday Park Alcorn St, Suffolk Park, 5km south Ⓣ 02/6685 3353, Ⓦ www.bshp.com.au/suffolk. Good location in a shady setting on Tallow Beach, with self-contained cabins with shower and toilet. Cabins ❹, sites ❶
Terrace Reserve Holiday Park Fingal St, Brunswick Heads Ⓣ 02/6685 1233, Ⓦ www.bshp.com.au/terrace. Shady spot by the river and near the beach, with fully self-contained cabins. Sites ❶, cabins ❹

The Town and around

There's plenty of opportunity to soak up local atmosphere – and the often bizarre mix of counter-cultures as surfie meets soap starlet meets hippie – simply by wandering the streets. Probably the best place to take it all in is on the first

Sunday of each month at the **market** on Butler Street behind the train station, a huge affair containing everything from leather handbags to organic veggies. If you want to explore, one of the first places to visit is the **lighthouse** on the rocky promontory of **Cape Byron**, where there's a small nature reserve (daily: March–Sept 8am–5.30pm; Nov–Feb 8am-7pm). The cape is the easternmost

Alternative and artistic Byron Bay

Byron Bay offers a huge variety of alternative therapies, New Age bookshops, crystals, palmists and tarot readers – all with a good dose of capitalism, as prices for massages and tarot readings are hiked up during the lucrative summer months. The alternative culture attracts artists and artisans in droves, and galleries and artists' studios abound.

Alternative therapies

The **Community Centre**, at 69 Jonson Street (ⓣ02/6685 6807, ⓔbbcc@mullum.com.au; closed Sun), opposite the train station in a brand new building, has great notice boards packed with information on everything from Celtic Shamanism to Tibetan healing workshops. At the rear of the *Belongil Beach House* on Childe Street, the **Relax Haven** (ⓣ02/6685 8304) has a flotation tank (1hr float $25) and massage available (float and massage $30); or the more central **Samadhi Flotation Centre**, 107 Jonson Street (ⓣ02/6685 6905), offers the same, plus classes, workshops and a resident naturopath and homeopath. **Quintessence**, Shop 8, 11 Fletcher Street (ⓣ02/6685 5533, ⓦwww.quintessencebyron.com.au), offers aromatherapy plus massage (30min; $45) as well as advice on detox and lymph draining. Heading off the deep end of the purple spectrum, **Ambaji Wellness Centre** at 6 Marvel Street (ⓣ02/6685 6620, ⓦwww.ambaji.com.au) is very New Age and offers a wide range of treatments from homeopathy, meditation (free) and yoga to tarot readings and crystal singing bowl vibrations – it's amazing how quickly the memories of past lives resonate through your chakras when a rubber striker is passed across the glass bowls. "Crystal dreaming" is even better: "Through bi-location and interaction with interdimensional beings, it is possible to retrieve ancient and future technologies for positive use now". Levitate down there, or get a copy of *Body and Soul* from the information centre for the full gamut of good vibes.

Arts and crafts

Local arts and crafts are on display at the **Byron Bay market**, held on the first Sunday of each month on Butler Street, behind the train station. There are others at The Channon and Alstonville on the second Sunday, Mullumbimby on the third Saturday, Uki and Ballina on the third Sunday and one at the showground at Bangalow, 13km southwest, on the fourth Sunday of each month. The **Arts Factory**, on Skinners Shoot Road, has several artists' workshops that you can visit (Tues–Sun 10am–3pm), and the **Byron Craft Market** is held here every Saturday (8.30am–3pm) with a courtesy bus (9.30am–3.30pm) from the community centre on Jonson Street. **The Epicentre**, on Border Street near Belongil Beach, has several outlets and resident artists and craftspeople, plus a large art gallery showing the work of local artists (open shop hours; $1 donation). Beyond here, 3km northwest of town, signposted off Ewingsdale Road (the road to the Pacific Highway), **Byron Bay Industrial Estate** has a host of artisans producing everything from leather goods to glassware. Back in town, Jonson Street is lined with shops selling crystals and locally made crafts, particularly jewellery.

Byron Bay is host to an Australian **Writers' Festival** for four days at the beginning of August; contact the Northern Rivers Writers' Centre, PO Box I846, Byron Bay, NSW 2481 ⓣ02/6685 5115, ⓦwww.byronbaywritersfestival.com.au.

point of the Australian mainland and is a popular spot to greet the dawn. There's an excellent circular **walking track** from the lighthouse, and with a bit of luck you'll see **dolphins**, who like to sport in the surf off the headland, or **humpback whales**, which pass this way heading north to warmer waters in June or July and again on their return south in September or October.

Main Beach in town is as good as any to swim from, and usually has relatively gentle surf. One reason why Byron Bay is so popular with surfers is because its beaches face in all directions, so there's almost always one with a good swell; however, you can usually find somewhere for a calmer swim. East of Main Beach, you can always find a spot to yourself (if you're learning to surf for example) on the less sheltered stretch of **Belongil Beach**, from where there's sand virtually all the way to **BRUNSWICK HEADS**, a quieter, more family-oriented resort located between the mouth of the Brunswick River and Simpson's Creek, with a long crescent of beach on the ocean side. The grassy riverfront area is a good spot for children, with several playgrounds and picnic areas.

Back in the other direction, Main Beach curves round towards Cape Byron to become **Clarkes Beach**. This and neighbouring **Wategos Beach** – beautifully framed between two rocky spurs – face north, and usually have the best surfing. On the far side of the cape, **Tallow Beach** extends towards the **Broken Head Nature Reserve**, 6km south of the town centre at Suffolk Park; there's good surf at Tallow just around the cape at Cosy Corner, and also at Broken Head. From the car park here, a short stroll through rainforest leads to the secluded, nudist **Kings Beach**, one of several isolated stretches of sand out this way.

The diversity of marine life in the waters of Byron Bay makes it a prime place to **dive**, though these are rock – rather than coral - reefs. Tropical marine life and creatures from warm temperate seas mingle at the granite outcrop of **Julian Rocks Aquatic Reserve**, 3km offshore; by far the most popular spot here is the **Cod Hole**, an extensive underwater cave inhabited by large moray eels and other fish. Between April and June is the best time to dive, before the plankton bloom (see "Listings" on p.332 for information on dive schools).

Eating

There's a multitude of places selling food in Byron Bay, and the standard is generally pretty high. Lots of alternative **cafés** offer delicious health foods and vegetarian dishes – although they don't usually stay open late except in the peak summer period.

Bay Kebabs Cnr Jonson and Lawson Sts. Generous falafel rolls and gourmet kebabs. Daily 10am until late.

The Beach Café Clarkes Beach. An excellent place for breakfast (from 7.30am), and also serves eclectic dinner choices in summer.

Belongil Beach House Cafe Childe St. Another great oceanfront place for breakfast, lunch and dinner. There are outside tables, and frequent avant-garde spoken word, cinema and music nights. BYO.

Buddha Bar At the *Arts Factory Backpackers Lodge*, Skinners Shoot Rd ☎02/6685 5833. Excellent veggie and meat dishes in 1950s-style booths, surrounded by artworks and hippies. There's also a cinema here, and the movie meal-deal is great value. BYO.

Byron Juice Bar Jonson St. Delicious smoothies and fantastic freshly squeezed juices are almost a meal in themselves at this popular place. They offer healthy snacks, too.

Café D.O.C. 7 Middleton St. Far from the madding crowds in a local bit of town, this great café is the best in the centre for huge bowls of muesli with fruit and other breakfasty things as well as nachos and burgers for lunch (noon to 3.30pm).

Earth 'n' Sea Pizzas Lawson St. Perennially popular pizzas – toppings are unusual and imaginative: try "Mullumbimby Madness" (with magic mushrooms). There's generous and affordable pasta too, and a $10 all-you-can-eat special on Wed nights. BYO and licensed. Daily from 5.30pm.

Fins At the *Beach Hotel*, cnr Jonson and Bay Sts ☎02/6685 5029. Award-winning and pricey

brasserie with an extensive verandah overlooking the ocean for people-watching. Mainly fish dishes, with Moroccan and southern European twists. Booking advised.
Fishmongers Bay Lane, behind the *Beach Hotel*. Locals rave about this place, which has some of the best seafood in Byron, at low prices.
Fresh 7 Jonson St. A very funky place. Try the oriental salads, excellent slices of tofu and juices, or simply hang out over a coffee. Evening meals are a delight.
Hulala Junction of Bangalow and Old Bangalow Rds. Cute and quirky Hawaiian/Mexican/Japanese café with some pretty weird dishes, like coconut shrimp.
The Rails Bistro Popular spot with great, affordable food and a good ambience.
Thai Noodle Bar Feros Arcade, off Jonson and Lawson Sts. Primarily a takeaway place, though there's a small bar-style eating area in which to enjoy moderately priced wok-fried noodles (you select the added ingredients), Malaysian-style *laksa* (noodle soup) and a good selection of vegetarian dishes. Mon–Sat 10am–6pm.
Twisted Sista Café Lawson St. Popular for its large portions of Mediterranean food, burgers and salads.

Entertainment and nightlife

The weekly free community newspaper, *The Byron Shire Echo*, has a comprehensive gig guide. There's plenty of activity in summer: **New Year's Eve** is such a big event that the council has taken to closing the town off – so come early. The huge outdoor **Blues and Roots Festival** (Easter weekend) takes over Red Devil park with several stages, a rave field, an all-night cinema, a food fair, market stalls and workshops; to find out exact dates, call the tourist information centre (☎02/6680 9271). Similarly, the **Splendour in the Grass** music festival (around July 20) brings in huge crowds. Tickets can be bought in advance from independent record outlets around Australia. At Pighouse Flicks, Old Piggery, Skinners Shoot Road, **The Byron Lounge Cinema** (☎02/6685 5828) shows the best newly released films, with the emphasis on the quirky, with two to three films nightly and seating on deck chairs or sofas. The price is $7 per film, or $14 with a meal from their great vegetarian restaurant.

Balcony Genteel cocktail lounge with a good location for people-watching above Jonson St.
Beach Hotel Cnr Jonson and Bay Sts ☎02/6685 6402. This huge, smart pub, superbly sited right opposite Main Beach, has a large terrace beer garden, bistro and restaurant and attracts a cross-section of locals. Live music (cover bands, often free), including jazz sessions on Sunday afternoon.
The Cheeky Monkey 115 Jonson St ☎02/6685 5886. This popular backpackers' hang-out has cheap food ($5 deals), loud music and a happy hour after 10pm. Open until 3am.
Great Northern Hotel Jonson St ☎02/6685 6454. This place has something for everyone: a front room with pool tables; a blokish public bar; and *The Backroom*, a large, stylish space that doubles as an Italian restaurant and a music venue for big-name Australian bands playing three or four times a week. Open till 1am.
La La Land Lawson St. If you've had enough of the tie-dye brigade, try sipping a cocktail at this chic Byron Bay branch of a Melbourne institution. Sushi, dips and pizza available for grazing. Daily 7pm–1am.
Rails At the Train Station. Some good local bands (mostly rock) rock the mike here a few times a week.

Listings

Bicycle and moped rental Many hostels have bikes which can either be used free or rented by guests; otherwise try Byron Bay Bicycle, 93 Jonson St, opposite Woolworths (☎02/6685 6067), which charges around $15 a day for a mountain bike (they also have rollerblades); or Byron Bay Bike Hire, opposite (☎0500 856 985). A cycling track runs from Byron to Suffolk Park via Broken Head nature reserve (8km one-way). Mopeds can be rented from *Ride On* (☎0429 144 963) from $43 a day.
Buses Book for Greyhound Australia, Kirklands and Premier through Byron Bus & Backpacker Centre, 84 Jonson St (☎02/6685 5517). Kirklands goes daily to Brisbane, and to Ballina (with stops at Murwillumbah and Tweed Heads), also daily to Lismore and Casino. Blanch's Coaches (☎02/6686 2144) runs around town, as well as south to Ballina via Suffolk Park, Bangalow and Lennox Head, and north to Mullimbimby – buy your ticket on the bus.

Car rental *Dolphins Motel* ⓣ02/6680 9577; Earth Car Rental, 11 Fletcher St ⓣ02/6685 7472; Hertz, Marvel St ⓣ02/6680 7925; Thrifty, Shirley St ⓣ02/6685 7925. Prices from $33 a day including 50km.
Diving Most dive schools offer complete scuba-diving courses, together with more affordable one-day courses and daily snorkelling boat trips (around $50). Byron Bay Dive Centre, 9 Marvel St (ⓣ02/6685 8333 or 1800 243 483, ⓦwww.byronbaydivecentre.com.au), does a good-value, one-day course for $130 including all equipment; Sundive, Middleton St (ⓣ02/6685 7755), is a small, friendly outfit. If you're already trained, one dive at Julian Rocks, with gear, costs from $75, two dives $145.
Environment Byron Bay Environment Centre, in the kiosk opposite the tourist information centre (same hours), at the train station.
Gay and lesbian information Tropical Fruits is a social group for gays and lesbians, holding dance parties every few weeks in halls around the area and Australia-wide; the Fruitline (ⓣ02/6622 6440, ⓦwww.tropicalfruits.org.au) gives recorded information on upcoming events.
Hang-gliding Tandem take-offs and lessons from $140 for 30min with the excellent Byron Airwaves (ⓣ02/6629 0354).
Horse riding Pegasus Park (ⓣ02/6687 1446) charges from $50 for one hour. Combined riding and canoeing trips cost $55 per hour. Seahorses Riding Centre (ⓣ02/6680 8155) offers lessons from $75 per half-day. Rides include beach, rainforest, sunrise and sunset tours.
Hospital Wordsworth St, off Shirley St ⓣ02/6685 6200.
Internet access Facilities are available all over town, but *Global Gossip*, by the tourist information centre on Lawson St (daily 8am–midnight), has the most reliable connections and the best rates ($4.50 per hr). Peter Pan's on Lawson St is the cheapest ($2 per hr).
Laundries You can use the laundry at most accommodation; otherwise try Byron Dry Cleaners and Laundrette, 42 Jonson St (daily 7am–7pm), with both self-service and service washes available, or the unattended self-service laundry on Marvel St (daily 7am–7pm).
Left luggage Byron Bus & Backpacker Centre, next to the tourist information centre, will mind bags for 24 hours for $5 (daily 7am–6.30pm).
Police 20 Shirley St ⓣ02/6685 9499.
Post office Next door to the Community Centre on Jonson St (postcode NSW 2481).
Skydiving Skydive Byron Bay (ⓣ02/6684 1323, ⓦwww.skydivebyronbay.com) offer Australia's highest jump (14,000ft) right onto the beach. $329.
Surfing Many hostels provide free boards. For surf lessons, one of the best outfits is Black Dog Surfing (ⓣ02/6680 9828), which rents out surf gear and offers 4hr lessons from $60 with free pick-up.
Taxi Byron Bay Taxi & Limousines ⓣ02/6685 5008, ⓦwww.byronbaytaxis.com. There's a taxi rank on Jonson St, opposite the *Great Northern Hotel*.
Travel agents There's a string of specialist outfits along Jonson St who can book adventure tours. Byron Bay Travel Centre, Shop 4, 52 Jonson St (Mon–Fri 9am–6pm, Sat & Sun 9am–4pm; ⓣ02/6685 6733), is a good general travel and STA agent which deals with bus bookings and passes, and also sells YHA and VIP membership. Jetset, corner of Jonson and Marvel streets (same hours; ⓣ02/6685 6554), can revalidate tickets and book international and domestic flights.

Tweed Heads

From Brunswick Heads, the Pacific Highway heads around 30km inland to Murwillumbah (see p.337), and then a further 30km to the coast at **TWEED HEADS**. Although officially still part of New South Wales, Tweed Heads – the twin city of Coolangatta in Queensland (see p.452) – is for all practical purposes part of the **Gold Coast**. It certainly looks the part: high-rise buildings, concrete apartment blocks and shopping centres vie for space with grandiose club buildings and a roadscape of advertising billboards in gaudy colours. From the shore, the jagged skyline of Surfers Paradise can be seen in the distance.

Tweed Heads has lots of places **to stay** (motels are cheaper here than further north), and even more opportunities to eat, drink and **gamble**, an activity which was once banned in Queensland, meaning that clubs and casinos relocated here to cash in. One of the biggest and longest-established places is the *Twin Towns RSL Club* (ⓣ07/5536 2277) on Wharf Street, whose special offers on cheap food, drink and live entertainment can be a good deal, so long as you don't lose too much in the machines along the way.

One of the few other attractions is the **Minjungbal Aboriginal Cultural Museum**, on Kirkwood Road in South Tweed Heads (daily 8.30am–4pm; $6, tours $10), where detailed exhibits and videos illustrate how Aboriginal people lived off this stretch of the coast; near the museum, a signposted boardwalk leads past an old bora ring – a sacred site used in initiation ceremonies. Ironically, the **Captain Cook Memorial Lighthouse** on **Point Danger** celebrates the very event that signalled the demise of Aboriginal culture in these parts: right at the state border, it was erected for the Cook bicentenary celebrations in 1970. Cook gave Point Danger its name after nearly running aground on it; **Mount Warning** (see below) was named at the same time to serve as a landmark for sailors navigating around the point.

Practicalities

The **Tweed Heads Visitors Centre** (Mon–Sat 9am–5pm; ⓣ1800 674 414, ⓦwww.tweedcoolangatta.com) is in the Tweed Mall, at the corner of Wharf and Bay streets; they also have information on the rest of the Gold Coast. From Coolangatta airport, **buses** generally make a beeline for the resort strip in Queensland; **long-distance buses** stop on Bay Street, near Tweed Mall; Surfside Buslines (ⓣ07/5574 5111, ⓦwww.surfside.com.au) runs local services up and down the Gold Coast, and to Murwillumbah.

If you want to **stay**, there are dozens of motels, caravan parks and holiday apartments strung out along the highway. *River Retreat Caravan Park*, 8 Philp Parade (ⓣ07/5524 2700, cabins ❸) is a good place, on the river and close to the beach, and with a bus service to all major attractions. There's even more choice if you continue on to Surfers Paradise for the full Gold Coast experience – if that's what you're after. For something less crass, head 20km south down the Coast Road to **Cabarita Beach** near Bogangar where you'll find the *Emu Park Lodge* (ⓣ02/6676 1190, ⓔemupark@norex.com.au; dorms $24, rooms ❷), a good **hostel** which has Internet access, a swap library, laundry, free bikes and boards, surfing lessons and trips to Mount Warning; pay for two nights and you get the third free. The village has a pub and several eating places. Back in Tweed Heads itself, it's not hard to find something **to eat**: if the clubs don't appeal, head for oceanfront Marine Parade, where there's everything from takeaway pizza to seafood restaurants.

Far North Coast Hinterland

The beautiful **Far North Coast Hinterland** lies between artist-filled **Lismore**, in the fertile Richmond River valley to the south, and **Murwillumbah**, in the even lusher valley of the Tweed River near the Queensland border. The Hinterland's three rainforest national parks, plus several reserves, are World Heritage-listed, protecting areas that the settlers never managed to log, and which protestors helped to save in the first successful anti-logging demonstration in Australia, in 1979.

Mount Warning – or Wollumbin ("cloud catcher") to the Bandjalung Aborigines – is the remains of the central magma chamber of a once enormous volcano, and its 1157-metre summit offers dazzling views of the area. **Mount Warning National Park** rises in the middle of a massive caldera eroded on the eastern side into a huge bowl, where the Tweed River flows to the sea through the valley's mostly agricultural patchwork of fields. The northwest rim section consists of the McPherson and Tweed ranges, covered by the **Border Ranges National Park**; the southern section lies within the **Nightcap National Park**, near counter-cultural **Nimbin** and **The Channon**, home to the largest and most colourful market in the area.

The local bus company, Kirklands (Ⓣ02/6622 1499), is based at Lismore, and the area is well served by **buses** from the coast, although there is no regular service on to Nimbin. A special shuttle bus runs three times daily to Nimbin from Byron Bay (Ⓣ02/6680 9189; $14).

Lismore and around

On the Bruxner Highway 65km inland from Ballina, **LISMORE** is the principal town of northeast New South Wales and the commercial focus of the fertile Richmond River valley, surrounded by prosperous dairy and farming country. This is one of the most densely populated rural areas in Australia, and has been since the early days of the colony. In the nineteenth century Lismore was an important river port for the **timber** trade, as lumberjacks cut their way through the valley's dense forest before moving up to the steep slopes of the McPherson Ranges near the Queensland border. Local red cedar was especially sought after. There's still a fair amount of forestry in the region, but these days the economic mainstay is dairy farming and cattle breeding, along with a rapidly growing tropical agriculture sector: bananas, sugar cane, avocados, tropical fruit and macadamia nuts. The Rainbow Region organic market takes place at the Lismore Showground on Tuesdays and Thursdays.

For all the intense agriculture, however, this is not your typical Ocker backwater; the city of 44,000 even has its own **Southern Cross University**, which includes a Koala Hospital on its grounds. Since the alternative-lifestyle seekers discovered the northeast in the 1970s, **cultural life** has flourished, with jewellers, potters, painters, graphic artists, sculptors and other arts-and-crafts people settling here and establishing a network of shops and galleries. Every first and third weekend they all come together for the region's **Car Boot Markets**; at other times the **Regional Art Gallery**, 131 Molesworth Street (Tues–Fri 10am–4pm, Sat & Sun 10.30am–2.30pm; donation), is the best place to get an overview, especially of sculpture. For a look at some local ceramics, drop into Art Aspects Gallery on 104 Woodlark Street. The **Historical Museum**, on the same street at no. 165 (Mon–Fri 10am–4pm; $2), houses an interesting, if somewhat motley, collection of pioneer relics and photographs. There are several festivals throughout the year, the most popular being the **Lantern Festival** in June (a huge procession of homemade lanterns) and the **Herb Festival** in August, where local music and local cuisine are the big draws.

Practicalities

Lismore is the home base of Kirklands **buses** (Ⓣ02/6622 1499), which, along with Premier (Ⓣ02/9281 2233), stop here on the Sydney–Brisbane route; their terminal is on Molesworth Street. Trains from Brisbane call in at Casino, 31km southwest (see p.335), from where there's a connecting bus. You can **fly** from Sydney with Regional Express (Ⓣ13 17 13); if you've booked accommodation, you'll normally be picked up from the airport. There are **car rental** desks at the airport and branches of the usual multi-national agencies on Dawson Street. For details of local events, head for the **Lismore Visitor Information Centre**, at the corner of Molesworth and Ballina streets (Mon–Fri 9.30am–4pm, Sat & Sun 10am–3pm; Ⓣ02/6622 0122, Ⓦwww.lismore.nsw.gov.au), which also has

Internet access ($5 per hr), an indoor rainforest display, a cultural gallery with the works of a hundred artists and craftspersons and a history exhibit.

There's a wide range of **accommodation** in the Lismore region, most of which can be booked through the Visitor Information Centre. The *Civic Hotel* at 210 Molesworth Street (ⓣ02/6621 2537; ❷) has some good pub rooms, as does the *Gollan Hotel* (ⓣ02/6621 2295; ❷) on the corner of Keen and Woodlark streets. A couple of kilometres south of town, the *Lismore Lake Caravan Park*, Bruxner Highway (ⓣ02/6621 2585; cabins ❷), has inexpensive campsites, a pool, barbecue, children's playground and a nice lake location. The excellent *Melvill House*, in the heart of town at 267 Ballina Street (ⓣ & ⓕ02/6621 5778; ❸–❺), is a relaxed guesthouse, stuffed full of local art and with a heated outdoor pool; some rooms are en-suite.

Lismore isn't a bad place to **eat**, and has a couple of excellent cafés and cosmopolitan restaurants. The favoured haunt of artists is *Caddies Coffee Company*, at 20–24 Carrington Street, which has excellent bagels, panini, salads and coffee, while retro fans should head for the *Mecca Café* in the mall on Magellan Street, which has kitsch furnishings and fresh sandwiches. Vegans and juice freaks will love *20,000 Cows Café*, 58 Bridge Street, and *Dr Juice*, a vegetarian healthy heaven, just round the corner at 142 Keen Street. There are also several good, mid-range Italian establishments, including *Paupiettes*, on Ballina Street (ⓣ02/6621 6135), and *Café Giardino*, on Keen Street (ⓣ02/6622 4664). *Mary Gilhooley's Irish Pub & Restaurant*, corner of Keen and Woodlark streets, has a vibrant atmosphere and inexpensive counter meals; it's also a good place for **live music** most nights and is home to the town's only **nightclub**, *One*. There's also live music at the *Gollan Hotel* and *Maggie Moore's* pub at 29 Molesworth Street.

Around Lismore

To explore the country **around Lismore** it's best to have your own vehicle, though there are tours from Byron Bay (see p.325). There's a **market** in at least one of the villages every Sunday, providing a taste of the area's colourful alternative lifestyle – the big ones are in the hilltop village of The Channon on the second Sunday of the month, and in Nimbin on the last. The halls in the various towns have dances and live music, and you may be lucky enough to be invited to a legendary hill party involving fire-eaters and drumming and dancing till dawn – there's usually one happening somewhere every weekend, normally in the same area as the market. Be warned though: there's a lot of live traditional music in the hills, so you might end up stripping the willow hand in hand with a village matriarch while the band fiddles up a storm.

CASINO, around 30km southwest of Lismore, is a small country town on the Richmond River from where route 91 follows the rail lines south towards Grafton, or north through **KYOGLE**, with its Buddhist temple and retreat, into Queensland. One of the most scenic drives in New South Wales is the short round-trip over the mountainous, winding country roads north and northeast of Lismore to Nimbin, The Channon, and Clunes, and then via Eltham and Bexhill, with superb views from the ridges and hilltops. Accessible via Nimbin, with the peak of Mount Nardi (800m) visible 12km beyond the town, is **Nightcap National Park**, a World Heritage-listed park and one of the loveliest in New South Wales.

Nimbin and around

NIMBIN, site of the famed Aquarius Festival that launched Australian hippie culture in 1973, is synonymous with Australian alternative culture. The surrounding area is dotted with perhaps as many as fifty communes, while the town is famous for live music, crafts, New Age therapies, marijuana and the surrounding rainforest. Try to come here for the Mardi Gras festival, when the town becomes a tent city, the rainforest rocks and the dreds dangle. Alternatively, aim to make it here on a market day (third Sunday of the month), where you'll catch some music, crafts and great food.

The centre of Nimbin itself is aglow with shopfronts painted in bright, psychedelic designs, while small stores sell health food, incense sticks and patchouli oil. You'll invariably be offered dope as soon as you set foot in town, and you'll see it smoked openly on the streets and in cafes. Something akin to a "hippie hall of fame", the **Nimbin Museum**, at 62 Cullen Street (hours as they please, but usually daily; $2), is certainly worth a visit. It's a weird and wonderful living museum run by hippies, with plenty of local history relating to the Aquarius Festival, Bundjalung Aboriginal culture, and a huge stone phallus in the centre of one room. Ask here about the **Annual Hemp Mardi Grass and Drug Law Reform Festival** (Ⓦwww.nimbinmardigrass.com), held on the first weekend in May. If you have Green leanings, the **Nimbin Environmental Centre**, also on Cullen Street, might be of interest: they campaign on environmental issues, and can arrange visits to the **Djanvung Permaculture Education Centre**, a showcase for a system of sustainable agriculture that is gaining ground worldwide. The **Hemp Embassy** (again, opens as it pleases; Ⓦwww.nrg.com.au/~hemp), down the lane next to the pub is worth a visit too for its display on the uses of hemp; its owners also run the *Hemp Bar* next door, and organize the town's Mardi Grass.

Practicalities

Nimbin has its own, small, **tourist information centre**, the Nimbin Tourist Connexion, at 8 Cullen Street (daily 9am–5pm; Ⓣ02/6689 1764, Ⓦwww.nimbinconnexion.com); staff can book accommodation and bus and train tickets, and there are bikes for rent and Internet access ($4.50 per hr). They also have details of the **Nimbin Shuttle Bus** up from Byron Bay (Ⓣ02/6680 9189; $14).

Accommodation

There are a number of **places to stay** in and near Nimbin, though during Mardi Grass the place is booked up well in advance, so be prepared **to camp**. All the hostels also have camping space.

Granny's Farm Backpackers & Camping Ⓣ02/6689 1333. In a peaceful farm setting a short walk from town, this is the most backpacker-oriented place in Nimbin, with two swimming pools and comfy doubles and the emphasis on beer and a good time. Dorms $20, rooms ❷

Grey Gum Lodge 2 High St Ⓣ & Ⓕ02/6689 1713. Right in town, this very comfortable and beautifully decorated place is about as smart as it gets hereabouts, with a saltwater swimming pool but no Nimbin vibe – which is a plus for some people. ❷

Klassic Lodge 413 Crofton Rd, 4km north of town near Nightcap National Park Ⓣ02/6689 9350. Cosy, if slightly twee, place. Also has a small pool. ❸

Nimbin Hotel and Backpackers Cullen St Ⓣ02/6689 1246. Very large, plain and clean place, with four-bed dorms for $25 per person, although if you're on your own or in a couple, there's a good chance you'll get a dorm all to yourself – in effect, a very cheap single/double room.

Nimbin Rox YHA 74 Thorburn St Ⓣ02/6689 0022, Ⓦwww.nimbinroxhostel.com. The pick of the hostels, this friendly, well-managed place has a range of accommodation with dorms, wood-and-canvas "lodges", doubles and tepees – plus a pool, flotation tank and massage room in its fruit garden. It's set in a superb hilltop location just outside town and named after the huge sacred rock monoliths which it overlooks. Dorms $24, "lodges", doubles and tepees ❷

Rainbow Retreat 75 Thorburn St ⓣ02/6689 1262. The hippiest place in town, with accommodation either in a dorm, an old VW combi, a gypsy wagon or a cheap double, plus camping space. It shares a stretch of Goolmanger Creek with the resident platypus, while horses munch between the tent spaces. Dorms $15, rooms ❷

Eating and nightlife

Nimbin's main strip, Cullen Street, is full of good **places to eat**, including the legendary *Rainbow Café*, which closes and then opens up again every couple of months. For great Indian veggie food, try *The Hub* opposite the tourist office on Cullen Street. The *Nimbin Café* has lots of tasty munchies – yummy savouries, hot chocolate, coffee and cakes – while *The E-Bar* offers Italian coffee, smoothies and excellent breakfast fare, as well as Internet access. Finally, the *Nimbin Trattoria & Pizzeria* serves up generous servings of pizza, pasta and salad nightly from 5pm (BYO). As ever, you'll get a man-sized feed for a few bucks at the Bowling Club, 1km out of town on the way to the Rainbow Power Station (signed from the main road).

For **nightlife and entertainment** there's the *Nimbin Hotel and Backpackers*, which sees plenty of live music (the bistro also serves good counter meals); the *Rainbow Retreat* also has live bands many nights a week. The small Bush Theatre (ⓣ02/6689 1111), located in an old butter factory over the bridge opposite *Granny's Farm Backpackers*, serves fabulous food and is home to the town's "Movie House" – films are shown here at weekends; call or check town notice boards for details.

The Channon

THE CHANNON, a 26-kilometre drive south of Nimbin, is a pretty village on the banks of **Terania Creek** with a well-known monthly market (every second Sunday of the month); the *Channon Tavern*, which serves good meals; and a teahouse, craft shop and art gallery in an old butter factory. A fourteen-kilometre drive along the unsealed Terania Creek Road brings you to **Protestors Falls** and a rainforest valley filled with ancient brush box trees, saved by a 1979 protest which was the first successful anti-logging campaign in Australia. The falls, named after the dispute, are a seven-hundred-metre walk from the picnic area; the waterhole underneath is perfect for swimming. Terania Creek is near the western edge of **Whian Whian State Forest**. On the forest's southeastern edge (reached via Mullumbimby or Dunoon), are the one-hundred-metre cascades of **Minyon Falls**.

You're allowed to **camp** for one night only at Terania Creek (no open fires allowed); alternatively, head either to the village campsite on the banks of the creek (ⓣ02/6688 6321) or to *Terania Park* (ⓣ02/6688 6121; cabins ❸), a scenic caravan park with cabins and campsites. For something a bit more comfortable, try the arty *Havan's B&B* (ⓣ02/6688 6108, ⓦwww.rainbowregion.com/havan; ❺), just off Terania Creek Road on Lawler Road overlooking the creek and rainforest.

Murwillumbah and around

After Ballina and Byron Bay, the next major stop on the Pacific Highway is **MURWILLUMBAH**, a quiet, inland town on a bend of the Tweed River, a little over 30km north of Byron Bay, which makes a good base for exploring some of the beautiful Tweed Valley and the mountains that extend to the Queensland border. Almost all buses on the north coast route stop here. The **tourist information** office is located in the **Rainforest Heritage Centre** on Alma Street (Mon–Sat 9am–4.30pm, Sun 9.30am–4pm;

Ⓦwww.tweed-coolangatta.com). It's well worth dropping by the **Tweed River Regional Art Gallery** at the corner of Tweed Valley Way and Minstral Road (Wed–Sun 10am–5pm; free), which displays the winners of the Doug Moran Portrait Prize, which originated here, as well as the work of local artists and travelling exhibitions.

The Tweed Valley and the surrounding area close to the Queensland border are among the most beautiful in New South Wales, ringed by mountain ranges that are actually the remains of an extinct volcano. Some twenty million years ago a huge shield **volcano** (a flat, shield-shaped landform rather than a cone-shaped peak) spewed lava through a central vent onto the surrounding plain. Erosion carved out an enormous bowl around the centre of the resultant mass of lava, while the more resistant rocks around the edges stood firm – these are now the **Nightcap**, **Border**, **Tweed** and **McPherson ranges**, the outer rim of a vast bowl. Right at its heart is **Mount Warning** (1150m), the original vent of the volcano, whose unmistakable, twisted profile rises like a sentinel from the Tweed Valley. A well-marked **bushwalking track** leads to the top from a car park just off the national park access road, itself a turn-off from the road to Uki, southwest of town. The path is extremely steep in its final stages (allow at least 4hr there and back) but you're rewarded by a sweeping view over the ranges of the volcanic rim and across the Tweed Valley to the Pacific.

There's a less strenuous, signposted 64-kilometre scenic drive through the **Tweed Valley**, which takes in some of its best features. A patchwork of sugar-cane fields and tropical fruit plantations is testimony to the fertility of the volcanic soil (there's even a tea plantation). Between the villages of Tumbulgum and Duranbah, the **big avocado** lures the wild-at-heart towards **Tropical Fruit World** (daily 10am–5pm; free) on Duranbah Road, a plantation which has been turned into a miniature theme park. The plantation grows avocados, macadamia nuts and many kinds of tropical fruit; for $25 you can ride around in open-air buses and miniature trains, or cruise around on man-made "tropical canals". There are canoes and aqua-bikes for rent, an animal park and playground, a restaurant and café (with exotic ice creams), as well as a fruit market selling plantation produce.

Slightly less commercial are the tours given during the cane-harvesting season at **Condong Sugar Mill** (Ⓣ02/6670 1700), on the Tweed River about 5km north of Murwillumbah (guided tours mid-June to Nov Tues–Thurs 9am–3pm; $7). The turn-off for the **Tree Tops Environment Centre** (daily 10am–5pm, but closed for renovations at the time of writing – call Ⓣ02 6672 3068 for latest information; free) is opposite the sugar mill; the centre is the home of Griffith Furniture, which creates beautiful designs from salvaged native timber using traditional timber-working techniques that you can observe in the workshop. Halfway between Nimbin and Murwillumbah, the pretty little village of **UKI** has a strong alternative bent, views of Mount Warning and a small, relaxed **market** on the third Sunday of each month.

Practicalities

Places to stay in Murwillumbah include the art deco *Imperial Hotel* at 115 Main Street (Ⓣ02/6672 2777; ❷), a grand old building right in the centre of town, with good-value singles and doubles, an excellent bistro, a kitchen for guests' use and local bands at weekends. *Mount Warning Riverside YHA Backpackers*, 1 Tumbulgum Road (Ⓣ02/6672 3763, Ⓦwww.yha.com.au; dorms $25, doubles ❷), is a truly wonderful find – a cosy hostel in a house leaning over the river. The hostel has private access for swimming, plus bikes for rent, free canoes and rowing boat, and free ice cream every evening at 8pm. Stay for two nights and you'll get a free trip to Mount Warning.

Alternatively, make the most of the countryside by staying in rural or **farm-stay** accommodation: *Midginbil Hill Country Resort* (Ⓣ02/6679 7158, Ⓦwww.bigvolcano.com.au/custom/midhill; bunkhouses ❶, lodges ❻, plus camping), a cattle station 30km west of Murwillumbah near Mount Warning, offers activities such as horse riding, canoeing and archery, and also has a pool, games room and tennis courts. *Mount Warning Forest Hideaway*, on Byrill Creek Road, near Uki (Ⓣ02/6679 7277, Ⓦwww.foresthideaway.com.au; ❺), occupies a hundred acres of lush forest and offers motel-style units with cooking facilities, plus a swimming pool. In Uki, you can stay at the clean *Uki Dreaming Guesthouse* (Ⓣ02/6679 5777, doubles ❷).

Places to eat include the old-fashioned *Austral Café*, an eat-in bakery on Main Street. *Margherita's Cantina*, also on Main Street, serves salads, lunches and breakfast from 7.30am. The *Imperial Hotel* on Main Street serves the best bistro food in town. It's also worth stopping at the *Mt Warning Hotel*, in the heart of Uki, for a country lunch, and there's locally grown organic coffee at the *Uki Trading Post* (daily 9am–5pm) right on the main road.

Lord Howe and Norfolk islands

Lord Howe Island, 700km northeast of Sydney, and roughly in line with Port Macquarie, is technically a part of New South Wales, despite its distance from the mainland. Its nearest neighbour is **Norfolk Island**, 900km further northeast, an external independent territory of Australia, though geographically it's closer to New Zealand. The approach to tourism of the two subtropical islands couldn't be more different: Lord Howe is the perfect eco-destination, attracting outdoor types with its rugged beauty, while Norfolk Island concentrates primarily on its status as a tax haven, and also on its fascinating history as a tough convict settlement and as the home for many of the descendants of the *Bounty* mutineers after they had left Pitcairn Island. Neither island caters to budget travellers.

Getting there

You can **fly to Lord Howe Island** with Qantas (Ⓣ13 13 13) from Sydney daily in summer, four times weekly from June to August, and from Coffs Harbour and Brisbane once weekly, for about $600 return; flights via Newcastle may be available in peak summer months. It's much easier to go on a **package tour**, but the lowest you can expect to pay for five nights is about $850 in winter, rising to $1600 in summer: try Oxley Travel (Ⓣ 1800 671 546 , Ⓦwww.oxleytravel.com.au) or Talpacific Holidays (Ⓣ13 27 47, Ⓦwww.talpacific.com); both operators also fly to Norfolk Island. Overseas visitors can fly to Lord Howe as an add-on fare on an air pass (see p.47).

The Qantas-linked Norfolk Jet Express (Ⓣ1800 816 947) flies to **Norfolk Island** from Sydney and Brisbane at weekends, while Flight West (Ⓣ1300 130

092, ⓦ www.flightwest.com.au) operates four flights a week from Brisbane and Sydney. Note that there's a $30 departure tax from Norfolk. **Packages** offer the best value, costing from $890 for five days. Air New Zealand flies twice weekly **from Auckland and Christchurch** to Norfolk Island, and a code-share agreement with Flight West means the destination can now be visited as a stop-over between New Zealand and Australia.

There are no flights between the two islands.

Lord Howe Island

I would strongly urge preserving this beautiful island from further intrusions of any kind...

Government Expedition, 1882

On the UNESCO World Heritage list since 1982 because of its rare birds, unusual plant life and coral reef, **LORD HOWE ISLAND** is a kind of Australian Galapagos, and an ultimate destination for ecotourists. The island's preservation was assured by Victorian-era descriptions of "this gem of the sea" when reports were brought back to the Australian mainland regarding the progress of the multi-racial settlers who had arrived in the 1830s. Even today only a tenth of the land has been cleared for cultivation or grazing, and two-thirds of the island is designated as **Permanent Park Reserve**. Just 11km long and not quite 3km across at its widest point, the crescent-shaped island's only industry other than tourism is its plantations of **kentia palms** (see p.341). With a population of just 350, the island can be visited by no more than 400 visitors at any one time; to enforce this limit, accommodation has to be booked in advance. Although some locals have vehicles, people get around mainly by bicycle, boat or on foot.

As you fly in, you'll get a stunning view of the whole of the volcanic island: the towering summits of rainforest-clad **Mount Gower** and **Mount Lidgbird** at the southern end, the narrow centre with its idyllic lagoon and a **coral reef** extending about 6km along the island's west coast, and a group of tiny islets off the coast at the lower northern end of the island providing sanctuary for the prolific **birdlife**.

The island is very easy-going and laid-back, and the emphasis is on tranquillity; most visitors are couples and families – there are no rowdy nightclubs here. Though it's expensive to get to the island, once here you'll find that cruises, bike rental and eating out are all relatively affordable. The island's **climate** is subtropical, with temperatures rising from an average low of 16°C to 19°C in winter, 26°C in the summer, and an annual rainfall of 1650mm. It's cheaper to visit in the winter, though some places are closed.

Some history

Lord Howe Island was discovered in 1778 by the ship *Supply* during a journey from Sydney to found a colony on Norfolk Island, though the island wasn't settled for another 55 years. These first **settlers**, who arrived in 1833, were three white men, with Maori women and boys, who provided whaling vessels with provisions. Other settlers arrived in the 1840s, but in 1853 two white men came with three women from the Gilbert Islands, and it is from this small group that many of Lord Howe's present population are descended. In the 1840s and 1850s the island continued to serve as a stopover for **whaling ships** from the US and Britain, with as many as fifty ships a year passing through. In 1882 a government

Lord Howe ecology

Seven million years ago a volcanic eruption on the sea floor created Lord Howe Island and its 27 surrounding islets and outcrops – the island's boomerang shape is a mere remnant of the massive shield volcano, mostly eroded by the sea. While much of the **flora** on the island is similar to that of Australia, New Zealand, New Caledonia and Norfolk Island, the island's relative isolation has led to the evolution of many **new species** – of the 241 native plants found here, 105 are endemic, including the important indigenous **kentia palm** (see below).

Similarly, until the arrival of settlers, fifteen species of flightless **land birds** (nine of which are now extinct) lived on the island, undisturbed by predators and coexisting with migrating seabirds, skinks, geckos, spiders, snails and the now-extinct giant horned turtle. However, in the eighteenth century Lord Howe became a port of call for ships en route to Norfolk Island, whose hungry crews eradicated the island's stocks of **white gallinule** and **white-throated pigeon**. The small, plump and flightless **woodhen** managed to survive, protected on Mount Gower, and an intensive captive breeding programme in the early 1980s saved the species (there are now about 200). About one million **seabirds** – fourteen species – nest here annually: and it is one of the few known breeding grounds of the providence petrel; the island also has the world's largest colony of red-tailed tropic birds and is the most southerly breeding location of the sooty tern, the noddy tern and the masked booby. Cats have now been eradicated from the island, as a result of which bird numbers have soared, and there's now also a plan to exterminate rats and mice too.

The cold waters of the **Tasman Sea**, which surround Lord Howe, host the world's southernmost **coral reef**, a tropical oddity that is sustained by the warm summer currents that sweep in from the Great Barrier Reef. There are about sixty varieties of brilliantly coloured and fantastically shaped coral, and the meeting of warm and cold currents means that a huge variety of both **tropical and temperate fish** can be spotted by snorkellers in the crystal-clear waters. Some of the most colourful species include the yellow moon wrasse and the yellow-and-black banner fish. Unique to Lord Howe is the doubleheader, with its bizarre, bulbous forehead and fat lips. Beyond the lagoon, the water becomes very deep, with particularly good diving in the seas around the Admiralty Islets, which have sheer underwater precipices and chasms. The diving season lasts from May to November (for information on dive companies, see p.346).

expedition from the mainland recommended that, in order to preserve the island, no one other than the present "happy, industrious" leaseholders and their families be allowed to make permanent settlement.

With the decline of whaling, economic salvation came in the form of the "thatch" palm, one of the four endemic species of the **kentia palm**. Previously used as roofing for the islanders' homes, it now began to be exported as a decorative interior plant, boosting the island's economy. The profits from the kentia trade were shared out equally amongst the island's residents, each of whom was in turn expected to take on an equal share of the, not overly hard, work on the kentia plantations. Between World Wars I and II this collective system made the island an egalitarian paradise whose legacy can still be seen today: no one locks their car (or even takes the key out), and you won't find a lock on your bike, or on your room door.

In 1918, however, the kentia industry was damaged by the appearance of **rats**, which escaped onto the island from a ship (true to form, the locals banded together into rat-catching parties with a bounty of one shilling for every ten rat's tails). **Tourism**, though, was eventually to become the mainstay of the island. Lord Howe had been a popular stopover on the cruise-ship circuit before World War II, and after the war it began to be visited by holiday-makers from Sydney, who came by seaplane.

Today, rats still pose a hazard to the palms, but the **kentia industry** is nonetheless in resurgence, with profits going towards the preservation of the island's unique ecosystem. Seeds are no longer exported but instead cultivated in the Lord Howe Island Board's own **nursery**, which sells two and a half million plants annually, mainly to Europe and North America; they also grow seedlings here for regeneration around the island. You can visit the nursery, as well as other parts of the island on guided walks with Ron's Rambles (ⓣ02/6563 2010). Ron will have you sniffing herbs, feeling rocks and believing some tall stories about the early islanders' bushcraft. Book at Thompson's General Store (see below).

Arrival, information and transport

There's no official transport from the **airport**, located in the narrow central part of the island, but wherever you're staying, you'll be met on arrival by your lodge-owner. The island's **visitors centre** (Mon–Fri & Sun 9am–4pm; ⓣ02/6563 2114 or 1800 240 937, ⓦwww.lordhoweisland.info) is located inside the Lord Howe Island Museum at the junction of Lagoon and Middle Beach roads; the centre runs an excellent twenty-minute audiovisual presentation on the island, gives out advice on weather conditions, and also has plenty of free brochures about wildlife and plants, as well as basic walking maps. A good buy for walkers is the useful *Ramblers Guide to Lord Howe Island* ($9), which covers all the walks on the island in much greater detail and is available from the visitors centre. The centre often hosts very good slide shows at 5.30pm (days vary, check at the visitor centre; $6) on island history and ecology.

Crossing the centre of the island to the north, Ned's Beach Road has a cluster of **shops** and **services**, including Thompson's General Store (ⓣ02/6563 2155), where you can book most activities – it's advisable to sign up in advance for cruises. You'll also find a community hall-cum-summer cinema and a **post office** (Mon–Fri 10am–3pm, Mon & Tues until 4pm) on this road which also acts as an agent for Commonwealth Bank account holders. Nearby, the Westpac **bank** agent (Mon & Fri 2–4pm, Tues–Thurs 10am–noon) also caters for some other cardholders. There are no ATMs on the island, although some establishments, including Larrups clothes and beachwear shop on Ned's Beach Road and Joy's store, give $50–100 cash out on eftpos or credit cards to customers. Basically, it's a good idea to bring all the cash you'll need with you to the island.

There are three places to buy **groceries** on the island: Thompson's General Store; the large Joy's Shop, opposite *Leanda Lei Apartments* on Middle Beach Road; and the Top Shop (Mon–Fri 9am–12.30pm & 4.30–6pm, Sun 9am–12.30pm), tucked away on Skyline Street off Mutton Bird Drive, where you can get fresh meat and vegetables, flown in daily from Port Macquarie. Inevitably, transport costs make things more expensive than on the mainland.

Transport

The island has only one **road** and relatively few cars. There are no streetlights so you'll need to bring a torch with you, or buy one from Joy's Shop, if you want to venture out at night. There's no regular bus service, but lodge owners and restaurants will usually pick up and drop off customers. Otherwise, Wilson's (see p.344) can do pick-ups and drop-offs. The most common ways to get around are by **bicycle**, boat or on foot. There are plenty of places to

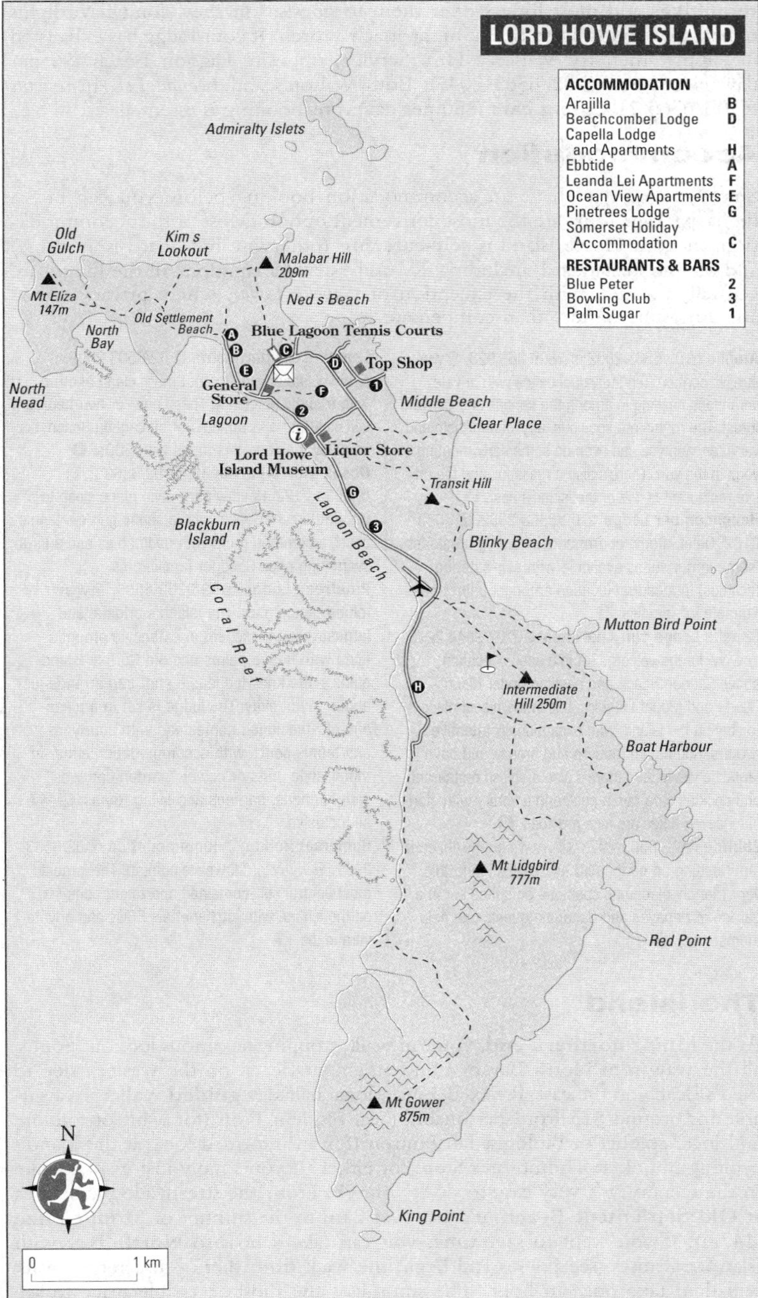

LORD HOWE ISLAND
ACCOMMODATION
Arajilla B
Beachcomber Lodge D
Capella Lodge and Apartments H
Ebbtide A
Leanda Lei Apartments F
Ocean View Apartments E
Pinetrees Lodge G
Somerset Holiday Accommodation C
RESTAURANTS & BARS
Blue Peter 2
Bowling Club 3
Palm Sugar 1
Admiralty Islets
Old Gulch
Kim s Lookout
Malabar Hill 209m
Mt Eliza 147m
Ned s Beach
Old Settlement Beach
North Bay
Blue Lagoon Tennis Courts
Top Shop
North Head
General Store
Middle Beach
Lagoon
Clear Place
Lord Howe Island Museum
Liquor Store
Transit Hill
Lagoon Beach
Blackburn Island
Blinky Beach
Coral Reef
Mutton Bird Point
Intermediate Hill 250m
Boat Harbour
Mt Lidgbird 777m
Red Point
Mt Gower 875m
N
King Point
0 1 km
Balls Pyramid (23 km)

rent bikes and most lodges offer them to guests, but they don't have lights either, so if you want to ride at night attach a torch. If your lodge has exhausted its supply, then try Wilson's Hire Service, opposite Lagoon Beach ($6 per day; closed Sat; T 02/6563 2045). Both Wilson's and *Leanda Lei Apartments* (T 02/6563 2195) rent **cars** ($50 per day); pre-booking is essential.

Accommodation

Since you need to have an accommodation booking before you can buy a flight, package tours are the most convenient option. Most of the accommodation on Lord Howe Island is **self-catering** (otherwise full board is available) and of a good standard, including TV and usually a laundry. All the lodges are centrally located, with the exception of *Capella Lodge*, where privacy, views and atmosphere more than compensate.

Arajilla T 02/6563 2002 or 1800 063 928, W www.arajilla.com.au. Ten individual suites with private verandahs nestling in among the kentias and Banyan forest. The rooms are spacious, airy, comfortable and very Zen, and you can even do some early morning yoga in the yurt. There's also a masseur, and the on-site restaurant is one of the island's best. 8

Beachcomber Lodge T 02/6563 2032, F 6563 2132. Quiet, studio apartments including breakfast (some larger suites available with self-catering facilities) in a central location amongst palm trees. Suitable for families. 7

Capella Lodge and Apartments T 02/9544 2273, W www.lordhowe.com. Set in a scenic location above Salmon Beach and nestling under Mount Gower and Mount Lidgbird, this is the nicest place to stay on the island, with exceptionally attentive owners. Rooms are modern and breezy, and have fantastic views, and there's also a stylish restaurant and cocktail café-bar, a pool, and a library with stunning views. Bikes are also provided. 8

Ebbtide T 02/6563 2023, W www.ebbtide-lhi.com.au. Nestling up on the cliff by Searles Point, this very friendly place has spacious en suites set in a garden of papayas and bananas (guests can help themselves). 7

Leanda Lei Apartments T 02/6563 2095, W www.leandalei.com.au. Smart, clean and run with friendly efficiency. These one- or two-bedroom self-catering apartments are by Lagoon Beach, set in nicely manicured grounds with BBQs. 7

Ocean View Apartments T 02/6563 2041, F 6563 2122. Holiday park-style place close to Old Settlement Beach, with a sunny garden, tennis court, a common room with pool tables and a large swimming pool. Good for families. 4

Pinetrees Lodge T 02/9262 6585, W www.pinetrees.com.au. The island's original and largest guesthouse, set in extensive grounds filled with native palms and old Norfolk Island pines – the knowledgeable staff can arrange just about any activity. The lodge is set in a pleasant, old-fashioned homestead with courtyard and tennis court, with accommodation either in motel-style units or newer "garden cottages" with kitchens, gardens and living rooms. 6–8 all inclusive.

Somerset Holiday Accommodation T 02/6563 2061, W www.lordhoweisle.com.au. The largest, most central self-contained apartment complex on the island, with kitchenettes, BBQs and private verandahs. 7

The island

At the island's **northern end**, you can walk, stopping at various lookout points, all the way from North Bay or Old Settlement Beach on the western side to Ned's Beach on the east. Relaxed, educational half-day **guided walks** are available for around $15 from personable local resident Ron (for a bit of folklore and local colour) or biologist Ian Hutton (for an informed look at the island's ecology); book at Thompson's Store for either. If you simply just want to take in the scenery, it's very easy to do it yourself. From the streamside picnic area at **Old Settlement Beach**, it's just over 2km to the summit of **Mount Eliza** (147m). If you want to save time, you can take a boat to **North Bay** with Islander Cruises (see p.346) and begin the walk from there – the return walk will then take only an hour. The summit is the most accessible place to see

sooty terns in their southernmost breeding grounds. When the colony visits the island between August and March each female lays a single speckled egg on the bare ground, which means that the actual summit has to be closed for the birds' protection.

Back at the base, a short five- or ten-minute walk through forest from **North Beach** (good for swimming and snorkelling on North Reef) leads to **Old Gulch**, a beach of boulders, where at low tide you can rock-hop to the **Herring Pools** at the base of the cliff front and examine the colourful marine life. From **Ned's Beach** the walk to **Malabar Hill** (209m) gives access to one of the world's largest nesting concentrations of **red-tailed tropic birds**, who between September and May make their homes in the crannies of the cliff face below, laying only one egg and looking after the chick for twelve weeks until it can fly. It's fascinating to watch the white birds' unusual and rather balletic backwards-dancing through the air during courtship. From the summit, you can just see Ball's Pyramid way to the south around the corner of Mount Lidgbird before heading along the cliff edge to **Kim's Lookout** (182m), which provides a good view of the settlement and the lagoon beaches and islets. From here it's just over a kilometre back to Old Settlement Beach (or you can continue to North Bay and Mount Eliza).

There are more walks in the **centre of the island**: from Middle Beach to Clear Place; from Blinky Beach, the island's main surfing spot, to **Transit Hill** (121m); and from near the airstrip to the summit of **Intermediate Hill** (250m); and two longer walks from the base of Intermediate Hill to **Boat Harbour** or to the base of **Mount Lidgbird** (777m). Less energetic is a trip to the **Lord Howe Island Museum**, opposite Lagoon Beach on the corner of Middle Beach and Lagoon roads, which details the history of the island from its discovery to the present day.

The ultimate view on the island is at its **southern end**, where the lofty summit of **Mount Gower** (875m) gives vistas over the whole island and out to sea towards **Balls Pyramid** (548m), a tall spike of volcanic rock which breaks dramatically up out of the ocean 23km from Lord Howe. Mount Gower is high enough to have a true **mist forest** on its summit, with a profusion of ferns, tree trunks and rocks covered in mosses. This very strenuous walk can be undertaken only with licensed **guide** Jack Shick (Ⓣ02/6563 2218; $35; BYO lunch). The track to the top was blazed by botanists in 1869, who took two days to get there, but they were rewarded with the discovery of a plant seen nowhere else on earth – the **pumpkin tree**, bearing fleshy orange flowers. You can see other rare endemic plants here, such as the island apple and the blue plum, as well as birds such as the providence petrel and the woodhen. On average, the return walk takes eight hours and you'll need to be fit. It's not for the faint-hearted, either: one section of the walk runs precariously along a narrow cliff face above the sea, and in parts the track is so steep that you must hang onto guide ropes. To join the walk, you have to be at the Little Island gate on the south of the island by 7.30am: transport there is available for an extra $6 round-trip from Whitfield Bus Tours (Ⓣ02/6563 2115), or it's about a half-hour cycle ride from the north of the island.

Slightly less energetic activities are available at the *Blue Lagoon Lodge*'s **tennis courts** on North Beach Road (balls and rackets available to rent from Thompson's Store), and the nine-hole **golf course** near *Capella Lodge* ($15 with your own clubs, $25 with theirs; balls $1); there's a chicken run competition held here on Friday afternoons.

Water-based activities

Besides bushwalks, the island has some sensational swimming, snorkelling and diving sites. The water's combined temperate and tropical sealife make local double-headed wrasse, lobsters and angelfish a common sight. Among the cruises on offer, the **glass-bottom boat cruises** from Lagoon Beach, which take about twenty passengers, are particularly good value at $25 for two hours (book at Thompson's General Store); included are opportunities to snorkel at **Erscotts Hole**, with gear and wet suits provided, and hand-feeding of fish, including a friendly old double-headed wrasse – you also see much more than on other, motorboat excursions. Islander Cruises (Ⓣ02/6563 2021, Ⓔislandercruises@bigpond.com.au) can take you to North Bay, combining a **snorkelling** excursion around the 1965 wreck of the *Favorite* (now colonized by three-stripe butterfly fish) with bushwalks or excellent beachcombing walks with naturalist Ian Hutton (Sept–June 10am–4pm; half/full day $25/35, including BBQ on full-day tour).

There's more stunning snorkelling at Sylphs Hole, off Old Settlement Beach, and on the east side of the island at Ned's Beach, where slightly musty snorkelling sets can be rented; sets are also available from most lodges, and Thompson's Store. Every day at 4pm for the last fifteen years, Ned's Beach has been the site of a **fish-feeding** frenzy, when a local man throws fish scraps into the water, attracting a throng of big trevally, kingfish and reef sharks; the beach is also home to a venerable sea turtle. Stay here until dusk and you can observe **muttonbirds** en masse darkening the sky as they come home to roost. They fly low through a forest of enormous **banyan trees** whose tangle of aerial roots descends to the ground.

Fishing trips can be arranged with Lulawai (Ⓣ02/6563 2195; $50 half-day), who guarantee you some fish, which the crew will prepare for you to barbecue later. Thompson's Store provides rods, reels, tackle and bait for those who already know what they're doing. If you're interested in **diving** in the waters around Lord Howe, contact Howea Divers (Ⓣ02/6563 2290, Ⓔhoweadivers@bigpond.com.au; boat dive plus gear $75, Ball's Pyramid dive plus gear $200), who are the most experienced and friendly outfit. As well as advanced dives and tuition, they offer novices the chance to dive either off boats or from the shore for $80, and they also run sensational dive trips to nearby Ball's Pyramid. Pro-Dive also has an outlet on the island, with packages bookable through their Sydney central reservations (Ⓣ02/9281 5066 or 1800 820 820, Ⓦwww.prodive.com.au). A cheaper way to see **Ball's Pyramid** is on a boat tour with Phasmid (Ⓣ02/6563 2287; $100). If you want to **kayak**, a double-canoe from Wilson's Hire costs $10 an hour (or $25/40 for a half/full day).

Eating and drinking

Bookings are necessary at all **eating** places for evening meals (and there's hardly any vegetarian food available, although you could try asking). An essential **lunch** or snack stop is the *Blue Peter* (daily 10am–5pm, also open for dinner on Fridays), a summer-only café on Lagoon Road, which offers affordable salads, speciality burgers, focaccia and daily fish specials. Thompson's General Store does inexpensive takeaway fish and beef burgers at lunch time, while the very pleasant *Palm Sugar* (Ⓣ02/6563 2120; daily 9am–4pm) on Skyline Drive does fish, pastries and antipasto plates. The best **restaurants** on the island are the restaurant at the *Arajilla* resort (Ⓣ02/6563 2002) and *Capella Lodge Restaurant* (Ⓣ02/6563 2008), both of which serve innovative modern Australian cuisine (though portions aren't huge) and excellent fish dishes. There's no pub on the island. The closest thing to a **bar** is the *Bowling Club* (daily 4.30–8pm); there's also a very popular disco here every Friday night (8pm–midnight).

Norfolk Island

Just 8km long and 5km wide, tiny, isolated **NORFOLK ISLAND**, an External Territory of Australia located 1500km due east of Brisbane, has had an eventful history, being linked with early convict settlements and later with the descendants of Fletcher Christian and other "mutiny-on-the-*Bounty*" rebels. It's a unique island, forested with grand indigenous pine trees, and with a mild subtropical climate ranging between 11°C and 18°C in the winter and from 19°C to 28°C in the summer. Nowadays the island's **tax-haven** status makes it a refuge for millionaires, and most visitors spend a fortune in the island's numerous **duty-free stores**. Norfolk is also said to have the world's **cleanest air** after Antarctica.

The island mainly attracts honeymooners or retired Australians and New Zealanders (known as the "newly weds and nearly deads"). All visitors require a **passport** to visit the island, which has its own Legislative Assembly. A thirty-day **visitor permit**, extendable to 120 days, is granted automatically on arrival. The island has no income tax, finances being raised from sources such as departure tax ($30) and a road levy included in the price of petrol. Most of the local people remain unaffected by tourism, maintaining their friendly attitude, ridiculous nicknames and the remnants of their dialect, **Pitcairn**, a mixture of old West Country English and Tahitian (see p.348).

Much of the land is cleared for cultivation, as islanders have to grow all their own fresh food; cattle roam freely on the green island and are given right of way, creating a positively bucolic atmosphere. At the centre of the island is its only significant settlement, **BURNT PINE** and on the south coast, picturesque **KINGSTON** is the sightseeing focus. Scenic winding roads provide access to the **national park** and the **Botanic Garden** in the northern half of the island, which together cover twenty percent of Norfolk's area with subtropical rainforest. Norfolk Island is also an ornithologist's paradise, with nine endemic **landbird** species, including the endangered **Norfolk Island green parrot**, with its distinctive chuckling sound. The two small islands immediately south of Norfolk, Nepean and Phillip islands, are important **seabird** nesting sites.

Some history

A violent volcanic eruption three million years ago produced the Norfolk Ridge, extending from New Zealand to New Caledonia (Norfolk Island's closest neighbour, 700km north), with only Norfolk Island and the smaller adjacent and uninhabited **Phillip** and **Nepean islands** remaining above sea level. **Captain Cook** "discovered" the islands in 1774, but it's now believed that migrating Polynesian people had lived here for hundreds of years prior. Cook thought the tall **Norfolk pines** might make fine ships' masts, with accompanying sails woven from the native flax. Norfolk Island was settled in 1788, only six weeks after Sydney. However, plans to use the fertile island as a base to grow food for the starving young colony of Australia foundered when, in 1790, a First Fleet ship, the *Sirius*, was wrecked on a reef off the island, highlighting the island's lack of a navigable harbour. This **first settlement** was unviable when the pines proved not to be strong enough for masts, and it was finally abandoned in 1814. Most of the buildings were destroyed to discourage settlement by other powers.

Norfolk's isolation was one of the major reasons for its **second settlement** (1825–55) – as a **prison**, described officially as "a place of the extremest punishment short of death". Some of the imposing stone buildings designed by Royal Engineers still stand in **Kingston**, on the southern coast of the island.

There were up to two thousand convicts on the island, overseen by sadistic commandants who had virtually unlimited power to run the settlement and inflict punishments as they saw fit.

Norfolk Island was again abandoned in 1855, but this time the buildings remained and were used a year later during the **third settlement**, which consisted of 194 Pitcairn Islanders (the entire population of the island), who left behind their overcrowded conditions to establish a new life here. The new settlers had only eight family surnames among them – five of which (Christian, Quintal, Adams, McKoy and Young) were the names of the original mutineers of the *Bounty*. These names – especially Christian – are still common on the island, and today about one in three islanders can claim descent from the mutineers. These descendants still speak some Pitcairn to each other: listen for expressions such as 'Watawieh yourle' (how are you) and 'Si Yourle Morla' (see you tomorrow). **Bounty Day**, the day the Pitcairners arrived, is celebrated in Kingston on June 8.

Information, transport and tours

The island's **airport** is on the western side of the island, just outside **Burnt Pine**, the main service town; the island's information centre, banks and post office are all in Burnt Pine. For information and bookings in advance, contact **Norfolk Island Tourism**, PO Box 211, Norfolk Island 2899 (Ⓣ6723/22147, Ⓦwww.norfolkisland.com.au), or consult Ⓦwww.pi-travel.com/norfolkisland – the most comprehensive of the many island information websites. All tourist facilities are based in the main town of **Burnt Pine**. Here, in the Bicentennial Complex on Taylor's Road, you'll find: the **Norfolk Island Visitor Information Centre** (Mon–Fri 8.30am–5pm, Sat 8.30am–1pm, Sun 8.30am–3pm; Ⓣ6723/22147, Ⓕ23109), which can book tours and activities; the liquor bond store, which sells discounted alcohol on production of your airline ticket; the **post office**; and the Communications Centre, where you need to go to make international **phone calls**. There are two **banks** on the main street, Westpac and Commonwealth; the Commonwealth has the island's only ATM.

There's no public transport on Norfolk Island, so getting around by **car** is much the best option. Many accommodation places offer a car as part of the package or give you a big discount on **car rental**. It's very cheap anyway, from just $20 (plus about $10 insurance) at the airport. No one's bothered about seat belts or even driving mirrors, and the maximum speed limit is only 50kph (40kph in town). There are also a limited number of **bikes** for rent, which can be arranged through the tourist office or your accommodation.

Tours

For **tours**, Pinetree Tours (Ⓣ6723/22424; Ⓦwww.pinetreetours.com), with an office on the main street next to the Commonwealth bank, offers a slew of pricey tours, including an extensive introductory half-day bus tour of the island ($20). Bounty Excursions (Ⓣ6723/23693, Ⓔbounty@norfolk.nf) covers a range of cultural and historic sites, including a Convict Ruins Tour (Mon 1pm & Fri 3pm; 3hr; $22) and a panoramic Norfolk Discovery Tour (Mon & Thurs–Sun; 3hr; $22). Culla & Co, on Rooty Hill Rd (Ⓣ & Ⓕ6723/22312), offers shire horse-drawn carriage rides of the island.

The island is surrounded by a coral reef and pristine waters, so at least one waterborne tour is a must; the volcanic seafloor is full of caves and swim-throughs and the whole area is a marine reserve – commercial fishing is banned. There are several glass-bottomed **boat cruises** ($20) on Emily Bay, including on the *Bounty Glass Bottomed Boat* (Ⓣ6723/22515) and *Christian's Glaas Bohtam Boet* (Ⓣ6523/23258). For fishing trips, ask at the tourist office. Bounty Divers at the Village Centre (Ⓣ6723/22751, Ⓦwww.bountydivers.nf) runs PADI courses ($425) and has **dive** charters ($85 per dive, including gear), **snorkelling** and **diving** gear, and guided reef walks. *Tropical Sea Kayaks* (Ⓣ6723/80508; Ⓦwww.seakayaking.nf) will take you on a 3.5-hour trip for $35.

Accommodation

A lot of **accommodation** is in comfortable 1970s-style motels. There are two faithfully restored five-star cottages. A central online **booking service** is available at Ⓦwww.norfolkislandaccommodation.com, or call Ⓣ6723/22255. The two most stunning places to stay are: *Christians* of Bucks Point (Ⓣ02/9525 7724, Ⓦwww.christians.nf; ❽), a whoppingly expensive historic property on the southeast coast, sleeping up to six, with floorboards and wooden doors from the original convict quarters in Kingston and car rental included in the price; and *Tintoela of Norfolk* (Ⓣ6723/22946, Ⓦwww.tintoela.nf; ❽), a large, luxury wooden house, and adjacent cottage sleeping up to ten, with panoramic views of Cockpit Valley and the ocean. *Anson Bay Lodge* (Ⓣ6723/22897, Ⓔansonbaylodge@norfolk.nf; ❹), a smaller property for two to four people, is the cheapest place, located on Bullock's Hut Road. Some of the more attractive **motels** include *Shearwater Scenic Villas* (Ⓣ6723/22539, Ⓦwww.shearwater.nf; ❺), with self-contained accommodation in extensive grounds with terrific water views near Bumbora Reserve. *Whispering Pines*, on Mount Pitt road (Ⓣ6723/22114; Ⓦwww.norfolk-pines-group.nf/whisper.html ❺) is another place that won't break the bank, with charming hexagonal timber cottages hidden in thickly wooded gardens. The attractive *South Pacific Resort* (Ⓣ6723/23154, Ⓦwww.southpacificresort.nlk.nf; ❻), close to Burnt Pine, has a bar, restaurant and swimming pool in pleasant green grounds.

The island

The island's main settlement, **BURNT PINE**, is a fairly modern affair crammed with shops selling everything from Lancôme cosmetics through to Sanyo stereos, all at duty-free prices; most shops are closed on Wednesday and Saturday afternoons and all day Sunday. **KINGSTON** is Norfolk's administrative centre, with the Legislative Assembly meeting in the military barracks and the old colonial Government House now home to the island's Administrator. There is an excellent view from the **Queen Elizabeth Lookout** over the **Kingston and Arthur's Vale Historic Area** and the poignant seafront **cemetery**, containing a number of graves from the brutal second settlement with detailed interpretive boards, but it's expensive to visit the remaining buildings and their museums: you can tour the buildings separately ($8) or with a combined ticket ($20), which allows multiple access to all sites spread over several days.

Quality Row bears some of the world's most impressive examples of Georgian **military architecture**, and looking at the buildings now it's difficult to imagine the suffering that took place behind their walls. Here is the place to come for a taste of Norfolk Island history; there are four museums housed under the umbrella of the **Norfolk Island Museum** (daily 11am–3pm; $8 per museum or $20 combined ticket; Ⓦwww.museums.gov.nf). The **Archeological Museum** is located in the basement of the former Commissariat which was built in 1835; the upstairs was converted by the Pitcairners to All Saints Church. Close by, in the **No. 10 House Museum**, there are examples of Norfolk pine furniture made by convicts. The worthwhile **Social History Museum** is located in the pier store and outlines the story of the island through its three settlements. Perhaps most interesting, though, is the **Maritime Museum**, in what was once the Protestant chapel; various artefacts recovered from the 1790 wreck of the *Sirius* are on display, including its huge anchor, but more compelling is the *Bounty*-related paraphernalia brought here by Pitcairners, including the ship's cannon and even the kettle that was used on Pitcairn Island for everything from fermenting liquor to boiling sea water for salt. The Kingston area is also the site of the island's main swimming **beaches**, protected by a small reef. Immediately in front of the walls of the ruined barracks is **Slaughter Bay**, which has a sandy beach dotted with interestingly gnarled and eroded basalt rock formations; the small hard-coral reef is excellent for **snorkelling**. At low tide you can take a cruise in a glass-bottomed boat (see "Tours", p.348) from nearby Emily Bay, which is also a safe swimming area, backed by a large pine forest.

In **Bumbora Reserve**, just west of Kingston, reached by car via Bumbora Road, you can see the natural regrowth of Norfolk pines; from the reserve you can walk down to Bumbora Beach, a shady little beach where you'll find some safe pools for children to swim in at low tide. There's another track down to **Crystal Pool**, which has more swimming and snorkelling.

West of Burnt Pine, along Douglas Drive, you'll find the exquisite **St Barnabas Chapel**, once the property of the Melanesian Mission (Anglican), which relocated gradually here from New Zealand between 1866 and 1921. The chapel's rose window was designed by William Morris, some of the others were designed by Sir Edward Burne-Jones, with the altar carved by Solomon Islanders – ancestral masters of the craft.

On the **west coast** there's a scenic picnic area with tables and barbecues high over **Anson Bay**, from where it's a satisfying walk down to the beach. Immediately north of here, the **national park** has 8km of walking trails, many of them old logging tracks. Many walks start from **Mount Pitt** (320m), a pleasing drive up a fairly narrow and winding sealed road surrounded by palms and trees – worth it for the panoramic views. The most enjoyable walk from here is the three-kilometre route to the **Captain Cook Memorial** (1hr 45min), which starts as a beautiful grassy path but soon becomes a downward-sloping dirt track with some steps. Just south of the national park, on Pitt Road, the rainforest of the **Botanic Gardens** is worth a tranquil stroll. Here you can observe the forty endemic plant species including the pretty native hibiscus, the native palm, and the island's best-known symbol, the **Norfolk pine**, which can grow as high as 57m with a circumference of up to 11m. Both parks are permanently open, but camping is not allowed in either. The island also has an ecotourism attraction, **A Walk in the Wild**, at Taylor's Road, Burnt Pine (daily 2–5pm; free), educating visitors about the fragile, disappearing rainforest and its birdlife.

Eating, drinking and entertainment

Norfolk Island **food** is plain and fresh, with an emphasis on locally caught fish and home-grown seasonal produce. Tahitian influence remains in the tradition of the big fish fries, and in some novel ways of preparing bananas. As most accommodation is self-catering, you'll want to head to the Foodland Supermarket in Burnt Pine (daily to 6pm). On Sunday afternoon fresh fish is sold at the Kingston pier.

The best, and most expensive, **restaurant** is *Mariah's*, at *Hillcrest Gardens Hotel* on Taylor's Road (☎6723/22255), for à la carte dining with spectacular views of Phillip Island. *Dino's* (ⓣ6723/24225), on Bumboras Road, is a quality licensed Italian place with a pleasant ambience. *James' Place* at New Cascade Road in Burnt Pine (ⓣ6723/23039) has innovative, Asian-influenced and vegetarian dishes. The *South Pacific Resort* puts on big fish fries, smorgasbord nights, roast carveries and musical shows at various times during the week; on other nights an ordinary brasserie menu is available from 5.30pm. A superb spot for **lunch** is the extremely popular *Café Pacifica* (ⓣ6723/23210) on Cutters Corn Road, set in a leafy nursery and serving exquisite brunches and afternoon teas.

The **clubs** on the island provide good places to eat, drink and mingle with the locals. Facing each other across Burnt Pine's main street are the *Sports and Workers Club* and the *Norfolk Island Bowling Club*. The *Golf Club* in Kingston has a popular bar that also serves meals. The only **pub** is the *Brewery*, opposite the airport, with local ales such as "Bee Sting" and "Bligh's Revenge", pool tables and a rough, late-night crowd that can be a bit intimidating for single women.

Travel details

Most public transport in New South Wales originates in Sydney, and the main services are outlined in the "Travel details" at the end of Chapter 1 on p.261.

Trains

All trains are run by Countrylink, which extends its network with additional bus services. For full details see ⓦwww.countrylink.nsw.gov.au or call ⓣ13 22 32.

- Sydney–Brisbane (2 daily; 14hr 10min), with stops including **Taree, Coffs Harbour** and **Grafton**.
- Sydney–**Canberra** (2 daily; 4hr 10min),
- Sydney–**Murwillumbah** (1 daily; 13hr 45min), via **Taree** (5hr 20min), **Wauchope** (6hr 30min), **Coffs Harbour** (8hr 40min), **Grafton** (10hr), **Lismore** (12hr) and **Byron Bay** (13hr).

Buses

Byron Bay to: Ballina (3–10 daily; 30min); Brisbane (10–13 daily; 2hr 15min); Coffs Harbour (5–8 daily; 3hr 50min); Murwillumbah (4–6 daily; 55min); Port Macquarie (6 daily; 7hr); Surfers Paradise (6–7 daily; 1hr 5min); Sydney (4–6 daily; 13hr 15min).

Canberra to: Albury (2 daily; 4hr 20min); Bairnsdale (3 weekly; 7hr); Batemans Bay (2 daily; 2hr 30min); Bega (2 daily; 3hr 40min); Bombala (3 weekly; 3hr 30min); Cooma (2 daily; 1hr 45min); Eden (1 daily; 4hr 20min); Griffith (1 daily; 6hr 35min); Melbourne (6 daily; 9hr 30min); Moruya (1–2 daily; 3hr 25min); Narooma (1 daily; 4hr 30min); Nowra (1 daily; 4hr 45min); Wagga Wagga (2 daily; 3hr); Wollongong (2 daily; 3hr 25min).

Coffs Harbour to: Byron Bay (5–8 daily; 3hr 50min); Grafton (5 daily; 1hr 10min); Nambucca Heads (6 daily; 50min); Port Macquarie (6 daily; 2hr 40min); Tweed Heads (1 daily; 6hr 10min).

Lismore to: Ballina (2 daily; 45min); Brisbane (3 daily; 3hr); Byron Bay (4–6 daily; 1hr 15min); Casino (1 daily; 25min); Murwillumbah (3–5 daily; 2hr); Nimbin (2–3 daily; 25min); Tweed Heads (3 daily; 2hr 45min).

Murwillumbah to: Tweed Heads (4–11 daily; 30min).

Port Macquarie to: Armidale (1 daily; 6hr 15min); Ballina (5 daily; 6hr); Bellingen (3 weekly; 3hr 15min); Brisbane (5 daily; 10hr 30min); Byron Bay (6 daily; 7hr); Coffs Harbour (6 daily; 2hr 40min); Dorrigo (3 weekly; 3hr 50min); Grafton (5 daily; 4hr 10min); Scone (3 weekly; 10hr 20min); Surfers Paradise (3–5 daily; 9hr); Tamworth (3 weekly; 8hr 30min).

Flights

Ballina to: Brisbane (4 daily; 45min); Sydney (4 daily; 1hr 50min).

Canberra to: Ballina (2–3 daily; 4hr 40min); Dubbo (5 daily; 2hr 15min); Grafton (1–2 daily; 2hr 30min); Lismore (1–4 daily; 4hr 10min); Moree (1–2 daily; 3hr 55min); Narrabri (1–2 daily; 3hr 15min); Newcastle (11 daily; 2hr 10min); Port Macquarie (3–9 daily; 2hr 25min); Sydney (20–25 daily; 35min); Tamworth (4–8 daily; 2hr 25min).

Coffs Harbour to: Brisbane (2 daily; 1hr); Sydney (6 daily; 1hr 15min).
Lismore to: Brisbane (2–3 daily; 25min); Sydney (5–8 daily; 1hr 50min).
Lord Howe Island to: Brisbane (6 weekly; 2hr); Sydney (1 daily; 2hr).
Norfolk Island to: Brisbane (4 weekly; 2hr 10min); Sydney (4 weekly; 2hr 30min).
Port Macquarie to: Brisbane (3–6 daily; 1hr); Coffs Harbour (2–3 daily; 25min); Sydney (6 daily; 1hr).
Tamworth to: Brisbane (4–12 daily; 2hr 20min); Cobar (8 weekly; 1hr); Melbourne (2–5 daily; 3hr 20min); Mildura (6 weekly; 1hr 30min); Sydney (3–8 daily; 1hr).
Taree to: Port Macquarie (Mon–Sat 1–2 daily; 20min); Sydney (3 daily; 55min).

3

Inland New South Wales

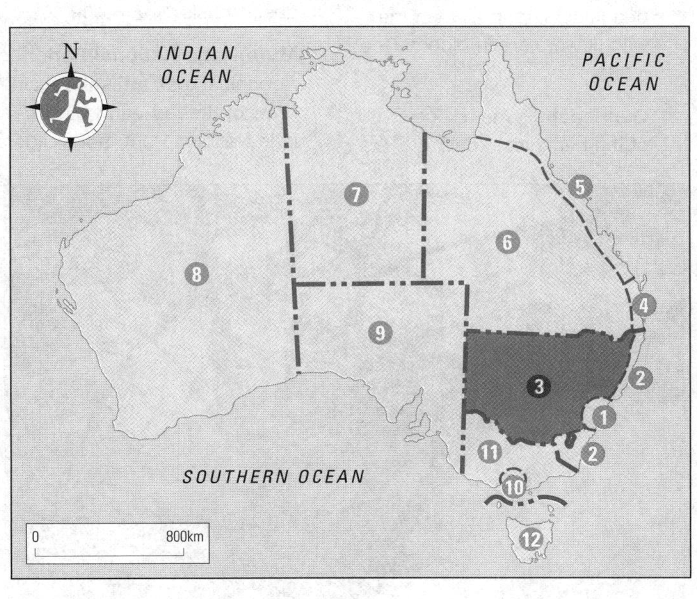

CHAPTER 3

Highlights

* **Tamworth Country Music Festival** Fans from all over the country descend on Tamworth for this famous annual festival. See p.380
* **Bald Rock** Climb the largest granite monolith in the world for unbeatable views. See p.387
* **Warrumbungle National Park** The rugged Warrumbungle National Park is especially beautiful in spring, when the wild flowers are in bloom. See p.389
* **Gunnedah** Home to one of the healthiest koala populations in the state, and a good place to spot them in the wild. See p.390
* **Broken Hill** Take a mine tour, visit the Royal Flying Doctor Service or browse the art galleries of this gracious Outback town. See p.397
* **Menindee Lakes** Boat through flooded red gum trees, among hundreds of water birds in this magical desert oasis. See p.408
* **Mutawintje National Park** Aboriginal rock art is the main draw of the red-earth Mutawintje National Park. See p.409

△ Koala spotting, Gunnedah

3

Inland New South Wales

Inland New South Wales is a very different proposition from the populous coast. Stretching inland for around a thousand kilometres, the state covers a strikingly wide range of landscapes, from the rugged slopes of the Great Dividing Range to the red-earth desert of the Outback, dotted with relatively small and scattered agricultural and mining communities. The **Great Dividing Range** itself runs parallel to the coastline – often very close – splitting the state in two.

West of the Great Dividing Range, towns such as **Bathurst** and **Dubbo** date back to the early days of Australian exploration, when the discovery of a passage through the Blue Mountains (see p.236) opened up the rolling plains of the west to free (non-convict) settlers, who appropriated vast areas of rich pastureland and made immense fortunes off the backs of sheep, establishing the agricultural prosperity which continues to this day. When gold was discovered near Bathurst in 1851, and the first **goldrush** began, New South Wales' fortunes were assured. Although penal transportations ceased the following year, the population continued to increase rapidly and the economy boomed as fortune-seekers arrived in droves. At much the same time, Victoria broke off to form a separate colony, followed by Queensland in 1859. The much-reduced borders that New South Wales has today were defined in 1863.

Agriculture also dominates the southern section of the state, where the fertile **Riverina** occupies the area between the three rivers of the Murrumbidgee, the Darling and the Murray (the last dividing New South Wales from Victoria). In the north of the state, falling away from the **Great Dividing Range**, the gentle sheep- and cattle-farming tablelands of the **New England** plateau extend from the northern end of the Hunter Valley to the border with Queensland.

Moving west away from the coast the land becomes increasingly desolate and arid as you head into the state's desert-like **Outback** regions, where the mercury can climb well above the 40°C mark in summer and where even places which look large on the map turn out to be tiny, isolated communities. The small town of **Bourke** is traditionally regarded as the beginning of the real Outback ("Back O'Bourke"), while other Outback destinations include the opal-mining town of **Lightning Ridge** and, in the far west of the state almost at the South Australian border, the mining settlement of **Broken Hill**, a surprisingly gracious city surrounded by the desert landscape of *Mad Max*.

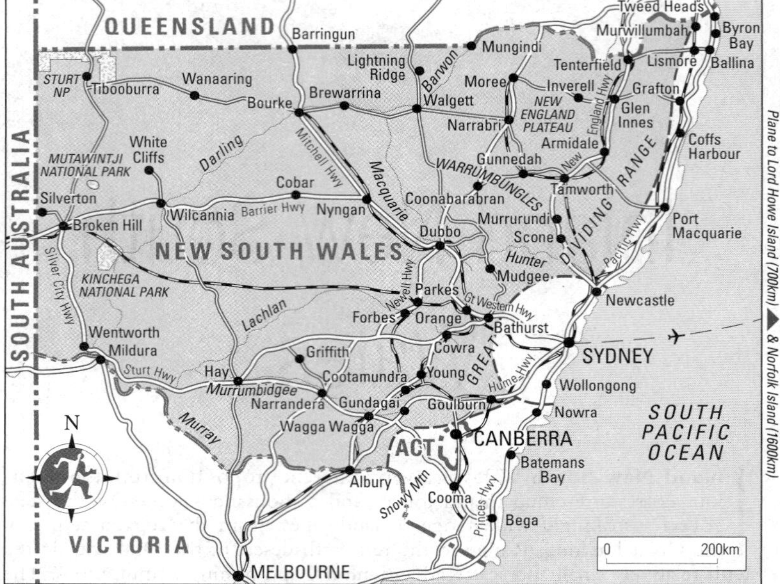

Out beyond the Blue Mountains, the **Great Western Highway** takes you as far as Bathurst; from there the **Mid-Western Highway** goes on to join the **Sturt Highway**, which heads, via Mildura on the Victorian border, to Adelaide. Any route west is eventually obliged to cross the **Newell Highway**, the direct route between Melbourne and Brisbane that cuts straight across the heart of central New South Wales.

Inland New South Wales still has a fairly extensive **rail** network, although the operator, Countrylink (Ⓦwww.countrylink.info; call Ⓣ13 22 32 for reservations), has replaced many train services with buses. Dubbo, Lightning Ridge, Broken Hill and Bourke are all accessible on Countrylink services. The train journey from Sydney to Broken Hill (about $250 return; 13hr each way) is a great way to see the red-earth desert in air-con comfort – if you're lucky the train will pass through one of the huge red sand storms that ravage the region from time to time. A one-month Backtracker pass ($198) will get you just about anywhere in the state on this system.

For details of the **National Parks and Wildlife Service** (NPWS) in New South Wales, including park entry fees, see p.267.

The central west: Bathurst, Dubbo and around

The **central west** of New South Wales is rich farmland, and the undulating green hills provide both seasonal work and picnicking spots for travellers. **Dubbo** is the region's major city, home to a famous zoo, while the scattered towns have their own rewards, not least **Mudgee**, with its surrounding vineyards.

Bathurst and around

The gracious city of **BATHURST**, elegantly situated on the western slopes of the Great Dividing Range 209km west of Sydney, is Australia's oldest inland settlement. Its beautifully preserved nineteenth-century architecture makes it worth a weekend visit from Sydney, to browse the antique shops and mellow out in one of the city's many cafés. The settlement was founded by Governor Macquarie in 1815, but Bathurst remained nothing more than a small convict and military settlement for years, only slowly developing into the main supply centre for the rich surrounding pastoral area. It was the discovery of **gold** nearby at the Lewis Ponds Creek at Ophir in 1851 (see p.360) and, later the same year, on the Turon River, which resulted in a goldrush that changed the life of the town and the colony forever. Soon rich fields of alluvial gold were discovered in every direction and, being the first town over the mountains for those on the way to the goldfields, Bathurst prospered and grew. The population increased dramatically: in 1885 Bathurst was proclaimed a city, and in the late 1890s it was even proposing itself as the site for the capital of the new Commonwealth of Australia.

Although there's still the odd speck of gold and a few gemstones (especially sapphires) to be found in the surrounding area, modern Bathurst has reverted to its role as the capital of one of the richest fruit- and grain-growing districts in Australia. It's also a tertiary education centre, with many students attending Charles Sturt University. In October and November, rev-heads turn up for the big annual motor-racing meetings – centred on the famous **Bathurst 1000** endurance race – at the Mount Panorama Racing Circuit. If V8 supercars do it for you, this is the place to be.

The City

Because of its cool climate – proximity to the mountains means it can be cold at night – and a scattering of grand nineteenth-century buildings, the town has a very different feel to anywhere on the baking plains further west. Pick up a map from the modern visitor information centre (see p.358) to help you find some of the stately mansions scattered around that bear testimony to Bathurst's former wealth; one of their pamphlets outlines an entertaining self-guided walk through the historic city centre. The old **courthouse** on Russell Street, built in 1880, makes a good place to start exploring, and there's also an interesting little **museum** tucked away in the east wing (Tues, Wed, Sat & Sun 10am–4pm; $2), which displays relics and archives of regional pioneer history along with some interesting Aboriginal artefacts.

The **Regional Art Gallery**, 70–78 Keppel Street (Tues–Sat 10am–5pm, Sun 11am–2pm; free), is a fine provincial art collection which has very good ceramics and paintings by Lloyd Rees, as well as regular special and travelling exhibitions. **Machattie Park**, further north up Keppel Street, on the corner of William Street, offers a chance to relax amid landscaped Victorian-era gardens with duck ponds and spreading shady trees. Look out, too, for the well preserved **Chifley Home** at 10 Busby Street (Sat, Sun & Mon 11am–3pm; $5), once the residence of Ben Chifley, Bathurst's most famous son, who was born to a blacksmith here in 1885 and served as prime minister of Australia between 1945 and 1949.

The **Fossil and Mineral Museum** at 224 Howick Street (Mon–Sat 10am–4pm, Sun 10am–2pm; $8) has some interesting crystals as well as Australia's only complete tyrannosaurus rex skeleton – a fearsome sight. **Sir Joseph Banks's Nature Park** (daily 9am–3.30pm; $4.40) occupies the summit of Mount Panorama and is home to wallabies, kangaroos and koalas. Not far away, the **Bathurst Goldfields**, at 428 Conrod Straight (call ⓣ02/6332 2022 or ask at the visitor centre for opening times; tours $10.20), a reconstruction of a former gold-mining area, are worth a visit if you're not going to make it to one of the actual gold towns further out. Goldrush mining methods are demonstrated, and you can even have a go at gold-panning.

Further afield, a drive up to **Mount Panorama** and its famous racing circuit provides panoramic views of the city; the **National Motor-Racing Museum** (daily 9am–4.30pm; $7), at Murray's Corner at the beginning of the racing circuit, features famous racing cars and bikes, plus photographs and memorabilia from the races. The **Bathurst Sheep and Cattle Drome** on Limekilns Road, 8km northeast of the city, has an entertaining and educational show (call ⓣ02/6337 3634 for show times; $11, children $7) covering everything you always wanted to know about sheepshearing and milking cows.

Practicalities

Countrylink **trains** and long-distance **buses** run to Bathurst from Sydney, with onward services to Broken Hill. The **Bathurst Visitor Information Centre** is at 1 Kendall Avenue (daily 9am–5pm; ⓣ02/6332 2333 or 1800 681 000, ⓦwww.bathurst.nsw.gov.au).

Accommodation

Accommodation is relatively expensive here, and if you visit on a race day prices rise by fifty percent and everywhere gets booked solid. There are a dozen or more motels along the highway, and **camping** at East Bathurst Holiday Park, on the highway in Kelso, 5km east (ⓣ02/6331 8286, ⓦwww.eastholidayparks.com.au; cabins ❷).

Commercial Hotel 135 George St ⓣ02/6331 4109, ⓦwww.geocities.com/commercialhotel-bathurst. Functional place with the cheapest rooms in town. Dorms $20, doubles ❷

Dinta Glen B&B 3 Strathmore Drive, Forest Grove ⓣ02/6332 6662. Tranquil and rustic place ten minutes' drive from the centre. ❹

Park Hotel 201 George St ⓣ02/6331 3399, ⓦwww.parkhotel.com.au. Comfortable B&B rooms and motel-style units. ❸

Royal Apartments 108 William St ⓣ02/6332 4920, ⓦwww.ix.net.au/-boshierd. The town's jewel-in-the-crown heritage building, with tasteful, fully serviced apartments – part modern, part antique. ❻

The Russells 286 William St ⓣ02/6332 4686, ⓦwww.therussells.com.au. Small family home offering four-star B&B rooms with log fires and generous cooked breakfasts. ❹

Eating, drinking and nightlife

There's a variety of **restaurants** in the city centre, including Thai, Indian and modern Australian cuisine. Most of the town's pubs also serve counter meals or have bistros at the back. For à la carte dining, try *Lamplighters* at 126–130 William Street (ⓣ02/6331 1448; closed Sun), with blackboard specials of steak and seafood in a wood-panelled setting. In the *Royal Apartments* building, the *Heritage Royal Coffee House* has superb coffee and cakes, while *Crêpes Royale*, 108 William Street, serves French-inspired dishes from morning tea to dinner (closed Mon). *The Crowded House Café* at 1 Ribbon Gang Lane (ⓣ02/6334 2300; closed Sun) offers good lunches and great Modern Australian cuisine in the evenings in the neo-Gothic Old School House; you can eat inside, or out in the leafy courtyard. If you're just after ice cream, try *Annies Old Fashioned Ice Cream Parlour*, on the corner of Church and George streets.

Due to the presence of so many students, Bathurst has a reasonable **nightlife**, centred mainly on pubs close to the university. Particularly popular is the *Oxford Tavern* on the corner of William and Piper streets, opposite the enormous *Leagues Club.* Friday is club night, featuring guest DJs at the *Site* on George Street ($7.50 entry).

Around Bathurst

The area **around Bathurst**, heading towards the Mudgee wine country, is dotted with semi-derelict villages and ghost towns dating back to the goldrushes of the nineteenth century. A scenic drive to the north via Peel and Wattle Flat leads to the tiny, picturesque village of **SOFALA**, 35km north of Bathurst on the Turon River, en route to Mudgee. Gold was found in the river here in 1851, just three weeks after the very first gold strikes in Australia, and today the narrow, winding main street still follows the course of the river. A good spot for a drink is the *Sofala Royal Hotel*, a very atmospheric, classic wooden pub with a big balcony; they also offer meals with a period flavour. You can stay at the *Old Gaol* on Barkley Street (ⓣ02/6337 7064; ❸), a rustic old hotel with a warm welcome and comfy beds.

From Sofala, a very narrow unsealed road follows the Turon River towards **HILL END**, an even more important goldrush site located on a plateau above the Turon Valley, 86km from Bathurst. In 1870, Hill End was the largest inland centre in New South Wales, a booming gold-mining town with a population of about twenty thousand, with 53 hotels, plus all the accoutrements of a wealthy settlement. Within ten years, however, gold production had faltered and Hill End became a virtual ghost town. It stayed that way until 1967, when the area was proclaimed a historic site and huge efforts were made to restore and preserve the town. You can pick up a leaflet at the NPWS **visitors centre** in the old hospital (daily 9.30am–12.30pm & 1.30–4.30pm; ⓣ02/6337 8206), where there's also a small museum ($3), and take a self-guided walk around the village, or rent some equipment and try your hand at panning or fossicking. There's an underground **mine tour** daily at 1pm ($6) and a gold-panning tour at 11am ($4). You can **stay** in the *Royal Hotel* here (ⓣ02/6337 8261, ⓕ6337 8393; ❷) and **eat** in the restaurant. There's also the four-star *Cooke's Cottage* B&B (ⓣ02/6332 5832; ❹), as well as **camping** areas run by the NPWS.

Another enjoyable excursion from Bathurst takes in the former gold-mining towns of **Rockley**, 35km south of Bathurst, and **Trunkey Creek**, and then continues to the spectacular **Abercrombie Caves**, 72km south of Bathurst in the middle of a large nature reserve. The principal and most impressive cavern, the **Grand Arch** (guided tours daily 10am–4pm; $14.50), is 221m long, about 39m wide at the north and south entrances, and in some places over 30m high – it's said to be the largest natural limestone arch in the southern hemisphere. More than eighty other caves are dotted around the reserve. In one of them, miners constructed a dance floor more than a century ago, and concerts and church services are still held here occasionally. Also within the reserve are old gold mines, and swimming holes in **Grove Creek**, which runs through the reserve, plunging 70m over the Grove Creek Falls at the southern edge. There's a **camping area** on the shore (ⓣ02/6336 1972; cabins ❷), complete with a public fossicking ground.

Orange, Forbes and Parkes

ORANGE, on the Mitchell Highway en route from Bathurst to Dubbo, is a pretty town on the eastern slopes of Mount Canobolas; coming from Bathurst, the drive is a pleasant one through undulating countryside, with the valley opening up before you. As befits the town's juicy name, fruit is the major local industry, although it's apples rather than oranges which are the mainstay, based in the orchards southwest of the town. You can find apple-picking **work** here from late February or early March for a period of about six weeks, while cherry picking takes place from late November to early January; contact the Employment National (see p.364). Many growers have rough accommodation on their properties but demand often outstrips supply, so bring a tent. If you want to sample the local produce rather than pick it, turn up for **Food Week** in the first week of April. The **Orange Visitors Centre**, on Byng Street in Civic Square (daily 9am–5pm; ⓣ02/6393 8226, ⓦwww.orange.nsw.gov.au), has information on local attractions including the **Ophir diggings**. The first gold field in Australia, established in 1851 and only 30km north of Orange, the site remains much as the diggers left it – beware of open shafts.

Orange prides itself on being rather cosmopolitan, and has quite a **café** society and some well-regarded **restaurants**. *Scottys on Summer* at 202 Summer Street does gourmet sandwiches, while the *Union Bank Café* at 84 Byng Street has a good range of vegetarian dishes and *Bodhi Garden* at 341 Summer Street has an exclusively veggie menu. The *Lakeside Café & Cellar* on Lake Canobolas Road (Mon–Fri 10am–3pm, Sat & Sun 10am–5pm; ⓣ02/6365 3456) is a very pleasant spot for lunch and local wines, while *Selkirks* at 179 Anson Street (ⓣ02/6361 1179; dinner Tues–Sat) offers pricy but highly recommended modern Australian cuisine.

A recommended place both **to stay** and eat is the *Metropolitan Hotel* at 107 Byng Street (ⓣ02/6362 1353; ❷), just up from the tourist office. It's a huge old-fashioned country pub built in 1872, with a wooden verandah where you can sit and eat barbecued dishes, baked potatoes, damper and salad. Hotel rooms have TV but no en-suite bathrooms; the more expensive motel suites come with all mod cons. The imposing *Duntryleague Guesthouse* (ⓣ02/6362 3822, ⓦwww.duntryleague.com; ❺) is a huge, heritage-listed Federation/Gothic mansion with modern rooms. There are lots of quality B&Bs around – one of the nicest central choices, with a bewitching garden, is *Marlene's Forget-Me-Not* at 69 Moulder Street (ⓣ02/6361 3711; ❹). There are two **caravan parks**, both a few kilometres from the centre: to the north, the *Colour City Caravan Park* on Margaret Street (ⓣ02/6362 7254; cabins ❷); and to the east, the *Canobolas Caravan Park*, 166 Bathurst Road (ⓣ02/6362 7279; cabins ❷).

West of Orange are the important regional towns of Forbes and Parkes. **FORBES**, on the Lachlan River, is a graceful old place famous as the stomping ground of the nineteenth-century bushranger **Ben Hall**, who is buried in the Forbes Cemetery. **PARKES**, 33km to the northwest along the Newell Highway, is well known for its **Observatory**, whose 64-metre radio telescope was used during the Apollo 11 mission to the moon, as well as in the 2000 film *The Dish*. The observatory's visitor centre (daily 8.30am–4.15pm; ⓦwww.parkes.atnf.csiro.au; free) has a 25-minute audiovisual presentation, *The Invisible Universe* (daily 8.30am–3.30pm, every 30min; $3) and a short 3D film. Just east of Forbes lies the small township of **Ellgowra**, where in 1962 Frank Gardiner and his gang pulled off the biggest gold heist in Australian history, taking a total of $3700 in cash and 77kg in gold from a mailcoach – worth an impressive $1.3 million at today's rates.

Mudgee and the wine country

About 120km north of Bathurst, the large, old country town of **MUDGEE** (meaning "the nest in the hills" in the Kamilaroi language) is the centre for an often-overlooked wine region. The town is set along the lush banks of the Cugewong River, and the countryside appears to have more grazing cows and sheep than vineyards. The wines have improved vastly since the days when they were referred to as "Mudgee mud" – the Cabernet Sauvignon and Shiraz are the tastiest, and the area's Chardonnays also have a good reputation. You can reach Mudgee via Hill End, but it's a bumpy unsealed route, and you're better off approaching via Sofala on an 88-kilometre sealed road (except for a small section) – watch out for sheep.

Countrylink runs a **bus** and **train** service to Mudgee from Sydney, changing at Lithgow, just east of Bathurst. The useful **tourist information centre** is at 84 Market Street (Mon–Fri 9am–5pm, Sat 9am–3.30pm, Sun 9.30am–2pm; Ⓣ02/6372 1020, Ⓦwww.mudgee.nsw.gov.au) and has detailed winery information and maps.

The award-winning *Grape Vine Restaurant* at *Lauralla Historic Guesthouse* (bookings essential; set meals $77) offers degustation menus. Otherwise, Mudgee doesn't have a great choice of places to **eat** – your best bet is the pub food at places like the inexpensive *Soldiers Club* brasserie at 99 Mortimer Street or the *Lawson Park Hotel*, a great old country pub on Church Street, which does roasts on Monday and Tuesday. You could also lunch at one of the wineries (see box on p.362).

Accommodation

Mudgee's proximity to Sydney means that **accommodation** is booked out at weekends, when it's best to call in advance. **Campers** should head for the *Mudgee Riverside Caravan and Tourist Park*, 22 Short Street (Ⓣ02/6372 2531, Ⓕ6372 7189; sites ❶, cabins ❷).

Bleak House 7 Lawson St Ⓣ02/6372 4888, Ⓦwww.geocities.com/bleakhousemudgee. 1860s heritage house with pool and private lace-ironwork verandahs overlooking the Cugewong River. ❻

Central Motel 120 Church St Ⓣ1800 457 222. Inexpensive but well-equipped motel, with tidy if slightly clinical rooms. ❸

Federal Hotel 34 English St Ⓣ02/6372 2150, Ⓔaussie@winsoft.net.au. Cleaner than you might expect, with small, basic rooms. ❷

Lauralla Historic Guesthouse Corner of Lewis and Mortimer Sts Ⓣ02/6372 4480, Ⓦwww.lauralla.com.au. Classic late Victorian-style home with quaint and cosy rooms. ❺

Parkview Guest House 99 Market St Ⓣ02/6372 4477 or 1800 621 531, Ⓦwww.parkviewmudgee.com.au. Quiet, centrally located B&B occupying a building of 1859 and boasting lots of period charm. Gay-friendly. ❺

Wanderlight Motel 107 Market St Ⓣ02/6372 1088. Central three-star motel with a pool and spa. ❹

Dubbo

DUBBO, named after an Aboriginal word meaning "red earth", lies on the banks of the Macquarie River, 420km northwest of Sydney and about 200km from Bathurst. The regional capital for the west of the state, it supports many agricultural industries and is located at a vital crossroads where the Melbourne–Brisbane **Newell Highway** meets the **Mitchell Highway** and routes west to Bourke or Broken Hill.

As such, it's well used to people passing through, but not staying long. If you do stop the only real attraction is the unique **Western Plains Zoo** on Obley Road, 5km south of town off the Newell Highway (daily 9am–5pm; $27; Ⓦwww.zoo.nsw.gov.au). The vast zoo-cum-safari park features expansive landscaped habitats in which many Australian animals are allowed to roam; other animals from five continents are kept in segregated enclosures. The zoo is crisscrossed by walking and cycling paths: the best idea is to start exploring

Mudgee wineries: five of the best

Botolabar Botolabar Lane (Mon–Sat 10am–5pm, Sun 10am–3pm; ⓣ02/6373 3840, ⓦwww.botobolar.com). Australia's first organic winery, known for its Marsanne among others, with self-guided tours (40min) and tastings on a shady terrace. There's also a picnic area and BBQs.

Huntington Estate Wines Cassilis Rd (Mon–Fri 9am–5pm, Sat 10am–5pm, Sun 10am–3pm; ⓣ02/6373 3825, ⓦwww.huntingtonestate.com.au). Huntington produces some of the region's most delicious wines. Particularly recommended are the young Semillons and the intense, heady Cabernet Sauvignon from 1995. An excellent annual chamber music festival takes place here in November.

Miramar Wines Henry Lawson Drive (daily 9am–5pm; ⓣ02/6373 3874; ⓦwww.miramarwines.com.au). Established by respected wine-maker Ian MacRae in 1977, this winery specializes in delicious whites, with atmospheric tastings among old cobwebbed casks. For no apparent reason, prices here are lower than at most other places.

Pieter Van Gent Black Springs Rd (Mon–Sat 9am–5pm, Sun 11am–4pm; ⓣ02/6373 3030, ⓦwww.pvgwinery.com.au). Tastings in a delightful setting: beautiful nineteenth-century choir stalls on cool earth floors, overshadowed by huge old barrels salvaged from Penfolds. Try their Pipeclay Port, a tawny port aged in wood. The winemaker is Dutch, and the herbs he uses in his traditional vermouth are specially imported from the Netherlands.

Poet's Corner Craigmoor Rd (Mon–Sat 10am–4.30pm, Sun 10am–4pm; ⓣ02/6372 2208, ⓦwww.poetscornerwines.com). Incorporating Craigmoor, Montrose and Poet's Corner wines. The original 1859 cellar, a vast space with a huge open fireplace, has a tin roof held up by tree-trunk beams. Upstairs is an equally characterful, though expensive, restaurant (ⓣ02/6372 4320; lunch daily 10.30am–2.30pm, Fri & Sat dinner from 6.30pm), while outside, views of hills and vineyards are fronted by a perfect cricket pitch and peaceful lawns fragrant with flowers. There's jazz in June, bush music in September and classical music in November.

early – by noon, the temperatures can become unbearable and the animals sometimes slink off out of sight into the shade. There's no public transport to the zoo, so cycling there, and around the zoo itself, is a good option: Wheeler Cycles, 193 Brisbane Street (ⓣ02/6882 9899), rents out bikes for $15 per day; electronic carts and bikes ($13 for 4hr) can be rented at the zoo itself. To walk there, follow the pleasant cycle track along the river – around an hour on foot from the city centre. Otherwise, take a taxi (Radio Cabs ⓣ13 10 08).

The state's largest **Livestock Market**, 3km north out of town on the Newell Highway, auctions sheep and cattle every Monday, Thursday and Friday (unloading from 8.30am). It's worth a visit just to see the local farmers decked out in their Akubra hats and Drizabone coats, and to get the authentic smell of country life. The YHA gives lifts to the market to its guests on request.

In the centre of town, **Old Dubbo Gaol** on Macquarie Street (daily 9am–4.30pm; $10) is worth an hour or so. A hundred years ago, this fortress-style building housed some of the most notorious criminals of the west, and today it glories in the details of nineteenth-century prison life, with loving attention to the macabre: the gallows, the hangman's kit and the careers of some of those who were executed here. In the cells, life-size animatronic models of convicted criminals tell the stories of their lives. Also worth a look-in is the National Trust property **Dundullimal Homestead** (daily 10am–5pm; $6), 2km past the zoo on Obley Road. An 1840s slab house with stone stables, it now houses a craft shop and mini farm, and you can sometimes see the odd jackeroo riding oxen rodeo-style.

The Dubbo **Regional Gallery** at 165 Darling Street (Tues–Sun 11am–4.30pm; free), has a kitsch collection of animals represented in art, including, surprisingly, an exceptional painting of a fox by the noted Australian artist Arthur Boyd. They also have a rotating cultural programme, including indigenous works at times.

Practicalities

Dubbo's 24-hour **bus** terminal, at the junction of the Mitchell and Newell highways, is busy with daily connections to Brisbane, Sydney, Melbourne, Adelaide, Canberra, Newcastle and Port Stephens. Just across the railway line is the **train station**, terminal for the XPT to and from Sydney. Countrylink (Ⓣ13 22 32) buses leave here for Bourke and Lightning Ridge. You can also **fly** daily to Dubbo with Regional Express (Ⓣ13 17 13), Airlink (Ⓣ1300 662 823) and Qantaslink (Ⓣ13 13 13) from Sydney. The tiny airport is 5km north-west of town. Regional Express also flies to Broken Hill and Coolangatta from here. Thrifty (at the train station) **rents cars** from $50 a day. The **Dubbo Visitors Information Centre** (daily 9am–5pm; Ⓣ02/6884 1422, Ⓦwww.dubbotourism.com.au) is set in a riverside park at the corner of Erskine and Macquarie streets, just off the Newell Highway.

Accommodation

As you'd expect, there are plenty of **motels**, with the majority on the Mitchell Highway (called Cobra Street as it passes through town).

Amaroo Hotel 83 Macquarie St Ⓣ02/6882 3533, Ⓕ6884 2601. The most salubrious pub-hotel in town, with large rooms and springy beds. ❸ including breakfast.

Castlereagh Hotel Corner of Brisbane and Tabralgar Sts Ⓣ02/6882 4877, Ⓕ6684 1520. This old hotel has the cheapest singles in town. The en-suite doubles aren't quite as good as you'd get in a motel, though they've got a lot more charm. ❸

Cattleman's Country Motor Inn Whylandra St, just south of the junction with Victoria St (Mitchell Highway) Ⓣ02/6884 5222, Ⓦwww.cattlemans.com.au. Good-value upmarket motel with two pools, a restaurant and well-furnished rooms. ❸

Dubbo Backpackers YHA 87 Brisbane St Ⓣ02/6882 0922, Ⓦwww.yha.com.au. The only hostel in town, this inviting family-run place is within walking distance of the train station and city centre. Dorms $22, rooms ❷

Dubbo Cabin & Caravan Parklands Ⓣ02/6884 8633, Ⓦwww.dubboparkland.com.au. The best of the town's caravan parks, occupying a green spot right on the river, though the luxurious cabins (some even have spas) are expensive. Also has camping space. Cabins ❹

Dubbo City Caravan Park Whylandra St, 2km west of the centre Ⓣ02/6882 4820, Ⓔddcp@dubbo.nsw.gov.au. Cheaper alternative to the *Dubbo Cabin & Caravan Parklands*, and though it looks a bit tired, it does the job for a quiet night's sleep. On-site vans ❶, cabins ❷

Formule 1 Whylandra St, just south of the junction with Victoria St (Mitchell Highway) Ⓣ02/6882 9211, Ⓕ6682 9311. The cheapest of the town's motels, this modern, ultra-clean place is very good value. ❷

Mayfair Cottage 10 Baird St Ⓣ02/6882 5226, Ⓔdonjstephens@bigpond.com. Centrally located B&B with very comfortable and well-decorated rooms in a separate guest wing, plus a pool. ❹ including breakfast.

Pastoral Hotel 110 Tabralgar St Ⓣ02/6882 4219. Characterful old hotel with a huge verandah; undergoing refurbishment at the time of writing. ❷

Eating and drinking

Dubbo has developed a bit of a **café society**. The self-consciously trendy *Echidna Café* at 177 Macquarie Street (closed Sun & Mon) serves expensive contemporary Australian cuisine, but you can just drop in for an excellent coffee. The *Grapevine Café*, 144 Brisbane Street, is more low-key – a relaxing place with a lovely, leafy courtyard, generous portions and breakfast served until noon at the weekend. *Chicken Spot*, on the corner of Macquarie and Tabralgar streets, is a good fast-food place with very nice sandwiches. For fresh bread and cakes, try the *Village Hot Bake* on Darling Street, by the railway station, a bustling bakery on two levels, also serving pies, fries and pizzas. If you crave the usual country-town fare such as steak and three veg, head to the *Amaroo Hotel*. There are also several **restaurants** at the bottom end of the main shopping area, including the gourmet pizza place *Sticks and Stones*, 215 Macquarie Street (daily from 6pm; ⓣ02/6885 4852).

Cowra

COWRA, on the banks of the Lachlan River, 107km southwest of Bathurst along the Mid-Western Highway, is famous as the location of the **Cowra Breakout** during World War II. August 5, 1944 saw the escape of 378 Japanese prisoners of war armed with baseball bats, staves, home-made clubs and sharpened kitchen knives – those who were sick and remained behind hanged or disembowelled themselves, unable to endure the disgrace of capture. It took nine days to recapture all the prisoners, during which four Australian soldiers and 231 Japanese died. The breakout was little known until the publication of Harry Gordon's excellent 1970s account *Die Like the Carp* (republished as *Voyage of Shame*).

You can see the site of the POW camp, now just ruins and fields, on Sakura Avenue on the northeast edge of town. The graves of the Japanese, who were buried in Cowra, were well cared for by members of the local Returned Servicemen's League, a humanitarian gesture that touched Japanese embassy officials who then broached the idea of an official **Japanese War Cemetery**. Designed by Shigeru Yura, the tranquil burial ground lies further north, on Doncaster Drive. The theme of Japanese–Australian friendship and reconciliation continued in Cowra with the establishment of the **Japanese Garden** (daily 8.30am–5pm; $8.50) in 1979 with funding from Japanese and Australian governments and companies. The large garden, designed to represent the landscape of Japan, is set on a hill overlooking the town, on a scenic drive running north off Kendal Street, the main thoroughfare. There's another anti-war symbol in the shape of the **World Peace Bell** on Civic Square, while an avenue of cherry trees connects the war cemeteries, the POW camp site and the Japanese Garden.

For more information, contact the very helpful **Cowra Visitor Information Centre**, at the junction of Olympic Highway, Laghlan Valley Way and the Mid-Western Highway (daily 9am–5pm; ⓣ02/6342 4333, ⓦwww.cowratourism.com.au). If you want to taste the local wine (the region is best known for its Chardonnays) head for the *Quarry Cellar Door and Restaurant*, 4km from Cowra on the Boorowa Road (Tues–Sun 10am–4pm; ⓣ02/6342 3650, ⓦwww.cowraregionwines.com); the attached restaurant (lunch Wed–Sun, dinner Fri & Sat) also does Devonshire teas and inexpensive light lunches of pasta and salads. If you're interested in the possibility of some **grape-picking** work, contact the Employment National (see below).

Young

Seventy kilometres southwest of Cowra along the Olympic Way, the hilly town of **YOUNG** is a good spot to pick up some **cherry-picking** work during the season (approximately six weeks from the first week of Nov) – being monotonous rather than strenuous, the work is popular with retired Queenslanders. To just pick your own and have a look at some orchards and packing sheds, head to any one of a number of places on the way into town from Cowra; you could also contact the Employment National on Boorowa

Street (ⓣ02/6340 2900). The long weekend in October generally coincides with the time when the **cherry blossoms** are in full bloom – a glorious sight – and there's even an annual Cherry Festival (late Nov/early Dec). There are also several vineyards on the slopes of the undulating area, which is becoming known as the **Hilltops wine region**. Two worth visiting are the small, family-run Lindsays Woodonga Hill Winery, 10km north of Young on Olympic Way (daily 9am–5pm), and Chalkers Crossing winery on Grenfell Road (daily 10am–4pm; ⓦwww.chalkerscrossing.com.au), where they also produce olive oils.

Young also has some significance as the site of the notorious **Lambing Flat Riots**. A former gold-mining centre known then as Lambing Flat, the town was the site of racist riots against Chinese miners in June 1861. As the gold ran out, European miners resented what they saw as the greater success of the more industrious Chinese. Troops had to be called in when the Chinese were chased violently from the diggings, beaten, their pigtails cut off, and their property destroyed. Carried at the head of the mob was a flag, painted on a tent flysheet, with the Southern Cross in the centre, and "Roll Up, Roll Up, No Chinese" lettered in the manner of a circus flyer. Following the riots, the Chinese Immigration Restriction Act was passed in 1861, one of the first steps on the slippery slope towards the White Australia Policy of 1901. You can see the original flag, and other exhibits relating to the riots, in the **Lambing Flat Folk Museum** (Mon–Sat 10am–4pm, Sun 10.45am–4pm; $2) in the Community Arts Centre, Campbell Street.

For more information, contact the **Young Visitor Information Centre**, 2 Short Street (Mon–Fri 9am–5pm, Sat & Sun 9.30am–4pm; ⓣ02/6382 3394, ⓦwww.young.nsw.gov.au). A recommended **farmstay** outside town on the Olympic Highway is *Old Nubba School House* (ⓣ02/6943 2513, ⓔnubba@dragnet.com.au; ④); the peaceful self-contained accommodation, a former schoolhouse in the grounds of the friendly family farm, sleeps up to eight.

The Hume Highway and the Riverina

The rolling plains of southwestern New South Wales, spreading west from the Great Dividing Range, are bounded by two great rivers: the **Murrumbidgee** to the north and the **Murray** to the south, the latter forming the border with the state of Victoria. This area is known as the **Riverina**, a name that conjures up a certain rural romance, suggesting a country Australia little visited by tourists. If you're looking for work on the land, you've a reasonable chance of finding it here.

The land the explorer John Oxley described as "uninhabitable and useless to civilized man" began its transformation to fertile fruit bowl when the ambitious **Murrumbidgee Irrigation Scheme** was launched in 1907, and the area around **Griffith** and **Leeton** now produces ninety percent of Australia's rice, most of its citrus fruits and twenty percent of its wine grapes. The capital of the central Riverina is **Wagga Wagga**, Australia's largest inland city. Along the Upper Murray, the main towns are on the Victorian side of the river (and are covered in the Victoria chapter), but you may drop into **Albury** en route to Melbourne on the Hume, or into **Wentworth** as a day-trip from Mildura or on the way to or from Broken Hill on the Silver City Highway. There are several interesting **festivals** in the region, including the Wagga Wagga Jazz

Festival in September and the Festival of Griffith, an orgy of Aussie wine, food and culture held every May.

If you want a quick route to Melbourne from Sydney, or vice versa, you'll inevitably end up on the rather tedious **Hume Highway**, which passes through the Southern Highlands, the Riverina and across the Murray River. Over the years the highway has been improved, but though this is one of Australia's main arteries between its two largest cities, it still narrows to one lane either way in parts. Choked with trucks, particularly at night, accidents are not infrequent, so keep your wits about you. While the highway itself may seem dreary, some of the nearby towns are truly and typically Australian; rich in food, wine, flora and fauna and friendly locals.

Goulburn and beyond

Now bypassed by the Hume Highway, **GOULBURN** is still the traditional stop-off point en route to Canberra. It's a large regional centre for the surrounding area, and for a quality **wool industry**, which was established in the 1820s. The town, with its wide streets, has a conservative country feel, but boasts some large and impressive public buildings. Goulburn's wool traditions have been immortalized by the **Big Merino** (daily 8am–8pm), a fifteen-metre-high sheep which stands proudly next to the Ampol service station on the Old Hume Highway; the first floor has a wool industry display, and on the third level you can look out over the town through the sheep's eyes. To get closer to the real thing and enjoy a glimpse into Australian country life, head for the long-established **Pelican Sheep Station** on Braidwood Road, 10km south of town (Ⓣ02/4821 4668, Ⓦwww.pelicansheepstation.com.au; bunkhouses ❶, house or cabins ❸, plus camping), which has been owned by the same family since 1827. Tours include a shearing demonstration and the chance to see sheepdogs being put through their paces, while kids can cuddle the lambs, newborn in April.

There are several historic places to visit in Goulburn, including the National Trust property **Riversdale**, an 1840 coaching inn on Maud Street (mid-Sept to mid-July Sat & Sun 10am–4.30pm, at other times by appointment on Ⓣ02/4821 9591; free), and the **Old Goulburn Brewery** on Bungonia Road (daily 9am–5pm; free), which has been brewing traditional ales and stouts since 1836. **The Cathedral of Saint Saviour**, completed in 1884, is one of the most attractive old churches in Australia, with some beautiful stained glass and a fine organ. You can get an informative pamphlet of walks and heritage buildings from the **Goulburn Visitors Centre** opposite the shady, flower-filled Belmore Park at 201 Sloane Street (daily 9am–5pm; Ⓣ02/4823 4492, Ⓦwww.igoulburn.com).

The Hume and Hovell Walking Track

This long-distance walk starts at **Gunning**, on the Hume Highway 50km east of Goulburn, and runs over 400km southwest **to Albury**, retracing as closely as possible the route taken on foot by the two eponymous explorers in the spring and summer of 1824 on their expedition from Sydney to Port Phillip, the site of what was to become Melbourne. The walk takes about fifteen to twenty days but the layout – a Bicentenary project – allows for half-day, full-day and weekend walks. There are several free leaflets detailing different chunks, available from the Department of Conservation and Land Management in Sydney (Ⓣ02/9228 6111), Goulburn (Ⓣ02/4823 0665) and Wagga Wagga (Ⓣ02/6921 2503); the *Hume and Hovell Walking Track Guidebook* by Harry Hill (Crawford House Press, Bathurst, $19.95) is also useful.

The classic place to **eat** in Goulburn is the *Paragon Café*, at 174 Auburn Street. A bastion of good, filling food including inexpensive breakfasts, great hamburgers, steaks, fish, veal, pasta and pizza, it's been here for around fifty years and retains its 1940s-era fittings; it's also licensed. A host of other good, multi-ethnic eateries can be found close by on the same street.

The most intriguing place to **stay** in the area is at the **Gunningbar Yurt Farm**, 20km out of town on Grabben Gullen Road (Ⓣ02/4829 2114; $20 as a helper with four-hours' work per day required, but all meals included; or as part of a WWOOF placement, see p.85). A yurt, in its original form, is a Mongolian round felt tent, though the ones here are mostly of wood and with solar power. Essentially a sheep property, the "yurt village" has several yurts, each with a different function, providing an educational centre for groups of children to help them become more self-sufficient and environmentally aware. If you want to stay, you must call in advance; if you don't have your own transport, someone can pick you up. **In town**, *Tattersalls Hotel*, 74 Auburn Street (Ⓣ02/4821 3088, Ⓕ4822 3505; $20), is a Nomad-affiliated hostel offering good and clean, if basic, dorm accommodation. The luxurious *Bentley Lodge* B&B on the edge of the town at 102 Clyde Street (Ⓣ02/4822 5135, Ⓦwww.bentlylodge.com; ⑤) hires out classic sports cars for a burn along the country lanes.

The **Bungonia State Recreation Area**, 25km east of Goulburn, covers a rugged strip of the Southern Tablelands containing some of the deepest **caves** in Australia, the spectacular limestone Bungonia Gorge and the Shoalhaven River. About an hour north of Goulburn via Taralga are the huge and more accessible **Wombeyan caves** (tours at 1pm and 2.30pm; $21; Ⓦwww.jenolancaves.org.au) which you can tour with a guide.

Yass and the Burrinjuck Waters State Park

YASS dates back to 1821 when Europeans first entered the area. Prior to this, the area had a high Aboriginal population, who gave the town its name, "yharr", meaning running water. On the outskirts of Yass as you exit the Hume Highway onto the Yass Valley Way from Goulburn (87km away) is the National Trust-owned **Cooma Cottage** (Mon & Thurs–Sun 10am–4pm; $4.40), a well-preserved nineteenth-century homestead which was the former home of the famous explorer **Hamilton Hume**. The cottage is now a museum, set in a hundred acres of rolling countryside and containing excellent material on Hume and his expeditions. Hume was different from many of his contemporaries in that he was born in Australia – in Parramatta, to free settlers in 1797 – and his explorations relied on his first-hand knowledge of the bush and of Aboriginal skills and languages. His first expedition was at the age of 17, accompanied by his brother and his Aboriginal friend Doual, and the trio discovered prime grazing lands in the Southern Highlands. Three years later he led the Goulburn Plains expedition, and pushing further afield in 1821 he discovered the rich and productive Yass Plains, where he settled in later life. Hume's best-known exploration was when he paired with Hovell, an English sea captain, to head for Port Phillip Bay; you can follow in their footsteps on the Hume and Hovell Walking Track (see box opposite). He also assisted Sturt in tracing the Murray and Darling rivers. The terrific **Visitors Centre** (Mon–Fri 9am–4.30pm, Sat & Sun 9am–4pm; Ⓣ02/6226 2557, Ⓦwww.yass.nsw.gov.au) has maps outlining a two-kilometre informative walk. The **Yass and District Museum** on Comur Street (call Ⓣ02/6226 4966 or ask at Visitors Centre to confirm opening times; $2) contains displays on what the town looked like back in the 1890s. The **Yass Valley Festival** (Nov 19–21) features food, wine and music, plus a flying dog competition. About 20km along the road to Gundagai at Gap Range is the gallery of the internationally renowned **glass sculptor** Peter Crisp (Ⓣ02/6227 6073, Ⓦwww.petercrisp .com.au), whose exquisite work is available for sale – if you can afford it. This is also a good area for **wine tours** (ask at the visitors centre).

There are some lovely **bed and breakfasts** in Yass. Two of the best are the elegant historical residence, *Kerrowgair*, 24 Grampian Street (Ⓣ02/6226 4932, Ⓦwww.kerrowgair.com.au; ❹), and *The Globe Inn*, 70 Ross Street (Ⓣ02/6226 3680, Ⓔstay@globeinn.com.au; ❺), which is run by two chefs. *The Australian Motel*, 180 Comus Street (Ⓣ02/6226 1744; ❷), is decent value, while at the very bottom of the range is the amazingly cheap *Club House Hotel*, 190 Comur Street (Ⓣ02/6226 1042; ❶) which is smelly, but they do clean the sheets. *Yass Caravan Park* (Ⓣ02/6226 1173; ❷) is pleasant and central, and there are lots of places **to eat** on Comur Street.

Continuing along the Hume Highway you'll reach a turn-off for the **Burrinjuck Waters State Park** after 27km, from where it's a 25-kilometre drive on a sealed road to the park set around the gigantic (2.5 times the size of Sydney Harbour) Burrinjuck Dam ($6 per car per day), with camping and picnic areas filled with kangaroos and chirping rosellas (Ⓣ02/6227 8114; on-site vans, units and tent sites ❷, cottages ❸). **WEE JASPER**, a picturesque village located on the backwaters of Burrinjuck Dam, has a basic **campsite** (Ⓣ02/6227 9626) and cabins (Ⓣ02/6227 9619; ❷). From here you can visit **Carey's Caves** (tours daily at noon & 1.30pm, Sat & Sun also at 3pm; $12) for a look at some of Australia's most spectacular limestone rock formations.

Turning off the Hume Highway at **Bowning** brings you to the peaceful village of **Binalong**. Australia's best-known poet, Banjo Patterson, spent much of his childhood here, attending the local school. Binalong railway station was used to transport gold from nearby Lambing Flat (Young), which made it a lucrative area for bushrangers. The grave of the daring bushranger "Flash" Johnny Gilbert lies alongside the road to Harden.

Gundagai and Holbrook

One hundred and four kilometres from Yass, **GUNDAGAI** sits on the banks of the Murrumbidgee, at the foot of the rounded bump of Mount Parnassus. The town was once situated on the alluvial flats north of the river, despite warnings from local Aborigines that the area was prone to major flooding. Proving them correct, old Gundagai was the scene of Australia's worst flood disaster in 1852, when 89 people drowned. The relocated Gundagai, on the main route between Sydney and Melbourne (until bypassed by the Hume Highway), became a favoured overnight stopping point amongst pioneers heading into the interior by bullock cart. A large punt was the only means of crossing the Murrumbidgee from 1849 until the **Prince Alfred Bridge** was erected in 1867; the pretty wooden bridge can still be used by pedestrians. Gold was eventually discovered here, and by 1864 Gundagai had become a boom town, preyed upon by the romantically dubbed bushranger **Captain Moonlight**.

Gundagai found immortality through a Jack Moses poem, in which "the dog sat on the tuckerbox, nine miles from Gundagai" and stubbornly refused to help its master pull the bogged bullock team from the creek. Somehow the image became elevated from that of a disobedient hound and a cursing teamster to a symbol of the pioneer with his faithful hound at his side. As a consequence, a **statue** of the dog was erected just outside town at **Five Mile Creek**, where pioneers used to camp overnight, and still a very pleasant spot to take an ice-cream break. Inside the **tourist centre** here, there's a range of cheerfully tacky souvenirs, and you can also send a postcard with a special "dog on the tuckerbox" postmark.

In the town itself, the **Gundagai Visitor Information Centre**, at 249 Sheridan Street (Mon–Fri 8am–5pm, Sat & Sun 9am–noon & 1–5pm; ⓣ02/6944 0250, ⓦwww.gundagaishire.nsw.gov.au), can help with accommodation and also sells CDs of folk songs featuring Gundagai, including *Along the Road to Gundagai*, from which every Australian remembers only the tuneful snatch "There's a track winding back, to an old-fashioned shack, along the road to Gundagai". If you want **to stay**, there's the *Kimo Homestead B&B*, Nangus Road (02/6944 1321; ❺), a few motels (❸) and the *Blue Heeler Guesthouse* on Sheriden Street (ⓣ02/6944 2286; dorms $15). The Gundagai District Services Club (daily noon–2pm & 5.30–9pm; ⓣ02/602944 1355) across the road from the visitors centre has good Chinese and Aussie **food**.

Sixty-eight kilometres south of Gundagai, **HOLBROOK** is a recommended food break on the drive to Melbourne (or Sydney), with two excellent bakeries on the Hume Highway as it heads through town. The *Holbrook Bakery* dishes out delicious beef and curry pies, and the *Scrummy Buns Bakery* across the road sells more unorthodox pies filled with crocodile, emu, kangaroo and rabbit – plus cappuccino and continental cakes. Perhaps these great bakeries are a legacy of a German past: settled by Germans in the 1860s, Holbrook was called Germantown up until World War I, when anti-German feeling resulted in a name change.

Wagga Wagga

WAGGA WAGGA, known simply as "Wagga" (and pronounced "Wogga"), is the most populous inland city in Australia and the capital of the Riverina region, with around 58,000 inhabitants, though despite its size it remains a green and pleasant place. Its curious name is thought to come from the Widadjuri, the largest of the New South Wales Aboriginal peoples: "wagga" means crow, and its repetition signifies the plural (though some claim it means "dancing men").

Wagga's main attractions are on the edge of the city. To the south, it's a half-hour walk to the impressive **Botanic Gardens** (daily: summer 7.30am–8pm; winter 7.30am–4.15pm; free) at the base of Willans Hill, a huge place with attractions including a walk-through bird aviary, a children's petting-zoo, bush trails and picnic areas, gardens of cacti and succulents, and a Chinese-style garden, plus a kiosk café. The **Historical Museum** (Tues–Sat 10am–5pm, Sun 2–5pm; free) on Lord Baden Powell Drive, by the Botanic Gardens, hosts a hotchpotch collection of old farm machinery, printing presses and a display of over 200 door-knockers.

Back in the centre, the **Wagga Wagga Regional Art Gallery** on Baylis Street (Mon–Sat 10am–5pm, Sun noon–4pm; free) is home to the National Art Glass collection, as well as touring exhibitions and over five hundred works by Australian printmakers from 1940 on. The adjacent **Museum of the Riverina** (Tues–Sat 10am–5pm, Sun 2–5pm; free) often hosts exhibitions on indigenous artists and local crafts. The **Willy Sheather Gallery**, 209A Edward Street (daily 9am–5pm; free; ⓦwww.wsg.net.au), displays Sheather's excellent and vivid work – bright, affectionate and sometimes comic scenes of local life.

On Sunday mornings a bit of life is sparked by the **market** (7.30am–noon) at the Myer car park on O'Reilly Street, which has secondhand clothes and books, crafts, local produce and cakes. There's also a farmer's market at Wollundry lagoon near the visitors centre on the second Saturday of each month. The city's **Charles Sturt University** boasts a well-regarded wine course and has its own on-campus **winery** (and cheesery) on Coolamon Road, both of which are open for tastings and sales (Mon–Fri 11am–5pm, Sat & Sun 11am–4pm; ⓣ02/6933 2435) – try the unusual lemon Myrtle cheese. You can also tour the heavenly Green Grove Organics **liquorice and chocolate factory** at 8 Lord Street in Junee, 50km away (tours Mon–Fri at 10.30am & 2.30pm; $4; ⓦwww.greengroveorganics.com). Ask at the visitors centre about **River Cruises**.

Practicalities

Roughly halfway between Sydney (470km) and Melbourne (435km), Wagga is just off the Sturt Highway, the main route between Adelaide and Sydney. Interstate Greyhound Australia **buses** heading to and from Brisbane, Sydney, Adelaide, Melbourne and Canberra all pass through, stopping at the train station, a little out of town. To **get around**, you can rent bikes from Kidson's Cycles at 107 Fitzmaurice Street (ⓣ02/6921 4474), or a car from Avis, on the corner of Edward and Fitzharding streets (ⓣ02/6921 9977). Baylis Street, the main strip (and Fitzmaurice Street, its continuation), extends from the train station to the bridge spanning the Murrumbidgee River.

The **Wagga Wagga Visitors Centre**, on Tarcutta Street, close to the river (daily 9am–5pm; ⓣ02/6926 9629, ⓦwww.tourismwaggawagga.com.au), is a mine of local information and maps and also books **accommodation** in town and on local **farmstays**.

Accommodation

Lawson Motor Inn 117–121 Tarcutta St ⓣ02/6921 2200, ⓦwww.thelawson.com.au. Well-run four-star motel with spacious, well-furnished rooms with satellite TV and kitchenettes. ❹

The Manor 38 Morrow St ⓣ02/6921 5962. Historic B&B next to the beautiful lagoon-front park, with heavy wooden furniture, old gramophones and pleasant communal areas. ❹–❻

Romano's Hotel Corner of Sturt and Fitzmaurice Sts ⓣ02/6921 2013, ⓦwww.romanoshotel.com.au. Old hotel with a nineteenth-century feel and rather bare rooms (single rates available). ❷–❸

Victoria Hotel 55 Baylis St ⓣ02/6921 5233, ⓦwww.vichotel.net. Good doubles (and $25 singles) with shared bathrooms – better rooms but none of the character of *Romano's*. ❷

Wagga Beach Caravan Park 2 Johnston St ⓣ02/6931 0603, ⓦwww.wwbcp.com.au. The town's best-situated caravan park, this shady and tranquil place has a free gas barbecue and a backpackers' dorm right on the town beach, five minutes' walk from the main shops. Dorms $22, en-suite cabins ❸

Eating, drinking and nightlife

In the town centre, the Baylis/Fitzmaurice strip and its side streets provide fertile **eating** ground. Wagga also has several huge **clubs**. *Wagga RSL*, on the corner of Dobbs and Kincaid streets, also has a Chinese restaurant and Friday-night piano bar. For drinking and dancing, the town's most popular spot is the lively *Victoria Hotel*, whilst *Maddison's* at 146 Fitzmaurice Street (Wed–Sat) is Wagga's venue for bands and irresponsible student shenanigans. The *Black Swan Hotel* (alias "The Muddy Duck") in North Wagga, close to the university, is eternally popular with the student population.

Indian Tavern Tandoori Restaurant 176 Baylis St ⓣ02/6921 3121. One up in the chilli stakes. Daily from 5.30pm. A popular spot with authentic tandoori dishes, though can be a bit liberal with the chilli sauce.

Montezuma's 85 Baylis St. Cosy wooden cantina with the best Mexican food in town. Lunch Wed–Fri, dinner Tues–Sun.

Romano's Hotel Corner of Sturt and Fitzmaurice Sts. This hotel has a good modern restaurant with lots of seafood and other dishes, plus decent espresso and all-day breakfasts.

Sugars Coffee Lounge 16 Forsyth St. Fresh and healthy focaccia and American-style bagels, as well as excellent coffee and a wide range of breakfast fare.

Victoria Hotel Good and extensive bistro menu; the upstairs balcony is open on Friday and Saturday nights.

Wagga Wagga Winery Oura Rd, a fifteen-minute drive from town ⓣ02/6922 1221, ⓦwww.waggawaggawinery.com.au. One of the best local places to eat. The wines themselves are nothing special, but the excellent local food (from $18 a head) and the setting, in an old pine log building with a large verandah and a garden area, is very pleasant. Daily 11am till late.

The Murrumbidgee Irrigation Area

Irrigation has transformed the area northwest of Albury, between the Lachlan and the Murrumbidgee rivers, into a fertile valley full of orchards, vineyards and rice paddies, cut through with irrigation canals. The **Murrumbidgee Irrigation Area** (or **MIA**) extends over two thousand square kilometres, a mostly flat and – from ground level at least – featureless landscape that is nonetheless responsible for producing most of Australia's rice, approximately eighty percent of New South Wales's wine grapes, and sixty percent of its citrus fruits. The water for the irrigation area is stored in Burrinjuck and Blowering dams and flows over 400km down the Murrumbidgee River to Berembed Weir, before being diverted into the main canal, which is 155km long and feeds a network of 1450km of supply canals – although the growing of such water-thirsty crops as rice in such a dry continent is becoming a contentious issue.

Probably the main reason you'll visit this off-the-beaten-track area is to find **work**, with abundant fruit picking available throughout the year. At the peak season there are up to three thousand jobs going begging. The season starts in August with oranges, which are picked right through to March, then onions in November, and stonefruit (peaches, apricots, plums), prunes and melons from December to March, overlapping with the grape harvest in February and March. Pay is calculated according to the amount picked. If you base yourself in Griffith or Leeton you'll need your own transport – if only a bicycle – since the orchards are up to 10km outside town. To avoid the possibility of a wasted trip due to a late season or a poor crop, it's essential to check with Employment National (see p.364) before turning up.

Griffith

Citrus orchards line the way into **GRIFFITH**, with a range of low hills in the background. The major centre of the MIA, it's known for its large **Italian population**, the descendants of immigrants who came in the 1920s, having already tried mining in Broken Hill, and again after World War II. Needless to say, a string of excellent Italian cafés and restaurants line the tree-filled main street of Banna Avenue, and the majority of **wineries** are run by Italian families. The city was designed by Walter Burley Griffin, the landscape architect from Chicago who was also responsible for Canberra.

The **Griffith Visitors Centre**, on the corner of Jondaryan and Banna avenues (Mon–Fri 9am–5pm; ⓣ02/6962 4145, ⓦwww.griffith.nsw.gov.au), can arrange trips on a school bus-run (7–9am & 3.30–5pm) to see the surrounding district, its rice paddies, citrus and stonefruit orchards and vineyards, for around a dollar. An even better way to get an overview of the area is to head for **Scenic Hill**, the escarpment that forms the northern boundary of the city. The **Sir Dudley de Chair's Lookout** gives a panoramic view of the horticultural enterprises below. Immediately beneath this rocky outcrop is the **Hermit's Cave**, where Valerio Recetti, an Italian immigrant, lived alone and undetected for ten years, working only at night and early in the morning with stone age tools to create a home in the caves. **Pioneer Park** (daily 9am–4.30pm; $7), in an extensive bushland setting 2km from the city centre, has 36 buildings recreating the era of the early MIA. The most interesting part is "Bagtown", a reconstruction of an early makeshift town built in 1910 to meet the needs of the Murrumbidgee Irrigation Area canal workers and pioneer farmers, and so-called because the homes were made of hessian cement bags with corrugated-iron roofs.

There are sixteen **wineries**, many Italian-run, in the area surrounding Griffith. Eleven are open to the public (some by appointment only); all are detailed in the *Griffith Visitors' Guide* booklet available from the visitors centre. The oldest winery, McWilliam's Hanwood Estate (Mon–Sat 9am–5pm), was established in 1913 and holds tastings in a building resembling a wine barrel, while one of the more celebrated vineyards is De Bortoli Wines (Mon–Sat 9am–5pm, Sun 9am–4pm), at De Bortoli Road, BilBul, the birthplace of the sensational Noble One Botrytis Semillon dessert wine, which has raked in over 300 gold medals all over the world. Several other wineries have been around for more than fifty years, dating from the 1920s influx of Italian immigrants. One of these is Rossetto Wines on Rossetto Road, off Leeton Road (Mon–Sat 8.30am–5.30pm), a friendly and down-to-earth concern known for its muscats and ports.

Accommodation

For **camping**, there's the cheap and basic campsite at the showground on the edge of town or the *Griffith Tourist Caravan Park*.

Area Hotel Banna Ave ⓣ 02/6962 1322. Simple, rather bare but clean hotel – although you're better off at the roomier *Victoria*. ❷

Griffith International Hostel 112 Binya St ⓣ 02/6964 4236, ⓦ www.griffithinternational.com.au. Very basic backpackers with communal kitchen and living room but little vibe. It's more of a functional base for fruitpickers than a fun place to hang out. Dorms $17, doubles ❷

Griffith Tourist Caravan Park 919 Willandra Ave, 2km south of the centre ⓣ 02/6964 2144, ⓕ 6964 1126. Popular with fruitpickers, this large bush block has well-maintained facilities and a peaceful ambience, as well as camping space. Cabins ❷

Ingleden Park Cottage Coghlan Rd ⓣ 02/6963 6527, ⓦ www.ingleden.com.au. One of the better local B&Bs, set on a working farm 15km from town, with modern rooms in a garden cottage. ❹

Victoria Hotel 384 Banna Ave ⓣ 02/6962 1299, ⓕ 6962 1081. A bit more comfortable than the town's other backpacker/fruitpicker places, with basic rooms, a TV lounge with free tea and coffee, a cool, covered courtyard, counter lunches downstairs, live entertainment (Wed–Sat) and quality bistro meals from Tuesday to Saturday. ❷, with cheap weekly rates.

Eating and drinking

There's no shortage of good Italian places to **eat and drink** on Banna Avenue. For gourmet picnic supplies, *Riverina Grove* on Whybrow Street is a fantastic deli stocking a wide range of regional produce like plums in port, local salami and cheeses. For drinking, the town convenes at the *Gemini Hotel* on Banna Ave, where you can sip a cocktail or down a schooner while listening to live music at the weekends.

Bassano Café Banna Ave. Hugely popular place. Sit at a pavement table and sample the excellent coffee and delicious focaccia, as well as pasta, home-made gelati, pastries and biscuits.

Belvedere Restaurant and Pizza 494 Banna Ave. Pizza and other Italian food in a relaxed atmosphere. Popular with travellers.

Bertoldo's Pasticerria 324 Banna Ave. Cheap, bakery-style place with inexpensive and filling pasta dishes.

Coro Club 20–26 Harward Rd. Large, cheap portions of Chinese food if you've had enough of all things Italian. Wed–Sun noon–2pm & 5.30pm–10pm.

Il Corso Café & Pizza 232 Banna Ave. Offers a range of Italian food beyond the familiar pasta dishes, including chicken and seafood dishes.

Romeo & Giulietta Pizza Restaurant 40 Mackay Ave. Delicious pizzas cooked in a wood-fired oven. Thurs–Sun from 6pm.

Around Griffith

Twenty-five kilometres northeast of Griffith is the **Cocoparra National Park** in the woodland-covered Cocoparra Range; for information about camping and bushwalking ask at the NPWS office at 200 Yambil Street in Griffith (Ⓣ02/6966 8100). Much further away, on the flat plains 185km northwest of Griffith, is **Willandra National Park**, reached via **Hillston** (64km from Griffith) on the unsealed Hillston–Mossgiel road. The park was created in 1971 from a section of the vast Big Willandra pastoral station, a famous stud merino property founded in the 1860s. As well as enabling you to experience the semi-arid riverine plains country at close quarters, a visit to the 1918 **homestead** gives an insight into station life and the wool industry. Wet weather makes all the roads to Willandra impassable, so check before you head out with the **park office** in Hillston (Ⓣ02/6967 8159); they also handle **accommodation bookings** for shared rooms in the shearers' quarters ($23 per person) – take extra supplies in case you get rained in.

Fifty-nine kilometres southeast of Griffith, **LEETON** is the third-largest town in the MIA, with a quarter of its population of Italian extraction. For information on the area and details of visiting its **rice mill**, head for the **Leeton Visitor Information Centre**, 10 Yanco Ave (Mon–Fri 9am–5pm, Sat & Sun 9.30am–12.30pm; Ⓣ02/6953 6481, Ⓦwww.leeton.visitnsw.com.au). There are two **caravan parks**, both 2km southeast: the *Leeton Caravan Park*, on Yanco Avenue (Ⓣ & Ⓕ02/6953 3323), caters for fruit-pickers with basic bunkrooms ($23 per person) and also has en-suite cabins with TV (❷); while *An Oasis Caravan Park* on Corbie Hill Road (Ⓣ02/6953 3882, Ⓕ6953 6256; vans ❶, cabins and spacious cottage ❷), caters more for tourists, with a better range of facilities. The large, tree-filled property at *Gilgal* is also a great spot to pitch a tent, with cheap rates for pickers. Despite the Italian population, Leeton feels less cosmopolitan than Griffith, but you can enjoy an Italian **meal** at the *MIA Social Club* on Racecourse Road (daily from 3pm; Ⓣ02/6953 4357).

Narrandera

Thirty kilometres southeast of Leeton, at the junction of the Sturt and Newell highways, **NARRANDERA** is a popular overnight stop en route from Adelaide to Sydney, or Melbourne to Brisbane. It's a very pleasant place to take a break, set on the Murrumbidgee River with streets lined with tall native trees; its white cedars, which blossom in November, are particularly beautiful. In mid-March the town hosts the **John O'Brien Festival** (Ⓦwww.johnobrien.com.au) of bush poetry and Irish music, a commemoration of the famous poet-priest who lived here in the early 1900s.

A good place to cool down is **Lake Talbot**, a willow-fringed expanse of water flowing from the Murrumbidgee River. Right next to the lake are the Lake Talbot Pools (Nov–April Mon–Fri 6am–9pm; adults $3), a family-friendly complex with picnic areas, barbecues, watery slides and an Olympic-sized **swimming** pool. Nearby, a reserve along the river has been declared a **koala regeneration area** for a disease-free colony of koalas; to get there, follow the **Bundidgerry Walking Track** around Lake Talbot and the Murrumbidgee

River. Free maps of the track are available at the friendly **Narrandera Tourist Information Centre**, in Narrandera Park on the Newell Highway (daily 9am–5pm; ⓣ02/6959 1766 or 1800 672 392, ⓦwww.narrandera.visitnsw.com.au). Fishing fanatics could try out the lake or river for some Murray cod, yellowbelly and redfin.

Practicalities

Aside from the *Historic Star Lodge* (lunch Thurs–Sat, dinner Tues–Sat), the best place for a **good meal** is the reliable Ex-Servicemen's Club opposite the information centre on Bolton Street. The *Murrumbidgee Hotel* also does good bistro meals.

Historic Star Lodge 64 Whitton St ⓣ02/6959 1768, ⓦwww.historicstarlodge.com.au. The best place to stay in Narrandera, this fine B&B boasts many original 1916 features, friendly owners and an award-winning restaurant. ❹

Lake Talbot Caravan Park Gordon St ⓣ02/6959 1302, ⓦwww.users/nex.net.au/users/fletcher. Quiet and shady caravan park, well positioned above the lake and pool, and with cabins and on-site vans. ❷

Mid Town Motor Inn Situated off the highway on the corner of East and Larmer Sts ⓣ02/6959 2122, ⓕ6959 3271. Clean, run-of-the-mill country motel rooms, and also has a swimming pool. ❸

Murrumbidgee Hotel 159 East St ⓣ02/6959 2011. The most appealing of the various classic country hotels, complete with iron-lace balconies, which line East St. The simple rooms are very good value. ❶

Narrandera Hotel 183 East St ⓣ02/6952 2122. Another of the old East Street hotels, this large, rambling building oozes country charm, though the rooms aren't quite as well furnished as the *Murrumbidgee Hotel*'s. ❶

Albury and around

The small city of **ALBURY** on the Murray River is a major stopover point on the route between Sydney and Melbourne, being roughly halfway between the two. It's twinned with Wodonga across the river in Victoria, and although Albury is the major centre, the principal information centre is on the Wodonga side – the **Albury Wodonga Visitor Information Centre** on the Hume Highway (daily 9am–5pm; ⓣ1300 796 222, ⓦwww.destinationalburywodonga.com.au). The **Albury Regional Museum** (daily 10.30am–4.30pm; free; ⓦwww.alburycity.nsw.gov.au/museum) on the Hume Highway occupies what was once the Turks Head Hotel – opportunistically sited here when the river was crossed by punt; changing exhibitions now focus on the social history of the region, including its Aboriginal heritage and previous status as a migrant work-camp.

The museum is set in **Noreuil Park**, a peaceful spot looking across to a bush-covered riverbank in Victoria. People lie about under the large gum trees – one of which was marked by the explorer Hovell at the point where he and Hume crossed the Murray – and swim in the river. You can also take to the water with a **cruise** on a replica paddle-steamer (book through the visitors centre; $16); there are two or three departures a day depending on the water level and demand. Another pleasant place is the **Albury Botanical Gardens** at the Dean Street end of Wodonga Place. Established in 1877, the gardens hold some impressive old trees, including a huge 41-metre Queensland kauri pine. The excellent **Albury Regional Art Centre** (Mon–Fri 10.30am–4pm, Sat & Sun 10.30am–5pm; free; ⓦwww.alburycity.nsw.gov.au/gallery), at 546 Dean Street in the decorative old town hall hosts periodic exhibitions and has a sizeable collection of sketches by Russell Drysdale (1912–81), who lived in the area in the 1920s and married into a local family. Wine de Tour (ⓣ02/6033 6366; daily at 11am; $49) run tours of the local **wineries**.

About 10km north of Albury on the Hume Highway, the larger-than-life **Ettamogah Pub** is like a parody of an Outback pub, straight out of a sketch by the Aussie cartoonist Maynard, although the precariously askew hotel really does serve drinks. Walk up the slanting staircase to the veering verandah where there are great views of the surrounding countryside. A touristy tin shack in the back flogs souvenirs.

Accommodation

Albury has a good range of places to stay. **Campers** are catered for at *Trek-31 Tourist Park*, 8km north on the highway (ⓣ02/6025 4355, ⓔtrek31@bigpond.com; cabins ❷).

Albury Backpackers 459 David St, near the train station ⓣ02/6041 1822, ⓔthecanoeguy@hotmail.com. Comfortable albeit wacky place, with half a combi van sticking out of one of the walls. The friendly owner rents out canoes (half-day $20, full day $30) and arranges overnight canoe trips ($60) down the mighty Murray. He can also help line up fruit-picking and farm work. Dorms $20, rooms ❷

Albury Motor Village YHA 372 Wagga Rd (Hume Highway), Lavington, 5km out of town ⓣ02/6040 2999, ⓔalbury@yhavic.org.au. This YHA is situated at a caravan park with a pool, but it's some way out of town and has the atmosphere of a morgue. Dorms $19.50, rooms ❷, cabins ❸

Carlton Country Comfort Corner of Dean and Elizabeth Sts ⓣ02/6021 5366, ⓦwww.countrycomfort.com.au. Plush motel with swimming pool, sauna, gym, spa and a corporate vibe. ❺

Gundowring B&B ⓣ02/6041 4437, ⓦwww.gundowringbb.com.au. Cosy four-star B&B in a restored Federation residence where you'll be plied with wine and given full country breakfasts served on the verandah. ❺

New Albury Just off the highway at 491 Kiewa St, about 2km north of the bridge over the Murray ⓣ02/6021 3599. This simple place is one of the best-value central hotels, and has its own Irish bar and a good bistro. ❸

Eating, drinking and nightlife

Dean Street is the main street for **food**. If you are ravenous and broke, head for *The Commercial Club*, which serves up one of the best deals in Australia, with all the pasta, steak, seafood and salad you can eat for $12. For something a little less functional, the retro *Electra Café* on the corner of Dean and Macaley streets serves a variety of internationally influenced meals on kitsch crockery (Mon–Sat 10am–10pm, Sun 10am–3pm; live music on Tues), while the licensed *Thai Lotus Flower Restaurant*, 610 Dean Street (ⓣ02/6041 3330), is a popular and smart dinner destination. *Trader Jack Seafood and Grill*, 645 Smollett Street (ⓣ02/6041 3055) also gets good reviews. **Nightlife** is a bit better than you might think. *The Bended Elbow*, 480 Dean Street (ⓣ02/6023 6266) which is a lively pub, and *Liquid* almost opposite (ⓣ02/6023 3433) have a band line-up on most Saturday nights. The *New Albury Hotel* has jazz on Sunday nights.

The lower Murray: Albury to Wentworth

Following the **lower Murray River** between Albury (see p.374) and the South Australian border, there's little of interest on the New South Wales side until the old port town of **Wentworth** and its surrounding storehouse of ancient Aboriginal history around **Lake Victoria** and in the remote **Mungo National Park**. The main centres are on the Victorian side of the river, Mildura (see p.1028) and Echuca (see p.1034) chief among them, although the New South Wales riverside towns of **Tocumwal** and **Corowa**, not far from Albury, are pleasant enough.

Corowa and Tocumwal

Following the river, it's 56km from Albury northwest to **COROWA**, across the Murray from Victoria's **Rutherglen wine region** (see p.1053). Blue flags flying all over town proclaim it to be the birthplace of Federation, since the Federation Conference of 1893 was held at Corowa's courthouse. Corowa also has the less romantic honour of being the largest pork producer in the southern hemisphere.

The **Corowa Tourist Information Centre** is at 88 Sanger Street (daily 9am–5pm; ⓣ02/6033 3221, ⓦwww.corowa-shire.visitnsw.com.au). There are stacks of **motels** in town offering very reasonable accommodation, such as the three-star, riverside *Corowa Golf Club Motel* (ⓣ02/6033 0634, ⓔmanager@corowagolfclubmotel.com.au; ❸). **Campers** could try the *Bindaree Motel and Caravan Park*, 454 Honour Avenue (ⓣ02/6033 2500, ⓔbindareecp@iprimus.com.au) which has riverside views as well as cabins (❸) and motel rooms with kitchenettes (❹). There are several places on the main street where you can get a **meal**, including the *Royal Hotel*, which serves up decent counter food; *D'Amico's* Italian restaurant; and the *Old Corowa Bakehouse*, a popular café-bakery that opens early.

On the way to Tocumwal, which is just under 80km from Corowa, there's a **boomerang factory** at **BAROOGA** called the Binghi Boomerang, where you can watch boomerangs being made and try them out yourself (call ⓣ03/5873 4463 for times). **TOCUMWAL** itself ("Toc" to locals) is a small, pleasant river town: its **Foreshore Park**, just behind the main street, is peaceful and shaded by large gum trees, and there's a sandy river beach only ten minutes' walk away. In front of the park is the **Tocumwal Visitor Information Centre** (daily 9am–5pm; ⓣ03/5874 2131 or 1800 677 271, ⓕ5874 3300), which provides information about the area and can book glider flights over the Murray.

Tocumwal has some classic old **country hotels**, most notably the very pleasant *Tocumwal Hotel* at 17–33 Deniliquin Street (ⓣ03/5874 2025, ⓔrealmac@dragnet.com.au; ❸), a hospitable hotel built in 1861 which has clean and simple self-contained motel units and also hosts live entertainment now and then. Next door is Central Store Antiques, which has good tearooms serving reasonably priced sandwiches and light meals. The best place to **camp** is the riverfront *Bushlands on the Murray Holiday Park* (ⓣ03/5874 2752, ⓦwww.tocumwalgolf.com.au/bushlands.htm; cabins ❸), a few minutes' walk from the beach.

Wentworth and Lake Victoria

Once a thriving river port, **WENTWORTH** is now a sleepy old town overshadowed by nearby Mildura, across the Murray River in Victoria. Located at the junction of the Murray and the Darling, the "two rivers" town was for seventy years the centre of river trade between New South Wales, Victoria and South Australia. The extension of the railway at the turn of the century bypassed Wentworth, however, and at the same time killed off much of the river trade.

Enquire at the **Wentworth Visitor Information Centre**, 28 Darling Street (Mon–Fri 9.30am–4pm, Sat & Sun 10am–2pm; ⓣ03/5027 3624, ⓦwww.wentworth.nsw.gov.au/tourism), about river cruises departing from Mildura Wharf aboard a period paddle-steamer (or call direct on ⓣ03/5023 2200; $14). The **Old Wentworth Gaol** on Beverly Street (daily 10am–5pm; $5) was built of handmade bricks in 1879, but the interpretive displays featuring bits of curling cardboard and dejected dummies are hardly worth the entrance fee. Opposite, **Pioneer World** (daily 10.30am–5pm; $5) is a folk museum exhibiting items related to Aboriginal and European history of the area, and models of giant, but extinct, Australian animals. There are some very good photos of old riverboats here. Perhaps the most interesting thing to do, however, is simply to drive down Old Renmark Road and have a look at the amazing, Sahara-like sand dunes.

The Aboriginal land council in Wentworth organizes visits to significant **Aboriginal sites** around Lake Victoria to the west, and Mungo National Park (see below) among the dry salt lakes to the northeast. The tours are run by Harry Nanya Tours at Shop 10, Sandych Street (Ⓣ03/5027 2076, Ⓦwww.harrynanyatours.com.au), and are accompanied by accredited Barkindji guides. In 1994, ancient Aboriginal graves were discovered at **Lake Victoria** – the Barkindji had always spoken of their existence. The partial draining of the eleven-square-kilometre lake revealed skeletons buried side by side and in deep layers; some of the estimated ten thousand graves date back six thousand years, in what is believed to be Australia's largest pre-industrial burial site – surpassing any such finds in Europe, Asia or North and South America. The site also challenges the premise that Aboriginal lifestyles were solely nomadic, suggesting that here at least they lived in semi-permanent dwellings around the lake.

Among the places to **stay** in Wentworth, the luxury apartments at the *Red Gum Lagoon Holiday Apartments*, 210 Adams Street (Ⓣ03/5027 2063; ❹), are wonderful, offering free use of canoes and rowboats on the lagoon itself. Another good waterfront choice is the *Willow Bend Caravan Park* on Darling Street (Ⓣ03/5027 3213, Ⓕ5027 3305; on-site vans ❶, cabins ❷), right near the shops but also at the confluence of the Darling and Murray rivers, where there are plenty of trees. You can get out on the water by renting one of the many **houseboats** (ask at the visitor centre). Prices start at about $180 per night for a four-berth. If you're looking for employment in the area, perhaps the best accommodation option is *Urumba Backpackers* at 81 Darling Street (Ⓣ02/5027 2499, ❶), where staff can help with finding work.

Mungo National Park

Mungo National Park, in the far southwest of New South Wales, is most easily reached from the river townships of Wentworth or Mildura (over the Victorian border, about 110km away – see p.1028); organized tours run to the park from both towns; if you want to tackle it on your own, you'll need a 4WD. The park is part of the dried-up **Willandra Lakes System**, which contain the longest continuous record of Aboriginal life in Australia, dating back more than forty thousand years. During the Ice Ages, between forty thousand and fifteen thousand years ago, the system formed a vast chain of freshwater lakes strung along Willandra Creek, then the main channel of the Lachlan River, flowing into the Murrumbidgee. The waters teemed with fish, attracting waterbirds and mammals, while Aborigines camped at the shores of the lake to fish and hunt, and buried their dead in the sand dunes. When the lakes started drying out fifteen thousand years ago, Aborigines continued to live near soaks along the old river channel. The park covers most of one of these dry lake beds, and its dominant feature is a great, crescent-shaped dune (a lunette), at the eastern edge of the lake, commonly referred to as the **Walls of China**.

There's an NPWS office (Ⓣ03/5021 8900) on the corner of the Sturt Highway at Buronga near Mildura, Victoria. The official **visitors centre** is by the southwest entrance to the park, and has a very informative display about the geological and Aboriginal history of the national park; nearby the impressive old **Mungo Woolshed** is open for inspection. From here it's a short drive to the lookout point on the rim of the lake, the former shore, from where you can look across the dry lake bed to the Walls of China. A signposted track takes you on a return trip across the lake floor to the Walls of China, then over the dune and on to the northwest part of the park. At sunset, or on nights with a full moon, the scenery takes on an eerie, otherworldly quality.

Beds in the former shearers' quarters and NPWS **campsites** in the park can be booked in advance through the visitors centre. Otherwise, try *Mungo Lodge* on the Mildura Road (☎03/5029 7297; ❸), which has motel units and self-contained cottages, plus a licensed restaurant.

The New England Plateau

The **New England Plateau** rises parallel to the coast, extending from the northern end of the Hunter Valley, some 200km north of Sydney, all the way to the Queensland border. At the top it's between 1000m and 1400m above sea level, and on the eastern edge an escarpment falls away steeply towards the coast. This eastern rim consists of steep slopes and precipitous cliff faces, deep gorges and thickly forested valleys, and because of its inaccessibility has remained a largely undisturbed wilderness. Streams and rivers from the highlands tumble over the rocks, and numerous mighty waterfalls pour into narrow gorges. On the plateau itself the scene is far more pastoral, as sheep and cattle graze on the undulating highland. Because of the altitude, the **climate** up here is fundamentally different from the subtropical coast, a mere 150km or so away: winters are cold and frosty, with very occasional snowfalls, while in summer the fresh, dry air can offer welcome relief after the heat and humidity of the coast. Even during a summer heatwave, when the daytime temperature might exceed 30°C, the nights will be pleasantly cool. Perhaps it was this that attracted the mainly Scottish immigrants who – despite the name – transformed the New England highlands into pastures in the nineteenth century.

The **New England Highway**, one of the main links between Brisbane and Sydney, passes all the major towns – **Tamworth**, **Armidale**, **Glen Innes** and **Tenterfield** – from where sealed and scenic side roads branch off towards the coast. Farms and stations all over the highlands provide **farmstay accommodation**, offering horse riding and other activities. The area is well served by **bus**: Greyhound Australia has daily services between Sydney or Canberra and Brisbane and between Brisbane and Melbourne, both via New England; Keans Travel (☎1800 043 339) operates daily between Sydney and Tenterfield via the Upper Hunter Valley; and Busways (☎1300 555 611) runs three times a week between Port Macquarie and Tamworth via Nambucca Heads, Coffs Harbour, Bellingen, Dorrigo, Armidale, Uralla and Walcha. There's also a daily **train** service between Sydney and Armidale via Tamworth.

The Upper Hunter Valley

The upper end of the Hunter Valley is Australia's main horse-breeding area – indeed it claims to deal in as much horseflesh as anywhere in the world, with at least thirty stud farms, and sires are flown in from all over the world to breed with the local mares. There are cattle- and sheep-breeding stations up here, too, while the fertile soils of the Upper Hunter also yield a harvest of cereals and fruits including, of course, grapes – see the box on p.228 for a sampling of Hunter Valley wineries.

The pretty township of **SCONE** is at the centre of the Hunter Valley horse trade, and you can get further details of the business from the **Scone Tourist Information Centre** on the corner of Susan and Kelly streets (daily 9am–5pm; ⓣ02/6545 1526, ⓦwww.horsecapital.com.au), which also has an excellent Internet café. The best time to visit is during the **Scone Horse Festival** – ten days in the middle of May – which features local prize specimens in horse shows, rodeos and races, along with more general cultural and artistic events. If you're planning to be in town at this time, be sure to book accommodation way in advance. At any time of year, ask at the tourist information centre about the regular races held in the area.

Lake Glenbawn, 15km east of Scone, makes a pleasant excursion. The dam holds back the waters of the Upper Hunter, storing up to 750 billion litres for irrigation purposes. **Recreation facilities** at the reserve here include a caravan park and boat rental: the lake is great for water-skiing, canoeing, sailing and fishing. Next to the kiosk, a small **museum** (open by appointment only – ask at the tourist information centre) exhibits relics from early pioneering days in the Hunter Valley. You can continue past the dam and climb to the plateau of the Barrington Tops (see p.307) to the national park of the same name.

Northeast of Scone is polo country, the haunt of mega-rich Australians. If you fancy seeing the elitist sport in action, there are polo grounds at **GUNDY** and at **ELLERSTON**. At Gundy, you can have a drink at the classic green-tin-roofed *Linga Longa Hotel*. In between Gundy and Ellerston, **Belltrees** is the family estate of the White family, who gave the world the Nobel prize-winning novelist **Patrick White**. Belltrees Station is a collection of buildings, including the 1832 Semphill Cottage, set among pepper trees; there's even a small school established in 1879. Further along is the White mansion where the family still live, and if you can afford it you can stay at the country house next door, or in the mountain retreat where in later life Patrick White used to escape when he returned home to visit; there are also a couple of cheaper self-contained **cottages** sleeping four people (country house from $198 per person per night, including breakfast, dinner and tour of the property; mountain retreat $245 per person per night, including all meals and 4WD transfers; cottages $70–110 per person per night; ⓣ02/6546 1123, ⓦwww.belltrees.com); polo tuition can be arranged.

Heading on towards the heart of the New England Plateau you'll pass **Burning Mountain**, about 20km north of Scone, near the village of Wingen. The smoking vents do not indicate volcanic activity but rather a seam of coal burning 30m under the surface: the fire was ignited naturally, perhaps by a lightning strike or spontaneous combustion, over a thousand years ago. The area, protected as a nature reserve, can be reached via a signposted **walking trail** that starts at the picnic grounds at the foot of the hill, just off the New England Highway; pick up the informative NPWS guide to the area's walking tracks from any NPWS office; the nearest one is in Scone. You might also see aquatic fossils on your walk – this area was once under the ocean. Fourteen kilometres north of Wingen, **MURRURUNDI** marks the end of the Upper Hunter Valley. It's a pretty spot, enclosed by the Liverpool Ranges; the *Café Telegraph* here makes a cheerful refreshment stop, with seats outside in the garden with the creek flowing past. The *Royal Hotel* is a good bet too, offering $5 lunch deals.

Practicalities

Countrylink **trains** run twice daily from Sydney to Scone and McCafferty's **buses** pass through. **Places to stay** in this area are widely scattered. Right in Scone the *Royal Hotel-Motel*, St Aubins Street (ⓣ02/6545 1722; ❶–❸), offers simple pub accommodation and fancier motel units – it also serves good counter meals. Right at the lake, the *Lake Glenbawn Holiday Village* (ⓣ02/6543 7752; ❸) has camping and three-bedroom cottages.

In nearby **Aberdeen**, a few kilometres south on the New England Highway, is the *Segenhoe* B&B, at 55 Main Rd (ⓣ02/6543 7382, ⓦwww.segenhoeinn.com; ❺), a charming sandstone residence from the early 1800s with large, period-style rooms; the staff can arrange a host of activities. Also recommended is the forested mountain-retreat *Craigmhor* (ⓣ02/6543 6394, ⓦwww.craigmhor.com.au; ❸), on upper Rouchel Road in the foothills of the Barrington Tops, 48km east of Aberdeen.

The best **food** is at the modern Australian *Quince*, 109 Susan Street (ⓣ02/6545 2286). If you're hungry for scones in Scone, then head to *Asser House Café* on Kelly Street – they also serve excellent coffee and tea.

Tamworth and around

TAMWORTH - the "City of Lights" – was the first in Australia to be fitted with electric street lighting, in 1888. To most Australians, however, Tamworth means **country music** – it's a sort of antipodean Nashville. The twelve-metre-high golden guitar in front of the **Golden Guitar Complex** (daily 9am–5pm; $6; ⓦwww.biggoldenguitar.com.au), on the southern edge of town, sums up the town's role as the country-and-western capital of Australasia. Inside the centre, you'll find waxwork figures of the great Australian country stars such as Chad Morgan, Buddy Williams, Smoky Dawson and his horse Flash, Slim Dusty, Reg Lindsay and Tex Morton. There's also a slightly incongruous collection of gems and minerals from the region – no rhinestones though. Afterwards, the **Longyard Hotel** next door is a handy place to weep in your beer for a while and, once a year, for a week in the second half of January, it becomes the focus of the **Tamworth Country Music Festival** when fans from all over the country descend, packing out camping spots. Every pub, club and hall in town hosts gigs, record launches and bush poetry, culminating in the presentation of the Australian country music awards – further information and bookings from Rural Press Events (ⓣ02/6762 2399, ⓦwww.countrymusic.asn.au) or the visitors centre (see opposite). There's more musical memorabilia at the corner of Brisbane Street and Kable Avenue, where the **Hands of Fame** cornerstone bears the palm-prints of more country greats. A glorious spoof, the Noses of Fame memorial, can be savoured over a beer at the *Tattersalls Hotel* on Peel Street.

Don't give up on Tamworth entirely if country music isn't your thing. The **Powerstation Museum** at 216 Peel Street (Tues–Fri 9am–1pm; $2.50), celebrates those pioneering street lights, and there are numerous art galleries and crafts studios around town – the **Tamworth City Gallery**, above the library at 466 Peel Street (Tues–Sat 10am–5pm, Sun noon to 4pm; free) has a good permanent exhibition and some local exhibits. Natural attractions include the **Oxley Lookout and Nature Reserve** at the end of White Street, with panoramic views of the city and the Peel River Valley; and **Lake Keepit**, 56km northwest of the city, where you can rent boats and mess about on the water.

The former gold-mining township of **NUNDLE** lies some 60km southeast of town in the "hills of gold" – people still visit with picks, shovels and sieves in the hope of striking it lucky, and you can join them for a day. You no longer need to buy a fossicking licence but it's still worth dropping by the General Store on Jenkins Street; they'll point you in the right direction to start digging.

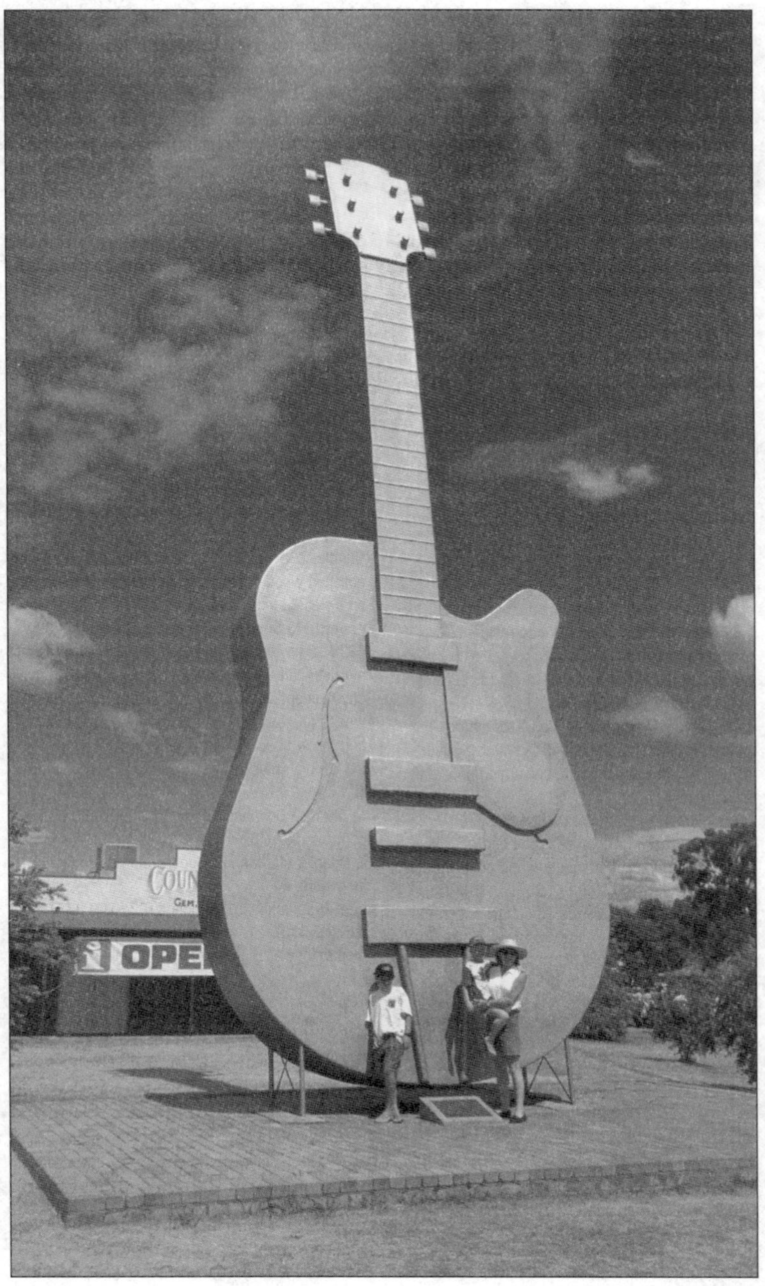

△ Golden Guitar, Tamworth

Practicalities

The big, guitar-shaped **Tamworth Visitor Information Centre** (daily 9am–5pm; ⓣ02/6755 4300, ⓦwww.tamworth.nsw.gov.au) is on the corner of Peel and Murray streets. Tamworth is well served by **bus**: McCafferty's runs daily from here to Sydney and Brisbane. **Local buses** can get you to Nundle (check with the tourist office), while Countrylink runs a daily **train** service from Sydney.

Accommodation

There's a fair spread of **accommodation** in town, though you might have trouble finding a room during the festival – you could try the string of **motels** on the New England Highway outside town.

Tamworth

Bunkhouse 118 New England Highway ⓣ02/6762 6300, ⓔbunkhouse@tpg.com.au. Entirely air-con hostel – spotless and inexpensive, if a bit clinical. Dorms $20, rooms ❷

Paradise Caravan Park Peel St ⓣ & ⓕ02/6766 3120. The closest place for campers and caravan-ers, on the river about five minutes' walk from the main part of town – very similar to the *Austin Caravan Park*. On-site vans ❷, cabins ❸

Passions B&B 118 Napier St ⓣ02/6766 4618, ⓔsjduncan@tpgi.com.au. Just about the only place in town with much character, set in a quiet but central location in a tree-lined residential neighbourhood. ❹

Quality Hotel Powerhouse Corner of East St and Armidale Rd ⓣ02/6766 7000, ⓦwww.qualityhotelpowerhouse.com.au. This smart motel has a corporate feel and five-star facilities, including room service, gym, swimming pool and sauna. ❺

Tamworth Hotel 147 Marius St ⓣ02/6766 2923, ⓔrumbler@ozemail.com.au. In the centre of town, with simple pub accommodation and good counter meals. ❷

Tamworth YHA 169 Marius St, opposite the rail-way station ⓣ02/6761 2600, ⓦwww.yha.com.au. Friendly place with a bit more atmosphere than *Bunkhouse*, plus friendly management and well maintained, if slightly old, facilities. Dorms $20, rooms ❷.

Around Tamworth

Austin Caravan Park 4km north of town off the New England Highway ⓣ02/6766 2380, ⓦwww.austintouristpark.com.au. Occupies a riverside spot with a pool and children's playground. Cabins ❷

Jenkins St Guest House 85 Jenkins Street, Nundle ⓣ & ⓕ02/6769 3239. Beautiful place with polished wood floors, fresh flowers in all rooms and an excellent local chef. ❻

Leconfield 50km east of Tamworth ⓣ02/6769 4328, ⓦwww.leconfield.com. If you want a taste of Australian country living, this place offers a five-day residential Jackeroo and Jilleroo school ($440) where you learn to ride and groom horses, shear and throw fleeces, lassoo, whip crack and go out mustering. They can also arrange pick-ups from Tamworth *YHA*.

Motel 359 Goonoo Goonoo Rd, 4km south of the centre ⓣ02/6762 4100, ⓕ6762 1789. This place is clean, if stark, and as good value as you'll find anywhere. ❷

Peel Inn Jenkins St, Nundle ⓣ02/6769 3377, ⓕ6769 3307. Historic hotel with rooms and hearty meals; they also organize gold-panning. ❷

Eating, drinking and entertainment

Outside festival time, you'll be disappointed if you think the town's **clubs and pubs** constantly resound to country-and-western. Probably the biggest venue (with no country outside festival time, but bands from Wednesday to Saturday) is the *Imperial Hotel* (ⓣ02/6766 2613) on the corner of Brisbane and Marius Streets. The *Central Hotel* (ⓣ02/6766 2160), on the corner of Peel and Brisbane streets, has bands from Thursday to Saturday and you can catch some acts on Thursday evening at the *Tamworth RSL Club* on Kable Avenue, and on the first Friday and third Sunday of the month in the *West's Diggers*.

Inland Café 407 Peel St. Cakes, focaccia and pasta, plus good coffee. Mon–Wed 7am–6pm, Thurs–Sat 7am–11pm, Sun 9am–5pm.

Longyard Hotel New England Highway. Pub restaurant serving large portions of good tucker such as meat and three veg and substantial pastas.

Daily noon–2.30pm, also Mon–Fri 6–8.30pm, Sat & Sun 6.30–8.30pm.
Old Vic Café 261 Peel St. Very metropolitan place, and a good people-watching spot, with fruit juices, pasta and pastries. Mon–Wed 7.30am–6pm, Thurs–Sat 7.30am–11pm, Sun 10am–4pm.
Quality Hotel Powerhouse Corner of East St and Armidale Rd. Good quality modern Australian mains ($30) in a very genteel setting.
Services Club 199 Marius St. Filling lunchtime buffets for around $9.
West's Diggers Club Corner of Bourke St and Kable Ave. Filling and inexpensive à la carte feeds of nachos, steak, chips and veggies in a pub-like environment.

Armidale and around

The city of **ARMIDALE** is home to the **University of New England**, which together with a couple of famous boarding schools gives an unexpectedly academic feel to a place so far up-country. Australia's highest city at around 1000m, Armidale is cooler than the surrounding plains and is also a place of considerable natural beauty, especially in autumn, when its many parks are transformed into a sea of red and golden leaves.

The central pedestrian mall, **Beardy Street**, is flanked by quaint Australian country pubs with wide, iron-lace verandahs – on the last Sunday of the month the street comes alive with an extensive **market** complete with buskers. The excellent **New England Regional Art Museum** on Kentucky Street (Tues–Sun 10am–5pm; free) includes fine surrealist work by Clifford Bayliss among others, as well as displays of work by Arthur Streeton, Tom Roberts and big-name temporary exhibits from Sydney. There are some lovely ceramics for sale in the shop. Next door, the arresting modern building with the distinctive ochre-coloured tin roof is the Aborigine-run **Aboriginal Centre and Keeping Place** (Mon–Fri 9.30am–4pm; Ⓣ02/6771 1242; $3), an educational, visual and performing arts centre which has displays of artefacts and interpretive material, plus special exhibitions. You might also want to visit the Armidale **Folk Museum**, at the corner of Rusden and Faulkner streets (daily 1–4pm; donation), which has a collection of artefacts from the New England region and displays on local history. There's more history at the **Saumarez Homestead** (daily 10am–4pm, closed mid-June to Sept; entry to homestead by guided tour only at 10:30am & 2pm daily, plus Sat & Sun 3pm & 4pm; $8), behind the

The Myall Creek massacre

In the first decades of the nineteenth century, when European settlers started to move up to the highlands and to use Aboriginal-occupied land on the plateau as sheep and cattle pasture, many of the local Aborigines fought back. Time and again bloody skirmishes flared up, though most were never mentioned in pioneer circles and have subsequently been erased from public memory. The **Myall Creek massacre** is one of the few that has found a place in the history of white Australia.

For Aboriginal people, expulsion from the lands of their ancestors amounted to spiritual as well as physical dispossession, and they resisted as best they could: white stockmen staying in huts far away from pioneer townships or homesteads feared for their lives. In 1837 and 1838, Aborigines repeatedly ambushed and killed stockmen near the Gwydir and Namoi rivers. Then, during the absence of the overseer at Myall Creek Station, near present-day Inverell, twelve farm hands organized a raid in retribution, killing 28 Aborigines. In court, the farm hands were acquitted – public opinion saw nothing wrong with their deed, and neither did the jury. The case was later taken up again, however, and seven of the participants in the massacre were sentenced to death on the gallows.

airport, a perfectly preserved dwelling dating from the 1800s. A two-hour **free bus tour** of the city with Heritage Tours departs from the visitor information centre daily (Mon–Fri 10am, Sat & Sun 10.30am).

One of the best ways to get around town is by **bike**: there's a signposted city tour, as well as a bike path to the **university campus**, 5km northwest of the city, where there are two small specialized museums (Antiquity and Zoology; both free), a kangaroo and deer park, and the historic Booloominbah homestead, built in the 1880s as a fashionable gentlemen's residence and now housing the university's principal administration office.

Practicalities

Armidale has a helpful **Visitor Information Centre** at 82 Marsh Street (Mon–Fri 9am–5pm, Sat 9am–4pm, Sun 10am–4pm; ⓣ02/6772 4655, ⓦwww.armidaletourism.com.au), which has information on accommodation, local sites and the area's national parks. The **bus** terminal is just by the information centre. Plenty of places offer **car rental**, among them Budget, at Ian Yates Service Centre, 2/270 Mann Street (ⓣ02/6771 1535), and Realistic Car Rentals, at Armidale Exhaust Centre, corner of Rusden and Dangar streets (ⓣ02/6772 8078). **Bikes** can be rented from Armidale Bicycle Centre, 244 Beardy Street (ⓣ02/6772 3718). For **taxis**, call Armidale Radio Taxis (ⓣ13 10 08).

Accommodation

Glenhope Homestead Red Gum Lane ⓣ02/6772 1940, ⓦwww.glenhopealpacas.com. For a real country feel, head 4km northwest of the city to this working alpaca farm. The self-contained doubles with kitchenette are modern, and have a scenic location overlooking the farm. ❹

Hideaway Motor Inn 70 Glen Innes Rd ⓣ02/6772 5177. Right in the centre of town, this clean motel is the cheapest around, with small but well-furnished rooms. ❸

Lindsay House 128 Faulkner St ⓣ02/6771 4554. This nineteenth-century residence is the nicest place to stay in Armidale, with large en-suite rooms and a bar and garden. ❺

New England Motor Inn 100 Dumaresq St ⓣ02/6771 1011, ⓦwww.newenglandmotorinn.com.au. Functional place in the town centre; rooms have bathtubs and satellite TV. ❹

Pembroke Tourist and Leisure Park 39 Waterfall Way, 2km east of town ⓣ02/6772 6470, ⓦwww.pembroke.com.au. This leisure park complex has good facilities including a swimming pool and tennis court, and is also home to a small YHA dormitory. Dorms $20, on-site vans ❷, cabins ❷

Poppy's Cottage Dangarsleigh Rd ⓣ02/6775 1277, ⓦwww.home.bluepin.net.au/poppyscottage. Olde worlde B&B set in a farm cottage five minutes' drive from town. ❹

Tattersalls Hotel 147 Beardy St ⓣ02/6772 2247; inexpensive and good-value singles and doubles in a central, quiet location. ❷

Eating, drinking and nightlife

Good, inexpensive **counter meals** are served at many of the grand old pubs on Beardy Street, including the *New England Hotel* and the *Imperial*. For entertainment in term time (March-Nov) head to the *St Kilda, Tattersalls, New England* or *Wicklows* hotels, all right in the centre for **live music** on Friday and Saturday nights. *Mojo's* **nightclub**, on the mall next to *Jean Pierre's* restaurant and the *University Bistro* have DJs at weekends.

Café Midalé Beardy St Mall. Light and airy place, popular with students and serving up Italian-style food – focaccia, panini and pasta of the day.

Jean Pierre's Beardy St. One of the town's better restaurants, serving modern Australian cuisine in a smart setting. BYO.

Jitterbug Mood 115 Rusden St ⓣ02/6772 2201. Lively spot with award-winning modern Australian cuisine and a long wine list, all at mid-range prices.

Lindsay House 128 Faulkner St ⓣ02/6771 4554. The best food in town, with an extensive gourmet

menu focusing on fresh Australian produce, and fabled desserts. Mains around $30. Bookings essential.
Rumours on the Mall Beardy St Mall. Another studenty place, with good, inexpensive meals and sandwiches, plus a decent breakfast (served until noon).
Upper Crust 133 Beardy St. Good fresh juice, gourmet sandwiches, kebabs and burgers (with veggie choices).

Around Armidale

Armidale makes for a good staging post north through the New England Plains or east to the coast through a hatfull of Australia's most beautiful national parks. If you don't mind dirt roads (mostly fine for 2WD in the dry), you can get to Coffs Harbour via hundreds of kilometres of rainforest roads, waterfalls and lookouts (get a map from the visitors centre). The exceptional **New England National Park**, 85km east on the Waterfall Way, and the several patchwork sections of the **Oxley Wild Rivers**, **Guy Fawkes River**, and **Cathedral Rock** national parks are full of ancient man ferns, towering canopy trees, gorges and spectacular **waterfalls** (although the falls may diminish to a trickle during prolonged dry spells). The most impressive are the **Wollomombi Falls**, among the highest in Australia, plunging 225m into a gorge just over 40km east of Armidale, off the road to Dorrigo. Nearby are the Chandler Falls, while **Ebor Falls**, a stunning double drop of the Guy Fawkes River, can be viewed from platforms just off Waterfall Way, another 40km beyond Wollomombi. Between Wollomombi and Ebor, **Point Lookout** in the New England National Park offers a truly wonderful panoramic view across the forested ranges – you'd be forgiven for thinking you were in the middle of the Amazon. The road to the lookout is unsealed gravel, but is usually in reasonable condition, and there are simple **cabins** and bush **campsites** where you can stay overnight: phone the NPWS in Armidale (Ⓣ02/6776 4260) for further information – it's essential you book in advance. The rest of the park is virtually inaccessible wilderness. Right on the edge of the park on Point Lookout Road is the *Yaraandoo Eco-Lodge* (Ⓣ02/6775 9219, Ⓦwww.yaraandoo.com.au; dorms $28, doubles ❹), where you can organize treks, kayaking, mountain bikes and horse rides.

On the way back to Armidale you could detour through the goldrush ghost town of **HILLGROVE**, where the old school has been converted into the **Rural Life and Industry museum** (daily 10am–5pm; $2) displaying old mining equipment and trying to recreate the lifestyle of the once-prosperous settlement. **URALLA**, 22km south of Armidale, is another old gold town, though in this case the town has managed to hang on, with a population of a couple of thousand. The Historic Building Walk will take you past the town's highlights, including **McCrossin's Mill Museum** (daily noon–5pm; $5), an old three-storey flour mill on Salisbury Street. Fossicking is still possible at the old Rocky River diggings: enquire at the **Uralla Visitor Information Centre**, New England Highway (daily 9.30am–4.30pm; Ⓣ02/6778 4496, Ⓦwww.uralla.com) or sign up for a tour with **Uralla Goldfield Tours** (Ⓣ02/6778 4850).

Gold apart, Uralla's other claim to fame is **Captain Thunderbolt**, the bushranger who terrorized the gold-rich New England region in the nineteenth century when the town was on the major Sydney-Brisbane route. A charismatic fellow, he had promised his aboriginal wife never to shoot anyone, and he never did. The police, however, had made no such promises, and Thunderbolt was apparently killed here in 1870 – although rumours abounded that the corpse was his brother's and that Thunderbolt was alive and well and plying his trade in California. There's a bronze statue of the bushranger and his horse on the corner of Bridge and Salisbury streets.

Southeast of Armidale, towards Walcha is **Dangars Lagoon**, a wetland region visited by more than a hundred different kinds of bird; a hide is provided for spotters. **Dangars Falls** and a network of twenty walking tracks and lookouts around **Dangars Gorge** are only 22km from Armidale on a minor road. Beyond these, about 20km east of Walcha, a turn-off from the Oxley Highway leads to **Apsley Gorge** and two more waterfalls in another section of the Oxley Rivers park. In **WALCHA** itself, 65km southwest of Armidale, there are the usual pioneer museums, but more interesting is the **Amaroo Museum and Cultural Centre** on Derby Street (Mon–Fri 9am–5pm; donation), which displays arts and crafts made by local Aboriginal people. Ask about these at the **visitor information centre**, 51 Fitzroy Street (daily 10am–4pm; ⓣ02/6774 2460). West of Armidale, 27km along the Bundarra Road, is the **Mount Yarrowyck Nature Reserve**, where an Aboriginal cave-painting site can be accessed via a three-kilometre circuit walk.

Glen Innes and around

GLEN INNES, the next major stop north on the New England Highway, about 100km from Armidale, is another pleasant town in a beautiful setting. Although agriculture is still important up here, you begin to see more and more evidence of the gemfields – sapphires are big business, as, to a lesser extent, is tin mining. In the centre, on Grey Street especially, numerous century-old public buildings and parks have been renovated and spruced up. There's some fine country architecture, including a couple of large corner pubs with iron-lace verandahs.

The **Land of the Beardies History House** (Mon–Fri 10am–noon & 1–4pm, Sat & Sun 1–4pm; $5), in the town's first hospital on the corner of Ferguson Street and West Avenue, displays pioneer relics, period room settings and a reconstructed slab hut. The name alludes to the two hairy stockmen who settled the area in the nineteenth century, and the Land of the Beardies title is one which the town is proud of, while the Scottish legacy of the original settlers is reflected in the name of the town itself and in many of its streets, which are rendered in both English and Gaelic. The local granite **Australian Standing Stones** at Martins Lookout, Watsons Drive, are based on the Ring of Brodgar in Scotland and are intended to honour the "contribution of the Celtic races to Australia's development". The stones are the site of a **Celtic Festival** (ⓦwww.australiancelticfestival.com) during the first weekend of May, when locals dust off their bagpipes, eat haggis, stage highland games and see the Celtic slaves take on the Roman legions.

The strongly Celtic nature of Glen Innes is counterbalanced by the town's department store, Kwong Sing & Co., which has been run by the same family of Chinese origin since 1886, when there were more Chinese here than Celts. While you're in the area, you might also consider a **horseback pub crawl** with Great Aussie Pub Crawls on Horseback (ⓣ02/6732 1599), one-hour to five-day horse-riding adventures through the bush with overnight stops at traditional Aussie pubs. A weekend trip costs $300, all inclusive. You can also go fossicking (sieving river silt in the faint hope of finding a sapphire) here – ask at the visitors centre.

In early November, Glen Innes celebrates the **Land of the Beardies Festival**, with everything from a beard-growing contest to dances, parades and arts-and-crafts exhibits.

Practicalities

The **Glen Innes & District Visitors Centre** is at 152 Church St, as the New England Highway is called as it passes through town (Mon–Fri 9am–5pm, Sat

& Sun 9am–3pm; ⓣ02/6732 2397, ⓦwww.gleninnestourism.com); they can help book accommodation and have a sapphire shop attached. Good **accommodation** options include the air-conditioned *Central Motel* on Meade Street (ⓣ02/6732 2200; ❸); the fancier (though not air-con) *Comfort Inn* on Church Street, 1km south of the centre (ⓣ02/6732 2255, ⓕ6732 1515; ❸), with a pool, spa and extensive landscaped grounds; and the well-equipped *Blue Sapphire Caravan Park*, 1km north of town off the New England Highway (ⓣ02/6732 1590; on-site vans ❶, cabins ❷). The nicest place by far, however, is the very welcoming 1920s *Mackenzie House* (ⓣ02/6732 1679, ⓔmackenzie.house@bigpond.com; ❹), quietly but conveniently situated right opposite the park in a lovely garden.

For **food** in the town, try the *Tea and Coffee Shop* on Grey Street, a cosy **tearoom** with loads of choice including Dutch pancakes, an array of interesting sandwiches, savoury croissants and hot breakfasts. Alternatively, there's modern Australian cuisine at the *Tasting Room* (closed Mon) and hefty feeds and $6 specials at the *Imperial Hotel* on Grey Street.

Inverell

The area between Glen Innes and **INVERELL**, 67km to the west, is one huge gemfield. Industrial diamonds, garnets, topaz, zircons and over half the world's sapphires are mined in the area. Inverell is also known as "Sapphire City", and at the **Dejon Sapphire Centre**, on the Gwydir Highway 18km east of town, you can watch gems being mined, washed, sorted and cut (daily 9am–5pm, mine tours 10.30am & 3pm; free). The showroom has a display of sapphires in 155 colours, from pale blue and green, to gold, lemon and pink.

If you want to try your own luck, you'll need to contact the **tourist office** on Campbell Street (Mon–Fri 9am–5pm, Sat 9am–1pm; ⓣ02/6728 8161, ⓦwww.inverell-online.com.au), which can direct you to the designated areas. If you want to **stay**, try the *Royal Hotel*, 260 Byron Street (ⓣ02/6722 2811; ❸), which has clean rooms with shared facilities, open fires and air-con, and counter meals; or the quiet, leafy *Sapphire City Caravan Park* on Moore Street (ⓣ02/6722 1830; on-site vans ❷, cabins ❸).

Tenterfield and around

Less than 20km from the Queensland border, **TENTERFIELD** marks the northern end of the New England Plateau. Although only a small town, it has a confirmed place in Australian history, being the birthplace of the Australian Federation, and in 2001 it played host to many centennial celebrations. Its title was earned when, in 1889, the Prime Minister of New South Wales, Sir Henry Parkes, made his famous Federation speech here, advocating the union of the Australian colonies; twelve years later the Commonwealth of Australia was inaugurated. A small **museum** (Wed–Sun 10am–4pm; $2) in Centenary Cottage recalls the occasion, and you'll still see the federation flag flown around town. Tenterfield's other claim to fame is as the birthplace of Peter Allen, the singer who penned the very popular "Tenterfield Saddler" (the saddlery is on Pelham Street) and "I still call Australia home" (he moved to the USA).

Tenterfield's real attractions lie outside town. Just 30km to the northeast is **Bald Rock**, in the national park of the same name, Australia's second-largest monolith after Uluru (see p.703), but a grey-granite version, 213m high. You can walk up the northeast side to the summit, from where there are breathtaking panoramic views well into Queensland.

The excursion to Bald Rock combines nicely with a visit to the nearby 210-metre-high **Boonoo Boonoo Falls**, also set in a national park of the same name, which is home to endangered brush-tailed rock wallabies. The road is sealed as far as Bald Rock, but there's a short unsealed road (passable in a 2WD) branching off before you reach the rock and running for around 2km to the falls. En route to Bald Rock on the left you'll pass **Thunderbolt's Hideout**, the rock shelter and stable of the bushranger Captain Thunderbolt (see p.385). The NPWS occasionally offers tours to both national parks: details are available from the **Tenterfield Visitors Centre**, 157 Rouse Street (Mon–Fri 9.30am–5pm, Sat 9.30am–4.30pm, Sun 9.30am–4pm; ⓣ02/6736 1082, ⓦwww.tenterfield.com).

Accommodation in Tenterfield includes a wide range of motels and pubs. The *Telegraph Hotel/Motel* on Manners Street (ⓣ02/6736 2888; ❷) is central and clean and also has good **counter meals**.

The northwest

From Dubbo, the **Newell Highway**, the main route from Melbourne to Brisbane, continues through the wheat plains of the northwest, their relentless flatness relieved by the ancient eroded mountain ranges of the **Warrumbungles**, near Coonabarabran, and **Mount Kaputar**, near Narrabri, with the **Pillaga Scrub** between the two towns. Clear skies and the lack of large towns make this an ideal area for stargazing, and large **telescopes** stare into space at both **Coonabarabran** and **Narrabri**. The thinly populated northwest has a relatively large percentage of Aborigines, peaking in the largest town of **Moree**. In 1971 Charles Perkins, an Aboriginal activist, led the **Freedom Ride**, a group of thirty people – mostly university students – who bussed through New South Wales on a mission to root out racism in the state. The biggest victory was in Moree itself when the riders, facing hostile townsfolk, broke the race bar by escorting Aboriginal children into the public swimming pool.

The **Namoi Valley** – extending from **Gunnedah**, just west of Tamworth, to Walgett – with its rich black soil, is **cotton country**. Beyond Walgett, just off the sealed Castlereagh Highway that runs from Dubbo, is **Lightning Ridge**, a scorching-hot, opal-mining town relieved by the hot **artesian bore baths** which are a feature of the northwest.

Coonabarabran and the Warrumbungles

COONABARABRAN is a touristy little town on the Castlereagh River, 160km north of Dubbo via the Newell Highway, and 465km northwest of Sydney. People come here to gaze at stars in the clear skies, or for bushwalking and climbing in the spectacular Warrumbungles, an ancient mountain range 35km to the west.

By virtue of its proximity to the **Siding Spring Observatory Complex** (daily 9.30am–4pm; $11 including tour; ⓦwww.sidingspringexploratory.com.au), perched high above the township on the edge of the Warrumbungle National Park, Coonabarabran considers itself the astronomy capital of Australia. The skies are exceptionally clear out here, due to the dry climate and a lack of pollution and population. The giant 3.9-metre optical telescope (one of the largest in the world) can be viewed close up from an observation gallery, and there's an astronomy exhibition, complemented by hands-on exhibits and a video show. There's no public transport here, but the school bus passes by – ask at the visitors centre (see below).

You can't actually view the stars at Siding Spring because, as a working observatory, it's closed at night. However the **Skywatch Observatory** (opening times vary; $5, night show $15; book before dusk on ⓣ02/6842 3303; ⓦwww.skywatchobservatory.com), on Timor Road, 2km from town on the way to the Warrumbungles, has night viewing through its modern telescope, plus a planetarium, theatre and "pathway to the stars" computer space-simulation programmes. On a different tack, Ukerbarley Tours (ⓣ02/6843 4446) run **cultural tours** focusing on the Gamilaroi Aboriginal history of the region.

Warrumbungle National Park

The rugged **Warrumbungles** are ancient mountains of volcanic origin with jagged cliffs, rocky pinnacles and crags jutting from the western horizon. The dry western plains and the moister environment of the east coast meet at these ranges, with plant and animal species from both habitats coexisting in the park. Resident fauna include four species of kangaroos, plus koalas and a variety of birds including wedgetail eagles, superb blue wrens, eastern spinebills and mountain galaxies.

Warrumbungle means "crooked mountains" in an Aboriginal language, and the park was in fact bordered by three different language groups – the Kamilaroi, the Weilwan and Kawambarai. Evidence of past Aboriginal habitation here is common, with stone flakes used to make tools indicating old campsites. The **Warrumbungle National Park** is spectacular, especially in spring when the wild flowers in the sandstone areas are in bloom. The most popular months with visitors are April, September and October: it's really just too hot for walking here in summer, and the cold winters occasionally bring light snow. If you do come in the hot months, remember to take plenty of water when you go walking, and something warm for the nights, which get quite cool.

The **National Park Visitors Centre**, in Coonabarabran at 56 Cassilis Street (daily 9am–4pm; ⓣ02/6825 4364), has hands-on displays and detailed maps of walking tracks. The wheelchair-accessible bitumen **Gurianawa Track** makes a short circuit around the centre and overlooks the flats where eastern grey kangaroos gather at dusk. Another good introduction to the park is the short **White Gum Lookout Walk** (1km), with panoramic views over the ranges – particularly dramatic at sunset. However, the ultimate – for the reasonably fit only – is the 14.5-kilometre (roughly 5hr) **Grand High Tops Trail** along the main ridge and back. The walk begins at the kangaroo-filled Camp Pincham and follows the flat floor of Spirey Creek through open forests full of colourful rosellas and lorikeets, and lizards basking on rocks. As the trail climbs, there are views of the three-hundred-metre-high Belougery Spire, and more scrambling gets you to the foot of the **Breadknife**, the park's most famous feature, a 2.5-metre-wide rock flake thrusting 90m up into the sky. From here the main track heads on to the rocky slabs of the Grand High Tops, with tremendous views of most of the surrounding peaks. Experienced walkers could carry on to climb Bluff Mountain and then head west for Mount Exmouth (1205m), the park's highest peak; both are great spots from which to watch the sunrise. The Warrumbungles are very popular with **rock climbers**, who are allowed to climb anywhere except the Breadknife; permits are required. There isn't any public transport to the Warrumbungles, so you'll need your own.

Practicalities

In addition to the National Park Visitors Centre on Cassilis Street (see above), Coonabarabran has its own **Visitor Information Centre** on the Newell

Highway, or John Street as it's called as it passes through town (daily 9am–5pm; ⓣ02/6842 1441 or 1800 242 881, ⓦwww.coonabarabran.com), where staff can organize visits to out-of-the-way places, including Aboriginal sites. Inside there's a free display of ancient megafauna – the large animals that used to roam the continent before human habitation, including a diprotodon – a wombat the size of a hippo.

Good **places to eat** in town include the wonderful *Woop Woop*, which has excellent modern cuisine in a cosy room of exposed brick and iron girders, situated in an alleyway just off John Street. Other establishments are all on John Street itself: the bright and airy *Jolly Cauli*, at no. 30, offers a wide choice of dishes, delicious coffee and home-made cakes, and also serves as the town's Internet café. The *Imperial Hotel* has the best counter meals.

Accommodation

Accommodation in the **national park** itself is limited to campsites, some of which have hot showers, electric barbecues and fireplaces (note that wood is not supplied, and while plenty of places sell it, there's a fine for collecting it in the park), and *Balor Hut*, an eight-bunk hut adjacent to the Breadknife. Bookings aren't necessary for any of the sites, but you may need to book the hut; mattresses aren't provided; bookings can be made at the National Park Visitors Centre. Anyone planning to stay in the park will need to bring provisions. There are plenty of alternative accommodation options **in town**.

In the national park

Tibuc Farm Timor Rd, 16km from town ⓣ02/6842 1740. Nestled under Bulleamble Mountain with three self-contained cabins varying from the decently equipped to the extremely basic (cold water only and no power). Mention when booking if you're not bringing your own linen. ❹ for up to four people.

Warrumbungles Mountain Motel & Cabins Timor Rd, 19km from town en route to the park ⓣ02/6842 1832, ⓦwww.warrumbungles.lisp.com.au. Set in bushland on the Castlereagh River. Rooms (BYO linen) have extra bunks and kitchens, so are good for families and small groups; there's also a small saltwater pool and facilities for tennis and basketball. Dorms $19, cabins ❸

In town

All Travellers Motor Inn John St ⓣ02/6842 1133, ⓦwww.alltravellers.com.au. Three-and-a-half-star motel with air conditioning and wheelchair-accessible rooms. ❸–❹

Elpaso Motel Newell Highway, 1km from the centre ⓣ02/6842 1722, ⓦwww.elpaso.com.au. One of the cheaper places to stay, but with good facilities including a large pool and licensed restaurant. ❸

Imperial Hotel John St ⓣ02/6842 1023. Excellent hotel which has a guest lounge, kitchenette, very reasonable singles and doubles, and a huge verandah with tables and armchairs. ❶

John Oxley Caravan Park 1.5km along the Oxley Highway ⓣ02/6842 1635. Shady and relaxing caravan park. On-site vans ❶, cabins ❷

The Namoi Valley: cotton country

On the Oxley Highway, 76km west of the New England city of Tamworth, **GUNNEDAH**, with a population of eight thousand, is one of the largest towns in the northwest. The town's claim to fame is as the inspiration for the Australian poet Dorothea MacKellar (1885–1968) and her patriotic verse *My Country*, in which she pledged her undying love for what was then – and still is now – a drought-stricken land. The opening stanza is familiar to most Australians, who learn it by rote at school:

I love a sunburnt country
A land of sweeping plains
Of ragged mountain ranges
Of drought and flooding rains...

Gunnedah has one of the healthiest **koala populations** in the state, and there is a semi-permanent resident bear in a eucalypt opposite the **information centre** (Mon–Fri 9am–5pm, Sat & Sun 10am–3pm; ⓣ02/6740 1564, ⓦwww.infogunnedah.com.au) in Anzac Park on South Street. The staff put out a "koala today" sign when he's home; otherwise you still have a high chance of seeing some on the Bindea Walking Track, a 7.4-kilometre walk from the information centre, or a 4.5-kilometre trek through the bush from the car park at Porcupine's Lookout; you'll also see wild kangaroos, and maybe even an echidna, but be careful because the track is quite overgrown and it's easy to get lost.

Gunnedah is a major beef cattle-selling centre, with auctions on Tuesdays. There are **markets** on the third Saturday of the month at Wolsely Park in Conadilly Street. The **Waterways Wild Life Park** (opening hours vary, check on ⓣ02/6742 1826; $4) 7km west of Gunnedah on the Mullaley Road (Oxley Highway) is a green lakeside which makes for an inviting pause from the highway and is home to emus, kangaroos, wombats, lizards and possums.

Should you want **to stay** in Gunnedah, try the friendly *Regal Hotel* at 298 Conadilly Street (ⓣ02/6742 2355; ❷), which has a laundry, a guest lounge with an open fire and entertainment on Friday and Saturday nights; or *Roseneath Manor* at 91 Maitland Street (ⓣ02/6742 1906; ❸), a historic nineteenth-century B&B with three cosy rooms and a cooked breakfast. The nearest caravan park is 1km east of town on Henry Street (ⓣ02/6742 1372; cabins and on-site vans ❶). Besides the usual pub bistros you can **eat** at the rather swish *Fiorella's Italian Restaurant*, 378 Conadilly Street (ⓣ02/6742 5004). *Pantry Creations*, *Classic Visions Café* and *Redgum Outdoor*, all on Conadilly Street, are good for coffee, cake and healthy luncheon fare.

Narrabri and Wee Waa

While Gunnedah does have some cotton crops, the slightly smaller town of **NARRABRI**, 97km northwest via the communities of Boggabri and Baan Baa, is recognized as the commercial centre of cotton growing. The **tourist information centre** is on the Newell Highway (Mon–Fri 9am–5pm, Sat & Sun 9am–2pm; ⓣ02/6799 6760, ⓦwww.narrabri-shire.visitnsw.com.au). The **Australia Telescope** complex lies 20km west on the Yarrie Lake road and consists of six antennas, five of which move along a three-kilometre railtrack. Opening times vary (ask at the tourist information centre), entry is free and there are lots of computer models to play with.

The other main attraction around Narrabri is **Mount Kaputar National Park**. The drive into the park to the 1524-metre **lookout** – with its panoramic views encompassing the vast Pillaga Scrub, the Warrumbungles and the New England Tablelands – is steep, narrow and partly unsealed (call ⓣ02/6792 1147 to check road conditions). There are eleven marked bushwalking trails in the park, with brochures available from the **NPWS office** at 100 Maitland Street in Narrabri (ⓣ02/6799 1740). The most striking geological feature of the park is **Sawn Rocks**, a basalt formation that looks like a series of organ pipes; it's reached via the northern end of the park on the unsealed road heading to Bingara. There are **camping** facilities at *Dawsons Spring*, with hot showers, and a couple of cabins sleeping a maximum of six, with bathroom, kitchen and wood stove (reservations via NPWS; cabins ❸). If you want to **stay** in Narrabri itself, or grab something to **eat**, try the good-value *Tourist Hotel* at 142 Maitland Street (ⓣ02/6792 2312; ❷), which offers homely and clean rooms, and has its own restaurant (closed Sun; ⓣ02/7672 1125).

The drive from Narrabri to **WEE WAA**, roughly 40km west, announces your entry into redneck territory with shattered bottles (thrown from speeding cars) which litter the roadside. Wee Waa was where the Namoi cotton industry began in the 1960s, and the large cotton "gins" or processing plants are located here. During the picking and growing season (April–July) free guided tours leave Namoi Co-op (daily 10.30am & 2.30pm; 1hr 30min–3hr 30min), but you'll need your own car to get around the various areas. If you can stand the rather raw, dispirited town and the blazing summer heat, you could earn some cash from the **cotton-chipping** work that's available here in abundance in December and January; ask at one of the two pubs on Rose Street, the main drag, and someone will send you in the right direction. From Wee Waa you can head west to Walgett and on to Lightning Ridge.

Lightning Ridge

The population of **LIGHTNING RIDGE**, 74km north of **Walgett** on the Castlereagh Highway (the road is fully sealed, but note that there's no place to stop for fuel between the two), is officially 4000 but unofficially it's reckoned to be about 10,000. It's a transient place, where people in their hordes pitch up in town lured by the town's one attraction: opal. Amid this harsh landscape scarred by holes and slag heaps, Lightning Ridge's opal fields are the only place in the world where the extremely valuable **black opal** can consistently be found. This lone enticement is heavily exploited by the town's opal galleries and **mines**, among them the Big Opal, 3 Mile Road (daily 9am–5pm; tours 10am; $12), which has demonstrations of opal-cutting and guided tours of an underground mine; and the Walk-in Mine, 1 Bald Hill Road (daily 9am–5pm; tours $7.50), which has tours to an underground mine and the opportunity to go fossicking. There's even an **opal and gem festival** in late July, which sees the population shoot up by another few thousand souls, plus the **Great Goat Race**, which is held down the main street over the Easter weekend; there's also a rodeo (with horses) on the Saturday. The effects of the opal obsession can also be seen in the gloriously crazy constructions of the few who have struck it rich; check out the **Bottle House**, 60 Opal Street, a bizarrely beautiful cottage and dog kennel built entirely from wine bottles set in stone.

There are clearly demarcated **fossicking areas** where you can try your luck at finding opals – but don't do it anywhere else, or you may stray onto others' claims (infringements are taken *very* seriously). Recover afterwards in the 42°C water of the hot **artesian bore baths** on Pandora Street (open 24hr; free); these tap into the great Artesian Basin, an underground lake of fresh water that's about the size of Queensland. More cooling is the Olympic Pool on Gem Street (end-Sept to Easter daily 10am–8pm), particularly appealing in the scorching heat since parts of the pool are shaded from the sun. **Bevan's Black Opal & Cactus** (Mon–Fri 10am–4pm; $5) has a good selection of opals for sale and an amazing cactus garden. The **Goondee Aboriginal Keeping Place** on Pandora Street (call ⓣ02/6829 2001 for opening times) has Aboriginal artefacts and information on bush tucker.

Practicalities

Countrylink runs **buses** to Lightning Ridge from Sydney and Dubbo daily. The **tourist information centre** is in the Miners Associated building on Morilla Street (ⓣ02/6829 1670, ⓦwww.lightningridge.net.au) and has opal-buying rooms attached – ask for the useful booklet *Walgett Shire and the Lightning*

Ridge Opal Fields, which contains a handy guide to buying opals. The centre can also fill you in on **accommodation** possibilities (all have air-con rooms), which include the central Black Opal Motel on Opal Street (Ⓣ & Ⓕ 02/6829 0518; ❸), and *Lightning Ridge Hotel Motel & Caravan Park*, a friendly pub on Onyx Street (Ⓣ02/6829 0304, Ⓦwww.lightning-ridge-hotel-motel.com; ❸), which also has cabins (❷) and van and tent sites (❶). The best place to **camp**, though, is *Crocodile Caravan and Camping Park*, Morilla Street (Ⓣ02/6829 0437, Ⓕ6829 2049; vans ❶, cabins ❷), which has a pool and spa and air-cooled cabins. Fossicking backpackers might also like to try the *Tram-o-tel* at 2 Morilla Street (Ⓣ02/6829 0448, ❶), which has basic bunk units and is within 300m of two opal mines. Full **banking** facilities are available at Westpac on Morilla Street or Commonwealth at the Post Office.

Back o' Bourke: the Outback

Travelling beyond Dubbo into the northwest corner of New South Wales the landscape transforms into an endless expanse of largely uninhabited red plain – the quintessential Australian Outback. The searing summer heat makes touring uncomfortable from December to February. **Bourke**, about 370km along the sealed **Mitchell Highway**, is generally considered the turning point; venture further and you're into the land known as "Back o' Bourke" – the back of beyond.

En route to Bourke, the Mitchell passes through **NYNGAN**, at the geographical centre of New South Wales, where the sealed **Barrier Highway** heads west for 584 sweltering kilometres, through Cobar and Wilcannia, to Broken Hill. Flood-prone Nyngan, on the eastern bank of the Bogan River, is a sizeable (compared to what you'll find beyond) and old-fashioned country town where you can refuel and freshen up. There's a small, shady park on Main Street where you can slump at picnic tables.

Bourke and around

BOURKE is mainly known for its very remoteness, and this alone is enough to attract tourists; once you've crossed the North Bourke Bridge that spans the **Darling River**, you're officially "out back". If you want to have a drink in the "Back o' Bourke" without pressing too far into the endless, scarcely populated plains all around, try the *North Bourke Hotel*, a shabby, wooden, green-tin-roofed Outback pub where bush poets congregate once a year during the annual **Mateship Festival** weekend, normally held in late September (details from the information centre). The lively festival began in 1993 to mark the centenary of the poet **Henry Lawson**'s stay in Bourke during a particularly harsh drought. Discovering mateship in hardship was a symbol for the fierce nationalism that arose in 1890s depression and drought-struck Australia. Work was scarce and Lawson often slept out in the town's Central Park, where a plaque is dedicated to him and to two other bush poets – Will Ogilvie and Breaker Morant – who lived here around the same time.

Bourke was a bustling river port from the 1860s to the 1930s, and there are some fine examples of riverboat-era architecture, including the huge reconstructed **wharf**, from where a track winds along the magnificent, tree-lined river. Thanks to irrigation with Darling River water, crops as diverse as cotton, lucerne, citrus, grapes and sorghum are successfully grown here despite the 40°C summer heat, while Bourke is also the commercial centre for a vast sheep- and cattle-breeding area.

With a population of three thousand (approximately twenty-five percent Aboriginal), Bourke acts as a base for regional services and welfare. Unfortunately, there is sporadic trouble involving alcoholism and aimless youngsters, and after dark the atmosphere can be intimidating. Visitors are best-off drinking in the very pleasant *Port of Bourke Hotel*, the *Oxley Club* or *Bowling Club*, and avoiding the *Post Office Hotel*.

Practicalities

An ongoing project to seal the roads in this corner of New South Wales has made it much more accessible than previously, but many lesser-travelled routes remain little more than dirt tracks. Up-to-date information can be found at Ⓦwww.backobourke.com.au. The **information centre**, inside the former train station on Anson Street (Easter–Oct daily 9am–5pm; Nov–Easter Mon–Fri 9am–5pm; Ⓣ02/6872 1222, Ⓦwww.visitbourke.com), can provide "**Mud Maps**" – roughly drawn maps marking places of interest off the beaten track in the surrounding area, though bear in mind that these destinations can be as far as 200km away. Staff at the centre can also arrange **tours** (Mon–Fri 2–5.30pm, Sat 9.30am–1pm; $22) covering orchards and vineyards in summer, and historical buildings and cotton farms in winter. You could also go for a **river cruise** aboard the old paddleboat *Jandra*, which operates between Easter and October. An hour's trip will cost $13.

Countrylink buses arrive here from Dubbo four times weekly, and you can also fly here with Airlink, four times weekly, from Sydney via Dubbo. **Accommodation** in town includes the pleasant *Port of Bourke Hotel* on Mitchell Street (Ⓣ02/6872 2544; ❸), which has a restaurant, air-conditioned rooms, some sharing a bath, some en-suite, but all opening out on to a sociable verandah; and the *Bourke Riverside Motel*, 3 Mitchell Street (Ⓣ02/6872 2539, Ⓕ6872 1471; ❹), boasting deluxe heritage cottages with king-size beds and a communal swimming pool. An ideal way to see how life is lived out here is to stay on an **Outback station**; the information centre has details of those that welcome visitors, among them *Comeroo Camel Station* (Ⓣ02/6874 7735; prices on application, but in the region of $25 per person self-catering and $60 full-board in the homestead), a unique experience with artesian hot bores, river waterholes with yabbying and fishing opportunities, and resident buffalo and ostriches. For those interested in **employment** in Bourke – harvesting tomatoes, onions and grapes between November and February and cotton-chipping between December and February – *Kidman's Camp Tourist Park* (Ⓣ02/6872 1612, Ⓕ6872 3107), 8km north of town on the Darling River, may be able to point you in the right direction.

The *Port of Bourke Hotel* is the best place in town for **food** and **drink** with fresh and healthy bistro meals, or counter meals out in the shady beer garden. The **Bowling Club Restaurant,** corner of Richard and Mitchell streets (Ⓣ02/6872 2190), has counter lunches from Tuesday to Sunday and dinner seven days a week. There's also Chinese food at the *Bowling Club* on the corner of Mitchell and Richard streets. **Internet** facilities are available free in thirty-minute slots in the library on Mitchell Street (Mon–Fri 9am–5pm). There's also a reasonable supermarket on Mitchell Street, and an IGA supermarket on the corner of Oxley and Sturt Streets.

West and north of Bourke

West of Bourke, it's 193km to the small settlement of **WANAARING**, past a reconstruction of **Fort Bourke**, built by Major Mitchell in 1835 as a secure depot to protect his stocks from Aboriginal people while he explored the Darling River. Near Fort Bourke is the kibbutz-like **Cornerstone Community**, a cotton-farming operation and teaching centre run by Christians; and where visitors are welcome.

Northwest, the road runs 215km to **HUNGERFORD**, on the Queensland border, and the **Dingo Fence** (see p.1194). The state border bisects Hungerford, which consists of little more than a couple of houses, a post office and a pub but was made famous (amongst Australians) by a Henry Lawson short story of the same name. Make sure you shut the steel dingo-proof fence behind you when you drive through: there's a $1000 fine if you don't. The heart of the town is the corrugated-iron *Royal Mail Hotel* (☎07/4650 4093; ❷), near the fence in Queensland: you can buy fuel, bread, milk and meat here, **meals** are served until 9pm, and the friendly owners are happy to give advice. You can also **stay** in the bedrooms running along the front verandah, the caravan or bunkroom in the back, or camp.

Heading directly **north** from Bourke, the sealed Mitchell Highway goes right up to just past Charleville in Queensland (see p.591). If you're passing this way, **BARRINGUN**, on the border 135km from Bourke, is worth a stop-off just to have a drink at the remarkably genteel *Tattersalls Hotel*, set amid a flower-scented garden. The hotel serves only snacks and doesn't have any accommodation. Across the road and closer to the border is the painted tin shed that comprises the *Bush Tucker Inn* (☎02/6874 7584; ❶), which has **meals**, rooms, fuel and camping space.

South and east of Bourke

Amidst the empty, featureless plains, the elongated **Mount Gunderbooka** (498m), about 70km southwest of Bourke en route to Cobar, appears all the more striking. Likened to a mini-Ayers Rock, the mountain was also of great cultural significance to the Aboriginal people of the area, with semi-permanent waterholes and caves; several **cave paintings** can be seen, contact the NPWS on Oxley Street in Bourke for details (☎02/6872 2744).

Twenty-eight kilometres **east** of Bourke, en route to Brewarrina, is a turn-off south to **Mount Oxley**, climbed by the explorers Sturt and Hume in 1829 to herald white settlement in the area. It's on private property, so you must first pick up a key from the information centre in Bourke, which also organizes tours here. The town of **BREWARRINA** (locals call it "Bree"), 100km east of Bourke on the Barwon River, has a large Aboriginal population and is a very pleasant Outback town, rather than the collection of sheds in the desert you might expect out here. In the days of riverboats, this was an important outpost, and the abundant fish stocks in the river made the area a natural fishery for the original Aboriginal population; the **stone fish traps** – a labyrinth of large, partly submerged boulders – can still be seen in the river. As many as five thousand Aborigines used to gather here to catch fish. The excellent **Aboriginal Cultural Museum** (Mon–Fri 9am–5pm, weekends by apointment; $6), located near the ancient fisheries in an earth-covered building similar to an Aboriginal shelter, explains the history of the area's Ngemba people and offers walkabout **tours**.

Cobar

Since copper was discovered here in 1869, **COBAR**, just under 160km south of Bourke and the first real stop on the Barrier Highway between Nyngan and Broken Hill, has experienced three mining booms. Today, it's home to the vast **CSA Mine**, said to be the most highly mechanized in Australia, extracting about 550,000 tonnes of copper every year. Earlier booms resulted in a number of impressive public buildings, among them the 1882 **courthouse** and the police station, as well as the *Great Western Hotel* on Marshall Street, whose iron-lace verandahs are said to be the longest in the state. Most people only stop here to refuel before the monotonous 250-kilometre stretch to Wilcannia; there is, however, a lovely picnic spot in Drummond Park, just off the highway on Linsley Street.

For more about the town, head for the excellent **Great Cobar Outback Heritage and Visitor Information Centre** (Mon–Fri 8.30am–5pm, Sat & Sun 9am–5pm; $6; Ⓣ02/6836 2448, Ⓦwww.outbacknsw.org.au/cobar) on Marshall Street. The museum has some great exhibits, like bush soap, made from kerosene, ashes and lard, and staff can tell you about above-ground tours of the CSA mine and provide Mud Maps showing places of interest around Cobar. Chief of these, and arguably one of the most significant Aboriginal rock-art locations in New South Wales, is the **Mount Grenfell Historic Site**, a 72-kilometre drive northwest of town. The rocky ridge contains three art sites with over 1300 motifs – human and animal figures, including the emus that you're still likely to see around the site, plus abstract designs and hand stencils. Older layers are visible beneath the more recent pigments, but there's no way to tell exactly how old the art is. The adjacent semi-permanent waterhole explains the significance of the site for the **Wongaibon people**. The NPWS in Cobar, at 19 Barton Street (Ⓣ02/6836 2692), hands out a leaflet about the site, plus a five-kilometre signposted return **walk** to the top of the ridge. To reach the site, head west along the Barrier Highway for 40km, then take the signed turn-off 32km north along a gravel road past Mount Grenfell Homestead to the picnic site.

There are lots of **motels** along the highway in Cobar. The *Cross Roads Motel*, at the corner of Bourke and Louth roads (Ⓣ & Ⓕ02/6836 2711; ❸), has air-conditioning and pools, while the *Cobar Caravan Park* (Ⓣ02/6836 2425; on-site vans ❶, cabins ❷) has smart cabins and shady trees. You can also stay at the charismatic and inexpensive *Great Western Hotel* (Ⓣ02/6836 2503; ❷), which has a good **restaurant** and all-you-can-eat breakfasts ($8). The tourist office can advise on **Outback bush stays**, such as the one at *Trilby Station* (Ⓣ02/6874 7420, Ⓦwww.trilbystation.com.au; campsites ❶, bunks $30, doubles ❹), two hours' drive distant.

Wilcannia and around

The next major town on the Barrier Highway is **WILCANNIA**, 260km west of Cobar. The former "Queen City of the West" was founded in 1864 and up until the early 1900s was a major port on the Darling River, from where produce was transported by paddle-steamers and barges down the Darling–Murray river system to Adelaide. Droughts, the advent of the railways and the motor car put an end to the river trade, and today the only reminders of that prosperous era are the ruins of the docks and the old lift-up bridge, along with a few impressive public buildings such as the post office, police station, courthouse, Catholic convent and Council Chambers on Reid Street, which houses the **tourist centre** (daily 9am–5pm; Ⓣ08/8091 5909). Nowadays Wilcannia survives as a service centre for a far-flung Outback population, with its banks, shops, motels and service stations, though problems with unemployment and alcoholism combine to give it a bit of a rough-town reputation.

Heading north or south of Wilcannia you can follow the river along one of Australia's last great 4WD adventures – **The Darling River Run** – 829km of Outback history, heritage and landscape running between Brewarrina and Wentworth. Further information on the run is available from Bourke Information Centre (see p.394).

You can travel the Darling River upstream **northwest** of Wilcannia all the way to Bourke, just under 300km, on unsealed roads that closely follow the east and west banks with crossings at the settlements of Tilpa and Louth. Station properties dot the riverfront, including Mount Murchinson Station, on the west side of the river 30km north of Wilcannia, said to have once been managed by the son of Charles Dickens. At **TILPA**, 130km north of Wilcannia, there's a classic Outback pub, the 1890s *Tilpa Hotel* (Ⓣ02/6837 3928, Ⓔtilpapub@bigpond.com.au; ❶), which has **meals** (the steak sandwiches are *huge*), **accommodation** and **fuel**; and for a $2 donation towards the Royal Flying Doctor Service, you can immortalize your name on the pub's tin wall. Ninety-three kilometres further on, at **LOUTH**, *Shindy's Inn* sells diesel and petrol and has basic accommodation in miniature cabins (Ⓣ02/6874 7422; ❷).

White Cliffs

From Wilcannia, you can head north off the Barrier Highway to the **opal fields** at **WHITE CLIFFS**, 98km away. Four kangaroo shooters found opals here in 1889 and four thousand miners followed. Besides opals, White Cliffs is famous for the extraordinary summer heat, and many of the two hundred residents live underground in "dug-outs". There are all sorts of underground attractions, as well as a solar power station that looks like something out of a space odyssey. For the authentic underground experience, there are two **places to stay**: the original and very friendly *White Cliffs Underground Motel* (Ⓣ08/8091 6647 or 8091 6677, Ⓔunderground.motel@telstra.com; ❹), which comes complete with licensed restaurant and outdoor swimming pool; and the only subterranean B&B, *PJs* (Ⓣ08/8091 6626, Ⓔpjsunderground@bigpond.com; ❺), with its underground spa bath and 64-million-year-old rock roof. You have to share a bathroom, but it's well worth it as this is one of the most unique places to stay in Australia. Cheaper, above-ground options include the *White Cliffs Hotel/Motel* (Ⓣ08/8091 6606; ❷) and the *White Cliffs Family Inn* at the post office (Ⓣ & Ⓕ08/8091 6645; ❸). If you can bear the heat, there's also **camping** (with hot showers) at *Opal Pioneer Reserve*, close to town (Ⓣ08/8091 6688). **Tourist information** is available on Keraro Road at the White Cliffs General Store (daily 8am–7pm; Ⓣ & Ⓕ08/8091 6611).

There are several **tours** to White Cliffs from Broken Hill (see box on p.405); otherwise you'll need your own transport to get here. The only fuel stop between Wilcannia and Broken Hill is at the *Little Topar Hotel*, roughly halfway along the 195-kilometre stretch of the Barrier Highway.

Broken Hill and around

The ghosts of mining towns that died when the precious minerals ran out are scattered all over Australia. **BROKEN HILL**, on the other hand, celebrated its centenary in 1988, and its famous "**Line of Lode**", one of the world's major lead-silver-zinc ore bodies and the city's *raison d'être*, still has a little life left in it after being mined continuously for over 110 years. Inevitably, Broken Hill revolves around the mines, but in the last decade it has also evolved into a thriving arts centre, thanks to the initiative of the **Brushmen of the Bush**, a painting school founded by local artists Pro Hart, Hugh Schulz, Jack Absalom, John Pickup and the late Eric Minchin. Diverse talents have been attracted to Broken Hill, and their works are displayed in galleries scattered all over town. Some may be a bit on the tacky side, but others are excellent, and it's well worth devoting some time to gallery browsing.

Almost 1200km west of Sydney and about 500km east of Adelaide, this surprisingly gracious Outback mining town – with a population of around 21,000 and a feel and architecture reminiscent of the South Australian capital – manages to create a welcome splash of green in the harsh desert landscape that surrounds it. Extensive revegetation schemes around Broken Hill have created grasslands that, apart from being visually pleasing, help contain the dust that used to make the residents' lives miserable. It's aided by a reliable water supply – secured for the first time only in 1953 – via a one-hundred-kilometre-long pipeline from the Darling River at Menindee. The city is also a convenient base for touring far northwest New South Wales and nearby areas in South Australia.

Remember to adjust your watch: Broken Hill operates on South Australian **Central Standard Time**, half an hour behind the rest of New South Wales. All local transport schedules are in CST, but you should always check.

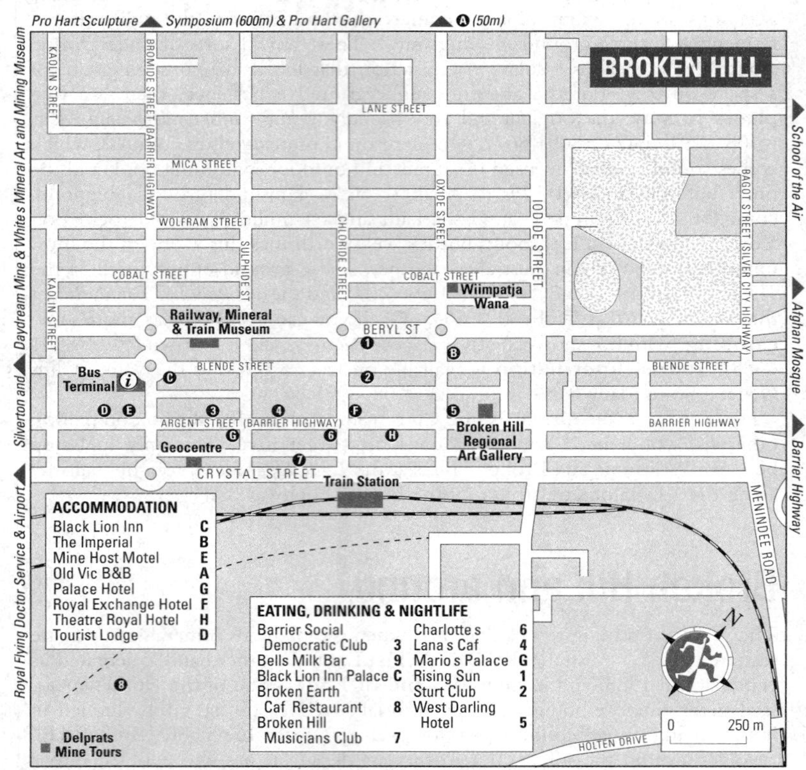

Arrival, information and accommodation

Arriving in Broken Hill by bus or train, you'll be centrally placed. The **bus terminal** (ⓣ13 20 30) is behind the useful **tourist information centre**, at the corner of Bromide and Blende streets (daily 8.30am–5pm; ⓣ08/8088 9700, ⓦwww.visitbrokenhill.com.au), where you can pick up a map ($3) for a self-guided heritage walk along Argent and Blende streets, or get information on the guided walking tour which delves into the city's history (Mon, Wed, Fri & Sat at 10am, no tours late Dec to early Feb; 1hr 30min–2hr; donation). The **train station** is on Crystal Street, just a block below Argent Street, although most Countrylink services arrive in town by bus. The **airport** is 5km south of town but there's no shuttle bus. Either catch a taxi (around $12) or arrange to have a rental car waiting (see p.406).

Accommodation

Black Lion Inn 34 Bromide St ⓣ08/8087 4801. Opposite the bus station. This is the town's cleanest and cheapest but simplest pub, with quiet rooms (some en-suite), including cheap singles ($24). ❷

The Imperial 88 Oxide St ⓣ08/8087 7444, ⓦwww.imperialfineaccommodation.com. The pick of the crop: a classy, four-and-a-half-star in a beautiful old building with huge verandah. The five spacious rooms have all mod-cons; there's also a kitchenette, free breakfast, a billiard room, a guest lounge, pool and garden. No kids allowed though. ❺

Lake View Caravan Park 1 Mann St, 3km northeast ⓣ & ⓕ08/8088 2250. A large site with disabled-access, en-suite cabins, a swimming pool and kiosk. On-site vans ❶, cabins ❷

Mine Host Motel 120 Argent St ⓣ08/8088 4044, ⓔminehost@ruralnet.net.au. Clean and functional and with a small pool, but little character. Central location right near the bus station, and close to clubs and pubs. ❹

Old Vic B&B 230 Oxide St ⓣ08/8087 1169, 0439 369 480. Farmhouse-style family guesthouse which is much cosier than it looks from the street. A good breakfast is included and all rooms share the bathroom. It's a 15min walk from the centre, though there are a couple of good pubs nearby for food. ❷

Palace Hotel 227 Argent St ⓣ08/8088 1699, ⓦwww.mariospalace.bigpond.com. Corner pub with one of the largest hotel balconies in New South Wales and a profusion of murals on every available surface, including a Botticelli-style *Birth of Venus* (painted by Mario, the landlord) which featured to hilarious effect in the film *Priscilla, Queen of the Desert.* All rooms have air-con, phone and a sink, and some are en-suite. ❷, *Priscilla* suite ❻

Royal Exchange Hotel 320 Argent St, cnr Chloride St ⓣ08/8087 2308, ⓦwww.royalexchangehotel.com. Plush, hotel-style en suites with smart furnishings and Internet data-ports. ❻

Theatre Royal Hotel 347 Argent St ⓣ08/8087 3318, ⓕ8087 3511. Nineteenth-century drinkers' pub with air-con, phone, fridge and TV in all rooms. Cheap singles and weekly rates available. ❷

Tourist Lodge 100 Argent St ⓣ08/8088 2086, ⓦwww.yha.com.au. Large YHA-affiliated hostel near the bus terminal – the only backpacker place in town. The shared kitchen/dining/TV room and common room are well-equipped, and there's a swimming pool and bikes available for rent. Dorms $22, doubles ❷

The City

Green it may be, but the huge slag heap towering over the city centre leaves you in no doubt that, above all, this is still a mining town. Take care shaking hands with anyone you suspect might have gripped a drill and shovel for 40 years; the old-timers can put a *serious* squeeze on you without noticing. The streets – laid out in a grid – are mostly named after chemicals. **Argent Street** (Latin for silver) is the main thoroughfare, with the highest concentration of historic buildings; parallel, on either side, are Crystal Street, with the train station, and Blende Street, while at right angles across the centre run Bromide, Sulphide, Chloride and Oxide streets. If you want to get an idea of what there is to see in the city centre, stop in at the tourist office for a heritage walk map or get information on the walking tour of the town (see p.399) – and look out for the interesting plaques commemorating important people and events all over town. An unexpected sight is the **Afghan Mosque** on the corner of Williams and Buck streets, on the site of the former camel camp where Afghan and Indian camel drivers loaded and unloaded their camel teams; you can visit it on Sunday at 2.30pm.

Murton's City Bus (ⓣ08/8087 3311) runs hourly or half-hourly along four routes through Broken Hill – the tourist office can provide a combined timetable and route map.

Mines and mining museums

One thing you shouldn't miss in Broken Hill is an underground mine tour. You can do it right in town at the disused Delprats mine, behind the railway station, or nearer Silverton at the Daydream Mine. At the excellent **Delprats** (tours Mon–Fri 10.30am, Sat 2pm, more during school holidays, arrive 10min before start; 2hr; $40) you don a miner's hat, and a heavy belt with batteries for your helmet light, before descending in the miners' cage – jammed in with fifteen people – 130m below the surface. Here, former miners working as guides will take you on a tour through the system of tunnels (stopes), demonstrating how miners used to work in the bad old days, and how the work is done now. The **Daydream Mine** (daily 10am–3.30pm; tours on demand; 1hr; $15), which operated between 1882 and 1889, is 20km out of Broken Hill on the Silverton Road – turn right at the sign and follow the dirt road for 13km; tours here are half as long as those at Delprats and a little tamer. Daydream can be booked through the tourist information centre, but without your own transport, you'll need to go on a bus tour (see box on p.405).

If you can't face going underground, take an overground tour of the old **South Mine**, reachable via Eyre Street in Broken Hill South, which commenced operations in 1888 and closed in 1972. The two-hour tours (ask at the tourist information centre for tour times; $11; ⓣ08/8088 6000, ⓦwww.lineoflodebrokenhill.org.au), which concentrate on the old ambulance room and BHP's rather horrific safety record, are rather haphazard and not particularly good value. Visits to South Mine can be easily combined with a visit to Photographic Recollections (see p.402).

There are three other mining-related attractions in the city. A visit to the bizarre but wonderful **White's Mineral Art and Mining Museum**, 1 Allendale Street, off Silverton Road (daily 9am–5pm; $4), might well be the next best thing to going underground. The art section is pretty extraordinary, consisting mainly of collages of crushed minerals depicting Broken Hill scenes, and at the back there's a walk-in underground mine, recreated so convincingly that it genuinely looks and feels like the real thing: inside, you're given an entertaining lecture, with videos and models, on the history of Broken Hill and its mines. A shop at the front of the museum sells minerals, opals, jewellery and pottery.

The **Railway, Mineral and Train Museum** (daily 10am–3pm; $2.50), opposite the tourist information centre, features an extensive mineral collection as well as old railway machinery and memorabilia including the fittings from the bedroom of the Maidens Hotel in Menindee where the explorers Burke and Wills stayed on their ill-fated expedition (see p.593). There are a few carriages and three glorious engines outside. Finally, the **Geocentre**, in a nineteenth-century bond store on the corner of Bromide and Crystal streets (Mon–Fri 10am–4.45pm, Sat & Sun 1pm-4.45pm; $3.50), looks at Broken

Mining and unionism in Broken Hill

The story of Broken Hill began in 1883 when a German-born boundary rider from Mount Gipps Station, Charles Rasp, pegged out a forty-acre lease of a "broken hill" that he believed was tin. A syndicate of seven was formed, founding the **Broken Hill Proprietary** (BHP) to work what turned out to be rich silver, lead and zinc deposits. Broken Hill's mines, dominated by BHP until they withdrew operations in 1939, have contributed greatly to the wealth of Australia: the deposit, more than 7km long and up to 250m wide, is thought originally to have contained more than three hundred million tonnes of silver, zinc and lead ores. Even now there's said to be ten years left in the "Line of Lode" currently being worked by the Perilya and CBH companies.

In the early years, living and working **conditions** for the miners were atrocious. The climate was harsh, housing was poor and diseases such as typhoid, scarlet fever and dysentery – to say nothing of work-related illnesses such as lead poisoning and mining accidents – contributed to a death rate almost twice the New South Wales average; there have been around eight hundred deaths in mining accidents since operations began. The mine and the growing town rapidly stripped the landscape of timber, leaving the settlement surrounded by a vast, bleak plain. Dust storms were common. Not surprisingly, perhaps, Broken Hill was at the forefront of **trade union** development in Australia, as the miners, many of them recent immigrants, fought to improve their living and working conditions. It was their ability to unite that ultimately won them their battles, above all in the Big Strike of 1919–20, when, after eighteen months of holding out against the police and strikebreakers, major concessions were won from BHP.

The unions typified the precious Australian concept of mateship – some miners literally died for each other, or worked for fifteen years side by side with the same partner. Not that the trade union movement at Broken Hill should be viewed through too-rosy glasses. The union, which effectively ran the town in conjunction with the mine companies, was also a bastion of racism and male supremacy – non-whites were not tolerated in town, nor were working women who happened to be married – and local attitudes remain strongly conservative.

Despite the life left in Broken Hill's mineral deposits, the future is none too certain. With modern mining technology the ore is removed faster, and the numbers employed are lower. Between 1970 and 1975, about 4000 people were employed in the mines. By the early 1980s this number had been reduced to 2500, and less than 600 work there now. The population continues to decrease gradually and every few years another of the city's many pubs closes down.

Hill's geology, mineralogy and metallurgy. One of the highlights is the spectacular **Silver Tree**, a 68-centimetre-high figurine, wrought of pure silver from the Broken Hill Mines, depicting five Aborigines, a drover on horseback, kangaroos, emus and sheep gathered under a tree.

Art galleries and sculpture parks

If you only go to one gallery in Broken Hill, make it the **Pro Hart Gallery**, at 108 Wyman Street (Mon–Fri 9am–5pm, Sun 1.30–5pm; $4; Ⓦ www.prohart.com.au). A former Broken Hill miner turned artist, Pro Hart's sculptures, etchings and prints typically depict Outback events and people such as race meetings, backyard barbecues and union leaders – look out for the fantastic ten-metre-long *History of Australia* showing scenes of Aboriginal life before the arrival of Captain Cook, the early pioneers, bush rangers and the founding of Broken Hill. The gallery's three levels are said to hold the largest private art collection in the southern hemisphere, with a truly astounding amount of the artist's own work as well as works by other Australian painters – Tom Roberts,

Sidney Nolan, David Boyd and Albert Namatjira among them, as well as (amazingly) originals by Salvador Dali, Picasso, Rembrandt, Turner, Constable and Monet. There's a collection of Hart's sculptures in a lot across the road which you can check out for free. If you're buying, you can get a print for $75; a small painting will set you back about $3500.

Broken Hill Regional Art Gallery in Sully's Emporium, 408 Argent Street (daily 10am–5pm; donation) has an excellent representative collection of artists from Broken Hill as well as Australian art in general. Established in 1904, it's the second-oldest gallery in the state – after the Art Gallery of New South Wales in Sydney – with a small collection of nineteenth- and early-twentieth-century paintings including works by Sidney Nolan, John Olsen, and the "Brushmen of the Bush" (though these are sometimes moved to make way for special exhibitions). Also on display are temporary photography exhibitions and sculptures created by artists who participated in the 1993 Sculpture Symposium at The Living Desert (see below).

Ant Hill Gallery (Mon–Sat 9am–5pm, Sun 1.30–5pm), at 24 Bromide Street just opposite tourist information, displays a small variety of local work. At 233 Rowe Street, just west of the centre, **D'Art De Main Gallery** (daily 9am–5pm; free) has a good collection of sculptures, portraits and landscapes by Geoff De Main, who also painted many of the wall murals you'll see around town. The central **Roxanna Minchin Gallery** at 105 Morgan Street (daily 11am–3/4pm) displays the artist's quasi-photographic work. The **Jack Absalom Gallery** at 638 Chapple Street (daily 9am–5pm; free) houses the original brushman's large, colourful Outback landscapes, as well as some beautiful opal jewellery. There's Aboriginal art – albeit with modern influence – at **Thankakali Cultural Centre**, corner of Beryl and Buck Streets (Mon–Fri 9am–4pm, Sat & Sun 10am–3pm; free).

There's a small photography gallery, **Images of Australia**, at 145 Sulphide Street (usually daily 9am–5pm; free), featuring colour prints of local landscapes and desert artefacts. **Photographic Recollections**, on Eyre Street (Mon–Fri 10am–4.30pm, Sat 1–4.30pm; $4.50), provides a pictorial history of Broken Hill, with over six hundred photographs accompanied by well-researched text that delves into mining, union and social history. The location itself, in the former **Central Power Station**, tells a story of the city's very Outback past; Broken Hill produced all its power here from the 1930s until as late as 1986, when it finally went onto the national grid.

Six kilometres out of town, the **Sculpture Symposium** in **The Living Desert Reserve** is the most dramatic of Broken Hill's art exhibits, a reserve in the eroded Barrier Ranges desert region containing a group of sculptures carved from Wilcannia sandstone boulders. The twelve artists involved in their creation were part of a sculpture symposium in 1993 and were drawn from diverse cultures – two from Mexico (including an Aztec Indian), two from Syria, three from Georgia (in the Caucasus), and five Australians, including two Bathurst Islanders – and this is reflected in the variety of their works. The pieces from the Georgian artists are particularly fine: Badri Sulushia's *Outback Madonna and Child*; Valerian Jiiya's Cubist interpretation; and Jumber Jikiya's horse's head, a tribute to the rare breed of Georgian horses slaughtered under Stalin's orders. Nastra Luna of Mexico badly injured his hands and his piece became a collective effort, depicting a soaring eagle, with the hands of the other sculptors who helped him imprinted in the rock. The Aboriginal artist Badger Bates, from Broken Hill, was inspired by the stone carvings of his ancestors, and his piece shows two rainbow serpents travelling north. The best time to visit the sculptures is at sunset on a clear evening, when the light

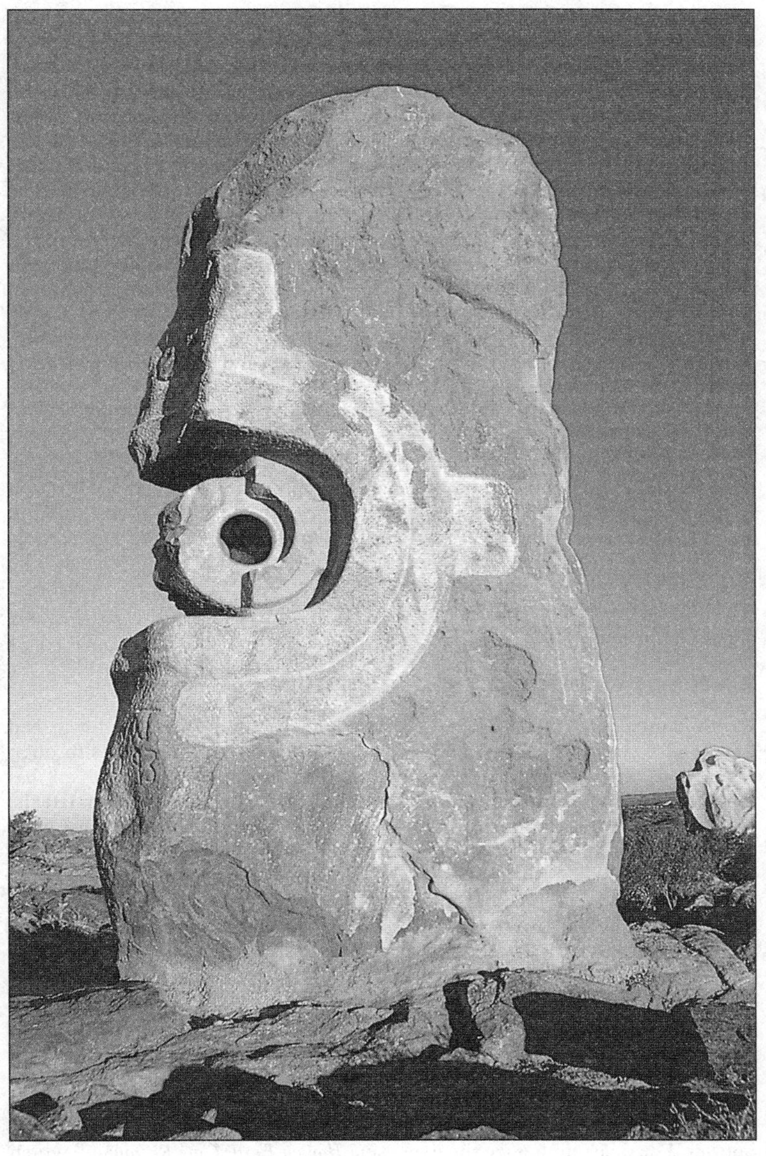

△ Sculpture symposium, Broken Hill

is magical and the rocks glow crimson. It's a pleasant fifteen-minute walk to the sculptures up the hill from the car park of the Living Desert Reserve. An information brochure ($1.10) about the sculptures is available from the tourist office.

The Royal Flying Doctor Service and the School of the Air

Broken Hill offers an excellent opportunity to visit two Australian Outback institutions: the Royal Flying Doctor Service (RFDS) and the School of the Air. The **Royal Flying Doctor Service**, at Broken Hill Airport, offers guided tours (Mon–Fri 9am–5pm, Sat & Sun 10am–4pm; $5.50; Ⓦwww.rfds.org.au), with an accompanying video and talk – it's best to buy your ticket in advance from the tourist office as places are limited. In the headquarters you'll see the radio room where calls from remote places in New South Wales, South Australia and Queensland are handled before going out to the hangar to see the aircraft. The popularity of the tours is due to the Australian television series, *The Flying Doctors*, which is shown worldwide, and since a third of the annual budget of $30 million has to come through fund-raising – the rest of the money is from the State and Federal governments – whatever you spend on the tour and at the souvenir shop here is going to a good cause.

In many ways the **School of the Air** is also indebted to the RFDS: lessons for children in the Outback, in a transmission area of 1.8 million square kilometres, were formerly conducted via RFDS two-way radio (these days it's all by webcam). The radio service was established in 1956 to improve education for children in the isolated Outback. You can still listen to the transmission in a schoolroom surrounded by children's artwork (Mon–Fri, term time only 8.30am; book in advance at the tourist centre; $3.30). It's frighteningly like being back at school, with jolly primary-school teachers hosting singalongs; what comes out of the radio is a static squawk, but the children in the far-flung areas seem to enjoy it.

Eating, drinking and nightlife

Restaurants aren't really Broken Hill's style – the town is famous for its bad food, and if your meal looks like it was trucked a thousand kilometres through a sandstorm to get here, that's because it probably was. Broken Hill still has the proverbial pub on every corner, and most of them serve **counter meals**, though they're not the best. The *West Darling Hotel* on the corner of Oxide and Argent streets has the not-monumental honour of serving the town's best pub lunch, according to locals. It's OK, but the *Sturt Club* on the corner of Blende and Chloride is the best of the lot, with various fish, meat, pasta and nachos-type meals (noon–9pm) for around $7–9. The *Barrier Social Democratic Club* (*Demo Club* to the locals), at 214 Argent Street, has an edible salad bar plus good, inexpensive breakfasts (7–9am). You could also vainly try the *Broken Hill Legion Club*, 166–170 Crystal Street (Ⓣ08/8087 4064); or the *Broken Hill Musicians Club*, 276 Crystal Street (Ⓣ08/8088 1777). These make most of their money out of gambling – with snooker tables, darts and endless parades of pokies machines – so they're happy to draw their customers in and keep them playing by tempting them with cheap food.

If you're looking for an alternative to the pubs and clubs, there are a few options. For smart dining try the expensive *Broken Earth Café Restaurant*, which is – literally and metaphorically – right on top of the heap on Federation Way, just past Delprats mine. The funky curved roof is visible all over town, the views are great and the modern Australian food and wine is . . . better than elsewhere. At no. 198 Argent Street, *Lana's Café* serves almost exclusively veggie fare, while cosy *Charlotte's* at no. 317, opposite the post office, has coffee and a range of cakes, muffins and slices. Top marks for effort, fun and originality go to *Bells*

Tours from Broken Hill

There is a big range of tours on offer, from scenic flights to 4WD tours, all of which can be booked from the tourist information centre (see p.399). Most include a pick-up and return service to and from your accommodation.

Air charters and scenic flights

If you have a bit of cash to spare, small aircraft are an excellent way of getting around, covering the enormous distances rather quickly and in relative ease and comfort.

Wetternet Air Airport Terminal ⓣ08/8088 5702. Tour flights to Tibooburra ($360 per person), White Cliffs ($250), over Lake Eyre and South Australia's Flinders Ranges ($550) as well as several more local scenic tours. Minimum of four people needed for most trips, unless you pay for the empty seats.

Bus tours

These tend to be overpriced, given that many tours merely provide transport to places that could be more enjoyably visited with a rental car or bike, or even by taxi. Tours are more frequent between early April and the end of November.

Silver City Tours ⓣ08/8087 6956, ⓔsctbhq@ruralnet.net.au. Excursions include Royal Flying Doctor Service ($23), School of the Air ($20), White's Mineral Art and Mining Museum ($20); half-day tours of city sights ($45), art galleries ($45), sunset Sculpture Symposium ($25), Silverton ($45); day-tours, including lunch, to White Cliffs ($130), Menindee Lakes by boat, Kinchega National Park and Tandou Irrigation Farm ($109), and Mutawintji National Park ($120).

John Arnold's Outback Safari Tours ⓣ & ⓕ08/8087 7701 or 0418 858 646 and **Hawke's City Sights Tours** ⓣ08/8087 2484 both offer similar tours to Silver City, though usually at slightly higher prices.

Four-wheel-drive tours

Broken Hill's Outback Tours ⓣ08/8087 7800 or 1800 670 120, ⓦwww.outbacktours.net. Offers a vast array of long-haul, fully inclusive tours including a five-day/four-night trip to all three national parks detailed in the following pages ($1680), and a six-day excursion to Flinders Ranges ($1540). Can provide customized tours too.

Corner Country Adventure Tours ⓣ08/8087 5142. Longer 4WD trips, including a four-day/three-night trip to Kinchega, Mutawintji and Sturt national parks ($1060), or tailor-made excursions as far afield as the Birdsville Track (see p.894).

Goanna Safari ⓣ08/8087 6057, ⓦwww.goanna-safari.com.au. Excellent tours with a well-informed, uniquely qualified and interesting guide who is never in too much of a rush; maximum four people in the group. One-day tours ($95) to: Poolamacca Station, a sheep station 60km north of Broken Hill; Menindee Lakes and Kinchega National Park; Mutawintji National Park including the Aboriginal art sites; the Dingo Fence; or closer to home a round-up of the Royal Flying Doctor Service, Silverton, and the Sculpture Symposium. Two-day safari to White Cliffs, staying in a dug-out motel ($340), or extending to three days and including Mutawintji ($510). Tibooburra and Camerons Corner are taken in on another two-day trip (also $340). Short trips out to The Living Desert sculpture site (minimum $10, cheaper depending on numbers) are also available.

Tri-State Safari ⓣ08/8088 2389, ⓦwww.tristate.com.au. A very highly recommended outfit who get right out back. Tours ranging from sunset sculptures and wine ($40) to one-day trips to Kinchega ($136, plus $53 for a river cruise) and mammoth Burke and Wills or desert tours, between four and eleven days in length (about $2000 for 11 days).

Milk Bar, all the way over in Patton Street on the south side of town. It's a great spot – a bit like the 1950s diner with a rock 'n' roll jukebox and vinyl booths. The multicoloured glass bottles of secret recipe sarsaparilla syrup and the like are on display along with sculptures made from hubcaps. They specialize in spiders (soda ice-cream floats), milkshakes and smoothies, but there's no food. For **grocery** supplies, visit the late-opening IGM behind the police station on Blende Street, or the large supermarkets in out-of-town Westside Plaza, Galena Street (open daily).

Drinking and nightlife

The city has always been a legendary **drinking** hole, and once had over seventy hotels. Many pubs have been converted to other uses, but there are still more than twenty licensed establishments and a pub crawl is highly recommended. Some places to include for an early drink are the kitsch-crammed *Mario's Palace*, 227 Argent Street, which memorably featured in *The Adventures of Priscilla, Queen of the Desert*; the *Rising Sun*, 2 Beryl Street, popular with younger locals on Friday nights when live bands play; the *Black Lion Inn*, 34 Bromide Street (open late, and on Fri & Sat till 4am), good any time but especially during happy hour (times vary) at the cocktail bar done out like an underground mine; and the *Mulga Hill Tavern*, on the corner of Oxide and Williams streets.

Another option is to sample the local culture at one of the numerous **clubs** mentioned above which often host live entertainment on Friday and Saturday nights. The Broken Hill Musicians Club has inherited Broken Hill's famous *Two Up School*, once an illegal back-lane gambling operation. The Broken Hill club was immortalized by Kenneth Cook's 1961 novel (and later film), *Wake in Fright*. Try to make it here on Fridays and Saturdays when the boys from the bush turn up in force to bet as much as $200 on one flip of a coin.

Listings

Airlines Qantas ⓣ13 13 13; Regional Express ⓣ13 17 13.
Bike rental Johnny Windham, 135 Argent St (ⓣ08/8087 3707), rents mainly mountain bikes: $5 per day, $25 per week, plus obligatory helmet $2; closed Sat & Sun. The *Tourist Lodge* rents bikes to guests at similar rates.
Bookshops ABC Centre, 309 Argent St (inside Cubans Radio), specializes in local history and the Outback (ⓣ08/8088 1177). For secondhand books, try Browzers Bookshop 345 Argent St (ⓣ08/8088 7221) or W Book Exchange, 320 Chloride St, cnr Thomas St (ⓣ08/8087 3383).
Car rental Avis, 121 Rakow St ⓣ08/8087 7532; Budget, 338 Crystal St ⓣ13 27 27; Hertz, at the tourist information centre ⓣ08/8087 2719; and Thrifty, 190 Argent St ⓣ08/8088 1928; all have desks at the airport too. You'll pay around $70/125 a day for a saloon car/4WD. Small cars are extinct here due to predation by utes with giant roo-bars.
Cinema Village Silver City Cinema, 41 Oxide St ⓣ08/8087 4569.
Hospital Broken Hill Base Hospital and Health Services, 176 Thomas St ⓣ08/8080 1333.
Internet access Bizbyte, 435 Argent St (Mon–Fri 9am–5.30pm, $3/30min); There's also free access at the library, on the corner of Blende and Chloride Sts, but you have to book.
Laundry Oxide St Laundrette, 241 Oxide St ⓣ08/8088 2022. Service washes available, with free pick-up and delivery.
Pharmacies Amcal Chemist, Westside Plaza, Galena St, has an after-hours emergency number (ⓣ08/8088 4800), but the most central pharmacy is Peoples CP Chemist, 323 Argent St.
Post office Cnr Argent and Chloride Sts, NSW 2880.
Swimming pool North Pool, north of the centre on McCulloch St (in theory, if not always in practice, open daily: April–Oct 6am–6pm; Nov–March 6–10pm; $2), is heated in winter.
Taxi Yellow Radio Cabs ⓣ08/8088 1144.
Tours See box on p.405.

Around Broken Hill

The ghost town of **SILVERTON**, just 25km northwest of Broken Hill on a good road, makes a great day out. If the scene looks vaguely familiar, you probably have seen it before: parts of *Mad Max II* were shot around here, and the **Silverton Hotel** (daily 8.30am–9.30pm, though they often close earlier) has appeared as the "Gamulla Hotel" in *Razorback*, "Hotel Australia" in *A Town Like Alice*, and "Juanita's Diner" in *Fiddlers Green* with Don Johnson. It also seems to star in just about every commercial – usually beer-related – that features an Outback scene. The stark impact of the pub, with barren, red earth stretching endlessly to the horizon, has been somewhat diminished by the greening of the desert, but it still makes a great photo. The pub has its own photo collection, the lower walls covered with snapshots from the 140 film shoots in which it has appeared, the upper walls piled high with an assortment of beer cans and old bottles. In some ways it feels like a milk bar, with a fridge full of cold soft drinks, a tea urn, and the only available food some limp sandwiches, pies and pasties, rather than the usual counter meals. But in the tradition of all Outback pubs, it has its own in-jokes; you'll find out what all the laughter is about if you ask to "take the test".

Taking the **Silverton Heritage Trail**, a two-hour stroll around town marked by white arrows, is a good way to work up a thirst, though it's far too hot to attempt in the summer. Along the way you'll pass the old **Silverton School Craft Centre** and the 1889 vintage **Silverton Gaol Museum** (daily 9.30am–4.30pm; $3), with the usual collection of relics from pioneer days and Outback stations, plus mining equipment. There's a burgeoning art scene here, too, with four galleries to browse through. **Peter Browne's Gallery** (daily 9am–5pm; Ⓦwww.outbackgalleries.com.au), in an 1884 house on a hill, is worth a look for its uniquely original decoration and the humorous paintings of bush scenes, koala-shearing, kookaburras boiling the billy, and Browne's trademark emus with huge, saucer-shaped eyes (they're all over the VW Beetle parked out the front). Also interesting is Albert Woodroffe's and Bronwen Woodroffe-Standley's **Horizon Gallery** (daily 9am–6pm; Ⓦwww.brokenhillartists.com), opposite the pub. The husband and wife team paint in a similar style, creating their trademark horizon paintings, mainly in pastels and acrylics – finely detailed works that really capture the sense of space and the seemingly endless skyline. A camel sticks its head out of the wall of the building so it's hard to miss.

One of the most enjoyable things to do in Silverton is to go on a **camel tour**. The Cannard family, who run the **Silverton Camel Farm** (daily 9am–4pm; Ⓦwww.silvertoncamels.com), come from a long line of camel trainers and have forty working camels. You can't miss the farm on the way into Silverton, with the shapes of camels looming like desert mirages. You can hop on for half an hour ($15), or trot for an hour along the nearby creek ($25). There's also a great sunset trek (2hr; $50), a ride to the Mundi Mundi Plain to look at the setting sun and a return trip under the night stars accompanied by a pack of lively dogs. Longer safaris into the desert – a day and a night out - are also available ($175 including meals).

Beyond Silverton, the road continues a further 14km to the **Umberumberka reservoir**, Broken Hill's only source of water until the Menindee Lakes Scheme was set up. There's a signposted lookout area that makes a nice picnic spot. A few kilometres further on you reach the **Mundi Mundi Plains Lookout**. Here, the undulating plateau you have been driving across descends gradually to a vast plain, and on clear days you can see in the distance the blurred outline of the northern Flinders Ranges in South Australia (this is the spot where, at the end of *Mad Max II*, Mel Gibson tipped the semi-trailer).

If you want to stay in Silverton, your only choice is to **camp** at Penrose Park, where there's a shower, toilets and barbecue – ask at the house there or call ⓣ08/8088 5307. Note that there's no **fuel** available at Silverton.

Kinchega National Park and the Menindee Lakes

Flat **Kinchega National Park** is situated among the beautiful **Menindee Lakes**, near the township of **MENINDEE**, southeast of Broken Hill, in an area of great natural beauty. There's a sealed road for the 110km to Menindee and the park entrance, and dirt roads thereafter (usually no problem for 2WD in the dry). Before you go, visit the Broken Hill NPWS at 183 Argent Street (ⓣ08/8088 5933) to check road conditions or ask at the **Menindee Tourist Information Centre** (Mon–Fri 9am–5pm, Sat & Sun 10am–1pm; ⓣ08/8091 4274), where you can get a free, detailed, hand-drawn "Mud Map" of the lakes area, showing areas of interest.

After the 110km drive through red desert from Broken Hill, the sight of the large red river gums on the creek bed, the spreading blue water, expanses of bright green grass in the flood plains and the bleached skeletons of old eucalypts in the lake is breathtaking. The Menindee "Lakes" are actually a series of flood plains fed by the Darling River, and the waters are a major habitat for **waterbirds**; there are over 210 species here in total, including numerous little black cormorants (shags), pelicans, ibis, white egrets and whistling kites. There's an **information** shelter 5km into the park and a normally unmanned visitor information centre about 10km further on near the historic and exceptionally well preserved **Kinchega Woolshed**, part of the Kinchega Station, which was one of the first pastoral settlements in the area when it was established in 1850, and which continued in operation until 1967; you can explore it by following the signposted **woolshed walk**.

Accommodation is available in shearers' sheds next to the old woolshed (book at Broken Hill NPWS), and there are also 35 **campsites** scattered throughout the woodland along the river. Campsite No.3 near Menindee Lake is the nicest actual site – right by the river amongst the gums – unless the lake is dry, in which case head for Burke and Wills' old base camp (they stopped here from October 1860 until January 1861 – a tree marks the spot) by Wethell Lake. The camping areas have composting toilets and seats, but you'll have to purify the water. A great way to see this area is on a **tour** with local fishing/bird-watching expert Geoff Looney, who can be contacted via the Menindee Tourist Information Centre; his three-hour boating trip ($40 each, minimum 2 people) is very informative and good value.

Burke and Wills stayed in Menindee at the *Maidens Hotel*, Yartla Street (ⓣ08/8091 4208; ❶), on their ill-fated trip north in 1860 (see box on p.593). Unfortunately the room in which they stayed is now full of poker machines, but there is some interpretive material in the hotel (the room's fittings are now in the Railway Museum in Broken Hill; see p.400), and the green courtyard is a good place for a drink or a counter meal. Otherwise, you can stay at the *Burke & Wills Motel* opposite (ⓣ08/8091 4313, ⓕ8091 4406; ❸), or camp in relative comfort at the *Menindee Lakes Park* on Lakes Shore Road, 5km northwest of town (ⓣ08/8091 4315, ⓕ8091 4325; on-site vans ❶), which has a kiosk and grocery store. If you don't have transport, you can take a **day-tour** out here from Broken Hill; the best is with Goanna Safari (see box on p.405).

Scotia Sanctuary

Halfway between Broken Hill and Wentworth, 163km south along the Silver City Highway, then 30km southwest, is **Scotia Sanctuary** (Ⓣ03/5027 1200), which protects the rare Mallee fowl in an environment of Mallee sand dunes. It was closed at the time of writing; call the number above to check the latest situation.

Mutawintji National Park

Mutawintji National Park, 130km northeast of Broken Hill in the Bynguano Ranges, has totally different and perhaps even more fascinating scenery to offer, with secluded gorges and quiet waterholes attracting a profusion of wildlife. The main highlights of the park are the ancient galleries of **Aboriginal rock art** in the caves and overhangs; you can only visit these accompanied by an Aboriginal tour guide (Wed & Sat 11am Eastern Standard Time; 2hr; $15; bookings required; special tours by arrangement on Ⓣ08/8088 7000) – there are no tours in the hot summer months. While on the tour you get to visit the **Mutawintji Cultural Resource Centre**, an amazing multimedia collaboration between indigenous Australians and the NPWS which tells of tribal history and myth in sound and pictures. There's a **camping** area at Homestead Creek, among river red gums at the entrance to Homestead Gorge, and a number of **walking trails** (including the short wheelchair-accessible Thakaaltjika Mingkana Walk). Access to and within the park is via unsealed gravel roads, and you'll need to bring extra fuel as none is available here. It's normally fine for 2WD vehicles, but check locally, as the roads can quickly become impassable after even a light rain; bring extra food just in case. The NPWS office in Broken Hill can provide other information. You can also get here from Broken Hill with Goanna Safari; a bushwalk (2hr 30min) is part of their excellent tour (see box on p.405).

Travel details

Most public transport in New South Wales originates in Sydney, and the main services are outlined in the "Travel details" at the end of Chapter 1 on p.261.

Trains

All trains are run by Countrylink, which extends its network with additional bus services. For full details see Ⓦwww.countrylink.nsw.gov.au or call Ⓣ13 22 32.

- Sydney–**Broken Hill** (2 daily; 13hr), via **Dubbo** (6hr 40min).
- Sydney–**Albury** (2 daily; 7hr 35min), via **Cootamundra** (5hr) and **Wagga Wagga** (6hr 10min).
- Sydney–**Armidale** (1 daily; 8hr 10min), via **Tamworth** (6hr 15min).
- Sydney–**Goulburn** (4 daily; 2hr 35min).
- Sydney–**Dubbo** (5 daily; 6hr 30min), via **Bathurst** (3hr 30min).
- Sydney–Melbourne (2 daily; 11hr), with stops at **Cootamundra** and **Wagga Wagga**.
- Sydney–**Moree** (1 daily; 9hr) via **Gunnedah** (6hr 20min) and **Narrabri** (7hr 45min).
- Sydney–**Scone** (2 daily; 4hr 20min).
- The New South Wales leg of the Indian Pacific linking Sydney and Perth via Adelaide takes in **Condobolin** (10hr 35min from Sydney), **Ivanhoe** (13hr 50min), **Menindee** (16hr 10min) and **Broken Hill** (18hr 55min).

Buses

Albury to: Canberra (2 daily; 4hr 20min); Corowa (4 weekly; 1hr); Cowra (1 daily; 4hr); Dubbo (3 daily; 8hr 30min); Echuca (4 weekly; 4hr 15min); Melbourne (3 daily; 3hr 45min); Tamworth (1 daily; 12hr 20min); Yass (3 daily; 4hr).

Armidale to: Brisbane (7 daily; 7hr 30min); Port Macquarie (1 daily; 6hr 15min); Melbourne (4 daily;

18hr 45min); Sydney (4 daily; 9hr); Tamworth (3 daily; 2hr 10min); Tenterfield (3 daily; 3hr).
Bourke to: Dubbo (3 weekly; 4hr 45min).
Broken Hill to: Adelaide (2 daily; 7hr); Cobar (3 daily; 5hr 20min); Dubbo (5 daily; 9hr 30min); Mildura (3 weekly; 4hr); Sydney (1 daily; 15hr 40min).
Coonabarabran to: Adelaide (3 daily; 12hr); Canberra (3 daily; 5hr 40min); Melbourne (5 daily; 7hr 30min); Sydney (6 daily; 8hr 30min–10hr).
Cootamundra to: Dubbo (6 weekly; 4hr 15min); Gundagai (6 weekly; 45min); Tumbarumba (6 weekly; 2hr 45min).
Dubbo to: Albury (3 daily; 8hr 30min); Bathurst (1 daily; 2hr 45min); Bourke (3 weekly; 4hr 45min); Brewarrina (3 weekly; 5hr 45min); Broken Hill (5 daily; 9hr 30min); Canberra (4 weekly; 6hr 10min); Cobar (3 daily; 3hr 40min); Coonabarabran (3–5 daily; 1hr 50min); Cootamundra (6 weekly; 4hr 15min); Cowra (2 daily; 3hr 20min); Forbes (2 daily; 2hr 35min); Griffith (2 daily; 4hr 45min); Gunnedah (1 daily; 4hr); Lightning Ridge (1 daily; 4hr 50min); Lithgow (1 daily; 4hr 35min); Moree (3 daily; 4hr 20min); Narrandera (1 daily; 5hr 15min); Orange (1 daily; 2hr 40min); Parkes (1 daily; 2hr 10min); Tamworth (3 daily; 4hr); Wagga Wagga (2 daily; 6hr).
Griffith to: Canberra (1 daily; 6hr 35min); Cootamundra (1 daily; 2hr 35min); Hay (1 daily; 3hr 50min); Leeton (2 daily; 50min); Narrandera (2 daily; 1hr 15min); Wagga Wagga (2 daily; 2hr 40min).
Lithgow to: Bathurst (3–6 daily; 1hr); Coonabarabran (6 weekly; 5hr 30min); Cowra (6 weekly; 2hr 40min); Dubbo (1 daily; 4hr 35min); Mudgee (1 daily; 2hr 35min); Orange (2–3 daily; 1hr 45min–2hr).
Tamworth to: Armidale (3 daily; 2hr 10min); Cessnock (1 daily; 4hr); Dorrigo (3 weekly; 4hr 10min); Dubbo (3 daily; 4hr); Gunnedah (2 daily; 1hr); Inverell (1 daily; 3hr 40min); Port Macquarie (3 weekly; 8hr 30min); Scone (2 daily; 2hr 15min); Tenterfield (2 daily; 4hr 30min).

Flights

Armidale to: Brisbane (4 daily; 3hr); Coolangatta (3 weekly; 50min); Sydney (5 daily; 1hr 15min).
Broken Hill to: Adelaide (1–4 daily; 1hr 40min); Dubbo (6 weekly; 2hr); Sydney (2–4 daily; 3hr 45min).
Dubbo to: Brewarrina (3 weekly; 1hr); Broken Hill (6 weekly; 2hr); Brisbane (2 weekly; 2hr 10min); Canberra (5 daily; 2hr 15min); Cobar (2 daily, Sun–Fri; 1hr); Coolangatta (2 weekly; 1hr 35min); Lightning Ridge (1 a day, Mon–Fri; 1hr 40min); Nyngan (4 weekly; 30min); Sydney (3–4 daily; 1hr); Walgett (5 weekly; 1hr 10min).

Southeast Queensland

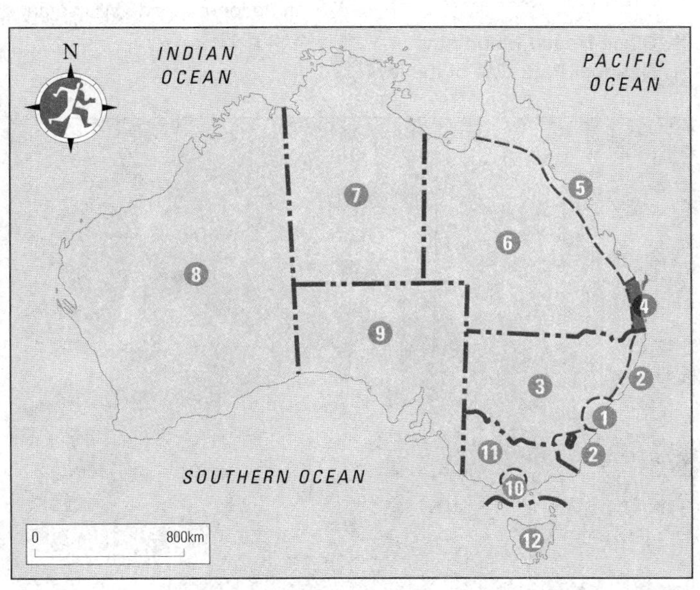

CHAPTER 4

Highlights

* **Gold Coast Entertainment** The bars, clubs and theme parks of Australia's prime domestic holiday destination provide raucous thrills around the clock. See p.449
* **Lamington National Park** Packed with beautiful jungle scenery and a huge variety of plants and animals, Lamington National Park is criss-crossed by dozens of enticing forest trails. See p.457
* **Glass House Mountains National Park** One of the few really special places on the Sunshine Coast; it's worth climbing at least one of the dramatic pinnacles for the fantastic views. See p.461
* **Surf at Noosa** Catch the waves at exclusive Noosa, popular with surfers since the 1960s. See p.466
* **Fraser Island** The giant dunes of beautiful Fraser Island are best explored on an action-packed 4WD safari. See p.474

△ Bushwalking in Lamington National Park

4

Southeast Queensland

Southeast Queensland comprises the 800-kilometre stretch between the New South Wales border and Fraser Island, and contains many of the classic features that lure visitors to Australia's second-largest state. **Surf** rolls in to long, sandy beaches, backed by vibrant towns in exotic settings; behind them, the land rises a thousand metres or more to lush, rainforest-clad plateaus. It's one of Australia's liveliest tourist hot spots, a factor that will be central to your impressions of the region: some love the hype and pace of its higher-profile attractions; others loathe it for the same reasons and despair of ever finding an untramped corner.

However, though parts of Southeast Queensland undoubtedly live up to their glitzy reputations, there's far more to the region than its popularity on the "drunken backpacker" trail would suggest. Set down towards the New South Wales border, the state capital **Brisbane** is an attractive, relaxed city with good work opportunities and a lively social scene, with some very underrated scenery within easy reach – the best of which are the giant, wooded, sand islands of shallow **Moreton Bay**. South of Brisbane, the **Gold Coast** is Australia's prime holiday destination; while its reputation was founded on some of Queensland's best surf, this now takes second place to a belt of beach-front high-rises, **theme parks**, and the host of bars and nightclubs surrounding **Surfers Paradise**. But even here there are quieter corners, such as the often almost empty beaches at the Gold Coast's southernmost town, **Coolangatta**. An hour inland, the Scenic Rim's green heights provide the perfect antidote to coastal concretions, with a chain of national parks packed with wildlife and endless hiking trails. Heading north of Brisbane, fruit and vegetable plantations behind the gentle **Sunshine Coast** benefit from rich volcanic soils and a subtropical climate. **Noosa** is the hub here, an up-and-coming resort town with more beaches and famous surf. Beyond looms **Fraser Island**, whose surrounding waters host an annual whale migration and where huge forested dunes, freshwater lakes and sculpted coloured sands form the backdrop for exciting 4WD safaris.

As a major tourist destination, Queensland's south coast seldom presents travel or accommodation problems, and in many places the only trouble is making some sort of choice between the vast array of options. However, during **busy periods** – the Easter and Christmas holidays, and at weekends – there are room shortages and price hikes in all accommodation except hostels.

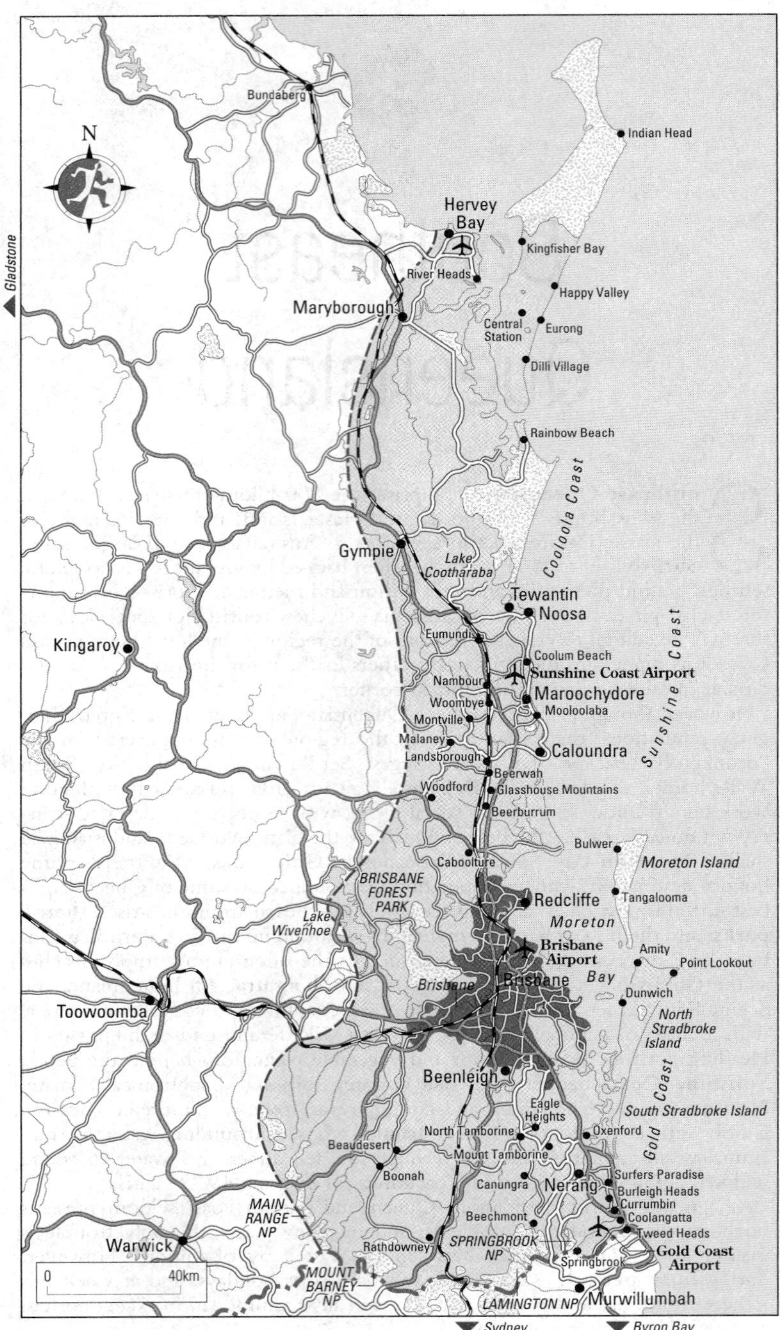
Bundaberg
N
Indian Head
Hervey Bay
Kingfisher Bay
River Heads
Happy Valley
Maryborough
Central Station
Eurong
Dilli Village
Rainbow Beach
Cooloola Coast
Gympie
Lake Cootharaba
Tewantin
Noosa
Kingaroy
Eumundi
Coolum Beach
Sunshine Coast Airport
Nambour
Maroochydore
Woombye
Mooloolaba
Montville
Sunshine Coast
Malaney
Caloundra
Landsborough
Beerwah
Woodford
Glasshouse Mountains
Beerburrum
Bulwer
Moreton Island
Caboolture
BRISBANE FOREST PARK
Redcliffe
Tangalooma
Moreton
Lake Wivenhoe
Brisbane Airport
Amity
Point Lookout
Bay
Brisbane
Brisbane
Dunwich
Toowoomba
North Stradbroke Island
Beenleigh
Gold Coast
Eagle Heights
South Stradbroke Island
North Tamborine
Oxenford
Beaudesert
Mount Tamborine
Boonah
Surfers Paradise
Canungra
Nerang
Burleigh Heads
MAIN RANGE NP
Currumbin
Beechmont
Coolangatta
Tweed Heads
Warwick
Rathdowney
SPRINGBROOK NP
Gold Coast Airport
Springbrook
0
40km
MOUNT BARNEY NP
LAMINGTON NP
Murwillumbah
Sydney
Byron Bay
Gladstone

This is most pronounced on the Gold Coast, though you'll find a degree of seasonal inflation throughout the region. Book in advance whenever possible, and don't be afraid to bargain outside the peak times.

Some history

In a way, Queensland's popularity as a holiday hotspot is surprising, as this is eastern Australia's most **conservative** state, often lampooned – somewhat unfairly – as being slow and regressive. There are, however, very physical and social divisions between the densely settled, city-oriented southeastern corner and the large, rural remainder, which is given over to primary industries such as mining and farming. These divisions date back to when Brisbane was chosen as capital on Queensland's separation from New South Wales in 1859; the city proved an unpopular choice with the northern pioneers, who felt that the government was too far away to understand, or even care about, their needs. These needs centred around the north's sugar plantations and the use of Solomon Islanders for labour, a practice the government equated with **slavery** and finally banned in 1872. Ensuing demands for further separation, this time between tropical Queensland and the southeast, never materialized, but the remoteness of northern settlements from the capital led to local self-sufficiency, making Queensland far less centralized than other states.

The darker side of this conservatism has seen Queensland endure more than its fair share of extreme or simply dirty politics. During the 1970s and early 1980s, the stranglehold of a strongly conservative National Party government, led by the charismatic **Sir Johannes Bjelke-Petersen** (better known as "Joh"), did nothing to enhance the state's image. Citing issues of law and order to justify granting the police sweeping powers, Joh created a repressive and domineering government, characterized by his own peculiar, slippery oratory. He finally became the victim of his own devices after initiating the Fitzgerald Inquiry – an investigation into government corruption – which implicated his cabinet in a variety of offences and forced him from office. But the following left-wing government was not without controversy, though state Labor leader Peter Beattie was re-elected as Premier for his third successive term and with a huge majority in 2004. The late 1990s were also blighted by the emergence from southeast Queensland of **Pauline Hanson** and her One Nation Party, whose shallow, racist outbursts won favour with a fair number of Australians who felt ignored by the main parties and threatened by a slowing economy and immigration issues.

Brisbane and around

By far the largest city in Queensland, **BRISBANE** is not quite what you'd expect from a state capital with over one-and-a-half million residents. Although there is urban sprawl, and high-rise buildings, slow-moving traffic, crowded streets and the other trappings of a business and trade centre, there's little of the pushiness that usually accompanies them. To urbanites used to a more aggressive approach, the atmosphere is slow, even backward (a reputation the city would be pleased to lose), but to others the languid pace is a welcome change and reflects relaxed rather than regressive attitudes.

Seen from the river or the top of Mount Coot-tha, it is an attractive enough place, with the typical features of any Australian city of a comparable age and size: a historic precinct, museums and botanic gardens. There's a confused blur of old and new, crammed in side by side rather than split into distinct districts, while new suburbs are blithely added to the shapeless edges as the need arises. The residents, too, have a spontaneous manner, partly because many are new to the area. In the early 1990s, economic malaise in Australia's southern states resulted in a steady northward migration of people seeking **work** – or at least finding Queensland a better place to be unemployed – and Brisbane was the obvious first stop. It's still a fairly easy place to find casual, short-term employment, and there's a healthy, unpredictable social scene, tempting many travellers to spend longer here than they had planned. As for exploring further afield, you'll find empty beaches and surf on **North Stradbroke Island** and **Moreton Island** – both easy to reach from the city – as well as subtropical woods in **Brisbane Forest Park**, a twenty-minute drive from the centre.

Some history

In 1823, responding to political pressure to shift the "worst type of felons" away from Sydney and the southeast – the further the better – the New South Wales government sent the Surveyor General **John Oxley** north to find a suitable site for a new prison colony. Sailing into **Moreton Bay**, he encountered three shipwrecked convicts who had been living with Aborigines for several months; they introduced Oxley to a previously unknown river. He explored it briefly, named it "Brisbane" after the governor, and the next year established a convict settlement at **Redcliffe** on the coast. This was immediately abandoned

Aboriginal Brisbane

John Oxley recorded that the **Brisbane Aborigines** were friendly; they had looked after the shipwrecked convicts and, in the early days, even rounded up and returned runaways from the settlement. In his orders to Oxley on how to deal with the indigenous peoples, Governor Brisbane admitted, though in a roundabout way, that the land belonged to them: "All uncivilized people have wants . . . when treated justly they acquire many comforts by their union with the more civilized. This justifies our occupation of their lands."

But future governors were not so liberal in their views, and things had soured long before the first squatters moved into the Brisbane area and began leaving out "gifts" of poisoned flour and calling in the Native Mounted Police to disperse local Aborigines – a euphemism for exterminating them. Bill Rosser's grim account in *Up Rode the Troopers – The Black Police in Queensland* tells the story through dialogues with the grandson of one of the last tribal members in the Brisbane area, and gives a good idea of how communities were split up and scattered by Queensland's **Protection Act**, which remained in force until the 1970s.

A trace of Brisbane's Aboriginal past is found at the **Nudgee Bora Ring** about 12km north of the centre at Nudgee Waterhole Reserve, at the junction of Nudgee and Childs roads. Last used in 1860, two low mounds where boys were initiated form little more than an icon today, and you'll probably feel that it's not worth the trip. More rewarding are the several **Aboriginal walking trails** at Mount Coot-tha; the City Hall information desk has leaflets on these which explain traditional uses of the area (see p.438).

in favour of better anchorage further upstream, and by the end of 1824 today's city centre had become the site of Brisbane Town.

Twenty years on, a land shortage down south persuaded the government to move out the convicts and free up the Moreton Bay area to settlers. Immigrants on government-assisted passages poured in and Brisbane began to shape up as a busy **port** – an unattractive, awkward settlement of rutted streets and wooden shacks. As the largest regional settlement of the times, Brisbane was the obvious choice as capital of the new state of Queensland on its formation in 1859, though the city's first substantial buildings were constructed only in the late 1860s, after fire had destroyed the original centre and state bankruptcy was averted by Queensland's first **gold** strikes at Gympie (see p.471). Even so, development was slow and uneven: new townships were founded around the centre at Fortitude Valley, Kangaroo Point and Breakfast Creek, gradually merging into a city.

After World War II, when General Douglas MacArthur used Brisbane as his headquarters to co-ordinate attacks on Japanese forces based throughout the Pacific, Brisbane stagnated, earning a reputation as a dull, underdeveloped backwater – not least thanks to the Bjelke-Petersen regime. As if to remove all trace of his rule, Brisbane underwent a thorough facelift before hosting the 1988 **World Expo**; not least for locals, who treated it as something of a coming-out party, the Expo provided a real boost after years of tedium. Development has continued to impress upon the city's skyline and since 2001 Brisbane has boasted the country's highest internal migration figures and a quarter of the national population growth, booming house prices and the resulting redevelopment of the dilapidated Brisbane River foreshore into upmarket apartments.

Arrival, information and city transport

Brisbane Airport is located 9km northeast of the centre, at the end of Kingsford Smith Drive. You'll find banks (including ATMs) and luggage lockers at both the domestic and the international terminals. To get to the city from either terminal, there's the speedy **Airtrain** ($10 one-way, Ⓦwww.airtrain.com.au), which takes just twenty minutes to reach Brisbane's Transit Centre; or the **Coachtrans bus** ($9 one-way, $15 return; Ⓣ13 12 30, Ⓦwww.coachtrans.com.au), which takes up to forty minutes but delivers direct to central accommodation as well as the Transit Centre. A taxi into the city costs around $30 for the half-hour trip. For the **Gold Coast**, Coachtrans delivers direct to accommodation for $18.50 one-way.

Long-distance buses and trains all end up at Brisbane's **Transit Centre**, located in the heart of the city on Roma Street. On the highest of the three levels are the **bus offices**, luggage lockers and a hostel information desk (daily 8am–5pm). The middle floor has fast-food joints, a bar, toilets and showers, a medical centre and ATMs, while on the ground floor is the arrival and departure point for local and interstate **trains**.

During the day, reaching your accommodation seldom poses any problems as **local buses** and **taxis** leave from just outside the Transit Centre, and most hosteliers either meet buses or will pick you up if you call them. You can't always rely on a pick-up late at night, however, when it's best to take a taxi. While Brisbane is not as dangerous as most European or American cities of its size, it's still not a good idea to wander around after midnight with your

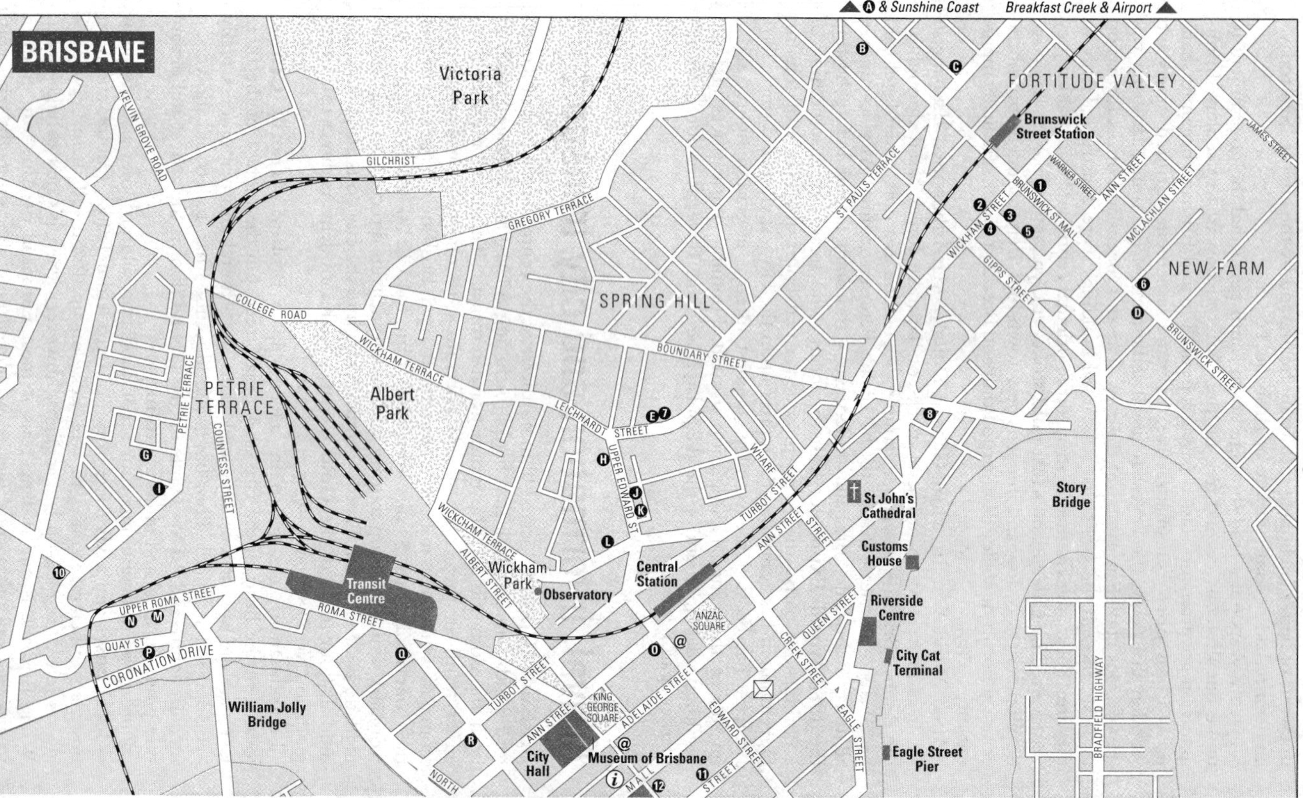
BRISBANE
A & Sunshine Coast
Breakfast Creek & Airport
F
Castlemaine Perkins Brewery & Mount Coot-tha
9
Sanctuary
Victoria Park
FORTITUDE VALLEY
NEW FARM
SPRING HILL
PETRIE TERRACE
Albert Park
Wickham Park
Observatory
Brunswick Street Station
Central Station
Transit Centre
St John's Cathedral
Customs House
Riverside Centre
City Cat Terminal
Eagle Street Pier
Story Bridge
William Jolly Bridge
City Hall
Museum of Brisbane
ANZAC SQUARE
KING GEORGE SQUARE
KELVIN GROVE ROAD
GILCHRIST
GREGORY TERRACE
COLLEGE ROAD
WICKHAM TERRACE
BOUNDARY STREET
LEICHHARDT STREET
UPPER EDWARD ST
ST PAULS TERRACE
WICKHAM STREET
BRUNSWICK ST MALL
WARNER STREET
ANN STREET
MCLACHLAN STREET
JAMES STREET
BRUNSWICK STREET
GIPPS STREET
WHARF STREET
TURBOT STREET
QUEEN STREET
CREEK STREET
EDWARD STREET
EAGLE STREET
ADELAIDE STREET
ALBERT STREET
ROMA STREET
UPPER ROMA STREET
QUAY ST
CORONATION DRIVE
COUNTESS STREET
PETRIE TERRACE
NORTH
MALL
BRADFIELD HIGHWAY

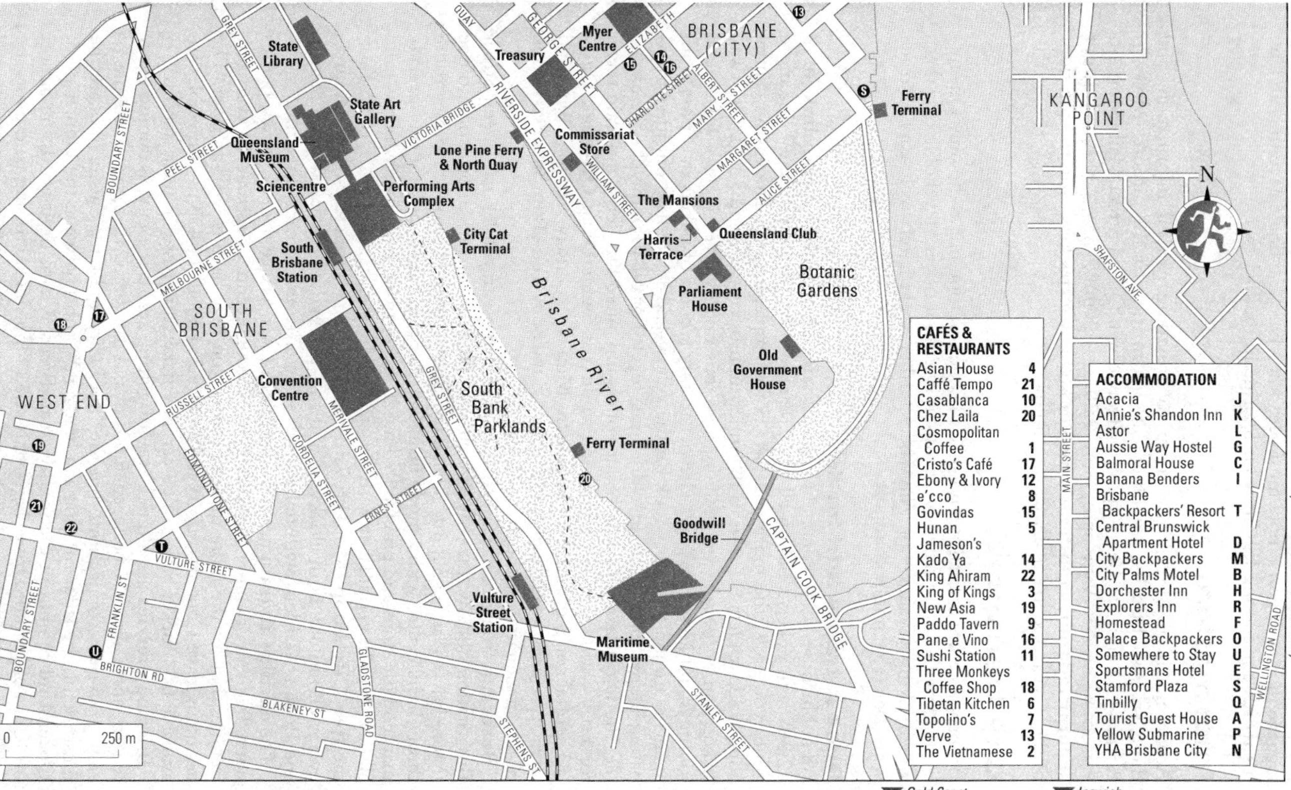
Ipswich, St Lucia & Lone Pine
Fort Lytton National Park & Manly
Gold Coast
Ipswich
BRISBANE (CITY)
KANGAROO POINT
SOUTH BRISBANE
WEST END
Brisbane River
Botanic Gardens
South Bank Parklands
State Library
State Art Gallery
Queensland Museum
Sciencentre
Performing Arts Complex
Lone Pine Ferry & North Quay
City Cat Terminal
South Brisbane Station
Convention Centre
Vulture Street Station
Maritime Museum
Goodwill Bridge
Ferry Terminal
Treasury
Myer Centre
Commissariat Store
The Mansions
Harris Terrace
Queensland Club
Parliament House
Old Government House
N
GREY STREET
PEEL STREET
BOUNDARY STREET
VICTORIA BRIDGE
RIVERSIDE EXPRESSWAY
QUAY
GEORGE STREET
ELIZABETH
CHARLOTTE STREET
ALBERT STREET
MARY STREET
MARGARET STREET
ALICE STREET
WILLIAM STREET
SHAFSTON AVE.
MAIN STREET
WELLINGTON ROAD
MELBOURNE STREET
RUSSELL STREET
MERIVALE STREET
CORDELIA STREET
ERNEST STREET
EDMONDSTONE STREET
VULTURE STREET
FRANKLIN ST
BRIGHTON RD
BLAKENEY ST
GLADSTONE ROAD
STEPHENS ST
STANLEY STREET
CAPTAIN COOK BRIDGE
0
250 m
CAFÉS & RESTAURANTS
Asian House 4
Caffé Tempo 21
Casablanca 10
Chez Laila 20
Cosmopolitan Coffee 1
Cristo's Café 17
Ebony & Ivory 12
e'cco 8
Govindas 15
Hunan 5
Jameson's
Kado Ya 14
King Ahiram 22
King of Kings 3
New Asia 19
Paddo Tavern 9
Pane e Vino 16
Sushi Station 11
Three Monkeys Coffee Shop 18
Tibetan Kitchen 6
Topolino's 7
Verve 13
The Vietnamese 2
ACCOMMODATION
Acacia J
Annie's Shandon Inn K
Astor L
Aussie Way Hostel G
Balmoral House C
Banana Benders I
Brisbane Backpackers' Resort T
Central Brunswick Apartment Hotel D
City Backpackers M
City Palms Motel B
Dorchester Inn H
Explorers Inn R
Homestead F
Palace Backpackers O
Somewhere to Stay U
Sportsmans Hotel E
Stamford Plaza S
Tinbilly Q
Tourist Guest House A
Yellow Submarine P
YHA Brisbane City N

luggage in tow. If you simply must get somewhere and don't have the cab fare, it's worth considering leaving your luggage in the lockers.

Information

Accommodation is well geared up to providing general information, and there are also **booths** providing city information at the airport (Mon–Fri 8.30am–4.30pm, Sat 10am–1pm), halfway down Queen Street Mall (Mon–Fri 9am–5.30pm, Sat 9am–5pm, Sun 9.30am–4.30pm).There's also a **budget accommodation counter** – aimed mostly at backpackers – on the top floor of the Transit Centre (daily 8am to 5pm).

City transport

Brisbane's centre is small and possible to cover on foot, but as the only Queensland city with a comprehensive transport system, it offers a level of luxury that's worth taking advantage of. Anywhere further afield is relatively easy to reach with private or public transport.

Buses, trains and ferries

All public buses, Citytrain and Council ferries are operated by **Translink** (Ⓣ 13 12 30) with tickets valid on all three. Fares are calculated by zone – the more zones you cross, the more you pay. For example, a single fare in the central zone is $2, while a ride out to the inner suburbs costs around $2.80. One-way tickets can be bought on your journey (bus drivers give change); for several journeys and longer stays it's cheaper to buy a book of tickets or a **pass** from agencies around the city – look for the yellow-and-white flags outside participating shops. Some passes give discounts for day or off-peak travel – for example, the **Day Pass** ($4 central zone) offers unlimited bus, ferry and train travel for a day within the zone purchased, ending at midnight; an **Off-Peak Daily** ($3 central zone) gives the same benefits Monday to Friday 9am to 3.30pm and after 7pm, and throughout Saturday and Sunday. A **Ten-Trip Saver** is a book of ten single fares for the price of eight.

Buses run from about 5am to 11pm, with most travelling via Queen Street Bus Station (below the Myer Centre). There's also an information office (Mon–Fri 8.30am–5.30pm). The **City Sights** blue bus tours a preset route through the centre with a guide from 9am to 5pm daily – look for the specially marked blue stops and purchase your $20 ticket from the driver which is valid all day. Another popular way to get around the Central Business District is on the **free City Loop** (Mon–Fri 7am–5.50pm). The distinctive red buses circle every ten minutes both clockwise and anti-clockwise between Central Station and Botanic Gardens with ten red bus stops en-route in each direction.

The electric **Citytrain** network provides a faster service than the buses, but it's not as frequent or comprehensive. Trains through central Brisbane run every few minutes, but for the more distant suburbs you may have to wait an hour. The last trains leave Central Station on Ann Street at about 11.45pm – timetables are available from ticket offices. You can buy tickets and passes at most stations.

Brisbane's **ferries** are a quick way of getting across the city. Running every ten to thirty minutes between 5.50am and 10.30pm, there are a couple of easy cross-river connections, but the Inner City and City Cat services are the most useful, the latter running at a bracing 27 knots between the University of Queensland campus in the southwest to Bretts Wharf, up towards the airport on Kingsford Smith Drive. Fares start at $2 for a single crossing, and passes are valid on all Council ferries. The central departure points for Inner City and

For all bus, train or ferry **information** call ⓣ13 12 30.

City Cat are from South Bank Parklands, Eagle Street Pier and North Quay, next to Victoria Bridge.

Taxis, cars and bikes

After dark, **taxis** tend to cruise round the clubs and hotels; during the day Roma Street is a good place to find one. To call a taxi, try B&W Cabs (ⓣ13 10 08) or Yellow Cabs (ⓣ13 19 24).

Driving is not much fun until you get your bearings. Unfortunately, signs just at junctions, rather than well before them, are typical not only of Brisbane but of all of Queensland, and you'd be well advised to get some sort of street directory as soon as possible. Once familiar with the city and its awkward one-way systems, there are no great problems, although parking is expensive and in short supply in the centre. For details of car-rental agencies, see "Listings", p.435.

Cyclists have a good number of bike routes from which to choose. Maps are available from some information sources (see p.436), libraries and city council offices. A few hostels loan bikes, or they can be easily rented elsewhere – again, see p.435.

Accommodation

Brisbane's inner-city **accommodation** is varied and excellent value. The most expensive places are in the city centre, though there are also some first-rate **motel** deals here. Beds are scarce only during major sports events including the annual Brisbane Cup horserace in June as well as the Royal Queensland Show (the "Ekka") in August. Prices at more upmarket places may also drop at weekends and outside peak season, due to the scarcity of business customers and competition from the Gold Coast.

Brisbane's abundant **backpackers' hostels** are scattered across town and out to the coastal suburb of Manly. Many have entertainment, cheap meals, Internet facilities, bikes for rent or loan, pools and courtesy buses on arrival (and sometimes departure), and can arrange work connections.

City centre and Petrie Terrace

Petrie Terrace is a ten-minute walk up the hill to the north of the Transit Centre – or take bus #144 from opposite the Transit Centre to stop 5.

Acacia 413 Upper Edward St ⓣ07/3832 1663, ⓕ3832 2591. Pleasant and central motel-like B&B with shared and en-suite rooms. ❸

Annie's Shandon Inn 405 Upper Edward St ⓣ07/3831 8684, ⓦwww.anniesinn.net. A cosy family-run B&B with single, double and en-suite rooms just a 5min walk from the city centre. ❸

Astor 193 Wickham Terrace ⓣ07/3144 4000, ⓦwww.astorhotel.com.au. Boutique hotel in a smart, renovated nineteenth-century colonial building with a range of en-suite rooms and fully serviced apartments. Doubles ❹, suites ❺, two-bedroom apartments ❻

Aussie Way Hostel 34 Cricket St ⓣ07/3369 0711, ⓔaussieway15@hotmail.com. Renovated nineteenth-century town house with quiet ambience, large pool, verandahs, balcony and period decor. Dorms $22, rooms ❷

Banana Benders 118 Petrie Terrace ⓣ07/3367 1157, ⓦwwwbananabenders.com.au. A small, friendly hostel with a homely, easy-going feel. There's a small kitchen and BBQ area, a casual TV-and-video lounge, deck-space for dining, and free entry to the local public pool. Dorms $21–23, rooms ❷

City Backpackers 380 Upper Roma St ⓣ07/3211 3221, ⓦwww.citybackpackers.com. One of

Brisbane's biggest hostels, this busy and well-run place has clean facilities, fair-sized rooms, own bar with budget meal deals and BBQ nights, swimming pool and free undercover parking. Dorms $16, en-suite rooms ❸

Dorchester Inn 484 Upper Edward St ⓣ07/3831 2967, ⓔdorchesterinn@bigpond.com.au. Comfortable, self-contained, serviced apartments with off-street parking. Singles/doubles ❸

Explorers Inn 63 Turbot St (cnr George St) ⓣ07/3211 3488, ⓦwww.explorers.com.au. Friendly boutique hotel and cheapest in the Central Business District but without parking. Standard rooms are good for single travellers, superior rooms have plenty of space – all rooms are non-smoking. ❸–❹

Palace Backpackers Cnr Ann and Edward streets ⓣ1800 676 340, ⓦwww.palacebackpackers.com.au. Huge hostel, purpose-built in 1911 but completely revamped (except for the ancient lift). Bang in the centre of town – which means that there's no parking space – with a restaurant and rowdy *Down Under Bar*, whose noise prompts some travellers to move elsewhere for some sleep. Poky singles, high-ceilinged and spacious doubles, and three- to nine-bed dorms. Dorms $22–25, rooms ❸

Sportsman's Hotel 130 Leichhardt St, Spring Hill ⓣ07/3831 2892 ⓦwww.sportsmanshotel.com.au. Gay-friendly pub with rooms; predominantly male clientele but both sexes welcome. ❷

Stamford Plaza Edward St ⓣ07/3221 1999, ⓦwww.stamford.com.au. Top-notch hotel with a grand mix of colonial and modern buildings overlooking the river and Botanic Gardens. ❽

Tinbilly Cnr George and Herschel streets ⓣ1800 446 646, ⓦwww.tinbilly.com. Modern party hostel and bar almost directly opposite the Transit Centre; facilities are good though doubles are expensive and the noise level can build through the evening. Dorms $22–27, rooms ❹

Yellow Submarine 66 Quay St ⓣ07/3211 3424. Small, comfortable hostel in a refurbished 1860s building with landscaped courtyard. Full kitchen facilities, laundry, BBQ and pool. The friendly owners put on free three-hour sailing trips every Wednesday around the bay and free BBQs at weekends, ensuring a sociable atmosphere. The staff can help out with work connections. Dorms $20–23, rooms ❷

YHA Brisbane City 392 Upper Roma St ⓣ07/3236 1004, ⓦwww.yha.com.au. Sterile but with excellent facilities, including a first-rate budget canteen (open to non-guests). Dorms $25.50, rooms ❸

Fortitude Valley and New Farm

The Valley's accommodation is well placed for clubs but the area can be seedy late at night, although the surrounding area of New Farm is quiet enough. Most buses travelling up Adelaide Street pass through the Valley, or you can take the train to Brunswick Street Station. For New Farm, take a bus (#177, #178, #167 or #168) from Adelaide Street.

Balmoral House 33 Amelia St, Fortitude Valley ⓣ07/3252 1397. A very quiet but slightly grubby hostel, with self-contained apartments, handy for Chinatown and Brunswick Street; not for partying. Dorms $17, rooms ❷

Central Brunswick Apartment Hotel 455 Brunswick St, Fortitude Valley ⓣ07/3852 1411, ⓦwww.centralbrunswickhotel.com.au. Gay-friendly accommodation in a sparkling red-brick building. Rooms are very comfortable, all with own bath and TV, some apartment-style with kitchen facilities. Shared amenities include spa and gym. ❺

City Palms Motel 55 Brunswick St, Fortitude Valley ⓣ1800 655 381. Only a short walk to Brunswick Street Mall and Chinatown, this modern place has spacious self-contained rooms and family units. ❸

Homestead 57 Annie St, New Farm ⓣ07/3358 3538 or 1800 658 344. A large house converted to a hostel, with quiet atmosphere, a pool shaped like a shamrock and plenty of outdoor space. There is free use of bikes and the hostel arranges trips to Mt Coot-tha. Dorms $17–20, rooms ❸

Tourist Guest House 555 Gregory Terrace, Fortitude Valley ⓣ1800 800 589, ⓦwww.touristguesthouse.com.au. One of Brisbane's converted Queenslanders (see p.425), this is a clean, quiet place with beautiful landscaping, some parking space, family rooms, laundry and kitchen. Dorms $22, rooms ❷–❸

South of the river and Manly

Brisbane Backpackers' Resort 110 Vulture St ⓣ 1800 626 452, ⓦwww.brisbanebackpackers.com.au. Soulless hostel complex with round-the-clock reception, video surveillance and all facilities, including a licensed travel agent. Courtesy bus into town and free pick-up from the Transit Centre. Dorms $19–22, rooms ❸

Moreton Bay Lodge 45 Cambridge Parade, Manly Harbour Village, Manly ☎ 1800 800 157, ⓦ www.moretonbaylodge.com.au. A 30min train ride from central Brisbane, this well-furnished antique pub out at Manly, on Moreton Bay, has great views of the bay and islands and small, clean rooms. It's just a stone's throw from Manly harbour and well geared up for sailing and island trips; there are plenty of shops and places to eat nearby. Pick-up from airport, or a 5min walk from Manly train station. Dorms $22, rooms ❸

Somewhere to Stay 45 Brighton Rd ☎ 1800 812 398, ⓦ www.somewheretostay.com.au. Reasonable facilities, but nonchalant staff; building and furnishings are showing distinct signs of wear. Worth paying extra for a room with a view over Brisbane's skyline rather than one of the basic dorms. Courtesy bus into town and free pick-up from the Transit Centre. Dorms $17–25, rooms ❷–❸

The City

The **city** is focused around the meandering loops of the **Brisbane River**, with the triangular wedge of the business centre on the north bank surrounded by community-oriented suburbs. At its heart are the busy, upmarket commercial and administrative precincts around **Queen Street** and **George Street**, an area of glass towers, cafés and century-old sandstone facades that extends to the **Botanic Gardens** on the river. Radiating **north**, the polish gives way to less conservative shops, accommodation and eateries around Spring Hill, Fortitude Valley and New Farm, and the aspiring suburbs of Petrie Terrace and Paddington. To the **west** is a blaze of riverside homes at Milton and Toowong and the fringes of Mount Coot-tha and Brisbane Forest Park. **Across the river**, the major landmarks are the Cultural Centre and the convention centre, and **South Bank Parklands**, which stretch to Kangaroo Point. Beyond are the open, bustling streets of **South Brisbane** and the **West End**, more relaxed than their northern counterparts.

Downtown

Queen Street is Brisbane's oldest thoroughfare, its southern section between George and Edward streets a pedestrian mall with the **Myer Centre** – a multistoreyed shopping complex – as its focus. Outside, the mall is always busy with people running errands, eating at any number of cafés, window shopping or just socializing. There's usually some kind of entertainment too: either informal efforts – acrobats, buskers and the occasional soap-box orator – or more organized events such as Aboriginal and Torres Strait Islander dancing or jazz sessions on the small stage about halfway down the street.

City Hall, Museum of Brisbane and Central Business District

North from the mall along Albert Street, you arrive at King George Square, with its fountains and bronze sculptures of swaggies, native wildlife and what look like large pieces of futuristic circuitry. Facing the square to the west is **City Hall**, a stately 1920s building ruined by an ugly clock tower. There's a reflection of its former policies in the triangular sculpture over the portico, which depicts the Aboriginal way of life "dying out before the approach of the white man". Inside, the **Museum of Brisbane** (daily 10am–5pm; free) has a smattering of paintings with regular exhibitions by prominent Australian artists and a social history gallery detailing the rather uneventful account of Brisbane's past and its rather more exciting aspirations for the future. There's a huge satellite image of the "200km City" plus an eclectic mix of television displays, retro posters and antique icons. The clock tower is open, too, if you want a view of the city centre (Mon–Fri 10am–3pm, Sat 10am–2pm; $2); access is through the City Hall foyer.

Flanked by roads further up Albert Street, tiny **Wickham Park** is overlooked by the grey cone of Brisbane's oldest building, a windmill known locally as the **Observatory**, built by convicts in 1829 to grind corn for the early settlement. The original wooden sails were too heavy to turn but found use as a gallows until being pulled off in 1850, and all grinding was done by a treadmill – severe punishment for the convicts who had to work it. After the convict era the building became a signal station and now stands locked up and empty, held together with a cement glaze.

East of here lies Brisbane's Central Business District which was heavily developed in the 1990s and left with a legacy of glassy high-rises sprouting alongside the restaurants and shops of the Riverside Centre; the few surviving old buildings are hidden among the modern ones. The copper-domed **Customs House** (daily 10am–4pm; free) at the north end of Queen Street, built in 1889, harbours a small collection of Chinese antiques and hosts free concerts given by the Queensland University Orchestra every month, while neo-Gothic **St John's Cathedral** (daily 9.30am–4.30pm; donation), on Ann Street, has some elegant stained-glass windows and the only fully stone-vaulted ceiling in Australia. Sunday morning is made lively by the **Eagle Street Markets** between the river and the road – too trendy for bargains, but not bad for jewellery and leatherwork, clothing and $25 massages.

The historic precinct

The area between Queen Street and the Botanic Gardens contains some of Brisbane's finest architecture, dating from the earliest days of settlement until the late nineteenth century. Between Elizabeth and Queen streets, occupying an entire block, is the former **Treasury** with its classical facade. Built in the 1890s, its grandeur reflects the wealth of Queensland's gold mines (though by this point most were on the decline) and was a slap in the face to New South Wales, which had spitefully withdrawn all financial support from the fledgling state on separation some forty years previously, leaving it bankrupt. With a twist typical of a state torn between conservatism and tourism, the building is now – appropriately enough – Brisbane's 24-hour **casino**.

South along William Street, the **Commissariat Store** is contemporary with the observatory, though in considerably better shape. Originally a granary, it is now a museum (Tues–Sun 10am–4pm; $4) and headquarters of the Royal Historical Society of Queensland; the knowledgeable staff pep up an otherwise dusty collection of relics dating back to convict times. Further south along George Street you pass **Harris Terrace** and **The Mansions**, two of the city centre's last surviving rows of Victorian-era terraced houses, the latter guarded by stone cats on the parapet corners. Nearby, on the corner of George and Alice streets, the **Queensland Club** was founded in 1859, just four days before the separation of Queensland from New South Wales. Heavy walls, columns and spacious balconies evoke a tropical version of a traditional London club; entrance and membership – women are still not allowed to join – are by invitation only. Diagonally opposite, **Parliament House** (Mon–Fri 9.30am–4pm, Sat–Sun 10am–2pm; free guided tours when Parliament not in session) was built to a design by Charles Tiffin in 1868 and presents an appealingly compromised French Renaissance style which incorporates shuttered north windows, shaded colonnades and a high, arched roof to allow for the tropical climate.

You can see the grand interior on an hour-long guided tour, and there's access to the chambers when there's no debate in progress.

South of Parliament House, George Street becomes a pedestrian lane along the western side of the Botanic Gardens and home to the Queensland University of Technology. Here you'll find **Old Government House** (Mon–Fri 10am–4pm; free), the official residence of Queensland's governors and premiers between 1862 and 1910. Another of Tiffin's designs, the building has been comprehensively restored to its stately early-twentieth-century condition, and is well worth a look for its furnishings.

The Botanic Gardens

Bordered by Alice Street, George Street and the river, Brisbane's **Botanic Gardens** overlook the cliffs of Kangaroo Point and, while more of a park than a botanic garden, provide a generous arrangement of flowers, shrubs, bamboo thickets and green grass for sprawling on, all offering an easy escape from city claustrophobia. Free **guided tours** (Mon–Sat 11am & 1pm except mid-Dec–Jan) leave from the rotunda, 100m inside the gardens' main entrance, halfway along Alice Street. Once a vegetable patch cultivated by convicts, formal gardens were laid out in 1855 by Walter Hill, who experimented with local and imported plants to see which would grow well in Queensland's then untried climate. Some of his more successful efforts are the oversized **bunya pines** around the Edward Street entrance at the east end of Alice Street, planted in 1860, and a residual patch of the **rainforest** that once blanketed the area, at the southern end of the park. Mangroves along the river, accessible by a boardwalk, are another native species more recently protected. During the day, cyclists flock to the park, as it's at one end of a popular cycling and jogging track that follows the north bank of the river south to St Lucia and the University of Queensland. At the southern end of the gardens, **classical music recitals** are held on an open-air stage in the summer, beyond which there's a **pedestrian bridge** over the river to South Bank Parklands.

The northern neighbourhoods

North of the river, just beyond Brisbane's central business district, are several former suburbs which have been absorbed by the city sprawl: Paddington and Petrie Terrace to the west, Spring Hill and Fortitude Valley to the north, and New Farm to the east. Houses in these areas are popular with Brisbane's aspiring professional class, and while office buildings and one-way streets are beginning to encroach, there's also an older character reflected in the high-set

Queensland houses

There can hardly be a more typical image of rural Queensland than a high-set "Queenslander" surrounded by green fields of sugar cane. A response to the northern climate, these houses come in all shapes and styles but the basic design is a wooden box on piles with a verandah or balcony – the idea being to have a cool flow of air underneath the house to reduce the humidity inside. Traditional colours, now more commonly seen in cities where it's becoming popular to renovate Queenslanders, are cream, red or green, while older buildings may have corrugated-iron awnings, red "bull-nosed" roofs and wooden latticework on porches and eaves. In Brisbane they're generally low-set, but tend to be raised further off the ground as you move up into the tropics – the exception to the rule is at Redcliffe, 12km north of Brisbane, where the pole houses have supports 10m high to compensate for a steep hill.

Queenslander-style houses (see box, p.425) still standing around Spring Hill, Petrie Terrace and the riverside setting of Breakfast Creek.

The Castlemaine Perkins Brewery

Just down the hill from Petrie Terrace, the **Castlemaine Perkins Brewery**, Milton Road, Milton (☎07/3361 7597), has been making Queensland's own beer since 1878. Their famous yellow-and-red XXXX emblem is part of the Queensland landscape: splashed across T-shirts and the roofs of Outback hotels, or on labels on countless discarded bottles and cans that litter everywhere from roadsides to the depths of the Barrier Reef. For enthusiasts, the brewery opens its gates for **tours** (Mon–Fri on-the-hour 10am–4pm; $18; bookings essential and you must wear fully-enclosed shoes), which incorporate a 1-hour rundown on the brewing process, followed by four free beers in the Ale House.

Fortitude Valley

While the other northern neighbourhoods are mainly residential, **Fortitude Valley** – better known as just "the Valley" – is a tangled mix of shops, restaurants, bars and clubs, comprising Brisbane's unofficial centre of artistic, gastronomic and alcoholic pursuits. An eclectic mix of the gay, the groovy and the grubby, the Valley is now in stage two of inner-city gentrification, which sees the urban-poor make way for hipsters, artists and students. Stage three – the arrival of yuppies and inflated real-estate prices – is looming, but in the meantime it's a great spot to enjoy an evening out among Brisbane's young, fun and adventurous. In less than a kilometre, the main thoroughfare of Brunswick Street has a dozen nightclubs, an Irish pub, a compact **Chinatown** complete with the usual busy restaurants and stores, and a burgeoning European street-café scene. It's best at weekends when cafés buzz and **live musicians** compete for your attention; on Saturday there's a secondhand **market** in the mall at no. 277. After dark the Valley's streets can be somewhat menacing, with an element of drug-related petty crime. Although there are usually crowds around until very late, if you've any distance to go on your own after the pubs close, take a taxi.

Breakfast Creek

Named by John Oxley, who tucked into a morning meal here in 1823 on his voyage of exploration upstream, **Breakfast Creek** has shops and a hotel marking an acute traffic bottleneck where the road bridges the creek between the upper reaches of Fortitude Valley and the route to the airport. A pretty, if noisy, spot, looking out over usually placid water to upmarket riverside apartments, the real estate in nearby Hamilton and Ascot is becoming quite exclusive. If you're out this way – perhaps going to the airport or heading north – consider looking around **Newstead House** (Mon–Fri 10am–4pm, Sun 2–5pm; $4.40), Brisbane's oldest residence. A low, solid brick-and-stone building with a slate roof, it was constructed as a private home in 1845 by convict labour, and became the Government House twelve years later. Enlarged by the governor, the house was the focus of social gatherings, and on the nights that balls were held armed police protected it from attacks by Aborigines. Restored and now open as a museum, both house and grounds are remarkably quiet. As you stand surrounded by century-old furniture, taking in the views across the creek from one of the elegant windows, it's easy to forget how close you are to the city. The house is in Newstead Park on the corner of Breakfast Creek and Newstead Avenue; to get there by public transport, take bus #300 or #302 to stop 12.

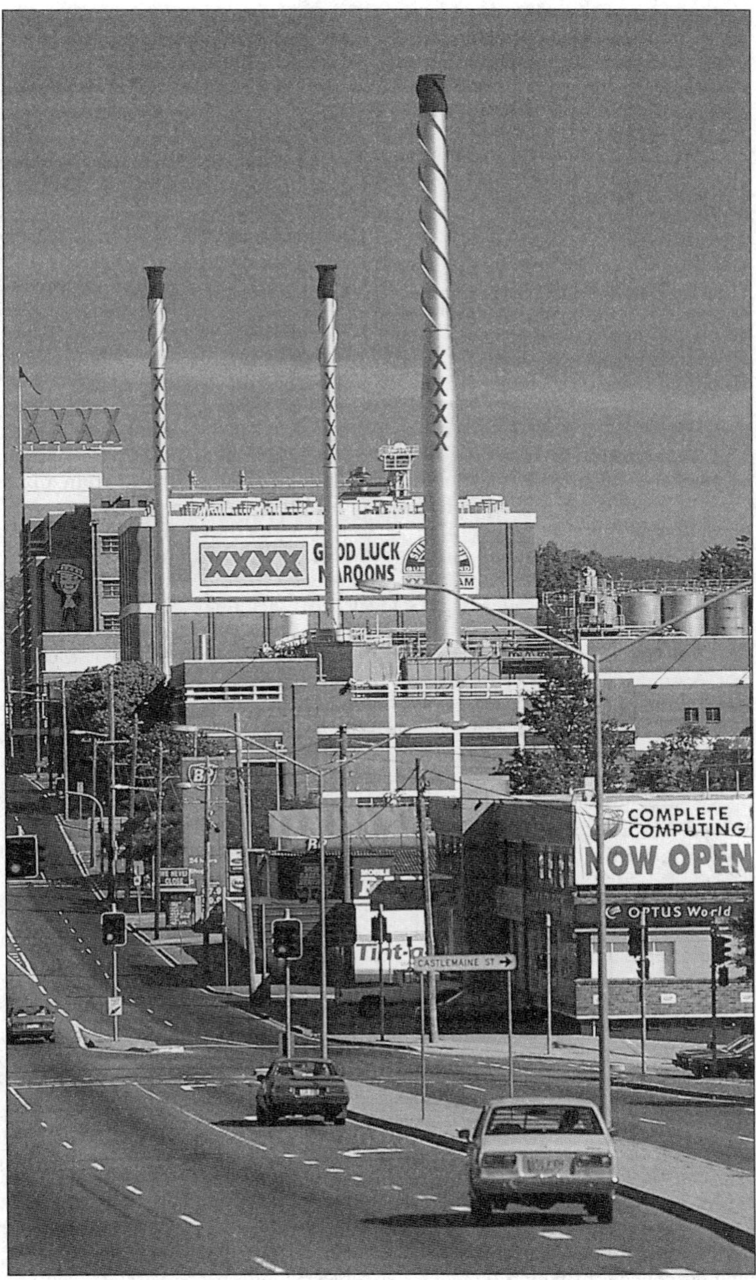

△ Castlemaine Brewery, Brisbane

South Brisbane

Across the river from the city centre, the **Cultural Centre** and its environs – comprising the state museum, library, gallery, performing arts complex, convention centre and South Bank Parklands – is Brisbane's most obvious tourist attraction. Immediately south of Victoria Bridge (itself a continuation of Queen Street), it's easily reached by train to South Brisbane Station, while plenty of buses from all parts of the city stop outside the station on Melbourne Street.

Beyond here, the **West End** is South Brisbane's answer to Fortitude Valley, with Boundary Street a similar ethnic mix – Asian, Greek and Italian – but with a more genteel atmosphere. There are no sights here as such, but it's worth a visit for the cluster of Asian stores and continental delicatessens, and for an escalating number of inexpensive restaurants and cafés around the hub at Boundary Road and Vulture Street, popular with students from the University of Queensland across the river at St Lucia; see pp.430–432 for details.

Queensland Museum and Sciencentre

The **Queensland Museum** (daily 9.30am–5pm; free, except for special exhibitions) is essentially a natural history museum, but it benefits from a bias towards unorthodox methods of presentation. Wedge-tailed eagles hover overhead, koalas climb the walls and, in the foyer, there's the unsettling experience of walking underneath full-scale models of a family of humpbacked whales suspended from the ceiling. There's an overview of the state's marine environment and western Queensland's fossil beds, including a reconstruction of Queensland's own Muttaburrasaurus and a section of the **Lark Quarry dinosaur trackways**. Above swings a furry pterodactyl, reflecting recent theories that Australia was subject to a cold climate during the era of the dinosaurs. Upstairs, the more recently extinct **megafauna** from the Darling Downs, just west of Brisbane, unexpectedly come to life – a breathing, twitching model of a marsupial lion lounging on a rock at the top of the escalators catches everyone by surprise. Rock hounds and prospective gem hunters will also be interested in the museum's **mineral collection** – dozens of multicoloured rocks from around the state together with information on identifying them in the field.

Ethnographic displays mostly relate to traditional life in New Guinea and Melanesia, with the glaring omission – apart from a handful of tools and a small section on the rainforest tribes from the north – of anything on Queensland's Aboriginal and Torres Strait Islander history. The displays are rounded off by miscellaneous items, including bits and pieces from aviation history and an eclectic collection of period furniture.

In the same building but with separate entrance facing Melbourne St, the **Sciencentre** (daily 10am–5pm; $9, family rate $28), is very therapeutic if you like to prod and dismantle exhibits instead of merely peering at them through a protective glass case. Great for children, favourites include the "perception tunnel", giving the impression of rotating although you remain stock still, and the "Thongophone", a set of giant pan pipes played by whacking the top with a flip-flop. It's all good rainy-day material.

State Art Gallery and Library

Queensland's **State Art Gallery** (Mon–Fri 9am–5pm, Sat–Sun 10am–5pm; free, except for special exhibitions) provides a large, airy space for its wide-ranging collection, which includes a sizeable exhibition of twentieth-century painters including visionaries such as Arthur Boyd and Sidney Nolan. Other

Australian works include the romantic paintings of Tom Roberts and the abstract canvases of Queenslander Ian Fairweather who was recently honoured with his own permanent gallery. One of the most interesting pieces in the gallery is a nineteenth-century stained-glass window depicting a kangaroo hunt – an Australian theme executed in a very European medium. In a museum with an increasing focus on **Aboriginal artists** there are some unusual (and very European) watercolour landscapes by Albert Namatjira (for more on the artist, see p.693), traditional papanya dot paintings by pioneer Clifford Possum Tjapaltjarri (see p.684), and rudimentary tribal items – dilly bags, headwear and shields – labelled as "art" but somehow out of place here.

The **John Oxley Library** (closed Sat), 996 Wynnum Road in Cannon Hill, records every aspect of Queensland's past in endless books, journals and photographs.

The South Bank Parklands

The sedate **South Bank Parklands** date back to just 1988 and were built on the former Expo site. Despite this, they're one of the nicest parts of the city – you can promenade under shady fig trees along the riverfront; picnic on lawns under rainforest plants and bamboo, lining the banks of shallow, stone-lined "streams" (which are convincing enough to have attracted large, sunbathing water dragons and birds); or make use of the artificial beach and accompanying saltwater pool. Bands play most Saturday nights on the outdoor stage, or at the *Plough Inn*, a restored, century-old pub in the reconstructed, cobbled high street; other attractions include exhibits at the **Maritime Museum** (daily 9.30am–4.30pm; $6), including a 90-year-old Torres Strait pearling lugger and the World War II frigate *Diamantina*, on show in the dry dock. Ferries and the City Cat stop at the Parklands, and there's also a pedestrian bridge from the Maritime Museum to the Botanic Gardens.

Along the river

The sluggish, meandering **Brisbane River** is, at four hundred million years old, one of the world's most ancient waterways. It flows from above Lake Wivenhoe – 55km inland – past farmland, into quiet suburbs and through the city before emptying 150km downstream into Moreton Bay, behind Fisherman Island. Once an essential trade and transport link with the rest of Australia and the world, it now seems to do little but separate the main part of the city from South Brisbane; though it's superficially active around the city centre, with ferries and dredgers keeping it navigable, most of the old wharves and shipyards now lie derelict or buried under parkland.

If the locals seem to have forgotten the river, it has a habit of reasserting its presence through **flooding**. In February 1893 cyclonic rains swelled the flow through downtown Brisbane, carrying off Victoria Bridge and scores of buildings: eyewitness accounts stated that "debris of all descriptions – whole houses, trees, cattle and homes – went floating past". This has since been repeated many times, notably in January 1974 when rains from Cyclone Wanda completely swamped the centre, swelling the river to a width of 3km at one stage. Despite reminders of this in brass plaques marking the depths of the worst floods at **Naldham House Polo Club** (1 Eagle St, near the markets), some of Brisbane's poshest real estate flanks the river, with waterfront mansions at Yeerongpilly, Graceville and Chelmer. They're all banking on protection from artificial Lake Wivenhoe, completed in 1984, which should act as a buffer against future floods.

Of the various ways to explore the river, the easiest is simply to take a return ride on the City Cat (though Fort Lytton and Lone Pine below are not on the Cat route) – such a popular, if unofficial, sightseeing trip that the service can be severely overcrowded during holidays.

Fort Lytton National Park

Surrounded by the pipes and chimneys of the Ampol oil refinery at Wynnum, **Fort Lytton National Park** (daily 10am–4pm; Museum open Sunday only, $4.50) is a product of the colonial struggles around the Pacific Rim at the end of the nineteenth century. Only a few days away from French forces on Nouméa (New Caledonia), Queensland felt threatened by competing European empires and developed a string of coastal defences during the 1880s. Brisbane received the best of these: by 1900, the river mouth at Fort Lytton bristled with artillery and a barrage of floating mines. However, the defences were never put to the test and modern warfare made them obsolete. The fort was downgraded to a secondary line of defence after World War I and abandoned altogether in 1945.

As a piece of military history, the buildings look the part: austere concrete bunkers dug into slopes and capped in grass, gun ports trained on the river and an underground tunnel for checking the mines running down to the water. The best time to visit is when the **Brisbane Garrison Battery** dresses up in period costume and fires the massive gun at Easter, and again on the Queen's birthday. The fort is at the end of Lytton Road, west of Wynnum at the mouth of Brisbane River; it is not possible to get here on public transport.

Lone Pine Sanctuary

Lone Pine Sanctuary on Jesmond Road, Fig Tree Pocket (daily 8am–5pm; $19), has been a popular day-trip upstream since first opening its gates in 1927. Here you can see a large number of native fauna in their natural state which, in the case of the sanctuary's hundred-odd **koalas**, means being asleep for eighteen hours a day. At close quarters they're revealed as grey cushions wedged into convenient forks in the trees, occasionally waking up for long enough to chew eucalyptus leaves and blink myopically at the crowds. In nearby cages you'll find other slumbering animals: Tasmanian devils, fruit bats, blue-tongued lizards and dingoes. Indeed, about the only lively creatures you'll see are birds and a colony of hyperactive sugar gliders in the nocturnal house. Alternatively, head for the outdoor paddock where tolerant wallabies and kangaroos allow themselves to be petted, fed and occasionally ruffled by visitors.

You can catch **bus** #430 from outside the Myer Centre on Elizabeth Street to Lone Pine, but the best way there is to take a ninety-minute **river cruise** past Brisbane's waterfront suburbs with Mirimar Cruises (daily departure 10am from North Quay beside Victoria Bridge, return 2.50pm; $44, including entry to Lone Pine). Free pick-up from your central accommodation is usually possible (for bookings call ⓣ1300 729 742).

Eating

Brisbane has no gastronomic tradition to exploit, but there's a good variety of bars and restaurants all over the city, with a trend towards "modern Australian" (creative use of local produce, with Asian and Mediterranean influences). Fortitude Valley has a dense grouping of Asian restaurants (and a fashionable café society), while South Brisbane's Boundary Street has more of a European flavour.

Counter meals and unlimited buffets at hotels are the cheapest route to a full stomach – aim for lunch at around noon and dinner between 5 and 6pm – or try one of the scores of **cafés** in the centre catering to office workers. The city's **restaurants** open from around 11am to 2pm for lunch, and from 6 to 10pm or later for evening meals; many are closed for one day a week (often Monday).

City centre

Ebony & Ivory cnr Albert St and Queen St Mall. Small informal family-owned café on an otherwise pretentious precinct, with hearty all-day breakfast. Most expensive item is the excellent goat and black-eyed peas at $17.50. Open 7am to 9pm, later at weekends.

e'cco 100 Boundary St ⓣ07/3831 8344, ⓦwww.eccobistro.com. Boasts an impressive awards list, not to mention publishing their own cookbook – you'll have to book, sometimes days ahead. Not cheap but good value, with most mains around $32. Open for lunch Tues–Fri, dinner Tues–Sat.

Govindas 1st floor, 99 Elizabeth St. Hare Krishna-run vegetarian food bar, with a $8.50 all-you-can-eat menu. Open Mon–Thu 11am–6.30pm, Fri 11am–8.30pm, Sat 11am–2.30pm; there's a $5 banquet every Sunday (5–7pm), but you'll have to sit through a lot of chanting before you actually get to eat.

Kado Ya Elizabeth Arcade, between Elizabeth and Charlotte streets. Most popular of several Asian fast-food restaurants in the arcade, serving up Japanese soups, noodle dishes and sushi rolls from about $7.

Pane e Vino Cnr Charlotte and Albert streets. Smart Italian café-restaurant with pavement tables, catering mainly to nearby office executives. Risottos from $16, main courses around $25.

Sushi Station 142 Elizabeth St, next to Wintergarden Food Court. One in a chain of BYO Japanese sushi bars where the selection of dishes parades around the tables on the back of a model train, featuring low-priced soups, rice, fish, seaweed and green-tea ice cream.

Topolino's 124 Leichhardt St. Cavernous budget Italian restaurant with huge pizzas, small but filling pasta favourites and very average salads. Pasta dishes under $12; pizzas $10–20.

Verve 109 Edward St. Modern Italian in an ambient basement cellar with funky music and art. Pastas and risottos $11–16, mains under $20 and excellent blackboard specials usually with the enticing goats' cheese gnocchi. Closed Sunday.

Petrie Terrace

Casablanca 52 Petrie Terrace. Inexpensive brasserie and café serving the young and pretentious. Tapas are served at the bar for around $12, and the food is excellent and mouthwateringly spicy, with genuine leanings towards North African cuisine. R&B hip-hop or live bands provide atmosphere at weekends and there's Latin dance classes in the cellar Tue–Fri.

Paddo Tavern 186 Given Terrace cnr Caxton St. Huge Irish pub with a dozen pool tables and beer & steak for $6.95. Live comedy acts downstairs.

Fortitude Valley

Asian House 165 Wickham St. Good, filling Chinese food at very reasonable prices – most mains, such as roast pork or greens in oyster sauce, are under $12.

Cosmopolitan Coffee 322 Brunswick St Mall. Relaxed place, something of an institution with Brisbane's café society; opens early for breakfast and is less pretentious than the surrounding competition.

Hunan Duncan St (halfway up Chinatown Mall, on the left). Stick to the "chef's suggestions" on the menu and you'll enjoy Brisbane's most authentic Chinese cuisine – though be warned, Hunanese cooking can use copious amounts of chilli and garlic. Try steamed beef in lotus leaf, fish in bamboo, or Mao's sliced pork – apparently a favourite dish of the late Chairman. Big portions, with mains $13–18.

King of Kings 169 Wickham St. Two restaurants with separate entrances, though in the same building; huge and tacky upstairs although popular with the local Chinese community thanks to its fine late-morning *yum cha* tea selections. Come prepared to queue at weekend lunchtimes. Open daily for lunch and dinner.

Tibetan Kitchen 454 Brunswick St ⓣ07/3358 5906. It's hard to resist any place that advertises "traditional Tibetan, Sherpa, Nepalese foods", and luckily the food here, including the Valley's best samosas ($5.90 for four) and curries, is tasty and cheap, and served in a very attractive setting. Mains $11–16. Open daily for dinner only; booking advisable at weekends.

The Vietnamese 194 Wickham St ⓣ07/3252 4112. With an interior as plain and unassuming as the name over the door, this is no-frills, genuine

Vietnamese cuisine – the steamboat is excellent, as are the chicken salad and Vietnamese spring rolls (self-assembled using a boiled rice-noodle wrapper). Most mains cost around $12; two can eat well for $30. Open daily 11am–3pm & 5–10pm; you'll need to book at the weekend.

South Brisbane

Caffé Tempo 181 Boundary St. Great Italian-style home cooking, with fresh salads and fine seafood pasta – even humble sandwiches come with a salad big enough to be a meal in itself. Most expensive dish costs around $15. Open daily 9am–late.

Chez Laila On the Boardwalk, South Bank Parklands. Smart, open-plan restaurant and bar with fine river views and Lebanese cuisine. Upmarket falafel, kebabs and *kibbi*, along with side dishes of stuffed vine leaves, hummus and *baba ghannouj* (grilled aubergine and tahini puree). Mains around $17.

Cristo's Café Cnr Melbourne and Boundary streets. Popular spot, sporting minimalist decor and Mediterranean colours inside, but with an open front that gives the feeling of pavement dining. Food is eclectic – tapas, antipasto, risotto, polenta and moussaka, alongside Asian noodles and spiced quail. Mains around $20.

King Ahiram 88 Vulture St. A long-running Lebanese takeaway and restaurant; not worth crossing town for, but good for kebabs and sticky Mediterranean desserts if you're in the area.

New Asia 153 Boundary St. Forget flashier Vietnamese restaurants in the neighbourhood, this is the best – prawns grilled on sugar cane, deep-fried quail, rice-noodle dishes – most for less than $8 a dish.

Three Monkeys Coffee Shop 58 Mollison St. Decorated with a funky assortment of African oddments; serves average coffee, awesome cakes, and effortlessly achieves the sort of bohemian atmosphere most coffee shops merely aspire to. Greek-influenced menu with plenty of vegetarian/lentil options, and nothing over $12. Open daily 9am–late.

Nightlife and entertainment

The city's entertainment horizons consist of an ever-fluctuating range of clubs, and a sound, if unadventurous, arts scene. That said, the city's best cross-section of attractions is not to be found in the centre, but rather north of the river in **Fortitude Valley**, which throbs with the nightclub crowd.

Pubs, clubs and live music

Brisbane nights were once a byword for boredom: the few places that offered after-dark entertainment were either illegal or lifeless and closed early, and locals headed to the coast for their weekends. Things have changed, however, and Brisbane has seen a recent explosion of home-grown musical talent, with bands such as Savage Garden, Regurgitator, Custard and Powderfinger putting the city firmly on the Australian pop-culture map. On Friday and Saturday evenings the centre is crowded, but the big push is out to the clubs, bars and restaurants (many with quality entertainment) of a reinvented and revamped Fortitude Valley. Live-music venues, however, are on the decline and tend to open and close in the blink of an eye; places listed below might be here to stay, but check with music stores such as Rocking Horse, 101 Adelaide St, or weekly **free magazines** for up-to-the-minute reviews and **listings**: *rave* for general info, *Time Off* for rock and live bands, and *Scene* for dance. There's no standard charge for club entry, and many places offer free nights and special deals.

City centre

Down Under Bar At *Palace Backpackers*, cnr Ann and Edward streets. Hugely popular and often overtly sexist get-drunk-throw-up-and-fall-down venue for travellers.

Victory Hotel 127 Edward St. Nice beer garden with braziers taking the chill off in winter and live bands Wed–Sun.

Petrie Terrace and Spring Hill

Milk Bar 2 Caxton St. The latest place in which to be seen, modern hip-hop club with live bands and guest DJs on weekends, jazz every Wednesday and mellow acoustic shows on Sunday.

Paddo Tavern 186 Given Terrace. Band and disco on Friday night and a sit down comedy club most days of the week.

Sportsmans Hotel 130 Leichhardt St. Gay, lesbian and straight crowds fill the two floors; pool tables, pinball, bands, bottle shop and bistro. Fantastic drag nights Thurs–Sun.

Fortitude Valley and New Farm

Arena 201 Brunswick St ⓣ07/3252 5690 for band info. Long-established venue hosting popular DJs and dance parties as well as local and international touring bands.

The Beat 677 Ann St. Small, crowded and sweaty pub with a beer garden outside where you can recharge your batteries on bar food. $10 cover charge is a bit off-putting, but it's one of the best techno/dance venues in town, and open until 5am. Upstairs is the *Cockatoo Club*, a stridently gay venue featuring both indoor and outdoor bars, with a penchant for commercial dance music. Open Wed–Sun.

Dooley's Cnr Brunswick and McLachlan streets. Rowdy, popular Irish pub hosting bands of variable quality; territorial male behaviour is the norm in the big pool-hall upstairs, and the police seem to get called in on a regular basis.

Phat Stuff 176 Wickham St. Predominantly a movement clothing outlet but hosts the "Strictly Battle Rhymes" live rapping competitions every Sunday from 1pm.

The Rev 25 Warner St. A renovated 120-year-old church, featuring funk and original live music. Next door at #27 is another church turned nightclub which for many years hosted blues and jazz. It's currently closed and for sale but the new owners might continue the tradition.

The Press Club In the *Empire Hotel*, cnr Brunswick and Ann streets. "Members only" club

Gay and lesbian Brisbane

Queensland has long had a reputation for repressive attitudes towards gays and lesbians, though anti-discrimination legislation is in force and Brisbane's gays and lesbians are revelling in a loud and energetic scene which gets better every year. In June the Pride Collective hosts the annual **Pride Festival**, a diverse three-week event, with a street march, fair, art exhibitions, a film festival, sports events, general exhibitionism and culminating with a dance party – the **Queen's Birthday Ball**. At the **Sleaze Ball** in November there's another opportunity to indulge in exhibitionism at this all-day party at their RNA Showgrounds.

The gay scene is largely clustered around the suburbs of Spring Hill, Fortitude Valley, New Valley, New Farm and Paddington. For up-to-the-moment **information**, listen to Queer Radio, station ZZZ 102.1FM (Wed 6–9pm) or pick up a copy of the fortnightly *Qnews* (ⓦwww.qnews.com.au) or *Queensland Pride* from gay nightclubs, street distributors and some coffee shops.

For gay-friendly **accommodation**, try *Central Brunswick Apartment Hotel*, or the *Sportsmans Hotel* (see p.422); nightlife focuses on *Cockatoo Club* above *The Beat*, *The Wickham Hotel* and *Sportsmans Hotel*– all listed under "Pubs, clubs and live music".

Support groups and information

AIDS Gladstone Road Medical Centre, 38 Gladstone Rd, Highgate Hill (ⓣ07/3844 9599), medical services and counselling; Queensland AIDS Council, 32 Peel St, South Brisbane (ⓣ07/3017 1777, ⓦwww.quac.org.au).

Books Bent Books, cnr of Vulture and Boundary streets, West End, is the longest established gay bookshop in Brisbane.

Medical Brunswick Street Medical Centre, 665 Brunswick St, New Farm (ⓣ07/3358 1977). Gay and Lesbian health service, open Mon–Sat from 8am.

The Pride Collective Organizers of the Pride Festival – contact them through ⓦwww.prideawards.org.au.

Queensland Pride PO Box 8151, Woolloongabba, QLD 4102 (ⓣ07/3392 2922). Free monthly publication covering Brisbane and the rest of the state.

(whatever that means); if you make it past the door gorillas, you'll find leather lounges, big "pouf" cushions to rest your feet on and a huge glam/industrial fan as the centrepiece, all of it enveloped in a relaxed and funky dance beat. Rather a "fabulous" crowd, out to see and be seen, with drinks prices to match. Closed Mon.

Ric's Bar 321 Brunswick St. Narrow, crowded place and overtly pretentious – getting to the bar takes some effort. Nightly mix of live Aussie bands downstairs and DJ-driven techno upstairs at the *Upbar*.

Waterloo Hotel Cnr Ann St and Commercial Rd. Manages to attract some big-name Australian touring bands, but almost always has good local talent Friday and Saturday nights.

The Wickham Hotel Cnr Wickham and Alden streets. Reputedly Queensland's most popular gay pub. Drag show on Thursday and DJs every night.

Zoo 711 Ann St. A hectic night out featuring dub or local bands, and Jazz every last Sunday of the month; Wed–Sun 5pm–late.

Film and theatre

Compared with the rest of the state, which tends to get only mainstream commercial successes, Brisbane has a varied programme of films. The Dendy, 346 George St (ⓣ07/3211 3244), Palace Centro, 39 James St, Fortitude Valley (ⓣ07/3852 4488), and Schonell, University of Queensland, St Lucia (ⓣ07/3377 2229), all show contemporary and vintage foreign-language and "offbeat" films. Even the multiscreen Hoyts cinema, upstairs at the Myer Centre, and the luxurious Regent, further down the mall, are worth checking for unexpected offerings. In August the **Brisbane International Film Festival** hosts a bundle of goodies from around the world shown over a week – contact one of the cinemas for details.

Big **theatrical productions** are staged at the Performing Arts Complex (ⓣ13 62 46) on the south bank in the Concert Hall, Optus Playhouse (home of the Queensland Theatre Company), Cremorne, or Lyric theatres; look out for lower-key, lunch-time performances, workshops and foyer exhibitions. The University of Queensland's Cement Box Theatre, over the river at their St Lucia campus (ⓣ07/3377 2240), offers more down-to-earth repertory fare, and there's also a newer venue in town at the Brisbane Powerhouse (ⓣ07/3358 8600), on the river next to New Farm Park in eastern Brisbane. A former power station, this once derelict building opened in 2001 as a centre for the performing arts, including the long-established La Boite Theatre and Vulcana Womens' Circus. Contact information outlets for performance details.

Sports and outdoor activities

Queensland's sporting obsession revolves around **rugby league**, though the Brisbane Broncos have lost their edge a little since their glory days in the early

Drinks for women: the Regatta Hotel

Though Australian pubs tend towards being all-male enclaves, women were once legally barred to "protect" them from the corrupting influence of foul language. On April 1, 1965, Merle Thornton (mother of the actress Sigrid Thornton) and her friend Rosalie Bogner chained themselves to the footrail of the **Regatta Hotel** bar at Toowong in protest; the movement they inspired led to the granting of "the right to drink alongside men" in the mid-1970s. The pink-and-white colonial hotel, now a trendy place for a drink after work on Fridays, is on the west bank of the river along Coronation Drive, about 2km from the city centre towards St Lucia.

1990s. Their stomping ground is at the Suncorp Stadium on Castlemains St, 5-minutes walk west of the city (tickets cost $24–43 available from Ticketek outlets or Ⓦwww.ticketek.com.au), and the event of the year is the State of Origin series in May or June. **Cricket** matches are played at "The Gabba" on Vulture Street, 3km southeast of the City, and the Queensland Reds **rugby union** team play at Ballymore Stadium (tickets cost $25–55 available from Ticketmaster 7 outlets or Ⓦwww.ticketmaster7.com).

To witness less commercial competition, visit the Royal Queensland Show (the "Ekka") in August, a huge agricultural expo with fairground attractions, stock shows, and wood-chopping contests; the show sees over half a million visitors descend on the RNA Showgrounds over the weekend event.

For something more hands on, Bay Dolphin (Ⓣ07/3207 9620, Ⓦwww.baydolphin.com.au) offers a full-day **sailing** between the mainland and North Stradbroke Island for $81 or you could treat yourself to a **scenic flight** over the city for $255 per person weekdays or $275 on weekends with Possum Air Tours (Ⓣ07/3397 0033, Ⓦwww.possumairtours.com.au; daily 7am and 9.45am from Archerfield Airport). For some plain Aussie weirdness, head west of town to the Australian Woolshed at 148 Samford Rd, Ferny Hills (Ⓣ07/3351 5366, Ⓦwww.auswoolshed.com, daily 8.30am–4.30pm; $17), where you can watch a highly polished performance including **trained sheep** (a rarity in itself), a shearing demonstration, morning tea and sheepdogs putting startled flocks through their paces.

Listings

Airlines Air New Zealand, 63 Adelaide St Ⓣ13 24 76, Ⓦwww.airnewzealand.com.au; Air Niugini, 99 Creek St Ⓣ1300 361 380, Ⓦwww.airniugini.com.pg; Air Vanuatu, Floor 5, 293 Queen St Ⓣ1300 780 737; Alliance Ⓣ1300 130 092; British Airways, 313 Adelaide St Ⓣ07/3238 2900; Garuda, 288 Edward St Ⓣ1300 365 330; Gulf Air, 217 George St Ⓣ07/3407 7282; Japan Airlines, Level 14, 1 Waterfront Place, Eagle St Ⓣ07/3229 9922; KLM Ⓣ1300 303 747; Korean Air, 400 Queen St Ⓣ07/3860 6000; Malaysia Airlines, 17th Floor, 80 Albert St Ⓣ13 26 27; Qantas, 247 Adelaide St Ⓣ13 13 13; Royal Brunei, 60 Edward St Ⓣ07/3017 5000; Singapore Airlines, 344 Queen St Ⓣ13 10 11; Thai International, 145 Eagle St Ⓣ07/3215 4700; United, 400 Queen St Ⓣ13 17 77; Virgin Blue, Level 7, Centenary Square, 100 Wickham St, Fortitude Valley Ⓣ07/3295 3000 or 13 67 89.

Banks Queensland banking hours are Mon–Fri 9.30am–4pm; major branches in the centre are around Queen and Edward streets.

Bike rental Valet Cycle Hire (Ⓣ0408 003 198) delivers bikes direct to your accommodation ($50 for one day, $70 for two, and $10 for each day thereafter), or Brisbane Bicycle, 87 Albert St (Ⓣ07/3229 2433) hires bikes from its premises for $20 for the day or $40 overnight.

Bookshops American Book Store, 173 Elizabeth St; Dymmocks, near the post office in Queen St; and Borders, near the Myer Centre, Elizabeth Street, all have a broad selection.

Camping supplies K2, 140 Wickham St, Fortitude Valley Ⓣ07/3854 1340; Silk Road, 128 Wickham St Ⓣ07/3257 4177; and Mountain Designs, 120 Wickham St Ⓣ07/3216 1866, all in a row for easy price comparisons, or Kathmandu, 728 Ann St Ⓣ07/3252 8054 for top-quality camping gear and information.

Car rental You'll pay around $40 for a single day's car rental; longer terms work out from $25–29 a day. Campervans start at $59 a day for long-term rental. Shop around and read rental conditions before signing. Most places will deliver; minimum age is 21. Abel (Ⓣ13 14 29); Integra, for campervans and one-way rentals to Melbourne, Sydney, Airlie Beach or Cairns (Ⓣ1800 067 414, Ⓦwww.integracar.com .au); Travellers Auto Barn, 2 Maud St, Newstead (Ⓣ07/3252 2638, Ⓦwww.travellers-autobarn.com), have campers for $60 a day and station wagons for $25 a day; U-Drive (Ⓣ1800 673 067 Ⓦwww.u-drive.com.au) offers standard cars at Brisbane airport from $33 a day; Wicked (Ⓣ1800 246 869, Ⓦwww.wickedcampers.com.au) specializes in discount long-term campervan rentals.

Consulates Britain, Level 26, 1 Eagle St Ⓣ07/3223 3200; Indonesia, 123 Eagle St Ⓣ07/3309 0888; Japan, 12 Creek St Ⓣ07/3221

5188; Papua New Guinea, 99 Greek St ⓣ07/3221 7915; Philippines, 23 Folkstone St, Newstead ⓣ07/3852 4440; Thailand, 87 Annerley Rd ⓣ07/3846 7771.
Hospitals/medical centres Roma Street Medical Centre, Level 2, Transit Centre (Mon–Fri 8am–5.30pm; ⓣ07/3236 2988); Royal Brisbane, Herston Rd, Herston (ⓣ07/3636 8111; buses #126, #144 or #172 from outside City Hall); and Travellers' Medical Service, Level 1, 245 Albert St (Mon–Fri 7.30am–7pm, Sat 9am–5pm, Sun 10am–4pm; ⓣ07/3211 3611), for general services, vaccinations and women's health.
Internet access Most hostels have terminals where you can log on from around $4 an hour; otherwise try City Email, 124 Adelaide St for $3 per hour.
Left luggage Not permitted at the airport but available at the Transit Centre for $6 per day per locker.
Maps The Royal Automobile Club of Queensland's series, free to members, or $5.50 each from the RACQ centre at 261 Queen St, covers everything from major highways to almost invisible 4WD-only tracks; and World Wide, 187 George St, stocks a comprehensive range of maps, atlases and travel guides for Queensland and beyond.
Markets Eagle Street (Sun until 3pm) and Brunswick Street Mall (Sat until 4pm) for bits and pieces; South Bank Parklands (Fri night, Sat & Sun until 5pm) for clothing, arts and crafts and a family atmosphere; King George Square Market in front of City Hall (Sun 8am–4pm) is small but has nice contemporary crafts; while the Riverside Centre (Sun only) is more "arty" than the rest.
QPWS 160 Ann St ⓣ07/3227 8186. Plenty of fluffy toys, brochures, books and general information about the state's national parks.
Pharmacies Transit Centre Pharmacy (daily 7am–6pm); and Day & Night Pharmacy, Queen Street Mall (Mon–Sat 8am–9pm, Sun 10am–5pm).
Police Queensland Police Headquarters is opposite the Transit Centre on Roma St ⓣ07/3364 6464.
Post office 261 Queen St (ⓣ13 13 18 poste restante); bring photo ID to collect poste restante. Mon–Fri 9am–5pm.
RACQ 261 Queen St (ⓣ13 19 05 breakdown service).
Telephones International payphones are located in the arcade beside the GPO at 261 Queen St; cheap international rates are also available through the Internet places near *Palace Backpackers* on Adelaide St.
Trains Queensland and interstate trains leave from the Transit Centre's ground floor; the ticket office and information centre there is open Mon–Fri 9am–5pm. For rail information call ⓣ13 12 30.
Travel agents Discounted air fares and other travel arrangements are available from: Backpackers World Travel, 131 Elizabeth St ⓣ1800 676 763; Flight Centre, 181 George St ⓣ07/3229 0150; cnr Creek and Queen streets ⓣ07/3227 1777; STA, 111 Adelaide St ⓣ07/3221 5722; Student Flights, 126 Adelaide St ⓣ07/3229 8449, ⓦwww.studentflights.com.au; Trailfinders, 91 Elizabeth St ⓣ07/3229 0887; and a YHA office opposite the Transit Centre at 154 Roma St (Mon–Fri 8.30am–6pm, Sat 9am–3pm; ⓣ07/3236 1680).
Work Popular with job-hunters, Brisbane offers fairly good employment prospects, if you're not too choosy. Many hostels run effective ad hoc agencies for their guests, or for out-of-town work, try Brisbane's WWOOF office at Banana Benders Backpackers, 118 Petrie Terrace (ⓣ07/3367 1157).

Moving on from Brisbane

Whilst Brisbane sprawls to the south towards the ever-popular **Gold Coast,** it comes to a rather abrupt halt north of the airport where farming quickly takes hold along with the quintessential countryside of the Glass House Mountains. Beyond are the region's most spectacular attractions of **Noosa Heads** and **Fraser Island**, which are between three and five hours' drive along the Bruce Highway.

Day-trips to the Gold Coast theme parks can be arranged from Brisbane, but there are so many accommodation options along the southern coast that there's little point in returning to the city. A forty-minute drive **south** on the Pacific Highway takes you to the turn-off for the Gold Coast Highway and the high-rise tourist sprawl of **Surfers Paradise**. The Pacific Highway continues south bypassing the congested coast and merges with the Gold Coast Highway 20km further south at the twin towns of **Coolangatta** and **Tweed Heads** which straddle the New South Wales border. Local buses to the Gold Coast towns

Tours from Brisbane

Most **tours** from Brisbane are pretty straightforward day-trips by bus to take in the highlights of Lamington, Tamborine Mountain, the Sunshine Coast or Gold Coast. Allstate Scenic Tours (☎07/3285 1777) has been running day-trips to Green Mountain at Lamington National Park for years (daily except Sat; $55), and you can arrange to be dropped off on one day and picked up another. Australian Day Tours (☎07/3236 4155) has a dozen or so day-tours to the Sunshine Coast, Gold Coast theme parks, or Lamington and Tamborine Mountain for $50–100; Coachliner (☎07/3236 1239) goes to Tamborine Mountain, Green Mountain or the Sunshine Coast ($45–90); while Far Horizons (☎07/3284 5475) operates day-trips to Lamington, the Glass House Mountains, or Hinterland cattle stations from around $60.

If you want a bit more depth to your trips, or to visit more distant regions, try the highly recommended Rob's Rainforest Explorer (☎0409 496 607, ⓦwww.robsrainforest.com) for day-trips to various parts of the Scenic Rim or Glass House Mountains, featuring plenty of wildlife, rainforests, bush tucker and swimming holes ($65); or Sunrover Expeditions (☎1800 353 717, ⓦwww.sunrover.com.au), for one- to three-day 4WD safaris to Moreton and North Stradbroke islands. Moreton Bay Escapes (ⓦwww.moretonbayescapes.com.au) offers one- to three-day tours of Moreton Island ($119–319; see p.441), and organizes one-day sailing trips out on the bay for $119.

and beyond include Kirkland's (☎1300 367 077), which runs eight times daily; and Coachtrans (☎13 12 30), which runs three services daily – most interstate services to Sydney with Greyhound Australia (☎13 20 30), and Premier Motor Coaches (☎13 34 10) also call in on the Gold Coast towns.

Travelling north, Suncoast Pacific (☎07/3236 1901) runs five services daily between the Transit Centre and all Sunshine Coast towns to **Noosa**. Most Greyhound Australia and Premier buses to Cairns call in at Sunshine Coast towns, before heading on to **Hervey Bay**, three and a half hours by road north of Brisbane but taking seven hours by bus on its meandering route.

Heading inland, Crisp's (☎07/4661 8333) has a daily service between the Transit Centre and Warwick, Moree and Tenterfield whilst Greyhound Australia runs daily to Mt. Isa via Toowoomba as well as to Stanthorpe and on to Sydney via the New England Highway.

Outer Brisbane and Moreton Bay

With the grossly hyped Gold Coast and Hinterland for competition, it's not surprising that few people bother with the country immediately surrounding Brisbane. Only 5km to the west, the city is hemmed in by **Mount Coot-tha**'s botanic gardens and the foothills of **Brisbane Forest Park**, which covers the green, wet heights of the D'Aguilar Range and stretches to the edge of Lake Wivenhoe.

In the opposite direction, coastal suburbs provide access to the shallow waters of **Moreton Bay**, famous throughout Australia as the home of the unfortunately named Moreton Bay Bug, which is actually a small, delicious lobster-like crustacean. While Brisbane is hardly noted for its beach life, with muddy shorelines attracting mangroves rather than sun worshippers, the largest of the bay's islands, **Moreton** and **North Stradbroke**, are generously endowed with sand, and are just the right distance from the city to make their beaches accessible but seldom crowded. The island of **St Helena** is not somewhere you'd visit for sun and surf, but its prison ruins recall the convict era and are an interesting day-trip. In the bay itself, look for dolphins, dugong (sea cows) and humpbacked whales, which pass by in winter en route to their calving grounds up north.

For organized **transport and tours** into the area, check the following individual accounts, as well as the box on p.437.

Mount Coot-tha

The lower slopes of **Mount Coot-tha** are the setting for Brisbane's second botanic gardens, a popular place for a Sunday picnic located on Sir Samuel Griffith Drive (daily 8am–5pm; free; bus #471 from Adelaide St runs hourly 9.15am–3.15pm). Careful landscaping and the use of enclosures create varying climates – dry pine and eucalypt groves, a cool subtropical rainforest complete with waterfalls and streams, and the elegant **Japanese Gardens** with bonsai and fern houses. In summer, the **tropical plant dome** seems an unnecessary feature in an already sweltering climate; inside, the floor is almost completely occupied by a pond – stocked with tropical lotus lilies and fish – and is overshadowed by tropical greenery dripping with moisture. Informative free one-hour guided walks depart from the info kiosk at 11am and 1pm daily.

The other dome in the gardens does duty as a **planetarium** ($11.50; Tue–Sun 10am–4.30pm with a late-night show on Saturday at 7.30pm; call ⓣ07/3403 8888 for programme and timetable of events). While the foyer display is dry and dated, the show itself, which you view lying back under the dome's ceiling, is an interesting observation of the key features of Brisbane's night sky.

After visiting the botanic gardens most people head up the road to the summit for panoramas of the city and, on a good day, the Moreton Bay islands. Walking tracks from here make for moderate hikes of an hour or two through dry gum woodland, and include several **Aboriginal trails** – the best of which branches off the Slaughter Falls track with informative signs pointing out plants and their uses as food, artefacts and hunting poisons. Pamphlets on the tracks are available from the botanical gardens Information library (Mon–Sat 10am-3pm), and the information desk in the foyer of Brisbane's City Hall.

Brisbane Forest Park

If your plans don't include seeing any other forests in the southeast, take advantage of **Brisbane Forest Park**'s proximity to the city. Covering approximately 280 square kilometres to the west of Brisbane, the park contains substantial tracts of virgin forest, and is well stocked with wildlife, pretty lookouts and easy walking tracks. A day is ample time to look around, or you could make the park the first stage of a scenic circuit from Brisbane via Lake Wivenhoe and Toowoomba (see p.582).

Highway 31 runs from the city centre via The Gap right through the park, with a half-dozen places to stop off and explore along the way. First of these is **Bellbird Grove** (4km into the park), containing another of the city's Aboriginal trails with an outdoor museum of bark huts and information on traditional plant uses. Around 12km along is **Boombana**'s one-kilometre rainforest circuit of moss-covered logs and towering buttressed trees, with the tiny township of **Mount Nebo** just beyond. From here it's a long run through gum woodland to similarly-sized **Mount Glorious**, and then you're at **Maiala National Park** (30km into the park), a fascinating tract of subtropical forest, where palms, figs and other giant trees compete for light, vines tangle up the forest floor and gullies guide fast-flowing creeks. Both townships sport tearooms.

There's plenty of **wildlife** to be encountered along the park's many kilometres of walking tracks. Catbirds snarl at each other in the rainforest, while dark-blue male **satin bowerbirds** woo females with an elaborate tunnel made from grass and decorated with blue objects – seeds and flowers are the natural choice, though given the opportunity the birds are happy to raid picnic tables and dustbins for blue plastic clothes-pegs, straws and even *Bushell's* teabags, which have a blue paper label attached to the string (Queensland dairies changed the colour of their plastic bottle-lids when it was suggested that bowerbirds might throttle themselves on them). At night, you'll see wallabies on verges, glider possums around flowering trees in open woodland, echidnas scraping through leaf litter for ants, and possibly the bandy-bandy, a timid, mildly poisonous snake boldly striped in black and white, which forms vertical hoops with its body when frightened.

Lake Wivenhoe, 85km beyond the Brisbane Forest Park, was created in the late 1970s to stop the Brisbane River flooding the city – the last of a series of floods struck in 1974. Its southern end is just visible from an outlook on the western edge of the **D'Aguilar Range**, about 10km west of Maiala, that gives a sweeping view down wooded hills to the drier country of the southwest. A road links the park with the Brisbane Valley Highway and if you're heading west, you can get to Toowoomba (see p.582) via the Wivenhoe Dam (140km) – a slower-paced, far more scenic route than the alternative Warrego Highway.

Practicalities

In general, spring (Sept & Oct) is the best time to visit Brisbane Forest Park; animals are active, many plants are in bloom and rain is infrequent. It can be cold and damp at night in winter, while fire bans can close sections of the park during prolonged dry spells (most frequently in November).

The park entrance and headquarters are at **Walkabout Creek Wildlife Centre** (daily 9am–4.30pm; ⓣ07/3300 4855), about 12km west of the city. You can reach Walkabout Creek by bus from the Myer Centre #385 (hourly Mon–Fri 9am–5pm, Sat & Sun 9am–4pm). Coming by car – the only way to explore more of the park other than walking – follow College Road west onto Route 31, and stay on it until you reach Walkabout Creek. Walkabout Creek makes a good first stop for free **maps**, information, details of bushwalking tours and, if you want to **camp** rough (there are no formal campsites), a permit. The Wildlife Centre itself (daily 9am–4.30pm; $5) is an idealized creek system where lungfish, turtles, snakes and frogs coexist with few of the stresses they'd encounter living this close together in the wild. Everything is well labelled and it's unlikely you'll ever get better views of crayfish mincing over the gravel at the bottom of the stream or water dragons sunning themselves on rocks. The centre also has a noisy walk-through aviary, as well as a collection of platypuses and a nocturnal house, and there's a smattering of wildlife in the surrounding gum forest.

Accommodation in the park needs to be booked in advance. At Mount Nebo, the *Railway Carriage* (ⓣ07/3289 8120; ⓔroselou@tpg.com.au; chalet ❹, car ❺) offers a night in a restored 1930s sleeper car, with bed, kitchen and en-suite, or a similarly equipped but more conventional chalet. At Mount Glorious, *Mt Glorious Getaways* (ⓣ07/3289 0172; ⓔbrownsm@gil.com.au; ❺) has several nicely designed and fully furnished self-catering cottages.

St Helena Island

Small, low and triangular, **St Helena Island** sits 8km from the mouth of the Brisbane River. Once the hunting ground of local tribes, the island took its name after an Aborigine known as Napoleon who was dumped here in 1828 when he became too troublesome for the jail at Dunwich on North Stradbroke Island. Forty years later, the spectre of overcrowding in mainland prisons prompted the government to turn St Helena Island into a penal settlement, and after clearing rainforest for timber and to prevent escapes, gardens were planted and houses built from coral blocks and clay. In some respects it was a model system, though conditions were still severe for the inmates: prisoners were taught a trade and were even paid for their labour, and there were only three escapes in its 65 years of operation. The government found it particularly useful for political troublemakers, such as the leaders of the 1891 shearers' strike and, with more justice, a couple of slave-trading "Blackbirder" captains.

A **tour** of the prison island, endearingly tagged the "Hell Hole of the South Pacific" during its working life, leaves you thankful you missed out on the "good old days". A clue as to why there were so few escapes is provided by the rusty swimming enclosure at the jetty, which was constructed to protect warders from the sharks whose presence was actively encouraged around the island. Evidence of the prisoners' industry and self-sufficiency is still to be seen in the stone houses, as well as in the remains of a sugar mill, paddocks, wells and an ingenious lime kiln built into the shoreline. The Deputy Superintendent's house has been turned into a bare museum (reached from the jetty on a mini-tramway), displaying a ball and chain lying in a corner and photographs from the prison era. Outside, the gardens that once produced prize-winning olive oil are now sparse, and the two cemeteries have been desecrated: many headstones were carried off as souvenir coffee tables, the corpses dug up and sold as medical specimens. The remaining stones comprise simple concrete crosses stamped with a number for the prisoners, or inscribed marble tablets for the warders and their children.

Cat-o'-Nine-Tails (Ⓣ07/3893 1240, Ⓦwww.sthelenaisland.com.au) offers **day-trips** (Mon–Fri departing 9.30am and returning 2.15pm, Sat & Sun departing 11am and returning at 4pm; $69 including lunch) and **night tours** (departs some Friday and Saturday nights; $79 includes three-course meal), the latter including a theatrical sound-and-light show on the island. Advance bookings are essential. Boats leave around 15km east of the city from the public jetty in the suburb of **Manly**, a ten-minute walk from Manly train station – from Brisbane, you can reach Manly direct from Roma Street, Central, South Brisbane and Vulture Street train stations.

Moreton Island

A 38-kilometre-long, narrow band of stabilized, partly wooded sand dunes 20km east of Brisbane, **Moreton Island**'s faultless beaches are distinctly underpopulated for much of the year – making it perfect for a day or two of surfing, fishing or camping. Most people cross to mid-point **Tangalooma Wild Dolphin Resort** on the daily **fast ferry** (departs 8am, 10am and 5pm; $56 open return) which leaves from the terminal 8km from the city at the end of Holt Street, off Kingsford Smith Drive at Pinkenba. They also offer extended day-trips from Brisbane to take in dolphin feeding (Sun–Fri; $85; returns after dark) and, from mid-June to late October, whale-watching tours ($195). A **courtesy bus** to the ferry terminal leaves daily at 9am from the Greyhound Australia coach bay on the third floor of the Roma Street Transit Centre, and returns you there afterwards (though extended day-trips return too late to catch it back and you'll need a taxi).

To take your own vehicle to the island, whose sand tracks are 4WD-only, contact the *Combie Trader* **vehicle barge** (ⓣ07/3203 6399; ⓦwww.moreton-island.com for timetables; $150 per car includes 4 passengers, foot passengers $35), which crosses from Scarborough Harbour to the tiny settlement of Bulwer on the island's north. The road rules are the same as on the mainland; check tide times before driving on the beach, and be aware that pedestrians may not hear you above the sound of the surf. Moreton Island Ferries (ⓣ07/3895 1000; ⓦwww.moretonventure.com.au for timetables; $135 per car includes two passengers, foot passengers $30) operates the new 400-passenger fast catamaran *MiCat* to Tangalooma and also offers 4WD day-tours along the beach for $103 including bush walks and sand-tobogganing. Alternatively, Sunrover Expeditions (ⓣ07/3203 4241, ⓦwww.sunrover.com.au) and Moreton Bay Escapes (ⓦwww.moretonbayescapes.com.au) run excellent **overnight camping tours** from Brisbane ($230–330 per person).

If you're planning to stay a while, note that **supplies** on the island are expensive, so you need to be self-sufficient and have enough water if you are camping. There are no banks. And before you go in the sea, remember that the beaches aren't patrolled and there are no shark nets. The worst times to visit are at Christmas and Easter, when up to a thousand vehicles crowd onto the island all at once.

The island has designated **campsites** at The Wrecks (just north of Ben-Ewa 3km towards Bulwer) and Comboyuro point (just north of Bulwer) on the west coast, and Blue Lagoon and Eagers Creek on the east side; you can also camp anywhere along beaches except where there are signs asking you not to, but you should first obtain a permit, available for $4 from barge operators or from the ranger based at Tangaloma Resort (ⓣ07/3408 2710).

Around the island

TANGALOOMA, a small settlement of wooden houses and a few shops midway along the island's west coast, is fronted by a set of wrecks, deliberately sunk to create an artificial harbour but now swamped in sand – a fine **snorkelling** site at high tide. Nearby, *Tangalooma Wild Dolphin Resort* (ⓣ07/3408 2666, ⓦwww.tangalooma.com; ❼) is a casual, upmarket affair with a range of rooms and units that incorporate parts of a former whaling station; they also organize daily dolphin feeding for wild dolphins who rock up every evening for a handout. Pleasantly shaded and busy at weekends and holidays, it's the only place on the island that has a **restaurant** and serves cold drinks – respectable dress required. There's also an QPWS campsite here (with water, showers and toilets), which gets as crowded as anywhere on the island. A three-kilometre track heads south from Tangalooma to the Desert, where the dunes are a great place to try sand-tobogganing. The resort lays on a short 4WD tour and sand-tobogganing trip for $20.

With your own vehicle, or if you don't mind hiking, take the ten-kilometre track from Tangalooma across to Moreton's more attractive eastern side; generally less crowded, the beach also has good surf. You end up at **Eagers Creek**, where there's another campsite and a five-kilometre return trip up sandy **Mount Tempest**'s 280-metre peak – an exhausting climb. Head 10km north up the beach, and you'll find **Blue Lagoon**, the largest of the island's freshwater lakes, only 500m from the beach and adjacent to the smaller, picturesque **Honeyeater Lake**. Blessed with shady trees, the dunes behind the beach make an ideal place to camp, and the site is supplied with water, showers and toilets. Dolphins come in close to shore – a practice that Moreton's Aborigines turned to their advantage by using them to chase fish into the shallows. Writing in the 1870s about his life in Brisbane, Tom Petrie reported that the Ngugi men would beat the surf with their spears, and:

By and by, as in response, porpoises would be seen as they rose to the surface making for the shore and in front of them schools of tailor fish. It may seem wonderful, but they were apparently driving the fish towards the land. When they came near, [they] would run out into the surf, and with their spears would jab down here and there at the fish, at times even getting two on one spear, so plentiful were they.

Moreton's northern end is about 9km wide, covered in ferns, grasstrees, paperbark and banksias around the shore, and dense scrub inland. The landing point here is **BULWER**, a cluster of weatherboard "weekenders" and a store stocking fuel and beer and providing basic **accommodation** in six-person units (ⓣ07/3203 6399; ❺). The beach is the only "road" south to Tangalooma, while vehicle tracks cut across to Honeyeater Lake and to the island's northeastern corner, **North Point**, where adjacent dunes form near-vertical cliffs, and fresh water, brown with tannin, seeps out into lagoons. Around from North Point, rocky Cape Moreton is capped by a red-and-white **lighthouse**, built between 1857 and 1928 and still operating. There's a museum in the house below and fine views down the east coast from adjacent cliffs.

The **south** of the island mostly consists of exposed dunes, some covered in scrub and others forming white "blows", which are destabilized, shifting hills that slowly roll over forests. Right at Moreton's southern tip, **KOORINGAL** is a sleepy version of Bulwer and has a **store** offering fuel, supplies and drinks from their bar (daily 8am–midnight), as well as **holiday units** that sleep up to ten (ⓣ07/3217 9965, ⓔmoretonbeach@optusnet.com.au; ❹–❺). From Kooringal, diversions include the twelve-kilometre return trip to **Big and Little Sandhills** via Toompani beach and eerie, long-dead stands of trees in the wake of the dunes. Take plenty of water.

North Stradbroke Island

North Stradbroke Island is, at 40km long, the largest and most established of the bay's islands, with sealed roads and the fully serviced townships of Dunwich, Amity and Point Lookout. Ninety percent of "Straddie" is given over to mining **rutile** (titanium dioxide), and the majority of the 3200 residents are employees of Consolidated Rutile Ltd. The mine sites south of Amity, and in the central west and south, are far from exhausted but their future is precarious, thanks to an oversupply on the world market. Other industries focus on timber, a by-product of preparing land for mining, and, increasingly, tourism.

Transport to the island leaves from Toondah Harbour at Cleveland, with Stradbroke Ferries (ⓣ07/3286 2666) crossing to Dunwich thirteen times daily (return fares $13 per person by water-taxi; $92 per car by barge). You can reach Cleveland by train from Brisbane, then catch the special red and yellow National Bus for 90cents to the harbour – phone Stradbroke Ferries for details. Also, watch out for package deals from various sources, such as the free courtesy bus (not including ferry fare) from Brisbane run on Monday, Wednesday and Friday by *Stradbroke Island Guesthouse* – call them first to book.

To **get around** the island, the Dunwich–Point Lookout **bus** connects with all water-taxis and costs $9 return, and various operators offer 4WD **safaris**: Sunrover Expeditions (ⓣ1800 353 717, ⓦwww.sunrover.com.au) and

Straddie Kingfisher Tours (ⓣ07/3409 9502; ⓦwww.straddiekingfishertours .com.au) both come recommended. Some roads on Stradbroke are open to mining vehicles only, so drivers should look out for the signs. Off-roading through the centre on non-designated roads is ill-advised: quite apart from the damage caused to the dune systems, the sand is very soft and having your vehicle pulled out will be very expensive. To drive on the beach, which requires 4WD, a permit must first be obtained from Stradbroke Island Tourism (ⓣ07/3409 9555) on Junner St in Dulwich or from Redlands Tourism, 152 Shore St, West Cleveland and costs from $10.60 for 48 hours.

Dunwich to Main Beach

Unless you need to fuel up or visit the bank, there's little to keep you at **DUNWICH**, Straddie's ferry port. Two sealed roads head out of town, east through the island's centre towards **Main Beach**, or north to Amity and Point Lookout. The road through the centre passes two **lakes**, the second and smaller of which, Blue Lake, is a national park and source of fresh water for the island's wildlife, which is most visible early in the morning. Beyond Blue Lake you have to cross the **Eighteen Mile Swamp** to reach Main Beach and, though there's a causeway, the rest of the route is for 4WDs only. You can **camp** behind the beach anywhere south of the causeway (north of it is mining company land), but be prepared for the mosquitoes that swarm around the mangroves; the southernmost point, looking over to South Stradbroke Island (see p.451), is an angling and wildlife mecca, with birdlife and kangaroos lounging around on the beaches.

The Top End

Heading north from Dunwich, it's 10km to where the road forks left to Amity and right to Point Lookout: **AMITY** is a sleepy place built around a jetty, while **POINT LOOKOUT** is where most visitors end up if they don't want to camp. Nineteen kilometres from Dunwich, Point Lookout spreads out around Stradbroke's single rock headland, overlooking a string of beaches. Stretched out along the road are a pub, takeaway pizza place, a store, some cafés and various types of **accommodation**. Top of the range are *Amity Bungalows* (ⓣ07/3409 7017; ⓦwww.amitybungalows.com.au; ❻), with thatch bungalows on a wooded property fronting the ocean, and *Samarinda* (ⓣ07/3409 8785; ⓦwww.samarinda.com.au; ❺), with motel rooms and two-bedroom units. At the other end of the scale, *Stradbroke Island Guesthouse* (ⓣ07/3409 8888, ⓦwww.stradbrokeislandscuba.com.au; dorms $25, rooms ❷) has dorm beds, plus surfboards, bikes and fishing gear for hire; they also organize scuba diving, 4WD, walking and trail-riding trips. *Stradbroke Tourist Park* (ⓣ07/3409 8127; ⓔladbroke@ecn.net.au; four- to six-person cabins ❸) is the best of the local **caravan parks**, or you can camp on the foreshore west of Rocky Point's beach access road, at the northwest corner of the island.

The **beaches** here are picturesque, with shallow protected swimming along the shore. **Flinders** runs west of Amity; **Home** and **Cylinder** between here and Cylinder Headland are both patrolled and, therefore, crowded during holiday weekends. If you don't mind swimming in unwatched waters, head for **Deadman's Beach** or **Frenchman's Bay**. On the headland above, there are fine views and the chance to see loggerhead turtles and dolphins; from the walking track around North Gorge down to Main Beach you might see whales – if you have binoculars. Stradbroke's **diving** – organized through *Stradbroke Island Guesthouse* – is renowned for congregations of the increasingly rare grey nurse shark, along with moray eels, dopey leopard sharks, and summertime manta rays.

The Gold Coast

Beneath a jagged skyline shaped by countless high-rise beachfront apartments, the **Gold Coast** is Australia's Miami Beach or Costa del Sol, a striking contrast to Brisbane, only an hour away to the north. Aggressively superficial, it's not the place to go if you're seeking peace and quiet: the endless succession of nightclubs, bars and theme parks provides raucous, relentless entertainment. It can be enjoyable for a couple of days – perhaps as a weekend break from Brisbane – but there's little variation on the beach and nightclub scene and if you're concerned that this will leave you jaded, bored or broke you would be better off avoiding this corner of the state altogether.

The coast forms a virtually unbroken beach 40km long, from **South Stradbroke Island** past **Surfers Paradise** and **Burleigh Heads** to the New South Wales border at **Coolangatta**. Surfers Paradise has the highest concentration of people and skyscrapers; as you head south through the strip of motels and shops the pace slows (relatively) and it's easier to find some unoccupied sand. The beaches are still touted as the main attraction, though they've become a backdrop to more commercial interests, and they swarm with bathers and board-riders all year round. **Surfing** blossomed here in the 1930s and still pulls in veterans and novices; Coolangatta, Burleigh Heads and South Stradbroke have the best waves and definitely the more serious surfies, but you'll find rideable swell all the way along the coast.

With around three hundred days of sunshine each year there's little "off-season" as such. **Rain** can, however, fall at any time during the year, including midwinter – when it's usually dry in the rest of the state – but even if the crowds do thin out a little, they reappear in time for the Gold Coast **Indy car race** in October, and then continue to swell, peaking over Christmas and New Year. The end of the school year in mid-November also brings on the phenomenon of **Schoolies Week**, when thousands of high-school leavers ditch exam rooms and flock to Surfers for a few days of hard partying, causing a budget accommodation crisis.

Getting there and around

From Brisbane, local **buses** from Roma Street Transit Centre to the Gold Coast include Kirkland's (☎1300 367 077), which runs about eight times daily to Southport, Surfers, Burleigh Heads, and Coolangatta; and Coachtrans (☎13 12 30), which runs three services daily – both cost around $35. Coachtrans also organizes Brisbane Airport transfers direct to accommodation as well as theme park transfers (☎07/3238 4700) from central Brisbane accommodation to Carrumbin Sanctuary, Dreamworld, Movie World, Wet 'n' Wild and Sea World. The **Citytrain** connects Brisbane Airport and City with Nerrang Station twice hourly for $18.50 with Surfside bus connections into Surfers Paradise.

Coming up **from New South Wales**, the coastal highway enters Queensland at Coolangatta, where you'll also find the **Gold Coast airport**. Gold Coast Tourist Shuttle (☎07/5574 5111) runs buses to all points between the airport and Surfers Paradise for $15 one-way. **Getting around**, the Gold Coast Highway from Tweed Heads and Coolangatta to Surfers Paradise, and all the theme parks, are covered by a **24-hour bus service** run by Surfside Buses, with up to seven services an hour between Surfers and Coolangatta. Their **passes** give unlimited travel for between one and fourteen days ($10–60). Otherwise you'll need to take a taxi or rent a vehicle; there are more details in accounts of the individual resorts.

Surfers Paradise

Spiritually, if not geographically, **SURFERS PARADISE** is at the heart of the Gold Coast, the place where its aims and aspirations are most evident. For the residents, this involves making money by providing services and entertainment for tourists; visitors reciprocate by parting with their cash. All around and irrespective of what you're doing – shopping for clothes, sitting on the beach, partying in one of the frenetic nightclubs or even finding a bed – the pace is brash and glib. Don't come here expecting to be allowed to relax; subtlety is non-existent and you'll find that enjoying Surfers depends largely on how much it bothers you having the party mood rammed down your throat.

Surfers' beaches have been attracting tourists for over a century, though the town only started developing along commercial lines during the 1950s when the first multistoreyed beachfront apartments were built. The demand for views over the ocean led to ever-higher towers which began to encroach on the dunes (not to mention shading them from mid-afternoon); together with the sheer volume of people attracted here, this soon caused serious **erosion** problems along the entire coast. Attempts to stabilize the foreshore with retaining walls, groynes and sand-pumping from offshore have had little long-term success. But none of this really matters. Though Surfers Paradise is a firm tribute to the successful marketing of the ideal Aussie lifestyle as an eternal beach party, most people no longer come here for the beaches but simply because everyone else does.

Arrival, information and security

Surfers' **bus station** (6am–10pm) is on Beach Road on the corner of the highway, one street down from Cavill Avenue. Here you'll find **luggage lockers**, **bus company desks** and an **accommodation information** counter. If the hostel you want isn't listed, call them for a free pick-up, and don't be surprised if, while walking around with your luggage, hostel minibuses stop for

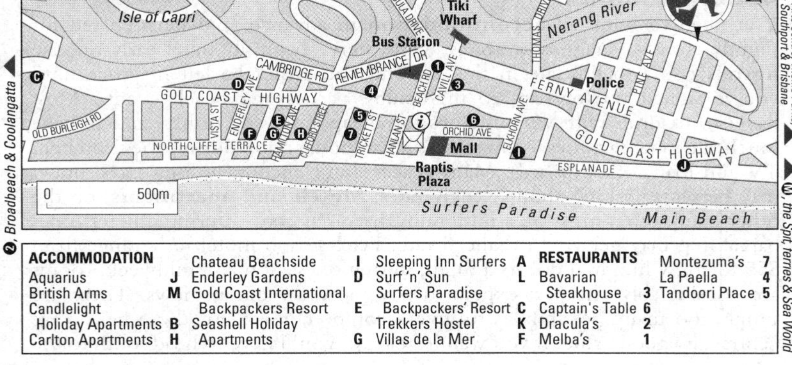

Surfing the Gold Coast

As locals will tell you, the Gold Coast has some of the **best surfing** beaches in the world. And in terms of consistency this might be true – on any given day there will be rideable surf somewhere along the coast – with 200-metre-long sand-bottom point breaks and rideable waves peaking at about four metres in prime conditions.

The area is known for its **barrels**, particularly during the summer cyclone season when the winds shift around to the north; in winter the swell is smaller but more reliable, making it easier to learn to surf. A rule of thumb for finding the best surf is to follow the wind: north when the wind blows from the north, south when it comes from the south. Generally, you'll find the best swell along the southern beaches, and on South Stradbroke Island. Sea **temperatures** range between 26°C in December and 17°C in June, so a 2–3mm wetsuit is adequate. Hard-core surfies come for Christmas and the cyclone season, though spring is really the busiest time. On the subject of **general safety**, all beaches as far north as Surfers are patrolled – look for the signs – and while sharks might worry you, more commonplace hostility is likely to come from the local surfies who form tight-knit cliques with very protective attitudes towards their patches.

For expert **tuition**, tours, or advice anywhere on the Gold Coast, contact locally based Surfaris (ⓣ1800 634 951, ⓦwww.surfaris.com) or Gold Coast Surfing Schools (ⓣ1800 787 337, ⓦwww.australiansurfer.com) – beginners pay around $45 for a two-hour session. **Competitions** or events are held somewhere along the coast on most weekends, advertised through local surf shops. To try your hand at **kitesurfing**, another popular Gold Coast pastime, contact Pureaqua (ⓣ07/5571 1622, ⓦwww.pureaqua.com) on the Broadwater at Stockport - beginners pay $185 for a three hour intro package.

you as they pass. The **tourist information office** is an open-air booth on Cavill Avenue (Mon–Fri 8.30am–5.30pm, Sat 8.30am–5pm, Sun 9am–4pm; ⓣ07/5538 4419).

Security is worth bearing in mind. Many people migrate to Surfers in search of an easier life, only to find themselves homeless and hard up. Others come to prey deliberately on tourists, especially around Christmas and Easter, or on teenagers during Schoolies Week in November. Don't leave vehicles unlocked at any time, don't take valuables onto the beach, and don't wander alone at night; muggings are common, especially around nightclubs – so take advantage of the courtesy buses run by hostels.

Accommodation

You need to book all **accommodation** in advance, and be prepared for slightly above-average room rates everywhere. Typically quiet early on, the **hostels** come to life late in the day and you won't be left in peace until you've signed up for trips to nightclubs, parties and beach events. Most have struck deals with various clubs for cheap entry and drinks, and all have much the same facilities – Internet at $5 an hour, pool, dormitories, kitchen, TV and loans of surfboards. Many places don't encourage long stays, but it may be worth asking about weekly rates. **Motels and apartments**, on the other hand, often insist on a minimum three-day stay – during quieter times bargaining may get you a reduced rate. Peak-season motel rates range from $55 to a few hundred dollars a night; during off-season and midweek, rooms are considerably cheaper; expect to pay more for ocean views. There are simply too many possibilities to give a comprehensive list; those below are central and good value. If you want to **camp**, you'll have to head south to the quieter sections of the Gold Coast – though all campsites get booked solid through the Christmas break.

Motels and apartments

Candlelight Holiday Apartments 22–24 Leonard Ave ⓣ07/5538 1277, ⓦwww.candlelightholidayapartments.com.au. Very pleasant, self-contained one-bedroom units in a quiet street close to the bus station with very helpful and friendly owners. Minimum three-night stay. ❺

Carlton Apartments Cnr Northcliffe Terrace and Clifford St ⓣ07/5538 5877, ⓦwww.carltonapartments.com.au. Self-contained double units in a seven-storey building on the beach. ❺

Chateau Beachside Cnr Esplanade and Elkhorn Ave ⓣ07/5538 1022, ⓦwww.chateaubeachside.com.au. Right in the heart of Surfers and overlooking the beach, this modern tower block is a great mid-range deal – rooms are a good size, and suites come with cooking facilities. ❻

Enderley Gardens 38 Enderley Ave ⓣ07/5570 1511, ⓦwww.enderleygardens.com.au. Self-contained units, one block away from the beach, ten minutes from the heart of Surfers. Facilities include pool, spa and tennis court. ❻

Seashell Holiday Apartments 12 Hamilton Ave ⓣ07/5539 0695. Spacious one- and two-bed self-contained apartments with 80s style decor. Friendly owners and ample parking help make this unbeatable value so close to the beach. ❹

Sleeping Inn Surfers 26 Peninsula Drive ⓣ1800 817 832, ⓦwww.sleepinginn.com.au. Close to the bus station, these nicely furnished self-contained units, all with TV, provide quality budget accommodation. Dorms $22, rooms ❸

Villas de la Mer Cnr Markwell Ave and Northcliffe Terrace ⓣ07/5592 6644, ⓦwww.villasdelamer.com.au. Attractive two- and three-bedroom apartments in a three-storey security complex, with ocean views from the upper levels. Simple but modern and well furnished. ❼

Hostels

Aquarius 44 Queen St, Southport ⓣ1800 229 955, ⓦwww.aquariusbackpackers.com.au. This hostel offers a tiny TV lounge on each floor, pool and communal kitchen, plus courtesy bus to/from Surfers. Small four- and six-bed dorms. Dorms $23, rooms ❸

British Arms 70 Sea World Drive ⓣ07/5571 1776 or 1800 680 269, ⓦwww.britisharms.com.au. A YHA property, close to Sea World about 5km north of the centre. Good facilities, plus a lively English bar and grill serving up pub fare, occasional entertainment and a range of beers till late. Dorms $27, rooms ❸

Gold Coast International Backpackers Resort 28 Hamilton Ave ⓣ1800 801 230, ⓦwww.goldcoastbackpackers.com.au. Secure, purpose-built hostel, with safe car park. Facilities include a small kitchen and a bar, but there's no pool and the place feels a bit sterile. Four-bed dorms $25, tiny doubles ❸

Surf 'n' Sun 3323 Gold Coast Highway ⓣ07/5592 2363 or 1800 678 194. Noisy, party hostel with cramped rooms and ordinary facilities, but it's close to the beach and centre. Five-bed dorms $20, twins ❷

Surfers Paradise Backpackers' Resort 2837 Gold Coast Highway ⓣ1800 282 800, ⓦwww.surfersparadisebackpackers.com.au. Purpose-built, sparklingly clean and efficient, with spacious rooms; the price per bed covers everything, including use of washing machines. Dorms $23, rooms ❷

Trekkers Hostel 22 White St, Southport ⓣ1800 100 004, ⓦwww.trekkersbackpackers.com.au. Beautifully restored, comfortable old house 3km from the centre with heaps of deals and trips. Staff are particularly friendly and welcoming, and their twice-weekly BBQ is cheap and good fun. Price includes a basic breakfast, with $6.60 meals at the nearby Royal Life Savers club. They have a courtesy bus, or you can catch local transport to the hostel. Dorms $23–26.

The City

Downtown Surfers Paradise is a thin ribbon of partially reclaimed land between the ocean and the **Nerang River** which – as the Broadwater – flows north, parallel with the beach, past the **Spit** and South Stradbroke Island into the choked channels at the bottom end of Moreton Bay. Reclaimed land in the river forms islands whose names reflect the fantasies of their founders – Isle of Capri, Sorrento, Miami Keys – and which have become much-sought-after real estate.

From its dingiest club to its best restaurant, Surfers exudes entertainment, and at times – most notoriously at New Year and Christmas – you can spend 24 hours a day out on the town. Another thing you'll spend is money; the only free venue is the beach and with such a variety of distractions it can be financial suicide venturing out too early in the day. The city is full of tourists staggering around at noon, with terrible hangovers and empty wallets, complaining how expensive their holiday has become. The area around **Cavill Avenue** is a bustle of activity from early morning – when the first surfers head down to the beach and the shops open – to after midnight, when there's a constant exchange of bodies between **Orchid Avenue**'s bars and nightclubs. If you spend any length of time in town, you'll get to know the district intimately. The block between the sea and Orchid Avenue is a **mall**, given over to snack bars, coffee houses and shopping arcades; you can pick up a cheap T-shirt or play a game of chess at one of the outdoor tables. **Raptis Plaza** here is a collection of upmarket fast-food joints overlooked by a replica of Michelangelo's *David*. The Gold Coast's latest attraction is **Spacewalker** (daily 10am–10pm; $29.90, ⓦwww.spacewalker.com.au), on Elkhorn Ave, which takes you on a journey through the Milky Way and a Black Hole amongst other galactic experiences.

Surfers' tower-block cityscape makes an immediate impression, but the stakes in who can build highest and so block their neighbours' view of the beach have just been upped considerably: on the highway near the corner of Hamilton Avenue, the 80-storey-high stylish Q1 building is currently under construction and, when opened in October 2005, will be the **world's tallest residential building**.

Across the Esplanade, the **beach** is all you could want as a place to recover from your night out. In early afternoon, the sun moves behind the apartment buildings, but you can escape the shadows by moving up to **Main Beach**. If you're feeling energetic, seek out a game of volleyball or head for the surf: the swell here is good in a northerly wind, but most of the time it's better for boogie-boards.

The theme parks

North of Main Beach, the Spit's attractions include the world's first "Versace hotel" – a six-star edifice fitted out with all things Versace – and **Sea World** (daily 10am–5pm; $58, ⓦwww.seaworld.com.au; access on the Surfside Bus from the highway), the longest running of the Gold Coast's theme parks. Besides various stomach-churning rides, the park features immaculately trained dolphins and killer whales, and helps rehabilitate stranded wild dolphins for later release.

The other theme parks are north out of town, all located on Surfside and Gold Coast Shuttle bus routes. **Dreamworld** (daily 10am–5pm; $58, ⓦwww.dreamworld.com.au), on the Pacific Highway at Coomera, 17km north of Surfers Paradise, has a violent double-loop roller-coaster and a fairground atmosphere, as well as a collection of hand-reared tigers in a large enclosure. **Movie World** (daily 10am–5pm; $58, ⓦwww.movieworld.com.au), also on the Pacific Highway, 14km north of Surfers, is a slice of Hollywood featuring studio tours, and Western and stunt shows. Near Movie World, **Wet 'n' Wild** (daily 10am–4.30pm or later; $36; ⓦwww.wetnwild.com.au) has a series of pools linked by vicious water slides – the back-breaking "twister" and the 25-metre-tall, high-speed slide alone are worth the entrance fee.

Eating

Surfers has somewhere to eat wherever you look, though most places are pretty forgettable. Some resorts offer bargain all-you-can-eat **breakfasts**, while during the rest of the day there's always something to eat at the **cafés** and snack bars along Cavill Avenue and the Esplanade. **Restaurants** range from fast-food to Asian and modern Australian; some places offer discounts on evening meals if you get in before a certain hour. More and more people are heading to convenient takeaway and burger joints out of Surfers to eat – south to the area around Broadbeach Mall, or north to Broadwater or Tedder Avenue, in Southport, where there's usually a Porsche or two parked along the trendy café strip. For **supplies**, there's a supermarket downstairs in the Centro Centre (on Cavill Avenue mall) and a 24-hour Night Owl store on the highway near Trickett Street.

Bavarian Steakhouse Cnr Gold Coast Highway and Cavill Ave ☎07/5531 7150. Wood-panelled theme restaurant on several floors, where you can wolf down steins of beer and plates of beef while staff dressed in leather and lace pump away on Bavarian brass instruments. Good fun if you're in the mood and fair value – about $22 for steak, salad and fries.

Captain's Table Upstairs 26 Orchid Avenue ☎07/5531 5766. Award-winning restaurant with excellent seafood variations. A $22 plate of delicious barbecued Moreton Bay Bugs should not be missed. Get in before 6.30pm for a discount and table with a view.

Dracula's 1 Hooker Blvd, Broadbeach ☎07/5575 1000, Ⓦwww.draculas.com.au. Well-designed and fun Gothic cabaret restaurant. Open Tues–Sat from 6pm; $59 per head ($65 on Sat); advance booking essential.

La Paella 3114 Gold Coast Highway. Tiny yet lively Spanish restaurant with excellent tapas for $15, Sangria by the bucket and sumptuous veal casserole for $20. Dinner only.

Melba's 46 Cavill Ave ☎07/5592 6922. Ambitious café-restaurant attached to the nightclub of the same name, with a mix of Mediterranean-style light meals and snacks served, unusually for Surfers, at pavement tables. Their seafood fettuccine and Moroccan duck are the chef's specialities with mains between $25–35. Opens at 7am for breakfast, closes at 5am.

Montezuma's 8 Trickett St, under the Aloha Tower ☎07/5538 4748. A cramped Mexican restaurant hung with luridly coloured, papier-mâché fiesta dolls, but serving fresh and spicy food. $20 will fill you up; open for lunch and dinner.

Tandoori Place 7–9 Trickett St ☎07/5592 1004. Fast-food ambience, but actually better than first impressions would suggest; their sweet curries are engagingly different, and they have a limited vegetarian menu. Most main dishes cost around $18.

Entertainment

Find out **what's on** through accommodation or by word of mouth; the free weekly magazines *Hello Gold Coast* and *Wot's On* are simply commercial business directories. For those desperate for an injection of culture amid all the brash goings-on, check out the programme at the **Arts Centre**, 135 Bundall Rd (☎07/5581 6900), where there's a theatre, gallery, restaurant and bar. You'll find **cinema** complexes on the corner of Clifford Street and Gold Coast Highway (☎07/5575 3355), as well as inside Pacific Fair Shopping Centre, Mermaid Beach (☎07/5575 3355), and Australia Fair Shopping Centre, Southport (☎07/5531 2200).

Realistically, though, it's Surfers' **clubs** that provide most of the nightlife. Initially, particularly if you're staying at a hostel or have picked up a **free pass** somewhere, your choice will most likely be influenced by the various deals on entry and drinks. The places listed below have a dependable reputation; none is especially chauvinistic, though places do change. Opening times are from around 6pm until 3am or later.

Cocktails and Dreams Orchid Ave. Nightly R&B, cheap drinks and extended happy hours; ladies nights on Tuesday to 11pm.

Fever 26 Orchid Ave. Best place for house and dance on the coast, with an ever-changing array of local and international DJs.

Howl at the Moon Upstairs at Centro Centre on Cavill Ave ☎07/5527 5522. Hugely popular

Gold Coast tours and cruises

Some hostels organize **tours** to the Scenic Rim, or try the following for day-trips to the **Hinterland** (Lamington, Natural Bridge, Tamborine Mountain and Binna Burra), **Sunshine Coast** (Noosa, The Big Pineapple or Mooloolaba) and **Brisbane**. Most offer free pick-ups. Bushwacker Ecotours (ⓣ07/5520 7238, ⓦwww.bushwacker-ecotours.com.au), highly recommended, day and night wildlife-spotting tours to Hinterland national parks; Coachliner (ⓣ07/5534 9977); Mountain Coach Company (ⓣ07/5524 4249); Pacific Tours (ⓣ07/5596 0350); Scenic Hinterland Tours (ⓣ07/5531 5536). Southern Cross (ⓣ1800 067 367, ⓦwww.sc4wd.com.au) runs 4WD day-tours around the Hinterland.

The following explore the **Nerang River** and **seafront** on one-hour to half-day cruises. Adventure Duck (ⓣ07/5557 8869, ⓦwww.adventureduck.com), a unique amphibious bus, departs eight times daily from Orchid Avenue for an hour-long trip ($45); Gold Coast Cruises (ⓣ07/5557 8888, ⓦwww.shangrila.com.au); Tall Ship (ⓣ07/5532 2444, ⓦwww.tallship.com.au), from two-hour calm-water cruises for $31.90 to day-trips to South Stradbroke at $99. See p.451 for more on trips to South Stradbroke Island.

restaurant, bar and nightclub with two live pianists performing their own sing-along renditions of popular hits. Open 8pm–2am, bookings advisable.
Meeting Place 26 Orchid Ave. Gold Coast's sole gay nightclub – though anyone is welcome – in the same building as *Embassy*.
Melba's 46 Cavill Ave. Big and relatively upmarket nightclub, with nightly happy hour until 10pm.
The Party At *The Mark*, Orchid Ave. Live rock bands on Friday and Sunday (with a $5 cover charge); DJs for the rest of the week.
Rose and Crown Raptis Plaza, Cavill Ave. Surfers' "local" pub; entertainment varies from decent local bands to DJs and strip shows (male and female).
Shooters Orchard Ave beside *Cocktails and Dreams*. Crowds heading for more serious dance spots start out here for a game of pool and a few drinks.
The Shack Orchid Ave. Popular pool sessions and live bands every Thursday.
Surfers Beergarden Cavill Ave, opposite Orchid Ave. Live music with local and interstate band talent on Thursday and Saturday nights.
Troccadero 7–9 Trickett St ⓣ07/5570 2100. Surfers' live-music mainstay, often attracting major Australian touring bands. There's also a packed and sweaty nightclub here between Thursday and Saturday nights with a cover charge of $6.

Listings

Banks and exchange Banks and ATMs are located right throughout Surfers, with most main branches around the Cavill Ave-Highway intersection. There are also several bureaux de change in Cavill and Orchid avenues, giving pretty much the same rates as the banks.
Buses Coachtrans to Brisbane (ⓣ13 12 30); Kirkland's to Brisbane, Byron Bay and Lismore (ⓣ1300 367 077); Greyhound Australia (ⓣ13 20 30); Premier (ⓣ13 34 10).
Car rental Competition keeps prices low, but advertised prices are often for long rentals, and exclude insurance and mileage charges: CY Rent a Car (ⓣ07/5570 3777), from $29 a day; East Coast Car Rentals (ⓣ07/5592 0444 or 1800 028 881), from $27 a day; Kanga Car and Moped (ⓣ07/5527 6044), old model cars from $19 a day; Red Back Rentals, inside the bus station, Beach Rd (ⓣ07/5592 1655), from $30 a day; Red Rocket (ⓣ07/5538 9074 or 1800 673 682), old model cars from $15 a day.
Hospitals and medical centres Gold Coast Hospital, Nerang St, Southport ⓣ07/5571 8211; Gold Coast Medical Centre, Centro Centre, on Cavill Avenue ⓣ07/5538 8099.
Internet There are many Internet cafés around the bus station on Beach Road and Gold Coast Highway charging upwards of $3.50 an hour.
Pharmacy Piaza Shopping Plaza, cnr Elkhorn Ave and Gold Coast Highway (7am–midnight).
Post office The main post office is in the Centro Centre on Cavill Avenue.
Surf rental Surfworld, Centro Centre, on Cavill Avenue ⓣ07/5538 4825. Typical prices are $25 a day for board rental, plus credit card deposit. For tuition see the box on p.446.
Taxis ⓣ13 10 08.

South Stradbroke Island

South Stradbroke Island is a twenty-kilometre-long, narrow strip of sand, separated from North Stradbroke Island by the 1896 cyclone and, as apartment buildings edge closer, doomed to become an extension of the Gold Coast. For now, though, South Stradbroke's relatively isolated and quiet beaches offer something of an escape from the mainland, though most day-trippers come over simply to get plastered in the bar at *South Stradbroke Island Resort* (Ⓣ07/5577 3311, Ⓦwww.ssir.com.au; rooms ❺, cabins ❻). Alternative accommodation is available at the new *Couran Cove Resort* (Ⓣ07/5597 9000, Ⓦwww.couran.com; cabins and rooms ❼), which offers a much more exclusive atmosphere, and doesn't welcome day-guests. There's also fine **surf** to enjoy along the southeast shore (though local surfies are notoriously protective), along with **fishing** in the Jumpinpin Channel between here and North Stradbroke.

Day-cruises via Sanctuary Cove to South Stradbroke Island Resort depart 9.30am from Marina Mirage on Sea World Drive and cost $75 including lunch, with evening booze cruises about $65; operators include Island Queen (Ⓣ07/5557 8800, Ⓦwww.islandqueen.com.au) and Shangri-La (Ⓣ07/5557 8888, Ⓦwww.shangrila.com.au). A cheaper alternative is the *South Stradbroke Island Resort* **ferry** ($49, includes lunch at the resort) which departs daily 10.30am from Runaway Bay Marina, 5km north of Surfers on Bayview Street, and returns between 2.30pm and 5pm depending on the day – bookings are essential.

Surfers Paradise to Currumbin

The central section of the Gold Coast lacks any real focus. Haphazardly developed and visually unattractive, it exists very much in the shadow of Surfers Paradise, but can't match its intensity. The highway is just a continuous maze of crowded, multi-lane traffic systems and drab buildings which lose momentum the further south you drive, but once you leave the road there are fine beaches, two **wildlife sanctuaries** and – unbelievable amid all the commotion and noise – a tiny **national park**, which preserves the coast's original environment.

Burleigh Heads National Park and around

Around 7km south of Surfers, **Burleigh Heads** consists of a traffic bottleneck where the highway dodges between the beach and a rounded headland; there can be very good surf here but the rocks make it rough for novices. Fifty years ago, before the bitumen and paving took over, this was all dense eucalypt and vine forest, the last fragment of which survives as **Burleigh Head National Park**. Entrance is on foot from the car park on the Esplanade, or turn sharply at the lights below the hill just south of the headland for the **visitors information centre** (daily 9am–4pm; Ⓣ07/5535 3032).

Geologically, Burleigh Heads stems from the prehistoric eruptions of the Mount Warning volcano (p.457), 30km to the southwest. Lava surfaced through vents, cooling to tall hexagonal basalt columns, now mostly tumbled and covered in vines. Rainforest colonized the richer volcanic soils, while stands of red gum grew in weaker sandy loam; along the eastern seafront there's a patch of exposed heathland bordered by groups of pandanus, and a beach along the mouth of Tallebudgera Creek. This diversity is amazing considering the minimal space, but urban encroachment has seriously affected the wildlife. **Butterflies** and **birds** are the most obvious inhabitants – on the heathland look out for the fairy wren's telltale black and red plumage – but the gums also support a small **koala** population (though, notoriously sensitive to disturbance, they often make themselves scarce). The area's natural resources once attracted Yugumbir

Aborigines, indicated by a few mounds of half-buried shells up on the headland, whose history is brought to life on a "Kaila" tour – book through the park visitors centre, or phone ⓣ07/5528 9744.

Less than 2km inland, the **David Fleay Wildlife Park**, West Burleigh Rd (daily 9am–5pm; $13; ⓣ07/5576 2411; take the Surfside Bus) is an informal park with boardwalks through forest pens and plenty of rangers at hand to answer your questions. The late David Fleay was the first person to persuade **platypus** to breed in captivity and the park has a special section devoted to this curious animal, along with crocodiles, koalas, plenty of birds and smaller animals. The free guided tours at 10am and 12.30pm are worthwhile; take advantage of their night spotlight organized through Aries Tours (ⓣ07/5594 9933) and, on Tuesday and Wednesday, their Aboriginal talk (call ahead for latest times).

Currumbin Beach and Sanctuary

A further 6km past Burleigh Heads, **CURRUMBIN BEACH** is a nice, relatively undeveloped stretch of coast between Elephant Rock and Currumbin Point, and with a breeze there are usually some decent rollers to ride. Just to the north, **PALM BEACH** is more sheltered. *Vikings*, in the surf-club building below Elephant Rock, serves Chinese food, or you can fill up on regular pub fare at the *Palm Beach Surf Club* along the beachfront.

Currumbin Sanctuary, on Tomewin Street (daily 8am–5pm; $23; night tours by arrangement ⓣ07/5534 1266, ⓦwww.currumbin-sanctuary.org.au), was started in 1946 by Alex Griffiths, who foresaw the decline of the coastal environment and developed the seventy-acre park as a wildlife refuge. Forest, lake and grassland fairly bustle with native fauna. There are the usual feeding times and tame kangaroos but the park's strongest point is the beautiful natural surroundings, best experienced from the elevated walkways through the forest, where you'll see koalas, tree kangaroos and birds at eye-level.

Coolangatta

On the Queensland-New South Wales border 10km south of Currumbin, **COOLANGATTA** merges seamlessly with Tweed Heads (in New South Wales; see p.332) along Boundary Road. With only a giant concrete plinth just off the main road marking the border, you'll probably make the crossing between states without realizing it. Unless it's New Year, when everyone takes advantage of the one-hour time difference between the states to celebrate twice, most travellers bypass Coolangatta completely; in doing so, they miss some of the best surf, least crowded beaches and the only place along the Gold Coast which can boast a real "local" community.

Coolangatta is set out one block back from the beach along **Griffith Street**, where you'll find banks, shops and little in the way of high-density development. Even the motel towers on Point Danger are well spaced, and the general ambience is that of a very small seaside town. Marine Parade fronts the shore, the view north over sand and sea ending with the jagged teeth of the skyscrapers on the horizon at Surfers Paradise.

Straddling the border at Point Danger, the **Captain Cook Memorial Lighthouse** forms a shrine where pillars enclose a large bronze globe detailing Cook's peregrinations around the southern hemisphere (see also p.1177). Twenty-five metres below, surfers in their colourful wet suits make the most of Flagstaff Beach's swell – at weekends this area is very crowded.

Coolangatta's daytime action is in the **surf**, the best being between Point Danger and Kirra Point (the latter nominated by world surfing champion

Kelly Slater as his favourite break), or at Flagstaff, across the state border in Tweed Heads – exactly where depends on the wind. **Greenmount**, effectively Coolangatta's town beach, is fairly reliable and is a good beach for beginners; Snapper Rocks and Point Danger further down the peninsula are for the more dedicated. For sun worshippers, **Coolangatta beach**, just north of Greenmount, is fine if you're staying nearby, but the six-kilometre stretch of sand further up, beyond Kirra Point, is wider and less crowded. **Surfing supplies and rentals** are available from Pipedream, Griffith Street (Ⓣ07/5599 1164), the best place for gear and information about local conditions and competitions, and from Mount Woodgee, 122 Griffith St (Ⓣ07/5536 5937). Surfboard and ski rental is around $20 a day plus credit-card deposit. All shops have decent secondhand boards for sale, though local boards tend to be too thin and lightweight to use elsewhere. You might also find a bargain in one of the pawnbroker's shops on Griffith Street. For **tuition**, see the box on p.446.

Practicalities

Griffith Street (the Gold Coast Highway) and the parallel, seafront **Marine Parade** run south for about a kilometre from the edge of town to the border, with a handful of short streets connecting them. At the border, Griffith Street kinks sharply inland as it enters Tweed Heads, while Boundary Street continues south (uphill) to Point Danger.

The **long-distance bus stop** is actually 150m over the border in Tweed Heads, just off the highway at Golden Gateway Travel, 29 Bay St (Mon–Sat 7.30am–5.30pm, New South Wales time; Ⓣ07/5536 1700) – there's no station as such, and if Golden Gateway is closed, you just get set down on the pavement. The **Gold Coast airport** (flight information on Ⓣ13 13 00) is 3km north of Coolangatta, and a taxi into Coolangatta costs around $8. Alternatively, the Airport Transit shuttle buses run to Coolangatta and all points to Surfers Paradise for $11 one-way and $16.50 return. Coolangatta's helpful **information centre** (Mon–Sat 8am–5pm, Sun 8am–2pm; Ⓣ07/5536 7765, Ⓦwww.goldcoasttourism.com.au) is on the corner of Warner and Griffith streets, about halfway down Griffith towards the border. **Taxis** can be booked on Ⓣ13 10 08 while **car rental** is available through Thrifty (Ⓣ07/5536 6955), at the Gold Coast airport, with prices starting at $35 a day.

Accommodation

Accommodation is strung out along the highway at Bilinga and Kirra, while the more expensive places are in the apartment buildings overlooking the sea on Marine Parade and Point Danger. For **camping**, try *Kirra Tourist Park*, Charlotte Street, Kirra (Ⓣ07/5581 7744).

Kirra Beach Hotel Across from the beach at Kirra Point Ⓣ07/5599 3400. Ideal location for board-riders although staff are indifferent. Some rooms are quite spacious, and all have bath, TV & fridge. Minimum 3-night stay. ❸

The Oaks 97 Griffith St Ⓣ1800 062 189, Ⓦwww.theoaksrhm.com.au. Modern and expensive resort hotel, with suites and two-bedroom penthouse apartments, right across from Greenmount Beach. ❼

On the Beach 118 Marine Parade, Greenmount Beach Ⓣ07/5536 3624. Single or double rooms and singles in self-contained apartments which are tidy and well placed for the town and the beach. ❹

Sunset Strip Budget Resort 199 Boundary St Ⓣ07/5599 5517, Ⓦwww.sunstrip.com.au. Good facilities, including family rooms and singles, huge kitchen and living areas (with three TVs), 20m pool and sun deck; no dorms. ❸–❹

YHA 3km up the coast at 230 Coolangatta Rd/Gold Coast Highway, Bilinga, near the airport Ⓣ07/5536 7644. Helpful management and nicely located for the quieter beaches, though a bit far from Coolangatta itself. ❷

Eating, drinking and nightlife

There are plenty of snack bars along Griffith Street, while **restaurants** include *Fresh* on Musgrave St near the *Kirra Beach Hotel*, a funky café with eight different tapas dishes and excellent salads, and *Café Uno* on Marine Parade, with sea views, pavement tables and a slightly overworked "Mediterranean" menu featuring mains from $22. The Surf Lifesaving Club down near the border at Greenmount Beach has good-value burgers, salads, sandwiches and cold drinks. If you're doing your own cooking, there's a 24-hour **convenience store** at the Showcase Shopping Centre beside the *Coolangatta Hotel* (corner of Griffith and Warner streets), and bigger **supermarkets** across the border at the main shopping centre on Wharf Street, in Tweed Heads (for further information on Tweed Heads, see p.332).

Coolangatta's **nightlife** centres around the pubs – you'll have to rely on posters to find out what's on. Best are live music sessions at the *Coolangatta Sands Hotel*'s fairly relaxed bar (corner of Griffith and McLean streets) and the *Coolangatta Hotel*'s nightclub, which also has live music and pool competitions.

The Hinterland and Scenic Rim

Inland from the coast's jangling excesses, the **Scenic Rim** forms a barrier between the coastal flatlands and the pastoral Darling Downs, encompassing a series of mountainous **national parks**. Here you'll find Queensland's largest expanse of subtropical rainforest and – the main attraction – the **Lamington Plateau**, packed with powerfully beautiful scenery, animals and birds. Whether you're a day-tripper, veteran hiker or just fancy camping in the same spot for a few days, it's not to be missed. Closest to the coast, **Springbrook**'s waterfalls or the rainforest suburbia at **Tamborine Mountain** make easy day-trips and are thus the most-visited destinations, while tough tracks at the region's extremes in the **Main Range** remain the prerogative of experienced bushwalkers.

The Eastern and Central Rim

The **Tamborine Mountain-Lamington** area is covered with a network of graded, well-trodden paths, so you don't have to be particularly skilled at bushwalking to enjoy the experience. Come prepared, though – tackling the longer or steeper routes requires some degree of fitness; test your endurance on shorter walks first. Paths are often well marked but sometimes narrow and slippery with little fencing along cliffs and waterfalls, so footwear should have a good grip and, ideally, be waterproof. **Rain** is a year-round possibility; the most comfortable weather conditions occur between June and November, though everything looks its best in the middle of the wet season with waterfalls in full flood and the greenery shockingly intense. If you do visit during the Wet (Jan–March), you'll have to endure rain, deep and fast-flowing rivers, occasionally closed paths and an unwelcome abundance of **leeches**.

Accommodation is largely limited to resorts and campsites, so if you're on a tight budget you'll need a tent. Nights in winter (July–Sept) are always cool enough to warrant a sleeping bag and pullover, though after-dark temperatures can drop even in midsummer. **Campsites** have water and stores nearby, but you'll save money by bringing your own supplies. A fuel stove is a good idea – collecting firewood in national parks is forbidden, although there are often barbecues with wood supplied. **Access** to the area is easy enough in itself but because of local geography there are few interconnecting roads, making back-tracking unavoidable if you want to visit more than one place. If you can, get hold of a vehicle – only Lamington and Tamborine Mountain have a regular bus service – and make sure you take a good road atlas along, as signposts to the parks are few and far between. Tours visit most locations – see accounts below and also the boxes on p.437 and p.450.

Tamborine Mountain

Tamborine Mountain is a rainforested volcanic plateau, about 40km inland as the crow flies from the Gold Coast, interspersed by the upmarket, compact satellite suburbs of northerly **Eagle Heights**, adjoining **North Tamborine** and **Mount Tamborine**, about 5km south. Once the haunt of the Wangeriburra Aborigines, Tamborine Mountain's forests were targeted by the timber industry in the late nineteenth century until locals succeeded in getting the area declared Queensland's **first national park** in 1908. Today, nine parks across the plateau protect a surprisingly diverse range of native forests from development.

Most of the parks surround North Tamborine. Just east between here and Eagle Heights, walking tracks at **Joalah National Park** head downstream through woodland to a (cold) swimming hole; look for giant epiphytic ferns in the canopy along the way and the Albert lyrebird, with its fantastically shaped tail and liquid song. There's more of the same – and fine views to the northwest – immediately north of North Tamborine at **Knoll National Park** (also a good place for a picnic). To the west are **Witches Falls**, where a three-kilometre track slaloms downhill through open scrub and rainforest. It's an easy walk, but is more rewarding for the views from the mountain than for the falls themselves, which are only a trickle that disappears over a narrow ledge below the lookout. Far more impressive is **Cedar Creek Falls**, another good swimming spot off the Brisbane road, though **Palm Grove** near Eagle Heights, the pick of the Parks, has the best views through the canopy of the Gold Coast, a few small creeks, and a limpid, eerie gloom created by an extensive stand of elegant piccabean palms. Hidden 20m up in the canopy are elusive wompoo pigeons, often heard but seldom seen – despite their vivid purple-and-green plumage and onomatopoeic call. Finally, down near Mount Tamborine, there's a stand of primitive, slow-growing cycads (see box on p.527) and a relatively dry climate at **Lepidozamia National Park**.

Practicalities

Ideally, you'll have your own transport for the mountain. Coming up **from Brisbane**, you'll be travelling either via Beenleigh and Oxenford to Eagle Heights, or via the lowland settlement of Tamborine township to North Tamborine; **from Surfers Paradise**, you ascend via Nerang to Mount

Tamborine. The sole **bus service** to the mountain is with the Mountain Coach Company (ⓣ07/5524 4249), which picks up daily from points along the Gold Coast between 8 and 9am and charges $42 for a day-trip, or $25 each way if you want to go up one day and back another. Once up here, you can get around with the Mountain Shuttle Service, which runs between settlements from 10am to 5pm on Saturday and Sunday only ($10 for the day).

NORTH TAMBORINE has most of the area's services, including a general store, post office, garage, ATMs (there are **no banks** up here) and a **visitors' information centre**, which has maps of walking trails; **EAGLE HEIGHTS** has another post office and a **tourist office** (daily usually 8.30am–5pm; ⓣ07/5545 1161); while **MOUNT TAMBORINE** is mostly residential. There's abundant **accommodation** on the mountain, generally of a romantic-getaway nature, including cosy rooms at *The Polish Place*, 333 Main Western Rd, North Tamborine (ⓣ07/5545 1603, ⓦwww.polishplace.com.au; self-contained chalet ❼); *Maz's Ambience Retreat*, 25 Eagle Heights Rd, North Tamborine (ⓣ07/5545 1766, ⓦwww.mazsretreat.com; ❻) which has suites with four-poster beds, plus a pool and surrounding forest; *The Cottages*, 23 Kootenai Drive, North Tamborine (ⓣ07/5545 2574; ❻–❼); the very stylish wooden pole-frame buildings at *Pethers Rainforest Retreat* (ⓣ07/5545 4577, ⓦwww.pethers.com.au; ❼); and *Tamborine Mountain Bed and Breakfast*, Witherby Crescent, Eagle Heights (ⓣ07/5545 3595, ⓦwww.tmbb.com.au; ❺) which offers sweeping views.

Springbrook National Park

Close to the coast along the New South Wales border, **Springbrook National Park** is comprised of three separate parks – Mount Cougal, Purling Brook Falls and Natural Bridge – which feature abundant waterfalls and swimming holes. Though grouped together, access to each section is by a different road with Purling Brook Falls being the most popular of the routes. **Mount Cougal** lies at the end of a road 21km west of Currumbin. Rainforest flanks the upper reaches of Currumbin Creek, and a path follows the stream to an abandoned sawmill, past pools and pretty cascades. For higher drama and a short, moderately demanding walk, head for **Purling Brook Falls**, a thirty-kilometre drive from Burleigh Heads via Mudgeeraba. There's a **campsite** outside the forest, near the top of the falls, with a store about 4km back along the main road. The 109-metre falls are very impressive after rain has swollen the flow; a four-kilometre track zigzags down the escarpment and into the rainforest at the base of the falls before curving underneath the waterfall (expect a soaking from the spray) and going back up the other side. In the plunge pool at the foot of the falls, the force of the water is enough to push you under; swimming is more relaxed in a couple of pools downstream, picturesquely encircled by lianas and red cedar. A ten-kilometre drive beyond the falls brings you to **Best of All Lookout** and a broad vista south to Mount Warning from the very edge of the Rim. On the lookout road, *Springbrook Mountain Lodge* youth hostel (ⓣ07/5533 5366, ⓔspringbrooklodge@ion.com.au; dorms $26–34, rooms ❸) has a good fireplace for cold winter nights and a fair claim to being the first place in Australia to see the sun each day – note that you should phone ahead for $20 transfer from the Gold Coast, and bring all your own supplies.

At the dark, damp and hauntingly eerie **Natural Bridge,** a collapsed cave ceiling beneath the riverbed has created a subterranean waterfall. An exciting but very dangerous leap down the falls will take you into the cave: several people have been killed trying it, and the recommended method is simply to walk in through the mouth, 50m downstream. From the back of the cave the forest outside frames the waterfall and blue plunge pool, surreally lit from above; glow worms illuminate the ceiling at night. The park is 49km from Burleigh Heads or Southport via Nerang and about 27km from Purling Brook. For a different tour of the area, Numinbah Valley Adventure Trails is highly recommended for 3-hour horseback rides from the base near Nerang to otherwise inaccessible volcanic caves ($65, pick-up from Surfers accommodation extra; book on ⓣ07/5533 4137, ⓦwww.numinbahtrails.com).

Lamington National Park

Lamington National Park occupies the northeastern rim of a vast 1156-metre high caldera centred on Mount Warning 15km away in New South Wales. An enthralling world of rainforest-flanked rivers, open heathland and ancient eucalypt woods, Lamington's position on a **crossover zone** between subtropical and temperate climes has made it home to a staggering variety of plants, animals and birds, with isolated populations of species found nowhere else.

There are two possible bases for exploring the park: **Binna Burra** on the drier northern edge, and **Green Mountain** (better known for the well-publicised **O'Reilly's Guesthouse**) in the thick of the forest. Routes come in from Canungra to Green Mountain (37km) and from Beechmont to Binna Burra (10km) – these are narrow, twisting roads cutting through patches of forest and cleared grazing land. From the Gold Coast, turn off at Nerang – roads to both Binna Burra and Green Mountain diverge from here; from Brisbane, leave the highway at Beenleigh – you pass through Canungra to reach Beechmont this way.

Buses run from the Gold Coast or Brisbane, although groups will find it's cheaper to rent a car. Green Mountain can be reached daily from Surfers Paradise with Mountain Coach Company (ⓣ07/5524 4249, call first to arrange pick-up; $45 return) and from Brisbane's Transit Centre with Allstate Scenic Tours (ⓣ1300 30 700; $44 return; no Sat service). Binna Burra's only bus is the *Mountain Lodge*'s Gold Coast service (ⓣ1800 074 260 for details). When you buy your bus ticket, make it clear whether you want to return the same day or another day: it's also possible to walk between Binna Burra and Green Mountain (see p.458 for details), so you might want to arrange to be dropped at one end and collected at the other.

Once here, Lamington has to be explored **on foot**: most of the tracks described below are clearly signposted and **free maps** are available from local QPWS ranger stations. If you're experienced and want to head off along less-defined paths, contact the rangers first for advice.

Binna Burra

It's some time since guests had to walk the last few kilometres through the steep forest to the tiny rustic **BINNA BURRA** base with their luggage on a horse. Today, upmarket *Mountain Lodge* (ⓣ07/5533 3622, ⓦwww.binnaburralodge.com.au; on-site tents ❸, cabins ❺) has wooden cabins with log fires, along with **on-site tents** and a **campsite** with hot showers up the road. Don't leave food unattended at the campsite – it's infested with brazen scrub turkeys. Hikers can **bushcamp** between February and November; for details contact the **park ranger** (daily 8am–4pm; ⓣ07/5533 3584) at the station, 1.5km before the lodge.

Both lodge and campsite overlook the Numinbah Valley from woodland on the crown of Mount Roberts, and walking anywhere always leaves you with an uphill return journey. The lethargic can simply wander 500m between the campsite and the lodge at night with a torch to be rewarded by the sight of groups of wallabies grazing on the verges; commotion in the trees betrays the presence of brushtail possums foraging for flowers and leaves. Try the lodge's **senses trail**: blindfolded and following a rope you become aware that there's more to the forest than just a blaze of green – or the 160m-long Flying Fox ride through the canopy for a possum's perspective of the environment.

Of the longer walks, try the easy five-kilometre **Caves Circuit**, which follows the edge of the Coomera Valley past the white, wind-sculpted Talangai Caves to remains of Aboriginal camps, strands of psilotum nudum, a rootless precursor of the ferns, and a hillside of strangler figs and red cedar. Plunging into another forest below the campsite, the harder **Ballunji Falls Track** is a compromise between access and terrain, with occasional vertical drops to test sure-footedness. Features on the way include views of Egg Rock from Bellbird Lookout, at its most mysterious when shrouded in dawn mists, and a stand of majestic forty-metre-tall box brush trees. Dedicated walkers can extend the track out to **Ships Stern**, an arduous and dry 21-kilometre return (allow a minimum of 8hr) with some wonderful views off the escarpment. **Dave's Creek Circuit** is similar but about half as long, crossing bands of rainforest and sclerophyll before emerging onto heathland. Look for tiny clumps of red sundew plants along the track, which supplement their nitrogen intake by trapping insects in sticky globules of nectar.

Other longer tracks can be joined together, allowing you to spend days hiking without ever returning to base. Most popular of these is the **Border Track**; a relatively easy 21-kilometre/nine-hour (one-way) path through rainforest linking Binna Burra with Green Mountain. If you need road transport between the two, the lodge usually runs a free weekly service to *O'Reilly's* for its guests, and will often take others for a fee if there's room – departures depend on demand, so all arrangements have to be made on site.

Green Mountain

Green Mountain's forests are Lamington at its best. With so much to dazzle the senses here the initial experience is confused, but gradually the various types of plants and trees become familiar, as do the distinct layers between the rainforest floor and canopy. Random rustles and trills resolve into wallabies thumping around tree roots, scrub turkeys scratching up leaf litter and a whipbird's cracking call; it's easy to become lost in the environment's complex structure.

The road from Canungra to Green Mountain ends at *O'Reilly's Guesthouse* (Ⓣ07/5544 0644, Ⓦwww.oreillys.com.au; ❼), a splendid and comfortable place opened in 1926 – bookings are advised at weekends and during holiday periods. The guesthouse has a very limited store (with EFTPOS facilities) and a moderately priced restaurant for meals and snacks throughout the day. There's also an exposed QPWS campsite with showers; call Ⓣ13 13 04 for essential advance booking. If you can't get in here, about 7km down the road the rustic *Cainbable Mountain Lodge* (Ⓣ07/5544 9207, Ⓦwww.cainbable.com; ❺) offers bed and breakfast in four-person cabins, or try the *Canungra Motel* (Ⓣ07/5543 5155, Ⓦwww.canungramotel.com; ❸) at the bottom of the range in Canungra settlement.

The **birdlife** around *O'Reilly's* is prolific and distracting: you can't miss the chattering swarms of crimson rosellas mingling with visitors on the lawn, and determined twitchers can clock up over fifty species without even reaching the forest – most spectacular is the black-and-gold regent bowerbird. But it's worth pushing on to the **treetop walk** just beyond the clearing, where a suspended walkway swings 15m above ground level. At the halfway anchor point you scale a narrow ladder to vertigo-inducing mesh platforms 30m up the trunk of a strangler fig to see the canopy at eye level. Soaking up the increased sunlight at this height above the forest floor, tree branches become miniature gardens of mosses, ferns and orchids. By night the walkway is the preserve of possums, leaf-tailed geckoes and weird stalking insects.

If you manage only one day-walk at Lamington, make it the exceptional five-hour **Blue Pool–Canungra Creek track** (15km) from Green Mountain, which features all the jungle trimmings: fantastic trees, river crossings and countless opportunities to fall off slippery rocks and get soaked. The first hour is dry enough as you tramp downhill past some huge red cedars to Blue Pool, a deep, placid waterhole where platypuses are sometimes seen on winter mornings; this makes a good walk in itself. After a dip, head upstream along Canungra Creek; the path traverses the river a few times (there are no bridges, but occasionally a fallen tree conveniently spans the water) – look for yellow or red arrows painted on rocks that indicate where to cross. Seasonally, the creek can be almost dried up; if the water is more than knee-deep, you shouldn't attempt a crossing and will need to retrace your steps. Follow the creek as far as **Elabana Falls** and another swimming hole, or bypass the falls; either way, the path climbs back to the guesthouse.

Another excellent trail (17.5km) from Green Mountain takes six hours via **Box Creek Falls** to the eastern escarpment at **Toolona Lookout**, on the Border Track to Binna Burra; rewards are a half-dozen waterfalls, dramatic views into New South Wales, and encounters with clumps of moss-covered **Antarctic beech trees**, a strange Gondwanan relict also found in South America. For seasoned, well-equipped walkers, there's a chance to delve into local history by way of an overnight hike to the **Stinson Wreck**. In February 1937 a plane bound for Sydney crashed into dense forest and the survivors were only located due to the incredible efforts of Bernard O'Reilly who, on his own, hiked from the plane to Green Mountain and returned with a rescue party. Nearby is **Westray's grave**, the burial place of one of the passengers who died looking for help, but it's difficult to reach. Today most of the wreck has been carted off by souvenir hunters or covered by jungle, but the guesthouse and park rangers can give you advice on the walk and may be able to put you in touch with bushwalkers who've been there.

The Western Rim

In contrast to the obvious charms of the Eastern Rim, the drier **Western Rim** is mainly given over to open eucalypt woods, with the steep peaks covered in heath. With few facilities, it's a place for serious bushwalkers; even "easy" routes are fairly demanding, with few neat paths or signposts – so come equipped, don't walk alone, and carry plenty of water. Access is along the Cunningham and Mount Lindesay highways from Boonah or Beaudesert in the east and **Warwick** (see p.584) from the west; there's no public transport.

Mount Barney, Main Range and Mount Mistake

Mount Barney's two peaks – the taller of which is a respectable 1359m above sea level – form an extremely rough region along the New South Wales border, 45km southwest of Beaudesert. From wherever you're approaching, aim for Rathdowney and then take Barney View Road past Bigriggen to Yellowpinch. You can stay south of Rathdowney at *Mt Barney Lodge*, an excellent old homestead at the foot of Mount Barney with camping, cabin and house **accommodation** (Ⓣ07/5544 3233, Ⓦwww.mtbarneylodge.com.au; cabins ❻; 2- to 8-person house $250 per weekend). The nearest supplies and alternative camping are at Rathdowney and Bigriggen.

From the car park 5km from Yellowpinch there's a distinct, hour-long track to the **Lower Portals**, a pool on Barney Creek flanked by vertical cliffs. The only other marked hike (though even for this you might need a topographic map) is the misleadingly named "tourist trail" along the south ridge to the saddle between Mount Barney's peaks: be prepared for an exhausting seven-hour return trip from Yellowpinch. Experienced walkers, with permits and advice from the QPWS about current conditions (write to PO Box 121, Boonah; Ⓣ07/5463 5041), could camp in the saddle at **Rum Jungle** and climb the peaks in the morning; the eastern peak is the easier of the two and has the better views across to Mount Lindesay's tor, poking above wooded slopes.

Main Range's precipitous terrain and sharp, progressively higher peaks are most directly accessible along the Cunningham Highway at Cunningham's Gap, between Brisbane and Warwick, about 90km from Boonah. Here you'll find some of the easier trails: tracks through rainforest along West Gap Creek and ascents of Bare Rock and Mount Mitchell, which you could complete in a couple of hours or a day, depending on your inclination. There's a QPWS **campsite** at the Gap (Ⓣ07/4666 1133); call in advance to check on conditions. **Mount Mistake** at the northern end of Main Range is an undeveloped park on the junction of three mountain ranges which form the northernmost extent of the Scenic Rim. Walking is said to be tricky but well worth the effort; if you're tempted, contact the QPWS at the number above.

The Sunshine Coast

The **Sunshine Coast**, stretching north of Brisbane to **Noosa**, is a more pedestrian version of the Gold Coast, where largely domestic tourist development is tempered by, and sometimes combined with, agriculture. Much local character is due to the lack of death taxes in Queensland – something which, together with the pleasant climate, attracts retirees from all over Australia. The towns tend to be bland places, lively enough at Christmas, but out of season you may be hard pushed to find much to do after dark. Even so, the beaches and surf are good, improving as you go further north and providing an excuse to linger for a few days. And though you'll find the hinterland far tamer than it is down south, it still has some arresting landscapes and scattered hamlets rife with Devonshire cream teas and weekend markets.

Without your own **transport**, the easiest way through the area is by **bus** – Sun Air Bus Service (Ⓣ07/5478 2811) and Suncoast Pacific from Brisbane (Ⓣ07/5443 1011) are the local alternatives to the national operators – or on a tour from Brisbane or the Gold Coast. Brisbane's **Citytrain** network can also take you into the region, with stops at the **Glass House Mountains**, **Woombye**, **Nambour** and **Eumundi**, from where there's a connecting bus to Noosa. There's also the **Sunshine Coast airport** just north of Maroochydore, serving Brisbane, Sydney and Melbourne. Once here, "the other car rental company" (Ⓣ07/5447 2831, Ⓦwww.noosacarrental.com) has the best in **car rentals** in the region, from runarounds to 4WDs for Cooloola and Fraser Island.

Woodford, the Glass House Mountains and Australia Zoo

The unremarkable town of **Caboolture** marks the start of the Sunshine Coast, 40km north of Brisbane. Though there's nothing to detain you here, 20km inland is the two-street town of **WOODFORD**, which draws thousands for the annual **folk festival** in December (Ⓦwww.woodfordfolkfestival.com/main/index.php). North from Caboolture is the **Glass House Mountains National Park**: nine dramatic, isolated pinnacles jutting out of a flat plain, visible from as far away as Brisbane. Catching sight of the peaks from the sea, Captain Cook named them after their shape and "elevation", a resemblance that's obscure today. To the Kabi Aborigines, the mountains are the petrified forms of a family fleeing the incoming tide; their names for the peaks – Tibrogargan, Tibberoowuccum and Beerwah, for instance – are far more evocative than Cook's. The peaks themselves vary enormously: some are rounded and fairly easy to scale, while a couple have vertical faces and sharp spires requiring competent climbing skills. It's worth conquering at least one of the easier peaks; the views are superb and the mountains are one of the few really special places on the Sunshine Coast. **Beerburrum**, overlooking the township of the same name, and **Ngungun**, near Glass House Mountains township, are two of the easiest to climb, with well-used tracks; the latter's views and scenery outclass some of the tougher peaks and it will take you only two hours there and back, though the lower parts of the track are steep and slippery. **Tibberoowuccum**, a small peak at 220m just outside the National Park boundary, must be climbed from the northwest, with access from the car park off Marsh's Road. The taller mountains – **Tibrogargan** and **Beerwah** (the highest at 556m) – are at best tricky, and **Coonowrin** should be attempted only by experienced climbers after contacting the QPWS Beerwah Office (Ⓣ07/5494 0150) on Bells Creek Road. For maps of the region and local climbing conditions, ask the experienced volunteers at the **visitor information centre** at the Matthew Flinders Park Rest Area 2km north of Beerburrum town.

At the northern end of the mountains between the hamlets of Beerwah and Landsborough, **Australia Zoo** (daily 8.30am–4pm; $29; Ⓣ07/5494 1134, Ⓦwww.crocodilehunter.com) has been made famous by the antics of zoo director Steve Irwin, otherwise known for his screen persona, "Crocodile Hunter". Irwin's zealous character has rubbed off on his gamekeepers, who offer great exhibitionism to the staged demonstrations, and it remains one of the largest and most enjoyable commercial zoos in Australia, with both foreign and native animals. The best way into the area is along the old highway 16km north from Caboolture or off the new one 10km north of Beerburrum; Citytrain stops at Beerwah (where zoo visitors can get a free pick-up, arranged in advance) and Glass House Mountains township. Noosa Hinterland Tours (Ⓣ07/5474 3366, call to arrange door-to-door pick-ups), and Australian Day Tours from Brisbane (Ⓣ07/3236 4155) offer regional **tours**. The most convenient **accommodation** in the area is at *Glasshouse Mountains Holiday*

Village (☎07/5496 9338; cabins ❸), south of Glass House Mountains township at the foot of Mount Tibrogargan.

Caloundra, Mooloolaba and Maroochydore

Coastwards and a little north of the Glass House Mountains, **CALOUNDRA** just manages to hold on to its small seaside-town atmosphere, and as such is unique along the Sunshine Coast where busy highways and beachfront over-development have long put paid to this elsewhere Even so, there are plenty of towering apartment blocks, though central **Bulcock Street** has only low-rise buildings and is lined with trees. Caloundra's **beaches** are very pleasant: the closest is Deepwater Point, just two streets south of Bulcock Street. **Shelley Beach** and **Moffat Beach**, about a kilometre distant, are much quieter. The **bus terminal** is on Cooma Terrace, one street south of Bulcock, where there's also an **information centre** (Mon–Fri 8.30am–5pm; ☎07/5491 2555). For **accommodation** try *Caloundra City Backpackers*, 84 Omrah Ave (☎07/5499 7655; dorms $17–20, rooms ❷), which is clean, well run, and just two minutes from Deepwater Point. *Estoril*, 38 McIlwraith St (☎07/4591 5988, Ⓦwww.estoril.com.au; ❹), offers self-catering apartments in a high-rise block right next to Moffat Beach and has a huge pool.

The stretch of coast north of Caloundra is taken up with Mooloolaba, Alexandra Headland, and Maroochydore: three beachside suburbs which fill the foreshore between the Mooloolah and Maroochy rivers with an amoeba-like blob of high-rise units and construction sites, though the beaches are pleasant and good for surfing. **MOOLOOLABA** features the kitsch, touristy Mooloolaba Wharf – from where you can organize sixty-minute **canal cruises** ($13.50), taking in some rather opulent waterfront real estate – and the pedestrianized seafront **Esplanade**, thick with boutique shops and restaurants. Nearby, on Parkyn Parade, **Underwater World** (daily 9am–6pm, last entry at 5pm; $22.50) has superb saltwater and freshwater tanks where barramundi – fish revered by Queensland anglers for their taste and legendary fighting spirit – and sharks, turtles and nonchalant freshwater crocodiles stare blankly at you through huge windows. For the real thing, Scuba World (☎07/5444 8595, Ⓦwww.scubaworld.com.au), just around the corner on Parkyn Parade, can train you or take you **diving** to local sandstone terrain, where you'll find nudibranch, soft corals and bottom-dwelling sharks, or up to **Wolf Rocks** – one of the best dive sites in Southeast Queensland – for bigger game. Mooloolaba has plenty of high-rise holiday apartments with weekly rates but there are only a few places that offer daily rates: *River Esplanade Motel* about 250m back from the waterfront at 73 Brisbane Rd (☎07/5444 3855 or 1800 807 399; rooms ❹) is the pick of a rather miserable collection of motels in the area or the excellent value en-suite rooms at *Mooloolaba Beach Backpackers*, (☎1800 020 120, Ⓦwww.mooloolababackpackers.com.au; dorms $22, rooms ❸), which organizes tours of the Sunshine Coast region (including skydiving and surfing tuition). **Eating** options are everywhere, though *Mooloolaba Surf Club*'s smart café, bar and restaurant on the Esplanade (daily noon–2pm & 6pm–late, Sun from 8am) is worth a visit for views out over the surf, and *Karakas*, opposite the entrance to Underwater World, has fiery Mexican cooking and live music through the week. *Mooloolaba Hotel*, on the Mooloolaba Esplanade, hosts rock bands every Friday and Saturday, and opens its doors as a nightclub on Sundays.

Most of the **other accommodation** options for independent travellers are 3km north of Mooloolaba, past Alexandra Headland, at the more relaxed settlement of **MAROOCHYDORE**. At the bottom end of the market, *Cotton*

Tree Caravan Park on Cotton Tree Parade, Maroochydore (Ⓣ07/5443 1253, Ⓦwww.maroochypark.qld.gov.au; cabins ❹) is right on the beach; for hostels there are *Cotton Tree Backpackers* at 15 Esplanade (Ⓣ07/5443 1755, Ⓦwww.cottontreebackpackers.com.au; dorms $21, rooms ❷), in the heart of town overlooking the ocean and with surf boards and kayaks for rent, and the rather hidden *YHA* close to the Maroochy River on Schirrmann Drive (Ⓣ07/5443 3151, Ⓦwww.yhabackpackers.com.au; dorms $24, rooms ❷), which has family rooms and offers a free pick-up from Maroochydore. The town's **dining** possibilities are on the thin side, though *Frozzy's*, 15 Esplanade, is a lively restaurant with melodic entertainment at weekends.

Nambour, the hinterland, and on to Noosa

Bisected by tramways from surrounding sugar plantations, the functional town of **NAMBOUR** sits inland from Maroochydore in the centre of the Sunshine Coast's farming region. There's not much in town to detain you, though five kilometres south between the highway and **Woombye** you'll find it hard not to at least pause and gawk at the renowned and ridiculous **Big Pineapple** which overshadows the eponymous plantation (daily 9am–5pm; free except tours and rides; Ⓣ07/5442 1333). Activities include trips around the plantation on a cane train and, of course, climbing the fibreglass fruit. Woombye is a stop on Brisbane's Citytrain network, or Sunshine Coast Coaches can bring you here from Nambour.

A two-hour circuit drive from Nambour along the Blackall Range takes you into the **hinterland**, a rural English-like idyll quite unexpected in subtropical Queensland, with fields dotted by herds of pied dairy cattle, and occasional long views out to the coast. Several settlements – such as **Montville** and **Mapleton** – have dolled themselves up as "villages" and suffer from an overdose of potteries and twee tearooms, though it's worth stretching your legs to reach a couple of respectably sized **waterfalls** up here: Kondalilla, 3km north from Montville towards Nambour, with swimming holes along Obi Obi Creek; and Mapleton Falls, just west of Mapleton, where the river plunges over basalt cliffs.

A much more genuine place is **MALENY**, whose ageing hippy population and single street of **cafés** (the *Upfront Club* has good food with a healthy inclination and live bands at weekends), a co-operative supermarket, and a short river walk all create a pleasantly "alternative" atmosphere. About 5km south out of town, **Mary Cairncross Park** (winter 10am–4pm, summer 9am–5pm; voluntary donation) is a small patch of **rainforest** inhabited by snakes, wallabies and plenty of birds; there's a fantastic view south over the Glass House Mountains from the entrance. Maleny's many **accommodation** options include *Maleny Palms Tourist Park* (Ⓣ07/5494 2933, Ⓦwww.malenypalms.com.au; cabins ❹) on Macadamia Drive, 1km west of town, and the wonderfully friendly and often full *Maleny Hills Motel* (Ⓣ07/5494 2551, Ⓦwww.malenyhills.com.au; ❸), which is about 5km east of town on the Montville road, beyond which you'll find a dozen or more B&Bs on the scenic road to Montville Village.

Back down near Nambour, you can reach Noosa by turning coastwards at **EUMUNDI**, a tiny town also on the Citytrain line best known for its Wednesday and Saturday **markets**, reputed to be the biggest and best in Australia, and as the original home of Eumundi Beer (now shifted elsewhere). An appealing place to overnight here is *Taylor's Damn Fine B&B* (Ⓣ07/5442 8685, Ⓦwww.taylorsbandb.com.au; ❼), an old Queenslander home filled with an extraordinary array of European "kitsch" and collectables – one separate guestroom is a beautifully renovated railway caboose. Otherwise, the turn-off for **Cooroy** sees you entering Noosa along the river via **Tewantin**. Approaching from Maroochydore up the coastal road, the journey is half as long, passing unevenly spaced townships; coming this way, *Coolum Beach Budget Accommodation* at 1862 David Low Way, Coolum (☎07/5471 6666; dorms $20, rooms ❸), is a very clean and well laid-out place to pull up for a couple of days of beach life.

Noosa

The exclusive end of the Sunshine Coast and an established celebrity "des-res" area, **NOOSA** is dominated by an enviably beautiful headland, defined by the mouth of the placid **Noosa River** and a strip of beach to the southeast. Popular since surfers first came in the 1960s to ride fierce waves around the headland, the setting compensates for the abundance of neon and concrete in town. It's also a starting point for trips to **Cooloola National Park** and **Fraser Island** directly north (see p.474), attractions that tend to overshadow Noosa's own sand, pleasant river scenery and tiny national park.

Information and accommodation

There are commercially driven **information booths** all over Noosa that are best avoided. For unbiased information head to the government-backed Noosa Information Centre run by volunteers on the roundabout at Hastings Street (daily 9am–5pm; ☎07/5447 4988), although even here only those companies that pay to be included are featured.

Hostels have courtesy buses for the beach, town and nightclubs, and all accommodation will help organize activities and tours, from surfing lessons to Cooloola and Fraser Island trips. **Motels** are concentrated along the river between Noosa Heads and Noosaville; some offer weekly rates which might add up to a free night, but prices double during school holidays. A group of

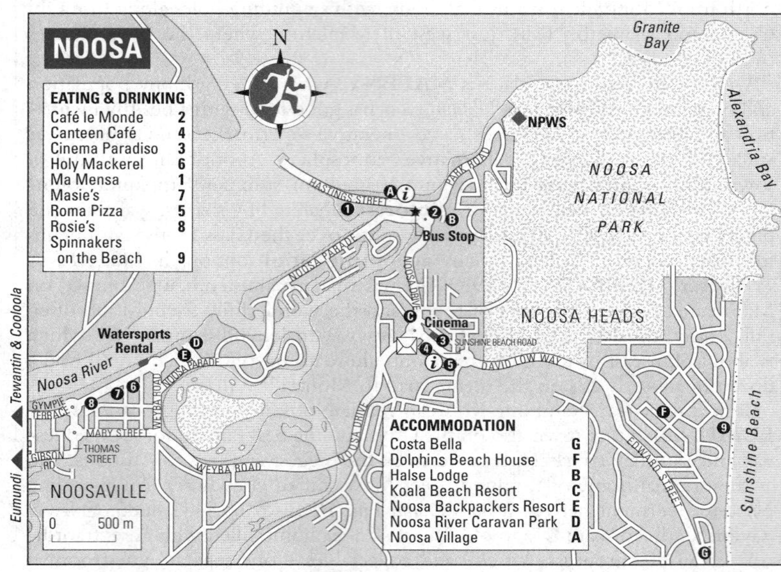

four staying a week or two may get better value – and a slice of luxury – by checking with Accom Noosa (Ⓣ07/5447 2224, Ⓦwww.accomnoosa.com.au) about deals on furnished apartments outside holiday periods. An alternative is to hire a houseboat for up to six people and explore the river and lakes at will – try Luxury Afloat based at the Memorial Park Jetty in Tewantin (Ⓣ07/5449 7611, Ⓦwww.luxuryafloatnoosa.com.au; min 2 nights from $595).

Dolphins Beach House 14 Duke St, Sunshine Beach Ⓣ1800 454 456, Ⓦwww.dolphinsbeachhouse.com. Self-contained units about a 5min walk from the sea with surfboards to hire. ❸

Gagaju Call ahead for directions or pick-up Ⓣ07/5474 3522. This is an authentic bush camp near Noosa, with a dozen bunk beds and space for campers. Created as an eco-friendly "bush experience", everything is built from recycled timber. Canoes and camping equipment, advice on hikes and canoe trips, and fireside bush-poetry readings are among the attractions. Their three-day independent canoe trip for $99 is highly recommended. Dorms $13.

Halse Lodge (YHA) 17 Noosa Drive, Noosa Heads Ⓣ1800 242 567, Ⓦwww.halselodge.com.au. Giant, sprawling, immaculate 1888 Queenslander building in large grounds close to Noosa Beach; definitely not for partying. Often full despite quantity of rooms, so book in advance. Dorms $28, rooms ❸

Koala Beach Resort 44 Noosa Drive, Noosa Heads Ⓣ07/5447 3355 or 1800 357 457, Ⓦwww.koalaresort.com.au. Central budget accommodation in dorms and motel units. Nowhere near the beach, and not especially clean, but the party atmosphere and live music might compensate. Dorms $22, rooms ❸

Melaluka Apartments 7 Selene St, Sunshine Beach Ⓣ1800 003 663, Ⓦwww.melaluka.com.au. A well-appointed high-rise development with excellent, self-contained apartment accommodation – one of the best deals in town. ❸

Noosa Backpackers Resort 9 William St, Noosaville Ⓣ1800 626 673, Ⓦwww.noosabackpackers.com.au. Converted motel units with small dorms and basic rooms but close to the activities centre on Gympie Terrace and free use of boogie-boards and surfboards. Dorms $21, rooms ❷

Noosa River Caravan Park Russell St, Noosaville Ⓣ07/5449 7050. Large campsite and van park with splendid river views, but with no cabins or on-site vans.

Noosa Village 10 Hastings St Ⓣ07/5447 5800, Ⓦwww.noosavillage.com.au. Unpretentious motel in the heart of Noosa's glitz with good-value deals in low season and weekdays; rooms are quiet but not huge, and some have balconies. ❻

The Town and around

"Noosa" is a loose term covering a seven-kilometre-long sprawl of merging settlements stretched along the south side of the Noosa River, culminating at **Noosa Heads**. This forms the core of the town, with a chic and brash shopping-and-dining enclave along beachside **Hastings Street**, and a far more down-to-earth area of shops, banks, and cafés, 1km inland along **Sunshine Beach Road**. Immediately east of this is the headland itself and **Noosa National Park**, worth a look for its mix of mature rainforest, coastal heath and fine **beaches** – Granite Bay and Alexandria Bay ("swimwear optional") have good sand pounded by unpatrolled surf – all reached along graded paths. These start from the picnic area at the end of Park Road (a continuation of Hastings Street), where you'll probably see **koalas** in gum trees above the car park. South of the headland and national park is the discreet suburb of **Sunshine Beach**, which features Noosa's longest and least crowded stretch of sand. All three suburbs are connected by a **bus service** (Sunbus), which goes by every twenty minutes or so between 5am and 9pm, with service extended to midnight at weekends.

West from Noosa Heads, **Noosaville** is a mainly residential district along the riverfront. In the late afternoon, half of Noosa promenades along **Gympie Terrace** as the sinking sun colours a gentle tableau: mangroves on the opposite shore, pelicans eyeing anglers for scraps and landing clumsily midstream, and everything, from cruise boats to windsurfers and kayaks, out on the water.

Noosa water activities

Noosa's original reason to be was the **surf**, and if you know what you're doing you'll find all the necessary gear at Surf World, 34 Sunshine Beach Rd, Noosa Heads (ⓣ07/5447 3538). The best surf is found around Noosa Heads, and if you're a novice and put-off by the crowds, try a lesson with Learn to Surf (ⓣ0418 787 577) or Wavesense (ⓣ07/5474 9076) – they can be hard to get hold of, but are worth the effort.

Most other water activities, including the popular **river cruises**, are based around Noosaville and Tewantin. Noosa River Cruises, Gympie Terrace, Noosaville (ⓣ07/5449 7362) and Everglades Waterbus, Harbour Town Complex, Tewantin (ⓣ07/5447 1838, ⓦwww.evergladeswaterbus.com.au) have day-tours on the river and lakes for around $70. To get as far as Lake Cootharaba, Beyond (ⓣ1800 657 666, ⓦwww.beyondnoosa.com.au) has six-hour cruises upriver for $69 and full-day tours for $129 including a cruise and a 4WD run along Rainbow Beach.

For **water sports**, Pro Ski, on the river bank at Gympie Terrace in Noosaville (ⓣ07/5449 7740), has water-skiing at $80 for thirty minutes, $125 for an hour, including instruction for novices, and jet skis at $60 for thirty minutes; next door, Pelican Boat Hire (ⓣ07/5449 7239) has small outboard boats for hire at $25 for the first hour ($12 for additional hours) as well as canoes and surf skis at $12 for the first hour ($6 for additional hours); Kingfisher Boat Hire (ⓣ07/5449 9353), at the Harbour Town Complex in Tewantin, rents out fishing boats with fuel, rods, bait pumps, crab pots, ice boxes and the rest, for around $25 an hour. In a different line, Kayanu, at the Noosa River Shopping Centre on Gympie Terrace (ⓣ0438 788 573, ⓦwww.kite-surf.com.au), has two-hour **kite surfing courses** ($140), and also rents out kayaks. Bikes can be hired from Noosa Bike Hire (ⓣ07/5474 3322), next door to Keyanu for $25 a full day including free delivery in the Noosa area or you may be tempted by their half-day downhill mountain adventures for $55.

With a spare day you can cruise or canoe (if you're energetic and start early enough) upstream to shallow lakes Cooroibah and Cootharaba (see p.469), or just paddle around, fish at the river mouth or rent a jet ski and have fun getting soaked (see box above for rental outlets). If you just want to take a quick ride along the river and don't want to fork out for a tour, hop on the **Noosa ferry**, which runs six times daily (10am–6pm) from the Sheraton Noosa Jetty off Hastings Street upstream to the suburb of **Tewantin**; it costs $10.50 for the hour-long return journey, or $14.50 for an all-day pass.

Eating, drinking and nightlife

Noosa's three communities – surfers, retirees and tourists – seldom share the same enthusiasms; evenings tend to be spent with your own crowd. This doesn't seem to affect the **nightlife**, though, and eating out in particular is pursued as a serious pastime. Hastings Street has long been the place to dine and be seen in Noosa, but soaring rents have seen some excellent eateries relocate to Noosaville, where you'll now find lots of casual diners checking out the places clustered along Gympie Terrace and Thomas Street.

Café le Monde Hastings St, Noosa Heads ⓣ07/5449 2366. Slightly snobbish street atmosphere and a mainly international menu – try the le Monde salad at $16. Open 7am for cappuccino; happy hour Mon–Fri 4–6pm and 9–10pm; live music Thurs–Sun.

Canteen Café Sunshine Beach Rd, Noosa Heads. Somewhere to slump over a big breakfast and good strong coffee, rather than be seen

Cinema Paradiso Sunshine Beach Rd, next to the cinema, Noosa Heads. Outdoor eating and good-sized portions of sirloin, rack of lamb and salads from around $13; check out the $17 meal-and-film deal.

Holy Mackerel 187 Gympie Terrace, Noosaville. Unquestionably the place for fish and chips – try

the sensational coconut prawns and handmade ice creams. Open 10am–late.
Ma Mensa Hastings St, Noosa Heads. Obligatory Italian bistro with outdoor tables; inexpensive for location. Very fine steamed mussels for $17; also specializes in pasta dishes around $15.
Masie's 247 Gympie Terrace, Noosaville. Excellent steak and seafood dishes served in a rather formal and airy setting with some outside tables. Try the seafood pie or pan fried veal. Mains around $25. Closed Monday.
Rosie's Gympie Terrace, near the corner of Albert St, Noosaville ⓣ07/5449 7888. Tiny and intimate BYO place, with a new menu every week. Popular with locals; mains around $24.
Spinnakers on the Beach Sunshine Beach Surf Club ⓣ07/5474 5177. Spacious bar and restaurant with unbeatable views. Seafood, steaks, pasta and salad – big servings, all in the $15–25 range. Courtesy bus from Noosa on Wed and Fri nights.

Listings

Banks Located along Sunshine Beach Rd, Noosa Heads.
Buses There's no actual bus station for long-distance buses. Drop-off and pick-up points are at the "Transit Centre" – just a bus shelter – at the junction of Noosa Parade and Noosa Drive.
Camping supplies and rental Outdoor Store, 28 Sunshine Beach Rd, Noosa Heads (ⓣ07/5447 2688), has all you'll need for Fraser Island and Cooloola.
Car rental Allterrain, 91 Noosa Drive, Noosa Heads (ⓣ07/5449 0877) and The Other Car Rental Company (ⓣ07/5447 2831, ⓦwww.noosacarrentals.com) have 4WD from $170 per day. For mokes and scooters try Big Kahuna (ⓣ07/5447 3777).
Cinema Sunshine Beach Rd, Noosa Heads ⓣ07/5449 2255.
Internet Internet Café, 9 Sunshine Beach Rd, has terminals from $5 an hour.
QPWS 240 Moorindil St, Tewantin ⓣ07/5447 3243.
Pharmacy Noosa Heads Day and Night Pharmacy, Hastings St. Daily until 9pm.
Police 48 Hastings St ⓣ07/5474 5255 or 5447 5888.
Post office Noosa Drive, Sunshine Beach Rd end (Mon–Fri 9am–5pm, Sat 9am–12.30pm).
Taxis ⓣ13 10 08.

The Cooloola Coast and Fraser Island

Halfway between Brisbane and the tropics, the **Cooloola Coast** and **Fraser Island** between them cover over 190km of the coastline north from Noosa, forming a world of giant dunes, forests, coloured sands and freshwater lakes where fishing and four-wheel driving take precedence over the more usual beach activities. But it doesn't have to be a macho tangle with the elements: for once it's relatively easy and inexpensive to rent tents and a 4WD and set off to explore in some comfort.

Europeans were initially unimpressed with this part of the coast, but abundant fresh water, seafood and plants must have supported a very healthy **Aboriginal population**; campfires along the beach allowed Matthew Flinders to navigate Fraser Island at night in 1802. Flinders labelled the region as "the **Great Sandy Peninsula**" on his maps, though he suspected that Fraser Island was in fact separated from the mainland. The Queensland government declared the area an Aboriginal reserve in the early 1860s but, with the discovery of **gold** at

Gympie in 1867, Europeans flocked in thousands into the region. This influx, and the economic boom that went with it, saved the fledgling Queensland from bankruptcy, but brought the usual racial conflicts, and the reserve gradually became little more than a holding pen for tribal survivors from all over the state. They were devastated by disease, and the last few were relocated to other reserves around Queensland at the start of the twentieth century so the area could be opened up for recreation.

Sand mining and **logging** are other incendiary topics here and there's a predictable split between conservationists and those people who count on local industries for their livelihood. **Forestry** is a particularly bitter issue; the mainland town of Maryborough was built on timber felling, and logging bans have aroused fury at what is seen as a sell-out to the Green movement. Locals, too, once drawn to the area for its natural appeal, now feel crowded out by regulations made to protect the coast from overuse by 4WDs and by drunken campers leaving piles of garbage behind them. While it's unlikely that visitors will become too entangled in these issues, a balance between protection and "development" – a word with almost religious connotations in Queensland – is far from being established.

Orientation and access

The first thing to decide is where to start. Cooloola comprises two regions: the inland region around **Cooroibah and Cootharaba lakes**, and the **Teewah Coloured Sands Beach** running north for 40km towards the lower end of Fraser Island and the small township of **Rainbow Beach**. The lakes and the southern end of the beach can be accessed directly from Tewantin, on the river 7km west of Noosa. Unless you drive up the beach from here – for which you'll need a 4WD – Rainbow Beach and northern Cooloola can only be reached 75km off Highway 1 from the inland town of Gympie, itself around 60km from Noosa. **Access to Fraser Island** is by ferry from Rainbow Beach (Inskip Point) in the south, or from the town of **Hervey Bay** in the north, 90km beyond Gympie.

Tours around the area run from Noosa, Rainbow Beach and Hervey Bay, though given the grand scale of the region they're inevitably rushed. The wildlife and overall serenity of the area are elusive, to say the least, unless you get away from the more popular places, camp for the night and explore early on in the day. Assembling a group and **renting a 4WD** is one way to do this, with hostels in Hervey Bay well experienced in arranging this type of tour for Fraser Island. Another is simply **walking**, an alternative ignored by almost all visitors, but one which allows unequalled access and intimacy with the region.

Unless you're on a tour, you'll definitely need **maps**, with many available from local garages and newsagents. Relevant sheets on national parks, available from the QPWS, supplement these. Drivers need **tide timetables**, as most beaches are only reliably negotiable at low tide. Rain won't ruin your stay – in fact it makes driving on sand far easier and enhances the colours – though in rough conditions services to Fraser might be cancelled, leaving you stranded.

The Cooloola Coast

The southern end of the Cooloola Coast, commonly referred to as **Noosa North Shore**, is dominated by features of the Noosa River which pools into lakes Cootharaba and Cooroibah as it nears Tewantin, while stands of commercial timber and dry sclerophyll woodland cover the interior, rising to dunes along the beach stabilized by scrubby heath. The beach runs straight north from Tewantin to **Double Island Point** and then curves west to Rainbow Beach township, where it's backed by vertical, coloured-sand cliffs whose weathered contours and tones constantly change with the shifting sun. Below, the windswept strip of sand separating land from sea becomes a 4WD highway at low tide, with brightly coloured flashes of canvas marking where the cliffs are low enough to form a protective foreshore suitable for camping. Most of the beach and interior north of Cootharaba is **national park**, as is the lake's shoreline.

Before you head in, note that **4WD** is essential for the beach, and the access roads leading to it – see Noosa "Listings", p.467 for car rental. Conventional vehicles can manage the lake road from Tewantin in the south, and Rainbow Beach from Gympie in the north – both of which are good places to use as bases for day-walks if you don't have the right vehicle. **Hiking**, you'll find the easiest path along the beach, but it makes things more interesting if you head inland at some stage. For the well equipped, walking tracks head upstream from Elanda Point, past the top of Lake Cootharaba and along the forty-kilometre **Cooloola Wilderness Trail**, or towards the coast – contact QPWS (Ⓣ07/5447 3243; daily 9am–3pm) on Moorindil St, Tewantin, just before the ferry access, first for camping permits, maps and an idea of conditions. For **tours** of the region, check operator details in the Noosa and Hervey Bay accounts.

The lakes

Cooroibah and its larger and more northerly neighbour **Cootharaba** are joined by a winding six-kilometre stretch of the Noosa River. Placid, and fringed with paperbarks and reedbeds, the lakes look their best at dawn before there's any traffic; they're saltwater and average just 1m in depth, subject to tides. At Cootharaba's top end, Kin Kin Creek and the Noosa River spill lazily into the lake through thickets of mangroves, hibiscus and ti-trees – the so-called **Everglades**. A boardwalk from **Kinaba**'s information centre at the northern end of the lake leads to a hide where you can spy on birdlife, and there's more on nearby Fig Tree Lake. The picnic area here is a former corroboree ground, which featured in the saga of Eliza Fraser (see p.475).

Beyond here, there's a footpath – or it's an easy paddle – on up the **Narrows** to **Harry Spring's Hut**. A campsite on the edge of the forest here is a gateway to Cooloola's interior: about another 8km upstream are navigable by canoe, and walking tracks mark the start of the Cooloola Wilderness Trail, a three-day hike up to the road at Rainbow Beach. Shorter trails also head across the river from here – you'll have to swim – and through forested dunes to the beach: an exhausting day-trip.

To reach the lakes from Tewantin, turn off the main road onto Werin Street at the school – there is a sign, but it's easy to miss – then turn left again and follow the signposts. The twenty-kilometre-long road follows the western side of the lakes to Kinaba, with turn-offs along the way to **Boreen Point** and **Elanda Point** townships, both on Cootharaba. **Accommodation** is at campsites in either, or there's bushcamping at Harry Spring's Hut (see above); at Boreen Point, *Lakeside Lodge* (Ⓣ07/5485 3127; ❸) has comfortable doubles. **Supplies** are available at Boreen Point – where there's fuel, a general store, hotel and telephones – or at Elanda Point's small general store. The township's campsites also **rent canoes** or flat-bottomed tinnies, or you can link up with a river tour from Noosaville (see box on p.466).

The coast

To reach the southern end of the beach from Tewantin, catch the **vehicle ferry** from the top of Moorindil Street (daily 5am–10pm; cars $5 one-way, pedestrians $1), which lands you across the Noosa River, about five minutes' drive from the sea and the **Great Sandy National Park**. There's **accommodation** 2km along near Lake Cooroibah's otherwise inaccessible eastern shore at *Noosa North Shore* (Ⓣ07/5447 1225; caravans ❸, suites/cottages ❻); family-oriented, and with every activity from horse riding to canoeing and tennis, they offer camping and caravans, as well as suites and cottages for up to eight people, plus all the associated facilities including a pub.

Otherwise, press on to the beach. The powdery foredunes at the end of the road look too small to worry about, but even in a 4WD you won't be the first to get stuck driving through them; the privately-run *Wilderness Campsite* (Ⓣ07/5449 7955) has fine views of Noosa, but this close to town things can get busy. From here you have a straight, 40-kilometre run of uninterrupted sand, backed by steep, forested dunes to play with – **camping** is permitted only after the 22km mark and only in designated areas; permits available from QPWS Tewantin. Just make sure you know what the local tides are doing, and remember that steep dunes mean that there are no exits off the beach until you reach the **Freshwater Creek campsite** (where there's a boggy patch of quicksand to be avoided), 30km along. For most of the way there's little to look out for in particular, though **coloured sands** are a feature of the region – particularly the northern end of the beach – caused by minerals leaching down the cliffs from above leaving broad bands of orange, red and white. There's also the **shipwreck** of the *Cherry Venture*, grounded just north of Freshwater Creek in 1973 and now eroded down to a rusting frame and funnel.

From Freshwater Creek you can reach Rainbow Beach by either negotiating a rutted, scarred track which runs up off the beach and inland through gum woodland to the township; or by carrying on up the beach, around its northern extremity at **Double Island Point** – when Fraser Island first fills the horizon – and then turning west along the sand for the final 5km or so.

RAINBOW BEACH itself is a small, slowly developing township at the end of the sealed road to Gympie. Most people come here for the challenging access at Inskip Point to Fraser Island's southern reaches. There's a post office, service station and shops, with **accommodation** at *Rainbow Beach Holiday Village* (Ⓣ07/5486 3222, Ⓦwww.beach-village.com; villas ❹), offering tents and villas; *Rainbow Beach Hotel* (Ⓣ07/5486 3125, Ⓦwww.rainbowhotel.com.au; ❸) has motel rooms; neighbouring *Rainbow Beach Backpackers* (Ⓣ1800 443 353, Ⓦwww.rainbowbeachbackpackersresort.com; dorms $19–22, rooms ❷) and *Rainbow Beach YHA* (Ⓣ1800 100 170, Ⓔrainbowbeachyha@bigpond.com; dorms $20, rooms ❸).

Accommodation can line up **Fraser Island safaris** from Rainbow Beach lasting one to three days, or contact Sun Safari Tours (Ⓣ07/5486 3227, Ⓦwww.fraser-is.com), who run day-trips to Central Station and Lake Birrabeen ($90). For **4WD rental**, many places to stay also rent out vehicles, or Safari (Ⓣ1800 689 819, Ⓦwww.safari4wdhire.com.au) offers five-seater off-roaders from about $135 per day, and can sort out packages including all vehicle and camping permits. The **Fraser Island ferry** leaves Inskip Point, 10km north of Rainbow Beach, for the fifteen-minute crossing to Hook Point on the island's south coast – first ferry leaves Inskip Point 6.30am, last ferry leaves Fraser 5.30pm; $65 per vehicle, foot passengers free – contact Manta Ray (Ⓣ0418 872 599) or Fraser

Island Barges (☎07/4125 2343). Drivers should note that this is a very difficult landing and should only be attempted if you have sound 4WD experience. Most 4WD companies outside Rainbow Beach do not permit crossings here – check with your rental agency first. You'll also need a **permit** for the island from the QPWS on the Rainbow Beach road (daily 7am–4pm; ☎07/5486 3160; see p.475 for more about Fraser Island permits and practicalities).

Heading on, Gympie and the highway are 80km away; if you don't have your own transport, there's a very slow local **bus** to Gympie (Mon–Fri 7.30am & 3.45pm, returning 6am & 1.30pm).

Hervey Bay

Back on the highway and heading north, it's a couple of hours to Hervey Bay past **Gympie** and **Maryborough**, historic gold and timber communities and now healthy market towns with handsome stone and wooden period buildings in their centres testifying to their wealthy past. **HERVEY BAY**, a rapidly

Whale-watching from Hervey Bay

Humpbacked whales are among the most exciting marine creatures to encounter: growing to 16m long and 36 tonnes, they make their presence known from a distance by their habit of "breaching" – making spectacular, crashing leaps out of the water – and expelling jets of spray as they exhale. Prior to 1952 an estimated ten thousand whales made the annual journey between the Antarctic and tropics to breed and give birth in shallow coastal waters; a decade later whaling had reduced the population to just two hundred animals. Now protected, their numbers have increased to over five thousand many of which pass along the eastern coast of Australia. An estimated two thirds enter Hervey Bay making it the best place to spot humpbacks in Australia. In Hervey Bay, the **whale-watching season** lasts from August to November, a little later than northern waters because Fraser Island leans outwards deflecting them away from the bay as they migrate north, but funnelling them in to the constricted waters when returning south.

The town makes the most of their visit with an August **Whale Festival**, and operators are always searching for new gimmicks to promote day-cruises and flights. In the early months you are more likely to see mature bulls who, being inquisitive, swim directly under the boat and raise their heads out of the water, close enough to touch. You may even see them fighting over mating rights with the chance to hear their enchanting mating songs, but of course you may see and hear nothing at all. The latter part of the season sees mothers and playful calves coming into the bay to rest before their great migration south, a good time to watch the humpbacks breaching. Whether all this voyeurism disturbs the animals is unclear, but they seem at least tolerant of the attention paid to them.

For **flights**, try Air Fraser Island (☎07/4125 3600); the cost is from $55 per person (depending on the number of passengers) for a thirty-minute buzz. **Cruises** last for a morning or a full day, costing between $75–85 per person, and are booked through an agent; some boats can take up to 150 passengers but this doesn't necessarily mean they feel overcrowded – check the boat size, the viewing space, speed of vessel and how many will be going before committing yourself. *Tasman Venture I*, *Hombre*, *Whalesong* and *Volante III* all come recommended, while *Spirit of Hervey Bay* has the bonus of having underwater portals to view the whales if they come close. For the added pleasure of sailing out to the whales, make arrangements with the yacht *Blue Dolphin* (☎07/4125 3727).

expanding sprawl of coastal suburbs – known locally as "God's Waiting Room" due to the large number of retirees living here – has no such pretensions, and the only reason to visit is to join the throng crossing to **Fraser Island**, or to venture into the bay to spot **whales** in the spring.

Orientation, arrival and information

Pialba is the commercial centre for this sprawling town and satellite suburbs, with shops strung along the **Esplanade** as it runs 7km from here east through **Scarness** and **Torquay** to **Urangan Harbour** and Marina; **barges and tours to Fraser Island** leave from here and from **River Heads**, 17km south. Approaching Hervey Bay from the south, turn off at Maryborough; from the north, leave the highway at Howard. The **bus station** is at Bay Central shopping complex, just off the main road into town about 1km from Pialba; the **airport** is about 5km south of Urangan off Booral Road, on the way to River Heads. Hervey Bay has a decent **local bus** service, circuiting around town from Bay Central between about 6am and 6pm, though you'll need a **taxi** for the airport (ⓣ13 10 08; $10–15). Almost every place to stay provides information and makes bookings, but you'll get more reliable, pressure-free help from the **tourist information office** inside the bus ticket office (Mon–Fri 6am–5.30pm, Sat & Sun 6.30am–1pm; ⓣ07/4124 4000) or from the official tourist information centre (daily 9am–5pm; ⓣ07/4125 9855) inconveniently located 3km out of town on the Fraser Coast Highway towards Maryborough.

Accommodation

Accommodation is packed during the whale-watching season (July–Oct) and at Christmas and Easter (when motel prices can double). Most places will pick you up from the bus station, and all can organize tours to Fraser, with the hostels specializing in putting together budget self-drive packages. If you're **camping**, the best van parks are fronting the beach on the Esplanade at Torquay (ⓣ07/4125 1578) and Scarness (ⓣ07/4128 1274).

Bay Bed & Breakfast 180 Cypress St, Urangan ⓣ07/4125 6919, ⓔbaybedandbreakfast@bigpond.com. Enormously friendly, home-style accommodation with excellent rooms and discounted weekly rates. ❹–❺

Bayview Motel 399 Esplanade, Torquay ⓣ07/4128 1134, ⓔbay.view.motel@optusnet.com.au. This historic guesthouse with wooden floors and colourful interior design boasts spotless rooms and friendly owners who can't do enough for you. ❸

Beaches 195 Torquay Rd, Torquay ⓣ1800 655 501, ⓦwww.beaches.com.au. Busy party hostel with lively bar/bistro and cheerful staff, one street back from the Esplanade. Dorms $20, rooms ❷

Beachside Motor Inn 298 Esplanade, Scarness ⓣ07/4124 1999, ⓔhosts@beachsidemotorinn.com.au. Comfortable motel units and family apartments with beach views but a bit out from town. ❺

Colonial Backpackers Resort (YHA) Cnr Pulgul St and Boat Harbour Drive, near Urangan Harbour, Urangan ⓣ1800 818 280, ⓦwww.coloniallogcabins.com. Tidy, comfortable and well run, though even double rooms are pretty bare, and you have to leave deposits for everything except the bed. Spacious grounds, with a bar, pool and restaurant, plus tame wildlife, might compensate. Dorms $25.50, rooms ❷, cabins ❸

Fraser Roving 412 Esplanade, Torquay ⓣ07/4125 6386, ⓦwww.oziroving.com.au. Barracks-like but clean and efficient backpackers with own bar and pool, specializes in Fraser trips. Dorms $20, rooms ❷

Friendly Hostel 182 Torquay Rd, Scarness ⓣ1800 244 107, ⓦwww.thefriendlyhostel.com.au. Relaxed intimate guesthouse, with comfy three-bed self-contained dorms and nice, family atmosphere. Dorms $20, rooms ❷

Koala Backpackers 408 Esplanade, Torquay ⓣ1800 354 535, ⓦwww.koalaresort.com.au. Large hostel with party atmosphere in a great location close to shops, with its own fleet of 4WDs. Dorms $22, rooms ❷

Mango Tourist Hostel 110 Torquay Rd, Torquay ⓣ07/4124 2832, ⓦwww.mangohostel.com.

Delightful old Queenslander with polished floors and just three rooms. The hosts are extremely knowledgeable on Fraser Island and can organize alternative nature-based walking tours, eco tours or sailing trips. Dorms $19, rooms ❷

Palace 184 Torquay Rd, Scarness ⓣ1800 063 168, ⓦwww.palacebackpackers.com.au. Excellent, purpose-built hostel with its own fleet of 4WDs; all units are roomy and come complete with kitchen and TV, and there's a pool too. Dorms $19, rooms ❸

Playa Concha 475 Esplanade, Torquay ⓣ07/4125 1544, ⓦwww.playaconcharesort.com. Comfortable, beachfront motel surrounded by palms and ferns, with a mix of single and double rooms and excellent-value serviced apartments sleeping up to six people. ❹

Eating and drinking

Apart from snack bars and fast-food joints in Pialba, most of the places to **eat** and spend the evening are along the Esplanade at Torquay.

Beachside Hotel Cnr Esplanade and Queens St, Scarness. Lively bar with retro furnishings and an open front for sea views, DJ Wed–Sat nights.

Black Dog Café Cnr the Esplanade and Denman Camp Rd, Scarness. An odd name for what is actually a small, smart restaurant with heavy Asian leanings – mostly Japanese. Udon soup, sushi, and beef teriyaki sit strangely alongside Cajun fish and Caesar salad. Good value, with mains at $12–18.

Curried Away 174 Boat Harbour Drive, Pialba ⓣ07/4124 1577. Half a dozen tables, 1960s musak, and takeaway ambience, but the food – genuine Sri Lankan curries – will get your mouth watering. Medium-sized portions of *rutu* chicken, vegetable samosas, dhal, *raita* and chutney – enough for two – will set you back $22; most mains are around $10. Dine in, take away or have it delivered for free.

Gringo's 449 Esplanade, Torquay. Good Mexican menu of enchiladas, chilli con carne and nachos, spiced to individual tolerances and with bean fillings as an alternative to meat. Main courses $17. Open daily from 5.30pm.

O'Reileys 446 Esplanade, Torquay. Savoury pizza, pasta and crepes, but best for fruit pancakes and cream. From $11. Open breakfast and dinner only; closed Monday.

Sails Cnr Fraser St and Esplanade, Torquay ⓣ07/4125 5170. Moderately upmarket Mediterranean/Asian brasserie, and a good place to splash out a little. Good choices are the Shanghai noodles and seafood risotto; some decent vegetarian options too, along with good old Aussie steaks. Alternatively, just plump for their tapas platter and a cocktail. Open daily 10am–midnight.

Thai Diamond 353 Esplanade, Scarness. Inexpensive yet filling dishes with cheerful service in an unassuming cafeteria-style setting, both licensed and BYO. Open daily 10am–midnight.

Listings

Airlines Air Fraser Island (ⓣ07/4125 3600); Sunstate (ⓣ07/4125 3488) for flights to Fraser and Brisbane. For Lady Elliot Island, contact the resort direct (see p.490).

Banks Most banks are in Pialba, with a few scattered along the Esplanade at Torquay.

Bicycles Rayz Pushbike Hire (ⓣ0417 644 814) rents out bikes at $12 a day, with free delivery and pick-up.

Camping equipment Some 4WD operators also rent camping equipment.

Car rental Nifty, 463 Esplanade (ⓣ1800 627 583), has decent runarounds from $29 a day. For 4WDs expect around $115 per day for two-seaters such as a Suzuki, $155 per day for an eight-seater Landrover Defender or Toyota Landcruiser, including insurance. Note that older ex-army Landrovers, while mechanically sound, are uncomfortable and best avoided unless you're trying to save money. Aussie Trax, 56 Boat Harbour Drive, Pialba (ⓣ07/4124 4433, ⓦwww.aussietrax.com) and Fraser Magic, Urangan (ⓣ07/4125 6612, ⓦwww.fraser-magic-4wdhire.com.au) are probably the most clued-up and longest-running operators in Hervey Bay and both put together good-value all-inclusive packages; Bay 4WD Centre, 54 Boat Harbour Drive, Pialba (ⓣ1800 687 178, ⓦwww.bay4wd.com.au), has been going nearly as long and offers much the same deal. If short on time, a fly/drive day or overnight tour package starting from $110 per person is available through Air Fraser Island (ⓣ07/4125 3600, ⓦwww.airfraserisland.com). For information about 4WD rental for Fraser Island, see box on p.476.

Internet access Several hostels can oblige, as can the tourist information near the bus station at Pialba's Bay Central shopping complex ($4 an hour).

Tours and cruises from Hervey Bay

Not surprisingly, all **tours** from Hervey Bay involve **Fraser Island**; day-trips start around $90, overnight camping trips from $195. Fraser Island Co (ⓣ1800 624 677, ⓦwww.fraserislandco.com.au) is a little pricey at $137, but gives the best one-day tour, with BBQ lunch, new vehicles and first-rate guides – it also seems to work out of phase with rival tours' schedules, so you don't keep bumping into busloads of other visitors. Alternatively, Fraser Venture Tours (ⓣ1800 249 122, ⓦwww.fraser-is.com) scores slightly higher for its overnight trips with accommodation at Eurong ($195). Otherwise try Wilderness Adventure (ⓣ1800 072 555, ⓦwww.cooldingotour.com), a two-day tour including accommodation at *Kingfisher Bay Resort* ($270); and Sand Island Safaris (ⓣ1800 246 911, ⓦwww.sandislandsafaris.com.au) for three days' worth covering most of the island (including accommodation at *Eurong Beach Resort*; $348).

Cruises include Stefanie Yacht Charters (ⓣ1800 689 610, ⓦwww.stefanie-charters.com.au), which spends two days or longer cruising around Fraser's western side, with the chance to see dolphins year-round, do some kayaking and land on the island. The cost is dependent on the number of passengers and the exact itinerary. Outside the whale season, Whalesong (ⓣ07/4125 6222, ⓦwww.whalesong.com.au) spends four hours around the bay looking for dolphins, turtles and – with real luck – dugong (sea cow) at $78 per person. Alternatively, Krystal Clear (ⓣ07/4124 0066) allows four to five hours for snorkelling, coral viewing, and a BBQ lunch on a small deserted sand island in the bay for $62. For whale-watching operators see box on p.471.

Laundry Cnr Esplanade and Frank St, behind *Dot's Food Bar*, Scarness (daily 7am–7pm).
Pharmacy Day and Night Pharmacy, 418 Esplanade, Torquay (daily 8am–8pm).
Police 146 Torquay Rd, Scarness ⓣ07/4128 5333.
Post office On the Esplanade, Torquay.
Scooter rental Horny's Scooter Hire (ⓣ0408 249 455) has scooters for $50 a day plus $100 deposit.
Taxi ⓣ13 10 08.
Water sports Torquay Beach Hire, 415 Esplanade at Torquay (ⓣ07/4125 5528), offers surf skis to windsurfers and outboard-driven tinnies for a day's fishing.

Fraser Island

With a length of 123km, **Fraser Island** is the world's largest sand island, but this dry fact does little to prepare you for the experience. Accumulated from sediments swept north from New South Wales over the last two million years, the scenery ranges from silent forests and beaches sculpted by wind and surf to crystal-clear streams and dark, tannin-stained lakes. The east coast forms a ninety-kilometre razor-edge from which Fraser's tremendous scale can be absorbed as you travel its length; with the sea as a constant, the dunes along the edge seem to evolve before your eyes – in places low and soft, elsewhere hard and worn into intriguing canyons. By contrast, slow progress through the forests of the island's interior creates more subtle impressions of age and permanence – a primal world predating European settlement – brought into question only when the view opens suddenly onto a lake or a bald blow.

The idyllic mood, however, is sobered by a number of factors, most alarming of which is the volume of traffic tearing along the beach and main tracks. In many ways the island has become the epitome of Queensland's environmental conflicts, with conservationists, tour operators, foresters and Aboriginal groups vying for control of resources – though the big problem of garbage-strewn foredunes has been solved by the introduction of large metal skips. In 1992, the entire island was recognized as a UNESCO World Heritage Site with all but a few pockets of freehold land and the tiny township of Eurong being National Park.

Some history

To the Kabi Aborigines, Fraser Island is **Gurri** (or K'gari), a beautiful woman so taken with the earth that she stayed behind after creation, her eyes becoming lakes that mirrored the sky and teemed with wildlife so that she wouldn't be lonely. The story behind the European name is far less enchanting. In 1836, survivors of the wreck of the *Stirling Castle*, including Captain Fraser and his wife Eliza, landed at Waddy Point. Though runaway convicts had already been welcomed into Kabi life, the castaways suffered "dreadful slavery, cruel toil and excruciating tortures", and after the captain's death Eliza was presented as a prize during a corroboree at Lake Cootharaba two months later. She was rescued at this dramatic point by former convict John Graham, who had lived with the Kabi and was part of a search party alerted by three other survivors from the *Stirling Castle*. The exact details of Eliza's captivity remain obscure as she produced several conflicting accounts, but her role as an "anti-Crusoe" inspired the work of novelist Patrick White and artist Sidney Nolan.

Practicalities

There are several ways to get to Fraser. If you're just after a quick day-trip and don't want to find yourself too far from civilization, take the **fast ferry** from Urangan Marina to *Kingfisher Bay Resort* on the island's west side ($35 includes return fare, lunch and brief ranger-guided walk; at least five trips daily between 8.45am and 4pm, with return ferries departing from Kingfisher Bay 7.40am–5pm).

For more serious explorations, you'll be crossing on one of three **barges**, which leave from three separate locations: Urangan Harbour, River Heads (a 10-minute drive north of Urangan) or Inskip Point (near Rainbow Beach – see p.470 for details), and you need to make arrangements for these in advance. The **Urangan Harbour–Moon Point** (central west coast) barge leaves at 8.30am and 3.30pm, returning at 9.30am and 4.30pm. The Moon Point landing is very difficult – unless you have sound 4WD experience and your rental company permits it, leave from River Heads. The **River Heads–Wanggoolba Creek** barge (access to Central Station) departs daily at 9am, 10.15am and 3.30pm, returning at 9.30am, 2.30pm and 4pm. Unless on an organized tour, you need a **barge ticket** (returns are $115 for vehicle including driver and 3 passengers, plus $6 for additional passengers), **vehicle permit** for the island if driving ($32.60), plus you'll have to pay **camping fees** in advance for national park sites if you're planning to camp ($4 per person per night). All these can be obtained where you rent your vehicle – and are usually covered in package deals – or from barge offices at Urangan and River Heads. It's essential to **prebook** barge services (Ⓣ07/4125 4444, Ⓕ4125 3357). Note that you can use return tickets only on the same barge; if you're planning a different exit from the island, you'll have to buy two one-way tickets.

There are a couple of **safety points** to bear in mind. As there have never been domestic dogs on the island, Fraser's **dingoes** are considered to be Australia's purest strain, and they used to be a common sight. Following the death by mauling of a child in 2000, however, dingoes which frequented public areas were culled and you'll probably not see many. If you do encounter some, keep your distance, back off rather than run if approached, and – despite their misleadingly scrawny appearance – don't feed them, as it's the expectation of hand-outs which makes them aggressive. You should also be aware that sharks and severe currents make Fraser a dangerous place to get in the sea; if you want to **swim**, stick to the freshwater lakes. Lastly, be sure to arrive well-stocked with **insect repellent**.

Getting around

Driving on the island requires a **4WD vehicle**. The east beach serves as the main highway, with roads running inland to popular spots. Other tracks, always slower than the beach, crisscross the interior; main tracks are often rough from heavy use, and minor roads tend to be in better shape. General advice is to lower your tyre pressures to around 12psi to increase traction on the sand, but this isn't generally necessary (if you get bogged, however, try it first before panicking). Rain and high tides harden sand surfaces, making driving easier. Most **accidents** involve collisions on blind corners, rolling in soft sand (avoid hard braking or making sudden turns – you don't have to be going very fast for your front wheels to dig in, turning you over), and trying to cross apparently insignificant creeks on the beach at 60kph – 4WDs are not invincible. Don't drive your vehicle into the surf; you'll probably get stuck and, even if you don't, this much saltwater exposure will rust out the bodywork within days (something the rental company will notice and charge you for). Noise from the surf means that pedestrians can't hear vehicles on the beach and won't be aware of your presence until you barrel through from behind, so give them a wide berth. Road rules are the same as those on the mainland.

Walking is an excellent way to see the island. There's only one established circuit, and even that is very underused, running from Central Station south past lakes Birrabeen and Boomanjin, then up the coast and back to Central Station via lakes Wabby and McKenzie; highlights are circumnavigating the lakes, chance encounters with goannas and dingoes, and the energetic burst up Wongi Blow for sweeping views out to sea. A good three-day hike that by each sundown renders you all but unconscious after all that walking across sand, it requires no special skills beyond endurance and the ability to set up

Renting a 4WD for Fraser Island

Fraser Island is simply too large and varied to appreciate fully on a day-trip, and with competition in Hervey Bay keeping prices to a minimum it's a great opportunity to learn to handle a 4WD. See p.473 for some recommended outfits, but a stipulation of the Fraser Coast 4 Hire Association is that the company should take time to protect both it and you with a full briefing on the island and driving practicalities.

Conditions include a minimum driver age of 21 and a $500 deposit, payable in plastic or cash – note that advertised prices are normally for renting the vehicle only, so tents, food, fuel, and **ferry** and **vehicle permit** for the island are extra, available separately or as part of a **package**. Fuel surcharge is also a point of contention – most hostels currently charge $30 extra per person, expensive considering a three-day trip would commonly use less than $100 of fuel. To help cut costs, you'll want to form a **group** of five or six. All hostels naturally want to sell you their tour but will usually fill the car to capacity (usually eight) to maximize their profits but this can be very uncomfortable on the bumpy tracks around Fraser. A three-day, two-night trip works out to about $135 a person plus extras.

camp before you pass out. If this is your thing, head to *Mango Tourist Hostel* (ⓣ07/4124 2832) in Torquay for more details.

Accommodation and supplies

Accommodation needs to be booked in advance. Top of the range is the plush *Kingfisher Bay Resort* (ⓣ07/4125 5511 or 1800 072 555, ⓦwww.kingfisherbay.com; ❼) on the west coast; the more down-to-earth *Fraser Island Wilderness Retreat* at Happy Valley on the east coast (ⓣ07/4127 9144, ⓦwww.fraserislandco.com.au; doubles ❻, five-bed lodge ❼) provides comfortable cabins and good food; while *Yidney Rocks Beachfront Units* (ⓣ07/4127 9167, ⓔyidneyrocks@bigpond.com; ❺), just to the south, has basic self-contained, one- and three-bedroom units aimed at fishing groups renting on a weekly basis. Further south, *Eurong Beach Resort* (ⓣ07/4127 9122, ⓦwww.eurongbeach.com; ❺–❻) has motel-style rooms, while *Dilli Village* (ⓣ07/4127 9130; ❹) has self-contained, four-bed bunkhouses.

With a permit, you can **camp** anywhere along the eastern foreshore except where signs forbid, or if you need tank water, showers, toilets and barbecue areas, use the **national park campsites** at Lake Allom, Dundubara and Waddy Point on the east coast and at Central Station and Lake Boomanjin (all booked through QPWS offices in the region). There are also **privately run campsites** at *Cathedral Beach Resort* (ⓣ07/4127 9177) and the nicer *Dilli Village* (see above).

For **supplies**, the east coast settlements of **Happy Valley** and **Eurong** have stores, telephones, bars and fuel; there's another store at *Cathedral Beach Resort* but no shops or restaurant at *Dilli*. You'll save money by bringing whatever you need with you – and make sure you take the empties home.

Around Central Station

Most people get their bearings by making their first stop at **Central Station**, an old logging depot with campsite, telephone and information hut under some monstrous bunya pines in the middle of the island, directly east of River Heads on the mainland. From the station, take a stroll along **Wanggoolba Creek**, a magical, sandy-bottomed stream so clear that it's hard at first to see the water as it runs across the forest floor. It's a largely botanic walk past some prehistoric angiopteris ferns to **Pile Valley**, where satinay trees humble you to insignificance as they reach 60m to the sky. They produce a very dense timber, durable enough to be used as sidings on the Suez Canal – and are consequently in such demand that the trees on Fraser have almost been logged out.

There are several **lakes** around Central Station, all close enough to walk to and all along main roads. Nine kilometres north (track distance), **McKenzie** is the most popular on the island, and often very crowded: ringed by white sand with clear, tea-coloured water reflecting a blue sky, it's a wonderful place to spend the day. To the south, **Birrabeen** (8km) is mostly hemmed in by trees, while **Boomanjin** (16km) is open and geologically "perched" in a basin above the island's water table. There's a fine campsite and communal fireplace here, attended by tame goannas.

Seventy-Five Mile Beach

Seventy-Five Mile Beach on the east coast is Fraser's main road and camping ground, one of the busiest places on the island. Vehicles hurtle along, pedestrians and anglers hug the surf, and tents dot the foredunes; this is what beckons the crowds over from the mainland. Sights along the way include **sand** in all its different forms: **Hammerstone Blow**, 6km north of Eurong, is slowly engulfing **Lake Wabby**, a small but deep patch of blue below the dunes with excellent swimming potential – another century and it will be gone. At **Rainbow Gorge**, about 5km south of **Happy Valley**, a short trail runs between two blows, through a hot, silent desert landscape where sandblasted trees emerge denuded by their ordeal. Incredibly, a dismal spring seeps water into the valley where the sand swallows it up; "upstream" are the gorge's stubby, eroded red fingers.

Six kilometres north of Happy Valley you cross picturesque **Eli Creek**, where water splashes briskly between briefly verdant banks before spilling into the sea. Sand-filtered, it's the nicest swimming spot on the island, though icy-cold. Back on the beach, another 4km brings you to the **Maheno**, wrecked in 1935 and now a skeleton almost consumed by the elements. More striking are the coloured cliffs known as the **Cathedrals**, which run north from the wreck. About 5km up the beach from here is the **Dundubara campsite**, behind which is the tiring, hot four-kilometre walk up **Wungul Sandblow** through what may as well be the Sahara; turn around at the top, though, and the glaring grey dunescape is set off by distant views of a rich blue sea.

Approximately 20km north from Dundubara, **Indian Head** is a rare – and pretty tall – rocky outcrop, the anchor around which the island probably formed originally. It's not a hard walk to the top, and on a sunny day the rewards are likely to include views down into the surf of dolphins, sharks and other large fish chasing each other; in season you'll certainly see pods of whales too, breaching, blowing jets of spray, and just lying on their backs, slapping the water with outstretched fins. From here there's a tricky bit of soft sand to negotiate for a final nine-kilometre run around to **Champagne Pools**, a cluster of shallow, safe swimming pools right above the surf line which mark as far north as vehicles are allowed to travel.

The interior, west coast and far north

Fraser's wooded **interior**, a real contrast to the busy coast and popular southern lakes, gets relatively few visitors. It encloses **Yidney Scrub**, the only major stand of rainforest left on the island, and although the name doesn't conjure up a very appealing image, the trees are majestic and include towering kauri pines. There's a circuit through Yidney from Happy Valley, taking in **Boomerang** and **Allom** lakes on the long way back to the beach near the Maheno. You can **camp** at Allom, a small lake surrounded by pines and cycads, and completely different in character from its flashy southern cousins. Further **north**, another road heads in from Dundubara township to **Bowarrady**, a not particularly exciting body of water famed for turtles who pester you for bread – if you can't imagine being pestered by a turtle, try refusing to hand it over.

The island's **west coast** is a mix of mangrove swamp and treacherously soft beaches, both largely inaccessible to vehicles. Access is via rough tracks which cross the island via Lake Bowarrady and Happy Valley to where the Urangan barge lands at Moon Point, though there's a better road to *Kingfisher Bay Resort* from the Central Station area.

Travel details

Trains

Main train routes out of Brisbane follow the Queensland coast north, covered at least daily by the *Sunlander*, *Queenslander*, and high-speed tilt train to Cairns, the *Spirit of the Tropics* to Townsville, and the *Spirit of Capricorn*, to Rockhampton. Southbound interstate services to Sydney also run daily. For Outback destinations from Brisbane, there's the *Westlander*, which heads inland twice a week to Toowoomba, Roma, and Charleville, and the *Spirit of the Outback*, another twice-weekly service via Rockhampton to Emerald and Longreach. For the twice-weekly *Inlander* to Charters Towers and Mount Isa, change at Townsville. All tickets – especially for sleepers – need to be booked as far in advance as possible.

Brisbane to: Ayr (6 weekly; 22hr 30min); Beenleigh (every 20min; 55min); Bowen (6 weekly; 21hr); Bundaberg (at least 1 daily; 4–6hr); Caboolture (every 20min; 1hr); Cairns (4 weekly; 31hr); Charleville (2 weekly; 16hr 25min); Cleveland, for Stradbroke Island (8 daily; 50min); Emerald (2 weekly; 15hr 15min); Eumundi (2 daily; 2hr 10min); Gladstone (at least 1 daily; 6–8hr); Glass House Mountains (every 2hr; 1hr 15min); Gympie (2 daily; 3hr); Ingham (4 weekly; 26hr 30min); Longreach (2 weekly; 24hr); Mackay (6 weekly; 16hr 30min); Maryborough (at least 1 daily; 3hr 45min–5hr); Proserpine (6 weekly; 19hr); Rockhampton (at least 1 daily; 7–12hr); Roma (2 weekly; 10hr 30min); Sydney (1 daily; 14hr); Toowoomba (2 weekly; 3hr 45min); Townsville (6 weekly; 24hr); Tully (4 weekly; 27hr 30min); Woombye (1 daily; 3hr).

Buses

The three main long-distance bus operators in Queensland are Greyhound Australia and Premier, who all follow the coastal highway; in addition, Greyhound Australia also run inland from Brisbane to Longreach and Mount Isa. Local operators include Kirkland's, which runs between Brisbane and Byron Bay via the Gold Coast; Suncoast Pacific Coaches, which runs between Brisbane and Noosa via the Sunshine Coast; and Crisp's, which runs due west from Brisbane to Toowoomba, Stanthorpe, Warwick and Goondiwindi.

Brisbane to: Airlie Beach (7 daily; 18hr); Ayr (8 daily; 21hr 30min); Beenleigh (8 daily; 40min); Bowen (8 daily; 19hr 30min); Bundaberg (5 daily; 6hr); Burleigh Heads (8 daily; 1hr 50min); Byron Bay (12 daily; 2hr 30min); Cairns (7 daily; 28hr 30min); Caloundra (8 daily; 2hr); Cardwell (7 daily; 24hr); Charleville (1 daily; 11hr); Childers (7 daily; 7hr); Coolangatta (8 daily; 2hr 10min); Gladstone (5 daily; 11hr); Gympie (10 daily; 4hr); Hervey Bay-Pialba (10 daily; 4hr 40min); Ingham (7 daily; 23hr 30min); Innisfail (7 daily; 27hr); Lamington National Park (1 daily; 3hr); Longreach (1 daily; 17hr); Mackay (8 daily; 15hr 30min); Maroochydore (5 daily; 2hr 5min); Maryborough (11 daily; 4hr); Mission Beach (5 daily; 26hr 25min); Mount Isa (1 daily; 25hr); Nambour (9 daily; 1hr 30min); Noosa Heads (7 daily; 2hr 50min); Rockhampton (7 daily; 12hr); Roma (2 daily; 7hr 45min); Surfers Paradise (every 30min; 1hr 30min); Sydney (10 daily; 16hr); Toowoomba (8 daily; 2hr 15min); Townsville (8 daily; 21hr 30min); Tully (7 daily; 25hr 30min); Winton (1 daily; 19hr).

Hervey Bay to: Airlie Beach (6 daily; 12hr 20min); Brisbane (8 daily; 4hr 40min); Bundaberg (5 daily; 1hr 40min); Cairns (6 daily; 22hr); Mackay (7 daily; 10hr); Mission Beach (5 daily; 20hr 30min); Noosa (5 daily; 3hr 15min); Rockhampton (7 daily; 5hr 30min); Townsville (7 daily; 16hr 25min).

Noosa to: Airlie Beach (4 daily; 15hr 50min); Brisbane (6 daily; 2hr 50min); Bundaberg (1 daily; 5hr); Cairns (2 daily; 25hr 45min); Hervey Bay (7 daily; 3hr 10min); Mackay (4 daily; 13hr 20min); Maroochydore (4 daily; 35min); Mission Beach (2 daily; 24hr); Rockhampton (4 daily; 9hr) Townsville (4 daily; 20hr).

Surfers Paradise to: Brisbane (every 30min; 1hr 30min); Burleigh Heads (every 10min; 30min); Coolangatta (every 10min; 1hr); Lamington National Park (2 daily; 1hr 30min); Sydney (8 daily; 15hr 30min); Tamborine Mountain (1 daily; 1hr); Toowoomba (2 daily; 3hr 30min).

Ferries

Brisbane to: Moreton Island (2 daily; 2hr); North Stradbroke Island (11 daily; 30min); St Helena (3 or more weekly; 2hr).

Hervey Bay to: Fraser Island (8 daily; 30min–1hr).

Rainbow Beach/Inskip Point to: Fraser Island (continually on demand; 15min).

Surfers Paradise to: South Stradbroke Island (3 or more daily; 30min).

Flights

The following are direct flights only.

Brisbane to: Adelaide (many daily; 3hr 30min); Alice Springs (2 daily; 4hr 30min); Bundaberg (2 daily; 50min); Cairns (many daily; 2hr 10min); Canberra (many daily; 2hr); Charleville (1 daily; 2hr); Darwin (2 daily; 3hr 40min); Emerald

(2 daily; 1hr 40min); Gladstone (4 daily; 1hr 15min); Hervey Bay (2 daily; 1hr 15min); Hobart (many daily; 3hr 50min); Longreach (1 daily; 3hr); Mackay (9 daily; 3hr); Maroochydore-Sunshine Coast (many daily; 30min); Melbourne (many daily; 2hr 25min); Mount Isa (2 daily; 4hr); Norfolk Island (4 weekly; 3hr 45min); Perth (many daily; 5hr); Proserpine (2 daily; 1hr 50min); Rockhampton (4 daily; 1hr 5min); Roma (1 daily; 1hr 10min); Sydney (many daily; 1hr 35min); Townsville (6 daily, 1hr 50min).

Gold Coast-Coolangatta to: Adelaide (many daily; 3hr 35min); Canberra (12 daily; 2hr 40min); Melbourne (many daily; 3hr 35min); Sydney (many daily; 1hr 15min).
Hervey Bay to: Brisbane (2 daily; 1hr 15min); Lady Elliot Island (2 daily; 35min).
Sunshine Coast-Maroochydore to: Brisbane (many daily; 30min); Melbourne (1 daily; 3hr); Sydney (1 daily; 1hr 45min).

5

Tropical Queensland and the Reef

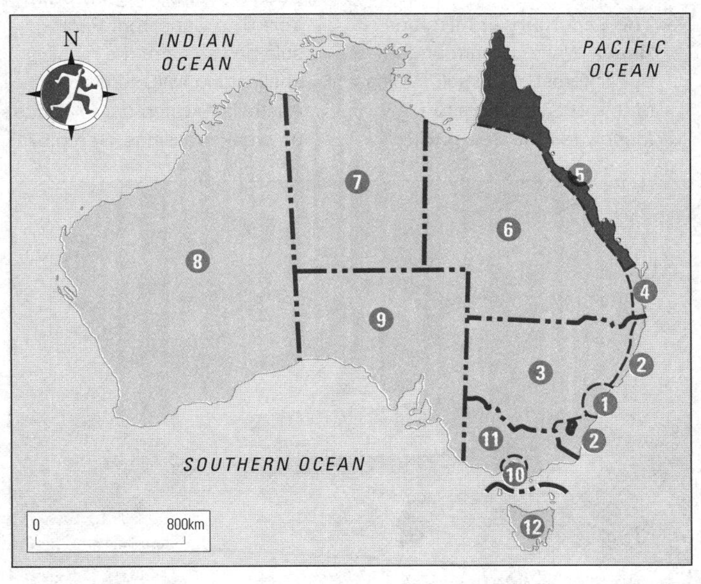

CHAPTER 5

Highlights

* **Great Barrier Reef** Scuba diving is the best way to explore one of the world's most beautiful coral complexes. **See p.486**

* **The Whitsundays** Lying just off the Great Barrier Reef, the rainforested peaks and long white beaches of the Whitsunday Islands offer some of the best diving and snorkelling in the world. **See p.509**

* **The Sanctuary at Mission Beach** Wake up surrounded by rainforest in the stilt cabins of this outstanding eco-friendly retreat. **See p.532**

* **Atherton Tablelands** The magnificent rainforest of the Atherton Tablelands brims with wildlife. **See p.551**

* **Aboriginal Dance Festival at Laura** In odd-numbered years, the sleepy town of Laura comes alive for two days in June for the fantastic Aboriginal Dance Festival. **See p.568**

* **Four-wheel driving on Cape York** The Cape York Peninsula has some of the most challenging 4WD territory in Australia – watch out for crocs on creek crossings. **See p.571**

△ Day-trip to the Great Barrier Reef

5

Tropical Queensland and the Reef

The move towards, and into, Queensland's **Tropical Coast** is more obvious than simply passing the Tropic of Capricorn marker at **Rockhampton**. North of Hervey Bay the landscape begins to brown as the temperature rises, and though there's still an ever-narrowing farming strip hugging the coast, the Great Dividing Range edges coastwards as it progresses north, dry at first, but gradually acquiring a green sward which culminates in the steamy, rainforest-draped scenery around **Cairns**. Along the way are scores of beaches, archipelagos of **islands** and regularly spaced cities, including **Townsville**, north Queensland's largest. There's also a wealth of **national parks**, some – such as Hinchinbrook Island – with superb walking trails, and others where you might encounter rare or unusual wildlife. Several places along the way are well set up for those with work visas to recharge their bank balances by **fruit and vegetable picking**; the best organized spots for this are the towns of Bundaberg, Bowen, Ayr and Innisfail. Moving north of Cairns, rainforested ranges ultimately give way to the savannah of the huge, triangular **Cape York Peninsula**, a sparsely populated setting for what is widely regarded as the most rugged 4WD adventure in the country.

Offshore, the onset of the tropics is marked by the appearance of the **Great Barrier Reef**, among the most beautiful and extensive coral complexes in the world. The reef, which begins to make its presence felt round the latitude of Bundaberg, drastically changes the nature of the coastline by blocking incoming surf and producing currents that deflect ocean-borne sand far out to sea. As a result, most **islands** north of Fraser are continental, formed when the peaks of ranges were drowned by rising waters at the end of the last Ice Age, creating abrupt coastlines and coral rubble beaches entirely different in character from the southeast's sandy formations. On the reef's outer edge, however, small isolated **cays** (sand islands) form, which tend to become encircled by fringing coral reef – these are particularly a feature of the southern reef. Further north, the cays thin out, while the main body of the reef thickens into thousands of individual shoals as it ventures nearer the coast. Whether cay or continental, many of these islands are close enough to ports for a day-trip, but for a real change of pace, try camping on one for a week or splashing out on a comfortable resort. **Divers** are well catered for, but novices needn't miss out on the best of the coral, which is within snorkelling range of the surface.

Access is along the more-or-less coastal Bruce Highway to Cairns, which is then briefly replaced by the Cook Highway, until notions of "main roads" begin to fall apart north of Mossman. Beyond here lie the jungles of the **Daintree**, the outpost of **Cooktown** and the beginnings of seasonal roads, humble tracks and the savannah wilderness of the Cape York Peninsula. Frequent **bus** and **train** services stop at all centres between Bundaberg and Cairns, but ideally you'll either be driving or willing to hitch to those places that the travel

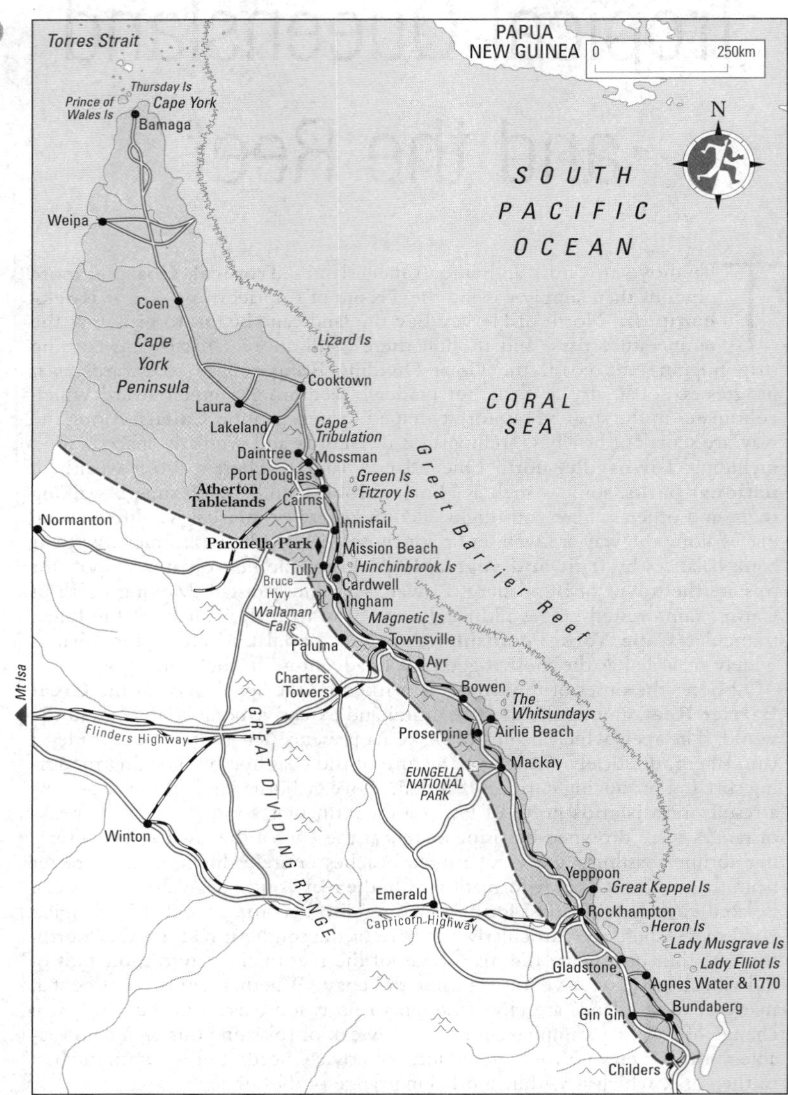

brochures have overlooked. Among the region's peculiar hazards are the slow, endless **sugar cane trains** that cross roads during the crushing season (roughly June–Dec); crossings are often (but not always) marked by flashing red lights.

Winters are dry and pleasant, but the summer climate (Dec–April) can be oppressively humid, with unpredictable **cyclones** bringing torrential rain and devastating storms, making roads on Cape York impassable and frequently even severing the coastal highway. To avoid the worst of the **crowds** at key places such as the Cairns region or the Whitsunday Islands, come as soon as the wet season is over (late April).

The Southern Reef

A string of cays about 80km offshore marks the southernmost section of the Great Barrier Reef: **Lady Musgrave Island** makes for a good day-trip, while there are resorts on **Heron** and **Lady Elliot** islands, and completely undeveloped campgrounds on several others. This section of the reef contains some of the better coral: being the furthest from land and surrounded by cool, deep water, it has suffered least from pollution and the El Niño-induced coral bleaching of recent years. Access is either from the ports of **Bundaberg** and **Gladstone**, or from the relatively remote coastal settlements of **Agnes Water** and **1770**. Bundaberg – along with the nearby hamlet of **Childers** – also lies at the heart of a rich sugar cane, fruit and vegetable farming area, and both are popular places to find short-term picking **work**.

Bundaberg is located 50km off the Bruce Highway from Childers (south) or Gin Gin (north); Agnes Water and 1770 can be reached either from Bundaberg or the highway; and Gladstone is 20km off the highway about 170km north of Gin Gin. Both Bundaberg and Gladstone are on the **train** line.

Childers

CHILDERS is a pretty, one-horse highway town, sadly known for the terrible fire which burned down the old *Palace Backpackers* in 2000, killing fifteen. The town has moved on, however: the site has been rebuilt as a tasteful, low-key memorial and **information centre** (Mon–Fri 9am–4pm, Sat–Sun 9am–3pm). Childers' core of old buildings offers an excuse to pull up and stretch your legs; these include the photogenic *Federal Hotel*, a wooden pub built in 1907, and the musty, bottle-filled and slightly dull **Childers Pharmaceutical Museum** (Mon–Fri 8.30am–4pm, Sat 8.30am–noon; $3). Just west of Childers, Flying High (daily 9am–4.30pm; $12.50) is a huge **aviary** with just about every type of Australian parrot and finch zipping around, squawking, or chewing the furnishings.

If you're after **farm work**, the new *Palace Backpackers* (Ⓣ07/4126 2244, Ⓦwww.childersbackpackers.com; $150/week) has numerous contacts and offers free transport to and from work but is often full so call ahead; alternatively the *Sugar Bowl Caravan Park* (Ⓣ07/4126 1521; three-bed bunk houses

The Great Barrier Reef

The **Great Barrier Reef** is to Australia what rolling savannahs and game parks are to Africa, and is equally subject to the corniest of representations. "Another world" is the commonest cliché, which, while being completely true, doesn't begin to describe the feeling of donning mask and fins and coming face to face with extraordinary animals, shapes and colours. There's so little relationship to life above the surface that distinctions normally taken for granted – such as that between animal, plant and plain rock – seem blurred, while the respective roles of observer and observed are constantly challenged by shoals of curious fish following you about.

Beginning with Lady Elliot Island, out from Bundaberg, and extending 2300km north to New Guinea, the Barrier Reef follows the outer edge of Australia's continental plate, running closer to land as it moves north: while it's 300km to the main body from Gladstone, Cairns is barely 50km distant from the reef. Far from being a continuous, unified structure, the nature of the reef varies along its length: the majority is made up by an intricate maze of individual, disconnected **patch reefs**, which – especially in the southern sections – sometimes act as anchors for the formation of low sand islands known as **cays**; continental islands everywhere become ringed by **fringing reefs**; and northern sections form long **ribbons**. All of it, however, was built by one animal: the tiny **coral polyp**. Simple organisms, related to sea anemones, polyps grow together like building blocks to create modular colonies – corals – which form the framework of the reef's ecology by providing food, shelter and hunting grounds for larger, more mobile species. Around their walls and canyons flow a bewildering assortment of creatures: large rays and turtles "fly" effortlessly by, fish dodge between caves and coral branches, snails sift the sand for edibles, and brightly coloured nudibranchs dance above rocks.

The reef is administered by the **Marine Parks Authority**, which battles against – or at least attempts to gauge – the effects of overfishing, pollution, environmental fluctuations and tourism. A popular villain, the polyp-eating **crown of thorns starfish** also causes severe destruction during cyclic plagues. All these things, sadly, are beginning to have a serious effect on the reef: the scorching, El Niño-inspired summer of 2001 saw extensive and widespread **coral bleaching** and subsequent die-back which, coupled with other stresses mentioned above, reduced many formerly colourful coral gardens to weed-strewn rubble. As of 2003, most badly hit areas were recovering, but it is becoming clear that if drastic measures are not taken soon to protect fish stocks, control agricultural run-off from sugar cane and banana farms, and reduce urban waste from being washed out to sea, the reef may have been irreversibly damaged within a generation. Don't let this put you off going – the reef is still unquestionably worth seeing, and if the government realizes how much tourism will be lost if the reef dies, they may get more involved in protecting it. In order to minimize damage, visitors should never stand on or hold onto reefs when snorkelling or diving; even if you don't break off branches, you'll certainly crush the delicate polyps.

Diving and other ways of seeing the reef

Scuba diving is the best way to come to grips with the reef, and **dive courses** are on offer right along the coast. **Five days** is the minimum needed to safely cover the course work – three days' pool and theory, two days at sea – and secure you the all-important C-card. The quality of training and the price you pay vary. Cheaper courses use island reefs or shore diving, instead of taking you to the main reef – though this isn't always a bad thing, as some of these sites are good. Before signing up, ask others who have taken courses about specific businesses' general attitude and whether they just seem concerned in processing as many students in as short a time as possible – you need to know that any problems you may encounter while training will be taken seriously. Another consideration is whether you ever plan to dive again: if this seems unlikely, **resort dives** (a single dive with an instructor) will set you back only $60 or so, and they're usually available on day-trips to the reef and island resorts. While the extra weight is a drag between dives, **qualified divers** can save on rental costs by bringing some gear along; tanks and weightbelts are covered in dive packages but anything else is extra. You need an alternative air source, timer, C-card and log book to dive in Queensland (the last is often ignored, but some places insist, especially for deep or night-time dives).

Snorkelling is a good alternative to diving: you can pick up the basics in five minutes and with a little practice the only thing you sacrifice is the extended dive time that a tank allows. If you think you'll do a fair amount, buy your own mask and snorkel – they're not dramatically expensive – as rental gear nearly always leaks. Look for a silicone rubber and toughened glass mask and ask the shop staff to show you how to find a good fit. If getting wet just isn't for you, try **glass-bottomed boats** or "subs", which can still turn up everything from sharks to oysters.

Reef hazards

Stories of shark attacks, savage octopuses and giant clams all make good press, but are mostly the stuff of fiction. However, there are a few things at the reef capable of putting a dampener on your holiday, and it makes sense to be careful. The best protection is simply to look and not touch, as nothing is actively out to harm you.

Seasickness and **sunburn** are the two most common problems to afflict visitors to the reef, so take precautions. **Coral and shell cuts** become badly infected if not treated immediately by removing any fragments and dousing with antiseptic. Some corals can also give you a nasty **sting**, but this is more a warning to keep away in future than something to worry about seriously. Animals to avoid tend to be small. Some dangerous **jellyfish** (see warning on p.42) are found at the reef during summer – wear a protective Lycra "stinger suit" or full wetsuit with hood. Conical **cone shells** are home to a fish-eating snail armed with a poisonous barb which has caused fatalities. Don't pick them up: there is no "safe" end to hold them. Similarly, the shy, small, **blue-ringed octopus** has a fatal bite and should never be handled. **Stonefish** are camouflaged so that they're almost impossible to distinguish from a rock or lump of coral. They spend their days immobile, protected from attack by a series of poisonous spines along their back. If you tread on one, you'll end up in hospital – an excellent argument against reef-walking. Of the larger animals, **rays** are timid, flattened fish with a sharp spine capable of causing deep wounds – don't swim close over sandy floors where they hide. At the reef, the most commonly encountered **sharks** are the black-tip and white-tip varieties, and the bottom-dwelling, aptly named carpet shark, or wobbegong – all of these are inoffensive unless hassled.

Environmental Management Charge

The Marine Parks Authority levies a fee commonly referred to as **reef tax** (currently $6 per person per day, though some tour operators add $4 extra for administration) to help fund monitoring and management of human impact on the reef. On most tours and boat trips, you will be required to pay the reef tax in addition to the cost of the tour. You may feel a little annoyed at having to fork out the extra money, especially if you've already paid quite a lot for your trip, but this is simply a "user-pays" system to help ensure that the reef is maintained for everyone to experience and enjoy.

$120/week) can arrange work though its management has drawn bad press from some travellers. Otherwise, *Hotel Childers* (☎07/4126 1719; ❷) is a great place to **stay**, with very cute "country-style" rooms, a spacious beer garden and the best **meals** in Childers – though *Laurel Tree Cottage*, on the main street at the Bundaberg end of town, comes a close second with traditional fare including delightful pies.

Bundaberg and around

Surrounded by canefields and fruit farms, **BUNDABERG** is famous for its **rum**, though the town is otherwise a humdrum place whose value as a jumping-off point for trips to Lady Elliot and Lady Musgrave **islands** is scarcely advertised. The adjacent coast is, however, an important place for **marine turtles**, who mass in huge numbers every summer to lay their eggs on the beaches; and those wanting **work** are virtually guaranteed seasonal employment (mostly Feb–Nov) picking avocados, tomatoes, snow peas and zucchini on farms in the area.

"Bundie" is synonymous with dark rum throughout Australia and if you believe their advertising pitch, the town's **rum distillery** on Whittered Street, about 2km east of the town centre along Bourbong Street (tours Mon–Fri 10am–3pm, Sat & Sun 10am–2pm; $9.90) accounts for half the rum consumed in Australia each year. A distillery **tour** allows fans to wallow in the overpowering pungency of raw molasses and ends, of course, with a free sample – though you probably won't need to drink much after inhaling the fumes in the vat sheds, where cameras are prohibited in case a flash ignites the vapour.

Flying 1270km from Sydney to Bundaberg in 1921, **Bert Hinkler** set a world record for continuous flight in a light aircraft (his flimsy wire and canvas Baby Avro), demonstrating its potential as transport for remote areas and so encouraging the formation of Qantas the following year (see p.602). In 1983, the

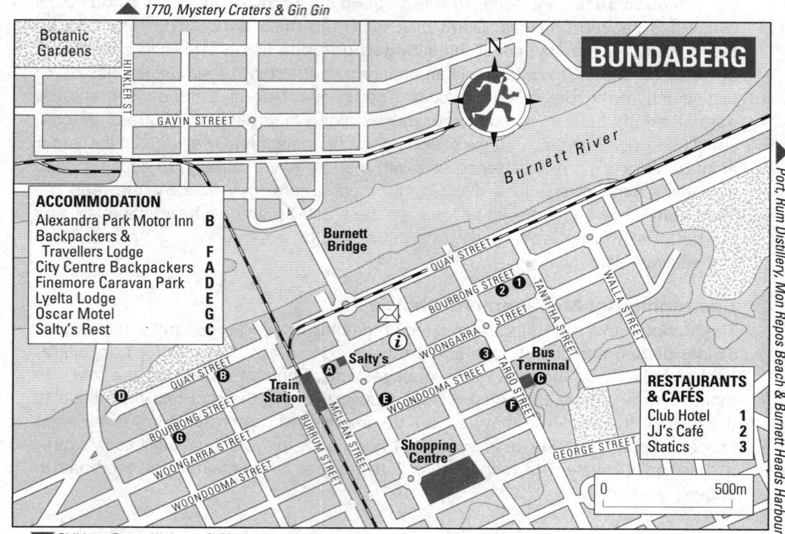

house where Hinkler lived at the time of his death in England was transported to Bundaberg and rebuilt in the Botanic Gardens, 4km from the centre over the Burnett Bridge towards Gin Gin, sharing its desirable surroundings with a Sugar Museum, Historical Museum and a steam train (all daily 10am–4pm; $5 for house). Outside the house, landscaped gardens flank ponds where Hinkler was supposedly inspired to design aircraft by watching ibises in flight.

Practicalities

Bundaberg lies south of the **Burnett River**, with the coast and quiet satellite suburbs – Bargara, Innes Park, Elliot Heads – about 15km to the east. Bourbong Street, the main thoroughfare, runs parallel to the river and is where you'll find several banks, the post office, and **Internet** cafés. The **bus terminal** is on Targo Street, and the **train station** (Ⓣ07/4153 9724, bookings Ⓣ13 22 32) is 500m west on McLean Street. The **airport**, for departures to Lady Elliot amongst other places, is 4km from the centre on the Childers Road; the **port**, for Lady Musgrave ferries, lies 10km east of the centre. The **tourist information** office (daily 9am–5pm; Ⓣ07/4153 8888) is at 271 Bourbong St.

Salty's, at 208 Bourbong St (Ⓣ1800 625 476, Ⓦwww.saltys.com.au), offers probably the cheapest four-day **dive course** in Australia ($169), though this uses shore dives with poor visibility and few fish; for $580 you get live-aboard boat diving around reefs and Lady Musgrave Island (qualified divers can get the same trip for $495 plus equipment rental). Bundaberg Coach Tours (Ⓣ07/4153 1037) runs **day-tours** featuring the rum distillery and other sights twice a week ($75), and twice-weekly day-tours to Agnes Water and 1770 ($75, minimum four people).

Central **accommodation** options include *Salty's Rest* (Ⓣ1800 625 476, Ⓦwww.saltys.com.au; dorms $18, rooms ❷), at the back of the bus terminal on Targo Street or the quieter but slightly seedy *Lyelta Lodge* on the corner of Maryborough and Woondooma streets (Ⓣ07/4151 3344; ❷). Most motels are just west of the centre: Friendly *Oscar Motel* at 252 Bourbong St (Ⓣ07/4152 3666, Ⓔoscarmotel@hotmail.com; ❸) has a pool and barbecue area, while *Alexandra Park Motor Inn* at 66 Quay St (Ⓣ07/4152 7255; ❸) is a modern Queenslander-style place with huge rooms. All places fill up over the Christmas holidays. For those looking for **farm work** try *Backpackers & Travellers Lodge*, opposite the bus terminal on Targo Street (Ⓣ07/4152 2080; dorms $20), and *City Centre Backpackers*, at 216 Bourbong St near the train station (Ⓣ07/4151 3501, Ⓔccbackpackers@hotmail.com; dorms $23, rooms ❷), although both hostels are reluctant to take advance bookings except in the quieter months from January to March. The closest **campsite** is *Finemore Caravan Park* on Quay Street (Ⓣ07/4151 3663; cabins ❷), which overlooks the river. At **Mon Repos Beach**, the first-rate beachfront *Turtle Sands Caravan Park* (Ⓣ07/4159 2340; cabins ❷) is right next to the turtle rookery and a kilometre of beach.

For **eating**, *JJ's Café* on Bourbong Street opens 6.30am for big breakfasts, while the nearby *Club Hotel* serves filling counter meals for lunch and evening, and sports a beer garden. For modern Italian, try *Statics*, on Targo Street. **Moving on**, trains and long-distance buses – Greyhound Australia (Ⓣ13 20 30) and Premier (Ⓣ13 34 10) – head up the coast to Gladstone and down to Childers and beyond; Greyhound Australia also runs to Agnes Water daily.

Mon Repos Beach and the turtle rookery

The Conservation Park at **Mon Repos Beach** is 15km east of Bundaberg, reached by initially following Bourbong Street out of town towards the port and looking out for small brown signposts for the beach (or larger ones for the *Turtle Sands Caravan Park*). Once the site of a French telegraph link to New Caledonia, today its reputation rests on being Australia's most accessible **loggerhead turtle rookery**. From October to March, female loggerheads clamber laboriously up the beaches after dark, excavate a pit with their hind flippers in the sand above the high-tide mark, and lay about a hundred parchment-shelled eggs. During the eight-week incubation period, the ambient temperature of the surrounding sand will determine the sex of the entire clutch; 28.5°C is the change-over point between male and female. On hatching, the endearing, rubbery-brown youngsters stay buried in the nest until after dark, when they dig themselves out en masse and head for the sea. In season, about a dozen turtles lay each night, and watching the young leave the nest and race towards the water like clockwork toys is both comical and touching – your chances of seeing both laying and hatching in one evening are best during January. The loggerhead's future doesn't look too bright at present: since 1980 Mon Repos' rookery population has halved, most likely due to net-trawling offshore. The QPWS runs nightly guided **tours** ($5.50) from November to March, when the beach is otherwise off limits between 6pm and 6am; most accommodation places can book you on a tour and transport package ($48), or contact Footprints Adventures (Ⓣ07/4152 3659, Ⓦwww.footprintsadventures.com.au) who organize specialist small group tours for $125.

Lady Elliot Island

The southern outpost of the Great Barrier Reef, **Lady Elliot Island** is a two-kilometre-square patch of casuarina and pandanus trees stabilizing a bed of coral rubble, sand and – in common with all the southern cays – a thick layer of **guano**, courtesy of the generations of birds which have roosted here. The elegant **lighthouse** on Elliot's west side was built in 1866 after an extraordinary number of wrecks on the reef; on average, one vessel a year still manages to come to grief here. Wailing shearwaters (muttonbirds) and the occasional suicide of lighthouse staff didn't endear Lady Elliot to early visitors, but a low-key **resort** and excellent reef have now turned the island into a popular escape.

Shearwaters aside, there's a good deal of **birdlife** on the island; residents include thousands of black noddies and bridled terns, along with much larger frigatebirds and a few rare red-tailed tropicbirds – a white, gull-like bird with a red beak and wire-like tail which nests under bushes on the foreshore. Both loggerhead and green **turtles** nest on the beaches too, and in a good summer there are scores laying their eggs here each night. The main reason to come to Lady Elliot, however, is to go **diving and snorkelling**: the best spots for diving are out from the lighthouse, but check on daily currents with the dive staff at the resort before getting wet. The Blowhole is a favourite with divers, with a descent into a cavern (keep an eye out for the "gnomefish" here), and there's also the 1999 wreck of the yacht *Severence* to explore. You've a good chance of encountering harmless leopard sharks, sea snakes, barracuda, turtles and gigantic manta rays wherever you go. Shore dives cost $29 per person, while boat dives are $39 ($49.50 for night dives), plus gear rental.

Lady Elliot can only be reached **by air** on daily flights from Hervey Bay or Bundaberg (day-return $239, including use of resort facilities, snorkelling gear and glass-bottom boat; resort guests $175; book through the resort). **Accommodation** on the island is with the comfortable *Lady Elliot Island Resort* (Ⓣ1800 072 200, Ⓦwww.ladyelliot.com.au; ❽), which has basic four-person tented cabins as well as motel-like suites with private bathrooms and ocean views. Breakfast and dinner (but not lunch or flights) are included in the rates; or enquire about discounted longer-term packages – but if you're not interested in underwater activities, a day or two is ample time to see everything and unwind.

Lady Musgrave Island

Lady Musgrave Island is another tiny, low island, this time covered in soft-leaved pisonia trees which host the usual throng of roosting birdlife, ringed by a coral wall which forms a large turquoise lagoon. Diving inside the lagoon here is safe but pretty tame (though snorkelling is good) – outside the wall is more exciting. Relatively easy, inexpensive access means that Lady Musgrave is the best of the southern cays on which to **camp** – there is no resort on the island, nor any facilities – though the island itself is off-limits during the tern nesting season (Oct–April).

From Bundaberg, *MV Lady Musgrave* departs from the Port Marina, about thirty-minutes' drive east from town (Mon, Thurs, Sat & Sun 8am; $145 single or day-return), taking three hours to reach the island. The booking office is at the marina (Ⓣ1800 072 110, Ⓦwww.lmcruises.com.au), and the staff here can organize a bus pick-up from your accommodation ($9). The island is also visited on Salty's dive trips (see "Practicalities", p.489). Alternatively, you can reach Lady Musgrave **from 1770 Marina** (see p.492) with the same company, whose ferry zips over to the island in just over an hour (Tues, Wed, Fri, Sat & Sun, 7.30am; $138 single or day-return). **Diving** from either vessel costs $30 for one dive or $40 for two, plus gear rental. **Campers** need camping **permits** from the Gladstone QPWS at 136 Goondoon St (Mon–Fri 8.30am–5pm; Ⓣ07/4971 6055) or book online at Ⓦwww.epa.qld.gov.au (see p.492); you can arrange for fresh provisions to be brought over by either ferry if you're planning a long stay – for practical details, see the "Island camping" box on p.493.

Agnes Water and 1770

On the coast 100km north of Bundaberg along the Rosedale road (or an additional 65km if coming from the north off the highway via **Miriam Vale**), the tiny settlements of **Agnes Water** and nearby **1770** mark where Captain Cook first set foot in Queensland on May 24, 1770. It's a pretty area, and one of the few undeveloped places along the Queensland coast that can be reached without a 4WD. If you don't have your own transport, Greyhound Australia operates a daily bus in both directions between Bundaberg and Agnes Water, stopping opposite Cool Bananas on Spring Road. Nearby attractions include the mangrove, fan palm and paperbark wetlands at **Eurimbula National Park**, and the coast at Agnes Water, which has Queensland's northernmost official **surfing**. 1770 is also the closest point on the mainland to the southern cays, with regular transport to several reefs.

AGNES WATER has undergone rapid development since the access road was sealed in 2000, and consists of a service station, two shopping complexes, several large resort villages and the *Agnes Water Tavern* – which does excellent **meals**. The town is fronted by a stunning, sweeping beach backed by sand dunes, and there are some delightful coastal walks in the area, including the 3km trail from Agnes Headland along the wooded ridge to Springs Beach, which is best reached from the Museum on Spring Road. For those with

4WD, there's access further south to **Deepwater National Park** and the **camping grounds** at Wreck Rock which are often fully booked during holidays (ⓣ07/4131 1600) – you can also explore the park with Discovery Coast Detours (ⓣ07/4974 9794; $28). **Accommodation** at Agnes Waters includes *1770 Getaway* (ⓣ07/4974 9329, ⓔgetaway1770@bigpond.com.au; ❹) on Spring Road set in four acres of landscaped gardens with over 65 species of tropical palms; *Agnes Palms Beachside Apartments* (ⓣ07/4974 7200, ⓦwww.barrierreef.net; ❸), on the road to 1770 and fronted by tropical bush just two hundred metres to the beach; *Escape* (ⓣ07/4902 1770, ⓔinfo@escapeat1770.com; dorms $25, rooms ❸), a smart homestay-style backpackers with complimentary breakfast and a pool with slivers of ocean views; and *Cool Bananas* (ⓣ07/4974 7660, ⓦwww.coolbananas.biz.com; dorms $22) on Spring Road which is a stopover for the Oz Experience and can get busy. Street Beat (ⓣ07/4974 7697), across the road, hires out scooters ($50 per day), cars ($55 per day) and 4WD vehicles ($75 per day).

1770 is even smaller, occupying the foreshore of a narrow promontory some 6km to the north. At the end of the road is windswept Round Hill with exposed walking trails and coastal views. **Reef boats** leave from the marina; Reef Jet runs day-trips to Fitzroy Reef lagoon ($125); see p.491 for details of how to reach Lady Musgrave Island. Among the more upscale **accommodation** options on hand, *The Beach Shacks* (ⓣ07/4974 9463, ⓔbeachshack@1770.net; ❻) are four hand-crafted bungalows facing the ocean; budget alternatives include the *Captain Cook Holiday Village* (ⓣ07/4974 9219; dorms $18, rooms ❸), which has a store, bar and bistro; and *1770 Campgrounds* (ⓣ07/4974 9286; cabins ❷), on the beach just beyond the marina. For **eating**, *Saltwater Café* overlooking the ocean on Captain Cook Drive does an excellent fish and chips with mains from around $20 – there's a lively bar next door.

Eurimbula National Park, on the west side of 1770 across Round Hill Creek, abounds with birdlife. You can **tour** the region aboard *The Larc* (ⓣ07/4974 9422; full day $95, sunset cruise $25), an amphibious bus which spends the day exploring the remote coastline. For road access to the park, head 10.5km back towards Miriam Vale from Agnes Water, where you'll see the track and national park sign to the north of the road. You can bushcamp about 15km inside the park in the dunes behind Bustard Beach but beware of prolific sand flies.

Gladstone and nearby islands

GLADSTONE is a busy port, and also the site of the Boyne Island processing plant, which refines aluminium from ore mined at Weipa on the Cape York Peninsula. Glaringly hot, there's no reason to stop here unless you're trying to reach the reef – if you're planning to camp on any of the southern cays, Gladstone is where you need to make arrangements through the **QPWS office**, at 136 Goondoon St (Mon–Fri 8.30am–5pm; ⓣ07/4971 6055 or book online at ⓦwww.epa.qld.gov.au). If you've time to spare, the **Tondoon Botanic Gardens**, about 7km south of town, comprise a part-wild spread of wetlands, woodlands, forests and native shrubs, all expertly laid out – you'll probably clock up wallabies and birdlife here too.

The main strip is Goondoon Street, where there's a "mall" – just the usual high-street shops, post office and banks – plus a couple of hotels and motels. You'll find a helpful **information centre** (Mon–Fri 8.30am–5pm, Sat–Sun

9am–5pm) inside the **ferry terminal** at the marina, about 2km north of the centre on Bryan Jordan Drive. *Gladstone Reef Hotel*, 38 Goondoon St (Ⓣ07/4972 1000; ❹), has ordinary motel rooms and good views from a rooftop pool. **Places to eat** include *Swaggy's Australian Restaurant*, 56 Goondoon St, with typical Aussie grills, and five buildings futher down at *Scotties*, which offers contemporary cuisine at gourmet prices.

Diving can be arranged through Gladstone Dive Centre, 16 Goondoon St (Ⓣ07/4972 9185), which runs irregular trips to Lamont, Llewellyn and Fitzroy reefs south of Heron. For longer trips, *Mikat* (Ⓣ07/4972 3415, Ⓦwww.mikat.com.au) caters to more serious divers and covers much of the southern reef from Lady Musgrave to Northwest islands.

Masthead and Northwest islands

Remote both in feel and location, **Masthead and Northwest islands** remain virtually undisturbed, with limited numbers of campers permitted at any one time. Both cays are around 500m long and 100m wide, with a good covering of pisonias; as the usual crowd of seabirds and turtles nest here, both are also closed during the nesting season (Oct–April). Even at other times, the ruckus generated by the birds can be quite disturbing, but in the right frame of mind this all becomes part of the experience. Don't overlook the reef's **snorkelling** or **fishing** if you have the gear, though bear in mind that certain sections of reef are protected zones where fishing is prohibited – check first with the QPWS in Gladstone.

The only way to reach Northwest and Masthead from Gladstone is by **charter boat**, and at $3000 minimum, you'll need to get a group together for it to be financially viable: operators include Robert Poulsson (Ⓣ07/4972 5166) and Curtis Endeavour (Ⓣ07/4972 6990), or contact the Gladstone Visitor Information Centre (Ⓣ07/4972 9000) at the Marina Ferry terminal for leads on other boats. Check the "Island camping" box below for practical details.

Heron Island

Famous for its diving, **Heron Island** escaped the depredations of guano hunters in the early twentieth century, though a turtle-canning factory operated on the island for several years. Small enough to walk around in an hour, half the cay is occupied by a comfortable **resort** and **research station**, the

Island camping

Campers intending to stay over on one of the undeveloped southern reef cays need to organize camping permits and transport well in advance, particularly for the Easter and September holiday periods, and to contact the boat operator a few days before departure to check on weather conditions – rough seas can suspend services to the islands. Note, too, that Lady Musgrave, Northwest and Masthead islands are **closed** to camping during the tern nesting season, between mid-October and mid-April. **Camping permits** cost $4 per person per night, and are only issued by the Gladstone QPWS (see opposite) or booking online at Ⓦwww.epa.qld.gov.au. You need to be entirely self-sufficient: take food, at least five litres of water per person per day, a fuel stove (wood fires are prohibited), waterproof tents and sand pegs, shovels, first-aid kit, a radio (for weather forecasts), spare batteries, garbage bags and emergency rations for at least two extra days.

rest covered in groves of pandanus, coconuts and shady pisonias, whose sticky seeds are unwittingly spread between islands on the backs of birds. Patches of long grass hide ground-dwelling rails (moorhen-like birds) which rocket from underfoot. Herons also stalk around the coral tops at low tide, fishing the pools – they're typically white, but a black species also frequents the area.

You can literally walk off the beach and into the reef's maze of coral, or swim along the shallow walls looking for action. The eastern edges of the lagoon are good for snorkelling at any time, but **diving** must be arranged through the resort (see below), which charges $48 for a standard dive, and $75 to venture out at night; equipment is extra. Dive **packages** save a few dollars if you're staying long enough to take advantage of them, and you can make two dives daily for free during June. A drift along the wall facing Wistari reef to Heron Bommie covers about everything you're likely to encounter. The coral isn't that good but the amount of life is astonishing: tiny boxfish hide under ledges; turtles, cowries, wobbegong, reef sharks, moray eels, butterfly cod and octopuses secrete themselves among the coral; manta rays soar majestically, and larger reef fish gape vacantly as you drift past. The Bommie itself makes first-rate **snorkelling**, with an interesting swim-through if your lungs are up to it, while the Tenements along the reef's northern edge are good for bigger game – including sharks.

There's a price to pay for all this natural wonder, namely no day-trips and no camping. The *Voyages Heron Island Resort* (reservations ⓣ13 24 69; island reception ⓣ07/4972 9055; ❽) is excellent, but its rates, coupled with the ferry charge ($180 return) place it well outside the budget bracket. **Ferries** leave from Gladstone Marina daily at 11am, except at Christmas; there's a car lockup here ($9 a day) operated by the tackle shop (8am–5pm).

The tropics: Rockhampton to Cape York

Rockhampton marks the start of the **tropics**, but with the exception of the Mackay region, it's not until you're well past the line and north of **Townsville** that the tropical greenery associated with north Queensland finally appears. Then it comes in a rush, and by the time you've reached **Cairns** there's no doubt that the area deserves its reputation: coastal ranges covered in rainforest and cloud descend right to the sea. Islands along the way lure you with good beaches, hiking tracks and opportunities for snorkelling and diving: the **Keppels** near Rockhampton, the **Whitsundays** off Airlie Beach, **Magnetic Island** opposite Townsville, and **Hinchinbrook** and **Dunk** further north. Cairns itself serves as a base for exploring highland rainforest on the **Atherton Tablelands** and coastal jungles in the **Daintree**, and for trips onto the **Cape York Peninsula** and, of course, out to the most accessible sections of the **Great Barrier Reef**.

Rockhampton

Straddling the Tropic of Capricorn, 100km north of Gladstone, **ROCKHAMPTON** was founded after a false goldrush in 1858 left hundreds of miners stranded at a depot 40km inland on the banks of the sluggish **Fitzroy River**; their rough camp below **Mount Archer** was adopted by local stockmen as a convenient port. The iron trelliswork and sandstone buildings fronting the river recall the balmy 1890s, when money was pouring into the city from central Queensland's prosperous cattle industry and the gold and copper mines 40km west at **Mount Morgan**. Today, however, despite hosting a large university campus, Rockhampton feels a bit despondent: the mines have closed (though before they did, they managed to fund the fledgling BP company), the beef industry is down in the dumps and the summers, unrelieved by coastal breezes, are appallingly humid. Bearing this in mind, the city is best seen as a springboard for the adjacent Capricorn Coast (see p.497), but with half a day to spare it's worth catching the Aboriginal version of history at the **Dreamtime Cultural Centre**; and there are a group of **limestone caves** to the north to poke around in.

Arrival and information

Rockhampton is divided by the Fitzroy River, with all services clustered directly south of the **Fitzroy Bridge** along Quay Street and East Street; the Bruce Highway runs right through town past two pairs of fibreglass bulls (repeatedly "de-balled" by pranksters). **Long-distance buses** stop at the coach station just north of the bridge on the highway; **local buses** to or from Yeppoon and the coast set down, amongst other places, along Bolsover Street.

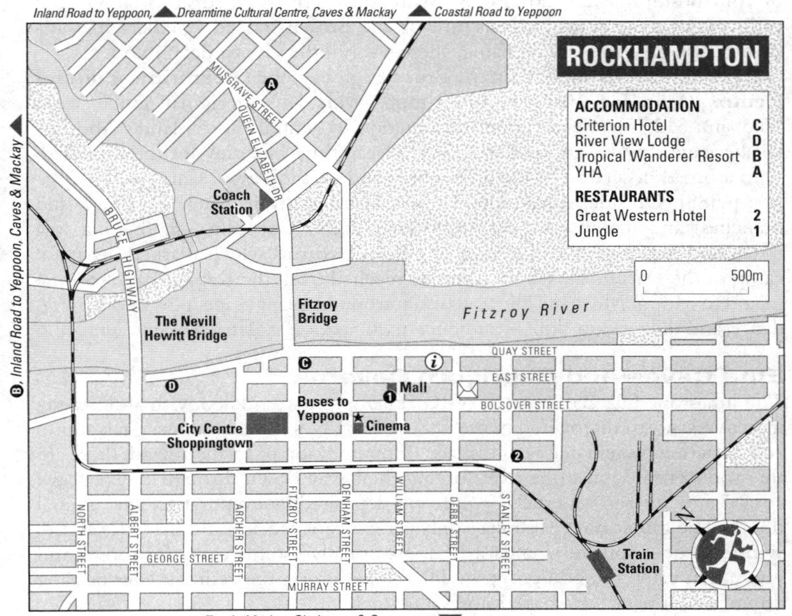

The **train station** is 1km south of the centre on Murray Street; the **airport** is 4km to the west at the end of Hunter Street. Banks, the post office and other services are mostly along East Street, and there's an **Internet** bar at *Jungle* (see opposite). **Tourist information** is available from the booth on the highway at the Tropic Marker, or at the more central **information centre** in the old customs house on Quay Street (Mon–Fri 8.30am–4.30pm, Sat–Sun 9am–4pm; ⓣ07/4922 5339). Recent reports of nasty incidents involving gangs of Aboriginal teenagers are unfortunately too numerous to ignore; there's no need for paranoia, but do follow local advice and don't walk alone at night.

Accommodation

The pick of the **accommodation** choices are the reasonably priced though often noisy suites above the pub at the historic *Criterion Hotel* on Quay Street (ⓣ07/4922 1225, ⓔryan@thecriterion.com.au; ❸), which overlooks the river. **Budget** options include *River View Lodge* at 48 Victoria Parade (ⓣ07/4922 2077, ❷) with shared facility rooms but in a pleasant and central location; the *YHA*'s well-appointed but dreary and isolated compound north of the river at 60 MacFarlane St (ⓣ07/4927 5288, ⓦwww.yha.com.au; $21.50); or the *Tropical Wanderer Resort*, on the highway 3km north of the river (ⓣ1800 815 563, ⓦwww.tropicalwanderer.com.au; cabins ❷, units ❸), with tent sites, cabins, motel units, a restaurant, and attractive gardens. If your only reason for being in Rockhampton is to get to Great Keppel, there's little reason to stay over, with Yeppoon and the ferry terminals so close by.

The City and around

It doesn't take long to look around the city. The **Tropic Marker**, 3km south of the river at Rockhampton's southern entrance, is just a spire informing you of your position at 23° 26' 30" S. Apart from a riverside stroll to take in the early twentieth-century architecture or the brown-stained boulders in midstream that gave the city its name, there's very little else to detain you.

About 5km north of town on the Bruce Highway, the **Dreamtime Cultural Centre** (Mon–Fri 10am–3.30pm; tours with an Aboriginal guide from 10.30am; $12.75) offers a good introduction to central Queensland's Aboriginal heritage. Inside, chronological and Dreamtime histories are intermingled, with a broad dissection of the archeology and mythology of Carnarvon Gorge (see p.588). Outside, surrounded by woodland, gunyahs (shelters of bark and branches) and stencil art, you'll find an unlikely walk-through dugong (sea cow), and the original stone rings of a **bora ground** which marked the main camp of the Darumbal, whose territory reached from the Keppel Bay coastline inland to Mount Morgan. The tour also introduces plant usage, plus boomerang, dance and didgeridoo skills – audience participation is definitely encouraged.

Etna Caves and Capricorn Caverns

The limestone hills 25km north of Rockhampton are riddled with an interesting **cave system** discovered in the 1880s. The caves have few classic stalagmites and stalactites, which need continuous dripping water to form; instead, there are tree roots encased in stone after forcing their way down through rocks, "cave corals" and "frozen waterfalls" – minerals deposited by evaporation after annual floods. The **ghost bat** (Australia's only carnivorous species) and the **little bent-winged bat** – both now endangered – seasonally use the caves for roosts, and you might catch the odd group huddled together on the ceilings, eyes peering down at you over leaf-shaped noses.

There are two sets of caverns open to the public, both reached by turning off the Bruce Highway at **The Caves** township: cross the rail line and bear left, and Etna Caves National Park is straight on past a council depot and around to the right; for Capricorn Caverns, turn right after the hotel and follow the billboards. The **Etna Caves** are undeveloped but none too extensive; between February and June you can explore on your own (6am–8pm; take a torch and durable shoes); between December and February you can go on a bat tour (four evenings a week; $7.60) with the QPWS – contact them for details (see below). The **Capricorn Caverns** (daily 9am–4pm; guided tour $16, adventure caving tour $60; ⓦwww.capricorncaves.com.au) are impressive, with plenty of spotlights illuminating their interiors. Bus tours to the Caverns leave at 9am on Monday, Wednesday and Friday from Kern Arcade (book first on ⓣ07/4934 2883; $40).

Eating and drinking

A **steak** of some kind is the obvious choice in Australia's "Beef Capital", and any of the hotels can oblige. There's a smattering of cafés around the mall, while the *Great Western Hotel*, over on Stanley Street (ⓣ07/4922 3888), serves quality 1884 steak, and has live country music and a weekly rodeo "out back" – call ahead for times as they change frequently. A perch at the *Criterion*'s bar on Quay Street overlooking the Fitzroy River is recommended for less flamboyant steak and beer, along with elbow-to-elbow closeness with a few locals. *Jungle*, on the corner of East and William streets, is a popular café-restaurant-bar which stays open late, and serves sandwiches and light meals for under $10 – the *Strutters* nightclub is upstairs.

Listings

Airlines Virgin and Qantas fly daily to Brisbane.
Buses Local buses serve the Capricorn Coast: Young's buses (ⓣ07/4922 3813; 6–12 daily) run from the stop beside the car park in Bolsover St, near the junction with William, to Yeppoon, Emu Park, and Rosslyn Bay. Greyhound Australia (ⓣ13 20 30) and Premier (ⓣ13 34 10) services all depart from the main bus terminal.
Car rental Network, 48 Fitzroy St (ⓣ1800 077 977); Red Spot Rentals, 302 Richardson Rd (ⓣ07/4922 7111).
Diving Capricorn Reef Diving, 189 Musgrave St, North Rockhampton (ⓣ07/4922 7720, ⓦwww.capricornreefdiving.com), gives certification courses from around $450 and offers dive courses around the Keppels.
Farmstays Myella Farm, The Eather Family, Myella, Barabala (ⓣ07/4998 1290, ⓦwww.myella.com), and Kroombit-Lochenbar, Valentine Plains Rd, Biloela (ⓣ07/4992 2186, ⓦwww.kroombit.com.au), are both a couple of hours out of town and offer accommodation, meals and participation in farm life from $250 for three days.
Hospital Base Hospital, Canning St, South Rockhampton ⓣ07/4920 6211.
QPWS The helpful QPWS office (ⓣ07/4936 0511) is situated 5km out of town on the Yeppoon–Rockhampton road.
Pharmacy CQ Pharmacy, 150 Alma St (daily 8am–10pm; ⓣ07/4922 1621).
Police Cnr Bolsover and Denham St ⓣ07/4932 1500.
Shopping City Centre Plaza on Bolsover St.
Taxi ⓣ07/4922 7111.
Trains Murray St ⓣ07/4932 0211.

The Capricorn Coast

Views from volcanic outcrops overlooking the **Capricorn Coast**, east of Rockhampton, stretch across graziers' estates and pineapple plantations to exposed headlands, estuarine mudflats and the **Keppel Islands**, 20km offshore. The coastal townships of **Yeppoon** and **Emu Park**, settled by cattle barons in the 1860s, were soon adopted by Rockhampton's elite as places to beat the summer heat, and retain a pleasantly dated holiday atmosphere, though **Great Keppel Island** is the coast's main draw.

Rockhampton to Yeppoon

First stop on the road to Yeppoon is about 25km from Rockhampton at **Koorana Crocodile Farm** (tours daily at 10.30am and 1pm; $15) where estuarine crocs are bred (koorana means "giving birth") to supply the leather industry and restaurants. If this doesn't bother you, the tours are interesting – despite a certain amount of showmanship involved in the feeding and meeting of Koorana's "stars". Some of the crocs are penned individually, but most are viewed en masse from the safety of protected boardwalks, raised over the mudflats and ponds where the reptiles bask. With luck you might see babies hatching, bleating as they squeeze themselves out of tiny eggs.

The sea appears suddenly at **EMU PARK**, a beach and breezy hillside covered by scattered Queenslander houses, where the wind howls mournful tunes through the wires of the **Singing Ship**, a peculiar monument to Captain Cook. **Budget beds** in a smart century-old building are offered at *Emu Park Beach House*, 88 Pattison St (ⓣ1800 333 349, ⓦwww.emusbeachhouse.com; dorms $18, twin rooms and family apartments ❷) – they also offer discount packages to Great Keppel from $69, and can collect from Rockhampton. A good alternative is the more motel-like *Endeavour Inn* on Hill Street (ⓣ07/4939 6777; ❸). One place to note between here and Yeppoon is **Rosslyn Bay**, where the cliffs have been weathered into hexagonal columns behind the **island ferry terminal** and **marina** (for details of getting to the islands, see below). Further on, **COOEE BAY** is virtually a suburb of Yeppoon, with an annual "Cooee Competition" when competitors give their tonsils a good airing from Wreck Point.

Yeppoon

YEPPOON's quiet handful of streets faces the Keppel Islands over a blustery expanse of sand and sea. All services are on **Normanby Street**, at right angles to seafront Anzac Parade. **Buses** pull into the depot on Hill Street, which also runs off Anzac Parade parallel with Normanby; the Young's Coaches **office** is just opposite. For **accommodation**, *Driftwood Motel*, 7 Todd Avenue (ⓣ07/4939 2446, ⓦwww.driftwoodunits.com.au; ❸), has self-contained rooms overlooking the beach, or there's basic dorm beds at *Yeppoon Backpackers*, 30 Queen St (ⓣ07/4939 8080; $20). The *Strand Hotel* (ⓣ07/4939 1301; ❸), on the corner of Anzac Parade and James Street, offers basic, four-bed units, while the *Poinciana Tourist Park* (ⓣ07/4939 1601; cabins ❷), just south of town off the Emu Park road, has self-contained cabins and shady tent sites.

Yeppoon prides itself on its fresh fish, and there are plenty of **restaurants** where you can sample it. The pick of the lot is *Seagulls Seafood* on Anzac Parade, which specializes in local Spanish Mackerel dishes, and its bucket of seafood is excellent value at $15. The nearby *Keppel Bay Sailing Club* has a cheaper bar with long views of the islands, while their restaurant offers budget all-you-can-eat lunches and dinners. Otherwise there's a legion of **cafés** to choose from along Normanby Street. For weekend **entertainment**, try *Bonkers Nightclub*, one road back from Anzac Parade on Hill Street.

The Keppel Islands

The eighteen **Keppel Islands** comprise a series of windswept hillocks covered in casuarinas and ringed by white sand so fine that it squeaks when you walk through it, while the sea is an invitingly clear blue – just right for a few days of indolence. Most of the islands are national parks and, with the exception of North and Great Keppel, are very small. Easy access, coupled with a resort and associated facilities, has made Great Keppel the most popular, but there are also reefs to snorkel and isolated camping spots on the other islands.

All access is from **ROSSLYN BAY**, just off the main road about 8km south of Yeppoon on the coastal route to Rockhampton, with departures from both the **ferry terminal** and the nearby **marina**. For **Great Keppel**, *Reef Cat* (Ⓣ07/4933 6744) from the terminal and *Freedom Fast Cat* (Ⓣ07/4933 6244) from the marina run a total of seven daily return services (the last leaves Great Keppel at 5.00pm); both charge $34 return. The marina is the place to find transport to other islands: *Prince Regal* is available for charter from $479 for two days, while the sailboat *Funtastic* offers day-cruises around the islands for $85 – for either call Ⓣ1800 336 244. The ferry terminal and marina both have exposed free parking, though for protection from salt spray, leave your car undercover at Great Keppel Island Security Car Park (Ⓣ07/4933 6670; $8 a day), opposite the Rosslyn Bay junction on the main road.

Great Keppel

Arriving at **Great Keppel**, the ferry leaves you on a spit near several **accommodation choices**; most offer packages or last-minute discounted packages (standby) if you ask for them. Closest to the spit, the *Pudley's on Keppel* (Ⓣ07/4933 6744; $24, cabins ❹) is a stark tent village with basic facilities and a military feel. Nearby, spruce and very friendly *Great Keppel Island Holiday Village YHA* (Ⓣ1800 180 235, Ⓦwww.gkiholidayvillage.com.au; dorms $27, tent cabins ❸, cabins ❺) has a first-rate kitchen and offers lodging in self-contained cabins, tents or dorms.

Along the beach, *Keppel Lodge* (Ⓣ07/4939 4251, Ⓦwww.keppellodge.com.au; ❹–❺) is a pleasant, **motel**-like affair; further down you come to the *Great Keppel Island Resort* (Ⓣ07/4939 5044 or 1800 245 658; ❽). This place changes its style on a regular basis; at present it's an 18–35 Contiki resort, with a lively bar and pool which may be open to non-guests. For **food**, there's a tearoom at the Shell House boutique on Fisherman's Beach. There's also a late-opening pizza shack – much frequented after the bar closes.

The main **beaches**, Putney and Fisherman's, are remarkably pleasant considering the number of people lounging on them at any one time, but a half-hour walk will bring you to more secluded spots. Reached on a woodland path past the resort, **Long Beach** attracts sun-worshippers, while snorkellers make the short haul over sand dunes at the western end to shallow coral on **Monkey Beach**. Middens (shell mounds) on Monkey Beach were left by Woppaburra Aborigines, who were enslaved and forcibly removed to Fraser Island by early settlers.

Other Keppels

The *Emu Park Beach House* in Emu Park on the mainland (see opposite) can set up trips to other islands, or contact the marina and enquire about boat charters (see opposite). None has provisions or reliable drinking water, so take your own. QPWS camping permits can be picked up at the Rockhampton (see opposite or book online at Ⓦwww.epa.qld.gov.au) or Rosslyn Bay offices. If you want to **scuba dive** around the islands, or simply get certified, contact Keppel Island Dive Centre on Great Keppel (Ⓣ07/4939 5022, Ⓦwww.keppeldive.com) – most dive sites are less than 15m deep, and there are abundant rays, turtles and sea snakes.

North Keppel is an undeveloped version of Great Keppel. There's a QPWS **campsite** on the west side of the island, behind the dunes at Considine Bay, with showers, toilets and a sporadic supply of tank water; take precautions against sandflies, which are abundant in sheltered spots here, and note that wood fires are banned. A walking track from the group of cabins at the southern end of Considine Beach leads to the reef at Maisy Bay.

Lightly wooded **Middle Island** has a QPWS camping area and **underwater observatory** complete with scenic Taiwanese junk. It's only a short hop from Great Keppel, and *Reef Cat* (☎07/4933 6744) runs daily snorkelling trips from Great Keppel for $25 return or you can visit as part of a Great Keppel day cruise from Rosslyn Bay for $55. **Humpy Island**, also off Great Keppel, is popular for fishing and has the best snorkelling reef of all the islands – a charter boat from Rosslyn Bay Marina will set you back $150. The hump doesn't do much to protect it from the southeasterlies, which are the main problem with camping here; facilities are similar to those on North Keppel.

Mackay and around

Some 360km north of Rockhampton along a famously unexciting stretch of the Bruce Highway, the fertile **Pioneer Valley** makes the **MACKAY** area a pleasant break from the otherwise dry country between Bundaberg and Townsville. Despite encounters with aggressive Juipera Aborigines, John Mackay was impressed enough to settle the valley in 1861, and within four years the city was founded and the first **sugar cane plantations** were established, attracting

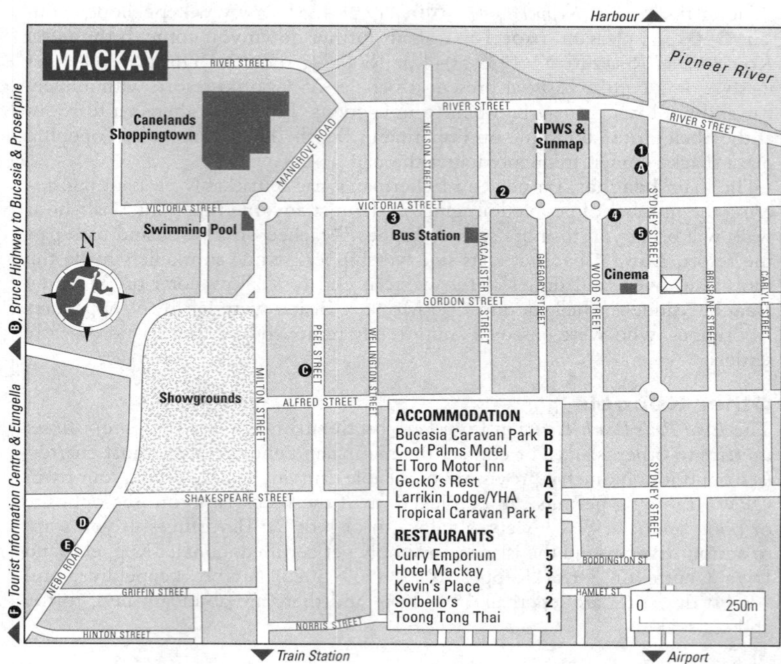

the migrant communities common to north Queensland – it's not unusual to hear English, Islander Pidgin and Maltese spoken within earshot of each other in town. Sugar and servicing mining operations centred inland on the Bowen Basin coalfields remain the core industries today, though both are facing uncertain futures: drought and viruses are ravaging crops, and the mines are gradually following new coal seams south and out of the region.

Mackay provides some welcome relief from the east coast "backpackers' pub crawl", and though it's only mildly geared up for tourism, the town's proximity to the delightful **Eungella** and **Cape Hillsborough** national parks makes it well worth a visit.

Practicalities

Mackay's centre straddles the crossroads of Victoria and Sydney streets, with the **bus station** just off Victoria on Macalister Street. Both **trains** (station on Connors Road, 3km south off Milton Street along Boundary Road or Paradise Street) and **planes** arrive south of town; a **taxi** into town from either terminal will set you back around $10. Mackay Travelworld at the bus station (Ⓣ07/4944 2144) is **ticket agent** for bus, train and air travel. The **tourist information** centre (Ⓣ07/4952 2677) is badly informed and poorly located 3km south of town along the Nebo Road (Bruce Highway); you're better off consulting the staff at wherever you're staying.

Accommodation

Most **accommodation** is either located in town or south along the Nebo Road, though for sun and sand, you need to take the highway towards Townsville and then turn off and follow the signs for **Bucasia**.

Bucasia Caravan Park Bucasia Esplanade, Bucasia Ⓣ07/4954 6375, Ⓔbucasia@bigpond.com. Beachfront camping and units with nice island views. Few amenities, although there's a nearby store. Units ❷

Cool Palms Motel 4 Nebo Rd Ⓣ07/4957 5477, Ⓕ4951 4660. Closest motel to town, quiet and inexpensive. ❷

El Toro Motor Inn 14 Nebo Rd Ⓣ1800 687 186, Ⓔeltoro@mackay.net.au. Not too far from the centre, with a friendly atmosphere and pool. ❸–❹

Gecko's Rest 34 Sydney St Ⓣ07/4944 1230, Ⓔinfo@geckorest.com.au. This central, modern hostel, set in a converted shopping arcade, has spacious rooms with a/c as well as a large, well-equipped kitchen, but little natural light. Dorms $20, rooms ❷

Larrikin Lodge/YHA 32 Peel St Ⓣ07/4951 3728, Ⓔlarrikin@mackay.net.au. Low-set, comfortable Queenslander house with a laid-back feel, two-minutes' walk from the bus station. The staff are very knowledgeable on the region, and the lodge runs its own bus to Eungella. Phone ahead to arrange check-in outside the office opening hours (7am–2pm & 5–8.30pm). Dorms $22, rooms ❷

Tropical Caravan Park Nebo Rd Ⓣ07/4952 1211. Two kilometres south from the centre, tidy *Tropical Caravan Park* has self-contained units in a garden setting. ❷

Eating

There is no shortage of good, cheap **places to eat** in Mackay. Several downtown pubs and restaurants also offer filling weektime lunch specials for around $5–10.

Curry Emporium 58 Sydney St. Open setting in a rather ordinary looking courtyard serving delicious Indian dishes – try the Durban Maharajah lamb, on the bone cooked in red curry. Everything under $20. Closed Sun & Mon.

Hotel Mackay Victoria St. As well as the usual grills, the hotel restaurant here has tasty Indian food, though the choices are limited. Expect to pay around $15 for a meal.

Kevin's Place Cnr Wood and Victoria streets Ⓣ07/4953 5835. Singaporean–Chinese restaurant with fixed-price lunches (try the *laksa* – a colossal bowl of noodles, seafood and spicy coconut soup) and à la carte dinners – around $22 – featuring

five-spice squid and whole fried fish. Closed Sun evenings.
Sorbello's 166 Victoria St. Good choice for pastas and other Italian dishes for around $20 per person.
Toong Tong Thai 10 Sydney St. Long-established Thai restaurant and takeaway with authentically hot and spicy food. There's a selection of appealing lunchtime specials, or it's around $25 a head for a full meal.

Listings

Airlines Virgin and Qantas have direct flights from Mackay to all the major cities between Cairns and Brisbane.
Banks Branches of all major banks are located around the intersection of Sydney and Victoria streets.
Camping equipment Mackay Camping World, 54 Gregory St.
Car rental Europcar, at the airport (☎07/4944 1188), offers the best rates in town.
Hospital Mackay Base Hospital, Bridge Rd ☎07/4968 6000.
QPWS Cnr Wood and River streets ☎07/4951 8788.
Pharmacy Day and Night Pharmacy, 65 Sydney St (daily 8am–9pm; ☎07/4957 3360).
Police Sydney St ☎07/4968 3444.
Post office 71–73 Sydney St.
Shopping Canelands Shoppingtown, across the road from the bus station, has everything you'll need.
Taxi ☎13 10 08.

Cape Hillsborough National Park

Cape Hillsborough, about an hour's drive north of Mackay, is the site of a pretty beachfront national park with tame wildlife, though you'll need your own vehicle to reach it. Head first up the highway towards Townsville and then take the signposted Seaforth road from **The Leap**, a small township at the base of a distinctively shaped hill which takes its name from events of 1866, when a settler was killed by Aborigines and the police drove an Aboriginal woman over the cliff during reprisals. The woman turned out to be holding a baby, which survived and was adopted by a local family. *The Leap*, one of Mackay's oldest **hotels**, is right underneath, and you can contest the details of the story over a cold beer if you're interested. From here the road passes the inevitable canefields on the way to Mount Jukes, before descending to coastal flats and turning off to Cape Hillsborough a couple of kilometres before **Seaforth** township.

The national park

The main area of the national park is set around a broad two-kilometre beach bounded by the wooded cliffs of Cape Hillsborough to the north and Andrews Point to the south; the shallow bay is good for swimming outside the stinger season. Local fauna include bush turkeys, pretty-face wallabies and some butch kangaroos – they're often on the beach in the early morning, males flexing muscles and chasing does in a parody of the stereotypical Aussie male. There's a ranger station here, with a small exhibition giving the rundown on local history and geology, but it's often closed. Hidden in bushland at the end of the road, the *Cape Hillsborough Resort* (☎07/4959 0152; ❸) has **tent sites and cabins**, plus an expensive and limited **store** (which closes at 6pm) and a restaurant. A good walk heads out 2km past here to **Hidden Valley**, a patch of cool, shady forest on a rocky beach where you'll find the outline of an Aboriginal fish trap; keep your eyes peeled for dolphins, turtles and pelicans out in the bay.

Five hundred metres back up the road towards Mackay, an excellent two-kilometre-long trail follows a **boardwalk** through coastal mangroves (bring insect repellent) and then snakes up to a ridge for views out over the area from open gum woodland peppered with grevillias, cycads (see box on p.527) and grasstrees – the latter identified by their tall, spear-like flower spike. There's also

Sugar cane on the Tropical Coast

Sugar cane, grown in an almost continuous belt between Bundaberg and Mossman, north of Cairns, is the Tropical Coast's economic pillar of strength. Introduced in the 1860s, the crop subtly undermined the racial ideals of British colonialists when farmers, planning a system along the lines of the southern United States, employed **Kanakas** – Solomon Islanders– to work the plantations. Though only indentured for a few years, and theoretically given wages and passage home when their term expired, Kanakas on plantations suffered greatly from unfamiliar diseases, while the recruiting methods used by "**Blackbirder**" traders were at best dubious and often slipped into wholesale kidnapping. Growing white unemployment and nationalism through the 1880s eventually forced the government to ban blackbirding and repatriate the islanders. Those allowed to stay were joined over the next fifty years by immigrants from Italy and Malta, who mostly settled in the far north and today form large communities scattered between Mackay and Cairns.

After cane has been planted in November, the land is quickly covered by a blanket of dusky green. Before cutting, seven months later, the fields are traditionally **fired** to burn off leaves and maximize sugar content – though the practice is dying out. Cane fires often take place at dusk and are as photogenic as they are brief; the best way to be at the right place at the right time is to ask at a mill. Cut cane is then transported to the mills along a rambling rail network. The **mills** themselves are incredible buildings, with machinery looming out of makeshift walls and giant pipes which belch out steam around the clock when the mill is in operation. Cane is juiced for raw sugar or molasses, as the market dictates; crushed fibre becomes fuel for the boilers that sustain the process; and ash is returned to the fields as fertilizer. **Farleigh Mill** (ⓣ07/4953 8400), north of Mackay, is open for **tours** (Mon–Fri, 1pm; $17) during the crushing season (June–Nov); sturdy shoes, long-sleeve shirt and long trousers are essential.

a huge **midden** up here, the remains of Aboriginal shellfish feasts, plus plenty of reptiles sunning themselves around the edges of the path.

Eungella National Park

At the end of the bitumen, 80km west of Mackay, magical rainforest and rivers would make **Eungella National Park** (pronounced "young-g'lla) worth the journey even if you weren't almost guaranteed to see **platypuses**. There are two separate sections: lowland swimming holes at **Finch Hatton Gorge** and highland forest at **Broken River**. Finch Hatton's rainforest is authentically tropical, while Broken River's plants are more closely allied with subtropical forests. The park's isolation has produced several unique species, including the Mackay tulip oak, the Eungella honeyeater and the much-discussed but probably extinct **gastric brooding frog**, known for incubating its young in its stomach.

Day-trips to both sections of the park can be arranged with Reeforest Tours from Mackay (ⓣ1800 500 353, ⓦwww.reeforest.com; $75) or the *Larrikin Lodge* (see p.501; $75) who also organize an overnight camping package for $145 including equipment, guided tour and two nights at their Mackay hostel before and after your visit to Eungella. With your own vehicle, head south down the Nebo Road/Bruce Highway to Mackay's city limits and follow the signs; if you're coming south down the highway from Proserpine, follow the signs just south of tiny **Kuttabul**, around 30km from Mackay.

Finch Hatton Gorge

The Eungella road passes through prime cane country as it runs the length of the **Pioneer Valley**; 35km along, call in at **Illawong Fauna Park** (daily 9am–5.30pm, except Jan–March closed Mon; $12, Ⓦwww.illawong-sanctuary.com) for a close look at a big slice of the local wildlife, from crocodiles and dingoes to koalas and the bizarre tawny frogmouth. Feeding time is 2.15pm, there's a pool to cool off in, one overnight **cabin** ($60 per person including bed, breakfast, dinner and park admission), and tickets are valid for unlimited entry all day.

Some 60km from Mackay, signposts just before Finch Hatton township mark the turn-off to **Finch Hatton Gorge**, 12km from the main road across several **fords** – access depends on the season, though generally it's negotiable by all vehicles. Immediately across the first creek, *Platypus Bush Camp* (Ⓣ07/4958 3204, Ⓦwww.bushcamp.net; dorms $20, cabins ❸), provides **camping** and basic cabin **accommodation**: mattress, pillow, amenities and kitchen are supplied; the rest (including food) is up to you. This is the most authentic rainforest experience you can have anywhere in Queensland: you'll see an astonishing array of bird- and animal-life (including the elusive platypus), sit by a fire under the stars, shower in the rainforest amidst fairy-like fireflies, and be lulled to sleep by a gurgling creek. About a kilometre and three creeks further you'll find *Finch Hatton Gorge Cabins* (Ⓣ07/4958 3281; dorms $16.50, cabins ❸) and a small **tearoom**. This is also the pick-up point for **Forest Flying** (advance booking essential on Ⓣ07/4958 3359; $45), which can take you for a ride 25m up through the tree tops (and a flying fox colony) on a wire-and-sling affair – much more secure than it sounds, and offering as close a view of the forest canopy as you'll ever get.

Another kilometre past the tearoom, the road ends at a picnic area, with **walking tracks** leading off into the forest. The gorge winds down the side of Mount Dalrymple as a rocky creek pocked with **swimming holes** and overshadowed by a hot jungle of palms, vines and creepers. **Araluen Falls** (1.5km from the picnic area), a beautiful, if icy, swimming hole and cascade, is the perfect place to spend a summer's day; further up (3km from picnic area) is an even more attractive cascade at the **Wheel of Fire Falls**, where you can sit up to your neck in the water.

Eungella township and Broken River

Past Finch Hatton township, the main road makes an unforgettably steep and twisting ascent. Take an immediate left at the top and stop for a drink or meal at *Eungella Chalet* (Ⓣ07/4958 4509; twins and doubles with shared bath ❸, suites ❹, five-person cabins ❻), whose back-lawn beer garden and swimming pool sit just metres away from a 700-metre drop into the forest, with a fantastic panorama down the valley. They've also installed a **hang-glider ramp** next to the pool that's used for the sporadically staged North Queensland Hang-gliding Championships (ask locally for dates). Around the corner, a general store, chip shop and couple of cafés form the rest of **EUNGELLA** township, while 5km further on, through patches of forest and dairy pasture, is **Broken River**. There's **accommodation** here at the excellent *Broken River Mountain Retreat* (Ⓣ07/4958 4528, Ⓦwww.brokenrivermr.com.au; doubles ❹, four-person self-contained cabins with fireplaces ❺) – they also run free guided **night walks** for their guests – or across the river at the QPWS **campsite** (cold showers and barbecues; self-registration). You can pick up free maps at the ranger's office (daily 8am–4.30pm; though not always attended, maps are available outside; Ⓣ07/4958 4552). Next door is a **kiosk** open daily for snacks and minimal supplies. Be prepared for rain: Eungella translates as "Land of Cloud".

Crowded during holidays and weekends, at other times the forest is quiet and cool, its interior chock full of wildlife and unusual plants. The best vantage points for **platypus-watching** are upstream from the road bridge on the purpose-built platform, or from the bridge itself. Normally fairly timid creatures, here they've become quite tolerant of people, and you can often see them right through the day. Wander around the picnic area after dark with a torch to see other **wildlife**: feathertail gliders, bettong, possums, grey kangaroos and owlet nightjars. Down by the river you're more likely to come across frogs, cane toads and platypuses in the evening, while squirrel gliders are sometimes seen in the huge gum trees up along the main road, and pythons use the warm verges to recover energy before a night's hunting.

The real star of Broken River, though, is the **forest** itself, whose ancient trees with buttressed roots and immensely high canopies conceal a floor of rich rotting timber, ferns, palms and vines. Local **cabbage palms**, with their straight trunks and crown of large, fringed leaves, along with huge, scaly-barked **Mackay cedar** and **tulip oaks**, are all endemic; many other shrubs and trees here are otherwise only found further south, indicating that Eungella may have been once part of far more extensive forests. It can be difficult to see animals in the undergrowth but the sun-splashed paths along riverbanks attract goannas and snakes, and you'll certainly hear plenty of birds. The best two **walking tracks** are either following the river upstream to Crediton, and then returning along the road (16km); or heading through the forest and down to the *Eungella Chalet* (13km return). If you're not that dedicated, there's also an easy forty-minute circuit from the picnic grounds upstream to **Crystal Cascades**.

On to Whitsunday

PROSERPINE, 123km north of Mackay, is a workaday sugar town on the turn-off from the Bruce Highway to Whitsunday, and a major transit point for the Whitsunday region. **Trains** and **planes** both service the town, as do the main **long-distance buses** – though they also have routes which detour daily to Airlie. Just south of town on the highway, **Whitsunday Information** (Ⓣ07/4945 3711) provides a fairly unbiased view of the area, something somewhat lacking at similar operations elsewhere in Whitsunday. If you wind up in town, Whitsunday Transit (Ⓣ07/4946 1800) runs a **local bus** six times daily between Proserpine and Whitsunday; contact them in advance to arrange pick-ups from the train station at the western end of town or airport (which is 10km south of town). Late arrivals can stay at the functional *Proserpine Motor Lodge*, 184 Main St (Ⓣ07/4945 1788; ❸), or the van park on Jupp Street.

Twenty kilometres east off the highway, **WHITSUNDAY** is the cover-all name for the increasingly sprawling communities of **Cannonvale**, **Airlie Beach** and **Shutehaven** (aka Shute Harbour). Until the early 1980s these were known only to locals and yachties, though following the discovery of the **Whitsunday Islands** (see p.509) by the mass tourist industry, the area boomed. Despite this, even now nobody comes to Whitsunday to spend time in town; it's just a place to be while deciding which island to visit. Airlie Beach and Cannonvale are the service centres; Shutehaven, from where island ferries generally leave, is 10km on from Airlie, past Cape Conway National Park. Other cruise and dive boats leave from **Abel Point Marina** between Cannonvale and Airlie. Whitsunday Transit runs a bus between Cannonvale, Airlie and Shutehaven roughly once an hour from around 6am to 10pm.

Cannonvale, Airlie Beach and Shutehaven

Coming from Proserpine, Whitsunday's first community is **CANNONVALE**, a scattering of modern buildings fringing the highway for about a kilometre or so, overlooked by luxury homes set higher up on the wooded slopes of the Conway Range. Just around the headland past Abel Point Marina, **AIRLIE BEACH** is nestled between the sea and pine forests, with just about everything crammed into one short stretch of **Shute Harbour Road** and the hundred-metre-long **Esplanade**. Despite the name, Airlie Beach has only a couple of gritty stretches of sand which get covered at high tide – though the view of the deep turquoise bay, dotted with yachts and cruisers, is very pretty. To make up the shortfall, there's a fine open-air landscaped **pool**, complete with showers, changing rooms, and a little sand, between Shute Harbour Road and the sea, which has gained local notoriety thanks to its nocturnal popularity with couples.

The main preoccupation in Whitsunday is organizing a **cruise**, but you can also rent **watersports** gear from the kiosk on the beach at Airlie; organize half-day to six-day **sea-kayaking** expeditions with Salty Dog (ⓣ07/4946 1388, ⓦwww.saltydog.com.au); or visit Bredl's **Wildlife Park** (daily 9am–4.30pm; $20), a ten-acre bush-zoo 4km from Airlie Beach towards Shutehaven, which has an excellent reptile collection. Otherwise, **Conway National Park** comprises a mostly inaccessible stretch of forested mountains and mangroves facing the islands, but there's a small picnic area on the roadside about 7km from Airlie on Shute Harbour Road, from where an easy walking track climbs **Mount Rooper** to an observation platform giving views of the islands' white peaks jutting out of the unbelievably blue sea. A final 3km on, **SHUTEHAVEN** (Shute Harbour) comprises a cluster of houses with stunning views overlooking the islands from wooded hills above Coral Point; it's one of Australia's busiest harbours, and most of the island ferries and bareboat charters depart from here. Those with cars will find limited **parking space** here; undercover facilities are available behind the Shell garage ($8 a day, or $14 for 24hr); there's an open-air grid at the harbour itself ($8 a day), and a free (but unguarded) area at the Lions Lookout up the hill from the Shell garage.

The Reef

The **Barrier Reef** sits about 50km northeast of Airlie, and contains some good sections with reasonably priced live-aboard dive charters – though if you're heading north, you'll find better-value day-trips to the reef available from Cairns. For a very easy couple of hours of snorkelling or diving, head for the pontoon at **Hardy reef** with Fantasea (ⓣ07/4946 5111, ⓦwww.fantasea.com.au; $161 includes snorkel equipment, $243 includes a one-tank dive). The popular **Bait reef** is visited by Reefjet (ⓣ07/4948 1212, ⓦwww.reefjet.com.au; $138 includes snorkel equipment, $198 includes a one-tank dive), though the lagoon here has been very hard hit by coral bleaching; bommies (isolated coral outcrops) on the outer edge make for better drift diving, and manta rays are occasionally seen too. The best sites – which are only visited by live-aboard dive boats (see "Listings", p.508) – are **Elizabeth**, **Seagull** and **Fairey**; Elizabeth and Seagull have great visibility, along with swarms of mackerel, trevally, humpheaded wrasse, sharks and juvenile reef fish hiding in the coral, while Fairey's strong currents make for exhilarating drift dives. Don't discount the fringing reefs around the islands either – see the island accounts for details of these.

Before heading out to the reef, make sure you catch **Reef Discovery**, a ninety-minute slide show and talk about the reef and its inhabitants given by local divers. Shows are held daily except Saturday at 6.15pm ($10) in the Reef Discovery building, towards the Shutehaven end of Shute Harbour Road; times are posted on the door.

Practicalities

Airlie's **long-distance bus terminal** is at the eastern end of town, off the Esplanade past the *Airlie Beach Hotel*. Staff at the town's hotels, hostels and other places offer limitless **information**, though don't expect it to be unbiased; the information office, airliebeach.com, up at the Cannonvale end of Airlie (ⓣ07/4946 5299, ⓦwww.airliebeach.com) is probably the most objective source, but it's a good idea to ask other visitors about which cruises they recommend before making a decision.

Accommodation

Unless you're in town during the September **Whitsunday Fun Race**, Christmas or New Year, you'll have little trouble finding **accommodation** – Cannonvale is a rather bland sprawling suburbia; Airlie Beach is busy and full of action; and Shutehaven is rural and extremely peaceful. All places act as tour agents, offering reductions or free nights if you book through them, although competition is ruthlessly cutthroat and some places eject guests found making bookings through other agents. Hostels are all cramped, but a pool, kitchen and room fridges are standard amenities. Motels and resorts often offer discounted rates of ten to twenty percent during the low season (roughly Feb to Easter and Oct to mid-Dec). For a campsite or cabins, try *Airlie Cove Van Park*, 3km towards Shutehaven on Shute Harbour Road (ⓣ07/4946 6727, ⓦwww.airliecove.com.au; cabins ❸).

Airlie Beach Hotel On the Esplanade, Airlie ⓣ07/4964 1999, ⓦwww.airliebeachhotel.com.au. This formerly seedy motel is now one of the smartest places to stay in Airlie. Refurbished older motel rooms ❹, new beachfront hotel rooms ❺

Airlie Beach YHA 394 Shute Harbour Rd, Airlie ⓣ07/4946 6312. Generally busy and somewhat crowded, with tidy dorms and doubles. Dorms $24.50, rooms ❸

Airlie Waterfront Backpackers Near the *Airlie Beach Hotel*, Airlie ⓣ07/4948 1300, ⓔawbpack@airlie.net.au. Apartments above a boutique shopping complex with private bedrooms and shared bathrooms and kitchens, sleeping six; also has dorms. Dorms $18–22, rooms ❸

Airlie Waterfront Bed and Breakfast Cnr Broadwater and Mazlin streets, Airlie ⓣ07/4946 7631, ⓦwww.airliewaterfrontbnb.com.au. One- or two-bedroom serviced apartments in a modern timber house with fantastic bay views; rooms are comfortably furnished; some have outdoor spa baths. ❻–❼

Backpackers By The Bay 12 Hermitage Drive, Airlie ⓣ07/4946 7267, ⓔbythebay@whitsunday.net.au. Small, comfortable place that's quieter than those in the centre of town and has nice bay views. Dorms $22, rooms ❷

Beaches 362 Shute Harbour Rd, Airlie ⓣ07/4946 6244 or 1800 636 630. Brash backpackers' hostel, with plenty of bunks and double rooms available. Dorms $20, rooms ❸

Coral Point Lodge 54 Harbour Ave, Shute Harbour ⓣ07/4946 9500, ⓕ4946 9469. Delightful and excellent value rooms and apartments with the best views in the Whitsundays. A bit hard to find though – turn up the hill immediately after the Shell garage and keep going to the end. The café-restaurant on hand is well worth a stop even if you're not staying here. ❹

Coral Sea Resort 25 Oceanview Ave, at the Cannonvale end of Airlie ⓣ07/4946 6458, ⓦwww.coralsearesort.com. Airlie's newest, most exclusive accommodation; rooms (some with ocean views) are all very smart, and there's a private jetty and a popular bar and pool area too. ❻

Koalas Shute Harbour Rd, at the Cannonvale end of Airlie ⓣ07/4946 6001 or 1800 800 421. Basic six-bed dorms, each with bathroom and TV. Facilities include a communal kitchen, volleyball court and large pool in pleasant landscaped grounds; you can also camp here. Dorms $16, rooms ❸

Magnums By the bridge on Shute Harbour Rd, Airlie ⓣ1800 624 634, ⓦwww.magnums.com.au. Tidy cabins with own bathrooms, pleasantly sheltered lawns, and a loud bar and nightclub next door. Dorms $12–18, rooms ❷

On the Beach Shute Harbour Road, Cannonvale end of Airlie ⓣ07/4946 6359, ⓔthebeach@whitsunday.net.au. Unpretentious central motel with self-contained serviced units looking over Airlie's artificial pool to the bay. ❹

Reef Oceania Village Resort ("Reef O's") 147 Shute Harbour Rd, Cannonvale ⓣ07/4946 6137 or

1800 800 795. The cheapest beds in the Whitsundays, but a bit out of town although a regular free shuttle-bus (6am–midnight) compensates. There's also a pool, inexpensive bar/bistro with live music, and a poorly equipped communal kitchen. Dorms $12–18, rooms ❷

Whitehaven Holiday Units 285 Shute Harbour Rd, Airlie ☎07/4946 5710, ⓔwhitsundayunits@wilput.com.au. Extraordinarily quiet, given its central location. Rooms are simply furnished and face out to sea. ❹

Eating and entertainment

You'll find a variety of places to **eat** in the area, though the majority of restaurants, as well as the liveliest nightclubs, are in Airlie, with a string of places along the Esplanade or Shute Harbour Road. Many of the smaller cafés open early and offer cheap breakfast specials. For self-caterers, there's a supermarket near the bridge.

Café Mykonos 287 Shute Harbour Rd, Airlie. Cheap and cheerful kebabs, souvlakia, dolmades and salads, with nothing over $9. Basically a takeaway, but there are a few tables and chairs if the nearby beach doesn't appeal.

Chatz Shute Harbour Rd, Airlie, across from Mykonos. Bar and brasserie serving mammoth helpings of grilled and basted meats for around $22. Top-value lunchtime deals for $6–10.

Deja Vu 303 Shute Harbour Rd, Airlie. Award-winning BYO restaurant, tucked away in a small courtyard, with a seasonal menu (around $30 per person). Dinner only (Tues–Sun).

Golden Temple 252 Shute Harbour Rd, Cannonvale. Popular and friendly Chinese restaurant with spacious dining and the usual takeaway menu. All mains under $20.

Hog's Breath Café Shute Harbour Rd, Airlie. The original of this chain of Tex-Mex grill restaurants, still serving good grub. Main courses around $24.

Juice Bar Cannonvale end of Shute Harbour Rd. Nightly grind 10pm–late.

KC's 50 Shute Harbour Rd, Airlie. Blowout on chargrilled steak, kangaroo, croc and seafood in noisy comfort; stays open until 3am and often has live bands. Mains around $20–25.

Morocco's Shute Harbour Rd, at the Cannonvale end of Airlie. Lively bar with a huge video screen, party atmosphere and cheap Mexican and Cajun dishes. Open daily 3pm–2am.

Paddy Shenanigan's Below the *Juice Bar*. Popular place to down a few pints and set the mood before heading upstairs.

Sailing Club Up past the bus stop off the Esplanade. Bar and decent pub food from 10am until late, with views out over the bay.

Listings

Airlines Island Air ☎07/4946 9933; Qantas ☎07/4945 1613 or ☎13 13 13.

Airports Long-distance flights use Proserpine; local flights to or around the islands depart from Whitsunday Airport, about halfway between Airlie and Shutehaven.

Banks NAB and Commonwealth in Airlie; ANZ and Westpac in Cannonvale.

Boat charters Unless you know exactly what you want, bookings are best made through an agent. Bareboat charters should be undertaken by experienced sailors only: average wind velocity in the Whitsundays is 15–25 knots, which means serious sailing. Five-person yachts start at around $400 a day; add another $100 during holiday seasons. Whitsunday Rent-a-Yacht ☎07/4946 9232, ⓦwww.rentayacht.com.au; and Queensland Yacht Charters ☎07/4946 7400, ⓦwww.yachtcharters.com.au have been going for years and are thoroughly reliable.

Car and scooter rental Airlie Beach Budget Autos, 285 Shute Harbour Rd, Airlie ☎07/4948 0300; Tropic Car Hire, 15 Commercial Close, Airlie ☎07/4946 5216.

Car lockup If you need to leave your vehicle in safe hands for a few days, contact Shute Harbour Secured Parking (☎07/4946 9666) or Whitsunday Airport Secured Parking, mid-way between Airlie and Shutehaven (☎07/4946 9998).

Diving Airlie's two most established operators are Oceania Dive, 349 Shute Harbour Rd ☎07/4948 1888, ⓦwww.oceaniadive.com; and Reef Dive, in the centre of town, near the post office ☎07/4946 6508, ⓦwww.reefdive.com.au. Both offer training (around $430 for a four-day open-water course, or $580 for a five-day course with up to eight dives) and live-aboard outings for qualified divers – three days and three nights work out at about $530 for ten dives. Weather, tides and currents will determine the most promising sites on any given day, but check first on how long is spent at the reef – often a couple of dives will be around an island. Island cruises and day-trips can often accommodate divers too – see the box on pp.512–513.

Doctor Opposite *McDonald's*, Shute Harbour Rd, Airlie (daily 8am–7pm; 24hr phoneline ⓣ07/4948 0900).

Flea market By the creek, for local produce and souvenirs (Sat 8am–noon).

Flights Island resort transfers aside, Air Whitsunday (ⓣ07/4946 9111, ⓦwww.airwhitsunday.com.au) offers a seaplane trip out to the reef and Whitehaven Beach (4hr; $295).

Internet If your accommodation can't help out, airliebeach.com, up near the *Hog's Breath* at the Cannonvale end of town, has a stack of terminals.

Left luggage There's a set of lockers with 24hr access on the corner of Shute Harbour Rd and the Esplanade ($4–6 per day).

QPWS Shute Harbour Rd, 3km out towards Shute on the left of the road (Mon–Fri 9am–4.30pm, Sat 9am–1pm; ⓣ07/4946 7022). Island camping permits and a small environmental display.

Pharmacy Airlie Day and Night Pharmacy (daily 8am–8pm).

Police Shute Harbour Rd, Cannonvale ⓣ07/4948 8888.

Post office In the centre of town, right behind *McDonald's*.

Taxi ⓣ13 10 08.

The Whitsundays

The **Whitsunday Islands** look just like the mountain peaks they once were before rising sea levels cut them off from the mainland six thousand years ago. They were seasonally inhabited by the Ngaro Aborigines when Captain Cook sailed through in 1770; he proceeded to name the area after the day he arrived, and various locations after his expedition's sponsors. Today, dense green pine forests and roughly contoured coastlines give the islands instant appeal, and the surrounding seas bustle with yachts and cruisers. Resorts first opened here in the 1930s and now number eight, but the majority of islands are still undeveloped and controlled by the QPWS, which maintains campsites on thirteen of them. Resorts aside, the few islands left in private hands are mainly uninhabited and largely the domain of local yachties. Those covered below all have regular connections to the mainland.

There are two ways to explore the Whitsundays: staying on the islands or cruising around them. **Staying** allows you to choose between camping and resort facilities, with snorkelling, bushwalks and beach sports to pass the time. **Cruises** spend one or more days around the islands, perhaps putting ashore at times (check this if it's the islands themselves you want to see) or diving and snorkelling. Don't miss the chance to do some **whale-watching** if you're here between June and September, when humpbacks (for more on which see p.471) arrive from their Antarctic wintering grounds to give birth and raise their calves before heading south again.

If you're planning to make use of the 34 **island campsites**, you'll first need to arrange transport, then obtain **permits** from the Whitsunday QPWS office who have full details of all campsites and facilities (see "Listings", see above or book online at ⓦwww.epa.qld.gov.au). At most, campsite facilities comprise a pit toilet, picnic tables and rainwater tanks, so take everything you'll need with you, especially insect repellent, a fuel stove (wood fires are prohibited) and **drinking water** – if you're planning a long stay, you can arrange for cruise boats to ferry in supplies. **Resorts** sometimes have a higher profile than the islands they're built on; though staying is often beyond most budget travellers' means, stand-by deals can slash prices and polite bargaining is always worth a try. Most, in any case, allow day-trippers to use their facilities.

The resort islands all offer relatively expensive return **ferry transfers** to and from the mainland. If you'd like to see more than one island, or plan to camp

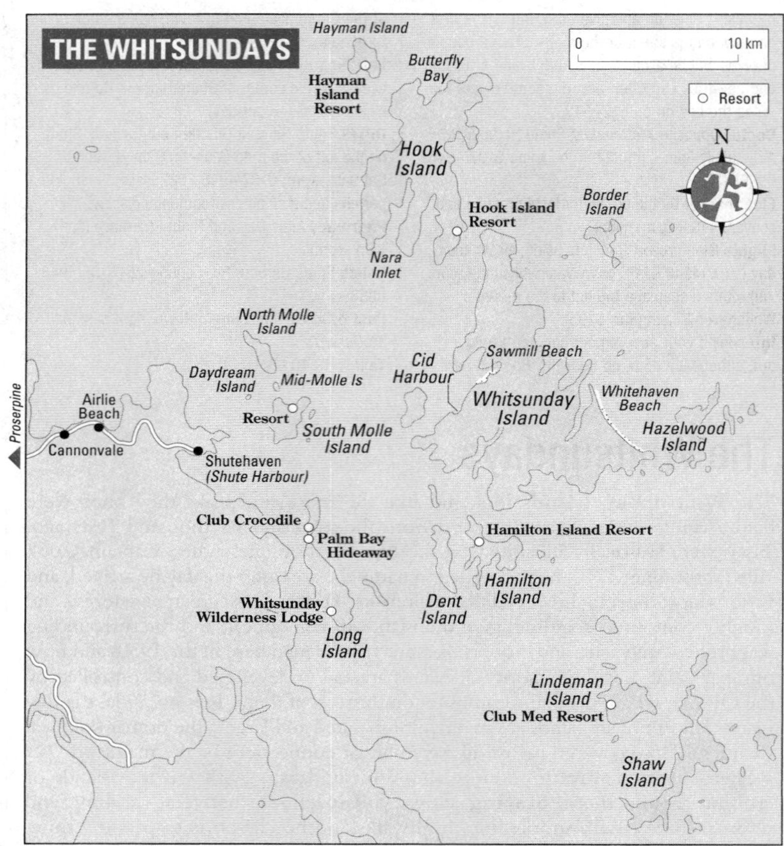

away from a resort, it's cheaper to choose some sort of a **cruise** – for details, see the box on pp.512–513. Once you've arranged everything else, check your **departure points**; most cruises and dive boats leave from Abel Point Marina, while resort ferries and island transfers tend to use Shutehaven – both stops on the Whitsunday Transit bus (see p.509).

Whitsunday Island

The largest island in the group, QPWS-run **Whitsunday Island** is also one of the most enjoyable. Its east coast is home to **Whitehaven Beach**, easily the finest in all the islands, and on the agenda of just about every cruise boat in the region. Long, white, and still clean despite the numbers of day-trippers and campers, it's a beautiful spot so long as you can handle the lack of distractions. The **campsite** here is above the tide line, with minimal shelter provided by whispering casuarinas. Snorkellers should head down to the far end of the beach facing Hazelwood Island. Blue Ferries runs a daily service to the beach.

Over on Whitsunday's west side, **Cid Harbour** is a quieter hideaway which lacks a great beach but instead enjoys a backdrop of giant granite boulders and tropical forests, with several more campsites above coral and pebble shingle. **Dugong Beach** is the nicest, sheltered under the protective arms and buttressed roots of giant trees; it's a twenty-minute walk along narrow hill paths from Sawmill Beach, where you're likely to be dropped off.

Hook Island

Directly north of Whitsunday, and pretty similar in appearance, **Hook Island** is the second largest in the group. The easiest passage to the island is on a transfer with *Voyager* from Shute Harbour ($40) to the low-key and fairly basic **resort** (ⓣ07/4946 9380, ⓦwww.hookislandresort.com, dorms $35, cabins ④–⑤) at the island's southeastern end, which offers cabins, dorms, and camping with fine views over the channel to Whitsunday, as well as a bar, a small **store** and a cafeteria serving meals and snacks. There are also several other **QPWS campsites** around the island, the pick of which is at southern **Curlew Beach** – sheltered, pretty and accessible only with your own vessel or by prior arrangement with a tour operator.

Cruises often pull into southern **Nara Inlet** for a look at the **Aboriginal paintings** on the roof of a small cave above a tiny shingle beach. Though not dramatic in scale or design, the art is significant for its net patterns – though the connection here seems obvious – which are otherwise found only at central highland sites such as Carnarvon Gorge (see p.588). On the rocks below the cave are some more recent graffiti, left by boat crews over the last thirty years.

Snorkelling on the reef directly in front of the resort is a must; snorkelling gear and surf skis are free (with deposit) to guests. The water is cloudy on large tides, but the coral outcrops are all in fairly good condition and there's plenty of life around, from flatworms to morays and parrotfish. Day-cruises run from Airlie to the snorkelling spots and visit the top-rate fringing coral at **Manta Ray Bay**, **Langford Reef** and **Butterfly Bay** on the northern and northeastern tips of the island – visibility can be poor here, but on a good day these sites offer some of the best **diving** in the islands.

Hayman Island

The extremely high price of accommodation at the **Hayman Island resort** (ⓣ07/4940 1244, ⓦwww.hayman.com.au; ⑧) pales into insignificance when compared with the resort's building costs, which topped $300 million. Guests indulge in lush rooms with extravagant and genuine Baroque and Renaissance furnishings, and staff move about through underground tunnels so that they don't get in the way. Not surprisingly, day-trippers aren't allowed anywhere near the place, although cruises and some dive trips stop off for a look at the coral off **Blue Pearl Bay** – which isn't actually that exciting – on the island's west coast.

The Molles and nearby islands

South Molle Island was a source of fine-grained **stone** for Ngaro Aborigines, a unique material for tools that have been found on other islands and may help in mapping trade routes. The slightly shabby **resort** (ⓣ1800 075 080, ⓦwww.southmolleisland.com.au; ⑥) in the north of the island offers heaps of extras – such as guided walks, and all sports and facilities – along with stand-by rates. **Walking tracks** from behind the golf course lead to gum trees and rainforest, encompassing vistas of the islands from the top of Spion Kop and Mount Jeffreys, and some quiet beaches at the south end. Fantasea-Blue Ferries runs daily from Shute Harbour ($44 return) if you just want a day out. South Molle's resort can sometimes organize a lift to the campsite on uninhabited **North Molle Island**,

Getting around the Whitsundays

Island transfers are offered by Fantasea-Blue Ferries and Whitsunday All Over, which between them operate daily ferry circuits between about half a dozen popular destinations; and Camping Whitsunday, which offers more remote drop-offs for campers. **Day-cruises** usually take in two or more islands, and offer the chance to experience the thrills of **boomnetting** – sitting in a large rope hammock stretched above the water at the front of the boat so that you can catch the full soaking force of the waves – and do some snorkelling; others may concentrate on a single theme, such as whale-watching, fishing or lazing on Whitehaven Beach. **Multi-day cruises** cover much the same territory but at a slower pace, and may give sailing lessons. Experienced groups might consider a **bareboat charter** (see "Listings" on p.508 for operators).

The list below is not exhaustive; word of mouth is the best method of finding out about who is still in business, what the current deals are and if operators live up to their advertisements. Check the length of trips carefully – "three days" might mean one full day and two half-days – along with how much time is actually spent cruising and at the destination, how many other people will be on the cruise, and the size of the vessel. There are scores of beautiful boats, so you'll be swayed by your preference for a performance racing yacht or a fun trip with lots of deck space on which to lounge. Bear in mind that a cheerful (or jaded) crew can make all the difference, and that weather conditions can affect destinations offered. Many yachts also have poor environmental practices and pump waste directly into the sea so it's wise to ask probing questions. Finally, if you want to save money, shop around as close to departure times as possible, when advertised prices tend to drop.

Island transfers

In addition to the following services, some island resorts have their own ferries or flights for guests.

Camping Whitsunday ⓣ07/4946 9330 or 0417 759 743. Return runs to beach campsites at North Molle, South Molle, Denman and Planton islands ($40 per person for a minimum of two people); they also offer good deals for transfers to campsites on Hook ($140) and Whitsunday ($95–120) and give free loans of water containers and snorkelling gear.

Fantasea-Blue Ferries Shute Harbour ⓣ07/4946 5111, ⓦwww.fantasea.com.au. Runs ferries several times daily to resorts on Long Island ($44), South Molle ($44), Hamilton ($57) and Daydream ($59), as well as day cruises to Whitehaven Beach ($77).

Day-trips: sailing

The following cost $69–99.

Illusions ⓣ07/4946 5255, ⓦwww.illusions.net.au. Catamaran trip to Hayman's Blue Pearl Bay includes snorkelling and boomnetting; scuba diving also available. Lunch is optional at $10 extra.

Maxi Ragamuffin ⓣ1800 454 777, ⓦwww.maxiaction.com.au. 24-metre-long racer to Blue Pearl Bay (Mon, Wed & Sat) and Whitehaven Beach (Tues, Thurs & Sun), for snorkelling; diving available. Lunch included.

only 2km away (or contact Camping Whitsunday; see box below); the beach here is made up of rough coral fragments, but the snorkelling is fairly good. There are another couple of campsites on **Mid-Molle Island**, joined to South Molle by a low-tide causeway about half a kilometre from the resort.

Day-trips: powered vessels

The following cost $76–99; includes lunch unless otherwise stated.

Mantaray ⓣ1800 816 365, ⓦwww.mantaraycharters.com. Fast and relatively roomy boat out to Whitehaven, where you spend around three hours at leisure before heading north to Mantaray Bay and some good snorkelling.

Ocean Rafting ⓣ07/4946 6848, ⓦwww.oceanrafting.com. Great value action-packed cruise on a zippy inflatable to Whitehaven Beach with options to visit either Hill Inlet or the aboriginal caves at Nara Inlet. Max 25 passengers.

Whitehaven Express ⓣ07/4946 7172, ⓦwww.whitehavenexpress.com.au. Trips to Whitsunday Island, stopping for scenery at Hill Inlet, before a snorkel and beach BBQ at Whitehaven.

Whitsunday Island Adventure Cruises ⓣ07/4946 5255. After a mandatory stop at Whitehaven Beach, this budget cruise proceeds to the resort areas at Hook and Long islands. Lunch $11 extra, or eat at the resorts.

Longer trips

The following cost $339–469 for two-night, three-day outings; trips departs at around 9am from Abel Point Marina, returning on day three about 4pm. The basic itinerary is to visit Hook Island via Nara Inlet, then move round to Whitehaven Beach on Whitsunday. There are two major sailboat companies in town, fronting for the majority of vessels: **Aussie Adventure Sailing** (ⓣ1800 359 554, ⓦwww.aussiesailing.com.au) specializes in classic tall and vintage-style ships; **Southern Cross** (ⓣ1800 675 790, ⓦwww.soxsail.com.au) puts the emphasis on maxi-yacht racers. Another large stable is owned by **Tallarook** (ⓣ1800 331 316, ⓦwww.tallarookdive.com.au), with a varied bag of vessels with mixed reports, all offering diving for certified divers.

Anaconda III (Koalas, ⓣ1800 466 444). The largest party yacht in the Whitsundays, taking up to 50 passengers, and fantastically comfortable.

Derwent Hunter (Tall Ship Adventures ⓣ07/4946 4195, ⓦwww.tallshipadventures.com.au). Ninety-foot schooner built in 1945 and totally refitted with timber decking and fittings after years spent as a research vessel, a film set and dubious activities in the South China Seas.

Iceberg (ⓣ1800 431 303, ⓔiceberg@tpg.com.au). Modern, fifteen-metre cruising yacht focusing on fun-filled adrenalin activities including kite surfing. Maximum of thirteen passengers and an enthusiastic crew.

Next Sailing (ProSail ⓣ1800 466 733, ⓦwww.nextsail.com.au). No fixed itinerary, small 12m yacht with maximum of 10 passengers aimed at budget travellers. BYO liquor keeps the cost down.

Schooner Friendship (ⓣ1800 677 119). Beautiful, romantic wooden schooner run by Aussie Adventure Sailing, and carrying just ten passengers.

Siska A 25-metre-long ocean maxi yacht with twenty passengers, owned by Southern Cross, winner of races between the UK and Australia.

Southern Cross The company's flagship: a high-speed, 21-metre-long America's Cup challenger accommodating fourteen passengers, aimed at couples.

Waltzing Matilda (Aussie Adventure Sailing). A more modern design than most of Aussie Adventure Sailing's fleet, this eighteen-metre ketch is not that roomy, but has a great atmosphere.

Daydream Island is little more than a tiny wooded rise between South Molle and the mainland, with a narrow beach running the length of the east side and coral to snorkel over at the north end. The **resort** (Ⓣ07/4948 8488, Ⓦwww.daydreamisland.com; ❽) offers fine food and hospitality, but its regimental lines dominate views of the island from the sea and detract from an otherwise very pretty scene. Fantasea-Blue Ferries offers day-trips for $59.

Tiny **Planton**, **Tancred** and **Denman** islands are just offshore from South Molle – with no facilities and limited camping at QPWS sites, they're about as isolated as you'll get in the Whitsundays. All three are surrounded by reef, but be careful of strong currents. Again, you may be able to arrange with Camping Whitsunday or cruise boats bound for Whitsunday Island to drop you off here.

Long Island

Long Island is exactly that, being not much more than a narrow, ten-kilometre ribbon almost within reach of the mainland forests. There are a few worthwhile hikes through the rainforest to Sandy Bay (where there's a QPWS **campsite**) or up Humpy Point, as well as three **resorts** on the island. *Club Crocodile Long Island* (Ⓣ07/4946 9400, Ⓦwww.clubcroc.com.au; packages including meals and transfers ❽), at Happy Bay, and *Peppers Palm Bay* (Ⓣ07/4946 9233, Ⓦwww.peppers.com.au; cabins and bungalows ❽), half a kilometre south at the island's waist, have similar attractions (a disco, parasailing, water-skiing and a dozen other sports). Fantasea-Blue Ferries runs daily **ferries** from Shute Harbour to *Club Crocodile* and *Peppers* ($59 return). For a real escape, *South Long Island Wilderness Lodge* (Ⓣ07/3221 7799, Ⓦwww.southlongisland.com; ❽) offers self-contained waterfront cabins, superb food and attentive service. It's only accessible by helicopter: contact the *Lodge* for package deals and transfers.

Hamilton and Lindeman islands

The apartment buildings dominating the view on **Hamilton Island** are the Gold Coast revisited, and it's interesting to speculate about what will happen to them during the next big cyclone. An enormous colony of fruit bats lives in the trees behind the waterfront and, apart from the flocks of cockatoos, seems to be the only native wildlife here. The island is privately owned, and its businesses operate under a lease: development includes a quaint colonial waterfront with hotel, bakery and various other stores, the *Hamilton Island Resort* (Ⓣ1800 075 110, Ⓦwww.hamiltonislandresort.com; ❼), a small zoo, and so many restaurants, pools, gift shops and sports facilities that the original character of the island has long since vanished. The twin towers of the resort loom over the beach complex, and give the best view of the whole area from one of the external glass lifts taken up to penthouse level. Inside the beach complex you'll find one of the pricier places to eat, and lots of signs in Japanese. Fantasea-Blue Ferries runs a daily service from Shute Harbour ($46 return for guests and $60 for day-trippers).

Lindeman Island suffered as a victim of feral goats, though their eradication has seen native plants making a comeback in a small melaleuca swamp and on the wooded northeast side. Mount Oldfield offers panoramic views, while other walking tracks lead to swimming beaches on the north shore. The *Club Med* **resort** (Ⓣ1800 258 263, Ⓦwww.clubmed.com; ❽), Australia's first, has all the services you'd expect and no day-trippers.

Bowen and the route to Townsville

BOWEN, a quiet seafront settlement 60km north of Proserpine, was once under consideration as the site of the state capital, but it floundered after Townsville's foundation. Today, stark first impressions created by the sterile bulk of the saltworks on the highway are offset by a certain small-town charm and some pretty beaches just off to the north. The main attraction for travellers though is the prospect of seasonal **farm work**: Bowen's mangoes and tomatoes are famous throughout Queensland, and there's a large floating population of itinerant pickers in town between April and January. The backpackers' hostels (see below) can help with finding work, though nothing's guaranteed.

Bowen's centre overlooks **Edgecumbe Bay**, at the harbour end of Herbert Street, where you'll find the usual range of services and a couple of old colonial exteriors on the *Grand View Hotel* and the Harbour Office. The **train station** is a few kilometres west of town near the highway, while **buses** stop outside Bowen Travel (Ⓣ07/4786 2835), just off Herbert on Williams Street, which can organize **tickets** for either. Budget **accommodation** – which should be booked in advance and is usually offered at weekly rates only – consists of *Bowen Backpackers* (Ⓣ07/4786 3433, Ⓔbowenbackpackers@bigpond.com; dorms $130/week, rooms ❷, closed Jan–March), right in town at the beach end of Herbert St; *Barnacles* (Ⓣ07/4786 4400, Ⓔbarnaclebackpackers@bigpond.com; dorms $131/week, rooms ❷), a little further out of town on Gordon Street; and *Reefers by the Beach* (Ⓣ07/4786 4199, Ⓦwww.reefers.com.au; dorms $22, rooms ❷), the most spacious hostel with a pool but located 3km from town near the beaches at 93 Horseshoe Bay Rd. **Mid-range** choices include *Castle Motor Lodge*, 6 Don St (Ⓣ07/4786 1322; ❸), about the closest option to the centre of town. You can **eat** at the *Grand View Hotel*, down near the Harbour Office on Herbert, or *McDees Café*, on the corner of Herbert and George streets; alternatively, stock up at Magees Supermarket on Williams Street and at the town's numerous fruit and vegetable stalls.

Bowen's attractive **beaches** lie a couple of kilometres north of the town centre. **Queens Beach**, which faces north, is sheltered and has a stinger net for the jellyfish season, but the best is **Horseshoe Bay**, small, and hemmed in by some sizeable boulders, with good waters for a swim or snorkel. *Horseshoe Bay Resort* (Ⓣ07/4786 2564; units ❸) makes an excellent base, two minutes' walk from the sea.

With your own transport, it might be worth skipping Bowen in favour of the ranch-style *Bogie River Bush House* (Ⓣ07/4785 3407, Ⓦwww.bogiebushhouse.com.au; dorms $20, rooms ❷), about 60km inland from town towards Collinsville. This splendid retreat offers rooms and backpacker dorms, as well as a pool and the chance to go horse riding, fishing, or to play with tame wildlife; you can also organize **farm work** here.

The Burdekin River, Ayr and Mount Elliot

Further on up the highway, 115km past Bowen, are the towns of **Home Hill** and **Ayr**, separated by a mill, a few kilometres of canefields and the iron framework of the **Burdekin River Bridge**. The river, one of the north's most famous landmarks, is still liable to flood during severe wet seasons, despite having to fight its way across three weirs and a dam. On the northern side, **AYR** is a compact farming town fast becoming another popular stop on the **farm work** trail. The highway – which runs through town as Queen Street – is where you'll find the bus stop and all essential services, as well as two workers' hostels which can find you employment picking and packing capsicums, amongst other things – *Ayr Backpackers* (☎07/4783 5837; phone in advance for pick-up; dorms $100/week; single nights are only available outside of the fruit picking season and on special request) on Willmington St is definitely the better option.

North of Ayr, **Mount Elliot** looms on the horizon, the only accessible section of the fragmented **Bowling Green Bay National Park**; turn off from the highway when you see the signs for **ALLIGATOR CREEK**, about 55km from Ayr. There's a QPWS ranger station and **campsite** (☎07/4778 8203 or book online at Ⓦwww.epa.qld.gov.au), in a valley at the end of the road (note that the road is open 6am–6pm only), from where the creek widens into a chain of rock pools and deeper channels. The pools become more private the further you get from camp and though swimmers might attract cruising eels and nibbles from freshwater shrimp, it's pretty idyllic.

Townsville

Hot and stuffy **TOWNSVILLE** sprawls around a broad spit of land between the isolated hump of Castle Hill and swampy Ross Creek. While cynics describe its two biggest attractions as **Magnetic Island** (just offshore) and Cairns, Townsville has undergone some tasteful development in recent years, and does have its moments – above all in its visible maritime history, in the sea views from the Strand promenade, and in the muggy, salty evening air and old pile houses on the surrounding hills, marking down Townsville as the coast's first really tropical city.

Townsville was founded in 1864 by John Melton Black and Robert Towns, entrepreneurs who felt that a settlement was needed for northern stockmen who couldn't reach Bowen when the Burdekin River was in flood. Despite an inferior harbour, the town soon outstripped Bowen in terms of both size and prosperity, its growth accelerated by **gold** finds inland at Ravenswood and Charters Towers (see p.608). Today, it's the gateway to the far north and transit point for routes west to Mount Isa and the Northern Territory; it's also an important military centre, seat of a university and home to substantial Torres Strait Islander and Aboriginal communities.

Arrival and information

Townsville's roughly triangular city centre is hemmed in by Cleveland Bay on the north, Ross Creek to the south and Castle Hill to the west. Oriented northeast and parallel with Ross Creek, **Flinders Street** is the main drag, sectioned into a downtown pedestrian **mall** before running its last five hundred metres as Flinders Street East. The **airport** is 5km northwest; a shuttle bus (book in advance on ☎07/4775 5544; $7 single, $11 return) meets most flights, stopping at points around town. **Long-distance buses** stop at the **Transit Centre** on the south side of Ross Creek on Palmer Street, while the **train station** is on the north side of the creek and east of the centre on Flinders Street.

Public **transport** serves the suburbs rather than the sights, though much of what there is to see is central; some hostels have bikes available. A very helpful **information** booth, with a separate counter handling (and booking) diving, cruises and tours, is located in Flinders Street Mall (Mon-Fri 9am–5pm, Sat & Sun 9am-1pm).

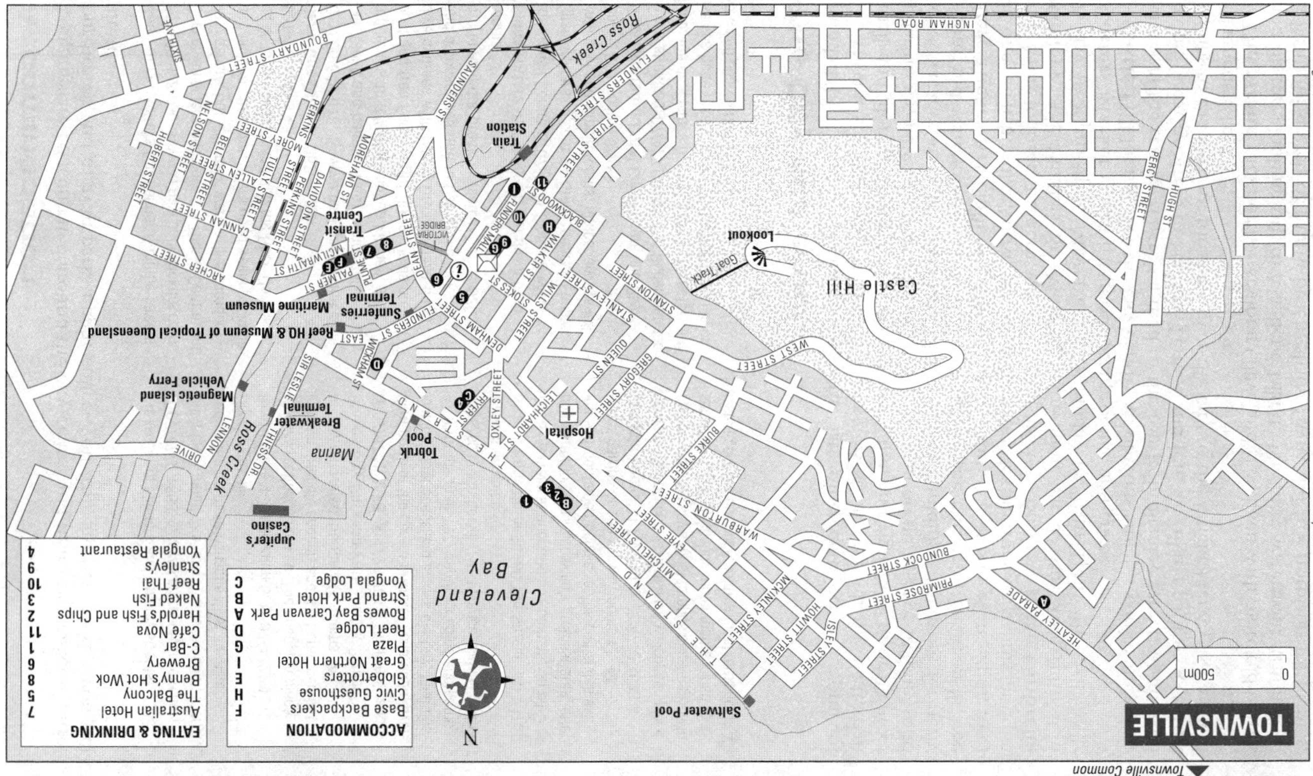
TOWNSVILLE
0
500m
ACCOMMODATION
Base Backpackers F
Civic Guesthouse H
Globetrotters E
Great Northern Hotel I
Plaza G
Reef Lodge D
Rowes Bay Caravan Park A
Strand Park Hotel B
Yongala Lodge C
EATING & DRINKING
Australian Hotel 7
The Balcony 5
Benny's Hot Wok 8
Brewery 6
C-Bar 1
Café Nova 11
Harold's Fish and Chips 2
Naked Fish 3
Reef Thai 10
Stanley's 9
Yongala Restaurant 4
N
Cleveland Bay
Saltwater Pool
Tobruk Pool
Jupiter's Casino
Marina
Breakwater Terminal
Magnetic Island Vehicle Ferry
Reef HQ & Museum of Tropical Queensland
Maritime Museum
Sunferries Terminal
Transit Centre
Train Station
Hospital
Castle Hill
Lookout
Goat Track
Ross Creek
Victoria Bridge
THE STRAND
HEATLEY PARADE
PRIMROSE STREET
BUNDOCK STREET
ISLEY STREET
HOWITT STREET
MCKINLEY STREET
MITCHELL STREET
EYRE STREET
WARBURTON STREET
BURKE STREET
GREGORY STREET
QUEEN ST
LEICHHARDT ST
OXLEY STREET
FRYER ST
WEST STREET
STANTON STREET
STANLEY STREET
WILLS STREET
STOKES ST
WALKER ST
BLACKWOOD ST
FLINDERS MALL
FLINDERS ST EAST
FLINDERS STREET
DENHAM STREET
WICKHAM ST
SIR LESLIE THIESS DR.
LENNON DRIVE
DEAN STREET
PLUME ST
PALMER ST
MCILWRAITH ST
MOREHAND ST
DAVIDSON STREET
PERKINS STREET
PERKINS ST
TULLY STREET
ALLEN STREET
CANNAN STREET
ARCHER STREET
BELL STREET
NELSON STREET
HUBERT STREET
MOREY STREET
BOUNDARY STREET
SIXTH AVE
SAUNDERS ST
STURT STREET
PERCY STREET
HUGH ST
INGHAM ROAD
Townsville Common
Airport
Ingham & Cardwell
Billabong Sanctuary, Charters Towers & Bowen

Accommodation

Lodgings are concentrated around the city centre and near the Transit Centre, but hostels and caravan parks might collect you from further afield if you call ahead.

Base Backpackers Cnr Palmer & Plume streets ⓣ1800 628 836, ⓦwww.basebackpackers.com. Conveniently located above the Transit Centre, and very secure, but with dark warren-like corridors and lacking character. Offers good-value package deals to Magnetic Island and the Reef. Dorms $21–23, rooms ❸

Civic Guesthouse 262 Walker St ⓣ1800 646 619, ⓦwww.backpackersinn.com.au. Clean and helpful, if not wonderfully modern, with a well-equipped kitchen, spa pool and free Friday night BBQs. Deals on dive courses with Diving Dreams (next door) and a sunset bus ride to Castle Hill lookout, or trip to Alligator Creek available. Dorms $20, rooms ❷

Globetrotters 45 Palmer St, just down from the Transit Centre ⓣ07/4771 3242, ⓦwww.globetrottersinn.com.au. Small, peaceful hostel with pool and simple rooms; almost always full. Dorms $21, rooms ❷–❸

Great Northern Hotel Cnr Flinders and Blackwood streets ⓣ07/4771 6191. Old Queenslander pub; the downstairs bar has lots of character, and serves huge meals from $10. Rooms have fan or a/c and shared bath. ❸

Plaza Cnr of Flinders and Stanley streets ⓣ07/4772 1888, ⓦwww.plazahotels.com.au. Downtown motel-like apartments, modern, friendly and with a bit more panache than the nearby *Holiday Inn*. ❹

Reef Lodge 4–6 Wickham St ⓣ07/4721 1112, ⓦwww.reeflodge.com.au. The cheapest place in town, friendly enough and a bit cramped but freshly renovated. Dorms $17, rooms ❷

Rowes Bay Caravan Park Heatley Parade ⓣ07/4771 3576, ⓕ4724 2017. Off The Strand, 3km north of the centre towards Pallarenda, overlooking Magnetic Island across the bay; take bus #7 from the mall. Very popular cabins and campsites, so worth booking in advance. Cabins (with or without en suite) ❸

Strand Park Hotel 59–60 The Strand ⓣ07/4750 7888, ⓦwww.strandparkhotel.com.au. Small boutique motel in Townsville's prettiest area, offering self-contained double rooms and suites with either garden or sea views. Rooms ❺–❻

Yongala Lodge 11 Fryer St ⓣ07/4772 4633, ⓦwww.historicyongala.com.au. A welcoming place, named after the city's most famous shipwreck, with spacious if slightly shabby motel rooms joined to a historic old Queenslander with original furnishings. ❹

The City and around

Funded by inland gold mines during the late nineteenth century, some of Townsville's architecture is quite imposing. A stroll through the pedestrian mall and along Flinders Street East, among the unimaginative assortment of pharmacies, newsagents and banks, will reveal a good number of stylishly solid stone facades and iron wrapround balconies on buildings that were formerly shops and warehouses. Along the mall and on the corner of Denham St, the **Perc Tucker Art Gallery** (Mon–Fri 10am–5pm, Sat & Sun 10am–2pm; free) is one such building, now featuring travelling exhibitions of mainly antique art. More offbeat, modern work by local artists is on view at the **Umbrella Gallery**, 482 Flinders St (Mon–Fri 9am–5pm, Sat & Sun 9am–1pm). On Friday (6.30pm–9pm, May–Dec) and Sunday (8.30am–1pm), the mall hosts **Cotters Market** which has good local produce and crafts.

Castle Hill looms over the city centre, an obvious target if you're after clear views of the region. There's a road to the top from Stanley Street; on foot go along Gregory Street to Stanton Terrace and join a walking path of sorts that climbs to the lookout for vistas over the city to the distant Hervey Range and Magnetic Island.

The Strand runs northwest along Cleveland Bay, lined with more old houses and fig trees looking out to Magnetic Island. The busy waterfront strip here is a beautiful stretch of palms, beach, shady lawns and free hotplates for picnics, plus cafés, a children's waterpark, and a specially built jetty for fishing from. Off the eastern end you'll find Townsville's **marina** (where most dive trips depart) and adjacent **Jupiter's Casino**; right down the western end is **Kissing Point**, a grassy headland with a stretch of sand and accompanying enclosed **saltwater pool** below – very welcome during the scorching stinger season.

The Reef HQ and Museum of Tropical Queensland

The **Reef HQ**, on Flinders Street East (daily 9.30am–5pm; aquarium $19.50, IMAX theatre $12, combined $29.50), houses a terrific aquarium and **IMAX theatre** (hourly shows), which projects films with a popular science theme onto a domed ceiling to create an overwhelming, wraparound image. The huge live tanks in the **aquarium** contain recreations of the reef, where you can watch schools of fish drifting over coral, clown fish hiding inside anemones' tentacles and myopic turtles cruising past. Between the main tanks are smaller ones for oddities: sea snakes, deep-sea nautiluses, baby turtles and lobsters. Upstairs, videos about the reef are shown, and you can handle some inoffensive invertebrates – tiny clams, sea slugs and starfish.

Next door to the Reef HQ, an innovative building houses the **Museum of Tropical Queensland** (daily 9.30am–5pm; $9.50), which showcases the Queensland Museum's marine archeology collection. The centrepiece is a full-sized, cut-away replica – figurehead and all – of the front third of the **Pandora**, a British frigate tied up in the tale of the **Bounty mutiny**, which sank on the outer reef in 1791 (see box overleaf for the full tale). Accompanying artefacts salvaged off the wreck since its discovery in 1977 include water jars and bottles, tankards owned by the crew, and the surgeon's pocket watch, with glass face and finely chased gold and silver mountings. Dioramas recreate life on board, with views into the cramped captain's cabin, and a dramatic reconstruction of the sinking; while a life-sized blueprint of the *Pandora*'s upper deck is mapped out on the carpet. You can also join in the twice-daily "Running Out the Gun", the loading and mock firing of a replica cannon from the *Pandora*. Other sections of the museum cover Outback Queensland's extensive **fossil** finds (including several life-sized dinosaur models), and touch on Aboriginal and Torres Strait Islander history.

The Maritime Museum

You'll find more about shipwrecks at the **Maritime Museum** (Mon–Fri 10am–4pm, Sat–Sun noon–4pm; $5), across Ross Creek near the Transit Centre on Palmer Street. Material here focuses on local shipwrecks. Most attention is given to the story of the **Yongala**, a hundred-metre-long passenger liner which went down with all hands during a cyclone in 1911, and was finally located intact in 1958; exhibits here are a must-see for scuba divers planning to dive the wreck (see p.521). Other wrecks covered include the Blackbirder vessel *Foam*, and the *Gothenburg*, a gold-miners' transport which sank near Bowen in 1875; ghoulish salvagers recovered the captain's safe and, assuming that corpses loaded with bullion had been eaten by sharks, began to fish for them, spurred on by the prospect of recovering gold from the carcasses.

Townsville Common and Billabong Sanctuary

The **Townsville Common Conservation Park** (daily 7.30am–7.30pm; free) is 6.5km north of the centre, on the coast at Pallarenda. The Bohle River pools into **wetlands** below the Many Peaks Range, a habitat perfect for wildfowl including the brolga, the stately symbol of northern marshes. Less popular – with rice farmers anyway – are huge flocks of magpie geese that visit after

The Bounty and the Pandora

In 1788, the British Admiralty vessel *Bounty* sailed from England to Tahiti, with a mission to collect **breadfruit** seedlings, intended to provide a cheap source of food for Britain's plantation slaves in the West Indies. But the stay in Tahiti's mellow climate proved so much better than life on board the *Bounty* that on the return journey in April 1789 the crew **mutinied**, led by the officer **Fletcher Christian**. Along with eighteen crew who refused to join in the mutiny, **Captain William Bligh** was set adrift in a longboat far out in the Pacific, while the mutineers returned to Tahiti, intending to settle there.

Things didn't go as planned, however. After an incredible feat of navigation over 3600 nautical miles of open sea, in June Bligh and all but one of his companions reached the Portuguese colony of Timor, emaciated but still alive, from where Bligh lost no time in catching a vessel back to England, arriving there in March 1790. His report on the mutiny immediately saw the Admiralty dispatch the frigate *Pandora* off to Tahiti under the cold-hearted **Captain Edwards**, with instructions to bring back the mutineers to stand trial in London.

Meanwhile in Tahiti, Christian and seven of the mutiny's ringleaders – knowing that sooner or later the Admiralty would try to find them – had, along with a group of Tahitians, taken the *Bounty* and sailed off into the Pacific. Fourteen of the *Bounty*'s crew stayed behind on Tahiti, however, and when the *Pandora* arrived there in March 1791, they were rounded up, clapped in chains and incarcerated in the ship's brig, a three-metre-long wooden cell known as "Pandora's Box".

Having spent a fruitless few months island-hopping in search of the *Bounty*, Captain Edwards headed up the east coast of Australia where, on the night of August 29, the *Pandora* hit a northern section of the Great Barrier Reef. As waves began to break up the vessel on the following day, Edwards ordered the longboats to be loaded with supplies and abandoned the ship, leaving his prisoners still locked up on board; it was only thanks to one of the crew that ten of them managed to scramble out as the *Pandora* slid beneath the waves.

In a minor replay of Bligh's voyage, the *Pandora*'s survivors took three weeks to make it to Timor in their longboats, and arrived back in England the following year. Edwards was castigated for the heartless treatment of his prisoners, but otherwise held blameless for the wreck. The ten surviving mutineers were court-martialled: four were acquitted; three hanged; and three had their death sentences commuted. Captain Bligh was later made Governor of New South Wales, where he suffered another mutiny known as the "Rum Rebellion" (see "History", p.1075). And the *Bounty*'s whole project proved a failure; when breadfruit trees were eventually introduced to the West Indies, the slaves refused to eat them.

Seventeen years later, the American vessel *Topaz* stopped mid-Pacific at the isolated rocky fastness of **Pitcairn Island** and, to the amazement of its crew, found it settled by a small colony of English-speaking people. These turned out to be the descendants of the *Bounty* mutineers, along with the last survivor, the elderly **John Adams** (also known as Alexander Smith). Adams told the *Topaz*'s crew that having settled Pitcairn and burned the *Bounty*, the mutineers had fought with the Tahitian men over the women, and that Christian and all the men – except Adams and three other mutineers – had been killed. The other three had since died, leaving only Adams, the women, and their children on the island. After Adams' death, Pitcairn's population was briefly moved to Norfolk Island in the 1850s (see p.347), where some settled, though many of their descendents returned and still live on Pitcairn.

rains and are a familiar sight over the city. You need a vehicle to reach the park, but once there you can get about on foot, although a car or bike makes short work of the less interesting tracks between lagoons. Camouflaged **hides** at Long

Swamp and Pink Lily Lagoon let you clock up a few of the hundred or more bird species: egrets stalk frogs around waterlilies, ibises and spoonbills strain the water for edibles and geese honk at each other, undisturbed by the low-flying airport traffic. Bring binoculars.

Seventeen kilometres south of Townsville on the highway, **Billabong Sanctuary** (daily 8am–5pm; $24 or $34 with transfers ⓣ07/4721 6489) is a well-kept collection of penned and wild Australian fauna laid out around a large waterhole. Amongst the free-ranging wildlife you'll find wallabies and flocks of demanding whistling ducks on the prowl for handouts; animals you'll probably be happier to see are caged include saltwater crocs, cassowaries (bred for release into the wild), dingoes, wedge-tailed eagles and snakes. A swimming pool and accompanying snack bar make the sanctuary a fine place to spend a few hours, and you can also tour the grounds with an Aboriginal guide and get an introduction to bush foods.

Eating, drinking and entertainment

There are plenty of good **eating** options in Townsville, with restaurants grouped in three main areas: in the centre on Flinders Street; south near the Transit Centre on Palmer Street; and out along The Strand. For evening entertainment, many of the town's hotels cater to the sizeable military and student presence and have regular live music, for which you might have to pay a cover charge.

Cafés and restaurants

Australian Hotel Palmer Street. This old wooden hotel is the place of choice for a decent steak and a drink in their attractive beer garden.

The Balcony Flinders Street Mall. Mediterranean-style salads and grills; also good coffee and cakes and a great view over the mall from upper-storey balcony tables. Mains $12–18.

Benny's Hot Wok Palmer St. Stylish and popular Singaporean and Asian café-restaurant, with tasty bowls of noodle soup for around $12, and Indonesian or Thai curries for about $18.

Brewery Cnr of Denham and Flinders. Café, bar and boutique brewery housed in the old post office building. The beer and ambience are good, though the outdoor tables are a bit noisy thanks to the adjacent main road.

C-Bar The Strand. One of the several café-restaurants in the area – right on the seafront with outside tables and a bar overlooking Magnetic Island. Good for anything from a coffee or beer to succulent char-grilled steak or lamb kebabs and salad. Happy hour daily from 5pm to 6pm, with live local bands on Sun evenings. Mains around $18.

Café Nova Cnr of Blackwood and Flinders streets, near the station. A student venue, with gener-

Diving and reef trips from Townsville

Sunferries (ⓣ1800 447 333, ⓦwww.sunferries.com.au) runs a day-trip to **John Brewer Reef** for snorkelling ($139) and optional diving. Townsville's best dive destination is the coral-encrusted **Yongala**, in 15–30m of water some distance offshore; this is a fabulous dive, particularly at night. However, tricky anchorage means that dives can only be made in good weather, and be aware that this is a demanding site – deep, with strong currents and startlingly big fish; it's best not to go unless you are an advanced diver with at least twenty dives. Operators include: Diving Dreams, 252 Walker St (ⓣ07/4721 2500, ⓦwww.divingdreams.com), who offer both day-trips to the *Yongala* (two dives, $185 plus gear) or three-day dive excursions including the *Yongala* (from $545); and Tropical Diving (ⓣ1800 776 150, ⓦwww.tropicaldiving.com.au), who do day-trips to the *Yongala* aboard their fast boat *Jazz II* (two dives, $189 plus gear). Both also offer dive courses from $235 to $595, depending on whether you opt for a live-aboard vessel or dive from shore.

ous helpings and meals for under $10. Serves huge and tasty salads, and offers a great movie and meal deal for the 5 Cinema across the street. Tues–Fri 10.30am–midnight, Sat & Sun 6pm–midnight.

Harold's Fish and Chips The Strand, opposite the *C-Bar*. If you can't catch your own from the nearby fishing jetty, console yourself with a takeaway from this excellent establishment.

Naked Fish Next door to *Harold's*. Upmarket modern seafood with mains from $20–30. Excellent calamari and broad wine list. Daily 5pm–late.

Reef Thai 455 Flinders St. Seafood green curry, *satays* and the chilli-packed beef dish known as "crying tiger". Mains around $14. Daily 5.30–10pm.

Stanley's Cnr Flinders and Stanley streets. Airy café and bistro serving early breakfasts, pasta, ornate sandwiches and grills.

Yongala Restaurant 11 Fryer St, in front of the *Yongala Lodge* ⓣ07/4772 4633. Historic, authentically furnished surroundings where you can enjoy live music and good, Greek-influenced food. Appropriately, the building's architect was on board the *Yongala* when it sank.

Pubs, bars and clubs

Bank Flinders St East. Drunken mix of military and locals makes this a sometimes heavy nightclub sporting Corinthian columns, spiked iron railings and bars on the windows.

Exchange Hotel Flinders St East. A real locals' watering hole in a rundown pub, with occasional live bands.

Mad Cow Flinders St East. Pool tables and dancing to "Top 40" tunes – packed on weekends.

Molly Malones Flinders St East. Standard Irish bar with stout on tap. Happy hour Mon–Fri 5–6pm, live bands Wed & Sat, and Irish dancing on Sun evenings.

Listings

Airlines Virgin Blue flies to Brisbane, and Qantas to everywhere else.

Banks All located on Flinders Street Mall; there are ATMs in most pubs and at the Transit Centre.

Bookshops Mary Who?, 414 Flinders St, has a fine range of just about everything.

Buses Greyhound Australia ⓣ13 20 30; Premier ⓣ13 34 10.

Car and scooter rental Independent, 25 Yeatman St (ⓣ1800 678 843, ⓦwww.independentrentals.com.au), has basic models from $30 a day; Townsville Car and Scooter Rentals, 12 Palmer St (ⓣ07/4772 1093), starts at $37 per day for a car, $33 for a scooter, and $10 for a pushbike; Europcar (ⓣ13 13 90) is the cheapest of the major car rental companies.

Hospital Townsville General Hospital, Eyre St ⓣ07/4781 9211.

Internet access At the Transit Centre, and at Umbrella Gallery at 482 Flinders St ($3–4 per hour).

Left luggage At the Transit Centre.

QPWS Marlow St, Pallarenda (Mon–Fri 8.30am–5pm; ⓣ07/4796 7777).

Police 30 Stanley St ⓣ07/4760 7777.

Post office Behind the Flinders Street Mall in Sturt St, near the junction with Stanley St.

Swimming Tobruk Swimming Pool, The Strand, in the parkland on the north side of the road, about 1km west of the junction with Wickham St.

Taxi There's a stand at Flinders Street Mall ⓣ13 10 08.

Tours Townsville Tropical Tours (ⓣ07/4721 6489, ⓦwww.townsvilletropicaltours.com.au) runs small, personalized 4WD day-tours to rainforest at Paluma ($120), the old gold-mining town of Charters Towers ($130), and more forest and waterfalls at Wallaman Falls ($130).

Magnetic Island

Another island named by Captain Cook in 1770 – after his compass played up as he sailed past – **Magnetic Island** is a beautiful triangular granite core about 12km from Townsville. There's a lot to be said for a trip: lounging on a beach, swimming over coral, bouncing around in a moke from one roadside lookout to another, and enjoying the sea breeze and the island's vivid colours. Small enough to drive around in half a day, but large enough to harbour several small settlements, Magnetic Island's accommodation and transfer costs are considerably lower than on many of Queensland's other islands, and if you've ever wanted to spot a **koala** in the wild, this could be your chance – they're often seen wedged into gum trees up in the northeast corner of the island.

Seen from the sea, the island's apex of **Mount Cook** hovers above eucalypt woods variegated with patches of darker green vine forest. The north and east coasts are pinched into shallow sandy bays punctuated by granite headlands and coral reefs, while the western part of the island is flatter and edged with mangroves. A little less than half the island is designated a **national park**, with the settlements of **Picnic Bay**, **Nelly Bay**, **Arcadia** and **Horseshoe Bay** dotted along the east coast. Shops and supplies are available on the island, so there's no need to bring anything with you.

Arrival and island transport

Two ferries operate between Townsville and Magnetic Island. **Sunferries** (Ⓣ07/4771 3855) leaves from the Flinders Street East terminal and the Breakwater terminal for the new multi-million dollar marina at Nelly Bay, midway along the east coast of Magnetic Island, at least ten times daily, with extra departures at weekends ($19.90 return); pick up a **timetable** from any information booth. There's no need to book, just buy a ticket at the jetty and hop on board. The **Magnetic Island Car Ferry** (Ⓣ07/4772 5422, Ⓦwww.magneticislandferry.com.au; $127 return for a car and up to three passengers; pedestrians $17 return) operates to Geoffrey Bay, Arcadia, at least four times daily from Ross Street, a ten-minute walk east along Palmer Street from the Transit Centre.

The island has 35km of road, including a dirt track to West Point and a sealed stretch between Picnic and Horseshoe bays. **Magnetic Island Bus Service** (Ⓣ07/4778 5130) meets all Sunferries and runs between Picnic Bay and Horseshoe Bay more or less hourly between 6.45am and 8.55pm with late services to 11.40pm on weekends; their day pass ($11) allows unlimited travel and can be purchased from the bus driver or at the Information Centre in the Nelly Bay Ferry Terminal. For your **own transport**, Moke Magnetic at Picnic Bay mall (Ⓣ07/4778 5377, Ⓦwww.mokemagnetic.com.au) rents out fun mini-mokes for a flat $65 a day, plus $100 deposit; MI Wheels at Horseshoe Bay (Ⓣ07/4778 5491) seems cheaper at $42 a day, though here you pay an additional $0.33 per kilometre and have to return the car with a full fuel tank. Both require a minimum driver age of 21, and ask that you stick to sealed roads. Various places on the island, including accommodation, rent out **bicycles** for about $15 a day, while Hooters Scooters (Ⓣ07/4778 5317), on Pacific Drive in Horseshoe Bay, has scooters from $30 a day.

Accommodation

Magnetic Island's **accommodation** is ubiquitous, with options for all budgets. Most lodgings have Internet access, rent out snorkelling gear, bikes, beach gear and watersports equipment, can make tour bookings and might pick you up if you call in advance.

Picnic Bay and Nelly Bay

Base Backpackers 1 Nelly Bay Rd, Nelly Bay Ⓣ1800 242 273, Ⓦwww.basebackpackers.com. Large modern backpackers' with lively atmosphere, large pool, bar and DJ, situated at the secluded southern end of Nelly Beach. Excellent facilities, and cheap meals served from its restaurant. Dorms $20 includes breakfast.

Magnetic Island Tropical Resort Yates St, Nelly Bay Ⓣ1800 069 122, Ⓦwww.magneticislandresort.com. Clean and comfortable chalet-style cabins with a/c and bathroom, in a lovely eight-acre bush setting attracting lots of birdlife. Reasonably priced evening steak and seafood restaurant and complimentary breakfast. ❺

Travellers Hideaway 32 Picnic St, Picnic Bay ⓣ1800 000 290, ⓦwww.travellersbackpackers.com. New location for one of the original backpackers', now set back one street from the beach in a converted motel block. Expect noisy disruptions from the adjacent construction site. Dorms $20, rooms ❷

Arcadia

Arkie's Resort 7 Marine Parade ⓣ1800 663 666, ⓦwww.arkiesmagnetic.com. Motel-style units set around a pool, with a cheap bistro and tacky nightlife. Dorms $15–23, doubles ❷

Beachside Palms 7 Esplanade ⓣ07/4778 5810. Four clean and spacious 1- and 2-bed apartments facing the beach at Geoffrey Bay with pool and laundry facilities. ❹–❺

Centaur House ⓣ1800 655 680, ⓦwww.bpf.com.au. Restored 1940s beach house, with fine bedrooms and shared bathrooms, but grubby kitchen and lounge area. Snorkelling is good across the road in Geoffrey Bay. Dorm $18, rooms ❷

Kooyong 13 Hayles Ave ⓣ07/4778 5132. Simple self-contained A-frame units in garden setting, a five-minute walk to picturesque Alma Beach. ❸

Marshall's 3 Endeavor Rd ⓣ07/4778 5112. Very friendly B&B with a family atmosphere and quiet garden close to walking trails; facilities are nothing special, but the owners more than make up for it. Three-day discounts are available. ❸

Horseshoe Bay

Bungalow Bay 40 Horseshoe Bay Rd ⓣ1800 285 577, ⓦwww.bungalowbay.com.au. Formerly *Geoff's Place*, re-established as a quiet retreat in a large wooded setting with pool, restaurant and a campsite. The owner feeds hundreds of wild lorikeets every afternoon. Dorms $22, rooms ❸

Maggie's Beach House Pacific Drive ⓣ1800 001 544, ⓦwww.maggiesbeachhouse.com.au. Large, purpose-built backpackers' complex overlooking the sea, with its own pool, budget restaurant, Internet facilities and bar. The place is well run, although you can't help feeling that this sort of high-density accommodation misses the whole point of Magnetic Island. Dorms $21–26, rooms ❸

New Friends Bed & Breakfast Horseshoe Bay Rd ⓣ07/4758 1220. Spacious, well-furnished apartments in large grounds a five-minute walk from the beach. ❺

Sails 13 Pacific Drive ⓣ07/4778 5117, ⓕ4778 5104. Self-contained apartments with a full range of modern amenities, including pool and outdoor BBQ area at the quiet end of Horseshoe Bay. One-bedroom apartments ❼, villas ❽

The island

Set on the southernmost tip of the island, **PICNIC BAY** is a languid spot, well shaded by surrounding gum woodland and beachfront fig trees, and offering a welcome contrast to Townsville's parched environment. Once the main ferry terminal (which since 2004 relocated to the new marina at Nelly Bay), this tiny settlement at the end of the tar-sealed road is now facing an identity crisis. Most

Magnetic Island tours and excursions

For a **tour** of the island, plump for a day out in a 4WD with Tropicana (ⓣ07/4758 1800, ⓦwww.tropicanatours.com.au; $132); the cost seems steep, but you'll be very well fed and looked after, plus you'll see just about all the island's beaches and bays. You could also spend a day **sailing** to hard-to-reach beaches and bays with *Jazza* (ⓣ1800 808 002, ⓦwww.jazza.com.au; $95), including snorkelling, lunch and afternoon tea; or try your hand **sea-kayaking** with Magnetic Island Sea Kayaks (ⓣ07/4778 5424; $49, including breakfast).

Relatively murky waters don't make Magnetic Island the most dramatic place to learn to **scuba dive**, but with easy shore access it's very cheap – certification courses start at $249 – and on a good day there's some fair coral, a couple of small shipwrecks and decent fish life. Operators include Pleasure Divers (ⓣ1800 797 797), and Dive Shack (ⓣ1800 100 066, ⓦwww.diveshack.com.au), both near *Arkie's Resort* at Arcadia; both can also arrange dives to the *Yongala* (see p.519).

of the small motels and backpacker hostels that thrived on the ferry business have closed down and the developers have pounced – a luxury 40-apartment resort is being constructed along the foreshore and the pedestrian mall has been whittled down to a small cluster of shops and a **post office**. For somewhere to **eat**, *Mermaid's* and *Feedja Café* (which uses only organic ingredients) serve tasty meals in a courtyard setting.

Nelly Bay, Arcadia and the Forts

On the east coast, north of Picnic Bay, **NELLY BAY** is thriving with the on-going development of the fashionable marina complex and ferry terminal. The bay itself comprises a sprawl of houses fronted by a good beach with a little reef some way out. Two streets back is a shopping complex with a supermarket, Mexican **restaurant** and coffee shop, while the **aquarium** (daily 9am–5pm; $2) just around the corner has tanks of giant clams – all part of a research project, and only open to the public as an afterthought. Alternatively, there's a **walking track to Arcadia** from here, though it can be hot work – start early and take plenty of water. A little further along the coast, **ARCADIA** surrounds **Geoffrey Bay** and counts the good-value *Banister's Seafood Restaurant* at 22 McCabe Crescent among its attractions. At Arcadia's northern end is the perfect swimming beach of **Alma Bay**, hemmed in by cliffs and boulders, and with good snorkelling over the coral just offshore. **Diving** here is marred by low visibility, but there are plenty of fish and brain coral, and a disintegrating shipwreck. A walking track from the end of Cook Road leads towards Mount Cook and the track to Nelly Bay, or up to **Sphinx Lookout** for sea views. At dawn or dusk you might see the diminutive island **rock wallaby** on an outcrop or boulder near Arcadia's jetty.

North of Arcadia the road forks, with the right branch (prohibited to rental vehicles) leading via tiny **Florence Bay** – one of the prettiest on the island – to **Radical Bay**, and the main road carrying on to Horseshoe. Leave your car at the junction and continue uphill on foot to **the Forts**, built during World War II to protect Townsville from attack by the Japanese. The walking track climbs gently for about 1.5km through gum-tree scenery to gun emplacements (now just deserted blockhouses) set one above the other among granite boulders and pine trees. The best views are from the slit windows at the command centre, right at the pinnacle of the hill. The woods below the Forts are the best place to see **koalas**, introduced to the island in 1930. They sleep during the day, so tracking them down involves plenty of wandering around – although if you hear ferocious pig-like grunts and squeals, then some lively koalas are not far away.

Horseshoe Bay and around

The road ends in the north at **HORSESHOE BAY** on the island's longest and busiest beach, half of which is developed and the other half remaining blissfully secluded, with views north beyond the bobbing yachts to distant Palm Island. The cluster of shops at the road's eastern end features a **general store** and bakery. Places to **eat** include the quaint *Sandbar Restaurant* with excellent seafood and the more flamboyant *Marlin Bar and Grill* with cheap steaks, several beers on tap and cocktails by the jug. The beach, which is good for swimming most of the year, is also a great place for activities – several beachfront operators here **rent** out jet skis, kayaks, surf skis and boats and provide joyrides on inflated tubes and water-skis. Other diversions include **horse rides** with the experienced Bluey's Horseshoe Ranch ($75 for the popular beach ride, $105 for a half-day ride; advance bookings necessary on ⓣ07/4778 5109). **Walking tracks** lead over the headland to Radical Bay by way of tiny **Balding Bay**, arguably the nicest on the island; you can spend a perfect day here snorkelling around the coral gardens just offshore and cooking on the hotplate provided. **Radical Bay** itself is another pretty spot, half a kilometre of sandy beach sandwiched between two huge, pine-covered granite fists.

Townsville to Cairns

Just an hour to the north of Townsville the arid landscape that has prevailed since Bundaberg transforms into dark green plateaus shrouded in cloud. There's superlative scenery at **Wallaman Falls**, inland from **Ingham**, and also near Cairns as the slopes of the coastal mountains rise up to front the **Bellenden Ker Range**. Forests here once formed a continuous belt almost to Cooktown, but logging has thinned them to a disjointed necklace of plantations and national parks. Even so, it seems that almost every side-track off the highway leads to a waterhole or falls surrounded by natural jungle – this is where it really pays to have your own vehicle. There's also a handful of islands to explore, including the wilds of **Hinchinbrook**, as well as the **Mission Beach** area between **Tully** and **Innisfail**, where you might find regular **work** on fruit plantations or further opportunities to slump on the sand.

Paluma and Jourama Falls

The change in climate starts some 60km north of Townsville, where the Mount Spec road turns west off the highway and climbs a crooked 21km into the hills to **Paluma** township. Halfway there, a solid stone **bridge**, built by relief labour during the Great Depression in the 1930s, spans **Little Crystal Creek**, with some picnic tables and barbeque hotplates by the road, and deep **swimming holes** overshadowed by rainforest just up from the bridge – beware of slippery rocks and potentially strong currents. Look out too for large, metallic-blue Ulysses **butterflies** bobbing around the canopy.

PALUMA itself consists of a handful of weatherboard cottages in the rainforest at the top of the range. A couple of **walking tracks** (from 500m to 2km in length) take you into the gloom, including a ridgetop track to **Witt's Lookout**; keep your eyes open for **chowchillas**, plump little birds with a dark body and white front which forage by kicking the leaf litter sideways; you'll also hear whipbirds and the snarls of the black-and-blue **Victoria riflebird**, a bird of paradise – they're fairly common in highland rainforest between here and the Atherton Tablelands, but elusive. For a good glimpse of these head for *Ivy Cottage Tearooms* (Tues–Fri 10.30am–4pm, Sat–Sun 10am–5pm), whose garden and birdtable is the local riflebird population's favourite afternoon haunt; their Devonshire cream teas aren't bad either. They also offer B&B **accommodation** (Ⓣ07/4770 8533; ❹); alternatives include self-contained cabins at *Misthaven Units* (Ⓣ07/4770 8607; ❸), and *Paluma Rainforest Cottages* (Ⓣ07/4770 8520, Ⓦwww.palumarainforest.com.au; ❺).

Past Paluma the range descends west, leaving the dark, wet coastal forest for open gum woodland. *Hidden Valley Cabins* (Ⓣ07/4770 8088, Ⓦwww.hiddenvalleycabins.com.au; ❷–❹), 24km beyond Paluma on a dirt road near Running River, provides everything you'll need: spa, pool, beer, meals and packed lunches. Nearby is **the Gorge**, a lively section of river with falls, rapids and pools – drive down in a 4WD or walk the last kilometre.

Back on the coastal highway heading north, you pass the *Frosty Mango* roadhouse (daily 8am–6pm), whose exotic fresh cakes and ice creams are made from locally grown fruit, before encountering more aquatic fun at **Jourama Falls**, 18km from the Paluma road. After turning west off the highway, the six-kilometre part-asphalt road to Jourama ends at a low-key QPWS campsite (contact Ingham QPWS ⓣ07/4776 1700 for booking details and key access) set amongst gum and wattle bushland peppered with huge **cycads**. From here an hour-long walking track follows chains across the rocky riverbed to more swimming holes surrounded by gigantic granite boulders and cliffs, finally winding up at the falls themselves – which are impressive in full flood but fairly insignificant by the end of the dry season.

Ingham and around

Home to Australia's largest Italian community, the small town of **INGHAM**, 110km north of Townsville, is well placed for trips inland to **Girringun National Park** – home to Australia's highest waterfall – and also gives access to the tiny port of **Lucinda**, the southern terminus for ferries to Hinchinbrook Island (p.529). Pasta and wine are to be had in abundance during the May **Italian Festival**, but the town is better known for events surrounding the former *Day Dawn Hotel* (now *Lee's Hotel*) on Lannercost Street, the legendary "**Pub with No Beer**". During World War II, Ingham was the first stop for serviceman heading north from Townsville, and in 1941 they drank the bar dry, a momentous occasion recorded by local poet Dan Sheahan and later turned into a popular ballad.

The highway curves through town as Herbert Street, though most services are located slightly to the west along Lannercost Street. Interstate **buses** stop ten times daily just where the southern highway meets Lannercost Street; **trains** stop 1km east on Lynch Street – you can buy tickets from Ingham Travel at 28 Lannercost St. Information is available at the well-informed **Hinchinbrook Visitor Centre** (Mon–Fri 8.45am–5pm, Sat & Sun 9am–2pm; ⓦwww.hinchinbrooknq.com.au), on the corner where the highway from Townsville meets Lannercost Street; they also stock brochures on local national parks.

Accommodation options include *Palm Tree Caravan Park* (ⓣ07/4776 2403; cabins ❸); straightforward pub rooms at *Lee's Hotel* (ⓣ07/4776 1503; ❸, including continental breakfast); or basic dorm beds at the *Royal Hotel* (ⓣ07/4776 2024; $14) on Lannercost Street. *Lee's* does filling budget **meals** – lunches are just $3.50 from Monday to Wednesday – and the bar hasn't run out of beer since the 1940s. The *Olive Tree Coffee Lounge*, just a few doors along from the Visitor Centre, is a great Italian place, with home-made pizza and pasta. The well-signposted **Tyto Wetlands Nature Walk** on the outskirts of town boasts 90 hectares of wetlands with over 200 species of birds, bird hides and walking trails. For the various sections of Girringun National Park, turn west down Lannercost Street and follow the road to **Trebonne** (lucidly marked, "This road

Cycads

Cycads are extremely slow-growing, fire-resistant plants found throughout the tropics, with tough, palm-like fronds – relics of the age of dinosaurs. Female plants produce bright orange seed cones which, in Australia, are eaten (and thus distributed) by emus. Despite being highly toxic to humans – almost every early Australian explorer made himself violently ill trying them – these seeds were a staple of Aborigines, who detoxified flour made from the nuts by prolonged washing. They also applied "fire-stick farming" techniques, encouraging groves to grow and seed by annual burning.

is not Route 1"); for Lucinda, follow the signs for Forest Beach and Halifax from the town centre.

Girringun National Park

Several disconnected areas of wilds west of Ingham together form **Girringun National Park**, formerly Lumholtz but now named after the mythical storyteller from the local Aboriginal tribes. The road from Ingham divides 20km along at Trebonne, with separate routes from here to either Mount Fox or Wallaman Falls. For **Mount Fox**, stay on the road for 55km as it crosses cattle country to the base of this extinct volcanic cone; the last two kilometres are dirt and can be unstable. A rocky, unmarked path climbs to the crater rim through scanty forest; it's hot work, so start early. The crater itself is only about 10m deep, tangled in vine forest and open woodland. With prior permission, you might be able to **camp** at the nearby township's cricket grounds – either ask at the school, or call ⓣ07/4777 5104.

The signposted **Wallaman Falls** route is a 40km run along a mostly sealed road up the tight and twisting range with cassowaries commonly sighted along the route. Tunnelling through thick rainforest along the ridge, the road emerges at a bettong-infested QPWS **campsite** before reaching the falls **lookout**. The falls – at 268m, Australia's highest – are spectacular, leaping in a thin ribbon over the sheer cliffs of the plateau opposite and appearing to vaporize by the time they reach the gorge floor. A walk down a narrow and slippery path from the lookout to the base dispels this impression, as the mist turns out to be from the force of water hitting the plunge pool. If you're staying the night, walk from the campsite along the adjacent quiet stretch of Stoney Creek at dawn or late afternoon to see **platypuses**.

Cardwell

Some 50km north from Ingham lies the modest little town of **CARDWELL** – not much more than a quiet string of shops on one side of the highway, with the sea on the other – though it's made attractive by the outline of Hinchinbrook Island, which hovers just offshore, so close that it almost seems to be part of the mainland. In recent years, Cardwell has become a bit of an environmental battleground as a result of the controversial **Port Hinchinbrook Marina**, which was built during the 1990s just south of town in a "protected" mangrove zone and dugong (sea cow) sanctuary. The resulting increase in marine traffic and the uncontrolled access to Hinchinbrook could be disastrous for this fragile area, and the numbers of once-common dugongs, and the sea-grass beds on which they feed, have already declined drastically.

Cardwell spreads for about 2km along the highway, with banks, the post office, supermarket and hotel all near or south of the **old jetty**, itself about halfway along the road. **Buses** pull up beside the BP service station and *Seaview Café* at the "Transit Centre" – actually just an open-sided bus shelter; the **train station** is about 200m further back. You can buy **tickets** at the agent next to the *Seaview Café* or, if they're closed, in the café itself (daily 8am until late). Just north of the jetty, the QPWS-run **Rainforest and Reef Centre** (daily 8am–4.30pm closed Sat–Sun, Dec–Mar; free; ⓣ07/4066 8601 or book online at ⓦwww.epa.qld.gov.au) issues **island permits** and has a walk-through rainforest and mangrove display.

The best of the **accommodation** is north of the jetty at the *Kookaburra Holiday Park*, 175 Bruce Highway (ⓣ07/4066 8648, ⓦwww.kookaburraholidaypark.com.au; dorms $18, cabins ❷, motel rooms ❸), which has tent sites and a self-contained backpackers' block, plus free use of fishing gear and bikes to hire. Alternatively, try the *Cardwell Beachfront Motel*, 1 Scott St (Ⓣ07/4066 8776, Ⓕ4066 2300; ❷–❸), a low-key, standard place facing the sea. For **food**, *Annie's Kitchen*, just up the highway from the bus stop, opens early and is the best of the town's numerous cafés; fish and chips can be had from *Seafood Fish & Chips* opposite the Rainforest Centre; if you're self-catering, head for 5 Star Supermarket on the north side of town.

As well as running to Hinchinbrook Island, Hinchinbrook Ferries (see Hinchinbrook Island "Practicalities" on p.530) also runs day-trips ($85) to the reef around **Garden** and **Goold islands** – you can camp on either. **Bareboats** from Hinchinbrook Rent a Yacht (Ⓣ07/4066 8007, Ⓦwww.hinchinbrookrentayacht.com.au) work out at around $90 per person per day in a group of six with a minimum four-day charter.

Hinchinbrook Island

Across the channel from Cardwell, **Hinchinbrook Island** looms huge and green, with mangroves rising to forest along the mountain range that forms the island's spine, peaking at **Mount Bowen**. The island's drier east side, hidden behind the mountains, has long beaches separated by headlands and the occasional sluggish creek. This was Giramay Aboriginal land, and though early Europeans reported the people as friendly, attitudes later changed and nineteenth-century "dispersals" had the same effect here as elsewhere. The island was never subsequently occupied, and apart from a single resort, Hinchinbrook remains much as it was two hundred years ago.

The island's main attraction is the 32-kilometre-long **Thorsborne Trail**, a moderately demanding hiking track along the east coast which takes in forests, mangroves, waterfalls and beaches. More adventurous, unmarked routes scale **Mount Straloch** – site of a USAF B24 plane wreck from World War II – and Mount Bowen; you'll need advice from the QPWS in Cardwell (see opposite) if you want to tackle these.

The Thorsborne Trail

The 32-kilometre **Thorsborne Trail** is manageable in two days, though at that pace you won't see much. **Trailheads** are at Ramsay Bay in the north and George Point in the south, and the route is marked with orange triangles (north to south), or yellow triangles (south to north). The north to south route is considered slightly more forgiving as it eases into ascents; although the advantage of ending up in the north is that the pick-up with Hinchinbrook Ferries includes a welcome few hours unwinding at the *Hinchinbrook Island Wilderness Lodge*'s bar and pool.

Boats **from Cardwell** take you through the mangroves of Missionary Bay in the north to a boardwalk that crosses to the eastern side of the island at **Ramsay Bay**. The walk from here to **Nina Bay**, which takes a couple of hours, is along a fantastic stretch of coast with rainforest sweeping right down to the sand and Mount Bowen and Nina Peak as a backdrop. If long bushwalks don't appeal, you could spend a few days camped on the forest's edge at Nina instead; a creek at the southern end provides drinking water and Nina Peak can be climbed in an hour or so. Otherwise, continue beyond a small cliff at the southern end of Nina, and walk for another two hours or so through a pine forest to **Little Ramsay Bay** (drinking water from Warrawilla Creek), which is about as far as you're likely to get on the first day.

Moving on, you scramble over boulders at the far end of the beach before crossing another creek (at low tide, as it gets fairly deep) and entering the forest beyond. From here to the next camp at **Zoe Bay** takes about five hours, following creek beds through lowland casuarina woods and rainforest, before exiting onto the beach near Cypress Pine waterhole. A clearing and pit toilets at the southern end of Zoe Bay marks the campsite, and water bottles can be filled just beyond. This is one of those places where you'll be very glad you brought insect repellent.

Next day, take the path to the base of **Zoe Falls** – the **waterhole** here is fabulous – then struggle straight up beside them to the cliff top, from where there are great vistas. Across the river, forest and heathland alternate: the hardest part is crossing **Diamantina Creek** – a fast-flowing river with huge, slippery granite boulders. **Mulligan Falls**, not much further on, is the last source of fresh water, with several rock ledges for sunbathing above a pool full of curious fish. Zoe to Mulligan takes around four hours, and from here to George Point is only a couple more if you push it, but the falls are a better place to camp and give you the chance to backtrack a little to take a look at the beachside lagoon at **Sunken Reef Bay**.

The last leg to **George Point** is the least interesting: rainforest replaces the highland trees around the falls as the path crosses a final creek before arriving at unattractive Mulligan Bay. The campsite at George Point has a table and toilet in the shelter of a coconut grove but there's no fresh water and nothing to see except Lucinda's sugar terminal, and little to do except wait for your ferry.

Practicalities

If you're not interested in a serious hike, Hinchinbrook Ferries (ⓣ1800 777 021, ⓦwww.hinchinbrookferries.com.au) offers an excellent **day-trip** ($90) departing 9am from the marina at Cardwell, cruising after dugong and stopping for a three-kilometre beach and rainforest walk before winding up with a dip in the pool at the *Hinchinbrook Island Wilderness Lodge* (ⓣ1800 777 021, ⓦwww.hinchinbrookresort.com.au; four-person cabins ❻, units ❼), which is where you'll find the island's only proper **accommodation**. The lodge is set on Cape Richards at Hinchinbrook's northernmost tip and makes a comfortable retreat, with either self-contained cabins or luxury treehouse units.

The Thorsborne Trail needs some **advance planning**. As visitor numbers to the island are restricted, the trail is usually booked solid: for the Christmas and Easter holidays, aim to book at least six months in advance. Also note that there are reduced ferries November to January and no ferries through February and March. The Cardwell QPWS office hands out trail **maps**, practical details, and **camping permits** ($4 per person per night), which can also be registered online at ⓦwww.epa.qld.gov.au. Since different **ferries** service the north and south ends of the island, you'll need to make two separate bookings if you're planning to enter and exit from separate ends of the trail. Hinchinbrook's north is served by Hinchinbrook Island Ferries from Cardwell's marina ($59 one-way). For the south, contact Phil & Kylie Menzies at Hinchinbrook Wilderness Safaris in Lucinda (ⓣ07/4777 8307; $46 one-way). Both operators also offer return fares for their ends of the island; contact them for prices.

Winter months (June–Oct) provide optimum hiking **conditions**, though it can rain throughout the year. Essentials include water-resistant footgear, pack and tent, a lightweight raincoat and insect repellent. Although streams with **drinking water** are fairly evenly distributed, they might be dry by the end of winter, or only flowing upstream from the beach – collect from flowing sources only. Wood fires are prohibited, so bring a fuel stove. Kookabura Holiday Park in Cardwell (see p.528) rents out essential **camping gear**. White-tailed rats and marsupial mice will gnaw through tents to reach food; the QPWS has installed metal food stores at campsites, though hanging anything edible from a branch may foil their attempts. Snakes are also common, if seldom encountered, and you should beware of crocodiles in lowland creek systems.

Edmund Kennedy National Park, Murray Falls and Tully

In May 1848, the **Edmund Kennedy expedition** landed just a few kilometres north of where Cardwell was later to be founded, and set off to walk to Cape York. Thick vegetation forced them to abandon their one hundred sheep and three carts, and, harassed by local tribes, the party gradually ran out of food; by December, Kennedy had left the others while he raced the last 100km with his Aboriginal companion, **Jackey-Jackey Galmarra**. Kennedy was killed by Jadhaigana Aborigines while negotiating a river within sight of the cape; Jackey managed to reach the waiting schooner *Ariel*, which set off down the coast to find only two of the other expedition members still alive. The little **Edmund Kennedy National Park**, down a short road off the highway 4km north of Cardwell, marks the spot where the doomed expedition struck inland, and you have to ponder the wisdom of trying to manoeuvre carts through the paperbark and mangrove thickets – romantically described by Kennedy's informant as "wooded hills and green valleys". There are boardwalks and trails through the park, and views across to Dunk and Hinchinbrook islands from the beach.

The road to the small but attractive **Murray Falls**, off the highway 20km further north, heads 20km inland past banana plantations to the edge of the Cardwell Range and the falls themselves. It's really just worth a look to break your journey, but there's a large **camping area** here (contact Cardwell QPWS Ⓣ07/4066 8601 or book online at Ⓦwww.epa.qld.gov.au) and tracks through the forest to permanent swimming holes and lookouts across the bowl of the valley. There's a basic store on the approach road, some distance from the falls, but it's best to stock up in Tully or Cardwell beforehand.

Some 45km north of Cardwell, **TULLY** lies to the left of the highway on the slopes of **Mount Tyson**, its 450-centimetre annual rainfall the highest in Australia. Settled by Chinese, who pioneered banana plantations here at the beginning of the twentieth century, it's a stopover for **white-water rafting** day-trips out of Cairns and Mission Beach on the fierce and reliable Tully River, 40km inland, but otherwise nothing special: cultivated lawns and flowerbeds back onto roaring jungle at the end of Brannigan Street, a constant reminder of the colonists' struggle to keep chaos at bay. Though most people drive the extra thirty minutes to Mission Beach (see below), there's **accommodation** here at *Green Way Caravan Park* (Ⓣ07/4068 2055; cabins ❸); while the well-managed *Banana Barracks* hostel at 50 Butler St (Ⓣ07/4068 0455, Ⓦwww.bananabarracks.com) has excellent **work** connections, plus free weekend beach trips and barbecues.

Mission Beach and Dunk Island

After branching east off the Bruce Highway a couple of kilometres past Tully, a loop road runs 18km through canefields and patches of rainforest to **Mission Beach**, the collective name for four peaceful hamlets strung out along a fourteen-kilometre stretch of sand – the area owes its name to the former Hull River Mission, destroyed by a savage cyclone in 1918. Not far offshore lies **Dunk Island**, whose idyllic beaches and rainforest track make it a pleasant day-trip.

Arrival and information

Long-distance buses set down outside the post office at Mission Beach, from where your accommodation might collect you if forewarned. Alternatively, a local **bus** (Ⓣ07/4068 5468) plies between South Mission and Bingil Bay roughly eight times daily between 8.30am and 8.30pm (restricted service Sat);

Tours from Mission Beach

Among the local **tours** worth seeking out, Raging Thunder's "Xtreme Team" (ⓣ1800 337 116, ⓦwww.rtextreme.com) is exclusive to Mission Beach and offers the best-value river rafting down the Tully River in small groups, getting to the river before the bus-loads arrive from Cairns. Skydive Mission (ⓣ1800 638 005, ⓦwww.jumpthebeach.com) can take you to eight thousand feet for freefall fun ($225), and also offers skydiving over Dunk Island ($390). If it's riverine wildlife you're after, Hinchinbrook Explorer (ⓣ07/4088 6154, ⓦwww.hexplorer.com.au) runs four-hour croc-spotting trips with dinner thrown in ($40), or you can go paddling with Coral Sea Kayaking (ⓣ07/4068 9154, ⓦwww.coralseakayaking.com; $89).

for a taxi call ⓣ07/4068 8155. The **Visitor Information Centre** (daily 9am–5pm) is just north of Mission Beach township along Porter Promenade. Behind the centre, the **Environmental Information Centre** (daily 10am–5pm) has a display on local habitat, along with a nursery growing seeds collected from cassowary droppings, with the aim of safeguarding the food supply for future generations of this giant bird.

Accommodation

Places to stay are fairly evenly distributed along the coast and cover everything from camping to resorts. All can provide information and book you on white-water rafting and other tours in the area. **Campsites** include the tidy *Coconut Village Caravan Park* at South Mission (ⓣ07/4068 8129, ⓔhideaway@austarnet.com.au; units ❷), and the *Hideaway Holiday Village* at Mission Beach (ⓣ07/4068 7104; cabins ❸).

Eco Village Clump Point ⓣ07/4068 7534, ⓦwww.ecovillage.com.au. Smart, motel-like accommodation set just back from the beach amongst pandanus, native nutmeg trees and tropical gardens with a natural rock pool. Luxury rooms have Jacuzzi. ❻

Honeyeater Homestay 53 Reid Rd, Wongaling ⓣ07/4068 8741, ⓦwww.honeyeater.com.au. Delightful, Balinese-inspired house, with lush tropical gardens surrounding the pool making the place look far larger and more secluded than it actually is. Only takes a maximum of six people. ❹

Licuala Lodge 11 Mission Circle, Mission Beach ⓣ07/4068 8194, ⓦwww.licualalodge.com.au. A tropical-style B&B with airy wooden verandahs and traditional, high-ceilinged interior; the landscaped garden and pool are worth a stay in themselves, and the huge breakfast will keep you going all day. ❹–❺

Mackays 7 Porter Promenade, Mission Beach ⓣ07/4068 7212, ⓦwww.mackaysmissionbeach.com. Standard Australian resort complex, with comfortable modern units arranged around gardens and a pool. ❻

Mission Beach Retreat Mission Beach ⓣ1800 001 056, ⓦwww.missionbeachretreat.com.au. Conveniently located next to the shops and bus stop in Mission Beach, close to the beach and with a small pool and laundry. Dorms $21, rooms ❷

Perrier Walk Guesthouse Perrier Walk, Mission Beach ⓣ07/4068 7141, ⓦwww.perrierwalk.nq.nu. Vivid tropical architecture, with a mix of Thai, Indonesian and Mexican elements in the guesthouse design and decor; friendly and very comfortable too, with pleasant gardens. Each room has its own verandah and outdoor shower. ❺–❻

Sanctuary Holt Rd, Bingil Bay ⓣ1800 777 012, ⓦwww.sanctuaryatmission.com. An outstanding operation set in fifty acres of thick rainforest. There's abundant wildlife – including cassowary – and a 700m forest track down to a beach. Huts are on stilts (and walled with fine-meshed netting, so you wake up surrounded by greenery), while cabins have verandahs; there's a bar, yoga lessons and an excellent-value restaurant. Note that hut access paths follow steep slopes, and some find the wildlife's proximity unsettling. Advance booking essential. Dorms $32.50, hut ❸, cabin ❺

Scotty's Beachhouse 167 Reid Rd, Wongaling ⓣ1800 665 567, ⓦwww.scottysbeachhouse.com.au. A popular backpackers' party place right across from the beach at Wongaling, with bunkhouses, a pool and a fine restaurant offering cheap meals. Dorms $18–22, rooms ❷

The Beach

Right down at the bottom end of the beach, **SOUTH MISSION** is a quiet, mostly residential spot, with a long, clean beach. Signposted off the main road on Mission Drive is a monument to the original site of the Hull River Mission; after the cyclone, the mission was relocated to safer surroundings on Palm Island. At the end of beachfront Kennedy Esplanade, the **Kennedy Walking Track** weaves through coastal swamp and forest for a couple of hours to the spot where Edmund Kennedy originally landed near the mouth of the Hull River – a good place to spot coastal birdlife and, quite likely, crocodiles.

Heading 4km north of South Mission takes you to **WONGALING BEACH**, a slowly expanding settlement based around a shopping centre and

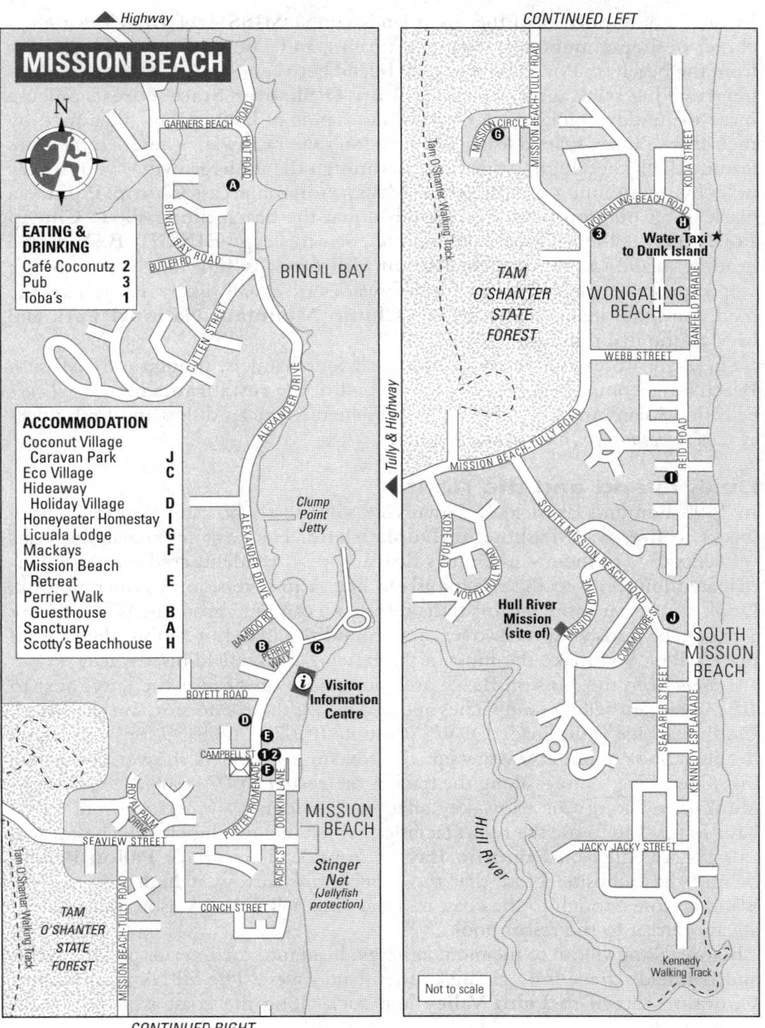

Cassowaries

Aside from the lure of the beach, forests here are a reliable place to spot **cassowaries**, a blue-headed and bone-crested rainforest version of the emu, whose survival is being threatened as their habitat is carved up – estimates calculate that there are only a couple of thousand birds left, all in tropical Queensland. Many larger trees rely on the cassowary to eat their fruit and distribute their seeds, meaning that the very makeup of the forest hinges on the bird's presence. Unlike the emu, cassowaries are not at all timid and may attack if they feel threatened: if you see one, remain quiet and keep a safe distance.

Mission's only **pub**. A further 4km lands you at **MISSION BEACH** itself, a cluster of shops, boutiques, restaurants, banks, and a post office one block back from the beach on Porter Promenade. Inland between the two, a six-kilometre-long walking track weaves through **Tam O'Shanter State Forest**, a dense maze of muddy creeks, vine thickets and stands of licula palms (identified by their frilly, saucer-shaped leaves). If you don't see cassowaries here – sometimes leading their knee-high, striped chicks through the undergrowth – you're very unlucky. Continuing 6km north of Mission township past **Clump Point** – a black basalt outcrop with views south down the beach sitting above **Clump Point Jetty** – the road winds along the coast to sleepy **BINGIL BAY** before heading inland to the excellent **Bicton Hill track**, a 4km hilly walk through wet tropics where encounters with cassowaries are equally likely. From here, the road continues inland alongside the **Clump Mountain National Park** and back to the main highway.

There are stores and places to **eat** at all four hamlets, though only Mission Beach has a comprehensive range – the best of the **restaurants** here are *Toba*'s eclectic "Asian" menu, and stylishly presented Mexican dishes and fresh juices at *Café Coconutz*, which also has a bar.

Dunk Island and the Reef

In 1898 Edmund Banfield, a Townsville journalist who had been given only weeks to live, waded ashore on **Dunk Island**. He spent his remaining years – twenty-five of them – as Dunk's first European resident, crediting his unanticipated longevity to the relaxed island life. A tiny version of Hinchinbrook, Dunk attracts far more visitors to its resort and camping grounds. While there's a reasonably satisfying track over and around the island, it's more the kind of place where you make the most of the beach – as Banfield discovered.

Vessels from the Mission Beach area put ashore on or near the jetty, next to *BB's* restaurant selling sandwiches and hot meals; there's no store on the island. On the far side is the shady QPWS campsite (Ⓣ07/4068 8199 for permits and details or book online at Ⓦwww.epa.qld.gov.au), with toilets, showers and drinking water. Five minutes along the track is the **resort** (Ⓣ07/4068 8199, Ⓦwww.dunk-island.com; ❼), a low-key affair well hidden by vegetation, but you'll have to pay $40 to use the resort facilities, which includes lunch. The best places to relax are either on **Brammo Bay**, in front of the resort, or **Pallon Beach**, behind the campsite. Note that the beaches are narrow at high tide and the island is close enough to the coast to attract box jellyfish in season, but you can always retreat to the resort pool.

Before falling victim to incipient lethargy, head into the interior past the resort and Banfield's grave for a circuit of the island's west. The full 9km up **Mount Cootaloo**, down to **Palm Valley** and back along the coast is a three-hour

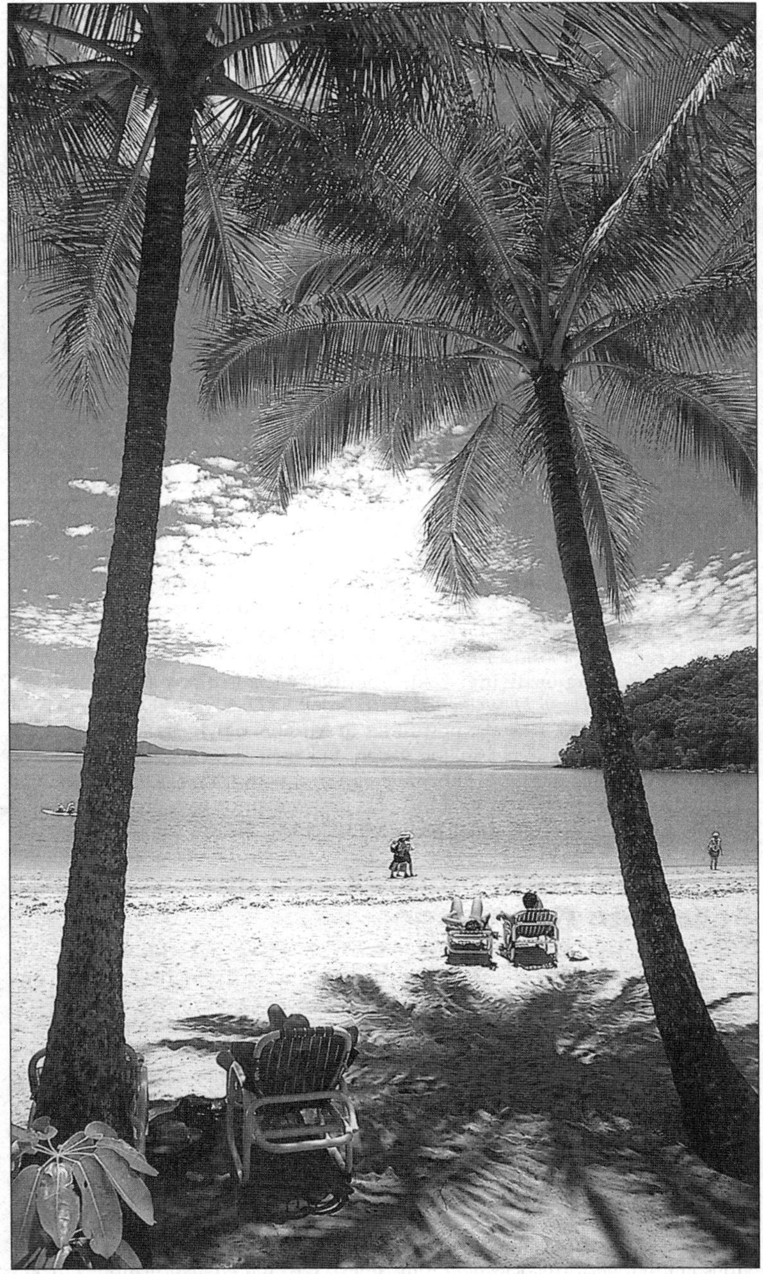

△ Dunk Island

Dunk Island and Reef ferries

All the ferries below run daily to Dunk for $40 return.

Dunk Island Ferry & Cruises Clump Point Jetty ⓣ07/4068 7211. Departs 8.45am and 10.30am, 40mins. Can also provide a coach pick-up from Cairns or Innisfail. For an extra $10 they provide a barbecue lunch at Dunk, and for a flat $64 you get the trip to Dunk, barbecue lunch, and an afternoon boomnetting around Bedarra Island.

Quick Cat Clump Point Jetty ⓣ07/4068 7289. Departs 8am, 10am and 2pm; 20mins. After dropping passengers at Dunk, continues out to Beaver Cay on the Barrier Reef for coral viewing, snorkelling and diving ($98; two dives $95 extra). On Wednesday and Sunday they also run a budget boat direct to the reef for $98, departing 11am.

Water Taxi Wongaling Beach ⓣ07/4068 8310. Departs 9.30am, 11am, 12.30pm, 2.30pm and 4.15pm; last boat leaves Dunk 4.45pm; 10mins. Free bus from Mission Beach accommodation available on request.

rainforest trek, best tackled clockwise from the resort. You'll see green pigeons and yellow-footed scrubfowl foraging in leaf litter, vines, trunkless palms and, from the peak, a vivid blue sea dotted with hunchbacked islands.

Ferries to Dunk cost $22 one-way (see box above for details), though occasional price wars between operators might save a few dollars; book directly or through your accommodation. The island is 5km – barely fifteen minutes – offshore, but even so the tiny water taxis are not really suitable if you have much luggage. **Camping gear** can be rented from the complex next to the post office in Mission Beach; you can also leave surplus equipment with them.

Some distance northeast of Dunk is **Beaver Cay**, the local section of the Barrier Reef, with a sand island and some very pretty coral gardens that make for easy **snorkelling** or **diving**. Aside from *Quick Cat* (see box above), you can dive with *Mission Beach Dive Charters* (ⓣ07/4068 7277; $200 plus gear rental for two dives and lunch), near the post office in Mission Beach, though they don't provide hot drinks or free drinking water, and their slow vessel gives a rough ride; a more reliable but more expensive option is with *Calypso Dive* (ⓣ07/4068 8432, ⓦwww.calypsodive.com; $260 plus gear rental for two dives and lunch) who offer a fast ride to the outer reef with toilet and shower facilities on board.

Paronella Park, Innisfail and the Bellenden Ker Range

Back on the highway around 25km north of Tully, tiny **Silkwood** marks the turning inland for the 23-kilometre run through canefields to **Paronella Park** (daily 9.30am–5pm; $20; ⓣ07/4065 3225, ⓦwww.paronellapark.com.au). This extraordinary estate was laid out by **José Paronella**, a Spanish immigrant who settled here in 1929 and constructed a **castle** complete with florid staircases, water features and avenues of exotic kauri pines amongst the tropical forests. Left to moulder for twenty years, the park was reclaimed from the jungle and restored during the 1990s, and now forms a splendidly romantic theme park, with half-ruined buildings artfully part-covered in undergrowth, lush gardens and arrays of tinkling fountains – all gravity-fed from the adjacent Mena Creek. A former walk-through aquarium has become the roost of endangered little bent-winged bats, and native vegetation includes a bamboo forest and dozens of *angiopteris* ferns, rare elsewhere. Fifteen-minute indigenous cultural performances held four times a day and educational bush tucker walking tours add to its appeal so you'll need a good couple of hours to do the place justice; it's possible to **camp** here and explore after dark – phone ahead for details. There's a **restaurant** on site, or you can eat across Mena Creek at the old pub.

The Paronella Park road and highway converge again 25km on at **INNISFAIL**, a busy town on the Johnstone River and a good spot to look for **work** picking bananas: *Innisfail Budget Backpackers*, on the highway just on the northern side of town (☎07/4061 7833; dorms $20), can help if you stay with them. Alternatively, try the much smarter *Codge Lodge* near the bright pink Catholic church on Rankin Street (☎07/4061 8055; dorms $20, rooms ❷). Innisfail is worth a quick stop anyway as a reminder that modern Australia was in no way built by the British alone: there's a sizeable **Italian community** here, represented by the handful of delicatessens displaying herb sausages and fresh pasta along the central Edith Street. The tiny red **Chinese Joss House** (and huge longan tree next to it) on Owen Street was first established in the 1880s by migrant workers from southern China, who cleared scrub and created market gardens here; and many of Innisfail's banana plantations have been bought up recently by **Hmong** immigrants from Vietnam.

Just beyond town, the Palmerston Highway turns off across the bottom end of the Atherton Tablelands, and at about the same point you begin to see the **Bellenden Ker Range**, which dominates the remaining 80km to Cairns. This coastal area of the tablelands includes Queensland's highest mountain, **Bartle Frere**. While the two-day return climb through **Wooroonooran National Park** to the 1600-metre summit is within the reach of any fit, well-prepared bushwalker, you should contact the park ranger (☎07/4067 6304) or the Cairns QPWS in advance (see "Listings", p.545) for accurate information about the route. To reach the start of the track, leave the highway 19km north of Ingham at one-house Pawngilly and continue for 8km, past Bartle Frere township, to **Josephine Falls**. Even without going any further, the falls – wonderfully enclosed jungle waterslides – are worth the trip. Marked with orange triangles, the climb to the peak passes through rainforest, over large granite boulders and out onto moorland with wind-stunted vegetation. Much of the summit is

Cane toads

Native to South America, the huge, charismatically ugly **cane toad** was recruited in 1932 to combat a plague of greyback beetles, whose larvae were wreaking havoc on Queensland's sugar cane. The industry was desperate – beetles had cut production by ninety percent in plague years – and resorted to seeding tadpoles in waterholes around Gordonvale. They thrived, but it soon became clear that toads couldn't reach the adult insects (who never landed on the ground), and they didn't burrow after the grubs. Instead they bred whenever possible, ate anything they could swallow, and killed potential predators with poisonous secretions from their neck glands. Native wildlife suffered: birds learned to eat non-toxic parts, but snake populations have been seriously affected. Judging from the quantity of flattened carcasses on summer roads (running them over is an unofficial sport), there must be millions lurking in the canefields, and they're gradually spreading into New South Wales and the Northern Territory – Kakadu received its first arrivals around 2000. Given enough time, they seem certain to infiltrate most of the country.

The toad's outlaw character has generated a cult following, with its warty features and nature the subject of songs, toad races, T-shirt designs, a brand of beer and the award-winning film *Cane Toads: An Unnatural History* – worth seeing if you come across it on video. The record for the largest specimen goes to a 1.8-kilogram monster found in Mackay in 1988.

blinded by scrub and usually cloaked in rain, but there are great views of the tablelands and coast during the ascent.

Further along the highway, there's a detour at **BABINDA** township – dwarfed by a huge sugar mill – to another waterhole at **the Boulders**, where an arm of Babinda Creek forms a wide pool before spilling down a collection of house-sized granite slabs. Cool and relatively shallow, the waterhole is an excellent place to swim, though it also has a more sinister reputation. Legend has it that an Aboriginal girl was raped here and in reprisal she cursed the pool against men; several deaths have been caused by subtle undertows dragging people over the falls – be very careful and stay well clear of the falls' side of the waterhole. You can also **camp** here for free.

Nearing the end of the range is **Gordonvale**, the place where the notorious **cane toad** was first introduced to Australia (see box p.537). From here, the tortuous Gillies Highway climbs from the coast to lakes Barrine and Eacham on the Atherton Tableland (for more on these see p.551). Marking the turn-off is **Walsh's Pyramid**, a natural formation which really does look like an overgrown version of its Egyptian counterpart. From here, the last section of the Bruce Highway carries you – in thirty minutes – through the suburbs of Edmonton and White Rock to Cairns.

Cairns and around

CAIRNS was pegged out over the site of a sea-slug fishing camp when gold was found to the north in 1876, though it was the Atherton Tablelands' tin and timber resources that established the town and kept it ahead of its nearby rival, Port Douglas (see p.559). The harbour is the focus of the north's fish and prawn concerns, and tourism began modestly when **marlin fishing** became popular after World War II. But with the "discovery" of the reef in the 1970s and the appeal of the local climate, tourism snowballed, and high-profile development has now replaced the unspoiled, lazy tropical atmosphere which was what everyone originally came to Cairns to enjoy.

For many visitors primed by hype, the city falls far short of expectations. However, if you can accept the tourist industry's shocking glibness and the fact that you're unlikely to escape the crowds, you'll find Cairns a convenient base with a great deal on offer, and easy access to the surrounding area – the Atherton Tablelands, Cape York and, naturally, the Great Barrier Reef and islands.

Arrival and information

Downtown Cairns is the grid of streets behind the Esplanade, overlooking the harbour and Trinity Bay. **Buses** arrive at the end of the Esplanade at Trinity Wharf Transit Centre – though with the upcoming redevelopment of Trinity Wharf the terminal will move, most likely to adjacent Reef Fleet Terminal. The **train station** is 750m away under the Cairns Central development between Bunda Street and McLeod Street. The **airport** is about 7km north, along the Cook Highway. A taxi from the airport into Cairns costs $12–15; a shuttle bus ($7) connects with most flights and delivers to all central accommodation. If you're staying in a hostel, you'll usually be **picked up** at the Trinity Wharf Transit Centre, and possibly from the train station and airport if you give advance notice.

The closest Cairns has to an official **Information Centre** is the Gateway Discovery Centre at 51 Esplanade (Ⓣ07/4041 3588), but this still runs purely as a commercial enterprise promoting only those tours that pay to be featured. Beware of the hordes of copycat information centres around town with misguided blue "i" signs to attract your attention – these are nothing but commercial high street agents selling high-paying commission products. Even the backpacker agents on Shield Street, which lure you in with free or very cheap Internet access, offer biased information and an unknowledgeable sales staff. Many tours offer **standby rates** the day or two before departure so if you don't mind taking a chance, it's worth waiting and contacting the tour company direct. *Cairns Discount Tours* (ⓣ07/4041 4677, ⓔtours@iig.com.au) specializes in these last-minute deals and comes highly recommended for its honest approach and thorough information planning.

Sunbus, the **local bus** service, is based at the **Transit Mall** on City Place (Lake St), and serves Cairns Northern Beaches as far as Palm Cove; daily, weekly and monthly **passes** are available, and you can get free timetables from the driver. You may also be able to **rent bikes** at your accommodation, or check out the rental outfits in "Listings" on p.545. If you want to buy or sell a **second-hand car**, head to Cairns Car Market (ⓣ07/4041 0332) on the roof car park above Tropical Arcade, corner of Abbott and Shields streets; cars for sale are also advertised on notice boards outside *Johno's* on the corner of Aplin and Abbott streets, and in an arcade beside the museum at City Place.

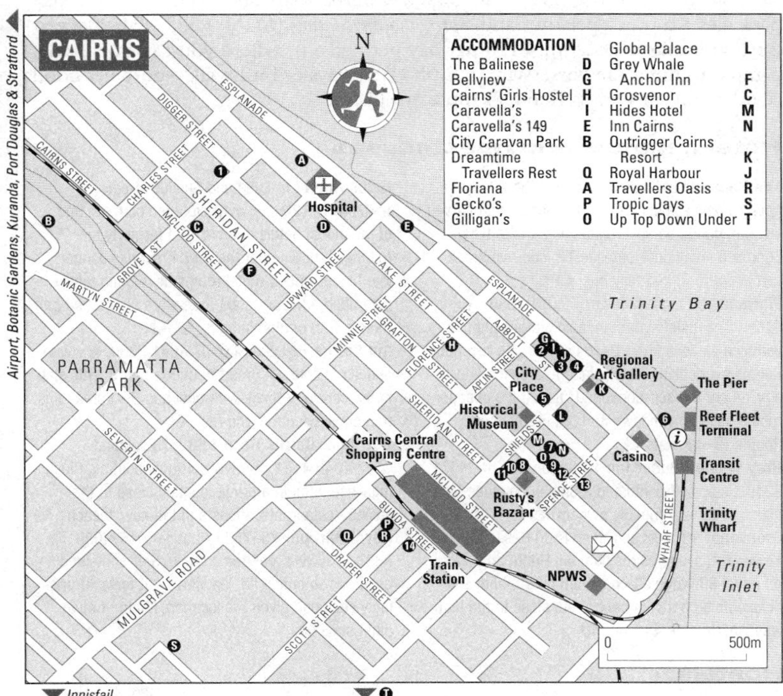

CAFÉS & RESTAURANTS

Café China	12	Curry Bowl	7	Green Ant	14	Phuket Thai	9	Swiss Cake and Coffee Shop	8	Yacht Club	6
Chapel	4	Dundees	13	La Fettuccina	10	Red Ochre	11	Woolshed	5		
Cock & Bull	1	Fetta's	2	Matsuri	3	Sports Bar	13				

Accommodation

Cairns has a prolific number of **places to stay**, and the following is just a selection of the best places. **Luxury** places favour views overlooking the sea, especially along the lower end of the Esplanade, an area which used to be the core of the city's **budget accommodation**. These are now spreading elsewhere; in particular, the area west of the train station is a focus for a number of smaller hostels, of which *Dreamtime* and *Tropic Days* are the pick. The nearest **campsite** to the centre is the *City Caravan Park*, at 14 Little St (Ⓣ07/4051 1467), though you can also camp at *Tropic Days* hostel. If bustling Cairns doesn't excite you but you want access to all its attractions, consider staying along the Cairns Northern Beaches (p.546), 15km north beyond the airport.

Expect seasonal **price fluctuations** at all accommodation, with Christmas and Easter as the busiest times, and February to March as the quietest; book ahead but beware of committing yourself to a special deal on a longer stay until you've seen the room – you probably won't be able to get a refund. All hostels have kitchens, most have a courtesy bus service, laundry and a pool, and offer special meal deals, usually at the *Woolshed* or *Sportsmans*. Note that hostels make most of their profits through commissions, not beds, so don't admit to making tour bookings elsewhere if you want your room to remain available.

For a change of pace, **farmstays** in the Cairns region include *Mount Mulligan Station* (Ⓣ1800 359 798, Ⓦwww.outbackfarmstay.com.au; three-day packages $160 per person), and *Springmount Station* (Ⓣ1800 333 004, Ⓦwww.springmountstation.com; $110 per day per person), where you can horse ride, camp out under the stars, swim in bush waterways or bushwalk – both get good reviews and provide a free pick-up from Cairns.

Hotels, motels and guesthouses

The Balinese 215 Lake St Ⓣ07/4051 9922, Ⓦwww.balinese.com.au. Stylish motel with carved wooden doors, bamboo blinds and lots of tiling. There's a small pool, satellite TV, inclusive breakfast and airport courtesy bus. ❹

Floriana 183 Esplanade Ⓣ07/4051 7886, Ⓔflori@cairnsinfo.com. Amiable old guesthouse with sea views and Art Deco decor in the reception. Rooms overlooking the Esplanade are nice and airy, as are the self-contained "flats"; the cheaper rooms have no windows and get pretty stuffy. Rooms ❷–❸, flats ❹

Grey Whale Anchor Inn 19 Gatton St Ⓣ07/4051 9249. Basic self-contained rooms in an older, quiet house, with very friendly owners. ❸

Grosvenor 188 McLeod St Ⓣ1800 629 179, Ⓦwww.grosvenorcairns.com.au. Bright and cheerful motel offering self-contained apartments and deluxe units; not very central but close to the highway. Apartments ❺, units ❻

Hides Hotel Cnr Lake and Shields streets Ⓣ07/4051 1266, Ⓦwww.clubcroc.com.au. One of the oldest hotels in town (and formerly the roughest), now under the *Club Crocodile* banner. The higher-priced motel rooms have been totally revamped; cheaper hotel rooms are unadorned pub rooms, with original fittings. ❸–❹

Inn Cairns 71 Lake St Ⓣ07/4041 2350, Ⓦwww.inncairns.com.au. Smart boutique apartments slap in the centre of town, with pool and BBQ area, plus rooftop views out to the reef. ❻

Outrigger Cairns Resort 53–57 Esplanade Ⓣ07/4046 4141, Ⓦwww.outrigger.com.au. Plush high-rise hotel in a prime location close to the casino, restaurants, shops and the new "beach". ❼

Royal Harbour 73–75 Esplanade Ⓣ07/4080 8888, Ⓦwww.breakfree.com.au. Self-contained hotel apartments with sea views – it feels surprisingly secluded given the location. Minimum two-night stay. ❻

Hostels

Bellview 85 Esplanade Ⓣ07/4031 4377, Ⓦwww.bellviewcairns.com.au. The quietest hostel on the Esplanade, with motel-like facilities and a range of rooms. Dorms $20, rooms ❷

Cairns' Girls Hostel 147 Lake St Ⓣ07/4051 2016, Ⓦwww.cairnsgirlshostel.com.au. Renovated 1930s Queenslander, with rambling rooms and a slightly dishevelled look. Can be hard to locate; look for the adjacent laundry. Dorms $16, rooms ❷

Caravella's 77 Esplanade ☎07/4051 2159, Ⓦwww.caravella.com.au. Busy and long-established hostel in the heart of the Esplanade, with good facilities but a warren of dark corridors with small dorm rooms. More spacious hostel at number 149 (☎07/4031 5680) at the quieter northern end of the Esplanade. Dorms $19, rooms ❷

Dreamtime Travellers Rest 4 Terminus St, behind the train station ☎07/4031 6753, Ⓦwww.dreamtimetravel.com.au. Small, friendly hostel with a keen owner and very relaxed tropical atmosphere about ten minutes' walk from the centre. They also offer Atherton Tablelands tour/accommodation packages with their sister hostel at Yungaburra (see p.556). Dorms $20, rooms ❷

Gecko's 187 Bunda St ☎1800 011 344, Ⓦwww.geckosbackpackers.com.au. Quaint hostel with wooden floors and dated furnishings in a restored 1920s house. Dorms $20, rooms ❷

Gilligan's 57–89 Grafton St ☎07/4041 6566, Ⓦwww.gilligansbackpackers.com.au. Massive and soulless backpackers' resort with CCTV cameras, 24-hr reception and every conceivable facility. Not a bad choice if you're looking for security but very impersonal. There's even a bar for 2000 people hosting DJs and live bands. Dorms $24–28, rooms ❸

Global Palace City Place, Lake St ☎07/4031 7921, Ⓦwww.globalpalace.com.au. This large, modern backpackers' place right in the centre of town has an industrial feel but is well organized and offers good facilities. Dorms $23, rooms ❷

Travellers Oasis 8 Scott Street ☎1800 621 353, Ⓦwww.travoasis.com.au. Low-key and very friendly family-run hostel in an old Queenslander – dorms a bit small but double rooms are spacious and some have balconies. Dorms $20, rooms ❷

Tropic Days 28 Bunting St ☎07/4041 1521, Ⓦwww.tropicdays.com.au. Though a little bit out of town, this is one of the best hostels in Cairns, with a big pool, nice gardens, colourful rooms and a highly sociable atmosphere. There's a small campsite too, and a courtesy bus through the day. Dorms $20, rooms ❷

Up Top Down Under 164 Spence St ☎1800 243 944, Ⓦwwwuptopdownunder.com.au. Quite a way from the centre, but the cheapest of Cairns' hostels, with inexpensive meals to match, helpful staff, a huge pool and enough space to relax. Dorms $18, rooms ❸

The City

Cairns' strength is in doing, not seeing: there are few monuments, natural or otherwise. This is partly because the Cape York goldfields were too far away and profits were channelled through Cooktown, and partly because Cairns was remote, lacking a rail link with Townsville until 1924; people came here to exploit resources, not to settle. Your best introduction to the region's heritage is at the **Cairns Historical Museum**, at the junction of Shields and Lake streets (Mon–Sat 10am–4pm; $5), which uses photos and trinkets to explore maritime history, the Tjapukai and Bama Aborigines from the tablelands, and Chinese involvement in the city and Palmer goldfields.

At **City Place**, the open-air pedestrian mall outside the museum, you'll find Cairns' souvenir-shopping centre, with a rash of cafés, and shops selling didgeridoos, T-shirts, paintings and cuddly toy koalas. Local performers do their best at the small **sound shell** here from time to time, and there are often more professional offerings in the evenings. Between Grafton and Sheridan streets, towards Spence Street, **Rusty's Bazaar markets** (Fri, Sat & Sun morning) sell a great range of local produce from crafts to herbs, fruit and veg, coffee and fish, with excellent deals on surplus produce around noon Sunday. Moving from the mall area down towards Trinity Wharf, the shops become more upmarket, though they're still selling essentially the same things; an increasing number of signs target the many Japanese visitors. **Trinity Wharf** itself is a collection of dormant offices, due for redevelopment, but the adjacent **cruise terminals** are where most sea trips out of Cairns begin. Next to the terminals and overlooking the marina, **The Pier** is a flashy shopping complex where many tour and cruise operators have booking offices ready to tempt you with brochures and videos of their activities.

Through the day and into the night, the **Esplanade** is packed with people cruising between accommodation, shops and restaurants. Grabbing an early-morning coffee here, you'll witness a quintessentially Australian scene: fig trees framing the waterfront, a couple of trawlers and seaplanes bobbing at anchor in the harbour, and drunks languishing on the benches. Joggers jog, and others promenade along the edge at low tide and watch birds feeding in the shallows – there's an identification chart in the park. Though originally fringed in mangroves and mud flats, developers have, after years of wrangles, created an **artificial beach** near the Pier; it's actually way above the tide-line, but encloses five landscaped **swimming lagoons** which are packed at weekends. Facing the lagoon on the far end of the Esplanade is the glass-domed casino and **Cairns Rainforest Dome** (daily 7am–6pm; $22), an equally artificial replica, this time of the rainforest with caged birds and several depressing looking crocodiles. The Esplanade's **night market** (daily 5pm until late), which runs through to Abbott Street, has a mix of fast-food courts, trendy tack and good-quality souvenirs, plus a great location near plenty of bars. Just around the corner from the Esplanade on Shields Street, **Cairns Regional Art Gallery** (Mon–Fri 10am–5pm, Sat & Sun 1–5pm; $4) is worth a look if Cairns' crasser commercial side is beginning to grate; exhibitions include both local artists' work and travelling shows.

Heading out of the centre, the city's natural attractions include the **Botanic Gardens** (Mon–Fri 8.30am–5.30pm; free guided walks Mon–Fri at 1pm) and the adjacent **Mount Whitfield Environmental Park** on Collins Avenue, off the highway near the airport (bus #7 from the City Place transit mall, or a dull forty-minute walk). Ringed by suburbia, the rainforest is dense enough for wallabies, and a raised boardwalk track through the wonderfully cool and tranquil atmosphere makes a fine escape from the city. Also worth a look are the **mangrove walks** on the airport approach road, whose boardwalks and hides give you a chance to see different varieties of mangrove trees, mudskippers and red-clawed, asymmetric fiddler crabs. Take some repellent or else you'll end up giving the flies a free lunch. Alternatively, Calm Water Tours (☎07/4031 4007; $49) **cruise** 34km along the waterways in search of birds and crocodiles.

Eating and nightlife

Cairns has no shortage of places to **eat**. Least expensive are the takeaways between the Esplanade's hostels serving Chinese food, falafel, kebabs and pasta. Some open early while others, such as *La Pizza* on the corner of Aplin Street, never close, switching from fast food during the day and evening to coffee and croissants at dawn. The night market also houses a fast-food plaza, with a choice ranging from fish and chips to pizza or sushi; alternatively, you can stock up at the **supermarkets** on Abbott Street or in Cairns Central.

Openly drinking on the streets is illegal in Cairns, but the **pub** and **club** culture thrives undaunted. Clubs open around 6pm, most charging $5 entry for bar and disco; more if there's a band playing. Many pubs also feature live music once a week – reviews and details are given in Cairns' free weekly **listings magazine**, *The Fly*; for some indigenous sounds, try to catch one of the up-and-coming local **Torres Strait Islander** performers, such as the Brisco Sisters. Try not to make yourself an obvious target for **pickpockets** and **bag-snatchers** who work the nightclubs, though the steady reports of drink-spikings, rapes and muggings are more worrying – don't hang around outside venues and get a taxi home.

Cafés and restaurants

Café China Cnr of Spence and Grafton streets. Two sections here cater to an increasing number of Chinese visitors to Cairns: an inexpensive noodle house on Spence Street with most dishes under $10, and a more sophisticated Cantonese restaurant on Grafton, with great roast meat or seafood dishes from $15, and daily *yum cha* sessions (best selection at weekends).

Chapel 94 Esplanade. Funky young atmosphere with alternative music, al fresco café and a larger restaurant upstairs with a menu to please everyone except those paying. Mains around $28. Daily 7am–late.

Cock & Bull 6 Grove St, cnr Grafton St. Keg Guinness, hearty counter meals (from around $15) and a pleasant garden atmosphere.

Curry Bowl In Mainstreet Arcade between Grafton and Lake streets, just south of Shields St. Very ordinary-looking fast-food counter, but the portions of (mostly vegetarian) Sri Lankan dahls and curries are large, cheap and pretty authentic.

Dundees 29 Spence St. Popular upmarket grill restaurant, with leanings towards native fauna – kangaroo, emu, crocodile – and seafood. Best dishes are the kangaroo satay and seafood platter (includes crays and mud crab). Mains around $28.

Fetta's 70 Abbott St. Lively family-run Greek restaurant with particularly tasty seafood. Most main dishes around $25; vegetable dishes from $18.

Green Ant 83 Bunda St. Cheap, cheerful and tasty evening meals with unbeatable drink deals. Mains – such as spicy chicken salsa or meat grills served with rice or chips – go for around $10, while the burgers will remind you what burgers used to be like before fast-food versions appeared. Daily 4pm–midnight.

La Fettuccina 41 Shields St ☎07/4031 5959. Superb home-made pasta and sauces for around $18, though very popular, so get in early or book – their "small" servings would be enough for most people.

Matsuri Next to the night-market entrance on Abbott St. Best place for sushi, noodle soups or other Japanese light meals in an authentic environment – popular with Japanese tourists. Most meals around $15. Closed Mon, and often on Tues.

Phuket Thai Grafton Street ☎07/4031 0777. Thai seafood and curries, with mains under $20 – highly rated by locals, and full most nights.

Red Ochre 43 Shields St ☎07/4051 0100. Long-running restaurant with Outback decor and a menu revolving around truly Australian ingredients such as kangaroo and crocodile – although emu meat seems to have been replaced by ostrich. Tasty, but some dishes a bit overworked. Mains $25 and up.

Sports Bar Spence St. Competition for the *Woolshed* at this bar, with light, reasonably priced meals, and plenty of satellite sports channels playing on the video screen. Evening specials on meals and drinks via vouchers from backpacker accommodation.

Swiss Cake and Coffee Shop 93 Grafton St. Top-notch patisserie with crisp strudels, rich cakes and fine coffee.

Woolshed 22 Shields St. Budget backpackers' diner, with huge and inexpensive meals, beer by the jug and party fever. Hostels give out vouchers for various discount meal deals here; it's worth "upgrading" these for a couple more dollars and getting a full-blown feed.

Yacht Club Esplanade. Opens 11am for drinks and enticing grill-and-salad meals at around $13; their "Sunset Special" (6.30–8.30pm) is a bucket of prawns and a beer for $13.

Nightlife

Casa De Meze Cnr Aplin St and the Esplanade. Open nightly, but best to come for Sun afternoon jam sessions of Latin and jazz.

Club Nu Trix 53 Spence St. Cairns' only dedicated gay club with drag shows on Saturday. Wed–Sun 9pm–late.

Johno's Cnr Abbott and Aplin streets. Traditional backpackers haunt, with a huge video screen and a youngish clientele. Live music, including international bands, most nights, and it's even worth catching Johno and the house band – they've been a Cairns' institution for decades.

Inbox Café 119 Abbott St. Good place to check out the local music scene with live gigs mixing with DJs on weekends and special promotions throughout the week.

P.J.O'Brien's City Place, next to Hides, Shields St. This Irish bar attracts a mix of locals and tourists, and is a popular place to meet and warm up before later club sessions. Best on Fri, Sat, and Sun nights.

Playpen Cnr Lake and Hartley streets. Nightclub and disco, with action on most nights and live bands some weekends.

Tropos Cnr Lake and Spence streets. Another hugely popular club with live dance shows, talent quests, DJs and three bars.

Activities

In addition to the tours covered in the box below, several operators offer more activity-led excursions. For **bushwalking**, Wooroonooran Safaris (ⓣ1300 661 113, ⓦwww.wooroonooran-safaris.com.au) spends a moderately strenuous day hiking through thick rainforest just north of Bartle Frere, where you're guaranteed to see wildlife and get wet crossing creeks ($119 all-inclusive, or $89 with your own gear and lunch); The Adventure Company (ⓣ07/4052 8300) spends two days in similar conditions ($275). If it's just **wildlife** you're after, Wildscapes Safaris (ⓣ07/4057 6272, ⓦwww.wildscapes-safaris.com.au) visits the Atherton Tablelands to spot platypus and rare nocturnal marsupials (day-tour $110, night-tour $140), as does Wait-a-While Spotlighting Tours (ⓣ07/4098 2422, ⓦwww.waitawhile.com) and Currawong (ⓣ07/4093 7287, ⓦwww.australiawildlifetours.com; $98–148).

Bicycle tours around the Atherton Tablelands are on offer four times a week with Bandicoot (ⓣ07/4055 0155; $98), or you can get stuck into some moderate to extreme off-road biking around Cairns and Cape Tribulation ($75–135) with Dan's Mountain Biking (ⓣ07/4032 0066) – both come highly recommended. Cairns' **bungee-jumping** venue is a purpose-built platform surrounded by rainforest in the hills off the coastal highway 8km north of Cairns; contact A.J. Hackett (ⓣ07/4057 7188; $109) which can also arrange parasailing at nearby York's Knob ($72) or for the latest adrenalin rush, try bungee jumping from the parasail ($190).

White-water rafting is organized on the reliable Tully River near Tully or the slightly less turbulent Barron River, behind Cairns, and is wild fun despite being a conveyor-belt business: as you pick yourself out of the river, the raft is dragged back for the next busload. A "day" means around five hours rafting; a "half-day" about two. Agents include RnR (ⓣ07/4041 9444, ⓦwww.raft.com.au) and Raging Thunder (ⓣ07/4030 7990, ⓦwww.ragingthunder.com.au); day-trips with either company cost from $88–145, multi-day expeditions $635–1200, with a compulsory rafting levy an extra, and often hidden, $25. For better value, consider the "Xtreme Team" packages available only from Mission Beach (see p.532) which gets you on the river before the Cairns day-trippers arrive and with smaller groups.

Tours from Cairns

Before exploring locally or around the Atherton Tablelands, Port Douglas and Cape Tribulation, bear in mind that the cheapest day-tours will set you back $80 per person, while it costs as little as $50 per day to rent a four-seat car – though you'll miss out on a tour guide's local knowledge. For the **Atherton Tablelands, the Daintree and Cape Tribulation**, the following come highly recommended: Uncle Brian ⓣ07/4050 0615, ⓦwww.unclebrians.com.au; Cape Trib Connections ⓣ07/4053 3833; Tropical Horizons ⓣ07/4058 1244, ⓦwww.tropicalhorizonstours.com.au; the backpacker-oriented Jungle Tours ⓣ07/4032 5600, ⓦwww.adventuretours.com.au; Queensland Adventure Safaris ⓣ07/4041 2418, ⓦwww.qastours.com; and Trek North Safaris ⓣ07/4051 4328, ⓦwww.treknorth.com.au. Wilderness Challenge ⓣ07/4035 4488, ⓦwww.wilderness-challenge.com.au visits the Daintree, Cape Tribulation and Mossman Gorge, and also goes to Cooktown and the Aboriginal rock-art sites around Laura. For **Cape York**, the following organize trips to the tip by 4WD, boat and plane, and enjoy reliable reputations: OZtours ⓣ07/4055 9535, ⓦwww.oztours.com.au; Billy Tea Bush Safaris ⓣ07/4032 0077, ⓦwww.billytea.com.au; and Exploring Oz ⓣ1300 888 112, ⓦwww.exploring-oz.com.au.

Finally, two places well worth looking into to arrange a spot of small-scale **fishing** for barramundi and other estuary fish are Paradise Sportfishing (☎07/4055 6088) and All Tackle (☎07/4034 2550) – both charge around $75 per person for a full day of shore-based fishing, or $140 from a boat.

For **diving**, see the box on pp.548–549.

Listings

Airlines Air New Zealand ☎1800 221 111; Air Niugini, 4 Shields St ☎07/4035 9888; Cathay Pacific ☎07/4013 1747; JAL, 15 Lake St ☎1800 177 884; Malaysia, 15 Lake St ☎07/4013 1627; Qantas ☎13 13 13; Singapore, 15 Lake St ☎07/4013 1011; Skytrans ☎07/4046 2462; Virgin Blue ☎13 67 89.

Banks and exchange Banks are scattered throughout the city centre, mostly around the intersection of Shields and Abbott streets and in Cairns Central. Some booths around the Esplanade also offer bureau de change facilities, though rates are lower than at the banks.

Bike rentals Bandicoot Bicycle Hire & Tours, 59 Sheridan St ☎07/4055 0155; bike rental $16.50 a day.

Books Exchange Book Shop, 78 Grafton St, has an excellent range of secondhand books to buy or exchange.

Buses Interstate services are operated by Greyhound Australia (☎13 20 30); and Premier (☎13 34 10) and leave from the Reef Street Terminal. Whitecar Coaches (☎07/4091 1855) run daily to Atherton from Spence St; Country Road Coachlines (☎07/4045 2794) run on Monday, Wednesday and Friday to Cooktown via Port Douglas and also to Karumba on Monday and Thursday; Coral Reef Coaches (☎07/4098 2800) and Sun Palm Coaches (☎07/4032 4999) both operate a daily service to Cape Tribulation via Port Douglas.

Camping equipment Adventure Equipment, 133 Grafton St (☎07/4031 2669), stocks and rents out all types of outdoor gear and even kayaks; City Place Disposals, cnr Shields and Grafton streets; Geo Pickers, 108 Mulgrave Rd, cnr Draper St; and Wolfies Disposals, 56 McLeod St, all have basic equipment and secondhand gear.

Car rental All the following offer discounts on long rentals; on a day-by-day basis you're looking at around $50 for a four-person runaround. Best of the bunch for general purposes is Minicar Rentals, 150 Sheridan St ☎07/4051 6288, ⓦwww.minicarrentals.com.au. Alternatively, try: A1 Car Rental, 141 Lake St ☎07/4031 1326; All Day, 151 Lake St ☎07/4031 3348, ⓦwww.cairns-car-rentals.com; Britz, 411 Sheridan St ☎1800 331 454, ⓦwww.britz.com, for 4WDs, motorhomes and campervans or Integra Car, 131 Lake St ☎1800 067 414, ⓦwww.integracar.com.au.

Cinemas There are multi-screens at BC City Cinemas at 108 Grafton St and in Cairns Central.

Hospital and medical centres Cairns Medical Centre, cnr of Florence and Grafton streets (☎07/4052 1119) is open 24hr for vaccinations and GP consultations (free if you have reciprocal national health cover). Hospitals include Base Hospital, northern end of the Esplanade (☎07/4050 6333), or, if you have insurance, Cairns Private Hospital (☎07/4052 5200) on the corner of Upward and Lake streets.

Internet access If your accommodation isn't connected, cheap access is offered by Peter Pan Travel on Shields Street 'though they'll try desperately to sell you a tour', or the more relaxed and friendly *Inbox Café* at 119 Abbott Street ($3 per hour).

Left luggage At the train and bus stations; around $5 a day.

QPWS At the southern end of Sheridan, just past the police station – look for the building with green and yellow trim (Mon–Fri 8.30am–5pm; ☎07/4046 6600). Staff are very helpful, and have plenty of free brochures on regional parks, plus books for sale on wildlife and hiking.

Pharmacy Cairns Day and Night Pharmacy and Medical Centre, 29b Shields St ☎07/4051 2466 (daily 8am–9pm).

Police 5 Sheridan St ☎07/4030 7000.

Post office 13 Grafton St, and upstairs in Orchid Plaza off the Transit Mall, Lake St.

Scenic flights Cairns Seaplanes offers spins over the Reef and islands for $299; Cape York Airlines (☎07/4035 9399, ⓦwww.capeyorkair.com.au) charges just $200 for a 1-hour flight or take the daily scenic mail flights to various parts of Cape York Peninsula for $300–890 depending on destination.

Shopping Tourist-oriented shops are concentrated close to the Esplanade and around City Place and Lake St, where Aboriginal art galleries have sprung up in profusion, though little is truly local – didgeridoos on sale here might have been made in Indonesia. Moving down Shields St the shops become more general, preparing you for what's on offer at the modern air-conditioned shopping complex in the Cairns Central development. Many shops don't open on Saturdays or Sundays.

Taxis The main cab rank is on Lake St, west of City Place. Alternatively, ring Black and White Cars on ⓣ13 10 08.
Trains Bunda St, under Cairns Central ⓣ13 22 32. Trains head south down the coast to Brisbane, up to Kuranda on the Atherton Tablelands (p.551), and west to Forsayth in the Gulf region (p.623).
Travel agents For budget travel and tours try: Flight Centre, 24 Spence St ⓣ07/4052 1077; STA, 9 Shields St ⓣ07/4031 4199; Trailfinders, next to *Hides Hotel*, Shields St ⓣ07/4041 1199.
Work You may be able to work a passage on barges going to Cape York; check "General Notices" in the Cairns Post for openings. For more regular employment try the backpacker contact points listed in the Cairns' "Arrival" section (p.538); there are often WWOOF placements available on the Atherton Tablelands.
Yacht Club 4 Esplanade ⓣ07/4031 2750. Worth contacting for hitching/crewing north to Cape York and the Torres Strait, south to the Whitsundays and beyond, and even to New Guinea and the Pacific.

Around Cairns

There's a fair amount to see and do **around Cairns** (unless otherwise stated, the areas below can be reached on Sunbus services from City Place; see p.541). About 12km northwest near Redlynch, **Crystal Cascades** (Wongalee Falls) is a narrow forest gorge gushing with rapids, small waterfalls and swimming opportunities – somewhere to picnic rather than explore. Don't leave valuables in your car, and heed warnings about the large, pale-green, heart-shaped leaves of the **stinging tree** (also known locally as "Dead man's itch"), common on the sides of the paths here; the stories may seem apocryphal but if stung you'll believe them all. Backtracking through **Kamerunga** township – as far as you'll get on the bus – there's a marked, fairly steep track through the **Barron Gorge National Park** up through forests to Kuranda (see p.551).

Cairns' variously developed **beaches** start 8km north of town just beyond the airport – most tour companies will arrange pick-ups from your accommodation. **Holloways Beach** is pretty enough but suffers from noise pollution lying directly in the path of ascending aircraft from Cairns airport – if you don't mind the noise, *Billabong B&B* on Caribbean Street (ⓣ07/4037 0162, ⓦwww.cairns-bed-breakfast.com, ❺ includes a sumptuous gourmet breakfast) is a delightful and secluded spot set on a man-made island surrounded by water and full of birdlife. **Yorkey's Knob,** on another access road 2km further north is a quiet residential setting alongside one of the best **kite surfing** beaches in Australia – Kiterite (ⓣ07/4055 7918) offers three-hour introductory lessons for $120. *Villa Marine* (ⓣ07/4055 8380, ⓦwww.villamarine.com.au, ❹) offers self-contained spacious units set fifty metres back from the beach in a cool patch of rainforest attracting wildlife and makes an ideal base for exploring the Cairns area – at 6.30am every morning pelicans are fed on the beach. You can **eat** at the popular and picturesque **marina** which doles out huge servings, and offers beer on tap and pokie machines.

About 12km north of Cairns, the township of **Smithfield** marks the starting point for the Kennedy Highway's ascent to Kuranda in the Atherton Tablelands. Shortly before, a large complex on the roadside houses both the Kuranda Skyrail cable-car terminus (see p.552) and the **Tjapukai Aboriginal Centre** (daily 9am–5pm; various packages $28–91, plus transfers). The centre's hefty admission price isn't bad value, as it includes entry to boomerang and didgeridoo displays, a fine museum, and three separate theatre shows featuring Dreamtime tales and dancing; it's not eye-opening stuff, but does offer a light-hearted and fully entertaining introduction to Aboriginal culture.

Beyond Smithfield is the more developed and up-market tourist area of Trinity Beach and Palm Cove, both with spotlessly clean, palm-fringed beaches and lots of luxury holiday apartments and beach resorts, cafés, boutique shops, restaurants and watersports. You can stay cheaply at **Trinity Beach** at the unusual looking *Casablanca Domes* (Ⓣ07/4055 6339, Ⓦwww.casablancadomes.com.au; ❹), resembling both an igloo and a seventies hippie camp. It's located along the Esplanade facing the beach and is very clean. Otherwise, expect to pay from $150 per night at the resorts with minimum stays enforced during the high seasons. *The Sebel Reef House* at **Palm Cove** (Ⓣ07/4055 3633, Ⓦwww.reefhouse.com.au; ❽) is the grandest of all the resorts along the coast whilst the most down-to-earth is *Kewarra Beach Resort* (Ⓣ07/4057 6166, Ⓦwww.kewarrabeachresort.com.au; ❽), tucked away in a secluded patch of rainforest on the quietest stretch of beach. **Cairns Tropical Zoo** (daily 8.30am–5pm; $26) back on the main highway offers close views of Australia's often-elusive fauna – their **night tour** (Mon–Thurs & Sat 7–10pm; $83 plus transfers) is particularly recommended. If you want to really escape for a few days, however, get out to **Ellis Beach**, thirty minutes north of Cairns on the way to Port Douglas (and unfortunately beyond the reach of bus services). You couldn't ask for a finer place to camp beside the beach, with tent sites and cabin accommodation at *Ellis Beach Caravan Park* (Ⓣ07/4055 3538; cabins ❸).

The Reef and diving

Seeing the **Great Barrier Reef**, either on a cruise or as a diver, is what attracts many visitors to Cairns, and there are so many ways to do this that making a choice can be very daunting. Broadly speaking, the reef can be classified into **three regions** – inner, outer and fringing – each somewhat different in character. The **inner reef**, a sheltered patchwork of coral and sea between the outer walls and Cairns, is flat and fairly shallow, a good place for novices. The **outer reef** borders the open sea, so has more dramatic appeal in the shape of walls, canyons, deeper water and bigger fish. **Fringing reef** surrounds **Green Island** and **Fitzroy Island**, and again has safe, easy access.

All regions are visited on **cruises**, with vessels ranging from old trawlers to racing yachts and high-speed cruisers; if you want to stay longer, check into an island **resort** or take an extended **dive trip**. One way to choose the right boat is simply to check out the **price**: small, cramped, slow tubs are the cheapest while roomy, faster catamarans are more expensive – though often better value. To narrow things down further, find out which serves the best **food**. Generally, if this is going to be your only visit, it's worth paying the extra. Before going (or even if you're not) take in the superb two-hour **Reef Teach** multimedia and interactive show in Cairns at the Bolands Centre, 14 Spence St (Mon–Sat 6.15pm; $13; Ⓦwww.reefteach.com.au), at which eccentric marine biologist Paddy Colwell gives more essential background than the dive schools and tour operators have time to impart – this is the most worthwhile thing you can do in Cairns.

You might be a little taken aback by the state of the Cairns **coral**: years of agricultural run-off and recent coral-bleaching events – not to mention the sheer number of visitors – is beginning to have a visibly detrimental effect. This is less apparent on the more remote sites, but becomes quite marked the closer you get to the coast. Having said that, even the most visited sites are still stocked with marine life, ranging from tiny gobies to squid, turtles, and big pelagic fish – though seasoned divers might come away disappointed.

Dive sites

The dozen or more **inner reef** sites are much of a muchness. Concentrated day-tripping means that you'll probably be sharing the experience with several

Reef trips and dive schools

The **reef cruises** and **diving** listings given below are not mutually exclusive – most outfits offer diving, snorkelling (usually free) or just plain sailing. **Prices** can come down by as much as thirty percent during the low seasons (Feb–April & Nov) and **standbys** on live-aboard boats can save even more. All dive schools run trips in their own boats, primarily to take students on their certification dives – experienced divers may want to avoid these. Paddy Colwell, a **marine biologist** at Reef Teach (see p.547), can organize a day-trip to the reef and accompany you on your dives ($200, all inclusive). Beware of **"expenses only"** boat trips offered to backpackers, which usually end up in sexual harassment once out at sea. If in doubt, find out from any booking office in town if you're dealing with an authorized, registered operator. In general, the outer reef provides better coral conditions and depending on your comfort level, you'll want to choose between trips to pontoon bases or to open-water reefs.

Reef cruises

SAILBOATS

Day-trips $89–170; three days (two nights) $380–500.

Ecstasea ⓣ07/4041 3055, ⓦwww.reef-sea-charters.com.au. Modern yacht aimed more for couples taking a maximum of twenty guests for trips to Upolu Cay, just south of Michaelmas; good food, and they'll let you have a go at sailing, too.

Ocean Free ⓣ07/4041 1118, ⓦwww.oceanfree.com.au. Budget day-trips to the reef around Green Island aboard a nineteen-metre rigged schooner.

Ocean Spirit II ⓣ07/4031 2920, ⓦwww.oceanspirit.com.au. Large vessel with 100 passengers – sails out to Michaelmas Cay, reputed for its clams, and motors back ensuring adequate time on the reef. Great presentation but one of the more expensive sailing trips.

Passions of Paradise ⓣ07/4050 0676, ⓦwww.passionsofparadise.com.au. Popular with backpackers, this roomy sail catamaran (very stable) cruises out to Upolu Cay.

Santa Maria ⓣ07/4031 0558, ⓦwww.reefcharter.com. Replica nineteenth-century, twenty-metre rigged schooner with maximum of 10 passengers for overnight trips to Thetford and Moore reefs.

POWERBOATS

$99–179 (day-trips only)

Great Adventures ⓣ1800 079 080, ⓦwww.greatadventures.com.au. Trips on a large, fast catamaran via Green Island to a private reef pontoon.

Osprey V ⓣ1800 079 099, ⓦwww.downunderdive.com.au. Speedy vessel to the outer Norman and Hastings reefs; comfortable boat, great crew and the best meals of any day-trip.

Reef Magic ⓣ1300 666 700, ⓦwww.reefmagiccruises.com.au. High-speed catamaran with five hours at Marine World in the outer barrier reef for snorkelling and glass-bottom boat trips.

Reef Quest ⓣ1800 612 223, ⓦwww.diversden.com. Stable, well-equipped catamaran which covers any number of sites depending on weather conditions.

Sunlover Cruises ⓣ1800 810 512, ⓦwww.sunlover.com.au. Fast catamaran to outer reefs of Moore and Arlington and Fitzroy Island; also offers packages including reef trips and overnight stays on Fitzroy.

Diving

DAY-TRIPS

$60–145; diving upwards of $50 for two dives, including gear rental.

Compass ⓣ1800 815 811, ⓦwww.reeftrip.com. Slow boat, not very stable in windy conditions but one of the cheapest with boomnetting on the way out.

Noah's Ark Too ⓣ07/4050 0677. Real budget diving at Michaelmas Cay and Hastings Reef; great value, but don't expect many creature comforts.

Sea Quest ⓣ1800 612 223. Very comfortable and speedy vessel running to Norman Reef with excellent crew.

Seastar II ⓣ07/4033 0333. Long-established family-run business with permits for some of the best sections of Hastings Reef and Michaelmas Cay – slow boat leaves at 7.45am to ensure adequate time on the reefs.

Super Cat ⓣ1800 079 099. Another well-organized budget option, though a faster, newer vessel than most in the price range.

Tusa ⓣ07/4031 1248, ⓦwww.tusadive.com. Purpose-built vessel holding a maximum of 28 passengers; a roving permit means each trip could go to any of ten separate reefs.

LIVE-ABOARDS

Live-aboard trips cater to more serious divers, last from three days upwards and cover the best of the reefs. Prices vary seasonally, with cheaper rates from February to June; standby rates only become available 48 hours or so before departure and have to be booked direct with the operator. All costs below include berth, meals and dives, but not gear rental. Remember that weather conditions can affect the destinations offered. For unbiased advanced **information**, check out Diversion Travel (ⓦwww.diversionoz.com) based in Cairns.

Diversity ⓣ07/4087 2100, ⓦwww.quicksilver-cruises.com. Speedy and very comfortable catamaran for trips to Cod Hole and Coral Sea. Two days $929; three and a half days $1749.

Mike Ball ⓣ07/4053 0500, ⓦwww.mikeball.com. Luxury diving with one of Queensland's best-equipped and longest-running operations; venues include Cod Hole and the Ribbons, Coral Sea sites and minke whale-watching expeditions, plus the *Yongala* near Townsville (see p.519). From $1050.

Nimrod Explorer ⓣ07/4031 5566, ⓦwww.explorerventures.com. Motorized catamaran with basic or plush cabins; four- to eight-day Cod Hole and Coral Sea trips cost $995–2545.

Serica ⓦwww.sericadiveaustralia.com. Luxury 22-metre sailboat to remote and pristine sections of the northern reef and Coral Sea. Five nights from $2700.

Spirit of Freedom ⓣ07/4040 6450, ⓦwww.spiritoffreedom.com.au. Huge 33-metre vessel with superlative facilities sailing to Cod Hole, the Ribbons and Coral Sea. Three days from $950; four days from $1050.

Taka ⓣ07/4051 8722, ⓦwww.takadive.com.au. New 30-metre fast vessel with four levels and facilities including digital photographic equipment rental and computers onboard. Four days at the Cod Hole and Ribbon reefs $900; five days (including Coral Sea sites) $1050.

Undersea Explorer ⓣ07/4099 5911, ⓦwww.undersea.com.au. Scientific research vessel where guests are allowed to participate in ongoing projects; destinations include Osprey Reef, Cod Hole and the Ribbons, and occasional trips to the historic *Pandora* wreck (see p.519). Seven days $2450.

Vagabond ⓣ07/4031 0784, ⓦwww.vagabond-dive.com. 20-metre yacht with maximum of 10 passengers and a roving permit to suit weather conditions. Two days from $275; three days from $395.

DIVE SCHOOLS

As always, ask around about what each **dive school** offers, though training standards in Cairns are pretty uniform. You'll pay around $325 for a budget Open-Water Certification course, diving lesser reefs whilst training and returning to Cairns each night;

Reef trips and dive schools ***Contd.***

and $550–650 for a four- or five-day course using better sites and staying on a live-aboard at the reef for a couple of days doing your certification. The following schools are long-established and have a sound reputation; certification dives are either made north at Norman, Hastings and Saxon reefs, or south at Flynn, Moore and Tetford.

CDC 121 Abbott St ⓣ07/4051 0294, ⓦwww.cairnsdive.com.au.

Deep Sea Divers Den 319 Draper St ⓣ07/4046 7333, ⓦwww.divers-den.com.

Down Under Dive 287 Draper St ⓣ07/4052 8300, ⓦwww.downunderdive.com.au.

Ocean Spirit Cruises 140 Mulgrave Rd ⓣ07/4031 2920, ⓦwww.oceanspirit.com.au.

Pro-Dive Cnr Abbott and Shields streets ⓣ07/4031 5255, ⓦwww.prodive-cairns.com.au.

other boatloads of people, with scores of divers in the water at once. On a good day, snorkelling over shallow outcrops is enjoyable; going deeper, the coral shows more damage, but there's plenty of patchily distributed marine life. **Michaelmas Cay**, a small, vegetated crescent of sand, is worth a visit: over thirty thousand sooty, common and crested terns roost on the island, while giant clams, sweetlips and reef sharks can be found in the surrounding waters. Nearby **Hastings Reef** has better coral, resident moray eel and Napoleon maori wrasse, as well as plenty of sea stars and snails in the sand beneath. The two are often included in dive- or reef-trip packages, providing shallow, easy and fun diving. Another favourite, **Norman Reef**, tends to have very clear water, and some sites preserve decent coral gardens with abundant marine life.

One of the cheaper options for diving the **outer reef** is to take an **overnight trip** (sleep on board) to nearby sections such as **Moore** or **Arlington** reefs, which take between ninety minutes and two hours to reach – rather generalized terrain, but the advantages over a simple day-excursion are that you get longer in the water plus the opportunity for night dives. **Longer trips** of three days or more venture further from Cairns into two areas: a circuit north to the Cod Hole and Ribbon reefs, or straight out into the Coral Sea. **Cod Hole**, near Lizard Island (see p.567), has no coral but is justifiably famous for mobs of hulking potato cod which rise from the depths to receive hand-outs; currents here are strong, but having these monsters come close enough to cuddle is awesome. **The Ribbons** are a two-hundred-kilometre string with some relatively pristine locations and good visibility, as are **Coral Sea** sites; these are isolated, vertically walled reefs some distance out from the main structure and surrounded by open water teeming with seasonal bundles of pelagic species including mantas, turtles and seasonal **minke whales**. The most visited Coral Sea sites are **Osprey** and **Holmes** reefs, but try to get out to **Bougainville Reef**, home to everything from brightly coloured anthias fish to fast and powerful silvertip sharks. For those heading south, the Whitsundays generally offer better value live-aboard excursions but more expensive day-trips than Cairns.

Green Island and Fitzroy Island

Heart-shaped, tiny and sandy, **Green Island** is the easiest of any of the Barrier Reef's coral cays to reach, making it a near-essential, if expensive, day-trip from Cairns. This, combined with the island's size, means that it can be difficult to escape other visitors, but you only need to put on some fins, visit the **underwater observatory** ($5; free admission with some ferry tickets) or go for a cruise in a glass-bottomed boat to see plentiful coral, fish and turtles. The five-star rooms at the **Green Island Resort** (ⓣ07/4031 3300, ⓦwww.greenislandresort.com.au; ❼) attract long-term guests, and there's a restaurant and pool open to day-trippers, plus plenty of sand to laze on. Daily **ferries** include *Big Cat* (ⓣ07/4051 0444, ⓦwww.bigcat-cruises.com.au; $58) which departs 9am from the Reef Fleet Terminal; and Great Adventures (ⓣ07/4044 9944; $56) departs 8.30am, 10.30am and 1pm from Trinity Wharf. Both run courtesy buses which will collect you from your accommodation. Day-trippers should bring their own **lunches**, as the resort's restaurant is very expensive. Alternatively, Ocean Free (ⓣ07/4041 1118; $89) offers sailing tours to Green Island with offshore snorkelling.

Fitzroy Island is a continental island, not a cay like Green Island, and sports a **resort** (ⓣ07/4030 7907, ⓦwww.fitzroyisland.com.au; bunkhouse $31, rooms ❺, cabins ❼) set in forest near the shore, from where you can dive on the island's reef. Fitzroy is actually quite large and, away from the resort, there are some worthwhile walks through highland greenery where you can escape the sunbathing hordes, notably the 2-hour trek to the Lighthouse for excellent views. Fitzroy Island Ferries (ⓣ07/4030 7907) operates three ferries a day from Reef Fleet Terminal (45min each way; $36 return), and also offers overnight package deals including the popular Party Night on Saturday ($17) with departures at 4pm and 7pm, returning late.

The Atherton Tablelands

The **Atherton Tablelands**, the highlands behind Cairns, are named after **John Atherton**, who made the tin deposits at Herberton accessible by opening a route to the coast in 1877. Dense forest covered these highlands before the majority was felled for timber and given over to dairy cattle, tobacco and grain. The remaining pockets of forest are magnificent, but it's the understated beauty that draws most visitors today, and though **Kuranda** and its markets pull in busloads from the coast, there are several quieter national parks brimming with rare species. You could spend days here, driving or hiking through rainforest to crater lakes and endless small waterfalls, or simply camp out for a night and search for wildlife with a torch. For a contrast, consider a side trip west to the mining town of **Chillagoe**, whose dust, limestone caves and Aboriginal art place it firmly in the Outback.

Drivers can reach the tablelands on the **Palmerston Highway** from Innisfail, the twisty **Gillies Highway** from Gordonvale, or the **Kennedy Highway** from Smithfield to Kuranda. Two stylish and unforgettable ways to ride up to the tablelands are by **train** from Cairns to Kuranda, which winds through gorges and rainforest; and in the green gondolas of the **Kuranda Skyrail** cable car, with a fantastic seven-kilometre (40min) aerial view of the canopy between Smithfield and Kuranda – either method costs $39.50 one-way or $60 return, excluding accommodation pick-up, and a "Skyrail up & train back" package is $98.50. Numerous **tours** run from Cairns (see box on p.544), and the **Kuranda bus service** costs just $2, though you really need your own transport to explore at leisure.

Kuranda and the Barron Gorge

A constant stream of visitors arriving from the coast has turned **KURANDA** into a stereotypical resort village – something, ironically, this once atavistic community was keen to escape. But despite overdevelopment and market-day tourism, it's hard not to like the place. The road comes in at the top of town, while **trains** and the **Skyrail** cable car arrive 500m down the hill, with essential services – post office, store (EFTPOS), bank, cafés – laid out between them along Coondoo Street. **Cafés** are legion, though pricey: *Annabel's Pie Shop*, across from the main markets, has excellent pasties and pies; the nearby Honey House has an on-site **beehive** and sells its honey, and if you're staying the night, *Billy's* at the *Middle Pub* (halfway down Coondoo) does tasty charcoal grill and salad fare.

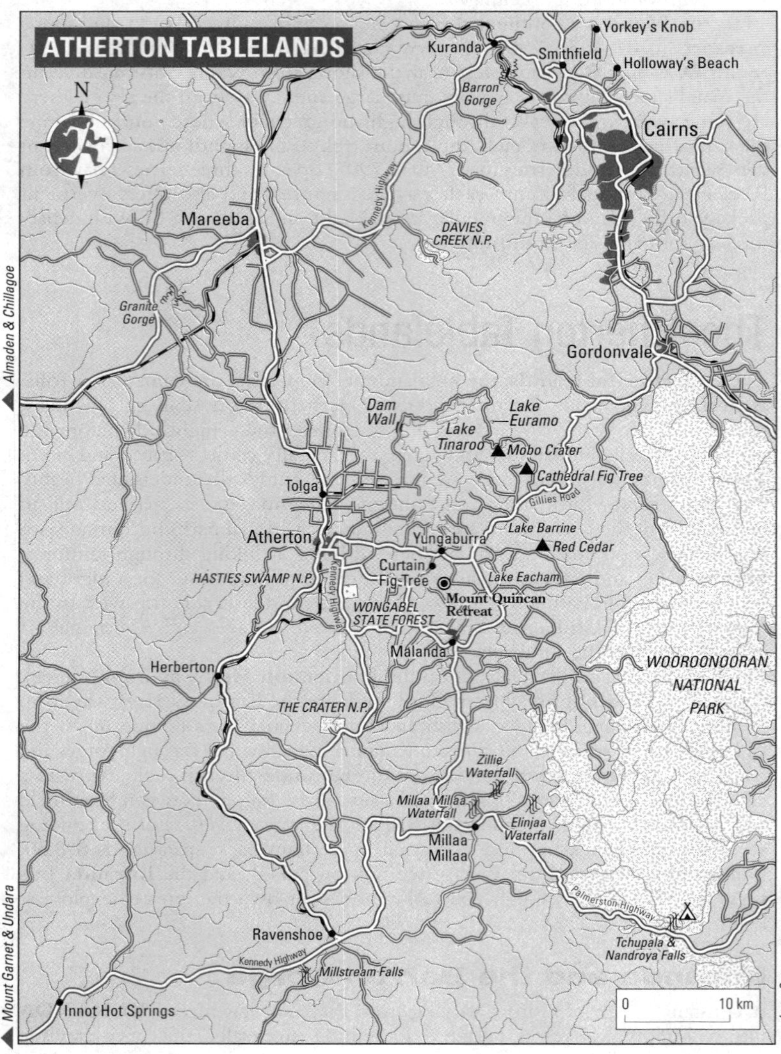

Wet tropics and World Heritage

Queensland's **wet tropics** – the coastal belt from the Paluma Range, near Townsville, to the Daintree north of Cairns – has been nominated under UNESCO **World Heritage** listing as containing one of the oldest surviving tracts of **rainforest** anywhere on earth. Whether this listing has benefited the region is questionable, however; logging has slowed, but the tourist industry has vigorously exploited the area's status as an untouched wilderness, constantly pushing for more development so that a greater number of visitors can be accommodated. The clearing of mangroves for a marina and resort at Cardwell is a worst-case example; Kuranda's Skyrail project was one of the few cases designed to lessen the ultimate impact (another highway – with more buses – was the alternative). Given the profits to be made, development is inevitable, but it's sadly ironic that a scheme designed to promote the region's unique beauty may accelerate its destruction.

Given its accessibility from Cairns, Kuranda isn't a place where many people stay overnight – it's virtually a ghost town after the markets close – and there's little **accommodation**. Just up from the cable-car terminus and orchid-shrouded train station, you'll find the quiet *Kuranda Backpackers' Hostel*, 6 Arara St (Ⓣ07/4093 7355, Ⓦwww.kurandabackpackershostel.com.au; dorms $18, rooms ❷), with a plentiful supply of bunks, large grounds, kitchen and laundry. Around the corner is *The Bottom Pub and Motel* (Ⓣ07/4093 7206; ❸), whose bar has more than a little atmosphere on Friday nights.

The main **street market** times are 8.30am to 3pm on Wednesday, Friday and Sunday, though the commercial **Heritage Market** is open daily. The street markets are best for crafts and clothes, but are not what they used to be, with a growing number of stallholders shying away from the regulated atmosphere here in favour of similar events at Yungaburra and Port Douglas. Nearby, forest fauna can be seen close up at the **Butterfly Sanctuary** (daily 10am–4pm; $13), a mix of streams and "feed trees" where giant ulysses and birdwing butterflies are the most obvious of the dozen local species protected by the breeding programme. **Birdworld**, behind the markets (daily 9am–4pm; $12), is a superb aviary with realistically arranged vegetation and nothing between you and a host of native and exotic rarities such as ecclectus parrots. At the **Koala Gardens** (daily 9am–4pm; $33) next door you can cuddle koalas and see wallabies, wombats, snakes and crocodiles in a rather bland environment. Look out for discounts to visit all three attractions.

Kuranda sits at the top of the **Barron Gorge**, spectacular in the wet season when the river rages down the falls, but otherwise tamed by a hydroelectric dam upstream. Cross the rail bridge next to the station and take a path leading down to the river, where Smiley's Adventure Hire (Ⓣ04/1277 5184, Wed–Sun), offers 45-minute **cruises** ($12) departing five times a day, and canoe rentals to explore the river at leisure. On foot, a newly prepared **walking track** descends to cold swimming spots along the railway and river from the lookout at the end of Barron Falls Road, 2km from town. Other trails follow the road beyond the falls through the **Barron Gorge National Park** and down to Kamerunga, near Cairns – see p.546 for details.

Mareeba and around

West of Kuranda, rainforest quickly gives way to dry woodland and tobacco plantations, quite a change from the coast's greenery. **Davies Creek** is at the end of a track branching off the road after 25km; paths lead from a campsite to where falls pour over a granite rock face to a pool surrounded by boulders and scrub.

The main road continues to **MAREEBA**, a quiet place and the tablelands' oldest town, founded in the 1900s after the area was opened up for tobacco farming. With the demise of the tobacco industry, farmers looked at other options and a thriving coffee industry sprung up. Coffee Works on Mason Street at the south exit of town (daily 9am–4pm) is one of several outlets in town where you can take a tour ($5.50), buy fresh beans, or try a brew at their café. More recently, tropical fruit plantations have become a profitable business with mangoes, avocados and lychees a particular favourite. To boost income, several farms are producing **tropical fruit wines** and have opened cellar doors to promote the unique mango wines, coffee liqueurs and banana brandy – try the award-winning Golden Drop Winery (daily 8am–6.30pm), 10km northwest of Mareeba off the highway at Biboohra.

Just beyond Biboohra, the **Mareeba Wetlands** (Wed–Sun 10am–4pm, closed Jan–March; $10; ⓣ07/4093 2514, ⓦwww.mareebawetlands.com.au), is a stunning 5,000-acre reserve of tropical savannah woodland with grass-fringed lagoons that attracts seasonal flocks of brolgas, jabiru storks and black cockatoos, along with resident wallabies and goannas. You can rent **canoes** here ($15 an hour), book twilight ranger-led **tours** ($48, advance bookings essential), or **camp** at Jabiru when not used by researchers. Another spot you could spend a few hours at is **Granite Gorge**, 12km southwest of town off the Chewko road; the last kilometre is a dirt track and entrance costs $5. At the gorge, a small river flows between a mass of house-sized granite boulders, creating plenty of swimming holes and opportunities for short hikes. To see the region from the air, take a hot-air balloon flight from Mareeba (ⓣ1800 677 444, ⓦwww.champagneballoons.com.au; $135 for 30 minutes).

Back in Mareeba, all the shops and banks can be found on Byrnes Street, with the **information centre** (daily 8am–4.30pm) at its southern end, marked by a memorial to James Venture Mulligan, the veteran prospector who discovered the Palmer River Goldfields (see p.568). Most of the **places to stay** are also at the southern end of town, including the rather shabby *Golden Leaf Motel*, 261 Byrnes St (ⓣ07/4092 2266; ❸) and the pleasant *Tropical Tablelands Caravan Park* (ⓣ07/4092 1158). Alternatively, *Arriga Park Farmstay* (ⓣ07/4093 2114, ⓦwww.bnbnq.com.au/arriga; ❹) is a colonial-style homestead and fruit farm about 15km west of town towards Chillagoe and offers personalized tours of Granite Gorge. **Leaving**, Atherton is 30km south, while the Peninsula Developmental Road heads north to Mount Molloy. For Chillagoe, follow signs from the northern end of town for Dimbulah.

West to Chillagoe

The 150-kilometre road to Chillagoe mysteriously alternates between corrugated gravel and isolated sections of bitumen, but poses no real problem during the dry season. Look for graffiti on boulders ("Top Cat Pass" is a gem) and enticing adverts for the *Almaden Hotel*, whose cool, mirrored, well-supplied bar and beer garden are an incredible oasis in ramshackle, dilapidated **ALMADEN**. From here until Chillagoe's inactive smelter chimney appears from behind an outcrop of rock, the road passes blocks of cut marble awaiting shipment to Italy.

CHILLAGOE dates from 1887, when enough copper ore was found to keep a smelter running until the 1950s; now a gold mine 16km west at Mungana seems to keep the place ticking over. Red dust, hillocks, a service station, oversized hotels and general store complete the picture. The **Hub Tourist Information Centre** (☎07/4094 7111) is on Queen Street, and can arrange **tours** of three of Chillagoe's caves (see below; daily 9am, 11am & 1.30pm; $11–13.75) – though check well in advance as the tours may be closed during the wet season and numbers are limited. **Accommodation** is available at the *Chillagoe Caves Lodge* on King Street (☎1800 446 375, ⓔcaveslodgechillagoe @bigpond.com; ❹), offering a pool and serves meals, or at *Chillagoe Cabins*, on the Mareeba edge of town (☎07/4094 7206, ⓦwww.chillagoe.com; ❹) with self-contained cabins in a pleasant garden atmosphere.

The caves

Chillagoe's **caves** are ancient coral reefs, hollowed out by rain and broken up into fluted masses half-buried in the scrub. Guides can take you through some, while you can explore others on your own, with instructions from the ranger. The caverns are noted for natural **limestone sculptures** caused by evaporation and, unusually for the location, some large stalagmites; the best formations are at **Royal Arch**, **Donna** and **Trezkinn**. Wildlife here includes grey swiftlets and agile pythons, which somehow manage to catch bats on the wing. A footpath leads through grassland between the caves, where you'll find echidnas, kangaroos, black cockatoos and frogmouths, the last odd birds whose name fits them perfectly. This is prime snake country, so wear solid shoes and trousers. **Balancing Rock** offers panoramic views, with the town hidden by low trees, while obscure Aboriginal paintings and engravings have been found near the **Arches**, west at Mungana. Past here, the road continues 500km to Normanton, Karumba and tracks up western Cape York – but it doesn't improve, and there's no fuel or help along the way.

Atherton and around

Thirty kilometres south of Mareeba and centrally placed for forays to most of the tablelands' attractions, **ATHERTON** is the largest town in the tablelands. It was founded in part by Chinese miners who settled here in the 1880s after being chased off the goldfields: 2km south of the centre, the corrugated iron **Hou Wang Temple** (daily 10am–4pm; $7) is the last surviving building of Atherton's old **Chinatown**, a once-busy enclave of market gardens and homes which was abandoned after the government gave the land to returning World War I servicemen. The temple was restored in 2000, with an accompanying **museum** containing photographs, and artefacts found on site.

The other main reason to come to Atherton is to catch the authentically grubby 1920s **steam train** to Herberton, which leaves from Platypus Park, just south of town (days and opening times are being rescheduled – contact the Atherton Information Centre on ☎07/4091 4222 for update); along the way you get to look at tunnels, forest and the pretty Carrington Falls, and then have an hour or so to look around Herberton (see p.557) before the return trip. Otherwise, you can clock up local birdlife at **Hasties Swamp**, a big waterhole and two-storey **observation hide**, about 5km south of town. While nothing astounding, it's a peaceful place populated by magpie geese, pink-eared ducks, swamphens and assorted marsh tiggets.

Atherton's banks, shops and early-opening **cafés** – *Chatterbox* is the most lively – can be found along Main Street, with a supermarket right at the south end past the post office. There's a friendly **information centre** (daily 9am–5pm) just south of the centre. **Accommodation** includes green and spacious **campsites** at the *Woodlands Tourist Park*, just at the edge of town on Herberton Road (☎07/4091 1407, ⓦwww.woodlandscp.com.au; cabins ❷–❸); the heavily tiled and hospitable *Atherton Travellers Lodge*, 37 Alice St, off Vernon Street (ⓣ07/4091 3552, ⓦwww.athertontravellerslodge.com; $18, rooms ❷), which specializes in finding **farm work**; and the very pleasant *Atherton Blue Gum* at 36 Twelfth Ave (ⓣ07/4091 5149, ⓦwww.athertonbluegum.com; ❹–❺), a modern timber B&B place which also runs regional tours.

Lake Tinaroo

At the village of Tolga, 5km north of Atherton, a turn-off leads to **Lake Tinaroo**, a convoluted reservoir formed by pooling the Barron River's headwaters. At the end of the 15km sealed road is the **dam wall** and nearby *Lake Tinaroo Holiday Park* (ⓣ07/4095 8232, ⓕ4095 8808; cabins ❷), which also rents out canoes at $33 a day. Past here, a gravel road runs 25km around the lake to the Gillies Highway, 15km east of Yungaburra, passing five very cheap **campsites** on the north shore before cutting deep into native forests. It's worth stopping along the way for the short walks to bright-green **Mobo Crater**, the spooky **Lake Euramo**, and the **Cathedral Fig**, a giant tree some 50m tall and 43m around the base; the thick mass of tendrils supporting the crown have fused together like melted wax.

Yungaburra and around

Just 13km east of Atherton at the start of the Gillies Highway to Gordonvale, the self-consciously pretty village of **YUNGABURRA**, consisting of the old wooden *Lake Eacham Hotel*, a store, a handful of houses and some quaint restaurants, makes an excellent base to explore the tablelands. The village is also the venue for a huge **market** held on the last Saturday of each month. Considering its diminutive size, Yungaburra has plenty of **places to stay**. The pine-and-slate *On the Wallaby Hostel*, 37 Eacham Rd (ⓣ07/4050 2031, ⓦwww.onthewallaby.com; dorms $20, rooms ❷), is very clued up on the area and organizes canoe and wildlife-spotting trips. The upmarket *Eden House* (ⓣ07/4095 3355, ⓦwww.edenhouse.com.au; ❺), and well-appointed motel rooms at the *Kookaburra Lodge* (ⓣ07/4095 3222, ⓦwww.kookaburra-lodge.com; ❸) are other good bets, or the delightful *Blue House* (ⓣ07/4095 2806; ❻), overlooking Peterson Creek beside the platypus trail. If you fancy a romantic weekend *Mt Quincan Crater Retreat*, on the Peeramon Road about 8km southeast of Yungaburra (ⓣ07/4095 2255, ⓦwww.mtquincan.com.au; ❽), has self-contained wooden units with spa baths which are built on tall poles looking into an extinct volcano crater; the place is also infested with tree kangaroos. For **eating**, *Flynn's Café* does an excellent breakfast, or try the bratwurst and rosti at *Nick's Swiss Italian Restaurant* (closed Mon). *Eden House* has an "Australian contemporary" menu and inexpensive set dinners; while the popular *Burra Inn* (ⓣ07/4095 3657) offers eclectic gourmet treats, from Tuscan lamb to kangaroo pie.

There's a **platypus-viewing platform**, set beside the road to Atherton on the western edge of Yungaburra, but the best place to spot the elusive mammals is early morning or late evening along the Wildlife and Botanical **walking trail** beside Peterson Creek best accessed from the end of Penda Street; you're likely to see **tree kangaroos** hopping along the branches, or well after dark to glimpse rare possums – call in at the Yungaburra Visitors Centre on Cedar Street (daily 9am–5pm; ⓣ07/4095 2416) for details of the trail. Another good place for wildlife spotting is the **Curtain Fig Tree**, another extraordinarily big parasitic strangler fig a couple of kilometres southwest on a minor road; the base is entirely overhung by a stringy mass of aerial roots drooping off the higher branches. If you prefer an informative wildlife walk, there are none better than

Alan's Nocturnal Tour (Ⓣ07/4095 3784, Ⓦwww.alanswildlifetours.com.au; $60) along the edge of a rainforest.

Lakes Eacham and Barrine

A few kilometres east of Yungaburra at the start of the Gillies Highway down to Gordonvale on the coast are the **crater lakes**, or "maars", of Barrine and Eacham – blue, still circles surrounded by thick rainforest. **Lake Eacham** has an easy four-kilometre trail around its shores, taking you past birds and insects foraging on the forest floor, along with inoffensive **amethystine pythons** – Australia's largest snake – sunning themselves down by the water. There's **accommodation** near the lake at *Lake Eacham Caravan Park* (Ⓣ07/4095 3730; cabins ❸), and cosy *Crater Lake Rainforest Cottages* (Ⓣ07/4095 2322, Ⓦwww.craterlakes.com.au; ❻), with four self-contained themed cottages set in a forest clearing. Some 5km further east on a dirt road, **Red Cedar** is another forest giant, a valuable timber tree somehow overlooked by nineteenth-century loggers; the tree's support roots are thicker than an average tree, and its straight, 35-metre-high trunk is two metres in diameter. For its part, **Lake Barrine** is relatively developed, with a **tearoom** overlooking the water serving good cream teas and canteen-style meals, and a **cruise boat** (daily at 10.15am, 11.30am, 1.30pm, 2.30pm & 3.30pm; $12) which spends an hour circuiting the lake. To get away from the crowds, head for the two enormous kauri pines which mark the start of an underused six-kilometre **walking track** around the lake; keep your eyes peeled for spiky-headed water dragons, and hordes of musky rat-kangaroos, which look exactly as you'd expect them to.

The Southern Tablelands

The Kennedy Highway continues 80km down from Atherton to Ravenshoe, the highlands' southernmost town, past easy walking tracks through **Wongabel State Forest**, and **the Crater** at Mount Hypipamee, a 56-metre vertical rift formed by volcanic gases blowing through fractured granite that's now filled with deep, weed-covered water. Picnic tables are on the site, as are ridiculously tame Lewins honeyeaters, but camping is prohibited. An alternative road from Atherton – and the train (see p.555) – circles west via **HERBERTON**, a quaint, one-time timber town without a modern building in sight. During the 1880s there were 30,000 people here (a century before Cairns achieved this population), and the railway from Atherton was built to service the town. If you're in Herberton at lunchtime on Sunday, there are huge outdoor **barbecues** at the *Royal Hotel*'s beer garden.

RAVENSHOE is mainly notable for the *Tully Falls Hotel*, Queensland's highest pub, and **Millstream Falls**, Australia's broadest waterfall, 5km away. There's also another **steam railway** here, with a train departing Saturday and Sunday at 1.30pm to the tiny siding of Tumoulin, Queensland's highest train station – check Ravenshoe's **Visitor Centre** (daily 9am–4pm, Ⓣ07/4097 7700) for bookings. If you get stuck here overnight, the *Old Convent B&B* (Ⓣ07/4097 6454; ❸) and *Tall Timbers Caravan Park* (Ⓣ07/4097 6325; motel rooms ❸) offer decent **accommodation**. Northeast, the road back to Atherton takes you past a blustery hillside sprouting an array of twenty long-stemmed **windmills**, part of a wind-generator power scheme. Southwest, the road drops off the tablelands past **Innot Hot Springs** – with its huge anthills and steamy upwellings behind the *Hot Springs Hotel* – and the township of **Mount Garnet**, to the start of the Gulf Developmental Road (see p.621).

Malanda, Millaa Millaa and the Palmerston Highway

About 25km southeast of Atherton, the **dairy** at **MALANDA** provides milk and cheese for the whole of Queensland's far north, plus most of the Northern Territory and even New Guinea. In the centre of town, the *Malanda Hotel* (☎07/4096 5488; ❷) was built in 1911 to sleep 300 people and claims to be the **largest wooden building** in the southern hemisphere; its old furnishings and excellent *1911* restaurant are worth a look even if you're not staying here, though the bar is so cavernous it always feels empty. Back less than a kilometre towards Atherton, there's a roadside swimming hole and short rainforest walk at **Malanda Falls Environmental Park**; the display at the **information centre** here (daily 9.30am–4.30pm; $2) gives a run-down on the tablelands' geology and its Aboriginal and settler history.

From Malanda it's about 20km south to **MILLAA MILLAA**, a quiet, 500-metre-long street with the usual hotel and general store. A waterfall circuit starts 2km east of the town, where a fifteen-kilometre road passes three small cascades: **Millaa Millaa Falls** consist of a ten-metre-high cascade over basalt columns into a cold, shallow pool, framed by gingers and tree ferns; **Zillie Falls** has good views from the top; and **Elinjaa Falls** has grassy picnic grounds and a short track through forest to the base of the falls. Past Millaa Millaa, the Palmerston Highway descends to the coastal highway near Innisfail; the road was named after **Christie Palmerston**, a fugitive who hid with Aborigines on the tablelands in the 1870s and pioneered the route. The **Palmerston section** of Wooroonooran National Park, which includes the Bellenden Ker Range (see p.537), occupies a huge area north of the highway and is worth a stopover to explore the most extensive, undisturbed spread of Atherton's rainforest, though you'll need some protection from summer flies. There's a QPWS **campsite** about 27km from Millaa Millaa, from where the best of the walking tracks lead to mossy **Tchupala Falls** and the impressive **Nandroya Falls**, while the highway descends 40km past the park to Innisfail.

Cairns to Cape Tribulation

Just a couple of hours' drive **north of Cairns** on the Cook Highway are the Daintree and Cape Tribulation, the tamed fringes of the Cape York Peninsula. The highway initially runs within sight of the sea to **Port Douglas** and **Mossman**, a beautiful drive past isolated beaches where hang-gliders patrol the headlands. North of Mossman is **the Daintree**, Australia's largest and the world's oldest surviving stretch of tropical rainforest. World Heritage listing hasn't saved it from development: roads are being surfaced, land has been subdivided, and there's an ever-increasing number of services in place, undermining the wild and remote brochure image. While this disappoints some visitors, the majestic forest still descends thick and dark right to the sea around **Cape Tribulation**, and you can explore paths through the jungle, watch for wildlife, or just rest on the beach.

Tours from Cairns will show you the sights, but you really need longer to take in the rich scenery and atmosphere – without your own transport, Sun Palm Express (☎07/4041 0578) and Country Road Coachlines (☎07/4050 0599) both run daily **shuttle buses** from Cairns to Cape Tribulation, picking up at Port Douglas and Mossman along the way.

Port Douglas and Mossman

Massive development in recent years has seen the once pretty fishing village of **PORT DOUGLAS**, an hour north of Cairns, turned into an upmarket tourist attraction, with a main street full of boutiques, shopping malls and holidaying hordes. However, the town does have a huge **beach**, along with plenty of distractions to keep you busy for a day or two, and it's getting to be as good a place as Cairns to pick up a regional tour or dive trip to the reef – though prices are steeper.

The town comprises a small grid of streets centred around Macrossan Street – which runs between Four Mile Beach and Anzac Park – with the **marina** a couple of blocks back. As in Cairns, a prolific number of businesses offer tourist **information** – the Port Douglas Tourist Information Centre at no. 23 (daily 8.30am–5.30pm; ⓣ07/4099 5599) can sort out everything from Aboriginal-guided tours of Mossman Gorge to sailing trips and buses to the Daintree. Between the end of Macrossan Street and the sea, **Anzac Park** is the scene of an increasingly busy Sunday morning **market**, good for fruit, vegetables and souvenirs. Near the park's **jetty** you'll find the whitewashed timber church of **St Mary's by the Sea**, built after the 1911 cyclone carried off the previous structure.

Out to sea, the Low Isles, Chinaman, Tongue and Opal **reefs** are all decent enough, though in much the same condition as popular sites off Cairns. *Quicksilver*, based at the marina (ⓣ07/4087 2100, ⓦwww.quicksilver-cruises.com), runs a sailing boat to the Low Isles ($124), while its high-speed catamaran will whisk you to the Agincourt Reef for the day ($180). You can organize

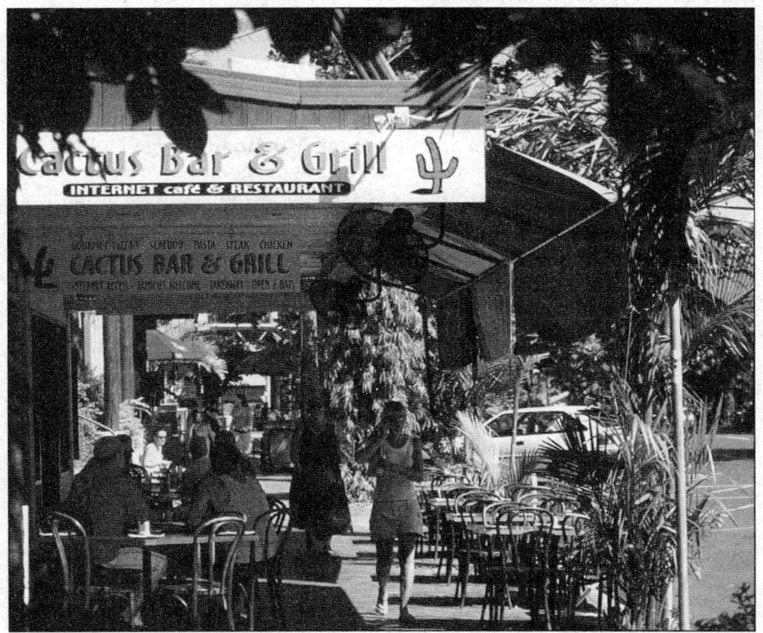

△ Macrossan street, Port Douglas

diving with them, but more serious divers should contact Poseidon Cruises, 34 Macrossan St (ⓣ07/4099 4772, ⓦwww.poseidon-cruises.com.au), or *Calypso Reef Charters* at Mirage Marina (ⓣ07/4099 4544, ⓦwww.calypsocharters.com.au), two fast vessels which make day-trips to less frequented sections for between $185 and $200.

The most upmarket of the town's **accommodation** options is the huge *Mirage Resort* (ⓣ07/4099 5888; ⓦwww.mirageresort.com.au; ❽), off Davidson Street on the way into town or there are more affordable units at the colourful *Pink Flamingo* (ⓣ07/4099 6622; ⓦwww.pinkflamingo.com.au; ❻), also off Davidson Street. Motel accommodation includes *Mango Tree Apartments*, 91 Davidson St (ⓣ07/4099 5677; ❺), just back from Four Mile Beach. Less flamboyant lodgings include the pleasant *Port O'Call Lodge/YHA* about one kilometre from town on Port Street (ⓣ07/4099 5422, ⓦwww.portocall.com.au; dorms $28, rooms ❸); and the central, multi-storey *Parrotfish Lodge* backpackers on Warner Street (ⓣ1800 995 011, ⓦwww.parrotfishlodge.com; dorms $23, rooms ❸).

Places to eat abound along Macrossan Street. Near the information centre, *EJ Seamarket* is a licensed fish-and-chip shop, so you can grab a cold beer while waiting for your meal to crisp. The *Iron Bar* has rough-cut timber furniture and a mid-range surf 'n' turf menu, while *Mango Jam Café* across the road opens late for wood-fired pizza, and the nearby *Star of Siam* has moderately priced Thai fare. *Catalina*, around the corner on Wharf Street (Tues–Sun 6.30pm–late; ⓣ07/4099 5287), occupies a beautiful setting, with a verandah shaded by two ancient mango trees, and serves sophisticated delicacies such as coral trout grilled in banana leaves. However, better views and certainly the best-value meals in town are at the *Combined Club* overlooking Dixon's Inlet on the waterfront.

Mossman

MOSSMAN, 14km past Port Douglas, is a quiet town which has hardly changed in the last thirty years; rail lines between the canefields and mill still run along the main street. Ten minutes inland, **Mossman Gorge** looks like all rainforest rivers should; the boulder-strewn flow is good for messing around in on a quiet day, but attracts streams of tour buses and car break-ins in peak season. Kuku Yalangi, the local community, put together the **Aboriginal walking trail** here and conduct **tours** (Mon-Fri 10am, noon & 2pm; $20; bookings on ⓣ07/4098 2595) of the gorge explaining its history and local plant usage. If you want **to stay** somewhere plush in the area, book in at the exclusive *Silky Oaks Lodge* (ⓣ1800 737 678, ⓦwww.silkyoakslodge.com.au; ❽), 12km from town through the canefields; there's not much rainforest here, but you get very well looked after.

Continuing north, the road splits left to Daintree township or right for the Daintree Ferry to Cape Tribulation. Backtracking southeast lets you leave the highway and climb to **Mount Molloy** and the **Peninsula Developmental Road** – the easier, inland route to Cooktown.

The Daintree

Set off the Mossman to Cape Tribulation road, the riverside **DAINTREE** township – a former timber camp – is now more or less just one big pub, a general store and a campground, though experienced 4WD hands can test their mettle on the **CREB Track** from here to Cooktown, erroneously marked as a proper road on some maps; you'll need tyre chains for steep, slippery gradients, and some practice at manoeuvering over large granite boulders. Most people skip all this, however, and instead follow the road to the **Daintree River Ferry** (6am–midnight; pedestrians $1 each way, vehicles $12) and the start of the mostly sealed 35-kilometre Cape Tribulation road. The river crossing can be very busy, with the cable ferry taking a dozen cars and tour coaches every fifteen minutes or so; you might want to take a **crocodile-spotting tour** with Bruce Belcher (ⓣ07/4098 7717; 1-hour; $20) or one of half a dozen other boats which prowl through the local mangroves in search of prey. For a more peaceful experience, if you don't mind getting up before the sun rises, Chris Dahlberg (ⓣ07/4098 7997) offers exceptional two-hour birding tours for $35.

The Cape Tribulation road

Across the river marks the start of the **Daintree National Park** and the 35km **scenic drive** to the tiny settlement of Cape Tribulation, beyond which the sealed road ends and becomes the alternative 4WD route to Cooktown. From the ferry crossing at Daintree River, it's 8km through rainforest over the convoluted Alexandra range to the **Jindalba Environmental Centre** (daily 8.30am–5pm; $20 includes informative 45-page booklet on the plants and wildlife), which features a five-level, 27-metre-high **tower** with identification charts for the plants and birds you're likely to see at each stage – the top also provides a fabulous view over the canopy. Trails head off into the forest from the car park beneath. Just up the road, **FLORAVILLE** has the regional **pub**, a café, and unexpected French cuisine – using Australian game meats – at *Le Bistrot* (ⓣ07/4098 9016); past here, a six-kilometre side road from the airstrip heads straight to the coast at **Cow Bay**, where there's an excellent **beach**. **Accommodation** along the Cow Bay road includes the open-plan, laid-back *Epiphyte Bed and Breakfast*, off a short track about 4km along (ⓣ07/4098 9039, ⓦwww.rainforestbb.com; ❷); and the jungle-clad cabins of *Crocodylus Village/YHA*, about 2km along (ⓣ07/4098 9166, ⓦwww.crocodyluscapetrib.com; dorms $20, rooms ❸) – meals here are healthy and inexpensive, and they arrange night walks, kayak trips to Snapper Island, and diving at the local reef.

Back on the Cape Tribulation road, another few kilometres lands you at *Fanpalm Café*, which marks the start of a **boardwalk** through a forest of fan palms, and the cabins, self-contained units and **camping** at *Lync-Haven Retreat* (ⓣ07/4098 9155, ⓦwww.lynchaven.com.au; ❸–❹) with 40-acres of rainforest walks. Moving on past a tea plantation and tiny **ALEXANDRA BAY** township, there's further **accommodation** up against the forest fence at *Deep Forest Lodge* (ⓣ07/4098 9162; ❹), which has well-furnished, self-contained cabins; and, inland off the main road in "boutique cabins" at *Heritage Lodge* (ⓣ07/4098 9138, ⓔheritage@c130.aone.net.au; ❼), which also sports a fancy restaurant, **insect museum** and more walking trails along Cooper Creek. Cape Tribulation Wilderness Cruises (ⓣ07/4098 9052; one-hour; $24), has an exclusive license to operate the Cape Tribulation section of the Daintree and cruises Cooper Creek four times a day in search of **crocodiles**. The next stop is 4km on at sandy **Thornton Beach**, where you'll find a licensed kiosk at *Café on Sea*; then it's another few kilometres to where concrete paths and boardwalks follow the creek through a mixture of forest to mangroves at the river mouth on the **Marrdja Botanical Walk** at **Noah Beach**. Look for spiky lawyer cane, lianas twisted into corkscrew shapes where they once surrounded a tree, and the spherical pods of the cannonball mangrove – dried and dismembered, they were used as puzzles by Aboriginal peoples, the object being to fit the irregular segments back together. The QPWS has a **campsite** (which must be pre-booked) in woodland behind the beach; it's big but prone

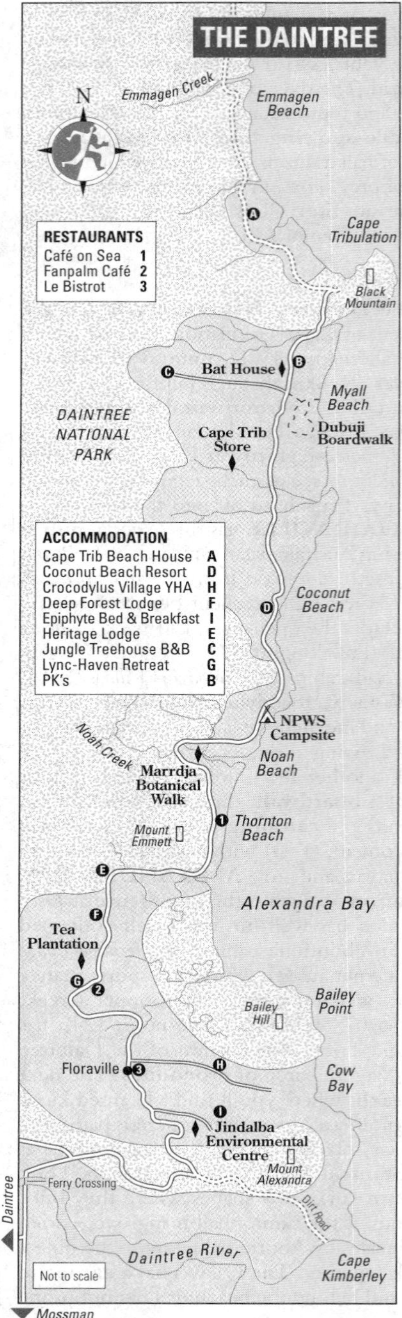

to be muddy and is closed during the wet season.

Just up the road is the exclusive beachfront *Coconut Beach Resort* (ⓣ07/4098 0033, ⓦwww.coconutbeach.com.au; ❽), with an extensive array of facilities including a huge A-frame restaurant ("smart tropical dress" required). North of here, the **Cape Trib Store** has a café and supplies, with a natural swimming hole in the forest close by. The café is also the base for Mason's Tours (ⓣ07/4098 0070, ⓦwww.masonstours.com.au), which organizes 4WD safaris and local day and night walks – they also publish a very detailed map of the Bloomfield Track to Cooktown if you're heading that way. Plants close in again a couple of kilometres beyond at **Dubuji Boardwalk**, a 1.2-kilometre-long replay of Marrdja, though with a greater variety of forests. Aside from fan palms, rainforest cycads and vines, look out for the very odd peppermint stick insect, which hides in pandanus leaves alongside the path; they're a strange blue-green colour, and squirt out a mint-scented spray when disturbed.

Cape Tribulation

Cape Tribulation – a forty-minute drive from the ferry crossing – was named when Captain Cook's vessel hit a reef offshore in June 1770. The cleared area below the steep, forested slopes of **Mount Sorrow** has a café, store, ATM, pharmacy and a **Bat House** (Tue–Sun 10.30am–3.30pm; $2), worth a visit to handle tame orphaned flying foxes. The beach here is attractive and accessed along a boardwalk from the township. **Beds** and **campsites** are available at the often noisy and overcrowded *PK's* hostel (ⓣ1800 232 333, ⓦwww.pksjunglevillage.com; dorms $25, rooms ④) with camping; alternatively, there's the *Jungle Treehouse* B&B (Ⓣ07/4099 5651, Ⓦwww.jungletreehousecapetrib.com.au; ⑤), set 200m up in the hills, as well as the friendly beachfront *Cape Trib Beach House*, 2.5km north (Ⓣ07/4098 0030, Ⓦwww.capetribbeach.com.au; dorms $25–32, cabins ③–④). All can organize horse riding, sea-kayaking, guided forest walks and the exhilarating experience of abseiling through the canopy with Jungle Surfing Tours (Ⓣ07/4098 0040, Ⓦwww.junglesurfingcanopytours.com; $99).

The area is best explored on foot – for the simple pleasure of walking through the forest with the sea breaking on a beach not five minutes distant. A **path** runs out to the cape, where you may see brilliantly coloured pittas (small, tail-less birds with a buff chest, green back and black and rust heads) bouncing around in the leaf litter, or even a crocodile sunning itself on the beach. One way to penetrate the undergrowth away from the paths is to follow small creeks: **Emmagen**, about 6km north, runs halfway up Mount Sorrow and is recommended for its safe swimming holes.

The Bloomfield Track

The scene of vicious confrontations in 1984 between construction crews and environmentalists who tried unsuccessfully to stop this alternative road to Cooktown being built through virgin forest, the **Bloomfield Track** is completely impassable after rain and otherwise requires a 4WD. Spanning 80km from Cape Tribulation to where the track joins the Cooktown Road at **Black Mountain**, the exciting section with drastic gradients lies below the halfway mark of the tidal **Bloomfield River**, which has to be crossed at low water. Beyond **Wujal Wujal Aboriginal community** on the north side, the road flattens out to run past *Bloomfield Cabins and Camping* (Ⓣ07/4060 8207, Ⓦwww.bloomfieldcabins.com; ③), where there's plentiful camping space and three basic cabins; and *Home Rule Rainforest Lodge* at **ROSSVILLE** (Ⓣ07/4060 3925; ②), which offers kitchen facilities and inexpensive meals. Alternatively, you could fork out for the reclusive *Peppers Bloomfield Lodge* (Ⓣ07/4035 9166, Ⓦwww.bloomfieldlodge.com.au; ⑦), though at a minimum of two nights at $586 per person – including transport from Cairns – it's not for everyone. Moving on, it's not far now to the more down-to-earth *Lions Den* pub with spacious pre-erected tents on stilts (Ⓣ07/4060 3911; ③), at **Helenvale** near Black Mountain (see p.565), about thirty minutes from Cooktown.

The Cape York Peninsula and Torres Strait Islands

The **Cape York Peninsula** points north towards the Torres Strait and New Guinea, and tackling the rugged tracks and hectic river crossings on the "Trip To The Tip" is an adventure in itself – besides being a means to reach Australia's northernmost point and the communities at **Bamaga** and **Thursday Island**, so far removed from southern attitudes that they could easily be in another country. But it's not all four-wheel driving across the savannah: during the dry season the historic settlement of **Cooktown**, the wetlands at **Lakefield National Park** and **Laura**'s Aboriginal heritage are only a day's journey from Cairns in any decent vehicle. Given longer you might get as far as the mining company town of **Weipa**, but don't go further than this without off-road transport; while some have managed to reach the Tip in family sedans, most who try fail miserably.

With thousands making the overland journey between May and October, a **breakdown** won't necessarily leave you stranded, but the cost of repairs

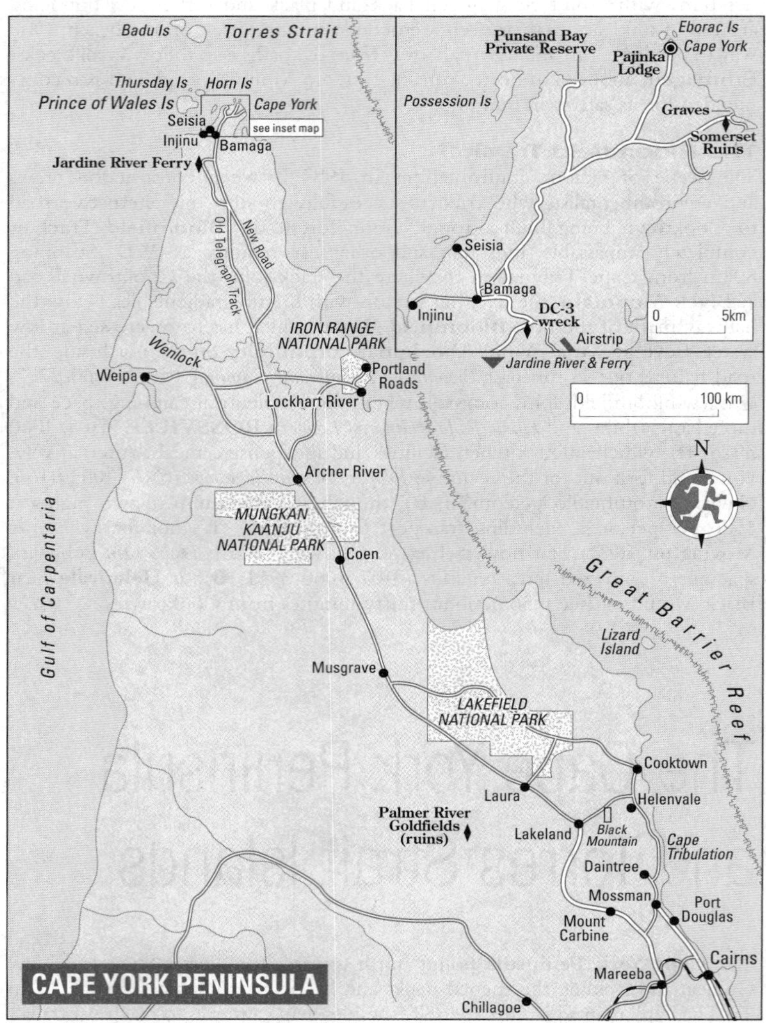

will make you regret it. **Bikers** should travel in groups and have off-roading experience. Those without their own vehicle can take overland **tours** right to the Tip; see box on p.544. From Cairns, it's also possible to **cruise** up to Thursday Island, aboard the *Trinity Bay* passenger and car ferry (Ⓣ07/4035 1234, Ⓦwww.seaswift.com.au). The ferry departs Cairns at 2pm every Friday, arriving in Thursday Island approximately 6pm on Sunday. Accommodation is in air-conditioned 4-bed cabins which cost $655 for one person private use, or $395 per person if three or four people travel together, whilst 4WD vehicles cost $800 and must be booked well in advance. You can also **fly** to various places on the Cape with Cape York Air (Ⓣ07/4035 9399, Ⓦwww.capeyorkair.com.au), which also does a one-day return postal run up to Thursday Island every Saturday for $890 from Cairns, stopping briefly at remote stations along the way.

You'll find a few roadhouses and motels along the way, but north of Weipa **accommodation** on the Cape is mostly limited to camping, and it's inevitable if you head right to the Tip that one night at least will be spent in the bush. Settlements also supply meals and provisions, but there won't be much on offer, so take all you can carry. Don't turn bush campsites into rubbish dumps: take a pack of bin liners and remove all your garbage. **Estuarine crocodiles** are present throughout the Cape: read the warning under "Wildlife dangers" in Basics (p.41) and see also p.650. There are few **banks**, so take enough cash to carry you between points – some roadhouses accept plastic. In Cairns, the QPWS stocks **maps** and brochures on the Cape's national parks, whilst the RACQ (Ⓦwww.racq.com) has up-to-date information regarding current road conditions. Vehicles heading to the Tip should carry a **first-aid kit**, a comprehensive tool kit and spares, extra fuel, and a tarpaulin for creek crossings. A winch, and equipment for removing, patching and inflating tyres may also come in handy.

Mossman to Cape York

Not as pretty as the coastal Bloomfield track but considerably easier, the 260-kilometre inland road to Cooktown and points north leaves the Cook Highway just before Mossman and climbs to the drier scrub at **MOUNT CARBINE**, a former tungsten mine whose roadhouse and *Mt Carbine Hotel* (Ⓣ07/4094 3108; ❷, with simple but clean rooms) fulfil all functions. The road beyond is sealed as far as **LAKELAND**, whose café, hotel and fuel stop marks the junction for routes north along the **Peninsula Developmental Road** to Laura (p.568), but the way to Cooktown lies east, past cataracts at the **Annan River Gorge**, and the mysterious **Black Mountain**, two huge dark piles of lichen-covered granite boulders near the road. Aborigines reckon the formation to be the result of a building competition between two rivals fighting over a girl, and tell stories of people wandering into the eerie, whistling caverns, never to return.

At this point it's worth making the four-kilometre detour south along the Bloomfield Track to the *Lions Den* at **HELENVALE**. The *Den* is an old-style pub playing up for tourists during the day, but one hundred percent authentic at night, from the iron sheeting and beam decor to those nasty exhibits in glass bottles on the piano. Those with 4WD vehicles can follow the track south from Helenvale to Cape Trib (see p.562), while back on the main road it's another twenty minutes to Cooktown past birdlife-filled waterholes at **Keatings Lagoon Conservation Park**, just 5km short of town.

Cooktown

After the *Endeavour* nearly sank at Cape Tribulation in 1770, Captain Cook landed at a natural harbour to the north, where he spent two months repairing the vessel, observing the "Genius, Temper, Disposition and Number of the Natives" and – legend has it – naming the kangaroo after an Aboriginal word for "I don't know". Tempers wore thin on occasion, as when the crew refused to share a catch of turtles with local Aborigines and Cook commented: "They seem'd to set no value upon any thing we gave them."

The site lay dormant until gold was discovered southwest on the **Palmer River** in 1873, and within months a harbour was being surveyed at the mouth of the **Endeavour River** for a tented camp known as **COOKTOWN**. A wild success while gold lasted, the settlement once boasted a main street alive with hotels and a busy port doing brisk trade with Asia through thousands of Chinese prospectors and merchants. But the reserves were soon exhausted and by 1910 Cooktown was on the decline. Today, the town's main drag, Charlotte Street, is neat but quiet, good for random wandering past the old wharves and **Endeavour Park**, the site of Cook's landing, now graced by a statue of the great navigator. Among monuments on the lawn are the remains of defences sent from Brisbane in the nineteenth century to ward off a threatened Russian invasion: one cannon, three cannonballs and two rifles. At the far end, the marina, Manta Marine (Ⓣ07/4069 5601, Ⓔmantam@bigpond.com) organizes two-hour **cruises** through the Endeavour River's mangroves ($25) and **fishing and diving** trips. Just outside town, 500m along Endeavour Valley Road, the half-wild **cemetery**'s Jewish, Chinese, Protestant and Catholic sections give a glimpse of how cosmopolitan the town once was. The cemetery's most famous resident is **Mary Watson** of Lizard Island (see p.567), whose grave near the entrance is decorated with seashells and a painting of a pietà.

The best **views** of the town and river are from the top floor of the old Sisters of Mercy Convent, now the **James Cook Museum** (daily 9.30am–4pm; $7) containing a bit of everything: artefacts jettisoned from the *Endeavour*; a reconstructed joss house; a display on pearling around Thursday Island; and an account of the "hopelessly insolvent" Cooktown–Laura railway. Not far away on the corner of Helen and Walker streets, the **Marine Museum** (daily 9.30am–5.30pm; closed Dec–Mar; $7) details the 1899 cyclones Mahina and Nachon, which collided north of Cooktown, sinking 76 vessels and killing 350 people.

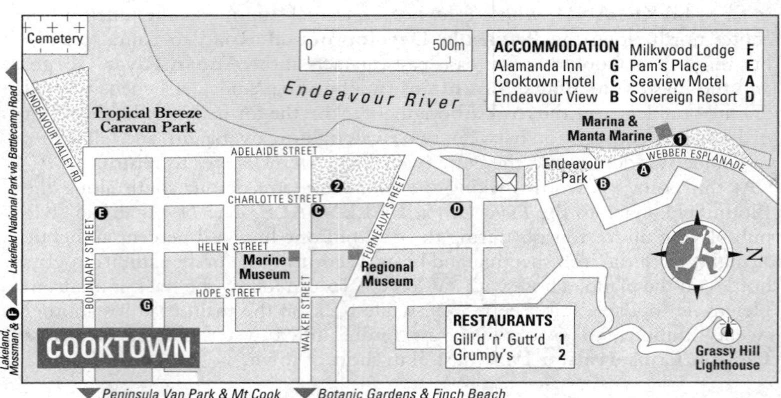

There are more views of the district from the red-and-white corrugated-iron cone of **Grassy Hill Lighthouse**, reached on a concrete track from the end of Hope Street. **Mount Cook** is a rather tougher proposition, a two-hour return hike through thick forest on meagre paths – follow the orange triangles from the nondescript starting point beyond Ida Street (you can pick up free maps of the route from the Council Offices next to the post office, open Mon–Fri 9am–4.30pm). At the end of Walker Street, the **Botanic Gardens** merge into original paperbark woodland, with a track running to **Finch Beach** on Cherry Tree Bay. Although it's sometimes rated as a safe swimming beach, you should heed the home-made warning signs in pidgin: "Dispela Stap Hia" and a picture of a croc.

Practicalities

The June **Discovery Festival** tends towards being a thorough piss-up, but even then **accommodation** shouldn't be too difficult to find. If you're camping, the *Tropical Breeze Caravan Park* near the cemetery is handy for town, or there are budget beds at *Pam's Place*, Charlotte Street (ⓣ07/4069 5166, ⓦwww.cooktownhostel.com; dorms $20–22, rooms ❷). For something a bit more lavish, *Alamanda Inn* (ⓣ07/4069 5203, ⓔphscott@tpg.com.au; ❸) on Hope Street offers quiet motel rooms and a big pool; the two-storey *Seaview Motel* (ⓣ07/4069 5377, ⓔseaview@tpg.com.au; ❹) is central and tidy; *Endeavour View B&B* (ⓣ07/4069 5676, ⓕ4069 6642; ❹) has self-contained wooden cabins; while the lavish *Sovereign Resort* (ⓣ07/4069 5400, ⓦwww.sovereign-resort.com; ❻) has a pool and café-bar-restaurant. Two kilometres out of town on a secluded hillside, *Milkwood Lodge* (ⓣ07/4069 5007, ⓦwww.milkwoodlodge.com; ❹–❺) offers self-contained cabins with verandah views out over the valley. There's delicious **food** at *Grumpy's Restaurant*, especially the barramundi, or riverside views from *Gill'd 'n' Gutt'd*, a chip shop at Fisherman's Wharf; the *Cooktown Hotel* (also known as the *Top Pub*) is the best spot for drink and bar meals. The **supermarket** is the last source of fresh provisions before Weipa, and the ATM at the **bank** here is the only one on the Cape.

Those continuing **up the Cape** have two options: vehicles other than 4WDs have to head southwest to Lakeland for Laura and points north; stronger sets of wheels can reach Lakefield National Park more directly by heading towards Hope Vale community and then taking the Battle Camp Road. The last **fuel** this way until Musgrave is about 33km from Cooktown at the *Endeavour Falls Tourist Park* (ⓣ07/4069 5431; self-contained units ❸), a nice spot in itself with a neighbouring waterfall, forest and an apparently croc-free swimming hole – though don't swim here without advice from the tourist park.

Lizard Island

Lizard Island is one of the most isolated resorts in Australia, a granite rise covered in stunted trees and heath, 90km north of Cooktown, and within sight of the outer reef – divers rave about the fringing coral here. The only regular access is on **flights** from Cairns with Qantas (around $500 return); those unable to afford the **lodge** (ⓣ07/4060 3999; ❼) – which has a bar and restaurant and comfortable, if simple, units – can use the QPWS **campsite** (permits from QPWS Cairns or book online at ⓦwww.epa.qld.gov.au; see p.545) down on Watson Beach. Campers should be self-sufficient in food and carry charcoal beads for cooking (gas cylinders and fuel are not allowed on the plane); unless in serious emergencies the lodge is off-limits, with the exception of its bar. There are far worse places to spend a few days in a tent, however, and there's sometimes fresh fish on sale to bulk out your supplies. The lodge can arrange diving for its guests.

Shell middens show that Lizard was regularly visited by Aboriginal peoples, but the island was uninhabited when **Robert Watson** built a cottage and started a sea-slug processing operation here in the 1870s, accompanied by his wife **Mary** and two Chinese servants. Aborigines attacked the house while Robert was at sea in October 1881, killing one of the Chinese and forcing Mary, her baby and Ah Sam to flee in a water tank; they paddled west for five days before dying of thirst. Her painfully matter-of-fact diary is kept at Brisbane's John Oxley Library, while the tank is on display at the Museum of Tropical Queensland in Townsville.

Quinkan Country: Laura and around

Back on the Peninsula Road, 60km north of Lakeland, **LAURA**'s store-cum-post office and roadhouse support the two-day **Aboriginal Dance Festival**, an electrifying assertion of Aboriginal identity, held in June of odd-numbered years. At any time of year you can visit the sandstone caves and ridges at **Split Rock**, 13km south of town, where a steep track leads to a two-hour gallery circuit. Paintings depict animals and startling spirit figures associated with sorcery: spidery, frightening **Quinkan** with pendulous earlobes, and dumpy Anurra, often with their legs twisted upwards. Other sites show scenes from post-Contact life, depicting horses, rifles and clothed figures; some caves were probably in use until the 1930s. You can find out more from Trezise Bush Service/Quinkan Tours (☎07/4060 3236), which has a camp west in the scrub at Jowalbinna, about an hour's drive from Laura.

Sites along the **Palmer River**, 80km (8hr) southwest of Laura along a terrible 4WD track, recall the gigantic 1873 **goldrush**. Mining life was volatile: Aborigines waged guerrilla warfare, and race riots erupted between whites and the Chinese – who at one time outnumbered the entire European population of Queensland and infuriated whites by doggedly extracting gold from "exhausted" claims. The settlements at Maytown and German Bar were abandoned once the gold had gone and today there's virtually nothing left except atmosphere; the Cairns QPWS (see p.545) stocks maps and permits.

Lakefield National Park

Ideally you'd take at least a week to absorb **Lakefield National Park**'s fifty thousand square kilometres of savannah and riverine flats, but even a single night spent here will give you a feel for the Cape's most accessible wilderness area. Apart from the **Old Laura Homestead** – built between 1892 and 1940 and standing abandoned in the scrub on the Laura River – the park's pleasures revolve around outdoor pursuits, fishing and exploring lagoons for wildlife. Lakefield's **crocodile-conservation** programme means you might see both fresh- and saltwater types; birdlife is plentiful and plenty of kangaroos put in an appearance. "**Magnetic**" **anthills** are a common landmark: the ants build flattened towers aligned north–south to prevent overheating in the noonday sun.

Vehicles other than 4WDs can sometimes manage the rough 170-kilometre track through the park between Laura township and Musgrave Roadhouse (see opposite), but only if there hasn't been any rain for a good while. High clearance is essential for other routes, including the Battle Camp road to Cooktown. **Ranger stations** (☎07/4060 3271) are located along the road at New Laura, at the southern end of the park, 50km from Laura; at Lakefield (central, 80km); and at Bizant (north, 100km). Popular places to camp and watch wildlife are **Horseshoe Lagoon** beyond Old Laura, **12 Mile Hole** near New Laura (4WD only), **Kalpowar Crossing** (near Lakefield, with showers and toilets) and **Hann Crossing**, in the north of the park.

Laura to Iron Range and Weipa

Following the main road, the 300km that stretches between Laura and Archer River passes in a haze of dust, jolts and roadhouses supplying fuel, food, beds and drink. First on the list is **MUSGRAVE** (135km from Laura; ⓣ07/4060 3229 for road condition check), a converted homestead where the track from Lakefield National Park joins the road; there's accommodation about 10km in towards the park at *Lotus Bird Lodge* (ⓣ07/4060 3295, ⓦwww.cairns.aust.com/lotusbird; ❻), whose spacious wooden cottages are surrounded by much the same scenery as you'll find in the national park. Back on the road north, the next two hours are a wild roller-coaster ride – look out for "Dip" signs warning of monster gullies – down to **COEN**, 107km from Musgrave. Coen's Ambrust General Store handles **camping**, provisions, fuel, post office business and an ATM machine at the *Exchange Hotel*. The *Homestead Guest House*, on Regent Street, has **beds** (ⓣ07/4060 1157; ❸) and can provide meals, while you can have any car problems fixed at Clark's workshop.

Some 25km further north, a 4WD track west heads into the dry woodland and rainforest of the **Mungkan Kaanju National Park**; the ranger station lies 75km along at Rokeby station (ⓣ07/4060 1137), with camping at undeveloped bush sites. Back on the main road north, it's 45km from the park turn-off to the **Archer River Roadhouse** (ⓣ07/4060 3266), which has a campsite and accommodation in units (❸), as well as the last reliable **fuel** on the main road before Bamaga, 400km away. Beyond are routes east to Iron Range (155km) and west to Weipa (190km) – covered below.

Iron Range

There's nothing else in Australia quite like the magnificent jungle at **Iron Range National Park**, a leftover from the Ice Age link to New Guinea, which hides fauna found nowhere else on the continent – the nocturnal green python and brilliant blue-and-red eclectus parrot are the best-known species. Four hours bouncing along a 110-kilometre 4WD track from the main road should bring you to a clearing where the army simulated a nuclear strike in the 1960s – fortunately using tons of conventional explosives instead of the real thing. Turning right at the junction here takes you past the **ranger station** (ⓣ07/4060 7170) to **LOCKHART RIVER**, an Aboriginal mission and fishing beach; supplies and fuel are sold here during weekday trading hours. The road left passes two **bush campsites** near the Claudie River and Gordon's Creek crossings before winding up at **PORTLAND ROADS** overlooking a monument to Edmund Kennedy (see p.531) and the remains of a harbour used by US forces in World War II – there are a few houses and beach accommodation at *Portland House* (ⓣ07/4060 7193, ⓦwww.portlandhouse.com.au; ❺), though there are no stores or any public services. There's further camping a few kilometres back towards the junction at **Chilli Beach**, a perpetually blustery, tropical setting backed by forest and coconut palms.

Next day, you have the chance to experience something unique on the mainland – sunrise and sunset over different seas – by taking **Frenchman's**

Road to Weipa. This starts 30km back from the Lockhart/Portland junction, crosses the difficult Pascoe and Wenlock rivers, and emerges on the Peninsula Developmental Road, 2km north of **Batavia Downs**. Head through Batavia and cross more creeks, which look worse than they are, to the main Weipa road; the trip coast to coast might take six to eight hours.

Weipa

Those without a 4WD will have to give Iron Range a miss, but can still take the road from Archer River to **WEIPA**, a town of red clay and yellow mining trucks dealing in kaolin and bauxite. The area was one of the first in Australia to be described by Europeans: Willem Janz encountered "savage, cruel blacks" here in 1606, a report whose findings were subsequently reiterated by Jan Carstensz, who found nothing of interest and sailed off to chart the Gulf of Carpentaria instead. Apart from a mission built at **Mappoon** in the nineteenth century, little changed until aluminium ore was first mined here in the 1950s, and Comalco built the town and began mining.

All traffic in Weipa gives way to the gargantuan mine vehicles and stays out of the restricted areas. The town comprises mostly company housing, but it does offer long-forgotten luxuries: you can pick up **spares** for your vehicle at the auto wreckers and service station on the way into town; and there's a **supermarket** and **post office** just in front of *Weipa Camping Ground* (ⓣ07/4069 7871, ⓦwww.campweipa.com; ❸–❹), a large campsite featuring hot showers and a laundry, as well as self-contained units, where you can unwind and swap tales about the rigours of the trip; fishing trips and mine tours can be arranged at the campsite office. The *Albatross Hotel* (ⓣ07/4097 6666, ⓔalbatrosshotel@bigpond.com; ❹–❺) up the road has rooms and bungalows, and its beer deck looks out over the western sea. Hardened **bikers** should try to catch the August **Croc Run**, Australia's richest and most challenging endurance race, which weaves its way through mangroves and creeks.

Around town, the library's **Cape York Collection** contains a unique collection of books and documents relating to the area, while the **Uningan Nature Reserve**, situated on the Mission River, preserves sixteen-metre-high **middens** composed entirely of shells left over from Aboriginal meals – some have been dated to sixteen hundred years ago. Driving is the only way to get here, and guidebooks are available from the campsite. Keep an eye out for crocs while walking around the reserve.

Leaving, there's a barge to Karumba and Normanton in the Gulf (see p.624) departing every Thursday – contact Gulf Freight Services (ⓣ07/4069 7309). Note that there is no reliable **fuel** between Weipa and Bamaga (340km).

North of the Wenlock

The seasonally deep, fast-flowing **Wenlock River**, an hour north of the Weipa junction on the main road, marks the start of the most challenging part of the journey north, with road conditions changing every wet season. Formerly requiring some skill and a bit of luck to cross safely, the Wenlock River itself has been tamed by a bridge. The road divides 42km further on, where die-hards follow the **Old Telegraph Track**, which has all the interesting scenery and creek crossings, though the telegraph lines have been dismantled, and many of the poles have been robbed of their ceramic caps by souvenir hunters. The first travellers of the year build simple rafts and log bridges to cross the creeks; as tracks dry and traffic increases, jarring corrugations and potholes are more likely to pose a problem, constituting a serious test of vehicle strength.

Crossing creeks by 4WD

While Cape York's crocs make the standard **4WD** procedure of walking creek crossings before driving them potentially dangerous, wherever possible you should make some effort to gauge the waters' depth and find the best route. Never blindly follow others across. Make sure all rescue gear – shovel, winch, rope, etc – is easy to reach, outside the vehicle. Electrics on petrol engines need to be waterproofed. On deep crossings, block off air inlets to prevent water entering the engine, slacken off the fan belt and cover the radiator grille with a tarpaulin; this diverts water around the engine as long as the vehicle is moving. Select an appropriate gear (changing it in midstream will let water into the clutch) and drive through at walking speed; clear the opposite embankment before stopping again. In deep water, there's a chance the vehicle might float slightly, and so get pushed off-track by the current – though there's not much you can do about this. If you stall, switch off the ignition immediately, exit through windows, disconnect the battery (a short might restart the engine) and winch out. Don't restart the vehicle until you've made sure that water hasn't been sucked in through the air filter – which will destroy the engine. If you have severe problems, recovery will be very expensive; see Basics, p.55.

There are some fine creeks on this route: **Bertie's** potholes are large enough to submerge an entire vehicle; **Gunshot's** three-metre vertical clay banks are a real test of skill (use low range first, and keep your foot off the brake); and the north exit at **Cockatoo** is deceptively sandy. Dozens wipe out on Gunshot every season; for the cautious there's a 24-kilometre detour via open scrub at **Heathlands** to the north side.

Those less certain of their abilities avoid the Old Telegraph Track and take the longer **New Road** to the east, consisting of 200km of loose gravel and bulldust. The two routes rejoin one another briefly after 75km, after which the New Road diverges left for 54km to the Jardine River Ferry crossing ($80 return, including use of the Injinu campsite at Bamaga), while the Telegraph Track ploughs on past beautiful clear green water and basalt formations at **Twin Falls**' safe swimming holes, through the deep Nolans Brook, before reaching the hundred-metre-wide **Jardine River**. This spot was once the only crossing point on the Jardine, but the river's width makes the crossing extremely testing, and the likelihood of crocodiles adds to the risks. However, it's worth the trip to camp (assuming you have enough fuel) before heading back to the ferry. From here, the last hour to Bamaga passes the remains of a **DC-3** that crashed just short of the airstrip in 1945.

Bamaga

BAMAGA, a community of stilt houses and banana palms founded by Saibai islanders in 1946, owes nothing to suburban values. Around the intersection you'll find a workshop and service station selling **fuel** (Mon–Fri 9am–5pm, Sat 9am–12.30pm, Sun 1.30–3pm), airline offices, a hotel and a **shopping centre** (fresh veggies, National Australia Bank agent, telephones, café and post office). For **accommodation**, there's the central *Resort Bamaga* (ⓣ07/4069 3050, ⓦwww.resortbamaga.com.au; ❷–❹), which has motel rooms and no-frills bungalows; turn left at the junction to **Injinu campsite** (Cowall Creek), or right past the shopping centre to the coast at **SEISIA** (Red Island Point). You can stay here in tents or cabins at the **Seisia Holiday Park** (ⓣ07/4069 3243, ⓔseisiaresort@bigpond.com; cabins ❹), under palms near the jetty, and take advantage of showers, laundry facilities, a canteen and fishing safaris. Peddells Passenger Ferry (ⓣ07/4069 1551; ⓦwww.peddellsferry.com.au; Mon, Wed &

Fri, 8am & 4pm; $41 one-way) departs from here to Thursday Island. Other services in Seisia include a roadhouse, tackle shop and 4WD rental.

Cape York and Somerset

To make local contacts, stay around Bamaga. To keep with the overland crowd, head 16km north to a road junction, then bear left for 11km to the idyllic beach at **Punsand Bay Private Reserve** (Ⓣ07/4069 1722; prefab tents $125 per person includes 3 meals), a just reward for the trials of the journey, with camping, meals and basic provisions. Around here you might spot the rare **palm cockatoo**, a huge, crested black parrot with a curved bill. You could spend a day recuperating on the beach, or return to the junction and take the seventeen-kilometre road past the Somerset fork to its end at another **campsite** (shower, water and kiosk), where the luxurious Aboriginal-owned **Pajinka Lodge** (Ⓣ07/4069 3252, Ⓦwww.pajinka.com) is awaiting redevelopment. Follow the footpath through vine forest onto a rocky, barren headland and down to a turbulent sea opposite the lighthouse on Eborac Island. A sign concreted into an oil drum marks the tip of mainland Australia and the end of the journey.

Somerset

Established on government orders in 1864 to balance the French naval station in New Caledonia, **Somerset** was founded by John Jardine, who was succeeded by his son Frank the following year. Frank became a legend on the Cape and tales of his exploits assume larger-than-life proportions (fearless pioneer to some, brutal colonial to others). Though envisaged as a second Singapore, Somerset never amounted to more than a military outpost under constant attack from termites and local tribes. In 1877, after the pearling trade in the Torres Strait erupted into lawlessness, the settlement was abandoned in favour of a seat of government closer to the problem at Thursday Island.

Today, only a few cannon, machine parts and mango trees testify to Somerset's former inhabitants; the buildings succumbed to white ants or were moved long ago. Frank and his wife Sana are buried on the beach directly below (standing up, say locals), next to a Chinese cemetery and traces of a jetty into the Adolphus Channel. Dogged exploration of the dense undergrowth above the beach to the left will uncover remains of a **sentry post** and a **cave** with stick-figure paintings, presumably Aboriginal. Past Somerset, a track continues onto another beach before circling back towards the main road.

The Torres Strait

Beyond Cape York, the 200-kilometre-broad, obstacle-strewn **Torres Strait** separates Australia from New Guinea; the strait was named after Luís Vaez de Torres, who navigated its waters in 1606. Prior to European contact, the Strait's islands had developed trade links with Australia and highland New Guinea, which supplied outrigger canoes – no suitable trees grow in the Strait – in exchange for oyster and trochus shell, and heads. Warfare between islands pervaded all aspects of life, and the eastern cult of Malo required human jaws as tribute. The early nineteenth century saw the first trade with Europeans, who soon discovered the Strait's rich pearl beds and occupied the islands as bases for the industry, decimating the islanders through violence and disease. Then on July 1, 1871, the **London Missionary Society** landed on Darnley Island.

Once the islanders realized that the mission protected them from the more piratical whites, they converted to Christianity at a speed that amazed even the missionaries. The advent of Christianity (known here as the "Coming of the Light") stabilized communities but also heralded the end of traditional life, as cults were undermined and wages and stores replaced the barter network. Another influential group were **South Sea Island** teachers, who brought their own dance styles and crops, and gradually intermarried with the locals.

The church created **island councils**, but Queensland held the real power with its **segregation laws**, which prevented emigration to the mainland. The only job in the Strait was pearling (for mother-of-pearl), and white boat-owners would have lost their labour pool if Islanders went south. Until World War II the islands made the best of it, but army service overseas gave returning recruits a better understanding of what they deserved from the government, and pressure removed some barriers to migration. The advent of plastics led to the collapse of the mother-of-pearl industry, and the unemployment that followed forced the government to drop all protectionist policies, with the result that by the mid-1970s half the Strait's former population was living on the mainland. The remainder formed a movement to establish an **Islander Nation**, which bore its first fruit on June 3, 1992, when the **Mabo Decision** acknowledged the Merriam as traditional owners of Murray Island, thereby setting a precedent for mainland Aboriginal claims and sending shock waves through the establishment.

Ferries cross regularly between Cape York and **Thursday Island**, the Strait's administrative centre – which, even on a brief visit, offers a fascinating glimpse into an all-but-forgotten corner of Australia. Travel beyond Thursday (except to neighbouring islands) is generally expensive, but many other islands do have guesthouses. There are twice-daily **flights** from Cairns to Horn Island with Skytrans (Ⓣ07/4046 2462, Ⓦwww.skytrans.com.au; $398 one-way) and Cairns to Yorke Island with Aero Tropics (Ⓣ1300 656 110, Ⓦwww.aero-tropics.com.au); with water taxi connections from both to nearby Thursday Island.

Thursday Island

A three-square-kilometre speck within sight of the mainland, between Prince of Wales, Hammond and Horn islands, **Thursday Island** wears a few aliases: coined "Sink of the Pacific" for the variety of peoples who passed through in pearling days, the local tag is Waiben or (very loosely) "Thirsty Island" – once a reference to the availability of drinking water and now a laconic aside on the quantity of beer consumed. The hotel clock with no hands hints at the pace of life and it's only for events like Christmas, when wall-to-wall aluminium punts from neighbouring islands make the harbour look like a maritime supermarket car park, that things liven up. Other chances to catch Thursday in carnival spirit are during the Coming of the Light festivities on July 1, and for the full-bore Island of Origin rugby league matches later in the same month – in one season 25 players were hospitalized, and one killed.

In town there are traces of the old **Chinatown** district around Milman Street, and a reminder of Queensland's worst shipping disaster in the **Quetta Memorial Church**, way down Douglas Street, built after the ship hit an uncharted rock in the Adolphus Channel in 1890 and went down with virtually all the Europeans on board. The Aplin Road **cemetery**, where two of the victims are buried, has tiled Islander tombs and depressing numbers of **Japanese** graves, all victims of pearl diving. As a byproduct of the industry, Japanese crews had accurately mapped the Strait before World War II and it's no coincidence that the airstrip was bombed when hostilities were declared in 1942; fortifications are still in place on Thursday's east coast. Bunkers and naval cannon at the **Old Fort** on the opposite side date from the 1890s.

Practicalities

There are **ferries** to Thursday Island every weekday morning from Punsand Bay (1hr 30min; $46 one-way) and three times a week from Seisia (1hr 15min; $41 one-way). Passing **Possession Island** on the way over, you come within sight of a plaque commemorating James Cook's landing here on August 22, 1770, when he planted the flag for George III and Great Britain. Then it's into the shallow channel between Horn Island (see below) and **Prince of Wales Island**, the Strait's largest island, stocked with deer and settled by an overflow population unable to afford Thursday's exorbitant land premiums.

The wharf on Thursday sits below the colonial-style **Customs House**, a minute from the town centre on Douglas Street. Here you'll find a post office with payphones, a **bank** and two of the island's **hotels**: the *Torres* just beats the neighbouring *Royal* as Australia's northernmost bar. Facing the water on Victoria Parade, the *Federal Hotel* (Ⓣ07/4069 1569, Ⓦwww.federalhotelti.com.au; ⑤) is fractionally quieter as lodgings on a busy night, while on Douglas Street, *Mura Mudh* (Ⓣ07/4069 2050; ①) is a cheap and cheerful **hostel** run by Thursday Islanders.

The **Gab Titui Cultural Centre** across from the ferry terminal provides an interesting insight into island affairs with a daily dance performance (Ⓣ07/4090 2130; Mon–Sat 9am–5pm, Sun 2–5pm, reduced opening times Jan–Feb; $6) and has the town's only **café** inside. Other facilities in town include a pharmacy and laundry on Douglas Street. Between June and October, Peddell's Buses (Ⓣ07/4069 1551) meets incoming ferries for a ninety-minute tour of the island ($25).

Other islands

Though you generally need permission from the local council, it's possible that you may be privately invited to other islands in the Strait. While some are within outboard range – "one drum trips" – you're looking at $400 or more each way to charter a five-seater plane to anywhere more distant – contact Aero Tropics (Ⓣ1300 656 110, Ⓦwww.aero-tropics.com.au). Torres Strait Tours on Thursday Island (Ⓣ1800 420 666, Ⓕ07/4069 1408) can arrange **water taxis** and island transfers if needed.

Just a few minutes from Thursday's wharf by water taxi ($15), **Horn Island** is another small chunk of land surrounded by mangroves and coral, the site of an open-cut gold mine and the regional **airport** (with regular flights to and from Cairns). The main reason to take a trip across is to visit the **pearling museum**, run by an ex-diver and stocked with his memorabilia – including an old-fashioned bronze dive helmet. He also owns Horn's sole place to **stay and eat**, the *Gateway Torres Strait Resort* (Ⓣ07/4069 2222; ⑤).

Of the remoter islands, eastern **Murray Island** (Mer) is enticing for its importance in island history; it was the centre for pre-contact religion, and it was over a land claim here that the Mabo Decision was handed down. To the north are **Badu**, centre of the Strait's burgeoning crayfish industry, and **Saibai**, a low deltaic island just 16km from the New Guinea mainland – the only place in Australia from where you can see another country.

Travel details

Trains

Bundaberg to: Ayr (6 weekly; 16hr); Bowen (6 weekly; 14hr); Cairns (4 weekly; 25hr); Gladstone (6 weekly; 2hr 30min); Ingham (4 weekly; 18hr); Innisfail (4 weekly; 21hr); Mackay (6 weekly; 11hr); Proserpine, for Airlie Beach (6 weekly; 13hr 30min); Rockhampton (6 weekly; 4hr 30min); Townsville (6 weekly; 17hr); Tully, for Mission Beach (4 weekly; 20hr).
Cairns to: Ayr (4 weekly; 9hr); Bowen (4 weekly; 11hr); Bundaberg (4 weekly; 25hr); Forsayth (1 weekly; 11hr 15min); Gladstone (4 weekly; 22hr); Ingham (4 weekly; 5hr); Innisfail (4 weekly; 2hr); Kuranda (1–2 daily; 1hr); Mackay (4 weekly; 13hr 20min); Proserpine, for Airlie Beach (4 weekly; 11hr 30min); Rockhampton (4 weekly; 19hr); Townsville (4 weekly; 4hr 40min); Tully, for Mission Beach (4 weekly; 3hr 15min).
Ingham to: Ayr (4 weekly; 3hr 30min); Bowen (4 weekly; 5hr); Bundaberg (4 weekly; 18hr); Cairns (4 weekly; 5hr); Gladstone (4 weekly; 16hr); Innisfail (4 weekly; 3hr); Mackay (4 weekly; 9hr); Proserpine, for Airlie Beach (4 weekly; 7hr); Rockhampton (4 weekly; 15hr); Townsville (4 weekly; 2hr); Tully, for Mission Beach (4 weekly; 2hr).
Mackay to: Ayr (6 weekly; 5hr); Bowen (6 weekly; 3hr); Bundaberg (6 weekly; 11hr); Cairns (4 weekly; 13hr 20min); Gladstone (6 weekly; 8hr); Ingham (4 weekly; 9hr); Innisfail (4 weekly; 12hr); Proserpine, for Airlie Beach (4 weekly; 2hr 30min); Rockhampton (6 weekly; 5hr 30min); Townsville (6 weekly; 7hr); Tully, for Mission Beach (4 weekly; 10hr 30min).
Proserpine to: Ayr (6 weekly; 2hr 40min); Bowen (6 weekly; 2hr); Bundaberg (6 weekly; 13hr 30min); Cairns (4 weekly; 11hr 30min); Gladstone (6 weekly; 10hr); Ingham (4 weekly; 7hr); Innisfail (4 weekly; 9hr 30min); Mackay (4 weekly; 2hr 30min); Rockhampton (6 weekly; 7hr 40min); Townsville (6 weekly; 4hr 40min); Tully, for Mission Beach (4 weekly; 8hr).
Rockhampton to: Ayr (6 weekly; 11hr); Bowen (6 weekly; 8hr 20min); Bundaberg (6 weekly; 4hr 30min); Cairns (4 weekly; 19hr); Gladstone (6 weekly; 1hr 30min); Ingham (4 weekly; 15hr); Innisfail (4 weekly; 18hr); Longreach (2 weekly; 12hr 30min); Mackay (6 weekly; 5hr 30min); Proserpine, for Airlie Beach (6 weekly; 7hr 40min); Townsville (6 weekly; 12hr); Tully, for Mission Beach (4 weekly; 16hr).
Townsville to: Ayr (6 weekly; 1hr 30min); Bowen (6 weekly; 3hr); Bundaberg (6 weekly; 17hr); Cairns (4 weekly; 4hr 40min); Gladstone (6 weekly; 14hr); Ingham (4 weekly; 2hr); Innisfail (4 weekly; 5hr); Mackay (6 weekly; 7hr); Mount Isa (2 weekly; 19hr); Proserpine, for Airlie Beach (6 weekly; 4hr 40min); Rockhampton (6 weekly; 12hr); Tully, for Mission Beach (4 weekly; 4hr).
Tully to: Ayr (4 weekly; 5hr 30min); Bowen (4 weekly; 7hr); Bundaberg (4 weekly; 20hr); Cairns (4 weekly; 3hr 15min); Gladstone (4 weekly; 18hr); Ingham (4 weekly; 2hr); Innisfail (4 weekly; 1hr 15min); Mackay (4 weekly; 10hr 30min); Proserpine, for Airlie Beach (4 weekly; 8hr); Rockhampton (4 weekly; 16hr); Townsville (4 weekly; 4hr).

Buses

Airlie Beach to: Ayr (7 daily; 2hr 20min); Bowen (7 daily; 1hr); Bundaberg (7 daily; 11hr 30min); Cairns (7 daily; 9hr 45min); Gladstone (7 daily; 10hr); Ingham (7 daily; 6hr); Innisfail (7 daily; 8hr 30min); Mackay (7 daily; 3hr); Mission Beach (5 daily; 8hr); Rockhampton (7 daily; 8hr 30min); Townsville (7 daily; 3hr 30min).
Bundaberg to: Airlie Beach (7 daily; 11hr 30min); Agnes Water/1770 (2 weekly; 2hr); Ayr (8 daily; 15hr); Bowen (8 daily; 13hr 30min); Cairns (8 daily; 21hr); Gladstone (8 daily; 3hr); Ingham (8 daily; 18hr); Innisfail (8 daily; 21hr); Mackay (8 daily; 9hr); Mission Beach (5 daily; 19hr); Rockhampton (8 daily; 4hr); Townsville (8 daily; 14hr 30min).
Cairns to: Airlie Beach (6 daily; 9hr 45min); Ayr (8 daily; 7hr 30min); Bowen (8 daily; 9hr); Bundaberg (8 daily; 21hr); Cape Tribulation (1 daily; 4hr); Gladstone (8 daily; 19hr 30min); Ingham (8 daily; 3hr 15min); Innisfail (8 daily; 1hr); Kuranda (1 daily; 35min); Mackay (8 daily; 12hr); Mission Beach (5 daily; 1hr 55min); Mossman (1 daily; 1hr 45min); Port Douglas (1 daily; 1hr 45min); Rockhampton (8 daily; 17hr); Townsville (8 daily; 4hr 45min).
Mackay to: Airlie Beach (7 daily; 3hr); Ayr (8 daily; 5hr); Bowen (8 daily; 4hr); Bundaberg (8 daily; 9hr); Cairns (8 daily; 12hr); Gladstone (8 daily; 6hr); Ingham (8 daily; 9hr); Mackay (8 daily; 11hr); Mission Beach (5 daily; 23hr); Rockhampton (8 daily; 4hr); Townsville (8 daily; 5hr 15min).
Mission Beach to: Airlie Beach (5 daily; 8hr); Ayr (5 daily; 5hr 30min); Bowen (5 daily; 7hr); Bundaberg (5 daily; 19hr); Cairns (5 daily; 1hr 55min); Gladstone (5 daily; 16hr); Ingham (5 daily; 2hr); Innisfail (5 daily; 2hr 45min); Mackay (5 daily; 23hr); Rockhampton (5 daily; 15hr); Townsville (5 daily; 4hr).
Rockhampton to: Airlie Beach (7 daily; 8hr 30min); Ayr (8 daily; 10hr); Bowen (8 daily; 10hr);

Bundaberg (8 daily; 4hr); Cairns (8 daily; 17hr); Gladstone (8 daily; 1hr 15min); Ingham (8 daily; 10hr); Innisfail (8 daily; 16hr); Longreach (3 weekly; 9hr); Mackay (8 daily; 4hr); Mission Beach (5 daily; 15hr); Mount Morgan (14 weekly; 2hr); Townsville (8 daily; 9hr 30min); Yeppoon (3 daily; 1hr 30min).
Townsville to: Airlie Beach (7 daily; 3hr 30min); Ayr (8 daily; 1hr); Bowen (8 daily; 3hr); Bundaberg (8 daily; 14hr 30min); Cairns (8 daily; 4hr 45min); Charters Towers (3 daily; 1hr 30min); Gladstone (8 daily; 13hr); Ingham (8 daily; 1hr 30min); Innisfail (8 daily; 3hr 45min); Mackay (8 daily; 5hr 15min); Mission Beach (5 daily; 4hr); Mount Isa (3 daily; 11hr 30min); Rockhampton (8 daily; 9hr 30min).

Ferries

Airlie Beach/Shute Harbour to: Daydream Island (1–2 daily; 45min); Hamilton Island (1–3 daily; 1hr); Hook Island (1–2 daily; 1hr 30min); Lindeman Island (2 daily; 1hr 30min); South Molle Island (2 daily; 45min); Whitsunday Island (1 daily; 2hr).
Cairns to: Thursday Island (1 weekly; 36hr).
Cape York to: Thursday Island (Mon–Fri 2 daily; 1hr 15min–2hr).
Cardwell to: Hinchinbrook Island (2 daily; 1–2hr).
Mission Beach to: Dunk Island (10 or more daily; 15min).
Rosslyn Bay to: Great Keppel Island (4–5 daily; 45min–1hr).
Townsville to: Magnetic Island (10 or more daily; 45min).
Weipa to: Normanton (1 weekly; 24hr).

Flights

Bundaberg to: Brisbane (3 daily; 1hr); Cairns (2 daily; 4hr 50min); Gladstone (1 weekly; 35min); Lady Elliot (daily; 45min); Mackay (1 daily; 2hr); Rockhampton (1 daily; 50min).
Cairns to: Bamaga (1 daily; 1hr 45min); Bundaberg (2 daily; 4hr 50min); Cooktown (1 daily; 45min); Dunk Island (1 daily; 45min); Lizard Island (2 daily; 1hr); Mackay (2 daily; 2hr 45min); Proserpine (6 weekly; 2hr); Rockhampton (2 daily; 3hr); Thursday Island/Horn Island (1–2 daily; 2hr); Townsville (2 daily; 1hr); Weipa (1 daily; 1hr 15min).
Gladstone to: Bundaberg (1 weekly; 35min); Rockhampton (5 weekly; 25min).
Mackay to: Cairns (2 daily; 2hr 45min); Rockhampton (2 daily; 45min); Townsville (4 daily; 1hr).
Rockhampton to: Cairns (2 daily; 3hr); Gladstone (5 weekly; 25min); Great Keppel Island (3 daily; 25min); Mackay (2 daily; 45min); Townsville (2 daily; 1hr 50min).
Townsville to: Cairns (2 daily; 1hr); Mackay (4 daily; 1hr); Rockhampton (2 daily; 1hr 50min).

6

Outback Queensland

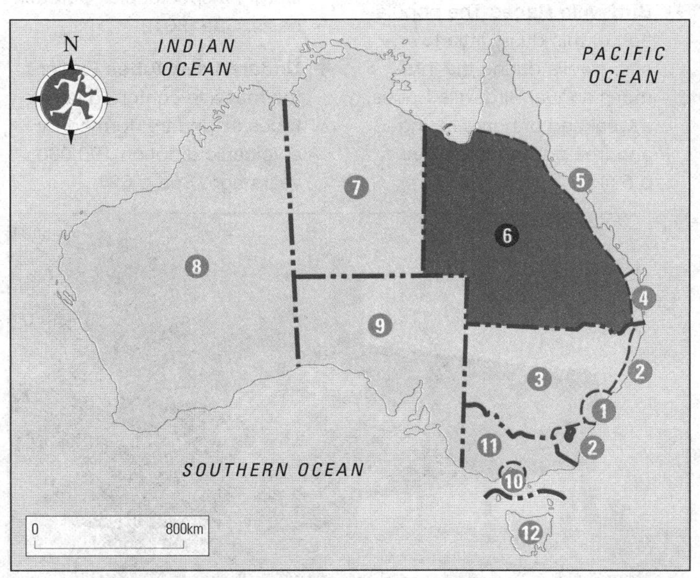

CHAPTER 6

Highlights

* **Artesian hot spa at Mitchell** The hot springs in single-street Mitchell make an enjoyable wallow on a cold winter's morning. See p.588

* **Carnarvon Gorge** Reach fantastic Aboriginal art sites with a hike through the verdant Carnarvon Gorge. See p.588

* **Birdsville Races** The population of this dusty little township swells during the infamous annual Birdsville Races, a weekend of horse racing and free-flowing beer. See p.594

* **Crayfish Derby at Winton** The winner nets $1500 and the runner-up gets to eat all the competitors at the biennial Australian Crayfish Derby, held in September in the archetypal frontier town of Winton. See p.604

* **Lawn Hill Gorge** Taking to the water is a wonderful way to explore the lush Lawn Hill Gorge, a spectacular Outback oasis. See p.619

* **Undara Lava Tubes** Explore the massive contorted lava tubes at Undara, formed by a volcanic eruption 190,000 years ago. See p.621

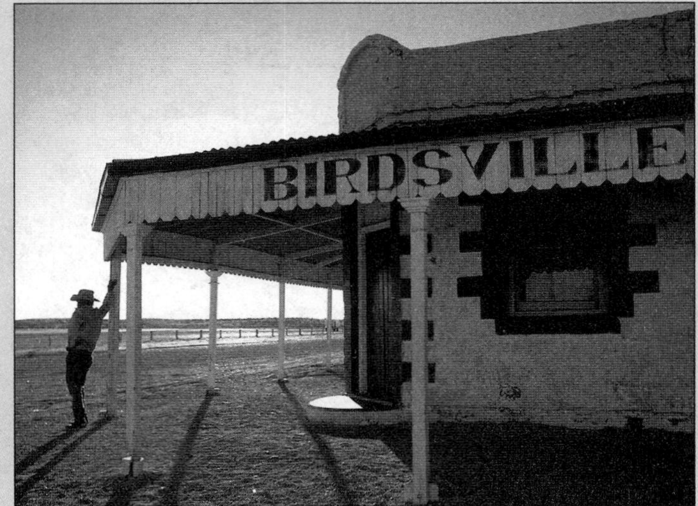

△ Birdsville hotel

6

Outback Queensland

Outback Queensland, the west of the state, is thinly populated by tenacious farming communities swinging precariously between famine and survival, and seems hard to reconcile with the lushness of the wet tropics in the east. The population is concentrated in the relatively fertile highlands along the **Great Dividing Range**, which run low behind the coast. On the far side, featureless plains slide over a hot horizon into the fringes of South Australia and the NT. Almost untouched by overseas visitors, the only places attracting tourists in any numbers are the **Stockman's Hall of Fame** at Longreach, the oases of **Carnarvon Gorge** in the Central Highlands and the northwest's **Lawn Hill Gorge**. But elsewhere the opportunities for exploration are immense, with **precious stones**, **fossils**, waterholes and **Aboriginal art** in abundance.

The region is responsible for producing some of Australia's most iconic imagery – **Banjo Paterson** first performed **Waltzing Matilda**, with its depiction of the "jolly swagman" (known more colloquially as a "swaggie"), in a hotel in Winton. Winton also tussles with nearby Longreach for the right to claim the honour of being the birthplace of **Qantas** airlines, and it was in the remote former mining town of Cloncurry that the Reverend John Flynn instigated the **Royal Flying Doctor Service**.

Choosing where to go is often determined by the most convenient starting point. **Main roads** and **trains** head west from the coast at Brisbane, Rockhampton and Townsville. Interstate **bus services** from Townsville are good, but otherwise the highways are only partially covered by public transport. If you're **driving**, your vehicle must be well maintained and you should carry essential spares, as even main centres often lack replacement parts.

Unless you're experienced and well equipped, you'll find that western **summers** effectively prohibit travel, as searing temperatures and violent flash floods can isolate regions (especially in the Channel Country on the far side of the Great Dividing Range) for days or weeks on end. Consequently, many tour companies, tourist offices and motels simply shut up shop between November and March, or at least during January and February. On the other hand, water revives dormant seeds and fast-growing desert flowers, which cover the ground to the horizon in good years. At other times, expect hot days and cool nights, plenty of dust and sparse landscapes.

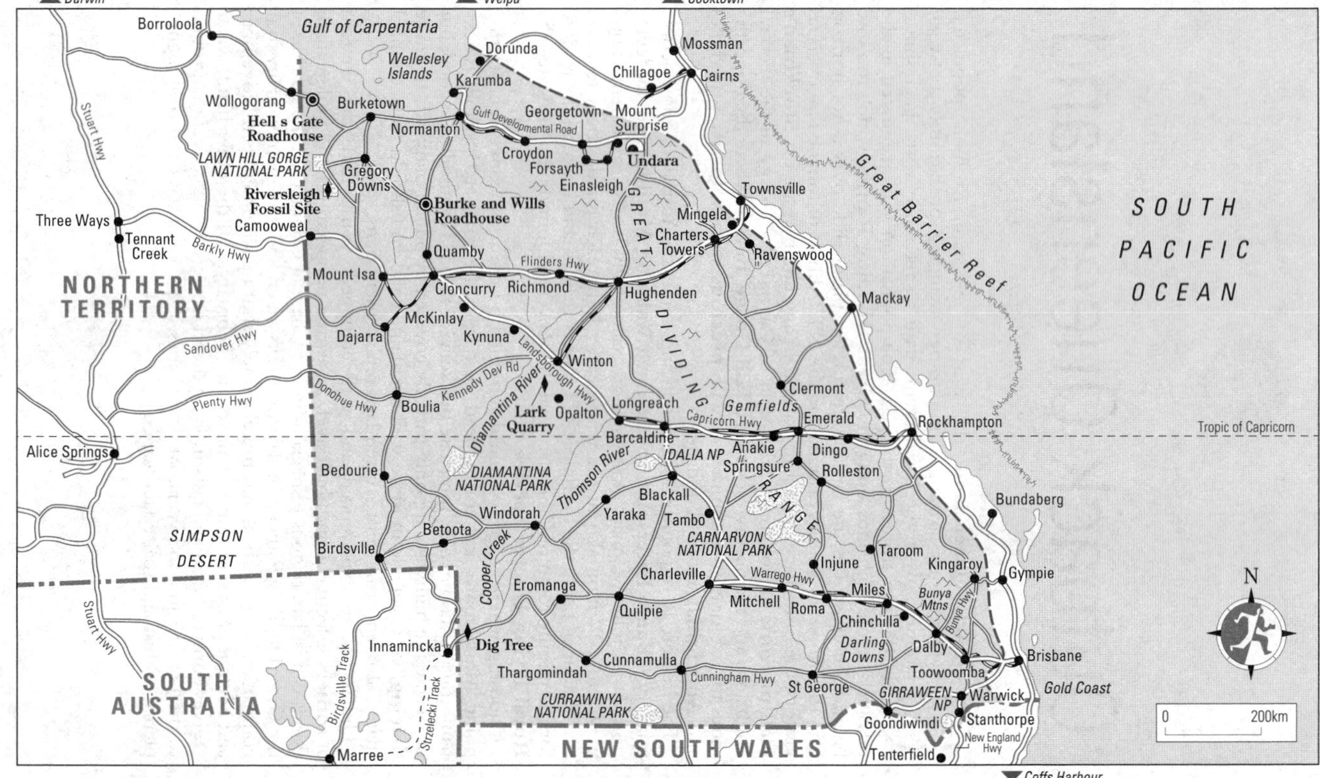
Darwin
Weipa
Cooktown
Coffs Harbour
Gulf of Carpentaria
Wellesley Islands
SOUTH PACIFIC OCEAN
Great Barrier Reef
Tropic of Capricorn
NORTHERN TERRITORY
SOUTH AUSTRALIA
NEW SOUTH WALES
SIMPSON DESERT
GREAT DIVIDING RANGE
Borroloola
Wollogorang
Hell s Gate Roadhouse
LAWN HILL GORGE NATIONAL PARK
Riversleigh Fossil Site
Burketown
Gregory Downs
Dorunda
Karumba
Normanton
Gulf Developmental Road
Georgetown
Croydon
Forsayth
Einasleigh
Mount Surprise
Undara
Chillagoe
Mossman
Cairns
Townsville
Mingela
Charters Towers
Ravenswood
Mackay
Burke and Wills Roadhouse
Three Ways
Tennant Creek
Barkly Hwy
Stuart Hwy
Camooweal
Quamby
Mount Isa
Cloncurry
Richmond
Flinders Hwy
Hughenden
McKinlay
Dajarra
Kynuna
Landsborough Hwy
Winton
Sandover Hwy
Plenty Hwy
Donohue Hwy
Kennedy Dev Rd
Boulia
Diamantina River
Lark Quarry
Opalton
Longreach
Gemfields
Clermont
Capricorn Hwy
Emerald
Rockhampton
Barcaldine
Anakie
Dingo
IDALIA NP
Springsure
Rolleston
Alice Springs
Bedourie
DIAMANTINA NATIONAL PARK
Thomson River
Blackall
Yaraka
Tambo
Windorah
CARNARVON NATIONAL PARK
Bundaberg
Taroom
Betoota
Birdsville
Cooper Creek
Charleville
Warrego Hwy
Injune
Kingaroy
Gympie
Eromanga
Quilpie
Mitchell
Roma
Miles
Bunya Mtns
Bunya Hwy
Chinchilla
Dalby
Innamincka
Dig Tree
Thargomindah
Cunnamulla
Cunningham Hwy
Darling Downs
Toowoomba
Brisbane
Gold Coast
St George
GIRRAWEEN NP
Warwick
Stanthorpe
Goondiwindi
New England Hwy
Tenterfield
CURRAWINYA NATIONAL PARK
Birdsville Track
Strzelecki Track
Marree
N
0
200km

Brisbane to Cooper Creek and Birdsville

The thousand-plus-kilometre haul from the comforts of the coast to Queensland's remote southwestern corner dumps you tired and dusty on the South Australian border, with some exciting routes down the Birdsville and Strzelecki tracks or through the hostile red barrier of the Simpson Desert yet to come. There are two ultimate targets – the outpost of **Birdsville**, with its annual horse races, and the **Dig Tree** at Nappa Merrie on Cooper Creek, monument to the Burke and Wills tragedy (see box on p.593). The highway scenery is as bleak as you'd expect: after crossing the fertile disc of the **Darling Downs**, the country withers and dries, marooning communities in isolation and hardship. Detour north through Queensland's **Central Highlands** however, and you'll find a landscape peppered with forested sandstone gorges and the Aboriginal sites at **Carnarvon National Park** – worth the journey even if you don't go any further.

The most practical route into the area from Brisbane is on the **Warrego Highway**, through Toowoomba, Roma and Charleville towards Quilpie. Roma is the jumping-off point for the Highlands and from Quilpie there are largely unsurfaced roads to Birdsville and the Dig Tree. The twice-weekly *Westlander* **train** runs in this direction from Brisbane to Charleville, as do daily buses en route from Brisbane to Mount Isa.

Running parallel to the Warrego to the south, the **Cunningham Highway** crosses the Downs between Warwick and Goondiwindi (the limit of the **bus** service in this direction), then heads out to Cunnamulla. West of Cunnamulla you're on your own, heading across oil, gas and opal fields towards the Dig Tree. **Four-wheel-drive vehicles** are preferable beyond the bitumen and are generally essential for reaching the Dig Tree.

The Darling Downs

The **Darling Downs**, a broad spread of prime agricultural land first explored by **Ludwig Leichhardt** in the 1840s, sprawl westwards from the back of the Great Dividing Range behind Brisbane, down to the state's southern boundaries. The Warrego Highway climbs a steep escarpment west to **Toowoomba**, **Kingaroy** and the **Northern Downs**, while the Cunningham Highway cuts through Cunningham's Gap to **Warwick** and the south. Highway towns west of Toowoomba – Dalby, Chinchilla and Miles – are unadorned farming centres with no specific sights. It's more the scenery along the Downs' fringes, particularly the **Bunya Mountains** in the north, or around the southeasterly **Granite Belt** (where there are also **wineries** and the possibility of **farm work**), which warrants a visit. Even if you tear across the Central Downs without stopping, you'll notice that the flat grasslands provide clear evidence of Aboriginal custodial practices; created by controlled burning designed to clear woodland and increase grazing land for game, they perfectly suited European pastoral needs. The Downs are relatively fertile and stud farms, dairy, cotton, wool and cereal farming have all been successfully tried at one time or another. Even unwanted plants thrive – during the 1920s millions of acres of land were infested by **prickly pear**, a South American cactus. It was finally brought to heel by the tiny parasitic *cactoblastis* moth in 1930 – a success story of biological control on a scale to match the later failure of the introduction of the cane toad (see box on p.537).

Toowoomba

TOOWOOMBA, 160km west of Brisbane, is a stately but staid university city perched on the edge of a six-hundred-metre escarpment, a promising setting that it doesn't quite live up to. Toowoomba's side streets and numerous gardens are pleasant enough however, the stylish houses and blaze of late-nineteenth-century sandstone architecture along central Main and Ruthven streets a reminder of its former business wealth. There's also a September **flower festival**, during which Toowoomba's tourist office (daily 9am–5pm; ⓣ1800 331 1155, ⓦwww.toowoomba.qld.gov.au), in James Street, hands out lists of exhibition gardens to visit. At other times the main attraction is the **Cobb & Co. Museum**, 27 Lindsay St (daily 10am–4pm; $8), 500m northeast of the centre across spacious Queens Park, which recalls the days when intrepid coaches bounced across the Outback delivering mail and passengers, between the 1860s and 1924. Aside from an impressive collection of these original coaches, the museum also houses interactive exhibitions on local history and flora and fauna, along with a working smithy at the back. If you've any spare time, **Picnic Point** at the top of Tourist Road, 2.5km east of the centre, is a pleasant spot on a warm day, offering a café, bar and restaurant as well as a picnic space, all with splendid views of the escarpment.

Downtown Toowoomba is a compact area based around the intersection of **Ruthven Street**, which runs north to south, and **Margaret Street**, which runs east to west. Around the intersection you'll find shops, **restaurants**, banks and a post office. The **bus station** is one block east of here on Neil Street (ⓣ07/4690 9888 for all companies), while the **train station** is 500m northwest on Railway Street. **Accommodation** prospects include the *Jolly Swagman Caravan Park,* 47 Kitchener Rd (ⓣ07/4632 8735; cabins ❶), about 1km southeast of the centre, *Range Motel* (ⓣ07/4632 3133; ❶) on Tourist Road, near the plateau's edge and with fine views, or the fairly quiet and central *Park Motel*, 88 Margaret St (ⓣ07/4632 1011; ❹). For food, *Jilly's Café* on Ruthven Street has a varied menu which includes vegetarian options – check for daily specials such as pumpkin and pinenut risotto, or five-spice chicken. **Moving on** from Toowoomba, the New England Highway runs 117km north to Kingaroy, plied by Polleys Coaches (ⓣ07/5482 9455, ⓦwww.polleys.com.au) and south to Warwick and Stanthorpe, covered by Greyhound Australia (ⓣ13 14 99, ⓦwww.greyhound.com.au) and Crisps (ⓣ07/3236 5266, ⓦwww.crisps.com.au). Goondiwindi is three hours southwest, again with Greyhound Australia, whose coaches follow the Warrego Highway west across the Central Downs to Charleville.

Around Kingaroy: the Northern Downs

KINGAROY, a small town in the heart of peanut country on the very fringes of the Downs, is a couple of hours' drive from Toowoomba and Dalby to the south, or Gympie on the coast. A cluster of castle-like **peanut silos** in the middle of town aptly symbolize the fame Kingaroy owes to **Johannes Bjelke-Petersen**, who farmed nuts here before becoming Queensland Premier in 1968, an office he held for nineteen years. His equally charismatic wife, Flo, also attained fame, making it onto postcards with her pumpkin scone recipe. Joh passed away in April 2005, but he and Flo are nevertheless in no danger of obscurity, with a dam, bridge, road and sportsground named after him, not to mention his ominous catch phrase "Don't you worry about that" still on everyone's lips. To get in touch with what Kingaroy is all about, take the free fifty-minute tour at the **Kingaroy Toasted Peanut Factory** (Mon–Fri 10.30am), 1km south of the centre on Kingaroy Street. Here, the scent of roasting is so seductive that you'll want to head back to the **Peanut Van** outside Lions Park, between the factory and town, which sells roasted nuts by the kilo. The last few years has also seen a rash of **wineries** springing up around Kingaroy, most open for tasting – and, of course, buying – daily. Stuart Range Estates (tours daily 10am & 2pm; $2; ⓣ07/4162 3711), just northeast of the centre at the end of William Street, has definite potential, though at present the wine is still a little green.

Kingaroy's tiny centre is built around the intersection of **Haly Street** and parallel **Youngman** and **Kingaroy** streets, which run north to south through town. The peanut silos are to the east, just along Haly Street, facing the **tourist office** (Mon-Fri 9am–5pm, Sat & Sun 10am–4pm; ⓣ07/4162 3199), which hands out a wineries map. For **somewhere to stay**, *Kingaroy Caravans* (ⓣ07/4162 1808; cabins ❶), 1km south near the peanut factory on Walter Road, has a variety of accommodation options in leafy surroundings. Otherwise, *Kingaroy Hotel-Motel* (ⓣ07/4162 1966; ❶) on the corner of Youngman and Haly streets, and the central *Club Hotel* (ⓣ07/4162 2204; ❶), on Kingaroy Street have good-value, similarly appointed rooms. The latter also offers occasional live music. Polleys Coaches (ⓣ07/5482 9455) leave daily from Kingaroy to Gympie and Toowoomba, while drivers can also take the Bunya Highway to Dalby.

The Bunya Mountains

Southwest of Kingaroy, a sixty-kilometre section of road twists through the **Bunya Mountains** before you reach **Dalby**, back on the Warrego Highway. Among the mountains' general greenery and clusters of unlikely flowers, you'll find stands of enormous **bunya pines**, which once covered the mountains and whose seeds were a valuable food source for local Aborigines, who gathered seasonally to gorge themselves. On his trip across the Downs in 1844, the indefatigable **Ludwig Leichhardt** witnessed the collection and roasting of nuts at such a feast and persuaded the government to make the area an Aboriginal reserve, free from logging or settlement. The decree was revoked in 1860, but today the Bunya Mountains still retain a significant stand of pines, along with orange-flowering **silky oaks** and ancient **grass trees**, with their three-metre-high, spear-like flower heads.

Two QPWS-run sites along the road at Burton's Well and Westcott make for good **bushcamping**, with another wallaby-infested site at the hamlet of Dandabah, where the ranger's office takes enquiries on all three (daily 2–4pm; ⓣ07/4668 3127; advance booking essential during holiday periods). Less frugal accommodation is also on hand about 500m north along the main road at the cosy and fun *Rice's Log Cabins* (ⓣ07/4668 3133; ❹), and the elegant *Bunya Mountain Lodge Guest House* (ⓣ07/4668 3134; ❺) nearby. Note that the mountains are generally several degrees cooler than the plains below, and it gets cold in winter. **Walking tracks** between the three campsites lead through the forest to orchid-covered lookouts and waterfalls – satin bowerbirds and paradise riflebirds, with their deep blue-black plumage and long curved beaks, are both fairly common here.

The Granite Belt

The southeastern edge of the Darling Downs along the New South Wales border, known as Queensland's **Granite Belt**, is a major **wine- and fruit-producing** area, which regularly records the state's coldest temperatures – on a winter's night it drops well below freezing here. Heading south from Toowoomba, you pass through the one-horse town of **NOBBY**, whose former resident **Steele Rudd** created archetypal Australian country characters in his "Dad and Dave" tales – commemorated at the *Nobby Hotel* in paintings and farm bric-à-brac.

Around 85km south of Toowoomba, **WARWICK** makes a fine base for exploring the region, and is known across the state for its **cheese**. Services are centred around Grafton and Palmerin streets, where sandstone buildings – which give the town a distinct "New South Wales" feeling – date back to the time when Warwick graziers competed fiercely with Toowoomba's merchants to establish the Downs' premier settlement. The October **rodeo** is about the only time you might experience trouble finding **accommodation** – try *Warwick Tourist Caravan Park*, 18 Palmer Ave (Ⓣ07/4661 8335; cabins ❶), 1.2km north of town on the highway, *Warwick Motor Inn*, 17 Albion St (Ⓣ 07/4661 1533, Ⓕ4660 5666; ❶), or *Country Rose Motel* (Ⓣ07/4661 7700, Ⓕ4661 1591; ❹). Alternatively, ask at the **tourist office** and art gallery (daily 8.30am–5pm; Ⓣ07/4661 3401) halfway down Albion Street.

The **Condamine River**, unimpressive where it flows through town, is part of Australia's longest river system. Originating from the highlands east of Warwick, it joins the Murray/Darling river system before emptying into the ocean near Adelaide. At **Queen Mary Falls**, 43km from Warwick beyond Killarney, a tributary exits the forest in a plunge off the top of the plateau. A two-kilometre-long track climbs to the escarpment at the head of the falls from the road, with a kiosk, **accommodation** and lunches provided by *Queen Mary Falls Tourist Park* (Ⓣ07/4664 7151, Ⓕ4664 7122; cabins ❶); you need your own transport to get here.

Heading on from Warwick, the New England Highway, served by Crisps Coaches (Ⓣ07/4661 8333, Ⓦwww.crisps.com.au) and Greyhound Australia (Ⓣ13 14 99, Ⓦwww.greyhound.com.au), runs south to Stanthorpe, then over the border to Tenterfield. The Cunningham Highway continues 200km west to Goondiwindi and the banks of the Macintyre River, which marks the state border with New South Wales.

Stanthorpe and Girraween National Park

Sixty kilometres south of Warwick along the New England Highway, **STANTHORPE** was founded in the 1880s around a **tin mining** operation on Quart Pot Creek, but really took off in the 1940s after Italian migrants started up the **fruit farms** and **wineries** that now throng the region. Today, it's a miniature version of Warwick, central **Maryland Street** sporting a couple of sandstone facades while retiree bungalows sprout on the hills above, and there's good opportunities for wine sampling and – in season – **fruit picking work**.

To start a **wine** tour, Heritage Wines (daily 9am–5pm; Ⓣ07/4685 2197), 15km north on the New England Highway – worth a visit alone for its huge, antique-laden reception room – and Ballandean Estate (daily 8.30am–5pm; Ⓣ07/4684 1226), the region's oldest vineyard, 20km southwest of town, both produce excellent wines and are open daily. A full list of wineries – and advice on the best – is available at the **tourist office** (daily 8.30am–5pm; Ⓣ07/4681 2057), overlooking the river just south of the centre on Leslie Parade. Staff can also help if you want to try **fossicking for topaz** (a semi-precious stone found near tin deposits), 13km northwest of Stanthorpe at **Swiper's Gully**; permits are available from the *Blue Topaz* caravan park (see below).

Stanthorpe has a good range of **accommodation**. For camping, *Blue Topaz Caravan Park* (Ⓣ07/4683 5279, Ⓕ4683 5280; cabins ❶), 5km south along the highway, can provide mining permits and *Top of Town* (Ⓣ07/4681 4888, Ⓕ4681 4222; dorms $16.50, cabins ❶), on the highway 2km north of town, has huge grounds. There are hostel beds at the excellent *Backpackers of Queensland*, 80 High St (Ⓣ07/4681 0999, Ⓦwww.backpackersofqueensland.com.au; dorms $16.50), while *Stannum Lodge Motor Inn* (Ⓣ07/4681 2000, Ⓦwww.stannumlodge.com.au; 3) on Wallangarra Road is a central motel with good facilities, including a swimming pool. If you're after **farm work**, contact the backpackers'.

The hills around Stanthorpe are granite, exposed as fantastic monoliths at **Girraween National Park**, 30km south down the New England Highway. Surrounding woodland suffered an appalling **bushfire** in October 2002, though as most plants in the region are fire-adapted, and regeneration is well under way, the park remains a worthwhile stopover. There's a QPWS **campsite** and ranger's office here (Ⓣ07/4684 5157) with showers and toilets – and the chance of seeing small, shy, active sugar gliders just after dark. Listen for claws clattering over bark and then shine your torch overhead to catch a glowing set of eyes in the spotlight.

With more energy than skill, you can climb several of the giant hills with little risk, as long as rain hasn't made them dangerously slippery – trails are well marked and free **maps** are available from the ranger's office. **Castle Rock** (2hr return) is entertaining: initially a gentle incline past lichen-covered boulders in the forest, the track follows a dotted white line into a fissure – look up and you'll see loose rocks balanced above you – before emerging onto a thin ledge above the campsite. Follow this around to the north side and clamber to the very top for superb views of the Pyramids, the Sphinx and Mount Norman poking rudely out of the woods. It's a further forty minutes' walk from the Castle Rock campsite to the **Sphinx** and **Turtle Rock**. Sphinx is a broad pillar topped by a boulder, while Turtle's more conventional shape means a scramble, with no handholds on the final stretch. Pat yourself on the back however, if you make it to the top of the completely bald **South Pyramid** (2hr return from Castle Rock) without resorting to hands and knees. Take a well-earned rest at the top and look across to the unscaleable North Pyramid from below Balancing Rock, an oval boulder teetering so precariously on its narrow end that you can see underneath to where the support is surely only a few years away from collapse. **Mount Norman**, the park's 1267-metre apex, lies an hour beyond Castle Rock and should only be attempted by experienced climbers – check details with the ranger at Girraween.

Goondiwindi and St George

Before European settlers put weirs on the Macintyre River in the **GOONDIWINDI** (pronounced "gundawindee") area, right on the New South Wales border some 180km west of Stanthorpe and 220km southwest of Toowoomba, it was little more than a string of waterholes and lagoons, attracting a lot of birdlife and inspiring the Aboriginal name Goonawinna – "birds' resting place". The irrigation weirs now supply the huge demands of the local cotton and wheat industries, but this hasn't dented the varied birdlife, despite the constant stream of road train transports rumbling through at all hours.

Goondiwindi is best known in Australia for the racehorse Gunsynd, alias the **Goondiwindi Grey**, who won over half of his races through the early 1970s.

There's a monument to him at the southern end of McLean Street, close to where the **Macintyre River** marks the state boundary. Nearby, also on McLean Street, the **Old Customs House Museum** (daily except Tues 10am–4pm; $3) has an eclectic gathering of anything old, from preserved snakes to steam engines. It predates the rest of the buildings in the town and even the wood-paved **Border Bridge** over the river.

The main road running east to west through town is Marshall Street, with shops, **banks**, a post office and most services nearby. The **tourist office** (daily 9am–5pm; ⓣ07/4671 2653, ⓦwww.goondiwindi.org) on Maclean Street has brochures galore, as well as **Internet** facilities. Inexpensive central **accommodation** can be found at *Rivergums*, 3 DeLacy St (ⓣ07/4671 1383; cabins ❶), a clean and friendly caravan park near the tourist office; *Gunsynd Motor Inn* (ⓣ07/4671 1555; ❶) on McLean Street, which has comfortable, if slightly austere-looking rooms; and at the recently renovated *Border Motel*, 126 Marshall St (ⓣ07/4671 1688; ❹). Be aware that during the November **cotton-chipping season**, places to stay are in very short supply. **Eat** at the *Victoria Hotel* on Marshall Street, whose counter meals feature a half-kilo steak buried under a mountain of vegetables.

Two hundred kilometres further west on the Barwon Highway, **ST GEORGE** sits on the banks of the Balonne River and is the administrative centre for the tranquil shire of Balonne. From St George, roads leave in almost every direction and on your way through the shire every town offers a taste of farming history, wildlife and a relaxed atmosphere. **Information** on the region is available from the Council Offices under the clock tower in the town centre (Mon–Fri 8.30am–5pm; ⓣ07/4620 8888, ⓦwww.balonne.qld.gov.au), and you can **stay** at the *Australian Hotel* (ⓣ07/4625 5000; ❶–❷) on the river bank; the pub rooms are typically basic, but you can pay a little extra for a motel-style suite. At the back of the Balonne Sports Store, a few doors down from the Council Offices, the proprietor has combined the woodcarving skills of his native Greece with the Aboriginal tradition of emu egg-carving and the wonders of electric lighting, producing a unique display of carved, illuminated emu eggs (daily 9am–5pm; $2).

The Central Downs and around

To break the unexciting journey northwest across the Downs from Toowoomba to Dalby, call in at **Jondaryan Woolshed** (daily 9am–4pm; $12.50; ⓣ07/4692 2229), 3km south of the highway from Jondaryan and about 45km from Toowoomba, to look around the collection of old buildings – all relocated from elsewhere, with the exception of the shed itself. Exhibits worth a closer look include a document dating from 1880, which itemizes some of the schoolmistress's tasks – including splinting broken legs, wallpapering buildings to keep out snakes and being able to fight off "swaggies" (hobos, or drifters) trying to sleep in the schoolhouse. Make sure you catch one of the **tours** (Mon–Fri 1pm, Sat, Sun & holidays 10.30am & 1.30pm) when the smithy is working and you can watch sheep shearers at work beneath the vast emptiness of the handcrafted woolshed roof, lit by a bare bulb – a very surreal tableau.

The next stops over the following 200km are **Dalby**, **Chinchilla** and **Miles**, rural centres devoid of much in the way of attractions but with the usual complement of places to stay. One place worth stopping at however, is *Possum Park* (ⓣ07/4627 1651; carriages ❶), some 20km north of Miles. A motel sited in World War II ammunition bunkers in prime bushland, **accommodation** here is in restored train carriages or your own tent – you'll have to provide your own meals.

Roma and Mitchell

ROMA, 140km west of Miles, was founded by settlers eager to occupy country made available by the opening up of the Darling Downs in 1862. Today, the town thrives on farming, supplemented by the **oil** and **gas fields** which have been exploited intermittently since the 1900s. Roma was also the venue for the 1871 trial of the audacious **Captain Starlight** (also known as Harry Redford), who stole a thousand head of cattle from a nearby property and drove them down through the South Australian deserts to Adelaide for sale. An unusual white bull in the herd was recognized and Redford arrested, but his pioneering of a new stock route won such popular approval that the judge refused to convict him.

Roma is a typical inland town – tidy, with streets lined with **bottle trees** (not only bottle-shaped but also full of sugary water for emergency stock-watering), and a slightly dated air lent by the iron decorations and wrapround balconies of its hotels. A useful place to stock up before heading north to Carnarvon National Park, it also has a reputation for its **cattle markets**, and the rodeo and carnival which is held every Easter. Romavilla Winery (Mon–Fri 8am–5pm, Sat 9am–noon & 2–4pm; Ⓣ07/4622 1822, Ⓦwww.romavilla.com) has been producing prize-winning **wine** since 1863; it's an eccentric, overgrown place about a kilometre north of town on the Carnarvon road, at Quintin Street.

The Warrego Highway runs through Roma as Bowen Street and it's here, on the eastern side of town, that you're greeted by the **Big Rig** (daily: Dec–March 10am–4pm; April–Nov 9am–5pm; $8, night show $5; Ⓣ07/4622 8676, Ⓦwww.thebigrig.com.au), originally a drilling tower left as a monument to the oil boom of the 1920s and now a $5 million complex exploring the history of Australia's oil and gas industry. It also doubles as the town's **tourist office**. Most of the town's shops, banks and businesses are one block north of Bowen Street, on parallel **McDowall Street**. Roma's **accommodation** choices include the *Starlight Motor Inn* (Ⓣ07/4622 2666, Ⓕ4622 2111; ❹), with standard motel beds, the less pricey *Bottle Tree Gardens* (Ⓣ07/4622 6111, Ⓕ4622 6499; ❶), on the corner of Bowen and Charles streets, and the *Big Rig Tourist Park*, 4 McDowell St (Ⓣ07/4622 2538; ❶), near the Big Rig, which has bright modern cabins and hot showers, welcome during sub-zero winter nights. **Restaurants** in Roma are fairly basic, though *Deano's*, at 77 Quintin St, does good steaks. For decent Chinese food, try *Golden Dragon* at 60–62 McDowall St.

The train station (Ⓣ07/4622 9411) is one block south of the highway on Station Street, at the corner of Charles Street, and the **bus terminal** is on Bowen Street by the more central of the two BP roadhouses. The **airport** is a small strip a few kilometres outside town. Tickets for all these can also be obtained from Harvey World Travel, 71 Arthur St (Ⓣ07/4622 1416). Heading north, the Carnarvon Developmental Road (take Quintin St from the town centre) gives access to Carnarvon National Park; otherwise, the next stops west along the highway are Mitchell and Charleville.

Mitchell

MITCHELL is a delightful, single-street town right on the western rim of the Downs, beside the Maranoa River, 88km west of Roma on the Warrego Highway. As with Roma, Mitchell has its local outlaw legend; the protagonists this time were the two **Kenniff Brothers**, who raided the district for cattle and horses in the early 1900s. After killing a policeman during one arrest attempt, they were finally ambushed south of town and dragged off for trial in Brisbane; unlike Captain Starlight, they were sentenced to death, though one brother had this commuted to a prison term.

There are two reasons to stop at Mitchell – either to follow the two-hundred-kilometre track north to Mount Moffat in Carnarvon National Park, or to make use of the town's **hot artesian springs**, which have been thoughtfully channelled into an open-air swimming pool and spa (daily 8am–7pm; $6) in the grounds of the old Kenniff Courthouse – good, steamy fun on a cold winter's morning. The courthouse itself now houses a **tourist office** (daily 8am–7pm; ⓣ07/4623 1133), where you can also arrange hour-long river cruises ($13.50), or 4WD day-tours to Mount Moffatt (minimum of four; contact Pop Wilson, ⓣ07/4623 1155). It also incorporates the *Healthy Byte Café*, an **Internet** terminal and a weekend cinema. For somewhere to **stay**, the excellent council-run campsite back across the Maranoa River allows you to pitch a tent free for two nights ($5.50 per tent per night thereafter); the *Mitchell Motel* (ⓣ07/4623 1355; ❶), on the western side of town, is the alternative. The central *Blue Pub* is a good place to eat and offers bargain $6 lunches.

Moving on, all transport and the Warrego Highway continue a further 180km west to Charleville. The **train station** is 500m from the courthouse at the western side of town, and the newsagent on the main street doubles as the **bus** agent.

Carnarvon National Park

North of Roma and Mitchell, Queensland's Central Highlands consist of a broad band of weathered sandstone plateaus along the Great Dividing Range, thickly wooded and spectacularly sculpted into sheer cliffs and pinnacles. It's an extraordinarily primeval landscape, and one still visibly central to Aboriginal culture, as poor pasture left the highlands relatively unscathed by European colonization. Covering a huge slice of the region, **Carnarvon National Park** includes **Carnarvon Gorge**, **Mount Moffatt** and the more remote sections further west. Most people head for Carnarvon Gorge, where you'll find the main facilities, the highest concentration of **Aboriginal art** and arguably the best scenery.

As there is **no public transport** to the park, you'll need your own vehicle: **access** to Carnarvon Gorge is from Roma to the south, or Emerald (see p.597) to the north, and to Mount Moffat from Roma or Mitchell. All these roads involve some stretches of dirt, making them impassable after heavy rain (most likely Nov–May). Always carry extra rations in case you get stranded for a while and – unless you're desperately short of supplies – stay put in wet weather, you'll only churn the road up and make it harder for others to use. Note too, that it is not possible to drive directly between the gorge and Mount Moffat sections (though you can hike with permission and advice from the rangers). Summer **temperatures** often reach 40°C, while winter nights will be below freezing. Gathering firewood is prohibited inside the park, so stop on the way in or bring a gas stove. The **QPWS district headquarters** are in Emerald (ⓣ07/4982 4555), and regional offices are listed below.

Carnarvon Gorge

To reach Carnarvon Gorge **from Roma**, head north 199km along the Carnarvon Developmental Road past Injune, then 45km west along a gravel access road to the ranger station, at the mouth of the gorge. **From Emerald**, the same access road is 230km south along the Gregory and Dawson highways through Springsure and Rolleston. From either direction, the **Consuelo Tableland**

Boomerangs

Curved throwing sticks were once found throughout the world. Several were discovered in Tutankhamun's tomb, Hopi Indians once used them and a twenty-three-thousand-year-old example made from mammoth ivory was recently found in Poland. Since that time the invention of the bow and arrow superseded what Aborigines call a **boomerang** or karli, but their innovation of a stick that returns has kept the boomerang alive, not least in people's imagination – they were originally used as **children's toys** but were then modified into decoys for hunting wildfowl. The non-returning types depicted in Carnarvon Gorge show how sophisticated they became as **hunting weapons**. Usually made from tough acacia wood, some are hooked like a pick, while others are designed to cartwheel along the ground to break the legs of game. Thus immobilized, one animal would be killed while another could be easily tracked to meet the same fate. Besides hunting, the boomerang was also used for digging, levering or cutting, as well as banging pairs together for musical or ceremonial accompaniment. At Carnarvon Gorge, the long, gently curved boomerangs stencilled on the walls in pairs are not repetitions but portraits of two weapons with identical flight paths; if the first missed through a gust of wind, for instance, the user could immediately throw the second, correcting his aim for the conditions. For the definitive book on the subject, check out Philip Jones' nicely illustrated *Boomerang: Behind an Australian Icon* (Wakefield Press).

stands out magnificently above dark forests as the road crosses the plains below, rising gradually to the foothills on the park's edge before terminating at the mouth of the gorge. The ranger station here (daily 8am–5pm; ⓣ07/4984 4505) has a payphone, an orientation model of the gorge, **free maps** and a library on the highlands and its wildlife.

Accommodation – best booked well in advance – is available either 2km before the ranger station at *Carnarvon Gorge Wilderness Lodge* (ⓣ1800 644 150, ⓦwww.carnarvon-gorge.com; ❽), where comfortable rooms are surrounded by a neat lawn and respectably sized cycad palms, or a further 2km away at the creekside *Takarakka* (ⓣ07/4984 4535, ⓦwww.takarakka.com.au; ❶), which has canvas-sided "cabins" and a big campsite. The *Wilderness Lodge* also has a bar and a **store** selling basics, fuel and LP gas refills. If both these are full, *Warremba Farmstay and Camping* (ⓣ07/4626 7175, ⓦwww.warrembafarmstay.com.au; ❶), on the access road 57km east of the gorge, has all-weather access, **homestay** accommodation and a campsite with hot showers, toilets, and big kitchen area.

Along the gorge

Carnarvon Creek's journey between the vertical faces of the gorge has created some magical scenery, where low cloud often blends with the cliffs, making them look infinitely tall. A three-kilometre trail heads downstream from near the *Wilderness Lodge*, crossing the creek a few times by means of stepping stones and fallen trees. If you're not prepared to get wet, you can't get past the frigid **swimming hole** here at the end of the trail. **Baloon Cave**, in woodland behind the *Lodge*, shelters some stencil art of hands and boomerangs – easy to reach if unimpressive compared with other sites in the park. Before setting off to find them, climb **Boolimba Bluff** from the *Takarakka* campsite for a rare chance to see the gorge system from above; it's a tiring climb but the views from the "Roof of Queensland" make the three-kilometre track worth the effort.

The day-walk (19km return from the ranger station) **into the gorge** takes some beating, along with its intriguing side gorges. The best of these are the **Moss Garden** (3.5km), a vibrant green carpet of liverworts and ferns lapping up a spring as it seeps through the rockface, and **Alijon Falls** (5km), which conceal the enchanting **Wards Canyon**, where a remnant group of angiopteris ferns hang close to extinction in front of a second waterfall and gorge, complete with bats and blood-red river stones.

Carnarvon's two major **Aboriginal art sites** are the **Gallery** (5.6km) and **Cathedral Cave** (at the end of the trail, 9.3km from the *Takarakka* campsite), both on the gorge track, though if you keep your eyes open there are plenty more to be found. These are Queensland's most documented Aboriginal art sites, though the paintings themselves remain enigmatic in their direct meaning. A rockface covered with engravings of vulvas lends a pornographic air to the **Gallery**, and other symbols include kangaroo, emu and human tracks. A long, wavy line here might represent the rainbow serpent, shaper of many Aboriginal landscapes. Overlaying the engravings are hundreds of coloured stencils, made by placing an object against the wall and spraying it with a mixture of ochre and water held in the mouth. Always personal and striking, hands – including children's – form the bulk of the designs, but there are also artefacts, boomerangs and complex crosses formed by four arms. Goannas and mysterious net patterns at the near end of the wall have been painted with a stick. **Cathedral Cave** is larger, with an even greater range of designs, including seashell pendant stencils – proof that trade networks reached from here to the sea – and engravings of animal tracks and emu eggs.

Beyond Cathedral Cave, there's a **bush campsite** (open only during Queensland Easter, summer and winter school holidays; bookings ⓣ07/4984 4505, ⓦwww.epa.qld.gov.au) and a number of little-visited canyons to explore plus – with advice and permission from the rangers – the possibility of hiking right through to Mount Moffatt.

Mount Moffatt

Mount Moffatt is part of an open landscape of ridges and lightly wooded grassland, at the top of a plateau to the west of Carnarvon Gorge. The area was the Kenniff Brothers' stomping ground: it was here that they murdered a policeman and station manager in 1902, events which were to lead to their being run to ground by a group of vigilantes. Years later in 1960, archeological excavations at their hideout, **Kenniff Cave**, were the first to establish that Aboriginal occupation of Australia predated the last Ice Age, and – though the cave is currently closed due to instability – there's plenty of evidence of previous Aboriginal tenure through the area.

From Roma, it's a 248-kilometre drive to the park boundaries via Injune, or 220km direct **from Mitchell**. Although the park perimeter can often be reached in 2WD vehicles, you'll need to rely on a 4WD or walking to get around once there. As there is **no fuel** or supplies of any kind available in the park, make sure you have enough before arrival – last sources for either are at Injune (150km) or Mitchell. There are four bush **campgrounds** in the park, two of which have drinking water.

Mount Moffatt's attractions are spread out over an extensive area. Entering from the south, the **Chimneys** area has some interesting sandstone pinnacles and alcoves, which once housed bark burial cylinders – look for the stencil of an entire body, arms spread-eagled. Around 6km on from here the road forks, and the right track continues 10km to the **ranger station** (ⓣ07/4626 3581, ⓕ4626 3651) where you can collect your **map** of the area, plan any bushwalking and book a campsite. The left track, meanwhile, runs 6km past **Dargonelly campsite** to **Marlong Arch**, a sandstone formation decorated with handprints and engravings. Five kilometres northeast from here, a trail leads to **Kookaburra Cave**, named after a weathered, bird-shaped hand stencil. A further 5km beyond the cave is **Marlong Plain**, a pretty expanse of blue grass surrounded by peaks, and another sandstone tower known as **Lot's Wife**. Ten kilometres north of Marlong Plain, a lesser track leads to several sites associated with the Kenniff legend, including the **murder scene**, and the rock where they are believed to have burned the evidence.

Finally, for pure scenery, head 15km due east of Marlong Plain to the **Mahogany Forest**, a stand of giant stringybark trees. Mount Moffatt itself and pink-walled Devils Canyon, in the park's southeast corner, are more difficult to reach – you need to carry reliable maps and have bushwalking skills.

Charleville to Cooper Creek and Birdsville

The last place of any size on the journey west from Roma is **CHARLEVILLE**, terminus for the **train** and a compact, busy country town with broad streets, shaded pavements and some solid buildings constructed when the town was a droving centre and staging post for Cobb & Co. It's well known as a victim of contradictory weather – in November 1947 a typical hot summer afternoon was interrupted for twenty minutes as the temperature plummeted and a blast of massive hailstones stripped trees, smashed windows and roofs and killed pets and poultry. In 1990 the town centre was struck by five-metre-deep floodwaters from the **Warrego River** – a dramatic end to years of drought. At the end of the twentieth century, attempts were made to end another dry spell with **Stiger Vortex Guns**, giant conical contraptions supposed to seed rainclouds. During trials, two of the six guns exploded and the meteorologist who recommended them was run out of town. Only two have survived – one is in the Queensland Museum in Brisbane and the other is outside the Scout Hut on Sturt Street, heading south towards Cunnamulla.

Around town, the QPWS complex and **fauna park**, east at Park Street on the Warrego Highway from Mitchell (Mon–Fri 9am–4pm; free), is dedicated to studying and breeding populations of rare local fauna such as the absurdly cute **bilby** (for more on which see the "Currawinya National Park" account) and the graceful **yellow-footed rock wallaby**, both of which are on show. The **Historic House** (Mon–Sat 9am–4pm; $4) on Galatea Street, originally a bank, is now a museum with some rooms decorated in period style and showing elegant architectural touches. **Anglers** can try their luck along the river, where the prize catch is large Murray cod, though perch and freshwater catfish are more likely.

The town is small but laid out in a confusing grid pattern. The **bus stop** (two services daily, east towards Brisbane and northwest as far as Mount Isa) is next to *Corones Hotel* on kilometre-long **Wills Street**, and the **train station** is at the street's southern end (two trains a week to Brisbane, Wed & Fri). Most services – banks, shops and post office – are also on this street. The **tourist office** (April–Sept daily 9am–5pm; Oct–March Mon–Fri 9am–5pm; ⓣ07/4654 3057, ⓦwww.murweh.qld.gov.au) is a kilometre south of town on Sturt Street. Three kilometres south of town, on Qantas Drive (off the Matilda Highway) is the **Cosmos Centre and Observatory** (April–Oct daily 10am–6pm; Nov–March daily except Sat 10am–5pm; night shows Mon, Wed, Fri & Sat 8–10pm; $19), which provides visitors with the opportunity to observe the night sky through powerful Meade telescopes – the lack of industrial light and pollution, combined with a low horizon, make the location ideal. During daylight hours, the centre has interactive displays and films explaining the history of astronomy and the formation of the universe, as well as a sun filter enabling closer inspection of the brightest star in the solar system. Booking is essential for the latter and also for night-time stargazing (Ⓣ07/4654 7771 or call in at the tourist office). **Motel** rooms can be found at the peaceful and modern *Charleville Motel* (Ⓣ07/4654 1566; ❹), near the train station on King Street, or the town's historic *Corones Hotel* (Ⓣ07/4654 1022, Ⓦwww.hotelcorones.com; hotel ❶, motel doubles ❶) on Wills Street. To **camp**, head for *Cobb & Co. Caravan Park*, on the eastern side of town off Alfred Street (Ⓣ07/4654 1053; cabins ❶), a pleasant spot with hot water, barbecues and a small shop (6am–8pm). There are the usual coffee shops, and generous **meals** at the *Corones Hotel*, whose dining rooms have been refurbished to original 1925 condition. **Moving on** from Charleville, roads head north to Blackall and Longreach (covered by Brisbane to Mount Isa buses), south via Cunnamulla to New South Wales, and further west to Quilpie. **Flights** to Brisbane leave from the tiny strip outside town. All transport bookings can be made with Western Travel Service at 37 Alfred St (Ⓣ07/4654 1260).

Cunnamulla and Currawinya National Park

CUNNAMULLA, a nondescript handful of service stations and motels 200km south of Charleville, is a trucking stop on the long run down the Mitchell Highway to Bourke in New South Wales. The town received recent notoriety thanks to Dennis O'Rourke's 2000 **documentary** *Cunnamulla*, which focused rather obsessively on the relationships of the town's more offbeat characters. There's a helpful **tourist office** (daily 9am–3pm; Ⓣ07/4655 2481) in the old schoolhouse on central Jane Street. **Accommodation** is just around the corner at the *Cunnamulla Hotel* (Ⓣ07/4655 1102; ❶) on Stockyard Street, or a short way south at *Jack Tonkin Caravan Park* (Ⓣ07/4655 1421; cabins ❶). Cunnamulla's Council Offices (Ⓣ07/4655 1131, Ⓦwww.paroo.info), on the corner of Stockyard and Louise streets, is the place to arrange a fossicking licence ($5.55, valid for a month) if you're planning to head 160km west to the **Yowah Opal Fields**, where shallow deposits yield much-sought-after Yowah Nuts – opalized ironstone nodules. Yowah Opal Festival takes place in mid-July for three days, with opal displays and mine tours. At the fields, beware of unfenced vertical shafts, which are practically invisible until you're on your way down – always look where you're going and never step backwards. Yowah has bore water, fuel and a **caravan park** (Ⓣ07/4655 4953; cabins ❶).

Two hundred kilometres southwest of Cunnamulla on minor roads, **Currawinya National Park** (Ⓦwww.epa.qld.gov.au) features lakes, wetlands and associated wildlife, in contrast to the semi-arid land more typical of the region. One animal to benefit is the highly endangered **bilby**, which, with its long ears and nose, looks like a cross between a rabbit and a bandicoot. Feral cats, rabbits, and grazing cattle have brought the bilby close to extinction, but a recently completed **fence** at Currawinya will keep all these pests out, allowing the new bilby population – reintroduced from the QPWS fauna centre in Charleville – to prosper. You can **camp** at Currawinya, but check on road conditions and practicalities with the QPWS ranger first (Ⓣ07/4655 4001). Past Currawinya is the tiny border town of **Hungerford**, where you can stock-up on fuel and groceries at the *Royal Mail Hotel*. From here it's a 200-kilometre run southeast on a largely unsealed road to Bourke.

Quilpie and the road to the Dig Tree

QUILPIE is a compact, dusty farming community 200km west of Charleville. The **tourist office** (Mon–Fri 8am–5pm, Sat & Sun 10am–4.30pm, closed Nov–March; ⓣ07/4656 2166, ⓦwww.quilpie.qld.gov.au) is on Brolga Street, and other amenities include a supermarket, baker, butcher and a fuel depot. The *Channel Country* **caravan park** is at 21 Chipu St (ⓣ07/4656 2087; cabins ❶) and there are also **beds** at the *Quilpie Motor Inn* (ⓣ07/4656 1277; ❹). The *Imperial Hotel* serves evening **meals** between 6 and 7.30pm, and there are a couple of cafés in town, which close at about 5.30pm.

As there are few signposts, a **map** is essential if you plan to drive from Quilpie to the Dig Tree at Nappa Merrie, 50km from Innamincka, over the border in South Australia. The last place to get fuel on the 490-kilometre, largely unsealed route lies an hour west of Quilpie at **EROMANGA**, a maintenance depot with a population of eighty souls whose *Royal Hotel* (ⓣ07/4656 4845; ❶) offers beer, food, information, and four **motel rooms**. From here you head across the stony plains above the huge **gas and oil** reserves of the Cooper Basin, past the cattle stations of Durham Downs and Karmona, lonely "nodding donkeys" and unaccountably healthy-looking droughtmaster cattle, to the **Dig Tree** on **Cooper Creek**.

The Burke and Wills saga

In 1860 the government of Victoria, then Australia's richest state, decided to sponsor a lavish expedition to make the first south to north crossing of the continent to the Gulf of Carpentaria. Eighteen men, twenty camels (shipped, along with their handlers, from Asia) and over twenty tons of provisions started out from Melbourne in August, led by **Robert O'Hara Burke** and **William John Wills**. Problems had already begun by the time the party reached Cooper Creek in December: Burke had impatiently left the bulk of the expedition and supplies lagging behind and raced ahead with a handful of men to establish a base camp on Cooper Creek. Having built a stockade, Burke and Wills started north, along with two other members of their team (Gray and King), six camels, a couple of horses and food for three months. Four men remained at camp, led by William Brahe, waiting for the rest of the expedition to catch up. In fact, most of the supplies and camels were dithering halfway between Cooper Creek and Melbourne, unsure of what to do next.

As Burke and Wills failed to keep a regular diary, few details of the "rush to the Gulf" are known. They were seen by **Kalkadoon Aborigines** following the Corella River into the Gulf, where they found that vast salt marshes lay between them and the sea. Disappointed, they left the banks of the Bynoe (near present-day Normanton) on February 11, 1861, and headed back south. Their progress slowed by the wet season, they killed and ate the camels and horses as their food ran out. Gray died after being beaten by Burke for stealing flour; remorse was heightened when they staggered into the Cooper Creek stockade on April 21 to find that, having already waited an extra month for them to return, Brahe had decamped that morning. Too weak to follow him, they found supplies buried under a tree marked "Dig", but failed to change the sign when they moved on, which meant that when the first rescue teams arrived on the scene, they assumed the explorers had never returned from the Gulf. Trying to walk south, the three reached the **Innamincka** area, where Aborigines fed them fish and nardoo (water fern) seeds, but by the time a rescue party tracked them down in September, only King was still alive. The full, sad tale of their trek is expertly told by Alan Moorehead in his classic work *Cooper's Creek*, a book well worth tracking down in your library (see "Books").

The site of Burke and Wills' stockade (see box on p.593), Depot Camp 65, is a beautiful shaded river bank alive with pelicans and parrots, and it's hard to believe that anyone could have starved to death nearby. The Dig Tree is still standing and protected by a walkway, but the three original blaze marks reading "BLXV, DIG 3FT NW, DEC 6 60-APR 21 61" have been cemented over to keep the tree alive. Burke's face was carved into the tree on the right by John Dickins in 1898, and is still clearly visible.

Pressing on, you'll be relieved to know that **Innamincka**'s pub is only 50km away at the top of the Strzelecki Track in South Australia.

Quilpie to Birdsville

The long road from Quilpie west to Birdsville is a relatively easy journey, manageable in good conditions without a 4WD, though depth markers along the road give an idea of how saturated this **Channel Country** becomes after rain. First stop is **WINDORAH**, a limp settlement of a dozen buildings offering fuel, a post office and an amazingly well-provisioned store. The *Western Star Hotel* (☎07/4656 3166; ④) is hard to pass by for a cold drink and a look at its collection of old photos; they also have tidy air-conditioned **rooms** and might let you **camp** out the back.

Ruins of the John Costello hotel lie 80km further on towards Betoota, opposite a windmill. Tired of riding 30km every morning to round up his stockmen from the bar, the manager of a nearby station had the local liquor licence transferred from the JC to his homestead in the 1950s. He pulled the roof off the hotel for good measure, and there's now little left beyond the foundations and some posts.

BETOOTA, 220km west of Windorah, is also on the verge of crumbling back into the dust, only coming to life once a year, in September, for the races and gymkhana. You can camp here at Brown's Creek, near the now defunct century-old adobe hotel. Beyond Betoota the country turns into a rocky, silent plain, with circling crows and wedge-tailed eagles the only signs of life, and it's hard to imagine what the occasional fenceline or grid is keeping apart. The red sand dunes visible on the horizon are the outer edges of the Simpson Desert. Driving can be hazardous here – you'll pass plenty of wrecks and shredded tyres – but with care (and good luck), the Diamantina River and Birdsville are just three hours away.

Birdsville and beyond

Famous for the **horse races** on the first weekend in September, when a few thousand beer-swilling spectators pack out the dusty little settlement, at other times **BIRDSVILLE** is something of an anticlimax, a handful of buildings where only the hotel and roadhouses seem to be doing business. But unless you've flown in, you'll probably be glad simply to have arrived intact. The **caravan park** (☎07/4656 3214; cabins ①) comprises a large patch of scrub by the creek with an amenities block, or you can camp for free along the artesian overflow, where huge flocks of raucous corellas seem to justify the township's name – though it's actually a corruption of "Burt's Ville", after the first storekeeper. Given the lack of alternatives, don't be surprised to find the comfy accommodation at the *Birdsville Hotel* full (☎07/4656 3244, Ⓦwww.theoutback.com.au; ④); during race weekend, all beds are reserved for the bar staff anyway, so you have to camp. For more on the **race weekend** check out Ⓦwww.birdsvilleraces.com, which gives a good breakdown of what to expect: alcohol and ponies, in that order – the hotel trades over 50,000 cans of beer in just two nights. **Provisions** and snacks can be bought from the general store. If you're organizing your own food, prepare the next day's meals after dark when the flies have settled down. You owe yourself at least one **drink** in the hotel's mighty bar; order by 5.30pm if you want a full evening meal – the "seven-course takeaway" is a pie and a six-pack.

The **Wirrarri Information Centre** (Mon–Fri 8.30am–4.30pm; ⓣ07/4656 3300, ⓔwirrari.centre@bigpond.com) on Billabong Boulevard will give you the lowdown on the state of the various Outback tracks if you're planning to use them, or ask at the **fuel station** (ⓣ07/4656 3236) across from the hotel. The Information Centre can also direct you to another tree blazed by Burke and Wills across the Diamantina, otherwise hard to locate among the scrub, or to attractions in town such as the old hospital. Originally built as a hotel and now just a stone shell, it operated as the original Australian Inland Mission between 1923 and 1927. The **Birdsville Working Museum** (daily 8am–6pm; $6; ⓣ07/4656 3259), as its name suggests, is more than just a collection of old stuff: all the exhibits, from petrol pumps and farm machinery to a complete blacksmith's shop, are fully restored and regularly operated.

Outside Birdsville, 14km north on the Bedourie road, there's a stand of slow-growing, old and very rare **Waddi trees**. They're about five metres tall and resemble sparse conifers wrapped in prickly feather boas with warped, circular seed pods. The wind blowing through the needles makes an eerie noise like the roar of a distant fire. For something more dramatic, head out west 33km to **Big Red**, at the start of the Simpson Desert crossing. Simpson's largest dune may seem unimpressive from below, but your opinion will change radically if you walk up or try to plant a 4WD on the top. If you're having a hard time getting up the long western face, there is a less steep track immediately on the right, which has a couple of quick turns near the summit. Two-wheel-drive vehicles can often reach the base (check with the police before setting off) and it's worth it to see the dunes, flood plains and stony gibber country (red desert, covered with loose stone) on the way.

North of Birdsville the next substantial settlement, Mount Isa, is a lonely 700km further on, with fuel available about every 200km. Those heading **west across the Simpson Desert** to Dalhousie Springs in South Australia need a Desert Parks Pass ($90) from the Birdsville QPWS office on Jardine Street (ⓣ07/4656 3272). Feasible in any sound vehicle during a dry winter, the 520-kilometre **Birdsville Track** heads from the racecourse down to Marree in South Australia (see p.894).

Rockhampton to Winton

Heading west from Rockhampton, the **Capricorn** and **Landsborough highways** run through the heart of central Queensland to Winton and ultimately Mount Isa. There's a lot to see here – just a couple of hours from the coast you'll find magical scenery atop the forested, sandstone plateau of the **Blackdown Tablelands**, while the town of **Emerald** offers the chance of seasonal farm work, and is also a gateway to Carnarvon Gorge and the **Gemfields**' sapphire mines. Continuing inland, both **Barcaldine** and **Longreach** are historically important towns, the latter hosting the archetypal Outback museum in the **Stockman's Hall of Fame**. Further west, **Winton** sits surrounded by a timeless, harsh orange landscape, with close access to some remote bush, unexpectedly imprinted with a dramatic set of dinosaur footprints at **Lark Quarry**.

Buses connect Rockhampton with Winton, and all main-town settlements west of Barcaldine are also on the Brisbane to Mount Isa bus run. Alternatively, you can catch the twice-weekly *Spirit of the Outback* **train** from Rockhampton as far as Longreach.

Into the Northern Highlands

As you move inland, the coastal humidity is left behind and the gently undulating landscape becomes baked instead of steamed. Passing the white rubble moonscape atop **Mount Hay** (36 km west of Rockhampton), where you can stay at the van park and fossick for agates, the road loops over low hills before adopting a pattern that becomes ever more familiar – straight for miles and then an unexpected bend. Bottle trees, with their bulbous, thick grey trunks and spindly, thinly leaved branches, herald the drier climate. Gradually, the deep-blue platform of the **Blackdown Tablelands** emerges from the horizon and, by the time you reach **Dingo**, dominates the landscape. Dingo is somewhere to stock up – there's a hotel, van park, fuel station and store, and a bronze monument to the town's namesake.

The Blackdown Tablelands

Floating 600m above the heat haze, the **Blackdown Tablelands**' gum forests, waterfalls and escarpments are a delight, a scenic refuge from the dry, flat lands below. A corrugated, unsealed twenty-kilometre access road is signposted on the highway, 11km from Dingo. National park campsite bookings can be made through the QPWS in Rockhampton (61 Yeppoon Rd; ⓣ07/4936 0511) or Emerald, or with the local **ranger** (ⓣ07/4986 1964, ⓕ4986 1325). Outside school holidays you could well have the place to yourself. There's no public transport into the park, but call in advance and catch the Greyhound Australia bus to Dingo, and **Namoi Hills Cattle Station** (ⓣ07/4935 9121, ⓕ4935 9234), set at the base of the tablelands, will pick you up at the drop-off point on the highway. They offer accommodation-and-meal packages, run tours round the station and onto the tablelands and regularly cater to the tour-bus crowd – phone ahead for costs and to check which days are booked if you want peace and quiet.

The access road from the highway runs flat through open scrub to the base of the range. The climb upwards is steep, twisting and slippery, as "pea gravel" puts in an appearance. Views over a haze of eucalyptus woodland are generally blocked by the thicker forest at the top of the plateau, but at **Horseshoe Lookout** there's a fabulous view north and, after rain, **Two Mile Falls** rockets over the edge of the cliffs. From here the road widens and runs past Mimosa Creek **campground** ($4 per person per night), dead-ending at the **Rainbow Falls** car park. The campground is excellent, shaded by massive stringybark trees with tank water, tables, toilets, fire pits and a creek to bathe in. At night the air fills with the sharp scent of woodsmoke, and the occasional dingo howls in the distance – with a torch, you might see **greater gliders** or the more active brushtail possum. Watch out for pied currawongs (crows) that raid unattended tables, tents and cars for anything, edible or not. Temperatures can reach 40°C on summer days, and drop below zero on winter nights.

Walks in the park include the short trip to **Officers Pocket**, a moist amphitheatre of ferns and palms with the facing cliffs picked out yellow and white in the late afternoon; a **circuit track** along Mimosa Creek, past remains of cattle pens and stock huts, to some beautifully clear **ochre stencils** of hands and weapons made by Gungaloo Aborigines over a century ago; and the park's finest scenery at **Rainbow Falls**, 6km past the campsite. At its glorious best around dawn, the track to the falls leads from the car park through an eerie gum forest to the top of the gorge, then follows around to where the creek seeps down steps into the greenery. From the edge you can spy on birds in the rainforest beneath and explosive thumps from below signal rock wallabies tearing across ledges hardly big enough for a mouse. A long staircase descends into a cool world of spring-fed gardens, ending on a large shelf about halfway into the gorge where Rainbow Falls sprays from above into a wide, clear pool. It may be pretty, but the water's paralyzingly cold; for a warmer dip, climb back up the stairs and follow the path to the top of the falls, where the creek runs in full sun and the bed has handy, bath-sized holes to sit in.

Emerald and around

The road west of Dingo crosses the lower reaches of the **Bowen Basin coalfields** at **Blackwater** then moves into **cotton country**, signalled by fluffy white tailings along the roadside around **YAMALA**, where you can take a tour of a working **cotton gin** (by appointment ⓣ07/4982 3888).

EMERALD is a misleadingly named place. This close to the Gemfield towns of Sapphire and Rubyvale, you'd think its origins could be traced to precious stones, but in fact the area was named Emerald Downs by a surveyor who saw the grassland here, atypically rich and green after heavy rains. A dormitory town for the Bowen Basin coal **mines** to the north, and set at the junction of routes north to Mackay and south to Carnarvon Gorge, Emerald is a busy place at the heart of a soundly productive district: the rich soil supports sunflowers, citrus trees, grape vines, lychees and rockmelons, all of which attract swarms of seasonal **fruit-pickers**. Despite being over a hundred years old, the town appears quite modern due to rebuilding after a series of disastrous fires in the 1950s.

Most essential services are on the Capricorn Highway, here called **Clermont Street**, where the main feature is the pristine train station, built in 1901 and restored in 1986. One road back from this is Egerton Street, where 250-million-year-old fossil tree trunks outside the town hall are preserved in great detail, right down to the texture of the bark. The **tourist office** (Mon–Sat 9am–5pm, Sun 10am–2pm; ⓣ07/4982 4142, ⓦwww.centralhighlandstourism.org.au) at the west end of Clermont Street has leaflets on local attractions. At the other end is the **bus station** for Emerald Coaches (ⓣ07/4982 4444), who run services to Longreach, Mackay and Rockhampton. **Accommodation** is plentiful, though during the April harvest or November cotton-chipping season there may be very little room available. The *Central Inn* (ⓣ07/4982 0800; ❶), near the station on Clermont Street, has a big kitchen, simply furnished rooms, and offers good advice for either farm work or visiting the Gemfields; the *Meteor Motel* (ⓣ07/4982 1166, ⓦwww.emeraldmeteormotel.com.au; ❹) on the corner of Opal and Egerton streets has a pool and a good steak restaurant; and the *Explorers Inn Motel* (ⓣ07/4982 2822; ❹) is in a quiet spot at the edge of town – it's newer than the rest with comfortable, well-appointed rooms and a saltwater pool.

South to Springsure

Ten kilometres south of Emerald, **Lake Maraboon** has been created by the Fairbairn Dam as the region's main water supply, though this being Australia you can also indulge in water sports, fishing and bird-watching here. All modern amenities and **accommodation** are provided by the *Lake Maraboon Holiday Village* (Ⓣ07/4982 3677, Ⓦwww.lakemaraboonresort.com.au, cabins ❶), which has fuel, a store (8am–6pm), a **restaurant** and a grassed camping area, which is pleasantly situated among trees by the lake.

The Carnarvon Gorge lies a further 200km or so south via the town of **SPRINGSURE**, set below the dramatic orange cliffs of Mount Zamia, also known as Virgin Rock – though weathering since it was named means you can barely see the likeness of the Madonna and Child. If you wind up here for the night, the *Zamia Motel* (Ⓣ07/4984 1455; ❶) has comfortable **rooms** and a **café**. It's worth pausing in the area to detour 10km southwest to **Rainworth Fort** (Mon–Wed & Fri 9am–2pm, Sat & Sun 9am–5pm; $6), to see how Aborigines put up a strong resistance to this district being settled. The fort is a squat stockade of basalt blocks and corrugated iron built by settlers for protection after "the **Wills Massacre**", when on October 17, 1861, Aboriginal forces stormed Cullin-la-ringo station and killed nineteen people in apparent retaliation for the slaughter of a dozen Aborigines by a local squatter. White response was savage, spurred on by vigilantes and a contingent of Native Troopers – newspapers reported that "a great massacre has been made among the blacks of the Nogoa [river district]". The fort, and newer structures of Cairdbeign School and Homestead at the same site, house a few relics of the period. Back on the Carnarvon road, it's 70km from Springsure to **Rolleston**, the last source of fuel, supplies and accommodation before the Carnarvon Gorge.

The Gemfields

The country an hour west of Emerald is sparse and always hot, the scrub interrupted only by ugly cleared patches covered in rubble, from mining operations. This wasteland masks one of the richest **sapphire fields** in the world and with hard work, the chances of finding some are good – though you're unlikely to get rich. The easiest fields to reach are the **Anakie Fields**, with facilities at Anakie, Sapphire and Rubyvale. Anakie township is off the highway about 45km from Emerald, Sapphire is 9km north of Anakie, and Rubyvale a further 8km north. Though well worked, the Anakie Fields are the best place for the newcomer to pick up tips; old hands proceed directly to **the Willows** (see p.600), 27km west of Anakie along the Capricorn Highway.

ANAKIE (a local Aboriginal word for "permanent water") has no gemfields itself, but gave its name to those at Sapphire and Rubyvale. Unusually pretty, it comprises a **van park** (Ⓣ & Ⓕ07/4985 4142; cabins ❶) with hot showers by the waterhole and a small shop open every day, backing onto a **pub**, post office and store. The **Gemfields Information Centre** (daily 8am–6pm; Ⓣ07/4985 4525, Ⓦwww.bigsapphire.com.au) near the highway has fuel, licences, rough maps and advice.

In contrast, the country around **SAPPHIRE** looks like a war zone. You'll find a post office and houses scattered along the road and a section of **Retreat**

Creek, where the first gems were found. *Sunrise Cabins* (☎07/4985 4281; ❶) has cabins and tent sites across the road from the medical centre, in sight of the creek. *Blue Gem Caravan Park* (☎07/4985 4162; ❶) has a **store**, fuel and fast food, or try a meal at *Thai & Chinese* next door. Towards Rubyvale is Pat's Gem Park (☎07/4985 4544) with a café, jewellery, craft displays and **fossicking lessons** for beginners. Forever Mine (☎07/4985 4616), a little further along Rubyvale Road, charges a seemingly steep $50 to fossick, though for this you get a tractor-scoop (about four buckets of wash) to pick through.

RUBYVALE has several shops, service stations and a few **mines** to look around. Tour groups tend to visit Miner's Heritage (daily 9am–5pm; $7), but equally interesting is Bobby Dazzler (daily 9am–5pm; $6), on the hill as you

Gem mining

Gems were first discovered in 1870 near Anakie, but until Thai buyers came onto the scene a century later operations were low-key, and even today there are still solo fossickers making a living from their claims. Formed by prehistoric volcanic actions and later dispersed along waterways and covered by sediment, the **zircons**, **rubies** and especially **sapphires** found here lie in a layer of gravel above the clay base of ancient riverbeds. This layer can be up to 15m down so gullies and dry rivers, where nature has already done some of the excavation for you, are good places to start digging.

Looking for surface gems, or **specking**, is best after rain, when a trained eye can see the stones sparkle in the mud. It's erratic but certainly easier than the alternative – **fossicking** – which requires a pick, shovel, sieve, washtub full of water and a canvas sack before even starting (this gear can be rented at all of the fields). Cut and polished, local zircons are pale yellow, sapphires pale green or yellow to deep blue, and rubies are light pink, but when they're covered in mud it's hard to tell them from gravel, which is where the washing comes in: wet gems glitter like fragments of coloured glass.

You have to be extremely enthusiastic to spend a summer on the fields, as the mercury climbs steadily to 42°C, topsoil erodes and everything becomes coated in dust. The first rains bring floods as the sunbaked ground sheds water, and if you're here at this time you'll be treated to the sight of locals specking in the rain, dressed in Akubras and Drizabones and shuffling around like mobile mushrooms. Conditions are best as soon after the wet season as possible (around May), when the ground is soft and fresh pickings have been uncovered – not surprisingly, this is also the busiest period.

If this all seems like too much hard work, try a **gem park** such as Pat's, where they've done all the digging for you and supply all the necessary gear for about $10. All you have to do is sieve the wash, flip it onto the canvas and check it for stones. There's an art to sieving and flipping, but you're pretty sure to find something, since park owners lace the wash with rejects. Gem parks will also value and cut stones for you. Another break from the business end of a pick is to pay $5, take a **mine tour**, and see if the professionals fare any better (contact Sapphire Safaris ☎07/4985 4388). In some ways they do – the chilled air 5m down is wonderful – but the main difference is one of scale rather than method or intent.

You need a **fossicker's licence**, available from shops and gem parks, which allows digging in areas set aside for the purpose or on no-man's-land. The $5.55 licence is valid for one month and gives you no rights at all other than to keep what you find and to camp at fossick grounds. To stake a claim and keep others away you need a **Miner's Right** from the field officer in Emerald (Department of Minerals and Energy, Clerana Centre, Clermont St; ☎07/4982 4011). This also carries obligations to restore the land to its original state and maintain it for two years after quitting the site.

approach town. The ground beneath each new development here has to be mined first; outdoor tennis courts and the surfaced road were built only after years of wrangling over whether the ground had given up all its treasures. Rubyvale also seems to be the place to pick up on apocryphal stories, such as the one about the largest star sapphire ever found being used as a doorstop. You'll hear plenty more during the annual **August Gemfest** which includes, in odd-numbered years, a **Wheelbarrow Race**. Here, in imitation of the first pioneering miners, all-comers push their one-wheeled transport, laden with pick and shovel, up the eighteen-kilometre track from Anakie to Rubyvale, pausing only at Sapphire to take on board a bucket of dirt. There's fuel, a general store and a good **van park** with campsites and cabins in Rubyvale (Ⓣ07/4985 4118; cabins ❶). The *New Royal Hotel* is a smart stone and timber building, with a mighty fireplace and tasty **food**.

The **Willows Gemfield**, part mining camp, part township, is the most recent designated fossicking area and fair-sized gems are rumoured to have been found. The immaculate *Willows Caravan Park* (Ⓣ & Ⓕ07/4985 5128; cabins ❶) is well shaded, has wangled a liquor licence and acts as a bank agent as well as supplying fuel and digging equipment. The gemfields are just down the track from the park.

Over the Range to Winton

Vistas from the rounded sandstone boulders at the top of the Great Dividing Range, west of the tiny railway stop of **Boguntungan**, reveal a dead-flat country beyond. Rivers flow to the Gulf of Carpentaria or towards the great dry lakes of South Australia, while unsealed roads run north to Clermont and south to Charleville. You'll notice an increase in temperature as flies appear from nowhere, tumbleweeds pile up on fences and trees never seem closer than the horizon. In terms of numbers, sheep are the dominant mammal in these parts, though there are some cattle and even a few people out here. Next stop on the road or rail line is the pleasant township of **Alpha**, where you can find fuel and a café or two, and **JERICHO**, one of the last places in Queensland with a **drive-in movie theatre**, which shows films on Saturday nights.

Barcaldine and Blackall

The only place of any size on the way to Longreach is **BARCALDINE**, 300km west of Emerald, an unassuming grid of quiet streets belying an important niche in Australian history. It was near here during the 1885 drought that geologists first tapped Queensland's **artesian water**, revolutionizing Outback development. The town further secured its place in history during the 1891 **shearers' strike** which – though a failure itself – ultimately led to the **formation of the Labor Party**. On the highway, outside the station which became the focus of the dispute, is a granite monument – sculpted to resemble the tips of a pair of shears – to shearers arrested during the strike. Right next to it, the sagging silver trunk of the **Tree of Knowledge**, a rallying point for shearers, struggles gamely to improve on its 170 years.

The **Australian Workers' Heritage Centre** (Mon–Sat 9am–5pm, Sun 10am–5pm; $12) is unmissable underneath a yellow and blue marquee on Ash Street. With an expanding collection of displays concentrating on the history of the workers' movement after the shearers' strike, as well as videos, artefacts and plenty of sepia-tinted photos covering themes including Outback women and Aboriginal stockmen, the museum acts as a useful counterpart to Longreach's Stockman's Hall of Fame. On the highway, the **tourist office** (Mon–Fri 8.30am–4.30pm; Ⓣ07/4651 1724) will direct you to other attractions such as the self-styled **Mad Mick's Funny Farm** (open most mornings April–Sept, or by arrangement Ⓣ07/4651 1172; adults $10, children $7), which has been restored to its early-twentieth-century condition and is inhabited by friendly, hand-reared animals; admission includes a ride in a Model-T Ford and tea and damper. For a closer look at Outback caves, waterholes, and **Aboriginal art** – much of it on private property – with a tall tale or two thrown in, contact Artesian Country Tours (Ⓣ07/4651 2211, Ⓦwww.artesiancountrytours.com.au). Their day-long "Aramac & Graceville" **tour** (Wed & Sat; $135 including all transport, lunch and tea) is highly recommended.

Banks and other services are mostly on Box Street, which runs south off the highway. **Accommodation** options include the *Ironbark Inn* (Ⓣ07/4651 2311; ❶), an "Outback-style" motel with attached steakhouse, *Barcaldine Motel* (Ⓣ07/4651 1244; ❶) and *Homestead Van Park* (Ⓣ07/4651 1308; cabins ❶), all on Box Street. Barcaldine has a disproportionate number of hotels, probably due to the hot summers – the *Artesian*, *Commercial* and *Union* hotels are three highway establishments all offering cold **drinks** and pub **meals**.

Blackall

One hour south of Barcaldine on the Landsborough Highway (and covered by Brisbane to Mount Isa buses), a sign at **BLACKALL** welcomes you to Merino Country. It was near here in 1892 that **Jackie Howe** fleeced 321 sheep in under eight hours using hand shears, a still-unbroken record. If you want to visit a **sheep station** to see modern shearers in action, it can be arranged by the **tourist office** (daily 9am–noon & 1–5pm; Ⓣ07/4657 4637), just off Shamrock Street on Short Street. There's more on the industry at the steam-driven **woolscour** (the plant where the freshly sheared fleeces are vigorously washed and cleaned), built in 1908 and in operation for seventy years; it has been restored recently and has guides on hand to show you around (daily 8am–4pm; $9.90).

In town, you could also track down the famous **black stump**, a surveying point used in pinpointing Queensland's borders in the nineteenth century and now the butt of many jokes; the original stump has been replaced by a more interesting fossilized one. Otherwise, pass time at the new **artesian spa** (Mon–Fri 6–10am & 2.30–6pm, Sat & Sun 11–6pm; $1.50), a large pool along the line of Mitchell's, at the town's Aquatic Centre on Salvia Street. Around 100km southwest of Blackall, **Idalia National Park** preserves one of Queensland's last groups of yellow-footed rock wallabies in the wild, though these can be seen more easily at the fauna park in Charleville, if you're heading that way. For details of access to Idalia, and possible guided **night tours** of the park, contact the ranger on Ⓣ07/4657 7333.

Blackall town sits on the banks of the often dry (but occasionally five-metre-deep) **Barcoo River**. Two-hundred-metre-long Shamrock Street, shaded by palms and bottle trees, is the main road on which you'll find banks, supplies and a few **places to eat** – if your dress is reasonably smart you can savour good food at the *Blackall Club*. The most central **places to stay** are the smart *Acacia Motor Inn* (Ⓣ07/4657 6022; ❹), on Shamrock Street, or at *Blackall Caravan Park* (Ⓣ07/4657 4816; cabins ❶) on Hart Lane, where you can yarn with other travellers around a huge campfire and be fed pot roasts, billy tea and damper for an extra fee. Long-distance **bus tickets** are available from Blackall Travel (Ⓣ07/4657 4422).

Longreach

LONGREACH, 110km west of Barcaldine and right on the Tropic of Capricorn, is different from other western towns – it's doing more than surviving. This is mainly due to the Stockman's Hall of Fame, an ambitious museum which pulls in busloads of tourists. Yet even before the museum, Longreach was an enterprising settlement with a firm place in history. Ever since the discovery of artesian water it has been a stronghold of cattle- and sheep-farming, but it really took off as the original headquarters of **Qantas** and is now home to a museum tracing the company's history.

On the highway 2km north of the town centre, the **Stockman's Hall of Fame** (daily 9am–5pm; $20; Ⓦwww.outbackheritage.com.au) is a masterpiece not just in architectural design – it's a blend of aircraft hangar and cathedral – but in being an encyclopedia of the Outback right in its heart. Since opening in 1988 its success has silenced critics, who underestimated the Outback's widespread appeal. A minor complaint might be that the displays themselves are fairly ordinary, but once you're here the Hall of Fame has achieved its dual aim of bringing people out west and providing background to the development of a vast portion of Australia.

Inside the museum, the Outback is romanticized through videos, slide shows, photographs and exhibits, but this isn't just another local museum where anything more than five years old is shown for its own sake. History starts in the Dreamtime and moves on, via a directory of those on the First Fleet (see "Contexts"), to early explorers and pioneers (including a large section on women in the Outback), before ending with personal accounts of life in the bush. Among more day-to-day features are some offbeat selections; if you thought barbed wire was just something to get stuck on, then check out the collection here, which has over a hundred types from the old hook design to modern razor wire. You'd be hard pushed not to find something of interest in the museum, be it boxing kangaroos, rodeos, bark huts or tall stories. The library and exhibitions by Outback artists (displayed in the art gallery) are also worth a browse.

Adjacent to the Hall of Fame is the new **Qantas Founders Outback Museum** (daily 9am–5pm; museum $16, 747 tour $12, combined ticket $26; Ⓣ07/4658 3737, Ⓦwww.qfom.com.au), whose prized possession is a decommissioned Qantas jumbo jet that can be viewed on a guided tour (booking advisable). An original 1922 hangar forms part of the exhibition, which also includes a beautiful collection of classic advertising posters.

Qantas

There's always been contention between Longreach and Winton as to which was the birthplace of **Qantas** (the Queensland and Northern Territories Aerial Service). Though the company officially formed at Winton, the first joy-flights and taxi service actually flew from Longreach in 1921, pioneered by Hudson Fysh and Paul McGinness. Their idea – that an airline could play an important role by carrying mail and passengers, dropping supplies to remote districts and providing an emergency link into the Outback – inspired other projects such as the Flying Doctor Service. Though the company's headquarters moved to Brisbane in 1930, Qantas maintained their offices at Longreach until after World War II – during the war US Flying Fortresses were stationed here – by which time both the company and its planes had outgrown the town.

Practicalities

Longreach is a more active version of Barcaldine, with plenty of spruce old buildings and a further abundance of watering holes. The main drag is south off the highway along **Eagle Street**, where you'll find hotels, cafés, banks, a cinema and a well-stocked **supermarket**. The **airport** is off the highway between town and the Hall of Fame and **trains** terminate at the station at the junction of Galah Street and the highway. **Buses** set down on Eagle Street at Longreach Outback Travel Centre (Ⓣ07/4658 1776, Ⓦwww.lotc.com.au), which can arrange all tickets, as well as **tours** of nearby sheep stations ($40), and waterway **cruises** on a paddle-boat ($44). The **tourist office** (April–Oct Mon–Fri 9am–5pm, Sat & Sun 9am–1pm; Nov–March Mon–Fri 9am–4.30pm, Sat & Sun 9am–noon; Ⓣ07/4658 3555) is in a replica of Qantas's original office, on the corner of Eagle and Duck streets opposite the post office.

There are two **campsites**: *Gunnadoo Van Park* (Ⓣ07/4658 1781; cabins ❶), on Thrush Road looking across to the Hall of Fame, and *Longreach Caravan Park* (Ⓣ07/4658 1770; ❶) on Ibis Street. *Hallview Lodge*, 81 Wompoo St (Ⓣ07/4658 3777; ❶), is a friendly B&B, or you can indulge in **motel** comforts at the *Albert Park Motel* (Ⓣ07/4658 2411, Ⓕ4658 3181; ❹) on Hudson Fysh Drive, or *Longreach Motor Inn* (Ⓣ07/4658 2322; ❹) on Galah Street. For **meals**, the *Longreach RSL Club* on Duck Street welcomes visitors. You can dine in their inexpensive restaurant (daily 10am–3pm & 5.30–8.30pm) or just settle into a chair in the lounge bar. Of Eagle Street's half-dozen hotels, try the *Lyceum* for counter food, or *Starlight's Hideout Tavern* for meals and nightlife.

Winton and beyond

Scenery doesn't come blander than on the 173-kilometre-long Longreach to Winton stretch: your only job as a driver is to keep your foot down and stay awake as the car cruises the empty Mitchell Plains. At the far end, **WINTON** is a real frontier town, and an excellent base for exploring this corner of the Outback. Dust devils blow tumbleweeds down the streets, and the main change over the last fifty years is that 4WDs have superseded the horse as a means of getting around. As Queensland's largest cattle-trucking depot, Winton has a constant stream of road trains rumbling through it, and conversations in hotel bars tend to revolve around problems of stock management. Winton has its share of history too: Qantas was founded here in 1920 and **Waltzing Matilda**, that evergreen ballad, premiered at the *North Gregory Hotel*. The surrounding countryside is an eerie world of windswept plains and eroded **jump-ups** – flat-topped hills layered in orange, grey and red dust – complete with **opal deposits** at Opalton and a stunning set of **dinosaur footprints** at Lark Quarry.

Winton's central drag is **Elderslie Street**, where you'll find banks, a post office and service stations. If there's a film on, treat yourself to a session in the **open-air cinema**, complete with canvas seats and original projector, at the corner of Elderslie and Cobb streets; the café here stays open until after dark. A few doors down, next to the *North Gregory Hotel*, the immense wooden **Corfield & Fitzmaurice building** (Mon–Fri 9am–5pm, Sat 9am–12.30pm; $3) opened as a store in 1916 and now houses a vast collection of rocks and fossils from around the world, along with a life-size diorama of the Lark Quarry dinosaurs – garbage bins around town are also shaped as dinosaur feet.

Further down Elderslie Street, opposite a tepid swimming pool and bronze statue of the jolly swagman, the **Waltzing Matilda Centre** (daily 8.30am–5pm;

Waltzing Matilda

The first public performance of "Banjo" Paterson's ballad **Waltzing Matilda** was held in April 1895 at Winton's *North Gregory Hotel*, and has stirred up gossip and speculation ever since. Legend has it that **Christina MacPherson** told Paterson the tale of a swagman's brush with the law at the Combo Waterhole near Kynuna while the poet was staying with her family at nearby Dagwood Station. Christina wrote the music to the ballad, a collaboration which so incensed Paterson's fiancée, Sarah Riley, that she broke off their engagement. While a straightforward "translation" of the poem is easy enough – "Waltzing Matilda" was contemporary slang for tramping (carrying a bedroll or swag from place to place), "jumbuck" for a sheep, and "squatters" refers to landowners – there is some contention as to what the poem actually describes. The most obvious interpretation is of a poor tramp, hounded to death by the law, but first drafts of the poem suggest that Paterson – generally known as a romantic rather than a social commentator – originally wrote the piece about the arrest of a union leader during the shearers' strike, and later toned it down. Either version would account for the popularity of the poem, which was once proposed as the national anthem – Australians readily identify with an underdog who dares to confront the system.

$14; ⓣ07/4657 1466) has some unusual items, including an indoor billabong, a fine display of Aboriginal artefacts featuring an entire tree with a boomerang half-carved out of its trunk, and a bottle collection covering everything from poisons to schnapps. The centre also doubles as a **tourist office** and sorts out **tours** to local sights – check with them too about road conditions before visiting Opalton, Lark Quarry, or national parks. For some really ludicrous fun, the **Australian Crayfish Derby**, part of the Outback Festival held in September in odd-numbered years, has to be worth a look; the owner of the winning crustacean nets $1500, and the runner-up gets to eat all the competitors. Every April the **Waltzing Matilda Festival** involves a rodeo and arts events, attracting bush poets to compete with "Banjo" Paterson.

Winton's **accommodation** prospects include the *Matilda Country Tourist Park* (ⓣ07/4657 1607; cabins ❶) on Chirnside Street, about 700km from Elderslie Street where the Landsborough Highway kinks into town, the nearby neat and trim *Banjo Motel* (ⓣ07/4657 1213; ❶) on Manuka Street, and the *North Gregory Hotel* (ⓣ07/4657 1375; hotel rooms ❶, motel rooms ❶), which has en-suite and shared bathrooms as well as some basic budget beds (❶) in the old shearers' quarters. The *North Gregory* is also one of the best places to **eat** in town, with the early-opening *Twilight Café* opposite. Leaving, there are two **buses** daily in each direction along the Landsborough Highway towards Mount Isa and Brisbane; the Gift and Gem Centre on Elderslie Street is the pick-up point and sells **tickets**.

Bladensburg National Park, Opalton and Carisbrooke

South of Winton, a 120-kilometre-long unsealed road runs down through the beautifully stark jump-ups, spinifex scrub, grassland and thin woods of Bladensburg National Park to the mining settlement of Opalton. The borders of **Bladensburg National Park** start just 8km from town, from where a rough track – generally negotiable in a conventional vehicle in dry weather – runs 15km in to **Skull Waterhole**, named after the "dispersal" of the Goa Aborigines by the Native Mounted Police in the late 1800s. Despite this sad history it's an interesting spot, as the water attracts kangaroos, budgerigars and ring-necked parrots. A further 10km south, via a **bush campsite**, is the southern boundary of the

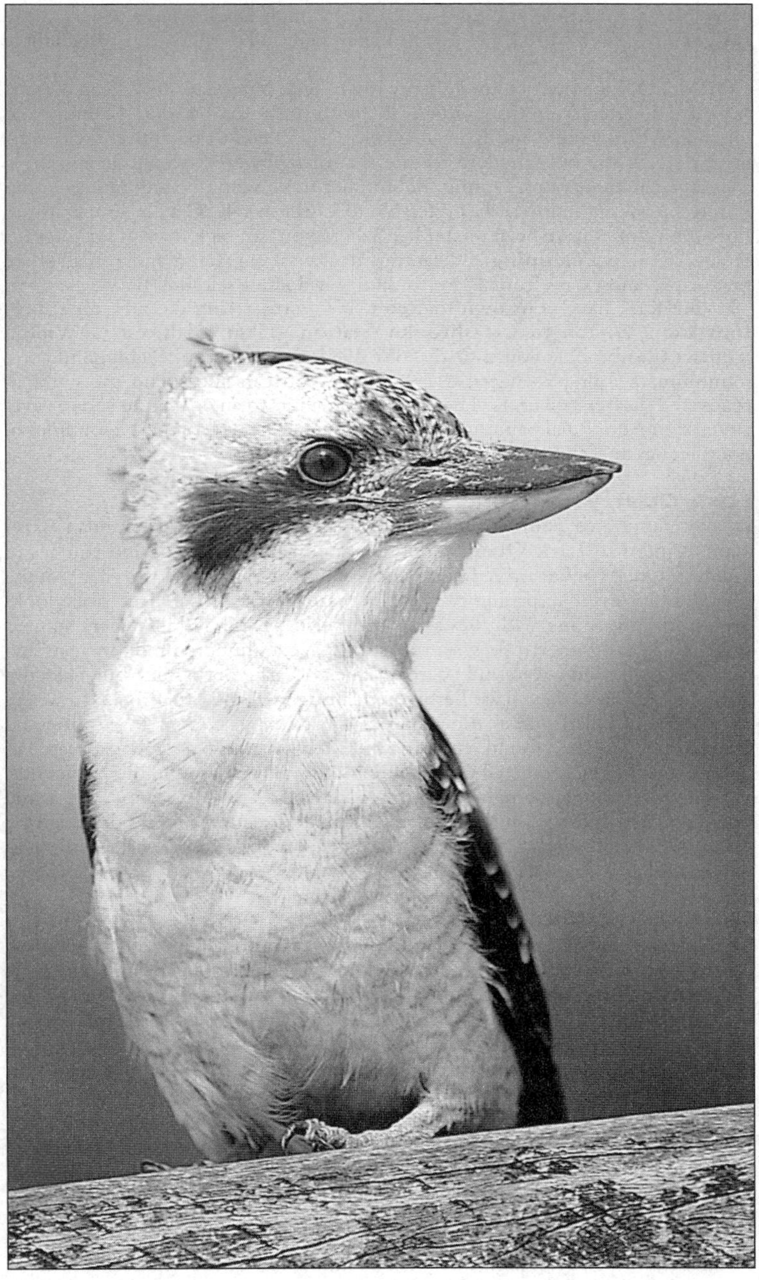

△ kookaburra

park, near a waterhole and the twenty-metre-high **Logan Falls**. Contact the **ranger** (Ⓣ07/4657 1192) before visiting and take all supplies, including ample drinking water, with you.

OPALTON is a multicultural shanty town, with Yugoslav and Czech miners, as well as deserters from Coober Pedy in South Australia, reworking century-old diggings with Chinese and Korean finance. You need to be entirely self-sufficient here, as the only modern feature is a solar-powered telephone and there isn't any drinking water. During the summer there won't be any miners either – hotels in Winton are easily preferable to Opalton's 40°C-plus temperatures. Fossicking zones have been established where you can pick over old tailings for scraps. There is a **camping** and caravan area, washing water, and a small **store** that's open most days from 10am to 2pm – it doesn't sell fuel, however.

If you don't have your own transport, it's worth seeing the area on a **day-tour** from Winton to **Carisbrooke Station**, 85km southwest of Winton (contact Carisbrooke Tours, Ⓣ07/4657 3984, Ⓔc.carisbrooke@bigpond.com; minimum of four passengers; $129), where you can also spend the night in renovated shearer's quarters. The trip includes visits to an opal mine and to caves covered in Aboriginal paintings – some abstract, others recognizable outlines of boomerangs and club-like nulla-nullas.

Lark Quarry

It takes about two hours to drive the 120km southwest on the Jundah Road from Winton to **Lark Quarry**, dodging kamikaze kangaroos and patches of bulldust. Once you've arrived there's no doubt that this is the rough heart of the Outback. Nor is it surprising to find **dinosaur remains** here: the place looks prehistoric, swarming with flies and surrounded by stubby hills where stunted trees and tufts of grass tussle with rocks for space. A hundred million years ago this was a shrinking waterhole across which a carnivorous dinosaur chased a group of various turkey-sized herbivores through the mud to a rockface where it caught and killed one as the others fled back past it. Over three thousand **footprints** have been found recording these few seconds of action, excavated in the 1970s and now protected by an awning and walkway around them. Indentations left by small, amazingly sharp, three-clawed feet – some very light as the prey panicked and ran on tiptoe – stream in all directions, while those left by the larger predator go only one way. Paths lead around to other, buried tracks where the chase ended.

West from Winton

The main route out of Winton follows the Landsborough Highway 340km northwest to Cloncurry, on the Townsville to Mount Isa road. Heading this way, the **Combo Waterhole**, 165km from Winton and just shy of Kynuna, provided the inspiration for "Banjo" Paterson's classic ballad "Waltzing Matilda". It's a fairly typical muddy soak, decorated by trees and beer cans, and with some solid stone weirs built at the start of the twentieth century by Chinese labourers. **KYNUNA**'s low-slung *Blue Heeler Hotel* (Ⓣ07/4746 8650; ❶) is also worth a stop, not least for its ice-cold beer. It's also possible to camp here. The other feature on the journey is the *Walkabout Creek Hotel* at **McKINLAY**, 75km past Kynuna, which you might recognize as the rowdy Outback pub in the film *Crocodile Dundee*. Since the film was shot, the whole building was moved 400m in order to make it more visible to passing tourists.

Heading due west of Winton, the Kennedy Developmental Road leads to Boulia, 367km away. The journey is a continuation of the Winton landscape, with fuel available every 150km and the chance to see the enigmatic **Min Min**

Light, an unexplained glowing oval reputedly seen bobbing around the bush at night. In case you miss it, thoughtful townspeople have erected a larger-than-life Min Min model. **BOULIA** consists of a hotel (☎07/4746 3144), van park and roadhouse. If you need a reason to visit, make it the annual **camel races** in July, when the town gets lively and inordinate quantities of beer are consumed. At quieter times of the year, drop in to the **Stonehouse Museum** (Mon–Fri 7am–5pm; $2) displaying regional finds, and the **Min Min Encounter Centre** (Mon–Fri 8.30am–5pm, Sat & Sun 9am–5pm; $12), a cross between a museum and sound-and-light show. Boulia's **tourist office** (daily 8.30am–6pm; ☎07/4746 3386) is here too, along with *Encounter's Café*, which claims to serve the Outback's best cappuccino – there's certainly no competition for a good many miles around. Some 200km southeast of Boulia, **Diamantina National Park** is a huge, pristine area with two **campsites**, rivers, waterholes, sand dunes, claypans, and heaps of wildlife, including **bilbies**. The park is very remote so come fully prepared and note that you might need 4WD – contact the **ranger** in Winton first (☎07/4652 7333).

From Boulia, Mount Isa is 300km north on bitumen, and Birdsville is 400km south on a mostly reasonable road. If you're really enjoying the ride, Alice Springs is 800km west on the Donohue and Plenty "highways" – a long stretch of dust and gravel. There's fuel every 250km or so, and track conditions improve once you're over the border into the NT.

Townsville to Lawn Hill

All the major settlements along the Townsville to Lawn Hill route are **mining** towns, spaced so far apart that precise names are redundant: **Mount Isa** becomes "the Isa", **Cloncurry** "the Curry", and **Charters Towers** "the Towers", as if nowhere else existed. Scattered across the vast tracts between are geological treasures waiting to be discovered, as well as traces of those who've tried before, and there's plenty to see as you head into the NT. Most people never stop to find out, grimly tearing along as fast as possible between Townsville and Three Ways along the Flinders and Barkly highways. It's a shame, because even if time is limited and you're relying on public transport, Charters Towers' century-old feel and Mount Isa's strange setting are worth a stopover. With the freedom of your own vehicle, there's untramped bush at the **Great Basalt Wall**, 80km west of Charters Towers, and **Porcupine Gorge**, north of Hughenden in the heart of dinosaur country, and the spectacular oasis of **Lawn Hill Gorge**, all a lifetime away from the coast's often banal spirit. With the highway forming the main link between Queensland and the NT, the major **bus lines** have at least daily services interstate between Mount Isa and Tennant Creek, or there's the twice-weekly *Inlander* **train** between Townsville and Mount Isa.

Gold country

There's little scenic variation over the two-hour journey from the coast to the heights of the inland range at the community of **Mingela**, but dry scrub at the top once covered seams of ore which had the streets of both **Charters Towers** and **Ravenswood** bustling with lucky-strike miners. Those times are long gone – though gold is still extracted from old tailings or sporadically panned from the creek beds – and the towns have survived at opposite extremes: connected by road and rail to Townsville, Charters Towers became a busy rural centre, while Ravenswood, half an hour south of Mingela, was just too far off the track and wasted to a shadow. Detours (☎07/4728 5311) runs day-trips from Townsville to one or the other for about $55.

Ravenswood

As the wind blows dust and dried grass around the streets between mine shafts and lonely old buildings, **RAVENSWOOD** fulfils ideas of what a ghost town should look like. Gold was discovered here in 1868 and within two years there were solid brick houses, a frenetic atmosphere and seven hundred miners on Elphinstone Creek working seams of gold, silver and lead ore. Every building on the main street was either a public house and dance house or a public house and general store.

The main attraction is to wander between the restored buildings, trying to imagine how the others must have looked. The curator of the **Court House Museum** (daily except Tues 10am–3pm; $2; ☎07/4770 2047 to book) gives entertaining **tours** of the museum, town and – with sufficient notice – current mining efforts. Built in 1879, the **post office** today doubles as the town's store and fuel supply. Unsurprisingly, the two most complete survivals are hotels, though how they both keep going with a scattered population of barely a hundred souls is anybody's guess. You'll probably end up in one as the day heats up; the *Railway* (☎07/4770 2144) seems to be the more popular, but though the *Imperial* (☎07/4770 2131; ❶) looks the worse for wear it has original wood panelling, mirrors and swing doors on the bar. Counter meals are available at either, while the *Imperial* also offers accommodation.

Charters Towers and around

Once Queensland's second-largest city, and often referred to in its heyday simply as "the World", **CHARTERS TOWERS** is a showcase of colonial-era architecture. An Aboriginal boy named **Jupiter Mosman** found gold here in 1871 and within twelve months three thousand prospectors had stripped the landscape of trees and covered it with shafts, chimneys and crushing mills. At first, little money was reinvested – the **cemetery** is a sad record of cholera and typhoid outbreaks from poor sanitation – but by 1900, despite diminishing returns, Charters Towers had become a prosperous centre. There's been minimal change since then and the population, now mainly sustained by cattle farming, has shrunk to about a third of what it was in its prime. Good times to visit are for the May Day weekend **Country Music Festival**, and the Easter **Rodeo**.

The town itself is worth about an hour of your time, with plenty of spruce old buildings along Gill and Mosman streets, including the pink-and-white headquarters of the *Northern Miner*, one of Queensland's oldest surviving newspapers on Gill Street, the classical elegance of the post office and the **World Theatre**, and the shaded country arcades outside the stores. The courtyard and glass roof at the former **Stock Exchange** and Assayer's Office now front some quiet shops and a lifeless **mining museum** (daily 9am–4pm; free). Next door, the solid facade of the town hall betrays its original purpose as a bank, which stored gold bars smelted locally, and the next bank along is now a grand facade for the World Theatre and Cinemas. Just down Mosman Street is the **Zara Clark Museum** (daily 10am–3pm; $4.40), housing an absorbing jumble of everything from old wagons to a set of silver tongs for eating frogs' legs. Further along the road there's plenty of shade under giant fig trees at **Lissner Park**, whose Boer

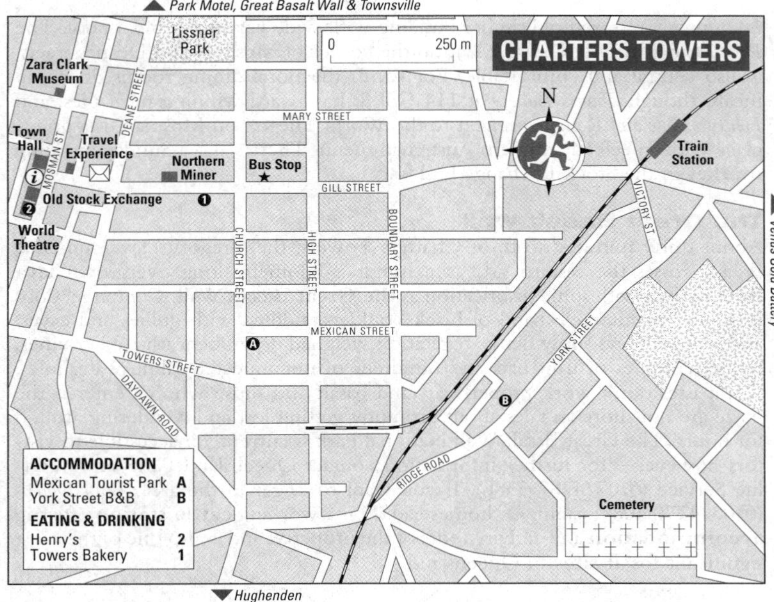

War memorial recalls stories of **Breaker Morant**, a local soldier executed by the British after shooting a prisoner.

The **Venus Gold Battery** (tours daily 10am & 2pm; $4.40), 5km out of town down Gill Street, is a fascinating illustration of the monumental efforts needed to separate gold from rock. Abandoned in 1972 after a century of operations, the battery is a huge, gloomy temple to the past, its machinery lying silent and piecemeal around the place. The intention is to restore it to full working order, presumably without recreating the actual conditions – it was a hideous place, a sweatbox filled with noxious fumes and noise. Ore was ground to a powder in one of the seven massive crushers, mixed with water and passed over a mercury screen. Any gold formed an amalgam and adhered to the mercury, which was then heated in a crucible to leave a pitted nugget and later remelted with flux to absorb any impurities. Sludge from the mercury screens was soaked in cyanide to leach out more gold, and then the cyanide was neutralized with sulphur and piled up outside. These mounds are now being reprocessed using modern methods to extract the last vestiges of the precious metal.

Practicalities

On the main Gill and Mosman streets, you'll find everything from supermarkets to banks. **Trains** stop at the far end of Gill Street and **buses** halfway along by the Caltex service station – **tickets** for either can be arranged through Travel Experience, 13 Gill St (Ⓣ07/4787 2622). The helpful **tourist office** (daily 9am–5pm; Ⓣ07/4752 0314) on Mosman Street, facing down Gill Street, has rough maps and advice on gold-panning **tours** in the area. For **accommodation**, the *Mexican Tourist Park* (Ⓣ07/4787 1161; on-site vans and cabins ❶), at the corner of Church and Mexican streets on the site of the once-busy Mexican Mine, is shaded and central. In tune with the local atmosphere is *York Street B&B* at 58 York St (Ⓣ07/4787 1028, Ⓔyorkstreetbb@httech.com.au;

❶), a nicely restored old timber building with wide verandahs and a pool. The *Park Motel* (Ⓣ07/4787 1022; ❶), on the corner of Mosman and Deane streets, is also central and comfortable. For **food**, the hotel dining rooms do cheap meals, though *Towers Bakery* at 114 Gill St has award-winning meat pies, and *Henry's Café and Restaurant*, next to the World Theatre on Mosman, is a pricey place with an eclectic modern Australian menu. There's also a Sunday morning **market** in the Stock Exchange building.

The Great Basalt Wall

About thirty minutes north of Charters Towers, the Gregory Developmental Road crosses the eastern side of a hundred-kilometre-long overgrown **lava flow** known with some justification as **the Great Basalt Wall**. Central sections form an impenetrable band of black boulders, riddled with gullies and caves, and aerial surveys show dense vegetation weighed down beneath rubber vines, hiding colonies of fruit bats and hundreds of unconnected saline waterholes. Compasses don't work properly around basalt and those who've entered the maze are not short on tales about promptly getting lost and wandering around for hours. The Great Basalt Wall National Park is currently inaccessible to visitors however – for further information contact Queensland Parks and Wildlife Service (Ⓣ07/4787 3388). If you want to linger in the area, *Bluff Downs* (Ⓣ07/4770 4084; cabins ❶, homestead ❻) is a working **cattle station** offering **accommodation** and activity tours of the property, and is also one of the most significant **fossil sites** in Queensland.

Dalrymple National Park

Dalrymple National Park, 46km north of Charters Towers and then 2.5km on a track, marks the site of the now-vanished **Dalrymple township**, founded in 1864 as the first official inland settlement in northern Australia. A gold-mining town, finds were rich enough to support five hotels during Dalrymple's very brief heyday. Completely demolished by a flood in 1870 however, today the remains include only the traces of pavements, foundations, and gravesites.

Dinosaur country

HUGHENDEN, 245km west of Charters Towers along the highway, looks big compared with some of the places you pass on the way there. A dozen wide streets, a supermarket, a couple of hotels and **banks** all conspire to make you feel that you've arrived somewhere. There are two places to spend time – the swimming pool on Resolution Street and the **Dinosaur Museum** and **information centre** (daily 9am–5pm; $3; Ⓣ07/4741 1021) on Gray Street. The display here focuses on the swamp-dwelling Muttaburrasaurus, bones of which were found south of town in 1963 and assembled into a ten-metre-long skeleton after souvenir hunters handed over pieces to the Queensland Museum in Brisbane. Though this family of dinosaurs was formerly believed to be vegetarian, Muttaburrasaurus' needle-like teeth have prompted a rethink about their possible diet. For **accommodation**, *Wrights Motel* (Ⓣ07/4741 1677, Ⓕ07/4741 1170; ❶) opposite the museum has reasonably priced rooms and a restaurant, and the *Rest Easi Motel* (Ⓣ & Ⓕ07/4741 1633; ❶), on the Flinders Highway to the west of the town centre, is quiet and also has camping facilities. *Pete's Country Café*, before the tracks on the other side of town, has good **burgers** and doubles as the **bus stop**, while *FJ Holden's Café* at 55 Brodie St is a 1950s-style diner complete with gingham tablecloths and Elvis memorabilia. Routes head out of Hughenden in all directions – aside from the highway west, there's the road north to Porcupine Gorge, or long stretches south to Winton or Longreach. You should fuel up before leaving town.

Porcupine Gorge is 70km north of Hughenden along the partially surfaced Kennedy Developmental Road, accessible only if you have your own vehicle (you can usually scrape by without a 4WD). A deep gash, completely invisible among the drab brown scrub until you're virtually in it, it's best seen at the start of the dry season (May to July) before the **Flinders River** stops flowing, when good swimming holes, beautifully coloured cliffs, flowering bottlebrush and banksia trees reward the effort of getting here. A **campsite** at the top of the gorge has limited cold water, toilets and nothing else. Look for wallabies on the walk into the gorge, which leads down steps and becomes an increasingly steep, rough path carpeted in loose stones. The white riverbed has been moulded by water into soft, elongated forms, curving into a pool below the orange, yellow and white bands of **Pyramid Rock**. This is the bush at its best – sandstone glowing in the afternoon sun against a deep-blue sky, with animal calls echoing along the gorge as the shadow of the gorge wall creeps over distant woods.

Richmond

More of the regional fossil record is on show 115km west of Hughenden along the highway at **RICHMOND**, whose **Fossil Museum** (daily 8.30am–4.45pm; $10) displays the petrified remains of hundred-million-year-old fish, long-necked elasmosaurs, and models of a kronosaur excavated in the 1920s by a team from Harvard University and now on show in the USA. Pride of the collection are a complete skeleton of a seal-like pliosaur – the most intact vertebrate fossil ever found in Australia – and the minmi ankylosaur, with its armour-plated hide.

Not many people hang around in Richmond, though it's by no means an unpleasant place – just very small. A roadside park makes a good spot to stretch your legs, with an original **Cobb & Co. coach** and views out across the Flinders River. There's **accommodation** at the *Richmond Lake View Caravan Park* (Ⓣ07/4741 3772; bunkhouse and cabins ❶), which also has tent sites and "backpacker" rooms with a communal kitchen ($40 for a twin share), or at *Entriken's Pioneer Motel* (Ⓣ07/4741 3188, Ⓔentrpion@tpq.com.au; ❶), opposite the museum. The fossil museum's **café** is the only one in town – otherwise head to the old wooden *Federal Palace Hotel* or one of the service stations for a feed.

Cloncurry and around

CLONCURRY, 280km west of Richmond, is caught between two landscapes, where the flat eastern plains rise to a rough and rocky plateau. Besides being the place where Australia's highest temperature (53.1°C) was recorded, Cloncurry offers glimpses into the mining history that permeates the whole stretch west to the larger and less personal settlement of Mount Isa. Copper was discovered here in 1867 but as the town lacked a rail link to the coast until 1908, profits were eroded by the necessity of transporting the ore by camel to Normanton. This meant that Cloncurry never reflected the quality of its mines – there are no traces of a wealthy past because there never was one. Even the current resurgence in mining hasn't had much effect on Cloncurry (aside from raising motel rates); miners are flown in from the coast to the mines, work their two-week shifts, then head home again, all without spending more than a couple of hours in town.

Buildings at the **Mary Kathleen Memorial Park Museum** (Mon–Fri 7am–4pm, Sat & Sun 9am–3pm; $5) were salvaged from Mary Kathleen, a short-lived uranium mining town between Cloncurry and Mount Isa. The museum is primarily of geological interest, a comprehensive catalogue of local ores, fossils and gemstones arranged in long cases, though Aboriginal tools and Burke's water bottle add some historical depth. The office gives out information on old mining camps and fossicking details if you feel inspired to try your luck hunting for garnets, copper and Maltese crosses (hard, reddish-brown staurolite crystals paired at right angles).

A positive side to Cloncurry's isolation is that it inspired the formation of the **Royal Flying Doctor Service**. Over on the corner of King and Daintree streets, John Flynn Place (Mon–Fri 7am–4pm, closed Dec–Feb; $8.50) is a monument to the man who pioneered the use of radio and plane to provide a "mantle of safety over the Outback". The exhibition explains how ideas progressed with technology, from pedal-powered radios to assistance from the young Qantas, resulting in the opening of the first Flying Doctor base in Cloncurry, in 1928. A combined Mary Kathleen and John Flynn ticket can also be purchased at either attraction ($12). A very different aspect of Cloncurry's past is also evident in the two foreign **cemeteries** on the outskirts of town. To the south of the highway, before you cross the creek on the way to Mount Isa, a hundred overgrown plots recall a brief nineteenth-century goldrush when the harsh conditions took a terrible toll on Chinese prospectors. Equally neglected are the unnamed graves of Afghanis at the north end of Henry Street, all aligned with Mecca. Afghanis were vital to Cloncurry's survival before the coming of the railway, organizing camel trains which carried the ore to Normanton whence it was shipped to Europe – a role now largely forgotten.

Practicalities

The highway runs through town as McIlwraith Street in the east, and **Ramsay Street** in the west. Most services – the usual banks, supermarket, half-dozen **bars** and a post office – are along Ramsay or the grid of streets immediately north. Cloncurry's **train station** is a couple of kilometres southeast of the centre, while **buses** drop off along Ramsay – you can buy **tickets** for either at Cloncurry Agencies, 45 Ramsay St (Ⓣ07/4742 1107). The best **campsite**, *Gilbert Park Tourist Village* (Ⓣ07/4742 2300; cabins ❶), is on the eastern edge of town off McIlwraith and has decent cabins. Otherwise, seek **accommodation** at the central *Wagon Wheel Motel* (Ⓣ07/4742 1866, Ⓔwagonwheelmotel@bigpond.com; ❶) on Ramsay Street, founded in 1867 with both older pub rooms and a new motel block, or the trendily eco-conscious *Gidgee Inn* (Ⓣ07/4742 1599, Ⓦwww.gidgeeinn.com.au; ❹) on McIlwraith Street, built from recycled timber and rammed earth. The latter also has a good restaurant, specializing in steak and seafood. The bars have counter meals, and *Cuppa's*, a café on Ramsay Street, is cool and spacious, and serves up strong coffee and good-value food. For entertainment, there's an **open-air cinema** one block north of Ramsay on Scarr Street, which screens films once or twice a week.

Moving on, the highway, buses and trains continue west for 118km to Mount Isa, while the **Burke Developmental Road** heads 380km north past forests of anthills and kapok trees to Normanton, via the one-pub settlement of **Quamby** (which also has races and an underwear-throwing competition in May), and the **Burke and Wills Roadhouse**. Aside from being a welcome break in the journey, with fuel pumps, a bar and canteen selling drinks, sandwiches and burgers, the roadhouse also marks the turning west on a sealed road to **Gregory Downs**, gateway to the oasis of Lawn Hill Gorge.

Onwards to Mount Isa: Mary Kathleen

The rough country between Cloncurry and Mount Isa is evidence of ancient upheavals which shattered the landscape and created the region's extensive mineral deposits. While the highway continues safely to Mount Isa past the **Burke and Wills monument** and the **Kalkadoon/Mitakoodi tribal boundary** at Corella Creek, forays into the bush will uncover remains of less fortunate mining settlements. About halfway to Mount Isa, a short and steadily crumbling road north to **MARY KATHLEEN** is marked with a small plaque. By all accounts, **uranium** was found here by accident when a car broke down; while waiting for help the driver and his friends tried fossicking and found ore. The two-street town was built in 1956 and completely dismantled in 1982 when export restrictions halted mining. Since then, once-manicured lawns have run riot, and an occasional bougainvillea and an unkempt row of casuarinas tangling along the access road are the only signs that there were gardens here – in a few years it will all have gone. About a kilometre past the old town the road becomes a dirt track and splits; a kilometre along the right fork a bumpy uphill track leads to the terraces of the open-cast **mine**, now reminiscent of a flooded Greek amphitheatre. On a cloudy day you can be sure that the alarming blue-green colour of the water is not simply a reflection of the sky. Locals maintain it's safe to swim here though, and some even claim health benefits.

Mount Isa and around

As the only place of consequence for 700km in any direction, the smokestacks, concrete paving and sterile hills at **MOUNT ISA** assume oasis-like qualities on arrival, despite being undeniably ugly. Though the novelty might have worn off by the time you've had a cold drink, the city has a few points to savour before heading on. There's evidence of the area's **Aboriginal heritage**, a couple of unusual **museums**, tours of the local mines, Australia's largest rodeo every August and last but not least, the fascinating situation and the community it has fostered.

The largest city in the world in terms of surface area – its administrative boundaries stretch halfway to Cloncurry – Mount Isa sits astride a wealth of zinc, silver, lead and copper, and owes its existence to these reserves and the need for a staging post for interstate travellers. The city's founding father was **John Miles**, who discovered ore in 1923, established **Mount Isa Mines** (MIM) the next year and began commercial mining in 1925. Originally a settlement of canvas and scrap wood, the city enjoyed a forty-year boom under the hegemony of MIM, until the late 1980s saw a decline in profits. Developments such as the Hilton Mine, north of the city, keep business ticking over, but mines further afield – as at Cloncurry – tend to be staffed by workers who live on the east coast and fly in for their shifts, staying on site until they take their money home, completely bypassing the Isa.

Arrival and information

With its two huge chimneys illuminated at night – the Rotary lookout on Hilary Street gives a good view – **MIM** is the city's major landmark, west of the often dry **Leichhardt River**. The Barkly Highway runs through town as Marian and Grace streets, with the city centre immediately south between Simpson and West streets; it then crosses the river and joins the Camooweal road in front of MIM. All **buses** pull in across the river at Campbell's Coach Terminal, **trains** terminate at the station below MIM; and the **airport** is 7km to the north, where taxis meet arrivals. The excellent **tourist office** (daily 8.30am–5pm; ⓣ07/4749 1555 or 1300 659 660) is located in the **Outback At Isa** complex on Marian Street and can make all tour bookings.

Accommodation

There's a good range of **accommodation** scattered all over Mount Isa, catering to most budgets.

Burke and Wills Resort ⓣ07/4743 8000, ⓔmercurehotelmtisa@bigpond.com. Upmarket and central motel on the corner of Grace and Camooweal. ❺

Moondarra Caravan Park ⓣ07/4743 9780. 4km from the city off Camooweal Rd, and close to a creek that draws plenty of local birdlife. The cabins are nothing special, but the shady, picturesque location compensates. Vans ❶, cabins ❶

Mount Isa Van Park (ⓣ07/4743 3252, ⓦwww.mtisacaravanpark.com.au. Situated on the eastern side of town just off Marian St, this is a well-kept campsite with pretty white and red cabins and a children's play area. Cabins with and without bathrooms ❶

Silver Star Motel ⓣ07/4743 3466, ⓔsilvstar@bigpond.net.au. East of centre, on the corner of Marian St and Doughan Terrace. Good facilities and a tree-lined pool, a welcome feature in this climate. ❶

Traveller's Haven ⓣ07/4743 0313, ⓦwww.users.bigpond.net.au/travellershaven. Hostel on the corner of Spence and Pamela sts – it's cool, quiet and staff can pick you up from the train and bus stations. Dorms $20, rooms ❶

The City

All the city's main attractions are handily grouped together in the award-winning **Outback At Isa** centre at 19 Marian St (daily 8.30am–5pm; ⓣ1300 659 660, ⓦwww.outbackatisa.com.au). The history of the region is explored in the **Isa Experience Gallery** ($10). The ground floor consists of a series of informative multi-media displays examining early prehistoric life, indigenous culture and the development of Mount Isa as a centre of mining activity, while the theatre on the upper level shows a surprisingly moving film focusing on the personalities who helped to build the city's multi-national community over the years. The entrance fee also includes access to the **Outback Park**, a rather lovely landscaped garden at the rear of the building. Those particularly interested in the prehistoric element of the gallery can investigate further in the excellent **Riversleigh Fossils Centre** ($10). The lime-saturated waters of the Gregory River at Riversleigh Station have been handily creating a fossil record since Australia was a teeming tropical forest. Paleontologists working there since the 1980s have discovered an incredible record of marsupial and mammalian evolution and environmental change between ten thousand and twenty million years ago, which is now all magnificently displayed here. Imaginative, life-sized dioramas and an informative video recreate the region at a time when it was a lush wetland, populated by ancestral platypus and koalas, giant snakes and emus, carnivorous kangaroos and the enigmatic "thingadonta". You can also visit the **laboratory** (guided tours daily at 10am & 1pm) out the back, where fossils are being prepared by soaking boulders collected at Riversleigh in weak acid, dissolving the rock but leaving bones, beaks and teeth intact. It's all essential viewing, particularly if you're planning to head out to Riversleigh itself.

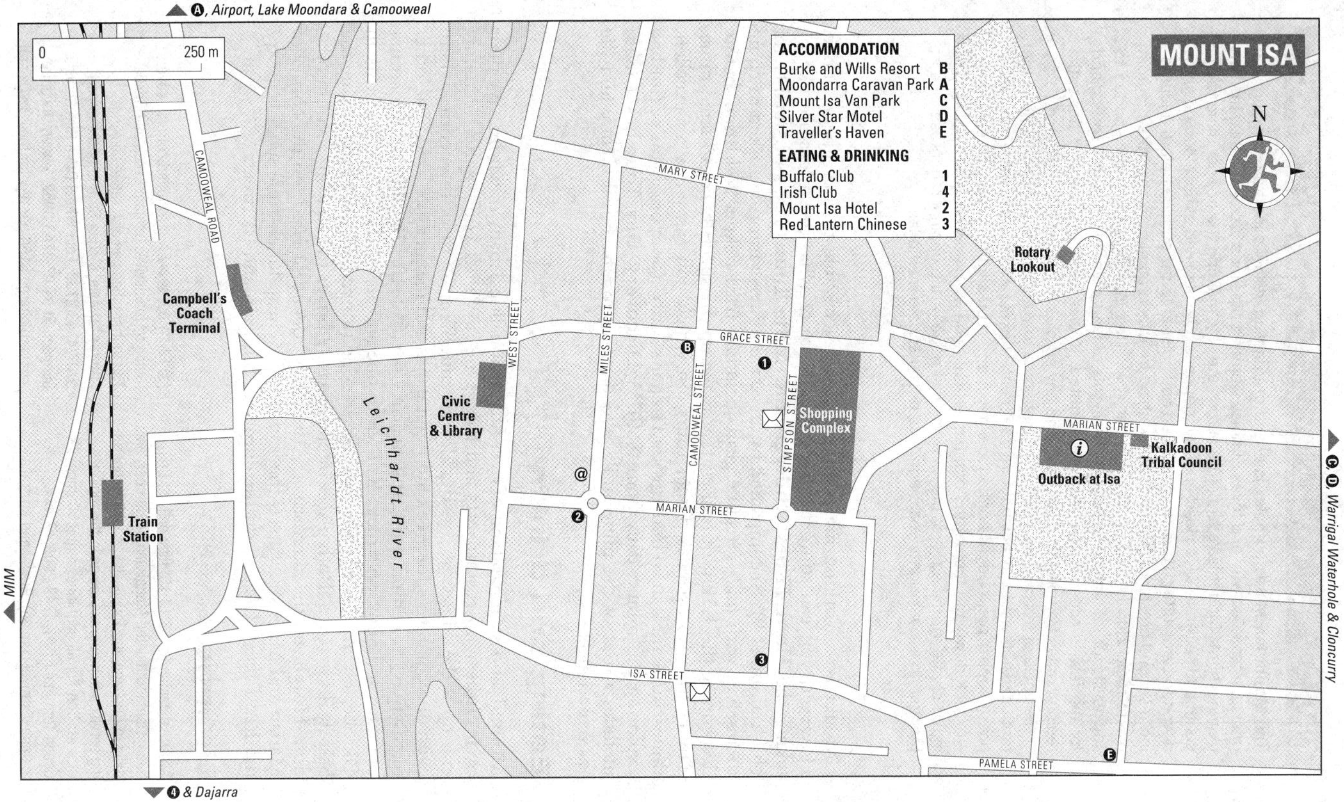

MOUNT ISA

A, Airport, Lake Moondara & Camooweal

C, D, Warrigal Waterhole & Cloncurry

4 & Dajarra

MIM

ACCOMMODATION

Burke and Wills Resort	B
Moondarra Caravan Park	A
Mount Isa Van Park	C
Silver Star Motel	D
Traveller's Haven	E

EATING & DRINKING

Buffalo Club	1
Irish Club	4
Mount Isa Hotel	2
Red Lantern Chinese	3

0 250 m

N

Camooweal Road
Mary Street
Grace Street
West Street
Miles Street
Camooweal Street
Simpson Street
Marian Street
Isa Street
Pamela Street
Leichhardt River
Campbell's Coach Terminal
Train Station
Civic Centre & Library
Shopping Complex
Rotary Lookout
Outback at Isa
Kalkadoon Tribal Council

MIM

The **Mount Isa Mines** complex is a land of trundling yellow mine trucks, mountains of slag, intense activity and miles of noisy vibrating pipelines. Above all this, the two chimneys trail Mount Isa's signature across the sky, marking the copper mine to the south and separate silver, lead and zinc deposits. Ore is mined almost 2km down by a workforce of 1200; it's roughly crushed and hoisted to the surface before undergoing a second crushing, grinding and washing in flotation tanks, to separate ore from waste rock. Zinc is sold as it is, copper is smelted into ingots and transported to Townsville for refining, while four-tonne ingots of lead/silver mix are sent to England for the few ounces of silver to be separated. Power for the mines and the entire region comes from MIM's own plant, and any surplus is sold to the state grid.

The scale of the process will be brought home to you if you stand under one of the mountains of tailings awaiting future treatment – next to which are humble mounds of green copper ore, bought from a local miner and representing maybe a year's effort – or look down into the depths of the open-cut mine, worked simply for rubble to fill in old shafts. At the edge of the mine the last ridge of the original Mount Isa, site of the first finds over eighty years ago, has been left as a memorial.

Mount Isa's working mines are no longer accessible to the general public. However, you can still get a fairly vivid taste of what the mines are like by taking the **Hard Times Underground Mine Tour** ($45; not suitable for children under 9). Accompanied by an actual miner, visitors are asked to equip themselves with full protective gear, including hard-helmet and torch, before descending the 1.2km of tunnels that make up the specially constructed mine. The centre also operates dinner tours, on which you can enjoy an excellent three-course meal in an underground miner's "crib" room once you've finished exploring the mines (daily 5pm; $69). A **Discovery Day Tour** ticket ($55) includes a tour of the mine and a two-day pass for the Fossil Centre and the Isa Experience.

Eating and drinking

Mount Isa boasts inhabitants of over fifty nationalities, many of whom have their own **clubs** with **restaurants** and bars. One in which you'll almost certainly end up is the *Irish Club*, on Buckley Avenue 2km south of the centre, where everyone converges for weekend night bands and inexpensive food. The other mainstay is the central and flashy *Buffalo Club* (Ⓣ0413 126 666), on the corner of Grace and Simpson streets. Known to one and all as "The Buffs", it hosts an Oktoberfest and has a comfy, heavily air-conditioned bar, and bistro serving the best steaks in town. Both places offer **courtesy buses** to and from accommodation. **Hotels** are the alternatives – the bulky *Mount Isa Hotel*, on the corner of Marian and Miles streets, sets the standard for cheap lunch-time specials, or try the *Red Lantern Chinese*, on the corner of Simpson and Isa streets.

Listings

Airlines Qantas (Ⓣ13 13 13) flies daily to Brisbane; Qantas-affiliated Macair (same number) flies daily to Brisbane and Townsville as well as operating services to numerous towns in the region.
Bus station For all enquiries, contact Campbell's Coach Terminal (Ⓣ07/4743 2006, Ⓦwww.campbellstravel.com.au). Greyhound Australia (Ⓣ13 14 99, Ⓦwww.greyhound.com.au) covers routes to Townsville, Tennant Creek and Brisbane. The tourist office can also make bookings.
Car rental Avis, Marian St (and at the airport) Ⓣ07/4743 3733; Four Wheel Drive Hire Service, Simpson St (Ⓣ07/4743 3962, Ⓦwww.4wdhire.com.au) charge $150 per day for their 4WDs and

also hire out camping gear ($300 per week for two people); Thrifty, cnr of Patricia and Miles streets ☎07/4743 2911.

Cinema Cnr Marian and West streets.

Hospitals 30 Camooweal St ☎07/4744 4444; Georgina Medical Centre, 71 Camooweal St ☎07/4743 1488.

Internet Back of Mt Isa newsagent at 25 Miles St; $5.50 an hour.

Pharmacy Corner Pharmacy, cnr Marian and Miles streets.

Police 7 Isa St ☎07/4744 1111.

Post office For poste restante, Isa St (☎07/4743 2454); there is another office on Simpson Street opposite the shopping complex.

Taxi ☎07/4743 2333.

Tours Campbell's (☎07/4743 2006, ⓦwww.campbellstravel.com.au) runs day-tours to local mines ($22), as well as three-day safaris to Lawn Hill Gorge between April and Oct ($660). Book through their office on Marian St, the bus station, or your accommodation.

Trains Queensland Rail operates a twice-weekly service back to Townsville. For information and bookings call ☎13 16 17, or check ⓦwww.qr.com.au.

Kalkadoon country

The scrub around Mount Isa is thick with abandoned mines, waterholes and Aboriginal sites. Either take a tour (see "Listings") or, if you're doing your own driving, check at the tourist office for the latest news on road conditions. The city marks the centre of the territory of the **Kalkadoons**, a tribe often compared with the Zulus for their fierce opposition to white invasion in the nineteenth century. After hounding squatters for ten years with guerrilla tactics, they were decimated in a pitched battle with an army of local settlers and Native Mounted Police near Kajabbi in 1884. Kalkadoon bones littered the battleground for years, but their stand gained them respect for their organized resistance to Europeans.

Numerous sites around Mount Isa attest to the Kalkadoons' abilities as prolific toolmakers and painters, and it's worth checking out their **Tribal Council office** (Mon–Fri 9am–5pm; ☎07/4749 3838), next to the Riversleigh Centre on Marian Street in Mount Isa, and talk to the staff. Bear in mind that although it's against the law to alter Aboriginal sites in any way, many local sites have been vandalized and you might find the council evasive.

Warrigal Waterhole, Poison Hole and Lake Moondarra

You need high clearance or great care to reach **Warrigal Waterhole**: drive 7km towards Cloncurry from the Tribal Council office on Marian Street in Mount Isa, turn south through the gate and bear left along a very rough track to reach a parking area 3.4km later, from where you walk past "ripple rocks" to the waterhole. One red figure with strange hair outlined in yellow on the left seems to have escaped damage but not so other figures and symbols, which have melted to ochre smears. The waterhole itself is hemmed in by sheltering rocks, which makes for a cool retreat from the sun.

A flooded open-cut mine, **Poison Hole**'s name comes from the surreal appearance of the water, coloured green by copper – it's actually safe to swim in, however. Tracks there change each year, but the hole is about ten minutes from the highway, and the turn-off should be roughly 25km back towards Cloncurry; look for signs spray-painted on the road. **Lake Moondarra**, 20km along on a good road (follow the signs from the highway heading towards Camooweal), is less offensively toned, and packed out with windsurfers and boats at weekends. During the week it's nearly deserted and other animals are attracted to the water – goannas, wallabies and flocks of pelicans. Beyond the dam wall at the north end of the lake, the unexpectedly green and shady **Warrina Park** is the unlikely home of peacocks and apostlebirds.

Camooweal and Lawn Hill

West of Mount Isa, the **Barkly Highway** continues to Camooweal and the NT. An unsealed road, a little over halfway to the state border, heads north off it, leading via Gregory Downs to **Lawn Hill Gorge National Park** and **Burketown**. If you're making for Lawn Hill, ensure you have a **campsite** booked and check the latest **road conditions** (Ⓣ1300 130 595, Ⓦwww.racq.com.au), as the route via Riversleigh is sometimes 4WD-only or closed, while the Gregory Downs road is fine for most cars if it's dry. Wherever you're driving, fuel up; it's two hundred monotonous kilometres to Camooweal and the fringes of the black-soil **Barkly Tablelands**, and at least twice that to Lawn Hill.

Camooweal and the Caves

There's no way to avoid **CAMOOWEAL** but you might wish there were – the township's atmosphere of lazy aggression is exacerbated by a total lack of charm. The highway from Mount Isa forms the main street, built in 1944 by American servicemen whose names are painted on a rock at the edge of town. You'll find a roadhouse, mechanic, general store (and Westpacbank agent), post office and hotel – a risky place for a last drink in Queensland. The store's old decor is worth a peek, and murals at the *Camooweal Roadhouse* (Ⓣ07/4748 2155; cabins ❶) should raise a chuckle. Around the back are **cabins** and a **campsite** with thick grass to raise a tent over. Otherwise, fuel up and move on.

The best features of the surrounding area are dolomite sinks known as **the Caves**; drive 8km down the Urandangie road south of Camooweal, then turn left and follow the dirt track for about thirty minutes. There's an NPWS **campsite** here, with toilets and a fence to keep out marauding cattle. Flocks of gibbering green budgerigars congregate around the creek and – if you can put up with their racket – it's preferable to a night in town. The park's nine caves are intriguing terraces, spiralling down 10m before tapering to vertical shafts. The district is riddled with them – one is a roost for **ghost bats**, and another has become famous for its coolibah trees. Caused by tunnels into the water table collapsing at the surface, the cave shafts continue straight down for anything between 18m and 75m before levelling out into an uncharted system. Instability makes approaching the mouths dangerous, so don't even think about exploring underground.

Heading on from Camooweal there's another track north to Lawn Hill, while 200km south beyond the Caves is **Urandangie** and a 650-kilometre 4WD "short cut", across to Alice Springs. West, it's a mere ten minutes' drive to the cattle grid separating Queensland from the NT's time zone and better roads. Next fuel is at the Barkly Homestead, 275km away.

Gregory Downs and Lawn Hill Gorge National Park

Hidden from the rest of the world by the Constance Range and a hot ocean of bleached grass, the red sandstone walls and splash of tropical greenery at **Boodjamulla (Lawn Hill) National Park** seem outrageously extravagant. There's little warning of this change in scenery; within moments, a land which barely supports scattered herds of cattle is exchanged for palm forests and creeks teeming with wildlife. There are two places to aim for, **Riversleigh Fossil Site** and **Lawn Hill Gorge**, connected to each other by a seventy-kilometre track. Most people base themselves at the gorge, which has the easiest access and the best facilities and scenery, though it's definitely worth making a trip to Riversleigh.

For Lawn Hill Gorge, routes from Cloncurry, Camooweal and Burketown all converge at **GREGORY DOWNS**, a tiny community of just nine inhabitants, a pub and general store, offering cold drinks, fuel, mechanical repairs, and a wild **canoe race** down the Gregory River each May Day weekend. From here, the gorge is 76km west along a decent gravel road, via the controversial **Century Zinc mine**, where work was halted when local Aborigines claimed traditional ownership of the region. After several years of negotiations, they finally accepted a substantial payment for use of the land and the mine reopened. While the situation has exacerbated the frustration felt by mining companies and farmers over the legal ambiguities surrounding the 1992 Mabo Decision (see "Contexts"), it's evidence that the wishes of Aboriginal communities are now being taken far more seriously.

Riversleigh Fossil Site

The Gregory Downs–Camooweal road to Riversleigh crosses the **Gregory River** three times around Riversleigh Station, which is why you need a 4WD on this route. The crossings are a foretaste of Lawn Hill – sudden patches of shady green and cool air in an otherwise hostile landscape. You can **camp** near the station from April until the end of October at *Campbell's Riversleigh Camp* (satellite phone ⓣ014 511 6441), where you'll also find on-site double tents (❶), hot showers, toilets and a barbecue area.

Like Lawn Hill, **Riversleigh** was once cloaked in rainforest supporting many ancestral forms of Australian fauna. The **fossil finds** here cover a period from twenty million to just ten thousand years ago, a staggering range for a single site, and one which details the transitional period from Australia's climatic heyday to its current parched state. Riversleigh may ultimately produce a fossil record of evolutionary change for an entire ecosystem, but don't expect to see much *in situ* as the fossils are trapped in limestone boulders which have to be carefully blasted out and treated with acid to release their contents. A roadside shelter houses a map of the landscape with fossil sites indicated on a rock outcrop nearby where, with some diligence, you can find bones and teeth protruding from the stones.

The Riversleigh Fossil Site lies halfway along an eighty-kilometre, 4WD-only track between Lawn Hill Gorge and the unsealed, 220-kilometre-long Gregory Downs–Camooweal road. Coming southwest from Gregory Downs on this road, the Riversleigh track starts 65km along, or it's 155km northeast from Camooweal.

Lawn Hill Gorge

When **Lawn Hill Creek** started carving its forty-metre-deep gorge the region was still a tropical wetland, but as the climate began to dry out, vegetation retreated to a handful of moist, isolated pockets. Animals were drawn to creeks and waterholes and people followed the game – middens and art detail an **Aboriginal culture** at least seventeen thousand years old. The NPWS **campsite** (tank water, showers, toilets) occupies a tamed edge of the creek at the mouth of the gorge and is booked solid between Easter and October (bookings on ⓣ07/4748 5572). An alternative campsite is at the pleasant **Adel's Grove** (ⓣ07/4748 5502, ⓦwww.adelsgrove.com.au), a Savannah Guides post 5km from the gorge, run by Barry Kubala, an expert on the gorge's vegetation.

Canoes are an excellent way of exploring the gorge from the inside – you can hire them for $10 an hour from Adel's Grove. An easy hour's paddle over calm green water takes you from the NPWS campsite between the stark, vertical cliffs of the Middle Gorge to **Indari Falls**, an excellent swimming spot with a ramp to carry your gear down. Beyond here the creek relaxes, alternating between calm ponds and slack channels choked with vegetation, before slowing to a trickle under the rockfaces of the Upper Gorge. Saltwater crocodiles are absent from the gorge, but you'll certainly see plenty of **birds** – egrets, bitterns and kites all put in an appearance. **Freshwater crocodiles** are hard to spot: since visitor numbers have increased, this timid reptile has retreated to the **Lower Gorge** – a sluggish tract edged in waterlilies and forest where goannas lounge during the day and rare **purple-crowned fairy wrens** forage in pandanus leaves.

In the creek itself are turtles, shockingly large catfish, and sharp-eyed **archer fish** that spit jets of water at insects above the surface. Just how isolated all this is becomes clear from the flat top of the **Island Stack**, a twenty-minute walk from the camp. A pre-dawn hike up the steep sides gives you a commanding view of the sun creeping into the gorge, highlighting orange walls against green palm-tops, which hug the river through a flat, undernourished country. The rocks along the banks of the Lower Gorge are daubed with designs relating to the Dingo Dreaming, a reminder of the sanctity of the gorge to the Waanyi people, who have inhabited the area for more than seventeen thousand years. In October 1994, a group of fifty people from local communities staged a month-long sit-in at the park, demanding joint management, a demand which was eventually met after several years of court procedures. The traditional Aboriginal name for the gorge, Boodjamulla, meaning Rainbow Serpent, has subsequently been adopted.

The Gulf of Carpentaria

The great savannahs and intricate river systems of western Cape York and the **Gulf of Carpentaria** were described in 1623 by the Dutch explorer Jan Carstensz as being full of hostile tribes – not surprising, since he'd spent his time here kidnapping and shooting any Aborigines he saw. The Gulf was ignored for centuries thereafter, except by Indonesians gathering sea-slugs to sell to the Chinese. Interest in its potential however, was stirred in 1841 by **John Lort Stokes**, a lieutenant on the *Beagle* (which had been graced by a young Charles Darwin on an earlier voyage), who absurdly described the coast as "Plains of Promise":

> **A vast boundless plain lay before us, here and there dotted with woodland isles . . . I could discover the rudiments of future prosperity and ample justification of the name which I had bestowed upon them.**

It took Burke and Wills' awful 1861 trek to discover that the "woodland isles" were deficient in nutrients and that the black soil became a quagmire during the wet season. Too awkward to develop, the Gulf hung in limbo as settlements sprang up, staggered on for a while, then disappeared – even today few places

Gulf trains

Two unconnected, anachronistic **railways** still operate in the Gulf region, mostly as tourist attractions. For advance bookings on either, call in to the relevant stations, or contact Queensland Rail (Ⓣ13 16 17).

The Savannahlander runs every Wednesday morning from Cairns to Almaden on the Chillagoe road, where it overnights before continuing to Forsayth, arriving Thursday afternoon. Friday morning it leaves Forsayth for Mount Surprise, arriving back in Cairns on Saturday evening. You spend the snails-pace journey being hauled over rickety bridges in carriages with corrugated-iron ceilings and wooden dunnies – a pastiche of Outback iconography. The trip costs $100 each way and you'll need to bring extra for hotel accommodation and meals.

The Gulflander runs once a week each way along an isolated stretch of line between Croydon and Normanton, a journey that takes a mere four hours (departs Croydon Thurs 8.30am, departs Normanton Wed 8.30am; $48 each way)

could be described as thriving communities. Not that this should put you off visiting – with few real destinations but plenty to see, the Gulf is a perfect destination for those who just like to travel. On the way, and only half a day's drive from Cairns, the awesome lava tubes at **Undara** shouldn't be missed, while further afield there are **gemstones** to be fossicked, the coast's birdlife and exciting **barramundi** fishing to enjoy, and the Gulf's sheer remoteness to savour.

Two sealed roads head through the region to Normanton and Karumba. The **Gulf Developmental Road**, which starts southwest of Ravenshoe on the Atherton Tablelands, and the **Burke Developmental Road** from Mount Isa. Coral Coaches (Ⓣ07/4031 7577) operates a bus service from Cairns to Mount Isa via Undara, and down the Gulf Developmental Road to Normanton and Karumba, where you need to change to take the Burke Developmental Road to Mount Isa, linking up with regional rail services. The Cairns to Normanton "road", via Chillagoe, is a shattering, unserviced, five-hundred-kilometre track best tackled by well-equipped off-road transport only, as are all the Gulf's remoter stretches. In the wet season, flying is the sole option for any travel. **Safaris** run from Cairns (see box on p.544) if you don't have the right vehicle, or you could get at least part of the way around on the Gulf's two rustic railways (see box above).

Most visitors to the Gulf need to be reasonably self-sufficient, as there are few banks and **accommodation** is limited for the most part to campsites or pricey motels. For **information** before you go, contact Gulf Savannah Tourism at 74 Abbott St, Cairns (Ⓣ07/4031 1631, Ⓦwww.gulf-savannah.com.au), which offers brochures and advice, though doesn't make bookings. Once in the region, you'll find the local QPWS is joined by the **Savannah Guides** (Ⓣ08/8985 3890, Ⓦwww.savannah-guides.com.au) a private ranger organization recently voted the best of its type in the world, which runs campsites with guides to show you around. On a more alarming note, you might also come face to face with the Gulf's two **crocodile** species – take care.

Undara Lava Tubes

The **Undara Lava Tubes** are astounding, massive tunnels running in broken chambers for up to 35km from the side of the volcano's low cone. It wasn't until 1989 that the majority of the caves were located and mapped and Undara declared an area of scientific interest. Currently run by the Savannah Guides but

NPWS-owned, Undara is on **Yarramulla Station**, 16km south off the Gulf Developmental Road, 130km from Ravenshoe. **Accommodation**, bar and **restaurant** at the *Lava Lodge* (Ⓣ07/4097 1411, Ⓦwww.undara.com.au; pre-fab tents $18 per person, cabins ❺) are in eleven restored railway carriages brought over from Mareeba and set up amongst a thin wattle forest – an eccentric but comfortable idea. Their swimming pool is an almost essential place to spend time during summer.

Because the tunnels are hard to enter – and some host a virulent lung fungus – you must take a tour. Although not cheap ($35 for a 2hr introduction, $65 half-day, $97 full day; for further information and bookings contact the *Lava Lodge*), these are good value considering that, as well as the chance to explore the tubes, you get an intimate rundown on local geology, flora, fauna and history from a member of the Collins family, who have lived on the station for more than a century. You can, however, make plenty of good short walks through woodland and up to lookout points in the low hills above the *Lava Lodge*, where you'll find wallabies and parrots during the day and plenty of nocturnal insects and reptiles.

Tubes and caves

When the Undara volcano erupted 190,000 years ago, the liquid lava followed rivers and gullies as it snaked northwest towards the Gulf. Away from the cone, the surface of these lava rivers hardened, forming insulating tubes which kept the lava inside in a liquid state and allowed it to run until the tubes were drained. These were then covered by later accumulations, and they'd still be unexplored if hot gases hadn't popped holes in the tube ceilings which eventually collapsed, creating a way in.

The edge of the flow is marked by darker soil and healthier vegetation; at cave mouths this becomes rampant, successfully concealing the entrances and making your first view of the tubes something of a shock – what looks like a bush at ground level turns out to be the top of a giant fig tree growing from the cave floor. The caves are decked in rubble and remnant pockets of thick prehistoric vegetation quite out of place among the dry scrub on the surface. Tool sites around the cave mouths show that Aborigines knew of their existence, though there's no evidence that they ever ventured in.

Once **inside**, the scale of the 52 tubes is overpowering. Up to 19m high and 900m long, their glazed walls bear evidence of the terrible forces that created them – coil patterns and ledges formed by cooling lava, whirlpools where lava forged its way through rock from other flows, and "stalactites" made when solidifying lava dribbled from the ceiling. Some end in **lakes**, while others are blocked by lava plugs. Animal tracks in the dust indicate the regular passage of kangaroos, snakes and invertebrates, and seasonally you'll encounter twittering colonies of bats clinging to the ceiling, but the overall scale of the tubes tends to deaden any sounds or signs of life.

Mount Surprise and around

MOUNT SURPRISE, 40km north of Undara, reputedly takes its name from the shock of the local Aborigines when they first saw whites. Aside from being a stop for the *Savannahlander* train on its weekly return leg to Cairns, there's little more here than the *Mount Surprise Tourist Park and Motel* (Ⓣ07/4062 3153, Ⓕ4062 3162; cabins ❶, motel rooms ❹), which has a gem shop, service station and the *Mount Surprise Hotel* (Ⓣ07/4062 3118; ❶). The main attraction lies a bumpy 40km north at **O'Briens Creek Topaz Field** (check on road conditions at Ⓦwww.racq.com.au or call Ⓣ1300 130 595), where you can camp at a waterhole known as **the Oasis**, and then organize a fossicking trip, although you will need to arrange a Fossickers Licence first. You might find a handful of topaz in a couple of hours and while it's not very valuable, there's pleasure in the hunt and it's beautiful when cut.

Beyond Mount Surprise the main road, which is the worst in all Queensland for stray cattle, crosses **the Wall**, where expanding gases in a blocked subterranean lava tube forced the ground above it up 20m into a long ridge. The same gaseous expulsion also seems to have cracked open a much deeper seam at **Ambo Springs** on Tallaroo Station (Easter–Oct daily until 4pm; $9; Ⓣ07/4662 1221). Formed by water 3km down becoming heated and forcing its way to the surface, the clear blue, sulphurous pools gradually accumulate a crusty grey collar around their vent from dissolved lime. This eventually closes the outflow, until the build-up of pressure explodes through to create a new spring. The water emerges at 92°C, but there are some cooler spas that are more comfortable for soaking in.

South of the main road near Ambo, there's a forty-kilometre detour down to **EINASLEIGH**, an ordinary handful of weatherboard and iron houses made memorable by the huge, delicious evening meals served at the *Central Hotel* (Ⓣ07/4062 5222; ❶), and summer dips in **Einasleigh Creek**'s deep basalt gorge. If you don't have your own vehicle (and you might need 4WD after rain), the *Savannahlander* **train** also passes this way.

Georgetown, Forsayth and around

Back on the main road about 90km west of Mount Surprise, **GEORGETOWN** is a similarly scaled, tidy town, home to the *Midway Caravan Park* (Ⓣ07/4062 1219, Ⓔbookings@midwayserro.com; cabins ❶), and the rather plusher, pink *Latara Resort Motel* (Ⓣ07/4062 1190, Ⓔlataramotel@bigpond.com; ❹), along with a couple of shops and **hotels** (*Wenaru* has the best meals). The area around Georgetown has a reputation as somewhere to fossick for **gold** nuggets – for **information** on likely places to try, head for **Terrestrial** (daily 10am–5pm; exhibition $10; Ⓣ07/4062 1485) on Low Street, which acts as both tourist office and home to the Ted Elliott Mineral Collection, an impressive display of precious stones.

Forty kilometres south off the highway down a decent gravel road is **FORSAYTH**, terminus for the *Savannahlander* **train** and home to the *Goldfields Hotel* (Ⓣ07/4062 5374; ❺ including dinner). It's also the last place to stock up before heading into the bush to two unusual locations. Two hours south in a 4WD through the scrub, the basic camp at **Agate Creek** (Ⓣ07/4062 5335; Easter–Oct) caters to agate hunters who scour the creek banks after each wet season for these semiprecious stones and rate this the best site in the world. This may be a matter of opinion but the colours, ranging from honey through to delicate blue, justify the time spent grubbing around with a pick looking for them. **Cobbold Gorge**, at Robinhood Station (Easter–Oct), 50km south of Forsayth on a passable dirt road, is a recently discovered and starkly attractive oasis inhabited by freshwater crocodiles and crayfish and surrounded by baking hot sandstone country. You can **camp** or stay in **cabins** here at *Cobbold Camping Village* (Ⓣ07/4062 5470, Ⓦwww.cobboldgorge.com.au; cabins ❶), which also organizes **tours**, including a 4WD trip around the station, fossicking for agates, lunch, and a scout up the kilometre-long gorge in a motorized punt (June, July & Aug only; $110) – an excellent way to experience a very remote corner of the Outback.

Croydon

CROYDON, 150km west of Georgetown along the main road, was the site of Queensland's last major **goldrush** after two station hands found nuggets in a fence-post hole in 1885. For a brief period the region received the attention it had always craved: within five years the railway was built and lucky miners whooped it up at Croydon's 36 hotels, but by 1900 chaotic management had brought operations to a close. Today, despite rumours of a new gold strike near town, the place is pretty sedate and most buildings predate 1920. The *Club Hotel* (the last of the 36), the general store and the restored old courthouse all have their original fittings and offer directions to other scattered relics. If you're tempted to stay, the aforementioned *Club Hotel* on Brown Street (Ⓣ07/4745 6184; ❶) has rooms, or you can pitch a tent at *Croydon Gold Van Park* (Ⓣ07/4745 6238) on the Georgetown side.

Moving on, buses and the main road plough on to Normanton, 154km west, as does the *Gulflander* **train**, which leaves Croydon on Thursday mornings from the station on Helen Street. When the rails and sleepers were unloaded at Normanton's wharves in the nineteenth century they were meant to form the first stage of a line to Cloncurry, but this was redirected to Croydon when gold was found. At the height of the gold rush the service carried two hundred passengers a week.

Normanton

Founded on the banks of the Norman River in 1868, **NORMANTON** was the Gulf's main port, connected to the Croydon goldfield by rail and Cloncurry's copper mines by camel train, though today the town lacks the air of faded splendour one might expect. Set in gritty, flat country, Normanton's fortunes declined along with regional mineral deposits and today there's only a thin collection of stores and service stations, a bank and post office, with shop awnings and a handful of trees providing scant shade. A worthy survivor of former times is the **Burns Philp Store** whose timber shell, built in the 1880s, covers almost an acre and remains upright (if empty) despite the attentions of a century's worth of termites. The **train** still runs once a week to Croydon.

Barramundi fishing (offered by Norman River Cruises; Ⓣ07/4745 1347, Ⓦwww.normanriverfishing.com.au) is beginning to brighten the area's prospects, a fact celebrated by the *Gulfland Motel* (Ⓣ07/4745 1290; rooms ❹), under the sign of the "Big Barra" at the south entrance to the town; the **motel** has pleasant rooms and a **campsite**. Alternative **accommodation** is at Normanton's lurid and recently refurbished *Purple Pub* (Ⓣ07/4745 1324, Ⓕ4745 1626; ❶). This is also a good place to **eat**, with a beer garden and tasty char-grilled steaks and fish. The town's other two hotels, the *Albion* and *Middle Pub*, are pretty raw watering holes. When you've had enough boozing, Karumba and routes on to western Cape York lie north, and Cloncurry is 400km south via the Burke and Wills Roadhouse. To the west is the fuel-less, 220-kilometre Burketown road, with features along the way including the site of Burke and Wills' northernmost camp near the Bynoe River, and the often difficult **Leichhardt River** crossing where the pocket-sized **Leichhardt Falls** contrasts with the aridity of the surrounding sand dunes, deposited each year when the river is in spate.

Karumba and the Gulf

Reached from Normanton across 70km of cracked, burning saltpan, patrolled by saurus cranes and jabiru storks, **KARUMBA**'s tidy gardens are, given the setting, ridiculously suburban. Set near the mouth of the **Norman River** and once an airforce base for Catalina flying boats moving between Brisbane and Singapore, today the town is overlooked by huge **sheds** storing slurry from the Century Zinc Mine near Lawn Hill Gorge; the slurry is fed through pipes to Karumba, then shipped overseas for refining. Karumba mostly survives on prawn trawling and fishing, however. Declining stocks of barramundi in the Gulf have inspired the **Barramundi Farm** (daily 1–5pm; $3), 2km from town along the river, which raises fish for release into the wild. One thing that will probably register is that there are few Aborigines in town – they shun the area, as many died in a tribal battle nearby.

Karumba comprises two separate areas – central Karumba itself, and Karumba Point, a couple of kilometres downstream near the estuary. The **centre** is along Yappar Street on the Norman River's south bank, with a supermarket, the *Karumba Café* (serving good barraburgers) and a post office. Popular fishing destination that it is, it's worthwhile booking ahead for **accommodation** in Karumba. *Gulf Country Van Park* (Ⓣ07/4745 9148; cabins ❶) is a shady campsite, *Matilda's End* (Ⓣ07/4747 6500, Ⓦwww.matildasend.com.au; ❶) has tidy units or there's the *Karumba Lodge* (Ⓣ07/4745 9121, Ⓦwww.karumbalodge.com.au; ❹), which started life as the airforce mess – the ramp that runs alongside the lodge down to the river was where the Catalina aircraft berthed. The *Lodge* has two **bars** – the ordinary *Suave Bar* and the infamous *Animal Bar*, which you should probably avoid unless you're extremely serious about drinking and don't mind occasional bouts of hand-to-hand combat. **Karumba Point** overlooks mudflats and mangroves along the river mouth and has a pool, campsites, and a twice-weekly free fish barbecue at the *Karumba Point Tourist Park* (Ⓣ07/4745 9306; cabins ❶). For outstanding sunsets, meals and ice-cold beer, head to the riverside *Sunset Tavern*.

To spot crocodile and birds, or **catch** something for the pot, contact Y-Not (Ⓣ07/4745 9316) or Katherine MII Fishing Charters (Ⓣ07/4745 9449). If you have your own tackle, Karumba Boat Hire (Ⓣ07/4745 9393) rents out four-metre-long tinnies from $50 for a half-day.

The Wellesleys and western Cape York

Gulf Freight Services on Yappar Street, Karumba (Ⓣ07/4745 9333) operates a weekly **barge** from Karumba to Weipa, near the tip of Queensland. The journey takes around thirty hours, leaving on Friday and returning Tuesday. A one-way trip costs $285 including meals and cabin. Prices for vehicles, which must be containerized, start at $490. Erratic services also go to the **Wellesley Islands**, which comprise two dozen windswept islands north of Burketown with excellent fishing around fragmented coral rubble. Never settled by whites, today they are **Aboriginal communities**, with an expensive but basic **resort** on **Sweers Island** (Ⓣ07/4748 5544, Ⓦwww.sweers.com.au; ❽), catering to serious fishermen. Transfers ($250 per person, minimum of four) can be booked with Gulf Line Aviation on Yappar Street, Karumba (Ⓣ1800 458 458, Ⓦwww.gulflineaviation.com.au), which can also fly you to Lawn Hill for the day ($300 per person, minimum of four).

Off-road drivers wanting to view wildlife might be tempted by superb **wetlands** on the western edge of the Cape York Peninsula, accessed from the Normanton to Karumba road off a 4WD-only, five-hundred-kilometre track which ultimately takes you to Chillagoe. Detouring north from the track, you'll find the coast thick with creeks, waterholes and animals. **Dorunda Station** (food, drink and limited fuel supplies; Ⓣ07/4745 3477; units ❺), about 180km up the road, is a working cattle property which arranges hunting safaris with cameras or .303s – targets are pigs, fish, birds and crocodiles. There's more of the same even further north at **Mitchell and Alice Rivers National Park**, via the Aboriginal community of **Kowanyama**. You'll need to take all supplies for this, as well as getting an NPWS permit and permission from the community (contact Cairns NPWS on ⓣ07/4052 3096 for details).

Burketown and on to the Territory

Set on the Albert River some 230km west of Normanton, **BURKETOWN** balances on the dusty frontier between grassland and the Gulf's thirty-kilometre-deep, unfriendly coastal flats. Styled Queensland's "Barramundi Capital" after the delicious sports fish, it has a huge road maintenance depot employing most of its 235 inhabitants. Despite lukewarm fame for providing background to Nevil Shute's *A Town Like Alice*, there's little beyond the welcoming and historic *Burketown Pub* (ⓣ07/4745 5104; units ❹), *Burketown Caravan Park* (ⓣ07/4745 5118, ⓦwww.burketowncaravanpark.com.au; cabins ❶), a hot artesian spring, a store, a couple of **fuel** pumps and a post office (Mon–Fri 9am–5pm; ⓣ07/4745 5111) which also acts as the **tourist office** and agent for day-flights to the Wellesley Islands. Accommodation can also organize **barra fishing**, or head 16km west to **Escott Barra Lodge** (ⓣ07/4748 5577, ⓕ4748 5649; units ❺) where you can also go riding, mustering, or tour one of the Gulf's precarious cattle stations. There's a restaurant and bar at the *Lodge*, but no store.

The Hell's Gate Track

The best road from Burketown heads south for about 120km to **Gregory Downs** and routes to Lawn Hill and Cloncurry. If you're serious about **fishing** and have a 4WD however, head 170km west from Burketown via the Aboriginal community at **Doomadgee**, to the **Hell's Gate Roadhouse** (ⓣ07/4745 8258), 50km from the NT. Fishing information and guided tours can be obtained from the Savannah Guides here, or you could try **Massacre Inlet**, reached from *Wollogorang Station* (ⓣ08/8975 9944; ❻) just on the Territory border; they will supply you with a $12 fishing permit as well as camping, motel rooms, meals, beer and the last fuel before Borroloola. Giant anthills, pandanus-frilled waterholes and irregular tides are the rewards – and the area is stacked with wildlife, including **saltwater crocodiless**.

The road on from Hell's Gate improves inside the Territory and once there you shouldn't have any trouble reaching Borroloola, 266km down the track.

Travel details

Trains

Barcaldine to: Emerald (2 weekly; 6hr); Longreach (2 weekly; 2hr); Rockhampton (2 weekly; 10hr).
Cairns to: Almaden (1 weekly; 6hr 30min); Forsayth (1 weekly; 2 days).
Charleville to: Brisbane (2 weekly; 17hr); Mitchell (2 weekly; 3hr 30min); Roma (2 weekly; 5hr); Toowoomba (2 weekly; 12hr).
Charters Towers to: Cloncurry (2 weekly; 11hr 30min); Hughenden (2 weekly; 5hr); Mount Isa (2 weekly; 20hr); Richmond (2 weekly; 7hr); Townsville (2 weekly; 2hr 30min).
Cloncurry to: Charters Towers (2 weekly; 11hr 30min); Hughenden (2 weekly; 8hr); Mount Isa (2 weekly; 4hr); Richmond (2 weekly; 5hr 30min); Townsville (2 weekly; 15hr).
Croydon to: Normanton (1 weekly; 4hr).
Emerald to: Barcaldine (2 weekly; 6hr); Longreach (2 weekly; 8hr); Rockhampton (2 weekly; 4hr 30min).
Forsayth to: Cairns (1 weekly; 2 days); Mount Surprise (1 weekly; 5hr 15min).
Hughenden to: Charters Towers (2 weekly; 5hr); Cloncurry (2 weekly; 8hr); Mount Isa (2 weekly; 11hr); Richmond (2 weekly; 2hr 10min); Townsville (2 weekly; 6hr).
Longreach to: Barcaldine (2 weekly; 2hr); Emerald (2 weekly; 8hr); Rockhampton (2 weekly; 12hr 30min).
Mitchell to: Brisbane (2 weekly; 14hr); Charleville (2 weekly; 4hr); Roma (2 weekly; 2hr); Toowoomba (2 weekly; 10hr).
Mount Isa to: Charters Towers (2 weekly; 15hr 30min); Cloncurry (2 weekly; 4hr 15min); Hughenden (2 weekly; 11hr); Richmond (2 weekly; 9hr); Townsville (2 weekly; 19hr).
Mount Surprise to: Cairns (1 weekly; 11hr).
Normanton to: Croydon (1 weekly; 4hr).
Richmond to: Charters Towers (2 weekly; 7hr); Cloncurry (2 weekly; 5hr 30min); Hughenden (2 weekly; 2hr 10min); Mount Isa (2 weekly; 9hr); Townsville (2 weekly; 9hr).
Roma to: Brisbane (2 weekly; 10hr 20min); Charleville (2 weekly; 5hr 10min); Mitchell (2 weekly; 2hr); Toowoomba (2 weekly; 11hr 40min).
Toowoomba to: Brisbane (2 weekly; 3hr 30min); Charleville (2 weekly; 12hr 30min); Mitchell (2 weekly; 10hr); Roma (2 weekly; 6hr 40min).

Buses

Barcaldine to: Blackall (1 daily; 1hr 15min); Brisbane (1 daily; 17hr); Chrleville (1 daily; 6hr); Cloncurry (1 daily; 8hr); Longreach (2 weekly; 2hr); Mitchell (1 daily; 13hr); Mount Isa (1 daily; 10hr); Rockhampton (2 weekly; 8hr); Roma (1 daily; 8hr); Toowoomba (1 daily; 13hr); Winton (1 daily; 6hr).
Charleville to: Barcaldine (1 daily; 6hr); Blackall (1 daily; 4hr 10min); Brisbane (2 daily; 10hr 40min); Cloncurry (1 daily; 13hr 30min); Longreach (1 daily; 6hr 30min); Mount Isa (2 daily; 15hr); Roma (2 daily; 3hr 40min); Toowoomba (2 daily; 8hr); Winton (1 daily; 9hr).
Charters Towers to: Camooweal (2 daily; 13hr); Cloncurry (2 daily; 8hr); Hughenden (2 daily; 3hr); Mount Isa (2 daily; 10hr); Richmond (2 daily; 5hr); Townsville (2 daily; 1hr 40min).
Cloncurry to: Camooweal (2 daily; 4hr 30min); Hughenden (2 daily; 5hr); Mount Isa (2 daily; 1hr 30min); Richmond (2 daily; 3hr 40min); Townsville (2 daily; 10hr).
Emerald to: Anakie (2 weekly; 35min); Barcaldine (2 weekly; 3hr 40min); Dingo (1 daily; 1 hr 35min); Longreach (2 weekly; 5hr 30min); Mackay (1 daily; 4hr); Rockhampton (1 daily; 3hr 30min).
Goondiwindi to: Brisbane (2 daily; 5hr); Toowoomba (2 daily; 3hr).
Longreach to: Barcaldine (1 daily; 1hr); Blackall (1 daily; 3hr 15min); Brisbane (1 daily; 16hr 10min); Charleville (1 daily; 6hr 30min); Cloncurry (1 daily; 6hr 30min); Dingo (2 weekly; 7hr 30min); Emerald (2 weekly; 5hr 30min); Mitchell (1 daily; 8hr); Mount Isa (1 daily; 7hr 50min); Rockhampton (2 weekly; 9hr 30min); Roma (1 daily; 10hr 25min); Toowoomba (1 daily; 14hr); Winton (1 daily; 2hr).
Mitchell to: Barcaldine (1 daily; 7hr); Blackall (1 daily; 5hr); Brisbane (2 daily; 9hr); Charleville (1 daily; 2hr 10min); Cloncurry (1 daily; 15hr); Longreach (1 daily; 8hr); Mount Isa (1 daily; 16hr); Roma (2 daily; 1hr); Toowoomba (2 daily; 6hr); Winton (1 daily; 11hr).
Mount Isa to: Barcaldine (1 daily; 9hr); Blackall (1 daily; 11hr 10min); Brisbane (1 daily; 25hr 20min); Charleville (1 daily; 14hr 40min); Charters Towers (2 daily; 9hr 50min); Cloncurry (2 daily; 2hr 35min); Hughenden (2 daily; 7hr); Longreach (1 daily; 8hr); Mitchell (1 daily; 16hr); Richmond (2 daily; 6hr); Roma (1 daily; 18hr 20min); Toowoomba (1 daily; 23hr); Townsville (2 daily; 12hr); Winton (1 daily; 6hr).
Richmond to: Charters Towers (2 daily; 5hr); Cloncurry (2 daily; 3hr); Hughenden (2 daily; 2hr); Mount Isa (2 daily; 4hr 30min); Townsville (2 daily; 7hr).
Roma to: Barcaldine (1 daily; 8hr); Blackall (1 daily; 7hr); Brisbane (2 daily; 7hr); Charleville (1 daily; 3hr

30min); Cloncurry (1 daily; 16hr 20min); Longreach (1 daily; 10hr); Mitchell (2 daily; 1hr); Mount Isa (1 daily; 18hr); Toowoomba (2 daily; 4hr 30min); Winton (1 daily; 12hr).
Stanthorpe to: Brisbane (1 daily; 5hr); Toowoomba (2 daily; 2hr 30min); Warwick (2 daily; 40min).
Toowoomba to: Barcaldine (1 daily; 13hr); Blackall (1 daily; 12hr); Brisbane (8 daily; 1hr 50min); Charleville (1 daily; 8hr); Cloncurry (1 daily; 21hr 30min); Goondiwindi (2 daily; 3hr); Kingaroy (1 daily except Fri; 3hr); Longreach (1 daily; 14hr 30min); Mitchell (2 daily; 6hr); Mount Isa (1 daily; 23hr); Rockhampton (1 daily; 12hr 45min); Roma (2 daily; 5hr); Stanthorpe (2 daily; 2hr 30min); Surfers Paradise (2 daily; 3hr); Warwick (2 daily; 3hr); Winton (2 daily; 16hr 30min).
Warwick to: Brisbane (2 daily; 3hr); Goondiwindi (1 daily; 2hr 30min); Stanthorpe (2 daily; 40min); Toowoomba (2 daily; 3hr).
Winton to: Barcaldine (1 daily; 3hr); Blackall (1 daily; 5hr 15min); Brisbane (1 daily; 19hr 25min); Charleville (1 daily; 9hr 20min); Cloncurry (1 daily; 4hr 30min); Longreach (1 daily; 2hr); Mitchell (1 daily; 11hr); Mount Isa (1 daily; 6hr); Roma (1 daily; 12hr 25min); Toowoomba (1 daily; 17hr).

Flights

Emerald to: Brisbane (2 daily; 2hr); Cairns (1–2 daily; 6hr 40min); Mackay (5 weekly; 5hr); Maroochydore (1 daily; 4hr 35min); Rockhampton (1–2 daily except Sun; 4hr); Townsville (1 daily except Sat; 4hr).
Longreach to: Brisbane (1 daily; 2hr 25min); Roma (5 weekly; 2hr).
Mount Isa to: Brisbane (1–2 daily; 2hr 15min); Burketown (1 weekly; 1hr 35min); Cairns (1–2 daily; 5hr 20min); Mackay (1 daily except Sun; 8hr); Mornington Island (5 weekly; 1hr 50min); Rockhampton (1–2 daily; 4hr); Townsville (1–3 daily; 2hr).
Roma to: Brisbane (1–2 daily; 1hr 10min); Longreach (4 weekly; 2hr).
Winton to: Townsville (2 weekly; 1hr 25min).

7

Northern Territory

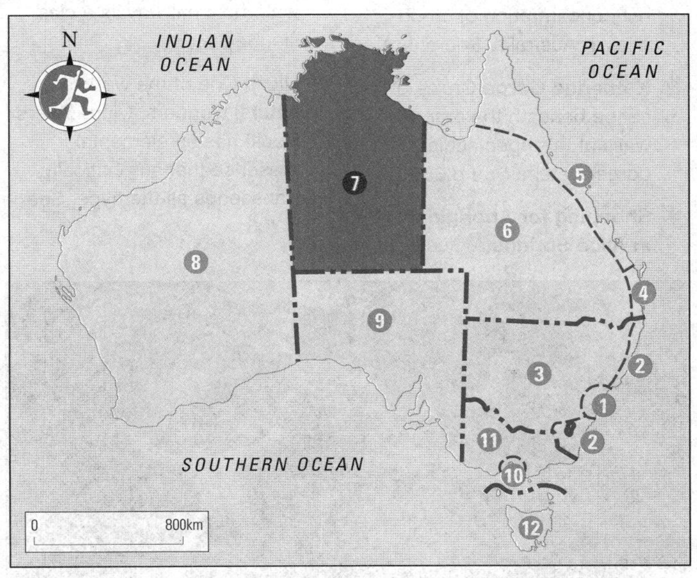

CHAPTER 7 Highlights

* **Aboriginal culture** You won't get all the answers, but the Territory is the best place to ask. See p.634
* **Kakadu National Park** Australia's largest national park is home to fascinating ancient rock art and an extraordinary diversity of flora and fauna. See pp.648–657
* **Top End crocs** The Mary River Wetlands have the highest concentration of crocodiles in Australia. See p.650
* **Katherine Gorge** Cruise or canoe beneath the orange walls of this spectacular gorge system. See p.665
* **Shopping for Aboriginal art in Alice Springs** A cluster of galleries in and around Todd Mall make finding a special souvenir easy. See p.684
* **Four-wheel driving in the Red Centre** Hop into your 4WD and explore the network of dirt tracks which radiate outwards from Alice Springs. See p.694
* **Kings Canyon** The two-hour walk around Kings Canyon, with a swim in a secluded waterhole halfway, is a classic. See p.697
* **Uluru** One of the world's natural wonders, Uluru (Ayers Rock) has an elemental presence that emphatically transcends all the hype. See p.703

△ Swimming in Kakudu National Park

7

Northern Territory

For the majority of Australians the **Northern Territory** – usually known as "the Territory", or simply "NT" – embodies the antithesis to the country's cushy suburban rim. Even the name conjures up a distant, frontier province – and, to an extent, this is still the case. Only around one percent of Australians inhabit an area covering a fifth of the continent, which partly explains why the Territory has never achieved full statehood. Territorians play up their tough, maverick image as outsiders in a land of "southerners", as well as the extremes of climate, distance and isolation that mould their temperaments. The Territory attracts those wanting to escape their past, and it's a place where people ask few questions. Most people were born elsewhere and that Australian institution, the "character", is in his element here, propping up the bars and bolstering the more palatable myths of the Territory's frontier history. The real "Crocodile Dundee" (see p.668) met his end here, and episodes like regular croc attacks and highway psycho killers help augment the Territory's untamed, Outback mystique.

The Territory's boundaries include some of Australia's oldest sites of Aboriginal occupation and some of the last regions to be colonized by Europeans. **Darwin**, the Territory's capital, is a prospering tropical town, while travellers from around the world flock here to explore the **Top End** (as tropical NT is known), primarily **Kakadu National Park**'s wildlife, waterways and Aboriginal art sites. Adjacent **Arnhem Land**, to the east, is also Aboriginal land – and out of bounds to casual visitors, although many tours now visit this never-colonized wilderness of scattered communities. Heading south you arrive at **Katherine**, where the main attraction is the nearby gorges within the **Nitmiluk National Park**.

By the time you reach **Tennant Creek**, 650km south of Katherine, you've left the interminable light woodland of the Top End and have begun to pass pastoral tablelands on the way to the central deserts surrounding **Alice Springs**. By no means the dusty Outback town many expect, Alice makes an excellent base to explore the region's natural wonders, of which that famous monolith, **Uluru** – or **Ayers Rock** – 450km to the southwest, is but one of many. This is one of the best areas to learn about the Aborigines of the Western Desert, among the last to come into contact with European settlers and the most studied by anthropologists.

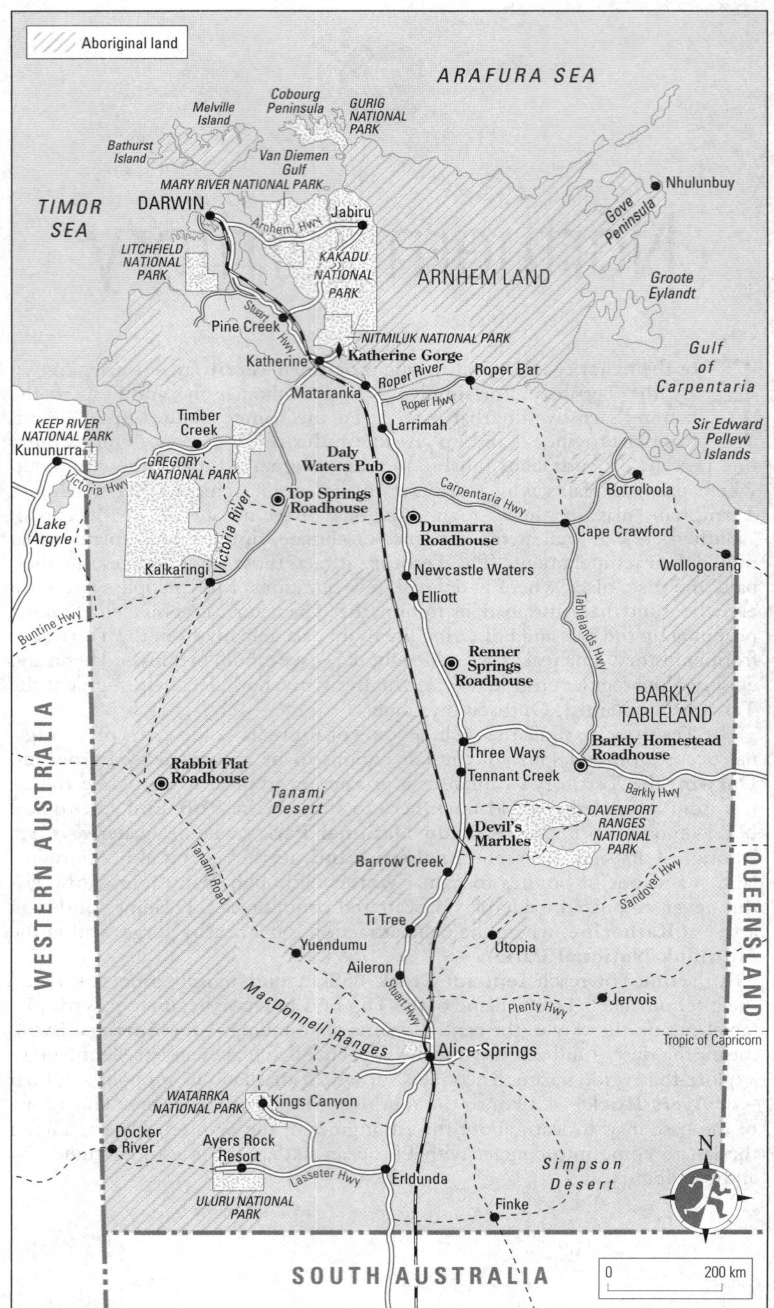
Aboriginal land
ARAFURA SEA
Cobourg Peninsula
Melville Island
GURIG NATIONAL PARK
Bathurst Island
Van Diemen Gulf
MARY RIVER NATIONAL PARK
TIMOR SEA
DARWIN
Jabiru
Arnhem Hwy
Nhulunbuy
Gove Peninsula
LITCHFIELD NATIONAL PARK
KAKADU NATIONAL PARK
ARNHEM LAND
Groote Eylandt
Stuart Hwy
Pine Creek
NITMILUK NATIONAL PARK
Katherine Gorge
Katherine
Gulf of Carpentaria
Roper River
Roper Bar
Mataranka
Roper Hwy
Larrimah
KEEP RIVER NATIONAL PARK
Timber Creek
Sir Edward Pellew Islands
Kununurra
GREGORY NATIONAL PARK
Daly Waters Pub
Victoria Hwy
Top Springs Roadhouse
Carpentaria Hwy
Borroloola
Lake Argyle
Victoria River
Dunmarra Roadhouse
Cape Crawford
Wollogorang
Kalkaringi
Newcastle Waters
Elliott
Buntine Hwy
Tablelands Hwy
Renner Springs Roadhouse
BARKLY TABLELAND
Three Ways
Barkly Homestead Roadhouse
Tennant Creek
Rabbit Flat Roadhouse
Tanami Desert
Barkly Hwy
DAVENPORT RANGES NATIONAL PARK
Devil's Marbles
WESTERN AUSTRALIA
Barrow Creek
Tanami Road
QUEENSLAND
Sandover Hwy
Ti Tree
Yuendumu
Utopia
Aileron
MacDonnell Ranges
Stuart Hwy
Jervois
Plenty Hwy
Tropic of Capricorn
Alice Springs
WATARRKA NATIONAL PARK
Kings Canyon
Docker River
Ayers Rock Resort
Lasseter Hwy
Erldunda
Simpson Desert
N
ULURU NATIONAL PARK
Finke
SOUTH AUSTRALIA
0
200 km

Darwin and the Top End

Darwin, the Territory's capital, lies midway along Australia's convoluted northern coast. Most tourists end up spending no more time here than it takes to visit nearby **Kakadu** and **Litchfield national parks**, continue their Australian circuit or maybe fly on to Indonesia. Even today the city possesses little appeal for short-term visitors, though it's a lot better than it used to be. Besides the two well-known parks mentioned above, the **Mary River National Park** offers a chance to explore a croc-infested wetland environment not accessible in Kakadu, while on the east side of Kakadu sits little known **Arnhem Land**, never colonized and slowly opening up to tourism. In the southwest, the **Daly River** region comprises small Aboriginal communities and riverside fishing haunts.

Darwin and around

Setting up a colonial settlement on Australia's remote northern shores was never going to be easy, and it took four abortive attempts in various locations over a period of 45 years before **DARWIN** (originally called Palmerston) was finally established in 1869 by the new South Australian state keen to exploit its recently acquired "northern territory". The early colonists' aim was to pre-empt foreign occupation and create a trading post, a "new Singapore", for the British Empire.

Things got off to a promising start with the arrival in 1872 of the **Overland Telegraph Line** (OTL), following the route pioneered by explorer **John McDouall Stuart** in 1862, that finally linked Australia with the rest of the world. **Gold** was discovered at Pine Creek while pylons were being erected for the OTL, prompting a goldrush and the construction of a southbound railway. After the goldrush ran its course, a cyclone flattened the depressed town in 1897, but by 1911, when Darwin adopted its present name, the rough-and-ready frontier outpost had grown into a small government centre, servicing the mines and properties of the Top End. Yet even by 1937, after being razed by a second cyclone, the town had a population of just 1500.

The first boom came with World War II after **Japanese air raids** destroyed Darwin once again at a cost of hundreds of lives, though this news was suppressed at the time, as was systematic looting by the army. The fear of invasion and an urgent need to get troops to the war zone led to the swift construction of the **Stuart Highway**, the first reliable land link between Darwin and the rest of the country.

Three decades of guarded postwar prosperity followed until Christmas Day, 1974, when **Cyclone Tracy** devastated Darwin. Fortunately a low tide limited storm surges and only 66 people lost their lives, but Tracy marked the end of old Darwin, psychologically as well as architecturally. The city was hastily and functionally rebuilt, but for many residents this was the last straw, and having been evacuated they never returned.

Since the mid-1990s Darwin has been making a concerted effort to take itself seriously as Australia's commercial "gateway" into Asia. With the help of the tourist boom, kicked off by Kakadu's exposure in the film *Crocodile Dundee* (as well as some long-overdue refurbishments in Mitchell Street and the Mall),

Aborigines in the Northern Territory

Over a quarter of the Territory's inhabitants are Aborigines, a far higher proportion than anywhere else in Australia. Most modern maps show that half of the Territory is now **"Aboriginal land"**, commercially unviable and returned to nominal Aboriginal control following protracted land claims. This uniquely Territorian demography is the result of a formerly sympathetic federal government's co-operation with the politically powerful Land Councils within the NT, established following the Land Rights Act of 1976. Excepting the national parks, most Aboriginal land is out of bounds to visitors without a permit or invitation, although some roads which cross them are exempt.

While the overwhelming majority of non-Aboriginal people tend to live in the two major urban centres of Darwin and Alice Springs, most Aborigines live in Outback communities, or occasionally in still more remote **outstations**: small satellite communities supporting a couple of families. While outstations replicate a nomadic, pre-Contact social group, the communities have been less successful, mixing clans who may have been enemies for eons.

Although snazzy interpretive centres in the national parks tend to concentrate on the eco-trendy close bond with nature, the truth is that Aboriginal society in the Territory and elsewhere in the north is imploding. The Territory is Australia's murder capital, chiefly led by men whose self-esteem as family providers and custodians of the Law (or even once poorly paid but respected stockmen) has been eliminated. The fact that Aboriginal men make up a disproportionately high percentage of the prison population is not solely due to widely assumed racism – although such attitudes may have driven them there in the first place. Furthermore the conditions in which many Aboriginal people live, along with their health, is worse than in many developing nations.

You will be reminded of these thorny and complex issues as you encounter the depressing spectacle of the Aboriginal fringe dwellers staggering around, most conspicuously in Katherine and Alice. Alienated from the affluent white society that busies itself around them, these people are the casualties of the clash of cultures which, in the Territory, is still within living memory. This chasm between two different cultures is actually far greater than most visitors realize. The failure of assimilation – the naive policy of the 1950s and 1960s – has been followed by the current failure of self-determination, while talk of Reconciliation or even land rights is merely symbolic and does little to improve actual living conditions.

Darwin is trying to shake off its bland feel of a "company town". Economic prospects were boosted still further by the completion in record time of the long-proposed **Darwin rail link** with Alice Springs in early 2004. Mining continues to flourish, though the surrounding land is agriculturally unviable and Top End beef is mediocre and mostly exported as live cattle to Asia.

Day-trips from Darwin include the popular Litchfield Park (see p.660) as well as the Aboriginal-owned Bathurst and Melville islands, a thirty-minute flight from town. Also worth a visit are either Crocodylus Park, on the edge of Darwin, or the Darwin Crocodile Farm, south of town, which makes a good day out when combined with the Territory Wildlife Park (see p.660). It takes more than a day to appreciate Kakadu; for tours there see p.644.

Arrival and information

Darwin Airport is 12km northeast of the city centre; a **shuttle bus** service (Ⓣ08/8981 5066 or 1800 358 945; $6) meets international flights and drops off passengers at all major hotels and the **Transit Centre** behind 69 Mitchell

Yet looking at the galleries of Alice Springs and the droning forests of didgeridoos, it would appear that Aboriginal **culture** is thriving. Some communities are inviting responsible tour operators to visit their settlements, or are setting up their own operations, so allowing you to experience something of their current and former way of life. It must be remembered, however, that even in the Territory no Aborigines live in or off the bush as they once did, although hunting and gathering is still a pastime to supplement conventional food sources.

Despite the often depressing realities, for those interested in getting to the heart of the enigmatic Australian wilderness, the Northern Territory offers enriching and memorable travel, providing an introduction to a land that has sustained a fascinating and complex culture for at least sixty thousand years.

Aboriginal tours

The term **"Aboriginal tour"**, while seeming to offer the promise of a privileged insight into the culture of indigenous Australians, can be misleading. Some tours will simply be focused on Aborigines and their culture, some will be offered by white-managed agencies but led by Aboriginal people (sometimes coerced into the role of guide), and some will be run by Aboriginal-owned organizations. Tours can often be no more than an opportunity for the operator to charge tourists over the odds to learn Aboriginal secrets and laws. Yet this secrecy, which was one of the pillars that supported traditional Aboriginal society, is exactly that, and what you learn on a tour can be a very watered-down version of the truth, from people reluctant to give away closely guarded customs.

As a tourist, meeting Aboriginal people by chance and getting to know them is difficult or takes some nerve, especially as Aboriginal land is, for the most part, out-of-bounds. Meaningful contact with Aborigines for the short-term visitor is therefore unlikely. Many Aborigines are weary of endless questions, well-meaning though they are, and an entirely different strategy in social dealings renders most exchanges awkward and superficial. In many cases then, it is from a knowledgeable and sympathetic non-Aboriginal guide (as well as from older, pre-PC-era books on the subject) that you can learn more about Aboriginal life and culture than which berries make good eating.

The message here is that you should not expect the earth by hopping onto an Aboriginal tour. In most cases it will only scrape the surface of a complex and arcane way of life, an experience that cannot easily be bought across a travel desk.

Street; a **taxi** (☎13 10 08, or see p.637) to town from the airport costs about $30. Given the proximity of Indonesia, Darwin is the cheapest place from which to leave Australia (see "Listings", p.646, for details).

On the other hand, Darwin is a long way from anywhere in Australia – the bus journey from Cairns takes a gruelling day and a half, including changes, and coming direct from Sydney, Melbourne or Perth, you're much better off flying. **Interstate buses** also arrive at the Transit Centre, where you can make reservations for onward journeys. Currently trains arrive at the forlorn **Darwin Passenger Rail Terminal** 20km from town, south of Berrimah, on Tuesday afternoons, heading back on the two-day journey to Adelaide on Wednesday mornings, though in peek season (May, June & July) this service runs twice-weekly. A shuttle bus ($9) ferries passengers between the Transit Centre and the rail terminal.

Five minutes' walk up from the Mitchell Street Transit Centre, the **Visitors Information Centre** (Mon–Fri 9am–5pm, Sat 9am–3pm, Sun 10am–3pm; ☎1300 138 886, Ⓦwww.tourismtopend.com.au) is the official tourist information outlet and has plenty of material on national parks throughout the NT. It's

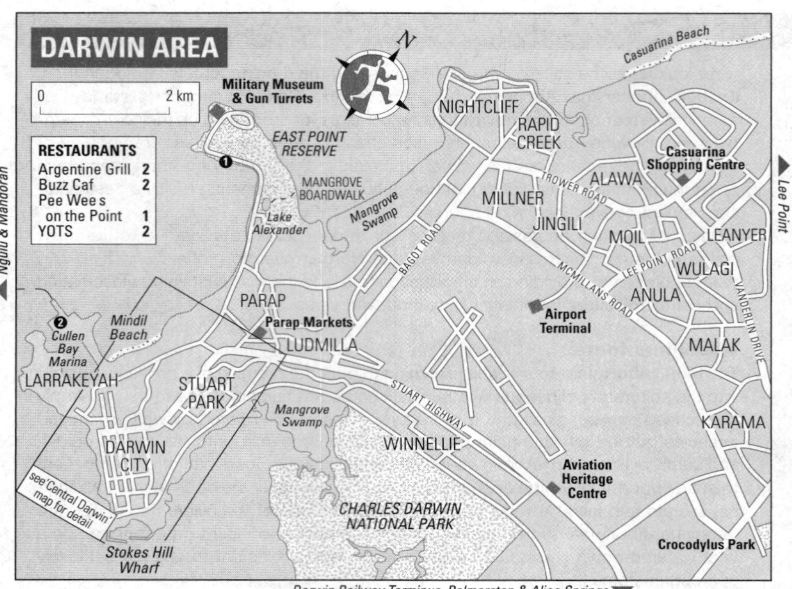

worth noting that local rental cars booked through the centre can come with unlimited kilometres (albeit at a higher rate), a deal which may not be available if you approach the rental agency direct. The free glossies *This Week In Darwin* and *Destination Darwin and the Top End* (the latter is the better of the two) can be picked up all around town – they're mostly rose-tinted advertorials, but are handy for their **maps**, including bus routes.

City transport

The city's inexpensive **bus service** can deliver you to most corners of Darwin. Services operate daily from around 7am to 8pm, with some routes running until after 11pm on Friday and Saturday. The **bus terminal** (ⓣ08/8924 7666) is on Harry Chan Avenue, at the bottom of Cavenagh Street, with a major **interchange** at the Casuarina shopping centre in the northern suburbs. A "Tourcard", offering unlimited travel for between one and seven days ($5–25), is available at both places. Buses leaving the city for the suburbs head out along Cavenagh Street, running out as far as Palmerston, and come back in along Mitchell and Smith streets.

Most hostels and some hotels rent out **bicycles** for around $18 a day. Although Darwin is flat, it's also perennially hot and humid, so East Point Reserve, 8km from the centre, is about as far as you'd want to ride for fun. If you feel confident a "twist and go" **scooter** is much more fun; you can rent them opposite the Transit Centre (ⓣ0418 892 885). To rent a 50cc moped ($40 per day; no passengers) you'll need to show a driver's licence. For a 125cc bike (from $70 per day) you'll require a motorcycle licence, although you can carry a passenger. A few local **car rental** outfits do battle along Mitchell and Smith streets, with prices starting at around $50 a day, plus mileage (see "Listings" on p.646, for more). **Taxis** work out at about $1.50 a kilometre and there are plenty

Top End weather

There is a certain amount of misunderstanding about the **tropical climate** of the Top End, usually summed up as the hot and humid "Dry" and the hotter and very humid "Wet". Give or take a couple of weeks either way, this is the pattern: the **Dry** begins in April when rains stop and humidity decreases – although this always remains high in the maritime tropics, whatever the season. It may take a couple of months for vehicular access to be restored to all far-flung tracks, but the bush never looks greener, while engorged waterfalls pound the base of the escarpments. From now until October skies are generally cloud-free, with daily temperatures reliably peaking in the low thirties centigrade, though June and July nights might cool down to 10°C – sheer agony for seasoned Top Enders but bliss for unacclimatized tourists.

From October until the end of the year temperatures and humidity begin to rise – the dreaded **Build Up**. Clouds accumulate to discharge brief showers, and it's a time of year when the weak-willed or insufficiently drunk can flip out and go "troppo" as the unbearable tensions of heat, humidity and dysfunctional air-con push them over the edge. Around November storms can still be frustratingly dry but often give rise to spectacular lightning shows (Darwin is the world's most lightning-prone city). While rain showers become longer and more frequent towards Christmas – the onset of the **Wet** – access on sealed roads is rarely a problem.

Only when the actual **monsoon** commences at the turn of the year do the daily afternoon storms quickly rejuvenate and then saturate the land. This daily cycle lasts for at least two months and is much more tolerable than you might expect, with a daily thunderous downpour cooling things off from the mid- to the low-thirties. Along with Queensland's Cape York, Darwin's proximity to the equator gives it a true monsoon. Two hundred kilometres south the rains are much less heavy, though a Wet is experienced along the coast as far southwest as Derby, WA, and Townsville on the north Queensland coast.

Coming in from the west, **cyclones**, sometimes just a week apart, occur most commonly at either end of the Wet and can dump 30cm of rain in as many hours, with winds of 100kph and gusts twice that speed. Frequent updates on the erratic path and intensity of these tropical depressions are given on national and state radio, so that most people are fully prepared if and when a storm actually hits. Some fizzle out or head back out to sea; others can intensify and zigzag across the land, as nearly every community between Exmouth, WA (1999) and Darwin (1974) has found to its cost.

cruising around: either hail one on the street or call ☎13 10 08, ☎08/8981 3777 or ☎08/8981 3300.

Accommodation

Darwin has **accommodation** ranging from luxury hotels to backpackers galore, and most of it is conveniently central. Rates in the town's apartments and more expensive hotels can drop by half from **late September through to March**, and even hostels drop a couple of dollars from their rates, especially for longer stays. Make sure you ring around or check the web sites before making a reservation during this period.

Hotels, motels and apartments

Most **hotels** and **motels** are right in the city centre, with the more prestigious examples found along the Esplanade offering views of the bay. If you're looking for self-catering accommodation, there are a couple of **apartment-hotels** in the centre, but for the most part they're further out.

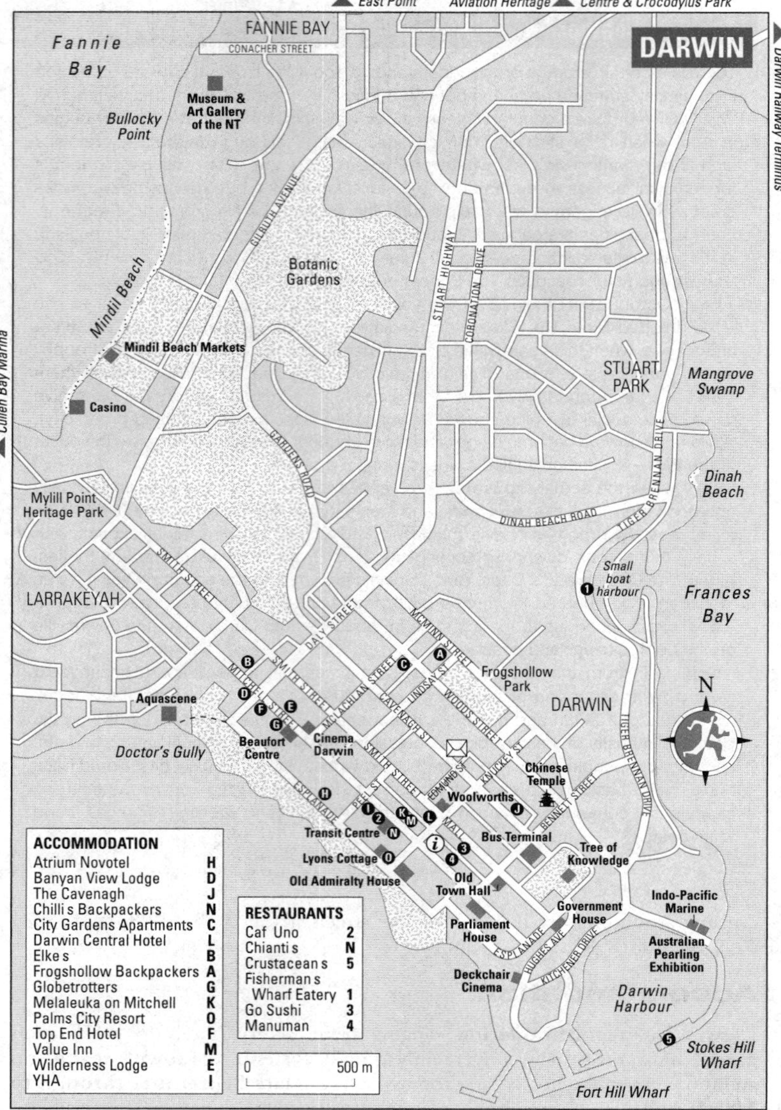

Atrium Novotel 100 Esplanade ⓣ08/8941 0755, ⓦwww.novoteldarwin.com.au. Upmarket hotel along the Esplanade with a foliage-draped atrium, bars, restaurants, a gym and pool as well as sea views and the popular *Zest* restaurant. ❻

City Gardens Apartments 93 Woods St ⓣ08/8941 2888 or 1800 891 138, ⓦwww.citygardensapts.com.au. Spacious, centrally located family units with a pool, two minutes' walk from Frogshollow Park, five minutes from town. ❻

Darwin Central Hotel Knuckey St ⓣ08/8944 9000, ⓦwww.darwincentral.com.au. Luxury high-rise modern hotel right by the Mall with spacious rooms, a choice of restaurants and bars, and great off-season rates. ❼

Palms City Resort 64 Esplanade, corner of Knuckey St ⓣ08/8982 9200, ⓦwww.citypalms.com. Set in its own mini-jungle in a good location at the city end of the Esplanade. Accommodation is in a block of motel rooms (basic or deluxe) or in a few detached duplex villas with some self-catering facilities and a deck. There's also a small pool. Breakfast from $15. ❺

Top End Hotel Cnr Mitchell and Daly streets ⓣ08/8981 6511 or 1800 626 151, ⓦtopend.bestwestern.com.au. Part of the *Best Western* chain, with low-rise motel-style rooms next to Darwin's famous *Sportsman's Bar*, complete with garden and pool. ❺

Value Inn 50 Mitchell St ⓣ08/8981 4733, ⓦwww.valueinn.com.au. No-frills motel with small en-suite rooms (TV, air-con and fridge) that sleep up to three – a real squeeze, but it's in a great location and there's a pool too. ❹

Backpackers and budget accommodation

Compared to the East Coast, you pay more for less in most of Darwin's **backpackers**, and staff aren't quite the cream of the hospitality industry (it's a Territory thing). Some places offer to pay for your airport shuttle if you book two nights or more, although as some backpackers are owned by tour operators staff may try to sell you tours whether you're interested or not. Unless you pay extra, most turn on the air-con (where available) only at night; without air-con a big, quiet fan is essential (and in fact can be preferable to noisy a/c units). Every backpackers features a tour desk and Internet facilities, but don't get too excited about offers of a "free breakfast": in most cases it's usually Z-brand tea or coffee, plus dried milk, bread and jam.

Banyan View Lodge 119 Mitchell St ⓣ08/8981 8644. Quiet YWCA (it accepts single males too) with twin rooms with fans and fridge but shared bathrooms and not much of a lounge area or an atmosphere. There's parking round the back. Four-bed dorms from $20, rooms ❸

The Cavenagh 12 Cavenagh St ⓣ08/8941 6383 or 1300 851 198, ⓦwww.thecavenagh.com. Converted old motel built around a swimming pool and superficially transformed with a smart new café-bar and deck out front and a big kitchen. Round the back it's not so flash, with sixteen-bed dorms (from $16) for the desperate, and much less congested four-bed en-suite dorms (from $23). Rooms ❸, motel rooms ❹

Chilli's Backpackers 69a Mitchell St ⓣ08/8949 9722 or 1800 351 313, ⓦwww.chillis.com.au. The town's original YHA, with airy decks where you can eat, chat or sunbake by the spas. It's very central and attracts a lively crowd. Dorms (four, six or eight beds) $20, rooms ❷

Elke's 112 Mitchell St ⓣ08/8981 6302 or 1800 816 302, ⓦwww.elkesbackpackers.com.au. Set in an old tropical house halfway down Mitchell Street. Its once excellent reputation seems to have slipped, though it's still a popular and reasonable option. There's a shady pool and garden area with off-street parking. Small four-bed dorms $22, rooms ❸

Frogshollow Backpackers 27 Lindsay St ⓣ08/8941 2600 or 1800 068 686, ⓦwww.frogs-hollow.com.au. A shady but comparatively cramped older purpose-built place, though it suffers from over-large dorms (8 or 12 beds), some of which only have fans. Dorms $20/22, rooms ❷

Globetrotters 97 Mitchell St ⓣ08/8981 5385 or 1800 800 798, ⓦwww.globetrotters.com.au. A free beer on arrival gives you an idea of what to expect from this shabby ex-motel. Also has a pool, bar and deck. Dorms (6 or 8 beds) from $20, rooms ❸

Melaleuca on Mitchell 52 Mitchell St ⓣ08/8941 7800 or 1300 723 437, ⓦwww.melaleucaonmitchell.com.au. This impressive-looking 400-bed "backpackers hotel resort" takes the processing of Darwin backpackers to a new level. There's accommodation in dorms (4 or 6 beds), doubles, triples and quads, while facilities include a flashy sundeck, pool, waterfall, and a bar with huge TV screen – though it's all rather soulless. Swipe card security tracks your every move, and there's also off-street parking and a women-only floor. Dorms $28, rooms ❸

Wilderness Lodge 88 Mitchell St ⓣ08/8981 8363 or 1800 068 886, ⓦwww.wildlodge.com.au. One of the better choices in the cheap 'n' cheerful category, set in a small, much-modified old building midway along Mitchell St with a good-sized pool, shady back lot and a rather cramped kitchen. Dorms from $21, rooms ❷

YHA 69 Mitchell St ⓣ08/8981 3995, ⓔdarwinyha@yhant.org.au. Well-designed backpackers right by the Transit Centre (though it's now overshadowed by the snazzy new *Melaleuca* over the road), with a spacious dining area overlooking the pool. Some rooms are en suite, although many are poorly ventilated and could do with a good clean. Eight-bed dorms £22, four-bed dorms $24, rooms ❸

Camping and caravan parks

The following places are both near the Stuart Highway in Winnellie, between 7km and 10km from the centre, a rather godforsaken light-industrial suburb, lying along the southern edge of the airport. Many of Darwin's caravan parks are pitched at long-term stays or touring retirees. Buses #5 and #8 both run here from the central bus terminal.

Hidden Valley Caravan Park 15 Hidden Valley Road, Berrimah ⓣ08/8947 1422, ⓦwww.hvtp.com.au. Caravan park with tent sites and self-contained units, plus a pool and kiosk. ❹

Shady Glen Caravan Park Cnr Farrell Crescent and Stuart Highway ⓣ1800 662 253, ⓦwww.shadyglen.com.au. Air-con cabins (❹) with TV, pool, kiosk, kitchen and Internet access.

The City

Present-day Darwin spreads north from the end of a stubby peninsula where the settlement was originally established on the lands of the Larrakeyah Aborigines. Over the years, suburbs have sprung up across the flat, mangrove-fringed headland, but for the visitor most of the action lies between the Wharf Precinct and East Point, 9km to the north. Tropical vegetation apart, it's not a good-looking city: huge tides create a warm, sludge-filled bay devoid of waves, while repeated destruction from cyclones, air raids and termites has put paid to most of the town's older architecture.

If you don't mind the humidity the city's attractions can all be reached on foot. Alternatively you could rent a car or scooter, or take the **Tour Tub** minibus (daily 9am–4pm; day-ticket $25, half-day $15; ⓣ08/8985 6322), a fun way to see most of the places detailed below over a day. It departs on the hour from Smith Street Mall, on Knuckey Street, and you can hop on and off as you please.

The City Centre

The city's shopping centre is **Smith Street Mall**, or the Mall as it's known these days. Kids love the walk-through fountain near the century-old **Hotel Victoria**, once Darwin's answer to a Wild West saloon, though it has now been subsumed by modern development so you'll hardly notice it's there. On and around the Mall, several art galleries and gift shops sell pearls, croc-skin products, classy Aboriginal crafts and tacky Australiana.

There are more old buildings further south along Smith Street as you cross Bennett Street. The **Old Town Hall**, built in 1883, was demolished by Cyclone Tracy, but its ruins are occasionally used as the location for outdoor performances by the theatre group based in the stone building, **Brown's Mart**, opposite. In the park behind Brown's Mart (opposite Darwin City Council) is a huge banyan tree known as the **Tree of Knowledge** marking the location of the former Chinatown, destroyed during the raids of World War II. At the beginning of the last century the industrious Chinese outnumbered Europeans three-to-one in the Top End, and were involved in everything from building the Pine Creek railroad to running market gardens. Backtracking up Bennett Street to Woods Street you'll find the ornate **Chinese Temple** (Mon–Fri 8am–4pm, Sat & Sun 8am–3pm; free) and **museum** (irregular times, try weekday mornings; free). The temple is another post-Tracy restoration, using the altar and statues from the 1887 original, and still serves Darwin's surviving Chinese population.

Walking back through the Mall, a left turn down Knuckey Street and over Mitchell Street leads to the Esplanade. On the left corner is the former **Admiralty House** (Mon–Sat 10am–5pm; free), a tropical-style 1920s house elevated on stilts which has managed to survive cyclones and air raids. Opposite is **Lyons Cottage** (daily 10am–5pm; free), a stone bungalow, dating from the same decade, which hosts changing photographic displays of early Territorian history. Back on Mitchell Street near the Transit Centre, the **Mitchell Street Tourist Precinct** is home to a welcome cluster of outdoor bars and cafés with occasional street entertainment.

Looking out over the harbour, the lawns along the **Esplanade** make for a pleasant stroll. Walking north along the Esplanade you'll end up at Daly Street, which marks the very end of the Stuart Highway. From here it's a straight 3000-kilometre run to Port Augusta in South Australia, with about half a dozen traffic lights on the way. Otherwise, a left turn down Doctor's Gully leads to the ever-popular **Aquascene** (see Ⓦwww.aquascene.com.au for tide-dependent opening hours or call Ⓣ08/8981 7837; $7), where at high tide scores of catfish, mullet and metre-long milkfish come in to be hand-fed on stale bread (supplied free). Heading in the opposite direction brings you to the modern white **Parliament House** (daily 8am–5pm; free 90min tours Sat 9am & 11am), at the southern end of the Esplanade, from where pathways along the shore lead to the Wharf Precinct.

The Wharf Precinct

At the southern end of town, **Stokes Hill Wharf** has become the focus of a wharfside tourist precinct with a couple of souvenir shops and a food court with quayside seating which comes to life every evening. Well worth a visit is the live coral display at **Indo-Pacific Marine** (daily: April–Oct 10am–5pm; Nov–March 9am–1pm; $18; Ⓣ08/8999 6573, Ⓦwww.indopacific.com.au), where the regular, informative talks will set you straight about corals – the Timor Sea north of Darwin is one of the world's richest and most diverse coral environments, though they're obscured from view by the tidal silt which feeds them. In the same building, the **Australian Pearling Exhibition** (daily 10am–5pm; $8) is a similarly imaginative display, describing Darwin's part in northwestern Australia's still-booming pearling industry. Round the other side of the harbour, a stairway up the cliff just past the Oil Storage Tunnels (on the Tour Tub itinerary, but about as interesting as they sound) leads up to a viewing point and to **Government House**, built in 1883 after the original residence was devoured by white ants. Rarely open to the public, it's nevertheless a good example of an elegant, though much restored, tropical building.

Cullen Bay Marina and the Fannie Bay museums

Walking north about 2km along the full length of Smith Street will bring you to a small roundabout and a sign pointing down to Cullen Bay Marina. Right by the roundabout you'll notice the so-called **Mylill Point Heritage Park**, a couple of pre-Tracy tropical houses, while down in **Cullen Bay Marina** itself you'll find some good restaurants (see p.645) in an attractive waterside setting.

From the marina roundabout it's a short hop north to the extensive **Botanic Gardens** (daily 7am–7pm; free). A further kilometre north brings you to the excellent **Museum and Art Gallery of the NT** (Mon–Fri 9am–5pm, Sat & Sun 10am–5pm; free) on Conacher Street overlooking Fannie Bay. The museum features an absorbing display of Aboriginal art by the Tiwi people of Bathurst and Melville islands, as well as Top End bark paintings and works from the central deserts in the familiar pointillist style. Elsewhere there are stuffed examples of everything that flies, swims and hops, skips or jumps in the Territory, while the maritime section comprises a massive boat shed housing craft as diverse as pearling luggers, Indonesian *praus*, Polynesian outriggers and the simplest of bark canoes. There's also an imaginatively designed exhibition commemorating Darwin's destruction by Cyclone Tracy, with a chilling film of the aftermath.

On to East Point

Continuing north, the main road (served by buses #4 and #6) curves right, while East Point Road continues straight up, entering **East Point Reserve**, an area of bushland that's home to around two thousand wallabies. A kilometre from the turn-off you pass **Lake Alexander**, a recreational saltwater lake suitable for year-round swimming and from where a **mangrove boardwalk** (currently under reconstruction) takes you out into the tidal environment.

The road ends at the **Military Museum** (daily 9.30am–5pm; $10) and **gun turrets**. Darwin was repeatedly bombed by the Japanese from 1942; at the time, news of both the air raids and the thirty thousand enemy troops massed on Timor was suppressed. The museum commemorates these events with a short video and some rather staid displays of uniforms, medals and other wartime memorabilia, while in the grounds a collection of aircraft engines and associated hardware quietly rusts away. **East Point** itself is also a good spot to observe the striking hues of Darwin's multichrome sunsets; if driving, watch out for the wallabies on the way back.

Aviation Heritage Centre, Crocodylus Park and Charles Darwin National Park

Set in a hangar off the Stuart Highway, on the southeastern edge of the airport, the non-profit **Aviation Heritage Centre** (daily 9am–5pm; $11; ⓦwww.darwinsairwar.com.au; bus #5 or #8) is dominated by the huge bulk of a B52 bomber on loan from the US Air Force and describes the engaging story of civil and military aviation in the region.

Further down the Stuart Highway, taking a left at the Berrimah traffic lights leads you to the crocodile research facility and farm of **Crocodylus Park** (daily 9am–5pm; tours at 10am, noon & 2pm; $25; bus #5) on McMillans Road. At the croc-filled lagoon here you can get within kissing distance of a three-metre man-eater; these usually dormant reptiles are coaxed into action during daily feeding sessions which coincide with tours led by guides. There's also an absorbing museum giving you the lowdown on the world of crocs.

Eating

There have been big improvements in Darwin's restaurant scene in recent years, and for a city of its size, there are plenty of good-quality options for every budget. The climate makes it likely that **seafood** will have been frozen, and so might as well be from Cape Cod as from the Timor Sea. That said, anglers are drawn to the Top End hoping to catch **barramundi**, an overrated "fighting fish", although **snapper** (aka Red Emperor) is much more flavoursome. Besides the places listed below don't forget Mindil Beach Markets (see p.646), especially on a Thursday night, and the varied range of inexpensive take-aways alongside the water at the end of Stokes Hill Wharf.

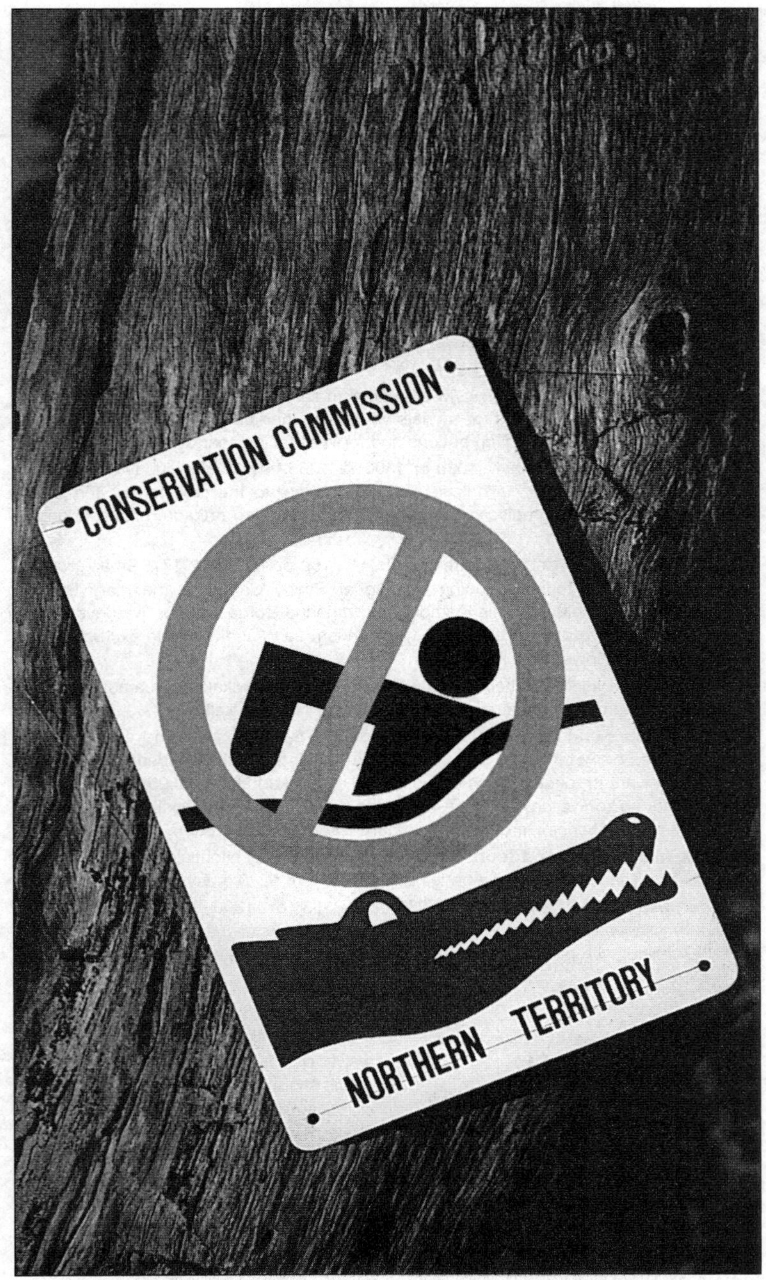

△ Crocodile warning

Tours from Darwin to the Top End

For most visitors, Darwin is simply a convenient base for trips into the surrounding countryside. **Kakadu** is the obvious draw, and for many is the main reason for visiting the Top End, but **Litchfield Park** is nearer and has several easily accessible swimming holes. While Litchfield remains a popular day-trip, most Kakadu tour operators offer two- to five-day tours, the latter including possible excursions into **Arnhem Land** or a return via Litchfield.

Note that the Territory and especially the Top End has not always attracted the cream of **tour guides** – budget operators used to try to out-do one another with dangerous practices designed to make tours more exciting and memorable. This trend came to a tragic end when a well-established guide led a group into a croc-filled billabong in Kakadu one night in 2002, resulting in the death of one woman. There are now moves to introduce proper training of guides, something that is long overdue. Operators listed below are recommended but be aware that the quality of the guides can vary. Expect to pay around $140 a day for your tour.

Billy Can ⓣ1800 813 484, ⓦwww.billycan.com.au. Small group tours (2–5 days) around the Top End catering for tourists who enjoy their comforts, with accommodated (as opposed to camping) options and forward-facing seats.

Darwin Day Tours ⓣ08/8947 4060 or 1300 721 365, ⓦwww.darwindaytours.com. Half-day tours (essentially a bus service plus cuppa) to the croc farms, Territory Wildlife Park and the jumping croc cruise, plus day-trips to Kakadu, Litchfield and Katherine ($100–150).

Gondwana Shop 6, Transit Centre ⓣ08/8941 7162 or 1800 242 177. Small-group three-day Kakadu tours (including boating at Shady Camp on the Mary River wetlands), four-day Mary River, Kakadu and Katherine Gorge trips (or five days with Litchfield), and five-day Kakadu tours with Arnhem Land and a unique excursion to Palumpa on the lower Daly River region.

Kakadu Dreams 50 Mitchell St ⓣ08/8981 3266, ⓦwww.kakadudreams.com.au. Low-cost full-on fun and games in packed 4WDs. "No oldies allowed".

Odyssey Tours and Safaris 50 Mitchell St ⓣ1800 891 190 ⓦwww.odysaf.com.au. Safari-tented or motel-based tours across the Top End and the Kimberley for those who don't want to rough it. Trips include three-day Kakadu tours ($695 tented, $895 in a lodge) up to five-day and one-week see-it-all trips from Manyallaluk, south of Katherine, to Katherine Gorge, Litchfield and Kakadu ($1465–1800).

Unique Indigenous Land Tours ⓣ08/8928 0022. One-day Litchfield tours and one- or two-day Kakadu tours with Aboriginal guides. From $220 a day.

Wilderness 4WD Adventures ⓣ08/8981 8363 or 1300 666 100, ⓦwww.wildernessadventures.com.au. Competitively priced tours (2–5 days) through Kakadu and Litchfield, with plenty of fun and action. The longer tours are a better deal.

City centre and the wharf area

Cafe Uno Mitchell St Tourist Precinct. Nice Italian café with daily lunchtime specials from $11 and dinners for around $20; there's a cocktail bar at the back. Daily 7.30am till late.

Chianti's Mitchell Centre, Mitchell St. Another quality Italian joint; the beef and mango salad, penne carbonara and ravioli funghi (all around $20) are popular. Daily 7.30am till late.

Crustacean's Stokes Hill Wharf ⓣ08/8981 8658. Set apart from the takeaway hoi-polloi at the end of the pier, this place does entrées like creamy seafood chowder and scallops in white wine (both around $15) and mains like seafood platters of crab, prawn, fish, lobster and Moreton Bay Bugs ($55 for two). Nightly from 6pm.

Fisherman's Wharf Eatery Fishermans's Wharf, Frances Bay Drive. Out of the centre, this long-established Darwinians' getaway does cheap seafood and chips for around $15. Mon–Sat 8.30am–8.30pm, Sun 10.30am–8.30pm

Go Sushi Mitchell St. All your rolled-up Japanese favourites plus vegetable tempura ($10), chicken yakatori ($15), Asahi beer and sake. Mon–Sat 10.30am–9pm

Hanuman 28 Mitchell St ⓣ08/8941 3500. One of Darwin's best restaurants, serving Indian, Nonya and Thai dishes such as wild barramundi and lemongrass ($24) and lamb Kerala ($19). Tues–Fri noon–2.30pm & 6.30pm–late, Sat & Sun 6.30pm–late.

Cullen Bay, Fannie Bay and East Point

Argentine Grill Marina Blvd, Cullen Bay. Aged steaks and game plus seafood. Start with something like smoked paprika and lemon whitebait on salad ($18) and move on to the Ocean Range: oven-baked chicken, prawns, barra and calamari in a saffron rice with a roast capsicum sauce ($34). Daily except Thursday from 6pm.

Buzz Cafe Marine Blvd, Cullen Bay. Popular quay-side café where starters include orange-glazed duck shanks ($14) while mains feature offerings like beer-battered barramundi with a lemon mayo salad ($24). Mon–Fri 11.30am till late, Sat & Sun 9am–late.

Pee Wee's on the Point East Point Road ⓣ08/8981 6868. Set on an outdoor terrace in the bush overlooking Fannie Bay, with starters featuring a daily-changing "seasonal showcase of Territorian dishes" ($30 for two). Follow that up with a crispy roasted duckling with sautéed garlic and rosemary potatoes ($32). Daily 5.30 till late.

YOTS Marina Blvd, Cullen Bay. For starters try Barra Spring Rolls ($15), then go for a dozen freshly shucked oysters ($22) or a kangaroo fillet ($27). Also does pasta and wood-fired pizzas. Daily 7.30am till late.

Drinking, nightlife and entertainment

Darwin's alcohol consumption is legendary, with **beer** being knocked back at around 230 litres per year per person – fifty percent more than in the rest of Australia (although consumption of soft drinks is also well above the national average).

Pubs, bars and entertainment

Darwin's Wild West atmosphere is long gone, in the city centre at least, and many **pubs** have transformed their functional frontier-town interiors into something more conducive to public servants and tourists – even central Darwin's loosest venue, the *Hotel Victoria* on the Mall, is calming down in its old age. For tourists and displaced southerners, the Guinness-serving *Shenannigan's* on Mitchell Street continues to strike the right chord, as does *Rourkes Drift* over the road, featuring a bit of wood and brass in its outdoor terrace instead of the once ubiquitous "galvo".

The free monthly newspaper *Fresh*, available around town or at the VIC, has **listings** of all locals events. **Mitchell Street** is the venue for most of Darwin's entertainment. **Live bands** appear most nights at *Lizards Bar and Grill* in the *Top End Hotel* on the corner of Mitchell and Daly streets, with DJs from 10pm, and from Thursday to Saturdays at *Duck Nutz* near the Cinema Darwin on Mitchell Street, where there's also blues and jazz on Sunday afternoons. The five-screen **Cinema Darwin** has cheap tickets on Tuesdays, while the *Darwin Entertainment Centre* opposite hosts acts from musicals to intimate revues from all over the country and even abroad. For an alternative to mainstream films, see what's on at the outdoor **Deckchair Cinema**, on the Esplanade below Parliament House (ⓣ08/8981 0700; ⓦwww.deckchaircinema.com; $12; closed Nov–March).

Festivals and events

The onset of the dry season sees an upsurge in activity as the city shakes off the languor of the Wet. As well as agricultural shows, rodeos and racing, August's **Festival of Darwin** sees bands, plays, parades and all sorts of happenings around the city, and is well worth catching. Early August is the time for the famous **Beer Can Regatta** in Fannie Bay – wacky boat races in sea craft made entirely from beer cans. A genuine manifestation of Territorian eccentricity, interest has picked up after a few slow years, but it's not the alcohol-fuelled celebration it used to be. Also in August, there's more nuttiness during the barefoot **Mud Crab Tying Competition**.

Markets

Every Thursday and Sunday night from 5.30pm (May–Oct only) **Mindil Beach Markets** attracts locals who park, unpack their eskies and garden furniture, and settle in for the sunset. A mouthwatering array of sizzling food stalls from all corners of the earth (but mostly Asia) tantalizes your nostrils, while stalls selling New Age remedies and handicrafts and performers round off one of Darwin's unmissable events. It's a three-kilometre walk from town through the Botanic Gardens, or a short ride on a #4 or #6 bus from the city centre; alternatively, a minibus service runs to and from most accommodation ($2.50 each way).

Parap's Saturday morning market, on Parap Road (bus #6), or **Rapid Creek market**, off Trower Road on Friday evenings and Sunday mornings (bus #6 or #10), are good year-round substitutes, with a smaller food selection, old books and knick-knacks.

Listings

Airlines The Flight Centre (Ⓣ13 16 00) in the Mitchell Centre or the YHA travel office at the Transit Centre can organize overseas flights and visits to Bali and the Palau Islands.
Banks All major banks are located in or near Smith Street Mall.
Bookshops Readback Book Exchange has branches on the Mall near Star Arcade and at 30 Cavenagh St.
Buses Greyhound Australia, Transit Centre, behind 69 Mitchell St Ⓣ08/8911 8700.
Camping equipment The NT General Store, 42 Cavenagh St, has everything you need for going out into the bush, from a new pair of Blunnies to mozzie nets, eskies, potties and billies.
Car and campervan rental Advance, 86 Mitchell St Ⓣ1800 002 227; Britz 4WDs and campervans, 44 Stuart Highway Ⓣ1800 331 454, Ⓦwww.britz.com; Europcar, 77 Cavenagh St Ⓣ1800 811 451 or 13 13 90; Kea Campers, kiosk on Mitchell St opposite the Transit Centre Ⓣ1800 252 555; Thrifty Rental Cars, 64 Stuart Highway Ⓣ13 61 39 (they also have an office at the *Value Inn* in Mitchell St).
Consulates Indonesia, 20 Harry Chan Ave (Mon–Fri 9am–1pm & 2–5pm; Ⓣ08/8941 0048).
Hospital Royal Darwin Hospital, Rocklands Drive, Casuarina Ⓣ08/8922 8888.
Internet access The best place by far is Didjworld, Harry Chan Arcade, off Smith St (daily 8am–9pm).
Permits for Aboriginal Land Northern Land Council, PO Box 42921, Casuarina 0811 Ⓣ08/8920 5100 Ⓦwww.nlc.org.au.
Pharmacy Amcal, next to the Woolworths between Smith and Cavenagh streets (Ⓣ08/8981 8522) is open until 8pm on weekdays. Coles, in the Mitchell Precinct, is open 24 hours.
Police Esplanade, end of Knuckey St Ⓣ08/8922 3344.
Post office 48 Cavenagh St, cnr Edmunds St.
Swimming The nearest decent-sized pool is at Ross Smith Ave, Parap (Ⓣ08/8981 2662); take bus #6 or #10 from the city centre. Or try Lake Alexander at East Point.
Vaccinations Carpentaria Medical Centre, 13 Cavenagh St (Ⓣ08/8981 4233); Cavenagh Medical Centre, 50 Woods St (Ⓣ08/8981 8566)

Bathurst and Melville islands

Around six thousand years ago, rising sea levels created **Bathurst and Melville islands**, 80km north of Darwin. Home of the **Tiwi** Aborigines, the islands are often collectively known as the Tiwi Islands. Differing significantly from mainland Aborigines, with whom they had only limited contact until the nineteenth century, the Tiwi people's hostility towards all intruders hastened the failure of **Fort Dundas**, Britain's first north Australian outpost (on Melville Island), which lasted just five years until 1829. The Tiwi word for white men, *murantani* or "hot, red face", probably originates from this time.

In just two generations, since a Belgian missionary cautiously established the present-day town of **NGUIU**, on Bathurst, the Tiwi have moved from a hunter-gatherer lifestyle to a commodity-based economy with much less difficulty than mainland Aborigines, though still not without social problems. **Tours** are the only way to see the islands. *Tiwi Tours* (Ⓣ1300 721 365, Ⓦwww.aussieadventure.com.au) will fly you over in thirty minutes for a day trip ($310, including return flight and permit, but not a pick-up to the airport). You can now also get there by high-speed ferry from Cullen Bay (Ⓣ08/8941 1991; from $219 plus $16 Land Council permit), taking two hours to cross Van Diemen Gulf to Nguiu. Either way it's all a bit of a shopping trip, inspecting Tiwi art and craft outlets such as Bima Wear's showroom, although lunch at Taracumbie Waterfall and a visit to an overgrown burial ground, where lopsided crosses mingle with carved *pukamani* burial poles, add some flavour. At around $564 the **overnight tours** are much more worthwhile. You'll get a chance to go food-gathering with local Tiwi, either offshore or through the bush, making it a refreshingly spontaneous encounter.

East along the Arnhem Highway

The **Arnhem Highway**, which runs east towards Kakadu, parts company with the main southbound Stuart Highway 10km beyond Howard Springs. Passing agricultural stations, farms and Humpdy Doo on the way east you'll see the turn-off to **Fogg Dam Conservation Reserve**. Originally established in the late 1950s as an experimental rice- and cotton-growing area that was to transform the Territory's economy, for various "operational" reasons, not least the passing birds which tucked into the crops, the whole scheme was a flop. Since then the dam has become more successful as a bird sanctuary, and driving across the barrage you'll easily spot jacanas, egrets and geese, and maybe even one or two of the countless pythons who feed on the water rats, goannas and wallabies. Being the first bit of wetland on the arid drive out of Darwin, it's restful on the eyes, and all the more pleasant if you follow the 3.6-kilometre boardwalk into the adjacent woodland or to the lagoon itself.

Back on the highway you'll spot the distinctive observation platform of the **Windows on the Wetlands Visitors Centre** (daily 7.30am–7.30pm), which overlooks the Adelaide River flood plain from the top of Beatrice Hill. On the top floor you can play with interactive displays describing the surrounding ecology. Unfortunately, what you have, in the words of one ranger, is a "window on the weedlands", since the floodplain has been infested by something called the "giant sensitive plant", one of many exotic plants that proliferate and choke out all other plant life and fish life, a problem nearby Kakadu also struggles with.

Adelaide River Jumping Crocs

Seeing crocodiles in their natural habitat is one of the Top End's undoubted highlights, but at the **Adelaide River Crossing**, 64km east of Darwin, you can go one better and join a **jumping crocodile cruise**. You'll have seen at least two other croc-jumping outfits along the road en route, but the *Adelaide River Queen* ($35 for a 90min cruise; up to four times daily; check times on Ⓣ08/8988 8144) is the original, involving enticing the river's numerous salties to surge out of the water and grab bits of boney offal on a string, making it easy and safe to snap great photographs. Sea eagles also sometimes swoop in to snatch the meat from the crocs' maws and, whatever your thoughts on the methods or wisdom of encouraging crocodiles to jump 2m out of the water, they are an amazing spectacle.

The Mary River

Continuing along the Arnhem Highway, you'll pass some huge cathedral **termite mounds** on the south side of the road, a popular tour bus photo stop. Twelve kilometres past the *Bark Hut Inn* roadhouse (camping), the **Jim Jim Road** leads southeast to Cooinda in Kakadu. Another 6km further along the Arnhem Highway, the Point Stuart Road turns north into the proposed **Mary River National Park**, ending at the point on Chambers Bay where the explorer Stuart was carried lame and blind to reach the sea in 1862. And it was here that legendary bushman Tom Cole made his living for a while, shooting crocs and buffalo, a tough life described with wry stoicism in his book, *Riding the Wildman Plains* – and where Rod Ansell (see p.668) briefly ran Melaleuca station.

The Mary River's attractions won't be giving Kakadu too much to worry about, but it does offer a rare chance to explore a wetland environment away from the crowds and get as close as you dare to some huge crocs. Try to find a copy of the *Mary River Wetlands* brochure/map in the "Discovery Trails" series produced by the visitors' centre in Darwin.

At present a sealed section turns off from the highway to reach another turn-off on the left for the Wildman Ranger Station (☎08/8978 8986), and **Couzens Lookout**, a basic campsite overlooking the river. Nearby **Rockhole** is a popular place to put a boat in for some barra fishing. From this point you can either backtrack to the main Point Stuart Road or follow the 32-km 4WD **Wildman Track** which rejoins Point Stuart Road further north. It's a great drive along a little-used trail amidst hopping marsupials, flocks of birds at the Mary River floodplains, huge termite mounds and, if you're observant, some crocs cruising among the lilies at Connellan Lagoon. With skilled driving a high-clearance 2WD will make it; if you're in a tall rental 4WD, beware of scratching the vehicle on overhanging trees. From Connellan Lagoon the Wildman Track gets sandier before it rejoins the Wildman Lodge Road (the old lodge is closed, though a new riverside resort is on the cards).

Further up Point Stuart Road is a turn-off for *Point Stuart Wilderness Lodge* (☎08/8978 8914), the only non-camping option in the area with a pool, bar and restaurant plus fan/air-con cabins (❸), four-share dorms ($25pp, minimum 3 share) and smart en-suite motel rooms with big bathrooms (❺). They also run wildlife cruises from Rockhole (call for times and prices). The road ends well before Point Stuart on the open sea at a place called **Shady Camp**, situated by a barrage which separates the Mary River's fresh water from the tidal reach. The choice of habitats seems to suit a whole lot of local crocs and a great way to meet them is by hiring a small outboard ($55 for 2hr with fuel; three people max; enquire at the Boat Hire nearby or call ☎08/8978 8943 or 0411 455 329 to reserve a boat). You're guaranteed to see several of these grisly reptiles lolling on the banks of either side of the barrage, as well as countless birds, including beautiful jabiru storks.

Kakadu National Park

Some 150km east of Darwin lies the World Heritage-listed **KAKADU NATIONAL PARK**. The park derives its name from the Bininj/Mungguy

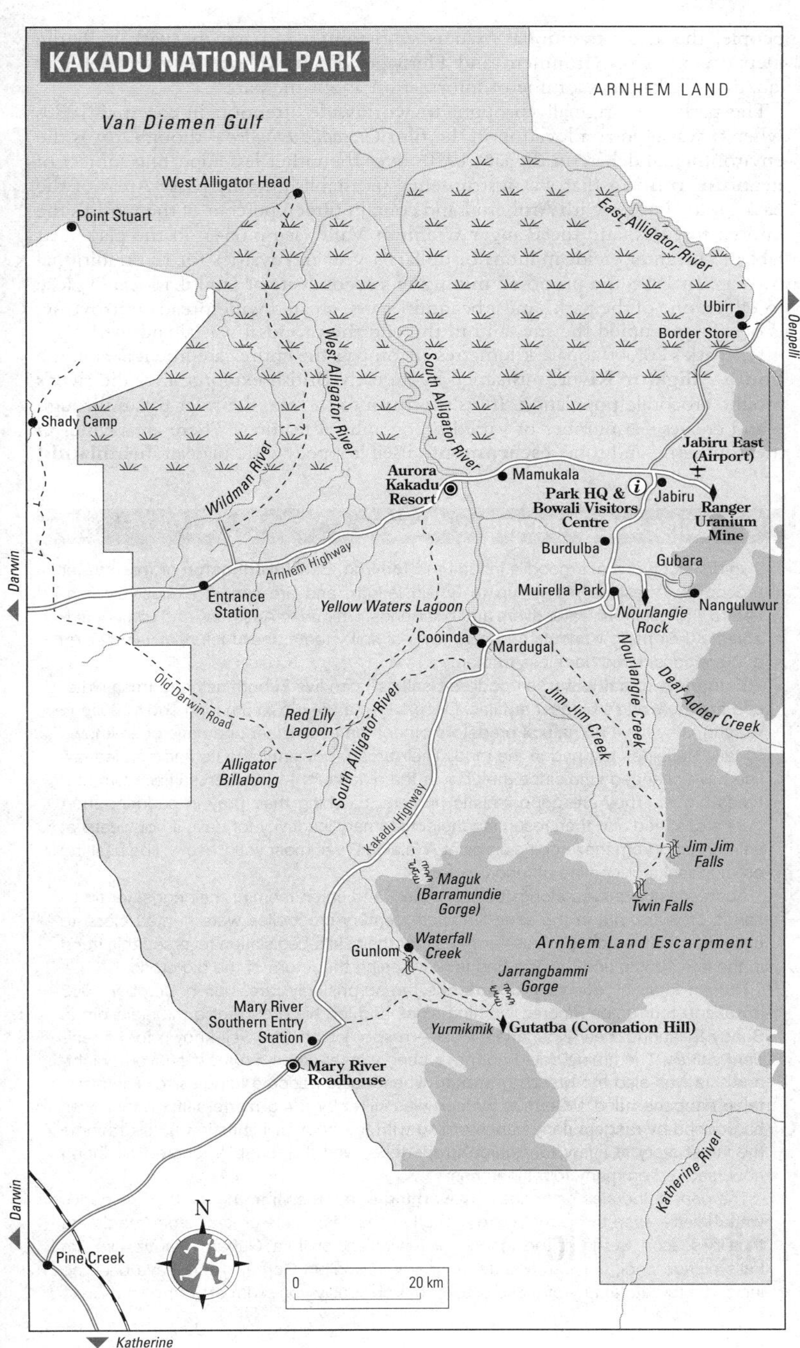

KAKADU NATIONAL PARK
ARNHEM LAND
Van Diemen Gulf
West Alligator Head
Point Stuart
East Alligator River
Ubirr
Border Store
Oenpelli
West Alligator River
South Alligator River
Shady Camp
Jabiru East
(Airport)
Wildman River
Aurora
Kakadu
Resort
Mamukala
Park HQ &
Bowali Visitors
Centre
Jabiru
Ranger
Uranium
Mine
Burdulba
Gubara
Darwin
Arnhem Highway
Entrance
Station
Muirella Park
Nanguluwur
Yellow Waters Lagoon
Nourlangie
Rock
Cooinda
Mardugal
Old Darwin Road
Nourlangie Creek
Deaf Adder Creek
Jim Jim Creek
Red Lily
Lagoon
South Alligator River
Alligator
Billabong
Kakadu Highway
Jim Jim
Falls
Maguk
(Barramundie
Gorge)
Twin Falls
Arnhem Land Escarpment
Gunlom
Waterfall
Creek
Jarrangbammi
Gorge
Mary River
Southern Entry
Station
Yurmikmik
Gutatba (Coronation Hill)
Mary River
Roadhouse
Katherine River
Darwin
N
Pine Creek
0
20 km
Katherine

people, the area's traditional owners who jointly manage the park with the Department of Environment and Heritage. Their website (Ⓦwww.deh.gov.au/parks/kakadu) is a mine of information about the park.

The park was originally brought to worldwide attention in the mid-1980s when it was used as a location in the film *Crocodile Dundee* – though it was the environmental debate in the late 1970s over the rather less appealing subject of **uranium mining** that was instrumental in establishing the park. Areas of the park on the border with Arnhem Land contain fifteen percent of the world's the known reserves, and the Ranger Uranium Mine (see p.654), in the park near Jabiru, currently yields millions of dollars a year in royalties for the traditional owners. In 1998 the proposed mining of a second site at Jabiluka located close to Ubirr, one of the park's most beautiful spots, created widespread controversy. Protestors occupied the site, and in the end the proposal was abandoned.

The park's 20,000 square kilometres encompass the entire catchment area of the **South Alligator River**, misnamed by an early British explorer after the river's prolific crocodile population. In its short run to the sea, the river passes through – and creates – a number of varied topographical features. There are ravines in the southern sandstone **escarpment**, itself topped with plateau **heathlands**,

Crocodiles and swimming in Kakadu

Two distinct types of crocodile inhabit the Top End. Bashful **Johnston** or **freshwater** crocodiles ("freshies") grow up to 3m in length, and are almost exclusively fish-eaters, living in freshwater rivers and billabongs. Unique to Australia, and distinguishable by their narrow snouts and neat rows of spiky teeth, they look relatively benign and are considered harmless to man.

Estuarine, or **saltwater**, crocodiles ("salties") can live in both salt and fresh water and are the world's biggest reptiles. Once fully mature (up to 6m long and 1000kg in weight), they have no natural predators other than each other and have been known to take buffaloes trapped in the mud. Their broad, powerful snouts and gnarled jaw line have changed little since the time of the dinosaurs – only then salties were four times bigger. They are opportunistic hunters, catching their prey in sudden, short bursts of speed and then resuming their customary inactivity for days if not weeks at a time. Apart from the jumping crocs at Adelaide River, most you'll see will be basking on mudbanks or cooling off underwater.

Aborigines have lived alongside crocodiles, and eaten them or their eggs, for thousands of years, but in the early twentieth century crocodiles were hunted close to extinction – either for sport, as vermin, or for their skin. Legislation reversed this trend in the late 1960s, and the Top End is now seeing the return of the big crocs.

Human fatalities due to **croc attacks** are surprisingly rare, but in October 2002 a Kakadu tour guide ignored warning signs and led his group for a midnight dip in Sandy Billabong, near Nourlangie Rock – a spot which was well-known for its resident salties. The timing could not have been worse: crocs are most active at night, and this was also the breeding season when males become aggressive. The inevitable happened and a German woman was killed by a 4.5-metre saltie (which was harpooned by rangers early next morning with the body still in its jaws). It's become the latest story in every tour guide's repertoire, with the formerly ignored billabong now featured on many tour itineraries.

The park authorities responded by **warning against swimming** in *all* of the park's waterholes – even those that were formerly considered safe or kept croc-free during the Dry season. Some visitors ignore this advice and swim at Gubara, Maguk, Jim Jim Falls plunge pool, Gunlom and Jarrangbarnmi (Koolpin Gorge). There have been no incidents to date at any of these places, but obviously you swim at your own risk.

while downstream the more commonly seen **savannah woodlands** merge into the paperbark **swamps**, tidal **wetlands** and the **mangroves** of the coastal fringe. There are also scattered pockets of monsoonal **rainforest**. Within these varied habitats an extraordinary diversity of flora and fauna thrives, including 2000 different **plants**, over 10,000 species of **insect**, half the Territory's species of **frog**, a quarter of Australia's **freshwater fish**, five out of the world's seven types of **turtle**, and over 75 different **reptiles** – more than you'll find in the whole of Europe (and some, such as the freshwater – or Johnston – crocodile, are unique to Kakadu). A third of Australia's **bird** species can also be found in Kakadu, including the elegant Jabiru stork, the similarly large brolga, with its curious courting dance, lily-hopping jacanas, white-breasted sea eagles, as well as galahs and magpie geese by the thousand. **Mammals** include kangaroos, wallabies, wallaroos, 26 bat species, and dingoes.

With so many interdependent ecosystems, maintaining the park's natural balance has become a full-time job. The **water buffalo**, brought in from Timor early in the nineteenth century (one of a dozen or so **feral species** found in the park), proliferated so successfully that their wallowing behaviour soon turned the fragile wetlands into saltwater mudbaths. Eradicating the buffalos, however, allowed their main food source, the *salvinia molesta* weed, to choke all other life out of the billabongs until a weevil was introduced to limit it. The long-feared arrival of the **cane toad** in 2002 was also a cause for concern, though scientists are working on a genetically engineered control. Yellow crazy ants are the latest introduced pest threatening the Kakadu habitat, but it is exotic **grasses** blown in from the east which pose the greatest ecological threat to the park, due to the higher temperature at which they burn and so the greater damage they cause. **Burning off** has long been recognized as a technique of land management by Aborigines who lit small, controllable fires as an aid to hunting and to stimulate new plant growth. Today, rangers imitate age-old Aboriginal practice, burning off the drying speargrass during June to preclude catastrophic fires at the end of the Dry, when the desiccated countryside could be devastated by a wildfire.

Visiting the park

In response to falling visitor numbers, as well as complaints over access, overpricing and the absence of the Aboriginal staff, in 2004 a new vision for the park's development was announced and **entry fees** were abolished.

It must be stressed that Australia's largest national park is a difficult place to appreciate in one short visit. Access to the park's diverse features is limited, and those expecting to find the bush humming with wildlife will be disappointed, especially if they stick to the two main sealed highways. Furthermore, at the most popular times of year for visitors, Kakadu is much **drier** than might be imagined, and most of the wildlife is active only during the early morning, in the evening or at night. Early-morning drives or walks along dirt tracks will certainly increase wildlife-spotting opportunities. The danger from crocodiles and the need to keep certain important Aboriginal sites secret – not to mention the harsh terrain and climate – mean that the wetlands and, especially, the most interesting escarpment country are difficult to fully appreciate, though it is something that is becoming easier in adjacent Arnhem Land (see p.657).

Although Kakadu's Aborigines distinguish six **seasons** throughout the year, to most people it's either the Wet, with up to 1600mm (just over five feet) of torrential rainfall between December and March, or the Dry, an almost complete drought. The **dry-season months** of June, July and August are the most popular times to visit the park, with acceptable humidity and temperatures

Ancient rock art

Up to five thousand **Aboriginal art sites** cover the walls of Kakadu's caves and sheltered outcrops, ranging in age from just thirty years old to over twenty thousand. Most of them are inaccessible to visitors, and many are still of spiritual significance to the three hundred or so Gagudju and other language groups who live in the park. The paintings include a variety of styles, from hand prints to detailed cross-hatched depictions of animals and fish from the rich **Estuarine period** of six thousand years ago. At this time, rising sea levels are thought to have submerged the land bridge by which Aborigines crossed into Australia. It is not unusual to see paintings from successive eras on one wall. **Contact period** images of seventeenth-century Macassar fishing *praus* and larger European schooners might be superimposed (a common feature of petroglyphs worldwide) over depictions of ancient and bizarre spirit-beings. Though partially understood at best and only really known by the individual artist, Kakadu's rock art provides a fascinating record of a culture that has been present in the Top End for over 60,000 years.

and fairly conspicuous wildlife. Towards the end of the Dry, birdlife congregates around the shrinking waterholes, while November's rising temperatures and epic electrical storms – known as the Build Up – herald the onset of the Wet. To see Kakadu during the **Wet** or the early Dry is, some say, to see it at its best. Water is everywhere and, while some sights are inaccessible and the wildlife dispersed, the land demonstrates the kind of verdant splendour that people often expect, but fail to find, in the most visited months.

Getting there and information

The **Arnhem Highway** leaves the Stuart Highway 43km south of Darwin, after which it's a fairly dull 210-kilometre drive to the Park HQ near Jabiru, past the entrance station (where they should give you a visitors' guide with a map). From Jabiru the sealed **Kakadu Highway** heads southwest through to Pine Creek on the Stuart Highway (an alternative entry point into the park if approaching from the south), passing Cooinda, which is pretty much at the heart of the park. The unsealed **Old Darwin Road** (also known as **Old Jim Jim**) starts 12km east of the *Bark Hut Inn* on the Arnhem Highway, but is passable for robust 2WD cars in dry conditions, and is a good alternative to slogging the full length of the Arnhem Highway. On the way you're bound to see some wildlife at Alligator Billabong and Red Lily Lagoon before joining the Kakadu Highway near Cooinda, 100km further on.

Without your own transport you'll have to rely on a **tour** (see box, p.644 for some recommended Darwin-based operators, or p.664 for places in Katherine). There are **buses** into the park: Greyhound Australia operates daily between Darwin, Jabiru and Cooinda, and the Kakadu Parklink (☎1800 089 113) runs between the *Kakadu Resort*, Jabiru and Cooinda. But make no mistake: trying to see the park using only a bus pass may leave you frustrated. To make the most of using the bus, try to organize some day-tours out of Jabiru or Cooinda, although this can take some planning. You're probably going to be in Kakadu only once, so do it properly: rent a car or join a tour. If you find yourself in the park and suddenly decide you need a car, **rental** can be arranged through the Thrifty office at the *Gagudju Crocodile Hotel* in Jabiru (☎08/8979 2552). The **map** you're given when you enter the park is handy, but details only the most popular areas; for the whole picture get yourself a copy of the HEMA 1:400,000 *Kakadu National Park* map.

At the eastern edge of the park, near the junction of the Arnhem and Kakadu highways, lies the excellently designed **Park Headquarters and Bowali Visitors Centre** (daily 8am–5pm; ⓣ08/8938 1123). Here you can pick up free notes covering all aspects of the park. A *What's On* pamphlet lists details of the **ranger-led walks** at many of the sites covered below, and the programme of **evening slide shows** at the caravan parks and resorts. An innovative walk-through **exhibition** takes you through a condensed Kakadu habitat, passing snakes and under a croc's belly. A café and gift shop round off the facilities.

Accommodation

Within Kakadu, most of the accommodation is at **Cooinda** or **Jabiru**. There are also a dozen free basic camping areas in the park, some accessible only along rough tracks where 4WD is best. There are also five better-equipped camping areas ($5.40 per person) at **Mardugal** near Cooinda, **Muirella Park** near Nourlangie Rock, **Merl** at Ubirr, **Garnamarr** near Jim Jim Falls and at **Gunlom**. In the Dry season, booking ahead at the Park HQ is advisable.

Aurora Kakadu Resort Arnhem Highway, 2.5km west of South Alligator Bridge ⓣ08/8979 0166, ⓔkakadu@aurora-resorts.com.au. Attractively landscaped resort with café, restaurant, and central pool area visited by birds and wallabies. There are pricey motel rooms (⑦) plus much better-value budget rooms – essentially a spacious en-suite motel room with a pair of bunk beds plus balcony or deck (④). Camping also available.

Gagudju Crocodile Holiday Inn Jabiru ⓣ08/8979 2800, ⓦwww.gagudju-crocodile.holiday-inn.com. Overpriced crocodile-shaped hotel, but nothing to sniff at if it's part of your package. ⑧

Gagudju Lodge Cooinda ⓣ08/8979 0145, ⓦwww.gagudjulodgecooinda.com.au. Near Yellow Waters and Warradjan Cultural Centre, but unless you're camping the worst budget choice in the park ($30–50pp in dorms or shared rooms) with cramped air-con cabins and no kitchen to speak of. There are also well-equipped motel units (⑦).

Kakadu Hostel Behind the Border Store near Ubirr ⓣ08/8979 2232 ⓔborderstore@hotmail.com. Aged hostel well past its prime and popular with mosquitoes, but the cheapest bed in Kakadu. Open all year subject to access. Six or twelve-bed air-con dorms from $25, rooms with fan ③

Lake View Park Lakeside Drive, Jabiru ⓣ08/8979 3144, ⓦwww.lakeviewkakadu.com.au. The best value on this side of the park, with a range of options. These include mesh-walled "bush bungalows" (④), sleeping four in a double bed and a bunk bed, plus fridge, tea and coffee and (external) private bathroom and shared BBQ area – though they are closely packed and noise carries through the mesh walls. The air-con/fanned double/twin rooms (⑤) around a communal kitchen and lounge area are quieter, though bathrooms are still shared. There are also fully equipped self-contained cabins sleeping four, with external private bathrooms (⑥).

Around the park

If your visit to Kakadu is short, seeing the **rock art** at Ubirr or Nourlangie Rock, taking a **cruise** at Guluyambi or Yellow Waters and checking out the Bowali Visitors Centre or Warradjan Cultural Centre will give you a taste of the park, and can just about be fitted into a long day. However, you can easily spend a week visiting all the spots detailed below, ideally followed by a return visit six months later to observe the seasonal changes. All the following places are reached off the **Kakadu Highway**. Unless indicated, all roads below are sealed and so accessible to rental 2WDs.

East along the Arnhem Highway

Soon after the entry station, a turn-off heads north 80km to **West Alligator Head**, currently the only place in Kakadu where you can get to the sea (via an increasingly rough track; allow at least two hours). The main attraction of the drive is the good chance it offers of seeing plenty of wildlife, especially early in the morning. In the Dry a regular 2WD can easily get to the two no-frills campsites (see below) along the Wildman River; if you want to get all the way to the coast (basic camping, so be prepared) you'll need a higher clearance 2WD or a 4WD.

On the way up you pass turn-offs to two **free campsites** on the Wildman River at **Two Mile Hole** (12km from the highway and slightly the nicer of the two) and **Four Mile Hole** (38km from the highway), but given that there are no toilets, little shade and a river full of crocs, there's not a whole lot to recommend them. Continuing north, about 60km from the Arnhem Highway you emerge onto a treeless flood plain for a kilometre or two. On re-entering the woodland the track narrows to two rough and corrugated ruts which can become quite numbing for the last 20km to West Alligator Head. It ends at the ruins of a former fish processing plant (where there are some toilets). Straight ahead you can camp on **Pocock's Beach**. Combing the beach is fun here, as jumping fish flutter across the water, but wander among the mangroves and eventually a croc will come cruising towards you. You'll find a bit more shade (but not much else) 4km further on at **Middle Beach**, a shallow, kilometre-wide bay, nice enough to walk along, but of course unsafe to swim in without sniper support. There's room for a couple of tents of visitors to camp in seclusion but no facilities.

Jabiru and the Ranger Uranium Mine

JABIRU, a couple of kilometres east of the Park HQ, is a company town, originally built to serve Kakadu's uranium-mining leases before the park was established. There are four mine leases in the park (and another in Arnhem Land) but only one or two are operating at present. As a result, Jabiru is less than half-full of mine workers and park employees. There's a **tourist information centre** (Ⓣ08/8979 2548), a small **supermarket**, a takeaway, bakery, post office and Westpac bank, all located in the **shopping plaza**. You'll also find a **health and dental clinic** (Ⓣ08/8979 2018) and a swimming pool (daily 9am–7pm; $3).

Kakadu Air (Ⓣ1800 089 113) operates out of the airport (6km east of Jabiru), offering thirty-minute **scenic flights** along the escarpment and wetlands from $80. Helicopter rides cost from $145 for twenty minutes. From Kakadu Air's office you can also take a one-hour tour of **Ranger Uranium Mine**. However, the mine consists of nothing more than a pit, pipelines and mysterious-looking buildings where the ore is processed, while the tour itself is largely a public-relations exercise.

Ubirr and the Guluyambi Cruise

The rock-galleries at **Ubirr** (Dry season 8.30am–sunset; Wet season 2pm–sunset), 43km north of the Park HQ, illustrate the rich food resources of the wetlands. Fish, lizards, marsupials and the now-extinct Tasmanian tiger or thylacine are depicted, as well as stick-like Mimi spirits, ancestral beings said to inhabit cracks in the rock and not unlike the "Bradshaw" or Gwoin Gwoin figures found in the Kimberley. The **Lookout** offers one of the park's most beautiful views across the East Alligator River to the rocky outcrops of Arnhem Land, while the six-kilometre return **Sandstone and River Walk** along the East Alligator River is one of the few longish walks in the park – a good way to escape the crowds.

Near the start of the Sandstone and River Walk you can take a ninety-minute **Guluyambi Cruise** ($35; 4 daily; Ⓣ1800 089 113) along the East Alligator River. A local Aboriginal guide takes you upstream to view the towering

Bushwalking in Kakadu

One of Kakadu's biggest disappointments is the lack of long-distance walking trails. A leaflet at the Park HQ lists twenty marked trails in the park, but most are short **nature trails**, such as the six-kilometre **Rockholes Walk** near Ubirr. Only the twelve-kilometre **Barrk Walk** – a three-hour trek (the sign claiming "allow 6–8 hours" can only exist to put people off) through Nourlangie Rock's backcountry – offers any challenge: a half-hour slog up the rock which you then cross, descend and circumnavigate. Although the trail is marked, it should not be undertaken lightly and is best done in the cool of early morning. No less energetic is the little-advertised two-hour walk up to the top of **Jim Jim Falls** for fine views across the escarpment see next page; walk now open again

In the often-overlooked southwest of the park near Gunlom, the **Yurmikmik** area on the edge of the escarpment offers a similar challenge in the unmarked **Motor Car Creek Walk** (11km) and **Motor Car and Kurrundie Creek Circle Walk** (14km; overnight stop recommended). Ask for the *Yurmikmik Park Notes* at the visitors centre. You're more than likely to have the faint track to yourself.

escarpment and rock paintings while demonstrating some canny bush trickery and even gives you a chance to set foot, albeit briefly, on Arnhem Land. The dramatic scenery makes it an enjoyable (if not necessarily superior) alternative to the better-known Yellow Waters option out of Cooinda.

Nourlangie Rock Area

Nourlangie Rock, Kakadu's most accessible and therefore most visited site, is 31km south of the Park HQ. It includes the **Anbangbang Rock Shelter**, where the dry ground preserves evidence of occupation stretching back twenty thousand years; dimples on boulders show where ochre was ground and then mixed with blood for painting. The **Anbangbang Gallery**, nearby, depicts the dramatic figures of Nabulwinjbulwinj, Namarrgon (the Lightning Man) and his wife Barrkinj. Unusually vivid, they were in fact repainted (a traditional and sometimes ritual practice) in the 1960s over similar but faded designs. The **Lookout** over the Arnhem Land escarpment, to the home of Namarrgon, is also the beginning of the twelve-kilometre **Barrk Walk** (see box above). Other places in the Nourlangie Rock area, all signposted and marked in the *Visitors' Guide* which you should have been given when you arrived in the park, include **Nanguluwur**, a less popular but fascinating art site 1.5km from the Nourlangie car park, which includes images from the Contact period when Aborigines first encountered explorers and settlers. **Nawulandja Lookout** has views onto the imposing hulk of Nourlangie Rock itself, which looms over **Anbangbang Billabong**, a *Crocodile Dundee* location. During the Dry, a two-and-a-half-kilometre track around circles the billabong.

Gubara, or Burdulba Springs, 13km along an unsealed track off the Nourlangie road, comprises a string of small pools along a palm-shaded creek, itself a hot forty-minute walk from the car park, but you can take a dip at the end of it (see box p.650).

Jim Jim Falls and Twin Falls

Although over 100km south of Park HQ, ending along a slow bumpy track, these two falls are definitely worth visiting. Allow two hours for the sixty-kilometre drive from the Kakadu Highway or go on a day-trip with an operator like Kakadu Gorge and Waterfall Tours (around $130; ⓣ08/8979 0145) from

Jabiru or Cooinda. The road there passes the Garnamarr campsite and a barrier which closes the road between 8.30pm and 6.30am.

Jim Jim Falls plunge 150m straight off the escarpment and are best caught from a plane in the Wet or in the early Dry as soon as the road reopens – they stop flowing later. A rocky, one-kilometre trail leads alongside the large pool (swimming at own risk; see box on p.650) to the base of the falls, while another track leads to the top of the cliffs, though it's quite a slog – ask at the Bowali Centre.

Twin Falls is a bumpy and sandy ten-kilometre drive from Jim Jim and includes the crossing of Jim Jim Creek, for which you'll genuinely require a 4WD. The bottom of the creek has been cobbled, but it's subsiding and should be driven across slowly. From the Twin Falls car park you once had to walk and then swim or paddle up the gorge for a kilometre to reach the idyllic beach by the plunge pool of Twin Falls, a rewarding mini-adventure that got you to one of the park's most perfect and popular spots. Now, using the possibility of crocs as a lame excuse, you must pay around $10 (the exact figure varies) to be ferried up the gorge and traipse along a boardwalk to the plunge pool (where you can't even swim). As an alternative the park authorities have improved the three-kilometre walk up to the top of Twin Falls which some tours have been using for years. To do the walk you need a free permit from the Bowali Centre or Garnamarr campsite, but once up here you can overlook the falls and swim in pools up to 2km upstream (but see box on p.650).

Yellow Waters and the Warradjan Aboriginal Cultural Centre

As Jim Jim Creek begins meandering into the flood plains close to the Cooinda resort, 50km southwest of Jabiru, it forms the inland lagoon of **Yellow Waters**. From the car park here, a short walk leads along the edge of the billabong from where popular **cruises** (5 daily; book in advance on ⓣ08/8979 0145) weave through the lushly vegetated waterways. The early morning cruise (2hr; $28) catches the lagoon and wildlife at their best: heat-of-the-day tours are thirty minutes shorter and a few dollars cheaper.

The turtle-shaped **Warradjan Aboriginal Cultural Centre** (daily 9am–5pm), on the Cooinda access road, offers unusually designed interpretive displays on the culture and lore of the local Aborigines, together with an arts and crafts shop. Interesting though it is, it has to be said that the display is not particularly effective at communicating its message and, unless you have some previous understanding of Aboriginal culture, you've forgotten much of what you've seen soon after leaving.

Maguk, Gunlom and other beauty spots

Robust 2WD cars can manage the twelve-kilometre corrugated track from the Kakadu Highway to **Maguk** (also known as Barramundie Gorge), which leaves the Highway 57km southwest of Cooinda. From the car park, a path leads along the creek to the large pool (swim at own risk; see box p.650). The pool is possibly still the home of a once-harassed freshie; for its sake rather than yours, keep away from the left bank. The top of the waterfall and more rock pools can be reached by clambering up the tree roots to the right of the falls.

Gunlom (also known as Waterfall Creek) is another *Crocodile Dundee* location, on a corrugated track 36km off the Kakadu Highway, close to the park's southwestern exit. Although the falls don't flow all year, it's a lovely paperbark-shaded place (swim at own risk; see box p.650), and as you can camp here it's well worth the diversion if entering or leaving via Pine Creek (if your car can

△ Yellow Waters wetlands

take it). The steep path to the top of the falls reveals still more pools (again, swim at own risk).

A right turn at the junction that leads to Gunlom follows on through Koolpin Creek to a locked gate and the **Koolpin** – or **Jarrangbammi** – **Gorge**. The key is available ($50 deposit) from the Southern Entry Station (ⓣ08/8975 4859) on the Pine Creek road, but you must also get a permit from Parks HQ which limits the number of visitors to forty vehicles per day. The track to the gorge crosses the creek again and requires 4WD. You can camp here or follow the escarpment on foot to the northwest for 3km to the narrow chasm of **Freezing Gorge** which, you'll be pleased to discover, lives up to its name. Five kilometres past the locked gate is Gutatba, a picnic site on the South Alligator River. Also known as Coronation Hill, this is the site of a former uranium mine. To local Jawoyn Aborigines this area is traditionally "Sickness Country", suggesting that even in its natural state uranium, as well as other toxic minerals found in the area, have proved harmful to human health.

Arnhem Land

ARNHEM LAND is geographically the continuation of Kakadu eastwards to the Gulf of Carpentaria, but without the infrastructure and picnic areas. Never colonized and too rough to graze, it was designated an Aboriginal reserve in 1931 and has stayed in Aboriginal hands since that time. In 1963 the Yirrkala of northwestern Arnhem Land appealed against the proposed mining of bauxite on their land. It was the first such protest of its kind, and included the presentation of sacred artefacts as well as a petition in the form of a bark painting to the government in Canberra. Although it didn't help in this particular case, their actions brought the issue of Aboriginal land rights to the public eye and paved the way for subsequent successful land claims in the Territory.

Except for two places, independent tourists are not allowed to visit Arnhem Land without an invitation, and by and large the twelve thousand Aborigines who live here prefer it that way. Little disturbed for over forty thousand years, Arnhem Land, like Kakadu, features thousands of rock-art sites and burial grounds. In recent years the mystique of this "forbidden land" has proved a profitable source of income for Arnhem Land's more accessible communities, and **tours**, particularly to the areas adjacent to Kakadu, are now offered in partnership with some operators. Prices reflect this exclusivity. Davidson's Arnhem Land Safaris (Ⓣ08/8927 5240, Ⓦwww.arnhemland-safaris.com) offer tours in the Mount Borradaile area for at least $600 a day with flights from Darwin, while Lord's Kakadu (Ⓣ08/8948 2200, Ⓦwww.lords-safaris.com) runs a day-trip into Arnhem Land from the Border Store in Kakadu for around $180. Despite the expense, a visit here, even for one day, is a special experience. You'll be shown amazing rock galleries and other sites which cannot be seen in adjacent Kakadu and have the chance to enjoy Arnhem Land's intangible allure; the sense of an ancient, untamed land that an over-managed national park can never imitate.

The only major settlement is **NHULUNBUY**, also known as **Gove**, in the northeast corner, a distant mining town of little appeal. Individual tourists are now permitted to make an unescorted day visit directly to the Injalak Arts and Crafts store (Mon–Fri 8am–5pm, also sometimes open June–Sept Sat 8am–noon; Ⓣ08/8979 0190, Ⓦwww.injalak.com) in the town of **OENPELLI** (or Gunbalanya), 15km over the East Alligator river crossing at the Border Store near Ubirr. A $12 permit must be obtained from the Northern Land Council (NLC; Jabiru Ⓣ08/8979 2410, Darwin Ⓣ08/8920 5100), which usually takes 24 hours. At the store you'll have a chance to buy locally-made items and watch them being made; it might also be possible to see the rock art on nearby Injalak Hill.

NLC permits are also issued to drive to Smith Point on the **Cobourg Peninsula**. Most visitors here are fishermen, and without a boat it's a long rough drive for comparatively little reward.

Along the Stuart Highway

From Darwin, the **Stuart Highway** passes old mining outposts and overgrown, but still commemorated, World War II airstrips. Along its length are a number of attractions which can be visited either as excursions from Darwin or as diversions on the journey to Katherine, 320km to the south. Don't expect to get to any of the places off the Highway without organizing local transport.

Darwin Crocodile Farm

South of the Arnhem Highway turn-off, 40km from Darwin, is the **Darwin Crocodile Farm** (daily 10am–4pm; $10), where crocodiles are studied, and also bred for their skins and meat (as they also are at Crocodylus Park near Darwin, see p.642). The lucky ones get scarred at an early age, rendering themselves unsuitable for conversion into handbags, and become breeding stock instead. Rogue crocs which turn nasty and harass local communities, as well

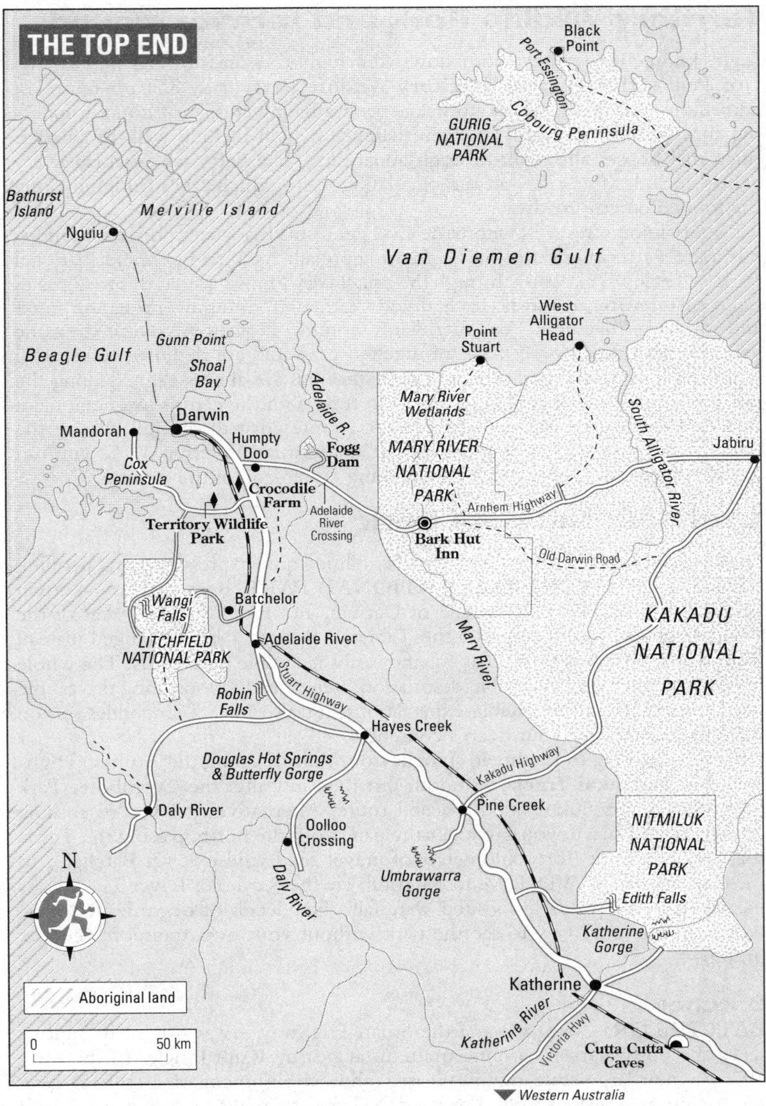

as the sixty-odd crocs which are caught annually in the traps around Darwin Harbour, are also relocated here.

Souvenirs (including photo opportunities to cradle baby salties) and croc burgers are available at the shop, and **guided tours** set off on the hour, when some of the eight thousand crocodiles and alligators also get fed. It's worth trying to catch the main feeding time (Mon–Fri 2pm, Sat & Sun noon & 2pm), since it's one of the few occasions when the crocs actually move.

Territory Wildlife Park and termite mounds

Eight kilometres further south down the highway, the turning west to the Cox Peninsula leads to the **Territory Wildlife Park** (daily 8.30am–6pm, last admission 4pm; $20), where you can spend a happy couple of hours wandering through a variety of Territorian habitats, which include walk-in aviaries, nocturnal houses and walk-through aquariums. The entry fee – worth every cent – includes free rides on the circulating train, which saves trudging along the four-kilometre roadway.

Twenty kilometres west before the Cox Peninsula road veers north to Mandorah there's a turning onto the northern approach track to Litchfield National Park (see below). Crossing through the usually dry Finniss River, this road passes fields of **termite mounds**, both fluted "cathedral" mounds, up to 4m high, and so-called "magnetic" or "meridian" mounds. Not often seen in the same vicinity, both designs are made of digested grass and are designed to create a regulated internal temperature. Magnetic mounds are always aligned along the polar axis and were once thought to be in tune with the earth's magnetic field. In fact, they're arranged so as to present a knife edge to the full heat of the midday sun, thus maintaining the habitat at a termite-preferred 30°C; you can feel the temperature difference by touching either side of the mound.

Litchfield National Park

"Kaka-don't, Litchfield-do" is an over-simplified quip expressing many people's preference for **LITCHFIELD NATIONAL PARK** over its better-known neighbour. Situated 100km south of Darwin, and roughly 16km west of the Stuart Highway, it encompasses the Tabletop Range, a spring-fringed plateau from which gush several permanent and easily accessible **waterfalls**. The whole park is a popular and enjoyable destination, free of restrictions, long drives, the need for 4WDs and intangible expectations. It's also free of crocodiles so you can splash around to your heart's content.

If you're driving to Litchfield straight from Kakadu along the Arnhem Highway, the **Marrakai Track**, a smooth dirt road just after the Corroboree Park Roadhouse, cuts 50km off the sealed route. Alternatively, if you're coming directly from Darwin you can enter the park from the north, passing the Territory Wildlife Park (forty kilometres of gravel road) and exit via Batchelor to the east or, with a 4WD, leave to the south via the Reynolds River Track passing some of the park's less visited waterfalls. For details of **organized tours**, which are the only way to see the park without your own transport, see box on p.644.

Batchelor

BATCHELOR – 8km west of the Stuart Highway – was originally built to serve the postwar rush to mine uranium at nearby Rum Jungle. In the early 1970s, when large-scale mining ceased, the establishment of Litchfield gave the town a new lease of life. For the traveller the town's only sight of note is a replica of the Gothic **Karlstein Castle**, next to the police station, built by a homesick Czech immigrant. There's no admission fee to enter the park, but no visitors' centre either, so get all the **information** you need (including a map) from the Parks and Wildlife Commission (P&WC) offices in either Batchelor (Ⓣ08/8976 0282) or at the visitors' centre' in Darwin. They also have information on extended **bushwalks** in Litchfield if you want to do more than hop from one waterfall to the next. There are a couple of **caravan parks** around Batchelor, but camping in the park is generally more appealing and convenient, though choose your time and place carefully, especially at weekends, when Litchfield is popular. For those who don't want to rough it, the *Rum Jungle Motor Inn* (☎08/8976 0123; ❺), on Rum Jungle Road in Batchelor, and the nearby *Jungle Drum Bungalows* (☎08/8976 0555; ❹) have cabin-style rooms.

Along Litchfield Park Road

Heading into the park from Batchelor you'll pass black-soil plains dotted with grey, tombstone-like termite mounds. The first chance for a splash is at the **Buley Rock Holes**, a string of easily accessible rock pools with basic camping nearby. Both the road and a 2.5-kilometre trail follow the Buley Creek to **Florence Falls**. A lookout surveys the twin twenty-metre falls from above, where a convoluted stairway drops right down to the shady plunge pool.

Back on the Litchfield Park Road (the main sealed road in the park which links all the most visited spots), a turn off south leads to the **Lost City**, a jumble of unusually weathered sandstone columns. Back on the main park road the uninteresting Tabletop Swamp is followed soon after by **Tolmer Falls**, probably the park's most photogenic waterfall, though you can only view it from the cliffs opposite due to the presence here of rare orange horseshoe bats. Look carefully above the chute and you'll notice a natural rock arch bridging the falls. From the clifftop lookout a half-hour walk leads back to the car park via the pools at the top of the falls, passing examples of ancient cycads (see p.527) on the way. From **Green Ant Creek** a one-hour return walk leads through pockets of rainforest to the top of the **Tjaetaba Falls**, with a pool to cool off in right on the lip of the cascade.

Packed out at weekends and during school holidays, **Wangi Falls**, on the west side of the park, has easy access past tree-shaded lawns and a café to a large plunge pool. Near the base of the left-hand cascade is a sun-warmed natural spa, but note the multilingual signs warning of the risk of drowning (the pool closes in the Wet when abnormal undertows develop). A trail leads through a rainforest boardwalk up over the falls and down the other side via a **lookout** – a good way to work off lunch.

The road leads north from Wangi out of the park to the rather grandly named **Litchfield Tourist Precinct**; basically a pair of caravan parks which can be quieter and marginally cheaper than those in the park, as well as being better equipped and less congested. *Litchfield Campground* has the log-cabin *Monsoon Café* and is a base for **helicopter flights** over the park's falls (☎08/8978 2077; from $89). You can also join twice-daily **billabong cruises** on the Reynolds River here (☎08/8978 2022).

You re-enter the park (without really knowing you left it) near **Walker Creek**, where there's a string of rock pools to wallow in and, upstream, eight secluded creekside **campsites** with room for just one or two tents; they can only be reached on foot (a walk of up to 2km). When paying their fees, campers are supposed to write on a board to indicate that they have occupied one of the sites, but no one seems to bother, so it may be worth seeing if there's one free before you lug in all your overnight gear. As in other parts of Litchfield, your chances of getting a free spot are much reduced on weekends.

Southern Litchfield: the Reynolds River Track

Near Green Ant Creek, the **Reynolds River Track** leads 44km south out of the park to the sealed Daly River Road. A half-metre-deep creek crossing near the start of the track discourages 2WDs from continuing, and if you want to get right through to Daly River you'll definitely need 4WD for the sandy section before Surprise Creek Falls, and some steep drops into possibly deep creek crossings. The track itself is fun, passing many huge termite mounds and burnt or recovering woodland, depending on the last bushfire, though the speed humps along its entire length can get annoying.

A few kilometres after the start of the track there is a turning left to the abandoned **Blyth Homestead**, which adds some token historic interest to the park. Back on the main track you soon reach the turn-off which leads a couple of kilometres to **Tjaynera Falls** campground (also known as Sandy Creek). From the campground car park it's a 1.7km walk to the falls above a large plunge pool. Nice though it is to strip off and dive in, the pool only gets the sun in the afternoon and there's virtually no room here to spread out in comfort. At the Tjaynera turn-off on the main track a sign warns that your 4WD may need a raised air intake to cross the Reynolds River, 6km further on, though in the late Dry the crossing is no drama. **Surprise Creek Falls** (camping), about twenty kilometres further on, are the highlight along the track. A short walk from the campsite car park leads to the sunny plunge pool and, tucked away on the rocks above, two perfectly positioned ten-metre-wide spa pools overlooking the whole scene. From this point it's about a twenty-minute drive over a few more speed humps to the junction with the Daly River Road.

Adelaide River and around

Established during the construction of the Overland Telegraph Line, the town of **ADELAIDE RIVER** was the supply head for Darwin's defence during World War II and consequently suffered sporadic Japanese bombing. Today the town, 110km south of Darwin, provides little more than a lunch-stop along the Stuart Highway, unless you want to visit the town's **war cemetery**, where many of the victims of the air raids are buried. Officially, 243 people died as a result of the eighteen months of Japanese bombing, which began in February 1942, but the cemetery has twice as many graves. The *Mobil Roadhouse* has **camping**, or try the *Adelaide River Inn* for rooms, dorms and a **restaurant**.

Just south of town, the old highway forks west along a rolling 75-kilometre scenic drive before rejoining the main road at *Hayes Creek* roadhouse. After the first 17km on this route you'll come to the turn-off for **Robin Falls**, a pretty little cascade reached after a ten-minute scramble up the creek bed from the car park. Seventeen kilometres south of Robin Falls turn-off, a road leads to **Daly River** community (passing a southern entrance into Litchfield Park; 4WD only), a dead-end favoured by barra fishermen; beyond is Aboriginal land.

Pine Creek and around

Site of the Territory's first goldrush, **PINE CREEK**, 230km from Darwin, is one of the Territory's oldest towns and has managed to hang onto an unreconstructed charm despite (or perhaps because of) its low touristic status. Gold was discovered here while digging holes for the Overland Telegraph Line pylons in 1871, and fools rushed in, hoping to pan their way to fortune. Unfortunately the gold was in the rock, not the riverbeds, requiring laborious crushing with heavy stamp batteries, which, for most prospectors, was too much like hard work for unpredictable returns. The subsequent labour shortage was solved by importing Chinese workers who kept the progressively poorer-quality ore coming for a few more years until fears of Asian dominance led to their being banned from the Territory in 1888. Ah Toys general store on Main Terrace is still run by the descendants of its original Chinese owner.

Around the town, the various time-worn buildings, such as the 1889 **Old Playford Hotel** and **Old Bakery**, may lead you to contemplate the crucial role of corrugated iron, or "galvo", in the colonial pioneering process. The **Miners Park**, at the northern end of town, displays crude mining hardware from over a century ago, and there's a **museum** (Mon–Fri 1–5pm; $3) on Railway Terrace, near the police station, and an old locomotive at the old train station itself. For **accommodation** there's a caravan park with camping, the *Pine Creek Motel and Laundromat* (☎08/8976 1442; ④) on Main Street, and the *Pine Creek Hotel* (☎08/8976 1288; ④) round the corner opposite the BP petrol station. If you want **to eat**, choose between the pub and the café next door.

From Pine Creek it's 200km along the sealed **Kakadu Highway** to Jabiru, in the heart of Kakadu National Park, passing the majority of the park's highlights on the way. Down the Stuart Highway, 91km south of Pine Creek, a turn-off leads 20km east to **Edith Falls** (Leliyn). Like Wangi in Litchfield, Edith Falls is popular on weekends with a kiosk and small waterfall at the back of the large pool. To get away from the recreational throng you can walk round to the secluded upper pools, on to Sweetwater Pool (9km return) or indeed all the way to Katherine Gorge along a 66-kilometre trail (see p.665).

Katherine to Alice

An obligatory stopover (at least for a couple of days) for visitors to the Top End, **Katherine** is a small but rapidly growing regional centre on the southern banks of the Katherine River. It's just 30km to **Katherine Gorge**, the town's primary tourist attraction and itself part of the larger **Nitmiluk National Park**.

West of Katherine, the **Victoria Highway** leads for 500km west to the WA border, passing Timber Creek and the entrance to **Gregory National Park** on the way. South of town is a vast touristic no-man's-land all the way to Alice. A dip in **Mataranka**'s thermal pool and a couple of "bush pubs" are the highlights of the 670km to **Tennant Creek**. South of Tennant Creek, only the rotund boulders of the **Devil's Marbles** brighten the string of roadhouses along the Stuart Highway, which rolls on for just over 500km to Alice Springs.

Katherine

Traditionally home of the Jawoyn and Dagoman people, the **Katherine River** area must have been a sight for explorer John McDouall Stuart's sore eyes as he struggled north in 1862. Having got this far, he named the river after a benefactor's daughter, Catherine, and within ten years the completion of the Overland Telegraph Line (OTL) encouraged European settlement, as drovers and prospectors converged on the first reliable water north of the Davenport Ranges. In 1926 a railway from Darwin finally spanned the river and "Kath-rhyne", as die-hard locals still call the town of **KATHERINE**, became established on its present site. It's essentially a "one-street" town, though in January 1998 that street found itself under two metres of water when two cyclones dumped a Wet season's worth of rain over southern Arnhem Land – a crocodile was spotted cruising lazily past the semi-submerged Woolworths.

The Town and around

The Stuart Highway becomes **Katherine Terrace**, the main street, as it passes through town. Along it lie most of the shops and services, including a big Woolworths, as well as several Aboriginal art galleries giving Katherine a compact and unexpectedly busy feel. If you're not doing the gorge and shooting through, the town is also a good place to pick up **casual work** on the stations and market gardens surrounding it.

If you want the full story on the town head 3km up Giles Street to the **Katherine Museum** (Mon–Fri 10am–4pm, Sat 10–1pm, Sun 2–5pm; $6), just before the original town site at Knotts Crossing, where a few original OTL pylons still remain upright. Inside are displays relating to Katherine's colonial history, including early medical instruments and a biplane from the time when the building did duty as a Flying Doctor base.

Some 27km south of town lie the **Cutta Cutta Caves**, with guided tours (hourly 9–11am & 1–3pm; closed at the height of the Wet; $12.50; ⓣ08/8972 1940) of the Limestone Cave and Cutta Cutta. These caves display subterranean karst features, as diverse as they are delicate. Cutta Cutta is the more visually impressive and is also the home of the rare orange horseshoe bat and rather alarming stalactite-climbing brown snakes.

Practicalities

The **airport** is 8km south of town, while the **train station** is the same distance west off the Victoria Highway; a **taxi** (call ⓣ08/8972 1777 or 8972 1999) from either to Katherine costs about $20. All buses arrive at the **Transit Centre**, at the south end of Katherine Terrace, next to the 24-hour *BP Roadhouse*. Katherine is a busy interchange for buses, with at least one daily arrival or departure for Darwin, Kununurra (WA) and Alice Springs. Just over the road you'll find the **tourist information centre** (Mon–Fri 8.30am–5pm, Sat & Sun 9am–2pm; ⓣ08/8972 2650 or 1800 653 142, ⓦwww.krta.com.au), with shelves groaning with leaflets. For more detailed information on Nitmiluk, Gregory and Keep River national parks call in at the **Parks and Wildlife Commission** (ⓣ08/8973 8770) on Giles Street, just over a kilometre from town, past O'Shea

Tours from Katherine

Campbells Trail Rides (ⓣ08/8972 1394) and **Brumby Tracks** (ⓣ08/8972 1425) both offer horse rides from a few hours to a few days.

Dreamtime Safari ⓣ08/8975 4277. Two days and three nights based in a remote but well-appointed Central Arnhemland bushcamp with a guide who's lived among the Aboriginal people since the 1980s. Thought-provoking and forthright, it raises issues rather than distracts you with bush lore. Special backpacker deals via the YHA in Darwin (see p.639).

Gecko Canoe Tours ⓣ08/8972 2224. ⓦwww.geckocanoeing.com.au. Two- to seven-day canoeing trips on the Katherine River system downstream of town for around $310 per day. Suitable for beginners, and in many ways far more satisfying than the rather crowded Katherine Gorge.

Kakadu Tours ⓣ1800 808 211. Katherine to Darwin over three days for $410, visiting all the sights including Twin Falls.

Manyallaluk ⓣ08/8975 4727 or 1800 644 727. Long-established Aboriginal culture tours; a fun day out with didgeridoo-playing, painting, spear-throwing and fire-lighting, all for $150 (or $110 self-drive).

Terrace. There's fast **Internet access** at the Katherine Art Gallery opposite Woolworths on Katherine Terrace, at the *Didj Café* round the corner, and the library on the main street, when it's open. To **rent a car** call Thrifty (ⓣ08/8972 3183 or 13 61 39), Hertz Rent-A-Car (ⓣ08/8971 1111; ⓦwww.hertznt.com) or Europacar (ⓣ1800 222 511). **Bikes** can be rented from the backpackers or the bike shop on the main street in town.

Accommodation and eating

There's a decent range of places to stay, though the town centre can get rowdy late at night. The tourist information centre provides a list and current prices of all the town's accommodation; the best options – and all the backpackers – are detailed below. There are also at least four caravan parks around town with en-suite cabins (from ❺). **Eating out** in Katherine is nothing to get excited about. The *Terrace Cafe* in the Woolworths Shopping Centre is a popular spot for a daytime snack; in the evening your best bet is a bar meal in the hotel/pubs or the *Mercure Inn*'s restaurant.

Backpackers

Kookaburra Lodge Cnr Lindsay and Third streets ⓣ08/8971 0257 or 1800 808 211, ⓦwww.kookaburrabackpackers.com.au. Katherine's best backpackers' choice, with well-converted motel units in spacious grounds with eight-bed air-con dorms and twins. Also has table tennis, free breakfast, a small pool and Transit Centre drop-offs. Dorms from $22, rooms ❸

Palm Court Backpackers Cnr Giles and Third streets ⓣ08/8972 2722 or 1800 626 722, ⓦwww.travelnorth.com.au. Old motel with a cramped kitchen and small pool. Dorms are mostly four-bed with fridge and en suite. Free breakfast. Dorms from $22, rooms ❸

Victoria Lodge 21 Victoria Highway ⓣ1800 808 875, ⓔvictorialodge@bigpond.com. Ten minutes' walk from the centre on the westbound highway eight- and four-bed dorms, plus twins. Quieter than the other two backpackers, but not always choosy about guests. Dorms from $22, rooms ❸

Motels

Beagle Motor Inn 2 Fourth St ⓣ08/8972 3998. The best choice in town for a basic, inexpensive motel room. ❸

Mercure Inn Katherine Stuart Highway ⓣ08/8972 1744, ⓔmercurekatherine@bigpond.com.au. Katherine's best motel, located four kilometres south of town and set back from the road (so you're guaranteed a good night's sleep). Also has a pool, bar and restaurant. ❹

Paraway Motel Cnr O'Shea and First streets ⓣ08/8972 2644. The most comfortable motel in the town centre. ❹

Nitmiluk National Park

The central attraction of the **Nitmiluk National Park** is the magnificent twelve-kilometre **Katherine Gorge**, carved by the Katherine River through the Arnhem Land plateau. Often described as thirteen gorges, it is in fact one continuous cleft, turning left and right along fault lines and separated during the Dry season by rock bars. The spectacle of the river, hemmed in by orange cliffs, makes for a wonderful **cruise** or canoe trip and, unlike Kakadu, Nitmiluk also welcomes bushwalkers along its many marked **trails**.

Travel North (ⓣ1800 089 103) operates **shuttle buses** along the sealed road between Katherine and the gorge for $22 return. Once at the gorge the **Park Visitors Centre** (daily 8am–7pm) has interpretive displays on the park's features from the local Jawoyn Aborigines' perspective (they own the park), and provides maps and further information on the trails, including the *Guide to Nitmiluk National Park* ($6.55) with topographical walking maps. It also includes a restaurant, gallery and a model of the gorge system which puts it all in perspective. As you sit on the terrace overlooking the river below, consider that in January 1998 you would have been under a metre of water.

If you want to do an extended **bushwalk** you'll have to register with the rangers. Trails include the 66-kilometre **Jatbula Trail** to Edith Falls, in the park's northwestern corner, for which you'll need at least three days, a minimum of two people and a $50 returnable deposit.

Exploring Katherine Gorge

Buses from Katherine terminate at the canoe ramp and jetty. Tickets for cruises are sold at the visitors centre. There is also safe swimming – you'll be pleased to know that saltwater crocs are virtually unknown in the gorge. While waiting for a cruise, you might want to take the steep, four-hundred-metre walk leading from the jetty to a superb clifftop **lookout** up the river.

Cruises ply the gorge in a series of boats. Travel North (☎1800 089 103) offers somewhat rushed two-hour cruises to the second gorge for $37, a four-hour cruise to the third gorge (the limit during the Wet season, when a more powerful jet boat is brought in) for $53, and an eight-hour "safari", which includes some rock-hopping that demands secure footwear, for around $92. The relaxed safari cruise includes a barbecue lunch, refreshments, plenty of time for swimming and a peep at the sixth gorge; it gets away from the rather busy downstream sections and is highly recommended. There are also exhilarating **helicopter flights** up the gorge from as little as $60 per person for fifteen minutes (☎08/8972 1253).

Canoeing up the gorge is an option for the more energetic, but don't expect to paddle up to the "thirteenth" in a day; canoeing is hard work for unaccustomed arms and shoulders, especially against the breeze which wafts down the gorge. Nitmiluk Tours (☎1800 089 103) rents solo canoes for $45 a day, $33 per half-day – add about fifty percent for two-person canoes (easier to control and a shared load for beginners). Waterproof containers are provided. The rental period is 8.30am to 4.45pm; overnight trips cost a bit less than an extra day's rental. Alternatively, put your own canoe on the river for a small fee payable at the visitors centre. Expect long sections of canoe-carrying over boulders and successively shorter sections of water as you progress up the gorges. Those determined to reach the thirteenth gorge (which, scenically speaking, is not really worthwhile) will find it easier to leave their canoe at the fifth and swim/walk the last couple of kilometres.

The first permissible overnight **campsite** is Smith's Rock in the fifth gorge (or anywhere upstream from there) – this is regarded as a fair day's paddling and portaging. The best time to canoe the gorge is early in the Dry season, when small waterfalls run off cliff walls and the water level is still high enough to reduce the length of the walking sections.

The Victoria Highway to Western Australia

The **Victoria Highway** stretches for 510km southwest of Katherine to Kununurra in Western Australia. South of the highway is the legendary Victoria River Downs (VRD) station, once the country's biggest cattle station. Known colloquially as the "Big Run", VRD was established in the great droving days of the 1880s when mobs of cattle were driven overland from Queensland over several months or even years. These days, like many unmanageable properties, it's owned by a business consortium better able to weather the market or, like the former Bradshaw station on the north side of the river, has been sold to become a US military training ground. VRD is also the base of Australia's biggest heli-mustering outfit, which pursues the daredevil practice of mustering widely dispersed stock with single-seater helicopters.

Around 150km from Katherine the Victoria Highway enters a picturesque spur of the Gregory National Park (see below). Just after the Victoria River crossing is the *Victoria River Wayside Inn* (❷–❹) which runs **river cruises** (daily April–Oct; 3hr; $55) on the Victoria River.

Timber Creek

Although little more than a pair of roadhouses-cum-bars with adjacent campsites, **TIMBER CREEK**, 300km west of Katherine, makes a welcome break on the long run to Kununurra. Lying on the Victoria River, in 1856 the explorer Augustus Gregory's ship ran aground and, forced to make repairs, Timber Creek was born, an inland port to serve the vast pastoral properties then being established throughout the region. This remote outpost was soon the scene of bitter disputes between Aborigines and the settlers, and in 1885 a **police station** was set up at Timber Creek, staffed by two policemen and a black tracker whose task was to patrol an area the size of Tasmania.

The **museum** (Mon–Fri 10am–noon; $3), housed in a previous police station west of the town, features the usual display of miscellaneous pioneering relics, dragged out of the surrounding undergrowth or abandoned homesteads and used to illustrate a pithy historical commentary about the region. On a different note, the town has the easternmost examples of the curious, bottle-trunked **boab trees**, similar to Africa's baobabs; according to Aboriginal mythology, the boab was a once-arrogant tree which was turned upside down to teach it a lesson in humility (interestingly, West African tribes subscribe to a similar myth to account for their baobabs). Behind one twin-trunked boab on the south side of the highway 4km west of town, lies the century-old grave of Tom Lawler who shot himself when the limited prospects of Timber Creek closed in on him.

Practicalities

Tourist information is dispensed from the Max River Cruise office between the two pubs (daily 8am–6pm; ⓣ08/8975 0850, ⓦwww.maxsvictoriarivercruise.com). Inside you'll find one of the finest selections of crocobilia north of the 26th parallel. Of special note is a rubber "Rude Croc" – squeeze one and see. A four-hour afternoon **boat tour** (daily 4pm; $60) runs 40km down the Victoria River to come back for sunset on the crags, meeting a few crocs, both polite and rude, on the way.

Accommodation can be found at the *Timber Creek Hotel* (ⓣ08/8975 0772; ❹), incorporating the *Gunamu Tourist Park* which has camping, cabins and motel rooms. The *Wayside Inn* (ⓣ08/8975 0732; ❹) also has camping and cabins, with shared bathrooms. The *Shell Roadhouse* here is open 24 hours. **Eating** options include whatever's going on at either of the two roadhouses or what you can dig up at the store next to Max's.

Gregory National Park

Gregory National Park, the Territory's second-largest park, is most easily reached via the Victoria Highway, 11km east of Timber Creek. Carved out from unviable pastoral leases, the park exhibits sandstone escarpments and limestone hills covered in light woodland. Because of its remoteness and rough terrain, it can only be explored in a suitable **4WD vehicle**, and it's a good idea to call at the **P&WC** office in Timber Creek (turn right just before Watch Creek, west of town; ⓣ08/8975 0888) to study the large map and get information about conditions.

Conventional cars with good clearance and up for a hammering can get as far as **Limestone Gorge**, on a corrugated track 47km south of the highway. Here you'll find a short walking trail looping up onto the surrounding escarpment, a croc-free billabong and a campsite. The stockyards and old homestead at Bullita, along with the ranger at Bullita Outstation (ⓣ08/8975 0833), are another 9km south of the Limestone Gorge turn-off where there's a phone to self-register. The seventy-kilometre **Bullita Stockroute** loops back northwards, crossing a couple of rivers and crawling over some extremely rocky terrain which will chew up your tyres. This takes a full day and scenically it's not worth it, although **camping** is permitted at designated spots along the way.

Alternatively, 4WDs can choose to leave the park south along the **Humbert River Track** – another rocky drive, allow at least six hours for the 112km to the park's eastern boundary, from where you can head east along station tracks. For another route continue circuitously south to the **Buntine Highway** and Kalkaringi via the **Broadarrow** or **Wickham tracks**. Both the stockroute

Life and Death of the real Crocodile Dundee

The survival story of **Rod Ansell** and his subsequent media exposure are generally agreed to be the inspiration for the character of Mick "Croc" Dundee in the popular 1980s films which portrayed a tough bushman as a "fish out of water" in the big city. In 1977, Ansell, then 27 years old, claimed he became marooned when his boat was overturned while fishing at the mouth of the Victoria River, northwest of Timber Creek. With just one oar he paddled a spare dinghy up the Fitzmaurice River to fresh water and survived for seven weeks using the bush skills he'd been brought up with. Living on a diet of feral cattle, berries and sharks, Ansell and his two bull terriers were found, emaciated but coherent, seven weeks later by stockmen. He played down his ordeal but the tale grew legs and, as in the film, a journalist, Rachel Percy, tracked him down and publicized his story in a TV documentary and later in a slim book, *To Fight the Wild*. Sensing an opportunity, Ansell hit the TV chat show circuit, where his story inspired the comedian Paul Hogan to co-write *Crocodile Dundee*. The film came out in 1985 and was a worldwide hit, helping to put Australia's Outback on the map.

Following the success of the film, Ansell took on a station near Shady Camp on the Mary River, but his tourist plans were foiled when he was barred from using the "Crocodile Dundee" epithet and his entire stock was subsequently shot as part of a bovine disease eradication programme. Under financial pressure, he lost his station and was later charged with assault and cattle stealing in Arnhem Land. Embittered by his own failure compared with the success of the film, Ansell broke up with his family and became a speed-addled recluse living near Roper Bar. In August 1999, weighing less than seven stone and in the grip of drug-induced paranoia, he shot at strangers near Berry Springs who he thought had kidnapped his sons, before shooting dead a policeman on the Stuart Highway. A shoot-out ensued, and when reinforcements arrived Ansell came out of hiding, firing, and was himself shot dead. Kate Finlayson's 2003 book *A Lot of Croc* describes a semi-fictionalized search to unravel the Rod Ansell story and, on the way. describes many definitively Territorian and politically-incorrect characters, encounters and situations.

and this route are **one-way** only from Bullita, and are closed from December to March.

Keep River National Park and the WA border

West of Timber Creek, the land flattens out into the evocatively named **Whirlwind Plains**, where the East and West Baines rivers frequently cut the Victoria Highway in the Wet. **Keep River National Park** lies just before the Western Australia border, 185km from Timber Creek. Accessible to all vehicles, it's an easily explored area of dissected sandstone ridges, shallow gorges and Aboriginal art sites, the best of which is **Nganalam**, 24km from the park entrance. Marked trails start from the two **campsites** in the park, and the ranger station (☎08/9167 8827), 3km from the highway, supplies details on longer walks and other attractions.

By now you can hardly have failed to get the message that Western Australia does not want any infested Territorian livestock, produce or honey. The intensively irrigated agricultural area around Kununurra is hoping to remain free from pests found elsewhere in Australia, so eat up your offending foodstuffs before the border or throw them away. If you're not sure what to get rid of, the guys at the checkpoint will put you right; the regulations are not as severe as they seem. Note too that **WA time** is an hour and thirty minutes behind the Territory. At the **border**, Kununurra (see p.794) is just 40km away.

South to Alice

The 1100km from Katherine, south down the "**Track**" (as the Stuart Highway is known) to Alice Springs, are something of a **no-man's-land** for travellers. A flat, arid plain rolls all the way from the Top End's big rivers to the waterholes of the Red Centre, and the white population here consists largely of individuals who are either passing through, slowly going "troppo" amidst the clatter of empty beer cans or involved in servicing the Aboriginal communities and outstations alongside the Track.

West of the Track, the vast Aboriginal lands of the Warlpiri and neighbouring groups occupy just about the entire **Tanami Desert**, while to the east are the grasslands of the **Barkly Tableland**, a declining pastoral region extending north to the seldom-visited coast of the **Gulf of Carpentaria**. The town of **Tennant Creek**, just over halfway, is an anti-climactic break to a journey; car drivers tend to press on down the Track before something breaks or wears out. The landscape as seen from the Stuart Highway encourages a kind of agoraphobic urgency (or just plain boredom), while the mind repetitively churns over such imponderables as "just how many anthills *are* there in the Northern Territory?"

Mataranka and the Roper River Region

MATARANKA – just over 100km from Katherine – is a small town, the capital of the repeatedly hyped "Never Never" country named after Jeannie Gunn's 1908 novel of a pioneering woman's life, *We of the Never Never*, set in the region. Site of reviled Administrator John Gilruth's planned Northern Territory capital, today the town is practically eclipsed by the nearby **Mataranka Homestead** resort, which lures in buses and passing tourists. South of town the

Elsey National Park road leads to the often-overlooked freshwater wetlands of the **Roper River**.

There's not much to the town itself, but as you come in a sign leads to the **Bitter Springs** enclave of Elsey National Park, where you can swim in the same lukewarm, minty blue (but not minty smelling) mineral waters which fill the Mataranka thermal pool (see below).

All **accommodation**, along with the supermarket, roadhouses, museum, café and craft shop, is lined up along **Roper Terrace**, the main highway, with a couple of new places on the Bitter Springs road. Both the *Shell* and *Mobil* roadhouses have basic cabins (❸). The *Old Elsey Roadside Inn* has basic motel rooms (❹) with something better at the *Mataranka Cabins* on the Bitter Springs road (Ⓣ08/8975 4838; Ⓦwww.matarankacabins.bigpondhosting.com; ❸).

Mataranka Homestead

Mataranka Homestead, 6km from town (Ⓣ08/8975 4544 or 1800 754 544; Ⓦwww.travelnorth.com.au), was established by Gilruth to raise sheep and horses and is now a bush resort. The palm-shaded **thermal pool**, actually in Elsey National Park but seemingly part of the resort, is the only attraction here: it's free, always open, teeming with people and the water is a pleasant 34°C. The resort has a **bar** and **bistro**, and free nightly entertainment (April–Sept only) as well as a tour-booking service. **Accommodation** includes rooms and self-catering cabins (❺) plus motel rooms, and three-bed en-suite rooms with air-con (❻). There is also a backpackers' (dorms $20) and a campsite. Overland **buses** stop at the homestead, which is signposted south of Mataranka.

Elsey National Park and the Roper River and Highway

A twelve-kilometre road into **Elsey National Park** (turn off just before the homestead) leads to a more secluded **campsite** with less of a holiday-camp atmosphere, offering canoe rental and swimming in the (almost croc-free) upper Roper River, as well as a small kiosk.

The **Roper River** itself is difficult to appreciate without your own boat, since it's barely developed, yet it's as scenic as the wetlands of Kakadu. **Cruises** are again operating along the Roper wetlands in the season (Ⓣ0427 754 804; from 4pm to sunset; $30). You'll be able to explore the river's so-called **Pandanus Avenue** and some "*African Queen*"-type channels into the beautiful **Red Lily Lagoon**, the most extensive freshwater wetlands in the Territory.

A couple of kilometres south of Mataranka, the **Roper Highway** leads east for 185km (the bitumen ends at around 140km) to the remote community store at **ROPER BAR** with self-catering cabins (❸) and a campsite. If you've got this far, you're probably heading for **Borroloola**, 380km away (see p.671), a corrugated track that is passable in the Dry for regular cars in good shape.

Down the Track to Three Ways

LARRIMAH, 72km south of Mataranka, was where the old Darwin railway terminated until 1976 when it closed for good following Cyclone Tracy. Up until then, Larrimah had been a busy road-rail terminus, receiving goods brought up from Alice Springs. Now it's just a fuel stop on the highway with a bit more history than most. The *Larrimah Hotel* is a typical **bush pub**, full of eccentricity, old bottles and half-melted Spitfire engines; you can **camp** here or take one of the hotel's inexpensive basic rooms (❷).

Another 89km south brings you to the **Daly Waters Pub**, situated 3km off the highway. Having held a "gallon licence" since 1893, it positively drips with memorabilia, including money and women's underwear pinned to the walls: you're welcome to contribute. During the 1930s, when Qantas's Singapore flights refuelled here, world-class aviators used to pop in for a pint, and these days tourists come to marvel at the nutty quaintness of it all and buy the famous tea towels. If you fancy a break there are cheap and basic **rooms** (❷).

Just beyond here, the **Carpentaria Highway** (technically the circumnational Highway 1) heads off east to Borroloola, 414km away (see p.671); the turn-off is at the *Highway Inn Roadhouse* (open 24hr). There's a second turn-off, further down the Track, just before *Dunmarra Roadhouse*, where the **Buchanan Highway** heads west to *Top Springs Roadhouse* (185km) and ultimately, if you turn off south, Halls Creek in Western Australia (see p.792) along almost 800km of mostly unsealed road.

Further down the Track, **NEWCASTLE WATERS** can't seem to make up its mind whether it's a historic droving township wanting to encourage tourists or a semi-abandoned ghost town. It's of little interest today except to nostalgic drovers.

Further south, **ELLIOTT** is little more than a string of roadhouses with cheap **camping** at the *Mobil Roadhouse* and slightly better facilities at the *Midland Caravan Park* (also the local post office). The *BP Roadhouse* and the *Elliott Hotel* (Ⓣ08/8969 2018; ❹) both offer simple **rooms**. There are a few shops serving the Jingili Aboriginal communities at either end of town, but apart from filling up with fuel or a counter meal at the pub, there's no reason to stop.

As you leave town to the south, the trees which have hidden the horizon for days recede into shrubs and soon disappear altogether as you approach the deserts of Central Australia. **Renner Springs** is another bush hotel with its insides plastered with eccentric knick-knacks and offering rooms (❸) and camping.

On the way to the roadhouse at **THREE WAYS** (open 24hr) watch out for the turn-off to a rocky profile of Churchill's Head and also the **Attack Creek Memorial** – where explorer Stuart was repelled by Aborigines on one of his expeditions. At Three Ways, the **Barkly Highway** heads east to Camooweal, Mount Isa and eventually Townsville, all in Queensland; it's 210km on the highway to the *Barkly Homestead* (6am–1am), a better-than-average roadhouse with all the usual services. From Three Ways, Tennant Creek (see p.672) is just 26km down the road.

Cape Crawford, Borroloola and the Tablelands Highway

Cape Crawford is nothing more than a highway junction with the *Heartbreak Hotel* roadhouse (Ⓣ08/8975 9928; ❸). From the roadhouse the single-width **Tablelands Highway** offers a bitumen alternative to the Gulf route, leading to western Queensland via the *Barkly Homestead* roadhouse.

Borroloola

Situated on the croc-infested **McArthur River**, **BORROLOOLA** has had a colourful history which reads like an exaggerated version of the familiar boom, bust and dribble pattern of so many Outback towns. The explorers Leichhardt and Gregory came this way in the mid-nineteenth century, reporting good pasture, and the cattle followed in droves. By the early 1880s, when Tennant Creek and Katherine were still just shacks on the Overland Telegraph Line, the settlement was a wild outpost that even the missionaries avoided. Ships that formerly supplied the OTL came upriver with provisions for the hard-living

The classics library and hermits of Borroloola

There are a number of more or less unlikely explanations for Borroloola's improbable **classics library**, including one which starts with a bored policeman's request for reading matter to New York's Carnegie Foundation. In truth, it was a gradual acquisition of nearly two thousand literary classics by the town's McArthur Institute at the beginning of the twentieth century. Termites tucked into the library, a cyclone destroyed the remains and only a handful of books survived, many in "private collections", gathering what must be enormous overdue fees.

In 1963 a boyish David Attenborough made a TV documentary about three **hermits** who had chosen to retreat to the 'Loo. Jack Mulholland came across as a slightly jaded recluse when pressed about "loneliness and... women", and the reputedly aristocratic "Mad Fiddler" was too deranged to face the camera, but **Roger Jose** was, and looked like, the real thing. Having devoured the library ahead of the ants, he lived in a water tank with his Aboriginal wife and was a humane if eccentric "bush philosopher" who once observed that "a man's riches are the fewness of his needs". He is buried at the end of the airstrip in Borroloola.

drovers, who were helping stock the pastoral leases right across the north of Australia.

Borroloola was proclaimed, or "gazetted", in 1885 and a new police station was established in an attempt to control the town's lawless urges. The end came when today's Barkly Highway became the favoured stock route, and by 1900 just a handful of Europeans remained in "The 'Loo". With their passing the four local Aboriginal groups comprising the Yanyuwa (see "Books", p.1215) have reclaimed the town and surrounding land, which now serves their communities.

The only original building to have survived the punch-ups, white ants and cyclones is the **Old Police Station**, now a museum (Mon–Fri 10am–4pm; free). With Borroloola's exceptional white history (see box above), the museum couldn't fail to be fascinating. Read, for example, E. Gaunt's hair-raising account of "The Birth of Borroloola", recalling the sporadic insanity of the early days; it seems the toxic home-brew known as "Come Hither", whose label showed a red-eyed Lucifer beckoning malevolently, was to blame. Not surprisingly, the coverage of local Aboriginal history is lightweight. All this history may tickle your fancy but don't be misled, Borroloola is a rough and depressing Aboriginal welfare town of interest only to those needing fuel and a feed on the coastal Gulf route.

There are a couple of basic **campsites** along the main road (cabins ❸–❺) and rooms in the pub (❺) which from the outside looks about as inviting as a detention centre. By road, Borroloola is easily accessible along the **Carpentaria Highway**, via the *Heartbreak Hotel* at Cape Crawford. Depending on who you ask, the **dirt road** to **Wollogorang** roadhouse and Hell's Gate in Queensland (see p.626) is either terrible or not bad, but it's bound to be an adventure.

Tennant Creek

Visitors expect to be disappointed by **TENNANT CREEK**, 26km south of Three Ways junction, and indeed its appeal to tourists is not immediately apparent. Hang around, however, and you'll discover an unpretentious Outback town, defying stagnation and hoping for prosperity.

John McDouall Stuart came through in the early 1860s, followed by the Overland Telegraph Line ten years later. Pastoralists and prospectors arrived from the south and east, and in 1933 Tennant Creek was the site of the last major **goldrush** in Australia. This was the time of gritty "gougers", such as Jack Noble and partner Bill Weaber (with one eye between them), who defied the Depression by pegging some of the town's most productive claims. Today mining corporations use modern methods to exploit marginal deposits, but the main business in Tennant these days is looking after the health, education and other needs of the region's Aboriginal communities.

Arrival and information

Tennant Creek is 504km from Alice and 664km from Katherine. The **airport** is about 3km from the centre, at the end of Davidson Street, and the **train station** is by the highway 7km south of town, though the train only stops if someone has a ticket for Tennant – getting off you'll feel like Spencer Tracy in the opening scene of *Bad Day at Black Rock*. The new train service has not been so good for the town as most people now shoot through to Darwin, some transporting their cars on the train. On Paterson Street (the town's main street, essentially the Stuart Highway) you'll find the usually empty hangar of the Transit Centre where interstate **buses** pull in – southbound buses come through at 3.30am, which also doesn't encourage stopovers. There's **Internet** access at *Switch* next to the Transit Centre and the *Talk of the Town* **café** next to that. The **visitors information centre** is out at Battery Hill (May–Sept Mon–Fri 9am–5pm & Sat 9am–noon; ⓣ08/8962 3388, ⓦwww.tennantcreektourism.com.au), 1.5km east along Peko Road.

Accommodation

There are motels at each end of town and one in the middle, but they occasionally fill up with contract workers if there is some exploration activity going on.

El Dorado Motor Inn Paterson St North ⓣ08/8962 2402. Motel at the north end of town with a licensed restaurant and nice pool area. ❹

Safari Backpackers Davidson St ⓣ08/8962 2207. The official YHA but don't expect anything fancy: four-bed dorms, doubles, kitchen, TV and functional air-con. Dorms $18, rooms ❷

Safari Lodge Motel Davidson St ⓣ08/8962 2207. Functional motel right in town centre, with *Fernanda's* next door. Deals with enquiries for the YHA opposite. ❹

TC Caravan Park Next to the Shell service station, Paterson St ⓣ08/8962 2325. One of three caravan parks in town, this one has good deals for camping; backpackers' bunkhouse and roomy cabins also available. Dorms $25, cabins ❷

Tennant Creek Tourist's Rest Leichhardt St ⓣ08/8962 2719; ⓦwww.touristrest.com.au. A time-worn row of two- and three-bed rooms with an authentic lived-in "Tennant" feel, plus a pool, free breakfasts and pick-ups off the bus. Also organises fossicking and Devil's Marbles tours (see p.674). Dorms $18, rooms ❷

The Town and around

In town, the **museum** (daily 3.30–5.30pm; $3), across the road from the *Memorial Club*, minutely details the history of Tennant Creek, using a chronological time scale starting from the year 0 "AS" (After Stuart). If you're heading to the visitors centre at **Battery Hill** you might as well take the sixty-minute tour of the mine site (up to 4 daily; $15), which includes an entertaining stroll through a specially-built show mine. There's also a chance to savour the din of the old stamp battery (2 tours daily; $15; both tours $24). The scale of the 1930s goldrush was not insignificant; for a year the equivalent of nearly a million dollars of gold came out of Tennant Creek each day.

Back in town, the recently built Nyinkka Nyunyu **Arts and Cultural Centre** (Mon–Fri 8am–5pm, Sat 9am–4pm, Sun 10am–2pm; ⓦwww.nyinkkanyunyu.com.au; $7.50), at the south end of Paterson Street, is similar in concept to the better-known cultural centres at Uluru and Kakadu. This one comes without the baggage of those glamorous locations, and instead gives a more rounded picture of a real community. Historical events are displayed in mini-dioramas alongside looped films of Warumungu talking about their experiences, as well as artefacts, bushtucker lore and some indifferent paintings. Particularly interesting is the story of the twenty-year land claim against an initially obstructive NT administration, which had only just gained self-government itself and was not yet disposed to giving large chunks of the Territory away.

Without your own vehicle, that's about it, although a couple of kilometres north of town is an old **telegraph station**, restored as a historic exhibit (Ⓣ08/8962 3388 for opening times). If you've come down the Track and not seen an OTL station yet, here's your chance.

Eating and drinking

You won't be surprised to hear that the Michelin **food guide** has overlooked Tennant Creek yet again. Your options are a counter **meal** in the *Tennant Creek Hotel*; the *Talk of the Town* café near the Transit Centre, which is open for daytime meals; and the Chinese a few doors up. Round the corner next to the *Safari Motel*, *Fernanda's* offers Mediterranean and seafood dishes, or you can sign in as a guest at the Memorial Club on Schmidt Street for a $15 feed and have a quiet drink afterwards.

Dedicated **drinkers** are well looked after, as the town boasts around thirteen licences and two pubs. Like a lot of pubs in Outback towns, front bars can be intimidating, while the carpeted back bars are for games of pool and benign socializing. Pubs are generally open from 10am to midnight. *Goldfields*, on Paterson Street, has a cleared front bar where you can get a good swing at your neighbour without breaking any of the fittings; the back bar is the place to take your mum for a sherry. Over the road, the *Tennant Creek Hotel* also has a back bar for a quiet drink.

Towards Alice and the Centre

If you're feeling a bit "Top Ended" then the 505km from Tennant to Alice offers some respite as the land opens out into the subtle hues of the central deserts. Unless you have a 4WD, only the Devil's Marbles are worth breaking the journey for, and if you've not got your own transport then they can be visited on a day-tour from Tennant Creek with Devil's Marbles Tours (Ⓣ0418 891 711; $60, 2 people minimum).

Eighty-seven kilometres from town, a sign points east towards the **Davenport Ranges National Park**. Here a track runs 160km east along the north side of the ranges before looping back west along the rougher but scenically more interesting southern side, passing a couple of waterholes, station homesteads and outstations on the way – a chance to see something of central NT other than the Stuart Highway. Ideally using a 4WD, you can expect to do the standard loop with an overnight camp and emerge about 100km further on down the Track. If you're interested, get a leaflet and map from Tennant Creek's visitor centre. Fuel and provisions are available at Kurundi and Murray Downs station stores on the way (both are on or near the main track).

South to Ti Tree

Right by the highway about 100km south of Tennant Creek, the **Devil's Marbles** (basic camping) are a genuine geological oddity, a scattering of huge rounded boulders thought by the local Warumungu Aborigines to be the eggs

Area 51 – Downunder

For decades there have been sightings of UFOs in the skies over Wycliffe Well. While the roadhouse has capitalized on this to the full with some kitsch alienobilia and a space ship on the forecourt, scores of newspaper articles in the restaurant attest to the regular sightings of UFOs, if not necessarily bug-eyed ETs. The location has certain parallels with Nevada's Area 51, a sparsely populated semi-desert, and the shady goings-on at the Pine Gap US military base near Alice Springs are just 400km to the south. Of course that's no distance at all for the latest remote orbiters fitted with the new generation plasma drives. Rationalizations of the sightings include that they are merely "glowing birds" or the "Min Min Light" (see p.606). Whatever the truth is, it would be unfair to suggest that Wycliffe Well's global selection of over 130 beers has any connection with the phenomenon, but it gives you something to do while you watch the skies and wait.

of the Rainbow Serpent. They're well worth a look as any excuse for a break is welcome. A short drive south of the Marbles is the old roadhouse/pub of **WAUCHOPE** (pronounced "Walkup"), which has a motel (❹) and budget rooms (❸) and a restaurant. **WYCLIFFE WELL**, a little further south, has the largest range of beer in Australia, which has to be worth a stop, as well as camping and rooms (❸).

BARROW CREEK, 60km further on, is one of the oldest roadhouses on the Track, originally a telegraph station, and remembered as the site of the Barrow Creek Massacre in 1874, when a local clan was all but wiped out in reprisal for the killing of the two men whose graves are in the forecourt. Fifty-four years later, the last of the Territory's massacres took place at Coniston, 100km to the southwest, when up to a hundred Aboriginal men, women and children were killed by a policeman following the death of a dingo trapper. The old pub is as characterful as they come along the Track, with walls daubed in coarse humour and foreign bank notes (a "bush bank"), as well as old rooms (❹) and cheaper cabins (❷–❸) out back.

At **TI TREE**, an Aboriginal community close to the middle of the continent, a couple of galleries sell keenly priced artefacts and paintings produced by the local Anmatjera and communities further afield, though as all over the Territory the quantity of indigenous art seems now to be in inverse proportion to its quality. After another 43km, the **AILERON** roadhouse (❺) has the last fuel before Alice and also sells Aboriginal art.

The Plenty Highway and Tanami Road

Heading towards Alice, the land finally begins to crumple as you near the MacDonnell Ranges. The **Plenty** and **Sandover highways**, which run off the Stuart Highway 66km south of Aileron, head northeast towards Queensland through the scenic Harts and Jervois ranges. Both are passable with sound, well-equipped conventional cars – the Plenty (which becomes the Donohue Highway in Queensland) is generally the busier and better maintained. If you're heading down to Birdsville or Winton this way (both in Queensland), the Donohue Highway short cut down to Boulia isn't half as bad as maps suggest.

Twenty kilometres north of Alice, the **Tanami Road** leads 1040km northwest to Halls Creek in Western Australia. The track is a dirt freeway up to the Granites mines just before the WA border, from where things can get a little rough and sandy. If you're heading from Alice to the Bungles (see p.792), the Tanami is quicker than the bitumen via Katherine, but pretty boring (although of course you need 4WD to get into the Bungles). The longest section without fuel is the 322km from Yuendumu to **Rabbit Flat** roadhouse (closed Tues–Thurs), with the next section to Billiluna station in WA nearly as long at 292km. You can also pop into the art gallery at the Aboriginal community of **Balgo Hills**, which sometimes has fuel, 31km south of the Tanami (the turn-off is about 88km on the WA side of the track); their garish and splodgy school of dot paintings is highly distinctive.

Before embarking on either route, it's worth checking out the condition of the tracks; phone RACQ for the Queensland sections (Ⓣ07/4775 3600), Emergency Services in Alice Springs (Ⓣ08/8951 6688) or the Main Roads Dept, Halls Creek (Ⓣ08/9168 6007); you can also check out up-to-date road conditions of desert tracks at Ⓦwww.exploreoz.com. Although they shouldn't be considered time-saving short cuts, the Plenty and Tanami tracks are both perfectly feasible in a tough, well-equipped 2WD vehicle.

Alice and the Centre

Set at what is just about the geographical centre of the continent, **Alice Springs** has a population of just 28,000, yet is still the largest settlement in the Australian interior. A modern and compact town in the midst of the MacDonnell Ranges, it makes an excellent base from which to explore the surrounding countryside.

The **Red Centre**, a marketing term coined to describe the area to the south, west and east of Alice Springs, is a historically rich and scenically spectacular region. It includes the lands inhabited by the "Anangu", the tourist-friendly epithet for the Aborigines from the Uluru region. Notwithstanding massacres as late as 1928, the **Aborigines of the central deserts** were fortunate in being among the last to come into contact with white settlers, by which time the exterminations of the nineteenth century had passed their peak and anthropologists like Ted Strehlow (see p.683) were hurrying to record a "dying race". As a result of this, their traditional way of life was well-documented, though their isolation is also said to have made their adjustment to modern life more difficult than Aborigines of the northern coast, who had contact with foreigners even before European colonization.

Ayers Rock – or **Uluru** – is Australia's most famous and most visited natural spectacle, and still the primary reason why most people come to the Centre. At first sight, even jaded "seen-it-all" cynics will find it hard to take their eyes away from its awesome bulk. But there's much more in the Centre than just the Rock, and it's rare in Outback Australia to find such a large region crammed with so many worthwhile and accessible places of interest. The **West MacDonnells**, a series of rugged ridges cut at intervals by slender chasms or huge gorges, start right on Alice's doorstep. In the other direction, the **Eastern MacDonnells** are less visited but no less appealing, with the remote tracks of the **Simpson Desert** to the south attracting the intrepid. To the west, **Palm Valley**, now linked to **Kings Canyon** via a good dirt road, can add a few days to a trip which, including the Rock, makes for probably the most memorable tour in the Outback. While most of these places certainly don't need a 4WD vehicle to get to, there are a few enjoyable and easy off-road tracks that can be fun in a rented 4WD; they're detailed in the box on p.694.

When to go and what to take

The aridity of the Centre results in seasonal extremes of temperature that are best avoided, if at all possible. In the midwinter months of July and August the air is lovely and clear, although **freezing nights**, especially around Uluru, are not uncommon. But there's no escaping the **summer heat**: in December and January the temperature may have reached 40°C by 10am and won't drop below 30°C all night. The transitional seasons of autumn (April–June) and Spring (Sept & Oct) are the best times to explore the region in comfort.

Rain is a rare and wonderful thing in the Centre. Whenever you visit, a sudden storm may temporarily transform the desert into a garden of wildflowers as well as cut off access along even the main roads, though as a rule it is **midsummer storms** which bring the most rain.

Out here a **wide-brimmed hat** is not so much a fashion accessory as a life saver, keeping your head and face in permanent shadow. All but the shortest of walks will also require a **water bottle** and loose, long-sleeved clothing plus lashings of **sun block** on any exposed skin. Australia's many venomous but rarely seen snakes and, more relevantly, rocky tracks and the carpet of prickly spinifex grass that covers a fifth of the continent, make a pair of **covered shoes or boots** the final precaution to safe and comfortable tramping around the Centre.

Alice Springs and around

Most visitors are surprised by the modern appearance of **ALICE SPRINGS**. The bright, clear desert air gives the Outback town and its people a charge that you don't get in the languid, tropical north. In Alice, the shopping centre is actually in the middle of town and not in some distant suburb, and so allusions to Nevil Shute's flyblown *A Town Like Alice*, or even Robyn Davidson's ockersome observations in *Tracks*, have long been obsolete.

The area has been inhabited for at least thirty thousand years by Aranda Aborigines, who moved between reliable water sources along the MacDonnell Ranges. But, as elsewhere in the Territory, it was only the Overland Telegraph Line's arrival in the 1870s that led to a permanent settlement here. Following **John McDouall Stuart**'s exploratory journeys through the area in the early 1860s, it was the visionary **Charles Todd**, then South Australia's Superintendent of Telegraphs, who saw the need to link Australia with the rest of the empire. The town's river and its tributary carry his name, and the "spring" (actually a billabong) and town that of his wife, Alice.

With repeater stations needed every 250km from Adelaide to Darwin to boost the OTL signal, the billabong north of today's town was chosen at the spot at which to erect the necessary buildings. When a spurious ruby rush led on to the discovery of gold at Arltunga in the Eastern MacDonnells, **Stuart Town** (the town's seldom-used official name in its early years) became a jumping-off point for the long slog to the riches out east. Arltunga's goldrush fizzled out, but the township of Stuart remained, a collection of shanty dwellings serving a stream of pastoralists, prospectors and missionaries.

In 1929 the **railway line** from Adelaide finally reached Stuart Town. Journeys that had once taken weeks by camel from the Oodnadatta railhead could now be undertaken in just a few days and by 1933, when the town officially took the name Alice Springs, the population had mushroomed to nearly five hundred Europeans. The 1942 bombing and subsequent evacuation of Darwin saw Alice Springs become the Territory's administrative capital and a busy military base, supplying the war zone in the north.

After hostilities ceased, some of the wartime population stayed on and Alice's fortunes continued to rise, boosted by the establishment of the US base, **Pine Gap**, southwest of town in the mid-1960s. The covert activities at the underground base conjure up many intriguing Roswell-esque theories (see box on p.792 or search the web), but the continued presence of around two thousand well-financed Americans in town has helped give Alice a purposeful, cosmopolitan feel, while greatly aiding the local service economy.

With the reconstruction of the poorly built rail link from Adelaide and the sealing of the Stuart Highway in the mid-1980s, Alice has only recently attained its present population of around 28,000. A tourist boom at that time, helped in no small measure by the massive publicity surrounding Azaria Chamberlain's abduction by a dingo at the Rock in 1980, took a knock when direct flights to Ayers Rock were established, but Alice and the surrounding area remain a worthwhile destination in their own right, even without the obligatory visit to the Rock.

Arrival, information and transport

The **airport** is 14km south of town. The airport shuttle (ⓣ08/8953 0310) meets incoming flights and costs $12, or $20 return, while a taxi (ⓣ08/8953 0979) will be about $25. **Buses** arrive at the Coles Complex at the western end of Gregory Terrace. Some of the keener backpacker hostels meet incoming buses (as well as some incoming flights). Alice's **train station** – open only when trains are due to arrive – is on George Crescent on the west side of the Stuart Highway, just off Larapinta Drive, about a fifteen-minute walk (or $5 taxi ride) from the town centre.

The **tourist information office** (Mon–Fri 8.30am–5.30pm, Sat & Sun 9am–4pm; ⓣ08/8952 5800 or 1800 645 199, ⓦwww.centralaustraliantourism.com) is at the river end of Gregory Terrace by the library and council offices. It features a well-organized range of brochures detailing the mind-boggling possibilities in Alice and around.

Transport

The centre occupies a compact area between the Stuart Highway and Leichhardt Terrace, along the dry Todd River, bordered to the north and south by Wills Terrace and Stott Terrace respectively. Bisecting this rectangle is **Todd Mall**, once the main street, now a relaxing pedestrian thoroughfare lined with alfresco cafés, galleries and souvenir outlets.

The town's sights are scattered, but you can still get around them all in a couple of days on foot. An alternative is to use the green and yellow **Alice Wanderer** (ⓣ08/8952 2111; day-ticket $25), a hop-on-hop-off bus service with commentary which visits most of the places of interest every seventy minutes. The Yeperenye Shopping Centre, on Hartley Street, is the terminus for the **suburban bus** network; it's best to check bus times before you set out (timetables are available from the tourist office or the council offices on Gregory Terrace). Of the four main routes, #1 West and #4 South are the most useful. Otherwise your best bet is to rent a **car** (see "Listings", p.686) or a **bicycle** from any of the hostels (around $20 a day). There's an enjoyable seventeen-kilometre **paved cycle track** through the bush to Simpson's Gap, starting at Flynn's Grave, 7km along Larapinta Drive, west of the town centre.

Accommodation

Most places in Alice (except the campsites) are either in the town centre area or along Todd Street and its southern continuation, **Gap Road** – a twenty-minute walk from the Mall which some find off-putting late at night. Booking ahead is advisable during the winter school holidays (June & July) or during special events like the Masters Cup in October. Note that the price codes given for

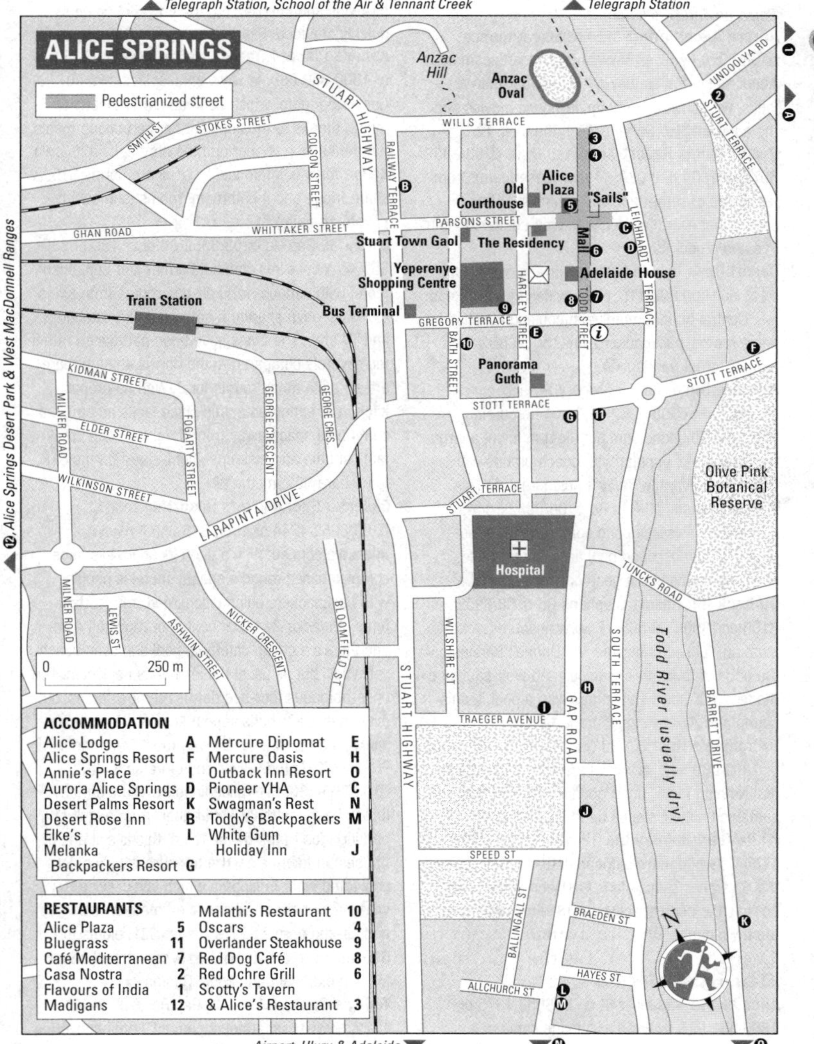

self-contained apartments are for a unit sleeping from four and six people; they often work out a better deal than a motel and are certainly more spacious. One day someone will invest in a purpose-built **backpackers**, but for the moment you get what you pay for from the selection of generally lacklustre converted motels listed below.

Motels and hotels

Alice Springs Resort 34 Stott Tce ⓣ08/8951 4545 or 1300 134 044; ⓦwww.voyages.com.au. Just over the river but not too far away, this plush four-star has all mod cons and the gourmand's *Barra-on-Todd* restaurant. ❼

Aurora Alice Springs 11 Leichhardt Terrace ⓣ08/8950 6666, ⓦwww.aurora-resorts.com.au. About as central as they get and better than it looks, with covered parking, in-house movies and the adjacent *Red Ochre Grill* on the Mall. ❺

Desert Palms Resort 74 Barrett Drive ⓣ08/8952 5977 or 1800 678 037, ⓦwww.desertpalms.com.au. Rows of semi-detached cabins in palmy setting just over the river, with well-equipped kitchens and a pool. ❺

Desert Rose Inn 15 Railway Terrace ⓣ08/8952 1411 or 1800 896 116, ⓦwww.desertroseinn.com.au. Central budget motel with cooking facilities in some rooms, backpacker twins (❷), a BBQ area and off-street parking. ❹

Mercure Diplomat 15 Gregory Terrace, cnr of Hartley St ⓣ08/8952 8977, ⓔmercureinn.diplomat@bigpond.com.au. Right in town, a large four-star motel popular with coach groups with a better than average *Keller's* Restaurant. ❺

Mercure Oasis 10 Gap Rd ⓣ08/8952 1444, ⓔmercureoasis@bigpond.com. Nicely laid-out motel with landscaped pool area, comfortable, spacious rooms and a good bar-restaurant. ❺

Outback Inn Resort Stephens Rd ⓣ08/8952 6100 or 1300 656 565, ⓦwww.novotel-outback.com.au. Tucked under the MacDonnell Ranges on the edge of town, this spacious and well-equipped modern four-star hotel comes with a pool, tennis courts and *Ainsley's* restaurant. ❺

Swagman's Rest 67–69 Gap Rd ⓣ08/8953 1333 or 1800 089 612, ⓦwww.theswagmansrest.com.au. Nothing fancy, but a good-value, fully self-contained option, sleeps up to six people. ❹

White Gum Holiday Inn 17 Gap Rd ⓣ08/8952 5144; ⓔwhitegum@bigpond.com. A notch below the *Swagman's*, this place has seen better days, but has the nearest self-contained motel units to the town centre. ❹

Backpackers

Alice Lodge 4 Mueller St ⓣ08/8953 1975 or 1800 351 925, ⓦwww.alicelodge.com.au. A converted house, not a motel, set in a quiet, residential street on the east side of the river all which makes for a mellow atmosphere. Nearer to the centre than it feels, there's a shady garden area and pool. Various aged caravans in the back cater for twins and doubles, but the tiny kitchen gets quickly crowded. Eight-share dorms $18, rooms ❷

Annie's Place 4 Traeger Ave ⓣ08/8952 1545 or 1800 359 089, ⓦwww.anniesplace.com.au. Converted motel which has had a great word-of-mouth thanks to the adjacent bar and cheap meals, but the kitchen is poor and the hard sell on its own *Mulga Tours* is infamous. Eight-share dorms $16 share fridge and a bathroom, rooms (some with private en-suite) ❸

Elke's 39 Gap Rd ⓣ08/8952 8422 or 1800 633 354, ⓦwww.elkes.com.au. Former self-contained motel with various-sized air-con rooms from twins to eights, each sharing a bathroom, tiny kitchen and TV area. The twins have been partitioned rather too severely compared to the dorms, though there are en-suite motel rooms for 3. With no proper kitchen or eating area, this place lacks an ambient communal space away from the pool. Free 'breakfast', shuttle and pick ups. Eight-share dorms $18, four-share $22, rooms ❷

Melanka Backpackers Resort 94 Todd St ⓣ08/8952 4744 or 1800 815 066 ⓦwww.melanka.com.au. With a good location, this huge complex based round a shabby motel is popular with backpackers being discharged from certain tours. *Melanka Party Bar* next door rages till 4am and there's a cheap cafeteria, pool and even beach volleyball, but as usual the kitchen is neglected. The once-notorious four-bed dorms are now threes, but even then the 8-beds appear spacious in comparison. All dorms $20, Small twin rooms with fridge ❸

Pioneer YHA Todd River end of Parsons St ⓣ08/8952 8855, ⓔalicepioneer@yhant.org.au. It may be a 'matronly' Y, but apart from a lack of parking (don't park by the river), this is still one of the best in town; a central but surprisingly quiet converted walk-in cinema which layout-wise, works a lot better than some ex-motels. Four-bed air-con dorms $23, sixes for $21, eights for $20 and even a sixteen at $19, plus a pool and a kitchen big enough to cope. Rooms ❸

Toddy's Backpackers 41 Gap Rd ⓣ08/8952 1322, ⓦwww.saharatours.com.au. Large converted motel next to *Elke's* feels neglected but gets by with cheap mixed, eight-bed dorms from $17, rooms from ❷ and motel rooms with bath, fridge and TV for ❸. There's also cheap beer and nightly BBQs plus free light breakfasts and shuttle/pick-ups make up for the twenty-minute walk to the town centre.

Caravan parks

Macdonnell Range Holiday Park Palm Place ☎08/8952 6111. Camping and cabins in a leafy setting on the south edge of town with all mod-cons and airport pick-ups. Cabins ❸

Stuart Tourist Park Opposite Araluen Centre, Larapinta Drive ☎08/8952 2547. The most central caravan park, about 2km west of town, with regular camping and powered sites. On-site vans ❸

Wintersun Caravan Park Stuart Highway, 3km north of town ☎08/8952 4080. Regular camping and powered sites. Cabins ❸

The Town

Start your tour of town by nipping up to **Anzac Hill** (off Wills Terrace) for a great view over Alice to the Heavitree Ranges beyond. In town, on Parsons Street is the **Old Courthouse** (daily 10am–5pm; $2.20) now home of the National Pioneer Women's Hall of Fame, a stirring photographic exhibit detailing the achievements of women such as Olive Pink (see below). Across the street is the **Residency** (Mon–Fri 9am–4pm, Sat 10am–4pm; free), a neat period dwelling and good place to cool off. Inevitably, a bit further down Parsons Street comes the **Stuart Town Gaol**, Alice's oldest building, dating from 1909.

From the "Sails" awning, a short stroll down the mall will take you past **Adelaide House** (March–Nov Mon–Fri 10am–4pm, Sun 10am–noon; $4), an ingenious convection-cooled building designed by the Reverend John Flynn, founder of the Royal Flying Doctor Service (RFDS). Adelaide House was the first hospital in Central Australia, and also the site of Flynn and Alf Treager's innovative radio experiments using portable, pedal-generated electricity. Inside you'll come across early medical and RFDS memorabilia.

Next door to Adelaide House is the **John Flynn Memorial Church** and, at 65 Hartley Street, you'll find **Panorama Guth** (Mon–Sat 9am–5pm, Sun noon–5pm; $5.50), a museum and art gallery displaying scores of Henk Guth's oiled landscapes, as well as original Albert Namatjira watercolours (see box on p.692 for more on Namatjira's life and the Hermannsburg school of painting he initiated). Much more curious is the collection of rare Aboriginal artefacts found here which you'll rarely see elsewhere, including some sacred and secret objects (*tjuringas*) once used during ceremonies. The panorama, from which the gallery takes its name, is a novel if unremarkable painting, 60m in circumference, showing the area around Alice, but the gallery below is a wonderfully comfy and congenial place to snooze through the regional home movies on show.

When you've had enough of artefacts and memorabilia, head out to the **Olive Pink Botanical Reserve** (daily 10am–6pm; donation), just across the causeway on Tuncks Road. Olive Pink was a passionate defender of Aboriginal rights long before the issue became fashionable. Like T.G.H. Strehlow (see p.683), with whom she briefly worked, Pink practised a kind of fanatical "inverted eugenics", working solely for the welfare and preservation of "full-blood" tribal Aborigines and their lore, while dismissing those of mixed blood as a lost cause. She also found time to collect native flora from the surrounding lands, all of which can be seen neatly labelled along pathways winding up through the reserve. Displays in the **visitors centre** (daily 10am–4pm) explain the various strategies the plants use to survive in the desert.

The Telegraph Station and School of the Air

The old **Telegraph Station** (daily 8am–5pm, picnic grounds until 9pm; $7) is tucked in the hills just to the north of town. Fully restored and accessible along a three-kilometre riverside walk from Wills Terrace (or off the Stuart Highway, 4km north of town), the historic reserve – situated right by the pool from which the town derives its name – faithfully recreates the settlement's earliest years. There are free and informative thirty-minute **tours** further detailing pioneering life at the telegraph station. All in all, it's a pleasant place to while away a quiet afternoon, with the surrounding picnic area giving a taste of the Outback on the edge of a city. The station is also the starting point of the **Larapinta Trail** bushwalk to Standley Chasm in the Western MacDonnells (see p.688).

On the other side of the Stuart Highway is the **School of the Air** (Mon–Sat 8.30am–4.30pm, Sun 1.30–4.30pm; closed during school holidays; $3.50), at 80 Head Street. Explanatory sessions are offered every thirty minutes on this famous Outback institution, through which children living on remote stations are taught over the radio. It's mostly visited by overseas schoolchildren and teachers. From town, take bus #3 and alight at stop 5 or 11.

Along Larapinta Drive to the Alice Springs Desert Park

Larapinta Drive heads out through the western suburbs to the **Alice Springs Cultural Precinct** (daily 10am–5pm; $8), some 2km from the town. The walk to the precinct isn't too bad, but check out the bus service if you're continuing to the Alice Springs Desert Park.

The precinct has brought together some of Alice's best attractions and is well worth the entry fee. The **Araluen Centre for Arts and Entertainment**, for example, is the focal point for the performing arts in the region with a 500-seat theatre, cinema, and art galleries that always have something on that is worth checking out. **The Central Australian Aviation Museum**, located in the Old Connellan Hangar, houses many of the aircraft in which Outback plane travel was pioneered and has a special memorial to the "Coffee Royale Incident" of 1929, in which rescuers searching for missing aviator Charles Kingsford-Smith perished in the northern Tanami Desert. Kingsford-Smith was accused of cynically staging the crash for publicity purposes, though this was never proved; the memorial poignantly displays the wreckage of the long-lost *Kookaburra* used in the search.

The **Museum of Central Australia** contains local fauna, including the largest bird that ever lived and an impressive display of locally found meteorites. In the same building the **Strehlow Research Centre** commemorates the life and work of T.G.H. Strehlow (see box opposite). Around the corner on Memorial Drive is the **Alice Springs Memorial Cemetery**, which includes the graves of pioneer aviator Eddie Connellan, artist Albert Namatjira and the reburied remains of the legendary, luckless prospector Harold Lasseter (see p.706), after whom the town's casino is rather ironically named.

Continuing from the precinct on Larapinta Drive you will come to one of Alice's premier attractions, the **Alice Springs Desert Park** (daily 7.30am–6pm; $20). Set right beneath the ranges topped by Mount Gillen, the park is an example of a thoughtful and imaginative design displaying various natural environments of the Territory. Allow at least two hours to fully appreciate the centre's ecology. Shown on the hour, the twenty-minute film is actually a little over-portentous, and the real highlight, after you've wandered through various aviaries and creek, sand-dune and woodland habitats, is the large **nocturnal house** where the Territory's varied, but rarely seen, fauna can be seen scurrying around in fake moonlight. The park succeeds in blurring the boundary between the surrounding bush and the fenced interior – there's as much birdlife darting

T.G.H. Strehlow

Theodore Strehlow was the son of a strict Lutheran missionary who grew up in Hermannsburg in the early 1900s among the uninhibited Aranda, a dualism which underpinned his life. Like his father before him, he became devoted to documenting Aranda lore as well as amassing their sacred *tjuringas*, handed over by elders convinced their way of life was doomed. Possessive of his knowledge, while resenting his lack of recognition, with the advent of Aboriginal rights in the 1970s he ignored demands to return the artefacts unless the price was right. Then, in a short-sighted attempt to raise awareness abroad, the embattled Strehlow sold photographs of secret initiation ceremonies to the German magazine, *Stern,* which were quickly resold to the trashy Australian *People* weekly, a humiliation which hastened Strehlow's death in 1978. An absorbing fifty-minute documentary about Strehlow plays every hour at the Strehlow Research Centre, filling you in on his early years, while skimming the above controversies. *Songs of Central Australia* (1971; out of print) is Strehlow's dense magnum opus, but his *Journey to Horseshoe Bend* (1967; for sale at the centre) is much more accessible, offering a revealing account of the 14-year-old Theo's journey south to try to save his dying father. Barry Hill's *Broken Song* (2002) is a rather incomplete biography.

about outside the aviaries as in, and now the park is beginning to grow into itself it's better than ever.

Eating, drinking and nightlife

The **eating** opportunities in Alice aren't at all bad. Todd Mall is lined with **cafés** with outdoor seating, and the **pubs** (see below) do counter meals for around $10. Besides the places listed below, the *Barra on Todd* at the *Alice Springs Resort* hotel and *Ainsley's* at the *Novotel* on Stephens Road are both very good.

Cafés and snack bars

Alice Plaza Todd Mall. Food halls with Asian- and Italian-inspired lunches.

Cafe Mediterranean Fan Arcade, Todd Mall. Tasty lunchtime concoctions of trans-Adriatic and Asian dishes plus shakes and smoothies.

Red Dog Café Todd Mall, south end. Along with place next door, a good spot for breakfast croissants and early morning people-watching.

Restaurants

Bluegrass cnr Stott Terrace and Todd St. Old colonial building hung with Aboriginal art makes *Bluegrass* one of the few places in town with some individual character and one of Alice's most popular restaurants. Starters include a prawn and veg tempura with sweet soy and ginger or spicy calamari, both for $16. Mains include a baby barramundi baked with dill and hollandaise sauce with prawns, avocados and potatoes for $28; a kangaroo steak for $22 has much more flavour. Good vegetarian selection too. Wed–Mon 6pm–late.

Casa Nostra Undoolya Road. Just over the river from Wills Terrace, a traditional *rizztorante* that's a little slice of wood-fired Sicily serving pizzas and the usual pastas with a variety of sauces for under $20. BYO and take-away, daily from 5pm.

Flavours of India 20 Undoolya Rd. All your favourite Indian dishes in a licensed restaurant Chicken Tikka or Lamb Pasanda from $16 and a good selection of vegetarian mains from $13. Mon–Sat from 6pm.

Oscars Todd Mall Cinema Complex. Among the better of the two or three modern Italian restaurants in the Mall, try seafood risotto for $22 or roast pumpkin salad for $18, but watch out for the cheap WA wines. Daily from 8am till late

Overlander Steakhouse 72 Hartley St. Long-established Alice favourite with tourists: the Drovers Blowout serves a selection of Territorian red meats on one plate for around $28 but there are some veggie options too. Daily 6pm till late.

Scotty's Tavern and Alice's Restaurant Todd Mall. Bar and restaurant serving typical Territorian food (including emu). Seven-dollar schnitzels with all the veg you can eat on Thursday nights.

Drinking, nightlife and entertainment

Like the surrounding desert, night-time Alice initially appears lifeless. However, something can be found going on somewhere most nights, particularly in the latter half of the week. The daily *Centralian Advocate* carries details of what's going on.

The *Todd Tavern*, at the top of Todd Mall, is the town's landmark **drinking** spot, complete with "unofficial" segregated bars. Thursday night at the enduringly popular *Bojangles Saloon* on Todd Street is all action. There's **jazz and blues** at *Scotty's* on Sunday afternoon from 1pm. *Sean's Irish Sibin* on Bath Street is a quieter option, while homesick Brits can head for the *Firkin and Hound*, on Hartley Street, a British theme pub that shows just what can be done with a multilevel car park and a little imagination. If nothing else tempts you, there's always the **cinema** at the top of Todd Mall, with cheap nights on Tuesday. Check the programme at the **Araluen Centre for Arts and Entertainment** (ⓣ08/8952 5022) on Larapinta Drive: you'll usually find a worthwhile play, film or concert. And if you're feeling lucky, *Lasseters Hotel Casino* on Barrett Drive along the river's east bank can accommodate you – but not in thongs and a tatty singlet.

Events

The more energetic activities tend to occur in the cooler months, starting with the **Bangtail Muster** on the first Monday in May, followed by May's **Heritage Week** celebrating Alice's history, a colourful and irreverent parade of silliness. The **Camel Cup races** in mid-July are Australia's biggest camel race meeting, ending in a huge fireworks display. The string of **rodeos** along the Track hits Alice in late August, while the town's most famous event, the wacky **Henley-on-Todd Regatta** kicks off in mid-September (ⓦwww.henleyontodd.com.au). Bottomless boats (or, to be honest, any contraption) are run down the dry riverbed; needless to say, the event is heavily insured against the Todd actually flowing. On the last Sunday in November there's the **Corkwood Festival**, a celebration of art, music and dance, with food and craft stalls in Todd Mall. There's also a rather uninspiring **market** every Sunday in the mall.

Shopping for Aboriginal art

Alice has become the country's foremost centre for **Aboriginal art and crafts**, and Todd Mall is full of galleries. Most distinctive are the **dot paintings**, which derive from temporary sand paintings once used to pass on sacred knowledge during ceremonies. The first dot paintings on canvas were produced in the early 1970s at Papunya, northwest of Alice, under the encouragement of a local teacher, Geoff Bardon. What was intended as a kind of constructive graffiti for youngsters was actually taken up by the elders and has since blossomed into one of the more positive aspects of Aboriginal self-determination as well as a highly lucrative industry.

Clifford Possum and Billy Stockman were among the earliest of the Papunya artists to find fame, but they've since been superseded by astute, commercially minded painters from communities throughout the central desert, the most successful of whom have experimented with innovative abstract and minimalist styles in their bid to woo international collectors. Alice's burgeoning number of art dealers and gallery owners have fanned the market, encouraging their top artists to churn out countless variations of their most marketable designs, supplying them with materials and studio space and even subbing them thousands of dollars when funds run low.

Some of the most sought-after **modernists** working in the Alice area include sisters Gloria and Kathleen Petyarre, and Minnie Pwerle, who all come from the famously productive Utopia community 270km northeast of Alice; Papunya artist George Tjungurrayi; the Pintupi Walala Tjapaltjarri, who only encountered white people for the first time in 1984 when he and his family emerged from the Gibson Desert; Kathleen Wallace of Santa Teresa's Keringke Arts Centre; and Alice-based Margaret Turner, daughter of Clifford Possum. Most of these artists are represented by more than one of Alice's top five galleries, and it only takes a few hours' browsing to become familiar with their idiosyncratic styles; their best works can sell for tens of thousands of dollars.

Buying and playing a didgeridoo

Didgeridoos, the simple wooden instruments whose eerie drone perfectly evokes the mysteries of Aboriginal Australia, have become phenomenally popular souvenirs, and even a New-Age musical cult to some. Authentic didges are created from termite-hollowed branches of stringybark, woollybark and bloodwood trees which are indigenous from the Gulf to the Kimberley. Most commonly they are associated with Arnhem Land, where they were introduced around 2000 years ago and are properly called *yidaka* or *molo* by the Yolngu people of that region. "Didgeridoo" is an Anglicized name relating to the sound produced.

Minuscule, bamboo and even painted pocket didges have found their way onto the market (anything under $120 has probably been drilled out in Bali), but a real didge is a natural tube of wood with a rough interior. Painted versions haven't necessarily got any symbolic meaning; plain ones can look less tacky and are cheaper. Branches being what they are, every didge is different but, if you're considering playing it rather than hanging it over the fireplace, aim for one around 1.3m in length with a 30–40mm diameter mouthpiece. Beeswax is often used to bring an oversize didge's mouthpiece down to an operable size, but a didge with a body of the right diameter and without wax can feel nicer to use. The bend doesn't affect the sound but the length, tapering and wall thickness (ideally around 10mm) does. Avoid cumbersome, thick-walled items which get in the way of your face and sound flat.

You'll be surprised that making the right sound instead of an embarrassing raspberry will take only a few minutes of persistence; the key is to hum while letting your pressed lips flap, or vibrate, with the right pressure behind them – it's easier using the side of your mouth. The tricky bit – beyond the ability of most uninitiates – is to master circular breathing; this entails refilling your lungs through your nose while maintaining the sound from your lips with air squeezed from your cheeks. A good way to get your head round this concept is to blow or "squirt" bubbles into a glass of water with a straw, while simultaneously inhaling through the nose. Unless you get the hang of circular breathing you'll be limited to making the same lung's worth of droning again and again.

Most outlets that sell didges also sell tapes and CDs and inexpensive "how to" booklets which offer hints on the mysteries of circular breathing and how to emit advanced sounds using your vocal chords.

The Sounds of Starlight show in Todd Mall (April–Nov Tues–Sat 7.30pm; $25) features Alice didge impresario Andrew Langford and friends and gives you a good chance to hear what can be done with a didge as well as being an entertaining night out. You'll also be given a free lesson afterwards, if you want.

And finally, remember that there is nothing magical about a didgeridoo; it's your lips that make the sound, which resonates through the tube – any tube. A length of grey 40mm PVC pipe from a hardware store may not have the same cachet or eerie timbre but produces a similar sound at around $5 a metre.

Of the two dozen **outlets for Aboriginal art** in Alice, the most serious, and expensive, include the Aboriginal co-operative Papunya Tula Artists, at 78 Todd Mall (Ⓦwww.papunyatula.com.au); the Aboriginal-owned Warumpi Arts, at 105 Gregory Terrace (Ⓦwww.warumpi.com.au); the Mbantua Gallery, at 71 Gregory Terrace (Ⓦwww.mbantua.com.au); Centralian Indigenous Art, just off Todd Mall on Reg Harris Lane (Ⓦwww.centralianart.com.au); and Gallery Gondwana, 43 Todd Mall (Ⓦwww.gallerygondwana.com.au), which also specializes in Tiwi sculptures and crafts. All of these are fun to browse even if you can't afford to buy. Reputable cheaper art shops on Todd Mall, where prices start at around $40, include Red Sand, Desert Art Gallery, and the Australian Aboriginal Dreamtime Gallery. Another place offering mediocre but inexpensive paintings and didgeridoos is The House of Oz, opposite *Melanka Backpackers Resort*. The more you spend, the more chance there is of making a deal, with free overseas postage and insurance usually offered at the bigger places. If you're heading north, there are galleries at Aileron, Ti Tree (see p.675) and Tennant Creek (p.672) too, though Alice has the best pieces and widest choice.

The better galleries supply labels of **authenticity** with each artwork to assure buyers they're getting the genuine article (some small, cheap pictures are produced in Indonesia and are identifiable both by their vague labels, stating "inspired by Aboriginal art", and a lack of the flaws that characterize genuine Aboriginal-produced canvases). Whatever style of painting you buy, at whatever price, it will definitely not hold the key to a dreaming or sacred site. Despite what some gallery owners might say, there is no such thing as a dreaming painting, though the male artists who own a particular dreaming may choose to present an interpretation that is appropriate for public consumption. Traditionally, women never paint dreamings, but are said to get inspiration from aerial landscapes, bushtucker and body painting.

Listings

Camping supplies Alice Springs Disposals, Reg Harris Lane, off Todd Mall.
Car rental Advance Car Rentals (ⓣ08/8953 3700) has good deals. Outback Rentals (ⓣ08/8952 1405 or 1800 652 133), at 78 Todd St opposite the council offices, has mopeds and Suzuki 4WD jeeps, as well as special deals, as does Thrifty (ⓣ08/8952 9999), on the corner of Hartley St and Stott Terrace. For 4WDs, Britz/Maui (ⓣ1800 331 454) is on the Stuart Highway north of Alice and has fully equipped Toyota Bushcampers sleeping two inside, or Adventurers sleeping four in two roof tents, as well as regular campervans..
Hospital Gap Rd ⓣ08/8951 7777.
Internet access Try the library on Gregory Terrace (one hour per day limit when busy); Outback Internet on the opposite corner (very cheap and open on Sundays, but with old equipment); or the JPC computer shop in the Coles complex off Bath St.
Maps The Map Shop, Alice Plaza, first floor (ⓣ08/8951 5393) for detailed maps of the Centre.
Permits for Aboriginal Land Central Land Council, 33 North Stuart Highway, PO Box 3321, Alice Spings 0871 ⓣ08/8951 6320, Ⓦwww.clc.org.au. Blank forms and subsequent permits can be faxed. For the WA section of the Great Central Road (see p.757) get your permit from the Ngaanyatjarra Council 58 Head St, next to *Sammy's Pizza*, ⓣ08/8950 1711, Ⓦwww.ngaanyatjarra.org.au.
Police Parsons St ⓣ08/8951 8888.
Post office Hartley St ⓣ08/8952 1020.

Sights south of Alice

Several sites of interest are located beyond **Heavitree Gap**, a couple of kilometres south of town. The museum, date garden and camel farm described below are within range of the #4 bus, which terminates at the **Old Timers Folk Museum** (April–Nov daily 2–4pm; $2), just off the Stuart Highway, and features yet another display of pioneering memorabilia. The remainder are easily reached by bike, or on the Alice Wanderer bus route.

Tours from Alice

A large number of **tour operators** offer adventurous, cultural or historic tours throughout the area. Just about every hotel and backpackers offers a tour-booking service, though be aware that not all of the latter do so impartially. Alternatively, you can try any of a number of travel shops which specialize in selling tours; there are a few around the corners of Todd Street and Gregory Terrace. Though Ayers Rock can be visited in a long day, your average Uluru tour is two to three days with a visit to Kings Canyon included and costs from as little as $250, though the $25 Uluru park entry fee isn't always included.

Austour ⓣ1800 335 009, ⓦwww.austourtravel.com. Daily one-day bus trips to Uluru from $195 and two-days visits from $295 in a tent or from $345–475 accommodated.

Ballooning Downunder ⓣ08/8952 8816 or 1800 801 601, ⓦwww.ballooningdownunder.com.au; **Outback Ballooning** ⓣ08/8952 8273 or 1800 809 790, ⓦwww.outbackballooning.com.au; **Spinifex** ⓣ08/8952 2862 or 1800 677 893, ⓦwww.balloonflights.com.au. Alice is Australia's ballooning capital and any of these three operators will take you up, up and away – and back down to a champagne breakfast (from around $200 for a 30min flight, or $300 for an hour). Don't wear your best clothes.

Frontier Camel Tours ⓣ08/8953 0444 or 1800 806 499, ⓦwww.cameltours.com.au. One-hour camel rides down the Todd River plus breakfast or dinner (up to $110), or short rides from $10. Also based at Ayers Rock.

Mulga Tours ⓣ08/8952 1545 or 1800 359 089, ⓦwww.mulgas.com.au. Cheap and cheerful three-day Rock tours sleeping in swags which can be a laugh with a good crowd.

Outback Experience ⓣ08/8955 2666, ⓦwww.outbackexperience.com.au. Four-wheel-drive day-trips to Chambers Pillar, Rainbow Valley and other spots in the northern Simpson for around $150.

Outback Quad Adventures ⓣ08/8953 0697, ⓦwww.outbackquadadventures.com.au. Fun quad-bike rides on a cattle station close to town using automatic machines: all you have to do is turn the throttle and steer. From $99 for an hour's ride to overnight tours Dress for extreme dust. There's another quad operation at Kings Creek Station (p.698).

Rockayer ⓣ08/8956 2345 and **Australian Outback Flights** ⓣ08/8952 4625. Flights to the Rock and back in a day for around $300. Don't dismiss a flight like this as you'll get to see some great scenery on the way.

Sahara Tours ⓣ08/8953 0881 ⓦwww.saharatours.com.au. Offers two-, three- and five-day camping tours through the West MacDonnells, to Kings Canyon and Uluru using comfortable minibuses and permanent campsites. As is often the case, the longer tours are the best value.

Wayoutback ⓣ08/8952 4324 or 1300 551 510, ⓦwww.wayoutback.com.au. Popular three- to five-day Rock and Canyon tours packed into a Troopcarrier for around $150 a day.

Out on Palm Circuit, the **Mecca Date Garden** (Mon–Fri 9am–5pm, Sat 9am–1pm; free) was Australia's first commercial date farm, set up in the 1950s. Dates themselves are believed to be the first plant to be cultivated by man, and the farm now produces around 4000kg of the fruit a year from trees introduced in the nineteenth century by Afghan camel drivers. You are offered a free sample on arrival. Tours of the farm – basically rows of date palms with an informative commentary – start on the hour.

A farm of a very different sort can be found a couple of kilometres down the Ross Highway. The **Frontier Camel Farm** (daily 8am–5pm; $6) offers short rides on camels, plus a camel and cameleering museum. Back down the Stuart

Highway just before the airport, about 10km south of town, the **Ghan Preservation Society** (daily 9am–5pm; $5.50) at MacDonnell Siding features a converted old train station housing a **museum** of Alice Springs' early rail years, and is also involved in the refurbishment of old Ghan locomotives and rolling stock which are used for train rides (Ⓣ08/8955 5047) along a short section of track. Next door the **National Transport Hall of Fame** (9am–5pm; $6) features a collection of old cars, trucks and motorbikes, including a cute red Fiat Tipo, something called the "Mulga Express" (not your average touring Kingswood) as well as the original 8WD road train that used to slog up to Darwin during the 1930s at a hot and noisy 30kph.

The MacDonnell Ranges

The **MacDonnell Ranges** are among the longest of the parallel ridge systems that corrugate the Centre's landscape. Their east–west axis, passing right through Alice Springs, is broken in many places by gaps carved through the ranges during better-watered epochs. It is these striking ruptures, along with the grandeur and colours of the rugged landscape – particularly west of Alice – which make a few days spent in the MacDonnells so worthwhile. The expansive **West MacDonnell Ranges National Park** is best appreciated with at least one overnight stay at any of the campsites mentioned below, while the often-overlooked **Eastern MacDonnells** have a more compact, intimate feel and are a better bet if your time is limited. Both ranges can be visited as part of a tour (see box on p.687) or with your own vehicle. Although some tracks are unsealed, 4WD vehicles are mostly unnecessary. However, because most rental companies don't like you driving conventional cars on corrugated tracks, you may end up renting one. If you do, then make the most of its all-terrain capabilities; check out the box on pp.682–683, as well as the **off-road driving advice** in Basics (p.50).

A better way still to get in touch with the West Macs is to do part of the **Larapinta Trail**, a long-distance footpath following the ranges which starts at the Telegraph Station north of Alice and ends 223km to the west on the 1347m summit of Mount Sonder. The walk is divided into around a dozen sections, but these sections do not necessarily delineate a day's walk. Trailside water tanks are situated no more than two days' walk or 30km apart. As a rule the more impressive but also more arduous sections are nearer town. Section 2 from Simpson's Gap to Jay Creek is 25km long – an overnight stop is advised, while the next section is a short but hard 14km to Standley Chasm with 350m of climbing. See Alice's tourist information office for latest details or print off the whole trail guide with maps from the PWCNT website (Ⓦwww.nt.gov.au/ipe/pwcnt; search for "Larapinta").

The West MacDonnell Ranges and Finke Gorge national parks

The **route** described below follows an anticlockwise loop out along Larapinta Drive and then Namatjira Drive to *Glen Helen Resort*, from where a 110-kilometre part-dirt road brings you past Gosses Bluff to the turn-off for Palm Valley, Hermannsburg and back to Alice – a total distance of 370km. The track passes through **Aboriginal land** on its return section, but no permit is required (unless stated), providing you keep to the road and camp at designated sites.

About 8km from town is a turning to **Simpsons Gap** (gates open daily 8am–8pm), the nearest and most popular of the West Macs' gaps, where a white, sandy riverbed lined with red and ghost gums leads up to a small pool. Agile rock wallabies live on the cliffs and there's a **visitors centre** and barbecues, as well as a seventeen-kilometre cycle track leading back to town. The first stage of the **Larapinta Trail** ends here – a 24-kilometre walk from the Telegraph Station in Alice.

Further along Larapinta Drive are the **Twin Ghost Gums**, immortalized in Albert Namatjira's definitive painting of the Centralian landscape; just beyond is a turn-off north to the tourist trap of **Standley Chasm** (daily 8am–6pm; $6), 50km from Alice. Situated on Iwupataka Aboriginal land, this is another popular spot, where a walk up the cycad palm-lined riverbed leads to a narrow chasm formed by the erosion of softer rock that once lay between the red-quartzite walls. Around noon both eighty-metre-high walls are briefly lit by the overhead sun. There is also a café with a terrace and a souvenir shop; black-footed rock wallabies are fed here daily at 9.30am.

Along Namatjira Drive

Another 6km along Larapinta Drive, **Namatjira Drive** turns north amid the West MacDonnell Ranges; continuing on Larapinta brings you to Hermannsburg and Palm Valley (see p.692). Along Namatjira Drive, a scenic 42km ahead is **Ellery Big Hole** (barbecues, toilets and camping), the biggest waterhole in the area which floods a large gap in the ranges. Nevertheless, caught between the brief ebb and flow of visiting bus tours, it's a great spot to splash about with the ducks, and if you can stand the cold water you can swim right through the gap to the far side. Eleven kilometres to the west is **Serpentine Gorge** (toilets but no camping): the only way to appreciate this gorge is to take the half-hour walk in and climb up the ridge on the right to a lookout. As with many concealed and perennial pools in Central Australia, the Aranda have nurtured a myth about the pool being the home of a serpent, and even today they visit the place reluctantly and never enter the water; Mutujulu waterhole beneath Uluru has a similar legend. In this way the myth acted as a device to ensure that the pool – a droughtproof source of water – was never polluted or carelessly used. Just down the road the **Serpentine Chalet** bush camping area is just that, with some pitches among the rather arid bushland and a relatively dull twenty-minute walk to a silted-up dam.

The **Ochre Pits**, signposted off Namatjira Drive, make an interesting diversion. The ochre, particularly the red variety, was a highly valued trading commodity and is still used by the Aranda for ceremonial purposes. From here there's a great walk to **Inarlanga Pass** (a narrow gorge on the Larapinta Trail), a most enjoyable two-hour hike along rounded ridges and through wooded valleys. Once at Inarlanga you will find a boulder-strewn creek bed framed by acutely twisted beds of rock.

Fourteen kilometres further west, **Ormiston Gorge** and **Pound National Park** (barbecues and camping) are also worth the effort. One of the most spectacular and easily accessible spots in the West Macs, the short ascent up to **Gum Tree Lookout** (the walk continues down into the gorge) gives a great view over the 250-metre-high gorge walls rising from the pools below – home to ducks and even the odd black swan. The three-hour **Pound Walk** includes some rock-hopping, and longer overnight walks can be undertaken by those who are properly equipped – ask the rangers at the Park Information Centre in the car park, who also organize occasional free slide-show evenings for campers.

Just west of Ormiston is **GLEN HELEN**, another wide chasm with a perennial reed-fringed waterhole in the bed of the ancient **Finke River**, which is

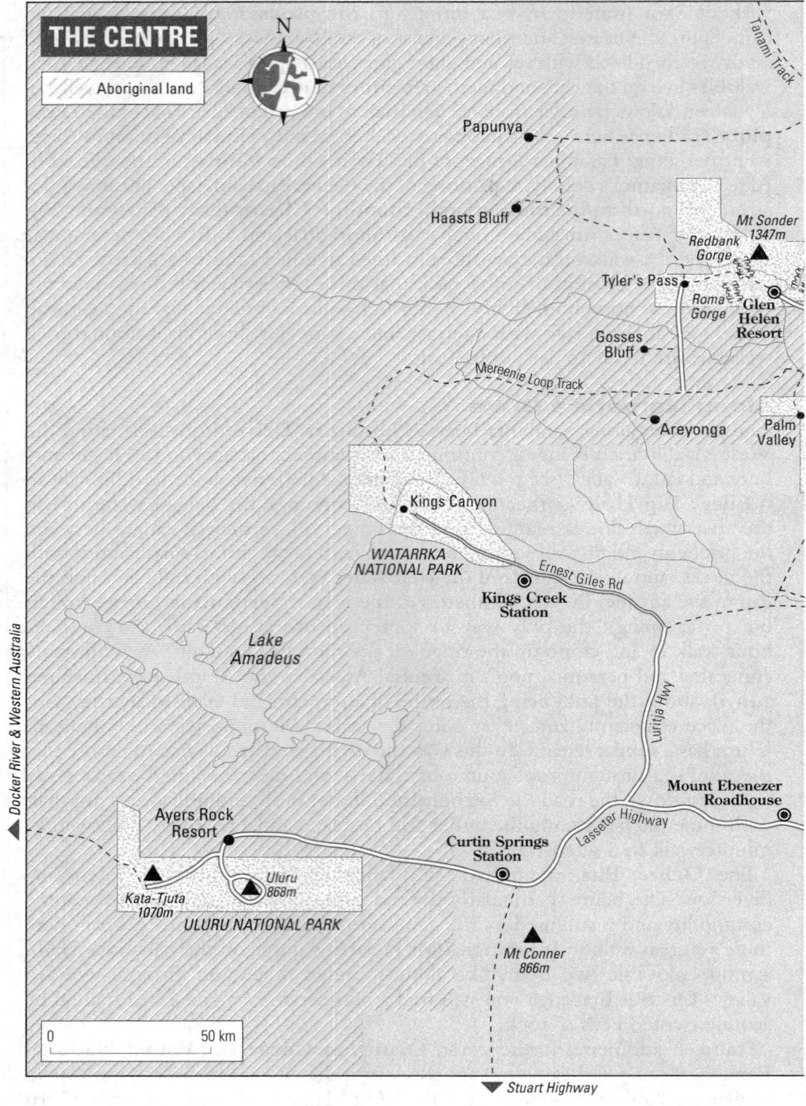

thought to have flowed along roughly the same course for over 100 million years and which, on the rare occasions when it flows, can reach as far as Lake Eyre in South Australia. *Glen Helen Resort* (ⓣ08/8956 7489, ⓦwww.glenhelen.com.au; four-share bunkhouse $80, rooms ❻) has fuel, camping space and accommodation and is a lovely place to spend a comfortable night out in the West Macs with a good restaurant and frequent live music in the bar. Helicopter flights over the nearby sites cost from $40. If you're heading towards Kings

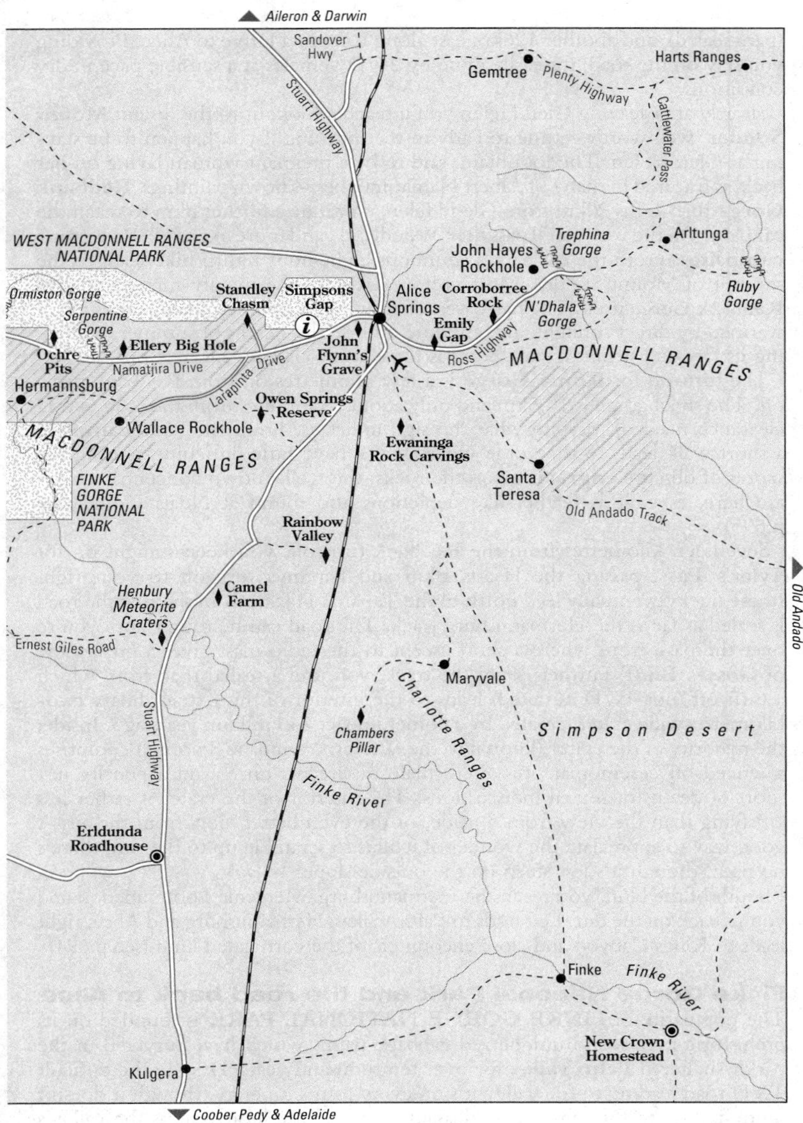

Canyon along the **Mereenie Loop Track** (see p.694) you're supposed to get your permit here ($2.50) though they're seldom checked. Make sure you have fuel for at least 250km.

Roma Gorge, Redbank Gorge and Gosses Bluff

Beyond Glen Helen the bitumen ends, but the natural spectacles continue. If you intend to complete the loop, it's about 107km to Hermannsburg (part-sealed), and another 126km east along Larapinta Drive to Alice. Providing you stay on the road, it's easily done by 2WD vehicles at a sensible pace in dry conditions.

Shortly after leaving Glen Helen you'll reach a lookout to the distant **Mount Sonder**, well worth getting to early in the morning if you happen to be staying at Glen Helen. The mountain, said to be a pregnant woman laying on her back, is featured in many of Albert Namatjira's best-known paintings. **Redbank Gorge** turn-off is 20km from Glen Helen; continue a further 8km to reach the car park. On the way you'll pass the "Woodland" and more exposed "Ridgetop" **campsites**. From the car park a strenuous eight-hour return hike leads to the summit of Mount Sonder. Most visitors settle for the twenty-minute hike to Redbank Gorge itself. The narrowest cleft in the West Macs, Redbank is never warmed by direct sunlight and, anytime outside the height of summer, exploring its freezing string of rock pools is for wetsuit-clad adventurers only.

The turn-off for **Roma Gorge** is a few kilometres on from Redbank turn-off. The small gorge is 10.5km and only about 25 minutes from the road (4WD clearance needed), despite what the sign indicates. From the basic **campsite** a short walk leads to the gorge where you'll have little difficulty spotting the scores of obscure **engravings** on the rocks; the well-known concentric circles are here, as well as feather-like depictions also found at Ndala Gorge (see p.696).

Seventeen kilometres from the Redbank turn-off, you keep straight on for **Tyler's Pass**, passing the Haasts Bluff and Papunya turn-off to your right (these tracks eventually lead north to the Tanami Track); from the pass the road is sealed as far as the Hermannsburg track. The road can be rough until you're over the pass, from where a short ascent to the radio mast gives a great view of **Gosses Bluff**. Further down the track, you join a sealed road from which a turn-off (not 4WD as stated) leads to the interior of this extraordinary two-kilometre-wide crater, created by a comet impact 140 million years ago. Inside, the majority of the crater (known to the Western Aranda as Tnorula) comprises a fenced-off ceremonial site where male miscreants once paid a penalty just short of death for sexual indiscretions. The interior of the crater is rather less satisfying than the view from outside, or the even better view from the air. A good way to appreciate the wonder of it all is to scramble up to the rim; there's no path, though it's less steep on the outside slope.

South of the bluff, you reach the Hermannsburg–Mereenie Loop junction and you're back on the dirt. Left leads to Palm Valley, Hermannsburg and Alice; right leads to Kings Canyon and close encounters of the corrugated kind (see p.694).

Finke Gorge National Park and the road back to Alice

The popularity of **FINKE GORGE NATIONAL PARK** is founded on its prehistoric cycads and unique red cabbage palms which have survived in the park's sheltered **Palm Valley** for over ten thousand years. Despite the difficult 4WD road leading to the valley it's on every tour's itinerary, though it doesn't quite live up to the hype. The pleasant forty-minute loop walk is the valley's highlight; visiting the rest of the park requires a 4WD vehicle and seems to be discouraged, as does the route along the Finke riverbed from Hermannsburg (see box on p.694). On the way in or out of the valley, you can climb up to the once-sacred **Initiation Rock**, giving a fine view over the Amphitheatre, a cirque of sandstone cliffs. The park has barbecues, toilets, solar-heated showers and camping.

HERMANNSBURG was originally a Lutheran mission established in the 1870s, making it among the oldest communities in the Centre. Unusually, you

Albert Namatjira

Born on the Hermannsburg Lutheran mission in 1902, Namatjira was the first of the Hermannsburg mission's much-copied school of landscape watercolourists. Although lacking much painting experience, Namatjira assisted Rex Battarbee on his painting expeditions through the Central Australian deserts in the 1930s during which his talent soon became obvious to Battarbee, who later became Namatjira's agent. Like all NT Aborigines at that time, Namatjira was forbidden to buy alcohol, stay overnight in Alice Springs or leave the Territory without permission, but at the insistence of southern do-gooders – and against his wishes – he was the first Aborigine to be awarded Australian citizenship, in 1956. This meant he could travel without limitations, but needed a permit to visit his own family on Aboriginal reserves, while the house in Alice he longed for was denied him for fear of the entourage he might have attracted. Following the success of his first exhibition in the south, which sold out in three days, he became a reluctant celebrity, compelled to pay taxes on his relatively huge earnings which were further depleted by the "share-it-all" kinship laws that still hamper successful Aboriginal artists today. A shy and modest man, much respected for his earnestness and generosity, he died in 1959 following a sordid conviction and short imprisonment for supplying alcohol to fellow Aborigines.

Critics could never make up their minds about his work, but his popular appeal was undoubted: exhibitions in the southern cities, which he rarely attended, persistently sold out within hours of opening, and today his paintings remain among the most valuable examples of Australia's artistic preoccupation with its landscape. Some Namatjira originals are exhibited at *Panorama Guth* in Alice.

are able to visit the town, or more specifically the **Historic Precinct** (daily 9am–4pm; $5), which features the original mission buildings converted into tearooms and an art gallery (tours $3.50). Your guide will rattle off his spiel on the history of the mission and the life and work of Albert Namatjira, and maybe also Theodore Strehlow, who were both born here (see boxes above and on p.683), although any observation about the "totemic faces" concealed in Namatjira's paintings should be taken with a pinch of salt. There is also a supermarket and fuel (cash only), but no accommodation.

Back towards Alice Springs, you'll pass the **Albert Namatjira Memorial** before reaching the small community of **Wallace Rockhole**, where there are one-hour tours (☎08/8956 7415; $10) of nearby Aboriginal petroglyphs, as well as a shop, fuel and camping. Continuing on towards Alice you'll pass the recently opened **Owen Springs Reserve** on the former cattle station of that name. For details see the box on p.695.

The Eastern MacDonnells and the northern Simpson Desert

Heading out of Alice through the **Heavitree Gap** and along the Ross Highway you soon reach **Emily Gap**, Alice's nearest waterhole, 10km from town. This is one of the most significant Aranda sacred sites, the start of the Caterpillar Dreaming trail. There are some interesting stylized depictions of the caterpillars on the far side of a pool that is worth wading through; you'll see the same image at **Jessie Gap**, a little further east. **Corroborree Rock**, 45km east of Alice, is an unusual, fin-like outcrop of limestone with an altar-like platform and two crevices piercing the fin. The rock was once a repository for sacred objects and a site of initiation ceremonies, or *corroborees*, and is now roped off.

John Hayes Rockhole and Trephina Gorge

John Hayes Rockhole and Trephina Gorge, by far the most satisfying of the accessible destinations in the Eastern MacDonnells, are just 80km from Alice.

Some 4WD tracks in the centre

While most us have little need to own a heavy, fuel-guzzling 4WD, renting one for a few days of off-road driving is fun and can get you to some beautiful corners of the central deserts. Below are some **4WD-only** routes close to Alice, which could all be linked into a memorable week in the dirt. Remember that 4WD vehicles are not invincible: when driven carelessly they can easily get stuck, become uncontrollable or damaged. They can also make a mess of the terrain if driven off main tracks; avoid wheel spins and tearing up vegetated ground which takes years to recover. Finally, make sure the outfit you're renting from understands and approves your proposed 4WD itinerary and, at the very least, read the advice and carry the gear recommended in "Basics", p.54. Ask at Alice's tourist office for the *4×4 Guide* booklet, which details other routes in the area. One problem with renting is that you're rarely supplied with any recovery gear; even a tow strap or second spare tyre have to be prised out of rental companies or must be rented as an extra item. Although most of the rental 4WDs are in good shape, it's in your own interest to make sure you are appropriately equipped, especially for travelling in remote areas. For recommended 4WD rental agents see the "Listings" for Alice on p.686.

Mereenie Loop Track

The main appeal of the Mereenie, linking the West Macs with Kings Canyon (around 200km, allow 3–4 hours), is that it avoids backtracking on the usual "Canyon and Rock" tour. However, scenically from the junction west of Palm Valley it's nothing special and the corrugations west of Areyonga can be fearsome. A further irritation is that, according to the mandatory permit issued either at Glen Helen or Kings Canyon, you're not allowed to stop, let alone camp, except for one so-so look-out just before the descent to the Kings Canyon Resort.

Finke River Route

With a day to spare and minimal experience with a 4WD, following the Finke riverbed from **Hermannsburg** down to the **Ernest Giles Road** offers an adventurous alternative to the highway and also saves some backtracking from Kings Canyon. Rewards include stark gorge scenery, a reliable waterhole and the likelihood that you'll have it all to yourself. Before you set off, seek out the ranger at Palm Valley (☎08/8956 7401) who'll fill you in on the state of the track and provide a handy **map** that clarifies all the junctions. When on the route follow the small signs for "Kings Canyon".

The hundred-kilometre track starts immediately south of Hermannsburg. After 10km of corrugated road you descend into the riverbed. From now on it's slow driving along a pair of sandy or pebbly ruts – you should deflate your tyres to at least 25psi/1.7bar and keep in the ruts to minimize the risk of getting stuck. The sole designated campsite is at **Boggy Hole**, much nicer than it sounds and around two hours (28.5km) from Hermannsburg. The campsite looks out from beneath river red gums to permanent reed-fringed waterholes, best seen at dawn as the sunlight creeps across the gorge and the ponds are alive with birdlife.

Beyond Boggy Hole, the track crisscrosses rather than follows the riverbed before the roller-coaster ride to the Giles Road across some low dunes thinly wooded with desert oaks – beware of oncoming traffic on blind crests. Boggy Hole to the Giles Road is 65km, so allow three hours. If you fancy taking the direct route to the Ernest Giles Road from the Tempe Downs station track, keep straight over the dunes just after a salt pan instead of turning sharply east; subsequent dunes can be avoided but

Both offer superb scenery and a selection of enjoyable walks, and there's a four-hour ridge walk linking the two. **John Hayes Rockhole** (limited camping space), reached along a rocky four-kilometre track requiring a high-clearance

the Palmer River crossing can be very sandy and may require further tyre deflation. Back on the road, keep speeds down until you can reflate your tyres.

Owen Springs Reserve

Not much to get excited about, at the moment all you have here is a thirty-kilometre 4WD track linking the Stuart Highway with Namatjira Drive (55km west of Alice) which crosses the **Hugh River** and its waterholes (camping) on the way.

Arltunga to Ruby Gap

Ask the ranger at the **Arltunga Visitors Centre** (☎08/8951 8211), 101km east of Alice, for the latest track conditions for this scenic, if bumpy, 53-kilometre drive (allow 2hr) through the ranges. It includes some steep creek crossings until you reach the sandy riverbed of the Hale and the **Ruby Gap Nature Park**. From here keep to the sandy ruts and inch carefully over the rocks for 7km to **Glen Annie Gorge**, a dead-end with maroon cliffs, bright green reeds and off-white sand.

Cattlewater Pass and the Harts Ranges

A less difficult track heads north from Arltunga past Claraville station and up over the Harts Ranges through the **Cattlewater Pass** to the Plenty Highway, 67km or three hours from Arltunga. It's a worthwhile and no less scenic way of returning to Alice from Ruby Gap via a different route and you're bound to see some hopping marsupials along the way. Once you reach the Plenty Highway it's an easy dirt road via Gemtree to the Stuart Highway and Alice, 150km away.

The Finke and Old Andado Tracks

More ambitious than the above is the 550-kilometre loop into the fringes of the Simpson Desert along the **Finke** and **Old Andado tracks** which diverge at Alice's airport and meet at the community of Finke. At the airport the Finke track is also known as the **Old Ghan Heritage Trail**, as it follows the route of the old railway all the way past Oodnadatta to Port Augusta in SA. On the way you'll pass stands of desert oak and may well see some feral camels, descendants of the original beasts led by Afghan cameleers before the Ghan train reached Alice in 1928. It passes Ewaninga Rock Carvings but before Maryvale detours east to the ruins of Rodinga sidings. The section from Rodinga to Finke is the best part of this route, either on the embankments of the actual railway or on the rougher track alongside it, passing other sidings with interpretive boards on the history of this pioneering overland route. As you near Finke the red sand ridges create some sandy passages, after which you cross the sandy Finke River itself and enter the community (fuel).

After Finke the nature of the route changes as you traverse overgrazed plains to New Crown station; you may prefer to call it a day here and turn west from Finke to Kulgera on the Stuart Highway. To complete the loop via Andado head east, recrossing the broad Finke, and follow the denuded pasturelands past Andado homestead and on to the ramshackle but still occupied Old Andado homestead, set between two dune ridges (basic accommodation and camping). North of here the track remains easy but gets bleaker still as the sand ridges thin out. After a while the ranges of the East Macs rise from the horizon and bring you back into vegetated and then wooded country for the rough final 150km past Santa Teresa community and the airport close to town.

vehicle, is a series of pools linked by (usually dry) waterfalls along a canyon. The ninety-minute "Chain of Pools" walk takes you to the top of the gorge and down through the pools – an ideal way to get hot, but with plenty of opportunities to cool off. Alternatively, the lower pools are accessible from the car park.

Trephina Gorge, perhaps the most impressive spot in the eastern part of the range, is a beautiful, sheer-sided sandy gorge whose rich red walls support slender, white-barked ghost gums and a small pool, while huge river red gums grow in the bed. There's a pleasant **campsite** and two enjoyable walks (the "Gorge" and "Panorama", both taking about 30min).

Arltunga and N'Dhala Gorge

Five kilometres beyond Trephina Gorge a turning northeast leads a corrugated 33km to **ARLTUNGA**, the site of Central Australia's first goldrush. The road here may still be long overdue for a grading, but a whole heap of money was spent on restoring the ghost town and providing it with a fancy **visitors centre** (daily 8am–5pm; ⓣ08/8951 8211). All the place needs now is some visitors; even the "loneliest pub in the scrub (which served grub) has closed down. Arltunga's story began in the 1890s, in the midst of the country's first economic depression, when gold was discovered by the miners originally drawn to the garnets at Ruby Gap (see below). Over the next fifteen years they regularly pushed barrows the 600km from Oodnadatta railhead to grope in desperate conditions for pitiful returns. Arltunga was never a particularly rich field and remains yet another abandoned testament to pioneering optimism. With a 4WD it's possible to continue on to Ruby Gap (see below) or north over the ranges to the Plenty Highway (see 4WD box).

Carrying on along the Ross Highway leads to the defunct Ross River Homestead and a turn right for an eleven-kilometre 4WD track to **N'Dhala Gorge**. On the way in you have a chance to appreciate the immense geological forces that have shaped the MacDonnell ranges, warping formerly horizontal beds by 90 degrees or more. The gorge itself is home to various **Aboriginal rock engravings** representing aspects of the Caterpillar Dreaming, with which other sites in the East Macs are also associated; the tall feather-like symbol (also found at Ruby Gorge) is said to represent the stages of a newly hatched moth taking flight.

About 4km before you arrive at N'Dhala a track to the left (signposted with the "Explorer Territory" logo) leads for a pleasant 13km south through a valley and over a couple of sandy river crossings to a less interesting station access track which joins the Ross Highway just before Jessie Gap.

Ruby Gap and Glen Annie Gorge

From Arltunga it's a fairly rough four-wheel drive out to Ruby and Glen Annie gorges (see box on p.695), both of them beautiful and wild places. Back in 1885 the explorer Lindsay discovered "rubies" while in the process of digging for water, thereby initiating the customary rush for what turned out to be worthless garnets. Crossing the sandy Hale riverbed leads into **Ruby Gap** and then **Glen Annie Gorges** (no facilities except camping). At the end of the day, even with the flies handing over to the mozzies, it's one of the most tranquil places you'll find in Central Australia.

The Old South Road and the northern Simpson Desert

Just 14km out of Alice, shortly after the airport turn-off, a sign indicates "Chambers Pillar (4WD)". This is the **Old South Road**, which follows the abandoned course of the Ghan and original Overland Telegraph Line to Adelaide, 1550km away; these days the sandy route has become part of the Old Ghan Heritage Trail which takes adventurous four-wheel drivers all the way to South Australia (see also box on p.695).

Ordinary cars can easily cover the 35km to **Ewaninga Rock Carvings**, a jumble of rocks by a small claypan (a dried-up pool). This sacred Aboriginal site is part of the Rain Dreaming, but we're told the meaning of the symbols is too dangerous to reveal.

Heading on past the store at **MARYVALE** (shop and fuel), you'll need a 4WD vehicle and to be in the mood for a thorough shaking if you want to get across the Charlotte Ranges and subsequent sand ridges all the way to **Chambers Pillar** (camping), a historic dead-end, 165km from Alice. Named by Stuart after one of his benefactors (who had natural features named after him and his family all the way to the Arafura Sea), the eighty-metre-high sandstone pillar was used as a landmark by early overlanders heading up from the railhead at Oodnadatta, in South Australia. The plinth is carved with their names as well as those of many others (including a certain J. Hendrix), and can be seen from the platform at the pillar's base. If you don't fancy renting your own vehicle, Outback Experience in Alice (see box p.687) has full-day tours to this area which include Chambers Pillar.

South to Kings Canyon

Kings Canyon is 320km southwest of Alice Springs, of which the hundred-kilometre section from the Stuart Highway turn-off towards Stockyard Homestead/Wallara is unsealed. From Stockyard, it's bitumen all the way to the Watarrka National Park which envelops Kings Canyon. If you're heading straight down the Track from Alice there's an increasingly barren run of nearly 700km to Coober Pedy (itself no oasis; see p.883) in South Australia.

Most **tours** of two days or more departing from Alice include Kings Canyon on their see-it-all itineraries, providing the easiest and cheapest way to enjoy the canyon. There are daily Greyhound Australia bus services from Alice Springs to Kings Canyon, or from Ayers Rock Resort with AAT Kings (see p.700).

The Stuart Highway to Kings Canyon

Around 76km from Alice, the turn-off to **Rainbow Valley** (basic camping) follows a twenty-kilometre dirt track (the very last bit may be sandy), to the "valley", actually a much-photographed outcrop set behind claypans which are said to produce rainbows following rain. More commonly, sunset catches the red-stained walls spectacularly and it's a wild place to spend the night, best followed in the morning by a climb up the crag.

You soon reach the Ernest Giles Road, where you turn off right for Kings Canyon; note that the first hundred kilometres are unsealed and in poor condition. Not far along this track there's another turn-off, to **Henbury Meteorite Craters**. The extra-terrestrial shower that caused these twelve depressions, from 2m to 180m in diameter, may have occurred in the last twenty thousand years, given that one of the Aranda's names for the place translates as "sun walk fire devil rock". A walk with interpretive signs winds among the craters, long since picked clean of any unearthly fragments. There is camping, barbecues and toilets.

The bone-shaking Ernest Giles Road heads west from here, joining the sealed Luritja Highway linking Ayers Rock Resort to Kings Canyon. Around here you'll see some nice shady groves of desert oak, the largest of the casuarina desert trees and related to the she-oaks of southwestern WA. The bitumen road continues west, past **Kings Creek station** (ⓣ08/8956 7474, ⓦwww.kingscreekstation.com.au), 35km from the canyon. Unlike most other pastoral properties in Australia, Kings Creek has taken to rounding up and raising the feral camels that other station owners regard as vermin. As meat they fetch the same price as cattle, but as racing camels sold to Arabia they are worth six times as much. There are various activities at Kings Creek, including quad rides (no experience necessary), helicopter flights over the canyon or beyond, and of course camel rides at sunrise or sunset. You'll also find a well-equipped campsite, pool, fuel and a shop/café, though the "canvas cabin" accommodation – a row of heavy-duty two-person tents baking in the sun – is expensive at $55 per person. Camp with your own gear or head for the better value Lodge at Kings Canyon Resort (see below).

Kings Canyon (Watarrka National Park)

As you cross the boundary of the **Watarrka National Park**, you'll see the turning to **Kathleen Springs**, a sacred Aboriginal waterhole which is an easy twenty-minute stroll away. It was once used to corral livestock and is now a good place to catch sight of colourful birdlife.

Another twenty minutes down the road is **Kings Canyon** itself. The big attraction here is the two-hour, six-kilometre **Rim Walk** up and around the canyon, one of the Centre's best and most popular hikes. **Early morning** is the best time to enjoy the walk, and for a couple of hours from just after sunrise visitors swarm out from the car park along the track. Undertaken in the now mandatory clockwise direction, the walk starts with a well-constructed stepped ascent (the toughest part of the walk), after which the trail leads through a maze of sandstone domes known as the **Lost City** where interpretive boards fill you in on the geology and botany. Don't miss the excursion to the vertiginous **Cotterill Lookout** overlooking the dramatic **southern wall**, with its curious "hieroglyphic" weathering patterns. Back on the signed track you soon clamber down into a palm-filled chasm known as the **Garden of Eden**, bridged by an impressive array of staircases. Coming up the far side there's an easily missed detour downstream to a shady **pool** where you can swim. The highlight of the walk, looking out from the throat of the canyon above a dry waterfall, is just a minute beyond, accessible either by wading knee-deep for a few steps round the right bank of the pool (or simply swimming across). Peering from the brink you get a perfectly framed **view** of the sunlit south wall and the canyon below. Returning to the staircase, the walk comes to the very edge of the south wall and then descends gently to the car park.

There have been some long-overdue improvements in facilities at the park (including a kiosk), but there is still no camping at Kings Canyon itself, although you can camp elsewhere in the park with a ranger's permit. Ten kilometres past the canyon, the *Kings Canyon Resort* (ⓣ08/8956 7442, ⓦwww.voyages.com.au) is a small resort with grassy **camping**, a pool and plenty of cooking and ablutions facilities. There's also an upgraded Lodge featuring four-bed bunkhouses (sleeping up to six; $38pp) with TV and a fridge and, at long last, a much-improved kitchen area. Over the road, the **hotel** (❽) offers privacy and great views but is rather over-priced when you can get a whole Lodge room to yourself for around $150. For something **to eat**, the service station has a pricey shop (daily 7am–7pm), while the daytime café (10am–3pm) next door serves sandwiches, burgers, salads and chips. In the evening the grill next to the bar has main courses from around $30, or try the $45 buffet at *Carmichaels*

Restaurant at the hotel over the road – actually a great deal when you clock the mouthwatering spread on offer.

Uluru–Kata Tjuta National Park and Ayers Rock Resort

Uluru–Kata Tjuta National Park encompasses **Uluru** (the Anangu name for **Ayers Rock**) and **Kata Tjuta** (or the **Olgas**). The park is the most visited single site in Australia and if you're wondering whether all the hype is worth it, then the answer is, emphatically, yes. The Rock, its textures, colours and not least its elemental presence is without question one of the world's natural wonders. Overt commercialization has been controlled within the park, designated by UNESCO in 1987 a World Heritage Site and other tourists can be avoided if you avoid the area and walks at the base of the climb.

Kata Tjuta (meaning "many heads") lies 45km west from the park entry station. A cluster of rounded domes divided by narrow chasms and valleys, it is geologically quite distinct from Uluru. Public access is limited to the "Valley of the Winds" walk and none of the domes, including Mount Olga, actually 200m higher than Uluru, can be climbed.

You can't camp in the park, nor can you go anywhere other than Uluru and Kata Tjuta or the Cultural Centre and the few roads and paths linking them, which can explain why some popular spots get crowded. Instead the **Ayers Rock Resort**, part of the settlement of Yulara, just outside the park, takes care of all tourists' needs.

Getting there

It's 210km from Alice to **ERLDUNDA**, a busy roadhouse (camping and cabins; ❹) on the Stuart Highway, from where the **Lasseter Highway** heads to Ayers Rock Resort, 247km to the west. After 56km is *Mount Ebenezer Roadhouse* and later the turning for the **Luritja Highway**, which leads 167km up to Kings Canyon. Road widening has taken place at the Yulara end, and all over the Centre road signs have appeared in four languages urging tourists in 4WDs (the most prone to accidents) to take it easy.

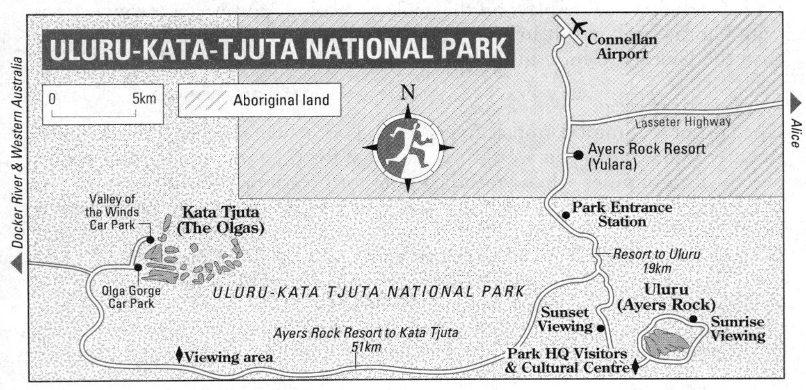

The next thing to catch your eye will be the flat-topped mesa of **Mount Conner**, sometimes mistaken for Uluru. *Curtin Springs Station* (☎08/8956 2906), 11km west of Mount Conner offers the last normal-priced accommodation (dustbowl camping free with $1 charge for showers; rooms ❷–❹) before Ayers Rock Resort. There's also a reasonably priced restaurant (daily 7–9am, 12.30–2pm and 6–8.30pm), fuel and a bar, plus scenic flights and 4WD tours to Mount Connor. You-know-what is now only 80km away.

Ayers Rock Resort (Yulara)

The purpose-built **AYERS ROCK RESORT** (aka Yulara) is far from the eyesore it could have been. Low-impact, environmentally aware design were not just buzz words, the resort was actually ahead of its time when it was built between 1983 and 1990, keeping building heights below the adjacent landscape, desalinating bore water (and recycling some of it to keep the gardens fresh), and using solar-powered electricity. Over the years it has aged well, helped along by occasional refurbishments and carefully considered extensions.

Practicalities

All the town's facilities branch off a central ring road called Yulara Drive around which a **free bus** circulates (every 20min; 10.30am–6pm & 6.30pm–midnight). Within this ring is a duned area crisscrossed with tracks and a couple of **lookouts**, scanning the Rock and Kata Tjuta on the horizon. In the **Shopping Square**, off the north side of Yulara Drive, you'll find a post office, supermarket (daily 8.30am–9pm), newsagent and an ANZ **bank** (Mon–Thurs 9.30am–4.30pm, Fri 9.30am–5pm) with an ATM, as well as cafés and restaurants. Apart from hotel bars, the only alcohol outlet is the **bottle shop** at the *Outback Pioneer Lodge*, where you'll also find the only **laundry**. There's also the all-important **Tours and Information Centre** (7.30am–8.30pm; ☎08/8957 7377) where you can rent a car and book everything that's going – see the box on p.702 for some ideas. You'll also find coin-operated **Internet access** here for a phenomenal $18 per hour.

Buses will either drop you off at your chosen accommodation, where you'll be given a town map, or at the Shopping Square, the hub of the resort. All incoming **flights** to Connellan Airport, 6km from town, are met by a free shuttle bus – **taxis** (☎08/8955 2152) cost about $15. The main Uluru–Kata Tjuta Cultural Centre (see below) is located within the park, but just as worthwhile is the **visitors information centre** (daily 8am–8pm), tucked out of the way between the Shopping Square and the *Desert Gardens Hotel*. In here you'll find absorbing visual displays on the geology, ecology and Anangu connections with Uluru – well worth an hour's browse and much more broadly informative than the Cultural Centre in the park.

Accommodation

The cost of accommodation at Ayers Rock Resort will come as a shock – two or three times what you would pay in Alice for the same standard of room, and even in summer when you're gasping for breath prices only drop by less than ten percent. But as visitor numbers continue to grow, you're advised to **book ahead** unless camping or visiting in midsummer, because the constant flow of tour groups from all over the world fills out the hotels quickly, and even the campground overflows at times. All accommodation is run by the Sydney-based Ayers Rock Resort (☎1300 134 044, ⓔreservations@voyages.com.au). To ring the actual hotels call ☎08/8957 7888 (or ☎08/8956 2055, ⓔcampground@voyages.com.au for the campground). All the places below are situated off Yulara Drive, and none is more than fifteen minutes' walk from the Shopping Square.

Ayers Rock Campground Offers electric BBQs, a small shop and swimming pool and does its best to keep the sites grassy for tents, with camping at $13pp. The campground also has a few air-con cabins ($150) which sleep six, with fully-equipped kitchens and TV – if you don't mind sharing bathroom facilities these are almost a good deal.

Desert Gardens Hotel Four-star hotel with a floral theme and well-appointed studio rooms ($439), which actually measure up pretty well compared to the *Lost Camel* and certainly the *Pioneer Lodge*.

Emu Walk Apartments Apartments with fully-equipped kitchens, a lounge and a balcony, close to the Shopping Square and with either one small ($439) or two ($528) bedrooms and a balcony.

Longitude 131° At $1650 per night and a minimum two-night stay, you won't be turning up here off-the-cuff. In fact you couldn't if you tried as this bank of super-luxury tented modules is hidden among the dunes with no signed access from the resort. Each is individually themed after a Centralian pioneer and has a direct view of the Rock. Meals are eaten communally in the central Dune House and all tours and other activities are thrown in. Realistically, you're likely to enjoy your room so much you may want to skip the tour programme, or stay an extra day or two.

Lost Camel Hotel Right behind the Shopping Square, pitched as a trendy boutique hotel, the *Lost Camel* features small one-bedroom units ($395) sleeping three at a pinch; with en-suite bathrooms and music centres but no TV, all set around an attractively tiled courtyard with a heated pool. The foyer has soft furnishings, a large TV screen and a small bar.

Outback Pioneer Lodge Most distant from the Shopping Square but with its own dining options and a bottle shop. Beds in the twenty-bed dorms (a record in the NT) go for $33 (also a record); more acceptable mixed four-bed dorms go for $41. The cheapest rooms ($167) are small and plain budget options with two bunk beds and air-con, TV, fridge, tea and coffee; the same unit with a bathroom costs $190. There are also conventional en-suite motel rooms with all the usuals, from $395.

Sails in the Desert Hotel Until recently the resort's flagship, with à la carte restaurants and galleries. It's still the favoured choice of upmarket package tour operators, who are probably paying a lot less than the $522 rack rate for a standard room.

Eating and drinking

Listed below are the resort's more moderately priced eating options. For the half-dozen, à la carte, expense-be-damned alternatives head to the restaurants, grills and bars at the *Sails* or *Desert Gardens* hotels.

Geckos Shopping Square. Mediterranean-style restaurant serving wood-fired pizzas, pastas, seafood and steak, all from around $15–25. Open 10am–10pm.

Outback Pioneer Lodge Yulara Drive. The kiosk (11am–9pm) here has various offerings, including fish and chips or burgers from around $7, as cheap a feed as you'll get here. A better deal is the cook-your-own BBQ (6.30–9.30pm) for around $16–20 including unlimited salad (note that they may insist on covered shoes). Opposite the pool is the *Bough House Restaurant* with an all-you-could-ever-want-to-eat buffet with countless meats, fish, salads and wobbling desserts for around $40 a head. A wheelbarrow ride back to your room is extra.

Quick Bites Shopping Square. Sandwich bar with an ice creamery nearby too. Open 9am–9pm.

Uluru-Kata Tjuta National Park

Even with our bus tours and our fully automatic cameras and our cries of "Oh, wow!", we still couldn't belittle it. I had come expecting nothing much, but by the power of the thing itself I had, like some ancient tribesman wandering through the desert and confronting the phenomenon [sunset on Uluru], been turned into a worshipper. Nobody was more surprised than I.

Geoff Nicholson, Day Trips to the Desert

The entry fee for **ULURU–KATA TJUTA NATIONAL PARK** (daily from one hour before dawn to one hour after dusk; $25, under-16s free) allows

Uluru National Park: tours from Ayers Rock Resort

All tours can be booked at your hotel desk or at the **Tours and Information Centre** in the Shopping Square, but note that most do not include the $25 park entry fee. **Car rentals** can also be booked at the Tours and Information Centre or directly from Hertz (☎08/8956 2244), Avis (☎13 63 33) and Thrifty (☎08/8956 2030) for around $100 a day, including 100km free mileage.

Anangu Tours ☎08/8956 2123, Ⓦwww.anangutours.com.au. Unchallenging cultural tours expanding on Dreamtime myths and bush tucker know-how along the Liru, Kuniya and possibly by now the Mala Walks at Uluru, led by a local Aboriginal guide and an interpreter from around $52 (self-drive $84) for a 4.5hr Kuniya Sunset tour with pick-ups. Unfortunately, the advertised "small groups" can consist of up to 35 people and the tours do not visit exclusive areas, so your tour can get invaded by other groups and curious individuals.

Ayers Rock Helicopters ☎08/8956 2472. Fifteen-minute helicopter rides over the Rock from $100, with longer options as far as Kings Canyon and Lake Amadeus salt lake for $340.

Discovery Ecotours ☎08/8956 2563, Ⓦwww.ecotours.com.au. Small group tours around Uluru and Kata Tjuta with local experts from $80. For $110 the *Uluru Walk* circling the Rock is particularly informative, covering both scientific and cultural aspect – perhaps the best tour in the park. The Spirit of Uluru (same price) covers a similar area but is vehicle-based. Both tours include a breakfast. Also has afternoon tours (3–4hr, including walks) to Kata Tjuta and Mount Conner from around $80 to $200 with dinner.

Frontier Camel Tours ☎08/8953 0444 or 1800 806 499; Ⓦwww.cameltours.com.au. Sunrise and sunset camel rides from $100.

Odyssey Tours & Safaris ☎02/1300 134 044 or 02/9339 1030. Offers visits to Cave Hill, just over the border in SA via Mount Conner, to hear the story of the cave's dreaming from a Yankunytjatjara custodian.

Scenic Flights ☎08/8956 2077. Scenic flights (40 min; from $135) over Uluru and Kata Tjuta, or add Kings Canyon and Lake Amadeus for $310 (2hr).

Uluru Express ☎08/8956 2152. Not really a tour but a small minibus that shuttles you from your accommodation to the Rock or the Olgas (from $35 for a sunrise/sunset trip to $140 for a three-day pass, including park entry fee).

Uluru Motorcycle Tours ☎08/8956 2019. Pillion rides round the Rock on the back of a Harley-Davidson. Passengers from $125, two-hour rental from $255.

unlimited access for up to three days, though it's easily extendable if you ask. Besides the two major sites of Uluru and Kata Tjuta the park incorporates the closed Aboriginal community of Mutujulu, near the base of the Rock, once site of the original pre-Yulara tourist resort.

The **Uluru–Kata Tjuta Cultural Centre** (daily: April–Oct 7.30am–5.30pm; Nov–March 7am–6pm; ☎08/8956 3138), situated 1km before the Rock, opened in 1995, on the tenth anniversary of the so-called "hand back" of Uluru to its traditional owners. The centre also houses a café, souvenir shop and two galleries, and all together you'd want to allow yourself at least an hour to look around. As in the Kakadu equivalent at Cooinda, the strikingly innovative design doesn't conceal the fact that you're getting a sanitized and superficial coverage of Aboriginal life which will leave you saturated with the usual Dreamtime myths, affirmations of land care and bushtucker know-how.

Otherwise, leaflets are available at the information desk on the park's geology, flora and fauna, as well as informative *Park Notes* on various topics and issues:

the park is also home to over 400 species of plants, 25 native mammals, 178 different birds and no less than 72 species of reptiles, and away from the two rocks features subtly diverse habitats from spinifex-covered sand hills to desert oak woodlands. Around the back, the two galleries sell arts and crafts from local artisans, though if you are looking for a painting, the best selection is in Alice. It's possible to walk the two kilometres from the Cultural Centre to the base of the climb along the **Liru path**.

Uluru

It is thought that Aboriginal people arrived at the Rock about 20,000 years ago, having occupied the Centre around 10,000 years earlier. These days **Uluru** straddles the ancestral lands of the people who still speak Yankunytjatjara and Pitjantjatjara dialects of what is called the Western Desert Language (the most used and, area-wise, most extensive Aboriginal language). They survived in this semi-arid environment in small mobile groups, moving from one waterhole to another. Water was their most valued resource, and so any site like Uluru or Kata Tjuta which had permanent waterholes and attracted game was of vital practical – and therefore religious – significance.

The first European to set eyes on Uluru was the explorer Ernest Giles, in 1872, but it was William Gosse who followed his Afghan guide up the Rock and so completed the first ascent by a European a year later, naming it **Ayers Rock** after a South Australian politician. With white settlement of the Centre came relocation of its occupants from their traditional lands to enable pastoralists' stock to deplete the fragile desert environment.

In 1958 the national park was excised from what was then an Aboriginal reserve and it wasn't long before tour operators succeeded in having most of the people who lived in the park relocated to a new community at Docker River (Kaltukatjarra), 300km to the west, close to the WA border. By the early 1970s the tourist facilities in the park were failing to cope and the purpose-built resort of Yulara was conceived and completed within a decade. At the same time the traditional custodians of Uluru began to protest about the desecration of their sacred sites by tourists, who at that time could roam anywhere. After a long land claim the park was subsequently returned with much flourish to the Yankunytjatjara and Pitjantjatjara people in 1985. Reclaimed, the site was initially unchanged under Aboriginal ownership, since it was a condition of hand-back that the park was leased straight back to the Department of Environment and Heritage who administer the park. Tourism continued unaffected but since that time, changes assisted by Aboriginal input have manifested themselves with characteristic subtlety, guiding the park's development. These days up to 400,000 tourists visit the relatively small park every year and, as most come in buses or tour groups, the place can sometimes feel crowded.

Anangu mythology

Uluru, Kata Tjuta and the surrounding desert are bound to a culture whose holistic cosmology sees the People – *anangu* – as having the Land and the Law – *tjukurpa* – as their central tenet of belief. A little confusingly, *tjukurpa* can also refer to the Time of Creation or Dreamtime. *Uluru* is actually the name of one of the many temporary waterholes near the summit. The *tjukurpa* seeks to provide its adherents with a connection with the past and a moral code by which to live and behave correctly, but in Aboriginal society these stories (which can sound simplistic when related to tourists) acquire more complex meanings as an individual's level of knowledge increases with successive initiations.

While Uluru is a key intersection along many "dreaming trails" (or "Songlines", as Bruce Chatwin's book described them) – principally those of the **Mala** (hare wallaby), **Liru** (poisonous snake), **Kuniya** (python) and **Kurpany** (monster dog) – it is not, as one often reads, the pre-eminent shrine to which Aborigines flocked like pilgrims from around the country. A muddy waterhole 200km away may be as significant. Uluru was once important to the Anangu as a reliable source of water and food as well as one of many landmarks incorporating ceremonial and burial sites along the trails created by the Anangu's Dreamtime ancestors. You can get a fuller version of these myths in the Cultural Centre or by joining an Anangu Tour.

Geology

The reason Uluru rises so dramatically from the surrounding plain is because it is a **monolith** – that is, a single piece of rock. With few cracks to be exploited by weathering, and the layers of very hard, coarse-grained **sandstone** (or arkose) tilted to a near-vertical plane, the Rock successfully resists the denudation of the landscape surrounding it. If one can visualize the tilted layers of rock, then Uluru is like a cut loaf, its strata pushed up to near-vertical slices so that from one side you look at the flat ends (the classic, steep-sided sunset profile). Elsewhere the separate vertical layers or slices are clearly evident as eroded grooves – the pronounced fluting and chasms along the Rock's southeast and northwest flanks. Brief, but spectacular, waterfalls stream down these channels following storms. In places, the surface of the monolith has peeled or worn away, producing bizarre features and many caves, mostly out of bounds but some accessible on the Kantju Gorge walk left of the car park by the start of the climb. The striking orangey-red hue, enhanced by the rising and setting sun, is merely superficial, the result of oxidation ("rusting") of the normally grey sandstone which can be seen in these caves.

Up and around Uluru

You can appreciate Uluru in any number of ways on various tours but to climb or not to climb. . . that is the question. "Anangu don't climb" is the oft-repeated message found at the base of the climb, along with the plea that "Anangu feel sad" when someone hurts themselves or dies on the Rock. That said, the Anangu have exclusive access to many more culturally significant sites along the base of the Rock than the summit climb.

Regardless of Anangu sentiment, many visitors to the Rock do attempt the hour-long **climb** to the summit, but make no mistake, if you do decide to climb it will be the greatest exertion you will undertake during your visit to Australia. Probably a third who try give up and, on average, one tourist a year dies, usually from a heart attack, with scores more needing rescuing. If you slip or collapse you'll roll straight back to the car park. But with a firmly attached hat, plenty of water, secure footwear and frequent rests, you'll safely attain the end of the chain from where the gradient eases off considerably and continues up and down gullies to the **summit**, often a windy spot, especially in the morning. Most people hang around only long enough for their legs to de-jellify and then climb back down; the daunting view into the car park can cause some freak outs. But the summit plateau is quite an interesting place. Gnarled trees survive in wind-scooped gullies and, while obviously maintaining caution near the edges, it's satisfying to explore the area away from the throng before they put signs up forbidding it. And in case you're wondering, yes mobile phones do work on the summit.

If you're at all unfit or are nervous about heights and exposed places, do not attempt the climb. These days the climb is regularly closed during high winds or by 8am if the temperature that day is expected to exceed 36°C, a precaution which often leads to disappointment amongst visitors. **Weather** statistics suggest that from September to December and in March you have a fifty percent chance of finding the climb closed due to winds, with April, August and, oddly enough January and February a ninety percent chance of the climb being open. Summer in fact is not as hot as you might think, with only six weeks above 40°C between October and April. At this time most of the average annual 300mm of rain falls in the park, though this figure is extremely variable and can be three times more or less in any year. Daily weather forecasts are posted in the Resort's accommodation and information centres and in the Park's Cultural Centre.

Far less strenuous, no less satisfying and certainly more in keeping with the spirit of the place are the **walks** one can take along the base of the rock. At the very least, the five-minute walk from the car park to **Mutitjulu**, a perennial pool, low-grade art site and scene of epic ancestral clashes, is recommended as long as you hit it between the waves of visiting tour groups. In the other direction from the base of the climb, the two-kilometre walk to **Kantju Gorge** (also known as the Mala Walk) is even better, passing unusually eroded caves, more rock art as well as pools shaded by groves of desert oaks, ending at the huge cliff above Kantju Gorge itself. Best of all is combining this with the nine-kilometre walk **around the Rock**, which takes an easy three hours, including time for nosing about. It offers a closer look at some Anangu sites (though most are closed – heed any warning notices) as well as a chance to appreciate the extraordinary textural variations and surface features you'll have noticed if driving round the rock. Remember though to take water, hat and appropriate footwear.

Kata Tjuta

The "many heads", as **Kata Tjuta** – or the **Olgas** – translates from the local Aboriginal language, are situated 51km from the resort or Uluru. This remarkable formation may have once been a monolith ten times the size of Uluru, but has since been carved by eons of weathering into 36 "monstrous domes", to use Giles' words, each smooth, rounded mass divided by slender chasms or broader valleys. The composition of Kata Tjuta – markedly different from Uluru's fine-grained rock – can be clearly seen in the massive, sometimes sheared, boulders set in a **conglomerate** of sandstone cement. Access to this fascinating maze is unfortunately limited to just two walks, in part because of earlier problems with over-ambitious tourists. Furthermore, the east of Kata Tjuta is said to be a site sacred to Anangu men and so is not accessible to the public.

The first of the permitted walks, the **Olga Gorge Walk**, is a rather pointless one-kilometre stroll into the dead-end chasm flanking Mount Olga (which, at 1070m, is the highest point in the massif). Better by far is the **Valley of the Winds Walk**, a seven-kilometre loop trail which takes about two hours, or the five-kilometre "there and back" walk to a **pass** between two domes. This is as much as you can see of Kata Tjuta's interior without a permit. It's worth knowing that the large tour buses tend to visit the Rock in the early morning and Kata Tjuta in the afternoon. By reversing this trend you might succeed in avoiding the worst of the crowds and enjoy either of these magical places in reasonable solitude.

The Great Central Road

From Kata Tjuta the **Great Central Road** leads west over 1100km to Laverton, 350km northeast of Kalgoorlie. The track is also known as the "Warburton Road" or, to tourism-marketing types, the "Outback Highway", and in 2004 commitments were again made to seal the road, so providing an all-weather link from southern WA to Ayers Rock and beyond. Until that happens, though, it's unsealed but in fairly good condition.

Two **permits** are needed to travel the Great Central Road, both free and easily obtained in Alice Springs or in Perth. The first is issued by the Central Land Council (CLC) in Alice overnight (or possibly while you wait); the second comes over the counter at the Ngaanyatjarra Council, which covers most of the WA section (for addresses see Listings p.686 – or, if coming from Perth, p.723). No one checks permits and so not everyone bothers with them, though showing the CLC permit at the entrance to Uluru national park allows non-stop transit through the park without paying the entry fee. Even once you're out of the park, both permits are for a **direct transit only**. Technically you're not supposed to stop anywhere along the way and only camp at the designated campsites next to roadhouses, but there are enough side tracks along the way to enable you to get out of sight without carving up the dense bush in a 4WD – definitely not acceptable.

As long as you don't get caught in a storm, a 4WD isn't necessary on the Great Central Road, but the usual precautions for driving on remote dirt roads should be taken: take more than enough fuel (note unleaded petrol restrictions), spare tyres and water, especially in summer, when it's not advisable to tackle this route alone in a old banger. Filling up at Yulara, the greatest diesel range needed is around 350km, while for modern vehicles specifically requiring unleaded petrol, it's a rather daunting 816km to **Tjukayirla roadhouse**. The restricted availability of petrol exists to curb the epidemic of petrol-sniffing which has claimed many lives in remote Aboriginal communities. **Avgas** is a non-stupefying substitute available at the Warakunna and Warburton roadhouses which works fine in older petrol engines not fitted with a catalytic converter in the exhaust system. If you run Avgas through a converter its emission-cleaning properties will be ruined but the car will probably still run OK. If you're confused, ask a mechanic. Fuel prices are about 25 percent higher than in Alice or Kalgoorlie.

Along the road

Scenically the first half of the route is more interesting, passing **Lasseters Cave** in the Petermann Ranges where the prospector **Harold Lasseter** sheltered with an Aboriginal family in 1931 after his camels bolted. He died trying to get to the Olgas and the location of the now legendary gold claim he had pegged went with him. Soon after, a dense woodland of desert oaks spreads across the valley leading to the forlorn community of **DOCKER RIVER** (or **Kaltukatjara**; store), 240km from Yulara (basic camping 2km down the road). Ten kilometres later you reach the WA border with the Rawlinson Ranges to the north and soon another nice stand of desert oaks.

Next up is **WARAKURNA** (**Giles**) community, where there's camping plus budget and self-contained motel rooms (☎08/8956 7344; ❷/❺), as well as a store, Avgas and diesel. West from here the land flattens all the way to **WARBURTON**, more or less halfway between Yulara and Laverton, where there's a roadhouse (☎08/8956 7656), Avgas and diesel, a store in the roadhouse and a campground round the back with budget and motel rooms (❷/❹). Just past the roadhouse is the Ngaanyatjarra shire office with a café and

gallery which is well worth a look (some local paintings are also on show at the Kalgoorlie's Mining Hall of Fame, see p.755). From Warburton the 255km to **Tjukayirla roadhouse** (unleaded petrol and diesel, plus camping and rooms for $30pp and $50pp respectively) and the following 320 kilometres to **LAVERTON** look very much like each other, especially if you're concentrating mainly on not joining the countless roadside wrecks. Laverton itself is not an overly noteworthy spot to rejoin civilisation – if you have it in you, **LEONORA** is just another 134km down the road.

Travel details

Trains

In peak season (May, June & July) the service between Alice and Darwin runs twice-weekly in both direction

Alice Springs to: Adelaide (Tues & Fri; 20hr); Port Augusta (Tues & Fri; 17hr; change for Sydney or Perth); Darwin (Mon; 22hr)

Darwin to: Alice Springs (Wed; 22hr) and on to Adelaide (2 days).

Buses

Alice Springs to: Adelaide (3–4 weekly; 27hr); Darwin (1 daily; 19hr); Katherine (1 daily; 15hr; change here for WA); Tennant Creek/Three Ways Roadhouse (1 daily; 6hr–6hr 30min; change at Three Ways for Queensland destinations); Yulara (1 daily; 5hr).

Darwin to: Alice Springs (1 daily; 19hr); Katherine (2 daily; 4hr; change for WA); Tennant Creek/Three Ways Roadhouse (2 daily; 13hr–13hr 30min).

Katherine to: Alice Springs (1 daily; 15hr); Darwin (2–3 daily; 4hr); Kununurra (2 daily; 6hr 30min); Tennant Creek/Three Ways Roadhouse (2–3 daily; 9hr 30min).

Tennant Creek to: Alice Springs (1 daily; 6hr); Darwin (2 daily; 13hr); Katherine (2–3 daily; 13hr); Townsville (1 daily; 12hr).

Domestic flights

Alice Springs to: Adelaide (1–2 daily; 3hr); Brisbane (1–2 daily; 3hr); Darwin (1–2 daily; 2hr); Melbourne (1–2 daily; 3hr); Sydney (1–2 daily; 3hr); Yulara (1–2 daily; 40 min).

Darwin to: Alice Springs (1–2 daily; 2hr); Brisbane (1–2 daily; 4hr); Broome (1 daily; 2hr); Cairns (1 daily; 3hr); Perth (1 daily; 4hr 30min).

Yulara (Ayers Rock) to: Alice Springs (1–2 daily; 1hr); Sydney (1–2 daily; 4hr 30min); Melbourne (1 daily; 4hr); Brisbane (1 daily; 4hr); Perth (3–5 weekly; 4hr 30min).

International flights

Darwin to: Brunei (2 weekly); Denpasar, Bali (3 weekly); Kuala Lumpur, Malaysia (1 direct weekly, or change at Singapore); Kupang and Dili, East Timor (4 weekly); Singapore (5–6 weekly).

8

Western Australia

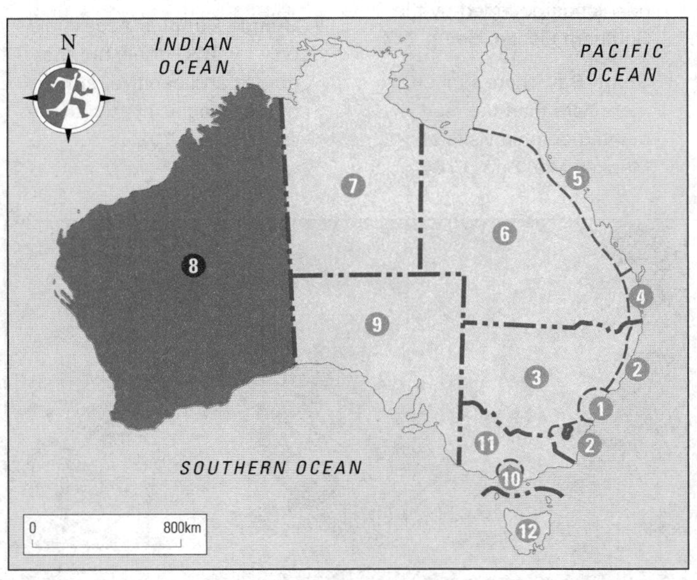

CHAPTER 8

Highlights

* **Fremantle** Eclectic, authentic and alive; worth more than the usual day-trip. See p.724
* **Tall Timber Country** Hike or cycle forest tracks, paddle the Blackwood River or drive among magnificent karri forests. See p.741
* **South Coast** Between Walpole and Cape Le Grand you'll find perfect sandy bays squeezed between granite headlands pounded by the Southern Ocean. See p.747
* **Shark Bay** There's much more here than the regimented dolphin visits at Monkey Mia. See p.764
* **Ningaloo Reef** "A barrier reef without the barriers". See p.770
* **Karijini National Park** Test your mettle exploring the banded chasms of the Hamersley Ranges. See p.776
* **The Kimberley** Barely populated and still untamed, the Kimberley is Australia's Alaska. See p.789
* **Bungle Bungles** Accessible only by 4WD or air, but the gorges and beehive domes of the Bungles are worth the effort. See p.792

△ Wandjina rock art, The Kimberley

8

Western Australia

Western Australia (WA) covers a third of the Australian continent; almost the size of India, yet with less than half a percent of that country's population. Conscious of its isolation from the more populous eastern states or indeed anywhere else, WA is ironically the most suburban of Australian states: almost all of its 1.9 million inhabitants live within 200km of Perth and most of the rest live in communities strung along the coastline.

Perth itself retains the leisure-oriented vitality of a young city, while the port of **Fremantle** resonates with a largely European charm. South of Perth, the wooded hills and trickling streams of the **southwest** support the state's expanding wine-growing and holiday-making area, and the giant **eucalyptus forests** around **Pemberton** further ripen a land fed by generous winter rains. East of the forests is the state's intensively farmed **wheat belt**, an interminable man-made prairie struggling against the saline soils it has created. Along the Southern Ocean's stunning storm-washed coastline, **Albany** is the primary settlement, part summer holiday, part retirement resort; the dramatic granite peaks of the **Stirling Ranges** just visible from its hilltops are among the most botanically diverse habitats on the planet. Further east, past **Esperance** on the edge of the Great Australian Bight, is the **Nullarbor Plain**, while inland are the Eastern Goldfields around **Kalgoorlie**, the only inland town of any size and sole survivor of the century-old mineral boom on which WA's prosperity is still firmly based.

While the temperate southwest of WA has been tamed by colonization, the north of the state is where you'll discover the raw appeal of the **Outback**. The virtually unpopulated inland deserts are blanketed with spinifex and support remote Aboriginal and mining communities, while the west coast's winds abate once you venture into the tropics north of **Shark Bay**, home of the amicable dolphins at **Monkey Mia**. From here, the mineral-rich **Pilbara** region fills the state's northwest shoulder with the dramatic gorges of the **Karijini National Park** at its core. Visitors also home in on the submarine spectacle of the easily accessible **Ningaloo Reef**, surrounding the North West Cape's beaches – some consider it superior to Queensland's Barrier Reef.

Northeast of the Pilbara, **Broome**, once the world's pearling capital, is indeed a jewel in the cyclone-swept coastline of the rugged "Nor'west", and an ideal preliminary to the **Kimberley**'s wilderness and hard-won cattle country. Cut off in the wet season, the Kimberley is regarded as Australia's last frontier, its convoluted and barely accessible coasts washed by huge tides and occupied only by secluded pearling operations, a handful of Aboriginal

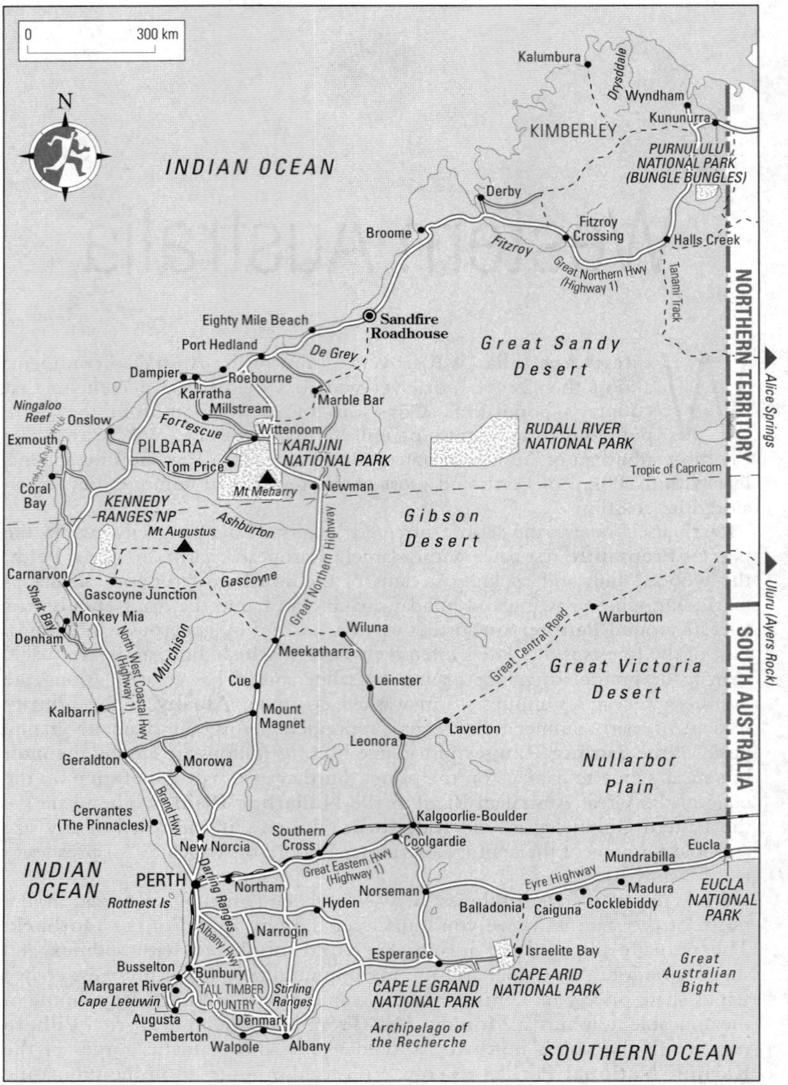

communities and crocodiles. On the way to the Northern Territory border is the surreal enigma of the World Heritage-listed **Bungle Bungles** – one of WA's greatest natural wonders.

Travellers never fail to underestimate the **massive distances** in WA, which is half the size of the USA. If you hope to explore any significant part of the state's million-and-a-half square kilometres, and in particular the remote Northwest, your own **vehicle** is essential, although you'll get to the most interesting places by combining local **tours** with buses. Either way, WA offers an essential mix of Outback grandeur, albeit more dispersed than elsewhere, and continues to attract tourists keen to break away from "the East", as the rest of Australia is known in these parts.

WA's **climate** is a seasonal mix of temperate, arid and tropical. **Winters** are cool in the south and wet in the southwest corner, while at this time the far north basks in daily temperatures of around 30°C, with no rain and tolerable humidity: this is the tropical dry season. Come the **summer**, the enervating wet season or "Wet" (from December to March) washes out the north while the rest of the state, particularly inland areas, crackles in the mid-40s°C heat. The southern coast is the only retreat for the heat-struck; the southwest coast is cooled by dependable afternoon sea breezes, known in Perth as the "Fremantle Doctor".

WA is eight hours ahead of GMT, one-and-a-half hours behind the Northern Territory and South Australia and two hours behind the other eastern states. From October to mid-March **time differences** increase by an hour, as New South Wales, Victoria, Tasmania, ACT and South Australia adopt daylight saving.

Some history

Aborigines had lived all over WA for around twenty thousand years by the time the seventeenth-century traders of the **Dutch East India Company** – and possibly the **Portuguese** before them – began wrecking themselves on the west coast in their quest for the valuable spices of the East Indies. A Dutch mariner, **Dirk Hartog**, was among the first of these and in 1616 he left an inscribed pewter plate on the island off Shark Bay that now bears his name. Recent evidence was also found hereabouts to suggest that the **French** claimed the whole continent just a few years before Cook. For the next two hundred years, however, WA's barren and waterless fringes remained – commercially at least – uninspiring to European colonists.

France's continued interest in Australia's southwest corner at the beginning of the nineteenth century brought a legacy of Francophone coastal features, and led the **British** to hastily claim the unknown western part of the continent in 1826. **Fredrickstown** (Albany) was established on the south coast in that year and the **Swan River Colony**, today's Perth, two years later. This **new colony** initially rejected convict labour and so struggled desperately in its early years, but it had the familiar effect on an Aboriginal population that was at best misunderstood and at worst annihilated. Aborigines and their lands were cleared for agriculture: these days black faces are rarely seen south of Perth.

Economic problems continued for the settlers until stalwart explorers in the mid-nineteenth century opened up the country's interior, leading to the goldrushes of the 1890s which propelled the colony into autonomous statehood in less than a decade. This **autonomy**, and growing antipathy towards the eastern states led to a move to secede from the federation in the depressed 1930s, when WA felt the rest of the country was dragging it down. However, following World War II the whole of white Australia – and especially WA – began to thrive, making money first from wool and later from huge iron ore and offshore gas discoveries that continue to form the basis of the state's wealth and today account for a quarter of the nation's entire economy. Meanwhile, most of WA's forty thousand Aborigines continue to live in squalid and remote communities, as if in another country.

National parks entry fees, walking times and school holidays

CALM (the government department of Conservation and Land Management) maintains WA's parks and also levies an **entry fee** or "pass" to the most-visited national parks in WA. The prices of the various passes are listed below. Throughout this chapter those CALM parks that require an entry fee have the phrase "CALM fee" placed in brackets after their names. You can obtain a pass from the entry station (often unattended), local CALM offices and some tourist offices. The CALM website (Ⓦwww.naturebase.net) contains details of all passes, as well as useful information about WA's national parks.

Day Pass: $9 per car, $3 per motorbike. For any number of WA parks visited on that day; useful in the Southwest.

Annual Local Park Pass: $17 per vehicle; gives unlimited access to parks in a given area for a year.

Holiday Pass: $22.50 per vehicle; allows entry into all WA parks for four weeks.

Annual All Parks Pass: $51 per vehicle; allows entry into all WA parks for a year.

Walking times

Right across the state (if not the entire country) signs for short walking trails consistently exaggerate a suggested duration time to the point where it dissuades many from even trying. Experience has shown that you can comfortably halve the indicated times and still factor in a picnic and a siesta. Where shown, the chapter gives **actual walking times**: the *minimum* time it takes to complete the walk at a normal pace without stops.

School holiday dates in southern WA

Summer: mid-December to the end of January
Easter: middle two weeks of April
Winter: middle two weeks of July
Spring: first two weeks in October

Perth and the South

South of the **Great Eastern Highway**, which joins **Perth** to **Kalgoorlie**, is the most climatically benign portion of WA, something you can only appreciate if you've spent much time up north. It supports intensive agriculture and coastal resorts, with all points eventually connected to Perth, the modern expression of the state's wealth. East of the state capital, the **Darling Ranges** offer a number of appealing day-trip destinations, while south of Perth, the **Margaret River Region**'s verdant landscape is especially attractive, supporting orchards, wineries and numerous home-like holiday hideaways in the giant karri forests around **Pemberton**. Both **Albany** and **Esperance** are engaging resort towns on the Southern Ocean's rugged coastline, where sea breezes take the edge off the summertime heat. They make ideal bases for exploration of their adjacent national parks, while the dreary **Wheatlands**, north of the coast, is a region to pass through rather than head for. **Kalgoorlie**, at the still-thriving heart of the **Eastern Goldfields**, is a colourful caricature of an Outback mining town and certainly deserves a stop if you're travelling east.

Perth

Although its absence of urban grime creates a favorable first impression, after visiting the other major Australian capitals it's hard to get too worked up – favorably or otherwise – about the sprawling suburban spread of **PERTH**. Western Australia's modern hub is home to nearly 1.5 million people and has a reputation for sunshine and an easy-going lifestyle – after work, people often go sailing, swimming or fire up a barbie on the south shore of the Swan River, which forms a broad lagoon ideal for recreation and sport. It's partly because of this contented detachment from the rest of the country (the city's on Western Standard Time, two hours behind the east coast), and partly because the original settlement sites of Fremantle and Guildford are now located 20km to either side, that central Perth lacks the charisma which makes a great city something more than just a clutch of skyscrapers and sweeping freeways.

The state's wave of mineral prosperity saw Perth change fast in the 1980s and considering its modest population, development continues today seemingly for development's sake. The city centre is essentially an uncovered shopping mall with museums, galleries and an adjacent Central Business District (CBD), but oddly fails to integrate the riverside frontage that's left to the joggers, cyclists and gulls. The real centre of the city is dispersed: **Northbridge** is the tourist restaurant and club district just north of the city centre; otherwise imitate the weekending locals and head for the hills, the beaches, the south shore of the river, the western suburbs of Leederville, Subiaco and Cottesloe, or last but not least the port of Fremantle, 20km from Perth's city centre.

Arrival and information

Perth's **international airport** (☎13 12 23) is 16km east of the city centre and the busier **domestic** terminal a few kilometres closer. **Shuttle buses** (international $20, domestic $11; ☎08/9277 7958) meet arrivals at both airports and take you to your chosen accommodation; don't let them influence your preference if you have one. Poorly signposted, but directly opposite the Qantas domestic terminal, you can also catch a green Transperth bus #200, #201, #202, #208 and #209 to the city, at least every forty minutes ($3). Otherwise, a trip by **taxi** to or from the international airport will take thirty minutes and cost around $25, or a bit less and faster from the domestic terminal. An airport shuttle runs to **Fremantle** (from $20 one-way; ☎08/9335 1614) once an hour.

Interstate **trains** and **buses** as well as Transco (formerly Westrail) **buses** serving rural WA use the **East Perth Rail and Bus Terminal**, three train stops east of the city central Transperth **Perth train station** on Wellington Street. Near the latter you will find the **Wellington Street Bus Station** for suburban services, and to confuse matters further there is also the **Esplanade Bus Station** on Mill Street (see p.717) by the Perth Conference Centre.

The main **tourist office** (Mon–Fri 8.30am–6.30pm, Sat 9am–1pm; ☎1300 361 351 or 1800 812 808, Ⓦwww.westernaustralia.net) is just across the road from the Transperth station in Forrest Chase precinct, and has numerous free city guides and maps, tour information and statewide promotional videos. An alternative is the **Travellers' Club Tour and Information Centre** (Mon–Fri 9am–5.30pm, Sat 10am–4pm; ☎08/9226 0660, Ⓦwww.travellersclub.com.au), down the road opposite the bus station at 555 Wellington St, with an information service for backpackers and budget travellers as well as inexpensive **Internet** access and notice boards for work and car sales.

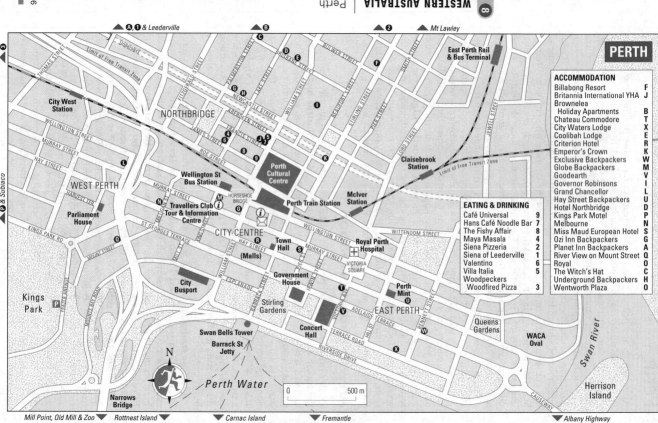

PERTH

ACCOMMODATION

Billabong Resort	F
Britannia International YHA	J
Brownelea Holiday Apartments	B
Chateau Commodore	T
City Waters Lodge	X
Coolibah Lodge	E
Criterion Hotel	R
Emperor's Crown	K
Exclusive Backpackers	W
Globe Backpackers	M
Goodearth	V
Governor Robinsons	I
Grand Chancellor	L
Hay Street Backpackers	U
Hotel Northbridge	D
Kings Park Motel	P
Melbourne	N
Miss Maud European Hotel	S
Ozi Inn Backpackers	G
Planet Inn Backpackers	A
River View on Mount Street	Q
Royal	O
The Witch's Hat	C
Underground Backpackers	H
Wentworth Plaza	O

EATING & DRINKING

Café Universal	9
Hans Café Noodle Bar	7
The Fishy Affair	8
Maya Masala	4
Siena Pizzeria	2
Siena of Leederville	1
Valentino	6
Villa Italia	5
Woodpeckers Woodfired Pizza	3

A, 1 & Leederville
B
2
Mt Lawley
3
P & Subiaco
Mill Point, Old Mill & Zoo
Rottnest Island
Carnac Island
Fremantle
Albany Highway

East Perth Rail & Bus Terminal
City West Station
Claisebrook Station
McIver Station
Perth Train Station
Perth Cultural Centre
Wellington St Bus Station
Travellers Club Tour & Information Centre
Horseshoe Bridge
Northbridge
West Perth
City Centre
East Perth
Parliament House
Town Hall
(Malls)
Government House
Royal Perth Hospital
Victoria Square
Perth Mint
City Busport
Stirling Gardens
Concert Hall
Queens Gardens
WACA Oval
Swan Bells Tower
Barrack St Jetty
Perth Water
Swan River
Herrison Island
Kings Park
Narrows Bridge
Limit of Free Transit Zone
Underpass
Thomas Street
Fitzgerald Street
Palmerston Street
Lake Street
Brisbane Street
William Street
Bulwer Street
Beaufort Street
Stirling Street
Pier Street
Smith Street
Lord Street
Jewell Street
Newcastle Street
Aberdeen Street
Francis Street
James Street
Roe Street
Wellington Street
Murray Street
Hay Street
Milligan St
King Street
St Georges Terrace
Mill St
Esplanade
Barrack Street
Irwin Street
Victoria Ave
Adelaide Terrace
Terrace Road
Riverside Drive
Hill St
Bennett Street
Wittenoom Street
Harvest Ter
Kings Park Rd
Mount Street
Mounts Bay Road
Frazer Avenue
Causeway
N
0 500 m

City transport

Transperth is Perth's efficient and inexpensive **suburban transport** network, with frequent **trains** to Fremantle and the northern, eastern and southern suburbs of Joondalup, Midland, Armadale and Mandurah, plus a fleet of **buses** filling in the gaps. The city centre has two suburban **bus stations**, one on Wellington Street, next to the central train station and, mostly for services south of the river, the Esplanade Bus Station, ten minutes' walk south at the bottom of Mill Street. Any southbound bus crossing the railway line at Horseshoe Bridge near the Wellington Street bus station goes to the Esplanade Bus Station. There are helpful Transperth **information offices** at both bus stations (Mon–Fri 7.30am–5.30pm, Sat 8am–1pm; ⓣ13 62 13).

Outside the **Free Transit Zone** (see box below), Perth is divided into eight concentric zones – zones 1 and 2 (tickets $3) are the most useful to visitors, incorporating Fremantle, the northern beaches and Midland. **Tickets** are available from bus conductors or vending machines at all (mostly unstaffed) stations; they are valid for up to two hours' (some for 1hr 30min) unlimited travel within the specified zones on Transperth buses, trains and the ferry to South Perth from Barrack Street Jetty. All-zone day-passes ($7.50) and ten-trip MultiRiders (from $17) are also available from certain newsagents. For a **taxi** call ⓣ13 13 30 or 13 10 08.

Perth has a far-reaching network of **cycle lanes**, which spread out to the suburbs and can make cycling a pleasant and viable option; the government agency Bikewest (ⓣ08/9216 8000) or the Bicycle Transportation Alliance (ⓣ08/9420 7210) can provide more information.

Accommodation

There's a full range of **accommodation** around the centre of Perth, much of it – from backpackers' hostels to hotels and apartments – inexpensive and conveniently close to, or even right in, the city centre. Self-contained apartments can be great value for groups of four or more. The nearest campsites are 7km from the city. Booking ahead for hotels and apartments is advisable in summer if you want to stay at the first place on your list.

Free transport in central Perth: the FTZ

Both of Perth's central bus stations, as well as the local train stations one stop on either side of the main Wellington Street train station, are within the **Free Transit Zone**, or **FTZ**. Most buses passing through the FTZ offer free travel within it, as do the snazzy "**CAT**" (Central Area Transit) buses serving the city centre. You can board the buses at special CAT stops to take you along two circular CAT routes with a third route, the **Yellow CAT** running up and down Wellington Street to East Perth; press a button and a voice tells you when the next bus is due. The **Blue CAT** runs from Barrack Street Jetty along the Foreshore and up Mounts Bay Road to Barrack Street and Aberdeen Street and then down William Street and over Horseshoe Bridge back to the river, while the **Red CAT** runs east to west along St Georges Terrace, the non-pedestrianized part of Hay Street and Wellington Street. All routes run from Monday to Thursday 7am to 6pm, Friday 7am to 1am, Saturday 8.30am to 1am and Sunday 10am to 5pm, with intervals of fifteen minutes at the most.

Hotels and self-contained apartments

Brownelea Holiday Apartments166 Palmerston St ⓣ08/9227 1710 or 1800 629 006, ⓦwww.brownlea.com.au. Part of the Budget chain – located north of Northbridge with a spa, pool and fully-equipped kitchens. ❹
Chateau Commodore 417 Hay St ⓣ08/9325 0461, ⓕ9221 2448. Good value for its position right in the centre of town, with parking, restaurant, bar and pool. ❹
City Waters Lodge 118 Terrace Rd ⓣ08/9325 1556, ⓦwww.citywaters.com.au. Small one- and two-bedroom apartments close to the river and ten minutes' walk from the centre. ❸
Criterion Hotel 560 Hay St ⓣ08/9325 5155 or 1800 245 155, ⓦwww.criterion-hotel-perth.com.au. Modernized grand-era hotel on the east side of central Hay St; rooms are on the small side but there's an in-house Italian restaurant and English-style theme pub. Internet access and some secure parking. ❹
Goodearth 195 Adelaide Terrace ⓣ08/9492 7777, ⓦwww.goodearthhotel.com.au. Superior motel close to the centre with a clean, contemporary look, views to the river and a range of good-value rooms, all with kitchenettes. ❹
Grand Chancellor 707 Wellington St ⓣ08/9327 7000 or 1800 999 144. Central four-star providing spacious rooms with minibar and in-house movies, as well as a gym, sauna and roof-top pool. ❻
Hotel Northbridge 210 Lake St ⓣ08/9328 5254, ⓦwww.hotelnorthbridge.com.au. Appealingly refurbished old-style hotel at the top end of Northbridge, which has good-value four-star rooms with a spa in all and some budget options. Off-street parking and three-bar pub below. ❺
Kings Park Motel 255 Thomas St, Subiaco ⓣ08/9381 0000, ⓦwww.kingsparkmotel.com.au. Good-value modern motel with spas in some rooms, five minutes from the city, on the edge of Kings Park and close to Subiaco shops and restaurants. ❹
Melbourne Cnr Hay and Milligan sts ⓣ08/9320 3333, ⓦwww.melbournehotel.com.au. Small, heritage-listed federation-era boutique hotel at the west end of Hay St. Well-equipped rooms with in-house movies, cable TV, Internet access, a café/bar and 24hr reception. Breakfast included. ❻
Miss Maud Swedish Hotel 97 Murray St ⓣ08/9325 3900, ⓦwww.missmaud.com.au. A pleasant variety of rooms, an interior with a Swedish/Alpine flavour and a spectacular smorgasbord breakfast included. ❺
River View on Mount Street 42 Mount St ⓣ08/9321 8963, ⓦwww.riverview.au.com. Comfortable, well-equipped units with kitchens, between the city centre and Kings Park. ❹
Royal Cnr Wellington and William sts ⓣ & ⓕ08/9324 1510, ⓔwentpert@fc-hotels.com.au. A tidy grand-era hotel with mostly shared facilities and with some big rooms which are better and less expensive than the *Wentworth Plaza* next door. ❸
Wentworth Plaza 300 Murray St ⓣ08/9481 1000, ⓔwentpert@fc-hotels.com.au. Part of the budget *Comfort Inn* chain. A plusher version of its sister, the *Royal* (above), with same central location, mix of en-suite and basin-only rooms plus 24hr reception and lifts. ❹

Backpackers'

Originally centred in **Northbridge**, Perth's backpackers' can now be divided into three categories: warren-like grand hotels or converted inner-city houses; the new breed of licensed backpacker resorts that cater to your every need and classy "boutique" backpackers' with a tranquil "guesthouse" feel. As a rule the further from central Northbridge the better the accommodation offered.

Free on-street daytime **parking** is no longer possible within Northbridge, but off-street parking is available at some accommodation and this is indicated in the reviews; there are plenty of inexpensive central car parks. The keener establishments meet incoming trains and buses at East Perth Rail and Bus Station and will also collect you for free from the airports, though some may insist on a two-nights minimum stay for this.

Northbridge and City Centre

Britannia International YHA 253 William St ⓣ08/9328 6121, ⓔbritannia@yhawa.com.au. Huge, three-storey warren in the heart of Northbridge, a stone's throw from the clubs and cafés but also affected by late-night noise and early morning garbage collection. By the time you read this the long-awaited new "gateway" YHA at 300 Wellington St, opposite Pier St, should have been converted and Britannia will become the "sink" hostel. You get little ambient communal space and some rooms have no windows although you do get little lounges here and there. 24hr reception, no parking. Eight- or six-share dorms from $24.50 (before YHA membership reductions), four-share $25.50, rooms ❸

Emperor's Crown 85 Stirling St ⓣ08/9227 1400 or 1800 991 553, ⓦwww.emperorscrown.com.au. Located in a bit of a corporate no-man's-land but close to the station, this is actually an outstanding all a/c boutique backpackers', setting a long-overdue new standard in Perth with a clean, modern interior, plasma-screen TV/DVD, latest Internet computers, a kitchen fit for cooking and an adjacent café. Standard six- or four-bed dorms at $24 and several double ❹ or triple ❹ configurations, some with en suite and all private rooms with TV/ DVD and fridges. Limited parking.

Globe Backpackers 553–561 Wellington St ⓣ08/9321 4080, ⓦwww.globebackpackers.com.au. Right next to Travellers Club information centre and as central as they come, with good security, a smallish kitchen, outdoor eating area and big TV rooms. Eight- and six- bed dorms cost $22, with the novelty of individual (as opposed to communal) bathrooms. Free breakfast and cheap Internet access. ❷

Along Newcastle Street

Ozi Inn Backpackers 282 Newcastle St ⓣ08/9328 1222, ⓦwww.oziinn.com. Another converted old house offering an "old-style" backpackers' which can feel a bit cramped or cozy depending on your attitude. Six-share dorms aren't too bad and go for $17, with a rather forlorn annexe over the road offering dorms from $14. Rooms ❷

Planet Inn Backpackers 496 Newcastle St ⓣ08/9227 9969, ⓦwww.club-red.com.au. The detached houses which make up this popular backpackers' are a bit far out of the centre, but there's a bar, mini-shop, and free breakfast plus apricots in season. More outdoor space than most and some parking. Eight- to six-share dorms from $16, rooms ❷

Underground Backpackers 268 Newcastle St ⓣ08/9228 3755, ⓔunderground@iinet.net.au. Mega-backpackers' that was a former hotel. There's a spacious foyer and a newer block at the back by the pool, which makes up for some windowless rooms. Free breakfast, bar, cheap Internet access, a/c rooms, video lounge, and 24hr reception. Twelve-share dorms $20, six-share $22 and four-share $24. Rooms for ❸ or $5 more with TV.

North of Newcastle Street

Billabong Resort 381 Beaufort St ⓣ08/9328 7720, ⓦwww.billabongresort.com.au. Former students' digs converted into a vast, palmy mega-resort that is among the best in town. The four-bed ($22) and eight-bed ($19) dorms all have an attached bathroom, while downstairs there's an appealing rather than token pool area. Just about every possible service is on offer, short of tucking you in at night. Free breakfast, plenty of parking and close to Mt Lawley shops. Rooms ❸

Coolibah Lodge 194 Brisbane St ⓣ08/9328 9958 or 1800 280 000, ⓦwww.coolibahlodge.com.au. Well-kept pair of colonial-era houses close to the *Northbridge* but just a touch too cramped for comfort. Small pool and a bar. Very limited parking. Eight-share dorms from $20, rooms ❸

Governor Robinsons 7 Robinson Ave ⓣ08/9328 3200, ⓦwww.govrobinsons.com.au. An old colonial house, beautifully converted with plenty of warm wood, a kitchen and bathrooms that won't make you squirm though there's no reception and no TV. Six-bed dorms ($20) with large lockers but mostly doubles, some en suite. ❸

The Witch's Hat 148 Palmerston St ⓣ08/9228 4228 or 1800 818 358, ⓦwww.witchs-hat.com. Distinctive heritage building in a residential area northeast of central Northbridge with wood interior, an attractive communal area, a few small doubles and some parking. Eight-, six- and four-bed dorms all at $22, rooms ❷

East of the Centre

Exclusive Backpackers 158 Adelaide Terrace ⓣ08/9221 9991, ⓦwww.exclusivebackpackers.com. Not always someone around to greet you but the attractive jarrah-wood interior, balcony and spacious dorms offer a touch of class. Off-street parking and a nice café next door supplement the rather inadequate kitchen. Five-bed dorms from $18 and comfortable twins or doubles. ❷

Hay Street Backpackers 266–268 Hay St ⓣ08/9221 9880. Well-positioned on the Red CAT route, *Hay Street* comprises nicely converted and well-maintained adjoined houses with two kitchens, small pool and parking possible by arrangement. Four- to six-bed dorms with a/c from $20 and twins/doubles at the back. ❷

Caravan parks

Central 38 Central Ave, 7km east of Perth ⓣ08/9277 5696. Located in Redcliffe, by the domestic airport. Closest good caravan park to the city centre. Cabins ❺

Scarborough Starhaven 18 Pearl Parade ⓣ08/9341 1770. Situated in a popular beach suburb, a 35min bus ride from the centre. On-site vans ❺

The City

The compact and walkable **central area** of Perth, from Wellington Street down to St Georges Terrace, and bounded vaguely by Hill Street to the east and Milligan Street to the west, is an easy-to-negotiate grid. Much of your time will be spent exploring the links between **Hay Street** and **Murray Street**, both of which are pedestrianized between William and Barrack streets and connected by numerous, glittering arcades. William Street runs north over the railway at **Horseshoe Bridge** and on into the restaurants and bars of Northbridge, while Barrack Street runs south to the **Barrack Street Jetty** on Perth Water, site of the millennial **Swan Bells Tower** (daily 10am–4.30pm; $6; Ⓦ www.swanbells.com.au). The distinctive tower houses the 280-year-old bells of London's St Martin-in-the-Fields church, presented to WA on the 1988 bicentenary. Perth Water is a lagoon on the **Swan River** formed by the bridged **Narrows** and popular with windsurfers, sailors and jet-skiers. From the jetty, a Transperth ferry (Sept–April 7am–9pm; May–Aug 7am–7pm) regularly crosses the Narrows to Mends Street Jetty on the south shore, while tourist ferries ply the river upstream to the Swan Valley wineries and downstream to Fremantle and **Rottnest Island** (see box on p.724).

Museums and old buildings

Situated just over the railway tracks in Northbridge, at the end of James Street, the **Perth Cultural Centre** comprises the **Art Gallery of Western Australia** (daily 10am–5pm; donation) and the state **museum** (daily 9.30am–5pm; donation), as well as the state library. The gallery's constantly changing displays include Aboriginal art, and other contemporary and classic works by Western Australian artists. There's always something worth seeing, the air conditioning is blissful in summer, and the free guided tours provide good information about the work displayed. The museum, part of the same complex, includes a floor devoted to Aboriginal culture, plus exhibitions of vintage cars, stuffed marsupials, meteorites, a diorama of a swamp and a reconstruction of an old jail.

Perth's surviving colonial-era buildings are so embedded in the modern infrastructure that they hold little interest. One exception is the **Perth Mint** (Mon–Fri 9am–4pm, Sat & Sun 9am–1pm; $8.80; Ⓦ www.perthmint.com.au), on the corner of Hill and Hay streets. Operating from its original 1899 base, Australia's principal specialist mint still trades in precious metals in bar or coin form and displays some large-scale replicas of gold nuggets and alluring 400-ounce ingots. Admission also gives visitors a chance to observe regular (on the hour) gold pouring as well as minting operations in the refurbished foundry, along with a guided tour.

Other than that, the **Old Mill** (daily 10am–4pm; $4; Transperth ferry from Barrack Street Jetty), situated at Mill Point, south of the Narrows and in the shadow of the Kwinana Freeway bridge, is an early building that has managed to retain its charm. A quaint, fairy-tale relic, the mill ground the colony's first flour and now houses a collection of pioneering bull-carts and period artefacts in its own attractive grounds.

Kings Park

The mostly wild, five-square-kilometre expanse of **Kings Park** is situated two-kilometres west of the centre down Mount Street (bus #33 or #5 from St Georges Terrace, free in the FTZ). Created with great foresight in 1872, along with the river, the park remains one of Perth's most popular recreational areas. It's enlivened by various flora and fauna, and although the park is small enough to enjoy on foot, you can rent **bicycles** from Koala Cycle Hire (Mon–Fri 9.30am–4pm, Sat & Sun 9.30am–6pm; $25) in the main car park on the park's east side, where there's a fine, tree-framed view over the city. There's a trail leading through the native bushland, a botanic and an aromatic garden, playgrounds, picnic areas, an elevated walkway through the trees and free guided tours from the **information centre** (daily 9.30am–3.30pm; ⓣ08/9480 3600) by the car park, which also provides maps of the park.

Eating and drinking

To eat well and inexpensively in Perth, stick to **Italian** and **Asian** places; these two cuisines cater for ninety percent of eateries and dominate the **food courts**, where you can easily get a decent meal for as little as $9. In Northbridge, food courts include the primarily Asian *Shang Hai* on James Street, while in the city you'll find *Metro* and the cosmopolitan *Carillon* off Hay Street Mall. At the other end of the scale, some of the better seafood restaurants may cost you $30 or more per head – still great value if you've come from Europe. **Northbridge**, especially around James and Lake streets, is the heart of Perth's tourist café and restaurant scene, with over forty establishments crammed into a square kilometre. Except for Sundays and Mondays Northbridge is very busy in the evenings, as people wander from place to place, eating and drinking until late.

It's also worth exploring options elsewhere, such as the strip of restaurants along Beaufort Street in Mt Lawley, north of Northbridge, lively Leederville to the west, Subiaco on the west side of Kings Park or of course **Fremantle**. All are fun places to dine without the congested, frenetic feel of Northbridge.

Café Universal 251 William St, Northbridge. Trendier place than most to enjoy cappuccinos, beers and street life, with food from 5pm including salads and focaccias for around $15. A Northbridge institution. Tues–Sat 4pm–late.

The Fishy Affair 132 James St, Northbridge ⓣ08/9328 3939, ⓦwww.fishyaffair.com.au. One of Northbridge's longest established restaurants with dishes like seafood chowder for $9, swordfish with vegetables from $23 and a seafood platter with an A-Z of marine life from $37 per person. Tues–Sun 11.30am–3pm & 5.30pm–late.

Hans Café Noodle Bar 245 William St, cnr Francis St, Northbridge. One of the many unpretentious Southeast Asian restaurants in the area with no noodle- or rice-based dish over $10. Daily 11am–10.30pm.

Maya Masala Cnr Lake and Francis sts, Northbridge ⓣ08/9328 5655. One of Perth's most popular Indian restaurants with *masala dosa* from $12, seafood *thali* for $13 and curries from $15. Tues–Sun 11.30am–2.30pm & 5.30pm–late.

Siena Pizzeria 500 Beaufort St, Mt Lawley ⓣ08/9227 6991, ⓦwww.sienas.com.au. Deservedly busy pair of restaurants with mouth-watering, wood-fired pizzas for around $16 and all your other Italian favourites like veal and calamari for around $22. Daily 5.30pm–late, plus Wed–Sun noon–3pm, Sat & Sun breakfast 7.30–10.30am.

Siena of Leederville 115 Oxford St, Leederville ⓣ08/9444 8844. Formerly connected with the above and still offering a similar range of mouth-watering Italian dishes. Daily 11.30am–late.

Valentino Cnr Lake and James sts, Northbridge. Italian restaurant with lunch specials, wood-fired pizzas and pastas for around $13, as well as a good range of cakes. Mon–Fri 7am–late, Sat 8am–late.

Villa Italia Cnr Aberdeen and William sts, Northbridge. Jazzy Italian café with a similar range of food as the *Valentino*. Mon–Fri 7am–late, Sat 8am–late.

Woodpeckers Woodfired Pizza 372 Hay St, Subiaco ⓣ08/9388 1122. Gourmet pizza and pasta from around $15. Daily 6pm–late.

Entertainment and nightlife

As with food, **Northbridge** is the focal point of after-dark action, with plenty of **pubs**, **bars** and teeming **dance clubs** concealed in improbable buildings.

In view of Perth's famed isolation, a night in Northbridge is the hottest spot for thousands of kilometres in any direction but there are also some lively bars in the city and inner suburbs. Perth's nightlife centres around alcohol and although the city is attempting to curb antisocial carousing and promote responsible behaviour, there's little chance of this with so many pubs and bars offering **free beer**, happy hours and other value-added incentives to tempt you. Late at night Northbridge can have an edge to it that some might find intimidating and many locals avoid the place these days.

The free weekly *X Press* newspaper available outside various central outlets has comprehensive **listings** on what's going on and who's playing where, or check out the entertainment section of Thursday's *West Australian* newspaper. For the lowdown on the **gay and lesbian scene**, see "Listings".

Pubs, bars and clubs

Aberdeen Hotel 84 Aberdeen St. Ever-popular meeting place in Northbridge, with a long-established gay night on Sundays.

Brass Monkey Cnr William and James sts. Enduringly popular pub with a good atmosphere in the heart of Northbridge. Live entertainment and a range of local beers.

Leederville Hotel Oxford St, cnr of Newcastle St, Leederville. The Sunday sessions are all the rage but you need to be smartly dressed. Mainstream bands and DJs.

Monkey Bar 393 Murray St. Live international alt-rock acts and DJs for an otherwise mainstream crowd.

Moon & Sixpence 300 Murray St. Popular English theme pub in the city centre.

Mustang Bar 46 Lake St. Big screen sports with free pool, cheap food, competitions and karaoke make this a favourite among partying backpackers.

Northbridge Hotel 198 Brisbane St. Quiet piano lounge and restaurant which does good breakfasts. Livelier public bar with Internet facilities.

Queens 520 Beaufort St, Mt Lawley. One of Perth's best bars, away from the Northbridge mania with a great atmosphere, locally brewed beers and a good restaurant for Sunday morning breakfasts.

Rosie O'Grady's James St, cnr of Milligan St. Irish theme pub with bands every night.

Universal Bar 221 William St. Live jazz and blues most nights.

Cinemas and theatres

Most of Perth's mainstream **cinemas** are located in the arcades off Hay and Murray streets in the city centre. Tuesday nights are cheap, with matinees also discounted at some places. Art-house cinemas close to the centre include Cinema Paradiso, in the Galleria complex on James Street. A little further out are the Art Deco-style Astor, at Mt Lawley on the corner of Beaufort and Walcott streets and the Luna on Oxford Street, Leederville, both a fifteen-minute walk west of Northbridge.

Any out-of-the-ordinary **shows** that visit Perth tend to set the city astir and are advertised and patronized heavily. The *Burswood International Resort and Casino* (Ⓣ08/9362 7777, Ⓦwww.burswood.com.au), just over the Causeway, southeast of the centre, is a do-it-all leisure complex comprising a five-star hotel, numerous restaurants and a huge dome hosting all sorts of sporting and show-business events. Otherwise try the Perth Concert Hall on St Georges Terrace (Ⓣ08/9231 9900, Ⓦwww.perthconcerthall.com.au) or Her Majesty's Theatre (Ⓣ08/9322 2929) on the corner of King and Hay streets.

Listings

Airline Skywest Ⓣ1300 660 088, Ⓦwww.skywest.com.au. Daily flights to the Goldfields, Esperance and Albany, Exmouth and Karratha.

Buses Greyhound Australia (Ⓦwww.greyhound.com.au) goes up along the coast to Darwin every day, less frequently to Port Hedland via Newman on the inland route, and once a week only to Adelaide and the east coast; Integrity Coach Lines (T 08/9226 1399 or 1800 226 339, W www.integritycoachlines.com.au) also heads north via Coral Bay/Exmouth (4 weekly) and as far as Broome (Mon & Fri); South West Coach Lines (T 08/9324 2333) has daily services to the Margaret River region as far as Augusta; and Transco (T 1300 662 205, W www.transwa.wa.gov.au) operates daily bus services as far as Esperance and, less frequently, north to Kalbarri and Meekatharra via Mullewa. They also do a four-week Southern Discovery Pass for around $155.

Car purchase For used vehicles, backpackers' notice boards and the many Internet cafés and travel shops like Travellers Club on 535 Wellington St are best for private sales. Try to avoid buying non-WA registered vehicles in WA as the change of ownership requires an inspection in the state of origin, or a local inspection prior to registration on WA plates, which might entail expensive repairs. Buying and running WA-plated cars within the state is simple as there is no annual roadworthy or change-of-ownership inspection; all you do is renew the annual vehicle registration document, or "rego".

Car rental Bayswater Car Rental, 160 Adelaide Terrace (T 08/9325 1000, W www.bayswatercarrental.com.au) also have offices at West Perth, Fremantle and Perth airport, and offer week-long unlimited kilometre deals from $24 a day; you could also try M2000, at 228 Lord St, East Perth (T 08/9227 0709, W www.m2000car.com.au) and four other city locations. They claim to undercut competitors with the cheapest new cars and unlimited kilometre deals. For **scooter rental** go to Scootaround, 127 Hill St, East Perth (T 08/9325 5100), or Modomio, Unit 4, 15 May Holman Dr, Bassendean (T 08/6278 4400, W www.modomio.com.au).

Cycle Hire About Bike Hire, Causeway Car Park, Riverside Drive. Mon–Sat 10am–5pm, Sun 9am–5pm T 08/9221 2665, E lhoffman@rideaway.com.au, or available from most backpackers' from $25 a day.

Gay and lesbian Perth The quickest way to plug into the scene is to pick up the weekly community paper *Out in Perth* and the monthly *Women Out West* (W www.womenoutwest.com.au), both free from Cinema Paradiso on James St or the Arcane Bookshop, 212 William St, Northbridge (T 08/9328 5073).

Hospitals Royal Perth, Victoria Sq T 08/9224 2244; Fremantle, Alma St T 08/9242 5544.

Maps Perth Map Centre, 900 Hay St (T 08/9322 5733), has a full range of topographic and touring maps.

Motoring associations RACWA, 228 Adelaide Terrace (T 08/9421 4444), offers a complete range of services, as well as maps.

Permits for Aboriginal Land Aboriginal Affairs Department, 197 St Georges Terrace T 08/9235 8000, W www.dia.wa.gov.au/Land/Permits/.

Police 2 Adelaide Terrace T 08/9222 111 or 13 14 44 for non-urgent calls

Post office Forrest Chase, opposite the train station. Mail collection service.

Trains The Indian-Pacific rail service (T 13 21 47, W www.trainways.com.au) now costs about the same as the equivalent bus fare, although it is no faster. Services leave on Wednesday and Sunday, getting to Sydney or Melbourne two days later, and there are great deals like half-price backpackers/overseas concessions and the six-month Great Southern Rail Pass ($590, conc. $450; for full details see p.49). Typical fares are Adelaide $309/conc. $155, Sydney $513/conc. $252 and Alice Springs $524/conc. $260 but over very long distances a flight becomes better value with the savings in travel time. Transco also has daily rail services south to Bunbury and twice on weekdays to Kalgoorlie. Both Transco and Indian-Pacific have offices at the Wellington St Bus Station

Around Perth

For excursions beyond central Perth, the port of **Fremantle**, at the mouth of the Swan River, should not be overlooked, nor should a trip over to **Rottnest Island**, an eighty-minute ferry ride from the city or half that from Fremantle. Perth's **beaches** form a near-unbroken line north of Fremantle, just a short train or bus ride from the centre, while with your own vehicle you can escape to wineries of the **Upper Swan Valley** and the **national parks** northeast of Perth, atop the **Darling Ranges**, which run parallel to the coast. Patchily forested hills, just half an hour's drive east of the city, the Ranges offer a network of cool, scenic drives and marked walking trails among the jarrah woodlands. Further afield, **Toodyay** and **New Norcia** can make a satisfying day-trip with a tour or in a rented car, as can visits to the old colonial settlement of **York**.

River cruises and tours from Perth

Commercial **ferry** operators are all based at Barrack Street Jetty and offer cruises up and down the Swan River from as little as $20 to Fremantle or $70 for a full-day upriver. Collecting you from your accommodation, **bus and 4WD** tours also leave daily in all directions from Perth. Popular **day-tours** include the peculiar Pinnacles, near Cervantes, the wineries of the Upper Swan Valley, New Norcia and Toodyay, York, Wave Rock and even the Tree Top Walk near Walpole – the last two being a *long* day on a bus.

For the Southwest **overnight tours** are better: three nights will typically pack in all the highlights in a loop via Albany. North of Perth the west-coast hot spots after the Pinnacles are Kalbarri, Shark Bay and then Coral Bay on the Ningaloo Reef, with four days or more being a good relaxed pace for the trip up. From here some tours shoot back down to Perth or head inland to Karijini National Park in the Pilbara, something that's well worth the effort if you've come this far north.

River cruises and Rottnest Island ferries

Captain Cook Cruises ⓣ08/9325 3341, ⓦwww.captaincookcruises.com.au. Offers a whole range of cruises including one upriver to some wineries ($65–100 with lunch), one down to Fremantle ($15; 3 daily) and some evening dinner cruises ($70–100) on the Swan River.

Golden Sun Cruises ⓣ08/9325 9916, ⓦwww.goldensuncruises.com.au. Cruises upriver to visit the National Trust property at Tranby House, faintly historic Guildford, and a day-cruise and bus tour around the Swan Valley wineries. Also downriver cruises to Fremantle from $20. **Oceanic Cruises** Perth ⓣ08/9325 1191, Fremantle ⓣ08/9430 2666, ⓦwww.oceaniccruises.com.au. Four daily Perth–Rottnest cruises from $60 and six daily from Fremantle to Rottnest from $45, as well as all-in Rottnest tours for $84 and overnight backpacker deals from $63. Also three daily Perth–Fremantle services for around $18.

Rottnest Express ⓣ08/9335 6406, ⓦwww.rottnestexpress.com.au. Up to ten Fremantle departures daily from $48, with overnight packages from $53 and bike rental from $10 a day.

Day tours

Feature Tours 26 St Georges Terrace ⓣ08/9475 2900 or 1800 999 819, ⓦwww.featuretours.com. Daily coach tours from Perth along the Swan Valley up to New Norcia and Toodyay as well as Margaret River, the Tree Top Walk and Wave Rock from $130–170.

Western Travel Bug ⓣ08/9204 4600 or 1800 627 488, ⓦwww.travelbug.com.au. Pinnacles, Wave Rock and Margaret River for under $100, all with plenty of activities.

Swan Valley wine tours

Various operators run **bus and boat tours** of the valley from Perth, among them

Fremantle

Although long since merged into the metropolitan area's suburban sprawl, Perth's port of **FREMANTLE** – "Freo" – retains a character that the city centre of Perth lacks. It's small enough to keep its energy focused, with a real working harbour instead of a fake marina, and it has an eclectic, arty ambience without too many upmarket pretensions.

Much of the convict-built dock, dating from the 1890s, was spruced up before the 1987 Americas Cup yacht race for an eagerly anticipated tourist boom that never quite materialized. Before that makeover Freo was as rough as any port – the period hotels were then "bloodhouses" full of brawling sailors – but today

Swan Valley Tours (Ⓣ08/9299 8667, Ⓦwww.svtours.com.au; around $70), Captain Cook Cruises (see opposite), who run a daily wine cruise from Barrack Street Jetty in Perth for around $100, and Out and About Wine Tours (Ⓣ08/9377 3376, Ⓦwww.outandabouttours.com.au) runs small group day-tours every day except Monday, including a three-course lunch, for $80.

Overnight tours

All Terrain Safaris Ⓣ08/9295 6680 or 1800 633 456, Ⓦwww.allterrain.com.au. Runs up the coast from $130 a day to Coral Bay, as well as Karijini and from Broome right into the northern Kimberley and the Bungles, to Kakadu. Also cheap "return the bus" runs back to Perth from Broome.

Easyrider Backpacker Tours 224 William St, Northbridge Ⓣ08/9227 0834, Ⓦwww.easyridertours.com.au. Hop on and off the yellow bus, with tickets valid from three days up to six months as far as Darwin via Coral Bay, Karijini and Broome, or over to Kalgoorlie, Esperance and Albany from as little as $70 per day plus food and lodging.

Planet Perth Tours Ⓣ08/9225 6622, Ⓦwww.planettours.com.au. Accommodated tours into the Southwest and five- to seven-day trips up to Exmouth and Broome from around $130 a day.

Red Earth Safaris Ⓣ08/9279 9011 or 1800 501 968, Ⓦwww.redearthsafaris.com.au. Monday departures for one-week coast runs up to Exmouth ($520) with the option of a fast return to Perth.

Southern Cross Safaris Ⓣ08/9574 4692 or 1800 000 881, Ⓦwww.scsafaris.com.au. Five-, eight-and nine-day adventure tours up to Coral Bay and over to Karijini in a 12-seater 4WD and sleeping in swags, from around $120 per day.

Westernxposure 179 William St, Northbridge Ⓣ08/9244 1200, Ⓦwww.westernxposure.com.au. Four-day Monkey Mia trips, three-day Southwest tours or ten-day jaunts via Exmouth and Karijini to Broome. Around $140 a day.

Surf tours

Lancelin Beach Surf School Ⓣ0417 905 789 after 4pm, Ⓦwww.surfschool.com.au. Picks you up early from Perth for up to four days, at around $90 a day with wetsuits, accommodation and food included.

H2Overland Ⓣ1800 010 515, Ⓦwww.h2osurfadventure.com. Day lessons off Perth's northern beaches from $45 for two hours, as well as a five-day surf tour to Exmouth.

Wedge Island Surf Co Ⓣ08/9336 6773, Ⓦwww.wedgeislandsurfco.com.au. Day-trips to Lancelin or a two-day tour to Wedge Island, including overnight camp and Pinnacles sunset for $190.

the town attracts a "latte and deck shoes" weekend crowd to its famed **markets** (worth planning your visit around) and the "cappuccino strip", as café-lined **South Terrace** is known. It's also worth noting that in the heat of summer Fremantle is often a breezy 5°C cooler than Perth, a mere 25 minutes away by train.

Arrival and information

Fremantle Station is located at the top end of Market Street, five minutes' walk north of the town centre. **Buses** (routes #102–106 and #151 from Perth's Esplanade Busport) also stop here; local **taxis** can be called on Ⓣ08/9335 3944. **Ferries** to Rottnest and Perth leave from the wharfside B Shed (behind the

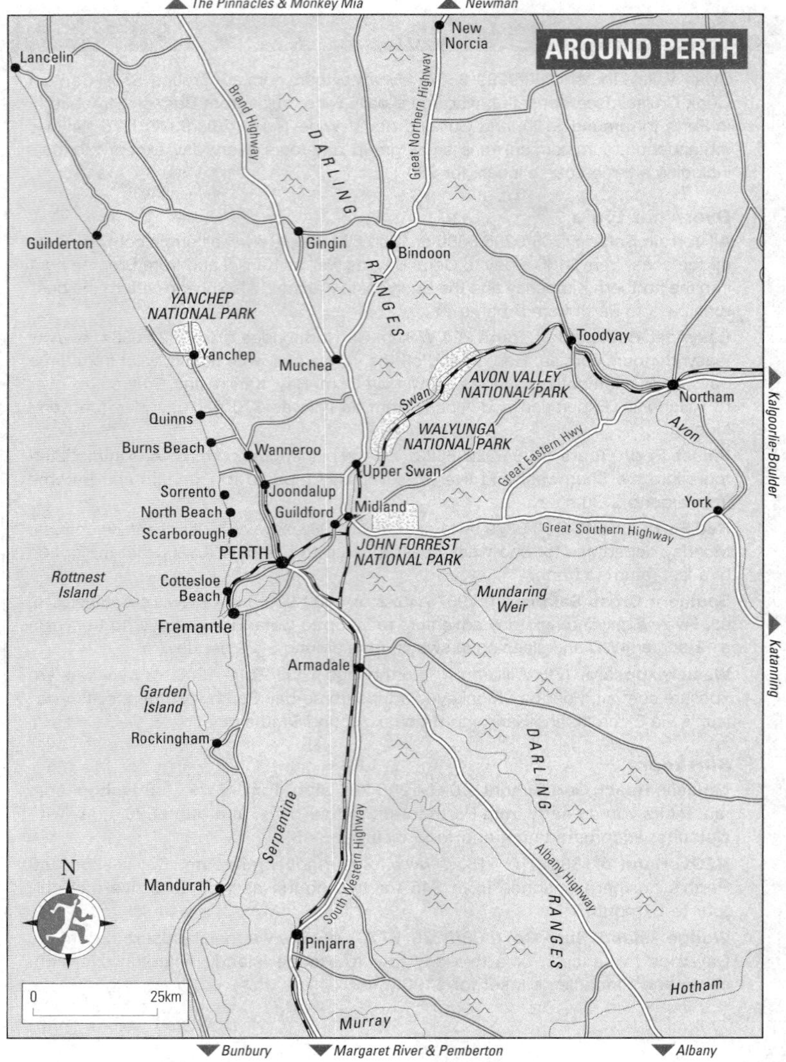

E Shed), which is ten minutes' walk from the station along Phillimore Street (see box on p.724 for details and prices). The orange **Fremantle CAT** is a free bus service which runs roughly every ten minutes along a figure-of-eight route that covers all places in the description below. You could also consider hopping aboard the **Fremantle Tram**, which offers informative commentaries on its various tours (daily 10am–4pm; from $10; hourly), and departs from outside the Town Hall on Kings Square. There's a small **tourist office** in the Town Hall on Kings Square (Mon–Fri 9am–5pm, Sat 10am–3pm, Sun 11.30am–2.30pm; ⓣ08/9431 7878, ⓦwww.fremantlewa.com.au).

Accommodation

Fremantle has no less than five backpackers' all within a kilometre of each other, as well as a caravan park. Grand-era hotels have been splendidly refurbished, their only drawback being shared bathrooms for most rooms. There are also plenty of B&Bs in and around the centre; check out the tourist office website above for some ideas.

Backpacker Inn YHA 11 Packenham St ⓣ08/9431 7065, ⓔbpinn_freo@hotmail.com. A good alternative to *Sundancer* around the corner and more spacious than anything you'll get in Perth. There's a massive kitchen, banks of computers and more than one spot to sit and chill. No parking. Four-, six- and eight-bed dorms from $20, rooms ❷

Fremantle Hotel Cnr High and Cliff sts ⓣ08/9430 4300, ⓕ9335 2636. Right by the Round House, this unpretentious old hotel has rooms with shared or en-suite facilities. ❹

Fremantle Village Caravan Park Cnr Cockburn and Rockingham rds, South Fremantle ⓣ08/9430 4866. The nearest campsite to the centre of town. On-site vans and cabins ❸

Norfolk Hotel 47 South Terrace ⓣ08/9335 5405, ⓕ9430 5909. Central non-pub hotel with mostly en-suite rooms plus a few budget options, all with a kettle and a fridge. Parking available. ❸

Old Fire Station Backpackers 11 Phillimore St ⓣ08/9430 5454, ⓦwww.old-firestation.net. Popular with young ravers and just two minutes from the station. Has a huge common room and women-only lounge and dorms, but it's a bit rough at the back. Four- to twelve-bed dorms from $18, rooms ❷

Pirates Backpackers 11 Essex St ⓣ & ⓕ08/9335 6635. Old backpackers' with a small kitchen but cosy lounge, outdoor area and bar. No parking. Dorms from $18, rooms ❷

Sundancer Backpacker Resort 80 High St ⓣ08/9336 6080 or 1800 061 144, ⓦwww.sundancer-resort.com.au. Newly transformed old pub and club; now colourfully decorated, with plenty of space and a bar. Limited parking (fee). Congested ten-bed dorms $16, four-bed $20 and rooms ❸

Tradewinds Hotel 59 Canning Highway ⓣ08/9339 8188, ⓦwww.tradewindshotel.com.au. Good-looking, federation-era hotel with well-equipped, self-contained apartments, close to the river and 2km from the centre. ❺

The Town

Exploring Fremantle on foot, with plenty of streetside café breaks, is the most agreeable way of visiting the town's compactly grouped sights. If you want to tick off all of them, start your appraisal on the relatively dull east side before moving down to the ocean to end up at the Fishing Boat Harbour, ready for a sunset seafood dinner.

Kick off with the hillside enclosure of **Fremantle Prison** (daily 10am–6pm; $14.90; ⓦwww.fremantleprison.com), whose entrance is on The Terrace, on the west side of the compound. Built by convicts in 1855, soon after the struggling colony found it couldn't do without their labour, the complex was only decommissioned in 1991. The high admission charge is offset by free tours (every 30min) of the prison buildings, sometimes guided by ex-wardens.

Not far from the prison are the more cheerful **Fremantle Markets** (Fri 10am–9pm, Sat & Sun 10am–5pm), on the corner of Henderson Street and South Terrace. A real locals' market that's not solely aimed at tourists, it's well worth a browse for some fresh food, unusual souvenirs from the many arts-and-crafts stalls, or New Age accessories. Moving down **South Terrace**, Fremantle's main street, you can revive your aching feet with some refreshment in one of the many inviting, alfresco **cafés** that give the town its Mediterranean atmosphere.

Suitably recaffeinated, head towards the "**West End**", as the old shipping office and freight district of Freo is known. A left-turn down the High Street will lead you past various art-and-crafts galleries and knick-knack shops to the **Round House** (daily 10am–5pm; donation), the state's oldest building and original jail, which boasts fine views back down into town and out to sea.

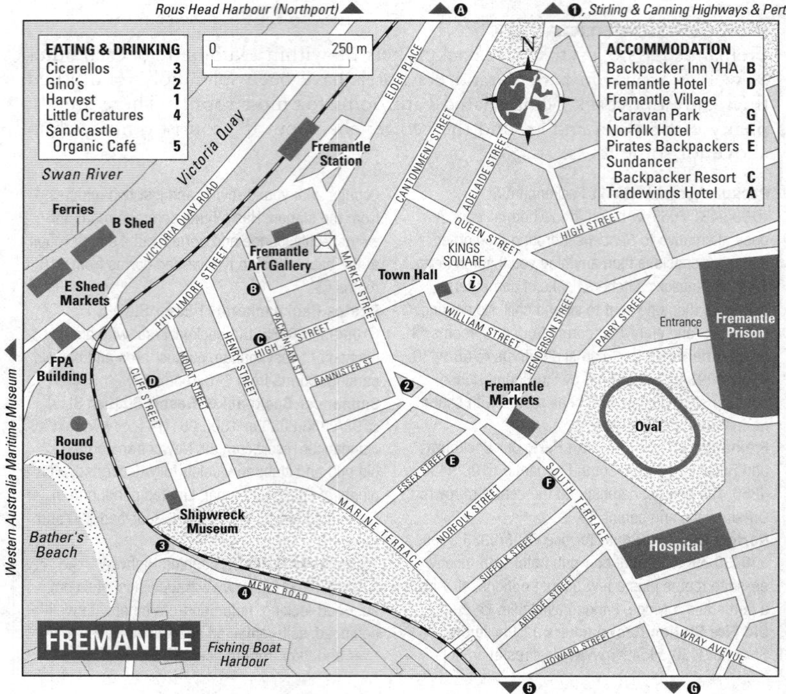

From here you can't miss the striking building housing the **Western Australian Maritime Museum** on Victoria Quay (daily 9.30am–5pm; $10 or $15 with submarine *Ovens*, and free every second Tues of the month; Ⓦwww.mm.wa.gov.au). The museum, with architectural overtones of the Sydney Opera House (though they don't like to admit it), features several galleries covering just about every nautical aspect of WA. Pride of place goes to the glossy-hulled *Australia II* yacht which won the America's Cup several times; alongside is the rather more weather-beaten *Parry Endeavour* belonging to many-times world circumnavigator John Sanders. Other highlights range from the very first Indonesian *prau* seized in WA for illegal fishing, right down to a boy's canoe made from a folded sheet of galvo. There are also displays on fishing, whaling, pearling and trade across the Indian Ocean. The **submarine** *Ovens* is round the back (same times; $8 or $15 with main museum entry; free tours on the half hour 10am–3.30pm).

Outside the Fremantle Port Authority building at the end of Phillimore Street, there's a statue to C.Y. O'Connor, who masterminded the rebuilding of the docks in the 1890s, as well as the construction of the vital water pipeline to Kalgoorlie. Nearby, where the Rottnest ferries berth, the **E Shed markets** (Fri 10am–9pm, Sat & Sun 10am–5pm) offer a food hall and a similar range of stalls to the better-known Fremantle Markets. The **Fremantle Motor Museum** (daily 9.30am–5pm; $9.50; Ⓦwww.fremantlemotormuseum.net) is in the B Shed opposite. Part of the York Motor Museum's collection, it houses a range of classic machines from the very first single-cylinder three-wheeled "automobile" built by Benz in 1886 to cars raced by the likes of Stirling Moss and Speedy Gonzales, as well as a few Harleys, new and old.

Fremantle's original maritime museum is on Cliff Street, and has now been renamed the **Shipwreck Museum** (daily 9.30am–5pm; donation). The centrepiece is the *Batavia*, the Dutch East Indiaman wrecked off present-day Geraldton over 375 years ago. As well as the ship's reconstructed stern, the exhibit includes the stone portico bound for the Dutch East India Company's unfinished fort at Batavia (modern-day Jakarta) and numerous corroded artefacts, together with a fascinating film about the extraordinary drama of the wrecking (and subsequent salvage) of the ship. The rest of the museum has collections from other Dutch vessels which regularly struck Australia's west coast on their way to the East Indies. Coming out of the Shipwreck Museum you find yourself on the grassy esplanade facing the numerous seafood restaurants on **Fishing Boat Harbour** – see "Eating", below.

Eating

Fremantle is a fun place to eat. **Seafood** restaurants overlook the Swan River or jut out into the Fishing Boat Harbour along Mews Road. In town, South Terrace and its adjacent streets are lined with predominantly **Italian** or **Asian** cafés and restaurants, none of them expensive and all adding to Freo's distinctive atmosphere. At the **Food Halls** (Thurs–Sun noon–9pm) on Henderson Street, next to the Markets, you'll find an array of global, but mostly Asian "pop foods".

Cicerellos Fishermans Wharf, 44 Mews Rd. Hugely popular restaurant which serves fish-and-chips right on the harbour. Platters are a good deal if there are a few of you, or go for a "Catch of the Day" or a "Seafood Tray" for around $13. Daily 8am–late.

Gino's 1 South Terrace. Like *Cicerellos*, a Fremantle institution. This enduringly popular and unpretentious sidewalk cafe serves great coffee and cakes as well as your traditional range of pasta with sauces from $15. Daily 8am–late.

Harvest 1 Harvest Rd, North Fremantle. Just over the Queen Victoria St bridge opposite *Mojos Bar*, this house has been converted into a small, relaxed restaurant with a few comfy sofas for weekend breakfasts. Starters for around $17 include prawn and scallop tournedos or beetroot-cured salmon, with mains like lamb rump with bacon, sprouts and salsa verde or veal rib with tomato mayo and wilted spinach for around $25. Tues–Fri 11am–late, Sat 8am–late, Sun 8am–3pm.

Little Creatures 40 Mews Rd, Fishing Boat Harbour ⓣ08/9430 5555, ⓦwww.littlecreatures.com.au. You sit amidst towering vats of fermenting pale ale in this old aircraft hangar, as the restaurant serves up wood-fired pizzas with inventive toppings such as harissa lamb or Atlantic salmon for around $17. The mussels in marinades of beer, chilli, lime, garlic or macadamia nut and herb crust for $17 are also popular, and there's a whole range of dishes including prosciutto-wrapped tiger prawns or marinated kangaroo with bush-tomato chutney that are designed to share. Mon–Fri 10am–midnight, Sat 9am–midnight, Sun 9am–11pm.

Sandcastle Organic Cafe 396 South Terrace, South Fremantle ⓣ08/9335 2445. At the very southern end of South Terrace, the all-organic menu includes scallop or squid starters from around $13 and daily tapas. Mains and vegetarian options include garlic and herb chicken and warm salads, and range from $25 to $30. Tues–Sat 6pm–late, Sun 8am–late.

Drinking and entertainment

Like the town itself, entertainment in Fremantle is generally a laid-back, easy-going affair, which at the same time produces a creative and diverse scene. Not a few of the country's eminent bands like the John Butler Trio and Eskimo Joe started out in Freo's pubs. The *Sail & Anchor* at 64 South Terrace is the town's main watering hole, serving a variety of "boutique" **beers** (a trend which originated in Fremantle). The *Left Bank Bar & Café*, at 15 Riverside Rd in East Freo is a good-looking and popular spot, usually packed on sunny weekends.

Bars with **live music** include *Rosie O'Grady's* at 23 William St and the *Newport Hotel*, 2 South Terrace. Just over the river, *Mojos Bar* at 237 Queen Victoria St is good for original music in a café bar setting, or try the *Swan Basement* at the Swan hotel down the road at no. 201. *Metropolis*, 52 South Terrace, is Fremantle's gigantic **nightclub**, offering a choice of bars and dance floors, while the *Fly By Night*, at the prison end of Queen Street, is a musicians' co-op airing local talent and makes an enjoyable, smoke-free change from pub venues.

Fremantle has no less than four **cinemas**, on Essex Street, William Street, Collie Street and Adelaide Street, all with cut-price tickets on Tuesday and for some matinees.

Rottnest Island

Eighteen kilometres offshore, west of Fremantle, **Rottnest Island** was so named by seventeenth-century Dutch mariners who mistook its unique, indigenous **quokkas**, beaver-like marsupials, for rats. Today, following an ignominious period as a brutal Aboriginal penal colony in the nineteenth century, Rottnest is a popular holiday destination, easily accessible from Perth or Fremantle by ferry and – at the very least – makes for a fun day out.

The island, inevitably abbreviated to "Rotto", is 11km long and less than half as wide, with one settlement, the main resort, stretching along the sheltered Thompson Bay on the east side. West of the settlement, a low heathland of salt lakes meets a coastline of clear, scalloped bays, small beaches and offshore reefs ending at the "West End", as the seaward "tail" of the island is known. Although well attuned to the demands of its 400,000 annual visitors, Rotto gets packed out during school summer holidays (for dates see p.714), especially around New Year when accommodation can be hard to find. Motorized traffic on the island is virtually non-existent, a real treat that makes **cycling** from bay to sparkling bay the best way to appreciate Rotto. Besides riding around the island, you can take a **train ride** up to Oliver Hill (5 trips daily; 2hr; $15), or get underwater with the help of the Dive Shop (daily 7.30am–6pm; ⓣ08/9292 5111), which organizes **dive trips** and rents out everything from snorkels and fins to full scuba-diving equipment. The diving and snorkelling off Rotto's beautiful coves are unlike anywhere on the adjacent mainland and a couple of days spent here, especially midweek when it's less busy, are well worth the excursion from Perth.

Practicalities

There are at least three **ferry** operators that service Rotto from the B Shed in Fremantle and Perth's Barrack Street Jetty. Prices have stabilized at around $40 day-return from Freo and $50 from Perth (see box on p.724 for details). The trip from Perth takes about eighty minutes and half as long from Fremantle, so to make the most of your day aim to board at the latter. You can also **fly** to Rotto in twenty minutes from Jandakot airport, about 20km south of Perth, with the Rottnest Air Taxi (ⓣ1800 500 006; from $80) among others. Rottnest Airport is a fifteen-minute walk from the settlement.

Ferries arrive at the jetty in Thompson Bay right in front of the island's **tourist office** (Mon–Sat 8.30am–5pm, Sun 10am–4.30pm; ⓣ08/9372 9752, ⓦwww.rottnest.wa.gov.au), which has maps and bus timetables and also serves as a **post office**. Daily two-hour **bus tours** depart from the bus stop behind the tourist office at varying times throughout the day ($22). There is also the more-or-less hourly Bayseeker **bus service** (Oct–April daily 9am–5pm; $7 day ticket) which takes you to the island's bays as far as the isthmus, Narrow Neck, 3km from the West End. The settlement has a general **store** with ATMs (daily 9am–5.30pm), a bakery, a takeaway and a **bistro**, with **bike rental** (daily 9am–1pm & 2–5pm; from $20 per day; ⓣ08/9292 5105) behind the hotel, a couple of minutes south of the tourist office.

Accommodation is found along Thompson, Longreach and Geordie bays, all adjacent to each other at the developed northeast end of the island and linked by the Bayseeker bus service. In early 2005 the facilities in Longreach Bay got a long overdue refurbishment, with the other two bays due to follow over the next year or two. The central reservations number for accommodation is ⓣ08/9432 9111; note that prices drop about twenty per cent in winter. A small YHA-associate **hostel** (ⓣ08/9372 9780, ⓔrottnest@yhawa.com.au; booking essential; dorms $22) is located in Kingstown Barracks at the southeastern end of Thompson Bay, 1km from the shops. Nearby, the *Rottnest Lodge Resort* (ⓣ08/9292 5161, ⓕ9292 5158; ❻) is a former prison converted into first-class motel units. **Camping** is available just behind the settlement (ⓣ08/9372 9730). Tents and mattresses can be rented (❶), or there are four- and six-bed self-contained cabins (❸). Camping is not permitted anywhere else on the island.

Perth's beaches

Perth's closest beaches extend along the **Sunset Coast**, 30km of near-unbroken sand and coastal suburbs stretching north of the Swan River, bordered by the Indian Ocean and cooled by afternoon sea breezes. There are also inshore beaches which are well worth a look along the **Swan River** at Crawley, Nedlands, Peppermint Grove and Mosman Bay on the north shore, and Como, Canning Bridge and Applecross on the south shore, and which are calm and safe for children.

Cottesloe Beach, 7km north of Fremantle, is the most popular city beach, with safe swimming. There are ice-cream vendors, cafés and watercraft-rental outlets a-plenty, all just a ten-minute walk from Cottesloe train station. Two kilometres north of here, **Swanbourne Free Beach** – cut off by army land in both directions but accessible from the road – has nude bathing. North of **Scarborough Beach**, itself another popular venue 6km north of Swanbourne, the surf and currents are more suited to wave-riding and experienced swimmers, though with fewer beachside facilities crowds are reduced. Bus #400 leaves from Perth's Wellington Street Bus Station for the 35-minute journey.

New Norcia and Toodyay

One of WA's most unusual architectural sights is **NEW NORCIA**, a monastic community dating from the nineteenth century, 130km northeast of Perth on the Great Northern Highway. This unexpected collection of Spanish-style buildings, bizarrely out of place in the Australian bush, is part of a community founded by Benedictine monks in 1846 with the aim of converting the local Aborigines to Christianity. Nowadays the community is a popular tourist attraction.

The community has a roadhouse with a restaurant, a **tourist office** (daily: Aug–Oct 9.30am–5pm; Nov–July 10am–4.30pm; ⓣ08/9654 8056) and a **museum and art gallery** (daily 9.30am–5pm; $6) which explains the Benedictines' motivations in coming here and displays a fine collection of religious art. The tourist office also runs two-hour **tours** of the town that leave at 11am and 1.30pm ($12.50). The **rooms** in the *New Norcia Hotel*

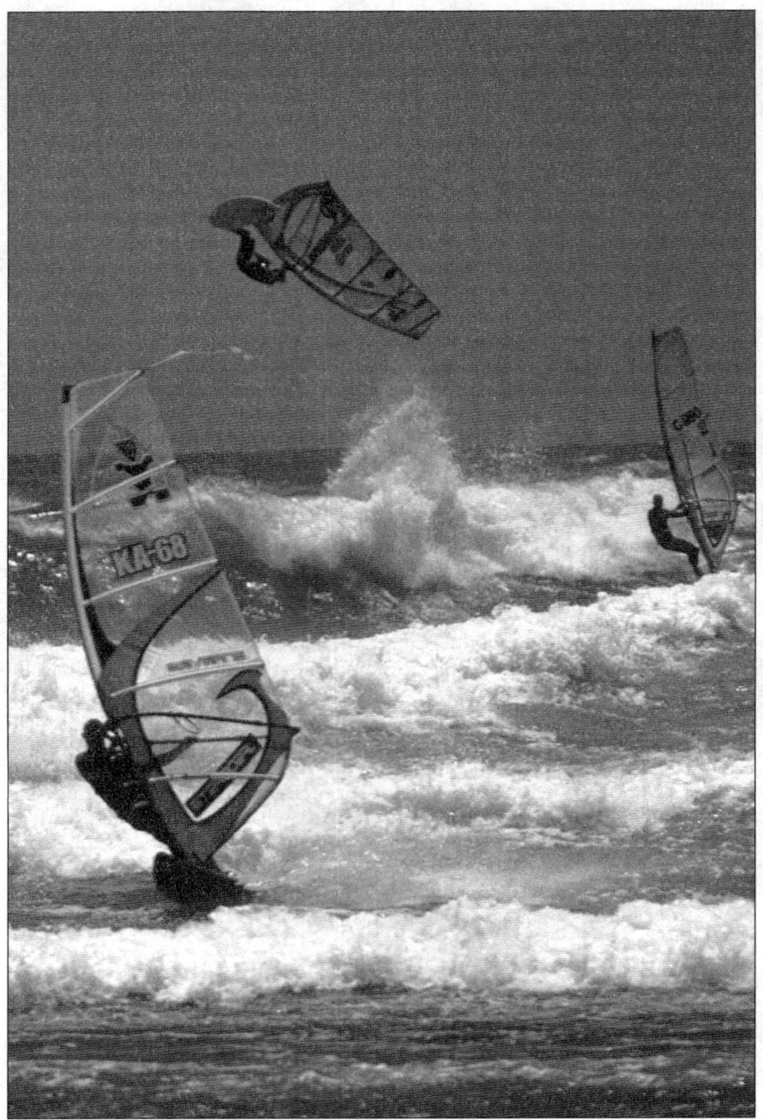

△ The Lancelin Ocean Classic windsurfing competition, Western Australia

(Ⓣ08/9654 8034, Ⓦwww.newnorcia.wa.edu.au; ❸) don't quite match the building's grand exterior, but they still offer an old-fashioned treat. The two-kilometre New Norcia **heritage trail** (guide leaflet available from the tourist office or museum; $5.50) begins here and takes you on a circuit past the community's impressive buildings.

The two most ornate buildings, on either side of the cemetery, are **St Gertrude's Residence for Girls** and **St Ildephonsus's for Boys**, the latter with striking Moorish minarets. Among other buildings, you can also visit the **Flour Mills** and the Abbey Church – both relatively ordinary in comparison, although you'll find the wood-fired **bread** made at the mills in Perth's best restaurants and at the retail outlet at 163 Scarborough Beach Rd, Mt Lawley.

Several bus-tour companies offer **day-trips** from Perth to New Norcia (see p.724), which is otherwise served only three times a week by Transco's rural bus service.

Toodyay

The old town of **TOODYAY**, set among the wooded hills of the Avon Valley, 85km northwest of Perth, makes an agreeable diversion on the way to – or from – New Norcia. The town was founded in 1836, making it one of the earliest inland settlements of the Swan River Colony, and a few buildings survive from that era. The **tourist office** (Mon–Sat 9am–5pm, Sun 10am–5pm; ⓣ08/9574 2435) is situated by the station behind **Connor's Mill** on Stirling Terrace, the town's main road. The mill houses a **museum** ($2.50), as does the **Old Newcastle Gaol** just over the rails on Clinton Street (Mon–Fri 10am–3pm, Sat & Sun 10am–4pm; $2). Other historic buildings include the riverside **St Stephen's Church**, opposite the mill, as well as the former Mechanics' Institute – now the **library** – on Stirling Terrace.

Guildford and the Swan Valley

North of the town of **GUILDFORD**, a thirty-minute drive northeast of Perth, is the **Upper Swan Valley** – WA's oldest wine-growing region. It makes for a pleasant day's **wine-tasting**, although the wines produced here reputedly don't match those of the Margaret River region, which themselves are not considered Australia's finest. **Guildford** itself is a historic town dating back to the earliest years of the colony, with several federation-era grand hotels to admire and Guildford Village Potters, at 22 Meadow St, acting as the town's **tourist office** (Mon–Fri 10am–3pm, Sat & Sun 10am–4pm; ⓣ08/9379 9400, ⓦwww.swanvalley.com.au). If you're heading up into the valley, pick up the *Swan Valley Wineries* guide from here, which details the area's attractions and its three-dozen or so wineries.

The Swan Valley Drive

Heading north from Guildford Village Potters, a clearly marked thirty-kilometre drive follows the west side of the river. Turning left down Banera Road will bring you to **Pinelli Wines** on Bennett Road (Mon–Sat 9am–6pm, Sun 10am–5pm), which offers two-litre flagons of decent table wine from $15. Further up Route 203, the **Little River Winery & Café** (daily 10am–5.30pm) is a small, independent winery with some award-winning wines and a pleasant café in which to enjoy them.

Driving down the valley's east side, several more wineries tempt you in: **Talijancich Wines** (Sun–Fri 11am–5pm), produces a rich muscat, while **Houghton's**, on Dale Road (daily 10am–5pm), is the area's biggest and most diverse producer of wines, with an art gallery and tended lawns on which to contemplate your tastings. The route returns to Guildford via Midland and thence to Perth, passing the Toodyay Road, which winds up into the Darling Ranges. For Swan Valley tours see p.724.

York

Stranded in the Avon Valley, 97km from Perth via the Great Southern Highway, **YORK** looks like a film set for an Australian western. The town is the state's most complete pioneering settlement, filled with attractive and well-preserved early architecture. The commercial centre of the Avon Valley until the railway – and with it the Great Eastern Highway – bypassed it 30km to the north, York is now an agricultural centre but also plays a historic role as a venerable museum of ornate nineteenth-century public buildings, coaching inns and churches. Be warned though: this inland region regularly bakes at 40°C in mid-summer.

The **Old York Gaol & Courthouse** (Tues–Sun noon–4pm; $3.50) on Avon Terrace harks back to the town's pioneer history while the **York Motor Museum** (daily 9.30am–4pm; $7.50), opposite the tourist office on Avon Terrace, capitalizes on York's antiquarian charisma with a large collection of vintage and classic vehicles – from a hundred-year-old single-cylinder tricycle to Ossie Cranston's 1936 Ford V8 racer. At the north end of the terrace are the **Sandalwood Yards**, where the perfumed wood – once prolific in WA and highly prized in the Orient – was stored during York's heyday. Near here you can take a walk down to the wobbly **suspension bridge** spanning the generally sluggish Avon River and take a look at the 1854 **Holy Trinity Church**, with its modern stained-glass designs by Robert Juniper, one of WA's foremost artists.

Practicalities

York's **tourist office** (daily 9am–5pm; ⓣ08/9641 1301, ⓦwww.yorktouristbureau.com.au) is at 105 Avon Terrace, the main road on which most of York's fine old buildings are located. A **town map** and information sheet is available here, which locates and briefly describes all of these structures as well as listing places to stay and eat. The *Imperial Inn*, 83 Avon Terrace (ⓣ08/9641 1010; ❹), is a restored, century-old **hotel** full of old-world charm, while the pricier *Castle Hotel* (ⓣ08/9641 1007; ❹) is even more splendid. There are several B&Bs in and around town; ask at the tourist office or check out their website.

The Southwest

The region south of Perth and west of the Albany Highway, known as **the Southwest**, is the temperate corner of the continent, where the cool Southern and warm Indian oceans meet to drop heavy winter rains. North of **Bunbury**, 180km from Perth, is a knot of industrial installations and satellite or retirement towns such as Rockingham and Mandurah; suburbs which offer little of interest to the visitor compared to what's ahead. South of Bunbury things improve greatly. The **Margaret River region** is WA's most popular holiday destination, famed for its wineries and surf. To the southeast is the so-called **Tall Timber Country**: towns set amid the remnants of the giant karri forests, offering a chance to experience one of the world's last stands of temperate old-growth forest.

At its best in spring and outside school holidays (dates on p.714), the Southwest's lush bucolic scenery is all the more appealing in that it can be enjoyed without donning a hat, water bottle and sunblock while swatting away flies, an experience augmented by several commendably untacky **galleries** and **woodcraft studios** displaying the work of local artisans, from boardroom tables to salad tongs – and at prices (even with overseas shipping) that are worth consideration.

There is also better-quality, and more varied **accommodation** in this region than the rest of the state put together and, backpackers' apart, the recommendations given below barely scratch the surface. Make the most of the tourist offices, and the large portfolios many of them have illustrating local places to stay.

South West Coach Lines serves Augusta via Margaret River and Busselton and Bunbury, as well as Collie, Donnybrook, Bridgetown and Manjimup. Transco has a similar provincial **bus** service as well as 28-day unlimited-travel **bus passes** for around $155, but the best way to get about is with a **car**, making use of Perth's inexpensive rental agencies. Expect to cover at least 2000km in a typical week's tour as far as Albany and note that some attractions and scenic drives take in unsealed roads which are probably not permitted in your rental contract.

An alternative is to follow parts of the **Bibbulmun Track**, a long-distance path which winds down 963km from Kalamunda, east of Perth, to Albany on the south coast. The full trek takes six to eight weeks, but some of the best sections of the track are found between the coastal inlets around Walpole and the forests and pastures south of Bunbury. You'll find more on the "Bib Track" at Ⓦwww.bibbulmuntrack.org.au.

Designated the "Mountain bikers' Bib", the **Munda Biddi Trail** (Ⓦwww.mundabiddi.org.au) is also lined with camp shelters and follows a similar route; south from Mundaring, 40km east of Perth, to Northcliffe, with the final stage to Albany soon to be completed in the next year or two.

Bunbury

Described as the capital of the Southwest, **BUNBURY**, the state's second-largest population centre, is clearly prosperous and content, but not the sort of place you'd cross oceans to see. A day's dallying here on the way south offers a chance to commune with the **dolphins** (found around The Cut on Leschenault Inlet, and in the inlets around Mandurah and Rockingham). It's a lot more fun than traipsing all the way up to Monkey Mia, although offering slightly less predictable sightings. They've made a better interpretive job of the Dolphin Discovery Centre too, situated on the beach off Koombana Drive (daily 8am–5pm; $4; Ⓣ08/9791 3088). Tours allow interaction with the dolphins from a boat ($35), or even by swimming with them, and there are also whale-watching trips in the summer months ($45).

Daily **bus services** from Perth (3hr) drop you at the well-stocked **tourist office** (Mon–Sat 9am–5pm, Sun 9.30am–4.30pm; Ⓣ08/9721 7922) in the old train station on Carmody Place. Shuttle buses to the town operate regularly from the **train station**, 3km from the centre, during the day and otherwise usually meet evening arrivals. The train from Perth takes two hours.

There is plenty of **accommodation** in and around town which includes the *Wander Inn* at 16 Clifton St (Ⓣ08/9721 3242, Ⓦwww.bunburybackpackers.com.au; dorms $20, rooms ❸), off Victoria Street, the main road. This is a nice backpackers' to hang out in after seeing the dolphins, and has bikes, boogie-boards and local tours available. On Molloy Street (on the corner with Clifton Street), you'll find the federation-era-style *Clifton* (Ⓣ08/9721 4300, Ⓦwww.theclifton.com.au; ❺), while the elegant *Rose Hotel* (Ⓣ08/9721 4533; ❺) on Victoria Street boasts a reasonable restaurant and a large range

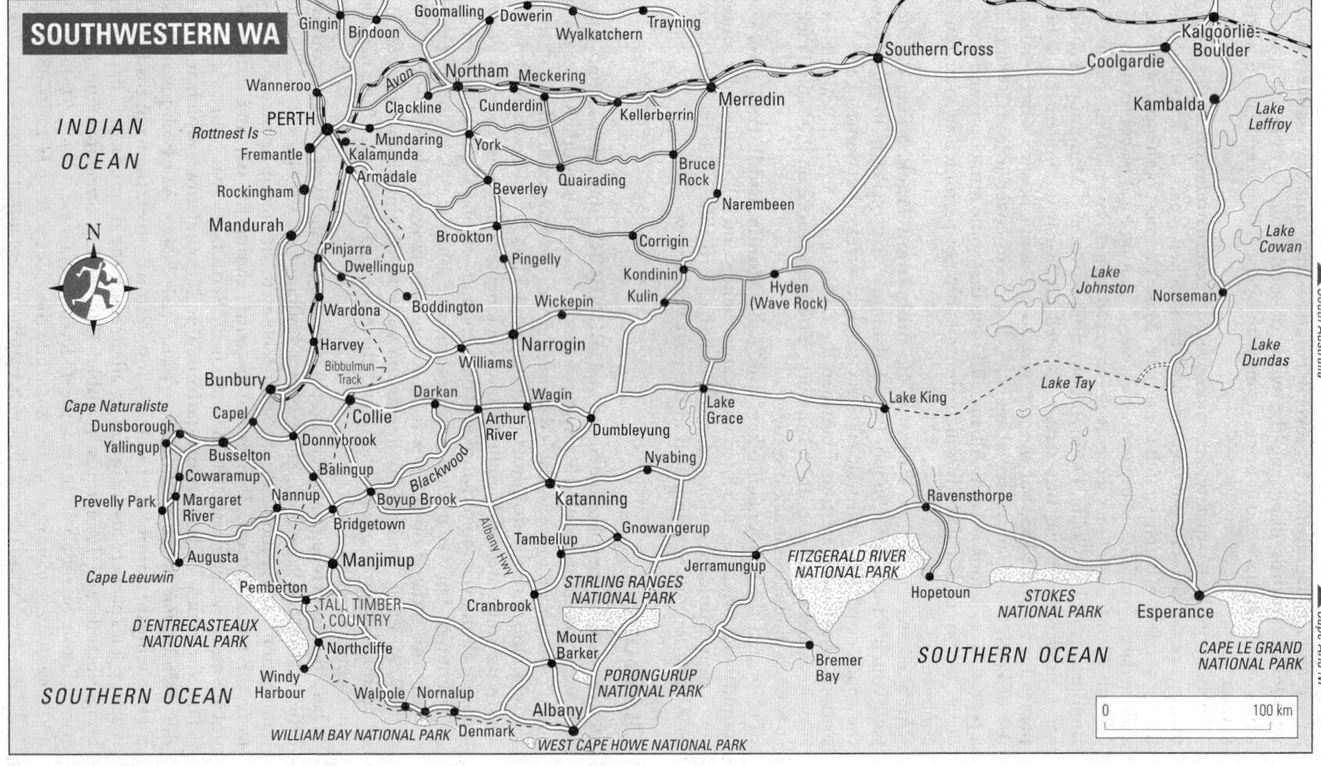
SOUTHWESTERN WA
Kanowna, Broad Arrow & Ora Banda
South Australia
Cape Arid NP
INDIAN OCEAN
SOUTHERN OCEAN
SOUTHERN OCEAN
N
Gingin
Bindoon
Goomalling
Dowerin
Wyalkatchern
Trayning
Southern Cross
Coolgardie
Kalgoorlie-Boulder
Kambalda
Lake Leffroy
Lake Cowan
Lake Johnston
Norseman
Lake Dundas
Lake Tay
Lake King
Wanneroo
PERTH
Rottnest Is
Fremantle
Rockingham
Mandurah
Avon
Northam
Meckering
Clackline
Cunderdin
Kellerberrin
Merredin
Mundaring
Kalamunda
York
Armadale
Quairading
Bruce Rock
Narembeen
Beverley
Brookton
Corrigin
Pingelly
Kondinin
Kulin
Hyden (Wave Rock)
Pinjarra
Dwellingup
Boddington
Wickepin
Wardona
Harvey
Bibbulmun Track
Williams
Narrogin
Bunbury
Darkan
Wagin
Lake Grace
Cape Naturaliste
Capel
Collie
Arthur River
Dumbleyung
Dunsborough
Yallingup
Busselton
Donnybrook
Nyabing
Cowaramup
Balingup
Blackwood
Prevelly Park
Margaret River
Nannup
Boyup Brook
Katanning
Ravensthorpe
Bridgetown
Albany Hwy
Gnowangerup
Tambellup
Augusta
Cape Leeuwin
Manjimup
Jerramungup
FITZGERALD RIVER NATIONAL PARK
Hopetoun
STOKES NATIONAL PARK
Esperance
Pemberton
TALL TIMBER COUNTRY
Cranbrook
STIRLING RANGES NATIONAL PARK
D'ENTRECASTEAUX NATIONAL PARK
Northcliffe
Mount Barker
Bremer Bay
CAPE LE GRAND NATIONAL PARK
Windy Harbour
Walpole
Nornalup
PORONGURUP NATIONAL PARK
Albany
0
100 km
WILLIAM BAY NATIONAL PARK
Denmark
WEST CAPE HOWE NATIONAL PARK

of boutique beers. There are plenty of sidewalk **cafés** and **restaurants** along Victoria Street.

Geographe Bay to Cape Naturaliste

South of Bunbury, the Bussell Highway curves west around **Geographe Bay** to **BUSSELTON**, named after a prominent pioneering family. The sprawling holiday town, sheltered from the ocean's currents and swells, is a popular "bucket and spade" resort where parents can be sure their kids won't inadvertently go searching for Nemo while splashing about. The town's foremost attraction is its famously long **jetty** (Ⓦwww.busseltonjetty.com.au; pedestrian access $2.50; jetty train $7.50, departs on the hour) right by the Fantasy Castle. With well over a century of maritime growth and soft corals adorning the two-kilometre-long jetty's supports, the **underwater observatory** (daily 9am–6pm; $12.50, or $20 with train ride) paints a vibrant picture of aquatic activity 8m below the surface.

Out of town the highway turns south towards Margaret River, though continuing west brings you to the small resort town of **DUNSBOROUGH**, 21km from Busselton. There's a YHA **hostel** (Ⓣ08/9755 3107, Ⓔdunsborough@yhawa.com.au; dorms $22, rooms ❸), 2km southeast of town (get off the bus at Quindalup) which is right on the beach. In the centre, the *Dunsborough Inn*, 50 Dunn Bay Rd (Ⓣ08/9756 7277, Ⓦwww.dunsboroughinn.com; dorms $20, rooms ❸–❹), has good-value, self-contained units and motel rooms. A step up in quality is the *Dunsborough Central Motel* (Ⓣ08/9756 7711 or 1800 097 711, Ⓦwww.dunscentralmotel.com.au; ❺), on the corner of Caves Road and Seymour Boulevard, which is also the town's only **pub**. Among other places *Café Ibis*, across the road from the post office, has interesting if pricey **meals**. With its sheltered position and minimal tides, Geographe Bay is ideal for **diving** – all the more so since the scuttling of the old *Swan* warship in 1997 in 30m of water (see p.78). Cape Dive, 222 Naturaliste Terrace, Dunsborough (Ⓣ08/9756 8778, Ⓦwww.capedive.com), is one of the dive outfitters visiting this and other dive sites in the bay.

Cape Naturaliste itself, 14km northwest of the resort, is the less impressive of the two capes which define the Margaret River region. Its truncated **lighthouse** (Mon & Wed–Sun 9.30am–4.30pm; $5) is open for inspection, and along the way there are turn-offs to secluded beaches and coves.

Along Caves Road to Margaret River and Cape Leeuwin

South of Dunsborough you head into the **Margaret River region** proper, characterized by caves, wineries, choice restaurants and snug hideaways all interspersed with woodcraft galleries, glass-blowing studios, potteries – and lots of fellow tourists. They've made sure there's plenty to see, do, taste and spend your money on here, but the region tends to dominate people's idea of the Southwest – delve a little deeper and you'll find plenty more out there.

Passing **Ngilgi Cave** you come to the turn-off for **YALLINGUP**, a small seaside resort with a lovely clean beach, populated by surfers bobbing around waiting for the big one. **Caves Road** leads south from here, passing the Gunyulgup Gallery (daily 10am–5pm), which has a particularly fine selection of pottery, glass, paintings and furniture by local artisans, and a lovely restaurant overlooking a lake. *Yallingup Forest Resort* (Ⓣ08/9755 2550, Ⓦwww.yallingupforestresort.com.au; ❻) on Hemsley Road, off Caves Road, would suit an extended stay in the area, offering large, self-contained chalets which sleep four, and the use of a pool and tennis court. The site also hosts the **Wicked Ale Brewery** (daily except Tues 10am–5pm; Ⓣ08/9755 2848) where chilli and chocolate beer, as well as the riveting "Bad Frog Citrus" variety are on tap. *Caves House Hotel* (Ⓣ08/9755 2131, Ⓦwww.caveshouse.com.au; ➎) is an inviting lodge dating from the 1930s, in the middle of town on Yallingup Beach Road.

Back on Caves Road a right turn leads, after 3km, to **Canal Rocks**, where the waves relentlessly pound the pink-granite outcrops into curious, scalloped forms. Further south are more turn-offs to the winery at **Abbey Vale Estate** (daily 10am–5pm) and **Bootleg Brewery** (daily 10am–4.30pm), which cheekily claims to be "a beer oasis in a desert of wine". Lager lovers should try the award-winning *Raging Bull* and *Wills Pils* brews but those intent on visiting some of the four-score wineries (and breweries) in the region should pick up the *Margaret River Regional Vineyard Guide* or the *Regional Map and Guide* from the Margaret River tourist office. With a new winery said to be opening somewhere in Australia every three days, you can rest assured that the choice is getting greater year by year.

Further down Caves Road you come to the crossroads leading 5km inland to the Margaret River township, while a right turn takes you to the oceanside resort of **PREVELLY PARK**, close to the estuary of the Margaret River. The Greek **Chapel of St John** will catch your eye: a memorial to the Preveli Monastery on Crete which sheltered Allied soldiers, Australians among them, in World War II. The turning opposite leads down to the blustery Prevelly beach where November's annual Margaret River Classic **surfing** championships are held.

Back at the chapel, the road continues down into the **resort**, where a boom in sea-view property over the last few years has seen private houses outnumber holiday chalets and caravan parks. With a better location than most, the spacious and well-equipped *Surfpoint Resort*, on Reidle Drive (Ⓣ08/9757 1777 or 1800 071 777, Ⓦwww.surfpoint.com.au; dorms $24, en-suite rooms ➍), is the best backpackers' in the region and does free pick-ups from Margaret River if you call ahead.

Margaret River

The wine-lovers' resort town of **MARGARET RIVER** and the surrounding region has been adopted by Perthian gastronomes as their weekend retreat from the urban rat race. Shared with a mix of docile holiday-makers, partying wave-riders and tourists drawn in by the hype, this buzzing town is handy for shopping (supermarket open till 9pm), eating out and browsing for crafty knick-knacks, though you may not want to stay here if it's rural bliss you're seeking. The **tourist office** (daily 9am–5pm; Ⓣ08/9757 2911, Ⓦwww.margaretriver.com), at the downhill end of the main road, embodies the swish, self-confident ethos of its preferred clientele, and can book you straight into accommodation and wineries, and also onto tours. Transco and South West Coach Lines **buses** visit daily from Perth, while local-guided wine-tasting **tours** with outfits like Wine For Dudes (Ⓣ08/9758 8699, Ⓦwww.winefordudes.com) cost from around $55. Bushtucker Tours (Ⓣ08/9757 1084, Ⓦwww.bushtuckertours.com; $55) offer just that from a canoe at the river mouth on Prevelly Beach, and the Margaret River Surf School (Ⓣ08/9757 1111, Ⓔmargaretriversurfschool@hotmail.com) gives daily two-hour lessons for $40 or a three-day course for around $95.

Apart from the two main backpackers', the range of **accommodation** is daunting, with scores of options in the immediate vicinity. The woodland settings out of town are the ones to go for; the tourist office has a big portfolio full of ideas. The reputation of the *Inne Town* backpackers' (ⓣ08/9757 3698; dorms $19, rooms ❸), down the road from the tourist office, seems to go up and down, while the purpose-built *Margaret River Lodge* (ⓣ08/9757 9532, ⓦwww.mrlodge.com.au; dorms $20, en-suite rooms ❹), 2km out on Railway Terrace, has a vast array of rooms, a pool and a volleyball court in spacious grounds, even if the location is a bit residential. All in all you might prefer *Surfpoint Resort* at Prevelly, out by the beach (see above). Those whose "dorming" days are behind them might prefer one of the three variously appointed *Bushy's Dream Cottages* (ⓣ08/9758 7130, ⓔbushysdreamcottages@bigpond.com; ❺), or *Bushy Lake Chalets* nearby (ⓣ08/9757 9677, ⓦwww.bushylake.com.au; ❺), on Rockboro Road 4km west of town. Note that around here many places charge a bit more on weekends when the place teems with polo-necked *bon viveurs*, and some insist on either a weekend's stay or minimum booking during holiday periods (see dates p.714). The *Margaret River* (ⓣ08/9757 2180; on-site vans ❸) and *Riverview* (ⓣ08/9757 2270; on-site vans ❸) **caravan parks** are both just a kilometre out of town.

The countryside surrounding Margaret River is dotted with charming **restaurants**, often attached to wineries, galleries or lodges. In town, and all situated along the main road, the best places to eat include *Goodfellas* for wood-fired pizzas, *Mammas* or *Margaret River Fish and Chips*. *VAT 107* is the town's premier gourmet restaurant for local seafood dishes or you can join the young crowd at *Settlers*, the town's main **pub**, which puts on live music in summer.

Augusta and Cape Leeuwin

Five kilometres southwest of Margaret River, on Boodjidup Road, one of the more interesting attractions vying for your attention is **Eagles Heritage** (daily 10am–5pm; $10; ⓦwww.eaglesheritage.com.au), a fascinating collection of birds of prey. Aviaries house huge wedge-tail and white-breasted sea eagles, peregrine falcons and a selection of owls.

Rejoining Caves Road, having passed the turning for the **Leeuwin Winery** (daily 10am–4.30pm) with its art gallery and restaurant, you head south into the silvery-barked **karri forest**. It's a magnificent sight and one well worth taking some time to appreciate, if you're not planning to visit Pemberton. Down the road are Mammoth and Lake caves (see box on p.740). If you visited the latter cave and noticed the stream that trickles out of its subterranean lake, you can catch up with it at the spring on **Cowup Bay** beach, 4km from the cave entrance along a dirt road, and with a campsite on the way. Back on Caves Road, Boranup Drive takes an off-road detour through the **Boranup Forest**, a great place for biking and riding, while *Boranup Gallery and Chalets* (ⓣ08/9757 7585, ⓦwww.boranupgallery.com; ❼) sells local art and gorgeous **furniture** made from local timbers, and offers accommodation in self-contained, rammed-earth **chalets** in bushland settings.

South of the forest, the Brockman Highway leads 90km east to Nannup, while continuing 3km south down Caves Road brings you to a turn-off to the old timber port of **Hamelin Bay**, which has a couple of shipwrecks that are ideal for snorkellers and scuba divers. There's a beachside **caravan park** (cabins ❸), which also offers bikes for rent.

Passing **Jewel Cave**, the Bussell Highway takes you 8km further to the small town of **AUGUSTA**, on the estuary of the Blackwood River – WA's oldest settlement after Albany and Perth. Little remains from those days, although the **museum** (daily: June–Sept 10am–noon; Oct–May 9am–5pm; $3) on Blackwood Avenue, the main road, retains some old relics and is more absorbing than you might expect. The **tourist office** (daily: June–Sept 10am–noon;

Margaret River caves

A band of limestone passing through the cape has created some 350 **caves** around Margaret River, four of which are open to the public. Most involve guided tours to avoid damage and accidents, with relatively high entrance fees and shuffling crowds rather detracting from the cavernous spectacle. Nevertheless, a visit to the region would be incomplete without seeing at least one. All are humid and include some long, stepped ascents, with temperatures around 17°C. Tours are less frequent from May to August – for more details about all except Ngilgi Cave, enquire at the tourist office in either Margaret River or Augusta. The **Cave Works Interpretive Centre** at Lake Cave (daily 10am–5pm; $3; ⓣ08/9757 7411) sells a **Grand Tour pass** for $40, which includes entry to Lake, Jewel and Mammoth caves; it also offers special discount options to visit all the caves except Ngilgi.

Jewel Cave (daily 9.30am–4pm; 7–12 tours per day, 60 min; $16). The best cave, featuring extraordinary and fragile formations such as five-metre "helictites" (delicate, straw-like formations) protected by breeze-proof doors. Also includes a two-hour tour of **Moondyne Cave** (daily at 2pm; $20, equipment supplied, maximum 10 people), a mildly adventurous and less rushed excursion with some belly crawling, although you won't miss any amazing features by not taking the tour. Enclosed footwear is compulsory.

Lake Cave (daily 9.30am–4pm; 7–12 tours per day, 45min; $16). A collapsed cavern, overgrown with huge karri trees, is the impressive entrance to the cave, where a unique "suspended table" hangs over the subterranean lake. The cave is also the site of the Cave Works Interpretive Centre (see above), dealing with all things speleological.

Mammoth Cave (daily 9am–4pm; self-guiding; $16). Large cavern and easy access, with some bones and fossils of extinct creatures inside; it would really be your last choice.

Ngilgi Cave (daily 9.30am–4.30pm; $16). Not visited on the cave tours but with plenty of nooks to explore and delicate features to admire.

Oct–May 9am–5pm; ⓣ08/9758 0166, ⓦwww.augusta-wa.com.au) is on Ellis Street. On Blackwood Avenue, the *Augusta Motel* (ⓣ08/9758 1944, ⓦwww.augusta-resorts.com.au; ❹) has great river views, as well as backpackers' dorms from $22. On the same road, the pristine *Baywatch Manor* (ⓣ08/9758 1290, ⓦwww.baywatchmanor.com.au), offers quality backpackers' accommodation for $22, self-contained chalets (❹) and also rents bikes and canoes. *Doonbanks Caravan Park* (on-site vans ❷, cabins ❷) is further up the road, and there are two more caravan parks south of town. You can **eat** at the *Colonial Restaurant* on the main road, or at the *Augusta Moon* Chinese restaurant on Allnutt Terrace.

Cape Leeuwin, 9km south of town, is probably why you've come this far, and it's worth the journey, giving a bleak, windswept "land's end" feel to this corner of Australia, especially on a mean and moody day. A Dutch captain named the cape after his ship in 1622, and Matthew Flinders began the onerous task of mapping Australia's coast right here, at the bottom left corner, in 1851. From the top of the still-working **lighthouse** (daily 9am–4pm; tours every 45min; $8), built in 1895, you can contemplate your position – halfway between the equator and the Antarctic coast. Nearby, an **old water wheel**, originally constructed for the lighthouse builders and now petrified in salt, is a well-known landmark.

Hikers may want to consider the 140-kilometre Cape Leeuwin to Cape Naturaliste **coastal walk**, though the less adventurous can tackle its five sections individually. The CALM office in Busselton (Ⓣ08/9752 1677) has detailed information on this, while the Cape Leeuwin lighthouse store has maps and advice.

Tall Timber Country

Sandwiched between the popular tourist areas of the Margaret River region and Albany's dramatic coast, the forests of the so-called **Tall Timber Country** are one of WA's greatest sights. Along with the sinuous **Blackwood River** (ideal for sedate canoeing, especially downstream of Nannup, below), the highlight of the region is the brooding, primeval majesty of the **karri forests**, known not as much for their arboreal gimmicks – of which the "climb-if-you-dare" **Gloucester Tree** near Pemberton is the best-known – as for the raw, elemental nature of the unique forest environment. Since the practice of literally tearing down or "clear-felling" the irreplaceable ancient forests was greatly reduced in 2001 (see box below), logging towns like Pemberton and Manjimup are adjusting to an economy based around sustainable tree plantations and tourism. Check out Ⓦwww.southernforests.com.au for further details on this area as far as Walpole.

The Blackwood River Valley and south

The northern part of the forest country is watered by the **Blackwood River** and divided by scenic roads which link the riverside mill towns. Though once a notoriously insular loggers' town which in the late-hippy era earned comparisons with New South Wales' Nimbin, these days **NANNUP**, 60km southeast of Busselton, is an idyllic settlement of wooden cabins nestling quietly among wooded hills. The **tourist office** (daily 9am–5pm; Ⓣ08/9756 1211, Ⓦwww.nannupwa.com.au) is on Brockman Street and has a portfolio of local **accommodation**. Set in a glorious permaculture garden, the *Black Cockatoo Traveller's Retreat* on Grange Road (Ⓣ08/9756 1035, Ⓦwww.blackcockatoo.nannup.net; dorms $20, rooms ❷) has no Internet or TV, bikes or tour desk, but is a haven of tranquillity in a class of its own. On the hill behind the *Cockatoo* is the smart and child-free B&B, *Holberry House* (Ⓣ08/9756 1276, Ⓦwww.holberryhouse.com; ❺), while lost among the jarrah 6km northwest of town, the *Nannup Bush Cabins* (Ⓣ08/9756 1170; ❹) are enchantingly situated hideaways.

Logging in Tall Timber Country

After a century and a half, the controversial logging of the Southwest's irreplaceable **old-growth forest** officially came to an end in 2001. Public debate over logging, and the sell-off of old-growth forests by CALM (the government department which also looks after WA's parks) to logging mills had grown ever more intense throughout the 1990s. Campaigners criticized CALM's sell-off as a display of mind-boggling environmental short-sightedness, pointing out that the centuries-old trees of old-growth forest predate colonization, and support a complex ecological system. As you explore the area along scenic drives you may assume the forest looks healthy and dense, but at times you're travelling in a 200m tree-lined corridor, outside of which lies an area still devastated by old-growth clear-felling. Quick to capitalize on a vote-winning issue, Labour won the 2001 state election by promising to outlaw the logging of old-growth forests. Some backtracking followed and loopholes remain, but since that time the recession predicted in the logging industry has not materialized, and fast-growing plantations of blue gum trees (aka Tasmanian oak) have been found to offer a viable future to sustainable plantation logging in WA.

The *Blackwood Café* opens all day for big breakfasts or local fish, or try the *Mulberry Café* up the road for something fancier. If not walking, then a great way to enjoy the region is in a **canoe**. Blackwood Canoeing (Ⓣ08/9756 1209, Ⓔblackwoodrivercanoeing@wn.com.au) have their own bush camp and offer self-guided one- to three-day **trips** on the lower Blackwood River, starting 27km south of town, from $35 a day. River levels vary with the seasons, making the overnight trips easier in the summer months.

From Nannup, a **scenic drive** winds 41km along the river to unremarkable Balingup, while the no less tree-lined Brockman Highway heads east 46km to **BRIDGETOWN**, a busy mill town with a large **tourist office** (daily 9am–5pm; Ⓣ08/9761 1740) on Hampton Street. Despite some token tea and craft shops, Bridgetown is really a place to get your ute serviced or chainsaw sharpened. By the river, where some pleasant bankside walks begin, the National Trust property of **Bridgedale House** (Mon & Thurs–Sun 10am–4pm; $5) rents out **canoes**.

Thirty-seven kilometres south of Bridgetown, **MANJIMUP** is the region's commercial centre, handy for shopping and other services but, apart from a visit to the **Timber Park** (daily 9am–5pm), behind the **tourist office** (daily 8.30am–5.30pm; Ⓣ08/9771 1831) on Rose Street (they both celebrate the local timber industry), it has little appeal. Graphite Road is a picturesque forest drive heading west 22km to **One Tree Bridge** and – after another couple of kilometres – to the magnificent **Four Aces**, a quartet of huge 350-year-old karri trees standing in a row. With a detailed map it's possible to spend all day driving around these gravelly and winding logging roads, but should you head south to Pemberton along the surfaced road you'll pass a turn-off to the **Diamond Tree**, where you can climb a fifty-metre lookout tree for free.

Pemberton and around

Though there may be quainter towns in the region, **PEMBERTON** is the most central base for Tall Timber touring. You'll find the **tourist office** (daily 9am–5pm; Ⓣ08/9776 1133, Ⓦwww.pembertontourist.com.au) halfway up the hill on Brockman Street, where you can pick up the *Pemberton–Northcliffe* map and guide ($1), as well as information on **horse riding**, **canoe** and **bike rental**, local **tours** and maps of **day-hikes** in the area, including part of the Bibbulmun Track. Behind here, the interactive Karri Forest Discovery Centre (daily 9am–5pm; donation) replicates the forest environment.

On Dickinson Street, Fine Woodcraft is one of the best craft galleries in the Southwest with everything you see, including the building itself, made from old-growth timber, either reclaimed or rejected by the mills. If you're interested, the owner can bring you up to date on the logging debate. A fun way of enjoying the surrounding forest is to take the **tram** (Ⓣ08/9776 1322, Ⓦwww.pemtram.com.au; from $14) from Pemberton to Warren Bridge (2 daily; 1hr 45min return) or better still as far as Northcliffe (Tues, Thurs & Sat; 5hr 30min return). The diesel tram rattles noisily along the old logging railway, over rustic timber bridges spanning tiny creeks, and visits the **Cascades**, a local beauty spot also accessible by road. In summer there's also a weekend **steam train** service up to Lyall Sidings, north of town.

The region's single most popular attraction is the **Gloucester Tree** (CALM fee; see box on p.714), situated on a clearly signposted road 3km southeast of town. At 61m, it's the world's tallest fire-lookout tree and its platform is accessible by climbing a spiral of horizontal stakes. Only a quarter of those who visit the tree actually climb up to the platform – the climb itself being more satisfying than the actual view.

The countryside all around is crisscrossed with peaceful walking trails and enchanting forest drives which venture deep into the karri woodlands. From **Beedelup National Park**, on the Vasse Highway 20km west of town, there's a short walk to a wobbly suspension bridge over **Beedelup Falls**, while the drive through the native karri forests of the **Warren National Park**, 10km southwest of town, will leave you in awe of these huge trees. The specially signed, 86km **Karri Forest Explorer** is a scenic drive that winds past many of the above attractions on a mixture of dirt and sealed roads. Otherwise, Pemberton Hiking and Canoeing (ⓣ08/9776 1559, ⓔpenhike@wn.com.au) or Pemberton Discovery Tours (ⓣ08/9776 0484, ⓔpdt@wn.com.au) can take you out for a day-trip which includes the D'Entrecasteaux dunes (see below).

As for **accommodation**, the *YHA Forest Stay* at Pimelea (ⓣ08/9776 1153, ⓔpemberton@yhawa.com.au; dorms $22, rooms ❷), 10km northwest of town, is a clutch of basic woodman's cabins with free pick-ups from town as well as bike rental. In town, *Pemberton Backpackers* (ⓣ08/9776 1105, ⓦwww.pembertonbackpackers.com.au; dorms $22, rooms ❸), right by the bus stop, has comfy doubles and a self-contained cottage (❸). Otherwise, besides the couple of motels in town (❹), the surrounding countryside abounds with tranquil self-contained woodland retreats, like *Karri Valley Hideaway Cottages* (ⓣ08/9776 2049, ⓦwww.karrivalleyhideaway.com.au; ❻), 21km west of town, or *Treenbrook Cottages* (ⓣ08/9776 1638, ⓦwww.treenbrook.com.au; ❺), 5km west, or the dozen or so rammed-earth cottages set among the *Warren River Resort* (ⓣ08/9776 1400, ⓦwww.warrenriverresort.com.au; ❺), off the Northcliffe road, 9km to the southwest. Campers can stay at the town's central **caravan park** (ⓣ08/9776 1300; cabins and five-bed cottages from ❹) or at any of the CALM-approved **campsites** in the surrounding forests. There are a couple of restaurants and cafés in town, but for trout or marron (freshwater crayfish), both local delicacies, try the restaurant at the *Eagle Springs Trout Hatchery*, signposted north of town.

Northcliffe and D'Entrecasteaux National Park

Thirty kilometres south of Pemberton, **NORTHCLIFFE** is a small, untouristed logging town (there's a hotel and caravan park with on-site vans ❷) while to the southwest is the long spread of coastal heathland and inland dunes making up the mostly inaccessible **D'Entrecasteaux National Park**. Driving south of Northcliffe you emerge from the forest and onto the heathland, passing a short steep walk up 187-metre Mount Chudalup for views of the Southern Ocean breaking against Sandy Island, which is 30km south of Northcliffe, just off **WINDY HARBOUR**. The tidy but seemingly deserted settlement has about fifteen permanent residents, no services and a few dozen weatherboard holiday homes. As long as you're suitably equipped, a grassy **campsite** in the centre of the hamlet makes an inviting stopover. West of the main bay you can walk to a broader, slightly more sheltered beach, also accessible from a car park off Old Lighthouse Road, a dead-end which leads west out of the settlement. From here it's possible to walk the 2km up the clifftop to **Point D'Entrecasteaux**, where a platform hangs out over the pounding surf below. You can also reach the Point in your car by following the Salmon Beach turn-off just before Windy Harbour. **Salmon Beach** itself is a wild, exposed strand below Point D'Entrecasteaux, facing the prevailing southwesterlies and therefore good for a hair-tussling stroll.

Albany and the southern coast

The alternating sheltered bays and rounded granite headlands of the **southern coast** or "Great Southern", around **Albany** were the site of WA's original colonial settlement. As elsewhere in the Southwest, the temperate climate (and changeable weather) creates a rural antipodean-English idyll unknown in the rest of WA, with wineries, craft galleries and tasteful restaurants.

Albany, 410km from Perth, is an agricultural centre and holiday destination, while **Denmark**, 54km to the west, is a twee, arty hamlet. **Walpole**'s bays and tingle forests mark the western limit of the southern coast. An hour's drive north of Albany lie the burgeoning wine-making region of Mount Barker and the mountainous **Porongurup** and **Stirling Ranges national parks**.

Perth's radial **bus services** to the main centres run on a frequent basis, but moving around by bus requires some planning to avoid inconvenient delays. Transco buses depart from Perth for Albany at least daily, either directly down the Albany Highway (6hr) or four times a week via Bunbury and twice-weekly via Pemberton (8hr). If you don't want to go on **tours** (see pp.724–725), then **car rental**, or shared lifts, are the best option for getting around.

Albany and around

In 1826, two years before the establishment of the Swan River Colony, the British sent Major Lockyer and a team of hopeful colonists to settle the strategic **Princess Royal Harbour**. It was a hasty pre-emptive response to French exploration of Australia's Southwest, and the small colony, originally called Fredrickstown, was allowed to grow at a natural pace – avoiding the vicissitudes of "Swan River Mania" that plagued Perth in the 1880s, when thousands of starry-eyed settlers poured into the riverside shanty town. Prior to the building of Fremantle Harbour in the 1890s, **ALBANY**'s huge natural harbour was a key port on the route between England and Botany Bay; a coaling station in the age of steamers. It was also the last of Australia that many Anzacs saw on their way to Gallipoli in 1914.

Now serving the southern farming belt, Albany has also become the centre of one of the Southwest's main holiday areas. Factors such as proximity to Perth, moderate summer temperatures, a surfeit of natural splendour and historical kudos all combine to make an agreeable and genuine destination, largely bereft of bogus tourist traps.

Arrival, information and accommodation

Transco **buses** arrive near the old train station on Lower Stirling Terrace, the location of the particularly clued-up **tourist office** (daily 9am–5.30pm; ⓣ08/9841 1088 or 1800 644 088, ⓦwww.albanytourist.com.au), which dispenses a handy local and regional **map**. Loves Bus Service (timetables at the tourist office, or call ⓣ08/9841 1211) provides in-town **public transport**: the #301 route between York Street, the town's main road, and Middleton Beach/Emu Point is particularly useful (Mon–Fri 9am–3pm, Sat 9.15–11am. For **car rental** try King Sound Vehicle Hire (ⓣ08/9841 1211, ⓦwww.kingsoundcars.com) among others.

Albany has several **guesthouses** and **B&Bs**, especially along Stirling Terrace near the harbour, as well as the customary range of highway-side motels and self-contained units, the latter found in the Middleton Bay area, 3km east of the centre. In the countryside, farmstays mix with cosy cottages and other pastoral retreats. The tourist office has a detailed photographic portfolio of the town's accommodation options. Note that prices drop by fifteen to fifty percent in winter, especially for apartments.

Motels, backpackers' and guesthouses

Albany Backpackers Cnr Stirling Terrace and Spencer St ⓣ08/9842 5255, ⓦwww.albanybackpackers.com.au. One of Albany's oldest buildings, now a warren of corridors and rooms with murals at every turn, plenty of amenities, space and a good atmosphere. Breakfast and a few minutes Internet free, plus coffee and cake every evening. Dorms $20, rooms ❸

Bayview YHA 49 Duke St ⓣ08/9842 3388, ⓔalbany@yhawa.com.au. Old wooden building 5min from the centre with dorms, twins, BBQs and some parking. Dorms $18, rooms ❸

Discovery Inn 9 Middleton Rd ⓣ08/9842 5535, ⓦwww.discoveryinn.net.au. An especially agreeable old guesthouse and restaurant, close to Middleton Beach, with breakfast included. ❹

Frederickstown Motel Cnr Frederick and Spence sts ⓣ08/9841 1600 or 1800 808 544, ⓦwww.albanyis.com.au/fredmtl. Good-value rooms close to town centre and the shops, with a restaurant. ❹

Travel Inn 191 Albany Hwy ⓣ08/9841 4144, ⓔcomfortinnalbany@iinet.net.au. Among Albany's better motels, with large comfortable rooms. ❹

Vancouver House 86 Stirling Terrace ⓣ08/9842 1071, ⓦwww.vancouverhouse.iitowns.com. Nineteenth-century guest house converted into a period-style B&B, with views onto the harbour and mostly en-suite rooms. ❸

Caravan parks

Emu Beach Emu Point, 7km from the town centre ⓣ08/9844 1147. Not a bad spot to stay for a few days. Amenities include trampolines and mini-golf. On-site vans ❸, cabins ❹

Middleton Beach Flinders Parade, Middleton Beach ⓣ08/9841 3593. Right on the weekend-posing drag and the sometimes windy beach. Cabins and on-site vans ❸

Mount Melville 22 Wellington St ⓣ08/9841 4616. Has a useful kitchen and is just 1km from town. On-site vans ❷, chalets from ❸

The Town and around

Albany's attractions are spread between the Foreshore, where the original settlers set up camp, the calm beaches around **Middleton Beach** and Emu Point on the still waters of Oyster Harbour. Driving east around the harbour brings you, after 40km, to the idyllic nature reserve at **Two Peoples Bay**, while the natural spectacles and attractions on the **Torndirrup Peninsula**, 20km southwest of town, along Frenchman's Bay Road, are also well worth a look.

On the **Foreshore** there's a replica of the *Amity* (daily 9am–5pm; $5), the brig that landed its sixty-odd settlers here on Boxing Day 1826, after six months at sea. Nearby is the **Old Gaol** (daily 10am–4.30pm; $4), so often the earliest surviving relic of European colonization right across Australia and the **Albany Residency Museum** (daily 10am–5pm; donation), which has meticulous displays of the town's maritime history, a section on Aboriginal bush medicines and an educational see-and-touch gallery for children upstairs.

Heading towards Middleton Beach, the curious tower on top of **Mount Melville Lookout**, off Serpentine Road, is colloquially known as "the spark plug". One of two lookouts in Albany, this one offers the better seaward vista. From here, backtrack to York Street, turn left and head 2km down Middleton Road to the **Old Farm**, Strawberry Hill (daily 10am–5pm; $3.30; closed June), tucked behind modern houses in its own enchanting gardens. Reminiscent of an English cottage, the farm (WA's first) provided the settlers with locally-grown produce, while the 1836 building here once housed the visiting Governor Stirling. Today it offers Devonshire teas and displays of domestic accoutrements.

Middleton Beach itself is dominated by Albany's upmarket *Esplanade Hotel*, and the town's main beach. From the beach, head up Marine Drive and turn right towards **Mount Clarence Lookout**, with its Anzac memorial and, on a clear day, a view as far as the Stirling Ranges, 80km to the north. On the way down you pass the **Princess Royal Fortress** (daily 9am–5pm; $4), an impressively restored naval installation dating from the end of the nineteenth century.

Eating

Fortunately, Albany shares the rest of the Southwest's laudable preoccupation with quality eating; several independent **restaurants** fill the gap between fast-food franchises and dreary motel dining rooms.

Beachside Cafe 2 Flinders Parade, Middleton Beach. Right on the beach, this café offers inexpensive alfresco by day and à la carte steak and seafood by night, from $25. Daily 7.30am–late.

Leonardos 166 Stirling Terrace West. The best Italian in town: pizzas from $15 are a safe bet but try the *osso bucco* – slow roasted veal shank for $27, followed by a chocolate *zabaglione* cherry cake. BYO. Mon–Sat 6.30pm–late.

Rustlers Steak House 63 Frederick St. All the meat you can eat: T-bones for $23 or try the sizzling chicken pesto for $24. Has a reasonable veggie selection too. Daily 5pm–late.

Rookleys Cnr Peels Place and York St. Deli-style café with focaccias for under $10 and decent coffee. Mon–Sat 8am–5.30pm.

Shamrock Café 184 York St. Full "Irish" breakfast with potato bread for $9, with meals from $12. Mon–Sat 7am–5pm, Sun 7am–4pm.

Listings

Bus Transco ⓣ13 10 53 or call into their office, next to the tourist office.

CALM 120 Albany Hwy (Mon–Fri 9am–5pm; ⓣ08/9841 7133). Information and passes for local national parks (see box on p.714).

Diving AlbanyDive.com (ⓣ08/9842 6886, ⓦwww.albanydive.com), on the corner of York St and Stirling Terrace, can take you to the local dive sites below from $85 with full gear rental. Albany may not be associated with an appealing tropical reef but the diving here is among the best in WA and the Leeuwin Current keeps things warmer than you might think. A lack of sediment in the natural harbours give a year-round visibility of over 30m (apart from a couple of weeks in January). In 2001, the scuttling of the *HMAS Perth* (live webcam at ⓦhmasperth.com.au) in King George Sound created what is now one of the most popular wreck dives in the country. Unlike the well-known *Swan* at Dunsborough, the *Perth* is not a gutted hulk but externally, a fully fitted ship. With its mast protruding just above the water, the wreck's surfaces have already become fully encrusted and colonized by a spectacular array of marine life. On nearby Michaelmas Island, the older wreck of the *Cheyne III* whaler is also a terrific dive site.

Post office Cnr Grey and York sts ⓣ08/9841 1811.

Taxi ⓣ08/9844 4444.

Tours and cruises Sail-A-Way (ⓣ0408 451 068) takes a catamaran into King George Sound for three hours of sunset cruising and whale watching, when in season, from $45. Escape Tours (ⓣ08/9844 1945) has day- and half-day tours around the region in a minibus from $65. Silver Star Cruises (ⓣ08/9842 9876, www.whales.com.au) can take you whale watching (June–Oct) in King George Sound for around $45.

Torndirrup National Park and Whaleworld

Frenchman's Bay Road leads onto a peninsula incorporating the **Torndirrup National Park** (CALM fees; see box on p.714) just 20km southwest of town, where a number of beaches, lookouts and other natural attractions await you. Passing various B&Bs, craft outlets and the **Wind Farm** with its ridge top boardwalk, the turn-off to **the Gap** and **Natural Bridge** are first on the list. Note that this area has claimed several lives, not just by slipping or getting blown into the sea but also as a result of **king waves** – huge waves which are indistinguishable in the swell and well up unexpectedly onto the shore all along the southern WA coast; play it safe, and don't go under the bridge or even over it on windy days. Returning from the car park, the sandy arc of **Cable Beach** on the right will catch your eye. A path leads down to the sloping granite shoreline from where – if the tide and the winds are right – you can get onto the beach itself.

From the beach you may be able to see the **Blowholes** doing their thing on the far side of the bay; for a closer look drive round and descend the steps to the headland. You won't get the reliable eruptions as found near Carnarvon (see p.767) and access to the vents is tricky on the sloping rock, but in the right conditions, the sound of the spray blasting out at 187kph could well make you jump.

Most tourists and tours visit the attractions above, but out of the summer season many places further along on the peninsula will be less crowded: check out the view from **Stony Hill** as well as tiny Misery Beach. Near here you can walk a kilometre up through a tunnel of shrubs to the summit of **Isthmus Hill**, in spring passing several varieties of orchids on the way; there's even one growing inside a stone shelter on the summit. A bracing half-day **walk** leads from the summit, culminating at Bald Head on the very tip of the Flinders Peninsula.

By now you'll have noticed the **unusually diverse flora** hereabouts: a couple of square metres of shrubbery will host over a dozen different plants, as well as the aforementioned orchids and other seasonal wildflowers. Much of this coast – from Windy Harbour up to the Fitzgerald River National Park and Hopetoun in the east – hosts a huge range of banksias, proteas and hakeas, originally catalogued by Joseph Banks in 1854 and which, like the forests to the east, are botanically unique to WA.

Frenchman Bay Road ends its orbit of the Princess Royal Harbour at sheltered **Frenchman's Bay** on the Torndirrup peninsula. Just before, you'll have passed the turn-off to **Whaleworld** (daily 9am–5pm; $18, conc. $14, free tours on the hour 10am–4pm; Ⓦ www.whaleworld.org), site of Australia's last whaling station which closed in 1978. Since that time the facility has been imaginatively developed into a world-class museum to the world's biggest creatures, who were once hunted to near extinction. The informative half-hour **tours** explain Australia's role in ending the hunting, though not before sharing the grisly details of the process (dismembering and boiling down the blubber and bones of a whale), and displaying the actual machinery that once did the job. Don't miss having a look around the towering *Cheyne IV* whale chaser which is beached right in the middle of the complex. Outbuildings house various other related exhibits, with further expansions planned in the years to come – and if nothing else the café has one of the best views in Albany.

Along the southern coast

An hour's drive west of Albany, **West Cape Howe National Park** is a coastal wilderness best suited to exploration by 4WD, while **William Bay National Park**, 15km west of Denmark, has many inviting coves which are accessible to regular vehicles. A few kilometres before Walpole, the **Valley of the Giants** is the home of the much-imitated **Tree Top Walk** and marks the edge of the giant tingle tree country. Transco buses run on Monday and Friday between Albany and Perth (via Bunbury; 6hr), but you won't see much this way – renting a car or arranging a lift is a better bet.

Denmark and William Bay National Park

DENMARK, set on the river of the same name, is a cute little country town and a great spot to enjoy a pleasant lunch, wander around some galleries, take a stroll or boat up the river. By the coast, the big lagoon of Wilson Inlet can turn an unappealing tannin colour if the moving sand bar happens to plug the lagoon's narrow mouth to the sea. Just outside the mouth of the lagoon is **Ocean Beach** (accessible via Ocean Beach Road on the west edge of town), with a spectacular view across the broad Ratcliffe Bay – here the swells sweep in to create ideal **surfing** conditions for learners. Contact South Coast Surfing for a one-to-one lesson (Ⓣ08/9848 2057 or 0401 349 854; 2hr; $50) or group sessions from one to three days (2hr per day, all including gear rental; $90).

Denmark's **tourist office** (daily 9am–5pm; Ⓣ08/9848 2055), on the corner of Strickland and Bent streets, can advise you on the array of **places to stay** in the vicinity and has a comprehensive free guide to the area. On Price Street. round the back of the **tourist office** is the small *Blue Wren Travellers' Rest* YHA (Ⓣ08/9848 3300, Ⓦhttp://bluewren.batcave.net; dorms $21, rooms ❷). The pristine *Edinburgh House* (Ⓣ08/9848 1477; ❹) is on the main road in the centre of town, while on Inlet Drive you'll find *Denmark Waterfront Motel and Cottages* (Ⓣ08/9848 1147, Ⓦwww.denmarkwaterfront.com.au), an idyllic hideaway on the water with shared budget rooms ($21), motel-style accommodation (❸) and great-value studios (❹). *Gum Grove Chalets* (Ⓣ08/9848 1877, Ⓦwww.gumgrove.com; ❹) are located on the way to Ocean Beach, on a hillside 3km south of town.

From Denmark town you can head west to the **William Bay National Park**, through the hills along **Shadforth Scenic Drive**, passing the **wineries** of West Cape Howe and Howard Park. Once at William Bay you'll find that the cove of **Green Pool** is one of the prettiest spots along the coast, with Madfish Bay and Waterfall Bay further west also worth a visit.

The Valley of the Giants' Tree Top Walk and Walpole

About 40km west of Denmark you can turn south to **Peaceful Bay**, a pleasant lunch stop with a caravan park and chalets. The forest of massive tingle and karri trees that make up the **Valley of the Giants** is now much better known for its **Tree Top Walk** (daily 9am–4.30pm; $8), an amazingly engineered six-hundred-metre walkway (accessible to wheelchairs), which sways on half a dozen pylons among the crowns of the karri trees, 40m above the ground. Ironically, the most exciting aspect of the walk is not the scrutiny of the tree canopy – which isn't especially dense, close or teeming with anything more exotic than crows – but rather the fairground thrill of actually treading along the quivering walkway. To gain a better impression of the surrounding forest, take the **Ancient Empire Walkway** which winds through the forest floor.

Back on the coastal highway, you pass through **NORNALUP**, which has a good roadside restaurant, with a riverside park for picnics and chalets nearby (Ⓣ08/9840 1107, Ⓦwww.valleyofthegiants.com.au/nornalupriversidechalets; ❹). You can take the track 6km west of town to the lovely Conspicuous Beach. **WALPOLE**, 10km from Nornalup, is the hub of many scenic drives to more towering forests, oceanic lookouts and sheltered inlets; there's a **tourist office** on the main road (Mon–Fri 9am–5pm, Sat & Sun 9am–4pm; Ⓣ08/9840 1111, Ⓦhttp://walpole.southernforests.com.au). There are a couple of **caravan parks** on the Walpole and Nornalup inlets, or for more creature comforts try *Hideaway Cottage* (Ⓣ08/9840 1138; ❹), 10km north of town, or the *Valley of the Giants Motel* (Ⓣ08/9840 0000; ❹) in the centre. Backpackers head for the *Tingle All Over* YHA (Ⓣ08/9840 1041, Ⓔtinglealllover2000@yahoo.com.au; 5-bed dorms $20, rooms ❸), at the west end of town. The hostel owns one of the biggest chess sets in the southern hemisphere and the owners also run a licensed taxi which is used by walkers for pick-ups and drop-offs. On Pier

Street is *Walpole Backpackers* (ⓣ08/9840 1244, ⓦwww.walpolebackpackers.com.au; dorms $20).

West of Walpole the **South Western Highway** starts its scenic run north-west – through more colossal forests – to Northcliffe (100km) and Pemberton (138km) at the heart of the Tall Timber Country.

The Porongurups and the Stirling Ranges

North of Albany lie the ancient granite highlands of the Porongurups and the impressive thousand-metre-high Stirling Ranges, 40km and 80km from Albany respectively. Both have been designated **national parks** and the CALM office in Albany provides further information and maps.

Porongurup National Park

The granite hills comprising the **Porongurup National Park** (CALM fees; see box on p.714) are often described as "among the oldest rocks on earth" and feature a dozen wooded peaks, whose protruding bald summits are over 600m high. The fifteen-kilometre-long ridge catches coastal moisture to support its isle of karri forests, thereby leaving the loftier Stirlings to the north dry and treeless.

Once at the park, most people are happy to do no more than take the five-minute stroll to **Tree in a Rock**, a natural oddity near the park's northern entrance. However, if you want to get your teeth into a good walk, head up the marked trail to **Devil's Slide** (671m) and, if you're up to it, return via Nancy and Hayward peaks; the full route needs at least half a day. **Balancing Rock**, at the eastern end of the park, can be reached in 45 minutes from the car park, with a cage on the exposed outcrop of Castle Rock providing safe viewing.

The Stirling Range National Park

Taking the Chester Pass Road north towards the looming **Stirling Range National Park** (CALM fees; see box on p.714), the distinctive profile of Bluff Knoll will, if you're lucky, reveal itself from the cloudbanks which often obscure its summit. Avid hillwalkers could spend a few days "peakbagging" here and come away well satisfied; the Stirlings are WA's best – if not only – mountain-walking area, with as many as five peaks over 1000m – although be aware that the area can experience blizzards as late as October. **Bluff Knoll** (1073m), the park's highest and most popular ascent, has a well-built path involving a three-hour-return slog. No matter how hot you may feel in the car park, rain falls often on the peak so be ready for the worst and take a sweater or a waterproof with you. Like much of the area, the floral biodiversity in the Range is exceptional, and often said to be greater than in the entire British Isles – something that's all the more evident at walking pace than if you're whizzing past at 100kph.

Having said that, the unsealed 45-kilometre Stirling Range **scenic drive** winds amid the peaks to Red Gum Pass in the west, where you can turn around and go back the same way (with superior views). Halfway along the drive **Talyuberup** (800m) is a short, steep ascent, with great vistas at the top, while **Toolbrunup** (1052m), accessed by a track next to the park campsite (see overleaf) is a short, steep three-hour round trip, with some exposed scrambling near the summit. Many other **trails** wander between the peaks and could link up into overnight walks. Before heading off through the bush discuss your plans with the **park ranger** (ⓣ08/9827 9230 or 9827 9278) at his residence, next to the *Moingup Springs* **campsite** off Chester Pass Road. With a lack of showers, the park campsite is a bit basic; more comfortable options are found at the *Stirling Range Retreat* (ⓣ08/9827 9229, ⓦwww.stirlingrange.com.au; cabins ❸, four-bed chalets ❸), just outside the park's northern boundary, opposite the Bluff Knoll turn-off. There's a café here too, which also sells CALM park passes and whose owners can fill you in on wildflower locales if you ask nicely. *Trio Park* campsite is on the park's south side on Salt River Road with inexpensive tent sites, a campers' kitchen and showers.

Esperance and the south coast

Esperance, 721km southeast of Perth, is at the western end of the **Archipelago of the Recherche**. Both town and archipelago were named after French ships which visited the area in the late eighteenth century, and whose persistent interest in the region precipitated the hasty colonization of WA by the edgy British. The archipelago is a string of haze-softened granite isles bobbing in the inky blue Southern Ocean, presenting an almost surreal seascape common to coasts washed by cold currents. The mild summer weather (rarely exceeding 30°C), fishing opportunities and surrounding national parks make the town a popular destination for heat-sensitive holiday-makers.

Fifty kilometres southeast of Esperance is the **Cape Le Grand National Park**, on the edge of the Great Australian Bight. Care should be taken all along this coastline, as unpredictable **king waves** frequently sweep the unwary away from exposed, rocky shores.

You can get to Esperance from Kalgoorlie with Transco's **bus service** (3 weekly; 5hr) or direct from Perth on the *Spirit of Esperance* service (6 weekly; 10hr). Albany, nearly 500km to the west along the South Coast Highway, can only be reached from Esperance direct on Mondays and Thursdays (connecting buses on Tues & Fri). To get from Albany to Esperance, it's best to arrange a **lift** with fellow travellers.

Esperance and around

The town of **ESPERANCE** prospered briefly as a supply port during the heyday of the Eastern Goldfields, and was revived after World War II when its salty soils were made fertile with the simple addition of missing trace elements. Now an established farming and holiday centre, the town lacks the charm promised by its name, but makes an ideal base from which to explore the south coast's dazzling beaches and storm-washed headlands.

Dempster Street is the town's main road, and site of the arts-and-crafts vending cabins which comprise the **Museum Village**. Nearby on James Street, the actual **museum** (daily 1.30–4.30pm; $5) is a surprisingly good repository of local memorabilia and is very proud of its Skylab display: the satellite disintegrated over Esperance in 1979 and NASA was reputedly fined $400 for littering.

Besides a walk along the Norfolk pine-lined esplanade and a round of mini-golf or go-karting, there's not much else to do in Esperance, so rent a bike or car and head out along the 36km **scenic loop** west of town. Travelling clockwise, you'll come first to the **Rotary Lookout** which overlooks the captivating seascape. You'll spot the **windfarm** on the way to **Twilight Beach**, an idyllic and sheltered spot which is much prettier than the town's more exposed beaches. From here settle in for more windswept grandeur (and a free nudist beach) at **Observation Point Lookout**, before the road turns inland towards **Pink Lake**. This is one of many lakes between here and Merredin which are sometimes so coloured by salt-tolerant algae, and whose seafaring cousins give the coastline its enchanting turquoise hue.

The hundred or so islands of the romantically named Archipelago of the Recherche – known as the **Bay of Isles** around Esperance – are chiefly occupied by seals, feral goats and multitudes of seabirds. Dolphins may also be seen offshore and Southern Right whales are commonly observed migrating to the Antarctic in spring. Mackenzies Island Cruises, 71 The Esplanade (Ⓣ08/9071 5757, Ⓦwww.woodyisland.com.au), offers daily trips with the possibility of overnight stays on **Woody Island** (summer only).

Practicalities

Transco **buses** stop in the town centre, with **taxis** available on Ⓣ08/9071 1782. The **tourist office** (Mon–Fri 8.45am–5pm, Sat 9am–4pm, Sun 10am–4pm; Ⓣ08/9071 2330) is in the Museum Village on Dempster Street and there is a **shopping centre** on Andrew Street, over the roundabout. The CALM office, at 92 Dempster St (Ⓣ08/9071 3733), provides information and passes for the national parks around Esperance. **Bicycles** are rented out from the tourist office or along the Esplanade. For inexpensive **car rental**, try Hollywood Hire (Ⓣ08/9071 3144) for old bangers, or the usual agencies. Esperance Diving and Fishing, 56 The Esplanade (Ⓣ08/9071 5111), runs **dive** charters and courses, and both hostels (see "Accommodation", below) have 4WDs for making informal runs along the coast, if there's enough in-house interest.

You can get a **meal** at *Ollie's*, 51 The Esplanade or in the evenings try the à la carte cuisine in the *Bay of Isles Motel*, 32 The Esplanade, where you can enjoy spectacular views while you dine. *Taylor Street Tearooms* by the jetty has an open fire, seafood and pasta and is not as stuffy as it sounds.

Accommodation

Although the self-contained units around town will almost certainly be booked out during school holiday periods (see p.714), there are a number of **other options** – especially given that air-conditioning is rarely necessary in Esperance. There are also at least three caravan parks in and around town.

Bayview Motel 31 Dempster St Ⓣ08/9071 1533, Ⓦwww.bayviewmotel.com.au. Central motel with some self-contained units. ❹

Blue Waters Lodge YHA Goldfields Rd Ⓣ08/9071 1040, Ⓔesperance@yhawa.com.au. Sprawling old hospital situated right on the bay, with pick-ups, bikes and possibly the largest hostel kitchen in the southern hemisphere. Can get inundated with school groups. Dorms $20, rooms ❸

Captain Huon Motel 5 The Esplanade Ⓣ08/9071 2383. Excellent small motel with some self-contained units and bike rental. ❹

Esperance Backpackers 14 Emily St Ⓣ08/9071 4724. The town's livelier hostel, with all the mod-cons, tours and pick-ups. Dorms $20, rooms ❸

Jetty Motel 1 The Esplanade Ⓣ08/9071 3333. Well-appointed, two-storey motel with ocean views. ❹

Old Hospital Motel William St Ⓣ08/9071 3587, Ⓔoldesp@emerge.net.au. Boutique-style establishment which offers an antidote to motel sterility with its tasteful decor. ❹

Cape Le Grand National Park

Once in Esperance, a visit to **Cape Le Grand National Park** (CALM fee; see box on p.714) is well worth the expense of renting a car or taking a tour; it's essentially a climb up a hill and a beach-hop – but on a good day they're the kind of beaches you want to roll up and take home with you. Once in the park, the climb to the summit of **Frenchman's Peak** (262m) is not as hard as it looks, and well worth the half-hour's exertion if you have a sturdy pair of shoes. The secret of its distinctive, hooked summit is an unexpected hole that frames the impressive view out to sea. Soon after the Frenchman's Peak turn-off, a track leads to **Hellfire Bay**; sheltered coves don't come any more perfect than this. From here you can take a tough, three-hour walk northwest to **Le Grand Beach** (limited camping), which is also accessible in a 4WD from Wylie Bay at the end of Bandy Creek Road if the tide is right. There is also a less demanding two-hour trek east to **Thistle Cove**, from where an easier trail leads to the broad arc of **Lucky Bay** further east (camping and water), with more sheltered swimming and unbelievable colours. **Rossiter Bay**, another 6km east from here, is distinctly unimpressive by comparison.

The Eastern Goldfields

Six hundred kilometres east of Perth, at the end of the **Great Eastern Highway**, are the **Eastern Goldfields**. In the late nineteenth century, gold was found in what still remains one of the world's richest gold-producing regions. Lack of fresh water made life very hard for the early prospectors, driven by a national economic depression into miserable living conditions, disease and, in most cases, premature graves. Nevertheless, boom towns of thousands, boasting grand public buildings, several hotels and a vast periphery of hovels, would spring up and collapse in the time it took to extract any ore.

In 1892 the railway from Perth reached the town of **Southern Cross**, just as big finds turned the rush into a national stampede. This huge influx of people accentuated the water shortage, until the visionary engineer C.Y. O'Connor oversaw the construction of a 556km **pipeline** from Mundaring Weir, in the hills above Perth, to Kalgoorlie in 1903. By this time many of the smaller gold towns were already in decline, but the Goldfields' wealth and boost in population finally gave WA the economic autonomy it sought in its claim for statehood.

In the years preceding the goldrush, the area was briefly one of the world's richest sources of **sandalwood**, an aromatic wood greatly prized throughout Asia as joss sticks, and still a staple in modern perfumery. Supplies in the Pacific had become exhausted, so by 1880 the fragrant wood was WA's second-largest exportable commodity after wool. Exacerbating the inevitable over-cutting was the goldrush's demand for timber to prop up shafts, or to fire the pre-pipeline water desalinators. Today the region is a pit-scarred and prematurely desertified landscape, dotted with the scavenged vestiges of past settlements, while at its core the **Super Pit** gold mine in Kalgoorlie gets wider and deeper year by year.

Moribund **Coolgardie** may have been the original goldrush settlement, but the Goldfields are now centred around the twinned towns of **Kalgoorlie-Boulder**, with Kalgoorlie being the thriving, energetic hub; this is Australia's richest town after Canberra. Even if you're not planning to pass through the Goldfields, there's enough to see in Kalgoorlie to make a couple of days excursion from Perth worthwhile – if for nothing else than the novelty of riding on the new "high speed" **Prospector**, the daily six-hour rail link between Perth and Kalgoorlie. **Buses** depart with similar regularity, taking about eight hours.

Coolgardie

Not quite dilapidated and abandoned enough to carry the name "ghost mining town", **COOLGARDIE** is more of a museum to itself, a town which – at its

Wave Rock

WA's best-known natural oddity is **Wave Rock** ($5 per car), 3km from the tiny farming settlement of **Hyden**, at the eastern edge of the Wheatlands prairie. At 15m high and 110m long, the formation resembles a breaking wave, an impression enhanced by the vertical water stains running down the overhanging face. While the rock, formed by wind and rain, is certainly unusual (though not unique) it's not worth the long day-trip from Perth. Even as a diversion south of the Great Eastern Highway (Merredin is 185km away and Southern Cross is 178km), its appeal is still overrated.

At the base of the rock a marked twenty-minute trail leads to another outcrop, **Hippo's Yawn**, while 21km from Wave Rock, on the way to Southern Cross, **Bates Cave** features Aboriginal hand paintings.

Beware that **accommodation** hereabouts is overpriced, including the *Wave Rock Caravan Park* (☎08/9880 5022; chalets ④), 5km east of town, and the *Hyden Wave Rock Hotel* on Lynch Street (☎08/9880 5052; ⑥).

peak – had twenty-three hotels, three breweries and six newspapers serving a population ten times greater than its present twelve hundred. Arthur Bayley cranked the gold fever up when he came into Southern Cross – then the easternmost extent of the rush – in 1892 with nearly sixteen kilos of gold. The ensuing wave of prospectors started within hours – ten thousand men rushed out of Southern Cross, culminating in a fourfold increase in WA's population by the end of the century.

The imposing **Wardens Court Building** on Bayley Street is a good point from which to start an appraisal of Coolgardie's numerous boom time relics. The building houses the **tourist office** (Mon–Fri 10am–5pm, Sat & Sun 10am–4pm; ☎08/9026 6090) and one of the most extensive provincial **museums** in WA (more or less same hours; $4). The grand upper floors are filled with an especially comprehensive collection of bottles, and the rest of the museum rewards a prolonged browse, giving you a feel for the dramatic effect the goldrush had on the area.

Outside the museum is an index to the 155 **historic markers** set around the town, and directly opposite you can't miss the varied miscellany and just plain old junk comprising **Ben Prior's Open-Air Museum** (free). Half a kilometre up Hunt Street, at the end of McKenzie Street, **Warden Finnerty's House** (daily except Wed 11am–4pm; $3) is the finely restored 1895 residence of the man whose unenviable job it was to set the ground rules for mining at the height of the rush. There's accommodation and places to eat in town but a far better range is available at Kalgoorlie, 40km down the road.

Kalgoorlie-Boulder

Whichever way you approach **Kalgoorlie**, the bustling gold capital of Australia officially twinned, municipally merged but still fervently distinct from **Boulder** (see p.754), it comes as a surprise after hundreds of kilometres of desolation. The conurbation possesses the idiosyncratic quality of places like Coober Pedy (see p.883) or Las Vegas. All three blithely disregard their isolation and bleak surroundings, so devoted is their attention to the pursuit of earthly riches – which, in Kalgoorlie's case, is **gold**.

Kalgoorlie

In 1893 **Paddy Hannan** (then 53 years old) and his mates, Tom Flannigan and Dan O'Shea, brought renewed meaning to the expression "the luck of the

Irish" when a lame horse forced them to camp by the tree which still stands at the top of Egan Street in **KALGOORLIE**. With their instincts highly attuned after eight months of prospecting around Coolgardie, they soon found gold all around them, and as the first on the scene enjoyed the unusually easy pickings of surface gold. Ten years later, when the desperately needed water pipeline finally gushed into the Mount Charlotte Reservoir, Kalgoorlie was already the established heart of WA's rapidly growing mineral-based prosperity. As sole survivor of the original rush, and revitalized by the 1960s nickel boom, Kalgoorlie has benefited from new technology that has largely dispensed with slow and dangerous underground mining. Instead, the fabulously rich "**Golden Mile**" reef east of town, near Boulder, is being excavated around the clock to create the vast, open-cast "Super Pit".

Proud of its history and continued prosperity, Kalgoorlie is one of the most parochial towns in Australia, a country that's full of them. Although the last decade has seen the encroachment of a suburban "shopping mall" lifestyle, "Kal" is first and foremost a "Working Man's Town" of twelve-hour, seven-day shifts, a testament to the ethos of hard work and hard play that flourished in Australia's Anglo-Celtic heyday. A pub without a half-dressed barmaid (known in WA as "skimpies") is the exception and in the sniggeringly louche red-light district of Hay Street, three of the infamous "tin shack" brothels remain conspicuously in business.

Start your tour of the town by taking a walk up to the top of Hannan Street to the bright red head-frame. This is the impressive entrance to the **Museum of the Goldfields** (daily 10am–4.30pm; donation), right next to the spot where Paddy and his crew found their first, auspicious nuggets. Inside is a modern display of Goldfields artefacts and history, with the very stuff that keeps the town going viewable in the basement vault. Aboriginal history and the sandalwood industry are also covered in this excellent introduction to the area, and there's a lookout over the town from the top of the red head-frame.

Hannan Street itself is one of Kalgoorlie's finest sights, with its superbly restored **federation-era architecture**, imposing public buildings and numerous flamboyant hotel facades. You're welcome to inspect the grandiose interior of the **town hall** (Mon–Fri 9am–4pm; free), with its splendid hall and less impressive art gallery. It's only when you stop to reflect that this is a remote, century-old town in the Western Australian desert that the stunning wealth of the boom years, which still continue, is brought home to you. Outside, a replica of a bronze **statue** of Paddy himself invites you to drink from his chrome-nozzled waterbag – the much vandalized original is now safely in the Mining Hall of Fame.

If it's merely your curiosity that's drawn you to Hay Street then *Langtrees 181* at no. 181 has found a novel and very successful way of perking up business in the quiet daylight hours – by offering **brothel tours** (1hr; $35). Although prostitution is illegal in WA, Kalgoorlie's "special needs" see a local policy of containment and toleration. This sordid industry is made slightly more palatable by the official ban on male control – investment benefits the entrepreneurial "madames" only. The tour itself leads you through the dozen or so themed rooms (some of which are more popular than others) while relating some of the not-so-lighthearted history of prostitution in WA, and answering all the questions you dare to ask.

Boulder and the Mining Hall of Fame

BOULDER, 5km south of Kalgoorlie, is much quieter and smaller than its twin – a place to visit rather than stay in. It was originally set up as a separate settlement to serve the Golden Mile but Boulder's heyday passed as Kalgoorlie's suburbs slowly expanded around it. Boulder has a similar collection of grand old buildings which – as in Kal – have received a face-lift, along with the pubs. One thing worth coming to Boulder for is a ride on the **Golden Mile Loopline**. The "Rattler", as it's known, once delivered workers to their pits around the clock but in 2004, the ever-expanding mining activities in the huge **Super Pit** (well worth a look from public viewing platforms) took a bite out of the Rattler's itinerary and it's still unsure when or if a diversion will be completed.

Just north of town are a couple more attractions without which a visit to Kalgoorlie–Boulder would not be complete. The **Mining Hall of Fame** (daily 9am–4.30pm; $20, surface only $15; Ⓦwww.mininghall.com) is an old mine site now transformed into a museum and mining theme park. Inside you can have a crack at gold panning or take a guided underground tour, led by former miners. This is probably as long as you'd want to spend down a mine – especially after you're given a brief demonstration of the pneumatic "air leg" drill. Back above ground, the Hall of Fame building has a comprehensive display of rocks and minerals, as well as Aboriginal art from the Warburton region where many mineral riches remain. The Prospectors Gallery is also fascinating, chiefly due to the life stories of Mark Creasly and Lang Hancock; an engaging documentary portrays Creasly as a lone prospector who doggedly scoured WA in his battered ute (displayed), until one day he finally struck it rich and sold out for millions. Lang Hancock is a better-known figure who established WA's iron-ore boom in the Pilbara, half a century ago, by prospecting from the air in a light plane, a replica of which hangs in another gallery. Conspicuous by its absence is the not-so-glorious blue asbestos chapter in WA's mining history with which Hancock was also involved (see p.780). Allow about two and a half hours for your visit.

Practicalities

Greyhound Australia (Ⓣ08/9021 7100 or 1300 662 205, Ⓦwww.greyhound.com.au) **buses** (incorporating the *Goldfields Express* service) arrive at Forrest Street in Kalgoorlie, opposite the **train station** (Transco; Ⓣ08/9021 2923). **Taxis** (Ⓣ13 10 08) meet the daily trains, which are no quicker than buses. Kalgoorlie's **tourist office** (Mon–Fri 8.30am–5pm, Sat & Sun 9am–5pm; Ⓣ08/9021 1966, Ⓦwww.kalgoorlie.com) is at 250 Hannan St, Kalgoorlie's main thoroughfare, and gives out informative sketch maps pinpointing Kal's dispersed attractions. There's an **Internet café** opposite and a post office just up the road at 204 Hannan St.

A local **bus service** operates between Kalgoorlie and Boulder every 25 minutes (Mon–Sat 8am–6pm; $2), with timetables available from Kalgoorlie's tourist office or the town hall. **Car rental** is expensive, though Halfpenny Rentals, 544 Hannan St Sth (Ⓣ08/9021 1804) try to live up to their name. Goldrush Tours (Ⓣ1800 620 440, Ⓦwww.goldrushtours.com.au) is the main local tour operator whose two-hour "History and Heritage" tour ($25) is recommended.

Accommodation

Although it's unlikely that Kalgoorlie will maintain your interest for more than a couple of days, the town does get busy with business travellers using the motels, and holiday-makers in the winter school holidays, so it's best to check room availability in advance. The many splendid hotel facades along Hannan Street deteriorate inside, but they all offer inexpensive rooms with either shared or en-suite facilities. You'll also find a couple of *Mercure* hotels at the top and bottom of Hannan Street (☎01300 656 565), with reduced weekend rates of around ❹ including breakfast. There are also several caravan parks around town with vans and cabins for around ❸.

Gold Dust Backpackers 192 Hay St ☎08/9091 3737, Ⓦwww.kalgoorliebackpackers.com. Purpose-built hostel with a/c, pool, free bikes, and pick-ups. Dorms $20, rooms ❷

Hannan's View Motel 430 Hannan St ☎08/9091 3333, Ⓦwww.hannansview.com.au. One of the best choices in town, with motel units, a pool, cheap breakfasts and some self-contained units. ❺

Kalgoorlie Backpackers 166 Hay St ☎08/9091 1482. Former brothel close to the centre with big kitchen, dorms and twins as well as a pool and bikes. Dorms $19, rooms ❷

Midas Motel 409 Hannan St ☎08/9021 3088 or 1800 813 088. Motel with nightclub, pool and self-contained rooms. ❺

York Hotel 259 Hannan St ☎08/9021 2337. Probably the best-looking facade on Hannan St. Shared bathrooms, but rates include breakfast. ❸

Eating and drinking

Starting at the cheap end, treat yourself to a good old **counter meal** at the *Star and Garter* pub on upper Hannan Street, or the *Kaoss Café* next to the Internet café in St Barbara's Square. Also at the top of Hannan Street, the spacious *Monty's Restaurant* is open around the clock and has leather sofas to spread out on and meals from around $20. At the other end of town, at 418 Hannan St, *Akudjura* restaurant serves seafood and steaks in a classy setting for around $25–30 a hit. For most locals, Kal's **nightlife** revolves around scantily-clad pub barmaids laying on beer jugs, so if you can't beat them, join them, with a crack at the "**Kal pub crawl**"; T-shirts from the tourist office are printed with a map linking the 32 pubs in Kalgoorlie-Boulder – handy if you lose your bearings halfway through. Otherwise there is a **cinema** complex on Oswald Street, halfway to Boulder.

The Goldfields Highway

North of Kalgoorlie, there are a number of mining and Aboriginal communities along the 726km stretch up to Meekatharra, itself halfway up the Great Northern Highway. Scenically the route hasn't got much to commend it, but it's useful if you're heading northeast to Alice via the Great Central Road (see p.706), or if you want to get from the Eyre Highway to northern WA in a hurry, avoiding Perth. It's worth knowing that most of the so-called **ghost towns** in this area – especially the ones closer to Kalgoorlie – are merely foundations of long-gone buildings, as all abandoned structures and materials were scavenged for reuse elsewhere. Nevertheless, the **Golden Quest Discovery Trail** self-guides tourists through the region as far as Leonora and Laverton – ask for the free map and guide at Kalgoorlie's tourist office.

Though it once boasted twelve thousand residents, two breweries and an hourly train to Kalgoorlie, you can give the rubble remains of **Kanowna** a miss. Even the two ghost towns of **BROAD ARROW** and **ORA BANDA** (respectively 38km and 66km from Kalgoorlie) have only a "bush pub" each to show for themselves. Broad Arrow is just a couple of dilapidated shacks and a **pub** that's popular with weekending Kal-Boulderians. At **Kookynie**, a short distance off the highway, is another bush pub, the *Grand Hotel* (❷), standing alone in the dust.

LEONORA, 237km north of Kalgoorlie, is a sprightly century-old mining town – a "one-horse" version of Kalgoorlie that survives with a federation-era main street and a couple of hotels (❹). Just south of town is the reconstructed **Gwalia** ghost town – an evocative scattering of galvo hovels, a general store and a museum (daily 10am–4pm; $4) at the top of the hill.

A sealed road branches northeast to **Laverton**, from where the **Great Central Road** is a straightforward if long track leading around 1100km to Yulara, NT (see p.706 for a full description). Back on the road to Meekathara, **LEINSTER** is another one of those bizarrely suburban-looking company towns, with a supermarket and a motel (❹), while **Wiluna**, 175km north of Leinster (hotel ❷) is the polar opposite, a century-old settlement that's now an Aboriginal welfare ghost town of quite intimidating desolation. Fueling up is the only reason you'd want to stop here. From Wiluna the long unmaintained **Gunbarrel Highway** winds east towards the NT border, while the **Canning Stock Route** runs northeast across the Great Sandy Desert for 1900km to Halls Creek; both routes are serious 4WD expeditions. The last 180km from Wiluna to Meekathara is a gravel road.

The Eyre Highway to South Australia

South of Kalgoorlie the Great Eastern Highway runs 190 kilometres to Norseman, at the western end of the **Eyre Highway**. The highway is named after the explorer John Eyre, who crossed the southern edge of the continent in 1841, a gruelling five-month trek which would have cost him his life but for some Aborigines who helped him locate water. Eyre crawled into Albany on his last legs but set the route for future crossings, the telegraph lines and the highway.

NORSEMAN was named after a prospector's horse which kicked up a large nugget in 1894 – a genuine case of lucky horseshoes. A bronze effigy of the nag now stands proudly on the corner of Roberts and Ramsay streets. Arrivals from South Australia may be eager to pick up their "I've crossed the Nullarbor" certificate from the **tourist office** (daily 9am–5pm; ⓣ08/9039 1071) on Roberts Street, which has a telecentre next door. There are two motels: the *Norseman Eyre Motel* on Robert St (ⓣ08/9039 1130; ❹) and a Great Western (ⓣ08/9039 1633; ❹) on Princep St (the main Kalgoorlie–Esperance road), where you'll also find budget rooms at *Lodge 101* (ⓣ08/9039 1541; dorms $20). If you've come from the east and are in a quandary about which route to take to Perth, consider nipping up to Kal but then return south and head west along the coast.

If you're heading back east on the Eyre Highway, it's about 730km to the South Australian border and another 480km from there to Ceduna, where the bleak **Nullarbor** section ends, though that still leaves 800km before you reach Adelaide – a drive of celebrated monotony. Although the longest stretch without fuel is only around 200km, do not underestimate the rigours of the journey in your own vehicle. Carry reserves of fuel and water, take rests every two or three hours and beware of kangaroos and other wildlife, especially between dusk and dawn. There are no banks between Norseman and Ceduna, and both towns have a quarantine checkpoint where a large range of prohibited animal and vegetable goods must be discarded.

BALLADONIA is 193km east from Norseman, with the *Balladonia Hotel* (ⓣ08/9039 3453; ❹) and its adjacent caravan park your choice for an overnight stop. Then, 200km of virtually dead-straight road further along, you reach **CAIGUNA**, which has a motel and caravan park (ⓣ08/9039 3459; on-site vans ❸, motel units ❹), and **COCKLEBIDDY**, another 66km further on (motel ❹). The place to stay in **MADURA**, 92km east of Cocklebiddy – and halfway between Perth and Adelaide if you're still counting – is the *Madura Pass*

Oasis Motel (☎08/9039 3464; ❹), while **MUNDRABILLA**, 116km further on and where you rise up into the actual Nullarbor plain, has a combined motel and campsite, the *Mundrabilla Motor Hotel* (☎08/9039 3465; ❸).

EUCLA, just 12km from the border, was re-established up on the escarpment after sand dunes exposed by overgrazing engulfed the original settlement by the sea. Only 4km away, the old telegraph and weather station are still visible above the sands, an eerie sight well worth a stroll. South of town is the **Eucla National Park** (CALM fee; see box on p.714), where the coastal cliffs can be seen extending east for 200km along the coast of South Australia. For accommodation, Eucla has a **caravan park** (bunkhouse ❶, on-site vans ❷), the *Eucla Motor Hotel* (☎08/9039 3468; ❹), or right on the border, there's the *Border Village* (☎08/9039 3474; ❸). For the South Australian section of this route, see p.880.

From Perth to Kununurra

The 4400-kilometre haul up Highway 1 along Western Australia's arching coastline from Perth to Broome, across the Kimberley and on to Darwin in the Northern Territory, is one of Australia's great road journeys. Even without detours, it's a huge, transcontinental trek between the country's two most isolated capitals, fringing the barely inhabited desert that separates them.

If any single trip across Australia benefits from independent mobility, it's this one: a car enables you to explore intimately and linger indefinitely. While some days in WA's **Northwest** will be punctuated by nothing more than road trains, road kill and roadhouses, there are several places where the climate, scenery and ambience may collectively conspire to subdue your road fever for a few days. If you're interested in discovering the wayside attractions, allow at least three to four weeks for the journey right through to Darwin. Otherwise, a fortnight will let you whizz through the highlights; anything less and you may as well fly.

The route is sealed all the way, but a glance at any map clearly shows the long distances between roadhouses, let alone settlements. Your vehicle should be in sound condition, particularly the tyres and the cooling system, both of which will be working hard in the heat of the Northwest. If you undertake the trip between January and March, expect very high temperatures as well as storms or even **cyclones**, with associated flooding and disruption. Following damage, roads and bridges on Highway 1 are repaired amazingly quickly, but if rain persists, back roads can be closed for weeks.

If you don't have a car, the rigid schedules and butt-numbing sectors of long-distance **bus** travel require a certain equanimity. Greyhound Australia and Integrity Coachlines offer a range of **regional passes** up the coast to Exmouth, Broome and Darwin. It should be noted that by doing the journey *from* Perth, schedules generally match connections to places off the highway with little delay. In the opposite direction, you are travelling "against the flow" of the timetable and can expect long waits unless heading directly back to Perth.

Up the coast to Broome

Ironically, nowhere along the 2400-kilometre drive to Broome will you glimpse vistas of frothing surf breaking temptingly onto golden beaches. The highway takes a more sheltered inland route with access to the ocean limited by private land, not to mention the sheer impenetrability of some of the terrain. Beach-camping your way up a deserted coast will more likely turn out to be bush camping, but there are just about enough attractions to make up for this, including the spooky **Pinnacles** near Cervantes, the idyllic resort of **Kalbarri**, and the **Shark Bay** Peninsula, with its chummy dolphins. Further north, the **Ningaloo Reef** running down the North West Cape should not be missed.

The Brand Highway

Travelling the **Brand Highway** (as Highway 1 is initially known), there's an obligatory detour to view the remarkable Pinnacles in **Nambung National Park** (CALM fee; no camping; see box on p.714), 250km from Perth and 70km west off the highway. A young crayfishing town, beaten by strong winds in summer, **CERVANTES** is the closest overnight stop. There are two caravan parks here, with tent pitches and on-site vans (❷), plus *Pinnacles Beach Backpackers* incorporating *Cervantes Lodge*, at 91 Seville St (Ⓣ08/9652 7377 or 1800 245 232, Ⓦwww.wn.com.au/pbbackpackers; dorms $18, rooms ❸), which has kitchen facilities, a laundry, TV/video lounge and barbecue. There's also the *Cervantes Pinnacles Motel* (Ⓣ08/9652 7145; ❺). You can eat at the *Lodge*, the *Tavern* or the *Thirst Point* pizzeria, all in town. Minibus **tours** to the park (daily 1pm plus 9.45am & 4.15pm depending on demand; $15; Ⓣ08/9652 7041) leave from the *Pinnacle Country Café*, which is also the **tourist office** (daily 8am–6pm), next to the Shell service station.

In the park, there's access to the ocean at **Kangaroo Point** and **Hangover Bay**, but the **Pinnacles** are the main attraction: a spread of limestone columns up to 3m high which were originally formed underground and have since been exhumed from the sands, like a terracotta army, by the perennial southwesterlies. A three-kilometre drive winds among them, but however lazy you're feeling, you'll find it hard not to park up and wander around this eerie expanse, sometimes enhanced by a "mist" of fine, windblown sand. Most day-tours from Perth arrive around midday, missing the evening sun's long shadows, which add still further to the Pinnacles' photogenic qualities.

After the Pinnacles there's really very little of interest until you get to the fishing town of **Dongara**, 150km north of Cervantes, with its fine Moreton Bay fig trees, and 40km later the tiny coastal resort of **GREENOUGH**, and its unusually well-restored nineteenth-century **Historical Hamlet** (daily 9.30am–4.30pm; $4 including guided tour; Ⓣ08/9926 1140). Up the road you'll notice Greenough's strange **leaning trees** – some bent almost flat against the ground by the prevailing salt-laden winds – as well as the imposing, three-storey bulk of **Clinch's Mill**, the **Pioneer Cemetery** and the **Pioneer Museum** (all daily except Fri 10am–4pm; $2; Ⓣ08/9926 1058), which records the area's heritage.

Geraldton

Situated in the middle of the **Batavia Coast**, 420km north of Perth, **GERALDTON** is a crayfishing, mining and pastoral centre whose town centre feels more like a busy Perth suburb than a country town. In fact, it's the state's second-largest city. The **Maritime Museum** (Mon–Sat 10am–4pm,

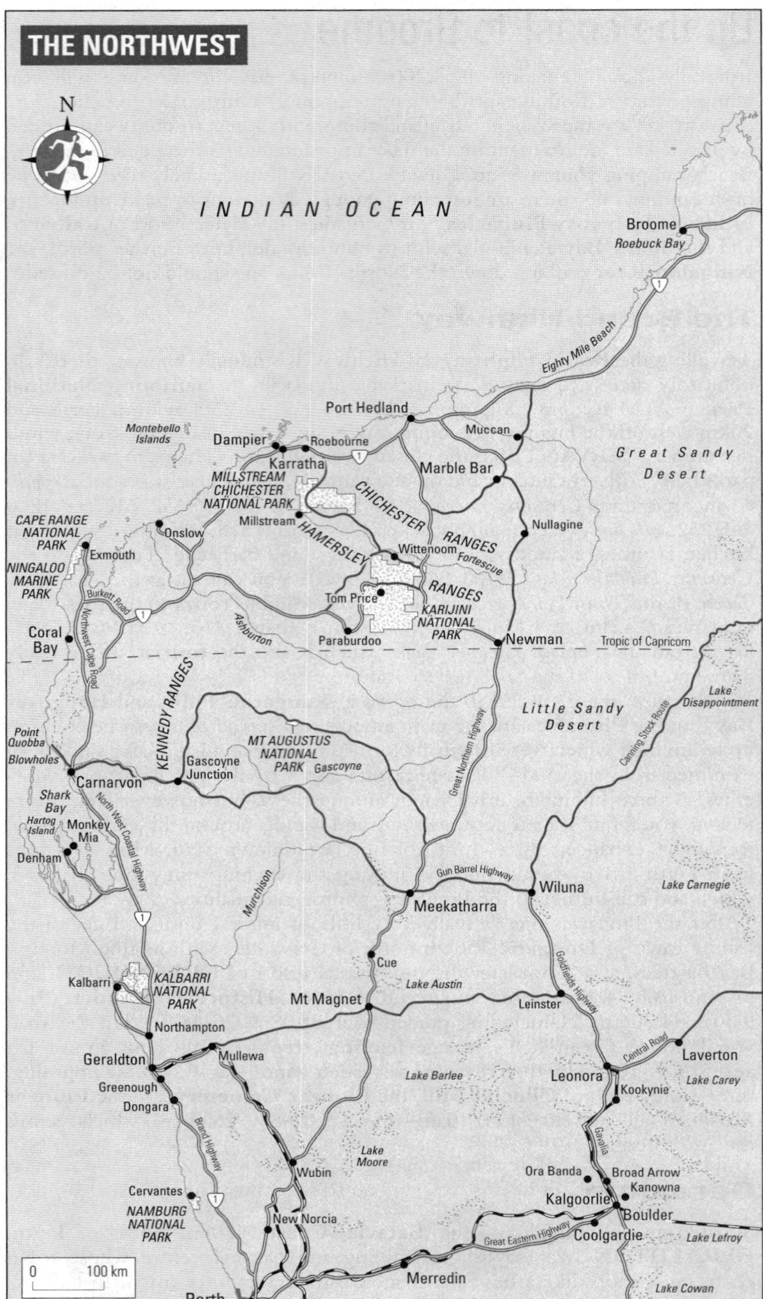
THE NORTHWEST
N
INDIAN OCEAN
Broome
Roebuck Bay
Eighty Mile Beach
Port Hedland
Muccan
Great Sandy Desert
Montebello Islands
Dampier
Roebourne
Karratha
Marble Bar
MILLSTREAM CHICHESTER NATIONAL PARK
CHICHESTER RANGES
Millstream
HAMERSLEY RANGES
Nullagine
CAPE RANGE NATIONAL PARK
Onslow
Exmouth
Wittenoom
Fortescue
NINGALOO MARINE PARK
Tom Price
KARIJINI NATIONAL PARK
Burkett Road
Northwest Cape Road
Coral Bay
Ashburton
Paraburdoo
Newman
Tropic of Capricorn
KENNEDY RANGES
Lake Disappointment
Little Sandy Desert
Canning Stock Route
Point Quobba
Blowholes
MT AUGUSTUS NATIONAL PARK
Gascoyne
Gascoyne Junction
Great Northern Highway
Carnarvon
Shark Bay
North West Coastal Highway
Hartog Island
Monkey Mia
Denham
Murchison
Gun Barrel Highway
Wiluna
Lake Carnegie
Meekatharra
Cue
Goldfields Highway
Lake Austin
Kalbarri
KALBARRI NATIONAL PARK
Mt Magnet
Leinster
Northampton
Central Road
Laverton
Geraldton
Mullewa
Lake Barlee
Leonora
Lake Carey
Greenough
Kookynie
Dongara
Brand Highway
Gavalia
Lake Moore
Wubin
Ora Banda
Broad Arrow
Kanowna
Cervantes
Kalgoorlie
NAMBURG NATIONAL PARK
New Norcia
Boulder
Great Eastern Highway
Coolgardie
Lake Lefroy
0 100 km
Merredin
Lake Cowan
Perth

Sun 1–5pm; donation) on Marine Terrace, by the yellow submarine, focuses on the fascinating *Batavia* tragedy (see p.729), which occurred on the Houtman Abrolhos islands, 100km offshore, as well as the contemporary crayfishing industry.

On Cathedral Drive, **St Francis Xavier Cathedral** was completed in 1938, the crowning glory of architect John Hawes' career. You'll find half a dozen examples of his unique Romanesque-Byzantine architectural style in the vicinity, of which the cathedral is his masterpiece. There are free tours on Mondays at 10am and Fridays at 2pm. If you're sufficiently impressed, ask at the tourist office (see below) about the **John Hawes Heritage Trail**, which leads you around some of his other works.

Practicalities

The tourist office is in the Bill Sewell Complex (Mon–Fri 8.30am–5pm, Sat & Sun 9am–4.30pm; ⓣ08/9921 3999, ⓦwww.geraldtontourist.com.au) on Chapman Road, 2km north of town, and will happily sort out all accommodation bookings. Greyhound Australia and Integrity buses arrive here daily and Transco buses alight at the old train station, just down the road. Recommended **restaurants** include seafood at the *Boatshed*, 357 Marine Terrace and *Skeetas*, 9 George Rd. For **accommodation**, *Batavia Backpackers* is behind the tourist office (ⓣ08/9964 3001, ⓔgeraldtonbackpackers@hotmail.com; dorms $18, rooms ❷) and *Foreshore Backpackers*, 172 Marine Terrace (ⓣ08/9921 3275, ⓔforeshorebp@hotmail.com; three- to four-bed dorms $20, rooms ❷) or there are motels from the *Best Western, Comfort Inn* and *Mercure* chains, among others (❹–❺).

Kalbarri and around

About 70 kilometres north of Geraldton, your curiosity may be aroused by a sign for the **Hutt River Principality**, a caravan park and old pastoral property that comes and goes as a goofy tourist attraction after it "ceded" from the Australian Commonwealth many years ago on an arcane legal technicality. The principality issues its own postage and passport stamps and has a chapel featuring religious paintings.

Situated on the mouth of the Murchison River nearly 600km north of Perth and 66km off Highway 1, **KALBARRI** is one of the best of the west coast's resorts. With no gimmicks or so much as a dreary old jail to shuffle through, it's a great place to do as much or as little as you like. With the dramatic scenery of Kalbarri National Park on its doorstep, few resorts can boast such an ideal location, together with good, inexpensive accommodation and a host of activities.

The area's history holds a few wonders of its own. In the 1920s a stockman discovered the remains of a **castaway's camp** on the clifftops north of Kalbarri and subsequent excavation revealed the wreck of the Dutch trader, *Zuytdorp*, at the base of the cliff, but no human remains. The fate of the survivors had been a three-hundred-year-old mystery until the diagnosis of the rare Ellis van Creveld Syndrome (endemic in the seventeenth-century Netherlands) among local children of Aboriginal descent suggested that some of the *Zuytdorp*'s castaways survived long enough to pass the gene on to the Aborigines of the area.

Arrival and information

Greyhound Australia **buses** from Perth drop passengers at the **Ajana turn-off** on Highway 1, to be met by a shuttle bus on Monday, Thursday and Saturday only. Transco buses from Perth come right into town in the middle of the

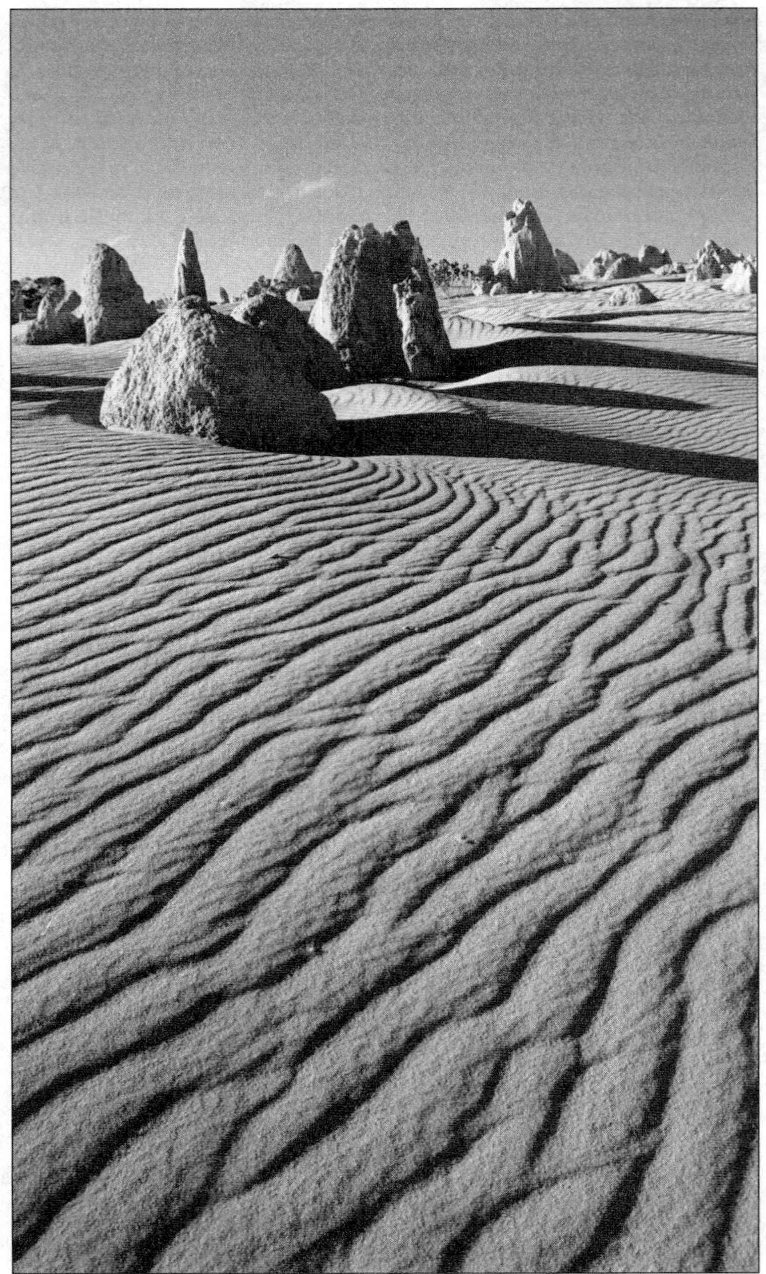

△ Pinnacles at Sunrise

night on Sunday, Monday, Wednesday and Thursday. The **tourist office** (daily 9am–5pm; ⓣ08/9937 1104 or 1800 639 468, ⓦwww.kalbarriwa.info) is in the Allen Centre on Grey Street; many local activities and tours can be booked here. The small **shopping centre** on Porter Street includes a bakery, supermarket and **post office**, with bank agencies and ATMs at various outlets around town. Suzuki **4WD jeeps** can be rented from *Kalbarri Backpackers'*; mileage is unlimited in Kalbarri and in the national park, and the drive up River Road at the town's northern end will give you a chance to fiddle with the transmission levers.

Accommodation

In the school holidays (see p.714) when Kalbarri is packed out, most holiday units insist on a minimum one-week's booking.

Kalbarri Backpackers 2 Mortimer St ⓣ08/9937 1430, ⓔkalbarribackpackers@wn.com.au. No competition but still spacious and tidy. Mixed dorms $18, rooms ❸

Kalbarri Beach Resort Off Clotsworthy St ⓣ08/9937 1061. Large resort with a pool, sauna and the *Zuytdorp Restaurant*. ❺

Kalbarri Palm Resort 8 Porter St ⓣ08/9937 2333 or 1800 819 029, ⓦwww.bestwestern.com.au/kalbarri. Good-value spacious rooms with pool and tennis courts. ❹

Kalbarri Seafront Villas 108 Grey St ⓣ08/9937 1025, ⓦwww.kalbarriseafrontvillas.com.au. Offers well-equipped units, some with ocean views. ❺

Kalbarri Sunsea Villas 38 Grey St ⓣ08/9937 1187, ⓦwww.kalbarrisunseavillas.com. Units by the river facing the sea with fully equipped units and a pool. ❺

Murchison Park Grey St ⓣ08/9937 1005. Well-shaded caravan park opposite the Foreshore. On-site vans ❸

The Town and around

For those not content to laze on **Chinaman's Beach** all day, there are plenty of more active pursuits on offer. An easy way to get yourself going is to take a **cruise** up the Murchison River on the *Kalbarri River Queen* (ⓣ08/9937 1104) or rent all sorts of **watercraft** on the Foreshore from Kalbarri Boat Hire & Canoe Safaris (ⓣ08/9937 1245). They can also take you up the lower Murchison to Gregory's Rock for a morning's canoeing, with a traditional bush breakfast on the way, for $50. Big River Ranch, 4km inland from Kalbarri (ⓣ08/9937 1214; pick-ups available), runs very popular **horse riding** trips for beginners and the experienced alike; the three-hour sunset ride ($45) through the river, along the beach and back again, is the memorable highlight. **Scenic flights** with Kalbarri Air Charter (ⓣ08/9937 1130; enquire at the gift shop at 28 Grey St) start from just $45 for the short but spectacular Coastal Cliffs run, and go up to $160 for the Grand Tour or a five-hour visit to Monkey Mia. Kalbarri Sports and Dive (ⓣ08/9937 1126) can organize **dives** if you ask, while the Reef Walker (ⓣ08/9937 1356) sets off on a variety of coastal cruises with diving or fishing opportunities from $35.

Eating and drinking

Don't leave Kalbarri without checking out *Finlay's Fish BBQ* (daily 11.30am–2pm & 5.30–8.30pm; ⓣ08/9937 1260) on Magee Crescent. With plate-spinning Captain Finlay's fresh fish, salad and damper for $12, and an unusual setting in an old ice works (plus occasional fireside ballads), *Finlay's* is a treat on a balmy night.

All the other **restaurants** can seem rather conventional by comparison; the *Zuytdorp* (daily 6–10pm) at the *Kalbarri Beach Resort* is a close rival, with a $19 smorgasbord, while in the same place *Jacks* is less formal. The *Black Rock Cafe* (daily 10am–8pm), on Grey Street, has views and seafood lunches, and *Rivers*

Café (same hours as the *Black Rock*), opposite the wharf, has takeaways and more fresh seafood. There's also a good health-food café inside the shopping centre. Of the two **pubs**, the *Kalbarri Hotel* on Grey Street is where the locals hang out, while the livelier *Gilgai Tavern* on Porter Street also serves meals.

Kalbarri National Park

Kalbarri National Park (CALM fee; see box on p.714), which surrounds the town, has two popular attractions: the serpentine **river gorge** of the upper Murchison River, reached off the Ajana road east of town, and the **coastal gorges** created by lesser creeks, a few kilometres south of Kalbarri and just about within cycling range. Kalbarri Coach Tours (Ⓣ08/9937 1161) visits both areas several times a week for around $50, with a range of more adventurous options also available.

The **coastal gorges** are accessible by tracks and short walks off the Kalbarri to Northampton road. **Red Bluff** is the prominent butte overlooking Jakes Corner, where there's good surfing, and the site of some barely discernible, prehistoric crustacean fossils. **Rainbow Valley** has some intriguing features exposed by weathering, as well as a coastal walk up to **Mushroom Rock**, the most interesting part of the coastline. Pot Alley is another lookout and Eagle Gorge has a tiny secluded beach, but the view from the cliffs above **Natural Bridge** (at 16km, the furthest from town) gives the impression that you are indeed perched on the edge of a vast continent.

Eleven kilometres east of Kalbarri on the Ajana Road, a corrugated track turns north for 25km to the **gorge** along the Murchison River, where at a junction you can go a few kilometres further north to **the Loop**, or south to **Z Bend**. It's possible to walk round the Loop (a horseshoe bend in the Murchison River) in about two hours although this may be prolonged by the abundance of swimming opportunities, birdlife and the odd, mean-looking feral pig; the walk is best undertaken early in the morning. Z Bend is the most dramatic lookout over the Murchison River far below, accessible down a steep track. Once here you can abseil, rap jump and climb up Z Bend's cliff; enquire at *Kalbarri Backpackers'* for all activities – no experience is necessary. Back on the Ajana road, heading inland for 30km from the Loop turn-off, Hawks Head and Ross Graham Lookout, both a few kilometres off the road, are less impressive but worth stopping for on the way out of Kalbarri if you're driving.

It is possible to **walk** from Z Bend to the Loop over a couple of days and from Ross Graham Lookout to the Loop in four days, but both are demanding treks so consult the **park ranger** (Ⓣ08/9937 1140) first.

Shark Bay

Shark Bay is the name given to the two prongs of land and their corresponding lagoons that comprise Australia's westernmost point, forming a roughly W-shaped coastline. **Denham**, the only settlement, is on the west side of the Peron Peninsula, while at **Monkey Mia Dolphin Resort**, on the sheltered east side of the peninsula, a family of dolphins has been coming in almost daily to meet people for nearly fifty years. The shallow, aquamarine waters of Shark Bay have earned it a World Heritage listing as a remarkable **ecological habitat**, a fact that tends to be overshadowed by the dolphins. It's worth noting that dolphins also "interact", albeit less reliably, at Rockingham, Mandurah and Bunbury south of Perth.

Greyhound Australia **buses** run to Monkey Mia from Perth twice daily on Monday, Thursday and Saturday (12hr): if you plan to visit, make sure your bus pass includes this excursion. Otherwise, if it's just the dolphins you want to see consider flying up from Perth with Skywest (☎08/9948 1247). Shark Bay **Taxi** Service (☎08/9948 1331) connects with interstate buses at the *Overlander Roadhouse*, which marks the turning off the highway to Shark Bay, charging $35 to Denham and $40 to Monkey Mia.

The road to Monkey Mia

It's 150km to Monkey Mia from the *Overlander Roadhouse*, a drive that's much like the rest of the coastline in this area – a dull dense mulga scrub punctuated with some unusual sights along the way. Twenty-eight kilometres west of the *Overlander*, a road leads 5km north to the **Old Telegraph Station** (daily 8.30am–5.30pm; $6; camping, on-site vans ❷) and **Hamelin Pool**. The Pool is home to an unusual community of **stromatolites**, colonies of sediment-trapping algae which are direct descendants of the earth's earliest life forms, dating back over three billion years. It is their ancestors we can thank for diligently oxygenating the earth's atmosphere, which eventually led to more complex life forms. Viewed from a platform, the 3000-year-old examples in Hamelin Pool flourish because no potential predator can handle the pool's hyper-saline water. The Old Telegraph Station has a pet "stromie" in a tank that can look more interesting than the actual colony unless the tide is right out.

Continuing on the main road towards Denham, you'll pass *Nanga Bay Resort* (☎08/9948 3992, Ⓔnangabay@wn.com.au; dorms $20, rooms ❹), with cabins and dorms in various formats; it's a popular fishing base but otherwise uninspiring. Across the isthmus – now spanned by an electric fence, which emits a recording of barking dogs (an attempt to scare feral animals off the peninsula) – is **Shell Beach**, composed of millions of tiny shells, several metres deep. Where they've consolidated under their own weight they're cut into blocks for local buildings. Twenty kilometres before Denham, **Eagle Bluff** is an impressive

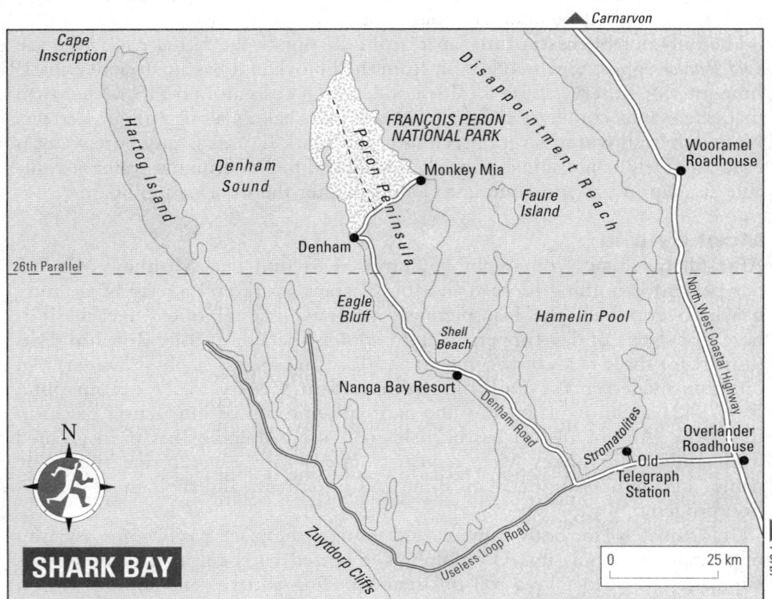

clifftop lookout where, if you're lucky, you might spot dugongs, dolphins and manta rays in the clear waters of Denham Sound below.

Denham

A small prawning port and holiday resort, **DENHAM** thrives in the lee of Monkey Mia's unflagging popularity. Between here and Monkey Mia (25km northeast), **François Peron National Park** (CALM fee; see box on p.714) is part of the Eden Project which – with the help of the aforementioned electric fence – is intended to re-establish native species by eradicating feral animals, particularly cats, with the aid of the herbal "1080" poison you see signed all over WA and to which native fauna is immune. The CALM office (ⓣ08/9948 1208) on Knight Terrace has more information about the park and other natural features in the Shark Bay area.

Denham's **tourist office** (daily 9am–5pm; ⓣ08/9948 1253, ⓦwww.ozpal.com/tourist) is on the town's main road at 71 Knight Terrace. The town also has a post office and a couple of supermarkets. **Buses** for Monkey Mia leave daily from 8am ($10). The MV *Explorer* (ⓣ08/9948 1246; from $90) operates cruises around Shark Bay, offering a good chance to see some of the clear-water bay's submarine wildlife. Shark Bay Charter Service's luxurious catamaran (ⓣ08/9948 1113) also makes for a great day out, and the company also runs **scenic flights** from $50.

It is important to call ahead when staying in the Shark Bay region as it can occasionally fill quickly if a coach tour arrives in town. **Places to stay** include *Bay Lodge*, 109 Knight Terrace (ⓣ08/9948 1278, ⓔbaylodge@wn.com.au; ❹), and the *Tradewinds Holiday Village* (ⓣ08/9948 1222; ❹), with units that sleep up to six people. The *Heritage Resort* (ⓣ08/9948 1133, ⓦwww.heritageresort.net.au; ❺), on the corner of Durlacher Street, is the town's best, and has a very pleasant bar and restaurant. Of the three **caravan parks** in town, the *Shark Bay Caravan Park*, 4 Spaven Way (ⓣ08/9948 1387; vans and cabins ❷–❸), is your best bet and has a big pool.

The only notable **restaurant**, apart from the one in the *Heritage Resort*, is the *Old Pearler* opposite, which is built from shell block and has an attractive maritime interior. It serves fresh local seafood, which costs around $15. Other than that, there are a couple of cafés, a pizza bar and a bakery along Knight Terrace. Note that fresh **water** is very precious in the Shark Bay area: salty bore water is used as widely as possible but locally desalinated public drinking water is available at a tap just as you come into Denham after the information board.

Monkey Mia

After all the hype, you might be surprised to find that **Monkey Mia** ($9 per person) is nothing more than a busy caravan park and a jetty by a pretty beach, overlooking the inauspiciously named Disappointment Reach. It is here that scores of day-trippers flock to witness the almost daily **dolphin** visits (usually for three feeds between 8am and 1pm and most reliably in winter). An intriguing video in the **Dolphin Information Centre** (daily 7.30am–4pm; ⓣ08/9481 3666) explains how the entirely unprompted interaction began in the 1960s. Almost all that has been learned about dolphins has been gleaned from studies of Monkey Mia's regular troupe of visitors, each one known by name, and numbering between three and six females and their third-generation progeny.

Unfortunately, for both dolphins and tourists, the place has become a victim of its massive popularity. The dolphins' repeated visits and their spontaneous familiarity seem to take a toll on their breeding patterns and for this reason calves, which lack immunity to human infections in their early weeks, are kept away from visitors. However, if you push into the right spot you do have a great opportunity to get a close-up shot of a dolphin.

More satisfying is a spin around the bay in one of the two catamarans berthed at the jetty, the best option being the stripped-down *Shotover* with **cruises** starting from $35 an hour – just turn up, and hop on. With luck, plenty of marine life (including prancing dolphins) can be observed and enjoyed.

The *Monkey Mia Dolphin Resort* (Ⓣ08/9948 1320 or 1800 653 611, Ⓦwww.monkeymia.com.au) is right on the beach: it has grassed campsites and, for backpackers, cramped old **caravans** with ancient kitchens (❷) or, a better option, safari tents (❸). There are also basic cabins, new budget beach-front units (❹), and motel **rooms** (❻). Also on site, there's a pool, spa, restaurant and small shop with basic groceries and takeaways.

Carnarvon and around

A centre for prawning fleets and the sheep stations of the Upper Gascoyne region, tropical **CARNARVON**, 900km from Perth, also supports a large agricultural zone, thanks to the superficially dry Gascoyne River's retrievable subterranean water. Unfortunately, the town continues to battle against a reputation for drink-related violence and crime and it's the only place between Perth and Katherine, in the NT, where you'll regularly see police cars on the prowl.

There's little in town to detain a passing traveller anyway, but a couple of diversions up the coast can make a fun day out. Six kilometres east of Carnarvon a bridge crosses the riverbed, passing the 65°C thermal well of Bibbawarra Bore and joins the sealed Blowholes Road, which leads to the **Blowholes** at Point Quobba, 65km from town. On all but the calmest days, incoming waves compress air through vents in the low cliff and erupt like geysers up to 20m into the air, a sight and sound well worth the detour. A couple of kilometres to the south is a basic campsite (no water) with sheltered snorkelling in the bay. Heading north past occasional tracks down to shell-lined beaches, you cross the private road linking the Dampier Saltworks at Lake MacLeod with the jetty at Cape Cuvier. Just north of the cape is the wreck of the *Korean Star*, beached here during a cyclone in 1988.

Practicalities

Carnarvon's ever-hopeful **tourist office** (Mon–Fri 8.30am–5pm, Sat & Sun 9am–2pm; Ⓣ08/9941 1146) is on the corner of Robinson Street and Camel Lane. **Buses** also arrive here, and the **post office** is just opposite. **Accommodation** in town includes the *Gateway Motel* on 379 Robinson St (Ⓣ08/9941 1532, Ⓔgatewaymotel@bigpond.com; ❹) and the *Hospitality Inn* (Ⓣ08/9941 1600, Ⓔcarnarvon@hospitalityinns.com.au; ❺) on West Street. *Carnarvon Backpackers*, on the foreshore, left at the end of Robinson Street (Ⓣ08/9941 1095; dorms $20), is the only choice in hostels and as good as you'd expect for this town. There are no fewer than seven **caravan parks** close to town catering for itinerant workers, and caravanners seeking the winter sun.

The North West Cape

Back on Highway 1 140km north of Carnarvon is the *Minilya Roadhouse* (daily 7am–9pm), from where a turning 6km later leads to the **North West Cape**. This hot, arid and often windy spike of land is notable for the 250-kilometre **Ningaloo Reef** which fringes its western edge, never more than 7km offshore and in places accessible right off the beach; "WA's barrier reef without the barriers" as some call it. **Exmouth** is the main settlement on the cape, located near its tip and growing year by year. However, the tiny resort of **Coral Bay**, 100km from the *Minilya*, is not only more convenient and pleasant, but the easiest place from which to view the reef.

Buses leave from Carnarvon every morning, stopping at Coral Bay on the way to Exmouth before returning to Carnarvon each afternoon. If you're heading northeast after an excursion to the Cape, you might as well go all the way back to Carnarvon and catch the bus you'd otherwise wait for at the *Minilya* – it's certainly more comfortable that way. Skywest **flies** between Perth and Exmouth (daily except Sat; 6hr), a better way of taking an excursion to the Cape if you don't want to make the 1300-kilometre drive from Perth.

Coral Bay

CORAL BAY is 12km west off the road to Exmouth and – school holidays excepted (see p.714) – can be a lovely spot from which to enjoy the reef. It's the idyllic beach resort many expect to find along the west coast, and here you can enjoy all the activities offered at Exmouth, but within walking distance of the sea. Little more than a couple of caravan parks and motels with mini shopping centres and other services, hot salty bore water and a lack of available land have held back large-scale development and although better water management arrived in 2005, the resort is not expected to grow noticeably. **Internet** access is widely available and there are **ATMs** in town, though it's worth noting that there is no official **tourist office** here; the many places displaying the familiar blue and white "i" logo are run – like almost everything else in Coral Bay – by one of the two business interests which between them own the resort.

All the **accommodation** and associated services are a few hundred metres apart along the resort's only road. On your right as you enter town is the *Ningaloo Club* backpackers' (ⓣ08/9948 5100, ⓦwww.ningalooclub.com; four- to eight-bed dorms $20–25, rooms from ❸), which has a big kitchen and games area, a small pool, nightly movies on widescreen TV and the *Club*'s own reef tours. Down the road on the left, the *Bayview Coral Bay* (ⓣ08/9942 5932, ⓦwww.coralbaywa.com) forms a large resort with shady but densely-packed powered sites for caravans and campervans ❶), various configurations of cabins, en-suite chalets, motel-type rooms and fully-equipped self-contained villas (❹–❻). Also onsite are a supermarket, **fuel** and *Fins* restaurant, which offers **Internet** access, serves good coffee, and has goldband snapper on the seafood menu. Ideally situated at the end of the road, the *Ningaloo Reef Resort* (ⓣ08/9942 5934, ⓦwww.ningalooreefresort.com.au) provides comfortable rooms in the *Coral Bay Hotel* ❻, with a **bar**, *Shades* restaurant and a popular takeaway, all by a grassed pool area with a great view over the bay. Adjacent is the *Peoples' Park Caravan Village* (ⓣ08/9942 5933, ⓔpeoplesparkcoralbay @bigpond.com), offering powered sites ❶, or motel-style cabins ❺. Like *Bayview Coral Bay*, this place is primarily set up for caravans rather than tents and they pack you in pretty tightly.

Two **glass-bottomed boats** operate several cruises daily over the reef (times depend on the tides and the included snorkelling gear can be kept for the rest of the day; from $35). The four-hour cruise, which takes you snorkelling on the more impressive outer reef, as well as visiting the Manta rays around the headland, is recommended. You'll see an amazing variety of fish, and soft and hard coral. Other fun **activities** at Coral Bay include catamaran cruises, resort dives or full PADI courses, scenic flights and sea kayaking. Your place of accommodation or either Coral Bay Adventures (ⓣ08/9942 5955, ⓦwww.coralbayadventures.com.au) or Coastal Adventure Tours (ⓣ08/9948

Ningaloo marine-spotters' calendar

Turtle hatching – January to March
Whale sharks – April to June
Manta rays – all year, Coral Bay
Coral spawning – March to April
Whale-watching – June to October
Turtle nesting – November to January

5190, Ⓦwww.coralbay.info/coastal.htm) in the shopping centre next to *Ningaloo Club* can organize it all for you. But even without all this activity and expenditure, you can still satisfy yourself just strolling up and down the beach and watching the dazzling white swell break over the reef, a few hundred metres off shore.

Exmouth

Back on the North West Cape Road on the way up to Exmouth, you pass Burkett Road, which cuts 150km from the journey if you're coming from the north. Turning north towards Exmouth, two roads lead up onto the emerging **Cape Range**: the Charles Knife Road climbs precipitously to the top of the range, 311m above sea level. From here it's possible to walk to the head of Shothole Canyon (allow 2hr), also accessible by car off the Exmouth road, though this is a far less dramatic introduction to the range.

EXMOUTH was built in 1967 to serve a former US Navy Communications Station and has since become a tourist base for visits to the Cape Range National Park and Ningaloo Marine Park. A high proportion of cloud-free days make the town a popular winter holiday-makers' resort, with tourist numbers increasing as the wonders of the Ningaloo reef become more widely known. Though far from being a west coast Cairns, diving and fishing charters, as well as marine wildlife-spotting tours (see box above) and other recreational activities all vie for your attention. Unlike Cairns, however, the ocean is a couple of kilometres away (a necessary cyclone precaution). The nearest place to see the reef is off Bundegi Beach (see overleaf), but the best of the **reef** and **beaches** are 50km away on the west side of the Cape.

Practicalities

Buses stop outside the **tourist office** (Mon–Fri 8.30am–5pm, Sat & Sun 9am–noon; Ⓣ08/9949 1176, Ⓦwww.exmouthwa.com.au) on the main Murat road opposite *Winstons/Ningaloo Caravan Resort*. Here, you can try to get your head around the range of offshore charters and tours offered. Note that if you are coming up to swim with the whale sharks, you can expect to pay a couple of hundred dollars a day for the privilege and will need both to be here at the right time of year (see box above) and have time to wait around for whale sightings.

The actual town centre is based around the apex of Maidstone Crescent; turn left at the Caltex fuel station. Here you'll find banks and the post office, supermarkets, a couple of cafes and public **Internet access**. A bus runs twice a week to Coral Bay and back (Ⓣ08/9949 4623; $50 return) and another service runs round the Cape once a day to just past the Cape Range National Park's Milyering visitors centre ($20 return, see p.771). Among other places, **cars** can be rented from *Exmouth Cape Tourist Village* or Allens Car Hire, 24 Nimitz St (Ⓣ08/9949 2403, Ⓔalscarhire@nwc.net.au). To make the most of this place you'll need some sort of transport.

When it comes to **eating** there are the usual takeaways and a Chinese in the shopping centre; other reliable favourites include *Whalers Café*, round the back on Kennedy Street and the *Sea Urchin*, behind the Caltex on Maidstone Crescent. The *Potshot* accommodates the town's main **pub**, with *Grace's Tavern* opposite the *Exmouth Cape Tourist Village*, south of the town centre.

Accommodation

Excape Backpackers Behind the *Potshot*, entrance in Payne St ⓣ08/9949 1201, ⓦwww.potshotresort.com. Central budget accommodation with small but en-suite dorms and a basic kitchen. Access to the resort's many other facilities. En-suite dorms $22, en-suite twins and doubles ❸

Exmouth Cape Tourist Village (Pete's Backpackers) Truscott Crescent ⓣ08/9949 1101 or 1800 621 101, ⓦwww.exmouthvillage.com. 2km south of town on the corner of Murat Road, this is really a spacious caravan park made up of rows of rather cramped prefab cabins with fitted kitchens serving backpackers. Tours, cruises, dives and car rental available, and the village also has a small pool and BBQ area, dorms $21.

Lighthouse Caravan Park Vlamingh Head ⓣ08/9949 1478. 16km north of town at the tip of the Cape. Basic chalets ❸, en-suite bungalows ❹ and fully featured "lookout chalets" on the hillside ❺. Powered sites ($13) and camping also available. Pool, tennis, small shop and fuel also onsite.

Ningaloo Club Market St ⓣ08/9949 1805, ⓦwww.ningalooclub.com. Situated by the new marina development 4km south of the town centre, this is a refreshing design of wood and canvas well suited to the climate. There's a choice between elevated safari tents sleeping six with attached open-air bathrooms $22pp, and some smaller twin-berth tents (deluxe, with TV ❸). There's also Internet access, a pool, bikes, a whale-watching platform and the beach is just over the dune.

Ningaloo Lodge Off Maidstone Crescent ⓣ08/9949 4949, ⓦwww.ningaloolodge.com.au. Centrally located hotel resort with well-equipped en-suite rooms, a kitchen and of course a pool. ❹

Potshot Hotel Resort Murat Road ⓣ08/9949 1200, ⓦwww.potshotresort.com. The town's main motel with restaurants and a pool. Offers a backpackers' ($22), budget motel rooms from ❹ and plusher serviced rooms from ❺

Winstons Backpackers Murat Rd, ⓣ08/9949 2377, ⓦwww.exmouthresort.com. A small block of four-bed dorms, which go for $20. Part of the *Ningaloo Caravan Resort*, offers self-contained cabins ❹, with a nice pool and some shaded camping too.

Cape Range and Ningaloo parks

These parks are adjacent land- and sea-conservation areas on the western edge of the North West Cape: to explore them from Exmouth you need either a vehicle, or to join one of the many tours sold around town. The proximity of the continental shelf is what gives the **Ningaloo Marine Park** such a stunning variety of marine life: over 500 species of fish and 220 species of coral have been recorded here which – among other things – is what attracts migrating whales and whale sharks. Heading north out of town for 14km past the Navy base, **Bundegi Beach** – just after the turn-off west and then south for Cape Range National Park, and set right below the huge antennae – is nicer than the town beaches; you can see a dark platform of **coral** just a couple of hundred metres offshore, so bring a snorkel. There are glass-bottomed coral viewing boats here too and the Navy Pier is reputed to be one of the best and most accessible dive sites in the area, teeming with sea life in shallow waters.

Backtracking to the turn-off for **Cape Range National Park** (CALM fee; see box on p.714), you pass a turn for the wreck of the *Mildura*, which clipped the reef in 1907 during a cyclone. There's also a fine **lookout** from Vlamingh Head lighthouse, from where you can see the **Muiron Islands** to the northeast (popular with turtles and diving charters). From here on south it's essentially a coastal drive past several deserted beaches, lagoons and rather congested campsites (book ahead at the CALM office in Exmouth, 22 Nimitz St ⓣ08/9949 1676 or at the park entrance). For snorkelling, the reef comes close again at the south point of **Turquoise Bay** where the wind and current tend to drift you north across the bay. Oyster Stacks, just to the south, is an alternative snorkelling venue, but you can pick pretty much any turn-off to enjoy a pristine beach and probably spot a few emus along the way.

CALM's Milyering **visitors centre** (daily 10am–4pm), 52km from Exmouth, is a solar-powered complex with videos and displays on the local ecology, and helpful staff. Another 30km past more bays and campsites brings you to **Yardie Creek**, a steep-walled canyon just a kilometre from the ocean. This is as far south as 2WDs can safely get in the park, but the walk up along the gorge's cliffs is worth the effort. The mouth of the creek sanded up a few years ago and as long as this does not change, 4WDs can easily continue south through the park past Ningaloo Homestead, enjoying beach camping or picnics all the way to Coral Bay, a drive that otherwise takes about half a day.

To Dampier and Karratha

Back on the North West Coastal Highway, it's over 500km from Carnarvon to the industrial twin towns of Dampier and Karratha, with just three roadhouses along the way. At *Nanutarra Roadhouse* (daily 6.30am–10pm) a sealed road heads east via the pristine company towns of **Paraburdoo** and **Tom Price** (70km dirt road or 131km sealed) and on to the fabulous Karijini National Park (see p.776). Further up the highway a road leads north 80km to the cyclone-battered **Onslow** (camping and a motel; ④), one of the Northwest's original settlements on the mouth of the Ashburton river, but now bypassed by the highway and most travellers too.

The two young towns of **DAMPIER** and **KARRATHA** are the Northwest's biggest industrial conurbation and population centre. Dampier was initially the export facility for Hamersley Iron's iron-ore mines at Tom Price, Paraburdoo and Marandoo, which are linked by a 350-kilometre railway. Karratha was established in 1968 when space ran out around Dampier and both grew dramatically when the **North West Shelf Natural Gas Project** got underway in the early 1980s. The project collects gas from offshore platforms 135km northwest of Dampier, from where it's piped 1500km to Perth or liquefied locally (LNG) for export to Japan and China. Offshore on the Montebello Islands, the British experimented with hydrogen bombs in the 1950s, before tests moved down to Maralinga in South Australia.

While useful for shopping centres, car repairs, accommodation and 24-hour fuel at the Caltex, the two towns have precious little to detain the passing traveller. Karratha's **tourist office** is on Karratha Road (ⓣ08/9144 4600, ⓔinfo@tourist.karratha.com), the access road off the Coastal Highway if approaching from the east. Of some interest are the **Aboriginal engravings** on the Burrup Peninsula on the northeastern outskirts of Dampier. You need a 4WD to get there but several examples can be easily seen at Deep Gorge, 1.1km before Hearson's Cove, where there's also good swimming at high tide.

Snappy Gum Safaris (ⓣ08/9185 2141, ⓦwww.snappygum.karratha.com) organizes **day-trips** from Karratha and Dampier to the Roebourne, Cossack and Point Samson area (see overleaf), further afield to Millstream and the Chichester National Park and also to Karijini (see p.772 and p.776 respectively). There are several pricey, business-oriented **motels** in Karratha like the *Best Western* (ⓣ08/9143 9888; ⑥) on Warambie Road. *Karratha Backpackers*, 110 Welland Way (ⓣ08/9144 4904; dorms $20), second right after the Shell, is a converted motel which struggles to get much business, so you might settle for a cabin or on-site van (⑤) at one of the caravan parks such as *Karratha Caravan Park*, off Karratha Road. **Internet** facilities are available at the town library or in the shopping centres.

Roebourne, Cossack and Port Samson

Established in 1864 and once the capital of the Northwest, **ROEBOURNE**, 40km east of Karratha, is the oldest surviving settlement between Port Gregory (near Kalbarri) and Darwin, though these days the town is mainly a centre for the Aboriginal population displaced by the pastoral settlement of the Northwest. As elsewhere, the **Old Gaol** was built to last and now houses the **tourist office** (Mon–Fri 9am–5pm, Sat & Sun 9am–4pm; ⓣ08/9182 1060) and **museum** (same hours, donation). Other nineteenth-century institutional buildings are dotted around the town. Next to the *Victoria Hotel* is *Mount Welcome Motel* (ⓣ08/9182 1282; ❺). There's also a caravan park (ⓣ08/9182 1063; on-site vans ❸) on De Grey Street, at the town's east end, but there are better options in Karratha or Cossack.

In Roebourne, a turn-off north leads a few kilometres to Wickham, Point Samson (see below) and passes another turn right to **COSSACK**, the small seaport which begat the town of Roebourne, and well worth a visit. All early settlers to the Northwest came through Cossack – pastoralists, pearlers as well as prospectors heading for the goldfields of the East Pilbara. At that time, the original tin and timber buildings used to be chained to the ground to weather the cyclones. But at the end of the nineteenth century, the inlet by the quay began silting up and the harbour was moved to nearby Point Samson until Port Hedland's became pre-eminent. By the 1940s Cossack was abandoned, its tramlines to Roebourne uprooted for scrap.

What's left of this historic "ghost port" has been finely restored, with interpretive signs filling you in on the origins and history of the place. The **courthouse**, with its museum of the settlement (for opening times ask at the cafe, next door; donation), is the most impressive building, both inside and out, while the former post and telegraph office is now a small art gallery (same access arrangements as for the courthouse, see above) displaying some fine local work. Hostel **accommodation** is available at the well-looked-after *Cossack Backpackers'* (ⓣ08/9182 1190; dorms $19), next door in the old police barracks. There's a café and pick-ups can be arranged from the Roebourne bus stop. Perseverance Street leads to the restored nineteenth-century **cemeteries**, both Christian and Asian, where the ages and occupations on the graves show how tough life here once was. The road continues on to **Settler's Beach**, a vast expanse of mudflat at low tide, where the pioneers came ashore before the quay was built. The original cast-iron lighthouse on **Jarman Island** is accessible by tour boat if visitor numbers and tides converge; ask at the café or the backpackers'.

Beyond Robe River Iron's oddly anachronistic company town of **Wickham** (handy for facilities and services, and a drive-in cinema), **POINT SAMSON** is a fishing port and a popular retirement and "wintering" centre. East of town is **Honeymoon Cove**, which has good swimming at high tide. Those weary of roadhouse meat pies will relish the **seafood** with a view at the *Trawlers Tavern* first-floor restaurant (daily 6–10pm), or from the pricier *Moby's Kitchen* takeaway on the ground floor (daily 11am–2pm & 5–9pm). **Places to stay** include chalets at the pricey *Point Samson Lodge*, 56 Samson Rd (ⓣ08/9187 1052; ❻), which also runs **boat charters**, or the small *Solveig Caravan Park* (ⓣ08/9187 1414; ❸) next to the *Trawlers Tavern*.

Millstream-Chichester National Park

Little more than a scenic drive and an inland oasis of palms and pools along the Fortescue River, the **Millstream-Chichester National Park** (CALM fee; see box on p.714), about 100km south of Karratha or Roebourne, is only worth a visit if you're coming or going from the Hamersley Ranges (a long fuel stage). Access from the north breaks off the coastal highway between Roebourne and Whim Creek, passing Pyramid Homestead soon after. Looking back north from the many lookouts in the park, atop the **Chichester Ranges**, you'll see why the homestead is so named; the view across this ancient Pilbara landscape is stirring and timeless.

Just inside the park, **Python Pool** is a striking waterhole backed with black and orange cliffs, where the silence is cut by the shriek of birds – well worth a photo stop. From this point it's a sixty-kilometre run south to **MILLSTREAM**, 150km from Roebourne and 183km from Wittenoom, where an old homestead has been converted into an unusually good **tourist office** (daily 8am–5pm; ⓣ08/9184 5144). A section predictably describes the rustic bliss of the Yinjibarndi Aborigines of Ngarrari (Millstream), but omits to mention that they were all cleared out by pastoralists. **Chunderwarriner Pool**, a short walk from the homestead, is a lily-dappled pool surrounded by palm trees. The date palms introduced by Afghan cameleers have overrun the indigenous Millstream palm, though this does not detract from the unexpectedly luxuriant scene. Black flying foxes hang from the palm fronds, and Millstream is also a haven for dragonflies and damselflies: 22 species have been recorded here. Walking trails up to 7km long follow the palm- and paperbark-lined Fortescue River to Crossing and Deep Reach pools, where you can **camp**.

Port Hedland and on to Broome

Whichever way you approach **PORT HEDLAND**, 1650km north of Perth via the inland Great Northern Highway, you'll spot the dazzlingly white stockpile of industrial salt at the Dampier Salt Works. It's particularly striking as red iron-ore dust coats everything else in the old town and port; even the pigeons are "enrouged". Pot Hedland is set on an island surrounded by mangroves and sludge. If you're travelling by bus, hopping off here will give you a chance to get to Karijini gorges. The detached suburb of South Hedland was the preferred residential area but these days is wracked by the same anti-social behaviour found in Broome.

The tourist office (see below) runs a daily town tour if there is enough interest, but more popular is the ninety-minute tour of the **BHP loading facility** (Mon, Wed, Fri & Sat 9.30am, Tues & Thurs 2.30pm; $18) where ships load up with 250,000 tons of iron ore at a time. In a bid to supply the huge demand in China, the port is busier than ever – exacerbating the dust problems for residents. Should you find yourself here in the wet season, whale- and turtle-watching tours are organized by the tourist office, with fishing, diving charters and harbour cruises available all year.

Practicalities

The **tourist office** where long distance **buses** stop is on Wedge Street (Mon–Fri 8.30am–4.30pm, Sat 10am–2pm; ⓣ08/9173 1711, ⓔphtbinfo@norcom.net.au). The **post office** is opposite, as are most banks. On Richardson Street, facing the shipping channel where the ore ships glide in, is *Frogs Backpackers'* ⓣ08/9173 3282; dorms $17). Like the *Harbour Backpackers'* round the corner in Edgar Street (ⓣ08/9173 4455; dorms $18, rooms ❷), these establishments are patched-up old buildings blending in with Hedland's unpretentious image. *Harbour's* has the only **sushi takeaway** north of Geraldton as well as a spa, and runs inexpensive but full-on Karijini tours (see p.777) and occasional **gold prospecting tours** ($50 a day). The *Pier Hotel* on the Esplanade no longer has the highest pub death rate in Australia but – as one local put it – at least you can see a punch coming, which is more than can be said for drinking holes in South Hedland. Next door, the *Esplanade Hotel* (ⓣ08/9173 1798; ❷-❹) has basic and en-suite motel rooms. Proper **motels** are pricey and located to the south, out of the dust zone, and include the *Best Western Hospitality Inn* (ⓣ08/9173 1044 or 13 17 79; ❺) on Webster Street and the *Mercure Inn* (ⓣ08/9173 1511; ❻), on the highway opposite the airport. There are less expensive options at the *Port Hedland Caravan Park* (ⓣ08/9172 2525; en-suite cabins ❸, motel rooms ❹), also on the highway, with similar prices at *Cooke Point Caravan Park* (ⓣ08/9173 1271), on Athol Street by the ocean, 8km from town.

Iron-ore dust can't do much for the taste buds, judging by Port Hedland's eateries. Good **restaurants** are confined to the motels like the *Mercure*. *Katz*, opposite the tourist office on Wedge Street, is roadhouse-grade mush. There are **Internet facilities** at the tourist office, and at the two backpackers'.

The strike that never ended

In 2002 a sculpture was unveiled in Port Hedland's Leak Park to commemorate the Aboriginal stockmen's strike of the 1940s. It acknowledged that Australia's once-legendary pastoral wealth was built on the backs of the Aboriginal people, on whose land and free or cheap labour it depended. Even John Forrest, WA's turn-of-the-twentieth-century premier, pastoralist and former explorer, conceded that "many of us could not be in the position we are today without native labour on our stations".

By the 1940s Australia was producing a sixth of the world's mutton and a quarter of its wool. In the Northwest, two million sheep grazed vast tracts of meagre land into the dustbowls of today, a marginal enterprise made economical by the low wages for black stockmen – barely $2 a week. The archaic **Native Administration Act** of the time protected the interests of rural industry by hampering mobility and sanctioning low or nonexistent pay for black workers.

Around this time **Don McLeod**, a white prospector, encouraged **Clancy McKenna** and **Dooley Binbin** to defy their conditions. After several years of painstaking preparation, eight hundred black workers simultaneously walked off their stations in the Port Hedland/Nullagine region on May 1, 1946. Police were instructed to harass the two camps established near Port Hedland and east of Marble Bar, and arrested McKenna and Binbin for communist subversion. Postwar food coupons were withheld, so the strikers returned to traditional ways of feeding and trading, amongst themselves. Port Hedland was at this time a small town with an "official" (white) population of just 150 and a "mob" of 400 strikers down the road. Jittery police arrested a visiting mediator, Padre Hodge, for being "within five miles of a congregation of natives", adding further support to the strike, coverage of which was largely censored from the national press.

In 1949 things came to a head, and a **station-to-station march** was organized, calling all remaining workers to join the strike. Arrest for such defiance was certain, and the strikers cheerfully offered to fill up the jail at Marble Bar and others throughout the Northwest. Only when the Seamen's Union banned the handling of "slave station" wool did the government hastily concede to McLeod's proposals – though they swiftly reneged on the deal. All through the 1950s, McLeod employed and assisted the strikers in mining ventures around Marble Bar, until the big mining companies began taking an interest in the Pilbara's mineral wealth and pushed them off their claims. The strikers never returned to the stations, demonstrating black assertion long before the 1960s civil rights campaigning in the USA, or the indigenous Australian land claims of the 1970s.

Port Hedland to Broome

The six-hundred-kilometre drive northeast from Port Hedland to Broome is one of world-class boredom, a dreary plain of spinifex and mulga marking the northern edge of the Great Sandy Desert. Halfway to Broome, the *Sandfire Roadhouse* (daily 6am–midnight) provides a welcome fuel stop before the 286-kilometre stretch to the *Roebuck Roadhouse* (daily 6am–10pm).

Despite your proximity to the ocean, beach access is only possible at the promisingly named **Eighty Mile Beach**. There's not much to do at the caravan park there (shop, fuel; cabins ❸), ten corrugated kilometres off the highway, but a drive along the beach at low tide is always exhilarating.

If you're coming south from Broome and heading for Karijini, there's an interesting dirt-road alternative that bypasses Port Hedland. One hundred kilometres after Sandfire, turn south onto the sandy Borehole Road, climb into the ranges at Shay Gap and then cross the De Grey River near Muccan station (ask at Sandfire if it's running deep). From here work your way through to **Marble Bar**, 270km south of Sandfire, where you'll find motels and fuel. After Marble Bar, head southwest to Hillside station and then west to Woodstock Community, where you soon rejoin the sealed road heading down to the *Munjina Roadhouse*, 250km from Marble Bar and 42km from Wittenoom. You only save 20km, but it's a lovely, if lonely, drive through the ochre ranges of the East Pilbara.

Inland to the Pilbara

About a thousand kilometres north of Perth are the ancient, mineral-rich highlands of the **Pilbara**, a geographical area including Mt Meharry, at 1249m the highest point in WA. The world's richest surface deposits of **iron ore** were developed here in the 1950s by Lang Hancock (see p.755) and rich discoveries continue to be made as private railroads cart the ore to the coast for shipping to Japan's – and lately China's – steel-hungry industries. Surrounding the huge open-cast mine sites are vast and arid pastoral properties, recovering from or surrendering to the early over-grazing, while in the centre of this region is the grandeur of the **Karijini National Park**, which boasts some of WA's most spectacular natural scenery.

The Great Northern Highway

Apart from the passage through the Hamersley Ranges north of Newman, scenically there's little to commend the **Great Northern Highway**'s 1600-kilometre inland section from Perth to Port Hedland – most people shoot through in two long days. But like the famed Nullabor, the monotony can have its own fascination as you pass from the wooded farmlands northward into ever more marginal sheep country, until the only viable commodity are the mineral riches below ground. Soon after New Norcia on the still narrow Great Northern Highway you'll encounter **road trains**, the iconic Outback transporters. North of Wubin they're made up into full-length trains up to 55m long, and run around the clock serving the Pilbara and the northwest coastal ports.

Unless you fancy overnighting in often-unhygienic roadside parking areas (ear plugs may help), note that **motels** and **hotels** can be up to 260km apart and are not necessarily the pick of the crop. **Buses** run three times a week between Perth and Port Hedland, stopping at the few places along the highway, including the *Munjina Roadhouse*, 190km north of Newman and 260km south of Port Hedland.

Among the half-dozen surviving towns along this inland route, semi-abandoned **CUE**, 650km north of Perth, retains some character from the goldrush era and, if nothing else, is a good place to stretch your legs. The **tourist office** on Robinson Road has displays on the town's history and details on nearby sites, including the Aboriginal rock paintings at **Walga Rock**, a few kilometres west of town. A night in the spacious jarrah interior of the *Queen of the Murchison Guest House* (ⓣ08/9963 1625; ❸), on the main road, beats any anodyne motel. The old building still echoes with the ghosts that presaged the town's decline, following World War II.

North of Cue the landscape outruns the south's rain-bearing fronts; claypans and scrub replace the trees and bloated or desiccated remains of roadkill proliferate. **MEEKATHARRA**, 115km north of Cue, is a mining and pastoral centre (though this makes it sound grander than it is), with a couple of century-old **hotels** like the *Royal Mail* on the main road (❹). The *Auski Inland Motel* (ⓣ08/9981 1433; ❺) is more salubrious, or you can listen to shunting road trains all night at the caravan park behind the *Ampol* service station. From Meekatharra, it's 180km of dirt east to forlorn Wiluna, then another 600km of dull bitumen south to Kalgoorlie-Boulder, while to the west Carnarvon (itself no paradise) lies at the end of a good seven-hundred-kilometre dirt road. Continuing north from Meekatharra on the Great Northern Highway, a road sign marks the **26th parallel**, welcoming you to the fabled "Nor'west", and clumps of the spiky spinifex grass which carpet Australia's interior deserts begin to appear.

NEWMAN, 350km north of "Meeka", is a company town built to serve what is now the world's largest open-cut iron-ore mine. Besides stocking up at the only Woolies between Port Hedland and Perth, the **mine tours** (Mon–Sat 8.30am & also Mon–Fri 1pm during peak season; 1hr 30min; enclosed shoes necessary; $12), departing from the **tourist office** (Mon–Sat 8am–5pm, Sun 9am–1pm; ⓣ08/9175 2964) on Newman Drive are the only other reason you'd want to stop here. The tours clearly demonstrate the simplicity and scale of the operation, as **Mount Whaleback** is gradually turned inside out and shipped to the Far East. Local companies run **tours** (see box opposite), lasting between half a day and three days, to local waterholes. The town has a pair of **motels** (❺) with bunkhouses (❸) and two **caravan parks** (dorms $28, en-suite cabins ❹).

Marble Bar

From Newman, a dirt road leads north for 300km through the scenic East Pilbara to **NULLAGINE** and **MARBLE BAR**. The latter (now linked to Port Hedland by a sealed road) was notorious for being Australia's hottest town, in 1923–24 clocking up 160 days over 38°C. This is the sole reason many visitors come to "the Bar", misnamed after a colourful bar of jasper by the Coolingan River 5km south of town. For an overnight stay, there's a **caravan park**, a **motel** (ⓣ08/9176 1166; ❸) and the town's famed, windowless *Ironclad Hotel* (ⓣ08/9176 1066; ❸) – a good place to get some drinking done or, if you're a "sheila", be stared at.

Karijini National Park

The **Karijini National Park** (CALM fee; see box on p.714) is WA's second largest park, with a vast unvisited section to the south, separated by the BHP

Yandicoogina mine railway. Apart from the impressive gorges, it's the distinctive blend of crooked, white-trunked snappy gums sprouting from the ox-blood red rock, over a carpet of pale green spinifex, which makes the eastern Pilbara more resplendent than the better known Kimberley, especially in July and August (also the busiest months). Most of the roads in the park are dirt, but barring cyclone-related storms in late summer, the park remains accessible throughout the year.

The **gorges** themselves cut through the north-facing escarpment of the Hamersley Ranges and can be broadly divided into three groups: those in the east near the tourist office; the central "Four Gorges" area; and those in the far west. All offer some **spectacular views** as well as short walks through their interiors. Some of these (detailed in the *Pilbara Walks* book available from CALM offices or the tourist office; $16) develop into challenging **canyoneering adventures** with immersions or swims through cold pools; not forbidden, but not encouraged without supervision. Take heed of the "Trail Risk [beyond this point]" **warning signs** in some of the gorges or better still take advantage of adventure tours and their guides' experience. If heading past the signs you must **inform a ranger** of your plans (via the campground host's radios or the tourist office) and report your safe return. Accidents occur regularly and fatalities are not uncommon but rangers are rarely seen. Currently the park lacks so much as a well-signposted day walk; you're either gazing down from lookouts or acting out Indiana Jones fantasies far below although there's talk of long-distance walks being developed in the next few years.

If you're driving through the park, note that **distances** can be deceptive; a full tour of all the gorges can involve a drive of over 250km. The nearest fuel and accommodation points are *Munjina Roadhouse* in the east (120km from the central gorges) or Tom Price in the west (84km). Most travellers without vehicles pick up tours (see box below) in Port Hedland, Tom Price or Karratha.

The visitors centre and the eastern gorges

On the east side of the park, around 36km from the turn-off on the Great Northern Highway is the **visitors centre** (daily 9am–5pm; ⓣ08/9189 8121). Constructed in massive iron plate, it symbolizes both the riches of the Pilbara

Tours of the Karijini

Make sure you enquire about the nature of these tours: the first two outfits below offer adventurous outings, depending on interest, while the latter two are more tame. Note too that if they are responsible, large groups of ten or more should have more than one guide for exploring deep into the gorge interiors.

Design-A-Tour (ⓣ08/9188 1670). Long-established Karijini operator with pick-ups at *Munjina Roadhouse* and Tom Price. Day-trips to all the gorges from around $100 with lunch.

Harbour Backpackers' (ⓣ08/9173 4455). Based in Port Hedland and run two- and three-day tours (dep. Sat) getting right into the gorges from around $100 a day. Wetsuits provided.

Lestok Tours (ⓣ08/9189 2032, ⓦwww.lestoktours.com.au). Operate out of Tom Price and offer scenic day-tours to all the gorge lookouts from around $100 with lunch.

Snappy Gum Safaris (ⓣ08/9185 2141, ⓦwww.snappygum.karratha.com). Based in Karratha, this outfit runs two- to four-day tours through the Pilbara from around $100 a day.

and, from above, a goanna or *bungarra* lizard of the local Banijima Aboriginal people. Inside, exhibits include some pioneering-era relics and captivating posters of the gorges as well as an "Aboriginal care-of-the-land" theme – a subject that is not actually pursued or explained anywhere else in the park. It's the selective view adopted by many national parks to underline their preferred eco-message while leaving visitors clueless as to the bigger picture of Australian indigenous culture.

Ten kilometres before the tourist office you'll have passed the **Dales Gorge** area, which has basic **camping** (toilets; gas barbecues) and is popular with caravanners. Here, the idyllic Fortescue Falls make a great lookout or a place to swim. With half a day to spare, a visit to the falls can be joined with a great six-kilometre walk to Fern Pool and Circular Pool beyond, with plenty of water to cool off in along the way. If you're still feeling energetic you can explore further up or down Dales Gorge.

The Four Gorges area

Just west of the tourist office, Bunjima Drive turns to gravel and soon you reach a turn-off leading north to **Kalamina Gorge**, with easy walks along its bed. Though pretty enough, Kalamina can be given a miss if you don't have much time. Back on Bunjima Drive, the next turn-off leads to an impressive lookout onto the tiered amphitheatre of **Joffre Falls** (usually just a trickle). The top of the "falls" can be easily reached and crossed along a spinifex-fringed path.

The dirt road winds on to end at **Knox Gorge** car park with another dramatic lookout platform nearby. Though not signposted, to the left of the notice board a narrow path leads through the spinifex for about a kilometre to a still more dramatic view into Red Gorge 100m below, near its confluence with Knox Gorge (beware of loose edges). Back at the car park, a loose rubbly track leads down into Knox Gorge itself. Just upstream is a nice pool, while heading downstream through pools or along ledges, the gorge suddenly narrows at a warning sign (allow 30min from the car park). Progress from here on gets awkward and ends at the exhilarating (to say the least) "Knox Slide", which is itself immediately followed by the potentially more dangerous 5m "Knox Jump" into a shallow pool. From here you can hop into the green waters of Red Gorge but the Slide and what follows should not be undertaken without equipment and either the know-how to get back up the Slide (rope ladders), or wet suits, other flotation aids and the commitment to swim up Red Gorge through cold pools up to 300m at a time to Junction Pool (allow an hour from the Slide, see below).

Back on Bunjima Drive, the next turning north passes the privately-run Savannah **Campground** (showers and gas barbecues available). The road ends at a car park on the spur between Hancock and Weano gorges. From here it's a short walk to **Oxer's Lookout**, which surveys the dramatic confluence of four gorges. Straight ahead is **Red Gorge**, which runs on into Wittenoom Gorge and Wittenoom itself. Returning from Oxer's Lookout on the Hancock Gorge (south) side of the spur is a more impressive viewing platform, which looks straight down to the mouth of Hancock Gorge as it runs into Junction Pool with its stand of tall cadjiput trees.

Back again from this viewing platform, and on the north side of the spur, steps drop down into **Weano Gorge** which, for most visitors, ends after a 15-minute walk along the bed of the gorge at **Handrail Pool**. If you're prepared to get wet and wild you can drop into the pool and carry on carefully downstream along narrow chasms and ledges, ending at a point where Weano Gorge drops 25m into Junction Pool. This is an exhilarating but not too dangerous way of appreciating the full drama of Weano Gorge, best undertaken with the guidance of a tour guide.

Back at the car park, the descent into **Hancock Gorge** – ending at a metal ladder – is no less impressive, as you enter a magical realm of banded iron walls washed smooth by passing floods. The warning signs start at **Kermit's Pool** (1hr return), from where some very tricky moves and slippery descents lead all the way down to **Junction Pool**. Unless led by tour guides, few visitors get to this point, where the former Miracle Mile used to lead up the cliff into the mouth of Weano Gorge. Tour operators are no longer permitted to go up the cliff (and so complete the true "Miracle Mile") though it must be said that, apart from one exposed step, the ascent of Weano cliff is technically much easier than some moves on the descent into Hancock. Following recent misadventures, the approved way out of Junction Pool is either back up Hancock, or up the freezing pools of Joffre Gorge to the first scree slope on the left, which leads 1.5km cross-country back to the Knox Gorge car park (a long way from Oxer's Lookout area where you may have started). From Junction Pool it's also possible to swim and walk all the way down Red Gorge, past Knox Gorge entrance at the Slide and out of the park into Wittenoom Gorge and eventually Wittenoom itself (allow a day and, if they ask, don't expect the blessing of the park rangers who toe the state line on Wittenoom, see below).

Mount Bruce, the western gorges and Tom Price

From the Four Gorges, Bunjima Drive continues across the roof of the Pilbara, to rejoin the sealed road between Tom Price in the west and the Great Northern Highway in the east. Overlooking the junction is **Mount Bruce**, at 1235m WA's second-highest peak and climbable along a six-kilometre path from where you can survey the Marandoo mine.

Depending on where you're going, it's now quite a detour to visit **Hamersley Gorge**, just outside the northwestern corner of the park, 48km west of Wittenoom and about 80km northeast of Tom Price. Should you make the effort you'll find its spa-like pool and acutely folded beds of blue-grey and orange rock unlike any of the other gorges. A bit of exploring up- and downstream could easily fill a day here. Just east of the Hamersley Gorge turn-off, the dirt road leading to Wittenoom passes through **Rio Tinto Gorge**, which bears an extraordinary resemblance to a box-canyon film set from 1950s westerns.

Given the pariah status of Wittenoom (for the full story see below), **TOM PRICE**, on the east side of the park, is the government-approved base for exploring Karijini. The **tourist office** (May–Sept Mon–Fri 8.30am–5.30pm, Sat & Sun 9am–noon; Oct–April Mon–Fri 8.30am–2.30pm, Sat 9am–noon; ⓣ08/9188 1112, ⓦwww.tompricewa.com.au), on Central Road has **Internet access** and organizes daily ninety-minute **tours** ($15) of Hamersley Iron's mine, time of departure dependant on when, and how many, people turn up. Accommodation is limited to the *Tom Price Hotel Motel* (ⓣ08/9189 1101; ❺) on Central Road or the caravan park below Mount Nameless on the Nanutarra Road (backpacker dorms $22, en-suite cabins ❹). Although it's not on the bus route, the town has all the services you'd expect, including the *Millstream Café* near the **supermarket**.

Wittenoom and Wittenoom Gorge

At each end of **WITTENOOM**, warning signs proclaim the possible health hazard incurred by setting foot in the town as a result of the asbestos mining carried out here up to 1966. It's estimated that one in ten ex-miners and former inhabitants have died of diseases associated with inhaling asbestos dust, so nowadays, for legal reasons the sole public call box is situated just outside the town's limits to be on the safe side.

In its natural state **blue asbestos** or crocidolite is a harmless and unusual fibrous mineral, readily found in the Yampire and upper Wittenoom gorges; it's only the **dust** produced during milling operations that can be lethal. Unfortunately, tailings from the mill were once used to make "sandpits" for the town's children, leaving all residents at the time susceptible to a virulent form of lung cancer. These days, resurfacing has long been completed and, unless you're burrowing into what's left of the tailings in Wittenoom Gorge, the town's air is no more harmful than most urban centres or indeed, active open-cut mines. Nevertheless the WA government has long been committed to shutting down Wittenoom, and have even deleted it from some maps and other information sources.

Partly because of its tragic history and partly due to its spectacular setting, the remainder of the town possesses an intangible ambience like few other places in WA. In the 1950s it was the biggest settlement in the Northwest – today the empty lots and roaming kangaroos speak of a ghost town not prepared to die just yet.

Three times a week, the Perth to Port Hedland **bus** stops at the *Munjina Roadhouse* (Ⓣ08/9176 6988; camping and motel rooms; ❹) on the Great Northern Highway, 42km east of town. If you call in advance, the *Guest House* (see below) may pick you up. As far as services in town go, there's a **post office** at the Gem Shop (daily 8am–6pm; Ⓣ08/9189 7096) on Sixth Avenue, which also dispenses basic groceries as well as a highly-recommended **sketch map** of the national park. If you're planning to stay a few days bring what you need.

There are two **places to stay** in Wittenoom, neither fancy but both cheap. *Wittenoom Holiday Homes* (Ⓣ08/9189 7096; enquire at the Gem Shop; ❷) offer complete three-bedroom houses for rent, or there's the charmingly basic *Wittenoom Guest House* (Ⓣ08/9189 7060; dorms $10, rooms ❷), the green bungalow by the "church" with camping in the well-kept garden or car park. The *Guest House* is the sort of place you'll come for a night and stay a week.

Wittenoom itself is at the mouth of **Wittenoom Gorge**, with Cathedral Pool on the left and Town Pool on the right, both around 6km south of town. At the end of the sealed road 5km further on are the foundations of the so-called Settlement, the former asbestos mining offices razed in 2003 as part of the clean-up operation; the same fate has befallen the ageing mill nearby, which may still be surrounded by the potentially lethal blue-grey tailings.

From the Settlement, it's possible to trek up to the impressive entrance of **Red Gorge** (2hr), and then walk and swim for another hour or so to **Junction Pool** (see p.779); all in all a hard day's adventuring.

Broome and around

"Slip into Broometime" used to be a well-worn local aphorism that still captures the tropical charm of **BROOME**, an ever more popular and – for the Northwest – uncharacteristically classy town with a population of fifteen thousand, which clings to a peninsula hanging over Roebuck Bay. William Dampier, the English buccaneer-explorer, passed through in 1699 while on the run from an irate Spanish flotilla, and 160 years later the local Aborigines repelled an early fleet of prospective pastoralists. Easily collected pearl shell heaped along Eighty Mile Beach led to the northwestern "**Pearl Rush**" of the 1880s, initially enabled by enslaved Aborigines. Later indentured workers from Asia had to seek the shell in ever-greater depths below the waves, boosted by the invention of hard-hat diving apparatus. Broome originated as a camp on sheltered Roebuck Bay where the pearl luggers "laid up" during the cyclone season. After a violent and raucous beginning common to many frontier towns of that era (see Borroloola, p.671), the port finally achieved prosperity which lasted until the outbreak of World War I.

It was actually the nacre-lined oyster shells, or **mother-of-pearl**, rather than extremely rare pearls themselves, which brought fortune to the town. By 1910, eighty percent of the world's pearl shell – used in the manufacture of buttons and cutlery handles amongst other things – came from Broome, by which time a rich ethnic mix and a rigidly racially stratified "plantation" society had developed. "Chinatown" teemed with riotous Kupangers, Filipinos and "Malays" (Southeast Asians) crewing for the predominantly Japanese divers – a boiling pot collectively termed "Saltwater Cowboys" in a well-known album by local musicians, the Pigram Brothers. Each season one in five divers died, several more became paralyzed and, as Broome's cemeteries steadily filled, only one shell in five thousand produced a perfect example of the silvery pearls unique to this area – a fascinating story vividly told in John Bailey's book *The White Divers of Broome*.

Stagnation followed both world wars, after which the wily Japanese – masters in the secret art of pearl culturing – returned and invested in the pearl-farming ventures around Broome's well-suited coastal habitat. Things improved with the sealing of the coastal highway from Perth in the early 1980s and the philanthropic interest of the English businessman Alistair McAlpine, who fell for Broome and subsequently kicked off its latter-day reinvention. He led the old town's tasteful development and refurbishment which capitalized on its oriental and pearling mystique. This rich history is enhanced by the sweeping expanse of **Cable Beach**, **Gantheaume Point**'s paprika-red outcrops and the Indian Ocean's breathtaking shade of turquoise. New beach resorts and housing developments continue to be built, and combined with the nearby Kimberley's "frontier" appeal, both aspiring lotus-eaters and visitors alike continue to be drawn in, and Broome's prosperity looks set to continue.

Arrival and information

Greyhound **buses** stop by the tourist office on the corner of Bagot Street and Broome Road (the main road into town from the coastal highway) where minibuses and taxis meet all arrivals. The interstate **airport terminal**, round the corner on McPherson Street, couldn't be more central, being less than a kilometre west of Chinatown and a short walk to the two main backpackers' and a motel. The clued-up staff at the **tourist office** (Mon–Fri 8am–5pm, Sat & Sun 9am–4pm; ⓣ08/9192 2222, ⓦwww.broomevisitorcentre.com.au) hand out local guides and town maps, to help you find your way around the initially confusing layout of Broome. The town's **bus service** ($3 per ride, Multirider tickets from $12 for 5 rides) runs between Chinatown and the end of Cable Beach Road from around 7am to 6pm, via most of Broome's accommodation centres. It's now supplemented by the Nightrider service which runs nightly from 6.30pm until just after midnight from April to December, and additionally until 3am Tuesday to Saturday from May to October ($3.50 per ride, Night Pass $6). For taxis and car, scooter and bike rentals, see "Listings".

Accommodation

Most of the **hotels** are in the southern part of town with the **backpackers'** located in and around Chinatown. Self-contained apartments are available in resort compounds located off Cable Beach Road. These **resorts** can represent good value if there's a group of you, though some don't have restaurants or bars. Prices are relatively expensive up here, but if you're stuck down south in winter and want to make a visit, it's possible to pick up package holidays to Broome aimed at the domestic market; ask at any travel agent. The southern winter is high season here, at which time you'll be advised to book ahead, although many Europeans escaping their own winter blues turn up in Broome's hot and humid season when they can expect prices lower than those listed below. There are five **caravan parks** in town, all marked on the map.

Hotels and resorts

Bali Hai Resort 6 Murray St, Cable Beach ⓣ08/9191 3100 or 1800 807 061, ⓦwww.balihairesort.com. Sumptuous and spacious luxury self-contained studios and two-bedroom apartments, outfitted in the style of a Balinese walled compound with outdoor shower and patio, all set around a shady pool. Ten percent reduction for three nights or more. ❻

Broome Motel Frederick St ⓣ08/9192 7775, ⓦwww.broomemotel.com.au. Set among tropical herbage, this is Broome's best value motel, with comfortable rooms. Short walk from the airport and Chinatown, and with good summertime reductions. ❹

Mangrove Hotel Carnarvon St ⓣ08/9192 1303 or 1800 094 818, ⓦwww.mangrovehotel.com.au. Very comfortable hotel, 5min from Chinatown and in a great position on a rise overlooking Roebuck Bay. The spacious terrace incorporating the *Tides* garden restaurant is a popular spot to view the "Staircase to the Moon". ❼

Ocean Lodge Cnr of Frederick St and Cable Beach Rd ⓣ08/9192 7700 or 1800 600 603, ⓦwww.oceanlodge.com.au. An average motel, part of the *Budget* chain located halfway between Cable Beach and Chinatown, opposite the town pool and near the shopping centre. Bus stop opposite. Rooms are in several blocks, all self-contained and including stoves. Set around a central pool. ❺

Palms Resort Hopton St ⓣ08/9192 1898 or 1800 094 848, ⓔpalmsresort@wn.com.au. Old complex of apartments and motel-style rooms in a large tropical garden setting. Three pools, two restaurants and bars, including the *Beer and Satay Hut*; close to the town beach and Seaview Shopping Centre. ❺–❻

Backpackers' and caravan parks

Broome's Last Resort Bagot St ⓣ08/9193 5000 or 1800 801 918, ⓦwww.broomeslastresort.com.au. Broome's original purpose-built backpackers' – close to a cinema and the tourist office but looks a bit cramped these days. You get a small landscaped pool, bar, bikes and coin-operated a/c. Dorms from $22, rooms ❸

Cable Beach Backpackers End of Sanctuary Rd ⓣ08/9193 5511 or 1800 655 011, ⓦwww.cablebeachbackpackers.com. Laid-back and spacious place away from the sometimes noisy central Broome alternatives. Has a pool, hammocks, bar, and big kitchen, as well as town shuttle bus and bus/airport pick-ups. Dorms ($22) are fanned and mostly four-bed with a few doubles. ❸

Cable Beach Caravan Park Millington Rd ⓣ08/9192 2066. One of Cable Beach's three caravan parks, 2km from the beach with self-contained cabins from ❹

Kimberley Klub Frederick St ⓣ08/9192 3233, ⓦwww.kimberleyklub.com. One of the best-designed backpackers' around; a purpose-built mini-resort that ticks all the boxes, although some dorms suffer from their proximity to late-night chatterboxes (dorms near the laundry are quieter). Spacious and breezy layout with volleyball, pool, bar, Internet access and fans, with coin-operated a/c in the four- to six-bed dorms. Dorms from $23, rooms ❸

Roebuck Bay Caravan Park Walcott St ⓣ08/9192 1366, ⓔroebuckbaycp@broomewn.com.au. The best-located caravan park in town, right next to the small town beach and Seaview Shopping Centre. Bike rental available. From April to Sept, camping is available in the adjacent mango field with kitchen, on-site vans ❸

The Town and around

Broome originally flourished around the old port area known as **Chinatown**, a misnomer as people from several, mostly Asian, cultures once lived here. This old quarter has seen much reconstruction of original buildings, with street signs in five languages and payphones topped with jaunty pagoda roofs. Trendy boutiques and cafés occupy most of the buildings, but Sun Pictures (see "Nightlife and events") on Carnarvon Street opened in 1916, which makes it as old as

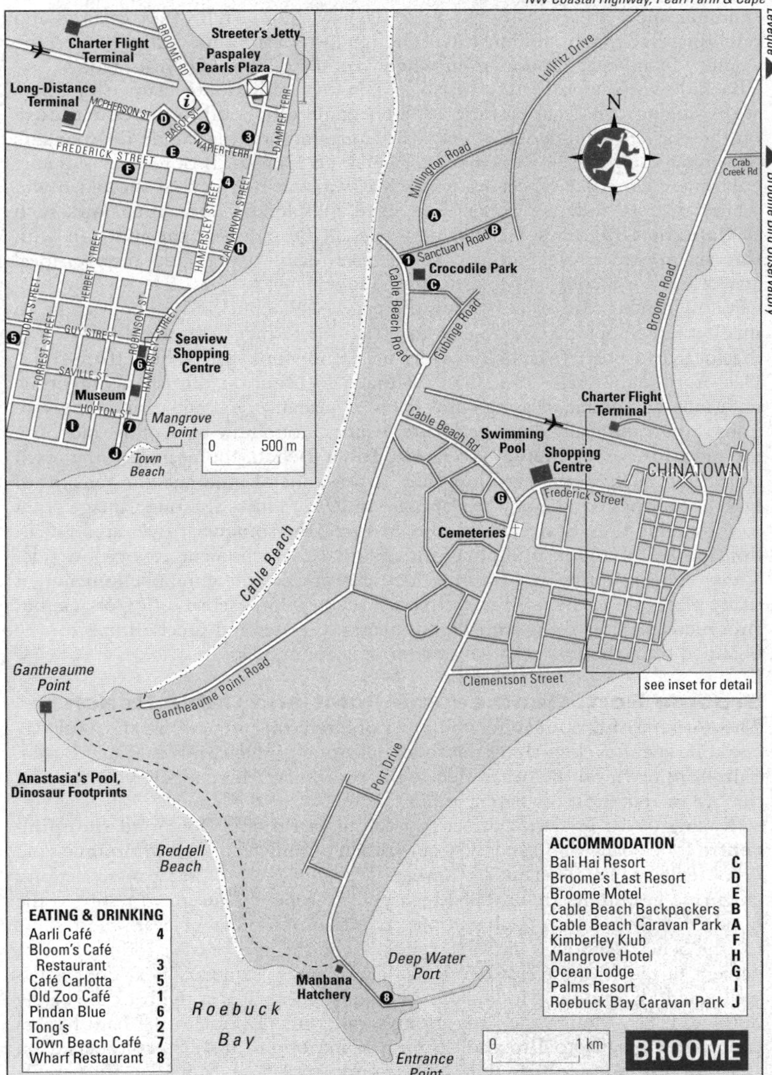

Hollywood itself. During the daytime you can take in the virtually unchanged interior and see photographs showing the segregated seating order of the bad old days. At the end of the street is the **post office** and the Paspaley Pearls Plaza **shopping centre** (supermarket open till midnight). A right turn leads to the renovated Streeter's Jetty, which runs into the mangroves off the end of Dampier Terrace. Conscious of the street's heritage, several **pearl dealers** have shops here, where you'll also find **Pearl Luggers** (daily 9am–5pm), a free exposition of Broome's pearling heritage, with a couple of dry-docked luggers and informative one-hour tours (three times daily; $18.50). **Johnny Chi Lane** runs between Dampier and Carnarvon streets; these days it's mostly full of art galleries and boutiques like much of Chinatown, though historical plaques fill you in on the events which begat Broome right where you stand, over 120 years ago.

Back down Napier Terrace past the Male Oval, a left onto Hamersley Street at the Shell garage leads past the 1888 telegraph office and to the **courthouse** on the corner of Frederick Street, whose grounds are the venue for **markets** on Sunday mornings – a good place to pick up prints of Broome's photogenic environs. Hamersley Street leads to what was the rich end of the old town, where masters and merchants once lived in splendid, airy bungalows such as **Captain Gregory's House**, now *Matso's Brewery* near the junction with Carnarvon Street. Next door, *Matso's Store* (daily 10am–5pm) displays local artwork and is a cool spot for an alfresco lunch.

Following the road round, along the edge of Roebuck Bay, you'll come to the Seaview Shopping Centre next to which the former Customs House houses the local **museum** (May–Nov Mon–Fri 10am–4pm, Sat & Sun 10am–1pm; Dec–April daily 10am–1pm; $3). Naturally focusing on the town's maritime traditions, and with a pleasing "junk shop" appearance, it could easily occupy an hour or two and really deserves a better venue. Round the back of the museum, the old **Pioneer Cemetery** overlooks **Town Beach**, the nearest to the town centre. From the jetty, very low tides reveal a lot of mud and the remains of Dutch seaplanes bombed by the Japanese in 1942. This is also one vantage point for observing the "**Staircase to the Moon**", the somewhat overrated reflections of the full moon rising over the mud flats, which occur at very low tides a few nights in spring and autumn. You can observe the same phenomenon at many places along the northwestern coast such as Port Hedland or Cossack, but Broome capitalizes on it with nightly markets. Dates and precise times can be obtained from the tourist office or at your accommodation.

Broome Port, Gantheaume Point and Cable Beach

The outskirts of Broome offer a number of interesting attractions, and a full day could be spent cycling along the following route, which ends at Cable Beach, 6km from town on the ocean side of the peninsula. Alternatively you can take the bus or rent a car, or better still, a scooter.

Heading down Frederick Street past the main Broome Boulevard **shopping centre** (open 8am–8pm) and the Cable Beach turning, you'll get to Broome's old **cemeteries** which filled quickly during the pearling years. The Japanese section's enigmatic headstones (refurbished by a philanthropic countryman) testify to the hundreds of lives lost in the hazardous collection of mother-of-pearl, mostly due to "the bends", although the 1908 cyclone took the lives of over 150 men – five percent of the workforce at that time. The Chinese cemetery next door is less well-cared for, and the Muslim and Aboriginal graveyards at the back are barely distinguishable, though the latter group's enslavement prior to the hard hat era contributed greatly to Broome's early pearling boom. It's a story touched on at **Manbana aquaculture hatchery** (tours April–Sept Mon–Sat 10.30am &

Tours around Broome

Although just hanging out in Broome can be satisfying, just about every permutation of recreational activity is becoming available in Broome, as the resort's popularity grows. Broome Day Tours (☎08/9192 1068) organize three-hour **historic tours** around the town (daily; $51), as do Pearl Town Tours (Mon, Tues, Thurs & Fri 2pm; ☎08/9192 6948; $50), which end with a free cocktail at *Matso's Brewery*. Three outfits: Ships of the Desert, Broome Camel Safaris and Red Sun Camels (all bookable via the tourist office) offer sunset **camel rides** along Cable Beach, from $65. At the other end of the beach, you can go **sea kayaking** around Gantheaume Point with Western Blue Sea Kayak (April–Nov up to twice daily; ☎1300 665 888, ⓦwww.westernblue.com.au; $65). Tours are undemanding, using stable "sit-on-top" kayaks with no experience required.

There are many worse places to watch the sunset than at sea on the *Pindan*, a traditional schooner built by its skipper (☎0408 884 440; BYO, plus snacks, 3pm–dusk; $65). Back in town Mamabulanjin Aboriginal Tours offer fun and informative three-hour cultural tours around Broome (☎08/9192 2660; $59). If none of that takes your fancy there are jaunts on Harley trikes, helicopters, hovercraft, motorised hang-gliders and hot-air ballooning, and that's just "h": the full alphabet of activities is available at the tourist office.

Broome is well positioned for **scenic flights** across the spectacular west Kimberly Coast which is only otherwise accessible by sea (and even then with difficulty due to the extreme tides). The Buccaneer Archipelago and the extraordinary spectacle of the **Horizontal Waterfall** where the huge tides tear back and forth through narrow openings into sea-flooded valleys are the highlights. Among others, Horizontal Falls Adventure Tours (☎08/9192 2885, ⓦwww.horizontalfalls.com.au; $340) offer a half-day flight in a high-wing seaplane which lands in Turtle Bay. Here, a small powerboat rides through the lesser rapids – a rare chance to see this far-flung corner of Australia from the air and sea. The flight returns via Cape Leveque with overnight stays on a houseboat moored in Turtle Bay, which will give you a chance to experience the tidal range and maybe see a crocodile.

Further afield

Luxury **cruise boats** pass along the convoluted inlets of the north Kimberley coast, but with some craft featuring à la carte menus and helidecks for incoming guests, prices will be as spectacular as the coastline. One-day road-based excursions include visits to **Windjana Gorge** and **Tunnel Creek** ($205) or **Geikie Gorge** ($232) with Australian Pinnacle Tours (☎08/9192 8080, ⓦwww.pinnacletours.com.au). Their buses are thoughtfully equipped with movies as it's a hefty 800km trip. Or you can do all three places in two days with Kimberley Wild Expeditions (☎08/9193 7778, ⓦwww.kimberleywild.com; from $375). Both the above outfits also do 1–3 day visits up to **Cape Leveque**, from $209 for the 470km round trip.

Between Broome and Kununurra, interstate buses run overnight so you won't see much of the Kimberley countryside; all the more reason to take an eastbound tour to Kununurra along the unsealed **Gibb River Road** (GRR, see p.796) instead. Outfits that are based in, or pass through Broome include Kimberley Wild (see above), who offer a four-day GRR tour from $770, and All Terrain Safaris (☎1800 633 456, ⓦwww.allterrain.com.au) who between May and October run seven- to twelve-day camping tours right across the GRR, including the remote Mitchell Plateau as well as the Bungles costing around $130 a day (longer tours continue to Darwin). Australian Adventure Travel (☎1800 621 625, ⓦwww.safaris.net.au) do a 5-day GRR in a big, comfy bus, ending in Kununurra, for $750. Finally, if you can get yourself to Derby you can hop on the *Gibb River Road River Express* which knocks out the 700km across the old stock route to Kununurra in one day (see p.797).

1.30pm; $15; ⓣ08/9192 3844), on Murakami Road near the end of Port Drive. Primarily a trochus shell hatchery (real shell buttons are back in vogue), with coral viewing aquariums and barramundi feeding, the tours also give an insight into the maritime cultures of the local Yawuru and Bardi people, who for millennia traded pearl shell right across Australia, as far away as current day NSW.

The turn off Port Drive continues to **Reddell Beach** on the Roebuck Bay side of the peninsula. Tides permitting, you can walk right along the shore, past the outcrops weathered by cyclones, to **Gantheaume Point**, where the dark red-sandstone formations contrast sharply with the pearly white expanse of Cable Beach and pastel blue ocean stretching northwards. The old **lighthouse** is now a beacon, but the pool built by the former keeper for his disabled wife, Anastasia, remains among the tidal rocks. A cast of some 120-million-year-old **dinosaur footprints** is set in the rocks – the originals are out to sea and visible at very low tides. In 1996 more dinosaur footprints were found on Aboriginal land north of Cable Beach, but were hewn from the rock by international fossil thieves.

Named after the nineteenth-century telegraph cable which came ashore here, **Cable Beach** extends for an immaculate 22km north of Gantheaume Point to Willie Creek. Regular 2WD cars and those with dogs can drive down a ramp onto the beach just before Gantheaume Point (where sea kayaking and some cruises commence – see "Tours" box on p.785). To the north, below the *Cable Beach Salt Bar and Grill* is the "children's" part of the beach (ie no cars, dogs or nudity). Windsurfers and sailboards are available on the beach during the season, though lately they've taken to corralling swimmers into a 100m-band of shore patrolled by a lifeguard. This is very comforting, but enough to drive you into the nude sunbathing area north of the rocks where cars (ideally 4WD) are also allowed again, all the way up to Willie Creek,

Broome is regarded as the westernmost limit of saltwater **crocodiles**; there's the odd sighting at the end of the Wet. The **Broome Crocodile Park** (April–Oct Mon–Sat 10am–5pm, Sun 2–5pm; guided feeding tours at 3pm; $15), on Cable Beach Road, can show you scores of these gruesome beasts at close quarters, including one-eyed Willie who was shot and eventually trapped in Willie Creek a few years ago.

The rich mudflats around Roebuck Bay are visited by thousands of migratory shore birds in late March – a third of Australia's species have been seen here. The **Broome Bird Observatory** (ⓣ08/9193 5600, ⓦwww.broomebirdobservatory.com; day entry $5, 1hr to full-day tours from $13 to $118, times dependent on tides and season), 25km north from town (last 15km dirt), welcomes day and overnight visitors and accommodation available includes camping, bunks from $36 and self-contained chalets ❹

Eating and entertainment

Gastronomically, Broome might almost be a trendy suburb of Perth; the cafés and restaurants are the best selection for a thousand kilometres or more so make the most of it. Contrary to expectations, but as in metropolitan Australia, the town's best cuisine tends to be Mediterranean rather than Oriental.

Aarli Café Hamersley Street, cnr of Frederick Street. Wood-fired pizzas and tapas, with fresh fish the speciality; check out the blackboard. Threadfin salmon, mangrove jack and, if you're lucky, coral trout make a change from the ubiquitous barramundi. Outdoor seating available. Daily 8am–late.

Bloom's Café Restaurant Carnarvon Street, Chinatown. Popular café with a fan-cooled jarrah interior, sandwiches, meals and the best big breakfast in town. Daily 7.30am–late.

Café Carlotta Jones Place off Dora Street, opposite Saville Street ⓣ08/9192 7606; BYO). With wood-fired pizzas, risotto and pasta, this is one of

Broome's most popular eateries so book ahead. Daily except Sun 5.30pm–late.

Old Zoo Café Challenor Drive, behind the Crocodile Park Cable Beach. Far and away your best bet out on Cable Beach. Among the many mouthwatering dishes, the steak with prawn sauce is the one to go for.

Pindan Blue Right by the Seaview Shopping Centre off Hamersley St. Sea views from the patio and when available, the sweet chilli mud crab is recommended. Daily 8am–late.

Tong's Napier Tce. May have missed out on the McAlpine makeover but said to be the best Chinese in town. Mon–Fri noon–2pm & 5.30pm–late, Sat & Sun noon–2pm.

Town Beach Café Town Beach, south end of Hamersley St. Great place for Sunday morning breakfasts. Mon–Sat 7.30am–late, Sun 7.30am–noon.

Wharf Restaurant Port Drive, south by the Deep Water Port. Broome's branch of Derby's acclaimed seafood restaurant. Eat in or takeaway. Daily noon–late.

Nightlife and events

Broome's raging **pub** is the *Roebuck Bay Hotel* on Napier Terrace, with live entertainment and happy hours. The least rough of the three bars here is the *Pearlers' Rest*. The *Divers' Camp Tavern* at Cable Beach comes a close second and usually gets the bands after the "*Roey*". Two **nightclubs** in Chinatown are open until the early hours and have not changed their names for years which says something about their endurung popularity: the *Nippon Inn* on Dampier Terrace draws in the backpackers, with *Tokyo Joe's* round the corner on Napier Terrace. If you prefer **real ale** to tinned lager, pay a visit to the Broome Brewery at *Matso's Store and Brewery* at the end of Hamersley Street, where all sorts of local fermentations await you.

For a uniquely "Broometime" experience, Sun Pictures '**walk-in cinema** in Chinatown is a real treat: watch the latest movies while mosquitoes nibble your ankles and the odd light aircraft comes in low across the screen. The town also has a conventional indoor twin-screen on the corner of Weld Street behind McDonalds.

The tourist office has information on various events, such as the **Broome Fringe Arts Festival**, a celebration of local artiness and culture usually held in early June. However, the big one is the week-long **Shinju Matsuri** in August or September, which attracts people from all over the country. The town celebrates its ethnic diversity, and the pearl that created it, finishing up with a huge fireworks display. Broome can get packed out for the Shinju, so unless you want to end up camping at the Bird Observatory, book your accommodation in advance. Exact dates for both festivals can be found at the tourist office.

Listings

Bicycle and scooter rental Broome Cycle Centre is next to the Shell garage in Chinatown and also outside the zoo on Cable Beach; bikes from $18 per day. Broome Scooter Hire (Ⓣ08/9192 6255) or Modomio (Ⓣ08/9193 5626, Ⓦwww.modomio.com.au) both rent scooters which are easy to start and ride from $39 per day (3-day deals). Driver's licence required.

Bookshop Napier Terrace in Chinatown, opposite the *Roebuck Bay Hotel*, with Woody's Book Exchange in Johnny Chi Lane.

Buses Greyhound Australia (Ⓣ13 14 99 or 08/9192 1561, Ⓦwww.greyhound.com.au) buses stop at Broome daily on its Darwin to Perth run. Book at the tourist office.

Car rental Besides the big names with offices at the airport (and who may offer relocation deals), Broome Discount Hire (Ⓣ08/9192 3100) at the airport delivers cars to your accommodation from $55 a day with 75km free mileage. Broome Car Rentals (Ⓣ08/9192 2110, Ⓦwww.broomebroome.com.au), next to the Shell on Hamersley St, does local runabouts with 50km free for $58 a day, up to full-size 4WD Land Cruisers for Cape Leveque or the Kimberley from $148.

Hospital Robinson St Ⓣ08/9192 9222.

Internet Telecentre in Chinatown at the top end of Dampier Terrace.

Police Ⓣ08/9192 0200.

Taxis Ⓣ08/9192 1133 or 13 10 08; Ⓣ1800 622 488; Ⓣ1800 880 330.

Willie Creek Pearl Farm

About 10km east of Broome, almost opposite the turn-off south for the Bird Observatory, a road leads north to the Aboriginal lands of the Dampier Peninsula, ending at Cape Leveque (see below). Thirty-eight kilometres north from Broome a turn-off from this road leads to the **Willie Creek Pearl Farm** (Ⓣ08/9192 6000, Ⓦwww.williecreekpearls.com.au; several tours daily with courtesy pick-ups in town $59, self-drive option $28, pre-booking essential), a popular day-tour from Broome. With the main showroom based on the banks of Willie Creek, most of the operation, which involves regularly cleaning and turning a quarter of a million shells by hand, has now moved offshore for security reasons. On arrival you get a very comprehensive presentation of the entire pearl farming process, information that was given up by the secretive Japanese only half a century ago. A boat tour in the creek follows, which inspects racks of seeded oysters that hang for two years at a time, building up layers of pearlescent nacre as they feed off the tidal nutrients. The fact that this process takes half the normal time and the local oysters are very large is what makes Willie Creek pearls among the finest and biggest in the world, a success story that has kick-started other pearling ventures all the way from Shark Bay to Darwin.

Exploring the Dampier Peninsula

Access to the isolated **beaches** on the southwest side of the Dampier peninsula and north of Broome is possible off the Cape Leveque road, about 10km north of the junction with the sealed highway or 20km from Broome. Some day-tours come here from Broome and camping is possible, although you ought to be well prepared as there are no facilities whatsoever. The first of the beaches is **Barred Creek**, to get to which you'll have to pass through a **sandy section** where most 2WDs get stuck. A few kilometres north up the coast is **Quondong Point**, overlooking the low red cliffs and a white rocky beach below. **Price Point**, after another 14km, is considered the pick of the points. Continue a few hundred metres past its signed turn-off and you'll find a ramp giving easy access to the beach and numerous coves below. From here it's around 40km back to the Cape Leveque road or 60km back to Broome.

Unless you don't mind giving your car a hammering, your best bet is to arm yourself with a solidly-built 4WD rental, or to join a tour for the corrugated two hundred-kilometre track all the way to **Cape Leveque**. With miles of pristine and **deserted beaches** and basic accommodation, this area is slowly opening up to low-key ecotourism. Note that if visiting any of the Aboriginal communities on the Cape you must **book your accommodation** in advance; free camping is not allowed and you should not wander uninvited into residential areas.

The Aboriginal community of **Beagle Bay** (fuel and store Mon–Fri; Ⓣ08/9192 4913; entry $5) is 125km from Broome. The highlight here is the **Sacred Heart Church**, built by German missionaries in 1918, a beautiful building with an unusual altar decorated with mother-of-pearl. After Beagle Bay the track to Cape Leveque gets narrower and sandier and you'll reach the turn-off leading after 33km to **Middle Lagoon** (no fuel; Ⓣ08/9192 4002, Ⓦwww.ibizwa.com/natureshideaway; entry $8), a lovely white-sand cove with camping, beach shelters (❷), partially equipped four-bed cabins (❺) and a six-bed self-contained cabin (❻). The bay offers sheltered swimming and good snorkelling. Up the road another 20km or so is the community of **Lombadina/Djarindjin** (no camping; fuel Mon–Fri; Ⓣ08/9192 4936, Ⓦwww.ibizwa.com/lombadina; entry $5), where you'll find well-equipped backpacker-style accommodation (❷), four-bed self-contained units (❻) and 4WD access to the beach over banks of soft sand (follow the signs). The wide shallow bay before you is again ideal for safe swimming.

A stay at the very popular *Kooljaman Resort* right at the tip of **Cape Leveque** (Ⓣ08/9192 4970, Ⓦwww.kooljaman.com.au; camping, beach shelters ❷, cabins ❺, safari tents ❻) is the reason why you've endured the last 211km. You'll find *Dinkas* **restaurant** and a small kiosk selling basic provisions. Situated right on the "sunrise" beach, the paperbark **cabins** and **beach shelters** (basically shade, a windbreak and a barbecue) are the pick of the accommodation – the fancier four-berth tents are up the hill. Come well-prepared however, as despite the prices, Kooljaman is no upmarket wilderness experience.

From Kooljaman you can rent a dinghy, try fishing, mud-crabbing, fishing and bushtucker **tours** and cruises to the old mission buildings on nearby Sunday Island. Ask at the resort for information.

The Kimberley

A region of tablelands, tropical woodland, big rivers and gorges about the size of Poland, the **Kimberley** is often romantically described as Australia's last frontier. It's a wilderness dotted with dormant or barely viable cattle stations, isolated Aboriginal communities and, increasingly, vast tracts of Aboriginal land, all capped with a ragged, tide-swept coastline inhabited chiefly by crocodiles, secluded pearling operations and a couple of exclusive, fly-in getaways.

With the difficulty of running cattle in a region wracked by floods or bushfires and subject to land claims, many stations have turned to tourism, though even this is not without its setbacks; one week of cyclonic rain washed out two properties in early 2002, and in 2005 winds of 280kph devastated *Faraway Bay* (see p.798) on the north coast. Even the full exploitation of minerals known to exist on the region's Mitchell plateau is made uneconomical by the climate and location; this alone says a lot about the Kimberley's remoteness.

The region has many examples of the enigmatic Wandjina-style rock paintings, which depict rows of mouthless beings with owl-like heads, or the slender Bradshaw figures, thought to be much older. When the dry season sets in around April, **tours** of the Kimberley resume, mainly between Broome and Kununurra (see boxes on p.785 and p.795) along the **Gibb River Road** (GRR), or down to the popular **Bungle Bungles**, south of the Highway 1, near Halls Creek. June to August are the coolest months and the best time to visit; by late September the heat is already building up and even Highway 1 closes periodically from January to March following storms or cyclones.

Derby to Fitzroy Crossing

Situated 36km north of the Highway 1, on a spur of land jutting into the mud flats of King Sound, **DERBY** is a mineral exploration base and a centre for local Aboriginal communities. For tourists there's not a whole lot going on short of taking a **scenic flight** over the impressive West Kimberley coastline (from $170; ask at the tourist office), and without your own transport you'll find the spread-out town hard work. The **tourist office** (Mon–Fri 8.30am–4.30pm, Sat 8.30–11.30am; Ⓣ08/9191 1426 or 1800 621 426, Ⓦwww.derbytourism.com.au) is at the top end of town on Clarendon Street, where **buses** also arrive. **Places to stay** took a big step forward in 2005 with the construction of *Derby Backpackers* right opposite the tourist office

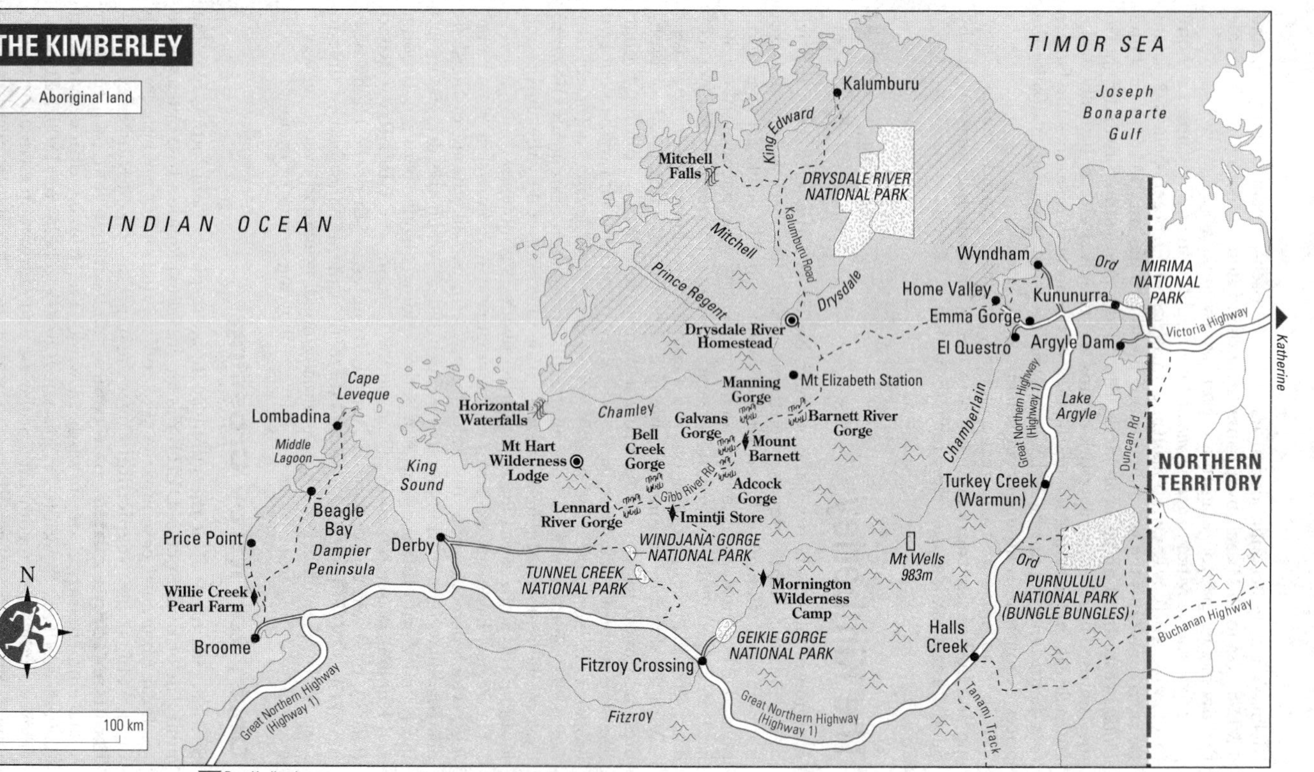
THE KIMBERLEY
Aboriginal land
TIMOR SEA
Joseph Bonaparte Gulf
INDIAN OCEAN
Kalumburu
King Edward
Mitchell Falls
DRYSDALE RIVER NATIONAL PARK
Kalumburu Road
Mitchell
Prince Regent
Drysdale
Drysdale River Homestead
Wyndham
Ord
MIRIMA NATIONAL PARK
Home Valley
Kununurra
Emma Gorge
Victoria Highway
Katherine
El Questro
Argyle Dam
Mt Elizabeth Station
Manning Gorge
Barnett River Gorge
Cape Leveque
Lombadina
Middle Lagoon
Horizontal Waterfalls
Chamley
Galvans Gorge
Bell Creek Gorge
Mount Barnett
Chamberlain
Great Northern Highway (Highway 1)
Lake Argyle
Duncan Rd
NORTHERN TERRITORY
Mt Hart Wilderness Lodge
King Sound
Gibb River Rd
Adcock Gorge
Turkey Creek (Warmun)
Lennard River Gorge
Imintji Store
Beagle Bay
Price Point
Derby
WINDJANA GORGE NATIONAL PARK
Mt Wells 983m
Dampier Peninsula
TUNNEL CREEK NATIONAL PARK
Ord
PURNULULU NATIONAL PARK (BUNGLE BUNGLES)
Mornington Wilderness Camp
Willie Creek Pearl Farm
Buchanan Highway
Halls Creek
GEIKIE GORGE NATIONAL PARK
Broome
Fitzroy Crossing
Tanami Track
N
0 100 km
Fitzroy
Port Hedland

(Ⓣ08/9191 1233; $22). *West Kimberley Lodge* at 17 Sutherland St (Ⓣ08/9191 1031; ❹) is a guesthouse with shared facilities, or there's the *Boab Inn* (Ⓣ08/9191 1044; ❹) on Loch Street. There are also two caravan parks. There's a good **restaurant** at the *Boab*, but for something special it's got to be the *Wharf* seafood restaurant out by the wharf (Tues–Sun from 6.30pm; closed Jan & Feb), which also does takeaways.

The **Gibb River Road** (full account p.796) starts just east of Derby and cuts straight across the Kimberley, passing many turn-offs for gorges prior to joining the sealed road between Wyndham and Kununurra, 667km further on. A great way to see the GRR is on the hop-on, hop-off *Gibb River Road River Express* (full details p.797), which runs between Derby and Kununurra. If you're heading east with your own vehicle and want to see the **Windjana Gorge** and **Tunnel Creek** national parks, follow the GRR for 119km to the Windjana turn-off. From here you rejoin the Great Northern Highway after 123km. This section is OK in dry weather in a 2WD and is only 30km longer than following the dull highway to Fitzroy Crossing, 256km from Derby.

Since the pastoral expansion into the Kimberley in the late nineteenth century, **FITZROY CROSSING** has been a small rest stop for travellers and a crucial crossing over the still-troublesome Fitzroy River. Today it's a "welfare town" serving the Aboriginal communities strung out along the Fitzroy Valley to the southwest. Because of its large catchment area, the Fitzroy River's run-off during flood peaks is second only to the Amazon, at which time two cubic kilometres of water a minute surge under the road bridge, spreading out across a flood plain 40km wide in places, before disgorging into King Sound.

As for the town, a Friday-night **drinking** session at the century-old *Crossing Inn* on Skuthorpe Road might give you the most memorable experience of the place, its having been brightly repainted by local children into something of a tourist attraction. The *Fitzroy River Lodge* (Ⓣ08/9191 5141; ❻), on the highway east of the bridge, caters comfortably for passing tours with **motel rooms**, canvas bushland lodges and grassy campsites, as well as a pool, restaurants and a bar. The *Crossing Inn* (Ⓣ08/9191 5080; cabins ❹) also has tent sites and the obligatory counter meals, while the *Tarunda Caravan Park*, next to the **supermarket/post office** on Forrest Road, has cheap tent sites and on-site vans ❸. The **tourist office** (daily 9am–5pm; Ⓣ08/9191 5355, Ⓔfitzroytb@bigpond.com) is on Flynn Drive, by the roadhouse, and can give you the lowdown on tours to the nearby national parks described below.

The Devonian Reef national parks

During the Devonian era, 350 million years ago, a large barrier reef grew around the then-submerged Kimberley plateau. The limestone remnants of this reef are today exposed in the national parks of **Geikie Gorge**, **Tunnel Creek** and, most spectacularly, **Windjana Gorge** (CALM fees apply for all; see box p.714), sometimes misleadingly described as the "West Kimberley", but of which they are just a dramatic and easily accessible fraction. All three parks are closed from December to April.

Geikie Gorge National Park

Eighteen kilometres upstream from Fitzroy Crossing, the river has carved out the five-kilometre **Geikie Gorge** through the exposed reef, best seen by **boat** with Darngku Heritage Cruises (Ⓣ08/9191 5552; 2–4hr; $50–110). Watermarks on the gorge's walls clearly show how high the river can rise, while below the surface harmless freshwater crocodiles jostle with freshwater-adapted stingrays and sawfish. Walking trails lead along the forested western banks, which are strategically dotted with picnic sites, barbecues and campsites.

Tunnel Creek and Windjana Gorge national parks

Going back along the highway, 42km west of Fitzroy Crossing, a dirt road turns north to follow the Napier Range (as the reef is known here) to **Tunnel Creek National Park** (no camping), 105km from Fitzroy Crossing. Here, Tunnel Creek has burrowed its way under the range, creating a 750-metre tunnel hung with bats and with who-knows-what in the pools. Although the collapsed roof illuminates the cavern halfway, the wade through the progressively deeper and colder water to the other end still takes some nerve – you'll need a torch and shoes that you don't mind getting soaked.

The most dramatic remainders of the reef are the towering ramparts of **Windjana Gorge** (camping), 135km from Fitzroy Crossing and 140km from Derby. A walking trail leads through a limestone crevice into a wide gorge splitting the Napier Range, lined with paperbark and Leichhardt trees. Freshwater crocodiles share the pools with various birds and can be seen sunning themselves in the afternoons.

Halls Creek and around

Further down the Great Northern Highway, **HALLS CREEK** is 288km east of Fitzroy Crossing. The gold rush of 1885 took place in the hills 17km south of town, and in less than four years a thousand prospectors succeeded in exhausting the area's potential, before stampeding off to Kalgoorlie. Today, new gold and diamond mines are opening up, even if for most the town is just another stop on the highway.

The **tourist office** (May–Sept: daily 8.30am–4.30pm; ⓣ08/9168 6262, ⓔvisitors@hcshire.wa.gov.au), has a café and is in the middle of town. **Internet access** is available next door in the library. For somewhere to **stay**, the *Halls Creek Caravan Park* (ⓣ08/9168 6169), on Roberta Avenue, has tent sites, grim single cabins ($25) and more spacious on-site vans (❸). The *Kimberley Hotel* (ⓣ08/9168 6101 or 1800 355 228, ⓦwww.kimberley-accom.com.au), opposite the caravan park, has pokey bunkhouses (beds $18) and expensive motel units (❺). It's also the only **pub** in town. The *Halls Creek Motel* on Duncan Road (ⓣ08/9168 6001; budget ❸, motel units ❺) is a better bet.

The gold-bearing hills to the southeast offer a few attractions for those with their own transport. **China Wall** is a block-like vein of quartzite rising above a toxic pool, 6km south of town. **Caroline Pool**, 9km further south, can be a bit fetid for swimming but **Palm Springs**, about 25km further on, is well worth a splash although you're better off spending the night by **Sawtooth Gorge**, a couple of kilometres further on; all bar the final creek crossing just before the gorge are manageable in a 2WD.

Purnululu National Park (Bungle Bungles)

The spectacular **Bungle Bungle** massif, seldom referred to by its official name, the **Purnululu National Park** (closed Jan–March; CALM fee – see box on p.714), is one of Australia's greatest natural wonders and in 2003 earned prestigious UNESCO World Heritage listing alongside the Pyramids, the Grand Canyon and the Great Barrier Reef. A couple of days spent exploring its chasms and gorges is well worth the effort and expense involved. Though visited by Europeans a century earlier, the Bungles were brought to prominence in the early 1980s and have quickly attracted a mystique matching that of Ayers Rock.

Due to the fragile nature of the banded rock domes as well as the difficulty in patrolling the remote park, road access from the Great Northern Highway is limited to 4WDs. The park was acquired in a severely over-grazed state (like much of the Northwest) but over the years CALM has worked hard to revive the soil and replace feral animals with indigenous wildlife. Note that the Bungles are always **hot**, with temperatures of 40°C possible in early September, so make sure you carry water and a wear a hat on the longer walks.

The **fly-drive tours** available from Kununurra (see box p.795), which involve flying to the park's airstrip and then being driven around in a 4WD, offer the best of both worlds. However, the half-hour doorless **helicopter flights** (turn up at the airstrip or call ⓣ08/9168 1811; $200) available in the park are permitted to fly much lower – if you've ever wanted to fly in a chopper, save your money for the Bungles: you won't be disappointed. Helicopter flights are also available from Turkey Creek.

From the highway it's a fun, 53-kilometre (two-hour) 4WD ride through station land to the **visitors centre** and entry station (daily 8am–1pm & 2–4pm; ⓣ08/9168 7300). Take it easy as the track is narrow and hilly, and expect oncoming traffic in the morning. From the entry station you can head to either of the two basic campsites on the north or south side of the park. **Kurrajong Camp** is the north site, 10km from the entry station and giving access to **Echidna Chasm**, a one-hour return walk into a slender chasm nearly a kilometre long and half as high. At times the cleft is less than half-a-metre wide and each time you think it's over, another chink opens up and you head further into the rock. **Frog Hole** (30min return) is a wider chasm, with a seasonal pool at the end, while **Mini Palms** is a longer walk along a creek bed to a palm-filled amphitheatre and then on over collapsed boulders to a viewing platform with a gorge below. At any point on these walks you can look up and see palms clinging to the rock walls hundreds of metres above you; the scale of the clefts is underlined when you realize the palms can be up to 20m high.

The geology of the Bungles

The weathered, beehive-like domes of the Bungles are a most unusual sight, exhibiting alternating sedimentary strata of iron oxide (orange) and cyanobacteria (grey-green or black), which itself forms a fragile crust over the sometimes powdery interior. The theory is that over millennia, sediments were deposited from two differing sources, creating alternating strata with varying mineral characteristics. The darker bands are marginally more porous (water bearing) and so support the lichen-like cyanobacteria – incidentally another name used for the stromatolite formations found at Shark Bay (see p.764).

You'll also notice the rocks on the higher, north side of the massif are conglomerate (stones set in a sand cement) and are actually older than the southern domes which were deposited on top of them. The whole range has been tilted to the south over time, exposing the older conglomerate.

Meanwhile, back on the south side, the maze of chasms dividing each "bungle" is being put down to an impact structure recently discovered on the roof of the plateau. At some stage a meteor is thought to have struck with such force that it sent fracture lines down through the rocks below. Over time the smashed upper strata have eroded exposing the splintered layers which were subsequently exposed and weathered into the well-known domes. The fact that there are "mini-bungle" formations elsewhere in the Kimberley, as well as the proven tilting of the massif and the current fashion for explaining epochal cataclysms with meteor strikes, makes this dramatic concept a little hard to swallow.

Wilardi Camp, on the south side of the park, is a better laid-out campsite, 25km from the entry station with access to the classic Bungle vistas. From the main car park, the short **Domes Walk** gets you among some bungles on the way to the half-hour walk into **Cathedral Gorge**, a huge overhanging amphitheatre with a seasonal pool whose rippled reflections flicker across the roof above.

Piccaninny Gorge is a tough, thirty-kilometre overnight walk for which you'll need to register and carry **large quantities of water**. Most people are understandably put off but it's quite possible to walk the seven kilometres along the creek to the **Elbow** and back in a day, following the creek. The rest of the park is currently inaccessible, the northeast being the ancestral burial grounds of the Djaru and Gidja people.

On to Wyndham

Halfway between Halls Creek and Kununurra is the roadhouse at **TURKEY CREEK** (bunkhouse $20, cabins ❹) next to the Warmun community, where a **helicopter** offers 45-minute flights (ⓣ08/9168 7337; $225) into the Bungles. Compared to the open helicopters used in the park, the faster, enclosed machine is a less exhilarating way of seeing the domes. Opposite the roadhouse is the Aboriginal Gidja Culture Centre displaying the art of and books on the original occupants of the region; there is also **Internet** access.

From Turkey Creek the road continues directly north, passing a roadhouse and the Argyle Diamond Mine (tours from Kununurra, see box p.795), source of most of the world's industrial diamonds. The scenery hereabouts takes on a rugged turn (especially at sunset) as you pass the Ragged and Carr Boyd Ranges to the junction with the Victoria Highway. At the junction, Kununurra is 46km to the east and Wyndham 51km northwest.

Strung out in three built-up areas along the muddy banks of the Cambridge Gulf, **WYNDHAM** was the port established to serve the brief goldrush at Halls Creek. The town was then well positioned to process and export East Kimberley beef until the meat works closed in 1985; these days the West Kimberley's only port ticks over quietly serving local Aboriginal people. At the top of the town is the **Crocodile Farm** (May–Nov daily 8.30am–4pm; feeding time 11am; $16). If you haven't been to one yet, here is your chance, but give the paltry crocodile sandwiches a miss. The biggest "salties" (for more see p.650) make the in-house Komodo Dragon look rather lame, although the pens packed with crocodile hatchings draped over each other might be said to possess a kind of hideous cuteness. You get a good aerial view of the farm and a whole lot more from the **Five Rivers Lookout** at the top of the 335-metre Bastion Ranges, overlooking the town on the east side. With the tide out you'll see the intricate web of creeks feeding into the muddy delta and the Cambridge Gulf.

The **tourist office** (daily 8am–5pm; ⓣ08/9161 1281, ⓦwww.eastkimberley.com.au) is on O'Donnell Street, and you can **camp** at the *Three Mile Caravan Park* (ⓣ08/9161 1064; on-site vans ❷) on Baker Street. The *Gulf Breeze Guest House* (ⓣ08/9161 1401; ❸) in the old post office on O'Donnell Street looks a bit of a long-termers' haunt. Opposite the *Gulf Breeze*, the *Wyndham Town Hotel* (ⓣ08/9161 1003, ⓔwyndham@bigpond.com; ❺) is as good as it gets and has the town's one **restaurant** – nothing special but better than gnawing on your shoe.

Kununurra and the Ord River

KUNUNURRA is the Kimberley's youngest town, built in the early 1960s to serve the **Ord River Irrigation Project**, fed by Lake Kununurra. The

Diversion Dam Wall, an impressive sight as you come in from the west, created this lake, essentially the bloated Ord River. Fifty kilometres upstream is a bigger dam, known as the Argyle Dam Wall, built in 1971 to ensure a year-round flow to the project, which has created **Lake Argyle**, the world's largest man-made body of water. The Ord River Irrigation Project was on the verge of expansion when it became mired in an inconclusive native title verdict in 2002. Lately, easy-to-produce sugar cane has become the most viable crop, backed up by the more labour-intensive water melons and other farmed produce which offer steady opportunities for menial **work**; see the backpackers' notice boards. Enhanced by the copious amounts of nearby fresh water which lends itself to recreational use, Kununurra escapes the listless feel of the older Kimberley towns.

A couple of kilometres east of town is **Hidden Valley** or Mirima National Park (CALM fee; see box on p.714), where a road leads into a narrow valley of "mini-bungles" and terminates with some short trails – you couldn't ask for a better walking area so close to town. Another popular spot is **Ivanhoe Crossing**, 13km north of town on the Ord River. Officially, the ford is closed to vehicles and you wouldn't want to try crossing it in anything less than a hefty 4WD. Downstream is saltwater crocodile country although some locals fish and bathe by the banks – just the sort of habitual behaviour salties go for. **Valentines Pool**, **Black Rock Falls** and **Middle Springs** are other waterholes on the far side of the Crossing (also accessible off the Wyndham highway), though all three get pretty soupy towards the end of the dry season.

Triple J Tours (ⓣ08/9168 2682; ⓦwww.triplejtours.net.au) offers speedy cruises from $65 up **Lake Kununurra** to Argyle Dam, while Diversion Cruises (ⓣ08/9168 3333) does a slower-paced three-hour sunset cruise ($40) around Lily Creek Lagoon, where you'll see crocodiles, fish, turtles and treefulls of bats, which all take to the air in a dramatic sky-darkening mass just after sunset. In fact, the lagoon is a great place to rent a canoe for a bit of exploring among the pandanus reeds; ask about rentals at the tourist office or Go Wild Adventure Tours (ⓣ0409 456 643 or 1300 663 369, ⓦwww.gowild.com.au), who lay on one- to three-day self-guided canoeing trips down the Ord River from $125 to $175 per person.

Practicalities

The **tourist office** (daily 8am–5pm; ⓣ08/9168 1177, ⓦwww.kimberley tourism.com/kununurra.htm) on Coolibah Drive has displays and videos on the area's many attractions, and details of all the tours that can take you there.

Regional tours from Kununurra

Although prices are as high per day as anywhere in Australia, Kununurra is the best base from which to visit the **Bungles** as well as the **Kimberley**. *Kununurra Backpackers'* (ⓣ1800 641 998) offers two- to three-day Bungles trips from around $150 a day. East Kimberley Tours (ⓣ08/9168 2213 or 1800 682 213, ⓦwww.eastkimberleytours .com.au) has a whole raft of options from one day in the Bungles to an eleven-day see-it-all GRR tour for over $2000 (including some flights). Slingair (ⓣ1800 095 500) visits the diamond mine in a day, along with a large range of other options, from $255. Alligator Air (ⓣ1800 632 533) has two-hour Bungle flights in high-wing aircraft for around $190 (no minimum numbers). Their six-hour "The Works" flight ($420) includes a stop on the Mitchell Plateau and is one of the best scenic flights over the Kimberley but needs a minimum of four passengers; call in advance if you're heading for Kununurra.

You'll find a **telecentre** next door and there's a perennially warm **swimming pool** ($3) over the road. The **post office** is also on Coolibah Drive. **Buses** arrive outside the BP **24-hour roadhouse**, passing through daily for Katherine, Darwin and Broome.

The only recommended **backpackers'** in town are the recently remodelled *Kimberley Croc* (☎08/9168 2702 or 1300 136 702, Ⓦwww.kimberleycroc.com.au; dorms from $19, twins and doubles ❷) on Konkerberry Drive, close to the pub and supermarket with a shaded pool and terrace, and *Kununurra Backpackers'* (☎08/9169 1998 or 1800 641 998, Ⓦwww.adventure.kimberley.net.au; dorms from $17) on 24 Nutwood Crescent. The hostel is made up of a couple of converted houses and a nice garden, and is in a quiet backstreet fifteen minutes' walk from town. It also has a small pool, TV room and a farm workers' annexe. Of the town's six **caravan parks**, the *Town* (☎08/9168 1763), on Bloodwood Drive, is the most central, while the *Kona* (☎08/9168 1031), right by Lake Kununurra, is 5km west of town; cabins in both cost from ❸. The *Mercure Inn* (☎08/9168 1455 or 1300 656 565; ❺), on the highway, is the town's best **motel**; you could also try the cheaper *Hotel Kununurra* (☎08/9168 0400, Ⓦwww.hotelkununurra.com.au; ❹) on Messmate Way.

Places to eat include *Kimberley in the Stars* on Cotton Terrace, and *Valentino's* (daily 5–10pm) on Papuana Street for pizzas. The bistro at *Gulliver's Tavern* is also recommended and gets the occasional band in the picking season.

Lake Argyle

When the **Argyle Dam** was completed in 1972, the Ord River managed to fill **Lake Argyle** in just one wet season; along with the neighbouring Victoria and the Fitzroy, these rivers account for a third of Australia's freshwater run-off and plans are often mooted to pipe it south where it's needed. Creating the lake was an engineer's dream: only a small defile needed damming to back up a shallow lake covering up to two thousand square kilometres. Since that time the fish population has grown over the years to support commercial fishing, as well as numerous birds and crocodiles, both estuarine and freshwater. When the lake was proposed, the Durack family's Argyle Homestead was moved to its present site, 2km from the tourist village (see below), and is now a **museum** (May–Oct daily 8.30am–4.30pm; $4) of early pioneering life in the Kimberley, as described in Mary Durack's droving classic, *Kings in Grass Castles*.

The long-established Lake Argyle Cruises (☎08/9168 7687, Ⓦwww.lakeargyle.com) and Argyle Expeditions (☎08/9168 7040) run **boat trips** from two to six hours (about $20 an hour) to show you wallaby caves, jabirus and other birds, as well as freshwater crocodiles.

The Gibb River Road

On the way to Wyndham you pass the start of the mostly unsealed **Gibb River Road** (or GRR) with its attendant warning sign. Originally built to transport beef out of the Kimberley to Wyndham and Derby, it cuts through the region's heart, offering a vivid slice of this vast and rugged expanse. At around 670km to Derby, it's 230km shorter than the Great Northern Highway, but although people have mistaken it as so, the "Gibb" is no short cut. The hammering from route's notorious corrugations depends partly on the quality of your suspension (letting some air out of the tyres helps greatly) but it's rare to get across without something breaking or falling off. Punctures are common (many stations can do repairs) and roll-overs are not that rare either. Heed the advice on off-highway driving on p.51.

Although as a scenic drive it's very satisfying, the attractions that make this route even more interesting – homesteads, gorges and their pools – are off the GRR and some are accessible only to robust, high-clearance vehicles, although unless stated a 4WD is not necessary in the places listed below. At times when your vehicle is vibrating so much it's drifting across the track, you may wonder if the trip is worth it. To absorb the experience it's best to plan to stop for a couple of days somewhere along the road at some of the places listed below; after all, you'll probably only be here once. Derby tourist office (see p.789) produces a comprehensive and annually updated *Travellers Guide* to the GRR ($4), including accommodation prices, which is also available at other local tourist offices. Distances given in brackets below are to destinations off the GRR.

If you're traversing the GRR west to east and want to spare your car the full ordeal, turn back at Manning Gorge and head down to the highway via Windjana Gorge, as the best GRR gorges are in the western half. **Tours** are available from Broome (see p.785) and Kununurra (see box on p.795). In 2004 the hop-on, hop-off **Gibb River Road River Express** bus service (Ⓣ08/9169 1880, Ⓦwww.gibbriverbus.com.au; $280 valid for three months) was introduced, running between Kununurra and Derby in about twelve hours while dropping you off and picking you up at many of the points listed below. Some enterprising **cyclists** are already using the service as a way of missing out or reducing the gruelling corrugation transits, while exploring the side tracks; it's possible the service may offer mountain bike packages on future runs. The problem is that without transport, getting to all but the nearest gorges and homesteads is quite a trek off the GRR (let alone carting provisions), although some stations will do pre-arranged pick-ups. Even then, doing the GRR in a day on the *Express* is surprisingly satisfying; the big-windowed bus gives great views and, with the driver's commentary, you'll be able to appreciate the great landscape a whole lot more without your teeth clenched and knuckles clamped around the wheel of your own vehicle.

The Karunjie Track

If you're starting the GRR from Wyndham consider taking the **Karunjie–King River Track**, which starts just out of town (follow signs for King River and *Drovers Rest*). The track is on El Questro station land and is more varied than the easternmost section of the GRR which you bypass, but you'll need a 4WD to get through the deep bull dust as you near the Gibb at the Pentecost River crossing, 85km from Wyndham – allow about three hours.

The track starts by heading out across a causeway to follow the King River, crossing it (it's usually dry) 30km from Wyndham by a Boab Prison Tree. Here the track divides: the left intercepts the GRR east of the Emma Gorge turn-off and the right leads west slowly round to the Cockburn Ranges, at one point crossing smooth, hardened mud flats before the going gets rough again as the track nears the Pentecost River. There are some washed-out sections and deep patches of bull dust that need to be churned through slowly. You join the GRR at the Pentecost crossing about 57km west of the Great Northern Highway.

The eastern Gibb River Road

The GRR proper starts halfway between Wyndham and Kununurra. The scenically impressive 250-kilometre eastern section up to the Kalumburu junction crosses many ranges and is crossed in turn by big rivers, the first of these being the King River, 17km from the sealed highway. Eight kilometres later is the turn-off for the plush mini-resort at **Emma Gorge** (2km; Ⓣ08/9161 4388; part of *El Questro Wilderness Park*; day-use pass $5.50; ❺ or ❻ en suite), a

The Northern Kimberley

Though a common destination in the dry season, the Northern Kimberley is a remote region where a well-equipped 4WD is essential. You'll find the **Kalumburu Road** junction 250km along the GRR, with a store and fuel at *Drysdale River Homestead* (59km; April–Nov daily 8am–noon & 1–5pm; ⓣ08/9161 4326, ⓦwww.drysdaleriver.com.au; units ④), which also offers cheap camping, a bar, meals and scenic flights over some remote northwest Kimberley waterfalls. The main attraction near here is the beautiful, four-tiered **Mitchell Falls**, 240km off the GRR and 70km west off the Kalumburu Road; turn-off at the King Edward River (camping, see below). This once remote spot is getting less so by the year and is now a **national park** (CALM fees apply, see p.714) with basic camping. There are also "exclusive" campsites at King Edward River and at Mitchell Falls car park run by APT/Kimberley Wilderness Adventures (June–Oct; ⓦwww.kimberleywilderness.com.au; half-board $120 per person) and used on their tours. From the Mitchell Falls car park it's a three-kilometre walk northwest to the falls themselves (passing Little- and Big Merten's Falls on the way) where a helicopter stands by (ⓣ08/9161 4512) to offer scenic flights in season from around $150. Just before you arrive at Mitchell Falls there's a turn-off to Surveyors Pool and Walsh Point (extremely rough, allow 3hr), right on the coast from where you may want to pre-arrange a pick-up to Kimberley Coastal Camp (see below) on the other side of the bay.

Kalumburu (276km; ⓣ08/9161 4300, ⓔkac10@bigpond.com; $35 vehicle permit) is an Aboriginal community with the languorous feel of a dispersed African village where ancient cars lie rusting and palms flap and sway in the tropical breeze. Buy your one-week vehicle permit on arrival from the community office (if there's anyone there), although you'll also need to get another (free) **permit** in advance from the Department of Indigenous Affairs (most easily done online at ⓦwww.dia.wa.gov.au or from Broome, Derby or the Kununurra tourist offices). As well as being able to get (expensive) fuel and basics from the store here, you can visit a mission set up in the nineteenth century by Benedictine monks. North of town along sandy tracks, there are basic campsites at pretty **McGowans Beach** (22km; contact owners on ⓣ08/9161 4386 to pay fees) and **Honeymoon Beach** (26km; owners on ⓣ08/9161 4366), the latter situated on a small bay and the better of the two, though lately a site at **Pago** (owners ⓣ08/9161 4394) has opened up too.

There are a couple of other accommodation options on the otherwise unpopulated Kimberley coast: exclusive, all-inclusive resorts like the *Kimberley Coastal Camp* (ⓦwww.kimberleycoastalcamp.com.au) southwest of Kalumburu, or *Faraway Bay* (ⓦwww.farawaybay.com.au) to the east, costing at least $600 a day and only accessible by air or sea.

manicured bush camp of tented cabins plus a restaurant, bar and pool. It's popular with coach parties, and there's a thirty-minute walk along Emma Creek to the fern-draped **gorge**, which is worth the entry fee. Better still if you're fit is the "Emma Dreaming Trail" which ascends the cliffs of the Cockburn Ranges behind Emma Gorge, passing pools and rock art sites on the way.

Further down the GRR is the turn-off for the station homestead or "township" of **El Questro Wilderness Park** (16km; ⓣ08/9169 4318, ⓦwww.elquestro.com.au; $12.50 day-use for all of ELQ), details from the reservations office in the Kununurra tourist office (ⓣ08/9169 1777). Uniformed "rangers" will guide or point out all sorts of activities, including heli-fishing and gorge cruises as well as various walks, gorges, rock art sites and drives over much of the million-acre property. They've spent a huge amount of money on making ELQ into a "see-it-all-here" private national park and for some it may all come across as a bit too commercialised compared to the other, more authentic station stays out here. Although you can do full-day tours from Kununurra for $165, it's much better to visit with your own vehicle (ideally a 4WD) and make the most of your day pass; the drive up to **El Questro Gorge** is recommended, as is Explosion Gorge. Affordable accommodation in ELQ includes secluded camping (some with distant washing facilities and so more suited to campervans), more central camping at the "Black Cockatoo" site, or en-suite bungalows (❼). There's also a bar, shop, fuel and restaurant.

From the *El Questro* turn-off, the Cockburn Range's cliffs lead you to the shallow but broad **Pentecost River** crossing. Eight kilometres on is *Home Valley Station* (1km; ⓣ08/9161 4322, ⓦwww.homevalley.com.au; ❶), a friendly, relaxed alternative to corporate *El Questro*, based around a breezy barn-like homestead that's more like the real thing, and boasting great sunset views across the Pentecost to the Cockburn Ranges. As well as camping, there are comfortable cabins for $125 half-board per person, a pool and an ever-growing network of 4WD tracks and walking trails to fishing spots.

West of Home Valley, the GRR has been rebuilt following the 2002 flood when the Durack River rose 24m in twelve hours and washed *Jack's Waterhole* (part of Home Valley) out into the Cambridge Gulf, never to be rebuilt. The track rattles away beneath your wheels for about 70km until *Ellenbrae Station* (5km; ⓣ08/9161 4322, ⓔellenbrae3@bigpond.com; meals available; gates locked 9.30am–2.30pm; camping, bungalows ❺), another million-acre property that's not had a cattle muster for years. The campground amenities area, like the main homestead itself, follow an "organic" open-plan design in stone and wood, a treat if you have it to yourself. Self-guide tour maps are available.

Kalumburu Road junction to Derby

After the Kalumburu Road junction, the turn-offs from the GRR to accessible gorges and waterholes increase. About 50km from the junction is a turn north to *Mount Elizabeth* (30km, ⓣ08/9191 4644, ⓔmt.elizabeth@bigpond.com; camping half-board $150 per person) with tours of the property available on set dates. Another 10km down the GRR is **Barnett River Gorge** (5km; basic camping), nothing too spectacular but with a couple of places where you can camp for free and swim in a billabong. Twenty kilometres after that is the *Mount Barnett Roadhouse* (May–Oct daily 7am–6pm; ⓣ08/9191 7007), where you can camp at Manning Gorge (7km), or take an hour's walk to the even nicer, multi-tiered **Upper Manning Gorge**. Further down the GRR both **Galvans** (700m) and **Adcock** (5km) gorges are less impressive by comparison.

Beverley Springs Station (ⓣ08/9191 4646, ⓔbeverleysprings@bigpond.com; camping with gorge access, bunkhouse $50, en-suite rondaval bungalows $143 per person half-board) is now open for visitors, 55km north off the GRR. As well as having access to other freshwater gorges, it's one of the few GRR stations from which you can get to the sea at Walcott Inlet, assuming the track is drivable ($50 fee per car, motorbikes half-price), though of course swimming here is not advisable.

Back on the GRR, a long 95km detour south brings you to *Mornington Wilderness Camp*, (ⓣ08/9191 7406 or 1800 631 946, ⓦwww.australianwildlife.org), a former station that, like Mount Hart (see below), has been bought out by a conservation organisation. Expect a few creek crossings in the final 15km after Glenroy Homestead. Washed out by the rain in 2002, the rebuilt *Mornington* now includes airy en-suite safari tents (full-board ❽) and creekside camping as well as a bar and restaurant. From the camp, you can access two impressive gorges on the Fitzroy River: **Sir John Gorge** (14km; 30min) has broad pools ideal for swimming and exploring upstream leads you to even greater grandeur.

To appreciate **Dimond Gorge** (23km; 1hr) you'll have to rent a canoe from the homestead ($50 per day) to paddle downstream beyond the sheer walls.

Back on the GRR just after Saddlers Creek is *Imintji Safari Camp*, run by APT/Kimberley Wilderness Adventures but open to passers-by (Ⓣ08/1800 675 222; half-board safari tents $120 per person). The **Imintji Store** (Ⓣ08/9191 5761) is just down the road and stocks fuel, ice, and a good supply of groceries, as well as carrying out basic vehicle repairs. Seven kilometres further on is the access track north to **Bell Creek Gorge** in the King Leopold Conservation Park (30km; vehicle entry fee, camping at two locations). Well worth some extra corrugations, this is the loveliest gorge along the GRR, although now very popular. Twenty-three kilometres further down the Gibb, on the far side of the King Leopold Ranges, is **Lennard River Gorge** (8km; last 3km 4WD), a dramatic cleft carved through tiers of tilted rock. Even in a 4WD you may find it quicker and certainly easier to walk the last two kilometres, which, unless they've been recently repaired, are very rough in parts.

A few kilometres on down the GRR is the turning north for *Mount Hart Wilderness Lodge* (50km; Ⓣ08/9191 4645, Ⓦwww.mthart.com.au; half-board $165 per person, lunch included if you stay more than one night, no camping or day visits). You need to book ahead but you can call from the Imintji Store or use the Lodge's private radio at the GRR turn-off. The former homestead has been cultivated into a cosy shaded retreat with a bar, comfortable indoor areas and a waterhole, and has private gorges to explore a few kilometres away. Scenic flights and helicopters use the lodge's airstrip to stop for lunch (and are available to visitors), but at other times it could be all yours.

Back on the GRR once more, you wind your way through the impressive **King Leopard Ranges** and soon come to the **Napier Ranges.** composed of the Devonian Reef, where a rock-chiseled profile of Queen Victoria's Head is evident as you pass through the gap. Nine kilometres from here a turn leads southeast to Windjana Gorge National Park (21km) and Fitzroy Crossing (165km). The last 62km to Derby is a sealed avenue of portly boab trees.

Travel details

Trains

Perth to: Bunbury (2–3 daily; 2hr); Kalgoorlie (1–2 daily; 6hr); Adelaide/Sydney (2 weekly; Adelaide 50hr, Sydney 60hr).

Buses

Kalgoorlie to: Adelaide (1 daily; 36hr); Esperance (3 weekly; 5hr); Leonora (2 weekly; 11hr); Perth (daily; 8hr).

Perth to: Adelaide (1 daily; 35hr); Albany (3 daily; from 6hr); Augusta (6 weekly; 6hr); Broome (daily; 32hr); Bunbury (1–2 daily; 2hr); Carnarvon (daily; 11hr); Dampier–Karratha (5 weekly; 21hr); Darwin (daily; 56hr); Denham (for Monkey Mia; daily; 12hr); Derby (3 weekly; 37hr); Esperance (4 weekly; 10hr); Exmouth (6 weekly; 6hr); Fitzroy Crossing (3 weekly; 40hr); Geraldton (2–4 daily; 6hr); Halls Creek (daily; 44hr); Hyden (for Wave Rock; 2 weekly; 5hr); Kalbarri (daily; 8hr); Kalgoorlie (daily; 8hr); Kununurra (daily; 49hr); Margaret River (3 daily; 5hr); Meekatharra (2 weekly; 10hr); Newman (2 weekly; 13hr); Port Hedland (1 daily; 25hr).

Flights

Perth to: Adelaide (6 daily; 4hr 15min); Alice Springs (5 weekly; 4hr); Ayers Rock Resort (3 weekly; 3hr 45min); Brisbane (3 weekly; 6hr 15min); Broome (1 daily; 2hr 30min); Darwin (1 daily; 6hr 15min); Esperance (2 daily; 1hr 50min); Kalgoorlie (1 daily; 1hr); Kununurra (6 weekly; 3hr 15min); Melbourne (12 daily; 5hr 15min); Sydney (12 daily; 6hr); Tom Price (1 daily; 2 hr).

9

South Australia

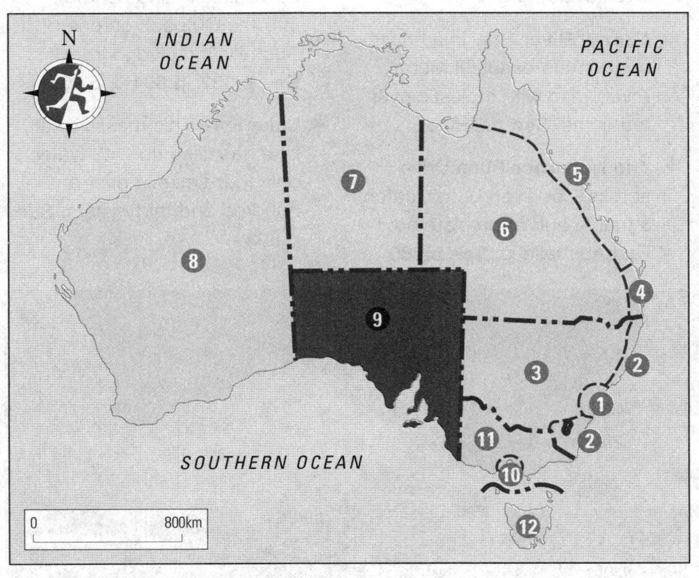

CHAPTER 9

Highlights

* **Adelaide Festival of Arts** The country's best-known and most innovative arts festival. **See p.824**
* **Barossa Valley** A popular day-trip from Adelaide, the Barossa Valley is home to some of Australia's finest wineries. **See p.834**
* **Kangaroo Island** Spectacular scenery and a huge range of wildlife. **See p.849**
* **Murray River** Stay in a house-boat on the beautiful Murray River, lined with majestic river red gums. **See p.866**
* **The Nullarbor Plain** Drive across – or, even better, catch a train – and appreciate how vast Australia is. **See p.880**
* **Coober Pedy** The inhabitants of scorching Coober Pedy live underground to escape the heat of summer. **See p.883**
* **Wilpena Pound** The main attraction of the Flinders Ranges National Park is the huge natural basin of Wilpena Pound. **See p.889**
* **The Strzelecki, Birdsville and Oodnadatta tracks** Fill up your tank and head off into the Outback on one of Australia's fabled journeys. **See p.892**, **p.894** & **p.894**
* **Lake Eyre** This massive salt lake has filled up with water only four times in over a hundred and thirty years. **See p.893**

△ Kangaroo Island

9

South Australia

South Australia, the driest state of the driest continent, is split into two very distinct halves. The long-settled southern part, watered by the Murray River, and with **Adelaide** as its cosmopolitan centre, enjoys a Mediterranean **climate** that makes it tremendously fertile and has been thoroughly tamed. The northern half, arid and depopulated, most definitely has not and as you head further north the temperature hots up to such an extreme that by Coober Pedy people live underground to escape the searing summer temperatures.

Most of southeastern South Australia lies within three hours' drive of Adelaide. Food and especially **wine** are among its chief pleasures: this is prime grape-growing and wine-making country. As well as its wineries the **Fleurieu Peninsula**, just south of Adelaide, has a string of fine beaches, while nearby **Kangaroo Island** is a great place to see Australian wildlife at its unfettered best. Facing Adelaide across the Investigator Strait, the **Yorke Peninsula** is primarily an agricultural area, preserving a little copper-mining history and some great fishing. The superb wineries of the **Barossa Valley**, originally settled by German immigrants in the nineteenth century, are only an hour east from Adelaide on the **Sturt Highway**, the main road to Sydney. This crosses the Murray River at Blanchetown and follows the fertile **Riverland** region to the New South Wales border. Following the **southeast coast** along the Princes Highway, you can head towards Melbourne via the extensive coastal lagoon system of the Coorong and enjoyable seaside towns such as Robe, exiting the state at **Mount Gambier**, with its crater lakes. The inland trawl via the **Dukes Highway** is faster but far less interesting. Heading north from Adelaide, there are old copper-mining towns to explore at Kapunda and Burra in the area known as the **mid-north**, which also encompasses the **Clare Valley**, a quieter, more down-to-earth wine centre than the Barossa Valley.

In contrast with the gentle and cultured southeast, the remainder of South Australia – with the exception of the relatively refined **Eyre Peninsula** and its strikingly scenic west coast – is unremittingly harsh desert, a naked country of vast horizons, salt lakes, glazed gibber plains and ancient mountain ranges. Although it's tempting to scud over the forbidding distances quickly, you'll miss the essence of this introspective and subtle landscape by hurrying. For every predictable, monotonous highway there's a dirt alternative, which may be physically draining but enables you to get closer to this precarious environment. The folded red rocks of the central **Flinders Ranges** and **Coober Pedy**'s post-apocalyptic scenery are on most agendas and could be worked into a sizeable circuit, but overall the Outback lacks any real destinations. Making

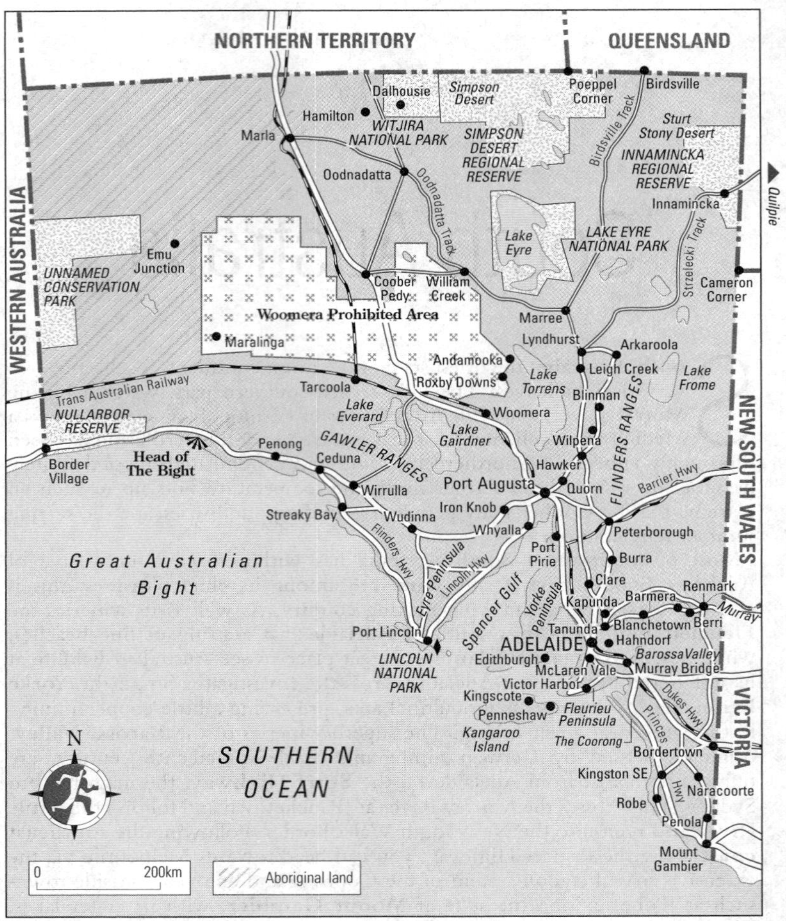

the most of the journey is what counts – the fabled routes to **Oodnadatta**, **Birdsville** and **Innamincka** are still real adventures, and not necessarily only for 4WDs.

Rail and **road** routes converge in Adelaide before the long cross-country hauls west to Perth via Port Augusta on the Indian Pacific, or north to Alice Springs and Darwin on the Ghan – both ranking as two of Australia's great train journeys.

Some history

The coast of South Australia was first **explored** by the Dutch in 1627. In 1792 the French explorer Bruni d'Entrecasteaux sailed along the Great Australian Bight before heading to southern Tasmania, and in 1802 the Englishman

Matthew Flinders thoroughly charted the coast. The most important expedition, though – and the one which led to the foundation of a colony here – was **Captain Charles Sturt**'s 1830 navigation of the Murray River from its source in New South Wales to its mouth in South Australia.

When South Australia was first settled by Europeans in 1836, it was home to as many as fifty distinct **Aboriginal groups**, with a population estimated at 15,000. Three distinct cultural regions existed: the Western Desert, the Central Lakes, and the Murray and southeast region. It was the people of the comparatively well-watered southeast who felt the full impact of white settlement, those who survived being shunted onto missions controlled by the government. Some Aboriginal people have clung tenaciously to their way of life in the Western Desert, where they have gained title to some of their land, but most now live south of Port Augusta, many in Adelaide.

South Australia was planned from the start: in the idealistic scheme of the English entrepreneur Edward Wakefield, there were to be no convicts here – instead, free settlers would be sold small units of land (rather than given large free land grants) in a state guaranteeing them civil and religious liberty. The success of the scheme was guaranteed when George Fife Angas formed the **South Australia Company** to finance it. In 1836, **Governor John Hindmarsh** landed at Holdfast Bay, now the Adelaide beachside suburb of Glenelg, with the first settlers; the next year Colonel William Light planned the spacious, attractive city of Adelaide, with broad streets and plenty of parks and squares. By 1839, Angas was assisting persecuted Lutheran communities from the eastern provinces of Prussia to settle in South Australia.

Early problems caused by the harsh, dry climate and financial incompetence (the colony went bankrupt in 1841) were eased by the discovery of substantial reserves of **copper**. The population of Adelaide boomed over the following decades, while the state's tradition of **libertarianism** continued; in 1894, South Australia's women were the first in the world to be permitted to stand for parliament and the second in the world to gain the vote (after women in New Zealand). Social improvement through slum clearances began after World War I, though of all the mainland states, the depressions and recessions of the interwar period hit South Australia the hardest, due in part to the three-year drought that preceded the Wall Street Crash of 1929. The situation eased following World War II, when new immigrants arrived, boosting the output of industry and injecting fresh life into the state.

The 1970s were the decade of **Don Dunstan**. The flamboyant Labor Premier was an enlightened reformer who had a strong sense of social justice: he abolished capital punishment, outlawed racial discrimination and decriminalized homosexuality. The state has been a duller place since his retirement in 1979, and a poorer one since the recession started to bite at the end of the 1980s. During recent years the largely unsuccessful privatizations of public utilities have added to South Australia's economic woes, while the state's image has been dominated by arguments over the siting of nuclear waste disposal facilities and the detention of asylum seekers, much to the chagrin of South Australians themselves, who feel that their state's attractions are being unfairly eclipsed by the lure of other Australian destinations.

Adelaide and the southeast

Adelaide is the state's transport hub, with good **bus** connections throughout the southeast, though there are more rewarding alternatives if you fancy travelling under your own steam. Much of the country is flat and great for **cycling**, and the principal route, the **Mawson Trail**, runs for 800km specifically planned for cyclists, extending from the Mount Lofty Ranges through the Barossa Valley and Flinders Ranges to the Outback town of Blinman. **Walkers** can follow a parallel route along the 1500-kilometre **Heysen Trail**, starting at Cape Jervis on the tip of the Fleurieu Peninsula and running up the coast before heading north over the Mount Lofty Ranges to the Flinders. The Heysen trail is closed between December and April – partly due to the high risk of fire, and partly as a result of an agreement with private landowners, through whose property some of the trail passes. Further information and maps for the trails are available from South Australian Travel Centre in Adelaide (see opposite).

Adelaide

ADELAIDE is always thought of as a gracious city and an easy place to live in, and despite a population of around one million and a veneer of sophistication, it still has the feel of an overgrown country town. It's a pretty place, laid out on either side of the **Torrens River**, ringed with a green belt of parks and set against the rolling hills of the **Mount Lofty Ranges**. During the hot, dry summer the parklands are kept green by irrigation from the waters of the Murray River on which the city depends, though there's always a sense that the rawness of the Outback is waiting to take over.

The original occupants of the Adelaide plains were the **Kaurna people**, whose traditional way of life was destroyed within twenty years of the landing of Governor John Hindmarsh at Holdfast Bay in 1836. The colony's surveyor general, **Colonel William Light**, had visionary plans for the new city. After a long struggle with Hindmarsh, who wanted to build around a harbour, Light got his wish for an inland city with a strong connection to the river, formed around wide and spacious avenues and squares. Postwar immigration provided the final element missing from Light's plan: the human one. Italians now make up the city's biggest non-Anglo cultural group, and in the hot, dry summers, Mediterranean-style alfresco eating and drinking lend the city a vaguely European air. Not surprisingly, one of Adelaide's chief delights is its **food** and **wine**, with South Australian vintages in every cellar, and restaurants and cafés as varied as Sydney's and Melbourne's, only much cheaper.

Outwardly conservative, Adelaide nonetheless takes advantage of South Australia's liberal traditions, with a nudist beach, relaxed drug laws and 24-hour hotel licences. It's the free and easy **lifestyle** within an ordered framework that's so appealing; Adelaide may not be an obvious destination in itself, but it's a great place for a relaxed break on your way up to the Northern Territory or across to Western Australia.

Arrival

Buses from out of town, including the airport bus, will drop you off at the basic **Central bus station**, on Franklin St. The international **airport**, 7km southwest from the centre, is small and modern, and has a currency exchange and information booth. The domestic terminal is about half a kilometre southwest. Both are serviced by the Skylink **airport bus** (daily 6am–9pm; 1–2 departures hourly; $7.50 one-way; to book a return trip or ask for a hotel pickup, ring ⓣ08/8332 0528), which will drop you off at most city accommodation on request; the bus also stops at Victoria Square and North Terrace, as well as the Central bus station. The airport bus also stops at the **Keswick Interstate** train terminal, about 1km from the city centre, from where it costs $4.00 to the city or airport; alternatively, walk across to the suburban platform and catch a train into **Adelaide train station**, situated on North Terrace in the city centre. A **taxi** from the airport costs around $17 to either the city or the beachside suburb of Glenelg; taxis to the city from the Keswick Interstate Terminal charge about $10.

Information

The first stop for information is the **South Australian Travel Centre**, at 18 King William St, between Rundle Mall and North Terrace (Mon–Fri 8.30am–5.00pm, Sat & Sun 9am–2pm; ⓣ1300 655 276, ⓦwww.southaustralia.com). This large modern office has helpful staff and masses of general information, including excellent free touring guides and maps of Adelaide and the state. Just around the corner on Rundle Mall itself is the **Rundle Mall Visitor Information Centre** (Mon–Thurs 10am–5pm, Fri 10am–8pm, Sat 10am–3pm, Sun 11am–4pm; ⓣ08/8203 7611, ⓦwww.adelaidecitycouncil.com), a smaller version of the above, offering brochures, maps and event guides - the friendly staff will answer any questions you may have about the city. Opposite the bus station at 110 Franklin St, the bright pink **Backpacker Transit and Travel Centre** (daily 8.30am–6pm; ⓣ08/8410 3000) can provide free maps and book all domestic tours; there's also a currency exchange, telephone, a good notice board, and Internet access ($3 for 1hr).

The **City of Adelaide Customer Centre**, 25 Pirie St (Mon–Fri 8.30am–5.30pm; ⓣ08/8203 7203, ⓦwww.adelaidecitycouncil.com), has a range of free maps and booklets, including the glossy fold-out *Art in Public Places Walking Guide*, which contains information on art throughout South Australia, and the monthly newspaper *About Adelaide*, which details all upcoming events and travelling exhibitions in the city.

City transport

The city centre is compact and flat, making walking an easy option, but if the heat becomes too much there are also two **free buses**. The **Bee Line** (#99B) runs from Victoria Square via King William Street, North Terrace and the train station to Hindley Street, then back again. Services run every five minutes during the week (Mon–Thurs 8am–6pm, Fri 8am–9.30pm) and every fifteen on Saturdays (10am–5pm). The **City Loop Bus** (#99C, same times; every 15min) takes in all the city's major cultural and commercial centres, beginning at Adelaide train station.

To explore further out of the city centre, you'll need to use the integrated **Adelaide Metro** system, which comprises buses, suburban trains and one tramline from the city to Glenelg. Metro buses and trains run until about

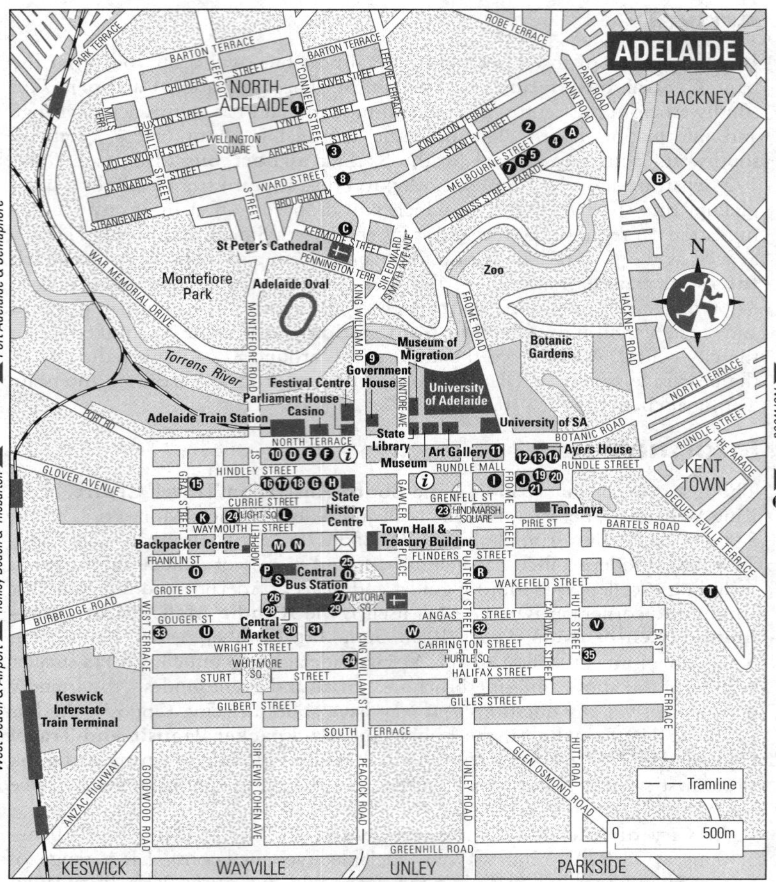

ACCOMMODATION

Adelaide Backpackers Inn	W
Adelaide Caravan park	B
Adelaide Central Backpackers	S
Adelaide Central YHA	L
Adelaide Meridien	A
Annie's Place	O
Austral Hotel	I
Backpack Oz	R
Cannon Street Backpackers	M
City Central Motel	G
The Cumberland	K
Director's Studios	U
East Park Lodge	V
Franklin Central Apartments	N
Greenways Apartments	C
Majestic Roof Garden Hotel	J
Mercure Grosvenor	D
Metropolitan Hotel	Q
Nomads Tatts Inner City	H
Norwood Apartments	T
Stamford Plaza Adelaide	F
Strathmore	E
Sunnys	P

EATING & DRINKING

Al Fresco Gelateria & Pasticceria	13
Amalfi Pizzeria Ristorante	11
Ambassadors Hotel	34
Apothecary 1878	10
Bacall's	6
Café Paradiso	37
Caffe Buongiorno	22
Cibo	8
Citrus	35
Cowley's	25
Earl of Aberdeen	32
Elephant Walk	4
Eros Ouzeri	19
Garage	24
Gaucho's	30
Govinda's	18
The Grange	27
Hawkers Corner	33
Irodori	20
Jasmin	23
Jerusalem	16
Jolleys Boathouse	9
Kwik Stix	3
Marcellina	15
The Melting Pot	36
Oostende	21
Oxford Deli Bar	1
Scoozi	14
Shibata	5
Star of Siam	31
The Store	7
T-chow	26
Tempo	17
Universal Wine Bar	12
Ying Chow	28
Zambracca	2
Zuma	29

11.30pm, with reduced services at night and on Sundays. The **Wandering Star** night bus service operates Fridays and Saturdays (12.30am–5am; $6). Four suburban **train** lines run from Adelaide train station, west to Grange and Outer Harbour and south to Noarlunga and Belair. The **tram** to seaside Glenelg (30min; $2) leaves from Victoria Square every fifteen to twenty minutes. The **O-Bahn** is a fast-track bus which runs on concrete tracks through scenic Torrens Linear Park, between the city (Grenfell St) and Tea Tree Plaza in Modbury, 12km northeast. Information on all of the above services as well as free timetables can be found at the **Passenger Transport InfoCentre** on the corner of King William and Currie streets (Mon–Fri 8am–6pm, Sat 9am–5pm, Sun 11am–4pm; ⓦwww.adelaidemetro.com.au); staff also sell tickets and hand out copies of *The Metroguide*, a free information booklet including a handy map of the system. You can also get transport info on ⓣ08/8210 1000 (daily 7am–8pm).

Tickets for the Metro system come in single-trip, multi-trip and day-trip permutations, and can be used on buses, trains and the tram; if you need to use more than one form of transport for a single journey, one ticket will suffice. Single tickets range in price from $1.90 to $3.40, depending on the time of day, and are valid for two hours. You can buy single-journey tickets from machines on board trains, buses and trams, as well as from train station ticket offices and the Passenger Transport InfoCentre. Other types of ticket, including the day-trip ticket ($6.40), can be bought from the Passenger Transport InfoCentre, train stations, post offices and some newsagents – look for the Metroticket sign.

Cycling is a popular and excellent alternative to public transport: the wide streets and level surfaces make riding a breeze, and there are several good cycling routes – including the **Torrens Linear Park track**, which goes from the sea at Westbeach to the hills at Athelston, weaving along the river. A map of this and other cycling routes is available from the City of Adelaide Customer Centre (see p.807); for bike rental outlets, see "Listings", p.827.

Accommodation

Adelaide has loads of **hostels**, and competition keeps prices low. Those on Gilles or Carrington streets, about ten minutes' walk southwest from the city centre, are generally cheaper than those closer to the city centre, and will pick you up from the bus or train station if you call ahead (several also send minibuses to scout for custom); some hostels will even come to the airport

Campsites in Adelaide

Adelaide's central **campsite** is at the *Adelaide Caravan Park*, Bruton Street, Hackney, on the Torrens River, 2km northeast of the centre (ⓣ08/8363 1566, ⓦwww.adelaidecaravanpark.com.au; cabins and two-bed holiday units ❹, villas with spas ❺). It's right on the Torrens Linear Park cycling route and can be reached by bus #281 or #282 from North Terrace, or on foot through parkland and along the river. For a beachfront setting, head to *Adelaide Shores Caravan Park*, Military Road, West Beach (ⓣ08/8356 7654, ⓦwww.adelaideshores.com.au; bus #278 from Currie St; cabins and on-site vans ❹), or the *Adelaide Beachfront Tourist Park*, 349 Military Rd, Semaphore (ⓣ08/8449 7726 or 1800 810 140, ⓦwww.adelaidebeachfront.com.au; cabins ❹), which has a swimming pool, recreation room, playground and a free shuttle bus service to West Lakes Mall and Ethelton train station. Both sites get very busy during summer. You could also pitch your tent on the rooftop of *Adelaide Central Backpackers* in the centre of the city.

if you call in advance. Otherwise, buses #171 or #172 from Victoria Square stop close to Gilles Street. There are cheap **hotel** rooms on Hindley Street, Adelaide's nightclub area and its tame version of a red-light district, though some women may find it threatening. The swankiest accommodation is along North Terrace. The only time you may have difficulty finding accommodation is during March when the annual **Womadelaide** festival and the **Arts Festival** (even years only) attract throngs of visitors – book ahead. Rooms also fill up quickly at weekends, especially at the more popular hostels around the Central bus station on Franklin Street and adjacent Waymouth Street. The seaside suburb of **Glenelg** and the nearby beach resorts (see p.819), about half an hour away from Adelaide by public transport, are good alternatives to the city centre, with plenty of self-catering apartments and one of Adelaide's liveliest hostels.

City centre

Hotels, motels and pubs

Austral Hotel 205 Rundle St ⓣ08/8223 4660, ⓦwww.theaustral.com. Basic rooms in one of Adelaide's best pubs on this "arty" street. Bands or DJs nearly every night, so it can be noisy. ❸

City Central Motel 23 Hindley St ⓣ08/8231 4049, ⓕ8231 4804. Centrally located budget motel. ❸

Director's Studios 259 Gouger St ⓣ08/8213 2500 or 1800 882 601, ⓦwww.savillesuites.com.au. A five-minute walk to Chinatown and the Central Market, this modern and very good-value hotel has well-furnished self-catering studio apartments and standard rooms. 24hr reception and free parking too. ❹

Franklin Central Apartments 36 Franklin St ⓣ08/8221 7050, ⓦwww.franklinapartments.com.au. Fully serviced one-, two- and three-bedroom apartments in a central location ideal for business or extended stays. 24hr reception. ❻

Majestic Roof Garden Hotel 55 Frome Street ⓣ08/8100 4499, ⓦwww.majestichotels.com.au. New, high-standard accommodation offering 120 very well appointed suites with surprisingly affordable rates. Facilities include room service, gym and Internet access. ❺

Mercure Grosvenor 125 North Terrace ⓣ08/8407 8888 or 1800 888 222, ⓔre1@mercuregrosvenorhotel.com.au. Dating from 1918, this genteel establishment recently underwent a $5 million makeover. Spacious, modern en-suite rooms come with air-con, and there's 24hr room service, a gym and sauna, bar and bistro and parking. Breakfast included. ❻

Metropolitan Hotel 46 Grote St ⓣ08/8231 5471, ⓕ8231 0633. Rather tacky locals' pub offering good-value meals, and basic clean rooms upstairs at bargain prices. Light breakfast included. ❷

Stamford Plaza Adelaide 150 North Terrace ⓣ08/8461 1111, ⓦwww.stamford.com.au/adelaide/adpla1bar.html. This central, high-rise luxury five-star hotel has all you'd expect: swimming pool, sauna, three restaurants, room service and views of the Festival Centre. Room rates are in excess of $200, though cheaper weekend packages are available. There's also a beachside equivalent, the *Stamford Grand Hotel*, at Glenelg. ❼

Strathmore 129 North Terrace ⓣ08/8212 6911, ⓦwww.strath.com.au. Smart, small hotel in a desirable location. The en-suite, motel-style rooms are small and have no views, though they come with all mod cons from air-con to room service. Free undercover parking. Breakfast included. ❺

Hostels

Adelaide Backpackers Inn 112 Carrington St ⓣ08/8223 6635 or 1800 247 725, ⓦwww.adelaidebackpackersinn.net.au. Shabby place in a converted pub, with a friendly ambience and helpful staff. There are six- to twelve-bed dorms and plenty of singles and doubles in a brighter, more modern air-con building. Generous breakfast thrown in and free apple pie in the evening. Internet access. Reception doubles as a travel agency, selling bus and train tickets. Dorms $22, rooms ❷

Adelaide Central Backpackers 128 Grote St ⓣ08/8231 0639 or 1800 804 133, ⓦwww.adelaidecmba.com.au. Friendly, clean and modern, with colourful murals decorating the entrance area, this is one of Adelaide's more sociable hostels. You can even pitch your tent on the roof, making this the cheapest spot in town. Travel agent service, BBQs, free bikes and an excellent notice board area available, and a light breakfast and linen are included. Dorms $19, rooms ❶

Adelaide Central YHA 135 Waymouth St ⓣ08/8414 3010, ⓔadlcentral@yhasa.org.au. Modern, rather ugly but extremely efficient youth hostel with over 200 beds in the heart of the city – though don't expect a lively atmosphere. Accommodation is in dorms (four- to eight-bed; all have lockers), doubles (some en suite) and two family rooms ($90). There are also well-equipped kitchens, a large laundry room, lockers, a comprehensive travel centre and Internet access next door. Some off-street parking spaces can be reserved. Dorms $23, rooms ❸

Annie's Place 239 Franklin St ⓣ08/8212 2668, ⓦwww.anniesplace.com.au. Welcoming, family-owned hostel in a beautifully restored Victorian house with a country-style kitchen and breakfast room, small bar and cosy plant-filled courtyard. Four-, six- and ten-bed dorms are available as well as immaculate doubles. Courtesy pick-up, free night tour and hearty continental breakfast included. Dorms $20, rooms ❸

Backpack Oz 144 Wakefield St, cnr Pulteney St ⓣ & ⓕ 08/8223 3551, ⓦwww.backpackoz.com.au. Converted from a nineteenth-century hotel, this low-key hostel has light, spacious rooms and dorms (four-, six- and ten-bed). There's a comfortable common room downstairs, plus bar (summer only), laundry and a small kitchen. Pick-ups from bus, train and airport available, and tours booked. Linen and a light breakfast included. Dorms $20, rooms ❸

Cannon Street Backpackers 110 Franklin Street, ⓣ 08/8410 1218 or 1800 069 731, ⓦwww.cannonst.com.au. One of the best hostels in town, this huge, warehouse-style place has a cool young feel and is very clean and well run. The big foyer has a travel centre, Internet access and a funky licensed bar though, while there's lots of noise and action downstairs, it's peaceful upstairs. Free light breakfast included, plus cheap day-membership at the gym around the corner, parking and bed linen. Dorms $17–20, rooms ❸

The Cumberland 205 Waymouth St ⓣ08/8231 3577, ⓕ8232 3578. Friendly hostel in a delightful, recently renovated Victorian hotel, but don't expect much peace and quiet – rooms are above a wine bar/dance club that's open 24 hours a day, seven days a week. Dorms $25, rooms ❷

East Park Lodge 341 Angas St ⓣ08/8223 1228 or 1800 643 606, ⓦwww.eastparklodge.com.au. Huge three-storey mansion with singles, doubles and four-bed dorms, all with air-con. The atmosphere is peaceful, with views of the hills from balconies and rooftop, and a pool to cool off in. Bus and train pick-ups if pre-booked; airport buses drop off here. Limited on-street parking. Free breakfast. Dorms $22, rooms ❸

Nomads Tatts Inner City 1st Floor, 17 Hindley St ⓣ08/8231 3225, ⓔtattscity@hotmail.com. Small, centrally located hostel above a heritage-listed hotel. A bit noisy, but it has good facilities, including a sunny verandah overlooking the main street, a well-equipped kitchen, pool table, Internet access, games and videos. Dorms $20–22, rooms ❸

Sunnys 139 Franklin St ⓣ08/8231 2430 or 1800 631 391, ⓦwww.sunnys.com.au. A friendly place in an old house next to the bus station. Six- to eight-bed dorms (bunks), plus one twin and a double, all with ceiling fans. Facilities include a pool table, sound system, TV and video, and train, bus and plane tickets are sold and tours booked. There's cheap Internet access too, plus off-street parking. Rates include linen, tea and coffee and a pancake breakfast. Dorms $22, rooms ❷

North Adelaide and Kent Town

Adelaide Meridien 21 Melbourne St, North Adelaide ⓣ08/8267 3033, ⓦwww.adelaidemeridien.com.au. Located on fashionable Melbourne St, this modern brick building is actually an eyesore and the 1980s decor is rather dated. Creature comforts include a sauna, spa and outdoor pool, and undercover parking is included in the rates. ❼

Greenways Apartments 41–45 King William Rd, North Adelaide ⓣ08/8267 5903, ⓦwww.greenwaysapartments.com. One-, two- and three-bedroom fully furnished self-catering units in an excellent location. ❹

Norwood Apartments 7 Wakefield St, Kent Town ⓣ08/8338 6555, ⓕ8336 4555. Five self-contained 2-person units, each containing kitchen facilities, washing-machine, tv, video and CD player. Good value and convenient location. ❹

Beach suburbs

Glenelg Beach Resort 1–7 Moseley St, Glenelg ⓣ08/8376 0007 or 1800 066 422, ⓦwww.glenelgbeachresort.com.au. Award-winning hostel near the beach. Lots of doubles and some singles and self-contained units available, as well as five- to six-bed dorms (no bunks). The lively common area downstairs has a bar open to the public, with loud music and activities ranging from bands, karaoke and comedians to pool comps and theme nights. No parking. Dorms $16–20, rooms ❷, self-contained units ❹

Glenelg Jetty Hotel 28 Jetty Rd, Glenelg ⓣ08/8294 4377, ⓕ8295 4412. Friendly, homely pub accommodation popular with country people visiting the city. Rooms are en suite or with shared bathroom. ❹

Glenelg Seaway Apartments 18 Durham St, Glenelg ⓣ08/8295 8503. Four basic and slightly run-down apartments in a quiet location close to the beach. ❸

Meleden Villa 268 Seaview Rd, Henley Beach ⓣ08/8235 0577, ⓦwww.meledenvilla.com. Good-value B&B one street back from the beach in a lovely old two-storey building with a pool and outdoor terrace. Downstairs rooms share a bathroom, while upstairs rooms, with balconies and sea views, are en suite. ❹

Oaks Plaza Pier Hotel 16 Holdfast Promenade ⓣ08/8350 6688, ⓦwww.theoaksgroup.com.au. The most recent development on the foreshore, this is quite the grandest hotel in Glenelg. Suites come with private balconies affording unspoilt ocean views, the sleek, modern rooms have all the comforts you'd expect at these prices, and facilities include a pool, gym, spa and sauna. ❼

Taft Motor Inn 18 Moseley St, Glenelg ⓣ08/8376 1233, ⓦwww.taftmotorinn.citysearch.com.au. Well-equipped motel units and one- and two-bedroom self-catering apartments near the beach; all have air-con and slightly dreary old-fashioned decor. Good for families, with a playground, garden and swimming pool (and toddler pool); baby-sitting available. 24hr reception. ❹

The City

Adelaide's city centre is laid out on a strict grid plan surrounded by parkland: at the heart of the grid is **Victoria Square**, and each city quarter is centred on its own smaller square. **North Terrace** is the cultural precinct, home to the city's major museums, two universities and the state library. **Hindley Street** is the liveliest in town, and the focus of the city's nightlife, while **Rundle Mall**, its continuation, is the main shopping area; **Rundle Street**, further east, is home to the city's arty café strip. West of Victoria Square between Grote and Gouger streets is the lively **Central Market** and the small **Chinatown**. The **Torrens River** flows to the north of North Terrace, while the Botanic Gardens and zoo are set on its south bank. Three main roads cross the river to the distinctive colonial architecture and café culture of **North Adelaide**.

Adelaide suffered numerous economic setbacks and built up its wealth slowly, and its well-preserved **Victorian architecture** has a reassuring permanence quite unlike the over-the-top style of 1850s Melbourne, with its grandiose municipal buildings funded by easy goldrush money. The bourgeois solidity of Adelaide's streets is enhanced by the fact that virtually every building, public or domestic, is made of **stone**, whether sandstone, bluestone, South Australian freestone or slate.

Gay- and lesbian-friendly accommodation

The beachfront **Semaphore Hotel**, 17 Semaphore Rd (ⓣ08/8449 4662, ⓕ8449 4626), in Semaphore (see p.819), a beach suburb about 15km northwest of the centre, is lesbian-run but also welcomes gay male guests and straights. The pleasant pub rooms share bathrooms (❸, weekly rates available), and there's a comfortable common room with a wood stove and pool table. The pub itself serves inexpensive meals and hosts live bands and DJs (Wed–Sun until 2am). Other, more central gay-friendly establishments include self-catering apartments at **Gurny Lodge**, 190–194 Gover St, North Adelaide (ⓣ08/8267 2500, ⓕ8239 2301; ❸) and **Greenways Apartments** (see p.811); and deluxe hotel rooms at the **Stamford Plaza Adelaide** (see p.810). Parkside Travel (ⓣ08/8274 1222) has an accommodation service, or check the ads in *Blaze* (see box, p.826).

The Botanic Gardens and Ayers House

There's really only one place to start your tour, and that's tree-lined **North Terrace**, a long heritage streetscape perfect for exploring on foot. At the eastern extremity is the main entrance to the **Botanic Gardens** (Mon–Fri 8am–dusk, Sat & Sun 9am–dusk; free guided tours operate daily from the kiosk by the main lake at 10.30am; Ⓦwww.environment.sa.gov.au/botanicgardens). Opened in 1857, the lovely gardens boast ponds, fountains, wisteria arbours, statues and heritage buildings – just like a classic English-style garden, but with plenty of native trees too. The elegant glass and wrought-iron **Palm House**, completed in 1877, was based on a similar building in Germany. Its role of displaying tropical plant species has been taken over by the stunning **Bicentennial Conservatory** (daily 10am–4pm, summer until 5pm; $3.50). This, the largest glasshouse in Australia, houses a complete tropical rainforest environment with its own computer-controlled cloud-making system. Make sure you pick up the leaflet *Walk with the Plants*, which gives detailed information about the glasshouse's contents. Other attractions include a fragrant herb garden, a rose garden and **Simpson House**, a pleasantly cool thatched hut containing palms and ferns beside a stream. When you've had enough, you can sit under shady trees by the duck-filled main lake outside the excellent licensed **kiosk** and have a beer or snack. At the northern entrance to the gardens, **North Lodge**, once the caretaker's residence, is now a shop (daily noon–4pm) that sells books on botany and gardening, plus other souvenirs.

Heading away from the gardens on North Terrace, the first notable building you come to is the National Trust-owned **Ayers House** (Tues–Fri 10am–4pm, Sat & Sun 1–4pm; $8). Home to the politician **Henry Ayers** who was premier of South Australia seven times between 1855 and 1897 and after whom the Rock was named, it began as a small brick dwelling in 1845 – the fine bluestone mansion you now see is the result of thirty years of extensions. Inside, it's elaborately decorated in late-nineteenth-century style, with portraits of the Ayers family.

The universities and the Art Gallery of South Australia

Between Frome Road and Kintore Avenue, a whole block of North Terrace is occupied by the University of Adelaide, and the art gallery, museum and state library. The **University of Adelaide**, the city's oldest, was established in 1874 and began to admit women right from its founding – another example of South Australia's advanced social thinking. The grounds are pleasant to stroll through: along North Terrace are **Bonython Hall**, built in 1936 in a vaguely medieval style, and **Elder Hall**, an early-twentieth-century Gothic-Florentine design now occupied by the Conservatorium of Music (concerts Fri 1.10pm; $5; Ⓣ08/8303 5925 for details). The highly decorative, Gothic-inspired **Mitchell Building** beside it constituted the entire original university; on the first floor is the **Museum of Classical Archeology** (Mon–Fri noon–3pm, term time only; free).

Overbearing Victorian busts of the upright founders of Adelaide line the strip between Bonython Hall and Kintore Avenue until you reach the two contemporary abstract sculptures outside the **Art Gallery of South Australia**, established in 1881 (daily 10am–5pm; free; guided tours Mon–Fri 11am & 2pm, Sat & Sun at 11am & 3pm; talks at 12.45pm most Tuesdays; Ⓦwww.artgallery.sa.gov.au). The gallery itself has an impressive collection of **Aboriginal art**, including many non-traditional works with overtly political content; major works by the Western Desert school of Aboriginal artists are on permanent display in Gallery 7. There's a fine selection of **colonial art**, too, and it's interesting to trace the development of Australian art from its European-inspired beginnings up to the point where the influence of the local light, colours and landscape began to take over. The collection of **twentieth-century Australian art** has some good stuff – Sidney Nolan, Margaret Preston, Grace Cossington-Smith – but a lot of dross too. There's also a large collection of twentieth-century British art, including paintings by Roger Fry and Vanessa Bell (Virginia Woolf's sister). The gallery has a good bookshop and coffee shop too.

The South Australian Museum and State Library

Next to the art gallery, a huge whale skeleton guards the entrance to the **South Australian Museum** (daily 10am–5pm; free; tours Sat & Sun at 2pm; Ⓦwww.samuseum.sa.gov.au). The museum's east wing houses the engrossing **Australian Aboriginal Cultures Gallery** (40min guided tours Wed–Sun; $10; book at the museum shop or on Ⓣ08/8207 7370), home to the world's largest collection of Aboriginal artefacts. Amongst the exhibits are a 10,000-year-old boomerang and the *Yanardilyi (Cockatoo Creek) Jukurrpa*, a huge painting by a collection of artists from across the continent recalling four important dreaming stories. The west wing focuses on **natural history and geology**, including an extensive collection of minerals from around the world (on level 3). There's also a permanent exhibition on local geologist **Sir Douglas Mawson** (1882–1958), who was commissioned by the museum to explore much of Australia in the early 1900s and who also undertook the historic Australasian Antarctic Expedition in 1911. Some of the animals he brought back from this expedition are still on display, along with others from around Australia. The **fossil gallery** includes a skeleton of Diprotodon, the largest marsupial ever to walk the earth, plus the **Normandy Nugget** (at the east wing entrance on the ground floor), the second-largest gold nugget in the world, weighing 26kg. For those wishing to gain a more comprehensive understanding of the museum's treasures, the **Science Centre** (Mon-Fri 10am–4pm) holds the Museum archives (booking essential, Ⓣ08/8207 7500) as well as the entire Douglas Mawson collection.

Next door to the museum, on the corner of Kintore Avenue, the 1884 **State Library** (Mon–Wed & Fri 9.30am–8pm, Thurs 9.30am–6pm, Sat & Sun noon–5pm; Ⓣ08/8207 7250, Ⓦwww.slsa.sa.gov.au) has everything from archives to newspaper and magazine reading rooms and free Internet access. It also holds the **Bradman Collection** (Mon–Fri 9.30am–5pm, Sat & Sun noon–5pm; free; Ⓦwww.bradman.sa.com.au), housing Sir Donald Bradman's personal collection of cricket memorabilia, including his own memoirs of the infamous Bodyline series with England. A large screen shows interviews and footage of his finest moments.

Around the corner on Kintore Avenue is the **Migration Museum** (Mon–Fri 10am–5pm, Sat & Sun 1–5pm; free; Ⓦwww.history.sa.gov.au), which takes you on a journey from port to settlement in the company of South Australia's settlers, through innovative, interactive displays and reconstructions – the "White Australia Walk", for example, has a push-button questionnaire giving you the red, green or amber light for immigration under the guidelines of the White Australia policy, which was in force from 1901 to 1958.

The government buildings and arts spaces

Continue west along North Terrace, past the War Memorial, to reach **Government House**, Adelaide's oldest public building, completed in 1855: every governor except the first has lived here. Across King William Road, two parliament houses, the old and the new, compete for space. The current **Parliament House**, begun in 1889, wasn't finished until 1939 because of a dispute over a dome, and while there's still no dome (and only half a coat of arms), it's a stately building all the same, with a facade of marble columns. Alongside is the modest **Old Parliament House** (closed to the public), built between 1855 and 1876.

On the corner of North Terrace and Morphett Street, the **Lion Arts Centre** is home to theatres, bars, a cinema, galleries and the **Experimental Art Foundation,** which houses artists' studios upstairs and provocative exhibitions in the gallery downstairs (Tues–Fri 11am–5pm, Sat 2–5pm). A short stroll south of here on Morphett Street, the **Jam Factory Craft and Design Centre** (Mon–Fri 9am–5.30pm, Sat & Sun 10am–5pm, Ⓦwww.jamfactory.com.au) displays beautiful objects (all of them for sale) made of leather, glass, wood and clay. A blue metal spiral staircase leads to a viewing platform above the **glass-blowing centre** (demonstrations Mon–Fri 9am–4pm, Sat & Sun 10am–4pm). A block west of here is the latest addition to Adelaide's contemporary art scene, the **Light Square Gallery** (Mon–Fri 10am–5pm; free) in the basement of the Roma Mitchell Arts Education Centre on Light Square. The focus here is on techno art and the digital age.

Along the Torrens River

The **Torrens River** meanders between central Adelaide and North Adelaide, surrounded by parklands. Between Parliament House and the river is the **Festival Centre**: two geometric constructions of concrete, steel and smoked glass, in a concrete arena scattered with abstract 1970s civic sculpture. The main auditorium, the Festival Theatre, has the largest stage in the southern hemisphere, hosting opera, ballet and various concerts; the foyer is often the venue for free Sunday afternoon concerts (2–4pm). The smaller Playhouse Theatre is the drama theatre, while the Space Theatre is often used for cabaret and stand-up comedy. Call Ⓣ13 12 46 for details of specific events.

A short walk across **Elder Park** is the river with its large fountain and black swans. **Popeye Cruises** to the zoo leave from here (Mon–Fri 1–3pm hourly; Sat & Sun 11am–5pm every 20min; $5 one-way, $8 return), and you can also rent paddleboats ($10 per 30min). Nearby, the green shed at **Jolleys Boathouse**, across King William Road, is an Adelaide institution, housing a restaurant (see p.822) and a cheaper kiosk, both with river views.

The most pleasant way to get to **Adelaide Zoo**, whose main entrance is on Frome Road (daily 9.30am–5pm; $15, children $9; free guided walks at 11am and 2pm; call Ⓣ08/8267 3255 for feeding times and keeper talks), is to follow the river, either by boat (see above) or on foot – a fifteen-minute stroll. Alternatively, walk from the Botanic Gardens through Botanic Park, entering through the children's zoo entrance on Plane Tree Drive, or take bus #272 or #273 from Grenfell or Currie streets. Opened in 1883, the country's second-oldest zoo (after Melbourne's) is more of a botanical garden than a zoo, with century-old European and native trees, including a huge Moreton Bay fig, and grounds full of picnic tables. The Victorian architecture is well preserved, and a few classic examples of the old-fashioned animal houses have survived, such as the **Elephant House**, built in 1900 in the style of an Indian temple. The zoo is best known for its extensive collection of **native birds**, with two large walk-through aviaries, while its newest section, the Southeast Asian Rainforest exhibit, has naturalistic settings that are home to sixteen animal species, including the endangered Malaysian tapir.

King William Street and Victoria Square

The city's main thoroughfare, **King William Street**, is lined with imposing civic buildings and always crowded with traffic. Look out for the **Edmund Wright House** at no. 59, whose elaborate Renaissance-style facade is one of Adelaide's most flamboyant. Inside the building, the **State History Centre** (Mon–Fri 9am–5pm, Sat & Sun noon–5pm) sometimes hosts free travelling exhibitions. On the other side of the street, and a couple of blocks south, the **Town Hall** (1866) is another of Edmund Wright's Italianate designs. The **General Post Office**, on the corner of Franklin Street, is yet another portentous Victorian edifice, this time with a central clock tower: look inside at the main hall with its decorative roof lantern framed by opaque skylights. Opposite, on the corner of Flinders Street, the **Old Treasury Building** retains its beautiful facade, although it now houses apartments.

Halfway down King William Street lies pleasant **Victoria Square**, a favourite Aboriginal meeting place and home to the Catholic **Cathedral of St Francis Xavier** (1856) and the imposing **Supreme Court**, on the corner of Gouger Street. Just to the west, the covered **Central Market** (Tues 7am–5.30pm, Thurs 11am–5.30pm, Fri 7am–9pm, Sat 7am–3pm) has been a well-loved feature of Adelaide for over a hundred years. Here you can find delectable European and Asian produce in a riot of smelly stalls and lively banter, as well as heaps of shops (open Mon–Sat), cafés, sushi and noodle bars and restaurants. Nearby Gouger and Grote streets also have good options for a meal or a coffee.

Rundle Mall and Rundle Street

The main shopping area in the central business district is the pedestrianized **Rundle Mall**, which manages to be bustling yet relaxed, enhanced by trees, benches, alfresco cafés, fruit and flower stalls, and usually a busker or two. The two main shopping centres are the **Myer Centre**, with over 120 speciality stores over five floors, and the **Adelaide Central Plaza**, dominated by the upmarket David Jones department store and a fantastic foodmart in the basement. Towards the east end of the mall is the decorative **Adelaide Arcade** and the Regent Theatre. By night, Rundle Mall is eerily deserted, a strange contrast to Hindley and Rundle streets on either side, which really come to life after dark.

Rundle Street was once the home of Adelaide's wholesale fruit and vegetable market, but was later appropriated by the alternative and arty, and by university students from the nearby campuses on North Terrace. It's now home to over fifty cafés and restaurants, many of them alfresco, several slick wine bars and two of the best pubs in town (*The Austral* and *The Exeter*, see p.821 and p.824). The disused **Adelaide Fruit and Produce Exchange** (1903) is worth a peek: a classically Edwardian building built of red brick with curved archways decorated with yellow plaster friezes of fruit, vegetables and wheat. The facade has remained, but the interior has been transformed into pricey apartments.

Tandanya: the National Aboriginal Cultural Institute

Tandanya, the National Aboriginal Cultural Institute, is situated opposite the classic old market buildings at 253 Grenfell St (daily 10am–5pm; $4; ⓣ08/8224 3200, ⓦwww.tandanya.com.au). The centre is managed by Aboriginal people, with the main focus on the visual arts, with temporary exhibitions of national significance and a permanent display of work called the "Desert Dream", created by Aboriginal communities from the Northern Territory. Displays cover Dreamtime stories, history and contemporary Aboriginal writing, while political paintings confront black deaths in custody and other issues. There are even a few scattered sand paintings around the floor representing the mortality of traditional art. The shop is an excellent place to buy Aboriginal products, original paintings, didgeridoos, tapes and books, as well as T-shirts and other souvenirs. There's also a 160-seat theatre for live performances – daily **didgeridoo** or **dance performances** are held at noon – and a café (Mon–Fri only) where you can try some bush tucker.

North Adelaide

North Adelaide, a ten-minute walk from the city centre, makes for an enjoyable stroll past stately mansions and small, bluestone cottages, or a good pub crawl around the many old hotels. There are three ways of getting there. The best walking route to North Adelaide is up King William Road past the Festival Centre (nearly every bus from outside the Festival Centre also goes this way). From Elder Park you cross the pretty 1874 Adelaide Bridge over the river to Cresswell Gardens, home of the **Adelaide Oval** cricket ground (guided tour Tues & Thurs except match days at 10am, Sun 2pm; 2hr; $10), which has a small **museum** of cricketing memorabilia (Tues & Thurs 10am–1pm; $2) and affords superb views of **St Peter's Cathedral** (daily 9am–5pm; free guided tours Wed 11am & Sun 3pm) on Pennington Terrace opposite Pennington Gardens. This Anglican cathedral was built in 1869 in French Gothic-Revival style, with an entrance suggestive of Notre-Dame in Paris. The *Cathedral Hotel* opposite, built in 1850, is Adelaide's second-oldest hotel. At the top of King William Road, the peaceful and shady **Brougham Gardens** boast palm trees set against the backdrop of the Adelaide Hills. If you continue straight up, you'll come to North Adelaide's main commercial strip, **O'Connell Street**, whose restaurant scene rivals that of Rundle Street.

The district's best range of early **colonial architecture** lies a block west of here along **Jeffcott Street**. Just south of the street in Montefiore Park is **Light's Vision**, a bronze statue of Colonel William Light pointing proudly to the city he designed. On Jeffcott Street itself is the neo-Gothic 1890 mansion **Carclew**, with its round turret, and the **Lutheran Theological College**, a fine bluestone and red-brick building with a clock tower and cast-iron decoration. Halfway up Jeffcott Street, on peaceful **Wellington Square**, lies the pretty 1851 *Wellington Hotel*, complete with its original wooden balcony. Turning into tree-lined **Gover Street** you'll find rows of simple bluestone cottages; in contrast, **Barton Terrace West**, two blocks west, has grand homes facing the parklands.

East of O'Connell Street is **Melbourne Street** (buses #204 and #209 from King William Street, #272 and #273 from Currie and Grenfell streets), an upmarket strip of good cafés, antique stores, restaurants, designer clothing boutiques and speciality shops. The **Banana Room**, at no. 125 is probably the best retro-chic clothes store in Australia, with an immaculate range of designer dresses from the 1920s through to the 1950s. Don't expect bargains – most things are over $100, but it's fascinating to browse.

The suburbs

Adelaide's **suburbs** spread a long way, and though they remain little visited, some of the inner suburbs – such as **Norwood** and **Thebarton** – have plenty of local character, inexpensive restaurants and out-of-the-ordinary shopping that's worth venturing out of the city centre for. West of the city lies a string of beaches, from **Henley** via **Glenelg** to **Brighton**, sheltered by the Gulf St

Vincent. Further north, **Port Adelaide** has some excellent museums to set off its dockside atmosphere.

Norwood and Thebarton

Norwood, just east of the city, has two interesting streets: **Magill Road** (bus #106 from Grenfell or Currie streets), with its concentration of antique shops, and **The Parade** (bus #123 and #124 from Grenfell or Currie streets), a lively shopping strip with some great cafés and pubs and good bookshops. At weekends the small **Orange Lane Market** (Sat & Sun 10am–5pm), at the corner of Edward Street and The Parade, is a sedate place to browse among secondhand and new clothes, books and bric-à-brac, or eat from Asian food stalls.

In **Thebarton**, west of the city, the lively **Brickworks Market** (Fri–Sun 9am–5pm; bus #110, #112 or #113 from Grenfell or Currie streets) spreads out from the 1912 Brickworks Kilns at 36 South Rd. There are plaza shops and indoor and outdoor stalls, mostly selling new clothes, and it's always busy with buskers and crowds of people.

Immediately south of the city, **Unley Road** (buses #190–198 from King William Street) is known for its antique shops and expensive boutiques. The parallel King William Road at **Hyde Park** (bus #203 from King William Street) is shaded by lots of trees, plants and vine-covered awnings, and has some good cafés to relax in.

Port Adelaide and Torrens Island

The unfortunate early settlers had to wade through mud at Port Misery when they arrived but thanks to William Light's visionary flair, **Port Adelaide** became the primary gateway to the state. Established not far from Port Misery in 1840, by 1870 it was a substantial shipping area with solid stone warehouses, wharves and a host of pubs. The area bounded by Nelson, St Vincent and Todd streets and McLaren Parade is a well-preserved nineteenth-century streetscape; several ships' chandlers and shipping agents show that it's still a living port, a fact confirmed by the many corner pubs (with pretty decorative iron-lace balconies) still in business. The **Port Adelaide Tourist Visitor Information Centre**, near the waterfront on the corner of Commercial Road and St Vincent Street (daily 9am–5pm; Ⓣ08/8405 6560), provides up-to-date details of attractions and information about local history.

To get here, take a train from the Adelaide train station or bus #151 (Mon–Sat daytime only) or #153 (evenings and Sun) from North Terrace, or #340 from Glenelg (Mon–Fri only). The best day to visit is Sunday or public holiday Mondays, when the **Fishermen's Wharf Markets** (9am–5pm) take over a large waterfront warehouse on Queens Wharf and several **cruises** are available on the water. The market (mainly bric-à-brac) adds some life to the waterfront, but the once-varied food stalls are now dominated by purveyors of meat pies and steak sandwiches. Outside is the quaint, red-painted metal **lighthouse** (daily 10am–4pm), dating from 1869, which can be climbed as part of a visit to the South Australian Maritime Museum (see below), as can the museum's two floating vessels moored 300m away, the steam tug *Yelta* and the coastal trader *Nelcebee*. There are Sunday afternoon trips to Glenelg from the lighthouse with Adelaide Cruises Ltd (Ⓣ08/8447 2366) and Port Adelaide River Cruises (Ⓣ08/8341 1194).

The pick of Port Adelaide's several museums is the **South Australian Maritime Museum** on Lipson Street (daily10am–5pm; Ⓦwww.history.sa.gov.au; $8.50, combined ticket with the National Railway Museum $15). Located in the old Bond Store, with its massive timber posts and wooden floors, the museum describes the story of the migrants who came through the port and the South Australian **coastal ketch trade**. Starting from the basement, the migration section has faithfully reconstructed three typical steerage or economy cabins from 1840, 1910 and 1950; you can wander through them, lie on a bunk, listen to sails creaking or hear "new Australians" remembering their journey. Level two explores South Australia's connections with the sea, from seaside scenes (with a working penny arcade) to pleasure cruises on the gulf, fishing and making model ships. On the ground floor you can board a real ketch; upstairs is a more traditional collection. Further along Lipson Street, the **National Railway Museum** (daily 10am–5pm; Ⓦwww.natrailmuseum.org.au; $10; combined ticket with the South Australian Maritime Museum $15) is a trainspotter's delight, with a collection of over twenty steam and diesel locomotives. A free train ride runs on demand.

A few kilometres north of Port Adelaide is **Torrens Island**. Apart from a lively fresh fish and produce market on Sunday (7am–2pm), its main attraction is its intricate **mangrove forests**, a tranquil habitat rich in marine life that can be explored on foot in the **St Kilda Mangrove Trail** (Tues–Sun 10am–4pm; $6.90; booking essential on Ⓣ08/8280 8172), which has an interpretive centre and a 1.7-kilometre boardwalk for self-guided tours; or by kayak with **Blue Water Sea Kayaking** (weekends and school holidays only; $40; booking essential; Ⓣ08/8295 8812), giving the chance to spot Port River dolphins along the way.

Semaphore to Henley Beach

On the coast just east of Port Adelaide, **Semaphore**, with its picturesque jetty and fine old buildings, was important as the site of Adelaide's signal station from 1856 until the mid-1930s, before becoming a desirable holiday spot. Its current incarnation is as a popular lesbian area (see box, p.826) with several gay- and lesbian-run cafés and a pub on **Semaphore Road**, a charming street running at right angles to the beach, with awnings, stained-glass shop and café windows, and an old-fashioned cinema. A Sunday steam train runs from Semaphore Jetty to **Fort Glanville** at 359 Military Rd (Sept–May every third Sun 1–5pm; $6), the only complete example of the many forts built in Australia in the mid-nineteenth century, when fear of Russian invasion reached hysterical heights after the Crimean War. To get to Semaphore by public transport, take a bus to Port Adelaide (see opposite) and then bus #333.

About 8km south of Semaphore, **Grange** is a charming beachside suburb, with a row of Victorian terraced houses facing the sands (bus #112 or #135 from Grenfell Street, 30min; Grange line train, 20min) and a popular pier with an upmarket kiosk. The next beach along is atmospheric **Henley Beach** (Mon–Sat bus #137, Sun #130, both from Currie Street, 20min; #286 or #287 from North Terrace, 35min), where the focus is **Henley Square**, opposite the long wooden pier. The square is lined with classic Federation-style buildings housing several popular restaurants and cafés. South of here, on the way to Glenelg, **West Beach** (#278 bus from Currie Street; 25min) is a rather soulless spot with a caravan park. It does have a good, long, sandy **beach** though.

Glenelg and Brighton

The most popular and easily accessible of the city's beaches is at **Glenelg**, immediately south of West Beach, and 11km southwest of the city. The thirty-minute tram ride here from Victoria Square is part of the experience: the beautiful 1929 trams have original fittings – red leather seats and leather hanging straps, and wood-panelled compartments. Glenelg was the site of the landing of Governor John Hindmarsh and the first colonists on Holdfast Bay; the **Old Gum Tree** where he read the proclamation establishing the government of the colony still stands on McFarlane Street (bus #167 or #168 from Currie or Grenfell streets), and there's a re-enactment here every year on Proclamation Day (Dec 28).

Nowadays, Glenelg is busy even off-season. **Jetty Road**, the main drag, is crowded with places to eat (for the obligatory seaside fish and chips, *Bay Fish Shop* at no. 27 is the best) and there's lots of accommodation (see p.811). The tram terminates at **Moseley Square**, with its elegant town hall and clock tower. On the opposite corner, the original Victorian *Pier Hotel*, now part of the imposing seafront *Stamford Grand Hotel*, is crowded with drinkers on Sunday, when Glenelg is at its most vibrant. From Moseley Square, the jetty juts out into the bay, and in summer the beach on either side is crowded with people swimming in the calm waters; it's also a popular windsurfing spot year-round. Facing the shore, **Glenelg Tourist Information** (daily 9am–5pm; ⓣ08/8294 5833, ⓦwww.holdfast.sa.gov.au) can help with the booking of accommodation, tours and rental cars; there's also a 24-hour touch-screen information terminal outside. Next door, **Beach Hire** (ⓣ08/8294 1477) rents out deck chairs, umbrellas, bikes, surf skis, body-boards and snorkel sets. Rollerblading and cycling are other popular activities in Glenelg, with a **bike track** south of the square – you can rent mountain and touring bikes from Beach Hire for around $35 per day. The foreshore is also overlooked by a modern marina development, a huge, but tastefully designed complex comprising apartments, waterfront restaurants and upmarket cafés.

South of Glenelg, **Brighton** has an old-fashioned, sleepy air, dominated by the stone Arch of Remembrance, flanked by palm trees, which stands in front of the long jetty. Running inland from the beach, Jetty Road has a string of appealing one- and two-storey buildings shaded with awnings that contain an assortment of art, craft and secondhand stores, and two popular alfresco cafés: *A Cafe Etc* and *Horta's*. Brighton is reached by train from Adelaide (25min) or bus #266 from Grote Street. For beaches further south, see p.844.

Eating and drinking

Adelaide has roughly one restaurant for every thirty people, so not surprisingly **eating out** is a local obsession, and it's wonderfully inexpensive compared to Sydney or Melbourne. One of the city's most popular places for a meal out is **Gouger Street** – many of the restaurants here are alfresco and at their busiest on Friday night, when the nearby Central Market stays open until 9pm. **Moonta Street**, right next to Central Market, is the home of Adelaide's small **Chinatown**, and has several Chinese restaurants and supermarkets, while the excellent **food plaza** off Moonta Street (daily 11am–4pm, Fri until 9pm) serves Vietnamese, Indian, Singaporean, Thai, Chinese and Malaysian food. **Hutt Street**, on the eastern edge of the city, has a string of fine Italian eateries and is a good place to go for breakfast. Café society is based around **Rundle Street** in the city, and **O'Connell Street** and the decidedly chic **Melbourne Street** in North Adelaide. Finally, eating in **pubs** doesn't just mean the usual steak and salad bar but covers the whole spectrum, from some of the best "contemporary" Australian food in town to bargain specials in several pubs along King William Street.

As for drinking, South Australian **wine** features heavily – which is just as well, since, by general consensus, **tap water** in Adelaide tastes dreadful, although it's perfectly safe – and thanks to the state's liberal licensing laws, even most cafés are licensed.

City centre

Cafés

Al Fresco Gelateria & Pasticceria 260 Rundle St. If you go to only one café in Adelaide, make it this one. Packed every night, the young Italian community have made it their own, and it's *the* place to people-watch and be seen, while treating yourself to the great coffee, *biscotti*, delicious home-made *gelati* and focaccia and calzone. Daily 6.30am until late.

Citrus 199 Hutt St. One of several Italian diners on this leafy street, *Citrus* benefits from a secluded outdoor eating area and one of the best breakfasts in town. Mon–Sat 7.30am–3pm, Fri & Sat 6pm–9.30pm.

Cowley's An Adelaide institution, this mobile pie cart takes up its position each night outside the GPO on Franklin St. It's famous for its pie floaters. Mon–Thurs & Sun 6pm–1am, Fri & Sat 6pm–3.30am.

Govinda's 79 Hindley St. Small vegetarian restaurant with Indian sweet cakes and an all-you can-eat lunch for $8.50. Lunch Mon–Sat 11.30am–3pm, dinner Tues–Sat 5.30–8.30pm.

Hawkers Corner 141 West Terrace, cnr Wright St. Something of a cheap-eats tradition, with Chinese, Thai, Malaysian and North Indian stalls – the Malay seafood laksa is highly recommended. Unlicensed and no BYO allowed. Tues–Sat 5–10pm, Sun 11.30am–8.30pm.

Jerusalem 131B Hindley St. Dimly lit Lebanese BYO that serves fresh and tasty Middle Eastern dishes. Daily noon until midnight.

Marcellina 273 Hindley St. This all-night pizza, steak and pasta bar is always full of people who have spilled out from the area's clubs and pubs. The pizzas are among the best in town; deliveries too (call ⓣ08/8211 7560). Mon–Thurs & Sun 11.30am–2am, Fri & Sat 11.30am–5am.

Scoozi 272 Rundle Street. A few doors east of *Al Fresco*, this popular licensed café does great Italian food – try the excellent wood-fired pizzas.

Tempo 91 Hindley St. Italian breakfasts and traditional trattoria-style cooking in the Art Deco foyer of a former cinema. The daily specials board is worth checking as is the modern wine list. Mon–Fri 9am–10pm, Sat 5.30pm–10.30pm.

Zuma 56 Gouger St. Locals flock here for the huge breakfasts, big salads, and filo parcels, bruschetta, focaccia and quiche baked on the premises. Mon–Thurs 7am–6pm, Fri 7am–10pm, Sat 7am–4am.

Pubs and wine bars

Ambassadors Hotel 107 King William St. Slightly sleazy pub that does a cheap, simple pub lunch, put on to attract people to play the pokies here.

Apothecary 1878 118 Hindley Street. Multi-level wine bar housed in a 19th-century pharmacy, one of the coolest venues in town. Tasty Italian bar snacks and decent cocktails add to the allure. Mon–Fri noon–midnight, Sat 6pm–2am.

Austral Hotel 205 Rundle St. Excellent, inexpensive bistro meals, including Malaysian, Thai, Mexican and Italian dishes, and good old Aussie steaks, burgers and seafood. There's also a pricier restaurant with an extensive wine list sourced from boutique wineries.

Earl of Aberdeen 316 Pulteney St, Hindmarsh Square ⓣ08/8223 6433. Set in a gazebo full of greenery this place serves huge portions of moderately priced, imaginatively cooked pasta, steak, fish and kangaroo. Attentive service too.

Oostende Ebenezer Place, off Rundle Street. Busy Belgian café, with loads of different Belgian beers (bottled and on tap) and food. Daily 10.30am until late.

Universal Wine Bar 258 Rundle St ⓣ08/8232 5000. Stylish that aims to educate people about South Australia's wines, with vintages by the glass or bottle, plus a small menu of delicious, moderately priced bistro food with a provincial French and Mediterranean slant. Live jazz on Sundays from 3.30pm. Mon–Sat 11.30am–late.

Restaurants

Amalfi Pizzeria Ristorante 29 Frome St ⓣ08/8223 1948. Upbeat, jazzy and young with a variety of moderately priced vegetarian dishes, innovative pasta sauces and traditional ones given a hot edge. Crowded, and open very late. Licensed. Closed Sat lunch & Sun.

Eros Ouzeri 275–277 Rundle St. Greek meze-style dining in a smart and airy setting in a renovated old building with high metal ceilings. The attached café serves Greek pastries and coffee. Licensed. Daily midday until late.

Garage 163 Waymouth St ⓣ08/8212 9577. Funky, moderately priced restaurant and bar in a converted garage warehouse with original brick walls. Great breakfasts and a lively lunch menu plus snacks served throughout the evening, when the focus turns to socializing, dancing and DJ music. Restaurant Mon–Fri 9.30am–3pm, Sun 11am–4pm, also dinner Mon 5.30–9.30pm.

Gaucho's 91 Gouger St ☎08/8231 2299. If you're after red meat, this Argentinian place serves some of the best steaks in town – just name your weight. Licensed and BYO. Closed Sat & Sun lunch.
The Grange *Adelaide Hilton*, 233 Victoria Square ☎08/8217 2000. European-style fine dining prepared by one of Australia's best chefs, Cheong Liew, who brings an Asian angle to already adventurous dishes. Very expensive. Dinner Tues–Sat, closed Dec & Jan.
Irodori 291 Rundle St ☎08/8232 6799. Modern, moderately priced Japanese restaurant specializing in sushi and *teppanyaki*. Some alfresco seating. BYO and licensed. Lunch Mon–Fri, dinner nightly.
Jasmin 31 Hindmarsh Sq ☎08/8223 7837. Highly regarded north Indian restaurant. The menu may not be overly adventurous, but the cooking is impeccable – try the magnificent beef vindaloo, or check for daily specials. Lunch Thurs–Fri, dinner Tues–Sat.
Jolleys Boathouse Jolleys Lane, off Victoria Drive next to City Bridge ☎08/8223 2891. Converted boathouse serving mouthwatering but pricey contemporary Australian cuisine. A popular venue for Sunday lunch. Licensed. Closed Sun night.
Star of Siam 67 Gouger St ☎08/8231 3527. Extremely popular, award-winning Thai restaurant with a superb, reasonably priced menu, including a good range of vegetarian dishes. Licensed. Lunch Mon–Fri, dinner Mon–Sat.
T-chow 68 Moonta St ☎08/8410 1413. Huge, popular and reasonably cheap Chinese restaurant serving Teochew regional specialities such as tender duck, shark's fin soup and green peppercorn chicken, plus quick noodle lunches for $5.
Ying Chow 114 Gouger St ☎08/8211 7998. Unpretentious and always crowded place, serving inexpensive northern Chinese cuisine, including specialities such as aniseed tea duck or scallops cooked with coriander and Chinese thyme. Vegetarians can enjoy delicious dishes such as bean curd with Chinese chutney. Licensed and BYO. Lunch Fri only, dinner nightly.

North Adelaide, Norwood and Unley

Cafés

Café Paradiso 150 King William Rd, Hyde Park, near Unley. A long-established Italian favourite, with great coffee and *biscotti* and alfresco dining out front. Licensed. Daily 8.30am–11.30pm.
Caffe Buongiorno 145 The Parade. Large, always lively café serving a wide variety of Italian food and drink which reaches a crowded and noisy crescendo on Sunday night. Daily 8am–1am or later.
Elephant Walk 76 Melbourne St. Lively but intimate place, with small private lounge areas divided by carved wooden elephants and bamboo screens. Daily 8pm–late.
Oxford Deli Bar At the *Oxford Hotel*, 101 O'Connell St, North Adelaide. Groovy and good-value pub, with plenty of meals for under $10 – try the Oxburger and fries.
The Store Level 1, 157 Melbourne St, North Adelaide ☎08/8361 6999. This corner location attracts a trendy, young clientele, has plenty of outdoor tables, and offers interesting breakfast and lunch menus. Daily 7am–7pm.

Restaurants

Bacall's 149 Melbourne St, North Adelaide ☎08/8267 2030. Cajun specialist with authentic oven-baked dishes and a lively New Orleans-style atmosphere. Book early if you want one of the few streetside tables. BYO and licensed. Tues–Sat 6–10pm.
Cibo 10 O'Connell St, North Adelaide. Woodfired pizzas, innovative pasta dishes and expensive Italian classics given a modern makeover using local ingredients. The location affords wonderful views across the city. Lunch Sun–Fri noon–2.30pm, dinner 5.30–9pm daily.
Kwik Stix 42 O'Connell St, North Adelaide ☎08/8239 2023. Spacious modern Asian restaurant with good-value meals, including excellent char-grilled and sizzling dishes from Laos, Korea and Malaysia (dinner only). Daily noon–2.30pm & 5–10pm.
The Melting Pot 160 King William Rd, Hyde Park, near Unley ☎08/8373 2044. One of the best modern French restaurants in Adelaide, with fantastic veal, spiced duck and seasonal fish, plus good wines and champagnes. Lunch Thurs & Fri, dinner Mon–Sat.
Shibata 131 Melbourne St, North Adelaide ☎08/8267 3381. Japanese restaurant specializing in moderately priced *nabe mono* (one-pot dishes). BYO and licensed. Dinner Tues–Sun.
Zambracca 94–98 Melbourne St, North Adelaide ☎08/8239 1345. A lively, licensed bistro crowded with Adelaide's smart set and dishing up superb, moderately priced Mediterranean food in slick, spacious surroundings. Daily 8am–late.

Beach suburbs

Cafés

Henley on Sea Immediately south of Henley Square, opposite the Henley Beach Life Saving Club ⓣ08/8235 2250. Relaxed café-brasserie – it was used as the location for *Moby Dick's* piano bar in the film *Shine* – with a summery atmosphere and views of the jetty and water, plus shaded tables outside. Food comprises light contemporary dishes with an emphasis on seafood. Licensed. Lunch & dinner daily from 11am; closed Tues.

Horta's 75–77 Jetty Rd, Brighton. Pretty licensed beachside place with pavement tables and a fish mosaic out front. Popular for lunch, with dishes ranging from pasta to Thai. Closed Mon. If it's full try the neighbouring *A Cafe Etc*, which does great all-day breakfasts and big salads.

The Lovin' Spoonful 69A Semaphore Rd, Semaphore. Gay- and lesbian-friendly café/restaurant with rich cakes, light vegetarian meals and Aussie bush tucker on the menu, plus cocktails in the quaint courtyard. Daytime only (opening hours change with the weather).

Sarah's 85 Dale St, Port Adelaide ⓣ08/8341 2103. Probably the best vegetarian restaurant in Adelaide. Without any menus, diners are asked to place their trust in chef Stuart Gifford's capable hands. Disappointment is unlikely. Lunch Wed–Fri, dinner Wed–Sat.

Stamford Grand Hotel The Foreshore, Glenelg ⓣ08/8375 0622. There are several good cafés and places to eat in this hotel, including the excellent café-style *Rickshaw's* restaurant, divided by an open kitchen where you watch the chefs at work: one side serves spicy Indian meals, the other a variety of Asian dishes. There's also a more upmarket contemporary restaurant, *The Promenade*, with great sea views.

Restaurants

Estias Henley Square, Henley Beach ⓣ08/8353 2875. Fun seaside place for casual dining on Greek meze amongst a playful modern Hellenic-themed decor, with reproduction classical sculptures and columns supporting the bar. Also serves more substantial, moderately priced dishes such as moussaka, and daily specials. Licensed and BYO. Closed Mon.

Lido On the Marina Pier Promenade at Glenelg. Reasonably priced Mediterranean-style restaurant, right on the water, with great views and an excellent atmosphere. Daily lunch & dinner.

Mama Carmella 4 Jetty Rd, Glenelg ⓣ08/8331 2288. Very popular, gleaming Italian café-pizzeria which is good for moderately priced lunches, a late meal or just coffee. Outside tables overlook the square. Daily 8am–late.

Salt Holdfast Shores Marina, Glenelg. Modern-designed restaurant and wine bar in an exclusive location. The bread and pasta are made on the premises and the oysters are fresh from Coffin Bay. Closed Mon.

Entertainment and nightlife

Adelaide may appear dead at night, but there's actually quite a lot going on – bands, clubs, film and theatre – if you know where to look. The best place to find out **what's on** is *The Guide*, which comes with Thursday's *Advertiser* and has film and theatre listings and reviews. There's also a thriving **free press**: top of the culture stakes is *The Adelaide Review*, a highbrow monthly covering the visual and performing arts, dance, film, literature, history, wine and food, available from bookshops such as Imprints on Hindley Street, museums, galleries and just about everywhere else. At the more populist end of the scale, *Rip It Up* is a gig listings magazine, out every Thursday, with film, theatre, club and music reviews and interviews; *db Magazine*, in the same vein, is published every two weeks on Wednesdays – both can be picked up at record stores such as B# Records, at no. 240 Rundle St and Muses at 112-118 Rundle Mall. Most big music events can be booked through Bass (ⓣ13 12 46, ⓦwww.bass.sa.com.au). B# Records sells tickets for underground events around town.

At night, the two spots to head for are **Rundle Street**, which boasts the most fashionable pubs and bars, and the more mainstream and rather sleazy **Hindley Street**, where you'll find several funky clubs and live-music venues east of Morphett Street catering for the nearby university crowd. For something a bit

The Adelaide Festival of Arts and Womadelaide

The huge **Adelaide Festival of Arts**, which takes over the city for three weeks from late February to mid-March in even-numbered years, attracts an extraordinary range of international and Australian theatre companies, performers, musicians, writers and artists. An avant-garde **Fringe** has grown up around the main festival, which for many people is more exciting than the main event. The official festival began in 1960 and has been based since 1973 at the purpose-built **Festival Centre** (see p.827). In addition, free outdoor concerts, opera and films are held outside the Festival Centre and at various other locations during the festival, while other venues around town host an "Artists' Week", "Writers' Week" and a small film festival. The 2006 Festival of Arts runs from March 3–19 (ⓦwww.adelaidefestival.org.au).

The **Fringe Festival** (ⓦwww.adelaidefringe.com.au) begins with a wild street parade on Rundle Street a week before the main festival, and events are held at venues all over town, with bands, cabaret and comedy at the Fringe Club, plus free outdoor shows and activities, while full use is made of the 24-hour licensing laws. **Advance programmes** for both the main and the fringe festival and further information is available from the offices of Tourism South Australia, or from all Bass outlets.

The annual **Womadelaide** world music weekend began in 1992 as part of the Arts Festival but has now developed its own separate identity, attracting over 30,000 people. Held in early March in the Botanic Park – four stages, two workshop areas, multicultural food stalls and visual arts – it's a great place to hear some of Australia's local talent, with a broad selection of Aboriginal musicians as well as internationally acclaimed contemporary and traditional artists from around the world. The full weekend (Fri night–Sun night) costs $168, but day and session passes are also available. Tickets are available from Bass (ⓣ13 12 46, ⓦwww.bass.sa.com.au). The 2006 Womadelaide runs from March 10–12. For advance information check out the website of Womadelaide (ⓦwww.womadelaide.com.au).

different, try the **Adelaide Casino** (Mon–Thurs & Sun 10am–4am, Fri & Sat 10am–6am; neat dress required), near the train station, complete with stunning domed marble entrance, glitzy gaming rooms and jaw-dropping Austrian crystal chandeliers.

Pubs and bars

Austral Hotel 205 Rundle St ⓣ08/8223 4660. More consciously arty and music-oriented than the *Exeter* (see below), the *Austral* is frequented by students for the independent local bands on Fri and Sat nights, and DJs Tues–Thurs & Sun nights. DJs are free, as is most of the music – when there's a cover charge, it's around $5. Fri & Sat open until 3am.

Archer Hotel 60 O'Connell Street, North Adelaide ⓣ08/8361 9300. This recently renovated pub now has chic retro decor, with a good range of Aussie beers on the ground floor and a cocktail bar upstairs. It's a good lunch venue too.

The Daniel O'Connell 165 Tynte St, North Adelaide ⓣ08/8267 4032. Huge Irish pub with a lovely beer garden set around an old pepper-tree plus a large restaurant. Live bands – sometimes Irish folk musicians – play on Fri and Sat nights, when the place is heaving.

Exeter Hotel 246 Rundle St ⓣ08/8223 2623. This spacious old pub with an iron-lace balcony is a long-established hangout for Adelaide's artists, writers and students, yet remains totally unpretentious. Good lunches served, and music nightly (no cover charge).

Grace Emily 232 Waymouth St ⓣ08/8231 5500. Relaxed atmosphere, a young, alternative crowd and a range of local acts to suit everyone. Nightly until late.

Worldsend 208 Hindley St ⓣ08/8231 9137. Large, multi-functional pub popular with the nearby university crowd and boasting two bars, a restaurant, cocktail bar, lounge, beer garden and live music at weekends. Licensed till 4am.

Clubs, comedy and live music

Cargo Club 213 Hindley St ☎08/8231 2327. Laid-back club featuring live jazz, spoken word, cabaret, soul, Latin, African and reggae acts and local and international DJs; the decor is a mix of classic cool and 1990s postmodernism, and there's something on most nights.

Church 9 Synagogue Place, off Rundle St ☎08/8223 4233. This industrial-chic club venue in a converted temple is the enduring focus for Adelaide's rave scene, with local and international DJs. Wed–Sat 9pm–5am.

Crown and Sceptre 308 King William St ☎08/8212 4159. A heritage-listed pub that's been groovified into one of Adelaide's best venues, complete with sparkly bar stools, cosy couches in the intimate band area and a busy espresso machine. Local bands Tues–Fri & Sun (usually free); Saturday is club night (until 5am; around $5), alternating weekly from *Comfy Club* (funk-beat oriented) to jungle and techno.

Enigma 173 Hindley St ☎08/8212 2313. Hip venue for the alternative university crowd. The small bar spills out into the street at weekends, and there's either funk or live grunge music upstairs. Wed–Sat till late.

Governor Hindmarsh 59 Port Rd, Hindmarsh ☎08/8340 0744, Ⓦwww.thegov.com.au. *The Gov*, as this Adelaide institution is affectionately known, is one of Adelaide's leading live venues (it survived a recent threat of closure after five thousand people marched to Parliament House to voice their concern). It currently hosts a broad range of live music and cabaret, with gigs on Wed, Thurs & Sat from 9pm, and jam sessions and Irish music Fri from 9pm.

Heaven 2 1 West Terrace ☎08/8216 5200. Huge dance club with a trashy teenage feel hosting resident DJs as well as visiting international acts and one-off events. Wed–Sat 9pm–5am.

The Planet 77 Pirie St ☎08/8359 2797. There's a whole world of entertainment crammed into this place, with a dance club hosting the best of local and international DJs, as well as a pool room, cocktail bar, wine bar and several cafés.

Rhino Room Upstairs at 13 Frome St ☎08/8227 1611. Underground club venue with an intimate lounge atmosphere: come casual or get glammed up, no one cares, though the regular clientele may make you feel as if you've barged into a private party. Comedy and poetry on Wed, local bands Thurs, funk on Fri and techno DJ on Sat. The cosy little bar provides a retreat from the performance. Wed–Fri 9pm–1am, Sat & Sun until 3am. Standard charge $5.

Royal Oak 123 O'Connell St, North Adelaide ☎08/8267 2488. Popular North Adelaide bar and restaurant with arty decor and a young crowd. Live jazz/Latin Sun and Wed, local bands Tues and Fri.

Supermild 182 Hindley St West ☎08/8212 9000. One of the best clubs in town, with a laid-back atmosphere, chilled tunes and good cocktails. Wed 9pm–1am, Thurs 9pm–3am, Fri–Sat 9pm–5am, Sun 9pm–midnight.

Gay and lesbian nightspots

Edinburgh Castle Hotel 233 Currie St ☎08/8410 1211. Friendly gay and lesbian-only venue with a dance floor Thurs to Sun, plus jukebox, bistro and beer garden with drag shows on Sun. Mon–Thurs 11am–midnight, Fri 11am–1.30am, Sat 11am–1am, Sun 2pm–1am.

Mars Bar 122 Gouger St ☎08/8231 9639. This Adelaide institution has been around for years and hosts drag acts for a big, friendly mixed crowd. Wed–Sat 9pm–late.

Film

Adelaide's reputation as a city of festivals was further enhanced with the inaugural **Adelaide Film Festival** in 2003. It seems certain to become a regular fixture, held in odd-numbered years and running for two weeks from late February to early March. Booking ahead is advisable (☎08/8271 1488, Ⓦwww.adelaidefilmfestival.org). As well as several city and suburban mainstream film complexes, Adelaide now has four art-house/retro cinemas. The main **discount day** for mainstream cinemas is Tuesday. In the summer, you can watch films outdoors at the **Moonlight Cinema** in the Botanic Gardens; bookshops around town have programmes or check out Ⓦwww.moonlight.com.au; tickets ($12.50) are available at the gate from 7.30pm onwards or through Bass (☎13 12 46, Ⓦwww.bass.sa.com.au).

Gay and lesbian Adelaide

South Australia was the first state to legalize gay sex and remains one of the most tolerant of lesbian and gay lifestyles, although Adelaide's gay scene remains more modest than Sydney or Melbourne. Apart from the city's more mainstream annual festivals, there are a few strictly gay and lesbian fiestas. The biggest and best is **Feast** (Ⓣ08/8231 2155, Ⓦwww.feast.org.au), launched in 1997, which runs for three weeks in November. Events include theatre, music, visual art, literature, dance cabaret and historical walks. plus a **Gay and Lesbian Film Festival** at the Mercury Cinema (see below). The festival culminates in **Picnic in the Park**, an outdoor celebration in the parklands that surround central Adelaide and which includes a very camp dog show. Earlier in the year, June's **Stonewall Celebrations** are less flamboyant, featuring serious talks and exhibitions in a number of venues. A popular male gay hangout is **Pulteney 431 Sauna**, 431 Pulteney St (Mon & Tues 7pm–1am, Sun, Wed & Thurs noon–1am, Fri & Sat noon–3am; Ⓣ08/8223 7506), with a spa, sauna, steam room, pool and snack bar.

To find out where the action is, pick up a copy of *Blaze* or check out other possibilities in the listings below. See p.812 for gay- and lesbian-friendly **places to stay**, and p.825 for gay and lesbian nightspots.

Useful organizations and publications

Blaze 213 Franklin St Ⓣ08/8211 9199, Ⓦwww.blazemedia.com.au. Fortnightly gay and lesbian newspaper, with news, features and listings. Free from venues and bookshops. *Blaze* also publishes the handy free *Lesbian & Gay Adelaide Map*.

Darling House Gay and Lesbian Community Library 64 Fullarton Rd, Norwood Ⓣ08/8334 1606. Fiction, non-fiction and newspapers. Mon–Fri 9am–5pm, Sat 2–5pm.

Liberation Monthly newsletter for lesbians – good for contacts and local events.

Murphy Sisters Bookshop 240 The Parade, Norwood. Ⓣ08/8332 7508. Gay/lesbian bookshop with a handy notice board. Wed–Sat only.

Parkside Travel 70 Glen Osmond Rd, Parkside Ⓣ08/8274 1222 or 1800 888 501. Gay owned and operated company offering hotel reservations, information and travel services.

Capri 141 Goodwood Rd, Goodwood Ⓣ08/8272 1177. Alternative and arty films complete with pre-show Wurlitzer organ on Tues, Fri and Sat evenings.

Chelsea 275 Kensington Rd, Kensington Park Ⓣ08/8431 5080. The latest releases and a "crying room" for parents and babies.

Mercury Cinema Lion Arts Centre, 13 Morphett St Ⓣ08/8410 1934, Ⓦwww.mercurycinema.org.au. A great art-house cinema showing short and foreign films.

Nova Cinema 251 Rundle St Ⓣ08/8223 6333. Arts cinema complex with three screens. Substantial backpacker discounts (with the relevant card).

Odeon Star Cinema 65 Semaphore Rd, Semaphore Ⓣ08/8341 5988. Quaint local beachside cinema showing mainstream films.

Palace East End 274 Rundle St Ⓣ08/8232 3434. Alternative venue showing foreign-language and art-house and other new releases. Discounts for backpackers.

Trak Cinemas 375 Greenhill Rd, Toorak Gardens Ⓣ08/8332 8020. Good alternative cinema with two screens. Bus #145 from North Terrace to stop 10.

Theatre and the performing arts

Out of festival time, mainstream theatre, ballet, opera, contemporary dance, comedy and cabaret continue to thrive at the **Festival Centre**. Classical concerts are held at the **Adelaide Town Hall** (usually performed by the Adelaide Symphony Orchestra) and at **Elder Hall** at the Conservatorium of Music on North Terrace. Almost anything that's on can be booked through Bass Ⓣ13 12 46, Ⓦwww.bass.sa.com.au.

Festival Centre King William Rd ⓣ08/8216 8600, ⓦwww.afct.org.au. Three major auditoriums and free music events in the foyer (Sun 2–4pm, winter only). See p.815 for more details.

Music House Lion Arts Centre, cnr Morphett St and North Terrace ⓣ08/8218 8400. The Lion Theatre is the main venue here, and there's always lots going on, from interstate performers and jazz bands to comedy line-ups. An irregular programme, so watch out for flyers.

Theatre 62 145 Burbridge Rd, Hilton ⓣ08/8234 0838. Two venues under one roof: the larger auditorium hosts mostly pantomime and sometimes a theatre-restaurant; the smaller Chapel theatre is used for more experimental productions.

Shopping

You can find most things you'll need in **Rundle Mall** (see p.816), which has three department stores, plus a handy Woolworths at no. 86 with a small supermarket attached. There's also a Coles supermarket at 21 Grote St (open daily), next to the Central Market. For **alternative fashion**, Rundle Street and, particularly, Miss Gladys Sym Choon at no. 235 is the place to go. For retro clothing visit Irving Baby, 33 Twin St, off Rundle Mall, or The Banana Room (see p.817). For **Aboriginal arts and crafts** try Tandanya (see p.816) or the Otherway Centre at 185 Pirie St. B# Records at 240 Rundle St and Krypton Discs, at 34 Jetty Rd, Glenelg, are both good for **records**.

There are several good **bookshops** around the city: Imprints, 80 Hindley St, is a good highbrow shop; the excellent Unibooks, at Adelaide University, provides an excuse to nose around the university; Angus & Robertsons, 138 Rundle Mall, is a large mainstream store; while the huge Borders, in Rundle Mall, has an excellent range of international newspapers and magazines and an in-store café. Adelaide Booksellers, 6A Rundle Mall sells good secondhand titles, as does O'Connell's Bookshop at 62 Hindley St – they also buy or exchange books.

Markets include Central Market (see p.816), Orange Lane Market, Brickworks Market, Port Adelaide Market and Torrens Island Fish and Produce Market (see p.816). East End Cellars, 22–26 Vardon Avenue, tucked away in a lane behind the excellent *Universal Wine Bar* (see p.821) on Rundle Street, is an excellent **bottle shop** if you want to buy some choice South Australian wines to take away.

Shopping hours are Monday to Saturday 9am to 5/6pm, with late-night shopping until 9pm on Friday in the city and Thursday in the suburbs, plus Sunday trading (11am–5pm) in the city only.

Listings

Airlines Air New Zealand ⓣ13 24 76; Alitalia ⓣ08/8306 8411; British Airways ⓣ08/8238 2138; Garuda ⓣ1300 365 330; Japan Airlines ⓣ08/8212 2555; Lufthansa ⓣ1300 655 727; Malaysia Airlines ⓣ08/8231 6171; Qantas ⓣ08/8407 2233; Singapore Airlines ⓣ08/8203 0800.

American Express Shop 32, Citi Centre, Rundle Mall (Mon–Fri 9am–5pm, Sat 9am–noon; ⓣ1300 13 90 60); 120 Jetty Rd, Glenelg (Mon–Fri 9am–5pm, Sat 9am–noon; ⓣ08/8376 7731).

Banks and foreign exchange All the major banks are located on King William St. Exchange services are available at the international airport, at American Express (see above) and at Travelex, 45 Grenfell St (Mon–Fri 9am–5pm; ⓣ08/8212 3354). Outside these hours, the casino (see p.824) or international hotels on North Terrace can help, but obviously the exchange rates will be poor.

Bikes and bike rental Flinders Camping, 187 Rundle St (ⓣ08/8223 1913), rents bikes for $15 per day and offers weekly rates; Linear Park Mountain Bike Hire at Elder Park (ⓣ08/8223 6271), situated near a section of the River Torrens Linear Park bike track, rents bikes by the hour or day at competitive prices; Bicycle SA, 46 Hurtle Square (ⓣ08/8232 2644), is a nonprofit cycling organization providing information and cycling maps and organizing regular touring trips.

Camping equipment and rental Rundle St is the place: for rental, try Flinders Camping at no. 187 (☎08/8223 1913), who can kit you out for the Flinders Ranges given 24hr notice – they are also the only place in town that repairs backpacks; Paddy Pallin at no. 228 sells a range of high-quality gear, plus maps; or there's Scout Outdoor Centre at no. 192.
Canoe rental and tours Adelaide Canoe Works, 74 Daws Road, Edwardstown (☎08/8277 8422), offer a range of courses and expeditions as well as very reasonably priced canoe and kayak hire.
Car rental Avis (☎13 63 33), Hertz (☎13 26 07) and Thrifty (☎08/8211 8788) have desks at the airport. Otherwise, small and friendly Access, 60 Frome Street (☎08/8359 3200 or 1800 812 580), does free airport deliveries and allows you to take their cars to Kangaroo Island; they also rent out sports cars. Other options include Action (☎08/8352 7044) or Excel (☎1300 551 164). Older, cheaper cars can be obtained from Cut Price Car Rentals (☎08/8443 7788), which also does one-way rentals and buy backs; or Rent-a-Bug (☎08/8234 0911). Britz Campervan, Car and 4WD Rentals (☎08/8234 4701 or 1800 331 454) have a full range of campervans for hire.
Disabled travellers Disability Information and Resource Centre, 195 Gilles St ☎08/8236 9555.
Environment and conservation The Conservation Council of South Australia, 120 Wakefield St (☎08/8223 5155), is a good place to find out what's going on. The Wilderness Society has its campaign office at 116 Grote St (☎08/8231 6586) and a shop in Victoria Square Arcade, Victoria Square (☎08/8231 0625).
Hospital Royal Adelaide Hospital, North Terrace ☎08/8222 4000; Dental Hospital, Frome Road ☎08/8222 8222.
Internet access There's limited-time free access at the State Library (see p.814; book in advance), and cheap access at Kiss Internet Cafe, 165 Hindley St and iNet Zone, 42 Grote St (both $5 per hour). Many of the backpackers' places now have Internet access for guests.
Laundries Adelaide Launderette, 152 Sturt St (daily 7am–8pm; service washes 8am–5pm); St Peter's Laundromat, 6th Avenue (daily 6am–10pm).
Left luggage Adelaide Train Station has 24hr lockers. There are also facilities at the Central Bus Station: Premier Stateliner ($2 per 24hr); Greyhound Australia (from $6 per 24hr).
Maps The Map Shop, 16A Peel St, between Hindley and Currie streets, has the largest range of local and state maps. If you're a member of an affiliated automobile association overseas, you can get free regional maps and advice on road conditions from the Royal Automobile Association, 55 Hindmarsh Square (☎08/8202 4540, ⓦwww.raa.net).
Medical centre City Centre Medical Clinic, 77 Gilbert Place ☎08/8212 3226.
Motorbike rental Show & Go Motorcycles, 236 Brighton Rd, Somerton Park ☎08/8376 0333.
Newspapers *The Advertiser* is very provincial and doesn't have good coverage of national and international news, but is useful on Thursday for entertainment listings, and Wednesday and Saturday for classifieds if you're looking for a car or other travel equipment. Alternatively, Melbourne's *The Age* is widely available. The best place to buy foreign and interstate newspapers is Rundle Arcade Newsagency, off Gawler Place, or Borders in Rundle Mall.
Pharmacy Midnight Pharmacy, 13 West Terrace (Mon–Sat 7am–midnight, Sun 9am–midnight). In Glenelg try Stephens Pharmacy, cnr Jetty Rd and Gordon St (daily 8.30am–10pm).
Police For emergencies call ☎000.
Post office GPO, 141 King William St, cnr Franklin St (Mon–Fri 8am–6pm, Sat 8.30am–noon); poste restante, Adelaide GPO, SA 5000.
Swimming pool Adelaide City Swim, 235 Flinders St (Mon 5.30am–8pm, Sat 6am–5pm, Sun 9am–1pm; $6 per hour). Adelaide Aquatic Centre, cnr Jeffcott Rd and Fitzroy Terrace, North Adelaide (daily 5am–10pm; swimming $5.50), is an indoor centre with pool, gym, sauna and spa; take bus #231 from North Terrace.
Taxis There's a taxi rank on the corner of Pulteney and Rundle streets, otherwise call Adelaide Independent ☎13 22 11; Suburban Taxi Service ☎13 10 08; or Yellow Cabs ☎13 22 27.
Telephones Rundle Mall has lots of phones, including ones that take credit cards. For peace and quiet, try the Phone Room in the GPO.
Tours The hop-on hop-off Adelaide Explorer City Sights Tour covers the city, Glenelg and West Beach, with departures from the Travel Centre, 14 King William St, daily at 9am, 10.30am, noon, 1.30pm & 3pm (☎08/8364 1933; $35; 3hr). Further afield, the majority of tours from Adelaide head for the Barossa Valley (see p.834), Kangaroo Island (see p.849) and the Fleurieu Peninsula (see p.842). General operators include Gray Line (☎1300 858 687, ⓦwww.grayline.com); Premier Day Tours (☎08/8415 5566, ⓦwww.premierstateliner.com.au); and Adelaide Sightseeing (☎08/8231 4144, ⓦwww.adelaidesightseeing.com.au). All of these can arrange trips further afield to the Murray River, Coorong and Flinders Ranges. Adelaide is also the home base for the excellent Wayward Bus, 115 Waymouth St (☎08/8410 8833 or 1800 882 823, ⓦwww.waywardbus.com.au), which does a good

one-way, small-group tour from Adelaide to Melbourne (or vice versa) via the scenic coastal route (three and a half days; $295 including breakfast, lunch and hostel accommodation). Wayward also runs one-way tours to Alice Springs taking in the Clare Valley, Flinders Ranges, Oodnadatta Track, Lake Eyre, Coober Pedy, Uluru, Kata Tjuta and Kings Canyon (eight days; $790 all-inclusive). Heading Bush 4WD Adventures (ⓣ08/8356 5501, ⓦwww.headingbush.com) does an epic ten-seater camping tour to Alice Springs taking in Flinders Ranges, Coober Pedy, the Simpson Desert and Uluru (ten days; $1400); while Camp Wild Adventures (ⓣ08/8132 1333, ⓦwww.campwild.com.au) offers an adventurous 4WD camping tour to Kangaroo Island (three days; $340 all inclusive), and another tour to Alice Springs via the Flinders Ranges (nine days; $1145 all inclusive).

Travel agents Adelaide YHA Travel, 135 Waymouth St ⓣ08/8414 3000; City Centre Travel, 75 King William St ⓣ08/8221 7246; Flight Centre, 54 King William St ⓣ08/8211 7246; Jetset, 23 Leigh St, off Hindley St ⓣ08/8212 7356; Peregrine Travel, upstairs at 192 Rundle St ⓣ08/8223 5905; STA Travel, 235 Rundle St ⓣ08/8223 2426; Thor Adventure Travel, upstairs at 228 Rundle St ⓣ08/8232 3071.

Work Information on work rights is available from the Department of Immigration and Multicultural Affairs ⓣ13 18 81, ⓦwww.immi.gov.au/employers. Unemployment is high in Adelaide itself, but it's a good place to find out about casual fruit-picking work in the Riverland. Hostels can help with finding work, and often provide a source of employment for young travellers.

Moving on from Adelaide

For **domestic flights** from Adelaide, Airlines of South Australia (ⓣ1800 018 234, ⓦwww.airlinesofsa.net) flies to Port Augusta, Leigh Creek and Port Lincoln; Emu Airways (ⓣ08/8234 3711, ⓦwww.emuairways.com.au) flies to Kangaroo Island; Jetstar (ⓣ13 15 38, ⓦwww.jetstar.com.au) flies to the Gold Coast, Melbourne and Hobart; Regional Express (ⓣ13 17 13, ⓦwww.rex.com.au) serves Broken Hill, Ceduna, Mount Gambier, Port Lincoln, Whyalla, Coober Pedy, Olympic Dam and Kangaroo Island; and Virgin Blue (ⓣ13 67 89, ⓦwww.virginblue.com.au) flies out of Adelaide to major cities countrywide.

The State Guide, available from the South Australian Travel Centre (see p.807) has route maps and timetables of all South Australia's **bus** routes. Most long-distance buses leave from the Central Bus Station on Franklin Street. Greyhound Australia (ⓣ1800 801 294) has a nationwide service that includes Alice Springs and Broken Hill in its destinations, while Firefly Express (ⓣ1300 730 740) runs to Melbourne and Sydney. V/Line (ⓣ08/8231 7620 or 13 61 96, ⓦwww.vline.vic.gov.au) also runs to Melbourne from Adelaide and Mount Gambier. State services are dominated by Premier Stateliner Coach Service (ⓣ08/8415 5544, ⓦwww.premierstateliner.com.au), which goes to the Riverland, Whyalla, Port Lincoln, Ceduna, Woomera, Roxby Downs and Olympic Dam, the Yorke and Fleurieu peninsulas and to Mount Gambier either inland or along the coast. Other local operators include the Barossa–Adelaide Passenger Service (ⓣ08/8564 3022), which stops at the main towns in the Barossa Valley en route to Angaston; the Yorke Peninsula Passenger Service (ⓣ1800 625 099), which runs from Adelaide to Yorketown, down the east coast via Ardrossan, Port Vincent and Edithburgh, and down the centre via Maitland and Minlaton; the Mid North Passenger Service (ⓣ08/8823 2375) via the Clare Valley and/or Burra to Peterborough; and the Murray Bridge Passenger Service (ⓣ08/8415 5555) to Pinnaroo via Murray Bridge and to Murray Bridge via Mannum and Meningie. Tickets can be purchased at the Central bus station. The **Bus Booking Centre** at Station Arcade, 52 Hindley St (ⓣ08/8212 5200), can arrange travel on any bus service.

There are three options for onward **train** travel - The *Overlander* to Melbourne, the *Ghan* to Darwin via Alice Springs and the *Indian Pacific*, which runs east to Sydney and west to Perth. Tickets can be booked through the Great Southern Railway Travel Pty (Ⓣ13 21 47, Ⓦwww.gsr.com.au), which produces a glossy brochure with current timetables. The Australian National Travel Centre, Station Arcade, North Terrace (Mon–Fri 8.30am–5.30pm; Ⓣ08/8231 4366), deals with interstate train enquiries and sells tickets; alternatively, call in at the Australian Rail Travel Centre, 18–20 Grenfell St (Mon–Fri 8.30am–5.30pm, Sat 9am–1pm; Ⓣ08/8231 4366).

Around Adelaide

Escaping Adelaide for a day or two is easy and enjoyable, with a tempting range of beaches, hills and wineries to choose from. Closest at hand are the **Adelaide Hills**, southeast of the city, which are popular for weekend outings and have numerous small national and conservation parks that are great for walking. To the south, the **Fleurieu Peninsula** extends towards Cape Jervis and has plenty of fine beaches and several small wineries. If wine is your priority, though, head for the **Barossa Valley**, Australia's premier wine-producing region, with over thirty excellent wineries within 50km of Adelaide. The valley is easily visited in a day from the city, but is also a great place to stop over and unwind. The **Yorke Peninsula**, across the gulf from Adelaide, is far less known, though many locals holiday here: as well as beaches, it has the remains of an old copper-mining industry and an excellent national park.

The Adelaide Hills

The beautiful **Adelaide Hills** are the section of the **Mount Lofty Ranges** that run closest to the city, just thirty minutes' drive away, and largely accessible by train and the Hills Transit bus service (Ⓣ08/8339 1191); several tours heading for the Fleurieu Peninsula also take in the area. Many people have set up home in the hills to take advantage of the cooler air, and there are some grand old summer houses here. The **Heysen Trail** long-distance walk cuts across the hills, with four quaint YHA hostels along it; most are run on a limited-access basis and you'll have to pick the key up first from the Adelaide office at 135 Waymouth St (Ⓣ08/8414 3010). Due to the high fire risk in midsummer, the trail is closed from mid-December to April. The **Adelaide Hills Visitors Information Centre** in Hahndorf (see p.832) is a good source of information about the area, and can also make accommodation bookings.

Leaving the city by Glen Osmond Road you join the **South Eastern Freeway**, the main road to Melbourne – there's an old tollhouse not far out of the city at Urrbrae and several fine old coaching hotels such as the *Crafers Inn*. At **CRAFERS** itself you can leave the freeway for the scenic Summit Road, which runs along the top of the hills, past the western side of the extensive **Mount Lofty Botanic Gardens** (daily 10am–4pm) to the **Mount Lofty Lookout**, the highest point of the range (727m). There's an **information centre** here (daily 9am–5pm; Ⓣ08/8370 1054, Ⓦwww.parks.sa.gov.au) with fantastic views and a café-restaurant and bar. Hills Transit buses #820, #821 and #822 run from Adelaide bus terminal or Currie Street via Crafers and up Piccadilly Road, from where you can access the eastern side of the Botanic Gardens. The free *Adelaide Hills Monthly* has information about local events and is available from the South Australia Travel Centre in Adelaide (see p.807) and other regional tourist information centres.

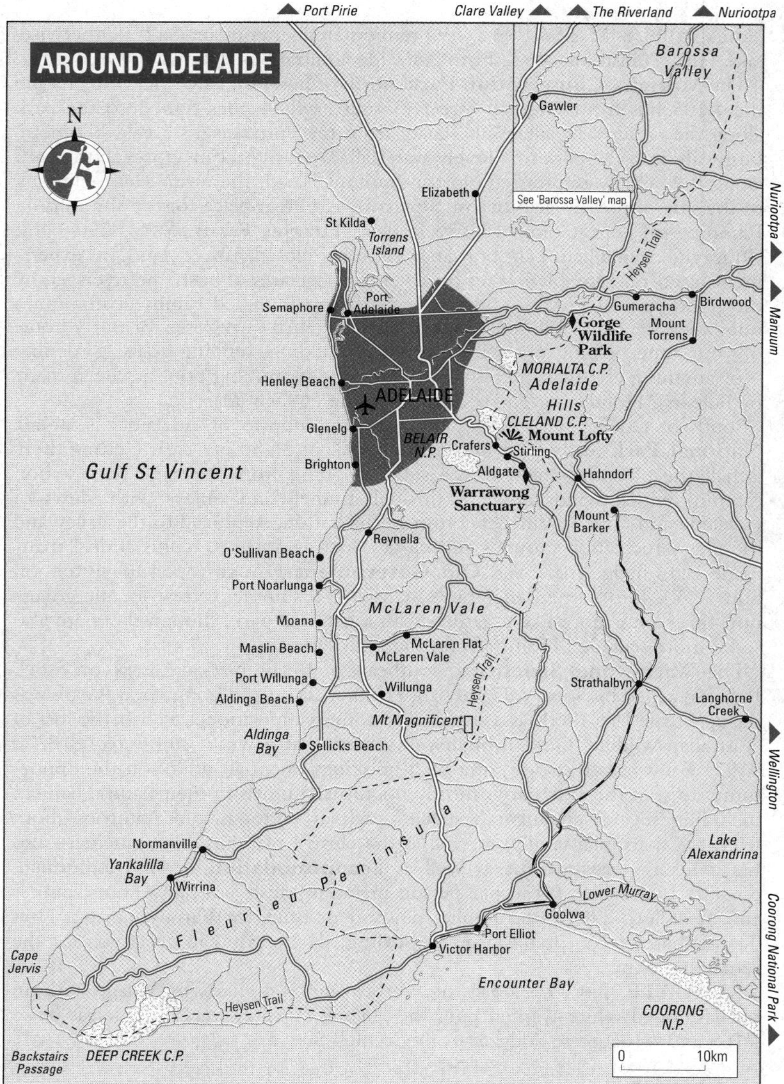

AROUND ADELAIDE

The turn-off to **Cleland Wildlife Park** (daily 9.30am–4.30pm; $13; Ⓦwww.cleland.sa.gov.au) is the first on the left after the lookout. Here you can cuddle a koala and see other Australian fauna in enclosures, and there are several good walking trails through native bush leading from the park into the surrounding Cleland Conservation Area. You can get up here as part of a tour with Gray Line (Ⓣ1300 858 687, Ⓦwww.grayline.com; $39), Adelaide Sightseeing (Ⓣ08/8231 4144, Ⓦwww.adelaidesightseeing.com.au; $49) or Premier Day

Tours (Ⓣ08/8415 5566, Ⓦwww.premierstateliner.com.au; $42). Otherwise, take Hills Transit bus #822 from Adelaide Central bus station.

The **Morialta Conservation Park**, north of here, is easily reached by taking the #105 bus from Grenfell Street (35min), which goes right into the park along the scenic Morialta Falls Road; from the entrance it's a two-kilometre bushwalk into the park to a lovely waterfall. By car you can approach the park along the equally impressive Norton Summit Road; the *Scenic Hotel*, clinging to the side of the hill at **Norton Summit**, is a great place to stop for a drink. Running off here, Colonial Drive leads to **Fuzzies Farm** (Ⓣ08/8390 1111, Ⓔfuzzyt@ozemail.com.au; bookings essential; closed July & Aug), an experiment in co-operative living set on seventeen hectares of bush and overseen by the philosophical Fuzzy. You can stay here in four-bed cabins (a minimum one-week stay costs $88 including meals); in return Fuzzy asks for thirty hours of your time helping out with carpentry, building, tending goats, gardening – or anything else that interests you (even the swimming pool has been made by helpers). Holidaying guests can stay in the cottage (❺).

South of Crafers, virtually in the southern suburbs of Adelaide, is **Belair National Park** (daily 8am till sunset; $2.70, or $6.50 per car). Getting there is half the pleasure – you take a suburban train from Adelaide train station (35min) which winds upwards through tunnels and valleys with views of Adelaide and Gulf St Vincent. From Belair station, steps lead to the valley and the grassy recreation grounds and kiosk. With its joggers, tennis courts, man-made lake, hedge maze and **Old Government House** (open to visitors on Sun 12.30–4pm), a residence built in 1859 as a summer retreat for the governor, this seems more like a garden than a national park, though there are also some more secluded bush trails through gum forests.

The **Warrawong Sanctuary**, southeast of Belair National Park on Stock Road, reached by Sturt Valley Road, Heather Road and Longwood Road, was set up in the late 1960s as a sustainable conservation model to halt the loss of Australian wildlife. Guided **bushwalks** starting at dawn or sunset (Ⓣ08/8370 9197, Ⓦwww.warrawong.com; $22; bookings essential) offer you the opportunity to spot the sanctuary's mostly nocturnal animals in their natural habitat, including several endangered species such as bettongs and potoroos (both from the marsupial family) as well as the elusive platypus. The sanctuary also has a licensed **restaurant** as well as **accommodation** in air-conditioned, en-suite tent-cabins ($150 per person including dusk and dawn tours, dinner and breakfast). There's no public transport or tours to Warrawong, but Hills Transit buses #166 or #193 go to Stirling, where you can get a taxi for the remaining 5km.

ALDGATE, just 3km north of Warrawong, is a charming village with an old-fashioned white-washed pub, the *Aldgate Pump Hotel*. Hills Transit buses #163 and #165 go to Aldgate from Grenfell Street.

Hahndorf

HAHNDORF, 28km southeast of the city, is the most touristy destination in the hills (frequent Hills Transit bus services from Central Bus Station; 40min) and is always crowded at weekends. Founded in 1839, it's Australia's oldest German settlement and still has the look of a nineteenth-century village. The Bavarian-style restaurants and coffee houses, crafts, antique and gift shops are thoroughly commercial, but it's still enjoyable, especially in autumn when the chestnuts and elms lining the main street have turned golden. The **Adelaide Hills Visitors Information Centre**, 41 Main St (daily 9am–5pm; Ⓣ08/8388 1185 or 1800 353 323, Ⓦwww.visitadelaidehills.com.au), has lots

B&B in the hills

Less than an hour from the city, the Adelaide Hills' many B&Bs in bush surroundings are well worth seeking out for a treat – but they aren't cheap. Adelaide Hills Country Cottages (ⓦwww.ahcc.com.au) lists a number of excellent B&Bs in and around Oakbank; alternatively, the South Australia B&B Association (ⓦwww.sabnb.org.au) has a useful brochure of places to stay, available from the South Australian Travel Centre in Adelaide (see p.807). One of the best places is *Apple Tree Cottage* in Oakbank (ⓣ08/8388 4193, ⓦwww.ahcc.com.au/apple_tree.html; ❼), a self-contained 1860 cottage beside an idyllic lake. In Aldgate, *Cladich Pavilions* are luxurious modern apartments set in native bushland (ⓣ08/8339 8248, ⓦwww.visitadelaidehills.com.au/cladich; ❻). For train enthusiasts, the 1880's *Mount Lofty Railway Station* (ⓣ08/8339 7400, ⓦwww.mlrs.com.au; ❹) in Mount Lofty has been converted into a sociable guesthouse-style B&B.

For **other accommodation** in the hills, try the *Warrawong Sanctuary* (see opposite), *Fuzzies Farm* (see opposite), or contact the Adelaide Hills Visitors Information Centre in Hahndorf (see opposite).

of information on B&Bs and other accommodation in the hills (no charge for bookings) and can provide information about the entire area, though you won't need much help in the village itself – there's basically just one street and all the buildings have blue plaques recounting their history. The **Hahndorf Academy** (Mon–Sat 10am–5pm, Sun noon–5pm; free) is a working artists' studio with a small collection of photographs, prints, displays and well-written interpretive boards that shed light on the lives of early German settlers, plus a few sketches by the town's most famous resident and one of Australia's best-known artists, **Hans Heysen**, who settled here in 1908. There's a more comprehensive collection of Heysen's paintings on display at his old home, **The Cedars**, about 2.5km northwest of the village, off Ambleside Road (Tues–Sun 10am–4pm; guided tours 11am, 1pm & 3pm; $8 studio and house; shop and garden free).

For a glass of authentic locally brewed pilsner, head for the lovely wooden bar of the *German Arms Hotel*, which has a log fire and photos of old Hahndorf, a reasonably priced bistro, and a more expensive **restaurant**. There are dozens of other places to eat - try *Muggletons General Store* on Main Street (open for lunch) where you can also buy delicious home-made jams and chutneys. *The German Cake Shop*, near the tourist office, just off the main street on Pine Avenue (daily 8.30am–6pm), is a crowded bakery and coffee shop where the speciality is *bienenstich*, a yeast cake topped with honey and almonds and filled with cream, butter and custard. For a picnic, the *Hahndorf Showcase Inn*, at the other end of the main street, stocks a tasty range of local produce.

Torrens River Gorge

Further north in the upper valley, the 27-kilometre **Gorge Scenic Drive** beside the Torrens River Gorge is one of the loveliest areas in the Adelaide Hills, but you'll need your own car to get there: take the Gorge Road off the A11 from Adelaide, a few kilometres past the suburb of Campbelltown. Fourteen kilometres along this road is the **Gorge Wildlife Park** (daily 9am–5pm; koala cuddling 11.30am, 1.30pm & 3.30pm; $10), a private park with mainly native birds and animals housed in walk-through enclosures. A few kilometres past the park, at Cudlee Creek, the Gorge Scenic Drive turns southeast away from the river and passes through picturesque valleys and vineyards to Mount Torrens. If you want to stick with the river, turn north before Cudlee Creek towards the Chain of Ponds, where the road connects after a few kilometres to the equally stunning **Torrens Valley Scenic Drive**.

GUMERACHA, the first town east of here, is home to **The Toy Factory**, 389 Birdwood Rd (daily 9am–5pm; ⓦwww.thetoyfactory.com.au), which sells wooden toys, games and puzzles and has a tacky eighteen-metre-high rocking horse which children (and adults) can climb up for good views of the countryside. At the eastern end of the Torrens Valley Scenic Drive is **BIRDWOOD**, home to the **National Motor Museum** on Shannon Street (daily 9am–5pm; $9) – Australia's largest collection of veteran, vintage and classic cars, trucks and motorcycles.

The Barossa Valley

The **Barossa Valley**, only an hour's drive from Adelaide, produces internationally acclaimed wines and is the largest **premium wine** producer in Australia. Small stone **Lutheran churches** dot the valley, which was settled in the 1840s by German Lutherans fleeing from religious persecution: by 1847 over 2500 German immigrants had arrived and after the 1848 revolution more poured in. German continued to be spoken in the area until World War I, when the language was frowned upon and German place names were changed by an act of parliament. The towns, however – most notably Tanunda – remain thoroughly German in character, even without the large doses of oompah tourist hype, and the valley is well worth visiting for the vineyards, wineries, bakeries and butcher's shops, where old German recipes have been handed down through generations. With up to 800,000 visitors per annum, the valley can seem thoroughly touristy and traffic-laden if you whizz through it quickly, but the peaceful back roads are more interesting, with a number of small, family-owned wineries to explore, many of which provide picnic areas and barbecues, and even children's playgrounds.

The first vines were planted in 1847 at the Orlando vineyards, an estate which is still a big producer. There are now over fifty **wineries**, from multinationals to tiny specialists. Because of the variety of soil and climate, the Barossa seems able to produce a wide range of wine types of consistently high quality; the white rieslings are among the best. The region has a typically Mediterranean climate, with dry summers and mild winters; the best time to visit is autumn (March–May), when the vines turn russet and golden and the harvest has begun in earnest. Much of the grape-picking is still done by hand and **work** is available from February. This is also the time of the week-long **Vintage Festival**, beginning on Easter Monday in every odd-numbered year (ⓣ08/8563 0600 for more information). Another local celebration is the **International Barossa Music Festival**, held annually for two weeks in early October and featuring mostly chamber music. Its headquarters are at Richmond Grove Winery on Para Road near Tanunda; other wineries act as venues, as do some of the area's pretty Lutheran churches.

Getting around the valley

The principal route from Adelaide to the Barossa Valley follows the Main North Road through Elizabeth and Gawler, and then joins the **Barossa Valley Highway** to Lyndoch. A more scenic drive takes you through the Adelaide Hills to Williamstown or Angaston, while from the **Sturt Highway** you can turn into the valley at Nuriootpa. Getting to the valley by **bus** is also reasonably easy: the Barossa–Adelaide Passenger Service (Mon–Sat 2 daily, Sun 1 daily;

Kapunda

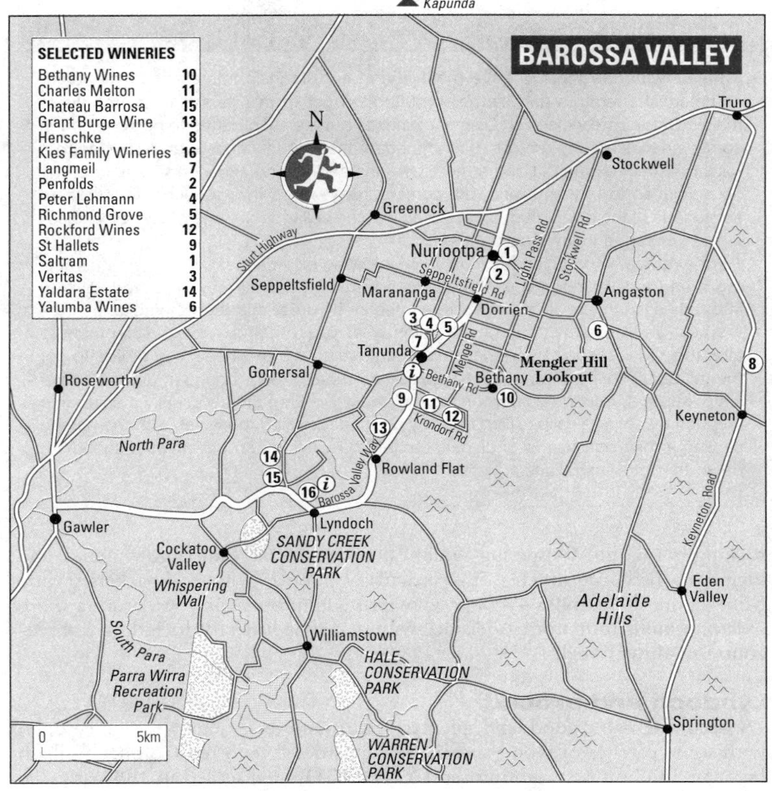

☎08/8564 3022) stops at the main Barossa towns en route to Angaston, while the daily Premier Stateliner (☎08/8415 5555) service to Riverland can drop you at Nuriootpa on request. If you're **cycling**, you might want to consider taking your bike on the standard train to Gawler, 14km from Lyndoch.

Driving isn't the ideal way to explore the Barossa, particularly if you want to enjoy tasting wines – once here, you can always rent a bike or take a tour. If you decide you do need a **car** to get around, you can rent one from the Caltex service station, 8 Murray St, Tanunda (☎08/8563 2677; $65 per day). A better way to experience the area is to **cycle**; there's a sealed bike track avoiding the busy highway between Tanunda and Nuriootpa and bike rental (around $10 a day) is available at *Zinfandel's*, 58 Murray St, Tanunda (☎08/8563 2822); *The Bunkhaus*, Barossa Valley Way, Nuriootpa (☎08/8562 2260); and *Barossa Caravan Park*, Barossa Valley Way, Lyndoch (☎08/8524 4262). Alternatively, you can take a two- to five-day **cycling tour** with *Ecotrek* (☎08/8383 7198, Ⓦwww.ecotrek.com.au), with an emphasis on wine-tasting, gourmet food and heritage accommodation. There's also a range of **sightseeing tours** from Adelaide offered by all the big commercial tour operators (see "Listings", p.827). For something different, try the small-group day-tour with Groovy Grape Getaways (☎1800 661 177, Ⓦwww.groovygrape.com.au; $65), which stops at Gumeracha's giant

Wine-tasting tips

Smaller wineries tend to have more charm and intrinsic interest than the larger commercial operators and it's here you'll often get to talk personally to the winemaker. Groups are welcomed by most wineries but are encouraged to book, although some wineries are too small to accommodate them. A few charge an **entry fee**, but for this expect extra staff and a more personalized tasting experience. You're under no obligation to buy any wine, but coming away with a few of your favourite taste sensations of the day – often only available at the cellar door – and a few fruity adjectives to describe them is part of the fun.

For a novice, wine-tasting can be an intimidating experience. On entering the **tasting area** (or cellar door) you'll be shown a list of wines that may be tasted, divided into reds and whites, all of which are printed in the order that the winemaker considers best on the palate. Unless you know what you're doing, it's not acceptable to alter this order, though by all means concentrate on red or white if you prefer. To get the full taste, sniff the wine first to appreciate the aroma or bouquet, and then take a sip, rolling it around on your tongue before swallowing; there's usually a spittoon if you don't want to swallow. Don't be shy about discussing the wines with the person serving – their purpose is to dispense chat and wisdom, and even wine snobs are down-to-earth Australians at heart.

rocking horse, the Whispering Wall near Lyndoch, and four large wineries, and includes a barbecue lunch – it's particularly popular with backpackers. Prime Mini Tours (Ⓣ08/8293 4900, Ⓦwww.primeminitours.com; $59) runs a more sedate minibus tour from Adelaide, with a similar itinerary including a three-course sit-down lunch.

Lyndoch and around

"A beautiful place, good land, plenty of grass and its general appearance open with some patches of wood and many kangaroos," reported Colonel William Light in 1837 on first sighting the **LYNDOCH** area; settled in 1839, it's one of the oldest towns in South Australia. Although vineyards were established from the outset, the primary activity until 1896 was the growing of wheat, when someone had the bright idea of converting a flour mill into a winery. Today there are ten wineries in the immediate Lyndoch area, from some of the smallest to one of the largest in the Barossa, all still family-owned. **Kies Family Wineries** on Barossa Valley Way provides free informal **tourist information** (daily 9.30am–5pm; Ⓣ08/8524 4110); their wine-tasting cellars (same hours) are in the same building.

Eight kilometres southwest of Lyndoch, off **Yettie Road**, is the **Whispering Wall**, a retaining wall for the **Barossa Reservoir**; it's shaped in such a way that words spoken on one side of the reservoir can be heard plainly on the opposite side 140m away. To the northeast, four kilometres along the Barossa Valley Way, the village of **ROWLAND FLAT** is dominated by the **Orlando Winery** complex, the oldest winery in the valley and home of some of Australia's best-known wines, sold under the **Jacob's Creek** label. Johann Gramp planted the first commercial vines at nearby Jacob's Creek in 1847, and forty years later his son expanded the winery and moved it to Rowland Flat. The **Jacob's Creek Visitor's Centre**, located on the banks of Jacob's Creek itself, has a tasting centre and restaurant with a gallery that includes information on production techniques, viticulture and the history of the area (daily 10am–5pm).

Four kilometres north of Rowland Flat, the peaceful **Krondorf Road/ Hallet Valley** area runs east of the Barossa Valley Way, with three charming wineries – Rockford, St Hallets and Charles Melton – each with its own philosophy of wine-making and tasting. Next to St Hallets Winery you can watch skilled coopers at work at the **Keg Factory**, St Hallet Road (Mon–Sat 8am–4.30pm, Sun 10.30am–4.30pm); the huge stainless steel fermentation tanks you'll see around the valley aren't suitable for all wines, many of which still need to be aged in wood to impart flavour.

Parallel to Krondorf Road to the north, Bethany Road runs east off the Barossa Valley Way to **BETHANY**, the first German settlement in the Barossa. The land is still laid out in the eighteenth-century Hufendorf style, with long, narrow farming strips stretching out behind the cottages, and the creek running through each property. Pretty gardens set off the old stone cottages, which remain well cared for. At dusk each Saturday the bell tolls at **Herberge Christi Church**, keeping up a tradition to mark the working-week's end, and Bethany – without even a pub or shop – retains its peaceful, rural village feel. The common where cattle grazed is now the Bethany Reserve, with a picnic spot by the creek.

Tanunda

TANUNDA is the Barossa's most quintessentially German town. The tree-lined main drag, **Murray Street**, boasts several old and beautiful buildings and proclaims its pedigree with German music wafting out of small wooden kegs above the shops. There's a more authentic atmosphere in the narrow streets on the western side of town, towards the river. Here, **Goat Square** was the site of the first town market and is bordered by the original cottages; the early market is re-enacted during the Vintage Festival (see p.834). Many **wineries** dot the town, the largest concentration being along **Para Road**, beside the Para River, including Stanley Brothers, Peter Lehmann, Richmond Grove, Langmeil and Veritas, all of which can be visited in the course of a pleasant stroll along the road and river.

For a good introduction to the wine-making industry, head for the **Barossa Wine and Visitor Centre**, 66–68 Murray St (Mon–Fri 9am–5pm, Sat & Sun 10am–4pm; wine centre daily 10am–4pm; $2; ⓣ08/8563 0600 or 1300 852 982, ⓦwww.barossa-region.org). The centre tells the history of the Barossa in an original way, on three tiers of cylinders, which you roll to read. Each group of cylinders represents a different historical period: spin the top tier for a background on world events, the middle tier for a specific Barossa chronology, and the bottom tier for Australia-wide happenings at the time to examine the Barossa's wine industry in the context of Australian and world history – it's quite engrossing. There are also engaging interpretive displays about wine making, and you can pick up some additional tips on wine-tasting etiquette. There are also lots of visitor information racks with brochures to thumb through. The low-key **Barossa Valley Historical Museum**, 47 Murray St (daily 10am–5pm; $2;), crams local history into a small quaint building which it shares with an antiques shop.

Three kilometres out of town, **Norm's Coolies**, at "Breezy Gully" off Gomersal Road (Mon, Wed & Sat 2pm; $8, children $2; ⓣ08/8563 2198), could only be in Australia: 28 sheepdogs are put through their paces by Norm and a herd of sheep. **Mengler's Hill Lookout**, east of Tanunda along Basedow Road and then the Mengler's Hill Road Scenic Drive, provides an unmatched view of the valley and its vineyards: there's a **sculpture garden** with white marble sculptures on the slopes below, and at night you can see the lights of Adelaide.

Barossa wineries

It's hard to choose between so many wineries, as almost all of them are worth a look. However, this selection should start you off.

Bethany Wines Bethany Rd, Bethany. A hillside winery set in an old quarry, with views over Bethany village (see p.837); five generations of the Schrapel family have grown grapes here. The ports are worth trying, especially the unusual white variety. Mon–Sat 10am–5pm, Sun 1–5pm.

Charles Melton Krondorf Rd, Tanunda. Small, friendly winery concentrating on a limited range of full-bodied reds that sell out fast. Informal tasting area in a wooden shed, where you sit at a long wooden table, with the door open to the vineyards and a friendly dog at your feet. Daily 11am–5pm.

Grant Burge Wines Barossa Valley Way, Jacob's Creek. Small, quality winery, established in 1988 to process wine from the area's oldest vineyards. Daily 10am–5pm.

Henschke Moculta Rd, Keyneton, 14km southeast of Angaston. Fifth-generation winemakers, the Henschke family's wines have won many international prizes. It's set in a peaceful setting off the beaten track and you'll need to ring the bell to rouse the amiable staff and start tasting. Mon–Fri 9am–4.30pm, Sat 9am–noon.

Langmeil Winery Langmeil Rd, near Tanunda. This was the original Langmeil village, built in the 1840s; the little vineyard you can see from the tasting area was planted in 1846. Prints of nineteenth-century photos on the walls document the local wine industry. With a slow and thoughtful approach to tasting and a small range (four reds, five whites and two tawny ports), you really get to know the wines – try the very peppery Grenache. Daily 10.30am–5pm.

Orlando Wines Steingarten Rd, Rowland Flat. Home of the famous Jacob's Creek range of wines and one of the oldest wineries in Australia. Daily 10am–5pm.

Peter Lehmann Para Rd, near Tanunda. Another pleasant spot for a bit of tasting in a homestead with vine-entwined verandahs surrounded by flowerbeds, gum trees and palms, overlooking a lawn leading down to the Para River; you're welcome to picnic here. Lehmann is as well known for his art collection as for his red wines, whose labels feature paintings by South Australian artists which are displayed here. Mon–Fri 9.30am–5pm, Sat & Sun 10.30am–4.30pm.

Richmond Grove Para Rd, near Tanunda. Large, historic winery sourcing grapes from around the Barossa and from other premier wine-growing areas in Australia – good if you want to compare the different regional characteristics of Australian wine. There's a lovely picnic area alongside the North Para River. Daily 10.30am–4.30pm.

Rockford Wines Krondorf Rd, Tanunda. No-nonsense approach and big unfussy wines by Robert O'Callahan, produced using old-fashioned techniques and including a good Basket Press Shiraz and an amazing fizzy Black Shiraz at around $50 a bottle. Mon–Sat 11am–5pm.

St Hallets Winery Krondorf Rd, Tanunda. Medium-size, quality producer. Its star wine is Old Block Shiraz, sourced from vines eighty to a hundred years old, with an intense flavour and a velvety softness. Daily 10am–5pm, lunch Sat & Sun.

Veritas Corner Stelzer Rd and Seppeltsfield Rd, near Tanunda. Established in the 1950s and known for its Hungarian-style wines, this family operation is a good place to come during harvest, around April, with tastings and sales in an unpretentious shed. Mon–Fri 10am–4.30pm, Sat & Sun 11am–4pm.

Yaldara Wines Gomersal Rd, Lyndoch. The ruins of a nineteenth-century flour mill have been transformed into a Baroque-style chateau complete with wine cellar and café (see p.841). Daily 9.30am–5pm.

Yalumba Wines Eden Valley Rd, Angaston. Largest and oldest family-operated Barossa winery, established in 1849, set in a lovely building and gardens. Daily 10am–5pm.

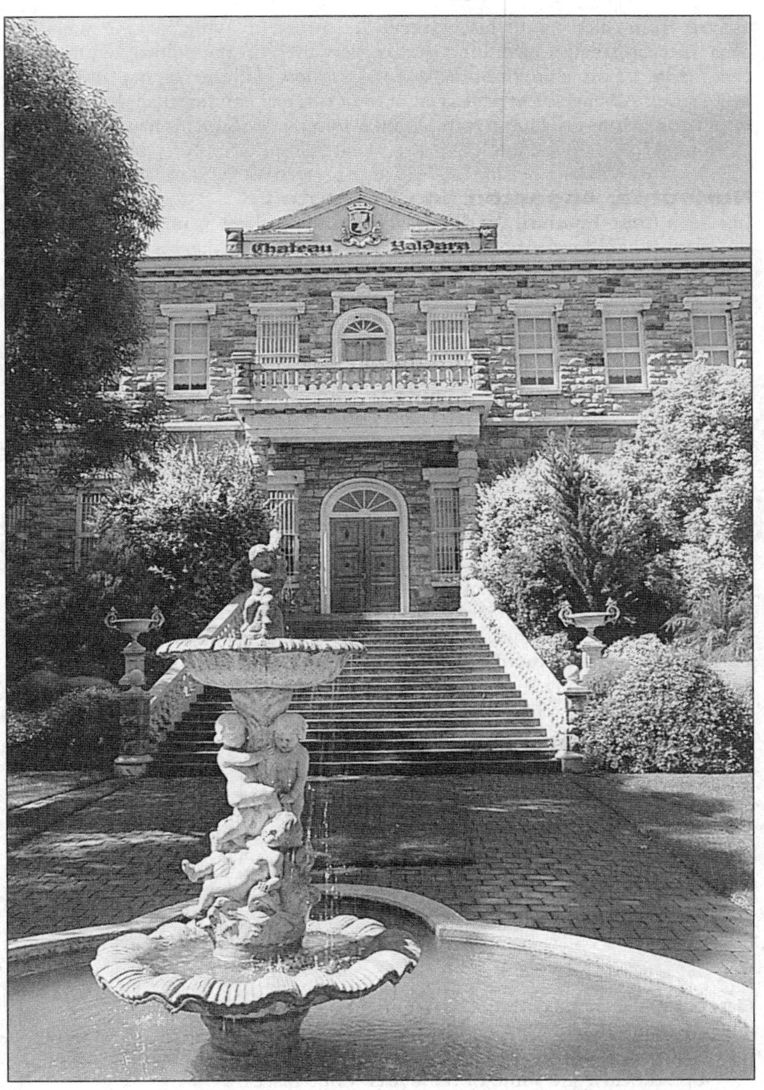

△ Chateau Yaldara Winery

Seppeltsfield, off the highway 4km northwest of Tanunda, must be, visually at least, the most spectacular of the wineries (tastings Mon–Fri 10am–5pm, Sat & Sun 11am–5pm). During the Great Depression the Seppelt family paid their workers in food to plant an avenue of date palms from Marananga to Seppeltsfield, and, on a hill halfway along the palm-lined avenue, stands the **Seppelt family mausoleum**, resting place of the male members of the family. The estate itself was founded in 1851 when Joseph Seppelt, a wealthy merchant, arrived from Silesia with his workers: he turned to wine making when his tobacco crop failed, establishing the largest winery in the colony, with everything from a port-maturation cellar to a distillery, vinegar factory and brandy bond store. All have been preserved in their original condition, and can be seen on a **tour** (Mon–Fri 11am, 1pm, 2pm & 3pm; Sat & Sun 11.30am, 1.30pm & 2.30pm; $7).

Nuriootpa, Angaston and Springton

Just 7km from Tanunda, **NURIOOTPA** is the valley's commercial centre: as the place where local Aborigines gathered to barter it takes its name from the word for "meeting place". It's not the most attractive of towns, dominated as it is by **Penfolds**, the Barossa's largest winery, which churns out mass-produced wines made with grapes from across South Australia. The finest building here is **Coulthard House**, a gracious, two-storey edifice commissioned by the area's first settler, William Coulthard. The town grew around his red-gum slab hotel, now the site of the *Vine Inn* community hotel. Together with the community store (where co-op members purchase shares and share in the profits), this finances many developments in the town, such as the excellent **swimming centre** in Coulthard Reserve by the shady, gum-lined North Para River. There's free **Internet access** at the public library, 10 Murray St (Mon, Wed & Fri 9am–5pm, Thurs 9am–7pm, Sat 9am–noon, Sun 2–4pm).

ANGASTON, southeast of Nuriootpa, is a pretty little town situated in the Barossa Ranges, an area of predominantly grazing land, red gums and rolling hills, although a few of the Barossa's oldest winemakers have been here for more than a century. This is the side of the Barossa that attracted the British pioneers, including George Fife Angas, the Scotsman after whom the town is named. The **Collingrove Homestead** (Mon–Fri 1–4.30pm, Sat & Sun 11am–4.30pm; $7.50; Ⓦwww.collingrovehomestead.com.au), 6km from town on Eden Valley Road, was one of his homes. Owned now by the National Trust, it's surrounded by lush gardens and offers accommodation (see opposite). Angas also lived at nearby Lindsay Park, now the private **Lindsay Park Stud**, Australia's leading racehorse breeding and training complex.

The major attraction at **SPRINGTON**, 20km south of Angaston, is the **Herbig family tree**, a hollowed-out gum tree in which a pioneer German couple lived for five years from 1855; they began their married life in the tree and had two of their sixteen children in it. Inevitably, Springton's old buildings have undergone the "boutiquing" process: the blacksmith shop is now a winery, and the old post office has been transformed into an arts and crafts gallery.

Barossa accommodation

There's comfortable accommodation in B&Bs and caravan parks throughout the valley, and you shouldn't have a problem finding somewhere decent to stay. Listed below are some of the better-value places.

Barossa Brauhaus Hotel 41 Murray St, Angaston Ⓣ08/8564 2014. Good-value basic rooms and cheap singles in a centrally located pub first licensed in 1849. Light breakfast included. ❸

Bunkhaus Travellers Hostel and Cottage Barossa Valley Way, 1.5km south of Nuriootpa Ⓣ & Ⓕ08/8562 2260. A comfortable, friendly, family-run hostel set in vineyards, with a cosy common room for winter and a swimming pool for summer. Bike rental available. Dorms $26, self-contained cottage ❷

Caithness Manor 12 Hill St, Angaston Ⓣ08/8564 2761, Ⓦwww.caithness.com.au. A former girls' grammar school whose lower storey has been transformed into a gracious guesthouse run by a friendly family. There's a sitting room complete with open fires, plus a swimming pool and spa. Each of the two spacious guest rooms has its own

bathroom and antique furnishings. Gourmet breakfast included. ❻
Collingrove Homestead Eden Valley Rd, 6km from Angaston ⓣ08/8564 2061, ⓦwww.collingrovehomestead.com.au. National Trust-listed B&B accommodation in old servants' quarters, set in English-style gardens. ❼
Langmeil Cottages Langmeil Rd, Tanunda ⓣ08/8563 2987, ⓦwww.langmeilcottages.com. German-style stone cottage with cooking facilities, peaceful setting and views of the Barossa Ranges; extras include champagne on arrival, breakfast provisions, free bicycles, heated pool and laundry facilities. ❻
Lawley Farm Krondorf Rd, south of Tanunda ⓣ08/8563 2141, ⓦwww.lawleyfarm.com.au. Restored stone cottages shaded by pepper-trees on a quiet road within walking distance of the best wineries. A full breakfast (included in room rates) is served in the farmhouse kitchen, and there's a hot spa in the garden. ❻
Seppeltsfield Holiday Cabins Seppeltsfield Rd ⓣ08/8562 8240, ⓕ8562 8563. These well-equipped log cabins, with wood fires, offer some of the best-value accommodation in the valley, set on a rural hillside overlooking the Seppelt winery. Standard rooms ❸, deluxe cabins with spa ❺
Tanunda Caravan and Tourist Park Murray St, Tanunda ⓣ08/8563 2784, ⓦwww.tanundacaravantouristpark.com.au. Set in parkland among beautiful waratah trees. On-site vans ❷, cabins ❸
Tanunda Hotel 51 Murray St, Tanunda ⓣ08/8563 2030 or 8563 2165. Built from local stone and marble in 1845, with Edwardian additions and decor inside. All rooms have TV, air-con, fridge, tea and coffee; some are en suite. ❸
Vine Inn Hotel Motel 14 Murray St, Nuriootpa ⓣ08/8562 2133, ⓦwww.vineinn.com.au. Spacious, modern motel-style units with air-con and queen-size beds; continental breakfast included. Spa and heated pool. ❺
Vineyards Motel cnr Stockwell and Nuriootpa roads, Angaston ⓣ08/8564 2404, ⓔvineyardsmotel1@ihug.com.au. Good location opposite the *Vintners Bar and Grill*, just a short walk away from Saltram Winery and its bistro. Modern units; facilities include room service, swimming pool and spa. ❸–❺

Barossa eating and drinking

There are excellent restaurants throughout the valley, as well as plenty of picnic spots and barbecue areas.

1918 Bistro and Grill 94 Murray St, Tanunda ⓣ08/8563 0405. Expensive but good fresh food using local ingredients cooked with a Mediterranean twist. Eat outside on the wide, plant-shaded verandah, or inside the beautiful old house, built in 1918, with a variety of nooks and corners for intimate dining. Local wines or BYO.
Barossa Bistro 37 Murray St, Angaston ⓣ08/8564 2361. Casual dining nightly with affordable, filling main courses including some interesting kangaroo dishes; lighter, cheaper meals at lunchtime. Licensed.
Barossa Wurst Haus and Bakery 86A Murray St, Tanunda. Specializing in traditional Barossa *Mettwurst* (German sausage), this delicatessen offers cheap but very tasty food. Good cappuccino. Daily 8am–5.30pm.
Barr-Vinum 8–10 Washington Street. Acclaimed chef Sandor Palmai serves up wondrous food in the restored 1840s home of Angaston's first doctor. The wine list is exemplary, the atmosphere relaxed and friendly. Expensive.
Cafe "Y" (Yaldara) Gomersal Rd, Lyndoch. Affordable prices aimed at families, with a children's menu too; pasta dominates, and they also do morning and afternoon tea. Daily 10am–4pm.
Harvesters Cafe 29D Murray St, Nuriootpa ⓣ08/8562 1348. Spacious, contemporary-style café with a nice courtyard serving great cooked breakfasts, homemade soups and a variety of vegetarian dishes. Tues–Sun 9am–5.30pm.
Lyndoch Bakery & Restaurant Barossa Valley Highway, Lyndoch. The best German bakery in the Barossa. The adjoining licensed restaurant serves hearty, moderately priced traditional dishes. Daily 8.30am–5.30pm.
The Park Restaurant/Café 2A Murray St, Tanunda ⓣ08/8563 3500. Affordable modern Australian cuisine in an 1840s stone villa set in a park, with either alfresco dining or indoor seating by the fire if it's cold.
Rendezvous House 22 Murray St, Angaston ⓣ08/8564 3533. Set in an old cottage with a small garden overlooking the pretty main street, this friendly organic café and restaurant serves vegetarian and meat dishes for around $10 and plenty of delicious tapas as well. Wed–Sun lunch, Fri–Sun dinner.
Salters Saltram Winery, Nuriootpa Rd, Angaston ⓣ08/8561 0222. Elegant bistro serving modern Australian-Italian cuisine, all fresh, deliciously prepared and reasonably priced. The attached

nineteenth-century winery specializes in full-bodied reds – try them at the cellar door before eating. Lunch only.

Vine Court Restaurant 49 Murray St, Nuriootpa. Serving simple but good Australian dishes and a few German specials, this place has the best-value meals in the valley: three courses for $15. Open daily for lunch and dinner.

Vintners Bar and Grill Cnr Stockwell and Nuriootpa roads, Angaston ⓣ08/8564 2488. A winemakers' hangout with expensive Mediterranean-style regional produce on the menu and a suitably impressive wine list. The decor is a mix of cool contemporary plus old stone walls, fireplaces and wooden beams, and there's a vine-covered courtyard for warm days. Wed–Sun lunch, Mon–Sat dinner.

Zinfandel Tea Rooms 58 Murray St, Tanunda. Popular place for hot, cooked breakfasts, German and Australian dishes for lunch and a delicious choice of strudels and cakes. You can sit inside the cosy cottage or out on the verandah. Daily 8.30am–6pm.

The Fleurieu Peninsula

The **Fleurieu Peninsula** (ⓦwww.fleurieupeninsula.com.au), thirty minutes south of Adelaide by car, is bounded by Gulf St Vincent to the west and the Southern Ocean to the south, the two connected by the Backstairs Passage at **Cape Jervis** (where ferries leave for Kangaroo Island, see p.849). There are fine beaches on both coasts and, inland, more wineries in the rolling **McLaren Vales**. It's a pleasantly undeveloped area, where many of the towns were settled from the 1830s, and there's a lot of **colonial architecture**, much of it now housing restaurants or B&Bs. For a round trip, leave the city via the Adelaide Hills and cut down through Mount Barker to well-preserved Strathalbyn and Goolwa, on the south coast, circling round through Victor Harbor, Yankalilla, Willunga and McLaren Vale. The peninsula is a good place to **cycle** – in addition to its roads it has two sealed bike paths: the 24km Encounter Bikeway (see box on p.846) follows the coast from Goolwa to just beyond Victor Harbor; another (shorter) path runs between Willunga and McLaren Vale. For **walkers**, the **Heysen Trail** starts at the southern tip of the peninsula at Cape Jervis and winds its way across the hilly countryside north to the Adelaide Hills and beyond. Although the trail is meant for long-distance walking, there are a number of well-signposted short walks along the way, including the 3.5-kilometre Deep Creek Waterfall Trail, just east of Cape Jervis with its wild coastal scenery. The Heysen Trail also passes through the Mount Magnificent Conservation Park, which contains a number of shorter walks offering excellent panoramic views.

If you're relying on **public transport**, Premier Stateliner (ⓣ08/8415 5555) makes four daily trips from Adelaide to Goolwa via McLaren Vale, Willunga, Victor Harbor and Port Elliot. There's also a sporadic service provided by the Southern Encounter and The Highlander **steam trains** (occasionally replaced by a diesel locomotive) which chug from Mount Barker to Victor Harbor and Strathalbyn respectively (first Sun of month June–Nov; ⓣ1300 655 991, ⓦwww.steamranger.org.au). Adelaide Sightseeing Tours run **tours** of the area (Mon, Wed & Sat 9.30am–5.30pm; ⓣ08/8202 8688, ⓦwww.adelaidesightseeing.com.au; $66), visiting Goolwa, Victor Harbor and McLaren Vale, connecting with Coorong Pelican cruises from Goolwa, with optional overnight stays at Victor Harbor to see the penguins returning to Granite Island.

The McLaren Vales

The fifty wineries of the **McLaren Vales**, in the northwest of the peninsula, are virtually in Adelaide, and the suburban fringes of the city now push right up to **REYNELLA**, where the first vineyards were planted in 1838. Among the earliest was Hardy's Reynella Winery on Reynell Road (Mon–Fri & Sun 10am–

McLaren Vale wineries

Listed below are half a dozen favourites from a wide choice of excellent wineries.

Chapel Hill Chapel Hill Rd, McLaren Vale, adjacent to the Onkaparinga Gorge. A small but very civilized winery in an old stone chapel with nice views over the vineyards. Winemaker Pam Dunsford was McLaren Vale's first Bushing Queen, and her wines have won several prizes. Daily noon–5pm.

D'Arenberg Osborn Rd, McLaren Vale. A family winery set up in 1928 and well known for its prize-winning reds. The first-rate restaurant is a good stop for lunch. Daily 10am–5pm.

Hoffman's Ingoldby Rd, McLaren Flat. Smallest of the wineries with only three labels to choose from, and these only available through the cellar doors or by mail order. A great place to sit in a peaceful setting and chat about wines with the friendly owners. Daily 11am–5pm.

Kay's Amery Vineyards Kays Rd, McLaren Vale. A wonderful family winery established in 1890; old photos of the family and the area cover the oak casks containing port. It's renowned for its Block 6 Shiraz from vines planted in 1892, though it sells out quickly. Also has a picnic area set amid towering gum trees. Mon–Fri 9am–5pm, Sat & Sun noon–5pm.

Scarpantoni Scarpantoni Drive, McLaren Flat. Small, prize-winning winery run by an Italian family, with a contemporary cellar more akin to a city wine bar. Mon–Fri 9am–5pm, Sat & Sun 11am–5pm.

Wira Wira McMurtie Rd, McLaren Vale. A large, classic ironstone building provides the setting for an impressive range of reds, whites and award-winning tawny ports, not forgetting the fortified Shiraz. Daily 9am–5pm.

5pm, Sat 10am–4pm), where the tasting room occupies the original ironstone and brick building, set in botanical gardens. There are several other wineries in Reynella, but the largest concentration – often in bush settings, though only an hour's drive from Adelaide – is around the small town of **McLAREN VALE**, which has about fifty wineries, mostly small and family-run. Since the 1960s there's been a trend for grape growers to switch from supplying winemakers to producing their own wine, and there's a swath of "boutique" wineries here as a result. More recently, the area has gained a reputation for its **olives**, and a number of shops have opened for tastings and sales. The Olive Grove (daily 9am–5pm), opposite the D'Arenberg winery, is the best, with excellent olives, oils, pestos and other sauces.

McLaren Vale is itself a "boutique" town, with many B&Bs and restaurants catering for the wine-buff weekend crowd. The liveliest time is in October, when the **Bushing Festival** celebrates the new wines, and the Bushing King or Queen, the winemaker who has produced the wine judged to be the best of the vintage, is crowned. A big part of the festival is the **craft market** held during the last weekend at Kay's Amery Vineyards, where there are fifty stalls manned by the artisans themselves, as well as food and entertainment. Information on this, and on the area's wineries, can be found at the **McLaren Vale and Fleurieu Visitor Centre** on Main Road, about 2km from the centre (daily 10am–5pm; ⓣ08/8323 9944, ⓦwww.visitorcentre.com.au) – it even has its own vineyard with a café and wine bar where you can sample wines from across the vale, including those wineries without cellar doors.

The centre can also book **accommodation**. Among the town's B&Bs are the historic *Claddagh Cottage*, Lot 8, Caffrey St (ⓣ08/8323 9806; ❺), within walking distance of the town centre; *Southern Vales*, 13 Chalk Hill Rd (ⓣ08/8323 8144;

❻), a more modern and hotel-like place with vineyard views; and *Samarkand*, Branson Road (Ⓣ & Ⓕ08/8323 8756; ❻), set in a large log cabin on a peaceful property complete with its own alpacas. Most **places to eat** in town are fairly fancy, and some of the wineries also have restaurants attached. For a more relaxed lunch, try *Blessed Cheese* at 150 Main Road, where aside from the divine dairy products, you can sample locally-grown olives and great coffee. The award-winning *Magnum Bistro* in the *Hotel McLaren*, 208 Main Rd (Ⓣ08/8323 8208), has delicious main courses, all reasonably priced. Across the road, at no. 201, the stylish *Oscar's* serves pizzas and Mediterranean salads (daily 11am–11pm; BYO). Restaurants include *The Barn*, on the corner of Main and Chalk Hill roads (Ⓣ08/8323 8618), where you can dine on moderately priced contemporary cuisine accompanied by local wines. On the corner of McMurtie Road, in the direction of Willunga, the award-winning *Salopian Inn* (Ⓣ08/8323 8769; lunch daily, dinner weekends only) is set in an atmospheric 1851 stone inn with a seasonally varying menu.

Gulf St Vincent beaches

A series of superb swimming beaches, often known as the **wine coast**, runs along the Gulf St Vincent shore roughly parallel to the McLaren Vales, from **O'Sullivan Beach** down to **Sellicks Beach**. All are easily accessible from Adelaide on public transport: take the train from Adelaide to Noarlunga Centre and bus #750 or #751 to the various beaches.

PORT NOARLUNGA is the main town, surrounded by steep cliffs and sand hills. Its jetty is popular with anglers and with wetsuit-clad teenagers who dive-bomb from it; at low tide a natural reef is exposed. Lifesavers patrol the local beaches, and you can rent surf and snorkelling gear at Ocean Graffix Surf and Skate Centre, 21 Salt Fleet Point. For the latest **surf report** call Ⓣ1902 241 018 (75¢ per min). **Moana**, two beaches south, has fairly tame surf that's perfect for novices. The southern end of **Maslins Beach**, south again, broke new ground by becoming Australia's first legal **nude** beach in 1975. The wide, isolated beach is reached by a long, steep walking track down the colourful cliffs from the Tait Road car park, deterring all but the committed. **Port Willunga**, the next stop down, offers interesting diving around the wreck of the *Star of Greece*, while just further south is **Aldinga Beach**, reached by the daily Adelaide–Cape Jervis Public Coach Service. From here there's a connecting bus to **Sellicks Beach** where, if you have your own car, you can drive along 6km of firm sand.

The coastal region south of here is more rugged, although there are some nice secluded beaches as well as the popular Heritage-listed sand dunes at **NORMANVILLE**. You can camp at *Normanville Beach Caravan Park* (Ⓣ08/8558 2038; en-suite cabins ❸). A few kilometres inland, the **Yankalilla Bay and Beyond Visitor Information Centre**, 104 Main Rd (Mon–Fri 9am–5pm, weekends 10am–4pm; Ⓣ08/8558 2999, Ⓦwww.yankalillabay.com), has a complete list of caravan parks and B&Bs along the coast. Ferries for Kangaroo Island (see p.849) depart from nearby Wirrina and Cape Jervis at the end of the Main South Road.

Victor Harbor

The old resort of **VICTOR HARBOR**, on Encounter Bay, is currently experiencing a resurgence in its fortunes, thanks principally to whales and penguins. In the 1830s there were three whaling stations here, hunting **southern right whales**, which came to Encounter Bay to mate and breed between June and September, heading close to shore, where they became easy targets.

Not surprisingly, their numbers began to decline, and by 1930 they had been hunted almost to extinction. Half a century later there were signs of recovery: in 1991, forty were spotted in the bay and eighty thousand people flocked to see them, while in 1998, sixteen females stayed in the bay to calf, and a dozen humpback whales were also spotted. A Heritage-listed former railway goods shed on Railway Terrace now houses the **South Australian Whale Centre** (daily 11am–4.30pm; $6), with excellent interpretive displays, exhibits and screenings on whaling and on the natural history of whales, dolphins and the marine environment. The centre also acts as a monitoring station, locating and tracking whales, and confirming sightings, which are most likely in June, July or August (call the hotline on Ⓣ1900 931 223, calls cost 75¢ per min; Ⓦwww.webmedia.com.au/whales). Two-hour whale cruises depart from Granite Island daily (June–Sept; Ⓣ0427 102 387; $55).

As well as whales, **Little Penguins** come to nest, roost and moult on **Granite Island**, which is linked to the esplanade by a narrow causeway. At dusk they come back from feeding – this is the best time to see them, on one of the ranger-led **penguin walks** run by Granite Island Nature Park (daily at dusk; 1hr; $13; booking essential on Ⓣ08/8552 7555). Before exploring the island you can visit the **Penguin Interpretive Centre**, which houses an audiovisual holographic display with a 3D park ranger giving the lowdown on daily penguin life (opens an hour before the start of a walk). You can walk across the 600-metre causeway to the island at any time, or get here on a traditional holiday ride with the Victor Harbor Horse Tram (daily 10am–4pm; $5, after which a shuttle bus takes over until 8.30pm; $6 return). The Granite Island Nature Park also has a small shark aquarium ($15), just offshore from the Penguin Interpretive Centre, and runs several cruises, including one to the West Island to spot the largest **sea-lion colony** in South Australia (minimum twelve people; $75; bookings essential on Ⓣ08/8552 7555).

Other local attractions include the **Cockle Train**, a Sunday steam train (sometimes diesel-hauled) which runs on the otherwise disused line along the coast to Goolwa via Port Elliot and back (every Sun & daily during school holidays; $23 return). If you're travelling with restless children, **Greenhills Adventure Park**, Waggon Road, alongside the Hindmarsh River (daily 10am–5pm, 6pm in summer; $20 adult, $15 child; Ⓣ08/8554 6554, Ⓦwww.greenhills.com.au), has activities from canoeing to waterslides. The Urimbirra **Wildlife Experience** (daily 9am–6pm; $8, child $4.50), 5km north on Adelaide Road, is an open-range park with native animals from all over the continent.

Practicalities

For further information on the area, head for the Victor Harbor **Tourist Information Centre** next to the causeway (daily 9.30am–4.30pm; Ⓣ08/8552 5738, Ⓦwww.victor.sa.gov.au); in the same building, the **Fleurieu & KI Booking Centre** (Ⓣ1800 088 552, Ⓔthebookingcentre@internode.on.net) can book accommodation and tours. The best **place to stay** is the *Anchorage*, 21 Flinders Parade (Ⓣ08/8552 5970, Ⓔanchoragevh@ozemail.com.au; ❹), a lovingly restored beachfront guesthouse with en-suite and spa facilities, a good restaurant attached, and an adjoining backpackers' hostel (dorms $18). Alternatives include the *Villa Victor Bed and Breakfast*, 59 Victoria St (Ⓣ08/8552 4258; ❹); and the *Family Inn Motel*, 300 Port Elliot Rd (Ⓣ08/8552 1941, Ⓕ8552 8645; ❸).

Good **places to eat** abound. The super *Cafe Bavaria* at 11 Albert Place is a gleaming venue with delicious fresh-baked German cakes and savouries at reasonable prices (closed Mon). If you're after Italian food, head for *Nino Solari's Pizzeria*, nearby at no. 16 (closed Mon), where you can plough into

The Encounter Bikeway

The **Encounter Bikeway** follows a scenic 24-kilometre stretch of coast between Victor Harbor and Goolwa. Parts of the route are on-road and slightly inland, but mostly it follows the coastline and is for cyclists and walkers only. The return trip can be completed comfortably in a day; the most scenic, and hilliest, section is between Dump Beach in Victor Harbor and the town of Port Elliot. **Mountain bike rental** is available at Goolwa Cycle Hire, Ampol Service Station, Cadell Street, Goolwa (ⓣ08/8555 1000; $22 per day), or Victor Harbor Cycle, 73 Victoria St, Victor Harbor (ⓣ08/8552 1417; $18 per day); alternatively, take your pick from a unique selection of brightly painted **tandem bikes**, some side-by-side and some with trailers, from Victor Bike Hire, 12 Flinders Parade, Victor Harbor (ⓣ08/8552 4458; from $10 per hour). Unfortunately, none offers a drop-off service for one-way journeys, but on Sundays you can take your bike on the Cockle Train (see below) between Victor Harbor and Goolwa and cycle back.

some generous portions of pasta and home-made *gelati*; for seafood, try the *Anchorage Café* on the beachfront Flinders Parade, a lively city-style café with an eclectic menu that's good for vegetarians; or for excellent fish and chips, the Victor Harbor Fish Shop, 20 Ocean St, is hard to beat. The best place to **drink** is on the Esplanade at the *Hotel Crown* which serves cheap bar meals, has streetside tables and big-name bands on Thursday and Friday and DJs on Saturday.

Port Elliot

PORT ELLIOT, just 5km east of Victor Harbor, is a pleasant little town with some good **coastal walks** along the cliffs at Freeman Knob and an attractive sandy beach with safe swimming at Horseshoe Bay. Campers can enjoy the beachside setting at the award-winning *Port Elliot Caravan & Tourist Park* (ⓣ08/8554 2134, ⓦwww.portelliotcaravanpark.com.au; cabins ❸, cottages ❺). A short stroll inland on the main Victor Harbor–Goolwa road, *Arnella by the Sea* (ⓣ08/8554 3611; dorms $22, rooms ❶) is a charming nine-bedroom guesthouse in a National Trust-listed building retaining its original wooden floorboards. For a superb (if expensive) meal overlooking the bay, head for the *Flying Fish Cafe* on The Foreshore. From here you can explore the coastal Encounter Bikeway (see box), or learn how to **surf** at nearby Middleton. For experienced surfers, Waitpinga Parsons and Chiton offer more thrills. Boards, wetsuits and fins can be rented from Southern Surf, 36 North Terrace (ⓣ08/8554 2375). For the latest surf report, call ⓣ08/8554 2047.

Goolwa

GOOLWA lies 14km east of Port Elliot, and 12km upstream from the ever-shifting sand bar at the mouth of the Murray River. Boaties love its position adjacent to vast Lake Alexandrina, yet with easy access to the Coorong (see p.856) and the ocean. Although so close to the coast, Goolwa feels like a real river town, and it thrived in the days of the Murray paddle-steamer trade, when it was the steamer's final offloading port – a rip-roaring place with almost a hundred taverns and the biggest police station in South Australia. The **railways** brought the good times to an end, and today only a few reminders of the boom times remain along Railway Terrace, with its old buildings painted in Federation colours. Steam trains make a comeback on Sundays, however, when the **Cockle Train** heads along the coast to Victor Harbor and

Cruises from Goolwa

Cruises to the mouth of the Murray and as far as Coorong National Park (see p.856) leave from the end of the wharf. Spirit of the Coorong Cruises (Ⓣ08/8555 2203, Ⓦwww.coorongcruises.com.au/) run two trips: the **Discovery Cruise** goes to the dune-covered Younghusband Peninsula, where passengers can alight and walk to the Southern Ocean (Mon & Thurs; also Tues & Sat Oct–May; 4hr; $70, or $120 from Adelaide); the **Adventure Cruise** consists of a 30-kilometre trip right into the national park (Wed; also Sun from Jun–Sept; 6hr; $84, or $124 from Adelaide).

back (every Sun & daily during school holidays; $20 return); and the **Southern Encounter** runs from the Adelaide Hills to Goolwa via Strathalbyn and Victor Harbor (see p.844). There are also frequent **coaches** from Adelaide to Goolwa run by Premier Stateliner (Mon–Fri 5 daily, Sat 2 daily, Sun 1 daily; Ⓣ08/8414 5555).

Overlooking the wharf beside the Hindmarsh bridge is **Signal Point Interpretive Centre** (daily 9am–5pm; $5.50), an innovative exhibition telling the story of the Murray and its river trade. The centre houses a small souvenir shop and café, as well as the helpful **Goolwa Tourist Information Centre** (daily 10am–4pm; Ⓣ08/8555 3488, Ⓦwww.visitalexandrina.com), which can book local river tours but not accommodation. For B&Bs, Cottages of Goolwa (Ⓣ08/8555 5880, Ⓦwww.cottagesofgoolwa.com) has a selection of self-catering cottages, including *Josephs* (❺), a luxurious historic cottage near the centre of town. The PS *Federal* on Barrage Road (Ⓣ08/8362 6229; minimum two-night stay; ❺) started life as a working paddle-steamer in 1902 and now provides comfortable, self-contained accommodation. *Riverport Motel* (Ⓣ08/8555 5033, Ⓕ8555 5022; ❹), on Noble Avenue 3km northeast of Goolwa, has motel units in a quiet setting beside the Lower Murray River, plus a pool, tennis court, bar and inexpensive dining room. Alternatively, try the *Corio Hotel* on Railway Terrace (Ⓣ08/8555 2011, Ⓕ8555 1109; ❸), which is also a popular **eating** place, along with the *Whistlestop Café* in Hays Street and *Woks 2 Eat*, an excellent licensed noodle bar on Cadell Street. **Campers** can head for *Goolwa Caravan Park*, Noble Avenue (Ⓣ08/8555 2737, Ⓕ8555 1095; cabins ❷).

Strathalbyn

The pretty town of **STRATHALBYN** sits quietly amongst rolling hills about 25km north of Goolwa and an hour's drive southeast of Adelaide. Settled in 1839 by Scottish immigrants, the historic town is the market centre for the surrounding farming community, but is also renowned for its antique shops, Heritage-listed buildings and serene atmosphere. Strathalbyn comes alive during its irregular but well-publicized **horse-racing** meetings and for a few traditional **festivals**: an antiques fair held in the third week of August, and an agricultural show and duck race in October. For a self-guided walking brochure of the town, head to the **Strathalbyn Tourist Information Centre** at the Old Railway Station, on South Terrace (daily 9am–5pm; Ⓣ08/8536 3508).

The best of the town's many **B&Bs** is *Watervilla House*, 2 Mill St (Ⓣ08/8536 4099, Ⓔwatervillahouse@triplei.net.au; ❺), a beautiful 1840s cottage overlooking landscaped gardens and the River Angas Park. Alternatively, the historic *Victoria Hotel* has quality motel rooms and a reasonable bistro (Ⓣ08/8536 2202, Ⓕ08/8536 2469; ❺). For **eating**, *Café Ruffino*, on the High Street, serves excellent home-made pastries and cakes, while *Jacks Bakery*, on the other side of the

High Street, has excellent coffee and an interesting gourmet menu. The only regular **public transport** is from Adelaide on Transit Bus #843 via Adelaide Hills (Mon–Fri only); alternatively, if your timing's right, the Southern Encounter steam train chugs in from Mount Barker and Goolwa on selected Sundays (see p.846).

The Yorke Peninsula

The **Yorke Peninsula** was almost the last section of the Australian coastline to be mapped by Matthew Flinders in 1802. Flat plains stretch out to the sea, so extensively cleared for farming that only tiny areas of original vegetation remain – in the Innes National Park at the very tip of the peninsula and in a couple of conservation parks. Much is now made of the northern peninsula's **Cornish heritage**, but the miners from Cornwall who flocked to the area when **copper** was discovered in 1859 have left behind little but their names and the ubiquitous Cornish pasty. The three towns of the Copper Triangle or "**Little Cornwall**" – Kadina, Wallaroo and Moonta – make the most of it at the Kernewek Lowender (Cornish Festival), held over the long weekend in May of odd-numbered years, though in fact the mining boom ended more than seventy years ago, and they've been plain country towns ever since.

Just two hours' drive from Adelaide, the peninsula offers a peaceful weekend break as well as good **fishing**. The east coast ports of Ardrossan, Port Vincent and Edithburgh on the Gulf St Vincent were visited first by ketches and schooners, and later by steamers transporting wheat and barley to England. Now the remaining jetties are used by anglers. They're all pleasant to visit, but **EDITHBURGH** offers the most facilities: once a substantial salt-production town and grain port, it still has a few fine old buildings and a long jetty. There's a tidal swimming pool set in a rocky cove, and from Troubridge Hill you can see across to the Fleurieu Peninsula and to **Troubridge Island Conservation Park**, with its 1850s iron lighthouse, migrating seabirds and Little Penguin population: guided tours are available (groups of four or more only; 2hr; $20; ⓣ08/8852 6290 for bookings and details; no tours July & Aug). **Accommodation** is available here in the lighthouse-keeper's cottage, which sleeps up to ten and a minimum of four – if you stay here you'll have the whole island to yourself, but it doesn't come cheap (arrange through the tour guide; minimum two-night stay; ❽).

In Edithburgh itself, more affordable **accommodation** options include foreshore motel units and comfortable two-bedroom apartments at *The Anchorage Motel and Holiday Units*, 25 O'Halloran Parade (ⓣ08/8852 6262, ⓕ8852 6147; holiday units and rooms ❸) and *Edithburgh Caravan Park* (ⓣ08/8852 6056, ⓦwww.edithburghcaravanpark.com) further along the foreshore, which has vans (❷) and en-suite cabins (❹). There are also motel units at the back of the *Troubridge Hotel* on Main Street (ⓣ08/8852 6013, ⓕ8852 6323; ❸); this faces the 1878 *Edithburgh Hotel* (ⓣ08/8852 6011), which is the best place for **meals** including local oysters. The *Location Café* on Edith Street (8am–4.30pm, Thurs–Mon) is a good option for a simple meal.

At the tip of the peninsula lies the **Innes National Park**, with its contrasting coastline of rough cliffs, sweeps of beach and sand dunes, and its interior of mallee scrub. The park is untouched except for the ruins of the gypsum-mining town of **Inneston**, near **Stenhouse Bay**. The **visitor centre** (ⓣ08/8854 3200) in the park sells entry permits ($6.50 per car) and **camping** permits ($6.50–$16 per car depending on which campsite you choose) and offers facilities such as hot showers. The main camping area is at **Pondalowie Bay**, which has some of the best **surf** in the state; there are several other good surfing spots around the park and north towards Corny Point. Other more sheltered coves and bays are good for **snorkelling**, with shallow reef areas of colourful marine life, while on land you might see emus, western grey kangaroos, pygmy possums and mallee fowl. The NPWS also operates five self-contained lodges around Inneston (ⓣ08/8854 3200, ⓕ8854 3299; minimum two-night stay; ❷). Alternatively, for a taste of luxury surrounded by wildlife, try the *Wilde Retreat* (ⓣ08/8854 1324, ⓦwww.wilderetreat.info; ❺), a tastefully designed and secluded cottage sleeping up to eight.

Premier Stateliner (ⓣ08/8415 5555) has a daily **bus** service from Adelaide to Moonta, via Kadina and Wallaroo. The Yorke Peninsula Passenger Service (ⓣ08/8391 2977) runs from Adelaide to Yorketown, alternating daily between the east coast via Ardrossan, Port Vincent and Edithburgh and the centre via Maitland and Minlaton. There's no transport to the national park itself.

Kangaroo Island

As you head towards **Cape Jervis** along the west coast of the Fleurieu Peninsula, **KANGAROO ISLAND**, only 13km offshore, first appears behind a vale of rolling hills. Once you're on the island, its size and lack of development – there's only one person for every square kilometre – leave a strong impression. This is actually Australia's third-largest island (after Tasmania and Melville Island, north of Darwin), with 450km of quite spectacular and wild coastline, and so takes some time to explore. To see all the island's unusual geological features and wildlife habitats, you'll need at least three days, though most people only visit the major attractions on the south coast – Seal Bay, Little Sahara, Remarkable Rocks and Flinders Chase National Park.

Although the island is promoted as South Australia's premier destination for tourism, it's still very unspoilt; only in the peak holiday period (Christmas to the end of Jan, when most of the accommodation is booked up) does it feel busy. Once out of the island's few small towns, there's little sign of human presence to break the long, straight stretches of road as they run through undulating fields, dense gum forests or mallee scrub. There's often a strong wind off the Southern Ocean, so bring something warm whatever the season, and take care when **swimming** – there are strong rips on many of the beaches. Safe swimming spots include Hog Bay and Antechamber Bay, both near Penneshaw; Emu Bay, northwest of Kingscote; Stokes Bay, further west; and Vivonne Bay, on the south side of the island.

Kangaroo Island is possibly the best place in Australia to see an astonishing range of **wildlife**, largely untroubled by disease or natural predators, and a third of the island is now protected in some form. When Matthew Flinders first sighted the island in 1802, "black substances" seen on shore in the twilight turned out to be **kangaroos**, prolific and easily hunted. Kangaroos still abound, as do wallabies. **Koalas** were introduced at Flinders Chase National Park in 1923 as a conservation measure. They have remained free of chlamydia, which is common in the mainland population, and have spread so widely that they are killing off many of the gum trees – calls for culling in the mid-1990s caused national controversy, so fertility control and relocation to other parts of Australia are being tried instead. Other animals found here include echidnas, platypuses, Little Penguins, fur seals, sea lions and, in passing, southern right whales. The island is also home to over two hundred other kinds of **birds**, as well as snakes.

Wild pigs and feral goats, the descendants of those left here by early seafarers, can also be found, while a pure strain of **Ligurian bees** brought by early settlers now forms the basis of a local honey industry. There are also over a million **sheep** on the island, most of them merino, while a sheep dairy here makes delicious cheeses. The latest local craze is for **marron farming**, with about 140 licensed producers of the freshwater crustacean, a bit like a cross between a lobster and a yabbie. Other diverse new industries include abalone farming, oyster and mussel production, olive-oil pressing and the revival of eucalyptus-oil distilling.

Getting to the island

Kangaroo Island Sealink **ferries** ply across the Backstairs Passage **from Cape Jervis to Penneshaw** – often a rough journey, though mercifully short. Two large vehicle ferries make the journey at least four times daily, and up to seven times during peak holiday periods, taking about forty minutes to cross: buses connect the service with Adelaide twice daily ($64 ferry return, $96 including bus from Adelaide, cars $138, motorbikes $44, bikes $11; ⓣ13 13 01, ⓦwww.sealink.com.au). At Penneshaw, connecting Sealink buses run to American River ($8 one-way) and Kingscote ($11), though they'll need to be booked in advance.

Alternatively, Kangaroo Island Ferries is a small and friendly operation which runs two daily crossings from Wirrina to Kingscote (2hr; $59.50 ferry return, $88.50 including bus from Adelaide, cars $128, motorbikes $44, bikes $10; ⓣ13 22 33, ⓦwww.kiferries.com). To get to Wirrina, take the turn-off from the Main South Road 11km south of Normanville. In addition, it's worth checking out various cheap **packages**, including accommodation and tours or car rental, often with special backpackers' rates. At one end of the scale, Sealink does a whirlwind $181 one-day coach tour leaving Adelaide at 7am and returning at 10.30pm, but it's pretty exhausting. A more leisurely option aimed at independent-minded budget travellers is with Kangaroo Island Ferry Connections (ⓣ08/8553 1233 or 1800 018 484, ⓦwww.ki-ferryconnections.com.au), which offers two-day, one-night small-group packages from Adelaide for about $295 per person with hostel accommodation in Penneshaw. Camp Wild Adventures (ⓣ08/8132 1333 or 1800 444 321, ⓦwww.campwild.com.au) has an excellent, more laid-back two-day 4WD tour from Adelaide, camping overnight in a secluded spot on the southern coast ($320 per person).

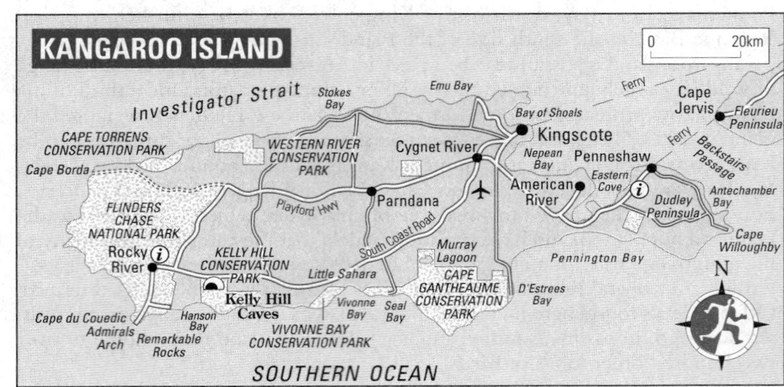

The Wayward Bus's two-day tour from Adelaide also takes advantage of an overnight stop near the Flinders Chase National Park, giving more time for viewing the spectacular sights there ($295 per person, or $335 to upgrade from dorm to twin or double room; ⓣ08/8410 8833 or 1300 653 510, ⓦwww.waywardbus.com.au).

It takes thirty minutes to **fly** to Kingscote on Kangaroo Island from Adelaide – costs vary, starting from $120 for a return ticket. For airlines that operate here, see p.829. There are **car rental** offices at Kingscote Airport, and a bus to town for about $10 with Airport Shuttle Services (ⓣ08/8553 2390).

Getting around, tours and activities

There's no public transport on the island, so without a tour or your own vehicle, hiring a car is pretty much essential. There are two **car rental** firms and it's best to book ahead to be sure of a vehicle – that way you'll also be met with the vehicle off the ferry or plane. Budget Rent a Car has an office at Penneshaw Ferry Terminal (ⓣ08/8553 3133; $55–85 per day, $385–510 per week), or you could try Kangaroo Island Rental/Hertz in Kingscote, on the corner of Franklin Street and Telegraph Road (ⓣ08/8553 2390 or 1800 088 296, ⓔhertzki@kin.net.au; $70 per day, $420 per week or $150 per day for 4WD).

Roads to most major attractions are bitumen-sealed, including the scenic eighty-kilometre **South Coast Road** from Cygnet River to the Flinders Chase National Park, Remarkable Rocks and Admirals Arch. The main drag is the **Playford Highway** from Kingscote through Cygnet River and Parndana to the western tip of the island at Cape Borda, although the last part of the highway along the northern edge of Flinders Chase National Park is not sealed and can be rough. At the eastern end of the highway, sealed roads feed off to the airport, Emu Bay, American River and Penneshaw. Most other roads are constructed of ironstone rubble on red dirt and can be very dangerous; the recommended speed on these roads is 60kph. Driving at night on all roads is best avoided due to the high risk of collision with kangaroos and wallabies. You'll see the carnage of animal remains alongside the road at depressingly short intervals – most are hit by speeding trucks. Cars have far less protection from impact and insurance excesses are often a mandatory $2000 for animal collision. The main roads are all good for **cycling** – for the island's best rental outlet, go to Bikes For Hire on Dauncey Street in Kingscote (ⓣ08/8553 2349; $27.50 per day).

Most people opt to visit the island on a **tour**, which can be good value if bought as part of a package (see p.828). There are several small-group tour companies based on the island: Adventure Charters of Kangaroo Island in Kingscote (ⓣ08/8553 9119, ⓦwww.adventurecharters.com.au), led by an ex-park ranger, offers 4WD tours with an emphasis on fine food, wine and accommodation as well as nature. There are also a couple of **dive** tour operators: Kangaroo Island Diving Safaris (ⓣ08/8559 3225, ⓦwww.kidivingsafaris.com), based at Telhawk Farm on the north coast, offers diving charters and residential dive courses with special backpackers' rates; and K.I. Diving on Beach Crescent, American River (ⓣ08/8553 1072, ⓦwww.kidiving.com) offers a three-day residential scuba course and certification ($415), as well as a half-day Discover Scuba course ($89).

Information and park entrance fees

With about one third of the island deemed a national or conservation park area, many of the parks charge entry fees and extras for guided tours. However, a one-year **Island Pass** ($42 per person) covers virtually all these costs (except for camping and the night-time penguin tours from Penneshaw and Kingscote, see p.853 and p.852), and is worth it if you're here for a while. The entry fees and tour prices quoted in the following accounts apply only if you don't have a pass – add up the cost of what you want to see and work out which is cheaper. Passes can be bought from the parks themselves or from the NPWS office on Dauncey Street, Kingscote (Mon–Fri 8.45am–5pm; ⓣ08/8553 2381, ⓦwww.environment.sa.gov.au); this office can also arrange camping permits and cottage accommodation in most of the national parks around the island. Passes can also be purchased from the **Kangaroo Island Gateway Visitor Information Centre**, at the edge of Penneshaw on the main road to Kingscote (Mon–Fri 9am–5pm, Sat & Sun 10am–4pm; ⓣ08/8553 1185, ⓦwww.tourkangarooisland.com.au), which also has an interpretive display on the island's history, geology and ecology and dispenses free maps.

The island

Coming by boat, you'll arrive at Kangaroo Island's eastern end, either at the small settlement of **Penneshaw** with its Little Penguin colony, or **Kingscote** a little further west, the island's administrative centre and also South Australia's second-oldest colonial settlement, though little remains to show for it. Between Penneshaw and Kingscote, sheltered **American River** is another good base. The airport is situated near **Cygnet River** – a quiet spot inland from Kingscote. From here, the **Playford Highway** and **South Coast Road** branch out to traverse the island, entering **Flinders Chase National Park** from the north and south respectively. The national park and surrounding wilderness protection area cover the entire western end of the island. The rugged **south coast** provides more wildlife-spotting and fine scenery: running west to east you can visit the aptly named Remarkable Rocks and Admirals Arch, both within the national park; go bushwalking in Hanson Bay; tour the limestone caves of Kelly Hill; camp at Vivonne Bay Conservation Park; play Lawrence of Arabia among the impressive sand dunes of Little Sahara; or roam amongst sea lions at Seal Bay. The quieter **north coast** has a series of sheltered beaches, including Emu Bay and Stokes Bay, and wild coastal cliff walks around Scotts Cove.

Kingscote and the north coast

With banks, shops, Internet access, a hospital, library and the only high school, **KINGSCOTE** is the island's main town. The coast here has been the scene of several shipwrecks – interpretive boards on the foreshore provide details. For more history, you can walk north along the Esplanade to the Reeves Point Historic Site, where boards commemorate the South Australia Company's first landing of settlers in July 1836, before they headed off to establish nearby Adelaide. The settlement never numbered more than three hundred people, and folded in 1839. Less than a kilometre up the hill above, on Seaview Road, is Hope Cottage Folk Museum (daily 1–4pm, Sat only in Aug; $5), the restored 1859 home of a pioneering family. Kingscote has a small colony of Little Penguins that were transported from Penneshaw during the building of the boardwalk there; not as impressive as Penneshaw's, they're best seen on the guided ranger talks that leave from the Marine Centre on the wharf (ⓣ08/8553 3112; April–Sept 7.30pm; Oct–March 8.30pm; $5). There's also pelican feeding around the Fisherman's Jetty with a small talk about their habits and habitat (daily 5pm; $2).

Established in 1907, the waterfront *Ozone Hotel* (ⓣ08/8553 2011 or 1800 083 133, ⓦwww.ozonehotel.com; ❺) is a local institution with comfortable rooms and a lively dining area. The best restaurant in town is *Bella* on Dauncey Street (ⓣ08/8553 0400), a cosy space where you can enjoy dishes such as local King George tempura whiting, or top-notch pizzas too (delivery service available). Also on Dauncey Street is the *Queenscliffe Family Hotel* (ⓣ08/8553 2254, ⓕ8553 2291; ❸), another old pub offering rooms and meals; next door is *PK's Lighthouse Cafe*, which has a varied menu, with vegetarian dishes and real coffee (closed Sun). Upmarket motel accommodation, with sea views, is found at *Wisteria Lodge*, Cygnet Road (ⓣ08/8553 2707, ⓦwww.wisterialodgeki.com; ❻). For the budget-conscious there's the *Kangaroo Island Central Lodge*, 19 Murray St (ⓣ08/8553 2787; dorms $20, rooms ❷), which has large clean dorms, a kitchen and common room. *Nepean Bay Caravan Park* (ⓣ & ⓕ08/8553 2394; on-site vans, cabins and cottages ❷–❸) at Brownlow Beach, 3km away, is the only place for campers. The Local Store (7.30am–7.30pm) near the entrance is handy for food and fuel.

The **beaches** on the north coast are more sheltered than those on the south. Emu Bay, 21km along a sealed road from Kingscote, is a secluded and quiet spot with a clean, sandy beach, a small penguin community, a few holiday homes and a couple of B&Bs – but no shops. *Wintersun Holiday Units* (ⓣ08/8553 5163, ⓔdmorris@kin.net.au) manages several self-contained cottages (❹) along the bay and in the nearby hills. For a touch of luxury, *Seascape* (ⓣ08/8553 5199, ⓦwww.seascape.ws; ❼) on Bates Road is a boutique-style B&B overlooking the bay. The friendly hosts can provide gourmet dinners on request as well as informative tours of the island. About 30km further west, secluded Stokes Bay is reached along a dirt road passing through a natural tunnel between overhanging boulders. There's a delightful calm rock pool – a perfect semicircle of rounded black stones which conveniently provides protection from the dangerous rip in the bay. Outside the tunnel, the *Rockpool Café* (summer only, daily 10am–5.30pm; ⓣ08/8559 2277) looks after the beachfront campsites and also sells milk and bread to campers.

Penneshaw

It's a 45-minute drive on a sealed road from Kingscote to **PENNESHAW**, set on low, penguin-inhabited cliffs. This is a popular base, with comfortable accommodation and plenty of places to eat. Penneshaw's crescent of sandy beach at Hog Bay curves from the rocks below the wharf, where the ferries come in, around to a wooded headland. The bay provides safe **swimming** and even a shady shelter on the sand. Above, there's a grassy picnic reserve with barbecues and the **Penguin Interpretive Centre**. Penneshaw Penguin Tours (daily 7.30pm & 8.30pm; $8; ⓣ08/8553 1103) provide an excellent informative commentary on the antics of the **Little Penguins** from the centre at dusk. This is the time they return from feeding in the unpolluted sea and cross the beach at Hog Bay to their cliffside burrows – a specially lit **boardwalk** provides a rookery viewing area.

Antechamber Bay, 10km southeast of Penneshaw, also has good, safe swimming. If you drive or cycle a further 10km along the unsealed dusty road you'll come to **Cape Willoughby Lighthouse**, at the eastern end of the island. Guided tours are offered by the NPWS (daily every 30min 10am–4pm; $10.50; ⓔcape.willoughby@saugov.sa.gov.au), and you can even stay in the sandstone homes of the original keepers. You'll find more safe swimming at **American Beach**, southwest from Penneshaw along the scenic road that hugs Eastern Cove.

The **Dudley Peninsula**, on which Penneshaw stands, is attached to the rest of the island by a narrow neck of sand; at the isthmus 511 steps lead up to **Mount Thisby** (Prospect Hill), a 99-metre hill of sand with views across to the mainland, to Hungry Beach, Pelican Lagoon and American River on the island's north coast, and in the opposite direction to **Pennington Bay**.

Practicalities

Penneshaw's Sealink office is at 7 North Terrace (Mon–Fri 8am–6pm, Sat & Sun 8am–1pm & 3–6pm; ⓣ08/8553 1122). There's no bank, but the **post office** (Mon–Fri 9am–5pm, Sat 9am–11pm) acts as an agent, and there's EFTPOS at Grimshaw's, the town's **general store** opposite the hotel (daily 8am–7pm, summer until 8pm). Penneshaw's accommodation options include the comfortable *Kangaroo Island YHA*, 33 Middle Terrace (ⓣ08/8414 3000, ⓦwww.yha.com.au/hostels; dorms $23, rooms ❸). The upmarket alternative is the friendly *Kangaroo Island Seafront Hotel* (ⓣ08/8553 1028, ⓦwww.seafront.com.au; ❺), set in landscaped gardens with motel-style rooms and fully equipped cabins, plus a heated pool, spa, sauna and tennis court, bar and restaurant. You can also stay in the two lighthouse-keepers' cottages at **Cape Willoughby** (ⓣ08/8559 7235, ⓕ8559 7268; BYO linen; ❹).

The best **restaurant** in town is *Sorrento's*, in the *Seafront Hotel*, specializing in seafood, steaks and local wines (ⓣ08/8553 1028). The nearby *Fish* (daily 4.30pm–8.30pm) is a neat black and white-tiled establishment cooking up a wonderful array of locally-caught produce such as lobster, marron, whiting and oysters. The tin-roofed bungalow of the *Penneshaw Hotel* is a small and friendly place to drink, with a verandah overlooking the water.

American River and Cygnet River

Facing Penneshaw across Eastern Cove, **AMERICAN RIVER** is actually a sheltered bay, where many small fishing boats moor, aiming to catch some of its abundant whiting. It's a peaceful place to stay, with a concentration of accommodation along the hilly shoreline and a general store. American River Rendezvous, the kiosk at the wharf (ⓣ08/8553 7150), provides a bit of a spectacle here with its raucous **pelican feeding** (daily 4.30pm; free). Boats can be chartered for local **fishing and sailing** from the kiosk or direct from Cooinda Charter Services (ⓣ & ⓕ08/8553 7063). *Matthew Flinders Terraces* (ⓣ08/8553 7100, ⓔkaykins@senet.com.au; ❻) is a beautifully situated **motel** with pool and spa; or try the *Wanderers Rest* (ⓣ08/8553 7140, ⓦwww.wanderersrest.com.au; ❼), an upmarket B&B with a quality seafood restaurant. Holiday units include the budget *Casuarina Coastal Units* (ⓣ08/8553 7020; ❸) and the more expensive *Ulonga Lodge* (ⓣ & ⓕ08/8553 7171; ❹), which also has a café.

CYGNET RIVER, at the junction of Playford Highway and the road from Penneshaw, boasts one of the best places to stay on the island: *Koala Lodge* (ⓣ & ⓕ08/8553 9006, ⓦwww.koalalodge.com; ❺), set amidst large gum trees, has personalized en-suite units near the river bank.

The south coast

There are several conservation parks strung out along the exposed south coast. The largest is **Cape Gantheaume**, an area of low mallee scrub supporting prolific birdlife around **Murray Lagoon**, the largest freshwater lagoon on the island (this is where you'll find the ranger station: daily 8am–5pm). The adjacent **Seal Bay Conservation Park** is home to almost six hundred **sea lions**, the third-largest breeding population in Australia. They are unusually tolerant of humans and you can walk quietly among the colony on the beach at Seal

Bay, accompanied by a national park guide (9am–4.15pm, until 7pm during summer holidays; every 15min in summer, every 45min in winter; $12.50; sunset tour $25), or take a stroll on the boardwalk ($9).

Vivonne Bay, with its long, sandy beach and bush setting, is a great place to camp. The beachside **campsite** (toilets, water, barbecues) is privately run ($4), and there's a well-stocked store and bottle shop 1km away on the main South Coast Road. It's safe to swim near the jetty or boat ramp or in the Harriet River, but the bay itself has a dangerous undertow. Between Seal Bay and Vivonne Bay, **Little Sahara** comprises 15km of perfect white-sand dunes rising unexpectedly out of mallee scrub.

The main features of the **Kelly Hill Conservation Park** are the **Kelly Hill Caves**, extensive limestone cave formations (NPWS guided tours daily: 9.30am–3.30pm; in summer until 4pm; $10.50). The tour explores only the largest cave – not the usual damp, bat-filled cavern, but very dry, with a constant temperature of 16°C. The NPWS runs adventure caving tours of three other caves ($26.50; ⓣ08/8559 7231 for details and booking). The eighteen-kilometre return **Hanson Bay Trail** goes from the caves to the sea, passing freshwater lagoons and dune systems: allow at least eight hours – longer, if you're tempted to stop for a swim. *Hanson Bay Sanctuary Homestead* (ⓣ08/8553 2603, ⓦwww.esl.com.au; ❻), just west of the Kelly Hill Conservation Park, is situated in a lovely secluded spot surrounded by bushland with excellent walking trails.

Flinders Chase National Park

Flinders Chase National Park, South Australia's largest, occupies the entire western end of the island. It became a park as early as 1919, and in the 1920s and 1930s koalas, platypuses and Cape Barren geese from the Bass Strait islands (see p.1133) were introduced. The land is mainly low-lying mallee forest, with occasional patches of taller sugar gum trees. The **Flinders Chase Visitors Centre** (daily 9am–5pm; ⓣ08/8559 7235, ⓔflinders.chase@saugov.sa.gov.au; park entry fee $7 per person) is surrounded by open grasslands where large numbers of kangaroos and wallabies graze. Koala signs lead to a glade of trees where you can see the creatures swaying overhead, within binocular range. Follow the **Platypus Waterhole Walk** for 3km to a platypus-viewing area, but be warned that to get a glimpse of the creatures requires endless patience. The winding sealed road through the park will take you to its most spectacular features, the huge and weirdly shaped, rust-coloured **Remarkable Rocks** on Kirkpatrick Point, and the impressive natural formation of **Admirals Arch**, where hundreds of New Zealand fur seals bask around the rocks. At the northern corner of the park, you can go on a guided tour of the 1858 **Cape Borda Lighthouse** (3–5 tours daily; $10.50; ⓣ08/8559 3257, ⓦwww.environment.sa.gov.au/parks/flinderschase/visit).

The main **camping** area is at Rocky River, or there are various **cottages** (❺) throughout the park – bookable through the Flinders Chase Visitors Centre – and several other good places to stay along the South Coast Road just outside the park. *Kangaroo Island Wilderness Resort* (ⓣ08/8559 7275, ⓦwww.austdreaming.com.au; dorms $40, rooms ❻) has large wood cabins set amidst bushland, plus an excellent restaurant – at dusk you can watch the nocturnal animals coming out to feed. Nearby, the *Western KI Caravan Park* (ⓣ08/8559 7201, ⓦwww.westernki.com.au; cabins ❹) is set in an expansive wildlife reserve, where you can camp under the tall gum trees and try to spot koala bears. By staying this end of the island you'll also see the spectacular coastal sights at their best – particularly Remarkable Rocks, which turn a deep orange with the setting and rising sun.

The southeast

Most travellers en route between Adelaide and Melbourne pass through southeast South Australia as quickly as possible. From Tailem Bend, just beyond Murray Bridge some 85km out of Adelaide, three highways branch out. The first, the **Ouyen Highway**, is the quintessential road to nowhere, leading through the sleepy settlements of Lameroo and Pinnaroo to the insignificant town of **Ouyen** in Victoria's mallee country (see p.1026). The second, the **Dukes Highway**, offers a fast and boring route to Melbourne via the South Australian mallee scrub and farming towns of **Keith** and **Bordertown**, before continuing in Victoria as the Western Highway across the monotonous Wimmera (see p.1025). It is, however, well worth breaking your journey to visit **the Coonawarra** and **Naracoorte**, in between the Dukes Highway and the coastal route: the former is a tiny wine-producing area that makes some of the country's finest red wine; the latter is a fair-size town with a freshwater lagoon system that attracts prolific birdlife, and a conservation park with impressive World Heritage-listed caves.

The third option, the **Princes Highway** (Highway 1), is much less direct but far more interesting. It follows the extensive coastal lagoon system of **the Coorong** to **Kingston SE**, and then runs a short way inland to the lake craters of **Mount Gambier**, before crossing into Victoria. There's another possible route on this last stretch – the **Southern Ports Highway** – which sticks closer to the coast, plus a potential detour along the Riddoch Highway into the scenic Coonawarra wine region. Premier Stateliner (Ⓣ08/8415 5555) serves two routes between Adelaide and Mount Gambier, one inland via Keith, Bordertown, Naracoorte, Coonawarra and Penola; the other along the coast via Meningie, Kingston SE, Robe and Millicent. The NPWS free newspaper, *The Tatler*, gives practical details relating to the southeastern coastal parks – pick up the latest copy from the Adelaide office (see p.807), or regional offices en route. Further information can be found at the regional visitor information website at Ⓦwww.thelimestonecoast.com.

Coorong National Park

From Tailem Bend, the Princes Highway skirts Lake Alexandrina and the freshwater Lake Albert before passing the edge of the **Coorong National Park**. The coastal saline lagoon system of the Coorong (from the Aboriginal *Karangk*, meaning long neck) is separated from the sea for over 100km by the high sand dunes of the **Younghusband Peninsula**. This is the state's most prolific **pelican breeding ground**, and an excellent place to observe these awkward yet graceful birds – there's a shelter with seating and a telescope focused on the small islands where some birds breed at Jacks Point, 3km north of Policemans Point on the Princes Highway. Without your own **transport**, one way to see the Coorong is to head off in a 4WD with a local naturalist from Coorong Nature Tours (day-trip $150 from Meningie, $200 from Adelaide; longer two- and three-day trips available; Ⓣ08/8574 0037, Ⓦwww.coorongnaturetours.com). You can also get to the park on a **cruise** from Goolwa (see box on p.847).

There are several designated **camping areas** with shelters, barbecues, toilets, running water (but no showers) and marked walking trails. The Coorong is also good for beach camping: with a permit (see opposite) you can camp anywhere along the beach, but cars must be parked in designated places, and you must bring your own drinking water, which can be collected outside the seldom-manned **Salt Creek NPWS ranger station** on the edge of the park. Elsewhere, **information** and **camping permits** ($6.50 per car) and maps of the park and campsites can be obtained at the national park **headquarters** at 32–34 Princes Highway, Meningie (Mon, Wed & Fri 9am–5pm; ⓣ08/8575 1200), the Melaleuca Information Centre, 76 Princes Highway (Mon–Fri 9am–5pm, Sat & Sun 10.30am–2.30pm; ⓣ08/8575 1278), and most petrol stations on the way to the park including Salt Creek's Shell petrol station, which has an outside notice board and a **café** serving delicious grilled Coorong mullet. There are **caravan parks** at Long Point, Parnka Point, Gemini Downs and 42-Mile Crossing – the only land access to the Younghusband Peninsula. If you're passing by, park your car at the 42-Mile Crossing information area and walk 1km along a sandy 4WD track for great views of the sand dunes and the wild Southern Ocean. This track runs alongside the beach all the way up the peninsula to Barkers Knoll and down to Kingston SE, with camping along the way. If you want to stay in more comfort, there are plenty of motels at the popular fishing centre of **Meningie**, by Lake Albert.

Camp Coorong, run by the Ngarrindjeri Lands and Progress Association, is 10km south of Meningie. This cultural centre attempts to explain the heritage and culture of the Ngarrindjeri Aborigines, once one of the largest groups in South Australia, occupying the land around the Coorong and the lower Murray River and lakes. There's a fascinating **museum** (Mon–Fri 9am–5pm; donation), and you can camp here or in the nearby Bush Reserve ($5 per group) or stay in the well-outfitted **cabins** (booking required on ⓣ08/8575 1557, ⓔnlpa@lm.net.au; ❸). A few kilometres further north is the Ngarrindjeri owned *Coorong Wilderness Lodge*, designed in the shape of a fish (ⓣ08/8575 6001, ⓔkuranga@lm.net.au; camping $10 per car, en-suite cabins ❸). The restaurant serves indigenous meals (booking essential), and if you want to learn more about Ngarrindjeri culture, the owners offer short tours, plus a comprehensive three-day wilderness and cultural tour.

Southern Ports Highway

KINGSTON South East (SE), on Lacepede Bay, is the first town past the Coorong: here the Princes Highway turns inland, while the **Southern Ports Highway** continues along the coast before rejoining the main road at Millicent. As the **Big Lobster** on the highway in Kingston suggests, the town has an important lobster industry: you can buy them freshly cooked at *Lacepede Seafood* by the jetty (daily 9am–6pm) for around $40 a kilo.

Lobsters apart, you're better off continuing down the coast. **ROBE**, on the south side of Guichen Bay, 44km from Kingston, was one of South Australia's first settlements, established as a deep-water port in 1847. After 1857, over sixteen thousand Chinese landed here and walked to the goldfields, 400km away, to avoid the poll tax levied in Victoria. As trade declined and the highway bypassed the town, Robe managed to maintain both dignity and a low-key charm, and during the busy summer period the population of less than eight hundred expands to over eleven thousand. Adelaidians love the place, with its well-preserved nineteenth-century streetscapes and its beach setting surrounded by lakes and bushland; some even drive the 366km for a weekend. Summer is also the season for Robe's other major industry, **crayfishing**. **Tourist information** is available inside the library on the corner of Smiley and Victoria streets (Mon–Fri 9am–5pm, Sat & Sun 10am–4pm; ⓣ08/8768 2465, ⓦwww.robe.sa.gov.au); they have walking and driving maps, and free, limited-time Internet access.

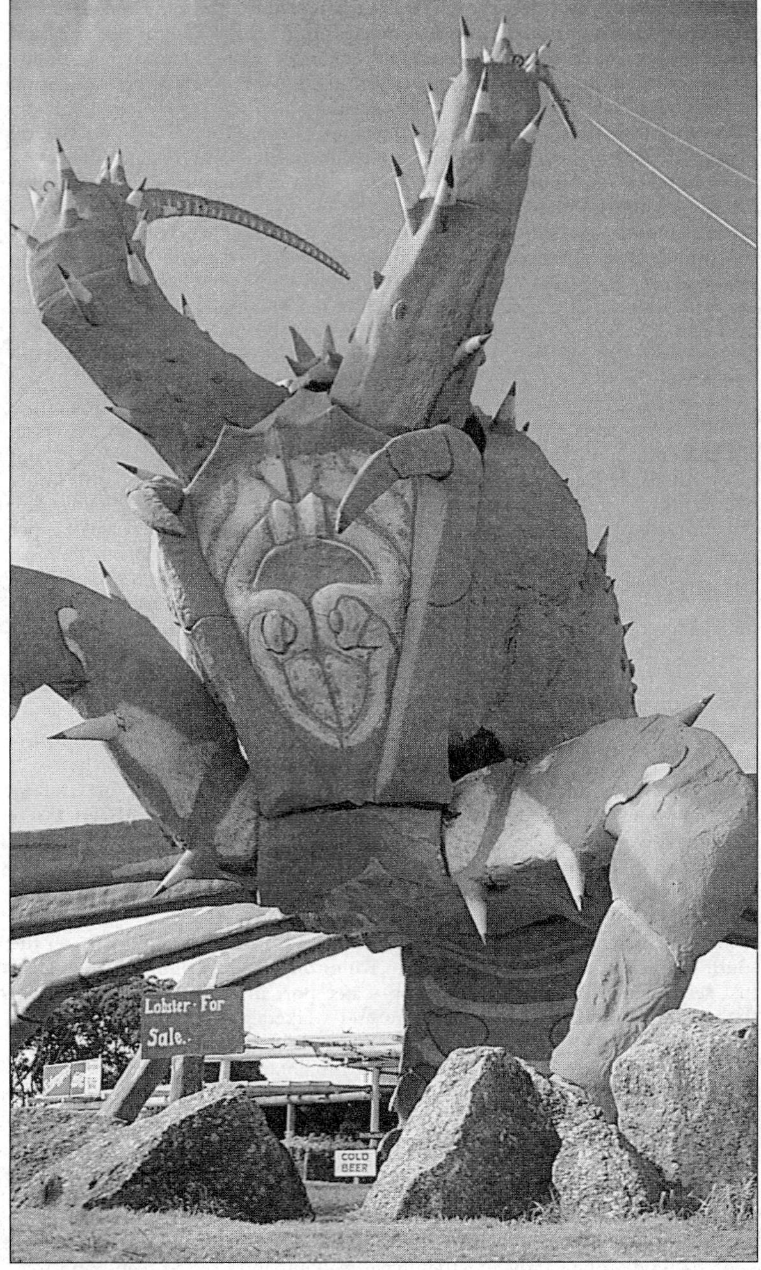

△ Larry the Big Lobster, Kingston

There are dozens of places to **stay**, most of which double up as places to eat. *Robe Hotel*, Mundy Terrace (ⓣ08/8768 2077, ⓕ8768 2495; ❹), is an old stone beachfront hotel with modern budget accommodation and en-suite motel-style rooms with views and spa units; the downstairs bars serve good bistro meals – lots of fish and a vegetarian dish of the day. The charming, ivy-covered *Caledonian Inn* on Victoria Street (ⓣ08/8768 2029, ⓦwww.caledonian.com.au; ❹ including breakfast) was first licensed in 1858 and wouldn't look out of place in an English village – it offers B&B accommodation upstairs or in homely cottages, and serves excellent food. Also on Victoria Street, *Guichen Bay Motel* (ⓣ08/8768 2001; ❹) has good-value, spacious rooms, some with kitchenette, as well as the licensed *Robetown Cottage Restaurant*, which has special crayfish dishes in season. *Sea Vu Caravan Park*, 1 Squire Drive (ⓣ08/8768 2273, ⓦwww.robeseavu.com; cabins ❹), is family-run and close to town, with a swimming beach right by it. The excellent *Bushland Cabins*, set in bushland southeast of the centre on Nora Criena Road (ⓣ08/8768 2386, ⓔbushland@seol.net.au; dorm $18, cabins ❸), has walking trails into the surrounding bush, including a one-kilometre clifftop track into Robe. There's also the award-winning *Robe Long Beach Holiday Park*, on the Esplanade (ⓣ08/8768 2237, ⓦwww.robelongbeach.com.au; cabins ❸). For **meals**, there's excellent café fare, all-day breakfasts and Italian coffee at *Wild Mulberry Cafe*, 46 Victoria St, opposite the Shell garage (daily 8am–5pm). *Robe Seafood and Takeaway*, 21 Victoria St, provides the ubiquitous fish and chips, while for self-caterers, Foodland Supermarket, opposite the Ampol petrol station, is open daily 7.30am–6.30pm, later in summer.

Between Robe and Beachport are four lakes: for part of the way you can take the Nora Criena Drive through **Little Dip Conservation Park**, 14km of coastal dune systems. The drive provides views of Lake Eliza and Lake St Clair before returning to Southern Ports Highway and the former whaling port of **BEACHPORT**, which boasts one of the longest jetties in Australia and many lobster-fishing boats at anchor on Rivoli Bay. Beachport has plenty of **accommodation**. *Bompas*, overlooking the bay at 3 Railway Terrace (ⓣ08/8735 8333, ⓔbompas@bigpond.com.au; dorms $18.50, en-suite rooms ❹), was the town's first licensed hotel in 1879, and is now a pleasing B&B guesthouse with a coffee bar, bistro and **restaurant** downstairs, with Thai, Malay, Italian and Australian dishes. There's also the *Southern Ocean Tourist Park* on Somerville Street, with panoramic bay views (ⓣ08/8735 8153; en-suite cabins ❸). For a snack, try *The Green Room* on Railway Terrace, which also rents out surf gear and golf clubs.

Continuing south on Southern Ports Highway, there are several turn-offs to **Canunda National Park** which has giant sand dunes, signposted coastal walking trails, an abundance of birdlife and camping facilities ($6.50 per vehicle; honesty box). The best place to explore the park is from **SOUTHEND** – you can pick up leaflets detailing the walks from the **National Park Headquarters** just beyond the town (Mon–Fri 8.30am–5pm; ⓣ08/8735 1177). The only **place to stay** apart from the campsites is the *Southend on Sea Tourist Park* on Eyre Street (ⓣ08/8735 6035; on-site vans ❷, cabins ❹). More accommodation is available in the rather ordinary town of **MILLICENT**, 15km to the south, which also has its own **Visitor Information Centre**, 1 Mt Gambier Rd (Mon–Fri 9am–5pm, Sat & Sun 10am–4pm; ⓣ08/8733 3205) and access to the park. The Southern Ports Highway rejoins the Princes Highway at Millicent.

Mount Gambier and around

Set close to the border with Victoria, **MOUNT GAMBIER** is the southeast's commercial centre. The small city sprawls up the slopes of an extinct volcano whose three craters – each with its own lake surrounded by heavily wooded slopes and filled from underground waterways – are perfect for subterranean diving. The **Blue Lake** is the largest of the three, up to 204m deep and 5km in circumference. From November to March it's a stunning cobalt blue, reverting to duller grey in the colder months. There are lookout spots and a scenic drive around the lake, and guided tours are offered by Aquifer Tours (Nov–Jan: daily on the hour 9am–5pm, Twilight Tour at 7pm; Feb–Oct: daily on the hour 9am–2pm; 45min; $6). The second-largest crater holds **Valley Lake** and a Wildlife Park (daily 7am–dusk; free), where indigenous animals range free amid native flora; there are lookouts, walking trails and boardwalks. West of the city centre, on Jubilee Highway West, is the extensive complex of underground caverns at **Engelbrecht Cave** (guided tours hourly 10am–3pm, check times in winter; 45min; $6). You can **dive** here in limestone waterways under the city, though you'll need a CDAA (Cave Divers Association of Australia) qualification to tackle these dark and dangerous waters. Contact the Mount Gambier NPWS office at 11 Helen St (Ⓣ08/8735 1177, Ⓦwww.adelaide.net.au/~ecave) for further information.

The centrepiece of Mount Gambier itself is **Cave Gardens**, a shady park surrounding a deep limestone cavern with steps leading some way down; the stream running into it eventually filters into the Blue Lake. At the rear of the park the municipal offices contain the Civic Centre, library and a small theatre. Fronting the park is the former Town Hall and the **Riddoch Art Gallery** (Tues–Fri 10am–5pm, Sat 10am–2pm; free) whose focus is the impressive Rodney Gooch collection of Aboriginal art from the Utopia region of the Northern Territory. In the same building, Studio One sells the work of local artists (Wed–Sun 11am–3pm). For more information on Mount Gambier's attractions, head for the excellent **Lady Nelson Victory and Discovery Centre**, on Jubilee Highway East (daily 9am–5pm; exhibition $10; Ⓣ08/8724 9750, Ⓦwww.mountgambiertourism.com.au), where the ecology, geology and history of Mount Gambier are explored from Aboriginal and European perspectives.

The CDAA (see above) issues permits for snorkelling in the crystal-clear waters of **Piccaninnie Ponds Conservation Park** and **Ewans Pond Conservation Park**, both south of Mount Gambier near Port Macdonnell. At Piccaninnie Ponds, a deep chasm with white-limestone walls contains clear water that is filtered underground from the Blue Lake – it takes five hundred years to get here. East of the city is **Umpherston Sinkhole** (open access), also known as the Sunken Garden, since it contains Victorian-era terraced gardens – they are floodlit at night when possums come out to feed.

Practicalities

Mount Gambier has heaps of places to **stay**, with motels lining the highway either side of town. The pick of them is the *Barn Motel & Apartments*, on Nelson Road (Ⓣ08/8726 8366, Ⓦwww.barnmotel.com; motel ❸, apartments ❺). *The Jail*, on Margaret Street (Ⓣ08/8723 0032, Ⓦwww.jailbackpackers.com; dorms $20), was built in the 1860s and is now a Heritage-listed building. The last inmates left in 1995 and you can stay in the original cells behind locked doors (some even have a solitary loo in the corner) or in the simple three-bed dorms. Meals are provided in the large common room, which also has a bar, and there are laundry facilities and Internet access. The central *Jens Hotel*, 40 Commercial St (ⓣ08/8725 0188, ⓔjens.town.hall.hotel@alhgroup.com.au; ❸), is a classic, wide-balconied old boozer with cheap bar and bistro meals, late opening hours and en-suite accommodation. Dining options are plentiful – pick of the bunch is the unassuming-looking *Sage and Muntries*, Commercial Street West, serving up fine Modern Australian cuisine. Alternatively, try the licensed *Café Capri Restaurant*, 53 Gray St (Mon–Sat 8.30am–10 or 11pm), or the award-winning *Caffe Belgiorno* on Percy St which specializes in classic Italian pizza and gourmet pasta. The town's **cinema** is next door in the Oatmill Building. The public library at the end of Watson Terrace (Mon–Fri 9am–4pm) has free limited-time Internet access.

Heading on to Melbourne from Mount Gambier, V/Line (ⓣ13 61 96) has a daily **bus** service via Portland, Warrnambool, Geelong and Ballarat.

The Coonawarra wine region

Directly north of Mount Gambier, the **Riddoch Highway** heads through the low-key and pretty **Coonawarra wine region**, and past some World Heritage-listed caves at Naracoorte, eventually linking up with the Dukes Highway at Keith. Most wineries are located on a ninety-kilometre stretch of highway between Penola and Padthaway. The region is renowned for the quality of its reds, which have been compared to those of Bordeaux. The soil and drainage is ideal, classic Terra Rossa over limestone, and the climate is perfect – and as the weather is not really variable from year to year, the wines are consistently good. Premier Stateliner (ⓣ08/8415 5544) stops daily at Penola and Naracoorte on its Adelaide to Mount Gambier inland service. Penola Coonawarra Tour Service (ⓣ08/8737 2779) offers restaurant transfers and winery tours around the area.

Penola

Twenty-two kilometres north of Mount Gambier, **PENOLA**, gateway to the Coonawarra wine region, is a simple but dignified country town of well-preserved nineteenth-century architecture. For information, head for **Penola Coonawarra Visitor Centre** in the historic Mechanics Institute Building (Mon–Fri 9am–5pm, Sat 10am–5pm, Sun 9.30am–4pm; ⓣ08/8737 2855, ⓕ8737 2251), which also houses a display featuring John Riddoch, pioneer of Coonawarra's vineyards, and hands out the free *Historic Penola and Coonawarra* map with details of the region's wineries.

Beside the 1857 Cobb & Co booking office (now a restaurant), **St Joseph's Catholic Church** looks like something out of an Italian village, a world away from the very modern **Mary MacKillop Interpretative Centre** (daily 10am–4pm; ⓣ08/8737 2092; $3.50) next door. Sister Mary MacKillop (1842–1909) was Penola's most famous resident, and Australia's first would-be saint – in 1995 Pope John Paul II pronounced her "Blessed", the last stage before full sainthood. MacKillop set up a school, created her own teaching method and, with Father Julian Tennyson Woods, co-founded the Sisters of St Joseph of the Sacred Heart, a charitable teaching order that spread throughout Australia and New Zealand. Dramatic episodes of alleged disobedience and excommunication give her story a certain oomph. There's an informative display in the centre, with Barbie-doll lookalike "nuns on the run" and dressed-up dummies in the original school room. Across the fields stand the National Trust-listed cottages of **Petticoat Lane**, where many of Mary's poverty-stricken students lived.

There are backpacker **beds** at the comfortable and centrally located *McKay's Trek Inn*, 38 Riddoch St (ⓣ0407 391 886; dorms $20), which caters for long-stay grape-pickers, so it's worth booking ahead. *Penola Caravan Park* on South Terrace (ⓣ08/8737 2381) has good-value on-site vans (❷) and en-suite cabins (❸). The focus of the town is the friendly, National Trust-listed *Heywood's Royal Oak Hotel*, 31 Church St (ⓣ08/8737 2322, ⓕ8737 2825; ❹), with four-poster doubles and some twin rooms.

The best place to **eat** is *Heywood's Royal Oak Hotel*, which has a beautiful beer garden and an excellent bistro. Otherwise, *Sweet Grape*, 48 Church St (daily 8.30am–4.30pm), dishes up affordable café favourites and international dishes. On the Riddoch Highway, *Hermitage Café and Wine Bar*, attached to Wetherall Winery (daily 11am–9pm; ⓣ08/8737 2122; bookings advised for dinner), focuses on local and organic produce.

Coonawarra Township

There isn't much to what is called **COONAWARRA TOWNSHIP**, a settlement that developed to house and service the adjacent Wynns Coonawarra Estate (see box), but it does make a good base if you're touring local vineyards. Cottage **accommodation** here includes *Coonawarra Country Cottages* (ⓣ08/8736 3304, ⓕ8736 3016; ❺), a quaint tin-roofed bungalow just around the corner from the old Coonawarra school, now *Nibs Bistro and Grill* (ⓣ08/8736 3006; licensed and BYO; bookings on Sat night recommended). Just out of town, on the Riddoch Highway, is the upmarket motel complex of *Chardonnay Lodge* (ⓣ08/8736 3309, ⓦwww.chardonnaylodge.com.au: ❻), set amongst lawns and rose gardens, with a swimming pool and an attached cafe-restaurant.

Naracoorte Caves

Midway between Penola and Padthaway, the **Naracoorte Caves Conservation Park** protects a World Heritage-listed system of limestone caves. Your first point of call should be the **Wonambi Fossil Centre** (daily 9am–5pm, summer until sunset; ⓣ08/8762 2340) which gives an insight into the area's archeological significance – important fossils of extinct Pleistocene megafauna,

Coonawarra wineries

There are twenty Coonawarra wineries that do tastings, most open Mon–Fri 9am–5pm, Sat & Sun 10am–4pm (for more information visit the Coonawarra Wine Association website at ⓦwww.coonawarra.org). A few favourites (arranged in order as if you were driving along the Riddoch Highway from Penola towards Coonawarra Township) include **Hollick Wines,** in a tiny restored 1870s slab wood and stone cottage; **Balnaves**, with its innovative architecture; **Leconfield**, with very well-regarded Cabernet Sauvignons and, unusually, a female winemaker; and **Zema Estate**, a small family-run winery with Italian roots and an old-fashioned, hands-on process. **Wynns Coonawarra Estate**, west of the Riddoch Highway on Memorial Drive at Coonawarra Township, is Coonawarra's longest-established (1896) and best-known winery. Continuing back on the Riddoch Highway towards Padthaway, **Brands** is an old family of winemakers who still make a sell-out Shiraz from the original vineyard, planted in 1896. The down-to-earth **Redman** family winery has also been making red wine for generations, focusing exclusively on just three varieties. Beyond Redman, the modern winery complex of **Rymill**, attractively located on Clayfield Road, west of the Riddoch Highway, includes a glass-walled tasting area overlooking the winery, and platforms upstairs for viewing the testing lab.

including giant kangaroos and wombats, were discovered here in the Victoria Fossil Cave in 1969. A walking trail from here leads to another notable feature, the **Bat Centre**, the only place in the world where you can watch bats inside a cave with the help of infrared remote control cameras.

The caves themselves are spread out over the Conservation Park: **Alexandra Cave** has the prettiest limestone formations (tours at 9.30am & 1.30pm; 30min), while **Victoria Fossil Cave** is popular for its fossils (10.15am & 2pm; 1hr). You can guide yourself through the **Wet Cave** (9am and 5pm), named after the very wet chamber at its deepest part; an automatic lighting system switches on as you walk through. **Admission fees** are $11 for one cave, $17.50 for two or $24 for all of them. There are also **adventure caving** tours in several other caves (2hr novice tours $27.50; 3hr advanced tours $200 per party, maximum six people; overalls can be rented for $5; lights and helmets supplied).

You can **camp** within the park ($19 per car), where facilities include powered sites, hot showers and even a free laundry, or stay in **dorms** at *Wirreanda Bunkhouse* (Ⓣ08/8762 2340; $14). More comfortable is the rural tranquillity at the *Cave Park Cabins* (Ⓣ08/8762 0696, Ⓕ8762 3180; ❸), only 1.5km from the caves. For **meals**, the licensed *Bent Wing Cafe* by the Fossil Centre is surprisingly sophisticated, dishing up everything from Greek salads to char-grilled kangaroo fillets with native plum chutney.

On the highway 12km west of the caves, the town of **NARACOORTE** is a small regional centre with a supermarket (open daily) and several places to eat and stay. *Naracoorte Hotel Motel*, 73 Ormerod St (Ⓣ08/8762 2400; ❸) has motel rooms and cheap meals; *Naracoorte Backpackers* (Ⓣ08/8762 3835, Ⓦwww.naracoortebackpackers.com.au; dorms $20) offers tours to the caves, has bikes for rent and 24-hour Internet access. A ten-minute walk north of town at 81 Park Terrace, *Naracoorte Holiday Park* (Ⓣ08/8762 2128, Ⓦwww.naracoorteholidaypark.com.au; cabins ❸) is set in a shady spot by a creek, close to a swimming lake.

The Riverland

The **Riverland** is the name given to the long irrigated strip on either side of the **Murray River** as its meanders for 300km from Blanchetown to Renmark near the Victorian border. The Canadian Chaffey brothers had already developed successful irrigation settlements in California when they were invited to Australia to look into possibilities for the Murray, establishing a colony at **Renmark** in 1887. The Riverland's deep red-orange alluvial soil – helped by extensive irrigation – is very fertile, making the area the state's major supplier of oranges, stone fruit and grapes. Fruit stalls along the roadsides add to the impression of a year-long harvest, and if you're after **fruit-picking work** it's an excellent place to start; contact the Harvest Labour Office on Riverland Drive in Berri (Ⓣ1800 062 332). The area is also Australia's major **wine-producing** region, though the hi-tech wineries here mainly make mass-produced wines for casks and export. Many are open to visitors, but their scale and commercialism make them less enjoyable than, say, the McLaren Vale's (see p.843).

The **Sturt Highway**, the major route between Adelaide and Sydney, passes straight through the Riverland. Premier Stateliner runs a twice-daily service along the highway from Adelaide to Renmark via Blanchetown, Waikerie, Barmera and Berri, and also goes daily (except Sat) to Loxton. Between

Waikerie and Renmark all the **towns** feel pretty much the same, with a raw edge, little charm or sophistication, and a yobbo culture (most apparent on drunken Friday nights). Each town has only one hotel, and these huge and mostly graceless **community hotels** are a feature of the Riverland: owned and run by the town, their profits are ploughed back into the hotel or channelled into the community, generally into sporting groups.

Blanchetown to Waikerie

BLANCHETOWN, 130km east of Adelaide, is the first Riverland town, and the starting point of the Murray's lock and weir system, which helps maintain the river at a constant height between the town and Wentworth in New South Wales (see p.376). Eleven kilometres west of town, **Brookfield Conservation Park**, a gift to South Australia from the Chicago Zoological Society, is home to the endangered **southern hairy-nosed wombat**; the creatures also thrive at nearby *Portee Station* (ⓣ08/8540 5211, ⓦwww.portee.com.au; ❻), a 200-square-kilometre sheep-grazing property where you can stay in the 1873 riverfront homestead. A range of tours (enquire for details) include river trips in a small boat to look at the prolific birdlife, and a 4WD station tour where you'll see wombats close up.

Following the river from Blanchetown, it's 36km directly north to **MORGAN**, one of the most attractive of the Riverland towns. At the height of the river trade between 1880 and 1915 Morgan was one of South Australia's busiest river ports, transferring wool from New South Wales and Victoria onto trains bound for Adelaide; parts of its mainly red gum and jarrah **river wharf** remain intact. You can wander through the riverfront park, past the old train station and the stationmaster's building, now a **museum** (Tues 2–4pm, on other days knock on the caretaker's door at the back of the museum or call ⓣ08/8540 2136), and up onto the wharves overlooking moored houseboats on the river to bushland beyond. The well-preserved nineteenth-century streetscape of **Railway Terrace**, the main street, sits above the old railway line and wharf, dominated by the huge Landseer shipping warehouse. There's standard **accommodation** in two adjacent old pubs: the *Terminus Hotel* (ⓣ08/8540 2006; ❷) and the *Commercial* (ⓣ08/8540 2107; ❸). A more comfortable option is the *Morgan Colonial Motel*, 1 Federal St (ⓣ08/8540 2277, ⓔmorganmotel@bigpond.com; ❹). You can also stay at the *Morgan Riverside Caravan Park* (ⓣ08/8540 2207, ⓔmorgancp@riverland.net.au; cabins ❸), in a great spot right in town by the river. For **food**, try the pubs or *Morgan Pizza Bar*, 17 Railway Terrace (ⓣ08/8540 2107; pizzas Fri–Sun from 5pm only, fish and chips from 5pm all week).

From Morgan the river takes a sharp bend east, meandering south to **WAIKERIE**; it's 32km from Morgan to Waikerie on a riverside road, with a free ferry crossing at Cadell. A less attractive drive from Blanchetown bypasses the river loop, reaching Waikerie by heading 42km northeast along the Sturt Highway. Waikerie is at the heart of the largest citrus-growing area in Australia; the first thing you notice is a huge complex owned by **Nippies** that takes up both sides of a street, allegedly the largest fruit-packing house in the southern hemisphere. A good base for **fruit-picking** work is *Nomads-on-Murray* (ⓣ08/8583 0211 or 1800 665 166; dorms $20, rooms ❷), on the Sturt Highway about 30km east of Waikerie.

Loxton

Some 35km east of Waikerie, the Murray makes another large loop away from the Sturt highway, with **LOXTON** at its southernmost reach, before twisting back north to Berri (see p.866). Leaving the highway at Kingston-on-Murray, you pass the **Moorook Game Reserve**, a large swamp fringed with river red gums and home to many waterbirds. In Loxton itself, the **Tourist & Art Centre**, at Bookpurnong Terrace (Mon–Fri 9am–5pm, Sat 9.30am–noon, Sun 1–4pm; ⓣ08/8584 7919, ⓦwww.loxtontourism.com.au), acts as an agent for Stateliner and can fill you in on local attractions such as the riverside **Loxton Historical Village** (Mon–Fri 10am–4pm, Sat & Sun 10am–5pm; $8), a replica of an early-twentieth-century Riverland town. Altogether more compelling is the **Katarapko Game Reserve**, opposite Loxton, where Katarapko Creek and the Murray have cut deep channels and lagoons, creating an island. Access from Loxton is by water only – perfect for canoeing and observing birdlife; to **camp**, you need a permit from the NPWS, 28 Vaughan Terrace, Berri (ⓣ08/8595 2111). *Loxton Riverfront Caravan Park*, Packard Bend (ⓣ08/8584 7862, ⓦwww.lrcp.com.au; cabins ❸), is a peaceful spot opposite the game reserve, with canoes for rent ($11 per hour, $55 per day).

Back in town, the only **accommodation** option is the overly glitzy *Loxton Hotel-Motel*, East Terrace (ⓣ08/8584 7266, ⓦwww.loxtonhotel.com.au; ❹), where you can get good bistro **meals** (noon–2pm & 6–8pm only) and all-day breakfasts on Sundays. Alternatively, cheap meals and free **Internet access** are available at the friendly *Loxton Club* (ⓣ08/8584 7353) at 27 Bookpurnong Terrace.

Barmera

If you haven't followed the river to Loxton, **BARMERA**, on the shores of Lake Bonney, is the next major stopping point along the highway. Its claims to fame are varied and dubious: at **Pelican Point**, on the lake's western shore, there's an official **nudist beach** (and a nearby nudist resort with camping, and on-site vans ❸; ⓣ08/8588 7366, bookings essential), while every June, the **South Australian Country Music Festival and Awards** are held in the lovely old Bonney Theatre. For more about the music awards, and **tourist information** in general, contact the Barmera Visitor Information Centre, Barwell Avenue (Mon–Fri 9am–5.15pm, Sat 9am–noon, Sun 10am–1pm; ⓣ08/8588 2289). The best bet for **accommodation** is the *Barmera Lake Resort Motel*, Lakeside Drive (ⓣ08/8588 2555, ⓔlakeresort@riverland.net.au; ❹), overlooking the lake, with a pool, laundry, games room, barbecue and *Cafe Mudz*, a bright and attractive café-wine bar serving breakfast, lunch and evening meals in an Australian country style. The extensive *Lake Bonney Holiday Park* is close by on Lakeside Drive (ⓣ08/8588 2234; cabins & cottages ❸). Eating options include the *Pagoda Chinese Restaurant* (ⓣ08/8588 3167; closed Tues). Riverland Leisure Canoe Tours, Thelma Road (ⓣ08/8588 2053), rents out **kayaks** for $15 per day, two-person **canoes** for $25 per day, and arranges day and overnight guided tours (phone for details).

Just under 20km from town towards Morgan, you pass a bend in the river dubbed **Overland Corner**, the former crossing point for the overland cattle trade heading to New South Wales. Opened here in 1859, the restful and delightfully isolated *Overland Corner Hotel* (ⓣ08/8588 7021, ⓔochotel@dodo.com.au; ❷ including continental breakfast), serves food (Tues–Sun) and has basic, old-fashioned **accommodation** – look, too, at the flood level from the incredible 1956 flood, practically up to the roof. You can camp and bushwalk in the adjacent **Herons Bend Reserve**, where an eight-kilometre trail (around 3hr) takes you past old Aboriginal campsites; a pamphlet detailing sites on the walk is available from the pub.

The Murray River

The **Murray River** is Australia's Mississippi – or so the American author Mark Twain declared when he saw it in the early 1900s. It's a fraction of the size of the American river, admittedly, but in a country of seasonal, intermittent streams it counts as a major river and, like the Mississippi, the Murray helped open up a new continent. Fed by melting snow from the Snowy Mountains, and by the Murrumbidgee and Darling rivers, the Murray flows through the arid plains, reaching the Southern Ocean southwest of Adelaide near Goolwa (see p.846). With the Darling and its tributaries, it makes up one of the biggest and longest watercourses in the world, giving life to Australia's most important agricultural region, the **Murray–Darling basin**. For much of its length it also forms the border between New South Wales and Victoria, slowing as it reaches South Australia, where it meanders through extensive alluvial plains and irrigation areas. Almost half of South Australia's water comes from the Murray: even far-off Woomera in the Outback relies on it.

Historically, the Riverland was densely populated by various **Aboriginal peoples** who navigated the river in bark canoes, the bark being cut from river red gums in a single perfect piece – many trees along the river still bear the scars. The Ngarrindjeri people's Dreamtime story of the river's creation explains how Ngurunderi travelled down the Murray, looking for his runaway wives. The Murray was then just a small stream, but, as Ngurunderi searched, a giant Murray cod surged ahead of him, widening the river with swipes of its tail. Ngurunderi tried to spear the fish, which he chased to the ocean, and the thrashing cod carved out the pattern of the Murray River during the chase.

The explorers **Hume** and **Hovell** came across the Murray at Albury in 1824. In 1830 **Sturt** and **Mitchell** navigated the Murray and Darling in a whale boat, Sturt naming it after the then Secretary of State for the Colonies (coincidentally, *Murrundi* was the Aboriginal name for part of the river). Their exploration opened up the interior, and from 1838 the Murray was followed as a **stock route** by "overlanders" taking sheep and cattle to newly established Adelaide. In 1853 the first **paddle-steamer**, the *Mary Ann*, was launched near Mannum. Goods were transported far inland, while wool

Berri

The **Big Orange** sets the scene in **BERRI**, announcing the fact that this is the town where the trademark orange juice comes from, and many travellers are drawn here between October and April by the prospect of **fruit-picking work**. The river is the main attraction, of course, with scenic river walks above coloured sandstone cliffs, as well as the **Wilabalangaloo Flora and Fauna Reserve** (Mon & Thurs–Sun 10am–4pm, daily during school holidays; $4), a native animal enclosure and a local history museum on the waterfront. You can also climb up the Big Orange for a good view of the Riverland, or watch the juice itself being produced in vast quantities at Berri Ltd. For more information, head for the **tourist office** on Riverview Drive (Mon–Fri 9am–5pm, Sat & Sun 10am–4pm; ⓣ08/8582 5511).

In terms of places to **stay**, in town the *Berri Resort Hotel*, Riverview Drive (ⓣ08/8582 1411, ⓦwww.berriresorthotel.com; ❺), is a huge riverfront pub that grows ever tackier and ritzier – though it's not a bad place to stay, with a swimming pool, tennis courts and good food. The excellent *Berri Backpackers* (ⓣ08/8582 3144; dorms $18, rooms ❶), 1km out of town towards Barmera on the Old Sturt Highway opposite the *Berri Club*, is the place to stay if you're fruit-picking, but is popular, so book ahead. Amenities include free bikes, Internet access, a sauna, swimming pool, gym, tennis and volleyball courts, plus two tree houses and a houseboat. For **food**, *Berri Canton Palace*, 1 Worman St (ⓣ08/8582 2818; closed Tues lunch), is a good Chinese restaurant; while the was carried to market. River transport reached its peak in the 1870s, but by the mid-1930s it was virtually finished, thanks to the superior speed of the railways.

Seeing the river

The best way to appreciate the beauty of the Murray – lined with majestic river red gums and towering cliffs that reveal the area's colourful soils – is to get out on the water. Several old **paddle-steamers** and a variety of other craft still cruise the Murray for pleasure – try the *Murray Princess* (Fri 6.30pm to Sun 2pm; $578 per person; 5-day package $1230 per person also available; ⓣ08/9206 1122, ⓦwww.captaincook.com.au), based at **Mannum**, one-hour's drive east of Adelaide (or take the Murray Bridge Passenger Service; Mon–Fri daily; ⓣ08/8532 2633). Other cruises from Mannum include sporadic trips on the paddle-steamer *Marion* (book at Mannum Tourist Information Centre, 67 Randell St; ⓣ08/8569 1303), and regular outings on the MV *Proud Mary* (morning tea cruises Mon 11am; 1hr 15min; 2-, 3- and 5-night cruises also available; ⓣ08/8231 9472, ⓦwww.proudmary.com.au, or book at Mannum Tourist Information Centre).

Renting a **houseboat** is a relaxing and enjoyable way to see the river. All you need is a driving licence, and the cost isn't astronomical if you get a group of people together and avoid the peak holiday seasons. A week in an eight-berth houseboat out of season should cost around $1200, in a four-berth $900. The South Australian Tourism Commission (ⓣ1300 655 276, ⓦwww.southaustralia.com) has pamphlets giving costs and facilities; they can also book for you; alternatively, contact the Houseboat Hirers Association (ⓣ08/8396 5266, ⓦwww.houseboat-centre.com.au).

A more hands-on way to explore the wetlands and creek systems is in a **canoe**, while the flat country, short distances between towns and dry climate are perfect for cycling – **bikes** can be rented at various hostels along the way.

For other Murray River accounts, see Goolwa (p.846), and the Victoria and New South Wales chapters (p.971 and p.353 respectively).

Mallee Fowl Restaurant, on the Sturt Highway 4km west of Berri (ⓣ08/8582 2096; lunch and dinner Thurs–Sat) serves excellent barbecue-style meals in a busy and characterful setting of Australiana.

Renmark

RENMARK, on a bend of the Murray 254km from Adelaide, is the last major town before the New South Wales border. As with the other Riverland towns, the main attraction of Renmark is the river and its surrounding wetlands, and there's not a great deal to see in the town apart from **Olivewood**, an interesting National Trust property on the corner of Renmark Avenue and 21st Street (Thurs–Mon 10am–4pm, closed Tues & Wed; $4). The former home of the Chaffey brothers, the Canadians who pioneered the irrigation and settlement of the Murray region, a palm-lined drive leads through a citrus orchard and olive trees to the house, which is a strange hybrid of Canadian log cabin and Australian lean-to. The attached museum is the usual hotchpotch of local memorabilia, unrelated to the Chaffeys or their ambitious irrigation project. The **Chaffey Theatre** on 18th Street (ⓣ08/8586 1800) has an impressive performing arts centre hosting amateur and professional plays, films and concerts.

The riverfront **Renmark Paringa Visitor Centre** on Murray Avenue (Mon–Fri 9am–5pm, Sat 9am–4pm, Sun 10am–4pm; ⓣ08/8586 6704) can book **river cruises**. The PS *Industry* – one of the few wood-fuelled paddle-steamers left on the Murray – is moored outside and cruises once a month (1hr

30min; $15; contact the tourist centre for times and bookings). Daily cruises are run by Renmark River Cruises (Ⓣ08/8595 1862, Ⓦwww.riverland.net.au/renriv/), which offers both motorized dinghy expeditions through the local backwaters (2hr; $59) and trips aboard the *Big River Rambler* (daily except Mon & Fri 2pm; 2hr; $28). It leaves from Renmark wharf and heads upstream for 7km past colourful river cliffs. The UNESCO-backed **Bookmark Biosphere Reserve**, a few kilometres from Renmark, manages nine thousand square kilometres of land. To explore this region by land or river, Bookmark Guides (details from the visitor centre) offer a variety of day and overnight tours from 4WD bush safaris to wine tasting.

The obvious **place to stay** in Renmark is the landmark *Renmark Hotel/Motel* (Ⓣ08/8586 6755, Ⓦwww.renmarkhotel.com.au; ❹), overlooking the river. Built in 1897 and given its facade in the 1930s, the hotel has been thoroughly modernized and has a large bistro, outdoor swimming pool and spa. The *Renmark Riverfront Caravan Park*, on Patey Drive 2km east of town (Ⓣ08/8586 6315; on-site vans ❷, en-suite cabins ❹), has an idyllic setting along 1km of riverfront. *Renmark Kebab & Pizza* (Tues–Sun 11am–8/9pm) at 31 Renmark Avenue is good for Greek-style food and pizzas; for Chinese, try *The Golden Palace*, 114 Renmark Ave (closed Tues).

The mid-north

Stretching north of Adelaide up to Port Augusta (see p.874) and the south Flinders Ranges is the fertile agricultural region known as the **mid-north**. The gateway to the region is the town of **Kapunda**, only 16km northwest of Nuriootpa in the Barossa Valley (see p.834), which became the country's first mining town when copper was discovered here in 1842. Kapunda can also be reached as a short detour from the **Barrier Highway** en route to Broken Hill in New South Wales, a route that continues through the larger mining town of **Burra**, and then to **Peterborough**, the self-proclaimed "frontier to the Outback". The centre of the mid-north's wine area, **Clare**, is 45km southwest of Burra, on the **Main North Road**, the alternative route to Port Augusta. Heading north to Port Augusta on **Highway 1** for the Northern Territory or Western Australia, you'll pass through the ugly lead-smelting city of **Port Pirie**, and from there on to the south Flinders Ranges.

Getting around the area by **bus** is problematic – while most of the major towns have transport links to Adelaide, there are virtually no buses between towns, however close they might be. The Greyhound Australia Adelaide to Broken Hill service goes via Burra, while the Mid North Passenger Service (Ⓣ08/8823 2375; no service Mon & Fri) from Adelaide takes in Burra, Peterborough and the main Clare Valley settlements. In addition, the Barossa to Adelaide Passenger Service (Ⓣ08/8564 3022) has a weekday service from Gawler – which can be reached by train – to Kapunda. All interstate buses to Darwin or Perth take Highway 1 through Port Pirie.

Kapunda and Burra

At the beginning of the 1840s South Australia was in serious economic trouble, until the discovery of **copper** at Kapunda in 1842 rescued the young colony and put it at the forefront of Australia's mining boom. The early finds at Kapunda were, however, soon overshadowed by those at **Burra**, 65km north: the Burra "**Monster Mine**" was the largest in Australia until 1860, creating fabulous wealth and attracting huge numbers of Cornish miners. The boom ended as suddenly as it began, as resources were exhausted – mining finished at Burra in 1877 and Kapunda in 1878.

Heading to **KAPUNDA** from the Barossa, the landscape changes as vineyards are replaced by crops and grazing sheep. As you come into town, you're greeted by a colossal sculpture of a Cornish miner entitled *Map Kernow* – "son of Cornwall". A place that once had its own daily newspaper, eleven hotels and a busy train station is now a rural service town, pleasantly undeveloped and with many old buildings decorated with locally designed and manufactured iron lacework.

If you have your own transport, you can follow a ten-kilometre **heritage trail** that takes in the ruins of the Kapunda mine, with panoramic views from the mine chimney lookout; details are available from the **Kapunda Information Centre** on Hill Street (Mon–Fri 9am–5pm, Sat 10am–1pm, Sun noon–3pm; ⓣ08/8566 2902, ⓦwww.kapunda-light.com). On the same street, the **Kapunda Museum** (June–Aug Sat & Sun 1–4pm; Sept–May daily 1–4pm; $5; ⓣ08/8556 2286) occupies the mammoth Romanesque-style former Baptist church. The best time to come to Kapunda is during the **Celtic festival**, held on the weekend before Easter, when Celtic music, bush and folk bands feature at the four pubs.

For **accommodation**, there's a colonial-style B&B at *Ford House*, 80 Main St (ⓣ & ⓕ08/8566 2280; ❹); the *Sir John Franklin Hotel*, also on Main Street (ⓣ08/8566 3233; ❷), has simple, clean rooms and is the most popular pub for inexpensive **meals**. Campers are catered for at *Kapunda Tourist and Leisure Park*, Montefiore St (ⓣ08/8556 2094, ⓦwww.kapundatouristpark.com; cabins ❸).

Burra

In 1851 the mine at **BURRA** was producing five percent of the world's copper, but when the mines closed in 1877, it became a service centre for the surrounding farming community, and nowadays takes advantage of its mining heritage to attract visitors. Plenty of money has been spent restoring and beautifying the place (even to the extent of topping up pretty, gum-shaded **Burra Creek** to ensure that it's always flowing), and the town's well-preserved stone architecture, shady tree-lined streets, great country pubs and upmarket home stores, art-and-craft and antiques shops, make it a popular weekend escape between March and November, before it gets too hot. The creek divides the town in two: the mine is in the north, while the southern section has the shopping centre, based around **Market Square**, where you'll also find the **Burra Visitors Centre** (daily 9am–5pm; ⓣ08/8892 2154, ⓦwww.visitburra.com). Its main function is to issue the **Burra Passport Key** to people driving the eleven-kilometre **heritage trail** ($15 per person, plus $5 deposit); the key gives you access to eight sites en route – and for an extra $9 you gain entry to all four museums (see below).

Heading north along Market Street you come to the **Burra Monster Mine** site, where there are extensive remains and interpretive walking trails, as well as the **Morphetts Enginehouse Museum** (Tues, Weds & Thurs 1pm–3pm, Sat & Sun 1pm–4pm; $4.50). Continuing north, the **Bon Accord Mine Complex** on Linkson Street (same opening hours as above; $4.50) was a short-lived failure compared to its hugely successful neighbour; there's a scale model of the monster mine and a shaft and mining relics on view. Other key-pass places in the northern section of the town are the old **police lock-up and stables, Redruth Gaol**, and **Hampton**, a now-deserted private township in the style of an English village. Back in the main part of the town, the pass gets you entry to the **Unicorn Brewery Cellars** (1873) and the fascinating two remaining **miners' dugouts**: by 1851, because of a housing shortage nearly two thousand people were living in homes clawed out of the soft clay along Burra Creek. There are two further museums: the **Market Square Museum** (daily 1–3pm; $3.50) was a general store, post office and home from 1880 to 1920; the **Paxton Square miners' cottages** on Kingston Street (Sat & Sun 2–4pm; $4.50) are decorated in 1850s style.

You can **stay** in other miners' cottages in Paxton Square, all overseen by the office in the former Methodist Chapel at the end of the row (ⓣ08/8892 2622, ⓕ8892 2508; ❹). There are 32 in all, although on weekends from mid-March to October they get quickly booked out by Adelaidians on short winter breaks. It can get very cold in the winter, but the cottages have fireplaces (free wood provided) and plenty of blankets, as well as modern kitchens; breakfast is available at the office. Other accommodation in town includes *Burra View House*, Mount Pleasant Road (ⓣ08/8892 2648, ⓕ8892 2150; ❺), and the tree-surrounded *Burra Motor Inn*, Market Street (ⓣ08/8892 2777; ❹), with contemporary-style rooms backing onto a creek, an indoor swimming pool and a well-priced restaurant. All the **hotels** in town have rooms, and most provide breakfast – try the down-to-earth *Commercial Hotel*, 22 Commercial Rd (ⓣ08/8892 2010; ❸). If you have a **tent** you could try the *Burra Caravan Park*, Bridge Terrace (ⓣ08/8892 2442; on-site vans ❶), in a pretty spot beside the creek, a couple of minutes' walk from the shops. *The Burra Hotel*, 5 Market St, does excellent **meals**, and there are several good cafés in town, notably *Polly's Kitchen* on Commercial Road (daily 9am–5.30pm), which has good coffee and a range of light meals, including a credible version of an authentic Cornish pasty.

The Clare Valley

The wine industry in the **Clare Valley**, west of the Barrier Highway between Kapunda and Burra, was pioneered by Jesuit priests at **Sevenhill** in the 1850s. There's no tourist overkill here: bus trips are not encouraged, and because it's a small area with just over thirty wineries, you can learn a lot about the local styles of wine (the area is especially recognized for its fine Rieslings). Often, too, you'll get personal treatment, with the winemaker presiding at the cellar door. In the cool uplands of the North Mount Lofty Ranges, Clare Valley is really a series of gum-fringed ridges and valleys running roughly 30km north from **Auburn** to the main township of **Clare**, on either side of the Main North Road. Huge sheep runs were established here in the nineteenth century and the area, which is prime merino land, still has a pastoral feel; several stations can be visited. There are also beautiful old villages and some well-preserved mansions, plenty of charming B&B accommodation and some superb restaurants attached to wineries. The big event of the year is the **Clare Valley Gourmet Weekend**, held in May at local wineries.

Between Clare and Auburn, the old railway line has been transformed into the **Riesling Trail**, a 27-kilometre cycling path; to cycle one way takes about two hours. Mountain **bikes** can be rented from Clare Valley Cycle Hire, 32 Victoria Rd, Clare ($22 per day; ⓣ08/8842 2782), which will deliver to anywhere in the valley.

Auburn to Watervale

Heading north through the valley, **AUBURN**, 120km from Adelaide, is the first settlement, small and village-like, which began life as a halfway resting point for wagons carrying copper ore from Burra to Port Adelaide. The *Rising Sun Hotel* (ⓣ08/8849 2015, ⓔrising@capri.net.au; ❹ including breakfast) is one of many great **pubs** in the valley, first licensed in 1850. It has small bedrooms in the hotel and mews-style accommodation in old stone stables, as well as a very affordable modern Australian menu and an appropriately long wine list. A more luxurious place to stay is *Dennis Cottage* (ⓣ08/8277 8177, ⓦwww.denniscottage.com.au; ❻), which has a spa, as well as paraphernalia associated with C.J. Dennis, the popular poet who was born here in 1876. *Tatehams*, on the Main North Road (ⓣ08/8849 2030, ⓔtatehams@chariot.net.au; ❻) is a very distinguished dining/guesthouse combination. There are two small **wineries** nearby: **Grossets** (Wed–Sun 10am–5pm) and **Mount Horrocks** (Sat & Sun 10am–5pm).

The next small village is **LEASINGHAM**, where you can camp or stay at *Leasingham Village Caravan & Cabins* (ⓣ08/8843 0136; cabins ❸), a popular place for **grape-pickers** from March to May. An attached restaurant serves simple, inexpensive weekend lunches (Thurs–Sun lunch and dinner; licensed or BYO). You can taste wines nearby at **Tim Gramp Wines** (Sat & Sun 10.30am–4.30pm). There are four small wineries at **WATERVALE**, 2km north: of them, **Crabtree of Watervale**, North Terrace (daily 11am–5pm, occasionally closed midweek), is one of the most enjoyable in the valley.

Mintaro

From Leasingham, you can turn off east to **MINTARO**, a village whose tree-lined streets and cottages are beautifully preserved from the 1850s, when it was a resting place for bullock teams travelling from the Burra copper mines. There's no general store or petrol supply here: the emphasis is on upmarket cottage accommodation, popular with Adelaide weekenders. The focus of the village is the *Magpie and Stump Hotel*, which is particularly lively on Sunday afternoons. Opposite, at **Reilly's Wines** (daily 10am–5pm), housed in an 1856 Irish bootmaker's building, you can taste vintages produced since 1994 from Watervale grapes; the **restaurant** here serves Italian food, with mains around $20 (dinner Mon & Fri–Sun; ⓣ08/8843 9013), and can also book **accommodation** in the nearby *Mintaro Pay Office Cottages* (❻ including breakfast). *Mintaro Mews*, on Burra Street (ⓣ08/8843 9001, ⓕ8843 9002; ❺), has upmarket B&B accommodation (no children) with an indoor heated pool and spa; Saturday nights are package only ($110 per person), including a four-course meal in the atmospheric restaurant. Southeast of the town lies the Georgian-style *Martindale Hall* (Mon–Fri 11am–4pm, Sat & Sun noon–4pm; $7; ⓣ08/8843 9088, ⓦwww.martindalehall.com; ❼ including breakfast); the mansion featured in the 1975 film *Picnic at Hanging Rock*. For $195 per person you can stay overnight and enjoy a four-course meal, cooked breakfast and the full run of the place – but it's freezing in winter.

Heading northwest from Mintaro to Sevenhill (see below) takes you through the rolling hills of the Polish Hill River area. About 8km along, **Paulett Wines** (daily 10am–5pm) has fabulous views, its verandah overlooking the "river" – a dry creek for eleven months of the year.

Sevenhill and the Spring Gully Conservation Park

The village of **SEVENHILL** has the valley's oldest winery, **Sevenhill Cellars**, on College Road (Mon–Fri 9am–5pm, Sat 10am–5pm). This is still run by a religious order and mainly makes sacramental wine, though the brothers have diversified into table wines, sweet sherry and port, doing everything from growing the grapes to bottling. The sandstone building has a tasting room with lots of character and history, and there's an old Catholic church in the grounds. Nearby, on College Road, *Thorn Park Country House* (Ⓣ08/8843 4304, Ⓦwww.thornpark.com.au; ❽) occupies an 1850 stone and slate building in a gorgeous setting; it offers **B&B** and a beautifully indulgent dinner – but at a price ($220 per person; B&B only costs $160 per person). *Sevenhill Hotel*, on the Main North Road, is a classic country pub serving popular inexpensive meals (daily except Sun).

To the west of the Main North Road, **Spring Gully Conservation Park** has the last remnant of red stringybark forest in South Australia. There are steep gullies, waterfalls, wildlife and, in spring, lovely wild flowers; free camping is allowed outside the fire-ban season (usually early December to the end of April). Nearby, attached to boutique wineries signposted from Sevenhill, are two excellent restaurants serving gourmet meals from deliciously fresh local produce at moderate prices. **Eldredge Wines**, Spring Gully Road (tastings daily 11am–5pm; lunch Thurs–Sun; restaurant bookings Ⓣ08/8842 3086) is located in a small farmhouse fronting a dam; **Skillogalee Winery** (daily 10am–5pm; Ⓣ08/8843 4311; lunch bookings advised) occupies a wonderful spot set against the backdrop of a clunking windmill, bushclad hill and vineyards, with meals and tastings by the fire in the 1850s cottage or on the verandah.

Clare

CLARE itself is a surprisingly ordinary town, with few concessions to the weekend visitors who pour in from Adelaide: it consists primarily of Main North Road, and virtually everything is closed on Sunday. The **tourist information** office, in the town hall at 229 Main North Rd (daily 10am–4pm; Ⓣ08/8842 2131, Ⓦwww.clarevalley.com.au), provides an excellent free visitors' guide and can book accommodation and restaurants. **Wineries** around town include Knappstein Wines, 2 Pioneer Ave (Mon–Fri 9am–5pm, Sat 11am–5pm, Sun 11am–4pm), an ivy-covered sandstone building with a verandah and an open log fire in winter; Jim Barry, a friendly, family-run place on the Main North Road (Mon–Fri 9am–5pm, Sat & Sun 9am–4pm); and Leasingham, 7 Dominic St (Mon–Fri 8.30am–5pm, Sat & Sun 10am–4pm), a large commercial winery established in 1893.

Some local sheep stations are open for tours, and **farmstays** are also available: pick of the bunch is *Bungaree Station* (Ⓣ08/8842 2677, Ⓕ8842 3004; BYO-bedding shearers' quarters $22, cottages B&B ❸), a working merino station 12km north of Clare on the Main North Road; one of the oldest and largest properties in the district, it has its own church as well as a swimming pool. *Geralka Rural Farm* (Ⓣ08/8845 8081, Ⓕ8845 8073; on-site vans ❷, units ❹) is a sheep and cereal property 25km north of Clare which offers weekend **farm activity tours** aimed at families (Sun & daily during school holidays 1.30pm, or by appointment; 2hr; $8, children $4).

Places to **stay** in Clare itself are all along Main North Road. Overlooking the hills, 2.5km south of the centre, is *Clare Valley Motel* at no. 74 (Ⓣ08/8842 2799, Ⓕ8842 3121; ❹); the *Clare Central Motel* is at the north end of town at no. 325 (Ⓣ08/8842 2277, Ⓕ8842 3563; ❺); both have pools. The best of the hotels are the friendly family-run *Bentleys*, 191 Main North Rd (Ⓣ08/8842 1700, Ⓕ8842 3474; motel rooms ❹), which also has a bistro; and the *Taminga Hotel* (Ⓣ08/8842 2808; ❶), offering basic pub rooms. You can **camp** 4km south of town at *Clare Caravan Park* on Main North Road (Ⓣ08/8842 2724, Ⓦwww.clare-caravan-park.com.au; on-site vans ❶, en-suite cabins ❸), which also has a swimming pool. Besides the pubs, you can **eat** well during the day at *Clare Fine Foods*, 279 Main North Rd (closed Sun), a small deli serving gourmet rolls and sandwiches and dishes such as Caesar salad or pasta; the espresso coffee here is the best in town. There's **Internet access** at Caprice Clare ($5 per 30min) in the Village Plaza on the Old North Road.

Port Pirie

From Clare, the Main North Road heads to Jamestown, 65km north. To the west, a road branches off towards Crystal Brook, where there's a hikers' lodge at Bowman Park providing basic overnight shelter for hikers on the Heysen Trail. From here it's not far up Highway 1 to **PORT PIRIE**, the fourth-largest urban centre in South Australia. An ugly industrial city, its skyline is dominated by smelters' chimneys: as the nearest seaport to Broken Hill, the lead and zinc smelting industry here dates back to the discovery of the rich vein of lead-silver-zinc found there in 1883. The **Port Pirie Tourism and Arts Centre** on Mary Elie Street (Mon–Fri 9am–5pm, Sat 9am–4pm, Sun 10am–3pm; ⓣ08/8633 8700 or 1800 000 424) has interpretive brochures and self-guided walking tours of the town if you're interested in **historic buildings** and the smelting industry. If not, there's little else to keep you here. Beyond Port Pirie, Telowie Gorge and Mount Remarkable National Park, in the southern stretches of the Flinders Ranges (see p.887), are within easy reach.

Outback South Australia

. . . a country such as I firmly believe has no parallel on earth's surface.

The explorer Charles Sturt, 1844.

Leaving behind the civilized south, the wild and vast expanses of South Australia's Outback can take some adjusting to. With little in the way of obvious destinations, the experience is the thing – few areas of the planet feel quite so isolated or hostile to human habitation. All routes radiate from Port Augusta, the commercial centre for the far north, and though buses cover the highways, elsewhere you'll need to have your own transport or take a tour. To the west, the **Eyre Highway** runs 950km to the border of Western Australia; the journey can be broken by taking a detour around the coast of the Eyre Peninsula, which has fine, sandy beaches and excellent fishing. Once past Ceduna, on the eastern edge of the Nullarbor Plain, there's little beyond you and the desert. The Indian Pacific train traverses the Nullarbor further inland, through even more extreme desolation. North, the **Stuart Highway** and **New Ghan rail line** link Port Augusta with the Northern Territory through 890km of progressively drier scenery, where regular markers along the roadside record the distance covered, as well as how far there is to go. **Prohibited zones** surround much of the highway, though about the only places you'd want to leave it anyway are at **Woomera** and the opal-mining town of **Coober Pedy** with its unusual underground dwellings; both lie outside the military areas and the boundaries of Aboriginal land.

All other roads north follow the route taken by the legendary but now defunct **Old Ghan** to the country towns of **Quorn** and **Hawker**, where routes diverge. To the northeast lie the **Flinders Ranges**, a series of spectacularly beautiful gorges and geological curiosities, most famous of which is Wilpena Pound. Continuing northeast will take you along the **Strzelecki Track** to **Innamincka** and beyond to Queensland. Heading due north takes you to **Marree**, at the head of the **Birdsville** and **Oodnadatta tracks**. Travel beyond Maree is not for the faint-hearted, but worth the effort for those wishing to experience the eerie silence and emptiness of Lake Eyre and the sheer isolation of the Dalhousie Hot Springs and the Simpson Desert.

A **Desert Parks Pass** is required for legal entry into Innamincka Regional Reserve, Lake Eyre National Park, Witjira National Park and the Simpson Desert: $90 per vehicle allows twelve months' unlimited access and use of campsites, with copies of the detailed NPWS *Desert Parks Handbook* and Westprint Heritage Maps' surveys thrown in. Passes are available from agencies throughout the north, or by post from the Port Augusta NPWS (PO Box 78, Port Augusta 5700; ⓣ1800 816 078). To find out about **road conditions** in these regions, call ⓣ1300 361 033, or check out the Desert Access **website**, ⓦwww.desertaccess.com.au.

Many roadhouses and fuel pumps have **EFTPOS** facilities. **Water** is vital: with few exceptions, lakes and waterways are dry or highly saline, and most Outback deaths are related to dehydration or heatstroke – bikers seem particularly prone. As always, stay with your vehicle if you break down. Summer **temperatures** can be lethally hot, winters pleasant during the day and subzero at night; rain can fall at any time of year, but is most likely to do so between January and May. RAA **road maps** are good but lack topographical information, so if you're spending any time in the north, pick up the excellent Westprint Heritage Maps and the cluttered *Landsmap Outback: Central and South Australia*. The South Australia Tourist Association issues a road map of the Flinders Ranges, but it's inadequate for walking; **hikers** traversing the Flinders on the Heysen Trail need topographic maps of each section and advice from the nearest NPWS office. Conditions of **minor roads** are so variable that maps seldom do more than indicate the surface type; local police and roadhouses will have current information.

Port Augusta and the west

How you see **Port Augusta** depends on where you've come from. Arriving from the Outback, the town's trees, shops and hotels can be a real thrill, but compared with the southeast of the state, it's pretty basic. However, being a transport hub has saved the town from destitution, and plans are afoot to make more of its seaside location. While you're deciding where to head next, there are a few things to see in town and some good **bushwalking** country around **Mount Remarkable**, at the tail end of the Flinders Ranges. The direct route west from Port Augusta, the **Eyre Highway**, begins its daunting journey towards Western Australia across the top of the **Eyre Peninsula**, but going this way you'll see virtually nothing. An alternative route detours around the peninsula's coastline (via the Lincoln and Flinders highways) before rejoining the highway at **Ceduna** on the brink of the **Nullarbor Plain**, while the rail line parallels the coast some 100km inland.

Port Augusta

Unkindly dubbed "Porta Gutter" by Adelaide's smart set, who paint dire pictures of a town rife with petty crime, **PORT AUGUSTA** sits at the tip of the Spencer Gulf and on the edge of everywhere else. Despite the name, the docks closed long ago and more recent employment mainstays such as the power station and railways were drastically scaled down during the 1980s – the former rail buildings have been converted to Employment Service offices.

During summer, you should make the most of the small **swimming beach** at the end of Young Street to escape the dust and heat – the old wooden pile crossing, now a footbridge, and a hundred-year-old jetty, all that remains of the port, make good perches for fishing. The chief source of **information** is the **Wadlata Outback Centre**, at 41 Flinders Terrace (Mon–Fri 9am–5.30pm, Sat & Sun 10am–4pm; ⓣ08/8641 0793, ⓦwww.portaugusta.sa.gov.au). This has a very helpful visitor information centre, an attractive café and an interesting permanent **exhibition** ($8.95). Audiovisual technology, didgeridoo loudspeakers and a giant model of Akurra, the Dreamtime snake, are deployed to explain Aboriginal bushcraft and Flinders Ranges' creation myths, while geological and mining displays give a scientific perspective. Human interest is provided by tales of the hardships suffered by nineteenth-century explorers Eyre and Sturt, plus short films (shown in continuous loops) which give a compelling account of early European settlement. You can also book a wide variety of **tours** from the centre including plane trips, fishing expeditions, 4WD tours and even golf. Internet access is also available ($5 for 30min).

The **Homestead Park Pioneer Museum**, east of the town centre on Elsie Street (daily 9am–4pm; $2.50), is centred around a log-built sheep station building. The 135-year-old homestead has been moved 100km from Yudnapinna and is filled with period furnishings, heaps of farm and railway machinery, plus animals, birds and a photographic museum in a vintage railway carriage.

Flanking the north side of town on the Stuart Highway is the new and ambitious **Australian Arid Lands Botanic Garden** (Mon–Fri 9am–5pm, Sat & Sun 10am–4pm; free entry, but it's worth taking the 1hr guided tour for $5.95, winter 11am, summer 9.30am), a showcase and research centre for regional and international desert flora, the slow-growing nature of which means that the garden's full splendour has yet to be realized, although a closer look will reveal a surprising wealth of species. The rain-gathering, solar-powered information centre, shop and café underline the ideals of the garden as an ongoing ecological project.

Practicalities

The centre of town overlooks the east side of the Spencer Gulf, more like a river where it divides the town. The **airport** (ⓣ08/8642 3100) is down Caroona Road, 5km west of the centre – taxis travel into the centre (ⓣ08/8642 4466). The **bus terminal**, serving Greyhound and Stateliner, is at 21 Mackay St (all services ⓣ08/8642 5055); **trains** pull in at Stirling Road (ⓣ08/8642 6699). Shops, banks and the post office are clustered along narrow Commercial Road. If you need **maps and information** beyond what's available at the Outback Centre, try the helpful **NPWS** at 9 Mackay St (ⓣ08/8648 5300) for park maps, info and permits; if you're a member, the RAA, at 91 Commercial Rd (ⓣ08/8642 2576), provides very good road maps. **Cars** can be rented from Budget, at 16 Young St (ⓣ08/8642 6040).

There are two central budget places to **stay**: *The Bluefox Lodge*, on National Highway One (ⓣ08/8641 2960, ⓔbluefoxlodge@ozzie.net; dorms $16.50, rooms ❸); and the friendly *Flinders Hotel*, 39 Commercial Rd (ⓣ08/8642 2544; dorms $14, rooms ❷). Alternatively, there are several **motels**, such as the comfortable *Poinsettia*, 24 Burgoyne St (ⓣ08/8642 2411; ❸), along the highway just across the gulf. The town's closest **campsites** are near here too, including the *Shoreline Caravan Park* at the end of Gardiner Avenue (☎08/8642 2965; cabins ❸) and the *Big 4 Holiday Park*, junction of Eyre and Stuart highways (☎08/8642 6455; cabins ❸).

Hotels are the place for **meals and entertainment**, but opening hours are vague and often depend on demand, which can be almost nonexistent during the week. The *Transcontinental*, Port Augusta's weekly rag, will have details of anything happening around town. Seafood addicts should head for the fish shop at the seaward end of Marryatt Street, which sells fresh fish and fish and chips; for Chinese, try the *King Po* restaurant at the other end of the street, near the Outback Centre. You'll find a few cafés for lunch and snacks along Commercial Road, while *Barnacle Bill's*, on Victoria Parade, 3km southeast of the town centre, has pretty good-value seafood and all the salad you can eat. The central *Commonwealth Hotel* on Commercial Road boasts an à la carte menu at weekends, while the *Hotel Augusta*, by the Westside Beach, serves meals with a fine view of sand, mangroves and the distant Flinders Ranges.

Mount Remarkable National Park

Mount Remarkable National Park lies in two sections, encircled by a ring road that starts 45km southeast of Port Augusta and runs via Wilmington, Melrose and Port Germein. The larger **western** slice contains Mambray Creek and Mount Cavern, and connecting tracks run from them to Alligator Gorge; Mount Remarkable and sections of the Heysen Trail rise to the **east** behind Melrose. If time is short, there are easy walks in **Alligator Gorge**, while the **Mount Cavern circuit** is considerably harder – both make good day-trips from Port Augusta. The only **campsite** with facilities is at Mambray Creek, but bush camping is allowed elsewhere with permission from the NPWS (☎08/8634 7068); you should also consult them in hot weather, as the park may be completely closed if there's a high risk of fire. Stateliner **buses** go daily to Mambray Creek, and three times weekly to Wilmington and Melrose.

Alligator Gorge, Melrose and Mount Remarkable

The eleven-kilometre dirt road from Wilmington to **Alligator Gorge** ($6.50 per car) ends at a picnic area perched on a spur above two bush campsites at Teal and Eaglehawk dams. Stairs descend into the gorge, with several walking options once you reach the gorge floor, including a three-hour circuit north to the ranger's office past the rippled **Terraces** (the remains of a fossilized lake shore), or an hour's trek south along the creek through a tight red canyon alive with frog calls, moss gardens and echoes (this section sometimes gets flooded, though there are usually enough stepping stones to avoid wet feet). For longer hikes down to Mambray Creek you'll need maps and approval from the NPWS.

Nearby, the quiet former copper-mining town of **MELROSE** has two hotels and a pleasant creekside **caravan park** (☎08/8666 2060; dorms $15, cabins ❸). **B&B** is available at *Bluey Blundstone's Blacksmith Shop* (☎08/8666 2173; ❹), carefully restored to its original 1865 condition. When the proprietor isn't producing decorative wrought-ironwork he serves cakes in a coffee shop at the back of the forge. The unremarkable summit of **Mount Remarkable** can be reached in three hours via the **Heysen Trail**, starting a couple of kilometres north of town from the showground.

Telowie Gorge, Mambray Creek and Mount Cavern

The small and appealing **Telowie Conservation Park** lies to the south off the Port Germein to Murray Town road. A very short path leads between the gorge walls, but, unless you're properly equipped for a long hike over to Wirrabara Forest and the Heysen Trail, you'll get more of a flavour of the area by camping along the creek and looking for rare wallabies at dawn and dusk.

The access track to **Mambray Creek** is east off the highway, halfway between Port Germein and the Wilmington road. Here you'll find a **campsite** (with water and toilets) and the national park headquarters. Mambray Creek is the start of some serious walks, either into the north part of the park along the **Battery Track** and **Alligator Creek**, or on the tough but shorter **Mount Cavern** circuit, which follows the path anticlockwise along the Black Range, giving spectacular views. The descent is down a loose stone slope held together by grasstrees, then entering cool woodland at Mambray Creek Gorge, where you might be able to get close to large groups of emus.

The Eyre Peninsula

Far from the rigours of the true Outback, and long appreciated by Adelaidians as an antidote to city stress, the **Eyre Peninsula**'s broad triangle is protected by the **Gawler Ranges** from the arid climate further north. The area began to be farmed in the 1880s, fishing communities sprang up at regular intervals and iron ore, discovered around 1900, is still mined around **Whyalla**. The detour **around the coast** passes imposing scenery and superlative **surfing** and **beach fishing**, especially where the Great Australian Bight's elemental weather hammers into the western shore – a chance to give your senses a workout before dealing with the Nullarbor's deadening horizons. Stateliner **buses** from Port Augusta run either across the top of the peninsula to Ceduna, or via Whyalla down the east coast to **Port Lincoln** at the southern tip, so you'll need your own transport to tackle the west side. Major **car rental** companies have outlets at both Whyalla and Port Lincoln which, if time is limited, are only fifty minutes by air from Adelaide. Note that locals don't rate Eyre Peninsula **tap water** as worth drinking; bottled water and filters are readily available in supermarkets.

Whyalla and the east coast

First visible an hour from Port Augusta as a smudge of grey over Long Sleep Plain, **WHYALLA**, the state's second most important city and headquarters of its heavy industry, isn't the prettiest of places. One Steel has its massive **steelworks** here (tours Mon, Wed & Sat 9.30am; 2hr; $8; book through the information centre) and tankers queue offshore to fill up at Santos' oil and gas refinery. Until it closed in 1978, the **shipyard** produced a few famous vessels, the first being the *Whyalla*, which now guards the northern entrance to town, having been dragged 2km from the sea in a complicated and expensive manoeuvre. The accompanying **information centre** and **maritime museum** (ⓣ08/8645 8900, ⓔvisitor.centre@whyalla.sa.gov.au; Mon–Fri 9am–5pm, Sat 9am–4pm, Sun 10am–4pm; $8 including ship tour) is largely occupied by a huge model of the oil refinery, as well as more relevant displays of shipping history. From the southwest, Whyalla presents a much greener aspect - at the junction of Broadbent Terrace and Playford Avenue an old aerodrome site has been landscaped into a series of ponds to recycle stormwater.

The highway curves through the old town under the name of Darling Terrace; you'll find a **post office**, **banks**, a **bus station** (ⓣ08/8645 9911), hotels and shops around the junction with Forsyth and Patterson streets, all periodically covered in (harmless) red fallout from the steelworks' mysterious pellet plant. **Accommodation** options include the *Foreshore Caravan Park* on Broadbent Terrace (Ⓣ08/8645 7474, Ⓦwww.whyalla-foreshore-caravan-park.com; cabins ❸) and *Derham's Motel* on Watson Terrace (Ⓣ08/8645 8877, Ⓦwww.derhamsforeshore.com.au; ❺), both a ten-minute walk from the centre along a surprisingly attractive beach, with Hummock Hill mercifully obscuring the view of the steelworks; people and pelicans find good fishing off the jetty. Otherwise, try your luck at one of the hotels: *Spencer* on Forsyth Street (Ⓣ08/8645 8411; ❸) has rooms, good food and weekend music. For **food**, seafood at *Spagg's*, 26 Patterson St, makes a welcome change from counter meals; after eating, walk past the rows of fifty-year-old workers' homes to the top of Hummock Hill for a view of the industrial complexes by night.

Beyond Whyalla, the east coast is an unassuming string of sheltered beaches and villages nestled beneath towering grain silos, the sort of places you could drive through without a second glance or else get waylaid beachcombing for a week. **COWELL** is known for its whiting and as the world's largest source of black "nephrite" jade, though not much of it is in evidence, since it's largely exported rough. **Arno Bay**, **Port Neil** and the larger **Tumby Bay** all boast clean, quiet beaches, good fishing and a range of accommodation – diversions include sundry museums and even a worm farm.

Port Lincoln

A tuna port and resort town built on a hillside above Boston Bay, **PORT LINCOLN** has the busiest atmosphere of anywhere on the peninsula. Its harbour is dotted with trawlers, and the main seafront streets of Tasman Terrace and Liverpool Street are full of eateries and far-from-genteel taverns. There's a **tourist information centre** here too (daily 9am–5pm; Ⓣ08/8683 3544 or 1800 629 911, Ⓦwww.visitportlincoln.net), between the post office and shopping mall; Stateliner **buses** (Ⓣ08/8682 1288) terminate a couple of streets away on Darling Terrace.

Porter Bay, until recently a swamp just south of town, has been transformed into a **marina** which has drawn many of the boats and some of the life away from the old town. The development includes a large, modern **leisure centre** (Mon–Fri 6am–9pm, Sat, Sun & holidays 9am–6pm; Ⓣ08/8682 3833). Entering town from the north, the Lincoln Highway (which later becomes Tasman Terrace and then London Street) affords splendid views of Boston Bay and presents you with myriad motel **accommodation** options, such as the luxurious *Limani Motel* (Ⓣ08/8682 2200, Ⓕ8682 6602; ❺). At the highway's far end lie the terraced tent sites of *Kirton Point Caravan Park* (Ⓣ08/8682 2537, Ⓦwww.kirtonpointcaravanpark.com.au; cabins ❸).

Most of Port Lincoln's attractions are underwater. You can get bait and tackle from any service station and **fish** off the town jetty, or for heavier game fishing contact Sea Charters (Ⓣ08/8682 2425), which can also take you on a cruise to **Dangerous Reef** for spotting seals, birdlife and sharks. The seas off Lincoln were once rated as the best place in the world to see **great white sharks** – footage for *Jaws* was filmed here – but trawling and hunting since the mid-1970s have placed this little-understood fish on the endangered species list. If this doesn't put you off **diving** – or if you just need advice on good places to fish or arrange a boat charter – contact Got One at 80 Tasman Terrace (Ⓣ08/8683 0021).

Around Port Lincoln

Lincoln National Park, just south of Port Lincoln, covers a rough peninsula of sandy coves, steep cliffs and mallee scrub, which is home to the discreet rock parrot. The NPWS at 75 Liverpool St (Ⓣ08/8688 3111) can supply maps and advice on road conditions. There's similar scenery 32km south at **Whalers Way**, a privately-owned stretch of road for which you'll need to collect a permit and key from the information centre in Port Lincoln ($25, plus $3 key deposit); the name derives from the whaling station which once operated at Cape Wiles – relics are stacked up around the gate. The power of the Southern Ocean is memorably demonstrated at **Cape Carnot**, in the southern section of the park, where giant waves and frosty blue surf force their way through blowholes which sigh as they erupt in sync with the swell.

Coffin Bay National Park, an hour's drive west from Port Lincoln, comprises a landscape of dunes and saltmarsh, mostly accessible only by 4WD, though parts are open to other types of vehicle – consult the NPWS in Port Lincoln before visiting. You'll be rewarded by isolation, sand sculptures at Sensation and Mullalong beaches, and the quality of the fishing. Semicircular stone walls on the northern shore are **Aboriginal fish traps** – fish were chased in at high tide and then the gaps in the side blocked with nets as the water receded. If you don't have your own 4WD, Great Australian Bight Safaris (Ⓣ08/8682 2750, Ⓦwww.greatsafaris.com.au) offers various day-trips ($60–$150), as well as longer camping and fishing adventures.

The picturesque setting of the town of **COFFIN BAY** is worth a look, though perhaps not during school holidays, when the caravan park (Ⓣ08/8685 4170; on-site vans ❷, cabins ❸) and abundant holiday cottages are full to bursting. A stroll along the coastal "Oyster Walk" takes you past the original fishermen's shacks, now mostly summer houses, and reveals a wealth of bird and plant life – a taste of Coffin Bay National Park to the west.

The west coast

To catch the best of the west coast and the townships along the way, you'll need to detour off the main road between Coffin Bay and Ceduna. The region's coastal communities are an unlikely mix of conservative farmers and "alternative" surfies who come to ride the endless succession of strong, hundred-metre-long crests rolling into Waterloo Bay at **ELLISTON**, one of the state's most highly regarded **surf beaches**. Bold **murals** at the Community Hall between the café and campsite address local themes – including a long-suppressed incident when Aboriginal people were driven over the cliffs. South of Venus Bay, rocks have been hollowed by the sea to form the **Talia Caves**, but the lengthy beach is more compelling, though camping is prohibited. Turning to the coast about 20km north of Port Kenny, you pass the strangely flared **Murphy's Haystacks**, a group of low granite monoliths that look like giant mushrooms. Pushing on to **Point Labatt** brings you to

The Acraman meteorite

In the mid-1980s a band of red earth from 600-million-year-old deposits in the Flinders Ranges was bafflingly identified as coming from the Gawler Ranges, 400km away. Investigations and satellite mapping suggested that 35-kilometre-wide **Lake Acraman** in the Gawler Ranges was an eroded **meteorite crater**, while Lake Gairdner and fragmented saltpans (such as Lake Torrens, see p.882) further east were set in ripples caused by the force of the strike. Estimates suggest that to have created such a crater the meteorite must have been 4km across; the mystery band in the Flinders was dust settling after impact. Though there is fossil evidence of animal life prior to this event – notably the Ediacaran fauna (see p.1193) – recent research indicates that the Acraman meteorite may well have killed it all. It's certainly true that the ancestors of almost all species living today evolved after this impact.

mainland Australia's only colony of **fur seals** – binoculars or a telephoto lens help to distinguish mother seals teaching pups to swim from the torpid, bulkier males basking on the rocks. Then it's back to the highway at **Streaky Bay** – the only place on the west coast that has a real centre – and then to drier country as you approach Ceduna and the Nullarbor.

The Eyre Highway and Gawler Ranges

Taking the **Eyre Highway** directly across the top of the peninsula from Port Augusta ensures an easy crossing to Ceduna, speeding past the mines at **Iron Knob** and dry scrub populated by green ring-necked parrots. Unusual geology appears around Wudinna in the form of isolated granite mounds (inselbergs) of various shapes and sizes. The largest, **Mount Wudinna**, 10km to the northeast, is second only to Uluru (Ayers Rock; see p.703) in monolithic magnitude, while 30km southwest lies **Ucontichie Hill**, whose curved natural formations include a **wave rock** similar to Hyden's in Western Australia (see p.753).

Iron Knob can be the start of forays along dirt tracks into the **Gawler Ranges**, before rejoining the highway at Wirrulla. While you might not need a 4WD, it's a remote area that requires advance preparation and advice from the NPWS. The ranges are low, rounded volcanic ridges coloured orange by dust, with occasional speckled boulders poking through a thin grass cover, and it's worth frightening the sheep and pink Major Mitchell cockatoos by walking up one of the peaks for a closer look. *Mount Ive Homestead* (Ⓣ08/8648 1817; ❷), 135km west of Iron Knob and right in the heart of the Ranges, has fuel, information and **accommodation** in basic rooms, plus camping space, but don't turn up unannounced. The track into the ranges passes **Lake Gairdner**, largest of the Gawler's **salt lakes**, with the ruins of Pondanna Homestead on a lonely plain at its southern end.

Ceduna and the Nullarbor Plain

You know where you are in **CEDUNA**: all the shops from camping store to supermarket are unambiguously named and a large signpost in the centre gives distances to everywhere between Perth and Port Augusta. Despite being small enough to walk around in twenty minutes, there's no lack of **caravan parks**, **banks** or **service stations**. It's a punishing 1200km west from here to the next town of any note, so this is the place to fill up the tank – not surprisingly competition for your custom is fierce, with almost every brand of fuel on offer and some places even handing out discount cards for use at their pumps along the way. The *Foreshore Van Park* on South Terrace (Ⓣ08/8625 2290; cabins ❸) and the *Ceduna Foreshore Hotel-Motel* on O'Loughlin Terrace (Ⓣ08/8625 2008 or 1800 655 300; ❹) are right next to the jetty – you can fish for whiting on the turn of the high tide. Before your early-morning start – it's a long way to anywhere – call in at the **information centre** on Poynton Street (Mon–Fri 9am–5.30pm, Sat & Sun 9am–5pm; Ⓣ08/8625 2780, Ⓦwww.ceduna.net) and the NPWS on McKenzie Street (Ⓣ08/8625 3144) for the latest on the Nullarbor's attractions. Incidentally, it almost never rains on the plain, and there's always a charge for **water**, which has to be distilled from underground reserves – so carry your own.

The Nullarbor Plain

Nullarbor may not be strictly correct Latin for "treeless", but it's an apt description of the plain which stretches flat and infertile for over 1200km across the Great Australian Bight. Taking the **train** brings you closer to the dead heart than does the **road**, which allows some breaks in the monotony of the journey to scan the sea for southern right whales and visit at least one Aboriginal site. From Ceduna to the Western Australian border it's 480km, which you can easily cover in under five hours if you want; Daliesque fridges standing along the highway in the early stages of the drive are actually makeshift mailboxes for remote properties. The last chance to catch some waves is at **Cactus Beach/ Point Sinclair** south of **Penong**, though its popularity took a dive after a surfer was killed by a great white here in 2000. Even for non-surfies it's worth the drive through white dunes, green shrubbery and blue lagoons to watch the extraordinary wave formations; there's a **campsite** with firewood provided (but no drinking water) and a basic store (12.30–2pm). In Penong itself, **accommodation** is provided by the *Penong Hotel* (ⓣ08/8625 1050; ❷) and *Penong Caravan Park* (ⓣ08/8625 1111, ⓔoatsfarm@bigpond.com; cabins ❷). There's also a general store and post office with EFTPOS (Mon–Fri 8am–5.30pm, weekends 9am–1pm).

Two hours from Penong you arrive at **Yalata Community**, settled by the Maralinga peoples cleared off their ancestral land by the British atomic bomb tests at Maralinga in the 1950s. At the roadhouse and White Well ranger station (ⓣ08/8625 2780) you can obtain permits to cross community borders and reach the **Head of the Bight**, the best place to see whales when they migrate up here between June and October. The Head is a stirring setting, where powdery dunes rise to absurdly melodramatic cliffs over just a couple of kilometres – you can't help feeling that this is how early cartographers must have envisaged the edge of the world – while southern right whales (see p.844) sport idly with their calves in the water below. Twenty minutes away is the **Nullarbor Roadhouse** (ⓣ08/8625 6271; ❶–❹), which has budget **beds**, motel rooms and a campsite, and is the last place to get fuel before Border Village. The famous triple yellow sign on the highway warning of camels, wombats and kangaroos marks the beginning of the run, which has absolutely no trees. Ironically, rabbits – no longer controlled by farmers now that the area is a national park – have almost crowded out the wombats.

Curiously enough for a land with minimal rainfall, the Nullarbor is undermined by partially flooded limestone **caverns**. From the outside, **Koonalda Cave** (just north of the *Nullarbor Roadhouse*) is a large hole with recently planted fruit trees growing in the mouth; inside, a tremendously deep network of tunnels leads to an underground lake, the shafts grooved by fingers being dragged over their soft walls. Although the patterns are clearly deliberate, their meaning is unknown. The cave is closed off to protect the engravings, but the Ceduna NPWS (see p.880) might be able to arrange a visit.

Border Village is just another roadhouse (ⓣ08/9039 3474; ❶–❹) with a natty fibreglass kangaroo in the car park – certainly the largest one between here and Antarctica. **Eucla** (see p.758) and the rest of the Nullarbor lie 16km over the border in Western Australia on a noticeably worse road and in a considerably earlier time zone.

The Stuart Highway: Woomera and beyond

Heading north of Port Augusta along the **Stuart Highway**, the first place of any consequence is **WOOMERA**, an uncharismatic but well-appointed barracks town two hours north of Port Augusta. The town has been in the news recently on account of its harsh **detention centre**, which houses political asylum seekers while their cases are being decided. In fact, the whole town was closed to the public until 1982, as it sits at the southeast corner of a five-hundred-kilometre corridor known locally as "the Range", ominously highlighted on maps as **Woomera Prohibited Area**. Don't expect to find out why at the mostly military **Heritage Centre** (daily 9am–5pm; $3), at the crossroads of Dewrang and Banool avenues. Models, rocket-relics and plenty of pictures detail the European Launcher Development Organisation's (ELDO) unsuccessful efforts to launch satellites here in the 1960s, but the reasons for the creation of the Prohibited Area – weapons-testing and the British-run 1950s **atomic bomb tests**, contaminated dust from which is still being scraped up and vitrified – are not mentioned. For a first-hand account, read Len Beadell's *Outback Highways*, cheerful tales of the bomb tests and the construction of "some sort of rocket range – or something" by the chief engineer. Currently, Australian, UK and US rocket prototypes are once again being tested here in the hope of turning Woomera into a launching centre.

There are two **places** to stay: the *Eldo Hotel* on Kotara Crescent (ⓣ08/8673 7867, ⓔwoomera.ess@bigpond.com; ❹), which also provides **meals** and booze; and the welcoming *Woomera Travellers Village* on Wirruna Avenue (ⓣ08/8673 7800, ⓦwww.woomera.com; ❸) – **camping** on the lawn is preferable to the beds in the dreary ex-barracks. The **shopping centre** has banks and other facilities, while next door **The Oasis** houses a small leisure centre with a café, bar and bowling alley. Greyhound Australia buses travelling on the Stuart Highway don't go into Woomera but will drop you off at the roadhouse at Pimba, 7km away; Stateliner services do, however, call in to the town.

Roxby Downs, Andamooka and Lake Torrens

Instead of returning to the highway, you might want to carry on past Woomera to the strangest two companion towns in Australia (a Stateliner **bus** goes from Woomera six nights a week). The first, **ROXBY DOWNS**, 80km away, is completely modern, a service centre built in 1986 for miners working the copper, gold, silver and uranium deposits at the nearby Olympic Dam Mine (tours Mon, Thurs, Sat 9am; 2hr; donation; bookings essential on ⓣ08/8671 2001). The friendly **Roxby Downs Cultural Precinct** on the main street (daily 9am–5pm; ⓣ08/8671 2001, ⓦwww.roxbydowns.com), has local information and a café. Another thirty minutes on along an unsurfaced road lies **ANDAMOOKA**, an opal-mining shantytown of block and scrap-iron construction whose red-earth high street becomes a river after rain. The soil proved to be too loose for the underground homes which became de rigueur at Coober Pedy (see p.883), but mud lean-tos, built in the 1930s, are still standing opposite the post office. **Facilities** include fuel, a supermarket, the *Tuckerbox Restaurant* (11am–late), two hotel/motels, two campsites, and the Opal Creek Showroom, which distributes maps and advice. If you fancy your luck "noodling", head to **German Gully**. Opals here are more strongly coloured than Coober Pedy's, but few have been found for years.

Another thirty-minute 4WD ride away is **Lake Torrens**, a sickle-shaped salt lake related to the Acraman meteorite (see box, p.879) which gets popular with bird-watchers in wet years. The lake is also renowned in paleontological circles for traces of the 630-million-year-old **Ediacaran fauna**, the earliest-known evidence of animal life anywhere on the planet, which was first found in Australia, and possibly wiped out by the meteorite. Delicate fossil impressions of jellyfish and obscure organisms are preserved in layered rock. The South Australian Museum in Adelaide has an extensive selection, but rarely issues directions to the site, which has been plundered by collectors since its discovery in 1946 by the geologist Reg Sprigg.

Coober Pedy

COOBER PEDY is the most enduring symbol of the harshness of Australia's Outback and the determination of those who live there. It's a place where the terrain and temperatures are so extreme that homes – and even churches – have been built underground, yet which has managed to attract thousands of opal prospectors. In a virtually waterless desert 380km from Woomera, and considerably further from anywhere else, the most remarkable thing about the town – whose name stems from an Aboriginal phrase meaning "white man's burrow" – is that it exists at all. **Opal** was discovered by William Hutchison on a gold-prospecting expedition to the Stuart Range in February 1915, and the town itself dates from the end of World War I, when returning servicemen headed for the fields to try their luck, using their trench-digging skills to construct underground dwellings.

In summer Coober Pedy is seriously depopulated but, if you can handle the intense heat, it's a good time to look for bargain opal purchases – though not to scratch around for them yourself: gem-hunting is better reserved for the "cooler" winter months. At the start of the year, spectacular **dust storms** often enclose the town for hours in an abrasive orange twilight.

The local scenery might be familiar to you if you're a film fan, as it was used to great effect in *Mad Max III*, *Pitch Black* and Wim Wenders' epic *Until The End Of The World*. There's not much to it, just a plain disturbed by conical pink mullock (slag) heaps, with clusters of trucks and home-made contraptions off in the distance, and **warning signs** alerting you to treacherously invisible, unfenced thirty-metre shafts. Be very careful where you tread: even if you have transport, the safest way to explore is to take a tour, examine a map, then go back on your own. Past the diggings, the **Breakaway Range** consists of a brightly coloured plateau off the highway about 11km north of town, with good views, close-ups of the hostile terrain, and bushwalking through two-hundred-year-old stands of mulga.

Wandering around the dusty streets, it can be hard to tell whether some of the odd machinery lying about is bona fide mining equipment or left-over film props. The **Big Winch Lookout** in the centre gives a grandstand view of the mix of low houses and hills pocked with ventilation shafts. The welded metal "tree" up here was assembled before any real ones grew in the area, though in the last few years there have been some attempts to encourage greenery with recycled waste water. For more on mining, there are several mine displays and museums in town: try **Old Timers Mine**, Crowders Gully Road (Ⓣ08/8672 5555; $10), or **Umoona** on Hutchison Street (Ⓣ08/8672 5288; entrance free, tours $10). There are numerous **tours** on offer, all of which feature a town drive, a spot of noodling and a visit to an underground home – which you might find embarrassingly like visiting a zoo. One of the best is Radeka's five-hour tour (Ⓣ08/8672 5223; $40), which includes a look at the Breakaway Range. Alternatively, book through your accommodation.

Coober Pedy has lately achieved a bit of a reputation for **violence**, which is perhaps not surprising given its extreme climate and the fact that most people have access to explosives. However, signs warning "no parking unless your

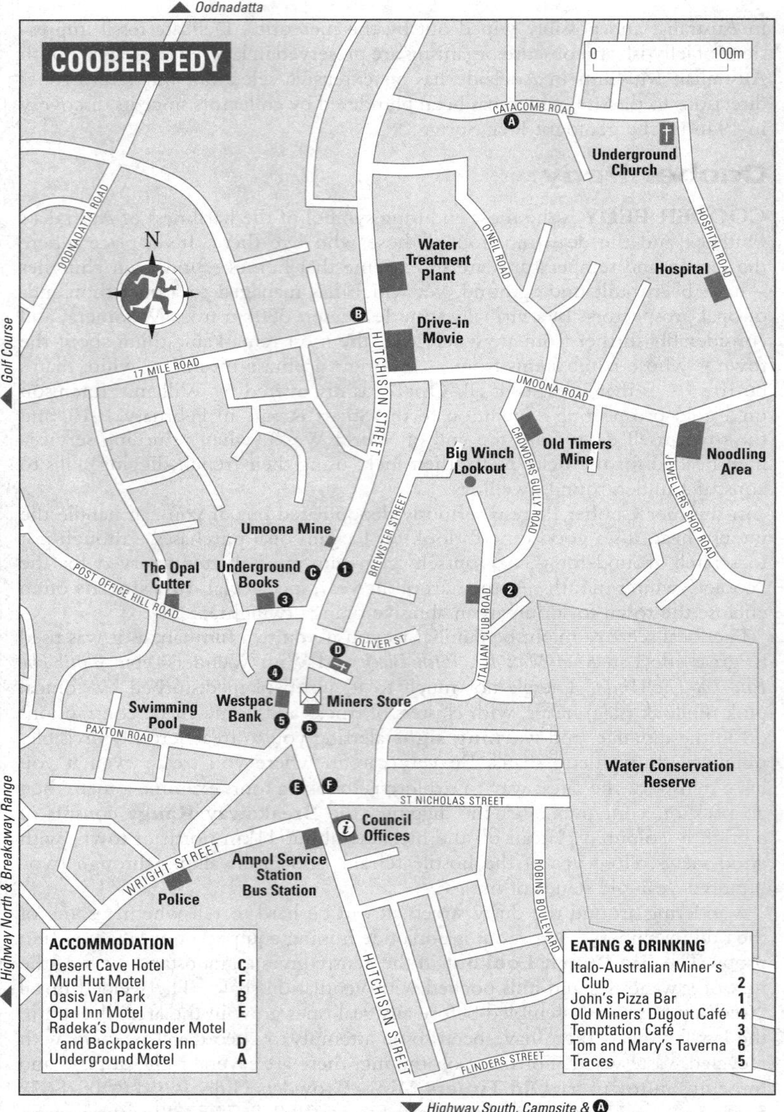

car is dynamite-proof" are really for amusement-value only, and visitors are unlikely to be the object of any discord.

Practicalities

Just about everything you'll need in Coober Pedy lies around the 500-metre strip between the *Opal Inn Hotel* and the water-treatment plant on **Hutchison Street** (also known as Main Street), which leads north off the highway. **Buses**

Finding and buying an opal

Opal is composed of fragile layers of silica and derives its colour from the refraction of light – characteristics that preclude the use of heavy mining machinery, as one false blow would break the matrix and destroy the colour. Deposits are patchy and located by trial and error: the last big strikes at Coober Pedy petered out in the 1970s, and though bits and pieces are still found – including an exceptional opalized fossil skeleton of a pliosaur (the reptilian equivalent of a seal) in 1983 – it's anybody's guess as to the location of other major seams (indeed, there may not be any at all). Because so much depends on luck, you'll hear little about mining technique and more about beating the system. For instance, it's now illegal to mine in town, but there's nothing to prevent "home extensions"; similarly, non-mining friends are often roped in to register claims and sidestep the "one per person" rule. Working another's claim (the "night shift") is a less honourable short cut.

Unless you're serious (in which case you'll have to pay $48.50 a year to the Mines Department for a **Miner's Permit** to peg your 50 x 50 metre claim), the easiest way to find something is by **noodling** over someone's diggings – ask the owner first. An area on the corner of Jewellers Shop and Umoona roads has been set aside as a safe area for tourists to poke about freely without danger of finding open mineshafts. Miners use ultraviolet lamps to separate opal from **potch** (worthless grey opal), so you're unlikely to find anything stunning – but look out for shell fossils and small chips.

The best time to **buy opal** is outside the tourist season, but don't deal through grizzled prospectors in the hotels unless you're very clued in. There are three categories: **cabochon**, a solid piece; **doublet**, a thin wafer mounted on a dark background to enhance the colour; and **triplet**, a doublet with quartz lens. While cabochons are most expensive and triplets least valuable, it takes some experience to price accurately within each category, as size, clarity, strength of colour, brightness and personal aesthetics all contribute. With about fifty dealers in town, it's up to you to find the right stone; reputable sources give full written guarantees. One of the best is The Opal Cutter on Post Office Hill Road (Ⓣ08/8672 3086, Ⓦwww.opalcutter.com.au) – the proprietors will tell you all you need to know about the precious stones and you can watch opals being cut on the premises.

drop you off at the Ampol service station (Greyhound Australia; Ⓣ08/8672 5151). From the **airport** you may be able to get a lift with one of the hostel buses that meet most flights, or make an advance reservation to ensure that someone meets you. *Desert Cave Hotel* (see p.886) is agent for Thrifty Car Rental; book well in advance.

The council offices on Hutchison Street (Mon–Fri 8.30am–5pm; Ⓣ1800 637 076, Ⓦwww.opalcapitaloftheworld.com.au), opposite the Ampol service station, are a mine of local **information**. Underground Books (Ⓣ08/8672 5558), on Post Office Hill Road opposite the Mobil service station, is a good alternative source – it stocks packs of local sketch maps which are a useful back-up to road maps. The Miners Store supermarket on Hutchison Street (Ⓣ08/8672 5051) is also the **post office** and Commonwealth **bank** agent (there's a Westpac branch opposite). The **hospital** is on Hospital Road, at the north end of town (Ⓣ08/8672 5009), and there's a **pharmacy** at the Medical Centre in the middle of Hutchison Street. Everyone shops on Thursday, as fresh meat and veggies arrive in a refrigerated lorry on Wednesday night and are scarce by the weekend. The **swimming pool** at the school on Paxton Road gives a welcome chance to cool down; it's open to the public for a few hours daily.

Accommodation

Coober Pedy relies heavily on tourist income, so finding **lodgings** shouldn't be a problem. To some people, the idea of sleeping underground is disturbing but, while not all accommodation is subterranean, it's worth spending at least one night in naturally cooled tunnels for the experience. Those wishing to camp might like to try *Riba's Caravan Park and Underground Camping* (ⓣ08/8672 5614, ⓔribascamping@hotmail.com) on William Creek Road, for the unique opportunity of pitching a tent beneath the earth's surface.

Desert Cave Hotel Hutchison St ⓣ08/8672 5688, ⓦwww.desertcave.com.au. This place offers a choice of below- or above-ground four-star accommodation. There's a swimming pool, and scenic flights, tours and car rental can be arranged. ❻

Mud Hut Motel Next to the council offices ⓣ08/8672 3003, ⓦwww.mudhutmotel.com.au. The bare, rammed-earth construction of this well-furnished motel gives a flavour of the subterranean without losing out on daylight. ❹

Oasis Van Park Opposite the water-treatment plant, Hutchison St ⓣ08/8672 5169, ⓔcooberpedybig4@ozemail.com.au. Spacious, air-conditioned cabins as well as camping facilities. Cabin rooms ❷

Opal Inn Motel Hutchison St ⓣ08/8672 5054. A standard motel block behind the hotel of the same name. ❹

Radeka's Downunder Motel and Back-packers Inn Oliver St ⓣ08/8672 5223, ⓔradekadownunder@ozemail.com.au. The best budget option in town. There are snaking tunnels downstairs with alcoves holding two to six beds – though it can be a long trek upstairs to the well-appointed kitchen and toilets – and a bar and pool table provide evening entertainment. Dorms $22, motel rooms ❹

Underground Motel Catacomb Rd ⓣ08/8672 5324, ⓔundergroundmotel@ozemail.com.au. Clean tiled rooms with views over the desert from the front porch. ❹ including breakfast.

Eating, drinking and entertainment

Restaurants in town are good value and portions are huge – beware of over-ordering; all those listed below are on the main street. The drive-in **cinema** on Hutchison Street shows a double bill most Saturday nights.

Italo-Australian Miners' Club Italian Club Road ⓣ08/8672 501. Big Italian dinners on Thursdays and Fridays, just below the Big Winch.

John's Pizza Bar Hutchison St. Popular pizza and fast food joint, serving decent coffee too.

Old Miners' Dugout Café Hutchison St. Atmospheric subterranean eaterie, where Eastern European dishes feature on the menu, alongside the likes of kangaroo and barramundi. Lunchtime budget specials.

Temptation Café Post Office Hill Road. Upmarket place with pavement tables, excellent pastries and coffee.

Tom and Mary's Taverna Hutchison St. ⓣ08/8672 5622. All the usual Greek staples, as well as a few Australian dishes.

Traces Hutchison St. ⓣ08/8672 5147. Greek grills, plus dancing. Daily 4pm–late.

Beyond Coober Pedy

The Stuart Highway ploughs 350km north from Coober Pedy to the state border. From **Marla** township (shop, post office and Commonwealth Bank at the roadhouse) you could head east to Oodnadatta across the **Painted Desert** at Arkaringa Hills, a larger version of the Breakaway Range, or 35km west into Aboriginal land to the state's newest opal strike at Mintabie – seek permission from Marla's police. If you want to get to **Oodnadatta**, there's also a direct two-hundred-kilometre dirt road from Coober Pedy across the pan of Giddi-Gidna (the **Moon Plain**), covered by the **mail run** which departs from Underground Books (ⓣ1800 069 911, ⓦwww.desertdiversity.com; $125) on a roughly twelve-hour triangular route to William Creek and Oodnadatta every Monday at 9am (anticlockwise) and Thursday (clockwise).

Australia's hottest 4WD journey has to be west from Coober Pedy to the **atomic bomb sites** at **Emu Junction**: concrete slabs cap pits where contaminated equipment lies buried, and sand fused into sheets of glass by the blasts covers the ground – the area is still highly radioactive and you'd be advised to pass through quickly. Beyond lies the virgin **Unnamed Conservation Park** and routes across the sand-dunes and Aboriginal land to the **Warburton Road** in Western Australia (see p.757). The NPWS at 11 McKenzie St in Ceduna (ⓣ08/8625 3144) supplies practical details and permits to 4WD convoys only.

The Flinders Ranges and northeast

If you're heading north from Port Augusta but want to avoid the Stuart Highway, an adventurous alternative route leads up to the spectacular **Flinders Ranges National Park** and beyond to the remote settlements of **Maree** and **Innamincka**.

Quorn and Hawker

The first stop between Port Augusta and the Flinders Ranges National Park is 50km northeast at **QUORN**, whose stone buildings and village atmosphere offer a last taste of the pastoral south before the austerities of the Outback set in. Best known for the **Pichi Richi railway**, the sole operational section of the old Ghan, Quorn was a major rail centre until the line was rerouted through Port Augusta in the 1950s. Enthusiasts restored the service twenty years later and started taking passengers on a two-hour return haul to Woolshed Flats through the **Pichi Richi Pass** – whose name has been variously attributed to a medicinal herb or an Aboriginal word for "gorge". Punctuated by a break at Woolshed Flats for a cream tea, it makes a relaxing and mildly scenic journey. Trains run only on a few weekends and holidays April–October; call ahead to check and book (ⓣ08/8658 6598 or 1800 440 101, ⓦwww.prr.org.au).

There's a **caravan park** in Quorn (ⓣ & ⓕ08/8648 6206; cabins ❸), but a night spent at the *Transcontinental Hotel* (ⓣ08/8648 6076; ❸) is much more congenial, with an easy-going crowd of truckies and drovers from the north for company. A good alternative is the *Andu Lodge* (ⓣ08/8648 6655; dorms $20, rooms ❸), which has excellent dorms and double rooms; they also run a host of one- to three-day **tours** into the different sections of the Flinders for between $119 and $299.

The main road through town is Railway Terrace, where you'll find the town's post office and hotels, which all do good-value **meals** but are quite strict about serving times. First Street and the block between it and Railway Terrace contain a few arts-and-crafts and secondhand shops to poke about in. The **tourist information** centre is at 3 Seventh St (ⓣ08/8648 6419).

There's good local bushwalking off the back road to Hawker along a string of ridges and cliffs, outrunners from the main body of the central Flinders, 100km north. Closest to Quorn is **Dutchmans Stern**, a solid day's hike for the reasonably fit from the car park to various lookouts. Less dedicated walkers will find **Warren**, **Buckaringa** and **Middle gorges** an easier proposition. Buckaringa's steep face is the most reliable place in the ranges to see the rare and ravishingly pretty **yellow-footed rock wallaby**, with its bushy, ringed tail and yellow paws – climb to the top at around 4pm and sit quietly until they appear. Closer to Hawker, it's also worth taking in the well-preserved remains

Flinders Dreaming and geology

The almost tangible spirit of the Flinders Ranges is reflected in the wealth of Adnyamathanha ("hill people") **legends** associated with them. Perhaps more obvious here than anywhere else in Australia is the connection between landscapes and Dreamtime stories, which recount how scenery was created by animal or human action – though, as Dreamtime spirits took several forms, this distinction is often blurred. A central character is **Akurra**, a gigantic maned serpent (or serpents) who guards waterholes and formed the Flinders' contours by wriggling north to drink dry the huge salt lakes of Frome and Callabonna. You may well prefer the Aboriginal legends to the complexities of geology illustrated on boards placed at intervals along the Brachina Gorge track, which explain how movements of the "Adelaide Geosyncline" brought about the changes in scenery over hundreds of millions of years.

of **Kanyaka Homestead**, abandoned after a drought in the 1880s, and **Yourambulla Cave**, which has some unusual charcoal symbols in a high overhang, reached by a ladder. Both are signposted from the road.

HAWKER itself, some 100km from Port Augusta, is somewhere to fuel up, make use of the last banks and shops, have a meal at the *Old Ghan Restaurant*, organize a **flight over the Flinders** through *Hawker Caravan Park* on the Wilpena exit (Ⓣ08/8648 4006), and acquire **Desert Park Passes** and advice about road conditions from the NPWS office at 60 Elder Terrace (Mon–Fri 8.30am–4pm; Ⓣ08/8648 4244). Once in Hawker, you'll have to decide whether to press on into the Flinders and the northeast or continue following the former Ghan line north towards Marree; the bitumen on the latter route extends past the Leigh Creek coalfields to Lyndhurst, at the start of the Strzelecki Track.

Flinders Ranges National Park

The procession of glowing red mountains at **Flinders Ranges National Park**, folded and crumpled with age, produces some of the Outback's most spectacular and timeless scenery, rising from flat scrub to form abrupt escarpments, gorges and the famous elevated basin of **Wilpena Pound**. The hard contrast between sky and ranges is softened by native cypresses and river red gums, and in spring the plains are burnished by **wild flowers** of all colours. Bushwalkers, photographers and painters flock here in their hundreds, but with a system of graded **walking tracks** ranging from a few minutes' length to several days – not to mention roads of varying quality – the park is busy without being crowded.

Nestling up against the edge of Wilpena Pound, **WILPENA** is a good place to orient yourself: it has a motel, campsite, gas, diesel and petrol pumps and an overpriced store. The NPWS **information centre** (daily 8am–6pm) is situated at the end of the bitumen where the main routes start into Wilpena Pound. Wilder places further into the park to set up camp for a few days include the national park campsites at **Bunyeroo** and **Brachina Gorge** in the west, **Trezona** and **Oraparinna** in the centre, and **Wilkawillana Gorge** in the extreme northeast, all accessible on unsealed roads. Even the more formal **lodgings** tend to be basic: for a longer stay you might consider renting a holiday cottage, which can be a bargain during the summer – Flinders Ranges Accommodation Booking Service (Ⓣ1800 777 880, Ⓦwww.frabs.com.au) offers a range of cabins (❷–❺) in the region.

Back at Wilpena, *Wilpena Pound Motel* (ⓣ08/8648 0004 or 1800 805 802, ⓦwww.wilpenapound.com.au; ❻) provides comfortable but expensive accommodation: there's a good, surprisingly exotic restaurant, however, and the chalet-like bar makes an atmospheric setting for an après-hike drink. Four-wheel-drive tours and flights over the Pound can also be arranged here. If you've a tent, the adjacent *Wilpena Campsite* (ⓣ08/8648 0004) is wooded and well equipped, and has standing tent accommodation. Other places to stay are dotted around the park: about 15km back towards Hawker, *Rawnsley Park* (ⓣ08/8648 0030, ⓦwww.rawnsleypark.com.au; cabins ❹, plus tent spaces) is beautifully located below Rawnsley Bluff and offers mountain bike rental and 4WD trips; *Willow Springs* (ⓣ08/8648 6282, ⓦwww.frabs.com.au/willowsprings.htm; ❹), 17km north of Wilpena before the Wilkawillana Gorge junction, is a working sheep station with blockhouse dormitories and cottage.

Most **walking tracks** lead into Wilpena Pound, though you can also pick up the Heysen Trail and follow it north from Wilpena for a couple of days around the ABC Range to **Aroona Ruins** on the northern edge of the park. The Wilpena NPWS offers booklets, maps (sometimes the 1:50,000 topographical series) and the latest information on routes; you're required to log out and back with them on any walk exceeding three hours. Realistically, hiking is restricted to the cooler winter months between May and October, as scant shade and reflective rocks raise summer temperatures above 40°C. Don't underestimate conditions for even short excursions: you'll need good footwear, a hat, sunscreen and **water** – at least half a litre per hour is recommended. **Camping out**, a waterproof tent, groundmat and fuel stove are essential, and note that the **weather** is very changeable; wind-driven rain can be a menace along the ridges and heavy downpours can make tracks dangerous.

Wilpena Pound

Wilpena Pound's two major hiking destinations are **St Mary's Peak** on the rim and **Edowie Gorge** inside the Pound – from Wilpena, allow nine hours for Edowie Gorge, eight hours for the ascent of St Mary's. Alternatively, an **overnight** trip through the Pound allows you to see all its major attractions. Leave the peak until last and head off across the Pound's flat, grassy bowl to the remains of **Hill's Homestead** – further evidence of the region's unsuitability for farming – then follow the track northwest to **Cooinda Camp**, about two hours from Wilpena. Assuming you left early enough, there's time to pitch a tent and spend the rest of the day following the creek upstream past **Malloga Falls** to **Glenora Falls** and views into Edowie Gorge before heading back to Cooinda – there might be places to swim after rain. Next morning it's a steep climb to **Tanderra Saddle** below the peak, followed by the last burst up to the summit of St Mary's Peak itself. The effort is rewarded by unequalled views west to Lake Torrens and north along the length of the ABC Ranges towards Parachilna; on exceptional mornings the peak stands proud of low cloud inside the Pound. The direct descent from the saddle back to Wilpena is initially steep, but shouldn't take more than three hours.

Shorter routes lead up **Mount Ohlssen Bagge** (a not-too-tiring four hours) and **Wangara Lookout** (2hr) for lower vistas of the Pound floor, and southwest across the Pound to **Bridle Gap** (6hr) following the Heysen Trail's red markers. Things to look out for are euro wallabies, emus and parrots inside the Pound, and cauliflower-shaped fossil **stromatolites** – algal corals – on the Mount Ohlssen Bagge route, similar to those still living at Hamelin Pool in Western Australia (see p.765).

Arkaroo Rock, Sacred Canyon and nearby gorges

Two **Aboriginal galleries** worth seeing are Arkaroo Rock and Sacred Canyon, both a short drive from Wilpena. **Arkaroo** is back off the main road towards Rawnsley Park and involves an hour's walk up the outside of Wilpena Pound to see mesh-protected rockfaces covered in symbols relating to an initiation ceremony and the Pound's formation, some dating back six thousand years. Snake patterns depict St Mary's Peak as the head of a male Akurra coiled round the Pound. To reach **Sacred Canyon**, briefly take the road from Wilpena into the north of the park, past the **Cazneaux Tree** – a river red gum made famous by Harold Cazneaux's prize-winning 1930 photograph *Spirit of Endurance* – before turning right and following a bumpy track to its end. Rock-hop up the narrow, shattered gorge to clusters of painted swirls covered in a sooty patina and clearer engraved emu prints and geometric patterns; the best examples are around the second cascade.

The main road through the park heads straight out to Blinman, but another track detours to **Bunyeroo** and **Brachina gorges** on the western limits. The gorges make good campsites: you have to walk into Bunyeroo but the track passes through Brachina on its way to the surfaced Hawker to Marree road. If you're pressing directly on to the Northern Flinders, you can avoid Blinman by turning right off the main road about 20km from Wilpena, heading to **Wirrealpa Homestead**.

The Northern Flinders

The Wilpena–Blinman road passes through a low group of hills, thin in timber but still swarming with wallabies, emus and galahs. **BLINMAN** comprises a few houses with well-tended gardens, three fuel pumps, and a hotel (Ⓣ08/8648 4867, Ⓦwww.blinmanhotel.com.au; ❸) with log fires, games room, pool and campsite; the keys to everywhere else in town are kept at the bar. The main track winds west through beautiful Parachilna Gorge, in the middle of which you could stay at **Angorichina** *Tourist Village* (Ⓣ08/8648 4842; dorms $18), which also has a campsite. The track meets the Hawker–Marree road at **Parachilna**, where there's great bush tucker at the *Prairie Hotel* (Ⓣ08/8648 4844, Ⓦwww.prairiehotel.com.au; ❺).

According to the Adnyamathanha, **coal** was made by Yoolayoola the kingfisher man, who built fires at Leigh Creek, halfway between Hawker and Marree. Today, 2.6 million tonnes of it are scooped out of the ground annually to be sent by rail and burnt at the power station in Port Augusta. At a car park just off the road you can climb around an old dragline crane and look over the edge of an open-cast mine; there are free **tours** daily (Ⓣ08/8675 2723). Coalworkers live either in the well-planned modern township of **Leigh Creek South** or at more traditional **Copley**, where *Tulloch's Bush Bakery* does a very civilized cappuccino and quandong pie. Fuel and camping sites are available at both towns.

The route into the Northern Flinders lies east, joining up with the direct road from Wilpena and then running north to the **Gammon Ranges National Park** and Arkaroola.

Chambers Gorge and Big Moro

On the road to the Gammon Ranges are the remote and little-visited sites of **Chambers Gorge** and **Big Moro**, worth every groan and twang of your vehicle springs for their stark beauty and Aboriginal significance. The ten-kilometre access track east into **Chambers Gorge** (28km after Wirrealpa) is decidedly dodgy after rain when you'll need a 4WD, but at other times 2WD vehicles – with care – should reach the natural campsite at the foot of **Mount Chambers**, within twenty minutes' walk of the gorge mouth. In a Dreamtime story, Yuduyudulya, the Fairy Wren spirit, threw a boomerang which split Mount Chambers' eastern end and then circled back to form the crown. An indistinct left fork before the gorge leads to a dense gallery of **pecked engravings**; most are circles, though a goanna stands out clearly on the right, facing the main body of art. Chambers Gorge itself is huge and silent, the broad stony entrance guarded by high, perpendicular cliffs and brilliant green waterholes that would take days to explore properly.

Big Moro is sacred to the Adnyamathanha as the residence of an Akurra. The creek trickles through a crumbling gorge into two clear green pools; limestone outcrops on the south side conceal miniature caves. The gorge lies west down an exceptionally tortuous fifteen-kilometre 4WD track opposite **Wertaloona Homestead**, 60km from the Mount Chambers junction. Pay attention to any signs and leave the three gates as you found them.

The Gammon Ranges

Arid and bald, the **Gammon Ranges** are the Flinders' last fling, a vicious flurry of compressed folds plunging abruptly onto the northern plains. Balcanoona is the NPWS headquarters for the otherwise undeveloped **Gammon Ranges National Park**, a thick band of sandstone cliffs – check with the Hawker NPWS (see p.888) for current conditions. There are two ways to experience the area: either carry on to Arkaroola (outside the park), or take the road west across the park through **Italowie Gorge** to Copley on the Hawker–Marree road. The steep red walls of the gorge are home to iga – native orange trees which symbolize the Adnyamathanha as a people. There are **bush campsites** here and shearers' quarters at **Balcanoona** (book through the Hawker NPWS ⓣ08/8048 4244; ❸).

On the northern edge of the park, **Arkaroola Wilderness Sanctuary** is a private wildlife sanctuary and **resort** (ⓣ08/8648 4848, ⓦwww.arkaroola.com.au; ❹), with a restaurant, caravan park and swimming pool. Scene of Australia's most recent volcanic activity, the area is a geologist's dream: **Paralana Hot Springs** (two hours away by 4WD) bubble out radioactive radon gas, and walks into the shattered hills surrounding the resort turn up fossils and semi-precious minerals. According to Aboriginal legend, the springs mark the site where a Dreamtime warrior extinguished his firestick after using it to kill a rival. The area is so rugged that conventional mining isn't really a profitable venture – drilling rigs are airlifted in, then ferried around on the lower half of a Chieftain tank. The resort's **Ridgetop Tour** ($85 per person) brings you closest to the heart of the scenery: four hair-raising hours in an open 4WD (wear something warm) following precipitous contours to **Sillers Lookout** and views east to the shimmering salt lakes of **Frome** and **Callabonna**. Remains of the hippopotamus-sized marsupial diprotodon have been found at Callabonna; the diprotodon survived well into Aboriginal times, but died out as the climate changed after the last Ice Age.

Arkaroola marks the limit of public transport, running its own connection to meet the Stateliner bus at Hawker on Monday and Friday. Some vehicles (with either high clearance or very careful drivers) can continue directly north to join the **Strzelecki Track** at Mount Hopeless, a little under half the distance to Innamincka. If you're unsure, the track can also be reached via Lyndhurst on the Hawker–Marree road, but this involves a three-hundred-kilometre detour from Arkaroola.

The Strzelecki Track

The 460-kilometre **Strzelecki Track** between Lyndhurst and Innamincka was pioneered in 1870 by **Harry Redford**, better known as Captain Starlight, who stole a thousand cattle from a property near Longreach in Queensland and drove them south across the Strzelecki Desert and down to Adelaide (see p.587 for more). Later used for more orthodox purposes, the track had a reputation as one of the roughest stock routes in the country, a serious obstacle for transport. Much of its epic nature has since been flattened, along with the road surface, by companies draining the **Moomba gas and oil fields**, and it's negotiable in any sound vehicle when dry.

Start at Lyndhurst by filling the tank – the next **fuel** is at the other end – and heading off around the northern tip of the Flinders; once past them, the journey becomes flat and pretty dull. At around the 105-kilometre mark you cross the 4850-kilometre-long **Dog Fence** (or Great Dingo Fence), designed to keep dingoes away from southern flocks, which stretches from the Nullarbor Plain east into New South Wales. Although its value is debatable, you do frequently see desiccated canine corpses poisoned by "1080" bait lying nearby. The road from Arkaroola connects within sight of **Mount Hopeless** (a pathetic hill, appropriately named); the next place to stop and perhaps camp is at the hot outflow from **Montecollina Bore**, 30km on. From here the scenery improves slightly as the road runs between dunes, and it's hard to resist leaving footprints along one of the pristine red crests.

At **Strzelecki Crossing** there's a choice of routes: you could abandon the track and head east to where Queensland, New South Wales and South Australia meet at **Cameron Corner**, where there's a store with **fuel**, a campsite (Ⓣ08/8091 3872) and a small bar; alternatively, you could continue to Innamincka either via Moomba or by following the direct but less-frequented **Old Strzelecki Track**. Cameron Corner and the old track are 4WD only, and all of the routes are crossed by straight **seismic test lines** which run off to dead ends in the bush – you risk becoming permanently lost if you accidentally follow one, so take care. **Moomba**'s jumble of pipes and lick of flame are sometimes marked as a township on maps but, though visible from the road, the refinery is closed to the public. Within an hour you've crossed into the **Innamincka Regional Reserve** and are approaching Innamincka's charms.

Innamincka

Cooper Creek, which runs through Innamincka, is best known for the misadventures of explorers Burke and Wills, who ended their tragic 1861 expedition by dying here (see box, p.593). **INNAMINCKA** was later founded on much the same spot as a customs house to collect taxes on stock being moved between Queensland and South Australia. Never more than a handful of buildings, it found fame mainly because John Flynn's Flying Doctor Service ran a mission here and because the hotel piled up decades of empties into a legendary 180-metre-long bottle dump before the town was abandoned in 1952. Lately, however, recreational four-wheel driving has led to a renaissance. The new *Innimincka Hotel* (Ⓣ & Ⓕ08/8675 9901; ④) has weekend barbecues, a video jukebox and impromptu dance sessions on Friday and Saturday nights, while the *Innamincka Trading Post* (Ⓣ08/8675 9900) has a couple of comfortable **cabins** (④), and stocks provisions and fuel. The mission was rebuilt in 1994 as a **museum** (for opening hours ask at the Trading Post), and there's a solar-powered telephone and spotless toilet/shower block opposite. Pelicans, parrots and inquisitive dingoes will be your companions if you camp out for free along the creek.

It only takes an hour to look around the museum and hunt for evidence of the bottle dump before you're ready for other distractions – you can take your pick from taking a walk, **fishing** for yellowbelly, bream and catfish, swimming in the creek, or renting a canoe from the hotel or the Trading Post. With a vehicle you could strike out 20km west to **Wills' grave** or 8km east to where **Burke** was buried (both bodies were removed to Adelaide in 1862). Another 8km beyond Burke's cairn is **Cullyamurra waterhole**, the largest permanent body of water in central Australia, and a footpath to rock engravings of crosses, rainbow patterns and bird tracks. With a 4WD you can also tackle the 110-kilometre track north to the shallow **Coongie Lakes**, where you can swim and watch the abundant birdlife. An hour's drive east of Innamincka along a rather poor track is Queensland, the Dig Tree and a fuelless route to Quilpie (see p.593).

The far north: Marree and beyond

MARREE is a collection of tattered houses which somehow outlived the old Ghan's demise in 1980, leaving carriages to rust on sidings and rails to be used for tethering posts outside the hotel. Although it was first a camel depot, then a staging post for the overland telegraph line, and finally the point where the rail line skirted northwest around **Lake Eyre**, today all traffic comes by road and is bound for the **Birdsville Track** into Queensland or the **Oodnadatta Track**, which follows the former train route to Oodnadatta and beyond into the Northern Territory or Simpson Desert.

Accommodation is limited to the hotel on the main street (☎08/8675 8344; ❸), which is also good for lunch or dinner, and the caravan park run by the *Oasis Café* (☎08/8675 8352; cabins ❸), a fairly well-stocked shop, fuel and fast-food outlet which was originally the telegraph relay station. The General Store (☎08/8675 8360), across the railway track towards Oodnadatta, doubles as a Commonwealth Bank agent and post office with fuel and EFTPOS. If it's open, visit the **Arabana Community Centre**, whose friendly staff will explain the uses of different types of boomerang.

Lake Eyre

Lake Eyre is a massive salt lake caught between the Simpson and Strzelecki deserts in a region where the annual evaporation rate is thirty times greater than the rainfall. Most years a little water trickles into the lake from its million-square-kilometre catchment area, which extends well into central Queensland and the Northern Territory, but floods have filled the basin only four times since white settlement of the region – most dramatically in 1974, when the lake expanded to a length of 140km. A hypnotic, glaring **salt crust** usually covers the southern bays, creating a mysterious landscape whose harsh surrounds are paved by shiny gibber stones and walled by red dunes – the crust was thick enough in 1964 to be used as a range for Donald Campbell's successful crack at the world land-speed record. Some **wildlife** also manages to get by in the incredible emptiness. The resident Lake Eyre dragon is a diminutive, spotted grey lizard often seen skimming over the crust, and the rare flooding attracts dense flocks of birds, wakes the plump water-holding frog from hibernation and causes the plants to burst into colour.

While you can **fly** over the lake (contact Wrightsair on ☎08/8670 7962; Ⓦwww.wrightsair.com.au; $150), only 4WDs can reach the shore 95km north of Marree, though the track to the campsite at a gum-shaded waterhole, just over halfway at **Muloorina Homestead**, is good. Timber at the lake is sparse and protected, which means that there's little shade and no firewood. There's no one to help you if something goes wrong, so don't drive on the lake's crust – should you fall through, it's impossible to extricate your vehicle from the grey slush below.

The Birdsville Track

Assuming there's been no rain, the 520-kilometre **Birdsville Track** is no obstacle to careful drivers during the winter: the biggest problem is getting caught in dried wheel ruts and being pulled off the road. Tearing north from Marree, the distant tips of the Flinders Ranges dip below the horizon behind, leaving you on a bare plain with the road as the only feature. Look for the **MV Tom Brennan**, a vessel donated to the area in 1949 to ferry stock around during floods, but now bearing an absurd resemblance to a large grey bathtub. Before the halfway house at Mungeranie Gap, a scenic variation is offered by the **Natterannie Sandhills** (150km), once a severe obstacle which has now been graded by digging out the soft sand and replacing it with clay. The **Mungeranie roadhouse** (ⓣ08/8675 8317; ❷) provides the only services on the track (fuel, beds and snacks), but seems to be unattended on Sundays, when you'll have to slog up the hill to the manager's house. In a 4WD you can head west from the roadhouse to **Kalamurina campsite** near Cowarie Homestead (58km) for the thrill of desert fishing on Warburton Creek.

Back on the track, a windmill at **Mirra Mitta bore** (37km from the roadhouse) draws piping-hot water out of the ground beside long-abandoned buildings; the water smells of tar and drains into cooler pools, providing somewhere to camp. By now you're crossing the polished gibber lands of the **Sturt Stony Desert**, and it's worth going for a walk to feel the cold wind and watch the dunes dancing in the heat haze away to the west. The low edge of **Coonchera Dune** to the right of the track (190km from the roadhouse) marks the start of a run along the mudpans between the sandhills; look for desert plants and dingoes. In two more hours you should be pulling up outside the Birdsville pub (see p.576).

The Oodnadatta Track

The road from **Marree to Oodnadatta** is the most interesting of the three famous Outback tracks, mainly because abandoned sidings and fettlers' cottages from the old Ghan provide frequent excuses to get out of the car and explore. Disintegrating sleepers lie by the roadside along parts of the route, otherwise embankments and rickety bridges are all that remain of the line. As with the roads to Birdsville and Innamincka, with care, any sound vehicle can drive the route in dry winter weather.

About 100km into the journey, near **Curdimurka ruins**, the road runs within sight of **Lake Eyre South**, giving a flavour of its bigger sister if you can't get out there. Twenty-five kilometres later, a short track south ends below three conical hills – two of which have hot, bubbling **mound springs** at the top, created when water escaping from the artesian basin deposits heaps of mud and minerals. The perfectly symmetrical **Blanche Cup** looks out across a plain – stripped of every shred of greenery by rabbits and cattle – to **Hamilton Hill**, an extinct spring, while further south the **Bubbler** gurgles a verdant stream into the desert where it evaporates after a couple of hundred metres. Important to the Arabana, these springs were used by Sturt in the 1850s and later by the telegraph and rail depots, but tapping the artesian basin for bore water has greatly reduced their flow.

One of these bores is not far up the road at **Coward Springs** (open daily 9am–5pm; $1), where a corroded pipe spilling into ponds beside the track has created an artificial environment of grasses and palms behind a **campsite** (April to late October; ⓣ08/8675 8336, ⓦwww.cowardsprings.com.au; cabins ❷) with toilet blocks and cabins built from sleepers. The ground can be boggy after rain but it's still a tempting stop. **WILLIAM CREEK**, 75km further, has a resident population of just ten – and is a source of fuel, camping and relaxation in the **hotel** (ⓣ08/8670 7880, ⓦwww.williamcreekhotel.net.au). Bar, walls and ceiling are heavily decorated with cards and photographs of 4WD disasters, and it also serves as a hangout for stockmen from **Anna Creek Station**, the world's largest cattle property, covering an area the size of Belgium. A solar-powered phone outside faces the battered remains of a Black Arrow **missile** dragged off the Woomera Range, just a few minutes' drive away. Off-road drivers can take a seventy-kilometre track from here to Lake Eyre's western shore; in the other direction is a more passable road to Coober Pedy, though there's almost nothing to see on the way except **Lake Cadibarrawirracanna**, a salt lake with permanent water and birdlife, at the halfway mark.

After William Creek the track gets rougher, crossing sand dunes and then moving into stony country cut by frequent creeks – shallow for most of the year. Hardy mulgas line the banks, their soft yellow blooms giving off a distinctive acrid scent. On the last stretch to Oodnadatta, look out for a sight of the extraordinary red and black crescent petals of **Sturt's desert pea**, the state emblem, growing by the roadside.

Oodnadatta

Unless you stay long enough to meet some locals, you'll probably feel that, like Marree, **OODNADATTA** survived the Ghan's closure with little to show for it. A few logically arranged but untidy streets lacking atmosphere or purpose, Oodnadatta was founded as a railhead in 1890, and mail and baggage for further north had to make do with camel trains from here until the line to Alice Springs was completed in 1928. Now that has gone, the town has become a base for the Aranda community – *utnadata* ("mulga blossom") is the Aranda name for a local waterway – and 4WD crews heading into the Simpson Desert. After rain you'll even need a 4WD for the last slippery kilometre into town, past the racecourse. If your visit coincides with the **race weekend** in May, helicopters will be circling the track on the left, trying to dry it out, and the town will be deserted, so stop at the track, buy a pass and join in. With neat clothes and some sort of tie, you'll even get into the "formal" ball afterwards.

You can camp at the **Pink Roadhouse** (ⓣ08/8670 7822, ⓦwww.pinkroadhouse.com.au), unless the relative luxury of a bed at the *Transcontinental Hotel* appeals (ⓣ08/8670 7804; ❸). The roadhouse acts as a store, bank, post office and café (home of the famous Oodnaburger, made to a "top secret" recipe), and sells detailed sketch maps of the area. The hotel holds the key to the **Railway Museum** opposite, where you'll find a strangely timeless photographic record of the town – scenes are hard to date because so little seems to have changed. Stock up with provisions and then check the Transport SA hotline (ⓣ1300 361 033) for road conditions and fuel supplies if you plan to head north towards Dalhousie Springs and the Simpson Desert (4WD only), or west to the Stuart Highway at Coober Pedy or Marla.

Dalhousie Hot Springs and desert crossings

Apart from the track out to the Stuart Highway, the area north of Oodnadatta is strictly for 4WDs, with **Dalhousie Hot Springs** in the Witjira National Park a worthwhile destination, or the **Simpson Desert** for the ultimate challenge. The route directly north, initially towards Finke and the Northern Territory, is relatively good as far as **Hamilton Homestead** (110km), though Fogarty's Claypan, around halfway, might present a sticky problem. From Hamilton the direct route east to Dalhousie Springs, shown on some maps, is now closed; take the longer route via **Eringa ruins** (160km) and **Bloods Creek bore** on the edge of **Witjira National Park**.

From there you can detour 30km north to **Mount Dare Hotel** (fuel, accommodation, food and provisions; ⓣ08/8670 7835, ⓦwww.mtdare.com.au; ❸).

The Simpson Desert crossing

Crossing the approximately 550km of steep north–south dunes through the **Simpson Desert** between Dalhousie in South Australia and Birdsville in Queensland is the ultimate challenge for any off-roader. In June, 4WD groups are joined by bikes attempting to complete the punishing **Simpson Desert Cycling Classic**. In winter, a steady stream of vehicles moves from west to east (the easier direction since the dunes' eastern slopes are steeper and harder to climb), but there's no help along the way, so don't underestimate the difficulties. Convoys need to include at least one skilled mechanic and, apart from the usual spares, a long-handled shovel and a strong tow-rope. While keeping weight to a minimum, you'll also need more than adequate food and water (six litres a day per person), and of course fuel – around a hundred litres of diesel if you take the shortest route, or two hundred litres of petrol. **Dune-ascent techniques** start with reducing tyre pressures to around 15psi to increase traction; select the gear and build up revs before starting. Don't attempt a gear change on the way up, and beware of oncoming vehicles on blind dune crests. If you don't make it over, slide down and try again; lighter vehicles may end up towing overburdened trucks. If all else fails, detours bypass many dunes.

The most testing, direct route follows the **French Line**, with the **Rig Road** detouring around the worst section but adding substantial distance (and fuel requirements) to the crossing. The enjoyment is mostly in the driving, though there's more than sand to look at: trees and shrubs grow in stabilized areas and at dusk you'll find dune crests patrolled by reptiles, birds, small mammals and insects. Photographers take advantage of clear skies at night to make timed exposures of the stars circling the heavens. **Purni Bore**, 70km from Dalhousie, is another uncapped spout (though this may change with growing concerns over diminished ground water), where birdlife and reeds fringe a 27°C pool; camping facilities here include a shower and toilet. A post battling to stay above shifting sand at **Poeppel Corner** (269km) marks the junction of Queensland, South Australia and the Northern Territory; salt lakes here vary in their water content and sometimes have to be skirted around. After the corner the dunes become higher but further apart, separated by claypans covered in mulga and grassland; you'll have to negotiate some of **Eyre Creek**'s channels too, which can be very muddy. **Big Red**, the last dune, is also the tallest; once over this it's a clear 41-kilometre run to Birdsville.

Note: A large area of the Simpson Desert outside the Witjira National Park and the Simpson Desert Conservation Park is now a Regional Reserve under the control of the NPWS, from whom you should seek advice and a **Desert Parks Pass** before setting out. Contact the NPWS at Port Augusta (ⓣ1800 816 078) or Hawker (ⓣ08/8648 4244).

In winter the homestead is busy with groups of 4WDs arriving from or departing for the desert crossing; it's at least 550km to the next fuel stop at Birdsville in Queensland. From the homestead it's a rough and bleak drive to Dalhousie Hot Springs.

The explorer Giles passed through this way in the 1870s, before the artesian basin had been extensively tapped by pastoralists, and described the scene:

The ground we had been traversing abruptly disappeared, and we found ourselves on the brink of limestone cliffs. . . From the foot of these stretched an almost illimitable expanse of – welcome sight – waving green reeds, with large pools of water at intervals, and dotted with island cones topped with reeds or acacia bushes.

Though reeds and water are less abundant today, Giles' account still rings true. The collection of over one hundred **mound springs** form Arabian-like oases, an impression enhanced by the green circle of date palms clustered around many of the pools. The largest spring, next to the **campsite** (which has showers and toilets), is cool enough to swim in and hot enough to unkink your back. What survives of the vegetation simmers with birdlife: budgerigars, galahs and the eye-catching purple, blue and red fairy wren. As nothing flows into the springs, the presence of **fish** – some, like the Dalhousie hardyhead, unique to the system – has prompted a variety of improbable explanations. One theory is that fish eggs were swept up in dust storms and later fell with rain at Dalhousie, but it's more likely that fish were brought in during an ancient deluge or that the population survives from when the area was an inland sea.

While the main springs area is flat and trampled by years of abuse from campers and cars – please stay on the marked paths here to avoid causing further erosion – trudging out to other groups over the salt and samphire-bush flats armed with a packed lunch and camera gives you an idea of what Giles was describing, and a good overview of the region from the top of well-formed, overgrown mounds. More views can be had from the stony hills to the west, and from **Dalhousie Homestead**, 16km south of the springs along the Pedirka road. The homestead was abandoned after the Ghan line was laid down, and today the stone walls, undermined by rabbit burrows, are gradually falling apart in the extreme climate.

Travel details

Trains

For all trains contact Great Southern Railway ⓣ 13 21 47, ⓦ www.gsr.com.au.

Adelaide to: Alice Springs (Ghan, 2 weekly; 20hr); Darwin (Ghan, 1 weekly; 47hr); Melbourne (Overlander, 4 weekly; 12hr 30min); Perth (Indian Pacific, 2 weekly; 38hr); Sydney (1 weekly, 23hr; Indian Pacific, 2 weekly; 26hr).

Buses

Further details of bus services can be found at ⓦ www.bussa.com.au.

Adelaide to: Alice Springs (1 daily; 18hr 30min); Barossa Valley (2 daily; 1hr 30min); Broken Hill (1 daily; 7hr); Ceduna (2 daily; 12hr); Clare (1 daily except Fri; 2hr 15min); Coober Pedy (1 daily; 10hr 30min); Goolwa (1–4 daily; 1hr 55min); Loxton (1 daily except Sat; 3hr 30min); Mannum (1 daily except Sat & Sun; 2hr 10min); McLaren Vale (1–3 daily; 50min); Melbourne (6 daily; 9hr 30min–14hr); Mount Gambier (1–3 daily; 6hr); Perth (1 daily; 34hr); Port Augusta (4–6 daily; 6hr); Port Lincoln (1 daily except Sat; 10hr); Renmark (2 daily; 4hr); Sydney (3 daily; 21–24hr); Victor Harbor (4 daily; 1hr 30min); Whyalla (4–6 daily; 5hr); Woomera (1 daily except Sat; 6hr); Yorke Peninsula (1 daily; 3–4hr).

Ceduna to: Adelaide (2 daily; 9hr 30min); Kalgoorlie (6 weekly; 26hr); Penong (6 weekly; 50min); Perth (6 weekly; 47hr); Port Augusta (2 daily; 5hr); Port Pirie (2 daily; 5hr 30min).
Coober Pedy to: Adelaide (at least 1 daily; 11hr); Alice Springs (at least 1 daily; 7hr); Oodnadatta (2 weekly; 5hr); Port Augusta (at least 1 daily; 6hr 10min).
Port Augusta to: Adelaide (at least 3 daily; 4hr 15min); Alice Springs (at least 1 daily; 14hr); Arkaroola (2 weekly; 7hr); Blinman (2 weekly; 3hr 15min); Ceduna (2 daily; 5hr); Coober Pedy (at least 1 daily; 6hr 10min); Hawker (3 weekly; 1hr 30min); Mambray Creek (for Mount Remarkable; several daily; 1hr); Marla (at least 1 daily; 10hr); Marree (2 weekly; 5hr); Melrose (2 weekly; 1hr); Port Lincoln (1–2 daily; 4hr 30min); Quorn (3 weekly; 40min); Roxby Downs (5 weekly; 3hr); Wilmington (2 weekly; 45min); Whyalla (1–2 daily; 50min); Woomera (5 weekly; 2hr).
Port Lincoln to: Adelaide (1 daily; 10hr); Port Augusta (1–2 daily; 4hr 30min); Whyalla (1–2 daily; 3hr 30min).

Flights

Adelaide to: Alice Springs (2 daily; 2hr); Ayers Rock Resort (2 daily via Alice; 3hr 45min); Brisbane (5–9 daily; 4hr); Broken Hill (1–2 daily; 1hr 40min); Cairns (1 daily; 4hr); Canberra (3 daily; 3hr 10min); Ceduna (1 daily except Sat; 1hr 30min); Coober Pedy (1 daily; 1hr 30min); Darwin (2 daily; 5hr); Kangaroo Island (8 daily; 30min); Leigh Creek (1 daily Mon–Fri; 2hr); Melbourne (11 daily; 1hr); Perth (3 daily; 5hr); Port Augusta (2–3 daily Mon–Fri; 1hr); Port Lincoln (5–7 daily; 30min); Sydney (9 daily; 2hr 10min); Whyalla (1–3 daily; 45min); Woomera (1 daily Tues, Wed & Thurs; 2hr).
Ceduna to: Adelaide (8 weekly; 1hr 20min).
Coober Pedy to: Adelaide (1 daily; 2hr).
Port Lincoln to: Adelaide (6 daily; 45min).

10

Melbourne and around

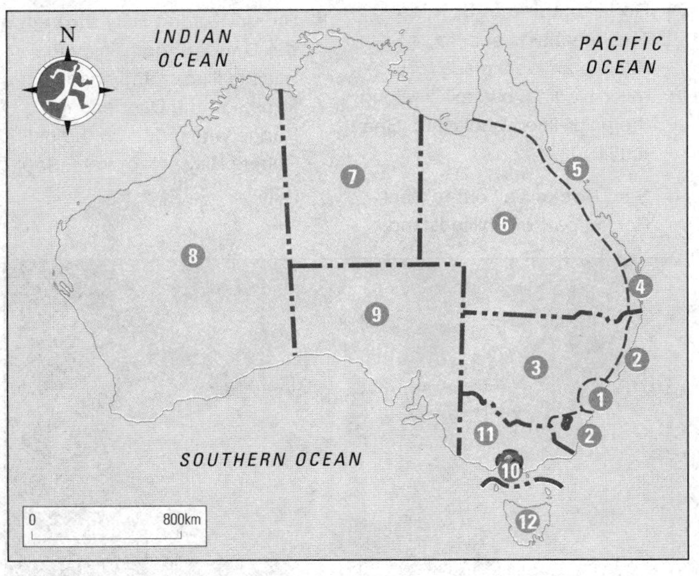

CHAPTER 10 Highlights

* **Chinatown** The low-rise, narrow streets of Melbourne's Chinatown haven't changed much since the nineteenth century, when a goldrush brought every corner of the world to this cosmopolitan city. See p.918
* **Aussie Rules match at the MCG** Join the cheering Melbourne crowds for an action-packed footy game at the MCG. See p.921
* **Roller-blading in St Kilda** The beachside suburb of St Kilda is an ideal place for roller-blading, especially along the palm-lined boulevard. See p.931
* **Seal Rocks** Sail out to Seal Rocks, part of Phillip Island Reserve, to see the largest known colony of Australian fur seals. See p.960
* **Yarra Valley** Victoria's answer to South Australia's Barossa Valley boasts pretty scenery and some great wineries. See pp.962–964
* **Healesville Sanctuary** Visit the beautifully located bushland zoo and wildlife sanctuary for injured and orphaned animals. See p.963
* **Riding Puffing Billy through the Dandenongs** Enjoy the quaint villages and shady forests of the Dandenong Range with a ride on the old Puffing Billy steam train. See p.964

△ Chapel Street tram

10

Melbourne and around

MELBOURNE is Australia's second-largest city, with a population of 3.5 million, around half a million less than Sydney. Rivalry between the two cities – in every sphere from cricket to business – is on an almost childish level. In purely monetary terms, Sydney is clearly in the ascendancy, having stolen a march on Melbourne as the nation's financial centre. However, as Melburnians never tire of pointing out, they have the incredible good fortune to inhabit what is often described as "one of the world's most liveable cities", and while Melbourne may lack a truly stunning natural setting or in-your-face sights, its subtle charms grow on all who spend time here, making it an undeniably pleasant place to live, and enjoyable to visit, too.

In many ways, Melbourne is the most European of all Australian cities: magnificent landscaped gardens and parks provide green spaces near the centre, while beneath the skyscrapers of the Central Business District (CBD), an understorey of solid, Victorian-era facades ranged along tree-lined boulevards present the city on a more human scale. The European influence is perhaps most obvious in winter, as trams rattle past warm cafés and bookshops, and promenaders dress stylishly against the chill. Not that Europe has supplied the city's only influences: large-scale immigration since World War II has shaken up the city's formerly self-absorbed, parochial WASP mindset for good. Whole villages have come here from Lebanon, Turkey, Vietnam and all over Europe, most especially from Greece, furnishing the well-worn statistic that Melbourne is the third-largest Greek city behind Athens and Thessaloniki. Not surprisingly, the immigrant blend has transformed the city into a **foodie mecca**, where tucking into a different cuisine each night – or new hybrids of East, West and South – is one of the great treats.

Melbourne's strong claim to being the nation's **cultural capital** is well founded: laced with a healthy dash of counterculture, the city's artistic life flourishes, culminating in the highbrow Melbourne International Arts Festival for two weeks in October, and its slightly more offbeat (and shoestring) cousin, the Fringe Festival. The city also takes pride in its leading role in Australian literary life, based around the Writers' Festival in August. Throughout the year, there are heavyweight seasons of classical music and theatre, a wacky array of small galleries, and enough art-house movies to last a lifetime. **Sport too**,

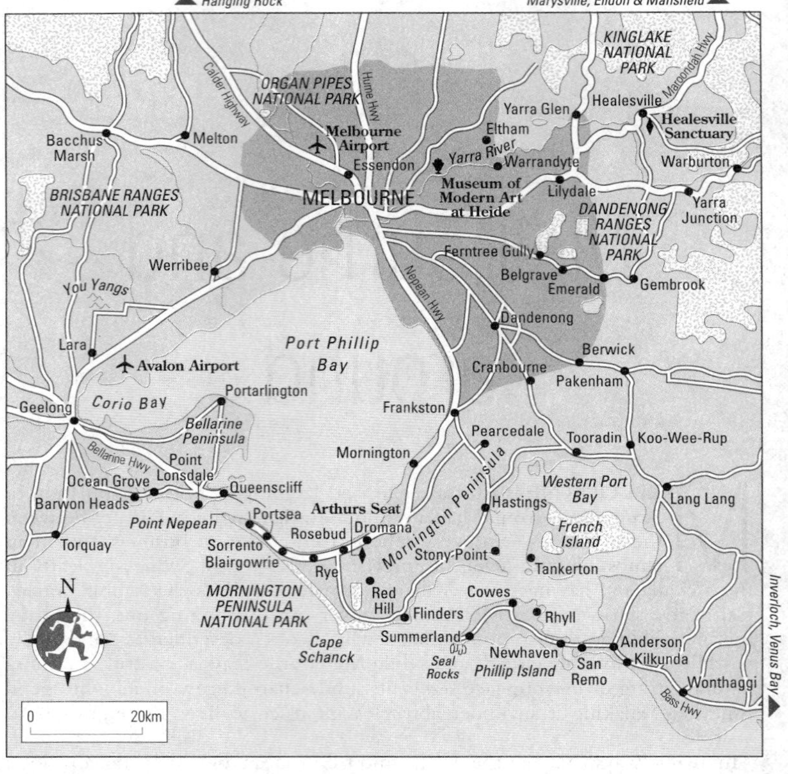

especially Australian Rules Football, is almost a religion here, while the Melbourne Cup in November is a public holiday, celebrated with gusto.

Melbourne is an excellent base for day-trips out into the surrounding countryside. Closest to Melbourne are the quaint villages of the eucalypt-covered **Dandenong Ranges**, while the scenic **Yarra Valley**, in the northeast, is Victoria's answer to South Australia's Barossa Valley, and one of many wine-producing areas around Melbourne. To the south, huge **Port Phillip Bay** is encircled by the arms of the Bellarine and Mornington peninsulas. **Mornington Peninsula** offers more opportunity for wine-tasting, and in addition to bucolic scenery there are beaches galore, the windswept ones popular with surfers, while the placid waters of the bay are good for swimming and messing about in boats. **Geelong** and most of the **Bellarine Peninsula** are maybe not quite so captivating, but Queenscliff near the narrow entrance to Port Phillip Bay, with its beautiful, refurbished grand hotels, is enjoying something of a comeback as a stylish (and expensive) weekend getaway.

Melbourne boasts a reasonably cool **climate** (although January and February are prone to barbaric hot spells when temperatures can climb into the forties).

Arrival and information

Melbourne Airport is 22km northwest of the city; the **Skybus Super Shuttle** (every 15min 6am–10pm, every 30min 10pm–1am and 5am–6am, hourly 1am–5am; $13 one way, $24 return, valid one year; ⓣ03/9670 7992; on-line ticket booking ⓦwww.skybus.com.au) will take you to Southern Cross station on Spencer Street on the west side of the city. A complimentary minibus service (Mon–Fri 6am–10pm, Sat & Sun 7.30am–6.30pm) picks up passengers from the coach terminal and drops them off at hotels in the city centre and the adjacent suburbs of Carlton, East Melbourne and South Melbourne. Travelling time between Melbourne Airport and the coach terminal is about thirty minutes. A taxi from Melbourne Airport costs around $35 to the city centre, $45 to St Kilda. Jetstar Airways, a budget subsidiary of Qantas, operates a limited number of **domestic flights** from **Avalon Airport**, located just off the Princes Freeway, 55km southwest of Melbourne. Transport is provided by **Sunbus** (ⓣ03/9689 6888; $12 one way), which meets all arriving Jetstar flights and drops off passengers at Spencer Street, and takes about an hour, depending on traffic.

Greyhound Australia buses arrive at the Greyhound Australia Coach Terminal on the north side of the city centre at Franklin St; Firefly and V/Line buses use the bus terminal at **Southern Cross Station**. At the time of writing, frantic construction work was going on here at what was formerly known as Spencer Street railway station, with the revamped interchange scheduled to open fully at the end of 2005 comprising a station for local, country and interstate **trains** and a coach terminal. Some hostels pick up from Southern Cross Station, as well as from the Tasmanian **ferry terminal** located about 4km southwest of the city centre at Station Pier in Port Melbourne. The terminal is served by the #109 tram to Collins Street in the CBD.

Information

The **Melbourne Visitor Centre**, housed underneath Federation Square, directly opposite Flinders Street station (daily 9am–6pm; ⓣ03/9658 9658, ⓦwww.thatsmelbourne.com.au), has brochures and maps galore about Melbourne and the rest of the state, in particular the pocket-sized *melbourne walks* series is probably the most useful: each one describes a themed, self-guided walk (1hr 30min–2hr 30min) around the city and has a good reference map. There's also information on public transport and major events and a tour and accommodation booking service (same hours; ⓣ03/9650 3663). Available at the centre is the discount sightseeing card, See Melbourne & Beyond Smartvisit Card (also sold online at ⓦwww.seemelbournecard.com), which provides free admission to more than 50 attractions in Melbourne and around and costs $99 for two days, $129 for three days and $199 for seven days. It's well worth the expense if you intend doing some serious sightseeing. A free **Greeter Service** matches up visitors with local volunteers for half a day, giving them an unparalleled insider's view of the city – book at least three days in advance (ⓣ03/9658 9658, ⓔgreeter@melbourne.vic.gov.au). **Information Victoria**, along Collins St (Mon–Fri 8.30am–5.30pm; ⓣ1300 366 356), has books and other publications on topics related to the state as well as the city's largest range of local maps, it also has a notice board of city events. **Tourism Victoria** (daily 8am–6pm; ⓣ13 28 42, ⓦwww.visitvictoria.com) is a phone and Internet service providing information on attractions, accommodation and upcoming events.

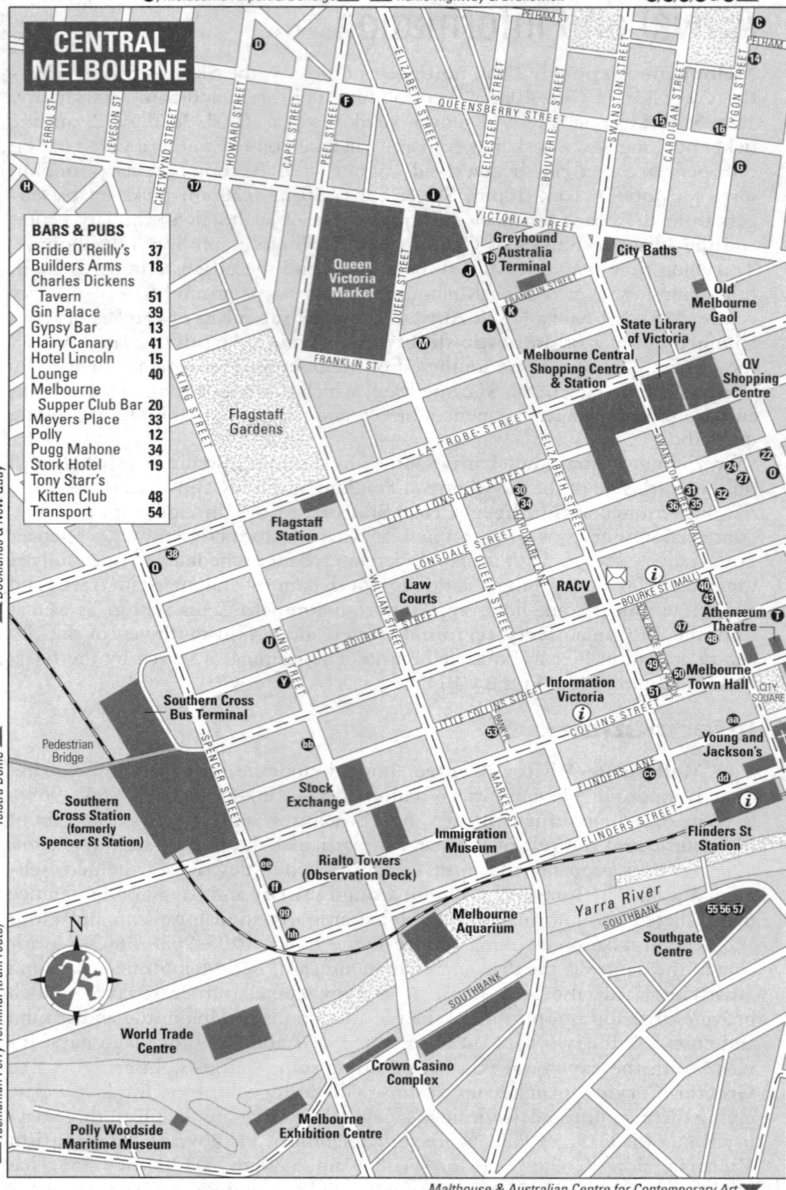

RESTAURANTS

Afghan Gallery	6	Camy Shanghai Dumpling and Noodle Restaurant	32	Crossways Food for Life	43	Il Solito Posto Basement	45
Babka Bakery Cafe	7	Chez Phat	27	eat drink bento	30	Jimmy Watson's	2
BearBrass	55	China Bar	22	Empress of China	23	Kenzan	44
Blue Train Café	56	Cookie	31	ezard at the Adelphi	52	Lemongrass	14
Brunetti	1			Flower Drum	25	Little Malaysia	21
				Grossi Florentino	26	Mario's	8

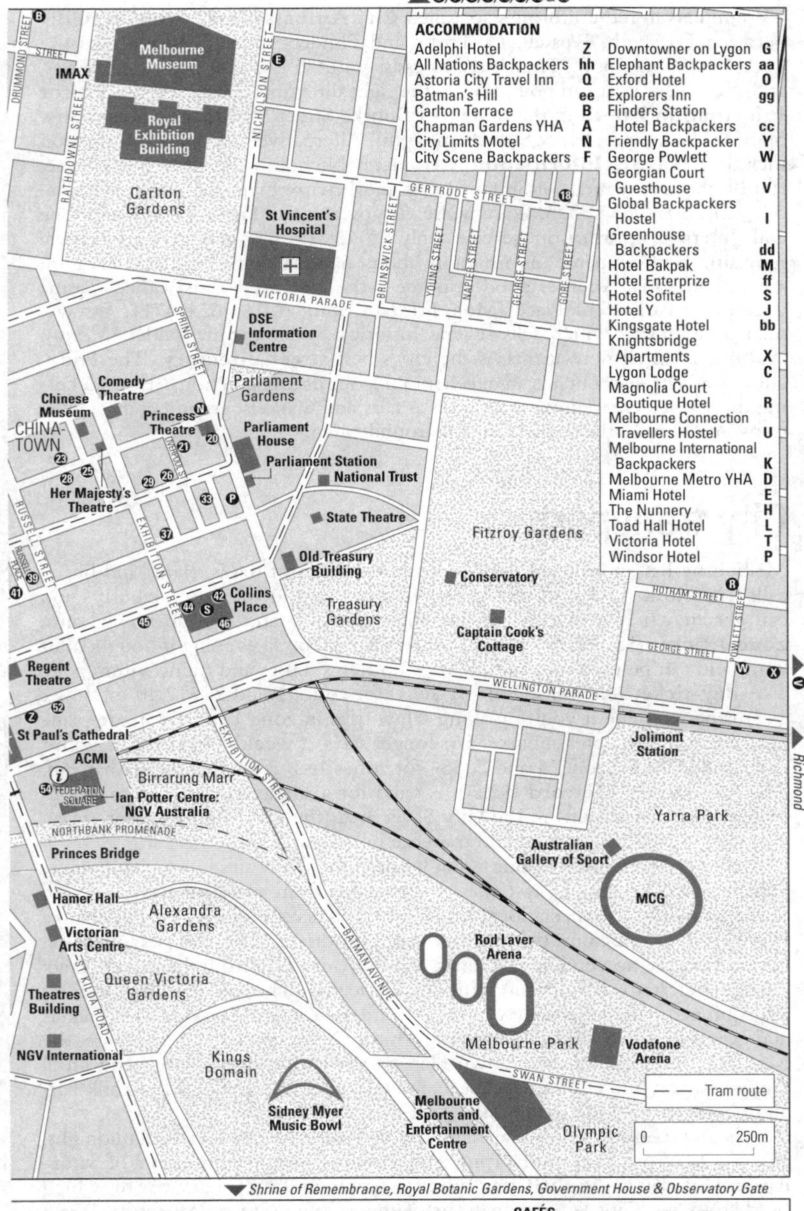

Mekong 36
Le Restaurant 46
Rhumbaralla's 9
Satay Inn 35
Shakahari 3
Shark Fin House 28
Syracuse 53
Thai Thani 10
Tiamo 1 4
Toofey's 5
Toto's Pizza House 16
The Vegie Bar 11
Walter's Wine Bar 57
Warung Agus 17
William Angliss College 38

CAFÉS

Cafe La 42
Cafe Segovia 49
Hopetoun Tea Rooms 50
Laurent Patisserie 47
Medallion Cafe & Cakes 24
Pellegrini's Espresso Bar 29

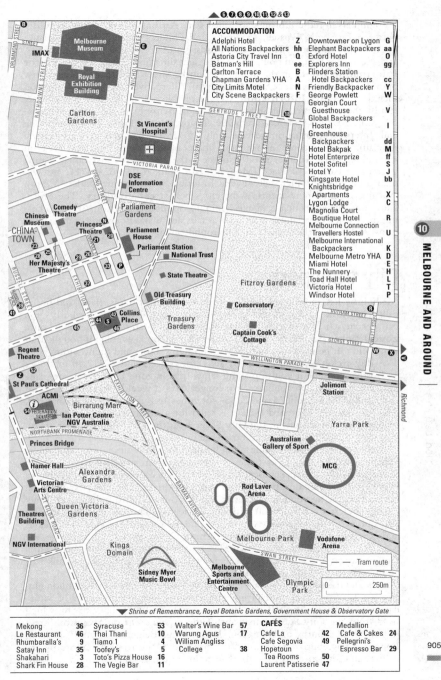

Volunteers in red uniforms – so-called **City Ambassadors** – roam the CBD between Elizabeth, Russell, La Trobe and Flinders streets (Mon–Fri 10am–4pm, Sat 11am–2pm). They'll try to assist with all kinds of tourist enquiries, and at the very least can point you in the right direction. There's also a **Visitor Information Booth** in the middle of Bourke Street Mall (Mon–Thurs 9am–5pm, Fri 9am–7pm, Sat & Sun 10am–5pm). Alternative sources of information include the **DSE Information Centre**, 8 Nicholson St, East Melbourne, run by the Department of Sustainability and Environment (Mon–Fri 8.30am–5.30pm; ⓣ03/9637 8325, ⓦwww.dse.vic.gov.au); and **Parks Victoria** (phone and Internet information service only: ⓣ13 19 63, ⓦwww.parkweb.vic.gov.au). Both dispense information about national parks and conservation areas in Victoria. Another good resource is the **National Trust** office, Tasma Terrace, 6 Parliament Place (Mon–Fri 9am–5pm; ⓣ03/9654 4711, ⓦwww.nattrust.com.au), which sells several historical walking-tour guides. *Melway,* available from all newsagents, is the city's best **street directory**. The Friday edition of *The Age* contains an excellent pull-out **listings** section, "EG", detailing the week's entertainment, as well as fairs and markets, art and craft exhibitions, sport, and other events in and around town.

City transport

Melbourne has an efficient public transport system of trams, trains and buses, called **metlink**. Unless you're going on a day-trip to the outer suburbs, you can get anywhere you need to, including St Kilda and Williamstown, on a **zone 1 ticket** ($3.10); this is valid for two hours (or all evening if bought after 7pm) and can be used for multiple trips on trams, buses and trains within zone 1. A **day-ticket** ($5.90 for zone 1; $9.50 for zones 1 and 2; $12.40 for zones 1–3) is better value if you're making a few trips in zone 1, or if you are planning a trip to the outer suburbs. For longer stays, a **weekly ticket** ($25.90 for zone 1; $43.70 for zones 1 and 2; $54 for zones 1–3) is an even better bargain. The **City Saver Metcard** ($2.20) is valid for a single trip on a tram or bus or between two stations in the City Saver area (the CBD and adjacent areas). Transfers between bus, tram and train are not possible with this card.

You'll need to **validate** your ticket by machine every time you board a new vehicle. Two-hour and day-tickets are available from **vending machines** on board trams and at train stations. Those on trams accept coins only, but change is given. You can't buy tickets from the tram driver. The reverse applies on buses: there are no vending machines, so buy your ticket from the driver (exact change preferred). Major train stations have staffed ticket offices; other stations are equipped with coins-only vending machines. You can also buy Met Tickets and get travel advice at the Melbourne Visitor Centre at Federation Square, the MetShop at the Melbourne Town Hall on the corner of Swanston and Little Collins streets, and at other shops, including most newsagents, a few milk bars and pharmacies – look for the flag with the metcard logo.

Train and tram services operate Monday to Saturday from 5am until midnight, and Sunday from 8am until 11pm, supplemented in the early hours of Saturday and Sunday by **NightRider buses** (every hour 12.30–4.30am; $6), which head from the City Square (in front of the *Westin Hotel* on Swanston Street to the outer suburbs of Frankston, Dandenong, Belgrave, Lilydale, Eltham, Epping, Craigieburn, St Albans, Werribee and Melton ($8.20), more or less in the same direction as the suburban train routes. Each bus has an onboard mobile phone, on which the driver can book a taxi to meet you at a bus stop (free call), or you can call a friend ($1) to meet you. For further information, call metlink (daily 6am–10pm, ⓣ13 16 38). For a range of public transport information including timetables and disability services, visit ⓦwww.metlinkmelbourne.com.au.

Trams

Melbourne's **trams** give the city a distinctive character and provide a pleasant, environmentally friendly way of getting around: the **City Circle** (see box below) is particularly convenient, and free. Trams run down the centre of the road, and stops are signposted (the "Central Melbourne" map shows the main routes in the centre); they often have central islands where you can wait: remember to keep an eye out for trams when crossing the road. Some trams can be boarded only at the front; others also have access via middle and rear doors.

Trains

Trains are the fastest way to reach distant suburbs. An underground loop system feeding into seventeen suburban lines connects the city centre's five train stations: **Southern Cross**, which also serves as the station for interstate and country trains; **Flagstaff**, on the corner of La Trobe and William streets; **Melbourne Central**, on the corner of Swanston and La Trobe streets; **Parliament**, on Spring Street; and **Flinders Street**, the main suburban station. Bikes can be carried free, but metlink asks people not to take bikes during peak periods (Mon–Fri 7–9.30am & 4–6pm).

Buses

Regular **buses** often run on the same routes as trams, as well as filling gaps where no train or tram lines run. Apart from the NightRider buses (see above), in general they are the least useful mode of public transport for visitors, with the possible exception of **Melbourne on the Move** (daily every 30min 10am–3pm; 24hr ticket $32; 48hr ticket $50; ⓣ1300 558 686, ⓦwww.melbourneonthemove.com.au), a privately run "explorer bus". It starts from City Square on Swanston Street and does a circuit of the city and adjacent

Melbourne's vintage trams

Some of Melbourne's trams are vintage wooden vehicles dating back as far as the 1930s (though none is quite as old as the system, which dates from 1885). Vintage **City Circle trams** (free) run in a loop along Flinders Street, Spring Street, Nicholson Street, La Trobe Street and Spencer Street (daily except Christmas Day and Good Friday every 12min 10am–6pm, Nov–March Thurs–Sat until 9pm). The **Colonial Tramcar Restaurant** (ⓣ03/9696 4000, ⓦwww.tramrestaurant.com.au) is a converted 1927 tram offering traditional silver- and white-linen restaurant service as you trundle around Melbourne. The service starts at Normanby Rd near the Crown Casino, South Melbourne; the restaurant (non-smoking) offers a three-course early dinner (daily 5.45–7.15pm; $66) and a five-course dinner ($104.50 Fri & Sat, $93.50 Mon–Thurs & Sun), plus a four-course lunch (Sun 1–3pm and other days subject to demand; $71.50). All drinks are included. You'll need to reserve at least two to three weeks ahead, or up to three or four months in advance for Friday and Saturday evenings.

Driving and cycling in Melbourne

Driving in Melbourne requires some care, mainly because of the trams. You can overtake a tram only on the left and must stop and wait behind it while passengers get on and off, as they step directly into the road (though there's no need to stop if there's a central pedestrian island). A peculiar rule has developed to accommodate trams at major intersections in the city centre: when turning right, you pull over to the left-hand lane and wait for the lights to change to amber before turning – a so-called "hook turn". Signs overhead indicate when this rule applies.

Cyclists should also watch out for tram lines – tyres can easily get wedged in them. This apart, Melbourne is perfect for cycling and you'll be in good company as it's a popular way of getting around. The friendly staff at **Bicycle Victoria** on Level 10, 446 Collins St (Mon–Fri 8.45am–5.15pm; ⓣ03/8636 8888) can assist with practical information; their website ⓦwww.bv.com.au has a list of organized bike rides in Victoria and interstate. The useful *Discovering Victoria's Bike Paths* ($18.95) is available at Bicycle Victoria or at newsagents. See "Listings", p.947, for **bike rental**. A good way of getting a handle on Melbourne is joining one of the guided, three-hour cycling tours run by **Real Melbourne Bike Tours** (ⓣ0417 339 203, ⓦwww.byohouse.com.au/biketours; $50 everything included; bookings necessary). They operate daily on demand and include a refreshment stop for coffee and cake.

suburbs, taking in the Arts Centre, the Botanic Gardens, the sports grounds and gardens of East Melbourne, the CBD and Carlton and stopping at twenty designated stops. Passengers buy a ticket on board which allows them to get on and off the bus as often as they want within 24 or 48 hours.

Accommodation

The most obvious areas with a concentration of accommodation places are the **city centre**, the adjoining suburbs of **North Melbourne**, **Carlton**, **Fitzroy**, **East Melbourne and Richmond**, and down by the bay around **St Kilda**. Some of the cheap accommodation areas on the fringes of the city centre are fairly dead at night, though they're within easy reach of all the action. St Kilda is very lively, if a bit rough around the edges, with a few hostels and quite a few motels and apartments. South of the CBD, **South Melbourne**, **Albert Park**, **South Yarra and Windsor** (see the "Melbourne Suburbs" map) offer a good compromise, handy for both the city centre and the beach, and with lots of good eating options.

The most exclusive **hotels** are in the centre, particularly around Collins Street and the leisure precincts of Southgate and the Crown Casino, while there's a collection of revamped hotels around Southern Cross Station. Melbourne has plenty of **backpacker accommodation**, ranging from fairly basic, even scruffy places to smart, custom-built hostels with all the mod cons. During winter, most hostel beds cost around $20, rising to around $26 in summer. Most hostels have separate dorms for females on request. Standard facilities include a kitchen, TV room, laundry, luggage storage and Internet access. The price codes given in the listings below are for the cheapest double room in summer.

For those with their own transport, **campsite** cabins and vans are an inexpensive option but they are located far from the city centre. You can book last-minute **discounted accommodation** in the city at ⓦwww.wotif.com.

Finally, if you plan on staying during the big **sporting events** you should be aware that virtually all accommodation (from five-star hotels to the scruffiest doss houses) tends to be booked out, usually for months, if not a year in advance. This applies particularly to the Australian Open Tennis in January and the Grand Prix (first or second weekend in March); other events and times to avoid or pre-book long in advance are the Melbourne Cup (first Tuesday in November and the preceding weekend) and the AFL Grand Final (second last Saturday in September).

City centre

Hotels and motels

Adelphi Hotel 187 Flinders Lane ⓣ03/9650 7555, ⓦwww.adelphi.com.au. Stylish hotel with a striking exterior and a sparse, ultramodern interior design that extends to the large guest rooms, all topped with a huge pool on the roof. ❼

Astoria City Travel Inn 288 Spencer St ⓣ03/9670 6801, ⓦwww.astoriainternational.com. Affordable and pleasant motel three blocks north of Southern Cross station, with spacious and bright units and an undercover car park; amenities include a saltwater pool and laundry. ❹

Batman's Hill 66 Spencer St ⓣ03/9614 6344, ⓦwww.batmanshill.com. An elegant Edwardian exterior belies a functional and modern interior. The wide range of facilities includes bars, a restaurant and 24hr room service, and it's handy for Southern Cross station, Telstra Dome, Docklands and the Casino Entertainment Complex just south of the river. ❺

City Limits Motel 20 Little Bourke St ⓣ03/9662 2544 or 1800 808 651, ⓦwww.citylimits.com.au. Motel-style units with en suite and the usual mod cons, on a quiet street just around the corner from Parliament station. Rates include continental breakfast. ❺

Explorers Inn 16 Spencer St ⓣ03/9621 3333 or 1800 816 168, ⓦwww.explorersinn.com.au. Renamed and redecorated medium-price hotel. Its lobby and café-bar decorated in groovy colours front pleasant if somewhat plain en-suite rooms. Internet access. ❺

Hotel Enterprize 44 Spencer St ⓣ03/9629 6991, ⓦwww.hotelenterprize.com.au. Solid hotel in central location opposite Southern Cross station with good, spacious superior rooms and smaller, but well-presented rooms in the budget section – the latter are particularly good value. Facilities include two restaurants and undercover parking ($5 per day). ❹–❻.

Hotel Sofitel 25 Collins St ⓣ03/9653 0000 or 1300 656 565, ⓦwww.sofitelmelbourne.com.au. An I.M. Pei-designed hotel, set on the top floors of a fifty-storey building, with marvellous views across Melbourne and surrounds, gloriously comfortable rooms and a good spread of cafés and restaurants, including the airy and reasonably cheap *Cafe La* (see p.934) and *Le Restaurant* (see p.935), a formal dining place with sensational vistas. ❽

Kingsgate Hotel 131 King St ⓣ03/9629 4171 or 1300 734 171, ⓦwww.kingsgatehotel.com.au. Huge, renovated old private hotel. En-suite rooms with colour TV, heating and air-con are good value; there are also inexpensive no-frills budget rooms with shared facilities and a few rooms for small groups or families (up to four beds). Facilities include a laundry, Internet access, a pleasant TV lounge and a bar and café (but no kitchen). Cheap breakfast available. ❸–❹

Miami Hotel 13 Hawke St, off the north end of King St ⓣ03/9321 2444 or 1800 132 333, ⓦwww.themiami.com.au. Renovated en-suite rooms with TV, wardrobe and ceiling fan, as well as simple, clean, standard rooms with shared facilities – good-value rates include a cooked breakfast. Also has a TV lounge, pool table, laundry and free off-street parking, but no kitchen. ❸

Victoria Hotel 215 Little Collins St ⓣ03/9653 0441 or 1800 331 147, ⓦwww.victoriahotel.com.au. Huge refurbished hotel in an unbeatable central location, with its own café, bar, a pool and sauna, and a wide range of rooms; the cheapest ones have shared facilities. Undercover parking available ($10 per day). ❸–❺

Windsor Hotel 103 Spring St ⓣ03/9633 6000 or 1800 033 100, ⓦwww.thewindsor.com.au. This luxurious, landmark Victorian-era hotel has 180 spacious, lavishly decorated rooms and suites. ❽

Budget hotels and hostels

All Nations Backpackers 2 Spencer St, at the corner of Flinders St ⓣ03/9620 1022 or 1800 222 238, ⓦwww.allnations.com.au. Big, rambling hostel renovated to a rather mediocre standard, though an in-house employment agency and a bar with free beer on arrival seem to keep the guests happy. There's 24hr reception and good security. Pick-up from airports 5.15am–1.30am; use courtesy phone at the airport. Rates include a light breakfast. Dorms (4–10 beds) $20–23.

Elephant Backpackers 250 Flinders St ⓣ03/9564 2616, ⓦwww.elephantbackpackers.citysearch.com.au. Very clean, well-equipped, secure and inexpensive hostel in an unbeatable central location. Singles and doubles are especially good value. The only drawbacks are a lack of complete privacy, as the walls between the rooms don't reach the ceiling, and the kitchen and small TV lounge are located in the rather dark basement. In winter you can get a twin room for the price of a dorm. Dorms $20, rooms ❷

Exford Hotel 199 Russell St ⓣ03/9663 2697, ⓦwww.exfordhotel.com.au. Secure, clean and good-value hostel set in an extremely central position above a refurbished pub, with friendly and helpful staff and the usual amenities, plus a tiny sundeck with BBQ. Accommodation is in two- to four-bed dorms, twins and doubles. Dorms $20–24, rooms ❸

Flinders Station Hotel Backpackers 35 Elizabeth St ⓣ03/9620 5100, ⓦwww.flindersbp.com.au. Large, but well-organized and clean hostel, centrally located in a former office block a few hundred metres from Flinders Street station. A spacious kitchen, sitting area, TV-lounge and pool table are all arranged around the reception desk on the third floor. Also a bar on the ground floor and one for in-house guests upstairs. Four-bed dorms with lockers under the beds $20; doubles with shared facilities ❸, spacious en-suite doubles ❸

Friendly Backpacker 197 King St ⓣ03/9670 1111 or 1800 671 115, ⓦwww.friendlygroup.com.au. Clean and secure hostel that lives up to its name. It has bright rooms with air-con and heating, a cosy small sitting area on each floor, a good kitchen and common room with TV near the reception in the basement, a well-organized noticeboard and very helpful staff. Convenient location close to Southern Cross station and Victoria Market. Dorms (mainly 4-bed) $26, rooms ❸

Greenhouse Backpackers 228 Flinders Lane ⓣ03/9639 6400 or 1800 249 207, ⓦwww.friendlygroup.com.au. Clean and very friendly place in a superb sixth-floor location amidst the characterful alleys and laneways of Melbourne's CBD. Sleeping is in spacious dorms (4–6 beds), or in singles and doubles. The big kitchen is well equipped with lots of cookers and plenty of storage space. In addition, there's a lounge, a big TV room, pool table, and a pleasant rooftop garden with BBQ. Staff can assist with finding work. A travel desk is located on the ground floor. Rates include breakfast and 30 min Internet access per day. Dorms $27, rooms ❸

Hotel Bakpak 167 Franklin St ⓣ03/9329 7525 or 1800 645 200, ⓦwww.bakpakgroup.com. Around six hundred beds in a converted former school building brightened up with colour co-ordinated paintwork, carpets and polished timber floors. In-house facilities include an employment agency, travel shop, café, cellar bar and a small cinema with free screenings plus internet access. All dorms (4–12 beds) have fans and lockers; female dorms available on request. There are also some spartan singles and doubles. Free pick-ups from bus terminals and airport between 6am and 8pm. Rates include light breakfast. Dorms $23–26, rooms ❸

Hotel Y 489 Elizabeth St ⓣ03/9329 5188 or 1800 468 359, ⓦwww.hotely.com.au. Close to Greyhound Australia Terminal and Victoria Market. The refurbished hotel has standard en-suite rooms with a small fridge, TV and a small desk; deluxe rooms also have air con and central heating. There's a microwave and a toaster in the bright, spacious guest lounge, and facilities also include a laundry and free access to the pool and gym at nearby City Baths. ❺

Melbourne Connection Travellers Hostel 205 King St ⓣ03/9642 4464. Convenient location close to Southern Cross station and Queen Victoria Market. A small, clean hostel – the polished wooden floorboards in the corridor are a nice touch – with TV-lounge and Internet room in the basement and a smallish but well-equipped kitchen on the ground floor. Rates including breakfast are dorms (4–14 beds) $22–27, rooms ❸

Melbourne International Backpackers 450 Elizabeth St ⓣ03/9662 4066, ⓦwww.melbourneinternationalbackpackers.com. Located just a few metres away from the Greyhound Australia Terminal, this is yet another hostel set in refurbished former offices. It's clean, wheelchair-friendly and secure, with rooms and dorms (mainly 4-bed), a big, well-equipped kitchen and a common room. Internet access. Reception 24hr. Dorms $20–$23, rooms ❸

Toad Hall Hotel 441 Elizabeth St ⓣ03/9600 9010, ⓦwww.toadhallhotel.com.au. Excellent budget choice close to Victoria Market and the Greyhound Australia Terminal. Clean dorms with en suite and private rooms, some with en suite. Friendly, cosy and secure, with a good kitchen, TV room, and a lovely, shaded courtyard out the back. Dorms $25, rooms ❸

North Melbourne, Carlton and Fitzroy

Carlton Terrace 196 Drummond St, Carlton ⓣ03/9662 2735 or 1800 035 388, ⓦwww.carltonterrace.com.au. Small guesthouse in a very pleasantly refurbished Victorian terrace house, handy to the city, Melbourne University and Carlton's cafés and restaurants. En-suite studio rooms with all mod cons, including a kitchenette. Very competitive rates for longer stays (5+ nights). Breakfast available. ❹

Chapman Gardens YHA 76 Chapman St, North Melbourne ⓣ03/9328 3595, ⓦwww.yha.com.au. More intimate than its sister hostel, the *Melbourne Metro YHA*, but further away from the city centre (3km) – take tram #50, #57 or #59 north from Elizabeth St, or Skybus drops off and picks up 50m from here. Mainly twins, a few singles, doubles and dorms (3–5 beds). Bicycle hire available. Dorms $22, rooms ❷

City Scene Backpackers 361 Queensberry St ⓣ03/9348 9525, ⓦwww.cityscene.com.au. Small friendly hostel next to a pub; the rooms and dorms (4 beds) come with heating and air con; rates include breakfast. Ring for airport pick-up. Dorms $18–20, rooms ❷

Downtowner on Lygon 66 Lygon St, Carlton ⓣ03/9663 5555 or 1800 800 130, ⓦwww.downtowner.com.au. Attractively refurbished rooms with all mod cons (some with spa) in the heart of Carlton. Undercover parking. ❺

Global Backpackers Hostel 238 Victoria St, North Melbourne ⓣ03/9328 3728 or 1800 700 478, ⓔglobalhostel@bigpond.com. Set above a pub opposite Queen Victoria Market, this small, simple and fairly pleasant hostel has dorms (mainly 4-bed), rooms, a TV lounge, kitchen, and a tiny courtyard. Dorms $19, rooms ❷

Lygon Lodge 220 Lygon St, Carlton ⓣ03/9663 6633. Good motel in central Carlton with attractive rooms, some with small kitchenette. Undercover car parking. ❺

Melbourne Metro YHA 78 Howard St, off Victoria St ⓣ03/9329 8599, ⓦwww.yha.com.au. An easy ten-minute walk from the bus terminal, this huge modern hostel – really more like a smart hotel – has family, double/twin and single rooms, with or without en suite, plus dorms (4–8 beds), and a host of other amenities: 24hr kitchen, rooftop garden with BBQ, Internet lounge, bicycle hire, car parking, plus a licensed cafeteria, currency exchange and an in-house travel agent. Skybus drops off and picks up here every half-hour. Dorms $25–28, rooms ❸

The Nunnery 116 Nicholson St, Fitzroy ⓣ03/9419 8637 or 1800 032 635, take #96 tram from Bourke St. The hostel section here has rather crammed dorms (4–12 beds), but the atmosphere is busy and friendly; there's also a big, cosy TV lounge, a kitchen and Internet access. The much more spacious guesthouse section next door has private rooms with shared facilities, plus a kitchen and lounge. Brunswick Street cafés and pubs are close to hand. Breakfast included. Dorms $23–27, hostel rooms ❸, guesthouse rooms ❹

East Melbourne

George Powlett Powlett St, cnr George St ⓣ03/9419 9488, ⓦwww.georgepowlett.com.au. Motel-style units off two central courtyards in a central location. Kitchenette with microwave and fridge, plus parking available. ❹

Georgian Court Guesthouse 21–25 George St ⓣ03/9419 6353. Standard rooms with shared facilities, and en-suite rooms equipped with TV, fridge and radio; all are bright, tastefully furnished and serviced daily. Rates include light breakfast. Quiet yet very central location. ❹

Knightsbridge Apartments 101 George St ⓣ03/9419 1333, ⓦwww.knightsbridgeapartments.com.au. Bright, serviced self-catering studio and two-bedroom apartments 1km from the centre, on a quiet street running off the east side of Fitzroy Gardens. Laundry and off-street parking. Excellent value. ❺

Magnolia Court Boutique Hotel 101 Powlett St ⓣ03/9419 4222, ⓦwww.magnolia-court.com.au. Elegant hotel in a quiet street, but within walking distance of Fitzroy Gardens, the CBD, MCG and Melbourne Park. Very tastefully furnished rooms with all facilities in two older, lovingly restored buildings as well as a new annexe. Breakfast available. ❺–❼

Richmond

Central Accommodation 21 Bromham Place, Richmond ⓣ03/9427 9826, ⓦwww.centralaccommodation.net. Touted as being more like a family home than a hostel, but with mainly dorms (4-bed), including a few doubles in a super-central location close to the lively pubs and shops of Bridge Rd; within walking distance (15min) of the MCG and Melbourne Park. Owners have good employment contacts in the area. Take tram #75 or #48 from Spencer St or Flinders St to stop no. 18. Weekly bookings only: dorms $125, doubles $145 per person.

Freeman Lodge 153 Hoddle St ⓣ03/8430 2978. Renovated, clean budget guesthouse with well-equipped rooms and dorms (maximum 4 beds) for a very low price. It's just around the corner from West Richmond station, within walking distance of Bridge Rd. Dorms $18–20, rooms ❷

Richmond Hill Hotel 353 Church St (between Bridge Rd and Swan St) ⓣ03/9428 6501 or 1800 801 618, ⓦwww.richmondhillhotel.com.au. Set in a stately Victorian mansion in a pretty garden, with spacious and cosy dining and sitting rooms. The guesthouse section offers B&B rooms with en-suite or shared facilities; the budget section has small, very clean dorms and good-value singles and twins (bunks), all with shared facilities and a kitchen. Tram #75 or #48 from Spencer St or Flinders St. Dorms $24–30, budget rooms ❸, guesthouse rooms ❹–❺

Albert Park, Middle Park, South Yarra and Windsor

The Beach Accommodation 97 Beaconsfield Parade, Albert Park ⓣ03/9690 4642, ⓦwww.thebeachaccommodation.com.au. Pleasant dorms, twins and doubles above a pub, everything completely refurbished, in a hard-to-beat location opposite a tram stop, overlooking the beach and handy for the Tasmanian ferry. Tram #1 from Swanston St to South Melbourne Beach. Dorms from $21, rooms ❸

Chapel Street Backpackers 22 Chapel St, Windsor ⓣ03/9533 6855 or 1800 613 333, ⓦwww.csbackpackers.com.au. Excellent, friendly hostel at the southern, quieter end of Chapel St, with very clean and comfy en-suite dorms (4–6 beds) and doubles. Small outdoor courtyard with BBQ. Opposite Windsor station (Sandringham line). Rates including a continental breakfast are dorms $26, rooms ❸

College Lawn Hotel 36 Greville St, Windsor ⓣ03/9510 6057, ⓦwww.collegelawnhotel.com.au. Simple, good-value backpacker accommodation above a great pub at the quieter end of Greville street. Small kitchen. Dorms $18, rooms ❸

The Como 630 Chapel St, South Yarra ⓣ03/9824 0400. Very upmarket accommodation with spacious suites in unusually bold colours and with all the amenities you'd expect in a five-star hotel, including indoor heated pool, sauna, spa, gym, valet parking, restaurant and a jazz bar. ❼

Gunn Island Brew Bar 102 Canterbury Rd, cnr Armstrong St, Middle Park ⓣ03/9690 1882. Inexpensive dorms and simple but pleasant rooms with shared facilities above a refurbished pub-cum-brewery, in a great location between beach and city. Take tram #96 from Spencer St. Close to the Aquatic Centre, beach and lots of restaurants and delis. Dorms $22, rooms ❷

Nomads Hotel Claremont 189 Toorak Rd, South Yarra ⓣ03/9826 8000 or 1300 301 630, ⓦwww.hotelclaremont.com. Three-star budget hotel with shared facilities; modestly priced, given the location in the heartland of chic South Yarra. Breakfast $4 extra. ❸

West End Hotel 76 Toorak Rd West, South Yarra ⓣ03/9866 3135. An old-fashioned B&B overlooking a shady park and close to the heart of exclusive South Yarra, with doubles and singles with shared facilities. Take tram #8, or the train to South Yarra. ❹

St Kilda

Annies B&B 93 Park St, St Kilda West, ⓣ03/8500 3755, ⓦwww.anniesbedandbreakfast.com.au. Small, family-run B&B in a renovated Edwardian house with a courtyard garden and BBQ facilities. Guests can use the front lounge with an open fireplace and TV/DVD player. Rooms have en-suite or private bathroom. ❺

Base 17 Carlisle St, St Kilda, ⓣ03/8598 6222. A swish, custom-built hostel with minimalist decor, bright colours and unusual features, such as the sunken fish tank beneath sturdy plate glass spanning the breezy common room (behind the reception area) like a covered stream. All dorms (great girls-only dorms) and rooms are en suite, scrupulously clean, with air con and drawers big enough to accommodate a backpack underneath the dorm beds. Other facilities include fast Internet access, a travel desk and a pleasant bar for drinks, budget meals and entertainment. The only slight drawback is the basement location of kitchen/dining room and TV area. Just around the corner from Acland Street; take tram #96 from the city. Dorms $23–30, rooms ❸

Gay and lesbian accommodation

For further accommodation possibilities other than those listed below, ring **Gay Share** (ⓣ 03/9691 2290), which arranges house shares for gays and lesbians, or visit ⓦ www.galta.com.au.

169 Drummond Street 169 Drummond St, Carlton ⓣ 03/9663 3081, ⓦ www.169drummond.com.au. Non-smoking B&B in a refurbished Victorian terrace house with en-suite rooms. ❺

California Motel 138 Barkers Rd, Hawthorn ⓣ 03/9818 0281 or 1800 331 166, ⓦ www.californiamotel.com.au. Gay-friendly motel accommodation close to the city; parking available. Take tram #109 or #42 from Collins St. ❼

Heathville House 171 Aitken St, Williamstown ⓣ 03/9397 5959, ⓔ heath@jeack.com.au. B&B in a pretty weatherboard house. Non-smoking. ❻

Palm Court B&B 22 Grattan Place, Richmond ⓣ 03/9427 7365. Spacious, moderately priced bedrooms in a Victorian mansion. Non-smoking. ❸

Boutique Hotel Tolarno 42 Fitzroy St ⓣ 03/9537 0200, ⓦ www.hoteltolarno.com.au. Pleasant small hotel in a restored building located right in the thick of things. Rooms with en-suite bathrooms, polished-timber floors and all mod cons are good value. ❺

Easystay Bayside 63 Fitzroy St ⓣ 03/9525 3833 or 1300 301 730, ⓦ www.easystay.com.au. Good, secure budget motel well situated for all the action and within a ten-minute walk of the beach. If you want quiet, book one of the units facing the car park out the back (which is locked at night). ❹

Jackson Manor Travellers Hostel 53 Jackson St ⓣ 03/9534 1877. Agreeable hostel in a renovated old mansion in a quiet location just off Grey St, with dorms and good-value doubles, a well-equipped kitchen and a comfy lounge room with wide screen TV and DVD player. Good security and free off-street parking. Dorms $22, rooms ❸

Olembia 96 Barkly St ⓣ 03/9537 1412, ⓦ www.olembia.com.au. Very comfortable budget guest-house in a fine old building with open fireplaces, a cosy lounge and dining room and a well-equipped kitchen. All the rooms are very appealing, and the singles are particularly good value. Off-street parking available. Dorms $24, rooms ❸

The Prince 2 Acland St ⓣ 03/9536 1111, ⓦ www.theprince.com.au. This boutique hotel is one of Melbourne's most elegant places to lay your head. The minimalistic bedrooms come with TVs and DVD players, Bose stereo radios, and a data connection for modem and fax. Other facilities include a day spa and relaxation centre, the elegant *Circa* restaurant (see p.939), the *Mink Bar* (see p.941), and a club/band room. ❽

Camping and caravan parks

There are no **campsites** anywhere close to the centre; the nearest is the *Melbourne Big 4 Holiday Park*.

Crystal Brook Holiday Centre Cnr Anderson's Creek and Warrandyte roads, East Doncaster ⓣ 03/9844 3637. Modern campsite and holiday park with tennis courts and a pool, 21km northeast of the city centre (20min via the Eastern Freeway). On-site vans and cabins ❸–❹

Melbourne Big 4 Holiday Park 265 Elizabeth St, Coburg East ⓣ 03/9354 3533 or 1800 802 678. Shady park 10km north of the city, with kitchen and a swimming pool. Take bus #526 to the city (daytime only, no service Sun). Cabins ❸

The City

Melbourne is a city of few sights but plenty of lifestyle, and you'll get to know the city just as well by sitting over a coffee or strolling in the park as by traipsing around museums or attractions. At the heart of the city lies the **Central Business District** (CBD), bounded by La Trobe, Spring, Flinders and Spencer streets, dotted with fine public buildings and lots of shops. Sights include the ghoulish **Old Melbourne Gaol**, just north of La Trobe Street, and the **Immigration Museum** in the Old Customs House, dedicated to Victoria's immigration history. The CBD is surrounded by gardens on all sides (save the downtown west): few cities have so much green space so close to the centre. To the north of the CBD a wander through lively, century-old **Queen Victoria Market** will repay both serious shoppers and people-watchers, while the **Melbourne Museum** in tranquil Carlton Gardens draws on the latest technology to give an insight into Australia's flora, fauna and culture. In the east, the CBD rubs up against Eastern Hill, home to **Parliament House** and other government buildings as well as the landscaped **Fitzroy Gardens**, from where it's a short walk to the venerable **Melbourne Cricket Ground (MCG)**, a must for sports fans.

Bordering the south side of the CBD, the muddy and in former decades much-maligned **Yarra River** lies at the centre of the massive developments which have transformed the face of the city, with new high-rises still popping up like mushrooms. The shift towards the Yarra River kicked off in the mid-1990s with the waterfront development of **Southgate**, **Crown Casino** and the **Melbourne Exhibition Centre**. The latest addition to Melbourne's cityscape is Federation Square on the north bank of the Yarra river opposite Flinders Street station; its adjacent park, Birrarung Marr, links Federation Square with the sports arenas further east. Continuing south of the river, the **Victorian Arts Centre** forms a cultural strip on one side of St Kilda Road, while on the other, Government House and the impressive Shrine of Remembrance front the soothing **Royal Botanic Gardens**.

Federation Square and around

Huge orange-and-brown **Flinders Street station**, the city's main suburban railway station, lies sandwiched between the southern edge of the CBD and the Yarra. "Under the clocks" – its entrance with a row of clocks detailing the times of all train departures – is still a traditional Melbourne meeting place. This famous old city landmark is now faced by **Federation Square** (or "Fed Square", as it's generally known), which occupies an entire block between Flinders Street and the Yarra River, and provides Melbourne with a single, central unifying focus it had always previously lacked. More recently it has become a popular after-work drinking spot, with the **Plaza** at its core, and it is here crowds gather to check out one of the many events staged throughout the month, including short art films, live music and dance parties. Rising up from St Kilda Road in a gentle incline, the Plaza narrows into a horseshoe-shape where it is hemmed in by buildings including the Ian Potter Centre, one of Melbourne's most interesting art museums (see below); and the Alfred Deakin Building which houses the Australian Centre for the Moving Image; there are also numerous cafés and restaurants. The underground Melbourne Visitor Centre (see "Information", p.903) is located at the northwestern end of the Plaza, directly across from Flinders Street Station.

On the north side of the Plaza, the **Australian Centre for the Moving Image** (daily 10am–6pm; free; Ⓦwww.acmi.net.au) is devoted to exploring the moving image in all its forms: film, television, games, video and digital media. Worth checking out is the Screen Gallery, an underground exhibition space spanning the entire length of Federation Square, and featuring changing exhibitions of screen-based art; and Memory Grid on the ground floor, which displays film work by students and participants in ACMI workshops (Mon-Fri

10am–5pm, Sat & Sun 10am–6pm; free). Two state-of-the-art cinemas screen themed programmes and host film festivals and events. Guided tours give a lot of background information on architectural and technological aspects of ACMI and Federation Square (daily 11am and 2pm, booking advised; $10; Ⓣ03/8663 2583, Ⓔtours@acmi.net.au).

Ian Potter Centre: NGV Australia

Walk from Flinders Street through the **Atrium** – a unique passageway of glass, steel and zinc – or from the Plaza through the similarly narrow **Crossbar** to reach the striking new home of the National Gallery of Victoria's collection of Australian art, the **Ian Potter Centre: NGV Australia** (Mon–Thurs 10am–5pm, Fri 10am–9pm, Sat & Sun 10am–6pm; free, except for special exhibitions; Ⓦwww.ngv.vic.gov.au), named in honour of Sir Ian Potter (1902–94), a local financier, philanthropist and patron of the arts. Occupying three floors, the centre showcases one of the best collections of Australian art in the country, with some seventy thousand works, of which about 1800 are usually on display (exhibits are rotated regularly). Traditional and contemporary indigenous art is displayed in four galleries on the ground floor; historic and modern Australian collections are housed on the second floor; while the galleries on the third floor are reserved for special temporary exhibitions. The artworks are complemented by interactive videos, which feature an overview of artists' works, with biographies and interviews.

The building itself is as much a work of art as its exhibits, constructed from two overlapping wings forming a slightly crooked X and offering constantly shifting views, with glimpses of the Yarra and the parklands through the glass walls in the southern part of the building. The best way to get a handle on the collection, as well as the building, is to participate in a **free guided tour** (Mon–Fri at 11am, noon, 2pm & 3pm, Sat & Sun at 11am & 2pm).

Galleries 1–4 on the ground floor give an excellent overview of the art produced in Australia's **indigenous communities**, showcasing works in both traditional and contemporary styles. Traditional art is represented by carved and painted figures from Maningrida, masks from Torres Straits Islands, Pukumani Poles from the Tiwi Islands north of Darwin, the Wandjina paintings from the north of Western Australia and bark paintings from Yirrkala and other places in Arnhem Land. One of the highlights is undoubtedly *Big Yam Dreaming* (1995), an enormous canvas by Emily Kam Kngwarray (c.1910–96) showing tangled, spidery webs of white against a black background, representing the pencil yam that grows along the creek banks at the artist's birthplace northeast of Alice Springs. In her brief career – she didn't take up painting until she was in her mid-70s – Emily produced a staggering three thousand-plus works, transcending the Western Desert-style dot paintings and developing a uniquely personal style, which, seemingly abstract and vibrantly coloured, is sometimes reminiscent of late Monet or Jackson Pollock.

On the second floor, galleries 5–11 contain paintings, sculptures, drawings, photographs and decorative arts from the mid-nineteenth century to the 1980s displayed in chronological order. One recurrent leitmotif is the harsh beauty of the Australian landscape, and (European) peoples' place in it. The early **colonial paintings** – with works by artists such as John Glover, Henry Burn, Frederick McCubbin and Tom Roberts – are particularly interesting, showing European artists struggling to come to terms with an alien land, as well as offering pictorial records of the growth of new cities and the lives of immigrants and pioneers.

Highlights of the twentieth-century collection include paintings by Albert Tucker, Russell Drysdale, John Perceval and, especially, **Sidney Nolan** (1917–92). Dissatisfied with his Eurocentric art training at Prahran Technical College, Nolan strived to express the Australian experience in a fresh style, exploring new ways of seeing and painting the nation's landscapes, as in his *Wimmera* painting of the 1940s; Nolan also showed a unique interest in the histories of convicts, explorers and bushrangers, resulting in pictures such as his well-known *Ned Kelly* series (1946–48). Another highlight is the gallery dedicated to the overwhelming *Pilbara* collection of Fred Williams, painted in 1979 in the Pilbara region of Western Australia.

The CBD

Seen from across the river, Melbourne's **Central Business District** presents a spectacular modern skyline; on close inspection, however, what you notice are the florid nineteenth-century facades, grandiose survivors of the great days of the goldrushes and after. The former Royal Mint on William Street near Flagstaff Gardens is one of the finest examples, but the main concentrations are south on **Collins Street** and along **Spring Street** to the east. At the centre of the CBD, trams jolt through the busy but somewhat tired-looking **Bourke Street Mall**. A stone's throw from these central thoroughfares, narrow lanes, squares and arcades with quaint, hole-in-the-wall cafés, small restaurants, shops and boutiques add a cosy and intimate feel to the city.

Collins Street

North of Fed Square, **Collins Street** is *the* smart Melbourne address, becoming increasingly exclusive as you climb the hill from the Spencer Street end. At the western end of Collins Street the Stock Exchange squares up to the Rialto Building opposite, an Italianate Gothic complex built in the 1890s which now houses the luxury *Meridien* hotel. The massive **Rialto Towers** is Melbourne's tallest structure, the reflective surface of its twin towers lending the skyline a bit of oomph. On clear days, especially at around dusk, a trip up to the **Melbourne Observation Deck** on the 55th floor is a must (daily 10am–late; $13.50; Ⓦwww.melbournedeck.com.au). There's a licensed café on the deck, and the admission fee includes the use of binoculars, and a twenty-minute film at the Rialto Vision Theatre at street level that highlights the best parts of Melbourne and Victoria. Nearby, at no. 333, the former **Commercial Bank of Australia** has a particularly sumptuous interior, with a domed banking chamber and awesome barrel-vaulted vestibule which you're welcome to admire during business hours.

Further up Collins Street, beyond the worthwhile diversion down William Street to the Immigration Museum in the Old Customs House (see below), shops become the focus of attention. The 1890s **Block Arcade**, at nos. 282–284, is one of Melbourne's grandest shopping centres, its name appropriately taken from the tradition of "doing the block" – promenading around the city's fashionable shopping lanes. Restored in 1988, the L-shaped arcade sports a mosaic-tiled floor, ornate columns and mouldings, and a glass-domed roof. **Australia on Collins** is a modern alternative next door with an upmarket food court and adjacent licensed restaurants and bars in its basement. Beyond this, on the corner of Collins and Swanston streets, the Neoclassical Melbourne **Town Hall** squats on City Square, a beleaguered space that never achieved its intended purpose: to provide Melbourne with a focal point. There is, however, an unmissable landmark on the south side of the square: the splendid **St Paul's**

Cathedral, built in the 1880s to a Gothic-revival design by English architect William Butterfield (who never actually visited Australia). Across from the cathedral on Swanston Street, the restored *Young and Jackson's Hotel* is now protected by the National Trust, not for any intrinsic beauty but as a showcase for a work of art which has become a Melbourne icon: **Chloe**, a full-length nude which now reclines upstairs in *Chloe's Bar and Bistro*. Exhibited by the French painter Jules Lefebvre at the Paris Salon of 1875, it was sent to an international exhibition in Melbourne in 1881 and has been here ever since.

Back on Collins Street, the pompous **Athenaeum Theatre** next to the Town Hall is an important ingredient in the rising streetscape leading up past **Scots Church**, whose Gothic-revival design merits a peek, though it's famous mainly as the place where Dame Nellie Melba first sang in the choir. Further up, beyond expensive boutiques and souvenir shops, Collins Place and the towering **Hotel Sofitel** next door dominate the upper part of Collins Street. The (male) toilet of *Le Restaurant* on the 35th floor of the *Sofitel* is known as the "loo with a view", but the view from the tables by the window isn't bad, either – though it doesn't come cheap (see "Eating"). Opposite, overshadowed by the *Sofitel* tower, stands one of the last bastions of Australian male chauvinism: the very staid, men-only **Melbourne Club**.

The Immigration Museum

At the corner of Flinders and William streets, just off the western stretch of Collins Street, the **Immigration Museum** (daily 10am–5pm; $6; Ⓦwww.immigration.museum.vic.gov.au) is dedicated to one of the central themes of Australian history. Housed in the beautifully restored Old Customs House, the museum builds a vivid picture of immigration history and personal stories using the spoken word, music, moving images, light effects and interactive screens, evoking the experiences of being a migrant on a square-rigger in the 1840s, a passenger on a steamship at the beginning of the twentieth century, or a postwar refugee from Europe. In the **Tribute Garden**, the outdoor centrepiece of the museum, a film of water flows over polished granite on which are engraved the names of migrants to Victoria, symbolizing the passage over the seas to reach these faraway shores. The names of all the Koorie people living in Victoria prior to white settlement are listed separately at the entrance to the garden.

Bourke Street and Chinatown

Bourke Street Mall extends west from Swanston Street to Elizabeth Street. The seventies-style mall is in desperate need of an overhaul and works are scheduled to start mid-2005, to be completed in time for the Commonwealth Games in 2006 (see p.75). After a fire gutted most of its interior in 2003, the Melbourne **General Post Office**, an imposing Victorian-era building at the corner of Elizabeth Street and Bourke Street, was restored, and reopened late 2004 as a light and airy shopping complex for high-end designer clothes and upmarket eateries. Running off Bourke Street Mall, the lovely **Royal Arcade** is Melbourne's oldest (1839), paved with black and white marble and lit by huge fanlight windows. A clock on which two two-metre giants, Gog and Magog, strike the hours adds a welcome hint of the grotesque. As you climb the hill east of here, Bourke Street keeps up the interest, with several cafés and bars that put out pavement tables at night – including *Pellegrini's*, Melbourne's first espresso bar and still buzzing – as well as late-opening book and record stores.

North of Bourke Street, and running parallel to it, is Little Bourke Street, with the majestic **Law Courts** by William Street at the western end, and **Chinatown** in the east between Exhibition and Swanston streets. Australia's oldest continuous Chinese settlement, Melbourne's Chinatown began with a few boarding-houses in the 1850s (when the goldrushes attracted Chinese people in droves, many from the Pearl River Delta near Hong Kong) and grew as the gold began to run out and Chinese fortune-seekers headed back to the city. Today the area still has a low-rise, narrow-laned, nineteenth-century character, and it's packed with restaurants and stores. The **Chinese Museum**, in an old warehouse on Cohen Place (daily 10am–5pm; $6.50), is concerned particularly with the Chinese role in the foundation and development of Melbourne. The museum organizes the **Chinatown Heritage Walk**, a two-hour guided tour of the building and Chinatown (hours vary depending on bookings; $15 or $31 including lunch; ⓣ03/9662 2888). The walk requires a minimum of fifteen people, but for one or two people it's still worth ringing as the museum might be able to slot you in with a larger group.

QV and the State Library of Victoria

North of the Chinese Museum rises the latest bulk development to change the structure and feel of the CBD: **QV** (Queen Victoria Village), which takes in almost the entire block between Russell, Lonsdale, Swanston and La Trobe streets, and is named after the Queen Victoria Women's Hospital which occupied this site from 1896 until the late 1980s, now houses a shopping complex with restaurants and bars. The building itself is an irregularly formed structure crisscrossed by open-air lanes and passageways with floor-to-ceiling glass walls. The basement houses a busy supermarket and a homeware chainstore, while the levels above offer a diverse range of shops, eateries and bars. The lanes themselves are dedicated to high-end fashion.

Aussie Rules aficionados may want to fork out the rather steep admission fee for the **AFL Hall of Fame and Sensation** (daily 9am–4.30pm; $22.50; ⓦwww.aflhalloffame.com.au), located at the QV, where visitors step into the imaginary shoes of a footy player and follow his journey through the build-up of Grand Final week, culminating in the finale on Saturday. For footy novices there's the **Australia's Own Game Theatre** on the ground floor where a short film explains the rules and the history of Australian Rules football (same hours; free admission). To the western edge of QV, along Swanston Street, is the **State Library of Victoria** (Mon–Thurs 10am–9pm & Fri–Sun 10am–6pm; closed public holidays; ⓦwww.slv.vic.gov.au). The building, dating from 1856, is a splendid example of Victorian architecture, and houses the state's largest research and reference library accessible to the public. The interior has been painstakingly refurbished and is well worth a visit, in particular the Cowen Gallery with a permanent display of paintings illustrating the changing look of Melbourne, the La Trobe Reading Room with its imposing domed roof and the Dome Gallery dedicated to the history of Victoria. Also worth mentioning is the **Chess Collection**; with almost 12,000 chess-related items it is reputedly one of the largest public collections in the world. You can play here, too.

Opposite the State Library is the refurbished **Melbourne Central** shopping complex mirroring the QV concept of alleys and passageways lined with cafés, sushi bars and boutiques.

Old Melbourne Gaol

The **Old Melbourne Gaol** (daily 9.30am–5pm; $12.50; ⓦwww.nattrust.com.au), on Russell Street, a block north of the State Library, is one of the most fascinating sights in the CBD. It's certainly the most popular, largely because Australian folk hero and bushranger **Ned Kelly** was hanged here in 1880 – the site of his execution, the beam from which he was hanged and his death mask are all on display (for more on Ned Kelly's exploits, see p.1050), as is assorted armour worn by the Kelly Gang. The "Melbourne Gaol Night Tour" (Wed, Fri, Sat & Sun: April–Oct 7.30pm, Nov–March 8.30pm; $20; advance bookings required with Ticketek ⓣ03/9299 9188) uses the spooky atmosphere of the prison to full effect.

The bluestone prison was built in stages from 1841 to 1864 – the goldrushes of the 1850s caused such a surge in lawlessness that it kept having to be expanded. A mix of condemned men, remand and short-sentence prisoners, women and "lunatics" (often, in fact, drunks) were housed here; long-term prisoners languished in hulks moored at Williamstown, or at the Pentridge Stockade. Much has been demolished since the jail was closed in 1923, but the entrance and boundary walls at least survive, and it's worth walking round the building to take a look at the formidable arched brick portal on Franklin Street.

The gruesome collection of **death masks** on show in the tiny cells bears witness to the nineteenth-century obsession with phrenology, a wobbly branch of science which studied how people's characters were related to the size and shape of their skulls. Accompanying the masks are compelling case histories of the murderers and their victims. Most fascinating are the women: Martha Needle, who poisoned her husband and daughters (among others) with arsenic, and young Martha Knorr, the notorious "baby farmer", who advertised herself as a "kind motherly person, willing to adopt a child". After receiving a few dollars per child, she killed and buried them in her backyard. The jail serves up other macabre memorabilia, including a scaffold still in working order, various nooses, and a triangle where malcontents were strapped to receive lashes by the cat-o'-nine-tails. Perhaps the ultimate rite of passage for visitors is the "Art of Hanging", an interpretive display that's part educational tool and part setting for a medieval snuff movie.

Queen Victoria Market

Opened in the 1870s, **Queen Victoria Market** (Tues & Thurs 6am–2pm, Fri 6am–6pm, Sat 6am–3pm, Sun 9am–4pm; ⓦwww.qvm.com.au) remains one of the best loved of Melbourne's institutions. Its collection of huge, decorative open-sided sheds and high-roofed halls is fronted along Victoria Street by restored shops, their original awnings held up with decorative iron posts. Although undeniably quaint and tourist-friendly, the market is a boisterous, down-to-earth affair where you can buy practically anything from new and secondhand clothes to fresh fish at bargain prices. Stallholders and shoppers seem just as diverse as the goods on offer: Vietnamese, Italian and Greek greengrocers pile their colourful produce high and vie for your attention, while the huge variety of deliciously smelly cheeses effortlessly draws customers to the old-fashioned deli hall. Saturday morning marks a weekly social ritual as Melbourne's foodies turn out for their groceries, while Sunday is for clothing and shoe shopping. The guided **Foodies Tour** (10am Tues, Thurs, Fri & Sat; $25 including food sampling, bookings essential) takes in all the culinary delights of the market. The market also runs regular day, evening and weekend cooking classes. For programmes and tour bookings call ⓣ03/9320 5835; details of the Cooking School programme are shown on the market's website.

Carlton Gardens and Melbourne Museum

At the CBD's northeast corner is **Carlton Gardens**, home to one of Melbourne's most significant historic landmarks – the **Royal Exhibition Building**. It was built by David Mitchell (father of Dame Nellie Melba) for the International Exhibition of 1880 and visited by 1.5 million people. In later years this is where Australia's first parliament sat in 1901, and the Victorian State Parliament from 1901–27. It was also used as a sporting venue for the 1956 Melbourne Olympics. The magnificent neoclassical edifice, with its soaring dome and huge entrance portal, is the only substantially intact example in the world of a Great Hall from a major exhibition; its scale and grandeur reflect the values and aspirations attached to industrialization. So much so that in 2004 Carlton Gardens and the Royal Exhibition Building were inscribed on the UNESCO World Heritage List. Ninety-minute tours of the building leave daily at 2pm ($4) from the Melbourne Museum next door.

Melbourne Museum (daily 10am–5pm; $6; Ⓦwww.melbourne.museum.vic.gov.au) is an ultramodern, state-of-the-art museum, which makes a dramatic contrast to its nineteenth-century neighbour, with its geometric forms, vibrant colours, immense blade-like roof and a greenhouse accommodating a lush fern gully flanked by a canopy of tall forest trees. The museum, which also houses a 400-seat amphitheatre, touring hall for major exhibitions and a shop, has been designed with the multimedia generation in mind – glass-covered display cabinets are few and far between; instead, there's a greater emphasis on digital culture with exhibition spaces exploring the way science and technology are shaping the future.

Highlights include the **Science and Life Gallery**, which explores the plants and animals inhabiting the southern lands and seas; **Bunjilaka**, the Museum's Aboriginal Centre, showcasing an extraordinary collection of Aboriginal culture from Victoria and further afield (curving for 30m at the entrance is "Wurreka", a wall of zinc panels etched with Aboriginal artefacts, shells, plants and fish); and the **Australia Gallery**, focusing on the history of Melbourne and Victoria, and featuring the legendary racehorse Phar Lap (reputedly Australia's most popular museum exhibit) and the kitchen set from the TV show *Neighbours*. Also of interest are the Evolution Gallery, which looks at the earth's history and holds an assortment of dinosaur casts, and the Children's Museum, where the exhibition gallery, "Big Box", is built in the shape of a giant, tiled cube painted in brightly coloured squares. One of the most striking exhibits is the **Forest Gallery**, a living, breathing indoor rainforest containing over 8000 plants from more than 120 species, including 25-metre-tall gums, as well as birds, insects, snakes, lizards and fish. Also part of the museum, the **IMAX Melbourne** boasts the world's biggest movie screen. Up to seven different IMAX films (daily on the hour 10am–10pm; $16, 3D films $17; Ⓣ03/9663 5454, Ⓦwww.imax.com.au) are projected each day; for some you need to don special liquid-crystal glasses for 3D action.

Parliament House and around

The Eastern Hill area beyond Spring Street has many fine public buildings, centred around **Parliament House**. Erected in stages between 1856 and 1930, the parliament buildings (guided tours on non-sitting days Mon–Fri on the hour between 10am & 3pm & at 3.45pm; free; Ⓣ03/9651 8569) have a theatrical presence, with a facade of giant Doric columns rising from a high flight of steps, and landscaped gardens either side. Just below, the Old Treasury Building from 1857 and adjacent State Government office, facing the beautiful

Treasury Gardens, are equally imposing. The **Gold Treasury Museum** in the Old Treasury features an audiovisual presentation, *Built on Gold*, shown in the old gold vaults deep in the basement (Mon–Fri 9am–5pm, Sat, Sun & public holidays 10am–4pm; $8.50), which illustrates the impact of the Victorian gold-rushes on the fledgling colony. A permanent exhibition on the social and architectural history of Melbourne shares the ground floor with temporary shows.

East of Parliament House, the broad acres of **Fitzroy Gardens** run a close second to Carlton Gardens as a getaway from the CBD. Originally laid out in the shape of the Union Jack flag, the park's paths still just about conform to the original pattern, though the formal style has been fetchingly abandoned in between. The flowers, statuary and fountains are best appreciated on weekdays, as at the weekend you'll spend most of your time dodging the video cameras of wedding parties. The gardens' much-touted main attraction is really only for kitsch nostalgists: **Captain Cook's Cottage** (daily: April–Oct 9am–5pm; Nov–March 9am–5.30pm; $3.70) was the supposed home of Captain James Cook, the English navigator who explored the southern hemisphere in three great voyages and first "discovered" the east coast of Australia; the flower displays at the **Conservatory** (daily 9am–5pm; free) might be more interesting to most people.

The MCG and around

East of Birrarung Park lies **Yarra Park**, containing the hallowed **Melbourne Cricket Ground (MCG)** – also easily reached by tram along Wellington Parade or train to Jolimont station. Hosting state and international cricket matches and some of the top Aussie Rules football games, the 'G', as it is affectionately referred to, is one of sportsmad Melburnians' best-loved icons. Home to the Melbourne Cricket Club since 1853, the complex became the centrepiece of the 1956 Olympic Games after it had been completely reconstructed - only the historic members' stand survived. Almost fifty years later, the MCG is undergoing another major transformation, to be completed in time for the Commonwealth Games in March 2006 (see p.75). **MCG City**, a new development in the northeast, will house galleries and exhibition spaces including the **Australian Gallery of Sport and Olympic Exhibition**, the **Australian Cricket Hall of Fame**, the **Sport Australia Hall of Fame** and the **Aussie Rules Exhibition.** At the time of writing, one-hour tours of the ground (hourly 10am–3pm; no tours on event days; $10; Ⓦwww.mcg.org.au) offer the chance to visit the players' changing rooms, coaches' boxes and cricket viewing areas and whatever is currently accessible; from 2006 the tours will include MCG City and the entry fee might go up accordingly.

From the MCG, three pedestrian bridges over Brunton Avenue lead to **Melbourne Park**, home to a further cluster of sporting venues. Rod Laver Arena and Vodafone Arena in Melbourne Park are the home of the Australian Open tennis championship in January – the latter can seat up to 10,500 people and has a retractable roof and moveable seating that allows for fully enclosed or open-air events such as cycling, tennis, basketball and concerts. On the other side of Swan Street lies the **Melbourne Sports and Entertainment Centre**, or "Glasshouse", as it's known locally; next door, Olympic Park is where the Melbourne Storm rugby league team play their matches.

Birrarung Marr

Melbourne's newest park, **Birrarung Marr**, forms a green link between the sports precinct of Melbourne Park and Federation Square, giving striking views of the city skyline, the sports arenas, river and parklands. Created from land previously used by railway lines, a swimming pool and a road, it now consists of grassy slopes, intersected by a long **footbridge** that crosses the entire park from the southeast to the northwest. The footbridge starts at a small, artificially created wetland area in the southeast by the river called the **Billabong** and leads over Red Gum Gully to the park's centrepiece, the **Federation Bells**, a collection of 39 bells ranging in size from a small handbell to one weighing a tonne, created to commemorate the Centenary of Federation in 2001. The bells are computer-controlled and normally ring every day from 8am to 9.10am, 12.30pm to 1.30pm and 5pm to 6.10pm.

The Yarra River and Southgate

Despite its nondescript appearance, the muddy **Yarra River** was – and still is – an important part of the Melbourne scene. Traditionally home to the city docks, tidal movements of up to two metres meant frequent flooding, a problem only partly solved by artificially straightening the river and building up its banks – this also had the incidental benefit of reserving tracts of low-lying land as recreational space, which are now pleasingly crisscrossed by paths and cycle tracks. Four **bridges** cross the river from the CBD: Spencer Street Bridge at the end of Spencer Street; Kings Bridge on King Street; Queens Bridge, not quite at the end of Queen Street; and Princes Bridge, which carries Swanston Street across. There's also a pedestrian bridge from the bank below Flinders Street station to the Southgate Centre. The best way to see the Yarra is on a **cruise** – see the box opposite.

On the south side of Princes Bridge you can **rent bikes** to explore the river banks (see "Listings", p.947); on fine weekends, especially, the Yarra comes to life, with people messing about in boats, cycling and strolling. Southgate, immediately west of Princes Bridge, is an upmarket shopping complex with lots of smart cafés, restaurants, bars and a huge food court with very popular outdoor tables; at lunchtime and weekends it's very hard to find a table, even indoors.

The Crown Casino, Docklands and Telstra Dome

Providing the Yarra's unavoidable focal point, the **Crown Casino** is Australia's largest gambling and entertainment venue, stretching across 600m of riverfront west of Southgate between Queens Bridge and Spencer Street Bridge. Next door, the **Melbourne Exhibition Centre** (known locally as "Jeff's Shed", a reference to Jeff Kennett, the former state premier behind its construction) is a whimsical example of the city's dynamic new architectural style: facing the river is an immense, 450-metre-long glass wall, while the street entrance has an awning resembling a ski jump propped up by wafer-thin pylons. The interesting **Polly Woodside Maritime Museum** (daily 10am–4pm; $11) is tucked into a small old dock next to the Exhibition Centre. The focus is the *Polly Woodside* itself, a small, barque-rigged sailing ship, built in Belfast in 1885 for the South American coal trade and retired only in 1968, when it was the last deep-water sailing vessel in Australia still afloat.

Opposite the Crown Casino, on the corner of Queenwharf Road and King Street, is the **Melbourne Aquarium** (daily: Jan 9am–9pm; Feb–Dec 9am–6pm; $19; Ⓦ www.melbourneaquarium.com.au). Resembling a giant fish-and-chip shop, the aquarium harbours thousands of creatures from the Southern Ocean. Part of it is taken up by the Oceanarium tank, which rests seven metres below the Yarra, holding over two million litres of water and containing 3200 animals from 150 species (there are over 550 species, or 4000 creatures, in the aquarium

River and Bay Cruises

Most cruises ply the **Yarra River** and the upper reaches of Port Phillip Bay (called Hobsons Bay) between St. Kilda and Williamstown at the mouth of the Yarra (see opposite). A cruise on the western suburbs **Maribyrnong River** reveals a side of Melbourne tourists don't usually get to see, and contrary to local (eastern suburbs) prejudices it is not all factory yards and oil storage containers either.

The main departure points in the city for cruises along the Yarra River are **Northbank Promenade**, at the southern end of Federation Square (sometimes still referred to as Princes Walk), **Southgate** and, further west, **Williamstown**. All cruises run weather permitting; in the cooler months (May–Sep) the last scheduled departures of the day may be cancelled.

Melbourne River Cruises (Ⓦwww.melbcruises.com.au) depart five to six times daily from Northbank Promenade near Princes Bridge. Tickets are available at the blue kiosks there or at Southgate, or call Ⓣ03/8610 2600. The Scenic River Garden Cruise (1hr 15min; $20) heads upriver past South Yarra and Richmond to Herring Island. The Port and Docklands Cruise (1hr 15min; $20) runs downriver past Crown Casino and Melbourne Exhibition Centre to the Westgate Bridge. Combined up- and down-river cruises cost $34. In addition, cruises to Williamstown and back (approx 1hr 15min; $29) leave daily every hour (10.45am–2.45pm, in the cooler months 10.45am, 12.45pm and 2.45pm – enquire at the office.

City River Cruises (Ⓣ03/9650 2214, Ⓦwww.cityrivercruises.com.au) operate similar Yarra cruises for a marginally cheaper price. Buy tickets at the green kiosk near the departure point at Northbank Promenade or on board. There are four departures daily between 10am and 2.30pm; additional departure in summer at 4pm.

Williamstown Bay and River Cruises (Ⓣ03/9682 9555, Ⓦwww.williamstownferries.com.au) ply the lower section of the Yarra between Williamstown and Southgate in the west of the city. Departures from Southgate daily every half-hour between 10.30am and 5pm, from Williamstown one hour later ($11, or $20 return). The company also runs six ferry services per day from St Kilda Pier to Williamstown on Saturdays, Sundays and public holidays, departing hourly between 11.30am and 3.30pm and from Gem Pier in Williamstown between 11am and 4pm ($6.50, or $11 return; tickets can be bought at the white ticket box at Southgate or from pier attendants and on board).

Maribyrnong Cruises (Ⓣ03/9689 6431, Ⓦwww.blackbirdcruises.com.au). Cruises depart from Wingfield Street and land at Footscray. The Maribyrnong River cruise passes Flemington Racecourse, Footscray Park and various other parklands to Essendon and shows the tranquil and pretty side of the supposedly drab Western suburbs (2hr; departs Tues, Thurs, Sat & Sun 1 pm; $14), while the Port of Melbourne cruise takes in the industrial aspects of the lower Maribyrnong and Yarra rivers plus the Docklands development (1hr; dep. Tue, Thur, Sat & Sun at 4pm; $7). Take the train to Footscray station (Sydenham/Werribee line) or take bus no. 219 from the city to Sunshine, and get off at bus stop 17.

Penguin Waters Cruises (Ⓣ03/9386 8488; Ⓦwww.penguinwaters.com.au). Departs from berth 1, Southgate, for a sunset cruise (2 hr, $55; includes. BBQ dinner and wine) along the Yarra to a structure in Port Phillip Bay, 4km from the mouth of the Yarra, where penguins come ashore. As this is the only cruise vessel permitted to visit the penguin colony and the exact location isn't publicized, you can see them without the crowds that congregate on Phillip Island (see p.958)

in total), as well as a sting-ray-filled beach with a wave machine and a fish bowl turned inside out where you can stand in a glass room surrounded by shark-filled water. The curved, four-storey building also houses a hands-on learning centre where children get a fish-eye view of life underwater, "Ride the Dive" platforms that simulate an underwater roller-coaster, lecture halls, an amphitheatre, cafés, shop and a restaurant.

Further downstream lies the **old dock area**, earmarked for grand-scale commercial, residential and leisure development as part of the **Docklands project**. Of all the city's new developments, this is likely to have the biggest impact on the look and feel of Melbourne: if all goes to plan, in ten to twelve years an entire new city district will stand by the waterfront here. For the time being, the area is still mostly an urban wasteland of warehouses, old docks and new roads cutting through empty open spaces. Squat in the middle of it all sits another of Melbourne's giant sporting venues, **Telstra Dome**, a 54,000-seater venue for AFL, cricket, and international soccer and rugby union matches, as well as concerts by big-name artists. A wide pedestrian footbridge crosses the railway tracks at Southern Cross station, connecting Telstra Dome and the Docklands district-in-the-making with Spencer Street and the older part of the city. The only completed waterside development to-date, **New Quay**, near the extension of La Trobe Street, opened in December 2002, and has a few residential blocks with cafés and restaurants on the ground floor. Its unique waterside location – within walking distance of the city centre, and with gorgeous panoramic views of Bolte Bridge to the west and the city's skyline to the east – seems to have worked its charm: on weekend evenings it is well-nigh impossible to find an empty parking space anywhere near.

Victorian Arts Centre

The **Victorian Arts Centre** (Ⓦwww.vicartscentre.com.au), on St Kilda Road, comprises Hamer Hall, the Theatres Building and the Sidney Myer Music Bowl, an open-air venue across St Kilda Road in Kings Domain (see below). At the top of the Theatres Building is a 162-metre-tall **spire** whose curved lower sections are meant to evoke the flowing folds of a ballerina's skirt; the mast at its peak turns an iridescent blue at night. A **guided tour** of Hamer Hall and the Theatres Building provides an insight into the history of the buildings and gives an overview of the architecture and design (Mon–Sat noon & 2.30pm; $11), while the **backstage tour** ventures behind the curtains, taking in the dressing rooms and costumes (Sun 12.15pm; $13.50, ticket from Theatres Building foyer). There are visual arts collections and other exhibits on display in the small **George Adams Gallery** and the basement of the Theatres Building (Mon–Sat 9am–11pm, Sun 9am–5pm; free).

The bluestone building next to the Theatres Building is home to the **National Gallery of Victoria** (NGV), Australia's oldest public art museum. After extensive refurbishments it was reopened in late 2003 and the gallery now houses a collection of international works under the name **NGV: International** (daily 10am–5pm; free, except for temporary exhibitions; Ⓦwww.ngv.vic.gov.au), having moved its Australian collection to its new domicile on Federation Square. Features such as the **Waterwall** at the entrance – a water curtain flowing down a glass wall twenty metres wide and six metres high – and the **Great Hall** on the ground floor, with a beautiful stained-glass ceiling, have been retained, and there's access to the landscaped **Sculpture Garden** via the Great Hall. In addition, individual galleries on the four levels were redesigned, and the overall exhibition space increased. The ground floor contains three large rooms for temporary exhibitions plus galleries dedicated to Oceanic Art, Pre-Columbian, Egyptian and Near Eastern, as well as Greek and Roman Antiquities. Level 1 has rooms displaying European paintings and sculpture from the fourteenth to the seventeenth century. Level 2 comprises paintings, sculpture and decorative arts from the seventeenth to the mid-twentieth century; the

△ Footbridge over Yarra River

Flemish and Dutch masters including the Rembrandt Cabinet being some of the highlights here, while the contemporary era is represented using installations and photos on level 3. There's also a pleasant *Garden Restaurant* (daily 10am-4pm) located in the Sculpture Garden. NGV has a regular programme of floor talks, lectures, discussions group, films and other activities – check out the gallery's *What's On* flyer or its website for details.

Further south, on Sturt Street, next to the Malthouse Theatre, the **Australian Centre for Contemporary Art** (ACCA; daily 11am–6pm; free) has consistently challenging exhibitions of contemporary international and Australian art.

On Sunday between 10am and 6pm the stalls of a good **arts and crafts market** line the pavement outside the Victorian Arts Centre, extending onto the footpath under the Princes Bridge.

Kings Domain

Across St Kilda Road from the National Gallery of Victoria, the grassy open parkland of **Kings Domain** encompasses the **Sidney Myer Music Bowl**, which serves as an outdoor music arena for the Victorian Arts Centre. South of the Bowl, and behind imposing iron gates with stone pillars and a British coat of arms, you can glimpse the flag flying over **Government House**, the ivory mansion of the governor of Victoria, set in extensive grounds. The

National Trust runs **guided tours** of the house (Mon, Wed & Sat, times by appointment; closed Dec 16–Jan 25 ⓣ03/9654 4711; $11), the highlight being the state ballroom, which occupies the entire south wing and includes a velvet-hung canopied throne, brocade-covered benches, ornate plasterwork and three huge crystal chandeliers.

Further south, on Dallas Brooke Drive, La Trobe's Cottage (Mon, Wed, Sat & Sun 11am–4pm; $2.20) has been re-erected as a memorial to Lieutenant-Governor La Trobe, who lived in this tiny house throughout his term of office (1839–54). The whole thing was sent over from England in prefabricated form, and makes a telling contrast to the later governor's residence. Inside there are interesting displays on La Trobe and the early days of the colony.

The Shrine of Remembrance, in formal grounds in the southwestern corner of the Domain, is aligned with St Kilda Road, which describes a gentle arc around it. Completed in 1934, it's a rather Orwellian monument, apparently half Roman temple, half Aztec pyramid, given further chill when a mechanical-sounding voice booms out and calls you in to see the symbolic light inside. The shrine is designed so that at 11am on Remembrance Day (Nov 11) a ray of sunlight strikes the memorial stone inside – an effect that's simulated every half-hour.

Royal Botanic Gardens

The **Royal Botanic Gardens** (daily: May–Aug 7.30am–5.30pm; April, Sept & Oct 7.30am–6pm; Nov–March 7.30am–8.30pm; free; ⓦwww.rbg.vic.gov.au) on Dallas Brooke Drive contain twelve thousand different plant species and over fifty thousand individual plants, as well as native wildlife such as cockatoos and kookaburras, in an extensive landscaped setting. Melbourne's much-maligned climate is perfect for horticulture: cool enough for temperate trees and flowers to flourish, warm enough for palms and other subtropical species, and wet enough for anything else. The bright and airy **visitors centre** (daily 9am–5pm) at Observatory Gate on Birdwood Avenue has displays, maps and brochures and is the best place to start your wanderings.

Highlights include the **herb garden**, comprising part of the medicinal garden established in 1880; the **fern gully**, a lovely walk through shady ferns, with cooling mists of water on a hot summer's day; the large ornamental **lake** full of ducks, black swans and eels; and various **hothouses** where exotic cacti and fascinating plants such as the Venus flytrap thrive. The *Observatory Gate Café* next to the visitors centre has indoor and outdoor sitting under sun sails and sells coffee, scrumptious cakes and sandwiches as well as light meals. The *Terrace Tearooms and Reception Centre* (daily 10am–4pm) by the lake is licensed and serves meals, or there's a snackbar next door. On summer evenings, plays are often performed in the gardens. Cinema buffs can also swap popcorn for picnic baskets each year from mid-December to mid-March when art-house, cult and classic films are projected onto a big outdoor screen at the Moonlight Cinema ($14; recorded info on ⓣ1900 933 899, or visit ⓦwww.moonlight.com.au). Enter at D Gate on Birdwood Avenue; films start at sunset. Don't forget to take an extra layer of clothing, a rug and, most importantly, insect repellent.

Guided walks (bookings essential; ⓣ03/9252 2300) start at the visitors centre: the Gardens Discovery Walk (Sun–Fri 11am & 2pm; $4.50), gives a fine introduction to the history and horticultural diversity of the gardens; and the Aboriginal Heritage Walk (Thurs & Fri 11am & second Sun of month 10.30am; $15.50) explores the traditional uses of plants for foods, medicine, tools and ceremonies. The painstakingly restored **Observatory Gate** complex, a group of Italianate buildings (originally built 1861–63) next door to the visitors centre can be visited on a self-guided tour (Mon & Fri–Sun 9am–4pm), or join a "Night Sky Experience tour" from the centre (Tues 7.30–9.30pm; during daylight-saving time 9–10.30pm; $15.50).

Melbourne suburbs

Far more than in the city centre, it's in Melbourne's **inner suburbs** that you'll really get a feel for what life here is really all about. Many have quite distinct characters, whether as ethnic enclaves or self-styled artists' communities. What's more, all can easily be reached by a pleasurable tram ride from the centre. Browsing through markets and shops, cruising across Hobsons Bay, sampling the world's foods and, of course, sipping espresso are the primary attractions of the suburbs. Café society finds its home to the north among the alternative galleries and secondhand shops of **Fitzroy**, while the Italian cafés on Lygon Street in nearby **Carlton** fuelled the Beat Generation with espresso, though there are now as many boutiques as bookshops. Grungy **Richmond**, to the east, can claim both Vietnamese and Greek enclaves, and a diverse music scene in its many pubs. South of the river is the place to shop until you drop, whether at wealthy **South Yarra**, self-consciously groovy **Prahran** or snobby **Toorak**. To the south, **St Kilda** has the advantage of a beachside location to go with its trendy but raucous nightlife. To firm up your itinerary with something more concrete, make for the well-designed Zoo in Carlton, or Scienceworks, a hugely enjoyable interactive museum in Spotswood. Also of interest is the Heide Museum of Modern Art in Bulleen and, a bit further along in the same direction, Eltham, with its artists' colony of Montsalvat.

Carlton

Carlton lies just north of the city (tram #1, #3 or #5 from Swanston Street) but, with its university presence and its long-established Italian restaurant scene, it could be a million miles away. **Lygon Street** is the centre of the action, and it was here, in the 1950s, that espresso bars were really introduced to Melbourne; exotic spots such as the *Caffe Sport*, *La Gina*, *University Caffe* and *Toto's* (which claims to have introduced pizza to Australia) had an unconventional allure in staid Anglo-Melbourne, and the local intelligentsia soon made the street their second home. Victorian terraced houses provided cheap living, and this became the first of the city's "alternative" suburbs. These days Carlton is no longer bohemian; its residents are older and wealthier, and Lygon Street has gone definitively upmarket, though the smart fashion shops still jostle with bookshops, excellent ethnic restaurants and cafés like *Tiamo* (see p.936).

Lygon Street itself is the obvious place to explore, but the elegant architecture also spreads eastwards to Drummond Street and, flanking Carlton Gardens, Rathdowne and Nicholson streets. Running along the western side of the university, Royal Parade gives onto Royal Park, with its memorial to the explorers Burke and Wills (see box, p.593), from where it's a short walk through the park to the Zoo.

Melbourne Zoo

When it opened in 1862, **Melbourne Zoo** (daily 9am–5pm; $16; Mon–Sat tram #55 from William Street, Sun tram #68 from Elizabeth Street, or train from Flinders Street station to Royal Park on the Upfield line; Ⓦwww.zoo.org.au) was the first in Australia. Some of its original features are still in evidence, including

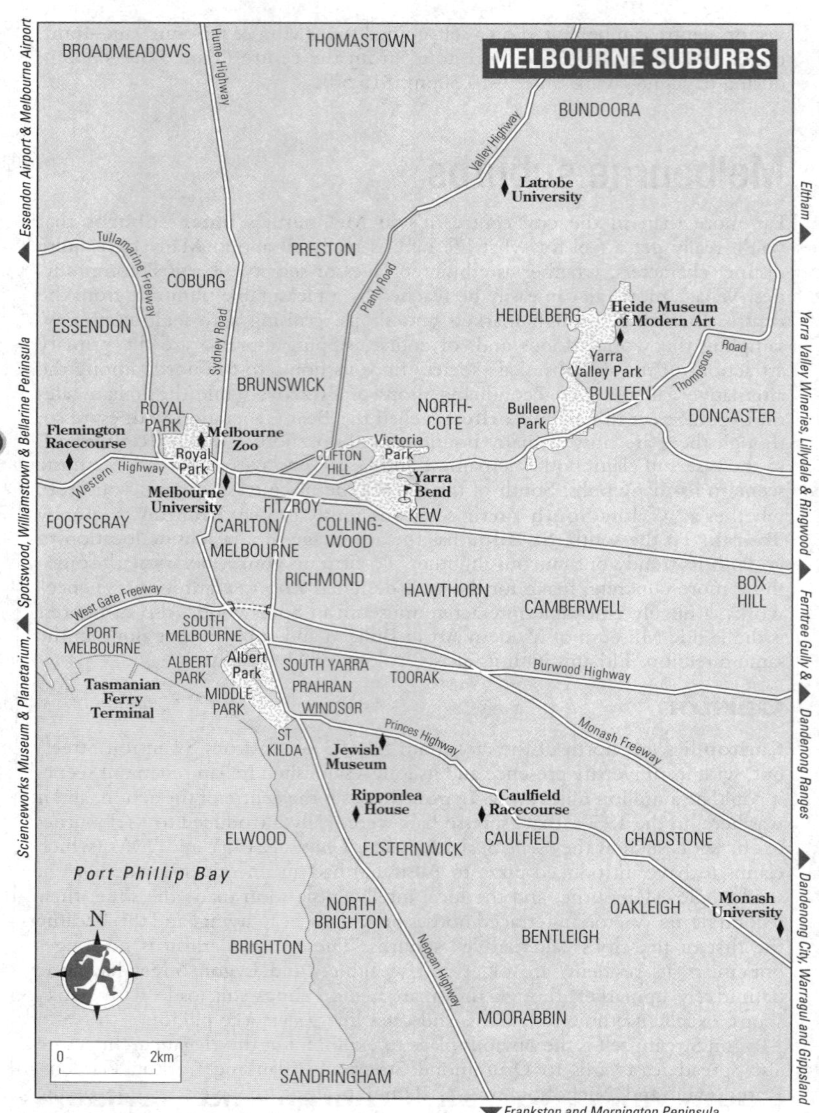

Australian and foreign trees, and landscaped gardens, but the animals have been rehoused in more natural conditions. The Australian area contains a central lake with waterbirds, open enclosures for koalas and other animals, and a bushland setting where you can walk among emus, kangaroos and wallabies. Strolling along the boardwalks of the **Great Flight Aviary** (daily 10.30am–4.30pm) you'll come across areas of rainforest, wetland, and a scrub area with a huge gum tree where many birds nest. The dark **Platypus House** (daily 9.30am–4.30pm) is also worth a look, since the mammals are notoriously difficult to see in the wild – even here there's no guarantee you'll be lucky. **Butterfly House** (daily 9.30am–4.30pm), a steamy tropical hothouse with hundreds of colourful Australian butterflies flitting about, is also highly enjoyable. In summer, the zoo stays open until 9.30pm on selected nights (usually weekends) for its Zoo Twilights music programme, which hosts live bands playing on the central lawn.

Fitzroy and Collingwood

In the 1970s, **Fitzroy** took over from Carlton as the home of the city's artistic community, and every year at the end of September, the colourful Fringe Parade and a street party on Brunswick Street usher in the **Fringe Festival**, the alternative scene's answer to the highbrow Melbourne International Arts Festival. The **International Comedy Festival** (April) and the **Next Wave Festival** (May, even-numbered years), two other notable arts events, also take place mainly in Fitzroy. The district's focus is **Brunswick Street** (tram #11 from Collins St), especially between Gertrude Street, home to Turkish takeaways, and Johnston Street, with its lively Spanish bars. In the shadow of Housing Commission tower blocks, welfare agencies and charity shops rub shoulders with funky secondhand clothes and junk shops, ethnic supermarkets and restaurants, cafés full of students and equally grungy artists, writers and musicians, and thriving bookshops that stay open late and are often as crowded as the many bars and music pubs. Most of the rough old hotels have been done up to match the prevailing mood: the *Provincial* is a good example, with its distressed paint-job and deli/café/bar inside.

Fitzroy's fringe art leanings are reflected in wacky "street installations" such as mosaic chairs, and sculptures like *Mr Poetry*. The eye-catching wrought-iron gate at the entrance to the Fitzroy Nursery at 390 Brunswick St, with its fairy-tale motif, sets the theme for the Artists Garden above the nursery, which exhibits sculptures and other decorative items for garden use. Fitzroy also boasts the unique Rose Street **Artists Market** (Oct–May Sat 11am–5pm) at 60 Rose St where fashion designers, painters, photographers, ceramicists, sculptors and other artists sell their work. The **Fitzroy Pool**, in the north of the suburb on the corner of Young and Cecil streets, is a summer meeting place where people occasionally swim between posing sessions.

While not as trendy as Brunswick Street, the partly shabby **Smith Street** (tram #86 from Bourke St), which forms the boundary between Fitzroy and Collingwood to the east, is forever catching up, but you'll still find quite a few charity shops, ethnic butchers and cheap supermarkets which the New Age bookshops, quirky little cafés and revamped pubs haven't managed to relegate to the edge. **Collingwood** and the adjacent suburb of Abbotsford have a large **gay** population, with a clutch of gay bars and clubs, particularly on Peel and Glasshouse streets.

South Yarra, Toorak, Prahran and Windsor

South of the river, the suburbs of **South Yarra**, **Prahran** and, to the east, **Toorak**, are home to the city's biggest **shopping** area, both grungy and upmarket. **Chapel Street** is the main drag: in South Yarra it extends for a Golden Mile of trendy shopping and *very* chic cafés; heading south beyond Commercial Road through Prahran and Windsor the stereotypically glossy streetscape takes on a refreshingly chequered, ruddier appearance. Crossing Chapel Street at right angles in South Yarra, Toorak Road boasts equally ritzy designer boutiques and, if that's possible, becomes even more exclusive east of

Grange Road, as it enters Toorak, a suburb synonymous with wealth. **Trams** #5, #6 and #72 from Swanston Street will get you from the city centre to Chapel Street.

South Yarra and Toorak

The **South Yarra** stretch of **Chapel Street** is awash with boutiques and speciality shops, bistro bars full of beautiful people and cooler-than-thou nightclubs. Amongst the wall-to-wall chic, it's worth making a beeline for the **Jam Factory** shopping complex, named after its former incarnation, as well as **Como Historic House and Gardens**, overlooking the river from Lechlade Avenue in South Yarra (daily 10am–5pm; $11). This elegant white mansion, a mixture of Regency and Italianate architectural styles, is a good example of the town houses built by wealthy nineteenth-century landowners. The admission fee includes a one-hour tour of the house; the last tour departs at 4pm. To reach the house, walk east along Toorak Road from Chapel Street, and then north on Williams Road; from the city centre, take tram #8 from Swanston Street.

Toorak has never been short of a bean: when Melbourne was founded, the wealthy built their stately homes here on the high bank of the Yarra, leaving the flood-prone lower ground for the poor; in addition, many European Jews who made good after arriving penniless in Australia celebrated their new wealth by moving to Toorak in the 1950s and 1960s. There's little to see or do in the suburb: the hilly, tree-lined streets are full of huge mansions in extensive private gardens, while so-called Toorak Village is stuffed with wickedly expensive designer boutiques.

Prahran and Windsor

Beyond Commercial Road in **Prahran** proper, Chapel Street still focuses on fashion, but in a more street-smart vein, becoming progressively more downmarket as it heads south. Landmarks include **Prahran Market** (Tues & Thurs dawn–5pm, Fri & Sat dawn–6pm), round the corner on Commercial Road, an excellent though expensive food emporium (fish, meat, fruit, vegetables and delicatessen) plus cafés and a few clothes shops. **Chapel Street Bazaar**, on the western side of Chapel Street, has good secondhand clothes, Art Deco jewellery, furniture and bric-à-brac. Just opposite, tucked away in Little Chapel Street, a lane off Chapel Street, **Chapel off Chapel** provides a venue for an eclectic mix of theatre performances, music and art exhibitions. Heading a further 100m south along Chapel Street brings you to **Greville Street**, in the heart of Prahran, which has taken over from Chapel Street as the corridor of cutting-edge cool, with retro and designer boutiques, music outlets, bookshops, and groovy bars and restaurants. Things really hot up over the weekend, and every Sunday the small **Greville Street Market** has arts, crafts and secondhand clothes and jewellery on the corner of Gratton Street in Gratton Gardens (noon–5pm).

As Chapel Street crosses High Street the suburb changes to **Windsor** and becomes more interestingly ethnic. Discount furniture and household appliance shops sit cheek by jowl with inexpensive Asian noodle bars, organic produce shops and up-and-coming café-bars. Busy Dandenong Road marks the boundary of Windsor and **St Kilda East**. Just across Dandenong Road on Chapel Street lies the **Astor Theatre**, a beautifully decorated cinema in an Art Nouveau building.

Prahran and Windsor can be reached by train; take the Sandringham train and get off at Prahran or Windsor Station, or by tram; all trams leave from Swanston Street and run along St. Kilda Road, turning left at some point: #72 turns left into Commercial Road, #6 turns left at High Street, #5 and #64 turn left into Dandenong Road; get off at the corner of these roads and Chapel Street.

South Melbourne and Albert Park

If it's the bay you're heading for, then St Kilda is the obvious destination; the quickest and most interesting way there is on the #96 tram from Bourke or Spencer streets, which runs on a light rail track via South Melbourne and Albert Park, past the Aquatic Centre with its five swimming pools (see "Listings", p.947). **South Melbourne**'s focus is the **South Melbourne Market** on the corner of Coventry and Cecil streets (Wed 8am–2pm, Fri 8am–6pm, Sat & Sun 8am–4pm), an old-fashioned, value-for-money place where you can browse stalls selling everything from fruit and vegetables to clothes and continental delicacies. Opposite here, a number of cafés and upmarket retail stores line **Coventry Street**; at no. 399, three portable iron houses, prefabricated residences constructed in England and shipped to Melbourne during the goldrush, have been preserved by the National Trust. At the other end of Coventry Street, **Clarendon Street** is South Melbourne's main shopping precinct, and a fine example of a nineteenth-century streetscape, with original Victorian awnings overhanging numerous cafés, clothing shops and restaurants.

Exclusive **Albert Park** has the feel of a small village, with many lovely old terraced houses and Dundas Place, a shopping centre of mouthwatering delis and bakeries. In the shadow of the St Kilda Road office buildings lies Albert Park itself, the home of the Australian Grand Prix (held in March).

St Kilda and around

The former seaside resort of **St Kilda** has an air of shabby gentility, which enhances its current schizophrenic reputation as a sophisticated yet seedy suburb, largely residential but blessed with a raging nightlife. Running from St Kilda Road down to the Esplanade, **Fitzroy Street** is Melbourne's red-light district – usually pretty tame, though late at night not a comfortable place for women alone – and epitomizes this split personality, since it's lined with dozens of thoroughly pretentious cafés and bars from which to gawp at the strip's goings-on. On weekend nights these and others throughout St Kilda are filled to overflowing with a style-conscious but fun crowd. During the day there's a very different feel, especially on **Acland Street**, with its wonderful continental cake shops and bakeries.

On Sunday, the **St Kilda Arts and Craft Market** (10am–4pm) lines the waterfront on Upper Esplanade. Going there is part of the ritual that includes taking a look at the beach, feeding your face, ambling into a few shops and listening to a busker.

St Kilda's most famous icon, **Luna Park** (Easter to Sept Sat & Sun 11am–6pm; Oct to Easter Fri 7pm–11pm, Sat 11am–11pm, Sun 11am–6pm; also Mon–Thur 11am–6pm school and public holidays; Ⓦwww.lunapark.com.au), is located on the Esplanade, entered through the huge laughing clown's face of "Mr Moon". Despite a couple of new attractions, there's nothing very high-tech about this 1912 amusement park: the Scenic Railway – the world's oldest operating roller-coaster – runs along wooden trestles and the Ghost Train wouldn't spook a toddler – but then that's half the fun. Wandering around is free, but you pay $7 for individual rides, or $33.95 for a day's unlimited rides. You can sit under the palm trees of **O'Donnell Gardens** next door, or nearby **St Kilda Botanical Gardens**, and eat your Acland Street goodies. The **beachfront** is a popular weekend promenade all year round, with separate cycling and walking paths stretching down to Elwood and Brighton, and a long pier thrusting out into the bay. Near the base of the pier is the botched redevelopment of a historic site, the **St Kilda Sea Baths**, which dates back to 1931, a heroically bad mix of shopping complex and function centre with a Moorish twist.

On Saturday, Sunday and public holidays, boat trips from the pier across Hobsons Bay to Williamstown (see box, p.933) give lovely views of St Kilda and the city.

Elwood and Elsternwick

The next stop south along the bay, **Elwood**, is a smaller, less colourful version of St Kilda, minus the seedy edge. With scores of high salaried twenty-somethings moving into the suburb's refurbished apartments in recent years, the slightly shabby, faintly alternative feel of Elwood has been replaced by yuppie bland. Ormond Road, the main street, is now lined with expensive café-restaurants and bars, designed and catering to the tastes of their clientele. Ormond Esplanade runs past parkland through which occasional paths run down to the beach. Take tram #96 to Acland Street in St Kilda, then walk south down Barkly Street towards Ormond Esplanade.

East of Elwood, **Elsternwick** (train to Ripponlea) is a largely Orthodox Jewish area. The original 1918 fittings and facade of Brinsmead Chemist at 73 Glen Eira Rd are protected by the National Trust, as is **Ripponlea House** at 192 Hotham St (daily 10am–5pm; $11), which shows how Melbourne's wealthy elite lived a century ago. The 33-room mansion has magnificent gardens, complete with ornamental lake and fernery, and a way-over-the-top interior. The grounds are popular for picnics at weekends, when the tearoom is also open (11am–4pm). Ten- to fifteen-minutes' walk away in East St Kilda, at 26 Alma Rd opposite the St Kilda Synagogue, is the **Jewish Museum of Australia** (Tues–Thurs 10am–4pm, Sun 11am–5pm; $7; tram #3 or #67 to stop 32 from Swanston Street in the city or from St Kilda Road). The museum's permanent exhibitions focus on Australian and world Jewish history, plus displays on Jewish beliefs and rituals, with a focus on festivals and customs. In addition, the museum regularly puts on special exhibitions that are well worth checking out.

Spotswood and Williamstown

Docks and industry dominate the area west of the city centre, reached by suburban train, by the Williamstown ferry (Williamstown Bay and River Cruises ⓣ03/9682 9555, ⓦwww.williamstownferries.com.au; for further details see box on p.923), or by heading out on the Westgate Freeway across the huge Westgate Bridge. A good reason for visiting **Spotswood**, the first suburb across the Yarra, is **Scienceworks and Melbourne Planetarium**, at 2 Booker St (daily 10am–4.30pm; $6, or $12.30 for combined Scienceworks and Planetarium ticket; additional charges for some exhibitions; ⓦwww.scienceworks.museum.vic.gov.au). Inside a Space Age building, set in appropriately desolate wasteland, the displays and exhibitions are ingenious, fun and highly interactive. Part of the museum consists of the original Spotswood Pumping Station, an unusually aesthetic early industrial complex with working steam pumps. The Planetarium features state-of-the-art digital technology, taking visitors on a virtual journey through the galaxy (Mon–Fri 2pm, Sat & Sun on the hour 11am–3pm; the 11am and noon shows are aimed at younger children).

On a promontory at the mouth of the Yarra, **Williamstown** is a strange mix of rich and poor: of industry, yachting marinas and working port. The street along the waterfront, confusingly named Nelson Place, is nowadays lined with expensive restaurants and cafés. **Williamstown Craft Market** is held along the waterfront (third Sun of each month, 10am–4pm). The most enjoyable way to get to Williamstown is by ferry from St Kilda or from Southgate in the city (both with Williamstown Bay and River Cruises; for details, see the box on p.923.

Bulleen and Eltham

Further afield in the northeastern suburbs lie two further attractions: the Heide Museum of Modern Art in **Bulleen** and Montsalvat in **Eltham** – you could make a day of it and visit them en route to the Yarra Valley wineries and the Healesville Sanctuary (see p.963).

The **Heide Museum of Modern Art** (Tues–Fri 10am–5pm, Sat & Sun noon–5pm; $5; Ⓣ03/9850 1500, Ⓦwww.heide.com.au) on Templestowe Road in Bulleen was the home of Melbourne art patrons **John Reed** (1901–81) and **Sunday Reed** (1905–81), who in the mid-1930s purchased what was then a derelict dairy farm on the banks of the meandering Yarra River. During the following decades the Reeds fostered and nurtured the talents of young unknown artists and played a central role in the emergence of Australian art movements such as the Angry Penguins, the Antipodeans and the Annandale Realists; the painters Sidney Nolan, John Perceval, Albert Tucker and Arthur Boyd were all members of the artistic circle at Heide at one time or another. Most of the museum is closed for refurbishment until March 2006 and the only building accessible to the public is the **Heide I Gallery** (same hours), set in the farmhouse where the Reeds lived from 1934 until 1967. The gallery exhibits pieces from the museum's extensive collection of paintings and other works purchased by the Reeds over four decades, including works by famous Australian artists of the mid- to late twentieth century, including Nolan, Tucker, Perceval and Boyd. Exhibits change every six months. The other feature of Heide I is its lovely, extensive gardens with whimsical sculptures and an enclosed herb patch, and is only partly accessible during the refurbishment. When the entire museum complex reopens it will boast much expanded gallery space, a new visitors car park and a licensed café-restaurant. The museum is located 14km from the city centre; take the suburban train to Heidelberg station (Eltham line) then bus #291 to Templestowe Road (frequent services).

Eltham, a bushy suburb further northeast, about 24km from the city, is known as a centre for **arts and crafts**. Its reputation was established in 1935 when the charismatic painter and architect Justus Jorgensen moved to what was then a separate town and founded **Montsalvat**, a European-style artists' colony. Built with the help of his students and followers, the colony's eclectic design was inspired by medieval European buildings with wonderful quirky results; Jorgensen died before it was completed and it has deliberately been left unfinished. He did, however, live long enough to see his community thrive, and to oversee the completion of the mud-brick Great Hall, whose influence is evident in other mud-brick buildings around Eltham. Today Montsalvat, a two-kilometre walk from Eltham station, contains a gallery and is still home to a colony of painters and craftspeople (gallery open daily 9am–5pm; $6.50; Ⓦwww.montsalvat.com.au).

Eating and drinking

Melbourne is Australia's premier city for **eating out**. Sydney may be more style-conscious and Adelaide comparatively cheaper, but Melbourne has the best food and the widest choice of it – and almost all of it is exceptionally good value. In the **city centre**, Greek cafés line Lonsdale Street between Swanston and Russell streets, while Little Bourke Street is the home of Chinatown. Lygon Street, in inner-city **Carlton**, is just one of many places across the city with a concentration of Italian restaurants. Nearby, Brunswick Street in **Fitzroy** and Smith Street in neighbouring **Collingwood** both have a huge variety of international cuisines as well as trendy bars and cafés. Indeed, Fitzroy and **St Kilda**, another gastronomically mixed bag, are the centres of bar and café society; St Kilda also has great restaurants, bakeries and delis, as does Jewish **Balaclava** (aka St Kilda East). In **Richmond**, Greek restaurants fill Swan Street while further north Vietnamese places dominate Victoria Street. In March each year, the city celebrates all this culinary diversity with a **Food and Wine Festival**, with food-themed street parties in the city's various different ethnic areas.

A lot of licensed restaurants still allow you to bring your own drink, though check first. It is worth noting, however, that most places only allow you to bring in wine, which usually incurs a corkage fee ($1–2 per person to $5–10 per bottle. If you're going to be around for a while, *The Age Cheap Eats in Melbourne*, and its more upmarket companion, *The Age Good Food Guide*, are worthwhile investments.

City centre

You can still find the odd old-fashioned **coffee lounge** in the city – the type of place where you can get a milky cappuccino and grilled cheese on toast – but stylish **cafés** with smarter decor and more diverse menus now set the scene. In the department stores, both the Myer and David Jones **food halls** are excellent for upmarket picnic ingredients, while the QV complex on Lonsdale St has several good eating places.

Cafés

Cafe La 35th Floor, *Hotel Sofitel*, cnr Collins and Exhibition streets ⓣ03/9653 7744. The café with the best views in Melbourne, and much more affordable than the exclusive *Le Restaurant* on the same floor (see below). Open daily for breakfast, lunch, dinner and afternoon teas.

Cafe Segovia 33 Block Place, off Little Collins St One of the oldest of the cafés in this fashionable lane between Little Collins St and Block Arcade, this Spanish-style place serves good coffee, breakfasts and light meals. Moderate. Licensed. Mon–Fri 7am–late, Sat 7.30am–late, Sun 9am–5pm.

Hopetoun Tea Rooms Block Arcade, 282 Collins St ⓣ03/9650 2777. Tea, scones and delicious cakes have been served in these elegant surroundings for more than one hundred years, but new-fangled delicacies such as focaccia with pesto sauce have now wheedled their way onto the menu. Moderate. Mon–Thurs 9am–5pm, Fri 9am–6pm, Sat 10am–3pm.

Laurent Patisserie 306 Little Collins St (between Collins and Elizabeth streets). Mouthwatering breads, cakes and pastries, as well as filled baguettes, croissants, soups for lunch. Licensed. Mon–Sat 8am–6pm, Sun 9am–5pm.

Medallion Cafe & Cakes 209 Lonsdale St. Popular Greek café, once shabby, now with an over-the-top, disco-style interior, but still serving authentic, cheap food. Daily 8am until late (3am Fri & Sat).

Pellegrini's Espresso Bar 66 Bourke St. Melbourne's first espresso bar, and still an institution, with classic 1950s interior and great cheap pasta. Mon–Sat 8am–11.30pm, Sun noon–8pm.

Restaurants

Cookie Level 1, 252 Swanston St ⓣ03/9663 7660. The place is a trendy nightspot as well as a restaurant; there are DJs every night. The restaurant serves moderately priced nibbles, salads and full meals, Asian-style, in an upstairs, roomy, modernized former Victorian dining hall. Licensed. Daily noon–11pm; bar until 3am.

Crossways Food for Life 123 Swanston St ⓣ03/9650 2939. Dirt-cheap, Indian-style vegetarian food prepared by Hare Krishnas. Mon–Sat 11.30am–2.30pm.

eat drink bento 115 Hardware Lane ⓣ03/9642 1136. This busy lunchspot serves bento boxes with contents such as sashimi, Peking duck pancakes, nori rolls, and is also open for dinner Thurs & Fri until 10pm. Licensed.

ezard at the Adelphi 187 Flinders Lane ⓣ03/9639 6811. This hip, dimly lit place is one of Melbourne's coolest eateries, with a tasty range of East meets West favourites. Expensive. Licensed. Mon–Fri noon–2.30pm & 6–10.30pm, Sat 6–10.30pm.

Grossi Florentino 80 Bourke St ⓣ03/9662 1811. A Melbourne institution. Choose between the cellar café-grill-restaurant, serving inexpensive, home-style pasta dishes, drinks and good coffee, and the very pricey, elegant Italian–French restaurant upstairs. Licensed. Mon–Sat 7.30am–1am, upstairs restaurant Mon–Fri lunch and dinner, Sat dinner only.

Il Solito Posto Basement 113 Collins St (off George Parade) ⓣ03/9654 4466. Charming basement location, casual atmosphere and good, no-fuss Italian food make for one of Melbourne's best dining experiences. Prices are moderate to expensive. Licensed. Mon–Fri 7.30am–11pm, Sat 9am–11pm.

Kenzan 45 Collins St ⓣ03/9654 8933. Sushi bar renowned for the freshness of its sushi and sashimi. Licensed. Moderate–expensive. Mon–Fri noon–2.30pm & 6–10pm, Fri & Sat 6–11pm.

Le Restaurant 35th Floor, *Hotel Sofitel*, cnr Collins and Exhibition streets ⓣ03/9653 0000. Luxurious restaurant with silver service and fantastic views over Melbourne and Port Phillip Bay. Serves carefully prepared seasonal dishes, together with Australian produce such as barramundi and yabbies. Expensive. Tues–Sat 7pm till late.

Mekong 241 Swanston St. One of many small Vietnamese cafés in the city specializing in *pho* (beef or chicken noodle soup). Excellent-value food (dishes about $6), but packed at lunchtime. Mon–Sat 9am–10pm, Sun 10am–10pm.

Satay Inn 250 Swanston St. Excellent, affordable Malaysian place, close to the big department stores. BYO. Daily 11am–11pm.

Southgate Across the river from Flinders Street station. With fine views of the river and the city skyline, this centre has developed into a very popular place to dine and drink – advance booking is essential for the restaurants on Friday and Saturday nights. Some of the best places are **BearBrass** (ⓣ03/9682 3799), lively, popular beer garden and restaurant; The **Blue Train Café** (ⓣ03/9696 0111), forever noisy and buzzy, which attracts a young, hip crowd and serves drinks and tasty, inexpensive light meals; and the more upmarket **Walter's Wine Bar** (ⓣ03/9690 9211)

Syracuse 23 Bank Pl ⓣ03/9670 1777. Mouthwatering tapas (served from 3pm) and lamb and leek sausages, along with fantastic cheeses, panforte and coffee. There's also an extensive wine list, a good selection of cigars and seductive atmosphere. Licensed. Mon–Fri 7.30am–11pm.

William Angliss College La Trobe St ⓣ03/9606 2111. Owned by a catering college, this cheap restaurant aims to dish up fine food and service, and usually succeeds, though occasional hiccups may occur. Bookings essential.

Chinatown

Yum cha (elsewhere known as dim sum, a series of small delicacies served from trolleys) is available at lunchtime almost everywhere; on Sunday it's a crowded ritual.

Camy Shanghai Dumpling and Noodle Restaurant Tattersalls Lane, between Little Bourke and Lonsdale streets, close to Swanston St ⓣ03/9663 8555. An extremely cheap, partly self-service place, dishing up very simple but delicious dumplings and noodles. No alcohol. Mon–Fri 11am–10pm, Sat & Sun 11am–9.30pm.

Chez Phat 7 Waratah Place ⓣ03/9663 0988. First-floor hideaway with a marvellous 1970s atmosphere. The interesting menu includes Jerusalem artichoke soup, porterhouse steak, and roast beetroot and duck neck sausages; tapas are served on Sunday. Licensed. Tues–Sat 6pm–midnight (Fri from noon, Sat from 10am), Sun 4–11pm.

China Bar 235 Russell St ⓣ03/9639 1633. Cheap chain with lots of Malaysian–Chinese noodle or rice fast-food classics such as won ton soup, *char kway teow* (fried rice noodles), *nasi lemak* (coconut rice); plus assorted claypot dishes and desserts. BYO. Other branches at 747 Swanston St, Carlton; and 500 Chapel St, South Yarra.

Empress of China 120–122 Little Bourke St

☎03/9663 1883. Expensive but good value, with lots of lesser-known dishes on offer. Licensed. Closed Sat lunchtime.

Flower Drum 17 Market Lane, between Bourke and Little Bourke streets ☎03/9662 3655. Outstanding Cantonese cuisine, including exquisite seafood and fish, an extensive wine list, excellent service and luxurious ambience. Naturally, this all comes at a price: expect to pay at least $70 per person for three courses. Licensed. Mon–Sat noon–3pm & 6–10pm, Sun 6–10pm.

Little Malaysia 26 Liverpool St ☎03/9662 1678. Cheap and good Malaysian hawker fare. Licensed and BYO. Daily 11.30am–3pm & 5.30–11pm.

Shark Fin House 131 Little Bourke St ☎03/9663 1555. Converted warehouse with three storeys devoted to about fifty kinds of yum cha. Very busy at lunchtime, especially at weekends. There's another branch at 50–52 Little Bourke St (☎03/9662 2681). Moderate–expensive. Licensed and BYO. Daily noon–3pm (Sat from 11.30am, Sun from 11am) & 5.30pm–1.30am.

Carlton and North Melbourne

Lygon Street, between Grattan and Elgin streets, is mainly wall-to-wall Italian pizza and pasta restaurants spilling out on the footpath, and on most evenings all but the most resolute looking passers-by are accosted by their touts. *Really* good restaurants are few and far between here, and cheap, Asian noodle bars, catering to the large number of Asian students at Melbourne Uni and the RMIT, are cropping up every month. To the southwest of Carlton, North Melbourne harbours an excellent Balinese restaurant.

Brunetti 198–204 Faraday St ☎03/9347 2801. An array of display cases filled with a mouthwatering selection of chocolates, pastries, biscuits and cakes, plus coffee. Licensed restaurant next door. Cakes and café daily 7am–10pm; restaurant Mon–Fri noon–3pm (Sat from 12.30pm); dinner Mon–Sat 6–10pm.

Jimmy Watson's 333 Lygon St ☎03/9347 3985. The strengths of this Lygon Street icon are its very good bar meals (modern Australian cuisine) in convivial, atmospheric surroundings, and a super wine list. Moderate prices. Licensed. Mon 10am–6pm, Tues–Sat 10am–9.30pm.

Lemongrass 174–176 Lygon St ☎03/9662 2244. Royal Thai cuisine in stylishly subdued surroundings. Moderate–expensive. Licensed. Daily noon–2.30pm & 5.30–10pm.

Shakahari 201–203 Faraday St ☎03/9347 3848. Excellent and imaginative Asian-influenced vegetarian food at moderate prices. Licensed. Mon–Sat noon–3pm & 6.30–9.30pm (Fri & Sat until 10pm), Sun 6.30–9.30pm.

Tiamo 1 303 Lygon St ☎03/9347 5759. One-time beatnik hangout and still popular with students, with layers of browning 1950s posters and a good-value blackboard menu. Next door is its sibling, *Tiamo 2*, which is more upmarket but still excellent value. Licensed and BYO. Mon–Sat 7.30am–11pm, Sun 9.30am–10pm.

Toofey's 162A Elgin St ☎03/9347 9838. Considered Melbourne's best seafood restaurant. The extremely fresh fish and seafood are prepared in a light, Mediterranean or Middle Eastern style. Expensive. Licensed. Tues–Fri noon–3pm & 6–10pm, Sat & Sun 6–10pm.

Toto's Pizza House 101 Lygon St ☎03/9347 1630. Melbourne's first pizzeria, dating from the 1950s – cheap, cheerful and noisy. Licensed. Daily 11am–11pm.

Warung Agus 305 Victoria St ☎03/9329 1737. Authentic Balinese restaurant with superb food at moderate prices. Licensed and BYO (wine only). Tues–Sat 6.30pm till late.

Fitzroy and Collingwood

Adjacent Fitzroy and Collingwood probably have the widest choice of cuisines in the city, and are good places to finish off a night on the town, as there's always lots going on.

Brunswick Street

Afghan Gallery 327 Brunswick St ☎03/9417 2430. Cheap and authentic Afghan food, popular with students, served up amidst Afghan hangings and rugs. Licensed and BYO. Daily 6–11pm.

Babka Bakery Cafe 358 Brunswick St ⓣ03/9416 0091. A deservedly popular place: the home-made bread and cakes are divine, and dishes from the changing blackboard menu are equally enticing. Try Russian blintzes for breakfast or *borsch* (a tangy, beetroot-based soup) and sourdough bread for lunch. Moderate. Licensed and BYO. Tues–Sun 7am–7pm.
Mario's 303 Brunswick St ⓣ03/9417 3343. European-style café where you can eat breakfast (until midnight), lunch and dinner or just have a coffee or a drink. Dauntingly smart staff and decor, but not expensive or dressy. The clientele is an interesting mixture of poseurs, celebrities and scruffs. Mon–Wed & Sun 7am–midnight, Thurs–Sat 7am–1am.
Rhumbaralla's 342 Brunswick St ⓣ03/9417 5652. The neon sign in the window is one of the street's landmarks, and the inside of this stylish café is just as vibrantly coloured. Breakfast until noon – the eggs Benedict are popular – then it's anything from focaccia to steak. Licensed and BYO. Daily 9am–1am.
Thai Thani 293 Brunswick St ⓣ03/9419 6463. One of Melbourne's best Thai restaurants, on two crowded levels, with moderate prices. Licensed and BYO (wine only). Daily 6–10.30pm.
The Vegie Bar 380 Brunswick St ⓣ03/9417 6935. Cheap, popular and hip (rather than hippie) place with simple, fresh vegetarian and vegan food. Licensed and BYO (wine only). Daily 11am–10pm.

Johnston Street and Smith Street

Gluttony – It's a Sin 278 Smith St ⓣ03/9419 2949. Good cakes, cooked breakfasts and meals. Popular with locals. Licensed and BYO. Tues–Sat 7am–11pm, Sun 10am–11pm.
Guru da Dhaba 240 Johnston St ⓣ03/9486 9155. Cheap and always packed Indian restaurant specializing in Punjabi cuisine – advance bookings are advised. BYO. Daily 5.30–11pm, Sat & Sun noon–3pm also.
Soul Food Cafe 273 Smith St ⓣ03/9419 2949. Comfortable cafeteria-style vegetarian café with wooden trestle tables. Mon–Thurs 8am–9pm, Fri–Sun 9am–6pm.

Richmond and Abbotsford

Swan Street, running from Church Street towards Wattle Park, is home to Greek restaurants, while **Victoria Street,** separating Richmond from Abbotsford, is lined with Vietnamese supermarkets, clothes shops and dozens of cheap, authentic restaurants.

Fenix 680–682 Victoria St, Richmond ⓣ03/9427 8500. Great views over the Yarra, especially in summer on the deck. As for the food, you can dive into steak, fish and steamed pudding, all of it decently priced and well presented. Mon–Fri 9am–11pm, Sat & Sun 8am–11pm.
Minh Minh 94 Victoria St, Richmond ⓣ03/9427 7891. Good, cheap Indochinese food (Vietnamese, Laotian and Thai dishes) served in surroundings that are a little bit more stylish than most on this street. BYO. Mon & Tues 4–10pm, Wed & Thurs & Sun from 11.30am, Fri & Sat 11.30am–11pm.
Salona 262A Swan St, Richmond ⓣ03/9429 1460. Long-established Greek restaurant – one of four in this block – serving good, plain and very reasonably priced dishes. Licensed and BYO. Daily noon–11.30pm.
Thy Thy 1 Upstairs at 142 Victoria St, Richmond ⓣ03/9429 1104. A very popular Vietnamese restaurant offering simple but tasty, inexpensive food. BYO. Daily 8am–10pm.
Ying Thai 235 Victoria St, Abbotsford ⓣ03/9419 1225. Authentic cheap Thai food – which means it can be a bit on the fiery side. Licensed and BYO. Tues–Sun noon–10pm.

South Yarra and Windsor

Caffe e Cucina 581 Chapel St, South Yarra ⓣ03/9827 4139. Still one of Melbourne's coolest eating spots, attracting a smart clientele and dishing up fantastic pasta. Licensed. Mon–Sat 7am–midnight.
Falafel House 196 Toorak Rd, South Yarra ⓣ03/9827 6236. Middle Eastern takeaway, perfect after pubbing or clubbing. Daily 9am–5am.
Globe Cafe 218 Chapel St, Windsor ⓣ03/9510 8693. Serves breakfast all day, and has great cakes and bread made on premises. Moderate. Licensed. Mon–Thurs 8.30am–10pm, Fri 8.30am–late, Sat & Sun 9am–late.

New Wind 106 Chapel St, Windsor ⓣ03/9827 1888. Pleasant Vietnamese-Thai bar-restaurant; lunch is particularly good value. BYO. Mon–Fri 11.30am–late, Sat & Sun 5pm–late.

Orange 125 Chapel St, Windsor ⓣ03/9529 1644. Epitomizes the grunge-chic of the Windsor-end of Chapel St. Great place to chill out; they serve breakfast all day, light meals for lunch and more substantial fare for dinner, or just chill out and sip cocktails until the wee hours. Licensed. Mon–Tues 7am–6pm, Wed–Fri & Sun until 2am, Sat until 3am.

Patersons Cakes & Café 117 Chapel St, Windsor ⓣ03/9529 8541. The long-established, renowned cake and pastry shop now also runs a good café on the premises. Mon–Fri 9.30am–5pm, Sat till 4pm.

South Melbourne, Albert Park and Port Melbourne

The night-time scene in these suburbs is rather low-key, but there are cafés and delicatessens aplenty dishing up a mouthwatering selection of food during the day.

Albert Park Hotel Cnr Bridport and Montague streets, Albert Park ⓣ03/9690 5459. Because of its corner position, this airy, breezy pub is a great spot for people watching – especially in warm weather when you can sit outside. They also do great lunches and dinners – kitchen closes Mon–Thurs 9.30pm, Fri & Sat 10pm, Sun 9pm.

Cafe Sweethearts 263 Coventry St, South Melbourne ⓣ03/9416 0091. Good for breakfast, and also has numerous (and some very exotic-sounding) varieties of sandwiches. Mon–Fri 7am–3pm, Sat & Sun 8am–3pm.

Dundas & Faussett Cnr Dundas Place and Faussett St, Albert Park ⓣ03/9645 5155. One of the many swish cafés in the heart of the Albert Park village. Daily 6am–7pm.

Feedings at Readings 253 Bay St, Port Melbourne ⓣ03/9681 9255. An irresistible bookshop with a café – browse, and read the first pages of your newly acquired book on the café terrace, perched a few steps above Bay Street. Licensed. Mon–Sat 8am–8pm, Sun 9am–8pm.

Misuzu's 7 Victoria Ave, Albert Park ⓣ03/9699 9022. Pleasant Japanese eatery and very modestly priced given the location. Open daily for lunch and dinner. Daily noon–3pm & 5.30pm–10pm.

Montague Park Foodstore & Café 406 Park St ⓣ03/9682 9680. Delicious dishes and desserts to take away or eat in – it's particularly pleasant in summer when tables are set out on the footpath. Daily 8am–5pm.

Villagio Dundas Place, Albert Park ⓣ03/9690 3144. Deli packed with Italian and continental goodies that's a bit of an Albert Park old-timer. There are tables outside where you can eat your selections and drink coffee. Mon–Sat 6am–6pm.

St Kilda

This suburb's café scene and nightlife revolves around **Acland Street** and **Fitzroy Street**. While the former is good for browsing in shops, for late breakfast and for pigging out on cakes, the latter, especially the block from Grey Street to the waterfront, arguably has the edge on vibrant nightlife.

Bala's 1D Shakespeare Grove, just off Acland St near Luna Park, St Kilda ⓣ03/9534 6116. Excellent, cheap Asian takeaway food, including lassis and lots of stir-fried dishes with ultra-fresh ingredients. There are a few tables if you want to eat in, though it gets very busy at lunch and dinner. Mon–Sat 4–10.30pm, Sun noon–10.30pm.

Big Mouth 201 Barkly St, St Kilda ⓣ03/9534 4611. A great spot for people-watching. The café downstairs is open for breakfast and light meals from 10am until late, while the upstairs restaurant (modern Australian cuisine) is open Monday to Friday 5pm–1am, Saturday 11am–late, and Sunday 10.30am till late. Licensed.

Cafe Ninety Seven 97 Fitzroy St, St Kilda ⓣ03/9525 5922. Cosy little café; in warm weather you can sit in the pleasant courtyard next to the café, its back framed by palm trees and the columned facade of a stately house. Cakes and light meals such as risotto and soups. Moderate. Daily 7.30am–midnight.

Chinta Blues 6 Acland St, St Kilda ⓣ03/9534 9233. Breezy, airy Malaysian eatery with very moderately priced food. Licensed and BYO. Open Mon–Sat noon–2.30pm & 6–10.30pm, Sun noon–10pm.

Cicciolina 130 Acland St, St Kilda ⓣ03/9525 3333. Friendly staff and moderately priced Italian food with an interesting twist keep this restaurant going from strength to strength, despite the number of tables crammed into the small space. Licensed. Mon–Sat noon–11pm, Sun noon–10pm.

Circa, the Prince, 2 Acland St, St Kilda ⓣ03/9536 1122. Part of *The Prince* establishment (see *Mink Bar* and *Prince Public Bar*) this is still one of Melbourne's best spots for fine dining, boasting a magnificently theatrical fit-out and excellent food and wine. Licensed. Tues–Thurs & Sat 6–11.30pm, Fri & Sun noon–3pm & 6–11.30pm.

Galleon Cafe 9 Carlisle St, St Kilda ⓣ03/9534 8934. Breakfast, served until 4pm, is the big attraction in this retro-style café, which is especially popular at weekends. Licensed and BYO. Mon–Fri 9am–11pm, Sat & Sun 8.30am–11pm.

Stokehouse 30 Jacka Blvd, St Kilda ⓣ03/9525 5555. Right by the beach (it gets packed in warm weather), this restaurant has two sections: a very affordable downstairs section with lots of unusual pizzas and pastas, fantastic cakes, coffee and wines; and a pricier upstairs section with superb views of the bay and excellent Italian-inspired food. Moderate–expensive. Licensed. Downstairs open Mon–Sat 11am–1am, Sun 10am–1am, upstairs daily noon–2.30pm & 6pm–10pm.

The Espy Kitchen, at the *Esplanade Hotel*, 11 Upper Esplanade, St Kilda ⓣ03/9534 0211. The restaurant has been dressed up a bit and the food is no longer only vegetarian, but it's still excellent and fairly reasonably priced. Mon–Fri 5–10pm, Sat & Sun from noon.

Topolinos 87 Fitzroy St, St Kilda ⓣ03/9534 4856. A dimly lit, noisy and smoky St Kilda institution, which churns out cheap pizzas, generous portions of pasta and good cocktails until very late. Licensed. Mon–Thurs noon–3am, Fri–Sun noon–6am.

Wild Rice 211 Barkly St, St Kilda ⓣ03/9534 2849. Vegan macrobiotic café with a lovely courtyard garden. Daily noon–10pm.

Elwood and Balaclava

Elwood's Ormond Street sports wall-to-wall trendy cafés, whereas **Balaclava**, along Carlisle Street, is catching up, but still manages to retain a bit of its old migrant atmosphere.

Beach House 63A Ormond Esplanade, Elwood ⓣ03/9531 7788. Friendly, if somewhat chaotic café next to the car park at Elwood Beach. Very good for breakfast, but *very* crowded on weekends, so book ahead. Licensed. Daily 9am–5.30pm.

Cafe Tarrango 15 Ormond Rd, Elwood ⓣ03/9531 7151. Indian-run café, with delicious organic, biodynamic vegetarian food at cheap prices, though there's not much atmosphere. Licensed and BYO. Mon 5–11pm, Tues–Sun 10am–11pm.

Glicks 330A Carlisle St, Balaclava ⓣ03/9527 2198. Friendly bakery renowned for bagels and traditional Jewish savouries: try the *kreplach*, *latkes* or gefilte fish. Mon–Thurs & Sun 6am–9pm, Fri until sunset. Closed Sat.

Jerry's Milk Bar 345 Barkly St, Elwood ⓣ03/9531 3078. Cornershop milk bar-cum-café brimming with old-fashioned trappings and locals who come for the cheap delicious soups, pasta and risotto. Daily 7am–6pm.

Turtle Cafe 34 Glenhuntly Rd, Elwood ⓣ03/9525 6952. Relaxed old corner café that attracts a faithful crowd for breakfast and light meals and snacks including bagels, focaccia, soups, salads. Moderate. Daily 7am–7pm.

Nightlife and entertainment

Melbourne has a rich arts and music scene, and there's always plenty to do in the evening. To find out **what's on**, check out *The Age* on Friday, when the newspaper publishes a comprehensive entertainment guide, "EG". *Melbourne Events* is a handy free monthly guide to all sorts of happenings, available at tourist information outlets. Also check out the free magazines *Beat* and *Inpress*, which you can pick up at most record shops, cinemas and cafés.

Annual **festivals** further enliven the scene: the **Melbourne International Arts Festival** (ⓦwww.melbournefestival.com.au) in October presents a selection of visual and performing arts, opera, and features individual performers from Australia and overseas, as well as a host of free events at Federation Square and other places around the city. The more innovative and cutting-edge **Melbourne Fringe Festival** (Ⓦwww.melbournefringe.com.au) starts in late September and overlaps a few days with the Melbourne Festival, while the **Melbourne Writers' Festival** (Ⓦwww.mwf.com.au) takes place in late August. The heavily promoted **Moomba Festival**, held in March, has a more commercial, "fun for the masses" approach, featuring events such as firework displays and dragon boat races on the banks of the Yarra River in Alexandra Gardens. Three music festivals take place in the first half of the year: the **Melbourne Music Festival** in February, one of the largest Australian festivals of contemporary music; the **Brunswick Music Festival** in the third week of March, concentrating on folk and world music; and the **Umbria Jazz Festival** (formerly known as the Melbourne Jazz Festival) which runs for eleven days in early May at various venues around the city centre and inner suburbs. The **Next Wave Festival**, held over two weeks in the second half of May, celebrates Victoria's young artists, writers and musicians.

Tickets for most venues can be booked through Ticketmaster7 (Ⓣ13 61 00, Ⓦwww.ticketmaster7.com) or Ticketek (Ⓣ13 28 49, Ⓦwww.ticketek.com.au); both take credit-card bookings only. You can buy tickets half-price on the day of performance from Half Tix at Melbourne Town Hall (Mon & Sat 10am–2pm, Tues–Thurs 11am–6pm, Fri 11am–6.30pm; cash only; Ⓣ03/9654 9420, Ⓦwww.halftixmelbourne.com).

Bars and pubs

Melbourne's fondness for a drink or three is reflected in its abundance of excellent **bars and pubs** – from places so obscure and cutting-edge you'll only know they exist by word of mouth to large establishments catering to broader and louder tastes. The push to revive Melbourne's once staid CBD has seen many older watering holes transformed into lively, youth-oriented venues, while cheap bar licences have meant that new spots are popping up each week. In addition, the relaxing of Melbourne's once draconian licensing laws has produced enlightened opening hours, meaning that it's now possible to drink from noon until dawn. A number of drinking places are also listed under "Live music" below.

City Centre

Bridie O'Reilly's 62 Little Collins St. Above-average theme pub, with lots of Irish gewgaws and hearty grub like stews, steaks and Guinness pies. There are two more branches: one at 29 Sydney Rd, Brunswick, the other at South Yarra (see below).

Charles Dickens Tavern Downstairs at Block Court, 290 Collins St. Comfy place for homesick Brits, with bitter and Guinness on tap, pint glasses, and live soccer and rugby on big-screen TVs.

Gin Palace 190 Little Collins St (entry via Russell Place). Glamorous subterranean joint with an upmarket drinks list specializing in cocktails – not cheap, but delicious and generous. Yummy food and good lounge music, too.

Hairy Canary 212 Little Collins St. This modern and stylish bar is a real people-puller, especially later in the week. An extensive menu is available most of the day, with a wide range of local and imported beers, wines by the glass and cocktails.

Lounge 243 Swanston St. Genuine all-rounder, attracting an arty-grungy crowd. The bar and nightclub have DJs and the upstairs restaurant serves good food – eat alfresco on the terrace.

Melbourne Supper Club Bar Level 1,161 Spring St. Lounge bar with comfy couches that manages to be elegant and laid-back at the same time. Cocktails range from affordable to expensive and there's an extensive wine list; a range of tasty snacks such as veal meatballs or polenta cakes will keep the hunger at bay.

Meyers Place 20 Meyers Place, off Bourke St. This swish, dimly-lit hole in the wall bar has proved a massive hit with those in the know and Melbourne's trendy office workers.

Pugg Mahone 106–112 Hardware St. Another Irish theme pub, with a great party atmosphere on Fridays and Saturdays, fuelled by house bands playing a mixture of folk and R&B.

Stork Hotel 504 Elizabeth St. Phlegmatic watering hole, located in a historic hotel from the goldrush era, featuring lovely Art Deco fittings, a mixed crowd of regulars and superb artwork on the walls from some of Australia's finest cartoonists, including Melbourne-based Michael Leunig.

Tony Starr's Kitten Club 267 Little Collins St. Sleek and stylish interior tricked out with slightly Oriental furnishings, conducive to lolling on comfy sofas and ottomans while cradling a cocktail and nibbling on Asian-inspired food from the grill.

Transport Federation Square. This new watering hole takes the zinc metal-jigsaw theme of its surroundings as its own decorative leitmotif and is a good spot either for after-work drinks or to finish off a night out. The windows of the airy ground-level pub look out on to St Kilda Rd – a great place for people-watching. The top floor lounge bar and restaurant, *Taxi*, features a Japanese-inspired menu.

Carlton and Fitzroy

Builders Arms 211 Gertrude St, Fitzroy. Groovy pub with guest DJs on weekends and the occasional weekday. Laid-back and unpretentious atmosphere.

Gypsy Bar 334 Brunswick St, Fitzroy. Intimate bar, usually packed, especially for jazz on Sunday night. Also great coffee and food.

Hotel Lincoln 91 Cardigan St, Carlton. Revamped pub where you can order inexpensive dishes from a blackboard menu in the dining room and wines by the glass from an excellent wine list.

Polly 401 Brunswick St, Fitzroy. Red velvet curtains give this cocktail bar a decadent feel, while cocktails bearing names like Kinky Miss Pinky veer towards the tacky. A popular hangout nonetheless.

Richmond and South Yarra

Belgian Beer Café Bluestone 557 St Kilda Rd, Windsor. A rare find in St Kilda Road's sterile office territory: a European-style beer hall in a historic bluestone building set back from the street. Convivial and comfortable in a rustic sort of way but definitely not downmarket. Unusual Belgian beers on tap and a food menu featuring well-prepared, solid European fare. Great beer garden in summer. Only drawback: prices are rather steep.

Bridie O'Reilly's 462 Chapel St, South Yarra. Irish-themed pub incongruously housed in an old church and saved from terminal tackiness by the pleasant front patio. Has meals and plenty of memorabilia from the Emerald Isle. Can get raucous on weekends, but it's fun if you're desperate for a Guinness or British beer.

Der Raum 438 Church St, Richmond. German for "the space", this is actually a small, groovy cocktail bar – the martinis, in particular, are well worth crossing town for.

St Kilda

Dog's Bar 54 Acland St, St Kilda. Chic setting attracting a dedicated clientele. The wine list is terrific (although there's a surprisingly small range of beers) and there's great tucker like bangers and mash, steak, pizza, pasta and chips.

The Esplanade Hotel 11 Upper Esplanade, St Kilda. Famous for its beachside views, this hotel is the epicentre of St Kilda's drinking scene and shouldn't be missed. Bands play every night and there are inexpensive meals from *The Espy Kitchen* at the rear, plus pool tables and pinball machines.

The George Public Bar 127 Fitzroy St, St Kilda. Very cool underground bar with an upbeat design. Favoured by locals, it has a large range of beers on tap, plus a pool table and free live music on Saturday afternoons. The service is friendly and the kitchen is open until late each night, serving a wide range of snacks and good-value meals. Table seats outside.

Mink Bar At *The Prince*, 2B Acland St, St Kilda. Refurbished hotel-bar-restaurant complex, this subterranean vodka bar has back-lit refrigerated shelves stacked high with an astonishing array of Russian, Polish, Swedish, Finnish, Lithuanian and – gulp – Japanese vodka. A great place for convivial quaffing and mellowing.

The Prince Public Bar 29 Fitzroy St, St Kilda. Defiantly local and no-frills, the downstairs public bar of *The Prince* (see above and *Circa, The Prince*) has an air of stubborn resistance in the face of St Kilda's freewheeling gentrification. Frequented in equal parts by colourful local identities and desperadoes, it's not for the faint-hearted.

Veludo Bar 175 Acland St, St Kilda. Magnet for St Kilda fashion plates, *Veludo* sports a bar downstairs with interesting and cheap food, and a smart restaurant upstairs overlooking Acland Street. Spacious and stylish, it really gathers steam at the weekends.

Live music

Melbourne has a thriving **band** scene, and just about every pub puts on some sort of music – often free – at some time during the week. Grungy Richmond has a big concentration of **music pubs**, and Fitzroy and St Kilda are also worthy areas to head to for a range of live music. Note the line between bars, music pubs and clubs is getting increasingly blurred; the pubs listed below are also good places for a drink and always have at least two bars, so you can escape the din if you want to. Most clubs have a **cover charge** of between $5 and $10. Some backpacker hostels give vouchers for reduced or free admission to a rapidly changing array of venues, or you can pick up the passes in music shops such as Gaslight at 85 Bourke Street.

Free **listings** magazines such as *Beat*, *Inpress* or *Zebra* are good sources of information about the local music scene, while local FM stations Triple R (102.7) and PBS (106.7) air alternative music and tell you what's on and where.

City centre and the northern suburbs

Barbukka 279 Smith St, Collingwood. Café-restaurant during the day that turns into a folk and world-music venue most nights.
Bennetts Lane 25 Bennetts Lane, off Little Lonsdale St in the CBD, between Exhibition and Russell streets. One of Melbourne's most interesting jazz venues, now expanded to include a larger back room to complement the original cramped, 1950s-style cellar.
Ding Dong Lounge 18 Market Lane, City. Small and busy place that plays host to jazz musicians, tribute bands and DJs.
Empress Hotel 714 Nicholson St, North Fitzroy. Lots of bands play here, the bar meals are big, if somewhat unsophisticated, and there's a great beer garden.
Grace Darling Hotel 114 Smith St, Collingwood. Pleasant watering hole, which sometimes hosts live jazz and R&B.
Lounge 243 Swanston St, City. Upstairs bar-restaurant-club that features bands and films, and has pool tables and a dance floor.
Manchester Lane Manchester Lane, just off Flinders Lane near Swanston St, City. The city's other good jazz venue. The drawback being most tables are for a dinner and show package: if you're there for the music only you are relegated to standing behind the diners.
The Rainbow 27 St David St, Fitzroy. Mellow atmosphere, interesting crowd and decor in an intimate bar with free music – R&B, funk and fusion – every night.

Richmond and the southern suburbs

Bridge Hotel 642 Bridge Rd, Richmond. Features jazz, reggae and African music.
Duke of Windsor 179 Chapel St, Windsor. Very nice dining room and a regular programme of blues and acoustics.
Corner Hotel 57 Swan St, Richmond. Alternative independent bands.
The Esplanade Hotel 11 Upper Esplanade, St Kilda. The "Espy" is the soul of St Kilda and of Melbourne's eclectic band scene (huge bouncers make it look rougher than it actually is), hosting an interesting nightly line-up of bands in the front bar (free) and Gershwin Room (small admission charge).
Lizard Lounge 90 Chapel St, Windsor. Alternative indie club.
The Prince Band Room At *The Prince*, 2 Acland St, St Kilda. Part of the refurbished *Prince* complex, this is another St Kilda icon which has undergone a facelift to fit in with the smart cafés and restaurants at this end of Fitzroy St. Upstairs late-night venue with good bands.

Clubs

Altitude Bar Bullens Lane (near the corner of Bourke and Russell streets), City. Trance and progressive house.
Brazen Lounge 169 Exhibition St, City. Spread over two storeys. The programme spans a wide range from indie/alternative; Brit pop, goth, house, R&B and funk.
Heat, Mercury Lounge and Club Odeon Crown Casino Entertainment Complex, south of the Yarra. Clubs on level 3 of the complex, playing mainstream pop from the 1980s onwards; occasional live bands.

Metro 20 Bourke St, City. Huge old theatre on three floors with eight bars and three dance floors, all very lavish. Expect an enormous queue of spivved-up kids on Friday night.

Monsoons Russell St, City. Upmarket club at the *Grand Hyatt. daFunk Club* for R&B, funk and soul.

Revolver 229 Chapel St, Prahran. Live music in the bandroom most weekends, while every night (Sundays from 7am) in the lounge room DJs spin electronic beats, reggae and dub sounds.

Viper Room 373 Chapel St, Prahran. Popular spot with Melbourne's dancing crowd.

Gay and lesbian venues and clubnights

Diva Bar 153 Commercial Rd, South Yarra. Cocktail and dance bar with a mixed crowd. Open Wed–Sun.

DT's Hotel 164 Church St, Richmond. Mixed crowd and popular pool competitions. Open Wed–Sun.

Glasshouse Hotel 51 Gipps St, Collingwood. Mainly for women, with DJs and a karaoke on Sunday. Open Thurs–Sun.

Laird Hotel 149 Gipps St, Collingwood. Well-equipped men-only venue, with two bars, DJs, a beer garden and games room; popular with the leather crowd. Open daily; cheap drinks until 10pm.

The Market 143 Commercial Rd, South Yarra. Excellent dance club with weekly menu of top-notch drag shows, karaoke nights and talent quests. No cover charge. Open Thurs–Sun.

The Peel 113 Wellington St (corner of Peel St), Collingwood. Dance floor, music videos and shows, drawing a large and appreciative crowd, mainly men. Open Wed–Sun.

Salon Kitty 399A High St, Northcote. Intimate lounge bar for women. Open Thurs–Sun.

Xchange Hotel 119 Commercial Rd, South Yarra. Mainly men. Open daily.

Comedy

Melbourne is the comedy capital of Australia, home of the madcap Doug Anthony All Stars, Wogs Out of Work and comedians from TV shows such as *The Big Gig* and *The Comedy Company*. The highlight of the comedy year is the **Melbourne International Comedy Festival** (Ⓦwww.comedyfestival.com.au) in April, based at the Town Hall in Swanston Street, with performances at several other venues around town. As well as local and interstate acts, you're likely to see some of the best stand-up comedians from overseas. For one-off performances and other venues, check out the "EG" supplement to *The Age* on Fridays.

Comedy Club 380 Lygon St, Carlton. Slick, cabaret-style space, which features largely mainstream comedians.

The Comics Lounge 26 Erroll St, North Melbourne. Comedy shows seven days a week; all formats from stand-up to cabaret. Tues & Wed nights host stand-up comedy newcomers. Pre-show dinner available Wed–Sat.

The Esplanade Hotel 11 Upper Esplanade, St Kilda. Stand-up shows each Tuesday and Sunday from 8pm.

Theatre

Melbourne offers a rich array of dramatic productions, from fringe to mainstream, with venues everywhere. Watch out for **outdoor performances** in summer, including alfresco Shakespeare and shows for children in the Royal Botanic Gardens from December until the end of February (Ⓣ03/9650 1500 for details; credit-card bookings with Ticketmaster7 Ⓣ1300 136 166).

Athenaeum Theatre 188 Collins St, City Ⓣ03/9650 1500. One of numerous small Victorian theatre buildings in the city, hosting guest performances – mainly plays and concerts.

Comedy Theatre 240 Exhibition St, City Ⓣ03/9209 9000. Not a comedy venue, but a small theatre hosting events similar to the Athenaeum.

Her Majesty's Theatre 219 Exhibition St, City Ⓣ03/9663 3211. Lavish musicals in a fabulously ornate old theatre.

Malthouse 113 Sturt St, South Melbourne Ⓣ03/9685 5111. A renovated malthouse containing two venues – the Beckett Theatre and the larger Merlyn Theatre – hosting guest performances, opera,

Gay and lesbian Melbourne

Melbourne's gay and lesbian scene may not be as in-your-face as Sydney's, but it's almost as big, and is also less ghettoized than in Sydney. Fitzroy, Collingwood and Carlton, north of the river, and St Kilda, South Yarra and Prahran, to the south, boast a strong **gay** presence; Fitzroy, Northcote and Clifton Hill are the city's recognized stomping grounds for **lesbians**. There are two free gay and lesbian **papers**: *Bnews* (Ⓦwww.bnews.net.au) and *MCV* (Melbourne Community Voice; Ⓦwww.mcv.com.au), both published weekly.

Big **events** are mostly organized by the ALSO (Alternative LifeStyle Organisation) Foundation, including one over the Australia Day weekend at the end of January: **Red Raw Resurrection**. The scene's annual highlight, however, is the fabulous **Midsumma Festival** (late Jan to early Feb; Ⓣ03/9415 9819, Ⓦwww.midsumma.org.au). Already in its 14th year, Midsumma provides an umbrella for a wide range of sporting, artistic and theatrical events. The Queen's Birthday public holiday in June is the time for the **Winterdaze** party, while Melbourne Show Day in September is marked by the **Show Off** dance party.

Organizations, support groups, bookshops and radio station

ALSO Foundation 1st Floor, 6 Claremont St, South Yarra Ⓣ03/9827 4999, Ⓦwww.also.org.au. Organizes events and publishes the *ALSO Directory*, free from community outlets, which lists everything from gay vets to lesbian psychologists.

Beat Books 157 Commercial Rd, Prahran Ⓣ03/9827 8748. Gay bookshop with a large range of magazines, books, sex toys and leather goods.

Gay and Lesbian Switchboard Ⓣ03/9827 8544 or 1800 631 493 (Mon, Tues, Thurs & Fri 6–10pm, Wed 2–10pm) for counselling, referral and information.

Joy 94.9 FM Ⓣ03/9699 2949, Ⓦwww.joy.org.au. Gay and lesbian radio station, with 24hr music ranging from classical to R&B and world music, plus news and updates about the arts and club scene.

Hares and Hyenas 135 Commercial Rd, Prahran Ⓣ03/9824 0110. Gay and lesbian bookshop.

Cafés and meeting places

Globe Cafe 218 Chapel St, Prahran Ⓣ03/9510 869. Good choice for a well-deserved treat after a hard morning's browsing on Chapel St. Mon–Fri 8.30am–late, Sat & Sun 9am–late.

Ice Café Bar 30 Cato St, Prahran Ⓣ03/9510 8788. Popular gay and lesbian meeting place in a small lane off Commercial Rd, opposite Prahran Market. Breakfasts are served daily until 4pm, with an extensive breakfast menu to choose from; plus light meals (pasta, risotto) and cocktails. Cheap–moderate. Daily 8am–late.

Jackie O 204 Barkly St, St Kilda Ⓣ03/9537 0377. Comfy, atmospheric surroundings complemented by relaxed service and value-for-money food. Daily 7.30am–6.30pm.

See also p.913 for gay- and lesbian-friendly places to stay and p.943 for gay and lesbian clubnights.

dance, concerts and readings. The resident Playbox company produces contemporary Australian plays.

La Mama 205 Faraday St, Carlton Ⓣ03/9347 6142. Plays by new writers, as well as poetry and play readings.

Playhouse Theatre Victorian Arts Centre 100 St Kilda Rd Ⓣ03/9281 8000. Mainstream productions, mainly from the Melbourne Theatre Company.

Princess Theatre 163 Spring St, City Ⓣ03/9299 9500. Small but lavish old-fashioned theatre which stages musicals and mainstream plays.

Regent Theatre 191 Collins St, near City Square, City Ⓣ03/9299 9500. This lovingly restored old theatre puts on productions of big-name musicals.

Theatreworks 14 Acland St, St Kilda Ⓣ03/9534 4879. Ground-breaking new Australian plays.

Classical music, opera and dance

The **Melbourne Symphony Orchestra** has a season from February to December based at Hamer Hall and the Melbourne Town Hall, while the **State Orchestra of Victoria** performs less regularly at Hamer Hall, often playing works by Australian composers. If you can't afford the ticket prices – expect to pay $40–80 for classical music performances, $60–130 for opera – you can listen to the Symphony Orchestra concerts on Tuesday at 7pm on Radio 3MBS (103.5FM).

Her Majesty's Theatre 219 Exhibition St, City ⓣ03/9663 3211. Occasionally hosts some of the great foreign ballet companies.

Malthouse Studio Victorian Arts Centre, 100 St Kilda Rd ⓣ03/9281 8000. Modern dance and plays.

Hamer Hall Victorian Arts Centre, 100 St Kilda Rd ⓣ03/9281 8000. Big-name concerts.

State Theatre Victorian Arts Centre, 100 St Kilda Rd ⓣ03/9281 8000. Venue for the Victoria State Opera and the Australian Ballet Company.

Film

Mainstream **cinemas** are concentrated on Bourke Street, where discount day is usually Tuesday. The Crown Casino has a number of cinemas showing blockbuster movies. In summer, watching a film under the stars at the Moonlight Cinema in the Botanic Gardens (see p.926) or at the Cinema at the Bowl (Sidney Myer Music Bowl) nearby can be a real treat (details from local press; bookings through Ticketmaster7 ⓣ13 61 00). The city's independent cinemas screen less obviously commercial US films and foreign-language films; these cinemas tend to offer discounts on Monday. The **Melbourne International Film Festival** in July (ⓦwww.melbournefilmfestival.com.au) has been going for over forty years, based at a number of cinemas around the city.

ACMI Federation Square ⓣ03/8663 2583, ⓦwww.acmi.net.au. Film-buff's cinema; often shows Australian movies.

Astor Theatre Cnr of Chapel St and Dandenong Rd, St Kilda ⓣ03/9510 1414, ⓦwww.astor-theatre.com. Classic and cult movie double bills in a beautiful Art Deco cinema.

Cinema Nova Lygon Court Plaza, 380 Lygon St, Carlton ⓣ03/9347 5331, ⓦwww.cinemanova.com.au. A rabbit warren of small, recently refurbished and comfortable cinemas showing the latest Hollywood releases, as well as arthouse movies. Cheap day Monday.

Como Gaslight Gardens, cnr of Toorak Rd and Chapel St, South Yarra ⓣ03/9827 7533, ⓦwww.palacefilms.com.au. Belongs to the Palace Cinemas chain, which shows latest releases of Hollywood movies as well as arthouse films.

IMAX Theatre Melbourne Museum complex, Rathdowne St, Carlton ⓣ03/9663 5454 ⓦwww.imax.com.au. Part of the Melbourne Museum complex (see p.920), with kitsch interiors and awesome technology, including a gigantic screen and film reels so big they require a fork-lift to move them. Shows both 2D and 3D films, usually lasting from 45min to 1hr, mostly documentaries on inaccessible places or anything involving a Tyrannosaurus Rex.

Kino Dendy 45 Collins St, City ⓣ03/9650 2100, ⓦwww.kinodendy.com.au. In the Collins Place atrium, with several cafés and bars in the complex.

Lumiere 108 Lonsdale St, City ⓣ03/9639 1055, ⓦwww.lumiere.com.au. The city's only independent cinema, screening a wide range of world cinema, with films from everywhere from Tunisia to Taiwan.

Westgarth Theatre 89 High St, Northcote ⓣ03/9482 2001. Art Deco period piece, decorated by the planner of Canberra, Walter Burley Griffin, showing quality mainstream films, cult classics and late shows.

Shopping

Melbourne's big two **department stores**, David Jones and Myer, are located off the Bourke Street Mall. **Shopping hours** are generally Monday to Friday

9am to 5.30pm, with late-night shopping till 7pm on Thursday and Friday evenings; many places also open at weekends from noon to 5pm.

Clothes

Some good, middle-of-the-road Australian brand names are Chelsea Girl, Country Road, David Lawrence, Jag, Rivers, Sportsgirl and Witchery. Dangerfield sells modern, funky clothes and great accessories. At the higher end of fashion look out for designer names such as Alanna Hill, Lisa Ho, Carla Zampatti and Saba. Some streets or precincts have clusters of shops of a particular type making it possible to go clothes hunting by district.

Bridge Road, Richmond (between Punt Road and Church Street). This is Melbourne's inner-city bargain district: lots of factory outlets, clothes and shoe shops selling seconds, samples and end-of-season stock. There's a lot of rubbish but enough good brand names if you do some extensive browsing.

Brunswick St, Fitzroy Interspersed with cafés, bars and "cutting edge" hairstylists you'll find lots of small, groovy clothes boutiques and accessories shops – great for unusual hats, costume jewellery and "lifestyle" bric-à-brac: unusually shaped wall clocks or whatever is the latest craze in interior decor.

Chapel St: South Yarra, Prahran and Windsor Many upmarket fashion outlets at the northern (South Yarra) end, getting progressively less expensive, younger and grungier towards Prahran and Windsor in the south.

City Arcades and Lanes Lots of boutiques and small shops, selling designer brands and unusual fashion and shoes, are tucked away in the laneways of the two city blocks bordered by Flinders, Swanston, Bourke and Elizabeth Streets.

Elizabeth St, City At the upper end between La Trobe and Franklin streets there are a few big shops selling samples and seconds (look out for Jump or Sportscraft labels).

GPO Centre, corner of Bourke St and Elizabeth St, City This grand, magnificently restored Victorian building is now home to high fashion outlets.

Greville St, Prahran (off Chapel St). A few big-name clearing centres.

Hardware St and Little Bourke St, City Lots of shops selling travel clothing and equipment. The place to head for if you want to kit yourself out for your skiing, hiking or rafting trip.

Lygon St, Carlton Mainly lined with cafés and restaurants, but there are also a few good shoe shops and fashion retail outlets, most of them at the northern end between Grattan and Elgin streets.

QV, City The latest city development with boutiques clustered in the "lanes" running from Russell St towards Swanston St selling high fashion designer labels.

Books

Academic and General Bookshop 259 Swanston St, City and at 196 Elgin St, Carlton. Secondhand bookshop selling a wide range of topics.

Angus & Robertson cnr of Bourke and Elizabeth streets, with other branches at 35 Swanston St, and 379 Collins St; all in the city. Mainstream bookshop.

Black Mask Books 78 Toorak Rd, South Yarra. Specializes in mystery and crime.

Book Affair 200–202 Elgin St, Carlton. Very good secondhand bookshop, particularly for novels.

Bookcity 205 Swanston St, City. Discount mainstream bookshop.

Border's, Jam Factory 500 Chapel St, South Yarra, also at Lygon Court Plaza, Lygon St, Carlton. Huge American chainstore with a superb range. Both branches have a café.

Brunswick Street Bookstore 305 Brunswick St, Fitzroy. Good independent bookseller.

Chronicles 91 Fitzroy St, St Kilda. Small, well-stocked independent bookseller.

Collins Booksellers 104 Elizabeth St, with branches also at 86 Bourke St and 401 Swanston St; all in the city. Mainstream bookshop.

Cosmos Books and Music 112 Acland St, St Kilda. Great independent bookshop with a good selection on politics and history as well as a small selection of CDs.

Grub Street Bookshop 379 Brunswick St, Fitzroy. Secondhand and antiquarian books.

Hill of Content Bookshop 86 Bourke St, City. Very small but very well-stocked.

Kill City 226 Chapel St, Prahran. Small bookshop specializing in mystery and crime.

Map Land 372 Little Bourke St, City. Good stock of maps and travel books.

Readers Feast Midtown Plaza, cnr of Bourke and Swanston streets, City. Big mainstream bookstore.

Readings Books & Music 309 Lygon St, Carlton, also at 253 Bay St, Port Melbourne. This independent bookshop is one of Melbourne's best. The Port Melbourne branch has a pleasant café-bar.

Music

Au-go-go 2 Somerset Place, City. Independent and rare recordings. Also displays notices for what's on and room shares.
Basement Discs 24 Block Place, off Little Collins St, City. Great range of jazz and world music.
Blue Moon Records 54 Johnston St, Fitzroy. Spezializes in world music, particularly Latin and Spanish.
Border's, Jam Factory See opposite. Large American bookstore with a big CD department.
Cosmos Books and Music 112 Acland St, St Kilda. Small music department, with a good selection of CDs; classical, jazz and world music.
Discurio 113 Hardware Lane, City. Classical music, jazz, blues and folk.
Gaslight 85 Bourke St, City. Superb range of everything except classical.
Metropolis Music Store Level 3, 252 Swanston St. A newcomer selling a good range of local and imported titles, some of which are very hard to come by.
Readings Books & Music See above. Very good CD department.
Rhythm and Soul Records 128 Greville St, Prahran. Funk, electronic, trance and techno grooves.
Thomas's Records 31 Bourke St, City. Small but with a very good range of music.

Markets

Camberwell Market Station St, Camberwell. Large flea market with lots of good secondhand clothes stalls, books, records, bric-à-brac, and plenty of food vans and cafés. Sun 7am–3pm; take the train to Camberwell.
Federation Square Book Market New and secondhand books are sold in The Atrium at Federation Square every Sunday 11am–4pm.
Gaslight Night Market. Held on the premises of the Queen Victoria Market. A lovely market with stalls selling unusual (and good) food, spices, deli items and gifts. Wed 5.30–10pm; end of November until end of February.
Prahran Market Commercial Rd, Prahran. Fresh produce market. Tues & Thurs dawn–5pm, Fri & Sat dawn–6pm.
Queen Victoria Market Probably the best loved of Melbourne's fresh produce markets. A huge range of products is available and the deli section is well worth visiting. Turns into a general clothes market on Sundays with only the fruit and veg section open also. Tues & Thurs 6am–2pm, Fri 6am–6pm, Sat 6am–3pm, Sun 9am–4pm; Ⓦwww.qvm.com.au.
South Melbourne Market Cecil St, South Melbourne. Fresh produce market. Wed 8am–2pm, Fri 8am–6pm, Sat & Sun 8am–4pm.
St Kilda Arts and Crafts Market A Melbourne institution and particularly nice in warm weather: retreat to the beach afterwards or to one of the cafés in Fitzroy or Acland Streets. Sun 9am–4pm, longer in summer.
Telstra Dome Concourse Market A new market selling arts and crafts. Sun 9am–4pm.
Victorian Arts Centre Crafts Market Good crafts market on the footpath alongside the Arts Centre, extending to the underpass towards Southgate. Sun 9am–4pm; in summer 10am–6pm.

Listings

Airlines (domestic) Jetstar Ⓣ03/8341 4901, Ⓦwww.jetstar.com.au; Qantas Ⓣ13 13 13, Ⓦwww. qantas.com.au; Virgin Blue Ⓣ13 67 89, Ⓦwww.virginblue.com.au.
Airlines (international) Alitalia Ⓣ03/9920 3799; British Airways Ⓣ03/8696 2633; Garuda Indonesia Ⓣ1300 365 330; Japan Airlines Ⓣ03/8662 8333; KLM Ⓣ1300 303 747; Lauda Air Ⓣ1800 642 438; Malaysia Airlines Ⓣ13 26 27; Qantas Ⓣ13 13 13; Singapore Airlines Ⓣ13 10 11; Thai Airways Ⓣ1300 651 960; United Airlines Ⓣ13 17 77.
American Express 233 Collins St and 260 Collins St (Mon–Fri 9am–5.30pm, Sat 9am–noon).
Banks and foreign exchange All major banks can be found on Collins St. Standard banking hours are generally Mon–Fri 9.30am–4pm (Fri until 5pm), although some branches of Westpac/Bank of Melbourne, including the one at 142 Elizabeth

St, are open on Saturday (9am–noon). Most banks have 24-hour ATMs, which accept a variety of cash, credit and debit cards. Branches of Travelex are at 257 Collins St, 233 Collins St and 261 Bourke St (Mon–Fri 9am–5.30pm, Sat 10am–4pm). There are Thomas Cook desks at arrivals at the international terminal of Melbourne Airport.

Bike rental Hire a Bicycle, a stall at Princes Bridge (daily 11am–5pm, weather permitting; ⓣ0417 339 203) has basic bicycles, mountain bikes and tandems ($15–17/2hr, or $26 per day; helmets, locks, maps and backpacks are provided). The owner also runs a three-hour Real Melbourne Bike Tour ($50 incl. bike hire, and coffee and cakes in

Tours from Melbourne

Melbourne can be used as a base for a wide variety of **tours** to the interior of Victoria or along the coast. Popular destinations are the Yarra Valley, the Great Ocean Road, the Grampians and the Penguin Parade at Phillip Island; sadly, only one operator offers walking tours of the gorgeous "Prom" (Wilson's Promontory). Given the distances, **day-trips** to all these destinations (except the Yarra Valley and Phillip Island) would be far too rushed. To get more than the most superficial impression, it is advisable to choose one of the **two-** to **four-day** excursions offered by various operators. The Great Ocean Road and the Grampians can also be visited on a one–way tour between Melbourne and Adelaide. Some of the smaller outfits do not operate during the winter months.

Adventure Tours Australia ⓣ1300 654 604, ⓦwww.adventuretours.com.au. A South Australia-based safari tour operator who has expanded enormously in the last few years. They do runs along the west coast from Perth to Darwin, Darwin to Adelaide and along the top of Australia from Darwin to Cairns and have Tasmania "stitched up". They also do a three-day one-way tour from Melbourne to Adelaide via the Great Ocean Road and the Grampians departing 2–3 times a week ($300). All the major sights are visited and there is a hop-on, hop-off option with accommodation upgrades possible.

Autopia Tours ⓣ03/9419 8878 or 1800 000 507, ⓦwww.autopiatours.com.au. Long-established outfit running popular day-trips by minibus along the Great Ocean Road ($75), to Phillip Island ($80) and the Grampians ($70), plus a combined tour to the Great Ocean Road and the Grampians (3 days, $170). They also offer one-way tours between Melbourne and Adelaide via the Great Ocean Road and the Grampians (3 days; $180), and from November to May between Melbourne and Sydney via the Snowy Mountains and Canberra (3–4 days; $200). Max. 22 people; prices do not include meals and accommodation.

Bunyip Bushwalking Tours ⓣ03/9531 0840. Nature-focused tours with – as their name implies – lots of bushwalking, mainly to Wilson's Promontory National Park (1–4 days; $80–345). For the longer trips you need to be reasonably fit and able to carry a pack with your own tent and supplies. The one- and two-day tours can be combined with the Phillip Island Penguin Parade on the way back to Melbourne. A two-day tour to the Grampians departs every Saturday ($170), and there are two departures mid-week for a trip to the Great Ocean Road and the forests and waterfalls of the Otways ($175). Very small groups.

Duck Truck Tours ⓣ03/5952 2548, ⓦwww.amaroopark.com. Based at the YHA in Cowes, Phillip Island, this long-established operator does day-trips from Melbourne to Phillip Island ($75), with very reasonably priced overnight options; in summer they also run day-trips from Cowes to the "Prom". Other day-trips include the Great Ocean Road ($60) and two-day trips to the Great Ocean Road and the Grampians ($125).

Echidna Walkabout ⓣ03/9646 8249, ⓦwww.echidnawalkabout.com.au. Long-running upmarket eco-tour operator, with very small groups and enthusiastic, extremely knowledgeable guides, focusing on native wildlife. The Savannah Walkabout day-tour goes to Serendip Sanctuary and the You Yangs, southwest of

Lygon St). In St Kilda, try the helpful St Kilda Cycles, 11 Carlisle St (Mon–Fri 9am–6pm, Sat 9am–5pm, Sun 10am–4pm; ⓣ03/9534 3074; full day $30, or $20 per half-day after 1pm), or the stand next to the cycle path near St Kilda Pier (ⓣ0412 445 575), which rents out bicycles on weekends, and daily during the summer holidays.

Consulates Canada, 1st Floor, 123 Camberwell Rd, Hawthorn East ⓣ03/9811 9999; UK, Level 17, 90 Collins St ⓣ03/ 9652 1600; USA, 553 St Kilda Rd ⓣ03/9526 5900.

Disabled travellers Paraquad Victoria, 208 Wellington St, Collingwood ⓣ03/9415 1200, ⓦwww.paraquad.asn.au. Assistance is available at

Melbourne, while longer trips head along the Great Ocean Road and to remoter parts of East Gippsland, and include bushwalks; accommodation is in B&Bs or very comfortable camps.

Eco Platypus Tours ⓣ1800 819 091, ⓦwww.ecoplatypustours.com. One very long day-trip along the the Great Ocean Road; going as far as Loch Ard Gorge and staying at the Twelve Apostles for the sunset. The return trip is along the faster inland route via Colac ($70).

Go West ⓣ1300 736 551, ⓦwww.gowest.com.au. This family-run tour company offers day-trips, primarily aimed for the backpacker market, on a 21-seater minibus travelling the Great Ocean Road ($70) and to Phillip Island ($70); tours are very good value, entertaining and informative.

Groovy Grape ⓣ1800 661 177, ⓦwww.groovygrape.com.au. One-way tour specialist offering regular trips between Melbourne and Adelaide via the Great Ocean Road and the Grampians (3 days; $295). In Adelaide you can join their day-tour to the Barossa valley ($65) and their one-way tour to Alice Springs (7 days; $770). Max. 20 people.

Let's Go Bush ⓣ03/9640 0826. Two-day trip to the Great Ocean Road ($99, plus $25 for overnight pub accommodation in Apollo Bay and food).

Macka and Dave's Out There Bus ⓣ03/9654 5432. Very relaxed three-day tour along the Great Ocean Road and to the Grampians, with activities such as surfing and walking thrown in to suit the group. Accommodation options include cabins or camping. Departures all year, 1–2 weekly, depending on the season. Drop-off in Melbourne or bus connection to Adelaide ($165 incl. breakfast).

Melbourne's Best Tours ⓣ1300 130 550, ⓦwww.melbournetours.com.au. More conventional half-day and full-day tours in a small (21-seater) luxury coach to various destinations including Mornington Peninsula ($130), Daylesford and Ballarat/Sovereign Hill ($110); Yarra Valley Wineries ($120); Healesville Sanctuary and the Dandenongs ($120).

Otway Discovery ⓣ03/9654 5432, ⓦwww.otwaydiscovery.primetap.com. Tours along the Great Ocean Road (one- or two-days; $65, with hop-on, hop-off option available), and to Phillip Island ($70 including BBQ dinner and wine-tasting).

Oz Experience ⓣ1300 300 028, ⓦwww.ozexperience.com.au. One-way trips from Melbourne to Adelaide and from Melbourne to Sydney are integral to this (almost) Australia-wide network backpacker bus company. Primarily attracts a very young, party crowd but a switch in their format to shorter day-long itineraries and more emphasis on hands-on activities such as surfing, hiking, mountain biking, might change this.

Wayward Bus ⓣ1300 653 510, ⓦwww.waywardbus.com.au. Long-established one-way specialist, their regular tours follow the coast all the way between Melbourne and Adelaide, running via the Great Ocean Road, Mount Gambier and The Coorong (3–4 days; $310 for hostel bed; $490 twin share). In Adelaide, you can join their Kangaroo Island tour or their trip to all the natural attractions of the Red Centre and the Northern Territory's Top End. Max. 21 people.

metropolitan, suburban, country and interstate stations, while relevant information for people with disabilities can be obtained by calling metlink on ☎13 16 38. Buses are progressively being replaced with low-floor wheelchair accessible models; however, passengers in wheelchairs still need to contact local bus operators for information. The Melbourne City Council produces a free mobility map of the CBD showing accessible routes and toilets in the city, available from the front desk of the Melbourne Town Hall. For wheelchair-accessible taxis, call Central Booking Service ☎1300 364 050. TADAS (Travellers Aid Disability Access Service), at Level 2, 169 Swanston St, near Bourke St Mall (Mon–Fri 9am–5pm, Sat & Sun 11am–4pm; ☎03/9654 7690), provides personal care and various services, including wheelchair rental; to get to the lifts, enter via alcove 2 shops south of Bourke St Mall.

Diving Underwater Victoria – Dive Industry Victoria Association (☎1800 816 151) has a list of members in the Greater Melbourne area who rent equipment, organize diving trips and offer dive courses.

Emergency ☎000 for fire, police or ambulance.

Employment Backpackers Resource Centre, at *Hotel Bakpak* (Mon–Fri 9am–5pm, Sat 9am–1pm; ☎03/9329 7525, ⓦwww.bakpak.com). Traveller's Work Centre at the *Coffee Palace*, 24 Grey St, St Kilda (☎03/9534 2003, Mon–Sat 10am–6pm). In addition Traveller's Contact Point (see "Travellers aid centre" opposite) has a noticeboard.

Environment and conservation Australian Trust for Conservation Volunteers ☎03/5333 1483 or 1800 032 501, ⓦwww.atcv.com.au; Department of Sustainability and Environment (DSE) Information Centre, 8 Nicholson St, East Melbourne ☎03/9637 8325, ⓦwww.dse.vic.gov.au; Parks Victoria telephone information service ☎13 19 63; Wilderness Society Shop, 247 Flinders Lane ☎03/9639 5455. The Melbourne Visitor Centre at Federation Square has a range of brochures on national parks.

Flat-hunting and sharing Check the Saturday edition of *The Age*, as well as the notice boards of hostels and cafés along Brunswick St in Fitzroy, the *Galleon Café* at 9 Carlisle St in St Kilda, Readings Books and Music, 309 Lygon St in Carlton, and at Traveller's Contact Point (see opposite).

Hospitals and medical centres Alfred Hospital, Commercial Rd, Prahran ☎03/9276 2000; Royal Children's Hospital, Flemington Rd, Parkville ☎03/9345 5522; Royal Melbourne Hospital, Grattan St, Parkville ☎03/9342 7000; and St Vincent's Hospital, Victoria Parade, Fitzroy ☎03/9807 2211. Melbourne Sexual Health Centre, 580 Swanston St, Carlton ☎03/9347 0244 or 1800 032 017 offers a free service. For vaccinations, anti-malaria tablets and first-aid kits contact the Travel Doctor (TMVC), 2nd Floor, 393 Little Bourke St ☎03/9602 5788, ⓦwww.tmvc.com.au.

Internet access There are plenty of cyber cafés throughout Melbourne with most charging between $4–7 per hour. Most backpacker hostels also have Internet access. Alternatively, in the city try Global Gossip, 440 Elizabeth St (Mon–Fri 8am–midnight; Sat & Sun 8am–9pm); FIFTYFIVE, 55 Elizabeth St (Mon–Fri 8am–3am, Sat 10am–3am, Sun 10.30am–11pm); Internet Café, 429 Elizabeth St (Mon–Sat 9am–11.30pm, Sun 10am–11.30pm); and Traveller's Contact Point, see opposite; in St Kilda: Hubway Internet Café, 9 Grey St (daily 9.30am–11pm).

Laundries Almost all of the hostels and hotels have their own laundry. Commercial self-serve coin laundries include Melbourne City Dry Cleaners, 244 Russell St, corner of Lonsdale St (Mon–Fri 7am–6pm, Sat 9am–3pm); City Edge Laundrette, 39 Errol St, North Melbourne (daily 6am–11pm); The Soap Opera Laundry & Cafe, 128 Bridport St, Albert Park (Mon–Fri 7.30am–7.30pm, Sat 8am–6pm, Sun 10am–6pm); and Blessington Street Launderette, 22 Blessington St, St Kilda (daily 7.30am–9pm).

Left luggage and luggage forwarding Most hostels and many hotels store luggage; hostels usually don't charge an extra fee for this service. Southern Cross station has lockers (daily 6am–10pm; $2; emptied nightly as does Flinders Street station (8am–8pm; $2). The lockers at the Greyhound Australia Terminal at Franklin St are accessible 24hr ($6–10). Traveller's Contact Point (see opposite) stores luggage, forwards it and/or sends it home.

Library The Redmond Barry Reading Room at the State Library of Victoria, 328 Swanston St (Mon–Thurs 10am–9pm, Fri–Sun 10am–6pm), has current Australian and overseas magazines; the Newspaper Room has Australian and overseas papers.

Motorbikes The northern end of Elizabeth Street in the city centre has a string of motorbike shops. Garner's Motorcycles, 179 Peel St, North Melbourne ☎03/9326 8676, ⓦwww.garnersmotorcycles.com.au, does rentals and may sell secondhand machines with buy-back deals.

Newspapers Melbourne's *The Age* is one of Australia's better papers; the pulpy *Herald Sun* is the city's only other daily. Foreign newspapers can be perused at the State Library (see above) or bought from McGill's Newsagency, 187 Elizabeth St.

Pharmacies Australian Unity Pharmacy, 286 Little Bourke St, next to the Myer department store

(Mon–Wed 9am–5.45pm, Thurs 9am–6.30pm, Fri 9am–9pm, Sat 10am–5pm; Mulqueeny's Pharmacy, cnr Swanston and Collins streets, opposite the Town Hall (Mon–Fri 8am–8pm, Sat 9am–6pm, Sun 11am–6pm).

Police Melbourne City Police Station, 637 Flinders St; ⓣ03/9247 6491; emergency ⓣ000.

Post office The GPO retail shop is located at 250 Elizabeth St (Mon–Fri 8am–6pm, including the *poste restante* counter). Other post offices are open Mon–Fri 9am–5pm. For voicemail and mail forwarding, contact Traveller's Contact Point (see "Travellers aid centre", below).

RACV The RACV outlet in the city is at 422 Little Collins St; it has good maps of Melbourne, Victoria and the rest of Australia (discounted for RACV members and members of affiliated overseas motoring associations; ⓦwww.racv.com.au). RACV also books accommodation listed in its guides and package holidays; members get special rates.

Skiing AUSKI Ski Hiring & Information Centre, 9–11 Hardware Lane ⓣ03/9670 1412, can advise on skiing conditions at Baw Baw, Buffalo, Mount Hotham, Buller, Falls Creek and at Thredbo in NSW.

Swimming pools City Baths, cnr of Swanston and Franklin streets (Mon–Thurs 6am–10pm, Fri 6am–8.30pm, Sat & Sun 8am–6pm; $4 for a swim, $8.50 including the sauna and spa, $16.50 for use of gym, pool, sauna and spa; ⓣ03/9663 5888), has a 30-metre heated indoor pool for swimming, plus a pool for water-aerobics and a gym. In the state-of-the-art Melbourne Sports & Aquatic Centre, Aughtie Drive, off Albert Park Rd in Albert Park, there's a choice between a wave pool, a 50-metre pool, a dive pool, a 25-metre lap pool, a 20-metre multi-purpose pool and a toddler area, plus a giant curling waterslide, spa, sauna and steam rooms (Mon–Fri 6am–10pm, 50-metre pool Mon–Fri 5.30am–8pm, Sat & Sun 7am–8pm; admission $5.70; $3.60 for spa, sauna and steam room; ⓣ03/9926 1555). Take tram #112 from Collins St or #96 from Bourke St in the city.

Taxis Taxi rank on Swanston St outside Flinders Street station, and plenty to flag down. Call Black Cabs Combined ⓣ13 22 27; Embassy Taxis ⓣ13 17 55; or Silver Top ⓣ13 10 08.

Telephones Melbourne has an abundance of public telephones and there are a plethora of discount phonecards around (such as ezycom, Unidial, iprimus and Green Card), which can be used in any payphone for dirt cheap international calls and are sold in lots of shops, as well as Internet cafés and some backpacker hostels. Read the fine print before buying – watch out for flagfall billing in units of 3min or more, and a too-short expiry date. The official Telstra rate for a call from a public phone is ridiculously expensive in comparison: to the UK it's about $1.60 per minute during peak hours (Mon–Fri 7am–7pm) and about 80¢ per minute off-peak; with one of the phonecards mentioned above, expect to pay about 1.5–5¢ per minute.

Transport For information on trams, suburban buses and trains, call metlink ⓣ13 16 38 (6am–10pm daily).

Travel agents For flight bookings: Flight Centre (ⓣ13 18 66) 19 Bourke St and 53 Elizabeth St, plus many branches throughout the city; STA Travel (ⓣ1300 360 960, ⓦwww.statravel.com.au), 273 Little Collins St, City and 142 Acland St, St Kilda, plus other branches throughout the city; Student Flights (ⓣ1800/046 462, ⓦwww.studentflights.com.au), many branches, including Shop 4, 250 Flinders St or 339 Swanston St; Travel agent: Backpackers World, Shop 1, 250 Flinders St (Mon–Fri 9am–6pm, Sat 10am–4pm; ⓣ03/9654 8477); Footprints Travel, 24 Grey St, St Kilda (Mon–Sat 10am–6pm, ⓣ03/9534 2003); Peter Pan Adventure Travel, 415 Elizabeth St (ⓣ1800/252 459, ⓦwww.peterpantravel.com); Traveller's Contact Point (see below); YHA Travel, 83 Hardware Lane (ⓣ03/9670 9611, ⓦwww.yha.com.au).

Travellers aid centre 2nd Floor, 169 Swanston St (Mon–Fri 9am–5pm, ⓣ03/9654 2600). As well as information there's also a café serving budget meals, nappy-changing facilities, showers (for a fee), toilets, lounge rooms, lockers, wheelchairs for rent and assistance for disabled and frail persons. Traveller's Contact Point, Level 1, 361 Little Bourke St (Mon–Fri 9am–6pm Sat 9am–1pm, ⓣ03/9642 2911, ⓦwww.travellers.com.au) sells backpacker discount cards, WWOOF memberships and has an employment noticeboard.

Moving on from Melbourne

Three **bus** services operate from Melbourne: V/Line buses (daily 7am–9pm; ⓣ13 61 96, ⓦwww.vlinepassenger.com.au) and Firefly (reservations daily 7am–8.30pm; ⓣ1300/730 740, ⓦwww.fireflyexpress.com.au) both have terminals at Southern Cross Station, while Greyhound Australia buses (reservation desk daily 6.30am–10.30pm; ⓣ13 20 30, ⓦwww.greyhound.com.au) depart from the Greyhound Australia Terminal on Franklin Street. For up-to-date **train** information, Southern Cross Station has a staffed information desk with all V/Line train (and bus) timetables and there is also a V/Line booking desk (6am–10pm ⓣ13 61 96). If you're travelling with a bicycle, come at least thirty minutes earlier to book it on the train. Suburban train information is available from metlink (see p.951). The **ferry** from Melbourne to Devonport in Tasmania, run by the *Spirit of Tasmania I* and *II*, takes ten hours. There's a nightly departure from Station Pier, Port Melbourne, at 9pm, plus additional departures at 9am (daily from mid-Dec to mid-Jan). The cheapest one-way fares range from $99 off-peak to $145 peak. The fare for standard cars and campervans is normally $10, but rises to $55 during the peak season (mid-Dec until late January). For motorbikes the cost is $5, and $38 during the peak season. Reservations with TT Line ⓣ13 20 10, ⓦwww.spiritoftasmania.com.au. To get to Station Pier take tram #109 from Collins Street in the city.

Finally, many **car rental** and campervan companies offer one-way rental (see listings below). Two used-car companies who offer cheaper rates are Rent-A-Bomb (ⓣ13 15 53) and Ugly Duckling in St Kilda (ⓣ03/9525 4010 or 1800 335 908).

Car rental companies

Apex ⓣ03/9330 3877
Ascot ⓣ13 24 94
Avis ⓣ13 63 33
Budget ⓣ13 27 27
Hertz ⓣ1300 132 607
Network ⓣ1800 736 825
Thrifty ⓣ1300 367 227

Campervan companies

Apollo Motorhomes ⓣ1800 777 779
Awesome Campers ⓣ1800 121 421
Backpacker Campervan Rentals ⓣ03/8379 8768
Britz ⓣ1800 331 454
Kea Campers Australia ⓣ1800 252 555
Maui ⓣ1300 363 800
NQ Australia Rentals ⓣ1800 079 529
Wicked Campers ⓣ1800 246 869

Around Melbourne

There are many possible day-trips out of Melbourne, mainly around the shores of the huge **Port Phillip Bay**, encircled by the arms of the Bellarine and Mornington peninsulas. The **Mornington Peninsula** on the east side has farmland and wineries on gently rolling hills and is home to some of the city's most popular beaches and surfing spots, packed on summer weekends. **Western Port Bay**, beyond the peninsula, encloses two fascinating islands – little-known **French Island**, much of whose wildlife is protected by a national park, and **Phillip Island**, whose nightly "Penguin Parade", when masses of Little penguins waddle ashore each night, is among Australia's biggest tourist attractions. The **Bellarine Peninsula** and the western side of Port Phillip Bay are less exciting, but they do give access to the west coast and the Great Ocean Road. A regular ferry service operates from Phillip Island and French Island to the Mornington Peninsula and from here on to the Bellarine Peninsula, making it possible to visit these places in one big loop before continuing along the Great Ocean Road, thus bypassing the need to backtrack to Melbourne. Even without your own car it is a do-able travel option but not one that gets much publicity in Melbourne.

Inland to the east, the **Yarra Valley** and the **Dandenong Ranges** offer beautiful countryside, wine-tasting and bushwalking.

The Mornington Peninsula

The **Mornington Peninsula** curves right around Port Phillip Bay, culminating in Point Nepean, well to the southwest of Melbourne. The shoreline facing the bay is beach-bum territory, though the well-heeled denizens of **Sorrento** and **Portsea**, at the tip of the peninsula, might well resent that tag. On the largely straight, ocean-facing coast, **Mornington Peninsula National Park** encompasses some fine seascapes, with several walking trails marked out. The western side of the peninsula facing the shallow waters of **Western Port Bay** (and French and Phillip Islands) has a much quieter, rural feel. Heading north from the pleasant township of **Flinders** the coastline of rocky cliffs flattens out to sandy beaches, while north of **Stony Point** are mudflats and saltmarshes lined by white mangroves; not particularly visually appealing but an internationally recognized and protected habitat for migratory waterbirds. Further inland, the area around **Arthurs Seat** and **Red Hill** is probably the most scenic: a bucolic landscape of rolling hills, orchards and paddocks. This is also where the bulk of the peninsula's 170 or so **vineyards** are located. They produce superb, if pricey, Pinot Noir and Shiraz wines, as well as good whites. As in the Yarra Valley, good restaurants, especially winery restaurants, have proliferated on the peninsula in recent years, some of them in truly spectacular settings. Two of the best are Crittenden at Dromana, Harrison's Road, Dromana (ⓣ03/5987 3800), which serves light lunches daily; and Max's at Red Hill, 52 Red Hill–Shoreham Road, Red Hill (ⓣ03/5931 0177), which has views over the hills and Western Port Bay; they serve lunches daily and dinners during the summer (Nov to Easter Thurs–Sat from 6pm). You could also try the equally scenic Montalto Vineyard and Olive Grove, 33 Shoreham Road, Red Hill South (ⓣ03/5989 8412) open for lunches daily and dinner Friday and Saturday, or the Hickinbotham Winery, 194 Nepean Highway, Dromana (daily 10am–5pm; ⓣ03/5981 0355), whose bakery-café serves soups, antipasto platters, focaccia and other breads. For more details, see the *Peninsula Wine Country Annual*, published by the Mornington Peninsula Vignerons Association; or *Wine Regions of Victoria*, available at tourist information centres.

As well as the beaches, the peninsula's **community markets**, selling local produce and crafts, attract many city dwellers: most are monthly affairs, so there's usually one every weekend. One of the biggest and best is the Red Hill Community Market, held on the first Saturday of every month (Sept–May 8am–1pm), at Red Hill Recreation Reserve, Arthurs Seat Road, 10km east of Dromana; others include the Farmers Market at Dromana Estate, 555 Old Moorooduc Rd, Tuerong, every fourth Saturday (year round 8am–1pm); Balnarring Racecourse Market at Colaart Rd, Balnarring, on the third Saturday of every month (Nov–April 8am–1pm); the Mornington Racecourse Market (year round every second Sunday 9am–2pm) at Racecourse Road, Mornington; and the Sunday Market at the Dromana Drive-in Cinema (year round 7am–1pm) on the Bittern-Dromana Rd, just off the Mornington Peninsula Freeway.

You can get to the peninsula by **public transport** from Melbourne to Frankston and from there to the main beach resorts and towns along the Nepean Highway on the northern side, but for a sightseeing trip taking in wineries, beaches and Arthurs Seat you'll need your own vehicle. Take a metlink train to Frankston and change there for Stony Point, or connect with a Portsea Passenger Service bus #788 from Frankston to Sorrento, stopping at the Peninsula Searoad Ferry terminal ($7.90) and Portsea ($8.20; for timetable information call ⓣ1800 115 666). From Sorrento there's a community bus to Dromana via Blairgowrie, Rye and Rosebud (4 daily Mon–Fri), but no transport to Arthurs Seat. The *Bayplay Adventure Lodge* (see opposite) in Blairgowrie runs a **transfer service** to and from Melbourne or Frankston once daily, picking up passengers early in the morning for various dive excursions, sea kayaking tours or other activities in the area, before returning them to Frankston or Melbourne in the evening (ⓣ03/5988 0188; Melbourne $25, Frankston $15 one-way).

The western coast

The peninsula starts at suburban **Frankston**, 40km from central Melbourne. From here on down, the western coast, flanked by the Nepean Highway, sports beach after beach, all crowded and traffic-snarled in summer. Twelve kilometres beyond Frankston, the fishing port of **Mornington** preserves some fine old buildings along Mornington Esplanade; there's a produce and craft market on Main Street every Wednesday. Five kilometres further on, near Mount Martha, **Briars Park** (daily 11am–4pm; $3.50) comprises an 1850s homestead complete with a collection of furniture and memorabilia given to the owner by Napoleon Bonaparte, and an enclosed wildlife reserve with woodlands and extensive wetlands (daily 9am–5pm; free). The **visitors centre** near the homestead has an audiovisual display giving you an overview of how the affluent upper crust lived in early pioneering days, as well as a rundown on the present-day facilities of the park. Two walkways through the woodlands start near the visitors centre; the adjacent **wetlands** are visited by more than fifty species of waterbirds, which can be observed at close distance from two bird-hides, accessible via a boardwalk from the visitor information centre.

Inland from Dromana, where seaside development begins in earnest, the granite outcrop of **Arthurs Seat State Park** rises 305m, providing breathtaking views of Port Phillip Bay. You can drive up the winding road, but for a leisurely enjoyment of the vista you can ride to the top with Arthurs Seat Chairlift (daily 11am–5pm; $8 one way, $12 return). At the summit, **Arthurs Seat Maze** (daily 10am–6pm; $12) combines four landscaped mazes with theme gardens, a sculpture park and a children's animal farm, and offers lots of family-oriented activities and a good restaurant. Alternatively, you can have a drink or a bite at the nearby revamped *Arthurs Seat Hotel*, with live jazz on Sunday afternoons.

Sorrento

Beyond Arthurs Seat, the peninsula arcs and narrows: the sands around Sorrento and Portsea offer a choice between the rugged surf of the ocean ("back" beaches) or the calmer waters of the bay ("front" beaches). With some of the most expensive real estate outside the Melbourne CBD, **SORRENTO** is the traditional haunt of the city's rich during the "season" from Boxing Day to Easter. Well-heeled outsiders also make it their playground in January and on summer weekends, flocking here to swim, surf and dive at the bay and ocean beaches. Exploring beautiful rock formations and low-tide pools, and swimming with bottlenose dolphins add to the attraction. The smell of money is everywhere – in the wide, tree-lined residential streets, the clifftop mansions boasting million-dollar views, and the town-centre cafés, restaurants, galleries and antique shops, running along Ocean Road down to the beach.

Sullivan Bay, 3km southeast, was in 1803 the site of the first white attempt to settle in what is now Victoria; the settlers struggled here for four months before giving up and moving on to what is now Tasmania. One of the convicts in the expedition was the infamous William Buckley who, having escaped, was adopted by the local Aborigines and lived with them for 32 years. When the "wild white man" was seen again by settlers he could scarcely remember how to speak English; his survival against all odds has been immortalized in the phrase "Buckley's chance". You can walk along the cliffs and around the pioneer cemetery; there's a signposted turn-off from the main road.

Swimming with dolphins and seals is one of Port Phillip Bay's prime attractions. Operators include the environmentally-conscious Polperro Dolphin Swims (Ⓣ03/5988 8437 or 0428 174 160, Ⓦwww.polperro.com.au), which takes the smallest groups; and Moonraker (Ⓣ03/5984 4211 or 0419 205 506, Ⓦwww.moonrakercharters.com.au). Both run, weather permitting, 3–4 hour trips twice daily during the season (Sept/Oct to April/May) for roughly the same prices: $100 for swimmers, including wetsuit and snorkelling equipment and $50 for sightseers. The *Bayplay Adventure Lodge* in Blairgowrie (see below) doubles as a PADI **dive resort** and offers dive courses (all levels) as well as a wide range of leisure dives for novices and experienced divers, they also run a guided sea-kayaking trip along the coast to Portsea (daily 4hr; $60–75, depending on the group size). On most days dolphins come to frolic around the boats and often seals and penguins can be sighted. They also provide a free booking service for all kinds of other outdoor activities around the peninsula including horse riding and surfing lessons.

Practicalities

A reliable **car and passenger ferry** service operated by Peninsula Searoad (Ⓣ03/5258 3244, Ⓦwww.searoad.com.au) runs across the mouth of the bay from Sorrento to Queenscliff on the Bellarine Peninsula all year round (hourly 7am–6pm, summer until 7pm). One-way fares for pedestrians are $9, while standard cars are $48–55 (depending on the season) for 2 passengers plus $5 for each additional passenger. Motorbikes plus a rider are $21–23. No advance bookings are necessary but cars should be at the terminal thirty to forty-five minutes prior to departure.

Accommodation

Bayplay Adventure Lodge 46 Canterbury Jetty Rd, Blairgowrie Ⓣ03/5988 0188, Ⓦwww.bayplay.com.au. Comfortable budget accommodation in a bushland setting near the beach, with a self-catering kitchen, free bicycles, Internet access and camping space. The lodge is also a PADI dive resort (see above) and offers daily transfers from and to Melbourne (see opposite). The Frankston-Portsea bus (#39) stops just out the front. Dorms $25, rooms ❸

Carmel of Sorrento 142 Ocean Beach Rd, Sorrento Ⓣ03/5984 3512. Charming, sandstone B&B (non-smoking) smack in the middle of town. ❻

Hotel Sorrento 5 Hotham Rd, Sorrento Ⓣ03/5984 2206, Ⓦwww.hotelsorrento.com.au. A charming 1871 limestone hotel located in a secluded spot on a hill above the jetty. ❺

Sorrento Hostel YHA 3 Miranda St, Sorrento Ⓣ03/5984 4323. Cosy place run by a friendly couple, with small dorms (some en suite), doubles and twin rooms and stacks of local information. Dorms $25, rooms ❸

Tamasha House 699 Melbourne Rd, Sorrento Ⓣ03/5984 2413. Modern B&B halfway between ocean and bay beaches. ❻

Eating and drinking

As is to be expected in this posh part of the peninsula, most eating places tend to be on the pricey side but some come with great water views as a bonus. In winter, a lot of eateries have restricted opening times or are only open at weekends.

The Baths 3278 Point Nepean Rd, Sorrento. Simple, but good café and fish & chips shop.
Buckley's Chance 174 Ocean Beach Rd, Sorrento ⓣ03/5984 2888. A relaxed pancake parlour, which also does burgers and steaks.
Continental Hotel 21 Ocean Beach Rd, Sorrento ⓣ03/5984 2201. This venerable old-timer has a good café with a range of Mornington Peninsula wines on its wine list, plus live music and a disco at weekends.
Loquat Restaurant and Bar 3183 Point Nepean Rd, Sorrento ⓣ03/5984 4444. A newcomer devoted to rather elaborate modern-Australian cuisine with Mediterranean influences; try the restaurant's signature dessert: steamed loquat and quince pudding. Dinner Thurs–Sun, lunch Sun.
Smokehouse Sorrento 182 Ocean Beach Rd ⓣ03/5984 1246. The restaurant's mainstay is its woodfired pizzas – it's a good idea to book for dinner as the place fills up quickly. Daily noon–late.
Hotel Sorrento 5 Hotham Rd ⓣ03/5984 2206. It has a casual hotel bar and a restaurant whose menu features seafood dishes, woodfired gourmet pizzas, steaks and similarly conventional fare – the prime attraction is the view across the Bay.
Shells Café 95 Ocean Beach Rd, Sorrento ⓣ03/5984 5133. This light-filled, breezy café serves good coffee and cakes plus the standard café fare, and is a prime spot for people-watching.

Portsea and Point Nepean

PORTSEA, just beyond Sorrento, is a mecca for divers, with excellent **dives** of up to 40m off Port Phillip Heads; trips operate from the pier throughout the summer and there are a couple of good dive shops. Portsea Front Beach, on the bay by the pier, is wall-to-wall beautiful people, as is Shelley Beach, which also attracts playful dolphins. On the other shore, Portsea Ocean Beach has excellent surfing, and a hang-gliding pad on a rock formation known as London Bridge. Back on the bay side, the extensive lawns of *Portsea Hotel*, a hugely popular drinking spot which features bands at weekends, overlook the beach.

The tip of the peninsula, with its fortifications, quarantine station and former army base is now privately operated under the name **Park at Point Nepean**, part of a patchwork of parks sprinkled over the southern end of the peninsula, collectively known as Mornington Peninsula National Park. The visitor centre and a car park are 1km west of Portsea (daily 9am–5pm; ⓣ03/5984 4276). Because of its fragile sandy environment, visitor numbers are limited, so if you want to visit on weekends and during school holidays it's advisable to book. Entrance to this part of the national park costs $7.20. To get to **Point Nepean,** 6km from the visitor centre, you can either rent a bike ($15 for 4hr) or board the Transporter "train" – actually a few carriages pulled by a tractor ($11 one-way, $13 return; these fares include the park admission fee). The Transporter departs from the visitor centre hourly between 9.30am and 12.30pm and at 2pm and 3pm. Alternatively, you can drive to Gunners car park, 2.5km into the park, and walk the rest of the way to Point Nepean.

The Transporter runs to the fortifications at Point Nepean, with four optional drop-offs for walks: the first, the **Walter Pisterman Heritage Walk** (1km), leads through coastal vegetation to the Port Phillip Bay shoreline; the second (1km) leads to the top of Cheviot Hill, where you can look across to Queenscliff, then continues to **Cheviot Beach** where on December 17, 1967, **Harold Holt**, Australia's then prime minister, went for a swim in the rough surf of Bass Strait and disappeared, presumed drowned: his body was never found. The third walk, the **Fort Pearce and Eagle's Nest Heritage Trail** (2km), crosses through defence fortifications. A fourth walk takes you around **Fort Nepean**, right at the tip of the peninsula. Built at the same time as Fort Queenscliff opposite to protect wealthy post-goldrush Melbourne from the imagined threat of Russian invasion, the fort comprises two subterranean levels, whose tunnels lead down to the Engine House at water level.

South and east coast

The rest of Mornington Peninsula National Park, which spreads along the ocean coast, is freely open to the public. An enjoyable two-day walk (27km) runs from London Bridge along the coast to **Cape Schanck**, site of an 1859 lighthouse. Here walkways lead down to the sea along a narrow neck of land, providing magnificent coastal views. The three **lighthouse keeper's cottages** offer the most scenic accommodation on the peninsula (Ⓣ0500 527 891, Ⓦwww.austpacinns.com.au; ❹–❺), each with a cosy lounge and kitchen. There's a small maritime museum ($8) at the lighthouse, which is open daily for tours (10am–4pm; $10).

The nearby **Bushrangers Bay Nature Walk** (6km; 2hr) heads from the cape to Main Creek, beginning as a leisurely walk along the clifftop, then leading down to a wild beach facing Elephant Rock. More energetic activities in this part of the peninsula include **horse rides** along Gunnamatta Beach or through bushland, organized by the Gunnamatta Equestrian Centre, Trueman's Rd, Rye (Ⓣ03/5988 6755), and **surfing** lessons, offered by the East Coast Surf School at various spots near Point Leo (daily year round; all levels $40 for 90min, equipment provided).

For a decent place **to stay**, the pleasant village of Flinders has a good B&B; *Samburu*, Eastern Grey Rise, off Meakins Rd, 14km west of Flinders (Ⓣ03/5989 0093, Ⓦwww.samburu.com.au; ❺) has a guest wing in the main farmhouse and a separate studio with great views. A cheaper option is the shady *Flinders Caravanpark* (Ⓣ03/5989 0458), which has tent sites and cabins (❸–❹).

Set in bushland 15km southeast of Frankston, near the northern end of Westernport Bay, **Pearcedale Conservation Park**, at 55 Tyabb-Tooradin Rd (Wed–Sun noon–5pm; $9; Ⓣ03/5978 7935, Ⓦwww.moonlit-sanctuary.com) is home to lots of kangaroos, wallabies, emus and waterbirds. However, the park's emphasis is on rare nocturnal Australian animals, so it's well worth coming late in the day to take part in their guided **Moonlit Sanctuary tour** (90min; $19.50; reservations essential). Starting at dusk, this tour offers the chance to see rare nocturnal Australian creatures such as eastern quolls, eastern bettongs, pademelons, gliders and tawny frogmouths in bushland enclosures.

French Island

FRENCH ISLAND, on the eastern side of the Mornington Peninsula, is well off the beaten track. A former prison farm, about two-thirds of the island is a national park, with the remaining third used as farmland. The island is renowned for its rich **wildlife**, especially birds of prey, and a flourishing koala colony. Virtually vehicle-free, it's a great place to cycle, an activity which is encouraged, with all walking tracks open to bikes. The French Island Tourist Association runs a telephone information service on Ⓣ03/5986 1239.

Places to stay include *McLeod Eco Farm and Historic Prison* (Ⓣ03/5678 0155; ❸), where you can sleep in former prison cells converted into twins with bunk beds, or in the former officers' quarters with queen-size beds – all have shared facilities. The farm is surrounded by national park and has 8km of beach frontage; the very reasonable rates include organic meals and transfer from the ferry jetty 29km away. Also in the national park is the small and basic *Fairhaven Campground* which has a pit toilet and tank water, but no showers. Camping is free, but must be booked in advance – two weeks ahead is advised during the summer school holidays and at Easter; at other times booking one or two days in advance will suffice (ⓣ03/5986 8987 or 13 19 63). Near the jetty, the small *Tortoise Head Guesthouse* (ⓣ03/5980 1234; ❺) offers B&B accommodation in guest rooms with shared facilities and four en-suite cabins with water views. Moderately priced lunches and dinners are also available. *French Island B&B* is a cottage with two bedrooms, operated by the general store, 2.5km from the jetty (ⓣ03/5980 1209; ❹) who also provide well-priced lunches and dinners. The *Bayview Chicory Kiln Tea Room* (10km from the jetty) has a private campsite with toilets and shower. In addition, scrumptious lunches and Devonshire teas are served here.

Inter Island Ferries (ⓣ03/9585 5730, ⓦwww.interislandferries.com.au) connects the Mornington Peninsula with French Island and Phillip Island (see below). Departing from **Stony Point**, on the eastern side of the Mornington Peninsula to **Tankerton jetty** on French Island (daily 8.30am & 4.15pm, noon Tues, Thurs, Sat & Sun, also 10am Sat & Sun). To get to Stony Point from Melbourne, take the Frankston train from Flinders Street station and a bus to Stony Point.

For a brief visit to French Island, it's best to book one of the afternoon tours covering the island's natural attractions and the historic prison. The **French Island Bus Tour** ($15 including Devonshire tea; ⓣ03/5980 1241, ⓦwww.frenchislandtours.com.au) operated by Lois Airs from the *Bayview Chicory Kiln Tea Rooms*, runs on Tuesdays, Thursdays and Sundays, and during school holidays also on Saturday. Alternatively, **French Island Eco Tours** ($25; ⓣ1300 307 054, ⓦwww.frenchislandecotours.com.au) runs tours on Thursday and Sunday with a two-course lunch available for $10 at McLeod Eco Farm, made from their organic produce. For both, take the Inter Island Ferry from Stony Point at noon to Tankerton Jetty; the tours meet the ferry and drop off at the jetty at the end of the tour.

Phillip Island

The hugely popular holiday destination of **PHILLIP ISLAND** is famous above all for the nightly roosting of hundreds of Little penguins at Summerland Beach – the so-called **Penguin Parade** – but the island also boasts some dramatic coastline, plenty of surfing (for more information, call the Phillip Island Surf Report on ⓣ1902 243 082), fine swimming beaches, and a couple of well-organized wildlife parks. **Cowes**, on the sheltered bay side, is the main town and a lively and attractive place to stay. Other, smaller, communities worth a visit are **Rhyll**, to the east, and **Ventnor**, just west of Cowes.

A daily **V/Line bus** to Cowes departs from Melbourne's Southern Cross Station in the afternoon, but there's no public transport on the island itself, so it can be tricky getting around and to the Penguin Parade, over 10km from Cowes. Joining a **tour** solves the transport problem. A few operators specializing in small groups (up to 20 people) run day tours of the island from Melbourne that include the Penguin Parade at dusk; the going rate is $70 including dinner and all entrance fees (see box on p.923 for a list of tour operators).

If you're **driving**, head southeast from Melbourne on the Princes Highway to Dandenong, then follow the South Gippsland Highway to Lang Lang and from there the Bass Highway to Anderson where the road heads directly west to San Remo and the bridge across to the island, a drive of approximately three hours in total. The scenic lookout about 3km before San Remo is worth stopping at, for fantastic views of Western Port Bay and the surrounding countryside. **SAN REMO** itself has lots of motels, a picturesque fishing fleet by its wharf and a co-operative selling fresh fish and crayfish. **NEWHAVEN**, the first settlement you come to after crossing the bridge, has a large tourist information centre (daily 9am–5pm; ⓣ1300 366 422, ⓦwww.basscoast.vic.gov.au), where you can book accommodation, pick up a free map and buy tickets for the Penguin Parade ($16), Churchill Island ($8.50), the Koala Conservation Centre ($8.50), or a combined ticket for all three ($28), as well as ferry cruises. **Churchill Island** (daily 10am–5pm; $8.50), 1km north of town, is mostly occupied by a working farm. A leisurely walk leads around the small island (2hr) from the Churchill Island Visitor Centre, with views of the unspoilt coastline; the visitor centre has a café, and nearby there's an historic homestead and a cottage in English-style gardens, surrounded by ancient moonah trees which are home to abundant birdlife.

Phillip Island Reserve and the Penguin Parade

The **Phillip Island Reserve** includes all the public land on the **Summerland Peninsula**, the narrow tip of land at the island's western extremity. The reason for the reserve is the **Little penguin**, smallest of the penguins, which is found only in southern Australian waters and whose largest colony breeds at Summerland Beach (around 2000 penguins in the parade area, and 20,000 on the island altogether). The **Penguin Parade** (nightly after dusk; $16; ⓣ03/5956 8300, ⓦwww.penguins.org.au) sounds horribly commercial – and with four thousand visitors a night at the busiest time of the year (around Christmas, January and Easter, when bookings are essential), it can hardly fail to be. Spectators sit in concrete-stepped stadiums looking down onto a floodlit beach, with taped narrations in Japanese, Taiwanese and English. But don't be too hard on it: ecological disaster would ensue if the penguins weren't managed properly, and visitors would still flock here, harming the birds and eroding the sand dunes. As it is, all the money made goes back into research and looking after the penguins, and into facilities such as the excellent **Penguin Parade Visitor Centre** (open from 10am; admission included in the parade ticket): the "Penguin Experience" here is a simulated underwater scene of the hazards of a penguin's life, and there are also interactive displays, videos and even nesting boxes to which penguins have access from the outside, where you can watch the chicks.

The parade itself manages to transcend the setting in any case, as the penguins come pouring onto the beach, waddling comically once they leave the water. They start arriving soon after dark; fifty minutes later the floodlights are switched off and it's all over, at which time (or before) you can move on to the extensive boardwalks over their burrows, with diffused lighting at regular intervals enabling you to watch their antics for hours after the parade finishes – they're active most of the night. If you want to avoid the worst of the crowds, the quietest time to observe them is during the cold and windy winter (you'll need water- or windproof clothing at any time of year). Remember too that you can see Little penguins close to St Kilda Pier in Melbourne and at many other beaches in southern and southeastern Australia, perhaps not in such large numbers, but with far fewer onlookers.

The Nobbies and Seal Rocks

At the tip of the Summerland Peninsula is **Point Grant**, where **The Nobbies**, two huge rock stacks, are linked to the island at low tide by a wave-cut platform of basalt, affording views across to Cape Schanck on the Mornington Peninsula. From the Point, a boardwalk leads across spongy greenery – vibrant in summer with purple and yellow flowers – along the rounded clifftops to a lookout over a blowhole. This is a wild spot, with views along the rugged southern coastline towards Cape Woolamai, a granite headland at the eastern end of the island. From September to April you may see muttonbirds (shearwaters) here – they arrive in September to breed and head for the same burrows each year, after an incredible flight from the Bering Strait in the Arctic Circle. Further off Point Grant, **Seal Rocks** are two rocky islets with the largest known colony of Australian fur seals, estimated to number around 16,000. It's possible to see seals here all year round, though their numbers peak during the breeding season between late October and December. **Cruises** to Seal Rocks are available from Cowes (see below).

Phillip Island Wildlife Park, the Koala Conservation Centre and Rhyll Inlet Boardwalk

Two further parks and a mangrove boardwalk complete Phillip Island's rich collection of wildlife attractions. **Phillip Island Wildlife Park**, on Thompson Avenue just 1km south of Cowes (daily 10am–5pm; $11), provides a shady sanctuary for Australian animals: beautiful pure-bred dingoes, Tasmanian devils, fat and dozy wombats, as well as an aviary and a koala reserve. There are also freely ranging emus, Cape Barren geese, wallabies, eastern grey kangaroos and pademelons.

The **Koala Conservation Centre**, on Phillip Island Tourist Road between Newhaven and Cowes (daily 10am–5.30pm; $8.50), aims to keep the koala habitat as natural as possible while still giving people a close view. A treetop walk through a part of the bushland park allows visitors to observe these marsupials at close range. At 4pm the rangers provide fresh gum leaves – a very popular photo opportunity. You can learn about koalas in the excellent interpretive centre.

The Conservation Hill Lookout, just off the Cowes–Rhyll Rd further north, provides a good view of the **Rhyll Inlet**, a significant roosting and feeding ground for migratory wading birds which come from as far as Siberia. A **boardwalk** starting at the car park takes visitors into the middle of the inlet, a landscape of mangroves, saltmarshes and mudflats. Unlike most other places on the island, the fishing village of **RHYLL** has managed to retain a sleepy charm. There are a couple of cafés and a tavern on the foreshore, with splendid views of the tranquil, shallow waters of Western Port Bay and the South Gippsland coast.

Cowes

Phillip Island's main town, **COWES**, situated at the centre of the north coast, is busy, touristy and even somewhat tacky, though the sandy bays are sheltered enough for good swimming and there are several decent places to eat and stay around **The Esplanade**, a lively strip facing the jetty. From November to April,

Wildlife Coast Cruises – confusingly still referred to by its old name Bayconnections – (ⓣ03/5952 3501, ⓦwww.bayconnections.com.au) offers various **cruises** from the jetty, the best being the trip to Seal Rocks (2hr 30min; $45) to see the Australian fur seals close up.

Inter Island Ferries (see p.958) runs transfers between Stony Point and Cowes and French Island, departing Stony Point daily 8.30am and 5pm, also noon Tues, Thurs, Sat & Sun ($9, bikes $4; one-way), and from Cowes daily at 9.10am and 5.25pm, and 12.40pm Tues, Thurs, Sat & Sun.

Accommodation

Out of season you shouldn't have any trouble finding somewhere **to stay**, but during the peak Christmas to Easter season accommodation nearly doubles in price and some places require weekly bookings. Note that B&Bs are very pricey all year round, and not all of them give value for money. A more reliable, if rather boring option is a motel. The Phillip Island tourist information centre in Newhaven handles accommodation bookings for the island.

Amaroo Park Cnr Church and Osborne streets ⓣ03/5952 2548, ⓦwww.amaroopark.com. Accommodation comprises a good YHA hostel and a caravan park; facilities include a convivial bar, heated swimming pool, cheap meals and bike rental. They also run tours of the island. Dorms $20, rooms ❸

The Castle – Villa by the Sea 7–9 Steele St ⓣ03/5952 1228. Delightful boutique hotel in a pleasant and quiet location just around the corner from the Esplanade. ❼

Coachman Motel 51 Chapel St ⓣ03/5952 1098, ⓕ5952 1283. Luxurious town house with motel units and suites. Facilities include a heated pool and spa for communal use. Rooms from ❸

The Continental Phillip Island 5–8 The Esplanade ⓣ03/5952 2316. A conveniently central hotel with en-suite rooms, some with seafront balconies, and a heated pool. ❹

Cowes Eco-Cottages Cnr Ventnor and Justice Rds ⓣ03/5952 6466. Three cottages set in a quiet bushland setting 3km out of town. ❺

Kaloha Holiday Resort Cnr Chapel and Steele streets ⓣ03/5952 2179. Motel units with cooking facilities, plus cabins, camping sites and facilities for on-site vans. Located in shady grounds giving onto a quiet swimming beach. ❸

Penguin Hill Country House B&B Cnr of Ventnor and Back Beach roads, Ventnor ⓣ03/5956 8777. A rural B&B with good ocean views. ❻

Rothsaye on Lover's Walk 2 Roy Court ⓣ03/5952 2057. A cosy, comfortable B&B. ❺

Seahorse Motel 29–31 Chapel St ⓣ03/5952 2003. An above average, centrally located motel. ❸

Eating and drinking

Carmichael's Restaurant 17 The Esplanade ⓣ03/5952 1300. Stylish place serving breakfast, lunch and dinner (mains $25–32) daily, with views from the wide balcony over the water.

Foreshore Tavern Beach St, Rhyll ⓣ03/5952 1300. A small, homely pub only a ten-minute drive away from the hustle and bustle of Cowes, The bistro serves great meals and the selection of wines is good too. Lunch and dinner daily, closed Mon and Tue in winter.

Isle of Wight Hotel The Esplanade ⓣ03/5952 2301. An old-fashioned Aussie pub with a couple of bars, a good-value bistro with sea views, a lively beer garden and entertainment in the summer at weekends.

Isola di Capri 2 Thompson Avenue, Cowes ⓣ03/5952 2435. Friendly, moderately priced, Italian restaurant at the corner of the Esplanade.

The Jetty The Esplanade ⓣ03/5952 2060. Relaxed restaurant specializing in fresh local seafood. Licensed.

The Yarra Valley and the Dandenongs

Northeast of Melbourne, the **Yarra Valley** stretches out towards the foothills of the Great Dividing Range, with **Yarra Glen** and **Healesville** the targets for excursions into the wine country and the superb forest scenery beyond. To the east, and still within the suburban limits, the cool **Dandenong Range** is as pretty as anywhere in Australia, with quaint villages, fine old houses, beautiful flowering gardens and shady forests of eucalypts and tree ferns.

To get to all these destinations and to have a good look round, you really need your own vehicle. From Monday to Saturday it's possible, although not exactly easy, to see the Dandenongs by **public transport** – for further details, enquire at metlink (Ⓣ13 16 38) in Melbourne. Trains run via Ferntree Gully to Belgrave, starting point of the **Puffing Billy** steam train (see p.964). **Bus #694** runs from Belgrave via Mt Dandenong Tourist Road to Olinda township in the Dandenong Ranges. **Bus #688** runs from Olinda via the northern part of Mt Dandenong Tourist Road to Croydon railway station, where you can catch a Met train back to Melbourne. **Healesville** comes within the orbit of the suburban transport system: take a train from Melbourne to Lilydale and then bus #685 (to visit the Healesville Sanctuary, it's best to take the daily bus departing from Lilydale). There's a daily V/Line service from Melbourne to **Eildon** via Healesville and Marysville; the V/Line service to **Mansfield** passes through Lilydale and Yarra Glen daily (for further information, call V/Line on Ⓣ13 61 96). There are local buses from Belgrave to **Emerald**.

The Yarra Valley

Just half an hour's drive from Melbourne, the **Yarra Valley** is home to around thirty of Victoria's best small **wineries**. The combination of good wine and fine food is really taking off in the valley, and in recent years quite a few winery restaurants have made a name for themselves in culinary circles. Wine country starts in outer suburbia north of the Maroondah Highway just before Lilydale (turn-offs are signposted). North of Lilydale, you can check out wineries (again, all signposted) along or near three routes – the Warburton Highway to the east, the Maroondah Highway to Healesville, and the Melba Highway, heading north past Yarra Glen. The brochure *Wineries of the Yarra Valley* contains a complete list of all local wineries and a map. Even better is the detailed booklet *Wine Regions of Victoria* – both are available at tourist information centres. If you intend to take a few swigs (and can't find a teetotal driver) it's best to join a **winery tour**: Backpacker Winery Tours (Ⓣ03/9877 8333, Ⓦwww.backpackerwinerytours.com.au) picks up from three locations in central Melbourne and two in St Kilda, visiting four wineries in the Yarra Valley ($85 including transport, tastings, a good restaurant lunch and a food platter in the afternoon).

The following are just a few of the wineries and restaurants in the Yarra Valley worth a visit. **Yering Station** (daily 10am–6pm; Ⓣ03/9730 0100), 32 Melba Highway, just south of Yarra Glen, is located on the site of the first vineyard planted in the area in 1838 (the cellar door operates from the original brick building) and has a glass-walled restaurant offering views across the valley, plus a wine bar and a shop selling regional produce. The grounds also host the lively **Yarra Valley Farmers' Market** (every third Saturday of the month 10am-3pm), selling fruit and vegetables, and other valley produce such as smoked trout, honey and jams. On the same property is the **Chateau Yering Historic House Hotel**. For real comfort and luxury, wine and dine at the hotel's more casual *Café Sweetwater* or the very posh *Eleonore's Restaurant*, then sink into a four-poster bed in one of the period-style rooms (Ⓣ03/9237 3333, Ⓦwww.chateau-yering.com.au; ❻). The **Yarra Valley Dairy** (daily 10.30am–5pm) at McMeikans Road, just south of Yering station, sells gourmet cheeses and serves tasty lunches. **De Bortoli** (bookings for the restaurant advisable on

(Ⓣ03/5965 2271) occupies an unbeatable location at Pinnacle Lane, off the Melba Highway at Dixon's Creek north of Yarra Glen, with views over gently rolling hills. This was one of the first places in the valley to offer gourmet food along with its wine – both cuisine and decor betray Italian influences.

Domaine Chandon, on the Maroondah Highway near the town of Coldstream, produces fine *méthode champenoise* sparkling wine, which you can sample ($7–9 per glass) in a modern, bright and airy tastings room with brilliant views. Free thirty-minute tours depart hourly from 11am to 4pm. **Eyton on Yarra** (Ⓣ03/5962 2119) winery and restaurant, further up towards Healesville at the corner of Maroondah Highway and Hill Rd, is known for its sparkling Pinot Chardonnay and specializes in locally produced food. There are four more wineries off the Warburton Highway, including **Yarra Burn** on Settlement Road at Yarra Junction; the restaurant here serves hearty Australian country cuisine (lunches daily; dinner Fri & Sat), and B&B accommodation is available in the homestead.

From Yarra Junction it's not far to **WARBURTON**, a pretty, old-fashioned town on the Upper Yarra River, and starting point for the **Upper Yarra Track**, which follows old timber tram and vehicle tracks upstream for over 80km. The track can be covered as a series of short walks or as a continuous five- to seven-day trek, finishing in the **Baw Baw National Park**, where it joins the Alpine Walking Track. For more information contact the DSE Information Centre in Melbourne (Ⓣ03/9637 8325) or the telephone information service run by Parks Victoria (Ⓣ13 19 63).

Wineries apart, **YARRA GLEN** also boasts the splendidly restored *Grand Hotel* (Ⓣ03/9730 1230, Ⓦwww.yarraglengrand.com.au; ❻) with very comfy en-suite rooms and suites, some of them with antique furniture and balconies, plus a café-bar, a bistro for moderately priced lunches and dinners (both open daily) and a more up-market restaurant (Thurs–Sat from 6.30pm and Sun 11.30am-2pm) and, not far away on the Melba Highway, the National Trust **Gulf Station** (Wed–Sun & public holidays 10am–4pm; $8), a collection of ten 1850s slab farm buildings set in a large area of farmland.

Healesville and beyond

HEALESVILLE is a small, pleasant town nestled in the foothills of the Great Dividing Range; there's a **visitor information centre** in the old courthouse building at the southern end of town, just off the Maroondah Highway (daily 10am–5pm). The town's main attraction is the renowned **Healesville Sanctuary** (daily 9am–5pm; $19; Ⓣ03/5957 2800, Ⓦwww.zoo.org.au), a bushland zoo with more than 200 species of Australian animals and a refuge for injured and orphaned animals, some of which are subsequently returned to the wild; those that stay join the sanctuary's programmes for education and the breeding of endangered species. It's a fascinating place in a beautiful setting, with a stream running through park-like grounds, dense with gum trees and cool ferns, and 3km of walking tracks. Many of the animals are in enclosures, but there are paddocks of emus, wallabies and kangaroos you can stroll through. The informative "meet the keeper" presentations are worth joining, especially the one featuring the birds of prey (noon & 2.30pm, weather permitting).

Continuing north on the Maroondah Highway over the Black Spur and Dom Dom Saddle towards Alexandra, the scenery becomes progressively more attractive. The **Maroondah Reservoir Lookout**, just off the highway 3km north of Healesville, is worth a brief stop, with picturesque views across the forest-fringed dam, and popular **picnic grounds** and **gardens** in the park on the southwest side of the reservoir. Soon after the reservoir, the highway meanders along bush-clad mountain slopes and enters luxuriant wet eucalypt forest with incredibly tall mountain ash, moss-covered myrtle beech, manna gum, gurgling creeks and waterfalls. The **Fernshaw Reserve and Picnic Ground** is a good place to stop and view the scenery. After the Dom Dom Saddle, 509m above sea level and 16km past Healesville, the highway descends towards Narbethong, where it enters drier country. Three kilometres past Narbethong there's a worthwhile detour down a turn-off to scenic **MARYSVILLE**, 9km off the highway. The village nestles in the foothills of the Great Dividing Range, with **Lake Mountain** (1400m), a very popular area for cross-country skiing and tobogganing, 20km further west. In summer, Marysville makes an excellent base for **bushwalking**, being surrounded by forests with many waterfalls. The best-known, **Steavensons Falls**, can be reached from the village by a walking trail or by road and is floodlit at night until 11pm. Just out of Marysville, the unsealed **Lady Talbot Forest Drive** turns off the Lake Mountain road and then winds 46km through the forest, past picnic areas and walking tracks (suitable for conventional vehicles, though after heavy rainfall it's best to check in Marysville for road conditions). Return to Marysville via the Buxton Road, or turn right and head north to Buxton, where you rejoin the highway. Further up, the Maroondah Highway passes the drier **Cathedral Range State Park**: west of the road here the mighty sandstone cliffs of Cathedral Mountain rise almost vertically behind the paddocks, overlooking the Acheron Valley.

The Dandenongs

As in the Blue Mountains of New South Wales, the **Dandenong** hills are enveloped in a blue haze rising from forests of gum trees which cover much of the area. Rain ensures the area stays cool and lush, while fine old houses and gardens add to the scenery. Easy bushwalks in the **Dandenong Ranges National Park** start from Ferntree Gully, accessible by train or by car via the Burwood Highway. A pleasant way to enjoy the forests and fern gullies is to take a ride on the **Puffing Billy** steam train (Ⓣ03/9754 6800, Ⓦwww.puffingbilly.com.au), which runs for 13km from the Puffing Billy station in Belgrave to Lakeside ($29.50 return) on Lake Emerald, stopping at Menzies Creek and Emerald: one train a day continues a further 9km from Lake Emerald to Gembrook ($40 return). The Puffing Billy station is a short, signposted walk from **Belgrave** station (suburban trains). The train has run more or less continuously since the early twentieth century, though its operation now depends on dedicated volunteers; on total fire ban days, diesel locomotives are used. Timetables vary seasonally but there are generally several services daily until late afternoon.

Just outside Emerald, man-made **Emerald Lake** has paddle-boats to rent and a swimming pool, as well as trails through bushland which continue into the nearby state reserve. *Emerald Backpackers*, 2 Lakeview Court (Ⓣ03/5968 4086; dorms $19, rooms ❷) caters mainly for people seeking farm work; the owners have local contacts. On weekdays and Saturday morning, bus #695 runs from the Belgrave train station to Emerald.

Geelong and the Bellarine Peninsula

Heading west towards Geelong – for the Bellarine Peninsula and Great Ocean Road – it's just a short detour off the Princes Freeway to **WERRIBEE**, home to the restored **Mansion at Werribee Park** (Mon–Fri 10am–3.45pm, Sat & Sun until 4.45pm; $12; ⓣ03/9741 2444 or 13 19 63), located on K Road. Built in 1874–77 by Scottish squatters Thomas and Andrew Chirnside, who struck it rich on the back of sheep, the sixty-room mansion is the largest private residence in Victoria. Guides in period costume show you around the ornate homestead and the Victorian-era gardens; alternatively, free audioguides are available at the entrance. The grand sandstone building is surrounded by ten hectares of formal gardens, including the **Victoria State Rose Garden** (free admission), which is at its best between November and April when the five thousand rose bushes are in bloom. Beyond the gardens are the extensive grounds of **Victoria's Open Range Zoo** (daily 9am–5pm; $19; ⓣ03/9731 9600, ⓦwww.zoo.org.au) where giraffes, cheetahs, rhinoceroses, hippopotamuses, monkeys, as well as kangaroos and emus, roam in large open enclosures. A fifty-minute **safari bus**, included in the admission price, takes visitors through the property (bus departs every 50min 10.30am–3.40pm). **Werribee Park Shuttle**, a private bus service, provides transport to Werribee Park (mansion and zoo) from Melbourne, departing from the Victorian Arts Centre, St Kilda Road at 9.30am ($20 return; advance booking required on ⓣ03/9748 5094). Southeast of here is the **Shadowfax Winery**, an impressive box-like structure that offers cellar-door sales (Sat & Sun from 10am), glimpses of the wine-making process and gourmet food.

Continuing along the freeway, you can detour west again through Little River to the **You Yangs**, small but rugged volcanic peaks which rise sharply out of the surrounding plains. Scramble to the top of the highest, **Flinders Peak** (348m), and you're rewarded with fine views of Geelong and Port Phillip Bay. The You Yangs, as well as the nearby **Brisbane Ranges**, are excellent places for spotting kangaroos, wallabies, koalas and possums at dusk. Alternatively, you can observe kangaroos, wallabies and emus, as well as numerous waterbirds, in their natural habitat at the little-known **Serendip Sanctuary**, 20km north of Geelong at 100 Windermere Rd, Lara (daily 10am–4pm; free; ⓣ03/5282 1584), which occupies a square kilometre of bush, marsh and wetlands. A refuge for threatened birds of the Western Plains of Victoria, the sanctuary is renowned for its captive breeding programme of brolgas, magpie geese and Australian bustards.

Geelong

Approaching **GEELONG** via its industrial outskirts, you can be forgiven for wanting to zip past the bland mélange of fast-food outlets, petrol stations and suburban housing to the beckoning seaside attractions of the Bellarine Peninsula and the Great Ocean Road beyond. However, in recent years, Geelong has made a big effort to shed its rust bucket image, mainly by revamping the waterfront it had previously turned its back on, and while still not warranting an extended stay, the city centre is a pleasant enough place to do some exploring, combined with a lunch stop.

The **National Wool Museum** (daily 10am–5pm; $7.30), housed in the Geelong Wool Exchange, a National Trust-listed building at the corner of Brougham and Moorabool streets, is worth a visit. The well set-up exhibition concentrates on the social history of the wool industry, with reconstructions of typical shearers' quarters and a millworker's 1920s cottage; wool is still auctioned off thirty days a year on the top floor of the exchange. Many of the town's best Victorian buildings are on **Little Malop Street**, including the elegant **Geelong Art Gallery** (Mon–Fri 10am–5pm, Sat & Sun 1–5pm;

free, but donation appreciated), which has an extensive collection of paintings by nineteenth-century Australian artists such as Tom Roberts and Frederick McCubbin, plus twentieth-century Australian paintings, sculpture and decorative arts. From Little Malop Street and Malop Street, Moorabool Street leads down to **Corio Bay** and the waterfront, with its renovated promenades, rotunda, fountains and lovely nineteenth-century carousel featuring over thirty sculpted wooden horses. There's a swimming enclosure at Eastern Beach. Notable waterfront eating places include the large **Cunningham Pier**. Nestled among the lawns and trees of Eastern Park around ten minutes' walk from the city centre are Geelong's **Botanic Gardens** (Mon–Fri 7.30am–5pm, Sat & Sun 7am–7pm; free). The entrance is through the latest addition to the gardens, the 21st Century Garden, which specializes in resilient native and exotic, dry climate plants. Beyond this are the historic gardens. Begun in the late 1850s they boast lawns, rare trees, a fernery and conservatory, fountains and sculptures, as well as the small *Tea House* (daily 11am–4pm).

On the way to Torquay, **Narana Creations** (Mon–Fri 9am–5pm, Sat 10am–4pm; free), an Aboriginal arts, crafts and cultural centre at 410 Torquay Rd (Surfcoast Highway) in Grovedale is worth a brief stop. Paintings and various arts and crafts are sold here, and visitors can sometimes listen to Dreamtime stories or didgeridoo playing.

Practicalities

In addition to the **visitor information centre** (daily 9am–5pm; ⓣ1800 620 888) at the Wool Museum, there's a helpful **tourist information stall** (Mon–Sat 9am–5pm) in the Market Square Shopping Centre at the corner of Moorabool and Malop streets. Both provide lots of brochures and free maps. The main **shopping** strip is along Malop Street.

To check out what's going on, pick up a copy of the free **listings magazine** *Forte*, available at music shops, and sometimes also at the visitor information centre. It covers the whole of southwest Victoria, and also has information on surfing, diving and other activities.

To get to the Bellarine Peninsula from Geelong, take a McHarry's Buslines **bus** (ⓣ03/5223 2111) from the Busport on Brougham Street (next to the Wool Museum) for Ocean Grove and Barwon Heads, Point Lonsdale via Queenscliff, St Leonards via Portarlington, and Grovedale via Torquay.

Accommodation

Irish Murphys 30 Aberdeen St, Geelong West ⓣ03/5221 4335, ⓦwww.irishmurphys.com. Backpacker accommodation above a pub; dorms from $18; rooms ❸

Riverglen Holiday Park Barrabool Road, Belmont ⓣ03/5243 5505, ⓕ5243 4760. Good caravan park on the south bank of the Barwon River, with shady tent sites and timber cottages ❹

Sundowner Geelong 13 The Esplanade ⓣ03/5222 3499, ⓦwww.sundownermotorinns.com.au. Upmarket accommodation with water views, a restaurant and bar, sauna and a pool. ❺

The Colonial Lodge Motel Fyans St, about 2km south of the city centre ⓣ03/5223 2266. Reasonably priced motel units ❸

Eating

Beach House Restaurant Eastern Beach Reserve ⓣ03/5221 8322. The café downstairs (open Mon–Sat from 10am, Sun from 9am; closed evenings) serves breakfast all day as well as other cheap fare, while the upmarket restaurant upstairs (Wed–Sun from 6pm; also Sun lunch) offers eclectic East-meets-West cuisine. Great views, especially from the restaurant. Moderate–expensive. Licensed.

Cats Bar Restaurant Lounge 90 Little Malop St ⓣ03/5229 3077. Big place with a polished cedarwood bar and moderately priced food – gets packed in the evenings. Licensed. Daily 10am–midnight.

Fishermen's Pier Seafood Restaurant Yarra St ⓣ03/5222 4100. Fish and seafood prepared in a range of styles, from Thai to Tuscan. Expensive. Licensed. Daily 11.30am–2.30pm & 5.30–9.30pm.

Irrewarra Sourdough Shop & Café 10 James St. Outlet of bakery based in Colac in the Otways. Sells their range of outstanding breads and serves delicious breakfasts and light lunches in the café section. Licensed. Moderate. Mon–Fri 7.30am–3.30pm.

Sailor's Rest Tavern 3 Moorabool St ⓣ03/5224 2241. Pleasant family restaurant with a menu of cheap to moderately priced warm and cold salads, risotto, pasta, steak and fish. Licensed. Daily 9am–9pm.

Tonic 5 James St ⓣ03/5229 8899. This restaurant-bar just around the corner from Little Malop St goes for cool, minimalist chic. The menu has a bit of everything: Cajun chicken salad, risotto, linguini, beef rendang, crispy lime battered fish, all available either as an entrée or main course. Moderate. Licensed. Mon–Sat lunch and dinner.

Wharf Shed Cafe 15 Eastern Beach Rd ⓣ03/5221 6645. Popular café-restaurant in a converted boatshed in Geelong's waterfront precinct that feeds cakes, pizzas, risotto, fish & chips to the masses coming here on a sunny weekend. Licensed. Mon–Fri 11am–late, Sat & Sun from 9am. Upstairs is the upmarket (and much pricier) *Le Parisien Restaurant* (ⓣ03/5229 3110), open for lunch and dinner daily.

Queenscliff and around

From Geelong, the Bellarine Highway runs 31km southeast to **QUEENSCLIFF** through flat and not particularly scenic grazing country. Queenscliff is essentially a quiet fishing village on Swan Bay – with several quaint cottages on Fishermens Flat – which became a favourite holiday resort for Melbourne's wealthy elite in the nineteenth century, then fell out of favour, and has only recently begun to enjoy something of a revival as a popular place for a weekend away or a Sunday drive. Queenscliff's position near the narrow entrance to Port Phillip Bay made it strategically important: a **fort** here faces the one at Point Nepean. Now the home of the Australian Army Command and Staff College, the fort and its museum can be visited on guided tours (Sat & Sun 1pm & 3pm; $4.40).

Full details of other things to do are available from the Queenscliff **Visitor Information Centre**, 55 Hesse St (daily 9am–5pm, ⓣ03/5258 4843). During school holidays and in summer, **Queenscliff Historical Tours** (ⓣ03/5258 3403) rents out bicycles ($20 per half day), as well as providing a map and audioguide to the town; you can either pick up a bike near the pier at the end of Symonds Road, or have it delivered to your accommodation. Other activities include kayaking ($27 for 2hr; ⓣ03/5258 2166; rentals from the marina on Larkin Parade) along the coast or further offshore; diving among wrecks and marine life with the **Queenscliff Dive Centre** (ⓣ03/5258 1188); and a cruise with **Sea All Dolphin Swims** (4hr; $100; twice daily in January, varying rest of the year; ⓣ03/5258 3889) visiting a seal colony, a gannet rookery and the chance to swim with dolphins in Port Phillip Bay.

Among the attractions is the **Queenscliff Maritime Museum**, Weerona Parade (Mon–Fri 10.30am–4.30pm, Sat & Sun 1.30–4.30pm; $4.40; ⓣ03/5258 3440), which concentrates on the many shipwrecks caused by The Rip, a fierce current about 1km wide between Point Lonsdale and Point Nepean. Outside, a tiny fisherman's cottage is set up as it would have been in 1870, and there's a shed where an Italian fisherman painted, in naive style, all the ships he'd seen pass through from 1895 to 1947 (imaginatively including the *Titanic*). Next door, the **Marine Discovery Centre** has a small aquarium stocked with local marine life (daily 10am–4pm during school holidays, other times by appointment; $5; ⓣ03/5258 3344, ⓦwww.dse.vic.gov.au/mafri/discovery); it also organizes a range of activities, mainly during the summer holidays, such as marine biology cruises, rock pool rambles and snorkelling tours. Every Sunday, the **Bellarine Peninsula Railway** operates steam trips from the old Queenscliff Railway Station to Drysdale, 20km northwest (11.15am & 2.30pm; $16; ⓣ03/5258 2069, ⓦwww.bpr.org.au).

The **Queenscliff Music Festival** (ⓦwww.qmf.net.au), held annually on the last weekend of November, features an eclectic mix of Australian contemporary music (folk, blues, world music, fusion) and draws ever-growing crowds.

Practicalities

Three grand **Victorian-era hotels** in Queenscliff are popular settings for romantic (but very expensive) breaks: the *Vue Grand*, 46 Hesse St (ⓣ03/5258 1544, ⓦwww.vuegrand.com.au; ❼) has a Spanish-style exterior and a fabulously ornate Victorian interior with a very expensive restaurant; the clifftop *Ozone Hotel*, 42 Gellibrand St (ⓣ1800 804 753, ⓦwww.ozonehotel.com.au; ❻ including breakfast), has sea views from its iron-lace verandahs and a gorgeous dining room; while the refined *Queenscliff Hotel*, 16 Gellibrand St (ⓣ03/5258 1066, ⓦwww.queenscliffhotel.com.au; ❽), is the best of all. **Budget alternatives** include the *Queenscliff Inn YHA*, 59 Hesse St (ⓣ03/5258 3737, ⓔqueenscliff@yhavic.org.au; dorms $23, rooms ❹), which is also a pleasant Victorian B&B guesthouse – the single rooms (❷) are particularly good value; and *Beacon Resort Holiday Park & Motel*, 78 Bellarine Highway (ⓣ03/5258 1133, ⓦwww.beaconresort.com.au), which has tent sites, cabins (❸), holiday units, motel rooms (❺) and a heated pool.

Among the town's **eating places**, the best fish and chips are at *Queenscliff Fish and Chips*, 77 Hesse St. Among the cafés there are *Café Cliffe*, 25 Hesse St, where locally produced wines by the glass and light lunches are served in the pleasant, Tuscan-style courtyard (Mon–Fri 11am-4pm, Sat & Sun 10am-4pm) and *38 South*, a café at the car ferry terminal with a fantastic view of the heads of the bay and the Mornington Peninsula. The *Royal Hotel* at 34 King Street has two moderately priced food outlets: *Zara's* upstairs does breakfasts, lunches and dinners (seafood, pasta, and meat from the grill), and the bar downstairs serves cheap bar meals. *Harry's*, a renowned old-timer, is now located on the balcony of the *Esplanade Hotel*, 2 Gellibrand St, and has a good wine list in addition to expensive, but excellent seafood (lunch Thurs–Sun, dinner Wed–Sat; daily in January; ⓣ03/5258 3750). Even pricier options include the gorgeous restaurants at the *Vue Grand* (lunch and dinner daily) and the *Queenscliff Hotel* (lunch daily, dinner Wed–Sat). The latter also has a cheaper courtyard restaurant. All are licensed.

Ferries run from Queenscliff across the mouth of Port Phillip Bay to Sorrento (see p.954)

Point Lonsdale and Portarlington

From Queenscliff it's about 5km to peaceful **Point Lonsdale**, whose most noticeable feature is its magnificent 1902 lighthouse, 120m high and visible for 30km out to sea. Below the lighthouse, on the edge of the bluff, is "Buckley's Cave" where William Buckley is thought to have lived at some stage during his thirty-year sojourn with the Aborigines. At **PORTARLINGTON**, which sits on Port Phillip Bay about 14km north of Queenscliff, there's a beautifully preserved steam-powered flourmill (Wed, Sat & Sun noon–4pm; $4; ⓣ03/5259 3847), four storeys of solid stone, owned by the National Trust.

Travel details

Trains

Melbourne to: Adelaide (5 weekly; 10hr); Alice Springs (1 weekly; 36hr); Ballarat (6–10 daily; 1hr 30min); Bendigo (5–11 daily; 2hr); Geelong (12–20 daily; 1hr); Perth (2 weekly; 60hr); Sydney via Albury (2 daily; 11hr); Warrnambool (1–3 daily; 3hr 15min).

Buses

Melbourne to: Adelaide (4 daily; 10hr); Brisbane (1 daily; 25hr); Perth via Adelaide (3 weekly; 47hr); Sydney via Bega (1 daily; 17hr); Sydney via Canberra (5–6 daily; 12–14hr)

Ferries

Melbourne to: Devonport, Tasmania (1–2 daily; 10 hr).

Flights

Qantas flies from **Melbourne** to: Adelaide (10–13 daily; 1hr 15min); Alice Springs (2 daily; 3hr 30min); Ayers Rock Resort (1–3 daily; 3hr 30min); Brisbane (12–15 daily; 1hr 55min); Cairns (7–11 daily; 3hr 15min direct); Canberra (5–7 daily; 1hr 5min); Coolangatta/Gold Coast (6–12 daily; 2hr); Darwin (3 daily; 4–5hr with one stopover); Hobart (4–7 daily; 1hr); Launceston (4 daily; 50min); Mackay (3–4 daily; 4hr 15min with one stopover); Perth (5–7 daily; 4hr); Rockhampton (6–7 daily; 3hr 30min with one stopover); Sydney (16–22 daily; 1hr 20min); Townsville (3–5 daily; 5hr with one stopover).

Jetstar flies from **Melbourne Tullamarine** to: Cairns (1–2 daily; 3hr 20min); Gold Coast (4–7 daily; 2hr); Hamilton Island (1 daily; 2hr 55min); Hobart (3–5 daily; 1hr 10min); Launceston (3–5 daily; 1hr); Newcastle (2 daily; 1hr 25min); Sunshine Coast (2 daily; 2hr 10min); and from **Melbourne Avalon** (near Geelong) to: Adelaide (1 daily; 1hr 15min); Brisbane (4 daily; 2hr); Sydney (4 daily; 1hr 15min).

Virgin Blue flies from **Melbourne** to: Adelaide (10–13 daily; 1hr 15min); Brisbane (8–9 daily; 2hr); Cairns (3–4 daily; 3hr 20min with one stopover); Canberra (2 daily; 1hr); Darwin (1 daily; 7hr with one stopover); Coffs Harbour (2 daily; 3hr 50min with one stopover); Gold Coast (6–8 daily; 2hr); Hobart (4 daily; 1hr 10min); Launceston (3 daily; 1hr); Mackay (1 daily; 4hr 10min with one stopover); Perth (4 daily; 4hr 15min); Sydney (13–18 daily; 1hr 20min); Townsville (3–4 daily; 6hr 30min with one stopover).

11

Victoria

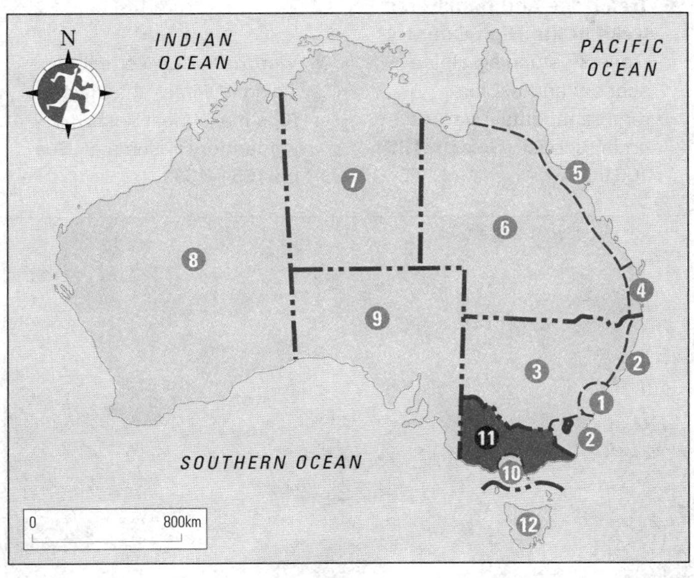
N
INDIAN OCEAN
PACIFIC OCEAN
SOUTHERN OCEAN
7
6
5
8
9
4
3
2
1
2
11
10
12
0
800km

CHAPTER 11

Highlights

* **Great Ocean Road** Wait until the sun is down and the crowds are gone and watch the fairy penguins come out to play at the Twelve Apostles. **See pp.977–997**
* **Goldfields** Mining memorabilia and grandiose architecture grace the old gold towns of Ballarat and Bendigo. **See pp.997–1014**
* **Trail rides and packhorse treks in the High Country** Traverse stunning alpine scenery and explore remote mountain valleys on horseback. **See pp.1054–1061**
* **Wilson's Promontory National Park** There's great bushwalking and fantastic coastal scenery at Victoria's favourite national park. **See pp.1038–1041**
* **Milawa Gourmet trail** Excellent local produce washed down with great wines from the Brown Brothers winery – all sampled against a backdrop of stunning scenery. **See p.1052**
* **Victorian Alps** Perfect for skiing in winter, the Victorian Alps make ideal bushwalking territory in summer. **See pp.1054–1061**

△ The Twelve Apostles

Victoria

Australia's second-smallest state, **Victoria** is the most densely populated and industrialized, and has a wide variety of attractions packed into a small area. It may not be a state to tour comprehensively, but Australians, at least, lap up the legends of their history that are thick on the ground: you're never too far from civilization, but everywhere there's a wild past of **gold prospectors** and **bushrangers**. All routes in the state radiate from **Melbourne**, bang in the middle of the coastline on the huge Port Phillip Bay, and no point is much more than seven hours' drive away. Yet all most visitors see of Victoria apart from its cultured capital is the **Great Ocean Road**, a winding 280km of spectacular coastal scenery. Others may venture to the idyllic **Wilsons Promontory National Park** (the "Prom"), a couple of hours away on the coast of the mainly dairy region of **Gippsland**, or to the **Goldfields**, where the nineteenth-century goldrushes left their mark in the grandiose architecture of old mining towns such as **Ballarat** and **Bendigo**.

There is, however, a great deal more to the state. Marking the end of the Great Dividing Range, the massive sandstone ranges of the **Grampians**, with their Aboriginal rock paintings and dazzling array of springtime flora, rise from the monotonous wheatfields of the **Wimmera** region and the wool country of the western district. To the north of the Grampians is the wide, flat region of the **Mallee** – scrub, sand dunes and dry lakes heading to the **Murray River**, where **Mildura** is an irrigated oasis supporting orchards and vineyards. In complete contrast, the **Victorian Alps** in the northeast of the state have several winter **ski slopes**, high country that provides perfect bushwalking and horse-riding territory in summer. In the foothills and plains below, where bushranger **Ned Kelly** once roamed, are some of Victoria's finest **wineries** (wine buffs should pick up a copy of the excellent hundred-page brochure, *Wine Regions of Victoria*, available from the visitor information centre in Melbourne and other towns). Beach culture is alive and well on this **coastline** with some of the best **surfing** in Australia.

The only real drawback is the frequently cursed **climate**. Winter is mild, and the occasional heatwaves in summer are mercifully limited to a few days at most, but the problem is that of unpredictability. Cool, rainy "English" weather can descend in any season, and spring and autumn days can be immoderately hot. But even this can be turned to advantage: as the local saying goes, if you don't like the weather, just wait ten minutes and it'll change.

Public transport, by road and rail, is with **V/Line** and subsidiary country bus lines. However, using your own vehicle is definitely a more convenient option, as train and bus services are fairly infrequent and quite a few places can be reached only with difficulty, if at all.

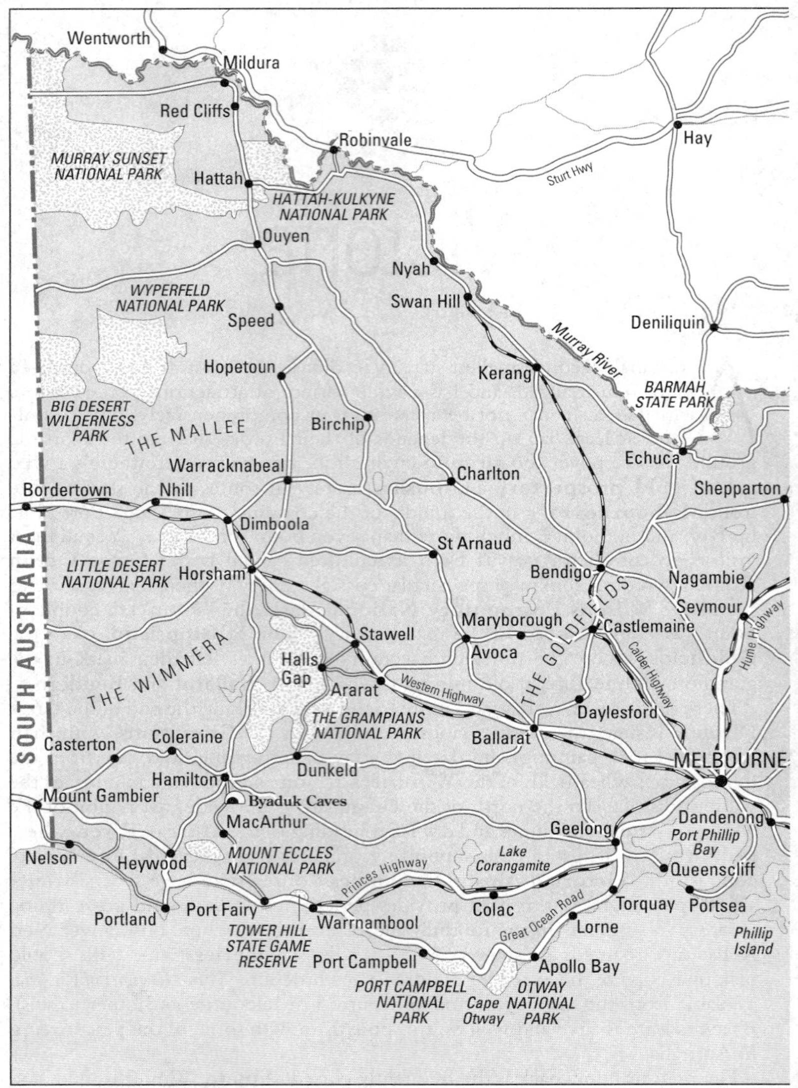

Some history

Semi-nomadic **Koories** have lived in this region for at least forty thousand years, and from earliest times developed sophisticated hunting and gathering methods, creating rock art, weaving baskets, making possum-skin cloaks to protect against the cold, and establishing semi-permanent settlements such as those of circular stone houses and fish traps found at Lake Condah in western Victoria.

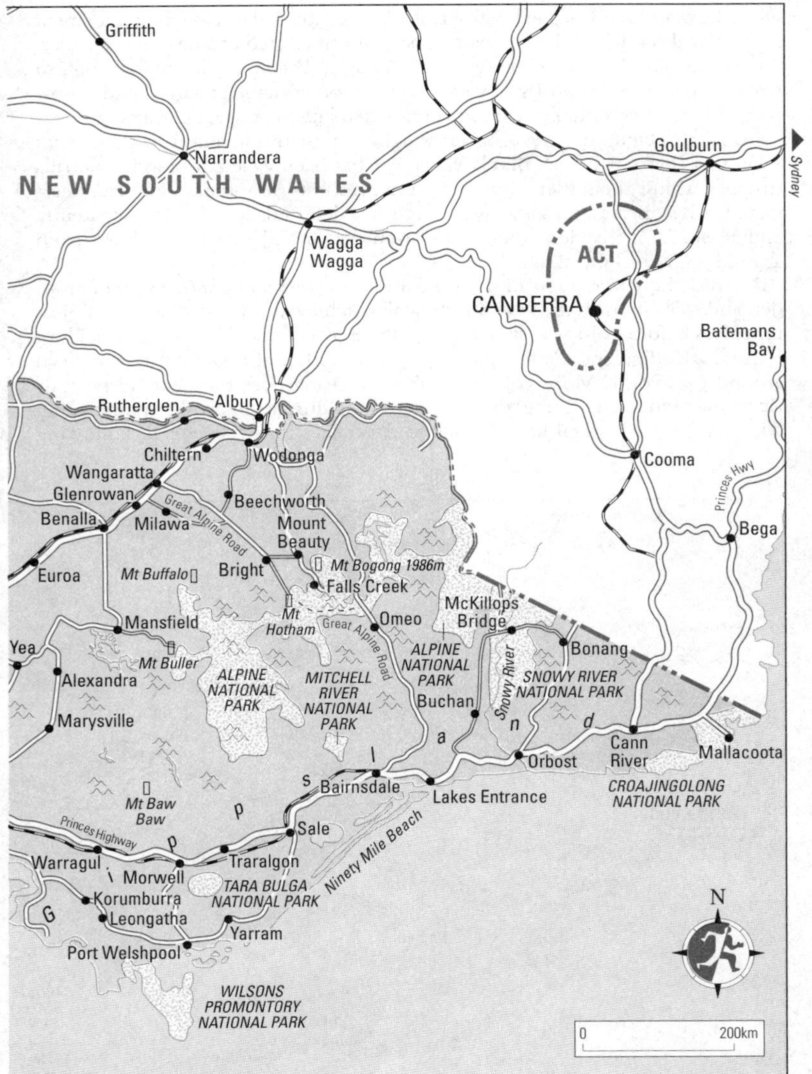

For the colonists, Victoria did not get off to an auspicious start: there was an unsuccessful attempt at settlement in the **Port Phillip Bay** area in 1803 but Van Diemen's Land (Tasmania) across the Bass Strait was deemed more suitable. It was in fact from Launceston that Port Phillip Bay was eventually settled, in 1834; other Tasmanians soon followed and **Melbourne** was established. This occupation was in defiance of a British government edict forbidding settlement in the territory, then part of New South Wales, but **squatting** had already begun the previous year when Edward Henty arrived with his stock to establish the first white settlement at **Portland** on the southwest coast. A pattern was created of land-hungry settlers – generally already men of means – responding to Britain's demand for wool, so that during the 1840s and 1850s what was to become Victoria evolved into a prosperous pastoral community with squatters extending huge grazing runs.

From the beginning, the Koories fought against the invasion of their land: 1836 saw the start of the **Black War**, as it has been called, a bloody guerrilla struggle against the settlers. By 1850, however, the Aborigines had been decimated – by disease as well as war – and felt defeated, too, by the apparently endless flood of invaders; their population is believed to have declined from around 15,500 to just 2300.

By 1851 the white population of the area was large and confident enough to demand separation from New South Wales, achieved, by a stroke of luck, just nine days before **gold** was discovered in the new colony. The rich goldfields of Ballarat, Bendigo and Castlemaine brought an influx of hopeful migrants from around the world. More gold came from Victoria over the next thirty years than was extracted during the celebrated California goldrush, transforming Victoria from a pastoral backwater into Australia's financial capital. Following

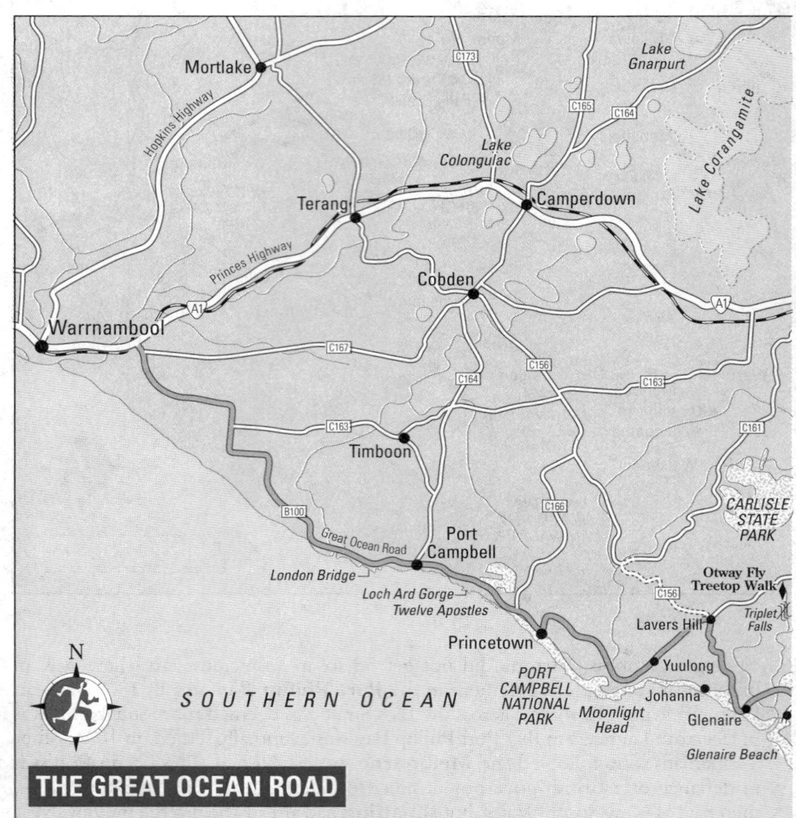

federation in 1901, Melbourne was even the political capital – a title it retained until Canberra became fully operational in 1927.

The Great Ocean Road and the far west coast

The **Great Ocean Road**, Victoria's famous southwestern coastal route, starts at Torquay, just over 20km south of Geelong, and extends 285km west to

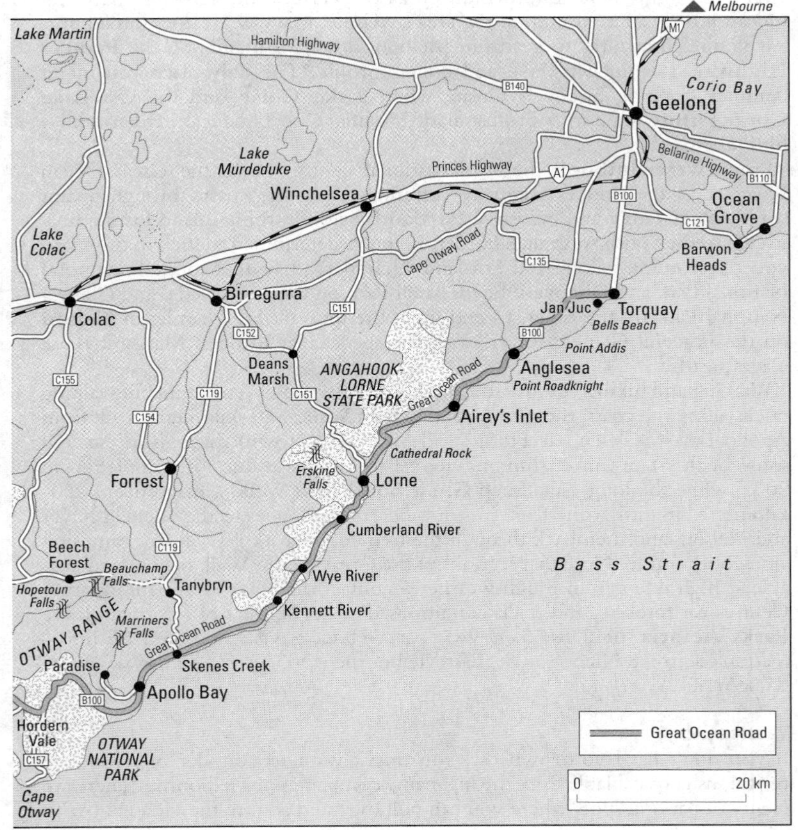

11 VICTORIA | The Great Ocean Road and the far west coast

Warrnambool. It was built between 1919 and 1932 with the idea of constructing a scenic road of world repute, equalling California's Pacific Coast Highway – and it certainly lives up to its reputation. The road was to be both a memorial to the soldiers who had died in World War I, and an employment scheme for those who returned. Over three thousand ex-servicemen laboured with picks and shovels, carving the road into cliffs and mountains along Australia's most rugged and densely forested coastline; the task was speeded up with the help of the jobless during the Great Depression. The road hugs the coastline between **Torquay** and **Apollo Bay** and passes through the popular holiday towns of **Anglesea** and **Lorne**, set below the Otway Range. From Apollo Bay the road heads inland, through the towering forests of the **Otway National Park**, before rejoining the coast at Princetown to wind along the shore for the entire length of the **Port Campbell National Park**. This stretch from Moonlight Head to Port Fairy, sometimes referred to as the "Shipwreck Coast", is the most spectacular – there are 200 known shipwrecks here, victims of the imprecise navigation tools of the mid-nineteenth century, the rough Southern Ocean and dramatic rock formations such as the **Twelve Apostles**, which sit out to sea beyond the rugged cliffs. The often windy and stormy weather enhances the jagged coastline, and even at the height of summer you can't rely on it being warm and sunny here. Information on all the villages and sights on the Great Ocean Road can be found on the area's website, Ⓦwww.greatoceanroad.org.

If you're in a hurry to get from Melbourne to Warrnambool, the **Princes Highway** is a much faster – and duller – route. The only place you might consider stopping briefly is Colac, where **Lake Colac** and the vast **Lake Corangamite** support a profusion of birdlife, with botanical gardens and a bird sanctuary.

From **Warrnambool**, the small regional centre where the Great Ocean Road ends, the Princes Highway continues along the coast, through quaint seaside **Port Fairy** and industrial **Portland**, before turning inland for the final stretch to the South Australian border. If you're determined to stick to the coast, you can continue along the Portland–Nelson road, with Mount Richmond National Park and Discovery Bay Coastal Park on the coastal side, and Glenelg National Park on the other, to end up at the unspoilt little hamlet of **Nelson** on the peaceful Glenelg River, with the spectacular Princess Margaret Rose Caves nearby.

Walking and hiking enthusiasts can choose between two magnificent walking tracks along the coast: the new **Great Ocean Walk**, a 91-kilometre track from Apollo Bay to Glenample Homestead (near Princetown) through forests and some of the state's most stunning coastal scenery, was due for completion in 2005; while the long-established **Great Southwest Walk**, a magnificent 250-kilometre circuit starting from just outside Portland, goes to the Glenelg River and Nelson, and then back through the two coastal parks. There are campsites along both routes. Note that sections of the Great Ocean Walk become impassable at high tide and in rough weather – contact the local Visitor Information Centres for forecasts and track conditions. Further sources of information are **Parks Victoria** (Ⓣ13 19 63, Ⓦwww.parkweb.vic.gov.au) and the DSE Information Centre, 8 Nicholson St, East Melbourne (Ⓣ03/9637 8325, Ⓦwww.dse.vic.gov.au).

Transport

If you don't have your own car, you might want to consider one-way **car rental**, usually available from the big-name companies in Melbourne. There are plenty of parking spots where you can pull over and admire the view, but with narrow roads, steep cliffs and incessant hairpin bends drivers need to keep their eyes glued to the road. In summer the road is filled with **cyclists**, and although the routes are exhilarating they are really only suitable for the experienced and adventurous.

V/Line (Ⓣ13 61 96, Ⓦwww.vline.com.au) has a "Great Ocean Road" **bus** service from Geelong to Apollo Bay, calling at Torquay, Anglesea, Lorne and points in between (Mon–Fri 4 daily; weekend twice daily). On Friday (and Mon in Dec & Jan) you can transfer in Apollo Bay to another V/Line bus along the Great Ocean Road to Warrnambool. There's a **train** service from Melbourne, via Geelong and Colac, to Warrnambool (3 daily, 2 services on Sun are combined train/bus services), with connecting buses to Port Fairy, Portland and Heywood (Mon–Sat 2 daily, Sun 1 daily) and on to Mount Gambier in South Australia (1 daily). From Warrnambool you can also return to Melbourne on the inland road, or go north to Ballarat. There's no public transport to Nelson.

Tours

One-way tours between Melbourne and Adelaide, via the Great Ocean Road, are a good way to take in the scenery. The backpackers' busline *Oz Experience* (Ⓣ1300 300 028, Ⓦwww.ozexperience.com) currently covers this route in three days, taking in the Great Ocean Road and the Grampians ($310, transport only) but duration, itinerary and price might change – so check. *Wayward Bus* (Ⓣ1300 653 510, Ⓦwww.waywardbus.com.au) sticks to the coast all the way to the Coorong in South Australia on its three-and-a-half-day tour (from $300, including hostel accommodation, breakfasts and lunches). With both you can get off the bus and continue your trip a few days later (booking required). The small and friendly *Groovy Grape* covers the Great Ocean Road–Grampians route in an all-inclusive three-day tour (Ⓣ1800 661 177, Ⓦwww.groovygrape.com.au; $260).

A few other reliable tour operators do **one- or two-day round-trips** from Melbourne to the Great Ocean Road, some with an extra Grampians option and/or possible transfer to Adelaide – see the box on pp.948–949.

Torquay

TORQUAY is the centre of **surf culture** on Victoria's "surf coast" and two local beaches, **Jan Juc** and **Bells Beach**, are solidly entrenched in Australian surfing mythology. If you're not here for the surf, then there's not really a lot happening: in hot weather the place is boisterously alive, but out of season it's somnolent and low-key. The big event here is the Rip Curl Pro Classic, held at Bells Beach at Easter, which draws national and international contestants and thousands of spectators (call Surf Victoria on Ⓣ03/5261 2907 or see Ⓦwww.ripcurlpro.com for details). Local **buses** run between Geelong and Torquay via Jan Juc – call McHarry's Buslines (Ⓣ03/5223 2111) for details.

As you come into Torquay along the Great Ocean Road you'll see the **Surf City Plaza** shopping centre on your right, one of the best places in town to rent and buy surf gear. The **Surfworld Museum** at the rear of the plaza (daily 9am–5pm; $6.50; Ⓦwww.surfworld.org.au), features a wave-making machine, interactive videos that explain how waves are created, and displays about the history of surfing. The museum doubles as the **Torquay Visitor Information Centre** (Ⓣ03/5261 4606), handing out a few leaflets and brochures. The **Mary Elliott**

Pottery, 80 Surfcoast Highway (open daily), is worth a look; it supplies tourist information as well. Turning left from the Great Ocean Road towards the beach, there's another cluster of shops, supermarkets and cafés around Gilbert Street.

A grassy public reserve shaded by huge Norfolk pines (with electric barbecues and picnic tables) runs along rocky **Fisherman's Beach** and **Front Beach**. The **Surf Beach** (or "back beach"), south of Cosy Corner (a headland separating Front and Surf beaches), is backed by rugged cliffs and takes a full belting from the Southern Ocean; it's patrolled in summer. **Jan Juc**, just south of Surf Beach across Torquay Golf Club, is also patrolled in season and has better swimming and surfing. The **South Coast Walk** to Aireys Inlet via Anglesea begins from here (25km; 8hr); the stretch to **Bells Beach** is a one-hour, three-kilometre walk.

Practicalities

Go Ride a Wave (Ⓣ1300 132 441, Ⓦwww.gorideawave.com.au), a long-established outdoors activities company based in neighbouring Anglesea with an outlet in Bell St, Torquay, offers **surfing lessons** (2hr/$60 or packages; gear included) as well as **sea kayaking** instruction and trips exploring the coastline. The Westcoast Surfing School runs surfing classes in Torquay and Anglesea (2hr/$50 or packages; gear included Ⓣ03/5261 2241, Ⓦwww.westcoastsurfschool.com). If you feel like taking to the air, **Skydive City**, east of Torquay at Barwon Heads (Ⓣ0414 686 722, Ⓦwww.skydivecity.com.au), offers a scenic flight over the Great Ocean Road concluded by a tandem jump out of the plane ($295). **Tiger Moth World Adventure Park**, a family amusement park 3km east of Torquay (daily 10am–5pm; $9.50; Ⓣ03/5261 5100, Ⓦwww.tigermothworld.com), has lots of mostly water-based attractions; they also offer skydives and **scenic flights** aboard vintage Tiger Moths, biplanes and modern aircraft – the latter fly as far west as the Twelve Apostles, following the rugged coastline (1hr 20min return, $200 per person, min 2 passengers).

Accommodation

Anita's Guesthouse, Cottage and Cabins 17 Anderson St Ⓣ03/5261 4732, Ⓦwww.torquaycottage.com.au. Budget cabins with shared facilities, as well as more upmarket rooms with en-suite bathrooms and a self-contained cottage with two bedrooms. Budget cabins ❸, en-suite rooms and cottage ❹

Bells Beach Backpackers 51–53 Surfcoast Highway Ⓣ03/5261 7070, Ⓦwww.bellsbeachbackpackers.com.au. Close to Surf City Plaza and painted with beach-house murals, this place is hard to miss. The small, clean and well-run hostel has dorms and a double, a nice back-yard for BBQs and volleyball, plus Internet access, bikes, boards and wetsuits for hire. Unsurprisingly, it's very popular – book at least a week in advance, 2–3 months for January. Dorms $20-$25, rooms ❸

Bernell Holiday Park Surfcoast Highway Ⓣ03/5261 2493, Ⓦwww.bernell.com.au. Tent and caravan sites, cabins and good facilities, including a heated saltwater pool, beach volleyball court and tennis courts. ❸

Torquay Hotel 36 Bell St Ⓣ03/5261 2001, Ⓦwww.torquayhotel.com.au. Very centrally located option, with good bistro fodder and live bands at the weekend too. ❹

Zeally Bay Caravan Park The Esplanade Ⓣ03/5261 2400, Ⓕ5261 2696. Few facilities and no pool but water views – including from some of the cabins – compensate. ❷

Eating and drinking

Bird Rock Bar & Bistro 2–4 Princes Terrace, Jan Juc. Popular hangout day and night.

Kuzies 57 Surf Coast Highway. Good for filling fare.

Nocturnal Donkey Shop 6/15 Bell Street. Good coffee, drinks and meals, including vegetarian options.

Pabs Tavern Stuart Avenue, Jan Juc. A pub, popular with surfers. Bar meals are available seven days a week.

Sandbah 21 Gilbert Street. This large and airy place is one of the nicest cafés on this street; they serve tasty breakfasts, cakes and lunches. Open 7.30am–6pm.

Scandinavian Ice Cream Company 34 Bell St. Great ice-cream option near the beach.

Anglesea and Aireys Inlet

On the way to Anglesea from Torquay, you can make a short but worthwhile detour to **Point Addis**; turn left just beyond Bells Beach. The road goes right out to the headland car park where you look down on the waves crashing onto the point. Steps lead down to an even better vantage point, with surf heaving below you and Bells Beach stretching to the northwest. Just before the headland, there's another car park from where an access track leads to the **Point Addis Koori Cultural Walk**. Interpretive signs along this one-kilometre trail point out the use of plants and other aspects of the traditional lifestyle of the Wathaurong clan who inhabited the Geelong region.

ANGLESEA itself is a pleasant place for a holiday, with the Anglesea River running through to the sea, and picnic grounds along its banks; its main claim to fame is a large population of **kangaroos**, which graze on the golf course. Despite tourist development, the beach has managed to retain its sand dunes and untouched aspect. Children can swim safely here, as the surf is fairly gentle, but the waves are high and powerful enough for body-surfers to enjoy. The small *Anglesea Backpackers Hostel* on 40 Noble St (ⓣ03/5263 2664; dorms $23, room ❸), located between the river and the golf course, has two six-bed dorms and an en-suite double. There are a few **cafés**: *Heathlands Teahouse* on the Great Ocean Road also has a gallery exhibiting photographs and other work by local artists (Wed–Sun, during school holidays daily, 10am–6pm). Two companies organize surfing and kayaking lessons here; see p.980.

From Anglesea the road goes inland for a few kilometres through scrubby bush. Beyond, a pretty white lighthouse with a red cap overlooks the small town of **AIREYS INLET**, where there's a general store, a café and craft shop near the lighthouse in what used to be the former lightkeeper's stables (7 Federal St; daily 9am–5pm). The horse-riding outfit Blazing Saddles operates rides through the Angahook Lorne State Park, beach rides and pony rides for kids (ⓣ03/5289 7322 or ⓣ0418 528 647, ⓦwww.blazingsaddles.com.au. For **accommodation** try *Aireys Inlet Caravan Park* on the Great Ocean Road (ⓣ03/5289 6230, ⓦwww.aicp.com.au; cabins ❸–❺) or *Split Point Cottages* at 40 Hopkins St (ⓣ03/5289 6566; ❺–❻), which features self-contained accommodation in four mud-brick cottages with two bedrooms. *Airey's by the Light*, 2 Federal St, on the way to the lighthouse (ⓣ03/5289 6134, ⓦwww.greatplacestostay.com.au/aireys/default.asp ❻–❼), is a very upmarket B&B with private decks and stunning sea views.

Lorne and around

Picturesquely set at the foot of the heavily forested **Otway Range**, on the banks of the Erskine River, **LORNE** has long been the premier holiday town of the Great Ocean Road. Only two hours' drive from the city, it's hugely popular with Melbourne weekenders who relish its well-established café society and whiff of 1960s counterculture overlaid on an essentially middle-class 1930s resort. To complete the picture, the **Angahook–Lorne State Park** (see p.983), with its walking tracks, plunging falls and fern gullies, surrounds the town.

About a thousand people live in Lorne, but from Christmas until the end of January twenty thousand more pour in; if you arrive unannounced, you'll have no hope of finding even a camping spot. The **Falls Festival** (ⓦwww.fallsfestival.com) on New Year's Eve is celebrated with a big rock concert that attracts droves of teenagers, followed eight days later by the Mountain to Surf Run and one day later by the highlight of the peak season, the **Pier to Pub Swim**. It is said to be the largest blue-water swimming event in the world and attracts as many as two and a half thousand competitors who race the 1200m from Lorne Pier to the main beach. The atmosphere surrounding these events is a lot of fun, but generally Lorne is much more enjoyable when it's less crowded, which means avoiding weekends and the peak summer season.

The town's beachfront is enlivened by the restored *Grand Pacific Hotel* with its 1870s facade, on a headland at the western end, and the modern, pink, terraced *Cumberland Resort*. Between the street and the beach is a foreshore with trampolines and a pool. The **surf beach** itself is one of the safest in Victoria, protected from the Southern Ocean by two headlands, but in summer it gets very crowded.

Practicalities

Lorne's **tourist office**, at 144 Mountjoy Parade (daily 9am–5pm; ⓣ03/5289 1152), is very helpful and has a good stock of leaflets packed with local information. Mocean Surfboards on Mountjoy Parade (daily 9.30am–5.30pm) rents out quality surf- and boogie-boards and wetsuits. Other services, such as banks, a post office and shops, are clustered primarily along Mountjoy Parade and parallel Smith Street.

Accommodation

Most accommodation is in the upper price bracket, and in December and January the majority rent by the week, with even B&Bs insisting on a three- or four-night minimum stay. To keep costs down, contact the Lorne Foreshore Committee, Ocean Road by Erskine Bridge (ⓣ03/5289 1382, ⓦwww.lorneforeshore.asn.au), which runs four **caravan parks** in the vicinity.

Anchorage Motel and Villas 32 Mountjoy Parade ⓣ03/5289 1891, ⓕ5289 2988. Motel units and two-storey villas with two bedrooms. Facilties include a pool and common spa. Units ❹, villas ❺

Erskine Falls Cottages Cora-Lynn Court, off Erskine Falls Rd, 4.5km north of town ⓣ03/5289 2666, ⓦwww.lornecottages.com.au. Spacious timber cottages (1–3 bedrooms) and units in the hills near Erskine Falls, with views of the ocean, big verandahs, fireplaces, a pool, a tennis court and a licensed café. ❺

Erskine on the Beach Mountjoy Parade ⓣ03/5289 1209, ⓦwww.erskinehouse.com.au. Once an old-fashioned, shabbily genteel guest-house, at the time of writing this place was being refurbished. It has a great location, with spacious lawns extending right to the beach. ❻

Grand Pacific Hotel 268 Mountjoy Parade, opposite the pier at Point Grey ⓣ03/5289 1609, ⓕ5289 2279. The restored and refurbished Victorian lives up to its name: it has great views over Loutit Bay from the dining room and the bar, and rooms have old-world charm but all the mod cons. It's worth shelling out a bit more for a room with sea views. ❺

Great Ocean Road Backpackers YHA 10 Erskine Ave ⓣ03/5289 1809, ⓔlorne@yhavic.org. This excellent, attractive hostel shares the grounds with *Great Ocean Road Cottages* (see below). The hostel section comprises two large timber cottages with balconies, and there's free use of laundry, bicycles and boogie boards. Dorm bed $20–25; rooms ❸

Great Ocean Road Cottages 3 Erskine Ave ⓣ03/5289 1070, ⓕ5289 2247. Well-designed, comfortable, self-catering cottages in a lovely forest setting beside the Erskine River. ❺

Sandridge Motel 128 Mountjoy Parade ⓣ03/5289 2180, ⓕ5289 2722. The standards of the motel units range from "simple" to "deluxe"; the latter feature private balconies facing the sea. ❹–❼

Eating, drinking and entertainment

There are great places to **eat** and **drink** everywhere in town – but they charge Melbourne prices and then some. Most licensed places allow you to BYO wine but charge a hefty corkage fee. *Kosta's* often has music in the evenings, while the *Lorne Hotel* has bands on Friday and Saturday nights. The Lorne Theatre, 78 Mountjoy Parade (☎03/5289 1272), screens films all week during summer and in the school holidays.

The Arab 94 Mountjoy Parade. An original beatnik hangout, which opened two weeks before the Olympic Games in 1956 and has been going strong ever since. It now sports minimalist decor and is still good for daytime snacks and fancier meals at night. Licensed and BYO wine. Daily 8.30am–late.

Ba Ba Lu Bar and Restaurant 6a Mountjoy Parade. Nice joint at the quieter eastern end of town with a great outdoor area. The restaurant follows a Spanish-Latin-American theme with tapas and mains such as *gambas a la plancha* (chargrilled prawns in a sherry sauce). There's also a good range of breakfasts and cheaper lunch items. Licensed and BYO. Daily 8.30am–late.

Erskine Falls Café Off Erskine Falls Rd, in the hills about 4.5km north of town. All-day breakfasts and light lunches. Open daily from 9am.

Kafé Kaos 54 Mountjoy Parade. Huge, delicious and healthy sandwiches, salads and wraps plus extensive (and much less healthy) breakfast options. Licensed and BYO wine. Mon–Thurs & Sun 8.30am–6pm, Fri & Sat until 11pm.

Kosta's 48 Mountjoy Parade. A popular, Greek-style bar and eating place, serving up good seafood as well as grilled meats. Licensed or BYO wine. Daily 9am–1am; closed mid-June to mid-July.

Lorne Hotel 176 Mountjoy Parade. Best pub meals in town, plus a dining room overlooking the ocean and live music on Fridays and Saturdays.

Lorne Pier Seafood Restaurant ☎03/5289 1119. An excellent seafood restaurant on the pier at Point Grey. Licensed and BYO. Open daily 6–9.30pm, longer in summer.

Mark's 124 Mountjoy Parade ☎03/5289 2787. A modern restaurant with a menu running from marlin steak to home-made gnocchi. Licensed and BYO wine. During summer holidays daily noon–3pm & 6pm–late; other times only evenings and Sat afternoon; closed May.

Mermaids Bed and Breakfast Café 22 Great Ocean Road. Just past the *Grand Pacific Hotel* at the western end of town, with its uninterrupted view of Lorne beach, this is a perfect little spot for coffee, breakfast or lunch. Licensed and BYO wine. Daily 8.30am–4pm, summer until 5pm.

Moon's Espresso Bar 108 Mountjoy Parade. A little taste of city life by the sea, this ultra-modern establishment serves excellent coffee and Mediterranean lunches and even has an attached cocktail bar.

Qdos Allenvale Rd ☎03/5289 1989. Tucked away in the eucalypt-clad hills above Lorne, this art gallery-cum-café serves light lunches, dinners and tasty home-made cakes and coffee in a relaxed atmosphere. Bookings advisable. Summer Thurs–Sun 10am–9pm, winter Fri–Mon 10am–6pm.

Angahook-Lorne State Park

Angahook–Lorne State Park extends along some 50km of coastline, from Aireys Inlet to Kennett River. Pockets of temperate rainforest, towering blue-gum forests, cliffs and waterfalls characterize the Lorne section of the park, south of the Erskine River. The **Erskine Falls**, one of the most popular attractions, drop 30m into a fern-fringed pool – you can reach them along a winding eight-kilometre road that ends with a short descent on a very steep but sealed section. From the car park the falls are a few minutes' walk through majestic trees and tall umbrella ferns; another 150m takes you down to the quiet, rocky Erskine River. It's also possible to walk through the bush from Lorne to the falls (7.5km one-way; 4hr), starting from the *Erskine River Caravan Park* (one of the four caravan parks run by the Lorne Foreshore Committee) next to the bridge over the Erskine River, just off the Great Ocean Road and following the river; after 1km you'll pass the Sanctuary, a natural rock amphitheatre, then Splitter Falls and Straw Falls, before reaching Erskine Falls.

Closer to Lorne, **Teddy's Lookout**, in Queens Park, is either a quick drive from the Great Ocean Road (up Otway Street, turn left at the roundabout into George Street), or a three-kilometre walk along the same streets; just follow the signposts. You end up high above the sea, with a view of the St George River below and the Great Ocean Road curving around the cliffs.

Apollo Bay and the Otway Ranges

Between Lorne and Apollo Bay wooded hills fall away steeply into the ocean. The road snakes along the coastline, becoming very narrow in places where it was literally gouged out of the rockface. The road descends to small bays at the mouths of the **Wye** and **Kennett** rivers and the small hamlets named after these rivers provide an idyllic setting for a few days of lazing around, fishing and bushwalking. There's **camping** at the *Wye River Foreshore Camping Reserve* (ⓣ03/5289 0412), *Wye River Valley Tourist Park* (ⓣ03/5289 0241, ⓦwww.wyerivervalleypark.com.au) and *Kennett River Caravan Park* (ⓣ03/5289 0272, ⓦwww.kennettriver.com), plus motel units at the *Rookery Nook Hotel* in Wye (ⓣ03/5289 0240; ❹) – their bistro serves good pub food too. You'll also find a host of self-contained cottages (bookings handled by Wye & Kennet River Getaways ⓣ03/5289 0486, ⓦwww.wyerivergetaways.com.au; ❺). The most impressive, though pricey, option is "the deckhouse" on 5 Sturt Court, Wye – it's perched right above the ocean, with stunning views and an equally stunning colour scheme inside the bright studio apartment (ⓣ03/5289 0222, ⓦwww.thedeckhouse.com.au; B&B ❻).

Inland lies a landscape of rolling hills and steep-sided valleys, much of it still covered in dense temperate rainforest – the **Otway Ranges** here get the highest annual rainfall in Victoria – large patches of which make up the Otway National Park.

Apollo Bay

APOLLO BAY enjoys a picturesque setting between pounding surf and gently rounded green hills. **Fishing** – commercial and recreational – is the main activity here. If you're interested in doing a bit yourself, enquire at Apollo Bay Fishing and Adventure Tours (ⓣ03/5237 7888 or 0418 121 784, ⓦwww.apollobayfishing.com.au), which offers fishing trips and scenic boat cruises. The town has an enjoyably alternative feel – a lot of artists and musicians live here and both local pubs often have music at weekends. Start your Saturday morning with a browse at the Foreshore Market (Sat 8.30am–4.30pm) which showcases locally produced arts and crafts as well as fresh produce. The annual Apollo Bay Music Festival takes place over a weekend in mid-March and features jazz, rock, blues and country, plus many workshops (information and bookings ⓣ03/5237 6761, ⓦwww.apollobaymusicfestival.com). For information on local activities, head for the Great Ocean Road Visitor Information Centre on the foreshore at the eastern end of town (daily 9am–5pm; ⓣ03/5237 6529), which has very helpful staff who can book accommodation.

Practicalities

Apollo Bay marks the start of the **Great Ocean Walk**, a 91-kilometre track through forests and some of the state's most stunning coastal scenery. Make sure you register with the Apollo Bay Visitor Information Centre which also provides updates on weather forecasts and track conditions as well as any other information. If you're interested in **horse riding**, book a trail ride with Wild Dog Trails, 225 Wild Dog Rd (ⓣ03/5237 6441; 90min $45/3hr $70); **cycling** enthusiasts can enquire about mountain-bike tours run by Otway Expeditions (ⓣ0419 007 586; minimum of two people required). **Flying** seems to be rather popular here, too: the Wingsports Flight Academy, in Evans Court (ⓣ0419 378 616, ⓦwww.wingsports.com.au), offers courses in hang-gliding and paragliding and allows those with no prior experience to fly with a fully qualified pilot along the coast in a powered hang-glider. Twelve Apostles Aerial Adventures (ⓣ03/5237 7370, ⓦwww.tigermothworld.com) and Cape Otway Aviation (ⓣ0407 306 065, ⓦwww.capeotwayaviation.com.au) both at the Apollo Bay airfield, south of town, do scenic flights to a variety of destinations, including nearby Cape Otway and the Twelve Apostles (from $80 for 10min), and as far afield as King Island, Tasmania; prices are per person and based on a minimum of three passengers. Sunroad Tours picks up people from their accommodation and takes them to view **glow-worms** on a private property near Apollo Bay (ⓣ03/5237 6080; 90min; $25) while Otway Natural Wonders operates out of the Otway town of **Forrest**, 37km north-west of Apollo Bay, and runs **canoe trips** in the densely forested hinterland to see platypus and glow-worms (ⓣ03/5236 6345; 2–6 people; 2–3hr; $85). For other sightseeing **tours** (4WD or normal vehicle) enquire at the Visitor Information Centre.

Accommodation

Numerous **accommodation** options can be found in the area, many of them picturesquely located in the hills and valleys surrounding the town – a scenic location is the **Barham River Valley** 8km west of town that has places in a lush rainforest setting. Apollo Bay's main street is lined with **motels**, most of them rather drab affairs dating from the 1970s.

There are several **caravan parks**, the closest to town being the *Waratah Caravan Park* at 7 Noel St (ⓣ03/5237 6562, ⓔinfo@waratahbaycaravanpark.com; cabins ❸–❹). Both the *Pisces Caravan Resort*, 2km north of the town centre (ⓣ03/5237 6749, ⓔpiscespark@hotkey.net.au; ❹), and the *Marengo Holiday Park* on Marengo Crescent in secluded surroundings on the foreshore (ⓣ03/5237 6162, ⓦwww.marengopark.com.au; ❸–❺), have cabins, some with en-suite facilities.

Arcady Homestead B&B 925 Barham River Rd, Barham River Valley ⓣ & ⓕ03/5237 6493. An old-fashioned, friendly guesthouse in bush surroundings, with four bedrooms, shared facilities. No heating in bedrooms but there are electric blankets and the roaring log fire in the guest lounge warms up the house. ❹

A Room with a View 280 Sunnyside Rd, Wongarra ⓣ03/5237 0218, ⓦwww.roomwithaview.com.au. Cosy, aptly named B&B accommodation, 14km east of town, with magnificent views of green rolling hills and the ocean, and gourmet breakfasts to set you up for the day. ❺

Eco Beach YHA 5 Pascoe St ⓣ03/5237 7899, ⓔapollobay@yhavic.org.au. Newly opened hostel with 4-bed dorms and lots of doubles, twins and singles. Central location near the cafés and shop too. Dorms $22, rooms ❸

Marriner's Falls Cottages 1090 Barham River Rd, Barham River Valley ⓣ & ⓕ03/5237 7494. Spacious and cosy cottages, built on a hillside, with spa, open fire, balconies and great views, but no TV. ❺

Otway Paradise Cottages 935 Barham River Rd, Barham River Valley ⓣ03/5237 7102, ⓦwww.otway-paradise-cottages.com.au. Five fully equipped, spacious cottages (1, 2 & 3 bedrooms) in a gorgeous rainforest setting. ❺

Skenes Creek Lodge Motel 61 Great Ocean Rd, Skenes Creek ⓣ03/5237 6918, ⓕ5237 6329. Good budget motel in a garden setting above the main road, with restaurant and ocean views. ❸–❺

Surfside Hostel Cnr of Great Ocean Rd and Gambier St ⓣ1800 357 263, ⓔsurfbakpak@greatoceanroad.org. A friendly place with small dorms and cheap doubles in a scenic location on a hill at the western side of town. Facilities include disabled access, outdoor BBQs and a large vinyl collection. The owner also rents cheap holiday units with en suite and cooking facilities at another location in town. Dorms $18–23, rooms and units ❷–❹

Eating

In town, the **eating** places are strung along the Great Ocean Road. To buy freshly caught seafood, go to the Fishermen's Co-op at the harbour (Mon–Thurs 9.30am–4.30pm, Fri until 5pm, Sat & Sun 10am–3pm).

Apollo Bay Hotel 95 Great Ocean Road. Recently renovated and extended pub that offers very good bistro meals.
Bay Leaf Café 131 Great Ocean Road ⓣ03/5237 6470. Good egg or pancake breakfasts, as well as nicely presented lunches and dinners. Open daily.
Buffs Bistro 51 Great Ocean Road. This reliable oldtimer serves light snacks, seafood and pasta.
La Bimba 125 Great Ocean Road ⓣ03/5237 7411. Cosy eatery on the first floor with an imaginative, eclectic and moderately expensive menu. Closed Mon & Tues May–Nov.
Chris's Sea-Grape Wine Bar & Grill 141 Great Ocean Road ⓣ03/5237 6610. The décor is a bit austere but you get good (if somewhat predictable) food here: standard brekkie and lunch fare during the day, grilled meat-and-salad combinations in the evening. Closed Mon May–Aug.
Chris's Beacon Point Restaurant 2km up Skenes Creek Road, Skenes Creek ⓣ03/5237 6411. The renowned restaurant in the hills above Skenes Creek features Mediterranean cuisine with a Greek accent and specializes in seafood – but it doesn't come cheap (mains $26–40).
Tanybryn Tea House and Gallery on the corner of Skenes Creek and Wild Dog roads. This place is worth the fifteen-minute drive from Apollo Bay township for its well-stocked craft shop, café and fine panorama (10am–5pm; closed July to mid-Sept).

Otway National Park

From Apollo Bay, the Great Ocean Road soon enters **Otway National Park**, curving and bending upwards through temperate rainforest and offering occasional glimpses of cleared hilltops and grazing sheep in the distance. From Maits Rest car park, 17km west of Apollo Bay, you can take an easy stroll through a lovely fern gully, which gives a feel of the dense rainforest that once covered the entire Otway Ranges. A little further down the road, towards Lavers Hill, you'll see a turn-off to the **Cape Otway Lighthouse**, 14km away on a sealed road, where there's a small café (daily 9.30am–4.30pm) and pleasant accommodation in two refurbished lighthouse keepers' residences, simply but tastefully decorated and fully equipped (ⓣ03/5237 9240, ⓦwww.lightstation.com; ❺). You can visit the lighthouse and the grounds on a self-guided tour (daily 9am–5pm; $10.50) or join a guided tour (times are subject to change; usually 11am, 2, 3 & 4pm daily; no extra fee). Three kilometres north of Cape Otway, the turn-off to Blanket Bay, is a good location for spotting koalas.

The only **caravan park** actually within the national park is *Bimbi Park* (ⓣ03/5237 9246, ⓦwww.bimbipark.com.au; cabins ❸–❹), about halfway along the road to the lighthouse. The facilities and some of the cabins are quite basic but the setting is gorgeous – on a small farm with paddocks surrounded by bushland – and the caravan park offers excellent **horse-riding** excursions, including a ride to Station Beach (1hr 30min; $40), a three-kilometre-long stretch of sand with freshwater springs and waterfalls.

Back on the Great Ocean Road, you momentarily return to the ocean at **Castle Cove**, a good lookout point across green, undulating dairy country. As you turn inland again, stepped hills rise sharply from the road as it passes turn-offs to **Johanna**, one of Victoria's best-known surf beaches, and winds up towards **LAVERS HILL**, the highest point in the Otway Ranges. The tiny town has three cafés: *Gardenside Manor* and *Blackwood Gully Tea Rooms* both serve light snacks and Devonshire teas daily from 10am, while the more contemporary *McDuffs Bakehouse & Café* sells pies, pasties, cakes and a tempting variety of breads – all made on the premises. There's motel accommodation at the *Otway Junction Motor Inn* (ⓣ03/5237 3295; ❹) and a small, cosy cottage at Fauna Australia Wildlife Retreat, a privately run Australian wildlife sanctuary – they also offer guided tours and serve refreshments (ⓣ03/5237 3234, ⓦwww.faunaaustralia.com.au; ❺).

Before continuing west, it's worth taking a detour to the region's latest tourist attraction, the **Otway Fly Treetop Walk**, about 10–15 minutes' drive east of Lavers Hill (daily 9am–5pm; $12.50; Ⓦwww.otwayfly.com) – just follow the road signs. A 600m steel-trussed walkway here allows you to walk through temperate rainforest at canopy level, 20–25m above the ground. If peering down from this height is not thrilling enough, you can climb on a narrow, see-through spiral staircase to the top of the Spiral Tower (47m), or walk to the end of the Cantilever, a beam extending from a tower and gently swaying above fern-fringed Youngs Creek. The Otway Fly Visitor Centre on top of the hill, 300m from the beginning of the walkway, has a good licensed café and a souvenir shop.

From Moonlight Head to Peterborough

The 130-kilometre stretch of coast between lonely, windswept Moonlight Head and Port Fairy is known as the **Shipwreck Coast**; it takes in the Twelve Apostles - something of an icon of the Great Ocean Road - and other well-known coastal formations such as Loch Ard Gorge and London Bridge. Most of the coast is protected within Otway National Park and **Port Campbell National Park**. At least 180 ships have come to grief in the coast's treacherous waters, and the **Historic Shipwreck Trail**, which links the sites of dozens of wrecks with informative plaques and signed walking paths, runs between Moonlight Head and Port Fairy. A brochure about the trail is available at all the visitor information centres in the region.

At the tiny hamlet of Princetown, *The 13th Apostle* (Ⓣ03/5598 8062; dorm bed $19–22; rooms ❸), a modern, purpose-built hostel, provides pleasant and clean budget accommodation. A general store and pub are across the road.

Beyond Princetown, the first worthwhile stop is steep and slippery **Gibsons Steps**, where you walk down to a kelp-covered beach beneath towering cliffs. From here on, the spectacle gets more and more extraordinary, with plenty of convenient stopping points from where you can admire the amazing formations. For a bird's-eye view of all this, take a helicopter ride with one of two companies in the area: PremiAIR Helicopter Services operate from the Twelve Apostles Centre (Ⓣ03/5598 8266), while 12 Apostles Helicopters are found on the Great Ocean Road near Loch Ard Gorge, just east of Port Campbell (Ⓣ03/5598 6161, Ⓦwww.12ah.com).

The most awe-inspiring formations are the **Twelve Apostles** – gigantic limestone pillars, some rising 65m out of the ocean, which retreat in rows as stark reminders of a wasting coastline (the cliff faces erode at a rate of about 2cm a year). The (unstaffed) Twelve Apostles Centre at the car park on the northern side of the road provides clean toilet facilities and welcome shelter from the rain and bone-chilling winds blowing off the Southern Ocean. It features wall-length panels of sailcloth with scripted poems about the Shipwreck Coast's awesome, dangerous beauty. Covered walkways lead through a tunnel under the road to the lookout points and a short walk along the clifftop. Sunset here (summer around 9pm, winter around 5.45pm) is a popular time for photographers and, unfortunately, crowds. Wait ten minutes or so after dusk, however, when the tourists have jumped back on their coaches and left, and you'll be treated to another fantastic spectacle, as hordes of fairy penguins waddle onto the shore in droves. Next stop is **Loch Ard Gorge**, where a small network of clifftop walks and a staircase leading down to a beach give you the chance to view the fantastic rock formations all around. It was here that the *Loch Ard*, an iron-hulled square rig, hit a reef and foundered while transporting immigrants from England to Melbourne in the spring of 1878. Of fifty-three people on board, only two survived: Eva Carmichael and Tom Pearce, both in their late teens. They were swept into a long gorge that had a narrow entrance, high walls and small beach, and Tom dragged Eva into a cave in the western wall of the gorge before going for help. A walkway leads down to the beach, covered with delicate pink kelp, and you can scramble over craggy rocks to the cave where Eva sheltered, now a nesting site for small birds. The Loch Ard cemetery, where the ship's passengers and crew are buried, is on the clifftop overlooking the gorge. As you drive further, you pass more scenic points, with resonant names such as the Blowhole and the Thundercave, before reaching Port Campbell.

Port Campbell and around

PORT CAMPBELL is a small settlement on the edge of the Port Campbell National Park. The **Port Campbell Information Centre** on Morris Street (daily 9am–5pm; ⓣ03/5598 6089) has displays and information about the area and its national parks, and can also book accommodation. Ask here too about the self-guided **Port Campbell Discovery Walk** (90min), which will take you along a clifftop to a viewpoint above Two Mile Bay.

Port Campbell **beach** is a small sandy curve, safe for swimming and patrolled in season – the town climbs the hill behind the beach.

If you're really fascinated by shipwrecks, *Port Campbell Boat Charters* at 32 Lord St (ⓣ03/5598 6411), offers **diving** to some wreck sites and can rent out snorkelling or diving gear to those who want to go it alone.

Practicalities

The town itself is a pleasant place to while away an evening, and with two hostels in town, **accommodation** needn't be expensive. In summer and for long weekends, however, it's advisable to book far ahead. The *Port Campbell YHA* (ⓣ03/5598 6305; dorms $23.50, rooms and cabins ❸) on Tregea Street is a pleasant, well-run place with a good kitchen, a spacious common room and TV lounge, bright dorms, double/twin rooms and two cabins. In comparison, *Ocean House Backpackers* (ⓣ03/5598 6942; dorm bed from $20) in an old house on Lord Street is rather dark and somewhat cramped. This hostel is operated by the *Port Campbell National Park Cabin & Camping Park* on Morris Street (ⓣ03/5598 6492); small groups are possibly better off booking into one of their beachside cabins ❸.

Port O'Call at 37 Lord St (ⓣ03/5598 6206, ⓔpoc@hotkey.net.au; ❹) is an agreeable motel with six inexpensive units, similar to the *Portside Motel* (ⓣ03/5598 6084, ⓔportsidemotel@bigpond.com.au; ❹), 62 Great Ocean Road, which has units with kitchenette facilities and private verandahs. Moving more upmarket, the *Comfort Inn Motel Port Campbell* (ⓣ03/5598 6231; ❻) also has a good licensed restaurant, *Napiers* (same phone number); likewise *Waves* (ⓣ03/5598 6101; ❻), a brand-new stylish apartment complex; both within coo-ee of each other on Lord Street.

Port Campbell offers plenty of choices for **eating places**, all close to each other on Lord Street. For regular Aussie fare, go to the good-quality bistro at the *Port Campbell Hotel* (daily lunch and dinner). *Timboon Fine Ice Cream* next to the Mobil petrol station sells delicious home-made ice cream, fruit sorbets and good coffee. *Nico's Pizza and Pasta* opposite serves pancakes, egg breakfasts and a huge variety of pizzas, some with very unusual toppings – "The Persian" comes with walnuts, feta, sliced pear, tomato and potatoes. Even more upmarket eateries include the above-mentioned *Waves* at no. 29, a licensed café/restaurant serving tasty breakfasts, lunch and dinner daily (booking advised on ⓣ03/5598 6111), and *20ate*, a restaurant and bar at no. 28 with a terrace. Breakfasts and light lunches are served daily in summer, otherwise Wed–Sun 8am–5pm. Next door is *Kooh Aah* on the ground floor, a café open for breakfast, lunch and dinner, and on the upper floor *The Splash Seafood Restaurant* (daily from 6pm; ⓣ03/5598 6408).

Port Campbell's expensive **general store** (daily: winter 8am–6pm; summer 7am–7pm) also has a bottle shop and an EFTPOS system that takes every type of card; it also functions as the post office and newsagent.

London Bridge, the Grotto and Timboon

Tourists could once walk across the double-arched rock formation known as **London Bridge**, a short distance west of Port Campbell, to the outer end facing the sea. In mid-January 1990, however, the outer span collapsed and fell into the sea, minutes after two very lucky people had crossed it – they were eventually rescued from the far limestone cliff by helicopter. As fate would have it, the couple were conducting an extra-marital affair, and fled from the waiting media as soon as the helicopter arrived. Another good place to stop, just before Peterborough, is the **Grotto**, where a path leads from the clifftop to a rock pool beneath an archway.

Moving on, you pass through undulating dairy country on the last stretch of the Great Ocean Road from Peterborough, on Curdies Inlet, to Warrnambool. There's little to detain you along the route, although if you're a cheese fan you might consider a detour to **TIMBOON**, 18km inland from Port Campbell: at **Timboon Farmhouse Cheese** on the corner of Ford and Fells roads (October–April daily; May–September Wed–Sun 10am–4pm), you can taste and buy excellent cheese, made from organic milk, and wine.

Warrnambool and onwards

Coming into **WARRNAMBOOL** on the Great Ocean Road you see the city's more pleasant aspects: its lovely coastal setting, with **Allansford Cheese-world** (Mon–Fri 8.30am–5pm, Sat & Sun 8.30am–4pm) indicating that this is the centre of rich **dairy country**. As well as selling cheese, it has tastings, a café serving teas and light meals, and a local history museum. However, if you approach Warrnambool from the northeast along the Princes Highway, you'll pass car lots, motels and an ugly factory belching smoke.

Lady Bay, where Warrnambool is sheltered, was first used by sealers and whalers in the early nineteenth century and was permanently settled from about 1839. **Southern right whales**, hunted almost to extinction, have begun to return in the last decade. Every year between June and September, female whales come to the waters off **Logans Beach** to calve. Often the whales swim very close to the shore and can be viewed from a specially constructed platform at Logans Beach.

The perils of shipping in the treacherous waters of the shipwreck coast are the theme at **Flagstaff Hill** at 23 Merri St (daily 9am–5pm; $14). The extensive grounds feature a recreated nineteenth-century coastal village, arranged around the original fort, erected in 1887 when the fear of a Russian invasion was widespread in Australia. Entry is via a new building housing the visitor information centre, an upmarket restaurant, a souvenir shop plus a theatrette and gallery. The walking tour starts at the Gravesend Theatre where a multimedia

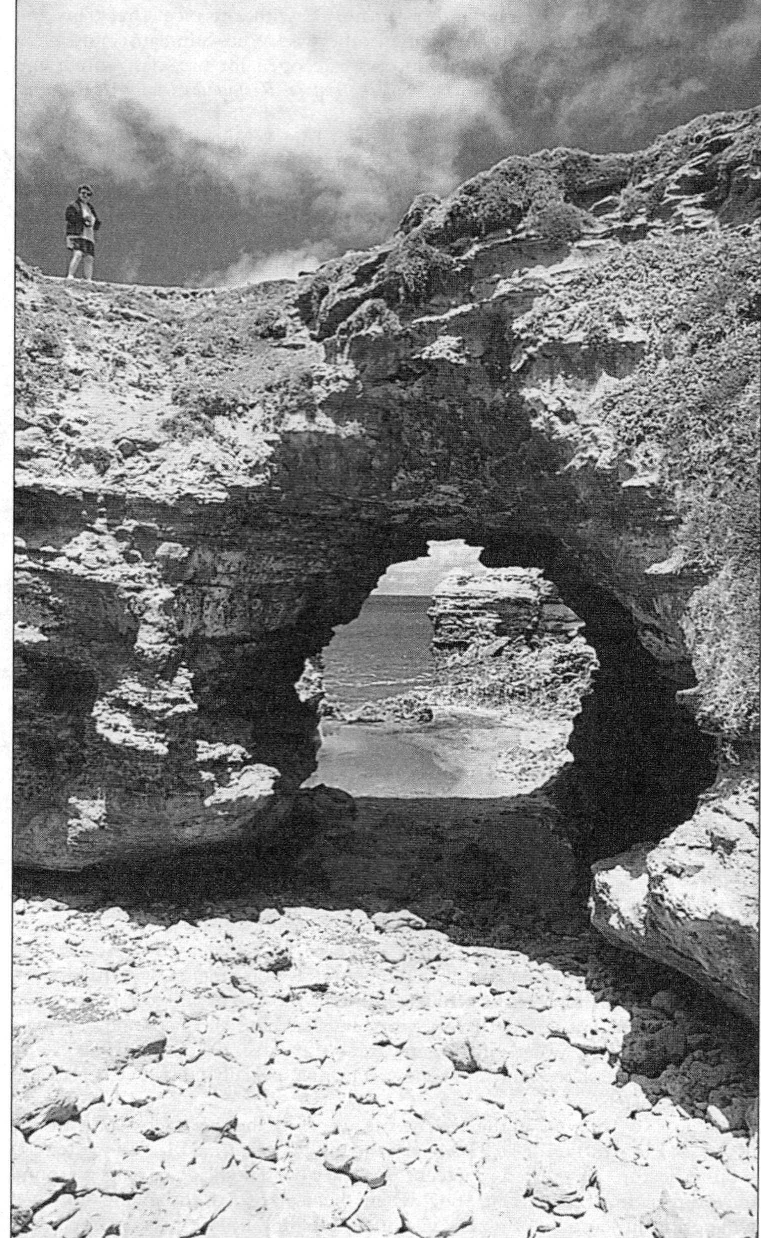

△ The Grotto, Port Campbell National Park

presentation about the perils of a voyage from England to Australia is screened, featuring extracts from a diary written by a migrant in 1863. Proceeding to the Grand Circle Gallery with its informative displays about nineteenth-century shipbuilding and, in particular, navigation, visitors learn why the western approach to Bass Strait was so dangerous to shipping in those days. Flagstaff Hill's pièce de résistance, however, is the multi-million-dollar sound and laser show **Shipwrecked** ($23; 70min, book at least 2 days in advance; ⓣ1800 556 111). Screened nightly after dusk, it recounts the story of the *Loch Ard* disaster (see p.987).

Warrnambool has a bustling downtown, with a major shopping centre on Liebig Street, several galleries and museums, and some fine old churches. Perhaps the best of the sights is the **Warrnambool Art Gallery** on Liebig Street (Mon–Fri 10am–5pm, Sat & Sun noon–5pm; free), a fine provincial gallery with collections of Western District colonial paintings and contemporary Australian prints. The **Botanic Gardens** on Botanic Road, designed in 1877 by William Guilfoyle, then Director of the Melbourne Botanic Gardens, are also worth visiting if you have some spare time. The classically designed, ornamental gardens are filled with winding paths and hills, and provide glimpses of the sea. There's also a fernery, a water-lily pond and a small rotunda.

Practicalities

The well-organized **Warrnambool Visitor Information Centre** (daily 9am–5pm; ⓣ03/5559 4620 or 1800 637 725) is part of the Flagstaff Hill complex at 23 Merri St. **Internet** access is available at Southern IT, 190 Timor St (ⓣ03/5561 4087) and at Flaherty's Chocolate Shop, 52 Kepler St. Southern Right Charters & Diving (ⓣ03/5562 5044) do **whale watching** cruises, scenic tours ($35/hr), **fishing and diving charters** as well as **dive courses** (PADI open water, 4 days, about $400); for **horse rides** along the beach contact Rundell's Mahogany Trail Rides (ⓣ03/5529 2303; about $4/90min.).

Accommodation

Backpackers at the Victoria Hotel Cnr of Lava and Liebig streets ⓣ03/5562 2073. Simple rooms above a pub in a central location. Dorms $20, rooms ❶

Girt By Sea B&B 52 Banyan St ⓣ03/5561 3162, ⓔgirtbyseabnb@hotmail.com. Three tastefully furnished bedrooms with their own bathroom in a restored historic house (built 1856). Convenient location between the town centre and the beach. ❺

Hotel Warrnambool Cnr of Koroit and Kepler streets ⓣ03/5562 2377, ⓕ5561 7248. Upmarket, refurbished place offering good B&B pub accommodation in the town centre; particularly good value for single travellers. ❷

Port Warrnambool Village 14A Pertobe Road, near the foreshore ⓣ03/5562 8063, ⓦwww.portwarrnamboolvillage.com.au. New self-contained apartments (2–4 bedrooms) with fully equipped kitchens; linen provided. There's also a lock-up garage and direct beach access. ❺

Stuffed Backpacker Operated by Flaherty's Chocolate Shop, 52 Kepler St ⓣ 03/5562 2459, ⓦwww.stuffed.com.au. No-frills accommodation just around the corner from the busy end of Liebig Street. Dorms $20, singles/doubles ❷

Warrnambool Beach Backpackers 17 Stanley St ⓣ03/5562 4874, ⓦwww.totaltravel.com.au/link.asp?fid=1036. The best backpacker hostel in town, less than 10 minutes' walk from the beach. It has comfy dorms with lockers (phone ahead for a female dorm) and doubles, some with en-suite, and a licensed bar and Internet access. Guests are picked up from the bus stop or train station in town on request. Dorms $20, en-suite rooms ❸

Warrnambool Surfside Holiday Park Pertobe Rd, opposite Lake Pertobe ⓣ03/5561 2611, ⓦwww.surfsidepark.com.au. Self-contained one- to three-bedroom cottages and cabins as well as camping right on the beach. ❹–❻

Warrnambool Whale View B&B 11 Logan Beach Rd, ⓣ & ⓕ03/5562 2484. A good choice in whale-watching season (May–Aug) as it's not far from the the beach and whale-watching platform, 5km southwest of town.

Eating and drinking

There are plenty of good places to **eat** and **drink**, most of them on Liebig Street. Out of town, two eating places near the water are worth seeking out: the licensed *Fishsails Café* near the southern end of Pertobe Street at the breakwater (a branch of the *Fishtales Café* on Liebig Street), and *Proudfoots on the River* at 2 Simpson St, in a refurbished historic boathouse on the Hopkins River, with tearooms, a smoke-free bistro and a tavern bar.

Balenas *Whalers Inn*, corner of Liebig and Timor streets. A trendy restaurant serving mod Oz cuisine. Open daily from 12noon. Moderate.
Beach Babylon 72 Liebig St. Pleasant place for pizza and pasta or just a glass of wine. Open daily from 6pm.
Black Olive Bar Restaurant & Cafe *Hotel Grand*, 158 Liebig St ⓣ03/5561 6106. The dinner menu features Mediterranean-inspired dishes and there's a good wine list. Open daily noon–late.
Caffe Regal 163 Timor St. Stylish lunch spot near the art gallery, with a basement bar that's a popular watering hole for Warrnambool's trendy set.
Figsellers Café 89 Liebig St. A simple joint with a tree-lined courtyard serving sandwiches, quiches and other snacks from 8.30am.
Fishtales Café 63 Liebig St. Funky place with an open courtyard, serving Asian curries, noodles, seafood and good coffee. BYO. Open daily 8am until late.
Freshwater Café 78 Liebig St ⓣ03/5561 3188. A renowned restaurant featuring modern Australian cuisine, using regional produce, especially seafood. Try the scallop wantons with native lemon myrtle sauce. Daily lunch & dinner.
Pippies by the Bay 23 Merri St ⓣ03/5561 2188. The new restaurant at the redeveloped Flagstaff Hill has views over Flagstaff Hill Maritime Village (see p.989) and Lady Bay. Licensed. Open daily for breakfast, lunch and dinner. Enquire about packages for the sound and laser show plus dinner at the restaurant.
Puds Pantry and Deli 60 Kepler St. Excellent home-made bread and pastries, as well as soups, pasta and curries to take away or eat in. Closed Sun.
Restaurant Malaysia 69 Liebig St. Oldtimer with faded photos of celebrities from the Eighties and Nineties in the window and inexpensive, good Southeast Asian cuisine on the menu.
Victoria Hotel Cnr of Liebig and Lava streets. This typical Aussie pub is good for bar meals; the steaks in particular are recommended.

Tower Hill Reserve and Koroit

About 13km west of Warrnambool along the Princes Highway, **Tower Hill State Game Reserve** is located in the crater of a volcano that last erupted about 25,000 years ago. In the nineteenth century, pioneer settlers stripped Tower Hill of its trees and used it as grazing land, but since the 1960s it has been reforested and wildlife has returned. If you visit the island in the middle of the crater lake, you'll encounter **emus**, **koalas** and, mostly at dusk, loads of **kangaroos** and **wallabies**. And several bird hides enable you to spy on the abundant birdlife. The game reserve is accessible all the time. The **Worn Gundidjidj Centre** (daily 10am–4pm) on the island has a small display area with information about the reserve and local Koorie culture, and a good shop selling Aboriginal bushtucker products as well as arts and crafts. There are also four self-guided short **walks** around the reserve (30min–1hr).

KOROIT, 7km to the north, is a tiny, old-fashioned town with Australia's largest concentration of people of Irish descent. The Catholic church is impressive, but the building that really dominates the town is the elegant two-storey **Koroit Hotel** on the main street, run by the same family since 1922. If you cut north from here to the Hamilton Highway you'll know you're getting into wool country when you see sheep walking down the main street of Woolsthorpe.

Port Fairy and Mount Eccles

PORT FAIRY, the next stop along the coast, was once an early port and whaling centre but is now a quaint crayfishing and tourist town with a busy jetty, a harbour full of yachts, and over fifty National Trust-listed buildings. Heavy southern breakers roll into the surrounding beaches, and on **Griffiths Island**, poised between the ocean and Port Fairy Bay, there's a **muttonbird** rookery with a specially constructed lookout where between September and April you can watch the birds roost at dusk. For a historic small town, it's quite a happening place, hosting numerous events. In summer the four-week-long **Moyneyana Festival** focuses on outdoor activities – with events such as a raft race on the Moyne River – reaching its climax with the Moyneyana New Year's Eve procession. At Easter the annual Queenscliff to Port Fairy **yacht race** ends here, with a huge party. **Music** is big too, with the Spring Music Festival in mid-October concentrating on classical music, with a bit of opera and jazz thrown in for good measure, and the huge **Port Fairy Folk Festival** over the Labour Day long weekend in March, which takes over the entire town, with Australian and overseas acts playing world, roots and acoustic music. Tickets are sold in early November, and usually sell out in two to three hours. For more information and festival bookings contact the **visitor information centre**, on Bank Street (daily 9am–5pm; ⓣ03/5568 2682, ⓦwww.myportfairy.com). The centre also produces an excellent 20¢ map of the Port Fairy Heritage Walk, which takes you on a route around town to admire the many fine buildings. The **History Centre**, in the old courthouse on Gipps Street by the river (Wed, Sat & Sun 2–5pm, daily during holidays; $3), displays costumes, historic photographs, shipwreck relics and other items relating to the town's pioneer history.

Port Fairy practicalities

With its village-like atmosphere and variety of excellent **accommodation** options, as well as good pubs, tearooms and restaurants, Port Fairy makes a good place to break your journey between Melbourne and Adelaide. The *Port Fairy YHA*, at 8 Cox St (ⓣ03/5568 2468, ⓦwww.portyfairyhostel.com.au; dorm bed $20, rooms ❸), is a well-run hostel in a lovely old house right in the town centre. The historic *Caledonian Inn* (ⓣ03/5568 1044, ⓦwww.caledonianinn.com.au; ❸), at the corner of Bank and James streets, has backpacker accommodation and affordable motel-style units, plus a good bistro. Going more upmarket, the *Comfort Inn* at 22 Sackville St (ⓣ03/5568 1082, ⓦwww.seacombehouse.com.au; ❸–❼), is one of many National Trust-listed buildings in the town, with cheaper hotel rooms, gorgeous but pricey modern motel units and historic cottages, and a good restaurant. There are also a number of B&Bs in quaint colonial cottages, amongst them *The Douglas*, by the river at 85 Gipps St (ⓣ03/5668 1016, ⓦwww.port-fairy.com/thedouglas/; ❹) and the *Merrijig Inn* at 1 Campbell St (ⓣ03/5568 2324, ⓦwww.merrijiginn.com; ❹). Full details of all cottages and B&Bs, and of Port Fairy's six caravan parks, can be obtained from the visitor information centre.

One of the best places to **drink** is the *Caledonian Inn* ("The Stump"), on the corner of Bank and James streets – it's the oldest continually licensed pub in Victoria (since 1844). In Sackville Street there are two good cafés – *Rebecca's* at no. 70 does breakfasts, light lunches, cakes and good coffee, while next door, sells delicious home-made ice cream. *JD's Surf Café* at no. 55 is open from 7am till late; in addition to breakfasts and light meals they also offer **Internet access**. Around the corner are a few more eateries: *Pelican's on Bank*, an atmospheric, upmarket café at 19 Bank St, and *Madagalli on Bank*, 24 Bank St (Wed–Sun 6pm till late; ☎03/5568 1829) for pizza and pasta; they also have a courtyard. *Portofino on Bank*, 26 Bank St (daily 6pm till late; ☎03/5568 2251) is a renowned and upmarket licensed restaurant, and also in the same category are the *Merrijig Inn* at 1 Campbell St (daily 6.30pm till late), and the *Stag Inn* at 22 Sackville St (Mon–Sat 6pm till late; ☎03/5568 3058). The renovated *Victoria Hotel*, 42 Bank St (☎03/5568 2891), has a highly recommended restaurant and a cheaper – but equally good – café (try the brunch for a real treat).

Mount Eccles National Park

Just over 50km northwest of Port Fairy is **Mount Eccles National Park**. Mount Eccles (although with an elevation of 168m it hardly deserves to be called a mountain) is an extinct volcano with lava caves, channels and a crater lake set in rugged, stony country; there used to be a quarry here and you can see the various layers of different lava flows where the mountain has been cut. **Lake Surprise** is the delightful crater lake, shimmering blue in summer. **Walks** – all of which begin from the picnic ground at the end of the entrance road – include a two-kilometre stroll around the rim of the crater, or you can descend and walk around the shoreline (with a chance to swim in the lake); there's also a two-hour walk along a lava canal leading to a cave. **Birdlife** is prolific here, the trees are loaded with koalas and there are lots of eastern grey kangaroos. Mid- to late spring is a good time for **wild flowers** – from orchids to native geraniums – and wattle. Look out for a tree in the southwest corner of the park that has had an Aboriginal shield cut out of it with a sharpened stone tool. You can **camp** in the park: there are toilets, hot showers, picnic tables and fireplaces (BYO wood; $14 per site per night; bookings required, ☎03/5576 1338).

Portland to Nelson

PORTLAND, the last stop on the Victoria coast going west on the Princes Highway, is an important industrial and fishing port. Portland likes to describe itself as the "Birthplace of Victoria". Indeed, there are quite a few historic buildings, but unlike Port Fairy, they don't add up to form a coherent, captivating townscape. **Nelson,** a friendly fishing village further west, or **Port Fairy** make for more atmospheric overnight stops on the coast route between Melbourne and Adelaide. The rugged coastal scenery to the southwest around Cape Nelson and Cape Bridgewater, however, is not to be missed.

Portland

If you want to learn what makes Portland tick, the comprehensive tour of the port and the Portland aluminium smelter at Point Danger, 5km from the foreshore, is well worth taking (dep. Mon, Wed and Fri at the Visitor Information centre; 2hr 30min–3hr; free but reservations necessary ☎1800 035 567). Portland Bay is the only deepwater port between Melbourne and Adelaide, and the **Port of Portland**, privately owned since 1996, transfers more than four million tonnes of goods per year, primarily grain and timber from the region.

At its inception, the **Portland aluminium smelter** had to contend with some local resistance, partly because of environmental concerns, partly because its proposed location at Point Danger comprised sites of cultural and spiritual significance to the local Aboriginal people, the Gunditj Mara. The construction finally went ahead and the smelter began operations in 1986, but Alcoa was forced to pay the Gunditj Mara compensation which they used to buy back land in the area of the Lake Condah Mission (see p.996). In the Nineties the smelter, nowadays jointly owned by the US-based firm Alcoa and Chinese and Japanese interests, developed the concept of a "smelter in the park". This entailed rehabilitation of parkland in the buffer zone around, and revegetation of areas within the smelter complex; the creation of wetlands and a rigorous waste minimisation programme aiming for zero waste entering landfill.

Back in town, the small **Maritime Discovery Centre** (admission $5; same hours as the visitor information centre) extends to the back of the information centre (see below) on the foreshore down from Bentinck Street. Its centrepiece is the skeleton of a 5.7m Great White Shark, caught eight miles west of Cape Bridgewater in 1982, the rest of the small collection a motley assemblage of boat-building tools, memorabilia of Life Saving Clubs, photos and information about local marine wildlife and the history of whaling and the port – but strangely, nothing of note on the Koori people who had lived in the region for a long time prior to white settlement.

A restored and modified vintage **cable tram** (daily 10am–4pm; $12) transports sightseers along the foreshore on a round trip of 7.5km, from the depot at Henty Park past the **Powerhouse Vintage Car Museum** with a good collection of vintage cars and motorbikes, mainly from the early to mid-1900s (daily 10am–4pm plus weekends during school holidays; $5) to **Fawthrop Lagoon** with plenty of water birds, including pelicans, then back through the **Botanic Gardens**, past the Maritime Discovery Centre to a World War II memorial lookout tower, and back the same route.

If you feel like walking, you can follow the **Historic Buildings Trail** (the visitor information centre has a brochure) which starts at the former Customs House in Cliff Street (near the southern end of Bentinck Street) and follows the grid of main streets in the CBD. There are about 200 nineteenth-century buildings in Portland, most of them bluestone houses of one or two storeys, and some weatherboard cottages. Apart from the **Old Town Hall** on Cliff Street which now serves as a small history centre and genealogical research centre (daily 10am–12noon; 2pm–4pm; $4; ⓣ03/5522 2266), they are now occupied by local businesses or are used as private residences.

Out of town, along the coast to the southwest around craggy **Cape Nelson** and stormy **Cape Bridgewater**, the scenery is stunning: caves, freshwater lakes close to the cliff coast, blowholes, a petrified forest of limestone columns where ancient trees used to stand, and the beach at **Bridgewater Bay**, which extends in a wide, sandy arc from one cape to the other. The best way to explore these features is along the walking tracks that start from the car park near the blowholes, signposted left off the road to Cape Bridgewater. Bring good walking shoes – the volcanic rocks can be very sharp – and food and drink. **Seal Point** at Cape Bridgewater is home to about 850 **fur seals**. Seals by the Sea tours (45min; $25) can be booked at the Beach Café and Information Centre (ⓣ03/5526 7155) at Bridgewater Bay. The licensed café is open daily for breakfast and lunch, Fri and Sat also for dinner.

Practicalities

The **visitor information centre**, part of the Maritime Discovery Centre (daily 9am–5pm; ⓣ03/5523 2671 or 1800 035 567, ⓦwww.portlandnow.net.au), has tourist pamphlets and maps galore, and the staff are happy to advise on local attractions, driving routes and the Great Southwest Walk which begins and ends in Portland (see opposite).

The Eumeralla War and Lake Condah Mission

Before the Southwest was permanently settled by whites, **clashes** between whalers and Aborigines resulted in massacres and the decimation of an entire tribe. The first squatters in Victoria, the Hentys, came to the Portland area in 1834 to pasture sheep on vast landholdings, and they too soon came into conflict with the Koories – from 1838 clans began to use their traditional burning-off process in an attempt to drive the Hentys away. During the 1840s a sustained guerrilla war, known as the **Eumeralla War**, was fought against settlers occupying land around Port Fairy, Mount Napier and Lake Condah. In the end it was only the deployment of the Aboriginal Native Police Corps in 1842 that finally broke the resistance – and even they took four years.

In 1867, a mission was established at **Lake Condah**, traditional Aboriginal lands with plentiful game and fish about 50km northeast of Portland, on the western edge of Mount Eccles. Surviving Aborigines were brought here but were forbidden to speak their own language or practise their culture. At its height in 1880 there were over twenty buildings of timber and stone. Although the mission was officially closed in 1919, a large community remained until the 1950s, when they were gradually dispossessed as land was given to returned World War II soldiers under the soldier settlement scheme. Perhaps the greatest injustice occurred when several Aboriginal returned soldiers, who had lived on Lake Condah, applied for land, only to be refused. With the money paid in settlement of the dispute about the location of the Alcoa smelter, Lake Condah was finally bought back in the 1980s.

There might be **guided tours** of the mission and the remnants of Gunditj Mara culture – call the Budj-Bim Tour and Hospitality Co at ⓣ03/5527 1699 or 0419 271 634.

For **accommodation**, there are lots of motels and a few B&Bs. At the more affordable end there are *Admella Motel,* 5 Otway Court, (ⓣ03/5523 3347, ⓕ03/5523 3589; ❹), with the standard mod cons you'd expect in a motel, and *Clifftop Accommodation B&B*, 13 Clifton Court (ⓣ03/5523 5100, ⓦwww.portland.au.com; ❹) with three spacious, light-filled rooms with ensuite and balconies overlooking Portland Bay; one room also has cooking facilities. Both are within walking distance of Percy Street, the central shopping strip.

At the southern end of the esplanade (Bentinck Street) is a cluster of **eating** options from where you can look out over the water and across to the busy port. Two notable ones are the very reasonably priced *Sully's Café and Wine Bar* at no. 55 and at no.79, *Kokopelli's,* a cool juice bar and café serving tapas, lunches and dinners. A few more eateries can be found at the main shopping strip (Percy Street) behind Bentinck Street. *Glenelg Adventure Services* at 67 Bentinck St ⓣ03/5523 7646) can kit you out for the Great Southwest Walk and other activities in the region: they sell camping accessories, all sorts of gear as well as bikes and canoes. **Internet** access is available at the library in Bentinck St (closed Wed).

Lower Glenelg National Park and Nelson

From Portland, the Princes Highway makes its uneventful way, via Heywood, to Mount Gambier in South Australia. After 120km it crosses the **Glenelg River** (which has its source in the Grampians) at Dartmoor, a popular point to begin a four-day canoeing trip down to the river's mouth at Nelson; ask about canoe rental at the Nelson Parks & Visitor Information Centre (see below). For most of the journey, the clear blue river flows through the unspoilt **Lower Glenelg National Park** in a sixty-kilometre gorge cut through limestone. The **Princess Margaret Rose Cave** (guided tours daily at 10am, 11am, noon, then hourly from 1.30pm to 4.30pm; $9.50; ⓣ08/8738 4171), a huge chamber of actively growing stalactites, stalagmites and other limestone formations, is the main cave in an extended system of limestone caves and the only one which is open to the public. It lies beside the river as it loops round by the South Australian border. It can be reached by canoe, car (unsealed roads from both sides of the border lead to the caves) or on a cruise from Nelson (see below).

NELSON, at the end of the coastal road and virtually on the Victoria/South Australia border, is well worth an overnight stay. A peaceful, friendly little hamlet, it feels caught in a time warp, and there's little to do but wander along the coast, read on the beach, and **fish** or **canoe** on the Glenelg. *Paestan Boat Hire*, 2km out of town on the Nelson–Winnap road (daily 8.30am–6pm; ⓣ03/5528 1481) and *Nelson Boat & Canoe Hire* on Kellet Street (daily 8.30am–6pm; ⓣ08/8738 4048) rent out canoes and kayaks. The latter also sells bait; you'll need a fishing licence, obtained from the Nelson Kiosk (daily 8am–6pm; ⓣ08/8738 4220), the local service station or post office. Fishing shelters line the river. Glenelg River Cruises on Old Bridge Road operates **cruises** to the Princess Margaret Rose Caves (daily in peak sesaon, other times Sat & Sun and on some weekdays; departs 1pm; 4hr; $22.50; ⓣ08/8738 4191, ⓦwww.glenelgrivercruises.com.au).

The **Nelson Parks & Visitor Information Centre** (daily 9am–5pm; ⓣ08/8738 4051, ⓦwww.parkweb.vic.gov.au) is signposted just off Leake Street; it also covers the Discovery Bay Coastal Park, which protects the shoreline almost all the way from Portland to the border. Here you can get camping permits for this and the Lower Glenelg National Park (book in advance in peak season) and information on walks and activities. *Ambience* is a new gallery/café/bar north of the highway on the Isle of Bags road (Mon–Tues & Thurs 10am–6pm, Fri & Sat 10am–8pm); very inexpensive counter meals are served at the one-storey *Nelson Hotel* on Kellet Street, a classic and untouristy pub that also has budget **rooms** (ⓣ08/8738 4011; ❸). Other cheap accommodation options include *Casuarina Cabins*, North Nelson Rd (ⓣ08/8738 4105; ❸); *Nelson Cottage B&B* on the corner of Kellet and Sturt streets (ⓣ08/8738 4161; ❸); *Kywong Caravan Park* on North Nelson Road (ⓣ08/8738 4174), which has cheap cabins (❷); and the four-bunk cabins at the *Margaret Rose Caves Campground* (ⓣ08/8738 4171; cold water only & BYO linen; ❷).

Central Victoria: the Goldfields

Central Victoria is classic Victoria: a rich pastoral district, chilly and green in winter and parched a brownish yellow in summer. Two grand provincial cities, **Ballarat** and **Bendigo**, whose fine buildings were funded by gold, draw large numbers of visitors, while, by contrast, the area's other centres such as **Maryborough** and **Castlemaine**, once prosperous gold towns in their own right, now seem too small for their extravagant architecture.

There's fairly good **transport** from Melbourne with regular V/Line trains and buses to Bendigo, Ballarat and the other major centres in the Goldfields, and a few local buses fill some gaps. However, as elsewhere in the state, your own transport is a big advantage. The easiest way to tour is to follow the **Goldfields Tourist Route**, whose chocolate-brown signs are marked by a distinctive circled capital G. The route links the major cities and towns – Bendigo, Castlemaine, Ballarat, Ararat and Stawell – with many smaller places in between.

Towards the Goldfields: the Calder Highway

Though you could take the Western Freeway or the train directly to Ballarat, the route along the **CALDER HIGHWAY** towards Bendigo, 150km northwest of Melbourne, is much more interesting. The railway to Bendigo, which continues to Swan Hill, follows the same route, calling at the main towns.

At Diggers Rest, 22km from Melbourne on the highway, a short detour to the east will take you to the tiny **Organ Pipes National Park** (Mon–Fri 8.30am–4.30pm, Sat & Sun & public holidays until 6pm), designated a national park for its outstanding geological interest. The rock formations here form a series of basalt columns, created by lava cooling in an ancient riverbed, and rising up to 20m above Jacksons Creek. The park can be explored along walking tracks and has picnic areas with tables. Back on the highway you'll come to **Gisborne**, 50km from Melbourne, developed as a coaching town for travellers on their way to the Bendigo and Castlemaine goldfields; it's dominated by **Mount Macedon**, an extinct thousand-metre volcano.

Fifteen kilometres or so from Gisborne, **Woodend** is a friendly, buzzing place with antique shops and cafés lined up along the main street, and also the jumping-off point for the **Hanging Rock Reserve**, 6km northeast (daily

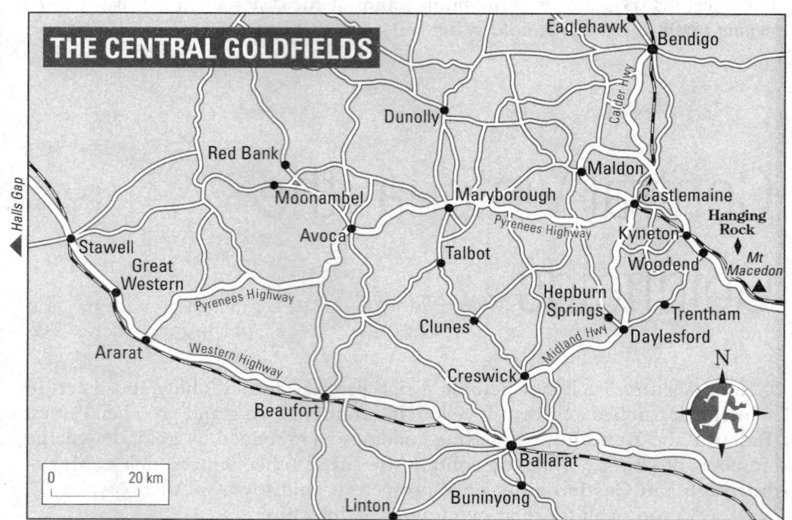

The goldrushes

The California goldrushes of the 1840s captured the popular imagination around the world with tales of the huge fortunes to be made gold-prospecting, and it wasn't long until Australia's first goldrush took place – near Bathurst in New South Wales in 1851. Victoria had been a separate colony for only nine days when gold was found at Clunes on July 10, 1851; the **goldrush** began in earnest when rich deposits were found in Ballarat nine months later. The richest goldfields ever known soon opened at Bendigo, and thousands poured into Victoria from around the world. In the golden decade of the 1850s, Victoria's population increased from eighty thousand to half a million, half of whom remained permanently in the state. The British and Irish made up a large proportion of the new population, but over forty thousand Chinese came to make their fortune too, along with experienced American gold-seekers and other nationalities such as Russians, Finns and Filipinos. Ex-convicts and native-born Australians also poured in, leaving other colonies short of workers; even respectable policemen deserted their posts to become "diggers", and doctors, lawyers and prostitutes crowded into the haphazard new towns in their wake.

In the beginning, the fortune-seekers panned the creeks and rivers searching for **alluvial gold**, constantly moving on at the news of another find. But gold was also deep within the earth, where ancient riverbeds had been buried by volcanoes; in Ballarat in 1852 the first **shafts** were dug, and because the work was unsafe and arduous, the men joined in bands of eight or ten, usually grouped by nationality, working a common claim. For deep mining, diggers stayed in one place for months or years, and the major workings rapidly became stable communities with banks, shops, hotels, churches and theatres, evolving more gradually, on the back of income from gold, into grandiose towns.

8am–6pm; $8 per car). The rock became famous because of the eerie 1975 film *Picnic at Hanging Rock*, about a group of schoolgirls who mysteriously go missing here after a picnic – a story which many people falsely believed to be true. More about that story, as well as scientific information about the geological history of the rock, can be gleaned from the displays in the new Hanging Rock Discovery Centre at its base; adjacent to it is a licensed café and a gift shop. You can walk around the base of the rock or climb to the summit with its massive boulders and crags in around an hour.

KYNETON, 15km further north, features **Piper Street**, a colourful strip lined with several fine historic bluestone buildings and the **Botanic Gardens**, scenically located above the Campaspe River, but the town lacks Woodend's inviting, friendly buzz.

Bendigo

Rich alluvial gold was first discovered in **BENDIGO** in 1851, and, once the initial fields were exhausted, shafts were sunk into a gold-bearing quartz reef. Bendigo became the greatest goldfield of the time, and had the world's deepest mine. Mining continued here until 1954, long after the rest of central Victoria's goldfields were exhausted, so it's a city that has developed over a prosperous century: the nationwide department store Myer began here, as did Australia's first building society in 1858. Although in many ways more magnificent than Ballarat, Bendigo is considerably lower-key. Its most visited sights are legacies of the mining days – the **Chinese Joss House** and the **Central Deborah Mine**.

Arrival, information and transport

Bendigo Airport Service provides a link to Melbourne's Tullamarine Airport (3 daily; $35 one way; booking essential on ⓣ03/5447 9006). V/Line **trains** and **buses** arrive at the train station on Railway Place, just south of the CBD, while Greyhound Australia buses stop at the Caltex service station in Golden Square, at the corner of High and Oak streets.

The **visitor information centre** on Pall Mall (daily 9am–5pm; ⓣ03/5444 4445 or 1800 813 153, ⓦwww.bendigotourism.com) has a free accommodation booking service and provides lots of brochures and maps, including the free *Bendigo Visitor Guide* booklet, complete with walking map. Wanting to give Bendigo a sophisticated air reminiscent of London, the newly prosperous citizens called its central crossroads **Charing Cross**. Pall Mall runs off to the east, while View Street, with many fine old buildings, climbs north off Pall Mall. Mitchell Street leads south to the **train station** and High Street (the Calder Highway) is the main exit west out of the city. The other important street is Hargreaves, parallel to Pall Mall one block south, with its impressive town hall and a revamped shopping mall. A good way to get an overall impression of the place is to take the **Vintage Talking Tram Tour** (daily 10am–3pm; daylight saving until 4pm; departures every hour, from the Central Deborah Goldmine; 1hr; $12.90). The tram tour ticket includes entrance to the **Bendigo Tram Museum**, located on Hargreaves Street at the opposite end of the route. **Buses** leave from the corner of Mitchell and Hargreaves streets and charge a flat fare of $1.65, valid for two hours.

Accommodation

In terms of atmosphere and style, the **B&B guesthouses** and **cottages** throughout Bendigo and the whole goldfields area are a much better option than the average, somewhat sterile motel room.

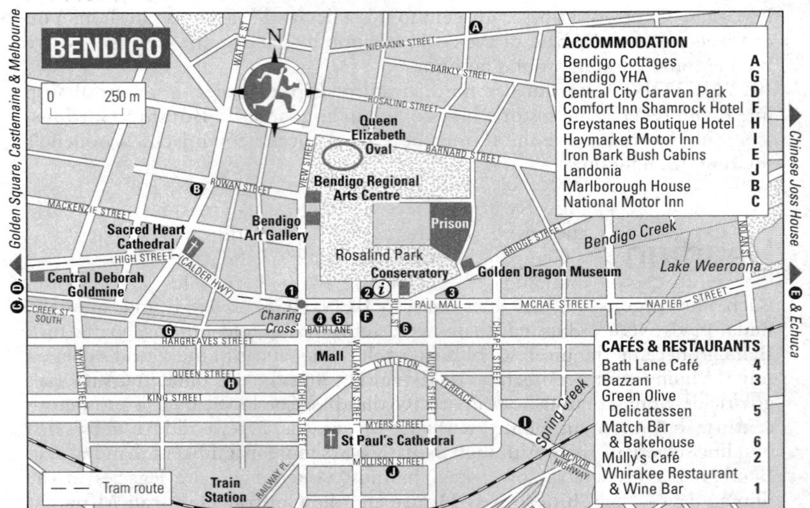

Bendigo Cottages Cnr of Niemann and Anderson streets ⓣ03/5441 5613, ⓦwww.innhouse.com.au/bendigocottages.html. B&B in two small, self-contained, charming weatherboard cottages. ❹

Bendigo YHA 33 Creek St South ⓣ03/5443 7680, ⓔbendigo@yhavic.org.au. Small, pleasant hostel right in the centre of town with dorms ($19), and two twin and two family rooms. Open fire in the lounge, and Internet access. ❷

Central City Caravan Park 362 High St, Golden Square ⓣ03/5443 6937, ⓕ5443 5605. Small caravan park with a new amenities block and a pool. Handy location 2.5 km southwest of the CBD; plus there's a bus stop to town just outside. En-suite cabins ❸

Comfort Inn Shamrock Hotel Cnr of Pall Mall and Williamson St ⓣ03/5443 0333, ⓕ5442 4494. Fabulous Victorian hotel that has a wide range of accommodation, from budget-priced rooms to executive suites. ❹–❻

Greystanes Boutique Hotel 57 Queen St ⓣ03/5442 2466, ⓦwww.greystanesmanor.com.au. Centrally located, beautifully appointed rooms in an elegant Victorian mansion with separate bar/lounge and open fires. ❻

Haymarket Motor Inn 5 McIvor Highway ⓣ03/5441 5654, ⓕ5441 5655. Ultramodern motel with a swimming pool and sauna, plus one accessible unit for disabled visitors. ❺

Iron Bark Bush Cabins Watson St ⓣ03/5448 3344. Self-contained cabins, also on a share basis for backpackers (bed $20), in a bushland setting a few kilometres out of town. Linen is supplied and there are cooking facilities and a licensed bar. Activity options include horse riding (trail rides from $30/hr) and a water slide ($8 for 10 rides). ❷

Landonia 87 Mollison St ⓣ03/5442 2183, ⓦwww.visitvictoria.com. A centrally located B&B in a Federation-style home, with separate guest entrance and an open fireplace in the lounge. ❺

Marlborough House 115 Wattle St ⓣ03/5441 4142, ⓦwww.marlboroughhouse.com.au. B&B in a goldrush-era mansion near the Sacred Heart cathedral, with stained-glass windows, marble fireplaces and a covered balcony. ❹

National Motor Inn 186 High St, 1km southwest, opposite the Central Deborah mine. ⓣ03/5441 5777. Decent motel with pool and spa as well as a bar and bistro. Units ❹–❻, suite ❼

The City

At the heart of Bendigo is the vast **Rosalind Park**, and three important religious buildings constructed with money from gold-digging – All Saints Church, St Pauls Cathedral and **Sacred Heart Cathedral**. Local Catholics imported stonemasons from Italy and England, and their craftsmanship can be seen in the design and details of Sacred Heart, begun in 1897 in English Gothic style. The interior has beautiful woodcarvings of the Twelve Apostles, and the crypt is the burial place of local bishops (daily 9am–5pm).

Many of Bendigo's finest goldrush buildings are along **Pall Mall**, including the law courts (1896) and the ornate Italianate (1887) edifice which now houses the visitor information centre – neither of which would seem out of place in a capital city. The amazingly decorative **Shamrock Hotel** stands opposite, four storeys of Victorian gold-boom architecture at its most extreme. **View Street**, climbing the hill beside Rosalind Park, has a few more elaborate goldrush buildings. The **Bendigo Regional Arts Centre** here is a massive Neoclassical pile, joined to the much more homely red-brick fire station that now serves as the Community Arts Centre. The **Art Gallery**, in another beautifully restored nineteenth-century building at no. 42 (daily 10am–5pm; gold coin donation ($1 or $2) appreciated), has an extensive collection of Australian painting from Bendigo's goldfield days to the present, as well as nineteenth-century British and European art acquired with all that gold. Several antique shops, restaurants and bars add to the arty feel of the street. The **Queen Elizabeth Oval**, with its old red-brick stadium, backs onto Rosalind Park, and you can watch Aussie Rules football here on winter weekends.

Bridge Street, one of the oldest in Bendigo, was once **Chinatown**, home to the Chinese who came by the thousands in the 1850s and who knew Bendigo as *dai gum san* ("big gold mountain"); when the gold ran out, many turned to market gardening in the area. Until as late as the 1960s old shops sporting faded Chinese signs were still in evidence, but now Chinese customs and ways of life are best seen in the **Golden Dragon Museum and Classical Chinese Gardens** on Bridge Street (daily 9.30am–5pm; $7), where there is an impressive collection of Chinese processional regalia including what are supposed to be the world's longest and oldest Imperial dragons, Sun Loong and Loong. An exhibition tells the full story of Bendigo's Chinese community since the days of the goldrush, whilst the attached gardens feature a temple to the goddess Kuan Yin. The National Trust-operated **Joss House**, on Finn Street in North Bendigo (daily 10am–5pm; $3), was built by the Chinese in the 1860s and is the oldest Chinese temple still in use in Australia. The route to the shrine passes man-made Lake Weeroona, whose picnic grounds are the setting for the lovely *Boardwalk Restaurant & Café* (daily 7am till late) in an old Chinese teahouse. To get to the Joss House, take bus #7 (approximately hourly Mon–Fri).

The Central Deborah Goldmine

The **Central Deborah Goldmine**, at the corner of Violet Street and the Calder Highway (daily 9am–5pm; Ⓦwww.central-deborah.com) was the last mine in the Central Goldfields to close. Exploring the area above ground is free: you can wander about and take a look at the engine room with its steam-driven air compressor. You can also see a room set up like a modest miner's house from the 1840s, a model of the mine itself, and a museum installed in the old changing rooms.

The sixty-minute underground **Mine Experience Tour** (6 times daily 10.10am–4pm; 11 times daily during school holidays; $16.90) is worth taking if you've never been down in a mine; everybody is issued with a reassuring hard hat, complete with torch and generator. You go down to a depth of 60m in a lift, which takes 85 seconds – it would take thirty minutes to reach the bottom of some of the deepest shafts. The further down you go the hotter it gets, but at 60m it's quite warm and airless, dripping with water and muddy underfoot. If you want to scramble around the mine a bit longer, climb ladders, perhaps operate a drill, you can join a longer **Underground Adventure** which also includes a meal (Morning Crib 9.30am–noon, Afternoon Crib 2.30–5pm, both $50; Lunch Tour noon–2pm, $58) For bookings, call Ⓣ03/5443 8322 or see the website.

Eating, drinking and nightlife

The town offers a fairly good choice when it comes to eating and drinking, and there's plenty of student-influenced nightlife during term time. Entertainment facilities at the LaTrobe University campus are open to all – call Ⓣ03/5444 7988 to find out what's happening. Several pubs have **bands** playing on Friday and Saturday nights, including the *Old Crown Hotel* at 238 Hargreaves St and *The Vine* at 135 King St, which also has an open-stage night on Mondays. Of the **Irish bars** in town, the Celtic-run *Brian Boru* on McIvor Road is by far the best, serving up decent Guinness and real Irish *craic* without the four-leaved clovers, while the *Shamrock Hotel* may not be Irish but is certainly popular for balcony drinking in the late afternoon. A young crowd congregates at the *Rifle Brigade Hotel* at 137 View St, a brewery pub with great food and beer and a wrought-iron verandah.

Bath Lane Café 13 Bath Lane. Local artwork is featured on the brightly painted walls and they serve good coffee, excellent breakfast, soups and other tasty snacks. Mon–Sat 7am–late.

Bazzani Howard Place Ⓣ03/5441 3777. Cosy restaurant at the end of the mall, renowned state-wide for the interesting, aesthetic and downright tasty dishes on the menu. Licensed. Daily noon–late.

Green Olive Delicatessen 11 Bath Lane. Fantastically cosy Italian-run café with outdoor seating, serving excellent coffee and desserts as well as gourmet deli fare to go. Open daily.
Match Bar & Bakehouse 58 Bull St. Stylish café-restaurant with lots of pasta, focaccia and pizza. Dinner daily, lunch daily except Sat.
Mully's Cafe and Colonial Bank Gallery 32 Pall Mall. In a grand, historic bank building from the 1880s, with an art gallery upstairs, this place has good breakfasts, brunches and afternoon teas. Licensed or BYO. Mon–Fri 7.30am–5pm, Sat & Sun from 8.30am.
Shamrock Hotel Café Cnr Pall Mall and Williamson St. This café-restaurant in the lovely, refurbished former public bar serves good breakfasts (home-baked bread) and has interesting, mainly modern Australian cuisine for lunch and dinner. Open daily.
Whirakee Restaurant and Wine Bar 17 View Point, at the beginning of View St, opposite the fountain ⓣ03/5441 5557. By now an old-timer, but still serving outstanding modern cuisine, with an excellent wine list. Lunch Wed–Fri, dinner Tues–Sat.

Castlemaine and around

CASTLEMAINE, 39 km southwest of Bendigo, is at the centre of the area once known as the Mount Alexander Goldfields. Between 1851 and 1861, when its gullies were among the richest in the world, 105,000kg of gold were found here (modest quantities are still found at Wattle Gully mine at nearby Chewton, the oldest working gold mine in Australia). Castlemaine became the headquarters of the Government Camp for the area in 1852, and its impressive buildings were built during the following ten years. With no deep mines to sustain it, however, Castlemaine has developed little since then. Some 19km northwest of Castlemaine lies the quaint, small historic town of **Maldon**.

Information and accommodation

The very helpful **Castlemaine Visitor Information Centre** is in the Market Building on Mostyn Street (daily 9am–5pm; ⓣ03/5470 6200 or 1800 171 888, ⓦwww.maldoncastlemaine.com) and can arrange accommodation in the area.

Places to stay include *Campbell Street Motor Lodge* at 33 Campbell St (ⓣ03/5472 2377; ❹), which has motel-style rooms in a historic, National Trust-listed house. The late-Victorian *Clevedon Manor* is centrally located at 260 Barker St (ⓣ03/5472 5212, ⓔclevedon@netcon.net.au; ❺), whereas the *Claremont Coach-House*, Burnett Rd (ⓣ03/5472 2281; ❺) provides accommodation in a double-storey stone cottage, 3km north of the CBD near the Botanic Gardens. Nearby, *Castlemaine Gardens Caravan Park*, on Doran Avenue, off Walker Street (ⓣ03/5472 1125; cabins ❷), is ideally located next to the open-air swimming pool (Dec–March only).

The Town

The town's finest building is the **Old Castlemaine Market** on Mostyn Street, a wonderfully over-the-top piece of Neoclassical architecture. The **Theatre Royal** on Hargraves Street, one of the oldest theatres in Australia, is also quite magnificent; it's said that when the famous Lola Montez performed here, miners threw nuggets of gold at her in appreciation. It's now a **cinema** (ⓣ03/5472 1196) incorporating a cabaret-style section and a licensed bistro downstairs, and more traditional movie-house seating upstairs. Theatre groups and live bands sometimes perform here, and there's even a sporadic disco.

Another unusual attraction, a short distance from the centre, is **Buda**, at 42 Hunter St (daily 9am–5pm; $7), a gracious nineteenth-century home and garden originally built in 1861 by a retired Baptist missionary in the style of an Indian villa. It was added to by its subsequent owner Ernest Leviny, a Hungarian silversmith, in the 1890s. The house and gardens give an insight into the good life enjoyed in the goldrush days, and much work by Leviny and his family is on display, including lampshades, carved woodhangings and embroidery made by his daughters, as well as early photography and the family's art and silverware collection. The **Castlemaine Art Gallery and Museum** on Lyttleton Street (Mon–Fri 10am–5pm, Sat & Sun noon–5pm; $5) is also worth a visit. It specializes in Australian photographs and paintings, featuring many works by the Heidelberg School, notably Frederick McCubbin and Tom Roberts. Partly because of the big **Castlemaine State Festival** which takes place over ten days in early April in odd-numbered years, this is quite an arty place, and there are several other galleries around town. In odd-numbered years lots of gardens in the Castlemaine district open their doors to visitors during the **Festival of Gardens**, which takes place during the Melbourne Cup week in November.

If you're here on a Saturday, trek the 2km out along the Melbourne Road to **Wesley Hill Market**, a giant flea market selling local produce and crafts (7am–1pm). Another tourist attraction is the **Dingo Farm** (daily, but call to confirm times and prices on ⓣ03/5470 5711) between Castlemaine and Chewton, where around a hundred dingoes are kept in fenced-in enclosures on bushland; signs along the Pyrenees Highway will direct you there.

Eating and drinking

Food in Castlemaine is excellent, with a wide variety of places to choose from. The best café is *Saff's* at 64 Mostyn St (daily 8am–late), which serves great breakfasts, smoothies and other feelgood fodder, and hosts special night-time events, including recitals and poetry readings, as well as live jazz most Sunday afternoons. *Togs Place* (breakfast and lunch daily; dinner Fri & Sat; booking recommended; ⓣ03/5470 5090) at 58 Lyttleton St provides good café-style food in a peaceful atmosphere, and has a courtyard where you can sit out in summer. The licensed *Globe Restaurant*, 81 Forest St (ⓣ03/5470 5171), also has a courtyard and an attached cheaper bistro serving a seasonally varied menu. The newest kid on the block is the hip *Fuel Restaurant* at 113 Mostyn St (Mon–Fri from 5pm, Sat and Sun 4pm; ⓣ03/5470 5000), dishing out an eclectic range of meals. It's fully licensed too. Or go for scrumptious pub meals at the *Criterion Hotel*, 163 Barker St, or the *Railway Hotel* at 65 Gingell St. Both have live music on weekends.

Maldon

MALDON, closely surrounded by low hills, is a tiny, peaceful town of quirky shops and a few B&Bs, a popular weekend getaway where you can simply relax and unwind. In 1965 the National Trust declared it the best-preserved gold-era settlement in Victoria. Gold was found here in 1853 and the rich, deep alluvial reefs were mined until 1926. The main shopping street largely preserves its original appearance, with single-storey shopfronts shaded by awnings and decorated with iron-lace work. Apart from the town's shops, cafés and architecture, there aren't many other points of interest, though you can take an underground tour at the stunning candlelit **Carman's Tunnel Goldmine**, off Parkin's Reef Road, 3km south of town (Sat, Sun, school & public holidays; tours depart every 30min between 1.30–4pm; 25min; $5).

During the long weekend before the Melbourne Cup (first weekend of November), things get a bit busier than usual as people head to town for the four-day **Maldon Folk Festival** (Ⓦwww.maldonfolkfestival.com). Since its inception in 1973 the event has steadily grown, and apart from traditional folk, it also features blues, bluegrass and world music as well as some theatre and dance. The main performance space is at the Tarrangower Reserve at the base of Mount Tarrangower, just out of town, but throughout the weekend there are also lots of things happening in town itself where you can listen for free. The weekend ticket for the festival is about $80 and includes bushcamping at the Tarrangower Reserve; a day ticket (Sunday only) is $35. Discounted "early bird" tickets are available two months in advance.

Practicalities

Public transport from Melbourne runs to Maldon on weekdays only and to a very limited timetable; take a train from Melbourne (Mon–Fri 8.40am & 3.50pm) to Castlemaine where you catch the connecting private Castlemaine Bus Lines service to Maldon. Return buses leave from Maldon post office to connect with trains back to Melbourne (Mon–Fri 9am and 4.40pm; to confirm call Ⓣ03/5472 1455). The Victorian Goldfields Railway, a tourist **steam train** (or diesel locomotive on days of total fire ban) runs between Maldon and Castlemaine (Sun, also Wed & Sat during school holidays and more frequently during the summer holidays; single trip $18; Ⓦwww.vgr.com.au).

For information on the town, check with the **Maldon Visitor Information Centre** in the Shire Gardens, High Street (daily 9am–5pm; Ⓣ03/5475 2569, Ⓦwww.maldoncastlemaine.com).

Places to **stay** include *Mount Hawke of Maldon B&B*, 24 Adair St (Ⓣ03/5475 1192, Ⓦwww.mounthawke.com.au; ❹), a cosy guesthouse, and the *Heritage Cottages*, 25 Adair St (Ⓣ03/5475 1094, Ⓦwww.heritagecottages.com.au; ❼), a selection of ten historical cottages, most with period furnishings and open fires. More affordable yet still a treat are *Agatha Panthers Cottages*, about 3km north-west of the town centre, near the Nuggetty Ranges (Ⓣ03/5475 1066, Ⓦwww.apcottages.com.au; ❹).

Eating places include *Café Maldon* at 52 Main St and *Berryman's Café* in an old bowling alley at 30 Main St. *McArthur's Coffee & Books*, further up at no. 43, has a very pleasant courtyard and also sells new and secondhand books (Wed–Sat 8.30am–5pm). The *Penny School Gallery Café* (daily 10am–5pm) further out at 11 Church St is a delightful place for a coffee, lunch or afternoon tea, after checking out the current exhibition at the gallery.

Maryborough and around

MARYBOROUGH was relatively late getting on the gold bandwagon – the first find here was in 1853, but it didn't take long to exploit it. The town, 47km west of Castlemaine on the Pyrenees Highway, is now a large, solid and rather dull country place, interesting only for remnants of architecture far too pompous for this quiet setting. When Mark Twain visited Maryborough he described it as a train station with a town attached. Nowadays the grandiose, renovated **Maryborough Railway Station** houses an **Antiques Emporium** and a café (daily except Tues 10am–5.30pm); a flour mill from the 1880s at the corner of Inkerman and Albert streets is now the **Flour Mill Gallery** which exhibits quality timber furniture and other arts and crafts. The Civic Centre at the heart of town is a classic nineteenth-century square with an elegant post office and gracious town hall and courthouse. For more information and accommodation bookings, turn to the **Central Goldfields Information Centre** at the Maryborough Resource Centre, corner of Nolan and Alma streets, just behind High Street (daily 9am–5pm; ⓣ03/5460 4511 or 1800 356 511, ⓦwww.centralgoldfields.com.au).

The *Bull & Mouth Hotel* at 119 High St (ⓣ03/5461 1002; ❸) has inexpensive pub **accommodation** and the bistro downstairs serves equally inexpensive **meals** (Tues–Sat); for B&B accommodation try *Bella's Country House*, 39 Burns St (ⓣ03/5460 5574; ⓦwww.weekendretreats.com.au/bellas/default.htm; ❹).

Twenty-one kilometres north of Maryborough is **DUNOLLY**, an attractive town filled with many distinctive old buildings and with kurrajong trees lining the main street. The goldfields here produced more nuggets than any in Australia, including the largest ever found: the 65-kilogram "Welcome Stranger" nugget, found in 1869 by two Cornish miners just 3cm below the surface as they were working around the roots of a tree, and valued at £10,000. Fourteen kilometres south of Maryborough, **TALBOT** is a tiny settlement consisting of little more than a pub and a corner store. It's hard to believe now that the town once had 56 hotels and a population of 33,000. Every third Sunday of the month, people congregate here to buy fresh produce at the **Talbot Farmers Market** (10am–2pm).

AVOCA, 26km southwest of Maryborough on the Pyrenees Highway, was another rich source of alluvial gold, and today boasts a collection of nineteenth-century buildings, including a chemist's shop established in 1854 and believed to be the oldest in Victoria. These days, the area around Avoca, known as the **Pyrenees region**, is increasingly known for its **vineyards**. A cluster of them is located in or near Moonambel, a hamlet 17km northwest of Avoca: one to aim for is the *Warrenmang Vineyard & Resort* on Mountain Creek Road (daily 9am–5pm; ⓣ03/5467 2233, ⓦwww.bazzani.com.au), which has a picturesque setting, an excellent restaurant, and offers resort-style accommodation in a homestead and timber lodges (dinner, bed and breakfast from $170 per person). Other well-known wineries in the area are Taltarni on Taltarni Rd, Moonambel (daily 10am–5pm; ⓦwww.taltarni.com.au) and Redbank, 18km north of Avoca (Mon–Sat 9am–5pm, Sun from 10am; ⓣ03/5467 7255, ⓦwww.sallyspaddock.com.au); they also do light lunches and rent out a cottage.

Daylesford and Hepburn Springs

The attractive, hilly country around Daylesford and Hepburn Springs is known as the "spa centre of Australia", with a hundred **mineral springs** within a fifty-kilometre radius. Daylesford grew from the Jim Crow gold diggings of 1851, but the large Swiss-Italian population here quickly realized the value of the water from the mineral springs, which had been bottled since 1850. People have been taking the waters at Hepburn Springs for almost as long – the spa complex was built in 1895. The new **Daylesford Visitor Information Centre**, servicing the whole area, is at 98 Vincent Street in Daylesford (daily 9am–5pm; ⓣ03/5348 1339); it has loads of brochures for the many places offering bed and breakfast and a board listing the vacancies at weekends, when places tend to fill up. V/Line has a direct **bus service** from Melbourne to Daylesford (Mon–Sat 2 daily, Sun 1 daily). Alternatively, Mon–Fri you can take a **train** from Melbourne to Ballarat and then transfer to a bus departing Ballarat in the early afternoon. This is the V/Line bus service between Geelong and Bendigo via Ballarat, Daylesford and Castlemaine (Mon–Fri 1 daily). For enquiries and bookings, phone ⓣ13 61 96 or go to ⓦwww.vline.com.au.

Daylesford

The town of **DAYLESFORD**, a popular weekend retreat for Melburnians, has a New Age, alternative atmosphere, with a large gay community. As a result, the town has several gay-friendly guesthouses, and on the second weekend in March it is the venue for **ChillOut**, Australia's largest rural gay and lesbian festival, featuring a street parade, music and cabaret, dance parties and a carnival at Victoria Park.

Daylesford's well-preserved Victorian and Edwardian streets rise up the side of Wombat Hill, where you'll find the Botanical Gardens, between Hill Street and Central Springs Road, whose lookout tower has panoramic views. Not far away, on the corner of Daly and Hill streets, is the **Convent Gallery** (daily 10am–5pm; $4), a rambling former convent that now has seven galleries selling high-quality arts, crafts and antiques, and a café and a bar. There's a great Sunday market (8am–2pm) just nearby, on the main road to Castlemaine. The town has "healing centres" aplenty; the spectrum of services ranges from natural therapies to the more esoteric, such as tarot readings – enquire at the visitor centre about a list.

Lake Daylesford, a short distance south from the town centre on Vincent Street, is the location of the Central Springs Reserve, which has several walking tracks and old-fashioned water pumps from which you can drink the mineral springs. The **Lake Daylesford Book Barn** here (open daily) is a picturesquely situated bookshop, with an extensive range of secondhand books. The charming *Boathouse Café* (breakfast & lunch daily, dinner Sat & Sun; ⓣ03/5348 1387) has lakeside dining, as well as dinghies, canoes and paddle-boats for rent. With your own transport there are two more options further afield: the **Lavandula Swiss Italian Farm** (daily 10.30am–5pm; $3) in nearby Shepherds Flat, 5km north of Hepburn Springs, where you can walk among the historic stone farmhouses, in the extensive gardens and lavender fields, and then have lunch or coffee and cake at *La Trattoria*, the farm's renowned Italian restaurant (ⓣ03/5476 4347); and **Tuki trout farm** (ⓣ03/5345 6233, ⓦwww.tuki.com.au) in Smeaton, 23km west of Daylesford via Creswick, where you can catch your own lunch and have it boned and cooked for you while you wait.

Practicalities

Internet access is available at the Hepburn Hub at the Neighbourhood House, 13 Camp St ($3 per 30min; Mon–Fri 9am–4pm) and at Daylesford Getaways, 123 Vincent St (Mon–Fri 9am–5pm).

Accommodation

You must book well in advance if you want **to stay** in Daylesford at the weekend. Bookings are handled by Daylesford Accommodation Booking Service (ⓣ03/5348 1448, ⓦwww.dabs.com.au), or try Daylesford Getaways (ⓣ03/5348 4422, ⓦwww.dayget.com.au).

35 Hill Street ⓣ03/5348 3878, ⓔjoanvdf@netconnect.com.au. Early Victorian brick cottage just below the Botanical Gardens, much-loved for its casual, friendly attitude. ❹

Ambleside on the Lake 15 Leggat St ⓣ03/5348 2691, ⓦwww.totaltravel.com.au/link.asp?fid=529887. Meticulously renovated Edwardian guesthouse overlooking Lake Daylesford. ❻

The Balconies 35 Perrins St ⓣ03/5348 1322, ⓦwww.spacountry.net.au/balconys/balconiesmain.htm. A rambling mansion with several balconies overlooking the lake: a favourite with gay visitors. ❺

Bergamo 51 Woolnoughs Rd ⓣ03/5348 7572, ⓦwww.bergamo.com.au. Two enchanting mud and timber cottages situated 12km northeast of town at Porcupine Ridge (travel along the Daylesford–Glenlyon Rd, and after 3km turn off to Porcupine Ridge). ❺

Royal Hotel Cnr of Vincent and Albert streets ⓣ03/5348 2205. Refurbished Victorian pub with ten pleasant, centrally heated rooms with en-suite facilities, some with spa bath. B&B ❹

Wildwood YHA 42 Main Rd, Hepburn Springs ⓣ03/5348 4435, ⓔdaylesford@yhavic.org.au. The best budget deal in town: a small and lovely renovated guesthouse with a homely kitchen and a deck overlooking a great garden area. If you're arriving by bus, phone ahead for a pick-up. Dorm bed from $20, rooms ❸

Eating and drinking

In such a gay-friendly place you can expect the local bars and eateries to be gay-friendly, too.

Altar Bar & Lounge Cnr of Hill and Daly streets at the Convent Galley. Good place for a wine or a cocktail with snacks available too. Fri & Sat 11am–midnight, Sun 11am–6pm.

Bad Habits Café Cnr of Hill and Daly streets at the Convent Galley. A Mediterranean-style café open daily 10–5pm.

Cliffy's Emporium 30 Raglan St. In a town of good cafés, this delightful deli-café/winebar rates a special mention for food and atmosphere. Mon–Thurs 10am–6pm, Fri–Sun till late.

D'bar Restaurant Club Lounge 74 Vincent St. Dine on scrumptious Mediterranean food in the first-floor winebar (Fri–Sun), listen to live jazz on Friday nights, or check out the DJs from 10pm on Saturdays.

Farmers Arms Hotel 1 East St. A great place to go for a drink (try a local ale), especially in the beer garden in summer, or a drink and dinner (Wed–Sun 6–9pm) – the cuisine is modern Australian and the servings are generous.

Frangos & Frangos Restaurant/Koukla Café Both at 82 Vincent St ⓣ03/5348 2363. The café serves excellent breakfasts and slightly simpler and cheaper lunches and dinners than the fine restaurant; in both the food is Mediterranean-inspired. Café open Mon–Tues 8am–4pm, Wed–Sun 8am–late; restaurant Mon & Tues 4pm–late, Fri and Sat 11am–late, Sun 11am–5pm.

Harvest Café 29 Albert St. A friendly, nonconformist haven that has an extensive menu (vegetarian, vegan and seafood), accompanied by folk and acoustic music on Sunday nights. Thurs–Mon 9am–9pm.

Lake House King Street near the lake ⓣ03/5348 3329. For a real splurge, try this outstanding but expensive restaurant; as well as dinner they do coffees and brunch. The menu changes according to the seasons; the cooking style is very sophisticated modern Australian and there is a strong emphasis on using local produce. Daily 8am–11am, noon–5pm & 7pm–late.

Sweet Decadence at Locantro 87 Vincent St. Chocolates, coffee and cake served up in a characterful old building. Daily 10–5pm.

Hepburn Springs

HEPBURN SPRINGS is not really a town at all, but a collection of guesthouses and a wonderful Art Deco **resort hotel** in a green, hilly and peaceful spot only 4km north of Daylesford. From the bus stop, walk through the shady Soldiers Memorial Park to the Mineral Springs Reserve, where you can taste three kinds of mineral water from old pumps and take advantage of the facilities at the ultra-posh **Hepburn Spa Resort** (Mon–Thurs 10am–7pm, Fri 10am–8pm, Sat 9am–8.30pm, Sun 9am–7pm; on long weekends until 8.30pm; ⓣ03/5348 2034, ⓦwww.hepburnspa.com.au). You can spend as long as you like here in the 34°C relaxation pool and 38°C mineral-water spa (both Mon–Fri $10; Sat, Sun & public holidays $15). Or indulge yourself by soaking in your own spa bath with essential oils (various options from $30 for 20min). The southern wing has massage, saunas, flotation tanks, and therapy and couch pools. Bookings must be made at least three (preferably six) weeks in advance, especially for weekends.

Practicalities

The Springs Retreat at the corner of Main Road and Tenth Street (ⓣ03/5348 2202, ⓦwww.thesprings.com.au; ❺) is a classic 1930s Art Deco resort with tastefully renovated en-suite rooms. There's a good-value buffet lunch in the dining room and a more expensive dinner menu; tasty counter meals are also available in the bar. *Dudley House*, at 101 Main Rd (Ⓣ03/5348 3033, Ⓦusers.netconnect.com.au/~dudley/; ❼, weekends ❽), is a lovely Federation-style weatherboard house with bed and breakfast and a fine restaurant. At the budget end of the scale is *Continental House*, 9 Lone Pine Ave (Ⓣ03/5348 2005, Ⓦwww.continentalhouse.com.au; ❷) a vegan retreat that offers basic accommodation, yoga classes and massages on request. The rambling house is located in a lovely garden setting on a hill above the Mineral Springs Reserve. In addition to small dorms (bed $22–25) and simple twins/doubles (BYO linen for all) there's a kitchen and several lounge rooms; a café offers vegan banquets on Saturday night.

A few eating places can be found along Main Street. The *Old Hepburn Hotel* at no. 236 is good for a drink in the beer garden or tasty pub grub (lunch and dinner Tues–Sun). For traditional Thai food go to *Jasmine Thai* at no. 114 (dinner daily except Tues; Ⓣ03/5348 1163), while *Misto* at no. 70 offers modern, Mediterranean cuisine (dinner Thurs–Mon, lunch Sun; Ⓣ03/5348 2843). The Art Nouveau *Palais* at no. 111 is a restaurant and bar (Wed–Sat eve) with an adjacent ballroom that's used for dance classes and as an entertainment venue – quite a few top-notch names from the Melbourne music scene and further afield perform here.

Ballarat and around

BALLARAT is a grandiose provincial city that makes a memorable first impression from whichever direction you approach. From the west, you enter via the Western Highway along the **Avenue of Honour**, lined on either side with over 22km of trees and dedicated to soldiers who fought in World War I. It ends at the massive **Arch of Victory**, through which you drive to enter Sturt Street and the city. Coming from the east, you approach the city on the Western Highway (Victoria Street), flanked by lawns, trees and colourful flowerbeds. Trains pull in to the elegant 1889 **station**, topped by a domed clock tower.

The Ballarat area was already settled before gold was discovered, and thus preserves a rural life for which the city is the supply centre. Nonetheless, it's gold that has marked the place indelibly: over a quarter of all **gold** found in Victoria came from Ballarat's fantastically rich reef mines before they were exhausted in 1918. Nowadays, in addition to the more obvious tourist attractions – especially Sovereign Hill – and fine **architecture**, the town is interesting in its own right, with a fairly large student population that lends some cultural presence and gives the city a reasonably active nightlife. Most people don't stay here overnight, however, as it's little more than an hour's drive from Melbourne.

Information and transport

The centrally located **Ballarat Visitor Information Centre**, on the corner of Sturt and Albert streets (daily 9am–5pm; Ⓣ03/5320 5741 or 1800 446 633, Ⓦwww.ballarat.com), has free **information** and maps of the town and can make accommodation bookings. Public **transport** in Ballarat and surrounding areas is handled by Davis Buslines (Ⓣ03/5331 7777; www.kefford.com.au); they charge a flat two-hour fare of $1.60. Buses to Sovereign Hill (#9, going to the suburb of Canadian) depart from the bus stop on Lydiard Street near the corner of Sturt Street; to the Eureka Centre (#8, going to Eureka) from Sturt Street in front of the Book City bookstore; to get to Lake Wendouree take bus #16 from Sturt Street near the Myer department store, going to Sturt Street West. The system extends as far as Buninyong, 10km south, and Creswick (see p.1014), 18km north.

Accommodation

There's an abundance of **accommodation** in all price ranges in Ballarat, from hostels to grand hotels, so you shouldn't have a problem finding a room to suit. Bear in mind that many places will be more expensive at weekends.

Ansonia 32 Lydiard St ⓣ03/5332 4678, ⓦwww.ballarat.com/ansonia.htm. Lovely boutique hotel in the historic precinct, with restaurant, library and guest lounge. ❺

Ballarat City Apartments 225 Lydiard St North ⓣ03/5332 6992, ⓦwww.ballarat.com/bca.htm. Five centrally located, self-contained apartments with one or two bedrooms, all with spas. ❹

Craigs Royal Hotel 10 Lydiard St South ⓣ03/5331 1377 or 1800 648 051, ⓦwww.craigsroyal.com. The accommodation at this grand Victorian-era hotel ranges from traditional pub rooms to luxurious suites – go for the wonderful two-level North Tower if your budget will allow it. ❹–❼

Eastern Station Guesthouse 81 Humffray Street ⓣ03/5338 8722, ⓦwww.ballarat.com/easternstation.htm. Reasonably priced comfortable doubles with shared kitchen and bathroom facilities. ❸

George Hotel 27 Lydiard St ⓣ03/5333 4866, ⓦwww.ballarat.com/george. Three-storey 1850s hotel with colonial-style decor, an inexpensive bistro and rooms, some with four-poster beds. ❸

Goldfields Holiday Park 108 Clayton St ⓣ03/5332 7888 or 1800 632 237, ⓦwww.ballaratgoldfields.com.au. Well located, right next to Sovereign Hill, this place has good facilities for campers, including a kitchen. Cabins ❸

Miners Retreat Motel 602 Eureka St ⓣ03/5331 6900, ⓦwww.ballarat.com/minersretreat.htm. Inexpensive standard motel units, just 100m from the site of the Eureka Centre; light breakfast included. ❸

Sovereign Hill Lodge YHA Magpie St ⓣ03/5333 3409, ⓔballarat@yhavic.org.au. This small hostel – part of a motel as well as part of Sovereign Hill theme park – has four rooms, a kitchen/dining area and a bar on site. Dorms from $20, rooms ❸, B&B in motel rooms ❺

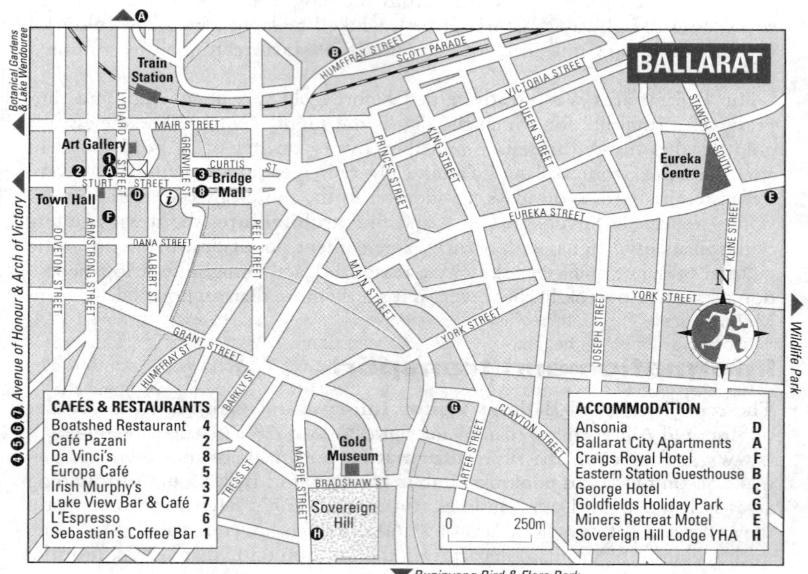

The City

Sturt and Victoria streets terminate on either side of the Bridge Mall, the central shopping area at the base of quaint **Bakery Hill** with its old shopfronts. Southeast of the city centre, Eureka Street runs off Main Street towards the site of the **Eureka Stockade**, with several museums and antique shops along the way. Main Street becomes Ballarat–Buninyong Road, and six blocks down is crossed by Bradshaw Street, where you'll find Sovereign Hill, the recreated gold town. Northwest of the centre, approached via Sturt Street, are the **Botanical Gardens** and Lake Wendouree.

The city centre

The most complete **nineteenth-century streetscape** is probably along Lydiard Street, which runs from the centre up past the train station; there are several two-storey terraced shopfronts, with verandahs and decorative iron-lace work, mostly dating from the mid- to late nineteenth century. The former **Mining Exchange** (1888) has been recently renovated to its former splendour, and the architecture of Her Majesty's Theatre (1875) also proclaims its goldrush-era heyday. The **Ballarat Fine Art Gallery** at 40 Lydiard St (daily 10.30am–5pm; free guided

The Eureka Stockade

The **Eureka Rebellion** is one of the most celebrated events of Australian history and generally regarded as the only act of white armed rebellion the country has seen – however, some historians argue that Aborigines were involved in it as well. It was provoked by conditions in the goldfields, where diggers had to pay exorbitantly for their right to prospect for gold (as much as thirty shillings a month), without receiving in return any right to vote, to have decent roads, transport or police protection, or to have any chance of a permanent right to the land they worked. Checks for licences were ruthless and brutal, and corruption rife. Protest meetings calling on diggers to refuse to pay drew huge crowds at Ballarat, Bendigo and Castlemaine; in response, in November 1853 the government made a small reduction in the fee.

The administration at Ballarat was particularly repressive, and in November 1854 local diggers formed the **Ballarat Reform League**, demanding full civic rights and the abolition of the licence fee, and proclaiming that "the people are the only legitimate source of power". At the end of the month a group of two hundred diggers gathered inside a **stockade** of logs, hastily flung together, and determined to resist further arrests for non-possession of a licence. They were attacked at dawn on December 3 by police and troops; thirty died inside, and five members of the government forces also lost their lives.

The movement was not a failure, however: the diggers had aroused widespread sympathy, and in 1855 licences were abolished, to be replaced by an annual **Miner's Right** which carried the right to vote and to enclose land. The leader of the rebellion, the Irishman Peter Lalor, eventually became a member of parliament.

The **Eureka Flag**, with its white cross and five white stars on a blue background, has become a symbol of the Left – and indeed of almost any protest movement: shearers raised it in strikes during the 1890s; wharfies used it before World War II in their bid to stop pig-iron being sent to Japan; and today the flag is flown by a growing number of Australians who support the country's transformation to a republic. On a deeper level, all sorts of claims are made for the Eureka Rebellion's pivotal role in forming the Australian nation and psyche. The diggers are held up as a classic example of the Australian (male) ethos of mateship and anti-authoritarianism, while the goldrush in general is credited with overthrowing the hierarchical colonial order, as servants rushed to make their fortune, leaving their masters and mistresses to fend for themselves.

tours daily 2pm, $5), another superb building, is the oldest provincial art gallery in Australia, established in 1884. The original, frayed **Eureka Flag** (see box) is on display here in a purpose-built space, with subdued lighting to protect the precious relic. The gallery's extensive collection is particularly strong on colonial and Heidelberg School paintings; displayed alongside are the watercolours of S.T. Gill, a self-taught artist who painted scenes of goldrush days in Ballarat. In another part of the gallery is a reconstruction of the drawing room of the famous Lindsay family (whose best-known members are the artist Norman and the writer Jack), from nearby Creswick, complete with several of their paintings. The new wing of the gallery, a striking structure with a curved zinc roof and a glass-encased staircase, extends out to former Camp Street, now renamed Alfred Deakin Place, and stands cheek by jowl with an 1880s red-brick building, a police station in its previous incarnation and now the *Gallery Café*. The visual and performing arts faculties of Ballarat University have been relocated to Deakin Place and are housed in new quarters of equally striking modern design. Walking from the Art Gallery along Lydiard Street to Sturt Street you'll see more nineteenth-century goldrush architecture: check out the imposing Classical-revival **town hall** on Sturt Street, which dominates the centre of the city.

There are still over forty **hotels** in Ballarat – survivors of the hundreds that once watered the thirsty diggers. Some of the finest are on Lydiard Street: *Craig's Royal Hotel* at no. 10 and the *George Hotel* at no. 27 are an integral part of Ballarat's architectural heritage. Sadly, during the 1970s, the council forced most of the old pubs to pull down their verandahs on the grounds that they were unsafe, so very few survive in their original form. One that does is attached to the *Golden City Hotel*, 427 Sturt St, which took the council to the Supreme Court to save its magnificent wide verandah with original cast-iron decoration.

The Botanical Gardens

The **Botanical Gardens**, laid out in 1858, cover about half a square kilometre alongside **Lake Wendouree**, just to the northwest of the city centre (#16 bus from Sturt St, near the Myer department store). Begonias grow so well in Ballarat that a **Begonia Festival** runs for ten days in March. The new **Conservatory** at the Botanic Gardens, an impressive glasshouse whose design was inspired by origami, is used to showcase them, and other floral displays, throughout the year (conservatory daily 9am–5pm; $3).

Other highlights are the **Avenue of Big Trees**, with a California redwood among its monsters, and the classical statuary, donated by rich gold miners, scattered about the gardens. Pride of place goes to Benzoni's *Flight from Pompeii*, housed in the Statuary Pavilion. Along Prime Minister Avenue you can see a bust of every prime minister of Australia.

Eureka and York streets

As you head east of the centre towards Eureka Street and the Eureka Stockade (bus #8 from outside the ANZ Bank on Sturt St), take a look at the unique shop facades on Main Street. The site of the Eureka Stockade is preserved in Eureka Gardens – to commemorate and honour the influential uprising (see box), the **Eureka Centre** (daily 9am–4.30pm; $8) was built on the western edge, on the corner of Eureka Street; its exhibits give detailed background information on the historic rebellion. Outside the centre, the big blue-and-white Eureka sail, shaped like a mining wind sail, is a Ballarat landmark.

Parallel to Eureka Street is York Street, where you'll find the **Ballarat Wildlife Park**, on the corner of Fussell Street (daily 9am–5.30pm; $15.50) which has kangaroos, as well as enclosures with wombats, Tasmanian devils, koalas, nonvenomous and venomous snakes and crocodiles. There's an emphasis on getting up close to the cuddlier animals and having your photo taken, and there are daily guided tours at 11am. Feeding times are also worth attending (weekends, daily during the school holidays: koalas 2pm, wombats 2.30pm, crocodiles 3pm, Tasmanian devils 3.30pm).

Sovereign Hill and the Gold Museum

The recreated gold-mining township of **Sovereign Hill** is located 1.5km southeast of the city centre, on Bradshaw Street (bus #9 from outside the ANZ Bank on Sturt St; daily 10am–5pm; $29 also includes admission to the Gold Museum; ⓣ03/5331 1944, ⓦwww.sovereignhill.com.au). Seventy buildings and shops here are modelled on those that lined Ballarat's main street in the 1850s, with a cast of characters wandering about in the dress of the period. The township was planned around an actual mine shaft from the 1880s, where guided underground tours are available. There are diggings where you can learn how to pan for gold (and perhaps get a small memento) and a mining museum filled with steam-operated machinery. Sovereign Hill puts on a spectacular outdoor **sound and light show**, "Blood on the Southern Cross" (two shows every night during school holidays, Mon–Sat rest of the year; 1hr 20min; $35, or joint ticket for show and Sovereign Hill, or for dinner and show, $60; bookings essential on ⓣ03/5333 5777), which makes use of the whole panorama of Sovereign Hill to tell the story of the Eureka Stockade.

Opposite Sovereign Hill, the **Gold Museum** (daily 9.30am–5.20pm, in summer until 6pm; $7.30 if not going to Sovereign Hill) offers a good overview of the recreated settlement. It has an outstanding display of real gold, and a large collection of coins that are arranged in displays exploring the history and uses of gold. The museum has also a small Eureka display which details life on the goldfields and explains the conditions that provoked the Eureka Stockade. Central to the display is a large painting of the rebellion by George Browning, a mid-nineteenth-century artist: it's interesting to see quite a few black faces portrayed in the stockade, which is generally labelled as the only white armed uprising to have taken place in Australia.

Eating and drinking

For its size, Ballarat has an astonishing number and variety of **eating places**, ranging from European coffee bars established by postwar immigrants to upmarket gourmet restaurants, not to forget more than forty **pubs**.

Ansonia 32 Lydiard St ⓣ03/5332 4678. Restaurant in a refurbished building that also houses a swish boutique hotel. The eclectic cuisine has influences from the Mediterranean to Southeast Asia. Licensed; open daily for breakfast, lunch and dinner (book for dinner).
Boatshed Restaurant 27 Wendouree Parade. Have a coffee or meal on the deck fronting Lake Wendouree. Licensed, open daily till late.
Cafe Pazani 102 Sturt St. Slick Italian café serving expensive food and excellent coffee. Licensed. Tues–Sat 9am–1am, Sun & Mon 9am–5.30pm.
Da Vincis 29 Sturt St. The best place for pasta in town: a lively atmosphere and generous, good-value servings, plus vegetarian options. Licensed. Daily10.30am–late.
Europa Café 411 Sturt St. A pleasant café serving good coffee, cakes and breads, and light meals. Mon–Wed & Sun 9am–6pm, Thurs–Sat 9am until late.
Irish Murphys 36 Sturt St. Big food at small prices, decent beer and frequent live music with minimal Irish kitsch combine to make this bar one of the most popular in town.
Lake View Bar & Café 22 Wendouree Parade. Excellent location overlooking Lake Wendouree, serving breakfasts, coffee and desserts; there is also an à la carte menu for full meals. Open daily from 7am till late.
L'Espresso 417 Sturt St. European-style, hip place for coffee and eclectic breakfasts; the

mains are good too, and very moderately priced. Daily 6.30am–6pm, also Thurs–Sun 6.30pm until late.

Sebastians Coffee Bar 58 Lydiard St North. Café-bar with cool minimalist decor opposite the Regent Multiplex cinemas. Open daily from 11am.

Entertainment and nightlife

Thanks to a burgeoning number of students – about 19,000 are enrolled at the University of Ballarat – the city has a lively **music** and **club** scene; for up-to-date information about what's on, check *The Courier* on Thursday. The bustling *21 Arms* at 21 Armstrong St, Ballarat North, is open until 5am and has four main areas ranging from a sofa lounge to the frenetic *Shed*; *Rattle 'n Hum* at 49 Mair St is another mainstay of the Ballarat club scene. The *Bridge Mall Inn* (locally known as *The Rat*) showcases **live bands** six nights a week, there's also the occasional gig at the *Thirsty Dog & Puppy Lounge*, 24 Lydiard St North and last, but not least, *Extremity*, the ever popular student uni bar at 12 Camp St, packs them in on weekends.

The elaborate Victorian-era Her Majesty's Theatre, at 17 Lydiard St (ⓣ03/5333 5800), stages all types of touring **productions**, and there's a three-screen **cinema** on the same street at no. 49 (ⓣ03/5331 1399).

Around Ballarat

The delightful, privately-run **Buninyong Flora and Bird Park** (daily 9am–5.30pm, $7; ⓣ03/5341 3843, ⓦwww.buninyong.com/birdpark) at 408 Eddy Ave, Mt Helen, 7km south of Ballarat, is worth a detour. It has 10 acres of landscaped bushland gardens, complete with a small rainforest and a waterfall, and about 150 parrots and cockatoos from Australia, Asia, Africa and South America, some of which were bred here.

Rich alluvial **gold** was found at **CRESWICK**, 18km north of Ballarat, in 1851, which made it an important mining centre. It's now a quiet little town, where the only reminder of earlier days is the grandiose Victorian architecture. The *American Hotel* and the *British Hotel* face each other across the main street, a hangover from mining days when miners of different nationalities stuck to their segregated groups. **CLUNES**, just beyond Creswick, to the northwest, was the site of the first worthwhile Victorian goldfield in 1851. The reefs here were too deep for small-scale mining, and the Port Phillip Company took over operations. The only profitable British gold mine in Australia, it was most productive between 1857 and 1881. The main street has many solid old buildings and rows of original shopfronts most of which are sadly vacant.

Western Victoria and the Mallee

Several roads run west from the goldfields to the South Australia border through the seemingly endless wheatfields of **the Wimmera**. To the west of the farming centre of **Ararat** is the major attraction of the area, **The Grampians National Park**, the southwestern tail-end of the Great Dividing Range. Stawell and **Horsham** – the latter regarded as the capital of the Wimmera – are good places to base yourself, but **Halls Gap**, in a valley and surrounded by national park, is even better. North of Horsham are **Nhill** and **Dimboola**, close to **Little Desert National Park** and, like **Warracknabeal** further north, wheat centres. Beyond here is the least populated part of the state, the wide, flat **Mallee** with its twisted mallee scrub, sand dunes and dry lakes. This region, with several state and national parks, extends from **Wyperfeld National Park** in the south, right up to Mildura's irrigated oasis on the Murray River. South of the Grampians is sheep country; following the Hamilton Highway from Geelong you'll end up at **Hamilton**, the major town and wool capital of the western district, also accessible via **Dunkeld** on the southern edge of the Grampians.

V/Line (Ⓣ13 61 96) has a **bus service** from Ballarat to Hamilton via Dunkeld (Mon–Sat 2 daily, Sun 1 daily; Mon–Fri the morning service continues to Mount Gambier in South Australia), and from Warrnambool to Hamilton and Casterton (Mon–Fri 1 daily). The Grampians Link consists of a **train service** from Melbourne to Ballarat and a connecting bus to Halls Gap, via Ararat and Stawell (1 daily). The Overland train service between Melbourne and Adelaide departs Melbourne Sun, Mon, Fri & Sat at 10.10pm, and arrives in Adelaide 11hr later; major stops en route in Victoria are Ararat, Horsham amd Dimboola (for details call Trainways Australia Ⓣ1300 13 21 47 or Ⓦwww.gsr.com.au). The Daylink connection (train from Melbourne to Bendigo, and from there a connecting bus via Horsham and Dimboola to Adelaide) departs Melbourne daily in the morning. Greyhound Australia and Firefly buses to Adelaide travel the Western Highway via Ballarat, Ararat, Stawell, Horsham, Dimboola and Nhill.

Ararat and the Western Highway

ARARAT, some 90km west from Ballarat, is still very much a goldfields town, with an overabundance of grandiose Victorian architecture and a main street laid out to show off the best profiles of the nearby mountains: **Mount Ararat** in the west and the **Pyrenees Range** with **Mount Cole** in the east. The town was founded in 1857, when a group of seven hundred hopeful Chinese from Guangdong province in southern China, making the slow trudge from the South Australian ports to the central Victorian goldfields, stumbled across a fabulously rich, shallow alluvial goldfield, the **Canton Lead**. The new multi-million-dollar **Gum San Chinese Heritage Centre** (daily 10am–4.30pm; $8; Ⓦwww.gumsan.com.au) pays homage to the fact that Ararat is the only town in Australia founded by the Chinese. It was designed by a Melbourne architect of Chinese origin and is a recreation of a two-storey southern Chinese temple set in a traditional Chinese garden. The exhibits recount the tale of the founding of the city and familiarize Western visitors with aspects of Chinese culture.

These days Ararat is the commercial centre for a sheep-farming and wine-producing area; local **wineries** include the Montara Winery, 3km south along the Chalamabar Road (Mon–Sat 10am–5pm, Sun noon–4pm), and Mount Langi Ghiran on Vine Road north of Buangor (turn north from the Western Highway towards Warrak; Mon–Fri 9am–5pm, Sat & Sun noon–5pm), renowned for its superb whites and reds. In the same direction, just north of Buangor, **Challicum**

Hills Wind Farm claims to be the largest in Australia; tours of the site depart from Buangor General Store ($14; phone to book ⓣ03 5354 5525).

Next door to Ararat town hall, with its clock tower and fountain, is the **visitor information centre** on High Street (Mon–Fri 9am–5pm; ⓣ03/5355 0281 or 1800 657 158, ⓦwww.ararat.asn.au), which provides information on the Grampians and can book accommodation in the area. The **Langi Morgala Museum** nearby (Sat & Sun 1–4pm; $2.20) occupies an old brick building banded with bluestone at the base and around the huge arched windows and doors. Along with the usual pioneering displays, there's an important collection of Aboriginal artefacts. A guided tour at **J Ward** further north across the railway tracks at Girdlestone St (Mon–Sat at 10am, 11am, 1pm & 2pm; additional tours on Sun and school holidays at noon and 3pm; $8; ⓦwww.jward.ararat.net.au), gives a chilling insight into one of the darker aspects of the area's social history. The 1859 building started out as a prison, but from the late 1880s it operated as a high-security ward of the Ararat Lunatic Asylum and criminally insane men were incarcerated here, in appalling conditions that were at the time considered acceptable. J Ward itself was closed as late as 1991.

For **food**, head for Barkly Street, where you'll find a supermarket, a bakery and a few good cafés. *Vines Café & Bar* at no 74 has good breakfasts, light meals and lots of local wines by the glass and is open daily 9am–6pm, Fri & Sat also 6.30pm–late. *Kerry's Café* at no 96 is a pleasant day-time place, open Wed–Sun 9am–6pm, and *Sicilian's Café-Bar-Restaurant* at no. 102 serves good pizza and pasta, open Mon–Wed 11.30am–9.30pm, Thurs-Sat till late. For bar meals head to the *Rex Hotel* at 129 Barkly St or the *Blue Duck Hotel* at no. 257. A good value-option is the bistro at the Ararat RSL club, 74 High St, which serves inexpensive meals daily.

Great Western and Stawell

Between Ararat and Stawell is the small settlement of **GREAT WESTERN**, the centre of a wine-producing area whose most famous historic **wineries** are right in town, on the Moyston Road. **Seppelt Great Western** (daily 9am–5pm), established in 1865, and **Best's Wines** (Mon–Sat 10am–5pm, Sun 11am–4pm) established in 1866, are both renowned for their sparkling *méthode champenoise* wines but they also produce a range of varietals including Shiraz, Cabernet Sauvignon, Riesling and Chardonnay. Best's has a timber winery building and an old underground cellar whereas Seppelt's boasts 1.5km of underground tunnels dug by miners in the late nineteenth century to aid sparkling-wine maturation. A tour of these tunnels, with subsequent wine tasting, is run Mon–Sat at 10.30am, 1.30pm & 3pm, during school holidays also on Sun (45min; $7.50).

STAWELL (pronounced "stall") is most famous for the **Stawell Gift**, a sprint race offering big prize-money that has been held here every Easter since 1877. It's also the closest major town to the Grampians and the departure point for the **bus** to Halls Gap. The helpful **Stawell & Grampians Visitor Information Centre** is at 52 Western Highway (ⓣ1800 246 880); the **Stawell Gift Hall of Fame** on Main Street (Mon–Fri 9–11am or by appointment; $2; ⓣ03/5358 1326) charts the history of the race itself. The town, with its winding main street, has a pleasant, old-fashioned feel, and it's a much less expensive place to stay than Halls Gap. The many motels along the highway all charge much the same (❸) for similar facilities. More expensive B&Bs and two caravan parks are the only real alternatives: *Walmsley B&B* in a historic house at 19 Seaby St (ⓣ03/5358 3164, ⓦwww.aussie-accommodation.com.au/Victoria/Stawell/WalmsleyBedBreakfast/ ❺) has five well-appointed rooms and a spa suite as well as an indoor pool, verandah and garden, while the *Stawell Grampians Gate Caravan Park* on Burgh Street 400m south of the Western Highway (Ⓣ03/5358 2376, Ⓕ5358 5275; cabins ❸), is the closest camping area to town.

The Grampians and around

Rising from the flat plains of western Victoria's wheat and grazing districts, the sandstone ranges of the **GRAMPIANS**, with their weirdly formed rocky outcrops and stark ridges, seem doubly spectacular. In addition to their scenic splendour, in the **Grampians National Park (Gariwerd)** you'll find a dazzling array of **flora**, with a spring and early summer bonanza of wild flowers; a wealth of **Aboriginal rock art**; an impressive **Aboriginal Cultural Centre**; **waterfalls** and **lakes**; and over fifty **bushwalks** along 150km of well-marked tracks. There are also several hundred kilometres of road, from sealed highway to rough track, on which you can make exciting **scenic drives** and **4WD** tours.

The **best times to come** are in autumn, or in spring and early summer when the waterfalls are in full flow and the wild flowers are blooming (although there'll always be something in flower no matter when you come). Between June and August it rains heavily and can get extremely cold; at that time many tracks are closed to avoid erosion. Summers are very hot, with a scarcity of water and the ever-present threat of bushfires. If you're undertaking extended walks in summer, carry a portable radio to get the latest information on the fire risk: on **total fire ban days** no exposed flames – not even that from a portable gas stove – are allowed.

HALLS GAP, 26km from Stawell, on the eastern fringes of the Grampians, is the only settlement actually surrounded by national park. Its setting is gorgeous, in the long flat strip of the Fyans Valley surrounded by the soaring bush and rock of the Wonderland, Mount Difficult and Mount William ranges; koalas are frequently seen in the surrounding trees. Packed with accommodation and other facilities catering to park visitors, this is the obvious place to base yourself, especially if you don't have your own transport.

Rock art in the Grampians

It's estimated that **Koorie** Aborigines lived in the area known to them as **Gariwerd** at least five thousand years ago. The area offered such rich food sources that the Koories didn't have to spend all their time hunting and food-gathering, and could therefore devote themselves to religious and cultural activities. Evidence of this survives in **rock paintings**, which are executed in a linear style, usually in a single colour (either red or white), but sometimes done by handprints or stencils. You can visit some of the rock shelters where Aborigines camped and painted on the sandstone walls, although many more are off-limits. In the northern Grampians one of the best is **Gulgurn Manja** (also known as Flat Rock), 5km south of the Western Highway near the Hollow Mountain campsite; from Flat Rock Road it's a signposted fifteen-minute walk. The name means "hands of young people", as many of the handprints here were done by children. In the southern Grampians is **Billimina**, a fifteen-minute walk above the Buandik campsite; it's an impressive rock overhang with clearly discernible, quite animated red stick figures. **Guided rock-art tours** are organized by the Brambuk Cultural Centre (see p.1019).

Information, tours and activities

The friendly staff at the **Halls Gap Visitor Information Centre** on Grampians Road next to the Mobil service station book accommodation, tours and activities (daily 9am–5pm; ⓣ03/5356 4616 or 1800 065 599). A few companies offer introductory climbing and abseiling; the going rate is about $60 for half a day and $110 for a full day. GMAC (Grampians Mountain Adventure Company; ⓣ03/5383 9218 or 0427 747 047, ⓦwww.grampiansadventure.com.au) are trained and accredited by the Australian Mountain Climbers Association; they also operate at Mt Arapiles and can cater for advanced levels. Hangin' Out in the Grampians (ⓣ03/5356 4535 or 0407 684 831, ⓦwww.hanginout.com.au) do similar things. In addition to climbing/abseiling tours, GAS (Grampians Adventure Services) at Shop 4, Stoney Creek Stores (ⓣ03/5356 4556) also offer canoeing and kayaking trips, guided nature and night-time spotlight walks as well as mountain bike tours; they sell outdoor gear and rent mountain bikes too ($40/day). The Grampians Horse Riding Centre (ⓣ03/5383 9255, ⓦwww.grampianshorseriding.com.au) at Brimpaen in the Wartook Valley on the northwestern side of the Grampians does trail rides through the bush 2–3 times a day (90min; $50). For a definitive overview of the mountain range turn to Grampians Scenic Flights (ⓣ03/5357 3234; Dec–June only; $150–200, depending on the number of passengers).

Internet access is at the Visitor Information Centre ($2/20min), as well as at the YHA and in a separate shack ("Internet Room") on the premises of *Ned's Beds*, 2 Heath St (at the southern end of the shopping strip; $3/30min – put your fee into the honesty box).

Accommodation

During school holidays, particularly in January and at Easter, the Grampians are packed, and although Halls Gap has lots of **accommodation** of every kind, you'll need to book in advance. Note that many places will insist on long stays, and prices rise at weekends.

A permit is required for the **campsites** in the National Park which must be obtained at the National Park Centre at Brambuk (see opposite). After hours you fill in a form and put your money into the box outside the centre. The fee is $11 per site per day. **Bushcamping** is allowed in the park, except in the Wonderland Range and within 100m of a dam, river or creek, or within 50m of a road; but the staff at the National Park Centre will want to be informed about where and when you are going to pitch your tent. Besides the basic park campsites, there are dozens of **caravan parks** in the vicinity. The most convenient, *Halls Gap Caravan Park* (ⓣ03/5356 4251, ⓕ5356 4421; cabins ❹, on-site vans ❸), is right opposite the shopping centre and so a bit noisy, but it's well equipped, and at the start of many walks. *Grampians Gardens Caravan Park* (ⓣ & ⓕ03/5356 4244, cabins and vans ❸, motel units ❹), 3km out of town at the corner of the Ararat and Stawell roads, is another good option.

Asses Ears Wilderness Lodge RMB 7351 Schmidt Road, Brimpaen ⓣ03/5383 9215, ⓦwww.assesearslodge.com.au. Great backpacker accommodation in timber cabins in a quiet location in the Wartook Valley on the northwestern side of the Grampians. There's a licensed bar, inexpensive restaurant, a swimming pool and a pool table, and you can hire mountain bikes ($20/day). The owners drop people off for hikes and organise loads of activities. Rates include continental breakfast and linen. Dorms $22–25, cabin ❸

Brambuk Backpackers Grampians Rd ⓣ03/5356 4250, ⓦwww.brambuk.com.au. This hostel, just opposite the Brambuk Centre, is well-designed, making judicious use of natural space and light, but already somewhat the worse for wear. Ask for a bed in the newer part of the hostel – the older section is in dire need of a spruce-up. Rates include light breakfast. Dorms $22, rooms ❷

Grampians Wonderland Cabins Ellis St, just off the Grampians Tourist Rd on the way to Brambuk Ⓣ & Ⓕ 03/5356 4264, Ⓔ Grampians–wonderland @netconnect.au. Beautiful two-bedroom timber cabins in a bushland setting. ❻

Grampians YHA Eco Hostel Grampians Rd Ⓣ 03/5356 4544, Ⓔ grampians@yhavic.org.au. Hostel built according to environmentally friendly principles, recycling waste water and using solar electricity and wood-heating stoves. It has excellent facilities, including Internet access. Dorms $20, rooms ❸

Grand Canyon Motel Less than 1km north of Halls Gap on Grampians Rd Ⓣ 03/5356 4280, Ⓔ grandcanyonmotel@bigpond.au. Cheap motel accommodation – very good for the price. ❹

Halls Haven Holiday Units Stawell Rd Ⓣ 03/5356 4304. About 2km out of town towards Stawell, the fully self-contained one-bedroom units here are probably the best value in town; plus there are a couple of two-bedroom cottages as well. The facilities include bbq, tennis court and a small solar-heated pool. ❹

Kookaburra Lodge 14 Heath St Ⓣ 03/5356 4395, Ⓦ www.grampians.net.au/kooka. One of the better motels in town, with a well-kept garden and pleasantly furnished rooms facing a patio hung with plants. ❺

Mountain Grand Boutique Hotel Grampians Rd, Halls Gap Ⓣ 03/5356 4232, Ⓦ www.mountaingrand .com.au. This elegant, refurbished 1930s-style guesthouse has comfortable en-suite rooms, some with spa. There's also a good licensed restaurant on the first floor. ❻

Neds Beds 2 Heath St, Halls Gap Ⓣ 03/5356 4296, Ⓦ www.grampiansbackpackers.com.au. Very small, family-run hostel. The central location near the shops, a BBQ area and outdoor verandah are pluses, but the rather cramped dorms with their wooden bunkbeds are just so-so. Rates include light breakfast. Dorms $22, double ❷

Tim's Place Grampians Rd, Halls Gap Ⓣ 03/5356 4288, Ⓦ www.timsplace.com.au. Small hostel with a lovely, homey feel. There are dorms in the main house, and in smaller buildings out the back, plus three doubles and a single. Rates include continental breakfast. Extras include cheap Internet access ($3/hr) and free use of mountain bikes. Dorms $22, rooms ❷

Brambuk The National Park and Cultural Centre

Just over 2km south of Halls Gap along the Grampians Road (also known as the Dunkeld Road or the Dunkeld–Halls Gap Road) is **Brambuk the National Park and Cultural Centre**, the best place to start your visit. It consists of two separate buildings: the first one (daily 9am–5pm; Ⓣ 13 19 63, Ⓦ www.parkweb .vic.gov.au) mainly dispenses information on the national park and sells guide books and maps; don't miss the display and videos that trace the development of the Grampians over four hundred million years.

Located behind this building is the original **Aboriginal Cultural Centre** (daily 9am–5pm; Ⓣ 03/5356 4381, Ⓦ www.brambuk.com.au) opened in 1989 as a place of learning for visitors and a cultural centre for the native peoples of Southwest Victoria and the Wimmera region. With its undulating red-ochre tin roof it blends in wonderfully with the backdrop of bush and rocky ridge; its design incorporates many symbolic features that are important to the five Koorie communities who own and manage the centre.

A small exhibition inside features a poignant photographic history of the area's orginal inhabitants, and there's a visual display on traditional Aboriginal foods and lifestyles. Downstairs, a shop sells Aboriginal music, books and souvenirs, while the small Gariwerd Dreaming Theatre features two presentations: *Gariwerd Dreaming* telling the region's creation story; and *Gariwerd – A Cultural Landscape* outlining the park's flora, fauna, geology, and Aboriginal and European history. The small *Bush Food Café* upstairs sells snacks and light meals; try a "wattlecino" (a cappuccino-style drink made from wattle seeds). Outside, the landscaped grounds are planted with examples of the major plant species found in the park.

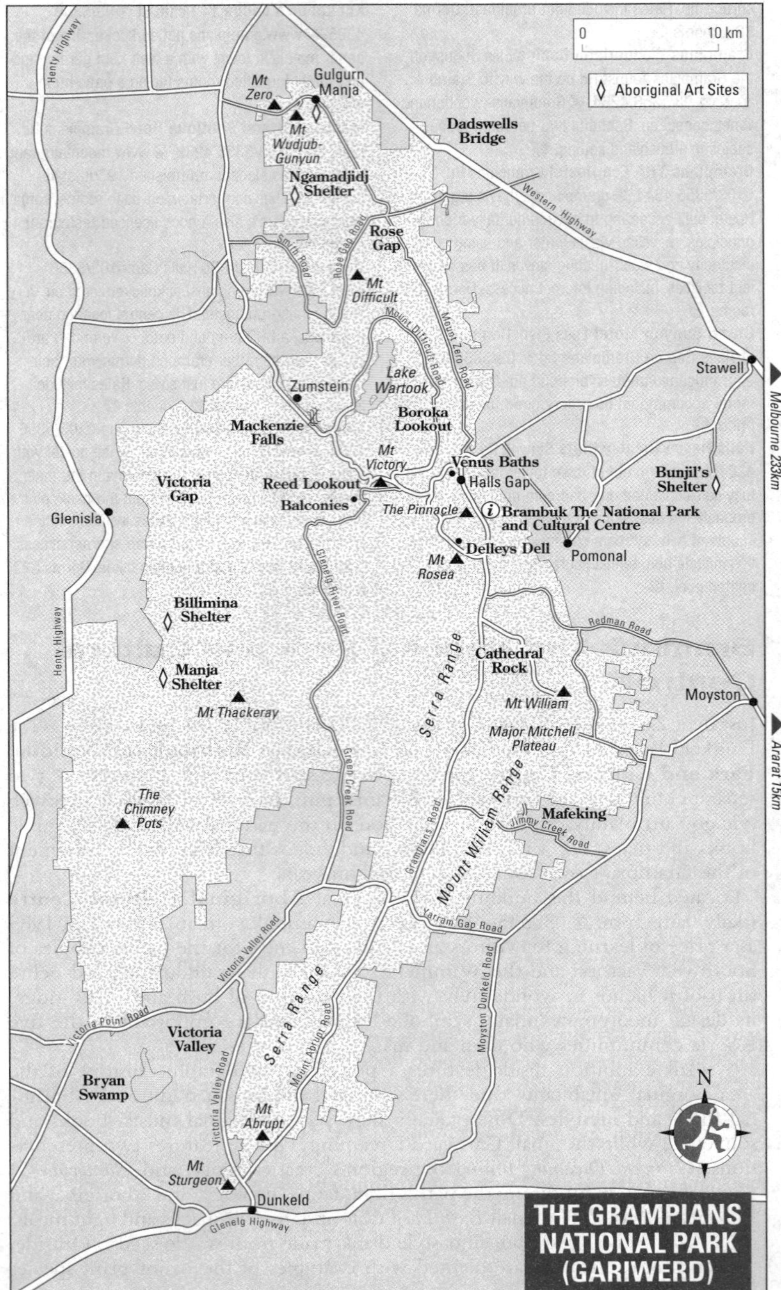
0
10 km
Aboriginal Art Sites
THE GRAMPIANS NATIONAL PARK (GARIWERD)
N
Henty Highway
Mt Zero
Gulgurn Manja
Mt Wudjub-Gunyun
Dadswells Bridge
Ngamadjidj Shelter
Western Highway
Rose Gap
Smith Road
Rose Gap Road
Mt Difficult
Mount Zero Road
Mount Difficult Road
Lake Wartook
Zumstein
Stawell
Melbourne 233km
Boroka Lookout
Mackenzie Falls
Mt Victory
Venus Baths
Halls Gap
Bunjil's Shelter
Victoria Gap
Reed Lookout
Balconies
The Pinnacle
Brambuk The National Park and Cultural Centre
Glenisla
Delleys Dell
Pomonal
Mt Rosea
Glenelg River Road
Henty Highway
Billimina Shelter
Redman Road
Cathedral Rock
Manja Shelter
Mt Thackeray
Mt William
Moyston
Serra Range
Major Mitchell Plateau
Ararat 15km
Green Creek Road
Mount William Range
The Chimney Pots
Mafeking
Grampians Road
Jimmy Creek Road
Victoria Valley Road
Yarram Gap Road
Serra Range
Mount Abrupt Road
Moyston Dunkeld Road
Victoria Point Road
Victoria Valley
Bryan Swamp
Victoria Valley Road
Mt Abrupt
Mt Sturgeon
Dunkeld
Glenelg Highway

There are short **rock-art tours** from the centre, as well as half- and full-day walks to other Aboriginal art sites in the national park. All tours are on demand only, must be booked at least 24hr in advance, and require a minimum of four people.

Bushwalks and scenic drives

The scenery and wildlife of the Grampians is tremendously varied, and the diversity of **vegetation** in the park is enhanced by the fact that this is the meeting place of the forested areas in the south and east of Victoria and the dry mallee country in the north. It's significantly warmer in the northern Grampians, an area of arid bushland filled with bent and twisted trees and scrubby undergrowth. In the cooler south, the vegetation ranges from stringybark forests and red-gum woodland in the wet Victoria Valley to luxuriant fern gullies such as Delleys Dell in the Wonderland Range. There are also subalpine communities of plants in exposed sites such as Mount William, as well as areas of stunted heaths on the Major Mitchell Plateau.

The National Park Centre at Brambuk hands out masses of free leaflets, walking guides and more detailed topographic maps; the excellent *Grampians Touring Guide* ($7.95) is a good all-rounder and handy for short walks. Although most walking tracks are clearly defined and well signposted, it's a good idea to buy Vicmap, or the walking maps published by Parks Victoria, and carry a compass if you're planning an overnight trek. Before beginning an extended walk, call into the centre and register. Some **walks** start from the campsite at Halls Gap, while others branch off the Victory and Grampian roads, making them difficult to get to without a car.

You can **drive** on roads through the park to major points and then get out and walk. The most popular section for visitors is the **Wonderland Range**, immediately to the west of Halls Gap. From the Halls Gap campsite you can head directly to **Venus Baths** (1.2km return). **The Pinnacle,** the most popular lookout in the Grampians, is usually accessed from the Wonderland Car Park (just off Mount Victory Rd; the turn-off is signposted). The 4.2 km return walk is easy, except for the slightly trickier Grand Canyon section where a series of steel ladders must be negotiated – as long as you wear sturdy shoes, are reasonably fit and don't suffer from vertigo, you'll be fine. **Delleys Dell** is another Wonderland walk (5km), through canopies of tree ferns: start at the Delleys Dell car park at the Rosea Campground (the turn-off from Mount Victory Rd is signposted). The other major features in the Grampians are the Balconies, Mackenzie Falls and Zumstein, all accessible via the Mount Victory Road northwest of Halls Gap. The walk to the **Balconies** (1.6km return), formerly known as the **Jaws of Death**, begins from the Reed Lookout car park (the turn-off is signposted) and goes for about ten minutes through a stand of lichen-covered tea trees until you have reached the lookout over the Victoria Valley and towards the Balconies. The much photographed, weird rock formation consists of one ledge above another, forming the image of a reptile's elongated, open jaw.

At **Zumstein** (5km east on Mount Victory Road) there's a picnic area and car park where western grey kangaroos stand passively, waiting for food. They're tame enough to pet, but can be a serious nuisance when you get out your food; don't encourage them by feeding them. A three-kilometre walk runs along the Mackenzie River Gorge from here to the base of **Mackenzie Falls**, which you can also reach more directly from Mount Victory Road. There's parking above the falls, and it's a short but strenuous walk to the base.

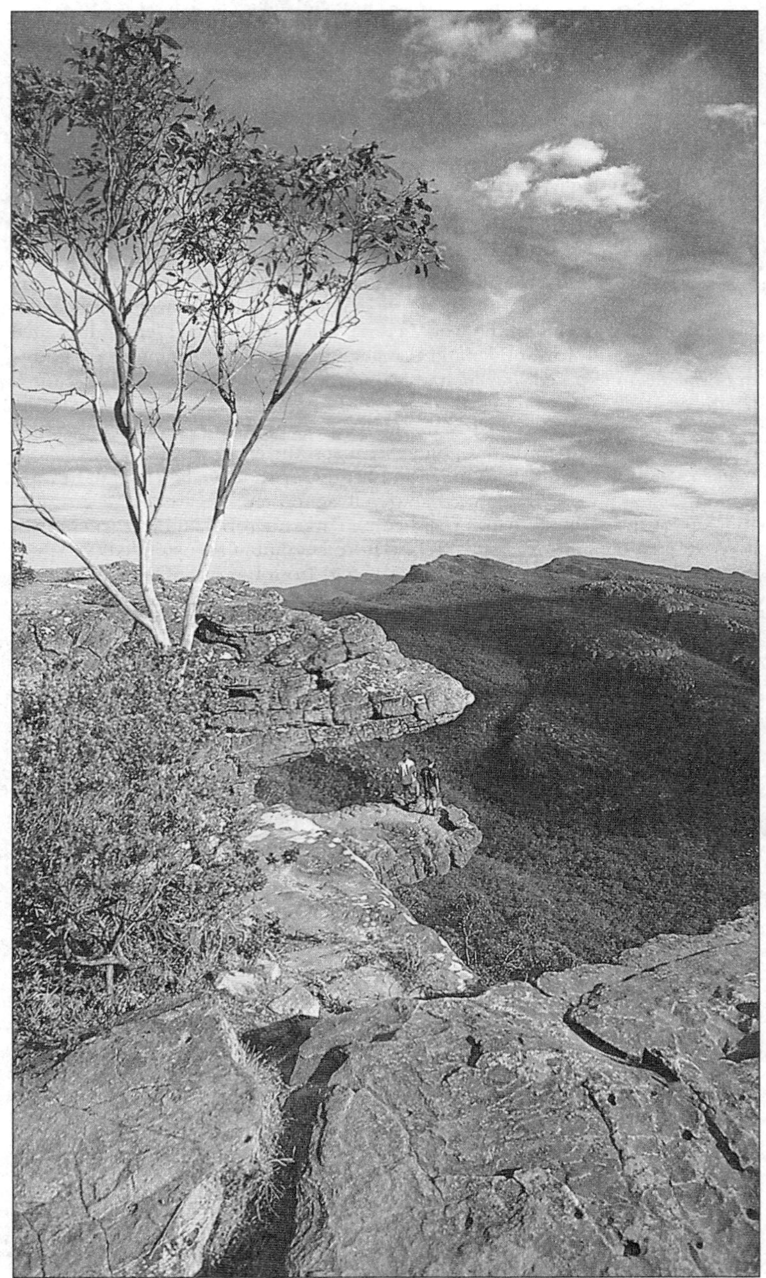

△ The Grampians

The Major Mitchell Trail

The first Europeans to reach the Grampians were **Major Thomas Mitchell** and his exploration party in 1836. Mitchell was the Surveyor General of New South Wales, and his glowing reports of the explorations subsequently attracted many squatters in the early 1840s. The **Major Mitchell Trail**, a signposted 1700-kilometre "long-distance cultural trail" along backroads and sometimes bush tracks, allows you to follow his route through Victoria, from Mildura along the Murray River to Swan Hill, then south to Horsham, detouring into the Grampians to ascend Mount William, and thence to the coast at Nelson and Portland. Heading back, it runs inland via Hamilton and Dunkeld on the southern edge of the Grampians, through central Victoria via Castlemaine, and then across the northeast part of the state via Benalla and Wangaratta, crossing back into New South Wales at Wodonga. A **handbook** of the walk is sometimes available at the DSE Information Centre or Information Victoria in Melbourne (see p.903), or enquire at the visitor information centres along the trail.

If you're reasonably fit, consider tackling the walk to the peak of **Mount William** (1168m; 3.5km return), the highest point in the park. This starts from the Mount William Road car park, for which you turn off 16km south of Halls Gap. More challenging overnight walks include one to the **Major Mitchell Plateau**, starting from the same car park but involving a difficult five-hundred-metre climb to the plateau, and the **Mount Difficult** walk, which starts from Rose Gap and goes across a large, undulating, rocky plateau.

Eating, drinking and entertainment

There's no shortage of places to **eat** in Halls Gap. A cluster of options can be found at the Stony Creek Stores complex on the main road which comprises *Coolas* for delicious home-made ice cream; the *Stony Creek Bakery* (daily 8am–5pm); the *Flying Emu Café* for cakes, snacks and light meals; the *Black Panther Café and Bar* (licensed and BYO) for breakfast, lunch, dinner and everything in between; and the popular *Toast to Us*, a pleasant restaurant with big windows facing a small reserve (open for lunch and dinner; licensed; book ahead for Saturday night ⓣ03/5356 4858).

Away from the stores, there are two good pub bistros serving moderately priced meals: the *Halls Gap Hotel and Family Bistro* (lunch and dinner daily) is 1km out of town on Stawell Road, while the *Halls Gap Tavern* (daily from about noon until late; lunch, dinner, morning and afternoon tea) is about 300m south of the shops on Lot 5, Dunkeld Road – the Tavern's "roast of the day" specials are particularly good value. The *Kookaburra Restaurant* on Grampians Road (ⓣ03/5356 4222) comes highly recommended for its inexpensive café-style dishes – mainly pasta and salads – and for its restaurant food, including baked duckling, kangaroo fillet and home-made ice cream. The *Balconies Restaurant* (ⓣ03/5356 4430) upstairs at the *Mountain Grand Guesthouse* offers elegant dining, good food and wines. *Darcy's* at the *Colonial Motor Inn* on Grampians Road (daily from 6.30pm, bookings advisable on ⓣ03/5356 3440) is a motel restaurant dishing up good grub including emu.

For entertainment, there's **live jazz** at the *Mountain Grand*: Saturday mornings (10am–1pm) at the *Café Grand* downstairs, and Saturday evenings from 7pm at their *Balconies Restaurant* upstairs. An alternative **film festival** comes to town at the beginning of November, and there's a jazz festival in mid-February.

Hamilton and around

Three highways converge at **HAMILTON**, a civilized little city where you can see the Grampians from the edge of the main street. Its main claim to fame is that it's the "Wool Capital of the World" – about six million sheep within a 80km radius yield about 10 percent of the world's wool production. The only reason you're likely to be here is if you're passing through, though there's a few things to distract you and the friendly **Hamilton Visitor Information Centre** on Lonsdale Street (daily 9am–5pm; ⓣ03/5572 3746 or 1800 807 056; ⓦwww.sthgrampians.vic.gov.au/tourism) can book accommodation if you decide to stay.

The most worthwhile of the town's five museums and galleries is the **Hamilton Art Gallery**, on Brown Street (Mon–Fri 10am–5pm, Sat 10am–noon & 2–5pm, Sun 2–5pm; donation), one of the finest provincial art galleries in the state. Its collection of eighteenth-century watercolours of English pastoral scenes by Paul Sandby is the largest outside Britain; among other gems are ninety engravings by William Hogarth and several pieces of eighteenth-century English furniture. The influence of the wealthy local Ansett family (of airline fame) is obvious; many of the excellent contemporary paintings were acquired through the Ansett Hamilton Art Awards.

Also in the town centre, but of marginal interest, is the **Hamilton History Centre** (2–5pm; closed Sat), located in the Mechanics Institute Building at 43 Gray St. East of town, on the Ballarat Road, is the **Sir Reginald Ansett Transport Museum** (daily 10am–4pm; $4), charting the history of the now defunct Ansett flight network which began here, while **The Big Woolbales** (daily 9.30am–4pm; daylight saving until 5pm) on Coleraine Road contain a small exhibition telling you about the wool industry of the Western district. There's also some refreshing greenery in the town centre: the Botanical Gardens are on the corner of French and Thompson streets, just one block from Gray Street, the main thoroughfare, while the banks of the **Grange Burn** are home to the eastern barred bandicoot, the only known population in mainland Australia. Grange Burn flows into man-made **Lake Hamilton**, which has a safe, sandy swimming beach and is filled with trout.

Practicalities

Hamilton features a wide variety of **accommodation**. Budget travellers can stay at the pleasantly sited *Lake Hamilton Caravan Park*, 8 Ballarat Rd (ⓣ & ⓕ03/5572 3855; cabins ❸). On the same road at no. 142 is the luxurious *Comfort Inn Grange Burn* (ⓣ & ⓕ03/5572 5755; ❺). The relaxed *Grand Central Hotel*, 141 Gray St (ⓣ03/5572 2899; ❸), is a good place both to eat and sleep: breakfast is included in the price of the motel-style rooms, there's an unpretentious bistro and bands play here at weekends.

The *Hamilton Strand* at 100 Thompson St (Mon–Sat 10am until late; licensed & BYO wine; ⓣ03/5571 9144) serves coffee, cakes and light snacks out the front and more substantial meals in the grand dining room behind. It has a good reputation, as does *Georgies Restaurant* at the *George Hotel*, 213 Gray St (daily lunch and dinner; ⓣ03/5572 1844). Other eating options are *127 Café-Bar-Restaurant* at 127 Thompson St (daily; ⓣ03/5571 1032) or for coffee and daytime refreshments the *Gallery Corner Café* at 175 Gray St.

Around Hamilton

Hamilton is situated on the fringe of an extensive volcanic plain that runs across western Victoria and into South Australia. The volcanic activities occurred fairly recently, from about 20,000 until 8,000 years ago. A tourist brochure, *Volcanic Discovery Trail*, describes a self-drive tour to the many remnants of this period of upheavals. Near Hamilton, Mount Napier (439m) to the south and Mount Rouse at Penshurst to the east were the sources of most of the lava flow now covering the area. Driving south towards Port Fairy, there's a very good view of Mount Napier directly ahead. The **Byaduk Caves** are located on the southwestern end of Mount Napier State Park – note that the Byaduk Caves Road turn-off from the Hamilton-Port Fairy Road, just north of the hamlet of Byaduk, is poorly signposted. The caves are actually fern-filled lava tubes; a walking path leads from the car park to viewing areas of cave entrances at collapsed roof sections. Harmans Cave 1 is the only one you can actually walk into. As you explore, watch out for stinging nettles and rough terrain, with frothy textured lava rocks scattered around, porous and covered in moss.

At Wannon on the Glenelg Highway, 15km west of Hamilton, there's a sign-posted turn-off to **Wannon Falls**, which are at their most impressive after a good winter rainfall season. A further 17km on, **COLERAINE** is picturesquely sited in the Wannon River Valley, between two tablelands. There you will find the **Peter Francis Point Aboretum** (open 24hr; free) and the **Eucalypt Discovery Centre** (Mon–Thurs 9am–5pm, Fri until 4.30pm, Sat 10am–4pm, Sun 11am–4pm; free), the nation's official eucalypt collection which has the largest number of species in the world. At **CASTERTON**, 29km further west on the Glenelg River, the 1843 **Warrock Homestead** (daily 10am–5pm; $6) is one of the most interesting in the country. The complex comprises more than thirty buildings – including the homestead, a blacksmith shop, shearers' quarters and a woolshed – and nowadays operates as a grazing property, but is open to visitors.

The Wimmera

The Wimmera, dry and hot, relies heavily on irrigation water from the Grampians for its vast wheatfields; before irrigation and the invention of the stump jump plough, the area was little more than mallee scrub, similar to the lands beyond **Warracknabeal**, the northernmost wheat-growing centre.

HORSHAM, capital of the wheatfields, makes a good stop-off point en route to Adelaide; it has an idyllic picnic spot, complete with barbecues, by the Wimmera River. There's little else to detain you, though the Grampians National Park (see p.1017) is within striking distance to the southeast, and **Mount Arapiles**, 40km west, is one of the most important **rock-climbing** centres in Australia – if you're interested contact The Climbing Company in Natimuk (Ⓣ1800 357 035), which can also organize **abseiling**. The **Horsham Visitor Information Centre**, at 20 O'Callaghan Parade (daily 9am–5pm; Ⓣ03/4382 1832 or 1800 633 218, Ⓦwww.horshamvic.com.au), books both accommodation and tours. One central, cheap **place to stay** is the *Royal Hotel*, 132 Firebrace St (Ⓣ03/5382 1255, Ⓔroyalpub@netconnect.com.au; rooms with shared facilities ❸), a grand old place established in 1881, which has retained many of its original features. *Moe's Mexicana*, 110 Firebrace St, is open daily from 6pm and has Mexican food as well as steaks and pasta on the menu, while *Café Bagdad* at 48 Wilson St has a very local, slightly arty alternative feel and serves espresso, cakes and ice cream, as well as big portions of cheap soups, salads and focaccia.

Continuing on the Western Highway, you come to **DIMBOOLA**, deep in the dreary flatlands; it's the sort of place that runs to its own dusty clock, frustratingly closing down for lunch just as interstate buses stop for a break. The *Dimboola Motel* (ⓣ03/5389 1177; ❹) and *Dimboola Hotel* (ⓣ03/5389 1380; ❹) are both on Horsham Road. **NHILL** and **Kaniva**, further along the highway, are similarly undistinguished. All three towns are within a few kilometres of **Little Desert National Park**, with Nhill being the best starting point if you plan to explore. *Little Desert Nature Lodge* (ⓣ03/5391 5232; dorms $20, rooms ❸), 16km southeast of the town on the Harrow Road, lies on the fringe of the park and runs good 4WD **tours**; it has camping, motel units and bunk rooms for groups. Far from being a desert, the national park has a great variety of plants, with colourful wild-flower displays in spring; much of the vegetation is low mallee scrub, among which the now rare mallee fowl can be spotted. There are three **campsites** within the national park: one on the Kiata South Road 13km from Kiata, east of Nhill – the others are at Horseshoe Bend and Ackle Bend, south of Dimboola (call Parks Victoria for more information on ⓣ03/5391 1255).

The Mallee

The Mallee, the most sparsely populated area of Victoria, begins north of Warracknabeal, from where the **Henty Highway** heads up to join the Sunraysia Highway and forge its way to Mildura, on the border with New South Wales. This is an area worth visiting only in winter, when it's drier and warmer than the rest of Victoria, but not too hot to make bushwalks unbearable. You really need your own transport to see anything; the only **public transport** is the small Henty Highway Coach that runs between Horsham and Mildura and mainly carries freight (departs Horsham BP service station Tues & Thurs at 9.15am and Fri at 5.45pm; Mildura train station Mon, Wed & Fri at 7.45am; 6hr; $60; ⓣ03/5023 5658 or 0427 865 379). Along the way are small dusty towns such as Brim, Bealah and **HOPETOUN** ("gateway to the Mallee"), whose shops still have their old awnings and apparently their original window displays too.

Fifty kilometres west of Hopetoun is **Wyperfeld National Park**, which at 3500 square kilometres is Victoria's third largest, with a chain of normally dry lake beds, mallee scrub, river red gum and black box woodlands, and rolling sand plains, with emus, kangaroos and mallee fowl among its wildlife. Bushcamping is not allowed in the park but a sealed road leads from Hopetoun via Yampeet to the *Wonga Campground*, where there's shady camping ($11 per site per night, max 6 people; payable by self-registration) and a picnic area with water and toilets. Another park, the Big Desert Wilderness is directly west of Wyperfeld but can be reached only by the Nhill–Murrayville track that runs between Broken Bucket, northwest of Nhill, and Murrayville, on the Mallee Highway west of Ouyen; there are no tracks, roads or facilities in the park, just more sand dunes, mallee scrub and lots of wildlife. You'll need a 4WD and considerable dedication to get the most out of it.

Beyond Hopetoun, the Henty Highway merges into the Sunraysia Highway. Heading north on the Sunraysia, you come to the small town of **SPEED**, which could hardly have a less appropriate name – tourist information is available at the general store. From here the mallee scrub clings to the edges of the highway, threatening to invade the red soil of cleared fields on either side. **OUYEN**, the "heart of the Mallee", is another small, undistinguished town where two highways meet. Heading west on the Mallee Highway, the access track to the picturesque **pink salt lakes** of the **Murray–Sunset (Yanga–Nyawi) National Park** leads north from Linga. Continuing north on the

Calder Highway from Ouyen, you pass the **Hattah–Kulkyne National Park**, just east of the highway; the park consists of dry mallee scrub, native woodland, and a lakes system lined with gums. Lake Hattah is reached by turning off the highway at Hattah, 34km north of Ouyen, onto the Hattah–Robinvale Road. From Hattah it's less than 70km to Mildura and the Murray River.

The Murray region

From its source close to Mount Kosciuszko high in the Australian Alps, the **Murray River** forms the border between Victoria and New South Wales until it crosses into South Australia (someone got a ruler out for the rest of the border to the coast), and although the actual watercourse is in New South Wales, the Victoria bank is far more interesting and more populous. After the entire length was navigated in 1836, the river became the route along which cattle were driven from New South Wales to the newly established town of Adelaide, and later in the century there was a thriving paddle-steamer trade on the lower reaches of the river, based at Wentworth on the New South Wales side (see p.376). In 1864, **Echuca** was linked by railway to Melbourne, stimulating the river trade in the upper reaches, and thus became a major inland port, the furthest extent of the navigable river. At the height of the paddle-steamer era, **Mildura** was still a run-down, rabbit-infested cattle station, but in 1887 the Chaffey brothers instituted irrigation projects that now support dairy farms, vineyards, vegetable farms and citrus orchards throughout northwestern Victoria. Between Mildura and Echuca, **Swan Hill** marks the transition to sheep, cattle and wheat country; the **Pioneer Settlement** here explores the extraordinarily hard lives of the early settlers. Above Echuca the Murray loses much of its magic as it flows through the more settled northeast.

Murray River red gums

The magnificent red gum forests of the Murray River floodplains are one of the major draws of the Murray River region, with evocative photographs gracing the pages of most tourist brochures. However, while these hardy trees are well adapted to the irregular cycles of drought and flood typical in Australia, human demand for water has created conditions of near-permanent drought they seem unable to cope with. In November 2004, a government report revealed that 75 percent of all red gums along the Murray are stressed, dying or dead. The cause is salinity and a lack of water, exacerbated by a 4-year natural drought. The infrequently released environmental flows are not sufficient to flush out the saline build-up and supply the trees with the water they need, and though the state and federal governments have agreed to let an additional 500 billion litres flow through the Murray some time after 2006, critics say this is just a third of what the river and the floodplains need in order to be moderately healthy. Time seems to be running out and, as the trees play a crucial part in maintaining the health of the river system, Australia stands to lose more than just an iconic landscape.

Nowadays **paddle steamers** cruise for leisure, and are the best way to enjoy the river and admire magnificent **river red gums** lining its banks, as well as the huge array of birds and other wildlife that the Murray sustains. Renting a **houseboat** is also a relaxing (if expensive) way to travel.

Mildura and around

MILDURA has a mirage-like aura, its vineyards and orange orchards standing out from a hot, dry landscape. To the southwest is the evocatively named **Sunset Country**, with nothing but gnarled mallee scrub, red sand and pink salt lakes (reached via Linga on the Mallee Highway). Mildura makes a good winter getaway, but summer can be stiflingly hot and it's best to avoid the area at this time if you can.

Deakin Avenue runs northwest through town to the river, with 7th Street and the train station facing the parklands that run along the river. Like any self-respecting small city, Mildura has a couple of malls, one running parallel to Deakin Avenue between 8th and 9th streets, and another, smaller one out of town at Deakin Avenue and 15th Street. The **Mildura Visitor Information and Booking Centre** is situated in the state-of-the-art Alfred Deakin Centre at Deakin Avenue and 12th Street (Mon–Fri 9am–5.30pm, Sat & Sun 9am–5pm; ⓣ03/5021 4424 or 1800 039 043, ⓦwww.visitmildura.com.au), which also houses a pool ($4.40) and gym, a decent café and a modern library, where

Cruises, tours and activities

The best **short river cruise** is on the PS *Melbourne* (daily 10.50am & 1.50pm; 2hr 10min; $22; ⓣ03/5023 2200), Mildura's only genuinely steam-driven paddle steamer. Built in 1912, it still has its original boiler and engine. The same company runs *Paddleboat Rothbury*, built in 1881 and in its day the fastest steamboat on the river; it's now been converted to diesel and takes people on cruises to local attractions, such as the Thursday cruise to Trentham Estate Winery ($48 including lunch and wine-tasting. *Paddleboat Coonawarra* (ⓣ03/5023 3366 or 1800 034 424) has **longer cruises**: four nights from $515 (depending on season). All cruises leave from **Mildura Wharf** at the end of Madden Avenue, west of the train station.

Away from the river, the most outstanding natural attraction is **Mungo National Park** (see p.377), 110km across the border in New South Wales. It's visited by tour operators from Mildura who charge about $80 a head: Junction Tours (ⓣ03/5027 4309 or 0408 596 438, ⓦwww.junctiontours.com.au) and Jumbunna Walkabout Tours (ⓣ03/5024 3406).

Koorie tour operators belonging to the Barkindji people also lend their perspective on the park with Harry Nanya Tours, based just over the border in Wentworth (Mon–Sat; ⓣ03/5027 2076, ⓦwww.harrynanyatours.com.au). They also do tours around Mildura, to Wentworth, and to other attractions and national parks in the surrounding area.

Camerons, 16 Olive Ave (ⓣ03/5021 2876 or 0427 793 297, ⓦwww.cameronsmildura.com.au), rents out sports gear and arranges **hot-air balloon flights** daily, weather permitting, for $230 per person for a 3hr 30min flight, including breakfast. Rainy days can be passed at the **Deakin Cinema Complex** at 98 Deakin Ave, while a back-to-nature alternative to the swimming pool on Deakin Avenue is available at the sandy **swimming beach** at Chaffey Bend. There are lifeguards in summer, but take local advice and beware of dangerous currents.

you can check your email ($2/30min). The visitor centre will book accommodation and supply free town maps: they also have particularly good information on the Murray–Sunset (Yanga–Nyawi) and Hattah–Kulkyne national parks.

Down on the river the seventy-year-old **Mildura Weir** system, designed to provide stable pools for irrigation and to enable navigation throughout the year, makes a pleasant place to while away an hour or so. Alternatively, wander down to the **Mildura Arts Centre**, 199 Cureton Ave (daily 10am–5pm; gallery $3), which consists of the historic home Rio Vista, the Mildura Regional Art Gallery, a theatre and a sculpture park. **Rio Vista** was built in 1890 for William Chaffey, who lived here with his first and second wives (both called Hattie Schell, the second the niece of the first) until he died in 1926. It's a lovely house, though rather ill-suited to the climate, and inside are various displays about the Chaffeys and the development of Mildura. The art gallery's most important piece is *Woman Combing Her Hair at the Bath*, a pastel by Edgar Degas; it also has some excellent sculpture by Australian artists.

Practicalities

Mildura is 555km from Melbourne, about as far as you can go in this small state; right on the border of New South Wales, and little over 100km from South Australia, it's ideally located for **onward transport** to either. Buses on the Sturt Highway, the major route between **Adelaide** and **Sydney**, pass through several times daily, with a Greyhound Australia service to Adelaide at 9.20am and a service to Sydney at 5.40pm, and a 4am Countrylink service to Sydney via Cootamundra. From Melbourne, there's also a V/Line train-bus connection via Bendigo or Swan Hill at least twice daily (call ⓣ13 61 96 to book). **Broken Hill**, north up Silver City Highway, can be reached by bus via Wentworth (departing Mildura train station Mon, Wed & Fri 9am; 3hr 30min; book at the visitor information centre). **Ballarat** is served once a day (except Sat) by V/Line, whilst you can get to **Albury**, via Swan Hill, Echuca and Rutherglen, on Wednesday, Thursday, Friday and Sunday. In terms of **local transport**, Coomealla Buslines runs a service across the river to Wentworth via Buronga (see p.1031), while the very regular Sunraysia Buslines (ⓣ03/5023 0274) services the centre from 7th to 15th streets, and to suburban areas further to the east and west, and to the south as far as Red Cliffs. Alternatively, you can **rent a car** from, among others, Budget at 7th Street and Etiwanda Avenue (ⓣ03/5021 4442).

Mildura has a good reputation as a place to find fruit-picking **work**, though the only guaranteed time is in February, when the grape harvest takes place. Unfortunately, this is also the time when the heat is most intense. If you think you can handle it, come around the end of January, the beginning of the eight-week season. Otherwise, there's a chance of picking up work during the citrus harvest in June and August, and possibly vine pruning. For details, call in at MADEC Jobs Australia/ Mildura Harvest Labour Office, 97–99 Lime Ave (Mon–Fri 7am–7pm; ⓣ03/5022 1797), or contact the National Harvest Labour Hotline (ⓣ1800 062 332, ⓦwww.jobsearch.gov.au/harvesttrail. Most of the town's backpacker hostels have contacts with a wide range of employers, will find a job for you, assist with the paperwork and provide transport to and from work.

Accommodation

Mildura has lots of reasonably priced **accommodation**, and an ever-increasing amount of hostels to cater to the hordes of hard-up backpackers that drift here looking for work. If you are staying longer, ask the hostel for their weekly rates – they come much cheaper. There's also a number of houseboats based in Mildura or across the river in Buronga or Wentworth. Ring the visitor information centre for information and bookings.

Adventure Houseboats Buronga ⓣ03/5023 4787, ⓦwww.adventure.ozland.net.au. Self-contained houseboats with laundry, CD player, TV and BBQ. Expect to pay from $400 off-peak for a 2-berth boat for 3 nights.
Burning Shores Backpackers 12 West Cliffs Ave, Red Cliffs ⓣ03/5024 2084, ⓦwww.burningshores.com.au. A small, family-run hostel with all the usual facilities, plus air conditioning and Internet access. The managers have good work contacts and provide transport from the bus stop and to work. One dorm (bed $20); the rest are twin/double and single rooms – the latter are particularly good value. ❶–❷
Mildura Grand Hotel 7th St, opposite the train station ⓣ03/5023 0511, ⓦwww.milduragrandhotel.com. Restored hotel, complete with ballroom, renowned gourmet restaurant, games room, spa, sauna and outdoor swimming pool. The sparsely decorated rooms range from basic to luxurious, with breakfast included. ❹–❼
Mildura International Backpackers 5 Cedar Ave ⓣ03/5021 0133, ⓔmildrabp@vic.ozland.net.au. Work-oriented hostel with recreation area, cable TV and laundry. The operators have work contacts, do all the paperwork required and organize transport too. Rooms are twin-, three- and four-bedded. Only weekly stays accepted; $120 per person per week.
Nomads Juicy Grape International Backpackers Block 446, Calder Highway, Sunnycliffs ⓣ03/5024 2112, ⓦwww.nomadsworld.com. Located 5km out of town, but there are free pick-ups from the bus stop and transport to jobs. They have Internet access, work registry and throw weekly BBQ parties. Dorms $22; rooms ❷
Riverboat Bungalow 27 Chaffey Ave ⓣ03/5021 5315, ⓦusers.mildura.net.au/bungalow/. The 1891 house is a work-and-play oriented place with work registry, Internet access, cable TV and a swimming pool in a large backyard near the river. Dorms $20, rooms ❷
Riverview B&B 115 Seventh St ⓣ03/5023 8975. Two rooms with en-suite in a 1950s-style house overlooking the river in a central location. ❹
Riviera Backpackers Motel 157 Seventh St ⓣ03/5023 3696 Working hostel in a centrally located former motel; units have been converted into 4-bed dorms with all mod cons; there's also a communal kitchen and a common room. Jobs and transport to work are arranged, and weekly rates ($130) are preferred.

Eating

Healthy food abounds in Mildura's **cafés and restaurants**, most of which are clustered on Langtree Avenue, just south of the mall. If you have your own transport, you can make an enjoyable outing to buy fruit and vegetables from surrounding farms. Otherwise, there are three excellent supermarkets, including a 24-hour Coles, surrounding Langtree Mall. In the upmarket bracket, there's the renowned restaurant *Stefano's* – resident chef Stefano de Pieri put Mildura on the culinary map of Australia with his cooking show on ABC TV.

27 Deakin Stefano's Good Food Store, Caffe and Bakery 27 Deakin Ave. A shrine to food that serves delicious breakfasts, lunches, coffee, cakes and bread as well as gourmet grocery items. Mon–Sat 8am–3pm, Sun 9am–3pm.
Hudak's Bakery Café 139 8th St & opposite Mildura Centre Plaza, 15th St. Good continental breads, pies, focaccias and cakes. Daily 7am–6pm.
Mildura Grand Hotel *The Grand*, as it's known, incorporates four eateries. Tucked away in the cellar is its crowning glory, *Stefano's* (dinner Mon–Sat; bookings essential ⓣ03/5023 0511). There's no menu but the northern Italian banquets (about $80 for 5 courses) are excellent. The other options include: *Dining Room One*, a bistro featuring Mediteranean cuisine; *The New Spanish Grill*, where you order your choice of grilled meat, side dishes and wine at the bar; and the *Grand Pizza Caffe and Wine Bar* for pasta and wood-fired pizzas.
Restaurant Rendezvous 34 Langtree Ave ⓣ03/5023 1571. Cheap lunches and other meals served in the bistro. There's also an upmarket restaurant, as well as a bar and courtyard seating. Lunch Mon–Fri, dinner Mon–Sat.
Sunraysia Wine Centre 34 Langtree Ave, next to the *Restaurant Rendezvous*. Sample local wines by the glass and have coffee and cake or snacks in the courtyard or on the terrace.
Taco Bills Langtree Ave. Cheap, substantial Mexican fare in cheery surroundings near the river. All main meals half-price on Tuesdays. Tues–Sun from 6pm.

Nightlife

Mildura's nightlife may not be the world's greatest, but there's enough to keep you occupied. Perhaps the best thing to do is to try out one of the **clubs**, where you can be signed in as a visitor; as an incentive to get you to the gambling machines, there's lots of inexpensive food and drink. The *Mildura Workingman's Club*, at 90 Deakin Ave between 9th and 10th streets, is one of many in town. Another good place for a drink is the vibrantly coloured, youth-oriented *Sandbar* at 43 Langtree Ave (nightly until 1am; light meals until 10pm; happy hour Mon–Fri 5–8pm), which has a courtyard and puts on live music weekly in the summer and at weekends the rest of the year.

Around Mildura

The easiest excursion from Mildura is to **RED CLIFFS**, some 15km south, with its vineyards and tree-lined streets. The huge **Lindemans Karadoc Winery** (daily 10am–4.30pm) is one of the largest **wineries** in Australia, where fifty thousand tonnes of grapes are crushed every year. The range of wines for tasting is extensive, prices are very reasonable and there's a café serving light lunches, coffee and cake (Mon–Fri 10am–3pm).

Across the Murray from Mildura at **BURONGA** (actually in NSW but more readily accessible from the Victoria side of the river), Boatmen Hire Boats next to the bridge (ⓣ03/5023 5874) rents out fishing boats for $25 per hour and canoes for $20 per hour. The nearby *Floating Cafe* (daily 10am–6pm) is a colourful pontoon moored in a lovely spot where there are lots of pelicans and ducks. Also at Buronga is the **BRL Hardy wine company** (Mon–Fri 10am–4pm, Sat 10.30am–4pm, Sun noon–4pm; ⓣ03/5018 9907), the largest cask winery in New South Wales, their most famous brand being Stanley Wines – you can taste the wine here or just pose for photos in front of the big wine cask outside. On a much smaller scale, **Trentham Estate Winery**, 10km down the Sturt Highway in an idyllic setting overlooking the river, has cellar door sales (Mon–Fri 9am–5pm, Sat & Sun 9.30am–5pm; and an upmarket restaurant (lunch Tues–Sun; dinner Sat; ⓣ03/5024 8888, ⓦwww.trenthamestate.com.au).

Swan Hill and around

Heading from Mildura or Red Cliffs for Swan Hill, you can go south down the Calder Highway, turning east at Hattah onto the Hattah–Robinvale Road and continuing past the Hattah Kulkyne National Park (see p.1027). Alternatively, you can cross the Murray into New South Wales and follow the Sturt Highway, recrossing the river at **ROBINVALE**, a small, rather characterless fruit-growing town, but idyllically situated within a great loop of the river. Wine buffs should make a stop at the **Robinvale Organic & Bio-Dynamic Winery**, Sea Lake Road (Mon–Sat 9am–6pm, Sun 1–6pm ⓣ03/5026 3955, ⓦwww.organicwines.com.au), where a wide range of wines, including some Greek varieties, are biodynamically produced.

Twenty-five kilometres from Swan Hill you reach the highly productive stone-fruit and vegetable-growing area of **NYAH**. Bushcamping (no water or facilities) is allowed in the nearby Nyah and Vinefera **state forests** along the Murray; contact Parks Victoria (ⓣ13 19 63). Eight kilometres beyond Nyah is the **Tyntynder Homestead** (open by appointment only on ⓣ03/5030 2754;

$8), a classic 1846 bungalow furnished in wealthy squatter style and set amid flowering gardens. Part of the homestead is a museum containing, among other things, a collection of Aboriginal artefacts.

As you approach **SWAN HILL** itself, the landscape changes – this is cattle and sheep country, with wheatfields further north. The Murray here is shallow and tricky to navigate, so there's not much river traffic. Swan Hill is a service centre for the pastoral industry and has a typically solid, conservative atmosphere. Surprisingly, it's quite a multicultural place, having ten percent of Victoria's Aboriginal population, and a large Italian community. The Pioneer Settlement is undoubtedly Swan Hill's main attraction, but while you're here, you could also visit the **Swan Hill Regional Art Gallery** (Tues–Fri 10am–5pm, Sat & Sun 11am–5pm; donation of $2 appreciated; free guided tour Sun 1.30pm), which specializes in folk and Aboriginal art, or take a guided tour to the **Murray Downs Homestead**, an impressive Victorian mansion at the heart of a forty-square-kilometre station – it's over the bridge in New South Wales, but barely 1km from town (tour bus leaves the Kookaburra booking office 2pm Tues–Thurs & Sat–Sun; $9; minimum numbers required; call to confirm ⓣ0428 500 417). The town's **swimming pool** on Monash Drive has several pools and a waterslide (Nov–March daily 11am–7pm; open for morning laps Mon, Wed & Fri 6am–8am; $3).

Pioneer Settlement

Swan Hill's **Pioneer Settlement**, a reconstruction of a pioneering community at Horseshoe Bend about 1km south of the train station, was the first of its kind in Australia and is still one of the best (daily 9am–5pm; $16; combination ticket for settlement, sound and light show and *Pyap* Cruise $34). The settlement may be closed for a short period every February; enquire on ⓣ03/5036 2410. The buildings are all authentic, having been transported from various sites near and far. One of the most interesting is the **Iron House**, an example of a nineteenth-century "kit home", many thousands of which were shipped out from Britain during the housing crisis that accompanied the gold-rush – cities and towns in Victoria had whole streets of them, and they were stiflingly hot in summer and freezing cold in winter. This particular example came from south Melbourne, where it was inhabited until 1967.

In the settlement's streets many of the **shops** are functional – the baker, the printer, the haberdashery and the porcelain doll shop – with assistants dressed in vaguely period costume. Generally, though, it's low-key and peaceful: buildings such as the barber's shop and the stock and station agents are open for you to wander around undisturbed. The pharmacy has a large collection of old medicines, with a gruesome dentist's surgery out back; the church is made from old bricks of the original courthouse; and there's even a rather creepy Masonic Lodge, which is still in use. The **Mechanics Institute** has a wonderful working "Stereoscopic Theatre" from 1895: the wooden cylinder has 25 viewfinders, each with a leather seat from which you can admire the 3D scenes. You can go on rides around the settlement in a 1924 Dodge or a horse-drawn carriage. In the evening, the **sound and light show** (nightly from dusk; $10) is strikingly effective.

The settlement is situated on the banks of the Marraboor River, a branch of the Murray, and a wooden bridge spans the river to Pental Island, which has an assortment of native flora and fauna. Otherwise, an old **paddle steamer**, the *Pyap*, cruises from the settlement upriver past Murray Downs every day at 10.30am and 2.30pm (1hr; $12), while the *Kookaburra* offers a longer luncheon cruise (1hr 30min; $29), departing at 12.30pm (Tues & Thurs–Sun).

Practicalities

The **Swan Hill Visitor Information Centre**, 306 Campbell St (daily 9am–5pm; ⓣ03/5032 3033 or 1800 625 373, ⓦwww.swanhillonline.com), has a free map of the town giving detailed information on local attractions; it also sells tickets for the Pioneer Settlement, its sound and light show and the MV *Kookaburra* and PS *Pyap* cruises. **Parks Victoria** at 1 McCallum St (Mon–Fri 8.30am–5pm; ⓣ03/5033 1290) can provide you with information on camping in the nearby Nyah and Vinefera state forests.

There's a strip of **motels**, all with swimming pools, along Campbell Street, where almost all the town's facilities are located. The most luxurious of the lot is the *Sundowner Swan Hill Resort* at no. 405 (ⓣ1800 034 220, ⓦwww.sundownermotorinns.com.au; ❺) which has an indoor and outdoor pool and spa, gym and other sports facilities; it's easily found because of its restaurant, the *Silver Slipper*, which has a huge rotating stiletto outside and even tackier decor inside. The *Paddle Steamer Motel* on the Murray Valley Highway, 3km south of the centre, has very good facilities and is much cheaper ⓣ03/5032 2151, ⓦwww.paddlesteamermotel.com.au; ❸). Also good value and much closer to the centre is *Jacaranda Holiday Units* at 179 Curlewis St (ⓣ03/5032 9077, ⓕ03/5033 1268; ❸). The *Riverside* at 1 Monash Drive (ⓣ03/5032 1494, ⓦwww.swanhillriverside.com.au; cabins ❸–❺) is a good, centrally located **caravan park** right on the riverfront.

Swan Hill **restaurants** still demonstrate an Italian culinary influence. *Bartalotta's Hot Bread*, at 178 Campbell St, is excellent, as is *Quo Vadis*, an authentic pizzeria at 255 Campbell St serving pasta and ribs too. A branch of the pizza-pasta restaurant chain *La Porchetta*, a newcomer in town, serves its very inexpensive pizza and pasta at no. 423, while *Teller's Restaurant & Bar* at no. 223 is a slick-looking, city-style brasserie in an old bank, open daily for lunch and dinner. *Café 202*, at 202 Beveridge St, serves tasty lunchtime options and good, strong coffee.

To Gunbower Island

From Swan Hill, the Murray Valley Highway heads southeast, away from the river, and follows the rail line past a series of about **fifty freshwater lakes,** collectively known as the Kerang Lakes or Wetlands. At the first of these, **Lake Boga**, 16km from Swan Hill, you'll find Lake Boga Jet Ski Hire and Parasailing. Also by the lake – follow the signs – is Best's St. Andrew's Vineyard, a large, commercial **winery**, the oldest in the Swan Hill region (Mon–Fri 9am–5pm, Sat 10am–4pm, Sun only during holidays noon–4pm; tours Mon–Fri 11am and 3pm; ⓣ03/5037 2154). The lakes peter out at Kerang, a sizeable town in a citrus-growing area on the Loddon River. Nearby Lake Reedy is one of the largest ibis-breeding grounds in Australia and has a viewing hide; the birds are widespread in the area, though, so you shouldn't have any trouble seeing some.

From Kerang, the Murray Valley Highway continues east to Cohuna, in a rich dairy-farming area, and from here towards **Gunbower Island**, a further 23km. The "island", encircled by the Murray River and Gunbower Creek, is a state forest of huge red gums and Gunnawarra wetlands, with 160 species of birds and a lot of wildlife. It's most easily approached from Cohuna (follow the signs on the Kerang–Koondrook road); for details of walks and camping contact Parks Victoria (ⓣ13 19 63).

Echuca and around

ECHUCA, a lively and progressive place, is the most easily accessible river town from Melbourne – it's only three hours or so by bus or car, making it a popular weekend getaway. Echuca became the largest inland port in Australia after the railway line connected it with Melbourne in 1864. When the **missions** began to close in the 1930s, many Aboriginal families, especially Yorta Yorta people from Cummeragunja mission, and Wemba Wemba from Moonacullah mission, migrated to the Echuca area. Since they weren't made welcome in the towns, the migrants were forced to live on the fringes in badly constructed, flood-prone housing, just close enough to be able to get to work and school. Women commonly worked in the canneries and hospitals, and the men packed fruit, sheared sheep and did other labouring jobs.

Arrival and information

The **tourist information centre**, 2 Heygarth St (daily 8am–5pm; ⓣ03/5480 7555 or 1800 804 446, ⓦwww.echucamoama.com), sells tickets to the port complex and for cruises, books accommodation and is an agent for V/Line and Countrylink **bus** tickets. V/Line runs up to six services between Melbourne and Echuca (train-bus and one direct train); there is also one daily connection with Sydney via Albury, and two to Adelaide (one direct, one via Bendigo).

Accommodation

As well as the **accommodation** options listed below, ask at the tourist office about the many **houseboats** available to rent in the area.

Echuca Caravan Park Crofton St, Victoria Park ⓣ03/5482 2157, ⓦwww.echucacaravanpark.com.au. A well-equipped caravan park right on the riverfront. Cabins ❸

Echuca Gardens YHA 103 Mitchell St ⓣ03/5480 6522 (8–10am & 5–10pm), ⓔechuca@yhavic.org.au. Budget accommodation in a restored Victorian worker's cottage – cosy atmosphere, but the dorms are cramped and tiny. The location on the edge of the Banyule Forest is very scenic though, and it's a ten-minute walk through red gums to sandy river beaches where it's safe to swim on the inner bends. Dorms $20, rooms ❷

Nomads Oasis Backpackers 410–424 High St ⓣ03/5480 7866, ⓔnomads@river.net.au. Centrally located, air-conditioned dorms as well as twins/doubles at an affordable price. There's a small kitchen and courtyard, and the owner has employment contacts and can provide transport to places of work. Dorms $21, rooms ❷

River Gallery Inn 578 High St ⓣ & ⓕ 03/5480 6902, ⓦwww.rivergalleryinn.com. Upmarket B&B accommodation in a pretty, historic home: seven of the eight self-contained rooms have open fire-places, and five have spas. ❻

Steam Packet Inn Cnr of Leslie St and Murray Esplanade ⓣ03/5482 3411, ⓦwww.steampacketinn.com.au. A National Trust-listed motel offering traditionally decorated rooms in the heart of the old port area. ❻

The town

Nowadays, **Port of Echuca**, with its massive wharves and collection of old buildings, is a major tourist attraction, and several cruises ply along the river from here. The town itself, however, is not too touristy, and has retained much of its charm. There are two principal streets: High Street, the former main street, leads to Murray Esplanade and the wharf, and is the centre of tourist activity, with lots of cafés and boutiquey shops, while Hare Street, the present-day main street, is lined with more commercial buildings.

To enter the old wharf area, dubbed the **Historic Wharf** (daily 9am–5pm), you'll need to pay a $11.50 entrance fee, which also allows entry to the *Star*

River cruises

A wide choice of **cruises with paddle steamers** is on offer, departing from berths just beyond the old wharf, best approached from High Street. One-hour port cruises are available on the PS *Alexander Arbuthnot*, PS *Pevensey* and the PS *Adelaide*, the latter, built in 1866, is the oldest wooden-hulled paddle steamer still operating in the world (about $19/hr; for all of them call ⓣ03/5482 4248). Other boats offering one-hour cruises are PS *Pride of the Murray* and PS *Canberra* (for both, call ⓣ03/5482 5244). The PS *Emmylou*, a wood-fired paddle steamer, has a variety of cruises (ⓣ03/5480 2237, ⓦwww.emmylou.com.au), while the MV *Mary Ann* (ⓣ03/5480 2200, ⓦwww.maryann.com.au) does lunch cruises (12.30pm; 2hr; $40) and dinner cruises (7pm; from $65). Kingfisher Cruises (ⓣ03/5480 1839) offers a two-hour eco-cruise through the Barmah wetlands some 30km upstream of the Murray, which contain the world's largest single stand of river red gums.

Hotel and the *Bridge Hotel*. Alternatively, you can combine a tour with a cruise on the *Pevensey* or the *Alexander Arbuthnot* (see box) for $24.50. The **Star Hotel** was first licensed in 1867 and is a typical pioneer pub, a tiny one-storey building with a tin roof and verandah. As the river trade declined, the *Star* was delicensed (in 1897), along with many of the other 79 hotels in town. Drinking on the premises became illegal, so the loyal clientele dug a tunnel to the street through which they could escape at the first hint of a police raid – you can examine this, along with the cellar and a small museum.

The magnificent red-gum **wharf** was a quarter of a mile long in its prime and is still fairly extensive. Three landing platforms at different levels allowed unloading, even during times of flooding, and there are wonderful views from the top, high over a bend in the river. Goods were transferred from train to steamer via this top level, and old train carriages sit on sidings here, piled high with trunks of red gum. You can wander below to the other levels, through a network of thick river-red-gum piles standing 12m high. At the lowest level, several **old paddle steamers** are moored, including the *Pevensey*, a 1911 cargo boat which you can wander aboard. In the wharf cargo shed there's a scale model of the working port and a ten-minute audiovisual presentation.

Back outside the wharf complex, along Murray Esplanade opposite Hopwood Gardens, is the **Bridge Hotel**, opened in 1858 but delicensed in 1916. It was built by the founder of Echuca, Henry Hopwood, an ex-convict who also started a punt service across the Murray; the story goes that if the pub wasn't doing well he'd close the ferry down for a few hours, leaving prospective passengers with little else to do but drink. Other attractions in the area include the **Red Gum Works** (daily 9am–5pm; free), housed in a large loading shed which is wonderfully scented by the wood as it's transformed from tree-trunk to souvenir; there's also a steam-operated sawmill and a blacksmith at work. The **Sharp Magic Movie House & Penny Arcade** screens silent movie classics continuously, and visitors can work the old gambling machines of the "penny arcade", all for a rather steep admission fee of $13.

Eating, drinking and nightlife

With hungry Melburnians to feed, there's no shortage of decent **eating places**. The small and friendly *American Hotel* is a good place to head for a **drink**, while the *Harvest Hotel*, 183 Hare St, draws a youngish crowd and plays host to live bands at weekends, as does the *Red Dog Saloon Bar* at the corner of Nish and Darling streets. The *OPT Entertainment Complex* at 273 Hare St has a restaurant, bar and pool tables; the nightclub here is open Friday and Saturday. The *Paramount Cinemas & Performing Arts Centre* at 392 High St has an auditorium and four cinemas with state-of-the-art facilities (Ⓣ03/5482 3399, Ⓦwww.echucaparamount.com). If you happen to be around in mid-February, look out for the **Jazz, Food and Wine Weekend**.

Echuca's **clubs** serve very cheap meals and drinks, presumably as an incentive to get you to their gambling machines – non-members can sign in as visitors. There are more clubs across the river in Moama.

Beechworth Bakery 513 High St. A branch of the original, very successful bakery from Beechworth; they sell a variety of breads baked in a wood-fired oven, sandwiches, pastries and other snacks, and there's a sun deck which is a good spot for breakfast or lunch. Daily 6am–7pm.

Black Pudding Delicatessen 525 High St. Scrumptious breakfasts and lunches that can be eaten in the lovely courtyard. Tues–Fri 8am–5pm, Sat & Sun 8am–3pm.

Bridge Hotel Hopwood Place. Coffee shop, bar and restaurant in the historic port area; good coffee, cakes and desserts, light lunches and mainly traditional Aussie dishes in the restaurant. Open daily for breakfast, lunch and dinner; the bar is open daily 7.30am–1am, Sun till 11.30pm.

La Porchetta 196 Annesley St Ⓣ03/5480 1130. Inexpensive pizza and pasta chain restaurant. Good-value meals. Licensed. Open daily 12noon–late.

Oscar W's Wharfside Murray Esplanade Ⓣ03/5482 5133. This restaurant serves excellent, superbly presented food to match the scenic setting next to the old Echuca Wharf, overlooking the Murray River. The moderately expensive cuisine is Mediterranean-inspired "mod Oz". Licensed. Open daily 11am–late.

Top of the Town High St, opposite the Aquatic Centre. Fish and chips shop selling excellent-quality, freshly cooked fish – including river fish. Daily 10am–8.30pm.

Wistaria Tearooms High St, opposite the *Shamrock Hotel*, or enter from the port. Lovely Victorian house where you can get breakfast and light meals, coffee and cakes. Licensed. Daily 8am–6pm.

Around Echuca

Thirty kilometres southeast of Echuca, Kyabram's main attraction is **Kyabram Fauna Park** (daily 9.30am–5.30pm; $11.50), a community-owned wildlife park divided into grassland for free-ranging kangaroos, wallabies, emus and other animals, and a huge wetland area. You can wander around the grassland area and through several aviaries; a two-storey observation tower affords views of the more than eighty species of native birdlife. Diamond pythons, tiger snakes, crocodiles and other not-so-pleasant creatures can be viewed from a safe distance at the Reptile House.

BARMAH, some 30km upstream on the Murray, is most easily reached by crossing into NSW at Echuca and heading north on the Cobb Highway, then turning east. This small river town is associated with red-gum milling, and with sleeper-cutting in the early railway days. The *Barmah Caravan Park* (Ⓣ03/5869 3225; ❶–❸) has a great site on the banks of the river among red gums, with a small, sandy beach for swimming and a few cabins. **Barmah State Park**, 10km out of town, has Australia's largest stands of **river red gum**, some of them 40m tall and five hundred years old. The forest runs along the Murray for over 100km and stands in an extensive flood plain – **canoeing** among the trees at flood time (July–Nov) is a magical experience; you can arrange transport and rent canoes from Echuca Boat and Canoe Hire (Ⓣ03/5480 6208, Ⓦwww.echucaboatcanoehire.com). During the wet season more than two hundred species of waterbird come here, and there's plenty of other wildlife; you might even see brumbies (wild horses). When it's dry you can use several well-established walking tracks: the place was of special significance to the Yorta Yorta Aborigines and you can still see fish traps, middens and scars on trees where the bark was used for canoes.

Yorta Yorta culture and lore are explained in the park's **Dharnya Centre** (daily 10.30am–4pm; ☎03/5869 3302), which also has archeological information and artefacts. A **cruise** in the MV *Kingfisher* leaves from the bridge near the centre (Mon, Wed, Thurs, Sat & Sun, plus other days during busy times; 2hr; $22; booking essential on ☎03/5840 1839) – a flat-bottomed boat that glides over Barmah Lake and through stands of red gum. Bushcamping is permitted in the park; contact Parks Victoria (☎13 19 63) for details.

Gippsland

GIPPSLAND stretches southeast of Melbourne from Western Port Bay to the New South Wales border, between the Great Dividing Range and Bass Strait. Green and well watered, it's been the centre of Victoria's dairy industry since the 1880s. **South Gippsland** is also, in contrast, the site of vast brown-coal deposits between Moe and Traralgon in the Latrobe Valley, where power stations generate more than 85 percent of the state's electricity while, offshore, Bass Strait wells exploit natural gas and crude oil reserves with several gas-processing and oil-stabilizing plants disfiguring the coastline. South Gippsland also has Victoria's most popular national park, **Wilsons Promontory**, or "The Prom", a hook-shaped landmass jutting out into the strait, with some superb scenery and fascinating bushwalks. In the east, around the **Gippsland Lakes** and **Ninety Mile Beach**, the region is unindustrialized; and just beyond Orbost–Marlo the unspoilt coastline of the **Croajingolong National Park** – with its rocky capes, high sand dunes and endless sandy beaches – stretches to the New South Wales border.

Transport

Having your own **car** is essential for getting off the highway to really experience the region's diverse highlights and to get to the unspoilt bush campsites on the coast. The Princes Highway itself is a very boring drive, particularly the stretch from the Latrobe Valley to Bairnsdale, but after Orbost the highway becomes more scenic as it goes through the tall, dense eucalypt forests of Far East Gippsland. If you don't have a car, you might want to consider travelling with Oz Experience, the **backpacker bus** company that covers the Sydney–Melbourne route in five days, via Phillip Island, Gippsland, the Snowy Mountains and Canberra.

V/Line **trains** run from Melbourne to Bairnsdale, basically following the Princes Highway through South Gippsland. From Bairnsdale, **buses** leave for Orbost, stopping at Lakes Entrance. The Sapphire Coast Link is a daily train–bus connection between Melbourne and Narooma on the south coast of New South Wales: take the train to Bairnsdale, then a connecting bus along the Princes Highway via Lakes Entrance, Orbost, Cann River and Genoa. On Mondays, Thursdays and Saturdays, the bus continues on to Batemans Bay. Similarly, the Capital Link train/bus service heads to Canberra via Bairnsdale on Monday and Thursday mornings, returning from Canberra Tuesday and Friday mornings. Bookings for all the above should be made through V/Line

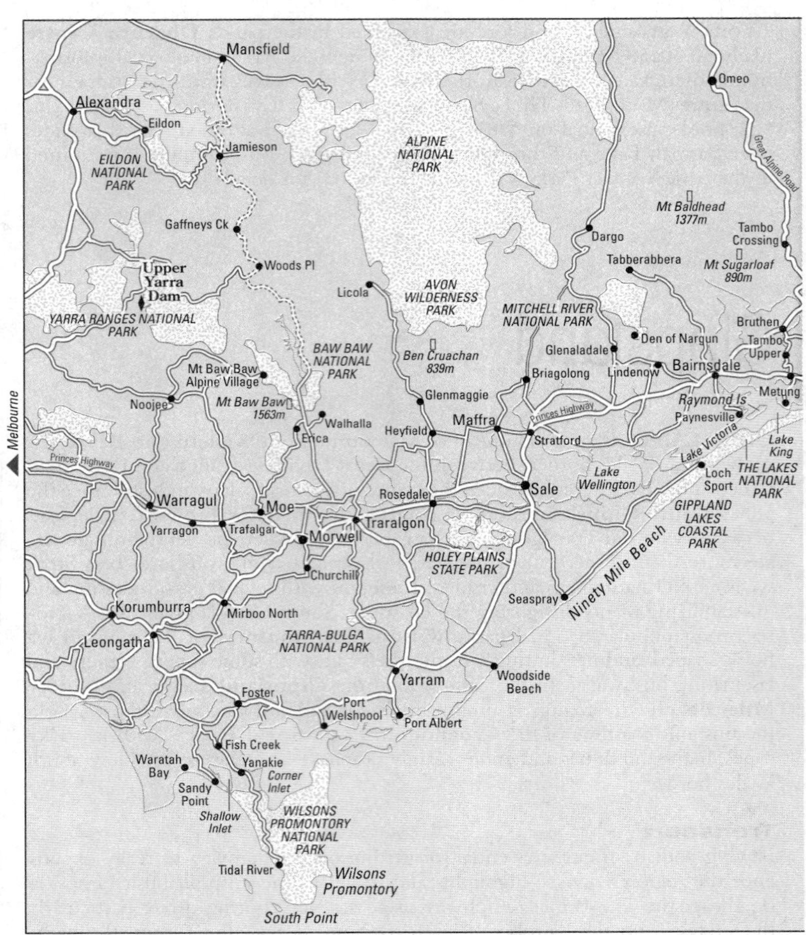

(☎13 61 96, ⓦwww.vline.com.au). Premier Motor Service (☎13 34 10), a NSW-based coach company, runs a daily service from Melbourne to Sydney along the coast but it's not very convenient if you want to get off at stops in East Gippsland: the bus leaves Melbourne at about 6pm, on Sat at 9.30pm, and gets to Lakes Entrance and Cann River in the early hours of the morning.

Wilsons Promontory and Tarra Bulga

WILSONS PROMONTORY, or "The Prom", the most southerly part of the Australian mainland, was once joined by a land bridge to Tasmania. Its barbed hook juts out into Bass Strait, with a rocky coastline interspersed with sheltered sandy bays and coves; the coastal scenery is made even more stunning

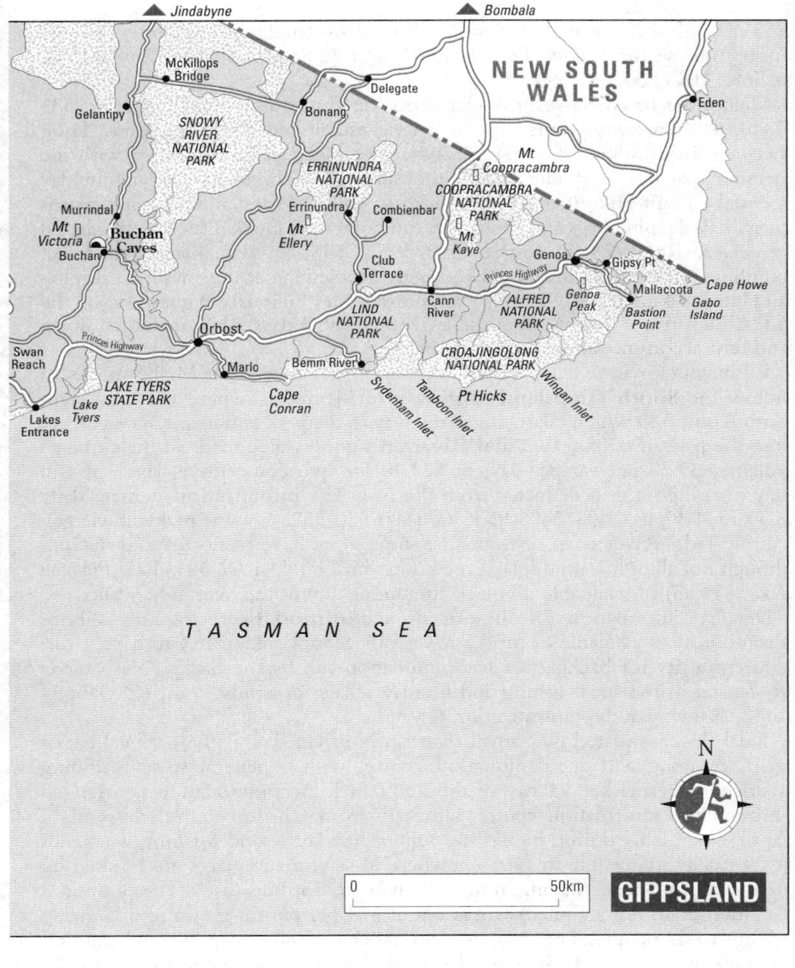

by the backdrop of granite ranges. It's understandably Victoria's most popular **national park**, and though the main campsite gets totally packed in summer, there are plenty of walking tracks and opportunities for bushcamping, and the park's big enough to allow you to escape the crowds. You can swim at several of the beaches and even **surf**: The Prom Surf School, based at Tidal River, operates courses in summer, for all ages and abilities, with all equipment provided (ⓣ03/5680 8512, ⓔpeck@pocketmail.com.au).

Arrival, information and accommodation

There's no public transport to Wilsons Promontory, so if you don't want to hire a car, you can take the evening V/Line bus from Dandenong to Yarram and get off at **FOSTER** on the South Gippsland Highway, from where the Foster Taxi Service transports people to the National Park and back (ⓣ03/5682 2188;

$85–90 one way for max. 5 people). For an overnight stay at Foster, try the motel units at the *Wilsons Promontory Motel* at 26 Station St (Ⓣ03/5682 2055, Ⓕ5682 1064; ❹).

Melbourne-based eco-tour operator Bunyip Bushwalking Tours (Ⓣ03/9531 0840, Ⓦwww.bunyiptours.com) is a long-established Prom specialist. Their two-day Bushwalking Tour ($255; twice weekly) can be combined with the penguin parade on Phillip Island; they also do a three-day and a four-day Coastal Circuit Hike (from $345; once weekly). All food and camping gear is provided, sleeping bags and backpacks can be rented. Duck Truck Tours, based at *Amaroo Park YHA* in Cowes (Ⓣ03/5952 2548, Ⓦwww.amaroopark.com), combine a tour of Phillip Island and penguin viewing at dusk with a camping and bushwalking trip to Wilsons Promontory; on Phillip Island guests stay at the YHA (departures from Melbourne twice weekly; 3 days; $325 including dorm and tent accommodation and some meals).

With your own vehicle, the easiest way to get here from Melbourne is to follow the **South Gippsland Highway** to Meeniyan, where you turn right onto Route 189 which takes you all the way to the park entrance. Once you get into the park, it's 30km to **Tidal River** on a good sealed road. At the entrance you pay $9.30 per car per day, or $14.40 for two consecutive days – if you stay overnight, this is deducted from the cost. The **information centre** (daily 8.30am–4.30pm; Ⓣ03/5680 9555 or 1800 350 552, Ⓦwww.parkweb.vic.gov.au) at Tidal River is an obvious first stop. They have plenty of information, though not all of it is on display, so ask: the small booklet *Discovering the Prom on Foot* ($14.95) is invaluable if you're attempting any of the overnight **walks**.

Detailed information on all sorts of **accommodation** close to Wilsons Promontory is available from Ⓦwww.promaccom.com.au. If you have a car, you could try for backpacker accommodation run by the *Sandy Point Café & Restaurant* in the small fishing and holiday village of Sandy Point (Ⓣ03/5684 1448, Ⓦwww.sandypointcafe.com; ❷).

Tidal River, situated by a small river on Norman Bay, is the national park's main camping and accommodation centre, with a general store including a pricey supermarket, takeaway food and fuel. Accommodation is arranged through the information centre, although from Christmas until the end of April – especially during public and school holidays – and for long weekends it's virtually impossible to get somewhere to stay; many places are booked up to a year in advance. Staying in the very basic motor huts (use of the campsite's facilities; linen not supplied) works out at $14 per person if you're in a group of four to six people. The camping area has about 480 non-powered campsites ($19.60 per night for 3 adults and 1 car; additional cars and people extra; max 8 people per site). Facilities include hot showers, a laundry and a summer outdoor cinema. There are also some very comfortable self-contained holiday cabins sleeping up to six people ($144 for two adults, plus $19.10 each extra adult).

Walks

Many short walks begin from Tidal River, including a track accessible to wheelchairs. One of the best is the **Squeaky Beach Nature Walk** (1hr return), which crosses Tidal River, heads uphill and through a tea-tree canopy, finally ending on a beach of pure quartz sand that is indeed squeaky underfoot. **The Lilly Pilly Gully Nature Walk** (3hr return) is very rewarding, as it affords an excellent overview of the diverse vegetation of "the Prom", from low-growing shrubs to heathland to open eucalypt forest, as well as scenic views. The walk starts at the Lilly Pilly Gully car park near Tidal River, follows a small valley and returns to the car park along the slopes of Mount Bishop. For **overnight camping** ($6.20 per person per night), you need to obtain a **permit** from the information centre at Tidal River (see opposite), as there is a restriction on the number of people allowed on the campsites. Half the sites at each camping area are reserved for advance bookings (at least 21 days in advance for holidays and long weekends; credit-card phone bookings accepted), while the remaining sites can be booked on arrival in the park. From September until the end of April, restrictions on the length of stay apply to the southern section of the park: only one night at each campsite, two at the *Roaring Meg* campsite. Hikers must use a gas-fuel stove as open fires are not allowed anywhere, and absolutely all rubbish must be carried out. Water from creeks is usually okay but the rangers recommend sterilizing it.

The tracks in the southern section of the park are well defined and not too difficult; the campsites here have pit toilets and fresh water. The most popular walk is the two- to three-day (37km) **Sealers Cove–Refuge Cove–Waterloo Bay** route, beginning and ending at the Mount Oberon car park. During summer holidays and at long weekends between November and the end of April, the tracks become extremely busy, so book well in advance or show up early. The remote north of the park is only suitable for experienced, properly equipped bushwalkers; there are no facilities (except for pit toilets at Tin Mine Cove) and limited fresh water.

Tarra Bulga National Park

Another good national park can be reached from Yarram, 50km beyond Foster on the South Gippsland Highway. **Tarra Bulga National Park**, in the heart of the Strzelecki Ranges, is dominated by forests of mountain ash and myrtle beech with a lower canopy of ferns – a cool green environment alive with colourful lyrebirds, crimson rosellas and yellow-breasted robins among the rich birdlife. The **visitors information centre** (Sat & Sun, daily in summer and Easter holidays, usually 10am–4pm; ⓣ03/5196 6166) at Balook on the Grand Ridge Road, between the two separate sections of the park, has information about the park (geology, history, flora and fauna) and the walks. The Grand Ridge Road (mostly unsealed and in parts quite rough) winds along the top of the Strzelecki Ranges through fern gullies and towering trees, affording gorgeous views of South Gippsland. The *Tarra Bulga Guest House* (ⓣ03/5196 6141, ⓦwww.tarrabulgaguesthouse.com; ❹), on Grand Ridge Road just 50m from the visitors centre, has every amenity, including a library and games room.

The Gippsland Lakes region

The **Gippsland Lakes**, Australia's largest system of inland waterways, are fed by the waters of the Mitchell, Nicholson and Tambo rivers, and are separated from the sea by Ninety Mile Beach. East of Yarram, the beach stretches long and straight towards **Lakes Entrance**, the tacky focal point of the area and one of Victoria's most popular holiday spots, with the foothills of the high country within easy reach to the north.

SALE, at the junction of the South Gippsland Highway and the Princes Highway, is a good point from which to head off to explore the coastal park and Ninety Mile Beach. From Seaspray, 35km south, a coastal road hugs the shore for 20km to Golden Beach, from where a scenic drive heads through the Gippsland Lakes Coastal Park to Loch Sport; here you're faced with the enviable dilemma of lakes on one side and ocean beaches with good surfing on the other. An unsealed road then continues on to Sperm Whale Head in the Lakes National Park. Sale's **tourist information centre** (daily 9am–5pm; ⓣ1800 677 520, ⓦwww.gippslandinfo.com.au), on the Princes Highway, can provide you with all the details. They can also give information about the **Bataluk Cultural Trail**, which starts in Sale and links sites of cultural and spiritual significance to the Gunai people, the original inhabitants of the Gippsland coast. The first stop on the trail, the Rahmayuck Aboriginal Corporation at 117 Foster St in Sale, sells arts and crafts, paintings and T-shirts (usually Mon–Fri 9am–5pm).

If you'd like to get friendly with the locals, opt for a stay off the beaten track at the small *Cambrai Backpackers* at 117 Johnston St in **Maffra,** a small dairy-farming town, 20km off the Princes Highway in the foothills of the Great Dividing Range. Located in a lovely, refurbished building right in the town centre, the hostel has dorms (4–6 beds) and doubles, a communal kitchen, comfy lounge and licensed bar. The owners pick up from the bus stop (pre-book), arrange walks in the high country and have work contacts (ⓣ1800 101 113, ⓦwww.maffra.net.au/hostel/; dorms $20-25, rooms ❸).

BAIRNSDALE is the next major town on the highway east of Sale and serves as another departure point for the lakes to the south. The efficient staff at the **tourist office** on Main Street (daily 9am–5pm; ⓣ03/5152 3444, ⓦwww.egipps.vic.gov.au/tourism/index.htm) will provide all the local information you'll need. A small exhibition at the **Krowathunkoolong Keeping Place**, parallel to the Princes Highway at 37–53 Dalmahoy St, explains the history of the Gunai people (usually Mon–Fri 9am–5pm; if closed, walk round the back to the admin section; $4).

For budget **accommodation** in Bairnsdale itself, try the *Grand Terminus Hotel* at 98 McLeod St (ⓣ03/5152 4040, ⓕ5152 3075; ❷). A gorgeous – if very pricey – alternative is the luxurious *Lake Gallery B&B* (ⓣ03/5156 0556, ⓦwww.lakegallerybedandbreakfast.com; ❼) in **Paynesville**, 16km south of Bairnsdale, which has two designer-decorated guest suites at the water's edge and its own jetty.

A short ferry ride away across the McMillan Straits from Paynesville is **Raymond Island** which, with its prolific birdlife, kangaroos and koalas, is an idyllic place to stay. The Raymond Island Ferry runs roughly every half-hour throughout the day (Mon–Thurs 7am–10.30pm, Fri & Sat 7am–midnight, Sun 8am–10.30pm; cars $5 return, foot passengers free). Accommodation options on the island are *Currawong Cottage*, 27 Currawong Close, ⓣ03/5156 7226; ❺), which sleeps up to four people, or a couple of two-bedroom flats at *Swan Cove Holiday Flats*, 390 Centre Road, (ⓣ03/5156 6716; ❸).

Forty-five kilometres northwest of Bairnsdale is another site on the Bataluk Cultural Trail, the **Den of Nargun** in the **Mitchell River National Park**. According to a Gunai legend, the small cave here was inhabited by a large female creature, a *nargun*, who would abduct people who wandered off on their own. As the Den of Nargun was a special place for Gunai women and may have been used for initiation ceremonies, the story served the purpose of keeping unauthorized people away. The cave is located in a small, beautiful valley; follow the loop track from the park picnic area via a lookout to the Mitchell River (30min), then take the track along Woolshed Creek to the cave and climb up the steep path back to the starting point (40min).

Lakes Entrance and Metung

LAKES ENTRANCE is named after the entrance to the Gippsland Lakes. A sandy barrier between the Gippsland Lakes and the sea formed about six thousand years ago, when first seen by white men in the 1840s the outlet was a seasonal, intermittent gap, unsuitable for reliable trade. In 1889 the present stable entrance was opened 6km east of the old one: the artificial entrance effectively cuts off the town's access to the length of **Ninety Mile Beach**.

As you might expect from the area's popularity, Lakes Entrance is a big, rather tawdry, tourist town, with loads of motels at either end of town as you enter from the highway. There are all sorts of attractions aimed at keeping holidaying children happy – from Fun Park to minigolf – on the Esplanade, which fronts onto an arm of Lake King. The **Griffiths Sea Shell Museum** at 125 Esplanade (daily 9am–5pm; $5), with its rather off-putting 1950s-style facade, has a huge collection of shells and marine life, as well as an aquarium containing an intriguing assortment of fish from the Gippsland Lakes. Lakes Entrance is also a big **fishing port**: the Fishermans Cooperative Wharf has a viewing platform where you can watch the catch being unloaded, as well as a tantalizing fish shop.

Beaches are obviously the big attraction here. Lakes Entrance Surf Beach, a substantial stretch of white sand patrolled in season by surf lifesavers, can be reached via a footbridge across the lake to Hummocks Reserve. A stand on the beach side of the footbridge hires canoes, paddleboats, aquabikes and catamarans. Of the many **lake cruises** on offer, one of the most popular is the trip from the *Club Hotel* jetty at the western end of town, up North Arm to the Wyanga Park Winery – the most famous local winery – on the fringe of the Colquhoun Forest, in the winery's own boat, the *Corque* (daily lunch cruise $40, Fri & Sat dinner cruise $60, Sun brunch cruise $30; book at Lakes Entrance Visitor Centre, or through the winery on ⓣ03/5155 1508). Other waterside activities are three-hour **fishing** trips with Mulloway Fishing Charters (ⓣ0427 943 154). At the time of writing, the environmentally friendly, electric-powered cruises with MB *Rubeena* on Lake Tyers, just east of Lakes Entrance, were not operating due to low water levels (enquiries ⓣ03/5155 1283).

Practicalities

Lakes Entrance Tourist Information (daily 9am–5pm; ⓣ1800 637 060), on the Esplanade, provides local advice and tickets for cruises on the lakes, and can also book accommodation, a useful service in summer when the place gets very crowded.

Accommodation

Coastal Waters Motel Esplanade ⓣ03/5155 1792, ⓦwww.coastalwaters.com.au. One of the better motels, with its own heated saltwater pool. ❺

Deja Vu Out of town at 17 Clara St ⓣ03/5155 4330, ⓦwww.dejavu.com.au. A rather special B&B in a pleasant location, with spacious en-suite rooms as well as separate 1- and 2-bedroom cottages overlooking the waterway of North Arm. ❼

Goat and Goose B&B 16 Gay St ⓣ03/5155 3079, ⓦwww.babs.com.au/goatandgoose. Recommended B&B in a timber house on a hill at the western end of town. There are great ocean views from the balconies, and three of the four suites come with a spa. Breakfast is huge and scrumptious, and, to top it all off, guests get a tour of Lakes Entrance in the owner's Rolls Royce. ❺

Kalimna Woods Kalimna Jetty Rd ⓣ03/5155 1957, ⓦwww.gippsland.com/web/KalimnaWoods/. Fully self-contained timber cottages, some with spas and log fires. ❺

Lazy Acre Log Cabins 35 Roadknight St ⓣ03/5155 1323, ⓦwww.lazyacre.com. A good bet, with a pool, BBQ, adventure playground, spa and facilities for disabled visitors. ❺

Riviera Backpackers YHA 5 Clarkes Rd ⓣ03/5155 2444, ⓔlakesentrance@yhavic.org.au. In the east end of town, this is a friendly place situated close to a beautiful stretch of lake. It has dorms and good en-suite rooms, a large kitchen/common room, Internet access, a laundry and a small pool with spa. Dorms $19, rooms ❷

Silver Sands Tourist Park 33 Myer St ⓣ03/5155 2343, ⓔmanager@ssands.com.au. A small, well-maintained caravan and camping park in a quiet location, a block behind the Esplanade, with en-suite cabins. ❸

Eating

At the **budget** end you'll find fish and chip shops such as the excellent *Fish-a-Fare* at no. 509 and *L'Ocean Fish & Chips* at 19 Myer St, just off The Esplanade, which serves its fish with gluten-free and wheat-free batter. For coffees, breakfasts and light meals, go for *Clearwater Café* at 23 Myer St and, back on The Esplanade, *Café Pelicano* at no. 171, *The Boathouse Licensed Café* at no. 213, *Lakes Patisserie Bakery* at no. 307. Inexpensive restaurants include the wonderfully named *A Moose on the Loose* for international and Thai cuisine at no. 567, *Adriano's Wood Oven* at no. 575 for Italian, and backpackers' favourite *Tres Amigos Mexican* for super-cheap stodge at no. 521.

Moving **upmarket**, *The Nautilus* (Ⓣ03/5155 1400) is a floating restaurant specializing in local seafood – arguably the best (and the most expensive) food in town. In addition to **wine-tasting**, the popular *Henry's Winery Cafe* at Wyanga Park Winery, 3km from town near North Arm (follow the signposts), also serves cakes and Devonshire **teas**, cheese platters and other meals; wines are available by the glass at cellar door prices (daily lunch & snacks noon–2.30pm, dinner Fri–Sat, in January and during the Easter holidays daily dinner from 6pm; bookings preferred on Ⓣ03/5155 1508).

Metung

If the commercialism of Lakes Entrance turns you off, head for the more refined charms of **METUNG**, a pretty, upmarket boating and holidaying village just 10km west along the shoreline. To get here, take the highway towards Bairnsdale, then turn south on the side road at Swan Reach.

A typically civilized **accommodation** option in Metung is *Maeburn Cottages*, 33 Mairburn Rd (Ⓣ03/5156 2736, Ⓦwww.gippslandlakes.com/maeburn; ❹), where you stay in three- to four-person cabins. *McMillans of Metung*, at 155 Metung Rd, has very comfortable, fully equipped cottages of different sizes in a garden setting, with a solar-heated pool, tennis court and a private jetty (Ⓣ03/5156 2283, Ⓦwww.mcmillansofmetung.com.au; ❺). *The Moorings at Metung*, 28 Main Rd (Ⓣ03/5156 2750, Ⓦwww.themoorings.com.au; ❺), are luxury apartments with sun decks and BBQs overlooking Bancroft Bay; their bistro menu offers everything from champagne brunch to coffee and cake. Cheaper is the *Metung Hotel* (Ⓣ03/5156 2206, Ⓦwww.metunghotel.com.au; ❸), which also offers food. The pleasant BYO *Little Mariners Café* at 57 Metung Rd serves breakfast, light **meals** and local seafood daily, while *Marrillee at Metung* on the same road at no. 50 (Ⓣ03/5156 2121) is pricier, licensed and specializes in local wines and fish. Both offer alfresco dining.

Buchan and the Snowy River Loop

Nowa Nowa is the inauspiciously named town where you turn north off the Princes Highway for the small town of **BUCHAN**, in the foothills of the Victorian Alps, and take a satisfying loop through the Snowy River National Park. Buchan boasts over six hundred **caves**, the most famous of which – the Royal Cave and the Fairy Cave – can be seen on **guided tours** (daily: April–Sept 11am, 1pm & 3pm; Oct–March 10am, 11.15am, 1pm, 2.15pm & 3.30pm; $12; booking advised on Ⓣ03/5155 9264). In the extensive park surrounding the caves there's an icy, spring-fed swimming pool, a playground, walking tracks and a campsite, plus lots of wildlife.

On the north bank of the Buchan River in the town is *Buchan Lodge* (Ⓣ & Ⓕ03/5155 9421; ❶), a smallish backpackers **hostel** with dorms, a country-style kitchen, laundry, log fire in winter, BBQ and a garden. The owner will advise about activities in the area, including caving, trail riding and rafting; for good pub grub head to the *Caves Hotel*.

The road continues north from Buchan through hilly country, following the Murrindal River and slowly winding its way up to the plateau of the Australian Alps. The sealed road ends at Wulgumerang, just before the turn-off to McKillops Bridge. You can continue straight up to Jindabyne in the Snowy Mountains of New South Wales – a spectacular drive – but about two-thirds of the road is unsealed and can be rough; check conditions before setting out.

Snowy River National Park

Turning right at Wulgumerang, about 55km north of Buchan, enables you to make a scenic arc through part of the **Snowy River National Park**, following the road towards Bonang (check road conditions in advance, as this is an unsealed road that can deteriorate badly in adverse weather conditions). **Little River Falls** are well worth a stop on this stretch: a short walk leads from the car park past snow gums to a lookout with breathtaking views of Little River Gorge and the falls. Equally stunning is the view from the second lookout from the top of the northeastern cliff face of **Little River Gorge** (about 10min from the car park).

Further on, you descend to the valley of the Snowy River, which you cross at **McKillops Bridge**, set in the landscape that inspired "Banjo" Paterson's famous ballad, *The Man from Snowy River*. The river's sandy banks are a favourite swimming spot, and are also the place to set out on a **rafting** trip through deep gorges, caves, raging rapids and tranquil pools; Snowy River Expeditions offers good-value river expeditions, as well as rafting, abseiling, rock-climbing, horse riding ($25/hr) and wild caving adventures ($35). They also run *Karoonda Park* (Ⓣ03/5155 0220, Ⓦwww.karoondapark.com; dorms $26, rooms ❸), a small country **hostel** situated on a beef and sheep farm in **Gelantipy**. Oz Experience buses pass through Gelantipy.

Bonang to Orbost

The road through the Snowy River National Park continues until it meets the Bonang–Orbost road. The general store at **Bonang**, a former goldrush town, sells takeaway food, groceries and fuel and has some information about the area. The rustic *Delegate River Tavern*, on the Monaro high plains about fifteen minutes' drive north from Bonang across the NSW border, is open daily for counter **meals** and has good-value B&B **accommodation** in log cabins (Ⓣ02/6458 8009; ❸).

The road down from the plateau to the coast, still mostly unsealed, leads past the **Errinundra National Park**, which protects magnificent wetland eucalypt forests containing giant, centuries-old specimens, as well as Victoria's largest surviving stand of **rainforest**. At **Errinundra Saddle**, in the heart of the park, there's a delightful picnic area and a self-guided boardwalk through the forest (about 40min). Take special care while driving, as all the roads in the area are heavily used by logging trucks.

The road from Bonang eventually leads to the old-fashioned town of **ORBOST**, on the Princes Highway where it crosses the Snowy River. There's a tranquil picnic spot opposite the *Snowy River Orbost Camp Park*, on the corner of Lochiel and Nicholson streets (Ⓣ03/5154 1097; cabins ❸), with huge gums lining one bank and cows roaming the paddocks on the other. The **Orbost**

Visitors Centre on Lochiel Street (daily 9am–5pm; ⓣ03/5154 2424) books accommodation and tours.

Lind and Croajingolong national parks

From Orbost to **Cann River**, the Princes Highway continues well inland, not to reach the coast again until Eden, across the border in New South Wales. For a drive through the warm temperate rainforest of **Lind National Park**, take the turn-off to the north (in the direction of Club Terrace and Combienbar) about 55km east of Orbost. After 4km along this road, and just 1km before the hamlet of Club Terrace, turn right onto the **Euchre Valley Nature Drive** which leads through a lush valley lined by tree ferns, following the Euchre Creek for about 6km until you get back to the Princes Highway. One third along the way in the national park, the **Growler picnic area**, equipped with tables, benches and a fireplace, is a very pleasant place to stop for a while.

The **Parks Victoria ranger office**, on the Princes Highway in Cann River (Mon–Fri 9am–noon & 12.30–3.30pm; ⓣ03/5158 6351), provides information on the **Croajingolong National Park**, which begins southeast of the town at Sydenham Inlet and continues for 100km along the coast to the state border. Within the park, foothills cloaked in warm temperate rainforest drop down to the unspoilt "Wilderness Coast". There's a good two-hour **hike** to Genoa Peak (access is from the Princes Highway a few kilometres west of Genoa; drive 8km to the car park and picnic spot which is the start of the walking track) which gives stupendous views over the forest and bay. There are several scenic camping spots in the park, which are very popular in summer and allocated way in advance by a ballot system. You can also stay in the lighthouse-keeper's cottage (entire cottage $250 for 6 people) or a bungalow (sleeps two; ❹) at *Point Hicks Lighthouse* at Point Hicks (ⓣ03/5158 4268). If you want to break your journey, Cann River itself offers very good-value accommodation; the least expensive is the *Cann River Motel* on the Princes Highway (ⓣ03/5158 6255; ❸ including breakfast), then there's *Cann Valley Motel* on the Princes Highway (ⓣ03/5158 6300; ❹-❺ , or try the *Cann River Caravan Park* at the junction of Princes and Cann Valley highways (ⓣ03/5158 6369; ❷), which has on-site vans for rent.

On a four-day **bushwalking safari** run by OzStyle Adventures (ⓣ1800 000 824, ⓦwww.ozstyle.net.au) you can experience the natural beauty of Croajingolong National Park without roughing it: there are five departures from Cann River in summer ($885; including one night luxury camping and two nights at a cottage at Point Hicks lighthouse and gourmet catering; minimum 6 people).

Mallacoota and around

MALLACOOTA is an unspoilt village in a gorgeous location surrounded by Croajingolong National Park, on the lake system of the **Mallacoota Inlet**. During the summer and Easter holidays the tranquil place turns into a bustling holiday resort. It's approached via Genoa, 47km east from Cann River along the Princes Highway. About 10km from Genoa, a turn-off to the left leads to **Gipsy Point**, an idyllic spot near the confluence of the Genoa and Wallagaraugh rivers on the upper reaches of the Mallacoota Inlet.

There's no tourist office in Mallacoota, but the people at the *Mallacoota Caravan Park* (see below) will do their best to help any visitors with enquiries. You can go on bushwalks and explore the beautiful waterways of the Mallacoota Inlet (Bottom Lake and Top Lake) on your own by renting a boat or canoe from Buckland's Jetty

Boat Hire (Ⓣ03/5158 0660). The **Parks Victoria office**, on the corner of Allan and Buckland drives (daily 9.30am–3.30pm; Ⓣ03/5158 0219, Ⓦwww.parkweb .vic.gov.au), has details of secluded camping spots and local bushwalks.

During the summer, Mallacoota, although seemingly remote, teems with holiday-makers. The population of just over a thousand trebles again for the Easter **Festival of the Great Southern Ocean**, which includes music, theatre and comedy, a community market, and fascinating sand sculptures.

Practicalities

Several **accommodation** options are located outside Mallacoota (and away from the summer crowds): try the friendly B&B *Mareeba Lodge*, 59 Mirrabooka Rd (Ⓣ03/5158 0378, Ⓕ5258 0407; ❹); *Karbeethong Lodge*, 16 Schnapper Point Drive (Ⓣ03/5158 0411, Ⓦwww.karbeethonglodge.com.au; ❹), a renovated, old-style weatherboard guesthouse with singles and doubles, most en suite; or *Adobe Flats*, mud-brick apartments on a former chicken farm at 17 Karbeethong Ave (Ⓣ03/5158 0329, Ⓦwww.adobeholidayflats.com.au; ❹). The last two are located in Karbeethong, 4km northwest of town, with beautiful views of Bottom Lake. In an area teeming with birdlife *Melaleuca Grove* (Ⓣ & Ⓕ 03/5158 0407; ❹) at the corner of Genoa and Morrabooka streets, has six motel units in a beautiful garden setting. In Mallacoota itself, the *Mallacoota Hotel* has accommodation in motel units (Ⓣ03/5158 0455; ❹) and dorms ($20) in a separate building out the back. Alternatively, you can pitch your tent at *Mallacoota Caravan Park*, right on the shores of the lake (Ⓣ & Ⓕ03/5158 0300) or rent a cabin at the *Beachcomber Caravan Park*, 85 Betka Rd (Ⓣ03/5158 0233, Ⓦwww.beachcombercaravanpark.com; ❷) or at the *Shady Gully Caravan Park*, Genoa Rd (Ⓣ03/5158 0362, Ⓦwww.mallacoota caravanpark.com; ❷); the latter has a solar-heated swimming pool.

Choices for **food** are very limited. The café next to the newsagent on Allan Drive serves brunch, light meals and good coffee, while the *Tide Restaurant & Cocktail Bar* on Maurice Avenue is the best place in town for dinner. Otherwise, counter meals are served at the *Mallacoota Hotel*, where there's **live music** every night in January. A summer cinema operates at the Mallacoota Community Centre, Allen Drive. There's a small Commonwealth Bank branch inside the post office next door; additionally, EFTPOS facilities are available at the Mobil service station and the supermarket.

Gipsy Point, about 20km northwest, has another good accommodation option, *Gipsy Point Lakeside Luxury Apartments*, set in a garden by the Wallagaraugh River (Ⓣ03/5158 8200 or 1800 688 200, Ⓦwww.gipsy.com.au; ❺), with attractive apartments, some with spa, and a heated pool. The *Gipsy Point Lodge*, nearby on MacDonald Street, has rooms (dinner, bed and breakfast) and cottages (Ⓣ1800 063 556, Ⓦwww.gipsypoint.com; rooms ❼, cottages ❺), with free use of canoes and rowboats; bird-watching and bushwalking excursions can be arranged.

The northeast

The **Hume Highway**, the direct route between Melbourne and Sydney, cuts straight through Victoria's northeast – an area that has become known as **Ned**

Kelly Country. **Euroa**, **Benalla** and **Glenrowan** (where he was finally seized after a bloody shoot-out) all have traces of the masked bushranger's activities, with Glenrowan wholeheartedly cashing in on his fame. West of the Hume, **Rutherglen**, right up against the state border, is Victoria's oldest established wine-producing region. There are also vineyards in the rich fruit-growing region of the **Goulburn Valley**, north along the Goulburn Valley Highway from **Seymour**. **Bushwalking** and **mountainbiking** in the Alpine region are most easily organized through outdoor tour operators such as the South Australia-based Ecotrek Bogong Jack Adventures, (Ⓣ08/8383 7198, Ⓦwww.ecotrek.com.au).

V/Line runs several **train and bus routes** through the northeast. The Melbourne–Albury train service goes via Seymour, Euroa, Benalla, Glenrowan, Wangaratta, Chiltern and Wodonga (at least 4 daily). There are also trains and buses from Melbourne to Shepparton, with connections to Cobram and Tocumwal in NSW (2–3 daily). Buses depart from Albury to Bendigo via Wangaratta and Benalla (Mon, Wed & Fri morning). The Murray Link bus service connects Albury with Mildura and runs via Rutherglen, Yarrawonga, Shepparton, Echuca, Kerang and Swan Hill (departing Albury Mon, Wed, Thurs & Sat mornings). There's a bus service from Wangaratta to Rutherglen (Mon–Fri), and one to Wahgunya and Corowa on the Murray. From Melbourne, you can catch a late afternoon train to Wangaratta (Wed, Fri or Sun) and take the connecting bus to Corowa via Rutherglen. For bookings and timetables call Ⓣ13 61 96.

The Goulburn Valley

The **Goulburn River** rises at Lake Eildon and flows through Seymour, Nagambie and Shepparton to join the Murray just east of Echuca. The rich plains of the Goulburn Valley yield much **fruit**, and there's an important fruit-canning industry based at Shepparton, as well as several **wineries**.

Seymour is the first major stop on the Hume Highway out of Melbourne; an important train interchange, it's an uninspiring place for the visitor. The Goulburn Valley Highway begins here, heading north to **NAGAMBIE** on the shores of the man-made Lake Nagambie. The town itself is uninteresting, but two prominent **wineries** nearby add some welcome flavour. **Tahbilk Winery** (Mon–Sat 9am–5pm, Sun 11am–5pm, Ⓦwww.tahbilk.com.au), 6km southwest, is the oldest continually operating winery and vineyard in Victoria; it opened in 1860, and the Shiraz and Marsanne are made from vines that have seen more than 140 harvests. The whitewashed buildings have been well preserved and there are extensive grounds to explore. In complete contrast is the ultramodern **Mitchelton Winery** (daily 10am–5pm; Ⓦwww.mitchelton.com.au), 14km southwest of Nagambie in Mitchellstown, off the Goulburn Valley Highway: its distinctive sixty-metre observation tower features on the Mitchelton label. The extensive riverside grounds have a pool and barbecues, which draw the crowds on Sunday. At the *Mitchelton Restaurant & Winebar*, overlooking the river, the wines are matched with outstanding food, using regional produce (daily 10.30am–3pm).

Goulburn River Cruises ply the Goulburn River between Chateau Tahbilk and the Mitchelton Winery (summer only; Ⓣ03/5794 2877). The **Nagambie Lakes Visitor Information Centre**, at 145 High St (daily 9am–5pm; Ⓣ03/5794 2647 or 1800 444 647), also deals with bookings for V/Line – or get your tickets at the newsagent at 310 High St. As few people stopover in town,

accommodation is very inexpensive: try the *Nagambie Goulburn Highway Motel*, 143 High St (Ⓣ & Ⓕ03/5794 2681; ❸), or the *Nagambie Caravan Park* next door (Ⓣ03/5794 2681; on-site vans ❷, holiday flats ❸).

The small city of **SHEPPARTON** is the operations centre for the SPC and Ardmona canned fruit companies, with peaches, pears, apples and plums tinned and exported worldwide. The **Greater Shepparton Visitor Information Centre** is located beside Victoria Park Lake in the south of town, at 534 Wyndham St on the Goulburn Valley Highway (daily 9am–5pm; Ⓣ03/5831 4400 or 1800 808 839, Ⓦwww.shepparton.vic.gov.au).

The Hume Highway and Kelly Country

Forty-seven kilometres beyond Seymour, **EUROA** is a small, friendly town with many fine Victorian and Federation-style red-brick buildings. The **Euroa Visitor Information Centre** is located on the Hume Highway (daily 9am–5pm; Ⓣ03/5795 3677 or 1300 134 610). The town's main shopping area, Binney Street, has a pleasant, old-fashioned feel: buildings with awnings and shop windows which don't seem to have changed much since 1975 or so. A good refreshment stop is the *Blue Dorset Café* at 14 Clifton St which serves fresh coffee, gourmet sandwiches and light meals.

BENALLA, 45km northeast of Euroa on the Hume Highway, is a civilized town on the lake of the same name, formed by the Broken River which runs through town and occasionally floods it. There's a rose festival held here every November, which transforms the town's picnic spots and gardens. The helpful **Benalla Visitor Information Centre**, 14 Mair St (daily 9am–5pm; Ⓣ03/5762 1749), has lots of pamphlets and information on the region, and can also book accommodation. In the same building, the **Costume and Pioneer Museum** ($3) displays a collection of women's dresses from the 1920s, ball gowns and male fashion from the late eighteenth century until the early twentieth century, and also a range of Ned Kelly relics, including the green silk cummerbund he was awarded as a child for saving a friend from drowning, and which he proudly wore when captured. The **Benalla Art Gallery**, in a lovely setting across the lake (daily 10am–5pm; free), has a fine collection of early twentieth-century and contemporary Australian art. Benalla is also Australia's main centre for **gliding** and is home to the biggest gliding club in the southern hemisphere; contact the Gliding Club of Victoria (Ⓣ03/5762 1058, Ⓦhttp://gliding-benalla.org) to find out about flights.

If you want **to stay**, the well-equipped *Trekker's Rest*, 1km out of town on the Kilfeera Road (Ⓣ03/5762 3535, Ⓦwww.trekkersrest.com.au; ❷–❸) has cheap rooms and en-suite apartments, all with heating and air conditioning. For something **to eat** during the day, there's the *Gallery Café* in a serene location at the Art Gallery by the lake (licensed; daily 10am–4pm), or in town, *Hides Bakery* at 111 Bridge St prepares excellent pies, salads and sandwiches and serves good coffee. In the evening three good choices are the very reasonable *Brigall's Restaurant* at the *Commercial Hotel* on Bridge Street, *Café Raffety's*, 55 Nunn St (Ⓣ03/5762 4066) where a blackboard menu features daily specials; and further up on the price scale, *Georgina's*, 100 Bridge St (lunch Thurs–Fri, dinner Mon–Sat; Ⓣ03/5762 1334) for excellent contemporary Australian cuisine.

Glenrowan and Kelly's last stand

GLENROWAN, 29km on from Benalla, was the site of the **Kelly Gang's last stand** and you're never allowed to forget it. A gigantic effigy of Ned Kelly, in full iron-armour regalia, greets you as you enter town, and there are lots of other tawdry attractions along the highway, such as the **Last Stand Show** (daily 9.30am–4.30pm; every half-hour; 40min; $18), a "computerized animated theatre" using dummies shuffling around on cue to dramatize the story of the siege – your money's better spent elsewhere. The last stand itself took place in Siege Street near the train station. Along the rail lines north of town, a small stone monument marks the spot where Kelly forced railworkers to rip up a section of the track, to try to derail the trainful of troopers he had lured to the town – though visitors are asked to stay away as the site is dangerous. Overlooking the town to the west is Mount Glenrowan, which the bushrangers used as a lookout.

The Ned Kelly story

Even before Ned Kelly became widely known, folklore and ballads were popularizing the free-ranging bush outlaws as potent symbols of freedom and resistance to authority. Born in 1855, **Ned Kelly** was the son of an alcoholic rustler and a mother who sold illicit liquor. By the time he was 11 he was already in constant trouble with the police, who considered the whole family troublemakers; constables in the area were instructed to "endeavour, whenever the Kellys commit any paltry crime, to bring them to justice . . . the object [is] to take their prestige away from them".

Ned became the accomplice of the established bushranger **Harry Power**, and by his mid-teens had a string of warrants to his name. Ned's brother, Dan, was also wanted by the police – hearing that he had turned up at his mother's, a policeman set out, drunk and without a warrant, to arrest him. A scuffle ensued and the unsteady constable fell to the floor, hitting his head and allowing Dan to escape. The following day warrants were issued for the arrest of Ned (who was in New South Wales at the time) and Dan for attempted murder; their mother was sentenced to three years' imprisonment.

From this point on, the **Kelly gang**'s crime spree accelerated and, following the death of three constables in a shoot-out at Stringybark Creek, the biggest manhunt in Australia's history began, with a £1000 reward offered for the gang's apprehension. On December 9, 1878 they robbed the bank at Euroa, taking £2000, before moving on to Jerilderie in New South Wales, where another bank was robbed and Kelly penned the famous **Jerilderie Letter**, describing the "big, ugly, fat-necked, wombat-headed, big-bellied, magpie-legged, narrow-hipped, splay-footed sons of Irish bailiffs or English landlords which is better known as Officers of Justice or Victoria Police" who had forced him onto the wrong side of the law.

After a year on the run, the gang formulated a grand plan: they executed Aaron Sherritt, a police informer, in Sebastopol, thus attracting a trainbound posse from nearby Beechworth; this train was intended to be derailed at Glenrowan with as much bloodshed as possible before the gang moved on to rob the bank at Benalla and barter hostages for the release of Kelly's mother. In the event, having already sabotaged the tracks, the gang commandeered the Glenrowan Inn and, in a moment of drunken candour, Kelly detailed his ambush to a schoolteacher who escaped, managing to save the special train. As the armed troopers approached the inn, the gang donned the home-made **iron armour** that has since become their motif. In the ensuing gunfight Kelly's comrades were either killed or committed suicide as the inn was torched, while Ned himself was taken alive, tried by the same judge who had incarcerated his mother, and sentenced to hang.

Public sympathies lay strongly with Ned Kelly, and a crowd of five thousand gathered outside Melbourne Gaol on November 11, 1880 for his execution, believing that the 25-year-old bushranger would "die game". True to form, his last words are said to have been "**Such is life**".

More interesting and far better value than the Last Stand Show is **Kate's Cottage and Ned Kelly Memorial** (daily 9am–5.30pm; $3), a replica of the Kelly home. With its bare earth floor, bark roof and newspaper-lined walls, it speaks volumes of the deprivation that drove the family to crime. An evocative audiotape narrates Ned's story from childhood and is interspersed with folk songs inspired by his life. The original homestead, 9km west along Kelly Gap Road, is now nothing more than rubble and a brick chimney.

Wangaratta

The small town of **WANGARATTA**, at the junction of the Ovens and King rivers, 16km from Glenrowan, is a convenient overnight stop between Sydney and Melbourne, but there are few reasons to linger unless you're here for the famous four-day **Wangaratta Festival of Jazz** (Ⓣ1800 803 944, Ⓦwww.wangaratta-jazz.org.au). Beginning on the Friday prior to the Melbourne Cup (the last weekend in Oct or the first weekend in Nov), this is one of the premier jazz events in the country, attracting national stars and international legends. Much of the city's accommodation is booked out two years in advance, so reserve ahead if you're planning to attend. The highway on either side of "Wang" is lined with motels, and the staff at **Wangaratta Tourist Information**, on the corner of Handley Street and Tone Road (daily 9am–5pm; Ⓣ03/5721 5711 or 1800 801 065), can book local tours and accommodation and give out stacks of leaflets about the area.

There's a vast range of **accommodation** in town. Good choices include the *Billabong Motel*, 12 Chisholm St (Ⓣ03/5721 2353, Ⓦwww.tourisminternet.com.au/wgbilla.htm; ❸), with good-value singles; *Millers Cottage Motel*, 26 Parfitt Rd aka Old Hume Highway (Ⓣ03/5721 5755, Ⓦwww.millerscottage.com.au/; ❹); and the modern *Parkview Sundowner*, 56 Ryley St (Ⓣ03/5721 5655; ❹); the latter two have a pool. In terms of **food**, *Scribbler's Cafe*, at 66 Reid St, serves good cakes and lunchtime fodder, while *Coffee.com*, at 84 Ovens St, has similar fare and Internet access. For dinner the renowned *Café Martini* at the *Bull's Head Hotel*, 87 Murphy St, has great but pricey wood-fired pizza, while the bistro at the *Vine Hotel* on Detour Road serves excellent local food and wine in a congenial setting (Ⓣ03/5721 2605). Out of town, the *Boorhaman Hotel*, a small country pub with an award-winning **microbrewery**, is worth a detour: they serve hearty country tucker, washed down with a lager, dark ale, or wheat beer produced by its *Buffalo Brewery*. It's on Boorhaman Rd, 16km north of Wangaratta towards the Murray Valley Highway – call Ⓣ03/5726 9215 for further directions.

Beechworth

Thirty-five kilometres east of Wangaratta, off the Ovens Highway (also known as the Great Alpine Road), is **BEECHWORTH**, once the centre of the rich **Ovens gold-mining region**. Sited picturesquely in the foothills of the Victorian Alps, the entire town has been acknowledged by the National Trust as being of historic significance, and the town and surrounding area have been designated a **Historic Park** by the Department of Sustainability and Environment. The **visitor information centre** is located in the fine old shire office on Ford Street (daily 9am–5pm; Ⓣ03/5728 3233 or 1300 366 321, Ⓦwww.beechworth.com/bworthinfo), and can book accommodation as well as provide you with pamphlets on places of interest, including the Gorge Scenic Drive (see p.1052). They also have Internet access.

As is true in so many other towns in the northeast, Beechworth is rich in **Ned Kelly** history. The **government buildings** on Ford Street house the

The Milawa Gourmet Region

The high country area of Victoria – and in particular the small town of **MILAWA**, 15km southeast of Wangaratta on the Snow Road – is renowned amongst foodies for the excellent quality of its locally produced food and wine, so much so that it has been dubbed the **Milawa Gourmet Region**, and even the most urban Melburnians have been known to make the two-hour trip just to stock up on dinner-party supplies.

If it's a tipple of something special you're after, try a tour of the **Brown Brothers Winery** (daily 9am–5pm; ⓣ03/5720 5500, ⓦwww.brown-brothers.com.au), situated about 2km from Milawa and clearly signposted; there's also a great café-restaurant here, the *Epicurean Centre* (daily 11am–3pm), which specializes in complementing Brown Brothers wines with unusual local foods. Back in the town, there's the **Milawa Cheese Factory** (daily 9am–5pm; ⓣ03/5727 3589) on Factory Road, where you'll find award-winning cheeses and another excellent restaurant. At the crossroads nearby, **Milawa Mustards** (10am–5pm, closed some Wednesdays) offers seventeen home-made seed varieties, while on the Snow Road **Whitehead's Mead** (daily 9am–5pm) sells a variety of meads made from Australian honey, a wide array of sticky, sweet honeys that put commercial brands to shame, candles and other honey products. The **Olive Shop** (Mon 10am–4pm, Thurs–Sun 10am–5pm) has locally grown olives and extra virgin olive oil. On the same road, **King River Café** (Wed–Sun 10am–late; ⓣ03/5727 3461) is a popular eatery specializing in local wines and good food – the cakes and coffee are excellent, too.

imposing HM Training Prison, where he and his mother were incarcerated, and the **courthouse** (daily 9am–5pm; $4) where his trial was held. Opposite, underneath the town hall, is the grim cell where he was imprisoned as a teenager (daily 10am–4pm; free). Other sights of interest in town include the **Burke Museum** on Loch Street (daily 10am–5pm; $6), which displays relics of the goldrush and tells the story of the Chinese miners who flocked here. The museum is dedicated to the explorer Robert O'Hara Burke, one-time Superintendent of Police in Beechworth, who perished with William John Wills on their historic journey from Melbourne to the Gulf of Carpentaria (see box on p.593). On Last Street the century-old **Murray Breweries** (daily 10am–4pm; free) is well worth a visit, not only for its free tastings and sales, but also for its National Trust display of twenty beautifully restored old carriages, including a Cobb & Co stagecoach.

The five-kilometre, one-way route of the **Gorge Scenic Drive** begins at Sydney Road and ends at Bridge Street, along the western edge of the town. It includes the famous Spring and Reid creeks, which supported eight thousand diggers in 1852, and an old storehouse for blasting powder known as the powder magazine, as well as natural features such as Flat Rock, Telegraph Rock and Woolshed Falls.

Practicalities

There's a very good choice of B&B **accommodation** in Beechworth: try *Beechworth Gorge Walk Guesthouse*, 10 Last St (ⓣ03/5728 2867, ⓦwww.beechworth.com/bgwalk; ❺); *Alba Country Rose Private B&B*, 30 Malakoff Rd (ⓣ & ⓕ03/5728 1107, ⓦwww.tourisminternet.com.au/bwalba.htm; ❺); or *Apple Tree Cottage*, 16 Frederick Street (ⓣ03/5728 1044, ⓦwww.inn.com.au/full/1058/19/1; ❺). A good-value place is *The Old Priory*, on Priory Lane (a continuation of Loch St), almost at the corner of Church Street (ⓣ03/5728 1024, ⓦwww.oldpriory.com.au/ ❸), a historic B&B with very reasonably priced singles. If you want peace and quiet, it's best to come at the weekend, when the school groups have gone. The *Empire Hotel*, on Camp Street (☎03/5728 1030; ❸), and *Tanswells Commercial Hotel*, 30 Ford St (☎03/5728 1480; ❸), are historic pubs that also offer accommodation. The latter has been continuously licensed since 1853 and has pleasant bars and bistro food.

For **food**, try the *Beechworth Bakery*, 27 Camp St (daily 6am–7pm). It's famous all over Australia for its delicious pies, bread, cakes and pastries, and on sunny days you can have breakfast on the balcony. *Gigis* at 69 Ford St is a very good café-restaurant (licensed; daily except Wed 9am–late, Sun until 6pm; ☎03/5728 2575) serving Northern Italian cuisine – the mains are bit pricey, though. Equally renowned is the stately *Bank Restaurant*, in the Bank of Australia building at 86 Ford St (licensed; daily from 6pm; ☎03/5728 2223).

V/Line has a **bus service** from Wangaratta to Beechworth (1 daily Mon–Fri) and an additional service to Bright via Beechworth (1 daily), and during school terms Beechworth Buslines has a service twice daily (☎03/5728 2182; Mon–Fri) from Beechworth to Albury and Wodonga.

Chiltern

CHILTERN, a sleepy former gold-mining centre with a well-preserved, mid-nineteenth-century streetscape, lies just off the Hume Highway about 40km from Wangaratta. The setting – with a bit of recent architectural licence on Conness Street – has been used in several period films. Although no longer licensed, the **Star Hotel** is still set up with the original bar and taps, an authentic background to a rather more ordinary souvenir and craft shop. For $2 you can gain access to the back (daily except Thurs) to look at a **monster vine**: planted in 1867 and reputedly Australia's largest, it once produced a single yield of over 6kg of grapes. The 1866 **Athenaeum** (Wed, Sat, Sun & public holidays 10am–4pm; $2) is now a local-history museum that features a collection of paintings by the obsessive local artist Alfred Eustace, who would use any available medium to paint on: paper, cardboard, even large gum leaves. **Dows Pharmacy Museum**, also on Conness Street (Sat & Sun 10am–4pm or by appointment ☎03/5726 1317; $2), has an extensive collection of old pharmaceutical equipment. Chiltern's most interesting attraction, however, is the National Trust-owned **Lake View Homestead** (most weekends 10am–4pm or by appointment ☎03/5726 1317; $2), on the shores of Lake Anderson, near the train station. Built in 1870, it was for a short period the home of the writer Ethel Florence Lindesay (1870–1946), who, under the pseudonym **Henry Handel Richardson**, immortalized the house in the novel *Ultima Thule*, the last book in *The Fortunes of Richard Mahoney* trilogy. For **refreshment**, stop in at the *Mulberry Tree Tearooms* on Conness Street.

Rutherglen

RUTHERGLEN, 18km west of Chiltern and 32km west of Wodonga on the Murray River Highway, is at the heart of Victoria's oldest wine-producing region, renowned for its excellent fortified wines, Rutherglen Muscat and Tokay. Thirteen **wineries** are situated in the area, most of them third- or fourth-generation establishments with cellars full of character. The landscape is rather disappointing, consisting largely of flat paddocks of cattle and sheep where you'd expect undulating vineyards. In fact, winemaking has always been just one of a range of farming activities in this area, where diversification remains the key to survival. The weather partly accounts for the quality of Rutherglen's fortified wines: the long, mild autumns allow the grapes to stay on the vines for longer, producing higher levels of sugar in the fruit. All the wineries are open for free **tastings** and cellar-door sales (Mon–Sat 10am–5pm; Sun hours differ from place to place).

The **Wine Experience Centre** at 57 Main St (daily 9am–5pm; ⓣ02/6032 9166 or 1800 622 871) is local history museum, shop, café and visitor information centre all in one – it has informative displays about the goldrush and agricultural history of the district, including winemaking. The shop sells local wines and arts and crafts, and there are stacks of brochures, including the informative *Rutherglen Touring Guide and Map* published by the winemakers of Rutherglen. They also rent mountain bikes ($22/day). On the Queen's Birthday weekend in June the town hosts the **Winery Walkabout** – one of Australia's biggest wine-tasting festivals, when the new season's releases are presented to the public. Another festive event, the **Tastes of Rutherglen**, is held over the Victorian Labour Day weekend in mid-March, and sees some of the best local restaurants guest-starring at the wineries.

Rutherglen is a popular weekend getaway from Melbourne, so **accommodation** can be hard to find at that time; during the week you'll have no problem. Right in the centre of town, is the *Poachers Paradise Hotel Motel*, 97 Murray St (ⓣ02/6032 7373, ⓦwww.poachersparadise.com.au; ❹), ten new motel units with air conditioning and the usual mod cons; two with a spa bath, are tucked away behind the 1860's hotel, whose bistro serves breakfast and hearty "pub grub" for lunch and dinner daily. Alternatively, a good-value B&B is *Country Cottage Accommodation*, 2 Moodemere St (ⓣ02/6032 8328, ⓕ6032 7328; ❺), or there's the *Walkabout Motel*, Murray Valley Highway (ⓣ02/6032 9572; ⓦwww.walkaboutmotel.com.au; ❹). The wineries all offer delicious, if expensive, gourmet **food**.

The Snowfields and the High Country

The **Victorian Alps**, the southern extension of the Great Dividing Range, bear little resemblance to their European counterparts; they're too gentle, too rounded, and above all too low to offer really great **skiing**. Nonetheless in July and August there is usually plenty of snow, and the resorts are packed out. Most people come here for the downhill skiing, though the **cross-country skiing**, which is rapidly growing in popularity, is excellent: **Lake Mountain**, 21km from Marysville, is the region's premier cross-country destination. **Snowboarding** was first encouraged at Mount Hotham and is now firmly established everywhere. **Falls Creek**, **Mount Hotham** and **Mount Buller** are the largest and most commercial skiing areas, particularly the last which is within easy reach of Melbourne; smaller resorts such as **Mount Baw Baw** are more suited to beginners. While you wouldn't come to Victoria especially to ski, you might as well give it a go if you're here at the right time of year, though be warned that accommodation is very pricey.

In summer, when the wild flowers are in bloom, the alps are ideal **bushwalking** territory with most of the high mountains (and the ski resorts) contained within the vast **Alpine National Park**. The most famous of the walks is the four-hundred-kilometre **Alpine Trail**, which begins in Baw Baw National Park, near Walhalla in Gippsland, and follows the ridges all the way to Mount Kosciuszko in the Snowy Mountains of New South Wales. If you are doing any serious bushwalking, you'll need to be properly equipped. Water can be hard to find, and the weather can change suddenly and unexpectedly: even in summer it can get freezing cold up here, especially at night. After prolonged dry spells,

bushfires can also pose a very real threat, as in early 2003, when fires, most likely ignited by a flash of lightning, blazed for six weeks across a large chunk of the high country in Victoria and southeastern New South Wales.

Mansfield and **Bright** are good bases for exploration of the Alps, and are great places to unwind. In summer the ski resorts can be ugly and only half the facilities are open, but there are often great bargains to be had on rooms. If you're **driving**, you'll need snow chains in winter (they're compulsory in many parts), and you should heed local advice before venturing off the main roads.

Mansfield and Merrijig

MANSFIELD is located at the junction of the Maroondah and Midland highways, just a few kilometres north of Lake Eildon, 140km east of Seymour and 63km south of Benalla. As the main approach to Mount Buller, it's a lively place with good pubs, restaurants and a cinema. The annual highlight is the **Mountain High Country Festival** in early November, which begins the weekend prior to the Melbourne Cup; activities include a picnic race known as the "Melbourne Cup of the bush". In the middle of April hundreds of hot-air-balloon pilots flock here for the three-day **Mansfield Balloon Festival**.

V/Line has a year-round **bus** service from Melbourne to Mansfield (Mon–Sat 2, Sun 1 daily; 3hr). The helpful **Mansfield Visitor Information Centre** on the Maroondah Highway (daily 9am–5pm; Ⓣ03/5775 1464 or 1800 060 686 for accommodation bookings, Ⓦwww.mansfield-mtbuller.com.au), has complete information on all sights and activities, including skiing and walks in the surrounding country. Out of the snow season, you have a choice of horse riding, hiking, climbing, abseiling, hang-gliding, rafting, canoeing or 4WD tours. Among the many local outfits are Stirling Experience (Ⓣ03/5775 3541, Ⓦwww.stirling.au.com) and Alpine 4WD Tours (Ⓣ03/5777 3709) for 4WD tours around Mount Buller and Mount Stirling (see p.1056).

The *Alzburg Inn Resort*, 39 Malcolm St (Ⓣ03/5775 2367 or 1800 033 023, Ⓦwww.alzburg.com.au; ❺), is a resort **hotel** with all mod cons, popular with skiers, while the neat and friendly *Mansfield Traveller's Lodge*, 116 High St (Ⓣ03/5775 1800, Ⓦwww.mansfieldtravellodge.com; dorm bed $23, rooms ❹), has motel rooms and a good backpackers' hostel in a separate building next door. There's also a good choice of **cottages** in Mansfield and around. *Mary's Place*, 5 Somerset Crescent, Mansfield (Ⓣ & Ⓕ03/5775 1928; ❹), offers B&B in a two-bedroom cottage in a beautiful garden setting. Out of town, *Burnt Creek Cottages* on Hanlons Road (Ⓣ03/5775 3067, Ⓦwww.greatplacestostay.com.au/burntcreek/default.asp; ❺) have great views, a tennis court and swimming pool; while *Willawong Bed & Breakfast and Cottage* at Lot 12, Mount Buller Road, Merrijig (Ⓣ03/5777 5750, Ⓦwww.willawongbnb.com.au; B&B ❹, cottage ❺) offers Bavarian-style accommodation in a gorgeous wooden house and a separate cottage in a lovely garden at the foot of the Alps.

Merrijig

The small town of **MERRIJIG**, a little under halfway to Mount Buller from Mansfield, is largely responsible for the great number of **riding** outfits in the area. The breathtaking high-country scenery nearby was used as the location for the 1982 film *The Man from Snowy River*, and visitors have been trying to live out their fantasies ever since. If you want to combine riding with lodge **accommodation**, try *Merrijig Lodge and Trail Rides*, Mount Buller Road (Ⓣ03/5777 5590, Ⓦwww.merrijiglodge.com.au; ❷).

Mount Buller and Mount Stirling

To reach **MOUNT BULLER ALPINE VILLAGE**, 48km from Mansfield, you ascend gradually upwards on the smooth, sealed Summit Road. With 7000 beds, 24 modern ski lifts and 80km of runs, the village has the greatest capacity of any Australian ski resort. In **winter**, during the ski season, Mansfield Mt Buller High Country Reservations books **accommodation** and dispenses **information** about all things snow-related (ⓣ1800 039 049, ⓦwww.mtbuller.com.au); in summer, call the Mansfield Visitor Information Centre on ⓣ03/5775 1464 or 1800 060 686.

ABOM Hotel & Bistro, on Summit Road (ⓣ03/5777 6091 or 1800 810 200, ⓦwww.mtbuller.com.au/abom; ❽), is the hub of the Alpine Village when open in winter. There are great views from here, and, further up on the **summit** of Mount Buller, there's an even more spectacular panorama west to Lake Eildon, north to farmlands and east to Falls Creek and Mount Hotham. The huge *Arlberg Hotel*, 53 Summit Rd (ⓣ03/5777 6260 or 1800 032 380, ⓦwww.mtbuller.com.au/arlberg/index.html; summer ❺, winter ❽), provides entertainment in ski season, and has everything from fast food to an expensive

Skiing practicalities

The official start of the **ski season** is the Queen's Birthday long weekend in June (though there may not be enough snow cover until August), lasting through to October. Day-trip or weekend **packages** are the best way to go, and are far cheaper than trying to do it yourself. The best value for money are trips organized by the *Alzburg Inn Resort* at Mansfield (ⓣ1800 033 023, ⓦwww.alzburg.com.au). The day tours leave Melbourne at 4am and arrive at Mount Buller at about 9am, giving the opportunity for a full day's skiing ($140, including entrance fees, a limited lift pass and a two-hour beginner's ski lesson or, for more advanced skiers, an Unlimited Day Lift Ticket); the 2 days/1 night package includes accommodation at the Alzburg Inn (from $220). It's also worth checking out the area around Hardware Street in Melbourne, where such companies as Auski at no. 9 (ⓣ03/9670 1412), and Mountain Designs at 373 Little Bourke St (ⓣ03/9670 3354) can advise on skiing conditions at the resorts, and sell or rent equipment. Other companies selling and renting out ski and snowboarding equipment are in the suburbs, e.g. Snowzone in Moorabbin, at 896 Nepeam Highway (ⓣ03/9553 4444).

During the snow season, an entry fee of $20–30 per car applies, depending on the resort. For **weather** and snow conditions, call the **Snow Reports Line** (ⓣ1900 912 990; $1.93 per min); or Snow Reports Updates (ⓣ1900 912 207; $1.05 per min). For accommodation, phone the central reservation hotlines of each mountain resort. The free *Australian Alpine News* is available at the visitor information centre in Melbourne as well as in the Alpine region. As a rough guide to **costs**, a lift ticket at Mount Buller is $85 per day, while **lessons** cost $85 for beginners (1-day limited lift and a 2hr lesson) and $120 for lower intermediate (1-day lift and a 3hr lesson). Full equipment rental is about $60 per day.

During the season, Mansfield–Mount Buller Bus Lines, 133 High St, Mansfield (ⓣ03/5775 2606), operates a **ski transport service** to Mount Buller once or twice daily; and Stirling Experience (ⓣ03/5777 3541) runs a daily service from Mansfield and Merrijig to Mount Stirling (booking essential; $40 return). In Bright, Adina Ski Hire, 15 Ireland St (ⓣ03/5755 1177, ⓦwww.adina.com.au), and Bright Ski Centre, 22 Ireland St (ⓣ03/5755 1093), rent out skiing and snowboarding equipment, offer package deals including off-mountain accommodation and transport to Mount Hotham, and have up-to-date snow reports and information on road conditions. There's no transport to Mount Buffalo.

restaurant; alongside its rooms there are some six-person, self-contained apartments (summer $250, winter $750 per day). More reasonably priced, although still excellent, is the B&B *Duck Inn* (ⓣ03/5777 6326, ⓦwww.mtbuller.com.au/duckinn/; summer ❹, winter ❻). In winter the truly budget-conscious can stay at the *YHA Lodge*, on The Avenue right in the centre of the village (ⓣ03/5777 6181, ⓔmountbuller@yhavic.org.au; open June–Oct; dorms $45–70), which has self-catering facilities; advance booking (available from May ❶) is essential. Enquire about transport, accommodation and ski/snowboard hire packages. The *Avalanche Alpine Lodge* (ⓣ03/9894 7375, ⓦwww.avalanchealpinelodge.com.au; ❼) has self-contained apartments and B&B rooms.

Mount Stirling, a few kilometres northeast, has more than 60km of maintained trails and is a good place for **cross-country skiing**. The only facility here is Mount Stirling Alpine Resort, a large complex at Telephone Box Junction, 9km from the turn-off left at Mirindah along Mount Stirling Road (ⓣ03/5777 6441, ⓦwww.mtstirling.com.au; entry $30 per vehicle; trail fees for bus passengers $9 per day); within the complex there's a visitor centre, a bistro, a ski school and ski rental is also available. As it's a day-resort, there's no accommodation in the complex itself, but the owners do have bunkroom and loft dormitories on a nearby farm, *Wairere Lodge* (ⓣ03/5777 3541, ⓦwww.stirling.com.au), about 45min from the mountain; in summer (Oct–June) there's a minimum booking of four people allowed ($20 per person); in winter, you'll have to rent the whole place (sleeps 24; $300 first night, $220 thereafter). All roads beyond Telephone Box Junction are open only from the beginning of November until the beginning of June, weather permitting. The fifty-kilometre **Circuit Road** from Telephone Box Junction circumnavigates Mount Stirling, and a 4WD access track from this road leads to **Craig's Hut**, which was used as a film set for *The Man from Snowy River*. As sections of Circuit Road are very rough for 2WD vehicles even in good weather conditions, you'll really need a 4WD for this route. In summer, Stirling Experience (ⓣ03/5777 3541, ⓦwww.stirling.com.au) does **4WD tours** to Craig's Hut and other destinations around the Mount Buller/Mount Stirling area as well as **fully supported bushwalks** (4 days; 1–3 departures per month).

Bright

BRIGHT is at the centre of the picturesque Ovens Valley, between Mount Buffalo and Mount Beauty about 75km southeast of Wangaratta on the Ovens Highway. It began life as a gold-mining town in the 1850s and today still has a faintly elegant air, with tall European trees lining the main street and filling the parks. A clear stream flows through Centennial Park, opposite the tourist information centre, and in autumn the glorious colours of the changing leaves make for a very un-Australian scene.

As the ski fields of Mount Hotham, Mount Buffalo and Falls Creek are less than an hour's drive away, the town is popular as a **ski base** in winter. In summer **outdoor activities** are on offer – such as paragliding, hang-gliding, bushwalking, horse riding and cycling. Alpine Paragliding, 6 Ireland St (ⓣ03/5755 1753, ⓦwww.alpineparagliding.com), organizes tandem flights for novices, and introductory and full courses leading to a licence. You could also take to the air in a powered hang-glider from Bright Micro-Lights (ⓣ03/5750 1555) or with the Eagle School of Micro-Lighting and Hang Gliding (ⓣ03/5750 1174 or 0428 570 168), which also does very enjoyable instructor-accompanied tandem flights.

For a change of pace, visit **Boynton's Winery Café** (daily 10am–5pm; ⓣ03/5756 2730), 10km northwest of Bright at Porepunkah, on the northeast slopes of the Ovens River Valley. Enjoy the spectacular views of Mount Buffalo while sampling a house wine – they specialize in cool-climate wines. A variety of Asian and Mediterranean dishes are on the menu, including Thai-style chicken curry and risotto. Alternatively, head south to nearby **Wandiligong**, a beautiful village that's entirely owned by the National Trust, where you'll find the *Wandiligong Café* and **maze** (Wed–Sun 10am–4.30pm; $8). The hedge maze itself is a lot of fun but the café, serving salads, freshly squeezed juices and home-made treats, and set in a tranquil garden at the end of a six-kilometre bushwalk from Bright, is a truly wonderful find.

Practicalities

V/Line operates a **bus** service to Bright from Wangaratta (1–2 daily; 1hr 15min). Bright **tourist information centre**, at 119 Gavan St (daily 9am–5pm; ⓣ03/5755 2275), has information on what's happening around town and also books accommodation. There's also an excellent **Internet café** in the same building.

To **get around**, you can rent a mountain bike from the Sports Centre, 47 Gavan St (ⓣ03/5755 5159) or Cyclepath, 74 Gavan St (ⓣ03/5750 1442) – both outfits also arrange biking tours. The new **Alpine Visitor Information Centre** in **Myrtleford** dispenses all sorts of information about the entire Alpine region from Wangaratta to Gippsland and books accommodation too (daily 9am–5pm; ⓣ1800 991 044); next door the *Alpine Enoteca*, a wine bar-café-restaurant, showcases regional produce and is open daily from 9am, Thurs–Sun until late; for bookings phone ⓣ03/5752 1155.

Accommodation

Alpine Hotel 7 Anderson St ⓣ03/5755 1366. Charming century-old place which is the focal point of town, with a rowdy bar, good-value bistro meals and excellent breakfasts; the back bar has bands on Friday night, and outside there's a sunny beer garden. ❸

Bright Hikers Backpackers 4 Ireland St ⓣ03/5750 1244, ⓦwww.brighthikers.com.au. One of the best budget places to stay, right in the centre of town. Its wide range of facilities includes a games room and an Internet lounge. Dorms $22, rooms ❸

Ellenvale Holiday Units at the eastern end of town at 68 Delany Ave ⓣ03/5755 1582, ⓦwww.ellenvale.com. A good place with a solar-heated pool and spa, tennis court and barbecues. ❹

Elm Lodge Holiday Motel 2 Wood St ⓣ1800 245 845, ⓕ03/5755 2206. Good-value and centrally located motel with a beautiful garden and a pool. Evening meals available. ❹

Freeburgh Cabins & Caravan Park 1099 Great Alpine Rd, Freeburgh, 10km south, ⓣ03/5750 1306, ⓦwww.freeburghcabins.com.au. Spacious holiday park with shady camp sites, a cottage and well-equipped cabins of various sizes, plus a large solar-heated pool, sheltered BBQs and a kiosk. Cottage ❹, cabins ❺

Mystic Valley Cottages 9 Mystic Lane, 2km southeast on the way to Wandiligong ⓣ03/5750 1502, ⓔmystic@brightvic.com. A good-value option, situated on a hill overlooking the beautiful Wandiligong Valley. ❹

Eating

Simone's at 98 Gavan St is one of the top Italian **restaurants** in Victoria; given the quality of the cooking the prices are very reasonable (Tues–Sun 6.30pm–late; licensed; ⓣ03/5755 2266). At *Sasha's of Bright*, 2d Anderson St, the Czech owner and chef cooks mainly hearty central European fare, and does it well and at moderate prices too: this is the place to come for Hungarian goulash, smoked pork neck with sauerkraut or crispy skinned duck (daily 6pm–late; licensed; ⓣ03/5750 1711)

Other good **places to eat** are the *Liquid Am-Bar Restaurant Cafe*, opposite the *Alpine Hotel*, which has a blackboard menu listing a variety of dishes and also serves good coffee; the *Riverdeck Café* at the tourist information centre, which sells great deli sandwiches; and the *Bright Bakery* at 80 Gavan St. Two cheap, casual family restaurants are *Tin Dog Café & Pizzeria* at 94 Gavan St, and *Cosy Kangaroo* across the street.

Mount Hotham and Dinner Plain

Heading southeast out of Bright on the Great Alpine Road, it's 18km to **HARRIETVILLE**, tucked just below **Mount Hotham** and Mount Feathertop. Originally a gold-mining town, it's now a pretty little village of wide, tree-lined streets, and is also a popular skiing base: there are outlets to rent skis and chains, a seasonal shuttle-bus service up to the resorts, and several places to stay and eat. Beyond Harrietville, it's a steep ascent to Mount Hotham in the Alpine National Park, the "powder snow capital of Australia". Because this is the state's highest ski area, the snow here can be marginally less sticky than elsewhere. **Dinner Plain**, a resort village 8km from the summit and about 1500m above sea level, has much more of a cosy, alpine village feel – complete with architect-designed timber houses that are meant to resemble cattlemen's mountain huts – than the somewhat unsightly Hotham resort. With 15km of groomed cross-country trails around the village and an 11km trail leading to Mt Hotham Dinner Plain is really the domain of cross-country skiers, but a regular shuttle bus ferries downhill skiers to Mt Hotham. Victorian **snowboarding** started at Hotham so there are lots of special facilities here, equipment rental and lessons. During the ski season, tractor-driven carts ferry you around the village and to the start of cross-country trails and skiing areas (all day until late; free), and helicopter shuttle flights in winter link Mount Hotham with Falls Creek, only a few minutes away by air (about $95 return) where you can ski or snowboard on the same lift pass. A few lodges stay open in summer, also the *General Hotel* which has a bar, bistro, bottle shop and fantastic mountain views. Following the establishment of a fully fledged airport at Horsehair Plain, 20km south of Mount Hotham where seventy-seater jets from Melbourne and Sydney can land, it's now easier than ever to get to Hotham and surrounding areas.

A few centres handle bookings for the mainly lodge-style **accommodation**: Mount Hotham Reservation Centre (ⓣ1800 354 555, ⓦwww.hotham.com.au); Mount Hotham Central Reservations (ⓣ03/5759 3522 or 1800 657 547, ⓦwww.ski.com.au); Mount Hotham Accommodation Service (ⓣ03/5759 3636 or 1800 032 061); Alpine Accommodation (ⓣ1800 246 462, ⓦwww.skihotham.com.au); and Dinner Plain Central Reservations (ⓣ1800 670 019, ⓦwww.dinnerplain.com). For general information about Dinner Plain, go to ⓦwww.visitdinnerplain.com.

Falls Creek

Thirty kilometres east of Bright, in the Upper Kiewa Valley, the town of **Mount Beauty** lies at the base of the state's highest peak, **Mount Bogong** (1986m). **FALLS CREEK**, 32km further along, on the edge of the Bogong High Plains, has a much more villagey feel than its sister resort at Mount Hotham, despite being Victoria's largest alpine resort. It also has probably Victoria's **best skiing**, with the largest snow-making system in Victoria to supplement any shortage of the real stuff, a wide variety of downhill pistes, and good cross-country trails. **Snowboarding** is really big here, too, and in addition there are rides on snowmobiles and snowbikes and a tube park for **snowtubing**. For **accommodation** bookings and information, contact Falls Creek Central Reservations (ⓣ1800 033 079, ⓦwww.fallscreek.com.au) or ask at the **Mount Beauty Visitor Information Centre** (daily 9am–5pm, ⓣ03/5754 4531 or 1800 808 277,

Ⓦwww.mtbeauty.com) on the Kiewa Valley Highway in the town. The budget-conscious would do best to stay in Mount Beauty and travel to Falls Creek for their skiing: enquire about packages at the Mount Beauty Accommodation Service (Ⓣ03/5754 1267). Accommodation options in the valley include *Mountain Creek Lodge* in Tawonga (Ⓣ03/5754 4247; motel units ❺); the wonderful *Braeview B&B* in Mount Beauty (Ⓣ03/5754 4746, Ⓦwww.braeview.com.au; ❺), which has two luxurious guest rooms, one self-contained studio apartment and a separate cottage, all in an established garden setting; and the well-designed and nicely furnished cottages at *Dreamers Mountain Village* (Ⓣ03/5754 1222, Ⓦwww.dreamers1.com; ❺).

Many of the pubs, **restaurants** and lodges in Falls Creek stay open in summer: some of the best are *The Cock 'n' Bull*, a pleasant English-style pub on the corner of Christie and Slalom streets; *The Man Hotel*, a cosy pub on Telemark Street; and the *Milch Café Wine Bar* on Schuss Street.

Apart from **bushwalks**, nature lovers can join Alpine Nature Rambles for informative short walks, studying the Alpine flora (Ⓣ03/5758 3492, Ⓦwww.rambles.com.au/rambles). Bogong Horseback Adventures (Ⓣ03/5754 4849, Ⓦwww.bogonghorse.com.au), a very professional and experienced **horse riding** operator based on a farm, specializes in three- to seven-day **packhorse tours** across the high plains which they run from December until the end of April (from $800 per person). They also run half-day ($70) and day rides ($140) through the Kiewa Valley and the lower levels of the Alpine National Park.

Another horse-riding outfit, *Packer's High Country Trail Rides* (Ⓣ03/5159 7241, Ⓦwww.dinnerplaintrailrides.com), operates from the small hamlet of **Anglers Rest**, further south towards Omeo. Their rides range from one and two hours ($55/$88) to overnight treks, and they also offer cheap lodge accommodation and a cottage (❹) at their farm, The Willows.

As for **festivals**, the entire village of Falls Creek, plus visitors, get together to celebrate "A Taste of Falls Creek" in mid-January.

Mount Buffalo National Park

Six kilometres northwest of Bright, back along the Ovens Highway, you can turn off into **Mount Buffalo National Park** ($9 per car in summer, $13 in winter), which encompasses a huge plateau around Mount Buffalo. **Skiing** here is for beginners to intermediates – and it's a gorgeous place to learn, among surreal-looking, snow-covered gum trees. Relatively inexpensive packages, including accommodation at the *Mount Buffalo Chalet* or the *Mount Buffalo Cresta Lodge* can be arranged through Mount Buffalo Reservations (Ⓣ1800 037 038, Ⓦwww.mtbuffalochalet.com.au/index.asp). The park looks at its best in summer, though, when there are wild flowers and waterfalls, and it's a great place for walking, water sports and other outdoor activities. Among the main attractions is the *Mount Buffalo Chalet* (Ⓣ03/5755 1500 or 1800 037 038, Ⓦwww.mtbuffalochalet.com.au/index.asp; full board ❽), a forty-minute drive on a sealed road from the Ovens Highway turn-off. Built by the Victorian government in 1910, it's very Australian in appearance, with a bottle-green tin roof, but is European in feel, and surrounded by flowers and magnificent views. You can play croquet on the lawn, and there's a sauna, billiard room, games room and tennis court, plus horse riding (summer only), and canoes and mountain bikes for rent. There are two **eating places**: the *Chalet Café* (daily 9.30am–5pm), a no-frills, no-views cafeteria – if you want to have a proper meal, reserve a place in the main dining room (Ⓣ03/5755 1500). The *Mt Buffalo Cresta Lodge* at the ski slopes of the Cresta Valley offers motel units and lodge rooms in winter and in peak periods

– enquiries and booking at ☎03/5755 1988 or at Mount Buffalo Reservations (see p.1060). On the way to the chalet you'll pass Lake Catani, where there's the only camping in the park (Nov–April; booking essential on ☎03/5755 1466, or through Parks Victoria on ☎13 19 63), as well as swimming, canoeing, kayaking and trout-fishing; the chalet rents out equipment.

Bent's Lookout, opposite the chalet, has tremendous views over the Ovens Valley, with small stone cabins doing duty as winter picnic areas. There's a hang-gliding ramp near here: if you're experienced and want to leap into the void, contact one of the operators in or near Bright (see p.1057). Beyond the chalet a sealed, not too steep road continues to Mount Buffalo itself (1721m).

Mount Baw Baw

The ski village at **MOUNT BAW BAW**, near the edge of the Baw Baw National Park, is considerably south of all the resorts and is, strictly speaking, in Gippsland. It's a quiet little place, commanding magnificent views south over much of Gippsland and consisting mainly of private lodges (reservations on ☎1800 629 578). Otherwise, try the *Cascades Apartments* (☎1800 229 229). The entry fee is $26 per vehicle per day. There are five ski lifts here, and a lift day-pass costs about $65, a much more reasonable price than at other resorts. As at Mount Buffalo, the ski runs are mainly for beginners and intermediates. In addition to downhill skiing and snowboarding, you can ski cross-country on 10km of groomed trails and snowtube at the Frantic Frog Super Tube Park. For more on Mount Baw Baw, see Ⓦwww.mountbawbaw.com.au.

Transport to and from the mountain has improved, though it's still far from ideal: in winter, Jindivick Charter & Tours (☎03/5165 1136) provides a bus service on Fridays and Mondays from Warragul Station to the resort ($40 return); they also run a luggage transport service from the day car park to the lodges ($15). If you drive yourself, access is via Noojee, 48km west of Mt Baw Baw. You get there from Melbourne either on the northeastern route via Lilydale and Yarra Junction, or on the Princes Highway via Dandenong and Pakenham, turning off at Drouin. The road between Nojee and the resort is narrow, steep and winding. To make matters worse, there are lots of logging trucks thundering along, so take care.

Travel details

V/Line monopolizes transport within Victoria, with a comprehensive combination of **train** and **bus** services; Melbourne, Ballarat and Geelong are the main interchanges. Following are the main V/Line Victorian services; local buses are detailed in the text. Timetables are subject to frequent change – call V/Line on ☎13 61 96 or consult Ⓦwww.vline.com.au for the latest information.

Trains

Melbourne to: Albury (4 daily; 3hr–3hr 40min); Bairnsdale (2 daily; 3hr 10min); Benalla (4 daily; 2hr–2hr 30min); Ballarat (6–10 daily; 1hr 30min); Bendigo (5–16 daily; 2hr); Castlemaine (5–16 daily; 1hr 35min); Colac (1–3 daily; 1hr 50min); Echuca (Fri & Sun 1 daily; 3hr 20min) via Bendigo (2hr); Geelong (11–25 daily; 1hr); Sale (2 daily; 2hr 45min); Shepparton (1–2 daily; 2hr 15min); Swan Hill (1 daily; 4hr 15min); Wangaratta (4 daily; 2hr 30min–3hr); Warrnambool (1–3 daily; 3hr 10min).

Buses

Apollo Bay to: Geelong (2–3 daily; 2hr 30min); Lorne (2–3 daily; 1hr); Port Campbell (Fri only; 1hr 55min); Torquay (2–3 daily; 2hr); Twelve Apostles (Fri only; 1hr 25min); Warrnambool (Fri only; 3hr 20min).

Bairnsdale to: Canberra (Capital Link 2 weekly; 2hr) via Lakes Entrance (30min), Orbost (1 hr 15min) and Cann River (2hr 15 min); Narooma/NSW (Sapphire Coast Link daily; 6hr) via Lakes Entrance (30min), Orbost (1hr 15min) and Cann River (2hr 15min).
Ballarat to: Bendigo (5 weekly; 2hr); Castlemaine (5 weekly; 1hr 30min); Daylesford (5 weekly; 45min); Geelong (2–4 daily; 1hr 25 min); Hamilton (1–2 daily; 2hr 20min); Horsham (1–2 daily; 2hr 20min); Maryborough (6 weekly; 1hr 5min); Mildura (6 weekly; 7hr 5min); Mount Gambier (5 weekly; 3 hr 30min); Warrnambool (5 weekly; 3hr).
Beechworth to: Bright (1–3 daily; 1hr); Wangaratta (1–4 daily; 30min).
Bendigo to: Echuca (1–3 daily; 1hr 20min); Geelong (5 weekly; 3hr 55min); Horsham (daily; 3hr 15min); Mildura (1–2 daily; 6hr); Swan Hill (1–2 daily; 3hr 5min).
Bright to: Beechworth (1–3 daily; 1hr); Wangaratta (1–3 daily; 1hr 25min).
Castlemaine to: Ballarat (5 weekly; 1hr 30min); Maryborough (1–4 daily; 55min).
Cowes to: Melbourne (1–2 daily; 3hr 15min).
Echuca to: Albury (1–2 daily; 3hr 45min–4hr 20min); Bendigo (1–3 daily; 1hr 20min); Melbourne (6–8 daily; 3hr); Mildura (4 weekly; 5hr 55min); Rutherglen (4 weekly; 3hr 40min–4hr 30min); Shepparton (4 weekly; 2hr 5min); Swan Hill (daily; 1hr 55min).
Foster (closest to Wilson's Promontory NP) to: Melbourne (daily; 2hr 40min).
Geelong to: Apollo Bay (2–3 daily; 2hr 55min) via Ballarat (2–4 daily; 1hr 25min); Ballarat (5 weekly 1hr 30 min); Bendigo (5 weekly; 4hr); Daylesford (5 weekly; 2hr 15min); Castlemaine (5 weekly; 3hr); Lorne (2–3 daily; 1hr 50min); Maryborough (4 weekly; 3hr 5min); Mildura (6 weekly; 9hr); Torquay (2–3 daily; 45min); Warrnambool (Coastlink via Apollo Bay; Fri only; 7hr).
Halls Gap (Grampians) to: Stawell (1 daily; 35min).
Hamilton to: Ballarat (1–2 daily; 2hr 15min); Warrnambool (1–2 daily except Sat; 1hr 40min).
Horsham to: Ararat (3–4 daily; 1hr 35min); Ballarat (1–2 daily; 1hr 20min); Stawell (3 daily; 55min).
Lakes Entrance to: Bairnsdale (1–3 daily; 35min); Canberra (Capital Link 2 weekly; 6hr) via Orbost (45min) and Cann River (2hr 15 min); Narooma/NSW (Sapphire Coast Link daily; 5hr 40min) via Orbost and Cann River.
Mansfield to: Melbourne (1–2 daily; 3hr); Mount Buller (snow season only; 1–2 daily; 1hr).
Maryborough to: Ballarat (5 weekly; 1hr); Castlemaine (1–4 daily; 55min).
Mildura to: Bendigo (1–2 daily; 6hr); Ballarat (6 weekly; 7hr 50min); Geelong (6 weekly; 9hr); Swan Hill (1–3 daily; 2hr 30 min–3hr).
Mount Beauty to: Wangaratta (2 weekly; 2hr 30min).
Mount Buller to: Mansfield (snow season only; 1–2 daily; 1hr).
Portland to: Mount Gambier (1–2 daily; 1hr); Port Fairy (1–2 daily; 1hr); Warrnambool (1–2 daily; 1hr 30min).
Shepparton to: Albury (1–3 daily; 2hr 20min); Melbourne (1–2 daily; 3hr).
Stawell to: Ballarat (5 weekly; 1hr 40min); Halls Gap (Grampians; 1 daily; 35min); Horsham (3 daily; 55min).
Swan Hill to: Albury (1–2 daily; 5hr 45min–6hr 20min); Bendigo (1–3 daily; 3hr); Echuca (1–2 daily; 2hr); Mildura (1–2 daily; 2hr 30min–3hr).
Wangaratta to: Beechworth (1–3 daily; 30min); Bendigo (3 weekly; 4hr 25min); Mount Beauty (2 weekly; 2hr 30min) via Bright (1hr 35min); Rutherglen (Sun–Fri 1 daily; 30min).
Warrnambool to: Apollo Bay (Fri only; 3hr 10min); Ballarat (5 weekly; 2hr 55min); Casterton (1–2 daily except Sat; 2hr 25min); Geelong (Coastlink via Apollo Bay; Fri only; 7hr); Hamilton (1–2 daily except Sat; 1hr 40min); Mount Gambier (1–3 daily; 3hr); Port Fairy (1–4 daily; 40min); Portland (1–3 daily; 1hr 30min).

Flights

Albury to: Melbourne (2–8 daily; 50min).
Mildura to: Melbourne (3–8 daily; 1hr 10min).
Portland to: Melbourne (1–3 daily; 40min).

12

Tasmania

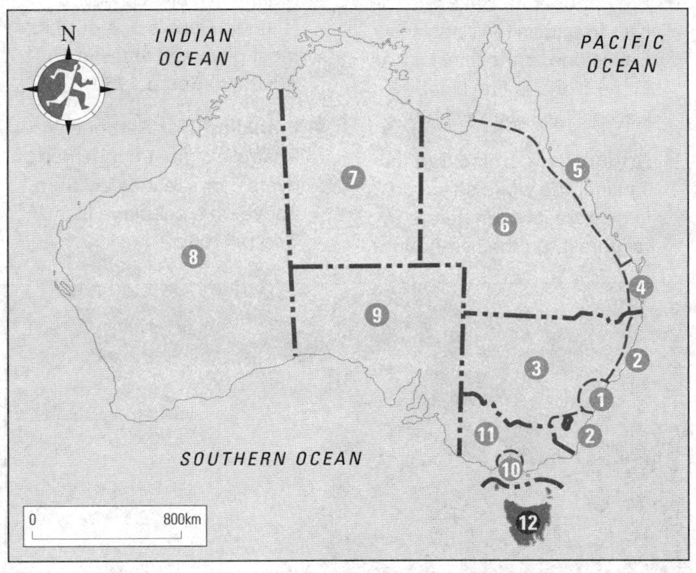
N
INDIAN OCEAN
PACIFIC OCEAN
SOUTHERN OCEAN
0
800km
1
2
2
3
4
5
6
7
8
9
10
11
12

CHAPTER 12 Highlights

* **Salamanca Market** Lined with old stone warehouses and characterful old pubs, Hobart's Salamanca Place comes alive for its colourful open-air Saturday market. **See p.1082**

* **Port Arthur** The infamous old penal settlement is the biggest draw on the wild, scenic Tasman Peninsula. **See p.1104**

* **Freycinet National Park** The hike to exquisite Wineglass Bay is one of the finest walks in the glorious Freycinet National Park. **See p.1109**

* **Arthur River cruise** See the Tarkine, the world's second largest tract of temperate rainforest, on the five-hour Arthur River cruise. **See p.1151**

* **Gordon River cruise** A cruise up the dark, brown Gordon River is the best way to get a glimpse of the World Heritage-listed wilderness. **See p.1158**

* **Cradle Mountain–Lake St Clair National Park** Famed for its gruelling Overland Track bushwalk, Cradle Mountain–Lake St Clair National Park is one of the most glaciated areas in Australia. **See p.1160**

* **Franklin River** Raft one of Australia's most dangerous rivers – or see it safely from above on a seaplane flight. **See p.1166**

△ Wine Glass Bay and wallaby, Freycinet National Park

12

Tasmania

There's an otherworldly quality to **Tasmania**, with its gothic landscape of rain clouds and brooding mountains. This was a prison island whose name, Van Diemen's Land, was so redolent with horror that when convict transport ended in 1852 it was immediately changed. Yet the island has another, friendlier side to it too, with distances comprehensible to a European traveller – it's roughly the size of Ireland – and resonant echoes of England: cream teas, old-fashioned B&Bs and amiable, homespun people. In winter, when the grass is green, the gentle and cultivated midlands, with their rolling hills, dry stone walls and old stone villages, are reminiscent of England's West Country. Town names, too, invariably invoke the British Isles – Perth, Swansea, Brighton and Somerset among them. It's a "mainlander's" joke that Tasmania is twenty years behind, and it's true that in some ways it is very old-fashioned, a trait that is by turn charming and frustrating. However, things are changing fast: with the rise of its cool-climate wine industry, foodie accolades for its superb local produce used in a newly sophisticated café and restaurant scene, booming real estate and immigration, and cheaper and more frequent ferries and flights creating an increase in new and luxurious accommodation.

Tasmania is the closest point in Australia to the Antarctic Circle, and the west coast is windswept, wet and savage, bearing the full brunt of the Roaring Forties – and Australia's **whale-stranding** hotspot. The southwest has wild rivers, impassable temperate rainforests, buttongrass plains, and glacially carved mountains and tarns that together form a vast World Heritage Area, crossed only by the Lyell Highway, providing some of the world's best wilderness walking and rafting. It's still one of the cleanest places on earth: a wilderness walk, breathing the fresh air and drinking freely from tannin-stained streams, is a genuinely bucolic experience.

A north–south axis divides the settled areas, with the two major cities, **Hobart**, the capital, in the south, and **Launceston** in the north. The **north-west coast**, facing the mainland across Bass Strait, is the most densely populated region, the site of Tasmania's two smaller cities, **Devonport** (where the Bass Strait ferries dock) and **Burnie**. Tasmania's **central plateau**, with its thousands of lakes, is sparsely populated, though full of weekender fishing shacks. The sheltered **east coast** is the place to go for sun and watersports activities; set against a backdrop of bush-clad hills, it has plenty of deserted beaches and is safe for swimming.

It rarely gets above 25°C in Tasmania, even at the height of summer, and the weather is notoriously changeable, particularly in the uplands, where it can sleet and snow at any time of year; the most stable month is February.

Winter (June–Aug) is a bitterly cold time to visit unless you choose the more temperate east coast; wilderness walks are best left to the most experienced and well-equipped at this time of year.

Some history

The Dutch navigator **Abel Tasman** sighted the west coast of the island in 1642. Landing a party on its east coast, he named it **Van Diemen's Land** in honour of the governor of the Dutch East Indies. Early maps show it connected to the mainland, and several eighteenth-century French and British navigators, including Bruny d'Entrecasteaux, William Bligh, and James Cook – who claimed it for the British – did not prove otherwise. Matthew Flinders' discovery of the **Bass Strait** in 1798 reduced the journey to Sydney by a week. In

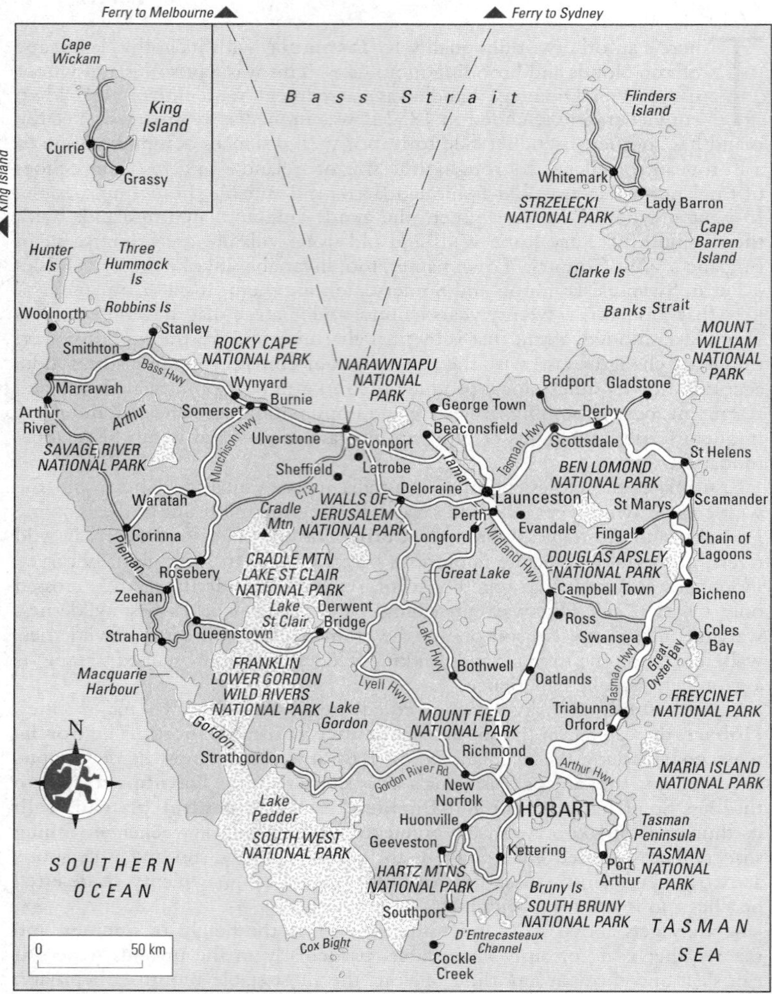

1803, after Nicholas Baudin's French expedition had been observed around the island's southern waters, it was decided to establish a second **colony** in Australia and Lieutenant David Bowen was dispatched to Van Diemen's Land, settling with a group of convicts on the banks of the Derwent River at Risdon Cove. In the same year, Lieutenant-Colonel John Collins set out from England with another group to settle the Port Phillip district of what would become Victoria; after a few months they gave up and crossed the Bass Strait to join Bowen's group. **Hobart Town** was founded in 1804 and the first **penal settlement** opened at Macquarie Harbour in 1821, followed by Maria Island and Port Arthur; they were mainly for those who had committed further offences while still prisoners on the mainland. Van Diemen's Land, with its harsh conditions and repressive, violent regime, became part of British folklore as a place of terror, a prison-island hell. Collins was Lieutenant-Governor of Van Diemen's Land until his death in 1810, but it is Lieutenant-Governor **George Arthur** (1824–36) who has the most prominent position in the island's history. His ideas were an influence on the prison settlement at Port Arthur and he was in charge at the time of the **Black Line**, the organized white militia used against the Aboriginal population.

Tasmania did not experience the postwar industrialization and immigration that transformed the mainland. A small, isolated and neglected state, it remains predominantly Anglo-Saxon in character, with an insular, often conservative, population. Its **natural resources** include forests – covering forty percent of the island – and water, and the mountainous terrain and fast-flowing rivers meant that hydroelectricity schemes began early here, under the auspices of the huge Hydro Electricity Commission (HEC). The flooding of **Lake Pedder** in 1972 led to the formation of the **Wilderness Society**, a conservation organization whose successful **Franklin Blockade** in 1982 saved one of the last wild rivers. Controversy over these issues still divides the state into "Greens" and a pro-logging, pro-dam working class worried about their jobs. By voting for the **Tasmanian Greens** in 1989, enough ordinary Tasmanians showed they didn't want Tasmania's natural assets destroyed, and the party held the balance of power in the state's parliament until 1992, and again in early 1996. The Tasmanian Greens party is represented federally by one senator, the famous environmental activist **Dr Bob Brown**. Ongoing conservationist campaigns are aimed at stopping old-growth logging in **The Tarkine** (see p.1151), **Styx Valley** (p.1101) and the **Blue Tier** (p.1114), and ending **woodchipping** (pulping trees for paper) for export to Japanese paper manufacturers; most wood taken from Tasmania's forests ends up this way, with Tasmania the only state in Australia that woodchips **rainforests**. Conservationists are also opposed to the practice of **clearfelling,** where native animals are poisoned with **1080 poison** to stop grazing on regrowth seedlings – it's even possible that the cancerous facial tumours decimating the **Tasmanian Devil** population could have been caused by 1080 in the food chain.

Tasmanian practicalities

Although it's small in Australian terms, make sure you give yourself enough time to see Tasmania; if you want to see only its cities you need no more than a few days, but to get a flavour of the countryside – the great outdoors is the real reason to come here – a couple of weeks or longer is necessary. Tasmanian Travel Centres, in Sydney at 60 Carrington St and in Melbourne at 259 Collins St (Ⓣ1300 655 145, Ⓦwww.tastravel.com.au), can provide **information** and also book all transport, tours and accommodation; their free information paper,

The Aboriginal peoples of Tasmania

The attempted genocide of the **Aboriginal peoples of Tasmania** is one of the most tragic episodes of modern history. Ironically, if it were not for American and British sealers and whalers who had operated from the shores of Van Diemen's Land since 1793, abducting Aboriginal women and taking them to the Furneaux Islands in the Bass Strait as their slaves and mistresses, the Tasmanian Aborigines would have disappeared without trace. Until recently, it was stated in schoolbooks that the last Aboriginal Tasmanian was **Truganini**, who died at Oyster Cove, south of Hobart, in 1876. However, a strong Aboriginal movement has grown up in Tasmania in the last thirty years.

The Aboriginal people of Tasmania appear to have been **racially distinct** from those of the mainland, although many of their beliefs and rituals were similar. About twelve thousand years ago, the thawing of the last Ice Age brought rising ocean levels, which separated these people from the mainland and caused their genetic isolation; it's thought that on the mainland new cultures probably entered ten thousand years ago. This isolation was also evident in **cultural development**: they couldn't make fire but kept alight smouldering fire sticks; their weapons were simpler – they didn't have boomerangs; and although seafood was a main source of food, eating scaly fish was taboo. In **appearance**, the men were startling, wearing their hair in long ringlets smeared with grease and red ochre, while women wore theirs closely shaved. To keep out the cold, they coated their bodies with a mixture of animal fat, ochre and charcoal; women often wore a kangaroo-skin cloak. Men decorated their bodies with linear scar patterns on their abdomens, arms and shoulders. Their **art** consisted of rock carvings of geometric designs, still to be seen in areas on the west and northwest coasts.

When the first **white settlement** was established in the early years of the nineteenth century there were reckoned to be about five thousand Aboriginal people in Tasmania, divided into nine main **tribes**. A tribe consisted of bands of forty to fifty people who lived in adjoining territory, shared the same language and culture, socialized, intermarried and – crucially – fought wars against other tribes. They also traded such items as stone tools, ochre and shell necklaces, and bands moved peaceably across neighbouring tribes' territory along well-defined routes at different times of the year to share resources: the inland Big River tribe, for example, would journey to the coast for sealing. Once they realized the white settlers were not going to "share" their

Tasmanian Travelways (Ⓦwww.travelways.com.au), is extremely useful, filled with detailed, comprehensive information on accommodation, attractions, bus timetables, car rental, adventure tours and national parks. It can also be picked up at local tourist offices in Tasmania. For general tourist information check out the government-funded Tourism Tasmania site Ⓦwww.discovertasmania.com.au. Available for purchase at tourist offices is the **See Tasmania Card** (3-day $149, 7-day $209, 10-day $279; more details Ⓦwww.seetasmaniacard.com), a passcard which provides entry to sixty tourist attractions.

It's easy to find **Internet access** in Tasmania, as most towns have a state-government funded Online Access Centre. The Tasmanian Communities Online website (Ⓦwww.tco.asn.au) gives locations of all the 64 centres as well as access to local town sites, often useful sources of information on local attractions and businesses.

Getting there

With so many airline companies offering competitive fares from the mainland to Tasmania, and the ferry company now with two routes (from Melbourne or Sydney), it's cheaper and easier to get to Tassie than it's ever been.

resources in this traditional exchange economy but were instead stealing the land, the nomadic people displayed a determination to defend it – by force, if necessary. Confrontation was inevitable, and by the 1820s the white population was in a frenzy of fear – though for every settler who died, twenty Aborigines met a similar fate. In 1828 Governor Arthur declared martial law, expelling all Aboriginal people from the settled districts and giving settlers what was, in practice, a licence to shoot on sight. Alarmed by these events, the British government planned to round up the remaining Aborigines and confine them to **Bruny Island**, south of Hobart Town. In 1830 a mass militia of three thousand settlers formed an armed human barrier, the **Black Line**, which was to sweep across the island, clearing Aborigines before them, in preparation for "resettlement".

The line failed; but unfortunately the final tactic was "divide and rule", in which the Aboriginal people themselves, with their superb tracking skills, were enlisted to help ensnare their tribal enemies. The 135 Aborigines who survived the Black Line were moved in 1834 to a makeshift settlement on exposed and barren Flinders Island. Within four years most of these people died of disease, or as a result of harsh conditions. In 1837 the 47 survivors were transferred to their final settlement at Oyster Cove, near Hobart, where – no longer a threat – they were often dressed up and paraded on official engagements. The skeleton of the last survivor, "Queen" Truganini, originally from Bruny Island, was displayed in the Tasmanian Museum until 1976, when her remains were finally cremated and scattered in the D'Entrecasteaux Channel, according to her final wishes.

The descendents of the original Aboriginal Tasmanians were given a voice with the establishment of the **Tasmanian Aboriginal Centre** (TAC) in the 1970s. The TAC's push for land rights has included the handing over of Wybalenna in Flinders Island. In the 1981 census, 2700 Tasmanians ticked the Aboriginal box; 16,000 did so in 2001. But this huge increase of people proclaiming Aboriginal heritage has ironically not pleased the TAC, whose sympathies lie with the long-documented and distinct Bass Strait communities. Many of those now identifying themselves as Aboriginal are from mainland Tasmania, but of these only descendents of Aborigines such as Fanny Cochrane (see p.1079) and Dolly Dalrymple can produce documents that trace a genealogy back to the time of white settlement.

By ferry

If you've bought a car to travel around Australia, you'll naturally choose to go by ship, and it's also the most romantic way to arrive. From the long-established Port Melbourne departure point, it's a potentially rough, ten-hour trip across the Bass Strait on the TT Line *Spirit of Tasmania* **ferries** to Devonport (daily Port Melbourne and Devonport departing 9pm, arriving 7am; also day sailings daily mid-December to mid-January departing 9am, arriving 7pm; bookings Ⓣ 13 20 10, enquiries Ⓣ1800 634 906, Ⓦwww.spiritoftasmania.com.au). Peak fares operate mid-December to late January, shoulder fares late January through April and September to mid-December, and off-peak fares May through August. On board, there are restaurants, bars and entertainment, and you can choose to sit up on reclining cruise seats (one-way: $99–145) or take a private en-suite cabin (pricier with portholes) ranging from basic twins (one-way per person: $210–273) and four-bunk cabins ($187–244) to luxury cabins ($295–383). Meals are extra on the Melbourne route, but on the longer, 21-hour Sydney to Devonport trip, dinner and brunch are included in the fare. Departures from Sydney, usually in the late afternoon to arrive in Devonport around lunchtime, are from 47–51 Hickson Rd, Darling Harbour; there are three weekly return sailings in the peak period, two per week in the shoulder season, and one per week off-peak. On the Sydney ferry, every passenger has a bed – the cheapest option is a multi-share hostel cabin ($160–190) and the dearest a porthole double cabin ($290–340).

Book in advance in summer, especially if you want to take a vehicle: standard-sized cars cost (one-way) $10 from Melbourne, $55 during peak season (motorbike $5/$38), and $55 from Sydney all year (bicycle $6; motorbike $38). Cheaper Apex return fares (21-day advance purchase) are available.

By air

Prices are very competitive for **flights** to Tasmania from the mainland with Virgin Blue (Ⓣ13 67 89, Ⓦwww.virginblue.com.au), with direct flights from Melbourne to Hobart and Launceston or flights via Melbourne including Sydney to Hobart from $120 or lower one-way, if you're prepared to leave early in the morning or later at night. Qantas' budget arm Jetstar (Ⓣ13 15 38, Ⓦwww.jetstar.com.au) has direct flights from Melbourne, Sydney and Brisbane to Hobart and Launceston; and Adelaide to Hobart; a typical fare is Melbourne to Launceston one-way at $240, although the price can go as low as $78. Qantas itself (Ⓣ13 13 13, Ⓦwww.qantas.com.au) also has (more comfortable) direct flights from Melbourne to Burnie, Devonport, Launceston and Hobart, and from Sydney to Hobart. **Fly-drive packages**, which include accommodation, can be particularly good deals: ask at travel agents. For flights to King and Flinders islands, see p.1133.

Getting around

With the vagaries of the public transport bus system and the difficulties of using it to get to all those out-of-the-way wilderness places that make Tasmania so attractive as a destination, the trend for travellers in the last few years is to hire a car, or for the more intrepid to motorbike or cycle. There are several good-value **tours** aimed at independent travellers that will get you off the beaten track and any number of **adventure expeditions** will provide transport from the cities as part of the deal (major tour and expedition operators are detailed in the box p.1072).

By bus

Six local **bus companies** and two charter services (detailed in the box opposite) reach most destinations on the island. You cannot use a mainland bus pass with any of these, and services are limited, often not running at weekends, especially on the east and west coasts; in winter and spring services are even further reduced.

Buying a local **bus pass** can be one way of cutting costs, but study timetables carefully before you buy. Redline's **Tassie Pass** comes in seven-, ten-, fourteen- and 21-day versions ($135/$160/$185/219) starting from the first day of use. TassieLink's **Explorer Bus Pass** has several formats: a seven-day pass valid for travel over ten days $172, ten-day for fifteen days $205, fourteen-day for twenty days $230, 21-day for 30 days $280. A YHA or VIP membership will give you substantial savings on all bus tickets and tours (see Basics, p.59).

By car and by bike

Renting a car is a sensible option, considering the vagaries of the transport system. Local operators offer reasonable weekly rates including basic insurance (see "Listings" in city accounts); as Tasmania is such a small island kilometres are usually unlimited, and you don't need a lot of petrol. Though distances seem short compared to the mainland, roads are often winding and mostly two-laned

Bus operators

"Tasmania's Own" Redline Coaches ⓣ03/6336 1446 or 1300 360 000, ⓦwww.tasredline.com.au. The island's largest operator, which we will refer to in the rest of the text as "Redline", offers frequent scheduled services between Hobart and Launceston via the east coast or direct via the Midland Highway, from Devonport to Hobart via Deloraine and Launceston, and along the northwest coast from Devonport to Burnie and on to Smithton and Stanley.

TassieLink ⓣ03/6271 7320 or 1300 300 520, ⓦwww.tassielink.com.au. Specializes in scheduled regional transport year-round and bushwalkers' "Wilderness Link" services for the South Coast Track and the Mount Anne Circuit from November to the end of March. Scheduled services run from Hobart to Burnie via Devonport and Launceston; Hobart to Strahan via Lake St Clair and Queenstown; Hobart to Port Arthur; Hobart south to Dover; Hobart up the east coast to St Helens; Launceston to Bicheno on the east coast via St Marys; and Launceston to Strahan via Devonport, Cradle Mountain and Queenstown.

Hobart Coaches ⓣ03/6233 4232, ⓦwww.hobartcoaches.com.au. Heads north out of Hobart to Richmond and New Norfolk, and south to Kingston, Snug, Kettering, Woodbridge and Cygnet.

Bicheno Coach Service ⓣ03/6257 0293. Runs between Coles Bay and Bicheno.

Broadby's ⓣ03/6376 3488. Runs between St Marys and St Helens and St Helens and Derby via Pyengana and Winnaleah.

Maxwell's ⓣ03/6492 1431. Provides a charter service based on a minimum of four passengers from Devonport and Launceston to and around the Cradle Mountain–Lake St Clair area and the Walls of Jerusalem National Park.

Tasmanian Tour Company ⓣ03/6423 4509, ⓦwww.tasmaniantourcompany.com.au. Bushwalking charter service from Devonport to Cradle Mountain, Frenchmans Cap and Walls of Jerusalem.

Tamar Valley Coaches ⓣ03/6334 0828. Launceston to Rosevears, Beaconsfield and Beauty Point.

– there are few freeways, except some short stretches on the outskirts of large cities – so **driving** can be slow and tiring. At dusk and night-time you have to be especially careful of animals darting in front of your car, as evidenced by the high number of dead native animals you'll see by the roadsides, and huge log trucks are unpleasant and sometimes scary road company. But with few cars, it's easy to relax and enjoy the scenery, also making **cycling** an attractive option, especially in summer, and on the flatter midlands and east-coast routes (otherwise, plenty of gruelling hills will keep you in shape). Several operators in Hobart, Launceston and Devonport rent bikes for touring.

National parks and bushwalking

All **national parks** in Tasmania charge daily (24hr) **entry fees**, often on an honour system, of $10 per pedestrian or cyclist, or $20 per vehicle (including up to eight passengers); if you plan to go bush for longer periods, then a **Parks Pass** will be better value. On offer are a two-month holiday pass (person, cyclist or motorcyclist $30, vehicle $50) or an annual pass for longer-stayers (car $42 for one park, $84 for all parks); camping fees are not included (though many sites are free anyway). Tasmania's wilderness has always attracted thousands of **bushwalkers**, and many of the churned-up tracks are gradually being boardwalked; keeping to set paths to avoid further erosion is just one of the national park's guidelines, available in a leaflet *Minimal Impact Walking*

Major tour and expedition operator contact details

Another way to get around the island is by taking a **tour**. The excellent Under Down Under Tours (ⓣ03/6362 2237 or 1800 064 726, ⓦwww.underdownunder.com.au), is a small-group eco-tourist outfit aimed at independent-minded travellers. Trips usually depart Launceston or Devonport and include bushwalking and wildlife spotting, hostel accommodation (which can be upgraded), and some but not all breakfasts and lunches. Their five-day tour (also ex-Hobart; $575) does a loop of the island including Cradle Mountain and the Freycinet Peninsula The two-day tour ($259) of the northwest includes the Arthur River cruise. Both can be combined into a seven-day trip ($759). Another five-day trip focuses on the wild west coast ($589). The eight-day ($799) version can be treated as a tour pass with the components done at your leisure.

The operators listed below offer trips and treks Tasmania-wide, detailed in the text.

Bottom Bits Bus ⓣ03/6234 5093 or 1800 777 103, ⓦwww.bottombitsbus.com.au.

Craclair Tours ⓣ03/6339 4488, ⓦwww.southcom.com.au/~craclair.

Island Cycle Tours ⓣ03/6239 1080, ⓦwww.islandcycletours.com.

Island Escape Tours ⓣ1800 133 555, ⓦwww.islandescapetours.com.

Rafting Tasmania ⓣ03/6239 1080, ⓦwww.raftingtasmania.com.

Roaring 40s Ocean Kayaking ⓣ03/6267 5000, ⓦwww.roaring40skayaking.com.au.

Tasmanian Expeditions ⓣ03/6334 3477 or ⓣ03/6339 3999, ⓦwww.tas-ex.com.

Tiger Trails ⓣ03/6234 3931, ⓦwww.tasmaniawalks.com.

from the **Tasmania Parks and Wildlife Service**, 134 Macquarie St, Hobart (ⓣ03/6233 2270, ⓦwww.parks.tas.gov.au). This, and all free walking and rafting notes referred to in this chapter, can be downloaded from their website. Detailed topographic **Tasmaps** ($9.10 each) of major walking tracks are available at the Service Tasmania shop at the same address and in all main towns (for locations ⓣ1300 13 5513 or ⓦwww.servicetas.gov.au). It must be emphasized that walking in the wilderness can be dangerous if you're ill-prepared: never go by yourself and always register your plans with a park ranger or inform others of your intentions. The downloadable brochure *Essential Bushwalking Guide and Trip Planner* gives information about the clothing and equipment needed in these parks, where the weather can change rapidly – even on a warm summer day hail, sleet or snow can suddenly descend in the highlands, and walkers who have disregarded warnings have died of hypothermia. As a minimum, you'll need wet-weather gear, thermal clothing, walking boots, a sturdy tent, warm sleeping bag, a fuel cooking stove, maps and a compass (which you should know how to use). Gear can be rented from outdoor shops in Hobart, Launceston and Devonport.

Festivals and events

The **Ten Days on the Island** festival is Tasmania's international arts festival, held biennially in March/April in venues around Tasmania (ⓣ03/6233 5700, ⓦwww.tendaysontheisland.org). The big music event is the **Cygnet Folk Festival** (see p.1092). On the sports front, the biggest deal is the finale of the **Sydney–Hobart yacht race** (see p.189), while **Targa Tasmania** is a car rally for GT and sports cars which takes over 2000km of the state's tarmacked roads for six days in April or May of each year (ⓦwww.targa.org.au).

Hobart and the east

From Lake St Clair in central Tasmania, the **Derwent River** flows past **Mount Field National Park**, Tasmania's oldest and most popular national park, through well-preserved **New Norfolk**, and towards **Hobart**, Tasmania's capital. Here, the river estuary widens to form a fine harbour before flowing into the waters of **Storm Bay** and out to the Tasman Sea. Hobart is Australia's most southerly city, battered by winter winds roaring in from the Antarctic, and surrounded by a jagged coastline. The hook-shaped **South Arm**, at the entrance to Storm Bay, is echoed on a larger scale by the **Tasman Peninsula**, with its infamous convict settlement at **Port Arthur**. To the south, the two tenuously connected halves of **Bruny Island** protect the waters of the **D'Entrecasteaux Channel**. On the mainland opposite Bruny Island is the fertile and cultivated **Huon Valley**, but as you head further south the coastline becomes increasingly wild: there are caves and thermal springs, the **Hartz Mountains National Park** inland, and the **Picton River**, where there's good rafting. The last settlement in this direction is **Cockle Creek**, the starting point for the South Coast Track which takes you towards the South West National Park (see p.1167), the great mass of wilderness forming Tasmania's southwest corner.

North of Hobart, the **east coast** of Tasmania is the tamest and most temperate part of the island, providing a popular cycling route past numerous sandy and deserted beaches and some lovely national parks. The **Tasman Highway** follows this coastline from Hobart to Launceston, heading inland through the northeast at **St Helens**, the east coast's largest town. The northeast corner is virtually unpopulated, and the **Mount William National Park** here is a haven for the Forrester kangaroo. Inland are some old tin-mining towns, and superb rainforest remnants and mountain scenery at **Weldborough Pass**, beyond which you pass through rich agricultural and forestry country to Launceston.

Hobart

HOBART is small but beautifully sited, and approaching it from any direction is exhilarating: speeding across the expressway on the Tasman Bridge over the wide expanse of the Derwent River, or swooping down the Southern Outlet with hills, harbour, docks and houses spread out below. The green- and red-tin-roofed timber houses climb up the lower slopes of Mount Wellington, snow-topped for two or three months of the year, and look down on the expansive harbour. It's a city focused on the water: the centre is only a few minutes' walk from the waterfront, where fresh seafood can be bought directly from fishing boats in Sullivans Cove, and yachties hang out at old dockside pubs or head for fish and chips served from the punts moored in Constitution Dock. South of Constitution Dock is Salamanca Place, a well-preserved streetscape of waterfront stone warehouses which is the site of a famous Saturday market, a Hobart highlight. Yacht races and regattas are held throughout the year, while at weekends the water is alive with boats; you can choose any type of craft for a harbour cruise – perfect in the summer when it's dry and not too hot. In winter, though, the wind roars in from the Antarctic and temperatures drop to 5°C and below.

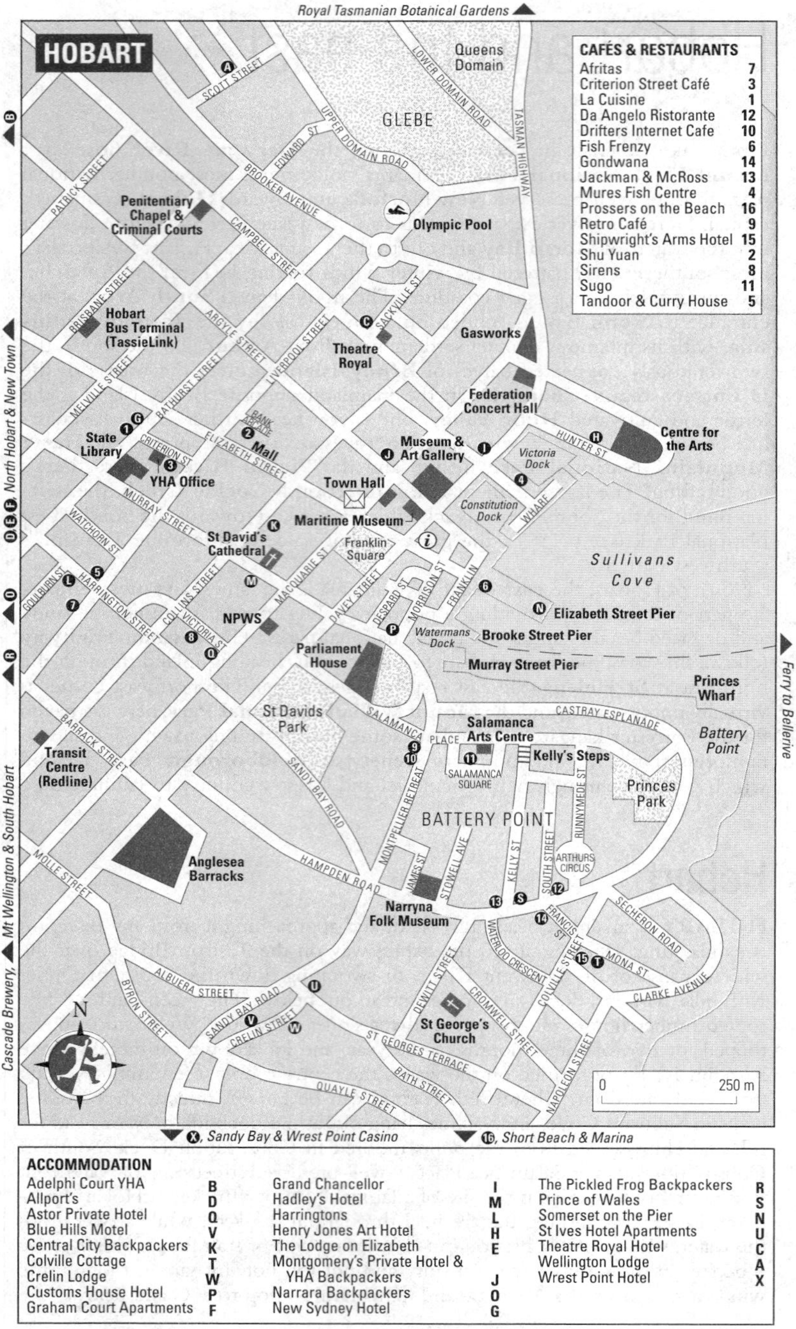

HOBART

Royal Tasmanian Botanical Gardens

CAFÉS & RESTAURANTS

Afritas	7
Criterion Street Café	3
La Cuisine	1
Da Angelo Ristorante	12
Drifters Internet Cafe	10
Fish Frenzy	6
Gondwana	14
Jackman & McRoss	13
Mures Fish Centre	4
Prossers on the Beach	16
Retro Café	9
Shipwright's Arms Hotel	15
Shu Yuan	2
Sirens	8
Sugo	11
Tandoor & Curry House	5

Queens Domain
GLEBE
Penitentiary Chapel & Criminal Courts
Olympic Pool
Hobart Bus Terminal (TassieLink)
Theatre Royal
Gasworks
Federation Concert Hall
State Library
YHA Office
Bank Arcade
Mall
Museum & Art Gallery
Centre for the Arts
Victoria Dock
Town Hall
Constitution Dock
Maritime Museum
St David's Cathedral
Franklin Square
Sullivans Cove
NPWS
Elizabeth Street Pier
Watermans Dock
Brooke Street Pier
Parliament House
Murray Street Pier
Princes Wharf
St Davids Park
Salamanca Arts Centre
Kelly's Steps
Salamanca Square
Battery Point
Princes Park
Transit Centre (Redline)
BATTERY POINT
Arthurs Circus
Anglesea Barracks
Narryna Folk Museum
St George's Church

Scott Street, Patrick Street, Edward St, Upper Domain Road, Lower Domain Road, Tasman Highway, Brooker Avenue, Campbell Street, Brisbane Street, Argyle Street, Sackville St, Liverpool Street, Bathurst Street, Melville Street, Criterion St, Elizabeth Street, Murray Street, Watchorn St, Hunter St, Wharf, Goulburn St, Harrington Street, Collins Street, Victoria St, Macquarie St, Davey Street, Despard St, Morrison St, Franklin, Salamanca Place, Castray Esplanade, Barrack Street, Sandy Bay Road, Montpellier Retreat, Runnymede St, Kelly St, South Street, Stowell Ave, James St, Hampden Road, Molle Street, Francis St, Secheron Road, Mona St, Waterloo Crescent, Colville Street, Clarke Avenue, Albuera Street, Byron Street, Crelin Street, Dewitt Street, Cromwell Street, St Georges Terrace, Bath Street, Quayle Street, Napoleon Street

Ferry to Bellerive

Cascade Brewery, Mt Wellington & South Hobart

B

D, E, F, North Hobart & New Town

O

R

0 250 m

N

X, Sandy Bay & Wrest Point Casino

16, Short Beach & Marina

ACCOMMODATION

Adelphi Court YHA	B
Allport's	D
Astor Private Hotel	Q
Blue Hills Motel	V
Central City Backpackers	K
Colville Cottage	T
Crelin Lodge	W
Customs House Hotel	P
Graham Court Apartments	F
Grand Chancellor	I
Hadley's Hotel	M
Harringtons	L
Henry Jones Art Hotel	H
The Lodge on Elizabeth	E
Montgomery's Private Hotel & YHA Backpackers	J
Narrara Backpackers	O
New Sydney Hotel	G
The Pickled Frog Backpackers	R
Prince of Wales	S
Somerset on the Pier	N
St Ives Hotel Apartments	U
Theatre Royal Hotel	C
Wellington Lodge	A
Wrest Point Hotel	X

Australia's second-oldest city after Sydney, Hobart has managed to escape the clutches of developers, and its early architectural heritage is remarkably well preserved – more so than any other antipodean city. There's a wealth of colonial Georgian **architecture**, with more than ninety buildings classified by the National Trust, sixty of which are on Macquarie and Davey streets. **Battery Point**, a village of workers' cottages and grand houses set in narrow, irregular streets, has hardly changed in the last 150 years.

Some history

In 1803 **Lieutenant John Bowen** led a party of 24 convicts from Sydney to settle on the eastern shores of the Derwent River at Risdon Cove. A year later **Lieutenant-Colonel David Collins** arrived, with about three hundred convicts, a contingent of marines to guard over them, and thirty or more free settlers including women and children, and founded Hobart Town on Sullivans Cove, 10km below the original settlement and on the opposite shore. Collins went on to serve as Lieutenant-Governor of the colony for ten years. For the first two years, food was scarce, and settlers had to hunt local game, creating an early culture based on guns that was later to have terrible effects on the Aboriginal population. The fine deep-water port helped make the town prosperous, and a merchant class became wealthy through whaling, shipbuilding and the transport of crops and wool. The period between the late 1820s and the 1840s was a golden age for building, with the government architect **John Lee Archer** and the convict **James Blackburn** responsible for some of Hobart's finest buildings.

Arrival, information and city transport

Hobart **airport** is 17km northeast of the city outside of Cambridge. Redline's **Airporter Shuttle Bus** ($9.70 one-way, $18 return; bookings ⓣ0419 383 462 or ⓣ0419 382 240), meets all flights, dropping off at central accommodation, as well as north to New Town and south to Sandy Bay. A **taxi** into the city centre costs around $25–30. Redline **coaches** arrive at the **Transit Centre**, 199 Collins St (ⓣ1300 360 000; left-luggage $1.50 per item per day; their airport service also drops off and picks up here). TassieLink disembarks at the **Hobart Bus Terminal**, 64 Brisbane St (ⓣ1300 300 520) where there's a free short-term left-luggage service for passengers (or $5 per bag for several days if you are going on a bushwalk) and a cafeteria.

Information

The first stop for general information is the **Tasmanian Travel and Information Centre** at 20 Davey St, corner of Elizabeth Street (Mon–Fri 8.30am–5.15pm, Sat & Sun 9am–4pm; ⓣ03/6230 8233), though it functions mainly as a travel, car-rental and accommodation-booking agency. The **National Trust Shop**, in the Penitentiary Chapel at the corner of Brisbane and Campbell streets (Mon–Fri 10am–2.30pm; ⓣ03/6231 0911), has inexpensive architectural guides detailing the bewildering range of listed buildings. On a more natural note, the **Tasmanian Environment Centre**, 102 Bathurst St (Mon–Fri 9am–5pm; ⓣ03/6234 5566, ⓦwww.tasmanianenvironmentcentre.org.au), is a relaxed resource space with lots of books and information to consult, a good selection of bushwalking guides for sale, and notice boards featuring environmental events, rooms to let and items for sale. For **bushwalking information** and a full range of Tasmaps, head for the Service Tasmania Shop at 134 Macquarie St (Mon–Fri 8.15am–5.30pm; ⓣ1300 135 513). Upstairs, the Parks and Wildlife Service (same hours and number) has information sheets and can refer you to a parks officer for advice; other general and bushwalking maps are stocked at the Tasmanian Map Centre, 100 Elizabeth St (ⓣ03/6231 9043).

City transport

Hobart's public transport system, the **Hobart Metro** (information ⓣ13 22 01, ⓦwww.metrotas.com.au), is useful for getting to less central accommodation and some more distant points of interest. The Metroshop, inside the GPO on Elizabeth Street sells Metro Tens (a pack of ten tickets giving a twenty percent saving) and provides timetables; the area outside – Elizabeth Street, Franklin Square and Macquarie Street – is the bus interchange. The handy yellow-painted **Busy Bee bus** does a circuit from Franklin Square through Battery Point and up Sandy Bay Road to the casino and back again. Single **tickets cost** from $1.60 (valid 1hr 30min); off-peak day-rover passes are $4.20. Captain Fell's Historic Ferries (see p.1081) offer a morning and evening commuter **ferry** to Bellerive on the eastern shore (Mon–Fri 7.50am & 5.25pm from Sullivans Cove, 8.15am & 5.40pm from Bellerive; $3.50; 20min). You can hail a **taxi** on the street, or there are taxi stands around the city; the major one is outside the Town Hall on Elizabeth Street.

Accommodation

There's plenty of **accommodation** in Hobart, but during the peak season from Boxing Day and throughout the first week of January, when the yachties hit town, prices can shoot up and places are hard to find. City and dockside **hotels** are the best option for clean, affordable private accommodation, and there's an increasing number of **hostels**; in the summer, student rooms are available at *Jane Franklin Hall* in South Hobart (ⓣ03/6223 2000). Battery Point is full of (sometimes pricey) **B&Bs**, and the area has several good self-catering holiday **apartments**, with costs comparable to a motel. Most **motels** are situated in Sandy Bay, about 3km south of the centre, or along the Brooker Highway, but B&Bs and guesthouses tend to offer better value.

Hotels and motels

Astor Private Hotel 157 Macquarie St ⓣ03/6234 6611, ⓦwww.astorprivatehotel.com.au. Central, old-fashioned, family-run hotel established in the 1920s. All rooms share bathrooms; rates include breakfast. The elegant *Astor Grill* at street level specializes in fine Tasmanian beef and seafood. ❹

Blue Hills Motel 96A Sandy Bay Rd, Battery Point ⓣ03/6223 1777 or 1800 030 776, ⓦwww.bluehillshobart.com. Pleasant motel with fantastic views of Mount Wellington from the west side of the building. Also one-bedroom apartments (sleeping four) with kitchen. ❺

Customs House Hotel Cnr Murray and Morrison streets, opposite Watermans Dock ⓣ03/6234 6645, ⓦwww.customshousehotel.com. Established in 1846, this waterfront pub opposite Parliament House with great views has been stylishly modernised; accommodation is now all en suite, and excellent value for the location. The pub bistro is well-regarded and it's a lively drinking spot. ❹, waterfront ❺

Grand Chancellor 1 Davey St ⓣ03/6235 4535 or 1800 75 33 79, ⓦwww.hgchobart.com.au. With an unfortunately ugly exterior, this is as close as Hobart gets to a five-star hotel (4.5 stars), in a great waterfront spot. Facilities include two restaurants, two bars including the elegant *Atrium*, and a health club. ❺–❽

Hadley's Hotel 34 Murray St ⓣ03/6223 4355 or 1800 131 689, ⓦwww.hadleyshotel.com.au. National Trust-listed hotel close to the waterfront, with an old-fashioned feel but modern facilities; in-house restaurant, café, bistro and bar. Room service, 24hr reception, and free parking. ❻–❼

Henry Jones Art Hotel 25 Hunter St ⓣ03/6210 7700, ⓦwww.thehenryjones.com. Combining the ambience of a nineteenth-century waterfront stone warehouse and jam factory with a luxury hotel-cum-contemporary art gallery, this is *the* place to stay in Hobart. Elegant touches include timber furnishings, sandstone walls, sensuous lighting, huge beds draped in vibrant silks, stunning opaque bathrooms, art by Tasmanian artists, LCD flat screen TVs and DVDs. There's dining at the hotel's *Steam Packet Restaurant* and the adjacent *IXL Bar* is very New York. ❼–❽

Harringtons 102 Harrington St ⓣ03/6234 9240, ⓔharringtons@harringtons.com.au. Small – only ten rooms on two floors – friendly and very modern hotel, handily located close to a concentration of cafés and restaurants. Good-value, small but colourful, nicely decorated and very clean rooms, plus some larger, more luxurious ones with marble bathrooms. ❹–❺

Prince of Wales 55 Hampden Rd, Battery Point ⓣ03/6223 6355, ⓔprinceofwaleshotel@bigpond.com. Ugly modern pub but in a great heritage location, with good motel-style rooms (but no phones) which either have views of the water or of Mount Wellington. Bathrooms all have tubs. Light breakfast in the bistro is included in the rate. Guest laundry; parking. ❹

Theatre Royal Hotel 31 Campbell St ⓣ03/6234 6925. A basic hotel, but in a great position across from the Theatre Royal, with plain but presentable rooms, some en suite; some singles available, and light breakfast included. Excellent bar and bistro downstairs. ❸–❹

Wrest Point Hotel 410 Sandy Bay Rd, Sandy Bay ⓣ03/6225 0112, ⓦwww.wrestpoint.com.au. Attached to the casino, this upmarket hotel has riverside rooms. Heated indoor pool, sauna and 24hr room service. Luxury tower or cheaper motel section. ❻–❽

B&Bs and guesthouses

Colville Cottage 32 Mona St, Battery Point ⓣ03/6223 6968, ⓦwww.colvillecottage.com.au. Peaceful Victorian weatherboard B&B, with en-suite rooms and a pleasant garden. ❻

The Lodge on Elizabeth 249 Elizabeth St, cnr Warwick St ⓣ03/6231 3830, ⓦwww.thelodge.com.au. Delightful guesthouse in an elegant National Trust-listed 1829 mansion; guest lounge with fireplace, games and complimentary port. All rooms en suite, some with spa. Also offers a self-contained cottage with spa (min. two nights). Light buffet breakfast included. ❺–❻, cottage ❻

Wellington Lodge 7 Scott St, Glebe ⓣ03/6231 0614, ⓦwww.wwt.com.au/wellingtonlodge. A Victorian-era weatherboard B&B (cooked breakfast served) classified by the National Trust, close to Queens Domain and the city centre, and with a pretty rose garden. All rooms either en suite or with own private bathroom nearby. ❹–❺

Hostels and budget accommodation

Adelphi Court YHA 17 Stoke St, New Town ⓣ03/6228 4829, ⓔadelphi@yhatas.org.au. Modern, motel-like hostel and guesthouse arranged around a courtyard, on a quiet suburban street, with the usual facilities. Far from the city (2.5km north), and a 10min walk to North Hobart's restaurant strip, but with plenty of parking. Bus #15 or #16 from Argyle Street, or #25–42, #100 or #105–128 from Elizabeth Street. Dorms $20–22, rooms ❸

Allport's 432 Elizabeth St, North Hobart ⓣ03/6231 5464, ⓦhttp://members.iinet.au/~allports. Heritage-listed 1850s mansion is now a very clean and comfortable hostel away from the centre but close to bars, cafés, restaurants and a cinema. Dorms and rooms are brightly painted with colourful duvets, simple pine furniture and telephones. The usual facilities plus loads of common areas, Internet access, and help-yourself veggie garden. Plenty of off-street parking. Dorms $20, rooms ❸

Central City Backpackers 2nd Floor, 138 Collins St, entrance off Imperial Arcade ⓣ03/6224 2404 or 1800 811 507, ⓦwww.centralbackpackers.com.au. One of Hobart's best hostels, in the spacious quarters of a once grand hotel. Friendly, efficient management. Dorms (three- to eight-bed, no bunks), singles ($42), twins or doubles; all heated; linen rental extra. Well set-up kitchen, pleasant dining area, TV and games rooms, Internet access and bike rental. No parking. Dorms $20–24, rooms ❷

Montgomery's Private Hotel & YHA Backpackers 9 Argyle St ⓣ03/6231 2660, ⓔmontys@southcom.com.au. Centrally located in a renovated old warehouse, this feels more impersonal hotel than friendly hostel. The tastefully decorated en suites have everything you'd get in a motel, including a phone but most dorms lack storage space and lockers. Very small kitchen/dining room, small lounge with TV. Bus and tour booking facilities, Internet, bike rental. Bag storage $2 per day. No parking. Dorms $20–22, rooms ❸, en suite ❹

Narrara Backpackers 88 Goulburn St ⓣ03/6231 3191, ⓦwww.narrarabackpackers.com. Attractive old house turned into a friendly, secure hostel, with an amiable live-in manager. The common room has pretty leadlight windows, a big table and comfy sofas; decent, well-equipped kitchen. Dorms, triples, twins and doubles, all very clean. Free Internet access. Off-street parking; bikes for rent. Dorms $19, rooms ❸

New Sydney Hotel 87 Bathurst St ⓣ03/6234 4516, ⓦwww.newsydneyhotel.com. Clean, central and small backpackers' above a pub with kitchen facilities and guest lounge plus Internet access. Noisy bands play downstairs six nights. Always lively, though, and budget pub meals are available. Parking $2 per day. Dorms $20, rooms ❷

The Pickled Frog Backpackers 281 Liverpool St ⓣ03/6234 7977, ⓦwww.thepickledfrog.com. Large hostel with young staff and a lively feel. The extensive communal area includes a bar/café selling cheap beers and meals, comfortable sofas, booths, pool table, wood fire, Internet access and industrial kitchen. Simple clean dorms (four- to eight-bed) and rooms; all have sinks and heating, though no storage. Light breakfast and linen included, bedding extra. Bike rental. Parking available. Dorms $20, rooms ❷

Caravan parks and self-catering apartments

Crelin Lodge 1 Crelin St, Battery Point ⓣ03/6223 1777, ⓦwww.bluehillshobart.com. Pleasant apartments with up to five beds, on a great perch in Battery Point. Most have views down the river. ❺

Graham Court Apartments 15 Pirie St, New Town ⓣ03/6278 1333, ⓦwww.grahamcourt.com.au. Comfortable, well-equipped one- to three-bedroom self-contained apartments set in a pleasant garden, but 2.5km north of the city centre. Disabled access. ❹–❺

St Ives Hotel Apartments 67 St Georges Terrace, off Sandy Bay Rd, Battery Point ⓣ03/6224 1044, ⓦwww.stivesmotel.com.au. Two-level two-bedroom apartments with full kitchen, TV/dining room, bathrooms with tubs, and neutral decor. Others are like standard motel rooms, but with full kitchen. All have balconies with water views. On four floors; luggage lift only. Rooms ❹, apartments ❺–❻

Somerset on the Pier Elizabeth St Pier ⓣ03/6220 6600 or 1800 766 377, ⓦwww.the-ascott.com. Waterfront apartment hotel – gorgeous split-level, spacious and light-flooded studio and one-bedroom apartments. Some have balconies, all have kitchen and laundry, and there's a gym and sauna. ❼–❽

Treasure Island Caravan Park 671 Main Rd, Berriedale ⓣ03/6249 2379. Large park 14km northwest of the city centre on the banks of the Derwent River; camp kitchen and pool. Vans ❷, en-suite cabins ❸

The City

Hobart is small and easy to find your way around, with the streets arranged in a grid pattern running southeast towards **Sullivans Cove**. You can walk anywhere in the city centre, which is mostly flat, although surrounded by some steep hills. The civic centre is **Franklin Square**, bounded by **Macquarie** and **Davey** streets, which between them have a concentration of listed buildings. The main shopping area is **Elizabeth Street Mall**, roughly in the centre of the **CBD** (the City Business District); Elizabeth Street slopes down from **North Hobart**, known for its many fine restaurants, to the Elizabeth Street Pier on **Franklin Wharf**. Here, at the harbour, fishing boats and yachts are moored, and cruises leave from Brooke Street Pier. **Salamanca Place**, with its row of Georgian warehouses, is on the waterfront on the south side of the cove; a steep climb up Kelly's Steps brings you to **Battery Point**, to the south. Following the Derwent River around from Battery Point, you reach salubrious **Sandy Bay**, with its casino and Royal Yacht Club. To the north of the centre are the parklands of the **Queens Domain**, with the **Royal Botanical Gardens** along the waterfront; from the Domain, the **Tasman Bridge** crosses the river to the residential eastern shore.

There are relatively few sights in Hobart other than the streets themselves, but these are enough to keep you wandering around for hours, stopping at a few museums and parks along the way. While walking through the city, it's worth glancing up occasionally to observe the **street signs**; the streets are often named after important local figures and the signs bear portraits and biographies. Around the docks area, and in Battery Point, interpretive boards point out historic and architectural features. Get self-guided walking maps from the Travel and Information Centre or go on one of the good historical walking tours (see p.1075).

Franklin Square

Set within a fountain in leafy **Franklin Square** is an imposing statue of Sir John Franklin, Governor of Van Diemen's Land between 1837 and 1843, and later posthumously famous as an Arctic explorer – his ill-fated 1845 expedition discovered the North West Passage. From the square, where a giant chess set gets plenty of use, you can walk south past many of the fine old buildings on Davey Street to **St Davids Park**, at the corner of Murray and Macquarie streets, originally the graveyard of St Davids Cathedral but converted to a park in the early twentieth century. It's a quiet spot containing some important monuments, among them a huge memorial to the first governor, David Collins. Other gravestones have been removed and set into two undulating sandstone walls at the bottom of the park.

Tasmanian Museum and Art Gallery and around

Just north of Franklin Square is the excellent **Tasmanian Museum and Art Gallery** at 40 Macquarie St (daily 10am–5pm; free but charge for some special exhibitions; free 50-minute guided tours Wed–Sun 2.30pm; Ⓦwww.tmag.tas.gov.au). The collection is, as the building's name suggests, a mixed bag. Much space is devoted to exploring Tasmania's tragic history, dwelling on penal cruelty, near genocide and the extinction of animal species.

As you enter, video-loop footage shows the last known **Tasmanian tiger** (**thylacine**), which died in captivity in Hobart Zoo in 1936. In 2003, in a collaborative purchase with Launceston's Queen Victoria Museum and Federal Hotels in Strahan, the museum acquired a unique, eight-skinned **thylacine rug** made in the late 1890s which the three will take turns exhibiting. The peculiar, flesh-eating, dog-like marsupial, which had a rigid tail, stripes and a backwards-opening pouch, was hunted out of existence by farming families fearful for their stock and encouraged by the 1888 to 1909 bounty on the creature's head (2184 were paid) – although unconfirmed thylacine sightings still occur. A project by Sydney's Australian Museum to resurrect the species using DNA from pickled specimens has recently been disbanded. A stuffed example is part of the unexciting taxidermy exhibition in the rest of the room, but the life-size reconstructions in an adjacent room of the Pleistocene-era **megafauna**, giant marsupials that once roamed Australia, are far more riveting.

On the next level above, the **Tasmanian Aboriginal room** displays cultural artefacts of the island's indigenous people, including some examples of the kind of exquisite shell necklaces that would have adorned "Queen" Truganini, reputed to be the last Aboriginal Tasmanian. The display gives a comprehensive account of the Aboriginal people, from their tragic near-extermination to recent events involving land rights campaigns. Particularly poignant is the recording of the voice of **Fanny Cochrane** (1834–1905) singing traditional songs; it is she who was probably the last full-blooded Aboriginal Tasmanian rather than Truganini as the myth relates.

The adjacent **art gallery** section has a display of colonial art featuring several 1830s and 1840s portraits of the well-known "final" Aborigines, including Manalargenna and Truganini by artists such as **Benjamin Duterrau** and **Thomas Bock**, as well as superb landscape paintings of Tasmania by the nineteenth-century artists including **John Glover** and **W.C. Piguenit**. There's also an excellent section on **convicts**: if you can't get to the convict ruins at Port Arthur or Richmond Gaol, this display will convince you of the brutality of the regime. At ground level, adjacent to the decent museum café, is a great **Children's Discovery Room**, and you can take some air at the café's pleasant outdoor courtyard.

Opposite the Museum and Art Gallery, the modest **Maritime Museum of Tasmania** (daily 9am–5pm; $6; Ⓦwww.maritimetas.org), in the red-brick Carnegie Building on the corner of Argyle and Davey streets, houses memorabilia, photographs and exhibits dominated by models of boats – the most impressive is a third-scale model of an open whaling boat. Arranged thematically, it provides an excellent introduction to the history of Hobart as a maritime city.

Northwest of Macquarie Street

There are several worthwhile sights along the straight streets that run north-west of Macquarie Street (running alongside Franklin Square), particularly Murray and Campbell streets. Three blocks northwest of Macquarie Street, on Murray Street at the corner of Bathurst Street, the **State Library** (Mon–Thurs 9.30am–6pm, Fri 9.30am–8pm, Sat 9.30am–12.30pm; Ⓦwww.statelibrary.tas.gov.au) holds the **Allport Library and Museum of Fine Arts** (Mon–Fri 9.30am–5pm, last Sat month 9.30am–2.30pm, and in Jan Sat 9.30am–12.30pm; free), the Allport family's private collection of eighteenth- and nineteenth-century furnishings, ceramics, silver and glass, paintings, prints and rare books relating to Australia and the Pacific made as a bequest to the library in 1965. *Zest*, the great little contemporary café at ground level, does good sushi.

The **Theatre Royal**, on Campbell Street at the corner of Sackville Street, is Australia's oldest surviving theatre, built in 1837. It has an intimate interior decorated in Regency style, best seen while attending a performance; otherwise, the staff might let you in for a peek. Further up, at the corner of Brisbane Street, the **Penitentiary Chapel and Criminal Courts** (daily tours except Aug 10am, 11.30am, 1pm & 2.30pm; 1hr; $7.70) comprise a complex of early buildings with two courtrooms, underground tunnels and cells. There's also a rather spooky ghost tour (nightly 8/8.30pm depending on season; $8.80; 1hr; bookings essential on Ⓣ0417 361 392).

The Waterfront

The focus of **Sullivans Cove** is busy **Franklin Wharf**, the first commercial centre of Hobart, where merchants erected large warehouses as the colony grew wealthier. In the 1830s, Hobart was one of the world's great whaling centres, and to cater for the growing volume of shipping, the New Wharf – **Princes Wharf** – was built, featuring a row of handsome sandstone warehouses on Salamanca Place. As the new wharf became the focus of port activity, the old wharf developed into an industrial centre of flour mills and factories. Part of the Henry Jones Jam Factory, between Victoria and Macquarie docks on Hunter Street, is now the **Centre for the Arts**, the University of Tasmania's art school. Beyond the original facade in a courtyard there are several large pieces of sculpture and the high-tech face of the art school. Inside, the **Sir James Plimsoll Gallery** (daily noon–5pm when there is an exhibition; free) has several shows a year featuring the work of contemporary Tasmanian artists. The rest of the old jam factory has been redeveloped and extended into a complex made up of the luxury *Henry Jones Art Hotel* (see p.1076) with a restaurant, bar, and art galleries featuring Aboriginal art and wood and furniture design. On the waterfront near the hotel, look out for the several sculptures and a plaque commemorating the links between Hobart and Antarctica, from the first 1840 expedition of the evocatively named *Erebus* and *Terror* under Captain Ross. Beyond this is the renovated old **Gasworks** on Macquarie Street in the former red-light slum district of **Old Wapping**. Its restored stone buildings are attractive enough, but the slick shops, restaurants and enterprises within – many are part of chains – try too hard to attract tourists. Opposite is the **Federation Concert Hall** (see p.1089), attached to the *Grand Chancellor* hotel and home to the Tasmanian Symphony Orchestra. The brass-clad building, opened in 2000, is oval-shaped, in keeping with the original gas cylinder in the old gasworks, and its acoustics are supposedly the best in Australia.

The old docks along Franklin Wharf are also thriving: at **Victoria Dock** lobster boats are moored, at **Constitution Dock** boats sell fresh and cooked seafood, and alongside is the Mures Fish Centre, a two-level complex of restaurants and cafés (see p.1087). The stylish development on Elizabeth Street Pier has a slew of trendy bars, eateries and luxury hotel apartments. From Brooke Street Pier and Watermans Dock, any number of **cruises** depart, while Murray Street Pier has been jazzed up with several restaurants. In summer, huge international cruise ships berth at the harbour, creating a rather glamorous backdrop to the waterfront pubs. Just behind the Travel and Information Centre, **Mawson's Place**, named after the Antarctic explorer Sir Douglas Mawson, uses wooden

Harbour cruises

Captain Fell's Historic Ferries Brooke Street Pier ⓣ03/6223 5893. A range of particularly good-value harbour cruises on the MV *Emmalisa*, all of which include meals of some kind ($15–$30). Also combined double-decker bus and harbour cruise (return leg) Cadbury's tour $42; departs Mon–Fri 10am or noon; includes lunch and wine.

The Cruise Company Brooke Street Pier ⓣ03/6234 9294, ⓦwww.thecruisecompany.com.au. Fast catamaran cruises. Their Cadbury's Cruise heads upriver to the chocolate factory at Claremont (Mon–Fri 10am; 4hr; $45 includes factory tour).

Derwent River Cruises Brooke Street Pier ⓣ03/6223 1914. The old MV *Cartela* used to bring apples from the Huon, but now offers Friday night dinner cruises with live music (depart 6.30pm; $5 cover charge plus meal and drink orders). The modern *Southern Cross Wanderer* cruises to the Derwent's upper reaches near Bruny Island (2hr 30min; Mon–Fri Wrest Point 10.40am, Brooke St 11am; $22); there's a shorter Harbour Highlights Cruise (1hr 30min; Mon–Fri: Hobart 1.30pm & 3pm, Wrest Point 1.10pm & 2.40pm; Sat & Sun: Hobart noon, 1.30pm, 3pm, Wrest Point 1.10pm, 2.40pm, 4.10pm; $15) as well as a cruise to the Cadbury Factory tour and Moorilla Estate Winery with a double-decker bus return (Mon–Fri Hobart 11am; 4hr 30min; $50 includes morning tea, wine- and cheese-tasting).

Lady Nelson Elizabeth Street Pier ⓣ03/6234 3348, ⓦwww.ladynelson.org.au. This replica of the brig in which Matthew Flinders made his exploratory journeys is a sail-training vessel, but also offers bargain pleasure trips most weekends year-round (call for times; 1hr 30min; $10).

The Peppermint Bay Cruise Brooke Street Pier ⓣ1300 137 919, ⓦwww.hobartcruises.com.au. Spectacular new cruise on a luxury catamaran (Oct–April daily noon, May–Sept Sun, Wed, Fri & Sat 11.30am; bow atrium $75, window $95, upper deck $125; gourmet-platter lunch included): south along the Derwent River and the D'Entrecasteaux Channel past Bruny Island to Woodbridge where there's a shore excursion to the stylish Peppermint Bay Hotel (see p.1092).

Port Arthur Cruises Brooke Street Pier ⓣ03/6224 0033 or 1300 134 561, ⓦwww.portarthurcruises.com.au. Cruises along the stunning, rugged coastline north to Port Arthur on the MV *Marana*, a 25-metre fast catamaran (departs 8am Sun, also Wed 26 Dec–May, no service Aug; 2hr 30min cruising, 3hr 30min at Port Arthur; Port Arthur site entry fee and return coach to Hobart leaving at 4pm included plus morning tea; $120, without return coach $85).

benches, glass screens and light towers to evoke a strong maritime theme sympathetic to its dockside location.

On **Salamanca Place** the old warehouses, shipping offices and storerooms are now full of arts-and-crafts galleries, speciality shops and cafés, interspersed with characterful waterfront pubs. At the end of Salamanca Place, on Castray Esplanade, the old silos have been converted into upmarket apartments. Salamanca Place comes alive for the open-air **Salamanca Market** (Sat 8am–3pm), an event with an alternative feel and wonderful local food, including colourful fruit and vegetable stands, and buskers; stalls focus on local crafts, particularly woodwork using distinctive Tasmanian timber (often recycled), and there's lots of bric-à-brac and secondhand books and clothes. Several of the narrow lanes and arcades in the area are worth exploring – with shops devoted to books, fairies and secondhand clothes and crafts – as is the **Salamanca Arts Centre**, a former jam-canning factory that's now home to a diverse range of arts-based organizations. Downstairs, the Peacock Theatre is the performance venue, and there are several galleries (daily 10am–5pm); upstairs, emerging contemporary artists show at the Long Gallery, with smaller displays in Sidespace.

Through the Arts Centre, Woobies Lane leads to lively **Salamanca Square**, a large public square with a fountain at its centre. The square is filled with cafés, restaurants and bars with outside seating, and some interesting shops including the Hobart Bookshop, which has a big Tasmania-related section.

A **guided walk** explores Sullivans Cove and Salamanca Place, starting from outside the Travel and Information Centre (daily 10am; 2hr; $20; bookings ⓣ03/6230 8233).

Battery Point

Kelly's Steps lead up from Salamanca Place to **Battery Point**, a district with an enduring village atmosphere. With the building of the new wharf in the 1830s, a working-class community grew up behind Salamanca Place; it takes its name from the battery of guns that were once sited on present-day **Princes Park**, protecting the harbour below. The area was first home to small cottages for waterfront workmen and, later, fine merchants' houses: the old pubs, with names such as the *Shipwright's Arms* and *Whalers Return,* leave no doubt about the nature of the population. Narrow streets, closely packed cottages, the flower-filled green of **Arthurs Circus** and the "corner-store" nature of the shops enhance the nineteenth-century village feel.

There's a particular concentration of early buildings on De Witt and Cromwell streets. **St George's Church**, on Cromwell, is the joint work of John Lee Archer (responsible for the nave, completed in 1838) and James Blackburn (the tower, added in 1847), the early colony's two best-known architects. **Hampden Road** has more fine nineteenth-century mansions, including one at no. 103 known as **Narryna** (Tues–Fri 10.30am–5pm, Sat & Sun 2–5pm; $5), a house museum furnished with period Georgian antiques.

If you want to become really acquainted with the history and architecture of the area, take the **Battery Point Walking Tour** (Sat 9.30am–noon, departing from the Wishing Well, Franklin Square; $10 including morning tea; bookings on ⓣ03/6223 7570), led by admirably knowledgeable National Trust volunteers.

Queens Domain and Royal Tasmanian Botanical Gardens

The **Queens Domain**, just north of the city centre, is a sparse, bush-covered hill traversed by walking and jogging tracks but positioned between two very busy highways. At the base of the hill on the Derwent, where the trees suddenly become lush and green, are the **Royal Tasmanian Botanical Gardens** (daily 8am–4.45pm), a formal collection of flower displays and orderly trees. Pick up a leaflet outlining the features of the gardens at any entrance, or from the **Botanical Discovery Centre** at the main entrance on the west side of the park (daily 10am–4.30pm, until 5pm Sept–April; free), where you'll find interactive games and exhibits as well as the **information centre**, café and restaurant. It's easy enough to walk to the Domain, following Davey Street or Liverpool Street from the city centre, but the gardens are quite far inside the grounds: from the city centre to the gardens should take you about thirty minutes. Bus #17 or any of the many buses to the Eastern Shore will drop you at Government House, in the centre of the Domain near the gardens, but there's no transport back.

Around the harbour

The estuary of the **Derwent River** is the deepest (and second-busiest) natural port in Australia. Just north of the Queens Domain, at **Cornelian Bay** in **New Town** you'll find cute fishing shacks and the well-regarded *Cornelian Bay Boat House Restaurant* (☎03/6228 9289) which also has a kiosk for coffees. A bike track runs here from the end of the Queens Domain below the Aquatic Centre (see p.1090). Heading upstream, the scenery becomes increasingly industrial, with a huge zinc-processing plant, but by Berriedale the setting is more unspoilt. Here, the **Moorilla Estate Winery**, off Main Road, has gorgeous river views from its landscaped grounds and from the huge windows of the wonderful **antiquities museum** whose collection includes African, Egyptian, Mesopotamian and pre-Columbian galleries as well as Roman mosaics (daily 10am–4pm; free; Bridgewater bus #X1). Established in 1958, it's one of Tasmania's oldest wineries; you can taste some of its fine cool-climate wines or eat lunch in its wonderful restaurant (bookings ☎02/6277 9900, Ⓦwww.moorilla.com.au). Beyond Berriedale lies Claremont and the riverfront **Cadbury's Factory**, dating from 1921, on Cadburys Road. The understandably popular factory tours include lots of chocolate-tasting (every 30min Mon–Fri 9am–1.30pm; 2hr; $12.50; booking essential on ☎03/6249 0333); from the city centre, take bus #37, #38 or #39 direct to the factory. Alternatively, you can cruise here (see the box on p.1081) or go on a guided coach tour with Tigerline (Mon, Wed & Fri 9.30am; 3hr; $46; ☎03/6272 6611).

The eastern side of the river is more residential, and looking across you'll see swelling, bush-clad hills with a modest line of homes below. The **Tasman Bridge** connects the eastern shore with the city: it was put out of action for over two years from January 1975, when the 20,000-tonne tanker *Lake Illawarra*, heading for the zinc-smelting works, crashed into it and destroyed two pylons. The ship is still at the bottom of the river, with its cargo of zinc concentrate, as are the bodies of seven crew members and five people in four cars.

The **Kangaroo Bluff Battery** at Bellerive, on the eastern shore – along with its counterparts at Sandy Bay (Alexandra Battery) and Battery Point (Mona Street Battery) – was erected in response to a Russian scare in the late nineteenth century, but it never saw active service. **Bellerive**, which you can reach by ferry from Brooke Street Pier (see p.1081), has a long, sandy beach at the Esplanade; some swim from it, although the water is somewhat polluted. The beach suburb is host to international test cricket at the modern **Bellerive Oval** on Derwent St (details on ☎03/6211 4000). There's cleaner water and surf beaches across the promontory from Bellerive at **Opossum Bay** (bus #296 or #300); while **Seven Mile Beach**, on Frederick Henry Bay, offers calmer swimming (bus #292 or #293). Ten kilometres north of Bellerive is **Risdon Cove**, site of the first European settlement of Van Diemen's Land; interpretive boards explain its early history (bus #267, #269 or #270).

Sandy Bay

Leafy, well-heeled **Sandy Bay**, a suburb just south of Battery Point, is home to a busy shopping centre on Sandy Bay Road. Near the shops, the Royal Yacht Club (where visitors can take a drink) fronts a marina, beside a beach and waterfront park. Further around the bay is the **Wrest Point Casino** on Sandy Bay Road. An ugly 1970s high-rise, the casino strives hard to be glamorous, but a rather downmarket tone is set by swarms of tour groups wearing name tags. More glamorous is the annual weekend **Sandy Bay Regatta** in January, when yachts are moored all around Sandy Bay's marinas, the river is filled with boats, and a funfair is held on the waterfront. At weekends throughout the year, too, hundreds of yachts are out on the water. Several buses go to Sandy Bay from the city centre, among them the yellow Busy Bee bus, and buses #52–56 and #60, #61 and #94.

Taroona to Kingston

South of the centre, what are defined as Hobart's suburbs terminate at beachside Kingston, reached speedily after 13km on the inland **Southern Outlet** or by a scenic, winding coastal drive via Sandy Bay Road and the **Channel Highway**. En route, at **Taroona**, 10km south of Hobart, the 48-metre-high **Shot Tower** (daily 9am–5pm; $4.50), built in 1870 to make lead shot, gives wonderful views of Hobart and the Derwent Estuary. **Kingston** is a residential suburb with wide, sandy **Kingston Beach**, which is 1km down Beach Road from the large and busy shopping centre. As all sea craft coming into Hobart have to go past the sheltered beach, it's a particularly good place to catch the end of the Sydney–Hobart yacht race. On the Esplanade there's a cluster of accommodation, including the homely *Kingston Beach Motel* (ⓣ03/6229 8969; all units with kitchenettes; ❹), a pub – the *Beachside Hotel* – serving good bistro meals (plus bands Thurs & Fri nights), and a nearby café, the recommended *Citrus Moon*, at 23 Beach Rd (daily 9/10am–5pm, Fri to 9pm). Heading south on the Channel Highway, the historical display at Australia's **Antarctic Division Headquarters** (Mon–Fri 9am–5pm; free), on the town's southern edge, can fill you in on Antarctic exploration; there's also a decent canteen. To get to Taroona, take bus #60 or #61; bus #61 continues on to Kingston; bus #67, #70 and #80 services Kingston.

Inland to Mount Wellington and Mount Nelson

Heading inland, the route southwest towards Mount Wellington via Davey and Macquarie streets takes you through **South Hobart**, on to Cascade Road and past the pretty **Cascade Gardens** and the nearby **Cascades Female Factory Historic Site** on Degraves Street. The sandstone walls here are all that remain of a prison built in 1827 to house recidivist convict women who were set to work washing and sewing; fascinating interpretative boards tell their story. It's free to visit, though the fudge factory and café beside it (daily 8am–4pm) offer guided tours to fund site conservation (Mon–Fri 9.30am plus Dec 26 to Easter Mon–Fri 2pm, Sat & Sun 9.30am; $9; 1hr 15min; bookings ⓣ03/6233 1559,

Ⓦwww.femalefactory.com.au). Beyond Cascade Gardens, at 140 Cascade Rd, the magnificent seven-storey **Cascade Brewery** is the oldest in Australia, still using traditional methods and taking advantage of the pure spring water that cascades – of course – down Mount Wellington. **Tours** (Mon–Fri 9.30am & 1pm; 2hr; $14; bookings essential on Ⓣ03/6221 8300) are at a fairly gruelling pace, but you're rewarded with a glass of draught beer at the end in the brewer's original residence. The small **museum** of brewing paraphernalia (Mon–Fri 9.15am–4pm; free) includes a few childhood pictures of the Hollywood actor Errol Flynn, who was brought up in the South Hobart area. If you miss the tour, you can visit the souvenir shop and museum and have a drink at the bar or in the beer garden. Take bus #43, #44, #46 or #49 to the brewery. Alternatively, you can walk or cycle all the way to Cascades Gardens and past the Female Factory along the pathway following the peaceful **Hobart Rivulet** (platypus are often seen here), starting from just behind the Village Cinema on Collins Street near the corner with Molle Street.

In any image of Hobart, **Mount Wellington** (1270m) is always looming in the background, sometimes snow-covered. Access is up winding Huon Road lined with houses as far as **Fern Tree**, from where Pillinger Drive turns into the steep and winding Pinnacle Road to the summit; the 19km drive provides several lookout points. Near the bottom of a walking route which goes right up the mountain (via Fernglade Track, Pinnacle Track and Zig Zag Track; 13km; 2hr 45min one-way; detailed in *Mount Wellington Walks*, $4 from Service Tasmania outlets), the *Fern Tree Tavern* offers teas, meals and views. There are picnic grounds with barbecues, shelters, toilets and information boards at the beginning of the track at Fern Tree, and about halfway up at **The Springs.** Pure, drinkable water cascades from rocks as you climb and the thick bush begins to gradually thin; by the top it's bare and rocky. Here, the stone **Pinnacle Observatory Shelter** (daily 8am–6pm) has details of the magnificent panorama of the city and harbour spread before you, which includes vast tracts of bush and grass plains, and views to Bruny Island to the south and as far as Maria Island to the north; there are toilets but no refreshments available at the top. Metro buses #48 or #49 run to Fern Tree, or The Mount Wellington Shuttle Bus Service can get you to the summit (Mon–Fri 9.30am, noon & 2.30pm, Sat & Sun 9.30am & 1.30pm; $25; 2hr tour includes 30min on top; Ⓣ0417 341 804), leaving from the Travel and Information Centre (see p.1075), or picking up from accommodation. Island Cycle Tours' three-hour trip includes a visit to the summit, and then a 20km downhill mountain-bike ride to Salamanca Place (city pick-ups; $55 includes drink and snack; see p.1072).

The views are also terrific from the Old Signal Station on **Mount Nelson** (340m) above Sandy Bay. The station was established in 1811 to announce the appearance of ships in Storm Bay and the D'Entrecasteaux Channel; the signalman's residence has been converted into tearooms (daily 9.30am–4.30pm), from where you get a panorama of the city below. To get to Mount Nelson, take bus #57 or #58.

Eating and drinking

Hobart's fare can't compare with the mainland cities' ethnically eclectic range of cuisines, but its dining scene is becoming more cosmopolitan; the greatest diversity of restaurants and cafés is found along the Elizabeth Street strip in North Hobart including Turkish, Indian, Sudanese, Indonesian, Mexican, Thai and several Italian places. In the city centre, there's a concentration of inexpensive ethnic eateries on Harrington Street between Collins and Liverpool streets, and then around the Liverpool Street corner – African, Cambodian, Thai,

Indian, Middle Eastern and Balinese. Superlative **seafood** can be had throughout the city, but especially in the restaurants by Victoria Dock and Elizabeth Street Pier, and from the permanently moored punts selling fresh and cooked fish and seafood in Constitution Dock. On Saturdays, the fresh produce and food stalls at **Salamanca Market** are excellent.

Cafés, pubs, bars and takeaways

Criterion Street Cafe 10 Criterion St. The pavement tables outside this relaxed, cosmopolitan café take in appealing Criterion Street, with its organic foodstore, groovy homeware and retro clothes stores. The Spanish omelette and the gourmet bacon sandwich are both very popular for breakfast, and lunchtime blackboard specials include soup, salad, risotto or savoury cheesecake and lots of vegetarian options; nothing over $12.50. Divine cakes and coffee too. Mon–Fri 7.30am–5pm, Sat 8.30am–3pm.

Drifters Internet Cafe 33 Salamanca Place, off Montpellier Retreat. Cosy, long nook of a café, its walls covered with Errol Flynn paraphernalia. Soups, toasted sandwiches, nachos, and jacket potatoes all come under $9. Several computers with Internet access ($1 per 10min, $5 per hour). Mon–Sat 10am–7pm, Sun 11am–7pm.

Jackman & McRoss 57–59 Hampden Rd, Battery Point and 32 Cross St, New Town. Two stylish eat-in bakeries, both serving excellent pastries and savouries such as gourmet baguettes and rolls. Mon–Fri 7.30am–6pm, Sat & Sun 7.30am–5pm.

Kaos Cafe and Lounge Bar 237 Elizabeth St, North Hobart. Trendy, gay-friendly late-night coffee spot, with groovy music and magazines to read. Focaccia, real fruit muffins and cakes plus delicious all-day breakfast. Now licensed, *Kaos* has its own very funky bar room, *Soak*, with plenty of relaxing lounge space, and on Fri and Sat nights there's a club atmosphere, with DJs spinning until the late hours. Mon–Thurs noon–midnight, Fri & Sat noon–2/3am.

La Cuisine 85 Bathurst St. Cafe-patisserie serving excellent French-style pastries and mounds of delicious, healthy salads. Mon–Fri 7am–5pm, Sat 8am–2pm.

Macquarie Street Foodstore 356 Macquarie St, South Hobart. For those en route to the Cascade Brewery or Mount Wellington, this colourful laid-back café, close to the Hobart Rivulet, is an essential stop for its legendary breakfast – big portions, free-range eggs, and huge and fluffy pancakes – served until 3pm. Mon–Fri 7.30am–6pm, Sat & Sun 8.30am–5pm. Licensed.

Retro Café 31 Salamanca Place. Relaxed, light and airy place serving the best espresso in town, plus wonderful breakfasts. Often full of politicians from the nearby State Parliament and other high-flyers meeting over coffee mid-week. Outside tables popular on market day (Sat). A good place to find out what's on – notices and flyers cover one wall. Mon–Sat 8am–6pm, Sun 8.30am–6pm.

Shipwright's Arms Hotel Cnr Colville and Trumpeter streets, Battery Point. Old pub, popular with the yachtie crowd. Dishes up a legendary fresh seafood platter.

Shu Yuan Bank Arcade, 64 Liverpool St. This tiny vibrant place, little more than a take-away, packs in the customers – many Asian – eager for its delicious vegetarian food from a Taiwan-trained chef who morphs mushrooms, gluten and tofu into delicious, filling creations (a lunch special of three dishes on rice costs $7). Also fresh fruit drinks. Mon–Thurs 10am–5.30pm, Fri 10am–4.30pm, Sat 11am–3pm.

Sugo Shop 9, Salamanca Square. Trendy café, with a dramatic red interior and big glass windows giving a view of the action-packed square. Despite appearances, it's not at all expensive. The Italian-styled coffee and food is excellent, and includes gourmet pizza (from $10), focaccia, salads, pasta and risotto. Breakfast, served until 11.30am, costs up to $12.50. Mon–Fri 8.30am–5pm, Sat & Sun 9am–5pm.

Restaurants and bistros

Afritas Restaurant 201 Liverpool St ☎03/6231 4999. Adorned with African art, this high-ceilinged former hall is the wonderful setting for a government employment initiative for Hobart's growing African refugee community. Dishes come from all over Africa, from Moroccan lamb with couscous to Dakar Duck (mains $17.50–26). Monday pizza night (think *merguez* sausage instead of pepperoni) is teamed with a jam session, and there's more African music nightly from 8pm. Lunch Tues–Fri, dinner Mon–Sat.

Annapurna 305 Elizabeth St, North Hobart ☎03/6236 9500. Popular, casual restaurant serving North and South Indian food. Great *masala dosai* plus curry-and-rice lunch specials for under $10. BYO. Closed lunch Sat & Sun.

Da Angelo Ristorante 47 Hampden Rd, Battery Point ☎03/6223 7011. A great village spot for an upmarket, tasty Italian meal including gourmet pizzas; generous portions and good service. Licensed and BYO. Dinner Mon–Sat.

Fish Frenzy Elizabeth Street Pier. A stylish, modern fish café – order your food at the counter and find a seat. The food is cheap and terrific ($12 fish and chips), the staff are friendly, and it's always packed. Open daily for lunch and dinner, continuously at the weekend from noon to 9pm. Licensed.

Gondwana Cnr Hampden Rd and Francis St, Battery Point ☎03/6224 9900. In an old cottage with village views, *Gondwana* is one of Hobart's best restaurants; the creative and innovative cuisine is sourced from quality fresh, local ingredients. Tasmanian wines available by the glass. Dinner bookings essential. Expensive – mains $26–33. Lunch Tues–Fri, dinner Mon–Sat.

Lickerish 373 Elizabeth St, North Hobart ☎03/6231 9186. Hobart's latest style-icon restaurant has food to match the decor. The top-quality Tasmanian produce comes with delicate accompaniments such as beetroot sorbet, or kumquat and cherry pickle. With mains between $21–26, it's well priced, too. Licensed. Dinner Tues–Sat.

Mures Fish Centre Victoria Dock. Set among yachts and fishing boats, this two-level food centre houses three restaurants, a fishmonger, a bakery (great scallop pies) and a café. *Mures Upper Deck* (☎03/6231 1999) is an upmarket restaurant which has lovely harbour views; *Mures Lower Deck* (☎03/6231 2121) has bistro food, with cheaper prices; *Orizuru* (☎03/6231 1790; closed Sun) serves authentic sushi – their salmon is delicious – and is Hobart's best Japanese option.

Prosser's on the Beach Long Point Beach Rd, Sandy Bay ☎03/6225 2276. In a relaxing spot in extensive Long Beach Reserve on Little Sandy Bay overlooking the Derwent River, this is Hobart's – and probably Tasmania's – best contemporary seafood restaurant utilising superb local fresh fish. Asian-influenced dishes vie with simple fish fillets on mash. Prices are very reasonable, with mains around $26–28. Licensed. Lunch Wed–Fri & Sun, dinner Mon–Sat.

Sirens 6 Victoria St ☎03/6234 2634. Upmarket vegetarian/vegan restaurant serving subtle Middle Eastern/North African-inspired food in a lovely plant-filled, high-ceilinged space that's a cross between Gothic and the Ottoman Empire. Licensed. Lunch Mon–Fri, dinner Tues–Sat.

Tandoor & Curry House 101 Harrington St ☎03/6234 6905. Good, authentic Indian eatery serving all the favourites and accompaniments with mains around $14. Licensed. Closed Sat lunch & Sun.

Vanidol's 353 Elizabeth St, North Hobart ☎03/6234 9307. A popular veteran, this casual, affordable place serves Thai, Indian and Indonesian food. BYO. Dinner Tues–Sun.

Entertainment and nightlife

A lively **nightlife**, though on a small scale, is centred around the waterfront. The focal point is *Knopwood's Retreat* (see overleaf), which attracts a large crowd on Friday and Saturday nights, and has a popular nightclub upstairs. The more conservative *Wrest Point Casino*, at 410 Sandy Bay Rd in Sandy Bay, is open late every night for gambling, drinking and dancing (☎03/6225 0112; casino Mon–Thurs & Sun 2pm–2am; Fri & Sat 2pm–3am, *Regine's* nightclub Wed–Sun 10pm–4am).

To find out **what's on**, check the gig guide in Thursday's *Mercury*. A local website Ⓦwww.nakeddwarf.com.au details the **live music** scene, sponsored by Aroma Records, 323 Elizabeth St, North Hobart, which has lots of flyers and info plus a great little café. There's free live music in the courtyard at Salamanca Place on Friday evenings (5.30–7.30pm). Also see *Trout Bar* (p.000) and *Customs House Hotel* (overleaf, p.1076). Tasmania is too small to lure many touring bands, so the ones that play the pubs are mainly local. For more compelling gigs, keep an eye on what's happening at the University of Tasmania campus at Sandy Bay (☎03/6220 2861). **Concerts** are staged by the Tasmanian Symphony Orchestra at the Federation Concert Hall (see p.1089) and by the Tasmanian Conservatorium of Music at the Conservatorium (5–7 Sandy Bay Rd; ☎03/6226 7306) or in churches around town. Most **tickets** can be booked via Centretainment, at 132 Liverpool St (☎03/6234 5998).

Bars, clubs and live music

Bar Celona 24 Salamanca Square. Renovated sandstone warehouse turned into a slick and spacious café (by day) and bar on two levels. The light lunches (from $8.50 to $15) can also be eaten at tables on the square. On Friday and Saturday nights DJs play laid-back lounge music on the mezzanine level (9pm–12.30am). Daily 9am–midnight, till 1am Fri & Sat.

Isobar 11 Franklin Wharf. Young and packed, the *Isobar* (Wed 5pm–midnight, Fri 6pm–2am, Sat 7pm–2am) is a weekend favourite with live music on Friday and Saturday; Wed attracts a student crowd. At *The Club* upstairs (Fri & Sat 10pm–5am; Fri $5, Sat $7 or free before 11pm; happy hour 11pm to midnight) DJs play commercial dance on the main floor and there's also an R&B room and the quieter *Back Bar*.

Knopwood's Retreat 39 Salamanca Place. A favourite with students, yachties and just about everyone else, this pub has a relaxed, coffee parlour/bar feel, with plenty of magazines and newspapers, plus outside tables. Lunch served Mon–Fri; open until 1am on Friday, when the pavement outside is packed.

The Lark Distillery 14 Davey St. A handy spot to recharge, with pavement tables overlooking Mawson Place. A range of spirits made on the premises can be tasted for free (the single malt whiskey has a $4 charge). Also a huge range of whiskey, and an all-Tasmanian wine list. Cheese platters to snack on (and soup in winter). Live folk music on Friday evenings (5.30pm–8pm; free). A cocktail bar operates nightly except Fri from 6pm to 2am. Mon–Thurs & Sun 10am–2am, Fri 9am–10pm.

New Sydney Hotel 87 Bathurst St (ⓣ03/6234 4516). Hobart's Irish pub, featuring live music nightly except Monday – from traditional Irish to blues and folk. Twelve beers on tap, including Guinness, and decent pub meals (no lunch Sun).

Queen's Head Cafe & Wine Bar 400 Elizabeth St, North Hobart ⓣ03/6234 4670. Colourful, spacious and casual venue hosting free live music nightly except Sun (from 8.30pm Mon–Thurs, 9.30pm Fri & Sat), from pub rock to reggae and jazz. Lunch menu ranges from a $5 soup to a $17 chargrilled steak, while dinner includes a $12.50 roast of the day and more meaty mains, including half a kilo of rib eye steak for $22.

Republic Bar & Café 299 Elizabeth St ⓣ03/6234 6954. Laid-back lounge atmosphere, funky decor

Gay and lesbian Hobart

Acts of male homosexuality were still a criminal offence in Tasmania until 1997. Founded in 1988, the **Tasmanian Gay and Lesbian Rights Group** (TGLRG) put persistent pressure on the government. Led by spokesperson **Rodney Croome**, their rally cry "We're here, we're queer, and we're not going to the mainland" certainly shook up conservative Tasmania; thousands signed the petition to urge the reform of the law. The federal government and the UN Human Rights Committee also pressed for change, and Tasmania's Upper House finally cracked, changing the law on May 1, 1997. Ironically, Tasmania now has Australia's best legislation to protect gay and lesbian rights: it's the only state that allows same sex couples to officially register their relationship to access the same rights as married couples under Tasmanian law.

The TGLRG can be contacted on ⓣ03/6224 3556 or check ⓦwww.tglrg.org.au. Working It Out (ⓣ03/6222 7688 ⓦwww.workingitout.org.au) is a state-funded gay and lesbian support and health agency, and there's a social and support group Gay and Lesbian Community Centre (GLC Inc). GLC Inc publishes a monthly newsletter, *CentreLines*, which is sold from the TGLRG stall at Salamanca Market and details events and occasional dance parties around town which they organise, details of which are available on their recorded **Gay Information Line** (ⓣ03/6234 8179, ⓦwww.glctas.org). There's also a specifically **Lesbian Line** (Thurs 6–10pm; ⓣ03/6231 4228). *GAYTAS*, a fold-out gay and lesbian visitor guide, is available from tourist offices. There's a monthly **gay and lesbian club night**, *La La Land Bar & Club*, at *Halo* 37a Elizabeth St Mall, on the first Saturday of the month (10pm–5am; $10; ⓣ0408 328 456 to check details, which change rapidly) playing progressive house and trance, and *Flamingos*, 60 Argyle St, has lately taken the place of the defunct club *Cruze*. The *Trade Hotel*, 24 Barrack St, is popular with both a gay and straight crowd, with a big gay crowd for the Sat night DJs (free) and other popular alternatives are *Kaos* (p.1086), *T-42°* (opposite) and *Syrup* (opposite).

and free music, usually blues and jazz, six nights a week (except Mon); attracts a good crowd, including plenty of students. Excellent meals too, with lots of seafood on the menu.

Rockerfeller's 11 Morrison St ⓣ03/ 6234 3490. Gay-friendly bar-restaurant. Cocktails, live jazz Sunday nights, a fun atmosphere and a contemporary Australian menu. Lunch Mon–Fri, dinner nightly.

Syrup 39 Salamanca Place ⓣ03/6224 8249. Often hosting international guest DJs, this trendy club is on two levels above *Knopwood's*. Different nights and different floors have changing sounds and themes: anything from Sixties theme nights, techno, house, drum'n'bass, and 1980s retro, to live disco and funk. Open from 9pm Thurs, 8pm Fri & Sat (until 6am) and with live bands on Saturday afternoon 3pm to 6pm. Cover charge around $7.

T-42° Elizabeth Street Pier ⓣ03/6224 7742. Stylish lounge bar in a great waterfront location – some tables on the pier – attracting a cross-section of trendies and young professionals. Half the place is an eating area serving well-priced Modern-Australian-style meals at lunch and dinner (mains from $18). A good place to try Tasmanian wines, with many available by the glass. Daily 11.30am–1.30am.

Trout Bar and Cafe *Eagle Hawk Inn*, Elizabeth St, cnr Federal St, North Hobart ⓣ03/6236 9777. Relaxed pub which feels more like an arty café. Small menu of pasta, salads, steaks, chicken and Asian curries. Music, often jazz or blues, usually free (or around $7), Thursday to Sunday nights in a friendly, chatty atmosphere. Lunch Wed–Fri, Sunday brunch 11am–3pm, dinner nightly.

Film, theatre, concerts and cabaret

Federation Concert Hall 1 Davey St, bookings ⓣ1800 001 190. Home to the Tasmanian Symphony Orchestra, with regular concerts.

The Playhouse Theatre 106 Bathurst St ⓣ03/6234 1536. The Hobart Repertory Theatre Society, an amateur not-for-profit group established in 1926, puts on at least five plays a year here plus a popular Christmas panto. Premises are also rented out to travelling shows.

Salamanca Arts Centre 77 Salamanca Place ⓣ03/6234 8414. Base of several performance companies, including the Terrapin Puppet Theatre, which puts on touring shows – including a puppet picnic at the end of December in St David's Park. Puppeteers are welcome to come in and look around. Specializing is contemporary works, the Peacock Theatre hosts performances by various local theatre companies.

State Cinema 375 Elizabeth St, North Hobart ⓣ03/6234 6318, ⓦwww.statecinema.com.au. Art-house and foreign films; reduced ticket prices Wednesday ($8). Licensed bar.

Theatre Royal 29 Campbell St ⓣ03/6233 2299, ⓦwww.theatreroyal.webcentral.com.au. This lovely old place (see p.1080) is not too expensive or stuffy, offering a broad spectrum of entertainment from comedy nights to serious drama. Tickets from $28 up to $75.

Village Cinema Centre 181 Collins St ⓣ03/6234 7288. Seven screens showing mainstream new releases; discount day is Tuesday.

Festivals and events

Hobart's premier event is the last part of the **Sydney–Hobart yacht race** (see also p.73). The two hundred or so yachts, which leave Sydney on December 26, arrive in Hobart around December 29, making for a lively New Year's Eve waterfront party complete with fireworks. The race coincides with the fortnight-long **Hobart Summer Festival** (Dec 27 to Jan 9; more information via ⓦwww.hobartcity.com.au), focused on waterfront Sullivans Cove. The major event is **The Taste of Tasmania** (daily 11am–11pm, Dec 28–Jan 3), a gourmet food-fest promoting Tasmanian food, wine and beer, held at Princes Wharf. The main festival features outdoor concerts in St David's Park (the kids' one is free), a circus, symphony concerts, children's theatre in the Botanical Gardens, the 1km Pier-to-Pier River Swim, a Tasmanian film festival, buskers, and night-time gallery openings. The **Australian Wooden Boat Festival** runs over three days in early February in odd-numbered years, marked by a host of boats moored around the docks; activities include theatrical and musical performances and boat-building courses (ⓣ03/6266 3486, ⓔinfo@awoodboatfest.com).

The week-long **Hobart Fringe Festival** in mid-February has visual arts, film and performance components (ⓦwww.hobartfringe.org; many events free). The whole city shuts down on October 24 during the **Royal Hobart Show** (Oct 23–26), an agricultural festival.

Listings

Airlines Jet Star ⓣ13 15 38; Par Avion Wilderness Tours, Cambridge Airport ⓣ03/6248 5390, ⓦwww.paravion.com.au; Qantas ⓣ13 13 13, or their travel centre at 130 Collins St; Tasair, Cambridge Airport ⓣ03/6427 9777 or 1800 062 900, ⓦwww.tasair.com.au; Virgin Blue ⓣ13 67 89.
American Express 74A Liverpool St ⓣ03/6234 3711.
Banks Branches of all major banks are on Elizabeth Street.
Bike rental and tours Several hostels rent bikes (see p.1077) as do Island Cycle Tours (see p.1072). Derwent Bike Hire (ⓣ03/6234 2910; $7 per hour, $20 per day, $90 per week) rents mountain bikes at the beginning of the bike track to Cornelian Bay, by the Cenotaph in the Regatta Grounds at the south end of the Queens Domain.
Bookshops Ellison and Hawker Bookshop, 90 Liverpool St, has an excellent travel section upstairs. Fullers Bookshop, 140 Collins St, and The Hobart Bookshop, 22 Salamanca Square, are Hobart's two best literary bookstores; Fullers has its own café. For a fine range of secondhand books, try Rapid Eye Books, 36–38 Sandy Bay Rd, Battery Point.
Bus companies "Tasmania's Own" Redline Coaches, Hobart Transit Centre, 199 Collins St ⓣ1300 360 000; TassieLink Hobart Bus Terminal, 64 Brisbane St ⓣ1300 300 520.
Campervan rental Tasmanian Campervan Hire, Cambridge Airport (ⓣ03/6248 9623 or 1800 807 119, ⓦwww.tascamper.com), from $80 per day off-peak to $110 in summer, minimum five-day rental.
Camping and outdoor equipment There is a concentration of camping gear shops on Elizabeth Street near Bathurst Street, including a big range at Jolly Swagman Camping World, 107 Elizabeth St; Paddy Pallin, 119 Elizabeth St, has quality outdoor equipment, and provides bushwalking information; Mountain Creek Great Outdoors Centre, 75–77 Bathurst St, has a big selection, from cheap to top of the range, and also rents out gear.
Car rental Autorent-Hertz, at the airport and 122 Harrington St (ⓣ03/6237 1111 or 1800 030 222, ⓦwww.autorent.com.au), also campervans; and Avis, at the airport (ⓣ03/6248 5424) have similar rates; Lo-Cost Auto Rent, at the airport and at 225 Liverpool St (ⓣ03/6231 0550 or 1800 647 060, ⓦwww.locostautorent.com) has older cars plus newer models; Marquee Car Rentals, 248 Argyle St (ⓣ03/6231 3820), offers very cheap weekly rates; Rent-A-Bug, 105 Murray St (ⓣ03/6231 0300, ⓦwww.rentabug.com.au), has low-priced VW Beetles.
Disabled travellers The Aged and Disability Care Information Service, 181 Elizabeth St (ⓣ03/6234 7448, ⓦwww.adcis.org.au), is an excellent source of information, providing free mobility maps of Hobart. Hobart City Council produces a free *Hobart CBD Mobility Map*, available from their HQ on the corner of Elizabeth and Davey streets (ⓣ03/6238 2711). Maxi Taxis (ⓣ03/6227 9577) has specially adapted vehicles.
Diving Southern Tasmanian Divers, 212 Elizabeth St (ⓣ03/6234 7243), organizes dive charters and rents out equipment; The Dive Shop, 42 Bathurst St (ⓣ03/6234 3428), runs PADI certification courses.
Environment To find out about or to volunteer for environmental conservation programmes, the Wilderness Society's campaign office is at 130 Davey St (ⓣ03/6224 1550, ⓦwww.wilderness.org.au/tas); its shop is at 33 Salamanca Place.
Hospitals Royal Hobart Hospital, 48 Liverpool St ⓣ03/6222 8308.
Internet access There's paid access at the State Library (see p.1080; free for Australian residents, $5.50 per 30min for overseas visitors) but the best rates are at hostels ($2–3 per hour) and at *Drifters Internet Cafe* ($5 per hour; also cheap phone cards for calling overseas; see p.68).
Laundrette 12 Salamanca Square is a combined café/laundry.
Pharmacy Macquarie Pharmacy, 180 Macquarie St (daily 8am–10pm; ⓣ03/6223 2339); North Hobart Pharmacy, 360–362 Elizabeth St (daily 8am–10pm; ⓣ03/6234 1136).
Post office GPO, cnr Elizabeth and Macquarie streets (Mon–Fri 8am–6pm). Poste restante: Hobart GPO, TAS 7000.
Swimming pool Tattersall's Hobart Aquatic Centre, cnr Liverpool St and Davies Ave (Mon–Fri 6am–10pm, Sat & Sun 8am–6pm; $4.85). Heated swim centre with waterslides and bubblejets. Also gym and fitness centre.
Taxis City Cabs Co-op ⓣ03/6234 3633; Combined Services ⓣ13 22 27.
Tours Tigerline (ⓣ03/6272 6611, ⓦwww.tigerline.com.au) runs large-group bus tours: their Hobart City Centre and Mount Wellington Tour covers the city, the dock area, Battery Point, Mount Wellington and the Royal Botanical Gardens (Tues & Thurs 2pm, Sun 9.30am; 3hr; $46). Tigerline also offers day-trips to Cascade Brewery and Mt Nelson, Mt Field National Park, Port Arthur, Richmond, Tahune Forest Airwalk and Bruny Island. The best tour to Bruny Island is with Bruny Island Ventures (book through Tigerline), which does a small-group day-tour led by a knowledgeable guide (8.30am,

returning 5.30pm; $130 including meals). The Bottom Bits Bus (see p.1072) offers a range of great small-group tours from Hobart (all $89), including Port Arthur and the Tasman Peninsula, Bruny Island and Mount Field National Park, Mount Wellington and the Tahune Forest AirWalk, and Freycinet National Park.

Women Women Tasmania, 140 Macquarie St (Ⓣ03/6233 2208), provides information services. Hobart Women's Health Centre, 25 Lefroy St North Hobart Ⓣ03/6231 3212.

YHA Tasmania Head Office, 28 Criterion St Ⓣ03/6234 9617, Ⓦwww.yha.com.au (Mon–Fri 9am–5pm).

Around Hobart

Picturesque channels, orchards and islands define the landscape south of Hobart. The D'Entrecasteaux Channel region and the Huon Valley form Tasmania's premier **fruit-growing** district, which once exported millions of apples to England; when the UK joined the European Community in the 1970s, however, two-thirds of the apple orchards were abandoned. The region is also heavily forested, and around **Geeveston** magnificent woodlands are still logged. **Hartz Mountains National Park** and the **Picton River** are easily accessible to the west of Geeveston and you can get wonderful views of both, and of old-growth forests, from the new **Tahune Forest AirWalk**. As you head down the coast, caves and thermal springs are all accessible en route to **Cockle Creek**, the southernmost point you can drive to in Australia, with foot access along a track into the South West National Park. Offshore, across the D'Entrecasteaux Channel from **Kettering**, **Bruny Island** – Truganini's birthplace – has deserted beaches and coastal bushwalks. To the north, you can head inland to **New Norfolk** and on to **Mount Field National Park**, while to the east lies historic **Richmond** and, on the Tasman Peninsula, the old penal settlement at **Port Arthur**.

South: the D'Entrecasteaux Channel, Huon Valley and beyond

The **Channel Highway** (B68) hugs the coastline south from Hobart and makes a lovely drive around the shores of the **Huon Peninsula**, circling back alongside the Huon River to Huonville. Heading to Huonville directly, it's a much shorter 37km on the **Huon Highway** (A6), which then heads south for 64km, terminating at Southport. An excellent free fold-out guide map, "The Huon Trail", is available from tourist offices; it outlines the **Huon Discovery Trail**, a series of signs and interpretative boards detailing points of interest off the Channel and Huon highways.

The Channel Highway

On the Channel Highway beyond Taroona and Kingston (see p.1084), **KETTERING**, 34km south of Hobart, is a thriving fishing port, with an attractive marina. It's from Kettering that you catch the ferry for Bruny Island (see p.1097). The unpretentious *Oyster Cove Inn* (Ⓣ03/6267 4446; rooms share bathroom; B&B ❸–❹) is right on the water, not far from the ferry terminal, and has fantastic views from its restaurant, and a quirky sculpture-cum-beer garden; it specializes in seafood and local produce. More upmarket, *Herons Rise Vineyard* on Saddle Road (Ⓣ03/6267 4339, Ⓦwww.heronsrise.com.au; ❺) has luxury self-contained cabins gazing across the marina. Inside the excellent **visitors centre** at the ferry terminal (see p.1097), the *Mermaid Cafe* has good food and great coffee (daily 9am–5pm; licensed); the centre has **Internet**

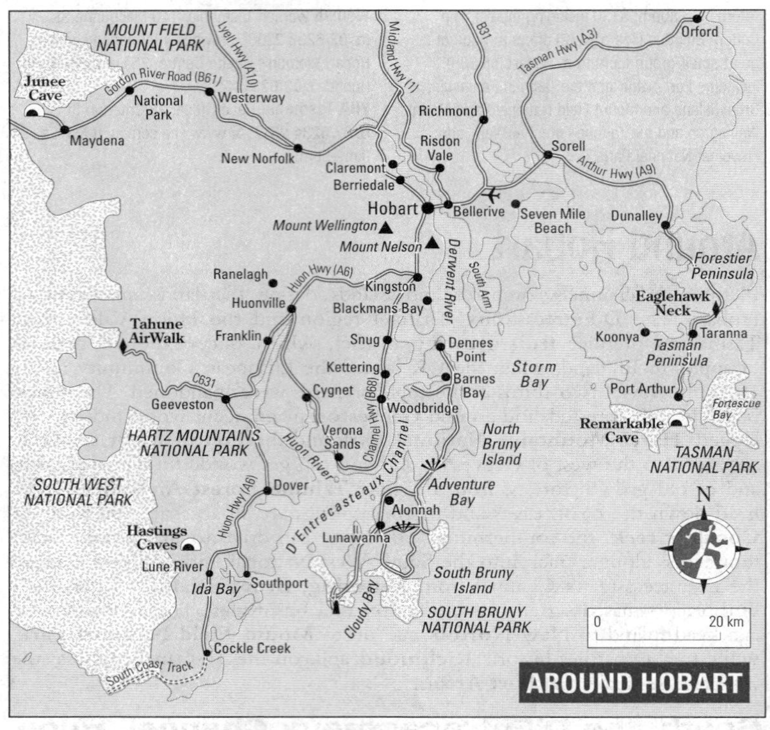

access. Roaring 40s Ocean Kayaking (see p.1072), based at the marina, rents **sea kayaks** (from $15 per hour, $55 per day), and also organizes day-trips to Bruny Island ($150) and weekend overnight tours to Recherche Bay ($225) and further afield.

The pretty village of **Woodbridge**, 4km further south, with its quaint general store and wooden meeting hall, had a big make-over when the Woodbridge Hotel was demolished in 2003 to make way for the $10 million *Peppermint Bay Hotel* (ⓣ03/6267 4088) with its fine food theme. The enviable waterfront location offers views across to Bruny in the upmarket restaurant and the deck attached to the bar (which also serves simpler food and coffee). A providore sells local Channel goods from cheese to smoked salmon, and there's an art gallery featuring Tasmanian artisans. You can **stay** in the *Old Woodbridge Rectory* (ⓣ03/6267 4742, ⓦwww.rectory.alltasmanian.com; ❹), an attractive B&B with disabled access. Woodbridge's **Online Access Centre** is at the West Winds Community Centre. You can get to Kettering and Woodbridge with Hobart Coaches on weekdays (4 daily).

From Woodbridge, you can continue around to the other side of the peninsula to Cygnet on the Channel Highway via **Verona Sands**, a pretty, sheltered beach, undeveloped except for the *Applejack Resort Motel* (ⓣ03/6297 8177, ⓦwww.applejack.com.au; ❹), which has tidy, spacious holiday units with full cooking facilities; a small on-site shop sells basic supplies. You could also take the gorgeously scenic inland route to Cygnet from Woodbridge on the

C627 through hilly, rural countryside, detouring after 5km for wine tastings at the **Hartzview Wine Centre** (daily 9am–5pm; ⓣ03/6295 1623, ⓦwww.hartzview.com.au; luxury three-bedroom homestead ❻), a further 2km along a well-graded dirt road.

CYGNET, at the centre of a major fruit-growing region, is a good spot to look for **fruit-picking work** in the busy apple-harvest season (March–May), but there's also the chance of finding strawberry- (Nov–May) or blueberry-picking (Dec–Feb) at other times. The town itself is very pleasant, backed by bush-covered hills; the appearance is sweetly old-fashioned but the town has an alternative cultural scene, the focus of which is the laid-back *Red Velvet Lounge Café* on Mary Street. It has a warm, communal atmosphere, sofas, a piano, affordable wholefood meals, great cakes, an in-house healthfood shop and useful notice board. Behind, the *fire bird bakehouse* serves woodfired pizzas (Thurs–Sun from 6pm). The more traditional, cosy *School House Coffee Shop* across the road does great scones, while all three pubs offer counter meals and you can also **stay** in clean rooms at the *Cygnet Hotel* (ⓣ03/6295 1267; ❷) or camp at the *Cygnet Holiday Park* both on Mary Street (ⓣ03/6295 1869). Two kilometres south out of town, right on the water, is the tranquil *Cygnet Bay Waterfront Retreat*, at Crooked Point (ⓣ03/6295 0980, ⓦwww.cygnetbay.com.au; ❺). *Nomads Huon Valley Backpackers*, at 4 Sandhill Rd just off the Channel Highway, 4km north at Cradoc (ⓣ03/6295 1551, ⓦwww.nomadsworld.com; dorms $20, rooms, some en-suite ❷–❸; pick-ups available if arranged in advance), on several rural acres, with river views, has all the necessary contacts for fruit-picking work. The weekend-long **Cygnet Folk Festival** (ⓦwww.cygnetfolkfestival.org; around $75 for the weekend; tickets through Centretainment), established in 1982, is the state's major folk, world and roots music event, and takes over the town in early January. Hobart Coaches (see p.1071) runs a limited service from Hobart to Cygnet (Mon–Wed & Fri 1 daily, Thurs 3 daily).

The Huon Highway: Huonville and around

The commercial centre of **HUONVILLE** is the focus of the region's apple industry, and another place where the prospect of finding work in the apple-harvest season (March–May) is good; it's also known for its delicious Huon Valley mushrooms. Once a rather redneck place, the town has developed a more alternative and upmarket edge, suited to its picturesque position on the Huon River. The handy **Parks and Wildlife Service information centre** and shop at 24 Main Rd (Mon–Fri 9am–4.30pm; ⓣ03/6264 8460) has information on all parks and reserves, and sells park passes, books, maps, and some walking gear. There's also a community-based drop-in **Environment Centre** at 17 Wilmot Rd (Tues–Fri 9.30am–4.30pm; ⓣ03/6264 1286), northwest of the roundabout near the Parks shop. There's a decent eat-in bakery, *Banjo's* opposite at no. 8 (daily 6am–6pm) or real café culture at *Cafe Moto* (closed Sat & Sun) back on Wilmot Road opposite the Environment Centre. Another good place to **eat** is *Huon Manor Bistro* (ⓣ03/6264 1311; closed Sat lunch & Sun dinner), a cosy, reasonably priced restaurant-cum-bar in a big federation-style riverfront homestead, just by the bridge into town.

There are opportunities to go for a ride on the river at Huonville with Huon River Cruises (ⓣ03/6264 1838, ⓦwww.huonjet.com), based at the **Huonville Visitor Information Centre** (daily 9am–5pm; same phone; Internet access $2 per 30min) on The Esplanade, as the Channel Highway is called coming into town from Cygnet. The *Southern Contessa* cruise visits Atlantic salmon fish farms and the Wooden Boat Centre at Franklin (Mon–Fri 10am; 2hr; $35); there are **jet-boat rides** (35min; $55), and pedal boats for hire (30min; $12). Huonville's **Online Access Centre** is at 23 Wilmot Rd. TassieLink runs a service from Hobart to Huonville.

At **GROVE**, 6km back towards Hobart on the Huon Highway (A6), the **Apple Heritage Museum** (daily 9am–5pm; $5) celebrates the local produce; the museum is surprisingly interesting, with hundreds of varieties of apples when in harvest season (March–May) and assorted apple paraphernalia from what was once a huge export industry.

Three kilometres northwest of Huonville via Wilmot Road, the picturesque hamlet of **RANELAGH** is home to the lauded *Matilda's of Ranelagh* at 44 Louisa St (Ⓣ03/6264 3493, Ⓦwww.matildasofranelagh.com.au), a B&B in an 1850 National Trust-listed mansion within English-style gardens with a characterful outhouse on the grounds. Just out of Ranelagh, the sleek vineyard-set winery/restaurant, **Home Hill**, at 38 Nairn St (winetasting daily 10am–5pm; lunch Wed–Sun, dinner Fri & Sat, morning and afternoon tea daily; Sun lunch bookings essential Ⓣ03/6264 1200), has a stunning backdrop of the peaks of Sleeping Beauty.

Southwest beyond Huonville, the road follows the west bank of the Huon for 8km to **FRANKLIN**, a bucolic community dating from 1839 with several fine old buildings and cute weatherboard homes facing the river and set against green hills. Franklin's chief attraction is the **Wooden Boat School**, where you can observe students (who come from around the world for the unique 18-month course) learning traditional wooden boat building and restoration (daily 9.30am–5pm; $5.50; Ⓦwww.woodenboatschool.com). You can **stay** in the colonial-era *Franklin Lodge* (Ⓣ03/6266 3506, Ⓦwww.franklinlodge.com.au; ❺) or in self-catering accommodation such as the friendly hilltop *Kay Creek Cottage* (Ⓣ03/6266 3524, Ⓦwww.kaycreekcottage.com.au; includes breakfast provisions). There's good-value bistro **food** at the 1853-established *Olde Franklin Tavern* and great coffee and cake and a varied modern menu opposite at the waterfront *Petty Sessions Gourmet Cafe* (daily 10am–5pm plus dinner Nov–April Wed–Sun, May–Oct Fri & Sat; licensed). In the evening, offerings at the well-regarded *Franklin Grill* include fresh Bruny Island oysters (dinner Wed–Sun; Ⓣ03/6266 3645; licensed & BYO; mains $20–26) or try *Franklin Woodfired Pizza* (from 5pm Mon–Fri, from 4pm Sat & Sun). *Tasmanian Seafood*, opposite the fire station, does tasty fish and chips, delicious tempura Huon Valley mushrooms and sweet-potato cakes.

Geeveston and around

Two huge upright logs act as an entrance to sleepy and solid **GEEVESTON**, a traditional logging town 18km south of Franklin and in the heart of the Southern Forest. Confrontation between conservationists and the timber industry here led to the so-called "Battle of Farmhouse Creek" in 1986, a dispute won by the conservationists, after which some of the forests were awarded World Heritage listing. The Forestry Commission was awarded millions of dollars in compensation, to be used on special forestry projects, one of which is the **Forest and Heritage Centre** in the town hall on Church Street (daily 9am–5pm; Ⓣ03/6297 1836, Ⓦwww.forestandheritagecentre.com.au; $5), which also has a **visitor information** centre. Displays explain how the Southern Forests grow, and look at the history of logging in the area – including the Farmhouse Creek dispute. There's also a gallery of local woodwork and a woodturner in residence (lessons are available). A related Forestry Tasmania project, the Tahune Forest AirWalk (see opposite), is 26km southwest along the now-sealed Arve Road. En route to the must-see AirWalk, on the drive along Arve Road, several boardwalks have been constructed through magnificent swamp gum and eucalypt forests – they're detailed on the free leaflet that's handed out.

Twenty-four kilometres southwest along Arve Road is the rugged **Hartz Mountains National Park**, with its glacial lakes, rainforests and alpine moorlands; a day-walk map is available from the Forest and Heritage Centre. From Arve Road, a stony, unsealed track winds up for 12km, with several stopping-off points; at the end of the track it's a couple of minutes' walk to Waratah Lookout, with great views over the Huon Valley and the Southern Forests. Another walk (4km) heads off to the sometimes snowcapped Hartz Peak (1255m); most of the trail is boardwalked, but parts are wet and boggy underfoot and there's the potential for fog to settle and icy winds and snow to sweep in at any time – recommended for well-prepared walkers only.

The **Picton River** skirts the Hartz Mountains from its source deep in the South West National Park; with its bouncy rapids, intermittent gentle sections and magnificent wilderness scenery, it's a popular, short (and affordable) **rafting** alternative to the Franklin River. Rafting Tasmania (see p.1072) runs year-round day-trips from Hobart for $145. The river continues towards the **Tahune Forest Reserve**, at the junction with the Huon River, just north of Hartz Mountains National Park. Here, the impressive $4.5 million **Tahune Forest AirWalk and Visitor Centre** (daily: April–Nov 9am–4.30pm; Dec–March 9am–8.15pm; $11; Ⓣ03/6297 0068, Ⓦwww.forestrytas.com.au) was opened in 2001. The 597-metre-long, steel-framed walkway is supported by twelve towers and suspended 25–48m in the air at the level of the tree canopy of the surrounding old-growth forest and, thrillingly, above the confluence of the rivers, with magnificent views across to the Hartz Mountains. For more thrills, the latest addition is the **Eagle Glide**, an aerial cable that whizzes you individually across the forest for an extra $33. Below, the riverside Huon Pine boardwalk provides an easy twenty-minute return stroll to huge and ancient Huon Pines. The visitor centre has a Forestry Tasmania interpretative display, while the attached licensed café focuses on local gourmet products. If you're picnicking, there are great shelters with roaring fires and gas barbecues for even the wildest day; camping is also allowed here.

You can **stay** at the *Geeveston Forest House*, a cottage hostel on the edge of town at 24 Arve Rd (Ⓣ03/6297 1102; dorms $20, room ❷). TassieLink has a Hobart–Geeveston service (four daily Mon–Fri, one daily Sat) but there's no transport to the AirWalk. Otherwise, the Bottom Bits Bus ($89; see p.1071) does a day-trip from Hobart which includes the Huon Valley and Hastings Caves.

Dover and around

DOVER, 21km from Geeveston, is an attractive fishing village on a large bay, **Port Esperance**, fed by the Esperance River. There are trees everywhere, and lush hills surround the village, backed by the clear, virtually triangular, outline of **Adamsons Peak** (1226m), snowcapped in winter. Boats moor off a jetty in the bay, where two tiny tree-covered islets are silhouetted against the sky at dusk.

The hub of Dover is the *Dover Hotel*, on the Huon Highway (Ⓣ03/6298 1210, Ⓔdoverhotel@bigpond.com; rooms ❸, motel units ❹), beside an apple orchard and rolling fields, with an old-fashioned dining room overlooking the water. Southern Wilderness Eco Adventure Tours (Ⓣ03/6297 6368; Ⓦwww.tasglow-wormadventure.com.au) offers a popular Glow Worm Adventure

Caving Trip (4hr; $65) departing from the hotel. The *Dover Beachside Tourist Park* on Kent Beach Road (Ⓣ03/6298 1301; vans ❷, cabins ❸–❹) is scenically sited near the jetty, beside a creek. Back up towards Geeveston, 12km north near picturesque Police Point, *Huon Charm* (Ⓣ03/6297 6314, Ⓦwww.huoncharm.com; ❹) consists of two waterfront cottages and is a more secluded alternative. Six kilometres south along the highway at **Strathblane** is the truly marvellous *Far South Wilderness Lodge and Backpackers* (Ⓣ03/6298 1922; Ⓦwww.farsouthwilderness.com.au; camping also available; TassieLink will drop off outside) sitting right on an inlet of the Esperance River in 80 acres of unspoilt forest. Activities include a nightly campfire, guided walks, mountain biking ($10 half-day; $15 full day) and kayaking hire ($15 hr; $45 day). A great place to **eat** in Dover itself is the excellent *Dover Woodfired Pizza* (Ⓣ03/6298 1908; Tues–Sun from 4pm; licensed), with wall-length windows looking down to the water; it's near the **Online Access Centre**. Although you can find fuel and supplies 20km south at **Southport** (the last place to get either), there's more choice and better value in Dover. TassieLink runs a service to Dover (Mon–Fri 1–2 daily plus extra services Dec–April).

Thirty-one kilometres from Dover are the Hastings Caves, in the foothills of Adamsons Peak, with the **Thermal Springs State Reserve** en route. The small, shallow and rather tepid springs, ranging from 20–30°C, are no great shakes, but the setting is lush and there are several walks in the grounds and there's a pleasant café and visitor centre (late Sept to end April daily 9am–5pm, end Dec to end Feb until 6pm, end April to early Sept 10am–4pm; $4.90 or cave ticket includes pool entry). Tickets to visit **Hastings Caves**, a few kilometres further on from the springs, must be bought from here: Newdegate Cave, the best, is open daily for tours (hourly 11am–3pm, with extra tours Oct–March; 45min; $19.50); it's always wet and cold inside, so bring something warm to wear. Also on offer are **adventure tours** of King George V Cave (6hr including BBQ and swim; $185), and a glow-worm display (Fri noon; 3hr; $69); these tours need to be booked in advance (Ⓣ03/6298 3209). Bottoms Bits Bus does a tour to Hastings Cave from Hobart (see above).

Cockle Creek

Beyond Ida Bay, the unsurfaced Cockle Creek Road takes you past picturesque sheltered bays and coastal forests, where wild flowers bloom in summer, to **COCKLE CREEK** on the lovely **Recherche Bay** (pronounced "research" by locals), so named because it was here that the French expedition under **Bruny D'Entrecasteaux**, sent to look for the missing Lapérouse expedition (see Sydney p.176), set up temporarily for four weeks in 1792 and again in 1793. As well as the important botanical research carried out by naturalist Labilladière, a garden was established and cordial meetings with the Aboriginal people were recorded. Given the site's cultural significance, there is currently a huge protest against proposed clearfelling in the area.

The only provision at the small settlement clustered around the Recherche Bay Community Centre is an emergency phone. Beyond, there are lots of free camping spots along the shore (one-month limit), as well as caravans inhabited semi-permanently by mainly fishing-obsessed retirees after the abundant crayfish, cockles and fish in the bay. Pit toilets and water are the only facilities. The wooden bridge across Cockle Creek leads to the **South West National Park** where an interpretative board outside the intermittedly-staffed office (to speak to a ranger contact Huonville NPWS p.1093) provides a fascinating history from Aboriginal, French, whaling and other perspectives. There's a five-minute walk to a waterfront bronze sculpture of a baby southern right whale and from here the easy Fishers Point walk takes you around the coast (4km round-trip; up to 2hr), but the most popular walk is the muddy but boardwalked first part of the **South Coast Track** to the beach at South Cape Bay and back (4hr return; moderate difficulty); the entire length of the track is for the very experienced only, but this portion gives you a small taste (see p.1170 for details of the whole walk). TassieLink has a "Wilderness Link" service to Cockle Creek from November to April.

Bruny Island

For beautiful lonely beaches and superb bushwalking, one of the best places in Tasmania is **Bruny Island**. Almost two distinct islands joined by a narrow isthmus (where you can sometimes see Little penguins from a specially constructed viewing platform), it's roughly 71km from end to end and has a population of only four hundred. The cost of taking a car across on the ferry deters casual visitors, so the island is never very full. The ferry from Kettering goes to substantially rural North Bruny, although most of the settlements, and places to stay and eat, are on South Bruny – the more scenic half, with its state forests and reserves.

Getting there, information and getting around

The **ferry from Kettering** (see p.1091) sails at least eight times daily (Mon–Sat 6.50am–6.30pm, till 7.30pm Fri, Sun 8am–6.30pm; 20min; ⓣ03/6267 4494 for times; $25 per car return or $30 public holidays, motorbikes $12.50, bikes $3.50, foot passengers free). The **Bruny D'Entrecasteaux Visitor Centre** at the Kettering ferry terminal on Ferry Road off the Channel Highway (daily 9am–5pm; ⓣ03/6267 4494, ⓦwww.tasmaniaholiday.com or www.brunyisland.net) books island accommodation, much of which is in self-catering cottages (it's best to stock up on groceries and petrol in Kingston, p.1084, as island prices are high and choice limited). It's best to book before going over, especially on the weekend when it's a popular weekend getaway, as people have had to sleep in their cars. The centre can also supply you with **information** on the island, including a good free fold-out map. As there is no public transport on the island, you'll need your own car or bike to get around unless you come on the excellent small-group day-tour from Hobart with Bruny Island Ventures (see p.1090), or Bruny Island Charters, which does very popular three-hour **wildlife cruises** exploring the south, around Fluted Cape, following the spectacular cliff line, to a seal colony; if you're lucky you'll see dolphins and maybe even a southern right whale, as well as the abundant birdlife in the area (Oct–April daily except Sat 11am from the jetty at Adventure Bay; $85; ⓣ03/6234 3336, ⓦwww.brunycharters.com.au). They also offer the cruise as part of a return trip from Hobart (Hobart pick-up 8.30am, returning 5/5.30pm; $145 including lunch).

If you're driving or riding yourself, be aware that many of the island's roads are unsealed, so expect some discomfort; even the stretch of speedy highway will suddenly become a dusty unsealed road for kilometres at a time. Petrol is only available at Dennes Point, Adventure Bay, Alonnah and Lunawanna. Hobart Coaches operates services from Hobart to Kettering that connect with a couple of the ferries (see p.1071).

Around the island

There's no town at **Roberts Point**, where the ferry docks on the north of the island, just a phone box, some public toilets, a post box and a fast-food van that takes advantage of cars arriving too early for the ferry. The main settlement on **North Bruny** is **DENNES POINT** at the northern extreme of the island, which has a general store (petrol sold) and attached café, and a jetty. This is a popular spot for weekend getaway 'shacks' for Hobart citizens fond of fishing. A detour off this route, 3km off the main road along an unsealed road, is the secluded settlement of **Barnes Bay**, where pretty Shelter Cove was the first "Black station" to be established for the forced resettlement of Aboriginal people (see box on p.1069). There's a small jetty which is a peaceful spot to contemplate the boats bobbing in the cove, and a pebbly beach, but no facilities – though you can **stay** here in the two-bedroom, very stylish *Bruny Beach House* (ⓣ03/5243 8486, ⓦwww.brunybeachhouse.com; ❺).

At the northern end of the isthmus connecting the two islands, the **Neck Game Reserve** (free) acts as a sanctuary for Little penguins and muttonbirds who inhabit rookeries in the sand dunes here. A wooden boardwalk (with stairs) descends over the burrows to the beach and an interpretative board provides information on the birds, best sighted between September and February as they return to their burrows after dusk. Atop the tallest sand dune here, reached by a high wooden stairway, is a small monument to **Truganini** (the "last" Tasmanian Aborigine, who was born here as one of the 70-strong Nuenonne band of the South East tribe), and you can take in superb views of the southern part of the island, where three former reserves have been turned into **South Bruny National Park**. You can see the Fluted Cape State Reserve region to the east of Adventure Bay; here, a steep climb to the top of the Cape (2hr 30min return) offers still better views. The Labillardière State Reserve area occupies the western "hook" of South Bruny Island; a winding, bumpy road leads to the **Cape Bruny Lighthouse** (guided tours by arrangement $8; ⓣ03/6298 3114), built in 1836 and manned until 1996; beyond this a seven-hour walking trail explores the peninsula. East of the hook, across **Cloudy Bay**, is the final chunk of the national park, with its great sweep of surf beach. You can do a spot of bushcamping here (pit toilet only, no water), and at Neck Beach about 1.5km from the isthmus viewing point (pit toilet, water, shelter with barbecue). For considerably more comfort, there's the secluded, self-catering beachfront *Cloudy Bay Cabin* (ⓣ03/6293 1171; ❺), powered by solar energy and gas. You can also stay just north of Cloudy Bay in the comfortable self-contained cottage at *Inala* (ⓣ03/6293 1217, ⓦwww.inalabruny.com.au; ❻), which doubles as the base for Inala Nature Tours (half-day to extended customized trips) run by a qualified biologist.

ADVENTURE BAY is the main settlement on the east coast of South Bruny, and the principal tourist centre strung along Adventure Bay Road. You can swim from the beautiful sandy sweep of beach, and there's a general store (petrol sold) with an ATM, and several accommodation choices. The **Bligh Museum of Pacific Discovery** (daily 10am–3pm; $4) charts Bruny's links with early explorers and seafarers (including Abel Tasman, Tobias Furneaux, James Cook, William Bligh, Bruny D'Entrecasteux and naturalist Labillardière, and Nicolas Baudin), for whom it provided a safe refuge after the arduous journey across the Southern Ocean, and the museum displays maps, documents, paintings and artefacts relating to landings here. The *Penguin Café* (daily 10am–5pm plus dinner Sat ⓣ03/6293 1352; licensed & BYO) does tasty casseroles, vegetarian dishes, gourmet burgers and serves yummy cakes and real coffee. A good place to **stay** nearby is the three-bedroom *Lumeah*, a comfortable homestead on Quiet Corner (ⓣ03/6293 1265; ⓦwww.morellaisland.com.au. ❺), with an outside spa and pretty garden. You can **camp** next to the beach at the *Captain James Cook Caravan Park* (ⓣ03/6293 1128; vans ❷, cabins

❹), which is closer to the shops but less attractive than the tree-filled *Adventure Bay Holiday Village* (Ⓣ03/6293 1270; dorms $20, vans ❶, cabins ❸, cottages ❹), a couple of kilometres further along, with the pleasant *Bay Cafe* and the island's only **hostel** accommodation. Just north of town, *Morella Island Retreats* (Ⓣ03/6293 1131, Ⓦwww.morella-island.com.au; ❻–❼) has several secluded, individual retreat cabins in their 25 acres of gardens; their *Hothouse Cafe* (bookings essential after 5.30pm) offers exotic dining in a hothouse amongst peacocks and parrots, surrounded by an abundant vegetable garden, with panoramic views across Neck Beach and all the way to Mount Wellington.

On the west coast, along the D'Entrecasteaux Channel, **ALONNAH** is the main settlement. As well as a general store and post office here (petrol sold) on Bruny Main Road, you'll find the *Hotel Bruny* (Ⓣ03/6293 1148; basic motel-style units ❸) next door; though it's unattractive, it has uninterrupted water views and offers good-value counter meals, and has the island's only bottle shop. Bruny Island's **Online Access Centre** is nearby on School Road. Near the settlement, *The Tree House* (Ⓣ03/5255 5147, Ⓦwww.thetreehouse.com.au; ❻) is a gorgeous all-wood, open-plan studio apartment (sleeps up to four) with wonderful water views.

Five kilometres south at **LUNAWANNA**, the Mangana Store (daily 8am–6/7pm) sells petrol, groceries and great fish- and hamburgers; the bakery next door bakes pizzas (Thurs only). You can stay at the excellent, well-maintained two-bedroom *Bruny Island Explorer Cottages* on Light House Road overlooking Daniels Bay (Ⓣ03/6293 1271, Ⓦwww.brunyisland.com; ❺); cottages have wood combustion fires and facilities include a communal laundry. From Lunawanna, it's a scenic drive south to Cloudy Bay (see p.1098).

New Norfolk, Mount Field National Park and Maydena

Heading inland from Hobart through the Derwent Valley towards Mount Field National Park, the A10 hugs the Derwent River for the 50km to the well-preserved colonial buildings of **NEW NORFOLK**. It was to here that the original settlers of Norfolk Island (see p.347) were moved between 1806 and 1814. The sizeable town has been at the centre of the hop-growing industry for 150 years, and there are still oast houses in the surrounding hop fields. The broad stretch of the Derwent here is clean, beautiful and swimmable, disturbed only by thrillseekers in jet boats: Devil Jet runs high-speed rides through the rapids (daily 9am–4pm; on the hour; 30min; $50 per person, minimum two people; Ⓣ03/6261 3460), leaving from the Esplanade. The river-facing *Bush Inn* at 49 Montagu St, the main road, claims to be Australia's oldest continuously licensed **hotel** (Ⓣ03/6261 2011; ❸), and with its stained wooden floorboards, huge stone fireplaces and a small ballroom with chandeliers and piano, it's a lovely place to stay, as is the antique-furnished *Old Colony Inn*, a simple, white-washed building on the same street at no. 21 (Ⓣ03/6261 2731; ❹). From New Norfolk, you can visit the **Salmon Ponds** (daily 9am–5pm; $5.50), 18km west on the Glenora Road in Plenty; established in 1864, this is Australia's oldest trout hatchery, set in beautiful formal gardens, with six display ponds and a restaurant.

Hobart Coaches has six **buses** on weekdays from Hobart to New Norfolk and three on Saturday; the buses leave from Metro Hobart's Elizabeth Street terminus. TassieLink also runs to New Norfolk (five weekly) on their scheduled year-round service to Queenstown. New Norfolk's **Online Access Centre** is on Charles Street.

Mount Field National Park

It's 37km through pretty rolling countryside full of hop fields from New Norfolk to **Mount Field National Park**, a high alpine area with tarns created by glacial activity where, in winter, there's enough snow to create a small ski field. At the base, the magnificent stands of **swamp gum** (the tallest species of eucalypt and the tallest hardwood in the world), along with the many **waterfalls**, help make this Tasmania's most popular park. Most people come here to see the impressive **Russell Falls**, which cascades in two levels. It's close to the park entrance and can be reached on an easy thirty-minute circuit walk. Longer walks continue on to **Horseshoe Falls** (1hr) and **Lady Barron Falls** (3hr return). The best short walk is the **Tall Trees Track** (1hr 30min), where huge swamp gums dominate; the largest date back to the early nineteenth century.

To get away from the tour-group mob, several shorter walks leave from various spots along the Lake Dobson Road, which leads high up to **Lake Dobson**, 16km into the park in the area of the alpine moorlands and glacial lakes. From the lake car park, you can go on plenty of longer walks, including treks along the tarn shelf that take several days, with huts to stay in along the way. The walk to **Twilight Tarn**, with its historic hut, is one of the most rewarding (4hr return), or you can continue on for the full tarn shelf circuit (6hr return). A shorter option is the **Pandani Grove Nature Walk** (with an accompanying leaflet available from the ranger station – see below), a forty-minute circuit of the lake, including a section of tall **pandanus** – the striking heath plant which, with its crown of long fronds, looks like a semi-tropical palm. You'll need your own transport to reach these higher walks, or you could come with the small-group Bottom Bits Bus (see p.1072) from Hobart on a Mt Field day-trip which includes a walk around Lake Dobson ($89). Tigerline (see p.1090) also operates day-tours from Hobart, visiting the Salmon Ponds (see p.1099) en route and allowing several hours to explore the park ($99 including morning tea).

Park practicalities

For information on the walks, to register for overnight hikes and to talk to the ranger, drop in to the **Mount Field Ranger Station** at the entrance to the park (daily 9am–4.30pm; ⓣ03/6288 1149), a complex also housing a café, shop and interpretive centre. An excellent range of free pamphlets details the natural environment alongside several of the walks in the park. There's also information here about walks in the South West National Park, several of which can be started from Scotts Peak Road, which runs off the Gordon River Road to the west of Mount Field (see p.1096). If you want to **stay** in the vicinity, head for the tiny settlement of **NATIONAL PARK** on Maydena Road, a ten-minute walk from the park, where there's basic ground-floor **pub** accommodation at the friendly *National Park Hotel* (ⓣ03/6288 1103; ❸ including breakfast), with popular **meals**; the former YHA hostel opposite may have reopened as a backpackers' by the time of publication. The pub has an EFTPOS facility, but the nearest fuel is 7km further on at Westerway. Just outside the entrance to the park are spacious 1950s-style self-contained units at *Russell Falls Holiday Cottages* (ⓣ03/6288 1198; ❹), while within the park itself there's a well-equipped **campsite** near the entrance.

Maydena and around

Nearby **Junee Cave State Reserve** is prime platypus-spotting territory; to get there head 11km southwest to **MAYDENA**, then right onto the narrow, winding Junee Road for 3.5km. A ten-minute walk from the reserve entrance through lush rainforest will bring you to **Junee Cave**, popular with cave divers.

In Maydena you can stay right on the Tyenna River at the highly recommended and very friendly *Giants' Table* (Ⓣ03/6288 2293, Ⓦwww.giantstable.com; rooms ❸, cabins ❺); there's a lodge with guest kitchen and lounge, or self-contained cottages. The characterful, licensed café (dinner Tues–Sat) serves delicious fresh-baked **meals**, with plenty for vegetarians. The lodge offers personalized 4WD ecotours of the surrounding area, as well as pick-ups and drop-offs for bushwalking. Maydena's **Online Access Centre** is in the Maydena Kindergarten on Holmes Street.

Out of Maydena, the **Styx Valley** is known as the "**Valley of the Giants**" after its huge swamp gum (eucalyptus regnans) – some of which are over 95 metres tall, five metres wide at the base and over 400 years old – in a large remnant of old-growth forest that's suffered damage from logging activities. A long-running conservationist campaign aiming to protect 150 square kilometres of this forest as the Styx Valley of the Giants National Park made international news in 2004, with a joint Greenpeace and Wilderness Society organised tree sit-in. Activists camped on a platform – the "Global Rescue Station" – 65m above ground around a giant tree dubbed Gandal's Staff, a Tolkien reference. A plaque at the base of the tree commemorates the five-month long campaign. Contact the Wilderness Society (p.1090) for campaign details and to get hold of a self-guided drive leaflet, or you can go on a full-day **tour** from Hobart with Tiger Trails ($99; see p.1072) which includes Russell Falls.

Richmond

RICHMOND, on the Coal River about 25km north of Hobart and surrounded by undulating countryside, scattered with wineries, is one of the oldest and best-preserved towns in Australia. Settlers received land grants in the area not long after the fledgling colony had been set up in 1803, and in 1824 Lieutenant-Governor Sorell founded the town, on the route between Hobart and the east coast. Soon, traffic to the new penal settlement at Port Arthur began to pass through, and Richmond's strategic location made it an important military post and convict station when Richmond Gaol was built in 1825; by the 1830s it was the third-largest town in Tasmania. In 1872, however, the **Sorell Causeway** was opened, bypassing Richmond, which became a rural community with little incentive for change or development. Most of the approximately fifty buildings – plain and functional stone dwellings – date from the 1830s and 1840s, and many are now used as galleries, craft shops, cafés, restaurants and guesthouses; the gorgeous village green is still intact. A free leaflet and map, *Let's Talk About Richmond*, is available at the gaol and details the buildings. Attractions along Bridge Street include the wooden **Richmond Maze** (daily 10am–5pm; $5.50) and the **Old Hobart Town Model Village** (daily 9am–5pm; $7.50), a large-scale outdoor model of Hobart in the 1820s.

Richmond's most authentic drawing card, however, is the sandstone, slate-roofed **Richmond Gaol** (daily 9am–5pm; $5.50), an intact example of an early prison. The prison's function was mostly to house prisoners in transit or those awaiting trial, and to accommodate convict road gangs working in the district; the east wing was designed to hold female convicts, who could not be accommodated at Port Arthur. Informative signs explain the various features of the gaol, which now seems incongruously pretty, set around a leafy central square. Richmond also has the distinction of having both Australia's oldest Roman Catholic church – that of **St John**, which dates in part from 1837 – and its oldest bridge. The graceful arched stone **Richmond Bridge** was constructed in 1823 under harsh conditions using convict labour; legend says that it's haunted by the ghost of the brutal flagellator, George Grover, who was beaten to death by the convicts and thrown into the river during its construction.

Practicalities

Hobart Coaches runs four **bus** services a day from Hobart (Mon–Fri; buses leave from Metro Hobart's Elizabeth Street terminus) and TassieLink also drops off on their Hobart to Swansea service (1 daily Mon–Fri during term time; Tues, Thurs & Sat only during school holidays). The Richmond Tourist Bus (ⓣ0408 341 804; $25) departs the tourist centre in Hobart (see p.1075) twice daily (9.15am & 12.20pm) and leaves Richmond 12.50pm & 3.50pm. The **Online Access Centre** is on Torrens Street. One of the best **places to stay** is *Prospect House* (ⓣ03/6260 2207, ⓦwww.prospect-house.com.au; ⑥), a Georgian country mansion set in extensive landscaped grounds, with its own well-regarded licensed restaurant open for dinner; it's on your left as you come into town on Cambridge Road. Further out, 6km from Richmond along Prossers Road, is *Richmond Country Bed and Breakfast* (ⓣ03/6260 4238; ④), a comfortable, reasonably priced homestead in a quiet rural setting. The central and pretty *Richmond Arms Hotel*, 42 Bridge St (ⓣ03/6260 2109, ⓦwww.richmondarms.com; ④), has characterful, self-catering accommodation in its converted mid-nineteenth-century stone stables; the hotel serves affordable meals. The cheapest place to stay is the *Richmond Cabin and Tourist Park*, on Middle Tea Tree Road on the outskirts of town (ⓣ03/6260 2192; vans ②, cabins ③), with shady grounds for camping and an indoor heated pool.

For **food**, there's an upmarket café-restaurant in the *Richmond Wine Centre*, 27 Bridge St, in an old weatherboard cottage set in pretty gardens with outside tables (ⓣ03/6260 2619; lunch daily, dinner Wed–Sat), where just about everything served is Tasmanian, including the wine. The award-winning Swiss-run *Richmond Bakery* on Edward Street, just off Bridge Street has an attached café; you can eat in the courtyard or take away to picnic tables on the village green.

The Forestier and Tasman peninsulas

The fastest route from Hobart to the **Tasman Peninsula** heads northeast along the Tasman Highway and then across the **Sorell Causeway** to the small town of **Sorell**, your last chance for shopping and banking; on the huge expanse of Pittwater, windsurfers are out in force on a sunny day. From Sorell, the Arthur Highway heads 34km southeast to **Dunalley** (fuel available), where a bridge crosses the narrow isthmus to the **Forestier Peninsula**. The bridge regularly opens to let boats through, which can cause delays. Once across, it's a further 42km to the infamous **Eaglehawk Neck**, the narrow point connecting the two peninsulas, once guarded by vicious dogs that in effect turned the Tasman Peninsula into a kind of prison island. Of the substantial military station here, only one building survives, the timber **Officers Quarters** dating from 1832. The NPWS have turned it into a fascinating mini-museum which provides a useful overview of Tasmanian history as well as detailing the site, and there's an entertaining eight-minute sound-and-silhouette diorama which tells the story of the infamous bushranger **Martin Cash**'s swimming escape from Eaglehawk Neck. Entry is free and the museum stays open as long as the nearby Officers Mess General Store, where there's an ATM, café and take-away.

Eaglehawk Neck Backpackers (ⓣ03/6250 3248; dorms $14), at 94 Old Jetty, 1km west of the Arthur Highway on the Forestier Peninsula side of Eaglehawk

Neck, is the perfect **place to stay** to explore the area – friendly, nonsmoking and green (in both senses of the word). Bikes are loaned (for a small donation) and there are canoes too. For a great deal more luxury, plus fantastic views and European hospitality, try the nearby *Osprey Lodge Beachfront Bed and Breakfast* at 14 Osprey Rd off Pirates Bay Drive (ⓣ03/6250 3629; ❻). The best place for something to **eat** is the excellent *Eaglehawk Cafe*, on the Arthur Highway near the turn-off to the blowhole (daily 9am–6pm; licensed & BYO), overlooking Norfolk Bay; the food is tasty and reasonably priced, utilizing local produce with a menu ranging from filled baguettes, platters of local produce to homemade pies (rabbit, venison, seafood), plus coffee and yummy cakes. At the Blow Hole car park, a cut-above-the-usual snack van (daily Oct–April) sells local oysters and seafood, crayfish pies, ice cream and strawberries, as well as hot drinks.

Southwest of Eaglehawk Neck at the small settlement of **Koonya**, **Cascades Historic Site** is a well-preserved 1840s Probation Station that has been owned by a farming family for five generations and now converted into self-catering cottages, most with open fires and one with a spa (*Cascades Colonial Accommodation*; ⓣ03/6250 3873, ⓦwww.cascadescolonial.com.au; ❺–❼). The peaceful, rural site has a half-hour waterfront walk. Nearby is the friendly *Seaview Lodge* (ⓣ03/6250 2766; dorms $19) on another farming property with sea views. The TassieLink Port Arthur service can drop you off near either accommodation.

Exploring the Tasman Peninsula

While Port Arthur, at the very bottom of the Tasman Peninsula, is the major attraction, the hardly developed peninsula has several good **bushwalks**, and some truly impressive rock formations on the rough ocean side. Some of the finest coastal features are around Eaglehawk Neck: just to the north, there's the **Tessellated Pavement**, onto which you can climb down at low tide; and to the south, off the highway, the fierce **Blowhole**, the huge **Tasman Arch**, and the **Devils Kitchen**, a sheer rock cleft into which the sea surges. Much of this area was proclaimed the **Tasman National Park** (ⓣ03/6250 3497) in 1999; the **Tasman Trail** is an exhilarating 16km coastal walk starting from the Devils Kitchen and ending at **Fortescue Bay**, which has a good camping area (otherwise, the bay is 12km down a dirt road east off the Arthur Highway). Download walking notes for the Tasman Trail on the NPWS website (see p.79), or if you're not confident, the excellent Tiger Trails offers a three-day guided walk (ex-Hobart; $499; see p.1072). South of Port Arthur, several walking tracks begin from **Remarkable Cave**: to Crescent Bay (5hr return), Mount Brown (5hr return) and Maingon Blowhole (3hr return).

The Eaglehawk Dive Centre, 178 Pirates Bay Drive (ⓣ03/6250 3566, ⓦwww.eaglehawkdive.com.au) offers **dive-boat charters** (equipment included) at low rates to caves, shipwrecks, kelp forests and nearby seal colonies with an underwater visibility of 15–30m. A glorious way to see the towering 190-metre cliffs and surging sea caves in southern Tasman Peninsula is from the water with Tasman Sea Charters (ⓣ1300 554 049, ⓦwww.tasmanseacharters.com; 10.30am daily; 3hr; $90; max 12), who hug the coast for over 20km. The commentary on geology is fantastic, but also expect to see and learn about giant kelp, jellyfish, sea eagles, the seals on Hippolyte Rocks, and if you're lucky, dolphins and even whales. Book in advance if possible, but the enthusiastic young operator waits daily at the Eaglehawk Neck Jetty (head towards the signposted Blow Hole), and if the morning trip is full he'll usually offer one in the afternoon. If you're interested in any other outdoor activities, **Hire it with Dennis** (ⓣ03/6250 3103) can deliver canoes, kayaks, dinghies, fishing lines, tents, sleeping bags and bicycles to the area, including Port Arthur.

Port Arthur

The most unceasing labour is to be extracted from the convicts . . . and the most harassing vigilance over them is to be observed.

Governor Arthur

PORT ARTHUR was chosen as the site for a **prison settlement** in September 1830, as a place of secondary punishment for convicts who had committed serious crimes in New South Wales or Van Diemen's Land itself, men who were seen to have no redeeming features and were treated accordingly. The first 150 convicts worked like slaves to establish a timber industry in the wooded surroundings of the "natural penitentiary" of the Tasman Peninsula, with narrow Eaglehawk Neck guarded by dogs. The regime was never a subtle one: **Governor George Arthur**, responsible for all the convicts in Van Diemen's Land, believed that a convict's "whole fate should be ... the very last degree of misery consistent with humanity". Gradually, Port Arthur became a self-supporting industrial centre: the timber industry grew into shipbuilding, there was brickmaking and shoemaking, wheat-growing, and even a flour mill. There was also a separate prison for boys – "the thiefs prison" – at **Point Puer**, where the inmates were taught trades. From the 1840s until transport of convicts ceased in 1853, the penal settlement grew steadily, the early timber constructions later replaced by brick and stone buildings. The lives of the labouring convicts contrasted sharply with those of the prison officers and their families, who had their ornamental gardens, drama club, library and cricket fields. The years after transport ended were in many ways more horrific than those that preceded them, as physical beatings were replaced by psychological punishment. In 1852 the **Model Prison**, based on the spoked-wheel design of Pentonville Prison in London, opened. Here, prisoners could be kept in tiny cells in complete isolation and absolute silence; they were referred to by numbers rather than names, and wore hoods whenever they left their cells. The prison continued to operate until 1877, by now incorporating its own **mental asylum** full of ex-convicts, as well as a geriatric home for ex-convict paupers. The excellent **interpretive centre**, housed in the new visitors centre (daily 9am–5pm), provides much more detail on the prison's sad history through artefacts and texts, and there's more fascinating information in the older museum, housed in what was the asylum.

In 1870 Port Arthur was popularized by Marcus Clarke's romantic tragedy, *For the Term of his Natural Life*. The public became fascinated by its buildings and the tragedy behind them, and soon after the prison closed, guided tours were offered by the same crumbling men who had been wrecked by the regime. In the 1890s the town around the prison was devastated by bushfires that left most buildings in ruins. A major conservation and restoration project began in the 1970s and today the **Port Arthur Historic Site** covers a huge area (office and most buildings daily 8.30am–dusk, grounds until about 11pm; $24 for a 48hr pass, including 40min guided tour; $10 for a pass after 4pm; for an extra $3 the pass lasts two years). The ticket office area houses a visitor information centre (Ⓣ03/6251 2371, Ⓦwww.portarthur.org.au). Several extra tours and cruises are available. There's a cruise on the MV *Marana* to explore the boys' prison at Point Puer (2hr; $10; daily except Aug) and another to the **Isle of the Dead** (1hr; $10; daily except Aug), Port Arthur's cemetery from 1833 to 1877, where you can view the resting places of 1100 convicts, asylum inmates, paupers and free men; the same company also runs a longer two-and-a-half-hour Tasman Island Wilderness Cruise from here to see the island's sheer cliffs and its sea birds and fur seals (Ⓣ03/6224 0033, Ⓦwww.portarthurcruises.com.au; Mon 8am, also Thurs 26 Dec–May, no service Aug; $49).

△ Old church in Penal Colony

The Port Arthur Historic Site houses more than sixty buildings, some of which – like the poignant **prison chapel** – are furnished and restored. Others, like the ivy-covered **church**, are picturesque ruins set in a landscape of green lawns, shady trees and paths sloping down to the cove. The beautiful setting makes it look more like a serene, old-world university campus than a prison, and indeed, the benign feeling of the place seems to have a capacity to absorb tragedy: another horrific chapter in Port Arthur's history occurred in April 1996, when the massacre of 35 tourists and local people by a lone gunman made international headlines. The café where most of the people were killed has been partially dismantled and a memorial has been built – a garden and reflecting pool laid out around the remaining walls. Visitors are requested to act sensitively and not ask the staff about the tragedy.

If you're staying overnight in Port Arthur (see p.1106 for accommodation), join the nightly lantern-lit **Historic Ghost Tour** (1hr 30min; $15.50; bookings on ⓣ03/6251 2310), which features lovingly researched and hauntingly retold tales of the settlement's past as you wander through the ruins.

Practicalities

If you don't have your own transport, and want to get to Port Arthur from Hobart on a **regular bus**, you'll usually have to stay overnight. TassieLink has a single afternoon service (Mon–Fri during school terms; Mon, Wed & Fri school holidays), stopping en route at Eaglehawk Neck, Koonya and other places on the Tasman and Forestier peninsulas. However, there are plenty of **bus tours** that sample some of the Tasman Peninsula sights along the way. The best is the small-group Bottom Bits Bus ($89; see p.1072), which also takes in peninsula walks and sights and the night-time ghost tour. Port Arthur Cruises also offers a pricey but spectacular cruise from Hobart (see box on p.1081) with an optional return coach trip. The Port Arthur Region Travel Shop, 49a Salamanca Place (ⓣ03/6224 5333, ⓦwww.portarthur-region.com.au; open daily) does bookings for the historic site and all related tours and accommodation.

There are various **places to stay** on the outskirts of Port Arthur. The *Comfort Inn Port Arthur* (ⓣ03/6250 2101, ⓦwww.portarthur-inn.com.au; ❺), overlooking the ruined church, is a pleasant place, with a bar open to the public – the only place nearby to drink – and reasonable counter meals. A little more expensive, the spacious *Port Arthur Villas* (ⓣ03/6250 2239, ⓦwww.portarthurvillas.com.au; ❺) has the amenities of a motel and kitchens in the units. Both are just across the road from the site on Safety Cove Road. Opposite the *Port Arthur Motor Inn* is the popular *Roseview YHA,* on Champ Street (ⓣ03/6250 2311, ⓔyhatas@org.au; booking essential Jan & Feb; dorms $19, rooms ❷–❸), in a former 1890s guesthouse. If it's full, 1km from the site, there are bunkhouse rooms and camping (including an excellent enclosed camp kitchen) at the tree-filled *Port Arthur Caravan and Cabin Park* at Garden Point (ⓣ03/6250 2340, ⓦwww.portarthurcaravan-cabinpark.com.au; dorms $15, en-suite cabins ❹).

Within the Port Arthur Historic Site, in the visitors centre, you can **eat** by day at the cafeteria-style *Port Cafe* (daily 9am–5pm) or spend more at the good *Felons Restaurant* at night (dinner only) or the *Museum Tea Rooms* in the old asylum; all three are licensed. In **Taranna**, 10km before Port Arthur on the A9, it's hard to miss the blue- and yellow-painted *The Mussel Boys Cafe* (Thurs–Sun; licensed), which serves fresh seafood done superbly – try the mussels in a dill coconut broth. Though you can come in for coffee and cake, it's really restaurant food and prices ($15–24); for a more relaxed atmosphere sit outside on the verandah and enjoy the water views.

The east coast: the Tasman Highway

For much of its length along the sunny **east coast**, the **Tasman Highway** gently rises and falls through grazing land and bush-covered hills. In summer there's something of an unspoilt Mediterranean feel about this stretch, with its long white beaches, blue water stretching to a cloudless sky, scenic backdrop of hills, and a thriving local fishing industry. Because the east coast is sheltered from the prevailing westerly winds and is washed by warm offshore currents, it has one of the most temperate climates in Australia. This, and the mainly safe swimming beaches, mean that it's a popular destination for Tasmanian families in the school holidays – prices go up and accommodation is scarce from Christmas to the middle of February. Even so, it's still relatively undeveloped and peaceful; there are four national parks, which include a whole island – **Maria Island** – and an entire peninsula – the glorious **Freycinet National Park**. The only blight on the landscape is the huge and controversial export **woodchip mill** at Point Home, one of four in Tasmania near Triabunna, which can be seen from the ferry to Maria Island.

The east coast is also Tasmania's best **cycling route**: it's relatively flat, and the winter climate is mild enough to tackle it in colder months, too. Distances between towns are reasonable, there's a string of youth hostels so you don't need to camp, and there are few cars. **St Helens** is the largest town on the east coast, with a population of just over a thousand; situated on **Georges Bay**, it makes a good base to explore the northeast corner and **Mount William National Park**. The oldest town, **Swansea**, lies sheltered in **Great Oyster**

Bay, facing the Freycinet Peninsula. To the north, the small fishing town of **Bicheno** offers fantastic diving, and it's a convenient place from which to visit both the Freycinet National Park (and its tiny settlement of **Coles Bay**) and the **Douglas Apsley National Park** inland. The highway detours inland at **St Marys**, although there's a more recently built road that allows you to follow the coast and enjoy spectacular views without having to tackle any hills.

Because the east coast is not heavily populated, **banking facilities** are rather inadequate, while small settlements have post offices that are also Commonwealth Bank agents. EFTPOS facilities are widely available in shops and service stations, but it's important to make sure you always have enough cash.

Transport services offered by Redline and TassieLink don't run to daily schedules, with big transport gaps on weekends – another good reason to cycle or drive – and various local bus services may need to be interchanged to get from one place to another. If you don't fancy getting stuck somewhere for a couple of days, check timetables carefully. **From Hobart**, TassieLink goes to Orford, Triabunna, Swansea, Bicheno, Scamander and St Helens via the Coles Bay turn-off for Freycinet National Park (1 daily Wed, Fri & Sun). **From Launceston**, Redline has services to the Coles Bay turn-off and Bicheno via towns along the Midlands Highway (1 daily Mon–Fri) and to Scottsdale (2 daily Mon–Fri, 1 daily Sun); Tassielink has a route to Bicheno via St Marys (1 daily Fri & Sun). Three local bus companies also operate: Stan's (☎03/6356 1662) between Scottsdale and Bridport; Broadby's (☎03/6376 3488) between St Helens and Derby via Pyengana and Winnaleah; and the Bicheno Coach Service (☎03/6257 0293) takes you to Coles Bay and the Freycinet National Park.

Another option is to go on a **tour**: Island Escape Tours (see p.1072) offers an active small-group four-day "East Coast Escape" departing from Launceston, which takes in the Blue Tier, a two-hour Bay of Fires walk, St Helens, Freycinet National Park, Maria Island, and the Tasman Peninsula and Port Arthur ($460; backpackers accommodation and most meals provided; three-day version without Port Arthur $360).

Maria Island National Park

As the Tasman Highway meets the sea at **ORFORD**, a small holiday resort on the estuary of the Prosser River, you get your first views across to **Maria Island**. The entire island, 15km off the east coast, is a national park, uninhabited save for its ranger. Its wide tracks are ideal for mountain biking, an activity encouraged here – because no other vehicles are allowed, you can ride in perfect safety (bike hire is available at Triabunna). The island's coastal road has no gradient, but inland there are a few hills to climb. **Birdlife** is prolific, with over 130 species; it's the only national park containing all eleven of the state's endemic bird species. The old airstrip is covered with Cape Barren geese, which you'll see if you walk to the **fossil cliffs**, a twenty-minute stroll from Darlington.

The ferry (see below) lands at **DARLINGTON**, where the structures of the former **penal settlement** (dating from 1825 and later a probation station until 1850) still stand, including the commissariat store with its visitor information boards, the convict barn, the cemetery, the mill house and the penitentiary. The penitentiary is now a **bunkhouse** ($22 per unit, sleeping six, or $8.80 per person in the "backpackers" bunkhouse); the basic units have wood stoves, table and chairs, and bunks with mattresses, but you'll need to bring your own cooking equipment and bedding. The units are often booked up well in advance, so call the ranger before turning up. The **campsite** here ($4.40 per person) is the island's best, with a public phone, toilets, fireplaces, cold water taps and tank water for drinking. As there is little water elsewhere on the island, free-range camping is best done at **Frenchs Farm** or the more picturesque **Encampment Cove**, two campsites with a rainwater supply and fireplaces.

You can take many short **walks** on the island, as well as longer bushwalks (though watch out for cyclists); a range of free pamphlets is available from the ranger's office at Darlington (Mon–Fri 4.15–5pm; ⓣ03/6257 1420). With a couple of days to spare, you can walk past the narrow isthmus to the rarely visited **southern end** of the island, which has unspoilt forests and secluded beaches. As there's no water here, be sure to bring supplies with you. Freycinet Adventures offers four-day **sea-kayaking and walking tours** of the island, departing from Hobart ($890; ⓣ03/6257 0500). The Maria Island Walk Tour (ex-Hobart $1549; max 8; ⓣ03/6227 8800, ⓦwww.mariaislandwalk.com.au) is a four-day guided walk skirting 25km of the coastline and staying in beachside wilderness camps and the late-nineteenth-century house of failed entrepreneur Diego Bernacchi in Darlington, with three-course meals each night. The well-regarded Tiger Trails ($599; see p.1072) offers a three-day bushwalking trip with basic camping and less gourmet emphasis.

Getting there: Triabunna

There's a choice of two **ferry services** to Maria Island. The more reliable service leaves from the *Eastcoaster Resort* at Louisville (ⓣ03/6257 1172), half-way between Orford and **TRIABUNNA** (reached by TassieLink from Hobart, Bicheno or St Helens); the *Eastcoaster Express* is a fast but noisy catamaran taking twenty minutes (bookings ⓣ03/6257 1589; 9.30am & 1.30pm; ex-Maria Island 12.30pm & 4pm; extra trips Nov–April; return $25, bikes and kayaks $2). From the main fishing wharf on the Esplanade at Triabunna itself, the quieter and steadier *Maria Island* ferry takes 45 minutes (bookings ⓣ0427 100 104; same times and prices). As well as the ferry fare, a $10 park entry fee is applicable in addition to camping fees – if you have a car pass, bring the receipt. It's not advisable to do Maria as a day-trip, as given the ferry times, you won't be able to really appreciate the walks, with probably just enough time to take in the convict ruins and the fossil cliffs.

The **visitor information centre** on the Esplanade in Triabunna (daily 10am–4pm; ⓣ03/6257 4772) is staffed by helpful volunteers and provides details on the island. Triabunna's **Online Access Centre** is on the corner of Vicary and Melbourne streets. A good base for day- and overnight trips to Maria Island is the friendly, relaxing and cosy *The Udder Backpackers YHA* on Spencer Street, 1km west of Triabunna (ⓣ03/6257 3439; dorms $18, rooms ❷). Well set-up for, and popular with, cyclists, it's located on a peaceful farm, where fresh organic fruit, vegetables and herbs are sold cheaply to guests; other food is sold in small cyclist-friendly amounts at the office and there's also a take-away liquor licence. Tents, sleeping bags and camping stoves are hired to take over to Maria Island (free ferry pick-ups and drop-offs). You can rent bikes to take over from On-Ya-Bike Bike Hire, 5 Vicary St (ⓣ03/6257 4086; $20 half-day, $33 per day). East Coast Eco Tours (ⓣ03/6257 3453) offers **boat trips** to local seal colonies and you might see dolphins, whales and sea eagles along the way.

Swansea

From Triabunna it's a fairly uneventful 50km drive north to **SWANSEA**, overlooking **Great Oyster Bay**, with views across to the Freycinet Peninsula.

If you're lucky, you might see dolphins frolicking in the bay from Franklin Street, the main strip that runs along the waterfront. One of Tasmania's oldest settlements, Swansea is an administrative centre, fishing port and seaside resort, with well-preserved architecture dating from the 1830s to the 1880s. The focus of town has always been **Morris's General Store**, on Franklin Street, run by seven generations of the family since 1868. Further evidence of Swansea's past can be found at the Glamorgan War Memorial Museum and Community Centre (Mon–Sat 9am–5pm; $3), also on Franklin Street, a former school now housing a miscellaneous collection including a billiard table built from a single log of blackwood ($2 for a game), and at the restored **Swansea Bark Mill**, 96 Tasman Highway (daily 9am–5pm; $5.50), once used to produce leather tanning agents from native blackwattle bark. Swansea's **Online Access Centre** is on Franklin Street.

Accommodation options include the *Swansea Motor Inn*, at 1 Franklin St (ⓣ03/6257 8102; ❸–❹), a waterfront red-brick motel and a bistro. *Freycinet Waters*, at 16 Franklin St (ⓣ03/6257 8080, ⓦwww.freycinetwaters.com.au; ❹–❺), is a light, refreshingly uncluttered seaside B&B in the old post office building; each en-suite room has its own private verandah overlooking the bay, while the nearby *Tubby and Padman* at no.20 (ⓣ03/6257 8901, ⓦwww.tubbyandpadman.com.au; ❺) is in an 1840s colonial homestead with a huge front verandah and contemporary-style self-contained units out back. Another B&B option is the gay-friendly *Meredith House*, 15 Noyes St (ⓣ03/6257 8119, ⓦwww.meredith-house.com.au; en suite ❻), an antique-filled guesthouse on a hill with views over the bay. On the waterfront are two **caravan parks** with excellent facilities: *Swansea Holiday Park* on Shaw Street, opposite the Old Bark Mill (ⓣ03/6257 8177; cabins ❸), and the friendly *Kenmore Caravan Park*, 2 Bridge St (ⓣ03/6257 8148; vans ❷, cabins ❸).

As for **food**, Swansea has a fair selection. The *Makepeace on the Bay* (Mon & Fri–Sun noon–9pm, Tues, Wed & Thurs 4pm–9pm; lunch $11.50–$19.50, dinner mains around $25; licensed), downstairs at the *Oyster Bay Guest House*, functions as a café-restaurant with outside tables and offers a varied European menu with lots of local seafood. There's a very smart restaurant specializing in seafood and game in the atmospheric 1846 *Schouten House*, 1 Waterloo Rd (dinner nightly; ⓣ03/6257 8564), with alfresco dining in summer. The *Left Bank Coffee & Food Bar*, in the old Commercial Bank of Australia building on the main street – look out for the red door (closed Tues, & Wed May–July; closed Aug), has a great atmosphere, outdoor dining, excellent coffee and fresh, simple food. *Kabuki By the Sea* (open daily for morning and afternoon tea and lunch; May–Nov Fri & Sat dinner, Dec–April Tues–Sat dinner; dinner bookings ⓣ03/6257 8588; ⓦwww.kabukibythesea.com.au) is a fine Japanese restaurant 12km south on the Tasman Highway with stunning views; it also has some guest cottages (❺).

The Freycinet Peninsula

Heading for Coles Bay and **Freycinet National Park**, you turn off the Tasman Highway 33km north of Swansea, following the Coles Bay Road. The drive from Swansea onwards is winding, with fantastic views of rural countryside contrasted with dramatic mountain- and sea-scapes. After about 8km along Coles Bay Road, you can turn left down a side road (3km unsealed) to the **Friendly Beaches**, part of the national park, taking in a length of unspoilt shoreline backed by eucalypt forest. If you're **cycling**, you can cut 40km from your journey by riding along Nine Mile Beach Road, at the end of which a ferry (book the night before on ☎03/6257 0239; $15; no service May–Sept) crosses the Swan River to **SWANWICK**, about 6km northwest of Coles Bay.

COLES BAY, on the north edge of the Freycinet National Park, is a sheltered inlet with fishing boats moored in the deep-blue water, all set against the striking backdrop of **The Hazards**, three pink-granite peaks – Amos, Dove and Mayson – rising straight from the sea. Since the 1930s the hamlet of Coles Bay has been the base for the park, and for fishing and recreation. As a result, there are numerous fishing shacks and **holiday houses** available to rent: call Freycinet Rentals (☎03/6257 0320), which also rents just about anything you might need for watersports, camping and walking. Just 3.5km west of Coles Bay, *The Edge of the Bay* (☎03/6257 0102, Ⓦwww.edgeofthebay.com.au; cottages ❻, suites ❼) has secluded, self-catering two-bedroom cottages set in bushland, or elegant Japanese-style suites with water views; rates drop considerably for a second and subsequent night's stay. There's also a restaurant and bar (dinner nightly). The *Iluka Holiday Centre*, in a great spot on the Esplanade across from Muirs Beach (☎03/6257 0115 or 1800 786 512, Ⓦwww.ilukaholidaycentre.com.au; dorms $20, rooms ❷, vans ❷, units ❸–❹), has a wide variety of accommodation, including a **YHA hostel** section. Nearby is a small supermarket, a tavern with bistro meals and the outstanding *Freycinet Cafe & Bakery* (daily 8am–7pm), an eat-in bakery selling European-style breads, pastries, pizza from 4pm, decent coffee and with outside tables looking across to the beachfront park. One kilometre from the *Iluka Holiday Centre*, overlooking The Hazards, supplies of all sorts are available at the **general store**, Coles Bay Trading, on Garnet Avenue (daily 8am–6pm, until 7pm Dec 26 to end Feb; ☎03/6257 0109), which also serves as the post office, service station and official tourist **information** centre; you can book accommodation, buy park passes, rent bikes ($11 half-day, $17 full-day) and use the public phones. Its coffee shop has great views of The Hazards. Next door you can get a wonderful seafood dinner at *Madge Malloy's* (dinner Tues–Sat; licensed; ☎03/6257 0399). For more information, check out the excellent website Ⓦwww.freycinetcolesbay.com.

Redline and TassieLink drop off 31km away from Coles Bay, at the turn-off on the Tasman Highway, connecting with the Bicheno Coach Service to Coles Bay (up to 3 daily; booking for off-peak times on ☎03/6257 0293), which can also take you right to the start of the walking tracks.

Freycinet National Park

The **national park office** (daily 9am–5pm; ☎03/6256 7000) is just 1km from Coles Bay, and sells maps and booklets on day-walks and has an interpretative display on the park. From here, the gravelled, disabled-access Great Oyster Bay path leads down to the beach (10min return). Opposite the centre, the powered national park **campsite**, with water and toilets but no showers, is in a sheltered location among bush and dunes behind Richardsons Beach; it's packed in holiday season, when you'll need to book well in advance through the park office. At the other end of Richardsons Beach, *Freycinet Lodge* (☎03/6257 0101, Ⓦwww.freycinetlodge.com.au; ❽) has luxurious wooden cabins spread through bushland and offers guided bushwalks; there's a bistro and a more upmarket restaurant with fabulous views overlooking the bay, both open all day and available to non-guests, and a tennis court. You can also stay at the basic *Coles Bay YHA* (no hot water) in the park itself, but only if you've booked in advance through the Hobart YHA office (see p.1091; dorms $10, rooms ❷); it's very popular during the summer months and Easter.

Tracks into the park begin at the **Walking Track Car Park**, a further 4km from the office. **Water** is scarce, so you must carry all you'll need, although the ranger can advise if there are any streams where the water is safe to drink. The shorter walks are well marked: the strenuous, gravelly walk up to the look-out to exquisite **Wineglass Bay**, with its perfect curve of white beach, is where most walkers head, and many continue on down to the beach itself (2.6km return to the lookout, 1–2hr; 5km return to the beach, 2hr 30min to 3hr 30min). The 27km **peninsula circuit** is a wonderful walk (10hr), best done over two days; it makes a good practice run for the big southwest hikes. There's a **campsite** at **Cooks Beach**, with a pit toilet, water tank, and a rough hut where you can stay.

Schouten Island, off the tip of the peninsula, is part of the national park: it's perfect for really secluded camping, as you're quite likely to have it all to yourself. Freycinet Sea Charters, in Coles Bay (Ⓣ03/6257 0355, Ⓦwww.freycinetseacharters.com), will drop you off here for around $66 per person return. They also offer a couple of small-group cruises: a two-hour sunset cruise around the island ($55) and a four-hour cruise to Winglass Bay (daily 10am; $88), or you could charter the boat for a day-trip which could take in a walk on the island and a visit to a nearby seal colony. There are campsites with pit toilet, a hut and two water tanks at **Moreys Bay**, and the creek at **Crocketts Bay** has reliable upstream water. Although there are no proper tracks on the island, walking is easy.

Freycinet Adventures (Ⓣ03/6257 0500) offers sea-kayaking tours on Coles Bay (2hr twilight trip $45; half-day morning $75, full-day $130), which can be extended to include overnight camping in the national park; they also run abseiling, rock-climbing and mountain biking trips. All Four Adventures (Ⓣ03/6257 0018) offers 4WD tours of the park.

Bicheno

Halfway up the east coast, **BICHENO** (pronounced "bish-eno"), sheltered in **Waubs Bay**, is a busy crayfishing and abalone port. The same conditions that make Bicheno ideal for fishing also make it a perfect spot for diving. Don't let the unattractive inland town centre on the Tasman Highway put you off; it has a beautiful bay setting and there's lots to do.

The 3.5km, one-way **Bicheno Foreshore Footway** runs from Redbill Point (reached via Gordon Street off the Tasman Highway at the western edge of town) and follows several points, bays and beaches, with views of **Governor Island Marine Nature Reserve**, and past the Blowhole. The usually clear waters are rich with a variety of marine life, and the reserve has spectacular large caves and extraordinary vertical rockfaces with swim-throughs and drop-offs. Bicheno Dive Centre, opposite the Sea Life Centre at 2 Scuba Court (Ⓣ03/6375 1138, Ⓦwww.bichenodive.com), offers dive courses and rents out gear. One of the most popular activities in Bicheno are the evening tours to a local **penguin** rookery with Bicheno Penguin Tours (Ⓣ03/6375 1333; nightly; $18). The French-owned Le Frog Trike Rides (Ⓣ03/6375 1777) runs a range of fun and thrilling three-wheeler tours, from $12 for a 10– to 15-minute ride to $170 for a 2hr ride to the Elephant Pass. Bicheno Glass Bottom Boats (Ⓣ03/6375 1294) offers one-hour, **glass-bottom boat tours** of the marine reserve ($18). The **Sea Life Centre** (daily 9am–5pm; $6.50), on the Tasman Highway, has a rather dingy aquarium but an excellent seafood restaurant (daily 9am–9pm; dinner bookings Ⓣ03/6375 1121). Bicheno's **Online Access Centre** is at The Oval, Burgess Street.

With a wide choice of **accommodation**, Bicheno makes a pleasant stopover. You can camp at the *East Coast Holiday Park* at 4 Champ St (Ⓣ03/6375 1999; vans ❶–❷, cabins ❸, apartments ❷–❸) or stay at the small, tidy and well-equipped *Bicheno Backpackers*, 11 Morrison St (Ⓣ03/6375 1651, dorms $18). For something really special, head for the *Bicheno Hideaway,* at 179 Harveys Farm Rd (Ⓣ03/6375 1312, Ⓦwww.bichenohideaway.com; ❹–❺), 3km south of Bicheno, where uniquely designed oceanfront self-contained chalets are set on six acres of natural bushland teeming with wildlife. Other options include the central *Beachfront Family Resort,* on the Tasman Highway (Ⓣ03/6375 1111; ❹), which has a swimming pool, and the *Bicheno Gaol Cottages,* on the corner of James and Burgess streets (Ⓣ03/6375 1430; ❺), with accommodation in the old prison and its converted stables. **Food**, too, is good in Bicheno. The formal *Cyrano French Restaurant,* at 77 Burgess St (dinner nightly; mains $20–24; Ⓣ03/6375 1137), is in the classic French vein, while the *Beachfront Tavern,* on the Tasman Highway, has the best counter meals: big servings and a great salad bar. The eat-in *Freycinet Bakery* (daily 8am–4pm) next to the post office is an excellent café, while across the grassy traffic island the *Cod Rock Cafe* cooks up fresh fish and other seafood (daily 10am–8pm). To sample some gourmet Tasmanian products, head for *Mary Harvey's Restaurant* in the gardens of the *Bicheno Gaol Cottages* (lunch & dinner daily Dec–April, dinner only Sept–June).

The Bicheno Coach Service (Ⓣ03/6357 0293) to Freycinet National Park leaves from the *Bicheno Takeaway* at 52 Burgess St.

The Douglas Apsley National Park to St Marys

Just 4km north of Bicheno on the Tasman Highway there's a turn-off to the **Douglas Apsley National Park**. Proclaimed in 1990, it's the location of the state's only remaining large dry sclerophyll forest. Because of the temperate weather of the east coast, the park's two-day walk, the **Leeaberra Track** – undertaken north to south – is a good one at any time of the year. Although facilities are being improved, this is a low-maintenance, untouristy park, so be prepared for basic bushcamping; get hold of the *Douglas Apsley Map and Notes* ($9.10).

Thirty kilometres north of Bicheno, just past Chain of Lagoons, the coastal Tasman Highway continues north to St Helens; turn off to the left for a spectacular climb with views of the surrounding coastline on a detour inland to **St Marys**, 17km away. You can stop at the dramatic **Elephant Pass** for pancakes, views and atmosphere at the *Mount Elephant Pancake Barn* (daily 8am–6pm), though the menu prices are high.

From Elephant Pass the road heads on to **ST MARYS**, a picturesque little Fingal Valley town surrounded by state forest and waterfalls best viewed from the 832-metre peak of logging-threatened **South Sister**, accessed 6km up unsealed and winding German Town Road. The place has a quiet, old-fashioned feel to it, but an alternative edge focused around the licensed *Escape Tasmanian Wilderness Cafe Gallery* at 21 Main St (Ⓣ03/6372 2444; Thurs & Sun 7.30am–9.30pm, Fri & Sat 7.30am–10.30pm; all day-breakfast and excellent coffee), with a pool table and regular live music and film screenings; and the fantastic little *Purple Possum Wholefoods Cafe* in the health food store (closed Sun) around the corner on Storey Street. The best place to stay is magical *Seaview Farm* (Ⓣ03/6372 2341, or 0417 382 876, Ⓦwww.seaviewfarm.com.au), 8km uphill on German Town Road; the hilltop position gives panoramic

South Sister and sea views. There's hostel accommodation in a comfortable cottage which has a big eat-in kitchen and cosy lounge with a wood stove, and the "dorms" are pretty rooms with beds not bunks (dorms $20, with linen and towel $25); or choose private accommodation in a row of en-suite rooms (❸) with verandah access providing fabulous views. You can arrange a pick-up in advance if you don't have your own transport. St Marys' **Online Access Centre** is at 23B Main St. There is full Commonwealth **bank services** in the post office at no. 36.

St Helens and the Bay of Fires

Heading downhill back to the coast, **ST HELENS** is the largest town on the east coast and the last before the Tasman Highway turns inland. It's situated on **Georges Bay**, a long, narrow bay with two encircling arms, and the surrounding coastline holds plenty of interest. Local **information** is available from the **St Helens History Room**, at 55 Cecilia St opposite the post office (Mon–Fri 9am–4pm & Sat 9am–noon, plus Sun 10am–2pm in summer; $2; ⓣ03/6376 1744), which details the area's mining history in the nearby Blue Tier (see p.1014) and provides maps and walk information. With a new resort hotel, new cinema, loads of great cafés, a health food store and even a vintage clothes store, St Helens is fast coming out of being a sleepy backwater, as the impressive beauty of the nearby Bay of Fires becomes more widely known and real estate prices rocket.

The southern arm of Georges Bay is the site of **St Helens Point Recreation Area**, where there's a large lagoon – Diana's Basin – which the highway skirts as it enters town. On the ocean side the **Peron sand dunes** stretch for several kilometres, and at the point there's good surfing at **Beer Barrel Beach**. **Binalong Bay**, 10km north of Georges Bay, is another popular surf spot (with a strong current, so beware); there's safer swimming in the large lagoon tucked behind, where people boat and water-ski. Binalong is the southern end of the mesmerisingly beautiful **Bay of Fires** (named for the many fires explorer Tobias Furneaux saw along the stretch in 1773), where the beach of bright sugary sand stretches for over 30km to Eddystone Point. Binalong Bay is an easy bike ride away from St Helens (hire bikes at the *YHA*), with only a couple of small climbs. From Binalong Bay, you can walk in around two hours along the beach to **Cosy Corner**; however, unless you want to walk back again you need to arrange to be picked up or go on a tour (see Island Escapes' "East Coast Escape" p.1072). There's accommodation, a shop and petrol, and you can **camp** here, as well as further along at Grants Lagoon in the **Bay of Fires Coastal Reserve** which stretches for 13km north alongside the partly sealed coastal drive to the scenic spot known as The Gardens.

To get to the lower half of **Mount William National Park** at the northern end of the Bay of Fires, take the road running inland north for 54km from St Helens to the pink-granite tower of the Eddystone Lighthouse. The northern end of the park is reached via Gladstone, by taking an unsealed track to **Great Musselroe Bay**, where there's a free basic **campsite**. There are no real tracks within the park itself, but plenty of beach and headland walking, and lots of Forrester kangaroos. **Bay of Fires Walk** leads a superb four-day guided coastal walk along the Bay of Fires and through Mount William National Park (ⓣ03/6331 2006, ⓦwww.bayoffires.com.au; $1595); packs and waterproof jackets are provided and accommodation is in luxury "ecotents" and a superbly designed ecolodge 40m above the sea with stunning views up and down the coast. Tiger Trails does a great Bay of Fires day-trip from Launceston – 3.5

hours of moderate guided coastal walking in Mt William National Park, picnic lunch included.

St Helens practicalities

There's a good range of **accommodation** to choose from in town. The *St Helens YHA*, at 5 Cameron St (ⓣ03/6376 1661; dorms $18, rooms ❷; bike hire $10 day, boards $5), is very homely and clean with friendly owners: expect a peaceful atmosphere with books, magazines, games and a wood stove to chat around; a self-contained flat is also available (❹). Across the road, *Dohertys* (ⓣ03/6376 1999, ⓦwww.dohertyhotels.com.au; ❻–❼) provides a sophisticated edge to the town, with the well-patronised *Deck on the Bay* café-bistro (daily 11am–9.30pm), pricier *Ocean View Restaurant* (daily breakfast & dinner), and *Lobby Bar*. Among the numerous B&Bs, the best value is *Artnor Lodge*, at 71 Cecilia St (ⓣ03/6376 1234; ❷, en-suite ❸). The *Bayside Inn*, at 2 Cecilia St (ⓣ03/6376 1466; all rooms en-suite ❸–❹), is a modern waterfront hotel/motel with a restaurant, pool and drive-in bottle shop. However, staying at Binalong Bay is much more scenic and relaxing, and there's plenty of choice, including the self-contained *Binalong Bungalows* (ⓣ03/6376 1720; ❸) and the upmarket B&B *Bed in the Treetops* (ⓣ03/6376 1318, ⓦwww.bedinthetreetops.com.au; ❻–❼) at 124 and 701 Binalong Bay Rd respectively. *Fidlers on the Bay*, facing Georges Bay at 2 Jason St (ⓣ03/6376 2444; daily 11am to late), is a highly regarded **café-restaurant** serving delicious local seafood and grills with a great Tasmanian wine list. For excellent coffee and a great menu featuring local organic produce, head for the cute *Milk Bar Cafe* at 57B Cecilia St (Mon–Sat 9am–5pm). Next door the reasonably priced *Wok Stop* (lunch Mon–Fri, dinner Mon–Sat) does curries, wok-fried noodles and fresh juices. The new **Forum Cinema** (ⓣ03/6376 1000) shows films Fri–Sun, plus there's a funky café-bar with couches, art exhibitions, live music on Fri nights, and an eclectic affordable menu. St Helens' bank is Westpac, at 41 Cecilia St, and its **Online Access Centre** is in the library at no. 61.

St Helens to Scottsdale: the Tasman Highway

From St Helens, the **Tasman Highway (A3)** cuts across the northeast highlands towards Launceston, 170km away. This is mostly dairy country, although there's the odd patch of surviving rainforest and the remnants of a tin-mining industry, based around the **Blue Tier**, a mountain plateau that experienced a mining boom in the 1870s. Many **ghost towns** were left after the mines finally closed in the 1950s.

Twenty-six kilometres northwest of St Helens on the A3 is the turn-off south for **PYENGANA** (1km) and St Columba Falls (a further 4km). In Pyengana it's worth touring **Healey's Pyengana Cheese Factory** (daily 9am–5pm; free), where you can watch the stuff being made (except Fri & Sat) and buy all the ingredients for a picnic at the falls, or have something to eat at the new café here. Further along, the one-storey *St Columba Falls Hotel* (ⓣ03/6373 6121) – the "Pub in the Paddock" – looks like a farmhouse; it's a real country local, serving huge steaks (from $16.50), and you can also **stay here** in cute tidy rooms with peaceful rural views (❸). At the end of the road (the last bit on dirt) is the **Columba Falls State Reserve**, an area of cool, temperate rainforest. The 1km return walk to the viewing platform at the base of **St Columba Falls** is easy, passing through a forest of manferns and under a canopy of sassafras and myrtle. At 110m, the falls are among the highest in

Tasmania, pouring with tremendous force over the cliffs – truly thunderous in winter.

Back on the A3 approaching the **Blue Tier**, Goshen is the first of the **ghost towns**, little more than an old school and the ruins of the Oxford Arms Inn. A little further on is the turn-off for **Goulds** Country, with the remaining buildings – all wooden – of what was once a town. Head through Goulds Country and past the site of another abandoned mining town, Lottah, and take the steep, unsealed Poimena Road to the site of Poimena. En route, there's "Hands Off The Blue Tiers" notices and other signs of the fierce environmental campaign against logging of the area, one of the few remaining old growth forests left in the northeast. The boardwalked 20-minute circuit **Goblin Forest Walk** (wheelchair accessible) provides fascinating interpretative boards which help to imagine the town once here. There's also a 30-minute walk to the 810-metre-high Blue Tier Summit, Mt Poimena, for views right across the northeast to the coast, and several other signposted walks taking between two to six hours. Get details on Blue Tier walks at St Helens History Room (see p.1113).

Returning to the Tasman Highway, the Weldborough Pass (595m) is probably the most beautiful part of the drive, with views across the valleys to the sea; it's worth taking the twenty-minute walk through the **Weldborough Pass Scenic Reserve**, predominately myrtle forest with manferns and occasional tall blackwoods. **WELDBOROUGH** itself, once the centre of a Chinese mining community, now consists of the isolated, characterful *Weldborough Hotel* (Ⓣ03/6354 2223; ❷), where you can get a **meal** (Mon–Sat) and a basic share-bathroom pub **room** for the night; there's also a campsite.

DERBY, on the Ringarooma River, was made prosperous by the profitable **Briseis Tin Mine** between 1876 and 1952. The **Derby Tin Mine Centre** (daily: June–Aug 10am–4pm; Sept–May 10am–5pm; $4.50) is now the only sign of development in a town that's been closing down since the 1950s: it has some interesting relics connected with the Chinese miners. **SCOTTSDALE**, 99km from St Helens, is a large, pleasantly situated town servicing the agricultural and forestry industries of the northeast. The **Scottsdale Forest EcoCentre**, on the outskirts of town at 88 King St (daily 9am–5pm; free) is yet another Forestry Tasmania public relations exercise; the unique, energy-smart building looks like a wooden spaceship that has landed and half-sunk into the ground. Inside, an "eco-walk" winds up the circular building, putting the local forest and forestry industry into historical and ecological context, and there's a pleasant café (daily 10am–3pm) and a **visitor information centre** (Ⓣ03/6352 6520). Scottsdale has good facilities, including a Westpac bank at 21 King St, supermarkets, the bustling *Cottage Bakery*, at 9 Victoria St, with a fresh sandwich bar and real coffee (closed Sun), and an **Online Access Centre** in the library at 51 King St. The classic Victorian-era *Beulah of Scottsdale*, 9 King St, set amongst flowery gardens, has attic bedrooms with mountain views, and a guest lounge and dining room (B&B ❻). There are some beautiful areas to visit nearby, including Ralph Falls in the Mt Victoria Forest Reserve and Evercreech Forest Reserve – get details from the EcoCentre, or Pepper Bush Peaks 4WD Adventure Tours (Ⓣ03/6352 2263, Ⓦwww.pepperbushcom.au; Launceston pick-ups) can take you off-road to visit some of these places. Tours include fine food and wine and range from a nocturnal wildlife tour with BBQ ($115) to a full-day tour ($275).

Twenty-one kilometres northwest, the fishing town and holiday spot of **BRIDPORT** has several places to **stay** including the modern, purpose-built *Bridport Seaside Lodge YHA Backpackers*, at 47 Main St (Ⓣ03/6356 1585, Ⓔbridportseasidelodge@hotmail.com; dorms $16, rooms ❷) right on the river estuary.

There's camping at *Bridport Caravan Park* (ⓣ03/6356 1227; sites only), which stretches for about a kilometre along Anderson Bay. The **beaches** in the area are lovely, especially the wide, sandy expanse where the Bird River flows among sand dunes and into the sea. *Bridport Seafoods* (daily 10am–7pm), attached to the fish-processing plant on Main Street, does excellent sit-down meals.

North and central Tasmania and the Bass Strait

The **north** of Tasmania is rich and settled agricultural country, and the fertile soil of the **Tamar Valley** in particular made this a prosperous area during the early colonial period. Thirty kilometres inland at the confluence of the Tamar and the North and South Esk rivers, **Launceston** quickly grew as a port and city; gracious early houses and well-preserved villages are still found around the area. Also settled early, due to its fine and open land, was the mostly flat, gently undulating **midlands** area between Launceston and Hobart; the **Midland Highway** more or less follows the old coaching route between the two cities. With its stone walls, hedgerows, haystacks, and small villages and towns, this rural stretch from the Tamar Valley to Hobart is softly appealing but not particularly exciting. In contrast, the area around **Deloraine**, 45km west of Launceston, is spectacular: the early colonial town is surrounded by rich farmland and dramatically located in hilly country below the crest of the **Great Western Tiers** – a mecca for bushwalkers. From Deloraine, the **Lake Highway** heads steeply south up over the Western Tiers and on to the **Central Plateau**, a sparsely populated lake-filled region dominated by the **Great Lake** and its fishing shacks.

Lying off the northern coast, in Bass Strait, are two islands worth visiting for their bushwalks and historic associations: **Flinders Island** in the northeast, largest of the Furneaux Islands, and **King Island** to the far northwest, part of the Hunter Island group. Both are reached by plane, with flights from Victoria or Tasmania.

Launceston and around

LAUNCESTON is dominated by the **Tamar River**, and approaching from the north along the Tamar Highway, zooming through haystack-filled countryside, it's a lovely sight, with grand Victorian houses nestling on hills above the banks. Approaching from the south on the dreary Southern Outlet, however, gives a slightly more accurate picture of the dull but worthy provincial town. Tasmania's second largest city, with a population of around 98,000, is however undergoing a shakeup by the youthful and progressive female mayor who's been at the helm since 2002.

As the third-oldest city in Australia, first settled in 1804, Launceston has hung on to disappointingly little of its elegant colonial Georgian architecture. What the city does have in abundance are many fine examples of colonial **Victorian architecture**: the 1870s and 1880s were prosperous times for Launceston, years of mineral exploration spurred on by the mainland goldrush, and a number of massive, dignified public buildings date from this boom period.

Launceston's real attractions, though, are its natural assets. It's situated at the confluence of the narrow **North Esk** and **South Esk rivers**, with the breathtaking **Cataract Gorge**, where the South Esk has carved its way through rock to reach the Tamar River, only fifteen-minutes' walk from the centre. Yachts and outboard motors ply the 50km of river, and the surrounding countryside of the **Tamar Valley**, with its wineries, strawberry farms and lavender plantations is idyllic. Beyond the eastern suburbs bush-covered hills fold back into the distance to **Ben Lomond**, a popular winter skiing destination just an hour's drive away.

Arrival, information and city transport

Launceston Airport is 20km south of the city, near the town of Evandale. The **Airport Shuttle Bus** (ⓣ0500 512 009) meets most flights and drops off at accommodation for $10. A **taxi** costs about $27, or you could **rent a car** – the main car companies have desks at the airport, or see "Listings" on p.1124. Long-distance **buses** arrive in the city centre at the **Cornwall Square Transit Centre**, on the corner of Cimitiere and St Johns streets, where both Redline (ⓣ1300 360 000) and TassieLink (ⓣ1300 300 520) have ticket offices; Redline has left luggage ($1.50 per 24hr) and there is a café plus tourist information. If driving, note that most streets operate on a **one-way system** and the length of Cameron Street is interrupted by Civic Square, and Brisbane Street by the Mall.

Information

For **information**, your first stop should be the **Gateway Tasmanian Travel Centre**, on the corner of St John and Paterson streets (Mon–Fri 9am–5pm, Sat 9am–3pm, Sun 9am–noon; ⓣ03/6336 3133, or 1800 651 827, ⓦwww.gatewaytas.com.au), which can also arrange car rental and book accommodation and travel tickets. The Wilderness Society Shop, at 174 Charles St, opposite Princes Square (ⓣ03/6334 2499), is a good source of information about wilderness issues and the environment and offers a summer walks programme into areas under threat by logging.

City transport

Launceston is very compact and most accommodation is within walking distance of the city centre, although **public transport** (the MTT) is useful for a couple of scattered attractions and some outlying accommodation (buses run until 6.15pm Mon–Thurs, 10pm Fri & Sat; restricted services Sun). The **MTT bus interchange** (information ⓣ13 22 01, ⓦwww.metrotas.com.au), where all buses arrive and depart, is on St John Street, on either side of the **Brisbane Street Mall**. Single fares are inexpensive, but it may be worth buying a Day Rover ($4.20) for unlimited off-peak travel (buy on board) or a ten-trip ticket (from $12.80; buy at Teagues Newsagency, opposite the post office).

Accommodation

Accommodation in Launceston is very good value, and rates don't tend to hike up in the busy December-to-February period, though **hostel** beds can be

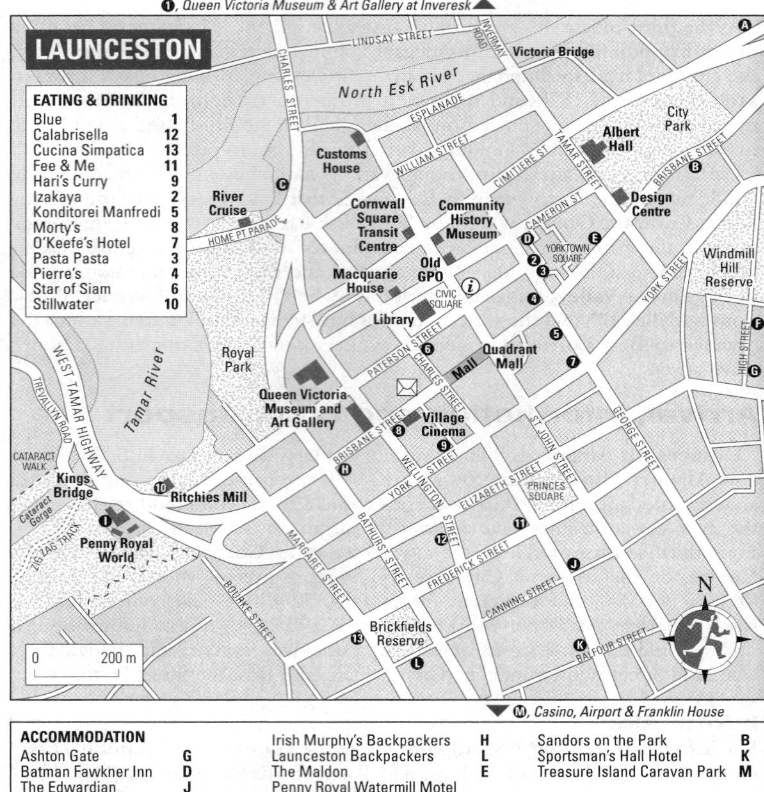

scarce then. A tragic fire at the YHA hostel on New Year's Eve 2004 led to its closure; contact the YHA office in Hobart (see p.1091) for the latest details of any new hostel. There's a concentration of **motels** along Brisbane Street and an abundance of **B&Bs** and self-catering accommodation.

Hotels, motels, B&Bs and self-catering

Ashton Gate 32 High St ⓣ03/6331 6180, ⓦwww.view.com.au/ashtongate. Classified by the National Trust, this weatherboard B&B has been taking guests for over forty years. Bedrooms are large and light; all are en suite, with TV and hot drinks. ❺–❻

Batman Fawkner Inn 35–39 Cameron St ⓣ03/6331 7222. This pleasant pub, established in 1822, offers bargain, single en-suite rooms with TV and phone ($45); larger, more attractive rooms have similar facilities. Light breakfast included. There's an Italian restaurant and bar meals, and a nightclub open on Fri & Sat nights, which makes it a bit noisy – better to stay here mid-week. ❹

The Edwardian 229 Charles St ⓣ03/6334 7771, ⓦwww.theedwardian.com.au. Lovely, two-storey red-brick Edwardian house near Princes Square, with self-contained self-catering suites. Breakfast provisions provided. Handy for the supermarket. No children. ❹–❺

Glebe Cottages 14A Cimitiere St ⓣ0500 500 581, ⓦwww.glebecottages.com.au. Good-value, spacious two- and three-bedroom self-contained cottages, in a convenient location near City Park. ❺

Hatherley House 43 High St ⓣ03/6334 7727, ⓦwww.hatherleyhouse.com.au. Recently voted one of the top 80 new hotels by *Condé Nast Traveller*, this gorgeous 1830s colonial mansion set in extensive English-style gardens (views stretch off to Ben Lomond) combines stunning original architectural features, tapestries, carvings and sculptures from India, Africa and the Orient with contemporary design and five-star luxury. Scrumptious breakfast served on the verandah, in the library café-bar or out in the garden. ⑦–⑧

The Maldon 32 Brisbane St ⓣ03/6331 3211. Elegant Victorian-era B&B, featuring iron-lace verandahs, chandeliers, engraved glass and a carved wooden staircase; en-suite rooms with modern facilities. ④

Penny Royal Watermill Motel and Village Apartments 145–147 Paterson St ⓣ03/6331 6699, ⓔpennyroyal@leisureinns.com.au. Built in 1840, this motel has a comfortable old-world charm, while the more modern self-contained apartments are spacious and reasonably priced. Close to the city centre and a short walk to the gorge and Cliff Grounds. Rooms ④, apartments ⑥–⑧

Peppers Seaport Hotel 28 Seaport Boulevard ⓣ03/6345 3333, ⓦwww.peppers.com.au. This brand-new resort has finally given Launceston a waterfont-lifestyle focus, with its cluster of bars, cafés and restaurants. In the hotel itself, rooms are very stylish, with natural wood furnishings and luxury fabrics. Spacious suites feature fully equipped kitchen and laundry. Most rooms have water views, but don't bother shelling out to stay here for a "city view" room which provides a very unattractive road vista. ⑦–⑧

Sandors on the Park 3 Brisbane St ⓣ03/6331 2055 or 1800 030 140. The best of a bunch of motels on this strip overlooking City Park – but not the most expensive –and just a short walk from the centre. Friendly professional service; guest laundry. Its bistro-style *Monkey Bar Café* opens noon–10.30pm. ④

Sportsman's Hall Hotel 252 Charles St ⓣ03/6331 3968. Pleasant pub with well-furnished, comfortable rooms (shared bathrooms). Breakfast included. Excellent, café-style bistro downstairs serving up very reasonably priced meals. ③–④

Hostels and caravan parks

Irish Murphy's Backpackers 211 Brisbane St ⓣ03/6331 4440, ⓦwww.irishmurphys.com.au. Hostel accommodation above a lively, centrally located pub. Facilities include TV lounge and a fully equipped kitchen but no laundry. Bedding $3 extra for dorms. Dorms $17, rooms ②

Launceston Backpackers 103 Canning St ⓣ03/6334 2327, ⓦwww.launcestonbackpackers.com.au. Launceston's best hostel is in a cheerfully painted, clean two-storey mansion with an adjoining modern annexe. Well-run without being regimental, the friendly much-travelled managers maintain a secure atmosphere. Good communal facilities include Internet access. Dorms come in three-, four- and six-bed varieties (sheet hire $2, blanket 50c), single rooms are available ($40), and some of the doubles (bedding included) have en-suites. Tours and bus tickets booked. Book ahead in summer. Dorms $18–20, rooms ②–③

Treasure Island Caravan Park 94 Glen Dhu St, South Launceston, 2km south of the centre ⓣ03/6344 2600. A small park, sloping up a hillside and looking right over a noisy freeway. Hard, uneven ground; crowded in summer. Camp kitchen with TV. Bus #21 or #24 to Wellington Street (stop 8). Vans ②, en-suite cabins ③

The City

The **Brisbane Street Mall** marks the centre of the city, which is arranged in a typical grid pattern around it. **Brisbane Street**, with the mall as its focus, is the main shopping precinct. The city is small and easy to get around, but if you want some background information, join Launceston Historic Walks (departs Mon–Fri 9.45am; 1hr 15min; $15; bookings ⓣ03/6331 3679) outside the Gateway Centre on Paterson Street.

City Park and the old wharf area

City Park (daily 8am–5pm), with its entrance of impressive wrought-iron gates on Tamar Street, is a real treasure. Established in the 1820s, the impression of a formally organized, very English park is reinforced by the **John Hart Conservatory**, full of flowers and ferns, and by the wrought-iron drinking fountain erected here for Queen Victoria's Diamond Jubilee in 1897. Referred to by the locals as "Monkey Park", it's the closest thing Launceston has to a zoo: its Japanese macaques (over twenty of them), romp around their small, moat-surrounded island.

Within City Park, on the corner of Tamar and Brisbane streets, is the **Design Centre of Tasmania** (daily 9.30am–5.30pm), established in 1976 to support and encourage Tasmanian designers. In a state that's always been perceived by the mainland as lagging behind, it's a source of pride that Tasmanian designers helped furnish the New Parliament House in Canberra. The Design Centre is now the home of the **Tasmanian Wood Design Collection** ($2.20), which showcases Tasmanian woodcrafts of some of these superb local designers, wood-workers and furniture-makers using native Tasmanian woods. Prices are beyond the range of most visitors, but the centre is also one of the best places to buy more portable **craft** items, such as woodwork, leatherwork and jewellery.

The wharves on the North Esk River have disappeared, but the massive Neoclassical **Customs House** is still there on The Esplanade, just east of the Charles Street Bridge. The **old wharf area**, around William Street and the Esplanade, has several interesting industrial buildings, including the 1881, still-operational **J. Boag & Son** brewery. Its popular brewery tours start in the **Boag's Centre For Beer Lovers**, opposite at 39 William St, which includes a **museum** (Mon–Fri 8.45am–4.30pm; free) and gift shop, and finish with a small tasting of four beers (Mon–Thurs 9am, 11.45am & 2.30pm; Fri 9am & 11.45am; 1hr 30min; $16; bookings ⓣ03/6332 6300, ⓦwww.boags.com.au).

The North Bank and Heritage Forest

Opposite the Esplanade, reached by Victoria Bridge from Tamar Street, and then a boardwalk along the river, is the **Queen Victoria Museum and Art Gallery at Inveresk** (daily 10am–5pm; free but charges for touring exhibitions; ⓦwww.qvmag.tas.gov.au), part of a multimillion-dollar redevelopment of the complex of old railway yards here. Opened in late 2001, the building's interior – two-thirds of which is home to the University of Tasmania's **Academy of Arts** – has an incredible sense of space. The art gallery is well worth visiting for its "Aspects of Tasmanian Art" exhibition, which notably contains landscapes by the nineteenth-century painter W.C. Piguenit, and "Strings Across Time – Tasmanian Aboriginal Shell Necklaces", which displays beautiful examples of the ancient women's art, including recent examples from the tradition of Cape Barren Islanders. From the art gallery you walk through to the former **Railway Workshops**, now transformed into a social history museum; the history of railways in Tasmania is hardly compelling stuff (though the Playzone for kids is great), but the walkway through the old Blacksmith Shop, complete with soundscape of machinery and voices, is eerie, and the exhibition on migration to the state, based on personal stories, gives a different angle on contemporary Tasmania. The sedate licensed café in the Railway Workshops has part of its seating in an old train carriage.

The railway yards site spans a large expanse of riverfront land dubbed by the council as the **Northbank Experience**. It includes the Tasmanian Conservation Workshops, the Exhibition Centre and the York Park Sports and Entertainment Centre (see p.1124), which has finally brought live AFL football to Launceston. Still to come is a visitor information centre and a clutch of cafés, restaurants and stores. The boardwalk to the art gallery continues along the North Esk River to **Heritage Forest**, parkland with walking, bike-riding and horse-riding trails.

Civic Square and around

Shady, grassy **Civic Square**, closed to traffic, does convey a tidy spirit of civic-mindedness. Here, **Macquarie House** was built as a warehouse in 1830 for Henry Reed, a wealthy merchant. **Cameron Street** was one of the first streets laid out after the city's settlement in 1806, and the stretch from Civic Square to Wellington Street is an almost perfectly preserved nineteenth-century streetscape, including the imposing Supreme Court building and, opposite, a row of fine Victorian red-brick terraced houses adorned with beautiful wrought-iron work.

South of Civic Square is the main shopping thoroughfare, the pedestrianized **Brisbane Street Mall**, a modest precinct taking up one small city block. Just off here is the arc of the **Quadrant Mall**, bounded by Brisbane and St John streets, with several lanes and an arcade leading from it. Gourlay's Sweet Shop here is a Launceston institution – for something really local, try the leatherwood honey drops. East of Quadrant Mall and one block north along George Street, **The Old Umbrella Shop** at no. 60 is a **National Trust information centre** (Mon–Fri 9am–5pm, Sat 9am–noon; ⓣ03/6331 9248) housed in an 1860s Tasmanian blackwood-lined shop.

The Queen Victoria Museum and Art Gallery

The **Queen Victoria Museum and Art Gallery**, on Wellington Street (daily 10am–5pm; free but charges for touring exhibitions; ⓦwww.qvmag.tas.gov.au), was opened in 1891 to mark half a century of Queen Victoria's reign. Its most valued possession is the Chinese joss house from Weldborough (see p.1115), constructed in the 1870s by Chinese workers introduced to the east coast tin mines to provide cheap labour. Elsewhere, other permanent **museum** exhibitions include: a history of mining in Tasmania; displays about the state's fauna, with big sections on the Tasmanian Tiger and the Tasmanian devil; accounts of the geology of Launceston and the local area; a **Planetarium** (Tues–Fri 3pm, Sat 2pm & 3pm; $5); and the "Discovery Plus" room, containing microscopes and specimen trays, as well as a display of live spiders and puzzles to play with. The **art gallery** section includes traditional and contemporary Aboriginal works, and decorative arts including costumes, textiles and ceramics, but most of the collection has moved to the Inveresk site. The *Queen Vic Café* is one of the best in Launceston.

Royal Park to Ritchies Mill Arts Centre

Behind the museum, and across Bathurst Street, **Royal Park** has extensive formal parklands running down to the Tamar River; there's even a croquet lawn here, if you were in any doubt about its English lineage. Between Royal Park and Cataract Gorge is a concentrated tourist area. **Ritchies Mill Arts Centre**, at 2 Bridge Rd on the Tamar River, has been converted from a nineteenth-century flour mill and millers' cottage and now contains two galleries and an alfresco café, *Stillwater* (see p.1123). Opposite Ritchies Mill, the overpriced **Penny Royal World** (daily 9.30am–4pm; $15) is a sort of historical funfair, developed on the site of an old bluestone quarry and based around an 1840 ironstone water mill and farmhouse – transferred to the site – and a replica of an 1825 wooden corn mill.

To the north of the park, **Tamar River Cruises** (ⓣ03/6334 9900, ⓦwww.tamarrivercruises.com.au) depart from Home Point, at the end of Home Point Parade, and head along the Tamar and into the mouth of beautiful Cataract Gorge, allowing a close-up view of the Launceston Yacht Club, as well as the wealthy suburb of **Trevallyn**, filled with classic Victorian mansions strung along the tree-covered hillside (Sept–May daily: hourly 9.30am–3.30pm; June & Aug hourly 11.30am–1.30pm; 50min; $15). A longer trip continues north up the Tamar as far as the Rosevears vineyards (see p.1127; Mon–Sat 3pm; 2.5hr; $35 including afternoon tea). Nearby, the **Old Launceston Seaport** on Seaport Boulevard is a lively new waterfront café, bar and restaurant precinct around the *Peppers Seaport Hotel* (see p.1119), a great spot with views over the yachts in the marina to the Trevallyn hillside.

Cataract Gorge and beyond

Few cities have such a magnificent natural feature within fifteen minutes' walk of the centre as Launceston. For a beautiful view of **Cataract Gorge**, turn left out of Penny Royal World and walk to the decorative wrought-iron 1863 **Kings Bridge**, which has a span of 60m. From the bridge the cliffs rise almost vertically from the smooth water of the South Esk River as it empties into the Tamar. The natural spectacle is even more dramatic when floodlit after dusk.

The **Zig Zag track** (25min one-way), on the Penny Royal World side of the bridge, is the more strenuous of the two walking routes along the gorge. The rock-stepped path shrouded by bush is satisfyingly secluded. The track runs steeply along the top of the gorge, from Kings Bridge to the **First Basin**, a large, deep canyon worn away by the river and filled with water. Across the Kings Bridge is the easier but busier **Cataract Walk** (40min one-way), which begins by the small tollhouse; the stroll is suitable for wheelchairs, and offers spectacular views of the gorge. From the trail, you'll see people canoeing, abseiling and even jumping off the cliffs into the water; Tasmania Expeditions offers abseiling trips here (see Tours, p.1125).

The Cataract Walk leads to the gardens of the **Cliff Grounds**, on the shady northern side of the gorge – genteel, English-style gardens with parading peacocks and arranged around a lovely 1896 rotunda, they make for a startling contrast with the gorge's wild beauty. *The Gorge Restaurant* (closed Mon; ⓣ03/6331 3330) in the grounds has stunning views over the First Basin; less expensive cream teas are served from the kiosk. If you enter the grounds from the First Basin end (where there's a car park; or take bus #51B), you'll find an enormous, unattractive **swimming pool**, built mainly to discourage people from swimming in the basin itself, where some have died.

To get across the First Basin to the Cliff Grounds, the **Launceston Basin Chair Lift** (daily 9am–4.30pm weather permitting; $7) takes an exhilarating six minutes to cover 457m – it's supposed to have the longest single span (308m) of any chair lift in the world. The views are wonderful, but if you're afraid of heights you might want to cross on foot via the **Basin Walk** directly underneath, although this route is impassable when the river is in flood. The other alternative, the narrow **Alexandra Suspension Bridge**, called the "swinging bridge" by locals, is even shakier when crowded with joggers.

A track starting from the Alexandra Suspension Bridge follows the river through unspoilt bush to the narrower **Second Basin** and the disused **Duck Reach Power Station** (90min return). From the station you could continue a bit further to the large **Trevallyn State Recreation Area** (daily 8am–dusk; no camping), on the South Esk River, and the **Trevallyn Dam**, 6km west of the city centre. To reach the area by road, go via the suburb of Trevallyn, following Reatta Road. In the recreation area at Aquatic Point, there's an **information centre**, summer canoe and windsurf boards rental, a playground, toilets and barbecues. The rest of the reserve consists of open eucalypt forest, with marked bushwalks and nature trails shared with horse riders.

Eating

Eating out in Launceston is a predominantly Anglo-Saxon affair, with **pubs** in particular offering decent meals. However, there are also a few excellent **cafés** and the odd ethnic place, and a new level of choice and sophistication at the Old Launceston Seaport surrounding *Peppers Seaport Hotel* (see p.1119). Options include the popular and very casual *Fish n' Chips* where you can sit at outside tables, the trendy *Mud Bar and Restaurant*, the rowdier *Dockside Cafe Winebar*, plus *Cube*, a funky little café and *Porthole*, a more traditional café-patisserie.

Blue Inveresk Railyards, off Invermay Rd. This café/bar, in a round and sunny former powerhouse, is a young, lively art college hangout. Classic, café meals for under $9, plus more substantial mains up to $16; also gourmet pizzas and $5.50 tapas menu to go with a drink. Outside tables prove very popular for the excellent weekend breakfast. Ambient DJs spin Friday night (from 7pm) and Sunday afternoons (2pm–5pm). Licensed. Mon–Sat from 8.30am (dinner Mon–Sat), Sun 8am–3pm.
Calabrisella 56 Wellington St ⓣ03/6331 1958. A crowded, noisy, atmospheric and affordable Italian restaurant. BYO. Dinner nightly except Tues.
Cucina Simpatica Cnr Margaret and Frederick streets, opposite Brickfields Reserve ⓣ03/6334 3177. Hip café with a colourful Mediterranean feel. Becomes a restaurant in the evening, with an eclectic, "contemporary" menu: delicious food (though pricey and small portions) and an emphasis on fresh local and organic produce. Licensed and BYO. Daily 10am until late.
Fee & Me 190 Charles St ⓣ03/6331 3195. Award-winning restaurant serving up expensive regional cuisine with an international flavour. Licensed. Dinner Mon–Sat.
Hari's Curry 152 York St ⓣ03/6331 6466. Very cheap, well-recommended Indian eatery – average main is $8.50 and there's nothing over $14. BYO. Dinner daily.
Izakaya Japanese Restaurant and Sushi Bar Yorktown Square ⓣ03/6334 2620. This excellent, long-established place serves all the favourite Japanese dishes: *ramen*, sushi, tempura, *bento*, though noodles are available lunchtime only. Mains average $15. Licensed (sake) and BYO. Lunch Wed–Fri , dinner Tues–Sun.
Konditorei Manfredi 106 George St. German cakes and pastries accompanied by delicious coffee; also a full menu of contemporary meals served on the smart upper level with its polished wood floors, licensed bar and outside courtyard. There's a sandwich bar for healthy takeaways. Mon–Sat 8.30am–5.30pm.
Morty's Cnr Brisbane and Wellington streets. Popular foodcourt near the cinema, with lots of Asian kitchens including Thai and Chinese. Also fish and chips, pancakes, and a juice bar. Licensed. Daily 10am–9.30pm.
O'Keefe's Hotel 124 George St. Popular pub meals, including a big range of international dishes such as curries and seafood are on offer, and there are cheap $9 lunch specials.
Pasta Pasta 75 George St. You can fill up here on freshly made pasta (small $8.30. medium, $12.40, large $13.50) with delicious and inventive as well as traditional sauces. There's plenty of choice for vegetarians, too, such as roasted vegetables in a napoli sauce, or pesto with pumpkin and pinenuts. Takeaway prices are substantially cheaper. Mon–Sat 10.30am–7.30pm, to 8.30pm Thurs–Sat.
Pierre's Coffee House and Restaurant 88 George St ⓣ03/6331 6835. Established in the 1950s by a French immigrant, *Pierre's* has the feel of a classic café-bistro. There's great coffee, fabulous hot chocolate, gorgeous cakes and Tasmanian wines by the glass. Mon–Thurs 10am–9pm, Fri 10am–10pm, Sat 10am–2pm & 6pm–10pm.
Star of Siam Cnr Charles and Paterson streets ⓣ03/6331 2786. Launceston's favourite Thai restaurant, worth booking on weekends. Mains average around $15. Licensed and BYO. Lunch Tues–Fri, dinner nightly.
Stillwater Ritchies Mill Arts Centre, Paterson St ⓣ03/6331 4153. Very popular riverside café/restaurant and wine bar (with an extensive local wine list) with a great atmosphere. During the day it's an alfresco café, with generous all-day breakfasts and board specials, while at night the menu is more upscale. Licensed and BYO. Daily 10am to late (book for dinner).

Entertainment and nightlife

The *Examiner*, based in Launceston, is the newspaper for the north of Tasmania – Thursday's entertainment section details weekly events. The **Princess Theatre**, 57 Brisbane St (ⓣ03/6323 3666), stages regular drama, opera, ballet and concerts, usually touring from interstate. Behind the theatre, the Earl Arts Centre, 10 Earl St (Ⓣ03/6334 5579), has fringe theatre productions, while the **Silverdome**, out of town on the Bass Highway at Prospect (Ⓣ03/6344 9999), is the venue for major exhibitions as well as entertainment and sports events. Hugely popular AFL football matches are held in **York Park Sports and Entertainment Centre** just near the Inveresk development (details and bookings Ⓦwww.aflintasmania.com), and you can gamble at the **Country Club Casino**, 9km out of town, off the Bass Highway at Prospect Vale (daily noon–1am, Fri & Sat until 4am; bus #61, #64, #65 Ⓣ03/6335 5777). The only **cinema**, the four-screen Village 4, at 163 Brisbane St (Ⓣ03/6331 5066), shows mainstream films. Check the Gay Information Line (see p.1088) for the latest details on the gay scene in Launceston.

Pubs, bars and clubs

Irish Murphy's 211 Brisbane St. Spirited Irish pub with Guinness on tap, live music (Wed to Sun) and pub meals.

Launceston Saloon 191 Charles St Ⓣ03/6331 7355. Always packed out on event nights with a young student crowd. The huge main *Saloon Bar* has pool tables, several plasma screens, local bands (Wed nights) and irregular interstate and international band events, and DJs nights on Friday and Saturday (9.30pm–5/6am; free) when the mezzanine-level becomes a karaoke bar. Big-screen TV and typical pub food served in the *Sports Bar*.

The Lounge Bar 63 St John St. Imposing corner stone building in a former bank is now a sophisticated bar-cum-club with lots of sofas and dance floors on two levels. Touring bands appear here regularly too. Wed & Thurs 6pm to late, Fri & Sat 5pm–5am.

Royal Oak Hotel 14 Brisbane St Ⓣ03/6331 5346. Popular, genial watering hole with live blues and jazz Thursday to Saturday nights. Crowded bistro serves Greek dishes as well as counter meals (mains $12–18). Mon–Sat until midnight, Sun until 10pm.

Royal on George 90 George St Ⓣ03/6331 2526. Renovated glass-fronted, light and colourful pub with an emphasis on food (from 8.30am for breakfast). A modern café-style menu – gourmet sandwiches and salads, pasta and risotto, plus classic but meaty mains. Live rock, jazz or acoustic music Friday and Saturday. Mon–Thurs & Sun until midnight, Fri & Sat to 3am.

Star Bar Café 113 Charles St Ⓣ03/6331 6111. Sophisticated bar with slick, modern decor and pavement tables; brasserie-style Mediterranean food available. There's also pleasant en-suite accommodation upstairs (❹). Daily 11am until late.

Listings

Banks and foreign exchange Commonwealth Bank, 97 Brisbane St; Travelex, 98 St John St (Mon–Fri 9am–5.30pm, Sat 10am–1pm).

Bike rental Bike Hire Tasmania, 83 George St Ⓣ03/6331 1311, Ⓦwww.bikehiretasmania.com.au rents city and touring bikes for $22 day, $123 per week.

Books Fullers Bookshop, 93 St John St.

Camping equipment A good option for renting or buying gear is Allgoods, with stores at 71–79 York St and 60 Elizabeth St. Paddy Pallin, 110 George St, focuses on the top end of the market and sells a wide range of freeze-dried foods, guidebooks and maps.

Car rental Europcar, airport and 112 George St (Ⓣ03/6331 8200 or 1800 030 118) also has 4WDs. Autorent-Hertz, airport and 58 Paterson St (Ⓣ03/6335 1111), also has campervans. For cheaper rates try: Economy Car Rentals, 27 William St (Ⓣ03/6334 3299) or Lo-Cost Auto Rent, 21 Wellington St (Ⓣ03/6334 6202).

Hospital Launceston General, Charles St Ⓣ03/6332 7111.

Internet access Launceston's Online Access Centre is on the ground floor of the State Library, Civic Square.

Motorbike rental Tasmanian Motorcycle Hire, 17 Coachmans Rd, Evandale (Ⓣ03/6391 9139, Ⓦwww.tasmotorcyclehire.com.au; from $115 per day, helmets included).

Pharmacy Amcal Centre Pharmacy, 84 Brisbane St (daily 9am–10pm; Ⓣ03/6331 7777).

Post office 170 Brisbane St, Launceston, TAS 7250.

Swimming The Launceston Swimming Centre, Windmill Hill Reserve (Mon–Fri 6am–7pm, Sat & Sun 9am–7pm except April to Oct daily from 11am; $3.20). Aquarius Roman Baths, 127–133 George

St (☎03/6331 2255), is a self-indulgent, opulent complex of therapeutic warm, hot and cold baths, sauna, steam rooms, gym, massage and solarium (Mon–Fri 9am–9pm, Sat & Sun 9am–6pm; admission to baths and saunas $24 or $40 per couple).

Taxis Taxi ranks are on George Street between Brisbane and Paterson streets, on St John St outside Princes Square. Central Cabs ☎13 10 08; Taxis Combined ☎13 22 27.

Tours Coach Tram Tour Company (☎03/6336 3133) offers city sights tours ($26; 3hr; Jan–April daily 10am & 2pm; May–Dec 10am) leaving from the Gateway centre. Tigerline (☎03/6272 6611 or 1300 653 633) has a programme of big commercial coach tours: Launceston city sights and Cataract Gorge (3hr; $49); Mole Creek caves and the wildlife park (full day $109); Seahorse World at Beauty Point and Hillwood Strawberry Farm (half-day; $69); and Cradle Mountain tour (full day $113), which gives 3hr 30min at the park. Tiger Wilderness Tours has the most interesting day-trips (☎03/6394 3212, Ⓦwww.tigerwilderness.com.au) including Tamar Valley Eco Tour, with a morning of four short walks (half-day; $60); Cradle Mountain including Mole Creek caves and Sheffield, and a walk around Dove Lake (full day $100); Meander Falls Remote Walk, including a 6hr return walk and lunch (full day $120). Tasmanian Expeditions (see p.1072) lead rock-climbing at Cataract Gorge (half-day $100, full day $180) and canoeing, as well as longer trekking, cycling and rafting tours.

Around Launceston

Before launching yourself into the beauty of the Tamar Valley, there are several fine Georgian farming estates and mansions around the well-preserved towns of **Evandale** and **Longford**, just 20-odd kilometres south of Launceston. If you're here in winter, you might consider joining the ski crowd who descend upon **Ben Lomond National Park**, southeast of Launceston; out of season, this is fine bushwalking country.

Evandale and Longford

Though no public transport runs to **EVANDALE**, 20km southeast of Launceston, this National Trust-classified town from the 1830s rewards a visit, particularly for its long-running Sunday market. At the **Evandale Tourism and History Centre** on High Street (daily 10am–3pm; ☎03/6391 8128), pick up a free *Heritage Walk* brochure. Otherwise, the map opposite the popular eat-in *Ingleside Bakery* (licensed), in restored 1867 council chambers, also on High Street, points out notable features – many of the old buildings bear descriptive plaques. The **Clarendon Arms Hotel**, on nearby Russell Street (☎03/6391 8181; ❷), was built in 1847 on the site of the former convict station; its mural-covered interior depicts the early history of Tasmania. The **Evandale Market**, held in Falls Park on Logan Road (Sun 8am–2pm), attracts large crowds to its varied hundred-odd stalls which include local organic produce. Once a year in late February, Evandale hosts the three-day-long **National Penny Farthing Championships** as part of its Village Fair; the races using the old bikes are quite a sight. Eight kilometres south of Evandale via the C416 and the C418 is the National Trust-owned **Clarendon Homestead** on the banks of the South Esk River (daily 10am–5pm, to 4pm June–Aug; $7.70), a grand white neo-classical-style country house built in 1838 for a wealthy wool grower and furnished in Georgian style; it's worth coming just for the lovely conservatory tea rooms at the front.

Australia's oldest continually running **racecourse** was established in 1847 at **LONGFORD**, 20km southwest of Launceston. It's a country classic, with the big event the New Year's Day Longford Cup. On the outskirts of town, along Woolmers Lane (C521), **Brickendon Estate** (Tues–Sun 9.30am–5.30pm; closed July & Aug; $8.25; ☎03/6391 1251) was set up from land granted to William Archer in 1824; fascinatingly, it's still run by Archers as a working sheep property. Generations of the family saw fit to preserve the early architecture and walking into the farm compound with its huge Dutch-style wooden barns is like setting foot into the film *The Girl With the Pearl Earring*. This ramshackle appeal is the setting for **accommodation** in absolutely charming old estate cottages (❺). William's brother Thomas Archer established his estate **Woolmers** in 1819 – just a few kilometres further along the hawthorn-hedgerow-lined Woolmers Lane – which lasted through six generations of Archers until 1994. The original Georgian bungalow with its dark warren of rooms still stands, as does the impressive Italianate villa that was adjoined in 1843. A guided tour of the house, with its grand dining room still set up as it was for a royal visit in 1868, is fascinating as much for the interiors as for the family story (daily 11am, 12.30pm, 2pm, 3.30pm; $18 includes Rose Garden). It's a scenic spot too, perched above the Macquarie River with views across the Great Western Tiers. The **National Rose Garden** (self-guided tour of grounds and garden $12), with over 4000 rose plants, has been set up in former orchards.

Ben Lomond National Park

The plateau of the **Ben Lomond Range**, over 1300m high and 84 square kilometres in area, lies entirely within **Ben Lomond National Park**, 50km southeast of Launceston. A small ski village sits below **Legges Tor** (1572m), the second-highest point in Tasmania, and can be reached in an hour from Launceston; above it the bumpy outline of the range's steep cliffs dominates the horizon. The **ski season** runs from mid-July to the end of September, and **accommodation** is limited to the *Ben Lomond Creek Inn* (Ⓣ03/6372 2444; bunk rooms ❹, half-board rooms ❽), which is usually booked out at weekends. However, the region's accessibility means there's no real need to stay. **Meals** are available at the inn, or there's fast food from the ski resort kiosk.

An all-day pass on the **ski lifts** costs around $40 (more details at Ⓦwww.ski.com.au/resorts/benlomond). Some ski rental is available on the mountain but there's a better range at Launceston Sports Centre, 88A George St (Ⓣ03/6331 4777). The Gateway Centre (see p.1117) can advise on ski packages and the **bus service** from Launceston which operates during the season. If you're driving, be warned that the final 20km to the ski village is unsealed and the last leg, **Jacobs Ladder**, is very steep, with hairpin bends, sheer drops and no safety barriers. You must carry wheel chains, which can be rented from the snowline. Otherwise, you can park just before the Ladder and take the **shuttle bus**. Outside the ski season, all services cease and the businesses close down, but the scenery and the alpine vegetation are magnificent enough to lure **bushwalkers**. There's a 12.5km track from Carr Villa, on the slopes of Ben Lomond, to Legges Tor. Bush **camping** is permitted anywhere in the national park, but Carr Villa is an informal camping area with a pit toilet. For more information, contact the ranger (Ⓣ03/6230 8233).

The Tamar Valley

To the north of Launceston is the beautiful **Tamar Valley**, where, for 64km, the tidal waters wind through orchards, vineyards, strawberry farms, lavender plantations, forested hills and grazing land. Only the Batman Bridge, near Deviot, and the APPM Wood Mill and Bell Bay Power Station, near the river's mouth, spoil the idyllic scenery.

West of the Tamar

The West Tamar Highway (A7) follows the line of the Tamar River from Launceston to Beauty Point and **Brady's Lookout State Reserve** provides magnificent views of the Tamar Valley and Ben Lomond; you can see as far as Low Head, 34km away. Rather than head straight along the highway, it's worth detouring for a stretch through **ROSEVEARS**, on a picturesque sweep of road along the riverbanks that's popular with cyclists. Along the way, stop at the **St Matthias Vineyard** (daily 10am–5pm) for some wine-tasting, Tasmanian cheeses and great views. In the village itself there's the **Waterbird Haven Trust** (daily 9am–dusk; $4), extending for half a kilometre along the waterfront, and the 1831 *Rosevears Tavern*, where you can have a drink. A few kilometres west of Rosevears is **Notley Gorge State Reserve**, a beautiful fern gorge with a number of walking tracks, reached by turning west off the highway at Legana. Back on the highway, **EXETER** has the useful **Tamar Visitor Centre** (daily 9am–5pm; ⓣ1800 637 989, ⓦwww.tamarvalley.com.au), an Online Access Centre on Main Road, and the excellent *Exeter Bakery*. Further north, **BEACONSFIELD** was once at the centre of Tasmania's former gold-mining area, and the mining ruins are still visible; two former mine buildings house the interesting, interactive **Grub Shaft Gold & Heritage Museum** (daily 10am–4pm; $8).

At gorgeous **Beauty Point**, the fascinating **Seahorse World** at Inspection Head Wharf (tours 9.30am–3.30pm, every 30min; $15; 45min–1hr; ⓦwww.seahorseworld.com.au) is the world's only commercial seahorse farm. By successfully harvesting the difficult-to-breed creatures for aquariums and the Chinese market, the farm is helping save those in the oceans from further depletion. The **Australian Maritime College** (AMC), established in Beauty Point in 1978, has developed the interpretative material at the farm, and there is also an interesting display about the AMC on the top floor, beside a café with stunning water views. There's more curious creatures next door in the **Platypus House** (daily 9am–4pm; ⓦwww.platypushouse.com.au; guided one-hour tour $15); platypus are elusive in the wild but you can catch a glimpse here (also Tasmanian frogs, butterflies and lizards). The AMC lends Beauty Point bags of atmosphere, with a big busy training ship moored at the marina by the *Beauty Point Hotel*. From the jetty here, the **Shuttlefish Ferry** crosses the Tamar to George Town (2–4 daily except Tues; $9 one-way, $16 return, bikes $1; 20 min; 2hr, $26 cruise to Low Head daily except Tues 11am; bookings ⓣ03/6383 4479). The faded motel units at the *Beauty Point Hotel* (ⓣ03/6383 4363, ⓔbeautypointhotel@bigpond.com.au; ❸) have fantastic river views. The pub itself is more upmarket, with tables outside on the water and views from the dining room, which has an excellent menu featuring a wide range of seafood. For somewhere really special to stay, *Pomona* (ⓣ03/6383 4073, ⓦwww.pomonabandb.com.au), just across the road on a rise above the river, has B&B accommodation (❺) in a charming federation-style house with great views from the verandah-cum-breakfast nook, or luxurious timber self-catering cottages (❻ includes breakfast hamper).

East of the Tamar: George Town and Low Head

Leaving Launceston and heading north along the East Tamar Highway, it's only a few minutes before you're zooming through scenic countryside, passing through Dilston where cows graze in paddocks at the base of bush-covered hills. After Hillwood and its famous strawberry farm, you're headed for the port of **GEORGE TOWN**, one of the oldest towns in Australia, where Colonel Paterson landed in 1804 to begin settlement of northern Tasmania. The **George Town Visitor Information Centre** is on Main Road on the way into town (daily 10am–4pm; ⓣ03/6382 1700); George Town's **Online Access Centre** is on Macquarie Street.

Despite its history, George Town isn't particularly compelling, with only one colonial building to look at, **The Grove**, an elegant stone Georgian mansion at 25 Cimitiere St (daily 10am–5pm; $6). More appealing is **LOW HEAD**, 5km north, with twenty-four National Trust-listed buildings, whitewashed cottages and rambling houses, all set amid extensive parkland. The original convict-built **Pilot Station** now houses a **museum** (daily 9am–5pm; $5), which has a display of maritime memorabilia. There's also a **Little penguin colony** at Low Head; guided tours are offered each evening at sunset (1hr; $14; bookings on ⓣ0418 361 860). Cruises to a nearby **fur seal** colony on Tenth Island are also on offer with Seal and Sea Adventure Tours (3–4 hours; $125; bookings ⓣ0419 357 028, ⓦwww.sealandsea.com). You can catch a ferry to Beauty Point from George Town with the Shuttlefish Ferry (see above).

George Town **accommodation** includes the *George Town Heritage Hotel*, at 77 Macquarie St (ⓣ03/6382 2655; ❹), the oldest pub in town but with few discernible traces of its early-nineteenth-century roots. On the warfront, the pretty wooden *Pier Hotel*, at 5 Elizabeth St (ⓣ03/6382 1300; rooms ❺, apartments ❻), has rooms upstairs in the old part, modern motel-style rooms on the waterfront, and self-catering units; the **food** here is good, from pasta to Asian curries. Opposite, at 4 Elizabeth St, is the *Traveller's Lodge* (ⓣ03/6382 3261; dorms $18, rooms ❷), a backpackers' in a pretty 1870 home, with a clean, modern interior.

In Low Head, you can stay in heritage-style cottage accommodation at the Pilot Station (see above; ⓣ03/6382 1143; ❹), and at *Belfont Cottages*, at 178 Low Head Rd (ⓣ03/6382 1841; ❺, with breakfast provisions supplied), or **camp** at *Low Head Caravan Park*, 136 Low Head Rd (ⓣ03/6382 1573; vans ❷, cabins ❸).

Around George Town: the Pipers River wine region

Heading east of George Town, a pleasant day can be spent exploring the **vineyards** around the **Pipers River area**, which produce distinctly flavoured, crisp and fresh cool-climate wines. The *Tamar Valley Wine Route* brochure, available from the information centres in Launceston (p.1117) and Exeter (see p.1127), covers twenty-one vineyards in the Tamar Valley and Pipers Brook area (virtually all open daily 10am–5pm) and offering free tastings. One of the best known is **Pipers Brook Vineyard** (Ninth Island is their other label), on the sealed C818, 2km off the B82. Established in 1974, the winery is housed in a modern, architect-designed complex, with self-guided tours. It also has a café (mains $15.50) and vine-covered courtyard. Nearby, also on the C818, lake-fronted **Janz** makes premium champagne; there's information on the wine-making process in the interpretive centre. The friendly, small-scale **Delamere Vineyard** on the B82, specializes in Pinot Noir and Chardonnay. Wine tours to the region operate from Launceston (see Tours, p.1125).

The Midland Highway

The **Midland Highway** is a fast three-hour route between Hobart and Launceston, more or less following the old coaching road, although you'll have to detour if you want to visit some of the towns on the way. Redline has several daily **bus** services between Hobart and Launceston, stopping at the major midland towns.

Campbell Town and Ross

Beyond **CAMPBELL TOWN** – a rather plain community originally settled by Scots but the Midlands' major centre – you drive south through sheep-grazing countryside, eventually turning off the highway to **ROSS**, 2km east. Also settled by Scots, this has a very secluded, rural feel; elm trees line the main Church Street, creating a beautiful avenue, while paddocks with grazing sheep stretch alongside. Old stone buildings along the idyllic street are well preserved, including the characterful sandstone *Man O'Ross Hotel*. From the grounds of St Johns Church of England, one of the town's three pretty churches, there are views of the Macquarie River, spanned by the sandstone **Ross Bridge**, designed by John Lee Archer and built by convicts in 1836; the intricate stone carvings on its three arches earned the convict stonemason a free pardon. A melancholy walk in the other direction from the church leads down to the original Ross burial ground and past the site of the **Female Factory**, actually a prison, where women convicts were held before being sent to properties as assigned servants. You can **stay** in several of the old cottages dotted about town: *Colonial Cottages of Ross* (Ⓣ03/6381 5354, ❺–❻ including breakfast provisions) has five to choose from. The *Man O'Ross Hotel* (Ⓣ03/6381 5445, ❸ including breakfast) has several intimate rooms in which to **eat or drink**, and shared-bathroom accommodation upstairs. There's **camping** at the pleasant *Ross Caravan Park* on Bridge Street (Ⓣ03/6381 5224; cabins ❶–❷). Two recommended **cafés** face each other across the main street: the cosy *Bakery Tea Rooms* and the more contemporary-style *That Place In Ross*. The Tasmanian Wool Centre on Church Street (daily 9am–5pm; Ⓣ03/6381 5466) acts as an **information centre** and also houses a wool exhibition and history museum (entry by donation) and has **Internet access**.

Oatlands

Back on the Midland Highway, it's 88km south from Ross to **OATLANDS**, which has Australia's greatest concentration of colonial **Georgian buildings**: 140 in two square kilometres, most built by convicts. Many are now occupied by antique and bric-à-brac shops, B&Bs and guesthouses. The most striking edifice is the **Callington Mill** and its outbuildings; the partly restored **windmill** was built in 1837 and remained in operation until 1892. From the top there are fine views of the town and the surrounding countryside; ask to go up to the adjacent **Dolls At The Mill** (daily 10am-4pm; $2), an extensive doll collection in the old mill residence. The best way to see the town is to go on one of Peter Fielding's guided **heritage walks** (Ⓣ03/6254 1135; $5), which visit several other buildings, including the Old Gaol and courthouse. His spooky evening **ghost tour** commences outside the mill (9pm during daylight savings, 8pm rest of year; $8).

For **food**, the cosy *Blossom's Georgian Tea Rooms*, 116 High St (Ⓣ03/6254 1516), serves scones and light lunches. The **Central Tasmania Tourism Centre**, 85 High St (daily 9am–5pm; Ⓣ03/6254 1212) can book **accommodation** from the many colonial-style B&Bs in the town; a good choice is the central *Oatlands Lodge*, at 92 High St (Ⓣ03/6254 1444; ❺). Oatlands' **Online Access Centre** is in the library at 68 High St.

The Great Western Tiers and Central Plateau

Deloraine, on the **Meander River**, is nestled in a valley of rich farmland dominated by **Quamby Bluff** (1256m) and the **Great Western Tiers**, where the Central Plateau drops abruptly to the surrounding plains. On the Bass Highway, it's roughly equidistant from Devonport (51km) and Launceston (48km). From Deloraine the **Lake Highway** begins, rising up over the Western Tiers to the Central Plateau, with its thousands of lakes. To the west of Deloraine are the extensive **cave systems** around **Mole Creek**, while **Walls of Jerusalem National Park** is accessed from **Western Creek**, 32km southwest of Deloraine.

Deloraine and around

DELORAINE is a delightful hilly town, often shrouded in mist, even on summer mornings, and divided into two parts by the bubbling **Meander River**. Although the area was settled by Europeans in the 1830s, Deloraine didn't really begin to develop until after 1846, and today it's a National Trust-classified town. **West Parade** follows the river, facing the park; at no. 17 the Georgian **Bonney's Inn** dates from 1830 and is the town's oldest remaining building (now a B&B; see opposite). At the next block, Westbury Place rises up steeply from West Parade; if you climb the hill you'll reach the tall spire-dominated **St Marks Church**, built in 1860, and there's a scenic **lookout** that gives a panoramic view over the town and the Western Tiers to the south. Deloraine has a café culture, plenty of secondhand and antique shops, and a small, alternative arts-and-crafts scene, witnessed regularly at the **market** on the first Saturday of every month across the river opposite the *Apex Caravan Park*, and at the annual **Tasmanian Craft Fair**, a huge event held over four days in early November.

Close to prime **bushwalking** areas in the Western Tiers, Deloraine is an established base for walkers. Popular tracks are the short walk to **Alum Cliffs**, overlooking the Mersey River Gorge (40min return), signposted on the road between Mole Creek and Chudleigh; a difficult walk to **Quamby Bluff**, renowned for its myrtle rainforest (6.5km; 6hr; beginning at Brodies Road, off the Lake Highway); the track to **Liffey Falls** (8km; 3hr; beginning at the picnic ground 5km west of the tiny community of Liffey), and the day-walk to **Meander Falls** through the Meander Forest Reserve, about 25km south of Deloraine, reached via the small settlement of Meander and Meander Falls Road (10km; 6–7hr; beginning from the picnic ground; Tiger Wilderness Tours does an excellent tour from Launceston – see p.1125). There's a walker registration and information booth at the Meander Falls car park. A free leaflet issued by Forestry Tasmania, *Visiting the Great Western Tiers*, has a map of the Meander Forest Reserve and tracks; you can pick it up from the Deloraine information centre (see opposite).

The western end of the Great Western Tiers overlooks **MOLE CREEK**, 24km west of Deloraine. Here, you can get up close to some Tasmanian devils at the **Trowunna Wildlife Park** (daily 9am–5pm; $14), or buy delicious local honey from **Stephen's Leatherwood Honey Factory** (Mon–Fri 8am–5pm). Surrounding the town, the **Mole Creek Karst National Park** has a network of over two hundred underground caves. About 14km west of Mole Creek are two rather spectacular ones: **Marakoopa Cave**, with huge caverns, streams, pools and glow worms (daily 10am, 11.15am, 1pm, 2.30pm & 4pm; 50–80min; $11); and 6km further west the smaller but more richly decorative **King Solomons Cave**, with stalactites and stalagmites (daily 10.30am, 11.30am, 12.30pm, 2pm, 3pm & 4pm; 40–60min; $11). Wild Cave Tours (Ⓣ03/6367 8142, Ⓦwww.wildcavetours.com) offers excellent $85 half-day and $170 full-day caving tours of the Mole Creek caves, underground streams and subterranean systems. Places to **stay** in **Mole Creek** range from an excellent campsite (Ⓣ03/6363 1150) to the congenial *Mole Creek Guest House* (Ⓣ03/6363 1399, Ⓦwww.molecreekgh.com.au; ❺), with its own restaurant and tourist information.

Deloraine practicalities

The two major **bus** companies both make regular stops in Deloraine. Redline stops daily on its Launceston–Devonport service, and its Launceston–Deloraine service which continues on to Mole Creek once daily on weekdays; and TassieLink on its Launceston–Queenstown service (3–4 weekly). The depot for Redline is the video shop by the roundabout at 29 West Church St (Ⓣ03/6362 2046); TassieLink is based at *Sullivans Restaurant*, at 17 West Parade. The **Great Western Tiers Visitor Information Centre**, at 98 Emu Bay Rd (daily 9am–5pm; Ⓣ03/6362 3471, Ⓦwww.greatwesterntiers.org.au), has maps, details on walking times and conditions, and makes free accommodation bookings; the centre is housed in an old inn with an attached folk museum ($7), which features a series of vast woven silk wall hangings, made by the local community. The **Online Access Centre** is behind the library at 21 West Parade.

Operators leading **outdoor activities** in the area include Cradle Wilderness on the Edge 4x4 Tours (Ⓣ03/6363 1173; half- and full-day tours; $75/$120); Jahadi Indigenous Experiences (Ⓣ03/6363 6172, Ⓦwww.jahadi.com.au; 4WD tours), and the Tasmanian Fly Fishing School (Ⓣ03/6362 3441, Ⓦwww.tasmanianflyfishing.com.au).

There's a wide range of **accommodation** choices in Deloraine. The popular, clean and well-run *Highview Lodge YHA Hostel*, at 8 Blake St (Ⓣ03/6362 2996, Ⓔbodach@microtech.com.au; dorms $19, rooms ❷; bike rental available), set on a hill commanding unparalleled views of Quamby Bluff; it's about a ten-minute walk from the information centre. In the centre of town, the big old *Deloraine Hotel* faces the river on the corner of Emu Bay Road and Barrack Street, and has shared-bathroom and en-suite rooms upstairs (Ⓣ03/6362 2022; ❸). Just across Barrack Street, a more upmarket choice is the Georgian *Bonney's Inn*, at 17 West Parade (Ⓣ03/6362 2974, Ⓦwww.bonneys-inn.com; ❺), which has spacious suites. A good motel on the outskirts of town is *Mountain View Country Inn*, 144 Emu Bay Rd (Ⓣ03/6362 2633; ❹), where the row of units affords great Tiers' views. *Bonney's Farm*, off Weetah Road, 4km northwest of Deloraine (Ⓣ03/6362 2122; ❹), has a guesthouse (B&B) and self-contained two- or three-bed units. The exquisite French-run guesthouse/restaurant *Calstock*, on the Lake Highway just outside Deloraine (Ⓣ03/6362 2642, Ⓦwww.calstock.net; ❼–❽), serves country-style meals created from local organic ingredients. You can **camp** at the riverside *Apex Caravan Park*, 51 West Parade (Ⓣ03/6362 2345).

In Deloraine there are plenty of informal **places to eat** on the main street, Emu Bay Road. The pick of the lot is the *Deloraine Deli* at no. 36 (Mon–Fri 9am–5pm, Sat 9am–2.30pm), a combination deli counter and tearoom with meals under $11 and great coffee. The best pub meals can be found at the *Deloraine Hotel*.

Walls of Jerusalem National Park

The **Walls of Jerusalem National Park** is on the western side of the Central Plateau, a series of five mountain peaks that enclose a central basin, an isolated area noted for its lakes, pencil pines and the biblical names of its various features. The best time to visit is November through to April; people have died of exposure here, so make sure you're well prepared. You'll need the *Walls of Jerusalem National Park Map and Notes* ($9.10; see p.1072).

As the Walls of Jerusalem is the only national park in Tasmania that you can't drive into, the walk in begins outside the park boundaries. From King Solomons Cave (see p.1131), head south, following the Mersey River and the unsealed road east of Lake Rowallan; the car park is at Howells Bluff. You walk through wilderness into the park, which is isolated and lacking even basic facilities, without a ranger (although rangers do patrol). However, the track is well kept, with boardwalks laid down over boggy areas, and there's plenty of clean water to drink from the streams and lakes. The few small leaky huts are really for emergencies only. If you just want to walk into the park to the central basin (through **Herods Gate**, with views of Barn Bluff and Cradle Mountain to the northwest), set up camp and then walk back, it's a 14km return hike, which takes seven or eight hours altogether, going at a steady pace over two days. The walk begins with a steep climb then levels out on the plateau. There are numerous routes to the various peaks and lakes – from **Damascus Gate** you get stunning views of Cradle Mountain–Lake St Clair National Park immediately west – and an experienced, well-equipped walker could spend a couple of days here. If you can afford the prices, you can always go on an **organized walk**: the recommended Tiger Trails (see p.1072) has a four-day expedition ($599) or a seven-day combination Cradle Mountain trip ($1399), both ex-Launceston, while Tasmanian Expeditions (see p.1072) offers a six-day circuit walk ($1190), departing from Launceston (Oct–April), as well as the combo. TassieLink can bring you to the beginning of the walk into the park on their summer-only (Nov–April) service from Launceston to Lake St Clair via Deloraine, Mole Creek and Marakoopa Cave, while Maxwell's operates on demand from Devonport ($180 1–4 people; $45 per person 5 or more people) and Launceston ($240/$60).

The Central Plateau

At its northern and eastern edges, the **Central Plateau** is rimmed by the long crest of the Great Western Tiers (1440m). At over a thousand metres above sea level, the plateau is often covered in frost and subject to sleet and snowstorms in winter. The **Great Lake** lies on the plateau about 8km from the escarpment, and only 40km from Deloraine, along the Lake Highway that continues to **BOTHWELL**, the plateau's only town, ending at Melton Mowbray, where it joins the Midland Highway. The major lakes can be reached from roads leading off the Lake Highway. To the west, between Cradle Mountain–Lake St Clair National Park and below the Walls of Jerusalem National Park, is the inaccessible "Land of Three Thousand Lakes".

The Central Plateau has few inhabitants – only around eight hundred live here year-long – but it's full of **fishing shacks**, and on a fine weekend the population sometimes swells to 25,000. It's also the base for the **Hydro Electricity Commission** (HEC): the countless high-altitude lakes are used as water storage for the generation of electricity. Several temporary HEC villages set up for hydroelectrical workers have been transformed into lodge-style accommodation. One is the *Bronte Park Highland Village* (Ⓣ03/6289 1126,

Ⓦwww.bronteparkhighlandvillage.com.au; dorms $20, cabins ❹, lodge ❹, spa cottages ❻), which also has a campsite, EFTPOS facilities, a dining room and bar, a store selling groceries and fuel, and is ideally situated for **Lake St Clair** (25km; see p.1160) and nearby **Lake Big Jim**, popular trout-fishing spots. Ausprey Tours (Ⓣ03/6330 2612, Ⓦwww.gotroutfishtasmania.com.au) offers **fly-fishing tuition**.

To reach the *Bronte Park Highland Village*, take the bone-shattering Marlborough Highway (B11), which runs southwest off the Lake Highway as it curves around the bottom of the lake to Miena. TassieLink drops off at the *Bronte Park* turn-off on the Lyell Highway on their Hobart–Queenstown scheduled service.

The Bass Strait Islands

Located in the rough waters of the Bass Strait, battered by the Roaring Forties, are two groups of islands: the Hunter group, dominated by **King Island** off the northwest tip of Tasmania, and the Furneaux group, the largest of which is **Flinders Island**, lying just beyond the northeast corner of the state. In the nineteenth century, sealers roamed the Bass Strait, but the two main islands now consist of low-key rural communities, while several tall lighthouses, and many shipwrecks offshore are testimony to the turbulence of the sea at King Island.

You can go by **ship** to Flinders Island from Bridport (see p.1115) on the northeast coast of Tasmania: Southern Shipping Co (ex-Bridport Mon, ex-Flinders Tues; departure times depend on tides; Ⓣ03/6356 1753) operates a car and passenger ferry. Car costs are prohibitive, but the return passenger fare of $88, which must be booked two weeks in advance, is good value, if you can put up with a possibly rough, eight-hour trip. **Airlines of Tasmania** (Ⓣ03/6359 2312 or 1800 144 460) flies to Flinders Island from Moorabbin Airport, just outside of Melbourne (one-way $200), and from Launceston (one-way $140). Tasmania's regional airline, Tasair (Ⓣ03/6248 5088 or 1800 062 900, Ⓦwww.tasair.com.au), flies daily to King Island from Burnie and Devonport ($180 one-way) with connecting Tasair flights from Hobart; Regional Express (REX; Ⓣ13 17 13) flies from Melbourne Tullamarine daily ($120 one-way).

King Island

King Island, smaller but more heavily populated than Flinders Island, is chiefly known for its rich dairy produce, with crayfish and kelp and wind farming as secondary industries. Green, low and windswept, it can't offer anything like Flinders Island's dramatic landscape, nor its history, though it did witness around sixty **shipwrecks** between 1801 and 1995, and there are several working lighthouses – **Cape Wickham Lighthouse** in the north is one of the tallest in the southern hemisphere. Many of the wreck sites can be dived with King Island Dive Charters (Ⓣ03/6461 1133, Ⓦwww.kingislanddivecharter.com.au).

The island's main town is **CURRIE**, which has a simple museum (daily 2–4pm, closed July & Aug; donation suggested). The bleak former tungsten mining village of **GRASSY** is on the eastern side of the island. The best thing about King Island is the food, with free-range lamb and pork and local beef and wallaby, as well as seafood and delicious creamy milk, which you can drink unpasteurized while on the island – a rare treat. Indeed, top of the list of things to do on the island is a visit to the **King Island Dairy** (Mon–Fri 8am–5pm, Sun 12.30–4pm), 8km north of Currie, for free tastings of the rich local dairy produce; the brie and the thick cream in particular have legendary gourmet status around Australia. The island's **kelp factory** is near Currie's golf course; the bull kelp is gathered from the surrounding shores and left to dry outside the factory on racks – you'll see it as you pass by. Once dry, the kelp is milled into granules and shipped to Scotland to be processed into alginates, used as a gelling agent in products like toothpaste and ice cream.

Practicalities

King Island Coach Tours, 95 Main St, Currie (Ⓣ03/6462 1138 or 1800 647 702), does prebooked **airport transfers** to Currie, which is less than 10km away ($20 for 1–4 passengers), and Grassy. They also run various coach, bushwalking and wildlife **tours**; the best is the short evening tour to see the **Little penguin** community at Grassy (Mon & Thurs; $40). Otherwise, to **get around**, Cheapa Island Car Rentals (Ⓣ03/6462 1603) and King Island Car Rental (Ⓣ03/6462 1282) both do airport drop-offs, or you can rent a **mountain bike** from The Trend, 26 Edward St, Currie ($18 per day). The Trend also provides **tourist information** (daily 8.30am–6.30pm; Ⓣ03/6462 1360) or you can contact **King Island Tourism Inc** (Ⓣ1800 645 014, Ⓦwww.kingisland.org.au).

The most obvious **places to stay** are around Currie. *King Island Gem Accommodation* (Ⓣ03/6462 1260 or 1800 647 702, Ⓦwww.kingislandgem.com.au; airport pick-up included) incorporates several styles and standards on North Road, 1.5km from town: *A-Frame Holiday Homes* (❺), *King Island Cosy Cabins* (❹) or **camping** at *Bass Caravan Park* (vans ❷). Right in the centre, *Parers Hotel* (Ⓣ03/6462 1633, Ⓔparers@kingisland.net.au; ❺) has en-suite, motel-style rooms and serves excellent meals in its bistro. Near the golf course, there's the immaculate *Wave Watcher Holiday Units*, 18 Beach Rd (Ⓣ & Ⓕ03/6462 1517; ❻). Nearby, the rooms at *Boomerang By the Sea* (Ⓣ03/6462 1288; Ⓦwww.bythesea.com.au; ❺) have stunning sea views – even better from the motel's glass-walled **restaurant**. Back in town, *King Island Bakery* makes delicious, gourmet-status pies – including crayfish and King Island beef – and hand-made breads, while *Nautilus Coffee Lounge* is Currie's best café and there's a supermarket (open daily), a bottle shop, a Westpac bank with an ATM, and an **Online Access Centre** at 5 George St.

Flinders Island

With a population of just 800 (nearly half of which are absentee landowners), **FLINDERS ISLAND** is nonetheless the largest of 52 named islands which make up the Furneaux group, first mapped by Tobias Furneaux in 1770. The islands became a base for seal hunters, who slaughtered seals in their tens of thousands and, so legend goes, lured many ships to their demise for a spot of piracy. Ironically, these rough men provided a vital link in the continuing survival of the Tasmanian Aboriginal people, by stealing women to work for them on the islands. When sealing ended, the Aboriginal communities survived by **muttonbird harvesting**, a seasonal industry that continues today with land rights claims in 1995 giving title to several outlying, though unoccupied, islands. In 2005 there was a further breakthrough when Tasmania's Legislative Council approved the handover of Aboriginal-occupied Cape Barren Island (population 75) and Clarke Island (population six), with the land to be managed by the Cape Barren Island Aboriginal Association.

Flinders Island itself played a large part in the tragedy of the Tasmanian Aboriginal people; between 1831 and 1834 the remnants of the Tasmanian tribes were persuaded or forced to accept relocation here. Settled at windswept **Wybalenna** on the west coast of the island, the Aborigines were without adequate food and shelter, and were forcibly Christianized, as their culture was expunged and their numbers dwindled. All that remains of the period of enforced Aboriginal settlement is the **chapel**, built in 1838 at Wybalenna, and the cemetery where only the white graves bear headstones. Of the 135 tribespeople who were sent here, only 47 were still alive when the settlement was abandoned in 1847 and moved to Oyster Cove, near Hobart. The chapel has been restored by the National Trust, but the Aboriginal people of Flinders Island succeeded with their land rights claim on Wybalenna, which was handed over in early 1999, and it is now up to them to decide how they'll run It. Due to political in-fighting, it's presently abandoned but can be visited.

There's a walk to Settlement Point from Wybalenna, where a viewing platform looks over an extensive **muttonbird** rookery – the sight and sound of hundreds of thousands of birds flying to the nesting islands each evening at dusk during the breeding season (Oct to late March) is extraordinary. The only commercial muttonbirding done by Aboriginal people now, however, is on Great Dog Island; in the grounds of **Emita Museum** just a few kilometres northwest of Wybalenna (Sat & Sun: summer 1–5pm; rest of year 1–4pm; $4), there's a replica of a typical **muttonbirding shed**, with its floor lined with tussock grass. Inside, shell necklaces made by the Aboriginal people of Cape Barren Island are displayed, and there are exhibits relating to sealing and shipwrecks.

History aside, isolated Flinders Island is very much a mecca for **bushwalkers** and **rockclimbers**. Only about half of the island is cultivated, and you can walk its entire length in about six days – you can arrange with Flinders Island Adventures to have food and water delivered en route – on the partially signposted north–south **Flinders Trail**, a route designed to provide a sampling of the various terrains. The best-known walk, however, is to the distinctive summit of **Mount Strzelecki** named after the Polish count, explorer and scientist who climbed it in 1842. The climb to the top starts about 10km south of Whitemark, signposted on Trousers Point Road – look out for a brown national park sign – the peak is in the **Strzelecki National Park** in the southwest corner (ranger ⓣ03/6359 2217). Though navigation is easy, it's a strenuous walk – about 5km return (3–5hr). The wind can be fierce at the summit, and mists roll in, so take something wind- and waterproof. **Trousers Point** itself, also in the park, is a good introduction to the delights of the island's deserted beaches. The site, with its fine, white sand and rust-coloured rock formations, is particularly spectacular, with Mount Strzelecki rising up behind the granite headland; there's a free camping area here, with a composting toilet, water tank and bins. Nearby, the **Healing Dreams Retreat** (ⓣ03/6359 4588, ⓦwww.healingdreams.com.au) with its retreat and day spa programmes, is a sign of the direction Flinders is heading. The **Flinders Island Ecology Trail** is a circuit designed to be followed in a car, with five stopping-points where interpretive material is provided. The Trail can be related to the excellent *Furneaux Ecological Notebook* ($7) available at the information office (below). **Walkers Lookout**, in the Darling Range, is a good starting point, offering the best panorama of Flinders and the surrounding islands, with signs pointing out all the landmarks; the other four points on the route highlight bird habitats. You can see the endemic protected **Cape Barren goose** everywhere and likewise the island's wombats.

Practicalities

There are two main bases on Flinders Island: **WHITEMARK**, the administrative centre on the west coast, and **LADY BARRON** in the south, the main fishing area and deep-water port, more picturesque but with few facilities. The post office in Whitemark houses the island's only **bank** – Westpac (Mon–Thurs 11am–2.30pm, Fri 11am–4/5pm) – with EFTPOS, but no ATM facilities. Whitemark's IGA **supermarket**, known locally as Walkers (ⓣ03/6359 2010, ⓔwalkers@vision.net.au; closed Sat afternoon and all Sun, but advance phone or email grocery orders delivered to accommodation), is opposite the pub. Look out for the locally made soaps and facial products for sale. The Lady Baron Multistore, tucked away on Henwood St, is hard to find: head uphill from the pub. It has EFTPOS and a post office plus petrol and is open daily. As there's no public transport, the best option is to **rent a car** and arrange to pick it up at the airport on arrival. Prices are quite reasonable with *Flinders Island Cabin Park* (ⓣ03/6359 2188), who also have mountain bikes for hire, or Bowman Lees Car Hire (ⓣ03/6359 2388). Unfortunately there's no 4WD hire though most of the roads are unsealed.

For general inquiries and **information** on activities such as cruises, scuba diving, fishing, bird-watching and scenic flights, and walking and climbing guides to the island, head for the Area Marketing and Development Office, as you come into Whitemark on Lagoon Rd (Mon–Fri 8.15am–5pm; ⓣ1800 994 477, ⓦwww.flindersislandonline.com.au). *Flinders Island Naturally*, a free visitors' guide with map, can be picked up here and at Tasmanian Travel Centres before you arrive on the island. Flinders Island's **Online Access Centre** is just opposite. Of the island's many available **tours**, one which comes very highly recommended is the good-value boat trip to observe the muttonbirds return to their nests at dusk with Flinders Island Adventures (Oct–March; 2hr 30min–3hr; $30 per person; ⓣ03/6359 4507, ⓔjamesluddington@bigpond.com) with the extremely knowledgable Luddingtons. They also offer several other half- or full-day trips, including cruises to the outer islands, fishing and diving trips and 4WD tours.

There's a **campsite** with water and showers (ⓣ03/6359 8560) and a shop at topaz-fossicking Killiecrankie Bay in the northwest of the island – or you can camp for free at the coastal reserves, or on any crown land as long as it's 500m from the road: designated sites are at Allports Beach, Lillies Beach, North East River and Trousers Point, and all have toilets and fireplaces, though only the last has water and a gas barbecue. You can also camp in more comfort a few kilometres out of Whitemark, near the airport, in pleasant sheltered grounds at the *Flinders Island Cabin Park* on Bluff Rd (ⓣ03/6359 2188; ❸), with tasteful, spacious and mostly en-suite cabins. In Whitemark itself, you can **stay** at the *Interstate Hotel* in the centre of town (ⓣ03/6359 2114; B&B ❸–❹), which has some en-suite rooms and serves huge throw-back-to-another-era meals in the popular bistro (except Sun); it also offers showers and laundry facilities to non-residents. The *Flinders Island Bakery* (closed Sun) has al fresco tables; delicious local wallaby and red wine pies are part of its repertoire and there's real coffee. Otherwise, apart from the pub (above), try the *Flinders Island Sports Club* at the end of the Esplanade for a reasonable meal in pleasant surroundings. In Lady Barron the *Furneaux Tavern*, overlooking Adelaide Bay on the dramatic Franklin Sound, has spacious and attractive cabin-style motel units set in pretty native gardens (ⓣ03/6359 3521; ❹), **meals** are served here in the upmarket *Shearwater Restaurant*, much Flinders Island's best place to eat, or there's simple bar meals in the convivial public bar. You could also try the excellent cabins with beautiful views at *Partridge Farm*, a ten-minute drive from Lady Barron at the end of the road to Badger Corner (ⓣ03/6359 3554; ❺).

The West

Except for the rich beef, dairy and vegetable-growing land along the northwest coast, the western half of Tasmania is untamed. The wild **west coast**, densely forested and battered by the rough Southern Ocean and the Roaring Forties, its shores strewn with huge dead trees washed down from the southwest's many rivers, would probably still be uninhabited if it weren't for the **logging** and **mining** industries. This part of the island is very densely populated (by Tasmanian standards), and the **Bass Highway**, which skirts the northwest coast, passes through two unattractive industrial cities, **Devonport** and **Burnie**. **Rocky Cape National Park** and the town of **Stanley** (originally built by the Van Diemen's Land Company – VDL – which still owns the northwest corner of the state) are the most interesting places for visitors.

Just south of Stanley the highway turns inland to **Smithton**, marking the beginning of a thickly forested region and a logging heartland. The Bass Highway ends at the tiny settlement of **Marrawah**, on the west coast (popular with surfers), where it meets the **Western Explorer** road, which runs south to sleepy **Arthur River** and then through the Arthur Pieman Protected Area to **Corinna**, where the road heads east via Savage River and Waratah onto the A10 (Murchison Highway). Alternatively, you can continue southwards, taking a barge across the Pieman River and then heading on to Zeehan (on the C249) and **Strahan** (on the B27), on the vast **Macquarie Harbour**. To reach Strahan on sealed roads, you have to go back to Marrawah and then to Somerset on the northwest coast, from where the Murchison Highway heads south through a copper- and lead-mining backwater. On the way you pass **Queenstown**, which has been subject to an ecological disaster; its surrounding rainforest has been destroyed, and in its place are bare and chalky hills.

Strahan sits on the edge of the **southwest wilderness**, an area of rugged coastlines, wild rivers, open plains, thick rainforest and spectacular peaks – the wettest part of Australia after the tropical lowlands of north Queensland. It's mostly inaccessible, except to very experienced and well-prepared bushwalkers, but **cruises** leave from Strahan to go up the **Gordon River**, offering a glimpse of its magnificent scenery. Some years ago, a plan to dam the Gordon River below the point where it joins the **Franklin River** put Strahan at the centre of a struggle between environmentalists and the state government. Eventually the federal government stepped in, and, following a landmark High Court ruling in 1983, the whole of the southwest – including the **South West National Park**, the **Franklin Lower Gordon Wild Rivers National Park** and the adjoining heavily glaciated **Cradle Mountain–Lake St Clair National Park** – became a vast, protected **UNESCO World Heritage Area**, occupying twenty percent of the state's land area. From Queenstown, en route to Hobart, the **Lyell Highway** provides limited access to the mainly inaccessible Franklin Lower Gordon park, and to Lake St Clair at **Derwent Bridge**.

The northwest coast

A succession of Tasmania's larger towns dot the conservative, agricultural **northwest coast**, including the cities of **Devonport** and **Burnie**, and the smaller community of older **Stanley**, on a peninsula jutting into the Bass Strait.

The **Bass Highway**, which connects them, becomes spectacularly beautiful beyond Wynyard, passing Table Cape, Boat Harbour Beach and Rocky Cape National Park, though it skirts the very northwest tip (privately owned by the Van Diemen's Land Company). At the end of the highway is **Marrawah**, from where you can head to Arthur River for a cruise. Redline runs daily services from Devonport to Burnie, and from Burnie to Smithton, stopping at all towns along the Bass Highway; there is no public transport to Marrawah or Arthur River.

Devonport and around

The industrial port of **DEVONPORT**, which in 1959 replaced Launceston as the terminal of the **Bass Strait ferry**, the *Spirit of Tasmania*, is not the most inspiring first point of contact with Tasmania. As the ship makes its slow progress up the Mersey River, you might almost think you're arriving at a 1950s English seaport, but for the tin-roofed weatherboard bungalows, the brittle quality of the light, the bush-covered hills to the east and a *McDonald's* on the waterfront. As a jumping-off point for Cradle Mountain, the Overland Track and the rugged west coast, Devonport has developed a significant tourism infrastructure – car-rental companies, bus companies, camping stores and backpacking information – and though it's hardly a destination in itself, it makes a good **base** for trips into the surrounding countryside.

Arrival and information

Thousands of people arrive in Devonport on the *Spirit of Tasmania* **Bass Strait ferries** (see p.1069) from Melbourne and Sydney; the ferries dock at the terminal in East Devonport, just across the Mersey River from the city centre. As the boats have their own tourist information and booking centre, you might have made all your arrangements on board. If not, there are company representatives and car hire desks in the terminal, and you can buy bus passes and tickets here. Most passengers head immediately for the waiting Redline and TassieLink **express buses** to Launceston and Hobart. Other bus routes leave from the depots in town (see Buses, p.1141). If you decide to stay, you can get to the city centre by walking north for a short distance to the bottom of Murray Street, where the ferry *Torquay* crosses the river (on demand Mon–Sat 7.45am–6pm; $2, bikes $0.50).

Devonport Airport is 10km east of the city; taxis into Devonport cost about $20 and it's a good idea to prebook (Taxis Combined ⓣ03/6424 1431). In town, staff at the **Tasmanian Travel and Information Centre**, 92 Formby Rd (daily 7.30am–5pm and until 9pm when day-sailings arrive; ⓣ03/6424 4466), book accommodation, tours and travel including car hire, sell bus passes, National Park passes, YHA membership, *See Tasmania* cards, fishing licences, and maps and specialist guides. For a full range of Tasmaps, bushwalking tips and local knowledge of the area visit the excellent **Backpackers Barn**, 10–12 Edward St (Mon–Sat 9am–6pm; ⓣ03/6424 3628, ⓦwww.backpackersbarn.com.au), which specializes in planning itineraries, booking bushwalking transport charters and tours to Cradle Mountain and other destinations with the in-house Tasmanian Tour Company (ⓣ03/6423 4509, ⓦwww.tasmaniantourcompany.com.au), and renting and selling equipment for bushwalkers; it also offers travellers a day-room, showers ($2) and huge lockers ($1 per day, $5 per week) and there's a great organic café, *Rosehip*. The huge Allgoods, at 6 Formby Rd (ⓣ03/6424 7099; closed Sun), sells and rents out gear, too. The Redline depot is opposite Backpackers Barn; TassieLink

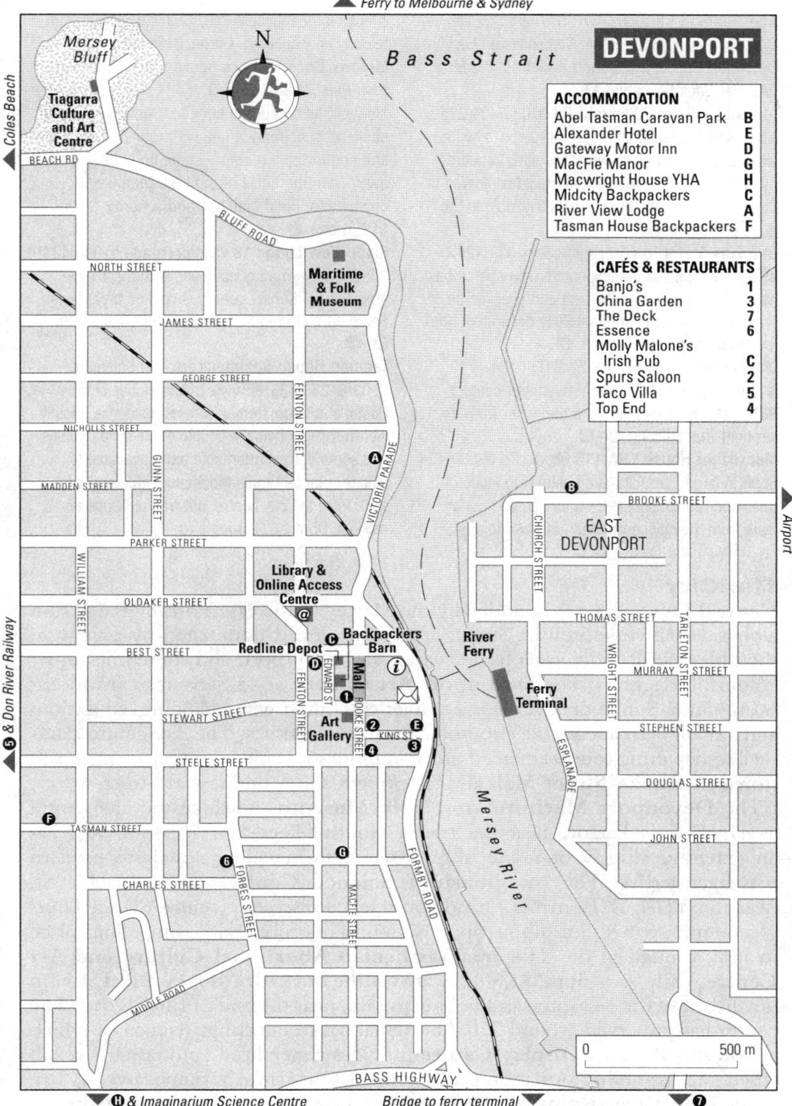

leaves from the tourist information centre, which sells tickets for both. Devonport's **Online Access Centre** is at the library at 21 Oldaker St.

Accommodation

Devonport has plenty of **accommodation**, mainly intended for ferry passengers. Hotels, motels and B&Bs take advantage of the summer trade to raise their prices.

Abel Tasman Caravan Park 6 Wright St, East Devonport ☎03/6427 8794. Campsites on East Devonport Beach, just a short walk from the ferry terminal. Vans ❷, cabins ❸

Alexander Hotel 78 Formby Rd ☎03/6424 2252. Neat, well-furnished, shared-bathrooms, all with sinks and some with views of the port. TV room, plus tea and coffee room; light breakfast served in the dining room and other meals available in the good pub bistro. ❷

Gateway Motor Inn 16 Fenton St ☎03/6424 4922. Quiet and centrally located, Devonport's best hotel offers views over the port and river mouth. Rooms are spacious and tastefully decorated. Bar, restaurant and room service. ❺

MacFie Manor 44 MacFie St ☎03/6424 1719. A rambling, two-storey, early-twentieth-century B&B that has distant views of the water from its wrought-iron balcony. ❹–❺

Macwright House YHA 115 Middle Rd ☎03/6424 5696. A large, barracks-like hostel with loads of rules and regulations. More than half an hour's walk from the city centre and not close to any shops, but the local Mersey Bus will get you from the city on weekdays. Dorms $13, rooms ❶

Midcity Backpackers Above *Molly Malone's Irish Pub*, 34 Best St ☎03/6424 1898, ⓔmollymalones@vantagegroup.com.au. Convenient backpackers' accommodation, with four-bed dorms and comfortable rooms – some en suite – well away from the noise of the Irish theme-pub downstairs. Good facilities and security. Dorms $15, rooms ❷

River View Lodge 18 Victoria Parade ☎03/6424 7357. A waterfront guesthouse with a convivial atmosphere. Serves generous cooked breakfasts. Some en-suite rooms but most share bathroom. ❸–❹

Tasman House Backpackers 169 Steele St ☎03/6423 2335, ⓦwww.tasmanhouse.com. Hostel in a large, former nurses' residence. Mostly well-furnished twins, a couple of en-suite doubles and some dorms. Affordable tours available to places such as Cradle Mountain. Fifteen minutes' walk from the city centre, but free pick-ups on request. Dorms $15, rooms ❷–❸

The City

Central Devonport is bounded by the Mersey to the east; Formby Road runs alongside it, while Stewart Street, at right angles, is dominated by a view of the bulky *Spirit of Tasmania* ferries when they're in port, and sometimes other colourful freighters. The **Devonport Art Gallery** at 45 Stewart St (Mon–Sat 10am–5pm, Sun 2–5pm; free) is a converted church with changing exhibitions and a small permanent collection of Tasmanian ceramics. The city centre caters well to departing tourists in need of last-minute souvenirs, with big-name chain stores on **Rooke Street Mall** and tasteful gift shops on Stewart Street.

The **Devonport Maritime and Folk Museum**, north of the city centre at 47 Victoria Parade, near the river's mouth (Tues–Sun 10–4pm; $3), has an extensive display of model ships ranging from sailing vessels to modern passenger ferries. The **Imaginarium Science Centre**, 19–23 MacFie St, near the *YHA*, is Tasmania's hands-on science discovery centre (Mon–Thurs 10am–4pm, Sat & Sun noon–5pm; $7.50). The only really compelling place to visit, though, is the **Tiagarra Tasmanian Aboriginal Culture and Art Centre** (daily 9am–5pm; $3.80), located at the dramatic **Mersey Bluff**, 1.5km northwest of the Maritime and Folk Museum, near the end of Bluff Road. The centre has preserved around 270 Aboriginal rock engravings (eleven of which are on show), and a **Display Centre** provides generalized (and rather rushed) taped background information on how the Tasmanian Aborigines lived.

The **Don River Railway**, using steam or diesel locomotives, runs excursions from Don Recreation Ground, west of town, along the Don River to the popular surfing spot of **Coles Beach** (hourly 10am–4pm; 30min; $10 return).

Eating, drinking and nightlife

Banjo's Rooke Street Mall. One of a Tasmanian chain of early-opening, eat-in bakeries offering inexpensive fresh-baked goods and unlimited tea and coffee. Daily 6am–6pm.

China Garden 33 King St ☎03/6424 4148. Popular Cantonese restaurant with $7.50 lunch specials. Licensed.

The Deck Cafe Restaurant 188–190 Tarleton St, East Devonport ⓣ03/6427 7188. Devonport's city-style waterfront hangout: you can relax on sofas with a coffee and cake, come for Sunday breakfast or have a beer outside watching the boats come in. By day there's sushi, pasta and risotto ($12.50–18.50), pizzas and gourmet sandwiches ($8.50). Lunch until 5pm segues into the pricier dinner menu, from a Tasmanian seafood plate ($26.50) to prime sirloin steaks. Fully licensed bar. Mon–Sat 10.30am until late, Sun 8.30am until late.
Essence 28 Forbes St ⓣ03/6424 6431. This big, old charming house offers the best of Tasmanian produce – traditional European standbys of venison, lamb, beef, trout, turkey and duck feature – with a contemporary edge. The crisp-skinned confit of duck is always popular. Mains around $24. You can just come in for a drink in the *Lounge Bar*, where several Tasmanian wines are available by the glass. Lunch Tues–Fri, dinner Tues–Sat.
Molly Malone's Irish Pub 34 Best St. Characterful and extensive Irish theme-pub with a great bistro. Lots of meaty pub favourites – including a roast of the day for $10 – and fish as well as vegetarian choices.
Spurs Saloon 18 King St ⓣ03/6424 7851. Lively bar and bistro (dinner Wed–Sun) with the Warehouse Niteclub attached. Also a venue for touring bands. Wed–Sun 5pm–late.
Top End 12 Rooke St. This light contemporary café has comfy sofas, magazines, a big spread of healthy food under glass counters and a fresh juice bar. Good coffee, pots of tea including chai, and yummy cakes. Vegetarian choices include curry samosas served with salad for $7.50. Licensed. Mon–Sat 7am–6pm.
Taco Villa Kempling St ⓣ03/6424 6762. Good Mexican food. BYO. Dinner Tues–Sun.

Listings

Bookshop Angus & Robertson Bookworld, 43 Rooke St ⓣ03/6424 2022.
Buses Redline and TassieLink both have ticket desks at the ferry terminal. Redline's depot is at 9 Edward St (ⓣ1300 360 000; left luggage $1 per item); TassieLink (ⓣ1300 300 520) services leave from the tourist office at 92 Formby Rd. Backpackers Barn (see p.1138) is the booking office and collecting point for Tasmanian Tour Companies on-demand bushwalking charter service to Cradle Mountain, Frenchmans Cap and Walls of Jerusalem. Also the similar Maxwells charter service is based in nearby Wilmot (ⓣ03/6492 1431).
Car rental Firms located at the airport and ferry terminal include Autorent-Hertz ⓣ03/6424 1013, Avis Tasmania ⓣ03/6427 9797 and Budget ⓣ03/6427 0650; among cheaper alternatives are Lo-Cost Auto Rent ⓣ03/6424 9922, ⓦwww.locostautorent.com and the popular Rent-A-Bug ⓣ03/6427 9304, ⓦwww.rentabug.com.au, both on Murray St by the ferry terminal, East Devonport.
Cinema C-Max Cinemas, 5–7 Best St (ⓣ03/6240 2111), is a four-screen cinema complex.
Post office Cnr Stewart St and Formby Rd, TAS 7310.
Taxi Taxis Combined ⓣ03/6424 1431.

Around Devonport

East of Devonport are some particularly rewarding spots on the **Rubicon River estuary**, where you'll find the seaside resort of **PORT SORELL**, roughly 19km from Devonport and across the river from the Narawntapu National Park (see overleaf). You can **stay** here in a self-catering three-bedroom solar-heated house at *Heron on Earth Organic Farm* (ⓣ03/6428 6144, ⓦwww.herononearth.com; ④), which lends out canoes for you to paddle across to the national park, and also bikes. More luxurious accommodation is provided 4km

The Tasmanian Trail

The **Tasmanian Trail** is a 480km multi-purpose recreational trail extending from Devonport on the north coast to Dover on the south coast. Created by connecting forestry roads, fire trails and country roads (often going through small towns) and at times traversing private land, it's primarily used for mountain biking and horse-riding. For more details consult ⓦwww.parks.tas.gov.au/recreaton/tstrail.html; or the *Tasmanian Trail Guidebook* is available from tourist offices and bookshops for $22.

northeast at **HAWLEY BEACH**, at the well-regarded, rather grand Victorian-era *Hawley House* (Ⓣ03/6428 6221, Ⓦwww.hawleyhousetas.com; ❻), which has a fine restaurant and its own vineyard producing chardonnay and pinot noir. From Hawley Beach there's a 10km return walk to Point Sorell.

To reach the western edge of the **Narawntapu National Park** (formerly Asbestos Range National Park), on the east side of the Rubicon River estuary, it's a meandering, 40km drive from Devonport. The remote park is worth the trip – particularly at dusk – for the chance to spot some wildlife: introduced **Forrester kangaroos** come down to feed at **Bakers Beach** at that time, and it's the best place in Tasmania to see **wombats**. The park is renowned for its occasional spectacular storms, accompanied by strong winds roaring along the beach. There's a self-registering **campsite** here, for which you pay a small fee (ranger Ⓣ03/6428 6277), and the beach is good for swimming, and for oyster-hunting from the rocks at low tide. You'll need your own transport to get out here.

The quirky town of **LATROBE**, just 5km south of Devonport, has put itself firmly on the map with the latest addition to Australia's list of "Big Things", a **Big Platypus** plonked on top of the Lucas Hotel at 45 Gilbert St. Inside, the **Platypus Experience** ($5) gives the lowdown on the platypus lifestyle, creatures you can often see at dusk at Kings Creek right by the hotel and in other spots near the town – the "experience" gives you the details, but the pub also has a **tourist information** centre that hands out free maps. Further along the street at no.139, **Reliquaire** is a vast and extraordinary toy/novelty shop hybrid that would probably even astonish in a big city.

SHEFFIELD, 30km south of Devonport, is a popular stop en route to Cradle Mountain. The cute, old-fashioned town, set amongst farmland made fertile by red volcanic soils, is situated near the base of Mount Roland (1231m) which provides a scenic backdrop. The town's rural economy was ailing when the community decided to reinvent itself through the medium of visual art; since the mid-1980s over thirty **murals** in various styles have been painted by several local artists, showing the history and folklore of the town. Next to the post office, the very efficient council-run **Sheffield Visitor Information Centre** (daily 9am–5pm; Ⓣ03/6491 1036) hands out a free pamphlet detailing the history of the murals project and a self-guided walking tour, which should take about an hour; they also book **accommodation** for free and offer **Internet** access; the **Online Access Centre** itself is in the high school on Henry Street. The best **eating** option in town is *Coffee on Main*, 43 Main St (Ⓣ03/6491 1893; BYO; Wed–Sun from 9.30am–5pm plus dinner Wed–Sat), which offers organic coffee made by trained baristas, inexpensive gourmet sandwiches and salads by day, and dinner mains ($14–22) from fresh local produce by the European-trained chef–owner.

Sixteen kilometres southwest of Sheffield at **GOWRIE PARK** at the base of **Mount Roland**, you can **stay** at *Mount Roland Budget Backpacker Rooms* (Ⓣ03/6491 1385; dorms $20) which has bunk-style quarters as well as the en-suite *Gowrie Park Wilderness Cabins* (❸). It makes a good base for walks up and around the summit (2hr return), which provide great views of Cradle Mountain. Adjacent, the rustic-feel *Weindorfers Great Food & Real Coffee* (daily Oct–May: 10am–9/10pm) is recommended.

You can get to Sheffield and Gowrie Park with TassieLink on their scheduled Launceston–Queenstown service via Cradle Mountain (3 weekly).

Ulverstone to Burnie

Redline buses follow the unremarkable coast from Devonport west to industrial Burnie, stopping at Ulverstone and Penguin. **ULVERSTONE**, 20km west of Devonport where the **Leven River** flows into the sea, is a popular family holiday centre with unpolluted **beaches**. A population of Little penguins comes to breed on the beach here between September and April, and the responsible Penguin Point Twilight Tours takes small groups from the Ulverstone Waterfront Inn out at dusk to see the penguins and their habitat (2–3hr; $15; bookings ⓣ03/6425 1599). The town's **accommodation** possibilities include the pleasant, two-storey B&B *Ocean View Guesthouse* at 1 Victoria St (ⓣ03/6425 5401; ❺), and the splendid 1903 red-brick *Furners Hotel* at 42 Reibey St (ⓣ03/6425 1488; en-suite B&B ❹), the latter complete with carved blackwood staircase and an excellent **bistro**; or you can camp at the waterfront *Ulverstone Caravan Park*, 1km east of the centre (ⓣ03/6425 2624; vans ❷, cabins and units ❸). The best place to **eat** is the riverside *Pedro's* on Wharf Rd (ⓣ03/6425 6663), the perfect spot for a seafood restaurant, with one of Tassie's most rated fish and chips shops attached. You can pick up free maps and information from the volunteer-run **Ulverstone Visitor Information Centre**, behind the post office (Mon–Fri 9.15am–3.30pm, Sat & Sun 10am–3pm; ⓣ03/6425 2839).

In the picturesque hop-growing countryside just under 25km south of Ulverstone, the **Gunns Plains Caves** (hourly tours daily 10am–4pm; 50min; $10), part of the **Gunns Plains State Reserve**, are worth visiting for their remarkable limestone formations which, when lit from behind, glow a succulent red. A permanent stream feeds an underground lake, and platypuses and possums enjoy the cool temperatures.

The best route west from Ulverstone follows the old Bass Highway (Penguin Rd) along the coastline, passing the Three Sisters and Goat Islands bird sanctuaries, Penguin Point where Little penguins roost, and a beautiful array of flowers as you come into **PENGUIN** itself, 12km along the highway. The eye-catching, neatly tended little town has three safe swimming beaches and a strong café culture. Cute blue-and-white penguin-shaped garbage bins line the beachfront main street, culminating in the two-metre-high **Big Penguin** in the foreshore park. The **Visitor Information Centre** (Mon–Fri 9am–4pm, Sat 9am–12.30pm; ⓣ03/6437 1421) can provide more details about things to do in the area including twilight penguin trips (1hr30min; ⓣ03/6437 2590; $12). Worth a visit in its own right, the *Groovy Penguin* (closed Mon & Tues; dinner available Fri night) is a fantastically colourful, cluttered and alternative-feel **café** with young and friendly owners – filling fare includes lentil burgers and lasagne. When it's closed, try the upmarket *Madsen Cafe*, in a former bank, with stylish bed and breakfast **accommodation** upstairs (ⓣ03/6437 2588, ⓦwww.themadsen.com.au; $150 to $180). Five kilometres south outside town, there are walking trails in the **Dial Range State Forest**.

BURNIE, on Emu Bay 15km west of Penguin, is an industrial and paper-manufacturing centre and container port, and Tasmania's third largest city with a population of nearly 20,000. The port, with its controversial pile of export woodchips and nearby paper mill, is unattractive but the city is situated amid rich farmland and beautiful rocky coves, and tourism is now being actively developed. The Redline depot is at 117 Wilson St and TassieLink departs from outside the **Tasmanian Travel and Information Centre** at the Civic Square precinct, off Little Alexander Street (Mon–Fri 8am–5pm, Sat & Sun 10am–4pm; ⓣ03/6434 6111). The Civic Centre on Wilmot Street is home to both the **Pioneer Village Museum**, with its reconstructed early-twentieth-century street (Mon–Fri 8.30am–5pm, Sat & Sun 9am–4pm; $6), and the **Burnie Regional Art Gallery** (Tues–Fri 10.30am–5pm, Sat & Sun 1.30–4.30pm; free). In complete contrast to the region's industrial base, the large-scale **Australian Paper Mill**, check out the wonderful community-based, non-profit **Creative Paper Mill**, on Old Surrey Rd (C112), 100m off the Bass Highway on the eastern side of Burnie (Nov–April daily 9am–4pm, tours 10am, noon & 2.30pm; May–Sept Mon–Sat Sat 10am–4pm, tours 11am & 2.30pm; 35–40min; $10; Ⓦwww.creativepapertas.com.au). The paper here is handmade and there's a product showroom, plus an art gallery. Three kilometres further along Old Surry Rd, **Lactos** is a prize-winning speciality **cheese factory** (tastings Mon–Fri 9am–5pm, Sat & Sun 10am–4pm; free), where you can sample and buy blends and variations of European cheeses, and also buy lunch. Forking off Old Surrey Rd just after the Creative Paper Mill, and just 1km from the city centre, **Fernglade** is a **platypus reserve** on a peaceful, forested stretch of the Emu River. The platypuses are easy to spot, particularly at dawn and after dusk. Burnie also has a free **penguin interpretative centre**, reached via a 1km boardwalk from the town centre; the long, thin building is open to the Little penguins who, lit by infra-red light, can be observed through windows via a periscope-style mirrored tunnel; the best time to view the penguins is after dusk between September and April. Conservationist William Walker (Ⓣ03/6435 7205) runs personalized nature-based scenic and cultural interpretive tours, visiting Fernglade and the penguins and other local points of interest, and specializing in day-walks with local gourmet food.

There's plenty of **accommodation**, should you decide to stay in Burnie; the information centre does free bookings. The *Burnie Holiday Caravan Park*, 253 Bass Highway, at Cooee on the pleasant, non-industrial side of town towards Wynyard (Ⓣ03/6431 1925; vans ❷, cabins ❸, motel ❹), has something to suit everyone with the attached *Ocean View Motel*, cabins, a **YHA hostel** section (dorms $18) and a campground. For more character, *Glen Osborne House*, at 9 Aileen Crescent (Ⓣ03/6431 9866; ❻), is a stylish Victorian-era B&B with en-suite rooms and a lovely garden of lawns, roses and fruit trees. **Food** choices include the veteran Italian, *Rialto Gallery*, at 46 Wilmot St (BYO; Ⓣ03/6431 7718), and the licensed *Cafe Europa,* corner Cattley and Wilson streets (Tues–Thurs 8.30am–9pm, Fri 8.30am–midnight, Sat 10am–midnight, Sun 10am–6pm), a cosmopolitan hangout, with some Greek Cypriot offerings on the Mediterranean menu (also good-value toasted Turkish sandwiches, snacks and lots of different kinds of coffee). The Metro Cinema, cnr Marine Terrace and Wilmot St (Ⓣ03/6431 5000, Ⓦwww.metrocinemas.com.au) is the **entertainment** focus. Burnie's **Online Access Centre** is at 2 Spring St.

Wynyard and around

WYNYARD, another 19km along the old Bass Highway from Burnie, snuggles into the lush pasturelands between the **Inglis River** and the sea. The wharf area, with its fishing boats and fresh fish shop, is just off bustling Goldie Street – the main street that parallels the river. There are over 12km of riverside walking tracks, starting from the riverfront park on the corner of Goldie and Hogg streets. It's an easy 3km walk to **Fossil Bluff** where layers of sedimentary rock containing fossilized seashells can easily be examined at low tide, and the beach itself has good views of the 170-metre seaface of **Table Cape**. A drive up to the **lookout** on Table Cape will reward you with magnificent views of the coast and hinterland, particularly pretty when the cape's **tulip fields** are in bloom around October.

Wynyard may well be the first place you see in Tasmania, since "Burnie" **airport** is actually just a five-minute stroll from the town centre. You can **rent a car** at the airport with Autorent-Hertz (Ⓣ03/6442 4444), Avis (Ⓣ03/6442

2512) or Budget (☎03/6442 1777). The Burnie Air-Bus connects the airport with Burnie ($9.90; ☎0439 322 466). MTT **public transport buses** connect Wynyard with Burnie, departing from 38 Jackson St. Redline calls at Gale's Auto Service, 28 Saunders St (☎03/6442 2205), en route from Burnie to Smithton via the turn-offs to Table Cape, Boat Harbour Beach and Rocky Cape.

The brand-new **Wynyard Tourist Information**, behind the intersection of Jackson and Dodgin streets (daily 9am–5pm; ☎03/6442 4143), has information on local activities and **accommodation**. There's camping at *Beach Retreat Tourist Park*, at 30B Old Bass Highway on the way out of town to Burnie (☎03/6442 1998; dorms $17, vans ❷, cabins ❸), and backpacker dorms. However, the best place to stay is *The Waterfront Wynyard*, 1 Goldie Street (☎03/6442 2351; ❹), in a fantastic riverfront spot right by the wharf. The recently done-up, very cute motel rooms are equipped with everything from satellite TV to DVD players, and the on-site café-restaurant (where the included light breakfast is served) is the best in town: couches, a river-view terrace, great coffee and cake served daily from 8am, and a pub-competitive restaurant at night (from $15 roast of the day to seafood curries). The takeaway fish and chip shop on the wharf is good, or try the tacky-looking *Buckaneers Restaurant*, at 4 Inglis St (☎03/6442 4104; lunch daily, dinner Thurs–Sun), which dishes up excellent fresh fish and seafood. Wynyard's **Online Access Centre** is at 21 Saunders St.

Boat Harbour Beach and Sister Beach

Eleven kilometres west of Wynyard, a turn-off from the Bass Highway winds down to **Boat Harbour Beach**, the prettiest on the northwest coast, with pale-blue water, white sand and very gentle waves. It's perfect for **diving**, too; equipment can be rented from the Scuba Centre at 62 Bass Highway in Wynyard (☎03/6442 2247), which also organizes excursions. *Jolly Rogers on the Beach* is a licensed cafe-restaurant right on the beach with tables out front; the kiosk does takeaways and rents **boogie-boards** and **wave skis**. Attractive **Sisters Beach**, closer to Rocky Cape, is much less developed (and there are no building works going on); you can stay at *Birdland Holiday Cottages*, 7 Bankisa Ave (☎03/6445 21471; ❹), set in forest. Back on the highway the Boat Harbour Store has petrol and a post office.

Rocky Cape (Tangdimmaa) National Park

Stretching for a mere 12km along the coast, from Sisters Beach to Rocky Cape, are the rugged hills and cliffs of **Rocky Cape (Tangdimmaa) National Park**, Tasmania's smallest national park, created in 1967 for the purpose of preserving some remarkable **Aboriginal archeological finds**. The mainly quartzite hills are pockmarked with caves, of which the two major ones, North Cave and South Cave, contain huge shell middens, bones and stone tools dating back as far as eight thousand years, when the sea was several fathoms below its current level.

Rocky Cape is now managed in consultation with the Tasmanian Aboriginal Land Council, and visitors are no longer allowed to enter the caves, although it's okay to reach the entrances. To reach North Cave it's a fifteen-minute walk there and back from the road, reached by driving 5km into the park and taking the left fork at the lighthouse – most people prefer just to walk along the various easy tracks. It takes seven hours to traverse the whole length of the park; there's no water, no toilets and camping is not allowed. Rocky pools, safe swimming beaches and picnic areas are scattered along the route, while in spring and summer there's a profusion of wild flowers on the scrubby heathland, including some unique native orchids. At dusk you may see wallabies, echidnas and various species of bird. Back on the highway, the *Rocky Cape Tavern* (ⓣ03/6443 4110) has camping and there's a petrol station nearby.

Stanley

It's a 31km drive from the Rocky Cape turn-off west along the Bass Highway (A2) to the fishing village of **STANLEY,** the original 1826 headquarters of the **Van Diemen's Land Company** and the first settlement in northwest Tasmania; the scenic coastal drive hugging the coast is marred only by the industrial scene at Port Latta. About 5km beyond here, a turn-off leads 27km south on the C225 to the must-see **Dip Falls Big Tree**, a gigantic eucalypt measuring 17m at its base and thought to be over 400 years old.

Back on the highway, long before you arrive at Stanley, 6km off the Bass Highway, you'll see your first breathtaking view of the **The Nut**, described by Matthew Flinders as a "cliffy round lump in form resembling a Christmas cake" that rises directly out of the ocean to a height of nearly 150m. **Circular Head**, as it's officially called (the name also for the surrounding municipality), is thought to be a volcanic plug, with the softer sediments around it having eroded away. The town itself is on a small, foot-shaped peninsula right at the base of The Nut, perched high above Sawyer Bay and Tallows Beach.

Information and tours

For **tourist information**, accommodation bookings and **Internet** access visit the Stanley Visitor Centre on the way into Stanley at 45 Main Rd (Mon–Fri 9am–5pm, Sat & Sun 10am–4pm; ⓣ03/6458 1330); it also serves as the Redline **depot** and sells bus tickets – Stanley is reached on the route between Burnie and Smithton (Mon–Fri 2 daily). The General Store is below the town centre on Wharf Road and has an ATM, while the newsagents' towards the end of Church St also has supplies and is an ANZ bank agent; there's more banking facilities a few doors up at the post office.

Stanley-based Wilderness to West Coast Tours (ⓣ03/6458 2038, ⓦwww.wildernesstasmania.com) offers a dusk platypus-viewing tour (2hr; $30) and a penguin tour (1hr; $15; both tours combined: $40). A wilderness 4WD tour explores the northwest tip, through farm country, temperate rainforest, gum forests and button-grass plains (5hr; $95); a longer version also visits the wild west coast (8.5hr; $195; both include morning tea and gourmet lunch). Stanley Seal Cruises on Wharf Road will take you to view the populous colony of the rare Australian **fur seal**, weather permitting (daily 10am; also April–June 3.30pm and Oct–March 1.30pm & 4.30pm; 1hr 10min; closed July; $40; ⓣ0419 550 134).

Accommodation

Stanley is now so packed with holiday **accommodation** it's hard for locals to find anywhere to rent, but this means competitive deals are available. In keeping with its historic ambience, Stanley has many "colonial" **B&Bs**, which are actually self-contained cottages with breakfast provisions supplied.

Beachside Retreat West Inlet Main Road (ⓣ03/6458 1350, ⓦwww.beachsideretreat.com. Two-and-a-half kilometres south of the town centre, some of the stunning designer cabins here have fantastic Nut views framed by huge porthole and picture windows, and there's access to a private beach. ❻

Dovecote Motel 1km along Dovecote Road ⓣ03/6458 1300, ⓦwww.dovecote.com.au. There's some of the best views of the Nut, across

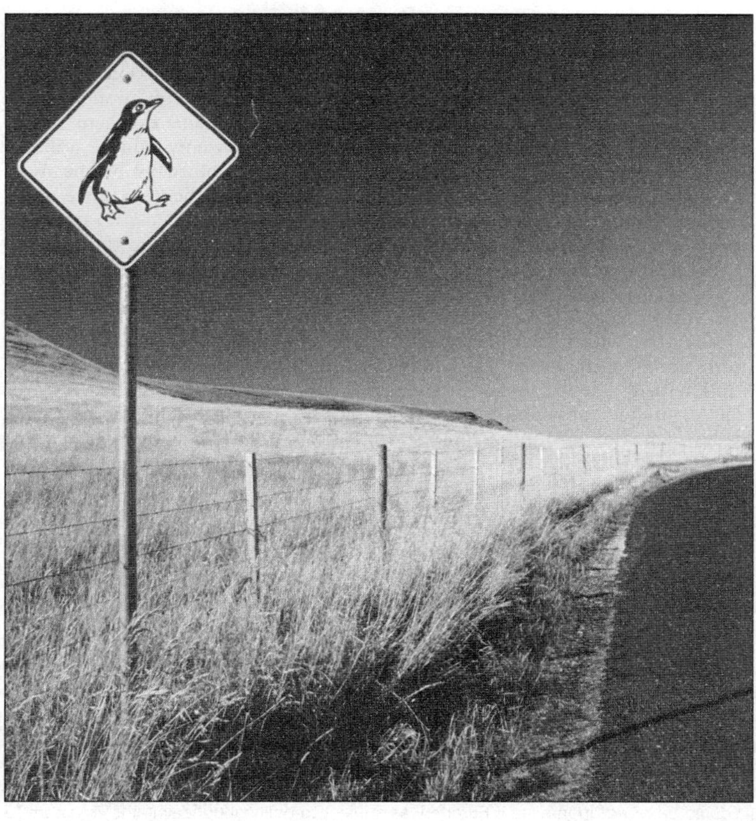

△ road crossing sign, near Stanley

the green fields of the Dovecote Estate, from the *Dovecote*'s spacious, well-appointed units (some self-catering); facilities include a bar and a restaurant. ❹–❺

Old Cable Station West Beach Rd, north of town, beyond Highfield House ⓣ03/6458 1312, ⓔcablestation@westnet.com.au. Once linking Tasmania with the mainland via King Island, this peaceful retreat is surrounded by a pretty flower-filled garden and has views stretching across fields to water. Choose from a spacious three-bedroom cottage, or two stylish en-suite rooms. Rooms ❺, cottage ❻

Palm Tree Spa Cottage 48 Alexander Terrace ⓣ1800 222 397. There's gorgeous Sawyer Bay views from the front verandah of this charming weatherboard self-contained house nestled under the Nut. The same management have several other excellent options, including *Abbeys Spa Cottage*, nearby at no. 34 (both ❺), and the modern, tiny but tidy and very good-value *Pol & Pen Holiday Chalets* close to Godreys Beach on Pearse St (❸).

Stanley Hotel Church Street ⓣ03/6458 1161. The recently renovated rooms at this sprawling, three-storey old pub are now brightly painted and quite smart, but still with good single rates ($35). Rooms ❸, en suite ❹

Stanley Cabin and Tourist Park and Stanley YHA Wharf Road ⓣ03/6458 1266. In a great absolute waterfront location opposite Marine Park, near the fishing wharf action and overlooking Tallows Beach with the general store nearby. The cabins have been recently renovated and the youth hostel has always been popular. There's also the option to camp. Dorms $20, rooms ❷, cabins ❸–❹

The Town

Stanley's main street, **Church Street**, runs below the foot of the Nut, and its restaurants and crafts shops – check out the contemporary wood designs in Stanley Artworks Studio Gallery near the post office – are high enough above the beach, wharves and the rest of the town to command excellent views. Although it's worthwhile doing the strenuous ten- to twenty-minute walk up the grassy **Nut** itself, you can get to the top more comfortably by means of an exhilarating **chair lift**, reached via the ramp opposite the post office (daily 9.30am–5pm, weather permitting; call ⓣ03/6458 1286 to check; no one-way tickets sold, $9 return). The licensed *Nut Rock Cafe*, next door to the chairlift, has fantastic views and decent coffee. A 2km circuit walk around the windy **Nut State Reserve** at the top affords views over the town and port, and southeast as far as Table Cape. Directly below is the exquisitely deserted **Godfrey's Beach** to the north, with its calm and translucent blue waters. Green Hills Road runs north alongside the beach and winds uphill to the original headquarters of the Van Diemen's Land Company, 2km north of the town, with superb views over Half Moon Bay. Though the rooms themselves of the **Highfield Historic Site** (daily 10am–4pm; grounds $2, house $6) are bare of artefacts, the interpretative boards provide a fascinating and honest history of the VDL Company and the North West, with lots from the Aboriginal perspective.

Below Church Street and Alexander Terrace, the foreshore area spreads alongside Wharf Road, with the curve of **Tallows Beach** stretching for kilometres

The Van Diemen's Land Company

. . . how is it that an absentee owner across the world got this magnificent and empty country without having paid one glass bead?

Cassandra Pybus

The **Van Diemen's Land Company (VDL)** was the brainchild of a group of prominent and well-connected individuals, who in 1824 managed to obtain by Royal Charter 250,000 acres of the mainly thickly forested, unexplored northwest corner of Tasmania. Their plan was to create their own source of fine wool in the colonies, which could be relied upon even if Europe was subject to political upheaval; the *Tranmere* arrived at Circular Head in 1826, with the personnel, livestock, supplies and equipment to create the township of Stanley.

The first flocks were grazed at Woolnorth on Cape Grim, a plateau of tussock grass and trees that might have been made for the purpose but, in fact, was prime Aboriginal hunting land. When hunting parties began to take the precious sheep, whites killed Aborigines in retaliation, and a vindictive cycle of killings began. The most tragic incident (a version of events denied by Woolnorth) was supposed to have occurred around 1826 or 1827: a group of Aboriginal men, seeking revenge for the rape of their women, speared a shepherd and herded one hundred sheep over the cliff edge. These deaths were ruthlessly avenged when a group of thirty unarmed Aborigines, hunting for muttonbirds near the same spot, were killed by shepherds and their bodies thrown over the cliff (now euphemistically called "Suicide Bay"). Ultimately, the Aboriginal people of the northwest were systematically hunted down: the last group, middle-aged parents and their five sons, were captured by sealers near the Arthur River in 1842 after the VDL's Chief Agent offered a £50 reward.

In the 1840s the company changed its emphasis from wool production to the sale and lease of its land, and it now holds just a fifth of its original land. Still registered on the London Stock Exchange, it is the only remaining company in the world operating under a Royal Charter; its major shareholder, who bought 87.5 per cent of the shares in 1993, is a New Zealand-based agribusiness in Dunedin.

southeast and the busy fishing port area, the marina full of colourful boats, to the west. By Marine Park, the slate-roofed **Van Diemen's Land Company Store** (now a B&B) was designed in 1844 by John Lee Archer, whose work can be seen notably in Hobart (see p.1075). From the nearby **port area**, at low tide, you can see the remnants of a 1923 **shipwreck**, a victim of the "furies" of the Bass Strait. On Fisherman's Dock, **Stanley Seaquarium** (daily 10am–4pm; $8) is full of creatures hauled up by fishermen. At feeding times, the Port Jackson and gummy sharks get so excitable they dance – it's a revelation that sharks can be so cute. The hands-on rockpool is fantastic, with sea stars, sea cucumbers and lots of shy hermit crabs in shells.

Eating

There's a good choice of places to **eat** within Stanley itself. *Hurseys Seafoods*, next to Marine Park on Wharf Road, is considered to be one of the best fish-and-chip shops in Tasmania. Inside are huge holding tanks from which you select live fish (around twenty kinds) and crayfish. Nearby at 15 Wharf Rd, *Stanleys on the Bay* is a well-regarded seafood and steak restaurant (ⓣ03/6458 1404; dinner Mon–Sat; closed July & Aug). Back on Church Street, the *Stanley Hotel* serves fresh seafood and other delicious pub fare in its lively lounge bar bistro with terrace dining and views; and the *Touchwood Coffee Shop* has expansive views from inside and outside tables, the best coffee in Stanley, seafood from octopus salad ($14.50) to crayfish rolls ($15.50), toasted sandwiches, and yummy biscuits, muffins and cakes.

Smithton and around

The only way to see Tasmania's rugged northwest tip, which remains under the control of the Van Diemen's Land Company, is by tour. Tours to **Woolnorth**, the original VDL cattle and sheep property, depart from the rather unattractive rural-industrial town of **SMITHTON**, 22km west of Stanley, at the mouth of the Duck River. The full-day **tour** to Woolnorth (daily; 3hr tour $45; day tour $95 including morning tea and lunch at the board table of the 1970s-built Directors Lodge) take in **Cape Grim** (see box opposite), where the air carried thousands of kilometres across the Great Southern Ocean by the Roaring Forties is reputed to be the cleanest in the world – it's the site of Australia's baseline air-monitoring station, the most sophisticated in a worldwide network, and Australia's largest **wind farm** taking advantage of these gusting winds. A couple of kilometres east of Cape Grim, you can stand at the point where Bass Strait meets the Southern Ocean and walk along the spectacular, rugged coastline.

What Smithton lacks in aesthetics it makes up for by its usefulness as a service centre, with supermarkets, fuel and banking facilities and an **Online Access Centre** on Nelson Street; the Redline **depot** is at 27 Victoria St. The resort-like *Tall Timbers Hotel Motel* on Scotchtown Road (ⓣ03/6452 2755, ⓦwww.talltimbershotel.com; ❺–❻), built from local timbers, has a vast and popular **bistro** and motel or self-catering **accommodation** and offers excellent 4WD tours. South of Smithton, ten **forestry reserves**, ranging from rainforests to blackwood swamps and giant eucalypt forests, are all accessible from a circular route, via Kanunnah Bridge and Taytea Bridge on the C218 (90km return). **Julius River Forest Reserve** and the **Milkshakes Hills Forest Reserve** are the most rewarding. The Forestry Commission, at the corner of Nelson and Smith streets (ⓣ03/6452 1317), provides maps and route information.

Marrawah

From Smithton the Bass Highway cuts across the northwest corner to the rich farming settlement of **MARRAWAH** on the west coast. Thirty kilometres along the way, Forestry Tasmania have come up with a startling public relations exercise: a Visitor Centre at the grumpily named **Dismal Swamp** (daily 9am–4pm; $10), where a 110-metre slide (not for kids though, over-13s only) can whiz you down to the blackwood sinkhole, where a trail through the swamp includes mazes and art installations. The centre makes a good stopping point, with really good coffee at the smart attached café. Marrawah itself has a general store/café with a post office and **petrol**, and the *Marrawah Tavern* serves plain but filling meals. **Greenpoint Beach**, which has been voted one of the three best **surfing** beaches in Australia, is 2km west from Marrawah and has a small **camping area** as well as the stylish *Ann Bay Cabins* (Ⓣ03/6457 1361; ❹). There's also excellent, spacious self-contained **accommodation** at *Glendonald Cottage* on the Arthur River Road, 3km south of Marrawah (Ⓣ03/6457 1191; ❹); the owner, Geoff King, is a passionate conservationist who is working to regenerate the coastal land and preserve its Aboriginal sites. Geoff knows a lot about natural, local and Aboriginal history and his Kings Run Wildlife Tours include fascinating nocturnal viewings of **Tasmanian devils** in the wild ($75; one hour before sunset until midnight).

The curve of Ann Bay here is shrouded by the hump of **Mount Cameron West** to the north. Three kilometres north of this bluff, at the end of a long exposed beach, is the most complex **Aboriginal art** site in Tasmania, now known as **Preminghana Indigenous Protected Area**: rock carvings of geometric or nonfigurative forms cover slabs of rock at the base of a cliff. Access is now restricted to a lookout.

Arthur River and the Arthur Pieman Protected Area

Just over 20km south of Marrawah, the scattering of holiday homes at **ARTHUR RIVER** marks the start of one of the Tasmanian coast's last great **wilderness areas**, where mighty trees that have been washed down the Frankland and Arthur rivers have crashed against the windswept shoreline. At one time the entire west coast looked like this, but the progressive damming of its rivers has left the **Arthur Pieman Protected Area**, part of the Tarkine, as a unique reminder, complete with a spectacular array of birdlife, such as black cockatoos, Tasmanian rosellas, orange-breasted parrots, black jays, wedge-tail eagles, pied heron and azure kingfishers. Trees on the steep banks of the never-logged river include myrtle, sassafras, celery-top pines and laurels, and there are giant tree ferns. From Gardiners Point – "**The Edge of the World**" – on the south side of the river mouth, the next land west is South America; it's a great vantage point to gaze on the battered coastline. It's obviously dangerous to swim here, due to extremely wild conditions and occasional freak waves – even walking along the beach can be an obstacle course, but it's possible to walk 9km to Sundown Point (arrange a pick-up vehicle or allow a full day to do the return walk).

As you come into the settlement on the sealed Arthur River Road, get the latest information on conditions (and camping permits) from the Parks and Wildlife office here (daily 9am–5pm; Ⓣ03/6457 1225). Opposite, the Arthur River Store (daily 7.30am–8pm; Ⓣ03/6457 1207) sells supplies and tickets for the Arthur River Cruise, and books **accommodation**. Also on Gardiner

Street is the spacious *Ocean View Holiday Cottage* (☎03/6457 1100; ❸–❹), right on the river mouth with stunning views, and the excellent but smaller *Sunset Holiday Villas* opposite (☎03/6457 1197; ❹). **Camping** at Arthur River is a truly pleasurable experience, with facilities that range from the fully serviced *Peppermint Campground* near the base office, to secluded areas among shady trees in the dips and hollows behind the dunes, equipped merely with water taps.

If you want to get out on the river, take a **cruise** (see below) or contact Arthur River Canoe & Boat Hire (☎03/6457 1312), which has canoes and boats available for rent.

The Arthur River Cruise

Perhaps the biggest attraction of the entire northwest coast is the excellent five-hour **Arthur River Cruise** on the MV *George Robinson* (daily 10am, returning 3pm, enquire about summer evening cruises; no trips June to beginning Sept; $65; bookings ☎03/6452 5088, Ⓦwww.arthurrivercruises.com; they will leave with only one person), which sails 14km upriver to the confluence of the Arthur and Frankland rivers at Turks Landing. The slow trip enables you to take in the tranquillity of the river and experience the transition from coastal scrub woodland to the edge of **the Tarkine** – the second largest tract of temperate rainforest found anywhere in the world; en route you cruise past a white-breasted sea eagles' nest, and see the enormous mating pair being fed. Morning tea on the boat includes rum-spiked hot chocolate if you're up to it. Before

The Tarkine

The Tarkine, covering 377,000 hectares in northwest Tasmania, was named after the Tarkiner band of Aboriginal people who once roved here. It's Tasmania's largest unprotected wilderness area – stretching from the wild west coast to Murchison Highway in the east and from the Arthur River in the north to the Pieman River in the south – though conservationists have been pushing for a Tarkine National Park since the 1960s and the area was recommended for UNESCO's world heritage list in the 1990s. Of its 240,000 hectares of forest, seventy per cent constitutes Australia's largest tract of **temperate rainforest**, second only in global significance to tracts in British Columbia. This "forgotten wilderness" of giant myrtle forests, wild rivers and bare granite mountains is the sort of place where the Tasmanian tiger, long thought extinct, might still be roaming – yet still its old-growth rainforests are under threat from logging.

Ignoring the protests of conservationists, the controversial **Western Explorer** "tourist road" through the Tarkine, from Arthur River all the way south to Zeehan, was constructed hastily and finished in 1996. A year before, an incredibly vast and ancient Huon pine was found in the area, as big as a city block and thought to date from around 8000 BC. Conservationists are apprehensive that "the road to nowhere", as they've called it, is being used as a cover to open up the area (currently state forest) to logging, thereby degrading it and reducing the likelihood of World Heritage listing in the future. If you choose to drive this route, pick up the *Western Explorer Travel Guide* pamphlet – issued by the Department of Infrastructure, Energy and Resources and available in information centres – and remember that the road is rough and Marrawah is the last fuel stop before Zeehan. Alternatively, the **Tarkine National Coalition**, based in Burnie (☎03/6431 2373, Ⓦwww.tarkine.org) produces guides to three self-drive Tarkine routes that don't involve the Western Explorer; these can be downloaded from their website. **Tiger Trails** (see box p.1072) specialises in Tarkine tours; there's a six-day expedition through giant myrtle forests ($849) or seven days on the battered west coast via Corinna and the Pieman River Cruise (ex-Launceston or Burnie; $1299).

a barbecue lunch (with wine) in a clearing, there's an informative half-hour guided bushwalk, where you'll learn about the rainforest species. The incredibly friendly crew even entertain with bush poetry on the trip back.

The A10 route to the west coast

From Somerset, a suburb of Burnie on the shores of Emu Bay, the A10 (called the Murchison Highway between here and the Zeehan turn-off) heads to **Queenstown**, in the heart of Tasmania's west-coast mining area. This major route to the west coast is relatively recent; prior to 1932 the coast was accessible only by sea. Following the highway, after 10km you pass **YOLLA**, a picturesque little town surrounded by rich farming country; you can get fuel here. A few kilometres past the Tewkesbury turn-off, the rural landscape ends and the road rises and winds through temperate rainforest to the **Hellyer Gorge State Reserve**. A walk leads through spicy ferns and dense myrtle forest to the Hellyer River and back on a wide and easy track (20min return).

West to Waratah and the Pieman River

Tiny, windswept **WARATAH**, set in mountain heathland 8km off the A10, reached its peak in the early twentieth century after thirty years of tin-mining at **Mount Bischoff**, when it was linked to Burnie by the **Emu Bay Railway**, built to facilitate access to the silver fields of Zeehan and Rosebery. Though the mine closed in 1935, Waratah is still a miners' town, with recent mining developments at the Que River. Little more than a scattered collection of scruffy weatherboard cottages, it's a pretty soulless place, but you can stop off for a **meal** at the big old pub on the hill and get **petrol**. Beyond Waratah, the last fuel stop on the road is the former mining town of **Savage River**, 45km along the B23.

The beautiful, unspoilt **Pieman River**, within the **Pieman River State Reserve**, is reached from the old gold-mining settlement of **CORINNA** on an unsealed road (C247) 26km south of Savage River. It's hard to believe that 2500 people once occupied what's now just a few shacks surrounded by dense bush. Corinna even had its own port, despite the difficulties of getting through the narrow **Pieman Heads** from the coastline. The river here is too dangerous for swimming, with an average drop of nearly 20m from the banks. The reserve used to be a logging area and it still holds one of the biggest stands of remaining Huon pine – saved because the water here was too deep to allow a dam to be built.

You can take a **cruise** on the river, all the way to the west coast, with **Pieman River Cruises** on the characterful Huon pine MV *Arcadia II* (daily 10.30am; 4hr; $50 including morning tea, $57.50 with picnic lunch; bookings essential ⓣ03/6446 1170). From its deck you can see Huon pine, leatherwood and pandanus ferns among the **temperate rainforest** of the river's north bank; the drier southern bank has mainly brown stringybark eucalypts. The trip allows you an hour to wander on your own along the wild west coast.

The cruise operators open the **kiosk** daily whenever they have time, but bring food along if you intend to use the **campsite** (no showers) or the cabins at the *Getaway Resort* (❸, linen extra). From the car park there's a walking track leading to a huge 600-year-old **manfern**, one of only four of such antiquity known to exist in Tasmania. A **barge** can take you across the Pieman River from here (daily 9am–7pm; $20 car, $10 bike), to continue on the C249 to Zeehan, and then on the B27 to Strahan.

South to Zeehan

Back on the A10, there's no fuel until tiny **TULLAH**, 40km south of Waratah. Fourteen kilometres further on, after crossing forest-covered **Mount Black**, the comparatively large zinc-mining town of **ROSEBERY** is a good place to stock up on supplies, with an ANZ bank (Mon, Tues & Fri 9.30am–noon, Wed 2–4pm) and an ATM outside the newsagents'. The comfortable motel-style B&B **accommodation** at *Mount Black Lodge* right next to the mine on Hospital Road (ⓣ03/6473 1039, ⓦwww.mountblacklodge.com; also licensed restaurant; ❹), attracts bushwalkers: the town is hemmed in by looming mounts Black, Read and Murchison, and there's also a fine walk to the 113-metre **Montezuma Falls** (3hr return), 8km south of the town.

From Rosebery, it's 23km to the turn-off to **ZEEHAN**, 6km southwest off the A10. The town became prosperous from the silver-lead mines that opened in the 1880s, and at its height boasted a population of eight thousand. However, the mines had already begun to fail by 1908, and the town was not to see a revival until the 1970s, when the Renison Bell tin mines were opened. Several boom-period buildings are still standing, including the elaborate facade of the **Gaiety Theatre**, once Australia's largest theatre, where Lola Montez once trod the boards. The outstanding **West Coast Pioneer Memorial Museum** on Main Street (daily 8.30am–5pm; $6) has displays on mining history and its own café. **Accommodation** is expensive, as Zeehan catches Strahan's overflow, and includes the *Heemskirk Motor Inn* (ⓣ03/6471 6107; ❹), and basic pub rooms at the *Hotel Cecil* on Main Street (ⓣ03/6471 6221; ❸), where you can get decent counter **meals**. The *Mount Zeehan Retreat Bed and Breakfast* provides evening meals on request (ⓣ03/6471 6424; no en-suites; B&B ❹). By far the cheapest option is the friendly *Treasure Island Caravan Park*, nicely situated 1km from the centre on Hurst Street (ⓣ03/6471 6633; vans ❷, cabins ❸). The ANZ **bank** has restricted opening hours (Mon & Tues 2–4pm, Wed 9.30am–noon, Thurs 9.30am–4pm & Fri 2–4pm), but there's an ATM at Vickers General Store on the main street.

From Zeehan it's possible to go straight to Strahan (47km) on a sealed road (B27), bypassing Queenstown and visiting the Henty Dunes (see p.1159) en route; or you could head back to the A10 (called the Zeehan Highway until Queenstown) and reach Strahan via Queenstown, another 32km along the highway. You can get to Rosebery and Zeehan on TassieLink's scheduled Launceston–Queenstown service via Cradle Mountain (3 weekly).

Queenstown

QUEENSTOWN is worth a visit, but not for reasons you might expect. Its infamous "**lunar landscape**" is chilling evidence of the devastation that single-minded commercial exploitation can wreak in such a sensitive environment. If you approach the town from Strahan you're confronted by the hideously ugly **copper mine**; from Hobart, the road winds down to the town around bare, reddish-brown rock.

Queenstown has been a mining centre since 1883, when gold was discovered at Mount Lyell, and it looks like a typical mining town, with its identical, pokey tin-roofed weatherboard houses. In 1893 the Mount Lyell Mining and Railway Company was formed and began to mine copper at Mount Lyell. The weird-looking mountains here, chalky white and almost totally devoid of vegetation, are the result of a lethal combination of tree-felling, sulphur, fire and rainfall. Since the smelters closed in 1969 there has been some regrowth on the lower slopes, but it's estimated that the damage already done has had an impact that will last some four or five hundred years. In late 1994 the Mount Lyell mine closed down, but the lease was taken over in 1997 by **Copper Mines of Tasmania**, which foresaw another ten years of operation with the remaining ore. Tailings from the mine are now dumped into a multimillion-dollar dam instead of the town's **Queen River**, where aquatic life is beginning to return. The Queen eventually flows into the **King River**, and its moonscaped banks all the way to the delta near Strahan attest to the lasting and wide-ranging environmental damage of the past century. Underground tours of the Mt Lyell mine are offered by Douggies Mine Tours, based at the *Empire Hotel*, below (daily 10am & 1pm; 2hr 30min; $58; ⓣ0407 049 612).

Next door to the mine is the **Parks and Wildlife Service office** (ⓣ03/6471 2511), the base for the Franklin Lower Gordon Wild Rivers National Park and the place to pick up the department's rafting and bushwalking guidelines. **Tourist information** is available from the reception desk of the **Galley Museum**

The West Coast Wilderness Railway

In 2002 the opening of the 35km **West Coast Wilderness Railway** between Queenstown and Strahan fulfilled the $30-million redevelopment of the old **Abt Railway**, which included the restoration or replacement of forty bridges and recreation of stations and associated buildings. Two of the four surviving locomotives from 1963 were restored and each carriage – replicas of old timber and brass models – was designed using different Tasmanian woods. The original railway was completed in 1896 to connect the Mount Lyell Mining Company in Queenstown with the port of Teepookana for the transport of copper ore, and in 1899 the line was extended to Regatta Point in Strahan. The railway closed in 1963, when it became more economical to transport by road, but years of lobbying finally led to the federal government financing its redevelopment. Reconstruction took three years; the original workers took six months less to hand-cut through the rugged rainforest terrain, struggling in the harsh, wet conditions. In fact, mining heritage is the main thrust of this trip and the informative commentary concentrates on it. The "wilderness" is something of a disappointing misnomer, though – at least for half of the journey the line follows slowly alongside the sadly polluted King River, its banks rusty from mine-tailings and lined with tree stumps. Most people take the trip from Strahan: from Dubbil Barril, as the train climbs over 200m up a 1:16 rack gradient using the restored rack and pinion track (a system invented by the Swiss engineer Dr Roman Abt), there are stunning gorge views and the train is immersed in up-close rainforest scenery. However, coming into Queenstown, the vision alongside the tracks is a shocking contrast – a shanty town of tin shacks and dilapidated wooden houses.

Trains leave from Queenstown at the reconstructed station on Driffield St, opposite the *Empire Hotel* (see opposite), and at Strahan from the original station at Regatta Point (see p.1157). There's a daily service in both directions, both of which provide a one-hour lunchstop at Dubbil Barril (packed lunch included) where there's a rainforest walk that takes five minutes. The train from Queenstown stops at the reconstructed historic settlement of Lynchford for half an hour for morning tea and a try at gold panning; the Lower Landing morning tea stop from Strahan is on the unscenic polluted King River and includes a lame mass honey-tasting exercise. Trains are hauled by steam between Queenstown and Dubbil Barril and diesel between here and Strahan. You can choose to go one-way from either Strahan or Queenstown with a coach return (with a 30min break in Queenstown or 1hr 30min in Strahan), or return from Dubbil Barril. The best return option is from Queenstown, as you avoid the ravaged river, enjoy a thrilling ascent and descent, get the steam train and a more enjoyable morning tea spot; the Strahan return trip is best avoided (departs Queenstown 10am, departs Strahan 10.15am; one-way 4hr; return 4hr 30min; $97 includes light lunch; extra $14 for 45min return coach; bookings necessary ⓣ1800 628 288).

housed in the old *Imperial Hotel* on Driffield Street, two blocks from the railway station (ⓣ03/6471 1483; Mon–Fri 10am–5pm, Sat & Sun 12.30pm–6pm; $4), whose extensive old photographic displays focus on West Coast life. Queenstown's **Online Access Centre** is nearby on the same street.

If you're **staying** in Queenstown, try the *Empire Hotel*, at 2 Orr St (ⓣ03/6471 1699, ⓔempirehotel@tassienet.au; rooms ❷, en suite ❸), a lovely, old-fashioned building noted for its National Trust-listed blackwood staircase; it has a good range of reasonably priced rooms and several budget singles ($30), plus good-value meals in the heritage dining room. *Mountain View Holiday Lodge*, at 1 Penghana Rd (ⓣ03/6471 1163; dorms $18, motel units ❸), across the river from the town centre, has been converted from the mine's single men's lodgings. For something special, *Penghana*, on The Esplanade at no. 32, provides B&B-style accommodation in an imposing stately mansion set in rainforest overlooking Queenstown (ⓣ03/6471 2560, ⓦwww.view.com.au/penghana; B&B ❻). There are **banking** facilities at the Commonwealth Bank on Orr St (closed noon–1pm), which has an ATM, and ANZ banking and an ATM at the Railway Express General Store on the same street. From Queenstown you can drive to Strahan on the B24 (42km), which starts as a steep, winding road through bare hills, or you continue along the A10 (called the Lyell Highway from Queenstown to Hobart) 88km east to the first fuel at Derwent Bridge, surrounded by the World Heritage Area (Franklin Lower Gordon Wild Rivers National Park, p.1165, and Cradle Mountain–Lake St Clair National Park, p.1160).

Strahan and around

STRAHAN, the only town and port on the west coast, sits in the huge **Macquarie Harbour** (over six times the size of Sydney's harbour), site of **Sarah Island**, a harsh secondary convict settlement in use between 1822 and 1830, which can be visited on a Gordon River cruise (see box p.1158). The entrance to Macquarie Harbour, named **Hells Gates** by arriving convicts, is only 80m wide. **Huon pine**, perfect for shipbuilding, grows abundantly in the area – logging and boatbuilding became the convicts' trade. After 1830 the timber continued to attract loggers, but it wasn't until 1882 that Strahan began life as a port for the nearby copper and lead fields. Although it was Tasmania's third-largest port in 1900, its unreliability led to its closure by 1970 and the population dwindled to three hundred. It's now a small **fishing village** for abalone, crayfish and shark, and commercial fish farming of rainbow trout and Atlantic salmon, though the main industry is tourism. The basing of the **Franklin Blockade** campaign here in 1982 shook up the town and brought the international media here for two months. **Cruises** on the **Gordon River** had already been running before this event, but the declaration of a **World Heritage Area** has meant that busloads of tourists now regularly descend upon Strahan to see the river, creating a hectic atmosphere while they're boarding and disembarking. The West Coast Wilderness Railway (see box opposite) was added to the list of attractions in 2003. Federal Resorts owns both the railway and Gordon River Cruises, and much of the central accommodation and the pub; since the general store recently left The Esplanade and moved up the hill, Strahan has ceased to seem "real", but there's no doubt that it's a beautiful town and the surrounding natural attractions are totally compelling.

Transport and services

The place to make enquiries and bookings for TassieLink **bus** services is the visitor centre (see p.1157). There's a scheduled service from Launceston and

Devonport via Cradle Mountain (3 weekly), connecting with a Queenstown–Strahan service (5 weekly), which connects with the service to Hobart via Lake St Clair. Airlines of Tasmania (Ⓣ03/6248 5490, Ⓦwww.airtasmania.com.au) has a new 45-minute Hobart–Strahan service (3 weekly; one-way $148). The Strahan Supermarket, 1km up the hill overlooking the centre on Reid St (Mon–Fri 7.30am–7pm, Sat & Sun 8am–6pm), has EFTPOS facilities and is an ANZ **bank** agent; otherwise, there's an ANZ **ATM** outside the *Fish Cafe* on The Esplanade. At The Esplanade's far end, the old **Customs House** contains the **post office** (also a Commonwealth Bank agent), and there is a **Parks and Wildlife** office (Mon–Fri 9am–5pm; Ⓣ03/6471 7122), where park passes are available, and an **Online Access Centre**.

Accommodation

If you've got your own transport to get there, you can **camp** for free at Ocean Beach and Henty Dunes (see p.1159); there are no facilities, but free hot showers can be had in town in the toilet block opposite the post office. **Accommodation** is expensive and gets booked up in the summer; to be safe, book ahead or bring a tent – otherwise you might have to head back to Zeehan or Queenstown. The Strahan Visitor Centre (see opposite) has a free accommodation booking service. For something different, you can also stay onboard West Coast Yacht (see p.1159; also enquire about their comfortable self-contained holiday units *The Crays* ❻).

Franklin Manor The Esplanade Ⓣ03/6471 7311, Ⓦwww.franklinmanor.com.au. Sedate and elegant two-storey weatherboard B&B, surrounded by trees and flowers. The interior is attractively decorated and lovingly maintained; classical music plays in the guest lounge, always filled with fresh flowers, and there's a classy restaurant run by an award-winning French chef (and co-owner). ❺–❼

Gordon Gateway Chalet Grining St, Regatta Point Ⓣ03/6471 7165, Ⓦwww.gordongateway.com.au. Peaceful harbourfront spot in over two acres of gardens looking across to the town and its fishing boats. Spacious studios with kitchenettes; gas BBQ site in the gardens. ❺

Risby Cove The Esplanade Ⓣ03/6471 7572, Ⓦwww.risby.com.au. An old sawmill, fully renovated using corrugated iron and Huon pine salvaged from the harbour, now houses upmarket one- and two-bedroom accommodation suites with kitchenette area. There's an on-site restaurant/café, gallery and even a digital film theatre (nightly 7pm; $9.50). ❺–❻

Strahan Backpackers Harvey St Ⓣ03/6471 7255. Located beside a bush-lined stream with its own resident platypus, this modern hostel has spacious but slightly neglected common kitchens, eating areas and a lounge. Well cared-for timber bedroom cabins (double or twin), some with TVs, share the hostel bathrooms and kitchens. Also a self-contained unit sleeping four (❹). It's 1km from the centre but TassieLink buses drop off. Dorms $20, rooms ❷, cabins ❸

Strahan Caravan & Tourist Park The Esplanade Ⓣ03/6471 7239. Well-positioned camping and cabins near the foreshore. Vans ❷, cabins ❸–❹

Strahan Colonial Cottages 7 Reid St Ⓣ03/6471 7019. Three beautifully renovated and well-equipped cottages, one a renovated church. ❻

The Strahan Village The Esplanade Ⓣ03/6471 7160 or 1800 628 286, Ⓦwww.strahanvillage.com.au. Among the various styles of Federal Hotels and Resorts' upmarket accommodation (all en suite) clustered along and above The Esplanade, best-positioned are the spacious "Terrace" rooms above the renovated 1930s *Hamers Hotel*, with private balcony access looking right over the boats ($200). There are a variety of "Village" units ($170–200) along the Esplanade, some of which look like cute cottages, but they're really only motel rooms. The most expensive "Hilltop" ($220–310) rooms command great views from the hill above, with the buffet-style *Macquarie Restaurant and Bar* also taking in the sights. The cheapest "Hilltop Garden View" rooms are tucked behind ($140). ❺–❽

Wheelhouse Apartments 4 Frazer St Ⓣ03/6471 7777, Ⓦwww.wheelhouseapartments.com.au. These unique two-storey apartments, with abundant use of local timbers and a stylish maritime theme, sit on the edge of a cliff above the harbour. Slanted wall-to-ceiling windows in the downstairs living room give a prow-of-a-ship feel and awesome views. Upstairs, there are less spectacular vistas from the spa in the master bedroom and from the second bedroom. Full kitchen and laundry in both apartments. $250 in peak season. ❽

The Town

Your first stop should be the innovative wooden and iron **Strahan Visitor Centre**, on The Esplanade (daily: Oct–March 10am–6pm, till 9pm Jan; April–Sept 11am–6pm; 24hr ticket $2; ⓣ03/6471 7622, ⓔstrahan@tasvisinfo.com.au), whose exterior design aims to echo the area's boatbuilding and timber industries. The interior features a waterfall, and a huge glass wall providing views of the harbour. The centre sets out its exhibits in a provocative and challenging way, under seven main themes: the Aborigines, convicts, logging, ecology, economy, wilderness and conflict. You can enter the foyer free of charge to pick up leaflets and information and take advantage of the **Internet access**. Outside, an **amphitheatre** is the early-evening venue for an entertaining two-man show, *The Ship That Never Was*, which retells – in slapstick audience-participation vein – the true story of an 1834 convict escape from Sarah Island (daily 5.30pm plus 8.30pm performance in Jan; $12.50).

Adjacent to the visitor centre the **Strahan Woodworks**, in a large, corrugated-iron shed (daily 8am–5pm), sells well-designed and crafted woodwork; you're also welcome to roam around Morrison's Saw Mill next door, and watch the Tasmanian timbers being processed. Also worth a visit is the **Forestry Tasmania Office**, next to Hamers pub (Mon–Fri 9am–noon & 1–5pm; ⓣ03/6471 7176), which has an amazing window display featuring a Huon pine log transforming itself into the bow of a boat; inside you can pick up leaflets describing the trees in the area, as well as other information.

The 1.7km **Strahan Historic Foreshore Walkway** is a pleasant gravel track following the shore of the harbour around to **Regatta Point** and its 1899 **train station** where the **West Coast Wilderness Railway** (see p.1154) leaves from; self-guided walk maps are available from the tourist office. En route you pass the **People's Park**, from where you can take the rainforest walk to **Hogarth Falls** (40min; 2km return).

Eating and drinking

On The Esplanade, *Hamers Hotel* (see opposite), is the focus of the town's social life, in the public bar at least, which is always a lively place for a **drink**; next door *Hamers Bar & Grill* is a fine bistro which serves up a varied selection of seafood, pasta, grills and curries (mains around $16) in a bustling atmosphere. Alongside, the *Fish Cafe & Take Away* (daily 11am–7.30pm) also makes great burgers while the smarter-than-usual *Banjo's Bakehouse* (daily 6am–8/9pm) has outside water-facing tables and does surprisingly good coffee to go with the pastries and the (pricey) cooked breakfasts (it also serves pizzas after 6pm). Just off The Esplanade on Harold St, the *Strahan Central Café* is a city-style café with views over the water from the outdoor deck and excellent coffee but restricted hours (daily noon–4pm). *Morrisons Seafood*, away from the tourist bustle at the southern end of The Esplanade past the Customs House, does the town's best fish and chips and divine wood-fired gourmet pizzas (from $10 small); there are tables in the park outside. Across the bay, Strahan's best **restaurant** is the dining room of the stylish *Franklin Manor* (see opposite), where you can sample innovative French cuisine in a pricey seven-course dégustation dinner menu ($110, with wine with each course $175), cooked by a Michelin-starred French chef. *Risby Cove* (see opposite) has an absolute waterfront café-restaurant (daily 10am through to dinner) where the contemporary Australian food has a good reputation and isn't too pricey.

Around Strahan

Six kilometres east of town, **Ocean Beach** is, at 30km, the longest beach in Tasmania but the wild waters are not safe to swim in. Come at dusk to observe

Cruising the Gordon River

The **Gordon River** is deep, its waters dark from the tannin leaching out of buttongrass plains – even the tap water in Strahan is brown (though perfectly fine to drink). Cruise boats used to travel as far as the landing at Sir John Falls, 30km upriver, but the speed at which the boats had to go was causing the riverbanks to erode – and they now travel only the 14km to **Heritage Landing**, where there's a chance to see a section of real **rainforest**: a boardwalk above the rainforest floor allows you to get close without disturbing anything. Trunks and branches of ancient myrtles and Huon pines provide homes for mosses, lichens and liverworts on their bark, and ferns and fungi grow from the trunks – even the dead trees support some forms of life, however lowly. The wet and swampy conditions are ideal for **Huon pines**, a threatened tree species found only in Tasmania: they're the second-oldest living things on earth after the bristlecone pines of western North America, with some trees found to be more than ten thousand years old. The massive pines, which may reach a height of 40m, can grow from seed but more often regenerate vegetatively, putting down roots where fallen branches touch the soil. The vast tree at the landing, reckoned to be around 2000 years old, split in two during 1997 – one half fell to the ground – but the trunk won't rot for up to one hundred years as it contains methyl eugenol oil which slows fungal growth. The oil content of the wood helps explain why it was so highly sought after as one of the few green Tasmanian timbers that floats: Huon pine logs were floated down to the boom camp and there fashioned into huge rafts to be rowed across Macquarie Harbour.

Two operators offer **river cruises**; both visit Sarah Island and make a thirty-minute stop at Heritage Landing. Gordon River Cruises have pre-designated seats, but there are floor-to-ceiling windows and you can move freely out on deck; to make the most of the experience on World Heritage Cruises, turn up early to bag a good seat. But for both, bring water- and windproof gear so you can brave the prow of the boat – much the most exhilarating spot when you whizz through Macquarie Heads (**Hells Gates**). Owned by Federal Resorts, **Gordon River Cruises** has one boat, the high-tech new *Jane Franklin II* (cruise departs 8.30am, returns 2pm, Nov–April extra cruise departs 2.30pm, returns 8pm; includes 1hr at Sarah Island; $50 including morning tea, bow-atrium seat $55, window seats $75, upper-deck seats including smorgasboard lunch $129; otherwise buffet lunch $12.50; ⓣ03/6471 4300 or ⓣ1800 628 288, ⓦwww.strahanvillage.com.au). Their booking office is located on the waterfront in a spacious complex, the Strahan Activity Booking Centre, where there's a photographic display of Strahan's history and interpretive material relating to the unique thylacine rug (see p.1079) which is exhibited in Strahan over the summer; the rug is displayed at 12.30pm and 4.30pm with an acccompanying talk (free). **World Heritage Cruises**, the local family-owned and -operated company with two day-trip boats (the *Wanderer II and Adventurer*), offers a slightly cheaper cruise, with a one-hour tour of the prison settlement Sarah Island, led by an actor telling convict tales (daily 9am–3pm; $65; snacks and $12 buffet meal available on board; licensed; ⓣ03/6471 7174, ⓦwww.worldheritagecruises.com.au). They also offer a similar afternoon cruise in summer (Jan–April; 2–8pm; $65), and a shorter morning cruise in the warmer months which doesn't stop at Sarah Island (Oct–April; 9am–1.30pm; $60). Their brand-new *Discovery*, a 33-metre small ship launched at the end of 2004, takes 24 passengers for three-day two-night luxury cruises on the Gordon River (overnight moored at Heritage Landing) and Macquarie Harbour (overnight moored at Sarah Island), with shore and kayaking excursions ($1995; 5-day package includes first night's and final night's luxury accommodation in Launceston or Hobart and transfers to and from Strahan).

the marvellous sunsets and to watch – from November to February – the migratory **muttonbirds** roost. It's an 11km drive on a gravel road, south off the road to Ocean Beach, to **Macquarie Heads** (Hells Gates). The extensive 30-metre high **Henty Dunes**, 12km north of town on the Zeehan Road (B27), are also worth seeing; two fun ways to experience them are by 4-wheel motorbike (see below) or by hiring sandboards from the Strahan Activity Centre (ⓣ1800 628 288; $30 per 2hr). You can **camp** for free at the picnic area or in other clearings and campfires are allowed. The **Teepookana Plateau** has an awe-inspiring stand of ancient Huon Pines (some nearly 2000 years old) visited via an elevated walkway which leads to a viewing tower offering 360-degree forest, mountain and harbour views; the only way to reach it and the namesake King River railway port ghost-town is by tour (see below).

To get around, you can rent **mountain bikes** from *Risby Cove* see p.1156; (half-day $10, full day $20). 4 Wheeler Bikes offers popular guided four-wheel motorbike tours of Henty Sand Dunes (40min; $40; bookings essential ⓣ03/6471 7622 or 0419 508 175) and longer tours to Teepookana. In addition to the Gordon River cruises (see box opposite) there's a wide choice of water-based **tours**. West Coast Yacht Charters, on The Esplanade (ⓣ03/6471 7422, ⓦwww.tasadventures.com/wcyc), runs evening **crayfish dinner sails** on Macquarie Harbour on a twenty-metre ketch, *Stormbreaker* (daily 6–8.30pm except May–Aug; $60 including dinner, $70 with crayfish when it's in season) and longer cruises up the Gordon River (leaving 6pm overnight to Sir John Falls for morning Franklin rafter pick-up; $150 includes accommodation on boat, breakfast and lunch; overnight Gordon river cruise to Sarah Island and Heritage Landing $290 including all meals, two nights $390); you can even stay on board the ketch for a water-borne B&B experience (❸). With Wild Rivers Jet, who have an office on The Esplanade (ⓣ03/6471 7174), you can blast up the already devastated **King River**, just south of Strahan (50min; $55), but a better option is the combined jet boat–4WD trip to the Teepookan Plateau (11am daily; 1hr 40min; $70). Strahan Marine Charters (ⓣ0418 135 983) offers private fishing or sightseeing tours.

Wilderness Air, on Strahan Wharf, runs spectacular **seaplane flights** over Macquarie Harbour and the wilderness area (daily from 9am; 1hr 20min; $129; bookings ⓣ03/6471 7280, ⓦwww.tassie.net.au/~wildair/), providing the unforgettable image of the smooth dark ribbon of the pristine Franklin River easing through dense forest. The highlight of the trip is the dramatic landing at **Sir John Falls Landing**, further upriver than the cruise boats can reach. They also have longer flights for viewing the rugged scenery around Frenchmans Cap ($149). Seair Adventure Charters (ⓣ03/6471 7718, ⓦwww.adventureflights.com.au) offers **helicopter flights** over Hells Gates and Macquarie Harbour ($95; 15min), and the Teepookana Forest, which includes a landing and walk to see the old growth Huon Pine ($165; 1hr).

The World Heritage Area

If we can revise our attitudes towards the land under our feet; if we can accept a role of steward, and depart from the role of conqueror; if we can accept the view that man and nature are inseparable parts of the unified whole – then Tasmania can be a shining beacon in a dull, uniform, and largely artificial world.

Olegas Truchanas, conservationist, 1971

It's the lure of the **wilderness** that attracts a certain type of traveller to Tasmania, to commune with nature at its most unspoilt. The state's vast wilderness areas of the South West National Park, Franklin Lower Gordon Wild Rivers

National Park and the adjacent Cradle Mountain–Lake St Clair National Park make up the **World Heritage Area**, recognized by UNESCO.

The future of the parks could have been very different had it not been for the bitterly fought battle waged by the environmentalists in the 1980s. In 1972 the flooding of the beautiful and unique **Lake Pedder** led to the formation, in 1976, of the **Wilderness Society**, which began a relentless campaign against the next plan for the southwest by the Hydro Electricity Commission (HEC), which was to build a huge dam on the Lower Gordon River that would efface Tasmania's last wild river, the Franklin. Pro-HEC forces included the then Tasmanian Premier Robin Gray. Years of protests and campaigns ensued, but in 1981 the whole southwest area was proposed for the World Heritage List. The **Franklin Blockade**, organized by the Wilderness Society and led by **Dr Bob Brown**, began on December 14, 1982, the day the southwest officially joined the list – a fact the Tasmanian government was choosing to ignore.

For two months, blockaders from all over Australia travelled upriver from their base in Strahan to put themselves in front of the bulldozers at the site, in non-violent protest. The **blockade** attracted international attention, notably when the British botanist David Bellamy joined in the protest and was among the twelve hundred or so arrested for trespassing. During the course of the campaign, Bob Hawke's Labor government was voted in, and in March 1983, following a trailblazing High Court ruling, the federal government forbade further work by the HEC. Though the blockade itself had failed to stop the preparatory work on the dam, it had changed, or at least challenged, the opinion of many Australians.

Cradle Mountain-Lake St Clair National Park

This must be a national park for the people for all time. It is magnificent, and people must know about it and enjoy it.

Gustave Weindorfer, botanist and mountaineer, 1910

Cradle Mountain–Lake St Clair National Park is Tasmania's best known, its northern **Cradle Mountain** end easily accessible from Devonport, Deloraine or Launceston, and its southern **Lake St Clair** end from Derwent Bridge on the Lyell Highway between Queenstown and Hobart. A popular route from Devonport is via Sheffield (see p.1142) on the B14, then the C132 via Wilmot, and for the final stretch to Cradle Valley, the C136. One of the most glaciated areas in Australia, with many lakes and tarns, the park covers some of Tasmania's highest land, with craggy mountain peaks such as **Mount Ossa** (1617m), the state's highest point. At its northern end, **Dove Lake**, backed by the jagged outline of Cradle Mountain, is a breathtaking sight, and at the park's southern end, Lake St Clair is the country's deepest freshwater lake at over 200m, occupying a basin gouged out by two glaciers. Between Cradle Mountain and Lake St Clair, the 80km **Overland Track** attracts walkers from all over the world, and is the best way to take in the stunning scenery – spread over five or more mud- and leech-filled days of physical, albeit exhilarating, exhaustion. However, you can do just part of the walk, or make several other satisfying day-walks around Cradle Mountain or Lake St Clair.

Transport to the park

TassieLink services both ends of the national park on two year-round **scheduled routes**, while The Overland Track summer service provides more

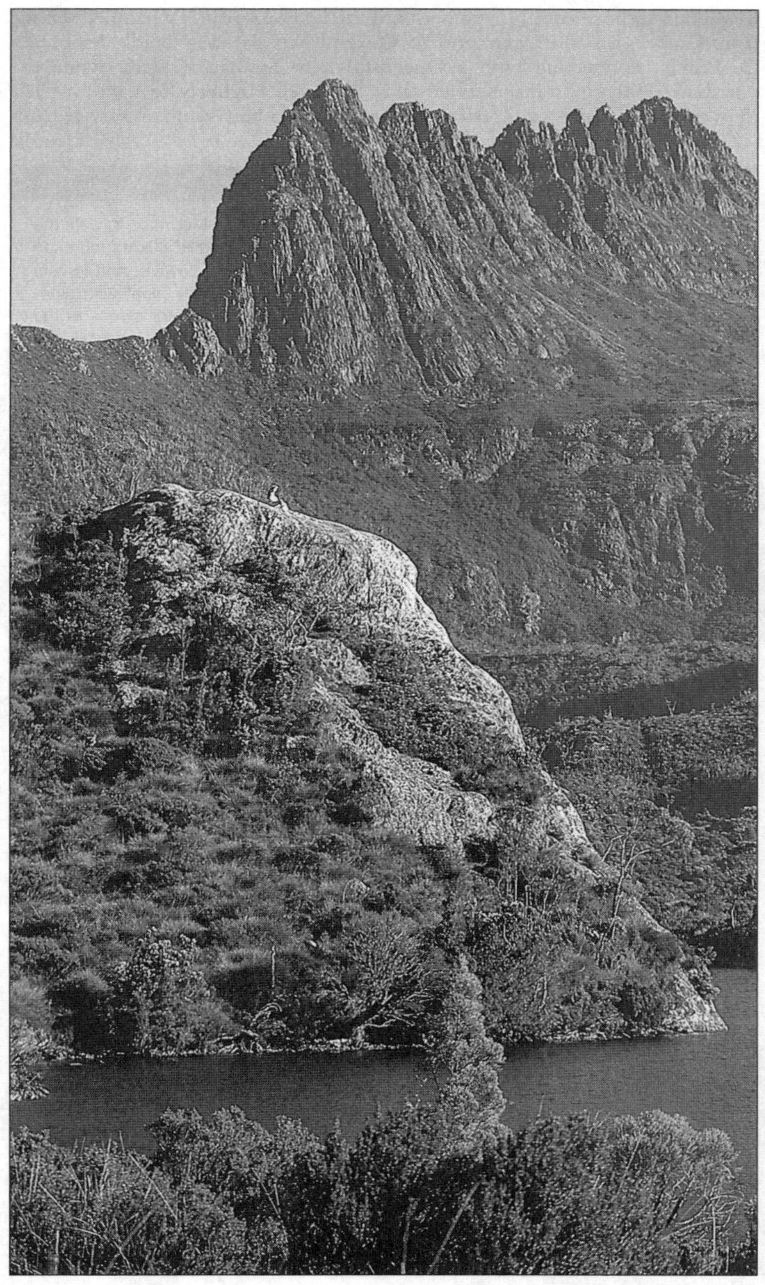

△ Cradle Mountain-Lake St Clair National Park

frequent transport from November until the end of April. A scheduled service from Launceston and Devonport to Queenstown goes via Cradle Mountain (3 weekly; connecting with a Queenstown to Strahan service), while the scheduled Hobart–Strahan service takes the Lyell Highway to Lake St Clair (5 weekly). A daily Launceston to Cradle Mountain summer service runs

The Overland Track

In summer and autumn, around 40 people a day depart Cradle Mountain to walk the **Overland Track**, probably Australia's greatest extended bushwalk: 80km, unbroken by roads and passing through buttongrass plains, fields of wild flowers, and forests of deciduous beech, Tasmanian myrtle, pandanus and King Billy pine, with side-walks leading to views of waterfalls and lakes and starting points for climbs of the various mountain peaks. Much of the track is frequently repaired boardwalk but you'll still end up ankle-deep in mud. Along the route are six basic coal-stove- or gas-heated huts (not for cooking – bring your own stove), with composting toilets outside. There's no guarantee there'll be space, so you should carry a good tent; a warm sleeping bag is essential even in the heated huts in summer.

The direct walk generally takes six days – five, if you catch a boat from Narcissus Hut across Lake St Clair; if you want to go on some of the side-walks, allow eight to ten days. On average, most walkers go for six to eight days. You should take enough food and fuel for the duration of your walk, plus extra supplies in case you have an accident or bad weather sets in; there's always plenty of unpolluted fresh water to drink from streams. Around 8000 people walk the track each year; most people come between November and April, but the best time is during February and March when the weather has stabilized, though it's bound to rain at some point, and may even snow. The track is at its most crowded from Christmas to the end of January. Because of overloading of the track during peak periods, from November 2005 a web-based booking system (Ⓦwww.overlandtrack.com.au) for departure dates will be introduced for the period between November and the end of April, and a fee of $100 per person in addition to the park entry fee will be applicable. Most people walk north to south, which is more downhill than up, and this will be the obligatory route direction between November and April. The rest of the year you can register at either end in the **national park offices** (see below and p.1164), where you receive an obligatory briefing and have your gear checked to make sure it's sufficient. The office sells last-minute camping gear and supplies: fuel stoves, meths, water bottles, trowels, warm hats and gloves. The *Cradle Mountain–Lake St Clair Map and Notes 1:100,000* ($9.10) is an essential purchase, and the *Overland Track – A Walkers Notebook* ($13.75) is a handy reference. Once you end up at Derwent Bridge (see p.1164), exhausted and covered in mud, you can use the hot showers at the campsite, for which there's a small charge.

The logistics of doing a one-way walk are smoothed by a couple of operators: Maxwell's Coaches (see above) and the Tasmanian Tour Company (see p.1138) can do **transfers** to get you back to your car, while TassieLink has special Overland Track fares that include transfers from Launceston to Cradle Mountain, and then back from Lake St Clair to Launceston ($104) or Hobart ($90) or Devonport ($79) or any two combinations. They can provide baggage transfer for an extra charge. **Guided tours** are available, the best offered by Craclair Tours (Oct–April; 8 days $1485, 10 days $1750; see p.1167); you'll still have to camp (except for comfortable cabin accommodation at the start and end) and carry a six-kilo pack. The easiest option is to go on a guided walk staying along the track at Cradle Huts, **private lodges** with hot showers, beds and delicious meals (6 days $2195 full board departing and returning Launceston; Ⓣ03/6331 2006, Ⓦwww.cradlehuts.com.au). Several operators combine Cradle Mountain with Walls of Jerusalem (see p.1132).

via Deloraine, Sheffield and Devonport. A Hobart to Lake St Clair summer service via Mount Field National Park runs daily. You can also try Maxwell's Coaches charter service (ⓣ03/6492 1431), which connects Devonport and Launceston to Lake St Clair ($70), and Launceston and Devonport to Cradle Mountain ($40).

Cradle Mountain

At **Cradle Mountain**, the impressive, modern **Cradle Mountain Visitor Centre** (daily 8am–5pm, later in summer; ⓣ03/6492 1133) provides information on the many day-walks available in this area of the park, and acts as a registration point for the Overland Track (see box opposite); it's worth buying the *Cradle Mountain Day Walks – Map & Notes* ($4) for more information. You can start here with a gentle ten-minute boardwalk circuit through rainforest and overlooking **Pencil Pine Falls**, ideal for wheelchairs or strollers. There's also the "Enchanted Walk" that follows the creek through rainforest to *Cradle Mountain Lodge* (1km one-way; 20min). Five kilometres into the park from the visitor centre, **Waldheim** ("Forest Home" in German) is the King Billy pine chalet built by the Austrian-Australian **Gustave Weindorfer** in 1912, and now a museum (open 24hr; free) devoted to the man who loved this wilderness area and helped to have it declared a national park; a fifteen-minute forest walk from the hut shows examples of ancient King Billy pine. Near the hut, there's a cosy heated day shelter where you can also picnic. There's a **shuttle bus** from the airstrip outside *Cradle Mountain Wilderness Cafe* (see below) and the Visitor Centre to Dove Lake, 2.5km on from Waldheim (Oct to mid-May every 15min daily 8am–5.20pm; mid-May to Sept Sat & Sun only); the bus is included in the park entry fee (see p.1071). Though you can still drive to the **Dove Lake car park**, in summer it's often full by 9am and the bus is the best alternative. The Dove Lake circuit (2–3hr) is an easy all-weather walk around the shore of the lake, or a popular, but steep and strenuous, day-walk from here to the summit of **Cradle Mountain** (6hr return; get advice from the ranger first). If you're feeling lazy, you can opt for a **helicopter scenic flight** (weather permitting) over the area with Seair ($185; 50min; landing at Fury Gorge with 20min on the ground; ⓣ03/6492 1132, ⓦwww.adventureflights.com.au), which is based by the *Cradle Wilderness Cafe* (see below). Further on from the café, at *Cradle Mountain Chateau* (see overleaf), the $2-million, nine-room **Wilderness Gallery** (daily 10am–5pm; $5, free for guests) features landscape photography – of Tasmania, Antarctica and the Pacific – from well-known and emerging local and international nature photographers, including the late, great Tasmanian, **Peter Dombrovskis**.

Just on the edge of the national park, and within walking distance of the visitor centre, the wonderful *Cradle Mountain Lodge* (ⓣ03/6492 1303, ⓦwww.cradlemountainlodge.com.au; cabins ❼) is the focus for **accommodation**, eating and drinking; it's definitely worth considering staying here as a treat after finishing the Overland Track. Scattered through the bush around the lodge are 96 luxurious serviced timber cabins, all with log fires and bathrooms (no cooking facilities but microwaves on request). At the lodge itself, guest facilities include lounges, a sauna, a massage room ($90 for 1hr), and you'll be treated to a slideshow about the area, a night-time wildlife documentaries, and a 45-minute walk. Other guided walks into the national park are available daily, ranging from $10 to $28. Non-guests can book in to eat at the classy **restaurant** (the buffet-style breakfast is well worth the cost – $24.95 full buffet and is included in the guest rate), or drop in to eat or drink at the cosy tavern **bar**. You can rent **bicycles** from the lodge ($15 half-day), arrange horse riding (1hr; $50), and there's a **general store** selling expensive groceries. In the national park there are eight basic self-catering **huts** (❸; linen extra $5.50 per person) at Waldheim (see above), which sleep four to eight people with generator electricity, pot-bellied stoves, no fridge or power points, and a shared amenities block – these are looked after by the National Park Visitor Centre. There's more accommodation at the cute *Cradle Mountain Highlander Cabins*, 1.5km from the park entrance on Cradle Mountain Road (ⓣ03/6492 1116, ⓦwww.cradlehighlander.com.au; ❺–❻). The newer *Cradle Mountain Wilderness Village,* next door, has a more antiseptic feel (ⓣ03/6492 1018, ⓦwww.cradlevillage.com.au; self-catering cabins ❻). Its licensed fast-food/bistro-style *Cradle Wilderness Cafe* also sells petrol and diesel (daily 8.30am–8pm, to 10.30pm in summer). *Cradle Mountain Tourist Park* (ⓣ03/6492 1395, ⓦwww.cosycabins.com/cradle), another half-kilometre back along Cradle Mountain Road, has a **campsite** with camp kitchen, a **YHA hostel,** *the Cradle Mountain Backpackers* in three heated bunkhouses (dorms $23, rising to $34 in summer), and some basic huts (❸), plus well set-up cabins sleeping up to six (❹). The campsite has a small **shop** and is linked to the lodge in summer by a shuttle bus. A little further on is the newest resort, the four-and-a-half star *Cradle Mountain Chateau* (ⓣ03/6492 1404 or ⓣ1800 130 002, ⓦwww.federalresorts.com.au; ❼–❽), which has ground-floor rooms in two adjoining guest wings, casual and upmarket restaurants, a bar serving snacks, a billiard room, tour desk, and an impressive photographic gallery directly opposite (see p.1163).

Lake St Clair and Derwent Bridge

Outside peak walking months (see p.1162), you can register to walk the Overland Track in the opposite direction at the ranger station at **CYNTHIA BAY** on **Lake St Clair** (daily 8am–5pm; ⓣ03/6289 1115), which houses an informative interpretive centre and an attractive bistro restaurant with views over the lake. Short and long **walks** around Lake St Clair are detailed on a board in the centre. You can go on a **cruise** on the MV *Idaclair,* which will drop you off at Narcissus Hut to begin the Overland Track from the southern end, or you can walk back to the centre (5–6hr); alternatively, get off at Echo Point and return on a three-hour bushwalk (summer: Cynthia Bay 9am, 12.30pm & 3pm; Narcissus Hut 9.30am, 1pm & 3.30pm; in winter the ferry runs on demand; round-trip 1hr 30min; to Echo Point $15; to Narcissus Hut $20 one-way, $25 return). Tickets (bookings essential) are sold at the restaurant, where you can also rent dinghies with outboard motors, canoes, kayaks and bicycles.

The restaurant also takes bookings for **accommodation**. *Lakeside St Clair Wilderness Holidays* (ⓣ03/6289 1137, ⓦwww.view.com.au/lakeside; ❻) has several expensive lodges, and also a backpackers' lodge (dorms $25). Compared to Cradle Mountain, the **campsite** here is poor – there's no kitchen and there's even a fee ($0.50 per 6min) to use the showers (though this is handy if you've come all muddy off the Overland Track, as you're welcome to wash here). For supplies (and takeaway alcohol), you have to go to **DERWENT BRIDGE**, 5km away on the Lyell Highway, served by Maxwell's Coaches (ⓣ03/6289 1125), whose $7 shuttle service runs on demand. At Derwent Bridge you can stay at the well-appointed self-catering *Derwent Bridge Chalets* (ⓣ03/6289 1000, ⓦwww.derwent-bridge.com; B&B ❺–❻), a couple of which are luxurious spa versions, where you'll be greeted by a welcoming fire, complimentary port and a friendly, considerate host; cheaper motel-style units, with limited kitchen facilities, are also available. The focus of the small community is the atmospheric pub, the *Derwent Bridge Wilderness Hotel* (ⓣ03/6289 1144; ❹), with its huge brick fireplace and high-ceilinged wood-raftered interior and generous, good-value bistro meals. You can stay in old-fashioned, lodge-style accommodation (some rooms en suite) or very basic hostel rooms (dorms $25; no kitchen) out back. Derwent Bridge is close to **Lake King William**, equivalent in size to Lake St Clair and popular with anglers.

Franklin Lower Gordon Wild Rivers National Park

The **Franklin Lower Gordon Wild Rivers National Park** was declared in June 1980 and by 1982 had been included with the adjoining parks on the World Heritage List. The park exists for its own sake more than anything, most of it being virtually inaccessible. You can cruise up the Gordon, or fly over it, but the really adventurous can explore by **rafting the Franklin** (see box on p.1166) and walking the **Frenchmans Cap Track**, both accessible from the **Lyell Highway**, which extends from Strahan to Hobart and runs through the park between Queenstown and Derwent Bridge. Plenty of short **walks** also lead from the highway to rainforest, rivers and lookouts.

The **Franklin River** is one of the great rivers of Australia, and the only major wild river system in Tasmania that's not been dammed. It flows for 120km from the Cheyne Range to the majestic **Gordon River**, from an altitude of 1400m down to almost sea level. Swollen by the storms of the Roaring Forties and fed by many other rivers, it can at times become a raging torrent as it passes through ancient heaths, deep gorges and rainforests. The discovery in 1981 of stone tools in the **Kutikina Cave** on the lower Franklin proved that during the last Ice Age southwest Tasmania was the most southerly point of human occupation on earth.

A **seaplane** from Strahan flies over the national park (see p.1159), and from it you can see the confluence of the two rivers – the planned site of the ill-fated dam – surrounded by thick forest, much of it impenetrable and probably never traversed by humans. The Gordon appears wide and slow compared to the narrow, winding Franklin.

Along the Lyell Highway (A10)

Heading east from Queenstown, the Lyell Highway (A10) enters the Franklin Lower Gordon Wild Rivers National Park, reaching Nelson River bridge after 4km, from where **Nelson Falls** is an easy twenty-minute return walk through temperate rainforest. From here, the road begins to wind and rise up to **Collingwood River**, the starting point for raft or canoe trips down the Franklin (see box p.1166), with some basic camping facilities.

In fine weather, the white-quartzite dome of Frenchmans Cap, looking a little like snow, can be seen from the highway. For a more spectacular viewpoint that takes in the Franklin River Valley, **Donaghy's Hill Wilderness Lookout Walk** begins further along the highway on the right. Walk from the parking area along the old road to the top of the hill, where a sign marks the beginning of the forty-minute return track. Further along the highway, the **walking track to Frenchmans Cap** (see below) begins with a fifteen-minute stroll to the suspension bridge over the river. Continuing on the Lyell, you have another opportunity to see the Franklin on a ten-minute **Nature Trail**, at a point where the river is tranquil, as it flows around large boulders; there's also a longer 25-minute circuit. At the start of the trail there's a picnic area and a wooden shelter with an **interpretive board** about the river. Beyond this point, open buttongrass plains take over, huge uninhabited expanses fringed

Rafting on the Franklin

One of the most rugged and inaccessible areas left on earth, the surrounds of the Franklin River can't really be seen on foot – few tracks lead through this twisted, tangled and wet rainforest. **Rafting** is the only way to explore the river and even this is possible only between December and early April. The Franklin is reached by rafting down the Collingwood River from the Lyell Highway, 49km west of Derwent Bridge. The full trip takes eight to fourteen days, ending at the Gordon River, where rafters head finally to Strahan by West Coast Yacht Charter (see p.1159) or seaplane with Wilderness Air (see p.1159) from Sir John Falls Camp.

One of the most dangerous Australian rivers to raft, with average **rapids** of grades 3 to 4 – and up to grade 6 in places – the Franklin requires an expedition leader with great skill and experience (though even guides have died in the rapids). It's also very remote, and in the event of an accident help can be days away. Despite this, the river's haunting isolation is part of the attraction for most visitors. The weather, too, can be harsh – and the water is cold. It's inadvisable to attempt the trip **independently** unless everyone in the party has white-water experience and the group leader has made a previous Franklin River trip; groups are required to have at least two rafts and to stay in contact with the **ranger** at Queenstown. Bear in mind that there's nowhere to rent rafting equipment in Tasmania. The **tour operators** don't require you to be experienced – just fit, with lots of stamina and courage. Prices are high, but this is an experience of a lifetime, with the seaplane flight back to Strahan usually included in the price. Water By Nature (ⓣ0408 242 941 or 1800 111 142, ⓦwww.franklinrivertasmania.com) who offer a five-day ($1390) on the Lower Franklin, a seven-day trip on the upper Franklin at $1690, or 10-day rafting the full navigable length of the river ($2250). The seven and ten-day trips include a day walk to Frenchmans Cap (see opposite) while the five and ten-day trips include a seaplane flight return to Strahan. Trips are also offered by Rafting Tasmania (see p.1072) and Tasmanian Expeditions (see p.1072).

The sketchy *Franklin River Rafting Notesheets* are available free from the Queenstown Ranger Station, PO Box 21, Queenstown, TAS 7467 (ⓣ03/6471 2511). There are **campsites** all along the Franklin, but most have room for only two or three tents.

The route

From the **Collingwood River**, it takes about three days to raft to the **Frenchmans Cap Track**. This is the **Upper Franklin**, alpine country with vegetation adapted to survive snow and icy winds. Watch out for two endemic pines, the **Huon pine** and **celery top pine**. There are lots of intermediate rapids along this stretch and a deep quartzite ravine and large still pool at Irenabyss.

The **Middle Franklin** is a mixture of pools, deep ravines and wild rapids as the river makes a 50km detour around Frenchmans Cap. Dramatic **limestone cliffs** overhang the **Lower Franklin**, which involves a tranquil paddle through dense myrtle beech forests with flowering leatherwoods overhead. The best raftable white water is here at Newlands Cascades. It's a short distance to **Kutikina Caves** and **Deena-reena**; only rafters can gain access to these Aboriginal caves.

with trees. This is **Wombat Glen**, which looks as though it's been cleared into grazing country until you step out into it and discover its bog-like nature.

At the foot of **Mount Arrowsmith**, the highway begins to ascend, winding around the mountain's southern side above the U-shaped glacial Surprise Valley. The **Surprise Valley Lookout** offers a good view of the valley and, across to the southwest, another excellent aspect of Frenchmans Cap. Continuing down, you come to King William Saddle, another fine lookout point with views of the **King William Range** to the south and **Mount Rufus** to the north.

The Frenchmans Cap Track

The most prominent mountain peak in the Franklin Lower Gordon Wild Rivers National Park is the white-quartzite dome of **Frenchmans Cap** (1446m). Its southeast face has a sheer five-hundred-metre cliff and from its summit there are uninterrupted views of Mount Ossa in the Cradle Mountain–Lake St Clair National Park, Federation Peak, Macquarie Harbour and, on a fine day, the whole of the southwest wilderness. It takes three to five days to do the 54-kilometre return trip to the summit, best done between December and March, though of the 700 who walk the track each year, only 600 do so between these months. Frenchmans Cap is much more demanding than the relatively straightforward Overland Track, as it has some very steep extended climbs and sections of mud, and should be attempted only by skilled bushwalkers – preferably with experience of other Tasmanian walks. The weather is temperamental: it rains frequently, and it can snow even in summer. Beyond Barron Pass, the track is above 900m and at any time of the year is subject to high winds, mist, rain, hail and snowfalls.

The track begins at the Lyell Highway, 55km from Queenstown, served by TassieLink's scheduled Hobart–Queenstown service (5 weekly), or you can charter Maxwell's Coaches (Ⓣ03/6492 1431) for $65 from Lake St Clair. A fifteen-minute walk from the road brings you to the suspension bridge across the river for the start of the walk. Record your plans in the registration book here and again in the logbook at the two **huts** at Lake Vera and Lake Tahune that provide basic accommodation (though this is usually full and you must bring tents and stoves with you); Frenchmans Cap is a proclaimed "Fuel Stove Only Area". There are composting toilets at both huts and plenty of camping spots along the way; water along the track is safe to drink. From the Franklin River to Lake Vera the well-defined track crosses plains and foothills, then becomes steep and rough as it climbs to Barron Pass – where there are magnificent views – becoming easier again on the way to Lake Tahune, close to the cliffs of Frenchmans Cap. From here it's a steep 1km walk to the summit, before returning the same way.

For further **information**, get the free *Frenchmans Cap Track Bushwalker Notes* and the *Frenchmans Cap Map and Notes* ($9.10); or contact the Queenstown Ranger Station (Ⓣ03/6471 2511). Craclair Tours (see p.1162), organizes seven-day guided treks (ex-Launceston $1325), and Tasmanian Expeditions offers a five-day trip (see p.1072; ex-Launceston; Dec–March; $1040).

The South West National Park

Tasmania's **South West National Park** is an area of contrast: arrow-sharp, crested ranges of white quartzite cut across buttongrass plains. The isolation, rough terrain and unpredictable weather, even in summer – the southwest has more than two hundred days of rain a year – means that this is an area for experienced bushwalkers only. Being able to use a compass and read a map are important, but so is a tolerance for trudging through deep mud and swampy buttongrass while heavily laden with supplies and plagued by leeches.

The map *South Coast Walks* ($9.10) covers the southern gateways to the World Heritage Area: Cockle Creek through Port Davey to Scotts Peak, as well as Moonlight Ridge and South West Cape, including notes on track conditions, weather and campsites. For the rest of the area you'll need to purchase Tasmap topographic **maps**.

Two airlines operate **flights** into the national park from Cambridge aerodrome, 15km from Hobart. **Par Avion** (ⓣ03/6248 5390, ⓦwww.paravion.com.au) offers a charter service to Melaleuca, weather permitting (45min; $145 one-way, $265 return); you can register your walk at the airstrip. They also offer a scenic flight over the southwest ($145), a combined scenic flight and boat trip on Melaleuca Inlet (4hr; $170) or Bathurst Harbour (full day; $275 including lunch). Par Avion also owns a luxury boat, the MV *Southern Explorer*, based on Bathurst Harbour with on-board accommodation, which cruises the harbour, Port Davey and the Davey River (2 days, 2 nights from $1400). Roaring 40s Ocean Kayaking (see p.1072) offers amazing **kayaking expeditions**: you're flown in to Melaleuca and then spend six days camping and kayaking on Port Davey and Bathurst Harbour ($1995; shorter 3-day trip $1300). **TasAir** (ⓣ03/6248 5088, ⓦwww.tasair.com.au) flies to Melaleuca or Cox Bight (both $150 one-way, $300 return), which can cut out the trudge from Melaleuca, and also offers joyrides over the whole of the World Heritage Area from Hobart for $176 (2hr 30min, includes a landing and refreshment at Cox Bight). If you're planning an extended walk, you can arrange for either airline to drop food supplies for you ($4.40 per kilo).

Unless you're flying in, or beginning a walk at **Cockle Creek**, south of Hobart, access to the South West National Park is via the **Gordon River Road,** which passes to the south of Mount Field National Park. The ranger for this (northern) end of South West National Park is based at Mount Field (see p.1100) and you should drop in or call to ask about conditions and to check that you're adequately prepared. The good sealed road heads through state forest and the South West Conservation Area, where the amazing craggy landforms of the **Frankland Range** loom above and signposts helpfully point out the names of the features, and past the drowned **Lake Pedder** (see box below) and the Gordon Dam's power station. The Hydro Tasmania-run **Gordon Dam Visitors Information Centre** is at the end of Gordon River Road, above the dam (Nov–April daily 10am–5pm; May–Oct 11am–3pm; ⓣ03/6280 1134). The Gordon Dam lookout here is breathtaking, and if you're after a thrill you can **abseil** down it with Aardvark Adventures (ⓣ03/6273 7722, ⓦwww.aardvarkadventures.com.au; 4–5 hours; $165) who will meet you at the site.

You can **stay** at Lake Pedder at the refurbished *Lake Pedder Chalet* (ⓣ03/6280 1166; shared-bathroom or en-suite rooms ❷–❹), a former staff house for the HEC that has lake views; facilities include a bar and bistro. Alternatively there are a number of free **campsites** in the area: just down the road on the shore

The flooding of Lake Pedder

To Senator Bob Brown, Tasmania's foremost Green activist, **Lake Pedder** "was one of the most gently beautiful places on the planet". The glacial lake, in the Frankland Range in Tasmania's southwest, had an area of 9.7 square kilometres until 1972, when it and the surrounding valleys were flooded as part of a huge hydroelectric scheme, creating a reservoir covering a massive 240 square kilometres and reached by the Lake Gordon Road via Maydena. Before then, the lake was so inaccessible that it could only be visited by light aircraft, which used to land on the perfect sand of the lake beach. In late 1994 a scientist revealed that, beneath the water, the sandy beach remained; in 1995 divers filmed underwater, revealing the still-visible impressions of light-aircraft tyre tracks. Certain scientists and conservationists, backed by the Wilderness Society, believe if Lake Pedder were drained it would revert to its former state, though it might take up to thirty years.

of Lake Pedder, *Ted's Beach* has a shelter shed, electric barbecues, water and toilets; and there are two more campgrounds at Scotts Peak at the southern end of Lake Pedder, where the Port Davey walk begins (see below). TassieLink runs a "Wilderness Link" service to Scotts Peak and to Condominium Creek from Hobart, via Mount Field (Dec–April).

Western Arthurs Traverse and Federation Peak

The most spectacular bushwalk in Tasmania, only 20km in length and 5km in width, **Western Arthurs Traverse** takes in 25 major peaks and 30 lakes. The last glacial period gouged into this range, leaving sharp quartzite ridges, craggy towers and impressive cliffs, and carving cirque valleys that are now filled by dark, tannin-stained lakes, surrounded by contrasting buttongrass plains. Violent storms, mists and continuous rain can plague the route in summer since it's in the direct path of the Roaring Forties. Crossing these ranges makes for a superb but difficult walk, taking between nine and twelve days, and camping areas are limited. Though there's no man-made track, the route, starting at Scotts Peak Road, is not difficult to follow; it involves scrambling over roots and branches and making short descents and ascents into gullies and cliff lines, and you'll need to use a rope at some point.

The **Eastern Arthur Range** is the location of the major goal for intrepid southwest walkers – **Federation Peak**, often considered the most challenging in Australia, with its steep, almost perfectly triangular outline rising starkly above the surrounding rugged peaks and ridges. It was named by a surveyor in 1901, the year of federation, when most of the major landmarks in the southwest were still unvisited; in fact, the peak was not successfully scaled until 1949, its thick scrub, forests and cliffs having kept walkers at bay. Although the walk is now easier since the terrain has been "broken in", each year many walkers are turned back by the worst weather in Tasmania, and one person has died tackling the route. All the ascents are extremely difficult, and most parties take between seven and ten days to reach the peak and return; minor rock climbing is required to get to the summit. The walk begins at the same point as the Port Davey Track.

Mount Anne Circuit

The highest peak in the southwest, **Mount Anne** (1423m) is part of a small range capped with red dolerite – a contrast to the surrounding white quartzite. Views from the summit are spectacular in fine weather, but even in summer the route is very exposed and prone to bad weather. It's suitable only for experienced walkers carrying a safety rope. The three- to four-day walk begins 20km along Scotts Peak Road at Condominium Creek (where there are basic camping facilities) and ends 9km south at Red Tape Creek; a car shuttle might be advisable, or you can be picked up and dropped off from Hobart with TassieLink's "Wilderness Link" service (Nov–April).

Port Davey Track

Going straight through the heart of the World Heritage Area, from Scotts Peak Dam south to Melaleuca (where you fly out, see p.1168), is the little-used 70km **Port Davey Track**, a wet, muddy four- to five-day trek over buttongrass plains, with views of rugged mountain ranges along the way. It's less interesting than some of the other walks in the area and most groups combine it with the South Coast Track for a ten- to sixteen-day wilderness experience, which requires a drop-off of food supplies. This combined walk is often called the **South West Track**. TassieLink offers a "Wilderness Link" (Nov–April) service to Scotts Peak.

South Coast Track

The **South Coast Track** is known for its magnificent **beaches** and spectacular coastal scenery of Aboriginal **middens**, rainforest and buttongrass ridges. At 85km, it's one of the longest tracks in the South West National Park – a six- to eight-day moderate to difficult walk, usually done from Melaleuca east to Cockle Creek. Since the route is mostly along the coast, the climate is milder than in many parts of the World Heritage Area but there is exposure to cold southerly winds and frequent rain; also, while crossing the exposed Ironbound Range (900m), even in summer it can sleet or snow. And though the track is regularly maintained, you do need to plough through sections of mud. There are no huts along the way, except at the Melaleuca airstrip. Around 1000 people do the walk each year, 75 percent of them between December and March. The best **approach** is to fly direct to Cox Bight with TasAir, cutting out the boring buttongrass plains walk from Melaleuca, then head for Cockle Creek where TassieLink provides a "Wilderness Link (Nov–April) service to Hobart. Alternatively, you can begin at Cockle Creek and fly out at Melaleuca with TasAir or Par Avion, or arrange for extra food supplies to be flown in at Melaleuca and continue along the Port Davey Track across the water, using the rowboats provided.

Tasmanian Expeditions (see p.1072) runs an extended **organized walk** of the South Coast Track (Nov–March; $1860). You need to be very fit for the nine-day trip, as each party member (maximum of ten) carries a share of the food and tents, a weight of 18–20kg. They also offer a 16-day trip ($2990) which combines the South Coast Track with the Port Davey Track, above. Tiger Trails' ten-day South Coast walk runs through the year (see p.1072; ex-Hobart $1599).

South West Cape

The granite South West Cape juts out for 3km into the wild Southern Ocean. **Walking** is fairly easy here, though the rough unmarked tracks across open countryside require sound navigation, and some high windy ridges have to be crossed. All routes start and end at Melaleuca or Cox Bight but there are a variety of ways to the cape and beyond, taking in different beaches and bays. Depending on which you choose, a simple route will take from three to seven days, and the full circuit between six and nine. Because of the growing popularity of the walks, they may be overcrowded in the summer months.

Travel details

Between Tasmania and the mainland states

Ferries

Spirit of Tasmania Bass Strait ferry from Port Melbourne to Devonport (1–2 daily; 10hr).
Spirit of Tasmania ferry from Darling Harbour, Sydney to Devonport (1–3 weekly; 21hr).

Flights

Mainly through Sydney's Mascot or Melbourne's Tullamarine airports, with smaller companies operating from Essendon and Moorabbin airports, on the fringes of Melbourne.

Flinders Island to: Launceston (2–4 daily; 45min); Melbourne (Moorabbin 4 weekly; 50min).
King Island to: Burnie (3 daily Mon–Fri, 2 daily Sat & Sun; 45min); Devonport (4 daily Mon–Fri, 2 daily Sat & Sun; 45min); Melbourne (Tullamarine 5 weekly; 45min).
Melbourne to: Burnie (4 daily; 1hr); Devonport (4 daily; 1hr); Flinders Island (Essendon 4 weekly; 50min); Hobart (10 daily; 1hr); King Island

(Tullamarine 5 weekly; 45min); Launceston (10 daily; 1hr).
Sydney to: Hobart (4–7 daily; 2hr 20min); Launceston (1–3 daily; 2hr 35min).

Transport on the island

Buses – scheduled services

Burnie to: Smithton via the northwest coast (1–3 daily Mon–Sat, 1 daily Sun; 1hr 30min).
Deloraine to: Devonport (3 daily; 40min); Hobart (2–4 daily; 4hr); Launceston (3–5 daily; 45min).
Devonport to: Burnie (3–6 daily; 50min); Cradle Mountain (3 weekly; 2hr 15min); Deloraine (3 daily; 40min); Hobart (2–4 daily; 5hr 30min); Launceston (3–5 daily; 1hr 30min); Queenstown (3 weekly; 7hr).
Hobart to: Bicheno (3–6 weekly; 4hr); Burnie (3–6 daily; 4hr 45min); Cygnet (3 on Thurs, 1 daily rest of week; 55min); Deloraine (2–4 daily; 4hr); Devonport (2–4 daily; 5hr 30min); Dover (2 daily Mon–Fri; 55min); Geeveston (4 daily Mon–Fri, 1 daily Sun; 1hr 15min); Kettering (Mon–Fri 4 daily; 40min); Lake St Clair (4 weekly; 3hr); Launceston (3–7 daily; 2hr 30min); New Norfolk (1–7 daily; 30min); Port Arthur (2 daily Mon–Fri; 2hr); Queenstown via New Norfolk, Lake St Clair and Frenchmans Cap with connections to Strahan (5 weekly; 7hr 45min); Richmond (5 daily Mon–Fri; 25min); St Helens (1–2 daily except Sat; 3hr); St Marys (1–2 daily except Sat; 3hr); Swansea (1–2 daily except Sat; 2hr 30min–3hr 30min).
Launceston to: Bicheno (3 daily except Sat; 2hr 40min); Burnie (3–6 daily; 3hr); Cradle Mountain (3 weekly; 4hr); Deloraine (2–5 daily; 45min); Derby (1–2 daily except Sat; 2hr 40min); Devonport (3–5 daily; 1hr 30min); Hobart (3–7 daily; 2hr 30min); Mole Creek (1 daily Mon–Fri; 1hr 30min); Queenstown (3 weekly; 7hr); St Helens via St Marys (1 daily except Sat; 2hr 45min).
Queenstown to: Strahan (5 weekly; 45 min).
Scottsdale to: Bridport (2 daily Mon–Fri; 30 min).

Ferries

Beauty Point to: George Town (2–3 daily Mon–Sat, 2 daily Sun; 15–20min).
Bridport to: Flinders Island (1 weekly; 8hr).
Kettering to: Bruny Island (10–11 daily Mon–Sat, 8 daily Sun; 20min).
Triabunna to: Maria Island (4 daily; 20–45min).

Contexts

Contexts

History 1175

Australia's indigenous peoples 1188

Wildlife 1193

Australia film 1198

Australian music 1207

Books 1215

Australian English 1227

History

The first European settlers saw Australia as *terra nullius* – empty land – on the principle that Aborigines didn't "use" the country in an agricultural sense, a belief which remained uncontested in law until 1992. However, decades of archeological work, the reports of early settlers and oral tradition have established that humans had occupied Australia for a minimum of forty thousand years – evidence that Aboriginal peoples shaped, controlled and used their environment as surely as any farmer. Even so, it's difficult for visitors to form an idea of pre-colonial times, as two centuries of European rule shattered traditional Aboriginal life, and evidence of those earlier times mostly consists of cryptic art sites and legends – though if you're lucky enough to get beyond the tourist image, you'll realize that Aboriginal culture, though being redefined, is far from confined to the past. The very simplified outline of Aboriginal history below is intended mainly as a background to accounts given in the Guide, followed by a fuller description of the years since European colonization.

From Gondwana to the Dreamtime

After the break-up of the supercontinent **Gondwana** into India, Africa, South America, Australasia and Antarctica, Australia moved away from the South Pole, reaching its current geographical location about fifteen million years ago. Though the mainland was periodically joined to New Guinea and Tasmania, there was never a land link with the rest of Asia, and the country developed a unique fauna. Most notably marsupials, or pouched mammals, became common, but a whole range of giant animals – the megafauna – also flourished, along with widespread rainforests, until about fifty thousand years ago. Subsequent Ice Ages dried out the climate; by six thousand years ago the seas had stabilized at their present levels and Australia's environment was much as it appears today: an arid centre with a relatively fertile eastern seaboard. **Humans** had been in Australia long before then of course, most likely taking advantage of low sea levels to cross the Timor Trough into northern Australia, or island-hop from Indonesia onto what is now the Cape York Peninsula via New Guinea. Exactly when this happened, how many times it happened and what the colonists did next are debatable. There's no direct evidence for either distinct or continuous migrations from Asia, but since the earliest dated sites are found in the south of Australia, it seems reasonable to believe that human occupation goes back further than scientists' current estimate of forty thousand years. The oldest known remains from central Australia are only 22,000 years old, so it's also fairly plausible that initial colonization occurred around the coast, followed by later exploration of the interior – though it's just as likely that corrosive rainforests, which covered the centre until about twenty thousand years ago, obliterated all trace of earlier human habitation. When the European settlers arrived, the **thylacine** (Tasmanian tiger) had disappeared from the Australian mainland but still lived in Tasmania, while the dingo, a descendant of the domesticated dogs introduced to Australia by Aborigines, was prevalent on the mainland but unknown in Tasmania. This indicates that there was a further influx of people and **dogs** more recently than twelve thousand years ago, after rising sea levels had separated Tasmania and it had become an island. The earliest inhabitants used crude **stone implements**, gradually replaced by a more refined technology based around lighter tools, **boomerangs**, and the use of core stones to flake "blanks", which were then fashioned into spearheads, knives and scrapers. As only certain types of stone were suitable for the process, tribes living further away from quarries had to trade with those living near them. **Trade networks** for rock, **ochre** (a red clay used for ceremonial purposes) and other products – shells and even wood for canoes – eventually stretched from New Guinea to the heart of the continent, following river systems away from the coast. **Rock art**, preserved in an ancient engraved tradition, and other more recent painted styles seem to indicate that cultural links also travelled along these trade routes – similar symbols and styles are found in widely separated regions.

It's probable that the disappearance of the megafauna was accelerated by Aboriginal hunting, but the most dramatic change wrought by the original Australians was the controlled use of **fire** to clear areas of forest. Burning promoted new growth and encouraged game, indirectly expanding grassland and favouring certain plants – cycads, grasstrees, banksias and eucalypts – which evolved fire-reliant seeds and growth patterns. But while the Aborigines modified the environment for their own ends, their belief that land, wildlife and people were an interdependent whole engendered a sympathy for natural processes, and maintained a balance between the population and natural resources. Tribes were organized and related according to complex kinship systems, reflected in the three hundred different **languages** known to exist at that time. Legends about the mythical **Dreamtime**, when creative forces shaped the landscape, provided verbal maps of tribal territory and linked natural features to the actions of these Dreamtime ancestors, who often had both human and animal forms. This spiritual and practical attachment to tribal areas was expedient in terms of use of resources, but was the weak point in maintaining a culture after white dispossession: separated from the lands they related to, legends lost their meaning, and the people their sense of identity.

The first Europeans

Prior to the sixteenth century, the only regular visitors to Australia were the **Malays**, who established seasonal camps while fishing the northern coasts for trepang, a sea slug, to sell to the Chinese. In Europe, the globe had been carved up between Spain and Portugal in 1494 under the auspices of Pope Alexander VI at the **Treaty of Tordesillas**, and all maritime nations subsequently kept their nautical charts secret, to protect their discoveries. It's possible, therefore, that the inquisitive **Portuguese** knew of **Terra Australis**, the Great Southern Land, soon after founding their colony in East Timor in 1516.

But while the precise date of "discovery" is contentious, it is clear that various nations were making forays into the area: the **Dutch** in 1605 and 1623, who were appalled by the harsh climate and inhabitants of Outback Queensland, and the **Spanish** in 1606, who were looking for both plunder and pagans to convert to Catholicism. The latter, guided by **Luis Vaes de Torres**, blithely navigated the strait between New Guinea and Cape York as if they knew it was there. As Torres hailed from Portugal it is indeed likely that he knew where he was; there's evidence that the Portuguese had **mapped** a large portion of Australia's northern coastline as early as 1536.

Later in the seventeenth century, the Dutch navigators **Dirk Hartog**, **Van Diemen** and **Abel Tasman** added to maps of the east and north coasts, but eventually discarded "New Holland" as a barren, worthless country. British interest was first stirred in 1697 by **William Dampier**, a buccaneer who wrote popular accounts of his visit to Western Australia. However, it wasn't until the British captured the Spanish port of Manila, in the Philippines, in 1762, that detailed maps of Australia's coast fell into their hands; it took them only six more years to assemble an expedition to locate the continent. Sailing in 1768 on the *Endeavour*, Captain **James Cook** headed to Tahiti, then proceeded to map New Zealand's coastline before sailing west in 1770 to search for the Great Southern Land – unsure whether this was New Holland or an as yet undiscovered landmass.

The British sighted the continent in April 1770 and sailed north from Cape Everard to **Botany Bay**, where Cook commented on the Aborigines' initial indifference to seeing the *Endeavour*. When a party of forty sailors attempted to land, however, two Aborigines attacked them with spears; the British drove them off with musket fire. Continuing on up the Queensland coast, the British passed Moreton Bay and Fraser Island before entering the treacherous passages of the Great Barrier Reef where, on June 11, the *Endeavour* ran aground off Cape Tribulation. Cook managed to beach the ship safely at the mouth of the Endeavour River (present-day Cooktown), where the expedition set up camp while the ship was repaired.

Contact between Aborigines and whites during the following six weeks was tinged with a mistrust that never quite erupted into serious confrontation, and Cook took the opportunity to make notes in which he tempered romanticism for the "noble savage" with the sharp observation that European and Aboriginal values were mutually incomprehensible. The expedition was intrigued by some of Australia's wildlife, but otherwise unimpressed with the country, and were glad to sail onwards on August 5. With imposing skill, Cook successfully managed to navigate the rest of the reef, finally claiming possession of the country – which he named **New South Wales** – for King George III on August 21, at Possession Island in the Torres Strait, before sailing off to Timor.

Convicts

The expedition's reports didn't arouse much enthusiasm in London however, and the disdainful attitude towards the Great Southern Land matched the opinion voiced by the Dutch more than a century before. However, after the loss of its American colonies after the **American War of Independence** in 1783, Britain was deprived of a handy location to offload convicted criminals. They were temporarily housed in prison ships or "hulks", moored around the country, while the government tried to solve the problem. Sir **Joseph Banks**, botanist on the *Endeavour*, advocated Botany Bay as an ideal location for a **penal colony** that could soon become self-sufficient. The government agreed (perhaps also inspired by the political advantages of gaining a foothold in the Pacific), and in 1787 the **First Fleet**, packed with over seven hundred convicts, set sail for Australia on eleven ships, under the command of Captain **Arthur Phillip**. Reaching Botany Bay in January 1788, Phillip deemed it unsuitable for his purposes and instead founded the settlement at **Sydney Cove**, on Port Jackson's fine natural harbour.

The early years at Sydney were not promising: the colonists suffered erratic weather and starvation, Aboriginal hostility, soil that was too hard to plough, and timber so tough it dented their axes. In 1790, supplies ran so low that a third of the population had to be transferred to a new colony on **Norfolk Island**, 1500 kilometres northeast. Even so, in the same year Britain dispatched a second fleet with a thousand more convicts – 267 of whom died en route. To ease the situation, Phillip granted packages of farmland to marines and former convicts before he returned to Britain in 1792. The first **free settlers** arrived the following year, and Britain's preoccupation with the French Revolutionary Wars meant a reduction in the number of convicts being transported to the colony, thus allowing a period of consolidation.

Meanwhile, **John Macarthur** manipulated the temporary governor into allowing his **New South Wales Corps**, which had replaced the marines as the governor's strong arm, to exercise considerable power in the colony. This was temporarily curtailed in 1800 by **Philip King**, who also slowed an illicit rum trade, encouraged new settlements, and speeded production by allowing convicts to work for wages. Macarthur was forced out of the corps into the wool industry, importing Australia's first **sheep** from South Africa. He continued to stir up trouble though, which culminated in the **Rum Rebellion** of 1808, when merchant and pastoral factions, supported by the military, ousted Governor **William Bligh.** Britain finally took notice of the colony's anarchic state and appointed the firm-handed Colonel **Lachlan Macquarie**, backed by the 73rd Regiment, as Bligh's replacement in 1810. Macquarie settled the various disputes – Macarthur had fled to Britain a year earlier – and brought eleven years of disciplined progress to the colony.

Labelled the "Father of Australia", for his vision of a country that could rise above its convict origins, Macquarie implemented enlightened policies towards former convicts or **emancipists**, enrolling them in public offices. He also attempted to educate, rather than exterminate, Aboriginal people and was the driving force behind New South Wales becoming a productive, self-sufficient colony. But he offended the landowner **squatters**, who were concerned that emancipists were being granted too many favours, and also those who regarded the colony solely as a place of punishment. In fact, conditions had improved so much that by 1819 New South Wales had become the major destination for voluntary emigrants from Britain.

In 1821 Macquarie was replaced as governor, and his successor, Sir Thomas Brisbane, was instructed to segregate, not integrate, convicts. To this end, when New South Wales officially graduated from being a penal settlement to a new British colony in 1823, convicts were used to colonize newly explored regions – Western Australia, Tasmania and Queensland – as far away from Sydney's free settlers as possible.

Explorers

Matthew Flinders had already circumnavigated the mainland in 1803 (and suggested the name "**Australia**") in his leaky vessel, the *Investigator*, and with the colony firmly established, expeditions began pushing inland from Sydney. In 1823 John Oxley, the Surveyor General, having previously explored newly discovered pastoral land west of the Blue Mountains, chose the **Brisbane River** in Queensland as the site of a new penal colony, thus opening up the fertile Darling Downs to future settlement. Meanwhile, townships were being founded elsewhere around the coast, eventually leading to the creation of

separate colonies to add to that of Van Diemen's Land (Tasmania), settled in 1803 to ward off French exploration: Albany and Fremantle on the west coast were established in 1827 and 1829 respectively, followed by the Yarra River (Melbourne, Victoria) in 1835, and Adelaide (South Australia) in 1836.

But it was the possibilities of the **interior** – which some maintained concealed a vast inland sea – which captured the imagination of the government and squatters. Setting out from Adelaide in 1844, **Charles Sturt** was the first to attempt to cross the centre. Forced to camp for six months at a desert waterhole, where the heat melted the lead in his pencils and unthreaded screws from equipment, he managed to reach the aptly named Sturt's Stony Desert before scurvy forced him back to Adelaide. At the same time, **Ludwig Leichhardt**, a Prussian doctor, had more luck in his crossing between the Darling Downs and Port Essington, near Darwin, which he accomplished in fourteen months. Unlike Sturt, Leichhardt found plenty of potential farmland and returned a hero. He vanished in 1848 however, while again attempting to cross the continent. In the same year, the ill-fated **Kennedy** expedition managed the trek from Tully to Cape York in northern Queensland, but with the loss of most of the party – Kennedy included – as a result of poor planning, starvation and attack by Aborigines. Similarly, **Burke and Wills**' successful 1860 south-to-north traverse between Melbourne and the Gulf of Carpentaria in Queensland was marred by the death of the expedition leaders upon their return south, owing to bad organisation and a series of unfortunate errors (see box on p.593 for the full story of their trek). Finally, Australia's centre was located by **John MacDouall Stuart** in 1860, who subsequently managed a safe return journey to Adelaide from the north coast the following year. Hopes of finding an inland sea were quashed, and the harsh reality of a dry, largely infertile interior began to dawn on developers.

Aboriginal response

British advances had been repulsed from the very first year of the colony's foundation; Governor Phillip reporting that "the natives now attack any straggler they meet unarmed". Forced off their traditional hunting grounds, which were taken by the settlers for agriculture or grazing, the Aborigines began stealing crops and spearing cattle. Response from the British was brutal; the relatively liberal Lieutenant-Governor George Arthur ordered a sweep of Tasmania in 1830, to round up all Aboriginal people and herd them into **reserves**, a symbolic attempt to clear "the uncivilized" from the paths of progress (see box on p.1068–1069). More direct action, such as the **Myall Creek Massacre** in 1838 (see box on p.383), when 28 Aborigines were roped together and butchered by graziers, created public outcry, but similar "**dispersals**" became commonplace wherever indigenous people resisted white intrusion. More insidious methods, such as poisoning waterholes or lacing gifts of flour with arsenic, were also employed by pastoralists angered over stock losses.

The Aboriginal people were not a single, unified society, and the British exploited existing divisions by creating the notorious **Native Mounted Police**, an Aboriginal force that aided and abetted the extermination of rival groups. By the 1890s, citing a perversion of Darwinian theory which held that Aboriginal people were less evolved than whites and so doomed to extinction, most states had followed Tasmania's example of "**protectionism**", relocating

Aborigines into reserves which were frequently a long way from their traditional lands – in Queensland, for instance, Rockhampton Aborigines were moved to Fraser Island, 500km away.

Gold

The discovery of **gold** in 1851 by Edward Hargraves, fresh from the California fields, had a dramatic bearing on Australia's future. The first major strikes in New South Wales and Victoria brought an immediate rush of hopeful miners from Sydney and Melbourne and, once the news spread overseas, from the USA and Britain. The British government, realizing the absurdity of spending taxes on shipping criminals to a land of gold when there were plenty of people willing to pay for their passage, finally **ended transportation** in 1853. Gold also opened up Australia's interior far more thoroughly than explorers had done; as returns petered out in one area, prospectors moved on into uncharted regions to find more. Western Australia and Queensland (which was saved from bankruptcy by the discovery of gold in 1867) experienced booms up until 1900 and, although mining initially followed in the path of pastoral expansion, the rushes began to attract settlements and markets into previously uncultivated regions.

A new "level society", based on a work-and-mateship ethic, evolved on the goldfields, where education had little bearing on an ability to endure hard work and spartan living conditions. Yet the **diggers** were all too aware of their poor social and political rights. At the end of 1854, frustrations over mining licences erupted at **Eureka** (see box on p.1011), on the outskirts of Ballarat in Victoria, where miners built a stockade and ended up being charged by mounted police. Twenty-two of the miners were killed in the event, which is commonly regarded as a turning point in Australian history. The surviving rebels – put on trial for high treason – were vindicated, and rights, including the vote, were granted to miners. The Victorian goldfields also saw **racial tensions** directed against a new minority, the Chinese, who first arrived there during the 1850s. Disheartened by diminishing returns and infuriated by the Chinese ability to find gold in abandoned claims, diggers stormed a Chinese camp at **Lambing Flat** in 1861. Troops had to be sent in to stop the riots, but the ringleaders were later acquitted by an all-white jury. Throughout the country, goldfields became centres of **nationalism** (despite the fact that the Chinese improved life by running stores and market gardens in mining towns), peaking in Queensland in the 1880s, where the flames were fanned by the importation of **Solomon Islanders** to work on sugar plantations. Ostensibly to prevent slavery, but politically driven by recession and growing white unemployment, the government forced the repatriation of Islanders, taxed the Chinese out of the country, and passed the 1901 Immigration Act – also known as the **White Australia policy** – which greatly restricted non-European immigration.

Federation and war

Central government was first mooted in 1842, but new states were not keen to return to the control by New South Wales, lose interstate customs duties, or share the new-found mineral wealth which had consolidated separation in the first place. But by the end of the century they began to see advantages to **federation**, not least as a way to control indentured labour and present a united front against French, German and Russian expansion in the Pacific. A decade of wrangling by the states, to ensure equal representation irrespective of population, saw the formation of a High Court and a two-tier parliamentary system consisting of a House of Representatives and Senate, presided over by a Prime Minister. Each state would have its own premier, and Britain would be represented by a Governor-General. Approved by Queen Victoria shortly before her death, the **Commonwealth of Australia** came into being on January 1, 1901.

It's notable that the Immigration Act (see opposite) was the first piece of legislation to be passed by the new parliament, and reflected the nationalist drive behind federation. Though the intent was to create an Australia largely of European – and preferably British – descent, the policy also sowed the seeds for Australian independence from the "Mother Country". The first pull away came as early as 1912, when the **Commonwealth Bank** opened; Australia was trying to become less financially reliant on Britain. Centred entirely on white interests, the White Australia policy ensured that Aboriginal people were not included in the national census, nor were they allowed to vote, until 1967. The new government did, however, give **women** the vote in 1902, and the Australian Labor Party, which had grown out of the economic recession and union battles with the government during the 1890s, established the concept of a **minimum wage** in 1907.

Defence had also been a positive force behind federation. But even though the war between Japan and Russia in 1904 had highlighted the need to build its own defence force, Australia was largely unprepared for the outbreak of hostilities in Europe a decade later, owning little more than a navy made up of secondhand British ships. Promising to support Britain to "the last man and the last shilling", there was a patriotic rush to enlist in the army, and an opportunistic occupation of German New Guinea by Australian forces. Surprisingly, the issue of compulsory conscription, raised by Prime Minister **Billy Hughes**, was twice defeated in referendums during World War I.

From the Australian perspective, the most important stage of the war occurred when Turkey gave its support to Germany in 1915. **Winston Churchill** formulated a plan to defend British shipping in the Dardanelles by occupying the **Gallipoli Peninsula**, and diverted Australian infantry bound for Europe. Between April and December 1915, wave after wave of Australian troops were mown down below Turkish gun emplacements, as they attempted to take control of the peninsula. By the end of the year it became clear that Gallipoli was not going to fall, and the survivors were evacuated to fight on the Western Front. The long-term effect of the slaughter was the first serious questioning of Anglo-Australian relations: should Australia have committed and sacrificed so much to defend a (geographically) distant country's interests? Conversely, Gallipoli, as Australia's debut on the world stage, is still to this day treated as a symbol of national identity and pride.

1918–39

After World War I, the Nationalist Party joined forces with the **Country Party**, to assume government under the paternalistic and fiercely anti-socialist guidance of **Earle Page** and **Stanley Bruce**. The Country Party was formed as a result of the widening divisions between the growing urban population and farmers, who felt isolated and unrepresented politically. Under the coalition, pastoral industries were subsidized by overseas borrowing, allowing them to compete internationally, and technology began to close the gap between the city and the Outback. Radio and aviation developments saw the birth of **Qantas** – the Queensland and Northern Territory Aerial Service – and the **Royal Flying Doctor Service** in Queensland's remote west. Development also occurred in the cities: work started on the Sydney Harbour Bridge, and the new Commonwealth capital, **Canberra**, was completed.

On the social front, the USA stopped mass immigration in 1921, deflecting a flood of people from depressed **Southern Europe** to Australia, which the government countered by encouraging British immigrants with assisted passages. While progressive in some areas – a dole was proposed for the unemployed, the sick, pensioners and mothers – the government overreacted to opposition, as exemplified by their response to the **seamen and dockers' strike** of 1928. Citing the arch-villain, "communism", as being behind the dispute, they attempted to stretch the scope of the Immigration Act to allow action to be taken against disturbances that were politically motivated. However, the implication that the law could be altered against anyone who disagreed with the government contributed to the downfall of Bruce and Page the following year. The themes of their rule, however – differences between rural and urban societies, questions of Australian identity, union disputes, and the effects of heavy borrowing to create artificially high living standards, unsupported by Australia's actual capabilities – are issues that are still relevant today.

As the **Great Depression** set in during the early 1930s, Australia faced the collapse of its economic and political systems, with all the parties divided. Pressed for a loan, the Bank of England forced a restructuring of the Australian economy. Adding to national embarrassment, politics and sports became blurred during the 1932 "**body-line**" cricket series: the loan was made virtually conditional on the Australian cricket authorities dropping their allegations that British bowlers were deliberately trying to injure Australian batsmen during the tour.

Meanwhile, worries about communism were succeeded by concern about the rise of fascism, as Mussolini and Hitler took power in Europe and Japanese forces invaded Manchuria – the **Tanaka memorial** in 1927 actually cited Australia as a target for a future conquest by Japan. Although displaying a certain ambivalence towards fascism, Australia assisted the immigration of refugees from central Europe, and – after a prolonged union battle – halted iron exports to Japan. When Prime Minister Joseph Lyons died in office, **Robert Menzies**, a firm supporter of British notions of civilization, was elected to the post, in time to side with Britain as hostilities were declared against Hitler in September 1939.

World War II and after

As happened in World War I, Australia developed its identity getting involved on a global scale in World War II, but this time without Britain's involvement. Menzies' United Australia Party barely lasted long enough to form diplomatic ties with the USA – in case Germany overran Europe – before internal divisions saw the government crumble, replaced by **John Curtin** and his Labor Party in 1941.

Curtin, concerned about Australia's vulnerability after the Japanese attack on Pearl Harbor, made the radical decision of shifting the country's commitment in the war from defending Britain and Europe to fighting off an invasion of Australia from Asia. After the **fall of Singapore** in 1942 and the capture of sixteen thousand Australian troops, Curtin succeeded in ordering the immediate recall of Australians fighting in the Middle East, despite opposition from Churchill, who wanted them for the Burma campaign. In February, the Japanese unexpectedly bombed Darwin, launched submarine raids against Sydney and Newcastle, and invaded New Guinea. Feeling abandoned and betrayed by Britain, Curtin appealed to the USA, who quickly adopted Australia as a base for co-ordinating Pacific operations under General **Douglas MacArthur**. Meanwhile, Australian troops in New Guinea halted Japanese advances along the **Kokoda trail** at Milne Bay, while the Australian and US navies slowed down the Japanese fleet in the **Battle of the Coral Sea** – which, thanks to modern cannons, was notable as the first naval engagement in which the two sides never even saw each other.

Australia came out of World War II realizing that geographically, the country was closer to Asia than Europe, that it could not count on Britain to help in a crisis (Churchill had been ready to sacrifice Australian territory to protect British interests elsewhere), and that it was able to form political alliances independent of the mother country. From this point on, Australia began to look to the USA and the Pacific, in addition to Britain, for direction. Another consequence of the war was that immigration was speeded up, fuelled by Australia's recent vulnerability. Under the slogan "Populate or Perish", the government reintroduced assisted passages from Britain – the "ten-pound-poms" – and also accepted substantial numbers of European refugees. Even Torres Strait Islanders, previously banned from settling on the mainland, were allowed to move onto Cape York in northern Queensland.

With international right-wing extremism laid low by the war, the old fear of **communism** returned. When North Korea, backed by the Chinese, invaded South Korea in 1950, Australia, led by a revitalized Menzies and his new Liberal Party, was the first country after the USA to commit troops to counter communist forces. Menzies also sent soldiers and pilots to Malaya (as it was known at the time), where communist rebels had been fighting the British colonial administration almost since the end of World War II, under the anti-communist SEATO (Southeast Asia Treaty Organization) banner. At home, he opened up central Australia to British **atomic bomb tests** in the 1950s, because – echoing the beliefs of the first European colonists – "nobody lived there". A number of Aborigines were moved to reserves but others – along with the British troops involved in the tests – suffered the effects of fallout and had their traditional lands rendered uninhabitable for the foreseeable future. Wrangles with the British government over compensation, and the clearing of the test sites at **Maralinga** and **Emu Junction** were finally settled in 1993.

Menzies was still in control when the USA became involved in **Vietnam**, and with conflict in Malaya all but over, Australia volunteered "advisers" to Vietnamese republican forces in 1962. Once fighting became entrenched, the government introduced conscription and – bowing to the wishes of the American president **Lyndon B. Johnson** – sent a battalion of soldiers into the fray in 1965, events which immediately split the country. Menzies quit politics the following year, succeeded by his protégé **Harold Holt**, who, rallying under the catchphrase "All the way with LBJ", willingly increased Australia's participation in the Vietnamese conflict. But as the war dragged on, world opinion shifted to seeing the matter as a civil struggle, rather than as a fight between democratic and communist ideologies, and in 1970 the government began scaling down its involvement. In the meantime, Aboriginal people were finally granted **civil rights** in 1967, and Holt mysteriously disappeared while swimming in the sea off the coast of Victoria, leaving the Liberals in turmoil and paving the way for a Labor win under **Gough Whitlam** in 1972.

Whitlam's three years in office had far-reaching effects: he ended national service and participation in Vietnam, granted independence to **Papua New Guinea**, recognized the People's Republic of China, and instituted free health care and higher education systems. In doing so however, he alienated the mostly conservative Senate, and when the government attempted to finance mining interests with an illicit overseas loan in 1975, the opposition prevented the Senate from functioning. In an unprecedented move, the Governor-General **John Kerr** (until then, a largely decorative representative of the Crown overseeing Australian affairs) dismissed the government – a move that shocked many into questioning the validity of Britain's hold on Australia – and called an election, which Labor lost. In contrast, the following eight years were uneventful, culminating in the return of Labor in 1983 under the charismatic Bob Hawke, a former trade union leader. Labor's subsequent thirteen years and record four terms in office, which produced surprisingly little lasting legislation, were suddenly brought to a close by the arrogant antics of Hawke's successor and former treasurer, **Paul Keating**. He was already widely unpopular for his scornful rhetoric and general lack of concern for the country's woes – particularly the effects of a massive foreign debt and crippling drought in eastern Australia – when news of a secret military agreement with Indonesia created a public backlash, resulting in a landslide victory for the **Liberal-National coalition**, led by **John Howard**, in 1996.

Current events

Previously dismissed by many as an ineffectual character, Howard's performance in office soon showed that his critics had underestimated his tenacity and consummate political skills, honed by 22 years in federal politics. In particular, his talent to quickly grasp any opportunity to rally (potentially flagging) support, thereby detracting from problems and scandals in his own government, combined with a superb sense of timing and, arguably, sheer good luck, enabled him to turn many potentially dangerous situations around in his favour. At the federal elections in October 2004, the Liberals scored a resounding victory and Howard was elected Prime Minister for the fourth time.

By December the same year, he was Australia's second-longest serving Prime Minister, surpassed only by Menzies' eighteen years in office. Winding back to 1996, Howard's stand against automatic firearms in the wake of the Port Arthur Massacre (see p.1105), having pushed through his legislation despite stiff opposition from gun lobbies and several state premiers, greatly reduced his feeble image. By 1998, Howard's political position was so secure that the coalition managed to be re-elected on what some considered a suicidal platform of **tax reform** through the implementation of a **GST**, or Goods and Services Tax. By mid-2001 however, Howard's prospects of winning the next election were slipping away. A GST-inspired rise in fuel costs had driven many farmers – traditional National Party supporters – to bankruptcy; businesses were reeling under the effects of the tax, consumers were having to pay more for their goods; and the Liberal-National coalition had been soundly trounced in state elections in Western Australia and Queensland. When on August 27, 2001, the Norwegian freighter *Tampa* requested permission to land on Christmas Island, northwest of Darwin, with 433 **refugees** on board, Howard used it as a chance to turn public opinion around. Howard successfully played on the time-honoured Australian fear of being "swamped" by hordes of immigrants. His political status was strengthened; the government's popularity soared, and the tribulations of the GST and the not-so-perfect shape of the economy were all but forgotten. The terrorist attacks on September 11 did nothing to assuage xenophobic fears, and when Australian soldiers were sent to Afghanistan to join the "war on terror" in mid-October 2001, this was also considered a show of appropriate strength. Buoyed by his good ratings in the opinion polls, Howard called a federal election for November 10. Predictably, it was a comfortable win for his coalition and the opposition Labor party was further diminished. The refugee question remained in the media spotlight for a few more months, until Australia's possible involvement in the US- and UK-led war on Iraq dominated the headlines. The carnage of the **car bomb in Kuta**, **Bali**, on October 12, 2002 – terrorist action targeted at Westerners but in particular, some argued, Australians – added urgency to the debate.

Defying public opinion, Howard vociferously supported the war in Iraq, UN-backed or not, and subsequently joined the "coalition of the willing" in the military attack on Iraq. In contrast to the government's emphatic rhetorical support, Australia's physical contribution to the war was actually quite small – two thousand troops, plus some warships and aircraft.

The domestic arena

Leadership struggles within the Australian Labor Party dominated the headlines throughout 2003, with Mark Latham finally emerging as the winner in a leadership contest against Kim Beazley in December.

When in 2004 it finally transpired that Saddam Hussein's arsenal of weapons of mass destruction, and the immediate threat it posed to international security, was a furphy, it failed to cause a public backlash in Australia. In his speech calling the election for October 9, 2004, Howard deftly sidestepped a debate about his government's sincerity, by saying voters had to decide whom they most trusted to look after Australia and its economic future. By pointing out that in eight and a half years the coalition government had delivered a strong and robust economy, and by warning that interest rates would be higher under a Labor government, Howard played on another kind of fear – the "hip-pocket nerve". From then on foreign affairs, in particular complex and sensitive topics like Iraq and national security, were practically off the radar screen and the election campaign was fought mainly on the theme of economic management. The strategy of playing the economy trump card paid off handsomely for Howard. Unforeseen by most opinion polls, the coalition achieved the biggest vote for any government seeking re-election since 1977: a clear-cut win of 52.75% of the two-party vote, over Labor's 47.25%. Furthermore, as of July 2005 it holds the absolute majority (39 of 76 of seats) in the Senate, enabling it to push through a raft of previously blocked legislation, notably in the area of industrial relations. John Howard's (and, should he choose to retire, Peter Costello's) conservative worldview will influence the shape and feel of Australian culture and society more than ever before. However, critics point out that the growth of Australia's economy since 2000 is not underpinned by a real increase in productivity, but stems primarily from borrowing money instead of earning it, as shown by the growing trade deficit (about $20 billion at the end of 2004). In short, it is a bubble bound to burst, an event which could finally prove the coalition government's undoing.

Foreign Policy

Looking beyond its shores, for most of the twentieth century Australia faced **Asia** with ambiguity, seeing it partly as a strategic threat, partly as an economic opportunity. The example of Japan is symptomatic: in the 1930s, Japan had become Australia's second-largest trading partner but during the 1940s Australia had to fight off an impending Japanese invasion. By the 1970s, with the White Australia policy coming to an end, Whitlam initiated a policy shift towards greater engagement with its neighbours in the region, which continued under the Fraser government and was intensified by the Hawke-Keating governments in the 1980s and early 1990s. This stance was based on the pragmatic recognition of Australia's economic interests, and led to an often appallingly conciliatory attitude to some Asian countries' more dubious actions against each other, as well as a pitifully weak response to regional human rights abuses. As was the case with most of his other political visions, Keating was unable to sell his orientation towards Asia to the general Australian public. The ubiquitous catchphrase of the 1990s: "**Australia is part of Asia**" confused and alienated voters. Howard capitalized on that during his first successful election campaign of 1996, with the recurring reproach that Keating was "obsessed with Asia" and out of touch with what ordinary Australians felt. The "part of Asia" notion did not wash with the countries in the area, either. Australia, with its predominantly white population and strong cultural and political ties to the Anglophone Western world (and a Prime Minister given to arrogant remarks and schoolmasterly lectures) would not be accepted as "Asian". Australia's most outspoken critic was Malaysia, under the rule of Dr Mahatir Mohamad (himself no stranger to schoolmasterly lectures), who continually vetoed Australia's attempts to join ASEAN, the regional trading bloc. The rough-hewn right-wing outbursts by **Pauline Hanson** and the (short-lived) rise of her **One Nation** party in 1996, which capitalized on widespread dissatisfaction with the major political groups, did nothing to enhance Australian credibility in the region.

From his first days in office, Howard's statements and actions in public signalled a backing off, if not complete reversal, from his predecessors' Asia policy. There was his refusal to distance himself emphatically from Pauline Hanson's spiteful, xenophobic – and, in particular, anti-Asian – utterances. In 1996, during his first state visit to Indonesia as Australian Prime Minister, he stated that Australia did not have to choose between geography and history. While Australia was geographically close to Asia and would eagerly pursue closer economic and security ties in the region, it did not want to be identified as an Asian nation. It would maintain its own culture and traditions, including a security alliance with the US and close ties to Europe.

The Australian-led UN intervention in the civil war in East Timor in 1999, instigated by pro-Indonesian militia, and covertly by members of the Indonesian armed forces, put a stop to the massacre and helped the emerging new nation stand on its own feet. Not surprisingly, Australia's relationship to Indonesia deteriorated badly as a result. Short of condoning a ruthless and murderous grab for power, it is hard to see how upsetting the sensibilities of Indonesians could have been completely avoided in this instance. However, subsequent noises about Australia taking a more pro-active role in maintaining regional security, and playing the role of America's deputy sheriff, added fuel to the fire and caused a furore across the entire region.

So too did remarks by Howard, made in 2002 and repeated during the election campaign of 2004, about Australia launching pre-emptive strikes against suspected terrorists in neighbouring countries if the need arose.

Forging closer links with the US has been the highest priority by the Howard government. Australia's participation in the war on Iraq and the signing of the Free Trade Agreement between Australia and the US are two examples of the importance attributed to the alliance with America.

Currently however, things have shifted yet again, both in Asia and Australia. The rancorous Mahathir retired in Malaysia, the conciliatory Yudhoyono has become president in Indonesia, and currently negotiations are under way to include Australia as a participant in a new East Asia summit in Kuala Lumpur, scheduled for December 2005, a forum which may well be the nucleus of an Asian bloc to rival the European Union. Australia's role in delivering aid to Indonesia's Aceh province, the region worst hit by the tsunami on Boxing Day 2004, has gone a long way towards creating goodwill, and counteracting Australia's "bullyboy" image. Ever the pragmatist, Howard has recognized the economic and strategic opportunities for Australia in these developments, and quietly readjusted his foreign policy. In an ironic twist, he might well pursue Keating's policy of close engagement with Asia – including a possible security treaty with Indonesia – that he so vehemently attacked ten years before.

Aboriginal Rights

In the domestic arena, there were some advances under Labor in the field of **Aboriginal rights**. An ineffectual inquiry into Aboriginal deaths in custody was overshadowed in June 1992, when the High Court handed down the landmark **Mabo Decision**, legally overturning the concept of *terra nullius*. Eddie Mabo's claim, set around Murray Island (Mer) in the Torres Strait, was granted, and the Merriam were acknowledged as traditional landowners. This decision led to the passing of the Native Title Act of 1993, after extensive discussions with indigenous representatives. Next came the **Wik Decision** in December 1996, which stated that native title and pastoral leases could coexist over the same area. The new Howard government initiated an alarmist debate about its implications, and triggered something of a public backlash against Aborigines. Support for One Nation increased as the party exploited people's fears to the hilt, contributing to Australia's racist image overseas. The government refused to negotiate with indigenous representatives who had sought to bring forward constructive proposals. In 1998, it introduced **Amendments** to the Wik decision, which wound back indigenous rights under the Native Title Act, whilst enhancing the rights of landholders and developers.

While Mabo and Wik had an effect in some instances – such as the handing back of the **Silver Plains** property on Queensland's Cape York to its traditional owners in 2000 – few similar land claims are likely to succeed. A **Native Title Tribunal** has been set up to consider each case, but given former resettlement policies, claimants have an uphill struggle as they need to prove constant association with the land in question since white occupation. Nonetheless, a growing acknowledgement that Aboriginal people were in fact the land's original inhabitants, and the perception that they will eventually be re-enfranchised, has seen mining companies, farmers, and notably – and ironically, given its past record – the Queensland government ignoring the political and legal wrangles and making private land-use agreements with, or handovers to, local communities. In this sense, Mabo and Wik have confirmed that Aboriginal people have land rights, despite the best efforts of the Howard government to undermine these.

Australia's indigenous peoples

White Australians have grouped the country's indigenous peoples under the term Aborigines, but are now coming to recognize many separate cultures as diverse but inter-related as those of Europe.

Today these cultures include urbanized Koorie communities in Sydney and Melbourne, semi-nomadic groups such as the Pintupi living in the western deserts, and the Yolngu people of eastern Arnhem Land, an area never colonized by settlers. If there is any thread linking these groups, it is the island continent they inhabit and, particularly in the north, the worsening state of health, education and opportunities they experience, despite the apparent revitalisation of Aboriginal culture.

Colonization

From 1788 the estimated 750,000 indigenous people of Australia were gradually dispossessed of their lands and livelihoods by the British colonists who failed to recognize them as legitimate inhabitants. Australia was annexed to the British Empire on the basis that it was *terra nullius*, or uninhabited wasteland. This legal fiction persisted until the High Court judged in the 1992 **Mabo** case that native title to land still existed in Australia unless it had been extinguished by statute or by some use of the land that was inconsistent with the continuation of native use and ownership. The **Wik Decision** of 1996 went a step further, acknowledging that native title continues to exist on pastoral leases, though with the proviso that "pastoral interest will prevail over native title rights, wherever the two conflict" (for more on the Mabo and Wik decisions, see "History", p.1187).

Upon deciding that the country was unoccupied, successive waves of new settlers hastened to make it so. Violent conflicts between indigenous and recently arrived Australians resulted in the decimation of Aboriginal groups. The most widely known of these conflicts was the **unofficial war** waged against Tasmania's Aboriginal peoples, which resulted in the near-destruction of indigenous Tasmanians (see also box on pp.1068–1069). Historians estimate that twenty thousand Aborigines may have died in these mostly unrecorded battles. Measuring the impact of colonization on the indigenous population has been hampered by a lack of information about conditions prior to colonization, as well as the failure of successive governments to record indigenous people as part of the population until the 1960s.

Australia's geographical isolation meant that the introduction of European **diseases** was also a powerful agent in decimating the indigenous populations. Whole populations were wiped out by smallpox and malaria epidemics, and the diaries from the First Fleet record the rapid destruction from smallpox of the Aboriginal camps in the Sydney hinterland within a few years of the establishment of the colony. Those who didn't die fled the area, unwittingly infecting neighbouring groups as they went. When Governor Hunter made the first exploratory expedition to western New South Wales in the 1820s, he recorded evidence of prior smallpox epidemics among Aboriginal groups who had not previously come into contact with European settlers. The lack of immunity to these introduced diseases was exacerbated by the trauma of dispossession, the lack of availability of – or access to – traditional food and water supplies, and the unhygienic consequences of being required to wear European-style clothing.

The **interruption of traditional food and water supplies** became progressively worse through the nineteenth and twentieth centuries as the pastoral industry expanded across rural Australia, and vast areas were stripped of vegetation to provide for grazing land. Grazing animals competed with local animals for food, drained established water sources and dug up the flora on the soil surface with their hooves, contributing to erosion and salinity and so creating dustbowls. Other European animals, originally introduced to make the countryside seem more like "home", rapidly multiplied and have now become ubiquitous throughout Australia. Foxes, and especially cats, have been blamed for the near extinction of small mammals and birds throughout arid Australia. Rabbit populations expanded to fill the niche the mammals vacated, and their destructive grazing habits have contributed to the increasing desertification of Australia's rangelands. Aboriginal people in central Australia have witnessed this ecological disaster within the last sixty years, and have lamented the loss of many animal species that once sustained them.

Australia's Aboriginal peoples have also been subjected to various forms of **incarceration**, ranging from prisons to apartheid-style reserves. Much of this systematic imprisonment was instigated between 1890 and 1950 as an official policy of **protection**, in response to the devastating impact of colonization. Missionaries and other well-meaning people believed that Aborigines were a dying race, and that it was a Christian duty to provide for them in their passing. Parliamentary records of the time reveal a harsher mentality. Aborigines were often viewed as a weak and degenerate people who exposed white settlers to physical and moral turpitude. For the wellbeing of Aborigines and settlers alike, state governments enacted legislation to appoint official **Protectors of Aborigines**, established reserves in rural areas and removed Aboriginal people to them. In some parts of Australia these reserves were established on traditional lands, allowing people to continue to live relatively undisturbed. Elsewhere, notably Queensland, people were forcibly removed from their home areas and relocated in reserves throughout the state. Families were broken up and the ties with the land and religion shattered. The so-called protectors had autonomy over those in their ward. For example, Aboriginal people required permits to marry or to move from one reserve to another, or were forced into indentured or simply slave labour to be paid in flour or tobacco. This treatment persisted in some areas until the late 1960s.

Aboriginal people are still ridiculously over-represented in Australia's prison population. In 1991, the situation led to a **Royal Commission into Aboriginal Deaths in Custody**, which reported to the Federal Parliament. It called for wide-ranging changes in police and judicial practice, and substantial changes to social programmes aimed at improving the lot of Aboriginal peoples in the areas of justice, health, education, economics and empowerment. But despite considerable government lip-service to the recommendations of the Royal Commission, it has not resulted in any substantial change to incarceration rates.

Since the 1920s, Aboriginal children fathered by Europeans but born to black mothers were removed and put into state institutions or with white foster parents as part of a policy of **assimilation**. The practice of "taking the children away" began in Victoria in 1886 and continued until 1969, and still haunts the lives of many Aboriginal Australians, now known as the **Stolen Generation**, who have lost contact with their natal families and their culture, and whose plight was depicted in the 2002 film *Rabbit-Proof Fence*. But despite the policy being the subject of a major government inquiry in 1997, and the subsequent media attention since the release of its report, the people are yet to receive an official national **apology**.

Revitalization

The **revitalization** of Aboriginal people and their culture effectively began in 1967, when a constitutional referendum overwhelmingly endorsed the rights of indigenous Australians as voting citizens, and gave the federal government the power to legislate for Aboriginal people. Prior to this referendum, Aboriginal people had the status of wards of each of the States. The referendum ushered in a new era of **self-determination** for Aboriginal people, evidenced by the establishment of the first Ministry for Aboriginal Affairs in the Whitlam Labor Government of 1972–75. After more than a hundred years of agitation, **land rights** were accorded to Aboriginal groups in the Northern Territory in 1976 under federal legislation. Since then, other states have legislated to vest title over various pieces of state-owned land to their traditional Aboriginal owners. All the mainland states and territories have now made provisions for Aboriginal land rights. Throughout the 1970s and 1980s successive federal governments set up various representative bodies, including the notorious **Aboriginal and Torres Strait Islanders Commission** (ATSIC: 1990–2004). This statutory authority gave elected Aboriginal representatives effective control over many of the federal funding programmes directed at Aboriginal organizations and communities. Substantial funds were directed towards training for employment and improved health education. Running at around two billion dollars per annum, this should have seen Aboriginal people thriving right across Australia. The reality was far different: corruption, nepotism and flawed or hare-brained projects all helped bring about ATSIC's abolition in 2004 and a return to greater federal government control (see "The future", below).

Along with ownership of land and some control over funding came opportunities for economic self-sufficiency and expansion previously unavailable to Aboriginal groups. In many parts of the country, this allowed Aborigines to buy the cattle stations on which they had worked without wages for many years. In central Australia, Aboriginal enterprises include TV and radio stations, transport companies, small airlines, publishing companies, tourist businesses and joint-venture mining operations.

Co-operative agreements with the Australian Nature Conservation Agency have led to Aboriginal ownership and joint management of two of Australia's most important conservation reserves, **Uluru–Kata Tjuta** and **Kakadu** national parks in the Northern Territory. These arrangements recognize that Aboriginal owners retain an enormous understanding about the ecology of their traditional lands that can be of great assistance in the development of land-management plans.

Citizenship and its problems

Despite these successes, Australia's indigenous peoples are struggling against considerable disadvantages. Along with citizenship in 1967 came a new-found unemployability (few station owners were willing to pay black workers the same wage as white people) along with the legal right to purchase **alcohol**, a disastrous combination. Institutionalized welfarism has compounded feelings of futility as well as shame towards one's Aboriginal origins and substance abuse is heavily implicated in the destructive spiral often observed by visitors to Outback towns (and some inner cities). The negative repercussions are evident in sickness and death, violence and despair, exclusion from education and meaningful employment, as well as families and communities in disarray. The vast overrepresentation of Aboriginal people in the criminal justice system is directly attributable to alcohol. **Poor health** continues to reduce substantially the life expectancy of Aborigines. Aboriginal women live approximately thirty years less than their white counterparts and in some places this gap is widening. Aboriginal infant mortality is three times higher than for white babies and the death rate from diabetes is eight times higher. As with most areas of social service, health services for Aboriginal peoples have been the province of white professionals until very recently; an essential focus of the new strategy is to empower Aboriginal people by giving resources to them directly.

On the **positive** side, many families and communities are confronting the problems that alcohol is causing. Between them they are putting pressure on problem drinkers to limit their drinking, and are now able to implement new laws to reduce the damage that alcohol is doing to the people around them.

The future

The process of **reconciliation** with its "rights"-based approach, as initiated by the Labor government under Keating, always has been anathema to Prime Minister John Howard. As he saw it, "symbolic measures" such as an apology or a treaty were an insult to the present generation of non-Aboriginal people who were not responsible for past mistakes, and did nothing to address problems in Aboriginal communities such as alcoholism, appalling health and lack of access to education. Upon his re-election in 1998, "**practical reconciliation**" was the new catchphrase and essentially meant the delivery of welfare services through mainstream programmes. Consistent with this approach, he steadfastly refused to give a formal apology, ignoring the widespread popular movement to that effect in 1999 and 2000. His government promised $63 million over four years of funding for counselling and "link-up" services for those who had been removed from their families. By 2004, only a small amount of the package had been spent.

In the same year the Howard government disbanded ATSIC and replaced it by a **National Indigenous Council** (**NIC**) of fourteen handpicked advisers, whose only function is to advise the government on the future direction of policies and programmes that will impact on every facet of Aboriginal lives. At the end of 2004, new buzz words frequently bandied about by the Howard government were "**mutual obligation**" and "**shared responsibility**". This rhetoric seems to align with Noel Pearson, the Aboriginal lawyer and community leader from the Cape York Peninsula, whose aim is to replace social welfare with social enterprise. On Cape York, he embarked on a community-based social renewal project, which includes having payments of benefits invested in enterprise activity rather than as an individual welfare cheque, with each individual and family making a commitment to contributing as well as receiving. The government has started to forge "**shared-responsibility agreements**" with Aboriginal communities. The first agreement released in December 2004 was with Mulan, a remote community in Western Australia. The government agreed to install a petrol bowser, and in return the community agreed to make sure their children showered daily and looked after other health issues.

A few prominent Aboriginal leaders such as Australian Labor Party vice-president Warren Mundine have welcomed agreements like this and more will be signed by other Aboriginal communities in the future. At first glance, it seems a common-sense approach. No more indiscriminate throwing of money at a problem, no more "one size fits all" solutions. However, the "mutual obligation" Pearson has in mind is paired with a vision of community self-determination and voluntary initiatives from below. It does not look very likely that a government that replaced ATSIC with a group of easily dismissible Aboriginal advisers is interested in the latter.

Underlying Howard's policy is the attitude that Aborigines should be assimilated into the mainstream of society. This is the same notion that was behind (now defunct) One Nation's petulant questions: why aren't they like us? Why should they get special treatment? While this might be achievable, if not necessarily desirable, for Aboriginal Australians living in the major cities, for others it may well mean severing cultural links with the past. Jackie Huggins, Queensland academic and Aboriginal, summed it up succinctly in a speech on reconciliation in November 2003: "The practical and the symbolic are impossible to separate because a sense of who you are and how you feel about yourself is intrinsic to how you behave and how you address your problems. If you believe you are an outsider you are an outsider. If you believe you're beaten you're beaten. If you believe the rest of Australia has no respect for your culture, then for all intents and purposes it doesn't."

Still, after two centuries of brutal mistreatment and almost four decades of mismanagement, it is tempting to envisage a better world, a world in which, in a few years' time, shared-responsibility agreements will have had a positive impact.

Wildlife

Despite forty thousand years of human pressure and manipulation, accelerated in the last two centuries by the effects of introduced species, Australia's ecology and wildlife remain among the most distinctive on earth. Nonetheless, they are also some of the most endangered: in the last two hundred years, more native mammals have become extinct here than on any other continent, and land clearing – particularly in Queensland – kills an estimated 7.5 million birds a year, bringing several species to the edge of extinction.

Australians love to tell stories about the **dangers** that the bush holds for the inexperienced traveller (see the "Health" section of "Basics" on pp.41–42, for general advice on coping with hazardous wildlife). In reality, fearsome "drop bears" lurking in gums, fallen tree trunks that turn out to be giant snakes, bloodthirsty wild pigs and other rampaging terrors are mostly confined to hotel bars, the product of suburban paranoia laced with a surprising naivety about the great outdoors. Apart from a couple of avoidable exceptions, there's little to fear from Australia's wildlife, and if you spend any time in the bush, you'll undoubtedly end up far better informed than the yarn-spinners.

Marsupials and monotremes

In the years after the demise of the dinosaurs, Australia split away from the rest of the world, and the animals here evolved along different lines to anywhere else. As placental mammals gained the ascendency in South America, Africa, Europe and Asia, it was the marsupials and monotremes which took over in Australia, alongside the megafauna (see box below). These orders may not be exclusive to Australia (they're also found in New Guinea and South America), but it's here that they reached their greatest diversity and numbers.

Marsupials are mammals that give birth to a partially formed embryo, which itself then develops in a **pouch** on the mother; this allows a higher breeding rate in good years. Easiest to find because they actively seek out people, **ringtail** and **brushtail possums** are common in suburbs and campsites, and

Ancient Australian wildlife

Australia has a **fossil record** which makes up in range what it lacks in quantity. Imprints of invertebrates from South Australia's **Ediacaran fauna**, dated to over 600 million years, are the oldest evidence of animal life in the world. On a larger scale, footprints and remains of several **dinosaur** species have been uncovered, and **opalized marine fossils** are unique to the country. Perhaps most intriguing is evidence of the **megafauna** – giant wildlife which included the twenty-metre-long, constricting snake montypythonides, flightless birds bigger than an ostrich, a rhino-sized wombat, carnivorous kangaroos, and thylacaleo, a marsupial lion – which flourished until about thirty thousand years ago, overlapping with Aboriginal occupation. Climatic changes were probably responsible for their demise, but humans definitely wiped out the **thylacine**, a dog-like marsupial with an oversized head, which vanished from the mainland after the introduction of dingoes but survived in Tasmania until 1936 – the year it received government protection.

often hard to avoid if they think there's a chance of getting some food. With a little persistence, you should encounter one of the several species of related **glider possums** on the edges of forests at dusk. **Kangaroos** and **wallabies** are the Australian answer to deer and antelopes, and range from tiny, solitary rainforest species to the gregarious two-metre-tall red kangaroo of the central plains – watching these creatures bouncing effortlessly across the landscape is an extraordinary sight. The arboreal, eucalyptus-chewing **koalas** and tubby, ground-dwelling **wombats** are smaller, less active and more sensitive to disturbance; this has made them more elusive, and has placed them on the endangered list as their habitat is cleared. Carnivorous marsupials are mostly shrew-sized today (though a lion equivalent probably survived into Aboriginal times, and fossils of meat-eating kangaroos have been found); two of the largest are spotted native cats or **quolls**, and Tasmania's indigenous **Tasmanian devil**, a terrier-sized scavenger.

Platypuses and echidnas are the only **monotremes**, **egg-laying mammals** that suckle their young through specialized pores. Once considered a stage in the evolution of placental mammals, they're now recognized as a specialized branch of the family. Neither is particularly rare, but being nocturnal, shy and, in the case of the platypus, aquatic, makes them difficult to find. Ant-eating **echidnas** resemble a long-nosed, thick-spined hedgehog or small porcupine, and are found countrywide; **platypuses** are confined to the eastern ranges and look like a blend of duck and otter, having a grey, rubbery bill, webbed feet, short fur, and a poison spur on males. This combination seemed too implausible to nineteenth-century biologists, who initially denounced stuffed specimens as a hoax, assembled from pieces of other animals.

Introduced fauna

Of the **introduced mammals**, **dingoes** are descended from dogs, introduced to Australia by Aboriginal people in the last twelve thousand years. To keep them away from flocks, graziers built "vermin fences", which were finally connected by the Australian government to form a 5400-kilometre-long, continuous fence, allegedly the world's longest. The **Dingo Fence** stretches from South Australia into northwest Queensland and down again to New South Wales. **Camels** have also become acclimatized to Australia since their introduction in the 1840s; they are doing so well in the central deserts that they are becoming a pest. Australia is the only place where dromedaries still occur in the wild, and they are regularly exported to the Middle East. The blight that **hoofed mammals** – horses, cows, sheep and goats – have perpetrated on Australia's fragile fauna is horrendous. Much of the country has been prematurely desertified by their eating habits, abrasive hooves and demand for water; once extracted from below ground, it is not replenished, which alters the mineral balance and kills remaining plant life. The damage caused by **rabbits** is equally pervasive, especially in the semi-desert areas where their cyclic population explosions can strip every shred of plant life from fragile dune systems. In an attempt to control the problem, the myxoma virus was introduced in the Fifties, and although a large part of the rabbit population was initially wiped out, the rabbits eventually developed a resistance and their numbers increased again in the following decades. Since 1996, another viral disease affecting the European rabbit, the rabbit calicivirus disease (RCD), has been released all over Australia, resulting in a dramatic reduction of rabbit numbers. It remains to be seen, however, whether the unsuccessful story of the myxoma virus will be repeated.

Feral **cats**, which hunt for sport as well as necessity, are currently one of the greatest threats to indigenous fauna, primarily small marsupials and birds. An introduced amphibian, however, has turned out to be the most insidious and rapacious invader of all. The highly poisonous **cane toads**, brought in to combat a plague of greyback beetles, have no natural enemies and for thirty years have been on a relentless march from the north Queensland sugar-cane fields, southwards along the coast and across northern Australia. In 2004 they invaded the lush Top End floodplains, which have more wildlife per square kilometre than the richest parts of Africa, Asia and the Americas. For more on the cane toad see p.537.

Reptiles, birds, bats and marine life

Australian **reptiles** come in all shapes and sizes. In the tropical parts of the country, the pale lizards you see wriggling across the ceiling on Velcro-like pads are **geckos**, and you'll find fatter, sluggish **skinks** – such as the stumpy blue-tongued lizard – everywhere. Other widespread species are **frill-necked lizards**, known for fanning out their necks and running on their hind legs when frightened, and the ubiquitous **goanna** family, which includes the monstrous perentie, third-largest lizard in the world. In central Australia, look out for the extraordinary **thorny devil** or moloch, an animal that seems part rock, part rosebush.

Crocodiles are confined to the tropics and come in two types. The shy, inoffensive **freshwater crocodile** grows to around 3m in length and feeds on fish and frogs. The larger, bulkier, and misleadingly named saltwater or **estuarine crocodile** can grow to 7m, ranges far inland (often in freshwater), and is the only Australian animal that constitutes an active threat to humans. Highly evolved predators, they should be given a very wide berth (see box on p.650 for specific precautions to take while in crocodile country). Despite their bad press, **snakes** are generally timid and pose far less of a problem, even though Australia has everything from constricting pythons through to three-quarters of the world's most venomous species.

With a climate that extends from temperate zones well into the tropics, Australia's **birdlife** is prolific and varied. Small **penguins** and **albatrosses** live along the south coast, while **riflebirds**, related to New Guinea's birds of paradise, and the **cassowary**, a colourful version of the ostrich, live in the tropical rainforests. The drabber **emu** prefers drier plains further west. Among the birds of prey, the countrywide **wedge-tail eagle** and the coastal **white-bellied sea eagle** are most impressive in their size. Both share their environment with the stately grey **brolga**, an Australian crane, and the even larger **jabiru stork**, with its chisel beak and pied plumage. **Parrots**, arguably the country's most spectacular birds, come in over forty varieties, and no matter if they're flocks of green budgerigars, outrageously coloured rainbow lorikeets or white sulphur-crested cockatoos, they'll deafen you with their noisy song. Equally raucous are **kookaburras**, giant kingfishers found near permanent water. The quieter **tawny frogmouth**, an incredibly camouflaged cousin of the nightjar, has one of the most disgruntled expressions ever seen on a bird.

Huge colonies of **bats**, of orange, ghost and horseshoe varieties, congregate in caves and fill entire trees all over Australia. The **fruit bat**, or flying fox, is especially common in the tropics, where evenings can be spent watching colonies of the one-metre-winged monsters heading out from their daytime roosts on feeding expeditions.

In addition to what you'll see on the Barrier Reef (covered in the Tropical Queensland chapter), **whales**, **turtles**, **dolphins**, **seals** and **dugongs** (sea cows) are part of the country's marine life, with humpback southern right whales recently making a welcome return to the coasts after being hunted close to extinction.

Flora

Australia's most distinctive and widespread **trees** are those that developed a **dependence on fire**. Some, like the seemingly limitless varieties of **eucalypts** or gum trees, need extreme heat to burst open button-shaped pods and release their seeds, and encourage fires by annually shedding bark and leaves, depositing a thick layer of tinder on the forest floor. Other shrubs with similar habits are **banksias**, **grevillias** and **bottlebrushes**, with their distinctive bushy flowers and spiky seed-pods, while those prehistoric survivors, palm-like **cycads** and **grasstrees**, similarly depend on regular conflagrations to promote new growth. For thousands of years, Aborigines used controlled burn-offs to make the land more suitable for hunting, thereby possibly enhancing these fire-reliant traits.

Despite the country having extensive arid regions, there is no native equivalent to the cactus, although the dry, spiky **spinifex**, or porcupine grass, the succulent **samphire** with its curiously jointed stem, and the aptly named **saltbush** come closest in their ability to survive extreme temperatures. After a rain, smaller desert plants rush to bloom and seed, covering the ground in a spectacular blanket of colour, a phenomenon for which Australia's Outback regions are well known.

On a larger scale, the Outback is dotted with stands of hardy **mulgas** and **wattles**, which superficially resemble scrawny eucalypts but have different leaf structures, as well as scattered groups of bloated, spindly-branched **bottle trees**, whose sweet, pulpy and moisture-laden cores can be used as emergency stock feed in drought conditions. The similar but far larger **boab**, found in the Kimberley and northeastern Northern Territory, is thought to be an invader from East Africa. **Mallee scrub** is unique to the southeastern Outback, where clearing of these tangled, bush-sized eucalypts for grazing has endangered both scrub and those animals which rely on it – the mound-building **mallee fowl** being the best known.

Mangrove swamps, found along the tropical and subtropical coasts, are tidal zones of thick grey mud and mangrove trees, whose interlocked, aerial roots make an effective barrier to exploration. They've suffered extensive clearing for development, and it wasn't until recently that their importance to the estuarine life-cycle won them limited government protection; Aboriginal people have always found them a rich source of animal and plant products.

Rainforest once covered much of the continent, but today only a small portion of its former abundance survives. Nevertheless, you'll find pockets everywhere, from Tasmania's richly verdant wilderness to the monsoonal examples of northern Queensland and the Top End in the Northern Territory.

Trees grow to gigantic heights, as they compete with each other for light, supporting themselves in the poor soil with aerial or buttressed roots. The extraordinary **banyan** and **Moreton Bay fig** trees are fine examples of the two types. They support a huge number of plant species, with tangled **vines** in the lower reaches, and **orchids**, **elkhorns** and other epiphytes using larger plants as roosts. **Palms** and **tree ferns**, with their giant, delicately curled fronds, are found in more open forest, where there's regular water.

Some forest types illustrate the extent of Australia's prehistoric flora. **Antarctic beech** or nothafagus, found south of Brisbane as well as in South America, along with native pines and **kauri** from Queensland, which also occur in New Zealand (the similarly-named Western Australian **karri** is also huge but unrelated), are all relict evidence of the prehistoric supercontinent. Gondwana. Other "living fossils" include primitive marine **stromatolites** – algae corals – still found around Shark Bay, Western Australia, and in fossilized form in the central deserts.

As long as you don't eat them or fall onto the pricklier versions, most Australian plants are harmless – though in rainforests you'd want to avoid entanglement with spiky **lawyer cane** or wait-awhile vine (though it doesn't look like it, this is a climbing palm). Also watch out for the large, pale-green, heart-shaped leaves of the **stinging tree**, a scraggly "regrowth" plant found on the margins of cleared tropical rainforest. Even a casual brush delivers an agonizing and prolonged sting; if you're planning on bushwalking in the tropics, learn to recognize and avoid this plant.

Australian film

All visitors to Australia these days will be aware of the popularity and respect for the Australian film industry since the early 1970s. It is generally agreed (with deference to a 1900 Salvation Army promo, *Stations of the Cross*) that *The Story of the Kelly Gang*, made by Charles Tait in 1906, was the world's first feature-length film. Australians' well-known antagonism towards figures of authority soon led to a hugely popular series of bushranger movies, eventually to be banned in 1912 by the New South Wales police on the grounds that their unsympathetic portrayal in these pictures was corrupting youngsters.

This **early heyday** of Australian film-making predated that of Hollywood and persisted with the production of various World War I morale boosters, despite the creation of a distribution duopoly (known as the "combine") which showed little interest in independent Australian films outside its control. With the ending of the war and its many cinematic testaments to the heroic disaster of Gallipoli, Australian silent cinema reached a creative peak. **Raymond Longford** was Australia's Spielberg of silents at this time, and his 1919 production of *The Sentimental Bloke* and its sequel, *Ginger Mick*, a year later, were popular and notably naturalist dramas about a woman's taming of her larrikin husband's proclivities. Along with the already established contempt for authority, Longford's films featured a distrust of sophistication and formality and, even then, the mythic spell of "the bush" began to make its mark on Australian productions.

Hollywood domination

The combine gradually squeezed the life from Australian cinema, which continued to decline as the powerful Hollywood studios got into their stride and entered the Golden Age of talkies. In 1933 the mildly reformed wild boy from Tasmania, **Errol Flynn**, starred in his first feature film, *In the Wake of the Bounty*, directed by **Charles Chauvel**, a leading figure in Australian film-making until the late 1950s.

During World War II there was a return to newsreels and documentaries, with the legendary cameraman, Damien Parer, earning **Australia's first Oscar** for his account of the fighting in New Guinea (*Kokoda Front Line*, 1942). Following the war, however, Hollywood's global domination of cinema was unassailed, and Australian cinema just about perished. Nevertheless, **Chips Rafferty** turned up as Australia's answer to John Wayne, appearing in an unremarkable series of formula films, such as the scenically superb epic of bovine migration, *The Overlanders* (1946).

In the 1950s the British Ealing Studios and the American MGM set up production companies in Australia, turning out the odd Outback drama which was watered-down for international consumption (but not success). This era produced few notable Australian films other than Cecil Holmes' return to the bushranger format in *Captain Thunderbolt* (1953), and his similarly leftist study of mateship, *Three In One* (1957). Chauvel's remarkable *Jedda, the Uncivilized* (1955) was more unusual in that it tackled the tricky issue of an Aboriginal girl's white upbringing, sexual temptation and subsequent abduction back to tribal life, where a tragic death inevitably awaited her. If there is one subject Australian cinema still has difficulty in dealing with (the New Wave having finally come to grips with women as individuals), it is that of the Aborigines.

Australia was by now nothing more than an exotic, marsupial-speckled location for "**kangaroo westerns**" and other dramas where British and American actors could exercise their skills. In 1959 Stanley Kramer directed *On the Beach*, Nevil Shute's post-Holocaust drama, with Ava Gardner, Gregory Peck and Fred Astaire tiptoeing through the fallout. A year later Fred Zinnemann directed Deborah Kerr and Robert Mitchum in *The Sundowners*, an affectionate classic of Outback itinerant labour.

The New Wave

The birth of the **New Wave** was a response to the burgeoning counterculture of the late 1960s. Among the many notable reforms of Gough Whitlam's Labor government was support for the long-neglected arts. Film-makers in particular were given a shot in the arm with the introduction of extremely generous grants to more than cover the cost of production. While in its early years this financial support helped produce some of the crassest male-fantasy "sex romps" ever seen (Tim Burstall's 1973 *Alvin Purple* and Terry Bourke's *Plugg* are matchlessly dire), the opening of the **Australian Film School** in 1973 allowed genuine talents such as Gillian Armstrong, Bruce Beresford and Paul Cox to flourish.

Two years later, the **Australian Film Commission** evolved from previous similar organizations to help produce and market Australian films, and although the grants have been regularly reduced ever since, their introduction kick-started the moribund industry so that there presently exists a diverse pool of directors and technicians to keep things going.

Peter Weir's unsettlingly eerie *Picnic at Hanging Rock* (1975) remains an early jewel, and the decade ended with further acclaim for his *Gallipoli*, Phillip Noyce's extraordinary *Newsfront* and Gillian Armstrong's first feature, *My Brilliant Career*. Auspicious futures were launched for Armstrong, and actors Sam Neill, Judy Davis and Mel Gibson, whose post-apocalyptic *Mad Max* trilogy saw a gradual stylistic evolution to suit the huge American market, though plans for a new *Mad Max*, which was to have been released in 2005, have been put on indefinite hold.

Contemporary Australian cinema is perhaps most exceptional for establishing a number of **women directors** and **producers** and providing a handful of strong women's roles. Inevitably, only the mainstream hits, such as the uplifting *Strictly Ballroom* and *Death in Brunswick*, have achieved wide overseas release, while many equally fine "small" films remain largely unseen. It is these quirky, uniquely Australian films of which the rejuvenated industry can be most proud. The prestige of numerous and consistent awards at the Cannes Film Festival and others proves that Australia's long-established cinematographic heritage has, more than any other art form, helped rid the country of its former philistine reputation. Confident and uncompromising films such as *Malcolm*, *Celia*, *Sweetie* and *The Year My Voice Broke* are just a few that complement their better-known siblings, with 1994 seeing a media-led "renaissance" in Australian film. Stephan Elliott's sartorially outrageous *The Adventures of Priscilla, Queen of the Desert* was the country's biggest box-office success up to that time and won international acclaim, while P.J. Hogan's wonderful *Muriel's Wedding* perfectly encapsulated the indigenous filmmaking idiom and proved that Australia still could make financially viable and idiosyncratic films.

Recent developments

By 1996, Australian film critics had grown weary of the trend in making "quirky, offbeat romances", such as Shirley Barratt's *Love Serenade* and Emma-Kate Croghan's 1996 Cannes hit *Love and Other Catastrophes*, although few would have much to complain about with Scott Hicks' globally acclaimed *Shine*. Since then, talented young writer-directors have focused on **crime stories**, often blackly comic, such as Gregor Jordan's first feature, the Sydney-set *Two Hands* (1999), which launched the career of Heath Ledger; Scott Roberts' *The Hard Word* (2002), with Guy Pearce and Rachel Griffiths; and Andrew Dominik's more graphic *Chopper* (2000), based on the autobiography of the very scary "Chopper" Read. Another trend is towards telling **Aboriginal stories**, with three major films coming out in the space of two years: Rolf de Heer's *The Tracker* (2002) and Phillip Noyce's *Rabbit-Proof Fence* (2002) both look back critically to the attitudes and atrocities of the 1920s and 1930s (respectively), dealing with the difficult subject matter of massacres (de Heer) and the "Stolen Generation" (Noyce); Stephen Johnson's *Yolgnu Boy* (2001), set in Arnhem Land, confronts contemporary indigenous adolescent experience, including graphic scenes of petrol sniffing. While other contemporary Australian films, such as the high-finance thriller *The Bank* by Robert Connolly (2001), starring American-based Anthony LaPaglia, could be set and told in any Western country, films such as *Rabbit-Proof Fence* and Ray Lawrence's bleak but brilliant *Lantana* show a distinctly Australian sensibility and landscape without exoticism, kitsch suburbia or cute and quirky characters, and reveal a new level of profundity and maturity in Australian cinema.

While the Liberal government has slashed funding to the Australian Film Commission and Film Finance Corporation, Australia's phenomenally successful **actors** now work mostly overseas where the pay, recognition and opportunities are much greater. These actors include Oscar-winners Russell Crowe (*Gladiator* and *Master and Commander*), Nicole Kidman (*Moulin Rouge* and *The Hours*) and Geoffrey Rush (*Shine* and *Quills*), and other major actors such as Judy Davis (*Naked Lunch* and *Celebrity*), Mel Gibson (*Braveheart* and *The Patriot*), Rachel Griffiths (*Blow* and the TV series *Six Feet Under*), Toni Collette (*The Sixth Sense* and *About a Boy*), Cate Blanchett (*The Aviator* and *The Lord of the Rings*), Sam Neill (*The Piano* and *Jurassic Park*), Anthony LaPaglia (*29th St* and *Lowdown*), Guy Pearce (*L.A. Confidential* and *Memento*), Richard Roxburgh (*Mission Impossible II* and *Moulin Rouge*), Hugh Jackman (*Kate & Leopold* and *Swordfish*), David Wenham (*Moulin Rouge* and *The Lord of the Rings*), Heath Ledger (*10 Things I Hate About You* and *A Knight's Tale*), Rose Byrne (*I Capture the Castle* and *Troy*) and Naomi Watts (*Mulholland Drive* and *The Assassination of Richard Nixon*). These actors do occasionally return home to star in films such as Gregor Jordan's 2003 *Ned Kelly* (featuring Geoffrey Rush, Naomi Watts and Heath Ledger), but this won't necessarily attract the locals: Australian films usually have short runs at home. In

1998 box office receipts hit a record A$629.2 million yet Australian films made up only two percent of that – and almost all lost money.

However, a low Australian dollar, skilled crews and Sydney's Fox Studios (see p.158), which opened in 1998, have attracted major productions such as *Dark City*, *The Matrix* trilogy, *Mission Impossible II*, *Star Wars Episode II* and *III*, *Moulin Rouge* and *The Quiet American* to Australia.

Films to watch out for

While you'd be lucky to catch all the recommendations below on the big screen (although keep an eye on the programmes of art-house, or repertory, cinemas in the major cities), many of the titles can be found in video-rental stores.

Humour, black comedy and satire

The Adventures of Priscilla, Queen of the Desert (Stephan Elliott, 1994). A queer romp across the Outback, prying into some musty corners of Australian social life along the way.

Babakiueria (Julian Pringler, 1988). A culture-reversing spoof beginning with Aborigines invading Australia during a roadside barbie and continuing with an anthropological-style study of white Australia. Rare, but well worth the search.

The Castle (Rob Sitch, 1997). A family's struggle to defend their home in the face of a trinity of suburban horrors: toxic-waste dumps, overhead power lines and airport developers.

Death in Brunswick (John Ruane, 1990). A black comedy about the misfortunes of a hapless dishwasher who becomes embroiled in a gangland killing.

The Hard Word (Scott Roberts, 2002). Three bank-robbing brothers (one played by Guy Pearce) are in cahoots with corrupt cops and a crooked lawyer. Their target: $100 million in cash held by Melbourne Cup bookies. Double and triple crossing has them on the run from everyone. Also stars Rachel Griffiths.

Malcolm (Nadia Tass, 1985). A charming, offbeat comedy about a slow-witted tram driver in Melbourne.

Muriel's Wedding (P.J. Hogan, 1994). Kleptomaniac frump Muriel wastes away in an Abba-and-confetti dreamworld until ex-schoolchum Rhonda masterminds Muriel's escape from her awful family and ghastly seaside suburb of Porpoise Spit. Great performances.

Adolescent and misfit romance

Better Than Sex (Jonathan Teplitzky, 2000). Josh, played by David Wenham (*The Boys*), has only three days left until he goes back to London, so a one-night, after-party fling with Cin (Susie Porter, *Mullet*) shouldn't hold any complications. A very sexy, warm and hilarious romantic comedy.

Flirting (John Duigan, 1989). This sequel to *The Year My Voice Broke*

Hot spots for film buffs and soap groupies

The majestic scenery of the Northern Territory has featured in many films. **Kakadu National Park** provided the setting for many of the scenes in *Crocodile Dundee*: familiar spots are possibly Anbangbang Billabong (see p.655) and Waterfall Creek (see p.656). *We of the Never Never* was set in the **Mataranka** region, which, predictably, has been rechristened "Never Never" country (see p.669); some costumes worn in the film are on display in the Old Courthouse and Residency in **Alice Springs** (see p.681).

Desolation and Outback grandeur have a stranglehold on the science-fiction and post-apocalyptic genres. Locations for *Mad Max II* include the **Silverton** area of New South Wales (see p.407); as his parting shot, Mel Gibson upscuttled the semi-trailer on the nearby **Mundi Mundi Plains**. In nearby **Broken Hill**, scenes from *The Adventures of Priscilla, Queen of the Desert* were filmed at the kitsch *Mario's Palace Hotel* (see p.406). In South Australia, the pockmarked scenery of **Coober Pedy** (see p.883) has found favour with many film-makers, including Wim Wenders, who made his epic *Until the End of the World* here, while the lunar-like landscape was also an invaluable element in creating the atmosphere of *Mad Max III*. And that Outback pub in *Crocodile Dundee* was none other than the *Walkabout Creek Hotel*, at **McKinlay** in Queensland (see p.606).

More lush surroundings have also caught the imagination: in Victoria the eponymous **Hanging Rock** (see p.998), which featured in *Picnic at Hanging Rock*, is within striking distance of **Woodend** (though the imposing mansion-school is actually in South Australia, the visitable Martindale Hall in the Clare Valley – see p.871).

The production of big-budget international films at Fox Studios in **Sydney** has provided locals with many location-spotting opportunities: *Mission Impossible II* provided the best haul, including scenes filmed at the **Bare Island** fortifications (see p.176). The soapy teenage angst and surfie bonhomie of *Home and Away* has long revolved around **Palm Beach** in Sydney's northern beaches (see p.175), with the **Barrenjoey Lighthouse** and headland regularly in shot. **Melbourne** is famous for being the filming location of *Home and Away*'s competitor, the veteran soapie *Neighbours*; Ramsay Street, Erinsborough is actually Pin Oak Court in Vermont South, while the cool international-hit TV series, *The Secret Life of Us* is filmed around St Kilda.

follows a young boy's adventures in boarding school. Superior coming-of-age film.

Lonely Hearts (Paul Cox, 1981). Following the death of his mother, 50-year-old Peter buys a new toupee and joins a dating agency.

A sensitive portrayal of the ensuing, at times awkward, relationship. Other Paul Cox features include *Man of Flowers*, *My First Wife* and *Cactus*.

Looking for Alibrandi (Kate Woods, 2000). Light yet surprisingly layered story of a teenage Sydney girl dealing with suicide, high school, new love and immigrant cultural identity.

Mullet (David Caesar, 2001). A slow-motion plot set in a New South Wales south-coast fishing town where nothing happens until a mysterious prodigal son (Ben Mendelsohn) returns to mixed receptions from his family, former friends and fiancée.

Strictly Ballroom (Baz Luhrmann, 1991). Mismatched dancers who, together, dare to defy the prescribed routines. A feel-good hit at Cannes and the box office, and the first feature from the highly successful director of *Moulin Rouge* (2001).

Urban dysfunctionals

The Boys (Rowan Woods, 1998). This tense drama follows Brett, played by rising star, David Wenham (*Better Than Sex*) as an ex-prisoner who terrorizes his dysfunctional family and coerces his unemployed brothers into a violent crime.

Careful, He Might Hear You (Carl Shultz, 1982). An absorbing tug-of-love drama set in 1930s Sydney.

Chopper (Andrew Dominik, 2000). Eric Bana brilliantly plays notorious, nihilistic Melbourne criminal Mark "Chopper" Read who ruthlessly dominates prison inmates and underworld associates alike. Based on Read's autobiography.

The Devil's Playground (Fred Schepisi, 1975). Burgeoning sexuality oozes between pupils and their tutors in a Catholic seminary.

Head On (Ana Kokkinos, 1998). Unemployed Ari (Alex Dimitriades) escapes living with his strict Greek parents by spending a hectic 24 hours nightclubbing, drug taking and graphically exploring his homosexuality.

Lantana (Ray Lawrence, 2001) A sometimes bleak but thought-provoking tale of trust and secrecy in marriage, set in Sydney. Coincidences and consequences bind lives of strangers together in ways that are as twisting, tangled and tough as the Australian plant that provides the film's title. The strong cast includes Geoffrey Rush and Anthony LaPaglia.

The Last Days of Chez Nous (Gillian Armstrong, 1991). A middle-aged woman slowly loses her grip on her marriage and family.

Romper Stomper (Geoffrey Wright, 1991). A bleak and pointless account of the violent disintegration of a gang of Melbourne skinheads, notable only as Russell Crowe's big-screen debut.

Sweetie (Jane Campion, 1988). Part black comedy, part bleakly disturbing portrait of a bizarre suburban family.

Ockerdom

The Adventures of Barry McKenzie (Bruce Beresford, 1972). Ultra-ocker comes to England to teach the "pommie sheilas about real men". Ironically, Barry Humphries' satire got beer-spurting ovations from the very people he despised and also set Beresford back a couple of years.

Crocodile Dundee (Peter Faiman, 1985). The acceptable side of genial, dinky-di ockerdom saw Paul Hogan sell Australian bush mystique to the mainstream and put Kakadu National Park firmly on the tourist agenda. Enjoyable once, but don't bother with the sequels.

Wake in Fright aka Outback (Ted Kotcheff, 1970). A horrifying gem in its uncut, 114min version; a real *Deliverance* Down Under. A coast-bound teacher blows his fare in Outback Hicksville and slowly degenerates into a brutal, beer-sodden nightmare.

Gritty and defiant women

Celia (Ann Turner, 1988). A wonderful allegory that mixes a 1950s rabbit-eradication programme with a communist witch-hunt. Stubborn Celia is determined to keep her bunny.

Dance Me To My Song (Rolf de Heer, 1998). A unique and moving film written by and starring cerebral palsy sufferer Heather Rose as she is abused by her carer and falls in love.

The Getting of Wisdom (Bruce Beresford, 1977). Spirited Laura rejects the polite sensibilities and snobbery of an Edwardian boarding school.

My Brilliant Career (Gillian Armstrong, 1978). An early feminist questions and defies the expectations of 1890s Victoria.

Puberty Blues (Bruce Beresford, 1981). Two teenage beach girls refuse to accept their pushchair-and-shopping-trolley destiny.

We of the Never Never (Igor Auzins, 1981). A good-looking version of Jeannie Gunn's autobiographical classic of early twentieth-century station life in the Top End.

Men in rugged circumstances

The Dish (Rob Sitch, 2000). Light-hearted take on how Australia saved NASA during the broadcasting of the 1969 Apollo 11 moon landing from New South Wales' Parkes Space Observatory (see p.360), and an aside on how the country's technological skills are often overlooked. Starring Sam Neill.

Gallipoli (Peter Weir, 1980). A deservedly classic buddy movie in which a young Mel Gibson strikingly evokes the Anzacs' cheery idealism and the tragedy of their slaughter.

The Last of the Knucklemen (Tim Burstall, 1978). Tensions build up in a remote Outback mine and explode in bare-fisted punch-ups.

The Man from Snowy River (George Miller, 1981). Men, horses and the land from A.B. ("Banjo") Paterson's seminal and dearly loved poem caught the overseas' imagination. A modern kangaroo western.

Plains of Heaven (Ian Pringle, 1982). A spookily atmospheric story of two weathermen in a remote meteorological station slowly losing their minds.

Sunday Too Far Away (Ken Hannam, 1973). A simple tale of macho shearers' rivalries in Outback South Australia.

Outback nightmares

Cunnamulla (Dennis O'Rourke, 2000). Controversial documentary of malaise in an isolated Outback town, 800km west of Brisbane, shot in a laconic style befitting Queensland, and featuring inhabitants' own stories of teen sex and hopelessness, frontier redneckery, racial tension, social dysfunction, and desperate longings for escape to distant cities.

Evil Angels (*A Cry in the Dark*) (Fred Schepisi, 1987). A dramatic retelling of the Azaria Chamberlain story; Ayers Rock (Uluru) and dingoes will never seem quite the same again.

Picnic at Hanging Rock (Peter Weir, 1975). A richly layered tale about the disappearance of a party of schoolgirls and its traumatic aftermath.

Razorback (Russell Mulcahy, 1984). Dark comedy exploiting urban paranoia of the Outback and featuring a remote township, a gigantic, psychotic wild pig, and some bloodthirsty nutters who run the local abattoir.

Walkabout (Nicolas Roeg, 1971). Following their deranged father's suicide during a bush picnic, two children wander through the wilderness until an Aboriginal boy guides them back to civilization.

About Aboriginal people

The Chant of Jimmie Blacksmith (Fred Schepisi, 1977). Set in the 1800s, when a mixed-race boy is forced onto the wrong side of the law. Based on the novel by Thomas Keneally.

Dead Heart (Brian Brown, 1996). A long-overdue and regrettably overlooked thriller, set on an Aboriginal community near Alice Springs. Bravely gets its teeth into some juicy political and social issues.

The Fringe Dwellers (Bruce Beresford, 1985). An aspiring daughter persuades her family to move from the bush into a suburban white neighbourhood, with expected results.

Jedda, the Uncivilized (Charles Chauvel, 1955). An orphaned Aboriginal girl brought up by a "civilized" white family cannot resist her "tribal" urges when she is semivoluntarily abducted by a black outlaw.

Manganinnie (John Honey, 1980). Set during the time of the "black drives" of 1830s Tasmania, a young Aboriginal girl gets separated from her family and meets a white girl in similar straits.

Rabbit-Proof Fence (Phillip Noyce, 2002). Very moving film, with beautiful cinematography, set in 1930s Western Australia and based on a true "Stolen Generation" story. Three girls, daughters of absent white fathers – construction workers of the fence itself – and black mothers, are taken from their families according to the policy of the all-powerful A.O. Neville, Chief Protector of Aborigines (Kenneth Branagh) to a settlement at Moore River, but manage to escape. The girls – Outback-cast unknowns giving emotive, natural performances – make their way over 2000km home following the fence, pursued by a tracker (David Gulpilil).

The Tracker (Rolf de Heer, 2002). Set in 1922, this is something of a fable told in an experimental way. Each character is a type: "The Fanatic", a police officer who will stop at nothing including cold-blooded massacre, leads "The Tracker" (the film is a star-vehicle for David Gulpilil), "The Follower" (a young green policeman), and "The Veteran", all in search of "The Accused", an indigenous man wanted for a white woman's murder. Violent massacre scenes are replaced by landscape paintings but with a painful soundtrack, while songs (performed by Aboriginal musician Archie Roach) and narration mostly convey the themes, creating a disturbing impression.

Yolgnu Boy (Stephen Johnson, 2001). In Yolgnu country in Arnhem Land, Lorrpu, Milika and Bortj have always been an inseparable trio. But when adolescence hits, 15-year-old Bortj's petrol-sniffing rampages land him in jail; as Lorrpu and Milika become tribally initiated, Bortj finds himself outside his own culture and unable to become a man, and friendships and loyalties are tested. When the three embark on a – beautifully shot – 500-kilometre overland trek to Darwin, living off the land, distress gives way to joy ... until they hit the city.

Portents of doom

Cane Toads: an Unnatural History (Mark Lewis, 1988). A very eccentric, original and amusing documentary about the mixed feelings Queensland's poisonous amphibians arouse and the real threat they may pose to Australia's ecology.

The Last Wave (Peter Weir, 1977). An eerie chiller about a lawyer defending an Aborigine accused of murder – and the powerful, elemental forces his people control.

Mad Max II (George Miller, 1981). The best of the trilogy, set in a near future where loner Max protects an oil-producing community from fuel-starved crazies. Great machinery and stunts.

Australian music

For a geographically isolated, sparsely inhabited island with a tiny market for its own recorded music, Australia has, with ever-more assurance, shouldered its way in to occupy a distinguished place in the international pop music hierarchy. In contrast with its fifty-year rock music heritage, the country's Aboriginal music boasts a creative presence of thousands of years. With a strong influence on contemporary Australian music, its importance in the ongoing reconciliation between black and white Australia can hardly be overstated.

Rock music

The story of Australian contemporary music closely parallels that of Britain and the US – rock'n'roll arrived in the 1950s, and each decade since has offered up its own revolutionary shift in the popular music landscape. Given the ubiquitous nature of Western popular culture, this is hardly surprising. Less predictable, however, has been the impact of Australian music on the global music scene, beginning in the 1970s with AC/DC, continuing in the 1980s with Midnight Oil and INXS, through to the more recent silverchair, Jet and The Vines.

The early years

Australia's very first rock star emerged in 1957 in the form of a lean, throaty, stage-strutting powerhouse named **Johnny O'Keefe**. All snake-hips and sex appeal, "The Wild One", as he became known, was one of the few early rock performers who could very nearly out-Elvis Elvis. Concert footage of his live performances is largely taken up by shots of women screaming, passing out and being carried from concert venues by sweaty police and exhausted security people. O'Keefe discovered early on that all the big players in the industry – performers, managers, promoters and record companies – were expert manipulators, and he quickly set about becoming one himself: legend has it that he bullied his way into his first recording contract by calling a press conference and announcing that the deal was done, guessing correctly that the publicity would leave the record company no option but to sign him.

Johnny O'Keefe was, to Australians, the embodiment of the defiant new brand of music that was then sweeping the world. He was to become synonymous with 1960s TV programmes that showcased Australian rock'n'roll talent, even as his own recording efforts were gradually swamped by the peace-love-hair movement of the time. O'Keefe remained a presence on television and radio until his death of a heart attack in 1978, aged just 43. In keeping with the requirements of rock god-dom, his last years were characterized by a series of breakdowns, bouts of depression and problems with alcohol. His rendition of the classic crowd-anthem **Shout** (1959) remains, to this day, an integral part of early rock'n'roll's global legacy (video footage of O'Keefe performing live also constitutes the opening sequence of the ABC's late-night music video programme *Rage*).

Surviving the Sixties

In company with the rest of the world, Australian music rode out the 1960s hanging onto the coat-tails of the massive British rock invasion. Overwhelmed by the omnipresent Beatles and Rolling Stones, Australia was to produce little ground-breaking rock music beyond the efforts of Billy Thorpe and the Aztecs, The Easybeats and Russell Morris, each of whom left behind a signature song forever embedded in the Australian psyche, and still played on commercial radio today: *Most People I Know (Think that I'm Crazy)* – Billy Thorpe and the Aztecs (1968); *Friday on My Mind* – The Easybeats (1966); *The Real Thing* – Russell Morris (1969).

The Seekers, however, were operating well clear of the crowded rock music mainstream, creating their own musical niche by building three-part harmonies around chords strummed on acoustic guitars, the two male voices cushioning the pristine power of lead vocalist Judith Durham. Songs such as *If I Had a Hammer* (1965) might sound like hippie anthems today, but The Seekers' brand of idealism appealed to millions of record-buyers, and several successful comeback tours show that their popularity has barely waned.

It was in 1967, though, that millions of Australians witnessed the decade's most significant music industry event – and not a single one of them even knew it. A young man named **Johnny Farnham** had appeared on television, performing a cute but innocuous ditty entitled *Sadie (the Cleaning Lady)* (1967). Good-looking and with a superb voice, as well as charming beyond his years, Farnham endeared himself immediately to Australian audiences; it was a promising debut, but nobody could have predicted how far he'd go. His name shortened these days to John, Farnham is now into his fifth decade as a performer, and continues to shift with apparently effortless ease between roles as rock star, stage-musical lead and TV personality. From 1982 to 1986 he was a popular frontman for the hugely successful Little River Band (having replaced Glen Shorrock), but it was in 1987 that his career peaked, with the release of his album *Whispering Jack*, which sold millions of copies worldwide, driven, appropriately enough, by the success of the single *You're the Voice* (1987).

Livin' in the Seventies

Having emerged from the shadows of the 1960s, Australian music began to find a voice of its own in the mid-1970s. For no obvious reason, **Glam Rock** was a phenomenon Australian bands not only embraced, but excelled at. Sherbet and **Skyhooks** pulled off the satin-jumpsuits-and-crazy-make-up combo with singular style. The "Mighty Hooks" were at all times the cheekier and sexier of the two. Singer "Shirley" Strachan famously performed in only a pair of tight satin trousers with a large, bright-red hand painted over the crotch; the other band-members were equally indulgent of their penchants for self-expression. There was no sacrifice of substance for style, however, with the band recording several of Australia's finest and most enduring pop songs, including such irresistible numbers as *You Just Like Me 'cause I'm Good in Bed* (1974), *Horror Movie* (1974), *Ego (Is Not a Dirty Word)* (1975), and *Women in Uniform* (1978).

Sherbet seemed almost serious by comparison, doing without the make-up and looking as though they only wore the satin pants, silly shoes and poncy scarves because that was what fashion dictated. It was a highly accomplished band no matter what they were wearing, and led by virtuoso pop vocalist Daryl Braithwaite, they recorded several standout tracks, including *Child's Play* (1976), *Howzat* (1976), *High Rolling* (1977) and *Summer Love* (1975). Although both bands flirted with overseas success, touring the US (and subsequently expressing bitterness at not having cracked the big time), history has conferred upon them the honour of having kicked open the rock music establishment's door, on behalf of an Australian music fraternity that had simply been waiting around for someone to show them "we're just as good as those bands from overseas".

Proof perhaps of the depth of talent concentrated in these two bands is the continued presence of individual members in Australian music and media today. Trivia buffs can still track down various Skyhooks alumni: former guitarist Red Symons is now a Melbourne radio announcer and is regularly cast as the villain on some of TV's nastier game shows, while Greg Macainsh is in high demand still as a bass player and songwriter; former lead singer Graeme "Shirley" Strachan was tragically killed in a helicopter crash in 2001, having enjoyed almost twenty years as a popular TV presenter. Stalwarts of Sherbet likewise have soldiered on: Daryl Braithwaite, the lead singer, is now a successful solo performer; Harvey James, one of the first Australian guitar-heroes, graduated to session musician and guitar-ace-for-hire; and Garth Porter, former keyboardist, has gone on to assume the unlikely mantle of producer/guru for many of Australia's top country music performers.

But even as Glam Rock was fading from cool to kitsch, a clannish group of young Scottish immigrants were beginning to play their own version of Chuck Berry-inspired blues-rock, only three times as loud and with heavily distorted guitars. **AC/DC** not only had the skills, the songs and the "muscle" to back it all up, they also boasted two figures who were destined to become universal icons of rock'n'roll rebellion: guitarist Angus Young's delinquent schoolboy persona had to share the adulation of wannabe rock rebels with singer Bon Scott, who was possessed not only of a genuine, self-destructive, live-hard-die-young ethos, but also sported the most mischievous grin ever seen in tandem with a microphone. It's unlikely anyone besides Bon could have delivered songs such as *Highway to Hell* (1979), *Whole Lotta Rosie* (1978), and *Dirty Deeds...Done Dirt Cheap* (1976) with the required sass to make them acceptable in a 1970s commercial market.

True to form, Bon died a rock star's death in London in 1980, poisoned by alcohol in the back seat of a car. It was, ironically, smack in the middle of a golden age for Australian music, when, during the period 1977–83, bands Men at Work, Midnight Oil, Cold Chisel, INXS, Air Supply and Little River Band were lining up right alongside AC/DC to take the pop music world by storm.

Oz music grows up

Even as AC/DC managed – in the space of a year following Bon's death – to recruit a new singer (Brian Johnston), settle permanently into life in Britain,

Top ten great Oz rock albums

1) *Livin' in the Seventies* Skyhooks. Mushroom Records, 1974.
2) *Howzat!* Sherbet. Sherbet Records, 1976.
3) *Goodbye Tiger* Richard Clapton. Infinity Records, 1977.
4) *Back in Black* AC/DC. Albert Records, 1980.
5) *East* Cold Chisel. WEA, 1980.
6) *Business As Usual* Men At Work. CBS, 1981.
7) *Kick* INXS. WEA, 1987.
8) *Diesel and Dust* Midnight Oil. CBS, 1987.
9) *Songs From the South: Paul Kelly's Greatest Hits* Paul Kelly. Mushroom Records, 1997.
10) *Highly Evolved* The Vines. Capitol Records, 2002.

and record the most acclaimed and successful heavy rock album of all time, *Back in Black* (1980), bands back in Australia suddenly found that the world was interested in them, too. **Little River Band**'s sound was so West Coast USA that commercial success in North America had long seemed inevitable; **Air Supply**, meanwhile, had the sort of stranglehold on the American easy listening love-song market to which Michael Bolton was perhaps, even then, beginning to aspire. More surprising was the impact made by **Men at Work**, a band whose well-crafted songs were invariably, if unfashionably, punctuated by arresting melodies played on a flute, and whose style came to be described as "white reggae". They announced their arrival in 1981 with the ska-ish *Who Can it Be Now?*, followed by *The Land Down Under*, both of which bombarded radio airwaves and shifted by the million.

During this period, Midnight Oil, Cold Chisel and INXS stayed closer to home, recognizing perhaps that their styles were less easily translatable from an Australian to a global audience. It is surely no coincidence that among these bands (all highly accomplished, and equally revered at home) the least identifiably "Australian" act – **INXS** – was the first to experience worldwide fame and fortune, when in 1987 their album *Kick* plundered the US charts. (This wave of success held tragic implications for singer Michael Hutchence; he would struggle to make the transition from rock star to rock superstar, suffering depression until his death by suicide in 1997.) Of the other two, most needs to be said about the band that had the biggest impact at home, and the least impact abroad – Cold Chisel. If the period three years either side of 1980 was to be remembered as the grand era of Oz "pub rock", then Chisel was the band that owned it, lock, stock and smoking barrel.

From Chisel to The Church

Formed in Adelaide in 1975, **Cold Chisel** was, like every great band from the Rolling Stones to U2, greater than the sum of its parts. Steve Prestwich (drums) and Phil Small (bass) made a compact and classy rhythm team, variously casting light and shadow about the more illustrious members of the group. Ian Moss's blues-rock guitar virtuosity and awesome soul voice made him a natural star on any stage, in lethal combination with lead singer Jimmy Barnes, Australia's self-styled wild man of rock and working-class hero. A great band must have great songs, and these were duly delivered by the immensely tall and serious man at the piano, **Don Walker**, arguably Australia's greatest songwriter.

Among hundreds of examples of Don Walker's craftsmanship in capturing the times/places/people/events poignant to Australians, *Khe Sanh* (1978) – a treatise on the Australian experience of surviving the war in Vietnam – remains a work without peer, while *Star Hotel* (1980) captures, in three verses and a chorus, the mood and events of September 19, 1979, when, in the working-class steel-town of Newcastle, police came to close down the city's main pub-rock venue, *The Star Hotel*, only to find themselves confronted by an angry crowd spoiling for a fight. Police cars were overturned and set alight in the course of a civil disturbance that echoed convict rebellions of two centuries earlier. The hotel was finally closed down, but the punters had made their point – and Chisel weren't going to let the police forget it.

Cold Chisel not only recorded the boozy summer nights, the trips up the coast, the girls, the fights, the pubs, the streets, the cities and towns, they sang it all back to the faithful in sweaty pubs and heaving stadiums night after night. When they called it a day in 1984, Chisel were Australia's greatest ever rock band, bar none. "Mossy" and "Barnesy" went on to fame and fortune as solo performers, but the band's long-awaited return did not come until 1998, when they released their first studio album in fourteen years *The Last Wave of Summer*; predictably, though, it failed to capture the power of the band in its heyday.

During this period, **Midnight Oil** by no means played second fiddle to Cold Chisel; rather, they had a different agenda, and their commitment and energy in delivering it live were never in question. Always highly political (lead singer Peter Garrett narrowly missed out on a Senate seat while he was leader of Australia's Nuclear Disarmament Party), "the Oils" brought Aboriginal land rights into the forum of pop culture, even as their uncompromising album *Diesel and Dust* (1987) brought them worldwide success. Twenty-five year veterans with fourteen albums to their credit (and often bracketed by critics with bands like Queen and U2 as the most powerful live act in the world), Midnight Oil's rage against the machine ended in 2002, with Peter Garrett leaving the band in order to resume his political career. In 2004, he was elected Labor member for Kingsford Smith, and stands on committees for indigenous people's affairs and the arts.

Among the distinguished musicians of the 1970s and 1980s, two songwriters stand (alongside Don Walker) above the rest as chroniclers of their culture and environment: **Richard Clapton** and **Paul Kelly**. Clapton's 1977 album *Goodbye Tiger* is unmatched as a celebration of the very fact of life in Australia – riding the city tram, searching for the perfect wave, soaking up the streetscapes of Oxford Street and Kings Cross. Paul Kelly is a more contemporary presence, and his songs go unerringly to the heart of the matter: *Have You Ever Seen Sydney From a 727 at Night?* (1985), *From St Kilda to Kings Cross* (1985) and *Adelaide* (1985) capture their respective subjects better than any photograph, while his ode to *Bradman* (1987) – written in homage to Australia's greatest Test cricket batsman Sir Donald Bradman ("The Don"), is the stuff of a true bard.

However, in order to appreciate the depth and diversity of Australian music as it reached **maturity**, one needs to take a stroll out to the fringes. With a well-established canon of "major" Australian bands now in place, others were finding looser creative environments in which to operate. The Triffids, The Birthday Party (with star alumnus Nick Cave), The Church and the Go-Betweens seemed tied to weirder and more eclectic influences (such as The Velvet Underground, David Bowie and Bob Dylan) than their "mainstream" counterparts. Although musically diverse, they held several characteristics in common: their songs seemed more poetic, or just more sensitive to light-and-shade; they were also far less commercially successful in Australia, yet all made a big impact in Britain and Europe. Among all of these, The Church alone continue to record and tour from various bases in Europe, while **Nick Cave** enjoys a position of enormous respect within the international music industry, thanks to several well received albums with his current band The Bad Seeds. Australia could boast, too, a white-hot outfit schooled in the nasty traditions of 1970s British punk: The Saints. Although known for their Sex Pistols-ish two-minute thrash exercises, The Saints were nevertheless real musicians, and survivors Chris Bailey and Ed Kuepper continue to record and perform songs of the highest quality.

The Nineties and beyond...

Strangest perhaps of all the facets of Australia's music industry has been its propensity for throwing up TV **soap stars** who mutated into pop stars. At last count there were no less than five ex-Neighbours cast members at large within the music industry: Kylie Minogue, Danii Minogue, Natalie Imbruglia, Holly Valance and Delta Goodrem. Australians have never known what to make of this, but both Natalie Imbruglia and Kylie Minogue have earned their stripes by recording fine pop albums; Holly Valance, meanwhile, has been widely dismissed as just another in a long line of soft-porn pop wannabes.

The roaring success of these soap-star singers goes some way to explaining the listlessness that afflicted the music community during the late 1980s to early 1990s. It seemed the moment **Kylie** was formally adopted by an adoring British public, Australian musicians breathed a collective sigh of relief, and got straight back to work. You Am I, The Whitlams, Powderfinger and The Cruel Sea had always been likely to show the way by writing and recording with passion and originality. By the mid-1990s, quality Australian bands were once again jostling for position in local and overseas markets, this time led by three scruffy-looking, fifteen-year-old schoolboys.

In 1994, Newcastle high-school trio Innocent Criminals sent a demo tape to radio station Triple J in response to a band competition, the prize for which was use of the station's recording facilities. The song, *Tomorrow*, had the Seattle grunge sound all over it, and an awesome rock vocal performance from singer/guitarist Daniel Johns. He didn't sound like a fifteen-year-old, although the band's written entry should have given some kind of clue; their "twenty-five-words-or-less" were written in green felt marker-pen on yellow cardboard: "We're not rap or hip-hop, we're rock and we love to play". *Tomorrow* arrived atop the Australian singles charts where it stayed for several weeks, and with the band renamed **silverchair**, their 1995 album *Frogstomp* took them into league – and onto a stage – with grunge giants like Pearl Jam and Soundgarden, even as the three "boys" were negotiating their last year of high school. Subsequent silverchair albums *Freak Show* (1997), *Neon Ballroom* (1999) and *Diorama* (2002) all met with solid sales and critical approval. Having fought the twin ravages of anorexia and a crippling bout of arthritis, Daniel Johns has since reinvented himself and is now writing and recording with prominent Aussie DJ Paul Mac; their style is a hybrid of rock chords and melodies with sampled sounds and keyboards, with the new band going by the name The Dissociatives. While silverchair has not been officially dissolved, it seems unlikely that their guitar-driven rock will ever again satisfy Johns' creative muse.

Not to be left out of the latest shift in the music biz, Australia has recently seen the emergence of two groups of precocious young rockers – **The Vines** and Jet. Having tapped into the retro-rock mood that reared its head in 2002 with bands like The Strokes, The White Stripes and The Hives (each of which mined the raw and rampant sound of The Who, The Stooges and The Ramones), The Vines exploded onto the world scene with such a rush that they scored both a recording deal and a hit album (*Highly Evolved*, 2002) after having played only a handful of live shows. Since then, beset by on-stage dramas and rumours of a split, their second album *Winning Days* (2004) has received mixed reviews. **Jet** soared into the hearts and minds of young rock fans, most notably in the UK, with their absurdly catchy guitar riffs and the kind of hard-living rock attitude that no doubt makes bands such as the Rolling Stones, Led Zeppelin and the Black Crowes (all influences emblazoned on Jet's leather-jacketed sleeves) fairly weep with pride. The album *Get Born* (2003) spent more than a year tearing up the charts worldwide, largely on the strength of the single *Are You Gonna Be My Girl?*, which has been a staple of several global television ad campaigns.

Australian rock music looks set to continue punching well above its weight. From Jet, The Vines and other rock outfits Powderfinger and Grinspoon to the thrashier Jebediah and The Living End, stylish and witty The Whitlams, and the rock/techno crossover work of Regurgitator, the latest array of talent is dizzying.

Aboriginal music

Aboriginal music is an increasingly powerful and invigorating seam in the fabric of world music. Its instruments and rhythms have a strong influence on contemporary Australian music, and there's probably no better example of the musical crossing of cultural boundaries than in the story of Australia's most recognizable instrument, the didgeridoo. Known also as a yidaki, or simply a "didge", this hollowed-out tree branch, when blown into, produces a resonant hum that can be punctuated by imitations of animal and bird noises. Its sound is uniquely evocative of the Australian landscape.

The big surprise for many visitors to Australia is the sheer **diversity** of Aboriginal music. From the big rock sound of the Warumpi Band, and the heartfelt guitar ballads of Archie Roach, to the cruisey island reggae of Saltwater and the echoes of an ancient culture in the work of Nabarlek (who sing mostly in their own language), there is no way of pigeonholing the music. The latest indigenous talent to hit the radio airwaves is a hip-hop group called The Wilcannia Mob, whose simple lyrics about days spent fishing and swimming are delivered by boys whose average age is twelve. It's no problem to see Aboriginal bands playing live, doing everything from metal to hip-hop and performing in all parts of the country, but there's really no better way to immerse yourself than by attending an indigenous music festival.

Festivals

Biggest of all the festivals is the **Barunga Sports & Cultural Festival**, which showcases up to forty bands, along with team sports, traditional dance, spear-throwing and didge-playing competitions. It's held at Barunga Community, 80km south of Katherine in the NT, over the Queen's Birthday holiday weekend in June (campsites with facilities are available); for information, phone the Barunga Community direct on ⓣ08/8975 4504. Also in the Top End, the **Milingimbi Cultural Festival** is purely a music event and, being harder to get to than Barunga, gets fewer white visitors. Dates for this one are hard to nail down, although it's always held sometime mid-year, on Milingimbi Island in the Crocodile archipelago. There are flights from Darwin, otherwise you need permission from the Northern Land Council (Darwin Head Office ⓣ08/8920 5100, ⓦwww.nlc.org.au) to drive across Arnhem Land to Ramingining to catch a barge. Traditional music and dance are featured, along with gospel bands and lots of Arnhem Land rock.

The festival held every odd-numbered year at **Laura** (next one is 2007), in far north Queensland, attracts high profile performers like the Warumpi Band and Christine Anu, plus all the local Murri bands. Held in June, there are usually quite a few backpackers and hippies about, as well as the local Murri community. It's about three hours' drive (on sealed roads) north from Cairns to Laura, a small town 60km west of Cooktown. Otherwise, another intriguing possibility on the west coast is the **Stompem Ground Festival**. First staged in Broome, Western Australia, in 1992, it drew on the strong and highly independent Aboriginal communities of the Kimberley region, attracting singers, dancers and bands into the incomparable beauty of Western Australia's far north, and is finally establishing itself on the Broome annual events calendar (Sept/Oct; ⓦwww.kimberleytourism.com) and is well worth checking out. Even if you find yourself stranded in the Big Smoke, you need not miss out; if you're in **Sydney** over summer, there's no better place to be on the Australia Day holiday

(January 26) than at "Survival", Waverley Oval, Bondi. This festival began as a highly political event, deliberately juxtaposed with the Australia Day festivities which mark the arrival of the First Fleet of "white invaders". It continues as a celebration of the survival of indigenous people and cultures in the face of white oppression, and draws many of the biggest names in indigenous music.

Artists

Most of the **bands** mentioned above have work available on CD, while other outstanding artists whose albums are widely available include Yothu Yindi, No Fixed Address, Tiddas, Kev Carmody and Coloured Stone. Compilation albums are worth looking into also, particularly those that cover a wide range of styles: *Meinmuk – Music from the Top End* (1996) and *Culture – Music from Black Australia* (2000) are Triple J compilations that showcase both the quality and diversity of aboriginal music – from rock, reggae and rap to gospel and metal. CAAMA (Central Australian Aboriginal Media Association) is an excellent source for the latest indigenous CDs and videos, all of which are available online at ⓦwww.caama.com.au.

Books

Australian writing came into its own in the 1890s, when a strong nationalistic movement, leading up to eventual federation in 1901, produced writers such as Henry Lawson and the balladeer A.B. "Banjo" Paterson, who romanticized the bush and glorified the mateship ethos, while outstanding women writers, such as Miles Franklin and Barbara Baynton, gave a feminine slant to the bush tale and set the trend for a strong female authorship. In the twentieth and twenty-first centuries, Australian novelists came to be recognized in the international arena: Patrick White was awarded a Nobel Prize in 1973, Peter Carey won the Booker Prize in 1988 and again in 2001, and Kate Grenville scored the 2001 Orange Prize for Fiction. Other writers who have made a name for themselves within Australia, such as David Malouf, Julia Leigh, Tim Winton (twice nominated for the Booker Prize), Thomas Keneally, Richard Flanagan, Chloe Hooper and Robyn Davidson have aroused curiosity further afield. Literary journals such as *Meanjin*, *Southerly*, *Westerly* and *Heat* provide a forum and exposure for short fiction, essays, reviews and new and established writers. The big prizes in Australian fiction include the Vogel Prize for the best unpublished novel written by an author under the age of 35, and the country's most coveted literary prize, the Miles Franklin Award.

Many of the best books by Australian writers or about Australia are not available overseas, so you may be surprised at the range of local titles available in Australian **bookshops**. A good website to check is that of Gleebooks (Ⓦwww.gleebooks.com.au), one of Australia's best literary booksellers, with a whole host of recent reviews; you can also order books online, to be posted overseas.

Travel and travel guides

★ **Peter Carey** *30 Days in Sydney: a wildly distorted account.* Part of Bloomsbury Publishers' "The Writer and the City" project, where "some of the finest writers of our time reveal the secrets of a city they know best". Based in New York, famous Australian writer Carey set himself a thirty-day time frame and gave it its aforementioned subtitle to defuse ideas that it might be a comprehensive guide. As he hangs out with old friends, it is their lives, the tales they tell and the often nostalgic trips around Sydney that form the basis of this vivid city portrait.

Bruce Chatwin *Songlines.* A semi-fictional account of an exploration into Aboriginal nomadism and mythology that turns out to be one of the more readable expositions of this complex subject, though often pretentious.

Sean Condon *Sean and David's Long Drive.* Australia's answer to Kerouac's *On the Road*, with humour in overdrive: Melbourne-based Condon and his friend David are fully fledged city dwellers when they set off on a tour around their own country, to come face to face with the dangers of crocs, tour guides and fellow travellers.

Robyn Davidson *Tracks.* A compelling account of a young woman's journey across the Australian desert, accompanied only by four camels and a dog. Davidson manages to break out of the heroic-traveller mould to write with compassion and honesty of the people she meets in the Outback and the doubts, dangers and loneliness she faces on her way. A classic of its kind.

Larry Habegger (ed) *Traveler's Tales Australia.* Excerpts and essays from some of the world's best travel writers – Bruce Chatwin, Tim Cahill, Jan Morris, Tony Horwitz, Pico Iyer and Paul Theroux – as well as new talents.

Howard Jacobson *In the Land of Oz*. Jacobson focuses his lucidly sarcastic observations on a round-Australia trip in the late 1980s that gets rather too close to some home truths for most Australians' tastes.

Tony Horwitz *One for the Road*. Married to an Australian, Pulitzer Prize-winning American author Horwitz comes to live in Sydney, but pines for adventure and sets off to hitchhike through the Outback. Along the way he encounters colourful characters from Aborigines to jackeroos, and hard-drinking men in a multitude of bush pubs. A comical yet highly perceptive account.

Mark McCrum *No Worries*. Knowing nothing of the country except the usual clichés, McCrum arrives in 1990s Australia and makes his way around by plane, train, thumb and Greyhound, meeting a surprising cast of characters along the way. As he travels, the stereotypes give way to an insightful picture of modern Australia.

Ruth Park *Ruth Park's Sydney*. Prolific novelist Park's 1973 guide to the city was fully revised and expanded in 1999. A perfect walking companion, full of personal insights, anecdotes and literary quotations.

Nicholas Shakespeare *In Tasmania*. During the seven years writing and researching a biography of Bruce Chatwin, British writer Shakespeare spent time in Australia following in his footsteps. Lured to Tasmania as one of the few remote places Chatwin had *never* been to, Shakespeare now lives there six months of the year. Discovery of a cache of letters written by the black sheep of the family revealed a Tasmanian connection: ancestor – and colourful villain Anthony Fenn Kemp. Researching his family history, Shakespeare found living Tasmanian relatives on his mother's side: two elderly spinsters who'd only once left their farm. A brilliantly Chatwinesque book, where historical tales weave in with the writer's own experiences.

Alice Thomson *The Singing Line*. The great-great-granddaughter of Alice Todd, the woman after whom Alice Springs was named, retraces her ancestor's journey to central Australia. Nice change from the usual male-centric view of the early pioneers.

Mark Whittaker and Amy Willesee *The Road to Mount Buggery: a Journey Through the Curiously Named Places of Australia*. Australia certainly has some unfortunate, banal and obscure place names, which Mark and Amy seek out on their journey, from Lake Disappointment to Cape Catastrophe. This entertaining, well-informed travelogue gives the fascinating stories behind the names.

Autobiography and biography

Julia Blackburn *Daisy Bates in the Desert*. For almost thirty years from 1913, Daisy Bates was Kabbarli, "the white-skinned grandmother", to the Aboriginal people with whom she lived in the desert. Blackburn's beautifully written biography interweaves fiction with fact to conjure up the life of one of Australia's most eccentric and misunderstood women.

Jill Ker Conway *The Road from Coorain*. Conway's childhood, on a drought-stricken Outback station during the 1940s, is movingly told, as is her battle to establish herself as a young historian in sexist, provincial 1950s Australia.

★ **Robert Drewe** *The Shark Net.* Accomplished novelist and journalist, Drewe has written a transfixing memoir of his boyhood and youth in Perth which segues into a literary true-crime story. Against a vividly drawn 1950s middle-class backdrop, Drewe shows how one man's random killing spree struck fear into the 'burbs of sunny, friendly and seemingly innocent Perth.

★ **Albert Facey** *A Fortunate Life.* A hugely popular autobiography of a battler, tracing his progress from a bush orphanage to Gallipoli, through the Depression, another war and beyond.

Eddie Mabo and Noel Loos *Edward Koiko Mabo: His Life and Struggle for Land Rights.* Mabo spent much of his life fighting for the autonomy of Torres Strait Islanders and in the process overthrew the concept of *terra nullius*, making his name a household word in Australia. Long interviews with the late black hero form the basis of this book and affectionately reveal the man behind the name.

David Malouf *12 Edmondstone Street.* An evocative autobiography-in-snatches of one of Australia's finest literary novelists, describing, in loving detail, the eponymous house in Brisbane where Malouf was born, life in the Tuscan village where he lives for part of each year, and his first visit to India.

Leah Purcell *Black Chicks Talking.* In an effort to overcome Aboriginal stereotypes, indigenous actor and writer Purcell gives insight into the lives of contemporary black women with this collection of lively, lengthy interviews, conducted with nine young females (all under 35), including the first Aboriginal Miss Australia (and now politician) Kathryn Hay, dancer Frances Rings, and actor Deborah Mailman.

Hazel Rowley *Christina Stead: a Biography.* Stead (1902–83) has been acclaimed as Australia's greatest novelist. After spending years in Paris, London and New York with her American husband, she returned to Australia in her old age.

Barry Hill *Broken Song: T.G.H. Strehlow and Aboriginal Possession.* As a child growing up on the Hermannsburg Mission in Central Australia, Strehlow had learnt the Aranda (Arrente) language. In 1932 the anthropologist began collecting Aranda songs, myths and *tjurunga* (sacred objects); his book *Songs of Central Australia* may have saved the Aranda language from extinction, and he was the first to really value the spirituality of Aboriginal religion. Resented by other anthropologists for his unique insight and access, Strehlow's was a fascinating career which ended in disgrace.

Society and culture

Richard Baker *Land is Life: From Bush to Town – the Story of the Yanyuwa People.* The Yanyuwa people inhabited the Gulf of Carpentaria before the Europeans arrived, but most now live in the town of Borroloola, 750km southeast of Darwin. Historian Baker, assigned a "skin" in the Yanyuwa kinship system, gathered the people's oral history and produced this fascinating story told from the Yanyuwa point of view and time.

★ **Geoffrey Blainey** *Triumph of the Nomads.* A fascinating account portraying Aboriginal people as masters and not victims of their environment. One of the best books on the subject.

Peter and Gibson Dunbar-Hall *Deadly Sounds Deadly Places.*

Comprehensive guide to contemporary Aboriginal music in Australia, from Archie Roach to Yothu Yindi; includes a handy discography.

Monica Furlong *Flight of the Kingfisher: a Journey Among Kukatja Aborigines.* Furlong lived among the Aboriginal people of the Great Sandy Desert; this is her account of Kukatja perceptions and spiritual beliefs.

Roslynn Haynes *Seeking the Centre: The Australian Desert in Literature, Art and Film.* The geographical and metaphorical impact of the desert on Australian culture is explored in this illustrated book as is the connection Aboriginal people have with the desert.

David Headon *North of the Ten Commandments.* An anthology of Northern Territory writings from all perspectives and sources – an excellent literary souvenir for anyone who falls for the charms of Australia's "one percent" territory.

Donald Horne *The Lucky Country.* This seminal analysis of Australian society, written in 1976, has yet to be matched and is still often quoted.

Peter Singer and Tom Gregg *How Ethical is Australia? An Examination of Australia's Record as a Global Citizen.* Australian Peter Singer, world-renowned philosopher and Professor of Bioethics at Princeton University, teams up with Tom Gregg to examine Australia's policies on foreign aid, the United Nations, overseas trade, the environment and refugees.

History and politics

Robyn Annear *Nothing But Gold: the Diggers of 1852.* With an eye for interestingly obscure details and managing to convey a sense of irony without becoming cynical, this is a wonderfully readable account of the goldrushes of the nineteenth century, a period in Australia's history which perhaps did more than any other to shape the country's national character.

Len Beadell *Outback Highways.* Extracts from Len Beadell's half-dozen books, cheerfully recounting his life in the central Australian deserts as a surveyor, and his involvement in the construction of Woomera and the atomic bomb test sites.

★ **John Birmingham** *Leviathan: the unauthorised biography of Sydney.* Birmingham's tome casts a contemporary eye over the dark side of Sydney's history, from nauseating accounts of Rocks' slum life and the 1900 plague outbreak, through the 1970s traumas of Vietnamese boat people – now Sydney residents, to scandals of police corruption.

Manning Clark *A Short History of Australia.* A condensed version of this leading historian's multivolumed tome, focusing on dreary successions of political administrations over two centuries, and cynically concluding with the "Age of Ruins".

Ann Curthoys *Freedom Ride: A Freedom Rider Remembers.* History professor Curthoys was one of the busload of young idealistic white university students who accompanied Aboriginal activist Charles Perkins (only 29 himself) on his revolutionary trip through northern NSW in 1965, to look at Aboriginal living conditions and root out and protest against racial discrimination.

David Day *Claiming A Continent: A New History of Australia.* Award-winning, general and easily readable history, concluding in 2000. The possession, dispossession and ownership of the land – and thus issues of race – are central to Day's narrative. Excellent recommended reading of recent texts at the end of each chapter will take you further.

Colin Dyer *The French Explorers and the Aboriginal Australians*. From Bruny d'Entrecasteaux's (1793) to Nicolas Baudin's (1802) expeditions, the French explorers and on-board scientists kept detailed journals which provide a wealth of information on Aboriginal Australians, particularly those of Tasmania who d'Entrecastaux noted "seem to offer the most perfect image of pristine society". Dyer provides engaging access to much recently translated material.

Bruce Elder *Blood on the Wattle: Massacres and Maltreatment of Aboriginal Australians Since 1788*. A heart-rending account of the horrors inflicted on the continent's indigenous peoples, covering infamous nineteenth-century massacres as well as more recent mid-twentieth-century scandals of the "Stolen Generation" children.

Tim Flannery (ed) *Watkin Trench 1788*. One of the most vivid accounts of early Sydney was written by a twenty-something captain of the marines, Watkin Trench, who arrived with the First Fleet. Trench's humanity and youthful curiosity shine through as he brings alive the characters who peopled the early settlement, such as the Aboriginal Bennelong.

★ **Robert Hughes** *The Fatal Shore*. A minutely detailed epic of the origins of transportation and the brutal beginnings of white Australia.

Dianne Johnson *Lighting the Way: Reconciliation stories*. Twenty-four very personal stories, written in a simple, engaging style, show Aboriginal and non-Aboriginal Australians working with each other, from community artworks to political activism. Positive and inspiring.

Mark McKenna *Looking For Blackfellas Point: An Australian History of Place*. This prize-winning book uncovers the uneasy history of Aboriginals and European settlers on the far south coast of NSW and widens its scope to the enduring meaning of land to both Aboriginal and white Australians.

Alan Moorehead *Cooper's Creek*. A historian's dramatic retelling of the ill-fated Burke and Wills expedition that set out in 1860 to make the first south-to-north crossing of the continent. A classic of exploration.

Sarah Murgatroyd *The Dig Tree: the Story of Burke and Wills*. Murgatroyd's recent retelling of the Burke and Wills story is gripping and immaculately researched – she journeyed along the route, and utilises the latest scientific and historical evidence, complemented by maps, photos and paintings.

Rosemary Neill *White Out: How Politics is Killing Black Australia*. Outspoken book that asserts the rhetoric of self-determination and empowerment excuses the wider society from doing anything to reduce the disparity between black and white Australian populations. Busting taboos about indigenous affairs, Neill criticises both left and right ideologies.

Cassandra Pybus *Community of Thieves*. Attempting to reconcile past and future, fourth-generation Tasmanian Pybus provides a deeply felt account of the near-annihilation of the island's Aboriginal people.

Henry Reynolds *The Other Side of the Frontier* and *The Law of the Land*. A revisionist historian demonstrates that Aboriginal resistance to colonial invasion was both considerable and organized. *The Whispering in Our Hearts* is a history of those settler Australians who, troubled by the treatment of Aboriginal people, spoke out and took political action. *Why Weren't We Told?* is his most personal, an autobiographical journey showing how he, like many generations of Australians, imbibed a distorted, idealized Australian history, and describing his path to becoming an Aboriginal history specialist; includes a moving story about his friendship with Eddie Mabo.

Portia Robinson *The Women of Botany Bay*. The result of painstaking research into the records of every female transported from Britain and Ireland between 1787 and 1828, as well as the wives of convicts who settled in Australia, Robinson tells with conviction and passion who these women really were.

Eric Rolls *Sojourners and Citizens* and *Flowers and The Wide Sea*. The first and second volumes of farmer-turned-historian Rolls' fascinatingly detailed history of the Chinese in Australia.

Anne Summers *Damned Whores and God's Police*. Stereotypical images of women in Australian society are explored in this ground-breaking reappraisal of Australian history from a feminist point of view.

Linda Weiss, Elizabeth Thurbon and John Mathews *How to Kill A Country: Australia's Devastating Trade Deal with the United States*. Australia's leading policy analysts examine the recent Free Trade Agreement with the United States, arguing that Australia's interests and identity will be damaged by the quest for a "special relationship".

Ecology and environment

★ **Tim Flannery** *The Future Eaters*. Palaeontologist Flannery poses that as the first human beings migrated down to Australasia, the Aborigines, Maoris and other Polynesian peoples changed the region's flora and fauna in startling ways, and began consuming the resources needed for their own future; the Europeans made an even greater impact on the environment, continuing this "future eating" of natural resources.

Josephine Flood *The Riches of Ancient Australia*. An indispensable and lavish guide to Australia's most famous landforms and sites. The same author's *Archaeology of the Dreamtime* provides background on the development of Aboriginal society.

Drew Hutton and Libby Connors *A History of the Australian Environmental Movement*. Written by a husband-and-wife team, Queensland academics and prominent in Green politics, this well-balanced book charts the progress of conservation attempts from 1860 to modern protests.

Ann Moyal *Platypus: the Extraordinary Story of How a Curious Creature Baffled the World*. When British and French naturalists were first introduced to the platypus, they were flummoxed: Was it bird, reptile or mammal? And did it really lay eggs? Moyal, a science historian, provides a captivating look at the platypus – and Australian nature – through European eyes.

Peter Latz *Bushfires and Bushtucker: Aboriginal Plant Use in Central Australia*. Handbook with photos, published by an Aboriginal-owned press.

Tim Murray (ed) *Archeology of Australia*. The last thirty-odd years have seen many ground-breaking discoveries in Australian archeology, with three sites in particular of great significance:

Kakadu in the Northern Territory, Lake Mungo in NSW, and South West Tasmania; a range of specialists contribute essays on the subject.

David Owen *Thylacine: the Tragic Tale of the Tasmanian Tiger.* Hunted to extinction, the last known Tasmania tiger died in Beaumaris Zoo in Hobart in 1936. But unconfirmed sightings continue: "The longer the thylacine stays dead, the greater the interest it arouses," writes Owen of the marsupial predator's now mythic status. Packed with fascinating facts and stories.

James Woodford *The Wollemi Pine: the Incredible Discovery of a Living Fossil from the Age of the Dinosaurs.* The award-winning environment writer at the *Sydney Morning Herald* tells the story of the 1994 discovery in Wollemi wilderness near Sydney. *The Secret Life of Wombats* begins as a fascinating account of the "wombat boy", a schoolboy so curious to find out about how wombats lived he crawled into their burrows. In *The Dog Fence: a Journey Through the Heart of the Continent* Woodford travels the 5400km length of the fence built to keep livestock safe from dingoes.

Mary White *The Greening of Gondwana.* Classic work on the evolution of Australia's flora and geography.

Contemporary fiction

Thea Astley *The Multiple Effects of Rainshadow.* On an Aboriginal island reserve in 1930, a white woman dies in childbirth, and her husband goes on a shotgun and dynamite rampage. The novel traces the effects over the years on eight characters who witnessed the violent events, ultimately exploring the brutality and racism in Australian life.

Murray Bail *Eucalyptus.* Beautifully written novel with a fairy-tale-like plot: NSW farmer, Holland, has planted nearly every type of eucalyptus tree on his land. When his extraordinarily beautiful daughter Ellen is old enough to marry, he sets up a challenge for her legion of potential suitors, to name each tree.

John Birmingham *He Died With A Felafel In His Hand.* A collection of squalid and very funny tales emerging from the once-dissolute author's experience of flat-sharing hell in Brisbane.

Anson Cameron *Tin Toys.* The Aboriginal "Stolen Generation" issue explored through the tale of Hunter Carolyn, an unintentional artist who can change skin colour at will.

★ **Peter Carey** *Bliss.* Carey's first and perhaps best novel is the story of a Sydney ad executive who drops out to New Age NSW. Other novels by Carey to look out for include his two Booker Prize winners *Oscar and Lucinda* and *The True History of the Kelly Gang*, about the bushranger Ned Kelly. Also worth a read are his bizarre short stories, *The Fat Man in History*, with which he launched his career.

Robert Drewe *The Savage Crows.* A writer, whose own life is falling apart in a cockroach-ridden Sydney of the 1970s, sets out to discover the grim truth behind Tasmania's "final solution".

Richard Flanagan *Death of a River Guide.* Narrator, environmentalist Aljaz Cosini, goes over his life and that of his family and forebears as he lies drowning in the Franklin River. Thoughtful writings about Tasmanian landscape, place, migration and the significance of history are the hallmark of Flanagan's novels. His nineteenth-century-set *Gould's Book of Fish: a novel in Twelve Fish* delves into Tasmania's past as the brutal penal settlement of Van Dieman's Land.

Tom Gilling *Miles McGinty*. Nineteenth-century Sydney comes alive in this riotous, entertaining love story of Miles, who becomes a levitator's assistant and begins to float on air, and Isabel, who wants to fly.

Kate Grenville *The Idea of Perfection*, set in the tiny, fictional NSW town of Karakarook, and about two unlikely characters who fall in love, won the 2001 Orange Prize for Fiction.

Chloe Hooper *A Child's Book of True Crime*. With a claustrophobia Tasmanian setting, this perverse, chilling novel is narrated by a young primary school teacher having an affair with the married father of her smartest pupil. His writer-wife's true-crime book, about a love triangle that disintegrates into murder, leads the anxious teacher into imagining a child's classic-Australian-literature-style version, with characters such as Kitty Koala and Wally Wombat.

Janette Turner Hospital *Oyster*. Disquieting novel set in the literally off-the-map, opal-mining, one-pub Queensland town of Inner Maroo, whose inhabitants are either rough-as-guts mining people, or religious fundamentalists.

Linda Jaivin *Eat Me*. Billed as an "erotic feast", this novel opens with a memorable fruit-squeezing scene (and this is only the shopping) as three trendy Sydney women (fashion editor, academic and writer) swap stories of sexual exploits.

Douglas Kennedy *The Dead Heart*. A best-selling comic thriller made into a film; an itinerant American journalist gets abducted by man-eating hillbillies in Outback Australia.

Julia Leigh *The Hunter*. Intriguing, internationally acclaimed first novel about the rediscovery and subsequent hunt of the Tasmanian tiger; a faceless biotech company after thylacine DNA plays the bad guy.

David Malouf *The Conversations at Curlow Creek*. One of Australia's most important contemporary writers charts the developing relationship between two Irishmen the night before a hanging; one is the officer appointed to supervise the execution and the other the outlaw facing his death. *Remembering Babylon* is the moving story of a British cabin boy in the 1840s who, cast ashore, lives for sixteen years amongst the Aboriginal people of far north Queensland, and finally re-enters the British colonial world.

Andrew McGahan *The White Earth* Set in Queensland's Darling Downs wheatfields; it's 1992, and the Mabo land rights case fills the news. After the death of his father, eight-year-old William and his unstable mother are invited to live on his ageing uncle's Kuran station, which has been his life's obsession to own. William, forced to prove himself worthy of inheritance, is drawn into his discontented uncle's White League. Questions of Aboriginal dispossession and white belonging reverberate.

Elliot Perlman *Seven Types of Ambiguity*. The chain of events, secrets and lies stretching back a decade that lead to Simon Heywood kidnapping his ex-girlfriend's son are related by seven different narrators. Probing middle-class anxiety in a consumeristic, market-driven society, Perlman's conscience-driven writing can be moralistic at times, but at its best is clever and insightful, providing an intense social portrait of contemporary Melbourne, from Toorak to St Kilda.

Tim Winton *Cloudstreet*. A wonderful, faintly magical saga about the mixed fortunes of two families who end up sharing a house in postwar

Perth. His latest novel, *Dirt Music*, again provides a wonderful evocation of the Western Australian landscape with a compelling narrative, and was short-listed for the 2002 Booker Prize.

Peter Goldsworthy *Three Dog Night*. It takes three dogs to keep a person warm on a desert night, an allusion to the love triangle which emerges when psychiatrist Martin Blackman returns to Adelaide after a decade in London with his new, much-loved wife, and visits his oldest friend, the difficult Felix, a once-brilliant surgeon dying of terminal cancer. Felix is an initiated man who has lived with Aborigines in the Central Australian desert; when Lucy accompanies him there, Martin must confront his insecurities.

Alex Miller *Journey to the Stone Country*. A betrayed wife leaves her middleclass Melbourne existence and returns to tropical North Queensland, setting out on a journey with a childhood Aboriginal acquaintance into the stone country which is his tribe's remote heartland. However, dark secrets from the lives of their grandparents threaten what future they may have together.

Danielle Wood *The Alphabet of Light and Dark*. Set evocatively on Bruny Island, in melancholy Tasmania gothic vein. Like the main character Essie, Wood's great-great grandfather was Superintendent of the Cape Bruny Lighthouse. Essie returns from Western Australia to the lighthouse after her grandfather's death to write her family history and becomes immersed in her ancestors' tragedies.

Australian classics

Barbara Baynton *Bush Studies*. A collection of nineteenth-century bush stories written from the female perspective.

Rolf Boldrewood *Robbery Under Arms*. The story of Captain Starlight, a notorious bushranger and rustler around the Queensland borders.

Marcus Clarke *For the Term of his Natural Life*. Written in 1870 in somewhat overblown prose, this romantic tragedy is based on actual events in Tasmania's once notorious prison settlement.

Miles Franklin *My Brilliant Career*. A novel about a spirited young girl in early-twentieth-century Victoria who refuses to conform.

May Gibbs *Snugglepot and Cuddlepie*. A timeless children's favourite: the illustrated adventures of two little creatures who live inside gumnuts.

Xavier Herbert *Capricornia*. An indignant and allegorical saga of the brutal and haphazard settlement of the land of Capricornia (tropical Northern Territory thinly disguised).

George Johnston *My Brother Jack*. The first in a disturbing trilogy set in Melbourne suburbia between the wars, which develops into a semi-fictional attempt to dissipate the guilt Johnston felt at being disillusioned with, and finally leaving, his native land.

Thomas Keneally *The Chant of Jimmie Blacksmith*. A prize-winning novel that delves deep into the psyche of an Aboriginal outlaw, tracing his inexorable descent into murder and crime. Sickening, brutal and compelling.

Henry Lawson Ballads, poems and stories from Australia's best-loved chronicler come in a wide array of collections. A few to seek out are: *Henry Lawson Bush Ballads*, *Henry Lawson Favourites* and *While the Billy Boils – Poetry*.

Norman Lindsay *The Magic Pudding*. A whimsical tale of some very strange men and their grumpy, flavour-changing and endless pudding; a children's classic with very adult humour.

Ruth Park *The Harp in the South*. First published in 1948, this first book in a trilogy is a well-loved tale of inner-Sydney slum life in 1940s Surry Hills. The spirited Darcy family's battle against poverty provides memorable characters.

A.B. ("Banjo") Paterson Australia's most famous bush balladeer, author of *Waltzing Matilda* and *The Man from Snowy River*, who helped romanticize the bush's mystique. Some of the many titles published include *Banjo Paterson's Favourites* and *Man From Snowy River and Other Verses*.

Henry Handel Richardson *The Getting of Wisdom*. A gangly country girl's experience of a snobby boarding school in early-twentieth-century Melbourne; like Miles Franklin (see above), Richardson was actually a female writer.

 **Nevil Shute** *A Town Like Alice*. A wartime romance which tells of a woman's bravery, endurance and enterprise, both in the Malayan jungle and in the Australian Outback where she strives to create the town of the title.

Christina Stead *For Love Alone*. Set largely around Sydney Harbour, where the late author grew up, this novel follows the obsessive Teresa Hawkins, a poor but artistic girl from a large, unconventional family, who scrounges and saves to head for London and love.

Randolph Stow *The Merry-go-round in the Sea*. An endearing tale of a young boy growing up in rural Western Australia during World War II.

Kylie Tennant *Ride on Stranger*. First published in 1943, this is a humorous portrait of Sydney between the two world wars, seen through the eyes of newcomer Shannon Hicks.

Patrick White Considered dense and symbolic – even visionary (though some claim misogynistic) – White's novels can be heavy going, but try and plough through *Voss*, *A Fringe of Leaves* or *The Twyborn Affair*, the latter a contemporary exploration of ambiguous sexuality.

Aboriginal writing

Faith Bandler *Welour, My Brother*. A novel by a well-known black activist describing a boy's early life in Queensland, and the tensions of a racially mixed community.

John Muk Muk Burke *Bridge of Triangles*. Powerful, landscape-driven images in this tale of a mixed-race child growing up unable to associate with either side of his heritage, but refusing to accept the downward spiral into despair and alcoholism adopted by those around him.

Evelyn Crawford *Over My Tracks*. Told to Chris Walsh, this oral autobiography is the story of a formidable woman, from her 1930s childhood among the red sandhills of Yantabulla, through her Outback struggles as a mother of fourteen children, to her tireless work, late in life, with Aboriginal students, combating prejudice with education.

Nene Gare *The Fringe Dwellers*. A story of an Aboriginal family on the edge of town and society.

Ruby Langford *Don't Take Your Love to Town*. An autobiography demonstrating a black woman's courage and humour in the face of tragedy and poverty lived out in northern NSW and the inner city of Sydney.

Sally Morgan *My Place*. A widely acclaimed and best-selling account of a Western Australian woman's discovery of her black roots.

David Mowaljarlai and Jutta Malnic *Yorro Yorro*. Starry-eyed photographer Malnic's musings while recording sacred Wandjina sites in the west Kimberley and, more interestingly, Mowaljarlai's account of his upbringing and Ngarinyin tribal lore.

★ **Mudrooroo** *Wildcat Falling*. The first novel to be published (in 1965) by an Aboriginal writer, under the name Colin Johnson, this is the story of a black teenage delinquent coming of age in the 1950s. *Doctor Wooreddy's Prescription for Enduring the Ending of the World* details the attempted annihilation of the Tasmanian Aborigines. Mudrooroo's three latest novels – *The Kwinkan* (1995), *The Undying* (1998) and *Underground* (1999) – are part of his magic-realist Master of Ghost Dreaming series.

Oodgeroo Noonuccal *My People*. A collection of verse by an established campaigning poet (previously known as Kath Walker).

Paddy Roe *Gularabulu*. Stories from the west Kimberley, both traditional myths and tales of a much more recent origin.

Kim Scott *Benang*. Infuriated at reading the words of A.O. Neville, Protector of Aborigines in Western Australia in the 1930s, who planned to "breed out" Aborigines from Australia, author Scott wrote this powerful tale of Nyoongar history using Neville's own themes to overturn his elitist arguments.

Archie Weller *The Day of the Dog*. Weller's violent first novel came out in an angry burst after being released, at 23, from incarceration in Broome jail. The protagonist, in a similar situation, is pressured back into a criminal world by his Aboriginal peers and by police harassment. Searing pace and forceful writing. His second novel, *Land of the Golden Clouds*, is an epic science-fiction fantasy, set 3000 years in the future, which portrays an Australia devastated by a nuclear holocaust and populated by warring tribes.

Specialist and wildlife guides

Jack Absalom *Safe Outback Travel*. The bible for Outback driving and camping, full of sensible precautions and handy tips for preparation and repair.

Catherine de Courcey and John Johnson *River Tracks: Exploring Australian Rivers*. A practical and up-to-date motoring guide to six river journeys, providing lots of insider insight and history too.

John Chapman and Monica Chapman *Bushwalking in Australia*. The fourth edition of this bushwalking bible, meticulously updated in 2003, has detailed notes for 25 of the best bushwalks Australia-wide, accompanied by colour topographic maps and photographs. The Chapmans also publish several other excellent walking guides, including the indispensable *South West Tasmania*.

David Clark *Big Things*. From the Big Banana to the Big Lobster, Clark provides a comprehensive guide to Australia's kitsch icons.

The Great Barrier Reef A Reader's Digest complete rundown on the Reef, lucid and lavishly illustrated. Available in coffee-table format and in a slighter, more portable, edited edition.

James Halliday *Australian Wine Companion*. Released every year, the venerable Halliday provides not only an authoritative guide to the best wines but to the wineries themselves with over 1865 wineries in the 2005 edition, making it a great accompaniment when visiting any of Australia's wine regions.

Tim Low *Bush Tucker: Australia's Wild Food Harvest* and *Wild Food Plants of Australia*. Guides to the bountiful supply of bushtucker that was once the mainstay of the Aboriginal diet; the latter is pocket-sized and contains clear photographs of over 180 plants, describing their uses.

Greg Pritchard *Climbing Australia: the Essential Guide*. Comprehensive guide for rock-climbers. Covers everything from the major climbing sites to the best websites, with easy-to-understand route descriptions.

Huon Hooke and Ralph Kyte-Powell *The Penguin Good Australian Wine Guide*. Released every year in Australia, this is a handy book for a wine buff to buy on the ground, with the best wines and prices detailed to help navigate you around the bottle shop.

Peter and Pat Slater *Field Guide to Australian Birds*. Pocket-sized, and the easiest to use of the many available guides to Australian birds.

Tyrone T. Thomas Regional bushwalking guides by local publisher Michelle Anderson Publishing. A series of ten local guides, from *50 Walks in North Queensland* to *120 Walks in Tasmania*, which make excellent trail companions.

Mark Warren *Atlas of Australian Surfing*. A comprehensive guide to riding the best of Australia's waves.

Nicola Wells et al *Cycling Australia*. Published in 2001, thirty-five popular cycling routes are described, from day rides to extended trips, with accompanying maps.

Australian English

The colourful variant of Australian English, or strine (which is how "Australian" is pronounced with a very heavy Australian accent), has its origins in the archaic cockney and Irish of the colony's early convicts as well as the adoption of words from the many Aboriginal languages. For such a vast country, the accent barely varies to the untutored ear; from Tasmania to the northwest you'll find little variation in the national drawl, with its curious, interrogative ending to sentences – although Queenslanders are noted for their slow delivery. One of the most consistent tendencies of strine is to abbreviate words and then stick an "-o" or, more commonly, an "-ie" on the end: as in "bring your cozzie to the barbie this arvo" (bring your swimming costume to the barbecue this afternoon). This informality extends to the frequent use of "bloody", "bugger" and "bastard", the latter two used affectionately. Attempting to abuse someone by calling them a bastard will most likely end up in an offer of a beer. There's also an endearing tendency to genderize inanimate objects as, for example, "she's buggered, mate" (your inanimate object is beyond repair) or "do 'im up nice and tight" (be certain that your inanimate object is well affixed).

The popularity of dire Australian TV soap operas has seen strine spread overseas, much as Americanisms have pervaded the English-speaking world. Popular strinisms such as "hang a U-ey" (make a U-turn) and the versatile and agreeable "no worries" are now commonly used outside Australia.

The country has its own excellent *Macquarie Dictionary*, the latest edition of which is the ultimate authority on the current state of Australian English. Also worth consulting: *The Dinkum Dictionary: The Origins of Australian Words* by Susan Butler and *Word Map* by Kel Richards, a dictionary of Australian regionalisms. What follows is our own essential list.

Akubra Wide-brimmed felt hat; a brand name.

Anzac Australia and New Zealand Army Corps; every town has a memorial to Anzac casualties from both world wars.

Arvo Afternoon.

Back o' Bourke Outback.

Banana bender Resident of Queensland.

Barbie Barbecue.

Battler Someone who struggles to make a living, as in "little Aussie battler".

Beaut! or you beauty! Exclamation of delight.

Beg yours? Excuse me, say again?

Beyond the Black Stump Outback; back of beyond.

Billabong Waterhole in dry riverbed.

Billy Cooking pot.

Bitumen Sealed road as opposed to dirt road.

Blowies Blow flies.

Bludger Someone who does not pull their weight, or a scrounger – as in "dole bludger".

Blue Fight; also a red-haired person.

Blundstones Leather, elastic-sided workmen's boots, now also a fashion item in some circles. Often shortened to "blundies".

Bonzer Good, a good thing.

Bottle shop Off-licence or liquor store.

Brumby Feral horse.

Buckley's No chance; as in "hasn't got a Buckley's".

Bugs Moreton Bay bug – type of crayfish indigenous to southern Queensland.

Bunyip Monster of Aboriginal legend; bogeyman.

Burl Give it a go; as in "give it a burl".

Bush Unsettled country area.

Bushranger Runaway convict; nineteenth-century outlaw.

Bushwhacker Someone lacking in social graces, a hick.
BYO Bring your own. Restaurant which allows you to bring your own alcohol.
Chook Chicken.
Chunder Vomit.
Cocky Small farmer; cow cocky, dairy farmer.
To come the raw prawn To try and deceive or make a fool of someone.
Coo-eee! Aboriginal long-distance greeting, now widely adopted as a kind of "yoo hoo!"
Corroboree Aboriginal ceremony.
Cozzies Bathers, swimmers, togs; swimming costume.
Crim Criminal.
Crook Sick or broken.
Crow eater Resident of South Australia.
Cut lunch Sandwiches.
Dag Nerd
Daggy Unattractive.
Daks or strides Trousers/pants.
Dam A man-made body of water or reservoir; not just the dam itself.
Damper Soda bread cooked in a pot on embers.
Dekko To look at; as in "take a dekko at this".
Deli Delicatessen, corner shop or sandwich bar.
Derro Derelict or destitute person.
Didgeridoo Droning musical instrument made from a termite-hollowed branch.
Digger Old-timer, especially an old soldier.
Dill Idiot.
Dilly bag Aboriginal carry-all made of bark, or woven or rigged twine.
Dinkum True, genuine, honest.
Disposal store Store that sells used army and navy equipment, plus camping gear.
Dob in To tell on someone; as in "she dobbed him in".
Drizabone Voluminous waxed cotton raincoat, originally designed for horse riding; a brand name.
Drongo Fool.
Drover Cowboy or station hand.
Dunny Outside pit toilet.
Esky Portable, insulated box to keep food or beer cold.
Fair dinkum or **dinky di** Honestly, truly.
Fossick To search for gold or gems in abandoned diggings.
Furphy A rumour or false story.
Galah Noisy or garrulous person.
Galvo Corrugated iron.
Garbo Garbage or refuse collector.
G'day Hello, hi.
Gibber Rock or boulder.
Give away To give up or resign; as in "I used to be a garbo but I gave it away".
Grog Alcoholic drink, usually beer.
Gub, gubbah Aboriginal terms for a white person.
Gutless wonder Coward.
Hoon A yob, delinquent.
Humpy Temporary shelter used by Aborigines and early pioneers.
Jackeroo Male station hand.
Jilleroo Female station hand.
Joey Baby kangaroo still in the pouch (also, less familiarly, a baby koala).
Koorie Collective name for Aboriginal people from southeastern Australia.
Larrikin Mischievous youth.
Lay by Practice of putting a deposit on goods until they can be fully paid for.
Lollies Sweets or candy.
Manchester Linen goods.
Mate A sworn friend, as essential as beer to the Australian stereotype.
Mexicans Residents of New South Wales and Victoria.
Milk bar Corner shop, and often a small café.
Moleskins Strong cotton trousers worn by bushmen.
Never Never Outback, wilderness.
New Australian Recent immigrants; often a euphemism for Australians of non-British descent.
No worries That's OK; It doesn't matter; Don't mention it.
Ocker Uncultivated Australian male.
Op shop Short for "Opportunity Shop"; a charity shop/thrift store.

Outback Remote, unsettled regions of Australia.
Paddock Field.
Panel van Van with no rear windows and front seating only.
Pashing Kissing or snogging, often in the back of a panel van.
Perve To leer or act as a voyeur; as in "What are you perving at?"
Piss Beer.
Piss head Drunkard.
Pissed Drunk.
Pokies One-armed bandits; gambling machines.
Pommie or **Pom** Person of English descent – not necessarily abusive.
Rapt Very pleased, delighted.
Ratbag An eccentric person; also a term of mild abuse.
Ratshit or **shithouse** How you feel after a night on the piss.
Rego Vehicle registration document.
Ridji Didge The real thing or genuine article.
Ripper! Rather old-fashioned exclamation of enthusiasm.
Rollies Roll-up cigarettes.
Root Vulgar term for sexual congress.
Rooted To be very tired or to be beyond repair; as in "she's rooted, mate" – your [car] is irreparable.
Ropable Furious to the point of requiring restraint.
Rouseabout An unskilled labourer in a shearing-shed.
Sandgroper Resident of Western Australia.
She'll be right or **she'll be apples** Everything will work out fine.
Shoot through To pass through or leave hurriedly.
Shout To pay for someone, or to buy a round of drinks; as in "it's your shout, mate".
Sickie To take a day off work due to (sometimes alleged) illness; as in "to pull a sickie".
Singlet Sleeveless cotton vest. The archetypal Australian singlet, in navy, is produced by Bonds.
Skivvy Polo neck.
Slab 24-can carton of beer.
Smoko Tea break.
Snag Sausage.
Speedo Famous Australian brand of athletic swimming costume; speedos (or sluggos) commonly refers to men's swimming briefs, as opposed to swimming trunks.
Spunk Attractive or sexy person of either gender; as in "what a spunk!" Can also be used as an adjective: spunky.
Squatter Historical term for early settlers who took up public land as their own.
Station Very large pastoral property or ranch.
Sticky beak Nosy person, or to be nosy; as in "let's have a sticky beak".
Stockman Cowboy or station hand.
Stubby Small bottle of beer.
Swag Large bedroll, or one's belongings.
Tall poppy Someone who excels or is eminent. "Cutting down tall poppies" is to bring overachievers back to earth – a national pastime.
Thongs Flip-flops or sandals.
Throw a wobbly Lose your temper.
Tinnie Can of beer, or a small aluminium boat.
Ute Short for "utility" vehicle; pick-up truck.
Wacko! Exclamation of enthusiasm.
Walkabout Temporary migration undertaken by Aborigines; also has the wider meaning of a journey. **Gone walkabout** To go missing.
Warm fuzzies Feeling of contentment.
Waxhead Surfer.
Weatherboard Wooden house.
Whinger Someone who complains – allegedly common among Poms.
Wog Derogatory description for those of Mediterranean descent.
Wowser Killjoy.
Yabber To talk or chat.
Yabbie Freshwater crayfish.
Yakka Work, as in "hard yakka".
Yobbo Uncouth person.

Travel store

Visit us online

roughguides.com

Information on over 25,000 destinations around the world

- **Read** Rough Guides' trusted travel info
- **Share** journals, photos and travel advice with other readers
- Get exclusive Rough Guide **discounts** and travel **deals**
- Earn membership points every time you contribute to the Rough Guide **community** and get **free** books, flights and trips
- Browse thousands of CD reviews and artists in our **music** area

STA TRAVEL
www.statravel.co.uk
For booking and enquiries:
0870 160 6070
To find fares, check availability, enter competitions, book online or find your local branch @
www.statravel.co.uk
450 BRANCHES WORLDWIDE · LOW COST FLIGHTS · ACCOMMODATION
INSURANCE · SKI · GAP YEAR · CAR HIRE · OVERLAND TRAVEL
ISIC/YOUTH CARDS · ROUND THE WORLD FLIGHTS · TRAVEL HELP

small print and Index

A Rough Guide to Rough Guides

In the summer of 1981, Mark Ellingham, a recent graduate from Bristol University, was travelling round Greece and couldn't find a guidebook that really met his needs. On the one hand there were the student guides, insistent on saving every last cent, and on the other the heavyweight cultural tomes whose authors seemed to have spent more time in a research library than lounging away the afternoon at a taverna or on the beach.

In a bid to avoid getting a job, Mark and a small group of writers set about creating their own guidebook. It was a guide to Greece that aimed to combine a journalistic approach to description with a thoroughly practical approach to travellers' needs – a guide that would incorporate culture, history, and contemporary insights with a critical edge, together with up-to-date, value-for-money listings. Back in London, Mark and the team finished their Rough Guide, as they called it, and talked Routledge into publishing the book.

That first *Rough Guide to Greece*, published in 1982, was a student scheme that became a publishing phenomenon. The immediate success of the book – with numerous reprints and a Thomas Cook Prize shortlisting – spawned a series that rapidly covered dozens of destinations. Rough Guides had a ready market among low-budget backpackers, but soon also acquired a much broader and older readership that relished Rough Guides' wit and inquisitiveness as much as their enthusiastic, critical approach. Everyone wants value for money, but not at any price.

Rough Guides soon began supplementing the "rougher" information about hostels and low-budget listings with the kind of detail on restaurants and quality hotels that independent-minded visitors on any budget might expect, whether on business in New York or trekking in Thailand.

These days the guides – distributed worldwide by the Penguin Group – offer recommendations from shoestring to luxury and cover more than 200 destinations around the globe, including almost every country in the Americas and Europe, more than half of Africa, and most of Asia and Australasia. Our ever-growing team of authors and photographers is spread all over the world, particularly in Europe, the USA, and Australia.

In 1994, we published the *Rough Guide to World Music* and *Rough Guide to Classical Music*, and a year later the *Rough Guide to the Internet*. All three books have become benchmark titles in their fields – which encouraged us to expand into other areas of publishing, mainly around popular culture. Rough Guides now publish:

- Travel guides to more than 200 worldwide destinations
- Dictionary phrasebooks for 22 major languages
- History guides ranging from Ireland to Islam
- Maps printed on rip-proof and waterproof Polyart™ paper
- Music guides running the gamut from Opera to Elvis
- Restaurant guides to London, New York, and San Francisco
- Reference books on topics as diverse as the Weather and Shakespeare
- Sports guides from Formula 1 to Man Utd
- Pop culture books from *Lord of the Rings* to Cult TV
- World Music CDs in association with World Music Network

Visit **www.roughguides.com** to see our latest publications.

Rough Guide credits

Text editors: Karoline Densley, Steven Horak, Helen Marsden, Gavin Thomas, Clifton Wilkinson
Layout: Umesh Aggarwal
Cartography: Ed Wright
Picture editor: Simon Bracken
Proofreader: Stewart Wild
Editorial: **London** Kate Berens, Claire Saunders, Geoff Howard, Ruth Blackmore, Polly Thomas, Richard Lim, Alison Murchie, Sally Schafer, Andy Turner, Ella O'Donnell, Keith Drew, Edward Aves, Nikki Birrell, Joe Staines, Duncan Clark, Peter Buckley, Matthew Milton, Daniel Crewe; **New York** Andrew Rosenberg, Richard Koss, AnneLise Sorensen, Amy Hegarty, Hunter Slaton
Design & Pictures: London Dan May, Diana Jarvis, Mark Thomas, Harriet Mills, Jj Luck, Chloë Roberts; **Delhi** Madhulita Mohapatra, Ajay Verma, Jessica Subramanian, Amit Verma, Ankur Guha
Production: Julia Bovis, Sophie Hewat, Katherine Owers
Cartography: **London** Maxine Repath, Katie Lloyd-Jones; **Delhi** Manish Chandra, Rajesh Chhibber, Jai Prakash Mishra, Ashutosh Bharti, Rajesh Mishra, Jasbir Sandhu, Karobi Gogoi, Animesh Pathak
Online: **New York** Jennifer Gold, Suzanne Welles, Kristin Mingrone; **Delhi** Manik Chauhan, Narender Kumar, Shekhar Jha, Rakesh Kumar, Lalit Sharma, Chhandita Chakravarty
Marketing & Publicity: London Richard Trillo, Niki Hanmer, David Wearn, Demelza Dallow, Louise Maher; **New York** Geoff Colquitt, Megan Kennedy, Milena Perez; **Delhi** Reem Khokhar
Custom publishing and foreign rights: Philippa Hopkins
Manager India: Punita Singh
Series editor: Mark Ellingham
Reference Director: Andrew Lockett
PA to Managing and Publishing Directors: Megan McIntyre
Publishing Director: Martin Dunford
Managing Director: Kevin Fitzgerald

Publishing information

This seventh edition published September 2005 by **Rough Guides Ltd**,
80 Strand, London WC2R 0RL
345 Hudson St, 4th Floor,
New York, NY 10014, USA
14 Local Shopping Centre, Panchsheel Park,
New Delhi 110017, India.

Distributed by the Penguin Group
Penguin Books Ltd,
80 Strand, London WC2R 0RL
Penguin Putnam, Inc.,
375 Hudson St, NY 10014, USA
Penguin Group (Australia)
250 Camberwell Road, Camberwell,
Victoria 3124, Australia
Penguin Books Canada Ltd,
10 Alcorn Avenue, Toronto, ON,
M4V 1E4 Canada
Penguin Group (New Zealand),
Cnr Rosedale and Airborne Roads,
Albany, Auckland, New Zealand

Typeset in Bembo and Helvetica to an original design by Henry Iles.

Printed in Italy by LegoPrint S.p.A

1256pp includes index

A catalogue record for this book is available from the British Library.

ISBN-13: 978-1-84353-475-4
ISBN-10: 1-84353-475-4

1 3 5 7 9 8 6 4 2

Help us update

We've gone to a lot of effort to ensure that the seventh edition of **The Rough Guide to Australia** is accurate and up to date. However, things change – places get "discovered," opening hours are notoriously fickle, restaurants and rooms raise prices or lower standards. If you feel we've got it wrong or left something out, we'd like to know, and if you can remember the address, the price, the time, the phone number, so much the better.

We'll credit all contributions, and send a copy of the next edition (or any other Rough Guide if you prefer) for the best letters. Everyone who writes to us and isn't already a subscriber will receive a copy of our full-colour thrice-yearly newsletter. Please mark letters: **"Rough Guide Australia update"** and send to: Rough Guides, 80 Strand, London WC2R 0RL, or Rough Guides, 4th Floor, 345 Hudson St, New York, NY 10014. Or send an email to **mail@roughguides.com**.

Have your questions answered and tell others about your trip at **www.roughguides.atinfopop.com**.

Acknowledgments

Margo Daly Special thanks to Linden Hyatt for so much kindness and support at home and in the Hunter Valley and Tasmania; also thanks to Margaret and Arthur Daly, Mahalya Middlemist and Janine Daly. Thanks to enthusiastic Sydney updaters Michael Schofield, Tania Paschen, Ann Mercer and Neal Drinnan, and tireless editors Karoline Densley, Steven Horak and Fran Sandham. In Tasmania, I'd like to thank Lalani Hyatt, Ross Patterson, Rosie Waitt and Tim Dub, Sha Sha Kwa and Caleb Gardner, Mike Callinan of YHA Tasmania, Phil McKenzie, Rodney Croome, Troy Baggett, Lisa Charles, Damian Connor, Gerard Walker, Ken Worsley and James Luddington. In NSW, thank you to Marie Blackmore, Rob McLauglin, Silke Kerwick of YHA NSW, and Megalong Books, Leura.

Anne Dehne As always, I'd like to thank all my friends for advice, support and companionship, especially Julie Gittus and Ashley McKeon. My thanks also go to helpful staff at visitor information centres in Victoria for patiently dealing with my queries, and to knowledgeable individuals and businesses for information and assistance.

Chris Scott Many thanks to Jeff Condon in Perth, Wayne in Darwin, Judith Watson at Lush PR, Neville on the Blackwood and the guys at the *Gibb River Express*.

Ian Osborn Special thanks are extended to Peter of Villa Marine in Yorkey's Knob for his valuable insight to the Cairns region, to Liby in Hervey Bay for her enthusiastic organising, to Harry and Sandy Davies of Fraser Magic for opening up the magic of Fraser Island to my family, and to Michael Nowland of Explorers Inn for his hospitality in Brisbane.

Michael Harcourt Special thanks to the South Australian Metropolitan Fire Service in Elizabeth, as well as the friendly staff of Outback at Isa. Thank you too to the people of Kangaroo Island whose ready willingness to share their knowledge and pride of their environment contributed greatly to that chapter. The whole venture would have been impossible without my partner (and chauffeur) Melissa Sultana, whose patience, energy and love were constant.

SMALL PRINT

Readers' letters

Thanks to all those readers of the sixth edition who took the trouble to write in with their amendments and additions. Apologies for any misspellings or omissions.

Carla Ambrose, Neil A. Baker, Marie Barbieri, Catherine Berry, Katherine Braithwaite, Lisa Brown, Laura Carleton, Stephen Costa, Ian Davey, Karis Dorrigan, Kenny Dryburgh, Joanne Fellows, Sarah Foat, Kip Freytag, Louise Gainford, Alan Gairey, Ali Gale, John Garratt, Suzanne Genever, Eimear Geraghty, Max Greenhalgh, Nat Greenway, Sharon Harris, Sue Heatt, Gillian Howell, Nick Humble, Lesley Hustinx, Ian Knowlson, Jan Kolaczinski, Aaro Kuivalainen, Craig Jackson, Susan Jackson, Alan and Liz Lewis, Tom Lloyd, Henry Long, Robyn Ludwig, Christine Luthy, Tracy Lynch, Monica Mackaness, Orlaith Mannion, Rachel Manson, Lorraine Mikhail, Lawrence Milton, Malcolm Mollison, Andrew Morris, Stephen Newborough, Alan Newman, Barney Newman, Chris Newton, Dave Payne, Sharon Peters, Emma Prineas, John Pritchard, Michael and Jackie Revell, P. Michael Rhodes, Sian Rosser, Ragnhild P. Sandvik, Rick Sarre, Leila Shabankarch, Sarah Smerdon, Heidi van Spaandonk, Gary Spinks, Jareen Summerhill, Vicky Tallon, Steve Taylor, Theresa Tuke, Beverly Tyler, Allan Tyrer, Erika R. Vogel, Ros Warburtons, Tricia Warby, Dean White, Karen Wilson, Emilia Wojanczyk, Len Woolley, Clifton Young.

Photo credits

Cover
Main front The Olgas, Kata Tjuta National Park © Alamy
small front top picture Sydney Opera House © Corbis
small front lower picture Kangaroo © Alamy
Back top picture Twelve Apostles, Great Ocean Road © Alamy
Back lower picture Brisbane River, Brisbane © Alamy

Title page
Children holding Australian flag, Western Australia, Australia © Frances Andrijich/WildLight

Full page
Dirt road, Northern Territory © Geoffrey Clifford/Getty

Introduction
Koala bear on tree branch © Jerry Driendl/Getty
Aborigine Baby Smoking Ceremony, Kimberley © Paul Chesley/Getty
Bill's Café © Robert Edwards/WildLight
Creek in rainforest, Yarra Ranges National Park, Victoria © Ern Mainka/Alamy
Hikers © Andrew Palmer/Alamy
Woman on Bondi Beach, NSW © D Harcourt Webster/Alamy
Semi-trailer and kangaroo crossing sign © Paul A. Souders/Corbis
Dream Painting, Walpiri tribe © Claire Leimbacht/Robert Harding

Things not to miss
01 Australia, Northern Territory, Ayers Rock © David Greenwood/Taxi/Getty
02 Humpback Whales © David Lomax/Robert Harding
03 Sailing in the Whitsundays © Lisa Nellis
04 Skiing in the Snowy Mountains © Tourism New South Wales
05 Witchetty grub in root of Acacia Kemeana Plant © John Miles
06 Paddle-steamer on the Murray River © Peter Wilson/Dorling Kindersley
07 Coober Pedy © John Miles
08 The Sanctuary Retreat, Mission Beach © K. Gillham/Robert Harding
09 Whitewater Rafting on the Franklin river © Tourism Tasmania
10 4WD vehicles on 75-Mile Beach, Fraser Island © Tourism Queensland
11 Geelong vs Melbourne, AFL match, MCG © Jerry Dennis
12 Salt Lakes, Yorketown © Peter Wilson/Dorling Kindersley
13 Tree Kangaroo and Joey © Anne Dehne
14 Campervans in The Kimberley, Western Australia © Frances Andrijich/WildLight
15 Beercan Croc, Darwin Beer Can Regatta © Chris Scott
16 Swimmer on Australia's Great Barrier Reef © Reuters/Corbis
17 Kangaroo Island © Paul A Souders/Corbis
18 Water Lily at sunrise, Kakadu National Park © Theo Allofs/Corbis
19 Performance at the Sydney Opera House © Tourism New South Wales
20 Woman in Kings Canyon © Sean Malyon/Alamy
21 Vineyards, Fleurieu © South Australia Tourism Commission
22 Crocodile, Northern Territory © Northern Territory Tourism
23 Melbourne Cup © Photolibrary.com
24 Wilpena Pound © South Australia Tourism Commission
25 The Twelve Apostles © Max Alexander/Dorling Kindersley
26 Bridgeclimb, Sydney Harbour Bridge © Bridgeclimb
27 Waterfall, Kimberley © WA Tourism
28 Magnetic anthills © David Leffman
29 Karijini Falls © Tony Yeates – Author
30 Manly Ferry, Sydney © Tourism New South Wales
31 Valley of the Giants Tree Top Walk © Department of Conservation and Land Management, Western Australia
32 Outback Track, South Australia © Anne Dehne
33 North Queensland tribes, Aboriginal Dance Festival © John Miles
34 Atherton Tablelands © Dave King/Dorling Kindersley
35 Royal Flying Doctor Service © Kit Kittle/Corbis
36 Birdsville Races © Julia Thorne / Robert Harding
37 Mutawintji National Park © Jerry Dennis
38 Wilsons Promontory National Park, Victoria © Jeff Drewitz/WildLight
39 4WD crossing a creek, Queensland © Chris Scott
40 Carnarvon Gorge © WA Tourism
41 Three Sisters, Blue Mountains © John Miles
42 Bondi Beach, Sydney © Rob Walls/Alamy
43 Sydney Gay and Lesbian Mardi Gras © Reuters/Corbis
44 Canoe in Katherine Gorge © Simon Grosset/Alamy
45 Cradle Mountain-Lake St Clair National Park © John Miles

Black and whites
p.100 Sydney Opera House © Lisa Nellis
p.111 Monorail on Pyrmont Bridge, Darling Harbour © David Wall/Alamy
p.157 Paddington Bazaar, Sydney © David Wall/Alamy
p.171 Manly beach, Sydney © David Hancock/Alamy
p.243 Flyway (formerly the Seniscender), Blue Mountains © Paul Cosgrave/Scenic World, Katoomba, Australia
p.264 Byron Bay, NSW © John Miles

p.275 Lake Burley Griffin, Canberra © Penny Tweedle/Corbis
p.325 Sandcastle, Byron Bay, NSW © Adam van Bunnens/Alamy
p.354 Koala in a eucalyptus tree © Darroch Donald/Alamy
p.381 Golden Guitar, Tamworth, NSW © Tom Keating/WildLight
p.403 Desert Sculptures, Broken Hill, NSW © Jerry Dennis
p.412 Bushwalking © Australian Tourist Board
p.427 Castlemaine Brewery, Brisbane © Neil Setchfield
p.482 Boat to Great Barrier Reef, Port Douglas © Jerry Dennis
p.535 Dunk Island © Jerry Dennis
p.559 Macrossan Street, Port Douglas © Nicholas Pitt/Alamy
p.578 Birdsville pub, Queensland © Morton Beebe/Corbis
p.605 Kookaburra © John Miles
p.630 Swimmers in a billabong, Kakadu National Park © Royalty-Free/Corbis
p.643 Putjamirra Camp croc warning © Jerry Dennis
p.657 Yellow Water wetlands © Grenville Turner/ WildLight
p.710 Wanjina Rock art © Chris Scott
p.732 The Lancelin Ocean Classic windsurfing competition, Western Australia © Gareth Lewis/Alamy
p.762 Pinnacles © Nick Ayliffe/Alamy
p.802 Kangaroo Island © Arco/M.Leder/ imagebroker/Alamy
p.839 Chateau Yaldara Winery © Neale Clark
p.858 Larry the giant lobster, Kingston © Lisa Nellis
p.900 Chapel Street tram, Melbourne © Christine Osbourne/Alamy
p.925 Footbridge over River Yarra, Melbourne © James Davies/Alamy
p.972 Great Ocean Road © Anne Dehne
p.990 The Grotto, Port Campbell NP, Great Ocean Road © Jerry Dennis
p.1022 The Grampians, Victoria © Jerry Dennis
p.1064 Wine Glass Bay and wallaby, Freycinet NP © Jerry Dennis
p.1105 church in Penal Colony, Tasmania © Dallas and John Heaton/Corbis
p.1147 Penguin road crossing sign, near Stanley, Tasmania © Rob Walls/Alamy
p.1161 Cradle Mountain-Lake St Clair NP, Tasmania © Tony Yeates

Index

Map entries are in colour

1770 491

A

Aberdeen 380
Aboriginal art 11, 684
Aboriginal Dance Festival (Laura) 21, 568
Aboriginal dreamtime stories 888
Aboriginal land rights 1190
Aboriginal People 634, 1068, 1188–1192
Aboriginal rock art, Grampians 1017
Aboriginal stockmen's strike, WA 774
Aboriginal, early resistance 1179
accommodation 57–60
ADELAIDE 806–829
Adelaide 831
- accommodation 809–812
- Adelaide, central 808
- Adelaide Central Plaza 816
- Adelaide Festival of Arts 824
- Adelaide Oval 817
- airlines 827
- arrival 807
- Art Gallery of South Australia 813
- Ayers House 813
- banks 827
- bars 824
- bike rental 827
- Botanic Gardens 813
- Bradman Collection 814
- Brighton 820
- buses 807
- camping 809
- camping equipment 828
- canoe rentals 828
- car rental 828
- cinema 825
- clubs 825
- comedy 825
- cycling 809
- disabled travellers 828
- drinking 820–823
- eating 820–823
- entertainment 823–825
- Festival Centre 815
- film 825
- gay and lesbian Adelaide 826
- gay and lesbian nightspots 825
- Glenelg 819
- Government House 814
- Henley Beach 819
- history 804
- hospital 828
- information 807
- internet access 828
- Jam Factory Craft and Design Centre 815
- Jolleys Boathouse 815
- King William Street 816
- laundries 828
- left luggage 828
- Light Square Gallery 815
- Lions Art Centre 815
- maps 828
- markets 827
- metro 807
- motorbike rental 828
- music 825
- Myer Centre 816
- National Aboriginal Cultural Institute (Tandanya) 816
- nightlife 823–825
- North Adelaide 817
- Norwood 818
- Old Parliament House 815
- Parliament House 815
- pharmacy 828
- police 828
- Port Adelaide 818
- post office 828
- pubs 824
- Rundle Mall 816
- Rundle Street 816
- Semaphore 819
- shopping 816, 827
- South Australian Museum 814
- State Library 814
- swimming 828
- Tandanya 816
- taxis 828
- telephones 828
- theatre 826
- Thebarton 818
- Torrens Island 819
- Torrens River 815
- tours 828
- trains 809
- transport 807
- travel agents 829
- universities 813
- Victoria Square 816
- Womadelaide 824
- work 829
- zoo 815

Adelaide Hills 818–822
Adelaide River 662
Adelaide River Crossing 647
Adventure Bay 1098
Agnes Water 491
AIDS organisations 43
Aileron 675
Aireys Inlet 981
Airlie Beach 506
airlines, domestic 48
Albany 744–746
Albury 374
Aldgate 832
Alice Springs 676–688
Alice Springs 679
Alien activity 675
Alligator Creek 516
Allonnah 1099
Almaden 554
Alpine National Park 1054
American River 854
Amity 443
Anakie 598
Andamooka 882
Angahook-Lorne State Park 983
Angaston 840
Anglesea 981
Anzacs 277
Apollo Bay 984
Ararat 1015
Arcadia 525
Archipelago of the Recherche 750
Arkaroola 891
Arltunga 696
Armidale 383–385
Arnhem Highway 647
Arnhem Land 657
Arthur River 1150
Ashes, the 74, 157
Atherton 555
Atherton Tablelands 21, 551–558
Atherton Tablelands 552
atomic bomb tests 1183
Auburn 870
Augusta 739
Aussie Rules football 74, 921
Austinmer 254
Australian Capital Territory (ACT) 267–285
Avoca (VIC) 1006
Avoca Beach 220

INDEX

Ayers Rock (Uluru)...13, 703
Ayers Rock Resort (Yulara) 700
Ayr 515

B

Babinder......538
Bairnsdale......1042
Bald Rock......387
Balgo Hills......676
Balladonia......757
Ballarat......1009–1014
Ballarat......**1010**
Ballina......323
Bamaga......571
banks......46
Barcaldine......600
Barmah......1036
Barmera......865
Barooga......376
Barossa Valley......21, 834–842
Barossa Valley......**835**
Barramundie Gorge (see Maguk)
Barrine, Lake......557
Barrington Tops National Park......307
Barringun......395
Barron Gorge National Park......546, 553
Barrow Creek......675
Bass Strait Islands 1133–1136
Batchelor......644
Batemans Bay......291
Bathurst......357–359
Bathurst Island......646
Beachport......859
Beaconsfield......1127
Beagle Bay......788
Beechworth......1051
Beedelup National Park......743
beer......65
Beer Can Regatta...17, 646
Bees, Ligurian......850
Bega......295
Belair National Park......832
Bellenden Ker Range...537
Bellingen......315
Ben Boyd National Park......297
Ben Lomond National Park......1126
Benalla......1049
Bendigo......999–1003
Bendigo......**1000**
Bermagui......294
Berri......866
Berrima......259
Berry......287
Bethany......837
Betoota......594
Bibbulman Track......735
Bicheno......1111
Big Banana......319
Big Merino......366
Big Orange......866
Bingil Bay......534
Binna Burra......457
birds......1195
Birdsville......594
Birdsville Races......22, 594
Birdsville Track......21, 595, 894
Birdwood......834
Birdworld, Kuranda......553
Blackall......601
Blackdown Tablelands......596
Blackheath......244
Blackwood River Valley......741
Bladensburg National Park......604
Blanchetown......864
Blinman......890
Bloomfield Track......563
Blue Mountains......23, 236–250
Blue Mountains......**238–239**
Blue Mountains National Park......237
Bonang......1045
Bondi Beach......24, 167
Booderee National Park......289
books......1215–1226
boomerangs......589
Boonoo Boonoo Falls...388
Booti Booti National Park......305
Borroloola......671
Bothwell......1132
Bouddi National Park...219
Boulder......754
Boulia......607
Bounty, ship......520
Bourke......393
Bournda National Park......296
Bowen......515
Bowling Green Bay National Park......516
Bowral......259
Bowraville......314
Braidwood......285
Brambuk......1019
Brewarrina......395
Bridge Climb......19, 131
Bridgetown......742
Bridport......1115
Bright......1057
BRISBANE......415–436
Brisbane......**418–419**
- Aboriginal Brisbane......416
- accommodation......421–423
- arrival......417
- bars......432
- bike rental......435
- Botanic Gardens......425
- Brisbane River......429
- car rental......435
- Castlemaine Perkins Brewery......426
- Chinatown......426
- City Hall......423
- clubs......432
- consulates......435
- Cultural Centre......428
- Downtown......423
- eating......430–432
- film......434
- Fort Lytton National Park......430
- Fortitude Valley......426
- gay and lesbian Brisbane......433
- Historic Precinct......424
- history......416
- hospitals......436
- information......420
- internet access......436
- Lone Pine Sanctuary......430
- Maritime Museum......429
- markets......436
- Museum of Brisbane......423
- music......432
- Observatory......424
- pubs......432
- Queensland Museum......428
- Sciencenter......428
- South Bank Parklands......429
- South Brisbane......428
- Sports......434
- St Johns Cathedral......424
- State Art Gallery......428
- theatre......434
- tourist office......420
- tours......437
- trains......436
- transport......420
- Wickham Park......424

Brisbane Forest Park......438
Brisbane Waters National Park......218
Brisbane, tours from.....437
Broad Arrow......756

Broken Hill....22, 397–406, 409
Broken Hill......................398
Broken Hill, tours from .405
Broome...............780–787
Broome........................783
Brunswick Heads 330
Bruny Island 1097
Buchan 1044
Budderoo National Park 257
Bulahdelah...................305
Bulwer 442
Bunbury......................735
Bundaberg..................488
Bundaberg..................488
Bundanoon..................259
Bundeena 253
Bundjalung National Park 323
Bungendore.................285
Bungle Bungles 792
Bunya Mountains 583
Burdekin River.............515
Burke and Wills 593
Burketown 626
Burleigh Heads............451
Burnie 1143
Burning Mountain.........379
Burnt Pine 349
Burnum Burnum..........295
Buronga.....................1031
Burra...........................869
Burrup Peninsula.........771
buses...........................49
bushtucker...............14, 62
bushwalking 76
Bushwalking, Kakadu...655
Busselton.....................737
Byron Bay........... 325–332
Byron Bay 327

C

Cable Beach................781
Caiguna 757
Cairns 538–546
Cairns.........................539
Cairns, tours from 544
Caloundra....................462
Camden 258
Camooweal 618
Campbell Town..........1129
campervans, rental......16, 51–53
camping.........................60
CANBERRA 268–283
Canberra......................270
accommodation........269–272
airlines............................ 281
airport............................ 268
ANU (Australian National University) 276
Anzacs 277
arrival 268
Australian Institute of Sport........................... 278
Australian National Botanic Gardens 277
Australian National University (ANU) 276
Australian War Memorial 276
banks 281
bike rental 269, 281
Black Mountain 277
books 281
buses 269, 282
cafés 278
camping 271
Canberra Nature Park 278
car rental 282
caravan parks 271
cinema 281
clubs 281
cruises........................... 283
diplomatic quarters 274
drinking 280
eating 278
embassies....................... 282
festivals 282
food............................... 278
Forrest........................... 274
galleries 282
golf................................ 282
Griffin, Walter Burley 268
guesthouses.................... 271
Hall of Memory 276
high commissions 282
High Court of Australia 272
horse riding 282
hospitals......................... 282
hostels........................... 271
hotels 271
information 268
internet access 282
jazz................................ 280
Jolimont centre 269
Lake Burley Griffin 274
markets 282
motels 271
music............................. 280
National Archives of Australia....................... 274
National Capital Exhibition....................... 276
National Gallery............... 273
National Library............... 272
National Museum of Australia....................... 276
National Portrait Gallery... 273
National Zoo and Aquarium 274
nature reserves 282
New Parliament House 274
nightlife.......................... 280
NRMA............................ 283
Old Parliament House...... 273
police 283
post office 283
Questacon....................... 272
restaurants 279
Royal Australian Mint....... 274
scenic flights................... 283
Screensound Australia..... 277
shopping 283
taxis............................... 283
Telstra Tower 278
Tent Embassy.................. 273
theatre 281
tourist information........... 269
tours 283
train station 268
trains 283
transport......................... 269
travel agents 283
Visitor Information Centre 269
Yarralumla 274
cane toads..........537, 1195
Cannonvale 505
canoeing, Katherine Gorge.................24, 666
Canunda National Park 859
Cape Hillsborough National Park............502
Cape Le Grand National Park 750
Cape Leeuwin 740
Cape Leveque 788
Cape Range National Park 770
Cape Tribulation 562
Cape Tribulation Road 561
Cape York...................572
Cape York Peninsula...564
Capricorn Coast 497–500
Captain Starlight 587
Captain Thunderbolt 385
Cardwell 528
Carey's Caves 368
Carnarvon...................767
Carnarvon Gorge....23, 588
Carnarvon National Park.................. 588–591
cars, buying and selling 53, 207
cars, rental....................51
Casino 335
cassowaries................534
Casterton...................1025
Castlemaine...............1003
caves, Chillagoe 555

caves, Margaret River (WA) 740
Ceduna.........................880
Central Plateau (TAS) 1132
Central Tilba.................294
Centre, The 690–691
Cervantes 759
Cessnock.....................227
Chambers Gorge..........890
Chambers Pillar............697
Channon, The...............337
Charleville....................591
Charters Towers 608
Charters Towers 609
chicko roll 63
Childers 485
children, travelling with ... 89
Chillagoe......................554
Chiltern 1053
Clare 872
Clare Valley 870–873
climate 11
Cloncurry.....................611
Clump Mountain National Park 534
Clunes 1014
Cobar...........................395
Cobourg Peninsula.......658
Cockle Creek.............1096
Cocklebiddy 757
Cocoparra National Park 373
Coen............................569
Coffin Bay.....................879
Coffs Harbour 317–321
Coffs Harbour 317
Coleraine 1025
Coles Bay..................1110
Commonwealth Games, Melbourne (2006) 75
convicts 1177
Conway National Park... 506
Coober Pedy 15, 883–886
Coober Pedy...............884
Cooee Bay....................498
Cook, Captain James 1177
Cooktown 566
Cooktown.....................566
Coolangatta 452–454
Coolgardie 752
Cooloola Coast ... 467–470
Cooma..........................300
Coonabarabran 388
Coonawarra township .. 862
Coonawarra wine region............... 861–863
Cooper Creek.......593, 892
Cooroibah Lake............469
Coorong National Park.. 856
Cootharaba Lake..........469
Coral Bay......................768
Corinna 1152
Corowa 376
Cossack.........................772
costs 44–47
Cotter Reserve 285
Cowell..........................878
Cowes 960
Cowra 364
Cradle Mountain.........1163
Cradle Mountain–Lake St Clair National Park.............. 1159–1171
Crafers 830
CREB Track 560
credit cards 46
Crescent Head 313
Creswick....................1014
cricket 74
Croajingolong National Park 1046
crocodiles.......19, 41, 565, 650
Crowdy Bay National Park 308
Croydon........................624
Crystal Cascades (Wongalee Falls) 546
Cue 776
Cunnamulla 592
Currawinya National Park 592
currency exchange.........46
Currie.........................1133
Currumbin Beach 452
cycads 527
cycling 78
Cygnet 1093
Cygnet River.................854
Cynthia Bay 1164

D

D'Entrecasteaux National Park 743
Daintree, The 560–563
Daintree, The 562
Dalhousie Springs 896
Dalrymple National Park 610
Daly River 662
damper 63
Dampier 771
Dampier Peninsula 788
Dandenong Ranges National Park 964
Dangars Lagoon 386
Darling Downs 581–588
Darling River Run 397
Darlington 1107
DARWIN.............. 633–647
Darwin area.................636
Darwin, central 638
- accommodation 637–640
- airlines 646
- airport............................ 634
- apartments 637–639
- Aquascene 641
- arrival 634
- Aviation Heritage Centre ... 642
- backpackers 639
- banks 646
- bars 645
- bookshops 646
- Botanic Gardens 641
- buses 635, 636, 646
- campervan rental 646
- camping 640
- camping equipment 646
- car rental 636, 646
- caravan parks 640
- Charles Darwin National Park 642
- cinema 645
- consulates 646
- Crocodylus Park 642
- Cullen Bay Marina............ 641
- cycles 636
- day-trips 634
- drinking 645
- East Point........................ 642
- East Point reserve............ 642
- eating 642–645
- entertainment 645
- Fannie Bay museums 641
- festivals 645
- food 642–645
- hospital 646
- hostels............................ 639
- hotels 637–639
- Indo-Pacific Marine.......... 641
- information 635
- internet access 646
- Lake Alexander 642
- markets 646
- motels 637–639
- nightlife........................... 645
- permits (for aboriginal land) 646
- pharmacy 646
- police 646
- post office 646
- pubs 645
- shuttle bus 634
- Smith Street Mall 640
- swimming 646
- tours (from Darwin to the Top End) 644
- transport......................... 636

vaccinations 646
Wharf Precinct 641
Daydream Island 514
Daylesford 1007
Deepwater National Park 492
Deloraine 1130
Denham 766
Denman Island 514
Denmark 747
Derby (TAS) 1115
Derby (WA) 789
Derwent Bridge 1164
Deua National Park 291
Devil's Marbles 674
Devonport 1138–1141
Devonport 1139
Dharug National Park 217
didgeridoo, buying and playing 685
Dig Tree 593
Dimboola 1025
Dingo 596
Dingo Fence 395, 1194
disabilities, travelling with 86–89
dive sites 78
diving, Cairns 547–550
diving, Great Barrier Reef 17, 486
diving, Townsville 521
dolphins
Bunbury (WA) 735
Monkey Mia (WA) 766
Nelson Bay (NSW) 305
Sorrento (Vic) 955
Dorrigo 316
Dorrigo National Park 316
Douglas Apsley National Park 1112
Dover 1095
drinking 64–66
driving 50–55
Dubbo 361–364
Dunk Island 534
Dunk Island, ferries 536
Dunolly 1006
Dunsborough 737
Dunwich 443

E

Eacham, Lake 557
Eagle Heights 455
Echuca 1034–1037
Eden 297
Edith Falls 663
Edithburgh 848
Edmund Kennedy National Park 531
Eighty-Mile Beach 775
Einasleigh 623
electricity 95
Ellerston 379
Ellgowra 360
Elliott 671
Ellis Beach 547
Elliston (SA) 879
Elsey National Park 670
embassies, Australian abroad 36
Emerald 597
emergencies 81
Emu Park 498
Encounter Bikeway 846
Entrance, The 220
Erldunda 699
Eromanga 593
Errinundra National Park 1045
Esperance 750
Eucla 758
Eucla National Park 758
Eumundi 463
Eungella 504
Eungella National Park 503–505
Eureka Stockade 1011
Eurimbula National Park 492
Euroa 1049
Eurong 477
Evandale 1125
Evans Head 323
Exeter 1127
Exmouth 769
explorers, maritime 1176
explorers, overland 1178
Eyre Peninsula 876–880

F

Falls Creek 1059
Faulconbridge 239
Federation 1180
Federation Peak 1169
festivals 71
film 1198–1206
Finch Hatton Gorge 504
Finke Gorge National Park 692
First Fleet 1177
Fitzroy Crossing 791
Fitzroy Island 551
Fleurieu Peninsula 842–848
flights
from Britain 28–30
from Ireland 29
from New Zealand 33
from North America 31–33
internal 47
Flinders Chase National Park 855
Flinders Island 1134–1136
Flinders Ranges 887–893
Flinders Ranges National Park 888–890
flora 1196
Floraville 561
food 61–64
Forbes 360
Forestier Peninsula 1102
Forsayth 623
Forster-Tuncurry 306
Foster 1039
four-wheel driving 23, 55
Cape York 563, 571
Central Australia 694
Fraser Island 15, 474
Kimberley 798
rental 51
Francois Peron National Park 766
Franklin 1094
Franklin Lower Gordon Wild Rivers National Park 1165–1167
Fraser Island 474–478
Fremantle 724–730
Fremantle 728
French Island 957
Frenchmans Cap Track 1167
Freycinet National Park 1109
Freycinet Peninsula 1109

G

gambling 95
Gammon Ranges National Park 891
Gawler Ranges 880
gay and lesbian life 91–93
Geelong 965
Geeveston 1094
Geikie Gorge National Park 791
gem mining 599

gemfields 598
Geographe Bay 737
George Town 1128
Georgetown 623
Geraldton 759
Gerringong 257
Gibb River Road ... 796–800
Gibraltar Range National Park 323
Ginnindera 285
Gippsland 1037–1044
Gippsland 1038–1039
Giraween National Park 584
Girringun National Park 528
Gladstone 492
Glasshouse Mountains .. 461
Glen Annie Gorge 696
Glen Helen 689
Glen Innes 386
Glenbrook 238
Glenrowan 1049
glossary 1212–1229
Gold Coast 444
gold country 607–610
goldfields (VIC) ... 997–1014
goldfields, central 998
goldrush 1180
goldrushes (VIC) 999
Goolwa 846
Goondiwindi 585
Gordon River 1158
Gordonvale 538
Gosford 218
Gosses Bluff 692
Goulburn 366
Goulburn Valley 1048
Gowrie Park 1142
Grafton 321
Grampians National Park 1017–1024
Grampians National Park 1020
Granite Belt 584
Grassy 1133
Great Barrier Reef 486, 547–550
Great Keppel Island 499
Great Ocean Road (VIC) 19, 977–997
Great Ocean Road 976–977
Great Western 1016
Green Island 550
Green Mountain 458
Greenough 759
Gregory Downs 619
Gregory National Park ... 667
Griffith 371
Grove 1094
Guildford 733
Gulf St Vincent beaches 844
Gumeracha 834
Gunbarrel Highway 757
Gunbower Island 1033
Gundagai 368
Gundy 379
Gunlom 656
Gunnedah 390
Gurri (see Fraser Island)

H

Hahndorf 832
Hall 285
Halls Creek 792
Halls Gap 1017
Hamelin Pool 765
Hamersley Ranges 775
Hamilton 1024
Hamilton Island 514
Hanging Rock (VIC) 998
Happy Valley 477
Harrietville 1059
Hartz Mountain National Park 1095
Hat Head National Park 313
Hattah-Kulkyne National Park 1027
Hawker 888
Hawkesbury River 216–218
Hawley Beach 1142
Hayman Island 511
Healesville 963
health 40–44
Heathcote National Park 253
Helenvale 565
Hells Gate Track 626
Hemp Embassy 336
Henbury Meteorite Craters 697
Hepburn Springs 1008
Herberton 557
Hermannsburg 692
hermits of Borroloola 672
Heron Island 493
Heron Island, camping .. 493
Hervey Bay 471–474
Hervey Bay, tours and cruises from 474
Heyson Trail 830, 842
Hill End 359
Hillgrove 385
Hinchinbrook Island 529
history 1075–1187
hitching 56
HOBART 1073–1091
Hobart 1074
- accommodation 1066–1068
- Allport Library and Museum of Fine Arts 1069
- arrival 1065
- bars 1077
- Battery Point 1072
- bike rental 1080
- buses 1080
- car rental 1080
- clubs 1077
- cruises 1071
- eating 1075
- festivals 1079
- Franklin Square 1068
- gay and lesbian Hobart ... 1078
- harbour 1073
- history 1075
- Hobart, around 1092
- information 1065
- internet access 1080
- Maritime Museum 1069
- Mount Nelson 1075
- Mount Wellington 1075
- music 1077
- Penitentiary Chapel and Criminal Courts 1070
- Queens Domain 1072
- Royal Botanical Gardens 1072
- Salamanca Market 1071
- Tasmanian Museum and Art Gallery 1069
- tourist office 1065
- tours 1080
- transport 1065
- waterfront 1070

Holbrook 369
holidays, national 71
Hook Island 511
Hopetoun (VIC) 1026
Horn Island 574
Horseshoe Bay 525
Horsham 1025
hostels 58–60
hotels 57
Hughenden 610
Hume and Hovell Walking Track 366
Hungerford 395
Hunter Valley, Lower 227–233
Hunter Valley, Lower 230
Huonville 1093
Huskisson 289
Hyden 753

I

Idalia National Park 601
Iluka 323
Ingham........................... 527
Innamincka 892
Innes National Park 848
Innisfail 537
insurance 38
internet access 69
Inverell 387
Iron Range National
Park 569

J

Jabiru........................... 654
jellyfish......................... 42
Jenolan Caves.............. 250
Jericho.......................... 600
Jervis Bay..................... 289
Jim Jim Falls 655
Jindabyne..................... 302

K

Kakadu National Park ... 17,
648–657
Kakadu National Park .. 649
Kalbarri............... 761–764
Kalbarri National Park... 764
Kalgoorlie 753
Kalumburu 798
Kanangra Boyd
National Park............. 250
Kangaroo Island 17,
849–855
Kangaroo Island 850
Kangaroo Valley............ 260
Kapunda 869
Karijini National Park... 20,
776–779
Karratha........................ 771
Karumba........................ 624
Kata Tjuta (the Olgas).... 705
Katherine 663–665
Katherine Gorge 665
Katoomba........... 241–243
Katoomba and Leura... 241
Keep River National
Park 669
Kelly, Ned 1050
Kempsey 313
kentia palm.......... 341, 342
Keppel islands............. 498
Kettering 1091
Kiama 256
Kiandra 302
Kimberley, The............... 20,
789–791
Kimberley, The............ 790
Kinchega National
Park 408
King Island.................. 1133
Kingaroy 582
Kings Canyon 18, 697
Kingscote 852
Kingston 349
Kingston SE 857
koalas 215
Kooringal 442
Koroit 992
Kosciusko National
Park 301
Kununurra..................... 794
Kuranda 551
Ku-Ring-Gai Chase
National Park 175, 214
Kyneton 998
Kynuna 606
Kyogle 335

L

Lady Barron................ 1136
Lady Elliot Island 490
Lady Musgrave Island ... 491
Lake Acraman 879
Lake Argyle.................. 796
Lake Barrine 557
Lake Condah Mission... 996
Lake Cooroibah 469
Lake Cootharaba.......... 469
Lake Eacham................ 557
Lake Eyre............... 16, 893
Lake Pedder 1168
Lake St Clair 1164
Lake Tinaroo................ 556
Lake Victoria................ 377
Lake Wallaga 295
Lake Wivenhoe 439
Lakefield National
Park 568
Lakeland 565
Lakes Entrance........... 1042
lamington 63
**Lamington National
Park**................... 457–459
Larapinta trail 688
Lark Quarry.................. 606
Larrimah 670
Launceston 1116–1125
Launceston 1118
laundries 95
Laura 568
Lavers Hill.................... 986
Lawn Hill National
Park 618
Leasingham 871
Leeton 373
Leinster........................ 757
Lennox Head 324
Leonora 756
Leura 240
Lightning Ridge 392
Lind National Park...... 1046
Lindeman Island........... 514
Lismore 334
**Litchfield National
Park**.................. 660–662
Lithgow 250
Little Desert National
Park 1026
Living Desert Reserve,
Broken Hill 402
Lizard Island 567
Lockhart River 569
Logging, WA 741
Lombadina 788
London Bridge.............. 989
Long Island 514
Longreach 602
**Lord Howe
Island** 339–346
Lord Howe Island 343
Lorne................... 981–983
Louth 397
Low Head.................... 1128
Lower Glenelg National
Park 996
Loxton 864
Lunawanna 1099
Lyndoch........................ 836

M

Mabo Decision ... 573, 1188
**MacDonnell
Ranges**............... 688–697
Mackay 500–502
Mackay........................ 500
Maclean 322
Macquarie Pass National
Park 256
Madura 757
Magnetic Island... 522–526
Magnetic Island, tours and
excursions 524

Maguk 656
Maiala National Park 438
Main Range 460
Major Mitchell Trail 1023
Malanda 558
Maldon 1004
Maleny 463
Mallacoota 1046
Mallee, The 1026
Manjimup 742
Mansfield 1055
maps 38
Marble Bar 776
Mardi Gras 24, 196
Mareeba 554
Mareeba Wetlands 554
Margaret River 738
Maria Island National Park 1107
Marla 886
Maroochydore 462
Marrawah 1150
Marree 893
marsupials 1193
Mary Kathleen 613
Mary River National Park 648
Maryborough (VIC) 1005
Marysville 964
Maryvale 697
Masthead Island 493
Mataranka 669
MCG 16, 921
McKinlay 606
McLaren Vale 843
Medlow Bath 244
Meekatharra 776
MELBOURNE 901–951
Melbourne 902
- accommodation 905–913
- airlines 947
- Albert Park 931
- aquarium 922
- arrival 903
- Aussie Rules football 921
- Australian Centre for the Moving Image 914
- banks 947
- bars 940
- bike rental 948
- Birrarung Marr 921
- Bourke Street 917
- Bulleen 933
- Captain Cook's Cottage 921
- Carlton 927
- Carlton Gardens 920
- CBD 916
- Chinatown 918
- clubs 942
- Collingwood 929
- Collins Street 916
- comedy 943
- Crown Casino 922
- cruises, Yarra River 923
- disabled travellers 949
- Docklands 924
- Eastern Hill 920
- eating 934–939
- Elsternwick 932
- Eltham 933
- Elwood 932
- employment 950
- Exhibition Centre 922
- Federation Square 914
- film 945
- Fitzroy 929
- gay and lesbian Melbourne 943, 944
- hospitals 950
- Ian Potter Centre 915
- IMAX 920
- Immigration Museum 917
- information 903
- internet access 950
- Kings Domain 925
- left luggage 950
- Luna Park 931
- markets 947
- MCG 16, 921
- Melbourne Central 918
- Melbourne Cup 19, 73
- Melbourne Museum 920
- Melbourne Observation Deck 916
- Melbourne, central 904–905
- Melbourne, suburbs 928
- motorbikes 950
- music 942
- National Gallery of Victoria 915, 924
- New Quay 924
- Old Customs House 917
- Old Melbourne Gaol 918
- Parliament House 920
- Prahran 930
- pubs 940
- Queen Victoria Market 919
- Queen Victoria Village (QV) 918
- RACV 951
- Royal Arcade 917
- Royal Botanic Gardens 926
- shopping 945–947
- South Melbourne 931
- South Yarra 930
- Spotswood 932
- St Kilda 931
- State Library 918
- swimming pools 951
- taxis 951
- Telstra Dome 924
- theatre 943
- Toorak 930
- tourist offices 903
- transport 906–908
- travel agents 951
- Victorian Arts Centre 924
- Williamstown 933
- Windsor 930
- Yarra River 922–927
- zoo 927

Melrose 876
Melville Island 646
Menindee 408
Menindee lakes 408
Meningie 857
Merimbula 296
Merrijig 1055
Metung 1044
Milawa Gourmet Region 1052
Mildura 1028–1031
Millaa Millaa 558
Millicent 859
Millstream-Chichester National Park 772
MIM 613, 616
Mimosa Rocks National Park 295
mining and unionism, Broken Hill 401
Mintaro 871
Mission Beach 531–536
Mission Beach 533
Mitchell 587
Mitchell and Alice Rivers National Park 626
Mitchell River National Park 1042
Mittagong 258
mobile phones, pre-paid 68
Mogo 291
Mole Creek 1130
Molles islands 511–514
Mon Repos Beach 489
money, wiring 47
Monkey Mia 766
monotrimes 1193
Montague Island 293
Mooloolaba 462
Moreton Island 440–442
Morgan 864
Mornington Peninsula 953–958
Mornington Peninsula National Park 953
Morton National Park 252, 290
Moruya 291
mosquitoes 41
Mossman 560
motels 57
motorbiking 55
motorhomes, rental 51–53
Mount Anne 1169
Mount Arapiles 1025
Mount Barney 459

Mount Baw Baw.........1061
Mount Buffalo National Park.........1060
Mount Buller.........1056
Mount Carbine.........565
Mount Coot-tha.........438
Mount Eccles National Park.........994
Mount Elliot.........516
Mount Field National Park.........1100
Mount Gambier.........860
Mount Glorious.........438
Mount Grenfell Historic Site.........396
Mount Gunderbooka.........395
Mount Hotham.........1059
Mount Isa.........613–617
Mount Isa.........615
Mount Isa Mines...613, 616
Mount Kaputar National Park.........391
Mount Mistake.........460
Mount Moffatt.........590
Mount Nebo.........438
Mount Remarkable National Park.........876
Mount Stirling.........1057
Mount Surprise.........622
Mount Tamborine.........456
Mount Victoria.........244
Mount Warning.........338
Mount William National Park.........1113
mountain biking.........78
Mudgee.........360
Mundrabilla.........758
Mungo National Park...377
Murray River (SA)...14, 866
Murray River (VIC).........1027–1037
Murray River, lower.........375–378
Murray-Sunset National Park.........1026
Murrumbateman.........285
Murrumbidgee Irrigation Area (MIA).........371–374
Murrurundi.........379
Murwillumbah.........337
Musgrave.........569
music.........1207–1214
Mutawintji National Park.........22, 409
Myall Creek Massacre...383
Myall Lakes National Park.........305
Mylestom.........315

N

Nagambie.........1048
Namagdi National Park.........284
Namatjira, Albert.........693
Nambour.........463
Nambucca Heads.........314
Nambung National Park.........759
Namoi Valley.........390–392
Nannup.........741
Naracoorte.........862
Naracoorte Caves.........862
Narawntapu National Park.........1142
Narooma.........292
Narrabri.........391
Narrandera.........373
National Park (TAS)...1100
national parks.........79
Nelly Bay.........525
Nelson.........997
Nelson Bay.........305
New England National Park.........385
New England Plateau...378
New Norcia.........731
New Norfolk.........1099
New South Wales (coastal) and ACT.........266
New South Wales, Inland.........356
Newcastle.........221–227
Newcastle.........222
Newhaven.........959
Newman.........776
newspapers.........69
Nguiu.........647
Nhill.........1026
Nhulunbuy.........658
Nightcap National Park.........334
Nimbin.........335–337
Ningaloo Marine Park...770
Nitmiluk National Park...665
Nobbies, The.........960
Nobby.........584
Noosa.........464–467
Noosa.........464
Noosa Heads.........465
Noosaville.........465
Norfolk Island.........347–351
Normanton.........624
Normanville.........844
Norseman.........757
North Stradbroke Island.........442
North Tamborine.........456
Northcliffe.........743
Northern Territory.........632
Northwest Island.........493
Northwest, the.........760
Nourlangie Rock.........655
Nowra-Bomaderry.........288
Nullagine.........776
Nullarbor.........757
Nullarbor Plain.........880
Nundle.........380
Nuriootpa.........840
Nyah.........1031
Nyngan.........393

O

Oatlands.........1129
Olgas, the (Kata Tjuta)...705
online information.........37
Onslow.........771
Oodnadatta.........895
Oodnadatta Track...21, 894
opals.........885
Opalton.........606
Ora Banda.........756
Orange.........359
Orbost.........1045
Orford.........1107
Ormiston Gorge.........689
Otway National Park...986
outdoor activities.........9, 75
Ouyen.........1026
Overland Track.........24, 1162
Oxley Wild Rivers National Park.........385
ozone hole.........40

P

package tours
from Britain.........30
from New Zealand.........34
from North America.........32
Palm Beach, QLD.........452
Palmer River.........568
Palmerston Highway...558
Paluma.........526
Pandora, ship.........520
Parkes.........360
Paronella Park.........536
Parramatta.........234–236
Patonga.........219
pavlova.........63
Paynesville.........1042
Pearl Beach.........219
Pemberton.........742
Penguin.........1143

penguins (TAS) 1111
penguins, little 845, 959
Penneshaw 853
Penola 861
Penrith 236
PERTH 715–723
Perth, around 726
Perth, central 716
  accommodation 702–704
  arrival 700
  Art Galley of Western
    Australia 705
  bars 707
  beaches 717
  buses 710
  car rental and purchase ... 710
  cinema 708
  clubs 708
  eating 706
  gay and lesbian Perth 710
  history 713
  information 700
  internet access 710
  Kings Park 706
  music 708
  Old Mill 706
  Perth Cultural Centre 705
  Perth Mint 705
  theatre 708
  tourist office 700
  tours 708
  trains 711
  transport 702
  zoo 706
Phillip Island 958–961
Picnic Bay 524
Picton 258
pie floater 63
Pine Creek 662
Pinnacles, the 759
Pioneer Settlement
  (VIC) 1032
Pittwater 214
Planton Island 514
Plenty Highway 675
Point Lookout 43
Point Samson 772
police 80
population 7
Porcupine Gorge 611
Porongurup National
  Park 749
Port Arthur 1104–1106
Port Arthur massacre .. 1105
Port Augusta 874–876
Port Campbell 988
Port Davey Track 1169
Port Douglas 559
Port Elliot 846
Port Fairy 993
Port Hedland 773
Port Lincoln 878
Port Macquarie ... 308–312
Port Macquarie 309
Port Noarlunga 844
Port Pirie 873
Port Sorell 1141
Port Stephens 305
Portarlington 968
Portland 994
Portland Roads 569
Portsea 956
Possession Island 574
postal services 67
Pound National Park 689
Prevelly Park 738
Prince of Wales Island ... 574
Pro Hart Gallery, Broken
  Hill 401
Proserpine 505
Purnunulu National
  Park 792
Pyengana 1114

Q

Qantas, origins of 602
Quamby 612
Quamby Bluff 1130
Queenscliff 967
Queensland houses 425
Queensland, outback ... 580
**Queensland,
  South East** 414
Queensland, tropical ... 484
Queenstown 1153
Quilpe 593
Quinkan 568
Quorn 887

R

radio 70
rafting, Franklin River
  (TAS) 15, 1166
Rainbow Beach 470
Rainbow Valley 697
Ranelagh 1094
Ravenshoe 557
Ravenswood 608
Red Cliffs 1031
red gums, Murray
  River 1027
Redbank Gorge 691
Renmark 867
Renner Springs 671
reptiles 1195
Reynella 842
Richmond TAS 1101
Richmond (QLD) 611
river cruises ... 14, 866, 1028,
  1035
Riverland (SA) 862–868
Riversleigh Fossil Site ... 618
Robe 857
Robinvale 1031
Rockhampton 495–497
Rockhampton 495
Rocky Cape National
  Park 1145
Roebourne 772
Roma 587
Roma Gorge 691
Roper Bar 670
Rosebery 1153
Rosevears 1127
Ross 1129
Rosslyn Bay 499
Rossville 563
Rottnest Island 730
Rowland Flat 836
Roxby Downs 882
Royal Flying Doctor
  Service 404
Royal National Park 252
Ruby Gorge 696
Rubyvale 599
rugby 74
Rutherglen 1053

S

Saibai Island 574
sailing, Whitsundays 14,
  512
Sale 1041
San Remo 959
Sanctuary, The, Mission
  Beach 15, 532
Sandover Highway 675
Sapphire 598
satellite phone 69
Scone 379
Scotia Sanctuary 409
Scotsdale 1115
scuba-diving 77
Seal Rocks (NSW) 305
Seal Rocks (Phillip Island)
  960
seasons 95
Seisia 571
Sevenhill 871
Seventy-Five Mile Beach,
  Fraser Island 477

sexual harassment........93
Shark Bay....................764
Shark Bay....................765
sharks, great white.......878
Sheffield......................1142
Shepparton.................1049
Shutehaven..................506
Silverton.......................407
Simpson Desert
Crossing....................896
Six Foot Track..............244
skiing..............................80
skiing, Ben Lomond.... 1126
skiing, Snowy
Mountains............14, 299
skiing, Victorian Alps
.................................1056
slang............... 1227–1229
Sliding Spring Observatory
Complex....................388
Slip, Slop, Slap.............40
Smithfield.....................546
Smithton....................1149
snakes.................41, 1195
Snowy Mountains......... 298–304
Snowy River National
Park........................1045
Sofala...........................359
Somerset......................572
Sorrento........................954
South Australia...........804
South Coast Track......1170
South Mission..............533
South Stradbroke
Island.......................451
South West Cape.......1170
South West National Park............... 1167–1170
South West Rocks........313
Southeast Asia, travel
from............................34
Southend......................859
Southern Cross............752
Southern Highlands......258
Southern Tablelands.....557
Southwest WA............736
Speed.........................1026
spiders............................41
sport, spectator...... 73–75
Springbrook National
Park.........................456
Springsure....................598
Springton......................840
Springwood...................239
St Albans......................217
St George.....................586
St Helena Island..........439
St Helens....................1113
St Marys......................1112
Stanley........................1146
Stanthorpe....................584
State of Origin...............74
Stawell........................1016
Stirling Range National
Park.........................749
Strahan........... 1155–1159
Strathalbyn...................847
stromatolites.................765
Strzelecki Track......21, 892
Stuart Highway
(SA)...................881–887
student cards.................95
sugar cane....................503
Sunshine Beach...........465
Sunshine Coast... 460–467
Surfers Paradise........... 445–450
Surfers Paradise..........445
surfing, the Gold
Coast........................446
Swan Hill.....................1032
Swan Valley.................733
Swanick......................1110
Swansea......................1108
SYDNEY................ 99–262
Sydney and around.....102
accommodation........110–125
airlines.......................... 206
airport buses.................. 105
Aquarium........................ 146
arrival............................. 104
art galleries..................... 201
Art Gallery of NSW.......... 143
Australian Museum.......... 140
Avalon Beach.................. 174
Balmain........................... 152
Balmoral.......................... 165
banks.............................. 206
Barrenjoey Peninsula....... 174
bars.........................188–192
beaches....................166–175
beer gardens................... 189
Birchgrove....................... 153
Bondi Beach...... 24, 167–170
Bondi Beach, Christmas Day
on.............................. 167
Botanic Gardens............. 143
Botany Bay.............175–178
Bradleys Head................ 164
Bridge Climb............. 19, 131
buses.............................. 108
camping equipment......... 206
campsites........................ 114
cars, buying and
selling........................ 207
CBD................................ 135
Centennial
Parklands..............156–158
Chinatown....................... 138
Circular Quay.................. 126
clubs.........................193–195
comedy........................... 199
consulates....................... 207
Coogee............................ 170
Cremorne Point............... 164
Cronulla.......................... 177
Customs House............... 127
cycling............................ 207
dance locations............... 198
Darling Harbour........144–149
Darling Harbour............... 145
Darlinghurst..................... 155
disabled travellers........... 208
diving.............................. 208
Domain, The.................... 142
Double Bay...................... 161
eating......................178–188
Elizabeth Bay.................. 161
ferries............................. 108
festivals........................... 202
film..........................199–201
foreign exchange............ 206
Fort Denison................... 134
Fox Studios..................... 158
Freshwater...................... 174
gay and lesbian Sydney... 121,
196–198
Glebe.......................149–151
Goat Island..................... 153
Gunnamatta Bay............. 178
Haberfield....................... 152
Harbour Bridge............... 130
harbour cruises............... 128
Haymarket & around Central
Station....................... 139
history............................ 103
holiday apartments.......... 123
horse racing.................... 203
hospitals......................... 208
Hyde Park............... 138, 140
Hyde Park Barracks......... 142
immigration..................... 208
information...................... 106
internet access................ 208
Justice and Police
Museum..................... 127
kids' Sydney.................... 134
Kings Cross..................... 158
Kirribilli........................... 163
Ku-Ring-Gai Chase National
Park.......................... 175
Kurnell Peninsula............ 177
La Perouse...................... 176
left luggage..................... 208
Leichhardt....................... 152
libraries........................... 208
Luna Park........................ 163
Macquarie Street............. 141
Manly.......................170–173
Manly Scenic Walkway.... 173
maps............................... 208
Mardi Gras................ 24, 196
markets........................... 205
Middle Harbour................ 165
Millers Point.................... 134
Mona Vale....................... 174
monorail.......................... 110
Moore Park...................... 156

Mosman Bay 164
Mrs Macquarie's Chair 143
Museum of Contemporary
Art 127
Museum of Sydney 136
music 192, 195–198
National Maritime
Museum 147
National Trust Centre 135
Neutral Bay 163
Newtown 151
Nielson Park 161
North Head 173
Observatory Park 135
Olympic Park 234
Paddington 155
Paddy's Market 138
Palm Beach 175
parks and wildlife
service 209
pharmacy (late-night) 209
police 209
post office 209
Potts Point 159
Powerhouse Museum 147
public holidays 209
pubs 188–192
Pyrmont 148
Queen Victoria Building
.... 137
Redfern 154
Rocks, The 131–135
Rocks, The 132
Rose Bay 161
Rozelle 152
Rushcutters Bay 161
scenic flights 209
sculpture walk 136
Shell Cove 164
shopping 203–206
Skytour 137
South Head 162
St Mary's Cathedral 141
surf lifesavers 168
surfing 209
Surry Hills 154
swimming pools 209
Sydney Cricket Ground
(SCG) 156
Sydney ferries 109
Sydney Harbour National
Park 173
Sydney Observatory 135
Sydney Opera House 18,
127–130
Sydney rail network 107
Sydney suburbs 150
Sydney Tower 137
Sydney, central 116–117
Taronga Zoo 164
taxis 110, 209
telephones 209
theatre 198–199
tourist offices 106
tours from Sydney 212
Town Hall 138
trains 108, 110
travel agents 209
travel passes 106, 112
Tumbalong Park 146
Ultimo 147
Vaucluse House 162
water sports 209
Watsons Bay 162
Whale Beach 175
women travellers 210
Woollahra 156
Woolloomooloo 159
work 210

T

Talbot 1006
Tall Timber Country 20,
741
Tam O'Shanter State
Forest 534
Tamar Valley 1126
Tamborine Mountain 455
Tamworth 380–383
Tamworth Country Music
Festival 380
Tanami Road 675
Tancred Island 514
Tangalooma 441
Tanunda 837
Taree 308
Tarra Bulga National
Park 1041
Tasman Peninsula 1102
Tasmania 1066
Tasmanian Trail 1141
Tathra 296
tax 85, 95
Taylors Arm 314
telephone codes,
international 68
telephones 67–69
television 70
temperature 12
Tennant Creek 672–674
Tenterfield 387
termite mounds 20, 660
Terrigal 219
Territory Wildlife
Park 660
Thirlmere Lakes
National Park 258
Thirroul 254
Thorsborne Trail 529
Thredbo 302
Three Ways 671
Thursday Island 573
Ti Tree 675
Tidbinbilla Nature
Reserve 284
Tilba Tilba 294
Tilpa 397
Timber Creek 667
Timboon 989
time zones 95
Tinaroo, Lake 556
tipping 95
Tiwi islands 646
Tjapaltjari, Clifford
Possum 684
Tocumwal 376
toilets, public 95
Tom Price 779
Toodyay 733
Toowoomba 582
Top End, the 659
Torndirrup Peninsula 746
Torquay 979
Torrens River Gorge 833
Torres Strait 572–574
tourist offices 37
Tower Hill State Game
Reserve 992
Townsville 516–522
Townsville 517
trains 48
trains, gulf (QLD) 661
Triabunna 1107
Tullah 1153
Tully 531
Tunnel Creek National
Park 792
Turkey Creek 794
Tweed Heads 332
Twelve Apostles 987
Twin Falls 656

U

Ubirr 654
UFOs 675
Uki 338
Ulladulla 290
Uluru (Ayers Rock) 13, 703
**Uluru-Kata Tjuta
(Ayers Rock)
National Park** ... 701–705
Uluru-Kata Tjuta
(Ayers Rock) National
Park 699
Ulverstone 1142
Undara Lava Tubes 621
Uralla 385
Urunga 315

V

Valley of the Giants 748
Van Diemen's Land Company 1148
vegemite 63
Victor Harbor 844
Victoria 974–975
Victorian Alps 1054
visas 35

W

Wagga Wagga 369–371
Waikerie 864
Walcha 386
Wallace Rockhole 693
Wallaga Lake 295
Walls of Jerusalem National Park 1132
Walpole 748
Walshpool National Park 323
Waltzing Matilda 604
Wanaaring 394
Wandiligong 1058
Wangaratta 1051
Waratah 1152
Warburton (VIC) 963
Warburton Road 887
Warren National Park ... 743
Warrnambool 989
Warrumbungle National Park 389
Warwick 584
Watarrka National Park 698
water sports 77
Watervale 871
Wauchope (NSW) 312
Wauchope (NT) 675
Wave Rock 753
weather 11
weather, Top End 637
websites, about Australia 37
websites, health 43
Wee Jasper 368
weights and measures 95
Weipa 570
Weldborough 1115
Wellesley Islands 625
Wenlock River 570
Wentworth 376
Wentworth Falls 239
Werribee 964
West Cape Howe National Park 747
West Coast Wilderness Railway 1154
Western Arthurs Traverse 1169
Western Australia 712
Western Explorer Route (TAS) 1151
Western Plains Zoo 361
Western Tiers .. 1130–1133
wet tropics 553
whales, Humpbacked ... 14, 471
whales, southern right ... 844
whale-watching, Hervey Bay 14, 471
White Cliffs 397
Whitemark 1136
Whitsunday 505–509
Whitsunday Island 510
Whitsunday islands 509–514
Whitsundays, The 510
Whyalla 877
Wik Decision 1188
Wilcannia 396
wildlife 1193–1197
Willandra Lakes System 377
William Bay National Park 748
William Creek 895
Wilpena 888
Wilpena Pound 19, 889
Wilsons Promontory National Park 1038
Wiluna 757
Wimmera, The 1025
Windjana Gorge National Park 792
Windorah 594
Windsor 217
Windy Harbour 743
wine tasting tips 836
wineries
- Avoca (VIC) 1006
- Barossa Valley (SA) ... 21, 838
- Coonawarra (SA) 862
- Goulburn Valley (VIC) 1048
- Great Western (VIC) 1016
- Hunter Valley 228–229
- Margaret River (WA) 738
- McLaren Vale (SA) 843
- Mildura (VIC) 1031
- Mudgee 362
- Pipers River (TAS) 1128
- Rutherglen (VIC) 1053
- Swan Hill (VIC) 1033
- Swan Valley (WA) 733

wines, Australian 65
Winton 603
Wisemans Ferry 216
witchetty grubs 63
Witjira National Park 896
Wittenoom 779
Wollogorang 672
Wollongong 254–256
Wombeyan Caves 367
women travellers 93
Wongalee Falls (Crystal Cascades) 546
Wongaling Beach 533
Woodbridge 1092
Woodend 998
Woodford (NSW) 238
Woodford (QLD) 461
Woolgoolga 321
Woolnorth 1149
Woomera 881
Wooroonooran National Park 537
working 82–86
Wycliffe Well 675
Wyndham 794
Wynyard 1144
Wyperfield National Park 1026

Yallingup 737
Yamala 597
Yamba 323
Yarra Glen 963
Yarra Valley 962–964
Yarrangobilly Caves 302
Yass 367
Yellow Waters 656
Yeppoon 498
Yolla 1152
York 734
Yorke Peninsula 848
Young 364
Yulara (Ayers Rock Resort) 700
Yungaburra 16, 556
Yuraygir National Park ... 323

Z

Zeehan 1153
Zig Zag Railway 250

Map symbols

Maps are listed in the full index using coloured text

Main road
Minor road
Unpaved road
Pedestrianized street (town maps)
Steps
Path/track
Railway
Ferry route
River
State/territorial boundary
Chapter division boundary
Point of interest
Mountain peak
Mountain range
Gorge
Viewpoint
Waterfall
Reef
Airport
Cave

Conservation hut
Chinese temple
Lighthouse
Golf course
Bus stop
Information office
Post office
Internet access
Campsite
Accommodation
Restaurant
Building
Church/cathedral
Aboriginal land
Prohibited area
Beach
Cemetery
Marsh
Park
Salt lake